TWENTIETH-CENTURY SCIENCE-FICTION WRITERS

EDITOR
CURTIS C. SMITH

ST. MARTIN'S PRESS
NEW YORK

First published in the United States of America
in 1981

All rights reserved. For more information, write:
St. Martin's Press, Inc.
175 Fifth Avenue,
New York, NY 10010

Library of Congress Cataloging in Publication Data
Main entry under title:

Twentieth century science fiction writers.

Bibliography: p.
1. Science fiction, American—Bio-bibliography.
2. Science fiction, English—Bio-bibliography.
3. Science fiction, American—History and criticism.
4. Science fiction, English—History and criticism.
I. Smith, Curtis C.
PS374.S35T89   016.813'0876'09   81-8944
ISBN 0-312-82420-3   AACR2

Twentieth-Century Writers of the English Language
already published:

   Twentieth-Century Children's Writers

   Twentieth-Century Crime and Mystery Writers

in preparation:

   Twentieth-Century Romance and Gothic Writers

   Twentieth-Century Western Writers

CONTENTS

PREFACE

As with so many things, science fiction was undergoing widespread changes in the late 1960's. It was a commonplace belief at that time that the boundaries between science fiction and so-called "mainstream" fiction were eroding. Pulp science-fiction writers had once been thoroughly conventional in literary technique; but now they were adopting multiple points of view, stream of consciousness, and surrealistic and expressionistic styles. The young writer-critics, such as Delany and Ellison, openly rejoiced at what seemed a definitive departure from the pulp ghetto. Science fiction, it was implied, was gaining status for itself and acceptance from the mainstream, and mainstream writers, for their part, were choosing science-fiction subject matter. The term "science fiction" was said to be outmoded; the 20th century had become so bizarre that the realism of science could not describe it, and only "speculative fiction," whether written by pulp or mainstream writers, could continue as a category.

Although there was some truth to this "New Wave" critical perspective, we can now see, as the 1970's become the 1980's, that science fiction as a term and as a distinct genre is resilient. Walk into any bookstore and it is easy to find the science fiction, separately shelved under a special sign. There *is* science fiction, and there *are* science-fiction writers, as most members of the Science Fiction Writers of America would tell you. The call for "speculative fiction" was issued from a frog perspective, from science-fiction writers and critics weary of being laughed at. The fact is that there are enough deficiencies in the mainstream literature of western countries that it would not altogether have been a triumph had science fiction merged with it. For all its own deficiencies, science fiction will best develop from self-acceptance.

Although science fiction is here to stay, this does not mean that we can define it. Publishers seem to have no problem deciding what to market as science fiction, but it is by now an old joke that every science-fiction convention features a panel discussion in which experts strive, in futility, to define the genre. I have been teaching science fiction in a university since 1969, and nearly every book in every version of my course is challenged by some student as not being "really science fiction." I won't add to the joke by trying to define science fiction here; I will refer the reader to Darko Suvin's *Metamorphoses of Science Fiction*, perhaps the most ambitious attempt yet at definition. But I do think it worthwhile to talk about why defining science fiction is both difficult and important. The term "science fiction" originated as late as the 1920's, and in some ways the science-fiction genre is in its youth; it could develop in a number of ways, and a part of the critical debate is over not what it is but what it could or should be. What does the word "science" in science fiction mean, anyway? Does it mean that there has to be accurate science, or plausible extrapolation of current theory, for a work to be considered science fiction? If we insist on this, a rather large part of what is now science fiction must be banished from the ghetto—all time-travel stories, for instance, since time travel cannot be presented as a reasonable extrapolation from current theory, despite Wells's impressionistic gymnastics in *The Time Machine*.

Suppose, then, we take the opposite tack and say that the science part of science fiction is a thin papering over a fantasy content. Science fiction, then, is a branch of fantasy. The problems with this view are severe. Modern adult fantasy has its own special history and conventions. More fundamentally, the best science fiction, by Wells, Stapledon, Lem, and Yefremov, does not seem to be describing a fantasy world but a world that bears an extrapolated resemblance to our own. New writers are not only imagining but thinking, and thinking in a way that has some relationship to science. The best science fiction is mimetic, and it is difficult to define science fiction because of the profundity of the meaning of mimesis in literature. Science fiction describes this world we live in, not some other; it is distinct enough as a genre to make such a book as this possible. Chronologically, this book's earliest authors are from the age of Wells. Of course there have been works arguably science fiction which predate Wells by thousands of years, from the Babylonian *Epic of Gilgamesh* to *The Odyssey* to Lucian's *A True Story*. A reader can examine Marjorie Hope Nicolson's *Voyages to the Moon* and J.O. Bailey's pioneer work *Pilgrims Through Space and Time* for discussion and summaries of science-fiction works from the Renaissance to the 19th century. Brian Aldiss argues convincingly in his *Billion Year Spree* that Mary Shelley's *Frankenstein* is the first science-fiction novel, and Shelley's book is certainly one of the works which has most influenced the direction of 20th-century science fiction. Doubtless there was science fiction before Verne and Wells, but these two great popular writers were decisive in creating a special audience for what until the 1920's was called the "scientific romance."

The English-language writers in this volume are, by a rather large majority, Americans; and this fact reflects the American domination, numerically, of the field. But by a curious paradox the United States has yet to produce a science fiction writer with the stature of a Wells, Stapledon, Capek, or Lem. Why is this so? Perhaps, as Franz Rottensteiner has speculated, it is precisely because these great European science-fiction writers have developed apart from the inbred self-congratulations of the American science-fiction ghetto. Stapledon, for example, wrote his first great future history, *Last and First Men*, without even knowing that there was such a literary category as science fiction: he had read only a few of the works of Wells. Even more fundamentally, perhaps in the American culture of the late 20th century there are deficiencies and blind spots that make the fiction of social and scientific speculation difficult. Lem has pointed out the scientific adsurdity of Asimov's laws of robotics, with their built-in assurances that robots—and by easy extension, technology—shall not harm humans. The assumption is that technology can be made safe by more technology (whatever "safe" is). All too often American science fiction has been public relations for technology, refusing to look at the potential dangers and the alternate social systems under which such dangers might be minimized. A telling critique of American science fiction comes from one of its ablest practitioners, Ursula K. Le Guin, in the November 1975 issue of *Science-Fiction Studies*. Le Guin contends that American science fiction has been singularly poor in presenting "the Other—the being who is different from yourself." The poor, the proletariat—and, until recently, women—have been conspicuous in American science fiction by their absence. Le Guin speaks of the domination of the masses by powerful elites in much American science fiction, and the assumption that wealth carries its own justification; she complains about the assumption that "competitive free-enterprise capitalism is the economic destiny of the entire Galaxy." A continuing weakness in American science fiction is the unwillingness or inability to imagine social change on the same scale as technological change.

Of course this is a generalization, perhaps an exaggerated one; Le Guin has said in a later context that she was speaking rhetorically.

Smith, Clark Ashton, *Planets and Dimensions: Collected Essays*, edited by Charles K. Wolfe.   Baltimore, Mirage Press, 1973.

Spelman, Richard C., *A Preliminary Checklist of Science Fiction and Fantasy Published by Ballantine Books 1953-1974.*   North Hollywood, Institute for Specialized Literature, 1976.

Spelman, Richard C., *Science Fiction and Fantasy Published by Ace Books 1953-1968.*   North Hollywood, Institute for Specialized Literature, 1976.

Stone, Graham, *Australian Science Fiction Index 1925-1967.*   Canberra, Australian Science Fiction Association, 1968; *Supplement 1968-1975*, Sydney, Australian Science Fiction Association, 1976.

Strauss, Erwin S., *The MIT Science Fiction Society's Index to the S-F Magazines 1951-1965.*   Cambridge, Massachusetts, MIT Science Fiction Society, 1966.

Strick, Philip, *Science Fiction Movies.*   London, Octopus, 1976.

Strickland, A.W., *Reference Guide to American Science Fiction Films.*   Bloomington, Indiana, TIS, 2 vols., 1980.

Summers, Montague, *A Gothic Bibliography.*   London, Fortune Press, 1941; New York, Russell, 1964.

Suvin, Darko, *Metamorphoses of Science Fiction.*   New Haven, Yale University Press, 1979.

Suvin, Darko, *Russian Science Fiction 1956-1974: A Bibliography.*   Elizabethtown, New York, Dragon Press, 1976.

Todorov, Tzvetan, *The Fantastic: A Structural Approach to a Literary Genre*, translated by Richard Howard.   Cleveland, Press of Case Western Reserve University, 1973.

Tuck, Donald H., *The Encyclopedia of Science Fiction and Fantasy Through 1968.*   Chicago, Advent, 2 vols., 1974-78.

Tymn, Marshall B., *American Fantasy and Science Fiction: Toward a Bibliography of Works Published in the United States 1948-1973.*   West Linn, Oregon, FAX, 1979.

Tymn, Marshall B., *Index to Stories in Thematic Anthologies of Science Fiction.*   Boston, Hall, 1978.

Tymn, Marshall B., Roger C. Schlobin, and L.W. Currey, *A Research Guide to Science Fiction Studies.*   New York, Garland, 1977.

Tymn, Marshall B., and Roger C. Schlobin, *The Year's Scholarship in Science Fiction and Fantasy 1972-1975.*   Kent, Ohio, Kent State University Press, 1979.

Urang, Gunnar, *Shadows of Heaven: Religion and Fantasy in the Writings of C.S. Lewis, Charles Williams, and J.R.R. Tolkien.*   Philadelphia, Pilgrim Press, and London, SCM Press, 1971.

Versins, Pierre, *Encyclopedie de l'Utopie des Voyages Extraordinaires et de la Science Fiction.*   Lausanne, L'Age d'Homme, 1972.

Walker, Paul, *Speaking of Science Fiction* (interviews).   Oradell, New Jersey, Luna, 1978.

Walsh, Chad, *From Utopia to Nightmare.*   New York, Harper, and London, Bles, 1962.

Warner, Harry, Jr., *All Our Yesterdays: An Informal History of Science Fiction Fandom in the Forties.*   Chicago, Advent, 1969.

Warrick, Patricia S., *The Cybernetic Imagination in Science Fiction.*   Cambridge, Massachusetts, MIT Press, 1980.

Weinberg, Robert, *The Weird Tales Story.*   West Linn, Oregon, Fax, 1977.

Weinberg, Robert, and Lohr McKinstry, *The Hero Pulp Index.*   Evergreen, Colorado, Opar Press, 1971.

Weinberg, Robert, and Edward P. Berglund, *Reader's Guide to the Cthulhu Mythos.*   Albuquerque, Silver Scarab Press, 1973.

Wells, Stuart, III, *The Science Fiction and Heroic Fantasy Author Index.*   Duluth, Purple Unicorn, 1978.

Wertham, Frederic, *The World of Fanzines: A Special Form of Communication.*   Carbondale, Southern Illinois University Press, 1973.

Williamson, Jack, editor, *Teaching Science Fiction: Education for Tomorrow.*   Privately printed, 1972.

Willis, Donald C., *Horror and Science Fiction Films: A Checklist.*   Metuchen, New Jersey, Scarecrow Press, 1972.

Wilson, Colin, *Science Fiction as Existentialism.*   Hayes, Middlesex, Bran's Head, 1978.

Wilson, Colin, *The Strength to Dream: Literature and the Imagination.*   London, Gollancz, and Boston, Houghton Mifflin, 1962.

Wolfe, Gary K., *The Known and the Unknown: The Iconography of Science Fiction.*   Kent, Ohio, Kent State University Press, 1979.

Wollheim, Donald A., *The Universe Makers: Science Fiction Today.*   New York, Harper, 1971; London, Gollancz, 1972.

Wymer, Thomas L., and others, *Intersections: The Elements of Fiction in Science Fiction.*   Bowling Green, Ohio, Popular Press, 1978.

2. Studies of Individual Authors

Allen, L. David, *Asimov's Foundation Trilogy and Other Works.*   Lincoln, Nebraska, Cliffs Notes, 1977.

Allen, L. David, *Herbert's Dune and Other Works.*   Lincoln, Nebraska, Cliffs Notes, 1975.

Allott, Kenneth, *Jules Verne.*   London, Cresset Press, 1940; Port Washington, New York, Kennikat Press, 1970.

Amory, Mark, *Biography of Lord Dunsany.*   London, Collins, 1972.

Barbour, Douglas, *Worlds Out of Words: The SF Novels of Samuel R. Delany.*   Frome, Somerset, Bran's Head, 1979.

Batchelor, John, *Mervyn Peake: A Biographical and Critical Exploration.*   London, Duckworth, 1974.

Bergonzi, Bernard, *The Early H.G. Wells: A Study of the Scientific Romances.*   Manchester, University Press, 1961.

Bergonzi, Bernard, editor, *H.G. Wells: A Collection of Critical Essays.*   Englewood Cliffs, New Jersey, Prentice Hall, 1976.

Boyd, Ian, *The Novels of G.K. Chesterton: A Study in Art and Propaganda.*   New York, Barnes and Noble, and London, Elek, 1975.

Breen, Walter, *The Gemini Problem: A Study in Darkover* (on Marion Zimmer Bradley).   Berkeley, California, Breen, 1973.

Brizzi, Mary T., *Philip José Farmer: A Reader's Guide.*   West Linn, Oregon, Starmont House, 1979.

Brown, E.J., *Brave New World, 1984, and We: Essays on Anti-Utopia.*   Ann Arbor, Michigan, Ardis, 1976.

Carpenter, Humphrey, *Tolkien: A Biography.*   London, Allen and Unwin, and Boston, Houghton Mifflin, 1977.

Carter, Lin, *Lovecraft: A Look Behind the Cthulhu Mythos.*   New York, Ballantine, 1972; London, Panther, 1975.

Chalker, Jack L., editor, *In Memoriam Clark Ashton Smith.*   Baltimore, Mirage Press, 1963.

Chesneaux, Jean, *The Political and Social Ideas of Jules Verne*, translated by Thomas Wikeley.   London, Thames and Hudson, 1972.

Clipper, Lawrence J., *G.K. Chesterton.*   New York, Twayne, 1974.

Cohen, Morton N., *Rider Haggard: His Life and Works.*   London, Hutchinson, 1960; New York, Walker, 1961.

Cook, W. Paul, *In Memoriam Howard Phillips Lovecraft: Recollections, Appreciations, Estimates.*   Privately printed, 1941.

Costa, Richard Hauer, *H.G. Wells.*   New York, Twayne, 1967.

Davenport, Basil, *An Introduction to Islandia* (on Austin Tappan Wright).   New York, Farrar and Rinehart, 1942.

De Bolt, Joseph W., editor, *The Happening Worlds of John Brunner.*   Port Washington, New York, Kennikat Press, 1975.

De Bolt, Joseph W., editor, *Ursula K. Le Guin: Voyager to Inner Lands and to Outer Space.* Port Washington, New York, Kennikat Press, 1979.

de Camp, L. Sprague, *Lovecraft: A Biography.* New York, Doubleday, 1975; London, New English Library, 1976.

de la Ree, Gerry, and Sam Moskowitz, editors, *After Ten Years: A Tribute to Stanley G. Weinbaum 1902-1935.* Westwood, New Jersey, de la Ree, 1945.

Derleth, August, *H.P.L.: A Memoir* (on H.P. Lovecraft). New York, Abramson, 1945.

Derleth, August, *Some Notes on H.P. Lovecraft.* Sauk City, Wisconsin, Arkham House, 1959.

Dickson, Lovat, *H.G. Wells: His Turbulent Life and Times.* London, Macmillan, 1969.

Dozois, Gardner, *The Fiction of James Tiptree, Jr.* New York, Algol Press, 1977.

Ellik, Ronald, and William Evans, *The Universes of E.E. Smith.* Chicago, Advent, 1966.

Ellis, Peter Berresford, *H. Rider Haggard: A Voice from the Infinite.* London, Routledge, 1978.

Evans, Robley, *J.R.R. Tolkien.* New York, Warner, 1973.

Foster, Robert, *A Guide to Middle-Earth* (on Tolkien). Baltimore, Mirage Press, 1971; revised edition, as *The Complete Guide to Middle-Earth*, London, Allen and Unwin, 1978.

Gardner, Martin and Russel B. Nye, *The Wizard of Oz and Who He Was.* East Lansing, Michigan State University Press, 1957.

Giannone, Richard, *Vonnegut: A Preface to His Novels.* Port Washington, New York, Kennikat Press, 1977.

Gibb, Jocelyn, editor, *Light on C.S. Lewis.* London, Bles, 1965.

Gillespie, Bruce, editor, *Philip K. Dick: Electric Shepherd.* Melbourne, Nostrilia Press, 1975.

Goble, Neil, *Asimov Analyzed.* Baltimore, Mirage Press, 1972.

Goddard, James, and David Pringle, editors, *J.G. Ballard: The First Twenty Years.* Hayes, Middlesex, Bran's Head, 1976.

Goldsmith, David H., *Kurt Vonnegut: Fantasist of Fire and Ice.* Bowling Green, Ohio, Popular Press, 1972.

Grant, Donald M., and Thomas P. Hadley, editors, *Rhode Island on Lovecraft.* Providence, Rhode Island, Grant Hadley, 1945.

Green, Roger Lancelyn, and Walter Hooper, *C.S. Lewis: A Biography.* London, Collins, and New York, Harcourt Brace, 1974.

Grotta-Kurska, Daniel, *J.R.R. Tolkien: Architect of Middle-Earth.* Philadelphia, Running Press, 1976.

Harbottle, Philip, *The Multi-Man: A Biographic and Bibliographic Study of John Russell Fearn.* Privately printed, 1968.

Helms, Randel, *Tolkien's World.* London, Thames and Hudson, and Boston, Houghton Mifflin, 1974.

Indick, Benjamin P., *The Drama of Ray Bradbury.* Baltimore, T-K Graphics, 1977.

Johnson, Wayne L., *Ray Bradbury.* New York, Ungar, 1980.

Jules-Verne, Jean, *Jules Verne: A Biography*, translated by Roger Greaves. New York, Taplinger, and London, Macdonald and Jane's, 1976.

Kagarlitsky, Julius, *The Life and Thought of H.G. Wells*, translated by Moura Budberg. London, Sidgwick and Jackson, 1966.

Keefer, Truman Frederick, *Philip Wylie.* Boston, Twayne, 1977.

Kilby, Clyde S., *Tolkien and the Silmarillion.* Wheaton, Illinois, Shaw, 1976; Berkhamsted, Hertfordshire, Lion, 1977.

Klinkowitz, Jerome, and John Somer, editors, *The Vonnegut Statement.* New York, Delacorte Press, 1973; London, Panther, 1975.

Kocher, Paul, *Master of Middle-Earth: The Fiction of J.R.R. Tolkien.* Boston, Houghton Mifflin, 1972; London, Thames and Hudson, 1973.

Kuehn, Robert E., editor, *Aldous Huxley: A Collection of Critical Essays.* Englewood Cliffs, New Jersey, Prentice Hall, 1974.

Lobdell, Jared, editor, *A Tolkien Compass.* La Salle, Illinois, Open Court, 1975.

Long, Frank Belknap, *Howard Phillips Lovecraft: Dreamer on the Nightside.* Sauk City, Wisconsin, Arkham House, 1975.

Lupoff, Richard A., *Barsoom: Edgar Rice Burroughs and the Martian Vision.* Baltimore, Mirage Press, 1976.

Lupoff, Richard A., *Edgar Rice Burroughs, Master of Adventure.* New York, Canaveral Press, 1965; revised edition, New York, Ace, 1968.

Mackenzie, Norman and Jeanne, *The Time Traveller: The Life of H.G. Wells.* London, Weidenfeld and Nicolson, 1973; as *H.G. Wells: A Biography*, New York, Simon and Schuster, 1973.

Manning, Audrey Smoak, *Bradbury's Works.* Lincoln, Nebraska, Cliffs Notes, 1977.

Mathews, Richard, *Aldiss Unbound.* San Bernardino, California, Borgo Press, 1977.

Metzger, Arthur, *A Guide to the Gormenghast Trilogy.* Baltimore, T-K Graphics, 1976.

Miesel, Sandra, *Against Time's Arrow: The High Crusade of Poul Anderson.* San Bernardino, California, Borgo Press, 1978.

Moore, Raylyn, *Wonderful Wizard, Marvelous Land* (on L. Frank Baum). Bowling Green, Ohio, Popular Press, 1974.

Moskowitz, Sam, *Hugo Gernsback.* New York, Criterion, 1959.

Noel, Ruth S., *The Mythology of Middle-Earth* (on Tolkien). Boston, Houghton Mifflin, and London, Thames and Hudson, 1977.

Nolan, William F., *The Ray Bradbury Companion.* Detroit, Gale, 1975.

Olander, Joseph D., and Martin H. Greenberg, editors, *Arthur C. Clarke.* New York, Taplinger, and Edinburgh, Harris, 1977.

Olander, Joseph D., and Martin H. Greenberg, editors, *Isaac Asimov.* New York, Taplinger, and Edinburgh, Harris, 1977.

Olander, Joseph D., and Martin H. Greenberg, editors, *Ray Bradbury.* New York, Taplinger, 1979.

Olander, Joseph D., and Martin H. Greenberg, editors, *Robert A. Heinlein.* New York, Taplinger, and Edinburgh, Harris, 1978.

Olander, Joseph D., and Martin H. Greenberg, editors, *Ursula Le Guin.* New York, Taplinger, and Edinburgh, Harris, 1979.

Panshin, Alexei, *Heinlein in Dimension: A Critical Analysis.* Chicago, Advent, 1968.

Parrinder, Patrick, *H.G. Wells.* Edinburgh, Oliver and Boyd, 1970; New York, Capricorn, 1977.

Parrinder, Patrick, editor, *H.G. Wells: The Critical Heritage.* London, Routledge, 1972.

Patrouch, Joseph F., Jr., *The Science Fiction of Isaac Asimov.* New York, Doubleday, 1974; London, Panther, 1976.

Pick, J.B., Colin Wilson, and E.H. Visiak, *The Strange Genius of David Lindsay.* London, Baker, 1970; as *The Haunted Man*, San Bernardino, California, Borgo Press, 1979.

Porges, Irwin, *Edgar Rice Burroughs, The Man Who Created Tarzan.* Provo, Utah, Brigham Young University Press, 1975; London, New English Library, 1976.

Porter, Andrew, editor, *Exploring Cordwainer Smith.* New York, Algol Press, 1975.

Powell, Lawrence Clark, *The Islandian World of Austin Wright.* Privately printed, 1957.

Rabkin, Eric S., *Arthur C. Clarke.* West Linn, Oregon, Starmont House, 1979.

American science-fiction writers, after all, now include Le Guin herself, Philip K. Dick, Mack Reynolds, Marge Piercy, Joanna Russ, Walter M. Miller, Jr., Robert Silverberg, Theodore Sturgeon, and Chan Davis. The very fact that such criticism as Le Guin's is being aired portends well for change.

Nowhere is change more evident than in the place of women writers and women characters in English-language science fiction. In the so-called "golden age" of the 1930's and 1940's, women were hard to find in the stories, present only as voluptuous and helpless objects on the lurid pulp covers. The "hard" science fiction of *Astounding* found some of its justification in getting teenage boys interested in science, and of course girls didn't count. E.E. "Doc" Smith found writing romantic scenes so difficult that he asked Mrs. Lee Hawkins Garby for help in these parts of *The Skylark of Space*. The relationships between men and women were seen as extrinsic to science fiction proper, something to be added on.

Character development remains a weak point in English-language science fiction, so that some of the best science fiction is still being written by writers not primarily associated with the field, such as Barth, Durrell, Pynchon, Anthony Burgess, and Lessing. But at least there are now women characters in science fiction, and an explosion of science-fiction writers who are women: consider Zenna Henderson, Pamela Sargent, James Tiptree, Jr., Ursula K. Le Guin, Joanna Russ, Lee Killough, Suzy McKee Charnas, Anne McCaffrey, Octavia Butler, Marge Piercy, and many others. These writers have brought speculation about the future of sex roles to science fiction. Science fiction, once totally the domain of men, has reversed itself and is now in the forefront of feminist thinking.

What now for science fiction? The field seems now more various than ever. Space opera is still around: good guys still wage intergalactic warfare against alien bad guys. Post-nuclear disaster scenarios, which proliferated in the field after 1945 and produced such classics as George R. Stewart's *Earth Abides* and Walter M. Miller, Jr.'s *A Canticle for Leibowitz*, are still being written by Bob Tucker, Christopher Priest, and others. But ecological disaster has tended to replace nuclear disaster in the works of such writers as John Christopher, Harry Harrison, Kate Wilhelm, Thomas M. Disch, and John Brunner. Although the New Wave has faded somewhat as a distinct movement, such writers as James Tiptree, Jr. and Gene Wolfe are carrying on experiments in style and structure. And a few writers, such as George Zebrowski, are carrying on the Wells-Stapledon-Lem tradition of prophetic extrapolation, writing poetry and philosophy on a gigantic scale.

The anti-utopian police state typified by *Brave New World* and *Nineteen Eighty-Four* dominated science fiction for decades, so that Kingsley Amis's early book on science fiction was appropriately called *New Maps of Hell*. Beginning, perhaps, with Le Guin's *The Dispossessed*, ambiguous utopias are challenging this domination. Marge Piercy has written an underrated utopia, *Woman on the Edge of Time*, which links the struggles of a minority woman of the present to a future utopia's efforts to preserve itself. Another underrated writer, Mack Reynolds, has updated Bellamy's *Looking Backward* (see Reynolds's entry for his comments on his work). Science fiction is returning to one of its historical origins, the utopian tradition.

In view of all these trends we can say that science fiction is one of the more protean literary genres in the late 20th century. People continue to turn to science fiction for escape and entertainment, as they should. But science fiction offers thought and involvement as well as escape. That there will be future conditions quite distinct from present ones is a proposition both disturbing and salutary. In the late 20th century the world is undergoing an even more profound transformation than is generally realized, and science fiction can help us to understand it.

CURTIS C. SMITH

READING LIST

1. **General Works**
Aldiss, Brian, *Billion Year Spree: A History of Science Fiction.*   London, Weidenfeld and Nicolson, and New York, Doubleday, 1973.
Aldiss, Brian, *Science Fiction Art.*   New York, Bounty, 1975; London, Hart Davis, 1976.
Aldiss, Brian, *Science Fiction as Science Fiction.*   Frome, Somerset, Bran's Head, 1978.
Aldiss, Brian, and Harry Harrison, editors, *Hell's Cartographers: Some Personal Histories of Science Fiction Writers.*   London, Weidenfeld and Nicolson, and New York, Harper, 1975.
Aldiss, Brian, and Harry Harrison, editors, *SF Horizons.*   New York, Arno Press, 1975.
Allen, Dick, *Science Fiction: The Future.*   New York, Harcourt Brace, 1971.
Allen, L. David, *The Ballantine Teachers' Guide to Science Fiction.*   New York, Ballantine, 1975.
Allen, L. David, *Science Fiction: An Introduction.*   Lincoln, Nebraska, Cliffs Notes, 1973; as *Science Fiction Readers Guide*, Lincoln, Nebraska, Centennial Press, 1974.
Amelio, Ralph J., *Hal in the Classroom: Science Fiction Films.*   Dayton, Ohio, Pflaum, 1974.
Amis, Kingsley, *New Maps of Hell: A Survey of Science Fiction.*   New York, Harcourt Brace, 1960; London, Gollancz, 1961.
Armytage, W.H.G., *Yesterday's Tomorrows: A Historical Survey of Future Societies.*   London, Routledge, 1968.
Ash, Brian, *Faces of the Future: The Lessons of Science Fiction.*   London, Elek, and New York, Taplinger, 1975.
Ash, Brian, editor, *The Visual Encyclopedia of Science Fiction.*   New York, Harmony, and London, Pan, 1977.
Ash, Brian, *Who's Who in Science Fiction.*   London, Elm Tree, and New York, Taplinger, 1976.
Ashley, Michael, editor, *The History of the Science Fiction Magazine.*   London, New English Library, 4 vols., 1974-76; vols. 1 and 2, Chicago, Regnery, 1976.
Atkinson, Geoffroy, *The Extraordinary Voyage in French Literature Before 1700.*   New York, Columbia University Press, 1920; *The Extraordinary Voyage in French Literature from 1700-1720*, Paris, Champion, 1922.
Bailey, J.O., *Pilgrims Through Space and Time: Trends and Patterns in Scientific and Utopian Fiction.*   New York, Argus, 1947.
Barnes, Myra, *Linguistics and Language in Science Fiction-Fantasy.*   New York, Arno Press, 1975.

Barron, Neil, editor, *Anatomy of Wonder*.   New York, Bowker, 1976.

Barron, Neil, and R. Reginald, *Science Fiction and Fantasy Annual 1980*.   San Bernardino, California, Borgo Press, 1980.

Baxter, John, *Science Fiction in the Cinema*.   New York, A.S. Barnes, and London, Zwemmer, 1970.

Berger, Harold L., *Science Fiction and the New Dark Age*.   Bowling Green, Ohio, Popular Press, 1976.

Bleiler, E.F., *The Checklist of Fantastic Literature*.   Chicago, Shasta, 1948; revised edition, as *The Checklist of Science-Fiction and Supernatural Fiction*, Glen Rock, New Jersey, Firebell, 1978.

Blish, James, *The Issue at Hand: Studies in Contemporary Magazine Science Fiction*.   Chicago, Advent, 1964; *More Issues at Hand*, 1970 (both books as William Atheling, Jr.).

Bova, Ben, editor, *Closeup, New Worlds*.   New York, St. Martin's Press, 1977.

Bova, Ben, *Notes to a Science Fiction Writer* (juvenile).   New York, Scribner, 1975.

Bova, Ben, *Through Eyes of Wonder: Science Fiction and Science* (juvenile).   Reading, Massachusetts, Addison Wesley, 1975.

Bova, Ben, *Viewpoint*.   Cambridge, Massachusetts, NESFA Press, 1977.

Bretnor, Reginald, editor, *The Craft of Science Fiction*.   New York, Harper, 1976.

Bretnor, Reginald, editor, *Modern Science Fiction: Its Meaning and Its Future*.   New York, Coward McCann, 1953; revised edition, Chicago, Advent, 1979.

Bretnor, Reginald, editor, *Science Fiction, Today and Tomorrow*.   New York, Harper, 1974.

Briney, R.E., and Edward Wood, *SF Bibliographies: An Annotated Bibliography of Bibliographical Works on Science Fiction and Fantasy Fiction*.   Chicago, Advent, 1972.

Brosnan, John, *Future Tense: The Cinema of Science Fiction*.   London, Macdonald and Jane's, 1978; New York, St. Martin's Press, 1979.

Brown, Charles N., and Dena Brown, editors, *Locus: The Newspaper of the Science Fiction Field*.   Boston, Gregg Press, 1978.

Calkins, Elizabeth, and Barry McGhan, *Teaching Tomorrow: A Handbook of Science Fiction for Teachers*.   Dayton, Ohio, Pflaum, 1972.

Cazedessus, C.E., Jr., editor, *Ghost Stories*.   Evergreen, Colorado, Opar Press, 1973.

Chauvin, Cy, editor, *A Multitude of Visions: Essays on Science Fiction*.   Baltimore, T-K Graphics, 1975.

Clarens, Carlos, *An Illustrated History of the Horror Film*.   New York, Capricorn, 1967; revised edition, as *Horror Movies*, London, Secker and Warburg, 1968.

Clareson, Thomas D., editor, *Extrapolation: A Science Fiction Newsletter 1959-1969*.   Boston, Gregg Press, 1978.

Clareson, Thomas D., *Many Futures, Many Worlds: Theme and Form in Science Fiction*.   Kent, Ohio, Kent State University Press, 1977.

Clareson, Thomas D., *Science Fiction Criticism: An Annotated Checklist*.   Kent, Ohio, Kent State University Press, 1972.

Clareson, Thomas D., *SF: A Dream of Other Worlds*.   College Station, Texas A and M University, 1973.

Clareson, Thomas D., editor, *SF: The Other Side of Realism: Essays on Modern Fantasy and Science Fiction*.   Bowling Green, Ohio, Popular Press, 1971.

Clareson, Thomas D., editor, *Voices for the Future: Essays on Major Science Fiction Writers*.   Bowling Green, Ohio, Popular Press, 2 vols., 1976-79.

Clarke, I.F., *The Pattern of Expectation 1644-2001*.   London, Cape, 1979.

Clarke, I.F., *The Tale of the Future*.   London, Library Association, 1961.

Clarke, I.F., *Voices Prophesying War 1763-1984*.   London, Oxford University Press, 1966.

Cockcroft, Thomas G.L., *Index to Fiction in Radio News and Other Magazines*.   Lower Hutt, New Zealand, Cockcroft, 1970.

Cockcroft, Thomas G.L., *Index to the Weird Fiction Magazines*.   Lower Hutt, New Zealand, Cockcroft, 2 vols., 1962-64.

Cole, Walter L., *A Checklist of Science-Fiction Anthologies*.   New York, Cole, 1964.

Contento, William, *Index to Science Fiction Anthologies and Collections*.   Boston, Hall, and London, Prior, 1978.

Crawford, Joseph H., Jr., James J. Donahue, and Donald M. Grant, *"333": A Bibliography of the Science Fantasy Novel*.   Providence, Rhode Island, Grandon, 1953.

Currey, L.W., *Science Fiction and Fantasy Authors: A Bibliography of First Printings of Their Fiction and Selected Non-Fiction*.   Boston, Hall, 1979.

Davenport, Basil, *Inquiry into Science Fiction*.   New York, Longman, 1955.

Davenport, Basil, editor, *The Science Fiction Novel: Imagination and Social Criticism*.   Chicago, Advent, 1964; revised edition, 1964.

Day, Bradford M., *Bibliography of Adventure: Mundy, Burroughs, Rohmer, Haggard*.   Denver, New York, Science Fiction and Fantasy Publications, 1964.

Day, Bradford M., *The Checklist of Fantastic Literature in Paperbound Books*.   Denver, New York, Science Fiction and Fantasy Publications, 1965.

Day, Bradford M., *The Complete Checklist of Science Fiction Magazines*.   New York, Science Fiction and Fantasy Publications, 1961.

Day, Bradford M., *An Index on the Weird and Fantastica in Magazines*.   Privately printed, 1953.

Day, Bradford M., *The Supplemental Checklist of Fantastic Literature*.   Denver, New York, Science Fiction and Fantasy Publications, 1963.

Day, Donald B., *Index to the Science-Fiction Magazines 1926-1950*.   Portland, Perri Press, 1952.

de Camp, L. Sprague, *The Conan Reader*.   Baltimore, Mirage Press, 1968.

de Camp, L. Sprague, *Science-Fiction Handbook*.   New York, Hermitage House, 1953; revised edition, with Catherine Crook de Camp, Philadelphia, Owlswick Press, 1975.

de Camp, L. Sprague, and George H. Scithers, editors, *The Conan Grimoire*.   Baltimore, Mirage Press, 1971.

de Camp, L. Sprague, and George H. Scithers, editors, *The Conan Swordbook*.   Baltimore, Mirage Press, 1969.

Delany, Samuel R., *The Jewel-Hinged Jaw: Notes on the Language of Science Fiction*.   Elizabethtown, New York, Dragon Press, 1977.

del Rey, Lester, *The World of Science Fiction 1926-1976: The History of a Subculture*.   New York, Ballantine, 1979.

Derleth, August, *Thirty Years of Arkham House*.   Sauk City, Wisconsin, Arkham House, 1970.

Eichner, Henry M., *Atlantean Chronicles.* Alhambra, California, Fantasy Publishing, 1971.

Eigruber, Frank, Jr., *Gangland's Doom: The Shadow of the Pulps.* Oak Lawn, Illinois, Weinberg, 1974.

Elliott, Robert C., *The Shape of Utopia: Studies in a Literary Genre.* Chicago, University of Chicago Press, 1970.

Elrick, George S., *The Science Fiction Handbook for Readers and Writers.* Chicago, Chicago Review Press, 1978.

Eshbach, Lloyd Arthur, editor, *Of Worlds Beyond: The Science of Science-Fiction Writing.* Reading, Pennsylvania, Fantasy Press, 1947; London, Dobson, 1965.

Eurich, Nell, *Science in Utopia: A Mighty Design.* Cambridge, Massachusetts, Harvard University Press, 1967.

Frank, Alan, *Sci-Fi Now: 10 Exciting Years of Science Fiction from 2001 to Star Wars and Beyond.* London, Octopus, 1978.

Franklin, H. Bruce, editor, *Future Perfect: American Science Fiction of the Nineteenth Century.* New York, Oxford University Press, 1966; London, Oxford University Press, 1968.

Franson, Donald, and Howard DeVore, *A History of the Hugo, Nebula, and International Fantasy Awards.* Dearborn Heights, Michigan, DeVore, 1975.

Freas, Frank Kelly, *The Art of Science Fiction.* Norfolk, Virginia, Donning, 1977.

Frewin, Anthony, *One Hundred Years of Science Fiction Illustration 1840-1940.* London, Jupiter, 1974; New York, Pyramid, 1975.

Friendly, Beverly, *Science Fiction: The Classroom in Orbit.* Glassboro, New Jersey, Educational Impact, 1974.

Gerani, Gary, and Paul H. Schulman, *Fantastic Television.* New York, Harmony, 1977.

Gerber, Richard, *Utopian Fantasy: A Study of English Utopian Fiction since the End of the Nineteenth Century.* London, Routledge, 1955; New York, McGraw Hill, 1973.

Gernsback, Hugo, *Evolution in Modern Science Fiction.* New York, Gernsback, 1952.

Gifford, Denis, *Science Fiction Film.* London, Studio Vista, and New York, Dutton, 1971.

Glut, Donald F., *The Frankenstein Legend.* Metuchen, New Jersey, Scarecrow Press, 1973.

Goulart, Ron, *Cheap Thrills: An Informal History of the Pulp Magazines.* New Rochelle, New York, Arlington House, 1972.

Gove, Philip Babcock, *The Imaginery Voyage in Prose Fiction.* New York, Columbia University Press, 1941; London, Holland Press, 1961.

Grant, Charles L., editor, *Writing and Selling Science Fiction.* Cincinnati, Writer's Digest, 1977.

Grebens, G.V., *Ivan Efremov's Theory of Soviet Science Fiction.* New York, Vantage Press, 1978.

Green, Roger Lancelyn, *Into Other Worlds: Spaceflight in Fiction from Lucian to Lewis.* London and New York, Abelard Schuman, 1957.

Griffiths, John, *Three Tomorrows: American, British, and Soviet Science Fiction.* London, Macmillan, 1980.

Gunn, James E., *Alternate Worlds: The Illustrated History of Science Fiction.* Englewood Cliffs, New Jersey, Prentice Hall, 1975.

Gunn, James E., *The Discovery of the Future: The Ways Science Fiction Developed.* College Station, Texas A and M University, 1975.

Gunn, James E., editor, *The Road to Science Fiction.* New York, New American Library, 2 vols., 1977-79.

Hall, H.W., *Science Fiction Book Review Index 1923-1973.* Detroit, Gale, 1975 (and later volumes).

Harrison, Harry, *Great Balls of Fire!* London, Pierrot, and New York, Grosset and Dunlap, 1977.

Hillegas, Mark R., *The Future as Nightmare: H.G. Wells and the Anti-Utopians.* New York, Oxford University Press, 1967.

Hillegas, Mark R., editor, *Shadows of Imagination: The Fantasies of C.S. Lewis, J.R.R. Tolkien, and Charles Williams.* Carbondale, Southern Illinois University Press, 1969.

Hoffman, Stuart, *An Index to "Unknown" and "Unknown Worlds" by Author and by Title.* Black Earth, Wisconsin, Sirius Press, 1955.

Holdstock, Robert, editor, *Encyclopedia of Science Fiction.* London, Octopus, and Baltimore, Hoen, 1978.

Hollister, Bernard C., and Deane C. Thompson, *Grokking the Future: Science Fiction in the Classroom.* Dayton, Ohio, Pflaum, 1973.

Index to Fantasy and Science Fiction in Munsey Publications. Alhambra, California, 1976(?).

Index to Perry Rhodan—American Edition. Cambridge, Massachusetts, NESFA Press, 2 vols., 1973-75.

Index to Science Fiction Magazines 1966-1976. Cambridge, Massachusetts, NESFA Press, 6 vols., 1971-77.

Isaacs, Leonard, *Darwin to Double Helix: The Biological Theme in Science Fiction.* London, Butterworth, 1977.

Johnson, William, editor, *Focus on the Science Fiction Film.* Englewood Cliffs, New Jersey, Prentice Hall, 1972.

Jones, Robert Kenneth, *The Shudder Pulps: A History of the Weird Menace Magazine of the 1930's.* West Linn, Oregon, FAX, 1975.

Ketterer, David, *New Worlds for Old: The Apocalyptic Imagination, Science Fiction, and American Literature.* Bloomington, Indiana University Press, 1974.

Knight, Damon, *The Futurians.* New York, Day, 1977.

Knight, Damon, *In Search of Wonder.* Chicago, Advent, 1956; revised edition, 1967.

Knight, Damon, editor, *Turning Points: Essays on the Art of Science Fiction.* New York, Harper, 1977.

Kyle, David, *The Illustrated Book of Science Fiction Ideas and Dreams.* London, Hamlyn, 1977.

Kyle, David, *A Pictorial History of Science Fiction.* London, Hamlyn, 1976.

Lasky, Melvin J., *Utopia and Revolution.* Chicago, University of Chicago Press, 1976.

Lawler, Donald L., *Approaches to Science Fiction.* Boston, Houghton Mifflin, 1978.

Lee, Walt, *Reference Guide to Fantastic Films.* Los Angeles, Chelsea Lee, 3 vols., 1972-74.

Le Guin, Ursula K., *The Language of the Night: Essays on Fantasy and Science Fiction*, edited by Susan Wood. New York, Putnam, 1979.

Leighton, Peter, *Moon Travellers: A Dream That Is Becoming a Reality.* London, Oldbourne, 1960.

Lester, Colin, editor, *The International Science Fiction Yearbook 1979.* London, Pierrot, 1979.

Locke, George, *Science Fiction First Editions.* London, Ferret Fantasy, 1978.

Locke, George, *Voyages in Space: A Bibliography of Interplanetary Fiction 1801-1914.* London, Ferret Fantasy, 1975.

Lowndes, Robert A.W., *Three Faces of Science Fiction.* Boston, NESFA Press, 1973.

Lundwall, Sam J., *Science Fiction: An Illustrated History.* New York, Grosset and Dunlap, 1978.

Lundwall, Sam J., *Science Fiction: What It's All About.* New York, Ace, 1971.

Magill, Frank N., editor, *Survey of Science Fiction Literature.*   Englewood Cliffs, New Jersey, Salem Press, 5 vols., 1979.

Malone, Robert, *The Robot Book.*   New York, Harcourt Brace, 1978.

Manlove, C.N., *Modern Fantasy: Five Studies.*   London, Cambridge University Press, 1975.

McGhan, Barry, *Sciencefiction and Fantasy Pseudonyms.*   Dearborn, Michigan, Misfit Press, 1973.

Menville, Douglas, *A Historical and Critical Survey of the Science-Fiction Film.*   New York, Arno Press, 1975.

Metcalf, Norm, *The Index of Science Fiction Magazines 1951-1965.*   El Cerrito, California, Stark, 1968.

Meyers, Walter E., *Aliens and Linguists.*   Athens, University of Georgia Press, 1980.

Moore, Patrick, *Science and Fiction.*   London, Harrap, 1957; Folcroft, Pennsylvania, Folcroft Editions, 1970.

Morton, A.L., *The English Utopia.*   London, Lawrence and Wishart, 1952.

Moskowitz, Sam, *Explorers of the Infinite: Shapers of Science Fiction.*   Cleveland, World, 1963.

Moskowitz, Sam, *The Immortal Storm: A History of Science Fiction Fandom.*   Atlanta, Atlanta Science Fiction Organization Press, 1954.

Moskowitz, Sam, editor, *Science Fiction by Gaslight: A History and Anthology of Science Fiction in Popular Magazines 1891-1911.*   Cleveland, World, 1968.

Moskowitz, Sam, *Seekers of Tomorrow: Masters of Modern Science Fiction.*   Cleveland, World, 1966.

Moskowitz, Sam, *Strange Horizons: The Spectrum of Science Fiction.*   New York, Scribner, 1976.

Moskowitz, Sam, editor, *Under the Moons of Mars: A History and Anthology of "The Scientific Romance" in the Munsey Magazines.*   New York, Holt Rinehart, 1970.

Mullen, R.D., and Darko Suvin, editors, *Science-Fiction Studies: Selected Articles on Science Fiction.*   Boston, Gregg Press, 2 vols., 1976-78.

Nicholls, Peter, editor, *Foundation: The Review of Science Fiction March 1972-March 1975.*   Boston, Gregg Press, 1978.

Nicholls, Peter, editor, *Science Fiction at Large.*   London, Gollancz, 1976; New York, Harper, 1977; as *Explorations of the Marvellous*, London, Fontana, 1978.

Nicholls, Peter, editor, *The Science Fiction Encyclopedia.*   New York, Doubleday, and London, Granada, 1979.

Nicolson, Marjorie Hope, *Voyages to the Moon.*   New York, Macmillan, 1948.

Okada, Masaya, *Illustrated Index to Air Wonder Stories.*   Nagoya, Japan, Okada, 1973.

Owings, Mark and Jack L. Chalker, *The Index to Science-Fantasy Publishers.*   Baltimore, Mirage Press, 1966; revised edition, as *Index to the SF Publishers*, 1979.

Panshin, Alexei and Cory, *SF in Dimension: A Book of Explorations.*   Chicago, Advent, 1976.

Parrinder, Patrick, editor, *Science Fiction: A Critical Guide.*   London, Longman, 1979.

Parrinder, Patrick, *Science Fiction: Its Criticism and Teaching.*   London, Methuen, 1980.

Parrington, Vernon Louis, *American Dreams: A Study of American Utopias.*   Providence, Rhode Island, Brown University, 1947.

Pavlat, Robert and William Evans, editors, *Fanzine Index.*   New York, Piser, 1965.

Pfeiffer, John R., *Fantasy and Science Fiction: A Critical Guide.*   Palmer Lake, Colorado, Filter Press, 1971.

Philmus, Robert, *Into the Unknown: The Evolution of Science Fiction from Francis Godwin to H.G. Wells.*   Berkeley, University of California Press, 1970.

Porter, Andrew, editor, *Experiment Perilous: Three Essays on Science Fiction.*   New York, Algol Press, 1976.

Rabkin, Eric S., *The Fantastic in Literature.*   Princeton, New Jersey, Princeton University Press, 1976.

Reginald, R., *By Any Other Name: A Comprehensive Checklist of Science Fiction and Fantasy Pseudonyms.*   San Bernardino, California, Borgo Press, 1980.

Reginald, R., *A Guide to Science Fiction in the Library of Congress Classification Scheme.*   San Bernardino, California, Borgo Press, 1980.

Reginald, R., *Science Fiction and Fantasy Literature: A Checklist 1700-1974.*   Detroit, Gale, 2 vols., 1979.

Reginald, R., *To Be Continued: An Annotated Bibliography of Science Fiction and Fantasy Series and Sequels.*   San Bernardino, California, Borgo Press, 1980.

Riley, Dick, editor, *Critical Encounters: Writers and Themes in Science Fiction.*   New York, Ungar, 1978.

Roberts, Peter, *Guide to Current Fanzines.*   Privately printed, 1978.

Rock, James A., *Who Goes There? A Bibliographic Dictionary of Pseudonymous Literature in the Fields of Fantasy and Science Fiction.*   Bloomington, Indiana, Rock, 1979.

Roemer, Kenneth M., *The Obsolete Necessity: America in Utopian Writings 1888-1900.*   Kent, Ohio, Kent State University Press, 1976.

Rogers, Alva, *A Requiem for Astounding.*   Chicago, Advent, 1964.

Rose, Lois and Stephen, *The Shattered Ring: Science Fiction and the Quest for Meaning.*   Richmond, Virginia, John Knox Press, and London, SCM Press, 1970.

Rose, Mark, editor, *Science Fiction: A Collection of Critical Essays.*   Englewood Cliffs, New Jersey, Prentice Hall, 1976.

Rottensteiner, Franz, *The Science Fiction Book: An Illustrated History.*   New York, Seabury Press, and London, Thames and Hudson, 1975.

Rovin, Jeff, *The Fabulous Fantasy Films.*   South Brunswick, New Jersey, A.S. Barnes, and London, Yoseloff, 1977.

Sadoul, Jacques, *2000 A.D.: Illustrations from the Golden Age of Science Fiction Pulps.*   Chicago, Regnery, and London, Souvenir Press, 1975.

Samuelson, David N., *Visions of Tomorrow: Six Journeys from Outer to Inner Space.*   New York, Arno Press, 1975.

Sargent, Lyman T., *British and American Utopian Literature 1516-1975.*   Boston, Hall, 1979.

Scholes, Robert, *Structural Fabulation.*   Notre Dame, Indiana, University of Notre Dame Press, 1975.

Scholes, Robert, and Eric S. Rabkin, *Science Fiction: History, Science, Vision.*   New York, Oxford University Press, 1977.

Schweitzer, Darrell, editor, *SF Voices.*   Baltimore, T-K Graphics, 1976.

Searles, Baird, and others, *A Reader's Guide to Science Fiction.*   New York, Avon, 1979.

Siemon, Frederick, *Science Fiction Story Index 1950-1968.*   Chicago, American Library Association, 1971.

Silverberg, Robert, *Drug Themes in Science Fiction.*   Rockville, Maryland, National Institute on Drug Abuse, 1974.

Reed, Peter J., *Kurt Vonnegut, Jr.* New York, Warner, 1972.

Roy, John Flint, *A Guide to Barsoom* (on Edgar Rice Burroughs). New York, Ballantine, 1976.

Schweitzer, Darrell, editor, *Essays Lovecraftian.* Baltimore, T-K Graphics, 1976.

Searles, Baird, *Stranger in a Strange Land and Other Works* (on Robert A. Heinlein). Lincoln, Nebraska, Cliffs Notes, 1975.

Schreffler, Philip A., *The H.P. Lovecraft Companion.* Westport, Connecticut, Greenwood Press, 1977.

Sidney-Fryer, Donald, *The Last of the Great Romantic Poets* (on Clark Ashton Smith). Albuquerque, Silver Scarab Press, 1973.

Slusser, George Edgar, *The Bradbury Chronicles.* San Bernardino, California, Borgo Press, 1977.

Slusser, George Edgar, *The Delany Intersection.* San Bernardino, California, Borgo Press, 1977.

Slusser, George Edgar, *The Farthest Shores of Ursula K. Le Guin.* San Bernardino, California, Borgo Press, 1976.

Slusser, George Edgar, *Harlan Ellison: Unrepentant Harlequin.* San Bernardino, California, Borgo Press, 1977.

Slusser, George Edgar, *Robert A. Heinlein: Stranger in His Own Land.* San Bernardino, California, Borgo Press, 1976.

Slusser, George Edgar, *The Space Odysseys of Arthur C. Clarke.* San Bernardino, California, Borgo Press, 1978.

Small, Christopher, *The Road to Miniluv: George Orwell, The State, and God.* London, Gollancz, 1975; Pittsburgh, University of Pittsburgh Press, 1976.

Steinhoff, William, *George Orwell and the Origins of 1984.* Ann Arbor, Michigan, University of Michigan Press, 1975; as *The Road to 1984*, London, Weidenfeld and Nicolson, 1975.

Sullivan, John, editor, *G.K. Chesterton: A Centenary Appraisal.* New York, Barnes and Noble, 1974.

Suvin, Darko, and Robert M. Philmus, editors, *H.G. Wells and Modern Science Fiction.* Lewisburg, Pennsylvania, Bucknell University Press, 1977.

Taylor, Angus, *Philip K. Dick and the Umbrella of Light.* Baltimore, T-K Graphics, 1975.

Tiedman, Richard, *Jack Vance: Science Fiction Stylist.* Wabash, Indiana, Coulson, 1965.

Tyler, J.E.A., *The Tolkien Companion.* London, Macmillan, and New York, St. Martin's Press, 1976; revised edition, as *The New Tolkien Companion*, Macmillan, 1979, St. Martin's Press, 1980.

Underwood, Tim, and Chuck Miller, editors, *Jack Vance.* New York, Taplinger, 1980.

Wagar, W. Warren, *H.G. Wells and the World State.* New Haven, Connecticut, Yale University Press, 1961.

Walker, Dale L., *The Alien Worlds of Jack London.* Grand Rapids, Michigan, Wolf House, 1973.

Watney, John, *Mervyn Peake.* London, Joseph, 1976.

Watt, Donald, editor, *Aldous Huxley: The Critical Heritage.* London, Routledge, 1975.

Weinberg, Robert, editor, *The Man Behind Doc Savage: A Tribute to Lester Dent.* Privately printed, 1974.

West, Richard C., *Tolkien Criticism: An Annotated Checklist.* Kent, Ohio, Kent State University Press, 1970.

Williams, Raymond, editor, *George Orwell: A Collection of Critical Essays.* Englewood Cliffs, New Jersey, Prentice Hall, 1974.

Williamson, Jack, *H.G. Wells, Critic of Progress.* Baltimore, Mirage Press, 1973.

Wise, S., *The Darkover Dilemma* (on Marion Zimmer Bradley). Baltimore, T-K Graphics, 1976.

Yoke, Carl B., *A Reader's Guide to Roger Zelazny.* West Linn, Oregon, Starmont House, 1979.

Zamyatin, Yevgeny, *A Soviet Heretic: Essays* (includes essay on Wells), translated by Mirra Ginsburg. Chicago, University of Chicago Press, 1970.

EDITOR'S NOTE

The selection of writers included in this book is based upon the recommendations of the advisers listed on page xvii.

The main part of the book covers English-language writers of science fiction since 1895. Appendices include selective representation of authors in other languages whose works have been translated into English, and of major fantasy writers.

The entry for each writer in the main part of the book consists of a biography, a bibliography, and a signed critical essay. Living authors were invited to add a comment on their work. The bibliographies list all books, including non-science-fiction works. Original British and United States editions of all books have been listed; other editions are listed only if they are the first editions. As a rule all uncollected science-fiction short stories published since the entrant's last collection have been listed; complete short story listings occur for writers whose reputations rest primarily on their short stories. Entries include notations of published bibliographies and manuscript collections. Other critical materials appear in the Reading List of secondary works on the genre.

I wish to thank Donald H. Tuck, Peter Nicholls, R. Reginald, William Contento, and Lloyd Currey for their now-indispensable reference books. Thanks go also to the many entrants who took the time to complete an extensive questionnaire. Finally, thanks are due to the University of Houston at Clear Lake City for the leave of absence which allowed me to lay the groundwork for this book.

ADVISERS

Brian Aldiss
John Brunner
Malcolm Edwards
John Eggeling
Charles Elkins
H.W. Hall
Lee Harding
Rosemary Herbert
Van Ikin
David Ketterer

Robert M. Philmus
Christopher Priest
Pamela Sargent
Robert Scholes
Baird Searles
Brian M. Stableford
Darko Suvin
Michael J. Tolley
Donald H. Tuck
Marshall B. Tymn

CONTRIBUTORS

Mitchell Aboulafia
Brian Aldiss
Rosemarie Arbur
Thomas D. Bacig
Douglas Barbour
George W. Barlow
Myra Barnes
Marleen S. Barr
Craig Wallace Barrow
Ruth Berman
E. R. Bishop
Michael Bishop
Russell Blackford
Bernadette Bosky
John P. Brennan
Peter A. Brigg
R.E. Briney
Mary T. Brizzi
John Brunner
Karen Burns
Peter Caracciolo
Steven R. Carter
Rosemary Coleman
T. Collins
Gary Coughlan
Richard Cowper
J. Randolph Cox
Michael Cule
Charles Cushing
Don D'Ammassa
David A. Drake
Grace Eckley
Karren C. Edwards
Alex Eisenstein
Peter Berresford Ellis
Eric A. Fontaine
Jeff Frane
Robert Froese
Alice Carol Gaar
John V. Garner
Walter Gillings
Stephen H. Goldman
Joan Gordon
Martin H. Greenberg
Colin Greenland
Rose Flores Harris
David G. Hartwell
Donald M. Hassler
Rosemary Herbert
Norman L. Hills
Terry Hughes

Elizabeth Anne Hull
Marvin W. Hunt
Van Ikin
Anne Hudson Jones
Robert L. Jones
Kenneth Jurkiewicz
Julius Kagarlitsky
Hilary Karp
George Kelley
John Kinnaird
David Lake
Donald L. Lawler
Michael M. Levy
James A. Livezey
Christopher Lowder
Robert A.W. Lowndes
Richard A. Lupoff
Peter Lynch
Andrew Macdonald
Gina Macdonald
Anthony Manousos
Patrick L. McGuire
Walter E. Meyers
Sandra Miesel
Richard W. Miller
Francis J. Molson
Lee Montgomerie
Will Murray
Susan L. Nickerson
William P. Nolan
Chad Oliver
Gerald W. Page
Diane Parkin-Speer
Michael Perkins
John R. Pfeiffer
Gene Phillips
Hazel Pierce
Nick Pratt
Bill Pronzini
Joseph A. Quinn
Eric S. Rabkin
Robert Reilly
Lawrence R. Ries
Natalie M. Rosinsky
Franz Rottensteiner
Joanna Russ
David N. Samuelson
Pamela Sargent
Harvey J. Satty
John Scarborough
Roger C. Schlobin

Darrell Schweitzer
Baird Searles
Kathryn L. Seidel
Susan M. Shwartz
Curtis C. Smith
Carol L. Snyder
Judith Snyder
Katherine Staples
Philippa Stephensen-Payne
Graham Stone
Leon E. Stover
C.W. Sullivan III
Judith Summers
Darko Suvin
Paul Swank
Norman Talbot
Robert Thurston
Michael J. Tolley
Frank H. Tucker
George Turner
Lisa Tuttle
Jana I. Tuzar

Marylyn Underwood
Steven Utley
W. Warren Wagar
Karl Edward Wagner
Ian Watson
Douglas E. Way
Karen G. Way
Jane B. Weedman
Mary S. Weinkauf
Dennis M. Welch
Fred D. White
Robert H. Wilcox
Cherry Wilder
David Wingrove
Gary K. Wolfe
Gene Wolfe
Anthony Wolk
Susan Wood
Martin Morse Wooster
Alice Chambers Wygant
Carl B. Yoke
George Zebrowski

Robert Abernathy
Mark Adlard
Brian Aldiss
Grant Allen
Kingsley Amis
Chester Anderson
Colin Anderson
Poul Anderson
F. Anstey
Piers Anthony
Christopher Anvil
Edwin L. Arnold
Fenton Ash
Isaac Asimov
Robert Asprin
John Atkins

J.G. Ballard
Arthur K. Barnes
Neal Barrett, Jr.
John Barth
T.J. Bass
Harry Bates
L. Frank Baum
John Baxter
Barrington John Bayley
Greg Bear
Charles Beaumont
Edward Bellamy
Stephen Vincent Benét
Gregory Benford
J.D. Beresford
Bryan Berry
Herbert Best
Alfred Bester
Lloyd Biggle, Jr.
Eando Binder
David F. Bischoff
Michael Bishop
Jerome Bixby
Christopher Blayre
James Blish
Robert Bloch
John Boland
Nelson S. Bond
J.F. Bone
Anthony Boucher
Sydney J. Bounds
Ben Bova
John Boyd
Leigh Brackett
Ray Bradbury
Marion Zimmer Bradley
Reginald Bretnor
Miles J. Breuer
Damien Broderick
Fredric Brown
James Cooke Brown
Rosel George Brown
John Brunner
Edward Bryant
Frank Bryning
Algis Budrys
Kenneth Bulmer
David R. Bunch
Eugene Burdick
Anthony Burgess
Edgar Rice Burroughs
William S. Burroughs
F.M. Busby
Octavia E. Butler
Samuel Butler

Martin Caidin
John W. Campbell, Jr.

Paul Capon
Terry Carr
Angela Carter
Lin Carter
Cleve Cartmill
Jack L. Chalker
A. Bertram Chandler
Louis Charbonneau
Suzy McKee Charnas
C.J. Cherryh
G.K. Chesterton
Robert Chilson
Charles Chilton
John Christopher
Arthur C. Clarke
Hal Clement
Mark Clifton
Stanton A. Coblentz
Theodore R. Cogswell
D.G. Compton
Richard Condon
Michael G. Coney
Robert Conquest
Edmund Cooper
Alfred Coppel
Lee Correy
Juanita Coulson
Robert Coulson
Jeni Couzyn
Richard Cowper
Erle Cox
Michael Crichton
Robert Cromie
John Keir Cross
John Crowley
Ray Cummings

Jack Dann
Arsen Darnay
Avram Davidson
Lionel Davidson
Hugh Sykes Davies
L.P. Davies
Chan Davis
Gerry Davis
L. Sprague de Camp
Miriam Allen deFord
Samuel R. Delany
Lester del Rey
Lester Dent
August Derleth
Gene DeWeese
Philip K. Dick
Peter Dickinson
Gordon R. Dickson
Thomas M. Disch
Sonya Dorman
Arthur Conan Doyle
Gardner Dozois
David A. Drake
Theodora DuBois
David Duncan
Lawrence Durrell

G.C. Edmondson
Geo. Alec Effinger
Max Ehrlich
Larry Eisenberg
Phyllis Eisenstein
Gordon Eklund
M. Barnard Eldershaw
Suzette Haden Elgin
Sumner Locke Elliott
Harlan Ellison
Carol Emshwiller

Sylvia Engdahl
George Allan England
Paul Ernst
Lloyd Arthur Eshbach
E. Everett Evans

Paul W. Fairman
Ralph Milne Farley
Philip José Farmer
Mick Farren
Howard Fast
Jonathan Fast
Edward Douglas Fawcett
John Russell Fearn
Jack Finney
Nicholas Fisk
Constantine FitzGibbon
Homer Eon Flint
Charles L. Fontenay
E.M. Forster
Alan Dean Foster
Gardner F. Fox
Pat Frank
Michael Frayn
Steve Frazee
Nancy Freedman
Gertrude Friedberg
H.B. Fyfe

Raymond Z. Gallun
Daniel F. Galouye
Randall Garrett
Jean Mark Gawron
Curt Gentry
Peter George
Hugo Gernsback
David Gerrold
Mark S. Geston
J.U. Giesy
Stephen Gilbert
Tom Godwin
H.L. Gold
Stephen Goldin
William Golding
Rex Gordon
Stuart Gordon
Phyllis Gotlieb
Felix C. Gotschalk
Ron Goulart
Charles L. Grant
Robert Graves
Curme Gray
Joseph Green
Sam Greenlee
George Griffith
Frederick Philip Grove
Wyman Guin
James E. Gunn
Lindsay Gutteridge

H. Rider Haggard
Isidore Haiblum
J.B.S. Haldane
Jack C. Haldeman
Joe Haldeman
Austin Hall
Edmond Hamilton
Lee Harding
Charles L. Harness
Vincent Harper
Harry Harrison
M. John Harrison
L.P. Hartley
Jon Hartridge
Jacquetta Hawkes

H.F. Heard
Robert A. Heinlein
Zenna Henderson
Joe L. Hensley
Frank Herbert
James Herbert
John Hersey
Philip E. High
James Hilton
Edward D. Hoch
Christopher Hodder-Williams
William Hope Hodgson
Lee Hoffman
James P. Hogan
Robert Holdstock
Cecelia Holland
H.H. Hollis
Robert Hoskins
William Dean Howells
Fred and Geoffrey Hoyle
L. Ron Hubbard
Zach Hughes
E.M. Hull
Evan Hunter
Aldous Huxley
C.J. Cutcliffe Hyne

John Jakes
Laurence M. Janifer
W.E. Johns
D.F. Jones
Langdon Jones
Neil R. Jones
Raymond F. Jones

Colin Kapp
David Karp
Anna Kavan
David H. Keller
Leo P. Kelley
William Melvin Kelley
Arthur Keppel-Jones
Alexander Key
Daniel Keyes
Lee Killough
Vincent King
Rudyard Kipling
Otis Adelbert Kline
Nigel Kneale
Fletcher Knebel
Damon Knight
Norman L. Knight
Arthur Koestler
Dean R. Koontz
C.M. Kornbluth
Michael Kurland
Henry Kuttner

R.A. Lafferty
David Lake
Sterling E. Lanier
Philip Latham
Keith Laumer
Tanith Lee
Ursula K. Le Guin
Fritz Leiber
Murray Leinster
Madeleine L'Engle
William Le Queux
Milton Lesser
Doris Lessing
Ira Levin
C.S. Lewis
Roy Lewis
Sinclair Lewis

Jacqueline Lichtenberg
Alice Lightner
David Lindsay
Alun Llewellyn
Jack London
Charles R. Long
Frank Belknap Long
Noel M. Loomis
H.P. Lovecraft
Robert A.W. Lowndes
Richard A. Lupoff
John Lymington
Elizabeth A. Lynn

John D. MacDonald
R.W. Mackelworth
Katherine MacLean
Pip Maddern
Charles Eric Maine
Barry N. Malzberg
Laurence Manning
George R.R. Martin
David I. Masson
Richard Matheson
Anne McCaffrey
Thomas McClary
J. Francis McComas
Vincent McHugh
J.T. McIntosh
Vonda N. McIntyre
Richard M. McKenna
Dean McLaughlin
Shepherd Mead
S.P. Meek
David Meltzer
Richard C. Meredith
Judith Merril
A. Merritt
Sam Merwin, Jr.
Roy Meyers
P. Schuyler Miller
Walter M. Miller, Jr.
Naomi Mitchison
Thomas F. Monteleone
Michael Moorcock
Brian Moore
C.L. Moore
Patrick Moore
Ward Moore
Dan Morgan
John Morressy
Janet E. Morris

Ray Nelson
Kris Neville
Simon Newcomb
Larry Niven
William F. Nolan
John Norman
Andre Norton
Alan E. Nourse
Philip Francis Nowlan

E.V. Odle
Andrew J. Offutt
Chad Oliver
Bob Olsen
George Orwell

Albert Bigelow Paine
Raymond A. Palmer
Edgar Pangborn
Alexei Panshin
Kit Pedler
Walker Percy

Emil Petaja
Rog Phillips
Marge Piercy
H. Beam Piper
Doris Piserchia
Charles Platt
Frederik Pohl
Arthur Porges
Jerry Pournelle
John Cowper Powys
Festus Pragnell
Fletcher Pratt
Christopher Priest
J.B. Priestley
Joe Pumilia
Tom Purdom
Thomas Pynchon

John Rackham
Ayn Rand
Marta Randall
John Rankine
Rick Raphael
Francis G. Rayer
Herbert Read
Tom Reamy
Kit Reed
Ed Earl Repp
Mack Reynolds
Walt and Leigh Richmond
Keith Roberts
Stephen Robinett
Frank M. Robinson
Spider Robinson
Ross Rocklynne
Richard Rohmer
Mordecai Roshwald
William Rotsler
Victor Rousseau
Joanna Russ
Bertrand Russell
Eric Frank Russell
Ray Russell

Fred Saberhagen
Margaret St. Clair
James Sallis
Sarban
Pamela Sargent
Richard Saxon
Josephine Saxton
Nat Schachner
Stanley Schmidt
James H. Schmitz
Thomas N. Scortia
Hank Searls
Arthur Sellings
Luis P. Senarens
Rod Serling
Garrett P. Serviss
Alan Seymour
Jack Sharkey
Richard S. Shaver
Bob Shaw
Robert Sheckley
R.C. Sherriff
M.P. Shiel
Wilmar H. Shiras
Nevil Shute
Alan Sillitoe
Robert Silverberg
Clifford D. Simak
Upton Sinclair
Curt Siodmak
B.F. Skinner

Kathleen Sky
John Sladek
Henry Slesar
William M. Sloane
Clark Ashton Smith
Cordwainer Smith
E.E. Smith
Evelyn E. Smith
George H. Smith
George O. Smith
Jerry Sohl
Norman Spinrad
Brian M. Stableford
Olaf Stapledon
Christopher Stasheff
Andrew M. Stephenson
Francis Stevens
George R. Stewart
Hank Stine
Frank R. Stockton
Leon E. Stover
Craig Strete
Theodore Sturgeon
Jeff and Jean Sutton
Leo Szilard

John Taine
Stephen Tall
Peter Tate
William F. Temple
William Tenn
Emma Tennant
Walter Tevis
D.M. Thomas
Robert Thurston
James Tiptree, Jr.
Arthur Train
Louis Trimble
E.C. Tubb
Wilson Tucker
George Turner
Lisa Tuttle
Mark Twain

Steven Utley

Jack Vance
Sydney J. Van Scyoc
A.E. van Vogt
John Varley
Roger Lee Vernon
A. Hyatt Verrill

Gore Vidal
Harl Vincent
Joan D. Vinge
Vernor Vinge
Kurt Vonnegut, Jr.

Edgar Wallace
F.L. Wallace
Ian Wallace
G.C. Wallis
J.M. Walsh
Hugh Walters
Donald Wandrei
Stanley Waterloo
William Jon Watkins
Ian Watson
Stanley G. Weinbaum
Manly Wade Wellman
H.G. Wells
Wallace West
Dennis Wheatley
James White
Ted White
Leonard Wibberley
Cherry Wilder
Kate Wilhelm
John A. Williams
Robert Moore Williams
Jack Williamson
Colin Wilson
Richard Wilson
Robert Anton Wilson
Jack Wodhams
Gary K. Wolf
Bernard Wolfe
Gene Wolfe
Donald A. Wollheim
Austin Tappan Wright
Harold Bell Wright
S. Fowler Wright
Philip Wylie
John Wyndham

Chelsea Quinn Yarbro
Laurence Yep
Michael Young
Robert F. Young

Arthur Leo Zagat
George Zebrowski
Roger Zelazny
Pamela A. Zoline

FOREIGN-LANGUAGE WRITERS

Kobo Abe
Jean-Pierre Andrevon
René Barjavel
Aleksandr Belyaev
Jorge Luis Borges
Pierre Boulle
Karin Boye
Johanna and Günter Braun
Valery Bryusov
Mikhail Bulgakov
Italo Calvino
Karel Capek
Camille Flammarion
Herbert W. Franke
Michel Jeury

Gérard Klein
Sakyo Komatsu
Kurd Lasswitz
Stanislaw Lem
André Maurois
Vladimir Mayakovsky
Josef Nesvadba
Maurice Renard
Albert Robida
Boris and Arkady Strugatsky
Vladimir Tendryakov
Abram Tertz
Alexey Tolstoy
Konstantin Tsiolkovsky
Ilya Varshavsky

Vercors
Jules Verne
Franz Werfel

Ivan Yefremov
Yevgeny Zamyatin

MAJOR FANTASY WRITERS

Lord Dunsany
E.R. Eddison
William Morris

Mervyn Peake
J.R.R. Tolkien

TWENTIETH-CENTURY
SCIENCE-FICTION
WRITERS

ABERNATHY, Robert (Gordon). American. Born in Geneva, Switzerland, in 1924. Educated at Princeton University, New Jersey, A.B. 1952; Ph.D. Served in the United States Army, 1946-48. Married Jean Clarke Montgomery in 1955; one daughter. Journalist: NBC Radio correspondent 1946-48; science editor. Professor of Languages, University of Colorado, Boulder. Since 1973, Trustee, Princeton University. Address: 2900 East Aurora, Apartment 154, Boulder, Colorado 80303, U.S.A.

SCIENCE-FICTION PUBLICATIONS

Uncollected Short Stories

"Mission from Arcturus," in *Science Fiction Quarterly* (Holyoke, Massachusetts), Spring 1943.
"Saboteur of Space," in *Planet* (New York), Spring 1944.
"When the Rockets Come," in *Astounding* (New York), March 1945.
"Failure on Titan," in *Planet* (New York), Winter 1947.
"Hostage of Tomorrow," in *Planet* (New York), Spring 1949.
"The Giants Return," in *Planet* (New York), Fall 1949.
"The Dead-Star Rover," in *Planet* (New York), Winter 1949.
"Peril of the Blue World," in *Flight in Space*, edited by Donald A. Wollheim. New York, Fell, 1950.
"The Ultimate Peril," in *Amazing* (New York), March 1950.
"The Tower of Babel," in *Amazing* (New York), June 1950.
"Righteous Plague," in *Science Fiction Quarterly* (Holyoke, Massachusetts), May 1951.
"Heritage," in *Omnibus of Science Fiction*, edited by Groff Conklin. New York, Crown, 1952.
"The Captain's Getaway," in *Orbit 1* (New York), 1953.
"The Four Commandments," in *Science Fiction Quarterly* (Holyoke, Massachusetts), February 1953.
"Lifework," in *Science Fiction Quarterly* (Holyoke, Massachusetts), May 1953.
"Professor Schlucker's Fallacy," in *Fantasy and Science Fiction* (New York), November 1953.
"The Record of Corrupira," in *Fantastic Universe* (Chicago), January 1954.
"Tag," in *Beyond* (New York), January 1954.
"When the Mountain Shook," in *If* (New York), March 1954.
"The Firefighters," in *Fantasy and Science Fiction* (New York), March 1954.
"The Thousandth Year," in *Astounding* (New York), April 1954.
"The Marvelous Movie," in *Future* (New York), August 1954.
"The Fishers," in *Fantasy and Science Fiction* (New York), December 1954.
"Heirs Apparent," in *Best from Fantasy and Science Fiction 4*, edited by Anthony Boucher. New York, Doubleday, 1955.
"Axolotl," in *Best Science Fiction Stories and Novels 1955*, edited by T.E. Dikty. New York, Fell, 1955; as " Deep Space," in *5 Tales from Tomorrow*, edited by Dikty, New York, Fawcett, 1957.
"World of the Drone," in *Imagination* (Evanston, Illinois), January 1955.
"The Guzzler," in *Science Fiction Quarterly* (Holyoke, Massachusetts), May 1955.
"The Year 2000," in *Fantasy and Science Fiction* (New York), January 1956.
"One of Them?" in *Science Fiction Quarterly* (Holyoke, Massachusetts), May 1956.
"The Laugh," in *Fantastic Universe* (Chicago), June 1956.
"Hour Without Glory," in *Fantasy and Science Fiction* (New York), July 1956.
"Grandma's Lie Soap, " in *SF: The Year's Greatest Science Fiction and Fantasy*, edited by Judith Merril. New York, Dell, 1957.
"The Canal Builders, " in *Every Boy's Book of Outer Space Stories*, edited by T.E. Dikty. New York, Fell, 1960.
"Junior," in *SF: The Best of the Best*, edited by Judith Merril. New York, Delacorte Press, 1967.
"Pyramid," in *Anthropology Through Science Fiction*, edited by Carol Mason, Martin H. Greenberg, and Patricia Warrick. New York, St. Martin's Press, 1974.
"Single Combat, " in *Sociology Through Science Fiction*, edited by

John W. Milstead and others. New York, St. Martin's Press, 1974.
"Strange Exodus," in *Space Odysseys*, edited by Brian W. Aldiss. London, Futura, 1974; New York, Doubleday, 1976.
"The Rotifers," in *Earth Is the Strangest Planet*, edited by Robert Silverberg. Nashville, Nelson, 1977.

*   *   *

Robert Abernathy is a thoroughly enjoyable writer with a number of strings to his bow. He is gifted with wit and sagacity, and his style is equal to any demand he makes on it (though he seldom goes in for verbal fireworks), but he has had no new stories published since the 1950's and no collection has appeared in book form.

Like many science-fiction writers, Abernathy began publishing early, and two of his earliest stories are excellent. "Heritage" is a study of the far future of the world and the question as to who shall succeed the degenerate human race; it is told by "the great time traveler, Nicholas Doody." "Peril of the Blue World" is a story of the Martian Expedition to Earth and why it failed: the tone is light and the narrator in perfect control; Anthony Boucher could do no better.

In "The Canal Builders" Earthmen have long been established on Mars, which they visit by teleportation; but when at last a manned interplanetary rocket is sent, the travellers find a ruined city they have never heard of. Another very different story set on Mars is "When the Rockets Come," which studies the harsh frontier society and the character of the hero. Vic Denning is a successor to Achilles or to Sir Bors: the hero who is never so happy as when his life is in danger. But "when the rockets come, it is not war"; valour and chivalry are obsolete.

Several stories contrast man with other races. In "Pyramid" man is imported to the planet Thegeth to dispose of an infestation of hamsters that have ruined the ecological balance. The thagatha, who have foolishly imported man, value above all else the balance of nature. Man, on the other hand, turns out to be an infestation without parallel; and the thagatha are completely unable to comprehend their motives. "The Rotifers," which takes place on Earth, features a 12-year-old boy who is examining pond life in his microscope. But as he does so, the rotifers also examine man, and are most displeased to learn of his existence. The sinister quality of this tale is admirable. "The Thousandth Year" contrasts man with an empire-ruling race of squidlike beings, this time much to man's advantage. The Ratk are taught never to trust anyone, and their constant suspicion is their downfall.

One of Abernathy's best and funniest stories, "Junior," deals with the generation gap. Most of what the earnest elders teach is based on experience, though not necessarily true. Junior, the rebellious polyp, manages to transcend the parental wisdom—emphatically. I pity anyone who tries to translate the new changes rung on old clichés in this story. "Axolotl" is a powerful story. It describes the first man to travel in space (some seven years early), and that part of the story has dated slightly. But the passages about the axolotl emerging from the ocean and undergoing a transformation it could not foresee remain powerful and moving. Space travel has not yet produced in us the transformation Abernathy describes; but the metaphor is immensely suggestive still.

Some of Abernathy's space opera remains lively: "The Dead-Star Rover," "Hostage of Tomorrow," "The Giants Return," and even "The Ultimate Peril," with its evil insect-like aliens who use one hundred percent of their brains. Other stories make more serious use of the author's strong sense of history: "Heirs Apparent" could have been a novel in other hands, but Abernathy wrote a long story of events on the Russian steppe after a Third World War, with expert cutting and no words wasted. "Hour Without Glory" is a fine short study of the military mind. And "One of Them?" is one of the most beautiful stories on the android theme that I have ever read.

Someone should bring out an Abernathy collection; his work is too good to remain buried in the reference libraries.

—Charles Cushing

ADLARD, Mark. British. Born in Seaton Carew, County Durham, 19 June 1932. Educated at Trinity College, Cambridge, 1951-54, B.A. 1954, M.A.; Oxford University, 1954-55; University of London, B.Sc. (extra-mural) in economics. Married Sheila Rosemary Skuse in 1968; one daughter and one son. Executive in the steel industry, in Middlesbrough, Yorkshire, Cardiff, and Kent, 1956-76. Since 1976, full-time writer. Agent: Ed Victor Ltd., 27 Soho Square, London W1V 6AY. Address: 12 The Green, Seaton Carew, Hartlepool, Cleveland TS25 1AS, England.

SCIENCE-FICTION PUBLICATIONS

Novels (series: Tcity in all books)

Interface. London, Sidgwick and Jackson, 1971; New York, Ace, 1977.
Volteface. London, Sidgwick and Jackson, 1972; New York, Ace, 1978.
Multiface. London, Sidgwick and Jackson, 1975; New York, Ace, 1978.

Uncollected Short Stories

"The Other Tradition" and "Theophilus," in *Beyond This Horizon,* edited by Christopher Carrell. Sunderland, Ceolfrith Press, 1973.

OTHER PUBLICATIONS

Novel

The Greenlander. London, Hamish Hamilton, 1978; New York, Summit, 1979.

Other

"Billion Year Spree: A Labour of Love," in *Foundation 6* (London), May 1974.

Mark Adlard comments:
One of my main pre-occupations is the importance of personal economic activity to "the good life." It seemed to me that various hypotheses about such matters could be explored fictionally, by presenting a future world in which economic activity had been largely made redundant. This fictional device would also make it possible to consider the moral dilemmas and responsibilities of managerial elites. It was considerations such as these, and not a previous enthusiasm for the genre, that induced me to write "science fiction."

*   *   *

Mark Adlard's Tcity trilogy, *Interface, Volteface,* and *Multiface,* makes up a whole less than the sum of its parts but it is nevertheless a highly interesting and readable work. The parts are considerable and the project ambitious. Reviewing *Multiface* for the *Times Literary Supplement,* T.A. Shippey noted the ironic contrast between the plots and characters of the first two books and those of Wagner's *Ring* and Dante's *Commedia* respectively: "Only the boldest writer would invite such comparisons....But Mark Adlard made a success of it, and has done so once more, in a novel based this time on *The Faerie Queene.*" Shippey is an over-bold reviewer, for his criticism is not just, although it does adumbrate a critical problem. For one thing, Spenser is only one among several important literary sources in *Multiface,* where the controlling reference (matching Wagner and Dante) is to Buddhism; for another, the relationships between the novels and their sources are not the same.

It seems likely that one of the problems is that the three novels were not all completed together. As literature, *Interface* is inferior to the later two. It is overloaded with exposition at the expense of narrative and, although Adlard is clearly aware of the problem (throughout the series, a stock joke is the blunt interruption of robotic exposition), information whether cultural or technological appears to be simply dropped into the text and does not resonate

within it. This is true of the Wagner references, which are only to Götterdämmerung, an odd choice for the first novel of a series. This novel concerns weaknesses at the interface between an enclosed society of drugged citizens and their benevolent, superior managers, weaknesses on both sides, which end in destruction for some but salvation for others. Adlard stands too far off from his characters, and, because the emotive level of the narrative is low, the climactic horrors and pathos fail somewhat in their effect. *Volteface* is much richer in texture, and the Dante references are both more numerous than the *Ring* ones and more deeply embedded in the text; The leading characters are more highly developed, and the narrative consequently more engaging, the ironies more piquant. In the failed Utopia of *Interface,* work had been denied the multitudinous citizens: in response to their discontent, work is reintroduced to Tcity by the executives, who deliberately create an old-fashioned (i.e., 20th-century) managerial structure, knowing this will be inefficient, merely to make work, i.e., the distribution of goods (trinkets) which are, of course, manufactured in fully automated factories. This scheme enables Adlard to write splendid satire as he traces both the collective volte-face and some individual reversals of life in Tcity. The *Inferno* of workfree pleasure is exchanged for a dubious *Purgatorio.* However, I would need to have the author explain to me just how his Dante-Beatrice pair (Twynne and Ventrix) are really illuminated by their source. Ventrix is an interesting character in her own right.

If idle pleasure was hell, work purgatory, then *Multiface* seems to be asking what is the ideal mode of life. The answer is that it depends on the individual life. Even Theravana Buddhism, practised by one saintly executive, may not suit all executives; Mahayana Buddhism, considered more suitable for the citizens, seems too perversely appropriate for the tormented Taggart, persuaded that in a lame dog he sees the reincarnation of his sadistic father, on which he exacts vengeance for this mother's suffering which has blighted the whole of his own life. As Jan Caspol puts it, "Men have different faces. There are no two alike, and you can't expect them to wear the same mask....Even Buddhas only point the way." Jan, though an executive, is the reader's choric companion throughout the series and he thus presumably voices the author's conclusion: but what consequences follow for the executives whose vast experiment has involved the beneficent control of a world society? The author seems to shy away from his bold socio-history, in favour of the predicaments of individuals. Their problems may be resolved for good or ill, but what of the further problems in Tcity? The trilogy seems to call for a further, maturer volume, one which will tell us what life is for, perhaps: we are at least provoked to consideration of this disturbing question. However, it may be in the intuition that life is open-ended, that there are no pat catastrophes, that the trilogy should properly end. One of its most appealing narratives is that of Osbert Osborne, discovering diversity and pattern in the apparently uniform stahlex beeblocks of Tcity (everything there is made of this remarkable versatile new material), yet knowing that he will never have time even to map his own multi-story block. Three faces can stand for the whole infinite polyhedron.

—Michael J. Tolley

AKERS, Alan Burt. *See* **BULMER, Kenneth.**

ALDISS, Brian (Wilson). British. Born in East Dereham, Norfolk, 18 August 1925. Educated at Framlingham College, Suffolk, 1936-39; West Buckland School, 1939-42. Served in the Royal Signals in the Far East, 1943-47. Married Margaret Manson in 1965 (second marriage); four children, two from previous marriage. Bookseller, Oxford, 1947-56; Literary Editor, *Oxford Mail,* 1958-69; Science-Fiction Editor, Penguin Books, London, 1961-64; Art Correspondent, *Guardian,* London. President, British Science Fiction Association, 1960-65; Co-Founder, 1972, and Chairman, 1976-78, John W. Campbell Memorial Award; Co-President, Eurocon Committee, 1975-79; Chairman, Society of Authors, London, 1978-79; Member, Arts Council Literature Panel, 1978-80. Since 1975, Vice-President, Stapledon Society; since 1977, Founding Trustee, World Science Fiction, Dublin. Recipient: World Science Fiction Convention citation, 1959; Hugo Award, 1962; Nebula Award, 1965; Ditmar Award (Australia), 1970; British Science Fiction Association Award, 1972, and Special Award, 1974; Eurocon Award, 1976; James Blish Award, for non-fiction, 1977; Cometa d'Argento (Italy), 1977; Prix Jules Verne, 1977; Pilgrim Award, 1978. Guest of Honour, World Science Fiction Convention, London, 1965, 1979. Agent: A.P. Watt Ltd., 26-28 Bedford Row, London WC1R 4HL. Address: Orchard House, Begbroke, Oxfordshire OX5 1RT, England.

SCIENCE-FICTION PUBLICATIONS

Novels

Non-Stop.   London, Faber, 1958; as *Starship,* New York, Criterion, 1959.
Vanguard from Alpha.   New York, Ace, 1959; as *Equator* (includes "Segregation"), London, Digit, 1961.
Bow Down to Nul.   New York, Ace, 1960; as *The Interpreter,* London, Digit, 1961.
The Male Response.   New York, Galaxy, 1961; London, Dobson, 1963.
The Primal Urge.   New York, Ballantine, 1961; London, Sphere, 1967.
Hothouse.   London, Faber, 1962; Boston, Gregg Press, 1976; abridged edition, as *The Long Afternoon of Earth,* New York, New American Library, 1962.
The Dark Light-Years.   London, Faber, and New York, New American Library, 1964.
Greybeard.   London, Faber, and New York, Harcourt Brace, 1964.
Earthworks.   London, Faber, 1965; New York, Doubleday, 1966.
An Age.   London, Faber, 1967; as *Cryptozoic!,* New York, Doubleday, 1968.
Report on Probability A.   London, Faber, 1968; New York, Doubleday, 1969.
Barefoot in the Head.   London, Faber, 1969; New York, Doubleday, 1970.
Frankenstein Unbound.   London, Cape, 1973; New York, Random House, 1974.
The Eighty-Minute Hour.   London, Cape, and New York, Doubleday, 1974.
The Malacia Tapestry.   London, Cape, 1976; New York, Harper, 1977.
Enemies of the System.   London, Cape, and New York, Harper, 1978.
Moreau's Other Island.   London, Cape, 1980; as *An Island Called Moreau,* New York, Simon and Schuster, 1981.

Short Stories

Space, Time, and Nathaniel: Presciences.   London, Faber, 1957; abridged edition, as *No Time Like Tomorrow,* New York, New American Library, 1959.
The Canopy of Time.   London, Faber, 1959; revised edition as *Galaxies Like Grains of Sand,* New York, New American Library, 1960.
The Airs of Earth.   London, Faber, 1963.
Starswarm.   New York, New American Library, 1964; London, Panther, 1979.
Best Science Fiction Stories of Brian Aldiss.   London, Faber, 1965; as *Who Can Replace a Man?,* New York, Harcourt Brace, 1966; revised edition, Faber, 1971.

The Saliva Tree and Other Strange Growths.   London, Faber, 1966.
Intangibles Inc. and Other Stories.   London, Faber, 1969.
Neanderthal Planet.   New York, Avon, 1970.
The Moment of Eclipse.   London, Faber, 1970; New York, Doubleday, 1972.
The Book of Brian Aldiss.   New York, DAW, 1972; as *Comic Inferno,* London, New English Library, 1973.
Excommunication.   London, Post Card Partnership, 1975.
Last Orders and Other Stories.   London, Cape, 1977.
New Arrivals, Old Encounters.   London, Cape, 1979; New York, Harper, 1980.

OTHER PUBLICATIONS

Novels

The Brightfount Diaries.   London, Faber, 1955.
The Hand-Reared Boy.   London, Weidenfeld and Nicolson, and New York, McCall, 1970.
A Soldier Erect; or, Further Adventures of the Hand-Reared Boy.   London, Weidenfeld and Nicolson, and New York, Coward McCann, 1971.
Brothers of the Head.   London, Pierrot, 1977; New York, Two Continents, 1978.
A Rude Awakening.   London, Weidenfeld and Nicolson, 1978; New York, Random House, 1979.
Brothers of the Head, and Where the Lines Converge.   London, Panther, 1979.
Life in the West.   London, Weidenfeld and Nicolson, 1980.

Play

Distant Encounters, adaptation of his own stories (produced London, 1978).

Verse

Pile: Petals from St. Klaed's Computer.   London, Cape, and New York, Holt Rinehart, 1979.

Other

"One That Could Control the Moon: Science Fiction Plain and Coloured," in *International Literary Annual 3,* edited by Arthur Boyars and Pamela Lyon.   London, Calder, 1961.
"Judgment at Jonbar," in *SF Horizons* (London), 1964.
"British Science Fiction Now," in *SF Horizons* (London), 1965.
Cities and Stones: A Traveller's Jugoslavia.   London, Faber, 1966.
The Shape of Further Things: Speculations on Change.   London, Faber, 1970; New York, Doubleday, 1971.
"The Wounded Land: J.G. Ballard," in *SF: The Other Side of Realism,* edited by Thomas D. Clareson.   Bowling Green, Ohio, Bowling Green University Press, 1972.
Billion Year Spree: A History of Science Fiction.   London, Weidenfeld and Nicolson, and New York, Doubleday, 1973.
"The Profession of Science Fiction 7: Magic and Bare Boards," in *Foundation 6* (London), May 1974.
Science Fiction Art, illustrated by Chris Foss.   New York, Bounty, 1975; London, Hart Davis, 1976.
"Dick's Maledictory Web: About and Around *Martian Time-Slip,*" in *Science-Fiction Studies* (Terre Haute, Indiana), March 1975.
"On Being a Literary Pariah," in *Extrapolation* (Wooster, Ohio), May 1976.
"What Dark Non-Literary Passions" (on Stanislaw Lem), in *Science-Fiction Studies* (Terre Haute, Indiana), July 1977.
Science Fiction as Science Fiction.   Frome, Somerset, Bran's Head, 1978.
"The Gulf and the Forest: Contemporary SF in Britain," in *Fantasy and Science Fiction* (New York), April 1978.
This World and Nearer Ones: Essays Exploring the Familiar.   London, Weidenfeld and Nicolson, 1979.
"The Hand in the Jar: Metaphor in Wells and Huxley," in *Foundation 17* (London), September 1979.

Editor, *Penguin Science Fiction*. London, Penguin, 1961; *More
Penguin Science Fiction*, 1963; *Yet More Penguin Science Fic-
tion*, 1964; 3 vols. collected as *The Penguin Science Fiction
Omnibus*, 1973.

Editor, *Best Fantasy Stories*. London, Faber, 1962.

Editor, *Last and First Men*, by Olaf Stapledon. London, Penguin,
1963.

Editor, *Introducing SF*. London, Faber, 1964.

Editor, with Harry Harrison, *Nebula Award Stories 2*. New York,
Doubleday, 1967; as *Nebula Award Stories 1967*, London, Gollancz, 1967.

Editor, *Farewell, Fantastic Venus*. London, Macdonald, 1968;
abridged edition, as *All about Venus*, New York, Dell, 1968.

Editor, with Harry Harrison, *Best SF 1967* [to *1975*]. New York,
Putnam, 7 vols., and Indianapolis, Bobbs Merrill, 2 vols., 1968-
75; as *The Year's Best Science Fiction 1-9*, London, Sphere, 9
vols., 1968-76.

Editor, with Harry Harrison, *The Astounding-Analog Reader*.
New York, Doubleday, 1972; London, Sphere, 2 vols., 1973.

Editor, *Space Opera*. London, Weidenfeld and Nicolson, 1974;
New York, Doubleday, 1975.

Editor, *Space Odysseys*. London, Futura, 1974; New York, Doubleday, 1976.

Editor, with Harry Harrison, *SF Horizons*. New York, Arno
Press, 1975.

Editor, with Harry Harrison, *Hell's Cartographers: Some Personal
Histories of Science Fiction Writers*. London, Weidenfeld and
Nicolson, and New York, Harper, 1975.

Editor, with Harry Harrison, *Decade: The 1940's*, The 1950's, The
1960's. London, Macmillan, 3 vols., 1975-77; *The 1940's* and
The 1950's, New York, St. Martin's Press, 2 vols., 1978.

Editor, *Evil Earths*. London, Weidenfeld and Nicolson, 1975;
New York, Avon, 1979.

Editor, *Galactic Empires*. London, Weidenfeld and Nicolson, 2
vols., 1976; New York, St. Martin's Press, 2 vols., 1977.

Editor, *Perilous Planets*. London, Weidenfeld and Nicolson,
1978; New York, Avon, 1980.

*

Bibliography: *Item Eighty-Three: Brian Aldiss: A Bibliography
1954-1972* by Margaret Aldiss, Oxford, Bocardo Press, 1972.

Manuscript Collection: Bodleian Library, Oxford University.

Brian Aldiss comments:

If you ask an author about his own work, you will get an earful of
propaganda, however beautifully camouflaged or phrased. For a
start I'll recommend interested parties to Richard Mathews' excellent and concise survey of my writing, *Aldiss Unbound* (San Bernardino, California, Borgo Press, 1977). Several other critical
works are being prepared, including a major evaluative work by
Professor Willis McNelly, which may relieve me of the necessity—
or even the ability—to write again.

I try to nourish people's imaginations: to imagine people, and to
people imagination. As when I began, so now: I wrote science
fiction because I saw in it a tremendous and dangerous freedom for
the writer. Freedom I craved, freedom from being confined to one
job or one country. So my books have ranged the spectrum of
science fiction and enlarged it; I am uncertain whether my most
richly textured novel, *The Malacia Tapestry*, should be regarded as
SF, fantasy, historical novel, allegory, or what—but that suits me,
and I hope it will suit some readers who, like me, hate categories.
One's work should embrace as much of the real world as possible.

My stories take place on many worlds, my central characters have
been of many nationalities. Consequently, speech is a major preoccupation; in my first novel, *Non-Stop*, I attempted to employ a sort
of heightened speech for my characters—in particular for Marapper
the Priest—and ever since, my people have addressed each other in a
variety of tongues. Perhaps because of this interest, I travel about
the world a good deal. The music of home-made varieties of English
refreshes a novelist's ear and his sense of humour.

If I'm one of the most travelled authors, I've also done most of the
odd jobs going in the SF field—often egged on by my old pal Harry
Harrison, who is as energetic as I am lazy. Book reviewing, film

reviewing, editing, anthologising, producing series, writing a history of the field, compiling a survey of SF art—in all these things,
curiosity rather than necessity has been the driving force. Now I
have "joined the opposition" and taken shares in a publishing
house.

Readers sometimes find it remarkable that I have written three
best-sellers (the Horatio Stubbs series, *A Hand-Reared Boy, A
Soldier Erect*, and *A Rude Awakening*) which have nothing to do
with science fiction. I do not see unbridgeable differences. My
fictions all concern underdogs in one disastrous situation or
another. However, it would be too easy to assume from this that my
view of life is gloomy, or that I regard myself as an underdog. My
life has been fortunate—not least in the fact that I immensely enjoy
writing (novels rather than this sort of thing) and regard the various
stages of creating a novel as a sensuous pleasure.

Much of my writing is humorous, or has a satirical edge. There is
little violence in my science fiction; I rarely blow worlds to pieces,
unless to make a reader feel sorry (rather than good) about it. I'm
told there is a certain amount of mysticism in my books, which
perhaps explains why they seem more popular in California than
the Eastern Seaboard. They are probably more popular in the UK
than the USA, because I use a touch of irony on my palette, a tone
with which the British are more familiar than the Americans, owing
to the lessons of history, etc. Post-Nixonians are catching up fast.

My novels are simple and accessible. *Non-Stop* is about a big
spaceship, *Hothouse* a big jungle, *Barefoot* a big trap, *The Malacia
Tapestry* a big town, and so on. My short stories, being shorter, are
about smaller things. Many of my novels are still quite dear to me,
even when I can see their faults, perhaps because they were built
with affection.

I would like to live in California or Hong Kong or Malaysia or
Sumatra or Jugoslavia or Italy or Denmark or Australia. Not
forever, of course; say a century in each place. Many of my novels
and stories make free with the time which is so economically dealt
out to us in real life.

*   *   *

In the Author's Note to his most recent collection, Brian Aldiss
says: "See, my stories are about human woes, non-communication,
disappointment, endurance, acceptance, love. Aren't those things
real enough?" They are, as are his stories, creating an *oeuvre* which
for breadth of vision and variety of formal experimentation is
unmatched in the genre. As one critic has proposed, Aldiss's two
gods are Proteus, the enigmatic shape-changer, and Prometheus,
the seeker of forbidden knowledge, fire-bringer, willing martyr in
the battle against the forces of tyranny. Thus his works not only
speak out against the repressive aspects of the human imagination
but by doing so in so many different and wittily stunning ways also
formally demonstrate the power of liberated creativity.

Some might argue that Aldiss's ability to write any kind of story
betrays a lack of a personal "voice," but they would be wrong. The
uniqueness of his voice partly inheres in his willingness to explore
imaginative forms, whether the early, classically perfect, stories of
The Canopy of Time or *Starswarm*, the extraordinary formal experiments of *Report on Probability A* (an SF version of the *nouvelle
roman*) and *Barefoot in the Head* (an attempt to use the language of
Joyce's *Finnegans Wake* to portray the mentality of a Europe
literally bombed by LSD into the "stoned" age), or the extraordinarily assured but never static forms of the recent stories and such
novels as *The Malacia Tapestry*. Like so many British writers,
Aldiss has never had to feel that he should either repeat himself or
apologize for writing SF. As a result, he has always been able to seek
the proper "style" with which to formulate his "content" most fully,
which is to say he has always recognized the ways in which style and
content are indivisible. From the beginning he has expanded his
knowledge of and ability to handle technique and recognized the
need to push against the conventional boundaries of the genre.

If he has refused to be held down by the conventionality of most
SF, Aldiss has never turned his back on it. Indeed, as his various
anthologies and *Billion Year Spree* show, he has always loved it all.
But he is fully aware of the negative imaginative effects of what he
calls "power-fantasy," and has sought as "a real writer" to transcend
the kind of writing which only transforms "a man into an organ of
conquest in a knocking-shop of wish-fulfilment." Thus, even in his

early works, set in far-distant futures of galactic empires or the end of the solar system (*Hothouse*), he tends to look at the human and emotional sides of events: the need individuals will always have for love and communication/community; the ways in which imaginative empathy can help people to face their lives; the qualities of courage and endurance we all need to survive, whether in the face of "ordinary" life or the end of all life as we know it.

Such a varied and multiplex *oeuvre* evades all simple systems of categorization. Certainly Aldiss always gives his readers rich and emotionally satisfying entertainment. And he always infuses his stories with powerful feelings, though the later fictions achieve far subtler nuances than the earliest stories do. From the very beginning, moreover, he reveals a particular capacity for a kind of elegiac vision, a quality of speech which uplifts even as it tells of the end of all we hold dear. It's a tone we might associate with Olaf Stapledon were Stapledon's works not so philosophically distanced. Still, Aldiss learned more from Stapledon than he did from Doc Smith, so that such memorable and moving fictions as "Who Can Replace a Man?," "Visiting Amoeba," "A Kind of Artistry," and, especially, the triumphant yet tragically muted "Old Hundredth" bear the full weight of human history and human endeavour. Nor has the elegiac vision ever fully disappeared from his work; it's just as powerfully present, with an even more complex use of SF technology-as-metaphor and greater, more dynamic gracefulness of style in "An Appearance of Life" (*Last Orders*). Here a "Prime Esemplastic Seeker," a sensitive with "a high serendipity factor," discovers in a vast galactic museum that humanity may just be "a projection" of an earlier great race, and, like the imprisoned holographic images of two earlier humans, is "drifting further apart, losing definition." But Aldiss doesn't end on this despairing note; his Seeker exercises the human will he no longer fully believes in to refuse to communicate his discovery to the rest of humankind, a highly moral act. This story and the somewhat similar (and also purely SF) "The Small Stones of Tu Fu" say rather depressing things about humanity's potentiality yet they are not depressing because their elegant and graceful style transcends their seemingly obvious "message" and develops through a complex and paradoxical tension their *real* message, the message of human creativity inherent in all great art.

As well as an elegiac vision, Aldiss has a special affinity for landscapes. From the beautiful evocations of "Old Hundredth," through such varied presentations as the almost hallucinatory visions of *An Age* or the renderings of early 19th-century Switzerland and the almost surreal final descriptions of the eternal ice in *Frankenstein Unbound*, to the deliciously sophisticated versions of city- and country-scapes in *The Malacia Tapestry*, Aldiss uses landscape in a highly coherent manner as metaphor and context rather than mere background.

Because Aldiss hates repeating himself, he continually pushes into new literary territory, yet he remains basically a writer of SF and fantasy (with the exception of the Stubbs series and some non-fiction). Beginning as a superior, though classically restrained, stylist, he moves through intense and brilliant experiments (*Report on Probability A*, *Barefoot in the Head*) and self-conscious fictions which explore both the conventions and the earlier classics of the genre (*Frankenstein Unbound* and *The Eighty-Minute Hour*), to emerge in the 1970's as an assured and elegant master of fictional forms whose power of characterization is sometimes overwhelming.

The writer of a glorious social comedy like *The Malacia Tapestry* and gnomic but captivating or frightening little fictions like the Enigmas in *Last Orders*, the "zeepee" stories, and the evocative, superbly civilized "The Small Stones of Tu Fu," Aldiss has now reached the point where it seems he could write anything he wishes to. He has done so by dint of a long and exhaustive apprenticeship to literature and language, a concern to "never cease exploring" either his medium or the realms of imagination which SF has claimed as its own; the results, at every stage of his career, are stories of great power and originality, stories which stand the test of critical re-reading better than most. And since Brian Aldiss is at the height of his art, it looks as if he will give us many more such stories in the years to come.

—Douglas Barbour

ALLEN, (Charles) Grant (Blairfindie). Also wrote as Cecil Power; Olive Pratt Rayner; Martin Leach Warborough. British. Born in Alwington, near Kingston, Ontario, Canada, 24 February 1848. Educated privately in New Haven, Connecticut; Collège Impériale, Dieppe; King Edward's School, Birmingham; Merton College, Oxford (Senior Classical Postmastership), 1967-70, B.A. (honours) 1871. Married Miss Jerrard in 1873 (second marriage); one son. Professor of Philosophy, Government College, Spanish Town, Jamaica, 1873-76; Tutor in Oxford, 1877; worked on the *Gazetteer of India*, Edinburgh, 1878; staff member, *Daily News*, London, 1879; lived in Surrey from 1880. *Died 28 October 1899.*

SCIENCE-FICTION PUBLICATIONS

Novels

Kalee's Shrine, with May Cotes. Bristol, Arrowsmith, 1886; New York, New Amsterdam, 1897; as *The Indian Mystery,* New Amsterdam, 1902
The Jaws of Death. London, Simpkin Marshall, 1889; New York, New Amsterdam, 1897.
The Great Taboo. London, Chatto and Windus, 1890; New York, Harper, 1891.
The British Barbarians: A Hill-Top Novel. London, Lane, and New York, Putnam, 1895.

Short Stories

Strange Stories. London, Chatto and Windus, 1884.
The Beckoning Hand and Other Stories. London, Chatto and Windus, 1887.
Ivan Greet's Masterpiece. London, Chatto and Windus, 1893.
The Desire of the Eyes and Other Stories. London, Digby Long, 1895; New York, Fenno, 1896.
A Bride from the Desert (includes "Dr. Greatrex's Experiment" and "The Back-Slider"). New York Fenno, 1896.
Twelve Tales, with a Headpiece, a Tailpiece, and an Intermezzo, Being Select Stories. London, Richards, 1899.

OTHER PUBLICATIONS

Novels

Philistia (as Cecil Power). London, Chatto and Windus, 3 vols., and New York, Harper, 1 vol., 1884.
Babylon (as Cecil Power). London, Chatto and Windus, 3 vols., and New York, Appleton, 1 vol., 1885.
In All Shades. London, Chatto and Windus, 3 vols., and Chicago, Rand McNally, 1 vol., 1888.
The Sole Trustee. London, SPCK, 1886.
For Maimie's Sake. London, Chatto and Windus, and New York, Appleton, 1886.
A Terrible Inheritance. London, SPCK, 1887; New York, Crowell, n.d.
This Mortal Coil. London, Chatto and Windus, 3 vols., and New York, Appleton, 1 vol., 1888.
The White's Man's Foot. London, Hatchards, 1888.
The Devil's Die. London, Chatto and Windus, 3 vols., and New York, Lovell, 1 vol., 1888.
The Tents of Shem. London, Chatto and Windus, 3 vols., and New York, Munro, 1 vol., 1889.
Dr. Palliser's Patient. London, Mullen, 1889.
A Living Apparition. London, SPCK, 1889.
Wednesday the Tenth. Boston, Lothrop, 1890; as *The Curise of the Albatross; or, When Was Wednesday the Tenth?,*1898.
Recalled to Life. Bristol, Arrowsmith, and New York, Holt, 1891.
What's Bred in the Bone. London, Tit-Bits, and Boston, Tucker, 1891.
Dumaresq's Daughter. London, Chatto and Windus, 3 vols., and New York, Harper 1 vol., 1891.
The Duchess of Powysland. London, Chatto and Windus, 3 vols., and Boston, Tucker, 1 vol., 1892.

The Scallywag. London, Chatto and Windus, 3 vols., and New York, Cassell, 1 vol., 1893.

Michael's Crag. London, Leadenhall Press, and Chicago, Rand McNally, 1893.

Blood Royal. London, Chatto and Windus, and New York, Cassell, 1893.

An Army Doctor's Romance. London and New York, Tuck, 1893.

At Market Value. London, Chatto and Windus, 2 vols., and Chicago, Neely, 1 vol., 1894.

The Woman Who Did. London, Lane, and Boston, Roberts, 1895.

Under Sealed Orders. London, Chatto and Windus, 3 vols., 1895; New York, New Amsterdam, 1 vol., 1896.

A Splendid Sin. London, F.V. White, 1896; New York, Buckles, 1899.

An African Millionaire. London, Richards, and New York, Arnold, 1897.

The Type-Writer Girl (as Olive Pratt Rayner). London, Pearson, 1897; as Grant Allen, New York, Street and Smith, 1900.

Linnet. London, Richards, 1898; New York, New Amsterdam, 1900.

The Incidental Bishop. London, Pearson, and New York, Appleton, 1898.

Rosalba: The Story of Her Development (as Olive Pratt Rayner). London, Pearson, and New York, Putnam, 1899.

Short Stories

The General's Will and Other Stories. London, Butterworth, 1892.

Moorland Idylls. London, Chatto and Windus, 1896.

Miss Cayley's Adventures. London, Richards, and New York, Putnam, 1899.

Hilda Wade. London, Richards, and New York, Putnam, 1900.

Sir Theodore's Guest and Other Stories. Bristol, Arrowsmith, 1902.

The Reluctant Hangman and Other Stories of Crime, edited by Tom and Enid Schantz. Boulder, Colorado, Aspen Press, 1973.

Verse

The Lower Slopes: Reminiscences of Excursions round the Base of the Hellicon. London, Mathews-Lane, and Chicago, Stone and Kimball, 1894.

Other

Physiological Aesthetics. London, King, 1877; New York, Appleton, 1878.

The Colour-Sense: Its Origin and Development: An Essay in Comparative Psychology. London, Trubner, and Boston, Houghton Osgood, 1879.

Anglo-Saxon Britain. London, SPCK, and New York, Young, 1881.

The Evolutionist at Large. London, Chatto and Windus, 1881; New York, Fitzgerald, 1882; Revised edition, Chatto and Windus, 1884.

Vignettes from Nature. London, Chatto and Windus, 1881; New York, Fitzgerald, 1882.

The Colours of Flowers, as Illustrated in the British Flora. London and New York, Macmillan, 1882.

Colin Clout's Calendar: The Record of a Summer, April-October. London, Chatto and Windus, 1882; New York, Funk and Wagnalls, 1883.

Flowers and Their Pedigrees. London, Longman, 1883; New York, Appleton, 1884.

Nature Studies, with others. London, Wyman and New York, Funk and Wagnalls, 1883.

Biographies of Working Men. London, SPEK, 1884.

Charles Darwin. London, Longman, and New York, Appleton, 1885.

Common Sense Science. Boston, Lothrop, 1887.

A Half-Century of Science, with T.H. Huxley. New York, Haumboldt, 1888.

Force and Energy: A Theory of Dynamics. London, Longman, 1888; New York, Humboldt, 1889.

Falling in Love, with Other Essays on More Exact Branches of Science. London, Smith Elder, 1889; New York, Appleton, 1890.

Individualism and Socialism. Glasgow, Scottish Land Restoration League, 1890 (?)

Science in Arcady. London, Lawrence and Bullen, 1892.

The Tidal Thames. London, Cassell, 1892.

Post-Prandial Philosophy. London, Chatto and Windus, 1894.

In Memoriam George Paul Macdonell. London, Lund, 1895.

The Story of the Plants. London, Newnes, 1895; as *The Plants,* New York, Review of Reviews, 1909.

The Evolution of the Idea of God: An Inquiry into the Origins of Religions. London, Grant Richards, and New York, Holt, 1897.

Tom, Unlimited: A Story for Children (as Martin Leach Warborough). London, Richards, 1897.

Paris. London, Richards, 1897; New York, Wessels, 1900; revised edition, 1906.

Florence. London, Richards, 1897; New York, Wessels, 1900; revised edition, 1906.

Cities of Belgium. London, Richards, 1897; New York, Wessels, 1900; as *Beligum: Its Cities,* Boston, Page 2 vols., 1903.

Venice. London, Richards, 1898; New York, Wessels, 1900.

Flashlights on Nature. New York, Doubleday, 1898; London, Newnes, 1899.

The European Tour: A Handbook for Americans and Colonists. London, Richards, and New York, Dodd Mead, 1899.

The New Hedonism. New York, Tucker, 1900.

Plain Words on the Woman Question. Chicago, Harman, 1900.

In Nature's Workshop. London, Newnes, and New York, Mansfield, 1901.

County and Town in England, Together with Some Annals of Churnside. London, Richards, and New York, Dutton, 1901.

Evolution in Italian Art, edited by J. W. Cruickshank. London, Richards, and New York, Wessels, 1908.

The Hand of God and Other Posthumous Essays. London, Watts, 1909.

Editor, *The Miscellaneous and Posthumous Works of H.T. Buckle,* abridged edition. London, Longman, 2 vols., 1885.

Editor, *The Natural History of Selborne,* by Gilbert White. London, Lane, 1900.

Translator, *The Attis of Caius Valerius Catulus.* London, Nutt, 1892

*   *   *

Besides his "progressive" novels flouting Victorian political and, especially, sexual taboos, such as the famous *The Woman Who Did,* Grant Allen was probably best known to the public through his series of historical guidebooks to Europe. Allen wrote a few SF stories, two of which are collected in *Strange Stores:*"Pausodyne" deals with revival after a century in suspended animation, and "The Child of the Phalanstery" with a future utopian society practicing euthanasia on deformed children. But his only major SF work is the novel *The British Barbarians* in which an enlightened visitor from the 25th-century looks on the culture, religious observances, and erotic proprieties of 1895 England as an anthropologist would on the customs of a primitive tribe. Befriending an unhappy woman, he is for his pains finally shot by her scandalized husband, and fades back to his future. For all its obviousness, the novel is still a very good satire of the peculiar English "propertarianism" and puritanism, and prefigures the anthropological vogue in sophisticated modern SF, mediated through his admirer Wells.

—Darko Suvin

AMIS, Kingsley (William).   Also writes as Robert Markham. British. Born in London, 16 April 1922. Educated at City of London School; St. John's College, Oxford, M.A. Served in the Royal Corps of Signals, 1942-45. Married 1)Hilary Ann Bardwell in 1948 (marriage dissolved, 1965), two sons, including the writer Martin Amis, and one daughter; 2) the writer Elizabeth Jane Howard in 1965. Lecturer in English, University College, Swansea, Wales, 1949-61; Fellow in English, Peterhouse, Cambridge, 1961-63. Visiting Fellow in Creative Writing, Princeton University, New Jersey, 1958-59; Visiting Professor, Vanderbilt University, Nashville, Tennessee, 1967. Recipient: Maugham Award, 1955; *Yorkshire Post* Award, 1974; Campbell Memorial Award, 1976. C.B.E. (Commander, Order of the British Empire), 1981. Agent: Jonathan Clowes & Co., 19 Jeffrey's Place, London NW1 9PP, England.

SCIENCE-FICTION PUBLICATIONS

The Anti-Death League.   London, Gollancz, and New York, Harcourt Brace, 1966.
The Alteration.   London, Cape, 1976; New York, Viking Press, 1977.
Russian Hide-and-Seek.   London, Hutchinson, 1980.

Uncollected Short Stories

"Hemingway in Space," in *Year's Best SF 6,* edited by Judith Merril. New York, Simon and Schuster, 1961; London, Mayflower, 1963.
"Something Strange," in *Five-Odd,* edited by Groff Conklin.   New York, Pyramid, 1964.
"Mason's Life," in *Best SF 1973,* edited by Brian Aldiss and Harry Harrison.   New York, Putnam, 1974; London, Sphere, 1975.

OTHER PUBLICATIONS

Novels

Lucky Jim.   London, Gollancz, and New York, Doubleday, 1954.
That Uncertain Feeling.   London, Gollancz, 1955; New York, Harcourt Brace, 1956.
I Like It Here.   London, Gollancz, and New York, Harcourt Brace, 1958.
Take a Girl Like You.   London, Gollancz, 1960; New York, Harcourt Brace, 1961.
One Fat Englishman.   London, Gollancz, 1963; New York, Harcourt Brace, 1964.
The Egyptologists, with Robert Conquest.   London, Cape, 1965; New York, Random House, 1966.
Colonel Sun: A James Bond Adventure (as Robert Markham). London, Cape, and New York, Harper, 1968.c
I Want It Now.   London, Cape, 1968; New York, Harcourt Brace, 1969.
The Green Man.   London, Cape, 1969; New York, Harcourt Brace, 1970.
Girl, 20.   London, Cape, 1971.
The Riverside Villas Murder.   London, Cape, and New York, Harcourt Brace, 1973.
Ending Up.   London, Cape, and New York, Harcourt Brace, 1974.
Jake's Thing.   London, Hutchinson, 1978; New York, Viking Press, 1979.

Short Stories

My Enemy's Enemy.   London, Gollancz, 1962; New York, Harcourt Brace, 1963.
Penguin Modern Stories 11, with others.   London, Penguin, 1972.
Dear Illusion.   London, Covent Garden Press, 1972.
The Darkwater Hall Mystery.   Edinburgh, Tragara Press, 1978.
Collected Short Stories.   London, Hutchinson, 1980.

Plays

Radio Plays: *Something Strange,* 1962; *The Riverside Villas Murder,* from his own novel, 1976.

Television Plays: *A Question about Hell,* 1964; *The Importance of Being Harry,* 1971; *Dr. Watson and the Darkwater Hall Mystery,* 1974; *See What You've Done* (*Softly, Softly* series), 1974; *We Are All Guilty* (*Against the Crowd* series), 1975; *Break In,* 1975.

Verse

Bright November.   London, Fortune Press, 1947.
A Frame of Mind.   Reading, Berkshire, University of Reading School of Art, 1953.
(Poems).   Oxford, Fantasy Press, 1954.
A Case of Samples: Poems 1946-1956.   London, Gollancz, 1956; New York, Harcourt Brace, 1957.
The Evans Country.   Oxford, Fantasy Press, 1962.
Penguin Modern Poets 2, with Dom Moraes and Peter Porter. London, Penguin, 1962.
A Look round the Estate: Poems 1957-1967.   London, Cape, 1967; New York, Harcourt Brace, 1968.
Wasted, Kipling at Bateman's.   London, Poem-of-the-Month Club, 1973.
Collected Poems 1944-1979.   London, Hutchinson, 1979; New York, Viking Press, 1980.

Recordings: *Kingsley Amis Reading His Own Poems,* Listen, 1962; *Poems,* with Thomas Blackburn, Jupiter, 1962.

Other

Socialism and the Intellectuals.   London, Fabian Society, 1957.
New Maps of Hell: A Survey of Science Fiction.   New York, Harcourt Brace, 1960; London, Gollancz, 1961.
"H.G. Wells," in *War of the Worlds, The Time Machine, and Selected Short Stories,* by Wells.   New York, Platt and Munk, 1963.
The James Bond Dossier.   London, Cape, and New York, New American Library, 1965.
"Science Fiction: A Practical Nightmare," in *Holiday* (Indianapolis), February 1965.
Lucky Jim's Politics.   London, Conservative Political Centre, 1968.
What's Become of Jane Austen? and Other Questions.   London, Cape, 1970; New York, Harcourt Brace, 1971.
Foreword to "The Game of Rat and Dragon" by Cordwainer Smith, in *The Mirror of Infinity,* edited by Robert Silverberg. New York, Harper, 1970.
On Drink.   London, Cape, 1972; New York, Harcourt Brace, 1973.
Kipling and His World.   London, Thames and Hudson, 1975; New York, Scribner, 1976.

Editor, with James Michie, *Oxford Poetry 1949.*   Oxford, Blackwell, 1949.
Editor, with Robert Conquest, *Spectrum [1-5]: A Science Fiction Anthology.*   London, Gollancz, 5 vols., 1961-65; New York, Harcourt Brace, 5 vols., 1962-67.
Editor, *Selected Short Stories of G.K. Chesterton.*   London, Faber, 1972.
Editor, *Tennyson.*   London, Penguin, 1973.
Editor, *Harold's Years: Impressions from the New Statesman and The Spectator.*   London, Quartet, 1977.
Editor, *The New Oxford Book of Light Verse.*   London and New York, Oxford University Press, 1978.
Editor, *The Faber Popular Reciter.*   London, Faber, 1978.

*

Bibliography: *Kingsley Amis: A Checklist* by Jack Benoit Gohn, Kent, Ohio, Kent State University Press, 1976.

Manuscript Collection: State University of New York, Buffalo.

Kingsley Amis has been a devotee of science fiction from the age of twelve. When he was invited to give the Christian Gauss Lectures at Princeton University, he selected science fiction as his subject. *New Maps of Hell* was based on those lectures and is a lucid and entertaining exposition of his criteria for good science fiction. The book was of importance in that it drew attention to the genre and went some way to establishing its "respectability" in the eyes of more conventional critics. It was widely acclaimed as a classic study of the field.

Following his establishment as an authority on science fiction Amis served on the editorial committee of the British Science-Fiction Book Club. Yet his own fictional forays into the media have been surprisingly few. "Something Strange," published in the London *Spectator* in 1960, and the novel *The Anti-Death League* failed to live up to Amis's own high criteria for "good science fiction." *The Alteration,* set in a world of 1976 in which the Reformation did not take place, centers on the question of castrating a talented young singer.

From 1961, working with novelist Robert Conquest, Amis edited the "Spectrum" series of anthologies of science fiction tales, including selections from many of the prominent names in modern science fiction.

—Peter Berresford Ellis

ANDERSON, Chester. American. Born in Stoneham, Massachusetts, 11 August 1932. Educated at the University of Miami, Coral Gables, 1952-56. Has worked as typesetter, janitor, proofreader, motel manager; Founding Editor, The Communication Company, San Francisco, 1967; Editor, *Crawdaddy,* 1968-69. Agent: Robert P. Mills Ltd., 156 East 52nd Street, New York, New York 10022. Address: P.O. Box 37, Villa Grande, California 93486, U.S.A.

SCIENCE-FICTION PUBLICATIONS

Novels

Ten Years to Doomsday, with Michael Kurland. New York, Pyramid, 1964.
The Butterfly Kid. New York, Pyramid, 1967.

OTHER PUBLICATIONS

Novels

The Pink Palace. New York, Fawcett, 1963.
Fox and Hare. Glen Ellen, California, Entwhistle, 1980.

Verse

Colloquy. San Francisco, Bread and Wine Press, 1960.
A Liturgy for Dragons. New York, Young, 1961.

Chester Anderson comments:
I am basically a poet. I write prose because that's what people read. I write science fiction because that's what *I* read. The only reason I write fiction at all is that my memory is so poor. Everything but *Ten Years to Doomsday* is autobiography plus exaggerations. Only the names are changed, because I can't remember them. I don't consider my writing science fiction except in the sense that all 20th-century writing must be either science fiction or dreck—even newspapers, teenage love letters, papal encyclicals. The future is now.

*   *   *

The Butterfly Kid, Chester Anderson's first solo performance as a science-fiction author, was nominated for the Hugo award in 1968, a significant honor for someone who had collaborated on his first science-fiction novel, *Ten Years to Doomsday,* only four years before. *Ten Years to Doomsday,* written with Michael Kurland, was a parody of some of Poul Anderson's novels. A small group of undercover agents for an interstellar empire accelerate the technological progress of a backwater planet to defeat an invasion by an unknown enemy. The denouement is rather perfunctory, and it is obvious that the authors enjoyed the creation of intricate plot twists and gave little thought to the resolution of the story. A certain lightness of tone in both the telling of the tale and the nature of the incidents related is apparent, and the same tone was used with more emphasis in *The Butterfly Kid.*

The Butterfly Kid is Anderson's celebration of the hippie life in Greenwich Village in the mid-1960's. Again the plot hinges on the defeat of an enemy of humanity, in this case a species of six-foot blue lobsters, who are intent on annexing the Earth into their empire. They intend to add a psychodelic drug to the water supply of New York City. The drug has the effect of materializing the takers' fantasies. Chester Anderson, the hero and narrator of the novel, and his friends foil the attempted conquest of Earth in a rather hurried conclusion. Anderson is particularly adept at depicting the social scene of Greenwich Village and his various friends and acquaintances who are the defenders of Earth.

—Harvey J. Satty

ANDERSON, Colin. British.

SCIENCE-FICTION PUBLICATIONS

Novel

Magellan. New York, Walker, and London, Gollancz, 1970.

OTHER PUBLICATIONS

Novel

Boon. London, Faber, 1964.

*   *   *

A short, complex novel in the tradition of *We* and *Brave New World* and full of the shifting realities associated with Philip K. Dick, *Magellan* is Colin Anderson's single science fiction work. Its first section portrays a post-catastrophe city of 50 million sitting in the middle of radioactive wastes. Gondolas travel Magellan's canals and art decorates its walls. Through TV dramas and Press Academy articles, people vicariously participate in others' lives. Disgustingly wise and intuitive social workers, Servants, try to keep everyone happy, working toward the ideal of everyman a genius. Euripides Che Fourthojuly 1070121, however, does not fit into society, though utilizing its drugs to endure. His wife, Chrys, is his only joy. Among the ruins of the space museum Euri gambles in the Old Town. In a game of luck opponents throw a silver ball at each other until one is badly hurt. On the night before Liberation, Euri kills a man. The next day, after he challenges and kills his Servant, he and Chrys flee just as Magellan is replaced by Chronophage, programmed to create a new order of perfect liberty from the Universal Society's tight controls.

Separated from Chrys, Euri has to cross a wasteland peopled with Magellanites who cannot cope with liberation. He resists solipsism, religion, and the pull of the power-mad Gubo to assert his own individuality. Finding peace in himself, he is reunited with Chrys to begin a struggle against cold, horror, and starvation when Chronophage deserts people to find Truth among the stars. Mankind is on its own to find real freedom without Magellan's artificiality. Chrys, Euri, and their baby, Ari, join the sea people to reestablish civilization. Beginning with decay and a skulking cat, *Magellan* ends with a sunlit sea and a free-wheeling hawk, symbolizing Euri's own experiences.

—Mary S. Weinkauf

ANDERSON, Poul (William). American. Born in Bristol, Pennsylvania, 25 November 1926. Educated at the University of Minnesota, Minneapolis, B.A. 1948. Married Karen Kruse in 1953; one daughter. Free-lance writer. President, Science Fiction Writers of America, 1971-72. Recipient: Hugo Award, 1961, 1964, 1969, 1972, 1973, 1979; Nebula Award, 1971, 1972; Tolkien Memorial Award. Guest of Honor, World Science-Fiction Convention, 1959. Agent: Scott Meredith Literary Agency, 845 Third Avenue, New York, New York, 10022. Address: 3 Las Palomas, Orinda, California 94563, U.S.A.

SCIENCE-FICTION PUBLICATIONS

Novels (series: Dominic Flandry; Trader Van Rijn)

Vault of the Ages (juvenile). Philadelphia, Winston, 1952.
The Broken Sword. New York, Abelard Schuman, 1954; London, Sphere, 1973.
Brain Wave. New York, Ballantine, 1954; London, Heinemann, 1955.
No World of Their Own. New York, Ace, 1955; as *The Long Way Home,* 1978.
Planet of No Return. New York, Ace, 1956; London, Dobson, 1967; as *Question and Answer,* Ace, 1978.
Star Ways. New York, Avalon, 1956; as *The Peregrine,* New York, Ace, 1978.
The Snows of Ganymede. New York, Ace, 1958.
War of the Wing-Men (Van Rijn). New York, Ace, 1958; London, Sphere, 1976; as *The Man Who Counts,* Ace, 1978.
Virgin Planet. New York, Avalon, 1959; London, Mayflower, 1966.
The War of Two Worlds. New York, Ace, 1959; London, Dobson, 1970.
We Claim These Stars! (Flandry). New York, Ace, 1959; London, Dobson, 1976.
The Enemy Stars. Philadelphia, Lippincott, 1959.
The High Crusade. New York, Doubleday, 1960.
Earthman, Go Home (Flandry). New York, Ace, 1960.
Twilight World. New York, Torquil, 1961; London, Gollancz, 1962.
Mayday Orbit (Flandry). New York, Ace, 1961.
Orbit Unlimited. New York, Pyramid, 1961; London, Sidgwick and Jackson, 1974.
Three Hearts and Three Lions. New York, Doubleday, 1961.
After Doomsday. New York, Ballantine, 1962; London, Gollancz, 1963.
The Makeshift Rocket. New York, Ace, 1962; London, Dobson, 1969.
Let the Spacemen Beware! New York, Ace, 1963; London, Dobson, 1969; as *The Night Face,* Ace, 1978.
Shield. New York, Berkley, 1963; London, Dobson, 1965.
Three Worlds to Conquer. New York, Pyramid, 1964; London, Mayflower, 1966.
The Corridors of Time. New York, Doubleday, 1965; London, Gollancz, 1966.
Flandry of Terra (omnibus). Philadelphia, Chilton, 1965.
The Star Fox. New York, Doubleday, 1965; London, Gollancz, 1966.
Ensign Flandry. Philadelphia, Chilton, 1966; London, Coronet, 1976.

The Fox, The Dog, and the Griffin: A Folk Tale Adapted from the Danish of Christian Molbech (juvenile). New York, Doubleday, 1966.
World Without Stars. New York, Ace, 1966; London, Dobson, 1975.
The Rebel Worlds. New York, New American Library, 1969; London, Coronet, 1972; as *Commander Flandry,* London, Severn House, 1978.
Satan's World. New York, Doubleday, 1969; London, Gollancz, 1970.
A Circus of Hells (Flandry). New York, New American Library, 1970; London, Sphere, 1978.
Tau Zero. New York, Doubleday, 1970; London, Gollancz, 1971.
The Byworlder. New York, New American Library, 1971; London, Gollancz, 1972.
The Dancer from Atlantis. New York, New American Library, 1971; London, Sphere, 1977.
Operation Chaos. New York, Doubleday, 1971.
There Will Be Time. New York, Doubleday, 1972; London, Sphere, 1979.
The Day of Their Return. New York, Doubleday, 1973; London, Corgi, 1978.
Hrolf Kraki's Saga. New York, Ballantine, 1973.
The People of the Wind. New York, New American Library, 1973; London, Sphere, 1977.
Inheritors of Earth, with Gordon Eklund. Radnor, Pennsylvania, Chilton, 1974.
Fire Time. New York, Doubleday, 1974; London, Panther, 1977.
A Midsummer's Tempest. New York, Doubleday, 1974; London, Futura, 1975.
A Knight of Ghosts and Shadows. New York, Doubleday, 1974; London, Sphere, 1978; as *Knight Flandry,* London, Severn House, 1980.
Star Prince Charlie (juvenile), with Gordon R. Dickson. New York, Putnam, 1975.
The Winter of the World. New York, Doubleday, 1975.
Mirkheim. New York, Berkley, 1977; London, Sphere, 1978.
The Avatar. New York, Berkley, 1978; London, Sidgwick and Jackson, 1980.
Two Worlds (omnibus). New York, Ace, 1978.
The Merman's Children. New York, Berkley, 1979.
The Devil's Game. New York, Pocket Books, 1980.

Short Stories

Earthman's Burden, with Gordon R. Dickson. New York, Gnome Press, 1957.
Guardians of Time. New York, Ballantine, 1960; London, Gollancz, 1961.
Strangers from Earth. New York, Ballantine, 1961; London, Mayflower, 1964.
Un-Man and Other Novellas. New York, Ace, 1962; London, Dobson, 1972.
Time and Stars. New York, Doubleday, and London, Gollancz, 1964.
Trader to the Stars. New York, Doubleday, 1964; London, Gollancz, 1965.
Agent of the Terran Empire (Flandry). Philadelphia, Chilton, 1965; London, Coronet, 1977.
The Trouble Twisters (Van Rijn). New York, Doubleday, 1966; London, Gollancz, 1967.
The Horn of Time. New York, New American Library, 1968.
Beyond the Beyond. New York, Doubleday, 1969; London, Gollancz, 1970.
Seven Conquests. New York, Macmillan, and London, Collier Macmillan, 1969.
Tales of the Flying Mountains. New York, Macmillan, 1970.
The Queen of Air and Darkness. New York, New American Library, 1973.
Homeward and Beyond. New York, Doubleday, 1975.
Homebrew. Cambridge, Massachusetts, NEFSA Press, 1976.
The Best of Poul Anderson. New York, Pocket Books, 1976.
The Book of Poul Anderson. New York, DAW, 1978.
The Night Face and Other Stories. Boston, Gregg Press, 1978.

Uncollected Short Story

"The Ways of Love," in *Destinies* (New York), January-February 1979.

OTHER PUBLICATIONS

Novels

Perish by the Sword.   New York, Macmillan, 1959.
Murder in Black Letter.   New York, Macmillan, 1960.
The Golden Slave.   New York, Avon, 1960.
Rogue Sword.   New York, Avon, 1960.
Murder Bound.   New York, Macmillan, 1962.
The Last Viking Book 2: The Road of the Sea Horse.   New York, Kensington, 1980.

Other

Is There Life on Other Worlds?   New York, Crowell Collier, and London, Collier Macmillan, 1963.
Thermonuclear Warfare.   Derby, Connecticut, Monarch, 1963.
"How to Build a Planet," in *SFWA Bulletin* (Sea Cliff, New York), November 1966.
The Infinite Voyage: Man's Future in Space.   New York, Macmillan, and London, Collier Macmillan, 1969.
"The Creation of Imaginary Worlds," in *Science Fiction, Today and Tomorrow,* edited by Reginald Bretnor.   New York, Harper, 1974.

*

Bibliography: *A Checklist of Poul Anderson* by Roger G. Peyton, privately printed, 1965.

Manuscript Collection: University of Southern Mississippi, Hattiesburg.

*   *   *

James Blish appropriately called Poul Anderson "the enduring explosion." The quality, quantity, and breadth of Anderson's achievements are unique in science fiction. Six Hugos and two Nebulas have been awarded to his novelettes, but 50 novels and 200 shorter works testify to his mastery of all story lengths. Over the course of more than 30 years he has explored an amazingly wide range of literary types from madcap comedy to grim tragedy in such a distinctive fashion that the term "poulanderson" was once suggested as a generic name.

Consider the following colors in Anderson's fictional spectrum: broad farce (the Hoka series written with Gordon R. Dickson and *The Makeshift Rocket*), adventure comedy (*Virgin Planet* and *The High Crusade*), action-adventure yarn ("The Longest Voyage" and the Van Rijn and Flandry series), socio-political drama ("Robin Hood's Barn," "Kings Who Die," and "No Truce with Kings"), "hard" science fiction (*The Enemy Stars*, "Epilogue," and *Tau Zero*), romantic fantasy (*Three Hearts and Three Lions* and *A Midsummer's Tempest*), and heroic fantasy (*The Broken Sword* and *Hrolf Kraki's Saga*).

Moreover, Anderson also writes songs, poems, parodies, essays, historicals, mysteries, and horror stories, and is a skillful translator of both prose and poetry from Scandinavian languages.

Science holds first place among Anderson's raw materials. His formal training in physics imparts a special rigor to his handling of any science. His research is thorough, his extrapolations imaginative. The most direct outlet for his scientific knowledge is the problem-solving story. Here characters must either discover a phenomenon ("The Sharing of Flesh" and "Hunter's Moon") or react to one that is already recognized (*Fire Time*). Linking objective physical problems parallel to subjective personal ones is Anderson's favorite literary structure. He builds these stories so well that they still succeed as fiction even after their scientific premises have been disproven—the Jupiter model in "Call Me Joe" (1957) has passed away; the appeal of its tenacious hero endures.

Furthermore, Anderson makes scientific problem-solving a vehicle for philosophical inquiry. For example, four marooned spacemen conduct an intense, self-conscious debate on the meaning of life in *The Enemy Stars*. In *Tau Zero*, which Blish has called "the ultimate hard science fiction novel," the crew of a crippled spaceship outmaneuvers fate on a slower-than-light odyssey beyond the end of time. Scientific phenomena likewise stimulate theological speculation in "The Martyr," "Kyrie," and "The Problem of Pain," and generate moral crisis in "Sister Planet." In Anderson's hands, the laws of nature assume poetic, symbolic, and even metaphysical significance.

A second source of Anderson's inspiration is history. "The Sky People" replays the age-old opposition between nomads and farmers; *The People of the Wind* is based on the Franco-Prussian War. Anderson also recreates the past with vivid authenticity (for example, lst-century Denmark in "The Peat Bog") and has produced superb time-travel stories ("The Man Who Came Early," *Guardians of Time,* and *There Will Be Time*). Furthermore, his interest in the historical process as such has led him to invent the longest-running and most elaborate future history in SF. His Technic Civilization series now stands at more than 40 separate items (including 11 novels) written over a period of 28 years that cover five millennia of galactic history. (See Sandra Miesel's chronological chart in the Gregg Press editions of the Flandry series, 1979 and "The Price of Buying Time," her afterword to the Ace editions of the same books.)

Thirdly, Anderson draws upon myth for truly heart-wrenching effects. He has both reassembled (*The Broken Sword* from *Volsunga Saga*) and reworked (*Hrolf Kraki's Saga*) Norse materials with all their Viking doom and pride intact. "Goat Song" is the definitive SF treatment of the Orpheus myth, a subject which had earlier inspired *World Without Stars*. Yet Anderson is not content simply to mine or rationalize mythology. He investigates the nature of mythmaking and analyzes its effects—tragic in *The Night Face* and mixed in "The Queen of Air and Darkness."

Anderson weaves science, history, myth, and other categories of learning together to fashion alien habitats and their fascinating inhabitants. Anderson is perhaps SF's finest world-builder, with inventions lovelier than Larry Niven's and more numerous than Hal Clement's. The lushness of Anderson's creations fit his sensuous style. (He has said that he tries to appeal to at least three senses in each scene.) His trademark use of poetic leitmotifs intensifies emotions still further—he would like to attain the lively color of his literary idol, Rudyard Kipling. These efforts produce a richer, larger-than-life quality to situations in his work: no real woods could be quite as enchanted as his fictional ones.

Anderson is a thoroughgoing romantic. His enthrallment with the beauty and terror of nature borders on pantheism. His complementary idealization of women is admitted gynolatry. The resonances between woman and universe work exquisitely well in *World Without Stars* because the Cosmic Goddess is kept offstage. Unfortunately, without this restraint *The Winter of the World* and *The Avatar* sink to the level of self-parody.

Anderson exalts experience over intellection, love over knowledge. He rejects, even fears, absolutes. For him, appreciating wonder is the purpose of life. The purest happiness is domestic. He emphasizes the joys of marriage and parenthood. Since children are the only certain pledge of immortality, building a better world for one's descendants is the best motive for achievement. The interaction between rational creatures and their environment is a matter of challenge and response. Anderson's heroes are always fallible beings who strive to meet life's challenges well. They are free, responsible persons sensitive to the needs of others—Anderson is no radical individualist like Robert A. Heinlein. They are willing to pay the price of doing "the right thing for the wrong reason," in Blish's phrase.

Yet however bravely heroes struggle, "nothing lasts forever." The supreme enemy is entropy. How are mortals to face certain doom? Anderson is not a Pelagian optimist like Gordon R. Dickson. He doubts that evolutionary progress will notably improve man's lot. Courage is the only fitting response. Unyielding endurance is a grim command in the language of the northern heroic tradition: "No man can escape his weird, but none other can take from him the heart wherewith he meets it." The author states it more gently in his own voice: "Life can be cruel, and is ultimately tragic, but mostly it is wonderful, or would be if we'd allow it to be." Anderson's stalwart personal creed is: "To hell alike with fatuous optimism and fashionable despair. Given guts and luck, we may still prevail; win or lose, the effort is infinitely worth making."

—Sandra Miesel

—————

ANSTEY, F. Pseudonym for Thomas Anstey Guthrie; also wrote as Hope Bandoff; William Monarch Jones. British. Born in London, 8 August 1856. Educated at King's College School, London; Trinity Hall, Cambridge. Called to the bar, 1880; worked briefly as a barrister. Regular contributor to *Punch,* London. *Died 10 March 1934.*

SCIENCE-FICTION PUBLICATIONS

Novels

Vice Versâ; or, A Lesson to Fathers. London, Smith Elder, and New York, Appleton, 1882; revised edition, Smith Elder, 1883; London, Newnes, 1901.
The Tinted Venus: A Farcical Romance. Bristol, Arrowsmith, and New York, Appleton, 1885.
A Fallen Idol. London, Smith Elder, and Philadelphia, Lippincott, 1886.
Tourmalin's Time Cheques (as Hope Bandoff). Bristol, Arrowsmith, 1891; as F. Anstey, New York, Appleton, 1891; as *The Time Bargain; or, Tourmalin's Cheque Book,* Arrowsmith, 1905.
The Statement of Stella Maberly (published anonymously). London, Unwin, and New York, Appleton, 1896.
The Brass Bottle. London, Smith Elder, and New York, Appleton, 1900.
In Brief Authority. London, Smith Elder, 1915; New York, Doran, 1916.

Short Stories

The Black Poodle and Other Tales. London, Longman, and New York, Appleton, 1884.
The Talking Horse and Other Tales. London, Smith Elder, and New York, United States Book Company, 1892.
Only Toys! London, Richards, 1903.
Salted Almonds. London, Smith Elder, 1906.
Humour and Fantasy (selection). London, Murray, and New York, Dutton, 1931.

OTHER PUBLICATIONS

Novels

The Giant's Robe. London, Smith Elder, and New York, Appleton, 1884.
The Pariah. London, Smith Elder, 3 vols., and Philadelphia, Lippincott, 1 vol., 1889.
The Travelling Companions. London, Longman, 1892; revised edition, 1908.
Under the Rose. London, Bradbury Agnew, 1894.
Lyre and Lancet. London, Smith Elder, and New York, Macmillan, 1895.
Love among the Lions: A Matrimonial Experience. London, Dent, 1898; New York, Appleton, 1899.
A Bayard from Bengal. London, Methuen, and New York, Appleton, 1902.

Short Stories

Slings and Arrows (as William Monarch Jones). Bristol, Arrowsmith, 1885.
Burglar Bill and Other Pieces for the Use of the Young Reciter. London, Bradbury Agnew, 1888; as *Mr. Punch's Young Reciter,* 1892.
The Man from Blankley's and Other Sketches. London, Longman, 1893.
Baboo Jabberjee, B.A. London, Dent, and New York, Appleton, 1897.
Puppets at Large: Scenes and Subjects from Mr. Punch's Show. London, Bradbury Agnew, and New York, Scribner, 1897.
Paleface and Redskin and Other Stories for Boys and Girls. London, Richards, and New York, Appleton, 1898.
Percy and Others: Sketches. London, Methuen, 1915.
The Last Load: Stories and Essays. London, Methuen, 1925.

Plays

Vice Versâ, adaptation of his own novel (produced Reading, Berkshire, and London, 1883). London, Smith Elder, and Boston, Baker, 1910.
Mr. Punch's Music-Hall Songs and Dramas. London, Bradbury Agnew, and New York, United States Book Company, 1892.
Mr. Punch's Pocket Ibsen (parodies). London, Heinemann, and New York, Macmillan, 1893; as *The Pocket Ibsen,* Heinemann, 1895.
The Man from Blankley's, adaptation of his own story (produced London, 1901).
A Short Exposure (produced London, 1901).
Lyre and Lancet, with F.K. Peile, adaptation of the novel by Anstey (produced London, 1902).
The Game of Adverbs (produced Liverpool and London, 1908). Published in *Another Book of Miniature Plays,* edited by Theodore Johnson, Boston, Baker, 1934.
The Brass Bottle, adaptation of his own novel (produced London, 1909). London, Heinemann, 1911.
A Fallen Idol, adaptation of his own novel (produced London, 1913).
The Would-Be Gentlemen, adaptation of a play by Molière (produced London, 1926). London, Secker, 1926.
The Imaginary Invalid, adaptation of a play by Molière (produced London, 1929). London, Hodder and Stoughton, 1929.
Four Molière Comedies (includes *The Miser, A Doctor Perforce, The Learned Ladies, The Misanthrope*). London, Hodder and Stoughton, 1931.
Three Molière Plays (includes *Tartuffe, Scapin the Trickster, The School of Wives*). London, Oxford University Press, 1933.

Other

Voces Populi (*Punch* articles). London, Longman, 2 vols., 1890-92.
A Long Retrospect (as T.A. Guthrie). London and New York, Oxford University Press, 1936.

*

Bibliography: *A Bibliography of the Works of F. Anstey* by Martin John Turner, privately printed, 1931.

*   *   *

F. Anstey was a major contributor to the English humorous magazine *Punch,* but is best known for his fantasy novels. In particular, *Vice Versâ* was not only a best-seller as a novel but was rewritten as a play and became an influential film comedy. *The Brass Bottle* had a similar history in the three media.

All Anstey's successful novels and short stories are fantastic comedies, based on the juxtaposition of smug bourgeois English "normal life" with exotic and magical power. The effect is both charming in its arbitrary extravagance and precisely satiric of the inert and stereotyped habits of mind on which normal social communications depend. When the power of magic overturns the foundations of the commonsense world, the unimaginative, the vulgar, and the selfish are revealed in all their stupidity and self-indulgence, while those capable of imaginative response, and therefore capable of sympathy, self-knowledge, and love, have earned a new chance when, as happens at the climax of each tale, the magical catalyst withdraws from the world. The comedy of *Vice Versâ,* for example, depends on th glibness with which a City businessman can mouth platitudes to his son about schooldays being the happiest of one's life, how much he envies the boy, and so forth. The mysterious talisman from the East grants his wish, and man and boy change places. Inevitably, and with excellent satiric point, the style and morality of the middle-aged businessman is totally inappropriate to a boarding-school, and Bultitude renders himself exquisitely miserable. When, at the climax, a second wish unites psychology and body correctly again, father and son are much improved.

The Brass Bottle evokes the extravagant and exotic gratitude of the Djinn released from his imprisoning bottle, and its effects upon the life and career of a talented but unknown young architect. Less pleasant protagonists, such as Tourmalin (*Tourmalin's Time Cheques*), find no inner resources and the magic therefore becomes "poetic justice" in revealing their self-indulgence. 19th-century techniques of flirtation have badly dated this novel and most of Anstey's stories about weak protagonists, such as *The Tinted Venus, A Fallen Idol,* and "The Magic H's" (in *Salted Almonds*). The Tinted Venus, a re-telling in contemporary terms of the story of the ring placed on the finger of a statue of Venus, has brilliant moments and a real sense of masculine sexual fear, but is marred by a note of naive snobbery at the expense of barbers (as well as by the laborious comedy about flirtation).

Anstey at times raises expectations of magic in order to tease his readers by denying that anything magical occurred, as in the excellent short story "The Gull" (in *Salted Almonds*) which ridicules sentimental versions of the transmigration of souls, or in the more flippant "The Talking Horse" (in *The Talking Horse and Other Tales*) where the madness of the narrator provides a kind of explanation. However, the most powerful juxtaposition of bourgeois "real life" with a total context of magic occurs in Anstey's last novel, *In Brief Authority,* where a smug English family and the younger governess are brought into the Märchenland, the world of the Grimm folktales. Brilliant episodes such as the testing of the ego of a Fairy Prince, or the applicability of Nietzsche's philosophy of the Ubermensch to the education of an ogre, give way in the final pages to an evocation of the trenches of the first World War. The cowardice, hypocrisy, smugness, and self-deception of upper-middle-class English life are seen as far more "the enemy" than the German tales, which test the bases of imaginative integrity.

Famous at one time for his translations of Moliére and critical parodies of Ibsen, as well as for his own plays and "scenes," Anstey is now forgotten as a playwright. The same fate has attended his "serious" novel *The Pariah,* but one of his best short stories is a fantasy about a "serious" novelist whose stereotyped characters come to life and move into his house; "Why I Have Given Up Writing Novels" (in *Salted Almonds*) in still a salutary experience for writers.

—Norman Talbot

ANTHONY, Piers (Piers Anthony Dillingham Jacob). British. Born in Oxford, 6 August 1934. Educated at Goddard College, Plainfield, Vermont, B.A. 1956; University of South Florida, Tampa, teaching certificate 1964. Served in the United States Army, 1957-59. Married Carol Marble in 1956; one daughter. Technical writer, Electronic Communications Inc., St. Petersburg, Florida, 1959-62; English teacher, Admiral Farragut Academy, St. Petersburg, 1965-66. Since 1966, free-lance writer. Recipient: Pyramid *Fantasy and Science Fiction* award, 1967. Agent: E.J. Carnell, 17 Burwash Road, London SE18 7QY, England. Address 1113 58th Street South, Gulfport, Florida 33707, U.S.A.

SCIENCE-FICTION PUBLICATIONS

Novels (series: Aton; Battle Circle; Cal, Veg, and Aquilon; Cluster; Tarot; Xanth)

Chthon (Aton). New York, Ballantine, 1967; London, Macdonald, 1970.
Omnivore (Cal, Veg, and Aquilon). New York, Ballantine, 1968; London, Faber, 1969.
The Ring, with Robert E. Margroff. New York, Ace, 1968; London, Macdonald, 1969.
All (Battle Circle). New York, Avon, 1978; as *Battle Circle,* n.d.
    Sos the Rope. New York, Pyramid, 1968; London, Faber, 1970.
    Var the Stick. London, Faber 1972; New York, Bantam, 1973.
    Neq the Sword. London, Corgi, 1975.
Macroscope. New York, Avon, 1969; London, Sphere, 1972.
The E.S.P. Worm, with Robert E. Margroff. New York, Paperback Library, 1970.
Orn (Cal, Veg, and Aquilon). New York, Avon, 1970; London, Corgi, 1977.
Prostho Plus. London, Gollancz, 1971; New York, Bantam, 1973.
Race Against Time (juvenile). New York, Hawthorn, 1973.
Rings of Ice. New York, Avon, 1974; London, Millington, 1975.
Triple Detente. New York, DAW, 1974; London, Sphere, 1975.
Phthor (Aton). New York, Berkley, 1975; London, Panther, 1978.
But What of Earth?, with Robert Coulson. Toronto, Laser, 1976.
Ox (Cal, Veg, and Aquilon). New York, Avon, 1976; London, Corgi, 1977.
Steppe. London, Millington, 1976.
Cluster. New York, Avon, 1976; London, Millington, 1978; as *Vicinity Cluster,* London, Panther, 1979.
Hasan. San Bernardino, California, Borgo Press, 1977.
A Spell for Chameleon (Xanth). New York, Ballantine, 1977.
Chaining the Lady (Cluster). New York, Avon, and London, Millington, 1978.
Kirlian Quest (Cluster). New York, Avon, and London, Millington, 1978.
Pretender, with Frances Hall. San Bernardino, California, Borgo Press, 1979.
The Source of Magic (Xanth). New York, Ballantine, 1979.
Castle Roogna (Xanth). New York, Ballantine, 1979.
God of Tarot. New York, BJ, 1979.
Vision of Tarot. New York, Berkley, 1980.
Thousandstar (Cluster). New York, Avon, 1980.
Faith of Tarot. New York, Berkley, 1980.
Split Infinity. New York, Ballantine, 1981.

Uncollected Short Stories

"Possible to Rue," in *Fantastic* (New York), April 1963.
"Quinquepedalian," in *Amazing* (New York), November 1963.
"Sheol," in *Analog* (New York), September 1964.
"Encounter," in *Fantastic* (New York), October 1964.
"Phog, " in *Fantastic* (New York), June 1965.
"Mandroid," with Andrew J. Offutt and Robert Margroff, in *If* (New York), June 1966.
"The Message, " in *Analog* (New York), July 1966.
"The Ghost Galaxies," in *If* (New York), April 1967.
"Within the Cloud, " in *Galaxy* (New York), April 1967.
"In the Jaws of Danger," in *If* (New York), November 1967.
"Beak by Beak," in *Analog* (New York), December 1967.
"The Alien Rulers," in *Analog* (New York), March 1968.
"Getting Through University," in *If* (New York), August 1968.
"The Life of the Stripe, " in *Fantastic* (New York), February 1969.
"None But I," in *If* (New York), October 1969.
"The Bridge," in *Worlds of Tomorrow 24* (New York), 1970.
"Equals Four," in *If* (New York), July 1970.
"Wood You?," in *Fantasy and Science Fiction* (New York), October 1970.
"Monarch," in *If* (New York), November 1970.
"In the Barn," in *Again, Dangerous Visions,* edited by Harlan Ellison. New York, Doubleday, 1972; London, Millington, 1976.

"Hard Sell," in *If* (New York), August 1972.
"Black Baby," in *If* (New York), October 1972.
"Hurdle," in *If* (New York), December 1972.
"Up Schist Creek," in *Generation*, edited by David Gerrold.   New
   York, Dell, 1972.
"Ki," in *Vertex* (Los Angeles), June 1974.

OTHER PUBLICATIONS

Novels with Roberto Fuentes

Klal.   New York, Berkley, 1974.
Mistress of Death.   New York, Berkley, 1974.
Bamboo Bloodbath.   New York, Berkley, 1975.

*

Manuscript Collection: Eastern New Mexico University Library,
Portales.

*   *   *

While Piers Anthony has been entertaining readers in a variety of
genres for nearly 20 years, he has also been instructing them. Frequently, his choices in life find fictive representation. In his early
years, Anthony had to face several dislocations, moves from England to Spain to the United States and the divorce of his parents. As
he said in an interview in *Science Fiction Review*, writing science
fiction was an answer to the depression resulting from these dislocations, the death of a cousin, and the memory of adolescent frailty.
The frailty of Cal in *Omnivore, Orn*, and *Ox* and the vegetarianism
of Veg thus have biographical roots, as does the interest in the
defensive strategy of judo in the Jason Striker martial arts novels
done with Roberto Fuentes. But the most persistent value advo-
cated in Anthony's novels is his concern for the environment, the
fear that "we cannot maintain our present trends without destroying
the world as we know it." This value usually surfaces as social satire
in Anthony's largely picaresque fantasies and science-fiction novels.

In *Chthon*, though the main action is the escape from the terrible
garnet mines on Chthon, part of the horror is due to ecological
problems. *Prostho Plus*, though a lighthearted spoof of bug-eyed
monster depictions of Dr. Dillingham's alien dental patients, nevertheless seriously deals with the sanctity of ecological chains. Even
The Ring deals with this ecological theme, as Jeff Font seeks his
father's lost fortune in an earthly society whose criminal behavior is
controlled by Skinnerian electronic rings. The respect that Jeff
begins to feel for the ring is Anthony's response to a need for control
beyond a rampant American individualism that sometimes is indistinguishable from the basest selfishness.

Macroscope continues to explore restraints on liberty in order to
promote the greater good. While the most capable brains using the
macroscope are destroyed, the destructive alien transmission is
particularly lethal for power brokers such as Senator Borland. Even
the entry testing which occurs as Afra, Ivo, Harold, and Beatryx
enter the alien space craft determines the fitness of the individual for
knowledge, the ability to bear knowledge responsibly. Not only
does the novel deal with environmentalism on earth and the effects
of disastrous population growth, but it shows the necessity for a
mental environmentalism in the group's interaction. Ivo must integrate his other personality, Schön, and Afra must balance competence by compassion. The flight from UN power and the quest for
the Traveller which make up the novel's double action enable
Anthony to explore physical and internal ecology.

Race Against Time appears to be a rebellion against the culture of
the Standard race on earth but winds up being an acceptance of that
race's ecological concern. The three pairs of genetically purebred
adolescent couples, on seeing the earth's former devastation, begin
to understand the genetic wisdom of racial preservation and peace.
Rings of Ice shows a new destruction of the earth by military forces
which hope to make energy use of ice rings from icy nebula. The
threat of tremendous flooding goes unrecognized, as the story
shows six people attempting to survive the apocalyptic destruction.
Again outer imbalance and psychological imbalance are both dealt
with in Anthony's novel: Thatch becomes aggressive; Gus masters
his fear of water; Zena overcomes her fear of men. *Triple Detente*

deals with environmental issues and war. Kazos and men avoid
battle by acting as conquerors of one another's planet, reducing
each planet's overpopulation. Similar strategies are used to avoid
battle with the Ukes, although their special racial instinct causes
both problem and solution.

The Battle Circle trilogy composed of *Sos the Rope, Var the
Stick*, and *Neg the Sword* is set after an atomic war. The trilogy's
action, showing a rebirth of big government in the tribe of Sol and
the monastic preservation of "crazy" technology and learning, cautions orderly development. Technology and learning must not over-
step moral and emotional development. That Sol seeks political
power to compensate for his sterility and Sos plans battles as
strategies for personal vengeance illustrates character but more
importantly social weakness. The state set up by Neq and the crazies
in the last novel occurs only after purgation of foolishness, pride,
and quick temper. When the cost of violence is tallied, such as the
needless death of the mutant Var, civilization begins. This Camelot
will not so easily be undone by sexuality, jealousy, and pride as the
original.

Omnivore, Orn, and *Ox* each deals with the preservation of the
planets and the preservation of the symbiotic relationship of Aquilon, Veg, and Cal. Only in *Ox* does Anthony provide Veg with his
own mate, the semi-clone Tamme, but in the two earlier novels, love
is controlled because the pairing of lovers is destructive to the trio.
Aquilon loves both men for different reasons, and neither man is
willing to cut out the other. The symbiosis of the group is paramount, as it is in *Rings of Ice* and other Anthony novels. The
conflicting claims of preservation and development are worked out
in each novel—the fungoid world of Nacre, the Paleocene planet of
Orn, and the high technology of Ox. The solution in each case
appears to be to control earth's appetite by controlling population.
Super agents such as Subble and Tamme become more than impe-
rialistic James Bonds. Violence is necessary in Anthony's novels,
but only to ensure species preservation. To alter the environment
unnecessarily is a major crime.

This is even true in Anthony's fantasies. *Hasan*, though a sexy
Arabian Nights series of picaresque adventures, is an ecologically
moral world. Magic is fine if magic is conserved. Since Bahram kills
young boys, he is killed in turn. Hasan, however, passes up violence
in refusing to kill the conquered Queen, making a happy resolution
possible. Hasan's foolish ignorance, which could precipitate needless violence, is mocked by those gifted in magical power, such as the
ifrit Dahnash.

The Xanth trilogy again focuses on conservation. Bink's quest in
A Spell for Chameleon to discover whether he has magic uncovers a
peculiar trait, resistance to magic's harm. The Magician Humfrey
believes in conserving his power, and even Trent says, prior to
renouncing force to gain a kingdom, "There is a balance of nature,
whether magical or mundane, that we should hesitate to interfere
with." In *The Source of Magic* Xanth learns conservation by temporarily losing its magic when Bink frees the demon. Again psychological ecology is important, as Grundy and Xanth learn about
feelings and lose their cool, and in the demon's case, formulaic
rationality. Scientific rationality is thus checked by feeling. In Dor's
quest in *Castle Roogna* conservation is also demonstrated.

The Cluster series, currently made up of four novels, *Cluster,
Chaining the Lady, Kirlian Quest*, and *Thousandstar*, makes much
use of the Tarot. While systems such as the *I Ching* have had a
bearing on some novels, the Tarot, from the time of *Macroscope*,
has been dominant in Anthony's symbol system. In *Chaining the
Lady*, for example, even the space craft have shapes common to
Tarot such as swords and cups. As a system, it appears to be
Anthony's answer to the age-old struggle between free will and
determinism. Basic to each of the novels is the conflict between
galaxies over galaxy-bonding energy. The means of preserving this
energy, necessary for the capitalist expansion of Andromeda, is
related to Kirlian aura transfer. It becomes Flint's job in *Cluster* to
give alien planets the secret of Kirlian transfer in order to protect the
Milky Way. As Flint enters the host body of each alien in carrying
out his mission, an appreciation of other cultures results. He learns
to appreciate alien differences and understand their validity; conquest is more often through sex than combat, even between Flint
and the Andromedan opposing him. *Chaining the Lady* echoes the
plot of *Cluster*, merely changing the sexes of the Milky Way and
Andromedan agents. The novel's end is again ecological as the will

of lesser auras is taken into consideration in transfer: civilization cannot be maintained by theft of massive new energy; development must be ecological. *Kirlian Quest* shows Herald of Slash assuming the roles of Flint and Melody of the previous novels. Rescue from the Amoeban menace turns out to be rescue from the ancients. What Anthony appears to be exploring is the psychology of bias, how sentients allow one gestalt to block another. The ancients/Amoebans seek to foster Kirlian sapience and fail to recognize it when they contact it. As Hweeh says about the difficulty of perception, "What we took as our ultimate salvation has been revealed as our ultimate threat. God and the Devil are one." The concern for rights of low Kirlian auras in the whole series may well be an extension of Anthony's concern for his eldest daughter's learning disability. *Thousandstar,* which tells of a race whose contestants are Kirlian auras and their host bodies, shows the effects of sexual cooperation and understanding in a manner similar to Le Guin's *Left Hand of Darkness,* as Jessica and Heem share the same body. The cooperation shown by the three hostile species is a paradigm for Anthony's environmentalism.

The Tarot sequence is an elaborate Tarot fantasy which connects to the Cluster series by the use of Kirlian auras and aliens from Cluster planets. Nonetheless, the action is allegorical, as Brother Paul seeks the God of Tarot in encounters with religious leaders, representatives of secular philosophies, and in visions having more in common with Dante, *Piers Plowman,* Bunyan, and Freudian dreams than with contemporary fantasy. While the communist leader, the Mormon, and the Quaker seem too easily reduced in this spiritual odyssey, the series still has much power, and the Tarot symbols are probably better to deal with in this fantasy guise than in science-fiction works, where the Tarot symbols frequently seem anthropomorphic when applied to alien cultures.

In Anthony's defense, however, it must be said that his portraits of aliens and their societies is one of his great strengths as a science-fiction writer. It is an achievement to describe not only an alien but his culture as well. One must credit this author with great powers of invention and logical consistency.

—Craig Wallace Barrow

ANVIL, Christopher. Pseudonym for Harry C. Crosby. American.

SCIENCE-FICTION PUBLICATIONS

Novels

The Day the Machines Stopped. Derby, Connecticut, Monarch, 1964.
Strangers in Paradise. New York, Belmont, 1969.
Pandora's Planet. New York, Doubleday, 1972.
Warlord's World. New York, DAW, 1975.

Uncollected Short Stories

"The Prisoner," in *Astounding* (New York), February 1956.
"Advance Agent," in *Galaxy* (New York), February 1957.
"Sinful City," in *Future* (New York), Spring 1957.
"Torch," in *Astounding* (New York), April 1957.
"Compensation," in *Astounding* (New York), October 1957.
"The Gentle Earth," in *Astounding* (New York), November 1957.
"Truce by Boomerang," in *Astounding* (New York), December 1957.
"Achilles Heel," in *Astounding* (New York), February 1958.
"Destination Unknown," in *Science Fiction Adventures* (New York), March 1958.
"Revolt," in *Astounding* (New York), April 1958.
"Top Rung," in *Astounding* (New York), July 1958.
"Cargo for Colony 6," in *Astounding* (New York), August 1958.
"Foghead," in *Astounding* (New York), September 1958.

"Nerves," in *Fantastic Universe* (Chicago), November 1958.
"Goliath and the Beanstalk," in *Astounding* (New York), November, 1958.
"Seller's Market," in *Astounding* (New York), December 1958.
"The Sieve," in *Astounding* (New York), April 1959.
"Leverage," in *Astounding* (New York), July 1959.
"Captain Leaven," in *Astounding* (New York), September 1959.
"The Law Breakers," in *Astounding* (New York), October 1959.
"Mating Problems," in *Astounding* (New York), December 1959.
"A Rose by Any Other Name...," in *Astounding* (New York), January 1960.
"Shotgun Wedding," in *Astounding* (New York), March 1960.
"A Tourist Named Death," in *If* (New York), May 1960.
"Star Tiger," in *Astounding* (New York), June 1960.
"The Troublemaker," in *Astounding* (New York), July 1960.
"Mind Partner," in *Galaxy* (New York), August 1960.
"A Taste of Poison," in *Astounding* (New York), August 1960.
"The Ghost Fleet," in *Analog* (New York), February 1961.
"Identification," in *Analog* (New York), May 1961.
"The Hunch," in *Analog* (New York), July 1961.
"No Small Enemy," in *Analog* (New York), November 1961.
"Uncalculated Risk," in *Analog* (New York), March 1962.
"The Toughest Opponent," in *Analog* (New York), August 1962.
"Sorcerer's Apprentice," in *Analog* (New York), September 1962.
"Gadget vs. Trend," in *Analog* (New York), October 1962.
"Philosopher's Stone," in *Analog* (New York), January 1963.
"Not in the Literature," in *Analog* (New York), March 1963.
"War Games," in *Analog* (New York), October 1963.
"Problem of Command," in *Analog* (New York), November 1963.
"Speed-Up," in *Amazing* (New York), January 1964.
"Rx for Chaos," in *Analog* (New York), February 1964.
"Hunger," in *Analog* (New York), May 1964.
"We from Arcturus," in *Worlds of Tomorrow* (New York), August 1964.
"Bill for Delivery," in *Analog* (New York), November 1964.
"Contract," in *Analog* (New York), December 1964.
"Merry Christmas from Outer Space," in *Fantastic* (New York), December 1964.
"New Boccaccio," in *Analog* (New York), January 1965.
"The Plateau," in *Amazing* (New York), March 1965.
"The Captive Djinn," in *Analog* (New York), May 1965.
"Duel to the Death," in *Analog* (New York), June 1965.
"High G," in *If* (New York), June 1965.
"Positive Feedback," in *Analog* (New York), August 1965.
"Untropy," in *Analog* (New York), January 1966.
"The Kindly Invasion," in *Worlds of Tomorrow* (New York), March 1966.
"Devise and Conquer," in *Galaxy* (New York), April 1966.
"Two-Way Communication," in *Analog* (New York), May 1966.
"Stranglehold," in *Analog* (New York), June 1966.
"Sweet Reason," in *If* (New York), June 1966.
"Missile Smasher," in *Analog* (New York), July 1966.
"Symbols," in *Analog* (New York), September 1966.
"Facts to Fit the Theory," in *Analog* (New York), November 1966.
"Sabotage," in *Fantasy and Science Fiction* (New York), December 1966.
"The Trojan Bombardment," in *Galaxy* (New York), February 1967.
"The Uninvited Guest," in *Analog* (New York), March 1967.
"The New Member," in *Galaxy* (New York), April 1967.
"Experts in the Field," in *Analog* (New York), May 1967.
"The Dukes of Desire," in *Analog* (New York), June 1967.
"Compound Interest," in *Analog* (New York), July 1967.
"Babel II," in *Analog* (New York), August 1967.
"The King's Legions," in *Analog* (New York), September 1967.
"The New Way," in *Beyond Infinity* (Hollywood), November 1967.
"A Question of Attitude," in *Analog* (New York), December 1967.
"Uplift the Savage," in *Analog* (New York), March 1968.
"Is Everybody Happy?," in *Analog* (New York), April 1968.
"High Road to the East," in *Fantastic* (New York), May 1968.
"The Royal Road," in *Analog* (New York), June 1968.
"Behind the Sandrat Hoax," in *Galaxy* (New York), October 1968.
"Mission of Ignorance," in *Analog* (New York), October 1968.
"Trap," in *Analog* (New York), March 1969.
"The Nitrocellulose Doormat," in *Analog* (New York), June 1969.

"The Great Intellect Boom," in *Analog* (New York), July 1969.
"Test Ultimate," in *Analog* (New York), October 1969.
"Basic," in *Venture* (Concord, New Hampshire), November 1969.
"Trial by Silk," in *Amazing* (New York), March 1970.
"The Low Road," in *Amazing* (New York), September 1970.
"The Throne and the Usurper," in *Fantasy and Science Fiction* (New York), November 1970.
"Apron Chains," in *Analog* (New York), December 1970.
"The Claw and the Clock," in *Analog* (New York), February 1971.
"The Operator," in *Analog* (New York), March 1971.
"Riddle Me This," in *Analog* (New York), January 1972.
"The Unknown," in *Amazing* (New York), July 1972.
"Ideological Defeat," in *Analog* (New York), September 1972.
"The Knife and the Sheaf," in *Future Kin*, edited by Roger Elwood. New York, Doubleday, 1974.
"Cantor's War," in *If* (New York), June 1974.
"Brains Isn't Everything," in *Analog* (New York), June 1976.

*   *   *

Christopher Anvil appeared more frequently in *Astounding/Analog* from the mid-1950's to the mid-1960's than any other author, yet he remains relatively unknown today. His novels are slight efforts, and do not compare with his finest short fiction.

At his best, in stories like "A Rose by Any Other Name," which skillfully examines the effect of certain words on international relations, the widely reprinted "Gadget vs. Trend," on the impact of one invention on the functioning of society, and "Positive Feedback," a hilarious story that illustrates the problem of adjusting systems while they are in action, he is an inventive and expert manipulator of social trends and processes. Indeed, he has been one of the very best SF observers (along with Mack Reynolds at *his* best) of the foibles and presumptuousness of social thinkers and social managers. He was perhaps too successful—he found a formula and worked it to death, and was one of the main reasons why the 1960's *Analog* always left you with the feeling that you had just read last month's issue again. He was a John Campbell writer who could be relied upon to hew to the formulas and fads of that editor, and like Randall Garrett became lost from public view through constant, unchanging exposure. Perhaps he might have flourished artistically in another market—some evidence for this possibility can be found in "Mind Partner," his finest work, and one of his few stories published in *Galaxy*. In several respects "Mind Partner" is a New Wave story, a powerful example of psychological science fiction at its best, written before anyone was arguing about the term or had even heard of it. The story has a nightmare quality about it that lingers long after the reading. The editor-writer relationship in science fiction is for the most part a mystery, and it is also possible that Campbell brought out the best in him.

Other notable stories include "Bill for Delivery," "The Captive Djinn," "The Great Intellect Boom," a major work that examines the effect of instant intellectuality on everyone in a society, "The Prisoner," and "Uncalculated Risk."

—Martin H. Greenberg

ARNOLD, Edwin L(ester Linden). British. Born in Swanscombe, Kent, in 1857; son of the writer Sir Edwin Arnold. Educated at Cheltenham College. Married 1) Constance Boyce, one daughter; 2) Jessie Brighton in 1919. Cattle breeder in Scotland, then worked in forestry in Travancore, India. *Died 1 March 1935.*

SCIENCE-FICTION PUBLICATIONS

Novels

The Wonderful Adventures of Phra the Phoenician. London, Chatto and Windus, 3 vols., and New York, Harper, 1 vol., 1890.
Lepidus the Centurion: A Roman of To-day. London, Cassell, 1901; New York, Crowell, 1902.
Lieut. Gullivar Jones: His Vacation. London, Brown Langham, 1905; New York, Arno Press, 1975; as *Gulliver of Mars*, New York, Ace, 1964.

Short Stories

The Story of Ulla and Other Tales. London and New York, Longman, 1895.

OTHER PUBLICATIONS

Novel

The Constable of St. Nicholas. London, Chatto and Windus, 1894.

Other

A Summer Holiday in Scandinavia. London, Sampson Low, 1877.
On the Indian Hills; or Coffee-Planting in Southern India. London, Sampson Low, 2 vols., 1881.
Coffee: Its Cultivation and Profit. London, Whittingham, 1886.
Bird Life in England. London, Chatto and Windus, 1887.
England as She Seems, Being Selections from the Notes of an Arab Hadji. London, Warne, 1888.
The Soul of the Beast. London, P.R. Macmillan, 1960.

Editor, *The Opium Question Solved*, by Anglo-Indian. London, Partridge, 1882.

*   *   *

Once a highly popular author, Edwin L. Arnold is little remembered and seldom read, and when read at all is generally examined as a possible source of inspiration for Edgar Rice Burroughs's Martian series rather than as an author of independent merit. Arnold's father, Sir Edwin Arnold, was one of the first Englishmen to study Eastern religion, philosophy, and culture. Very likely as a result of his father's influence, young Arnold became interested in Asian philosophy, in particular in theories of reincarnation and the cyclical nature of existence.

These theories are visible in Arnold's first and most successful novel, *The Wonderful Adventures of Phra the Phoenician*. Phra is described as a man appearing about 30 years of age, but in fact having no recollection of ever having been younger. His most ancient memory is of life in classical Phoenicia, but even in that recollection he was a man, not a child. Over the ages, Phra has lived and (apparently) died repeatedly. He describes himself as a simple military man, although he admits to being a great swordsman. As an early colonist in Britain he met and fell in love with the Princess Blodwen. Following her death he too "died" and encountered her ghost in the spirit world, but after many years Phra recovered, his undecayed body as good as ever, and resumed his life. This cycle is repeated numerous times, down to the present (Victorian) era. The book is an excellent example of Victorian fantasy, closest in spirit to Haggard's *The World's Desire*, written with Andrew Lang. To modern readers *Phra* will seem slow-paced, florid, and overlong, but it is still readable.

The Story of Ulla and Other Tales is a collection of Arnold's shorter fiction. Several of the stories contain fantastic elements, for the most part of rather conventional nature (i.e., ghost stories). Most relevant is "Rutherford the Twice-Born," in which Arnold reverts to the reincarnation/resurrection theme. *Lepidus the Centurion* is still another treatment of the resurrection/reincarnation theme. A Roman legionnaire revives from suspended animation in contemporary England, and then proceeds to acclimate himself to polite Victorian society, learning to play tennis and the like. *Lepidus* is the least of Arnold's novels in actual interest for the present-day reader. The author attempts the comedy of manners in style, but the result is poor.

Lieut. Gullivar Jones: His Vacation was Arnold's final novel, and the most interesting to the modern reader of science fiction. Jones, a lieutenant in the US navy, comes into possession of a magic carpet while on leave. He is carried to Mars where he encounters a race of cultured urban dwellers attempting to preserve a high ancient civilization against the maraudings of savage desert nomads. He rescues the civilized Princess An from the nomads, travels to an icy River of Death (compare Haggard and Burroughs), and has other adventures among the Martians before returning to earth. By combining the setting and plot elements of *Gullivar Jones* with the heroic figure of *Phra the Phoenician*—and with the addition of elements from such works as *A Journey to Mars* by Pope and *Zarlah the Martian* by Grisewood—one assembles the full recipe of Burroughs's Barsoomian saga, at least of the early volumes.

Although Arnold's last book was published in 1905, he lived until 1935, well into the period of modern "pulp" science fiction, but there appears to be no record of his attitude toward the works of later writers, including Burroughs.

—Richard A. Lupoff

ASH, Fenton. Pseudonym for Frank Atkins; also wrote as Fred Ashley; Frank Aubrey. British. Grew up in South Wales. Studied engineering. Wrote serials for boys' papers in 1900's; film critic for a London Sunday paper.

SCIENCE-FICTION PUBLICATIONS

Novels

The Radium Seekers; or, The Wonderful Black Nugget. London, Pitman, 1905.
The Temple of Fire; or, The Mysterious Island (as Fred Ashley). London, Pitman, 1905.
A Trip to Mars (juvenile). London, Chambers, 1909; New York, Arno Press, 1975.
By Airship to Ophir (juvenile). London, Shaw, 1911.
The Black Opal (juvenile). London, Shaw, 1915; New York, Arno Press, 1975.

Novels as Frank Aubrey (series: Monella)

The Devil-Tree of El Dorado (Monella). London, Hutchinson, 1896; New York, New Amsterdam, 1897.
A Studio Mystery. London, Jarrolds, 1897.
A Queen of Atlantis (Monella). London, Hutchinson, and Philadelphia, Lippincott, 1899.
King of the Dead. London, Macqueen, 1903; New York, Arno Press, 1978.

Short Stories as Frank Aubrey

Strange Stories of Hospitals. London, Pearson, 1898.

* * *

At the turn of the century, Frank Atkins, using the Fenton Ash and other pen-names, was writing a genre of fiction which contained elements of what critics today broadly term speculative fiction. To call Atkins a science-fiction writer, however, would be to push him into a category which his writing fits only at certain key points: in theme and plot, in characters, and in style. Atkins's work suits his time and place, but in at least one novel, *A Trip to Mars,* he explores possibilities only being hinted at by a few other writers and cinematic directors of his time.

Atkins stretches coincidence to the limit in certain areas. He hypothesizes lost civilizations on earth—the remains of Atlantis in the middle of the Sargasso Sea, El Dorado on a mountain top in an unexplored region of South America—in four books, and only in *A Trip to Mars* does he move beyond the earth. He frequently postulates long-lost relatives; the conflict often revolves around the good characters overcoming powerful forces of evil. But Atkins's outcomes are pat, and he prepares his reader well with very broad hints for any "surprise."

Atkins strives for believability in his settings, giving lengthy descriptions with numerous footnotes, of the flora and fauna both in South America and in the Sargasso Sea, though there are many descriptions of the fantastic in all his books—giant flowers, fruits, animals, huge dazzling jewels and massive amounts of gold. He also frequently hypothesizes seers who make accurate, if non-specific, predictions, usually astrologically. Atkins's only real speculative scientific developments occur in his "red ray" (*King of the Dead*) and space ship (*A Trip to Mars*). "Hard" scientific developments play minimal part in his books.

Most of Atkins's characters are, at best, stereotypes. His infrequent attempts at light-heartedness generally occur when he introduces a lower-class Englishman (usually a sailor) with a droll, "uneducated" accent, uttering malapropisms. His "evil" characters are in all senses malevolent and frequently seem to be in league with some never-explained Dark Power. Only in *King of the Dead* does he portray directly a Power of Evil, called Mahrimah, who resembles a fallen angel. All the books have as protagonists male "chums" who are young, adventuresome, and typically British. Of lesser importance are the young women, generally the love interests of one or both of the "chums"; some are exotic, some are classically British, but they are without exception coy and beautiful, and are frequently endangered by natural or human foes. This is true even for Vanina, the queen of *A Queen of Atlantis,* who actually plays a very passive role in the plot. While in all of Atkins's books the good characters consistently behave nobly, most of the books contain a totally noble figure as well. In his Monella novels this character is Monella himself, a noble figure of great age who is roaming the world until he can regain his throne in El Dorado; in *King of the Dead* the noble figure is Lorenzo, né Manzoni, who is even more enigmatic than is Monella. They are consistently wise, strong, compelling, and remote, and both also have to atone for some "sin" (primarily caused by his leaving of his people and venturing into the "real" world) by admitting his error and setting things to rights.

Atkins's style is probably the most interesting feature of his books. Atkins uses the common technique of ending each chapter with a hint of what is to come, and it does serve its purpose—to keep the reader reading. Atkins uses much description in his books, which is fortunate since his dialogue is often formal and stilted. Atkins's point of view is consistently third-person, but the particular outlook of each chapter varies determined by whom Atkins chooses to focus through. Atkins is at his best when describing the exotic features of his setting—costly and beautiful architecture, elaborate costumes, wonderful jewels. He excels at choosing exotic names for people, places, animals, and Gods—Ivanta, Alondra, Mellenda, Ulama, Lyostrah, Morveena. The tension in his novels frequently revolves around encounters with natural but terrifying animals, such as cuttlefish, enormous snakes, gorilla-type animals, pumas, and most of his novels feature supernatural monsters such as zombies, vampires, and, most particularly, the devil-tree in the novel of that name. The devil-tree, a huge tree which seizes its victims in tentacle-like branches and conveys them to its maw, a hollow trunk, is fully as terrifying and loathesome as any creation of current writers of horror novels or directors of horror movies. After the tree consumes its victims, it releases them, or what is left of them, to be carried off and eaten by crocodile-like monsters who live in a pond at its base. In the climactic scene at the end of the novel, the evil priests are all seized and eaten, some by the tree, and some by being torn to bits by the monsters as the priests are held in the tree's tentacles awaiting their turn in its maw. The nightmarish effectiveness of this description is such that its image remains vivid in the reader's mind long after he has finished the book itself.

In fact, if Atkins's writing is akin to speculative fiction, it is certainly supernatural and horror fiction which it most resembles. He does work with settings which are largely unknown to his world, but it is their exotic quality rather than any science-fiction aspect which he develops. Only in *A Trip to Mars* does Atkins extrapolate any scientific devices, and these are fanciful, based on principles long since outdated. Additionally, the Mars which Atkins depicts is so similar to his exotic settings on earth as to be interchangeable, and his Martian characters are certainly no less human, in physical features or in outlook, than the characters in his earth-based novels. Nevertheless, Atkins's books are still interesting reading, particularly in editions which contain the quaint original illustrations, as period pieces.

—Karren C. Edwards

ASIMOV, Isaac. Also writes as Dr. A.; Paul French. American. Born in Petrovichi, U.S.S.R., 2 January 1920; emigrated to the United States in 1923; naturalized, 1928. Educated at Columbia University, New York, B.S. 1939, M.A. 1941, Ph.D. 1948. Served in the United States Army, 1945-46. Married 1) Gertrude Blugerman in 1942 (divorced), one son and one daughter; 2) Janet Opal Jeppson in 1973. Instructor in Biochemistry, 1949-51, Assistant Professor, 1951-55, and since 1955 Associate Professor, Boston University School of Medicine. Recipient: Edison Foundation National Mass Media Award, 1958; Blakeslee Award, for non-fiction, 1960; World Science Fiction Convention Citation, 1963; Hugo Award, 1963, 1966, 1973, 1977; American Chemical Society James T. Grady Award, 1965; American Association for the Advancement of Science-Westinghouse Writing Award, 1967; Nebula Award, 1972, 1976. Guest of Honor, World Science Fiction Convention, 1955. Address: 10 West 66th Street, New York, New York 10023, U.S.A.

SCIENCE-FICTION PUBLICATIONS

Novels (series: Foundation; Trantorian Empire)

Triangle (Empire). New York, Doubleday, 1961; as *A Second Isaac Asimov Omnibus*, London, Sidgwick and Jackson, 1969.
  Pebble in the Sky. New York, Doubleday, 1950; London, Corgi, 1958.
  The Stars, Like Dust. New York, Doubleday, 1951; London, Panther, 1958; as *The Rebellious Stars,* New York, Ace, 1954.
  The Currents of Space. New York, Doubleday, 1952; London, Boardman, 1955.
Foundation Trilogy. New York, Doubleday, 1963(?); as *An Isaac Asimov Omnibus*, London, Sidgwick and Jackson, 1966.
  Foundation. New York, Gnome Press, 1952; London, Weidenfeld and Nicolson, 1953; abridged edition, as *The Thousand-Year Plan,* New York, Ace, 1956.
  Foundation and Empire. New York, Gnome Press, 1952; London, Panther, 1962; as *The Man Who Upset the Universe,* New York, Ace, 1955.
  Second Foundation. New York, Gnome Press, 1953.
The Caves of Steel. New York, Doubleday, and London, Boardman, 1954.
The End of Eternity. New York, Doubleday, 1955; London, Panther, 1958.
The Naked Sun. New York, Doubleday, 1957; London, Joseph, 1958.
Fantastic Voyage (novelization of screenplay). Boston, Houghton Mifflin, and London, Dobson, 1966.
The Gods Themselves. New York, Doubleday, and London, Gollancz, 1972.
The Collected Fiction: The Far Ends of Time and Earth, Prisoners of the Stars. New York, Doubleday, 2 vols., 1979.

Novels (juvenile) as Paul French (series: Lucky Starr in all books)

David Starr, Space Ranger. New York, Doubleday, 1952; Kingswood, Surrey, World's Work, 1953.
Lucky Starr and the Pirates of the Asteroids. New York, Doubleday, 1953; Kingswood, Surrey, World's Work, 1954.
Lucky Starr and the Oceans of Venus. New York, Doubleday, 1954; as *The Oceans of Venus,* as Isaac Asimov, London, New English Library, 1973.
Lucky Starr and the Big Sun of Mercury. New York, Doubleday, 1956; as *The Big Sun of Mercury,* as Isaac Asimov, London, New English Library, 1974.
Lucky Starr and the Moons of Jupiter. New York, Doubleday, 1957; as *The Moons of Jupiter,* as Isaac Asimov, London, New English Library, 1974.
Lucky Starr and the Rings of Saturn. New York, Doubleday, 1958; as *The Rings of Saturn,* as Isaac Asimov, London, New English Library, 1974.

Short Stories

I, Robot. New York, Gnome Press, 1950; London, Grayson, 1952.
The Martian Way and Other Stories. New York, Doubleday, 1955; London, Dobson, 1964.
Earth Is Room Enough. New York, Doubleday, 1957; London, Panther, 1960.
Nine Tomorrows: Tales of the Near Future. New York, Doubleday, 1959; London, Dobson, 1963.
The Rest of the Robots. New York, Doubleday, 1964; London, Dobson, 1967.
Through a Glass, Clearly. London, New English Library, 1967.
Asimov's Mysteries. New York, Doubleday, and London, Rapp and Whiting, 1968.
Nightfall and Other Stories. New York, Doubleday, 1969; London, Rapp and Whiting, 1970.
The Early Asimov; or, Eleven Years of Trying. New York, Doubleday, 1972; London, Gollancz, 1973.
The Best of Isaac Asimov (1939-1972). London, Sidgwick and Jackson, 1973; New York, Doubleday, 1974.
Have You Seen These? Cambridge, Massachusetts, NESFA Press, 1974.
The Heavenly Host (juvenile). New York, Walker, 1975; London, Penguin, 1978.
Buy Jupiter and Other Stories. New York, Doubleday, 1975; London, Gollancz, 1976.
The Dream, Benjamin's Dream, Benjamin's Bicentennial Blast. Privately printed, 1976.
The Bicentennial Man and Other Stories. New York, Doubleday, and London, Gollancz, 1976.
Good Taste. Topeka, Kansas, Apocalypse Press, 1976.

OTHER PUBLICATIONS

Novels

The Death Dealers. New York, Avon, 1958; as *A Whiff of Death,* New York, Walker, and London, Gollancz, 1968.
Murder at the ABA. New York, Doubleday, 1976; as *Authorized Murder,* London, Gollancz, 1976.

Short Stories

Tales of the Black Widowers. New York, Doubleday, 1974; London, Gollancz, 1975.
More Tales of the Black Widowers. New York, Doubleday, 1976; London, Gollancz, 1977.
Casebook of the Black Widowers. New York, Doubleday, and London, Gollancz, 1980.

Verse

Lecherous Limericks. New York, Walker, 1975; London, Corgi, 1977.
More Lecherous Limericks. New York, Walker, 1976.
Still More Lecherous Limericks. New York, Walker, 1977.

Asimov's Sherlockian Limericks. Yonkers, New York, Mysterious Press, 1978.

Limericks: Too Gross, with John Ciardi. New York, Norton, 1978.

Other

Biochemistry and Human Metabolism, with Burnham Walker and William C. Boyd. Baltimore, Williams and Wilkins, 1952; revised edition, 1954, 1957; London, Ballière Tindall and Cox, 1955.

The Chemicals of Life: Enzymes, Vitamins, Hormones. New York, Abelard Schuman, 1954; London, Bell, 1956.

Races and People, with William C. Boyd. New York, Abelard Schuman, 1955; London, Abelard Schuman, 1958.

Chemistry and Human Health, with Burnham Walker and M.K. Nicholas. New York, McGraw Hill, 1956.

Inside the Atom. New York and London, Abelard Schuman, 1956; revised edition, New York and London, Abelard Schuman, 1958, 1961, 1966, 1974.

Building Blocks of the Universe. New York, Abelard Schuman, 1957; London, Abelard Schuman, 1958; revised edition, 1961, 1974.

Only a Trillion. New York and London, Abelard Schuman, 1957; as *Marvels of Science,* New York, Collier, 1962.

The World of Carbon. New York and London, Abelard Schuman, 1958; revised edition, New York, Collier, 1962.

The World of Nitrogen. New York and London, Abelard Schuman, 1958; revised edition, New York, Collier, 1962.

The Clock We Live On. New York and London, Abelard Schuman, 1959; revised edition, New York, Collier, 1962; Abelard Schuman, 1965.

The Living River. New York and London, Abelard Schuman, 1959; revised edition, as *The Bloodstream: River of Life,* New York, Collier, 1961.

Realm of Numbers. Boston, Houghton Mifflin, 1959; London, Gollancz, 1963.

Words of Science and the History Behind Them. Boston, Houghton Mifflin, 1959; London, Harrap, 1974.

Breakthroughs in Science (juvenile). Boston, Houghton Mifflin, 1960.

The Intelligent Man's Guide to Science. New York, Basic, 2 vols., 1960; revised edition, as *The New Intelligent Man's Guide to Science,* 1 vol., 1965; London, Nelson, 1967; as *Asimov's Guide to Science,* New York, Basic, 1972; London, Penguin, 1975.

The Kingdom of the Sun. New York and London, Abelard Schuman, 1960; revised edition, New York, Collier, 1962; Abelard Schuman, 1963.

Realm of Measure. Boston, Houghton Mifflin, 1960.

Satellites in Outer Space (juvenile). New York, Random House, 1960; revised edition, 1964, 1973.

The Double Planet. New York, Abelard Schuman, 1960; London, Abelard Schuman, 1962; revised edition, 1966.

The Wellsprings of Life. New York and London, Abelard Schuman, 1960.

Realm of Algebra. Boston, Houghton Mifflin, 1961; London, Gollancz, 1964.

Words from the Myths. Boston, Houghton Mifflin, 1961; London, Faber, 1963.

Fact and Fancy. New York, Doubleday, 1962.

Life and Energy. New York, Doubleday, 1962; London, Dobson, 1963.

The Search for the Elements. New York, Basic, 1962.

Words in Genesis. Boston, Houghton Mifflin, 1962.

Words on the Map. Boston, Houghton Mifflin, 1962.

View from a Height. New York, Doubleday, 19663; London, Dobson, 1964.

The Genetic Code. New York, Orion Press, 1963; London, Murray, 1964.

The Human Body: Its Structure and Operation. Boston, Houghton Mifflin, 1963; London, Nelson, 1965.

The Kite That Won the Revolution. Boston, Houghton Mifflin, 1963.

Words from the Exodus. Boston, Houghton Mifflin, 1963.

Adding a Dimension: 17 Essays on the History of Science. New York, Doubleday, 1964; London, Dobson, 1966.

The Human Brain: Its Capacities and Functions. Boston, Houghton Mifflin, 1964; London, Nelson, 1965.

Quick and Easy Math. Boston, Houghton Mifflin, 1964; London, Whiting and Wheaton, 1967.

A Short History of Biology. Garden City, New York, Natural History Press, 1964; London, Nelson, 1965.

Planets for Man, with Stephen H. Dole. New York, Random House, 1964.

Asimov's Biographical Encyclopedia of Science and Technology. New York, Doubleday, 1964; London, Allen and Unwin, 1966; revised edition, Doubleday, 1972; London, Pan, 1975.

An Easy Introduction to the Slide Rule. Boston, Houghton Mifflin, 1965; London, Whiting and Wheaton, 1967.

The Greeks: A Great Adventure. Boston, Houghton Mifflin, 1965.

Of Time and Space and Other Things. New York, Doubleday, 1965; London, Dobson, 1967.

A Short History of Chemistry. New York, Doubleday, 1965; London, Heinemann, 1972.

The Neutrino: Ghost Particle of the Atom. New York, Doubleday, and London, Dobson, 1966.

The Genetic Effects of Radiation, with Theodosius Dobzhansky. Washington, D.C., Atomic Energy Commission, 1966.

The Noble Gases. New York, Basic, 1966.

The Roman Republic. Boston, Houghton Mifflin, 1966.

From Earth to Heaven. New York, Doubleday, 1966.

Understanding Physics. New York, Walker, 3 vols., 1966; London, Allen and Unwin, 3 vols., 1967.

The Universe: From Flat Earth to Quasar. New York, Walker, 1966; London, Penguin, 1967; revised edition, Walker, 1971; revised edition, as *The Universe: From Flat Earth to Black Holes—and Beyond,* Walker, 1980.

The Roman Empire. Boston, Houghton Mifflin, 1967.

The Moon (juvenile). Chicago, Follett, 1967; London, University of London Press, 1969.

Is Anyone There? (essays). New York, Doubleday, 1967; London, Rapp and Whiting, 1968.

To the Ends of the Universe. New York, Walker, 1967; revised edition, 1976.

The Egyptians. Boston, Houghton Mifflin, 1967.

Mars (juvenile). Chicago, Follett, 1967; London, University of London Press, 1971.

From Earth to Heaven: 17 Essays on Science. New York, Doubleday, 1967; London, Dobson, 1968.

Environments Out There. New York, Abelard Schuman, 1967; London, Abelard Schuman, 1968.

"There's Nothing Like a Good Foundation," in *SFWA Bulletin* (Sea Cliff, New York), January 1967.

Science, Numbers, and I: Essays on Science. New York, Doubleday, 1968; London, Rapp and Whiting, 1969.

The Near East: 10,000 Years of History. Boston, Houghton Mifflin, 1968.

Asimov's Guide to the Bible: The Old Testament, The New Testament. New York, Doubleday, 2 vols., 1968-69.

The Dark Ages. Boston, Houghton Mifflin, 1968.

Galaxies (juvenile). Chicago, Follett, 1968; London, University of London Press, 1971.

Stars (juvenile). Chicago, Follett, 1968.

Words from History. Boston, Houghton Mifflin, 1968.

Photosynthesis. New York, Basic, 1968; London, Allen and Unwin, 1970.

The Shaping of England. Boston, Houghton Mifflin, 1969.

Twentieth Century Discovery (juvenile). New York, Doubleday, and London, Macdonald, 1969.

Opus 100 (selection). Boston, Houghton Mifflin, 1969.

ABC's of Space (juvenile). New York, Walker, 1969.

Great Ideas of Science (juvenile). Boston, Houghton Mifflin, 1969.

To the Solar System and Back. New York, Doubleday, 1970.

Asimov's Guide to Shakespeare: The Greek, Roman, and Italian Plays; The English Plays. New York, Doubleday, 2 vols., 1970.

Constantinople. Boston, Houghton Mifflin, 1970.

The ABC's of the Ocean (juvenile). New York, Walker, 1970.

Light (juvenile). Chicago, Follett, 1970.

"F & SF and I," in *Twenty Years of Fantasy and Science Fiction,* edited by Edward Ferman and Robert Mills. New York, Putnam, 1970.

Best New Thing (juvenile). Cleveland, World, 1971.

The Stars in Their Courses. New York, Doubleday, 1971; London, White Lion, 1974.

What Makes the Sun Shine. Boston, Little Brown, 1971.

The Isaac Asimov Treasury of Humor. Boston, Houghton Mifflin, 1971; London, Vallentine Mitchell, 1972.

The Sensuous Dirty Old Man (as Dr. A.). New York, Walker, 1971.

The Land of Canaan. Boston, Houghton Mifflin, 1971.

ABC's of Earth (juvenile). New York, Walker, 1971.

The Space Dictionary. New York, Starline, 1971.

More Words of Science. Boston, Houghton Mifflin, 1972.

Electricity and Man. Washington, D.C., Atomic Energy Commission, 1972.

The Shaping of France. Boston, Houghton Mifflin, 1972.

Asimov's Annotated "Don Juan." New York, Doubleday, 1972.

ABC's of Ecology (juvenile). New York, Walker, 1972.

The Story of Ruth. New York, Doubleday 1972.

Worlds Within Worlds. Washington, D.C., Atomic Energy Commission, 1972.

The Left Hand of the Electron (essays). New York, Doubleday, 1972; London, White Lion, 1975.

Ginn Science Program. Boston, Ginn, 5 vols., 1972-73.

"Why Read Science Fiction?," in *3000 Years of Fantasy and Science Fiction,* edited by L. Sprague de Camp and Catherine Crook de Camp. New York, Lothrop, 1972.

How Did We Find Out about Dinosaurs [The Earth Is Round, Electricity, Vitamins, Germs, Comets, Energy, Atoms, Nuclear Power, Numbers, Outer Space, Earthquakes, Black Holes, Our Human Roots Antarctica] (juvenile). New York, Walker, 15 vols., 1973-79; 6 vols. published London, White Lion, 1975-76.

The Tragedy of the Moon (essays). New York, Doubleday, 1973; London, Abelard Schuman, 1974.

Comets and Meteors (juvenile). Chicago, Follett, 1973.

The Sun (juvenile). Chicago, Follett, 1973.

The Shaping of North America from the Earliest Times to 1763. Boston, Houghton Mifflin, 1973; London, Dobson, 1975.

Please Explain (juvenile). Boston, Houghton Mifflin, 1973; London, Abelard Schuman, 1975.

Physical Science Today. Del Mar, California, CRM, 1973.

Jupiter, The Largest Planet (juvenile). New York, Lothrop, 1973; revised edition, 1976.

Today, Tomorrow, and.... New York, Doubleday, 1973; London, Abelard Schuman, 1974; as *Towards Tomorrow,* London, Hodder and Stoughton, 1977.

"When Aristotle Fails, Try Science Fiction," in *Speculations,* edited by Thomas D. Sanders. Beverly Hills, California, Glencoe Press, 1973.

The Birth of the United States 1763-1816. Boston, Houghton Mifflin, 1974.

Earth: Our Crowded Spaceship. New York, Day, and London, Abelard Schuman, 1974.

Asimov on Chemistry. New York, Doubleday, 1974; London, Macdonald and Jane's, 1975.

Asimov on Astronomy. New York, Doubleday, and London, Macdonald, 1974.

Asimov's Annotated "Paradise Lost." New York, Doubleday, 1974.

Our World in Space. Greenwich, Connecticut, New York Graphic Society, and Cambridge, Patrick Stephens, 1974.

The Solar System (juvenile). Chicago, Follett, 1975.

Birth and Death of the Universe. New York, Walker, 1975.

Of Matters Great and Small. New York, Doubleday, 1975.

Our Federal Union: The United States from 1816 to 1865. Boston, Houghton Mifflin, and London, Dobson, 1975.

The Ends of the Earth: The Polar Regions of the World. New York, Weybright and Talley, 1975.

Eyes on the Universe: A History of the Telescope. Boston, Houghton Mifflin, 1975; London, Deutsch, 1976.

Science Past—Science Future. New York, Doubleday, 1975.

"Is There Hope for the Future?," in *The Best from Galaxy 3,* edited by James Baen. New York, Award, 1975.

Alpha Centauri, The Nearest Star (juvenile). New York, Lothrop, 1976.

I, Rabbi (juvenile). New York, Walker, 1976.

Asimov on Physics. New York, Doubleday, 1976.

The Planet That Wasn't. New York, Doubleday, 1976; London, Sphere, 1977.

The Collapsing Universe: The Story of Black Holes. New York, Walker, and London, Hutchinson, 1977.

Asimov on Numbers. New York, Doubleday, 1977.

The Beginning and the End. New York, Doubleday, 1977.

Familiar Poems Annotated. New York, Doubleday, 1977.

The Golden Door: The United States from 1865 to 1918. Boston, Houghton Mifflin, and London, Dobson, 1977.

The Key Word and Other Mysteries (juvenile). New York, Walker, 1977.

Mars, The Red Planet (juvenile). New York, Lothrop, 1977.

Life and Time. New York, Doubleday, 1978.

Quasar, Quasar, Burning Bright. New York, Doubleday, 1978.

Animals of the Bible (juvenile). New York, Doubleday, 1978.

Isaac Asimov's Book of Facts. New York, Grosset and Dunlap, 1979; London, Hodder and Stoughton, 1980.

Extraterrestrial Civilizations. New York, Crown, 1979; London, Robson, 1980.

A Choice of Catastrophes. New York, Simon and Schuster, 1979; London, Hutchinson, 1980.

Saturn and Beyond. New York, Lothrop, 1979.

Opus 200 (selection). Boston, Houghton Mifflin, 1979; as *Opus,* London, Deutsch, 1980.

In Memory Yet Green: The Autobiography of Isaac Asimov 1920-1954. New York, Doubleday, 1979.

The Road to Infinity. New York, Doubleday, 1979.

In Joy Still Felt: The Autobiography of Isaac Asimov 1954-1978. New York, Doubleday, 1980.

The Annotated Gulliver's Travels. New York, Potter, 1980.

Editor, *The Hugo Winners 1-3.* New York, Doubleday, 3 vols., 1962-67; *1* and *3,* London, Dobson, 2 vols., 1963-67; *2,* London, Sphere, 1973.

Editor, with Groff Conklin, *Fifty Short Science Fiction Tales.* New York, Macmillan 1963.

Editor, *Tomorrow's Children: 18 Tales of Fantasy and Science Fiction,* New York, Doubleday, 1966; London, Futura, 1974.

Editor, *Where Do We Go from Here?* New York, Doubleday, 1971; London, Joseph, 1973.

Editor, *Nebula Award Stories 8.* New York, Harper, and London, Gollancz, 1973.

Editor, *Before the Golden Age: A Science Fiction Anthology of the 1930's.* ·New York, Doubleday, and London, Robson, 1974.

Editor, with Martin H. Greenberg and Joseph D. Olander, *100 Great Science Fiction Short-Short Stories.* New York, Doubleday, and London, Robson, 1978.

Editor, with Martin H. Greenberg and Charles G. Waugh, *The Science Fictional Solar System.* New York, Harper, 1979; London, Sidgwick and Jackson, 1980.

Editor, with Martin H. Greenberg and Charles G. Waugh, *Thirteen Crimes of Science Fiction.* New York, Doubleday, 1979.

Editor, with Martin H. Greenberg, *The Great SF Stories 1-4.* New York, DAW, 4 vols., 1979-80.

Editor, with Martin H. Greenberg and Joseph D. Olander, *Microcosmic Tales: 100 Wondrous Science Fiction Short-Short Stories.* New York, Taplinger, 1980.

Editor, with Martin H. Greenberg and Joseph D. Olander, *Space Mail.* New York, Fawcett, 1980.

Editor, with Martin H. Greenberg and Joseph D. Olander, *The Future in Question.* New York, Fawcett, 1980.

Editor, with Alice Laurance, *Who Done It?* Boston, Houghton Mifflin, 1980.

Editor, with Martin H. Greenberg and Joseph D. Olander, *Miniature Mysteries: 100 Malicious Little Mystery Stories.* New York, Taplinger, 1980.

Editor, with Martin H. Greenberg and Charles G. Waugh, *The Seven Deadly Sins of Science Fiction.* New York, Fawcett, 1980.

*

Bibliography: *Isaac Asimov: A Checklist of Works Published in the United States March 1939-May 1972* by Marjorie M. Miller, Kent, Ohio, Kent State University Press, 1972; in *In Memory Yet Green*, Doubleday, 1979.

Manuscript Collection: Mugar Memorial Library, Boston University.

*   *   *

The world's most prolific science writer, Isaac Asimov is responsible for some of the best-known science fiction ever published. Usually avoiding melodramatic action, Asimov's fiction focuses on puzzle-solving that seeks to educate the reader in science and technology. The frequent conflict between his generally optimistic and detached tone and the plot lines and concepts of his stories might be troubling for someone who laid more claims to being an "artist." It may be less important, however, for a superior self-taught craftsman whose fictions have entertained millions over more than 40 years.

In many of Asimov's short stories, the gimmick is everything, and it may be no more than a pun or a surprise ending. Sometimes the gimmick is clever but repetitious, as in three stories about societies so technologically sophisticated that something we take for granted today has to be rediscovered: writing in "Someday," mathematics in "The Feeling of Power," walking outdoors in "It's Such a Beautiful Day." A certain amount of repetition is also apparent in Asimov's robot stories and mysteries. Sometimes the gimmick is memorable, as in "Franchise" which extrapolates polling methods to their logical conclusion—computer elections with toss-ups decided by a scientifically chosen average citizen. Similarly "What If?" poses an image of time as fixed but fluid, with variant means producing the same end; this is exhibited through newlyweds' indulging their curiosity to find out what might have happened if they hadn't met as they did.

Even longer stories may be gimmick-oriented, though the best surmount their origins. "Profession," for example, is interesting as a reduction to the absurd of trends in accelerated education. While everyone else is secure in knowing that he will find his niche through programming suited exactly to his brain pattern, the protagonist discovers that he, as a really creative individual, must educate himself. But an interstellar civilization's dependence on one world's ritual "Reading Day," "Education Day," and job-seeking "Olympics" is hardly credible, nor is the secret conspiracy of creative individuals. The same objection to a conspiracy of silence can be raised about "The Dead Past," but its extrapolative source has a sharper satirical edge, relating grants for scientific research to the spectre of government control of curiosity. Unable to get clearance for direct observation of ancient Carthage, a historian persuades a physicist to build a time-viewer from classified data, a task which the scientist's own specialty makes simple. Before the government can act, these well-meaning rebels make public a surveillance technology extending to the most recent past, which completely eliminates privacy in the present. If the interests of science and public policy clash in that story, the interests of science and basic human ethics are at odds in "The Ugly Little Boy." If not Asimov's best, this is certainly his most emotional story, contrasting the imperative for scientific research with that drive's effects on individual human beings, especially the little Neanderthal boy who has been snatched into the present, and the nurse who views with deadly seriousness her job of taking care of him.

Other human interest stories also stand out in Asimov's short fiction. "Dreaming Is a Private Thing" gives impressionistic glimpses of a literal dream-industry from an entrepreneur's viewpoint. "The Martian Way" is at first glance another gimmick story. Martian colonists, who depend on water as reaction mass for their spaceships, are endangered by an Earth-first political movement's threat to cut off their supply. The answer is simple, for a Martian: bring water from the rings of Saturn. But this novella, too, transcends its gimmick to propagandize for human progress, to display The making of a new kind of civilization, and to take a satirical poke at recurrent demagogic types in America.

Although Asimov's best work comes from the 1950's, his most popular fiction stems from the previous decade. Written when he was barely 21, "Nightfall" may be the most popular short story in all of science fiction. It creaks with pulp clichés of the 1930's, including the stock characters who people a distant planet. The premise is implausible, that this "alien" race experience darkness only once every two thousand years. Still, "Nightfall" is a classic of science-fictional perspective and sense of wonder. The astronomical situation is theoretically possible, although fundamentally unstable. The panic resulting from darkness is a credible metaphor standing for the periodic fall of civilization. And the viewpoint of the scientists poses a suggestive antidote, studying rather than worshipping the strange phenomena. Curiosity is conquered by fear, however, raising the same note of ambivalence toward science which provides an undercurrent in other Asimov fictions.

The robot stories (begun in 1940) which overflow three volumes, *I, Robot, The Rest of the Robots,* and *The Bicentennial Man,* gave rise to the "Three Laws of Robotics," formulated with *Astounding*-editor John W. Campbell, Jr. Asimov devised these control mechanisms to offset a "Frankenstein complex" he saw in science fiction. Puzzle-stories, exploring limits and loopholes in the Three Laws, they sometimes trivialize rather than defuse the modern fear of and antipathy toward technological civilization which are their subtext. Although some of the short works rise above the mass, notably "Liar," "Reason" and "The Last Question," his best robot stories are the two detective novels *The Caves of Steel* and *The Naked Sun,* set three thousand years in the future when man has settled a limited number of outer planets but people on Earth have little to do with them. Examples of classic mystery form, they posit the necessity of man-machine cooperation if man is to achieve his "manifest destiny" in space. The six juvenile novels about David "Lucky" Starr are concerned with the settling period. Mostly puzzle-stories set in the solar system as it was understood in the 1950's, these have been reissued recently with disclaimers about their outmoded astronomical speculations. That same passion for scientific accuracy informs his film-novelization, *Fantastic Voyage,* which rationalizes everything but the fundamental impossiblity at the movie's core: a subminiaturized vehicle and five humans that enter a scientist's bloodstream to remove a blood clot from his brain.

As a novelist, however, Asimov is best-known for *The Foundation Trilogy.* Loosely based on historical parallels with the Roman Empire, these stories and novellas speculate on the possiblility of a deterministic psycho-history that calls into question the free will decisions of his anti-heroic protagonists. In a crumbling Galactic Empire, they try to keep alive the spirit of scientific inquiry throught a Dark Age until civilization can again be consolidated. Not the first to examine such an empire, Asimov's work was different in its focus on decision-making rather than blood-and-thunder action, and its assumption—a compromise with editor Campbell's insistence that aliens be inferior—of a humans-only civilization. Three novels taking place in earlier stages of the Empire—*Pebble in the Sky, The Stars, Like Dust,* and *The Currents of Space*—are significant for their portrait of a radioactive Earth reviled and neglected by her far-flung children, but less rewarding than most of Asimov's work. Loosely connected to the same future history, *The End of Eternity* is Asimov's closest approach to a conventional love story. In it, the overthrow of an organization, Eternity, which functions through time travel to stabilize 70 thousand centuries of Earth's history, brings about a temporal universe in which Earth's Galactic Empire can come into being.

In a different vein *The Gods Themselves* suggests a more "serious" Asimov in terms of artistry and contemporary social relevance. At issue, in part, is an impending energy crisis temporarily solved by drawing energy from an alternate universe. The major interest for Asimov-watchers, however, is the para-universe itself and his largely successful creation of an alien civilization and consciousness. Unfortunately, the aliens are abandoned in the conclusion, and the energy crisis is shifted away from their cosmos to still another para-universe in a feat of auctorial sleight-of-hand.

Although his latest work does not break major new ground, it shows the continued potentiality for growth in a writer who could well afford to rest on previous accomplishments. Having brought into the field a low-key anti-melodramatic style, a love for playfully solving puzzles and problems, and an air of scientific detachment and respectability, Asimov has written a body of work already one of the cornerstones of modern science fiction.

—David N. Samuelson

ASPRIN, Robert (Lynn). American. Born in St. Johns, Michigan, in 1946. Attended the University of Michigan, Ann Arbor, 1964-65. Served in the United States Army, 1965-66. Married Anne Brett; one daughter and one son. Accounts clerk, 1966-70, payroll analyst, 1970-74, and cost accountant, 1974-78, University Microfilm, Ann Arbor. Since 1978, free-lance writer. Agent: Kirby McCauley, 60 East 42nd Street, New York, New York 10017. Address: 204 South Fourth Avenue, Ann Arbor, Michigan 48104, U.S.A.

SCIENCE-FICTION PUBLICATIONS

Novels

The Cold Cash War. New York, St. Martin's Press, and London, New English Library, 1977.
Another Fine Myth. Virginia Beach, Donning, 1978.
The Bug Wars. New York, St. Martin's Press, 1979.
Tambu. New York, Ace, 1979.
Mirror Friend, Mirror Foe, with George Takei. Chicago, Playboy Press, 1979.

OTHER PUBLICATIONS

Other

Myth Conceptions. Virginia Beach, Donning, 1979.

Editor, *Thieves' World.* New York, Ace, 1979.

*   *   *

One of the more energetic and interesting writers to emerge since the late 1970's, Robert Asprin compiled a most impressive record for productivity in his early years. His first book, *The Cold Cash War,* introduced themes present in most of his later works, and which can be traced, at least in part, to Asprin's pre-literary occupation. He had been a cost accountant for a large "high-tech" corporation, and was thoroughly familiar with corporate procedures and the problems of management and personal rivalries within the corporate environment.

In *The Cold Cash War,* Asprin posits growing impatience and dissatisfaction on the part of large corporations with governmental mandates and unresponsiveness. In this situation, the corporations form private armies; when the government, through its "official" army, tries to suppress this odd rebellion, the corporations triumph as a result of possessing superior technology and more effective means of troop-motivation. The book is somewhat limited in characterization and plot, but shows excellent powers of technological and sociological extrapolation, at least in the near-future range.

The Bug Wars, Asprin's second science-fiction novel (a fantasy novel of very different nature intervened), continued the military theme, and is a worthy experiment, but unfortunately fails seriously. Asprin portrays an interplanetary struggle between a race of highly advanced, highly militaristic, intelligent reptiles and a coalition of huge insects. The narration is from the viewpoint of the reptiles, and it is uncertain to both the reptiles and the reader whether the insects are truly intelligent or not. A background rationale involves a mysterious elder race which had been instrumental in the spread of the insects through space. There is also passing mention of small warm-blooded animals, the reader being free to speculate as to whether these are pre-human beings, true humans of a degraded culture, or simply warm-blooded animals. A novel told completely from the viewpoint of a reptilian alien and involving no identifiable human characters was a most ambitious undertaking. The result, unfortunately, was a thoroughly one-dimensional book devoted almost entirely to the military details of battle; without characters suitable for reader empathy or identification, the volume makes poor reading. It is further marred by numerous minor solecisms and clichés. Asprin has suffered from poor editing.

Tambu shows marked improvement. It is the story of a band of professional pirate-hunters, laid against the background of a future interstellar trading culture. The structure of the book is unnecessarily cluttered with excerpts from a supposed interview at the end of

Tambu's career, between which Asprin intersperses major incidents in his life. But the story-telling is brisk, the characterization indicates considerable progress, and a feel is achieved, at least sporadically, that is reminiscent of the old *Planet Stories* or E.E. Smith space operas.

Asprin's collaborative novel, *Mirror Friend, Mirror Foe,* was written with George Takei, the actor best known for his continuing role in the *Star Trek* series. In this novel, against a background of intercorporate espionage and cold-war, the authors place a corporate spy within a robot-manufacturing concern. The spy's heritage derives from the Japanese *ninja;* this, presumably, is Takei's contribution while Asprin's is the corporate situation. From a promising start, the book unfortunately degenerates into cliché as the robots, escaping from their normal conditioning, go lurching and clanking about a planet murdering every human being they encounter.

Asprin's fantasy novel, *Another Fine Myth,* is a work of high humor in the tradition of de Camp and other veterans of the *Unknown* era. It is an Arabian Nights fantasy, with *jinni,* spells, dragons, homunculi, and a green-haired whore with a heart of gold, and is altogether charming albeit trivial.

—Richard A. Lupoff

_____

ATKINS, John (Alfred). British. Born in Carshalton, Surrey, 26 May 1916. Educated at Bristol University, B.A. (honours) in history 1938. Served in the Royal Artillery, 1944-46. Married Dorothy J. Grey in 1940; Two daughters. Interviewer, Mass Observation, London, 1939-41; Literary Editor, *Tribune,* 1942-44; District Organiser, Workers' Educational Association, Bristol, 1948-51; teacher, Ministry of Education, Sudan, 1951-55 and 1958-64; Head of the Department of English, Higher Teacher Training Institute, Omdurman, Sudan, 1965-68; Senior Lecturer in English, University of Benghazi, Libya, 1968-70; Docent in English Literature, University of Lodz, Poland, 1970-76. Recipient: Arts Council Award, 1970. Agent: David Higham Associates Ltd., 5-8 Lower John Street, London W1R 4HA. Address: Braeside Cottage, Mill Lane, Birch Green, Colchester CO2 0NG, Essex, England.

SCIENCE-FICTION PUBLICATIONS

Novel

Tomorrow Revealed. London, Spearman, 1955; New York, Roy, 1956.

Uncollected Short Stories

"The Theft of the Sun," in *English Story 4,* edited by Woodrow Wyatt. London, Collins, 1943.
"The Light of the World," in *English Story 5,* edited by Woodrow Wyatt. London, Collins, 1944.
"Climbing the Princess," in *English Story 9,* edited by Woodrow Wyatt. London, Collins, 1949.

OTHER PUBLICATIONS

Novels

Cat on Hot Bricks. London, Macdonald, 1950.
Rain and the River. London, Putnam, 1954.
A Land Fit for 'Eros, with J.B. Pick. London, Arco, 1957.

Short Story

The Diary of William Carpenter. London, Favil Press, 1943.

Verse

Experience of England.   London, Favil Press, 1943.

Other

The Distribution of Fish.   London, Fabian Society, 1941.
Walter de la Mare: An Exploration.   London, Temple, 1947; Folcroft, Pennsylvania, Folcroft Editions, 1973.
The Art of Ernest Hemingway: His Work and His Personality.   London, Nevill, 1952; New York, Roy, 1954.
George Orwell: A Literary Study.   London, Calder, 1954; New York, Ungar, 1955.
Arthur Koestler.   London, Spearman, and New York, Roy, 1956.
Aldous Huxley: A Literary Study.   London, Calder, and New York, Roy, 1956; revised edition, London, Calder and Boyars, 1967; New York, Orion Press, 1968.
Graham Greene.   London, Calder, and New York, Roy, 1957; revised edition, London, Calder and Boyars, 1966; New York, Humanities Press, 1967.
Sex in Literature:
   1. *The Erotic Impulse in Literature.*   London, Calder and Boyars, 1970; New York, Grove Press, 1972.
   2. *The Classical Experience of the Sexual Impulse.*   London, Calder and Boyars, 1973.
   3. *The Medieval Experience.*   London, Calder and Boyars, 1978.
Six Novelists Look at Society: An Enquiry into the Social Views of Elizabeth Bowen, L.P. Hartley, Rosamond Lehmann, Christopher Isherwood, Nancy Mitford, C.P. Snow.   London, Calder, and Dallas, Riverrun Texas, 1977.

*   *   *

John Atkins's *Tomorrow Revealed* is cast some thousands of years in the future. When most people are living a mindless existence, the son of a star-gazer, who has been taught to read and write by his father, writes a history of the earth and the planets visited by earthlings, the facts culled from such authors as Wells, Graves, Orwell, C.S. Lewis, Bradbury, Kuttner, Heinlein, van Vogt, and others. The novel is cast in the form of historical narrative, and the narrator is responsible for much unconscious humor as he attempts to fabricate a plausible history of mankind incorporating the various sources he uses. Much of the delight of this novel for the reader conversant with the major works of speculative fiction derives from his recognition of the sources, his knowledge of contemporary history, and the often disastrous conclusions drawn by the future historian, who is often guilty of distorting facts to fit his theory. The basic orientation of Atkins's book is theological, though it is far from doctrinaire theology. At the conclusion of his history, the narrator is convinced that history "is nothing unless it is an adjunct of theology." He concludes from his fascinating reading of the "sources" that there is a theological significance to human destiny. As he says, "I am convinced of a purpose."

Atkins is very articulate and well-versed in speculative fiction; he has written a book which is marvellous entertainment. There is a great deal of humor in this book, an element all too often absent from speculative fiction. Its basic weakness is that the entire novel is narrated; there is not one dramatized scene, or any character development or interaction—simply the dispassionate voice of the historian.

—Joseph A. Quinn

AUBREY, Frank.   *See* ASH, Fenton.

AVERY, Richard.   *See* COOPER, Edmund.

AYRE, Thornton.   *See* FEARN, John Russell.

BAHL, Franklin.   *See* PHILLIPS, Rog.

BALLARD, J(ames) G(raham).   British.   Born in Shanghai, China, 15 November 1930. Educated at Leys School, Cambridge; King's College, Cambridge. Served in the Royal Air Force. Married Helen Mary Matthews in 1953 (died, 1964); three children. Agent: John Wolfers, 3 Regent Square, London WC1H 8HZ. Address: 36 Charlton Road, Shepperton, Middlesex, England.

SCIENCE-FICTION PUBLICATIONS

Novels

The Wind from Nowhere.   New York, Berkley, 1962; London, Penguin, 1967.
The Drowned World.   New York, Berkley, 1962; London, Gollancz, 1963.
The Burning World.   New York, Berkley, 1964; revised edition, as *The Drought,* London, Cape, 1965.
The Crystal World.   London, Cape, and New York, Farrar Straus, 1966.
Crash!   London, Cape, and New York, Farrar Straus, 1973.
Concrete Island.   London, Cape, and New York, Farrar Straus, 1974.
High-Rise.   London, Cape, 1975; New York, Holt Rinehart, 1977.
The Unlimited Dream Company.   London, Cape, and New York, Holt Rinehart, 1979.

Short Stories

The Voices of Time and Other Stories.   New York, Berkley, 1962.
Billenium and Other Stories.   New York, Berkley, 1962.
The Four-Dimensional Nightmare.   London, Gollancz, 1963.
Passport to Eternity and Other Stories.   New York, Berkley, 1963.
The Terminal Beach.   London, Gollancz, 1964; abridged edition, New York, Berkley, 1964.
The Impossible Man and Other Stories.   New York, Berkley, 1966.
The Disaster Area.   London, Cape, 1967.
The Day of Forever.   London, Panther, 1967.
The Overloaded Man.   London, Panther, 1967.
The Atrocity Exhibition.   London, Cape, 1970; as *Love and Napalm: Export USA,* New York, Grove Press, 1972.
Chronopolis and Other Stories.   New York, Putnam, 1971.
Vermilion Sands.   New York, Berkley, 1971; London, Cape, 1973.
Low-Flying Aircraft and Other Stories.   London, Cape, 1976.
The Best Short Stories of J.G. Ballard.   New York, Holt Rinehart, 1978.

OTHER PUBLICATIONS

Play

The Assassination Weapon (produced London, 1969).

Other

"Some Words about *Crash,*" in *Foundation 9* (London), November 1975.

*

Bibliography: in *J.G. Ballard: The First Twenty Years* edited by James Goddard and David Pringle, Hayes, Middlesex, Bran's Head, 1976.

* * *

Of all the British writers of the New Wave, J.G. Ballard is undoubtedly the most original and distinctive. Though nourished by masterpieces of literature (from Homer and the Bible through Shakespeare to Coleridge and Melville) and the arts (from Bosch to Dali and Leonor Fini), his style is as distinctive as a signature: the abrupt openings, which plunge the reader straight into the action, as if he were already perfectly acquainted with the circumstances —outlandish though they may be—and with the whereabouts and idiosyncrasies of the characters—even though they may border on aberration or mania; the painter's eye which fixes things, land-scapes, and even living beings into striking pictures of both geomet-rical precision and coruscating beauty; the rich comparisons, through which, so often, paragraphs, instead of being concluded (i.e., closed upon themselves), are prolonged by mysterious harmo-nies and correspondences far and wide into space and time.

But if Ballard's usual approach is characteristic, his evolution is also conspicuous and coherent. His first stories still played with traditional SF situations, for example, the time paradox in "The Gentle Assassin," or warned of future exacerbation of present-day problems, such as unbridled urbanisation and overpopulation in "Build-Up" and "Billenium," later eminently illustrated by John Brunner. Yet even in the first collections (*The Voices of Time, Billenium, Four-Dimensional Nightmare*) are already to be found two dominant features of his later works: fascination for objects, especially the products of technology—clocks in "Chronopolis," invading metal in "Mobile"—and interest in the deviating psyche —one story of 1962 is entitled "The Insane Ones."

In the series of stories (1960 to 1967) set in Vermilion Sands—a decadent seaside resort which, as the soon-decaying materialisation of wild dreams, may be called an "inner landscape"—fascination and insanity are indeed allied in the various heroines: an actress who continues her murderous career beyond death, a poetess who wants a young admirer to repeat the sacrifice of Corydon to the muse Melandra, a rich and beautiful widow who has her portrait sculpted in the clouds. Extraordinary creatures (flying rays, singing orchids) or artefacts (a psychotropic house, a metal sculpture that sings and grows, clothes that live and feel) reflect and amplify the inner and mutual conflicts of those glamorous lamias and their suicidal woo-ers, in a baroque symphony of art, love, and death.

Meanwhile Ballard was writing a series of novels, each about a great natural catastrophe, in which he expressed his fascination with the awful beauty of the raging elements (air, water, fire, and "earth"—i.e., petrification—in succession, but often mingling: for example, *The Drought* is paradoxically full of references to ship-wrecks) and with the exceptional personalities who take advantage of those terrible situations to fulfil their perverse desire, inordinate ambitions, or suicidal manias. It is the last of these, *The Crystal World,* that goes furthest in picturing a cataclysm entirely unpredic-table and irremediable (a "time leak" causes matter to extend in space in the form of crystals), and both deadly and dazzling, and wilful characters for whom it is the occasion of romantically pursu-ing fatal ambitions devoid of any rational motivation.

As if Ballard had exhausted the treasures of his poetic imagina-tion by throwing them all into *The Crystal World,* the 1970's show a sudden turn towards bareness, both in his style—soberer descrip-tions, fewer far-flung comparisons—and in his material—no more

inordinate power and ambition in men, like Hardoon the modern Pharaoh, no more divine charm and exactingness in women, like Leonora Chanel the modern Medea, no more remote deadliness and beauty in the landscapes, like the all-invading hurricane, jun-gles, sands, or gems of the four previous novels. The characters are, rather, on the level of the reader and of the writer (some of them very much like him indeed; and with recurring names, Catherine, Helen, Maitland, Robert, to underline their commonness) in settings which present-day humanity has created for itself: the world of the auto-mobile (*Crash!*), of an environment forcefully adapted to traffic (*Concrete Island*), of gigantic apartment-buildings (*High-Rise*). These views of the present are not less dreadful than the previous views of the future, but more so, as is plain in the title of the collection of short stories which served as a sketchbook for the novels, *The Atrocity Exhibition.* In all four books, the monstrosity of our society is thrown into a crude light by bringing together some of its apparently irrelevant aspects—political murder and sport in "The Assassination of J.F. Kennedy Considered as a Downhill Motor Race," promiscuous sex and traffic hazards in *Crash!*—or just by heaping up instances of its worst consequences: the victims of car-mania horribly maimed in mind as well as in body, the most perverse and obsessive sexual pursuits, the most ruthless conflicts raging among the inmates of vertical "concentration camps" or among the wretched "Robinsons" that survive in the ruins lapped against by the ocean of traffic.

These descriptions are made even more unbearable by the de-tachment of the writer: before wounds as well as sexual organs—the two kinds of openings through which the flesh is reached by the most exquisite pain and pleasure—he remains cool and precise. There is a kind of morbid fascination in his attitude, which he ascribes to his taking part, as much as his fellow-men—in the worship of the new Moloch. Both the meaning and the outcome remain obscure: Ballard is fond of interpreting the most incongru-ous marks (of sperm as well as blood) in terms of mysterious alphabets, but "the writing on the wall" never finds its Daniel. Ballard sees us all, himself included, as carried away helplessly to some dark and terrible doom; all his characters, more or less will-ingly, bungle their escapes.

The writer himself seems to be the prisoner of his system of thought: in a more recent collection, *Low-Flying Aircraft and Other Stories,* whenever he imagines what the survivors could do after the collapse of our society, he invariably focuses his interest on those who madly attempt to resuscitate the old technological and social system, though—or maybe because—it was the very cause of the failure. In passing from the natural catastrophes of tomorrow to the man-made cataclysms of today, perhaps Ballard has not forsaken science fiction, since he claims to see in our environment "the fossils of the future" and reveals what is apocalyptic about it (he has coined the word "autogeddon" in parallel to the biblical "Armageddon," the cosmic battle at the end of time). But can there be any more science-fiction writing when the horizon is blocked—to borrow one of Ballard's favourite metaphors: as by a stranded whale—by the corpse of our own contemporary civilisation?

—George W. Barlow

BARNES, Arthur K(elvin). Also wrote as Dave Barnes; Kelvin Kent. American. Born in Bellingham, Washington, in 1911. Educated at the University of California, Los Angeles, B.A. (Phi Beta Kappa). Free-lance writer. *Died in 1969.*

SCIENCE-FICTION PUBLICATIONS

Short Stories (series: Gerry Carlisle)

Interplanetary Hunter. New York, Gnome Press, 1956.

Uncollected Short Stories (series: Gerry Carlisle)

"Lord of the Lightning," in *Wonder Stories* (New York), December 1931.
"Challenge of the Comet," in *Wonder Stories* (New York), February 1932.
"Guardians of the Void," in *Wonder Stories Quarterly* (New York), September 1932.
"The Hole Men of Mercury," in *Wonder Stories* (New York), December 1933.
"Emotion Solution," in *Wonder Stories* (New York), March 1936.
"The House That Walked" (as Dave Barnes), in *Astounding* (New York), September 1936.
"Prometheus," in *Amazing* (New York), February 1937.
"Green Hell" (Carlisle), in *Thrilling Wonder Stories* (New York), June 1937.
"The Dual World" (Carlisle), in *Thrilling Wonder Stories* (New York), June 1938.
"The Energy Eaters" (Carlisle; with Henry Kuttner), in *Thrilling Wonder Stories* (New York), October 1939.
"Day of the Titans," in *Thrilling Wonder Stories* (New York), February 1940.
"Waters of Wrath," in *Thrilling Wonder Stories* (New York), October 1940.
"Forgotten Future," in *Science Fiction* (Holyoke, Massachusetts), January 1941.
"The Little Man Who Wasn't There," in *Thrilling Wonder Stories* (New York), March 1941.
"Guinea Pig," in *Captain Future* (New York), Spring 1942.
"Fog over Venus," in *Thrilling Wonder Stories* (New York), Winter 1945.
"Grief of Bagdad," in *My Best Science Fiction Story,* edited by Leo Margulies and Oscar J. Friend. New York, Merlin Press, 1949.

Uncollected Short Stories as Kelvin Kent

"Roman Holiday" (with Henry Kuttner), in *Thrilling Wonder Stories* (New York), August 1939.
"Science Is Golden" (with Henry Kuttner), in *Thrilling Wonder Stories* (New York), April 1940.
"Knight Must Fall," in *Thrilling Wonder Stories* (New York), June 1940.
"The Greeks Had a War for It," in *Thrilling Wonder Stories* (New York), January 1941.
"De Wolfe of Wall Street," in *Thrilling Wonder Stories* (New York), February 1943.

OTHER PUBLICATIONS

Other

"It's a Science," in *Writer's Digest* (Cincinnati), May 1945.

*   *   *

Arthur K. Barnes is virtually unknown to the modern reader of science fiction; not a word of his considerable output in the field has seen print in a quarter of a century, and it has been more than 30 years since his last original story was published. To the reader of pulp "scientifiction" in the 1930's and 1940's, however—particularly to the reader of *Thrilling Wonder Stories*—Barnes was well known and popular, both for his own work and for his collaborations with Henry Kuttner. Nearly all of Barnes's fiction was either space opera or science fantasy. Although more or less solidly based on scientific knowledge of the period, his stories relied on farcical humor and rapid action for their effects. By today's standards they seem rather juvenile. Nevertheless, when viewed in historical perspective they are both interesting and entertaining.

The most popular of Barnes's space opera was a series about Gerry Carlisle, Tommy Strike, and the crew of *The Ark,* all of whom were employed by the "London Interplanetary Zoo" to trap and bring back alive nonintelligent alien life forms; the best of these novelettes were collected in Barnes's only book, *Interplanetary Hunter.* Much of his science fantasy involves time-travel into the past, and was co-authored with Henry Kuttner.

—Bill Pronzini

———————

BARRETT, Neal, Jr. American. Formerly worked in public relations; now a full-time writer. Address: 2032 Kipling, Houston, Texas 77098, U.S.A.

SCIENCE-FICTION PUBLICATIONS

Novels (series: Aldair)

Kelwin. New York, Lancer, 1970.
The Leaves of Time. New York, Lancer, 1971.
The Gates of Time. New York, Ace, 1972.
Highwood. New York, Ace, 1972.
Stress Pattern. New York, DAW, 1974.
Aldair in Albion. New York, DAW, 1976.
Aldair, Master of Ships. New York, DAW, 1977.
Aldair, Across the Misty Sea. New York, DAW, 1980.

Uncollected Short Stories

"Made in Archerius," in *Amazing* (New York), August 1960.
"To Tell the Truth," in *Galaxy* (New York), August 1960.
"The Stentorii Luggage," in *Galaxy* (New York), October 1960.
"The Graybes of Raath," in *Galaxy* (New York), June 1961.
"The Game," in *Amazing* (New York), July 1963.
"I Was a Spider for the SBI," in *Fantastic* (New York), November 1963.
"To Plant a Seed," in *Amazing* (New York), December 1963.
"In the Shadow of the Worm," in *Amazing* (New York), October 1964.
"Starpath," in *If* (New York), December 1966.
"By Civilized Standards," in *If* (New York), November 1969.
"Grandfather's Pelts," in *If* (New York), July 1970.
"Greyspun's Gift," in *Worlds of Tomorrow* (New York), Winter 1970.
"A Walk on Toy," in *Fantasy and Science Fiction* (New York), September 1971.
"Survival Course," in *Galaxy* (New York), January 1974.
"Happy New Year, Hal," in *Amazing* (New York), December 1974.
"Nightreat," in *Epoch,* edited by Roger Elwood and Robert Silverberg. New York, Berkley, 1975.
"The Talking," in *Lone Star Universe,* edited by George W. Proctor and Steven Utley. Austin, Texas, Heidelberg, 1976.
"The Flying Stutzman," in *Fantasy and Science Fiction* (New York), July 1978.
"Hero," in *Fantasy and Science Fiction* (New York), September 1979.

*   *   *

Neal Barrett, Jr., is blessed with the ability to create both an articulate, perceptive witness and an alien world worth witnessing. The combination is rarer in science fiction than it should be, and a true delight when found. Barrett devises original, self-consistent cultures, and then sends in someone who must try to understand. His victims are usually first-person narrators. They respond to their situation with humorous mixtures of wit and panic, and they endeavor intelligently to undo the puzzles they face. The solutions are never facile or predictable; Barrett has a real talent for setting up what he calls "completely alien rules of order."

He creates his alienness not by wholesale invention but by systematic alterations of familiarity. An early example is *The Leaves of Time*, where the protagonist, Jon DeHaviland, is thrown across reality-lines from an Earth conquered by rapacious Gorgons, to a peaceful Earth where the Vikings settled North America. The modern Norwegian-American culture is nicely detailed, along with subtle changes in the history and names of other countries. The puzzle in this book is not the civilization but the identity of the Gorgon who followed DeHaviland, and who is perfectly disguised as a citizen of the new world. The resulting hunt, taking place on not-quite-familiar ground, is an effective blend of suspense thriller and science fiction—effective because the suspense comes directly from the science-fiction aspects of the plot, and is not just complicated by them.

The alien world of *Stress Pattern* is closer to wholesale invention. Barrett creates a desert ecology so coherently simple that both its simplicity and its coherence are part of its puzzle. The narrator is a marooned economics professor who trudges in search of under standing, armed with indignation and a dry self-mockery. Occasional echoes of *Dune*—huge worms and sand— are deceptive; this is a lonelier and stranger world. One of its strangest aspects is the natives' method of reproduction, where the male carries the embryo on a string, and patterns it not by genes but by subconscious image. The results, for the economics professor, are harrowing and wonderful; like a science-fiction writer, he must face and live with the embodiments of his own imagination.

The puzzle and humor of *Stress Pattern* are combined with the altered Earths of *The Leaves of Time* in Barrett's most successful books, the Aldair series. The first book opens in a crowded medieval marketplace. The narrator, Aldair, booted and carrying his family sword, seems the appropriate protagonist of barbaric fantasy, until a series of casual clues reveals that though he walks on two feet and has hands, he is actually a pig, a thinking beast in a world without humans, where wolves, bears, sheep and other animals have evolved warring civilizations. It is a measure of Barrett's talent that the humor of this revelation fades into acceptance, until the comrade ships and enmities of the beasts form the stuff of genuine heroic fantasy, to the extent that the reader can share with Aldair the horror and shame of the first moment when he himself realizes he has the shape of what ancient men called "beasts." The hidden origin of the animals becomes Aldair's quest, a set of journeys filled with wild fights, exotic ruins, unique friendships, and Aldair's own understated humor. The reader, while trying to figure out the major puzzle, can work on the minor ones of telling one animal from another and deciphering the geography of Europe behind the distorted place names. Because the Aldair books finally offer a technological and historical explanation, they are in effect fantasy for science-fiction readers, but it is hard to imagine a reader of any kind who would not enjoy them.

Barrett's skills are exhibited separately in his many short stories, ranging from the slapstick comedy of "The Stentorii Luggage" to the chilling richness of "Nightreat." Most of his stories are told in the first person, a mode Barrett handles extraordinarily well. Actually, a first-person narration, humorous or not, is common in science fiction, along with ecological riddles. What makes Barrett special is the originality and high development of his imagination. His puzzles are always worth the solving.

—Karen G. Way

BARTH, John (Simmons). American. Born in Cambridge, Maryland, 27 May 1930. Educated at the Juilliard School of Music, New York; Johns Hopkins University, Baltimore, A.B. 1951, M.A. 1952. Married 1) Anne Strickland in 1951, one daughter and two sons; 2) Shelley Rosenberg in 1970. Junior Instructor in English, Johns Hopkins University, 1951-53; Instructor to Associate Professor of English, Pennsylvania State University, University Park, 1953-65; Professor of English, State University of New York, Buffalo, 1965-73. Since 1973, Centennial Professor of English and Creative Writing, Johns Hopkins University. Recipient: Brandeis University Creative Arts Award, 1965; Rockefeller grant, 1965; American Academy grant, 1966; National Book Award, 1973. Litt.D.: University of Maryland, College Park, 1969. Address: c/o Writing Seminars, Johns Hopkins University, Baltimore, Maryland 21218, U.S.A.

SCIENCE-FICTION PUBLICATIONS

Novel

Giles Goat-Boy; or, The Revised New Syllabus. New York, Doubleday, 1966; London, Secker and Warburg, 1967.

Short Stories

Chimera. New York, Random House, 1972; London, Deutsch, 1974.

OTHER PUBLICATIONS

Novels

The Floating Opera. New York, Appleton Century Crofts, 1956; revised edition, New York, Doubleday, 1967; London, Secker and Warburg, 1968.
The End of the Road. New York, Doubleday, 1958; London, Secker and Warburg, 1962; revised edition, Doubleday, 1967.
The Sot-Weed Factor. New York, Doubleday, 1960; London, Secker and Warburg, 1961; revised edition, Doubleday, 1967.
Letters. New York, Putnam, 1979; London, Secker and Warburg, 1980.

Short Stories

Lost in the Funhouse: Fiction for Print, Tape, Live Voice. New York, Doubleday, 1968; London, Secker and Warburg, 1969.

Play

The Tragedy of Taliped Decanus, adaptation of his novel *Giles Goat-Boy* (produced New York, 1977).

*

Manuscript Collection: Library of Congress, Washington, D.C.

Bibliography: *John Barth: A Descriptive Primary and Annotated Secondary Bibliography* by Joseph Weixlmann, New York, Garland, 1975.

* * *

John Barth's first two novels, *The Floating Opera* and *The End of the Road,* which some might think realistic or mimetic, predict his later distance from realism and his approach to a narrative so aware of itself that later novels and stories frequently resemble science fiction or fantasy. While *The Floating Opera* appears to be a realistic story about Todd Andrews's decision to commit suicide, his failure, and subsequent change of mind on suicide's necessity, the manner of narration is a harbinger of Barth's later disaffiliation with realism. As Todd writes, edits, and arranges notes for his inquiry into his father's suicide in seven peach baskets over 16 years, he sees that "Everything, I'm afraid, is significant, and nothing is finally important." Taken to an extreme, this philosophy wreaks havoc on narrative form, for if one cannot determine significance, how can novels be plotted or characters drawn? Even determining what one should summarize and what make into a scene becomes a problem, a problem Jake Horner, protagonist-narrator of *The End of the Road* continually confronts. After a speech by Joe Morgan, a rationalist believer in relative values, Jake says, "it may well be that Joe made no such long coherent speech as this all at once; it is certainly true that during the course of the evening this was the main thing that got said, and I put it down here in the form of one uninterrupted whiz-bang for convenience sake." In addition to literal detail, literary character is undermined in both novels as Todd cannot determine the motive of his father's suicide, Jane's love, or his own decision to pursue life or death. Similarly, the focus of the plot in *The End of the Road* is Rennie's and Jake's motives for sexually betraying Joe, motives that cannot be determined. The doctor of the Remobilization Farm even reduces consistency of character to the Mythotherapy of role playing, so that, instead of mimesis and realism, Barth is led to myth and "the artifices of narrative."

One such artifice, *The Sot-Weed Factor*, is a "representation of a representation of life," or Barth's representation of an 18th-century novel. Like Fielding's Tom Jones, who learns to control his wild good nature by good sense, Ebenezer Cooke, Virgin and Poet, learns the value of experience after an innocence much like Jake Horner's paralyzing Cosmopsis. Burlingame, similar to both the doctor in *End of the Road* and a Smollett picaro, searches for his father while initiating much intrigue through disguise. Biography and history are also Barthian aims. Since Ebenezer Cooke is a real 18th-century poet of Maryland, Barth imagines a life around the known facts and poetic texts and also recreates an impossible-to-untangle history of early Maryland. Like Eben, the reader finds it difficult to evaluate the merits of Lord Baltimore and John Coode. The psychological gap between the 20th-century world and the 18th is frequently pregnant with mythical comparisons, comparisons that make the reader rethink positions, although Ebenezer's introduction to the contextuality of experience, his earning his estate, and learning responsibility to others, such as Joan Toast, are instructive also.

Giles Goat-Boy is a self-consciously mythic and allegorical novel, with George Giles, the goat-boy, moving through a series of heroic encounters as Grand Tutor of a university. Barth has structured the mythical and allegorical encounters in imitation of heroic stages outlined by such works as Lord Raglan's *The Hero*, Joseph Campbell's *The Hero with a Thousand Faces*, and Otto Rank's *The Myth of the Birth of the Hero*. Thus it is not by accident that George's birth resembles Christ's and Oedipus's or that his heroism is frequently congruent to classical mythology. Because Barth has collapsed world history into the history of the university, the allegory frequently has suggestive historical parallels—Campus Riots I and II are World Wars I and II, for instance. Figures in the allegory frequently match historical personages—Enos Enoch is Jesus Christ and Lucky Rexford John Kennedy. Occasionally characters in the novel link to several historical figures; Max, for example, touches Robert Oppenheimer and Sigmund Freud. The allegory is basically reductive, however, and is not as powerful as the mythic comparisons to George's actions—at most one can see a better relation between thought and power because of it. George's struggles with WESCAC the all-ruling computer, his love of Anastasia, and his conflict with the false Harold Bray, who values answers over thought process, are at the heart of the novel, causing George to shift from "the clear distinction between Passage and Failure" to "failure is passage" and finally to passage and failure as interdependent and distinct. As in the earlier novels, the action is seen through many narrative filters, with cover letters by editors, publisher, and J.B., unknown revisions by them and the computer, a posttape, postscript, and footnote to the postscript.

Lost in the Funhouse, a series of linked short stories showing protagonists from sperm to old age, may be John Barth's most experimental fiction. That this work is for "Print, Tape, Live Voice" is no joke, since Barth has performed many stories on college campuses. "Frame-Tale" is an endlessly revolving Moebius strip repeating, "ONCE UPON A TIME THERE WAS A STORY THAT BEGAN...." "Night-Sea Journey," which may recount the union of the sperm and egg that produces Ambrose Mensch, protagonist of several stories, is the tale of the sperm's journey, wittily recreating Western philosophy as the sperm and its brothers meditate the meaning of existence. More conventionally "Ambrose His Mark" recounts the narrator's naming and the quest to capture a hive of bees. The three characters in "Autobiography" are Barth as Father, a tape machine as mother, and the story unwillingly conceived by both pondering the terms of its being. "Water Message" shows Ambrose in grade school, bullied but gifted with words,

sexually confused but given a task to fill the blank in a message from a bottle, a vocation to write. "Petition" a letter from a Siamese twin to Prajadlipok, King of Siam, parallels the situation between Peter and Ambrose, in that the letter-writer pleads for an operation to separate the spirituality of one from the carnality of the other; failure to separate will lead to a threat of death for both, ending a love triangle common in Barth's fiction. The title story, "Lost in the Funhouse," illustrates two dilemmas; Ambrose at 13 is lost in both an Ocean City funhouse maze and a sexual one, while the narrator is lost in a maze of fictional technique. Ambrose ends his problem by determining to "construct funhouses for others," thereby gaining a false sense of control. "Echo," another story for tape, is a marvelous use of narrative point of view; since Echo repeats the words of others in the story, its meaning changes depending on whether Tiresias, Echo, Narcissus, or Barth is the center of interest. Following "Two Meditations," "Title" is a debate by an imaginary author, possibly Ambrose, meant to be performed on multitrack tape about the possibility of writing a meaningful story and finding the significance of a love affair. "Life-Story" further twists self-conscious technique, as its main character is trapped in a fiction he does not like and wishes to tell his own story. "Menelaid" and "Anonymiad" look forward to *Chimera*. Mene laus, or Proteus in disguise, tells a story about driving Helen away by refusing to accept but wanting to know her reason for love, while "Anonymiad" again deals with the problem of the writer and his craft through a marooned Homeric minstrel as *Lost in the Funhouse* moves full circle from approaching birth to approaching death.

Chimera, composed of the novellas "Dunyazadiad," "Perseid," and "Bellerephoniad," continues Barth's interest in the tale within a tale, the relation of sexuality and narrative, and new uses of old myths. Dunyazade, sister of Scheherazade, is in a similar plight, and, with the help of a genie-like Barth from the 20th century, tells the tale of the composition of a *1001 Nights* as her entertainment for her lover, with death again the ultimate critic and day the end of climax and denoument. Perseus tells of his attempt at middle age to go adventuring again, and once he shakes his stodgy heroic status for adventure winds up in the stars, surrounded in love by the shell-like beauty of his story's constellation. Bellerephon, unable to get off the ground with Pegasus for a long time, is punished for flying too near Olympus and is transformed into a confused story of himself, as the vanity of a former hero falls to a Maryland marsh.

Many of Barth's previous characters appear in *Letters*, along with Barth himself and a new character, Lady Amherst, a heroine in distress similar to Fielding's Lady Booby and Richardson's Clarissa. Several motives generate the work: Barth's wish to revive the epistolary novel, his wish to write sequels for each of his previous works, and his ambition to write his version of historical fiction, the history of Maryland and the United States. Literary, local, and national politics help stitch *Letters* together, as the awarding of an honorary doctorate, a Fellini-like film supposedly made from several novels, and the political demonstrations of 1969 cause much of the novel's actions to occur. Passions of the heart, love, envy, and jealousy, sometimes political and sometimes personal, stimulate the rest of the novel: Ambrose Mensch for Lady Amherst, Jake Horner for Marsha Blank, Todd Andrews for Jane Mack, and Jerome Bray, Burlingame-Castine-Cook and Reg Prinz for all available women. Sexual confusion, particularly in the middle of *Letters*, imitates Fielding's scenes at inns as well as abductions in Richardson's *Clarissa* and *Pamela*, as Barth recapitulates his career, still more concerned with the manner than the object of imitation.

—Craig Wallace Barrow

BASS, T.J. Pseudonym for Thomas J. Bassler. American. Born in Clinton, Iowa, 7 July 1932. Educated at St. Ambrose College, Davenport, Iowa, B.A. 1955; State University of Iowa, Ames, M.D. 1959. Married Gloria Napoli in 1960; three daughters and three sons. Deputy medical examiner, Los Angeles, 1961-64. Since 1964, in private practice as a pathologist. Since 1972, Editor, *American Medical Joggers Newsletter.* Address: 27558 Sunnyridge Road, Palos Verdes Peninsula, California 90274, U.S.A.

SCIENCE-FICTION PUBLICATIONS

Novels

Half Past Human. New York, Ballantine, 1971.
The Godwhale. New York, Ballantine, 1974; London, Eyre Methuen, 1975.

Uncollected Short Stories

"Star Seeder," in *If* (New York), September 1969.
"A Game of Biochess," in *If* (New York), February 1970.
"Song of Kaia," in *If* (New York), November 1970.
"Rorqual Maru," in *The 1973 Annual World's Best SF,* edited by Donald A. Wollheim and Arthur W. Saha. New York, DAW, 1973.

*   *   *

T.J. Bass's novels, *Half Past Human* and *The Godwhale,* give a vivid picture of a horrifying future society, of a world-wide Earth Society ("the big ES") that controls every detail of life in the planet-sized hive that Earth has become. Three trillion people, degenerate "Nebishes," live in warrens beneath the surface, every inch of which is devoted to crops. These shrunken souls live short and regimented lives, are processed at their deaths for the proteins that sustain their fellows, and even have puberty postponed until the CO—the Class One computer—decides they are ready for sexual maturity.

Yet these novels are not cautionary tales of the sort of Harry Harrison's *Make Room, Make Room,* although some have read them so: rather, their concerns are teleological, like C.S. Lewis's Perelandra Trilogy or Walter M. Miller's *A Canticle for Leibowitz.* Assuming a kind Providence and a personal God, these works ask, what is the end of man? While *Half Past Human* and *The Godwhale* do not directly address the question, they do show a Providence that cares about the fall of a sparrow—or a Nebish. If the hand of God has not been noticed in Bass's works, it is because the author shows God using unfamiliar instruments. In the Perelandra trilogy or in *A Canticle for Leibowitz* God works through human beings; here, His ambassadors are machines so intelligent that they have personalities. Not that God makes robots and sends them hurtling toward Earth: the machines in Bass's novels are the artifacts of earlier stages of human civilization, providentially appearing when Mankind has most need of them.

In *Half Past Human* we see the plight of those few remaining real humans who live outside, apart from ES; like animals, they are hunted for sport. But in their vigor and resilience lies more hope for the future than in the Nebishes, whose machines are crumbling around them. However, even the Nebishes are not negligible or less than human: some among them can survive when circumstances remove them from the womb of their society. The novel is the story of a new beginning on a new planet for the humans living outside and for the Nebishes adaptable enough to accept it.

Both novels show an impressive command of biological knowledge, and indeed sometimes the flow of jargon obscures rather than communicates. But the point may be that most people in the society are treated (and regard themselves) just as mechanically as the many robots that work for them. Still, knowledge is regarded as good, and machines are good when they serve rather than control. This point is strongly argued in *The Godwhale,* named for a huge plankton harvester. Like the huge automated spaceship that is the *deus et machina* of *Half Past Human,* the Godwhale is an artifact of a freer, more expansive past. Although these machines are so powerful that they are regarded as "cyberdeities," they are purposeless without free humans to direct them. In *The Godwhale* that direction comes partly from the chosen few, true humans who have adapted to life in the sea, and partly from a superman bred by Nebishes to command the harvester. "Miracles" occur at opportune times in both novels:

the rescue of the outsiders in *Half Past Human,* and the regeneration of marine life in *The Godwhale.* Whereas the first shows the hope of a new society among the stars, the second gives promises of a regeneration of life on Earth.

Together, *Half Past Human* and *The Godwhale* are rewarding novels, rich both in characterization and in scientific detail, yet concerned with still larger matters. That *The Godwhale* offers a new proof of the existence of God shows just how large that concern is.

—Walter E. Meyers

BATES, Harry (Hiram Gilmore Bates III).   Also writes as Anthony Gilmore; A.R. Holmes; H.G. Winter.   American.   Born in Pittsburgh, Pennsylvania, 9 October 1900. Educated at Allegheny College, Meadville, Pennsylvania, 1917-18; University of Pennsylvania, Philadelphia, 1919-20. Clockmaker, 1914-17, 1920-22; reporter, Philadelphia *Enquirer,* 1923; assistant cameraman, Whitman-Bennett Studios, 1924; Editor for Clayton magazines, including *Astounding Stories,* 1930-33, and *Strange Tales,* 1931-32; Editor, *Technocracy,* 1935-37, and for the WPA art and writers projects; actor and machinist; Story Analyst, Columbia Pictures, 1958-59, and David O. Selznick, 1960. Recipient: Midamericon World Science-Fiction Convention Award, 1976. Agent: Forrest J. Ackerman, 2495 Glendower Avenue, Hollywood, California 90027. Address: 207 Eighth Avenue, New York, New York 10011, U.S.A.

SCIENCE-FICTION PUBLICATIONS

Novel

Space Hawk: The Greatest of Interplanetary Adventures (as Anthony Gilmore), with D.W. Hall. New York, Greenberg, 1952.

Uncollected Short Stories

"The City of Eric" (published anonymously), in *Amazing Stories Quarterly* (New York), Spring 1929.
"The Slave Ship from Space" (as A.R. Holmes), in *Astounding* (New York), July 1931.
"A Matter of Size," in *Astounding* (New York), April 1934.
"Alas, All Thinking," in *Astounding* (New York), June 1935.
"The Experiment of Dr. Sarconi," in *Thrilling Wonder Stories* (New York), July 1940.
"Farewell to the Master," in *Astounding* (New York), October 1940.
"A Matter of Speed," in *Astounding* (New York), June 1941.
"Mystery of the Blue God," in *Amazing* (New York), January 1942.
"Death of a Sensitive," in *Science Fiction Plus* (Philadelphia), May 1953.
"The Triggered Dimension," in *Science Fiction Plus* (Philadelphia), December 1953.

Uncollected Short Stories as H.G. Winter, with D.W. Hall

"The Hands of Aten," in *Astounding* (New York), July 1931.
"The Midget from the Island," in *Astounding* (New York), August 1931.
"Seed of the Arctic Ice," in *Astounding* (New York), February 1932.
"Under Arctic Ice," in *Astounding* (New York), January 1933.

OTHER PUBLICATIONS

Other

"So Help Me!" (as S.F. Whozis), in *Science Fiction Quarterly* (Holyoke, Massachusetts), February 1956.
"Editorial Number One," in *A Requiem for Astounding,* by Alva Rogers.   Chicago, Advent, 1964.

Harry Bates comments:

Astounding Stories (now *Analog)* was born to the publisher William Clayton and one of his editors—me—in a now unimaginable world populated by a single science-fiction magazine, Hugo Gernsback's *Amazing Stories,* which published amateurishly written "gadget" stories. The *Amazing* writers got one-tenth of a cent a word after publication; the writers for the Clayton empire were professionals, getting the very-high-for-those-days minimum of two cents on acceptance. I agreed with Clayton that *Astounding* had to have competent professional writing with strong plots and physical action; but its stories had also, of course, to contain tinges of science and binges of excitements and moreover be astounding—and where was any body of writers to cook to this recipe?

I had to create one. Because they had already sold to me I called on the writers in adventure magazines of which I already was editor, coaxing them to attempt this very different new field. Almost to a man they knew no science, and to use their stories at all I had (when possible) to correct and amplify what they turned in. I gave out story ideas right and left and did enormous amounts of hurried rewriting. Eventually almost all of these writers quit trying, for they had to eat, and there was no second market for the stories I had to reject.

The public in those days had never heard the term science fiction and had to be educated to it. *Amazing* often used the ugly term scientifiction, which I had as quickly as possible to suppress from the genre. Physical action remained an *Astounding* requisite. No one then dreamed what today's science fiction of way-way-out imaginings—fantasy—would be; if one of today's stories had been submitted to me then I'd probably have had to turn it down so as not to estrange the readers we aimed for and were accumulating. In time *Astounding*, in spite of its minimum of two cents a word, all but got out of the red, so that it was instantly profitable when Street & Smith with its much lower word rate took it over.

The stories I wrote in collaboration with my assistant D.W. Hall during those infant years were the product of sheer necessity, to avoid filling out the magazine with worse. The first Hawk Carse story was written as an example to my writers of the wanted element of character, and it was its extreme success that demanded the writing of the several that followed. All the stories published later under my own name were written hastily for a quick buck after my separation from *Astounding*, my prime interests lying elsewhere. I remember that in each case I hesitated at using my own name rather than a pseudonym; but its added value all but guaranteed the quick sale, however sloppy the writing. Who might have guessed that one day there would come into being such a phenomenon as museums of science-fiction—anthologies!—necropolises!—and that such imperfect stories as mine would be resurrected to populate them? There, now, they live again, after a fashion—zombies, all their sores still upon them.

The worst occurred with my "Not Understanding," which Gernsback characteristically renamed "The Triggered Dimension." When his *Science Fiction Plus* folded, his editor, wanting to squeeze into the last issue this last long story of mine, attempted the impossible, cutting out almost completely its very necessary central scene—the scene which gave reason for story and my title—and shortening the last sentence of paragraph after paragraph so as to save single lines. So one day I rewrote the story with the care I wish heartily I'd given it in the first place and with the cut-out parts restored—and then while I was at it I rewrote half of the others that had appeared under my own name. One, "A Matter of Speed," became "Oh Outrage!," a longish novel of very different mood which bad health has so far not let me quite finish.

Friends who since have read my "Alas, All Thinking" have asked me how I ever could have projected *Homo terminal* with mental processes so degenerated. The reason lies not quite in the realm of pure fantasy. Beginning when quite young (and having what I thought was a good body) I remained aware always that *Homo* of my day thoroughly forgets he is an animal with the body of an animal and early loses all inborn capacity to enjoy the *moving* of his body, coming almost always to overvalue the non-moving brain. I had merely to extrapolate. It happens that upon rereading the story I found I'd given no solid examples of his degenerated thinkings, so when I rewrote it I gave many, too many, Book-an-hour Devourers will say. But perhaps there exists somewhere a reader or two who, like me in the writing, will find pleasure in my assortment of bad thinkings. It is for *these*—educated *adults*—that I put a few strictly unnecessary extra ones in. Devourers, I do not rewrite stories for *you.*

*   *   *

Building on his experience as an editor of action-adventure pulps for William Clayton, Harry Bates began his career in science fiction as founding editor of the magazine whose name—*Astounding*—would become under later leadership synonymous with hard science fiction. But Bates has said that his first writers of stories for *Astounding* in 1930 were "almost wholly ignorant of science and technology." He named the magazine. He enlisted and cajoled professional pulp writers to add a science veneer to action and adventure narratives. He rewrote and wrote pseudonymously much of the material himself, and he paid professional rates. The result was a wider readership and a wider professional base for the genre that had begun hardly as literature with the Gernsback "scientifiction." Under the name Anthony Gilmore, Bates and his fellow editor D.M. Hall began the highly popular Hawk Carse series. The literary qualities of fast-paced action tale in this series helped establish the space-opera characteristics in science fiction that have to this day balanced the hard descriptions of scientific speculation and technology in order to make the genre exciting and popular as well as speculative and futuristic. The stories in the Hawk Carse series were collected as *Space Hawk.*

Bates edited the first 34 issues of *Astounding* as well as a few issues of a rival for *Weird Tales* entitled *Strange Tales,* but he continued to publish important science-fiction stories under his own name after his editing work had ended. Apparently the added speculative and scientific thoughts that he had worked up in the Clayton offices in order to capture more of the pulp market took a permanent hold on his imagination, and so Bates himself is representative of the professional pulp writers with little original scientific training who helped to create the genre. "Alas, All Thinking" expresses a classic theme of early science fiction with a tone and writing style that also embody the best and the worst characteristics of the genre. The theme is ultimately from the 18th-century enlightenment, and one wonders what has been the source of transmission from the *philosophes* to the New York pulp writers. But somehow the theme is intact: a fear of too much rationality and the ironic sense of progress leading to actual degeneration in humanness. The theme is mingled with the Golden Age/Iron Age myths in which life appears richer, more fertile, more heroic in the past; and the time-travel gimmick of super science facilitates the use of the present even as an heroic past so that satire fuses in the story with the myth of lost innocence. Bates's writing does not understate the theme, and when he tries to heighten emotion at the end the tonal effect is stiff. The story, like many others of this decade, is at the same time poignant, rich, and primitive.

Bates's single most well-known story (filmed in 1951 as *The Day the Earth Stood Still*) also first appeared in *Astounding*—this time the Campbell magazine of 1940. "Farewell to the Master" is a story rich with influence on the genre and less over-written than much of Bates's other work. The tapestry of the story weaves elements ranging backward in indebtedness to Mary Shelley's *Frankenstein* and forward in apparent influence to Walter Tevis's *Mockingbird* (1980). It is fascinating to think of the old pro pulp editor reaching backward to the romantics and influencing as academic a writer as Tevis several decades later. Bates tells the story of a technologically made creature who transcends his creators in competence so that he becomes the master, and yet there is an enigmatic sadness inherent in this future hero who is somehow more incomplete than his more primitive makers. The accomplishment of Bates illustrates how the genre which began in the practicalities of the pulp markets has progressed through a fine web of influence and allusion.

—Donald M. Hassler

BAUM, L(yman) Frank. Also wrote as Floyd Akers; Laura Bancroft; John Estes Cooke; Hugh Fitzgerald; Suzanne Metcalf; Schuyler Staunton; Edith Van Dyne. American. Born in Chittenango, New York, 15 May 1856. Educated at schools in Syracuse, New York, and Peekskill Military Academy, New York. Married Maud Gage in 1882; four sons. Reporter, New York *World*, 1873-75; Founding Editor, *New Era*, Bradford, Pennsylvania, 1876; actor (as Louis F. Baum and George Brooks), theatre manager, and producer, New York and on tour; poultry farmer in the 1880's; salesman, Baum's Castorine axle grease, 1886-88; Owner, Baum's Bazaar general store, Aberdeen, Dakota Territory, 1888-90; Editor, *Saturday Pioneer*, Aberdeen, 1890-91; Reporter, Chicago *Post*, Buyer, Siegel Cooper and Company, Chicago, and Salesman, Pitkin and Brooks, Chicago, 1891-97; Founder, National Association of Window Trimmers, 1897, and Founding Editor and Publisher, *The Show Window* magazine, Chicago, 1897-1902; Founding Director, Oz Film Manufacturing Company, Los Angeles, 1914. *Died 6 May 1919.*

SCIENCE-FICTION PUBLICATIONS

Novels (juvenile; series: Oz)

The Master Key: An Electrical Fairy Tale. Indianapolis, Bowen Merrill, 1901; London, Stevens and Brown, 1902.
Ozma of Oz. Chicago, Reilly and Britton, 1907; as *Princess Ozma of Oz,* London, Hutchinson, 1942.
The Emerald City of Oz. Chicago, Reilly and Britton, 1910.
Tik-Tok of Oz. Chicago, Reilly and Britton, 1914.

OTHER PUBLICATIONS

Novels

The Fate of a Crown (as Schuyler Staunton). Chicago, Reilly and Britton, and London, Revell, 1905.
Daughters of Destiny (as Schuyler Staunton). Chicago, Reilly and Britton, 1906.
Tamawaca Folks (as John Estes Cooke). Macatawa, Michigan, Macatawa Press, 1907.
The Last Egyptian (published anonymously). Philadelphia, Stern, and London, Sisley, 1908.

Plays

The Maid of Arran, music and lyrics by Baum, adaptation of the novel *A Princess of Thule* by William Black (also director: produced Gilmore, Pennsylvania, and New York, 1882).
Matches (produced New York, 1882).
Kilmourne; or, O'Connor's Dream (produced Syracuse, New York, 1883).
The Wizard of Oz (juvenile), music by Paul Tietjens, lyrics by Baum, adaptation of the novel by Baum (produced Chicago, 1902; revised version, as *There Is Something New under the Sun,* produced New York, 1903).
The Woggle-Bug (juvenile), music by Frederic Chapin, adaptation of the novel *The Marvelous Land of Oz* by Baum (produced Chicago, 1905).

The Tik-Tok Man of Oz (juvenile), music by Louis F. Gottschalk, adaptation of the novel by Baum (produced Los Angeles, 1913).
Stagecraft: The Adventures of a Strictly Moral Man, music by Louis F. Gottschalk (produced Santa Barbara, California, 1914).
The Uplift of Lucifer; or, Raising Hell, music by Louis F. Gottschalk (produced Santa Barbara, California, 1915). Edited by Manuel Weltman, privately printed, 1963.
The Uplifters' Minstrels, music by Byron Gay (produced Del Mar, California, 1916).
The Orpheus Road Company, music by Louis F. Gottschalk (produced Coronado Beach, California, 1917).

Screenplays: *The Fairylogue and Radio-Plays,* 1908-09; *The Patchwork Girl of Oz,* 1914; *The Babes in the Wood,* 1914; *The Last Egyptian,* 1914; *The New Wizard of Oz,* 1915.

Verse (juvenile)

By the Candelabra's Glare. Privately printed, 1898.
Father Goose, His Book. Chicago, Hill, and London, Werner, 1899.
The Army Alphabet. Chicago, Hill, 1900.
The Navy Alphabet. Chicago, Hill, 1900.
The Songs of Father Goose, music by Alberta N. Hall. Chicago, Hill, 1900.
Father Goose's Year Book: Quaint Quacks and Feathery Shafts for Mature Children. Chicago, Reilly and Britton, 1907.

Other (juvenile)

The Book of the Hamburgs: A Brief Treatise upon the Mating, Rearing, and Management of the Different Varieties of Hamburgs (for adults). Hartford, Connecticut, Stoddard, 1886.
Mother Goose in Prose. Chicago, Way and Williams, 1897; London, Duckworth, 1899.
The Art of Decorating Dry Goods Windows and Interiors (for adults). Chicago, Show Window Publishing Company, 1900.
A New Wonderland. New York, Russell, 1900; as *The Surprising Adventures of the Magical Monarch of Mo,* Indianapolis, Bobbs Merrill, 1903.
The Wonderful Wizard of Oz. Chicago, Hill, 1900; as *The New Wizard of Oz,* Indianapolis, Bobbs Merrill, 1903; London, Hodder and Stoughton, 1906.
American Fairy Tales. Chicago, Hill, 1901; London, Constable, 1978; augmented edition, Indianapolis, Bobbs Merrill, 1908.
Dot and Tot of Merryland. Chicago, Hill, 1901.
The Life and Adventures of Santa Claus. Indianapolis, Bowen Merrill, and London, Stevens and Brown, 1902.
The Enchanted Island of Yew. Indianapolis, Bobbs Merrill, 1903.
The Marvelous Land of Oz. Chicago, Reilly and Britton, and London, Revell, 1904.
Queen Zixi of Ix. New York, Century, 1905; London, Hodder and Stoughton, 1906.
The Woggle-Bug Book. Chicago, Reilly and Britton, 1905.
John Dough and the Cherub. Chicago, Reilly and Britton, 1906; London, Constable, 1974.
Annabel (as Suzanne Metcalf). Chicago, Reilly and Britton, 1906.
Sam Steele's Adventures on Land and Sea (as Hugh Fitzgerald). Chicago, Reilly and Britton, 1906; as *The Boy Fortune Hunters in Alaska* (as Floyd Akers), 1908.
Twinkle Tales (Bandit Jim Crow, Mr. Woodchuck, Prairie-Dog Town, Prince Mud-Turtle, Sugar-Loaf Mountain, Twinkle's Enchantment) (as Laura Bancroft). Chicago, Reilly and Britton, 6 vols., 1906; as *Twinkle and Chubbins,* 1911.
Sam Steele's Adventures in Panama (as Hugh Fitzgerald). Chicago, Reilly and Britton, 1907; as *The Boy Fortune Hunters in Panama* (as Floyd Akers), 1908.
Policeman Bluejay (as Laura Bancroft). Chicago, Reilly and Britton, 1907; as *Babes in Birdland,* 1911.
The Boy Fortune Hunters in Egypt [China, Yucatan, the South Seas] (as Floyd Akers). Chicago, Reilly and Britton, 4 vols., 1908-11.
Dorothy and the Wizard in Oz. Chicago, Reilly and Britton, 1908.
The Road to Oz. Chicago, Reilly and Britton, 1909.
L. Frank Baum's Juvenile Speaker (miscellany). Chicago, Reilly

and Britton, 1910; as *Baum's Own Book for Children*, 1912.
The Sea Fairies. Chicago, Reilly and Britton, 1911.
The Daring Twins. Chicago, Reilly and Britton, 1911.
Sky Island. Chicago, Reilly and Britton, 1912.
Phoebe Daring. Chicago, Reilly and Britton, 1912.
The Patchwork Girl of Oz. Chicago, Reilly and Britton, 1913.
The Little Wizard Series (Jack Pumpkinhead and the Sawhorse, Little Dorothy and Toto, Ozma and the Little Wizard, The Cowardly Lion and the Hungry Tiger, The Scarecrow and the Tin Woodsman, Tik-Tok and the Nome King). Chicago, Reilly and Britton, 6 vols., 1913; as *Little Wizard Stories of Oz*, Reilly and Britton, 1914; London, Simpkin, 1939.
The Scarecrow of Oz. Chicago, Reilly and Britton, 1915.
Rinkitink in Oz. Chicago, Reilly and Britton, 1916.
The Snuggle Tales (Little Bun Rabbit, Once upon a Time, The Yellow Hen, The Magic Cloak, The Ginger-Bread Man, Jack Pumpkinhead). Chicago, Reilly and Britton, 6 vols., 1916-17; as *Oz-Man Tales*, 6 vols., 1920.
The Lost Princess of Oz. Chicago, Reilly and Britton, 1917.
The Tin Woodman of Oz. Chicago, Reilly and Britton, 1918.
The Magic of Oz. Chicago, Reilly and Lee, 1919.
Glinda of Oz. Chicago, Reilly and Lee, 1920; London, Armada, 1974.
Our Landlady (for adults; *Saturday Pioneer* columns). Mitchell, South Dakota Writers' Project, 1941.
Jaglon and the Tiger Fairies. Chicago, Reilly and Lee, 1953.
A Kidnapped Santa Claus. Indianapolis, Bobbs Merrill, 1961.
Animal Fairy Tales. Chicago, International Wizard of Oz Club, 1969.
The Purple Dragon and Other Fantasies, edited by David L. Greene. Lakemont, Georgia, Fictioneer, 1976.

Other (juvenile) as Edith Van Dyne

Aunt Jane's Nieces [Abroad, at Millville, at Work, in Society, and Uncle John, on Vacation, on the Ranch, Out West, in the Red Cross]. Chicago, Reilly and Britton, 10 vols., 1906-15.
The Flying Girl [and Her Chum]. Chicago, Reilly and Britton, 2 vols., 1911-12.
Mary Louise [in the Country, Solves a Mystery, and the Liberty Girls, Adopts a Soldier]. Chicago, Reilly and Britton, 4 vols., and Reilly and Lee, 1 vol., 1916-19.

*

Bibliography: in *The Annotated Wizard of Oz* edited by Michael Patrick Hearn, New York, Potter, 1973.

*   *   *

Known and loved for his Oz books, L. Frank Baum animates America's conflict between technology and pastoralism in his children's fantasy. In Oz, Ozma and Glinda use magic to negate technological dangers. After the Nome King and his forces tunnel beneath the desert, they are routed with the Water of Oblivion. Technology (like magic) is good or bad, but always interesting.

Before Baum invented Oz he wrote a column, "Our Landlady," for the Aberdeen *Saturday Pioneer.* Mrs. Bilkins looked forward to people hoisting signal flags to call airships or escape in them to count ballots. One column describes a farm where electricity powers chairs, lights cigars, serves 14-course dinners, dresses people, and shows movies. The farmer-scientist even smiles by electricity. Already Baum's humor, gentle satire, wild circumstances, and exaggerated characters are obvious.

Many science-fiction devices enliven Baum's children's books. At the end of *The Emerald City of Oz* Glinda forever separates Oz from the world, creating a lost place. Dystopian, eccentric tyrants like the Nome King and the Boolooroo of Sky Island abound, but reform easily. The Phanfasms, who control minds and disguise their magnificent city as a rock heap, are described in a passage reminiscent of Stanislaw Lem or Philip D. Dick. Marvelous creations like the Tin Woodman, Scarecrow, Sawhorse, Patchwork Girl, and Pumpkinhead are accepted without the reservations human beings hold about robots' and androids' eternal souls. Although most owe their sentience to the Powder of Life, Tiktok is made of copper and

clockwork. Dorothy observes, "his machinery makes him just as good as alive." H.M. Wogglebug, who entered society through Professor Nowitall's magnifying glass, feeds his students School Pills invented by the Wizard to provide correct doses of knowledge.

The Master Key exemplifies boys' science fiction. Rob evokes the Demon of Electricity, who demonstrates to him the potentiality and dangers of electrical inventions. Only in Oz, however, are people wise and kind enough to use such power, Baum intimates.

—Mary S. Weinkauf

BAXTER, John. Also writes as Martin Loran. Australian. Born in Sydney, New South Wales, 14 December 1939. Educated at Waverly College, Sydney, 1944-54. Married 1) Merie Elizabeth Brooker in 1962 (divorced, 1967); 2) Joyce Allison Agee in 1978. Staff Controller, New South Wales State Government, Sydney, 1957-67; Publicity Director, Australian Commonwealth Film Unit, Sydney, 1967-70; Presenter, *Understanding Films* series, 1969; film critic, *Kaleidoscope* programme, BBC Radio, London, 1972-80. Lecturer, United States Embassy, London, 1973-74, and for United States Government in Europe, 1974-75, and Hollins College, Virginia, 1975-76, and London Campus, 1976-78. Recipient: Australian Film Award, 1969; Kranz Film Festival Award, 1970; Benson and Hedges prize, for TV documentary, 1970; Ditmar Award, 1971. Agent: Ed Victor Ltd., 27 Soho Square, London W1V 6AY. Address: Flat 1, 3 The Park, London N.6, England.

SCIENCE-FICTION PUBLICATIONS

Novels

The Off-Worlders. New York, Ace, 1966; as *The God Killers*, Sydney, Horwitz, 1968.
The Hermes Fall. London, Panther, and New York, Simon and Schuster, 1978.

Uncollected Short Stories

"Vendetta's End," in *Science Fiction Adventures* (London), December 1962.
"Eviction," in *New Worlds* (London), March 1963.
"Interlude," in *New Worlds* (London), November 1963.
"Toys," in *New Worlds* (London), January 1964.
"The New Country," in *Science Fantasy* (Bournemouth), April 1964.
"Testament," in *New Writings in SF 3*, edited by John Carnell. London, Dobson, 1965; New York, Bantam, 1967.
"Takeover Bid," in *New Writings in SF 5*, edited by John Carnell. London, Dobson, 1965; New York, Bantam, 1970.
"The Hands, " in *New Writings in SF 6*, edited by John Carnell. London, Dobson, 1965; New York, Bantam, 1971.
"The Traps of Time," in *The Best of New Worlds*, edited by Michael Moorcock. London, Compact, 1965.
"More Than a Man," in *New Worlds* (London), February 1965.
"Tryst," in *New Writings in SF 8*, edited by John Carnell. London, Dobson, 1966; New York, Bantam, 1971.
"Skirmish," in *New Worlds* (London), April 1966.
"Apple," in *New Writings in SF 10*, edited by John Carnell. London, Dobson, 1967.
"The Case of the Perjured Planet" (as Martin Loran, with Ron Smith), in *Analog* (New York), November 1967.
"An Ounce of Dissension" (as Martin Loran, with Ron Smith) and "The Beach," in *The Pacific Book of Australian Science Fiction*, edited by John Baxter. Sydney, Angus and Robertson, 1968; London, Angus and Robertson, 1969.
"Memories of the Future," in *Vision of Tomorrow* (Newcastle upon Tyne), July, August, and September 1970.

OTHER PUBLICATIONS

Novels

Adam's Woman (novelization of screenplay).   Sydney, Horwitz, 1970.
The Bidders.   Philadelphia, Lippincott, 1979; as *Bidding*, London, Granada, 1980.

Plays

Screenplays (documentaries): *Beyond the Pack Ice,* 1968; *Golf in Australia,* 1969; *After Proust,* 1969; *Australian Diary* series, 1969-70; *Top End,* 1970; *The Magic Years of Cinema* (1 episode), 1976.

Television Documentaries: *Understanding Film* series, 1969; *No Roses for Michael,* 1970.

Other

Hollywood in the Thirties.   New York, A.S. Barnes, and London, Zwemmer, 1968.
Science Fiction in the Cinema.   New York, A.S. Barnes, and London, Zwemmer, 1970.
The Australian Cinema.   Sydney and London, Angus and Robertson, 1970.
The Gangster Film.   New York, A.S. Barnes, and London, Zwemmer, 1970.
The Cinema of Josef von Sternberg.   New York, A.S. Barnes, and London, Zwemmer, 1971.
The Cinema of John Ford.   New York, A.S. Barnes, and London, Zwemmer, 1971.
Hollywood in the Sixties.   New York, A.S. Barnes, and London, Tantivy Press, 1972.
Sixty Years in Hollywood.   South Brunswick, New Jersey, A.S. Barnes, and London, Tantivy Press, 1973.
An Appalling Talent: Ken Russell.   London, Joseph, 1973.
Stunt: The Story of the Great Movie Stunt Men.   London, Macdonald, 1973; New York, Doubleday, 1974.
King Vidor.   New York, Monarch Press, 1976.
The Hollywood Exiles.   New York, Taplinger, and London, Macdonald and Jane's, 1976.
The Fire Came By: The Riddle of the Great Siberian Explosion, with Thomas Atkins.   New York, Doubleday, and London, Macdonald and Jane's, 1976.

Editor, *The Pacific Book of Australian Science Fiction.*   Sydney, Angus and Robertson, 1968; as *The Pacific Book of Science Fiction,* London, Angus and Robertson, 1969.
Editor, *The Second Pacific Book of Australian Science Fiction.*   Sydney, Angus and Robertson, 1971; as *The Second Pacific Book of Science Fiction,* London, Angus and Robertson, 1971.

John Baxter comments:
Ted Carnell discovered and encouraged many young writers in the 1960's; almost alone among them I moved away from SF as I entered professional writing, a defection Ted tried hard, though unsuccessfully, to approve. He would probably be happy that, almost 20 years after he accepted my first story, I have drifted, in a roundabout way, back to the field he loved so much. Had he lived I might have convinced him that the cinema, to which I have given so much of my energy, combined technology and aesthetics in a form analogous to the best science fiction. In any event, it is this synthesis from which I hope to produce a third decade of writing—fictional, critical, and perhaps a combination of the two.

*   *   *

As editor of the first two major anthologies of Australian SF writing, John Baxter laid some of the foundations for its growth. He exerted a twofold influence upon Australian SF of the 1970's. Rejecting the concept that science fiction must be prophetic, Baxter emphasized "insight rather than intelligent guessing," arguing that "a story which tells us that a rose is a rose and explains why is far more worthwhile than one which states that E equals MC squared

and leaves it at that." Baxter also esteemed the literary qualities of science fiction, publishing material that was innovative in style and structure, yet neither ignoring nor denigrating stories written in a more traditional narrative style. In short, he ran up the flag for an Australian science fiction that was literate, thoughtful, and original.

Baxter's own short stories reflect these criteria. They are original and ambitious, reflecting influences from both traditional and new wave SF. One of his best-known stories, "Apple," is a traditional man-meets-monster story—except that the encounter takes place in a surrealistic setting, and the story evolves from imagery and setting rather than action. A gigantic apple lies cradled in a valley, the juices dripping from its sides as men tunnel into its core. The central character is a professional Moth Killer who battles with the grubs that lurk in the apple's core. It is suggested that the apple-world may be the result of atomic warfare, but for Baxter the explanation is incidental; his story conveys its own inner logic, and that is enough. The same is true of the more experimental story "The Beach." Described as "a first sketch of what an *Australian* SF story might be like," it employs distinctively Australian symbols of life and nature, and abandons conventional narrative structure in order to emphasize mood and imagery. The style and symbolism are evident in the closing lines: "Without fear, he swam towards the sea mountains, the peaks of which even now he could see gilded beyond the green. There, he knew, he would find his grail, the sunken, brooding sun."

Unlike his stories, Baxter's two science-fiction novels have little to commend them. *The Off-Worlders* is set on the planet Merryland in the year 2833 and deals with a rustic community which is suspicious of technology and has rejected God, turning instead to Satan. *The Hermes Fall* is based on *The Fire Came By,* Baxter's nonfiction work on the famous Siberian "meteorite" of 1908 (written with Tom Atkins). Despite its well-researched background, *The Hermes Fall* is merely a conventional "disaster" novel using science-fiction effects, in this case an asteroid on collision course with the Earth.

—Van Ikin

———————

BAYLEY, Barrington John.   British.   Born in Birmingham, Warwickshire, 9 April 1937. Educated at a grammar school in Shropshire. Served in the Royal Air Force, 1955-57. Married Joan Lucy Clarke in 1969; one son and one daughter. Reporter, Wellington *Journal,* early 1950's; civil servant, Ministry of War, London, 1954-55; in Australian Public Service, London, 1957-58; has also worked as a clerk, typist, and coal miner. Agent: Scott Meredith Literary Agency, 845 Third Avenue, New York, New York, 10022, U.S.A.; or E. J. Carnell Literary Agency, Rowneybury Bungalow, Sawbridgeworth, near Old Harlow, Essex CM20 2EX. Address: 48 Turreff Avenue, Donnington, Telford, Shropshire TF2 8HE, England.

SCIENCE-FICTION PUBLICATIONS

Novels

Star Virus.   New York, Ace, 1970.
Annihilation Factor.   New York, Ace, 1972; London, Allison and Busby, 1979
Empire of Two Worlds.   New York, Ace, 1972; London, Hale, 1974.
Collision Course.   New York, DAW, 1973; as *Collision with Chronos,* London, Allison and Busby, 1977.
The Fall of Chronopolis.   New York, DAW, 1974; London, Allison and Busby, 1979.
The Soul of the Robot.   New York, Doubleday, 1974; London, Allison and Busby, 1976.
The Garments of Caean.   New York, Doubleday, 1976; London, Fontana, 1978.
The Grand Wheel.   New York, DAW, 1977; London, Fontana, 1979.
Star Winds.   New York, DAW, 1978.

Short Stories

The Knights of the Limits.   London, Allison and Busby, 1978.
The Seed of Evil.   London, Allison and Busby, 1979.

Barrington John Bayley comments;

I have no personal philosophy as regards my work; I write according to my ability and interest. I regard myself as a genre SF writer—that is, as a traditionalist.

*   *   *

Barrington John Bayley is author of a number of *sui generis* short stories and of equally *sui generis* novels. His stories introduce, with a conjuror's panache, whole alternative ontologies. What if the universe were composed of solid rock, and worlds were hollow spaces within it ("Me and My Antronoscope")? What if a ship could literally sail the "surface" of space just as we sail the surface of the sea? What, then, would our own astronauts' fish-eye-view be of such a ship sinking ("The Ship That Sailed the Sea of Space")? His yoking of metaphysical speculation with pulp adventure themes—sometimes stylized, sometimes natural—is reminiscent of Borges's intersection of detective and horror formulas with metaphysics. For the philosophers of Borges's subjective planet which displaces ordinary reality (in "Tlön, Uqbar, Orbis Tertius") "metaphysics is a branch of the literature of fantasy." For Bayley, likewise (or perhaps more truly for Bayley, fantasy, including SF, is a branch of metaphysics!). His novels are thus metaphysical space operas, drawing upon the grand old pulp tropes of space battles—groaning overdrives, the dense worlds of the Hub, intrepid captains, cynical adventurers with pearl-handled laser pistols—and transmuting the cosmic ding-dong into a witty, technicolour, eccentric, experimental philosophy.

Thus in *Star Virus* space freebooters capture a crystal ball constructed by ancient alien beings — or by extra-dimensional entities — which contains the original of our own galaxy within it, ours being merely the macroscopic copy. (The novel ends with the lovely rallying cry, not parody so much as perfect simulation: "Did you hear that, you trash? Do you know where we're going? Andromeda! Andromeda!") *Star Winds* presumes that all our contemporary science is a looney misconception and that the ether actually exists — so that one can sail schooners and windjammers from world to world; not boring old ram-jets but proper sailing ships — and, what's more, that the alchemists were right about the nature of reality after all, so that the philosopher's stone can be achieved. *The Garments of Caean* develops the old adage that "clothes make the man" into the ultimate persuasive absurdity of sentient suits which control people and are part of a galactic takeover by vegetable fibre — tossing in, along the way, cultures who aren't even aware that they possess bodies. *The Soul of a Robot* explores the Lemian theme of existential cybernetics, by way of a quest, while its climax — though ironic — contains a note of un-Lemian transcedence (as does *Star Winds*, with its achievement of the alchemist's goals) true to the pulp tropes but true also to the exuberant metaphysical playfulness of Bayley.

—Ian Watson

BEAR, Greg(ory Dale).   American.   Born in San Diego, California, 20 August 1951. Educated at San Diego State University, 1968-73, A.B. in English 1973. Married Christina M. Bear in 1975. Part-time Lecturer, San Diego Aerospace Museum, 1969-72; technical writer and planetarium operator, Reuben H. Fleet Space Theater, San Diego, 1973; bookstore clerk, 1974-75. Since 1975, free-lance writer. Agent: Richard Curtis Agency, 156 East 52nd Street, New York, New York 10022. Address: Summitview Lane, Spring Valley, California 92077, U.S.A.

SCIENCE-FICTION PUBLICATIONS

Novels

Hegira.   New York, Dell, 1979.
Psychlone.   New York, Ace, 1979
Beyond Heaven's River.   New York, Dell, 1980.

Uncollected Short Stories

"Destroyers," in *Famous Science Fiction* (New York), Winter 1967.
"Webster," in *Alternities,* edited by David Gerrold.   New York, Dell, 1974.
"The Venging," in *Galaxy* (New York), June 1975.
"Perihesperon," in *Tomorrow,* edited by Roger Elwood.   New York, Evans, 1975.
"A Martian Ricorso," in *Analog* (New York), February 1976.
"Sun-Planet," in *Galaxy* (New York), April 1977.
"Scattershot," in *Universe 8,* edited by Terry Carr.   New York, Doubleday, 1978; London, Dobson, 1979.
"Mandala," in *New Dimensions 8,* edited by Robert Silverberg. New York, Harper, 1978.
"The Wind from a Burning Woman," in *Analog* (New York), October 1978.
"The White Horse Child," in *Universe 9,* edited by Terry Carr. New York, Doubleday, 1979.

OTHER PUBLICATIONS

Other

"The Space Theater," in *Vertex* (Los Angeles), 1974.
"Future Vision," in *Galileo 3* (Boston).

Greg Bear comments:

Ideally, science fiction and fantasy should give a writer extraordinary freedom; in practice, that freedom is somewhat limited by the demands of commercial fiction. Used properly, however, the demands of commercial fiction—ease of reading, entertainment—can act as beneficial restraints, causing fiction—like a bansai tree—to expand beautifully within a limited format. Today, unfortunately, the demands of commercial fiction are inhibited by emphasis on "the commercial" and de-emphasis on "the fiction." This is not just the fault of publishers—good writers make their publishers as much as the publishers shape them. Within my own work, I try to contradict the obvious. A character's clichéd or "commercial" response rankles me—I will not bend character or story to fit a format. The story determines its own outcome. These may seem simple and obvious requirements, but much of the successful fiction being published today consists of deliberate distortions and lies to soothe readers, rather than to stimulate or irritate them. I cannot serve up placebos. As for science fiction in general, my tendency in the past has been to emphasize the cosmic, humans working within and against a complex but somehow directed universe; in the future, I intend to explore the inward, mirror-image universe we all enclose. Ultimately, I don't think I'll find much difference between macro and micro—but who knows?

*   *   *

A man of many talents, Greg Bear has taught science fiction, written newspaper features on SF movies, done illustrations for SF magazines, and published a dozen novels and stories in just over five years of work. Ranging from arty fantasy and revamped myths to hard science extrapolation and far-future space opera, his writing, like his art work, is never less than competent, and shows considerable development over a short span.

An old maid gets her man literally from the dictionary in the whimsical "Webster." Story-telling is passed on in a mysterious manner in "The White Horse Child." Another bookish story is "Scattershot," mixing humor and derring-do in a Flying Dutchman story that constitutes a commentary of sorts on the literary mélange called science fiction. A certain amount of bookish pretentiousness is also evident in Bear's novel *Hegira.* Wanderers on an immense artificial planet explore variations on terrestrial experience, centered on scientific and religious attitudes toward learning. Quest survivors penetrate the sphere, literally shifting perspective to find the meaning of it all. The style is often ponderous, ill-matching the Arabian Nights illustrations of Stephen Fabian. A youthful speculation (written in 1973) on the destiny of man, the book foreshadowed a continuing preoccupation with sensory detail and mythic significance.

Psychlone is much better written. In this para-psychological thriller, Bear speculates on the dubious dangers to the living posed by the focussed psychic energy of the dead. Though guilt over victims of nuclear attack gives social relevance to the metaphor, the scientific rationalizations for both problem and solution are fuzzy. Contemporary settings, believable characters, intense sensory detail and a fast-paced style are done so well, however, that readers may forgive the flaws in argumentation.

Among tamer extrapolation, "A Martian Ricorso," follows the first manned expedition to the Red Planet, where Martian life forms pose a danger not only to doomed crew members but also to human preconceptions about intelligence and civilization. An abortive melodramatic threat to crash an asteroid spaceship into Earth is at the center of "The Wind from a Burning Woman," but of greater interest is the background of a misguided "post-technological" society. "Perihesperon" is tightly focussed on two (temporary) survivors of a starship accident; though the result is more sentimental than tragic, their feelings are exquisitely realized. This story is linked, by reference to the long-lived Baroness Anna Sigrid-Nestor, with a coherent fictional future man shares with other intelligent races. Set early in the cycle, "The Venging" postulates black holes as sacred objects for a three-brained alien race. Their "burial ground," the Pafloshwa Rift, having been despoiled by human scientific experiments, one of the three-brained Aighors seeks revenge, driving the human scientist through a black hole's field into another universe where he and his crew, hopelessly marooned, discover the truth of Sartre's observation: "Hell is other people."

After the Aighors have been annihilated by the Perfidisians, humans are challenged, in "Sun-Planet" (illustrated by Bear), to abandon an artificial world the creators of which are long extinct. Aided by "setties" (Cetaceans), whale-like creatures redesigned by man, humans are beginning to decipher information encoded in the planet's structures. In a race against time, their quest bears fruit, making possible a sharing agreement with the Perfidisians and self-realization for the protagonist.

Other elements of the saga may be discerned, combined with UFOlogy and World War II elements, in *Beyond Heaven's River*. Given the growth of Bear's style and sensibilities and the scope provided by this future canvas, it should be a major addition to his canon. Bear's future bears watching.

—David N. Samuelson

BEAUMONT, Charles. Pseudonym for Charles Nutt; also wrote as Keith Grantland. American. Born in Chicago, Illinois, 2 January 1929. Served in the United States Army for one year. Married Helen Louise Brown in 1949; one son and two daughters. Radio writer, actor, illustrator, and animator. Recipient: Jules Verne Award, 1954; *Playboy* award, for non-fiction, 1961. *Died 21 February 1967.*

SCIENCE-FICTION PUBLICATIONS

Short Stories

The Hunger and Other Stories. New York, Putnam, 1957; as *Shadow Play*, London, Panther, 1964.
Yonder. New York, Bantam, 1958.

Night Ride and Other Journeys. New York, Bantam, 1960.
The Magic Man and Other Science-Fantasy Stories. New York, Fawcett, 1965; London, Fawcett, 1966.
The Edge. London, Panther, 1966.

OTHER PUBLICATIONS

Novels

Run from the Hunter (as Keith Grantland, with John E. Tomerlin). New York, Fawcett, 1957; London, Boardman, 1959.
The Intruder. New York, Putnam, 1959.

Plays

Screenplays: *Queen of Outer Space*, with Ben Hecht, 1958; *Burn, Witch, Burn (Night of the Eagle)*, with Richard Matheson and George Baxt, 1962; *The Wonderful World of the Brothers Grimm*, with David P. Harmon and William Roberts, 1962; *The Premature Burial*, with Ray Russell, 1962; *The Haunted Palace*, 1963; *7 Faces of Dr. Lao*, 1964; *The Masque of the Red Death*, with R. Wright Campbell, 1964; *Mister Moses*, with Monja Danischewsky, 1965.

Television Plays: for *Twilight Zone* series.

Other

Remember? Remember? New York, Macmillan, 1963.

Editor, with William F. Nolan, *Omnibus of Speed: An Introduction to the World of Motor Sport.* New York, Putnam, 1958; London, Stanley Paul, 1961; as *When Engines Roar*, New York, Bantam, 1964.
Editor, *The Fiend in You.* New York, Ballantine, 1962.

*   *   *

Charles Beaumont was a consummate craftsman of the popular market short story—perhaps the most accomplished writer of this type of fiction to publish in the 1950's and early 1960's. He wrote extensively for *Playboy* and other magazines, including many in the science-fiction field, and often blended elements of humor, horror, psychological suspense, and extrapolative SF. If much of his subject matter is grim, and many of his stories basically downbeat in resolution, his smooth and upbeat writing style keeps his work from being negative or oppressive.

Among his more than 50 stories (and articles) of science fiction and fantasy is "The Vanishing American," an allegorical tale about a man who becomes invisible to his fellow men, and perhaps Beaumont's finest short story. Others of quality include "Free Dirt," "The Love Master," "The Quadriopticon," and, the best of a number with a jazz music background, "Black Country."

His tragic death at 37, of a rare aging disease which had ravaged him and kept him from writing for three years, cut short a career which might have progressed to major stature.

—Bill Pronzini

BELLAMY, Edward. American. Born in Chicopee Falls, Massachusetts, 26 March 1850, and lived there for most of his life. Educated at local schools; Union College, Schenectady, New York, 1867-68; travelled and studied in Germany, 1868-69; studied law: admitted to the Massachusetts Bar, 1871, but never practised. Married Emma Sanderson in 1882. Associate Editor, *Union*, Springfield, Massachusetts; Editorial Writer, *Evening Post*, New York, 1878; Founder, with his brother, Springfield *Daily News*, 1880; after 1885 devoted himself to writing and propagation of Socialist ideas: lectured throughout the United States; founded *New Nation*, Boston, 1891. *Died 22 May 1898.*

SCIENCE-FICTION PUBLICATIONS

Novels

Dr. Heidenhoff's Process. New York, Appleton, 1880; Edinburgh, Douglas, 1884.
Looking Backward 2000-1887. Boston, Ticknor, 1888; London, Reeves, 1889.
Equality. New York, Appleton, and London, Heinemann, 1897.

Short Stories

The Blindman's World and Other Stories. Boston, Houghton Mifflin, and London, Watt, 1898.

OTHER PUBLICATIONS

Novels

Six to One: A Nantucket Idyl. New York, Putnam, and London, Sampson Low, 1878.
Miss Ludington's Sister: A Romance of Immortality. Boston, Osgood, 1884; London, Reeves, 1890.
The Duke of Stockbridge: A Romance of Shays' Rebellion. New York, Silver Burdett, 1900.

Other

Edward Bellamy Speaks Again! Articles, Public Addresses, Letters. Kansas City, Peerage Press, 1937.
Talks on Nationalism. Chicago, Peerage Press, 1938.
Religion of Solidarity. Yellow Springs, Ohio, Antioch, 1940.
Selected Writings on Religion and Society, edited by Joseph Schiffman. New York, Liberal Arts Press, 1955.

*

Bibliography: in *Bibliography of American Literature* by Jacob Blanck, New Haven, Connecticut, Yale University Press, vol. 1, 1955.

*   *   *

In *Looking Backward*, Edward Bellamy observed that both the "working classes" and "true and humane men and women, of every degree, are in a mood of exasperation, verging on absolute revolt, against social conditions that reduce life to a brutal struggle for existence." In its sequel, *Equality*, he added the ruin of prairie farmers by capitalist mortgages, the degradation of women through economic exploitation, the recurrent economic crises, and the concentration of three-quarters of national wealth into the hands of 10% of the population. Bellamy's utopianism was the point at which all these deep discontents intersected with the American religious and lay utopian tradition and the world socialist movement. As the spokesman of the "immense average of villagers, of small-town-dwellers" who believed in "modern inventions, modern conveniences, modern facilities" (Howells), in Yankee gadgetry as white magic for overcoming drudgery, he accepted the financial trusts as more efficient and changeable from private waste and tyranny to a Yankee communism or "Associationism": the nation "organized as the one great corporation...in the profits and economies of which all citizens shared."

Bellamy's new frontier is the future. It offers not only better railways, motor carriages, air-cars, telephones, and TV, but also a classless brotherhood of affluence socializing these means of communication and other upper-class privileges to achieve comfort and security for everyone through a reorganized "economy of happiness." Universal high education, work obligation from 21 to 45, equal and guaranteed income for everyone including the old, the sick, and children, flexible planning, and public honors reduce government to a universal civic service called the Great Trust or the Industrial Army. The generals of each guild or industrial branch are chosen by the retired alumni of the guild, and the head of the army is president of USA. Doctors and teachers have their own guilds, and a writer, artist, journal editor, or inventor is exempted from the army if enough buyers sign over a part of their credit. Individuality is fostered and objectors can "work out a better solution of the problem of existence than our society offers" in a reservation (the first use of this escape-hatch of later utopias).

Bellamy's economic blueprint is integrated into the story of Julian West, who wakes from a mesmeric sleep of 1887 into the Boston of 2000, is informed about the new order by Dr. Leete, and falls in love with Leete's daughter. This system of epoch-constrasts is reactualized in the nightmarish ending when Julian dreams of awakening back in the capitalist society of 1887. He meets its folly and repulsiveness with an anguished eye which supplies to each place and person a counterpossibility; the utopian estrangement culminates in the hallucination about "the possible face that would have been actual if mind and soul had lived" which he sees superimposed upon the living dead of the poor quarter. The lesson is that living in this nightmare and "pleading for crucified humanity" might yet be better than reawakening into the golden 21st century—as, in a final twist, Julian does. *Looking Backward*—intimately informed by Bellamy's constant preoccupation with human plasticity, memory and identity, brute reality and ideal possibility—reposes on a balance of world-times. Its plot is Julian's change of identity. In two of Bellamy's later stories, "The Blindman's World" and "To Whom This May Come," the alienated Earthmen are contrasted to worlds of brotherhood and transparency where men are "lords of themselves." As the anxious idealist becomes an apostate through a healer's reasonable lectures and his daughter's healing sympathy, the construction of a social system for the reader is also the reconstruction of the hero. This radical-democratic innovation, in which a changed world is accompanied by changing people's "nature," is epoch-making for future utopias and SF.

However, Bellamy retreated from this discovery. Just as Julian is the mediator between two social systems for the reader, so Edith Leete is the steadying emotional mediator for Julian, a personal female Christ of earthly brotherhood. Bellamy's "sunburst" of a new order is validated equally by socialist economics, ethical evolution, and Christian love; his future brings a purified space and man. The friendly house of Dr. Leete is the hearth of spacious, clean, classless Boston, with Edith as the Dickensian cricket on the hearth. Hard-headed civic pragmatism is the obverse of a soft-hearted petty-bourgeois "fairy tale of social felicity." Bellamy expects a nonviolent, imminent, and instantaneous abandonment of private capitalism by recognition of its folly. With telling effect he extrapolated the Rationalist or Jeffersonian principles and institutions to a logical end-product of universal public ownership. But he also remained limited by such ideals. His fascination with the rationally organized army should perhaps not be judged by our reaction today, since it was acquired under Lincoln and translated into peaceful and constructive terms. Further, any utopia before automation had to be harsh on recalcitrants, and Bellamy evolved toward participatory democracy in *Equality*. But even there he continued to stress State mobilization, "public capitalism," and technocratic regimentation *within* economic production as opposed to ideal classless relations outside it, dismissing "the more backward races" and political efforts by "workingmen."

Uncomfortable with sweeping changes of life-style, Bellamy is at his strongest in the economics of everyday life outside a capitalist framework—dressing and love, distribution of goods, cultural activities, democratic supply and demand (e.g., in organizing a journal or in solving brain-drain between countries). Here he is quite free from centralized State Socialist regulation. When contrasting such warm possibilities with stultifying private competition, he presents exempla of great force, as the initial allegory of the Coach, the parables of the Collective Umbrella and of the Rosebush, or (in *Equality*) the parables of the Water-Tank and of the Masters of the Bread. All such impressive and sometimes splendid apologues come from a laicized and radicalized New England pulpit style rather than from genteel fiction. Their ethical tone and the sentimental plot addressed themselves to women and all those who felt insecure and unfree in bourgeois society. Bellamy's homely lucidity made his romance, with all its limitations, the first authentically American socialist anticipation tale.

Bellamy's success fuses various SF strands and traditions. He interfused the preceding, narratively helpless tradition of utopian anticipations—tales culminating in Hale and Macnie, Cabet—with an effective Romantic system of correspondences. His ending, refusing the alibi of dream, marks the historical moment when this lay millenialism came of age: the new vision achieves, within the text, a reality *equal* to that of the author's empirical actuality. Bellamy links thus two strong American traditions: the fantastic one of unknown worlds and the practical one of organizing a new world— both of which translate powerful biblical themes into economics. His materialist view of history as a coherent succession of changing human relationships and social structures was continued by Morris and Wells and built into the fundamentals of subsequent SF. Equally the plot educates the reader into acceptance of the strange by following the protagonist's puzzled education. Modern SF, though it has forgotten this ancestor, builds on *Looking Backward* much as Dr. Leete's house was built on the remnants of Julian's house and on top of his sealed sleeping chamber, excavated by future archeology.

Traits from Bellamy's other works also drew from and returned into the SF tradition. The Flammarion-like, cosmically exceptional blindness of Earthmen and the transferral by spirit to Mars are found in "The Blindman's World," and despotic oligarchy as the alternative to revolution in *Equality*. Most immediately, the immense ideologico-political echo of *Looking Backward* reverberated around the globe through a host of sequels, rebuttals, and parallels. Bellamy had hit exactly the right note for a time searching for alternatives to ruthless plutocracy, and close to 200 utopian tales expounding or satirizing social democracy, State regulation of economy, Populist capitalism, or various uncouth combinations thereof were published in the US from 1888 to 1917 (notably Donnelly's *Caesar's Column*, Howell's *A Traveller from Altruria*, and London's *The Iron Heel*). In Britain the echo was felt in Morris's answer, *News From Nowhere*, in Wells, and in Germany in three dozen German utopian or anti-utopian tales.

—Darko Suvin

BENÉT, Stephen Vincent. American. Born in Bethlehem, Pennsylvania, 22 July 1898; brother of the poet William Rose Benét. Educated at Summerville Academy; Yale University, New Haven, Connecticut (Chairman, *Yale Literary Magazine,* 1919), A.B. 1919, M.A. 1920; the Sorbonne, Paris. Married Rosemary Carr in 1921; one son, two daughters. During the Depression and war years became an active lecturer and radio propagandist for the liberal cause. Editor, Yale Series of Younger Poets. Recipient: Poetry Society of America Prize, 1921; Guggenheim Fellowship, 1926; Pulitzer Prize, 1929, 1944; O. Henry Award, 1932, 1937, 1940; Shelley Memorial Award, 1933; National Institute of Arts and Letters Gold Medal, 1943. D.Litt.: Middlebury College, Vermont, 1936; Honorary Degree: Yale University, 1937. Vice-President, National Institute of Arts and Letters. *Died 13 March 1943.*

SCIENCE-FICTION PUBLICATIONS

Short Stories

Thirteen O'Clock: Stories of Several Worlds.   New York, Farrar and Rinehart, 1937; London, Heinemann, 1938.
The Short Stories of Stephen Vincent Benét: A Selection.   New York, Armed Services Editions, 1942.

OTHER PUBLICATIONS

Novels

The Beginning of Wisdom.   New York, Holt, 1921; London, Chapman and Dodd, 1922.
Young People's Pride.   New York, Holt, 1922.
Jean Huguenot.   New York, Holt, 1923; London, Methuen, 1925.
Spanish Bayonet.   New York, Doran, and London, Heinemann, 1926.
James Shore's Daughter.   New York, Doubleday, and London, Heinemann, 1934.

Short Stories

The Barefoot Saint.   New York, Doubleday, 1929.
The Litter of the Rose Leaves.   New York, Random House, 1930.
The Devil and Daniel Webster.   Weston, Vermont, Countryman Press, 1937.
Johnny Pye and the Fool-Killer.   Weston, Vermont, Countryman Press, 1938; London, Heinemann, 1939.
Tales Before Midnight.   New York, Farrar and Rinehart, 1939; London, Heinemann, 1940.
Twenty-Five Short Stories.   New York, Sun Dial, 1943.
O'Halloran's Luck and Other Short Stories.   New York, Penguin, 1944.
Selected Stories.   London, Fridberg, 1947.

Plays

Five Men and Pompey: A Series of Dramatic Portraits.   Boston, Four Seas, 1915.
The Headless Horseman, music by Douglas Moore (broadcast, 1937).   Boston, Schirmer, 1937.
The Devil and Daniel Webster, music by Douglas Moore, adaptation of the story by Benét (produced New York, 1939).   New York, Dramatists Play Service, 1939.
Elementals (broadcast, 1940-41).   Published in *Best Broadcasts of 1940-1941,* edited by Max Wylie.   New York, Whittlesey House, 1942.
Freedom's a Hard-Bought Thing (broadcast, 1941).   Published in *The Free Company Presents,* edited by James Boyd.   New York, Dodd Mead, 1941.
Nightmare at Noon, in *The Treasury Star Parade,* edited by William A. Bacher.   New York, Farrar and Rinehart, 1942.
A Child Is Born (broadcast, 1942).   Boston, Baker, 1942.
They Burned the Books (broadcast, 1942).   New York, Farrar and Rinehart, 1942.
Dear Adolf (broadcast, 1942).   New York, Farrar and Rinehart, 1942.
All That Money Can Buy (screenplay), with Dan Totheroh, in *Twenty Best Film Plays,* edited by John Gassner and Dudley Nichols.   New York, Crown, 1943.
We Stand United and Other Radio Scripts (includes *A Child Is Born, The Undefended Border, Dear Adolf, Listen to the People, Thanksgiving Day—1941, They Burned the Books, A Time to Reap, Toward the Century of Modern Man, Your Army).*   New York, Farrar and Rinehart, 1945.

Screenplays: *Cheers for Miss Bishop,* with Adelaide Heilbron and Sheridan Gibney, 1941; *All That Money Can Buy,* with Dan Totheroh, 1941.

Radio Plays: *The Headless Horseman,* 1937; *The Undefended Border,* 1940; *We Stand United,* 1940; *Elementals,* 1940-41; *Listen to the People,* 1941; *Thanksgiving Day—1941,* 1941; *Freedom's a Hard-Bought Thing,* 1941; *Nightmare at Noon; A Child Is Born,* 1942; *Dear Adolf,* 1942; *They Burned the Books,* 1942; *A Time to Reap,* 1942; *Toward the Century of Modern Man,* 1942; *Your Army,* 1944.

Verse

The Drug-Shop; or, Endymion in Edmonstoun.   Privately printed,
   1917.
Young Adventure.   New Haven, Connecticut, Yale University
   Press, 1918.
Heavens and Earth.   New York, Holt, 1920.
The Ballad of William Sycamore.   New York, Brick Row Book
   Shop, 1923.
King David.   New York, Holt, 1923.
Tiger Joy.   New York, Doran, 1925.
John Brown's Body.   New York, Doubleday, and London,
   Heinemann, 1928.
Ballads and Poems 1915-1930.   New York, Doubleday, 1931;
   London, Heinemann, 1933.
A Book of Americans, with Rosemary Carr Benét.   New York,
   Farrar and Rinehart, 1933.
Burning City.   New York, Farrar and Rinehart, 1936; London,
   Heinemann, 1937.
Ballad of the Duke's Mercy.   New York, House of Books, 1939.
Nightmare at Noon.   New York, Farrar and Rinehart, 1940.
Tuesday, November 5th, 1940.   New York, House of Books, 1941.
Listen to the People: Independence Day 1941.   New York, Council
   for Democracy, 1941.
Western Star.   New York, Farrar and Rinehart, 1943; London,
   Oxford University Press, 1944.
The Last Circle: Stories and Poems.   New York, Farrar Straus,
   1946; London, Heinemann, 1948.

Other

My Favorite Fiction Character.   Privately printed, 1938.
We Stand United (speech).   New York, Council for Democracy,
   1940.
A Summons to the Free.   New York, Farrar and Rinehart, and
   London, Oxford University Press, 1941.
Selected Works of Stephen Vincent Benét.   New York, Farrar and
   Rinehart, 1942; as *The Stephen Vincent Benét Pocket Book,* New
   York, Pocket Books, 1946.
America.   New York, Farrar and Rinehart, 1944; London,
   Heinemann, 1945.
Selected Poetry and Prose, edited by Basil Davenport.   New York,
   Holt Rinehart, 1960.
Selected Letters, edited by Charles A. Fenton.   New Haven, Con-
   necticut, Yale University Press, 1960.
*Stephen Vincent Benét on Writing: A Great Writer's Letters to a
   Young Beginner,* edited by George Abbe.   Brattleboro, Ver-
   mont, Greene Press, 1964.

Editor, with others, *The Yale Book of Student Verse 1910-
1919.*   New Haven, Connecticut, Yale University Press, 1919.

*

Bibliography: "Stephen Vincent Benét: A Bibliography" by Gladys
Louise Maddocks, in *Bulletin of Bibliography* (Boston), September-
December 1951 and January-April 1952.

*   *   *

The poet Stephen Vincent Benét wrote only a few works which
might be thought of as science fiction. "By the Waters of Babylon"
belongs to the history of science fiction as one of the earlier stories of
the world after the destruction of our present civilization: it depicts
the ruined, poisoned city and the man who tries to discover how the
ancients lived. It has many cousin-stories, from Poul Anderson's
Vault of the Ages to John Crowley's *Engine Summer,* and when it is
looked at in comparison with these it may well seem lacking in
individuality. Though certainly appealing, it is not Benét's best
story. Many of Benét's strongest stories have a historical theme,
often with a slight flavour of legend and the supernatural. *The Devil
and Daniel Webster* is a brilliant tribute to Daniel Webster as a
great American and jurist. Daniel Webster is defending a fellow
New Hampshireman against the devil, Mr. Scratch; the judge is the
ghost of that Justice Hawthorne (of the Salem witch trials) who was

Nathaniel Hawthorne's ancestor. In this story the author never puts
a foot wrong, and the grimness and the humour are beyond praise.
"The Curfew Tolls" could perhaps be claimed for science fiction,
since it is a "World of If" story. The narrator is a crusty and
conventional English military man who has met a Sardinian adventurer in the 1780's; though the Sardinian has had little chance of
military action himself, he makes trenchant analyses of the campaigns of Clive and Dupleix. As the narrator meets the incredible
family of the Sardinian, the reader begins to realize who the adventurer is: a Napoleon born too early, dying before the Revolution
even begins, and unable to leave his mark on history.

In the late 1930's and early 1940's Benét produced a number of
poems and stories that reflect what was happening in the world
around him. "The Last of the Legions" is an account of the retreat of
the last legion to leave Britain, when Alaric began attacking Rome.
It is as solidly alive as Kipling's stories of Roman Britain, and it asks
a question relevant to Benét then, and to us now: what should a
dying civilization wish to leave behind it? "By the Waters of
Babylon" is seen to best advantage when read with this story, and
with the nightmare poems "Notes to Be Left in a Cornerstone,"
"Metropolitan Nightmare," "Nightmare Number Three," and
"Nightmare for Future Reference."

—Charles Cushing

———————

BENFORD, Gregory (Albert).   American.   Born in Mobile,
Alabama, 30 January 1941. Educated at the University of Okla-
homa, Norman, B.S. in physics, 1963; University of California, San
Diego, M.S. 1965, Ph.D. 1967. Married Joan Abbe in 1967; one
daughter and one son. Fellow, 1967-69, and Research Physicist,
1969-72, Lawrence Radiation Laboratory, Livermore, California.
Assistant Professor, 1971-73, and since 1973, Associate Professor of
Physics, University of California, Irvine. Visiting Professor, Cam-
bridge University, 1976. Recipient: Nebula Award, 1974. Agent:
Richard Curtis, 156 East 52nd Street, New York, New York 10022.
Address: Department of Physics, University of California, Irvine,
California 92717, U.S.A.

SCIENCE-FICTION PUBLICATIONS

Novels

Deeper Than the Darkness.   New York, Ace, 1970; revised edition,
   as *The Stars in Shroud,* New York, Berkley, 1978; London,
   Gollancz, 1979.
Jupiter Project.   Nashville, Nelson, 1974.
If the Stars Are Gods, with Gordon Eklund.   New York, Berkley,
   1977; London, Gollancz, 1978.
In the Ocean of Night.   New York, Dial Press, 1977; London,
   Sidgwick and Jackson, 1978.
Find the Changeling, with Gordon Eklund.   New York, Dell,
   1980.
Timescape.   New York, Simon and Schuster, and London, Gol-
   lancz, 1980.
Shiva Descending, with William Rotsler.   New York, Avon, 1980.

Uncollected Short Stories

"Stand-In," in *Fantasy and Science Fiction* (New York), June 1965.
"Representative from Earth," in *Fantasy and Science Fiction* (New
   York), January 1966.
"Flattop," in *Fantasy and Science Fiction* (New York), May 1966.
"Sons of Man," in *Amazing* (New York), November 1969.
"Inalienable Rite," in *Quark 1,* edited by Samuel R. Delany and
   Marilyn Hacker.   New York, Paperback Library, 1970.
"The Scarred Man," in *Venture* (Concord, New Hampshire), May
   1970.

"The Prince of New York," in *Fantastic* (New York), June 1970.

"3:02 P.M., Oxford," in *If* (New York), September 1970.

"The Movement," in *Fantastic* (New York), October 1970.

"Nobody Lives on Burton Street," in *World's Best Science Fiction 1971*, edited by Donald A. Wollheim and Terry Carr. New York, Ace, and London, Gollancz, 1971.

"West Wind, Falling," in *Universe 1*, edited by Terry Carr. New York, Ace, 1971; London, Dobson, 1975.

"But the Secret Sits," in *Galaxy* (New York), March 1971.

"Battleground," in *If* (New York), June 1971.

"And the Sea Like Mirrors," in *Again, Dangerous Visions*, edited by Harlan Ellison. New York, Doubleday, 1972; London, Millington, 1976.

"2001 Hypothesis," in *Vertex* (Los Angeles), April 1973.

"Icarus Descending," in *Fantasy and Science Fiction* (New York), April 1973.

"Threads of Time," in *Threads of Time*, edited by Robert Silverberg. Nashville, Nelson, 1974; London, Millington, 1975.

"Man in a Vice," in *Amazing* (New York), February 1974.

"Nobody Lives Around There," in *Vertex* (Los Angeles), February 1974.

"Cambridge, 1:58 A.M.," in *Epoch*, edited by Roger Elwood and Robert Silverberg. New York, Berkley, 1975.

"John of the Apocalypse," in *Tomorrow Today*, edited by George Zebrowski. Santa Cruz, California, Unity Press, 1975.

"White Creatures," in *New Dimensions 5*, edited by Robert Silverberg. New York, Harper, 1975.

"Beyond Greyworld," in *Analog* (New York), September 1975.

"Doing Lennon," in *The Best Science Fiction of the Year 5*, edited by Terry Carr. New York, Ballantine, and London, Gollancz, 1976.

"Seascape," in *Faster Than Light*, edited by Jack Dann and George Zebrowski. New York, Harper, 1976.

"What Did You Do Last Year?," in *Universe 6*, edited by Terry Carr. New York, Doubleday, 1976; London, Dobson, 1978.

"Marauder," in *Alien Worlds*, edited by Charles N. Brown. London, Mews, 1976.

"How It All Went," in *Amazing* (New York), March 1976.

"Knowing Her," in *New Dimensions 7*, edited by Robert Silverberg. New York, Harper, 1977.

"Hellas in Florida," in *Fantasy and Science Fiction* (New York), January 1977.

"Homemaker," in *Cosmos* (New York), May 1977.

"A Snark in the Night," in *Fantasy and Science Fiction* (New York), August 1977.

"Nooncoming," in *Universe 8*, edited by Terry Carr. New York, Doubleday, 1978; London, Dobson, 1979.

"Starswarmer," in *Analog* (New York), September 1978.

"Old Woman by the Road," in *Destinies* (New York), November-December 1978.

"Calibrations and Exercises," in *New Dimensions 10*, edited by Robert Silverberg. New York, Harper, 1979.

"A Hiss of Dragon," with Marc Laidlaw, in *The Best Science Fiction of the Year 8*, edited by Terry Carr. New York, Ballantine, and London, Gollancz, 1979.

"Time Shards, in *Universe 9*, edited by Terry Carr. New York, Doubleday, 1979.

"In Alien Flesh," in *The 1979 Annual World's Best SF*, edited by Donald A. Wollheim. New York, DAW, 1979.

"Time Guide," in *Destinies* (New York), January-February 1979.

"Redeemer," in *Analog* (New York), April 1979.

"Dark Sanctuary," in *Omni* (New York), June 1979.

"Titan Falling," in *Amazing* (New York), August 1980.

Gregory Benford comments:

I am a resolutely amateur writer, preferring to follow my own interests rather than try to produce fiction for a living. And anyway, I'm a scientist by first choice and shall remain so.

I began writing from the simple desire to tell a story (a motivation SF writers seem to forget as they age, and thus turn into earnest moralizers). It's taken me a long time to learn how. I've been labeled a "hard SF" writer from the first, but in fact I think the job of SF is to do it *all*—the scientific landscape, peopled with real persons, with "style" and meaning ingrained. I've slowly worked toward that goal, with many dead ends along the way. From this comes my habit of

rewriting my older books and expanding early short stories into longer works (sometimes novels). Ideas come to me in a lapidary way, layering over the years. Yet, it's not the stirring moral message that moves me. I think writers are interesting when they juxtapose images or events, letting life come out of the stuff of the narrative. They get boring when they preach. To some extent, my novels reflect my learning various subcategories of SF—*Deeper Than the Darkness* was the galactic empire motif; *Jupiter Project* the juvenile; *If the Stars Are Gods* and *In the Ocean of Night* both the cosmic space novel, etc. *Timescape* is rather different, and reflects my using my own experiences as a scientist. Yet short stories, where I labored so long, seem to me just as interesting as novels. I learned to write there. Nowadays, my novels begin as relatively brisk plotlines and then gather philosophical moss as they roll. If all this sounds vague and intuitive, it is: that's the way I work. So I cannot say precisely why I undertake certain themes. I like Graham Greene's division of novels into "serious" and "entertainment," though I suspect the author himself cannot say with certainty which of his own is which.

It seems to me my major concerns are the vast landscape of science, and the philosophical implications of that landscape on mortal, sensual human beings. What genuinely interests me is the strange, the undiscovered. But in the end it is how *people* see this that matters most.

*   *   *

En route from teenage fanzine editor to University of California physicist, Gregory Benford evolved in the 1970's into a major writer of hard science fiction, moving from derivative melodrama to original low-key narratives partly won from experience. His best work combines the scientist's respect for data and verisimilitude and an artist's flair for construction and style. With some frequency, this involves combining, even rewriting earlier pieces, as his artistry improves.

No simple label for social or mythological straw figures, the "alien" in Benford's fiction is fundamentally unknowable without the observer also changing. The term encompasses the nature of the universe and the face of the future, which both scientist and SF writer must grapple with and assimilate. This preoccupation is evident from the forgettable "Flattop" to such a moving and technologically complex narrative as "White Creatures."

Jupiter Project, Shiva Descending, and *Find the Changeling* are relatively routine novels, a juvenile exploration story, a catastrophe novel and a mystery-melodrama, respectively. Benford's other novels are more substantial, demanding more of the reader.

If the Stars Are Gods is an episodic work (the eponymous novella won a Nebula). It and the section published separately as "The Anvil of Jove" are the best of a series of alien encounters by Bradley Reynolds, an aging astronaut who seeks the alien in part because of his own alienation from a youth-oriented society.

Another alien-seeker, Nigel Walmsley, encounters emissaries of an ancient and probably hostile machine civilization in *In the Ocean of Night*. Alienated from a world deteriorating socially and ecologically, a world which is not just bare background but lived in, he rejects an artificial religion in favor of a different kind of faith. Unable to understand fully the alien in human terms, Nigel gradually incorporates the alien viewpoint, coming to see the essential bond between any two sparks of intelligence in a hostile universe.

A more popular success, *The Stars in Shroud* is a stylish space opera, incorporating East-West and human-alien dichotomies as does *In the Ocean of Night*, to which it is now the sequel, once-removed, in a planned tetralogy. Elements of the missing links may be found in "And the Sea Like Mirrors," "In Alien Flesh," and "Starswarmer."

His best novel, *Timescape*, is a sensitive treatment of an original viewpoint on a significant theme. It is set in La Jolla, California (1962-63), where Benford attended graduate school, and Cambridge, England (1998), where he has also lived and worked. The novel concerns attempts by future physicists to warn their predecessors in time to avert a world-wide ecotastrophe. But it is also about people embedded in society, staving off quiet desperation, and most of all it concerns "doing science," with all of its political, economic, and personality clashes.

Some of Benford's work has little or no "alien" slant, such as

"Doing Lennon." But even such minor pieces as "Nooncoming," "Time Shards," and "Old Woman by the Road" grapple with our attempts, deliberate or inadvertent, to change the present into the future.

—David N. Samuelson

BERESFORD, J(ohn) D(avys). British. Born in Castor, Northamptonshire, 7 March 1873. Educated at Oundle School, Northamptonshire, and at a school in Peterborough; articled to Lacey W. Ridge, architect, London, 1901. Married Beatrice Roskams; three sons and one daughter. Practised architecture in the early 1900's. *Died 2 February 1947.*

SCIENCE-FICTION PUBLICATIONS

Novels

The Hampdenshire Wonder. London, Sidgwick and Jackson, 1911; as *The Wonder,* New York, Doran, 1917.
Goslings. London, Heinemann, 1913; as *A World of Women,* New York, Macaulay, 1913.
Revolution: A Story of the Near Future in England. London, Collins, and New York, Putnam, 1921.
Real People. London, Collins, 1929.
The Camberwell Miracle. London, Heinemann, 1933.
What Dreams May Come.... London, Hutchinson, 1941.
A Common Enemy. London, Hutchinson, 1942.
The Riddle of the Tower, with Esmé Wynne-Tyson. London, Hutchinson, 1944.

Short Stories

Nineteen Impressions. London, Sidgwick and Jackson, 1918; Freeport, New York, Books for Libraries, 1969.
Signs and Wonders. Waltham St. Lawrence, Berkshire, Golden Cockerel Press, and New York, Putnam, 1921.
The Meeting Place and Other Stories. London, Faber, 1929.

OTHER PUBLICATIONS

Novels

Stahl Trilogy:
  The Early History of Jacob Stahl. London, Sidgwick and Jackson, and Boston, Little Brown, 1911.
  A Candidate for Truth. London, Sidgwick and Jackson, and Boston, Little Brown, 1912.
  The Invisible Event. London, Sidgwick and Jackson, and New York, Doran, 1915.
The House in Demetrius Road. London, Heinemann, and New York, Doran, 1914.
The Mountains of the Moon. London, Cassell, 1915.
These Lynnekers. London, Cassell, and New York, Doran, 1916.
W.E. Ford: A Biography, with Kenneth Richmond. London, Collins, and New York, Doran, 1917.
House-Mates. London, Cassell, and New York, Doran, 1917.
God's Counterpoint. London, Collins, and New York, Doran, 1918.
The Jervaise Comedy. London, Collins, and New York, Macmillan, 1919.
An Imperfect Mother. London, Collins, and New York, Macmillan, 1920.
The Prisoners of Hartling. London, Collins, and New York, Macmillan, 1922.
Love's Pilgrim. London, Collins, and Indianapolis, Bobbs Merrill, 1923.

Unity. London, Collins, and Indianapolis, Bobbs Merrill, 1924.
The Monkey-Puzzle. London, Collins, and Indianapolis, Bobbs Merrill, 1925.
That Kind of Man. London, Collins, 1926; as *Almost Pagan,* Indianapolis, Bobbs Merrill, 1926.
The Decoy. London, Collins, 1927.
The Tapestry. London, Collins, and Indianapolis, Bobbs Merrill, 1927.
The Instrument of Destiny: A Detective Story. London, Collins, and Indianapolis, Bobbs Merrill, 1928.
All or Nothing. London, Collins, and Indianapolis, Bobbs Merrill, 1928.
Love's Illusion. London, Collins, and New York, Viking Press, 1930.
Seven, Bobsworth. London, Faber, 1930.
An Innocent Criminal. London, Collins, and New York, Dutton, 1931.
Three Generations Trilogy:
  The Old People. London, Collins, 1931; New York, Dutton, 1932.
  The Middle Generation. London, Collins, 1932; New York, Dutton, 1933.
  The Young People. London, Collins, 1933; New York, Dutton, 1934.
The Next Generation. London, Benn, 1932.
The Inheritor. London, Benn, 1933.
Peckover. London, Heinemann, 1934; New York, Putnam, 1935.
On a Huge Hill. London, Heinemann, 1935.
The Faithful Lovers. London, Hutchinson, and New York, Furman, 1936.
Cleo. London, Hutchinson, 1937.
The Unfinished Road. London, Hutchinson, 1938.
Strange Rival. London, Hutchinson, 1939.
Snell's Folly. London, Hutchinson, 1939.
Quite Corner. London, Hutchinson, 1940.
The Benefactor. London, Hutchinson, 1943.
The Long View. London, Hutchinson, 1943.
Men in the Same Boat, with Esmé Wynne-Tyson. London, Hutchinson, 1943.
If This Were True—. London, Hutchinson, 1944.
The Prisoner. London, Hutchinson, 1946.
The Gift, with Esmé Wynne-Tyson. London, Hutchinson, 1947.

Short Stories

The Imperturbable Duchess and Other Stories. London, Collins, 1923.
Blackthorn Winter and Other Stories. London, Hutchinson, 1936.

Plays

The Compleat Angler: A Duologue, with A.S. Craven (produced London, 1907). London, French, 1915.
The Royal Heart, with A.S. Craven (produced London, 1908).
The Veiled Woman (produced London, 1913).
Howard and Son, with Kenneth Richmond (produced London, 1916).
The Perfect Machine, with A.S. Craven, in *English Review 26* (London), May 1918.

Verse

Poems by Two Brothers, with Richard Beresford. London, Erskine Macdonald, 1915.

Other

H.G. Wells. London, Nisbet, and New York, Holt, 1915.
Taken from Life, photographs by E.O. Hoppé. London, Collins, 1922.
Writing Aloud. London, Collins, 1928.
The Case for Faith-Healing. London, Allen and Unwin, 1934.
The Root of the Matter: Essays, with others, edited by H.R.L. Sheppard. London, Cassell, 1937; Freeport, New York, Books

for Libraries, 1967.
What I Believe.   London, Heinemann, 1938.
The Idea of God.   London, Clarke, 1940.

*

Bibliography: "J.D. Beresford: A Bibliography" by Helmut E. Gerber, in *Bulletin of Bibliography 21* (Boston), January-April 1956.

*   *   *

J.D. Beresford, born just seven years after H.G. Wells, had affinities of imagination with the older writer, and similarities of style and theme may have dimmed the Beresford flame in the Wellsian glare. All his excellent science fiction is forgotten save *The Hampdenshire Wonder.* The neglect is regrettable because his attitudes were almost diametrically opposed to those of the politicising and romanticising Wells. Beresford's superficially gentler treatments show, on examination, an appreciation of the grimmer aspects of human nature which Wells tended to gloss in comedy or satire.

The first of Beresford's science fiction novels, *The Hampdenshire Wonder* may stand for most of the qualities and methods of its successors. As the story of a super-intelligent child born to working-class parents (one of the few major science-fiction themes Wells never attempted) it is an obvious forerunner of Stapledon's *Odd John,* but is superior in handling to the later book. The story of the lonely child (unwanted by all except his doting mother, and in his intellectual solitude having little use for her) making his misunderstood way through childhood to an ironical death at the hands of the village idiot illumines the theme of "difference" more clearly than, for example, Sturgeon's melodramatic *More Than Human.* Beresford's viewpoint is peculiar to himself. He was not primarily concerned, like more modern practitioners, with the symptoms and displays of transcendent genius so much as with the effect of this doomed creation's existence on those about him. The child is strongly drawn, with considerable understanding of the requirements of super-intelligence, but the characters who remain with the reader are the father, an uneducated county cricketer and workman who deserts child and wife when he can no longer bear the child's "unnatural" presence, and the mother, whose devotion to the self-absorbed genius is given without any return of affection or understanding. The two, supremely human, emphasise the child's alienness and eeriness in a fashion denied to our "mind-blowing" contemporary writers. Also, they demonstrate that characterisation in depth is possible in a genre which prefers to offer types as symbols of humanity confronting "difference." Beresford presents, without strain, rounded personalities who also manage to symbolise humanity dealing with the incomprehensible.

Goslings recalls Wells's *War of the Worlds* in its portrait of a plague-ridden, deserted London, but again the emphasis is on the reactions of people. Wells's stricken city is a symbol of trampled mankind; Beresford's is a challenge to the ordinary, unschooled but individual people who must live in and defeat it. *The Camberwell Miracle* has a faith healer (if that be the phrase for the talent) as central character, and here Beresford gives love and serenity to a portrait one can only imagine Wells handling with pragmatic savagery. *The Riddle of the Tower* (with Esmé Wynne-Tyson) again invades Wellsian territory, via bomb blast into an alternate space-time, to discover a human culture reminiscent of the hive or the termitary. Again the treatment is thoughtful rather than dramatic or satirical, though the warning against technological excess is clear.

These novels stand comparison with the best of current science fiction, and, in literary quality, head and shoulders above most. Beresford published over 40 mainstream novels and it is his mainstream approach to science-fiction problems of structure and balance that give his romances a unique flavour.

—George Turner

—————————

BERRY, Bryan.   Also wrote as Rolf Garner.   British.   Born in 1930. Worked in publishing; wrote for advertising agencies and educational films. *Died in 1955.*

SCIENCE-FICTION PUBLICATIONS

Novels

And the Stars Remain.   London, Panther, 1952.
Born in Captivity.   London, Panther, 1952.
Dread Visitor.   London, Panther, 1952.
The Venom Seekers.   London, Panther, 1953.
From What Far Star?   London, Panther, 1953.
Return to Earth.   London, Panther, n.d.

Novels as Rolf Garner (series: Venus in all books)

Resurgent Dust.   London, Panther, 1953.
The Immortals.   London, Panther, 1953.
The Indestructible.   London, Panther, 1954.

Uncollected Short Stories

"Aftermath," in *Authentic* (London), August 1952.
"The Final Venusian," "Groundling," and "The Imaginative Man," in *Planet* (New York), January 1953.
"Ancient City," in *Authentic* (London), May 1953.
"Mars Is Home," in *Planet* (New York), May 1953.
"Mission to Marakee," in *Two Complete Science Adventure Books* (New York), Summer 1953.
"The Tree," in *Authentic* (London), August 1953.
"The Adaptable Man," in *Authentic* (London), September 1953.
"Hidden Shepherds," in *Authentic* (London), February 1954.
"The Toy," in *Planet* (New York), March 1954.
"World Held Captive," in *Two Complete Science Adventure Books* (New York), Spring 1954.
"Savious," in *Authentic* (London), June 1954.
"Strange Suicide," in *Authentic* (London), April 1955.

*   *   *

The similarity of Bryan Berry's early stories to those of Ray Bradbury probably accounts for his initial success in *Planet Stories* (one issue carried three of his stories). Bradbury and other leading professionals had recently deserted the pulp magazine for better paying markets, and Berry's stories were unabashed space opera, an area the editor of the magazine, Jack O'Sullivan, liked and one in which Bradbury had been inactive for some time.

Berry's *Planet* stories weren't bad, but they hardly justified special attention. In "The Imaginative Man" space explorers encounter Venusians who appear to be mythological beasts. In "Groundling" a man's desire to go into space drives him to murder his wife. "The Final Venusian" tells of an earthman and two androids, the last sentient beings after a war has destroyed Earth and its planetary colonies. The story bears a resemblance to Bradbury's "Dwellers in Silence," and that, coupled with the special treatment singled out by O'Sullivan for Berry's *Planet* debut, led to some anti-Berry letters from readers. Berry's letter of reply stated that his favorite SF writer was not Bradbury but Clifford D. Simak; other favorites were van Vogt, Sturgeon, Russell, del Rey, and the "rising young star" E.C. Tubb.

As a writer, Berry could claim a fairly good style, somewhat more straightforward and less mannered than Bradbury's, but also lacking in Bradbury's verve. Even so, the Bradbury touch was definitely evident in much of his work. His novel "World Held Captive" is a typical sociological SF novel of oppressive government and secret underground organizations, and the world his characters move in is compatible enough with the one described in Bradbury's *Fahrenheit 451.* In his letter Berry described himself as an unabashed romantic with a taste for the melancholy, which probably accounts for a lot of the Bradbury flavor—that and the natural tendency of a beginning writer to fall under the influence of others. It can also be argued that for a relatively inexperienced writer forced to grind out scores of novels to make a living in a market dominated by prolific adventure writers, this was probably a very intelligent approach. British readers must have found Berry's stories a nice contrast to the often slambang fiction of John Russell Fearn.

Not all of Berry's fiction falls easily into the Bradbury pattern, however. "The Adaptable Man" is a highly simplified van Vogtian superman story with its protagonist caught up in a far-reaching plot of which, it turns out, he is the key figure. It's a well-done story, but not nearly so compelling as those more driven and irrational efforts of van Vogt himself. "The Toy" is a well-plotted time-travel story with a stronger ending than most of his stories boasted. "Mars Is Home" also has a strong plot, though weakened by a poor climax.

Berry died at the age of 25. He left a relatively large body of writing behind him, and we can readily discern his lucidity and the fact that in most of his fiction his concerns appear to be the familiar concerns of everyday life; even when his fiction draws its apparent inspiration from van Vogt, the characters remain rather domesticated creatures, not at all like the flamboyant archetypes of either van Vogt or Bradbury. Berry's case is complicated, however, by the fact that much of his fiction is buried under house names that can't be properly identified as belonging to him, though we know he wrote the well-received Venus trilogy as Rolf Garner. Because we can never really know what Berry might have become, it's impossible to read his fiction without regret.

—Gerald W. Page

BEST, (Oswald) Herbert.   British.   Born in Chester, Cheshire, 25 April 1894. Educated at King's School, Chester; Queens' College, Cambridge, LL.B. 1914. Served in the Royal Engineers, 1914-19: Lieutenant. Married the writer and illustrator Evangel Allena Champlin (pseudonym Erick Berry) in 1926 (died, 1974). District Officer, British Colonial Civil Service, Nigeria, 1919-32. Address: Sharon, Connecticut 06069, U.S.A.

SCIENCE-FICTION PUBLICATIONS

Novel

The Twenty-Fifth Hour.   London, Cape, and New York, Random House, 1940.

OTHER PUBLICATIONS

Novels

The Mystery of the Flaming Hut.   London, Cassell, and New York, Harper, 1932.
The Skull Beneath the Eaves.   London, Grayson, 1933.
Winds Whisper.   London, Hurst and Blackett, 1937.
Low River.   London, Hurst and Blackett, 1937.
Whistle, Daughter, Whistle.   New York, Macmillan, 1947.
The Columbus Cannon.   New York, Viking Press, 1954.
Diane.   New York, Morrow, 1954; London, Museum Press, 1955.
A Rumour of Drums.   London, Cassell, 1962; New York, McKay, 1963.

Other (juvenile)

Garram the Hunter.   New York, Doubleday, 1930; London, Lane, 1935.
Son of the Whiteman.   New York, Doubleday, 1931.
Garram the Chief.   New York, Doubleday, 1932; London, Lane, 1935.
Flag of the Desert.   New York, Viking Press, 1936; Oxford, Blackwell, 1937.

Tal of the Four Tribes.   Oxford, Blackwell, and New York, Doubleday, 1938.
Gunsmith's Boy.   Chicago, Winston, 1942; London, Newnes, 1944.
Concertina Farm.   London, Joseph, 1943.
Young'un.   New York, Macmillan, 1944; London, Cape, 1945.
Border Iron.   New York, Viking Press, 1945; London, Newnes, 1946.
Writing for Children (for adults), with Erick Berry.   New York, Viking Press, 1947; revised edition, Coral Gables, Florida, University of Miami Press, 1964.
The Long Portage.   New York, Viking Press, 1948; as *The Road to Ticonderoga,* London, Penguin, 1954.
Watergate: A Story of the Irish on the Erie Canal.   Philadelphia, Winston, 1951.
Not Without Danger.   New York, Viking Press, 1951.
Ranger's Ransom.   New York, Aladdin, 1953.
The Sea Warriors.   New York, Macmillan, 1959.
Desmond's First Case.   New York, Viking Press, 1961.
Bright Hunter of the Skies.   New York, Macmillan, 1961.
Carolina Gold.   New York, Day, 1961.
Desmond the Dog Detective: The Case of the Lone Stranger.   New York, Viking Press, 1962.
The Webfoot Warriors: The Story of UDT, the US Navy's Underwater Demolition Team.   New York, Day, 1962.
Parachute to Survival.   New York, Day, 1964.
Desmond and the Peppermint Ghost.   New York, Viking Press, 1965.
Desmond and Dog Friday.   New York, Viking Press, 1968.
The Polynesian Triangle.   New York, Funk and Wagnalls, 1968.
Men Who Changed the Map: A.D. 400 to 1914, with Erick Berry.   New York, Funk and Wagnalls, 1968.

*   *   *

The reputation of Herbert Best is as a writer of young adult stories and popularized history rather than of science fiction. Nevertheless, his very fine novel *The Twenty-Fifth Hour* takes its place among the good science-fiction stories of post-catastrophe sociology. It was published in 1940, and its subject matter made it timely. In the mid-20th century Ann Shillito of Chicago survives the man-invented disease that exterminates the populations of the Americas. The British officer Hugh Fitzharding survives a European war that has reduced men to lone hunters who prey cannibalistically upon one another. They meet improbably on the coast of France and sail to North Africa where they find a somewhat utopian civilization re-emerging, and live happily. The contrived happy ending does not neutralize the novel's realism. Hemp and cotton ropes and clothing soon weaken and rot (among the reminders to the modern reader that Best wrote before the age of plastic and synthetics). Perversion is coolly inventoried. Cannibalism, incest, casuasl rape, women as chattel (Best's position on women is enlightened), and torture and murder for fun are endemic. That North Africa is the location of rising civilization is both plausible and symbolically satisfying. However, the message is gloomy. High technology seduces men into losing basic survival competence; it makes uncontrolled biological warfare possible. Complex and ingenious, it makes mankind powerful and insane. The novel's desolate picture of western civilization is an emblem of its disastrously bankrupt culture.

The stature and interest of *The Twenty-Fifth Hour* is well measured by the excellence and importance of earlier and later examples of this class of novel. It looks back to Mary Shelley's *Last Adam,* Wells's *Time Machine,* and M.P. Shiel's *The Purple Cloud,* and it forms a remarkable diptych with L. Ron Hubbard's *Final Blackout.* It looks forward to works by George R. Stewart, John Bowen, Pat Frank, John Christopher, Alfred Coppel, Brian Aldiss, and Philip Wylie.

—John R. Pfeiffer

BESTER, Alfred. American. Born in New York City, 18 December 1913. Educated at the University of Pennsylvania, Philadelphia, B.A. 1935. Married Rolly Goulko in 1936. Free-lance writer: book reviewer, *Fantasy and Science Fiction*, New York, 1960-62, radio and TV writer, and staff member, *Holiday*, New York. Recipient: Hugo Award, 1953. Agent: Robert P. Mills Ltd., 156 East 52nd Street, New York, New York 10022, U.S.A.

SCIENCE-FICTION PUBLICATIONS

Novels

The Demolished Man. Chicago, Shasta, and London, Sidgwick and Jackson, 1953.
Tiger! Tiger! London, Sidgwick and Jackson, 1956; as *The Stars My Destination*, New York, New American Library, 1957.
The Computer Connection. New York, Berkley, 1975; as *Extro*, London, Eyre Methuen, 1975.
Golem. New York, Simon and Schuster, and London, Sidgwick and Jackson, 1980.

Short Stories

Starburst. New York, New American Library, 1958; London, Sphere, 1968.
The Dark Side of the Earth. New York, New American Library, 1964; London, Pan, 1969.
Starlight. New York, Doubleday, 1976; as *The Great Short Fiction of Alfred Bester: Star Light, Star Bright* and *The Light Fantastic*, New York, Berkley, 2 vols., 1976; London, Gollancz, 2 vols., 1977-78.

Uncollected Short Stories

"Galatea Galante," in *Omni* (New York), April 1979.
"MS Found in a Coconut," in *Analog* (New York), June 1979.
"Fondly Fahrenheit," in *Fantasy and Science Fiction* (New York), October 1979.

OTHER PUBLICATIONS

Novel

Who He? New York, Dial Press, 1953; as *The Rat Race*, New York, Berkley, 1956.

Other

"Gourmet Dining in Outer Space," in *Holiday* (New York), May 1960.
The Life and Death of a Satellite. Boston, Little Brown, 1966; London, Sidgwick and Jackson, 1967.
"My Affair with Science Fiction," in *Hell's Cartographers*, edited by Brian W. Aldiss and Harry Harrison. London, Weidenfeld and Nicolson, 1975; New York, Harper, 1976.
"Writing and *The Demolished Man*," in *Experiment Perilous*, edited by Andrew Porter. New York, Algol Press, 1976.

*   *   *

Alfred Bester has not been a prolific writer of science fiction. His career has generated so far only a handful of novels and short stories spanning some 35 years. In the space of a limited output, however, Bester has achieved a rare importance in the field. Two of his novels are classics, and a younger generation of writers already acknowledges his influence. Despite this stature, Bester still considers himself an outsider to the genre, and speaks of his "affair" with science fiction. Much of his life has been spent writing for comics, radio, television, and general magazines. Science fiction has remained for him primarily "a safety valve, an escape hatch, therapy."

Bester is the grand master of what has come to be called the "pyrotechnic" science-fiction novel. His works are fast-paced adventures, full of surprises, and brought together by remarkably intricate convergences of characters, events, and ideas. The manner is a little reminiscent of space opera, but Bester has been subject to more immediate influences in his "action-packed" comic book and broadcast media work. His novels, moveover, are vastly more sophisticated than simple adventure stories.

As a science fiction writer, Bester is more interested in people than in science. In his preface to "The Pi Man" (*Starlight*), he comments, "I'm not much interested in extrapolating science and technology; I merely use extrapolation as a means of putting people into new quandaries which produce colorful pressures and conflicts." Consequently, the science predominating in Bester's fiction is psychology. His short stories typically assume the focus of extravagant case studies, and — if we can judge from the prefaces — much of their substance derives from the author's habit of analyzing himself (which is perhaps the basis of Bester's "therapy" in science fiction). Bester's favorite character type is the compulsive, the driven man. His stories center on such figures as sources of interest and motivation. Bester calls them his "anti-heroes," but they are usually constructed of heroic material. He endows them with extraordinary powers and sets them loose to interact with their environments in significantly perverse ways. Other characters — representatives of social stability — hunt, observe, and manipulate them, or are in turn manipulated. There is a lot of intrigue in Bester's fiction and a lot of detective work.

When Bester made his move to long fiction, he found a medium well-suited to his compulsive leading characters. *The Demolished Man* makes no significant departure technically from his shorter fiction. The characters, however, have more room to move around. Bester doesn't waste the opportunity. *The Demolished Man* presents a more heterogeneous picture of a culture than was usual for an early 1950's science-fiction novel. Though its leading characters are the cream of an enlightened society — the unmistakable beings of romance—they do not remain insulated from their inferiors. Bester brings them into slums, houses of illusion, and the underworld. Some of this is for exotic contrast, but the willingness at least to recognize the seamy side of a future civilization is refreshing.   On one level, *The Demolished Man* is a mystery story. A man commits a murder in the 24th century, when telepathy has made crime discoverable in advance and therefore preventable. How could such a man escape detection? Ben Reich, the murderer, is a powerful man with access to all the technology, brain power, and social deference necessary to legal immunity. He is also ironically a pawn of archetypal patterns, a man whose elaborate criminal strategy blinds him to his own motive.   The representative of justice — the first-class telepath Prefect Lincoln Powell — finds himself faced with a predictable dilemma: the conviction and punishment of Reich, while necessary to the continuing order, will not bring satisfaction. Reich, who embodies the best as well as the worst in humanity, must somehow be reclaimed. In 24th-century technology, Bester allows for such a process.

Bester's second novel, *Tiger! Tiger!*, is generally regarded as his greatest success and as a pinnacle achievement in the field. It is itself an epic success story: the account of a man — bleakly ordinary, abandoned, and near death in space — who manages to save himself, and, with the sole motive of revenge, acquires wealth, knowledge, and eventually the power to defeat his enemies, only to find on the brink of success that his goals no longer make sense to him. This failure of resolve is in effect his final test. He becomes a changed man, a saint instead of a tiger, aspiring to lead others on the road to self determination. In this novel, Bester ranges even further into the sordid future of poverty, crime, and vice. The protagonist, Gulliver Foyle, is himself a graduate of the gutter, who speaks a common dialect and moves easily among the dregs of 25th-century civilization. During his quest for vengeance, Gully passes through diseased cities and the marketplace of vice. He visits a slave labor camp and spends time in prison, and encounters an array of minor characters that would do well in a wax museum. It is, as Bester warns, "an age of freaks, monsters, and grotesques."

The variety of setting and abundance of ideas in Bester's longer fiction are an important outcome of structure and of method: his novels are episodic, moving as the term "pyrotechnic" suggests like explosions in series. Successive episodes introduce new surprises rather than resolving old conflicts, up to the eventual climax when the weight of ideas and events finally forces a synthesis. The method takes careful planning and a wealth of raw material. Bester's special talent as a writer is the art of constellation. He draws upon an awesome array of apparently incongruous materials, and proceeds to make connections until he has fabricated a tightly knit and interesting story.

The Computer Connection has the same kind of construction. Some of its social content has been updated in that the heroes include American Indians, blacks, and women who are not beautiful. The characterizations abound in stereotypes, however, and Bester pointedly pokes fun at the social movements of the early 1970's so it is difficult to see any clear social statement. While neither the approach nor the ideas in The Computer Connection are as fresh as in his 1950's classics, the novel is still entertaining reading. Bester now confronts the problem facing any major author, of having to write in the context of his own earlier achievements and those of younger writers who have learned from him.

—Robert Froese

BEYNON, John. *See* **WYNDHAM, John.**

BIGGLE, Lloyd, Jr. American. Born in Waterloo, Iowa, 17 April 1923. Educated at Wayne University, Detroit, 1941-43, 1946-47, A.B. (honors) 1947; University of Michigan, Ann Arbor, 1947-53, M.M. in music literature 1948, Ph.D in musicology 1953. Served in the United States Army, 1943-46: Sergeant. Married Hedwig T. Janiszewski in 1947; one daughter and one son. First Secretary-Treasurer, 1965-67, Chairman, Board of Trustees, 1967-71, and Founder of the Regional Collections, Science Fiction Writers of America. Founder, and since 1979, President, Science Fiction Oral History Association. Agent: Kirby McCauley Ltd., 60 East 42nd Street, New York, New York 10017, U.S.A.

SCIENCE-FICTION PUBLICATIONS

Novels (series: Cultural Survey; Jan Darzek)

The Angry Espers. New York, Ace, 1961; London, Hale, 1968.
All the Colors of Darkness (Darzek). New York, Doubleday, 1963; London, Dobson, 1964.
The Fury Out of Time. New York, Doubleday, 1965; London, Dobson, 1966.
Watchers of the Dark (Darzek). New York, Doubleday, 1966; London Rapp and Whiting, 1968.
The Still, Small Voice of Trumpets (Survey). New York, Doubleday, 1968; London, Rapp and Whiting, 1969.
The World Menders (Survey). New York, Doubleday, 1971; Morley, Yorkshire, Elmfield Press, 1973.
The Light That Never Was. New York, Doubleday, 1972; Morley, Yorkshire, Elmfield Press, 1975.
Monument. New York, Doubleday, 1974; London, New English Library, 1975.
This Darkening Universe (Darzek). New York, Doubleday, 1975; London, Millington, 1979.
Silence Is Deadly (Darzek). New York, Doubleday, 1977; London, Millington, 1980.
The Whirligig of Time (Darzek). New York, Doubleday, 1979.

Short Stories

The Rule of the Door and Other Fanciful Regulations. New York, Doubleday, 1967; as The Silent Sky, London, Hale, 1979.
The Metallic Muse. New York, Doubleday, 1972.
A Galaxy of Strangers. New York, Doubleday, 1976.

OTHER PUBLICATIONS

Other

"Science Fiction Goes to College: Groves and Morasses of Academe," in Riverside Quarterly (Regina, Saskatchewan), April 1974.
"Quantum Physics and Reality," with Michael Talbot, in Analog (New York), December 1976.
"The Morasses of Academe Revisited," in Analog (New York), September 1978.
"The Arts: Media," in Analog (New York), January 1980.

Editor, Nebula Award Stories 7. London, Gollancz, 1972; New York, Harper, 1973.

*

Manuscript Collection: Spencer Research Library, University of Kansas, Lawrence.

* * *

The best-known creations of Lloyd Biggle are the Council of Supreme and its extensions, the agents of the Galactic Synthesis, the Cultural Survey, and the Interplanetary Relations Bureau, known for mottoes such as "Democracy Imposed from Without Is the Severest Form of Tyranny." Supreme is a vast computer that is fed information by its eight councilors; the only human is number ONE, Jan Darzek, who ironically was recruited by Supreme from uncertified Earth (i.e., not fit for social intercourse with civilized planets because its inhabitants tell lies) through Rok Wllon, who eventually becomes EIGHT. EIGHT dislikes ONE personally but they unite in common cause against the Dark Force, the Udef, which threatens the universe.

Supreme is not a ruler but an advisor, though people tend to accept its wisdom without hesitation since it eventually always proves reliable. Supreme—the ultimate in impartial democratic justice—fails in its function only when it is deprived of data input or asked the wrong question, thus simultaneously demonstrating the old programmers' wisdom "Garbage in; garbage out" and suggesting the need for an informed electorate of enlightened self interest.

Always highly readable, Biggle narrates the adventures of Jan Darzek as he saves Earth in All the Colors of Darkness, the galaxy in Watchers of the Dark, and a large part of the universe in This Darkening Universe, as well as two individual worlds in Silence Is Deadly and The Whirligig of Time. In The World Menders and The Still, Small Voice of Trumpets the Cultural Survey officers must cope with bureaucracy while solving the problems of how to bring an uncertified world into the Galactic Synthesis of self-rule and trade with other planets. Monument and The Light That Never Was also deal with the place of art and beauty in human culture and civilization.

Biggle's characterization is generally drawn with vivid broad strokes in the literary tradition of Charles Dickens; e.g., Darzek's assistant is a little old lady, Miss Schlupe ("Schluppy"), who loves the comfort of her rocking chair as she makes beer out of whatever exotic vegetation is available wherever she lands in the galaxy. The chief interest in Biggle's stories is not character motivation, but puzzle solving, understanding the nature of the universe so that it can be managed intelligently. Throughout his stories, intelligent life in whatever form it appears (even a giant vegetable computer) earns respect. In the ironic tradition of Jonathan Swift, humanoid-appearing creatures may turn out to be sub-human animals (The World Menders), as determined by their lack of culture, particularly religion and the arts. Repeatedly Biggle dramatizes the need for a holistic understanding of a culture, including the ecological balance of a planet and the physical strengths and weaknesses of its inhabitants. Tolerance and respect for differences between species is demonstrated to benefit all intelligent beings, and Biggle uses gentle satire to provide moral instruction as he delights.

His greatest strength is in creating believable alien worlds and civilizations, complete with native flora and fauna, linguistic idiosyncrasies, customs of courtship and marriage, provisions for raising children, social intercourse and folkways (always inseparable from economic trade and business affairs), religion, systems of government, and culture in its most inclusive sense. Because of this complexity, it is unfair to limit his stories with the label juvenile—even though neither his heroes nor his villains ever use expletives stronger than "drat"—but his clear-cut pro-life moral tone is particularly suitable for young readers.

Unfortunately Biggle is currently writing very little short fiction, but some of the best of his stories are available in three collections; *A Galaxy of Strangers* contains the prefect gem "And Madly Teach."

—Elizabeth Anne Hull

BINDER, Eando. Pseudonym for Otto Oscar Binder (and his brother Earl Andrew Binder until 1934); also wrote as John Coleridge. American. Born in Bessemer, Michigan, 26 August 1911. Studied science and chemical engineering at Crane City College, Northwestern University, Evanston, Illinois, and the University of Chicago for three years. Married Ione Frances Turek in 1940; one daughter. Clerk, Central Scientific Company, Chicago, 1930-31; assistant to Science Librarian, Crerar Library, Chicago, 1931-32; free-lance writer after 1932: reader of manuscripts, Otis Kline Literary Agency, 1936-38; comic book writer from 1941; Editor, *Space World*, New York, 1962-63. *Died 14 October 1974.*

SCIENCE-FICTION PUBLICATIONS

Novels

Lords of Creation.   Philadelphia, Prime Press, 1949.
Enslaved Brains.   New York, Avalon, 1965.
The Avengers Battle the Earth-Wrecker.   New York, Bantam, 1967.
The Impossible World.   New York, Curtis, 1967.
Menace of the Saucers.   New York, Belmont, 1969.
The Double Man.   New York, Curtis, 1971.
Five Steps to Tomorrow.   New York, Curtis, 1971.
Get Off My World.   New York, Curtis, 1971.
Night of the Saucers.   New York, Belmont, 1971.
Puzzle of the Space Pyramids.   New York, Curtis, 1971.
Secrets of the Red Spot.   New York, Curtis, 1971.
The Mind from Outer Space.   New York, Curtis, 1972.

Short Stories

The New Life (as John Coleridge).   New York, Columbia, 1940.
Martian Martyrs (as John Coleridge).   New York, Columbia, 1940.
Adam Link—Robot.   New York, Paperback Library, 1965.
Anton York—Immortal.   New York, Belmont, 1965.

Uncollected Short Stories

"All in Good Time," in *Signs and Wonders,* edited by Roger Elwood.   Old Tappan, New Jersey, Revell, 1972.
"Any Resemblance to Magic," in *Long Night of Waiting,* edited by Roger Elwood.   Minneapolis, Lerner, 1974.
"Better Dumb Than Dead," in *Journey to Another Star,* edited by Roger Elwood.   Minneapolis, Lerner, 1974.
"The Missing World," in *The Missing World,* edited by Roger Elwood.   Minneapolis, Lerner, 1974.

OTHER PUBLICATIONS

Play

Television Play: *I, Robot,* 1964.

Other

The Golden Book of Space Travel [*Atomic Energy, Jets and Rockets*] (juvenile).   New York, Golden Press, 3 vols., 1959-61.
The Moon, Our Neighboring World (juvenile).   New York, Golden Press, 1959.
Planets: Other Worlds of Our Solar System (juvenile).   New York, Golden Press, 1959.
Victory in Space.   New York, Walker, 1962.
Careers in Space.   New York, Walker, 1963.
Riddles of Astronomy.   New York, Basic, 1964.
What We Really Know about Flying Saucers.   New York, Fawcett, 1967.
Mankind, Child of the Stars, with Max H. Flindt.   New York, Fawcett, 1974; London, Coronet, 1976.

*   *   *

Though the unique name Eando is formed from "E and O," representing Earl and Otto Binder, for all practical purposes Eando was Otto Binder; the early, collaborative stories comprise a very minor component of the Binder works, both qualitatively and quantitatively. Binder maintained that a real professional could write anything, from the libretto of an opera to a technical manual. While not embracing quite this broad a range, his works were sufficiently varied to give the notion strong support. In addition to his science fiction, Binder produced weird-horror fiction, gothic romance, and considerable non-fiction, as well as hundreds of comic book and comic strip "scripts."

Binder's most important single story is generally regarded to be "I, Robot," published in the January 1939 *Amazing.* (The Isaac Asimov book, *I, Robot,* appeared in 1950. Its title was as much a tribute to Binder as anything else; in his autobiography, Asimov attributes the inspiration of his famous "positronic robot" stories to a meeting with Binder and the reading of Binder's "I, Robot.") The significance of Binder's story lies in its sympathetic, even emotional, portrayal of the robot Adam Link. This effect is heightened by the first-person narration. The story was hugely successful and led to a series of popular sequels. Lester del Rey's equally significant "sympathetic robot" story, "Helen O'Loy," was written independently and simultaneously with Binder's "I, Robot," and actually reached print in *Astounding* a month before Binder's story. Del Rey abandoned the theme after a single effort, while Binder, Asimov, and shortly thereafter Eric Frank Russell (with his Jay Score stories) continued the development of the theme.

Binder's stories collected as *Anton York—Immortal* were also highly popular in their day, although lacking in the seminal significance of the Adam Link series. The Anton York stories are concerned with the impact of immortality on a lone man (eventually joined by an immortal wife) and on society. A number of Binder's other stories and novels achieved popularity in their time, but have little present readership. Their loss of popularity is probably due to Binder's stylistic limitation. Though a perfectly competent writer, he did not often succeed in bringing a sense of excitement to his prose; an illuminating comparison is E.E. Smith, whose unbounded energy totally transcended the limitations of his weak prose style.

Binder's "Via Etherline" tales were later collected as *Puzzle of the Space Pyramids.* Prior to the appearance of these stories, space travel and interplanetary exploration were almost always portrayed as glamorous, romantic activities. Binder instead portrayed them as grimy, difficult, dangerous, and often boring tasks. The stories were echoed in the realistic/predictive space fiction of Arthur C. Clarke, e.g., *Prelude to Space, Sands of Mars, A Fall of Moondust.*

In the 1940's and 1950's, Binder devoted most of his efforts to writing comic book continuity. As the principal writer for the *Captain Marvel* feature, he was chiefly responsible for the humorous, satirical, and often science-fiction elements that best characterized that altogether superior feature. In the 1960's, he developed an interest in UFOs and possible space-visitors, and three of his last works were devoted to these themes. One other series of stories by Binder is noteworthy. These are the tales about Jon Jarl, a young officer in the space patrol of the future. Binder wrote literally scores of these stories as text filler in the *Captain Marvel Adventures* comic book. As juvenile science fiction, they are charming, succinct, and stimulating. They have, unfortunately, never been collected.

—Richard A. Lupoff

BISCHOFF, David F(rederick). American. Born in Washington, D.C., 15 December 1951. Educated at the University of Maryland, College Park, B.A. 1973. Worked as dishwasher, soda-jerk, clerk; Associate Editor, *Amazing,* New York. Since 1974, staff member, NBC-TV, Washington, D.C. Secretary, 1978-80, and since 1980, Vice-President, Science Fiction Writers of America. Agent: Henry Morrison Inc., 58 West 10th Street, New York, New York 10011. Address: 2004 Erie Street, Adelphia, Maryland 20783, U.S.A.

SCIENCE-FICTION PUBLICATIONS

Novels

The Seeker, with Christopher Lampton. Toronto, Laser, 1976.
Tin Woodman, with Dennis R. Bailey. New York, Doubleday, 1979; London, Sidgwick and Jackson, 1980.
Nightworld. New York, Ballantine, 1979.
Star Fall. New York, Berkley, 1980.

Uncollected Short Stories

"Top Hat," in *Fantastic* (New York), December 1977.
"Alone and Palely Loitering," in *Chrysalis 3,* edited by Roy Torgeson. New York, Kensington, 1978.
"A Forbidden World," with Ted White, in *Amazing* (New York), January 1978.
"In Medias Res," in *Fantastic* (New York), April 1978.
"Outside," in *Fantasy and Science Fiction* (New York), April 1980.

OTHER PUBLICATIONS

Other (juvenile)

Quest. Milwaukee, Raintree, 1977.
Strange Encounters. Milwaukee, Raintree, 1977.
The Phantom of the Opera. New York, Scholastic, 1977.

*   *   *

David F. Bischoff's work tackles a wide range of subjects and situations. While his ease at creating lively dialogue—or mono-logue—is recognizable throughout his solo and collaborative writing, some of his most memorable fiction shows a flair for taking a quotation, character, or situation from literary history and playing with it in science-fiction terms. His writing has a youthful quality about it; his work often features dreamers, young or old, or young people whose naivety is charming or, in more somber work, moving.

Bischoff's first solo full-length novel, *Nightworld,* is a light-hearted, effervescent tale of a youthful prince and his discovery of the realities behind the apparitions of evil in his world. The novel supposes that an intelligent computer "who" has modelled "herself" after Queen Victoria has been so pleased with the simulacrum or "mandroid" of Prince Albert designed for her that she "peoples" her empire—now expanded to galactic proportions—with other historical mandroids. Nightworld is itself a resort colony patterned after medieval England, equipped with electricity and other modern

conveniences including a master computer unfortunately taken over by a madman who fancies himself to be Satan. It takes a 600-year-old mandroid of H.G. Wells to help Prince Oliver Dolan overcome Satan's legions—including mandroidal werewolves and vampires—and to prepare a dark-age society for the awesome possibilities of the future.

"Alone and Palely Loitering" takes its title and inspiration from the poetry of John Keats. This futuristic love story is the monologue of Ensign Henry Loftus, a young disillusioned space navigation officer who finds that he has been blind in more ways than one regarding a seemingly perfect blind date. Loftus falls in love at first sight with his "Genevieve" but during an "ideal" honeymoon the couple visits the Plateau of Plato, a tourist spot which reveals "flickering shadows of True Reality." Here Loftus meets an apparition of John Keats who warns "La belle dame/ Sans merci/ Hath thee in thrall!" The bride disappears, finally to be revealed as an android created to reflect the dreams of its partner.

The Seeker, written with Christopher Lampton, focuses on the inner needs of Gordon Ames, a minister in a small midwestern town who faces his own personal crisis of faith at the same time as the quiet life of his community is shaken by the crash landing of an alien space craft. Ames's friendship with the alien Trebar alienates him from his own people but brings him to a fuller awareness of his own identity as a seeker of truth and a man of love existing in a community of people blinded by hate and ignorance.

Tin Woodman, written with Dennis R. Bailey, also turns its attention to questions of alienation. This novel, with its emphasis on strong characterization, portrays the tortured loneliness of two young "Talents"—individuals with the supranormal ability to read minds and emotions—who are paradoxically alienated from their fellows even as they have access to their innermost thoughts and feelings. Contact with an alien—essential to the success of star cruiser Pegasus's voyage—must be entrusted to the unstable adolescent Talent Div Harlthor, who finds communion—literally and figuratively—on his mission of first contact. Meanwhile another young Talent, Mora Elburn, must intrepret the far-reaching implications of Div's actions, which in a sense provide a human heart to an alien being.

—Rosemary Herbert

BISHOP, Michael. American. Born in Lincoln, Nebraska, 12 November 1945. Educated at the University of Georgia, Athens, B.A. in English 1967 (Phi Beta Kappa), M.A. 1968. Served in the United States Air Force as English Instructor, Air Force Academy Preparatory School, 1968-72: Captain. Married Jeri Ellis Whitaker in 1969; one son and one daughter. English Instructor, University of Georgia, 1972-74. Since 1974, free-lance writer. Recipient: Deep South Con XV Phoenix Award, 1977; Clark Ashton Smith Award, for verse, 1978. Agent: Virginia Kidd, Box 278, Milford, Pennsylvania 19337. Address: Box 646, Pine Mountain, Georgia 31822, U.S.A.

SCIENCE-FICTION PUBLICATIONS

Novels

A Funeral for the Eyes of Fire. New York, Ballantine, 1975; London, Sphere, 1978.
And Strange at Ecbatan the Trees. New York, Harper, 1976; as *Beneath the Shattered Moon,* New York, DAW, 1977; London, Sphere, 1978.
Stolen Faces. New York, Harper, and London, Gollancz, 1977.
A Little Knowledge. New York, Berkley, 1977.
Catacomb Years. New York, Berkley, 1979.

Transfigurations. New York, Berkley, 1979; London, Gollancz, 1980.
Under Heaven's Bridge, with Ian Watson. London, Gollancz, 1980.

Short Stories

Blooded on Arachne. New York, Berkley, 1980.

OTHER PUBLICATIONS

Verse

Windows and Mirrors. Tuscaloosa, Alabama, Moravian Press, 1977.

Other

"On Reviewing and Being Reviewed," in *Shayol 1* (New York), November 1977.
"Evangels of Hope," in *Foundation 14* (London), September 1978.
Introduction to *Ubik,* by Philip K. Dick. Boston, Hall, 1979.
"Conversation with Furthermore B. Hayves," in *Thrust 12,* Summer 1979.

*   *   *

In Michael Bishop's novel *A Little Knowledge* one of the characters refers to the medieval theological concept of *haecceitas* "or thisness, the specialness of each individual attribute of God's creation as a means of understanding the whole." Bishop has a fine sense of the "thisness" of existence, in his case of alien or future existences which may be metaphors for the here and now, but which establish themselves uniquely well; it is notable that Bishop, almost alone among writers, pays special and constant attention to the *eyes* of his aliens as visible extensions of their inner selves.

"Thisness" limits one's understanding of what life can be about, yet at the same time is the only tool for discovering meaning, the search for which Bishop delineates in a richly textured inventive prose, coining a host of neologisms and employing a whole gamut of rhetorical devices. This is a little obtrusive in his first novel, *A Funeral for the Eyes of Fire,* but more subtle in subsequent works where the rhetoric hints at archetypal mythic patterns acting themselves out through literary style (juxtaposition, invocation, repetition, paradox, hyperbole, zeugma, oxymoron) rather than through the overt mythologizing of, say a Zelazny. Thus, in *And Strange at Ecbatan the Trees* one feels that the main characters are protagonists at the same time as they are real, suffering, learning humans or humanoids; within the fabulous territory of SF, another level of fable is being generated just beneath the surface (as the syntax of a poem by itself forms its own interior fable), providing an articulate energetic substructure. It's surely no accident that Bishop christened his *Eye of Fire* world Trope (literally a figure of speech).

Yet there is nothing artificial here; the striving is less for effect than for understanding, for a kind of transcendence or salvation—the painful search for which is often characterized by strange mutations and transformations. Thus, in Bishop's shorter fiction a man may become a prosthetic machine, alien to himself and other flesh-life ("The House of Compassionate Sharers"), or turn into a planet-sized tomato ("Rogue Tomato"); or a semi-mutant man who fails to become sufficiently alien to his heritage suffers anguish by contrast with the evolved Parfects ("The White Otters of Childhood"). One of the last men alive tries to revive the race, only to create mocking vegetable effigies ("Effigies"), and the armless aliens of a paradise world stretch themselves to snapping point for the sake of a lost human, bringing about an awe-ful, misconceived apotheosis ("Cathadonian Odyssey"). Bishop's art here is of the exotic parable, handled with an intensity of presence which renders the strange familiar to us without robbing it of its essential strangeness.

His novels, too, constitute searches—for oneself, in alien or alienated surroundings. *A Funeral for the Eyes of Fire* tells of the painful self-discovery of a younger brother during the politically expedient destruction of an alien religious kibbutz; *And Strange at Ecbatan the Trees* of a distant planet where human beings are preserved by the superior Parfects—and preserved *from themselves*

by the genetic suppression of emotion. The story intersects an upsurge of violence caused by barbarian renegades with a scientist-artist's ritual dramas before silent, emotionally "masked" audiences, involving reanimated corpses—for only the dead may show emotion.

Another kind of simulation, another deceit, and another search for salvation motivate *Stolen Faces,* where demoted Lucian Yeardance is exiled to a leper colony on a world that masks itself in Aztec motifs, to discover that the lepers are scapegoats of the world's conscience, deliberately mutilating and degrading themselves—a discovery which drives Lucian to his own King Lear-like abasement, for he is a scapegoat as surely as they are.

A Little Knowledge and *Catacomb Years* are both set (the former capsuled chronologically within the latter) in the domed future city of Atlanta which has gone into internal religious exile (along with the other perhaps more secular Urban Nuclei of this alienated future America) while the rest of the world has gone out to the stars. Enigmatic aliens from 61 Cygni are introduced into Atlanta as a hopeful picklock for the self-prisoned city in *A Little Knowledge,* and a moment of revelation occurs to two of the Atlantans presenting the aliens as reincarnated humans higher up an evolutionary psychic ladder; however, the events that lead to the eventual dismantling of the dome in *Catacomb Years* are more public and political, though when the dome is breached, in a typical Bishop paradox, it is the *night* that is reborn: the mystery of the wider universe.

Transfigurations is the novelization of Bishop's bravura novella "Death and Designation among the Asadi," introducing a genetically enhanced "neo-chimp" to break through the communication barrier with an alien race who communicate by eye-signals, and upon whom the heart-rent anthropologist of the earlier tale has projected his own dilemmas. In the process Bishop transfigures the earlier fable's ambiguous exotica into literal events which illuminate discomfortingly our own deep racial past. Discovery of the alien, again, mediates a self-discovery.

—Ian Watson

BIXBY, Jerome (Lewis). American. Born in Hollywood, California, 11 January 1923. Studied piano and composition at the Juilliard School of Music, New York. Served in the Medical Corps, United States Army Air Corps, during World War II: Private. Married 1) Sarah Reader in 1946; 2) Linda Burman in 1967 (divorced); three children. Editor, Fiction House, 1949-51, *Planet Stories* and *Two Complete Science Adventure Books,* 1950-51, *Action Stories* and *Frontier Stories,* Standard Publications, 1951-53, Galaxy Publications, 1953-54; Owner, Exoterica mail-order business, 1963-64, and Walden Realty Company, 1964-65, both in Bullhead City, Arizona. Agent: O. Klement, 9772 Olympic Boulevard, Beverly Hills, California 90212. Address: 315 East Gilbert, San Bernardino, California 92404, U.S.A.

SCIENCE-FICTION PUBLICATIONS

Novel

Star Trek: Day of the Dove. New York, Bantam, 1978.

Short Stories

The Devil's Scrapbook. New York, Brandon House, 1964.
Space by the Tale. New York, Ballantine, 1964.

OTHER PUBLICATIONS

Plays

Screenplays: *It! The Terror from Beyond Space*, 1958; *Curse of the Faceless Man*, 1958; *The Lost Missile*, with John McPartland and Lester William Berke, 1958; *Fantastic Voyage*, with others, 1966.

Television Plays: *Mirror, Mirror*, 1967, *By Any Other Name*, with D.C. Fontana, 1967, *Day of the Dove*, 1968, and *Requiem for Methuselah*, 1968, all in *Star Trek* series.

*   *   *

With second careers as editor, screenwriter, TV writer, real estate developer, and with a serious interest in musical composition, Jerome Bixby has not taken good enough care of his work as a science-fiction writer or pushed his own editors and publishers hard enough to get his work into print for access by the contemporary reader. Only one volume of collected SF, *Space by the Tale*, and one of horror and fantasy tales, *The Devil's Scrapbook*, have been published. Beyond these only occasional tales in anthologies, led by Bixby's most famous story, "It's a *Good* Life" (1953), form the surface portion of an iceberg of over 300 SF stories and 1000 other stories.

Space by the Tale is an indirect compliment to Bixby as an editor, for his own selection captures the range of the skills of this most interesting and whimsical of short story producers. All of the stories, except perhaps the slightly laboured "The Bad Life," are models of Bixby's characteristic light, clean, quick style and of a story told clearly and quickly. For style and story-telling alone "It's a *Good* Life" fully deserves its classic status. In a series of short, macabre comic scenes Bixby sketches a mid-American farming town where little Anthony, a mutated "baby," is born with godlike powers of telekinesis, telepathy, and the ability to make and destroy the material universe. He has isolated the town, possibly destroying the rest of creation, and both as "baby" and "boy" he has struck back unconsciously when hate is directed at him, neatly planting in a cornfield the destroyed persons and animals which he first changes in unspeakable ways. The story is brilliantly paranoid, as no one alive in the town can *think* ill of Anthony, his acts, or their situation, for at any moment they may catch his attention and be struck down. The story has a pervasive air of inevitability and horror.

"It's a *Good* Life" is typical of Bixby's best stories in three ways. First, it presents a model of an omniscient god and poses the question of the morality of godhead. Anthony has immense powers but wholly immature moral judgement, which puts him part way between the omnipotent Judeo-Christian god and the capricious Greek Olympians. Bixby has written numerous fantasy stories about God and the Devil in conflict, which, however whimsical in the Stephen Vincent Benét tradition, are at heart moral tales. In "It's a *Good* Life" he asks what the universe would be like with a malevolent, child-like god who simply holds personal comfort and pleasure above any standard of his own behaviour. That "child-like" Anthony reminds the reader of Bixby's second gift, his skill at observing human beings. His young god is capable of malice but also of bored benevolence and even kindness. The frightened townspeople are very real, very typical, yet slight variations in their reactions stamp their experiences as authentic, heightening the terror. This same care with the creation of characters is of assistance when Bixby writes his more whimsical stories, giving a delicacy of shading to the humour. The third way in which "It's a *Good* Life is characteristic of Bixby's SF work is that it is not a "hard" science story. Bixby can write such stories ("Small World" and "The Bad Life" in *Space by the Tale*), but his forte really lies at the juncture of SF, fantasy, and the moral tale, where a generalised scientific concept provides a base for a story of human nature. Anthony is a typical creation. His conception is not explained and his powers are described in general rather than technical terms. Anthony can "think" people into a cornfield, "do the thing" to separate the town from the rest of the world, and "change" people in horrible but undescribed ways. Stories such as these are fantasies but they are based on concepts accepted by SF. *Space by the Tale*, for example, contains "The Draw," in which telekinesis creates the fastest of all western gunmen; "The Young One," about a family of werewolves

settling in the midwest with their son; "Angels in the Jets," about a planet where something in the atmosphere drives everyone crazy in a liberating fashion; and "Laboratory," about gigantic creatures whose laboratory asteroid is wrecked when two humans blunder into its invisible environs.

Bixby's best stories have an energetic twist. The resident imp in "The Magic Typewriter" is bound to bring to pass everything typed on the machine, which is marvellous until its owner goes out for cigarettes and his horribly ugly landlady sits down and types an illiterate yet deadly letter making him her lover and taking over the typewriter. The Devil in "Trace" actually does a favour for a lawyer whose car has broken down. In this sly allegory about the sudden kindnesses of the rich at their summer places Bixby proves that even the Devil has his good moments. When the Devil finds out that he is helping a lawyer his murmured, "Ah. Then perhaps we may meet again" is typical of the quiet wit of this charming and skillful craftsman.

—Peter A. Brigg

———————————

BLADE, Alexander. *See* **GARRETT, Randall.**

———————————

BLAYRE, Christopher. Pseudonym for Edward Heron-Allen; also wrote as Nora Helen Warddel. British. Born in London, 17 December 1861. Educated at Harrow School. Served with the Staff Intelligence Department of the War Office during World War I. Married 1) Marianna Lehmann in 1891; 2) Edith Pepler in 1903, one daughter. Admitted as a Solicitor of the Supreme Court, 1884. Lived in the United States, 1886-89; gave frequent lectures on protozoology. Editor, with E. Polonaski, *Violin Times*, London, 1893-1907. Fellow, Royal Society, 1919. *Died 28 March 1943.*

SCIENCE-FICTION PUBLICATIONS

Novel

Some Women of the University, Being a Last Selection from the Strange Papers of Christopher Blayre. London, Stockwell, 1934.

Short Stories

The Purple Sapphire and Other Posthumous Stories. London, Philip Allan, 1921; revised edition, as *The Strange Papers of Dr. Blayre*, 1932; New York, Arno Press, 1976.
The Cheetah-Girl. Privately printed, 1923.

OTHER PUBLICATIONS as Edward Heron-Allen

Novels

The Princess Daphne. London, Drane, 1885; Chicago, Belford Clarke, 1888.
The Romance of a Quiet Watering-Place (as Nora Helen Warddel). Chicago, Belford Clarke, 1888.

Short Stories

Kisses of Fate. Chicago, Belford Clarke, 1888.
A Fatal Fiddle. Chicago, Belford Clarke, 1890.

Verse

The Love-Letters of a Vagabond.   London, Drane, 1889.
The Ballades of a Blasé Man.   Privately printed, 1891.

Other

De Fidiculis Opusculum.   Privately printed, 9 vols., 1882-1941.
Chiromancy; or, The Science of Palmistry, with Henry Frith.   London, Routledge, 1883.
Codex Chiromantiae.   Privately printed, 3 vols., 1883-86.
Violin-Making, As It Was and Is.   London, Ward Lock, 1884; Boston, Howe, 1901.
A Manual of Cheirosophy.   London, Ward Lock, 1885.
Practical Cheirosophy: A Synoptical Study of the Science of the Hand.   New York and London, Putnam, 1887.
De Fidiculis Bibliographia, Being an Attempt Towards a Bibliography of the Violin and All Other Instruments with a Bow.   London, Griffith Farran, 2 vols., 1890-94.
Prolegomena Towards the Study of Chalk Foraminifera.   London, Nichols, 1894.
Some Side-lights upon Edward FitzGerald's Poem "The Ruba'iyat of Omar Khayyam."   London, Nichols, 1898.
Nature and History at Selsea Bill.   Selsey, Sussex, Gardner, 1911.
Selsey Bill: Historic and Prehistoric.   London, Duckworth, 1911.
The Visitors' Map and Guide to Selsey.   Selsey, Sussex, Gardner, 1912.
The Foraminifera of the Clare Island District, Co. Mayo, Ireland, with Arthur Earland.   Dublin, Clare Island Survey, 1913.
Protozoa (report for the 1910 Antarctic expedition), with Arthur Earland.   Privately printed, 1922.
Barnacles in Nature and Myth.   London, Oxford University Press, 1928.
The Gods of the Fourth World, Being Prolegomena Towards a Discourse upon the Buddhist Religion.   Privately printed, 1931.
The Parish Church of St. Peter on Selsey Bill, Sussex.   Privately printed, 1935.

Editor, *Edward FitzGerald's Ruba'iyat of Omar Khayyam, with the Original Persian Sources.*   London, Quaritch, 1899.
Editor, *The Second Edition of Edward FitzGerald's Ruba'iyyat of 'Umar Khayyám.*   London, Duckworth, 1908.
Editor, with Arthur Earland, *The Fossil Foraminifera of the Blue Marl of the Côte des Basques.*   Manchester, Literary and Philosophical Society, 1919.
Editor, *Memoranda of Memorabilia,* by Madame de Sévigné.   Privately printed, 1928.
Editor, *The Further and Final Researches of Joseph Jackson Lister upon the Reproductive Processes of Polystomella crispa (Linné).*   Washington, D.C., Smithsonian Institution, 1930.

Translator, *The Science of the Hand,* by C.S. d'Arpentigny.   London, Ward Lock, 1886.
Translator, *The Ruba'iyat of Omar Khayyám.*   London, Nichols, 1898.
Translator, *The Lament of Bába Táhir.*   London, Quaritch, 1902.
Translator, *Quatrains of Omar Khayyám.*   London, Mathews, 1908; revised edition, 1908.
Translator, *The Ruba'iyat of Omar Khayyám the Poet: The Literal Translation of the Ousley Manuscript.*   London, Lane, 1924.

*   *   *

Christopher Blayre remains an enigmatic figure. His extraordinarily versatile life in varied scientific and artistic fields is mostly well recorded—he did research in marine biology and palaeontology, horticulture, music, occultism, Persian literature, history, and bibliography—but the names under which he wrote some of his unacknowledged fiction have not been discovered, and how much more he may have written of possible interest is not known. What we do have is a quite interesting group of stories, mainly on supernatural themes, and a few with a place in science fiction's formative stage. The weird stories use familiar elements of ghosts and apparitions, possession, visions, and curses, but the treatment is modern.

There is some effective satirical humor, as in the immortal Wandering Jew succumbing to modern medicine, and a visit to an annex to Hell with an institution for completing unfinished works.

"Aalila" concerns a visit to Venus by matter transmission. The Venerians, who inevitably resemble humans, have an incompatible culture, and the experimenter's inevitable sexual involvement with Aalila leads to the expected disaster. It is an effective tale for all its familiarity. "The Cosmic Dust" is a sequel, and must be among the earliest stories on the interplanetary transmission of life in spores. This was a very important concept and raises questions that remain open. "The Mirror That Remembered" has another idea often suggested, a device for visualising past scenes. A marginal item is "The Blue Cockroach," where a temporary change in personality follows an insect bite.

The Cheetah-Girl, dropped by the publisher at the last moment from *The Purple Sapphire,* is a more ambitious work, a serious story of a macabre project—the creation of a human-cheetah hybrid, and its consequences. The rationale is logical, considering the elementary state of genetics in 1920. These stories compare very favorably with the better known proto-science fiction of the period. The style is easy, assured, and fresh.

—Graham Stone

———————

BLISH, James (Benjamin).   Also wrote as William Atheling, Jr.   American.   Born in East Orange, New Jersey, 23 May 1921. Educated at East Orange High School; Rutgers University, New Brunswick, New Jersey, 1938-42, B.Sc. 1942; Columbia University, New York, 1945-46. Served in the United States Army, 1942-44. Married 1) Virginia Kidd in 1947; 2) Judith Ann Lawrence in 1964; two children. Editor of a trade newspaper, New York, 1947-51; public relations counsel, New York and Washington, D.C., 1951-68. Editor, *Vanguard Science Fiction,* New York, 1958; Co-Editor, *Kalki: Studies in James Branch Cabell,* Oradell, New Jersey. Vice-President, Science Fiction Writers of America, 1966-68. Recipient: Hugo Award, 1959. *Died 29 July 1975.*

Science-Fiction Publications

Novels (series: Cities in Flight)

Jack of Eagles.   New York, Greenberg, 1952; London, Nova, 1955; as *ESP-er,* New York, Avon, 1958.
The Warriors of Day.   New York, Galaxy, 1953; London, Hutchinson, 1978.
Cities in Flight (revised edition).   New York, Avon, 1970.
   Earthman, Come Home.   New York, Putnam, 1955; London, Faber, 1956.
   They Shall Have Stars.   London, Faber, 1956; as *Year 2018!,* New York, Avon, 1957.
   The Triumph of Time.   New York, Avon, 1958; as *A Clash of Cymbals,* London, Faber, 1959.
   A Life for the Stars.   New York, Putnam, 1962; London, Faber, 1964.
A Case of Conscience.   New York, Ballantine, 1958; London, Faber, 1959.
VOR.   New York, Avon, 1958; London, Corgi, 1959.
The Duplicated Man, with Robert A.W. Lowndes.   New York, Avalon, 1959.
The Star Dwellers (juvenile).   New York, Putnam, 1961; London, Faber, 1962.
Titans' Daughter.   New York, Berkley, 1961; London, New English Library, 1963.
Mission to the Heart Stars (juvenile).   New York, Putnam, and London, Faber, 1965.

A Torrent of Faces, with Norman L. Knight.   New York, Doubleday, 1967; London, Faber, 1968.

Welcome to Mars! (juvenile).   London, Faber, 1967; New York, Putnam, 1968.

Black Easter; or, Faust Aleph-Null.   New York, Doubleday, 1968; London, Faber, 1969.

The Vanished Jet (juvenile).   New York, Weybright and Talley, 1968.

Spock Must Die! A Star Trek Novel.   New York, Bantam, 1970.

The Day after Judgment.   New York, Doubleday, 1970; London, Faber, 1972.

...And All the Stars a Stage.   New York, Doubleday, 1971; London, Faber, 1972.

Midsummer Century.   New York, Doubleday, 1972; London, Faber, 1973.

The Quincunx of Time.   London, Faber, 1975.

Short Stories

The Seedling Stars.   New York, Gnome Press, 1957; London, Faber, 1967.

Galactic Cluster.   New York, New American Library, 1959; London, Faber, 1960.

So Close to Home.   New York, Ballantine, 1961.

Best Science Fiction Stories of James Blish.   London, Faber, 1965; revised edition, 1973.

Star Trek 1-12 (from the TV series; vol. 12 with J.A. Lawrence).   New York, Bantam, 12 vols., 1967-77; London, Corgi, 12 vols., 1972-78.

Anywhen.   New York, Doubleday, 1970; London, Faber, 1971.

The Best of James Blish, edited by Robert A.W. Lowndes.   New York, Ballantine, 1979.

OTHER PUBLICATIONS

Novels

The Frozen Year.   New York, Ballantine, 1957; as *Fallen Star,* London, Faber, 1957.

The Night Shapes.   New York, Ballantine, 1962; London, New English Library, 1963.

Doctor Mirabilis.   London, Faber, 1964; New York, Dodd Mead, 1971.

Other

The Issue at Hand: Studies in Contemporary Magazine Science Fiction (as William Atheling, Jr.).   Chicago, Advent, 1964.

"Is This Thinking?," in *SF Horizons 1* (London), 1964.

"S.F.: The Critical Literature," in *SF Horizons 2* (London), 1965.

"On Science Fiction Criticism," in *Riverside Quarterly* (Regina, Saskatchewan), August 1968.

More Issues at Hand: Critical Studies in Contemporary Science Fiction (as William Atheling, Jr.).   Chicago, Advent, 1970.

"The Tale That Wags the Dog: The Function of Science Fiction," in *American Libraries* (Chicago), December 1970.

"The Development of a Science Fiction Writer," in *Foundation 2* (London), June 1972.

"Moskowitz on Kuttner," in *Riverside Quarterly* (Regina, Saskatchewan), February 1972.

"A Surfeit of Lem, Please?," in *Foundation 6* (London), May 1974.

Editor, *New Dreams This Morning.*   New York, Ballantine, 1966.
Editor, *Nebula Award Stories 5.*   New York, Doubleday, and London, Gollancz, 1970.
Editor, *Thirteen O'Clock and Other Zero Hours,* by C.M. Kornbluth.   New York, Dell, 1970; London, Hale, 1972.

*

Bibliography: *James Blish: A Bibliography 1940-1976* by Judith A. Blish, privately printed, 1976.

*   *   *

James Blish can be seen as the complete man of letters for the young genre of science fiction from his early days of fandom in the 1930's until his untimely death from cancer in 1975, and one wonders whether Blish, if he had lived, might not eventually have published the masterpiece he insisted the genre would be incapable of producing. Out of such ironies often come great works of art; and Blish had a consuming and scholarly interest in great art—from music, James Joyce, and Ezra Pound to the best science-fiction writers. The irony is that Blish as a writer came directly out of the pulp and fan tradition with all its variety, and even at the end of his career, when he was producing his best theorizing about the genre, he was also grinding out the highly commercial *Star Trek* novelizations. Blish was a steady producer of short fiction for the pulps who later learned to write superb novels and series. He saw the need for continuing critical writing and theorizing about the new genre of science fiction and produced masterful examples of both. He was a fan, an agent, an editor; and he was both beloved and feared for his totally comprehensive involvement with the genre. Blish's first editor, fellow Futurian, and friend, Robert A.W. Lowndes, develops the argument (in his introduction to *The Best of James Blish*) that Blish learned to write and to admire science fiction that was crafted "the hard way." His work, then, demonstrates both the scope and the artistic depth that was possible in science fiction during his lifetime.

Several of Blish's most often used themes and the ironies and tensions inherent in those themes can serve as illustration. *The Seedling Stars,* a full-length fiction made from shorter pieces about microscopic life, convinces the reader that mankind inhabits an infinite universe where the possibilities for protean form-changing and new and dynamic adaptations (the real mainstream of science fiction) are seemingly limitless and also necessary. At the end of the book, this Stapledonian view is summed up as follows, "There's no survival value in pinning one's race forever to one set of specs." And yet within the same period of his writing, Blish is continually looking for the one set of eternal specifications that govern human existence. Perhaps his most effective novel, *A Case of Conscience,* serves as the concluding part of a trilogy in which each of the protagonists is Christian; and the eternal battle between good and evil throughout the trilogy seems much more real and absolute than the open-ended relativism of adaptive evolution. Blish juggled these themes, and the comic tension from the resulting balance produces a high seriousness that (though the works appeared at first in the pulps) deserves to be treated as literature.

Another theme that apparently fascinated Blish because it appears often through his work (from a juvenile such as *The Star Dwellers* to the epic ending of his tetralogy *Cities in Flight*) is the catastrophism of the explosive first moments of creation seen also as the end of all things. The awesome fecundity of the moment of death is Blish's most sublime image. I believe it appears frequently and interestingly enough in his work to allow a thoroughly Freudian analysis of Blish's fascination with death and with catastrophism. The point is that, though he is as completely at home with the intentions and the conventions of the pulps as one is with his hometown, the true territory that Blish explores extends into the most profound speculations of our time. He was a good scholar and a good critic who would be delighted to know that future scholars and critics will also value his fictions.

Blish's own late theorizing about the genre maintains that variety and a kind of comic fecundity constitute its strength and reason for existence at this time in our history. He bases his theory on the historical speculations of Oswald Spengler; and R.D. Mullen has argued (in his afterword published with the gathered sections of *Cities in Flight*) that that tetralogy is grounded in Spenglerian theory. What Blish denies, of course, following from Spengler is that at this late date in our history and in this genre in particular, which best represents the variety of our time, no new synthesizing masterpieces (or epics) will appear. His own attempts are lengthy. *Cities in Flight* contains four novels. The trilogy that he intended to entitle *After Such Knowledge* contains the magnificent historical novel on Roger Bacon, *Doctor Mirabilis,* two novellas, and the science fiction novel *A Case of Conscience.* One would like to think that the theorist doth protest too much. But the trilogy was left unconnected at Blish's death, and the effect also of the tetralogy may be more centrifugal than centering. In any case, the work of Blish is rich with these dilemmas and tensions and, always, the art.

—Donald M. Hassler

BLOCH, Robert. Also writes as Collier Young. American. Born in Chicago, Illinois, 5 April 1917. Educated in public schools. Married 1) Marion Holcombe; 2) Eleanor Alexander; one daughter. Worked as copywriter, Gustav Marx Advertising Agency, Milwaukee, Wisconsin, 1943-53. Editor, *Science-Fiction World,* New York, 1956. President, Mystery Writers of America, 1970-71. Recipient: Evans Memorial Award, 1959; Hugo Award, 1959; Ann Radcliffe Award, 1960, 1966; Mystery Writers of America Edgar Allan Poe Award, 1960; Trieste Film Festival Award, 1965; Convention du Cinéma Fantastique de Paris Prize, 1973; World Fantasy Convention Award, 1975. Guest of Honor, World Science Fiction Convention, 1948, 1973; World Fantasy Convention, 1975; Bouchercon I, 1971. Agent: Scott Meredith Literary Agency, 845 Third Avenue, New York, New York 10022. Address: 2111 Sunset Crest Drive, Los Angeles, California 90046, U.S.A.

SCIENCE-FICTION PUBLICATIONS

Novels

This Crowded Earth, and Ladies' Day. New York, Belmont, 1968.
Sneak Preview. New York, Paperback Library, 1971.
Reunion with Tomorrow. New York, Pinn, 1978.

Short Stories

Atoms and Evil. New York, Fawcett, 1962; London, Muller, 1963.
Bloch and Bradbury, with Ray Bradbury. New York, Tower, 1969; as *Fever Dream and Other Fantasies,* London, Sphere, 1970.
Fear Today, Gone Tomorrow. New York, Award, 1971.
The Best of Robert Bloch. New York, Ballantine, 1977.

Uncollected Short Stories

"Picture," in *Shadows,* edited by Charles L. Grant. New York, Doubleday, 1978.
"The Spoiled Wife," in *Chrysalis 3,* edited by Roy Torgeson. New York, Kensington, 1979.
"Freak Show," in *Fantasy and Science Fiction* (New York), May 1979.
"The Bald-Headed Mirage," in *Fantastic* (New York), July 1979.
"Nina," in *The Best from Fantasy and Science Fiction 23,* edited by Edward L. Ferman. New York, Doubleday, 1980.

OTHER PUBLICATIONS

Novels

The Scarf. New York, Dial Press, 1947; as *The Scarf of Passion,* New York, Avon, 1948; revised edition, New York, Fawcett, 1966; London, New English Library, 1972.
The Kidnapper. New York, Lion, 1954.
Spiderweb. New York, Ace, 1954.
The Will to Kill. New York, Ace, 1954.

Shooting Star. New York, Ace, 1958.
Psycho. New York, Simon and Schuster, 1959; London, Hale, 1960.
The Dead Beat. New York, Simon and Schuster, 1960; London, Hale, 1961.
Firebug. Evanston, Illinois, Regency, 1961; London, Corgi, 1977.
The Couch (novelization of screenplay). New York, Fawcett, and London, Muller, 1962.
Terror. New York, Belmont, 1962; London, Corgi, 1964.
The Star Stalker. New York, Pyramid, 1968.
The Todd Dossier (as Collier Young). New York, Delacorte Press, and London, Macmillan, 1969.
It's All in Your Mind. New York, Curtis, 1971.
Night-World. New York, Simon and Schuster, 1972; London, Hale, 1974.
American Gothic. New York, Simon and Schuster, 1974; London, W.H. Allen, 1975.
There Is a Serpent in Eden. New York, Kensington, 1979.
Strange Eons. Browns Mills, New Jersey, Whispers Press, 1979.

Short Stories

Sea-Kissed. London, Utopian, 1945.
The Opener of the Way. Sauk City, Wisconsin, Arkham House, 1945; London, Spearman, 1974.
Terror in the Night and Other Stories. New York, Ace, 1958.
Pleasant Dreams—Nightmares. Sauk City, Wisconsin, Arkham House, 1960; London, Whiting and Wheaton, 1967; as *Nightmares,* New York, Belmont, 1961.
Blood Runs Cold. New York, Simon and Schuster, 1961; London, Hale, 1963.
More Nightmares. New York, Belmont, 1962.
Yours Truly, Jack the Ripper: Tales of Horror. New York, Belmont, 1962; as *The House of the Hatchet and Other Tales of Horror,* London, Tandem, 1965.
Horror-7. New York, Belmont, 1963; London, Corgi, 1965.
Bogey Men. New York, Pyramid, 1963.
Tales in a Jugular Vein. New York, Pyramid, 1965; London, Sphere, 1970.
The Skull of the Marquis de Sade and Other Stories. New York, Pyramid, 1965; London, Hale, 1975.
Chamber of Horrors. New York, Award, 1966; London, Corgi, 1977.
The Living Demons. New York, Belmont, 1967; London, Sphere, 1970.
Dragons and Nightmares. Baltimore, Mirage Press, 1969.
Cold Chills. New York, Doubleday, 1977; London, Hale, 1978.
The King of Terrors. Yonkers, New York, Mysterious Press, 1977; London, Hale, 1978.
Out of the Mouths of Graves. Yonkers, New York, Mysterious Press, 1979; London, Hale, 1980.
Such Stuff as Screams Are Made of. New York, Ballantine, 1979; London, Hale, 1980.
Mysteries of the Worm. New York, Kensington, 1979.

Plays

Screenplays: *The Couch,* with Owen Crump and Blake Edwards, 1962; *The Cabinet of Caligari,* 1962; *Strait-Jacket,* 1964; *The Night Walker,* 1964; *The Psychopath,* 1966; *The Deadly Bees,* with Anthony Marriott, 1967; *Torture Garden,* 1967; *The House That Dripped Blood,* 1970; *Asylum,* 1972.

Radio Plays: *Stay Tuned for Terror* series (39 scripts), 1944-45.

Television Plays: contributions to *Lock-Up,* 1960; *Alfred Hitchcock Presents,* 1960-64; *Thriller,* 1961-62; *I Spy,* 1964; *Run for Your Life,* 1965; *Star Trek,* 1966-67; *Journey to the Unknown,* 1968; *Night Gallery,* 1971.

Other

The Eighth Stage of Fandom: Selections from 25 Years of Fan Writing, edited by Earl Kemp. Chicago, Advent, 1962.
"Imagination and Modern Social Criticism," in *The Science Fiction*

Novel, edited by Basil Davenport.   Chicago, Advent, 1969.
The Laughter of a Ghoul: What Every Young Ghoul Should Know.
West Warwick, Rhode Island, Necronomicon Press, 1977.

Editor, *The Best of Fredric Brown.*   New York, Ballantine, 1977.

*

Bibliography: in *Robert Bloch Fanzine* (Los Altos, California),
1973.

Manuscript Collection: University of Wyoming Library, Laramie.

Robert Bloch comments:

Although I have had upwards of 100 short stories and novelets
published in science-fiction magazines, I am primarily a writer of
fantasy and mystery-suspense fiction: the bulk of my work falls
within these two genres, as does my writing for screen, television,
and radio. As a result my work has been almost entirely ignored by
science-fiction critics and historians—thank God! Having somehow managed to survive as a professional writer over a period of 45
years, I'd hate to blow it now. I am still fascinated by the SF field
and by the people in it.

*   *   *

Although Robert Bloch has been associated with science fiction
since his first fan-magazine appearance at the age of 15, he has never
been regarded as a main-line science-fiction writer. As he says,
"Through the years, most of my work has been on the peripheral
edges of science fiction proper—fantasy, weird-horror and suspense, together with a smattering of humor. To the extent that
psychopathology is classifiable as a branch of medical science, my
other novels...all contain these elements as they pertain to an examination of subjective reality." Nonetheless, for five decades Bloch
has made a positive impact and been a popular figure in the science
fiction community, and has contributed scores of stories to the field.

The earliest period of his professional career was dominated by
the influence of H.P. Lovecraft; Bloch corresponded with Lovecraft
and sent him drafts of his earliest stories for comment. Among his
early *Weird Tales* stories was "The Shambler from the Stars," in
which he killed Lovecraft quite gorily; Frank Belknap Long had
done the same to Lovecraft in a story several years before, and
Lovecraft killed off Bloch (renaming him "Robert Blake") in his
turn. It was all good fun, and made rather good horror fiction as
well. Bloch moved shortly to a series of horror stories with Egyptian
motifs; titles such as "The Brood of Bubastis," "The Eyes of the
Mummy," "Fane of the Black Pharaoh," and "The Secret of Sebek"
speak for themselves. Still later works fall into the horror-suspense-
crime area, with heavy emphasis on psychopathology. These
include "House of the Hatchet," "The Skull of the Marquis de
Sade," "Enoch," "Lizzie Borden Took an Axe," and others, including Bloch's best known and most successful novel, *Psycho.* Another
recurrent theme in Bloch's works is that of Jack the Ripper. Bloch's
most successful short story is "Yours Truly—Jack the Ripper"; a
later use of the theme was in "A Toy for Juliet." Among other
notions, Bloch suggests that Jack was a sort of vampire who pro-
longs his existence through his crimes. Bloch returned to his early
enthusiasm for Lovecraft with *Strange Eons.* In this novel he collects numerous Lovecraftian themes, including the Cthulhu Mythos,
and projects them into a future world-catastrophe, thereby providing a marginally scientific basis for the material.

Fondly remembered by many veteran readers are Bloch's "Lefty
Feep" stories. Some 22 of these appeared in *Fantastic Adventures*
(1942-46). All are pun-filled, wise-cracking, parodistic works. Once
more, titles are indicative of content: "Time Wounds All Heels,"
"The Weird Doom of Floyd Scrilch," "Stuporman," and (reflecting
Bloch's topicality) "The Pied Piper Fights the Gestapo." Some of
Bloch's works, however, have been thoroughly serious. The majority of these have been in the psychopathological vein, but some,
such as "The Cloak" and "That Hell-Bound Train," have been
"real" science fiction or fantasy. (The latter story won a Hugo
award, a rare achievement for a fantasy story.) In the science-fic-

novella "This Crowded Earth" Bloch suggested the miniaturization
of the human species as a solution for overpopulation problems;
Vonnegut's *Slapstick* duplicates Bloch's device.

—Richard A. Lupoff

————————

BOLAND, (Bertram) John. British. Born in Birmingham,
Warwickshire, 12 February 1913. Educated privately. Served in the
Royal Artillery, 1939-45. Married Philippa Carver in 1952. Worked
as a farm labourer, deckhand, lumberjack, railroad and factory
worker, and salesman, 1930-38; advertising signs and automobile
parts salesman, 1946-55; Chairman, Writers Summer School, 1958-
60. Chairman, Associates Branch, 1960-61, and Radio Committee,
1966-70, Writers Guild of Great Britain; Chairman, Crime Writers
Association, 1963. Recipient: Writers Guild of Great Britain Zita
Award, for radio play, 1968. *Died 9 November 1976.*

SCIENCE-FICTION PUBLICATIONS

Novels

White August.   London, Joseph, 1955; New York, Arcadia House,
1965.
No Refuge.   London, Joseph, 1956.
Operation Red Carpet.   London, Boardman, 1959.

Uncollected Short Stories

"Herma," in *Science Fantasy* (Bournemouth), December 1956.
"The Man from Toombla," in *New Worlds* (London), May 1957.
"Fabulous Photographer," in *New Worlds* (London), June 1957.
"Manhunter," in *New Worlds* (London), August 1957.
"Doat Age," in *Galaxy* (New York), September 1957.
"Straight from the Horse's Mouth," in *Science Fantasy* (Bourne-
mouth), October 1957.
"The Wire Tappers," in *Science Fantasy* (Bournemouth), December
1957.
"Secret Weapon," in *New Worlds* (London), March 1958.
"The Picture," in *Fantastic* (New York), November 1958.

OTHER PUBLICATIONS

Novels

Queer Fish.   London, Boardman, 1958.
The League of Gentlemen.   London, Boardman, 1958.
Mysterious Way.   London, Boardman, 1959.
Bitter Fortune.   London, Boardman, 1959.
The Midas Touch.   London, Boardman, 1960.
Negative Value.   London, Boardman, 1960.
The Gentlemen Reform.   London, Boardman, 1961; New York,
Macmillan, 1964.
Inside Job.   London, Boardman, 1961.
Vendetta.   London, Boardman, 1961.
The Golden Fleece.   London, Boardman, 1961.
The Gentlemen at Large.   London, Boardman, 1962.
Fatal Error.   London, Boardman, 1962.
Counterpol.   London, Harrap, 1963; New York, Walker, 1965.
The Catch.   London, Harrap, 1964; New York, Holt Rinehart,
1966.
Counterpol in Paris.   London, Harrap, 1964; New York, Walker,
1965.
The Good Citizens.   London, Harrap, 1965.
The Disposal Unit.   London, Harrap, 1966.
The Gusher.   London, Harrap, 1967.
Painted Lady.   London, Cassell, 1967.
Breakdown.   London, Cassell, 1968.

The Fourth Grave. London, Cassell, 1969.
The Shakespeare Curse. London, Cassell, 1969; New York, Walker, 1970.
Kidnap. London, Cassell, 1970.
The Big Job. London, Cassell, 1970.
The Trade of Kings. Crowborough, Sussex, Forest House, 1972.

Plays

Swag (produced London, 1971).
Gottle (produced London, 1972).
Murder in Company, with Philip King (produced Bexhill, Sussex, 1972). London, French, 1973.
Elementary, My Dear, with Philip King (produced Worthing, Sussex, 1976). London, French, 1975.
Who Says Murder?, with Philip King (produced Cheltenham, 1978). London, French, 1975.

Radio Plays: *Bait,* 1962; *The Character,* 1965; *The Gentlemen Back in League* (serial), 1967; *Uncle Guy,* 1968; *The Burden,* 1969.

Television Plays: *The Fifth Victim; The Smoke Boys,* 1963.

Other

Free-Lance Journalism. London, Boardman, 1960.
Short-Story Writing. London, Boardman, 1960; revised edition, as *Short Story Technique,* Crowborough, Sussex, Forest House, 1973.

*   *   *

Using a basic plot worthy of Ian Fleming, John Boland in *White August* describes a steady radioactive snowfall in August on the British Isles. The scientist William Barnaby Garrett tries to determine the source of the snowfall and to eradicate it; he is aided by a Churchill-like prime minister, Charles Henry Warburton, who attributes the snowfall to the misanthrope Hans Bruderhof, a mad scientist who once boasted he had discovered how to control the weather and could use radio waves to make snow. With a university professor measuring the radioactivity and determining when the snow will become lethal, Garrett eventually succeeds in building a portable Extra Ultra High Frequency Radio/Transmitter, and discovers the source of the snow to be four or five hundred miles toward the west. A reconnaissance aircraft discovers moving fog in the Atlantic, and the British send destroyers in line abreast into the fog to destroy the enemy transmitter; but Warburton must finally call upon the United States, which drops one small atomic bomb and destroys the enemy. A minor subplot reveals the eagerness with which one citizen becomes a small dictator; Bruderhof is never revealed, nor the supposition that he is the enemy ever ascertained.

In *No Refuge* Robert Claymore, a British bank manager and former RAF pilot, persuades Geoffrey Leary, a Canadian aircraft ferrier, to arrange a refuge for them in Alberta and then robs his bank. With Leary in drunken sleep, Claymore makes an emergency landing in the north of Greenland. At first the country of Yademos, a crater ringed by mountains and inaccessible from the outside, seems to be a utopia having 4000 years of history and advanced technology with no war, no sickness, no poverty. Ten "Servants," five men and five women, rotate yearly as Ministers of army, engineering, education, justice, history. All ten are engineers, doctors, and lawyers and "serve" 25 years until the next "election." Modestly claiming they "lack the education to appreciate" whatever motivates the others, they serve a populace of Masters aided by attendants who have no standing. All but the Servants are drugged, programmed, and controlled to perform given tasks at prescribed levels of skill. Through discs over the ears and boxes on the chests providing music and incense respectively, the Masters perform like automata. Awaiting repair of the plane, Claymore gradually learns that the "army" is children who clean sewers, that marriage is outlawed and population controlled, that he and Leary have been spied on constantly by three-dimensional television, that justice for a rebel is a trial by ordeal with death the only punishment and with escape impossible. Only the Servants are "beneath the law." Tannui, the place of retirement, actually functions for the administration of

euthanasia through drugged sleep and cremation. Finally, he learns, the Servants have immortality; after 25 years each one chooses the body of an exceptional child, transfers all knowledge to that person by means of a circular disc on the scalp, and goes to Tannui to be "reborn." At a Servant's suggestion, Claymore believes he consents to Leary's extermination, but, as he tries to escape, Leary meets him at the plane and kills him. Leary's craft, however, has been rigged and explodes in flame.

A borderline science fiction work by Boland, *Operation Red Carpet,* imagines a future in which Russia tries to conquer Britain.

—Grace Eckley

———————

BOND, Nelson S(lade). American. Born in Scranton, Pennsylvania, 23 November 1908. Educated at Marshall University, Huntington, West Virginia, 1932-34. Married Betty Gough Folsom in 1934; two sons. Public relations field director, government of Nova Scotia, 1934-35. Free-lance writer and philatelic researcher; now a book dealer. Associated with the Roanoke Community Theatre. Recipient: International Stamp Exhibition Award, for non-fiction, 1960. Address: 4724 Easthill Drive, Sugarloaf Farms, Roanoke, Virginia 24018, U.S.A.

SCIENCE-FICTION PUBLICATIONS

Novel

Exiles of Time. Philadelphia, Prime Press, 1949.

Short Stories

Mr. Mergenthwirker's Lobblies and Other Fantastic Tales. New York, Coward McCann, 1946.
The Thirty-First of February. New York, Gnome Press, 1949.
The Remarkable Exploits of Lancelot Biggs, Spaceman. New York, Doubleday, 1950.
No Time Like the Future. New York, Avon, 1954.
Nightmares and Daydreams. Sauk City, Wisconsin, Arkham House, 1968.

OTHER PUBLICATIONS

Plays

Mr. Mergenthwirker's Lobblies, adaptation of his own story (televised). New York, French, 1957.
State of Mind. New York, French, 1958.
Animal Farm, adaptation of the novel by George Orwell. New York, French, 1964.

Author of screenplays for government agencies, some 300 radio plays, and television plays for *Philco Playhouse, Kraft Theatre, Studio One,* and other series.

Other

The Postal Stationery of Canada: A Reference Catalogue. Shrub Oak, New York, Herst, 1953.

*   *   *

Nelson S. Bond's only novel published in book form is *Exiles of Time,* and it actually constitutes the fourth volume of a tetralogy; the earlier works in the series, *Sons of the Deluge, Gods of the*

Jungle, and *That Worlds May Live,* were published in *Amazing. Exiles of Time,* though written in a clear, readable style, suffers from too great a reliance on stereotyped characters. It's the story of a time traveller who encounters Ragnarok, and the epilogue quotes from the Elder *Edda,* giving the reader considerable insight into Bond's skill at plotting. It's an impressive demonstration. The ability to plot is one of Bond's strongest points, and he was never more sure or ingenious than here.

By and large, Bond's best fiction remains his short stories, and he has displayed a remarkable range with them. During his years as a regular contributor to the pulps he wrote not only for Ray Palmer's *Amazing* and *Fantastic Adventures,* but for John Campbell's more demanding *Astounding* and *Unknown.* He also wrote for *Thrilling Wonder Stories, Weird Tales,* and especially for *Planet Stories.* "The Castaway" (*Planet,* Winter 1940) is an almost perfect example of Bond's ability to take a formula story and raise it above its own limits. A spaceship crew rescues a man marooned on an asteroid. Subsequent events suggest he's a jinx and suicidal to boot, with the ship finally zooming out of control at a speed that will cause it to burn when its hits Earth's atmosphere. The castaway devises a way to save the ship and its crew, but the real surprise lies in his actual identity.

"The Castaway" fits into a future history that includes most of Bond's space stories. These stories seem to take place mostly in the 23rd century, with the solar system explored and colonized by Earthmen, and most of them center on members of the Solar Space Patrol or a space transport company called IPS. While Bond wrote a number of character series within this frame, the Lancelot Biggs series is probably the most important, and in many ways the most typical. Biggs is the eccentric and likeable first officer of the IPS ship *Saturn,* and he divides his time between getting on his captain's nerves and producing scientific miracles to save the ship from certain disaster. About half these stories were included in *The Remarkable Exploits of Lancelot Biggs, Spaceman.*

While there is no denying Bond's talent with the short story, many of his novelets and short novels are excellent. Two *Planet* novelets from 1941 demonstrate his skill with space opera. Both center on the adventures of the young, clean-cut spaceman Chip Warren and his partners Syd Palmer and "Salvation" Smith. "Shadrach" has them discovering a rich lode of "ekalastron," an almost impervious metal, rare and valuable, that plays a part in several of Bond's future history stories. "The Lorelei Death" pits them against space pirates, but, though the better action story, it's marred by some questionable science in its ending. "Pawns of Chaos" (*Thrilling Wonder Stories,* April 1943) is based on the sort of idea popular with editors almost everywhere at that time, invaders from another dimension where the political system bears some similarity to that of Nazi Germany. Bond obviously had fun writing it, especially those sections describing battles in and around his home town of Roanoke, Virginia. "Pawns of Chaos" doesn't fall into Bond's future history sequence, nor do the Meg the Priestess stories which constitute what is probably the best work he did in the SF pulps. In the Meg stories, civilization has virtually collapsed and humanity exists in scattered tribes, a few of which preserve knowledge of writing and reading through a matriarchal leadership, although their ideas of the past are distorted as myths and legends. In "Pilgrimage" (*The Thirty-First of February*) Meg becomes priestess of her clan in Virginia and travels west to consult the gods carved on Mount Rushmore. "Magic City" (*Astounding,* February 1941) has her visit the city of death—New York—to confront its goddess.

Bond's penchant for writing action scenes in settings he knows produced a superior story in "The Ultimate Salient" (*Planet,* Fall 1940). A science-fiction writer receives a manuscript purporting to tell future events: the democracies fall to totalitarian forces in 1963 and the survivors flee to the moon where they face almost certain death because they lack the knowledge to synthesize chlorophyl. Since they are known to have taken a number of old SF magazines along, the writer is asked to use the manuscript as the basis of a story, ending it with the formula for chlorophyl that the survivors need. The story was later completely rewritten as "The Last Outpost," and is included in *No Time Like the Future.* The new version sets up a revolt against a world dictatorship, with neither the minions of the dictatorship nor the rebels being very desirable. Disaster befalls both sides but a third group flees to Venus—where the item needed for their survival is the formula for vitamin A.

Bond has claimed he was never actually a science-fiction writer but a fantasist who wrote for the SF magazines. Certainly his first big success (in 1937) was the fantasy "Mr. Mergenthwirker's Lobblies," about a gentle man who acquires the companionship of two invisible beings who foretell the future. Such stories as this were probably the prototypes of the sort of light fantasies Ray Palmer sought for *Fantastic Adventures.* It should be noted that Bond wrote a number of SF stories for his ostensibly fantasy markets, including *Blue Book,* and expressed pride in such stories as "To People a New World," "Martian Caravan," and the Pat Pending stories, about the inventor of a succession of incredible gadgets.

Bond's prose was polished enough for the prestige markets of the 1940's without being too slick to remain palatable today. By turns he can be humorous, serious, or adventurous, handling each approach with equal skill. But it remains plotting where he really shines. His story "The Cunning of the Beast" (*The Thirty-First of February*) may be that most overworked of stories, the Adam and Eve story, but it's the most cleverly plotted of them. A number of his yarns spring from Biblical or mythological sources, usually with happy results. "Uncommon Castaway" (*No Time Like the Future*) is a twist on the story of Jonah and the whale. Much of Bond's fiction resembles that of Saki or John Collier. "And Lo! The Bird" presents the Earth as an egg about to be hatched, and "Conqueror's Isle" tells of an outpost of supermen waiting for the passing of homo sapiens (both in *No Time Like the Future*).

Bond's knack for the off-beat is shown not only in his humor and his variety of approach, but also in a handful of stories written as poems. Two of them from *Planet,* "The Ballad of Blaster Bill" and "The Ballad of Venus Nell," show a touch of Robert Service (though to be honest, "Blaster Bill's" tempo is borrowed from Kipling's "Gunga Din").

—Gerald W. Page

BONE, J(esse) F. American. Born in Tacoma, Washington, 15 June 1916. Educated at Washington State University, Pullman, B.A. 1937, D.V.M. 1950; Oregon State University, Corvallis, M.S. 1953. Served in the United States Army, 1937-46, and Army Reserve, 1946-66: Lieutenant Colonel. Married 1) Jayne M. Clark in 1942 (divorced, 1946), one daughter; 2) Felizitas Margarete Endter in 1950, one daughter and two sons. Instructor, 1950-52, Assistant Professor, 1953-57, Associate Professor, 1958-65, and Professor of Veterinary Medicine, 1965-79, Oregon State University. Fulbright Lecturer in Egypt, 1965-66, and Kenya, 1980-81. Recipient: Department of Health, Education, and Welfare award, 1969. Agent: Scott Meredith Literary Agency, 845 Third Avenue, New York, New York 10022. Address: 3329 Cascade Avenue S.W., Corvallis, Oregon 97330, U.S.A.

SCIENCE-FICTION PUBLICATIONS

Novels

The Lani People.   New York, Bantam, and London, Corgi, 1962.
Legacy.   Toronto, Laser, 1976.
The Meddlers.   Toronto, Laser, 1976.
Gift of the Manti, with R. Myers.   Toronto, Laser, 1977.
Confederation Matador.   Virginia Beach, Donning, 1978.

Uncollected Short Stories

"Survival Type," in *Galaxy* (New York), March 1957.
"Quarantined Species," in *Super Science Fiction* (New York), December 1957.
"Assassin," in *If* (New York), February 1958.
"The Tool of Creation," in *Super Science Fiction* (New York), April 1958.

"The Sword," in *Fantastic Universe* (Chicago), September 1958.
"Triggerman," in *Astounding* (New York), December 1958.
"The Fast-Moving Ones," in *Super Science Fiction* (New York), December 1958.
"Nothing But Terror," in *Fantastic* (New York), January 1959.
"Second Chance," in *Satellite* (New York), February 1959.
"Insidekick," in *Galaxy* (New York), February 1959.
"Cultural Exchange," in *If* (New York), January 1960.
"The Issahar Artifacts," in *Amazing* (New York), April 1960.
"Fireman," in *Fantastic* (New York), May 1960.
"Noble Redman," in *Amazing* (New York), July 1960.
"To Choke an Ocean," in *If* (New York), September 1960.
"The Missionary," in *Amazing* (New York), October 1960.
"A Question of Courage," in *Amazing* (New York), December 1960.
"A Prize for Edie," in *Astounding* (New York), April 1961.
"Weapon," in *Amazing* (New York), June 1961.
"Special Effect," in *Fantastic* (New York), November 1961.
"Pandemic," in *Analog* (New York), February 1962.
"Founding Father," in *Galaxy* (New York), April 1962.
"For Service Rendered," in *Amazing* (New York), April 1963.
"On the Fourth Planet," in *Galaxy* (New York), April 1963.
"A Hair Perhaps," in *If* (New York), January 1967.
"The Scent of It," in *Infinity 2*, edited by Robert Hoskins. New York, Lancer, 1971.
"Gamesman," in *Crisis*, edited by Roger Elwood. Nashville, Nelson, 1974.
"High Priest," in *Strange Gods*, edited by Roger Elwood. New York, Pocket Books, 1974.
"Technicalities," in *Amazing* (New York), January 1976.

OTHER PUBLICATIONS

Other

Observations on the Ovaries of Infertile and Reportedly Infertile Dairy Cattle.... Corvallis, Oregon State College, 1954.
Animal Anatomy. Corvallis, Oregon State College Cooperative Association, 1958; revised edition, as *Animal Anatomy and Physiology,* 1975.

Editor, *Canine Medicine.* Wheaton, Illinois, American Veterinary Publications, 1959; revised edition, 1962.
Editor, with others, *Equine Medicine and Surgery.* Wheaton, Illinois, American Veterinary Publications, 1963; revised edition, 1972.

*   *   *

J.F. Bone made a considerable impact with the publication of his first novel, *The Lani People*, along with several first-rate shorter works. Unfortunately, his career faltered for approximately ten years; very few works appeared under his name, and none of them particularly memorable.

The Lani People came perilously close to being a narrated lecture, for it quite obviously intended to comment unfavorably upon man's tendency to dehumanize others. In the future, a race of humanoids exists, differing from normal humanity because of the addition of a prehensile tail. They are considered less than human, property in fact, and have virtually no rights under the law. Despite the plot-the slow realization by the protagonist of the essential evil inherent in the situation-Bone was inventive enough to maintain reader interest throughout.

Of Bone's later novels, *Legacy* was a rather routine story of a marooned man who joins a police force on a far world and becomes involved with the effort to suppress a dangerous new drug, Tonocaine. Although not actively bad, the novel's trivial nature and trite plot were disappointing to those who had remembered Bone's earlier work. The two other Laser novels were even more insignificant. In *The Meddlers* the human race is engaged in conscious manipulation of alien cultures for its own benefit. In *Gift of the Manti* the situation is just the opposite, with secretive aliens manipulating human culture for our own good, offhandedly wiping out 90 percent of the human race along the way. Both novels are underwritten and unbelievable and totally forgettable.

Bone did better with *Confederation Matador,* although that novel also has serious flaws. After the collapse of a human interstellar empire, a new confederation has arisen, which is carefully trying to rebuild human technology. An agent is sent to one world colonized by Spanish-speaking peoples to discover why that colony is slowly losing its technological base, despite an absence of external pressures. The agent discovers that superhuman aliens have established a base and are systematically exterminating the human colonists. Although the novel has sections that are quite well done, Bone has added some unnecessary and confusing subplots that distract attention from the main issue.

There is a considerable body of shorter pieces by Bone, most of which remain quite readable. Of particular note is "Founding Father," a novella in which stranded reptilian aliens use mental control to force humans to refuel their ship, and a strange relationship grows between the two species. Another excellent story is "Triggerman" which calmly presents the man with the ultimate power to cause or avert a nuclear war, and his dispassionate reaction to a world crisis. "On the Fourth Planet" is not as ambitious as the other two, but this tale of a Martian slowly eating his way across the surface of his planet, and his unhappy encounter with a human probe is extremely inventive and, within its limited structure, possibly the most successful of Bone's stories.

—Don D'Ammassa

BOUCHER, Anthony. Pseudonym for William Anthony Parker White; also wrote as H.H. Holmes. American. Born in Oakland, California, 21 August 1911. Educated at Pasadena Junior College, California, 1928-30; University of Southern California, Los Angeles, B.A. 1932; University of California, Berkeley, M.A. 1934. Married Phyllis May Price in 1938; two sons. Theatre and music critic, *United Progressive News,* Los Angeles, 1935-37; science fiction and mystery reviewer, San Francisco *Chronicle,* 1942-47; mystery reviewer, *Ellery Queen's Mystery Magazine,* 1948-50 and 1957-68, and *New York Times Book Review,* 1951-68; fantasy book reviewer, as H.H. Holmes, for Chicago *Sun-Times,* 1949-50, and New York *Herald Tribune,* 1951-63; reviewer for *Opera News,* 1961-68. Editor, *Magazine of Fantasy and Science Fiction,* 1949-58, and *True Crime Detective,* 1952-53; edited the Mercury Mysteries, 1952-55, Dell Great Mystery Library, 1957-60, and Collier Mystery Classics, 1962-68. Originated *Great Voices* program of historical recordings, Pacifica Radio, Berkeley, 1949-68. President, Mystery Writers of America, 1951. Recipient: Mystery Writers of America Edgar Allan Poe Award, for non-fiction, 1946, 1950, 1953. *Died 31 October 1968.*

SCIENCE-FICTION PUBLICATIONS

Novel

Rocket to the Morgue (as H.H. Holmes). New York, Duell, 1942.

Short Stories

Far and Away: Eleven Fantasy and Science-Fiction Stories. New York, Ballantine, 1955.
The Compleat Werewolf and Other Stories of Fantasy and Science Fiction. New York, Simon and Schuster, 1969; London, W.H. Allen, 1970.

Uncollected Short Story

"A Shape in Time," in *The Future Is Now*, edited by William F. Nolan. Los Angeles, Sherbourne Press, 1970.

OTHER PUBLICATIONS

Novels

The Case of the Seven of Calvary. New York, Simon and Schuster, and London, Hamish Hamilton, 1937.
The Case of the Crumpled Knave. New York, Simon and Schuster, and London, Harrap, 1939.
The Case of the Baker Street Irregulars. New York, Simon and Schuster, 1940; as *Blood on Baker Street,* New York, Mercury, 1953.
Nine Times Nine (as H.H. Holmes). New York, Duell, 1940.
The Case of the Solid Key. New York, Simon and Schuster, 1941.
The Case of the Seven Sneezes. New York, Simon and Schuster, 1942; London, United Authors, 1946.
The Marble Forest (as Theo Durrant with others). New York, Knopf, and London, Wingate, 1951; as *The Big Fear,* New York, Popular Library, 1953.

Plays

Radio Plays: for *Sherlock Holmes* and *The Case Book of Gregory Hood* series, 1945-48.

Other

Ellery Queen: A Double Profile. Boston, Little Brown, 1951.
"The Publishing of Science Fiction," in *Modern Science Fiction,* edited by Reginald Bretnor. New York, Coward McCann, 1953.
"Science Fiction Still Leads Science Fact," in *New York Times Magazine,* 1 December 1957.
"Fantasy and/or Science Fiction," in *The Wall Around the World,* by Theodore R. Cogswell. New York, Pyramid, 1962.
"In Step with Science," in *New York Times Book Review,* 27 February 1966.
Multiplying Villainies: Selected Mystery Criticism 1942-1968, edited by R.E. Briney and Francis M. Nevins, Jr. Boston, Bouchercon, 1973.
Sincerely, Tony/Faithfully, Vincent: The Correspondence of Anthony Boucher and Vincent Starrett, edited by Robert W. Hahn. Chicago, Catullus Press, 1975.

Editor, *The Pocket Book of True Crime Stories.* New York, Pocket Books, 1943.
Editor, *Great American Detective Stories.* Cleveland, World, 1945.
Editor, *Four and Twenty Bloodhounds.* New York, Simon and Schuster, 1950; London, Hammond, 1951; abridged edition, as *Crime-Craft,* London, Corgi, 1957.
Editor, with J. Francis McComas (first 3 vols. only), *The Best from Fantasy and Science Fiction 1-8.* Boston, Little Brown, 2 vols., 1952-53; New York, Doubleday, 6 vols., 1954-59.
Editor, *A Treasury of Great Science Fiction.* New York, Doubleday, 1959.
Editor, *The Quality of Murder.* New York, Dutton, 1962.
Editor, *The Quintessence of Queen: Best Prize Stories from 12 Years of Ellery Queen's Mystery Magazine.* New York, Random House, 1962; as *A Magnum of Mysteries,* London, Gollancz, 1963.
Editor, *Best Detective Stories of the Year: 18th* [through *23rd*] *Annual Collection.* New York, Dutton, and London, Boardman, 6 vols., 1963-68.

*

Bibliography: "Anthony Boucher Bibliography" by J.R. Christopher, Dean W. Dickensheet, and R.E. Briney, in *Armchair Detective* (White Bear Lake, Minnesota), nos. 2, 3, 4, 1969.

* * *

Anthony Boucher brought both style and sophistication to popular fantasy and science fiction, two qualities in rather short supply during the 1940's and 1950's. Boucher enjoyed successful careers in all three phases of popular literature: he was a critic, an author, and an editor.

Boucher wrote both fantasy and science fiction stories. Many of his best stories were published in Campbell's *Astounding Science Fiction* and *Unknown,* and in *Weird Tales.* Boucher's talent ran to the kind of fantasy or fantastic science fiction associated with *Unknown* in the 1940's and *Beyond* in the 1950's. His stories tend to be comic treatments of ordinary people involved in situations and actions that run contrary to their customary, common-sense approach to life. Boucher seems to imply that most people, and certainly his truly sympathetic characters, possess an innate disposition to believe in supernatural forces. As was the case with most characteristic *Unknown* stories, mythic themes are treated lightly with a comic and often ironic distance. That is certainly the case with Boucher's most successful stories. "Q.U.R.," "Robinc," and "We Print the Truth" may be taken as illustrating Boucher's manner in science-fiction stories. The first two stories are bar-room tales, similar to Henry Kuttner's Galloway Gallegher tales and Arthur Clarke's *Tales from the White Hart.* They share characteristic themes with some of Heinlein's stories of the private inventor and of proprietory business enterprise as illustrated in "We Also Walk Dogs." Boucher's hero, Dugglesmarther H. Quinby, changes the world with a revolution in android technology, making the androids more efficient by making them less like humans. Boucher thus lightly shows two of his virtues as a writer: effective comic reversal of clichés or worn-out formulas to produce surprise and delight, and a humanistic and often literary resonance.

The best of his fantasy tales may be the most famous of his stories, the novella "The Compleat Werewolf." The title suggests distantly perhaps yet fittingly a parallel to the Michael Shea adventures of L. Sprague de Camp and Fletcher Pratt. Many of the storytelling concepts are the same: an academic setting; a strong courtship subplot; comic anachronism involving a modern character caught up in mythic or legendary adventures but retaining a modern, skeptical sense of incongruity; the concomitant farcical employment of magic; and the obligatory happy ending in which the hero returns to the prosaic world with a fuller appreciation of its homely values or at least its familiar comforts. Best of all, he returns to a world in which he fits. Boucher's 1942 tale includes a little Nazi espionage to spice up the plot. Professor Wolfe Wolf, the hero in spite of himself who ends with the right girl despite an earlier unsuitable preference for a co-ed Venus, is the pattern of the modern, domesticated hero that has run remarkably true to form now for more than a quarter century.

Two or three other fantasy tales may be noted here briefly as representative of Boucher's range. "Snulbug" is Boucher's tale of modern demonology told with a more comic perspective than C.S. Lewis's *Screwtape Letters,* which it recalls. In Boucher's story, the human race is preserved from additional mischief by the incompetence of a conjurer and the third-rate demon he manages to call up to work his will. "They Bite" is an effective suspense-horror story making use of the familiar formula in which modern, skeptical men find themselves the unbelieving victims of legendary desert ogres. "We Print the Truth" is loosely based on the familiar theological chestnut of the contradiction between divine foreknowledge and free will. Boucher's fictional equivalent of divine foreknowledge is the *Grover Sentinel,* whose stories become true for all who read them. Boucher's working out of the problem which involves speculations of wish fulfillment and something he terms "variable truth" is characteristically ingenious and amusing, very much like the armchair mysteries he wrote under the name of H.H. Holmes. It was under the same name that Boucher wrote one of the most amusing science-fiction mystery *roman à clef* novels, *Rocket to the Morgue,* which is also a pastiche of styles, mannerisms, and familiar formulas of the main science-fiction writers of the dominant eastern establishment.

Boucher's best known SF story, "The Quest for St. Aquin" (1951), has lost none of its original luster after more than a quarter century. If anything, its stature has grown by virtue of the works it has to some degree inspired: James Blish's *A Case of Conscience* (1958), Walter M. Miller, Jr.'s *A Canticle for Leibowitz* (1960), and Robert Silverberg's "Good News from the Vatican" (1970). The quest takes place in a post-nuclear catastrophe California in which religious worship of any kind is officially suppressed by the ruling Technarchy through its KGB style "Loyalty Checkers." The quest ends with the paradoxical revelation that the fabled Saint Aquin is in fact the one perfect android of legend that had proved by its faultless logic the existence of God, and whose present lifeless state proves that existence in quite another way. The virtues of the story are many, including the economy with which Boucher creates his repressive, future world in which religious persecution is once again a fact of life for all believers and the finely realized humanity of the story's characters from the pope who must hide his fisherman's ring in the heel of his shoe to the Jewish "good Samaritan" on whom the irony of his rescue of the questing priest is hardly lost. The central action, however, depends of Boucher's skill in creating two characters: the young, unsophisticated priest sent on the quest by the pope to discover whether the cult of St. Aquin is orthodox, and the priest's mechanical "robass," who turns out to be none other than Old Nick himself back at the tempting game in a new form. The confrontation is altogether enchanting and somehow satisfying theologically at the same time. Among the story's many achievements as prophetic SF entertainment, the reader should consider that it is one of those stories of the 1950's, and one of the earliest, to dramatize the future brotherhood of all people of faith, whatever their religious affiliation. A quarter century ago that seemed a far more radical notion than it does today.

Perhaps Boucher's most important contribution to the literature of popular fantasy and SF came not as an author but as co-editor and later editor of *The Magazine of Fantasy and Science Fiction,* which made its debut before the public without "science fiction" on the masthead in 1949. The magazine has proven to be the healthiest and most consistently influential competition to the *Astounding/Analog* tradition of science fiction/science fact literature. Boucher and McComas established their magazine as a quality pulp that was more concerned with literary standards than with literary ideology. It has continued to publish stories in both genres and mixtures of the two that are distinguished by literary, that is mainstream, writing. Something must be added also about the affection and respect that Boucher won by his amiable disposition and urbane wit. His was one of the more important benign influences on the encouragement and development of many of the New Wave writers with whom he probably had less in common than with the Golden Age writers of his own salad days.

—Donald L. Lawler

BOUNDS, Sydney J(ames). Also writes as Wes Saunders. British. Born in Brighton, Sussex, 4 November 1920. Served in the Royal Air Force during World War II. Worked for London Transport until 1951, then free-lance writer.

SCIENCE-FICTION PUBLICATIONS

Novels

Dimension of Horror. London, Panther, 1953.
The Moon Raiders. London, Foulsham, 1955.
The World Wrecker. London, Foulsham, 1956.
The Robot Brains. London, Digit, 1957; New York, Arcadia House, 1967.

Uncollected Short Stories

"Too Efficient," in *New Worlds 5* (London), 1949.
"The Spirit of Earth, " in *New Worlds* (London), Winter 1950.
"The City," in *Other Worlds* (Evanston, Indiana), May 1951.
"A Matter of Salvage," in *New Worlds* (London), January 1952.
"The Flame Gods," in *New Worlds* (London), March 1952.
"The Treasure of Tagor," in *Science Fantasy* (Bournemouth), Spring 1952.

"Frontier Legion" (6 episodes), in *Authentic* (London), October 1952-March 1953.
"Liaison Service," in *Laurie's Space Annual.* London, Laurie, 1953.
"The Adaptable Planet," in *Nebula* (Glasgow), Autumn 1953.
"Weather Station," in *Nebula* (Glasgow), April 1954.
"Portrait of a Spaceman," in *New Worlds* (London), October 1954.
"Project Starship," in *Nebula* (Glasgow), October 1954.
"It's Dark Out There," in *Authentic* (London), November 1954.
"First Trip," in *Science Fantasy* (Bournemouth), December 1954.
"John Brown's Body, " in *Authentic* (London), December 1954.
"Sole Survivor," in *New Worlds* (London), February 1955.
"The Active Man," in *New Worlds* (London), March 1955.
"Time for Murder," in *Authentic* (London), October 1955.
"The Beautiful Martian," in *Nebula* (Glasgow), November 1955.
"Leave," in *Authentic* (London), January 1956.
"Grant in Aid," in *Authentic* (London), March 1956.
"Frontier Encounter," in *Nebula* (Glasgow), March 1956.
"Act of Courage," in *Authentic* (London), April 1956.
"Reaching for the Stars," in *Fantastic Universe* (Chicago), June 1956.
"First Lesson," in *New Worlds* (London), July 1956.
"Mutation," in *New Worlds* (London), September 1956.
"We Call It Home," in *New Worlds* (London), November 1956.
"Random Power," in *Science Fantasy* (Bournemouth), December 1956.
"The Wayward Ship," in *New Worlds* (London), June 1958.
"Outside," in *New Worlds* (London), July 1958.
"The Mules," in *New Worlds* (London), August 1958.
"Out There," in *Science Fiction Adventures* (London), September 1962.
"Scissors," in *Science Fantasy* (Bournemouth), February 1964.
"Private Shape," in *New Worlds* (London), October 1964.
"World of Shadows," in *New Worlds* (London), June 1966.
"Public Service," in *New Writings in SF 13,* edited by John Carnell. London, Dobson, 1968.
"The Ballad of Luna Lil," in *New Writings in SF 14,* edited by John Carnell. London, Dobson, 1969.
"Throwback," in *New Writings in SF 16,* edited by John Carnell. London, Dobson, 1969.
"World to Conquer," in *Vision of Tomorrow* (Newcastle upon Tyne), November 1969.
"Ward 13," in *Vision of Tomorrow* (Newcastle upon Tyne), January 1970.
"One of the Family," in *Vision of Tomorrow* (Newcastle upon Tyne), February 1970.
"Limbo Rider," in *Vision of Tomorrow* (Newcastle upon Tyne), April 1970.
"The Ghost Sun," in *Vision of Tomorrow* (Newcastle upon Tyne), May 1970.
"Musicale," in *Vision of Tomorrow* (Newcastle upon Tyne), June 1970.
"No Grater Love," in *Vision of Tomorrow* (Newcastle upon Tyne), July 1970.
"The Possessed," in *New Writings in SF 21,* edited by John Carnell. London, Sidgwick and Jackson, 1973.
"Monitor," in *New Writings in SF 22,* edited by Kenneth Bulmer. London, Sidgwick and Jackson, 1973.
"Hothouse" and "The Mask," in *Frighteners,* edited by Mary Danby. London, Fontana, 1974.
"The Animators," in *Tales of Terror from Outer Space,* edited by R. Chetwynd-Hayes. London, Fontana, 1975.
"Starport," in *The Best of Science Fiction Monthly,* edited by Janet Sacks. London, New English Library, 1975.
"Talent Spotter," in *New Writings in SF 25,* edited by Kenneth Bulmer. London, Sidgwick and Jackson, 1975.
"The Guardian at Hell's Mouth," in *The First Armada Book of Monsters,* edited by R. Chetwynd-Hayes. London, Armada, 1975.
"The Hanging Tree," in *The Seventh Armada Ghost Book,* edited by Mary Danby. London, Armada, 1975.
"Homecoming," in *The Ninth Fontana Book of Great Horror Stories,* edited by Mary Danby. London, Fontana, 1975.
"A Complete Collection" and "An Eye for Beauty," in *Frighteners 2,* edited by Mary Danby. London, Fontana, 1976.

OTHER PUBLICATIONS

Novels

Vengeance Valley (as Wes Saunders).   Leicester, Fiction House, 1953.
The Yaqui Trail.   London, Hale, 1964.
Gun Brothers.   London, Hale, 1966.
Lynching at Noon City.   London, Hale, 1967.

*   *   *

Sydney J. Bounds produced only four science-fiction novels in his career as a writer, all of which are generally dismissed as routine potboilers. To a certain extent, this is true, and the plots sound very much like story ideas for a series of very bad films. There is also a certain amount of injustice in the charge, not only because Bounds was writing what his audience wanted to read, but also because he has unfairly been lumped with Vargo Statten, Gil Hunt, Robert Fanthorpe, and other British writers who churned out endless streams of highly forgettable fiction.

The Robot Brains is unashamedly melodramatic, with a trio of macrocephalic villains from the future returning to our time with a weapon that disintegrates the heads of its victims. Bounds seems to have borrowed heavily from *The Time Machine,* for the malformed future men live in underground cities, and mate with women who are no longer intelligent. But the novel is more than mere crash and bang adventurism. The protagonist contacts another group of future humans which possesses scientific knowledge more than adequate to prevent the plot to alter history. But there is more complexity than one might think, for the latter is subject to an ethical code that eschews the use of violence, even in self defense. Similarly, *Dimension of Horror* is more convoluted than appears on the surface. Ostensibly it is the story of alien intervention to foment a war between Earth and the human colonists of Venus. But once more the hero is faced with two factions among the aliens, and the moral dilemma involved in taking action against one's own race.

The most disappointing novel is *The Moon Raiders* wherein batlike aliens possessed of science far in advance of our own invade our world for its minerals. At first they resort to stealth, but when finally revealed they broadcast an ultimatum: surrender your metals or have atomic bombs teleported into your cities. *The World Wrecker* makes use of many of the elements of the first three novels. This time we have a human scientist driven insane by an accident that disfigures his face. Wandering in the South American jungles, he discovers a hoard of alien devices which make him the most powerful man on Earth, literally capable of destroying the entire world. Once more an ethical question dominates the story. The aliens return, but cannot decide whether to intervene, and in what fashion. But even their continued inaction is tantamount to intervention, and they hover indecisively as events proceed rapidly toward disaster.

There is no question that Bounds is far from being an influence in the field. His books are largely forgotten, his short stories almost never reprinted, and there is certainly nothing of an enduring quality in his fiction. Nevertheless, he should not be dismissed as easily as he often is; melodrama has its place in genre fiction, and his novels are still of a higher qualtiy than much that appears each year.

—Don D'Ammassa

BOVA, Ben(jamin William). American. Born in Philadelphia, Pennsylvania, 28 November 1932. Educated at Temple University, Philadelphia, B.S. 1954. Married Rosa Cucinotta in 1953; one son and one daughter. Editor, *Upper Darby News,* Pennsylvania, 1953-56; technical editor on Vanguard Project, Martin Aircraft Company, Baltimore, 1956-58; screenwriter, Physical Science Study Committee, Massachusetts Institute of Technology, Cambridge,

1958-59. Since 1960, science writer, Avco-Everett Research Laboratory, Everett, Massachusetts. Editor, *Analog,* New York, 1971-78. Since 1978, Editor, *Omni,* New York. Recipient: Hugo Award, for editing, 1973, 1974, 1975, 1976, 1977, 1979. Agent: Scott Meredith Literary Agency, 845 Third Avenue, New York, New York 10022, U.S.A.

SCIENCE-FICTION PUBLICATIONS

Novels (series: Exiles)

The Star Conquerors (juvenile).   Philadelphia, Winston, 1959.
Star Watchman (juvenile).   New York, Holt Rinehart, 1964; London, Dobson, 1972.
The Weathermakers (juvenile).   New York, Holt Rinehart, 1967; London, Dobson, 1969.
Out of the Sun (juvenile).   New York, Holt Rinehart, 1968.
The Dueling Machine (juvenile).   New York, Holt Rinehart, 1969; London, Faber, 1971.
Escape! (juvenile).   New York, Holt Rinehart, 1970.
The Exiles Trilogy (juvenile).   New York, Berkley, 1980.
  Exiled from Earth.   New York, Dutton, 1970.
  Flight of Exiles.   New York, Dutton, 1972.
  End of Exile.   New York, Dutton, 1975.
THX 1138 (novelization of screenplay).   New York, Paperback Library, 1971; London, Panther, 1978.
As on a Darkling Plain.   New York, Walker, 1972.
The Shining Strangers (juvenile).   New York, Walker, 1973.
When the Sky Burned.   New York, Walker, 1973.
The Winds of Altair (juvenile).   New York, Dutton, 1973.
Gremlins, Go Home! (juvenile), with Gordon R. Dickson.   New York, St. Martin's Press, 1974.
The Starcrossed.   Radnor, Pennsylvania, Chilton, 1975.
City of Darkness (juvenile).   New York, Scribner, 1976.
Millennium.   New York, Random House, and London, Macdonald and Jane's, 1976.
The Multiple Man.   Indianapolis, Bobbs Merrill, 1976; London, Gollancz, 1977.
Colony.   New York, Pocket Books, 1978; London, Magnum, 1979.

Short Stories

Forward in Time.   New York, Walker, 1973.
Maxwell's Demons.   New York, Baronet, 1979.
Kinsman.   New York, Dial Press, 1979; London, Sidgwick and Jackson, 1980.

OTHER PUBLICATIONS

Other

The Milky Way Galaxy: Man's Exploration of the Stars.   New York, Holt Rinehart, 1961.
Giants of the Animal World (juvenile).   Racine, Wisconsin, Whitman, 1962.
Reptiles Since the World Began (juvenile).   Racine, Wisconsin, Whitman, 1964.
The Uses of Space (juvenile).   New York, Holt Rinehart, 1965.
Magnets and Magnetism (juvenile).   Racine, Wisconsin, Whitman, 1966.
In Quest of Quasars: An Introduction to Stars and Starlike Objects (juvenile).   New York, Collier, 1970.
Planets, Life, and LGM (juvenile).   Reading, Massachusetts, Addison Wesley, 1970.
The Fourth State of Matter: Plasma Dynamics and Tomorrow's Technology.   New York, St. Martin's Press, 1971.
The Amazing Laser (juvenile).   Philadelphia, Westminster Press, 1971.
The New Astronomies.   New York, St. Martin's Press, 1972; London, Dent, 1973.
Starflight and Other Improbabilities (juvenile).   Philadelphia, Westminster Press, 1973.
Man Changes the Weather (juvenile).   Reading, Massachusetts,

Addison Wesley, 1973.

Survival Guide for the Suddenly Single, with Barbara Berson. New York, St. Martin's Press, 1974.

The Weather Changes Man (juvenile). Reading, Massachusetts, Addison Wesley, 1974.

Workshops in Space (juvenile). New York, Dutton, 1974.

Notes to a Science Fiction Writer (juvenile). New York, Scribner, 1975.

Through Eyes of Wonder (juvenile). Reading, Massachusetts, Addison Wesley, 1975.

Science—Who Needs It? (juvenile). Philadelphia, Westminster Press, 1975.

The Seeds of Tomorrow (juvenile). New York, McKay, 1977.

Viewpoint. Cambridge, Massachusetts, NESFA Press, 1977.

Editor, *The Many Worlds of SF.* New York, Dutton, 1971.

Editor, *Analog 9.* London, Dobson, 1973.

Editor, *Science Fiction Hall of Fame 2.* New York, Doubleday, 1973.

Editor, *The Analog Science Fact Reader.* New York, St. Martin's Press, and London, Millington, 1974.

Editor, *The Best of Astounding.* New York, Baronet, 1977.

Editor, *Closeup, New Worlds.* New York, St. Martin's Press, 1977.

Editor, *Exiles.* New York, St. Martin's Press, 1978.

Editor, *Aliens.* New York, St. Martin's Press, 1978.

Editor, *The Best of Analog.* New York, Baronet, 1978.

Editor, with Don Myrus, *The Best of Omni.* New York, Omni, 1980.

*

Manuscript Collection: Pennsylvania State University Library, University Park.

*   *   *

Ben Bova's science fiction—with emphasis on *correct* science—can be likened to a schematic diagram in which each work is a component in a master design. Many of his characters reappear to interlock his works. This repetition, coupled with his themes, produces a mosaic unmistakably contrived. The design can be evidenced by grouping his works into three categories: "pure romps," Earth-based stories, and star stories.

The "pure romps" (Bova's own designation) show that people are often motivated by misguided principles, and include stories such as "The Secret Life of Henry K.," "The Great Supersonic Zeppelin Race," and the novels *Gremlins, Go Home!* (a delightful juvenile work written with Gordon R. Dickson) and *The Starcrossed* (on Hollywood's bickering, bantering, and bedlam).

The Earth-based stories establish man's move to the stars as essential because of the mishandling of his Earth home. A Few juvenile stories (many are included in *Forward in Time*) and novels fit in this category. For instance, in the short story "Blood of Tyrants" and in a longer work, *Escape,* the background is the chaotic ghetto to which the protagonist Danny Romano reacts or from which he tries to excape. *City of Darkness* deals with the same theme: youths are left to fend for themselves against insensitive, insane odds. Forced to live a quasi-life in overcrowded conditions, they rebel—violently.

Besides articulating the theme of overpopulation (perhaps Bova's most often used theme), he treats three other major themes: politics, the military establishment, and scientific progress. *Out of the Sun* is strictly military, introducing Frank Colt (who also figures in *Millennium* and *Colony*). *The Dueling Machine* portrays an inventor whose machine relieves tension but which inadvertently creates the setting for a murder. A telepathic but fumbling hero makes this readable novel one of Bova's best. *The Multiple Man* deals with cloning and politics. Bova's training as a journalist is obvious: the President's press secretary confronts a conflict of duty. As investigative reporter, he uncovers a fantastic story that he must either bury or make known to the public. *The Weathermakers* relates the encounter of a typical Bovan protagonist with bureaucratic folderol and military arrogance.

Bova's male protagonists possess an instinct to lead and a sense of rightness that defies bureaucracies and decries anti-science sentiment. They succeed, though often at high personal loss. One exceptional piece is based on a screenplay by George Lucas, *THX 1138*, in which the main character, drug-encapsulated, is not an heroic figure. Instead, he is part of an human-less society in which emotions are sacrificed and love becomes a death trap. His escape to a world made healthy again by the near absence of man expresses an insightfulness about 20th-century issues.

The star stories situate man's move outward. Unable to solve his problems on Earth, man "island hops," escaping the old world and founding new ones, and discovering some older ones that nearly destroy him. Though the major themes apply, man's environment and his ability to use scientific technology to benefit himself are important sub-themes. The *Exiles* trilogy belongs in this group. Dramatic and adventuresome, the books trace the fate of a group of 2000 molecular geneticists and biochemists and their families, banned from Earth, who journey to a new star system. Of the three, *End of Exile* is the most suspenseful, involving superstition, a juvenile protagonist, a real crisis and last-second salvation.

The *Kinsman* stories and *Millennium* and *Colony* represent the placing of man in the universe. From his first meeting with this daring individual, the reader recognizes near superhuman qualities in the astronaut Chet Kinsman who has one flaw, lending credibility to his heroic stature. Reared a Quaker, he cannot expiate the guilt he experiences from having killed a woman. In *Millennium,* because of his disregard for policy and regulation, Kinsman declares Selene (Moonbase) a nation and averts a holocaust on Earth. Kinsman's death wish in *Millennium* is for man to mine the moon for its resources. *Colony,* an involved novel, continues the conflict of power begun in *Millennium.*

When a solar flare destroys Earth, Moonbase survivors become slaves to their environment in *When the Sky Burned.* Like modern man, they have no concern for the future, except as it directly affects them. In *The Winds of Altair,* scientists probing an alien planet almost make the very human mistake of destroying life which already exists on the planet in order to make it more habitable for man. The boy protagonist *feels* the wrong being committed against the planet's creatures and convinces his elders.

The most far-reaching star stories are those which stem from the discovery of the Titan machines and the Others. In *As on a Darkling Plain,* Dr. Sidney Lee goes back to the Jupiter moon of Titan to uncover the purpose of the machines placed there by unknown beings one million years earlier. Lee comments: "They're not beyond the scope of human intelligence. *That's* the most important discovery of all." In his *Notes to a Science Fiction Writer,* Bova says, "at the core of all good SF is the very good fundamental faith that we can use our intelligence to understand the world and solve our problems."

The other two major works in the Titan group are *The Star Conquerors* and its sequel, *Star Watchman.* Having defeated the Masters, a superior intelligence and culture, man now controls the Empire. *How* he will handle his responsibility is the Masters' question—and seems to be Bova's. The Masters temporarily retreat, but the ultimate question surrounds the Others: Who are they? And, if and when they return, what will they do to man? Answering the first question provides a provoking answer to the second when Dr. Lee makes the frightful discovery that the Others were men. Man's quest has been and continues to be one of destruction, mishandling, and unconcern, Bova's scheme illustrative of that quest.

The short story "Stars, Won't You Hide Me?" provides another answer to the question of the Others. After fleeing from them for billions of years, Holman (whole man) seems on the verge of losing, but at the moment of man's—Holman's—end, the universe also ends. The story concludes with a note of optimism and hope. Indeed, as long as man survives, hope remains.

—Marylyn Underwood

BOYD, John. Pseudonym for Boyd Bradfield Upchurch. American. Born in Atlanta, Georgia, 3 October 1919. Educated in Atlanta, Fulton County, Georgia, and St. Paul, Minnesota, public schools; Atlanta Junior College, 1938-40; University of Southern California, Los Angeles, A.B. 1947. Served in the United States Navy, 1940-45: Lieutenant Commander; mentioned in Royal Navy despatches. Married Fern Gillaspy in 1944. Production Manager, Star Engraving Company, Los Angeles, 1947-71; free-lance writer, 1971-79. Agent: Charles Neighbors Inc., 240 Waverly Place, New York, New York 10014. Address: 1151 Aviemore Terrace, Costa Mesa, California 92627, U.S.A.

SCIENCE-FICTION PUBLICATIONS

Novels

The Last Starship from Earth. New York, Weybright and Talley, 1968; London, Gollancz, 1969.
The Pollinators of Eden. New York, Weybright and Talley, 1969; London, Gollancz, 1970.
The Rakehells of Heaven. New York, Weybright and Talley, 1969; London, Gollancz, 1971.
Sex and the High Command. New York, Weybright and Talley, 1970.
The Organ Bank Farm. New York, Weybright and Talley, 1970.
The Gorgon Festival. New York, Weybright and Talley, 1972.
The I.Q. Merchant. New York, Weybright and Talley, 1972.
The Doomsday Gene. New York, Weybright and Talley, 1972.
The Andromeda Gun. New York, Berkley, 1974.
Barnard's Planet. New York, Berkley, 1975.
The Girl with the Jade Green Eyes. New York, Viking Press, and London, Penguin, 1978.

Uncollected Short Story

"The Girl and the Dolphin," in *Galaxy* (New York), March 1973.

OTHER PUBLICATIONS

Novels

The Slave Stealer. New York, Weybright and Talley, 1968; London, Jenkins, 1969.
Scarborough Hall. New York, Berkley, 1975.

*

Manuscript Collection: University of California, Fullerton.

John Boyd comments:
Insofar as any writer consciously erects a schema for the body of his work, my intentions in science fiction have been generally to take mythic themes and find—ideally to strike—their echoes in the modern world. I attempt, without pedantry, to be didactic and, above all, entertaining. A story without some moral theme, either expressed or implied, is usually frivolous, but an apparently frivolous tale with a strong moral basis can be a gem. In telling my tales, when the substance weakens, I attempt to beguile the reader with stylistic wiles.

*   *   *

In addition to romances of the historical and contemporary South, John Boyd has published 11 science-fiction novels. Triumphs of style over substance, they are witty and sensuous, inventive in details if not major premises. Stylish variations on familiar SF themes, these tall tales kid the conventions of romance and science fiction, while satirizing human fatuousness.

The Last Starship from Earth depicts a dystopian alternate present, from which two star-crossed lovers are eventually exiled. A fast shuffle shows that exiles on the planet Hell have manipulated the romance, involving the young mathematical rebel in a time-travel story. Changing history, he fails to benefit from it, but lives on into our present as the Wandering Jew. Romantic courtship rituals come

in for a ribbing, as do the "rational" practices of a rigid behaviorist society, and the whole is imbued with allusions to, and the spirit of, English Romantic poetry.

Positing intelligent vegetable life, *The Pollinators of Eden* is a more lyrical tale of a repressed female scientist, ending with a complicated defloration and impregnation by her fiancé *and* the orchids of the planet Flora. Partially balanced by satire of scientific grantsmanship and politics, titillation is the book's prime object, accomplished with poetic allusions and complicated metaphorical connections. *The Rakehells of Heaven* also involves carnal contact with aliens, as two astronauts educate university students on a distant planet in human culture. The natives of Harlech (Heaven) adopt our vices as well as our virtues, culminating in crucifixion of one scout and expulsion of the other. The satire is still broader, the plot more unwieldy, in *Sex and the High Command,* as the U.S. Navy officers and other bumbling males in high places fall prey to the world's women who have learned, with the aid of chemistry, how to manage quite well without men. Like the protagonist of *Rakehells,* the hero parodies Southern manhood, representing rigid values unprepared for change.

In post-catastrophe California a brilliant neurosurgeon is brought to *The Organ Bank Farm* to perform brain transplants while pursuing his "hobby" of trying to cure autistic children. Amid the trappings of music therapy and behaviorist computers, his sense of decency is engaged, especially on behalf of a beautiful girl lost in an imaginary medieval world. Love and sex and poetry are present in profusion, capped by a bewildering but plausible surprise ending.

Revolutions in *The Gorgon Festival* and *The I.Q. Merchant* result from discoveries in chemistry. Rejuvenated older women fail in the first, amid the paraphernalia of rock music, motorcycle gangs, racism, and the generation gap. Flirting with sexual taboos named for Oedipus and Electra, the second emphasizes family drama. Estranged from his alcoholic wife and formerly retarded son, the inventor sees events pass him by as his intelligence-booster transforms society. Then with his youthful lover he leapfrogs simple genius into communal ESP in another tricky ending.

The Doomsday Gene projects bitterness toward a world of high technology and scientific irresponsiblility, seen largely through the eyes of a repressed clairvoyant girl. Unusual for Boyd, it is stiffly written, internally inconsistent, even incoherent in places, though not lacking in poetic allusions. A further decline is visible in *Andromeda Gun,* a spoof on conventions of the old West, in which an alien intelligence tries to reform the mind of a Southern rebel turned rabid outlaw.

Barnard's Planet revisits old haunts with an exploratory mission to an Edenic world where vegetable evolution has outstripped animal. Amid five "cluster-educated" multiple-discipline geniuses, representing national interests, the captain is an atavism. Unwilling to subject this world to Earth's warring interests, he discovers himself as the saboteur (and poet) he's under orders to defeat.

The protagonist of Boyd's next book has a similar narrow escape. Bumbling bureaucrats and military men almost achieve what they are trying to prevent: takeover by a high-technology, hive-like alien race, temporarily marooned on Earth. Loving and loved by the queen, for whom Boyd's lyricism scales new heights, the hero escapes the fate of a discarded drone, to recall fondly *The Girl with the Jade Green Eyes.*

Freed from the sexual taboos and stylistic limitations of a previous era, Boyd approaches science fiction as entertainment, with literary tolls and aims. Viewed whole, his books are lightweight confections, their component parts wildly implausible. If one is prepared, however, in the act of reading, to trace interwoven motifs and allusions, while trying to outguess the turns of plot, Boyd generally supplies a superior diversion.

—David N. Samuelson

BRACKETT, Leigh (Douglass). American. Born in Los Angeles, California, 7 December 1915. Married Edmond Hamilton, *q.v.*, in 1946 (died, 1977). Free-lance writer from 1939. Recipient: Jules Verne Award; Silver Spur Award, 1963. *Died 24 March 1978.*

SCIENCE-FICTION PUBLICATIONS

Novels

Shadow over Mars. London, Consul, 1951; as *The Nemesis from Terra,* New York, Ace, 1961.
The Starmen. New York, Gnome Press, 1952; London, Museum Press, 1954; as *The Galactic Breed,* New York, Ace, 1955; as *The Starmen of Llyrdis,* New York, Ballantine, 1976.
The Sword of Rhiannon. New York, Ace, 1953; London, Boardman, 1956.
The Big Jump. New York, Ace, 1955.
The Long Tomorrow. New York, Doubleday, 1955.
Alpha Centauri—or Die! New York, Ace, 1963.
People of the Talisman, The Secret of Sinharat. New York, Ace, 1964.
The Ginger Star. New York, Ballantine, 1974; London, Sphere, 1976.
The Book of Skaith. New York, Doubleday, 1976.
  The Hounds of Skaith. New York, Ballantine, 1974; London, Sphere, 1976.
  The Reavers of Skaith. New York, Ballantine, 1976.

Short Stories

The Coming of the Terrans. New York, Ace, 1967.
The Halflings and Other Stories. New York, Ace, 1973.
The Best of Leigh Brackett. New York, Doubleday, 1977.

OTHER PUBLICATIONS

Novels

No Good from a Corpse. New York, Coward McCann, 1944.
The Long Tomorrow. New York, Doubleday, 1955.
The Tiger among Us. New York, Doubleday, 1957; London, Boardman, 1958; as *Fear No Evil,* London, Corgi, 1960; as *13 West Street,* Corgi, 1962.
An Eye for an Eye. New York, Doubleday, 1957; London, Boardman, 1958.
Rio Bravo (novelization of screenplay). New York, Bantam, and London, Corgi, 1959.
Follow the Free Wind. New York, Doubleday, 1963.
Silent Partner. New York, Putnam, 1969.

Plays

Screenplays: *The Vampire's Ghost,* with John K. Butler, 1945; *Crime Doctor's Manhunt,* with Eric Taylor, 1946; *The Big Sleep,* with William Faulkner and Jules Furthman, 1946; *Rio Bravo,* with Jules Furthman and B.H. McCampbell, 1959; *Gold of the Seven Saints,* with Leonard Freeman, 1961; *Hatari!,* with Harry Kurnitz, 1962; *El Dorado,* 1967; *Rio Lobo,* with Burton Wohl, 1970; *The Long Goodbye,* 1973; *Star Wars II: The Empire Strikes Back,* 1979.

Television Plays: for *Checkmate* and *Suspense* series, and *Terror at Northfield* for *Alfred Hitchcock* series.

Other

Editor, *The Best of Edmond Hamilton.* New York, Ballantine, 1977.

Ghost Writer: *Stranger at Home* by George Sanders, New York, Simon and Schuster, 1946; London, Pilot Press, 1947.

*

Manuscript Collection: Special Collections, Eastern New Mexico University Library, Portales.

* * *

Leigh Brackett was during the late 1940's and early 1950's the uncontested "Queen of Space Opera." As a girl, she spent summers exploring the beaches near Santa Monica; the majesty of the Pacific by day and its bio-luminescence by night, and her reading of Edgar Rice Burroughs provided much of the imagery that was to make her science fiction unique. In a *Planet Stories* "Feature Flash" in 1942, she admitted her addiction to things dramatic, repeatedly describing herself as "a ham." This quality served her well when she worked in films, very often "writing before the camera"—that is, revising dialogue on the basis of actors' performances in prior scenes. Her facility with character and dialogue (in the "tough" detective novel, *No Good from a Corpse*) got her the movie job, and, later prompted Pauline Kael to suppose that most of her dialogue in *El Dorado* was improvised by the actors because it seemed too realistic to have come from any script.

All these aspects of her personal and professional self found ready expression in the kind of science fiction that made her famous. At present, space opera is a derogatory term, denoting impossibly larger-than-life characters, melodramatic incidents, and flights of fancy quite distant from straight extrapolative science fiction. In the 1940's and early 1950's, however, space opera was the staple of most of the pulp magazines, partly because it was an escape from ordinary life, partly because it evoked a "sense of wonder" just by its portrayal of alien beings, awesome settings, and heroic acts, and partly because of the literary skills of Brackett herself.

The Sword of Rhiannon is perhaps the apex of Brackett's career as a writer of space opera. It begins with a renegade archeologist's being thrown back a million years by a strange "bubble of time" within the tomb of the ancient god-like Martian, Rhiannon. Once in the past, Brackett's hero finds himself involved in all sorts of adventures (he, with Rhiannon's help, frees ancient Mars of the tyranny of one race, the serpent-evolved Dhuvians, and wins the love of the princess of a human Martian race). The way Brackett tells this story gives it much greater literary quality than the space-opera label suggests. Her setting—verdant Mars with a luminous ocean—and her characters—of several Martian races, each independently evolved to the level of human culture—allow the reader a glimpse of Mars as a vital world, not the dying one the Terrans find when they arrive just before the beginning of our third millennium. In this novel, Brackett masterfully interweaves the melodramatic heroism of space opera with imaginative postulation of three sapient life-forms besides the native human race of Martians.

Before *Rhiannon,* Brackett produced two space-opera master-pieces, "Enchantress of Venus" and "The Lake of the Gone Forever." Afterwards, she turned to more conventional science fiction with *The Long Tomorrow,* a post-Destruction narrative considered by many to be Brackett's best, and stories like "The Tweener" and "The Queer Ones." Then she turned to making novels of previously published novelettes; "Queen of the Martian Catacombs" and "Black Amazon of Mars"—both, incidentally, featuring not just extraordinary women characters but the literary "original," Eric John Stark—became *The Secret of Sinharat* and *People of the Talisman.*

Considering the excitement of her narratives and the immediate pleasure to be derived from them, one might assume that Brackett's science fictions are fun to read, even lessons in the use of English prose, but basically light entertainment. However, one can perceive three serious aspects of her fiction, whether it is space opera or not.

One, illustrated best in the stories and novels about Eric John Stark, is a thematic interest in the essential goodness of most forms of natural life. Stark, son of Earthborn humans who died on Mercury, struggles for survival among a supportive group of non-human Mercurians and only later is returned to civilization. Stark is a renegade and mercenary, a "criminal" only because he does not recognize the authority of artificial laws; whenever he finds himself in a situation calling for heroic action, the "primal ape" in him seems set apart from the civilized human. Nevertheless, both his natural and civilized selves—demonstrated by his consistent sympathy for the wronged, whatever their species may be—seek the good.

Another is Brackett's thematic egalitarianism and, along with it and Stark's appetite for the good, a strong sense of respect for other living things. The care with which she treats her native Martians and Venusians—though alien, they are persons, too—makes this evident. *The Starmen* is the tale of the quest for equality on a galactic scale; respect for other life runs just below the surface of "The Tweener," evoking sad sympathy from the reader. And "All the Colors of the Rainbow" is, like Le Guin's *The Word for World Is Forest*, a cruelly bitter satire of racist and other mean prejudices, set forth by paradoxically delicate prose.

Then there is Brackett's growth as a writer, helped along by her husband, Edmond Hamilton; as she influenced his deepening characterization, he influenced her growing ability to structure fiction with a strong yet uncontrived plot. This growth is evident in her Skaith series. Besides the technical expertise with plotting, Brackett had, by the time she wrote about Skaith, evidently rethought the biology in *Rhiannon*; on Skaith as on ancient Mars there are at least three non-human sapient races, but these have evolved from a single stock, each seeking survival by accommodating itself differently to life beneath the dying ginger sun.

From February 1940 when "Martian Quest" appeared in *Astounding*, almost until the day she died in March 1978. Brackett's love for science fiction was self evident in her works. Her last work was the first full draft of the screenplay for *Star Wars II*.

—Rosemarie Arbur

BRADBURY, E.P. *See* **MOORCOCK, Michael.**

BRADBURY, Ray(mond Douglas). American. Born in Waukegan, Illinois, 22 August 1920. Educated at Los Angeles High School. Married Marguerite Susan McClure in 1947; four children. Full-time writer since 1943. President, Science-Fantasy Writers of America, 1951-53. Member of the Board of Directors, Screen Writers Guild of America, 1957-61. Recipient: O. Henry Prize, 1947, 1948; Benjamin Franklin Award, 1954; National Institute of Arts and Letters Grant, 1954; Boys' Clubs of America Junior Book Award, 1956; Golden Eagle Award, for screenplay, 1957; Gandalf Award, 1980. D. Litt.: Whittier College, California, 1979. Agent: Don Congdon, Harold Matson Company, 22 East 40th Street, New York, New York 10016. Address: 10265 Cheviot Drive, Los Angeles, California 90064, U.S.A.

SCIENCE-FICTION PUBLICATIONS

Novels

Fahrenheit 451. New York, Ballantine, 1953; London, Hart Davis, 1954.
Something Wicked This Way Comes. New York, Simon and Schuster, 1962; London, Hart Davis, 1963.

Short Stories

Dark Carnival. Sauk City, Wisconsin, Arkham House, 1947; London, Hamish Hamilton, 1948.
The Martian Chronicles. New York, Doubleday, 1950; as *The Silver Locusts*, London, Hart Davis, 1951.

The Illustrated Man. New York, Doubleday, 1951; London, Hart Davis, 1952.
The Golden Apples of the Sun. New York, Doubleday, and London, Hart Davis, 1953.
The October Country. New York, Ballantine, 1955; London, Hart Davis, 1956.
A Medicine for Melancholy. New York, Doubleday, 1959; as *The Day It Rained Forever*, London, Hart Davis, 1959.
The Small Assassin. London, Ace, 1962; New York, New American Library, 1973.
The Machineries of Joy. New York, Simon and Schuster, and London, Hart Davis, 1964.
The Vintage Bradbury. New York, Random House, 1965.
The Autumn People. New York, Ballantine, 1965.
Tomorrow Midnight. New York, Ballantine, 1965.
Twice Twenty-Two (selection). New York, Doubleday, 1966.
I Sing the Body Electric! New York, Knopf, 1969; London, Hart Davis, 1970.
Bloch and Bradbury, with Robert Bloch. New York, Belmont, 1969; as *Fever Dreams and Other Fantasies*, London, Sphere, 1970.
(Selected Stories), edited by Anthony Adams. London, Harrap, 1975.
Long after Midnight. New York, Knopf, 1976; London, Hart Davis MacGibbon, 1977.
The Stories of Ray Bradbury. New York, Knopf, 1980.

OTHER PUBLICATIONS

Novel

Dandelion Wine. New York, Doubleday, and London, Hart Davis, 1957.

Short Stories

The Last Circus, and The Electrocution. Northridge, California, Lord John Press, 1980.

Plays

The Meadow, in *Best One-Act Plays of 1947-48.* New York, Dodd Mead, 1948.
The Anthem Sprinters and Other Antics (produced Los Angeles, 1968). New York, Dial Press, 1963.
The World of Ray Bradbury (produced Los Angeles, 1964; New York, 1965).
The Wonderful Ice-Cream Suit (produced Los Angeles, 1965). Included in *The Wonderful Ice-Cream Suit and Other Plays*, 1972.
The Day It Rained Forever. New York, French, 1966.
The Pedestrian. New York, French, 1966.
Christus Apollo, music by Jerry Goldsmith (produced Los Angeles, 1969).
The Wonderful Ice-Cream Suit and Other Plays (includes *The Veldt* and *To the Chicago Abyss*). New York, Bantam, 1972; London, Hart Davis, 1973.
The Veldt (produced London, 1980). Included in *The Wonderful Ice-Cream Suit and Other Plays*, 1972.
Leviathan 99 (produced Los Angeles, 1972).
Pillar of Fire and Other Plays for Today, Tomorrow, and Beyond Tomorrow (includes *Kaleidoscope* and *The Foghorn*). London, Bantam, 1975.
The Foghorn (produced New York, 1977). Included in *Pillar of Fire and Other Plays*, 1975.
That Ghost, That Bride of Time: Excerpts from a Play-in-Progress. Privately printed, 1976.
The Martian Chronicles, adaptation of his own stories (produced Los Angeles, 1977).
Farenheit 451, adaptation of his own novel (produced Los Angeles, 1979).

Screenplays: *It Came from Outer Space,* with David Schwartz, 1952; *Moby-Dick,* with John Huston, 1956; *Icarus Montgolfier Wright,* 1961; *The Picasso Summer,* 1967.

Television Plays: *The Jail,* 1962; *The Life Work of Juan Diaz,* 1963.

Verse

Old Ahab's Friend, and Friend to Noah, Speaks His Piece: A Celebration.   Privately printed, 1971.
When Elephants Last in the Dooryard Bloomed: Celebrations for Almost Any Day of the Year.   New York, Knopf, 1973; London, Hart Davis MacGibbon, 1975.
That Son of Richard III: A Birth Announcement.   Privately printed, 1974.
Where Robot Mice and Robot Men Run round in Robot Towns: New Poems, Both Light and Dark.   New York, Knopf, 1977; London, Hart Davis MacGibbon, 1979.
The Bike Repairman.   Northridge, California, Lord John Press, 1978.
The Author Considers His Resources.   Northridge, California, Lord John Press, 1979.
The Aqueduct.   Glendale, California, Squires Press, 1979.

Other

"Day after Tomorrow: Why Science Fiction?," in *Nation* (New York), 2 May 1953.
Switch on the Night (juvenile).   New York, Pantheon, and London, Hart Davis, 1955.
"Literature in the Space Age," in *California Librarian* (Sacramento), July 1960.
R Is for Rocket (juvenile).   New York, Doubleday, 1962; London, Hart Davis, 1968.
S Is for Space (juvenile).   New York, Doubleday, 1966; London, Hart Davis, 1968.
"At What Temperature Do Books Burn?," in *The Writer* (Boston), July 1967.
"An Impatient Gulliver above Our Heads," in *Life* (New York), 24 November 1967.
Teacher's Guide: Science Fiction, with Lewy Olfson.   New York, Bantam, 1968.
The Halloween Tree (juvenile).   New York, Knopf, 1972; London, Hart Davis MacGibbon, 1973.
Mars and the Mind of Man.   New York, Harper, 1973.
Zen and the Art of Writing, and The Joy of Writing.   Santa Barbara, California, Capra Press, 1973.
"Science Fiction: Before Christ and after 2001," in *Science Fact/ Fiction.*   Chicago, Scott Foresman, 1974.
"Henry Kuttner: A Neglected Master," in *The Best of Henry Kuttner.*   New York, Doubleday, 1975.
The Mummies of Guanajuato, photographs by Archie Lieberman.   New York, Abrams, 1978.

Editor, *Timeless Stories for Today and Tomorrow.*   New York, Bantam, 1952.
Editor, *The Circus of Dr. Lao and Other Improbable Stories.*   New York, Bantam, 1956.

*

Bibliography: in *The Ray Bradbury Companion* by William F. Nolan, Detroit, Gale, 1975.

*   *   *

Ever since the remarkable critical and popular success of *The Martian Chronicles* in 1950, Ray Bradbury has been among the most visible of science-fiction writers, and although he has not produced a major work in several years he remains the most widely recognized spokesman for the genre, and particularly for the romantic attitudes toward space flight and technology which it sometimes embodies. In some sense this is ironic, since Bradbury's best works—dating from the early 1950's—are powerful indictments of unchecked technological progress and question humanity's ability to deal creatively with the new worlds of which science and technology hold promise.

Bradbury is above all a humanist, and this humanism is evident throughout his career, which might be divided into three general periods roughly corresponding to the 1940's, the 1950's, and the 1960's to the present. The first of these periods sees the youthful Bradbury move from an adolescent science-fiction fan making his first professional sales (the first was the story "Pendulum" written with Henry Hasse) to a mature stylist who had become one of the most popular science-fiction writers in America. Bradbury's first book, the collection of stories *Dark Carnival,* was not science fiction at all, but rather ranged from satirical horror (such as "The Handler" which concerns a mortician who plays practical jokes on his "clients") to sensitive portrayals of lonely or pathetic individuals—a wife incapacitated with horror at her own mortality after viewing Mexican mummies ("The Next in Line"), a "normal" boy alone in a family of friendly vampires ("The Homecoming"). Many of the stories had originally appeared in *Weird Tales,* a horror pulp that represented a market Bradbury would soon abandon, but it was in these tales that he developed his craft to maturity, and many of them remain among his strongest work.

The Martian Chronicles began the second and most prolific phase of Bradbury's career. A series of stories, linked by bridge passages, concerning the colonization and exploitation of Mars by what seem to be exclusively citizens of small midwestern American towns, the book owed much to the American tradition of frontier literature, and quickly consolidated Bradbury's reputation as one of science fiction's leading stylists. Although the portrayal of the Martians ranges from sensitive, essentially ordinary families ("Ylla") to shapeless monsters ("The Third Expedition"), they soon fade into the background as the stories focus on different types of earth settlers—romantics, misfits, opportunists, idealists, even fugitive Blacks (in "Way in the Middle of the Air"). In the end, an atomic war sends most of the settlers back to earth to join their families, leaving only a few isolated families such as that depicted in "The Million-Year Picnic," whose father vows to start a new world on Mars without the prejudices and regimentation that had come to characterize life on earth.

The Illustrated Man appeared in the following year, and again connected the stories by a frame narrative; in this case, each story is presented as a tattoo come to life. A few of the stories retain the Martian setting of the *Chronicles,* and one of these, "The Fire Balloons," is an early attempt at treating a serious religious issue in science fiction—the question of whether a benign alien life form can be said to have achieved Christian grace. Other stories explore themes that had become familiar to Bradbury readers. The amorality of children which appeared as a theme in a few *Dark Carnival* stories here returns in stories in which children murder their parents in a mechanical playroom ("The Veldt") or assist invading aliens ("Zero Hour"). Mexico, which had fascinated Bradbury since a trip he took there in 1945, is the setting of "The Fox in the Forest" and "The Highway." And the romantic attitudes toward space travel that were to remain a Bradbury staple are evident in "The Rocket," "No Particular Night or Morning," and "Kaleidoscope, " a tale of the crew of an exploded spaceship drifting slowly to their deaths, which Bradbury later dramatized.

Fahrenheit 451, a dystopian satire of a totalitarian state in which "firemen" are professional bookburners who set fires rather than put them out, is the only science-fiction work of Bradbury's to approach *The Martian Chronicles* in popularity, and the only novel-length science-fiction work he has yet produced. *Fahrenheit 451* is as much an attack on mass culture as it is a satire of McCarthy-era censorship; the enforced illiteracy of this future society, we are led to believe, is at least in part due to the desires to avoid offending special interest groups in the mass media and to the rise of television (which Bradbury had already effectively satirized in "The Pedestrian"). The novel is as simple as a parable, and few attempts are made to offer a realistic portrait of an imagined society. The police state, it seems, exists almost solely to burn books, and the society of outcasts that the hero Montag finally escapes to join seems curiously incapable of political action, choosing instead to preserve literary culture by memorizing all the great books.

Of the other four collections Bradbury published during the 1950's, none was primarily science fiction. *The Golden Apples of the Sun* introduced what was to become a familiar Bradbury mix of small-town tales, fantasies, Mexican stories, science fiction, and crime tales. *The October Country* reprinted most of the contents of *Dark Carnival* and added four stories, and *Dandelion Wine* was a collection of sketches based on Bradbury's own boyhood in Waukegan, Illinois. *A Medicine for Melancholy* repeated the mix of *The Golden Apples of the Sun,* introducing in book form a new theme for Bradbury, Irish life and character, which had come to fascinate the author while he was in Ireland in 1954.

Bradbury's long-awaited full-length novel *Something Wicked This Way Comes* is a fantasy concerning an evil carnival that influences the lives of people in a small midwestern town. Despite occasional touches of real power, the novel is overwritten and self-conscious, and many readers regard it as the beginning of a third phase of Bradbury's career, characterized by a decreasing output of fiction, a tendency of that fiction to be self-imitative, and an increased turning to such new forms as the drama and poetry. Two new collections, *The Machineries of Joy* and *I Sing the Body Electric!,* suggested little in the way of new directions or artistic growth, despite some excellent stories. Bradbury's only new collection of the 1970's, *Long after Midnight,* contained several excellent stories—but many of them had been written prior to 1955. Other volumes of poetry and plays appeared, and Bradbury must be recognized for his efforts to introduce science fiction into forms that had seldom seemed amenable to it, but he has yet to produce a major work in either of these forms.

Whatever the final assessment of Bradbury's later work, his historical importance both in popularizing science fiction and making it respectable cannot be denied. Though the genre had produced excellent craftsmen before Bradbury, his finely tuned style and humanistic concerns exerted a profound influence on a generation of later writers and helped significantly to reduce the barriers that had long isolated science fiction from more traditional literary culture.

—Gary K. Wolfe

BRADLEY, Marion Zimmer. Also writes as Lee Chapman; John Dexter; Miriam Gardner; Valerie Graves; Morgan Ives. American. Born in Albany, New York, 3 June 1930. Educated at New York State College for Teachers, 1946-48; Hardin-Simmons University, Abilene, Texas, B.A. 1964; University of California, Berkeley. Married 1)Robert A. Bradley in 1949 (divorced, 1963), one son; 2) Walter Henry Breen in 1964, one son and one daughter. Singer and writer. Agent: Scott Meredith Literary Agency, 845 Third Avenue, New York, New York 10022. Address: Box 352, Berkeley, California, 94701, U.S.A.

SCIENCE-FICTION PUBLICATIONS

Novels (series: Darkover)

The Door Through Space (Darkover).   New York, Ace, 1961.
Seven from the Stars.   New York, Ace, 1962.
The Planet Savers, The Sword of Aldones (Darkover).   New York, Ace, 1962; London, Arrow, 2 vols., 1979.
The Colors of Space (juvenile).   Derby, Connecticut, Monarch, 1963.
The Bloody Sun (Darkover).   New York, Ace, 1964; London, Arrow, 1978.
Falcons of Narabedla (Darkover).   New York, Ace, 1964.
Star of Danger (Darkover).   New York, Ace, 1965; London, Arrow, 1978.
The Brass Dragon.   New York, Ace, 1969; London, Methuen, 1978.
The Winds of Darkover.   New York, Ace, 1970; London, Arrow, 1978.
The World Wreckers (Darkover).   New York, Ace, 1971; London, Arrow, 1979.

Darkover Landfall.   New York, DAW, 1972; London, Arrow, 1978.
Hunters of the Red Moon.   New York, DAW, 1973; London, Arrow, 1979.
In the Steps of the Master.   New York, Grosset and Dunlap, 1973.
The Spell Sword (Darkover).   New York, DAW, 1974; London, Arrow, 1978.
Endless Voyage.   New York, Ace, 1975; revised edition, as *Endless Universe,* 1979.
The Heritage of Hastur (Darkover).   New York, DAW, 1975; London, Arrow, 1979.
The Shattered Chain (Darkover).   New York, DAW, 1976; London, Arrow, 1978.
The Forbidden Tower (Darkover).   New York, DAW, 1977; London, Prior, 1979.
Storm Queen (Darkover).   New York, DAW, 1978.
The Ruins of Isis.   Virginia Beach, Donning, 1978.
The Survivors, with Paul E. Zimmer.   New York, DAW, 1979.
The House Between the Worlds.   New York, Doubleday, 1980.
Two to Conquer.   New York, DAW, 1980.
Survey Ship.   New York, Ace, 1980.

Short Stories

The Dark Intruders and Other Stories.   New York, Ace, 1964.
The Keeper's Price.   New York, DAW, 1980.

OTHER PUBLICATIONS

Novels

I Am a Lesbian (as Lee Chapman).   Derby, Connecticut, Monarch, 1962.
Spare Her Heaven (as Morgan Ives).   Derby, Connecticut, Monarch, 1963; abridged edition, as *Anything Goes,* Sydney, Stag, 1964.
Knives of Desire (as Morgan Ives).   San Diego, Corinth, 1966.
No Adam for Eve (as John Dexter).   San Diego, Corinth, 1966.
Castle Terror.   New York, Lancer, 1966.
Souvenir of Monique.   New York, Ace, 1967.
Bluebeard's Daughter.   New York, Lancer, 1968.
Witch Hill (as Valerie Graves).   San Diego, Greenleaf, 1972.
Dark Satanic.   New York, Berkley, 1972.
In the Steps of the Master.   New York, Grosset and Dunlap, 1973.
Can Ellen Be Saved?   New York, Grosset and Dunlap, 1975.
Drums of Darkness.   New York, Ballantine, 1976.
The Catch Trap.   New York, Ballantine, 1979.

Novels as Miriam Gardner

The Strange Woman.   Derby, Connecticut, Monarch, 1962.
My Sister, My Love.   Derby, Connecticut, Monarch, 1963.
Twilight Lovers.   Derby, Connecticut, Monarch, 1964.

Other

Songs from Rivendell.   Privately printed, 1959.
A Complete, Cumulative Checklist of Lesbian, Variant, and Homosexual Fiction.... Privately printed, 1960.
Men, Halflings, and Hero-Worship.   Baltimore, T-K Graphics, 1973.
The Necessity of Beauty: Robert W. Chambers and the Romantic Tradition.   Baltimore, T-K Graphics, 1974.
The Jewel of Arwen.   Baltimore, T-K Graphics, 1974.
The Parting of Arwen.   Baltimore, T-K Graphics, 1975.
"Experiment Perilous: The Art and Science of Anguish in Science Fiction, " in *Experiment Perilous,* edited by Andrew Porter. New York, Algol Press, 1976.

Editor, *Elbow Room.*   New York, Ballantine, 1980.

Translator, *El Villano in su Rincon,* by Lope de Vega.   Privately printed, 1971.

*

Bibliography: *The Gemini Problem: A Study in Darkover* by Walter Breen, privately printed, 1973; *The Darkover Dilemma: Problems of the Darkover Series* by S. Wise, Baltimore, T-K Graphics, 1976.

Manuscript Collection: Boston University.

Marion Zimmer Bradley comments:

The secret of life is to do what you enjoy doing most, and to get someone to pay you enough so you don't actually have to starve while you're doing it. People who want other things, money and status, baffle me. I write professionally because it's the only thing I can do well, and every other job I have had has either bored or frustrated me past tolerance; and since I write compulsively and would no matter what else I was doing, it's wonderful that I can get paid for it.

* * *

Marion Zimmer Bradley is a writer almost impossible to categorize. By the time she was 16 she had written two science-fantasy novels, neither of them published though both indicative of her interest in psychology and psionic abilities that was to find mature expression in her well-known Darkover novels. Her early works indicate no favorite theme or subject. Some are extrapolative science fiction typical of the time, like "Year of the Big Thaw," "The Crime Therapist," and "Exiles of Tomorrow." Some are science fantasy, like "Jackie Sees a Star" and *Falcons of Narabedla*. And others, like "Women Only" and "Centaurus Changeling," are notable for the intrusion of women characters into what was considered, C.L. Moore and Leigh Brackett notwithstanding, "a man's field."

After more than 25 years of writing science fiction professionally, Bradley remains difficult to pin down. As early as 1958, in "The Planet Savers," she introduced a Free Amazon belonging to a group of women who have by oath renounced all dependence on men. From this character one might infer that Bradley is a feminist, yet in *Darkover Landfall* she authorially denies one of the protagonists the right to terminate an unwanted pregnancy. Then not a feminist? But *Endless Voyage* is a novel absolutely without sex-roles for its male and female characters. *The Shattered Chain*, set on Darkover with its male-supremacist cultures, is a probing and sensitive treatment of women's need to live according to their own decisions. Thus Bradley shows how women characters should be presented as strong human beings, but regards fiction in which they are strong because of the contrived absence of men as demeaning and, generally, propagandistic.

Bradley excels at writing well-plotted, exciting adventure narratives, like *Hunters of the Red Moon*, a novel with an astonishing yet credible assortment of human and non-human sapient characters. *Endless Universe*, too, is an adventure story on a cosmic scale, with the opening up of new-found worlds complemented by the maturation and interaction of its principal characters. Every one of the Darkover novels is some kind of adventure, and *The Ruins of Isis* combines the excitement of archeological searching for what may have been the first intelligent race with the sometimes agonizing adventures of a heterosexual couple trying to conform to the customs of a rigidly structured Matriarchate.

Although most of her novels—particularly those set on Darkover and others written since 1970—deserve reading for their story-telling, their thematic content is at least as significant as their plots. *Hunters of the Red Moon* and *Endless Universe* embody, respectively, themes of racial and individual tolerance and respect; *The Ruins of Isis* is clearly an indictment of any kind of sexual chauvinism. The Darkover novels test various attitudes about the importance of technology, and more important, they study the very nature of human intimacy. This latter "experiment," having been initiated more than 20 years ago, is as unique as it is vitally important.

First, however, Bradley's "test" of technologies. By postulating a Terran Empire the main features of which are advanced technology and bureaucracy, and a Darkover that seems technologically backward and is fiercely individualistic, Bradley sets up a conflict to which there is no "correct" resolution. As Terrans ourselves, we see the good of many of the Empire's technological marvels. But the Darkovans are human, too, and evoke our sympathy, especially when we learn that their lack of technical "progress" is deliberate,

for in the barely remembered past their psionically based technology very nearly annihilated their world. Bradley does not take sides; she allows her readers almost complete freedom to decide which of the technologies, or which combination of the two, is the more humanly practical solution.

Bradley's "experiment" with human intimacy relies, for its science, on an extrapolated psychology of telepaths. As early as 1964, in *The Bloody Sun,* she drew readers into a world in which sexual intimacy is clearly secondary to the nearly total union felt by telepaths working in close rapport. In *The Heritage of Hastur* she illustrates the psychical and physical results of repression: as a boy, Regis Hastur expressed his love for Lew Alton and, in fear and guilt about what he thought was immoral intimacy, he blocked his telepathic powers so that their inevitable awakening very nearly killed him. He comes into his "heritage" when he accepts his androgynous nature. *The Forbidden Tower* explores the "nakedness" of one telepath to another, and affirms the interdependence of mental and physical intimacy when the four principal characters, already intimate from having shared telepathic rapport, share their bodies in sexual lovemaking as a natural extension of their already profound love and respect for one another.

While the intimacies shared by Bradley's characters are fictional, they are nonetheless correlatives of both real relationships between persons and the psychical integration of female and male qualities within a self. That Bradley writes ("so boldly," some may think) science fiction that deals openly with what is to us most mysterious and wonderful—the human psyche and, more, the human being rendered whole—fully justified Theodore Sturgeon's assessment of the young-fan-now-mature: Marion Zimmer Bradley is "one of the Big Ones."

—Rosemarie Arbur

BRETNOR, Reginald. Also writes as Grendel Briarton. American. Born in Vladivostok, Russia, 30 July 1911; emigrated to the United States in 1920. Attended college in California and New Mexico. Married l)Helen Harding in 1949 (died, 1967); 2) Rosalie Leveille in 1969. Writer for the office of War Information and the State Department Office of International Information and Cultural Affairs, 1943-47. Since 1947, free-lance writer. Address: Bŏx 1481, Medford, Oregon 97501, U.S.A.

SCIENCE-FICTION PUBLICATIONS

Short Stories

Through Space and Time with Ferdinand Feghoot (as Grendel Briarton). Berkeley, California, Paradox Press, 1962; augmented edition as *The Compleat Feghoot*, Baltimore, Mirage Press, 1975.
The Schimmelhorn File. New York, Ace, 1979.

OTHER PUBLICATIONS

Novel

A Killing in Swords. New York, Pocket Books, 1978.

Other

Decisive Warfare: A Study in Military Theory. Harrisburg, Pennsylvania, Stackpole, 1969.

Editor, *Modern Science Fiction: Its Meaning and Its Future.* New York, Coward McCann, 1953; revised edition, Chicago, Advent, 1979.
Editor, *Science Fiction, Today and Tomorrow.* New York,

Harper, 1974.
Editor, *The Craft of Science Fiction: A Symposium on Writing Science Fiction and Science Fantasy.* New York, Harper, 1976.
Editor, with James P. Baen, *The Future at War.* New York, Ace, 1979.

Translator, *Moncrief's Cats,* by François-Augustin Paradis de Moncrif. London, Golden Cockerel Press, 1961; Cranbury, New Jersey, A.S. Barnes, 1962.

*   *   *

Reginald Bretnor's career as a science-fiction writer is minor. Of his three works of fiction, only two are SF, the third, *A Killing in Swords,* being a *hommage* to the mysteries of Anthony Boucher. *The Schimmelhorn File* collects Bretnor's series about an eccentric Pennsylvania Dutch inventor of the future. These stories show Bretnor's talents for fast-paced comedy, but are otherwise forgettable. The stories about Ferdinand Feghoot include Bretnor's most influential fictions, a series of short anecdotes that conclude with an intricate pun. This form has proven popular with fans and editors, and has been copied by such authors as John Brunner and Damon Knight.

Bretnor's important work is as an editor. He has proven his skill as an anthologist with *The Future at War,* but his editorial talents are for criticism rather than fiction. His *Modern Science Fiction: Its Meaning and Its Future* was the first attempt by a writer within the field to treat SF as a movement of social history, rather than an *ars nova* unique unto itself. Including major essays by Asimov, de Camp, and others, *Modern Science Fiction* is *the* primary document for understanding the climate of opinion that produced the SF of the 1950's. Its two successors, *Science Fiction, Today and Tomorrow* and *The Craft of Science Fiction,* are no less important to an understanding of the science fiction of the 1970's. Together, the trilogy is a pinnacle of analytical thought that will be studied long after Bretnor's own fiction is forgotten.

—Martin Morse Wooster

BREUER, Miles J(ohn). American. Born in Chicago, Illinois, in 1888. Educated in public schools in Crete, Nebraska; University of Texas, Austin; Rush Medical College, Chicago, M.D. Served in the Medical Corps during World War I: Lieutenant. Married; two daughters and one son. Practiced medicine, specializing in diagnosis and internal medicine, in Lincoln, Nebraska. *Died in 1947.*

SCIENCE-FICTION PUBLICATIONS

Novel

The Girl from Mars, with Jack Williamson. New York, Stellar, 1929.

Uncollected Short Stories

"The Stone Cat," in *Amazing* (New York), September 1927.
"The Riot at Sanderac," in *Amazing* (New York), December 1927.
"The Puzzle Duel," in *Amazing Stories Quarterly* (New York), Winter 1928.
"Buried Treasure," in *Amazing* (New York), April 1929.
"The Book of Worlds," in *Amazing* (New York), July 1929.
"Rays and Men," in *Amazing Stories Quarterly* (New York), Summer 1929.
"The Fitzgerald Contraction," in *Science Wonder Stories* (New York), January 1930.
"The Driving Power," in *Amazing* (New York), July 1930.
"The Time Valve," in *Wonder Stories* (New York), July 1930.

"Paradise and Iron," in *Amazing Stories Quarterly* (New York), Summer 1930.
"Inferiority Complex," in *Amazing* (New York), September 1930.
"A Problem in Communication," in *Astounding* (New York), September 1930.
"The Birth of a New Republic," with Jack Williamson, in *Amazing Stories Quarterly* (New York), Winter 1930.
"On Board the Martian Liner," in *Amazing* (New York), March 1931.
"The Time Flight," in *Amazing* (New York), June 1931.
"The Demons of Rhadi-Mu," in *Amazing Stories Quarterly* (New York), Fall 1931.
"The Einstein See-Saw," in *Astounding* (New York), April 1932.
"Mechanocracy," in *Amazing* (New York), April 1932.
"The Perfect Planet," in *Amazing* (New York), May 1932.
"The Finger of the Past," in *Amazing* (New York), November 1932.
"The Strength of the Weak," in *Amazing* (New York), December 1933.
"Millions for Defense," in *Amazing* (New York), March 1935.
"The Chemistry Murder Case," in *Amazing* (New York), October 1935.
"Mr. Dimmitt Seeks Redress," in *Amazing* (New York), August 1936.
"The Company or the Weather," in *Amazing* (New York), June 1937.
"Mr. Bowen's Wife Reduces," in *Amazing* (New York), February 1938.
"The Raid from Mars," in *Amazing* (New York), March 1939.
"The Disappearing Papers," in *Future* (New York), November 1939.
"The Oversight," in *Comet* (Springfield, Massachusetts), December 1940.
"Child of Neptune," with Clare Winger Harris, in *Tales of Wonder* (Kingswood, Surrey), Spring 1941.
"Lady of the Atoms," in *Tales of Wonder* (Kingswood, Surrey), Autumn 1941.
"Breath of Utopia," in *Tales of Wonder* (Kingswood, Surrey), Spring 1942.
"The Sheriff of Thorium Gulch," in *Amazing* (New York), August 1942.
"Mars Colonizes," in *The Garden of Fear and Other Stories,* edited by William L. Crawford. Los Angeles, Crawford, 1945.
"A Baby on Neptune," with Clare Winger Harris, in *Away from the Here and Now,* edited by Harris. Philadelphia, Dorrance, 1947.
"The Man with the Strange Head," in *The Big Book of Science Fiction,* edited by Groff Conklin. New York, Crown, 1950.
"The Gostak and the Doshes," in *Science Fiction Adventures in Dimension,* edited by Groff Conklin. New York, Vanguard Press, 1953; as *Adventures in Dimension,* London, Grayson, 1955.
"The Hungry Guinea-Pig," in *Science Fiction Adventures in Mutation,* edited by Groff Conklin. New York, Vanguard Press, 1955.
"The Captured Cross-Section," in *Fantasia Mathematica,* edited by Clifton Fadiman. New York, Simon and Schuster, 1958.
"The Appendix and the Spectacles," in *The Mathematical Magpie,* edited by Clifton Fadiman. New York, Simon and Schuster, 1962.
"Man Without an Appetite," in *Great Science Fiction about Doctors,* edited by Groff Conklin and Noah D. Fabricant. New York, Macmillan, 1963.

*   *   *

Miles J. Breuer wrote some of the most intriguing tales that appeared in the early volumes of *Amazing Stories.* Like David H. Keller, he gave much of his attention to psychological themes and was more interested in the possible effects of machines on humankind than in mechanical marvels or life on other worlds. His stories often pointed a moral, yet were never mere parables; his characters were genuinely human rather than superhuman, and he wrote with a conviction that was rare in those days. He was also something of a poet.

Though he had a weakness for plots involving relativity and the fourth dimension, as in "The Captured Cross-Section" and "The Book of Worlds," he produced some novel variations on other familiar themes, such as "The Hungry Guinea-Pig," depicting the drastic results of an experiment in growth stimulation. "Buried Treasure" was remarkable for presenting a code diagram enabling readers to decipher a cryptogram which figured in the story; later he adapted the same idea to "The Chemistry Murder Case." But his most striking contribution was "The Gostak and the Doshes," which satirised extreme nationalism and in its treatment of semantics was several years in advance of Korzybski. "Rays and Men" graphically portrayed the reactions of a man of 1930 to the strictly logical, emotionless world of 2180. "Paradise and Iron" drew a realistic picture of two future cities, in one of which art and beauty flourished at the expense of the other, where the workers were menaced by thinking machines. "The Birth of a New Republic" recounted the events which followed the colonisation of the Moon in the 24th century, when the miners and other settlers fought for their independence against the combined forces of Earth's powerful corporations. This was produced in collaboration with Jack Williamson, who did most of the actual writing under the strict guidance of Breuer, from whom he learned much about the techniques of storytelling.

Breuer also collaborated with Clare Winger Harris, the first woman writer to be featured in *Amazing*, in "A Baby on Neptune." In "The Fitzgerald Contraction" and its sequel, "The Time Valve," he departed from his usual economical construction to concoct a disordered mixture of science and adventure. The first story was based on the premise that survivors of the lost continent of Mu had repaired to the Moon. In the sequel, the author took up the tale to present a gloomy picture of the human race reverting to savagery after an atomic war—200,000 years hence. It was hardly Breuer at his best.

He continued to write almost exclusively for *Amazing* over more than a decade, his contributions becoming less frequent—and, generally, less impressive—during the years of its decline under its venerable editor, T. O'Conor Sloane. He appeared only twice in the revitalised magazine before he withdrew from the scene in 1942, leaving little trace of his work beyond the confines of the outdated pulps.

—Walter Gillings

BRODERICK, Damien. Australian. Agent: Virginia Kidd, Box 278, Milford, Pennsylvania 18337, U.S.A. Address: 69 Phillip Street, Balmain, New South Wales 2041, Australia.

SCIENCE-FICTION PUBLICATIONS

Novel

Sorcerer's World. New York, New American Library, 1970.

Short Stories

A Man Returned. Sydney, Horwitz, 1965.

Uncollected Short Stories

"The Disposal of Man," in *International* (New York), November 1967.
"The Vault," in *Vision of Tomorrow* (Newcastle upon Tyne), August 1969.
"The Star-Mutants," in *Vision of Tomorrow* (Newcastle upon Tyne), March 1970.
"The Ultimate Weapon," in *Vision of Tomorrow* (Newcastle upon Tyne), August 1970.

"Incubation," with John Romeril, and "Growing Up," in *The Zeitgeist Machine,* edited by Damien Broderick. London, Angus and Robertson, 1977.
"Passage in Earth," in *Rooms of Paradise,* edited by Lee Harding. Melbourne, Quartet, 1978; New York, St. Martin's Press, 1979.

OTHER PUBLICATIONS

Other

Editor, *The Zeitgeist Machine: A New Anthology of Science Fiction.* London, Angus and Robertson, 1977.

*   *   *

Damien Broderick is widely recognized as the editor of *The Zeitgeist Machine,* an important anthology of Australian science fiction. This anthology has in fact deserved more attention from Australian SF readers. Broderick is also the writer of some of the most literate science fiction currently being produced. He shows a wide-ranging literary interest; his stories draw on sources as disparate as *Finnegans Wake* and the French structuralists.

In his collection *A Man Returned* Broderick displays many of the qualities which have marked his work: a tendency toward black humour; a concern with investigating human nature and, often, human sexuality; and a willingness to write stories which attempt to develop literary qualities. Many of the stories in the collection are simply black jokes. "The Disposal of Man" works on the premise that we are literally property—stage property in a cosmic drama. Occasionally a piece of property has to be disposed of; this process is carried out by bikini-clad girls who take corpses to the bath owned by the narrator's aunt. The title story of the collection is a comparatively trivial piece. It postulates the extinction of humanity by a plague; Dr. Keith McNaughton returns to Earth from the stars, and is told what has happened by civilized robots. The situation is potentially poignant, but Broderick's handling of it is almost wilfully insensitive. It is explained to McNaughton that a lone woman has been cryogenically preserved to play the role of new Eve to his Adam; however, the woman proves to be a signally ill-designed robot which falls apart when he touches it. The best story of the collection is "There Was a Star." Surprisingly enough in the same collection with a number of stories which spoof religion, this one is a sensitive and literate celebration of the incarnation of Christ. The collection as a whole seems to reveal a sensibility profoundly divided in its attitude towards religious feelings.

Something of Broderick's versatility is demonstrated by his science-fantasy novel, *Sorcerer's World.* This novel shows some of Broderick's characteristic strengths and weaknesses. He is able to inject some interest into an old idea: the bringing of science-fiction concepts into a sword and sorcery ambience. Broderick makes a great effort to transform the science-fantasy form with vivid prose; however, the result is often mere overwriting. At times the novel falls uneasily between parody and unredeemed cliche. The result can be bathetic, such as when a horseman exclaims, "By the Vial! An interstellar transport!"

Broderick has shown a keenness to emphasize his more recent work, but this often demonstrates the same qualities as the earlier stories. The two Broderick stories in *The Zeitgeist Machine* show Broderick's usual concern for style and craft. "Incubation" (written with the well-known Australian playwright John Romeril) is a well-crafted story which uses the proven device of setting up an unsympathetic protagonist and giving him his come-uppance—in this case along with the rest of humanity. "Growing Up" is a more self-consciously literary work. It deals with, among other things, the recapitulation of the life of the human species in that of the individual, and with the relationship between human freedom and the development of technology. Unfortunately, the story is flawed in its structure and overwritten.

A finer example of Broderick's recent work is "Passage in Earth." Broderick investigates the myths of cyclical recurrence so dear to such literary modernists as Yeats and Joyce. The story provides an engaging glance at *Finnegans Wake,* with Joyce's Shaun and Shem providing the names of alternating world-rulers in a distant future. The letters "HCE," which denote Joyce's central character, come to stand for "Holistic Cybersystem Executive." The story is entertaining and accessible to any reader, not just to esoteric Joyceans. In this case, Broderick's stylistic experiments are wholly successful. It is to be hoped that his forthcoming novel, *The Dreaming Dragons,* will add to this intelligent writer's reputation as one of the genuine stylists of science fiction.

—Russell Blackford

BROWN, Fredric. American. Born in Cincinnati, Ohio, 29 October 1906. Educated at the University of Cincinnati; Hanover College, Indiana. Married Elizabeth Chandler (second wife); two children by first marriage. Office worker, 1924-36; journalist on Milwaukee *Journal;* free-lance writer after 1947. Recipient: Mystery Writers of America Edgar Allan Poe Award, 1948. *Died 11 March 1972.*

SCIENCE-FICTION PUBLICATIONS

Novels

What Mad Universe. New York, Dutton, 1949; London, Boardman, 1951.
The Lights in the Sky Are Stars. New York, Dutton, 1953; as *Project Jupiter,* London, Boardman, 1954.
Martians, Go Home. New York, Dutton, 1955.
Rogue in Space. New York, Dutton, 1957; London, Boardman, 1958.
The Mind Thing. New York, Bantam, 1961.

Short Stories

Space on My Hands. Chicago, Shasta, 1951; London, Corgi, 1953.
Angels and Spaceships. New York, Dutton, 1954; London, Gollancz, 1955; as *Star Shine,* New York, Bantam, 1956.
Honeymoon in Hell. New York, Bantam, 1958.
Nightmares and Geezenstacks: 47 Stories. New York, Bantam, 1961; London, Corgi, 1962.
Daymares. New York, Lancer, 1968.
Paradox Lost and Twelve Other Great Science Fiction Stories. New York, Random House, 1973; London, Hale, 1975.
The Best of Fredric Brown, edited by Robert Bloch. New York, Ballantine, 1977.

OTHER PUBLICATIONS

Novels

The Fabulous Clipjoint. New York, Dutton, 1947; London, Boardman, 1949.
The Dead Ringer. New York, Dutton, 1948; London, Boardman, 1950.
Murder Can Be Fun. New York, Dutton, 1948; London, Boardman, 1951; as *A Plot for Murder,* New York, Bantam, 1949.
The Bloody Moonlight. New York, Dutton, 1949; as *Murder in Moonlight,* London, Boardman, 1950.
The Screaming Mimi. New York, Dutton, 1949; London, Boardman, 1950.
Compliments of a Fiend. New York, Dutton, 1950; London, Boardman, 1951.
Here Comes a Candle. New York, Dutton, 1950; London, Boardman, 1951.
Night of the Jabberwock. New York, Dutton, 1950; London, Boardman, 1951.
The Case of the Dancing Sandwiches. New York, Dell, 1951.
Death Has Many Doors. New York, Dutton, 1951; London, Boardman, 1952.

The Far Cry. New York, Dutton, 1951; London, Boardman, 1952.
The Deep End. New York, Dutton, 1952; London, Boardman, 1953.
We All Killed Grandma. New York, Dutton, 1952; London, Boardman, 1953.
Madball. New York, Dell, 1953; London, Muller, 1962.
His Name Was Death. New York, Dutton, 1954; London, Boardman, 1955.
The Wench Is Dead. New York, Dutton, 1955.
The Lenient Beast. New York, Dutton, 1956; London, Boardman, 1957.
One for the Road. New York, Dutton, 1958; London, Boardman, 1959.
The Office. New York, Dutton, 1958.
Knock Three-One-Two. New York, Dutton, and London, Boardman, 1959.
The Late Lamented. New York, Dutton, and London, Boardman, 1959.
The Murderers. New York, Dutton, 1961; London, Boardman, 1962.
The Five-Day Nightmare. New York, Dutton, and London, Boardman, 1963.
Mrs. Murphy's Underpants. New York, Dutton, 1963; London, Boardman, 1965.

Short Stories

Mostly Murder: Eighteen Stories. New York, Dutton, 1953; London, Boardman, 1954.
The Shaggy Dog and Other Murders. New York, Dutton, 1963; London, Boardman, 1964.

Plays

Television Plays: for *Alfred Hitchcock* series.

Other

"Why I Selected Nothing Sirius," in *My Best Science Fiction Story,* edited by Leo Margulies and O.J. Friend. New York, Merlin Press, 1949.
Introduction to *Human?,* edited by Judith Merril. New York, Lion, 1954.
Mickey Astromouse (juvenile). New York, Quist, 1971.

Editor, with Mack Reynolds, *Science-Fiction Carnival.* Chicago, Shasta, 1953.

*

Bibliography: "Paradox and Plot: The Fiction of Fredric Brown" by Newton Baird, in *Armchair Detective* (San Diego), October 1976-January 1978.

*   *   *

Fredric Brown's novels and short stories are primarily satiric spoofs of more decorous science fiction. In a genre that often takes itself too seriously, Brown's works are delightful departures from sober convention. His novels are fast-moving and often very funny. The characters tend to be larger than life and are marred by only one comic flaw, overconfidence.

The humor in Brown's classic first novel, *What Mad Universe,* develops from his satiric approach to the parallel-universe theme so popular in much of 1940's SF. The protagonist, Keith Winton, somehow falls out of time and space after an explosion demolishes the house where he is staying. He wanders through a myriad of possible universes, each more absurd than the last, with dragons, purple monsters, and the threat of an inter-planetary war with an extra-terrestrial race from arcturus. The novel is a superior blend of broad farce and subtle satire. In *Rogue in Space* Brown ridicules the taciturn, macho space cadet, a stock character in early SF. And in *Martians, Go Home* Brown pokes fun at the over-used convention of little green men invading the earth. In this work Brown creates excellent satire of the xenophobia so pervasive in early fiction dealing with alien contact.

Some of Brown's later fiction reflects a more introspective prose style. In *The Lights in the Sky Are Stars* he creates a serious theme and complex characterizations. Man Andrews, the protagonist, must deal with internal conflicts which revolve around his inability to resume his career in space exploration when he is grounded after an accident. The major characters in the novel are believable, and its principal theme of personal deterioration has universal validity. Still, Fredric Brown remains primarily a comic writer. He has the unique talent of making funny what is serious.

—Karen Burns

BROWN, James Cooke. American. Born in Tagvillarin, Bohol, Philippines, 21 July 1921. Educated at the University of Minnesota, Minneapolis, B.A. (cum laude) 1946, Ph.D. 1952. Served in the United States Army Air Force, 1941-45: First Lieutenant; Distinguished Flying Cross, Purple Heart, Air Medal. Married Lujoye Fuller in 1959; one son and two daughters. Instructor in sociology, Wayne University, Detroit, 1949-50, and Indiana University, Bloomington, 1950-52; Assistant Professor, University of Florida, Gainesville, 1955-62. Since 1962, Director, Loglan Institute, Gainesville. Visiting Professor of Philosophy, University of Florida, 1970-71. Address: Route 2, Box 386A, Gainesville, Florida 32601, U.S.A.

SCIENCE-FICTION PUBLICATIONS

Novel

The Troika Incident. New York, Doubleday, 1970.

OTHER PUBLICATIONS

Other

Loglan, with L.F. Brown. Gainesville, Florida, Loglan Institute, 5 vols., 1963-75.

*   *   *

James Cooke Brown's only attempt at fiction, *The Troika Incident,* has a genesis unlike the usual utopian novel. Science fiction appears in the work only as a means of getting three astronauts from our own time into the future, a century or so hence. There they find a world in which people are happy, well-fed, well-adjusted, engaged in pursuits that interest and enrich them. Crime has disappeared, as have family problems; international tensions no longer exist, though something like nations do; pollution and labor problems are absent, though industry continues. To the three travelers, the new society seems heaven on earth.

The cause of this angelic transformation of human nature has been the adoption of a universal second language called "Panlan." The language was invented by beginning with a search for the most basis concepts in the most widespread natural languages. These concepts are then embodied in words whose sounds will suggest the native words to the speakers of those languages: for example, "good" in Panlan is *gudbi,* supposedly an amalgamation of German *gut,* Endlish *good,* Spanish *bien,* and Russian *dobryi.* When the words are joined in a syntax reminiscent of symbolic logic, Panlan facilitates thinking and resolves misunderstandings. And when misunderstandings go, the author argues, so do all human problems.

The language described in the novel exists: it is Loglan (for "*logical language*"), an invention of Brown's; it was originally designed to test the Whorf hypothesis, that the language one speaks constrains what one can think. But as Brown himself has written, his

interest in Loglan rapidly outstripped his intention to use it as a tool for research. He saw it as a desirable end in itself, one which *The Troika Incident* was written to promote.

—Walter E. Meyers

BROWN, Rosel George. American. Born in New Orleans, Louisiana, 15 March 1926. Educated at Tulane University, New Orleans, B.A. 1946; University of Minnesota, Minneapolis, M.A. 1950. Married W. Burlie Brown in 1946; one son and one daughter. Worked as welfare visitor in Louisiana, for three years. *Died in November 1967.*

SCIENCE-FICTION PUBLICATIONS

Novels

Earthblood, with Keith Laumer. New York, Doubleday, 1966; London, Hodder and Stoughton, 1979.
Sybil Sue Blue. New York, Doubleday, 1966; as *Galactic Sybil Sue Blue,* New York, Berkley, 1968.
The Waters of Centaurus. New York, Doubleday, 1970.

Short Stories

A Handful of Time. New York, Ballantine, 1962.

Uncollected Short Stories

"And a Tooth," in *Fantastic* (New York), August 1962.
"Fruiting Body," in *Fantasy and Science Fiction* (New York), August 1962.
"The Artist," in *Amazing* (New York), May 1964.

*   *   *

Many science-fiction writers have a sense of humor that enables them to populate a universe of their own creation with a myriad of creatures both homely and fantastic. Rosel George Brown had this and another rarer ability, the ability to portray men and women who are believable, sympathetic, and winning.

Her first published story, "From an Unseen Censor," describes a search for a missing inheritance from the narrator's uncle Isadore. Finding clues planted by his uncle, the young man finds the fabulously rare perfume trees that are his uncle's bequest. Humor derives from Brown's use of Poe's "The Raven" as a model for burlesque, with Isadore filling the place of the "lost Lenore." Another young man, a space traveler, finds love on a Utopian planet where time seems to stand still ("Of All Possible Worlds"). Distraught when the whole race throws itself lemming-like from a cliff into the sea, the man has to adjust to a world that has no more meaning for him.

Brown's male characters are not the only ones with which she deals so carefully. In *Earthblood,* written with Keith Laumer, there are kindly extra-terrestrials like Iron Robert, a hugh stone-like creature who has been taught the meaning of love and compassion by the earth-bred Roan. And there are well-drawn women characters, earthly and alien, who are more than the stock sex-objects that fill lesser fiction. An example is Stellaire, who is only half human genetically, but fully human in her love and understanding of Roan. By her death Roan is finally freed to find the earth from which the seed that engendered him came so long before. Another woman ready to love and work is the mail-order bride of "Virgin Ground." A tough, self-sufficient girl, she faces a surly, unwilling groom. Cruelly left to die in a Martian sandstorm, she saves herself and then takes the farm from the boorish man who deserted her. An ending twist finds the heroine five years later faced with an eager groom sent out to share in the farm she has worked alone. Other women likely to be familiar to a reader are the harassed mother of "Car-pool," who finds that hungry earth children are likely to eat a gentle alien child who rides to the "Play Place" with them, and the garden club member who wants to make a prize-winning entry in "Flower Arrangement."

Rosel Brown's most memorable character, however, is Sybil Sue Blue, the tough earth policewoman, whose job in the novel named for her is finding the Centaurian drug pushers who are killing earth teenagers. Since widowed by the death of her explorer husband, Sue has been plagued by guilt that her daughter has "had to raise herself." Of course, the girl Missy has done no such thing, because the love and concern of Sue for her daughter is apparent whether she is worrying about Missy's being injured in retribution for Sybil's work, or thinking that things would have been different if her husband had lived. *The Waters of Centaurus* shows Sybil's further resourcefulness, not only at handling threats to interstellar peace, but at handling crises between generations, as Missy falls in love with a young alien.

Only a dozen of Rosel Brown's stories have been separately published, in *A Handful of Time;* but the collection and her novels show her remarkable growth as a writer in her use of character. Her early death was one of the most regrettable in the history of modern science fiction.

—Walter E. Meyers

BRUNNER, John (Kilian Houston). Also writes as Keith Wood-cott. British. Born in Preston Crowmarsh, Oxfordshire, 24 September 1934. Educated at Cheltenham College, Gloucestershire, 1948-51. Served in the Royal Air Force, 1953-55. Married Marjorie Rosamond Sauer in 1958. Technical abstractor, Industrial Diamond Information Bureau, London, 1956; Editor, Spring Books, London, 1956-58. Writer-in-Residence, University of Kansas, Lawrence, 1972. Founder, Martin Luther King Memorial Prize, 1968; Past Chairman, British Science Fiction Association. Recipient: British Fantasy Award, 1965; Hugo Award, 1969; British Science Fiction Association Award, 1970, 1971; Prix Apollo (France), 1973; Cometa d'Argento (Italy), 1976, 1978; Europa Award, 1980. Agent: Leslie Flood, E.J. Carnell Literary Agency, Rowneybury Bungalow, Sawbridgeworth, near Old Harlow, Essex CM20 2EX, England; or, William Reiss, Paul R. Reynolds Inc., 12 East 41st Street, New York, New York 10017, U.S.A.

SCIENCE-FICTION PUBLICATIONS

Novels (series: Galactic Empire: Zarathustra Refugee Planet)

Threshold of Eternity. New York, Ace, 1959
The World Swapper. New York, Ace, 1959.
Echo in the Skull. New York, Ace, 1959; revised editon as *Give Warning to the World*, New York, DAW, 1974.
The Hundredth Millennium. New York, Ace, 1959; revised edition, as *Catch a Falling Star*, 1968.
The Atlantic Abomination. New York, Ace, 1960.
Sanctuary in the Sky. New York, Ace, 1960.
The Skynappers. New York, Ace, 1960.
Slavers of Space. New York, Ace, 1960; revised edition, as *Into the Slave Nebula*, New York, Lancer, 1968; London, Dawson, 1980.
Meeting at Infinity. New York, Ace, 1961.
Secret Agent of Terra (Planet). New York, Ace, 1962; revised edition, as *The Avengers of Carrig*, New York, Dell, 1969.
The Super Barbarians. New York, Ace, 1962.
Times Without Number. New York, Ace, 1962; Morley, Yorkshire, Elmfield Press, 1974.
The Space-Time Juggler (Empire), *The Astronauts Must Not Land.*

New York, Ace, 1963; *The Astronauts Must Not Land* revised as *More Things in Heaven*, New York, Dell, 1973.
Castaways' World (Planet), *The Rites of Ohe.* New York, Ace, 1963; *Castaways' World* revised as *Polymath*, New York, DAW, 1974.
The Dreaming Earth. New York, Pyramid, 1963; London, Sidgwick and Jackson, 1972.
Listen! The Stars! New York, Ace, 1963; revised edition, as *The Stardroppers*, New York, DAW, 1972.
Endless Shadow. New York, Ace, 1964.
To Conquer Chaos. New York, Ace, 1964.
The Whole Man. New York, Ballantine, 1964; as *Telepathist*, London, Faber, 1965.
The Altar on Asconel (Empire). New York, Ace, 1965.
The Day of the Star Cities. New York, Ace, 1965; revised edition, as *Age of Miracles*, Ace, and London, Sidgwick and Jackson, 1973.
Enigma from Tantalus, The Repairmen of Cyclops. New York, Ace, 1965.
The Long Result. London, Faber, 1965; New York, Ballantine, 1966.
The Squares of the City. New York, Ballantine, 1965; London, Penguin, 1969.
A Planet of Your Own. New York, Ace, 1966.
Born under Mars. New York, Ace, 1967.
The Productions of Time. New York, New American Library, 1967; London, Penguin, 1970.
Quicksand. New York, Doubleday, 1967; London, Sidgwick and Jackson, 1969.
Bedlam Planet. New York, Ace, 1968; London, Sidgwick and Jackson, 1973.
Stand on Zanzibar. New York, Doubleday, 1968; London, Macdonald, 1969.
Father of Lies. New York, Belmont, 1968.
Double, Double. New York, Ballantine, 1969; London, Sidgwick and Jackson, 1971.
The Jagged Orbit. New York, Ace, 1969; London, Sidgwick and Jackson, 1970.
Timescoop. New York, Dell, 1969; London, Sidgwick and Jackson, 1972.
The Evil That Men Do. New York, Belmont, 1969.
The Dramaturges of Yan. London, Ace, 1971; London, New English Library, 1974.
The Wrong End of Time. New York, Doubleday, 1971; London, Eyre Methuen, 1975.
The Traveler in Black. New York, Ace, 1971; London, Severn House, 1979.
The Sheep Look Up. New York, Harper, 1972; London, Dent, 1974.
The Stone That Never Came Down. New York, Doubleday, 1973; London, New English Library, 1976.
Total Eclipse. New York, Doubleday, 1974; London, Weidenfeld and Nicolson, 1975.
Web of Everywhere. New York, Bantam, 1974; London, New English Library, 1977.
The Shockwave Rider. New York, Harper, and London, Dent, 1975.
Interstellar Empire. New York, DAW, 1976.
The Infinitive of Go. New York, Ballantine, 1980.
Give Warning to the World. London, Dobson, 1980.
Players at the Game of People. New York, Ballantine, 1980.

Novels as Keith Woodcott

I Speak for Earth. New York, Ace, 1961.
The Ladder in the Sky. New York, Ace, 1962.
The Psionic Menace. New York, Ace, 1963.
The Martian Sphinx. New York, Ace, 1965.

Short Stories

No Future in It and Other Science Fiction Stories. London, Gollancz, 1962; New York, Doubleday, 1964.
Now Then! London, Mayflower-Dell, 1965; New York, Avon, 1968.

No Other Gods but Me.   London, Compact, 1966.
Out of My Mind.   New York, Ballantine, 1967; London, New English Library, 1968.
Not Before Time: Science Fiction and Fantasy.   London, New English Library, 1968.
From This Day Forward.   New York, Doubleday, 1972.
Entry to Elsewhen.   New York, DAW, 1972.
Time-Jump.   New York, Dell, 1973.
The Book of John Brunner.   New York, DAW, 1976.
Foreign Constellations.   New York, Everest House, 1980.

OTHER PUBLICATIONS

Novels

The Brink.   London, Gollancz, 1959.
The Crutch of Memory.   London, Barrie and Rockliff, 1964.
Wear the Butcher's Medal.   New York, Pocket Books, 1965.
Black Is the Color.   New York, Pyramid, 1969.
A Plague on Both Your Causes.   London, Hodder and Stoughton, 1969; as *Backlash,* New York, Pyramid, 1969.
The Devil's Work.   New York, Norton, 1970.
The Gaudy Shadows.   London, Constable, 1970; New York, Beagle, 1971.
Good Men Do Nothing.   London, Hodder and Stoughton, 1970; New York, Pyramid, 1971.
Honky in the Woodpile.   London, Constable, 1971.

Play

Screenplay: *The Terrornauts,* 1967.

Verse

Trip: A Cycle of Poems.   London, Brunner Fact and Fiction, 1966; revised edition, Richmond, Surrey, Keepsake Press, 1971.
Life in an Explosive Forming Press.   London, Poets' Trust, 1971.
A Hastily Thrown-Together Bit of Zork.   South Petherton, Somerset, Square House, 1974.

Other

Horses at Home.   London, Spring, 1958.
"The Genesis of *Stand on Zanzibar* and Digressions into the Remainder of Its Pentateuch," in *Extrapolation* (Wooster, Ohio), May 1970.
"The Development of a Science Fiction Writer," in *Foundation 1* (London), March 1972.
"The Science Fiction Novel," in *The Craft of Science Fiction,* edited by Reginald Bretnor.   New York, Harper, 1976.
"A Different Kick; or, How to Get High Without Going into Orbit," in *The Book of John Brunner.*   New York, DAW, 1976.
"Science Fiction and the Larger Lunacy," in *Science Fiction at Large,* edited by Peter Nicholls.   London, Gollancz, 1976; New York, Harper, 1977.

Editor, *The Best of Philip K. Dick.*   New York, Ballantine, 1977.

Translator, *The Overlords of War,* by Gérard Klein.   New York, Doubleday, 1973.

*

Bibliography: "A Brunner Bibliography" by Joseph W. De Bolt and Denise De Bolt, in *The Happening Worlds of John Brunner,* edited by Joseph W. De Bolt, Port Washington, New York, Kennikat Press, 1975.

John Brunner comments:
For me, the essence both of science fiction and of the necessity for it can be summed up by quoting the opening sentence of L.P. Harley's *The Go-Between:* "The past is a foreign country; they do things differently there." Given that we are all being deported willy-nilly towards that foreign country, the future, where we shall ultimately die, I'd rather make the journey as a tourist with no matter how fallible a Baedeker, than be deported as a refugee. This is, I suppose, the chief reason why my SF has tended to become more and more concentrated on that portion of the future I may reasonably expect to survive into myself, and less and less concerned with the unbridled fantasy of space opera.

Concurrently, I'm told, it has also become more difficult. In a case like *Stand on Zanzibar,* this is hardly surprising—I generally tell prospective readers to remember that it should be read like a newspaper, not like a novel, for we are used to snippets about a dozen subjects on the front page, each continued elsewhere. But, much as a jazzman can keep on coming home to the blues during a playing career of half a century or more, I retain enormous respect for the conventional narrative forms and use them for the great majority of my fiction. Rules must be learned before one can judge when they may safely be broken, even (one might say especially) in our so-called "fiction of the future"—which of course, like all fiction, is actually about you and me and the here-and-now.

Let me therefore suppose that someone has chanced on this brief entry in this monumental work, and being unacquainted with SF but interested in exploring the subject, decides that a good place to start would be with those writers who have won the field's major awards. What would I commend of my own work by way of an introduction? Three books above all: *Quicksand* because of its totally contemporary setting and ambiguous SF element; *The Squares of the City* because as long ago as 1960 I was there discussing the depersonalisation we are all now acquainted with in the computer age; and *The Whole Man* because it would give a new reader some insight into the proper function of SF's standard devices, such as—in this instance—telepathy, a metaphor for total communication. It has been well said that the great contribution of SF to the corpus of literature is "the future as metaphor." I entirely agree, and though in the past I have had my doubts I do not currently feel that I shall ever exhaust the possibilities opened up to us by that discovery.

But in *Stand on Zanzibar, The Jagged Orbit, The Sheep Look Up,* and *The Shockwave Rider* I've done my best to put on the page everything I as an individual could garner and combine into a credible narrative, concerning that tomorrow we are doomed to endure. Every day necessarily alters it; SF, like all printed fiction, belongs to the past.... But even metaphors drawn from an obsolete future can be invaluable in preparing us for eventual reality, whatever form—out of an infinite number—it may actually take.

*   *   *

Though a comparative newcomer, John Brunner is one of the most famous SF writers, not only in his own country but also in the U.S.A. and even in non-English-speaking countries, France especially. This may be due in part to his abundant production: he sold his first novel when still at secondary school, and ever since (except for a couple of years) has lived by his pen exclusively, having therefore at times "to churn out an astonishing amount of wordage per year." But a prolific writer is not necessarily a great one. Had Brunner been content with turning out space operas by the dozen, such as those he produced in the 1960's (Zarathustra Refugee Planet and Galactic Empire series, *Slavers of Space,* etc.), he could have made a good livelihood, but he would certainly not have attracted such attention from critics or won such an impressive array of awards.

In fact, even Brunner's minor works—those in which he treats traditional SF themes and aims at thrilling as many readers as possible through simple devices, such as suspense and exoticism—are not negligible and, according to Donald A. Wollheim, would be worthy of an in-depth analysis, for they already contain, if only implicitly, the great problems developed in his more elaborate novels (e.g., *Polymath,* a 1974 revision of *Castaways' World,* 1963). Besides, Brunner was more than once carried away by an idea or a character that demanded to be dealt with more thoroughly: the best example is *The Whole Man,* a very fine, rich, and personal treatment of telepathy which originated as a mere recipe for turning out a whole batch of heroic fantasy (*The City of the Tiger*). And even some of Brunner's major works sometimes failed at first to be recognized as such by critics and publishers, who saw in them only the shallow tricks of a clever but uninspired craftsman. For instance, *The Squares of the City,* completed as early as 1960, was not published until 1965: converting into a story, move for move, a game of chess actually played in 1892 could seem a mere amusement, at best superficial, at worst inhuman, though it was in fact the most effective means of unveiling to deceived—and self-deceiving—city-dwellers the fact that modern town-planning rests on their being treated as pawns.

Not that Brunner is adverse to being called a "craftsman": indeed his favourite self-definition is as a "wordsmith" (a notion not alien to the choice of his early pen-name John Loxmith). Both as a recognized poet and as a gifted linguist, he is highly aware that words are the material with which he works—and plays. All the resources of the language are put to use in his novels, from puns ("The Warp and the Woof-Woof") to poems (in *The Sheep Look Up* especially) through literary allusions (such titles as "Wasted on the Young" or *The Productions of Time*). If such devices may sometimes seem to be enjoyed for their own sake, they generally aim at conveying as forcefully as possible the nature of the characters and the portent of the story.

Brunner's style is not as plainly recognizable as Ballard's, for instance: that is because he does not want to stamp it permanently as his own, but to adapt it to the changing demands of the subjects. For that purpose he may borrow from other writers, past or present, quite freely—and very consciously too. In his early writings he inevitably came under certain influences—that of van Vogt is very perceptible in *Threshold of Eternity,* a story of super-human beings warring through time as well as space. But he deliberately chose to transpose the technique of mixing factual indications and fictional invention used by Dos Passos in his fresco of American society in the early 20th century (*U.S.A.*) to a comprehensive picture of the all-too-possible dramas of overpopulation and over-exploitation in 2010 (*Stand on Zanzibar*) and to imitate Sterne's purposeful divagation in *Tristram Shandy* the better to express the paranoia of a nation whose inner conflicts (personal as well as racial) are not solved but magnified by mass-media. (*The Jagged Orbit*).

More than formal innovation—which too often has been the sole contribution of so-called New Wave SF writers—it is this development of present-day problems into the tragedies of the near-future that characterizes Brunner's proper approach to science fiction: the poisoning of a continent in *The Sheep Look Up* or computerized enslavement in *The Shockwave Rider.* And the same determination to face, and make us face, the worst possible consequences of today's irresponsible attitudes equally appears in stories which take place in the present world with hardly any transposition at all—for example, racism in *A Plague on Both Your Causes* and *Black Is the Color,* both published as mystery novels—or in a far more distant future and make use of conventional SF situations—ecological concerns in *Bedlam Planet* or the fatal danger of pure reason as the unique basis of social organisation in *Total Eclipse.*

Yet it would be misleading to reduce Brunner's works to these recurring warnings: even in the great novels in which they are predominant, one is also struck by the masterliness with which the plot, or more often than not several plots together, are driven to a conclusion that is both inescapably logical and pleasantly unexpected (*The Dreaming Earth* where salvation springs from what is at present a great evil, escapism through drugs); by the richness of invention and the power of realistic vision through which the most daring flights of imagination are given credibility (*The Dramaturges of Yan* in which the soul of a whole planet comes to life); by the multiplicity, complexity, and veracity of the characters (who, some critics complain, sometimes take precedence over SF as a literature of ideas, as in *Quicksand,* a penetrating study in sexual frustration, or *The Productions of Time,* a conflict between personal vices and the need for human communication); by the depth of the philosophical implications (the title *More Things in Heaven* speaks for itself: though an agnostic, Brunner is highly conscious of man's transcendental aspirations, and often gives new forms to old religious beliefs, whether in the whole structure of a book like *Age of Miracles* or in a messianic character like Austin Train in *The Sheep Look Up*).

If I were to sum up in a single word Brunner's dominant attitude towards the tenets of the past, the problems of the present, and the possibilities of the future, the word would be open-mindedness.

—George W. Barlow

BRYANT, Edward (Winslow, Jr.). American. Born in White Plains, New York, 27 August 1945. Educated at the University of Wyoming, Laramie (General Motors scholar; Ford Foundation fellow), B.A. in English 1967, M.A. 1968. Broadcaster, disk jockey, and news director, KOWB-Radio, Laramie, 1965-66; worked as rancher and in a stirrup buckle factory; Columnist ("The Screen Game"), *Cthulhu Calls,* Powell, Wyoming, 1973-77. Free-lance writer and lecturer. Recipient: Nebula Award, 1979, 1980. Agent: Robert P. Mills Ltd., 156 East 52nd Street, New York, New York 10022. Address: P.O. Box 18162, Denver, Colorado 80218, U.S.A.

SCIENCE-FICTION PUBLICATIONS

Novels

Phoenix Without Ashes, with Harlan Ellison. New York, Fawcett, 1975; Manchester, Savoy, 1978.
Cinnabar. New York, Macmillan, 1976; London, Fontana, 1978.

Short Stories

Among the Dead and Other Events Leading Up to the Apocalypse. New York, Macmillan, 1973.
Particle Theory. New York, Pocket Books, 1980.

OTHER PUBLICATIONS

Plays

Radio Play: *Breakers,* 1979.

Television Play: *The Synar Calculation,* with Edward Hawkins, 1973.

Other

"Breaking Waves: The Latest Look of Science Fiction," in *Science Fiction: Education for Tomorrow,* edited by Jack Williamson. Philadelphia, Owlswick Press, 1980.

Editor, with Jo Ann Harper, *2076: The American Tricentennial.* New York, Pyramid, 1977.

*

Bibliography: *Edward Bryant Bibliography,* Los Angeles, Swigart, 1980.

Edward Bryant comments:
I find considerable contradictions at this time in my life and career (each, for the time, indistinguishable from the other). I love the glittering attractions of cities, but find the east and west coasts claustrophobic. I love the spaciousness and low population density of the mountain west, but don't wish the situation of a hermit. I love being a westerner, but have no nostalgic aspirations of living on a ranch again as I did when I was younger. The wide open spaces liberate, but do not trigger me to hunt or fish or ski. But I notice the metaphor of the mountain west creeping increasingly into my work.

People seem continually bent on telling me I don't truly write "real" SF, whatever that is, but then I continue to read and admire what I consider to be the best of other people's SF, and then go on to write more of the fiction I feel I'd like to encounter as an SF reader.

I seem to be a minority writer in SF, like Avram Davidson, Thomas Disch, and Carol Emshwiller (I don't pretend to place myself in their bracket—I simply admire the work of all three tremendously). All of us seem to communicate—at best—with perhaps 30 to 40 per cent of the great mass of SF readers. For me, that's a little frustrating—but not sufficiently that I plan a pragmatic campaign to include more telepathic dragons, mightily thewed barbarians, Empire blockade runners, or other crowd-pleasers in my fictions. I expect to continue swimming my own way.

Although the boredom quotient (a facet of Sturgeon's law) in SF is still rather high, I'm excited about where the best of the field seems to be heading in the 1980's. I think finally there are a decent number of literate writers of SF who have an eclectic grounding in the arts and humanities as well as in science and technology. They are articulate and genuinely inquisitive about the interrelationship between human beings and universe. They are blessed with minimal knee-jerk prejudices about science and technology. Many of them have been practicing and cogitating, perhaps consolidating their craft, during the past two decades. I may have my doubts about the future of the universe itself, but I'm sanguine about the prospects for science fiction.

*   *   *

Like one of his best-known and most important mentors, Harlan Ellison, Edward Bryant has thus far tended to write short fictions. In fact, his only novel is an adaptation of Ellison's original prize-winning television script for the doomed *Starlost* series, *Phoenix Without Ashes.* Again, like Ellison, Ray Bradbury, and some of his contemporaries, Bryant is essentially a fabulist, a writer of fantasy who uses science-fiction trappings in his work for their metaphorical effect rather than as realistic background. He is the very opposite of a "hard" science-fiction writer, someone like Larry Niven, say, who believes in a fiction of ideas and specific extrapolation. He is also a more adventurous stylist than most traditional hard science-fiction writers.

Bryant's vision can be extremely dark, as his first collection of mostly nightmarish fables, *Among the Dead,* demonstrates. A portrayal of a world sliding on good intentions and nothing else into the deepest of pits, this collection is full of sad and terrifying glimpses of human ennui and failure of nerve. Entropy is the reigning god, and metaphors of decay, death, and Sisyphusian effort appear everywhere. Many of the stories are set in a bleak near-present, but the far future of "Love Song of Herself" and indeterminate time/space of "Dune's Edge" are no more hopeful. Nevertheless, and this is one of the marvelous paradoxes of good writing, the formal energy and black wit of the best of these stories often overcome their thematic sense of utter depression.

Phoenix Without Ashes is a collaboration in the best sense of the word. Taking Ellison's screenplay as his basic story, Bryant has written a novel which effectively works out some nice variations of the conventional SF "closed universe" theme, previously handled by writers as disparate as Heinlein and Aldiss. Characterization is minimal (it was to be a TV series, after all), but the story moves with a certain grandeur to its ending as new beginning, and it's an entertaining book, though not special the way *Cinnabar* so definitely is.

Bryant calls *Cinnabar* a "mosaic novel," a richly evocative description for this sequence of interlocking stories. It takes another grand old SF metaphor, the city *at* the end of time and *as* the end of human endeavor, and, in a tour de force of colourful, glitteringly *fin de siècle* stylization, explodes the conventional possibilities of the metaphor in a grand fireworks display. The way the whole context alters its individual parts can be seen in the changes "Gray Matters"—also in *Among the Dead*—undergoes when it's set into the glamorous mosaic of *Cinnabar.* Although it remains a tale of sexual and emotional ennui, its focus shifts from the victims to the strong and positive personality of Tourmaline Hayes who figures energetically throughout *Cinnabar.*

Cinnabar may be a "doomed city of hope" as Bryant says; but as he also says, "all things considered, I know *I* would rather be in Cinnabar," and that desire informs the dazzling and energetic writing in the book. Anything is possible in this city at the centre and terminus of time because its brightest and most complex inhabitants joyfully recognize the profoundly human potentiality of the argument that "biologically speaking, there are no imperatives," though moral choice remains a centrally human act. Only a few of Cinnabar's near-immortal citizens accept the challenge to seek and grow implicit in the city's multiplex presence. Most suffer from ennui, emotional and spiritual entropy, but Bryant wisely keeps them well in the background while focussing on Tourmaline, the compleat tourist, Obregon, the always curious non-specialist, Leah Sand, the melancholy media artist, Jad Blue, the computer-created cat-mother, and Harry Blake, the 1963 university student who falls down a temporal rabbit hole and learns to view human potentiality anew. And then there's Terminex, the central computer slowly going crazy trying to run the city and hold all its different time zones

in place. The style, grace, and wit apparent throughout *Cinnabar* mark it as a brilliant example of speculative fantasy at its best, and suggest that Bryant will continue to offer us high entertainment in his future work.

—Douglas Barbour

<hr>

BRYNING, Frank (Francis Bertram Bryning).   Also writes as F. Cornish.   Australian.   Born in Fairfield, Victoria, 2 August 1907. Educated at Fairfield State School, 1912-20; University High School, Melbourne, 1921-24. Married Henrietta Edna Ewell in 1935; one daughter. Clerk, Harrisons Ramsay Importers, Melbourne, 1925-26; worked for news agency and library, 1926-28, and as an electrical appliance salesman, 1928-31, Melbourne; free-lance journalist and editor, Melbourne and Sydney, 1932-49: Editor, *Flax Newsletter,* Sydney, 1942-49; Editor, *Architecture, Building, Engineering* and *Queensland Building Yearbook,* both Brisbane, 1950-57; Editor, *Hardware Trader, Brisbane Building Yearbook, Queensland Fruit and Vegetable News,* and *Australian Electrical World,* all Brisbane, 1957-73. Agent: Leslie Flood, E.J. Carnell Literary Agency, Rowneybury Bungalow, Sawbridgeworth, near Old Harlow, Essex CM20 2EX, England.

SCIENCE-FICTION PUBLICATIONS

Uncollected Short Stories (series: Joan Buckley; Vivienne Gale)

"Operation in Free Flight" (Gale), in *Australian Monthly* (Melbourne), March 1952; as "Operation in Free Orbit," in *Fantastic Universe* (Chicago), February 1955.
"Action-Reaction" (Gale), in *Australian Monthly* (Melbourne), June 1952.
"Space Doctor's Orders" (Gale), in *Australian Monthly* (Melbourne), January 1953.
"On the Average," in *Forerunner,* April 1953.
"Jettison or Die!," in *Australian Monthly* (Melbourne), August 1953.
"The Gambler" (Buckley), in *Australian Monthly* (Melbourne), October 1954; as "Coming Generation," in *Fantastic Universe* (Chicago), July 1955.
"Pass the Oxygen," in *Future* (New York), October 1954.
"Daughter of Tomorrow" (Buckley), in *Australian Monthly* (Melbourne), February 1955.
"Poor Hungry People," in *Etherline,* August 1955.
"Infant Prodigy" (Buckley), in *Fantastic Universe* (Chicago), November 1955.
"Consultant Diagnostician" (Buckley), in *Fantastic Universe* (Chicago), December 1955.
"And a Hank of Hair" (Gale), in *Australian Journal* (Melbourne), May 1956.
"The Robot Carpenter," in *Australian Journal* (Melbourne), July 1956.
"Power of a Woman," in *Australian Journal* (Melbourne), January 1957.
"I Did, Too, See a Flying Saucer!," in *Amazing* (New York), August 1958.
"Place of the Throwing-Stick," in *Coast to Coast.*   Sydney, Angus and Robertson, 1959.
"Escape Mechanism," in *Sunday Mail,* October 1967.
"For Men Must Work," in *The Pacific Book of Australian Science Fiction,* edited by John Baxter.   Sydney, Angus and Robertson, 1968; London, Angus and Robertson, 1969.
"The Visitors," in *Vision of Tomorrow* (Newcastle upon Tyne), March 1970.
"Election," in *Vision of Tomorrow* (Newcastle upon Tyne), June 1970.
"Lost Explorer," in *Science Fiction Monthly* (London), August

1975.
"Beyond the Line of Duty," in *Void* (St. Kilda, Victoria), August 1976.
"The Homecoming of Haral," in *Void* (St. Kilda, Victoria), August 1977.
"Nemaluk and the Star-Stone," in *Envisaged Worlds,* edited by Paul Collins. St. Kilda, Victoria, Void, 1977.
"Mechman of the Dreaming," in *Other Worlds,* edited by Paul Collins. St. Kilda, Victoria, Void, 1978.

Uncollected Short Stories as F. Cornish

"The Vase with the Character of a Flower Pot," in *Australasian* (Melbourne), September 1944.
"Bloodthinker," in *The World's News,* January 1945.
"Miracle in the Moluccas," in *Pocket Book Weekly,* January 1950.

OTHER PUBLICATIONS

Other

"What Has Science Fiction to Say?," in *Meanjin* (Melbourne), Winter 1954.
"Mouses Will Make Moons," in *Australian Journal* (Melbourne), April 1957.
"Australian Writers and Science Fiction," in *Overland* (Melbourne), August 1975.

Frank Bryning comments:
In science fiction my prejudice is in favour of "hard-core," or "scientific fiction." I hold that the essential problem or conflict in the lives of the characters in a science-fiction story will derive from their involvement in some event in the natural universe—some biological, psychological, sociological, techological, cosmological activity. Their experiences, however unusual or mystifying, will be explicable, ultimately, according to that accumulation of precise factual knowledge and verifiable experience and the logically reasoned theories and speculations based on it that we call "science."

This as distinct from "fantasy"—from fiction of the "super"-natural, from fairy tale, fable, legend, myth (religious or otherwise), magic, witchcraft, the occult, or ghoulies and ghosties and things that go boomp in the night. In fantasy I have always found much profit and delight. I still do. I yield to no one in my capacity to find enjoyment there, or moral lesson. From fantasy I do not expect believable premises, strictly logical progression of cause and effect, or any real conviction, yet I consider those fantasies most satisfying which are internally logical after one suspends disbelief in their mystical premises.

I would like to think that the sum total of all my writing—fiction and non-fiction, plus my work as staff writer and editor—would designate me as a realist rather than a surrealist. Almost all my work has been to present the "rational" viewpoint, I believe. My fiction is concerned mainly with the doings of typical everyday people in the everyday world (including, perhaps, the world of tomorrow in my science fiction) rather than with "exploring" so-called "alternative realities" or fantasising about "other planes of existence." I want to be on the side of enlightenment rather than obfuscation, of rationalism rather than mysticism. I hope readers, of my science fiction in particular, and my fellow writers, may agree that I am.

*   *   *

Having grown up on Wells, Verne, and Bellamy, Frank Bryning naturally turned to writing SF stories, and it was natural that he should become a writer who stresses the *science* in science fiction. Bryning is best known for his Aboriginal stories "Place of the Throwing-Stick" (his best story), "Nemaluk and the Star-Stone," and "Mechman of the Dreaming." Bryning regards the Australian Aborigines as "the most distinctively Australian phenomenon one might use," and these three stories reflect the theme of "the 'Aboriginal possessor of the land' versus the colonial invader." In "Place of the Throwing-Stick" the Aboriginal Munyarra attacks the most recent of the white man's importations—the rocket. The confrontation takes place at Australia's real-life Woomera Rocket Range, allowing Bryning to link the Stone Age past with the Space Age

present through the name "Woomera" (Aboriginal for "spear-throwing stick").

Bryning's long-time membership in the British Interplanetary Society is reflected in his cycle of Commonwealth Satellite Space Station stories, embracing items written from the 1950's to the present. Eschewing the Americanization of SF, Bryning posits a near future in which the Commonwealth of Australia has established a network of space stations. The emphasis is upon character and realistic situations, with the ten stories being linked by the central character, Dr. Vivienne Gale. Plots are generated by the humdrum daily life in space, and many stories deal with space medicine and the problems of weightlessness.

There is nothing flashy or sensational about Bryning's stories. They are solidly and conventionally constructed, and their extrapolations are never allowed to outstrip the author's knowledge. As future histories, they are modest. But their strengths and merits lie in their quiet, dogged realism, their guarded optimism, and their compassion for the man with a day's work to complete.

—Van Ikin

_____

BUDRYS, Algis (Algirdas Jonas Budrys).   Also writes as Frank Mason.   Lithuanian.   Born in Konigsberg, Germany, 9 January 1931. Educated at the University of Miami, 1947-49; Columbia University, New York, 1950-51. Married Edna Frances Duna in 1954; four sons. Clerk, American Express, New York, 1950-51; editorial positions at Gnome Press, 1952-53, *Galaxy,* 1953, *Venture SF,* 1957, *Fantasy and Science Fiction,* 1957, *Ellery Queen's Mystery Magazine,* 1957, *Car Speed and Style, Custom Rodder,* and *Cars Magazine,* all 1958-59, Regency Books, 1961-63, Playboy Press, 1963-64, and Commander Publications, 1966; public relations positions, Theodore R. Sills Inc., Chicago, 1966-67, Geyer-Oswald Advertising, 1967-68, and Young and Ribicam, 1969-73; Operations Manager, Woodall Publications, 1973-74. Since 1974, President, Unifont Company, Evanston, Illinois. Science fiction reviewer and columnist, *Galaxy,* 1966-70, *Fantasy and Science Fiction,* 1975-79, *Locus,* 1977-79, Washington *Post,* 1978, and Chicago *Sun-Times,* 1979; Instructor, Columbia College, Chicago, 1977; visiting writer, Clarion Science Fiction Writing Workshop, 1977-79, and Evanston schools, 1978-79. Recipient: Mystery Writers of America award, 1966; Science Fiction Writers of America Hall of Fame award. Address: Unifont Company, 824 Seward Street, Evanston, Illinois 60202, U.S.A.

SCIENCE-FICTION PUBLICATIONS

Novels

False Night. New York, Lion, 1954; as *Some Will Not Die,* Evanston, Illinois, Regency, 1961; London, Mayflower, 1963.
Man of Earth. New York, Ballantine, 1958.
Who? New York, Pyramid, 1958; London, Gollancz, 1962.
The Falling Torch. New York, Pyramid, 1959.
Rogue Moon. New York, Fawcett, 1960; London, Muller, 1962.
The Amsirs and the Iron Thorn. New York, Fawcett, 1967; as *The Iron Thorn,* London, Gollancz, 1968.
Michaelmas. New York, Berkley, and London, Gollancz, 1977.
Blood and Burning. New York, Berkley, 1978; London, Gollancz, 1979.
The Life Machine. New York, Berkley, 1979.

Short Stories

The Unexpected Dimension. New York, Ballantine, 1960; London, Gollancz, 1962.
Budrys' Inferno. New York, Berkley, 1963; as *The Furious Future,* London, Gollancz, 1963.

Uncollected Short Stories

"Cerberus," in *Fantasy and Science Fiction* (New York), December 1967.
"Die Shadow," in *The Second If Reader of Science Fiction,* edited by Frederik Pohl.   New York, Doubleday, 1968.
"Be Merry," in *On Our Way to the Future,* edited by Terry Carr.   New York, Ace, 1970.
"Now Hear the Word of the Lord," in *Best SF 1969,* edited by Harry Harrison and Brian Aldiss.   New York, Putnam, and London, Sphere, 1970.
"The Ultimate Brunette," in *The Fiend.*   Chicago, Playboy Press, 1971.
"Players at Null-G," with Theodore R. Cogswell and Ted Thomas, in *Fantasy and Science Fiction* (New York), July 1975.
"A Scraping at the Bones," in *Best SF 1975,* edited by Harry Harrison and Brian Aldiss.   Indianapolis, Bobbs Merrill, and London, Weidenfeld and Nicolson, 1976.
"The Silent Eyes of Time," in *The Best Science Fiction of the Year 5,* edited by Terry Carr.   New York, Ballantine, and London, Gollancz, 1976.
"The Nuptial Flight of Warbirds," in *Analog* (New York), May 1978.

OTHER PUBLICATIONS

Play

Radio Play: *Rogue Moon,* from his own novel, 1979.

Other

Truman and the Pendergasts (as Frank Mason).   Evanston, Illinois, Regency, 1963.
Bicycles: How They Work and How to Fix Them.   Evanston, Illinois, Unifont, 1976.

*

Manuscript Collection: Spencer Research Library, University of Kansas, Lawrence.

Algis Budrys comments:
My work, when found, speaks for itself. I think a piece of creativity is its own justification. However, if a rationale is desired, then the theoretical underpinning of my SF is that speculative fiction is drama made more relevant by social extrapolation. That is, I proceed on the assumption that, by certain fortuitous strokes of talent, some prose artists can create conditional realities in which recognizably human behavior occurs under illuminating circumstances which are not yet known to have occurred in what we have agreed to call reality. The proposition is that a few members of the readership will be inspired to look about them anew and draw conclusions of benefit to mankind's continuing endeavor to escape extinction. I seriously doubt that any critical analysis of my work, however accurate, will have much relevance to my necessarily minor role in that endeavor. I commend to his or her god whatever hominid organism is eventually able to overcome the darkness, and I rest my case.

*   *   *

Like Nabokov and Solzhenitsyn, Algis Budrys is ours by courtesy of Communism. I have been told that his real name means something like John Sentry, a pseudonym he has in fact employed. A sentry he is, if the brave who watched the stockade, the alien walls of the invader, may be called a sentry. A warrior he is by any definition. He understands more of the psychology of the man who fights—not the man who dies—than any other writer I know. Every age and every genre produce a few writers too good for them, authors who pour oceans into their wine cups or summon Sigurd and Fafnir in person to entertain the nursery. Budrys is one of these. He is, in the best sense, too serious a writer for science fiction.

Who? is the book that made him famous. It is perhaps as fine a study of dehumanization and alienation as science fiction will ever produce. A brilliant American scientist is torn by a laboratory explosion and repaired with what we would now call "bionic" parts by the Soviets. He is returned to the US—but the US cannot be sure of that. So much of him is gone that what remains cannot be identified. All this is simple enough. It is even—if you like—a retelling of L. Frank Baum's story of the Tin Woodman, who when he had sliced his "meat" (humanity) completely away could no longer recall his true name (which was Nick Chopper). The difference lies in intent, and in the treatments that result from it. Baum was manufacturing a paradox to amuse children, one not really much different from the rhyme about the Gingham Dog and the Calico Cat who ate each other up. Budrys is intensely concerned with the effect of technology—and particularly the technology of the Cold War—on our humanity. He asks if the Soviets were really doing the West a favor when they restored Martino, since he cannot be identified and thus cannot be of use. *Can* they do the West a good office, when all they do *must* be suspect? SF offers few figures of the symbolic intensity of this faceless, maimed scientist, the man who could prove ten thousand things, if only he could prove who he is.

Budrys's writing falls into two distinct periods, the first ranging from 1952 to the middle 1960's, the second from the middle 1970's to the present. The best work of his earlier period is surely *Rogue Moon,* which he wished to call *The Death Machine,* a vastly better title in *Rogue Moon* a "matter transmitter" has been invented in a near future in which rocketry is still primitive; and an unmanned probe has managed to drop a transmitting and receiving station on the far side of the moon. The first explorers to go through the transmitter discover an alien construct millions of years old, a thing compounded of building, machine, and hallucination. It soon kills everyone who ventures inside. This alien construct is perhaps the biggest and best red herring in all SF, because it is not really what *Rogue Moon* is about. It is about Hawks, the brilliant, compassionate, iron-souled scientist who has developed the "matter transmitter" and is determined to have the construct analyzed, and Barker, the death-obsessed Saturday afternoon hero he gets to do the exploring—through a score of deaths. Like *Who?* it is about the nature of identity. It is also about the nature of life, about what it is to live and have lived.

When a writer of Budrys's calibre is silent for so long as Budrys was silent, silenced not by the knouts and jails of totalitarian authority but by his own frustrations, his readers are entitled to expect him to be a different and even better writer if he chooses to write again. Budrys's justification is *Michaelmas,* his best novel and the book that has brought him considerable recognition outside SF. If *Rogue Moon* was cinematic, *Michaelmas* is bibliomatic—a story that can be told well only in a book. Americans are apt to find a certain glamour in kings and queens, princes and princesses—an amiable weakness. We are sometimes even liable to find an attraction in tyrants of one sort or another, in Napoleon, Caesar, and even Stalin—though we should know much better. But numbed by a parade of crooks and nonentities, we seem to have forgotten the romance of a President, of the good citizen elevated by his own efforts and the admiration of his fellows to a pre-eminence in the state, the romance our great grandfathers sensed so strongly in the embodiment of the Republic. Budrys, a Lithuanian refugee and the son of refugees, has not. G.K. Chesterton once said that a sword was the most glorious object in the world, but that a pocket-knife was more glorious than a sword, because it was a secret sword. Laurent Michaelmas is a secret President, the secret President of the Earth. In the hands of any other writer, he would almost certainly be a tyrant, and, no doubt in the hands of most, an insane tyrant. In Budrys's, as he struggles with human treachery and an alien visitor of awesome power, he remains an eminently sane and decent man, as lonely and as sad as our society's sane and decent men must always be. In flatly and persuasively denying the inevitable corruption of power, *Michaelmas* may well be the most optimistic book of the latter 20th century. It is certainly one of the best, as Budrys himself is one of its best—and least characteristic—storytellers.

—Gene Wolfe

BULMER, (Henry) Kenneth. Also writes as Alan Burt Akers; Ken Blake; Ernest Corley; Arthur Frazier; Adam Hardy; Kenneth Johns; Philip Kent; Bruno Krauss; Neil Langholm; Karl Maras; Manning Norvil; Charles R. Pike; Andrew Quiller; Richard Silver; Tully Zetford. British. Born in London, 14 January 1921. Educated at Catford Central School, London. Served in the Royal Corps of Signals, 1941-46. Married Pamela Kathleen Buckmaster in 1953; two daughters and one son. Worked for paper merchandising and office equipment firms, 1936-54. Address: Waterdown House, 51 Frant Road, Tunbridge Wells, Kent TN2 5LE, England.

SCIENCE-FICTION PUBLICATIONS

Novels

Space Treason, with A.V. Clarke. London, Panther, 1952.
Cybernetic Controller, with A.V. Clarke. London, Panther, 1952.
Encounter in Space. London, Panther, 1952.
Space Salvage. London, Panther, 1953.
The Stars Are Ours. London, Panther, 1953.
Galactic Intrigue. London, Panther, 1953.
Empire of Chaos. London, Panther, 1953.
World Aflame. London, Panther, 1954.
Challenge. London, Curtis Warren, 1954.
Zhorani (as Karl Maras). London, Comyns, 1954.
Peril from Space (as Karl Maras). London, Comyns, 1954.
City under the Sea. New York, Ace, 1957; London, Digit, 1961.
The Secret of ZI. New York, Ace, 1958; London, Digit, 1961; as *The Patient Dark,* London, Hale, 1969.
The Changeling Worlds. New York, Ace, 1959; London, Digit, 1961.
The Earth Gods Are Coming. New York, Ace, 1960; as *Of Earth Foretold* (includes "The Aztec Plan"), London, Digit, 1961.
Forschungskreuzer Saumarez. Munich, Moewig, 1960; as *Defiance,* London, Digit, 1963.
No Man's World. New York, Ace, 1961; as *Earth's Long Shadow* (includes "Strange Highway"), London, Digit, 1962.
Beyond the Silver Sky. New York, Ace, 1961.
The Fatal Fire. London, Digit, 1962.
The Wind of Liberty (includes "Don't Cross a Telekine"). London, Digit, 1962.
The Wizard of Starship Poseidon. New York, Ace, 1963.
The Million Year Hunt. New York, Ace, 1964.
Demon's World. New York, Ace, 1964; as *The Demons,* London, Compact, 1965.
Land Beyond the Map. New York, Ace, 1965.
Behold the Stars. New York, Ace, 1965; London, Mayflower, 1966.
Worlds for the Taking. New York, Ace, 1966.
To Outrun Doomsday. New York, Ace, 1967; London, New English Library, 1975.
The Key to Irunium. New York, Ace, 1967.
Cycle of Nemesis. New York, Ace, 1967.
The Doomsday Men. New York, Doubleday, and London, Hale, 1968.
The Key to Venudine. New York, Ace, 1968.
The Star Venturers. New York, Ace, 1969.
The Wizards of Senchuria. New York, Ace, 1969.
Kandar. New York, Paperback Library, 1969.
The Ulcer Culture. London, Macdonald, 1969; as *The Stained-Glass World,* London, New English Library, 1976.
The Ships of Durostorum. New York, Ace, 1970.
Blazon. New York, Curtis, 1970; as *Quench the Burning Stars,* London, Hale, 1970.
Star Trove. London, Hale, 1970.
Swords of the Barbarians. London, New English Library, 1970; New York, Belmont, 1977.
The Hunters of Jundagai. New York, Ace, 1971.
The Electric Sword Swallowers. New York, Ace, 1971.
The Insane City. New York, Curtis, 1971; London, Severn House, 1978.

The Chariots of Ra. New York, Ace, 1972.
On the Symb-Socket Circuit. New York, Ace, 1972.
Roller Coaster World. New York, Ace, 1972; London, Severn House, 1978.

Novels as Philip Kent

Mission to the Stars. London, Pearson, 1953.
Vassals of Venus. London, Pearson, 1954.
Slaves of the Spectrum. London, Pearson, 1954.
Home Is the Martian. London, Pearson, 1954.

Novels as Alan Burt Akers (series: Dray Prescot in all books)

Transit to Scorpio. New York, DAW, 1972; London, Futura, 1974.
The Suns of Scorpio. New York, DAW, 1973.
Warrior of Scorpio. New York, DAW, 1973.
Swordships of Scorpio. New York, DAW, 1973; London, Futura, 1975.
Prince of Scorpio. New York, DAW, 1974.
Manhounds of Antares. New York, DAW, 1974.
Arena of Antares. New York, DAW, 1974.
Fliers of Antares. New York, DAW, 1975.
Bladesman of Antares. New York, DAW, 1975.
Avenger of Antares. New York, DAW, 1975.
Armada of Antares. New York, DAW, 1976.
The Tides of Kregen. New York, DAW, 1976.
Renegade of Kregen. New York, DAW, 1976.
Krozair of Kregen. New York, DAW, 1977.
Secret Scorpio. New York, DAW, 1977.
Savage Scorpio. New York, DAW, 1978.
Captive Scorpio. New York, DAW, 1978.
Golden Scorpio. New York, DAW, 1978.
A Life for Kregen. New York, DAW, 1979.
A Sword for Kregen. New York, DAW, 1979.
A Fortune for Kregen. New York, DAW, 1979.
A Victory for Kregen. New York, DAW, 1980.
Beasts of Antares. New York, DAW, 1980.
Rebel of Antares. New York, DAW, 1980.
Legions of Antares. New York, DAW, 1981.

Novels as Tully Zetford (series: Ryder Hook in all books)

Whirlpool of Stars. London, New English Library, 1974; New York, Pinnacle, 1975.
The Boosted Man. London, New English Library, 1974; New York, Pinnacle, 1975.
Star City. London, New English Library, 1974; New York, Pinnacle, 1975.
The Virility Gene. London, New English Library, 1975; New York, Pinnacle, 1976.

Novels as Manning Norvil (series: Odan in all books)

Dream Chariots. New York, DAW, 1977.
Whetted Bronze. New York, DAW, 1978.
Crown of the Sword God. New York, DAW, 1980.

Uncollected Short Stories (series: Earth-Shurilala-Takkat War)

"First Down," in *Authentic* (London), April 1954.
"Some Other Time, in *Authentic* (London), May 1954.
"All Glory Forgotten," in *New Worlds* (London), June 1954.
"Bitter the Path," in *New Worlds* (London), August 1954.
"It Takes Two," in *Authentic* (London), October 1954.
"The Black Spot," in *New Worlds* (London), February 1955.
"Ordeal," in *Authentic* (London), March 1955.
"Asylum," in *New Worlds* (London), April 1955.
"Psi No More," in *Science Fantasy* (Bournemouth), June 1955.
"The Day of the Monster," in *Authentic* (London), July 1955.
"Total Recall," in *New Worlds* (London), August 1955.
"Know Thy Neighbour," in *Authentic* (London), September 1955.
"Come to Prestonwell," in *Authentic* (London), November 1955.
"Plaything" in *New Worlds* (London), November 1955.

"Sunset," in *Nebula* (Glasgow), November 1955.
"The Old Firm," in *Authentic* (London), February 1956.
"Quarry," in *Infinity* (New York), February 1956.
"The Smallest Ally," in *New Worlds* (London), March 1956.
"Sunk," in *New Worlds* (London), April 1956.
"Mr. Culpeper's Baby," in *Authentic* (London), April 1956.
"Project Pseudoman," in *Nebula* (Glasgow), July 1956.
"The City Calls," in *New Worlds* (London), October 1956.
"The Great Armadas," in *Nebula* (Glasgow), December 1956.
"Recreation," in *Authentic* (London), December 1956.
"Their Dreams Remain," in *Fantastic Universe* (Chicago), December 1956.
"Prestige," in *Authentic* (London), January 1957.
"Child's Play," in *Authentic* (London), February 1957.
"Three-Cornered Knife," in *Infinity* (New York), February 1957; as "Ambiguous Assignment," in *Authentic* (London), September 1957.
"The Day Everything Fell Down," in *Fantasy and Science Fiction* (New York), August 1957.
"Native Law," in *New Worlds* (London), August 1957.
"Mission One Hundred," in *New Worlds* (London), September 1957.
"The Ties of Iron," in *Nebula* (Glasgow), September 1957.
"Reason for Living," in *Science Fantasy* (Bournemouth), October 1957.
"There's No Business," in *Nebula* (Glasgow), October 1957.
"By the Beard of the Comet," in *Fantastic Universe* (Chicago), December 1957.
"Never Trust a Robot," in *New Worlds* (London), January 1958.
"The Great Game," in *Nebula* (Glasgow), February 1958.
"The Unreluctant Tread" (War), in *New Worlds* (London), February 1958.
"Advertise Your Cyanide," in *Nebula* (Glasgow), April 1958.
"Out of Control," in *Science Fantasy* (Bournemouth), April 1958.
"Wisdom of the Gods," in *Nebula* (Glasgow), July, August, September, and October 1958.
"Space Command" (War), in *New Worlds* (London), August 1958.
"The Bones of Shoshun," in *Science Fantasy* (Bournemouth), October 1958.
"Survey Corpse," in *Nebula* (Glasgow), February 1959.
"The Gentle Approach," in *New Worlds* (London), June 1959.
"Castle of Vengeance," in *Science Fantasy* (Bournemouth), November 1959.
"The Halting Hand," in *Science Fiction Adventures* (London), December 1959.
"Profession, Spaceman," in *New Worlds* (London), March 1960.
"Greenie Gunner," in *New Worlds* (London), December 1960.
"Flame in the Flux Field," in *New Worlds* (London), March 1962.
"The Contraption," in *Science Fantasy* (Bournemouth), July 1964.
"A Case of Identity," in *Science Fantasy* (Bournemouth), August 1964.
"Draft Dodger," in *If* (New York), March 1966.
"Not Human," in *Alien Worlds* (Manchester), August 1966.
"Inside Out," in *Impulse* (London), December 1966.
"The Adjusted," in *Best from Fantasy and Science Fiction 16,* edited by Edward L. Ferman. New York, Doubleday, 1967; London, Gollancz, 1968.
"Swords for a Guide," in *Vision of Tomorrow,* (Newcastle upon Tyne), August 1969.
"Shapers of Men," in *Vision of Tomorrow* (Newcastle upon Tyne), November 1969.
"Station HR972," in *Nightmare Age,* edited by Frederik Pohl. New York, Ballantine, 1970.
"The Scales of Friendship," in *Vision of Tomorrow* (Newcastle upon Tyne), May 1970.
"Culpable in Glass," in *Vision of Tomorrow* (Newcastle upon Tyne), August 1970.
"A Memory of Golden Sunshine," in *New Writings in SF 19,* edited by John Carnell. London, Dobson, 1971.
"Aquaman," in *Space Two* edited by Richard Davis. London, Abelard Schuman, 1974.
"The Fowling," in *Beyond This Horizon,* edited by Christopher Carrell. Sunderland, Ceolfrith Press, 1974.
"Wizard of Scorpio" (as Alan Burt Akers), in *The DAW Science Fiction Reader,* edited by Donald A. Wollheim. New York, DAW, 1976.
"Psycho Sis," in *Fantasy and Science Fiction* (New York), April 1978.

OTHER PUBLICATIONS

Novels

White-Out (as Ernest Corley). London, Jarrolds, 1960.
The Dark Return (as Neil Langholm). London, Sphere, 1975.
By Pirate's Blood (as Richard Silver). New York, Pinnacle, 1975.
Jaws of Death (as Richard Silver). New York, Pinnacle, 1975.
Trail of Blood (as Neil Langholm). London, Sphere, 1976.
The Land of Mist (as Andrew Quiller). London, Mayflower, and New York, Pinnacle, 1976.
Sea of Swords (as Andrew Quiller). London, Mayflower, and New York, Pinnacle, 1976.
Brand of Vengeance (as Charles R. Pike). London, Mayflower, 1978.
Blind Run. London, Severn House, 1980.

Novels as Adam Hardy

The Press Gang. London, New English Library, and New York, Pinnacle, 1973.
Prize Money. London, New English Library, and New York, Pinnacle, 1973.
The Siege. London, New English Library, 1973; as *Savage Siege,* New York, Pinnacle, 1973.
Treasure. London, New English Library, 1973; as *Treasure Map,* New York, Pinnacle, 1974.
Powder Monkey. London, New English Library, 1973; as *Sailor's Blood,* New York, Pinnacle, 1974.
Blood for Breakfast. London, New English Library, 1974; as *Sea of Gold,* New York, Pinnacle, 1974.
Court Martial. London, New English Library, and New York, Pinnacle, 1974.
Battle Smoke. London, New English Library, 1974; New York, Pinnacle, 1975.
Cut and Thrust. London, New English Library, 1974; New York, Pinnacle, 1975.
Boarders Away. London, New English Library, and New York, Pinnacle, 1975.
Fireship. London, New English Library, 1975; New York, Pinnacle, 1976.
Blood Beach. London, New English Library, 1975.
Sea Flame. London, New English Library, 1976.
Close Quarters. London, New English Library, 1977.

Novels as Arthur Frazier

Oath of Blood. London, New English Library, 1973.
The King's Death. London, New English Library, 1973.
A Flame in the Fens. London, New English Library, 1974.
An Axe in Miklagard. London, New English Library, 1975.

Novels as Ken Blake

Where the Jungle Ends. London, Severn House, 1978.
Stake Out. London, Barker, 1978.
Hunter Hunted. London, Barker, 1978.
Long Shot. London, Severn House, 1979.
Blind Run. London, Sphere, 1979.
Fall Girl. London, Sphere, 1979.
Dead Reckoning. London, Sphere, 1980.

Novels as Bruno Krauss

Steel Shark. London, Sphere, 1978.
Shark North. London, Sphere, 1978.
Shark Pack. London, Sphere, 1978.
Shark Hunt. London, Sphere, 1980.

Other

The True Book about Space Travel (juvenile; as Kenneth Johns, with John Newman).   London, Muller, 1960.
Pretenders (juvenile).   London, New English Library, 1972.

Editor, *New Writings in SF 22-30.*   London, Sidgwick and Jackson, 8 vols., 1973-76, and London, Corgi, 1 vol., 1977.
Editor, *New Writings in SF Special 1-3.*   London, Sidgwick and Jackson, 1975-78 (vol. 1 edited with John Carnell).

Kenneth Bulmer comments:

If in an unwary moment I open one of my early books I find great difficulty in identifying with the writer. The immediate purpose of the writer appears plain enough; he is dazzled by a vision of what this literature called SF might achieve, and is concerned to express this vision in terms then available to him. There is genuine feeling; but he is handicapped by environment, editorial prejudice, and lack of data. There is an unfortunate assumption that other people will readily share his insights, that the vision is so self-evident it must be conveyed. His own interests in the fascinating details of, for instance, the future, space and time travel, the interactions and potentialities of the human mind and spirit, appear to overshadow what he is driving at. Imperceptive, top-of-the-head critics have said that most of the writer's work is space opera; a closer reading will reveal this statement to be untenable. The vision of what SF might achieve remains, dimmed a little, it is true, by the current state of general SF, and this writer has in recent years turned to other interests, including the Fox books (as Adam Hardy) and adult fantasy, both, incidentally, sharing that imaginative exploration of worlds unknown to the present day.

I have said many times, and will re-iterate, that SF is not respectable but is responsible. I remain unconvinced that this statement has been grasped by those to whom it is addressed. If poetry and non-establishment fiction are literatures of revolt, then SF is also. But it is more than merely a literature against, for example, the dead hand of authoritarianism or outmoded sexual mores: it is a literature against the spoliation of man by mankind's creations, which is by inference by man himself. This is not quite the same order of protest. This does not mean that SF is less as literature but more, for it incorporates more of life and, to enlarge a cliché, the felt responses within the emotional reactions to the human condition.

One underlying theme in my work is the exploration of the feelings and reactions of people forced, by the environment, other people, or inner compulsions, to perform acts and live lives far removed from what they would desire. As an introduction to my work I would instance the observation of a recent correspondent who remarked of my novels that they are filled with compassion all too often lacking in other works of SF.

*   *   *

If any single writer could epitomize the formularized science-fantasy milieu of Donald A. Wollheim's Ace Books, Kenneth Bulmer would be a good choice. Inasmuch as American adventure pulps took most of their formulaic elements from British adventure fiction, it might be fitting if Ace, Wollheim's tribute to the adventurous side of SF, were typified by a British writer who seemed devoted to formula for formula's sake.

It should be stressed, of course, that no author of narrative prose escapes formulaic elements—in fact, one measure of "art" might be that an artist emphasizes his meaning, his theme, to the extent that the story transcends its formulaic devices, as Conrad's stories rise above the classification of sea stories. A formula writer, however, emphasizes those devices—the plot, the action, the characters, (and in SF, the "idea" or paranormal concept)—and then he either ignores potential theme or gives it moderate attention at best. Ace Books did in fact print many SF adventures of the latter type—by Emil Petaja, whose theme involves the regeneration of ancient myth and myth-figures, and Leigh Brackett, whose theme evokes the tragedy and beauty of dying cultures. Yet Bulmer, a writer of the former mold, really represents Ace's virtual concentration on simple, diverting fantasy more aptly, though he cannot quite be dismissed as a "hack." Bulmer did for Ace's science-fantasy line what Edgar Wallace did for mysteries, and what Seabury Quinn did for

supernatural tales—that is, by the bulk of his efforts he demonstrated that the formula alone, followed in ritualistic manner, still had entertaining potentiality by sheer virtue of its diverse (though meaningless) imagery. In other words, unthematic but prolific writers like Bulmer, Wallace, and Quinn sustain a certain interest for the critic of their sub-genres approximate to that of Pop Art's importance in the scheme of modern art.

Bulmer's plots are his works' weakest components. Other formula elements can be, and have been, neglected in science-fantasy without necessarily diluting the significance of the potential theme. Jack Williamson might use stereotyped characters, Burroughs might overemphasize frenetic action, and Philip José Farmer might employ ideas of little originality, but in each case a mastery of strong plotting could carry at least a moderate thematic commitment. The plot of any adventure tale must be intricate enough to suggest a more intriguing version of reality, but the formlessness of Bulmer's plots suggests more the freewheeling absurdity of comedy. Instead of intensely focusing on the progress of the conflict, Bulmer lets his characters get sidetracked into smaller, distantly related episodic conflicts which serve little purpose but to delay the conclusion of the main conflict.

The Million Year Hunt does not suffer too badly from this but it shows the pattern in that a young man vows vengeance on the man who murders his sweetheart, but haphazardly gets transported to a planet where a discorporate alien intelligence becomes linked with him, and prods the hero to aid the alien's quest, whereby the hero serendipitously acquires both vengeance and a new girl. Less successful are *The Key to Irunium* and *The Key to Venudine,* which deal with confused humans who become involved in dimension-hopping conflicts between opposing factions, and *Cycle of Nemesis* in which a group of humans tries to imprison an ancient alien "demon" into his confining crypt, while the demon delays them by hurling them through time into different periods. This kind of bizarre scene-shifting was probably Bulmer's solution for the dull conventionality that pervades early novels like *The Secret of ZI* and *Behold the Stars.*

His best novel is probably the well-plotted *The Wizard of Starship Poseidon,* sort of an outer-space *Topkapi* or burglary caper. There is even a pro-scientific theme in the story of a scientist dedicated to reproducing scientifically the germinal process of life but who, deprived of a grant, decides to steal his funds from a military payroll. (Wittily enough, the grant is given to a literary theorist who hopes to prove that Shaw and Wells were the same person.) In this effort, Bulmer's tendency to overstock his stories with eccentric characters is a benefit, and he managed several good plot-twists without becoming vague. A runner-up for best work might be *The Star Venturers* in which a soldier-of-fortune is forced to track down an abducted prince by the prince's sister, not knowing that she intends to kill him and thereby keep the throne. The hero is motivated by an artificial life-form implanted in his skull which causes him pain if he does not seek the prince—which he does, in wild escapades against formidable odds. Bulmer was always a writer of good abilities, but has never quite found his metier—as in his later novels, which attempt to break from the adventure format into social satire, resulting in interesting but unoriginal works like *On the Symb-Socket Circuit* and *Roller Coaster World.*

—Gene Phillips

BUNCH, David R(oosevelt). American. Born in Lowry City, Missouri. Educated at Central Missouri State College, Warrensburg, B.S. 1946; Washington University, St. Louis, M.A. 1949; State University of Iowa, Iowa City, 1951-52. Served in the United States Army Air Force, 1942-46. Married Phyllis Geraldine Flette in 1951; one living daughter. Worked in cafeteria, as clerk and warehouseman, mail handler, druggist; staff member, Wagner Electric Company, St. Louis, 1953-54; civilian cartographer, Air Force Aeronautical Chart and Information Center, St. Louis, 1954-

73. Agent: Virginia Kidd, Box 278, Milford, Pennsylvania 18337. Address: P. O. Box 12233, Soulard Station, St. Louis, Missouri 63157, U.S.A.

SCIENCE-FICTION PUBLICATIONS

Novel

Moderan.   New York, Avon, 1971.

Uncollected Short Stories

"Routine Emergency," in *If* (New York), December 1957.
"That High-Up Blue Day That Saw the Black Sky-Train Come Spinning," in *Fantasy and Science Fiction* (New York), March 1968.
"In the Land of the Not-Unhappies," in *Fantastic* (New York), June 1970.
"Holdholtzer's Box," in *Protostars,* edited by David Gerrold and Stephen Goldin.   New York, Ballantine, 1971.
"Price of Leisure," in *Galaxy* (New York), May 1971.
"The Joke," in *Fantastic* (New York), August 1971.
"Doll for the End of the Day," in *Fantastic* (New York), October 1971.
"The Lady Was for Kroinking," in *Generation,* edited by David Gerrold.   New York, Dell, 1972.
"Training Talk No. 12," in *Fantasy and Science Fiction* (New York), January 1972.
"Two Suns for the King," in *If* (New York), April 1972.
"Up to the Edge of Heaven," in *Fantastic* (New York), April 1972.
"The Good War," in *Fantastic* (New York), December 1972.
"Breakout in Ecol 2," in *Nova 3,* edited by Harry Harrison.   New York, Walker, 1973.
"Seeing Stingy Ed," in *The Haunt of Horror* (New York), June 1973.
"Moment of Truth in Suburb Junction," in *Fantastic* (New York), September 1973.
"Helping Put the Rough Works to Jesse," in *Eternity 3* (Sandy Springs, South Carolina), 1974.
"Among the Metal-and-People People," in *New Dimensions 4,* edited by Robert Silverberg.   New York, New American Library, 1974.
"How Xmas Ghosts Are Made," in *Alternities,* edited by David Gerrold.   New York, Dell, 1974.
"Report from the Colony," in *SF Directions,* edited by Bruce McAllister.   Christchurch, Edge Press, 1974.
"Alien," in *Fantastic* (New York), January 1974.
"Short Time at the Pearly Gates," in *Fantastic* (New York), March 1974.
"In the Land That Aimed at Forever," in *Fantastic* (New York), May 1974.
"At Bugs Complete," in *Fantastic* (New York), July 1974.
"Why Not Some Hint?," in *Eternity 4* (Sandy Springs, South Carolina), 1975.
"End of a Singer," in *Fantastic* (New York), April 1975.
"The Strange Case of the Birds," in *Fantastic* (New York), December 1975.
"Mr. Who?," in *Fantastic* (New York), April 1978.
"Send Us a Planet?," in *Fantastic* (New York), July 1978.
"Pridey Goeth," in *Fantastic* (New York), October 1978.
"When the Metal Eaters Came," in *Galaxy* (New York), June-July 1979.
"New Member," in *Fantastic* (New York), July 1980.
"The Strange Rider of the Good Year," in *Amazing* (New York), November 1980.

David R. Bunch comments:

I do not write mainly to glorify the scientific accomplishments of mankind or to predict how more and more unbelievably astounding those accomplishments are apt eventually to be. And they are, I am convinced, destined to be astounding, increasingly frightening. But I am much haunted by many questions and a wistful wondering concerning the true worth of man in his spaceship outbound for the stars. Aren't "stars" right here the main stars we should be true-

headed for and in-bound toward? Is not that elusive Light of Godly humanness locked and hidden in the obscured soul of man our main objective? And shouldn't the other stars whirling "out there" be regarded as the inscrutable business of God?

But because I do have these heart questionings and this wistful wondering concerning importances, it must make of my science fiction writings something other than a glorification of hard science. I write what the trade knows as "soft" science fiction, wherein social statement is as important as the soul-less telling of how a piece of machinery behaves. In many ways I am almost anti-science in my science-fiction writings. I believe we have upped too much our search for greater and still greater technological triumphs and lessened to our loss the quest for a clearer and brighter understanding of that sometimes blinding Light which is, or should be, our very sacred souls.

So I write not to shout-scream the glories of our great science breakthroughs, or to predict even greater thrusts. I write with more urgent business in mind: to make the reader "see," through my sometimes grim social statements and my often stark satirical comments—both apt to be perverse, even cynical—what worship of science may do in irretrievable detriment to Man and his Earth.

Did human kind come this far on our faltering, seeking, sometimes glorious course only to dehumanize ourselves and become of no greater significance than the machines themselves that once we used as an aid in our search for significances?

*   *   *

David R. Bunch's short, idiosyncratic stories have, almost invariably, been met with varying degrees of outrage from readers unwilling to work with his convoluted prose to reach the plot that to most is opaque. In his own way Bunch is one of the most original and creative writers in the genre, and it is unfortunate that the conservative bent of most readers is such that he is not given the attention he deserves.

The bulk of his work has been a loosely organized series set against the background of Moderan, several dozen of which have been collected as a book under that title. Moderan is a thoroughly repulsive future to rank with the Nebishes of T.J. Bass. Humans have acquired immortality, or as near to it as matters, through replacement of most of their body parts with metal. In fact, only a few flesh strips remain, the tiniest traces of humanity. Their physical transformation is matched by their emotional one. Most humans live in highly armed castles, called Strongholds. The protagonist of most of the series is Stronghold Ten, a man who early in the series is fitted with metallic limbs and organs, and makes use of his determination to make himself the foremost warmaker in the land. He alternates between highly mechanized combat and resting in his hip-snuggie chair within his stronghold, watching the sky change color as each month a new vapor shield is erected, or gazing out across his garden of metal flowers.

The series does much better as a whole than as individual stories, most of which are extremely episodic. Several do stand fairly well alone, particularly "Was She Horrid?" wherein Stronghold Ten is visited by a female, "The Walking, Talking I-Don't-Care Man" in which he has a male visitor, and "How It Ended" which concludes the first cycle of Moderan stories. An uncollected Moderan story, "Two Suns for the King," is as good as anything in the collection; Stronghold Ten is struck with an undeniable urge to grow something organic, and can find no unpolluted soil to work with.

There are literally dozens of stories not in the Moderan series, some of which fall into a lesser series of "Training Talks" by a male parent to his two young children. In one of his more straightforward stories, "Holdholtzer's Box," a scientist invents a box wherein he expects to entice people to their deaths. The interface between man and machine, so obvious in the Moderan stories, is present in much of his other work. A road clearing crew fails to distinguish between auto wreckage and human flesh in "Routine Emergency," for example, and people are lobotomized to happiness in "In the Land of the Not Unhappies."

The best single story may well be "That High-Up Blue Day That Saw the Black Sky-Train Come Spinning." In a style reminiscent of the best of R.A. Lafferty, Bunch introduces us to a group of aging nonconformists who decide that children need to be saved from the horrible fate of growing up. And they succeed. Another story that is extremely effective, though enigmatic, is "The Strange Case of the Birds" wherein an increasing number of people begin to see a malformed bird shape outlined against the moon.

Bunch often assails human vanity, rarely as well as in "Pridey Goeth," in which a town is taken in by a clever potion purveyor, and literally falls mortally wounded as the result. His clear-sighted view of the narrowmindedness of humanity is reinforced to a certain extent by the general reaction to his work, but it appears that Bunch is far more interested in making the statements he feels necessary than in gaining critical acclaim.

—Don D'Ammassa

BUPP, Walter. *See* GARRETT, Randall.

BURDICK, Eugene (Leonard). American. Born in Sheldon, Iowa, 1 January 1918. Educated at Stanford University, California, B.A. 1942; Magdalen College, Oxford (Rhodes Scholar), Ph.D. 1950. Served in the United States Navy, 1942-46: Lieutenant Commander; Navy-Marine Corps Cross. Married Carol Warren in 1942; two daughters and one son. Staff Member, Naval War College, Newport, Rhode Island, 1950-51; staff member, then Professor of Political Theory, University of California, Berkeley, 1951-65. Recipient: Houghton Mifflin Literary Fellowship, 1956. *Died 26 July 1965.*

SCIENCE-FICTION PUBLICATIONS

Novel

Fail-Safe, with Harvey Wheeler.   New York, McGraw Hill, 1962; London, Hutchinson, 1963.

OTHER PUBLICATIONS

Novels

The Ninth Wave.   Boston, Houghton Mifflin, and London, Gollancz, 1956.
The Ugly American, with William J. Lederer.   New York, Norton, 1958; London, Gollancz, 1959.
The 480.   New York, McGraw Hill, and London, Gollancz, 1964.
Sarkhan, with William J. Lederer.   New York, McGraw Hill, 1965; London, Putnam, 1966.
Nina's Book.   Boston, Houghton Mifflin, and London, Putnam, 1965.

Short Stories

A Role in Manila: Fifteen Tales of War, Postwar, Peace, and Adventure.   New York, New American Library, 1966.

Other

The Blue of Capricorn.   Boston, Houghton Mifflin, 1961; London, Gollancz, 1962.

Editor, with Arthur J. Brodbeck, *American Voting Behavior.* Glencoe, Illinois, Free Press, 1959.

* * *

Eugene Burdick, author of numerous and very successful works of political intrigue, seems, at first glance, an odd inclusion in a discussion of science fiction. To begin with, *Fail-Safe,* the only work of his that could be so classified, is a collaborative effort. Harvey Wheeler's contribution, however, is merely technical and he functions mainly as political advisor in much the same capacity as William J. Lederer in other works. The literary talent is Burdick's, and it is he who is usually accepted as author.

It is not easy to pin *Fail-Safe* down as science fiction in the general sense. Burdick claimed that *Fail-Safe* is not science fiction, but "true," and that its events "ultimately will occur," an opinion, he admits, based only on unclassified material. Even more amazingly he stated in one interview that the holocaust is "inevitable." Moreover the scientific reliability of the novel is questionable. We read of miles instead of knots per hour, of navigating by the stars instead of by instruments, of missile launchings that are counted down instead of immediately activated and warheads that travel too fast for sub-orbital flight. Indeed, the thread of the plot, that a lowly condensor in a single computer could trigger a unilateral thermonuclear assault by a superpower is more than a little presumptuous. In fact, in November 1979 and several times in June 1980, just this type of near-accident occurred without apocalyptic results. But very often what is technically absurd reality can be very good science fiction. However, as one would assume, where there is trouble with science there is likely to be trouble with fiction. Burdick tends to manipulate his characters, flat and stereotypical though they are, with all the glee of the scientist inventing devious behavioral predicaments for his specimens. These situations, unfortunately, become the plot.

Fail-Safe, then, reflects the major problem of much of the new science fiction (*The Manchurian Candidate,* for example, or Peter Bryant's *Two Hours to Doom*)—it comes too close to reality to be just fiction but not close enough to be anything else. These authors risk, at some point, losing the advantage of artistic distance that placing their work in the past or future might give them. And, unlike other examples of contemporary SF, there is little fantasy and considerably less wonder, once considered indispensable elements of the genre.

It is easy to see, then, that it is not literary merit but theme that remains the novel's most important contribution to science fiction. The attitude that man, a very fallible creature, is incapable of building a machine that is itself infallible, a perfectible extension of his own mind, is a common one in SF, as is the theme of the possible (inevitable?) destruction of mankind. But the considerable originality of the novel is the assumption that what usually chills a reader when actualized on strange planets and distant galaxies will be intensified when placed here now. This has proved true. This novel and others like it (*On the Beach, Alas Babylon,* etc.) have created a new and socially important brand of science fiction with their concern not with prescient fantasy and technical razzle-dazzle but with certain human truths more familiarly associated with "literary" fiction. Burdick has described a society where men of authority and power are bereft of feeling and devoid of morality and, even worse, impotent and inept. It is a society where politicians care only for electoral results and scientists for cold facts, where military men are conditioned to mindless obedience far beyond grandiose thoughts of self-preservation, and technicians treat their work as an art form with no thought of the ultimate outcome of a job well done.

Burdick's vision is clear and his message plain: man decreases his tenuous control of the world as he increasingly complicates it. By ever more reliance on computerization he gives away his powers of thought to thoughts of power. His programmed alter egos are shadowy logicians created to free their inventors not merely from the rigors of calculation and precision but, more insidiously, from conscience and morality. This is Burdick's warning—mankind is reaching a period of technological dependence where it may become no longer safe to fail.

—James A. Livezey

BURGESS, Anthony. Pseudonym for John Anthony Burgess Wilson; also writes as Joseph Kell. British. Born in Manchester, Lancashire, 25 February 1917. Educated at Xaverian College, Manchester; Manchester University, B.A. in English 1940. Served in the British Army Education Corps, 1940-46: Sergeant-Major. Married 1)Llewela Isherwood Jones in 1942 (died, 1968); 2) Liliana Macellari in 1968, one son. Lecturer, Extra-Mural Department, Birmingham University, 1946-48; Education Officer and Lecturer, Central Advisory Council for Adult Education in the Forces, 1946-48; Lecturer, Ministry of Education, 1948-50; English Master, Banbury Grammar School, Oxfordshire, 1950-54; Colonial Service Education Officer, Malaya and Brunei, 1954-59. Writer in Residence, University of North Carolina, Chapel Hill, 1969-70; Professor, Columbia University, New York, 1970-71; Visiting Fellow, Princeton University, New Jersey, 1970-71; Distinguished Professor, City University of New York, 1972-73. Since 1972, Literary Adviser, Guthrie Theatre, Minneapolis. Also composer. Fellow, Royal Society of Literature, 1969. Address: 44 Rue Grimaldi, Monaco.

SCIENCE-FICTION PUBLICATIONS

Novels

A Clockwork Orange. London, Heinemann, 1962; New York, Norton, 1963.
The Wanting Seed. London, Heinemann, 1962; New York, Norton, 1963.
The Eve of Saint Venus. London, Sidgwick and Jackson, 1964; New York, Norton, 1970.
1985. London, Hutchinson, and Boston, Little Brown, 1978.

Uncollected Short Story

"The Muse," in *Best SF 1969,* edited by Brian Aldiss and Harry Harrison. New York, Putnam, and London, Sphere, 1970.

OTHER PUBLICATIONS

Novels

Time for a Tiger. London, Heinemann, 1956.
The Enemy in the Blanket. London, Heinemann, 1958.
Beds in the East. London, Heinemann, 1959.
The Right to an Answer. London, Heinemann, 1960; New York, Norton, 1961.
The Doctor Is Sick. London, Heinemann, 1960; New York, Norton, 1966.
The Worm and the Ring. London, Heinemann, 1961; revised edition, 1970.
Devil of a State. London, Heinemann, 1961; New York, Norton, 1970.
One Hand Clapping (as Joseph Kell). London, Davies, 1961; as Anthony Burgess, New York, Knopf, 1972.
Honey for the Bears. London, Heinemann, 1963; New York, Norton, 1964.
Inside Mr. Enderby (as Joseph Kell). London, Heinemann, 1963.
Nothing Like the Sun: A Story of Shakespeare's Love-Life. London, Heinemann, and New York, Norton, 1964.
The Malayan Trilogy (includes *Time for a Tiger, The Enemy in the Blanket, Beds in the East*). London, Pan, 1964; as *The Long Day Wanes,* New York, Norton, 1965.
A Vision of Battlements. London, Sidgwick and Jackson, 1965; New York, Norton, 1966.
Tremor of Intent. London, Heinemann, and New York, Norton, 1966.
Enderby Outside. London, Heinemann, 1968.
Enderby (includes *Inside Mr. Enderby* and *Enderby Outside*). New York, Norton, 1968.
MF. London, Cape, and New York, Knopf, 1971.
Napoleon Symphony. London, Cape, and New York, Knopf, 1974.

The Clockwork Testament; or, Enderby's End. London, Hart Davis MacGibbon, 1974; New York, Knopf, 1975.
Beard's Roman Women. New York, McGraw Hill, 1976; London, Hutchinson, 1977.
Abba Abba. London, Faber, 1977; Boston, Little Brown, 1978.
Man of Nazareth. New York, McGraw Hill, 1979; London, Magnum, 1980.
Earthly Powers. London, Hutchinson, and New York, Simon and Schuster, 1980.

Short Story

Will and Testament: A Fragment of Biography. Verona, Plain Wrapper Press, 1977.

Plays

Cyrano, music by Michael J. Lewis, lyrics by Burgess, adaptation of the play by Rostand (produced Minneapolis, 1971; New York, 1973). New York, Knopf, 1971.
Oedipus the King, adaptation of a play by Sophocles (produced Minneapolis, 1972; Southampton, Hampshire, 1979). Minneapolis, University of Minnesota Press, 1972; London, Oxford University Press, 1973.

Television Plays: *Moses the Law-giver,* 1975; *Jesus of Nazareth,* with Suso d'Amico and Franco Zeffirelli, 1979.

Verse

Moses: A Narrative. London, Dempsey and Squires, and New York, Stonehill, 1976.
A Christmas Recipe. Verona, Plain Wrapper Press, 1977.

Other

English Literature: A Survey for Students (as John Burgess Wilson). London, Longman, 1958.
The Novel Today. London, Longman, 1963; Folcroft, Pennsylvania, Folcroft Editions, 1971.
Language Made Plain. London, English Universities Press, 1964; New York, Crowell, 1965; revised edition, London, Fontana, 1975.
Here Comes Everybody: An Introduction to James Joyce for the Ordinary Reader. London, Faber, 1965; as *Re Joyce,* New York, Norton, 1965.
The Novel Now: A Student's Guide to Contemporary Fiction. London, Faber, and New York, Norton, 1967; revised edition, Faber, 1971.
Urgent Copy: Literary Studies. London, Cape, 1968; New York, Norton, 1969.
"H.G. Wells," in *New York Times Book Review,* 3 August 1969.
Shakespeare. London, Cape, and New York, Knopf, 1970.
Joysprick: An Introduction to the Language of James Joyce. London, Deutsch, 1973; New York, Harcourt Brace, 1975.
Obscenity and the Arts (lecture). Valletta, Malta Library Association, 1973.
A Long Trip to Teatime (juvenile). London, Dempsey and Squires, 1976; New York, Stonehill, 1978.
New York, with the editors of Time-Life books. New York, Time, 1976.
Ernest Hemingway and His World. London, Thames and Hudson, and New York, Scribner, 1978.
The Land Where Ice Cream Grows (juvenile). Tonbridge, Kent, Benn, and New York, Doubleday, 1979.

Editor, *Coaching Days of England.* London, Elek, 1966.
Editor, *A Journal of the Plague Year,* by Daniel Defoe. London, Penguin, 1966.
Editor, *A Shorter Finnegans Wake,* by James Joyce. London, Faber, 1966; New York, Viking Press, 1967.
Editor, with Francis Haskell, *The Age of the Grand Tour.* London, Elek, and New York, Crown, 1967.
Editor, *Malaysian Stories,* by W. Somerset Maugham. Singapore, Heinemann, 1969.

Translator, with Llewela Burgess, *The New Aristocrats,* by Michel de Saint-Pierre. London, Gollancz, 1962.

Translator, with Llewela Burgess, *The Olive Trees of Justice,* by Jean Pelegri. London, Sidgwick and Jackson, 1962.

Translator, *The Man Who Robbed Poor Boxes,* by Jean Servin. London, Gollancz, 1965.

*

Bibliography: *Anthony Burgess: An Enumerative Bibliography* by Paul Boytinck, Norwood, Pennsylvania, Norwood Editions, 1974.

Manuscript Collection: Mills Memorial Library, Hamilton, Ontario.

*   *   *

Anthony Burgess's critical survey of fiction *The Novel Now* devotes a chapter to science fiction; he has paid some attention to it as a book reviewer, and even used science-fiction bits and pieces in several novels. His own works of science fiction are melodramatic but not comfortable adventures with cardboard cutouts in rocket-ships; they are studies of character, language, society, and the possibility of morality in a world which declares it meaningless. Burgess's world-view is agnostic in doubting God's presence, but Manichean in hypothesizing a conflict between evil and good.

The makings of a dystopian future are present in the social stupor and mindless violence of England in *The Right to an Answer,* the double-think and sexual ambiguity of Russia in *Honey for the Bears,* and the East-West conflict of his "eschatological spy novel," *Tremor of Intent,* all set against the backdrop of imminent nuclear holocaust. Precognition in *One Hand Clapping* is Howard Shirley's means to gain enough money to show his wife, Janet, that the material life is not worth living; he fails, and her narration shows why, but the science fiction is peripheral. It is even more so in *Inside Mr. Enderby,* whose protagonist finds his poem about a minotaur has been made into a dreadful movie, *Son of the Beast from Outer Space.*

That may have been prescient, since Stanley Kubrick brought fame to Burgess with his movie adapted from *A Clockwork Orange* (it departed considerably from the book, and earned the novelist only a consultant's fee). In a neo-Orwellian future, there are men on the moon but youth gangs mug and rape the old and young at will, provoking police-state responses. The kids drink narcotic-laced milk, speak a Russian-rooted slang, "Nadsat," and may be subjected to perfected aversive conditioning. After treating us to his version of the joys of sex (a mechanical "in-out in-out"), of the "ultra-violent," and of classical music (especially the last movement of Beethoven's Ninth), Alex explains how his buddies ("droogs") got him arrested for beating up ("tolchocking") an old woman ("starry ptitsa"), whose death gets him imprisoned. To get out, he volunteers for the "Lodovico treatment," which conditions him to avoid all three loves, leaving him helpless. Victimized by old victims, he is befriended by one of them, unaware. Author of an essay, "A Clockwork Orange," this man, F. Alexander, uses Alex to change his political party from "outs" to "ins." "Cured," Alex returns to his old ways, unless we accept as canonical the last chapter of the first (English) edition, which rounds out his life, death, and resurrection. This controversial episode shows Alex thinking of growing up and settling down; solving his problem, perhaps, it does not help us choose between his crimes and those of the State. Both cure and disease are repugnant to Burgess (Kubrick is less equivocal); the State is more culpable, but its manipulation is only a step beyond that which made Alex a "clockwork orange" in the first place.

The symmetry of the original three seven-chapter sections, pointed inversions of victims and victimizers, parallels between Alex and his benefactor, "Lodovico," and "Ludwig van," show Burgess's conscious artistry, but his most striking device is "Nadsat." To understand Alex, the reader literally must learn his language, not that difficult in context though most editions now dilute the effect with a glossary. Verbal violence both shields the reader from and exposes him to physical violence, while learning to understand Alex leads to condoning his behavior, and accepting the conditioning effects of society in general. Although Alex accepts matter-of-factly his own allegiance not to goodness, but to "the

other shop," the question of good-and-evil is both raised and rendered all but moot.

Burgess later labelled this book "too didactic, too linguistically exhibitionistic," but his other major dystopian novel, *The Wanting Seed,* employs a comparable amount of violent melodrama and stylistic versatility to display the Manichean dilemma. Treated here in historical context, it involves a "Pelphase" (Pelagian perfectibility), an "Interphase" (chaotic brutality), and a "Gusphase" (Augustinian contrition). Fantastically accelerated, this cycle takes little more than a year to go from an overpopulated age in which homosexuality is the key to advancement and unauthorized fertility a fatal offense to a plague-ridden world sacrificed to by massacre, orgies, and cannibalism mocking Christian communion. A return to actual Christianity, outlawed in the Pelphase, and active heterosexuality is witnessed by Tristram Foxe, his wife Beatrice-Joanna, and his brother (her lover) Derek. Flamboyantly homo, Derek becomes dutifully hetero, maintaining his executive rank as his Ministry changes from Infertility to its opposite. In prison, then the army, where he alone lives through a massacre, Tristram goes through Hell to return to his unfaithful wife. Having run away to bear twins, she is a living monument to ambivalence, naming them Derek and Tristram and claiming both men as fathers, husbands, and lovers. Less grounded in realism, more obviously a fable, this book has been taken by some critics to be more optimistic than the other. But the restoration of fertility is not an improvement, rather a restatement of the individual-State conflict in the context of a future crisis.

Burgess revisited dystopia in *1985,* not a novel but a critique of Orwell's "cacotopia" (and his own), partly in fictional form. A loosely strung essay discusses the strengths, flaws, contemporary sources, and historical roots of *Nineteen Eighty-Four,* explicitly relating them to Pelagian and Augustinian theology. The talky story concerns the abortive fight of common man Bev Jones against the system, suggesting what the next seven years might bring to England in the form of economic chaos, breakdown in human relationships, and Arab-dominated return to religion (Islam, of course), with practically none of the invention, wit, or style of its predecessors.

If that vein was played out, another one he might have mined is suggested by a short story reflecting his continued preoccupation with fate, language, and artists who care about both. Next to Joyce, his favorite subject is Shakespeare, about whom Burgess has written a biography and a novel (pastiching Elizabethan style), *Nothing Like the Sun.* In "The Muse" Shakespearean scholar Paley visits a parallel Earth's Renaissance England to prove that actor didn't write those plays. Hallucination, if not madness, awaits him, but his point is proven, though he doesn't know it; the plays he, like previous visitors, has brought with him Shakespeare takes to revise for performance in his own time. A jape, not a serious accounting for that "impossible" genius, this story, with its surrealistic effects and its subjugation of scientific theory and technological expense to extravagant fantasy, was right at home in the New Wave of English science fiction.

On balance, Burgess's science fiction may be said to lack verisimilitude and extrapolative exactness, and to suffer from obsession with a single theme. But his fables are prophetic in an Old Testament way, and what he had done with style and invention almost with one hand dwarfs the accomplishments of many other writers' lifelong careers.

—David N. Samuelson

———————————

BURKE, Ralph. *See* **GARRETT, Randall.**

———————————

BURROUGHS, Edgar Rice. Also wrote as John Tyler McCulloch. American. Born in Chicago, Illinois, 1 September 1875. Educated at the Harvard School, Chicago, 1888-91; Phillips Academy, Andover, Massachusetts, 1891-92; Michigan Military Academy, Orchard Lake, 1892-95. Served in the United States 7th Cavalry, 1896-97; Illinois Reserve Militia, 1918-19. Married 1) Emma Centennia Hulbert in 1900 (divorced, 1934), two sons and one daughter; 2) Florence Dearholt in 1935 (divorced, 1942). Instructor and Assistant Commandant, Michigan Military Academy, 1895-96; owner of a stationery store, Pocatello, Idaho, 1898; worked in his father's American Battery Company, Chicago, 1899-1903; joined his brother's Sweetser-Burroughs Mining Company, Idaho, 1903-04; railroad policeman, Oregon Short Line Railroad Company, Salt Lake City, 1904; Manager of the Stenographic Department, Sears Roebuck and Company, Chicago, 1906-08; Partner, Burroughs and Dentzer, advertising contractors, Chicago, 1908-09; Office Manager, Physicians Co-Operative Association, Chicago, 1909; Partner, Stace-Burroughs Company, salesmanship firm, Chicago, 1909; worked for Champlain Yardley Company, stationers, Chicago, 1910-11; Manager, System Service Bureau, Chicago, 1912-13; free-lance writer after 1913; formed Edgar Rice Burroughs Inc., publishers, 1913, Burroughs-Tarzan Enterprises, 1934-39, and Burroughs-Tarzan Pictures, 1934-37; lived in California after 1919; Mayor of Malibu Beach, 1933; also United Press Correspondent in the Pacific during World War II, and Columnist ("Laugh It Off"), *Honolulu Advertiser,* 1941-42, 1945. *Died 19 March 1950.*

SCIENCE-FICTION PUBLICATIONS

Novels (series: Mars; Pellucidar; Venus)

A Princess of Mars. Chicago, McClurg, 1917; London, Methuen, 1919.
The Gods of Mars. Chicago, McClurg, 1918; London, Methuen, 1920.
The Warlord of Mars. Chicago, McClurg, 1919; London, Methuen, 1920.
Thuvia, Maid of Mars. Chicago, McClurg, 1920; London, Methuen, 1921.
The Chessmen of Mars. Chicago, McClurg, 1922; London, Methuen, 1923.
At the Earth's Core (Pellucidar). Chicago, McClurg, 1922; London, Methuen, 1923.
Pellucidar. Chicago, McClurg, 1923; London, Methuen, 1924.
The Master Mind of Mars. Chicago, McClurg, 1928; London, Methuen, 1939.
The Monster Men. Chicago, McClurg, 1929.
Tarzan at the Earth's Core (Pellucidar). New York, Metropolitan, 1930; London, Methuen, 1938.
Tanar of Pellucidar. New York, Metropolitan, 1930; London, Methuen, 1939.
A Fighting Man of Mars. New York, Metropolitan, 1931; London, Lane, 1932.
Jungle Girl. Tarzana, California, Burroughs, 1932; London, Odhams Press, 1933; as *The Land of Hidden Men,* New York, Ace, 1963.
Pirates of Venus. Tarzana, California, Burroughs, 1934; London, Lane, 1935.
Lost on Venus. Tarzana, California, Burroughs, 1935; London, Methuen, 1937.
Swords of Mars. Tarzana, California, Burroughs, 1936; London, New English Library, 1966.
Back to the Stone Age (Pellucidar). Tarzana, California, Burroughs, 1937.
Carson of Venus. Tarzana, California, Burroughs, 1939; London, Goulden, 1950.
Synthetic Men of Mars. Tarzana, California, Burroughs, 1940; London, Methuen, 1941.
Land of Terror (Pellucidar). Tarzana, California, Burroughs, 1944.
Escape on Venus. Tarzana, California, Burroughs, 1946; London, New English Library, 1966.
Beyond the Farthest Star. New York, Ace, 1964.

Short Stories

The Land That Time Forgot. Chicago, McClurg, 1924; London, Methuen, 1925.
The Eternal Lover. Chicago, McClurg, 1925; London, Methuen, 1927; as *The Eternal Savage,* New York, Ace, 1963.
The Cave Girl. Chicago, McClurg, 1925; London, Methuen, 1927.
The Moon Maid. Chicago, McClurg, 1926; London, Stacey, 1972; abridged edition, as *The Moon Men,* New York, Canaveral Press, 1962; augmented edition, London, Tandem, 1975.
Llana of Gathol. Tarzana, California, Burroughs, 1948; London, New English Library, 1967.
Beyond Thirty. Privately printed, 1955; as *The Lost Continent,* New York, Ace, 1963.
The Man-Eater. Privately printed, 1955.
Savage Pellucidar. New York, Canaveral Press, 1963.
Tales of Three Planets. New York, Canaveral Press, 1964.
John Carter of Mars. New York, Canaveral Press, 1964.
The Wizard of Venus. New York, Ace, 1970.

OTHER PUBLICATIONS

Novels

Tarzan of the Apes. Chicago, McClurg, 1914; London, Methuen, 1917.
The Return of Tarzan. Chicago, McClurg, 1915; London, Methuen, 1918.
The Beasts of Tarzan. Chicago, McClurg, 1916; London, Methuen, 1918.
The Son of Tarzan. Chicago, McClurg, 1917; London, Methuen, 1919.
Tarzan and the Jewels of Opar. Chicago, McClurg, 1918; London, Methuen, 1919.
Tarzan the Terrible. Chicago, McClurg, and London, Methuen, 1921.
Tarzan and the Golden Lion. Chicago, McClurg, 1923; London, Methuen, 1924.
The Girl from Hollywood. New York, Macaulay, 1923; London, Methuen, 1924.
Tarzan and the Ant Men. Chicago, McClurg, 1924; London, Methuen, 1925.
The Bandit of Hell's Bend. Chicago, McClurg, 1925; London, Methuen, 1926.
The Tarzan Twins (juvenile). Joliet, Illinois, Volland, 1927; London, Collins, 1930.
The Outlaw of Torn. Chicago, McClurg, and London, Methuen, 1927.
The War Chief. Chicago, McClurg, 1927; London, Methuen, 1928.
Tarzan, Lord of the Jungle. Chicago, McClurg, and London, Cassell, 1928.
Tarzan and the Lost Empire. New York, Metropolitan, 1929; London, Cassell, 1931.
Tarzan the Invincible. Tarzana, California, Burroughs, 1931; London, Lane, 1933.
Tarzan Triumphant. Tarzana, California, Burroughs, 1931; London, Lane, 1933.
Tarzan and the City of Gold. Tarzana, California, Burroughs, 1933; London, Lane, 1936.
Apache Devil. Tarzana, California, Burroughs, 1933.
Tarzan and the Lion-Man. Tarzana, California, Burroughs, 1934; London, W.H. Allen, 1950.
Tarzan and the Leopard Men. Tarzana, California, Burroughs, 1935; London, Lane, 1936.
Tarzan and the Tarzan Twins, with Jad-Bal-Ja, The Golden Lion (juvenile). Racine, Wisconsin, Whitman, 1936.
Tarzan's Quest. Tarzana, California, Burroughs, 1936; London, Methuen, 1938.
The Oakdale Affair; The Rider. Tarzana, California, Burroughs, 1937.
Tarzan and the Forbidden City. Tarzana, California, Burroughs, 1938; London, W.H. Allen, 1950.
The Lad and the Lion. Tarzana, California, Burroughs, 1938.

The Deputy Sheriff of Comanche County. Tarzana, California, Burroughs, 1940.
Tarzan and the Foreign Legion. Tarzana, California, Burroughs, 1947; London, W.H. Allen, 1949.
Tarzan and the Madman. New York, Canaveral Press, 1964; London, New English Library, 1966.
The Girl from Farris's. Kansas City, Missouri, House of Greystoke, 1965.
The Efficiency Expert. Kansas City, Missouri, House of Greystoke, 1966.
I Am a Barbarian. Tarzana, California, Burroughs, 1967.
Pirate Blood (as John Tyler McCulloch). New York, Ace, 1970.

Short Stories

Jungle Tales of Tarzan. Chicago, McClurg, and London, Methuen, 1919.
Tarzan the Untamed. Chicago, McClurg, and London, Methuen, 1920.
The Mucker. Chicago, McClurg, 1921; as *The Mucker* and *The Man Without a Soul,* London, Methuen, 2 vols., 1921-22.
The Mad King. Chicago, McClurg, 1926.
Tarzan the Magnificent. Tarzana, California, Burroughs, 1939; London, Methuen, 1940.
Tarzan and the Castaways. New York, Canaveral Press, 1964; London, New English Library, 1966.

Other

Official Guide of the Tarzan Clans of America. Privately printed, 1939.

*

Bibliography: in *Edgar Rice Burroughs, The Man Who Created Tarzan* by Irwin Porges, Provo, Utah, Brigham Young University Press, 1975; London, New English Library, 1976.

*   *   *

While best known for his long series of jungle adventure tales featuring the character Tarzan, both in their original prose form and in uncounted motion pictures, television series, comic strips, and other adaptations, Edgar Rice Burroughs was in fact a very important and very popular science-fiction writer. In a lifetime output of more than 70 books, essentially equal numbers were devoted to jungle adventures and to science fiction. Burroughs's remaining output was widely distributed among westerns, Graustarkian romances, historical novels, and a few decidedly unsuccessful attempts at contemporary realism. The last group, most notably *The Girl from Hollywood,* are of interest for their autobiographical content. As a science-fiction writer Burroughs may be regarded as a descendant of Verne. His emphasis was on wonders: wonderful planets, strange creatures, magnificently melodramatic plots. Burroughs was himself of plebeian origins, but his works more often display a bias in favor of aristocracy. His heroes are generally noblemen and/or wealthy, e.g., Lord Greystoke (Tarzan), John Carter (Confederate cavalry captain and plantation owner), David Innes (scion of Connecticut gentry). His heroines are often princesses, most notably Dejah Thoris, eventual consort of John Carter. (Exceptions include the hoodlum hero of *The Mucker* and the prostitute heroine of *The Girl from Farris's.*)

It is important to note that Burroughs was not a significant creator in his writing, but rather was a synthesist of immeasurable natural talent. Every major theme in Burroughs's fantastic fiction (i.e., science fiction and jungle adventures) was anticipated in earlier works. Burroughs's genius lay in his ability to invest familiar material with such energy that it attained new heights of popularity. He did not invent the feral-man novel, the hollow-earth novel, the interplanetary romance, or any other significant fantastic form. He *did* write some of the most successful, most completely developed, most colorful, energetic, and suspenseful examples of each. Burroughs's science fiction divides into three major series, one minor series, and several independent works, two of which are of major importance.

Burroughs's literary career began, at least as far as published fiction is concerned, with the first of his interplanetary romances, *A Princess of Mars.* This novel and its sequels concern an earthly hero of somewhat equivocal and mysterious immortality who is transferred to Mars by a means that suggests astral projection. On Mars ("Barsoom") the hero discovers a dying world containing an ancient, decadent civilization, roving nomadic tribes, and a complex mixture of races, species, and traditions. Through a series of some 11 volumes John Carter rises to the supreme Warlordship of Barsoom, marries the incomparably beautiful red-skinned Princess Dejah Thoris (who lays eggs but is otherwise wholly human), becomes a father and grandfather, travels extensively upon Barsoom, visits one of its moons, and ultimately journeys to the planet Jupiter. There he presumably remains (he was in the midst of an uncompleted adventure when Burroughs died). While some of Burroughs's more ardent admirers consider Barsoom and all its associated material a brilliantly original creation, it was in fact the very opposite. The character of John Carter is virtually identical to that of Phra the Phoenician, while the basic rationale of Barsoomian history and culture closely resembles that of the planet Mars in a book called *Lieut. Gulliyar Jones: His Vacation;* both books are by Edwin Lester Arnold. More of the Barsoomian culture and many of the plotting devices used by Burroughs appear in *Journey to Mars* by Gustavus Pope, in *Across the Zodiac* by Percy Greg, and even in some of the strange Theosophical teachings of Helena Blavatsky (as pointed out by L. Sprague de Camp). And the dueling, kidnapping, impersonating, court-intrigue ridden Barsoomian society, possibly borrowed from Pope, in itself is more than suggestively reminiscent of the court at Zenda as recorded by Anthony Hope, who might well have borrowed from Mark Twain!

Burroughs's second most significant science-fiction series was the Pellucidar books, beginning with *At the Earth's Core.* While the later books of this series are of inferior quality, the first two or three are among Burroughs's best work. Here the essential notion is that of an earth-boring machine accidentally breaking through the planet's crust to discover that the earth is hollow, illuminated by a miniature interior sun, and inhabited by a wide variety of species including primitive humans and paleontological survivals. Once again, elements derive from numerous earlier works, certainly including Holberg's *Nils Klim* and Verne's *Journey to the Center of the Earth,* and very likely (the name itself is suggestive) Bradshaw's *The Goddess of Atvatabar.* While the Pellucidar series does let down in quality, it contains numerous fascinating features. One of these is a speculation—this one more likely original to Burroughs—on the nature of time and the timeless condition of a world of eternal daylight. There is considerable humorous and satirical material in the books. Also of interest is the so-called "series cross-over" volume, *Tarzan at the Earth's Core,* in which the two separately created universes of Tarzan's jungle world and the hollow earth, are merged—or at least, one may say, their separation is bridged via dirigible.

Burroughs's final science-fiction series details the adventures of Carson Napier on Venus. The books of this sequence date from late in Burroughs's career and are derivative of his Martian cycle without ever quite duplicating its spirit. There is also a degree of likelihood that the Venus books were written to strike back at Otis Adelbert Kline, who had written a series of interplanetary romances laid on Venus, under heavy influence of Burroughs's Martian cycle. (This theory is advanced by Sam Moskowitz, and is circumstantially persuasive although unfortunately is in no way documented.)

The Land That Time Forgot is one of Burroughs's major non-series science-fiction works (in some editions it is divided into three very slim volumes, corresponding with its original magazine serialization, and is consequently regarded as a small series itself). Opening with a sequence of submarine warfare in the first World War, the action quickly shifts to the island of Caspak (also known as Caprona), a place remarkably reminiscent of both Verne's *Mysterious Island* and Peter Wilkins's island retreat in the novel of Robert Paltock. There follow numerous incidents involving primitive and violent life-forms, intriguing speculation on evolutionary processes, and a final confrontation with a chilling post-human winged form (again reminiscent of Paltock). The paleontological elements in this book, like those in Burroughs's hollow-earth novels, are remarkably detailed and authentic. They derive from Burroughs's involvement with the subject at first as a student and later as an instructor at the Michigan Military Academy.

The Moon Maid, Burroughs's second major independent science-fiction work, is also divisible into three more-or-less self-sustained segments. It ties into Burroughs's Martian cycle, as a spaceship named *Barsoom* travels from the earth to the moon. The moon is found to be hollow and inhabited, with access to the inner regions obtained through lunar craters. All of this, of course, is strangely like the moon of Wells's *The First Men in the Moon.* In later sequences, using technology introduced from the earth, lunar forces invade and conquer our planet. At this point Burroughs's novel turns into a saga spaced over many generations. Burroughs handled the challenges of the form astonishingly well, and *The Moon Maid* is one of his most successful works.

His other works of science fiction have received relatively little attention. *The Monster Men* is a charmingly creaky cross of jungle adventure, desert island romance, mad scientist, and *Frankenstein*-monster plots. This last element occurs also in several of Burroughs's Martian novels, most notably *Master Mind of Mars* and *Synthetic Men of Mars. Beyond Thirty* is a surprisingly effective story of a future war-torn Europe reverting to barbarism—anticipating L. Ron Hubbard's *Final Blackout.*

Burroughs's Tarzan stories and other jungle adventures, while not essentially works of science fiction, contain many elements derived from science fiction and allied forms. After feralism itself, the next most common theme in the books is that of the lost race, tribe, city, or country. These are handled well if somewhat repetitiously by Burroughs; it should be noted that this form of adventure writing was perfected by Haggard, whose works seem likely to have influenced Burroughs. The theme of feralism is itself very old in literature and folklore; it was best known prior to the creation of Tarzan in the *Jungle Books* of Kipling. The Tarzan novels also include Atlantean themes, immortality serums, paleontological survivals, at least one city of intelligent gorillas, and at least one satirical novel (*Tarzan and the Ant Men*) apparently based on Swift.

As Burroughs borrowed from many earlier writers, he in turn was read by and influenced uncounted later writers. The briefest smattering of these must include H.P. Lovecraft, Robert E. Howard, Edmond Hamilton, Leigh Brackett, Ray Bradbury, Gore Vidal, and J.R.R. Tolkien. Direct imitators of Burroughs range from his contemporaries J.U. Giesy and William L. Chester, to many present-day writers including Lin Carter, Michael Resnick, Anne McCaffrey, John Norman, and Philip José Farmer. In most cases, where the imitation of Burroughs is very literal the result is a rather lifeless pastiche; where Burroughs's influence is less specific and the later writer uses Burroughs as a wellspring of color, verve, and suspense, the result is often admirable.

—Richard A. Lupoff

BURROUGHS, William S(eward). Also wrote as William Lee. American. Born in St. Louis, Missouri, 5 February 1914. Educated at John Burroughs School and Taylor School, St. Louis; Los Alamos Ranch School, New Mexico; Harvard University, Cambridge, Massachusetts, A.B. in anthropology 1936; studied medicine at the University of Vienna; Mexico City College, 1948-50. Served in the United States Army, 1942. Married Jean Vollmer in 1945 (died); one son. Has worked as a journalist, private detective, and bartender; now a full-time writer. Heroin addict, 1944-57. Recipient: American Academy Award, 1975. Lived for many years in Tangier; now lives in New York City. Agent: Peter Matson, Literistic Ltd., 32 West 40th Street, New York, New York 10018, U.S.A.

SCIENCE-FICTION PUBLICATIONS

Novels

The Naked Lunch. Paris, Olympia Press, 1959; London, Calder, 1964; as *Naked Lunch,* New York, Grove Press, 1962.
The Soft Machine. Paris, Olympia Press, 1961; New York, Grove Press, 1966; London, Calder and Boyars, 1968.
The Ticket That Exploded. Paris, Olympia Press, 1962; revised edition, New York, Grove Press, 1967; London, Calder and Boyars, 1968.
Nova Express. New York, Grove Press, 1964; London, Cape, 1966.
The Wild Boys: A Book of the Dead. New York, Grove Press, 1971; London, Calder and Boyars, 1972; revised edition, London, Calder, 1979.
Exterminator! New York, Viking Press, 1973; London, Calder and Boyars, 1974.

OTHER PUBLICATIONS

Novels

Junkie: Confessions of an Unredeemed Drug Addict (as William Lee). New York, Ace, 1953; London, Digit, 1957.
Dead Fingers Talk. London, Calder, 1963.
Short Novels. London, Calder, 1978.
Blade Runner: A Movie. Berkeley, California, Blue Wind Press, 1979.
Cities of the Red Night: A Boy's Book. London, Calder, 1980; New York, Holt Rinehart, 1981.
Port of Saints. Berkeley, California, Blue Wind Press, 1980.

Play

The Last Words of Dutch Schultz. London, Cape Goliard Press, 1970; New York, Viking Press, 1975.

Other

The Exterminator, with Brion Gysin. San Francisco, Auerhahn Press, 1960.
Minutes to Go, with others. Paris, Two Cities, 1960; San Francisco, Beach, 1968.
The Yage Letters, with Allen Ginsberg. San Francisco, City Lights, 1963.
Roosevelt after Inauguration. New York, Fuck You Press, 1964.
Valentine Day's Reading. New York, American Theatre for Poets, 1965.
"The Hallucinatory Operators Are Real," in *SF Horizons 2* (London), 1965.
Time. New York, "C" Press, 1965.
Health Bulletin: APO-33: A Metabolic Regulator. New York, Fuck You Press, 1965; revised edition, as *APO—33 Bulletin,* San Francisco, Beach, 1966.
So Who Owns Death TV?, with Claude Pelieu and Carl Weissner. San Francisco, Beach, 1967.
The Dead Star. San Francisco, Nova Broadcast Press, 1969.
Ali's Smile. Brighton, Unicorn, 1969.
Entretiens avec William Burroughs, by Daniel Odier. Paris, Belfond, 1969; translated as *The Job: Interviews with William S. Burroughs* (includes *Electronic Revolution*), New York, Grove Press, and London, Cape, 1970.
The Braille Film. San Francisco, Nova Broadcast Press, 1970.
Preface to *Love and Napalm: Export U.S.A.,* by J.G. Ballard. New York, Grove Press, 1972.
Brion Gysin Let the Mice In, with Brion Gysin and Ian Somerville, edited by Jan Herman. West Glover, Vermont, Something Else Press, 1973.
Mayfair Academy Series More or Less. Brighton, Urgency Press Rip-Off, 1973.
White Subway, edited by James Pennington. London, Aloes, 1974.
The Book of Breeething. Ingatestone, Essex, OU Press, 1974; Berkeley, California, Blue Wind Press, 1975; revised edition,

Blue Wind Press, 1980.
Snack: Two Tape Transcripts, with Eric Mottram. London, Aloes, 1975.
Sidetripping, with Charles Gatewood. New York, Strawberry Hill, 1975.
Ah Pook Is Here and Other Texts: The Book of Breeething, Electronic Revolution. London, Calder, 1979.

*

Bibliography: *William S. Burroughs: An Annotated Bibliography of His Works and Criticism* by Michael B. Goodman, New York, Garland, 1975; *William S. Burroughs: A Bibliography 1953-73* by Joe Maynard and Barry Miles, Charlottesville, University Press of Virginia, 1978.

*   *   *

One of the most important members of the American Beat movement, William S. Burroughs has repeatedly used science-fiction situations and images in his bizarre novels of protest against social control. Critical opinion is widely divided on Burroughs: Eric Mottram's *The Algebra of Need* is an apocalyptic eulogy, and Burroughs is often considered to be among the select few major contemporary authors; however, Martin Seymour-Smith represents a strong minority critical response in his reference to Burroughs's "monumental stupidity." In fact, Burroughs demonstrated his ability to write with conventional intelligence in his first novel. *Junkie* is an autobiographical confession of a morphine addict. It is also a map of Hell, attacking a spiritless society and its gratuitous abuses of power. Despite the autobiographical element, Burroughs shows ironic control over his narrator, an unsettled picaro who sometimes interprets himself as an idealistic quester.

Burroughs's reputation rests mainly upon the four novels *The Naked Lunch, The Soft Machine, The Ticket That Exploded,* and *Nova Express.* These form a tetralogy which attacks the obsessive need for control which Burroughs sees as having gripped our planet. That obsession is often given its focus in such science-fiction images as the dystopias and advanced behavioural technologies of *The Naked Lunch,* and the ubiquitous fantasy of metamorphosis into arthropod form to represent the dehumanization of both controller and controlled. Especially in *The Ticket That Exploded* and *Nova Express,* Burroughs presents the extended metaphor of an invasion by aliens—the Nova Mob—whose members act through and control humans who share their weaknesses and predilections. *The Ticket That Exploded,* the more accessible of these two novels, makes it clear that the aliens are a metaphor for controlling powers on Earth, presented as if they could only be a Manichean force of evil from space.

It would be easy to condemn these novels for their frequent opacity and the paranoid sensibility which they seem to reveal. However, Burroughs does write with admirable confidence and power; where the prose is readable at all, the phrasing is sharp, and the dialogue is usually convincing. The difficulty is that, as Burroughs admits in *The Job,* a series of interviews with Daniel Odier, the prose is sometimes "simply not readable." This is mainly the result of Burroughs's so-called "cut-up" and "fold-in" techniques: the mechanical rearrangement of sliced-up pages and the juxtaposition of words from quite different texts. Both Burroughs's admirers and his detractors have over-emphasized the genesis of the prose in these techniques, rather than the patterns of meaning which (sometimes) result on the page.

Since the publication of *Nova Express,* Burroughs has increasingly appeared to be a sage—an unsympathetic philosopher of life—rather than a creative artist. Unfortunately, he has not been a very good sage. Looking through his interviews and theoretical works, one finds the occasional insights hidden amid such obsessive and often inhumane pronouncements as this, on women: "I think they were a basic mistake, and the whole dualistic universe evolved from this error."

Eric Mottram has given extravagant praise to the recent novella "Ah Pook Is Here"; however, it is difficult to see how that work seriously adds to the experience described in, especially, *The Soft Machine.* Perhaps the most interesting of the later works, for science-fiction readers, is *The Wild Boys.* This novel begins as a series of linked apocalyptic vignettes. These are pulled together as the story emerges of packs of homosexual specialist warriors who are able to outfight conventional armies, and who ravage their near-future world. The book is a projection of the need which Burroughs feels to destroy all present-day institutions, including the family and the national state.

—Russell Blackford

BUSBY, F.M. American. Born in Indianapolis, Indiana, 11 March 1921. Educated at Washington State University, Pullman, B.Sc. 1946, B.Sc.E.E. 1947. Served in the National Guard, 1940-41, and United States Army, 1943-45. Married Elinor Doub in 1954; one daughter. Project Supervisor, Alaska Communication System, Seattle, 1947-53; telegraph engineer, 1953-70. Since 1970, free-lance writer. Recipient: Hugo Award, for editing, 1960. Address: 2852 14th Avenue West, Seattle, Washington 98119, U.S.A.

SCIENCE-FICTION PUBLICATIONS

Novels (series: Barton; Rissa)

Cage a Man (Barton). New York, Doubleday, 1973; London, Hamlyn, 1979.
The Proud Enemy (Barton). New York, Berkley, 1975.
Rissa Kerguelen. New York, Berkley, 1976.
The Long View (Rissa). New York, Berkley, 1976.
Rissa Kerguelen (omnibus). New York, Berkley, 1977.
All These Earths (Barton). New York, Berkley, 1978.
Zelde M'Tana (Rissa). New York, Dell, 1980.

Uncollected Short Stories

"A Gun for Grandfather," in *Future* (New York), Fall 1957.
"Here, There, and Everywhere," in *Clarion 2,* edited by Robin Scott Wilson. New York, New American Library, 1972.
"Of Mice and Otis," in *Amazing* (New York), March 1972.
"The Puiss of Krrlik," in *Fantastic* (New York), April 1972.
"Proof," in *Amazing* (New York), September 1972.
"The Real World," in *Fantastic* (New York), December 1972.
"Play It Again, Sam" and "Road Map," in *Clarion 3,* edited by Robin Scott Wilson. New York, New American Library, 1973.
"Tell Me All about Yourself," in *New Dimensions 3,* edited by Robert Silverberg. New York, Avon, 1973.
"Once upon a Unicorn," in *Fantastic* (New York), April 1973.
"Three Tinks of the House," in *Vertex* (Los Angeles), June 1973.
"2000½: A Spaced Oddity," in *Vertex* (Los Angeles), August 1973.
"Pearsall's Return," in *If* (New York), August 1973.
"The Learning of Eeshta," in *If* (New York), October 1973.
"If This Is Winnetka, You Must Be Judy," in *Universe 5,* edited by Terry Carr. New York, Random House, 1974; London, Dobson, 1978.
"I'm Going to Get You," in *Fantastic* (New York), March 1974.
"What Was That?," in *Amazing* (New York), April 1974.
"Getting Home," in *Fantasy and Science Fiction* (New York), April 1974.
"Time of Need," in *Vertex* (Los Angeles), August 1974.
"Collateral," in *Vertex* (Los Angeles), August 1974.
"Retroflex," in *Vertex* (Los Angeles), October 1974.
"Misconception," in *Vertex* (Los Angeles), April 1975.
"The Signing of Tulip," in *Vertex* (Los Angeles), June 1975.
"Advantage," in *Vertex* (Los Angeles), August 1975.
"Search," in *Amazing* (New York), December 1976.
"Never So Lost," in *Amazing* (New York), October 1977.

"Come to the Party," with Frank Herbert, in *The 1979 Annual World's Best SF*, edited by Donald A. Wollheim.   New York, DAW, 1979.

*   *   *

F.M. Busby's true skill lies in depicting the process of orientation—showing how a mind dropped into a totally unprecedented situation gets its bearings and adjusts. Busby uses this skill in its purest form in his short stories, and as a result these stories are challenging, convincing, and often brilliantly successful. He also writes extended novels in which his main characters carry their orienting ability into larger contexts, and there his success, while adequate, is not so consistent.

The alarming situations which Busby's characters most often face are not made of swirling atmospheres or alien ruins, but of changes in identity itself. In "Getting Home" the protagonist wakes up from a drug trip to find his identity is lodged in someone else's mind. Every time he sleeps, he moves into the mind of a different person, and by the time he returns to what he thinks is his own body, he has had to adjust to being an old man, several women, a child abuser, two children, and a homosexual male. The final turn of the tale, as he reaches "home," is Busby at his best. In other stories, the disorienting factor is time. "Road Map" presents a 52-year-old man who wakes to find he has been reincarnated as his wife, at her birth. After he adjusts, first to being a baby with an adult mind, and then to being female, the husband's knowledge of the wife's past become the "road map," which with love and determination he/she extends. In "If This Is Winnetka, You Must Be Judy" the protagonist is a man who lives his life non-sequentially—jumping without warning in and out of his different ages, trying to keep track of the parts he has yet to live. Again, it is a bond of love and loyalty, this time with a wife who also lives non-sequentially, which allows them to gain control over their temporal geography.

Busby's Barton trilogy begins with just such an exercise in orientation, though the context is somewhat more conventional. Barton, an otherwise undistinguished human being, is captured by evil aliens and placed in a featureless grey cage for eight years. Through a variety of psychological methods the aliens attempt to change his identity to one of their race, the lobster-like Demu. He fights back, though, never forgets who he is, and escapes. This first part of the plot, originally published as the story "Cage a Man," is exciting and closely focussed. Barton becomes a compelling and believable hero whose escape the reader applauds. But once Barton is back on earth, assembling the revenge fleet, dealing with bureaucrats and arranging the surgical restoration of the alien woman he loves, the story bogs down and never really recovers. Though the fleet visits several alien planets and eventually discovers the galactic origin of humanoid life, the actual narration is composed of interminable boardroom meetings, each relentlessly complete with agenda, dialogue, and refreshments. Busby also seems paternally determined that his characters find sufficient occasions for (undetailed) sex, producing an astoundingly boring repetitiveness. As Barton, prickly individualist with a heart of toleration, finally sets off for the stars, one may wish he would encounter something more interesting.

Yet Busby is by no means an amateur writer, and though his subsequent novels do not change much in content, he has improved pace and local color. *Rissa Kerguelen, The Long View* and *Zelde M'Tana* all describe the same galaxy—ruled by a totalitarian corporation, forcing uniformity on its victims, and resisted by a space-pirate underground. The main difference in these books is that the Barton-ish characters are female, giving Busby a chance to do some reorienting of his own. And though the rebels still run their ship like a corporation, with meetings, refreshments, and no aliens, there are occasional confrontations that revive interest.

One sometimes suspects that Busby creates worlds where, once located, he himself cannot escape, or even notice the conventionality of the walls. Yet he is capable of true imaginative power—the story "Tell Me All about Yourself," which calmly depicts a brothel for necrophiliacs, is as chillingly bizarre as the genre allows, and a first-hand experience in disorientation for the reader. Yet even in that world, however horribly, connections of individual loyalty hold when all else dissolves. Busby has the talent to set his characters and readers truly adrift, and the conviction that only human

networks can give accurate directions. When he lets the drift be far enough, the shock of location is a real award.

—Karen G. Way

————————————

BUTLER, Octavia E(stelle).   American.   Born in Pasadena, California, 22 June 1947. Educated at Pasadena College, 1965-68, A.A. 1968; California State University, 1969. Since 1970, free-lance writer. Address: Box 6604, Los Angeles, California 90055, U.S.A.

SCIENCE-FICTION PUBLICATIONS

Novels (series: Patternists in all books except *Kindred*)

Patternmaster.   New York, Doubleday, 1976; London, Sphere, 1978.
Mind of My Mind.   New York, Doubleday, 1977; London, Sidgwick and Jackson, 1978.
Survivor.   New York, Doubleday, and London, Sidgwick and Jackson, 1978.
Kindred.   New York, Doubleday, 1979.
Wild Seed.   New York, Doubleday, and London, Sidgwick and Jackson, 1980.

Uncollected Short Stories

"Crossover," in *Clarion*, edited by Robin Scott Wilson.   New York, New American Library, 1971.
"Near of Kin," in *Chrysalis 4*, edited by Roy Torgeson.   New York, Kensington, 1979.

Octavia E. Butler comments:
I began writing fantasy and science fiction because these seemed to be the genres in which I could be freest, most creative. I had in mind from my first novel a series, a fictional history of people called Patternists who are, by mutation and selective breeding, developing psionic abilities. The books of this series are, in the order of the events they cover, *Wild Seed*, which begins in 1690, *Mind of My Mind* (present-day), *Survivor* (near future), and *Patternmaster* (distant future). The books are stories of power—adjustment to power, struggle for power, corruption by power. I bring together multiracial groups of men and women who must cope with one another's differences as well as with new, not necessarily controllable, abilities within themselves.

A non-Patternist novel, *Kindred*, tells the story of a young black woman of the 1970's who is shifted back in time to the ante-bellum South where she is enslaved and forced to fend for herself in a world almost as hostile and alien to her as another planet.

*   *   *

In her first novels, Octavia E. Butler creates a future history, beginning in the present with *Mind of My Mind*, moving to the future of *Patternmaster* and *Survivor*. Dealing with the bonding of people with para-normal abilities, Butler combines adventure with social commentary. Her work shows the influence of Theodore Sturgeon's *More Than Human*.

Butler's Patternist society is the subject of *Mind of My Mind* and *Patternmaster*, and referred to in *Survivor*. While telepathic powers are common in SF, a society of linked telepaths controlled by the most powerful of them is not. *Patternmaster's* vagueness is clarified in *Mind of My Mind*, which tells of the dynasty's founding at Forsyth, California. Living 4,000 years, deliberately breeding for telepathic ability, Doro succeeds through his daughter Mary. References to Los Angeles, child-beating, shop-lifting, revivals, and everyday names like Rachel, Karl, and Jon indicate the present. The Prologue, in fact, breaks the commonplace by the simple statement that Doro (an uncommon name) was wearing a new body. Until her transition from latent to active, Mary is a disturbed, sullen slum child. Just before she reaches full power, Doro marries her to a wealthy telepath, Karl Larkin. At first repelled, they form a strong attachment and become the "First Family" after Mary gathers such diverse telepaths as a healer, artist, and teacher who have led unhappy lives. She forms potential enemies into a pattern of minds attached to hers like threads. Before long they have rescued latents from squalor, crime, and death, making them into a Southern California network of 15,500. Eventually, a duel to the death between Mary and Doro is inevitable.

Mind of My Mind explains much of the other books. The art practiced by Amber in *Patternmaster* grows from Rachel's faith healing. The system of arranging patternists into separate houses with the Patternmaster in Forsyth emerges. Why brothers and lovers kill each other becomes apparent. Sensitive to children's chaotic minds, patternists are unfit parents, often neglectful or homicidal. The use of "mutes," non-telepaths, as servants and the code of honor that prevents their mistreatment grows out of the immature latent's tendency to maim or kill inferiors. Although the other books can be read separately, the society is established here.

Patternmaster leads toward the inevitable duel of Teray and Coransee to determine their father's successor. It is told in a bare straightforward narrative. Mary's pattern has developed so that there are housemasters controlled by a Patternmaster. Low-level patternists manage mutes, and healers repair mental and physical damage. The young mature in schools, and after transition are attached to housemasters, learning skills, or become outsiders, remaining inferiors. The enemy Clayarks are mutants with lion-like bodies and human heads. They use rifles and protective gloves, speak, and capture mutes. Their hatred leads to Rayal's death from the incurable disease they are driven to transmit, a result of organisms the starship *Clay's Ark* brought to Earth. The plot is remarkably like *As You Like It* in conflict, escape from society, and the dynamic heroine, Amber. Its conclusion suggests a renewal of society through the union of patternists who show concern even for the Clayarks.

Survivor deals with mutes whose goal is to spread the concept of man's superiority through the universe. Encountering people who communicate not only verbally but through changing the color of their fur, they misjudge them. Soon they are dominated by the Garkohn, who enslave them with the drug meklah. Before being adopted by the missionary leader, the Afro-Asian Alanna lived off the land as a wild human. When captured by the enemy Tehkohn, she alone survives withdrawal from meklah. In fact, Alanna adapts so well she becomes an honored hunter and wife of their highest judge. Returning to the missionaries, she and her husband help them to freedom. The irony of the missionaries' plight is that, seeking freedom from patternists and Clayarks, they find themselves dominated by the so-called animals they hoped to enslave. Their prejudices endanger their survival. Because she is willing to change, Alanna is a survivor, achieving greatness through trial, as the patternists endure traumatic transition before assuming power.

Butler too is a survivor. She has developed a consistent world and is contemporary in her choice of themes, protests, and strong women and minority characters. Her works show a conscious attempt to improve narrative technique and create vivid, detailed, unique societies. Already her books have the depth of classics.

—Mary S. Weinkauf

BUTLER, Samuel. Also wrote as Cellarius. British. Born at Langar Rectory, near Bingham, Nottinghamshire, 4 December 1835. Educated at Shrewsbury School, Shropshire, 1848-54; St. John's College, Cambridge 1854-58, B.A. (honours) 1858; studied painting at Heatherley's School, London, 1865. Sheep farmer, Rangitata district, New Zealand, 1859-64; settled in London, 1864; exhibited paintings at the Royal Academy, London, 1868-76; studied and composed music. *Died 18 June 1902.*

SCIENCE-FICTION PUBLICATIONS

Novels

Erewhon; or, Over the Range. London, Trubner, 1872; revised edition, 1872; London, Richards, 1901; New York, Dutton, 1910.
Erewhon Revisited Twenty Years Later. London, Richards, 1901; New York, Dutton, 1910.

OTHER PUBLICATIONS

Novel

The Way of All Flesh, edited by R.A. Streatfeild. London, Richards, 1903; New York, Dutton, 1910.

Plays

Narcissus: A Dramatic Cantata, words and music by Butler and Henry Festing Jones. London, Weekes, 1888.
Ulysses: A Dramatic Oratorio, words and music by Butler and Henry Festing Jones. London, Weekes, and Chicago, Summy, 1904.

Verse

Seven Sonnets and A Psalm of Montreal, edited by R.A. Streatfeild. Privately printed, 1904.

Other

A First Year in Canterbury Settlement. London, Longman, 1863; revised edition, edited by R.A. Streatfeild, London, Fifield, 1914; New York, Dutton, 1915.
The Evidence for the Resurrection of Jesus Christ As Given by the Four Evangelists, Critically Examined (published anonymously). Privately printed, 1865.
The Fair Haven: A Work in Defence of the Miraculous Element in Our Lord's Ministry upon Earth. London, Trubner, 1873; New York, Kennerley, 1913.
Life and Habit: An Essay after a Completer View of Evolution. London, Trubner, 1878; New York, Dutton, 1911.
Evolution Old and New. London, Hardwicke and Bogue, and Salem, Massachusetts, Cassino, 1879.
Unconscious Memory. London, Bogue, 1880; New York, Dutton, 1911.
Alps and Sanctuaries of Piedmont and the Canton Ticino. London, Bogue, 1881; New York, Dutton, 1913.
Selections from Previous Works. London, Trubner, 1884.
Gavottes, Minuets, Fugues, and Other Short Pieces for Piano, with Henry Festing Jones. London, Novello, 1885.
Holbein's "Dance." London, Trubner, 1886.
Luck or Cunning as a Main Means of Organic Modification? London, Trubner, 1887.
Ex Voto: An Account of the Sacro Monte or New Jerusalem at Varallo-Sesia. London, Trubner, 1888; revised edition, 1889.
A Lecture on the Humour of Homer. Cambridge, Metcalfe, 1892.
On the Trapanese Origin of the Odyssey. Cambridge, Metcalfe, 1893.
The Life and Letters of Dr. Samuel Butler. London, Murray, 2 vols., 1896.
The Authoress of the Odyssey. London, Longman, 1897; New York, Dutton, 1922.
Shakespeare's Sonnets Reconsidered, and in Part Rearranged. London, Longman, 1899; New York, Dutton, 1927.
Essays on Life, Art, and Science, edited by R.A. Streatfeild. London, Richards, 1904; Port Washington, New York, Kennikat Press, 1970.
God the Known and God the Unknown, edited by R.A. Streatfeild.

London, Fifield, 1909; New Haven, Connecticut, Yale University Press, 1917.

The Note Books of Samuel Butler: Selections, edited by Henry Festing Jones.   London, Fifield, 1912; New York, Kennerley, 1913.

The Humour of Homer and Other Essays, edited by R.A. Streatfeild.   London, Fifield, and New York, Kennerley, 1913.

The Collected Works [Shrewsbury Edition], edited by Henry Festing Jones and A.T. Bartholomew.   London, Cape, and New York, Dutton, 20 vols., 1923-26.

Butleriana, edited by A.T. Bartholomew.   London, Nonesuch Press, 1932; as *Samuel Butler's Note Books: Some New Extracts,* New York, Random House, 1932.

Samuel Butler's Note Books: Further Extracts, edited by A.T. Bartholomew.   London, Cape, 1934.

Letters Between Samuel Butler and Miss E.M.A. Savage, edited by Geoffrey Keynes and Brian Hill.   London, Cape, 1935.

The Essential Samuel Butler, edited by G.D.H. Cole.   London, Cape, and New York, Dutton, 1950.

Samuel Butler's Note Books: Selections, edited by Geoffrey Keynes and Brian Hill.   London, Cape, 1951.

Correspondence of Butler and His Sister May, edited by Daniel F. Howard.   Berkeley, University of California Press, 1962.

The Family Letters 1841-1886, edited by Arnold Silver.   London, Cape, and Stanford, California, Stanford University Press, 1962.

The Book of the Machines (as Cellarius).   London, Quarto Press, 1975.

Translator, *The Iliad of Homer.*   London, Longman, 1898; New York, Dutton, 1921.

Translator, *The Odyssey.*   London, Longman, 1900; New York, Dutton, 1922.

Translator, *Hesiod's Works and Days.*   Privately printed, 1923.

*

Bibliography: *The Career of Samuel Butler: A Bibliography* by Stanley B. Harkness, London, Lane, 1955.

*   *   *

Samuel Butler was the son of an Anglican rector, whom he later immortalized in his grim autobiographical novel of Victorian family hypocrisy *The Way of All Flesh.* He graduated from Cambridge in classics, then worked for one season among the poor in London, as a result of which he did not become a clergyman but moved instead to New Zealand. From 1859 to 1864, he managed there a sheep-ranch, began to write about the country and about the new and sensational theory of evolution, and gathered the elements for his novel *Erewhon.* His other writings attacked received opinion in religion, biology, philology, and child-rearing, proposing alternatives which are today generally seen as eccentric, though the controversy around his Neo-Lamarckism is by no means over.

Though Butler's literary masterpiece is *The Way of All Flesh,* some reversals from his country of Erewhon (itself to be read backwards as most other names in the novel) are as interesting and more modern. This civilization, found (as the subtitle has it) "over the range," in an unexplored part of the traditionally upside-down Antipodes, is used for satirical discussions; most importantly, the Erewhonians establish to their satisfaction that machines are using mankind as a means for their indirect evolution and ban all of them, beginning with clocks and watches. Other exposures of the ulterior moral motives, and thus of the hypocrisy of Victorian bourgeois society are the perfectly logical value-transferral between illness and crime, Unreason and Reason, or religion and banking. Unfortunately, Butler's overall stance is not at all consistent: for a crucial example, if the time-quantifying tool of clocks is banned, the basic agent of quantifying in modern civilization, money, should logically also be banned instead of being promoted as the religion of Musical Banks. Thus the various elements of Erewhon become mutually incompatible as the sketch of a believable alternative. As Edmund Wilson remarked, "Butler, though he could be most amusing about people's mercenary motives, was too much a middle-class man himself to analyze the social system, in which...he occupied a privileged position" (*The Shores of Light,* New York, 1967). The novel

dissolves into a string of more or less unrelated satires of the surfaces of Victorian civilization, hesitating between Swiftian bite and middle-class propriety, mildly diverting paradox and cynical justification (though, beside the amusing passages, the fable of the Unborn—who foster the libido of their parents in order to incarnate—retains a certain Platonic charm).

The continuation, *Erewhon Revisited,* is more coherent but less broadly relevant, focussing as it does on the religious cult that has sprung up in Erewhon around the totally misunderstood narrator of the first novel, now promoted to "Sun-child" in a clear parody of Christ (making this novel a continuation of Butler's *Fair Haven* at least as much as of the earlier satire). What is worse, this sequel retracts even the partial estrangement of *Erewhon,* as well as its own satire on the founding of religions, by its final horizon of salvation through annexation to the British Empire.

Butler's SF, thus, remains incidentally amusing reading, especially in the first book. However, its primary importance is in the satirical prefiguration of what will later become a much more anguished and wider debate on reification and "machine consciousness" in cybernetics, as well as in the general argument about controlled evolution. Butler had therefore an important influence on subsequent SF, from such Victorians as his friend R.E. Dudgeon through J. Carne-Ross, W.J. Roe, and W. Grove to G.B. Shaw's drama-cycle *Back to Methuselah* and some American SF. But his main problems will be picked up and brought to a more sophisticated level by Wells, Zamyatin, and Capek. There remain the striking freshness and irreverence of Butler's best satirical passages.

—Darko Suvin

———

CAIDIN, Martin.   American.   Born in New York City, 14 September 1927. Served in the merchant marine, 1945; United States Air Force, 1947-50: Sergeant. Married Grace Caidin in 1952; one son and one daughter. Consultant, correspondent, and broadcaster on aviation and civil defense: Associate editor, *Air News* and *Air Tech;* consultant to New York State Civil Defense Commission, 1950-62, Air Force Missile Test Center, Cape Canaveral, 1955, and Federal Aviation Agency, 1961-64; correspondent, Metropolitan Broadcasting (radio and TV), 1961-62. Founder, Martin Caidin Associates Inc. Address: 44 Netto Lane, Plainview, New York 11803, U.S.A.

SCIENCE-FICTION PUBLICATIONS

Novels (series: Steve Austin)

The Long Night.   New York, Dodd Mead, 1956.

Marooned.   New York, Dutton, and London, Hodder and Stoughton, 1964

The Last Fathom.   New York, Meredith Press, and London, Joseph, 1967.

No Man's World.   New York, Dutton, 1967.

Aquarius Mission.   New York, Bantam, 1968.

Four Came Back.   New York, McKay, 1968.

The God Machine.   New York, Dutton, 1969.

The Mendelov Conspiracy.   New York, Meredith Press, 1969; London, W.H. Allen, 1971; as *Encounter Three,* New York, Pinnacle, 1978.

The Cape.   New York, Doubleday, 1971.

Cyborg (Austin).   New York, Arbor House, 1972; London, W.H. Allen, 1973.

Operation Nuke (Austin).   New York, Arbor House, 1973; London, W.H. Allen, 1974.

High Crystal (novelization of TV play; Austin).   New York, Arbor House, 1974; London, W.H. Allen, 1975.

Cyborg IV (Austin).   New York, Arbor House, 1975; London, W.H. Allen, 1977.

OTHER PUBLICATIONS

Novels

Devil Takes All. New York, Dutton, 1966; London, W.H. Allen, 1968.

Anytime, Anywhere. New York, Dutton, 1969; London, W.H. Allen, 1970.

Almost Midnight. New York, Morrow, 1971; London, Bantam, 1974.

Maryjane Tonight at Angels Twelve. New York, Doubleday, 1972.

The Last Dogfight. Boston, Houghton Mifflin, and London, Weidenfeld and Nicolson, 1974.

Three Corners to Nowhere. New York, Bantam, and London, Corgi, 1975.

Whip. Boston, Houghton Mifflin, 1976; London, Corgi, 1977.

Other

Jets, Rockets, and Guided Missiles, with David C. Cooke. New York, McBride, 1951; revised edition, as *Rockets and Missiles, Past and Present,* 1954.

Rockets Beyond the Earth. New York, McBride, 1952.

Worlds in Space. New York, Holt, and London, Sidgwick and Jackson, 1954.

Zero!, with M. Okumiya and J. Horikoshi. New York, Dutton, 1956; London, Cassell, 1957.

Vanguard! New York, Dutton, 1957.

Samurai!, with Saburo Sakai and Fred Saito. New York, Dutton, 1957; London, Kimber, 1959.

Air Force: A Pictorial History of American Airpower. New York, Rinehart, 1957.

Countdown for Tomorrow. New York, Dutton, 1958.

Thunderbolt!, with Robert S. Johnson. New York, Rinehart, 1958.

The Zero Fighter, with M. Okumiya and J. Horikoshi. London, Cassell, 1958.

Spaceport, U.S.A. New York, Dutton, 1959.

War for the Moon. New York, Dutton, 1959; as *Race for the Moon,* London, Kimber, 1960.

Let's Go Flying! New York, Dutton, 1959.

Boeing 707. New York, Dutton, 1959.

X-15: Man's First Flight into Space. New York, Rutledge, 1959.

Black Thursday. New York, Dutton, 1960.

Golden Wings: A Pictorial History of the United States Navy and Marine Corps in the Air. New York, Random House, 1960.

The Astronauts. New York, Dutton, 1960; revised editon, 1961.

The Night Hamburg Died. New York, Ballantine, 1960; London, New English Library, 1966.

A Torch to the Enemy: The Fire Raid on Tokyo. New York, Ballantine, 1960.

Man into Space. New York, Pyramid, 1961.

Thunderbirds! New York, Dutton, 1961.

The Long, Lonely Leap, with Joseph W. Kittinger. New York, Dutton, 1961.

Cross-Country Flying. New York, Dutton, 1961.

Test Pilot (juvenile). New York, Dutton, 1961.

This Is My Land, photographs by James Yarnell. New York, Random House, 1962.

I Am Eagle, with G.S. Titov. Indianapolis, Bobbs Merrill, 1962.

Rendezvous in Space. New York, Dutton, 1962.

Aviation and Space Medicine, with Grace Caidin. New York, Dutton, 1962.

The Man-in-Space Dictionary. New York, Dutton, 1963.

The Moon: New World for Men. Indianapolis, Bobbs Merrill, 1963.

Red Star in Space. New York, Crowell Collier, 1963.

The Power of Decision. New York, Dell, 1963.

Overture to Space. New York, Duell, 1963.

The Long Arm of America. New York, Dutton, 1963.

By Apollo to the Moon (juvenile). New York, Dutton, 1963.

The Silken Angels: A History of Parachuting. Philadelphia, Lippincott, 1964.

The Winged Armada. New York, Dutton, 1964.

Hydrospace. New York, Dutton, 1964.

Everything But the Flak. New York, Duell, 1964.

The Mission, with Edward Hymoff. Philadelphia, Lippincott, 1964.

Wings into Space. New York, Holt Rinehart, 1964.

The Mighty Hercules (juvenile). New York, Dutton, 1964.

Why Space? New York, Messner, 1965.

Barnstorming. New York, Duell, 1965.

The Greatest Challenge. New York, Dutton, 1965.

The Ragged, Rugged Warriors. New York, Dutton, 1966.

Flying Forts. New York, Meredith Press, 1968.

Me 109: Willy Messerschmitt's Peerless Fighters. New York, Ballantine, 1968; London, Macdonald, 1969.

Fork-Tailed Devil: The P-38. New York, Ballantine, 1971.

Destination Mars. New York, Doubleday, 1972.

When War Comes. New York, Morrow, 1972.

Bicycles in War, with Jay Barbree. New York, Hawthorn, 1974.

Planetfall. New York, Coward McCann, 1974.

The Tigers Are Burning. New York, Hawthorn, 1974.

Wingborn. New York, Bantam, and London, Corgi, 1979.

The Saga of Iron Annie. New York, Doubleday, 1979.

Star Bright. New York, Ballantine, 1979.

Kill Devil Hill: Discovering the Secret of the Wright Brothers, with Harvey B. Combs. Boston, Houghton Mifflin, 1979.

Editor, *The DC-3: The Story of the Dakota,* by Carroll V. Glines and Wendell F. Moseley. London, Deutsch, 1967.

*   *   *

Martin Caidin builds on his numerous non-fiction works concerning aviation and aerospace technology to provide convincing background for his speculative fiction. This fiction, set in the present or near future, consistently warns that America's naive idealism about peaceful cooperation in outer space should be tempered by a realistic awareness of nationalistic competition, that our technological capabilities are outstripping our emotional and psychological controls, and that a technological, materialistic, and empirical approach to phenomena fails fully to account for and control such phenomena.

Some of Caidin's books explore what could go wrong with a space flight: personal problems that affect efficiency (nagging wives, wayward children, secret affairs, drugs, and blackmail) in *The Cape,* the possiblility of foreign sabotage on the ground (*The Cape, No Man's World*) or with laser beams in space (*Cyborg IV, The Mendelov Conspiracy*), technical and mechanical difficulties (*Marooned*), bombardment by meteors and invasion of alien bacteria *(Four Came Back)*, and hostile confrontation on arrival (Russian and Chinese in *No Man's World*). Minor characters and anecdotes from one book become major characters and events in another. For example in the background of several books is a boorish newspaper man who intrudes where he doesn't belong, but who gets his story and ultimately helps out. In *Marooned* this brash, intuitive reporter breaks through NASA security to learn the truth of an astronaut's plight; in *The Mendelov Conspiracy* he investigates UFO's that prove part of an international scientists' plot to force the world to nuclear disarmament.

The Long Night, a terse and vivid step-by-step portrait of a family and town confronted with an atomic explosion and resultant firestorm, demonstrates Caidin's interest in how people react to disaster or panic. Caidin believes a military elite must use force if necessary to quell irresponsible, destructive mobs born of irrational fears—a theme in *Four Came Back* where earthlings fear alien bacteria, *The Long Night* where rumors of radiation send hordes flying, and *The Mendelov Conspiracy* where mobs attack nuclear stockpiles. To teach his audience about sea and space and disaster, Caidin relies on digressions, flashbacks, reverie, and experts explaining to neophytes, techniques that provide a wealth of interesting material, but which occasionally reduce the effectiveness of the plot. Caidin blends fact and fiction, the feasible and the speculative. His forte is his reliance on quotes by real men to make his tales of the emotions and conflicts of the near future seem perfectly natural and credible.

A Caidin hero is a tough, well-trained military man. He is proud of his work, devoted to his country, a man who can face up to and control his fear while those around him panic or succumb. Usually a one-time test pilot, he works hard and plays hard. His is a world of machines, whether in outer space or hydrospace. He is often excited and inspired by a strikingly beautiful, intelligent, and independent woman (secret agent, archaeologist, oceanographer, bionics expert, astronaut), but usually this romance remains unresolved or the woman dies suddenly, violently.

Caidin is fascinated by the idea of man and machine becoming a harmonic single entity—either in terms of sensitive reaction time or else literally as in the Steve Austin series. In *The God Machine* the ultimate computer is designed to interact with human operators and to mimic and transcend human logic, but a programming fault results in the horror of logic being carried out to literal, absurd, and inhuman ends. In *The Last Fathom* the developer of a revolutionary submarine maneuvers at incredible depths to prevent the devastation of the free world. *Cyborg* is a fascinating and highly technical dramatization of the reconstruction of a test pilot's body, with microscopic units replacing the nervous system, and a fusion of bone and metal replacing missing legs and arm until the man becomes more than mere man, capable of gruelling (and incredible) missions to expose Russian submarine bases and steal experimental planes. *Operation Nuke* and *High Crystal* feature further cyborg wonders as Austin plays fugitive to infiltrate a terrorist organization dependent on nuclear arms and then races to find the power source of an ancient Indian civilization—a giant crystal. In *Cyborg IV* Austin, linked symbionically to his space vehicle to control it with thought and reflex action, attacks Russians in space to protect military security. Such missions are the price his country demannds as payment for not leaving him a helpless paraplegic.

In general, Caidin's best pieces describe specific disasters to make the reader aware of the full horror of nuclear wars and other modern technological dangers. While emphasizing the courage and strength needed for controlling and surviving in experimental machinery, Caidin also demythologizes the glamour by focusing on practical, minute-to-minute detail. Perhaps his greatest contribution is in illuminating the relationship between man and machine to show that man must avoid becoming machine-like if he is to remain human.

—Andrew and Gina Macdonald

CAMPBELL, John W(ood), Jr. American. Born in Newark, New Jersey, 8 June 1910. Educated at Blair Academy; Massachusetts Institute of Technology, Cambridge, 1928-31; Duke University Durham, North Carolina, B.S. 1933. Married 1) Dona Stuart in 1931; 2) Margaret Winter in 1950; four children. Car and gas heater salesman; worked in the research department of Mack Truck, Hoboken Pioneer Instruments, and Carleton Ellis chemical company; Editor, *Astounding*, later *Analog*, 1937-71, *Unknown*, later *Unknown Worlds*, 1939-43, and *From Unknown Worlds*, 1948. Recipient: Hugo Award, for editing, 1953, 1955, 1957, 1961, 1962, 1964, 1965. Guest of Honor, World Science Fiction Convention, Philadelphia, 1947, San Francisco, 1954, London, 1957. *Died 11 July 1971.*

SCIENCE-FICTION PUBLICATIONS

Novels (series: Arcot, Morey, and Wade)

The Mightiest Machine. Providence, Rhode Island, Hadley, 1947.
The Incredible Planet. Reading, Pennsylvania, Fantasy Press, 1949.
The Moon Is Hell. Reading, Pennsylvania, Fantasy Press, 1951.

Islands of Space (Arcot, Morey, and Wade). Reading, Pennsylvania, Fantasy Press, 1957.
Invaders from the Infinite (Arcot, Morey, and Wade). New York, Gnome Press, 1961.
The Ultimate Weapon. New York, Ace, 1966.

Short Stories

Who Goes There? Chicago, Shasta, 1948; as *The Thing and Other Stories*, London, Cherry Tree, 1952; as *The Thing from Outer Space*, London, Tandem, 1966.
Cloak of Aesir. Chicago, Shasta, 1952.
The Black Star Passes (Arcot, Morey, and Wade). Reading, Pennsylvania, Fantasy Press, 1953.
Who Goes There? and Other Stories. New York, Dell, 1955.
The Planeteers. New York, Ace, 1966.
The Best of John W. Campbell. London, Sidgwick and Jackson, 1973.
The Best of John W. Campbell, edited by Lester del Rey. New York, Doubleday, 1976.
The Space Beyond. New York, Pyramid, 1976.

OTHER PUBLICATIONS

Other

"Concerning Science Fiction," in *The Writer* (Boston), 1946.
The Atomic Story. New York, Holt, 1947.
"Science of Science Fiction," in *Atlantic* (Boston), May 1948.
"Value of Science Fiction," in *Science Marches on*, edited by James Stokley. New York, Washburn, 1951.
"The Future of Science Fiction," in *Modern Science Fiction*, edited by Reginald Bretnor. New York, Coward McCann, 1953.
"Science-Fiction and the Opinion of the Unwise," in *Saturday Review of Literature* (New York), 12 May 1956.
"Science Fact: Science Fiction," in *The Writer* (Boston), August 1964.
Collected Editorials from Analog, edited by Harry Harrison. New York, Doubleday, 1966.
"Science Fiction We Can Buy," in *The Writer* (Boston), September 1968.

Editor, *The Astounding Science Fiction Anthology*. New York, Simon and Schuster, 1952; shortened version, as *The First [and Second] Astounding Science Fiction Anthology*, London, Grayson, 2 vols., 1954, and as *Astounding Tales of Space and Time*, New York, Berkley, 1957; complete version, as *The First [and Second] Astounding Science Fiction Anthology*, London, New English Library, 2 vols., 1964-65.
Editor, *Prologue to Analog.* New York, Doubleday, 1962; London, Panther, 1967.
Editor, *Analog 1-8.* New York, Doubleday, 8 vols., 1962-71; London, Panther, 2 vols., 1967; London, Dobson, 4 vols., 1968.
Editor, *Analog Anthology.* London, Dobson, 1965.

*   *   *

Had it not been for John W. Campbell, Jr., science fiction as a publisher's category might have perished with the demise of the pulp industry. As editor of *Astounding* (later *Analog*) *Science Fiction*, from September 1937 to December 1971, he demanded good writing and sometimes got it. That is his achievement (never mind his cranky indulgence in Dianetics and the Dean Drive), and he set the standard with the better of his own stories. As a result, his magazine attracted enough story-tellers that it and the science-fiction genre remain in existence today. (The stories of reasoned fantasy he published as editor of *Unknown Worlds* are, however, no longer current.)

His early stories take off from the space operatics of E.E. Smith, but with that extra something-to-say that interested the industrial scientists who became his chief readers. The something that must have interested them was the idea of professional colleagueship which stressed the intellectual value of shared discovery; the outcome of the research and development was not a new consumer product, but something to save the species.

Campbell's first story, "The Voice of the Void" (1930), set the pattern. Men ten billion years in the future prepare to leave the planets of the solar system because the sun is dying. By this time, science had become central to the human way of life and a scientist in training takes a 70-year course at an engineering school, where making inventions is part of the curriculum. Graduates from such schools have been gathering for generations to meet the growing emergency of the sun's death. At last they develop a matter transmitter that sends fleets of spaceships to another system of planets orbiting the giant star Betelgeuse. They accomplish this in a spirit of professional association, men of pure science called to salvationist duty, but in just those fields—aviation and broadcasting—under commercial development at the time of writing. Likewise in "Twilight" a time traveller from the far future asks what are the most important inventions of the day, and the answer is "airplanes and radio."

The pulp tradition of SF that Campbell elevated above adventure fiction—the last refuge of rugged individualism in American letters—was a world of "pooled mental resources." His intellectual hero was attractive to the young student or professional scientist in industry whose job was anything but free to explore wherever the research team's curiosity might lead.

Two groups of Campbell stories follow through with a standard set of heroes. The more popular one is the Arcot, Morey, and Wade series. Dr. Richard Arcot, a world-famous physicist, works for the research laboratories of Transcontinental Airways, selling it his inventions under the patronage of its president, who happens to be the father of Arcot's colleague, the mathematician Morey. Wade, introduced during the course of the first story, "Piracy Preferred," is an air pirate who preys on Transcontinental's great 30,000-passenger superplanes with a device for making his marauding aircraft invisible, but after being captured he joins Arcot's lab staff. Fuller, an aeronautical design engineer, joins the group in "Solarite," and proves his worth in *Islands of Space* by designing a faster-than-light ship on a principle discovered by Arcot. All four then make a tour of the cosmos. The title islands are island universes, galactic nebulae. Financing a tour of these is more than even Transcontinental can afford, so its president helps Arcot raise the rest in popular support from "the wealth of two worlds," Earth and Venus. All this is spent on a fantastic adventure of observational science. But the debt is repaid when the group is able to deal with an alien threat in *Invaders from the Infinite*.

The other story series is *The Planeteers*, dealing with Penton and Blake, a pair of cosmic explorers who land on various worlds and solve exotic puzzles. But again this has survival value. Curiosity is a tough-minded quality because what observation reveals is that "change is the natural order of things." Science is "a method of thinking" that can meet "goals ahead larger than those we know" by knowing how, when the problem is upon us, "to produce that which never existed." Science is the way mankind educates itself to meet the challenge of necessity.

Campbell's test of survival is nowhere dramatized more forcibly than in *The Moon Is Hell*. The first rocketship to the moon crashes and its crew of research scientists, stranded on the dead rock, win from the object of their curiosity food, water, and air. This is the research and development process glamorized in a power fantasy that makes its most important business the winning of life itself. "Machines and gadgets aren't the end and goal; they are the means to the true goal." The commercial products of the technological revolution are but objects of practice on which to learn and organize the skills of innovative group thinking, come the day of unexpected crisis.

Curiosity is the mainspring of human adaptability, and may very well drive the products of man's inventions when he himself is gone. In "The Last Evolution" Campbell introduces an original concept or robots, heretofore imagined only as workers or slaves. He has them become man's evolutionary descendants. They are "science machines" that make other machines. They supercede man, but surprisingly they end by recreating him. The machine brings to perfection man's urge to explore and do research and create that which never before existed.

A technology that outlives its makers is also the theme of Campbell's most famous story, "Twilight." 88 million years in the future,

man is extinct, but his great automatic cities are still in place. The deathless cities go on with "the tireless, ceaseless perfection their designers had incorporated in them."

Perhaps the best work of fiction Campbell ever wrote is "Who Goes There?" An alien monster is found frozen in the Antarctic ice, buried with its ship, by a team of scientists doing weather research. Once thawed, it gets loose in their camp and changes form by imitating one or more of the sled dogs and one of the men, down to their cells and memories. The dogs are killed, but the problem remains how to discover by some test which man is the monster before it takes over the camp and then the whole world. The leader of the expedition is the tough-minded scientist who has the intellectual prowess to do just that. He devises a blood test, taking a sample from each man and touching it in turn with the tip of a hot needle. The monster not only replicates any body it takes over, it reduplicates itself in every cell of that body. The test is this: when irritated the monster's *blood* will live—and crawl away." It does, and the man whose sample it is reveals himself in hideous form. Alert for the transformation with poised axes, the others hack their false colleague to pieces. These few men, outnumbered by millions of life cells, all intelligent, were not defeated. Humanity is *real*, monsterhood is false. Humans have "not an imitated, but a bred-in-the-bone instinct, a driving, unquenchable fire that's genuine."

The monster is no villain: it is a problem. And to be conquered it must be understood, as must all the other unpredictable threats of nature in a universe of constant change. It is deadly to *adapt* to nature, a lazy, undisciplined way that leads to digestion by the cosmic process; survival means *control* of nature. The monster is the opposite of humanity because it goes with nature, not against it. For curiosity it has mere cunning, for pooled mental resources collective imitation. And here is the political note in Campbell's thinking, often sounded in his magazine editorials. For him, collectivism is a monstrous thing that would devour human ideals, but should not be able to do so as long as the superior strength of individuals is united in free association.

—Leon E. Stover

CAPON, (Harry) Paul. Also wrote as Noel Kenton. British. Born in Kenton Hall, Suffolk, 18 December 1912. Educated at St. George's School, Harpenden, Hertfordshire. Served in the Royal Army Service Corps, 1940; Technical Director, Soviet Film Agency, 1941-44. Married 1) Doreen Evans-Evans in 1933, one daughter and one son; 2) Amy Charlotte Gillam in 1956. Free-lance film editor and scriptwriter for London Films, 1931-32, Gaumont British, 1933-35, Warner Brothers, 1936-37, British National 1944-48, Walt Disney, 1955-58, and Granada Television, 1959-62; Head of Film Production, Independent Television News, London, 1963-67. *Died 24 November 1969.*

SCIENCE-FICTION PUBLICATIONS

Novels (series: Antigeos)

The Other Half of the Sun (Antigeos). London, Heinemann, 1950.
The Other Half of the Planet (Antigeos). London, Heinemann, 1952.
The World at Bay (juvenile). London, Heinemann, 1953; Philadelphia, Winston, 1954.
Down to Earth (Antigeos). London, Heinemann, 1954.
Phobos, The Robot Planet (juvenile). London, Heinemann, 1955; as *Lost—A Moon*, Indianapolis, Bobbs Merrill, 1956.
The Wonderbolt (juvenile). London, Ward Lock, 1955.
Into the Tenth Millennium. London, Heinemann, 1956.
Flight of Time (juvenile). London, Heinemann, 1960.

OTHER PUBLICATIONS

Novels

Battered Caravanserai.   London, Heinemann, 1942.
Brother Cain.   London, Heinemann, 1945.
The Hosts of Midian.   London, Nicholson and Watson, 1946.
Dead Man's Chest.   London, Nicholson and Watson, 1947.
The Murder of Jacob Canansey.   London, Heinemann, 1947.
Fanfare for Shadows.   London, Boardman, 1947.
O Clouds Unfold.   London, Ward Lock, 1948.
Image of a Murder.   London, Boardman, 1949.
Toby Scuffell.   London, Ward Lock, 1949.
Threescore Years.   London, Ward Lock, 1950.
Delay of Doom.   London, Ward Lock, 1950.
No Time for Death.   London, Ward Lock, 1951.
Death at Shinglestrand.   London, Ward Lock, 1952.
Death on a Wet Sunday.   London, Ward Lock, 1953.
In All Simplicity.   London, Heinemann, 1953.
The Seventh Passenger.   London, Ward Lock, 1953.
Malice Domestic.   London, Ward Lock, 1954.
Thirty Days Hath September.   London, Ward Lock, 1955.
Margin of Terror.   London, Ward Lock, 1955.
Amongst Those Missing.   London, Heinemann, 1959.
The Final Refuge.   London, Harrap, 1969.

Other (juvenile)

The Cave of Cornelius.   London, Heinemann, 1959; as *The End of the Tunnel,* Indianapolis, Bobbs Merrill, 1959.
Warriors' Moon.   London, Hodder and Stoughton, 1960; New York, Putnam, 1964.
The Kingdom of the Bulls.   London, Hodder and Stoughton, 1961; New York, Norton, 1962.
Lord of the Chariots.   London, Hodder and Stoughton, 1962.
The Golden Cloak.   London, Hodder and Stoughton, 1963.
The Great Yarmouth Mystery: A Chronicle of a Famous Crime (for adults).   London, Harrap, 1965.
Roman Gold.   Leicester, Brockhampton Press, 1968.
Strangers on Forlorn.   London, Harrap, 1969.

Translator, *Surrealism,* by Yves Duplessis.   New York, Walker, 1963.
Translator, *Sexual Reproduction,* by Louis Gallien.   New York, Walker, 1963.
Translator (as Noel Kenton), *Animal Migration*, by René Thévenin.   New York, Walker, 1963.
Translator, *The French Wines,* by Georges Ray.   New York, Walker, 1965.

*   *   *

Paul Capon's novels have had very little distribution in the United States and he is generally unknown there, which is surprising in view of the large number of inferior writers whose works have been reprinted from their original European appearance. He received most attention with the Antigeos trilogy, portions of which were broadcast on the BBC. Antigeos is a twin world to the Earth, located at the opposite side of Earth's orbit, hidden from us by the bulk of the sun. This impossiblility has recurred frequently in the genre, and is just plausible enough to be fascinating to casual readers.

Antigeos is a Utopia of sorts, or at least it is until the unscrupulous Earth humans arrive. In the first volume the initial contact is made, but the unpleasant results don't become evident until the middle volume where human vanities and greeds begin to work their way on Antigeos. In the final volume a group of financiers plot to exploit the newly discovered world as an involuntary colony, until they are thwarted by the true at heart.

The rest of Capon's adventure novels have been dismissed as juveniles, and two at least very definitely are, *The Wonderbolt* and *Flight of Time.* But Capon's excellent narrative ability makes some of them of interest to adult readers as well. There is an alien invasion from Poppea in *The World at Bay,* for example, unique in that the aliens arrive in diminutive space stations. *Phobos, The Robot Planet* has as its central character the entire Martian moon, which we learn to be a gigantic robot spaceship which wanders around kidnapping people out of curiosity rather than malice. This latter novel is lighter in tone than the others, and has its moments of genuine humor.

Paul Capon went on to write one major adult novel, *Into the Tenth Millennium,* and made use of one of the oldest of science fiction plots—the journey into the future to visit a Utopian society. Capon transports three modern-day humans via drugs to a future society which does seem to have solved most of the significant societal problems, and we are treated to an unusually entertaining tour of that society. Never ignoring the need to sustain interest, Capon avoids preachiness, and portrays for us a world that is realistic as well as Utopian, a goal never achieved by most of the "classic" works of this type.

Capon was not particularly prolific and attracted little attention with his books, all of which are presently out of print. This is surprising because his narrative technique is masterful and his plots, while familiar, are not more so than many another far more successful novel. The predominance of young protagonists may well have stereotyped Capon as a writer of juveniles, making it impossible for him to reach a more adult audience with is more serious work.

—Don D'Ammassa

CARR, Terry (Gene).   Also writes as Norman Edwards.   American. Born in Grants Pass, Oregon, 19 February 1937. Educated at the City College of San Francisco, 1954-57, A.A. 1957; University of California, Berkeley, 1957-59. Married 1) Miriam Dyches in 1959 (divorced, 1961); 2) Carol Newmark in 1961. Associate Editor, Scott Meredith Literary Agency, New York, 1962-64; Editor, Ace Books, New York, 1964-71; Editor, *SFWA Bulletin,* 1967-68; Founder, Science Fiction Writers of America Forum, 1967-68. Since 1971, free-lance writer, editor, and lecturer. Recipient: Hugo Award, for editing, 1959, for non-fiction, 1973. Address: 11037 Broadway Terrace, Oakland, California 94611, U.S.A.

SCIENCE-FICTION PUBLICATIONS

Novels

Warlord of Kor.   New York, Ace, 1963.
Invasion from 2500 (as Norman Edwards, with Ted White). Derby, Connecticut, Monarch, 1964.
Cirque.   Indianapolis, Bobbs Merrill, 1977; London, Dobson, 1979.

Short Stories

The Light at the End of the Universe.   New York, Pyramid, 1976.

Uncollected Short Story

"Virra," in *Fantasy and Science Fiction* (New York), October 1978.

OTHER PUBLICATIONS

Other

Editor, with Donald A. Wollheim, *World's Best Science Fiction 1965 (to 1971).*   New York, Ace, 7 vols., 1965-71; *1968 to 1971* vols. published London, Gollancz, 4 vols., 1969-71; first 4 vols. published as *World's Best Science Fiction: First* [to *Fourth*] *Series,* Ace, 1970.
Editor, *Science Fiction for People Who Hate Science Fiction.* New York, Doubleday, 1966.

Editor, *New Worlds of Fantasy 1-3.* New York, Ace, 3 vols., 1967-71; vol. 1 published as *Step Outside Your Mind,* London, Dobson, 1969.
Editor, *The Others.* New York, Fawcett, 1968.
Editor, *Universe 1-10.* New York, Ace, 2 vols., 1971-72; New York, Random House, 3 vols., 1973-74; New York, Doubleday, 5 vols., 1976-80; London, Dobson, 10 vols., 1975-80.
Editor, *The Best Science Fiction of the Year 1-9.* New York, Ballantine, 9 vols., 1972-80; vols. 4-8 published London, Gollancz, 1975-80.
Editor, *This Side of Infinity.* New York, Ace, 1972.
Editor, *An Exaltation of Stars.* New York, Simon and Schuster, 1973.
Editor, *Into the Unknown.* Nashville, Nelson, 1973.
Editor, *Worlds Near and Far.* Nashville, Nelson, 1974.
Editor, *Creatures from Beyond.* Nashville, Nelson, 1975.
Editor, *The Ides of Tomorrow* (juvenile). Boston, Little Brown, 1976.
Editor, *Planets of Wonder: A Treasury of Space Opera* (juvenile). Nashville, Nelson, 1976.
Editor, *To Follow a Star* (juvenile). Nashville, Nelson, 1977.
Editor, *The Infinite Arena* (juvenile). Nashville, Nelson, 1977.
Editor, *Classic Science Fiction: The First Golden Age.* New York, Harper, 1978; London, Robson, 1979.
Editor, *The Year's Finest Fantasy 1-2.* New York, Berkley, 2 vols., 1978-79.
Editor, *The Best Science Fiction Novellas of the Year 1-2.* New York, Ballantine, 2 vols., 1979-80.
Editor, *Beyond Reality.* New York, Elsevier Nelson, 1979.
Editor, *Dream's Edge: Science Fiction Stories about the Future of the Planet Earth.* San Francisco, Sierra Club, 1980.

*

Terry Carr comments:

I've never been prolific as a fiction writer: most of my "career" has been devoted to editing, first as an editor for Ace Books, where I founded the "Ace Science Fiction Specials" series, 1968-71, and more recently as an editor of anthologies.

As a writer I'm known best for stories about alien creatures ("The Dance of the Changer and the Three," "Hop-Friend," *Cirque,* etc.), but in truth this is an outgrowth of my interest in communication between *all* kinds of "people." Short stories such as "Touchstone" and "They Live on Levels" are examples that don't include aliens: the novel *Cirque* has an important alien character but it's mostly about communication between the human characters. Another "theme" in my stories is transcendental experience: see particularly the novella "The Winds at Starmont" and the novel *Cirque.*

*   *   *

Terry Carr's career clearly illustrates the versatility of many science-fiction personalities. Like other major writers and editors—including Robert Silverberg, Ted White, Gregory Benford, and Harlan Ellison—Carr first gained prominence in the fan community of the 1950's. (His first Hugo Award was for editing the amateur news magazine *Fanac* with Ron Ellik.) This and other amateur magazines helped to launch his career as a professional editor. He also became known for humorous, ironic writing, a significant feature of much of his professional fiction.

In 1961, Carr began writing science fiction professionally. His early novels, *Invasion from 2500* (with Ted White) and *Warlord of Kor,* are clearly potboilers. However, Carr's short stories from the 1960's reveal both literary polish and a fascination with alien beings characteristic of his later work, especially as shown by the millipede in *Cirque.* These qualities are shown in "Hop-Friend," a witty variation on Weinbaum's "A Martian Odyssey."

Carr's mature fiction includes "The Dance of the Changer and the Three" which provides an evocative study of an alien culture as told through one of its myths; "Ozymandias" linking Egyptian burial rituals with cryonics; and "They Live on Levels" in which cultures and characters are gradually revealed through messages between them. All display polish and a wide-ranging imagination.

These qualities also characterize *Cirque.* Carr utilizes the convention of a crisis in the far-future city of Cirque to force his disparate characters to change their lives. The novel, thus structured, adheres to the traditional unities of place, time, and action. It relies heavily on coincidence, yet characters and events are made plausible. The city itself is a near-Utopia, maintained by a literal rejection of filth which must be confronted and accepted. Thus the novel is both a psychological study of the need for change, growth, and acceptance, and a religious allegory of the power of love.

Carr's major importance in the sf field has been as an editor. *Classic Science Fiction* is his most important collection, since it offers not only stories from the Golden Age of the early 1940's but also Carr's meticulously researched background notes on the authors and the period. For his *Universe* series, and the "best of the year" collections, he has become respected as "the editor with impeccable taste."

—Susan Wood

———————

CARTER, Angela (Olive, née Stalker). British. Born in Eastbourne, Sussex, 7 May 1940. Educated at the University of Bristol, 1962-65, B.A. in English 1965. Married Paul Carter in 1960 (divorced, 1972). Journalist, Croydon, Surrey, 1958-61. Arts Council Fellow in Creative Writing, University of Sheffield, 1976-78. Recipient: Rhys Memorial Prize, 1968; Maugham Award, 1969; Cheltenham Festival prize, 1979. Agent: Deborah Rogers Ltd., 5-11 Mortimer Street, London W1N 7RH, England.

SCIENCE-FICTION PUBLICATIONS

Novels

The Magic Toyshop. London, Heinemann, 1967; New York, Simon and Schuster, 1968.
Heroes and Villains. London, Heinemann, 1969; New York, Simon and Schuster, 1970.
The Infernal Desire Machines of Dr. Hoffman. London, Hart Davis, 1972; as *The War of Dreams,* New York, Harcourt Brace, 1974.
The Passion of New Eve. London, Gollancz, and New York, Harcourt Brace, 1977.

Short Stories

Fireworks: Nine Profane Pieces. London, Quartet, 1974.
The Bloody Chamber and Other Stories. London, Gollancz, 1979; New York, Harper, 1980.

OTHER PUBLICATIONS

Novels

Shadow Dance. London, Heinemann, 1966; as *Honeybuzzard,* New York, Simon and Schuster, 1967.
Several Perceptions. London, Heinemann, 1968; New York, Simon and Schuster, 1969.
Love. London, Hart Davis, 1971.

Plays

Radio Plays: *Vampirella,* 1976; *Come unto These Yellow Sands,* 1979; *The Company of Wolves,* from her own story, 1980.

Verse

Unicorn. Leeds, Location Press, 1966.

Other

Miss Z, The Dark Young Lady (juvenile).   London, Heinemann,
   and New York, Simon and Schuster, 1970.
The Donkey Prince (juvenile).   New York, Simon and Schuster,
   1970.
Comic and Curious Cats, illustrated by Martin Leman.   London,
   Gollancz, and New York, Crown, 1979.
The Sadeian Woman: An Exercise in Cultural History.   London,
   Virago, 1979; as *The Sadeian Woman and the Ideology of Por-
   nography,* New York, Pantheon, 1979.

Translator, *The Fairy Tales of Charles Perrault.*   London, Gollancz, 1977; New York, Avon, 1978.

Angela Carter comments:
   Speak as you find.

                    *   *   *

Angela Carter describes herself as a Gothic writer, which in her
case puts her in the distinguished company of Mary Shelley and
Brian Aldiss. In her persuasive "Polemical Preface" to *The Sadeian
Woman,* she proposes a "moral pornographer" as an artist who
demystifies the flesh to reveal "the real relations of man and his
kind." More generally, I think she might see her work as that of a
"moral mythographer" who creates myths to destroy myths, pornographic writing being one of her weapons. She, more properly than
Sade, to whom she applied the phrase, is "a terrorist of the imagination": he is too boring and disgusting to be terrifying and she is
over-deferential as well as patronizing in her critique of this writer,
who really only serves as her stalking-horse.

   Most of Carter's fiction may be classed as fantasy, and even the
delightful mainstream comedy, *Several Perceptions,* uses fantasy as
its subject. Three of her novels are in the SF genre, two of which are
concerned with the harnessing of science in the service of fantasy, so
that "science fantasy" describes them with particular felicity.

   In the post-holocaust world of *Heroes and Villains,* civilization
has been reduced to ivory towers guarded by Soldiers (the heroes)
and menaced by barbarians and mutants. The heroine Marianne, a
Professor's daughter, rescues one of the Villains during a raid (he
happens to be her brother's murderer) and flees with him: he rapes,
then marries her. The account of their ensuing love-hate relationship is a kind of anti-romance, in which the ambivalent barbaric
nastiness and beauty are vividly paraded before us. One of the
novel's key themes is the treacherous nature of appearances, yet
possibly the book exists principally for the sake of one apparition, a
strange déjà-vu effect whereby Henri Rousseau's painting, *The
Sleeping Gypsy,* is magically recreated (an effect requiring thorough
preparation, for instance the provision of conditions in which it is
feasible for lions to roam the English countryside).

   The Infernal Desire Machines of Dr. Hoffman, in which an
embodiment of Sade actually appears in one of its Grand Guignol
episodes, is a much more powerful and ambitious work in which the
author's evidently wide reading among the great satiric fantasists is
everywhere apparent. The picaresque hero, Desiderio (a desirer), is
on a mission to kill Dr. Hoffman, generator of mirages that drive
men mad, and a quest to find and possess Hoffman's daughter,
Albertina. The rational but impressionable hero is a reluctant exorcist and the end to his adventure seems of less importance than the
erotic and horrific sideshows which distract him on the way.
Although her coldblooded "mad scientist" villain is sufficiently evil,
his chilling nature is matched by the resolute sangfroid of the
author, even while describing multiple buggery, rape, cannibalism,
or eye-juggling; the excessive violence is not accompanied by a
commensurable emotional response. One of the best episodes is in a
relatively low key, Desiderio's night of love with the somnambulist
daughter of an absentee mayor, his subsequent arrest for her
murder, and his escape by climbing one-handed up a chimney. The
writing is so good in this novel that one wishes it were better as a
whole, that it had more humour and more seriousness, as with Swift
or even Beckford.

   The Passion of New Eve achieves a better balance of horror and
humour, wit and pathos, self-indulgent fantasy and cool iconoclasm. The hero, Evelyn, is an Englishman precipitated into the

American nightmare. Not a nice man himself, he mistreats his black
mistress in New York, once "a city of visible reason" but now in
Ballardian decay. Fleeing to the desert, Evelyn becomes New Eve
when captured by lesbian guerrillas; fleeing from them she is raped
by the petty tyrant Zero and becomes one of his harem, of lower
status than his pigs. She accompanies the nihilist Zero on his
mission to kill the film idol Tristessa, whom Evelyn had worshipped. Tristessa is revealed as transvestite, impregnates Eve, kills
Zero, is killed in error by soldiers while Southern California burns
in apocalyptic warfare, leaving Eve, after passage through an Earth
womb, to escape American shores bearing her child, committed to
the sea like a female Prospero. Machismo is mocked splendidly in
both male and female in this satiric anti-mythic novel, a bravura
performance.

   A few of the tales in *Fireworks* fall sufficiently within the genre to
serve as an excuse for reading the whole fantastic collection. In the
Afterword the author refers to her Gothic tradition as retaining a
singular moral function, "that of provoking unease." She understands the quality of her own art perfectly here.

                                                    —Michael J. Tolley

                    _____

CARTER, Lin(wood Vrooman).   American.   Born in St. Peters-
burg, Florida, 9 June 1930. Educated at Columbia University, New
York, 1953-54. Served in the United States Army Infantry, 1951-53.
Married Noel Vreeland in 1964. Advertising and publishers copy-
writer, 1957-69. Since 1969, free-lance writer: editorial consultant,
Ballantine Books Adult Fantasy. Recipient; Nova Award, 1972.
Agent: Henry Morrison Inc., 311½ West 20th Street, New York,
New York 10011. Address: 100-15 195th Street, Hollis, Long Island,
New York 11423, U.S.A.

SCIENCE-FICTION PUBLICATIONS

Novels (series: Callisto; Conan; Great Imperium; Green Star;
   Thongor; World's End; Zarkon)

The Wizard of Lemuria.   New York, Ace, 1965; revised edition, as
   Thongor and the Wizard of Lemuria, New York, Berkley, 1969.
Thongor of Lemuria. •New York, Ace, 1966; revised edition, as
   Thongor and the Dragon City, New York, Berkley, 1970.
The Star Magicians.   New York, Ace, 1966.
The Man Without a Planet (Great Imperium).   New York, Ace,
   1966.
Destination: Saturn, with David Grinnell.   New York, Avalon,
   1967.
The Flame of Iridar.   New York, Belmont, 1967.
Thongor Against the Gods.   New York, Paperback Library, 1967.
The Thief of Thoth.   New York, Belmont, 1968.
Conan of the Isles, with L. Sprague de Camp.   New York, Lancer,
   1968.
Tower at the Edge of Time.   New York, Belmont, 1968.
Thongor at the End of Time.   New York, Paperback Library,
   1968; London, Tandem, 1970.
Thongor in the City of Magicians.   New York, Paperback Library,
   1968.
Conan the Wanderer, with Robert E. Howard and L. Sprague de
   Camp.   New York, Lancer, 1968; London, Sphere, 1974.
The Purloined Planet.   New York, Belmont, 1969.
Giant of World's End.   New York, Belmont, 1969.
Conan of Cimmeria, with Robert E. Howard and L. Sprague de
   Camp.   New York, Lancer, 1969; London, Sphere, 1974.
Lost World of Time.   New York, New American Library, 1969.
Tower of the Medusa.   New York, Ace, 1969.
Star Rogue (Great Imperium).   New York, Lancer, 1970.

Thongor Fights the Pirates of Tarakus.   New York, Berkley, 1970;
  as *Thongor and the Pirates of Tarakus,* London, Tandem, 1971.
Conan the Buccaneer, with L. Sprague de Camp.   New York,
  Lancer, 1971.
Outworlder (Great Imperium).   New York, Lancer, 1971.
Black Legion of Callisto.   New York, Dell, 1972; London, Futura,
  1975.
Under the Green Star.   New York, DAW, 1972.
The Quest of Kadji.   New York, Belmont, 1972.
The Black Star.   New York, Dell, 1973.
Jandar of Callisto.   New York, Dell, 1973.
The Man Who Loved Mars.   New York, Fawcett, and London,
  White Lion, 1973.
Sky Pirates of Callisto.   New York, Dell, 1973; London, Futura,
  1975.
When the Green Star Calls.   New York, DAW, 1973.
The Valley Where Time Stood Still.   New York, Doubleday, 1974.
Time War.   New York, Dell, 1974.
By the Light of the Green Star.   New York, DAW, 1974.
The Warrior of World's End.   New York, DAW, 1974.
The Nemesis of Evil (Zarkon).   New York, Doubleday, 1975.
Invisible Death (Zarkon).   New York, Doubleday, 1975.
Mad Empress of Callisto.   New York, Dell, 1975.
Mind Wizard of Callisto.   New York, Dell, 1975.
Lankar of Callisto.   New York, Dell, 1975.
As the Green Star Rises.   New York, DAW, 1975.
The Enchantress of World's End.   New York, DAW, 1975.
The Volcano Ogre (Zarkon).   New York, Doubleday, 1976.
The Immortal of World's End.   New York, DAW, 1976.
In the Green Star's Glow.   New York, DAW, 1976.
The Barbarian of World's End.   New York, DAW, 1977.
Conan of Aquilonia (collection), with L. Sprague de Camp.   New
  York, Ace, 1977; London, Sphere, 1978.
Ylana of Callisto.   New York, Dell, 1977.
The City Outside the World.   New York, Berkley, 1977.
Renegade of Callisto.   New York, Dell, 1978.
The Wizard of Zao.   New York, DAW, 1978.
The Pirate of World's End.   New York, DAW, 1978.
Conan the Swordsman, with L. Sprague de Camp.   New York,
  Bantam, 1978; London, Sphere, 1979.
Conan the Liberator, with L. Sprague de Camp.   New York, Ban-
  tam, 1979.
Journey to the Underground World.   New York, DAW, 1979.
Tara of the Twilight.   New York, Kensington, 1979.
Lost Worlds.   New York, DAW, 1980.

Short Stories

King Kull, with Robert E. Howard.   New York, Lancer, 1967.
Conan, with Robert E. Howard and L. Sprague de Camp.   New
  York, Lancer, 1967; London, Sphere, 1974.
Beyond the Gates of Dream.   New York, Belmont, 1969.

Uncollected Short Stories

"The Dweller in the Tomb" and "Shaggai," in *Dark Things,* edited
  by August Derleth.   Sauk City, Wisconsin, Arkham House,
  1971.
"The Higher Heresies of Oolimar," in *Flashing Swords!,* edited by
  Lin Carter.   New York, Doubleday, 1973.
"Black Hawk of Valkarth, " in *Fantastic* (New York), September
  1974.
"The Vale of Pnath" and "Out of the Ages, " in *Nameless Places,*
  edited by Gerald W. Page.   Sauk City, Wisconsin, Arkham
  House, 1975.
"The Twelve Wizards of Ong," in *Kingdoms of Sorcery,* edited by
  Lin Carter.   New York, Doubleday, 1975.
"The City in the Jewel," in *Fantastic* (New York), December 1975.
"The Curious Custom of the Turjan Seraad," in *Flashing Swords! 3,*
  edited by Lin Carter.   New York, Dell, 1976.
"Zoth-Ommog," in *The Disciples of Cthulhu,* edited by Edward P.
  Berglund.   New York, DAW, 1976.
"The Martian El Dorado of Parker Wintley," in *The DAW Science
  Fiction Reader,* edited by Donald A. Wollheim.   New York,
  DAW, 1976.

"People of the Dragon," in *Fantastic* (New York), February 1976.
"Black Moonlight," in *Fantastic* (New York), November 1976.
"The Pillars of Hell," in *Fantastic* (New York), December 1977.

OTHER PUBLICATIONS

Verse

Dreams from R'lyeh.   Sauk City, Wisconsin, Arkham House,
  1975.

Other

Tolkien: A Look Behind "The Lord of the Rings."   New York,
  Ballantine, 1969.
Lovecraft: A Look Behind the "Cthulhu Mythos."   New York,
  Ballantine, 1972; London, Panther, 1975.
Imaginary Worlds: The Art of Fantasy.   New York, Ballantine,
  1973.
Middle-Earth: The World of Tolkien.   New York, Centaur, 1977.

Editor, *Dragons, Elves, and Heroes.*   New York, Ballantine, 1969.
Editor, *The Young Magicians.*   New York, Ballantine, 1969.
Editor, *The Magic of Atlantis.*   New York, Lancer, 1970.
Editor, *Golden Cities, Far.*   New York, Ballantine, 1971.
Editor, *The Spawn of Cthulhu.*   New York, Ballantine, 1971.
Editor, *New Worlds for Old.*   New York, Ballantine, 1971.
Editor, *Discoveries in Fantasy.*   New York, Ballantine, 1972;
  London, Pan, 1974.
Editor, *Great Short Novels of Adult Fantasy 1-2.*   New York,
  Ballantine, 2 vols., 1972.
Editor, *Flashing Swords! 1-4.*   New York, Doubleday, 2 vols.,
  1973; New York, Dell, 2 vols., 1976-77.
Editor, *The Year's Best Fantasy Stories 1-4.*   New York, DAW, 4
  vols., 1975-78.
Editor, *Kingdoms of Sorcery.*   New York, Doubleday, 1975.
Editor, *Realms of Wizardry.*   New York, Doubleday, 1976.

*   *   *

Writing in the tradition of Edgar Rice Burroughs and A. Merritt,
Lin Carter has become a leading practitioner of Sword and Sorcery
fiction-fantasies and sagas involving superheroes, magicians, fair
damsels, interplanetary pirates, and cosmic adventurers. The recipe
for typical Lin Carter fare has been aptly summed up in *Science
Fiction Review:* "Take a pinch of Flash Gordon, add some Barba-
rella, a little John Carter, a touch of *Dying Earth,* and you have Lin
Carter." If this smorgasbord seems rehashed or stale at times,
fantasy fans don't seem to mind: he has more devoted readers and
more books in print than many a novelist with more serious pretensions and aspirations. However, Carter has let it be known (in
Realms of Wizardry) that he doesn't consider his work "mere juvenile escapism." Although he concedes that "fantasy began to go out
of fashion about two hundred years ago" and we are "still mired
down in the Age of Realism," the great tradition of fantasy has
flourished in writers like William Morris, Lord Dunsany, E.R.
Eddison, H.P. Lovecraft and, more recently, in Jack Vance, Clifford Ball, and Roger Zelazny. Whether one hears in Lin Carter's
work "echoes of a wild, rarer music" or a former advertising copywriter letting off steam depends on one's taste and judgment.

While it is impossible to summarize a writer so prodigiously
prolific, a sampling of his major series will give the flavor of his
work. The most fantastic and exotic is World's End, an epic set on
the gigantic continent of Gondwane in the unimaginably distant
future (700 million years from now, in the Aeon of the Falling
Moon). After an "azure deluge" an artisan-priest and his non-
human wife discover a newly created giant named Ganelon Silver-
mane wandering naked and helpless. The miraculous appearance of
this superhero sets the stage for half a dozen novels depicting his
Gilgameshian struggles against evil. Equally fabulous, but more
contemporary, is Prince Zarkon, the leader of a band of adventurers
with gangster movie monsters ("Scorchy" Muldoon, "Ace" Har-
rigon, "Doc" Jenkins). Written out of nostalgia for the pulp fiction
of the 1930's, particularly *Doc Savage* and *The Avenger,* these files
of the "Nemesis of Evil" involve high-level crime fighting and

intrigue. In the Green Star sequence, Carter uses a first-person narrator who is rich, handsome, but unfortunately crippled with polio. His romantic dreams of glory and adventure frustrated, the narrator turns to Eckankar, the Tibetan art of soul-travel, in order to voyage beyond his physical body to the fantastic world of the Green Star. There he finds adventures galore: he evades the snares of a mad scientist, searches for his beloved princess, and struggles with monsters and malefactors for another half-dozen volumes.

Carter has also written single novels like *The Wizard of Zao*, a picaresque "heroic fantasy" that blends humor and adventure. The green-skinned wizard is a colorful old codger whose first act is to purchase a voluptuous "Wild Girl" on sale at a slave market in the impoverished Kingdom of Ning. With this ludicrously naive companion, he sets off on a series of improbable adventures, battling evil and having fun, until he finally returns to Magicians Mountain to "hobnob with his fellow wizards."

Carter's novels suggest not only the unquenchable appeal of fantasy but also self-conscious nostalgia that makes all he writes seem derivative. By straining to make myths, epics, and legends easily palatable, Carter has whetted the appetite but provided little solid fare to nourish our hunger for the truly marvelous, ideal, and transcendent.

—Anthony Manousos

CARTMILL, Cleve. Also wrote as Michael Corbin. American. Born in Platteville, Wisconsin, in 1908. Married; one son. Accountant, newspaperman, radio operator; invented the Blackmill system of high-speed typography. *Died 11 February 1964.*

SCIENCE-FICTION PUBLICATIONS

Short Stories (series: Jake Murchison)

The Space Scavengers. Chatsworth, California, Major, 1975.

Uncollected Short Stories

"The Shape of Desire," in *Unknown* (New York), June 1941.
"No News Today," in *Unknown* (New York), October 1941.
"Bit of Tapestry," in *Unknown* (New York), December 1941.
"Prelude to Armageddon," in *Unknown* (New York), April 1942.
"No Graven Image," in *Unknown* (New York), February 1943.
"Guardian" (as Michael Corbin), in *Unknown* (New York), February 1943.
"The Persecutors," in *Super Science* (Kokomo, Indiana), February 1943.
"Forever Tomorrow," in *Astonishing* (Chicago), April 1943.
"Murderer's Apprentice," in *Science Fiction* (Holyoke, Massachusetts), April 1943.
"The Darker Light," in *Super Science* (Kokomo, Indiana), May 1943.
"Let's Disappear," in *Astounding* (New York), May 1943.
"Wheesht!," in *Unknown* (New York), June 1943.
"Clean-Up," in *Unknown* (New York), October 1943.
"The Link," in *Adventures in Time and Space*, edited by Raymond J. Healy and J. Francis McComas. New York, Random House, 1946; London, Grayson, 1952.
"Deadline," in *The Best of Science Fiction*, edited by Groff Conklin. New York, Crown, 1946.
"With Flaming Swords," in *A Treasury of Science Fiction*, edited by Groff Conklin. New York, Crown, 1948.
"Visiting Yokel," in *My Best Science Fiction Story*, edited by Leo Margulies and O.J. Friend. New York, Merlin Press, 1949.
"Cabal," in *Super Science* (Kokomo, Indiana), January 1949.
"Bells on His Toes," in *Fantasy and Science Fiction* (New York), Fall 1949.

"Punching Pillows," in *Astounding* (New York), June 1950.
"Captain Famine," in *Thrilling Wonder Stories* (New York), December 1950.
"Number Nine," in *Great Stories of Science Fiction*, edited by Murray Leinster. New York, Random House, 1951; London, Cassell, 1953.
"The Green Cat," in *The Outer Reaches*, edited by August Derleth. New York, Pellegrini and Cudahy, 1951; London, Consul, 1963.
"You Can't Say That," in *New Tales of Space and Time*, edited by Raymond J. Healy. New York, Holt, 1951; London, Weidenfeld and Nicolson, 1952.
"Overthrow," in *Journey to Infinity*, edited by Martin Greenberg. New York, Gnome Press, 1951.
"At Your Service," in *Thrilling Wonder Stories* (New York), August 1951.
"The Huge Beast," in *Best from Fantasy and Science Fiction*, edited by Anthony Boucher and J. Francis McComas. Boston, Little Brown, 1952.
"Nor Iron Bars," in *Fantasy and Science Fiction* (New York), August 1952.
"My Lady Smiles," in *Fantasy and Science Fiction* (New York), November 1953.
"Age Cannot Wither," in *Beyond 10* (New York), 1955.
"Youth, Anybody?," in *Fantasy and Science Fiction* (New York), November 1955.
"Hell Hath Fury," in *Hell Hath Fury*, edited by George Hay. London, Spearman, 1963.
"Oscar," in *Fifty Short Science Fiction Tales*, edited by Isaac Asimov and Groff Conklin. New York, Macmillan, 1963.
"The Bargain," in *The Unknown 5*, edited by D.R. Benson. New York, Pyramid, 1964.
"Some Day We'll Find You," in *Dimension 4*, edited by Groff Conklin. New York, Pyramid, 1964.

OTHER PUBLICATIONS

Other

"Why I Selected 'Visiting Yokel,' " in *My Best Science Fiction Story*, edited by Leo Margulies and O.J. Friend. New York, Merlin Press, 1949.

*   *   *

Some writers in science fiction, as in other fields of literature, achieve notoriety not for their body of work but for a single story or novel. Tom Godwin ("The Cold Equations") is one such writer. Another is Cleve Cartmill, for "Deadline" (*Astounding*, March 1944). Although "Deadline" has dubious literary merits (predictable plot, pedestrian handling), the story is unique in that it describes, in considerable scientific detail, the manufacture and use of an atomic bomb a year before the United States dropped the first genuine atomic bombs on Hiroshima and Nagasaki. Its publication did not cause an immediate furor in science-fiction circles; it did, however, cause one in the War Department.

Shortly after the novelette appeared, Cartmill was visited by a representative of Military Intelligence and questioned at some length; his file of correspondence with the editor of *Astounding*, John W. Campbell, concerning "Deadline" was also confiscated. Cartmill was later cleared of any wrong-doing, although he was told that he had "violated personal security" in wartime by publicly disseminating the facts contained in the story. These facts, however, were a matter of public record, as Campbell himself pointed out to the Military in denying their request not to publish any further speculation on nuclear fission. Following the close of World War II, "Deadline" became a link in the argument that science fiction is a valid medium for predicting the future. It was also pointed to with pride as an example of science fiction as a "serious" art form for adults, rather than improbable escapism for juveniles, thereby worthy of consideration not only by members of the scientific community but by the heads of government.

Despite the fact that Cartmill's rather extensive output of science fiction and fantasy is largely forgotten today, at least some of it is of a quality to interest the serious student. His best work, perhaps, is the highly imaginative short novel "Hell Hath Fury". Other excellent efforts include his first published story, "Oscar," and a grim little tale called "The Bargain." Cartmill also wrote space opera; popular in the 1940's was his "Space Salvage" series featuring Jake Murchison and his crew of the spaceship *Dolphin* who tackled "impossible" problems and made fantastic rescues in space. The best of these stories were posthumously collected as *The Space Scavengers*, the only book to bear Cartmill's name.

—Bill Pronzini

CHALKER, Jack L(aurence). American. Born in Norfolk, Virginia, 17 December 1944. Educated at Towson State College, Baltimore, B.S. 1966; Johns Hopkins University, Baltimore, M.L.A. 1969. Served in the United States Air Force 135th Air Commando Group, 1968-71, and the Maryland Air National Guard, 1968-73: Staff Sergeant. Married Eva C. Whitley in 1978. English, history, and geography teacher in Baltimore high schools, 1966-78. Since 1961, Founder-Director, Mirage Press, Baltimore. Agent: Eleanor Wood, Blassingame McCauley and Wood, 60 East 42nd Street, New York, New York 10017. Address: 4704 Warner Drive, Manchester, Maryland 21102, U.S.A.

SCIENCE-FICTION PUBLICATIONS

Novels (series: Well of Souls)

A Jungle of Stars. New York, Ballantine, 1976.
Midnight at the Well of Souls. New York, Ballantine, 1977.
Dancers in the Afterglow. New York, Ballantine, 1978.
The Web of the Chosen. New York, Ballantine, 1978.
Exiles at the Well of Souls. New York, Ballantine, 1978.
Quest for the Well of Souls. New York, Ballantine, 1978.
A War of Shadows. New York, Ace, 1979.
The Identity Matrix. New York, Berkley, 1979.
And the Devil Will Drag You Under. New York, Ballantine, 1979.
Twilight at the Well of Souls. New York, Ballantine, 1980.

Uncollected Short Stories

"No Hiding Place," in *Stellar 3*, edited by Judy-Lynn del Rey. New York, Ballantine, 1977.
"In the Wilderness," in *Analog* (New York), July 1978.
"Dance Band on the Titanic," in *The 1979 Annual World's Best SF*, edited by Donald A. Wollheim. New York, DAW, 1979.
"Stormsong Runner," in *Whispers 2*, edited by Stuart David Schiff. New York, Doubleday, 1979.

OTHER PUBLICATIONS

Other

The New H.P. Lovecraft Bibliography. Baltimore, Mirage Press, 1962; revised edition, with Mark Owings, as *The Revised H.P. Lovecraft Bibliography*, 1973.
The Index to the Science-Fantasy Publishers, with Mark Owings. Baltimore, Mirage Press, 1966; revised edition, as *Index to the SF Publishers*, 1979.
The Necronomicon: A Study, with Mark Owings. Baltimore, Mirage Press, 1967.
An Informal Biography of Scrooge McDuck. Baltimore, Mirage Press, 1974.

Editor, *In Memoriam Clark Ashton Smith.* Baltimore, Mirage Press, 1963.
Editor, *Mirage on Lovecraft.* Baltimore, Mirage Press, 1964.

*

Bibliography: in *Program Book*, Paracon 1, State College, Pennsylvania, 1978.

Jack L. Chalker comments:

Although I have a technical background, my degrees are in the social, not the pure, sciences, and my work generally reflects this. My stories are about people, mostly ordinary people, caught up in extraordinary circumstances and usually changed by them. They use the fun-house mirror reflection of science fiction to examine people and culture, including ideology, as I see them today. The themes are anti-dogmatic: ideologies and human preachments are taken apart, examined, and generally found wanting. For this reason, a lot of my work has been taken as anti-utopian and downbeat, but there is a strain of optimism there because, no matter what, mankind copes with adversity and overcomes, although never without cost. There is an inherently absurdist streak in man which has caused him, over six thousand years of recorded history to kill, torture, and maim, mostly in the name of the people. Man adapts, advances, and grows despite this.

On the individual level, my stories examine the way human beings treat each other, generally brutalizing those most in need of help, and those individuals' quests for their own better life. For these themes, and others, interwoven in my stories, science fiction provides the perfect metaphors. I am a strongly political writer, without ideology, only hope. And yet all my stories are superficially plots of twist and turn, diverting entertainments, problems to be solved. Pacing is all important to me; I want the reader to turn to the next page, to keep reading, and to have a good time as my serious themes creep into the entertainment but never get in its way.

*   *   *

Jack L. Chalker's novels combine a number of genres from which SF arises: fantasy, detective fiction, Utopian fiction, and scientific extrapolation. The Well of Souls novels stress fantastic metamorphoses of aliens and mystery-thriller elements, while Utopian concerns, expecially the communalism of Plato's city of pigs versus radical independence, combine philosophically with the mystery-thriller and an increasing concern for scientific mimetic detail in later works.

A Jungle of Stars is a frame novel, a story within a story that Chalker frequently uses to begin his alien novels. In this case he uses a realistic Viet Nam patrol as a contrast to the fantastic struggle between the two aliens, the Bromgrev and the Hunter, both of whom are failed gods. Chalker sensitively handles the Viet Nam patrol, the romance between Paul Savage and Jennifer Barron, but leaves the assumption of power by Paul at the end unsettled. No choice is made between the dictatorship of the Hunter and the communal totalitarianism of the Bromgrev; Paul's vengeance ethic may be modified by love, but his assumption of power leaves major questions unsettled.

Midnight at the Well of Souls further explores this question of what to do with power through the dilemma of another set of failed gods, the Markovians, whose answer is the creation of the Well World with hexes serving a prototypes for the universe's population. The metaphysical search which should be undertaken by Nathan Brazil is deflected by an adventure-quest to the Markovian brain by those thirsting for power and by a fascination with the different alien cultures of the hexes. Personality and character are cleverly matched to a species and an ecological environment. The threat to control the universe in *Exiles at the Well of Souls* and *Quest for the Well of Souls* is no longer directly through the Markovian brain but through the recreation of the Well World's transforming powers on New Pompeii. As in the previous novels, power for that purpose is subordinate to a quest, this time for rockets which crash land on the hexes of the Well World. The struggle to recover a rocket to travel to New Pompeii is the motive for the plots of both novels; *Exiles* ends when one rocket is destroyed by the Gedemondans; in *Quest* the struggle for the rocket is successful, but the use of the combined power of a sentient Obie and New Pompeii becomes subordinate to Mavra Chang's thirst for exploration, delaying again the answer to the metaphysical problem.

What to do with absolute power becomes a more limited political question in *The Web of the Chozen*: how to respond to human force and hegemony with a virus capable of changing humans to Choz. While becoming free of Mozes, the computer, and controlling the virus occupy much of the plot, the struggle between Choz and human results in conquest and a new apocalyptic beginning for social institutions. Bar Holiday, the transformed scout, grows as bored with the new Choz society as he was by the bureaucratic fascism of human society however. *Dancers in the Afterglow* uses an alien conquest and defeat further to explore Utopian alternatives. Ondine, a resort planet, is a test case for two systems roughly akin to Maoist communism, where "we" replaces "I," and capitalist individualism. While the work camps established by the alien robots resemble the worst Cambodian experiments, the result does produce a mindless happiness. Though no one fares well in the psychic competition of pre-conquest Ondine, the loss of individuality may not be worth the happiness. *A War of Shadows* deals with this same political struggle in which the left and right victimize the United States, although the left is merely an extension of a conservative fascist conspiracy in government itself. Chalker handles the science, in this case viral research and recombinant DNA, better than in any previous novel, and the political forces are nicely characterized; however, the book resembles the science thriller *The Andromeda Strain* far more than it does science fiction.

As in all fiction, the journey is more significant than the conclusion. Chalker, however, has learned to leash some of the big questions that leave his early novels hanging inconclusively—ideas have become taken over by life, but he has done so by reducing the protean life forms that fascinate him.

—Craig Wallace Barrow

CHANDLER, A(rthur) Bertram. Australian. Born in Aldershot, Hampshire, England, 28 March 1912. Educated at Peddar's Lane Council School, and Sir John Leman School, Beccles, Suffolk. Married 1) Joan Chandler; 2) Susan Schlenker; two daughters and one son. Apprentice, rising to Third Officer, Sun Shipping Company, London, 1928-35; Fourth Officer, rising to Chief Officer, Shaw Savill Line, London, 1936-55; Third Officer, rising to Master, Union Steam Ship Company of New Zealand, Wellington, 1956-75. Recipient: Ditmar award (Australia), 1969, 1971, 1974, 1976; Seiun Sho award (Japan), 1975; Invisible Little Man Award, 1975; Australian Literature Board Fellowship, 1980. Agent: Scott Meredith Literary Agency, 845 Third Avenue, New York, New York 10022, U.S.A.; or, E.J. Carnell Literary Agency, Rowneybury Bungalow, Sawbridgeworth, near Old Harlow, Essex CM20 2EX, England; or, Curtis Brown (Australia) Pty. Ltd., 86 William Street, Paddington, New South Wales 2021, Australia. Address: Flat 23, Kanimbla Hall, 19 Tusculum Street, Potts Point, New South Wales 2011, Australia.

SCIENCE-FICTION PUBLICATIONS

Novels (series: Empress Irene; John Grimes; Rim Worlds)

Bring Back Yesterday (Rim Worlds). New York, Ace, 1961.
Rendezvous on a Lost World (Rim Worlds). New York, Ace, 1961; as *When the Dream Dies*, London, Allison and Busby, 1980.
The Rim of Space (Rim Worlds). New York, Avalon, 1961; London, Allison and Busby, 1980.
Beyond the Galactic Rim, The Ship from Outside (Rim Worlds). New York, Ace, 1963.
The Hamelin Plague. Derby, Connecticut, Monarch, 1963.
Glory Planet. New York, Avalon, 1964.

The Deep Reaches of Space. London, Jenkins, 1964.
Into the Alternate Universe (Grimes), *The Coils of Time.* New York, Ace, 1964.
The Empress of Outer Space (Empress), *The Alternate Martians.* New York, Ace, 1965.
Space Mercenaries (Empress). New York, Ace, 1965.
The Road to the Rim (Grimes). New York, Ace, 1967.
Contraband from Otherspace (Grimes). New York, Ace, 1967.
Nebula Alert (Empress). New York, Ace, 1967.
Spartan Planet (Grimes). Sydney, Horwitz, and New York, Dell, 1968.
Catch the Star Winds (Rim Worlds). New York, Lancer, 1969.
The Sea Beasts. New York, Curtis, 1971.
To Prime the Pump (Grimes). New York, Curtis, 1971.
The Inheritors, The Gateway to Never (Grimes). New York, Ace, 1972.
The Bitter Pill. Melbourne, Wren, 1974.
The Big Black Mark (Grimes). New York, DAW, 1975.
The Broken Cycle (Grimes). London, Hale, 1975; New York, DAW, 1979.
The Way Back (Grimes). London, Hale, 1976; New York, DAW, 1978.
Star Courier (Grimes). London, Hale, and New York, DAW, 1977.
The Far Traveller (Grimes). London, Hale, 1977; New York, DAW, 1979.
To Keep the Ship (Grimes). London, Hale, and New York, DAW, 1978.
Matilda's Stepchildren. London, Hale, 1979.
Star Loot (Grimes). New York, DAW, 1980.

Short Stories (series: John Grimes in all books)

The Rim Gods. New York, Ace, 1968.
The Dark Dimensions, Alternate Orbits. New York, Ace, 1971; *Alternate Orbits* published separately as *Commodore at Sea*, 1979.
The Hard Way Up. New York, Ace, 1972.

Uncollected Short Stories (series: Rim Worlds)

"The Last Hunt" (Rim Worlds), in *Galaxy* (New York), March 1973.
"On the Account" (Rim Worlds), in *Galaxy* (New York), May 1973.
"Hard Luck Story," in *Void 1* (St. Kilda, Victoria), 1975.
"The Hairy Parents," in *Void 2* (St. Kilda, Victoria), 1975.
"Rim Change," in *Galaxy* (New York), August 1975.
"Kelly Country," in *Void 3* (St. Kilda, Victoria), 1976.
"The Mountain Movers," in *The Zeitgeist Machine*, edited by Damien Broderick. London, Angus and Robertson, 1977.
"The Long Fall," in *Amazing* (New York), July 1977.
"No Room in the Stable," in *Asimov's Choice: Astronauts and Androids.* New York, Dale, 1978.
"The Sleeping Beast" (Rim Worlds), in *Amazing* (New York), January 1978.
"Grimes at Glenrowan" (Rim Worlds), in *Isaac Asimov's Science Fiction Magazine* (New York), March-April 1978.
"The Hairy Parents," in *Fantastic* (New York), October 1978.
"Doggy in the Window," in *Amazing* (New York), November 1978.
"Journey's End," in *Amazing* (New York), February 1979.
"Grimes and the Great Race," in *Isaac Asimov's Science Fiction Magazine* (New York), April 1980.

*

Bibliography: "Bibliography of the Works of A. Bertram Chandler" by Ross Pavlac, in *Marcon XIII* (Columbus, Ohio), March 1978.

A. Bertram Chandler comments:

Quite a few years ago Robert Heinlein said, "Only people who know ships can write convincingly about spaceships." At the time I thought that this was very true. I have not changed my opinion. I believe that the crews of the *real* spaceships of the future, vessels going a long way in a long time, will have far more in common with today's seamen than with today's airmen. I freely admit that my stories are essentially sea stories and that John Grimes, my series character, is descended from Hornblower. At a book-signing recently in Fukuoka I felt flattered when one of my Japanese faithful readers gave me one of Forester's Hornblower novels to autograph.

* * *

In the years since World War II A. Bertram Chandler has established himself as one of the most prolific of science fiction's adventure novelists. During the 1950's he wrote many short stories for the pulps, but since 1961 his output has consisted chiefly of novels, and an assessment of his place among the writers of the genre will depend on an evaluation of those longer works.

At least 16 of his novels and collections of stories have a similar locale and, for the most part, a common core of characters. A few of the novels concern the adventures of a future space-traveller, Derek Calver (e.g., *The Rim of Space, The Ship from Outside*), but the great majority of Chandler's works detail the exploits of John Grimes—naval officer, merchant captain, center of controversies and conflicts, and ladies' man. By design, the life of John Grimes owes much to C.S. Forester's naval hero Horatio Hornblower. Both authors picture the rise from obscure origins to fame of ship commanders, with the obvious difference being, of course, that the ships which Grimes captains sail through space centuries from now. Readers interested in following the internal chronology of the novels to observe the career of John Grimes should begin with *The Road to the Rim*, in which Ensign Grimes, fresh from the academy of the Federation Survey Service, begins his star-travelling. The book serves as a pattern for the plots of the longer works: typically, Grimes is given a mission, sets forth, and is plunged into difficulties by misadventure or malice; he then extricates himself from his troubles, usually by resourcefulness (but sometimes by chance), and returns to face his exasperated superiors. This blueprint of events marks even the longest tales, for instance, that of *The Dark Dimensions*, which, when set in motion, is resolved only in its sequel, *The Way Back*.

Grimes's advancement up the ladder of rank continues in *The Hard Way Up*, by the end of which he has promoted to Lieutenant Commander. But he has not long to serve in the Earth-based Federation: in *The Big Black Mark*, the crew of Grimes, now a Commander, mutinies and sets him adrift (à la Captain Bligh of the *Bounty*); he brings himself and a few loyal crew-members through a hazardous journey to safety (again like Bligh). At the end of the story, Grimes realizes that his career with the Federation Survey Service is at an end, and resolves to head for the most important locale of the series—the Rim Worlds.

"The Rim" is one part of the rim of the Milky Way Galaxy, and the Rim Worlds are those relatively few planets clustered around the lonely stars at the edge of the spiral arm in which Earth is located. By the middle of Grimes's career, the Rim Worlds are organized into a loose confederation; their limited man-power leads Grimes to conclude that his officer's skills will be welcomed there. After an interlude as a merchant captain (in *To Keep the Ship*), Grimes joins the Rim Worlds Navy and rises to positions of power and authority.

Chandler's fiction is certainly not serious, and it would be a mistake to evaluate it as if it were; rather, his works are what Graham Greene called "entertainments," books intended to be read for the pleasure of a fast-moving plot, likeable central characters (whom one gets to know well after a dozen novels or so), and well-realized scenes of shipboard life, even if those ships ply the vaster oceans of space.

—Walter E. Meyers

CHARBONNEAU, Louis (Henry). Also writes as Carter Travis Young. American. Born in Detroit, Michigan, 20 January 1924. Educated at the University of Detroit, A.B. 1948, M.A. 1950. Served in the United States Army Air Force, 1943-46: Staff Sergeant. Married Hilda Sweeney in 1945. Instructor in English, University of Detroit, 1948-52; copywriter, Mercury Advertising Agency, Los Angeles, 1952-56; staff writer, Los Angeles *Times*, 1956-71; free-lance writer, 1971-74; Editor, Security World Publishing Company, Los Angeles, 1974-79. Agent: Scott Meredith Literary Agency, 845 Third Avenue, New York, New York 10022, U.S.A.

SCIENCE-FICTION PUBLICATIONS

Novels

No Place on Earth. New York, Doubleday, 1958; London, Jenkins, 1966.
Corpus Earthling. New York, Doubleday, 1960; London, Digit, 1963.
The Sentinel Stars. New York, Bantam, 1964; London, Corgi, 1964.
Psychedelic-40. New York, Bantam, 1965; as *The Specials*, London, Jenkins, 1967.
Down to Earth. New York, Bantam, 1967; as *Antic Earth*, London, Jenkins, 1967.
The Sensitives. New York, Bantam, 1968.
Barrier World. New York, Lancer, 1970.
Embryo (novelization of screenplay). New York, Warner, 1976.

OTHER PUBLICATIONS

Novels

Night of Violence. New York, Torquil, and London, Digit, 1959; as *The Trapped Ones*, London, Barker, 1960.
Nor All Your Tears. New York, Torquil, 1959.
The Time of Desire. London, Digit, 1963.
Way Out. London, Barrie and Rockliff, 1966.
Down from the Mountain. New York, Doubleday, 1969.
And Hope to Die. New York, Ace, 1970.
From a Dark Place. New York, Dell, 1974.
Intruder. New York, Doubleday, 1979.

Novels as Carter Travis Young

The Wild Breed. New York, Doubleday, 1960; as *The Sudden Gun*, London, Hammond, 1960.
The Savage Plain. New York, Doubleday, 1961; London, Hammond, 1963.
Shadow of a Gun. London, Muller, 1962.
The Bitter Iron. New York, Doubleday, 1964; London, Ward Lock, 1965.
Long Boots, Hard Boots. New York, Doubleday, 1965; London, Ward Lock, 1966.
Why Did They Kill Charley? New York, Doubleday, and London, Ward Lock, 1967.
Winchester Quarantine. New York, Doubleday, 1970.
The Pocket Hunters. New York, Doubleday, 1972.
Winter of the Coup. New York, Doubleday, 1972.
The Captive. New York, Doubleday, 1973.
Guns of Darkness. New York, Doubleday, 1974.
Blaine's Law. New York, Doubleday, 1974.
Red Grass. New York, Doubleday, 1976.

* * *

A sort of philosopher's stone, the secret of good writing has been sought for centuries. This secret has been revealed in part by Louis Charbonneau, who offers the simple but unacceptable formula: write. Most writers today could do worse than to emulate his example of journalist-advertising copywriter regimen to achieve the smooth, fluid word manipulation which makes for engrossing reading. Charbonneau's years of smithing language into informative patterns give his science fiction a pace and clarity which are too seldom found in the turgid New Wave.

With his first novel, *No Place on Earth*, Charbonneau took what might have been a trite topic—population control—and infused it with reportorial excitement. While his characters are not especially complex, what he does with them is identifiable and convincing. There is a hero, but he is unheroic in defying the laws of population control promulgated by Malthus, the First Leader. There is irony in his work with the Propaganda Section, where the hero is urged to THINK BIG to accomplish BIG THINGS. And there is, here and there, sparkling humor as needed—he takes his girl on a helicopter joyride to feast on wine and sirloin capsules. Charbonneau's style is terse and fast. Even the philosophical passages are compressed and economical. He leans heavily upon dialogue for both advancing the plot and revealing his characters. The novel is arresting right at the start, as the reader is whirled into the center of things with the explosive return of our hero's memory.

A charge of pelvic fascination might be leveled against Charbonneau, particularly in such works as *Corpus Earthling*. The theme is intriguing: occupation by aliens of Earth's citizens. An instructor at UCLA taps into a telepathic conversation between two of these aliens, Martians who have leaked into human forms to set up a conduit for their fellows back home. When these aliens detect his intrusion, they attempt to wipe him out to protect their secret. He in turn tries to narrow down their probable habitations among, of course, three toothsome coeds. Much of his research takes place in bed—objectionable to some readers, but difficult to improve upon as a means of turning up intimate details that reveal how the tenants control the owners.

Charbonneau's fascination with control is drawn forward a couple of centuries in *The Sentinel Stars* to a world into which each individual is born with a debt to the Internal Revenue Service. That unfortunate population must spend all its years working off the debt—almost impossible in light of essential costs. But the hero, TRH-247, an aberrant in this computer-run society, kicks over the traces. Skipping work obligations, he picks up a girl, carries on a rooftop love affair, and is consigned to a "correction" camp. Obviously, the genetic computer suffered a slight relapse when designing TRH—and a few others, it turns out. Again, we see the journalist's focus upon a trend. The power to tax IS the power to destroy, literally, and the reader derives a savage delight from learning there is no safety in numbers—in or out of the machine.

Louis Charbonneau is both a child and mentor of his times. His topics come from the practical world, but he touches them with his own peculiar magic. Like other writers, he takes liberal advantage of his right to extrapolate and to enlarge upon what may appear to be insignificant trends in the real world. His prose is muscular and nimble. It's a pity he ceased his science-fiction writing with *Barrier World* a decade ago.

—Robert H. Wilcox

CHARNAS, Suzy McKee. American. Born in New York City, 22 October 1939. Educated at New York High School of Music and Art; Barnard College, New York, B.A. in economic history 1961; New York University, M.A. Married Stephen Charnas in 1968; two step-children. Peace Corps English and history teacher, Girls' High School, Ogbomoso, Nigeria, 1961-62; Lecturer in Economic History, University of Ibadan, Ife, Nigeria, 1962-63; English-History Core Teacher, New Lincoln School, New York, 1965-67; worked for Community Mental Health organization, New York, 1967-69. Since 1969, free-lance writer. Agent: Virginia Kidd, Box 278, Milford, Pennsylvania 18337. Address: 8918-B Fourth Street NW, Albuquerque, New Mexico 87114, U.S.A.

SCIENCE-FICTION PUBLICATIONS

Novels

Walk to the End of the World. New York, Ballantine, 1974; London, Gollancz, 1979.
Motherlines. New York, Berkley, 1979; London, Gollancz, 1980.
The Vampire Territory. New York, Simon and Schuster, 1980.

Uncollected Short Story

"The Ancient Mind at Work," in *Omni* (New York), February 1979.

OTHER PUBLICATIONS

Other

"Symposium on Women and SF," in *Khatru 3-4* (Baltimore), 1975.
"The Good Rape," in *Kolvir* (Baltimore), 1978.
"Interview," in *Algol* (New York), Winter 1978-79.

* * *

When Iago says to Brabantio, "you'll have your daughter covered with a Barbary horse...you'll have coursers for cousins, and gennets for germans," an exemplar of malevolence addresses a symbol of patriarchal power. These two representational essences are fused in Suzy McKee Charnas's first novel, *Walk to the End of the World*, where masculine hegemony is synonymous with unmitigated evil. Iago's utterance also illuminates its sequel, *Motherlines*, in which daughters are indeed covered by horses who are thought to be the near kinsmen of their mistresses. As *Othello* explores the effects of exaggerated personality traits, Charnas's fiction presents an exaggerated vision of sexism's consequences.

Walk to the End of the World is set in "the Holdfast," a limited environment populated by survivors of "the Wasting," or nuclear holocaust. This postwar society is a paradise for white male misogynic bigots: the entire population is Caucasian, and the men are taught that "females themselves brought on the Wasting of the world." Holdfast "fems" supposedly "had no souls, only inner cores of animated darkness shaped from the void beyond the stars. Their deaths had no significance. Some men believed that the same shadows returned again and again in successive fem-bodies." We, with our Eve, Pandora, and cultures where women are fuel for the flames of their husbands' funeral pyres, cannot feel smug after encountering a Holdfast myth. In this manner, Charnas's fiction continuously echoes reality.

The structure, as well as much of the content of *Walk to the End of the World*, reflects women's secondary status. Before encountering Alldera, the heroine, readers are familiar with the Holdfast's notions of "fem-taint," "cunt-hunger," institutionalized rape, and girl children who must scratch for survival in the straw of the "kit-pen." Alldera's situation is immediately apparent: as a woman, she must satisfy all the demands of her male masters. Even a slave cannot be completely controlled by an oppressor. Since Alldera possesses mental acuteness and training as a runner, she can sometimes use her mind and body to suit her own best advantage. Her circumstances resemble those of an intelligent, talented Black person in the Jim Crow south. The novel's plot corrects the Holdfast's negative view of the feminine. For example, the text clarifies its own prologue: women certainly did not cause the Wasting of the world. Rather, "subhuman" men cause the wasting of women. Happily, something positive does manage to coincide with the sombering aspects of this novel and women's reality. Alldera has the opportunity to flee the Holdfast; some women have the pleasure of knowing that when they approach their house yard gate, they are not walking to the end of their world.

In *Motherlines* the open plains lying beyond the men's sphere of influence sharply contrast with the Holdfast's defined boundaries. Women completely control this terrain. In fact, to cite another example of Charnas's penchant for creating extreme circumstances, men never enter the domain of escaped "free fems" and the indigenous riding women of the motherline tribes. This women's world is not a Utopia for sterotypically peace-loving, nurturing females. The tribes routinely raid each other, one powerful woman dictates her will to the free fems, and the riding women's method of raising children reminds Alldera of the Holdfast's "kit-pen." Although the tribal women are imperfect, they possess impressive attributes: self-sufficiency, an identification with matrilineal relationships, and racial tolerance. Alldera and her free fem companion are allowed to live in the tribe with dignity. She no longer has the negative self-image described in *Walk to the End of the World*, where she feels "hollow in body...hollow in mind, for there was nothing else she might imagine, feel, or will that a man could not wipe out of existence by picking her up for his own purposes." This transformation is of primary importance in *Motherlines*.

Another aspect of the novel is a secondary concern. "Oh...We mate with our horses," is the answer to Alldera's question about reproduction in a completely female society. Those who judge this information to be a flippant, sarcastic retort react prematurely. The woman who answers Alldera speaks the truth about a situation which expands the definition of "perversion." Charnas's characters are not presented solely to titillate an audience. Although the sexuality of the motherline tribes is bizarre, they always mate to fulfill their natural reproductive purpose. And the women are in total control of the sexual arena. In contrast, human heterosexuality can be degrading and destructive.

In the real world, the idea of a totally independent woman is, using Harlan Ellison's term, a "dangerous vision." Many readers, men and women, might be taken aback by the controversial content of Charnas's novels.

—Marleen S. Barr

* * * * *

CHERRYH, C.J. Pseudonym for Carolyn Janice Cherry. American. Born in St. Louis, Missouri, 1 September 1942. Educated at the University of Oklahoma, Norman, 1960-64, B.A. in Latin 1964 (Phi Beta Kappa); Johns Hopkins University, Baltimore (Woodrow Wilson Fellow, 1965-66), M.A. in classics 1965. Taught Latin and ancient history in Oklahoma City public schools, 1965-76. Recipient: Hugo Award, 1979. Address: 11217 North McKinley, Oklahoma City, Oklahoma 73114, U.S.A.

SCIENCE-FICTION PUBLICATIONS

Novels (series: Faded Sun; Morgaine)

The Book of Morgaine. New York, Doubleday, 1979.
  Gates of Ivrel. New York, Doubleday, 1976; London, Futura, 1977.
  Well of Shiuan. New York, DAW, 1978.
  Fires of Azeroth. New York, DAW, 1979.
Brothers of Earth. New York, DAW, 1976; London, Futura, 1977.
Hunter of Worlds. New York, Doubleday, and London, Futura, 1977.
The Faded Sun: Kesrith. New York, DAW, 1978.
The Faded Sun: Shon'Jir. New York, DAW, 1979.
Serpent's Reach. New York, DAW, 1979.
Hestia. New York, DAW, 1979.
The Faded Sun: Kutath. New York, DAW, 1980.

Uncollected Short Stories

"The Dark King," in *The Year's Best Fantasy Stories 3*, edited by Lin Carter. New York, DAW, 1977.
"The Dreamstone," in *Amazons*. New York, DAW, 1979.
"Cassandra," in *The 1979 Annual World's Best SF*, edited by Donald A. Wollheim. New York, DAW, 1979.

* * *

C.J. Cherryh learned her craft not at the expense of the reader, but during long years of collecting rejection slips. In consequence, the high quality of her first novel made it immediately clear that someone special had appeared on the scene of imaginative fiction. This novel, *Gates of Ivrel*, carried an introduction by Andre Norton in which the older writer, with enviable generosity (and honesty), declares that Cherryh already writes better than she herself ever did. Cherryh's early promise of things to come is already in the process of realization.

Cherryh has remained inside the established limits of her own chosen tradition, that of science fiction and related fantasy. However, she has made her tradition more human and more real. She breathes life into the standard character types of soldiers, spacefarers, and interstellar diplomats, of sorcerers, slaves, and princesses; she gives each of them individual psychologies and individual problems. Her extra-terrestrials too take on corporality—and not merely as representatives of a species with instincts, motivations, and cultures differing from ours, but as individuals within such a species.

Like a number of other SF writers, Cherryh often deals with intercultural conflict. The features here which raise her work above the average include, first, the fascinating and realistic complexity of the interactions she depicts (which seem to involve a dead minimum of three cultures and two intelligent species), and, second, the elegance with which she incarnates these cultural complexities in the minds and actions of her characters. Cherryh usually plunges these characters into a situation where their lives (and sometimes much more than lives) depend on their coming to terms with beings whose standards of conduct (even basic instincts) differ radically from their own. And for the most part they do come to terms, coexist, and even love one another. Their success is never complete, and it has a price, but it is success even so. Cherryh is basically an optimistic writer, and her optimism is the more persuasive because it arises not out of ignorance of suffering and evil (which are vividly, even gruesomely, depicted), but instead out of a spiritual victory over them.

Cherryh's success has already been sufficient to establish her as a popular full-time writer, but even so her work is still in the process of consolidation. Ironically enough, this comes as a result of the very depth and complexity of Cherryh's creative vision. Often her stories are of such labyrinthine complexity that they require many volumes for their unfolding. For example, the three volumes in her science-fantasy series about the "sorceress" Morgaine and her liegeman Vanye are sufficiently rounded off to be called a trilogy, yet the story is far from finished. For another aspect of the problem, we might consider a work complete in one volume, one Cherryh has said is closest to her own heart, *Hunter of Worlds*. Some readers and critics have complained that the novel is needlessly obscure, chiefly because of the heavy use of words from various non-human languages to convey concepts which lack simple expression in English. Cherryh herself has noted that many readers have imputed human psychological motivations to the nonhuman characters in place of the meticulously elaborated extra-terrestrial psychologies which comprise a large part of the novel's raison d'être. In the Faded Sun trilogy we find a decrease in obscurity, but also a certain decrease in the richness of the cultures portrayed. More experience may well teach Cherryh how to bring the entire richness of her imagination unimpeded to the reader.

—Patrick L. McGuire

* * * * *

CHESTERTON, G(ilbert) K(eith). British. Born in London, 28 May 1874. Educated at Colet Court School, London; St. Paul's School, London (Editor, *The Debater*, 1891-93), 1887-92; Slade School of Art, London 1893-96. Married Frances Blogg in 1901. Worked for the London publishers Redway, 1896, and T. Fisher Unwin, 1896-1902; weekly contributor to the *Daily News*, London, 1901-13, and the *Illustrated London News*, 1905-36; Co-Editor, *Eye*

Witness, London, 1911-12, and Editor, *New Witness*, 1912-23; regular contributor to the *Daily Herald*, London, 1913-14; leader of the Distributist movement after the war, and subsequently President of the Distributist League; convert to Roman Catholicism, 1922; Editor, with H. Jackson and R.B. Johnson, Readers' Classics series, 1922; Editor, *G.K.'s Weekly*, 1925-36; Lecturer, Notre Dame University, Indiana, 1930; radio broadcaster in the 1930's. Also an illustrator: illustrated some of his own works and books by Hilaire Belloc and E.C. Bentley. Honorary degrees: Edinburgh, Dublin, and Notre Dame universities. Fellow, Royal Society of Literature. Knight Commander with Star, Order of St. Gregory the Great, 1934. *Died 14 June 1936.*

SCIENCE-FICTION PUBLICATIONS

Novels

The Napoleon of Notting Hill.   London and New York, Lane, 1904.
The Man Who Was Thursday: A Nightmare.   Bristol, Arrowsmith, and New York, Dodd Mead, 1908.
The Ball and the Cross.   New York, Lane, 1909; London, Wells Gardner, 1910.
The Flying Inn.   London, Methuen, and New York, Lane, 1914.

Short Stories

The Man Who Knew Too Much and Other Stories.   London, Cassell, and New York, Harper, 1922.
Tales of the Long Bow.   London, Cassell, and New York, Dodd Mead, 1925.
The Coloured Lands (includes non-fiction).   London and New York, Sheed and Ward, 1938.

OTHER PUBLICATIONS

Novels

Manalive.   London, Nelson, and New York, Lane, 1912.
The Return of Don Quixote.   London, Chatto and Windus, and New York, Dodd Mead, 1927.

Short Stories

The Tremendous Adventures of Major Brown.   London, Shurmer Sibthorp, 1903.
The Club of Queer Trades.   London and New York, Harper, 1905.
The Innocence of Father Brown.   London, Cassell, and New York, Lane, 1911.
The Perishing of the Pendragons.   New York, Paget, 1914.
The Wisdom of Father Brown.   London, Cassell, 1914; New York, Lane, 1915.
The Incredulity of Father Brown.   London, Cassell, and New York, Dodd Mead, 1926.
The Secret of Father Brown.   London, Cassell, and New York, Harper, 1927.
The Sword of Wood.   London, Elkin Mathews, 1928.
(Stories).   London, Harrap, 1928.
The Poet and the Lunatic: Episodes in the Life of Gabriel Gale.   London, Cassell, and New York, Dodd Mead, 1929.
The Moderate Murderer, and The Honest Quack.   New York, Dodd Mead, 1929.
The Ecstatic Thief.   New York, Dodd Mead, 1930.
Four Faultless Felons.   London, Cassell, and New York, Dodd Mead, 1930.
The Floating Admiral, with others.   London, Hodder and Stoughton, 1931; New York, Doubleday, 1932.
The Scandal of Father Brown.   London, Cassell, and New York, Dodd Mead, 1935.
The Paradoxes of Mr. Pond.   London, Cassell, 1936; New York, Dodd Mead, 1937.
The Vampire of the Village.   Privately printed, 1947.

Father Brown: Selected Stories, edited by Ronald Knox.   London, Oxford University Press, 1955.
Selected Stories, edited by Kingsley Amis.   London, Faber, 1972.

Plays

Magic: A Fantastic Comedy (produced Eastbourne and London, 1913; New York, 1917).   London, Martin Secker, and New York, Putnam, 1913.
The Judgment of Dr. Johnson (produced London, 1932).   London, Sheed and Ward, 1927; New York, Putnam, 1928.
The Surprise (produced Hull, 1953).   London, Sheed and Ward, 1953.

Verse

Greybeards at Play: Literature and Art for Old Gentlemen: Rhymes and Sketches.   London, R. Brimley Johnson, 1900.
The Wild Knight and Other Poems.   London, Richards, 1900; revised edition, London, Dent, and New York, Dutton, 1914.
The Ballad of the White Horse.   London, Methuen, and New York, Lane, 1911.
Poems.   London, Burns Oates, 1915; New York, Lane, 1916.
Wine, Water, and Song.   London, Methuen, 1915.
A Poem.   Privately printed, 1915.
Old King Cole.   Privately printed, 1920.
The Ballad of St. Barbara and Other Verses.   London, Palmer, 1922; New York, Putnam, 1923.
(Poems).   London, Benn, and New York, Stokes, 1925.
The Queen of Seven Swords.   London, Sheed and Ward, 1926.
The Collected Poems of G.K. Chesterton.   London, Palmer, 1927; revised edition, New York, Dodd Mead, 1932.
Gloria in Profundis.   London, Faber and Gwyer, and New York, Rudge, 1927.
Ubi Ecclesia.   London, Faber, 1929.
The Grave of Arthur.   London, Faber, 1930.
Greybeards at Play and Other Comic Verse, edited by John Sullivan.   London, Elek, 1974.

Other

The Defendant.   London, R. Brimley Johnson, 1901; New York, Dodd Mead, 1902.
Twelve Types.   London, Humphreys, 1902; augmented edition, as *Varied Types*, New York, Dodd Mead, 1903; selections as *Five Types*, Humphreys, 1910; New York, Holt, 1911; and as *Simplicity and Tolstoy*, Humphreys, 1912.
Thomas Carlyle.   London, Hodder and Stoughton, 1902; New York, Pott, n.d.
Robert Louis Stevenson, with W. Robertson Nicoll.   London, Hodder and Stoughton, and New York, Pott, 1903.
Leo Tolstoy, with G.H. Perris and Edward Garnett.   London, Hodder and Stoughton, and New York, Pott, 1903.
Charles Dickens, with F.G. Kitton.   London, Hodder and Stoughton, and New York, Pott, 1903.
Robert Browning.   London and New York, Macmillan, 1903.
Tennyson, with Richard Garnett.   London, Hodder and Stoughton, 1903; New York, Pott, n.d.
Thackeray, with Lewis Melville.   London, Hodder and Stoughton, and New York, Pott, 1903.
G.F. Watts.   London, Duckworth, and New York, Dutton, 1904.
Heretics.   London and New York, Lane, 1905.
Charles Dickens.   London, Methuen, and New York, Dodd Mead, 1906.
All Things Considered.   London, Methuen, and New York, Lane, 1908.
Orthodoxy.   London and New York, Lane, 1908.
George Bernard Shaw.   London and New York, Lane, 1909; revised edition, London, Lane, 1935.
Tremendous Trifles.   London, Methuen, and New York, Dodd Mead, 1909.
What's Wrong with the World.   London, Cassell, and New York, Dodd Mead, 1910.
Alarms and Discursions.   London, Methuen, 1910; New York, Dodd Mead, 1911.

William Blake. London, Duckworth, and New York, Dutton, 1910.

The Ultimate Lie. Privately printed, 1910.

A Chesterton Calendar. London, Kegan Paul, 1911; as *Wit and Wisdom of G.K. Chesterton*, New York, Dodd Mead, 1911; as *Chesterton Day by Day*, Kegan Paul, 1912.

Appreciations and Criticisms of the Works of Charles Dickens. London, Dent, and New York, Dutton, 1911.

A Defence of Nonsense and Other Essays. New York, Dodd Mead, 1911.

The Future of Religion: Mr. G.K. Chesterton's Reply to Mr. Bernard Shaw. Privately printed, 1911.

The Conversion of an Anarchist. New York, Paget, 1912.

A Miscellany of Men. London, Methuen, and New York, Dodd Mead, 1912.

The Victorian Age in Literature. London, Williams and Norgate, and New York, Holt, 1913.

Thoughts from Chesterton, edited by Elsie E. Morton. London, Harrap, 1913.

The Barbarism of Berlin. London, Cassell, 1914.

London, photographs by Alvin Langdon Coburn. Privately printed, 1914.

Prussian Versus Belgian Culture. Edinburgh, Belgian Relief and Reconstruction Fund, 1914.

Letters to an Old Garibaldian. London, Methuen, 1915; with *The Barbarism of Berlin*, as *The Appetite of Tyranny*, New York, Dodd Mead, 1915.

The So-Called Belgian Bargain. London, National War Aims Committee, 1915.

The Crimes of England. London, Palmer and Hayward, 1915; New York, Lane, 1916.

Divorce Versus Democracy. London, Society of SS. Peter and Paul, 1916.

Temperance and the Great Alliance. London, True Temperance Association, 1916.

The G.K. Chesterton Calendar, edited by H. Cecil Palmer. London, Palmer and Hayward, 1916.

A Shilling for My Thoughts, edited by E.V. Lucas. London, Methuen, 1916.

Lord Kitchener. Privately printed, 1917.

A Short History of England. London, Chatto and Windus, and New York, Lane, 1917.

Utopia of Usurers and Other Essays. New York, Boni and Liveright, 1917.

How to Help Annexation. London, Hayman Christy and Lilly, 1918.

Irish Impressions. London, Collins, and New York, Lane, 1920.

The Superstition of Divorce. London, Chatto and Windus, and New York, Lane, 1920.

Charles Dickens Fifty Years After. Privately printed, 1920.

The Uses of Diversity: A Book of Essays. London, Methuen, 1920; New York, Dodd Mead, 1921.

The New Jerusalem. London, Hodder and Stoughton, 1920; New York, Doran, 1921.

Eugenics and Other Evils. London, Cassell, 1922; New York, Dodd Mead, 1927.

What I Saw in America. London, Hodder and Stoughton, and New York, Dodd Mead, 1922.

Fancies Versus Fads. London, Methuen, and New York, Dodd Mead, 1923.

St. Francis of Assisi. London, Hodder and Stoughton, 1923; New York, Dodd Mead, 1924.

The End of the Roman Road: A Pageant of Wayfarers. London, Classic Press, 1924.

The Superstitions of the Sceptic (lecture). Cambridge, Heffer, and St. Louis, Herder, 1925.

The Everlasting Man. London, Hodder and Stoughton, and New York, Dodd Mead, 1925.

William Cobbett. London, Hodder and Stoughton, 1925; New York, Dodd Mead, 1926.

The Outline of Sanity. London, Methuen, 1926; New York, Dodd Mead, 1927.

The Catholic Church and Conversion. New York, Macmillan, 1926; London, Burns Oates, 1927.

Selected Works (Minerva Edition). London, Methuen, 9 vols., 1926.

A Gleaming Cohort, Being Selections from the Works of G.K. Chesterton, edited by E.V. Lucas. London, Methuen, 1926.

Social Reform Versus Birth Control. London, Simpkin Marshall, 1927.

Culture and the Coming Peril (lecture). London, University of London Press, 1927.

Robert Louis Stevenson. London, Hodder and Stoughton, 1927; New York, Dodd Mead, 1928.

Generally Speaking: A Book of Essays. London, Methuen, and New York, Dodd Mead, 1928.

(Essays). London, Harrap, 1928.

Do We Agree? A Debate, with G.B. Shaw. London, Palmer, and Hartford, Connecticut, Mitchell, 1928.

A Chesterton Catholic Anthology, edited by Patrick Braybrooke. London, Burns Oates, and New York, Kenedy, 1928.

The Thing (essays). London, Sheed and Ward, 1929.

G.K.C. as M.C., Being a Collection of Thirty-Seven Introductions, edited by J.P. de Fonseka. London, Methuen, 1929.

The Resurrection of Rome. London, Hodder and Stoughton, and New York, Dodd Mead, 1930.

Come to Think of It: A Book of Essays. London, Methuen, 1930; New York, Dodd Mead, 1931.

The Turkey and the Turk. Ditchling, Sussex, St. Dominic's Press, 1930.

At the Sign of the World's End. Palo Alto, California, Harvest Press, 1930.

Is There a Return to Religion?, with E. Haldeman-Julius. Girard, Kansas, Haldeman Julius, 1931.

All Is Grist: A Book of Essays. London, Methuen, 1931; New York, Dodd Mead, 1932.

Chaucer. London, Faber, and New York, Farrar Rinehart, 1932.

Sidelights on New London and Newer York and Other Essays. London, Sheed and Ward, and New York, Dodd Mead, 1932.

Christendom in Dublin. London, Sheed and Ward, 1932; New York, Sheed and Ward, 1933.

All I Survey: A Book of Essays. London, Methuen, and New York, Dodd Mead, 1933.

St. Thomas Aquinas. London, Hodder and Stoughton, and New York, Sheed and Ward, 1933.

G.K. Chesterton (selected humour), edited by E.V. Knox. London, Methuen, 1933; as *Running after One's Hat and Other Whimsies*, New York, McBride, 1933.

Avowals and Denials: A Book of Essays. London, Methuen, 1934; New York, Dodd Mead, 1935.

The Well and the Shallows. London and New York, Sheed and Ward, 1935.

Explaining the English. London, British Council, 1935.

Stories, Essays, and Poems. London, Dent, 1935.

As I Was Saying: A Book of Essays. London, Methuen, and New York, Dodd Mead, 1936.

Autobiography. London, Hutchinson, and New York, Sheed and Ward, 1936.

The Man Who Was Chesterton, edited by Raymond T. Bond. New York, Dodd Mead, 1937.

Essays, edited by John Guest. London, Collins, 1939.

The End of the Armistice, edited by F.J. Sheed. London and New York, Sheed and Ward, 1940.

Selected Essays, edited by Dorothy Collins. London, Methuen, 1949.

The Common Man. London and New York, Sheed and Ward, 1950.

Essays, edited by K.E. Whitehorn. London, Methuen, 1953.

A Handful of Authors: Essays on Books and Writers, edited by Dorothy Collins. London and New York, Sheed and Ward, 1953.

The Glass Walking-Stick and Other Essays from the Illustrated London News 1905-1936, edited by Dorothy Collins. London, Methuen, 1955.

G.K. Chesterton: An Anthology, edited by D.B. Wyndham Lewis. London and New York, Oxford University Press, 1957.

Essays and Poems, edited by Wilfrid Sheed. London, Penguin, 1958.

Lunacy and Letters (essays), edited by Dorothy Collins. London and New York, Sheed and Ward, 1958.

Where All Roads Lead.   London, Catholic Truth Society, 1961.
The Man Who Was Orthodox: A Selection from the Uncollected Writings of G.K. Chesterton, edited by A. L. Maycock.   London, Dobson, 1963.
The Spice of Life and Other Essays, edited by Dorothy Collins.   Beaconsfield, Buckinghamshire, Finlayson, 1964; Philadelphia, Dufour, 1966.
G.K. Chesterton: A Selection from His Non-Fictional Prose, edited by W.H. Auden.   London, Faber, 1970.
Chesterton on Shakespeare, edited by Dorothy Collins.   Henley on Thames, Oxfordshire, and Chester Springs, Pennsylvania, Dufour, 1971.
The Apostle and the Wild Ducks, and Other Essays, edited by Dorothy Collins.   London, Elek, 1975.

Editor, *Thackeray* (selections).   London, Bell, 1909.
Editor, with Alice Meynell, *Samuel Johnson* (selections).   London, Herbert and Daniel, 1911.
Editor, *Essays by Divers Hands 6*.   London, Oxford University Press, 1926.
Editor, *G.K.'s* (miscellany from *G.K.'s Weekly*).   London, Rich and Cowan, 1934.

*

Bibliography: *Chesterton: A Bibliography* by John Sullivan, London, University of London Press, 1958, supplement, 1968.

Manuscript Collection: Humanities Research Center, University of Texas, Austin.

*   *   *

G.K. Chesterton, who is perhaps most familiar to today's reader as the creator of the Father Brown detective stories, typified the prolific man of letters of his day, confidently turning his talents to poetry, novels, and literary and social criticism. A background in journalism and a religious conversion from agnosticism to Anglo-Catholicism colored his works which always retained a journalistic flair for snaring the reader's attention, and was more often than not decidedly preoccupied with religious and moral questions. Both his fiction and non-fiction are notable for defending views of modern civilization in philosophical disagreement with such of his contemporaries as G.B. Shaw and H.G. Wells. Chesterton became an apologist for religion, a champion of individual freedom and free will, a critic of industrialization, and most characteristically a soldier for the forces of optimism, finding in the small ordinary details of living a reassuring anchor for man's great spiritual achievements.

Chesterton, who never referred to any of his works even as "scientific romances," would be astonished to have any of them, however fantastic, categorized as "science fiction," although some of the allegorical works do share, in common with some science fiction, a firm belief that there *is* a future in store for mankind, a concern with the long-range effects of scientific advances, and a predilection for extrapolating upon political and social trends by means of envisioning future worlds in which they are carried to an extreme. It must be emphasized, however, that even in his portrayal of future societies, Chesterton (even more so than a writer such as C.S. Lewis) is far more concerned with religious questions than with building fantastic worlds. The fantastic, for Chesterton, is an engaging means to a moralistic end; descriptions of new worlds are secondary in importance to his aim of achieving religious allegory. His work may sometimes depict a future, yet it can hardly be termed "futuristic."

Symbols, imagery and overall messages are repetitive in Chesterton's fiction. The enigmatic *Man Who Knew Too Much*, in the spirit of Father Brown, solves apparently inexplicable puzzles and resolves paradoxes, re-establishing order in temporarily stunned English country settings. A suspicious automobile accident can take on great proportions. "As they drew near there seemed a sort of monstrous irony in the fact that the dead machine was still throbbing and thundering busily as a factory, while the man lay so still." Amiable intellectual non-conformists are featured in more "tall stories" collected in *Tales of The Long Bow*, a work which portrays an old world society of masculine friendship as the basis of sensible

"lunacy" as a group of friends mature and learn to stand up for their beliefs, in the face of blind British convention or greedy industrialization of the English countryside. Irony can be biting when Chesterton's implied utopia of a green countryside England is threatened. Pollution of a beloved fishing spot is likened to a serpent entering the Garden of Eden. Ironically, this "alien" pollution is the result of the manufacture of "some kind of new and highly hygienic cosmetics." The "soul of England" is Chesterton's ideal, discovered not by regarding the surface or materialistic view of things but by looking at the commonplace from an original angle, as in the reflected "tranquil topsy-turvydom" of a fishing pool. More earnest "lunatics" are portrayed in *The Ball And The Cross*, a distinctly allegorical work which portrays the triumph of God over the devil and spiritual reason over intellectual atheism in an almost picaresque tale told of two Scotsmen, a Catholic and an atheist, who battle with words and swords over the atheist's "blasphemy." Saint Paul's architectural dome, topped with the cross, provides substance for the title and heavy-handed symbolism, while a flying ship which appears but briefly in dreamlike sequences, represents without subtlety "Science" and is operated by one Captain Lucifer.

The Napoleon of Notting Hill and *The Flying Inn* are extrapolative works set in a future which seems old fashioned to today's reader. The former supposes a London "almost exactly like what it is now" except for the fact that the "people had cheated the prophets of the twentieth century." A lackadaisical population has lost all faith in change or revolution. One man is so like the next that even the rule of the nation can rest in anyone's hands; the king is chosen by rotation. A foppish new king, and the society he rules over, are galvanized by a young man who fights for the small neighborhood state, who raises (literally) a sword for Notting Hill. Again the power of ordinary people is championed. *The Flying Inn* imagines a future England in which the posting of inn signs is outlawed (and traditional English values and rights threatened); paradoxically, alcohol may only be consumed beneath the non-existent inn signs. Humphrey Pump, the landlord of one such threatened establishment, and Patrick Dalroy, a Catholic Irishman, fly (on foot) throughout the British countryside, planting their sign and undermining the forces of Lord Ivywood, a Nietzschean hero who denies all human limitations and wishes to mesh English values with orientalism and Mohammedanism. Almost anticipating Orwell's notion of Newspeak, the Turk who influences Ivywood uses cant and false logic to support his views; in particular he cites the example of numerous pubs being named "The Saracen's Head" as evidence that English and Turkish heritage must be shared.

The Man Who Was Thursday is Chesterton's most readable fantasy and most subtle allegory concerning the struggle between forces of civilization and anarchy, order and chaos, optimism and pessimism. A league of anarchists turns out to be composed entirely of policemen infiltrators while the leader, a man known as Sunday, turns out to be an enigmatic "god." This rich book wrestles with the paradox of evil in a universe created by God and seems to say that even the incomprehensible forces of terror and apparent chaos may have a place in society in that they provide a challenge which makes man value civilization all the more. Interestingly, in this work civilization is sometimes represented by the machine, in contrast with those works by Chesterton showing the machine as a threatening force.

—Rosemary Herbert

CHILSON, Robert.   American.   Born in Ringwood, Oklahoma, 19 May 1945. Educated in Appleton City High School, Missouri. Since 1967, free-lance writer. Agent: Richard Curtis, 156 East 52nd Street, New York, New York 10022. Address: 6109-A East 152nd Street, Grandview, Missouri 64030, U.S.A.

SCIENCE-FICTION PUBLICATIONS

Novels

As the Curtain Falls.   New York, DAW, 1974.
The Star-Crowned Kings.   New York, DAW, 1975.
The Shores of Kansas.   New York, Popular Library, 1976; London, Hale, 1977.

Uncollected Short Stories

"The Mind Reader," in *Analog* (New York), June, 1968.
"The Big Rock," in *Analog* (New York), October 1969.
"The Wild Blue Yonder," in *Analog* (New York), January 1970.
"The Fifth Ace," in *Analog* (New York), February 1970.
"Per Stratagem," in *Analog* (New York), July 1970.
"Excelsior!," in *Analog* (New York), August 1970.
"In the Wabe," in *Analog* (New York), November 1970.
"Ecological Niche," in *Analog* (New York), December 1970.
"In His Image," in *Analog 8*, edited by John W. Campbell, Jr.   New York, Doubleday, 1971.
"Compulsion Worse Confounded," in *Analog* (New York), November 1971.
"Truck Driver," in *Analog* (New York), January 1972.
"Forty Days and Forty Nights," in *Analog* (New York), August 1973.
"The Devil and the Deep Blue Sky," in *Beyond Time*, edited by Sandra Ley.   New York, Pocket Books, 1976.
"The Tame One," in *Galileo* (Boston), September 1976.
"People Reviews," in *Universe 7*, edited by Terry Carr.   New York, Doubleday, and London, Dobson, 1977.
"Adora," in *Galileo* (Boston), April 1977.
"O Ye of Little Faith," in *Cosmos* (New York), November 1977.
"Moonless Night," in *Galaxy* (New York), March 1978.
"Written in Sand," in *Isaac Asimov's Science Fiction Magazine* (New York), December 1979.

*   *   *

Most of Robert Chilson's early stories appeared in *Analog*, and were little distinguished from the usual technophilic, politically reactionary fiction in which the magazine specialized. The most promising of these is "Per Stratagem," a tale of human-alien contact in which the alien entity's biology and culture are imaginatively rendered, despite the tired plot of humans outwitting aliens, proving racial superiority.

Chilson's later novels are somewhat more adventurous, even lyrical. *The Shores of Kansas* is a moderately successful formula story about time-travel, while *The Star-Crowned Kings* resembles the typical Andre Norton plot of a young protagonist coming into manhood. *The Star-Crossed Kings* is interesting in that it posits a stellar civilization in which psychically endowed humans called Starlings rule the rest of mankind. Young Race Worden, however, learns that he also possesses psychic powers, which, in most such adventures, is usually the impetus for the hero to "take on" the establishment. Chilson avoids that cliché, but substitutes instead another cliché less often used but familiar to *Analog* writers—the concept that the establishment (Starlings) is basically benign except for a dangerous few, who are the only ones Race Worden must fight. While this is less melodramatic than a similar Andre Norton tale of a psychic's persecution by authority (*Forerunner Foray*), it is also less exciting as an adventure-story; Chilson is also formula-bound in following his hero's personal growth, so that the book also fails as a character study. One remark is interesting: "It shocked him to realize that many of the inequities were as much the fault of the underdogs as of the overlords." The concept itself is not objectionable, but the phrasing, as well as the circumstances of the observation, seems to express sympathy for the overlords, whereas a more radical writer, Harlan Ellison, might express a similar sentiment with tacit sympathy for the underdogs.

Unquestionably, Chilson's best accomplishment is *As the Curtain Falls*. Its format resembles the Dying Earth stories of Jack Vance, in which organized civilization has completely decayed, succeeded by barbaric cultures and weird mutations of humanity. In many places, the novel approaches parody of the Vance style, but for the most part Chilson's colorful descriptive prose, attention to detail, and deep sense of his world's history serve the primary purpose of telling a vivid adventure story. *As the Curtain Falls* centers on the attempts of a young prince, Trebor of Amballa, to establish in his fumbling way a world-empire, and, although most of the novel follows his adventures in rescuing his reluctant bride, he does accomplish his task at novel's end with the help of man's former heritage, a functional computer. As with *Star-Crowned Kings*, the plot is extremely loose, but this is compensated for by Chilson's plethora of bizarre cultures and place-names, wild characters (such as Lyantha, the pulchritudinous witch-queen who becomes immortal with the sacrifice of young men), and strange inventions (such as a battle between opposing fleets of ships built to sail on dry salt beds). The essential quality of Vance that Chilson lacks is a fascination with alien mentalities, altered states of mind, abstruse philosophies, and magic. In this regard, Chilson again betrays a reactionary consciousness in the way he chooses to satirize the world of effete artists, in that he presents no alternative (as Vance might) to the pretentiousness that passes in literary circles for an "altered state of mind."

Yet, unusually enough, a recent Chilson story, "Moonless Night," concerns a female dancer whose personal artistry is beyond reproach. The gimmick of this tale is the brief encounter of the female and a male trader, whose bodily proteins are so alien to hers that a touch results in mutual cellular destruction, and a painfully short romance. In essence, Chilson is a writer who has striven to strike a balance between lyricism and irony, but has not truly devoted himself to either.

—Gene Phillips

———————

CHILTON, Charles (Frederick William).   British.   Born in London in 1917. Educated at Thanet Street Church of England School, London. Married to Penelope Colbeck; two sons and one daughter. Free-lance writer and journalist, and radio producer for the BBC, London; devised and wrote *Riders of the Range* annual, from 1953. Recipient: Western Heritage Award, for children's book, 1963. Address: 27 Commonside, Keston, Kent, England.

SCIENCE-FICTION PUBLICATIONS

Novels (series: Jet Morgan in all books)

Journey into Space (novelization of radio series).   London, Jenkins, 1954.
The Red Planet (novelization of radio series).   London, Jenkins, 1956.
The World in Peril (novelization of radio series).   London, Jenkins, 1960.

OTHER PUBLICATIONS

Plays

Oh What a Lovely War, with the Theatre Workshop, London (produced London and New York, 1964).   London, Methuen, 1965.

Radio Plays: *Riders of the Range, Journey into Space*, and *The World in Peril* series in the 1950's.

Other

Riders of the Range (juvenile).   London, Juvenile Productions, 1951.
Second Round-Up with Riders of the Range (juvenile).   London, Juvenile Productions, 1952.

The Riders of the Range Square Dance Manual. London, Hutchinson, 1953.
The Book of the West: The Epic of America's Wild Frontier and the Men Who Created Its Legends. London, Odhams Press, 1961; Indianapolis, Bobbs Merrill, 1962.
Discovery of the American West (juvenile). London, Hamlyn, 1970.

*   *   *

For science-fiction enthusiasts who grew up in the Britain of the 1950's, the name of Charles Chilton is held in special esteem. Chilton was the writer and producer of the first modern space-age adventure series to be broadcast on BBC Radio (on what was then the Home Service). Children and even adults would ensure that they were at their radio sets by 6:15 p.m. to tune in to *Journey into Space* which featured the space adventures of Jet Morgan and his comrades Mitch, Doc, and Lemmy.

The series started with a very authentic scientific basis, the four intrepid explorers being launched in a moon-shot, though later time-travel and flying saucers piloted by aggressive aliens gave a fantasy edge to the story. However, there was no doubt about the widespread enthusiastic response from the audience. The name of Charles Chilton became a byword for juvenile science-fiction. In a second series, *The Red Planet*, Morgan and his crew journey to Mars and find themselves fighting against evilly disposed aliens who seek to invade the Earth. *The World in Peril* continued Jet Morgan's fight against the Martians who, in this tale, plot to use a giant asteroid to invade earth.

Chilton has never ventured back into the world of *Journey into Space*, nor, apparently, written more science fiction. However, his contribution was a major one in encouraging and shaping the attitude of a generation of British youngsters towards science fiction.

—Peter Berresford Ellis

CHRISTOPHER, John. Pseudonym for Christopher Samuel Youd; also writes as Hilary Ford; William Godfrey; Peter Graaf; Peter Nichols; Anthony Rye. Born in Huyton, Lancashire, in 1922. Educated at Peter Symonds' School, Winchester. Served in the Royal Signals, 1941-46. Married in 1946; five children. Recipient: Rockefeller-Atlantic award, 1946; *Guardian* Award, for children's book, 1971. Agent: David Higham Associates Ltd., 5-8 Lower John Street, London W1R 4HA, England.

SCIENCE-FICTION PUBLICATIONS

Novels (series: Tripods)

The Year of the Comet. London, Joseph, 1955; as *Planet in Peril*, New York, Avon, 1959.
The Death of Grass. London, Joseph, 1956; as *No Blade of Grass*, New York, Simon and Schuster, 1957.
The Caves of Night. London, Eyre and Spottiswoode, and New York, Simon and Schuster, 1958.
The Long Voyage. London, Eyre and Spottiswoode, 1960; as *The White Voyage*, New York, Simon and Schuster, 1961.
The World in Winter. London, Eyre and Spottiswoode, 1962; as *The Long Winter*, New York, Simon and Schuster, 1962.
Sweeney's Island. New York, Simon and Schuster, 1964; as *Cloud on Silver*, London, Hodder and Stoughton, 1964.
The Possessors. London, Hodder and Stoughton, and New York, Simon and Schuster, 1965.
A Wrinkle in the Skin. London, Hodder and Stoughton, 1965; as *The Ragged Edge*, New York, Simon and Schuster, 1966.
The Little People. London, Hodder and Stoughton, and New York, Simon and Schuster, 1967.
The White Mountains (juvenile; Tripods). London, Hamish Hamilton, and New York, Macmillan, 1967.
The City of Gold and Lead (juvenile; Tripods). London, Hamish Hamilton, and New York, Macmillan, 1967.
The Pool of Fire (juvenile; Tripods). London, Hamish Hamilton, and New York, Macmillan, 1968.
Pendulum. London, Hodder and Stoughton, and New York, Simon and Schuster, 1968.
The Lotus Caves (juvenile). London, Hamish Hamilton, and New York, Macmillan, 1969.
The Guardians (juvenile). London, Hamish Hamilton, and New York, Macmillan, 1970.
The Prince in Waiting (juvenile). London, Hamish Hamilton, and New York, Macmillan, 1970.
Beyond the Burning Lands (juvenile). London, Hamish Hamilton, and New York, Macmillan, 1971.
The Sword of the Spirits (juvenile). London, Hamish Hamilton, and New York, Macmillan, 1972.
Dom and Va (juvenile). London, Hamish Hamilton, and New York, Macmillan, 1973.
Wild Jack (juvenile). London, Hamish Hamilton, and New York, Macmillan, 1974.
Empty World (juvenile). London, Hamish Hamilton, 1977; New York, Dutton, 1978.

Short Stories

The Twenty-Second Century. London, Grayson, 1954; New York, Lancer, 1962.

Uncollected Short Stories

"Conspiracy," in *Gateway to the Stars*, edited by E.J. Carnell. London, Museum Press, 1955.
"Manna," in *New Worlds* (London), March 1955.
"The Gardener," in *Tales of the Frightened* (New York), Spring 1957.
"The Noon's Repose," in *Infinity* (New York), April 1957.
"Doom over Kareeta," in *Satellite* (New York), October 1957.
"A World of Slaves," in *Satellite* (New York), March 1959.
"Winter Boy, Summer Girl," in *Fantastic* (New York), October 1959.
"A Few Kindred Spirits," in *Best from Fantasy and Science Fiction 16*, edited by Edward L. Ferman. New York, Doubleday, 1967; London, Gollancz, 1968.
"Communication Problem," in *Beyond Infinity* (Hollywood), November 1967.
"Specimen," in *Fantasy and Science Fiction* (New York), December 1972.
"The Long Night," in *Galaxy* (New York), October 1974.

OTHER PUBLICATIONS

Novels

Giant's Arrow (as Anthony Rye). London, Gollancz, 1956; as Samuel Youd, New York, Simon and Schuster, 1960.
Malleson at Melbourne (as William Godfrey). London, Museum Press, 1956.
The Friendly Game (as William Godfrey). London, Joseph, 1957.
A Scent of White Poppies. London, Eyre and Spottiswoode, and New York, Simon and Schuster, 1959.
Patchwork of Death (as Peter Nichols). New York, Holt Rinehart, 1965; London, Hale, 1967.

Novels as Samuel Youd

The Winter Swan. London, Dobson, 1949.
Babel Itself. London, Cassell, 1951.
Brave Conquerors. London, Cassell, 1952.
Crown and Anchor. London, Cassell, 1953.
A Palace of Strangers. London, Cassell, 1954.
Holly Ash. London, Cassell, 1955; as *The Opportunist*, New York, Harper, 1957.

The Choice.   New York, Simon and Schuster, 1961; as *The Burning Bird*, London, Longman, 1964.
Messages of Love.   New York, Simon and Schuster, 1961; London, Longman, 1962.
The Summers at Accorn.   London, Longman, 1963.

Novels as Peter Graaf

Dust and the Curious Boy.   London, Joseph, 1957; as *Give the Devil His Due*, New York, Mill, 1957.
Daughter Fair.   London, Joseph, and New York, Washburn, 1958.
Sapphire Conference.   London, Joseph and New York, Washburn, 1959.
The Gull's Kiss.   London, Davies, 1962.

Novels as Hilary Ford

Felix Walking.   London, Eyre and Spottiswoode, and New York, Simon and Schuster, 1958.
Felix Running.   London, Eyre and Spottiswoode, 1959.
Bella on the Roof.   London, Longman, 1965.
A Figure in Grey (juvenile).   Kingswood, Surrey, World's Work, 1973.
Sarnia.   London, Hamish Hamilton, and New York, Doubleday, 1974.
Castle Malindine.   London, Hamish Hamilton, and New York, Harper, 1975.
A Bride for Bedivere.   London, Hamish Hamilton, 1976; New York, Harper, 1977.

Other

"Decline and Fall of the Bug-Eyed Monster," in *Fantasy and Science Fiction* (New York), October 1956.
"Science and Anti-Science," in *Fantastic Universe* (Chicago), June 1958.
"Not What-If But How-He," in *The Writer* (Boston), November 1968.
In the Beginning (juvenile).   London, Longman, 1972.

*   *   *

The reputation of John Christopher as a writer of science fiction for both adult and younger readers is solidly established. Perhaps the greatest single exposure was the film version in the early 1970's of the novel *The Death of Grass*. The elements present in this relatively early piece are a hallmark for all of his science fiction. Taken together, it forms all kinds of answers to the question "What do people do when things fall apart?" An account of his work may fall rather naturally into three parts: the early short fiction and "Managerial" stories; novels of crises, catastrophe and survival; and novels for younger readers.

The Twenty-Second Century conveniently displays Christopher's apprenticeship period. Six of the stories in the collection feature Max Larkin, a Director in one of the "corporations" that govern earth in place of political institutions in the not-too-distant future. Read along with the fuller exposition of this state of affairs in *Planet in Peril*, the stories present the proposition that political institutions will bring civilization to ruin and that government by enlightened commercial interests may do better. The case for this is epitomized in the laid-back character of Larkin, the unmarried, late-middle-aged corporate director, whose manipulative genius is time and again effective in world crises where armies and doomsday weapons have always failed. The 14 additional stories are something of an index of the novels that would follow. Sterility doom in "The New Wine," a medieval level of technological survival in "Weapon," and the panorama of 20th-century ruin in contrast to the garden of a new Eden in "Begin Again" provide glimpses of the worlds of the catastrophe novels. Beyond these, imprisonment by adaptive necessity in a lunar vivarium in "Christmas Roses," the interdiction of books in "A Time of Peace," and the humanity-saving wholesomeness recognized by enlightened aliens in a human village dedicated to a technologically simple way of life in "Blemish" are typical of the settings and subjects of the juvenile pieces. At least one more story,

"Rock-a-Bye," featuring the super-child born of a relationship between a Martian woman and a man from Earth is beautiful in its own right and deserves larger treatment. At this stage in his career Christopher's narrative craft is nearly mature. With minor refinements it is what it will be for the works to follow. He does not experiment with style. He tells stories with pace, suspense, sanity, and clarity. Moreover, unlike that of many writers, his strength is not in the short story but in the longer narrative work.

Two exceptions to the sort of novel for which Christopher is best known are *The Possessors*, wherein a group of people at a remote ski lodge are savaged by "body-snatching" aliens, and *The Little People*, wherein a group of vacationers at a remote old mansion are savaged by dwarves created by Nazi geneticists. Both are excursions in science-fiction gothic. The strength of both lies in the plausible behaviors of small groups of people in short-term crises.

But is is to scenarios of planet-wide catyclysm and survival in a world that will never be the same again that the most famous stories direct us. *The Death of Grass*, reminding us that corn, wheat, and rice are "grass," has a blight on all the species of grass cause a world famine. *The World in Winter* shows European civilization destroyed by a new ice age. *A Wrinkle in the Skin* presents earth devastated by the effects of continent-heaving earthquakes. *Pendulum* varies the cause of disaster from that of nature run amok to human society run amok—an obvious fictional response to the social transformations taking place in western civilization during the late 1960's. But with few alterations the effect is the same. More people survive. Yet once more society is reduced to savagery, to endure again the insanity and agony of social evolution that in past history did not teach their lessons well enough. These pieces are variations upon several principal themes. Human civilization is fragile and vulnerable. It cannot survive catastrophe either from natural causes or incompetent government. In the event of catastrophe the few who survive will be winnowed again by good health, knowledge of basic tools and nature, and the ability to kill other human beings, however reluctantly, out of necessity. Simultaneously, they must have the ability to love and form, once again, wholesome social contracts. Billions die in these stories, but hope and human potentiality have the final determination in each of them. Somehow mankind will recover and rebuild, though *Pendulum*, the latest of the novels, insists that it will not be swift.

With a sensible selection against the more baldly brutal and explicit details of violence and sexual behavior these themes are produced again in the novels for younger readers. There is an evenness of quality in all these works, so that a few may represent them all. The most famous are those that form the Tripod Trilogy, featuring Will Parker. Will is born in a backwoods village on a future earth conquered and enslaved by alien invaders who travel on land and water in vehicles with three immensely long terrain-gobbling legs. They are reminiscent of the Martian craft in Wells's *War of the Worlds*. The aliens employ the very strongest young humans as body servants. The remainder are mere breeders, forbidden more than a medieval level of technology and, ultimately, little more than vermin who will be exterminated when the aliens convert earth's atmosphere and gravity to their own. It doesn't happen, of course. Will and two friends have a principal role in returning earth to humans. The theme is the meaning of individual freedom and honor. Knowledge and curiously daring enough to see beyond popular mythology, self-discipline, respect for other people—especially odd ones—and the courage to act in the face of pain and under threat of death earn freedom. Finally, a single work called *The Guardians* refreshes these propositions about freedom in a post-catastrophe story of a boy who, learning of a conspiracy by aristocratic "guardians" to keep the mass of men at a stuporous level of existence in the cities, determines to join a revolution to free them. The work received the *Guardian* Award in 1971. Indeed, in terms of narrative art, Christopher's stories for young readers may be his finest achievement.

—John R. Pfeiffer

CLARKE, Arthur C(harles). British. Born in Minehead, Somerset, 16 December 1917. Educated at Huish's Grammar School, Taunton, Somerset, 1927-36; King's College, London, B.Sc. (honours) in physics and mathematics 1948. Flight Lieutenant in the Royal Air Force, 1941-46; served as Radar Instructor, and Technical Officer on the first Ground Controlled Approach radar; originated proposal for use of satellites for communications, 1945. Married Marilyn Mayfield in 1954 (divorced, 1964). Assistant Auditor, Exchequer and Audit Department, London, 1936-41; Assistant Editor, *Physics Abstracts,* London, 1949-50. Since 1954, engaged in underwater exploration and photography of the Great Barrier Reef of Australia and the coast of Sri Lanka. Director, Rocket Publishing, London, Underwater Safaris, Colombo, and Spaceward Corporation, New York. Has made numerous radio and television appearances, and has lectured widely in Britain and the United States; commentator, for CBS-TV, on lunar flights of Apollo 11, 12, and 15. Recipient: International Fantasy Award, 1952; Hugo Award, 1956, 1974, 1980; Unesco Kalinga Prize, 1961; Boys' Clubs of America award, 1961; Franklin Institute Ballantine Medal, 1963; Aviation-Space Writers Association Ball Award, 1965; American Association for the Advancement of Science Westinghouse award, 1969; *Playboy* award, 1971; Jupiter Award, 1973; Nebula Award, 1973, 1974, 1980; Campbell Memorial Award, 1974; American Institute of Aeronautics and Astronautics award, 1974; Boston Museum of Science Washburn Award, 1977. D.Sc.: Beaver College, Glenside, Pennsylvania, 1971. Chairman, British Interplanetary Society, 1946-47, 1950-53. Guest of Honor, World Science Fiction Convention, 1956. Fellow, Royal Astronomical Society; Fellow, King's College, London, 1977; Chancellor, Moratuwa University, Sri Lanka, 1979. Agent: David Higham Associates Ltd., 5-8 Lower John Street, London W1R 4HA, England. Address: 25 Barnes Place, Colombo 7, Sri Lanka.

SCIENCE-FICTION PUBLICATIONS

Novels

Prelude to Space. New York, Galaxy, 1951; London, Sidgwick and Jackson, 1953; as *Master of Space,* New York, Lancer, 1961; as *The Space Dreamers,* Lancer, 1969.
The Sands of Mars. London, Sidgwick and Jackson, 1951; New York, Gnome Press, 1952.
Islands in the Sky (juvenile). London, Sidgwick and Jackson, and Philadelphia, Winston, 1952.
Against the Fall of Night. New York, Gnome Press, 1953.
Childhood's End. New York, Ballantine, 1953; London, Sidgwick and Jackson, 1954.
Earthlight. London, Muller, and New York, Ballantine, 1955.
The City and the Stars. London, Muller, and New York, Harcourt Brace, 1956.
The Deep Range. New York, Harcourt Brace, and London, Muller, 1957.
Across the Sea of Stars (omnibus). New York, Harcourt Brace, 1959.
A Fall of Moondust. London, Gollancz, and New York, Harcourt Brace, 1961.
From the Oceans, From the Stars (omnibus). New York, Harcourt Brace, 1962.
Dolphin Island (juvenile). New York, Holt Rinehart, and London, Gollancz, 1963.
Prelude to Mars (omnibus). New York, Harcourt Brace, 1965.
2001: A Space Odyssey (novelization of screenplay). New York, New American Library, and London, Hutchinson, 1968.
The Lion of Comarre, and Against the Fall of Night. New York, Harcourt Brace, 1968; London, Gollancz, 1970.
Rendezvous with Rama. London, Gollancz, and New York, Harcourt Brace, 1973.
Imperial Earth. London, Gollancz, 1975; New York, Harcourt Brace, 1976.
The Fountains of Paradise. London, Gollancz, and New York, Harcourt Brace, 1979.

Short Stories

Expedition to Earth. New York, Ballantine, 1953; London, Sidgwick and Jackson, 1954.
Reach for Tomorrow. New York, Ballantine, 1956; London, Gollancz, 1962.
Tales from the White Hart. New York, Ballantine, 1957; London, Sidgwick and Jackson, 1972.
The Other Side of the Sky. New York, Harcourt Brace, 1958; London, Gollancz, 1961.
Tales of Ten Worlds. New York, Harcourt Brace, 1962; London, Gollancz, 1963.
The Nine Billion Names of God: The Best Short Stories of Arthur C. Clarke. New York, Harcourt Brace, 1967.
The Wind from the Sun: Stories of the Space Age. New York, Harcourt Brace, and London, Gollancz, 1972.
Of Time and Stars: The Worlds of Arthur C. Clarke. London, Gollancz, 1972.
The Best of Arthur C. Clarke 1937-1971, edited by Angus Wells. London, Sidgwick and Jackson, 1973.

Uncollected Short Story

"Quarantine," in *Isaac Asimov's Science Fiction Magazine* (New York), Spring 1977.

OTHER PUBLICATIONS

Novel

Glide Path. New York, Harcourt Brace, 1963; London, Sidgwick and Jackson, 1969.

Play

Screenplay: *2001: A Space Odyssey,* with Stanley Kubrick, 1968.

Other

Interplanetary Flight: An Introduction to Astronautics. London, Temple Press, 1950; New York, Harper, 1951; revised edition, 1960.
The Exploration of Space. London, Temple Press, and New York, Harper, 1951; revised edition, 1959.
"In Defense of Science Fiction," in *Unesco Courier 15* (New York), November 1952.
"Science Fiction: Preparation for the Age of Space," in *Modern Science Fiction,* edited by Reginald Bretnor. New York, Coward McCann, 1953.
The Young Traveller in Space (juvenile). London, Phoenix House, 1954; as *Going into Space,* New York, Harper, 1954; as *The Scottie Book of Space Travel,* London, Transworld, 1957; revised edition, with Robert Silverberg, as *Into Space,* New York, Harper, 1971.
The Exploration of the Moon. London, Muller, 1954; New York, Harper, 1955.
Foreword to *Authentic Book of Space,* edited by Herbert J. Campbell. London, Panther, 1954.
The Coast of Coral. London, Muller, and New York, Harper, 1956.
The Making of a Moon: The Story of the Earth Satellite Program. London, Muller, and New York, Harper, 1957; revised edition, Harper, 1958.
The Reefs of Taprobane: Underwater Adventures Around Ceylon. London, Muller, and New York, Harper, 1957.
Voice Across the Sea. London, Muller, 1958; New York, Harper, 1959; revised edition, London, Mitchell Beazley, and New York, Harper, 1974.
Boy Beneath the Sea (juvenile). New York, Harper, 1958.
The Challenge of the Spaceship: Previews of Tomorrow's World. New York, Harper, 1959; London, Muller, 1960.
The First Five Fathoms: A Guide to Underwater Adventure. New York, Harper, 1960.
The Challenge of the Sea. New York, Holt Rinehart, 1960; London, Muller, 1961.

Indian Ocean Adventure. New York, Harper, 1961; London, Barker, 1962.

Profiles of the Future: An Enquiry into the Limits of the Possible. London, Gollancz, 1962; New York, Harper, 1963; revised edition, Harper, 1973; Gollancz, 1974.

The Treasure of the Great Reef. London, Barker, and New York, Harper, 1964; revised edition, New York, Ballantine, 1974.

Indian Ocean Treasure, with Mike Wilson. New York, Harper, 1964; London, Sidgwick and Jackson, 1972.

Man and Space, with the editors of *Life.* New York, Time, 1964.

Voices from the Sky: Previews of the Coming Space Age. New York, Harper, 1965; London, Gollancz, 1966.

The Promise of Space. New York, Harper, and London, Hodder and Stoughton, 1968.

"When Earthman and Alien Meet," in *Playboy* (Chicago), January 1968.

Foreword to *Three for Tomorrow.* New York, Meredith, 1969; London, Gollancz, 1970.

First on the Moon, with the astronauts. London, Joseph, and Boston, Little Brown, 1970.

Report on Planet Three and Other Speculations. London, Gollancz, and New York, Harper, 1972.

The Lost Worlds of 2001. London, Sidgwick and Jackson, and New York, New American Library, 1972.

Beyond Jupiter: The Worlds of Tomorrow, with Chesley Bonestell. Boston, Little Brown, 1972.

Technology and the Frontiers of Knowledge (lectures), with others. New York, Doubleday, 1975.

The View from Serendip (on Sri Lanka). New York, Random House, 1977; London, Gollancz, 1978.

Editor, *Time Probe: Sciences in Science Fiction.* New York, Delacorte Press, 1966; London, Gollancz, 1967.

Editor, *The Coming of the Space Age: Famous Accounts of Man's Probing of the Universe.* London, Gollancz, and New York, Meredith, 1967.

*

Bibliography: in *Arthur C. Clarke* by Eric S. Rabkin, West Linn, Oregon, Starmont House, 1979.

Manuscript Collection: Mugar Memorial Library, Boston University.

*   *   *

With 16 very popular novels to his credit, Arthur C. Clarke is one of the small handful of writers who have shaped science fiction in our century. His persistent spiritual—and sometimes lyrical—optimism concerning the place of humanity in the universe and his enthusiastic faith in technology gather together both the hard and soft sides of the genre in works of classic importance. Clarke's love of the details of technology also enlivens his highly regarded work as a science writer. By his own count, Clarke has produced "approximately five hundred articles and short stories" including "The Star," a Hugo-winning response to Wells's belittling of humanity in his famous story of the same name.

One can take a preliminary survey of Clarke's work by examining his short fiction. *Tales from the White Hart* gains coherence by establishing a tavern frame within which Harry Purvis tells one tall tale after another, displaying Clarke's energetic—and sometimes outrageous—sense of humor, a sense epitomized in the pun-ishing ending of his later story called "Neutron Tide." Many of Clarke's novels and short stories have been repackaged in other volumes. In *The Nine Billion Names of God* Clarke collects his 25 favorites among his then-published short stories. The majority of his most famous pieces are here, including the almost pastoral title story in which Western science and Eastern religion confront each other and eternity, "Rescue Party" in which the would-be saviors of a doomed Earth are startled by humanity's self-reliance, "Superiority" in which a space war is lost by too much cleverness, "The Sentinel" which is often thought of as the germ for *2001,* and "The Star." One must turn to *The Wind from the Sun* to find "A Meeting with Medusa," a Nebula-winning novella that includes the discovery of

life in the dense atmosphere of Jupiter, and Clarke's own choice for his single best piece of fiction, "Transit of Earth." This story tells of an astronaut on Mars who knows his life supports cannot long sustain him but who nonetheless sets up the equipment necessary to record for posterity the first human observation of Earth passing across the disc of the sun, a mythic moment typical of Clarke that holds both sunrise and sunset in suspense. This story is also typical of Clarke in depending upon technical detail for its setting and dramatic situation and in balancing a symbol of demise with one of rejuvenation. Clarke's characteristically isolated hero joyfully and paradoxically greets the future by rushing toward Bach, a beauty from the past: "Johann Sebastian, here I come."

Clarke's faith in technology is profound; he is quite proud "to know several astronauts who became astronauts through reading my books." He is also justifiably proud to have first proposed (1945) geosynchronous communication satellites, an innovation that has already changed our world and will continue to move us toward the single community Clarke's heroes always contemplate when looking back at Earth from space. The majority of Clarke's novels are highly technological, human characters being invented primarily to provide occasion for humor, to put life at stake, or to locate a coherent point of view from which to explore in imaginative and thrilling detail the wonders of science and of the future universe. *Islands in the Sky* and *Dolphin Island* are juvenile novels employing teenaged boys as observers, the former presenting a grand tour of many sorts of satellites and space stations and a lunar fly-by and the latter showing science reaching out to the aliens with whom we share our planet, intelligent mammals of the sea. *Prelude to Space, The Sands of Mars, Earthlight, The Deep Range, Imperial Earth,* and *The Fountains of Paradise,* though more adult, are still primarily exciting guided tours rather than compelling dramas. In each of these the technology is amazingly detailed; the plot is admirably thickened by political impediments to the implementation of the technology; and these impediments are excitingly but predictably overcome. Within this general scheme, *Prelude to Space* concentrates on the development and launching of the first rocket to leave our atmosphere; *The Sands of Mars,* one of the two psychologically strong novels in this group, concerns first contact and the establishment of viable human colonies on a terraformed Mars; *Earthlight* studies political changes on the Earth and colonized planets as lunar technology develops, including that needed for self-defense and efficient mineral recovery; *The Deep Range* follows the development of whaleherding and its philosophical shift from a meat to a milk industry; *Imperial Earth,* the other psychologically strong novel and Clarke's favorite, also concerns the effect of technology on the social systems on several solar worlds and the personal and political maturing of a man bound to lead the people of Titan through necessary cultural adaptations; and *The Fountains of Paradise* chronicles the building of the "space elevator" that will effectively free humanity from the Earth.

Three other heavily technological novels need mention. *Glide Path,* Clarke's only non-science fiction novel, follows the very important World War II development of Ground Controlled Approach radar. Clarke was in charge of English GCA operations and this novel has interest not only for its technology but for its quasi-autobiographical detail. *A Fall of Moondust* concerns a tourist "boat" trapped within a lunar sea of microscopic dust. This highly effective novel compellingly challenges the reader to try to beat the fictional technicians to a plan for rescue while all the time anoxia and mechanical failures threaten the passengers. And finally, *Rendezvous with Rama* combines the absolutely fascinating exploration of an extra-solar vessel come into our system with profound philosophic questioning of the significance of humanity, of biological life, and of intelligence. This is the only work ever to win all major science fiction awards: Hugo, Nebula, Campbell, and Jupiter.

The questioning in *Rendezvous with Rama* recalls Clarke's novels of cultural exploration. *The Lion of Comarre,* the most like a fairy tale of Clarke's works, traces the quest of a young man to find the geniuses of the past, to destroy the enchanted city keeping them in pacified torpor through technologically induced pleasures, and to open the static pastoral land to science. A similar plot structures *Against the Fall of Night* and *The City and the Stars,* the one an earlier version of the other. These works are more convincingly written than *Comarre* and improve upon it by having the city and country cultures both static, but for different reasons, by creating in Alvin a central character with whose growing pains we can identify, and by casting the drama of terrestrial rejuvenation against a cosmic context. That cosmic context provides the overall power of *Childhood's End,* Clarke's most popular novel and his first great testament of faith in human evolution to a higher plane. His last great testament, *2001: A Space Odyssey,* combines motifs and attitudes spanning Clarke's entire career to produce a technologically compelling story of the next generation's space program, a humanly moving story of struggle and courage against harsh interplanetary space and computers gone awry, and a philosophically moving study of the evolution of humanity and our meaning in the universe. This book, done while Clarke collaborated with Stanley Kubrick on the screenplay for the film *2001,* is the best summation both intellectual and artistic of Clarke's career. The film is perhaps the most widely important work of science fiction ever produced.

In his love of technical detail and his efforts to use science correctly in constructing his novels of adventure, Clarke has been perhaps the foremost writer of his generation to carry on the work of Verne and the editorial policies of Campbell; but in his abiding concern for society and philosophy, Clarke is also the foremost heir of Wells and Stapledon. Clarke has won himself a unique and towering position in science fiction by combining the enthusiasm of one camp with the breadth of vision of the other. Clarke has written that his youthful reading of Stapledon's *Last and First Men* (1930) "transformed my life." That book, chronicling the evolution and demise of humanity, ends with the suggestion that "we shall make after all a fair conclusion to this brief music that is man." Stapledon's line reminds us of the farewell of the astronaut in "Transit of Earth," but with a difference: Stapledon sees the music as a conclusion; Clarke sees it as an embrace in something greater than man. This spiritual faith in Clarke comes not from religion, however, but from science itself. As a character says in *The Fountains of Paradise,* the book with which Clarke claims he has retired from writing, "he could not understand how anyone could contemplate the dynamic asymmetry of Euler's profound yet beautifully simple [equation] without wondering if the universe was the creation of some vast intelligence." Even for the reading generation that began with Hiroshima, Clarke in his fiction marshals the intimations of intelligence to justify human hope.

—Eric S. Rabkin

CLEMENS, Samuel Langhorne. *See* **TWAIN, Mark.**

CLEMENT, Hal.   Pseudonym for Harry Clement Stubbs.   American.   Born in Somerville, Massachusetts, 30 May 1922. Educated at Harvard University, Cambridge, Massachusetts, B.S. in astronomy 1943; Boston University, M.Ed. 1947; Simmons College, Boston, M.S. 1963. Served as a bomber pilot with the 8th Air Force during World War II: Air Medal, with four oak leaf clusters; since 1953, served in the Air Force Reserve: Lieutenant Colonel. Married Mary Elizabeth Myers in 1952; two sons and one daughter. Since 1949, science teacher, Milton Academy, Massachusetts. Technical Instructor, Special Weapons School, Sandia Base, New Mexico, 1951. Member of the Milton Warrant Committee; Chairman of the District Board of Review, Boy Scouts of America. Address: 12 Thompson Lane, Milton, Massachusetts 02187, U.S.A.

SCIENCE-FICTION PUBLICATIONS

Novels (series: Mesklin)

Needle.   New York, Doubleday, 1951; London, Gollancz, 1961; as *From Outer Space,* New York, Avon, 1957.
Iceworld.   New York, Gnome Press, 1953.
Mission of Gravity (Mesklin).   New York, Doubleday, 1954; London, Hale, 1955.
The Ranger Boys in Space (juvenile).   Boston, Page, and London, Harrap, 1956.
Cycle of Fire.   New York, Ballantine, 1957; London, Gollancz, 1964.
Some Notes on Xi Bootis.   Chicago, Advent, 1959.
Close to Critical.   New York, Ballantine, 1964; London, Gollancz, 1966.
Star Light. (Mesklin).   New York, Ballantine, 1971.
Ocean on Top.   New York, DAW, 1973; London, Sphere, 1976.
Through the Eye of a Needle.   New York, Ballantine, 1978.

Short Stories

Natives of Space.   New York, Ballantine, 1965.
Small Changes.   New York, Doubleday, 1969; as *Space Lash,* New York, Dell, 1969.
The Best of Hal Clement.   New York, Ballantine, 1979.

OTHER PUBLICATIONS

Other

"Whirlagig World," in *Astounding* (New York), June. 1953.
"The Creation of Imaginary Beings," in *Science Fiction, Today and Tomorrow,* edited by Reginald Bretnor.   New York, Harper, 1974.
"Hard Science and Tough Technologies," in *The Craft of Science Fiction,* edited by Reginald Bretnor.   New York, Harper, 1976.

Editor, *First Flights to the Moon.*   New York, Doubleday, 1970.
Editor, *The Moon,* by George Gamow.   London, Abelard Schuman, 1971.

*   *   *

A continuous fan since his mid-teens of physical science and of the fictional extrapolations from it that the genre has labeled "hard" science fiction, Hal Clement published his first story in John Campbell's *Astounding* in 1942 when he was an astronomy major at Harvard. He has gone on to become one of the most highly admired scientific extrapolators and lovers of the tight demands of logic in the genre despite the fact that he is not a full-time writer. Clement and his classic fictions are mentioned whenever the discussion of science in the genre comes up; and hence he represents both the full maturing of the Campbell engineering effect on science fiction and the limitations of that approach. Campbell demanded a good story, of course, and Clement's stories are carefully constructed and often convey a certain excitement and suspense. But their distinguishing characteristic is that a problematic condition in physical reality, or simply a condition of difference such as an increase or decrease in heat or gravity, must be elaborated upon, explained, and taken through certain plot changes so that the reader can simply understand the problem or the difference. This is a literature of total imitation, or mimesis, in which the facts of the universe are what is mimed. Often in Clement's work, words themselves seem secondary to the phenomena. It is no coincidence that Clement loves, and, in fact, himself paints—as George Richard—astronomical art works of the phenomenal universe. At the end of his most famous novel, *Mission of Gravity,* the alien hero who is trying cleverly to acquire a more useful science for his truly phenomenal planet, Mesklin, that orbits the double star 61 Cygni, comments, "They finished up with the old line about words not really being enough to describe it. What else beside words can you use, in the name of the Suns?" His second-in-command answers, "this quantity-code they [humans] call Mathematics." Furthermore, for Clement himself any symbols seem to reside not in the words but in the Suns themselves—or in their mathematics.

The literary effect of hard science fiction that makes it good reading derives not so much from its accuracy (although Clement has written non-fiction essays in which he challenges the reader to catch his fictions in an inaccuracy thus implying that the puzzle element is central) as from its ability to tell how science can show difference. The sublime effect of the varied and infinite universe does not require the fanciful imagination in science fiction but can be, to paraphrase Wordsworth who wanted science and imagination linked, the simple produce of the common day if you are an astronomer. The planetary environments are main characters in Clement's fictions, major sources of the sublime, from the variable high-gravity world of Mesklin to the giant and peculiar planet Dhrawn that the Mesklinites explore in *StarLight,* to a variety of other worlds in which differences in atmospheric components, in mass, in heat all demonstrate that scientific extrapolation is not dry as dust. But not only does scientific extrapolation discover exciting differences in environment; it also assumes and sets about to demonstrate, in Clement's work, that life forms would evolve differently in different environments. Clement is fascinated by alien viewpoints, and the non-human characters are the most interesting characters in most of his fiction. This commitment to difference, not only in environments but also in life forms, makes Clement a far more interesting—and more accurate—extrapolator than his fellow hard science-fiction writer, Isaac Asimov, who peoples the galaxy with humans. But beneath the strange morphological surfaces and beyond the alien body chemistry, Clement's extra-terrestrials still seek humanlike goals, most often the goal of more knowledge and more scientific control. Thus Captain Barlennan of Mesklin can seem both strange and familiar as he connives to learn flight and even space travel under conditions far different from those given to us to learn the same things. The emphasis in Clement is on learning, movement, and difference—not on any symbolic revelation of oneness.

One of his first aliens can illustrate perhaps most vividly the strengths and the weaknesses of Clement's brand of hard science fiction. This creature, the hero in *Needle* and reappearing in *Through the Eye of a Needle,* evolved from viruses rather than from protozoan cells into a highly intelligent life form in which only the memory cells are specialized. The other cells are continually changing into various organs as need arises; but usually the creature lives most efficiently as a friendly parasite, or symbiont, insinuating its small virus-like cells easily among the larger protozoan-like cells of its host. In *Needle* the creature has come to Earth in hot pursuit of a criminal member of its race. They come from light years away, of course, representing Clement's one bow to illogic—faster-than-light travel. The creature, called simply The Hunter, adopts as his host a teenage boy. They become the best of friends in a delightful and carefully detailed symbiosis. Clement has the enemy or adversary creature adopt the boy's father as its host. The story then unfolds as an exciting tale of detection with a lot of biological extrapolation worked in, but Clement adds nothing suggestive nor psychologically extrapolative about the basic filial conflict that readers of Wordsworth, Joyce, and even Thomas Wolfe might expect. In several different places, Clement has written sarcastically about "amateur psychoanalysts"; and it is almost as though he invented this story, which contains one of his nicest and most different aliens, deliberately to demonstrate that hard science fiction extrapolates only with the physical.

—Donald M. Hassler

CLIFTON, Mark (Irvin). American. Born in 1906. Trained as a teacher, but worked for 25 years as a personnel officer: compiled 200,000 case histories. Recipient: Hugo Award, 1955. *Died in 1963.*

SCIENCE-FICTION PUBLICATIONS

Novels

They'd Rather Be Right, with Frank Riley, New York, Gnome Press, 1957; as *The Forever Machine,* New York, Galaxy, 1967.
Eight Keys to Eden. New York, Doubleday, 1960; London, Gollancz, 1962.
When They Come from Space. New York, Doubleday, 1962; London, Dobson, 1963.

Short Stories

The Science Fiction of Mark Clifton, edited by Barry N. Malzberg and Martin H. Greenberg. Carbondale, Southern Illinois University Press, 1980.

*   *   *

Mark Clifton had a brief ten year writing career, but in that short span he had an enormous impact on science fiction. Most of Clifton's work was sold to *Astounding* in the form of two series.

The first series was about Bossy, the first of the super computers, and it was clearly developed in the novel *They'd Rather Be Right.* As Bossy follows its program to "heal" and "perfect" humans, the treated humans develop psi powers and immortality. However, society fears these "perfected" humans and sets off a witch hunt to destroy the treated humans and Bossy. Although there's plenty of action, the novel's plot concentrates on society's fears of the unknown, even if the unknown might provide great benefits. This book has subtlety and rare sophistication.

The second series features Ralph Kennedy, an extraterrestrial psychologist who manages—in glib, light stories—to save Earth from alien invasions. *When They Come from Space* satirizes bureaucracy when Earth is menaced by the terrible alien Black Fleet. Kennedy is drafted to confront the invasion and manages to discover the secret of the Black Fleet. The plot is clever and the wit is as dry as a martini.

Clifton's only novel not a part of any series is the underrated *Eight Keys to Eden.* This is a puzzle story dealing with a situation first developed by Clarke's *Childhood's End.* An E-man (or Extrapolator) is sent to investigate the colony on the planet Eden when the colony mysteriously stops communicating with Earth. The E-man must solve the ecological-psychological problem which becomes, in Clifton's treatment, a critique of Earth civilization.

—George Kelley

CLIVE, Dennis. *See* **FEARN, John Russell.**

COBLENTZ, Stanton A(rthur). American. Born in San Francisco, California, 24 August 1896. Educated at the University of California, Berkeley, A.B. 1917, M.A. 1919. Married Flora Bachrach in 1922. Feature writer, San Francisco *Examiner,* 1919-20; book reviewer, New York *Times* and New York *Sun,* 1920-38; Founding Editor, *Wings: A Quarterly of Verse,* New York, then Mill Valley, California, 1933-60. Address: 5380 Cribari Crest, San Jose, California 93135, U.S.A.

SCIENCE-FICTION PUBLICATIONS

Novels

The Wonder Stick.   New York, Cosmopolitan, 1929.
Next Door to the Sun.   New York, Wings Press, 1936.
When the Birds Fly South.   Mill Valley, California, Wings Press, 1945.
The Sunken World.   Los Angeles, Fantasy, 1948; London, Cherry Tree, 1951.
After 12,000 Years.   Los Angeles, Fantasy, 1950.
Into Plutonian Depths.   New York, Avon, 1950.
The Planet of Youth.   Los Angeles, Fantasy, 1952.
Under the Triple Suns.   Reading, Pennsylvania, Fantasy Press, 1955.
Hidden World.   New York, Avalon, 1957; as *In Caverns Below,* New York, Garland, 1975.
The Blue Barbarians.   New York, Avalon, 1958.
The Runaway World.   New York, Avalon, 1961.
The Last of the Great Race.   New York, Arcadia House, 1964.
The Lizard Lords.   New York, Avalon, 1964.
The Lost Comet.   New York, Arcadia House, 1964.
The Moon People.   New York, Avalon, 1964.
Lord of Tranerica.   New York, Avalon, 1966.
The Crimson Capsule.   New York, Avalon, 1967; as *The Animal People,* New York, Belmont, 1970.
The Day the World Stopped.   New York, Avalon, 1968.
The Island People.   New York, Belmont, 1971.

Uncollected Short Stories

"The Gas-Weed," in *Amazing* (New York), May 1929.
"The Making of Misty Isle," in *Science Wonder Stories* (New York), June 1929.
"The Radio Telescope," in *Amazing* (New York), June 1929.
"The Wand of Creation," in *Amazing* (New York), August 1929.
"Reclaimers of the Ice," in *Amazing Stories Quarterly* (New York) Spring 1930.
"A Circle of Science," in *Amazing* (New York), May 1930.
"Missionaries from the Sky," in *Amazing* (New York), November 1930.
"The Man from Tomorrow," in *Amazing Stories Quarterly* (New York), Spring-Summer 1933.
"The Men Without Shadows," in *Amazing* (New York), October 1933.
"The Confession of Mr. DeKalb," in *Astounding* (New York), January 1934.
"Manna from Mars," in *Astounding* (New York), March 1934.
"The Green Plague," in *Astounding* (New York), April 1934.
"The Radio Mind-Ray," in *Astounding* (New York), July 1934.
"In the Footsteps of the Wasp," in *Amazing* (New York), August 1934.
"The Truth about the Psycho-Tector," in *Astounding* (New York), October 1934.
"Beyond the Universe," in *Amazing* (New York), December 1934.
"Riches for Pluto," in *Astounding* (New York), December 1934.
"Older Than Methuselah," in *Amazing* (New York), April 1935.
"Triple-Geared," in *Astounding* (New York), April 1935.
"An Episode in Space," in *Astounding* (New York), May 1935.
"The Golden Planetoid," in *Amazing* (New York), August 1935.
"The Glowworm Flower," in *Astounding* (New York), June 1936.
"Denitro," in *Amazing* (New York), February 1937.
"The Reign of the Long Tusks," in *Astounding* (New York), February 1937.
"Gravity, Unaffected," in *Astounding* (New York), September 1937.
"Exiles from the Universe," in *Amazing* (New York), February 1938.
"Through the Time Radio," in *Marvel* (New York), August 1938.
"Rout of the Fire Imps," in *Marvel* (New York), November 1938.
"Death in the Tubeway," in *Amazing* (New York), January 1939.
"The Weather Adjudicator," in *Marvel* (New York), February 1939.
"The Man from Xenern," in *Thrilling Wonder Tales* (New York), August 1939.

"The Purple Conspiracy," in *Fantastic Adventures* (New York), November 1939.
"Planet of the Knob Heads," in *Science Fiction* (Holyoke, Massachusetts), December 1939.
"Missionaries of Mars," in *Tales of Wonder* (Kingwood, Surrey), Spring 1940.
"Fire Gas," in *Famous Fantastic Mysteries* (New York), April 1940.
"Sunward," in *Thrilling Wonder Stories* (New York), April 1940.
"Headhunters of Nuamerica," in *Comet* (Springfield, Massachusetts), March 1941.
"Over the Space-Waves," in *Startling* (New York), April 1941.
"Enchantress of Lemuria," in *Amazing* (New York), September 1941.
"The Crystal Planetoids," in *Amazing* (New York), May 1942.
"The Phantom Armada," in *Fantastic Adventures* (New York), May 1942.
"The Scarlet Rollers," in *Fantastic Adventures* (New York), September 1942.
"The Stygian Terror," in *Fantastic Adventures* (New York), November 1942.
"The Cosmic Deflector," in *Amazing* (New York), January 1943.
"Ard of the Sun People," in *Amazing* (New York), February 1943.
"The Sun Doom," in *Fantastic Adventures* (New York), June 1943.
"The Siderial Time-Bomb," in *Startling* (New York), Winter 1944.
"The Odyssey of Battling Bert," in *Amazing* (New York), December 1944.
"The Nemesis of the Astropede," in *Thrilling Wonder Stories* (New York), Fall 1945.
"Titan of the Jungle," in *Thrilling Wonder Stories* (New York), Summer 1946.
"Flight Through Tomorrow, in *Fantasy Book 1* (Los Angeles), 1947.
"Time Trap," in *Fantasy* (London), August 1947.
"The Universe Ranger," in *Fantasy Book 6* (Los Angeles), 1950.
"The Way of the Moth," in *Thrilling Wonder Stories* (New York), December 1951.
"The Revolt of the Scarlet Lunes," in *Spaceway* (Alhambra, California), December 1953.
"The Midgets of Monoton," in *Spaceway* (Alhambra, California), February 1954.
"Microcosm," in *Fantastic Universe* (Chicago), April 1958.

OTHER PUBLICATIONS

Verse

The Thinker and Other Poems.   New York, White, 1923.
The Lone Adventurer.   New York, Unicorn Press, 1927; revised edition, San Jose, California, Redwood Press, 1975.
Shadows on a Wall.   New York, Poetic Publications, 1930.
The Enduring Flame.   New York, Paebar, 1932.
Songs of the Redwoods.   Los Angeles, Overland Outwest, 1933.
The Merry Hunt.   Boston, Humphries, 1934.
The Pageant of Man.   New York, Wings Press, 1936.
Songs by the Wayside.   New York, Wings Press, 1938.
Senator Goose.   Mill Valley, California, Wings Press, 1940.
Winds of Chaos.   Mill Valley, California, Wings Press, 1942.
Green Vistas.   Mill Valley, California, Wings Press, 1943.
Armageddon. Mill Valley, California, Wings Press, 1943.
The Mountain of the Sleeping Maiden.   Mill Valley, California, Wings Press, 1946.
Garnered Sheaves: Selected Poems.   Mill Valley, California, Wings Press, 1949.
Time's Travelers.   Mill Valley, California, Wings Press, 1952.
From a Western Hilltop.   Mill Valley, California, Wings Press, 1954.
Out of Many Songs.   Mill Valley, California, Wings Press, 1958.
Atlantis and Other Poems.   Mill Valley, California, Wings Press, 1960.
Redwood Poems.   Healdsburg, California, Naturegraph, 1961.
Aesop's Fables.   Norwalk, Connecticut, Gibson, 1968.
Selected Short Poems.   San Jose, California, Redwood Press, 1974.
Strange Universes: New Selected Poems.   San Jose, California, Redwood Press, 1977.

Sea Cliffs and Green Ridges. Happy Camp, California, Naturegraph, 1979.

Other

The Decline of Man. New York, Minton Balch, 1925.
Marching Men: The Story of War. New York, Unicorn Press, 1927.
The Literary Revolution. New York, Frank Maurice, 1927.
The Answer of the Ages. New York, Cosmopolitan, 1931.
Villains and Vigilantes. New York, Wilson Erickson, 1936.
The Triumph of the Teapot Poets. Mill Valley, California, Wings Press, 1941.
An Editor Looks at Poetry. Mill Valley, California, Wings Press, 1947.
New Poetic Lamps and Old. Mill Valley, California, Wings Press, 1950.
From Arrow to Atom Bomb: The Psychological History of War. New York, Beechhurst Press, 1953.
The Rise of the Anti-Poets. Mill Valley, California, Wings Press, 1955.
Magic Casements: A Guidebook for Poets. Mill Valley, California, Wings Press, 1957.
The Long Road to Humanity. New York, Yoseloff, 1959.
My Life in Poetry. New York, Bookman Associates, 1959.
The Swallowing Wilderness. New York, Yoseloff, 1961.
The Generation That Forgot to Sing. Mill Valley, California, Wings Press, 1962.
Avarice: A History. Washington, D.C., Public Affairs Press, 1964.
Ten Crises in Civilization. Chicago, Follett, 1965; London, Muller, 1967.
Demons, Witch Doctors, and Modern Man. New York, Yoseloff, 1965.
The Paradox of Man's Greatness. Washington, D.C., Public Affairs Press, 1966.
The Poetry Circus. New York, Hawthorn, 1967.
The Pageant of the New World. Berkeley, California, Diablo Press, 1968.
The Power Trap. South Brunswick, New Jersey, A.S. Barnes, 1970.
The Militant Dissenters. South Brunswick, New Jersey, A.S. Barnes, 1970.
The Challenge to Man's Survival. South Brunswick, New Jersey, A.S. Barnes, 1972.

Editor, *Modern American* [and *British*] *Lyrics.* New York, Minton Balch, 2 vols., 1924-25; as *Modern Lyrics,* New York, Loring and Mussey, n.d.
Editor, *The Music Makers.* New York, Ackerman, 1945.
Editor, *Unseen Wings.* New York, Beechhurst Press, 1949.
Editor, *Poetry Today.* Mill Valley, California, Wings Press, 1955.
Editor, *Poems to Change Lives.* New York, Association Press, 1960.

*   *   *

In the earliest days of the science-fiction magazines, most of the stories were reprinted from other sources; shortly, however, new works began to appear in *Amazing, Science Wonder Stories,* and the others. One of the first of these "new" authors, along with such writers as Jack Williamson and E.E. Smith, was Stanton A. Coblentz.

Coblentz's work was unusual for these magazines, as most of the material utilized science fiction as a vehicle for transmitting "hard science" (i.e., the Verne tradition), or a device for establishing melodramatic adventure situations (i.e., the Burroughs tradition). Coblentz, by contrast, utilized the standard devices of science fiction—space travel, time displacement, discovery of lost races—in order to establish a satiric mirror in which to reflect the foibles of contemporary society and/or timeless modes of human conduct. In this sense, Coblentz worked in the tradition of Lucian, Cyrano, Swift, and, to a substantial extent, H.G. Wells. Almost alone among Coblentz's contemporaries, David H. Keller exhibited similar attitudes and utilized similar techniques. Coblentz thus provided a

model for such later humorists and satirists as William Tenn, Robert Sheckley, Frederik Pohl, and C.M. Kornbluth. Pohl, at least, of this group, has expressed his admiration for and debt to Coblentz.

Coblentz's first published science fiction was the novel *The Sunken World.* A modern submarine discovers survivors of the classical Atlantis living an idyllic existence in a glass dome on the ocean bottom, but they are destroyed through the inadvertent influence of the submariners.

In *Hidden World* a contemporary traveller finds his way into an unknown civilization hidden in giant caverns beneath the earth. This theme is one Jules Verne had used as a device for travelogue-like exploration of imaginary geography, and Edgar Rice Burroughs had used it, in his Pellucidar series, as a background for adventure tales with primitive human and non-human creatures. Coblentz's book harkened back to Ludvig Holberg's *Nils Klim* in using the inhabited hollow earth as a site for satirical events. In *Hidden World,* the traveller becomes caught up in a society at war for no comprehensible issue, except for the possible purpose of reducing unemployment and stimulating economic activity. *Into Plutonian Depths,* dealing with society on the planet Pluto, posits a situation in which men and women past child-bearing age aspire to become surgically neutered, these neuters being the pampered and powerful rulers of Plutonian society. The cover of the Avon edition described the novel as dealing with "the third sex" (a widely utilized euphemism for homosexuality at the time), to which Donald Wollheim, Avon's editor, later ascribed the success of the edition.

Many other works by Coblentz contain satirical matter, most often reflecting Coblentz's revulsion against war, consistently portrayed as senseless and ignoble, and his distress with the oppression and materialistic greed manifested in human institutions. *After 12,000 Years* portrays a future world in which armies of insects have been bred to giant and ferocious stature and enslaved for service in warfare. This anticipates *The Dragon Masters* (1962) by Jack Vance, a distant cousin of Coblentz's. It should be noted that Coblentz has had a long and varied literary career, of which his science fiction represents only one aspect. Two novels approaching science fiction are *The Wonder Stick,* a pleasantly done story of primitive life, and *When the Birds Fly South,* a beautifully realized novel of an unknown race in the Himalayas, this book being somewhat comparable to James Hilton's *Lost Horizon.*

—Richard A. Lupoff

———————

COGSWELL, Theodore R. American. Born in Coatesville, Pennsylvania, 10 March 1918. Educated at the University of Colorado, Boulder, B.A. 1947; University of Denver, M.A. 1948, graduate study, 1956-57; University of Minnesota, Minneapolis, 1949-53; Latin Institute, Brooklyn College, 1973. Served as a statistical control officer, United States Army Air Force, 1942-46: Captain; Order of the Cloud and Dragon, Republic of China. Married 1) Marjorie Mills in 1948, two daughters; 2) Coralie Norris in 1964. Boulder correspondent, United Press, 1941-42; Instructor, University of Minnesota, 1949-53, and University of Kentucky, Lexington, 1953-56, 1957-58; Assistant Professor, Ball State University, Muncie, Indiana, 1958-65. Since 1965, Professor, Keystone Junior College, La Plume, Pennsylvania. Since 1959, Executive Director, and Editor of Proceedings, Institute for 21st Century Studies. Editor, *SFWA Forum,* 1970-71, 1973-76; book reviewer, Minneapolis *Tribune,* 1970-72; Editor, I.C.S., Scranton, Pennsylvania, 1975-78; Editorial Consultant, Sandvik Inc., Fair Lawn, New Jersey, 1978. Secretary, Science Fiction Writers of America, 1973-74. Agent: Kirby McCauley, 60 East 42nd Street, New York, New York 10017. Address: 108 Robinson Street, Chinchilla, Pennsylvania 18410, U.S.A.

SCIENCE-FICTION PUBLICATIONS

Novel

Spock Messiah (novelization of TV play), with Charles A. Spano.
New York, Bantam, 1976; London, Corgi, 1977.

Short Stories

The Wall Around the World. New York, Pyramid, 1962.
The Third Eye. New York, Belmont, 1968.

Uncollected Short Stories

"Early Bird," with Ted Thomas, and "Probability Zero! The Popu-
lation Implosion," in *Astounding,* edited by Harry Harrison.
New York, Random House, 1973.
"Paradise Regained," with Ted Thomas, in *Saving Worlds,* edited
by Roger Elwood. New York, Doubleday, 1973.
"Faex Delenda Est," in *Best SF 1972,* edited by Harry Harrison and
Brian Aldiss. New York, Putnam, and London, Sphere, 1973.
"Lentil Soup," in *Cooking Out of This World,* edited by Anne
McCaffrey. New York, Ballantine, 1973.
"Players at Null-G," with Ted Thomas and Algis Budrys, in *Fantasy
and Science Fiction* (New York), July 1975.
"Grandfather Clause," in *Fantasy and Science Fiction* (New York),
September 1975.

OTHER PUBLICATIONS

Plays

Some Call It Heads (produced Denver, 1948).
Operation Tel Aviv (produced Foothills, California, 1949).
Contact Point, with G.R. Cogswell, in *Six Science Fiction Plays,*
edited by Roger Elwood. New York, Washington Square
Press, 1976.

Television Play: *Red Dust* (*Tales of Tomorrow* series), 1952.

Verse

The Roper (song), music by John Jacob Niles. New York,
Schirmer, 1955.

*   *   *

Theodore R. Cogswell's work ranges in mood from horror to
irony and spoof, in form from novellas to short stories, poetry, and
drama, and in quality from expert and meaningful story-telling to
juvenile fantasy.

While portions of his stories (like "Test Area") are chilling,
Cogswell's best horror story is probably "The Burning," which is
about a demonic god (a terrible matriarch) who demands love and
obedience from her "children"—and also eats them alive. Often
horror is mixed with irony in Cogswell's work, as in "Emergency
Rations" where cannibals are trapped in a Trojan horse scheme and
literally cooked alive since they "can't feel nothing"; "Thimgs"
where the unscrupulous main character demands vitality in his
bargain with a "Guardian" for longer life—only to find that the lives
"spliced" on to his are those leading to horrible sudden deaths; and
"Wolfie" where Peter Vincent bargains with a warlock to be turned
into a werewolf in order to kill his cousin and collect on his will, but
is transformed into a mangy toothless mutt that must be put out of
its "misery." In these three stories the would-be victimizers become
victims, for as the Guardian says in "Thimgs," "the ethical universe
is just as orderly as the physical one." Occasionally, Cogswell's
mood borders on spoof, as in "Probability Zero! The Population
Implosion" which manipulates statistics in order to "prove" that
England's population has declined since the year 1000 from 275
billion to 44 million at the present time. So, the story advises
ticklishly, if you hear doomsayers of the population bomb, you need
remember only that "statistics show . . . you have nothing to worry
about." "Probability Zero!" illustrates what a Pirandello character
says of a statistic: it's "like a sack; it won't stand up till you've put

something in it." Unfortunately, what we put into it is interpretation, which is usually debatable and rarely definitive.

Cogswell is quite adept in the various literary genres. His first
novella, "The Spectre General," is an accomplished story in the
Heinlein tradition, involving delightful situational and understated
humor and an alternating chapter/scene plot structure, which deals
with the revival of a dying empire by technologists. *The Wall
Around the World* is a fine reworking of the Icarus myth, blending
and contrasting magic and technology in its main character, Porgie.
Cogswell's shorter works are also expert, as I have implied above
and as the story "Early Bird" reveals. The most imaginative of all his
fictions, this piece depicts a fascinating symbiotic relationship
between the main character, Kurt Dixon, and his ship's mother
computer and between "her" and two incredibly adaptive, semi-
organic monsters on a planet Kurt was forced to retreat to during
his battle with the gigantic, people-eating Kieriens. Cogswell's poetry, although different in theme and mood from his other work, is
quite good, as his Swiftian lambast against contemporary poets
("sparrow farts" and "word kickers") in "Faex Delenda Est" suggests. Finally, his drama is also impressive. For example, *Contact
Point,* written with his wife, has an excellent sense of timing and
action, dealing with the first space crew to reach a star and their
anxieties and conflicts in bringing back a deadly radioactive organism. At first convinced that earth's doctors can save him, and
willing to endanger the rest of humanity, the main character undergoes a dramatic change whereby he challenges earthlings to reunite
and stop fighting among themselves in order to annihilate him and
his ship before it lands.

Although Cogswell sometimes stoops to puerile fantasy as in
"The Masters" (a vampire story), he is a versatile writer who usually
makes a point. Even in "The Masters" we see that just as the ethical
universe is orderly so is the physical one, so that we never know if we
will need some endangered species (the snaildarter?) to help us in
our afflictions.

—Dennis M. Welch

COMPTON, D(avid) G(uy). Also writes as Guy Compton; Frances Lynch. British. Born in London, 19 August 1930. Educated
at Cheltenham College, 1940-48. Served in the British Army, 1948-
50. Married 1) Elizabeth Tillotson in 1952 (divorced, 1969), two
daughters and one son; 2) Carol Savage in 1971, one step-daughter
and one step-son. Worked as stage electrician, furniture maker,
salesman, docker, and postman; Editor, Reader's Digest Condensed
Books, London 1969-81. Lives in the United States. Recipient: Arts
Council bursary, 1964. Agent: Virginia Kidd, Box 278, Milford,
Pennyslvania 18337, U.S.A.

SCIENCE-FICTION PUBLICATIONS

Novels

The Quality of Mercy. London, Hodder and Stoughton, and New
York, Ace, 1965; revised edition, Ace, 1970.
Farewell, Earth's Bliss. London, Hodder and Stoughton, 1966;
New York, Ace, 1967.
The Silent Multitude. New York, Ace, 1966; London, Hodder
and Stoughton, 1967.
Synthajoy. London, Hodder and Stoughton, and New York, Ace,
1968.
The Electric Crocodile. London, Hodder and Stoughton, 1970; as
The Steel Crocodile, New York, Ace, 1970.
Chronocules. New York, Ace, 1970; as *Hot Wireless Sets, Aspirin
Tablets, The Sandpaper Sides of Used Matchboxes, and Some-
thing That Might Have Been Castor Oil,* London, Joseph, 1971.
The Missionaries. New York, Ace, 1972; London, Hale, 1975.

The Unsleeping Eye. New York, DAW, 1973; as *The Continuous Katherine Mortenhoe,* London, Gollancz, 1974.
A Usual Lunacy. San Bernardino, California, Borgo Press, 1978.
Windows. New York, Berkley, 1979.
Ascendancies. London, Gollancz, and New York, Berkley, 1980.

Uncollected Short Stories

"It's Smart to Have an English Address," in *World's Best Science Fiction 1968,* edited by Donald A. Wollheim and Terry Carr. New York, Ace, 1968; London, Gollancz, 1969.
"Bender, Fenugreek, Slatterman, and Mupp," in *Interfaces,* edited by Ursula K. Le Guin and Virginia Kidd. New York, Ace, 1980.

OTHER PUBLICATIONS

Novels as Guy Compton

Too Many Murderers. London, Long, 1962.
Medium for Murder. London, Long, 1963.
Dead on Cue. London, Long, 1964.
Disguise for a Dead Gentleman. London, Long, 1964.
High Tide for Hanging. London, Long, 1965.
And Murder Came Too. London, Long, 1966.
The Palace (as D.G. Compton). London, Hodder and Stoughton, and New York, Norton, 1969.

Novels as Frances Lynch

Twice Ten Thousand Miles. London, Souvenir Press, and New York, St. Martin's Press, 1974; as *Candle at Midnight,* New York, Dell, 1977.
The Fine and Handsome Captain. London, Souvenir Press, and New York, St. Martin's Press, 1975.
Stranger at the Wedding. New York, St. Martin's Press, and London, Souvenir Press, 1977.
A Dangerous Magic. London, Souvenir Press, and New York, St. Martin's Press, 1978.
In the House of Dark Music. London, Hodder and Stoughton, 1979.

Plays

Radio Plays: *Chez Nous,* 1961; *Bandstand,* 1962; *Blind Man's Bluff,* 1962; *Fully Furnished,* 1963; *Always Read the Small Print,* 1963; *If the Shoe Fits,* 1964; *Mandible Light,* 1964; *A Turning off the Minch Park Road,* 1965; *Time Exposure,* 1965; *The Real People,* 1966; *Island,* 1968; *Surgery,* 1968; *The Respighi Inheritance,* 1973.

Other

"The Profession of Science Fiction 16: By Chance Out of Conviction," in *Foundation 17* (London), September 1979.

D.G. Compton comments:

Possibly the best introduction to any writer's work is to know why he does it. The reason I write what people have been kind enough to call SF ("kind enough" because the label makes possible a large and informed readership for stuff that otherwise would probably sink without trace) is that I'm basically a rather embarrassed sort of person, afraid of admitting to commitment, who welcomes SF's distancing mechanisms. After all, it's far safer to dare to care about one's characters when the situation in which one places them isn't quite "real."

Also, I've led what is sometimes known as a "sheltered life." For which read "limited." Thus I know very little about the commonalities of human existence: commerce, golf, brick-laying, what you will. This same sheltered life, however, has involved me in close and prolonged—and often painful—contact with just a few very positive individuals (mostly women, let's face it), and from these individuals I've learned a lot. So I try to write about that of which I know at least something, people, while setting them discreetly in worlds of my own devising (about which I may also be expected to know something). Future worlds, for convenience's sake, but always closely tied to my own muddled understanding of the present world around

me. In general terms I don't much like this present world, and developing it a few years on is a good way of finding out why. And perhaps even of seeing how to change it.

*   *   *

D.G. Compton's science-fiction novels usually lead to extremes of reaction from their readers. Some are strongly attracted to his mature themes, richly fluent prose, strong concentration on character, and realistic appreciation of the seamier side of human existence. Others are dismayed by the density of his prose, the ineffectualness of many of his characters, the underlying distrust of technology as a cure for all of humanity's ills, the absence of much physical action, and the frequently bizarre nature of his situations. But it appears that Compton is beginning to win over an ever larger share of readers as he continues to skewer human foibles and failings.

Two of his more popular novels deal with our delight in vicarious experience of another's life. *Synthajoy* created a minor controversy because of the dissolute nature of its characters. The story concerns the development of a means to record the life experiences of an individual, to be played back at another time for an interested audience. Although there are obvious beneficial aspects to such an invention, it is almost immediately subverted. Compton returned to this theme in *The Unsleeping Eye.* In a world where disease and pain are virtually unknown, Katherine Mortenhoe has contracted a terminal disease that leaves her only weeks to live. The entertainment world is quick to realize that this provides a possibly unique opportunity to produce a profitable bit of entertainment, and they employ a man with cameras surgically implanted in one eye. The cameraman manipulates Katherine so that she is emotionally dependent upon him, totally unaware that he is filming her agony for an unfeeling audience. But as time passes, his feelings for her become genuine, and there is a dawning realization that he too is being manipulated.

Compton's most accomplished work is *The Electric Crocodile,* set in an ultra-secret research institute. The protagonist rapidly realizes that more is transpiring within the research group than is apparent. Eventually it is revealed to him that the authorities fear that blind technological progress is too dangerous, and they have created a computer bank to monitor and even interfere with scientific developments. They are blithely unaware that they have surrendered their destiny to the very technology they hoped to control. This complexity of philosophy and plot is rarely found in any genre, and Compton's ability to control his work has rarely been equalled.

The Silent Multitude is perhaps his most controversial work. A spore from space attacks concrete, and most artifacts of man's civilization are crumbling. Against the background of a deserted city, Compton presents a small cast of characters, reflecting their personal decay against the collapse of the city itself. Even without the brilliant characterization, this would remain a memorable novel, for Compton's description of the dissolution is haunting.

The isolated research organization appears again in *Chronocules,* also presented as an island of hope in a crumbling society. It is clear that the collapse of the present society is accelerating and will come within the lifetimes of the protagonists, so they desperately seek a means to escape into the future. Although an excellent novel in itself, it suffers when compared to *The Electric Crocodile* and *The Silent Multitude,* to both of which it is thematically similar. *The Missionaries* should have been a very controversial novel, but attracted little attention. A small group of aliens arrives on Earth, preaching the religion of Ustiliath. Compton makes it quite clear that, for all practical purposes, the aliens are absolutely correct in their beliefs, and that conversion to their religion is the only logical course. But humanity reacts with fear and loathing, and the aliens reach the same fate that greeted many Christian missionaries in their efforts to bring "enlightenment" to the "savages."

Two of Compton's early novels are highly competent, but neither is of the quality of his later work. *The Quality of Mercy* is a low-key examination of the tensions brought to bear on a group of military personnel when it becomes clear that something, perhaps a nuclear war, is imminent. In many ways, this is a forerunner of *The Electric Crocodile. Farewell, Earth's Bliss* makes use of one of science fiction's most well-traveled plots, the penal colony on Mars, to present a cast of misfit humans against a kaleidoscopic background where reality and fantasy aren't always distinguishable.

Compton has written few short stories, possibly because he is not able to develop his characters at that length. Certainly for those who enjoy his style and presentation, Compton's characters are a significant element in the appreciation of his work. Compton seems to have eschewed the traditional concerns of science fiction, using the plots he borrows only as the frame upon which to hang his real interests, the morality of science, the peculiarities of humanity, and our ability to control our own destinies.

—Don D'Ammassa

CONDON, Richard (Thomas). American. Born in New York City, 18 March 1915. Educated in public schools in New York. Served in the United States Merchant Navy. Married Evelyn Hunt in 1938; two children. Worked briefly in advertising; publicist in the American film industry for 21 years: worked for Walt Disney Productions, Hal Horne Organization, Twentieth-Century Fox, Richard Condon Inc., and other firms; theatrical producer, New York, 1951-52. Agent: Harold Matson Company Inc., 22 East 40th Street, New York, New York 10016, U.S.A.; or, A.D. Peters Ltd., 10 Buckingham Street, London WC2N 6BU, England. Address: Rossenarra House, Kilnoganny, County Kilkenny, Ireland.

SCIENCE-FICTION PUBLICATIONS

Novel

The Manchurian Candidate. New York, McGraw Hill, 1959; London, Joseph, 1960.

OTHER PUBLICATIONS

Novels

The Oldest Confession. New York, Appleton Century Crofts, 1958; London, Longman, 1959; as *The Happy Thieves,* New York, Bantam, 1962.
Some Angry Angel: A Mid-Century Faerie Tale. New York, McGraw Hill, 1960; London, Joseph, 1961.
A Talent for Loving; or, The Great Cowboy Race. New York, McGraw Hill, 1961; London, Joseph, 1963.
An Infinity of Mirrors. New York, Random House, and London, Heinemann, 1964.
Any God Will Do. New York, Random House, and London, Heinemann, 1966.
The Ecstasy Business. New York, Dial Press, and London, Heinemann, 1967.
Mile High. New York, Dial Press, and London, Heinemann, 1969.
The Vertical Smile. New York, Dial Press, 1971; London, Weidenfeld and Nicolson, 1972.
Arigato. New York, Dial Press, and London, Weidenfeld and Nicolson, 1972.
The Star-Spangled Crunch. New York, Bantam, 1974.
Winter Kills. New York, Dial Press, and London, Weidenfeld and Nicolson, 1974.
Money Is Love. New York, Dial Press, and London, Weidenfeld and Nicolson, 1975.
The Whisper of the Axe. New York, Dial Press, and London, Weidenfeld and Nicolson, 1976.
The Abandoned Woman: A Tragedy of Manners. New York, Dial Press, and London, Hutchinson, 1977.
Bandicoot. New York, Dial Press, and London, Hutchinson, 1978.

Death of a Politician. New York, Marek, 1978; London, Hutchinson, 1979.
The Entwining. New York, Marek, 1980.

Plays

Men of Distinction (produced New York, 1953).

Screenplays: *A Talent for Loving,* 1965; *The Summer Music,* 1969; *The Long Loud Silence,* 1969.

Other

And Then We Moved to Rossenarra; or, The Art of Emigrating. New York, Dial Press, 1973.
The Mexican Stove: What to Put on It and in It, with Wendy Bennett. New York, Doubleday, 1973.

Editor, with Burton O. Kurth, *Writing from Experience.* New York, Harper, 1960.

*

Manuscript Collection: Mugar Memorial Library, Boston University.

*   *   *

The Manchurian Candidate, Richard Condon's famous bestseller, is a capable mixture of science fiction and thriller, a satisfying, if strange, brew of Pavlov, Sophocles, and Raymond Chandler. This novel is, at once, a satire on cold-war politics, a who-done-it, and a crypto-psychoanalytic oedipal tale of a mother and son. Above all, however, it is an original and oddly compelling work of science fiction.

It belongs to that category of post-war SF that is more concerned with the world in which we live than that of the past or future, more concerned with the use of known technology (in this case, brainwashing and post-hypnotic suggestion) than the hypothetical science of the future. Condon, however, very cleverly disguises the border between the plausible and the implausible so that many readers may be unaware precisely when they have passed into the realm of fantasy.

As in other science-fiction works of this kind (*Fail-Safe,* for example), our own all-too-recognizable society is shown to be decaying and dangerous, driven to the brink by the very brilliance of its own advances and their inevitable misuse. We see man, both individually and collectively, tested and found wanting in his clashes with the new technology. Not only is Raymond Shaw compelled to act against his own natural impulses, but an entire people, in this case McCarthy-America, is whipped into a media-induced orgy of commie hunting, temporarily blinded to the irresponsibility, dishonesty, and, in some cases, illegality of their actions. It is, however, the story of Man as an individual entity slowly dehumanized by technology that is the focal point of this novel. For a variety of reasons, Raymond Shaw is an emotional bankrupt, a mannekin unable to feel in any normal way, an automaton who bases his actions and responses on the behavioral patterns of those around him. He is depicted as the wasteland figure so often spawned by modern society and so familiar in 20th-century literature. But Condon is not merely retelling the old story of a man's essential humanity dissociated by technology. It is because Shaw was *already* an extreme case of the wasteland man that he is chosen as the best psychological guinea pig for metamorphosing into the perfect assassin. But even so, Condon tells us, the humanity of the man eventually will overcome even the most intensive bombardment of scientific mischief. All the monstrous psychoanalytic resources of the medical community are brought to bear on the already fractured psyche of the most receptive specimen available, and still the plans ultimately fail.

If Condon is expressing optimism, it is more subtle than it seems: Shaw escapes the hold on him only through suicide. And the rather bleak picture of our world is one dominated by technology, dependent on science, and sophisticated beyond common understanding. Yet all this will never be able to overwhelm completely the most precious qualities of the simple human creature: an understanding of good and evil, a capacity for independent thought, a compulsion to be free, and a sense of honor which, one hopes, eventually will prevail.

—James A. Livezey

CONEY, Michael G(reatrex). British. Born in Birmingham, Warwickshire, 28 September 1932. Educated at King Edward's School, Birmingham, 1944-49. Served in the Royal Air Force, 1956-58. Married to Daphne Coney; two sons and one daughter. Auditor, Russell and Company, Birmingham, 1949-56; Senior Clerk, Pearce Clayton Maunder, Dorchester, Dorset, 1958-61; Accountant, Pontins, Bournemouth, 1962; Tenant, Plymouth Breweries, Totnes, Devon, 1963-66; Accountant, Peplow Warren Fuller, Newton Abbot, Devon, 1966-69; Manager, Jabberwock Hotel, Antigua, West Indies, 1969-72. Since 1973, Management Specialist, British Columbia Forest Service, Victoria. Recipient: British Science Fiction Award, 1976. Address: 2082 Neptune Road, R.R. 3, Sidney, British Columbia, Canada.

SCIENCE-FICTION PUBLICATIONS

Novels

Mirror Image. New York, DAW, 1972; London, Gollancz, 1973.
Syzygy. New York, Ballantine, and Morley, Yorkshire, Elmfield Press, 1973.
Friends Come in Boxes. New York, DAW, 1973; London, Gollancz, 1974.
The Hero of Downways. New York, DAW, 1973; London, Futura, 1974.
Winter's Children. London, Gollancz, 1974.
The Jaws That Bite, The Claws That Catch. New York, DAW, 1975; as *The Girl with a Symphony in Her Fingers,* Morley, Yorkshire, Elmfield Press, 1975.
Hello Summer, Goodbye. London, Gollancz, 1975; as *Rax,* New York, DAW, 1975.
Charisma. London, Gollancz, 1975; New York, Dell, 1979.
Brontomek! London, Gollancz, 1976.
The Ultimate Jungle. London, Millington, 1979.
The Human Menagerie. London, Millington, 1980.

Short Stories

Monitor Found in Orbit. New York, DAW, 1974.

Uncollected Short Stories

"Bartholomew & Son (and the Fish Girl)," in *New Writings in SF 27,* edited by Kenneth Bulmer. London, Sidgwick and Jackson, 1975.
"Starthinker 9," in *Andromeda 1,* edited by Peter Weston. London, Futura, 1976; New York, St. Martin's Press, 1979.
"Trading Post," in *SF Digest 1* (London), 1976.
"The Cinderella Machine," in *Fantasy and Science Fiction* (New York), August 1976.
"Those Good Old Days of Liquid Fuel," in *The 1977 Annual World's Best SF,* edited by Donald A. Wollheim. New York, DAW, 1977.
"Just an Old-Fashioned War Story," in *Ascents of Wonder,* edited by David Gerrold. New York, Popular Library, 1977.
"Catapult to the Stars," in *Fantasy and Science Fiction* (New York), April 1977.
"Sparklebugs, Holly, and Love," in *Fantasy and Science Fiction* (New York), December 1977.
"In Search of Professor Greatrex," in *Pulsar 1,* edited by George

Hay. London, Penguin 1978.
"Penny on a Skyhorse," in *Galileo 11-12* (Boston), 1979.
"The Summer Sweet, The Winter Wild," in *Interfaces,* edited by Ursula K. Le Guin and Virginia Kidd. New York Ace, 1980.

Michael G. Coney comments:
My purpose is to entertain myself as well as my readers. Each of my novels has been an experiment in style and content with one consistent trait: they are all mystery stories. Love is there too, and human psychology, and biology, and a little "hard" science, but my main intent is to keep the reader guessing. I think my earlier novels were too conservative; they were all hung on hooks of known science and "real" reality—which is odd, since as an SF reader my preference is for the persuasively fantastic: the "sense of wonder" story. My short stories are normally written as vehicles for ideas, situations, and characters which I intend to use in my novels—I find it much easier to work this way than to plunge into a novel cold. Other short stories have been written for specific purposes, generally to use up one-off ideas before I forget them.

*   *   *

Michael G. Coney has produced a substantial body of work remarkably quickly. From the beginning he was taking well-worn themes and quietly stamping his own mark on them, Philip K. Dick perhaps the model in *Mirror Image,* the post-holocaust novel in *Winter's Children,* the Heinleinian micro-universe story in *The Hero of Downways,* Asimov's "Nightfall" in *Syzygy.* An impression of modest achievement may have been fostered by Coney's interest in small or local communities, but this was a false impression: cumulatively, the work appears large and individual. The best way of reading Coney is probably to absorb him quickly, culminating in the prize-winning *Brontomek!* which takes up many ideas from the earlier stories: the amorphs from *Mirror Image,* the heroine's name and personality from Susanna in *Charisma,* the brontomeks from a monstrous agricultural machine in a grim tale, "Esmeralda," which also has the idea of post-hypnotic suggestion. The works are sufficiently light and varied for them to be easily digested and the food is certainly not bland: in the short stories, particularly, there are piquant horrors; and the rich syrup of romantic love, often an ingredient which may offend some palates, is usually mixed with bitters at the close of each course. Coney likes to study the reactions of a small group to a large threat, whether natural but alien, as in *Hello Summer, Goodbye* and *Syzygy,* or social but inhuman, as in *Syzygy*'s sequel, *Brontomek!* Solutions are not likely to be achieved by technological means but, after valiant efforts, may be granted by special grace; to some problems escape or outgrowth is the only solution.

Coney is not a pessimistic writer but he is suspicious, yet suspicious of suspicion. One of his leading themes is credulity, but it is treated ambivalently. The framing chapters of *Syzygy* point up that novel's concern about group vulnerability to suggestion; yet it seems in *Brontomek!* that it may sometimes be better to be happily deceived, as individuals are by the amorphic "Tes" (thous, ideal companions). Coney hates manipulators: his sympathetic characters are often their victims; yet it is not easy for his characters to find someone to blame. In *Brontomek!* the immoral Organization stamps on a whole planet, yet its own agents are clearly victims too, and there is something sublimely admirable in the irresponsible force of its symbol, the rogue brontomek, which malignly rampages only for a time, then pathetically loses its motive power, to be found dying at the end of the book, "betrayed by its own mechanical weaknesses." Human manipulators and strong egotists are similarly seen with horrified admiration (Carioca Jones or Hector Bartholomew in the Peninsula stories, Strang in *Brontomek!*), and their devoted lovers (Joanne, who gladly gives her hand to Carioca, or Mrs. Strang) are seen with baffled disgust. However, if the author identifies, for narrative purposes, with such lovers, they are presented with strong sympathy (in both *Charisma* and *The Jaws That Bite, The Claws That Catch* Coney seems over-tolerant of some repellent features of his heroes, concomitant on their devotion). Alien manipulators are also presented sympathetically (their control is accidental in *Syzygy;* accidents are rectified by benevolent fostering in "The Tertiary Justification" and "Symbiote"; they show wise control of beasts in "Oh, Valinda!"). So disposed, Coney gives us one of the genre's sweetest heroines in the alien Pallahaxi Brown-eyes (*Hello Summer, Goodbye*), and seems to envy the self-containedness of his multi-individual aliens (Kli a' Po in *Brontomek!* and the amusing Vegan in "Trading Post"); his humans find it hard to relate to other individuals.

There is strong dystopian satire in *Friends Come in Boxes* (which offers a radical solution to people over 40) and *The Jaws That Bite, The Claws That Catch* (prisoners reduce their sentences by voluntary bondage). In the case of the latter novel, it is noticeable that the narrator, Joe Sagar, takes a softer line towards prisoners than he does in the short Peninsula stories; it's unfortunate that the best of these stories, "Bartholomew & Son ..." and "The Cinderella Machine," are omitted from the novel version. As a dystopian writer Coney's animus is principally against the notion that utility or justice should outweigh compassion. Coney's plots often draw upon those of other popular fiction: like Bester's *The Demolished Man, Charisma* has an SF variant of the locked-room mystery, for instance, and "Monitor Found in Orbit" wickedly plays on the spy thriller, while fully justifying its employment of stream-of-consciousness narrative. Coney appreciates that the SF form can be used to cast old problems in high relief; in my favourite of his novels, *The Hero of Downways,* he studies heroism as it were in a clinical laboratory situation—and takes a fresh look at such SF standards as clones, the multi-individual self, mutations, and miniaturized people. Others may enjoy Coney more for his presentation of lively new sea and air vehicles, or unusual tidal conditions on strange planets; I see no reason why he should not become a highly popular writer in the genre.

—Michael J. Tolley

CONQUEST, (George) Robert (Acworth). Also writes as J.E.M. Arden. British. Born in Great Malvern, Worcestershire, 15 July 1917. Educated at Winchester College; Magdalen College, Oxford, B.A. 1939; University of Grenoble. Served in the Oxfordshire and Buckinghamshire Light Infantry, 1939-46. Married 1) Joan Watkins in 1942 (divorced, 1948), two sons; 2) Tatiana Mihailova in 1948 (divorced, 1962); 3) Caroleen Macfarlane in 1964 (divorced, 1978); 4) Elizabeth Neece in 1979. Member of the U.K. Diplomatic Service, 1946-56; Fellow, London School of Economics, 1956-58; Lecturer in English, University of Buffalo, 1959-60; Literary Editor, *The Spectator,* London, 1962-63; Senior Fellow, Columbia University, New York, 1964-65; Fellow, Woodrow Wilson Center, Washington, D.C., 1976-77; Senior Research Fellow, Hoover Institution, Stanford, California, 1977-79; Visiting Scholar, Heritage Foundation, Washington, D.C., 1980. Editor, *Soviet Analyst,* London, 1971-73. Recipient: P.E.N. prize, 1945; Festival of Britain prize, 1951. M.A. 1972, and D.Litt. 1974: Oxford University. Fellow, Royal Society of Literature, 1972. O.B.E. (Officer, Order of the British Empire), 1955. Address: 28 Shawfield Street, London S.W. 3, England.

SCIENCE-FICTION PUBLICATIONS

Novel

A World of Difference. London, Ward Lock, 1955; New York, Ballantine, 1964.

Uncollected Short Stories

"The Veteran," in *Analog* (New York), October 1965.
"A Long Way to Go," in *Analog* (New York), November 1965.
"No Planet Like Home," in *Galaxy* (New York), April 1970.

OTHER PUBLICATIONS

Novel

The Egyptologists, with Kingsley Amis. London, Cape, 1965; New York, Random House, 1966.

Verse

Poems. London, Macmillan, and New York, St. Martin's Press, 1955.
Between Mars and Venus. London, Hutchinson, and New York, St. Martin's Press, 1962.
Arias from a Love Opera. London, Macmillan, and New York, Macmillan, 1969.
Casualty Ward. London, Poem-of-the-Month Club, 1974.
Coming Across. Menlo Park, California, Buckabest, 1978.
Forays. London, Chatto and Windus, 1979.

Other

"Science Fiction," in *New Statesman* (London), 20 March 1954.
Where Do Marxists Go from Here? (as J.E.M. Arden). London, Phoenix House, 1958.
The Soviet Deportation of Nationalities. London, Macmillan, and New York, St. Martin's Press, 1960.
Common Sense about Russia. London, Gollancz, and New York, Macmillan, 1960.
Courage of Genius: The Pasternak Affair. London, Collins-Harvill Press, and Philadelphia, Lippincott, 1961.
Power and Policy in the U.S.S.R. London, Macmillan, and New York, St. Martin's Press, 1962.
The Last Empire. London, Ampersand, 1962.
"Science Fiction and Literature," in *Critical Quarterly* (Manchester), Winter 1963.
Marxism Today. London, Ampersand, 1964.
Russia after Khrushchev. London, Pall Mall Press, and New York, Praeger, 1965.
The Great Terror: Stalin's Purge of the Thirties. London, Macmillan, and New York, Macmillan, 1968; revised edition, 1973.
"Beyond the Moon," in *Encounter* (London), June 1969.
Foreword to "Specialist" by Robert Sheckley, in *The Mirror of Infinity,* edited by Robert Silverberg. New York, Harper, 1970.
The Nation Killers: The Soviet Deportation of Minorities. London, Macmillan, and New York, St. Martin's Press, 1970.
Where Marx Went Wrong. London, Stacey, 1970.
Lenin. London, Fontana, and New York, Viking Press, 1972.
Kolyma: The Arctic Death Camps. London, Macmillan, and New York, Viking Press, 1978.
Present Danger: Towards a Foreign Policy. Oxford, Blackwell, and Stanford, California, Hoover Institution, 1979.
The Abomination of Moab. London, Temple Smith, 1979.
We and They. London, Temple Smith, 1980.

Editor, *New Lines 1-2.* London, Macmillan, 2 vols., 1956-63.
Editor, *Back to Life* (anthology). London, Hutchinson, and New York, St. Martin's Press, 1958.
Editor, with Kingsley Amis, *Spectum [1-5]: A Science Fiction Anthology.* London, Gollancz, 5 vols., 1961-65; New York, Harcourt Brace, 5 vols., 1962-67.
Editor, *Soviet Studies Series.* London, Bodley Head, 8 vols., 1967-68; New York, Praeger, 8 vols., 1968-69.
Editor, *Pyotr Yakir.* London, Macmillan, 1972; New York, Coward McCann, 1973.
Editor, *The Robert Sheckley Omnibus.* London, Gollancz, 1973.
Editor, *The Russian Tradition,* by Tibor Szamuely. London, Secker and Warburg, 1974; New York, McGraw Hill, 1975.

Translator, *Russian Nights,* by Alexander Solzhenitsyn. London, Collins-Harvill Press, 1977; New York, Farrar Straus, 1978.

*   *   *

Robert Conquest is best known as a non-fiction writer on Soviet affairs, but he is also highly regarded in the close and intense world of contemporary poetry, both as an editor and writer. His most influential work in this category was *New Lines,* a small anthology of poetry that he edited in 1956 signalling the emergence of techniques and themes that soon became known as "The Movement." However, another project that he invested with attention and energy was *Spectrum: A Science Fiction Anthology* which he edited, with Kingsley Amis, for five years. This played an important role in helping science fiction gain a respectable foothold on the somewhat stodgy English literary turf. The yearly prefaces that Amis and Conquest prepared were apologies for the genre: "There are kinds of ingenuity, kinds of invention, kinds of question [sic], ways of putting such questions, notions of possibility, effects of irony and wit, of wonder and terror that only science fiction offers and can offer." By following these prefaces, a reader can gauge with some accuracy the state of "that American Art," science fiction, in England during the early 1960's.

Conquest's own writings in the field are rather meager. Besides a handful of short stories, he wrote one science-fiction novel in the mid-1950's, *A World of Difference.* This work was written while he was still in the foreign service and reflects concerns from that area of his life. The theme of the novel is the preservation of individual liberties in a future age when the government has at its command the means to control minds. A group of citizens, "The Watch-dogs," have established an underground system of protecting these liberties, but as they move towards a confrontation with the government, the watch-dogs ironically prove more oppressive in protecting the citizens than the government was. The book is cast as a rather heavy moral lesson, but this is relieved by some occasionally light touches, such as having the spaceships named after "Movement" poets: the Gunn, the Larkin, the Enright, and the Holloway.

—Lawrence R. Ries

COOPER, Edmund. Also writes as Richard Avery. British. Born in Marple, Cheshire, 30 April 1926. Educated at Manchester Grammar School, 1937-41; Didsbury Teachers Training College, Lancashire, 1946-47. Served as a radio officer in the British Merchant Navy, 1939-45. Married 1) Joyce Plant in 1946, one daughter and three sons; 2) Valerie Makin in 1963, two sons and two daughters; 3) Dawn Freeman-Baker in 1980. Journalist, British Iron and Steel Research Association, London, 1960-61, and Federation of British Industries, London, 1962; staff writer, Esso Petroleum, London, 1962-66. Since 1967, regular science-fiction reviewer, *Sunday Times,* London. Address: Stammers, Madehurst, Arundel, Sussex, England.

SCIENCE-FICTION PUBLICATIONS

Novels

The Uncertain Midnight. London, Hutchinson, 1958; as *Deadly Image,* New York, Ballantine, 1958.
Seed of Light. London, Hutchinson, and New York, Ballantine, 1959.
Transit. London, Faber, and New York, Lancer, 1964.
All Fools' Day. London, Hodder and Stoughton, and New York, Walker, 1966.
A Far Sunset. London, Hodder and Stoughton, and New York, Walker, 1967.
Five to Twelve. London, Hodder and Stoughton, 1968; New York, Putnam, 1969.
Sea-Horse in the Sky. London, Hodder and Stoughton, 1969; New York, Putnam, 1970.
The Last Continent. New York, Dell, 1969; London, Hodder and Stoughton, 1970.

Son of Kronk. London, Hodder and Stoughton, 1970; as *Kronk,* New York, Putnam, 1971.
The Overman Culture. London, Hodder and Stoughton, 1971; New York, Putnam, 1972.
Double Phoenix, The Firebird. New York, Ballantine, 1971.
Who Needs Men? London, Hodder and Stoughton, 1972; as *Gender Genocide,* New York, Ace, 1972.
The Cloud Walker. London, Hodder and Stoughton, and New York, Ballantine, 1973.
The Tenth Planet. London, Hodder and Stoughton, and New York, Putnam, 1973.
The Slaves of Heaven. New York, Putnam, 1974; London, Hodder and Stoughton, 1975.
Prisoner of Fire. London, Hodder and Stoughton, 1974; New York, Walker, 1976.
Merry Christmas, Ms. Minerva! London, Hale, 1978.
A World of Difference. London, Hale, 1980.

Novels as Richard Avery (series: The Expendables in all books)

The Death Worms of Kratos. London, Coronet, and New York, Fawcett, 1975.
The Rings of Tantalus. London, Coronet, and New York, Fawcett, 1975.
The War Games of Zelos. London, Coronet, and New York, Fawcett, 1975.
The Venom of Argus. London, Coronet, and New York, Fawcett, 1976.

Short Stories

Tomorrow's Gift. New York, Ballantine, 1958; London, Digit, 1959.
Voices in the Dark. London, Digit, 1960.
Tomorrow Came. London, Panther, 1963.
News from Elsewhere. London, Mayflower, 1968; New York, Berkley, 1969.
The Square Root of Tomorrow. London, Hale, 1970.
Unborn Tomorrow. London, Hale, 1971.
Jupiter Laughs and Other Stories. London, Hodder and Stoughton, 1979.

OTHER PUBLICATIONS

Other

Wish Goes to Slumber Land (juvenile). London, Hutchinson, 1960.

Edmund Cooper comments:

I believe, along with people like Kurt Vonnegut and J.G. Ballard and earlier illustrious writers such as George Orwell, Aldous Huxley, and H.G. Wells, that science fiction is the perfect medium for making a social or political statement. I am not interested greatly in gadgetry. I am interested passionately in the future of mankind. People matter to me far more than machines or innovations, which is why I concentrate on characterization in my novels. I try to entertain and believe I am successful in doing this; but basically I want to put up ideas for consideration by my readers. Voluminous correspondence assures me that I have succeeded in this end.

*   *   *

From the publication of his earliest novels and stories of the late 1950's, Edmund Cooper quickly established himself as an urbane stylist whose sometimes almost visionary grasp of science fiction's key themes and images could distinguish his best fiction and almost redeem his lesser works. There is always a moment in a Cooper story when the "sense of wonder," so often cited as the basic emotional stance of science fiction, becomes concretized in a dramatic image or action, whether it be an encounter with a god who turns out to be a spaceship (*A Far Sunset*) or simply an epiphanal moment of self-discovery on a distant planet ("M81—Ursa Major").

Cooper's plots and characterizations do not always match his style and vision. His early stories and novels sometimes read almost as practice exercises in traditional science-fiction themes: the revolt of androids in a "utopian" society (*That Uncertain Midnight*), time-travel paradoxes ("Repeat Performance"), generations-long space voyages (*Seed of Light*), the pitting of humans against a rival culture in a setting alien to both (*Transit*). Each of these themes had been treated in earlier, classic science-fiction stories, but for the most part Cooper succeeded in working his own variations on them. *That Uncertain Midnight,* for example, is unusual in its sympathetic portrayal of the dilemma of the androids, and *Transit* focuses sensitively on the character and emerging relationships of the four humans who find themselves stranded on an unknown planet. Though *Transit* shows that Cooper is capable of developing complex characterizations, he all too often reverts to the near-superman genius-hero of traditional pulp science fiction for his protagonists.

Perhaps the most persistent theme in Cooper, though it seldom emerges as more than background, is that of nuclear war. Nuclear war is the cause of the rise of the androids in *That Uncertain Midnight,* the dystopian state in "Tomorrow's Gift" (one of his finest short stories), the escape from earth in *Seed of Light,* the destruction of the entire human race in *The Overman Culture,* the anti-technological society of *The Cloud Walker,* and the dominion of satellite cities over Earth in *The Slaves of Heaven.* Though it might be misleading to categorize Cooper as a simple technophobe, his cautionary attitude toward technology is also revealed in a number of stories in which "primitive," non-technological societies are shown to be morally superior to decadent technological ones. This is a theme of "The Enlightened Ones," *A Far Sunset,* and *The Slaves of Heaven. A Far Sunset,* in particular, stands as one of the more anthropologically sophisticated treatments of a primitive alien society and its mythology in recent science fiction.

Cooper's later fiction reveals a more sophisticated and complex understanding of the themes of science fiction as the themes become increasingly subordinated to his concerns as a storyteller and stylist. *The Overman Culture,* for example, begins as an enjoyably surrealistic portrait of a London in which Queen Victoria reigns, Churchill is prime minister, and the young protagonist is Michael Faraday. The explanation, when it comes, is ingenious and satisfying, yet does not destroy the sense of playful fantasy established in the opening chapters. Like many science-fiction writers, Cooper often begins with such an entertaining proposition that there is a risk that the final rationalization will disappoint the reader. Increasingly, he has come to master this technique, and as a result has established a clear identity for himself as a literate and frequently witty novelist.

—Gary K. Wolfe

COPPEL, Alfred. Also writes as Sol Galaxan; Robert Cham Gilman; Derfla Leppoc; A.C. Marin. American. Born in Oakland, California, 9 November 1921. Educated at Menlo College, Menlo Park, California; Stanford University, California, 1939-42. Served in the United States Army Air Force, 1942-45: First Lieutenant. Married Elizabeth Ann Schorr in 1943; one son and one daughter. Writer for Philco, Palo Alto, California, 1957-58; Public Relations Executive, Cerwin Group, 1958-61, and Reynolds Advertising, 1961-62, both in San Francisco. Since 1962, free-lance writer. Agent: Robert Lescher, 155 East 71st Street, New York, New York 10021. Address: 614 Westridge Drive, Portola Valley, California 94025, U.S.A.

SCIENCE-FICTION PUBLICATIONS

Novels

Dark December. New York, Fawcett, 1960; London, Jenkins, 1966.
Thirty-Four East. New York, Harcourt Brace, and London,

Macmillan, 1974.
The Dragon. New York, Harcourt Brace, and London, Macmillan, 1977.
The Hastings Conspiracy. New York, Holt Rinehart, and London, Macmillan, 1980.

Novels as Robert Cham Gilman (juvenile; series: Rhada)

The Rebel of Rhada. New York, Harcourt Brace, 1968; London, Gollancz, 1970.
The Navigator of Rhada. New York, Harcourt Brace, 1968; London, Gollancz, 1971.
The Starkahn of Rhada. New York, Harcourt Brace, 1970.

Uncollected Short Stories

"Age of Reason," in *Astounding* (New York), December 1947.
"Jinx Ship to the Rescue," in *Planet* (New York), Winter 1948.
"Runaway," in *Planet* (New York), Spring 1949.
"The Starbusters," in *Planet* (New York), Summer 1949.
"Secret Weapon," in *Astounding* (New York), July 1949.
"Captain Midas," in *Planet* (New York), Fall 1949.
"Flight from Time," in *Planet* (New York), Winter 1949.
"Goldfish Bowl," in *Fantasy Book 6* (Los Angeles), 1950.
"The First Man on the Moon," in *Planet* (New York), Spring 1950.
"My Brother's Keeper," in *Amazing* (New York), June 1950.
"Warrior Maid of Mars," in *Planet* (New York), Summer 1950.
"The Metal Smile," in *Super Science* (Kokomo, Indiana), July 1950.
"Half Life," in *Super Science* (Kokomo, Indiana), September 1950.
"The Last Two Alive," in *Planet* (New York), November 1950.
"Star Tamer," in *Super Science* (Kokomo, Indiana), November 1950.
"The Terror," in *Future* (New York), November 1950.
"Earthbound," in *Fantastic Adventures* (New York), December 1950.
"Task to Luna," in *Planet* (New York), January 1951.
"Forbidden Weapon," in *Marvel* (New York), February 1951.
"The Awful Weapon," in *Future* (New York), May 1951.
"The Brain That Lost Its Head," in *Fantastic Adventures* (New York), June 1951.
"Tydore's Gift," in *Planet* (New York), September 1951.
"Wreck of Triton," in *Planet* (New York), November 1951.
"Double Standard," in *Galaxy* (New York), February 1952.
"The Subversive," in *Marvel* (New York), May 1952.
"Welcome," in *Science Fiction Quarterly* (Holyoke, Massachusetts), August 1952.
"Mother," in *Fantasy and Science Fiction* (New York), September 1952.
"The Hunters," in *Fantastic Story* (New York), Fall 1952.
"Death Is Never Final," in *Fantastic Adventures* (New York), October 1952.
"...and Goal to Go," in *Amazing* (New York), November 1952.
"Defender of the Faith," in *Science Fiction Quarterly* (Holyoke, Massachusetts), November 1952.
"Legion of the Lost," in *Future* (New York), November 1952.
"The Magellanics," in *Two Complete Science Adventure Books* (New York), Winter 1952.
"Love Affair" (as Derfla Leppoc) and "Homecoming," in *Vortex 1* (New York), 1953.
"The Dreamer," in *The Best Science-Fiction Stories 1953,* edited by E.F. Bleiler and T.E. Dikty. New York, Fell, 1953.
"The Peacemaker," in *Prize Science Fiction,* edited by Donald A. Wollheim. New York, McBride, 1953.
"What Goes Up," in *Science and Sorcery,* edited by Garret Ford. Los Angeles, Fantasy, 1953.
"Divided We Fall," in *Fantastic Story* (New York), January 1953.
"For Humans Only," in *Avon Science Fiction and Fantasy Reader* (New York), January 1953.
"The Invader," in *Imagination* (Evanston, Illinois), February 1953.
"Turnover Point," in *Amazing* (New York), May 1953.
"Preview of Peril," in *Planet* (New York), September 1953.
"The Flight of the Eagle" (as Sol Galaxan), in *Planet* (New York), September 1953.
"The Guilty," in *Cosmos* (New York), November 1953.

"Turning Point," in *If* (New York), November 1953.

"The Exile," in *Stories for Tomorrow,* edited by William Sloane. New York, Funk and Wagnalls, 1954; London, Eyre and Spottiswoode, 1955.

"Meb," in *Fantastic Story* (New York), Spring 1954.

"Mars Is Ours," in *Fantasy and Science Fiction* (New York), October 1954.

"Community Property," in *If* (New York), December 1954.

"Touch the Sky," in *Startling* (New York), Summer 1955.

"The Last Night of Summer," in *The End of the World,* edited by Donald A. Wollheim. New York, Ace, 1956.

"The Hills of Home," in *Future 30* (New York), 1956.

"The Fifth Stone," in *Fantastic* (New York), December 1956.

"Blood Lands," in *Way Out,* edited by Ivan Howard. New York, Belmont, 1963.

"For Sacred San Francisco," in *If* (New York), November 1969.

"The Rebel of Valkyr," in *Galactic Empires 1,* edited by Brian Aldiss. London, Weidenfeld and Nicolson, 1976; New York, St. Martin's Press, 1977.

OTHER PUBLICATIONS

Novels

Hero Driver. New York, Crown, 1954.

Night of Fire and Snow. New York, Simon and Schuster, 1960.

A Certainty of Love. New York, Harcourt Brace, 1966.

The Gate of Hell. New York, Harcourt Brace, 1967.

Order of Battle. New York, Harcourt Brace, 1968; London, Hutchinson, 1969.

Between the Thunder and the Sun. New York, Harcourt Brace, 1971.

The Landlocked Man. New York, Harcourt Brace, 1972; London, Macmillan, 1975.

Novels as A.C. Marin

The Clash of Distant Thunder. New York, Harcourt Brace, 1968.

Rise with the Wind. New York, Harcourt Brace, 1969; London, Heinemann, 1970.

A Storm of Spears. New York, Harcourt Brace, 1971; London, Hale, 1973.

*

Bibliography: in *Fiction! Series One* edited by Dan Tooker and Roger Hofheins, New York, Harcourt Brace, 1976.

Manuscript Collection: Boston University.

Alfred Coppel comments:

I began writing in the SF genre for two reasons: first, it was a field that did not limit the imagination (untrained though it might be) of a young writer, and second, I had read SF since early youth—and I believed then (as I still do) that a writer should write what he enjoys reading.

I have since turned to writing "general" novels, but I am told there is still a bit of the SF writer's mark on my work. I accept this with pride. Those of us who learned our craft in the hard school of the SF magazines learned early on to be professionals. To my mind, there is no higher praise that can be bestowed on a writer.

*   *   *

Although Alfred Coppel has done most of his writing in other fields, his few contributions to science fiction have been almost invariably among the better attempts in the field. His novel *Dark December,* for example, is one of the best post-nuclear war novels ever to appear, far superior to many whose titles are better known.

His more straightforward novels in the genre consist of the Rhada trilogy written under the pseudonym of Robert Cham Gilman. Man's interstellar empire has collapsed into a feudal society that is a mixture of science and magic, spaceships and incantations. Against this background, Coppel wrote three adventures of young men attempting to come to grips with the stresses and internal contradictions of their society. Although writing ostensibly for younger readers, Coppel has not pulled any punches. The novels deal explicitly with the seamier side of human acquisitiveness and the urge for power. The cyclic drive to self-destruction is an almost ever-present backdrop against which the characters play out their lives.

Coppel uses his settings and plots to examine his characters, rather than just employing characters as animated tour guides of exotic landscapes. The protagonist of *Dark December* is a fighter pilot who wanders across an America torn by nuclear bombs, plagues, famine, and human savagery. But it is not his adventures with which the reader is concerned but the effects of those adventures on him as he grows increasingly desperate to discover the fate of his missing family.

In recent years, Coppel's closest approach to science fiction has consisted of a pair of excellent near-future political novels. In *Thirty-Four East,* the world is on the brink of conflagration as the President is apparently assassinated, and the Vice-President is held hostage by Arab terrorists intent upon the destruction of Israel. In Washington, the generals move to fill the power vacuum, while across the ocean a weak Premier of the Soviet Union begins to succumb to pressure from his own generals. The only chance to sidetrack the headlong movement toward war is to rescue the Vice-President. The situation is similar in *The Dragon.* The Red Chinese have developed a new weapon which gives them effective superiority over the Russians. Unless the President can somehow restore the balance of power, a war between the two Communist giants is inevitable, and it is just as certain that the rest of the world will be drawn into the confrontation. In both cases, Coppel has captured the reins of suspense firmly, and linked them to a credible sequence of political and personal events. Each novel is complex and satisfying, and it is interesting to speculate about Coppel's possible achievements had he devoted his efforts primarily to science fiction, rather than remaining as diversified in his interests as he has.

There has been a considerable number of short stories as well, almost all of them above average. Possibly his most successful is the depressingly realistic "The Last Night of Summer." Stellar evolution has caused a change in the energy output of the sun, and an astronomical event is imminent that will briefly make the Earth uninhabitable. Except for a limited number granted a place in shelters constructed underground, the entire human population will be wiped out within a few days. The hero of this story murders his wife and sacrifices his own chance for survival in order to provide a chance for life to his two daughters. It is one of the most effective world disaster stories of all times, accomplishing more in a few pages than have many novels.

—Don D'Ammassa

CORBETT, Chan. *See* **SCHACHNER, Nat.**

CORNISH, F. *See* **BRYNING, Frank**

CORREY, Lee. Pseudonym for G(eorge) Harry Stine. American. Born in Philadelphia, Pennsylvania, 26 March 1928. Educated at University of Colorado, Colorado Springs (Editor, *The Window,* 1948-49), 1946-50; Colorado College, Colorado Springs, B.A. in physics 1952. Married Barbara Ann Kauth in 1952; two daughters and one son. Chief of the Propulsion Branch, Controls and Instruments Section, 1952-55, and Chief of Range Operations division and Navy Flight Safety Engineer, 1955-57, White Sands Proving Ground, New Mexico; Design Specialist, Martin Company, Denver, 1957; President and Chief Engineer, Model Missiles, Denver, 1957-59; Vice-President and Chief Engineer, MicroDynamics, Broomfield, Colorado, 1959; Design Engineer, Stanley Aviation, Denver, 1959-60; Assistant Director of Research, Huyck Corporation, Stamford, Connecticut, 1960-65; free-lance consultant, 1965-73; Marketing Manager, Flow Technology, Phoenix, 1973-76. Since 1976, free-lance consultant and writer. Editor, *Missile Away!,* 1953-57; Columnist ("Conquest of Space"), *Mechanix Illustrated,* 1956-57; Editor, *The Model Rocketeer,* 1957-64 and since 1976. Founder and past President, National Association of Rocketry; Associate Fellow, American Institute of Aeronautics and Astronautics. Agent: Blassingame McCauley and Wood, 60 East 42nd Street, New York, New York 10017. Address: 616 West Frier Drive, Phoenix, Arizona 85021, U.S.A.

SCIENCE-FICTION PUBLICATIONS

Novels

Starship Through Space (juvenile). New York, Holt Rinehart, 1954.
Contraband Rocket. New York, Ace, 1955.
Rocket Man (juvenile). New York, Holt Rinehart, 1955.
Star Driver. New York, Ballantine, 1980.

Uncollected Short Stories

"Galactic Gadgeteers" (as G. Harry Stine), in *Astounding* (New York), May 1951.
"Greenhorn" (as G. Harry Stine), in *Fantastic Story* (New York), Fall 1952.
"Pioneer," in *Astounding* (New York), August 1953.
"The Day the Rocket Blew Up," in *Saturday Evening Post* (Philadelphia), 15 August 1953.
"Ill Wind," in *Astounding* (New York), December 1953.
"Amateur," in *Astounding* (New York), February 1954.
"Design Flaw," in *Astounding* (New York), February 1955.
"The Plains of San Augustine," in *Astounding* (New York), April 1955.
"Satellite Wild," in *American Legion* (New York), July 1955.
"The Brass Cannon," in *Fantasy and Science Fiction* (New York), November 1955.
"Wireroad," in *Fantastic Universe* (Chicago), September 1956.
"The Education of Icky," in *Astounding* (New York), January 1957.
"Landing for Midge," in *Fantastic Universe* (Chicago), July 1957.
"Coffin Run," in *Fantastic* (New York), August 1957.
"Homecoming," with Lewis J. Stecher, in *Fantastic Universe* (Chicago), November 1958.
"Letter from Tomorrow," in *Fantastic Universe* (Chicago), May 1959.
"And a Star to Steer Her By," in *Every Boy's Book of Outer Space Stories,* edited by T.E. Dikty. New York, Fell, 1960.
"The Test Stand," in *The Expert Dreamers,* edited by Frederik Pohl. New York, Doubleday, 1962.
"The Easy Way Out," in *Analog 6,* edited by John W. Campbell, Jr. New York, Doubleday, 1968.
"Something in the Sky," in *Encounters with Aliens* edited by George W. Early. Los Angeles, Sherbourne Press, 1969.

OTHER PUBLICATIONS as G. Harry Stine

Other

"The Truth of the Matter," in *Fantasy and Science Fiction* (New York), November 1956.
Rocket Power and Space Flight. New York, Holt Rinehart, 1957.
Earth Satellites and the Race for Space Superiority. New York, Ace, 1957.
"How to Think a Science Fiction Story," in *The Year's Best Science Fiction 6,* edited by Judith Merril. New York, Simon and Schuster, 1961.
"Time for Tom Swift," in *Analog* (New York), January 1961.
"Science Fiction Is Too Conservative," in *Analog* (New York), May 1961.
Man and the Space Frontier. New York, Knopf, 1962.
Handbook of Model Rocketry. Chicago, Follett, 1965; revised edition, 1967, 1970, 1976.
"How to Make a Star Trek," in *Analog* (New York), February 1968.
The Model Rocket Manual. New York, Sentinel, 1970; revised edition, New York, Arco, 1977.
The Third Industrial Revolution (juvenile). New York, Putnam, 1975.
Shuttle into Space: A Ride in America's Space Transportation System (juvenile). Chicago, Follett, 1978.

*   *   *

Even the most cursory exposure to the science fiction of Lee Correy would indicate clearly his preoccupation with space travel and its importance to the human race. Most of his novels and short stories deal with space travel not just as a plot element, common to a large minority of the field, but as the central focus of the story.

Contraband Rocket demonstrates that if the government is not willing to exert time and money on space travel, then perhaps private citizens will. The idea that a collection of idealists could refurbish an old rocket for a moon flight has become obsolescent in the face of the complex reality of space travel, but this early novel exudes the optimistic self-confidence of its time. Correy tried to make the same basic concept more palatable in the recent *Star Driver.* A small company develops a working anti-gravity unit and mounts it in a commercial aircraft in order to make a dramatic presentation of its possibilities and enable them to evade government regulation. Unfortunately, the situation remains implausible, and Correy's pedagogic concerns interfere with the plot as well.

Although not as pedantic, his juvenile novels also reflect Correy's interest in space exploration, with the first mission to Alpha Centauri in *Starship Through Space,* and the second expedition to Mars in *Rocket Man.* Paradoxically, these latter are more effective in conveying the fascination with travel to other worlds because Correy has spent more effort on plot than in his novels aimed at an older audience.

For the most part, Correy's short stories deal with the mechanics of space exploration. In "The Test Stand," for example, a man's view of his own career and relation to death is revised when he is nearly killed preventing an accident during a test firing. The importance of the human factor in even the most sophisticated aspects of space flight are demonstrated in "Coffin Run" wherein a substitute pilot must be retrained rapidly to complete a necessary flight, despite the objections of some of the authorities. Neither story descends into lecture, but it is clear in each that Correy is attempting to humanize the mechanical nature of the space program. Correy's best short story is "The Easy Way Out." Alien invaders land in a remote part of Earth, and set out to discover how susceptible the planet is to invasion. They encounter a number of animals, and rate each on a "Ferocity Index," eventually retreating in utter terror when they witness the bullying of a pet wolverine by a pair of human children. Although the basic concept is amusing, the story encompasses an inherent flaw; it is unlikely that a race that had conquered large chunks of the universe would automatically assume that every animal it encountered was a separate intelligent species, that no preliminary survey from space would have identified the nature and technological level of humanity. Less ambitious but more successful is a very mild but well-handled story, "Something in the Sky." A test missile veers away from its intended target and strikes something invisible in space, constructed of materials unknown on this planet. In just a few thousand words and with considerable restraint, Correy conveys a mood of mystery and wonder.

Although Correy now seems more concerned with non-fiction advocating space travel, as in *The Third Industrial Revolution,* he has displayed the potentiality to be an interesting writer of fiction.

—Don D'Ammassa

COTTON, John. *See* **FEARN, John Russell.**

COULSON, Juanita (née Wellons). Also writes as John J. Wells. American. Born in Anderson, Indiana, 12 February 1933. Educated at Ball State University, Muncie, Indiana, B.S. 1954; M.A. 1963. Married Robert Coulson, *q.v.,* in 1954; one son. Elementary school teacher, Huntington, Indiana, 1954-55; collator, Heckman Book Bindery, North Manchester, Indiana, 1955-57; publisher, *SFWA Forum,* for two years. Since 1953, Editor, with Robert Coulson, *Yandro* fan magazine; since 1963, free-lance writer. Recipient: Hugo Award, for editing, 1965. Guest of Honor, World Science Fiction Convention, 1972. Agent: Virginia Kidd, Box 278, Milford, Pennsylvania 18337. Address: Route 3, Hartford City, Indiana 47348, U.S.A.

SCIENCE-FICTION PUBLICATIONS

Novels

Crisis on Cheiron. New York, Ace, 1967.
The Singing Stones. New York, Ace, 1968.
Unto the Last Generation. Toronto, Laser, 1975.
Space Trap. Toronto, Laser, 1976.
The Web of Wizardry. New York, Ballantine, 1978.
The Death God's Citadel. New York, Ballantine, 1980.

Uncollected Short Stories

"Another Rib" (as John J. Wells), with Marion Zimmer Bradley, in *Fantasy and Science Fiction* (New York), June 1963.
"A Helping Hand," in *If* (New York), November-December 1970.
"Wizard of Death," in *Fantastic* (New York), February 1973.
"The Dragon of Tor-Nali," in *Fantastic* (New York), February 1975.
"Unscheduled Flight," in *Beyond Time,* edited by Sandra Ley. New York, Pocket Books, 1976.
"Intersection Point," in *Star Trek: The New Voyages,* edited by Sondra Marshak and Myrna Culbreath. New York, Bantam, 1976.
"Uraguyen and I," with Miriam Allen deFord, in *Cassandra Rising,* edited by Alice Laurance. New York, Doubleday, 1978.

OTHER PUBLICATIONS

Novels

The Secret of Seven Oaks. New York, Berkley, 1972.
Door into Terror. New York, Berkley, 1972.
Stone of Blood. New York, Ballantine, 1975.
Fear Stalks the Bayou. New York, Ballantine, and Skirden, Lan-

cashire, Magna, 1976.
Dark Priestess. New York, Ballantine, 1977.
Fire of the Andes. New York, Ballantine, 1979.

Other

"Of (Super) Human Bondage," in *The Comic-Book Book,* edited by Richard A. Lupoff and Don Thompson. New Rochelle, New York, Arlington House, 1974.

Juanita Coulson comments:

Before I could write, my mother transcribed my earliest attempts at story telling. For my 8th Christmas, she gave me a typewriter, compounding the felony. In a sense, I have been writing fiction since before I could write. My only interest was in concocting characters and adventures that satisfied an audience of one—me. It wasn't until I was in my 30's that Marion Zimmer Bradley insisted I should submit my work professionally. Without her encouragement, I never would have made the effort. I am still surprised to find that some kind people actually pay me for writing the stories I wrote so long ago solely for my own entertainment. Other than the fun of creating, my aims are to follow two maxims: There Are No Simple Answers and Take The Long View. To some degree, I share Marion Bradley's theory that a villain is just a protagonist with a different point of view; the story *might* have been told from the villain's position, *if* he (or she) is a valid character to start with. And in any story, I don't think all the questions can be answered—certainly not completely. People—and characters—are too complex. As for The Long View, it's a humbling rule to write by, but it serves me equally in science fiction, contemporary woman's genre fiction, or a historical romance set in 1770 B.C. The Long View ought to be an essential ingredient of all science fiction, especially considering the past and future history of humanity *and* of other species, known and unknown, and cosmology. Putting us in our place in that immense scheme of things is, for me, the foundation of a sense of wonder.

* * *

Since her first appearance in professional print in 1963, Juanita Coulson's writing has included science fiction of both the speculative and the adventurous varieties, heroic fantasy, romantic suspense ("Gothics"), and historical romances, as well as occasional non-fiction.

Her first story, "Another Rib," a collaboration with Marion Zimmer Bradley, tells of a group of men, the only survivors of a destroyed Earth, and what happens when alien medical technology offers them an unconventional way of perpetuating the human species. The theme is handled with skill and delicacy, resulting in a memorable story.

Coulson's first novel, *Crisis on Cheiron,* deals with the struggle of a small band of allies to save an underdeveloped planet from economic and ecological ruin at the hands of an unscrupulous Terran corporation. In *The Singing Stones* another world is in peril: Pa-Liina, with its quasi-telepathic Stones of Song, suffering under the domination of its decadent sister world Deliyas. In both novels the alien environment is well thought out and convincingly portrayed, and the scientific underpinnings are given colorful settings and action reminiscent of the work of Leigh Brackett and Marion Zimmer Bradley. The theme of an alien world suffering the unwelcome attentions of Earthmen is also present in "A Helping Hand": this time the Earthmen's intentions are benevolent, but their complete misunderstanding of the world they are trying to help leads to disaster.

Unto the Last Generation is the story of a future Earth where population control has been all too successful, rendering most of mankind infertile. The young battle with the old for the inadequate supplies of food distributed by a military government, while a group of scientists work in secret, trying to ensure humanity's survival. *Space Trap* deals with the first contact between Earthmen and a telepathic civilization from across the galaxy, as representatives of both groups battle for control of a remote planet on which they are trapped.

"Unscheduled Flight" is more anecdote than story: it sets up an interesting parallel-worlds situation but does nothing with it. Two long fantasy novels, *The Web of Wizardry* and *The Death God's*

Citadel, are both set in the same imaginary world, in which sorcery and the presence of supernatural beings are facts of everyday existence. The backgrounds (geographical, cultural, and lingusitic) are worked out in detail; the characters are interesting, the action well-paced, resulting in two very entertaining adventures. Two earlier short stories, "Wizard of Death" and "The Dragon of Tor-Nali," are set in the same world as the novels.

—R.E. Briney

COULSON, Robert (Stratton). Also writes as Thomas Stratton. American. Born in Sullivan, Indiana, 12 May 1928. Educated at Silver Lake High School; studied electrical engineering, International Correspondence School, 1960. Married Juanita Coulson, *q.v.* in 1954; one son. Cemetery caretaker, 1941-43; wool bagger, 1944; house painter, 1945-47; bookbinder, Heckman Book Bindery, North Manchester, Indiana, 1947-57. Draftsman, 1965-76, and since 1976, order writer, Overhead Door of Indiana, Hartford City. Since 1953, Editor, with Juanita Coulson, *Yandro* fan magazine. Recipient: Hugo Award, for editing, 1965. Guest of Honor, World Science Fiction Convention, 1972. Agent: Virginia Kidd, Box 278, Milford, Pennsylvania 18337. Address: Route 3, Hartford City, Indiana 47348, U.S.A.

SCIENCE-FICTION PUBLICATIONS

Novels (series: Joe Karns)

The Invisibility Affair (as Thomas Stratton, with Gene DeWeese). New York, Ace, 1965.
The Mind-Twisters Affair (as Thomas Stratton, with Gene DeWeese). New York, Ace, 1965.
Gates of the Universe (Karns), with Gene DeWeese. Toronto, Laser, 1975.
Not You See It/Him/Them...(Karns), with Gene DeWeese. New York, Doubleday, 1975; London, Hale, 1976.
To Renew the Ages. Toronto, Laser, 1976.
But What of Earth?, with Piers Anthony. Toronto, Laser, 1976.
Charles Fort Never Mentioned Wombats (Karns), with Gene DeWeese. New York, Doubleday, 1977; London, Hale, 1978.

Uncollected Short Stories

"The Tracy Business," with Gene DeWeese, in *Fantasy and Science Fiction* (New York), February 1970.
"John Carter and His Electric Barsoom," with Gene DeWeese, in *The Conan Grimoire,* edited by L. Sprague de Camp and George H. Scithers. Baltimore, Mirage Press, 1971.
"By the Book," with Gene DeWeese, in *Amazing* (New York), May 1971.
"Soy la Libertad," in *Beyond Time,* edited by Sandra Ley. New York, Pocket Books, 1976.

OTHER PUBLICATIONS

Other

"From Conciliabule to Congestion, with a Touch of Condescension," in *Midamericon Program Book,* 1976.

Robert Coulson comments:
First of all, I don't write because I have any burning desire to tell stories, or to influence the masses, or even to be admired (though I suppose the last might have some bearing on my writing). I write professional fiction because it's the most enjoyable way I've found to make money. Not the most reliable—which is why I work at a regular job and write as a sideline—but the most enjoyable. Since writing is extra income, rather than my living, I can afford to write pretty much what I like. What I like, mostly, is humor: puns, incongruities, parody, satire (not farce: I seldom find farce particularly funny). Basically, I don't take writing—my own, or anyone else's—very seriously, and I'll make fun of a writer who shows that he takes himself overly seriously. I try to be entertaining, and any profundities will be slipped in gently and (I hope) well hidden. Any influencing of the reader in a work of fiction should be subtle.

Fortunately for our co-authorship, Gene DeWeese has much the same sense of humor that I have; once one of our books is finished and in print, it's impossible even for us to remember exactly who wrote what. Saves a lot of disagreement during the writing.

*   *   *

Robert Coulson has been a science-fiction fan since the 1940's and has been involved in amateur SF journalism for more than 25 years. His journalism work has been entirely non-fiction: humorous articles and the incisive reviews which he still writes for his and his wife's magazine *Yandro.* Coulson has remained active as an SF fan even after becoming a professional writer.

Most of Coulson's science-fiction writing has been done in collaboration with his long-time friend, Gene DeWeese. In 1967, under the name Thomas Stratton, Coulson and DeWeese wrote two paperback spinoffs from *The Man from U.N.C.L.E.* TV series. *The Invisibility Affair* involved THRUSH's use of an invisible dirigible in their latest plan for conquest. One of the chapter titles from the book ("Charles Fort Never Mentioned Sandbags") would turn up ten years later, transmuted into the title of another Coulson/DeWeese collaboration. In *The Mind-Twisters Affair,* Napoleon Solo and Illya Kuryakin foil a THRUSH attempt to control the minds of world-famous scientists. Both books feature the unlikely situations and off-beat humor which made the television series so popular.

The Coulson/DeWeese novel *Gates of the Universe* is the story of a bulldozer operator and would-be science fiction writer, Ross Allen, who is accidentally whisked from Earth to the planet Venntra through a Probe Gate, a means of alien interstellar transportation. Both the Bulldozer and Allen's SF background aid him in coping with the dangers of a world threatened by the antics of an apparently mad computer. *Now You See It/Him/Them...,* a combination murder mystery and SF novel of psi powers, is set at a science-fiction convention. A follow-up novel, *Charles Fort Never Mentioned Wombats,* takes place in Australia, among a group of science-fiction fans on their way to attend the World Science Fiction Convention in Melbourne. The trip is complicated by assorted encounters with extra-terrestrials.

All of the Coulson/DeWeese collaborations, as well as Coulson's solo work, involve standard SF ingredients, handled with skill, humor, and occasionally a refreshing irreverence. They also employ the practice of "Tuckerizing," named after the SF fan and writer Wilson Tucker: using the names of family, friends, and well-known SF figures for characters in the story. This is not noticeable to the general reader, but can prove distracting to those who are familiar with the names.

Coulson's only solo works to date are *To Renew the Ages* and "Soy la Libertad." The novel is set in a sparsely populated North America after a nuclear war, and chronicles the hero's battle against an unknown telepathic menace which is threatening the safety of the scattered pockets of civilization. His search for the source of the danger leads him into contact with the remarkable heroine, Tamara Bush, and the matriarchal society which she represents. "Soy la Libertad" is an alternate-world story, telling of the aftermath of a political assassination in a version of North America where Texas, the Confederacy, the Five Indian Nations, and the Mormons' Deseret are separate countries, not part of the United States. Based on the author's broad knowledge of history and told with a nicely calculated irony, it is a memorable story.

Coulson's name also appeared as co-author on *But What of Earth?* but Coulson merely revised a manuscript submitted by Piers Anthony. The result, after further changes by editorial hands, was unsatisfactory to both writers.

—R.E. Briney

COUZYN, Jeni. South African. Born in South Africa, 26 July 1942. Educated at the University of Natal, B.A. 1962, B.A. (honours) 1963. Drama Teacher, Rhodesia, 1964; Producer, African Music and Drama Association, Johannesburg, 1965; Teacher, Special School, London, 1966; Poetry Organiser and Gallery Attendant, Camden Arts Centre, London, 1967. Since 1968, freelance poet, lecturer, and broadcaster. Writer-in-Residence, University of Victoria, British Columbia, 1976. Recipient: Arts Council grant, 1971, 1974; Canada Council grant, 1977. Address 117 Rosebery Road, London N.10, England.

PUBLICATIONS

Verse

Flying. London, Workshop Press, 1970.
Monkeys' Wedding. London, Cape, 1972.
Christmas in Africa. London, Heinemann, 1975.
House of Changes. London, Heinemann, 1978.
The Happiness Bird. Victoria, British Columbia, Sono Nis Press, 1978.
A Time to Be Born. London, Heinemann, 1981.

Other

Editor, *Twelve to Twelve: Poems Commissioned for Poetry D-Day, Camden Arts Festival 1970.* London, Poets' Trust, 1970.

Jeni Couzyn comments:

In a very early poem I wrote: "As I tumble in the cold / from the sheer edges of my mind / from the edge of this / tiny body / gapes the big sky." This stumbling fragment sums up my sense of myself as an astonished thinking speck in a vast and mysterious universe, and it is from this perspective that I discovered and became excited by science fiction. Science fiction asked the right questions, aggravated my mind in the right way, and its images explored, though never answered, the questions in ways that stretched my imagination.

I owe much to science-fiction writers, although my attention has moved in other directions in recent years. John Brunner I discovered in my late twenties, and as a result of his work I developed a huge hunger for any SF writer who questioned what we are, and speculated about what we might be. All my books have at least one SF poem. *Monkeys' Wedding* has a whole SF section called "Notes to the Designer," and *Christmas in Africa* has six poems based directly on stories by Brian Aldiss. I choose science fiction as a form for my poems when I need its qualities of distancing, or the havoc it plays with figure/ground formation to heighten perception.

* * *

Jeni Couzyn's poetry reflects her international background. She was born in South Africa in 1942, came to England during the 1960's, and moved to Canada during the 1970's. Her first book of poems, with illustrations by the author, was *Flying* (1970). Since then, Couzyn's poetry has developed steadily. It remains pruned yet diverse, slowly coming to deal, in central images, with her central concerns: "Shabbiness drops off me like old rags / in your company." There is no shabbiness in the naked poetry, however, only a fear that ultimately shabbiness might prevail. Against shabbiness and defeat there are strong defences. Couzyn's poetry is a poetry of extremes; for this reason its tone is often incantatory. Spells and chants and graces abound. The lady knows she is a witch; incantation works.

This attraction for extremity has drawn Couzyn towards science fiction, which so frequently traffics with the exaggerated case, the *ne plus ultra.* In *Flying* there is the "Preparation of Human Pie" poem, supposedly an extract from a cookery article in the *Encyclopaedia Galactica.* The grave tone conceals a delight in the gruesome details of how to prepare genital sauce. By later standards, the poem, for all its conceits, is callow. The collection *Monkeys' Wedding* banishes Grand Guignol in favour of deeper understandings and symbolisms. It includes a poem about the hospital which follows the narrator wherever she goes: "Then I opened my eyes and saw / The hospital, striding over the hills towards me." The most memorable

poem of the collection, also infused with a thinking that is recognisably science fictional, is "There Are Some Creatures Living in My Body." Cool precision of language curbs an underlying river of feeling.

More recent collections, *Christmas in Africa* and *House of Changes,* reveal transformations: the ardent climber has become a mountain goat. Couzyn is now an established poet, with a fusion of thought, feeling, and language which is individual without being quirky. Although many poems are brilliantly successful in their own right, one now senses an integrated meta-world behind the poems. The suffering is still there, rendered as vividly as ever, but is placed within a wider spectrum of emotion—and of life, for spirits, animals, and androids crowd the verse. It is a mistake to place too much emphasis on the pain: quite as remarkable in Couzyn's work are a note of rejoicing and a sardonic wit, which are as often turned on the narrator as on her subject matter.

Such honesty is alarming as well as pleasing. Honesty isolates. Seeking extremes, the poet turns naturally to Africa. Africa forms a background to many poems. With its luxuriance and its nearness to the bone, it becomes universalised. Couzyn's is an animist world, full of fertility. We still need spells against many things, leprechauns, barrenness, and tidal waves—not that tidal waves, being part of nature, are unwelcome. "Fill my lake deeply, but carry me not away." People come and go, desiring freedom.

The symbolist-like freedom of science fiction is explored in both these collections. In particular, they contain poems based on stories by SF writers: in "Christmas in Africa," by Brian Adiss, in "House of Changes," by Philip K. Dick. In "Do Androids Dream" the androids have the same hungers as flesh, and the same cry: "Let me live." The poems in the earlier collection form an interesting binary group, based either directly on the original stories ("The Moment Eclipses," "Marapper the Priest," "We Embark for Cythera," "The Lizard Touches Down," and "What Can We Make to Replace a Man") or from an original idea that has been developed in a poetic form ("The Cell Attempts to Communicate with the Giant," "Inside Outside," "The Giant Sleeps").

Here an incantatory note is extremely effective, for instance in "Marapper the Priest," carried through with fine cutting edge:

> may our hands grow quicker
> our eyes sharper our arms stronger our tempers fiercer
> that we may overcome all who oppose us
>
> may we scatter the entrails of the mad captain
> through the length and breadth of the world.
> *May the long journey end*
>
> *may the ship come home.*

Jeni Couzyn is one of a number of poets who use science fiction themes. With her tenderness and astringency, she draws from them a terse music which, while being entirely her own, also pierces to the essence of SF's divinatory experience.

—Brian Aldiss

COWPER, Richard. Pseudonym for Colin Middleton Murry. British. Born in Bridport, Dorset, 9 May 1926; son of the writer John Middleton Murry. Educated at Rendcomb College, Gloucestershire, 1937-43; Brasenose College, Oxford, 1948-50, B.A. (honours) in English 1950; University of Leicester, 1950-51. Served in the Royal Navy Fleet Air Arm, 1944-47. Married Ruth Jezierski in 1950; two daughters. English Master, Whittinghame College, Brighton, 1952-67; Head of the English Department, Atlantic World College, Llantwit-Major, Glamorgan, 1967-70. Agent: A.P. Watt Ltd., 26-28 Bedford Row, London WC1R 4HL; or, James Brown Associates, 25 West 43rd Street, New York, New York 10036, U.S.A. Address: Landscott, Lower Street, Dittisham, near Dartmouth, Devon TQ6 OET, England.

SCIENCE-FICTION PUBLICATIONS

Novels

Breakthrough.   London, Dobson, 1967; New York, Ballantine, 1969.
Phoenix.   London, Dobson, 1968; New York, Ballantine, 1970.
Domino.   London, Dobson, 1971.
Kuldesak.   London, Gollancz, and New York, Doubleday, 1972.
Clone.   London, Gollancz, 1972; New York, Doubleday, 1973.
Time Out of Mind.   London, Gollancz, 1973.
The Twilight of Briareus.   London, Gollancz, and New York, Day, 1974.
Worlds Apart.   London, Gollancz, 1974.
The Road to Corlay.   London, Gollancz, 1978; New York, Pocket Books, 1979.
Profundis.   London, Gollancz, 1979.

Short Stories

The Custodians and Other Stories.   London, Gollancz, 1976.
The Web of the Magi.   London, Gollancz, 1980.
Out Where the Big Ships Go.   New York, Pocket Books, 1980.

OTHER PUBLICATIONS

Novels as Colin Murry

The Golden Valley.   London, Hutchinson, 1958.
Recollections of a Ghost.   London, Hutchinson, 1960.
A Path to the Sea.   London, Hutchinson, 1961.
Private View.   London, Dobson, 1972.

Play

Radio Play: *Taj Mahal by Candlelight* (as Colin Murry), 1966.

Other

One Hand Clapping: A Memoir of Childhood (as Colin Middleton Murry).   London, Gollancz, 1975; as *I at the Keyhole,* New York, Stein and Day, 1975.
"Backwards Across the Frontier," in *Foundation 9* (London), November 1975.
Shadows on the Grass (autobiography; as Colin Middleton Murry).   London, Gollancz, 1977.
"A Rose Is a Rose Is a Rose" (on Roger Zelazny), in *Foundation 11-12* (London), March 1977.

Richard Cowper comments:
First and foremost, in my writing, I aim to please *myself.* Experience in the form of some 15 novels has taught me that if I do this I usually contrive to please some other people too. That's just as well, for to write books that did not give me pleasure in the writing would be a grim sort of punishment and I'd very soon pack writing in altogether. But having said that I feel bound to add that I am profoundly conscious that I am in the entertainment business where "those who live to please must please to live."
My ambition has always been to write fine novels. By that I mean novels in which, as it were, I contrive to put the beat of the human heart on to the printed page—to make the reader endure and enjoy the whole gamut of human experience through the medium of my imagination. I contend that, to have its full impact, science fiction must be presented in human terms and allow the reader scope for imaginative identification with the characters in the stories.

*   *   *

Richard Cowper entered the SF genre from the mainstream with *Breakthrough,* which used a contemporary setting to unravel the story of "passengers" in the minds of his characters, survivors of a more perfect, poetical age. This emphasis upon the "dream state," central to Cowper's work, is used in a different manner in *Phoenix,* where a youth, Bard, wakes after suspended animation and finds himself two thousand years in the future, in a simpler, post-

holocaust society. Like the protagonist of *Breakthrough* (and, indeed, like many of Cowper's protagonists) he is possessed of special paranormal powers, which are unknown to him at the book's outset and which he discovers and eventually learns to use with sensitivity. These powers are evident again in *Domino,* where the young protagonist (still at school), Christopher Blackburn, finds himself pursued by people from the future who are trying to stop him from experimenting in genetics, experiments which are to change the face of future society, making a master-slave arrangement. The interaction between different realities witnessed in these three books is to be seen in his later work as a strong theme.
In 1972 the satiric *Clone* launched Cowper upon the SF reading public. It is marked by its hostility to the technophilic direction man is taking, and by a distaste for modern living in general. It is all delivered with humour, and follows the picaresque adventures of the young innocent, Alvin, who remains morally intact despite the gross advances of the world to him. He discovers he is part of a four-man Clone which develops immense paranormal powers but, as in all of Cowper's books, disposes of these powers in a humane, almost mystical manner. *Time Out of Mind* said little more than had been already stated in *Domino,* and is another tale of future interference in present (or near-present) society. *Kuldesak* is a far better book, showing us man in degeneration, living beneath the ground at the command of robots and computers, becoming (literally) vegetables as the years pass. Mel, the inquisitive young protagonist of this story, goes to the surface and changes it all, leading man out of his rut and back to the sane path of existence.
The Twilight of Briareus is probably Cowper's finest SF novel, written in a consummately elegant style and building to a powerful and emotive climax. Man becomes sterile as an after-effect of a nearby nova which sweeps the Earth and, as a result of the nova, "passengers" are discovered in the minds of several people. The new "aliens" and the old man struggle to take control of man's destiny, and the peaceful resolution of this contest in the mind of Calvin Johnson, the central character of the book, brings the book to a close, even as Johnson himself dies in the snow. Like the earlier books it is set in a near-contemporary England and most of the critical events are internal ones, arising from the tension between the "dream state" and "reality": "So that moment joined my previous glimpse of the sun-sculpted hills as just another strand of the elusive web that had drawn us here, and, as I stumbled forward beside her up to the house, I had the wierdest feeling that I was a fugitive in limbo fleeing between two worlds, one dead, the other powerless to be born." Johnson's words echo a feeling that is prevalent in many of these books, and he is perhaps the most subtly drawn of all Cowper's characters and the nearest to the author, involved, as so many of Cowper's protagonists are, in watching the external world crumble around him as the internal landscape of his mind opens up to display previously unguessed paranormal powers. *Twilight of Briareus* is the definitive exploration of this inner conflict and its resolution.
Worlds Apart breaks from this serious lyricism and satirises SF writers in a most direct manner. George Cringe, an unimportant junior science teacher, writes an SF tale about Chnass while a Chnassian, Zil Bryn, writes a tale about George. Its humorous contrast between the mundane and the sublime is beautifully done and its comic delights are many.
It was after this comic break that Cowper first tried his hand at SF short stories and produced "The Custodians," the first of a series of delicately imagined and richly written stories. It deals with prescience and the nuclear holocaust but dwells, almost paradoxically, on the medieval past. There is a wealth of emotion in these stories and while "Paradise Beach" is flawed, "The Hertford Manuscript" and "Drink Me, Francesca" possess the same poetic lilt. The most important of these stories, however, is "Piper at the Gates of Dawn" which deals with the birth of a new religion. A novella of immense wealth and power, it brings to mind Le Guin's Earthsea books; its post-holocaust setting is similar to that of *Phoenix.* The young boy, Tom, has the gift of joining men together in a brotherhood through the music of his flute and the image of the White Bird. These images, picked up 18 years later, when the "kinsmen" of Tom's "religion" are being persecuted, form the basis of *The Road to Corlay.* It is a sensuous book that pampers both heart and mind and, as in both *Breakthrough* and *Twilight,* has a "passenger" in the mind of one of its contemporary characters. Carver, a 20th-century scientist, sees

through the eyes of Thomas of Norwich, an inhabitant of the world of Corlay — AD 3018 — and through the "double-vision" Cowper emphasises once again that it is only by shedding man's present direction (which, he infers, can only be achieved by some natural or unnatural catastrophe which robs man of almost everything) and assuming a new life-style, that any future can exist for *Homo sapiens.*

Profundis is once again in the vein of *Clone,* with an innocent protagonist, Tom Jones, re-enacting the Christ myth in a beserk computer-run submarine, *HMS Profundis,* which has already denuded the Earth "above surface" by causing global war. As black comedy it is not as effective as *Clone,* but it is, perhaps, much more profound in its message.

—David Wingrove

COX, Erle (Harold). Australian. Born in Melbourne, Victoria, 15 August 1873. Educated at Melbourne Church of England Grammar School. Farmer, then journalist: drama critic for *Argus* and *Australasian,* both Melbourne, 1918-46. Recipient: *Lone Hand* prize, for short story, 1910. *Died 20 November 1950.*

SCIENCE-FICTION PUBLICATIONS

Novels

Out of the Silence. Melbourne, Vidler, 1925; London, John Hamilton, 1927; New York, Henkle, 1928.
Fools' Harvest. Melbourne, Robertson and Mullens, 1939.
The Missing Angel. Melbourne, Robertson and Mullens, 1947.

* * *

Originally a farmer, Erle Cox graduated from free-lance writing to professional metropolitan journalism in his forties. His early short stories in Australian magazines were never collected, and he is known only for three novels. He never gained literary recognition: orthodox criticism ignores him and comprehensive literary histories give him a bare mention.

Yet *Out of the Silence* had great popular appeal, though Cox had to finance the 1925 edition himself. An earlier human race, destroyed in a world catastrophe 27 million years ago, left time-capsule spheres preserving their culture and chosen representatives in stasis. Found and revived in modern Victoria, the superwoman Earani prepares to take over the world and recreate her highly developed, rational, heartless civilisation. Her intellectual stature and enormous personal magnetism give good prospects of success, certainly with the other survivor she detects in the Himalayas revived as well. The book is well told, if slow and wordy by later standards, maintaining suspense as the mystery and menace unfold. The atmosphere of middle-class rural Australia about 1910 contrasts strangely with the threatened scientific tyranny. Earani is a terrible figure: a prodigy not of evil but of self-assured virtue without compassion. Characteristically her program includes genocide of inferior elements, including the colored races. The grotesque racism, almost too absurd to be abhorrent, was perfectly acceptable in the Australia of 60 years ago and caused no comment. No longer a book to sympathise with, it has historic importance.

Cox's other books are quite different. *Fools' Harvest* is a typical warning of foreign conquest of Australia, forseeing the scale of World War II atrocities but without scientific interest. *The Missing Angel* is a light satire about the Devil in Melbourne's polite society.

—Graham Stone

CRICHTON, (John) Michael. Also writes as Michael Douglas; Jeffery Hudson; John Lange. American. Born in Chicago, Illinois, 23 October 1942. Educated at Harvard University, Cambridge, Massachusetts, A.B. (summa cum laude) 1965 (Phi Beta Kappa); Harvard Medical School, M.D. 1969; Salk Institute, La Jolla, California, 1969-70. Married 1) Joan Radam in 1965 (divorced, 1971); 2) Kathleen St. Johns in 1978. Recipient: Mystery Writers of America Edgar Allan Poe Award, 1968, 1980; Association of American Medical Writers Award, 1970. Agent: International Creative Management, 8900 Beverly Boulevard, Los Angeles, California 90048. Address: 9200 Sunset Boulevard, Suite 1000, Los Angeles, California 90069, U.S.A.

SCIENCE-FICTION PUBLICATIONS

Novels

The Andromeda Strain. New York, Knopf, and London, Cape, 1969.
Drug of Choice (as John Lange). New York, New American Library, 1970; as *Overkill,* New York, Centesis, 1970.
Binary (as John Lange). New York, Knopf, and London, Heinemann, 1972.
The Terminal Man. New York, Knopf, and London, Cape, 1972.
Westworld. New York, Bantam, 1975.

OTHER PUBLICATIONS

Novels

A Case of Need (as Jeffery Hudson). Cleveland, World, and London, Heinemann, 1968.
Dealing; or, The Berkeley-to-Boston Forty-Brick Lost-Bag Blues (as Michael Douglas, with Douglas Crichton). New York, Knopf, 1971; London, Talmy Franklin, 1972.
The Great Train Robbery. New York, Knopf, and London, Cape, 1975.
Eaters of the Dead. New York, Knopf, and London, Cape, 1976.
Congo. New York, Knopf, 1980; London, Allen Lane, 1981.

Novels as John Lange

Odds On. New York, New American Library, 1966.
Scratch One. New York, New American Library, 1967.
Easy Go. New York, New American Library, 1968; London, Sphere, 1972; as *The Last Tomb,* as Michael Crichton, New York, Bantam, 1974.
The Venom Business. Cleveland, World, 1969.
Zero Cool. New York, New American Library, 1969; London, Sphere, 1972.
Grave Descend. New York, New American Library, 1970.

Plays

Screenplays: *Westworld,* 1973; *Coma,* 1978; *The First Great Train Robbery,* 1978.

Other

"Sci-Fi and Vonnegut," in *New Republic* (Washington, D.C.), 26 1969.
Five Patients: The Hospital Explained. New York, Knopf, 1970; Cape, 1971.
"Approaching Ellison," in *Approaching Oblivion,* by Harlan Ellison and Ed Bryant. New York, Walker, 1974; London, Millington, 1976.
Jasper Johns. New York, Abrams, and London, Thames and Hudson, 1977.

Theatrical Activities:

Director: **Films** — *Westworld,* 1973; *Coma,* 1978; *The First Great Train Robbery,* 1978. **Television** — *Pursuit,* 1972.

Michael Crichton comments:

I am interested in the quality of verisimilitude and how it is and sustained in fiction. All of my work, both science fiction and other writing, has tended to revolve around issues of what we believe and why. In recent years a good deal of my work has been devoted to films, which I direct as well as write.

*   *   *

Michael Crichton's primary science-fiction works are: *The Andromeda Strain, Binary,* and *The Terminal Man.* Classified as "soft" science fiction, each of these books is set in what is essentially contemporary society. In each case, though, a science-fiction element has been introduced upon which the subsequent development of the plot depends. In *The Andromeda Strain,* for example, a mutating micro-organism brought back from the upper atmosphere by a satellite kills all but two people in a small northern Arizona town and then threatens the rest of humanity. In *Binary* the tapping into a "closed code computer mechanism" to determine the time and route of a shipment of nerve gas permits a psychopathic multimillionaire to concoct a devious plot to assassinate the President. In *The Terminal Man* psychosurgery permits the connection of a psychopathic patient's brain to a computer and turns him into a living time bomb. It is, of course, their nearness to real life that makes these three novels believable and frightening. The novels are highly technical, and the narrative is laced with graphs, charts, diagrams, and computer printouts. Some of the information is real; the rest of it is fictionalized but dressed up to raise the level of credibility. Jargon from the appropriate scientific field adds to the realism. The drama of the stories develops from the threat of imminent disaster and the subsequent efforts to prevent it.

The Terminal Man and *Binary* are clearly less effective than *The Andromeda Strain,* but interesting and entertaining nonetheless. The terminal man himself is a psychotic named Harry Benson, who believes that machines are taking over the world. He becomes a threat when he is chosen for a unique experiment that connects his brain to a miniaturized computer which is powered by an atomic pack containing 37 grams of radioactive plutonium. Though the pack is implanted under his skin, if Benson breaks it open, he will kill himself and expose anyone in the immediate area to deadly radiation. Benson's physical problem is psychomotor epilepsy, and the computer is supposed to stop his seizures with a counteracting electrical shock. Because the sensation produced is more pleasurable than several orgasms, however, he learns to increase the frequency of the shocks through biofeedback techniques. Benson, in fact, becomes an electronic junkie. Though the novel produces a believable female lead in Dr. Janet Ross, a psychiatrist working on the project, it fails successfully to build tensions between the major characters, and much of the potential drama remains undeveloped. Moreover, the sense of a threat never really materializes because Benson is more pathetic than dangerous.

Pacing is Crichton's strongest quality, and *Binary* is much better in that regard. A more complicated plot and a high level of suspense—a State Intelligence Agent, John Graves, unravels a complicated puzzle created for him by John Wright, the insane right-wing multimillionaire, before a half-ton of ZV nerve gas kills the President and more than a million other people in San Diego—make *Binary* a more compelling book. Wright is a much more worthy adversary than Benson, and more deadly. He is both intelligent and clever. His anticipation of every move that Graves makes creates an eerie drama, a sense of frustration, and genuine "daylight" horror. When Graves finally figures out the puzzle and prevents the binary gasses from mixing to create ZV, it brings a sigh of relief.

The best of Crichton's books, without question, is *The Andromeda Strain.* Though the antagonist is a micro-organism, drama is achieved by the fact that its properties are unknown and that it has great potentiality to kill. It is heightened when the mutating organism eats through the rubber seals in one of the workrooms and contaminates that level of the underground laboratory. This sets the self-destruct mechanism of the complex into operation. Unless countermanded, the mechanism will set off an atomic bomb which will destroy the complex and disperse the deadly organism over the Earth's surface: the key to the spectacular success of the work lies in its pacing. Suspense is built with each development. Clues to the

nature of the organism are so interwoven with plot impediments that the reader is compelled to read on. Though the characters are only moderately interesting as people, the roles they play in the development of the drama are important and add to the suspense.

In general, Crichton's style is clinical. His narrative is lean and well-adapted to the fast action, dialogue, and rapid pacing upon which he relies. There is some social commentary in the novels as they depict the follies of man's self-assurance. Lack of judgment or planning combines with deadly technology in all three cases to remind man that he is often his own worst enemy.

—Carl B. Yoke

CROMIE, Robert.   British.   Born in 1856. *Died in 1907.*

SCIENCE-FICTION PUBLICATIONS

Novels

For England's Sake.   London, Warne, 1889.
A Plunge into Space.   London, Warne, 1890; Westport, Connecticut, Hyperion Press, 1976.
The Crack of Doom.   London, Digby Long, 1895.
The Next Crusade.   London, Hutchinson, 1896.
A New Messiah.   London, Digby Long, 1902.

Short Stories

The King's Oak and Other Stories.   London, Newnes, 1897.

OTHER PUBLICATIONS

Novels

The Lost Liner.   London, Newnes, 1899.
Kitty's Victoria Cross.   London, Warne, 1901.
The Shadow of the Cross.   London, Ward Lock, 1902.
El Dorado.   London, Ward Lock, 1904; as *From the Cliffs of Croaghaun,* Akron, Ohio, Saalfield, 1904.

Short Stories

The Romance of Poisons, Being Weird Episodes from Life, with T.S. Wilson.   London, Jarrolds, 1904.

*   *   *

All that is known about Robert Cromie is that from 1889 to 1904 he published 11 books of fiction (one with T.S. Wilson), a number of which are SF. The list begins with *For England's Sake,* which cashed in on the patriotic popularity of the "future war" tale by transferring it to India, where loyal natives headed by heroic maharajah defeat dastardly Russian invasion. Its continuation is *The Next Crusade,* whose battles and love entanglements are not as interesting as Cromie's Preface, briefly discussing "the history of the future" and with a too easy facetiousness concluding that as against the history of the past it contains fewer errors (Cromie's Britain allied with Austria occupies Constantinople, so that he may have been co-responsible for Churchill's disastrous World War I venture against the Dardanelles). Two other novels are more important. *A Plunge into Space* is an interplanetary novel halfway between Vernes and Wells (the second edition in 1891 has a brief and unrevealing preface by Verne) detailing how a scientist discovers anti-gravity, how his explorer-friend helps him to cast a steel globe in Alaska in spite of Indian attacks and sullen half-breeds, and how the two with four more friends—again characterized by profession— fly to a desert Mars. Vegetation and a decaying utopian civilization (which has TV and aircraft but no politics or money) are found near its polar sea. A love affair between one of the heroes and a beautiful Martian coyly named Mignonette results in the latter first becoming a stowaway in their spacecraft on return and then sacrificing her life; the craft is destroyed. *The Crack of Doom* has one of the first mad scientists in SF planning to use the secret of atomic energy to blow up our planet. The plot flounders through lots of genteel Victorian love melodrama, telepathy, hypnotism, secret societies, stereotyped characters, vague echoes of drawing-room Schopenhauerism, and a sentimental happy ending. A final SF novel, *A New Messiah,* also leans on a melodramatic plot.

—Darko Suvin

CROSS, John Keir. Also wrote as Stephen Macfarlane; Susan Morley. British. Born in Carluke, Lanark, 19 August 1914. Clerk and entertainer in the 1930's; radio writer for BBC, London, from 1937. *Died 22 January 1967.*

SCIENCE-FICTION PUBLICATIONS

Novels (juvenile)

The Angry Planet. London, Lunn, 1945; New York, Coward McCann, 1946.
The Owl and the Pussycat. London, Lunn, 1946; as *The Other Side of Green Hills,* New York, Coward McCann, 1947.
The Flying Fortunes in an Encounter with Rubberface. London, Muller, 1952; as *The Stolen Sphere,* New York, Dutton, 1953.
SOS from Mars. London, Hutchinson, 1954; as *The Red Journey Back,* New York, Coward McCann, 1954.

Short Stories

The Other Passenger: 18 Strange Stories. London, Westhouse, 1944; Philadelphia, Lippincott, 1946.

Uncollected Short Stories

"The Best Holiday I Ever Had" (juvenile), in *Laurie's Space Annual.* London, Laurie, 1953.
"Mothering Sunday," in *Best Black Magic Stories,* edited by John Keir Cross. London, Faber, 1960.

OTHER PUBLICATIONS

Novels

Mistress Glory (as Susan Morley). New York, Dial Press, 1948; as *Glory,* as John Keir Cross, London, Laurie, 1951.
Juniper Green. London, Laurie, 1952; (as Susan Morley), New York, Dial Press, 1953.

Plays

Radio Plays: *The Kraken Wakes,* from the novel by John Wyndham; *The Archers* series, with others, 1962-67; *The Brockenstein Affair,* from a work by George R. Preedy, 1962; *The Free Fishers,* from the novel by John Buchan, 1964; *Bird of Dawning,* from the novel by John Masefield, 1965; *Be Thou My Judge,* from a work by James Wood, 1967.

Television Play: *She Died Young,* 1961.

Other (juvenile)

Studio J Investigates. London, Lunn, 1944.
Jack Robinson. London, Lunn, 1945.
The Man in Moonlight. London, Westhouse, 1947.
The White Magic. London, Westhouse, 1947.
Blackadder. London, Muller, 1950; New York, Dutton, 1951.
The Dancing Tree. London, Hutchinson, 1955.
Elizabeth in Broadcasting. London, Chatto and Windus, 1957.
The Sixpenny Year. London, Hutchinson, 1957.

Other (juvenile; as Stephen Macfarlane)

The Blue Egg. London, Lunn, 1944.
Detectives in Greasepaint. London, Lunn, 1944.
Lucy Maroon, The Car That Loved a Policeman. London, Lunn, 1944.
Mr. Bosanko and Other Stories. London, Lunn, 1944.
The Strange Tale of Sally and Arnold. London, Lunn, 1944.
The Story of a Tree. London, Lunn, 1946.

Other

Aspect of Life: An Autobiography of Youth. London, Selwyn and Blount, 1937.

Editor, *The Children's Omnibus.* London, Lunn, 1948.
Editor, *Best Horror Stories.* London, Faber, 1957; *Best Horror Stories 2,* Faber, 1965.
Editor, *Best Black Magic Stories.* London, Faber, 1960.

*   *   *

A short story writer in the tradition of Saki and John Collier, a popular anthologist of horror stories, and an occasional writer of science-fiction and fantasy dramas for the BBC, John Keir Cross is especially noteworthy for his juvenile science fiction. *The Angry Planet* was among the first modern science-fiction novels directed at a young audience, and is interesting for the manner in which it reworks themes from Wells and C.S. Lewis into a context more readily accessible to younger readers.

The Angry Planet involves a group of three children who travel to Mars by hiding on an experimental rocket ship. The life they find there is elegantly portrayed, and reveals Cross's familiarity with earlier science fiction as well as intelligent speculation. Martian society is dominated by intelligent plant life, the major forms of which are called the Beautiful People and the Terrible Ones. This opposition of two divergent strains of the same evolutionary path calls to mind the Morlocks and Eloi from Wells's *The Time Machine,* and the moral values attached to each race calls to mind C.S. Lewis's *Out of the Silent Planet.* The relatively sophisticated multiple viewpoint narrative adds further interest to the tale and helps to maintain suspense. A sequel, *SOS from Mars,* describes subsequent journeys to Mars. Another juvenile science-fiction novel, with the unlikely title *The Flying Fortunes in an Encounter with Rubberface,* concerns the launching of an artificial earth satellite, and may be the first juvenile treatment of this theme except for Arthur Clarke's 1952 *Islands in the Sky.* Cross's adult fiction, represented by the collection *The Other Passenger,* tends more toward fantasy and the occult than science fiction, but includes the classic *doppelgänger* story "The Other Passenger." Cross's short fiction is distinguished by sensitive style and psychological insight.

—Gary K. Wolfe

CROSS, Polton.   *See* FEARN, John Russell.

———————

CROWLEY, John.   American.   Born in Presque Isle, Maine, 1 December 1942. Educated at Indiana University, Bloomington, B.A. 1964. Photographer and commercial artist, 1964-66. Since 1966, free-lance writer. Address: 71 Lexington Avenue, New York, New York 10010, U.S.A.

SCIENCE-FICTION PUBLICATIONS

Novels

The Deep.   New York, Doubleday, 1975; London, New English Library, 1977.
Beasts.   New York, Doubleday, 1976.
Engine Summer.   New York, Doubleday, 1979; London, Gollancz, 1980.

Uncollected Short Stories

"Where the Spirits Gat Them Home," in *Shadows,* edited by Charles L. Grant.   New York, Doubleday, 1978.
"The Reason for the Visit," in *Interfaces,* edited by Ursula K. Le Guin and Virginia Kidd.   New York, Ace, 1980.

*   *   *

John Crowley applies the lore of the Middle Ages to the problems of earth's future in his brilliantly structured novels *The Deep* and *Beasts.*

The Deep shows the elaborate social system of a medieval society; the scholarly, monastic Greys, a feudal Red faction pitted against a feudal Black one, and the Just, sworn defenders of the common folk, systematically assassinate the leaders of both Reds and Blacks. Only the guns of the Just suggest the prior existence of a modern technology. Otherwise, life is primitive and warfare heroic in this world of Norse myth, a disk mounted on a pillar founded in the Deep. Guarded below by Leviathan and above by the Heavens, deeply embroiled in its own conspiracies, this Middle Earth has forgotten its myths and its origins. An android visits this world, but, damaged in landing, cannot remember the purpose of its journey. Its superhuman strength and mental powers bring this Visitor in contact with all factions in this warring Middle Earth. By discovering fragments of lore, the Visitor learns its quest: to observe the ways of men and then seek Leviathan at the ends of the Earth. Only from Leviathan can the Visitor learn the truth: the Maker, worshipped by men, transplanted them and all things common to them to their small Middle Earth. The Byzantine treacheries, the elaborate sexual intrigues, the unending wars, all are the Maker's plan; the Just, who consider themselves social avengers by choice, are the Maker's ultimate regulatory device. Quest fulfilled, the Visitor returns through space to the Maker, leaving behind one of the Just to prophesy the reality of a forgotten God. *The Deep* asserts that in man's elaborately self-absorbed world, the Reds and the Blacks are pawns, not players, in a larger game than they imagine.

Beasts likewise plays on the idea of order based on conflict: Nature, itself threatened by the technology and politics of man. Set in the 21st century, the novel borrows the theme of medieval beast epics, placing it in an almost totally industrialized world. The kingly lion and the sly fox, part human as a result of genetic experiments, appear as major characters. The savagery of the wolf is represented by the members of USE, the Union of Social Engineering, dedicated to the restoration of a totalitarian Federal Government and the ultimate subjection of the environment. Painter, leader of the lion-men, and Counselor Reynard, the grotesque fox-man, turn to a charismatic human leader, Sten, son of a politician and student of an ecologist. The central theme of *Beasts* is the hunt. The characters,

beasts and men, all hunt; Crowley's ethical and thematic distinction lies between those whose hunting is in harmony with Nature and those whose prey is Nature itself. Young Sten's coalition of wise beasts which ends the novel suggests that Nature—helped by its own—may still survive.

The Deep and *Beasts* are structured to introduce the reader to all parts and all points of view of the moral and physical world each novel develops. Crowley's characters are both plausible and symbolic; action and symbol develop simultaneously. Although a few readers may find Crowley's literary allusions, structure, and symbolism confusing, the reader who appreciates craft, imagination, and talent will respect Crowley's contribution to science fiction.

—Katherine Staples

———————

CUMMINGS, Ray(mond King).   American.   Born in New York City, 30 August 1887. Educated at Princeton University, New Jersey, one year. Married Gabrielle W. Cummings; one son and one daughter. Worked on oil wells in Wyoming and in placer mines in British Columbia and Alaska; arranged record albums and wrote labels for Edison Records in the 1920's. *Died 23 January 1957.*

SCIENCE-FICTION PUBLICATIONS

Novels (series: Halijan; Matter, Space, and Time; Tama)

The Girl in the Golden Atom (Matter, Space, and Time).   London, Methuen, 1922; New York, Harper, 1923.
The Man Who Mastered Time (Matter, Space, and Time).   Chicago, McClurg, 1929.
The Sea Girl.   Chicago, McClurg, 1930.
Tarrano the Conqueror.   Chicago, McClurg, 1930.
Brigands of the Moon (Halijan).   Chicago, McClurg, 1931; London, Consul, 1958.
The Shadow Girl (Matter, Space, and Time).   London, Swan, 1946; New York, Ace, 1962.
The Man on the Meteor.   London, Swan, 1946(?).
The Princess of the Atom (Matter, Space, and Time).   New York, Avon, 1950; London, Boardman, 1951.
Beyond the Vanishing Point.   New York, Ace, 1958.
Wandl the Invader (Halijan).   New York, Ace, 1961.
Beyond the Stars.   New York, Ace, 1963.
A Brand New World.   New York, Ace, 1964.
The Exile of Time (Matter, Space, and Time).   New York, Avalon, 1964.
Explorers into Infinity.   New York, Avalon, 1965.
Tama of the Light Country.   New York, Ace, 1965.
Tama, Princess of Mercury.   New York, Ace, 1966.
The Insect Invasion.   New York, Avalon, 1967.

Short Stories

Into the Fourth Dimension and Other Stories.   London, Swan, 1943.

Uncollected Short Stories

"Battle of the Solar System," in *Thrilling Wonder Stories* (New York), Spring 1944.
"The Gadget Girl," in *Thrilling Wonder Stories* (New York), Fall 1944.
"Juggernaut of Space," in *Planet* (New York), Fall 1945.
"Up and Atom," in *Startling* (New York), September 1947.
"The Simple Life," in *Startling* (New York), May 1948.
"Ahead of His Time," in *Thrilling Wonder Stories* (New York), June 1948.
"The Little Monsters Come," in *Planet* (New York), Winter 1948.

"A Fragment of Diamond Quartz," in *Super Science* (Kokomo, Indiana), January 1950.

"The Planet Smashers," in *Out of This World Adventures* (New York), July 1950.

"Science Can Wait," in *Fantastic Story* (New York), Fall 1952.

"He Who Served," in *Fantastic Universe* (Chicago), September 1954.

"The Man Who Could Go Away," in *Fantastic Universe* (Chicago), July 1955.

"Requiem for a Small Planet," in *Saturn* (Holyoke, Massachusetts), March 1958.

"The Dead Who Walk," in *Magazine of Horror* (New York), April 1965.

*   *   *

Ray Cummings had a long writing career, but it must be said that he long outlived his originality, and was noted for shamelessly rehashing a few early stories. Established as one of the trailblazers before the advent of *Amazing Stories,* he was the only one of them to carry on as a prominent name. His output was exceeded only by Hamilton and Kuttner, but he did not move with the movement, and was soon dated.

The early tales that made his name had sketchy but strongly suggestive scientific foundations. Though he showed his debt to Wells by borrowing his narrative frame from *The Time Machine* more than once, his stories were closer to Haggard's or Burroughs's. Usually visitors from 20th-century New York in a strange setting with a vague pre-industrial society resolved a conflict and helped pave the way for more advanced thinking.

His first and favorite inspiration was sub-microscopic, even sub-atomic life—atoms or sub-atomic particles as worlds. The idea dated from Nicholas Odgers's *The Mystery of Being; or, Are Ultimate Atoms Inhabited Worlds?* (1863), but Cummings added the idea of reducing one's size indefinitely to penetrate such a realm—later reversing it to visit a super-world in which we inhabit a particle. It is a tribute to his skill that a story based on such an idea could be a popular success. The unnamed chemist in *The Girl in the Golden Atom* (Rogers in the sequel) sees with his super-microscope an infinitesimal human race, including a nubile wench. (Compare Fitz-James O'Brien's *The Diamond Lens.*) But instead of agonising over the unattainable he devises size-changing drugs. (Compare *Alice in Wonderland.*) The relativity of size and the experience of changing size are vividly evoked. The book was fresh and exciting then, and it still reads well, and rates as a classic—though it is not precisely science fiction. (Incidentally, this adventure does not reach the level of an atomic world, despite the title; G.P. Wertenbaker has the doubtful honor of first taking the idea that far in "The Man from the Atom," in *Science and Invention,* August 1923.)

In the extended book version the villain was called Targo, and many later evildoers were named alliteratively—Taro, Toroh, etc. They are typically greedy megalomaniacs, usually gross or deformed, good at sneering and cynical laughter. Subtleties of character and motivation are not displayed, but human relations were simplified and fogged with romantic myths in most science fiction then. The writing is direct and conversational. To modern eyes there was much overstating the obvious, especially in the novels, but there were mystery and suspense supporting the action for the original audience.

Cummings was an early exploiter of time travel, scarcely touched since Wells, in *The Man Who Mastered Time, The Shadow Girl,* and others, though mostly for change of scene only. *Explorers into Infinity* reversed the exploration of the inconceivably small to visit a vastly greater sphere. *The Man on the Meteor* told of a tiny worldlet in Saturn's ring with seas and aquatic microscopic humans. *Tarrano the Conqueror* had a future of interplanetary affairs and a new Napoleon. In *The Sea Girl* an undersea people threatened the land. *A Brand New World* had a new extra-Solar planet entering the system. *Brigands of the Moon* moved into the kind of future interplanetary traffic early magazine SF postulated and helped establish space piracy as a popular theme. Cummings wrote many routine space adventure shorts thereafter. In "Jetta of the Lowlands" (*Astounding,* 1930) new nations grew from settlements on the dry sea bed after the oceans receded. Not to be overlooked were some robot stories of interest, particularly "Zeoh-X" (*Thrilling Wonder*

Stories, April 1939) and "XI-2-200" (*Astounding,* September 1938); 16 stories featuring the character "Tubby" carried some gentle satire on many of his own plots and concepts.

—Graham Stone

———

DANN, Jack. American. Born in Johnson City, New York, 15 February 1945. Educated at Hofstra University, Hempstead, New York, 1963; State University of New York, Binghamton, 1965-68, B.A. in social science and political science 1968; St. John's Law School, New York, 1969-71. Taught writing and science fiction at Broome Community College, Binghamton, 1972, and Cornell University, Ithaca, New York, summer 1973; Managing Editor, *SFWA Bulletin,* 1970-75. Free-lance writer and lecturer. Agent: Joseph Elder Agency, 150 West 87th Street, No. 6-D, New York, New York 10024. Address: P.O. Box 555, Johnson City, New York 13790, U.S.A.

SCIENCE-FICTION PUBLICATIONS

Novel

Starhiker.   New York, Harper, 1977.

Short Stories

Timetripping.   New York, Doubleday, 1980.

OTHER PUBLICATIONS

Verse

Christs and Other Poems.   Binghamton, New York, Bellevue Press, 1978.

Other

Introduction to *Showcase,* edited by Roger Elwood.   New York, Harper, 1973.

"Fumfuttings and Prognostications," in *SFWA Bulletin* (Sea Cliff, New York), Fall 1974.

"The Science Fiction Novel," with Gardner Dozois, in *Fiction Writer's Handbook,* edited by Hallie and Whit Burnett.   New York, Harper, 1975.

Editor, *Wandering Stars: An Anthology of Jewish Fantasy and Science Fiction.*   New York, Harper, 1974; London, Woburn Press, 1975.

Editor, with Gardner Dozois, *Future Power.*   New York, Random House, 1976.

Editor, with George Zebrowski, *Faster Than Light: An Anthology of Stories about Interstellar Travel.*   New York, Harper, 1976.

Editor, *Immortal.*   New York, Harper, 1977.

Editor, with Gardner Dozois, *Aliens!*   New York, Pocket Books, 1980.

*

Manuscript Collection: Temple University, Philadelphia.

*   *   *

Jack Dann, a serious and somewhat intellectual writer, has specialized in speculative fiction that explores cultural perceptions and mindsets beyond the confines of ordinary human consciousness.

Starhiker, Dann's first novel, depicts the odyssey of a wandering minstrel named Bo, a dharma bum who yearns for a new way of life free from the benign despotism of earth's current rulers, the Hrau. Since earth is a second-rate space colony for these superior beings, Bo stows away on one of their craft in order to begin "star-hiking." His journey becomes increasingly inward as he crosses the boundaries of the imagination into worlds and cultures at the very core of the galaxy and the self. Influenced by Eastern religion, higher mathematics, and philosophers ranging from Leibniz to Buckminster Fuller, *Starhiker* presents an ambitious and sometimes perplexing itinerary. With its spare and yet poetic style, the novel attempts to move the reader to the frontiers of language and thought, sometimes becoming overly prolix, tangled, or abstract when the writing falters.

In his latest work-in-progress, *Amnesia,* Dann examines the problem of fringe religious groups and such phenomena as glossalia, or speaking in tongues. As the pressures of technology increase, certain people, called Screamers, develop a strange psychosis that allows them to communicate telepathically when they get together in a group. After his wife becomes a Screamer and is killed, a guilt-ridden painter decides to go along with a cult whose chief religious practice consists of "plugging into" recently dead Screamers and voyaging into the collective unconscious. This macabre story suggests the cultural and spiritual malaise of modern society through the private agonies of its main characters.

—Anthony Manousos

DARNAY, Arsen. American.

SCIENCE-FICTION PUBLICATIONS

Novels

A Hostage for Hinterland. New York, Ballantine, 1976.
The Karma Affair. New York, St. Martin's Press, 1978.
The Siege of Faltara. New York, Ace, 1978.

Uncollected Short Stories

"The Eastcoast Confinement," in *Galaxy* (New York), October 1974.
"Such Is Fate," in *If* (New York), October 1974.
"The Splendid Freedom," in *The Best from Galaxy 3,* edited by James Baen. New York, Award, 1975.
"The Politics of Patricide," in *Galaxy* (New York), March 1975.
"Gut in Peril," in *The Best from If 3,* edited by James Baen. New York, Award, 1976.
"Plutonium," in *Galaxy* (New York), March 1976.
"Salty's Sweep," in *Stellar 3,* edited by Judy-Lynn del Rey. New York, Ballantine, 1977.
"The Mildews of Mars," in *Analog* (New York), January 1977.
"The Phermonal Fountain," in *Galaxy* (New York), August 1977.
"The Tank and Its Wife," in *Analog* (New York), January 1978.
"The Golden Fleece," in *Fantastic* (New York), April 1978.
"The Man Who Drove to Work," in *Analog* (New York), July 1978.

OTHER PUBLICATIONS

Other

The Role of Nonpackaging Paper in Solid Waste Management 1966 to 1976, with William E. Franklin. Rockville, Maryland, Solid Waste Management Office, 1971.

Salvage Markets for Materials in Solid Wastes, with William E. Franklin. Washington, D.C., Environmental Protection Agency, 1972.
Recycling Assessment and Prospects for Success. Washington, D.C., Environmental Protection Agency, 1972.
"Through Innocent Eyes," in *Galaxy* (New York), January 1976.

*   *   *

Arsen Darnay works in two modes, serious and wryly humorous. "Gut in Peril" is an example of wry humor. It is an allegorical fantasy involving the pursuit by Lard Fatta Gut of the ultimate conquest of Mighty Matz, who lives in Kosher Castle. Gut conquers by devouring everything in his path, and is ultimately saved from destruction by Al Kasell, a fizzy foaming tablet in a goblet of cool water. Darnay's other attempts at humor include his stories of the adventures of Mandraid Friday, a "PSIchic surrogate," which is apparently a very sophisticated robot. In "The Mildews of Mars" Friday (named, as Darnay has him point out, after the 20th-century detective) uncovers a nefarious plot to destroy the world's supply of a new type of fuel. In "The Pheromal Fountain" Friday pursues criminals who have loosed a psychedelic substance, cleverly disguised as pigeon droppings, on an unsuspecting public. Whether or not Darnay's wry humor is enjoyable is a matter only the reader himself can decide.

Darnay's serious fiction is much more palatable. One common denominator pervades all his fiction: levitron, a substance which powers gravitron generators which provide anti-gravity. Levitron is made from helium. In most of Darnay's fiction, the worlds in which levitron exists are post-holocaust worlds. "The Eastcoast Confinement" is set in a not-so-distant post-holocaust world in which a religious government is in power in the United States. Some short stories are set far in the future: in "The Splendid Freedom" a young man of gypsy origin returns from a far-distant planet to encounter a disillusioning, overpopulated earth which sustains its economy by providing tourists with holographic presentations of "old" earth and by offering artificial sense-stimulations of all kinds. *A Hostage for Hinterland* works most heavily with the levitron-gravitron idea. In this novel the United States consists of a number of levitron-generated cities and tribes scattered around the remainder of old America, now returned to its natural state. The cities, luxurious and corrupt, ultimately are destroyed, when tribesmen cut the supply of helium and the towers literally fall. Led by Mical Bono, an innocent tribesman who has come into one of the cities, and by Regina, a princess-turned-priestess, some refugees do flee from the city shortly before it begins to collapse, and at the end of the book Bono and Regina begin the process of re-forming a society which will presumably be much like that existing today. *The Karma Affair* is a somewhat muddled novel whose plot centers around a scientist's development of a device for transmuting souls from body to body, generation to generation, an idea first explored in "Plutonium." The novel concerns the interaction of three Karma-bound souls as they pass through a series of transmutations in a period from World War II Germany through Nixonian Washington into an endless future.

The Siege of Faltara is an excellent adventure novel involving the attempts of a secret agent, Ronald Frederick, working for a galaxy-wide commercial "government," to infiltrate and destroy the ruling faction of the planet Fillippi, and in particular of the city of Faltara. This he ultimately does, with the help of two young, carefully drawn Fillippians, Jan Rigg and his sweetheart Sophie. Jan is the trainer of an absolutely delightful species of e-t beast, the tapfa: "It is a cross between a horse and a camel, but it has six legs, red eyes, and its fur is blue. To look at it you would think that it cannot walk, and it can't. It just hobbles about like a man on crutches. Yet it is the fastest land animal in Outermost. When aroused, its humps secrete a hormone, and the legs move so rapidly that they make a blurr." In the climactic scene, Frederick rides a tapfa in jousts with the ruling prince's six clones, defeats each of them, and sparks the revolution that will win him his freedom from personal bondage to his own galaxy-wide service.

In his article "Through Innocent Eyes" Darnay discusses at some length his journey from casual reader to professional writer of science fiction. The account is interesting, instructive, and humorous. Darnay's essay and his more serious fiction prove him to be a capable writer.

—Karren C. Edwards

DAVIDSON, Avram. American. Born in Yonkers, New York, 23 April 1923. Educated at New York University, 1940-42, 1947-48; Yeshiva University, New York, 1947-48; Pierce College, Canoga Park, California, 1950-51. Served in the United States Navy, 1941-45. Married Grania Kaiman (divorced); one son. Editor, *Fantasy and Science Fiction* magazine, New York, 1962-64. Recipient: Hugo Award, 1958; Ellery Queen Award, 1958; Mystery Writers of America Edgar Allan Poe Award, 1961; World Fantasy Award, 1979. Agent: E.J. Carnell Literary Agency, Rowneybury Bungalow, Sawbridgeworth, near Old Harlow, Essex CM20 2EX, England.

SCIENCE-FICTION PUBLICATIONS

Novels

Joyleg, with Ward Moore. New York, Pyramid, 1962.
Mutiny in Space. New York, Pyramid, 1964; London, White Lion, 1974.
Rogue Dragon. New York, Ace, 1965.
Rork! New York, Berkley, 1965; London, Rapp and Whiting, 1968.
Masters of the Maze. New York, Pyramid, 1965; London, White Lion, 1974.
The Enemy of My Enemy. New York, Berkley, 1966.
Clash of Star-Kings. New York, Ace, 1966.
The Kar-Chee Reign. New York, Ace, 1966.
The Island under the Earth. New York, Ace, 1969; London, May-flower, 1975.
The Phoenix and the Mirror; or, The Enigmatic Speculum. New York, Doubleday, 1969; London, Mayflower, 1975.
Peregrine: Primus. New York, Walker, 1971.
Ursus of Ultima Thule. New York, Avon, 1973.

Short Stories

Or All the Seas with Oysters. New York, Berkley, 1962; London, White Lion, 1976.
What Strange Stars and Skies. New York, Ace, 1965.
Strange Seas and Shores. New York, Doubleday, 1971.
The Enquiries of Dr. Eszterhazy. New York, Warner, 1975.
The Redward Edward Papers. New York, Doubleday, 1978.
The Best of Avram Davidson, edited by Michael Kurland. New York, Doubleday, 1979.

Uncollected Short Story

"The New Zombies," with Grania Davis, in *Interfaces,* edited by Ursula K. Le Guin and Virginia Kidd. New York, Ace, 1980.

OTHER PUBLICATIONS

Other

Editor, *Best from Fantasy and Science Fiction 12-14.* New York, Doubleday, 3 vols., 1963-65; London, Gollancz, 2 vols., 1966; Panther, 1 vol., 1967.

*   *   *

Avram Davidson is primarily a writer of fantasy and fantasy SF. His best stories are comic or ironic, and he is also a master of the mystery and weird fantasy and SF story. In structure if not in style

and thought, Davidson writes in the O. Henry tradition. But though his stories possess a familiar pattern of development, Davidson gives the impression of being unpredictable and eccentric. In part, this view may rest on Davidson's sometimes oblique method of developing his stories, deliberately omitting anticipated transitions so as to heighten contrasts and increase tension. It is a technique which a mystery writer may be expected to favor. It is particularly effective in his Hugo-winning story "Or All the Seas with Oysters," a tale based on the premise of the animated machine, in this case a red French racing bicycle, and the contrasting reactions of the two main characters to the discovery of such an alien being. The story has a finely developed sense of narrative irony, which is one of the characteristics of Davidson's best fiction.

A related type of science fantasy in Davidson's repertory is the comic tale rooted in Jewish humor. "The Golem" is a deservedly famous story in which Davidson combines comic formulas of traditional ethnic humor with an overlay of modern SF. The contrasting expectations of each tradition makes for the special comic sense of the story. Davidson also displays a fine talent for parody in such literary stories as "Author, Author," in which the reader is treated to some delicious echoes of the Asimov story of the same title as well as to a burlesque of the detective mystery/fantasy ending in a bittersweet reversal of poetic justice. Davidson takes his place as a writer of popular fantastic SF in the tradition that comes prominently to the surface with Poe and continues in the 20th century with Merritt, Lovecraft, and the *Weird Tales* and *Unknown* schools on the one hand, and such diverse writers of comic fantasy as Cabell and the Yiddish master Isaac Bashevis Singer on the other. In tone as well as intention, however, Davidson is closer to popular and even commerical pulp writers like L. Sprague de Camp and Fletcher Pratt than to either Poe or Cabell.

Davidson has also written many novels, some of which fall into familiar categories. There have been the SF pot boilers dealing with alien invaders, alternate universes, and other fantastic SF premises (*Masters of the Maze, Clash of Star-Kings, The Kar-Chee Reign*). Related to these are the space operas *Mutiny in Space, Rogue Dragon, Rork!,* and *The Enemy of My Enemy.* Of these, *Masters of the Maze* is clearly the most accomplished work. More successful have been the mock heroic fantasy *Peregrine: Primus* and the heroic romance fantasy *The Phoenix and the Mirror* (part of a projected series provisionally titled *Virgil Magus*). Both works are distinguished by a level of popular scholarship found in the Harold Shea stories of de Camp and Pratt. The wit and satire that animate the picaresque misadventures of Peregrine, bastard son of the king of Sapodilla, are absent from the more seriously intended *Phoenix and the Mirror,* and the latter romance suffers in consequence. Each, however, is notable for Davidson's attempt at introducing premises for romance that lie outside the familiar Christian traditions. Indeed, Davidson's invention and treatment are intended to be contrary to Christian-oriented legends, offering the reader an unspoken but also an unmistakable dissent from the tradition that has dominated heroic fantasy since the middle ages. It is too bad that it does not work.

Perhaps the most curious of all Davidson's fantasy prose fictions is *The Enquiries of Dr. Eszterhazy,* a collection of linked stories in which the master detective and doctor of everything, Engelbert Eszterhazy, stands in as the amused and amusing hero of a series of mysterious affairs taking place in and about the fictitious triune monarchy of Sythia-Panmonia-Transbalkania. Curiously, it seems that Davidson's experimental form of blending the internal narrative context of fantasy with the quite external tone and viewpoint of the implied modern narrator is responsible for the failure of the book to win either the popular support or the critical acclaim it deserves. The book seems destined to enjoy the status of underground classic, as a fantastic parody of the detective story that will serve to identify cognescenti among readers and those with a refined if still largely popular taste for the deliberately fantastic and artificial.

—Donald L. Lawler

DAVIDSON, Lionel. British. Born in Hull, Yorkshire, 31 March 1922. Served in the Royal Naval Submarine Service, 1941-46. Married Fay Jacobs in 1949; two sons. Free-lance magazine journalist and editor, 1946-59. Recipient: Crime Writers Association Golden Dagger, 1961, 1967, 1979. Agent: Curtis Brown Ltd., 1 Craven Hill, London W2 3EP, England.

SCIENCE-FICTION PUBLICATIONS

Novel

The Sun Chemist. London, Cape, and New York, Knopf, 1976.

OTHER PUBLICATIONS

Novels

The Night of Wenceslas. London, Gollancz, 1960; New York, Harper, 1961.
The Rose of Tibet. London, Gollancz, and New York, Harper, 1962.
A Long Way to Shiloh. London, Gollancz, 1966; as *The Menorah Men,* New York, Harper, 1966.
Making Good Again. London, Cape, and New York, Harper, 1968.
Smith's Gazelle. London, Cape, and New York, Knopf, 1971.
The Chelsea Murders. London, Cape, 1978; as *Murder Games,* New York, Coward McCann, 1978.

Other

Under Plum Lake (juvenile). London, Cape, and New York, Knopf, 1980.

*   *   *

Lionel Davidson is a distinguished novelist whose place in this book has to be defended rather than assumed. He is the unique holder of three Golden Dagger Awards for crime novels. Although his novels often contain important fantasy elements, that is to say, things not known to exist, these things are presented with unusual "scientific" care. If we take Delany's categories in his essay "About Five Thousand One Hundred and Seventy Five Words" as our guide, whereby SF concerns "events that have not happened," naturalistic fiction "events that could have happened," and fantasy "events that could not have happened," then we find several of Davidson's novels overlapping the contingent borders of all three categories. *The Rose of Tibet* looks like an updated Rider Haggard adventure in form and includes one or two actions that the harder-headed reader would say could not have happened, but it is presented as if it did happen, and it includes, for instance, a map reference to a secret pass to Tibet sufficiently plausible to have persuaded some Indian readers of its veracity. *Smith's Gazelle* concerns a small flock of a supposedly extinct gazelle that take shelter in a ravine on the Israeli border. The Six-Day War threatens the gazelle's survival. If Smith's Gazelle were, say, a Kraken or a small band of mutants, it would clearly belong to SF, but being neither wondrous nor threatening, its place seems rather to be in mainstream fiction. Does an improbability have to be outrageous before it belongs in SF or fantasy? Does not Davidson rather, with his superb mastery of formal realism, suggest one way of refining and subtilizing prose fantasy?

From the SF standpoint, *The Sun Chemist* has the strongest claim of Davidson's work to be included in the genre. It satisfies Asimov's proviso that SF should be about scientists, and concerns the rediscovery of an invention which—so the author assures us —really works. Also it is the brainchild of a real scientist, the great Zionist leader Chaim Weizmann. The idea of Israel laying hands on a source of relatively cheap energy, the humble potato, is an exciting one. Had the novel been published ten years ago, it would clearly have seemed SF. However, it was marketed as a thriller. A distinction should nevertheless be made between this novel, in which the science is presented seriously, and thrillers such as the Bond novels, in which the treatment of the science element is perfunctory. Here

the science, and the character of the real scientist, are of major interest, the hero being a historian engaged in editing some of Weizmann's correspondence.

—Michael J. Tolley

DAVIES, Hugh Sykes. British. Born in Wales in 1909. Educated at St. John's College, Cambridge, B.A. (honours) in classics 1930, in English 1931. Worked with the Ministry of Food during World War II. Fellow of St. John's College, 1933-76. Recipient: Le Bas Essay Prize, 1933.

SCIENCE-FICTION PUBLICATIONS

Novel

The Papers of Andrew Melmoth. London, Methuen, 1960; New York, Morrow, 1961.

OTHER PUBLICATIONS

Novels

Petron. London, Dent, 1935.
No Man Pursues. London, Lane, 1950.
Full Fathom Five. London, Lane, 1956.

Other

Realism in Drama. Cambridge, University Press, 1934.
Surrealism, with others, edited by Herbert Read. London, Faber, 1936; New York, Praeger, 1971.
The Poets and their Critics:
    1. *Chaucer to Collins.* London, Penguin, 1943; revised edition, London, Hutchinson, 1960.
    2. *Blake to Browning.* London, Hutchinson, 1962; revised edition, 1966.
Grammar Without Tears. London, Lane, 1951; New York, Day, 1953.
Trollope. London, Longman, 1960; in *British Writers and Their Work 9,* Lincoln, University of Nebraska Press, 1969.
Browning and the Modern Novel (lecture). Hull, University of Hull, 1962; Folcroft, Pennsylvania, Folcroft Editions, 1969.
Thomas De Quincey. London, Longman, 1964.

Editor, with George Watson, *The English Mind: Studies in the English Moralists Presented to Basil Willey.* Cambridge, University Press, 1964.

*   *   *

Apart from his literary criticism, Hugh Sykes Davies is the author of three unusual novels. The tiny extravaganza *Petron* is the first genuine surrealist novel in English, and specifically owes much to that branch of surrealism associated with the paintings of Salvador Dali. In particular, it is remarkable for elaborated, clearedged, and heavily symbolic landscapes, apparently baseless violence of incident, and a defiantly anti-logical sequence of events and episodes. Much later, *Full Fathom Five* reverses the approach. A Jamesian density of characterisation and point of view makes the "realistic" situation, actions, and motivation eventually more spectacular than any supernatural range of possibilities that might have been derived from the juxtaposition of research on an enigmatic line of ancient monoliths and modern salvage operations. Apart from these seductive and rejected possibilities, the novel has little right to be called science fiction.

The Papers of Andrew Melmoth becomes a genuine science-fiction study, authoritatively expressing the isolation of the genuinely scientific and analytical genius from the glib assumptions of society. *Full Fathom Five* involved a "criminal" with an appalling background, juxtaposed with scientists and salvage officers; the consciousness of the scientist Andrew Melmoth combines the traumatic ordeal of his childhood with genuine and meticulous scientific integrity. Melmoth's study of the relationship between rats and the refuse-systems of human cities convinces him that rodent intelligence, communication, and social organisation are much underestimated by humans. Later he becomes certain that the rats' view of the world is superior to both the emotional chaos spread by an individual neurotic "cultured" woman and the elegant intellectual and privileged distance maintained by other major characters, including "HSD," the narrator. Melmoth's decision to join the rats, though no surprise, is subtly and acutely developed, utilising an excellent portrait of a somewhat lonely rat-catcher. If there are still readers who believe that psychological acuity cannot mix well with scientific method—or science fiction—*The Papers of Andrew Melmoth* is an excellent corrective.

—Norman Talbot

DAVIES, L(eslie) P(urnell). Also writes as Leslie Vardre. British. Born in Crewe, Cheshire, 20 October 1914. Educated at Manchester College of Science and Technology, University of Manchester, qualified as optometrist 1939 (Fellow, British Optical Association). Served in the British Army Medical Corps in France, North Africa, and Italy, 1939-45. Married Winifred Tench in 1940. Dispensing pharmacist, Crewe, Cheshire, 1930-39; free-lance artist in Rome, 1945-46; postmaster, West Heath, Birmingham, 1946-56; Optician in private practice, and gift shop owner, Deganwy, North Wales, 1956-75. Since 1975, has lived in Tenerife. Agent: Howard Moorepark, 444 East 82nd Street, New York, New York 10028, U.S.A.; or, Carl Routledge, Charles Lavell Ltd., 176 Wardour Street, London W1V 3AA, England. Address: Apartment K-1, Edificio Alondra, El Botanico, Puerto de la Cruz, Tenerife, Canary Islands, Spain.

SCIENCE-FICTION PUBLICATIONS

Novels

The Paper Dolls. London, Jenkins, 1964; New York, Doubleday, 1966.
The Artificial Man. London, Jenkins, 1965; New York, Doubleday, 1967.
The Lampton Dreamers. London, Jenkins, 1966; New York, Doubleday, 1967.
Psychogeist. London, Jenkins, 1966; New York, Doubleday, 1967.
Twilight Journey. London, Jenkins, 1967; New York, Doubleday, 1968.
The Alien. London, Jenkins, 1968; New York, Doubleday, 1971; as *The Groundstar Conspiracy,* London, Sphere, 1972.
Dimension A. London, Jenkins, and New York, Doubleday, 1969.
Genesis Two. London, Jenkins, 1969; New York, Doubleday, 1970.
What Did I Do Tomorrow? London, Barrie and Jenkins, 1972; New York, Doubleday, 1973.

Uncollected Short Story

"End Game," in *The Tenth Ghost Book,* edited by Aidan Chambers. London, Barrie and Jenkins, 1974.

OTHER PUBLICATIONS

Novels

Man Out of Nowhere. London, Jenkins, 1965; as *Who Is Lewis Pindar?,* New York, Doubleday, 1966.
Tell It to the Dead (as Leslie Vardre). London, Long, 1966; as *The Reluctant Medium,* as L.P. Davies, New York, Doubleday, 1967.
The Nameless Ones (as Leslie Vardre). London, Long, 1967; as *A Grave Matter,* as L.P. Davies, New York, Doubleday, 1968.
Stranger to Town. London, Jenkins, and New York, Doubleday, 1969.
The White Room. New York, Doubleday, 1969; London, Barrie and Jenkins, 1970.
Adventure Holidays Ltd. New York, Doubleday, 1970.
The Shadow Before. New York, Doubleday, 1970; London, Barrie and Jenkins, 1971.
Give Me Back Myself. New York, Doubleday, 1971; London, Barrie and Jenkins, 1972.
The Silver Man (in Swedish). Stockholm, Wahlströms, 1972.
Assignment Abacus. London, Barrie and Jenkins, and New York, Doubleday, 1975.
Possession. London, Hale, and New York, Doubleday, 1976.
The Land of Leys. New York, Doubleday, 1979; London, Hale, 1980.

*   *   *

Combining suspense, mystery, and science fiction, L.P. Davies's hybrid novels reflect his own variegated background. His first novel, *The Paper Dolls,* was praised by Anthony Boucher (in *The New York Times*) as a "vigorous man-against-the-unknown adventure story, with touches of horror all the more effective for their being underplayed."

The Artificial Man begins with a quiet English village, a mild-mannered science-fiction writer, and pleasant townsfolk—all of which soon proves monstrously illusory. The placement of SF and suspense motifs within a commonplace setting lends itself easily to cinematic treatment, and the book was filmed as *Project X.*

The key to L.P. Davies's technique is that neither reader nor characters can ever be sure whether memories and dreams are portents, flashbacks, or messages from other worlds and times. The psychological, supernatural, and psychokinetic overlap, revealing unexpected horror and dangers lurking at the fringes of the mind. Ordinary events and situations are turned inside out to disclose terrible secrets. Because Davies plays fast-and-loose with SF and mystery conventions, a novel like *The Alien* that seems to involve extra-terrestrials actually turns out to be a whodunit, while an apparently gothic mystery like *Psychogeist* can be rationalized as speculative science fiction.

Since plot and suspense are everything in Davies's work, discussion of his novels must be sketchy lest their endings be given away. *Psychogeist* concerns a man whose bizarre dreams about the planet Andrida have frightening consequences. In *Dimension A* a young man follows his scientist uncle into a parallel world where the seemingly primitive Toparians and the mind-reading Varteds compete for survival—and have designs on earth. In *Genesis Two* an outing in the Lake Country becomes a terrifying voyage into a steamy tropical jungle, man's last refuge after technological disaster. All of these novels include murder and intrigue.

Although Davies is not a particularly stimulating or innovative writer, his fusions of SF and suspense result in competent thrillers that are as hard to put down as they are to take seriously.

—Anthony Manousos

DAVIS, (Horace) Chan(dler). American. Born in Ithaca, New York, 12 August 1926. Educated at Harvard University, Cambridge, Massachusetts, B.S. 1945, M.A. 1947, Ph.D. in mathematics 1950. Served in the United States Naval Reserve, 1944-46. Married Natalie Zemon in 1948; one son and two daughters. Instructor in mathematics, University of Michigan, Ann Arbor, 1950-54; Director of Experimental Research, Kenyon and Eckhardt advertising company, New York, 1955-57; Associate Editor, *Mathematical Reviews,* Providence, Rhode Island, 1958-61. Since 1962, Associate Professor, then Professor of Mathematics, University of Toronto. Served six month prison sentence for refusing to answer questions before the House Un-American Activities Committee, 1960. Member of the Institute for Advanced Study, Princeton, New Jersey, 1957-58. Agent: Virginia Kidd, Box 278, Milford, Pennsylvania 18337, U.S.A. Address: 52 Follis Avenue, Toronto M6G 1S3, Canada.

SCIENCE-FICTION PUBLICATIONS

Uncollected Short Stories

"To Still the Drums, " in *Astounding* (New York), October 1946.
"The Journey and the Goal," in *Astounding* (New York), May 1947.
"The Nightmare," in *A Treasury of Science Fiction,* edited by Groff Conklin. New York, Crown, 1948.
"The Aristocrat," in *Astounding* (New York), October 1949.
"Blind Play," in *Planet* (New York), May 1951.
"Share Our World," in *Astounding* (New York), August 1953.
"Letter to Ellen," in *Science Fiction Thinking Machines,* edited by Groff Conklin. New York, Vanguard Press, 1954.
"It Walks in Beauty," in *Star Science Fiction Stories 4,* edited by Frederik Pohl. New York, Ballantine, 1958.
"The Statistomat Pitch," in *Infinity* (New York) January 1958.
"Adrift on the Policy Level," in *Star Science Fiction Stories 5,* edited by Frederik Pohl. New York, Ballantine, 1959.
"Last Year's Grave Undug," in *Great Science Fiction by Scientists,* edited by Groff Conklin. New York, Macmillan, 1962.
"Hexamnion," in *Nova 1,* edited by Harry Harrison. New York, Delacorte Press, 1970.

Chan Davis comments:
There is so much that needs saying about our real and impending predicaments and ironies, and science fiction allows one to say it in ways less bogged down in the past—given this opportunity, why should the writer reject it by producing stories which merely ask the reader to suspend disbelief? One can comment by parables set on concocted planets; by extrapolations; or, most powerfully, by the "higher cautionary tale, " in which a potentiality in our own future is brought into relief by magnifying it. Not escape is offered, but engagement. Some suspension of disbelief is required, but not suspension of compassion, not suspension of curiosity or common sense. Let this note stand as introduction to the few stories I wrote in my youth and the many I wish yet to write.

*   *   *

Chan Davis has produced a small number of superior stories, beginning with "The Nightmare," one of the first post-Hiroshima science-fiction works to focus on the dangers and effects of nuclear war. Although he is a mathematician, most of his stories either explicitly or implicitly examine social themes. Other notable stories include "Adrift on the Policy Level," arguably the finest treatment of bureaucracy and the bureaucratic mind in all of science fiction, and "Letter to Ellen," which, because of a very superficial thematic resemblance to the earlier "Helen O'Loy" by Lester del Rey, never attained the classic stature due it.

—Martin H. Greenberg

DAVIS, Gerry. Address: c/o W.H. Allen, 44 Hill Street, London W1X 8LB, England.

SCIENCE-FICTION PUBLICATIONS

Novels with Kit Pedler

Mutant 59, The Plastic Eaters. London, Souvenir Press, 1971; New York, Viking Press, 1972.
Brainrack. London, Souvenir Press, 1974; New York, Pocket Books, 1975.
The Dynostar Menace. London, Souvenir Press, and New York, Scribner, 1975.

Novels (series: Doctor Who)

Doctor Who and the Cybermen. London, Target, 1974.
Doctor Who and the Tenth Planet. London, Target, 1976.
Doctor Who and the Tomb of the Cybermen. London, W.H. Allen, 1978.

OTHER PUBLICATIONS

Plays with Kit Pedler

Television Plays: *Doctor Who* series (3 plays); *Doomwatch* series (39 plays); *Galenforce.*

See the essay on Kit Pedler.

———————

de CAMP, L(yon) Sprague. American. Born in New York City, 27 November 1907. Educated at California Institute of Technology, Pasadena, B.S. in aeronautical engineering 1930; Massachusetts Institute of Technology, Cambridge, summer 1932; Stevens Institute of Technology, Hoboken, New Jersey, M.S. 1933. Served in the United States Naval Reserve, 1942-45: Lieutenant Commander. Married Catherine A. Crook in 1939; two sons. Instructor, Inventors Foundation Inc., New York, 1933-36; Principal of School of Inventing and Patenting, International Correspondence Schools, Scranton, Pennsylvania, 1936-37; Editor, Fowler-Becker Publishing Company, New York, 1937-38, and American Society of Mechanical Engineers, New York, 1938; Assistant Mechanical Engineer, Naval Aircraft Factory, Philadelphia, 1942; radio scriptwriter, *The Voice of America* series, 1948-56; publicity writer, Gray and Rogers, Philadelphia, 1956. Free-lance writer. Member of the Advisory Board, Society for the History of Technology. Recipient: International Fantasy Award, 1953; Tolkien Fantasy Award, 1976; Science Fiction Writers of America Grand Master Award, 1979. Address: 278 Hothorpe Lane, Villanova, Pennsylvania 19085, U.S.A.

SCIENCE-FICTION PUBLICATIONS

Novels (series: Conan; Viagens Interplanetarias)

Lest Darkness Fall. New York, Holt, 1941; London, Heinemann, 1955.
Divide and Rule. Reading, Pennsylvania, Fantasy Press, 1948.
Genus Homo, with P. Schuyler Miller. Reading, Pennsylvania, Fantasy Press, 1950.
Rogue Queen (Viagens). New York, Doubleday, 1951; London, Pinnacle, 1954.
Cosmic Manhunt (Viagens). New York, Ace, 1954; as *A Planet Called Krishna,* London, Compact, 1966; as *The Queen of Zamba,* New York, Dale, 1978.
The Return of Conan, with Björn Nyberg. New York, Gnome Press, 1957; as *Conan The Avenger,* New York, Lancer, 1968.
The Tower of Zanid (Viagens). New York, Avalon, 1958.

The Glory That Was. New York, Avalon, 1960.
The Search for Zei (Viagens). New York, Avalon, 1962; as *The Floating Continent,* London, Compact, 1966.
The Hand of Zei (Viagens). New York, Avalon, 1963.
Conan the Adventurer, with Robert E. Howard. New York, Lancer, 1966.
Conan the Warrior, with Robert E. Howard. New York, Lancer, 1967.
Conan the Conqueror, with Robert E. Howard. New York, Lancer, 1967.
Conan the Usurper, with Robert E. Howard. New York, Lancer, 1967.
Conan the Freebooter, with Robert E. Howard. New York, Lancer, 1968.
Conan the Wanderer, with Robert E. Howard and Lin Carter. New York, Lancer, 1968; London, Sphere, 1974.
Conan of the Isles, with Lin Carter. New York, Lancer, 1968.
Conan of Cimmeria, with Robert E. Howard and Lin Carter. New York, Lancer, 1969; London, Sphere, 1974.
Conan the Buccaneer, with Lin Carter. New York, Lancer, 1971.
Conan of Aquilonia (collection), with Lin Carter. New York, Ace, 1977; London, Sphere, 1978.
The Hostage of Zir. New York, Berkley, 1977.
The Great Fetish. New York, Doubleday, 1978.
Conan the Swordsman, with Lin Carter. New York, Bantam, 1978; London, Sphere, 1979.
Conan the Liberator, with Lin Carter. New York, Bantam, 1979.

Short Stories

The Wheels of If. Chicago, Shasta, 1948.
The Tritonian Ring and Other Pusadian Tales. New York, Twayne, 1953; London, Sphere, 1978.
The Continent Makers and Other Tales of the Viagens. New York, Twayne, 1953.
Sprague de Camp's New Anthology of Science Fiction, edited by H.J. Campbell. London, Panther, 1953.
Tales of Conan, with Robert E. Howard. New York, Gnome Press, 1955.
A Gun for Dinosaur and Other Imaginative Tales. New York, Doubleday, 1963.
Conan, with Robert E. Howard and Lin Carter. New York, Lancer, 1967; London, Sphere, 1974.
The Best of L. Sprague de Camp. New York, Doubleday, 1977.
The Purple Pterodactyls. Huntington Woods, Michigan, Phantasia Press, 1979.

OTHER PUBLICATIONS

Novels

The Incomplete Enchanter, with Fletcher Pratt. New York, Holt, 1941; London, Sphere, 1979.
Land of Unreason, with Fletcher Pratt. New York, Holt, 1942.
The Carnelian Cube, with Fletcher Pratt. New York, Gnome Press, 1948.
The Castle of Iron, with Fletcher Pratt. New York, Gnome Press, 1950.
The Undesired Princess. Los Angeles, Fantasy, 1951.
Solomon's Stone. New York, Avalon, 1957.
An Elephant for Aristotle. New York, Doubleday, 1958; London, Dobson, 1966.
Wall of Serpents, with Fletcher Pratt. New York, Avalon, 1960.
The Bronze God of Rhodes. New York, Doubleday, 1960.
The Dragon of the Ishtar Gate. New York, Doubleday, 1961.
The Arrows of Hercules. New York, Doubleday, 1965.
The Goblin Tower. New York, Pyramid, 1968; London, Sphere, 1979.
The Golden Wind. New York, Doubleday, 1969.
The Clocks of Iraz. New York, Pyramid, 1971.
The Fallible Fiend. New York, New American Library, 1973; London, Remploy, 1974.
The Compleat Enchanter: The Magical Adventures of Harold Shea (includes *The Incomplete Enchanter* and *The Castle of Iron*),

with Fletcher Pratt. New York, Doubleday, 1975; London, Sphere, 1979.
The Virgin and the Wheels. New York, Popular Library, 1976.

Short Stories

Tales from Gavagan's Bar, with Fletcher Pratt. New York, Twayne, 1953; expanded edition, Philadelphia, Owlswick Press, 1978.
The Reluctant Shaman and Other Fantastic Tales. New York, Pyramid, 1970.

Verse

Demons and Dinosaurs. Sauk City, Wisconsin, Arkham House, 1970.
Phantoms and Fancies. Baltimore, Mirage Press, 1972.

Other

Inventions and Their Management, with Alf K. Berle. Scranton, Pennsylvania, International Textbook Company, 1937; revised edition, as *Inventions, Patents, and Their Management,* Princeton, New Jersey, Van Nostrand, 1959.
The Evolution of Naval Weapons. Washington, D.C., Department of the Navy, 1947.
Lands Beyond, with Willy Ley. New York, Rinehart, 1952.
Science-Fiction Handbook: The Writing of Imaginative Fiction. New York, Hermitage House, 1953; revised edition, with Catherine Crook de Camp, Philadelphia, Owlswick Press, 1975.
Lost Continents: The Atlantis Theme in History, Science, and Literature. New York, Gnome Press, 1954.
Engines (juvenile). New York, Golden Press, 1959; revised edition, 1961, 1969.
The Heroic Age of American Invention. New York, Doubleday, 1961.
Man and Power (juvenile). New York, Golden Press, 1961.
Energy and Power (juvenile). New York, Golden Press, 1962.
The Ancient Engineers. New York, Doubleday, and London, Souvenir Press, 1963.
Ancient Ruins and Archaeology, with Catherine Crook de Camp. New York, Doubleday, 1964; London, Souvenir Press, 1965; as *Citadels of Mystery,* London, Fontana, 1972.
Elephant. New York, Pyramid, 1964.
Spirits, Stars, and Spells: The Profits and Perils of Magic, with Catherine Crook de Camp. New York, Canaveral Press, 1966.
The Story of Science in America, with Catherine Crook de Camp. New York, Scribner, 1967.
The Great Monkey Trial. New York, Doubleday, 1968.
The Conan Reader. Baltimore, Mirage Press, 1968.
The Day of the Dinosaur, with Catherine Crook de Camp. New York, Doubleday, 1968.
Darwin and His Great Discovery (juvenile), with Catherine Crook de Camp. New York, Macmillan, 1972.
Scribblings. Cambridge, Massachusetts, NESFA Press, 1972.
Great Cities of the Ancient World. New York, Doubleday, 1972.
"Up and Away from the School of Invention: The Development of a Science Fiction Writer," in *Foundation 4* (London), July 1973.
Lovecraft: A Biography. New York, Doubleday, 1975; London, New English Library, 1976.
Literary Swordsmen and Sorcerers: The Makers of Heroic Fantasy. Sauk City, Wisconsin, Arkham House, 1976.
Heroes and Hobgoblins. Forest Park, California, Heritage Press, 1978.

Editor, *Swords and Sorcery.* New York, Pyramid, 1963.
Editor, *The Spell of Seven.* New York, Pyramid, 1965.
Editor, *The Fantastic Swordsmen.* New York, Pyramid, 1967.
Editor, with George H. Scithers, *The Conan Swordbook.* Baltimore, Mirage Press, 1969.
Editor, *Warlocks and Warriors.* New York, Putnam, 1970.
Editor, with George H. Scithers, *The Conan Grimoire.* Baltimore, Mirage Press, 1971.
Editor, with Catherine Crook de Camp, *3000 Years of Fantasy and Science Fiction.* New York, Lothrop, 1972.

Editor, with Catherine Crook de Camp, *Tales Beyond Time.*   New York, Lothrop, 1973.

Editor, *To Quebec and the Stars,* by H.P. Lovecraft.   West Kingston, Rhode Island, Donald M. Grant, 1976.

*   *   *

L. Sprague de Camp's earliest SF story, "The Isolinguals," embodies an interesting concept (modern folk suddenly begin to speak and act like their remote ancestors), but is rather disjointed. Other very early stories are minor. However, by 1939 he had clearly hit his stride, first with "Divide and Rule" and, most especially, with his first novel, *Lest Darkness Fall.* Other worthwhile stories from this period include the Johnny Black series, about an intelligent talking bear (this series ran out quickly because, as de Camp has explained, in the first story Johnny Black saved the world; by the fourth story, he merely saved his boss's job; there was nowhere to go); "The Merman," a scientifically rigorous account of the problems faced by a man who is able to breathe water; and "The Gnarly Man" about an immortal Neanderthal found working in a circus sideshow.

Lest Darkness Fall is one of de Camp's most famous works, now a classic. It achieved the distinction, unusual for pulp material of the period, of being published as a book by a large publisher. *Lest Darkness Fall,* far superior to the usual run of 1939 pulp fiction, is essentially a realistic *Connecticut Yankee,* in which a modern man finds himself in the real 6th century (not that of legend, as Twain used) and takes it upon himself to prevent the Dark Ages. He succeeds in a manner which will surprise most readers. De Camp apparently did a great deal of thinking about how such a man would fit in and make his way in the society of post-Imperial Rome, and what 20th-century marvels he would actually be able to produce in such a milieu (it starts with double-entry book-keeping). The characterization in the novel is also far superior to that in most SF of the period. Though his characters don't involve the reader intensely, they are not one-dimensional stereotypes; it is possible to sit back and watch, and believe that these are real people.

Typical features of de Camp's best fiction, as demonstrated in *Lest Darkness Fall,* are intelligent conception and development, and an enormously readable style. The intent in most of his fiction seems to be to provide light but not insubstantial entertainment, and he succeeds at a high level of sophistication. Most of his works also display a lively wit, which at times leads him to somewhat formless stories filled with jokes for their own sake, rather in the manner of P.G. Wodehouse or Thorne Smith (whom de Camp acknowledges as a major influence).

Humor is particularly evident in his collaborations with Fletcher Pratt, especially the Harold Shea series. Of these, *The Incomplete Enchanter* is probably de Camp's best-known work. The hero is a psychologist who has found a way to transport himself into the worlds of myth. In "The Roaring Trumpet" he encounters the Norse gods. In "The Mathematics of Magic" he battles the enchanters of Spenser's *Faerie Queene.* Again, the development is rigorously logical, but the premises are impossible. Much of the humor results from the incongruity. Other stories in this series include *The Castle of Iron* (the world of *Orlando Furioso*), "The Wall of Serpents" (the *Kalevala*), and "The Green Magician" (the Ireland of Cuchulain).

Other collaborations with Pratt are less successful. The Gavagan's Bar series are in the manner of Lord Dunsany's Jorkens, with each tale told in a bar, usually by one of a regular round of customers, but the stories tend to stop just as the fantastic premise is presented. Thus they are exactly as good as the idea, which makes them uneven and rather anecdotal.

De Camp ceased writing during World War II, and published very little fiction until "The Animal Cracker Plot" in 1949. This, while rather slight in itself, was the first of the Viagens Interplanetarias series, which constitute the largest body of his science fiction. The common background involves a Brazilian-dominated world, which causes Portuguese to be the language of space travel. The stories vary widely in complexity and intent. "Calories," for instance, makes a specific scientific point, that meat-eating is far more fuel efficient than vegetarianism. Thus the hero is able to escape across a glacier from vegetarian foes because he is able to carry more food than they are. *Cosmic Manhunt* and *The Hand of Zei* are swashbuckling adventures, something of an attempt to do an

Edgar Rice Burroughs type of story plausibly. *Rogue Queen,* the most notable of the group, involves a rigid matriarchy patterned after bees. It is one of the earliest SF stories in which sex roles play any important part, though a modern feminist would hardly be pleased. All these stories move briskly and give a good idea of how the various societies work without stopping to lecture the reader at length. There are countless small details which add versimilitude.

De Camp continued to write science fiction until about 1960. Outstanding stories from this period include "A Thing of Custom," "Aristotle and the Gun," and "A Gun for a Dinosaur." However, he devoted most of his efforts during this period, and in the following decade, to historical novels and scientific non-fiction. He returned to fantasy with his renewed involvement in the Conan series of Robert E. Howard, and in the 1960's he edited the entire series. As a result Howard became one of the most popular authors in English. Credit must be given to de Camp for creating the sword and sorcery boom of the period. During this time he completed more Howard fragments, sometimes in collaboration with Lin Carter, and wrote new Conan stories. These pleased some fans and displeased others, possibly because de Camp, a far more rational and experienced person, was never able to match Howard's psychotic intensity or narrowness of outlook. His own sword and sorcery fiction, *The Tritonian Ring, The Goblin Tower,* and *The Clocks of Iraz,* are more sophisticated, with frequent humorous touches.

In the 1970's de Camp got away from Conan and wrote another Viagens novel, *The Hostage of Zir,* and the "Willy Newbury" series, about a banker whose humdrum life is constantly being interrupted by supernatural occurrences. The best of these make skillful use of autobiographical material. The most successful work of this period is *The Great Fetish,* enormously readable, full of fascinating situations, and enlivened with satire. For example, the schoolteacher hero, before his wife runs off with a man he must then hunt down and kill because his society expects nothing less from him, is in trouble with the authorities for *not* teaching evolution. The heresy is that the world is a lost colony of Earth. This turns out to be true.

In de Camp's fiction human foibles and pretenses are prominently displayed, but rational, sensible types always prevail. If there is any message, it is that reason is the only effective way to solve problems. A de Camp hero never gets anywhere until he starts using his head. Then the results surprise everyone, particularly the reader.

—Darrell Schweitzer

---

deFORD, Miriam Allen.   American.   Born in Philadelphia, Pennsylvania, 21 August 1888. Educated at Wellesley College, Massachusetts; Temple University, Philadelphia, A.B. 1911; University of Pennsylvania, Philadelphia. Married 1) Armistead Collier in 1915 (divorced, 1921); 2) Maynard Shipley in 1921 (died, 1934). Feature writer, Philadelphia *North American,* 1906-11; editorial staff member, Associated Advertising, 1913-14; Editor of house organ, Pompeiian Oil Company, Baltimore, 1917; Claims Adjuster, 1918-23; Staff Correspondent, Federated Press, 1921-56; Editor, Federal Writers Project, 1936-39; Staff Correspondent, *Labor's Daily,* California, 1956-58; Contributing Editor, *The Humanist.* Lecturer and Member of the Board, San Francisco Senior Citizens Center, 1952-58. Member of the Board, Mystery Writers of America, 1960, 1963. Recipient: Committee for Economic Development Essay Prize, 1958; Mystery Writers of America Edgar Allan Poe Award, 1961. *Died in 1975.*

SCIENCE-FICTION PUBLICATIONS

Short Stories

Xenogenesis.   New York, Ballantine, 1969.
Elsewhere, Elsewhen, Elsehow: Collected Stories.   New York, Walker, 1971.

Uncollected Short Stories

"Vooremp, Spy," in *Infinity 3*, edited by Robert Hoskins. New York, Lancer, 1972.

"Lone Warrior," in *Two Views of Wonder*, edited by Thomas N. Scortia and Chelsea Quinn Yarbro. New York, Ballantine, 1973.

"A Way Out," in *The Alien Condition*, edited by Stephen Goldin. New York, Ballantine, 1973.

"5,000,000 A.D.," in *Future City*, edited by Roger Elwood. New York, Simon and Schuster, 1973.

"Uraguyen and I," with Juanita Coulson, in *Cassandra Rising*, edited by Alice Laurance. New York, Doubleday, 1978.

OTHER PUBLICATIONS

Novel

Shaken with the Wind. New York, Doubleday, 1942.

Verse

Penultimates. New York, Fine Editions Press, 1962.

Other

Cicero as Revealed in His Letters. Girard, Kansas, Haldeman Julius, 1925.
The Life and Poems of Catullus. Girard, Kansas, Haldeman Julius, 1925.
The Augustan Poets of Rome. Girard, Kansas, Haldeman Julius, 1925.
The Facts about Fascism. Girard, Kansas, Haldeman Julius, 1926.
Latin Self Taught. Girard, Kansas, Haldeman Julius, 1926.
The Truth about Mussolini. Girard, Kansas, Haldeman Julius, 1926.
Love Children: A Book of Illustrious Illegitimates. New York, Dial Press, 1931.
Children of Sun. New York, League to Support Poetry, 1939.
Who Was When? A Dictionary of Contemporaries. New York, Wilson, 1940; revised edition, 1950; revised edition, with Joan S. Jackson, 1976.
They Were San Franciscans. Caldwell, Idaho, Caxton, 1941; revised edition, 1947.
The Meaning of All Common Given Names. Girard, Kansas, Haldeman Julius, 1943.
The Facts about Basic English. Girard, Kansas, Haldeman Julius, 1944.
Facts You Should Know about California. Girard, Kansas, Haldeman Julius, 1945.
Psychologist Unretired: The Life Pattern of Lillien J. Martin. Palo Alto, California, Stanford University Press, 1948.
Uphill All the Way: The Life of Maynard Shipley. Yellow Springs, Ohio, Antioch Press, 1956.
The Overbury Affair: The Murder That Rocked the Court of James I. Philadelphia, Chilton, 1960.
Stone Walls: Prisons from Fetters to Furloughs. Philadelphia, Chilton, 1962.
Murderers Sane and Mad: Case Histories in the Motivation and Rationale of Murder. London and New York, Abelard Schuman, 1965.
Thomas Moore. New York, Twayne, 1967.
The Real Bonnie and Clyde. New York, Ace, 1968.
The Old Worker Comes Back. San Francisco, Old Age Counselling Center, n.d.
On Being Concerned: The Vanguard Years of Carl and Laura Brannin. Privately printed, 1969.
The Real Ma Barker. New York, Ace, 1970.

Editor, *Space, Time and Crime.* New York, Paperback Library, 1964.
Editor, *The Theme Is Murder: An Anthology of Mysteries.* New York, Abelard Schuman, 1967.

*   *   *

Miriam Allen deFord, better known for her mystery stories, wrote about 30 science-fiction stories in a span of 30 years. The best collection of her work is *Xenogenesis* which includes two of her best stories, "The Children" and "The Absolutely Perfect Murder." Both stories illustrate the skill deFord possessed when writing about time travel. "The Children" tells of a many-thousand-year-old experiment with time travel and the effect it has on the children of the experimenter. In "The Absolutely Perfect Murder" a harried husband of the future decides to murder his nagging wife, and after much thought comes up with a perfect murder plan: the husband will take advantage of the Government's new time-machine travel program and go into the past with the intent to murder his wife's father—so she never could be conceived. All goes according to plan, but deFord manages a brilliant twist at the story's conclusion. *Elsewhere, Elsewhen, Elsehow* is inferior to her first collection, but it includes one of her best-known stories, "The Monster." DeFord will be remembered for her story-telling ability and her early development of the themes of post-holocaust society, sex roles, and time paradoxes, and the fusion of the crime story and science fiction.

—George Kelley

DELANY, Samuel R(ay). American. Born in New York City, 1 April 1942. Educated at the Bronx High School of Science, New York; City College of New York (Poetry Editor, *The Promethean*), 1960, 1962-63. Married the poet Marilyn Hacker in 1961 (separated, 1974); one daughter. Butler Professor of English, State University of New York, Buffalo, 1975; Fellow, Center for Twentieth Century Studies, University of Wisconsin, Milwaukee, 1977. Recipient: Nebula Award, 1966, 1967 (two awards), 1969; Hugo Award, 1970. Address: c/o Bantam Books Inc., 666 Fifth Avenue, New York, New York 10019, U.S.A.

SCIENCE-FICTION PUBLICATIONS

Novels (series: Fall of the Towers)

The Jewels of Aptor. New York, Ace, 1962; revised edition, Ace, and London, Gollancz, 1968.
The Fall of the Towers. London, Sphere, 1971; New York, Ace, 1972.
   Captives of the Flame. New York, Ace, 1963; revised edition, as *Out of the Dead City*, London, Sphere, 1968; Ace, 1977.
   The Towers of Toron. New York, Ace, 1964; London, Sphere, 1968.
   City of a Thousand Suns. New York, Ace, 1965; London, Sphere, 1969.
The Ballad of Beta-2. New York, Ace, 1965.
Empire Star. New York, Ace, 1966.
Babel-17. New York, Ace, 1966; London, Gollancz, 1967.
The Einstein Intersection. New York, Ace, 1967; London, Gollancz, 1968.
Nova. New York, Doubleday, 1968; London, Gollancz, 1969.
Dhalgren. New York, Bantam, 1975.
Triton. New York, Bantam, 1976; London, Corgi, 1977.
The Ballad of Beta-2, and Empire Star. London, Sphere, 1977.
Empire: A Visual Novel, illustrated by Howard V. Chaykin. New York, Berkley, 1978.

Short Stories

Driftglass: 10 Tales of Speculative Fiction. New York, Doubleday, 1971; London, Gollancz, 1978.
Tales of Nevèryon. New York, Bantam, 1979.

OTHER PUBLICATIONS

Novel

The Tides of Lust. New York, Lancer, 1973; Manchester, Savoy, 1979.

Other

"About Five Thousand One Hundred and Seventy Five Words," in *Extrapolation* (Wooster, Ohio), May 1969.
"The Profession of Science Fiction 8: Shadows, Part 1," in *Foundation 6* (London) May 1974.
"When Is a Paradox Not a Paradox?" and "The Profession of Science Fiction 8: Shadows, Part 2," in *Foundation 7-8* (London), March 1975.
The Jewel-Hinged Jaw: Notes on the Language of Science Fiction. Elizabethtown, New York, Dragon Press, 1977.
The American Shore: Meditations on a Tale of Science Fiction by Thomas M. Disch—"Angouleme." Elizabethtown, New York, Dragon Press, 1978.
Heavenly Breakfast: An Essay on the Winter of Love (memoir). New York, Bantam, 1979.

Editor, with Marilyn Hacker, *Quark 1-4.* New York, Paperback Library, 4 vols., 1970-71.
Editor, *Nebula Award Winners 13.* New York, Harper, 1980.

*   *   *

Samuel R. Delany has been delighting, and occasionally outraging, SF readers for close to two decades and yet he is still perceived as one of the young turks of the genre. One of a group including Ursula K. Le Guin, Joanna Russ, Roger Zelazny, and, in England, Brian Aldiss, J.G. Ballard, and Michael Moorcock, who turned the field over in the early 1960's, he shares with those writers a common dedication to the *art* of writing *and* the popular energy and ideology of science fiction. Delany, for example, is widely read in contemporary poetry and structuralist criticism yet he also contends that SF offers wider literary possibilities to the serious writer than any other area. Indeed, Delany has said that he wrote his first novel, *The Jewels of Aptor,* because, even at 19, he felt he could write a more complex and human story than those he was reading at the time. It's a good first novel, still enjoyable today, and it contains most of the literary obsessions he has explored in every work since: problems of communication and community; new kinds of sexual/loving/family relationships; the artist as social outsider (the Romantic vision of the artist as criminal); cultural interactions and the exploration of human social possibilities these allow; mythic structures in the imagination.

In *The Jewels of Aptor,* as in all his works up to *Nova,* the archetypal quest serves as a narrative structure, in this case under the aegis of a White Goddess lifted right out of Robert Graves's poetic theology. His basic characters appear here, too, especially the youthful questor who is seeking both knowledge of self and a valid purpose in life. And although the post-holocaust world is a fairly standard one in SF, the young writer at least attempts to fill in his social and cultural background in a believable manner.

The Fall of the Towers trilogy represents a double-barrelled attempt to write a good SF anti-war novel and to create a complex future society. Though only partially successful, the trilogy demonstrates Delany's commitment to making complete "new worlds" in his SF and, in the ruminations of the social historian, Rolth Catham, his concern to explain the cultural and historical background of his future societies. In the books that follow, he develops narrative strategies for integrating vast amounts of such information into his fast-paced plots while deepening their ideological content. Indeed, since his questors are always seeking information rather than simple material rewards, their ruminations and encounters with other thinkers are necessary aspects of their adventures.

The first major turning point in Delany's development as a writer is the small but delightfully "multiplex" (the whole novel is an explanation of the term) *Empire Star.* Actually written after the award-winning *Babel-17,* whose explorations of the interface between language and perceived reality were fairly new in SF, it pushes the concepts of language and reality through a series of Borgesian changes in a delightfully light manner. It is a significant work because its structure *is* its plot, a story which turns in upon itself like a moebius strip as the narrative point of view remains a central character who is simply a point of view in a fiction which insists that in order to comprehend your self and your place in "this vast multiplex universe" you must be able to perceive both from as many points of view as possible. A circular narrative of novella length which "contains" an epic novel, *Empire Star* marks a consolidation of Delany's growing writing talents.

His next two novels represent further growth and consolidations. In *The Einstein Intersection* he explores first-person narrative in the context of a search for the mythic ground to personality. In *Nova,* one of the finest and most multiplex space operas ever written, he pushes the stylistic pyrotechnics of Alfred Bester's *The Stars My Destination* even further out; transforms the myths of Prometheus and Indra's Freeing of the Waters into SF terms; recreates something of the feel of Greek tragedy in the epic battle for control of the galaxy between Lorq Von Ray and the Reds; subtly and dramatically explores character interaction on a variety of social levels; creates one of the most complete, intelligent, and multiplex renderings of a future galactic society in all SF, including a serious investigation of political and economic power and an intellectually satisfying history of that society; makes an engaging and intriguing comparative study of two types of the artist; and writes one of SF's bolder self-conscious fictions, a novel containing an apprentice novelist who not only explains many of the narrative patterns it uses (like the Tarot/Grail Quest) but, it appears, eventually "writes" the book we are reading. It's a superb accomplishment, and one on which to rest a reputation, but Delany has never stopped exploring his medium.

At the time *Nova* appeared and he was beginning his five-year struggle with what was to become *Dhalgren,* Delany gave a lecture on SF in which he stated, contradicting a major dictum of pulp science fiction—a "fiction of ideas" only—that "put in opposition to 'style,' there is no such thing as 'content'." In the same essay and elsewhere since then, he has also attempted to discover the particular structures of science-fiction discourse. Two books of criticism demonstrate the care with which he has explored the theory and practice of SF writing.

Dhalgren is not only huge, it *is* SF, but it's also a novel concerned to explore the minutiae of a perceived life. Delany provides a series of phenomenological close-ups of the perceptual surround which the lost city of Bellona and its varied inhabitants offer the kid, another of his questing artist figures, perhaps the final version. Although difficult and in many ways pretentious, *Dhalgren* rewards the careful reader with a vast array of marvelously realized characters, intense personal relationships, explorations of the nature of art and reality, and much else. Simply in terms of its explorations of style and form it is an important work, even if one finally dislikes it.

Triton is much more obviously a work of science fiction, but it's also one which could only have been written by the author of *Dhalgren.* A much shorter book, it nevertheless packs an incredible amount of speculation and information into its pages. It contains one of SF's most convincing future societies and is full of immensely provocative sexual, psycho/social, philosophical, and artistic speculations. In it Delany for the first time deliberately creates a protagonist too rigid, too locked into a particular system of perceptions, to be capable of adapting to the processes by which his civilization exists, and in showing us why he offers both a profound psychological portrait and a complex critique of our own society and what Michel Foucault would call its "episteme."

What is so exciting about Delany's whole *oeuvre,* including the stories I've not even mentioned, is the way they constantly reveal an artist in a creative struggle with the conventional limitations of his chosen genre. Delany has enlarged the possibilities of SF, and for that alone, if not for the superb entertainment he has provided along the way, he deserves our praise and thanks.

—Douglas Barbour

del REY, Lester.   *See* **FAIRMAN, Paul W.**

---

del REY, Lester (Ramon Felipe San Juan Mario Silvio Enrico Alvarez-del Rey).   Also writes as Edson McCann; Philip St. John; Erik Van Lhin; Kenneth Wright. American. Born in Clydesdale, Minnesota, 2 June 1915. Educated at George Washington University, Washington, D.C., 1931-33. Married the writer and editor Judy-Lynn Benjamin (fourth marriage) in 1971. Sheet metal worker, McDonnell Aircraft Corporation, St. Louis, 1942-44; author's agent, Scott Meredith Literary Agency, New York, 1947-50; Editor, *Space Science Fiction,* London, 1952-53; Publisher, as R. Alvarez, 1952, and Editor, as Philip St. John, 1952-53, *Science Fiction Adventures;* Associate Editor, as John Vincent, 1953, and as Cameron Hull, with Harry Harrison, 1953, *Fantasy Fiction;* Editor, as Wade Kaempfert, *Rocket Stories,* 1953; Managing Editor, *International Science Fiction,* 1968; Managing Editor, 1968-69, and Features Editor, 1969-74, *Galaxy* and *If;* Editor, *Worlds of Fantasy,* 1968. Fantasy Editor, 1975-77, and since 1977, Editor, Del Rey Books (Ballantine Books). Since 1974, Book Reviewer, *Analog.* Taught fantasy fiction, New York University, 1972-73; Editor, Garland Press science-fiction series, 1975. Recipient: Boys' Clubs of America Science Fiction Award, 1953. Guest of Honor, World Science Fiction Convention, 1967. Agent: Scott Meredith Literary Agency, 845 Third Avenue, New York, New York 10022. Address: 160 West End Avenue, New York, New York 10023, U.S.A.

SCIENCE-FICTION PUBLICATIONS

Novels

Marooned on Mars (juvenile).   Philadelphia, Winston, 1952; London, Hutchinson, 1953.
Rocket Jockey (juvenile; as Philip St. John).   Philadelphia, Winston, 1952; as *Rocket Pilot,* London, Hutchinson, 1955.
The Mysterious Planet (juvenile; as Kenneth Wright).   Philadelphia, Winston, 1953.
Attack from Atlantis (juvenile).   Philadelphia, Winston, 1953.
Battle on Mercury (juvenile; as Eric Van Lhin).   Philadelphia, Winston, 1953.
Step to the Stars (juvenile).   Philadelphia, Winston, 1954; London, Hutchinson, 1956.
Rockets to Nowhere (juvenile; as Philip St. John).   Philadelphia, Winston, 1954.
Preferred Risk (as Edson McCann, with Frederik Pohl).   New York, Simon and Schuster, 1955.
Mission to the Moon (juvenile).   Philadelphia, Winston, and London, Hutchinson, 1956.
Police Your Planet (as Eric Van Lhin).   New York, Avalon, 1956; revised edition, as Lester del Rey, New York, Ballantine, 1975; London, New English Library, 1978.
Nerves.   New York, Ballantine, 1956; revised edition, 1976.
Day of the Giants.   New York, Avalon, 1959.
Moon of Mutiny (juvenile).   New York, Holt Rinehart, 1961; London, Faber, 1963.
The Eleventh Commandment.   Evanston, Illinois, Regency, 1962; revised edition, 1970.
The Sky Is Falling, Badge of Infamy.   New York, Galaxy, 1963; *Badge of Infamy* published London, Dobson, 1976.
Outpost of Jupiter (juvenile).   New York, Holt Rinehart, 1963; London, Gollancz, 1964.
The Runaway Robot (juvenile), with Paul W. Fairman.   Philadelphia, Westminster Press, 1964; London, Gollancz, 1967.
Rocket from Infinity (juvenile).   New York, Holt Rinehart, 1966; London, Faber, 1967.
The Scheme of Things, with Paul W. Fairman.   New York, Belmont, 1966.

The Infinite Worlds of Maybe.   New York, Holt Rinehart, 1966; London, Faber, 1968.
Siege Perilous, with Paul W. Fairman.   New York, Lancer, 1966; as *The Man Without a Planet,* 1969.
Tunnel Through Time (juvenile), with Paul W. Fairman.   Philadelphia, Westminster Press, 1966.
Prisoners of Space (juvenile), with Paul W. Fairman.   Philadelphia, Westminster Press, 1968.
Pstalemate.   New York, Putnam, 1971; London, Gollancz, 1972.
Weeping May Tarry, with Raymond F. Jones.   Los Angeles, Pinnacle, 1978.

Short Stories

...and Some Were Human.   Philadelphia, Prime Press, 1948.
Robots and Changelings.   New York, Ballantine, 1958.
Mortals and Monsters.   New York, Ballantine, 1965; London, Tandem, 1967.
Gods and Golems.   New York, Ballantine, 1973.
Early del Rey.   New York, Doubleday, 1975.
The Best of Lester del Rey.   New York, Ballantine, 1978.

OTHER PUBLICATIONS

Other

It's Your Atomic Age.   New York, Abelard Press, 1951.
A Pirate Flag for Monterey (juvenile).   Philadelphia, Winston, 1952.
Rockets Through Space (juvenile).   Philadelphia, Winston, 1957; revised edition, 1960.
The Cave of Spears (juvenile).   New York, Knopf, 1957.
Space Flight (juvenile).   New York, Golden Press, 1959.
The Mysterious Earth [*Sea, Sky*].   Philadelphia, Chilton, 3 vols., 1960-64.
Rocks and What They Tell Us (juvenile).   Racine, Wisconsin, Whitman, 1961.
"Flying Saucers in Fact and Fiction," in *Flying Saucers in Fact and Fiction,* edited by Hans S. Santesson.   New York, Lancer, 1968.
"A Game of Futures: An Introduction," in *Children of Infinity,* edited by Roger Elwood.   New York, Watts, 1973.
"Forty Years of C.L. Moore," in *The Best of C.L. Moore.*   New York, Doubleday, 1975.
The World of Science Fiction 1926-1976: The History of a Subculture.   New York, Ballantine, 1979.

Editor, with Cecile Matschat and Carl Carmer, *The Year after Tomorrow.*   Philadelphia, Winston, 1954.
Editor, *Best Science Fiction Stories of the Year.*   New York, Dutton, 5 vols., 1972-76.

*   *   *

The key to understanding the achievement of Lester del Rey is to place his work and standards in the context of his times as a writer and the formative influence of the ubiquitous John W. Campbell. Del Rey produced much of his early work in his spare time. Once established as a writer he created vast volumes of material and clearly thought of authorship as a craft rather than as a vocation. His standard is the orderly, well-told tale of the magazine writer, stamped by commercial necessity. Del Rey's writing balances commercial motives, excellence in the context of his times, and an ongoing faith in science.

Del Rey's early period can be dated 1938-54, from his first published short story, "The Faithful," to his first adult novel, *The Sky Is Falling.* For the first ten years he submitted *only* to Campbell and published at least 38 stories. They contain the detailed imagining Campbell liked and narrative briskness for an editor who wanted a story but paid by the word. The two best-known stories from this period are "Helen O'Loy" and *Nerves.* "Helen O'Loy" is a witty tale about bachelor room-mates, a robot-repair wizard and a doctor, who improve a robot by adding emotions. Helen then patterns her emotions after television soap operas and falls for Dave, the repairman, who eventually marries her. The story is filled with touches of futuristic imagination. For example, Phil, the doctor, is called to give counterhormones to a wealthy old lady's son and the servant with whom he is infatuated. In the plot proper del Rey generates humour by juxtaposing soap opera romanticism and the robot: "Helen's technique may have lacked polish, but it had enthusiasm, as he found when he tried to stop her from kissing him. She had learned fast and furiously—also, Helen was powered by an atomotor." *Nerves* is more dated in scientific terms but it has an exciting plot about a blowout in a nuclear plant. Though radiation burns are erroneously described, *Nerves* is suspenseful, and touches like a motor needle for surgical sutures and sterilization by supersonic sound provide excellent decoration. The story sets up good characterisation within the limits of its form, stressing an elder doctor-younger doctor relationship. The title focuses the theme of control under stress.

The early stories cover many topics. Some are fantasies, such as "Hereafter, Inc." in which a hypocritical puritan refuses to accept that he is in heaven because the people he secretly hoped were damned sinners are with him. Others are nostalgic, such as "Though Dreamers Die" in which Jorgen, the last man, realises that the robots who have helped him travel through space after a plague on Earth will carry on man's dreams and aspirations. Some deal with hard science, such as "Habit" about a rocket race won by slingshotting around Jupiter to gain velocity.

After 1952 del Rey became a regular writer of juvenile SF, a form well suited to his abilities. He generally features a hero just turning 18 who ventures into space to help build a satellite station, explore the Moon, or investigate a strange planet. True to form for such tales the boy usually stows away on a rocket ship and takes some foolish initiative, creating trouble for everyone until he extricates himself by a clever manoeuvre. Rather than the projection of any powerful ethical goal or cautionary extrapolation del Rey's ability lies in telling a good story, so it follows that these juveniles are very successful. They are laden with presumptions about women, the merit of individual initiative, and the benefits of American democracy, but this reflects del Rey's innate beliefs and his times rather than propaganda intent.

The Sky Is Falling is a sport among del Rey's works. It describes an alternate universe where magic dominates but is in danger because the sky and its zodiacal symbols are cracking and falling. The hero, mistaken for his engineer uncle, is revivified (after a fatal accident on Earth) to fix the sky. The detail of this novel is fascinating: individuals' energies wax and wane with their planets and the scientific method is shown to resemble that of the magicians. It sparkles with imaginative exuberance in its denial of conventional reality (when pieces of sky crush people) and in zany turns of plot.

The two most interesting novels from del Rey's later work are *Police Your Planet* and *Siege Perilous*. The former deals with a frontier Mars riddled with poverty and crime where the police extort mountains of graft and people live in terror. Bruce Gordon, a reporter exiled from Earth for exposing the truth, struggles for survival and eventually the liberation of this vividly awful world. Del Rey is really painting a subtle picture of urban decay on Earth, where violence is the law. The novel is awkwardly imagined in places (air is held in Marsport by a fabric-covered dome) but it has power, energy, and much lightly buried compassion. On the other hand, *Siege Perilous* is a novel which swings from a Martian invasion horror story to the wildly ridiculous. America's orbiting satellite, a scientific station and weapons base, is invaded by Martians who fear man will invade Mars and intend to destroy Earth first. The three humans who evade the initial gas attack eventually outwit the Martians. This basic story is riotously decorated by the Martians' knowledge of Earth having come exclusively from television broadcasts. 26 invasion-of-Mars movies have motivated the attack which is carried out in a mixture of Wild West, Ronald Coleman, Chicago gangster, and grade-D science-fiction styles. Earth triumphs in an old-fashioned shootout while the heroine awaits torture. Del Rey has great fun with the clichés and patterns. Yet even while letting go in this action romp he manages to insert interesting minor ideas such as the satellite refining of pure crystalline metals and the balancing of the space station by pumping a water ballast.

In a long, steady career ranging from 1938 to the present, Lester del Rey has become most skillful in his craft. Like many writers of his period he fills out imaginative detail around solid plots to capture the excitement of the scientific universe. His weaknesses lie in the sentimentality of his message stories and the impression that

he does not write from a coherent or socially critical view of the universe. A virtuoso craftsman whose love is the story itself, he may not meet recent expectations as a "committed" writer and may therefore lack the "heart" which lifts a writer from the good to the great.

—Peter A. Brigg

DENT, Lester. Also wrote as Kenneth Robeson; Tim Ryan. American. Born in La Plata, Missouri, 12 October 1904. Studied telegraphy at Chillicothe Business College, Missouri, 1923-24. Married Norma Gerling in 1925. Taught at Chillicothe Business College, 1924; telegrapher, Western Union, Carrolton, Missouri, 1924, and Empire Oil and Gas Company, Ponca City, Oklahoma, 1925; telegrapher, then teletype operator, Associated Press, Tulsa, 1926; journalist for Tulsa *World*; house-writer for Dell, publisher, 1930; Free-lance writer from 1930, and also dairy farmer and aerial photographer. *Died 11 March 1959.*

SCIENCE-FICTION PUBLICATIONS

Novels as Kenneth Robeson (series: Doc Savage in all books)

Quest of the Spider. New York, Street and Smith, 1933.
The Man of Bronze. New York, Street and Smith, 1933.
The Land of Terror. New York, Street and Smith, 1933.
The Thousand-Headed Man. New York, Bantam, 1964
Meteor Menace. New York, Bantam, 1964.
The Polar Treasure. New York, Bantam, 1965.
Brand of the Werewolf. New York, Bantam, 1965.
The Lost Oasis. New York, Bantam, 1965.
The Monsters. New York, Bantam, 1965.
The Land of Terror. New York, Bantam, and London, Tandem, 1965.
Quest of Qui. London, Bantam, 1965; New York, Bantam, 1966.
The Mystic Mullah. New York, Bantam, 1965; London, Bantam, 1966.
The Phantom City. New York, Bantam, 1966.
Fear Cay. New York, Bantam, 1966.
Land of Always-Night. New York, Bantam, 1966.
The Fantastic Island. New York, Bantam, 1966; London, Bantam, 1967.
The Spook Legion. New York, Bantam, 1967.
The Red Skull. New York, Bantam, 1967.
The Sargasso Ogre. New York, Bantam, 1967.
Pirate of the Pacific. New York, Bantam, 1967.
The Secret of the Sky. New York, Bantam, 1967; London, Bantam, 1968.
The Czar of Fear. New York, Bantam, 1968.
Fortress of Solitude. New York, Bantam, 1968.
The Green Eagle. New York, Bantam, 1968.
Death in Silver. New York, Bantam, 1968.
The Mystery under the Sea. New York, Bantam, 1968; London, Bantam, 1969.
The Deadly Dwarf. New York, Bantam, 1968.
The Other World. New York, Bantam, 1968; London, Bantam, 1969.
The Flaming Falcons. New York, Bantam, 1968; London, Bantam, 1969.
The Annihilist. New York, Bantam, 1968; London, Bantan, 1969.
Hex. London, Bantam, 1968; New York, Bantam, 1969.
The Squeaking Goblin. New York, Bantam, 1969.
Mad Eyes. New York, Bantam, 1969.
The Terror in the Navy. New York, Bantam, 1969.
Dust of Death. New York, Bantam, 1969.
Resurrection Day. New York, Bantam, 1969.
Red Snow. New York, Bantam, 1969.

World's Fair Goblin. New York, Bantam, 1969.
The Dagger in the Sky. New York, Bantam, 1969.
Merchants of Disaster. New York, Bantam, 1969.
The Gold Ogre. New York, Bantam, 1969.
The Man Who Shook the Earth. New York, Bantam, 1969.
The Sea Magician. New York, Bantam, 1970.
The Midas Man. New York, Bantam, 1970.
The Feathered Octopus. New York, Bantam, 1970.
The Sea Angel. New York, Bantam, 1970.
Devil on the Moon. New York, Bantam, 1970.
The Vanisher. New York, Bantam, 1970.
The Mental Wizard. New York, Bantam, 1970.
He Could Stop the World. New York, Bantam, 1970.
The Golden Peril. New York, Bantam, 1970.
The Giggling Ghosts. New York, Bantam, 1970.
Poison Island. New York, Bantam, 1971.
The Munitions Master. New York, Bantam, 1971.
The Yellow Cloud. New York, Bantam, 1971.
The Majii. New York, Bantam, 1971.
The Living Fire Menace. New York, Bantam, 1971.
The Pirate's Ghost. New York, Bantam, 1971.
The Submarine Mystery. New York, Bantam, 1971.
The Motion Menace. New York, Bantam, 1971.
The Green Death New York, Bantam, 1971.
Mad Mesa. New York, Bantam, 1972.
The Freckled Shark. New York, Bantam, 1972.
The Mystery of the Snow. New York, Bantam, 1972.
Spook Hole. New York, Bantam, 1972.
The Mental Monster. New York, Bantam, 1973.
The Seven Agate Devils. New York, Bantam, 1973.
The Derrick Devil. New York, Bantam, 1973.
Land of Fear. New York, Bantam, 1973.
The South Pole Terror. New York, Bantam, 1974.
The Crimson Serpent. New York, Bantam, 1974.
The Devil Ghengis. New York, Bantam, 1974.
The King Maker. New York, Bantam, 1975.
The Stone Man. New York, Bantam, 1976.
The Evil Gnome. New York, Bantam, 1976.
The Red Terrors. New York, Bantam, 1976.
The Mountain Monster. New York, Bantam, 1976.
The Boss of Terror. New York, Bantam, 1976.
The Angry Ghost. New York, Bantam, 1977.
The Spotted Men. New York, Bantam, 1977.
The Roar Devil. New York, Bantam, 1977.
The Magic Island. New York, Bantam, 1977.
The Flying Goblin. New York, Bantam, 1977.
The Purple Dragon. New York, Bantam, 1978.
The Awful Egg. New York, Bantam, 1978.
Tunnel Terror. New York, Bantam, 1979.
The Hate Genius. New York, Bantam, 1979.
The Red Spider. New York, Bantam, 1979.

Uncollected Novels as Kenneth Robeson (series: Doc Savage in all works; all works appeared in *Doc Savage* magazine, New York)

"The Men Vanished," December 1940; "The All-White Elf," March 1941; "The Golden Man," April 1941; "The Pink Lady," May 1941; "Mystery Island," August 1941; "Birds of Death," October 1941; "The Invisible Box Monsters," November 1941; "Peril in the North," December, 1941; "Men of Fear," February 1942; "The Too-Wise Owl," March, 1942; "Pirate Isle," May 1942; "The Speaking Stone," June 1942; "The Man Who Fell Up," July 1942; "The Three Wild Men," August 1942; "The Fiery Menace," September 1942; "The Laugh of Death," October 1942; "They Died Twice," November 1942; "The Devil's Black Rock," December 1942; "The Time Terror," January 1943; "Waves of Death," February 1943; "The Black, Black Witch," March 1943; "The King Of Terror," April 1943; "The Talking Devil," May 1943; "The Running Skeletons," June 1943; "Mystery on Happy Bones," July 1943; "Hell Below," September 1943; "The Goblins," October 1943; "The Secret of the Su," November 1943; "The Spook of Grandpa Eben," December 1943; "According to Plan of a One-Eyed Mystic," January 1944; "Death Had Yellow Eyes," February 1944; "The Derelict of Skull Shoal," March 1944; "The Whisker of Hercules," April 1944; "The Three Devils," May 1944; "The Pharaoh's Ghost," June

1944; "The Man Who Was Scared," July 1944; "The Shape of Terror," August 1944; "Weird Valley," September 1944; "Jiu San," October 1944; "Satan Black," November 1944; "The Lost Giant," December 1944; "Violent Night," January 1945; "Strange Fish," February 1945; "Ten Ton Snakes," March 1945; "Cargo Unknown," April 1945; "Rock Sinister," May 1945; "The Terrible Stork," June 1945; "King Joe Cay," July 1945; "The Wee Ones," August 1945; "Terror Takes Seven," September 1945; "The Thing That Pursued," October 1945; "Trouble on Parade," November 1945; "The Screaming Man," December 1945; "Measure for a Coffin," January 1946; "Se-Pah-Poo," February 1946; "Terror and the Lonely Widow," March 1946; "Five Fathoms Dead," April 1946; "Death Is a Round Black Spot," May 1946; "Colors for Murder," June 1946; "The Exploding Lake," September 1946; "The Devil Is Jones," November 1946; "Danger Lies East," March 1947; "No Light to Die By," May 1947; "The Monkey Suit," July 1947; "Let's Kill Ames," September 1947; "Once Over Lightly," November 1947; "I Died Yesterday," January 1948; "The Pure Evil," March 1948; "Terror Wears No Shoes," May 1948; "The Angry Canary," July 1948; "The Swooning Lady," September 1948; "The Green Master," Winter 1949; "Return from Cormoral," Spring 1949; "Up from Earth's Center," Summer 1949.

OTHER PUBLICATIONS

Novels

Dead at the Take-Off. New York, Doubleday, 1946; London, Cassell, 1948; as *High Stakes,* New York, Ace, 1953.
Lady to Kill. New York, Doubleday, 1946; London, Cassell, 1949.
Lady Afraid. New York, Doubleday, 1948; London, Cassell, 1950.
Lady So Silent. London, Cassell, 1951.
Cry at Dusk. New York, Fawcett, 1952; London, Fawcett, 1959.
Lady in Peril. New York, Ace, 1959.
Hades and Hocus Pocus, edited by Robert Weinberg. Chicago, Pulp Press, 1979.

Play

Screenplay: *Bowery Buckaroos (*as Tim Ryan), with Edmond Seward, 1947.

*

Bibliography: "The Secret Kenneth Robesons" and "The Duende Doc Savage Index" by Will Murray, in *Duende 2* (North Quincy, Massachusetts), 1977.

*   *   *

Science fiction, as it manifested itself in the early pulp magazines, did not always appear in SF publications, or even in works which were primarily of that genre. Quite often, the various single-character magazines such as *The Shadow* and *Doc Savage* featured interesting science fiction in the guise of adventure and detective fiction. The novels of Kenneth Robeson fall into this catagory. Kenneth Robeson was a house pseudonym used by Street and Smith in their *Doc Savage* and *Avenger* magazines between 1933 and 1949. It masked a number of writers, including Ryerson Johnson, Harold A. Davis, William G. Bogart, Alan Hathway, Paul Ernst, and Emile C. Tepperman. The Robeson byline, however, was most frequently used by, and identified with, Lester Dent, the creator and author of most of the Doc Savage novels.

The Doc Savage novels were not predominately science fiction except, perhaps, in their premise of Doc Savage himself, a man raised and trained by a host of world experts to be a physical and mental superman, to whom fantastic abilities are attributed.

With the exception of space and time travel, the Doc Savage adventures employed most of the themes common to early SF: mind transference (*Mad Mesa*); teleportation (*The Vanisher*); robots (*The Seven Agate Devils*); anti-gravity (*The Secret of the Sky*); biological mutation (*The Monsters*); invisibility (*The Spook Legion*); force fields (*The Motion Menace*); raising the dead (*Resurrection Day*); and destructive rays (*The Deadly Dwarf*). Structurally, the stories are formula. Doc Savage contends with criminals or power seekers who possess and attempt to pervert new technological discoveries toward their own ends.

Lost worlds were a popular Doc Savage theme. *The Land of Terror* and "The Time Terror" postulated pockets of dinosaurs in remote areas. *The Mental Wizard* and "The Green Master" concerned lost Egyptian colonies in South America. There were submarine cities (*The Red Terrors*) and subterranean worlds (*Land of Always-Night*). *The Other World* combined the subterranean civilization with surviving dinosaurs. Many adventures employed myths and legends as their bases. The Fountain of Youth and Aladdin's Cave are the goals in *Fear Cay* and *The Majii*. Lester Dent often created his own folk myths to lend color to his antagonists in *The Feathered Octopus* and *The Squeaking Goblin*. Doc Savage, the "Man of Bronze," is himself a mythic character who possesses all the prerequisites of a culture hero—wisdom, great strength, and near-magical scientific powers. He is a champion who defends humanity against the menace of technology in evil hands. His enemies, appropriately enough, are evocative of man's superstitious fear of the unknown (in this case, scientific advancement) and call themselves by such titles as The Sargasso Ogre, The Roar Devil and The Purple Dragon. The mythological theme is carried as far as a traditional descent into Hell by the hero in the final Doc Savage novel, "Up from Earth's Center," a fantasy.

Although primarily juvenile in its appeal, Lester Dent's work combines a fertility of invention with a vividness of imagination seldom surpassed. His best efforts include *Meteor Menace, The Thousand-Headed Man, Land of Always-Night,* and *Resurrection Day.* The later Doc Savage stories are considerably more mature in theme and tone. Among these, "The Whisker of Hercules," *The Red Spider* and "Up from Earth's Center" are exceptional.

—Will Murray

DERLETH, August (William). Also wrote as Stephen Grendon; Tally Mason. American. Born in Sauk City, Wisconsin, 24 February 1909. Educated at St. Aloysius School; Sauk City High School; University of Wisconsin, Madison, B.A. 1930. Married Sandra Winters in 1953 (divorced, 1959); one daughter and one son. Editor, Fawcett Publications, Minneapolis, 1930-31; Editor, *The Midwesterner,* Madison, 1931; Lecturer in American Regional Literature, University of Wisconsin, 1939-43. Owner and Co-Founder (with Donald Wandrei, 1939-42), Arkham House Publishers (including the imprints Mycroft and Moran, and Stanton and Lee), Sauk City, 1939-71. Editor *Mind Magic,* 1931; Literary Editor and Columnist, Madison *Capital Times,* 1941-71; Editor, *The Arkham Sampler,* 1948-49, *Hawk and Whippoorwill,* 1960-63, and *The Arkham Collector,* 1967-71, all Sauk City. Recipient: Guggenheim Fellowship, 1938; *Scholastic* award, 1958; Midland Authors award, for poetry, 1965; Ann Radcliffe Award, 1967. *Died 4 July 1971.*

SCIENCE-FICTION PUBLICATIONS

Short Stories

Harrigan's File. Sauk City, Wisconsin, Arkham House, 1975.

OTHER PUBLICATIONS

Novels

Murder Stalks the Wakely Family. New York, Loring and Mussey, 1934; as *Death Stalks the Wakely Family*, London, Newnes, 1937.
The Man on All Fours. New York, Loring and Mussey, 1934; London, Newnes, 1936.

Three Who Died. New York, Loring and Mussey, 1935.
Sign of Fear. New York, Loring and Mussey, 1935; London, Newnes, 1936.
Still Is the Summer Night. New York, Scribner, 1937.
Wind over Wisconsin. New York, Scribner, 1938.
Restless Is the River. New York, Scribner, 1939.
Sentence Deferred. New York, Scribner, 1939; London, Heinemann, 1940.
The Narracong Riddle. New York, Scribner, 1940.
Bright Journey. New York, Scribner, 1940.
Evening in Spring. New York, Scribner, 1941.
Sweet Genevieve. New York, Scribner, 1942.
The Seven Who Waited. New York, Scribner, 1943; London, Muller, 1945.
Shadow of Night. New York, Scribner, 1943.
Mischief in the Lane. New York, Scribner, 1944; London, Muller, 1948.
No Future for Luana. New York, Scribner, 1945; London, Muller, 1948.
The Shield of the Valiant. New York, Scribner, 1945.
The Lurker on the Threshold. Sauk City, Wisconsin, Arkham House, 1945; London, Gollancz, 1948.
Fell Purpose. New York, Arcadia House, 1953.
Death by Design. New York, Arcadia House, 1953.
The House on the Mound. New York, Duell, 1958.
The Hills Stand Watch. New York, Duell, 1960.
The Trail of Cthulhu. Sauk City, Wisconsin, Arkham House, 1962; London, Spearman, 1974.
The Shadow in the Glass. New York, Duell, 1963.
Mr. Fairlie's Final Journey. Sauk City, Wisconsin, Mycroft and Moran, 1968.
The Wind Leans West. New York, Candlelight Press, 1969.

Short Stories

Place of Hawks. New York, Loring and Mussey, 1935.
Any Day Now. Chicago, Normandie House, 1938.
Country Growth. New York, Scribner, 1940.
Someone in the Dark. Sauk City, Wisconsin, Arkham House, 1941.
Something Near. Sauk City, Wisconsin, Arkham House, 1945.
"In Re: Sherlock Holmes"—The Adventures of Solar Pons. Sauk City, Wisconsin, Mycroft and Moran, 1945; as *Regarding Sherlock Holmes,* New York, Pinnacle, 1974; as *The Adventures of Solar Pons,* London, Robson, 1975.
Sac Prairie People. Sauk City, Wisconsin, Stanton and Lee, 1948.
Not Long for This World. Sauk City, Wisconsin, Arkham House, 1948.
Three Problems for Solar Pons. Sauk City, Wisconsin, Mycroft and Moran, 1952.
The House of Moonlight. Iowa City, Prairie Press, 1953.
The Survivor and Others, with H.P. Lovecraft. Sauk City, Wisconsin, Arkham House, 1957.
The Return of Solar Pons. Sauk City, Wisconsin, Mycroft and Moran, 1958.
The Mask of Cthulhu. Sauk City, Wisconsin, Arkham House, 1958; London, Consul, 1961.
The Reminiscences of Solar Pons. Sauk City, Wisconsin, Mycroft and Moran, 1961.
Wisconsin in Their Bones. New York, Duell, 1961.
Lonesome Places. Sauk City, Wisconsin, Arkham House, 1962.
Mr. George and Other Odd Persons (as Stephen Grendon). Sauk City, Wisconsin, Arkham House, 1963; as *When Graveyards Yawn,* London, Tandem, 1965.
The Casebook of Solar Pons. Sauk City, Wisconsin, Mycroft and Moran, 1965.
Praed Street Papers. New York, Candlelight Press, 1965.
The Adventure of the Orient Express. New York, Candlelight Press, 1965; London Panther, 1975.
Colonel Markesan and Less Pleasant People, with Mark Schorer. Sauk City, Wisconsin, Arkham House, 1966.
The Adventure of the Unique Dickensians. Sauk City, Wisconsin, Mycroft and Moran, 1968.
A Praed Street Dossier. Sauk City, Wisconsin, Mycroft and Moran, 1968.

The Shadow Out of Time and Other Tales of Horror, with H.P. Lovecraft. London, Gollancz, 1968.
A House above Cuzco. New York, Candlelight Press, 1969.
The Chronicles of Solar Pons. Sauk City, Wisconsin, Mycroft and Moran, 1973; London, Robson, 1975.
The Watchers Out of Time and Others, with H.P. Lovecraft. Sauk City, Wisconsin, Arkham House, 1974.
Dwellers in Darkness. Sauk City, Wisconsin, Arkham House, 1976.

Verse

To Remember, with *Salute Before Dawn*, by Albert Edward Clements. Hartland Four Corners, Vermont, Windsor, 1931.
Hawk on the Wind. Philadelphia, Ritten House, 1938.
Elegy: On a Flake of Snow. Muscatine, Iowa, Prairie Press, 1939.
Man Track Here. Philadelphia, Ritten House, 1939.
Here on a Darkling Plain. Philadelphia, Ritten House, 1941.
Wind in the Elms. Philadelphia, Ritten House, 1941.
Rind of Earth. Prairie City, Illinois, Decker Press, 1942.
Selected Poems. Prairie City, Illinois, Decker Press, 1944.
And You, Thoreau! New York, New Directions, 1944.
The Edge of Night. Prairie City, Illinois, Decker Press, 1945.
Habitant of Dusk: A Garland for Cassandra. Boston, Walden Press, 1946.
Rendezvous in a Landscape. New York, Fine Editions Press, 1952.
Psyche. Iowa City, Prairie Press, 1953.
Country Poems. Iowa City, Prairie Press, 1956.
Elegy: On the Umbral Moon. Forest Park, Illinois, Acorn Press, 1957.
West of Morning. Francestown, New Hampshire, Golden Quill Press, 1960.
This Wound. Iowa City, Prairie Press, 1962.
Country Places. Iowa City, Prairie Press, 1965.
The Only Place We Live. Iowa City, Prairie Press, 1966.
By Owl Light. Iowa City, Prairie Press, 1967.
Collected Poems, 1937-1967. New York, Candlelight Press, 1967.
Caitlin. Iowa City, Prairie Press, 1969.
The Landscape of the Heart. Iowa City, Prairie Press, 1970.
Listening to the Wind. New York, Candlelight Press, 1971.
Last Light. New York, Candlelight Press, 1971.

Recordings: *Psyche: A Sequence of Love Lyrics*, Cuca, 1960; *Sugar Bush by Moonlight and Other Poems of Man and Nature*, Cuca, 1962; *Caitlin*, Cuca, 1971.

Other

The Heritage of Sauk City. Sauk City, Wisconsin, Pioneer Press, 1931.
Consider Your Verdict: Ten Coroner's Cases for You to Solve (as Tally Mason). New York, Stackpole, 1937.
Atmosphere of Houses. Muscatine, Iowa, Prairie Press, 1939.
Still Small Voice: The Biography of Zona Gale. New York, Appleton Century, 1940.
Village Year: A Sac Prairie Journal. New York, Coward McCann, 1941.
Wisconsin Regional Literature. Privately printed, 1941; revised edition, 1942.
The Wisconsin: River of a Thousand Isles. New York, Farrar and Rinehart, 1942.
H.P.L.: A Memoir (on H.P. Lovecraft). New York, Abramson, 1945.
Oliver, The Wayward Owl (juvenile). Sauk City, Wisconsin, Stanton and Lee, 1945.
Writing Fiction. Boston, The Writer, 1946.
Village Daybook: A Sac Prairie Journal. Chicago, Pelligrini and Cudahy, 1947.
A Boy's Way: Poems (juvenile). Sauk City, Wisconsin, Stanton and Lee, 1947.
Sauk County: A Centennial History. Baraboo, Wisconsin, Sauk County Centennial Committee, 1948.
It's a Boy's World: Poems (juvenile). Sauk City, Wisconsin, Stanton and Lee, 1948.

Wisconsin Earth: A Sac Prairie Sampler (selection). Sauk City, Wisconsin, Stanton and Lee, 1948.
The Milwaukee Road: Its First 100 Years. New York, Creative Age Press, 1948.
The Country of the Hawk (juvenile). New York, Aladdin, 1952.
The Captive Island (juvenile). New York, Aladdin, 1952.
"Contemporary Science Fiction," in *College English* (Urbana, Illinois), January 1952.
Empire of Fur: Trading in the Lake Superior Region (juvenile). New York, Aladdin, 1953.
Land of Gray Gold: Lead Mining in Wisconsin (juvenile). New York, Aladdin, 1954.
Father Marquette and the Great Rivers (juvenile). New York, Farrar Straus, 1955; London, Burns and Oates, 1956.
Land of Sky-Blue Waters (juvenile). New York, Aladdin, 1955.
St. Ignatius and the Company of Jesus (juvenile). New York, Farrar Straus, and London, Burns and Oates, 1957.
Columbus and the New World (juvenile). New York, Farrar Straus, and London, Burns and Oates, 1956.
The Moon Tenders (juvenile). New York, Duell, 1958.
The Mill Creek Irregulars (juvenile). New York, Duell, 1959.
Wilbur, The Trusting Whippoorwill (juvenile). Sauk City, Wisconsin, Stanton and Lee, 1959.
Arkham House: The First Twenty Years—1939-1959. Sauk City, Wisconsin, Arkham House, 1959.
Some Notes on H.P. Lovecraft. Sauk City, Wisconsin, Arkham House, 1959.
The Pinkertons Ride Again (juvenile). New York, Duell, 1960.
The Ghost of Black Hawk Island (juvenile). New York, Duell, 1961.
Walden West (autobiography). New York, Duell, 1961.
Sweet Land of Michigan (juvenile). New York, Duell, 1962.
Concord Rebel: A Life of Henry D. Thoreau. Philadelphia, Chilton, 1962.
Countryman's Journal. New York, Duell, 1963.
The Tent Show Summer (juvenile). New York, Duell, 1963.
Three Literary Men: A Memoir of Sinclair Lewis, Sherwood Anderson, Edgar Lee Masters. New York, Candlelight Press, 1963.
The Irregulars Strike Again (juvenile). New York, Duell, 1964.
Forest Orphans (juvenile) New York, Ernest, 1964; as *Mr. Conservation*, Park Falls, Wisconsin, MacGregor, 1971.
Wisconsin Country: A Sac Prairie Journal. New York, Candlelight Press, 1965.
The House by the River (juvenile). New York, Duell, 1965.
The Watcher on the Heights (juvenile). New York, Duell, 1966.
Wisconsin (juvenile). New York, Coward McCann, 1967.
The Beast in Holger's Woods (juvenile). New York, Crowell, 1968.
Vincennes: Portal to the West. Englewood Cliffs, New Jersey, Prentice Hall, 1968.
Walden Pond: Homage to Thoreau. Iowa City, Prairie Press, 1968.
Wisconsin Murders. Sauk City, Wisconsin, Mycroft and Moran, 1968.
The Wisconsin Valley New York, Teachers College Press, 1969.
Thirty Years of Arkham House: A History and a Bibliography 1939-1969. Sauk City, Wisconsin, Arkham House, 1970.
The Three Straw Men (juvenile). New York, Candlelight Press, 1970.
Return to Walden West. New York, Candlelight Press, 1970.
Love Letters to Caitlin. New York, Candlelight Press, 1971.
Emerson, Our Contemporary. New York, Crowell Collier Press, 1971.

Editor, with R.E. Larsson, *Poetry Out of Wisconsin*. New York, Harrison, 1937.
Editor, with Donald Wandrei, *The Outsider and Others*, by H.P. Lovecraft. Sauk City, Wisconsin, Arkham House, 1939.
Editor, with Donald Wandrei, *Beyond the Wall of Sleep*, by H.P. Lovecraft. Sauk City, Wisconsin, Arkham House, 1943.
Editor, with Donald Wandrei, *Marginalia*, by H.P. Lovecraft. Sauk City, Wisconsin, Arkham House, 1944.
Editor, *Sleep No More: Twenty Masterpieces of Horror for the*

Connoisseur. New York, Farrar and Rinehart, 1944; abridged edition, London, Panther, 1964.

Editor, *The Best Supernatural Stories of H.P. Lovecraft.* Cleveland, World, 1945; revised edition, as *The Dunwich Horror and Others,* Sauk City, Wisconsin, Arkham House, 1963.

Editor, *Who Knocks? Twenty Masterpieces of the Spectral for the Connoisseur.* New York, Rinehart, 1946; abridged edition, London, Panther, 1964.

Editor, *The Night Side: Masterpieces of the Strange and Terrible.* New York, Rinehart, 1947; London, New English Library, 1966.

Editor, *The Sleeping and the Dead.* Chicago, Pelligrini and Cudahy, 1947; as *The Sleeping and the Dead* and *The Unquiet Grave,* London, New English Library, 2 vols., 1963-64.

Editor, *Dark of the Moon: Poems of Fantasy and the Macabre.* Sauk City, Wisconsin, Arkham House, 1947.

Editor, *Strange Ports of Call.* New York, Pelligrini and Cudahy, 1948.

Editor, *The Other Side of the Moon.* New York, Pelligrini and Cudahy, 1949; abridged edition, London, Grayson, 1956.

Editor, *Something about Cats and Other Pieces,* by H.P. Lovecraft. Sauk City, Wisconsin, Arkham House, 1949.

Editor, *Beyond Time and Space.* New York, Pelligrini and Cudahy, 1950.

Editor, *Far Boundaries: 20 Science-Fiction Stories.* New York, Pelligrini and Cudahy, 1951; London, Consul, 1965.

Editor, *The Outer Reaches: Favorite Science-Fiction Tales Chosen by Their Authors.* New York, Pelligrini and Cudahy, 1951; as *The Outer Reaches* and *The Time of Infinity,* London, Consul, 2 vols., 1963.

Editor, *Beachheads in Space.* New York, Pelligrini and Cudahy, 1952; London, Weidenfeld and Nicolson, 1954; abridged edition, as *From Other Worlds,* London, New English Library, 1964.

Editor, *Night's Yawning Peal: A Ghostly Company.* Sauk City, Wisconsin, Arkham House, 1952; London, Consul, 1965.

Editor, *Worlds of Tomorrow: Science Fiction with a Difference.* New York, Pelligrini and Cudahy, 1953; London Weidenfeld and Nicolson, 1954; abridged edition, as *New Worlds for Old,* London, New English Library, 1963.

Editor, *Time to Come: Science-Fiction Stories of Tomorrow.* New York, Farrar Straus, 1954; London, Consul, 1963.

Editor, *Portals of Tomorrow: The Best Tales of Science Fiction and Other Fantasy.* New York, Rinehart, 1954; London, Cassell, 1956.

Editor, *The Shuttered Room and Other Pieces by H.P. Lovecraft and Divers Hands.* Sauk City, Wisconsin, Arkham House, 1959.

Editor, *Fire and Sleet and Candlelight: New Poems of the Macabre.* Sauk City, Wisconsin, Arkham House, 1961.

Editor, *Dark Mind, Dark Heart.* Sauk City, Wisconsin, Arkham House, 1962; London, Mayflower, 1963.

Editor, *When Evil Wakes: A New Anthology of the Macabre.* London, Souvenir Press, 1963.

Editor, *Over the Edge.* Sauk City, Wisconsin, Arkham House, 1964; London, Gollancz, 1967.

Editor, *At the Mountains of Madness and Other Novels,* by H.P. Lovecraft. Sauk City, Wisconsin, Arkham House, 1964; London, Gollancz, 1966.

Editor, *Dagon and Other Macabre Tales,* by H.P. Lovecraft. Sauk City, Wisconsin, Arkham House, 1965; London, Gollancz, 1967.

Editor, with Donald Wandrei (3 vols.) and James Turner (2 vols), *Selected Letters,* by H.P. Lovecraft. Sauk City, Wisconsin, Arkham House, 5 vols., 1965-76.

Editor, *The Dark Brotherhood and Other Pieces,* by H.P. Lovecraft and others. Sauk City, Wisconsin, Arkham House, 1966.

Editor, *A Wisconsin Harvest.* Sauk City, Wisconsin, Stanton and Lee, 1966.

Editor, *Travellers by Night.* Sauk City, Wisconsin, Arkham House, 1967.

Editor, *New Poetry Out of Wisconsin.* Sauk City, Wisconsin, Stanton and Lee, 1969.

Editor, *Tales of the Cthulhu Mythos,* by H.P. Lovecraft and others. Sauk City, Wisconsin, Arkham House, 1969.

Editor, *The Horror in the Museum and Other Revisions,* by H.P. Lovecraft. Sauk City, Wisconsin, Arkham House, 1970; abridged edition, London, Panther, 1975.

Editor, *Dark Things.* Sauk City, Wisconsin, Arkham House, 1971.

*

Bibliography: *100 Books by August Derleth,* Sauk City, Wisconsin, Arkham House, 1962.

Manuscript Collection: State Historical Society of Wisconsin Library, Madison.

*   *   *

During his 47-year literary career, August Derleth contributed to a wide variety of literary categories, always with skill and frequently with distinction. His output included contemporary novels, historical novels, award-winning short stories, regional history, biography, nature essays, poetry, literary criticism, fiction and non-fiction for young readers, detective novels, Sherlock Holmes pastiches, true crime essays, and a large body of weird and supernatural fiction. It was in the latter area that he began his career at 16, with the story "Bat's Belfry." This was the first of more than a hundred stories to be published in *Weird Tales,* with nearly as many more appearing in other fantasy and science-fiction magazines, and collected in 11 volumes. The best of these stories, such as "Mrs. Manifold" and "The Lonesome Place," display a macabre inventiveness and a sure talent for inducing cold chills. Derleth's contributions to the field of science fiction were made primarily in his roles as editor and publisher. Arkham House Publishers preserved and popularized not only H.P. Lovecraft's works and those of Clark Ashton Smith, Robert E. Howard, Henry S. Whitehead, Robert Bloch, William Hope Hodgson, Algernon Blackwood, and A.E. Coppard, but published the first books of Ray Bradbury, Fritz Leiber, and A.E. van Vogt. Between 1948 and 1954 Derleth edited nine popular collections of science fiction, including *Beyond Time and Space,* one of the first attempts to provide science fiction with a literary pedigree by including excerpts from Plato, Lucian of Samosata, Sir Thomas More, Rabelais, and Francis Bacon. Derleth's literary tastes and his broad view of what constituted science fiction gave his anthologies a distinctive flavor that set them apart from the work of other compilers.

Of Derleth's hundreds of short stories, the only ones classifiable as science fiction are the 17 tales which make up *Harrigan's File.* These stories recount a succession of odd encounters between Tex Harrigan, a skeptical newspaper reporter, and an assortment of eccentric characters, crazy inventions, scientific experiments gone awry, and visitors from other planets or dimensions. Always low-key, some of the tales are quietly effective, but others are marred by surprisingly heavy-handed satire. (One story contains references to a Pernsback-Galmer—read Gernsback and Palmer—Lunar Expedition and to SF writers named Van Heingeon and Spragsimov Pouldersen.) One cannot help but feel that these products of Derleth-the-author would have been disdained by Derleth-the-editor, whose sights were always set high and whose accomplishments not infrequently matched his intentions.

—R.E. Briney

DeWEESE, Gene (Thomas Eugene DeWeese). Also writes as Jean DeWeese; Thomas Stratton. American. Born in Rochester, Indiana, 31 January 1934. Educated at Valparaiso Technical Institute, associate degree in electronics 1953; also studied at the University of Wisconsin, Madison, Indiana University, Bloomington, and Marquette University, Milwaukee. Married Beverly Joanne Amers in 1955. Electronics technician, Delco Radio, Kokomo, Indiana, 1954-59; technical writer, especially on space navigation, Delco Electronics, Milwaukee, 1959-74. Since 1974, free-lance writer. Agent: Larry Sternig Literary Agency, 742 North Robertson, Milwaukee, Wisconsin 53213. Address 2718 North Prospect, Milwaukee, Wisconsin 53211, U.S.A.

SCIENCE-FICTION PUBLICATIONS

Novels (series: Joe Karns)

The Invisibility Affair (as Thomas Stratton, with Robert Coulson). New York, Ace, 1967.
The Mind-Twisters Affair (as Thomas Stratton, with Robert Coulson). New York, Ace, 1967.
Gates of the Universe (Karns), with Robert Coulson. Toronto, Laser, 1975.
Now You See It/Him/Them... (Karns), with Robert Coulson. New York, Doubleday, 1975; London, Hale, 1976.
Jeremy Case. Toronto, Laser, 1976.
Charles Fort Never Mentioned Wombats (Karns), with Robert Coulson. New York, Doubleday, 1977; London, Hale, 1978.
Major Corby and the Unidentified Flapping Object (juvenile). New York, Doubleday, 1979.
The Wanting Factor. Chicago, Playboy Press, 1980.
The Adventures of a Two-Minute Werewolf (juvenile). New York, Doubleday, 1980.

Uncollected Short Stories

"The Tracy Business," with Robert Coulson, in *Fantasy and Science Fiction* (New York), February 1970.
"John Carter and His Electric Barsoom" (as Thomas Stratton, with Robert Coulson), in *The Conan Grimoire,* edited by L. Sprague de Camp and George H. Scithers. Baltimore, Mirage Press, 1971.
"By the Book," with Robert Coulson, in *Amazing* (New York), May 1971.
"The Spaceship," in *Strange Encounters.* Milwaukee, Raintree, 1977.
"When You Wish upon a Star," in *Stellar 3,* edited by Judy-Lynn del Rey. New York, Ballantine, 1977.
"The Midnight Bicyclist," with Joe L. Hensley, in *The Best of Galileo,* edited by Charles C. Ryan. New York, St. Martin's Press, 1979.

OTHER PUBLICATIONS

Novels as Jean DeWeese

The Reimann Curse. New York, Ballantine, 1975.
The Carnelian Cat. New York, Ballantine, 1975.
The Moonstone Spirit. New York, Ballantine, 1975.
The Doll with Opal Eyes. New York, Doubleday, 1976; London, Hale, 1977.
Cave of the Moaning Wind. New York, Ballantine, 1976.
Web of Guilt. New York, Ballantine, 1976.
Nightmare in Pewter. New York, Doubleday, 1978.
Hour of the Cat. New York, Doubleday, 1980.

Other

Making American Folk Art Dolls, with Gini Rogowski. Radnor, Pennsylvania, Chilton, 1975.

*   *   *

Gene DeWeese was an active science fiction fan in the early 1950's and contributed fiction to a number of the amateur publications of the time. His first professional fiction, written with Robert Coulson (as Thomas Stratton), was two novels in the Man from U.N.C.L.E. series, *The Invisibility Affair* and *The Mind-Twisters Affair.* The first of these, revolving around an invisible dirigible, is the more successful in catching the wacky atmosphere of the TV series. Both books have the humor and in-group references (such as naming characters after friends and acquaintances) which are present in almost all DeWeese/Coulson collaborations. DeWeese and Coulson published two short stories in the early 1970's: "The Tracy Business," a brief private-eye/fantasy amalgam, and "By the Book," an ironic fable on an ecological theme. These novels feature reporter Joe Karns and his encounters with psi phenomena and UFO's in company with a varying crowd of science fiction fans, both real and fictional.

DeWeese's solo *Jeremy Case* is the story of the title character and a "companion," an alien symbiote which not only regenerates Jeremy's body after a plane crash but gives him the power to heal others. Far from becoming a superman, Jeremy remains a troubled victim of his new power and of the people who want him to misuse it. The book is a low-key but solidly satisfying work. DeWeese describes the plot of *The Wanting Factor* as "The Man in Half Moon Street turns out to be Christ."

DeWeese has also produced (as Jean DeWeese) a series of entertaining novels in the modern publishing category of the Gothic. While observing the usual conventions of the form, the novels generally feature intelligent and independent heroines, well-realized backgrounds, and menaces which are often genuinely supernatural. The books are not entirely free from the same kind of in-group references that appear in the SF novels—for example, in *The Doll with Opal Eyes* the author disposes of a character named Thomas Stratton, *Nightmare in Pewter* contains a minor character named Joe Karns—but they are less likely to be noticed by the intended audience.

—R.E. Briney

———————

DICK, Philip K(indred). American. Born in Chicago, Illinois, 16 December 1928. Educated at Berkeley High School, California, graduated 1945. Married five times; two daughters and one son. Has worked as a record store manager and an announcer on KSMO-AM radio, Berkeley. Recipient: Hugo Award, 1963; Campbell Memorial Award, 1975. Agent: Scott Meredith Literary Agency, 845 Third Avenue, New York, New York 10022. Address: 408 East Civic Center Drive, Apartment 301, Santa Ana, California 92701, U.S.A.

SCIENCE-FICTION PUBLICATIONS

Novels

Solar Lottery. New York, Ace, 1955; as *World of Chance,* London, Rich and Cowan, 1956.
The World Jones Made. New York, Ace, 1956; London, Sidgwick and Jackson, 1968.
The Man Who Japed. New York, Ace, 1956; London, Eyre Methuen, 1978.
Eye in the Sky. New York, Ace, 1956; London, Arrow, 1971.
The Cosmic Puppets. New York, Ace, 1957.
Time Out of Joint. Philadelphia, Lippincott, 1959; London, Sidgwick and Jackson, 1961.
Dr. Futurity. New York, Ace, 1960; London, Eyre Methuen, 1976.
Vulcan's Hammer. New York, Ace, 1960; London, Arrow, 1976.
The Man in the High Castle. New York, Putnam, 1962; London, Penguin, 1965.
The Game-Players of Titan. New York, Ace, 1963; London, Sphere, 1969.
Martian Time-Slip. New York, Ballantine, 1964; London, New English Library, 1976.
The Simulacra. New York, Ace, 1964; London, Eyre Methuen, 1977.
The Penultimate Truth. New York, Belmont, 1964; London, Cape, 1967.

Clans of the Alphane Moon. New York, Ace, 1964; London, Panther, 1975.

The Three Stigmata of Palmer Eldritch. New York, Doubleday, 1965; London, Cape, 1966.

Dr. Bloodmoney; or, How We Got Along after the Bomb. New York, Ace, 1965; London, Arrow, 1977.

The Crack in Space. New York, Ace, 1966; London, Eyre Methuen, 1977.

Now Wait for Last Year. New York, Doubleday, 1966; London, Panther, 1975.

The Unteleported Man. New York, Ace, 1966; London, Eyre Methuen, 1976.

Counter-Clock World. New York, Berkley, 1967; London, Sphere, 1968.

The Zap Gun. New York, Pyramid, 1967; London, Panther, 1975.

The Ganymede Takeover, with Ray Nelson. New York, Ace, 1967; London, Arrow, 1971.

Do Androids Dream of Electric Sheep? New York, Doubleday, 1968; London, Rapp and Whiting, 1969.

Ubik. New York, Doubleday, 1969; London, Rapp and Whiting, 1970.

Galactic Pot-Healer. New York, Doubleday, 1969; London, Gollancz, 1971.

A Maze of Death. New York, Doubleday, 1970; London, Gollancz, 1972.

Our Friends from Frolix 8. New York, Ace, 1970; London, Panther, 1976.

We Can Build You. New York, DAW, 1972; London, Fontana, 1977.

Flow My Tears, The Policeman Said. New York, Doubleday, and London, Gollancz, 1974.

Deus Irae, with Roger Zelazny. New York, Doubleday, 1976; London, Gollancz, 1977.

A Scanner Darkly. New York, Doubleday, and London, Gollancz, 1977.

The Divine Invasion. New York, Pocket Books, 1981.

Valis. New York, Bantam, 1981.

Short Stories

A Handful of Darkness. London, Rich and Cowan, 1955; Boston, Gregg Press, 1978.

The Variable Man and Other Stories. New York, Ace, 1956; London, Sphere, 1969.

The Preserving Machine and Other Stories. New York, Ace, 1969; London, Gollancz, 1971.

The Book of Philip K. Dick. New York, DAW, 1973; as *The Turning Wheel and Other Stories,* London, Coronet, 1977.

The Best of Philip K. Dick, edited by John Brunner. New York, Ballantine, 1977.

The Golden Man. New York, Berkley, 1980.

Other Publications

Novel

Confessions of a Crap Artist. Glen Ellen, California, Entwhistle, 1978; London, Magnum, 1979.

Other

"(Unpublished) Foreword to *The Preserving Machine,*" in *Science-Fiction Studies* (Terre Haute, Indiana), March 1975.

"Man, Android, and Machine," in *Science Fiction at Large,* edited by Peter Nicholls. London, Gollancz, 1976; New York, Harper, 1977.

"A Clarification" (on Stanislaw Lem), in *Science-Fiction Studies* (Terre Haute, Indiana), March 1978.

"The Profession of Science Fiction 17: The Lucky Dog Pet Store," in *Foundation 17* (London), September 1979.

*

Bibliography: in *Philip K. Dick: Electric Shepherd* edited by Bruce Gillespie, Melbourne, Norstrilia Press, 1975; in *Science-Fiction Studies* (Terre Haute, Indiana), March 1975.

Manuscript Collection: California State University, Fullerton.

*   *   *

Generically, there are two phases to Philip K. Dick's writing career. There is the early profusion of short stories, 73 published from 1952 to 1955, and then the spate of novels from 1962. The cause of the division and whether it is qualitative are two vital concerns.

Dick is not at all an easy writer in the later stage, despite the lurid covers and titles like *The Zap Gun* or *Do Androids Dream of Electric Sheep?* Typically, point of view is divided among a variety of characters (as many as 15 in *The Simulacra*), and the characters are anti-heroic. Barney Mayerson in *The Three Stigmata of Palmer Eldritch* is rarely called by his right name and can easily be viewed as a failure according to the values prevalent in his society. Dick's characters at their best are survivors under conditions which are disastrous both physically and psychologically. Through them we see the constructive forces of humanity and empathy struggling with entropy, with the Form Destroyer. Bruno Bluthgeld may have released the bombs for the Third World War, time may have begun to go backwards, or a Neanderthal heritage may be forthcoming, but Dick's "minor man" (a TV repairman or a used flapple salesman) is coping and even contributing. This survival works in two ways: the personal—a Mr. Tagomi (in *The Man in the High Castle*) discovers resources unsuspected in himself, though the pain of the choice leads to a heart attack—and the societal—Tagomi helps to avert, for a time, a genocidal massacre of the Japanese by their German allies. In a letter (9 September 1970) Dick observes that "the enormous process of decline is pushed back slightly. Enough so that it matters. What Mr. Tagomi has done matters. In a sense, there is nothing more important on all Earth than Mr. Tagomi's irritable action." Tagomi cannot perceive what ultimate effect his small ripple will have. The resolution remains open-ended. Similarly, when the estranged Juliana Frink telephones her husband Frank, a sign of forthcoming conjugal and perhaps societal harmony, the phone rings without being answered, a test of the reader's faith.

Dick uses the traditional material of SF—psionics, robots, space flight, futuristic weaponry, alternative universes, aliens, other worlds. But he is interested not in a space opera plot but in his characters. Consequently, in *Galactic Pot-Healer* we see the initial despair of Joe Fernwright—thinking that he "ought to give up and take some other line of work," that his "work isn't good enough," and considering suicide. A master-repairer of pottery who has never tried to make his own pot, Joe is resigned to playing absurdist games from his tiny cubicle. Enter the god-like Glimmung, who assembles a group of misfits into a purposeful society with the goal of raising the sunken cathedral Heldscalla. Intermeddled in the parable is hilarious material, Willis, the free-lance writing robots, the Glimmung himself, a god who falls to the basement through the several floors of the hotel where the project is ensconced. It is typical of Dick's subtle manipulation of the success/survival theme that when Joe's first pot comes from the kiln, it is "awful." Awful or awe-ful, there's no knowing—it's the last word of the novel.

Galactic Pot-Healer is one of the easier novels in terms of character. When the focus is divided among several characters, the reader has more to weigh. *Martian Time-Slip* has Norbert Steiner's suicide, the mad greed of Arnie Kott, the timeless understanding of the Martian autochthone Heliogabalus, Sylvia Bohlen's empty loneliness, and Jack Bohlen's enduring a schizophrenia inherent both in the self and its society. The novel ends with "patience" as Jack and his father search the Martian night for the distraut Erna Steiner. Ursula K. Le Guin observes that Dick's "characters are ordinary.... That some of them have odd talents such as precognition makes no difference, since they inhabit a world where precognition is common; they're just ordinary neurotic precognitive slobs." What counts is their "honesty, constancy, kindness, and patience."

The policeman Felix Buckman in *Flow My Tears, The Policeman Said* collects antique snuff boxes and old postage stamps and his love is regressive and self-centered; he delegates the responsibility for executing Jason Taverner to a subordinate. Yet Dick's system is not at all stilted. Rick Deckard in *Do Androids Dream of Electric Sheep?* is a bounty hunter who gains our sympathy. Inevitably, somewhere, sometime, a Dick protagonist will have an existential moment of choice. Joe Chip in *Ubik* announces an intention to make such a choice (a homeostatic coffeeshop has just refused him service): " 'One of these days,' Joe said wrathfully, 'people like me will rise up and overthrow you, and the end of tyranny by the homeostatic machine will have arrived. The day of human values and compassion and simple warmth will return, and when that happens someone like myself who has gone through an ordeal and who genuinely needs hot coffee to pick him up and keep him functioning when he has to function will get the hot coffee whether he happens to have a poscred readily available or not.' "

Dick, especially since 1962, uses the vocabulary and world view of the Swiss existential psychologists (Ludwig Binswanger, for instance); Rollo May's collection of articles in *Existence: A New Dimension in Psychiatry and Psychology* (1958) may have been instrumental for a shift in Dick's writing. Earlier stories already indicated a strong interest in psychology; "Exhibit Piece" asks what is real, and the language of psychiatry contributes to the story. But in the later works the vocabulary is explicitly existential: the umwelt, the mitwelt, the eigenwelt, and a contrast of the tomb world with the chthonic and the ethereal. The existentialists, for instance, describe in a case study the severity of anankastic schizophrenia, its compulsion and its "blocked energies." Dick transforms this material to SF in the person of psychokinetic pianist Richard Kongrosian (*The Simulacra*). There the extreme pressures of his being-in-the-world find a release for this blocked energy in Art and ultimately in the wider political sphere. Similarly Dick's treatment of autism and the warped perception of time in *Martian Time-Slip* has its roots in the same school.

The structure of a Dick novel can be tantalizing with so many diverse elements, plots, characters, bizarre events and moments—talking taxis, autonomic wrist watches, messages left in toilet bowls by quasi-gods, Heliogabalus reading *Life* and cooking a bouillabaisse, the Wind God George Walt (one body with two heads), vugs, flapples, bibs, wubs, can-D, chew-Z, bes and ges. Yet the humor is vital and the events and characters cohere thematically. Loose ends and inconsistencies are rare in his extensive corpus. It is worth mentioning another way in which Dick is an economical writer. He frequently draws from his early short stories for novel material. *The Penultimate Truth* for instance, reshapes "The Defenders," "The Mold of Yancy," and "The Unreconstructed M." This recycling of older material works so well, perhaps, because of the consistency of Dick's vision, and because, as Le Guin puts it, his "language [is] appropriate to what he wants to say, to us, about ourselves."

If there is an area where Dick is open to criticism, it is his handling of female character. Protagonists are nearly always male (Juliana Frink in *The Man in the High Castle* is an exception). In Dick's defense, he sees us living in an era dominated by the "solar-centric masculine deities," a world of "rocket ship space probes" rather than a realm of the "mother, the woman, the Earth, the chthonic world of the Cyrenaican Aphrodite" (*A Scanner Darkly*). Hence Juliana Frink is described as a "daemon" and Donna Hawthorne *(A Scanner Darkly)* seems to vanish "like fire or air, an element of the earth back into the earth."

—Anthony Wolk

DICKINSON, Peter (Malcolm de Brissac). British. Born in Livingstone, Zambia, 16 December 1927. Educated at Eton College (King's Scholar), 1941-46; King's College, Cambridge (exhibitioner), B.A. 1951. Served in the British Army, 1946-48. Married Mary Rose Bernard in 1953; two daughters and two sons. Assistant Editor and reviewer, *Punch*, London, 1952-69. Recipient: Crime Writers Association Golden Dagger, 1968, 1969; *Guardian* Award, for children's book, 1977; *Boston Globe-Horn Book* Award, for children's book, 1977; Whitbread Prize, 1979; Carnegie Medal, for

children's book, 1980. Agent: A.P. Watt Ltd., 26-28 Bedford Row, London WC1R 4HL. Address: 33 Queensdale Road, London W11 4SB, England.

SCIENCE-FICTION PUBLICATIONS

Novels (series: The Changes)

The Changes (juvenile).   London, Gollancz, 1975.
   The Weathermonger.   London, Gollancz, 1968; Boston, Little Brown, 1969.
   Heartsease.   London, Gollancz, and Boston, Little Brown, 1969.
   The Devil's Children.   London, Gollancz, and Boston, Little Brown, 1970.
The Green Gene.   London, Hodder and Stoughton, and New York, Pantheon, 1973.
The Gift (juvenile).   London, Gollancz, 1973; Boston, Little Brown, 1974.
The Poison Oracle.   London, Hodder and Stoughton, and New York, Pantheon, 1974.
King and Joker.   London, Hodder and Stoughton, and New York, Pantheon, 1976.
The Blue Hawk (juvenile).   London, Gollancz, and Boston, Little Brown, 1976.

OTHER PUBLICATIONS

Novels

Skin Deep.   London, Hodder and Stoughton, 1968; as *The Glass-Sided Ants' Nest*, New York, Harper, 1968.
A Pride of Heroes.   London, Hodder and Stoughton, 1969; as *The Old English Peep Show*, New York, Harper, 1969.
The Seals.   London, Hodder and Stoughton, 1970; as *The Sinful Stones*, New York, Harper, 1970.
Sleep and His Brother.   London, Hodder and Stoughton, and New York, Harper, 1971.
The Lizard in the Cup.   London, Hodder and Stoughton, and New York, Harper, 1972.
The Lively Dead.   London, Hodder and Stoughton, and New York, Pantheon, 1975.
Walking Dead.   London, Hodder and Stoughton, 1977; New York, Pantheon, 1978.
One Foot in the Grave.   London, Hodder and Stoughton, 1979; New York, Pantheon, 1980.

Plays

Television Plays (for children): *Mandog* series, 1972; *The Changes*, 1975.

Other (juvenile)

Emma Tupper's Diary.   London, Gollancz, and Boston, Little Brown, 1971.
The Dancing Bear.   London, Gollancz, 1972; Boston, Little Brown, 1973.
The Iron Lion.   Boston, Little Brown, 1972; London, Allen and Unwin, 1973.
Chance, Luck, and Destiny (miscellany).   London, Gollancz, 1975; Boston, Little Brown, 1976.
Annerton Pit.   London, Gollancz, and Boston, Little Brown, 1977.
Hepzibah.   Twickenham, Middlesex, Eel Pie, 1978; Boston, Godine, 1980.
Tulku.   London, Gollancz, and New York, Dutton, 1979.
The Flight of the Dragons.   London, Pierrot, and New York, Harper, 1979.
City of Gold and Other Stories from the Old Testament.   London, Gollancz, and New York, Pantheon, 1980.

Editor, *Presto! Humorous Bits and Pieces.*   London, Hutchinson, 1975.

Peter Dickinson comments:

I regard all my fiction as SF (that's to say I write it as if it were), though usually the S bulks much smaller that the F. Classic detective stories (which I try to write) usually have to be restricted to a closed world, which I tend to invent as if it were an alien planet. Indeed, inventing even a normal human character seems to me to demand an effort of the same kind as inventing an alien species; this may account for the fact that my characters have a tendency towards the grotesque. The children's books are straightforward soft SF; *The Green Gene* began as a satire about apartheid, or rather about outsiders' attitudes to it, but acquired directions and energies of its own. My attitude to SF is much more influenced by the pulp I read in the 1940's then by anything more recent, or in book form.

*   *   *

Peter Dickinson has never written a book which has been published initially with the science-fiction label attached to it. Yet over his many books for children and adults the aura of fantasy and SF is constantly present, and in recent years many of his earlier works have been reissued as SF. Dickinson's reputation for more than a decade has been as the author of mystery and detective novels for adults and fantasy books for the young. Of the latter, *The Weathermonger* and *The Blue Hawk* are notable successes.

His style is precise, elegant, and erudite; his works evince a truly Dickensian fascination with characterization, and esoterica, and a very modern sense of politics and anthropology. His plots often emerge from or turn upon an imagined world created in detail analogous to the world of a fantasy or SF novel. It is his creation of contained and consistent worlds which has caused him to be widely read in the SF community. The whole Pibble series is founded upon the character of the thoughtful detective who is always given the odd cases—and strange they are, too: an alien culture is living in the heart of London (one of the last surviving members of a primitive New Guinea tribe is murdered); contemporary and 18th-century history is revised (a murder on the country estate of a nobleman and war hero involves a killer lion and a number of layers of disillusionment with the British past); a religious cult buys an island upon which they are building the city of God (but many of the members are criminals); strange doings in a research hospital for cathypnics (an invented children's disease which causes its sufferers to become telepathic before coma and death). And of his other mysteries, one is set in an alternate near-future universe in which all the Celtic racial groups are bright green (*The Green Gene*) and another is set in an alternate present universe involving a different ruling family of England (*King and Joker*). A third, *Walking Dead*, requires the reader to accept Voodoo magic as true. *The Poison Oracle*, set in an imagined Arab country, involves a strange culture of marsh-dwelling primitive indigenes who consider poison as magic.

Whether or not a science-fiction world is created by Dickinson in his mystery fiction, the plight of his central character is that he is confronted with a world which must be understood, appreciated, and accepted as real in order to solve the mystery. This is as true of the world of politics and real estate in *The Lively Dead* or the world of the Greek island of Hyos in *The Lizard in the Cup* as it is of the world of the cathypnics in *Sleep and His Brother* or the Voodoo world of *Walking Dead*.

Dickinson is certainly influenced by the contemporary literature of science fiction and fantasy, and exerts some reciprocal force. Quite obviously, several of his novels are clearly fantasy or SF and read as such. Even those which contain only certain elements of SF are satisfying to many SF readers. Dickinson remains aloof and unclassifiable, but one of our important writers.

—David G. Hartwell

DICKSON, Gordon R(upert). American. Born in Edmonton, Alberta, Canada, 1 November 1923; emigrated to the United States at age 13. Educated at the University of Minnesota, Minneapolis, B.A. 1948, and graduate study, 1948-50. Served in the United States Army, 1943-46. Since 1950, free-lance writer. Recipient: Hugo Award, 1965; Nebula Award, 1966. President, Science Fiction Writers of America, 1969-70. Address: Box 1569, Twin City Airport, Minnesota 55111, U.S.A.

SCIENCE-FICTION PUBLICATIONS

Novels (series: Dorsai; Robby Hoenig)

Alien from Arcturus. New York, Ace, 1956.
Mankind on the Run. New York, Ace, 1956; as *On the Run,* 1979.
The Genetic General. New York, Ace, 1960; London, Digit, 1961; expanded edition, as *Dorsai!,* New York, DAW, and London, Sphere, 1976.
Time to Teleport. New York, Ace, 1960.
Secret under the Sea (juvenile; Hoenig). New York, Holt Rinehart, 1960; London, Hutchinson, 1962.
Naked to the Stars. New York, Pyramid, 1961; London, Sphere, 1978.
Delusion World, Special Delivery. New York, Ace, 1961.
Necromancer (Dorsai). New York, Doubleday, 1962; London, Mayflower, 1963; as *No Room for Man*, New York, Macfadden, 1963.
Secret under Antarctica (juvenile; Hoenig). New York, Holt Rinehart, 1963.
Secret under the Caribbean (juvenile; Hoenig). New York, Holt Rinehart, 1964.
Space Winners (juvenile). New York, Holt Rinehart, 1965; London, Faber, 1967.
The Alien Way. New York, Bantam, 1965; London, Corgi, 1973.
Mission to Universe. New York, Berkley, 1965; London, Sphere, 1978.
The Space Swimmers. New York, Berkley, 1967; London, Sidgwick and Jackson, 1968.
Planet Run, with Keith Laumer. New York, Doubleday, 1967; London, Hale, 1977.
Soldier, Ask Not (Dorsai). New York, Dell, 1967; London, Sphere, 1975.
None But Man. New York, Doubleday, 1969; London, Macdonald, 1970.
Wolfling. New York, Dell, 1969.
Spacepaw (juvenile). New York, Putnam, 1969.
Hour of the Horde (juvenile). New York, Putnam, 1970.
The Tactics of Mistake (Dorsai). New York, Doubleday, 1971; London, Sphere, 1975.
Sleepwalker's World. Philadelphia, Lippincott, 1971; London, Hale, 1973.
The Outposter. Philadelphia, Lippincott, 1972; London, Hale, 1973.
The Pritcher Mass. New York, Doubleday, 1972.
Alien Art. New York, Ace, 1973; London, Hale, 1974.
The R-Master. Philadelphia, Lippincott, 1973; London, Hale, 1975.
Gremlins, Go Home! (juvenile), with Ben Bova. New York, St. Martin's Press, 1974.
Star Prince Charlie (juvenile), with Poul Anderson. New York, Putnam, 1975.
Three to Dorsai! (omnibus). New York, Doubleday, 1975.
The Dragon and the George. New York, Doubleday, 1976.
The Lifeship, with Harry Harrison. New York, Harper, 1976.
Time Storm. New York, St. Martin's Press, 1977; London, Sphere, 1978.
The Far Call. New York, Dial Press, and London, Sidgwick and Jackson, 1978.
Home from the Shore. New York, Sunridge Press, 1978; London, Dobson, 1980.
Lost Dorsai. New York, Ace, 1980.
Masters of Everon. New York, Ace, 1980.
The Star Sailors. New York, St. Martin's Press, 1980.

Short Stories

Earthman's Burden, with Poul Anderson. New York, Gnome Press, 1957.
Danger—Human. New York, Doubleday, 1970; as *The Book of Gordon R. Dickson,* New York, DAW, 1973.
Mutants. New York, Macmillan, 1970.
The Star Road. New York, Doubleday, 1973; London, Hale, 1975.
Ancient, My Enemy. New York, Doubleday, 1974; London, Sphere, 1978.
Gordon R. Dickson's SF Best. New York, Dell, 1978.
In Iron Years. New York, Doubleday, 1980.

OTHER PUBLICATIONS

Other

"Plausibility in Science Fiction," in *Science Fiction, Today and Tomorrow,* edited by Reginald Bretnor. New York, Harper, 1974.

Editor, with Poul Anderson and Robert Silverberg, *The Day the Sun Stood Still.* Nashville, Nelson, 1972.
Editor, *Combat SF.* New York, Doubleday, 1975.
Editor, *Nebula Winners 12.* New York, Bantam, 1979.

*   *   *

Evolution is Gordon R. Dickson's pre-eminent subject. He delights in showing consciousness emerging, developing, and perfecting itself in pursuit of god-like powers. "Man's future is upward and outward," says this writer. He presents an open-ended universe filled with limitless possibilities ready to be seized by whatever beings are bold enough. Dickson, a Pelagian humanist, maintains that intelligent life-forms can direct their own destiny. Ultimately, this capacity for continuous growth will surpass the static excellence of divinity, even that of a deity mighty enough to make the sun stand still ("Things That Are Caesar's"). Nature is the milieu in which this drama unfolds, not a participant in the action. Dickson is no romantic pantheist like Poul Anderson, a writer with whom he is often incorrectly linked. Rather, it might be said of him as was said of the Persian poet Firdowsi: "He celebrates the exploits of men, the action is man to man, the thought is of men about men; men are raised to the level of supermen."

Taken together, Dickson's works are simply variant readings of a single epic adventure—Life's quest for transcendence. He proclaims the victories of tenacious, creative, morally responsible people who can reshape heaven and earth by sheer force of will. Right makes might. Goodness must prevail. Mind conquers matter. The author's idealism and boundless confidence are qualities so traditional as to seem novelties in this gloomy era.

Thus, Dickson's favorite literary structure is the initiatory scenario. His protagonists learn, not only for themselves, but on behalf of their group, culture, or species. For example, the hero of *The Pritcher Mass* spearheads the collective aspirations of all living things on Earth. The typical Dickson plot exemplifies mythologist Joseph Campbell's heroic monomyth: a young, obscure, or otherwise lightly regarded individual discovers and masters his own unique abilities. Despite misunderstanding from friends and opposition from foes, he confounds conventional wisdom (often in some juridical confrontation), and thereby averts disaster.

This pattern persists in Dickson's juveniles: an exceptionally mature boy and girl save their planet from ruthless developers in *Alien Art.* It even shapes his humorous works like the Dilbian series (humans earning the respect of huge, roughneck aliens), *The Dragon and the George* (an English professor adjusting to life as a medieval dragon), and the works written with Poul Anderson (a diplomat coping with compulsively imitative aliens). Dickson's comedies center on rational beings struggling to function in preposterously irrational situations.

However, Dickson usually stages his initiations as action-adventure tales. Some have objected to the frequency of military or quasi-military settings but these critics are reading a political intent

into the work that is not there—Dickson is not Robert A. Heinlein. Although he sees an evolutionary advantage in humanity's pack-hunting instinct, his backgrounds are largely dictated by convenience. Traditionally, soldiers and explorers have been obvious subjects for life-and-death dramas of fortitude, daring, and loyalty. Yet Dickson is innovative by making his heroes cerebral and empathic as well as endowing many of them with his own talents for poetry, music, and art. "Call Him Lord" and "Jean Dupres" are about courage, not killing. They are mirror-image studies in manhood: a prince is executed for cowardice to forestall an evil reign; a colonial boy's death in battle brings peace within his people's grasp. These two stories illustrate the technical mastery and absolute economy of his best work.

Although Dickson's elegance and limpidity are better displayed at shorter lengths, he is always a deliberate craftsman. (He was formally trained in writing by Robert Penn Warren, among others, and has made it his sole profession.) He has even developed his own approach to science fiction, the "consciously thematic novel." This is Dickson's way of making a philosophical statement without resorting to the crudities of propaganda. As he explains: "The aim is to make the theme such an integral part of the novel that it can be effective upon the reader without ever having to be stated explicitly...."

Dickson's philosophical purpose imparts a peculiarly relentless-quality to his prose. Every element is concentrated along the cutting edge of the blade. Nothing in his stories exists for its own sake except the message. Although he is a dedicated researcher who experiences as well as studies his backgrounds, he never inserts decorative color or extraneous details. Consider the degree of control imposed on complex raw materials in *The Far Call,* the finest realistic novel about the space program yet written. Dickson welds his stories together with symbols. These are typically grouped in pairs and triads that seek some ultimate unity—salvation is integration. Dualities exist worldwide but Dickson's trinities are best interpreted according to the structuralist theories of Indo-European mythologist Georges Dumézil. Thus, Dickson's design manages to be both universal and specifically Western. The tidiest and most accessible examples of his symbolism occur in *Home from the Shore* and its sequel, *The Space Swimmers.*

The Dorsai or Childe Cycle is the major showcase for Dickson's ideas and artistry. For the past 20 years, he has been constructing a mighty epic tracing the course of human evolution from the 14th to the 24th centuries. (The results published to date should be viewed as works-in-progress since the author plans to revise all of them.) When completed, the Cycle will consist of three historical, three contemporary, and six science-fiction novels. In these novels, the same hero passes through three incarnations, developing intuition as a Man of War, empathy as a Man of Philosophy, and creativity as a Man of Faith, until he assimilates the qualities of his Twin enemy and becomes the first Responsible Man, integrating the unconscious/conservative and the conscious/progressive halves of the racial psyche within himself. The level of aesthetic achievement varies. *Dorsai!* is notable for introducing a thoroughly sympathetic superman and for loading a military action yarn with mythic archetypes. The murkiness and subtlety of *Necromancer* make severe demands on the reader. *Soldier, Ask Not* attains wrenching emotional impact by using its villain as the viewpoint character. *The Tactics of Mistake* is as stilted as an animated war game. However, the short "illuminations" that accompany the Cycle proper ("Warrior," "Brothers," "Amanda Morgan," and *Lost Dorsai*) are uniformly excellent both in content and execution.

Yet despite decades of steady accomplishment, Dickson is less admired than he ought to be. His reputation as a novelist was tainted by early pulpish efforts like *Time to Teleport* and hasty potboilers like *The R-Master.* Anti-war backlash during the 1960's and 70's distorted reactions to the Cycle. Stories of man's indomitability ("Danger: Human") drew charges of Heinleinian human supremacy. But this criticism overlooks Dickson's sensitive portraits of aliens ("Black Charlie" and *The Alien Way*) and his pleas for interspecies empathy ("Dolphin's Way"). Complaints against Dickson's ineptitude with women characters have more validity. Too many of these are nonentities who exist only to frustrate and misunderstand his heroes. Only masculine interactions are important. However, in recent years he has systematically worked to correct this weakness by deepening characterizations and revising old formulas. The triad in *Time Storm* is the Man of Philosophy, the Woman of War, and the Animal of Faith. The complementary Twins in *The Far Call* are no longer men but a pair of male-female couples. "Amanda Morgan" is a sample of the strong women's roles due in future installments of the Cycle.

At its serious best, Dickson's writing strikes the mind like remembered strains of half-heard music or swift torrents of icy water. C.S. Lewis's description of Norse myth applies equally well to Dickson: "cold, spacious, severe, pale, and remote."

—Sandra Miesel

DISCH, Thomas M(ichael). Also writes as Thom Demijohn; Leonie Hargrave; Cassandra Knye. American. Born in Des Moines, Iowa, 2 February 1940. Educated at New York University, 1959-62. Part-time checkroom attendant, Majestic Theatre, New York, 1957-62; copywriter, Doyle Dane Bernbach Inc., New York, 1963-64. Since 1964, free-lance writer and lecturer. Recipient: O. Henry Prize, 1975; John Campbell Memorial Award, 1980. Agent: Marie Rodell-Frances Collin Agency, 141 East 55th Street, New York, New York 10022. Address: 31 Union Square West, No. 11E, New York, New York 10003, U.S.A.

SCIENCE-FICTION PUBLICATIONS

Novels

The Genocides.   New York, Berkley, 1965; London, Whiting and Wheaton, 1967.
Mankind under the Leash.   New York, Ace, 1966; as *The Puppies of Terra,* London, Panther, 1978.
Echo round His Bones.   New York, Berkley, 1967; London, Hart Davis, 1969.
Camp Concentration.   London, Hart Davis, 1968; New York, Doubleday, 1969.
The Prisoner.   New York, Ace, 1969; London, Dobson, 1979.
334.   London, MacGibbon and Kee, 1972; New York, Avon, 1974.
On Wings of Song.   New York, St. Martin's Press, and London, Gollancz, 1979.
Triplicity (omnibus).   New York, Doubleday, 1980.

Short Stories

One Hundred and Two H-Bombs.   London, Compact, 1966; New York, Berkley, 1971; as *White Fang Goes Dingo,* London, Arrow, 1971.
Under Compulsion.   London, Hart Davis, 1968; as *Fun with Your New Head,* New York, Doubleday, 1971.
Getting into Death.   London, Hart Davis MacGibbon, 1973; New York, Knopf, 1976.
Fundamental Disch.   New York, Bantam, 1980.

OTHER PUBLICATIONS

Novels

The House That Fear Built (as Cassandra Knye, with John Sladek). New York, Paperback Library, 1966.
Black Alice (as Thom Demijohn, with John Sladek).   New York, Doubleday, 1968; London, W.H. Allen, 1969.
Clara Reeve (as Leonie Hargrave).   New York, Knopf, 1975.
Neighboring Lives, with Charles Naylor.   New York, Scribner, 1981.

Verse

Highway Sandwiches, with Marilyn Hacker and Charles Platt. Privately printed, 1970.
The Right Way to Figure Plumbing.   New York, Basilisk Press, 1971.

Other

"The Embarrassment of Science Fiction," in *Science Fiction at Large,* edited by Peter Nicholls.   London, Gollancz, 1976; New York, Harper, 1977.

Editor, *The Ruins of Earth: An Anthology of the Immediate Future.*   New York, Putnam, 1971; London, Hutchinson, 1973.
Editor, *Bad Moon Rising.*   New York, Harper, 1973; London, Hutchinson, 1974.
Editor, *The New Improved Sun: An Anthology of Utopian Science Fiction.*   New York, Harper, 1975; London, Hutchinson, 1976.
Editor, with Charles Naylor, *New Constellations.*   New York, Harper, 1976.
Editor, with Charles Naylor, *Strangeness.*   New York, Scribner, 1977.

*   *   *

At first sight, there seems to be a strange gap between Thomas M. Disch's short stories and his novels. Certainly, both are bathed in the same dark atmosphere—at worst pessimism, at best grim humour. But the novels deal with conventional SF themes—invasion of Earth by superior beings and reduction of human beings to animals, tamed (*Mankind under the Leash*) or even exterminated (*The Genocides*); jailing of, and experimenting on, pacifists and liberals by the authoritarian government of the US at war (*Camp Concentration*); instantaneous transmission and parallel worlds (*Echo round his Bone*); the horrors and absurdities experienced in a decadent New York of the near future (*334*). In many of the stories, on the contrary, especially those collected in *Getting into Death*, not only are the usual views of the future missing, but even the logical coherence which is the very spirit of SF: little details of everyday life are magnified and strange correspondences appear, which little by little become more real than our rational conventions. Indeed, A. Dorémieux, a French SF critic, has noted that Disch no longer *needs* all the paraphernalia of the genre to express his personality and his view of the world. But, even if we stick to those of his writings which can undoubtedly be classified as SF, don't we find, through the usual themes, the same philosophical concerns?

As a transition between the two, let us consider *The Prisoner,* better known perhaps as a TV serial than in book form. The theme is akin to that of *Camp Concentration,* but all the "historical" context which accounted for the imprisonment and ruthless intellectual exploitation on the characters is here omitted, so that it appears as a general parable of the absurd suspicion in which *any* society holds its members, as in Kafka's *Trial* and *Castle.* Neither is the "reciprocator," which allowed the prisoners to transmit their egos into their jailers' bodies, any longer necessary to convey the notion that each of us is both a victim and a tormentor, an accomplice of the social system which deprives him of his liberty and, more often than not, dignity. Other steps towards a more profound and original view of this human tragedy are taken in the short stories. First, the evil is not necessarily arbitrary tyranny: the hero of "Flight Useless, Inexorable the Pursuit" vainly tries to escape mechanized pity; in "The City of Penetrating Light" happiness is compulsory; and in "The Affluence of Edwin Lollard" the worst crime is poverty. Very significantly, it is in a well-stocked store that the hero of "Descending" start going down endless stairs to hellish solitude and death. But it is not only our consumer society which is at fault: any producers' society is; and no more inexorable indictment could be conceived than "Thesis on the Social Forms and Social Controls in the USA," in which it is mathematically proved that the best possible organisation of the community rests on schizophrenia, induced in the individual so that, when he is aristocratically satisfying his needs and desires, he may remain ignorant of the time (one year out of five) he spends democratically toiling in his turn.

However, a society in which all material problems are solved once and for all would perhaps be even more inhuman, as in "Now Is Forever" in which the "reprostat" makes it possible to produce as many copies as wanted, not only of the necessaries and amenities of life, but of oneself so as to dodge death: these people who should be completely free are in fact totally enslaved to the endless repetition of meaningless scenes that they are not even conscious of having already enacted. "Assassin and Son" expresses, somewhat less metaphysically, the similar idea that your free choice of the moment immediately turns into your constraining self-definition. In other words, each of us builds his own "squirrel's cage"—an image which appears in several stories besides the one which bears that title, and in which the hero—"Disch"!—never knows whether he is being studied by scientists or extra-terrestrials, but is sure of one thing: it would be much worse if he were suddenly set free!

The paradox of this confinement is that it is both self-imposed and unbearable: society is hell, but so is our own company! Two stories transpose this on the social plane: "Problems of Creativeness" in which Birdie Ludd is denied what he aspires to because he is unable to reach original self-expression, and "The Man Who Had No Idea" in which Barry Riordan finds it extremely difficult to get a communication license. The pangs of creation and those of communication are indeed Disch's main obsession *as a writer*, but also as a clear-sighted witness of man's condition: when (in "Come to Venus, Melancholy") Selma—a girl whose diseased body has been replaced by a machine—tries to share her poetic tastes with John, he laughs at her, and she shuts herself up for five days, only to find herself dreadfully shut off forever; in "The Number You Have Reached" Justin, who has good reason to believe he is the last survivor of mankind on Earth, falls back on numbers, and when Justine—perhaps a mere figment of his unhinged imagination—rings him up and asks to see him, he commits suicide; after Marcia has lived alone in New York for months, her horror for "Roaches" turns into a perverse passion; and in "Linda and Daniel and Spike" the ugly heroine not only gives herself an imaginary lover but a child by him, who makes her suffer, for he somehow (how?) is a cancer—and that is perhaps the story that goes farthest from both the conventions and the rationality of SF and deepest into the psychological and philosophical foundations of human nature.

Once you have gone so deep, nothing of what was built above stands solid any longer: confronted with solitary death, the Russian cosmonaut in "Moondust, The Smell of Hay, and Dialectic Materialism" realises nothing is worth dying for; and in "Doubting Thomas" a former scientist and Christian now back among his African tribe and levitating, crashes to his death as he becomes aware that all depends on faith. No certainty is unshakable at that level, not even that of one's own identity: the average American in "The Beginning of April or the End of March" is sure neither of his name nor of the number of his children, and the hero of "The Asian Shore," who has gone to Turkey to verify his ideas about the arbitrariness of architecture, eventually elects to become one with Yavuz, a native. Not even Descartes's *cognito* is proof against doubt: in "The Sightseers" Jimmy and Ramona, who plan to be the new Adam and Eve after the decadence and disappearance of the human race, are, without knowing it, artificial creatures; and in *Echo round His Bones* Professor Panofsky's double is convinced he has no soul: machines can also think, and if his invention could create an "echo" of reality, only God can create souls—and how could the reader be sure either that he is living in *the* real world (a question asked by Plato among others, with his myth of the cave)?

It is indeed those philosophical implications which are characteristic of Thomas M. Disch: he may occasionally use science fiction to explore future possibilities and thus denounce present tendencies, as in *334*, but he mainly uses it to explore human nature and the human condition, just as ancient thinkers used myths. And SF proves such a corrosive instrument that it leaves nothing but the bones... with just a rather absurd echo round them.

—George W. Barlow

DORMAN, Sonya (née Hess). American. Born 6 April 1924. Attended agricultural college, one year. Married Jack Dorman (second marriage) in 1950; one daughter. Has worked as stable maid, kennel owner, receptionist, cook, dancer, greenhouse assistant, and housekeeper. Recipient: MacDowell Colony fellowship (five); Science Fiction Poetry Association Rhysling Award, 1978. Lives in Connecticut. Agent: John Schaffner, 425 East 51st Street, New York, New York 10022, U.S.A.

SCIENCE-FICTION PUBLICATIONS

Novel

Planet Patrol (juvenile). New York, Coward McCann, 1978.

Uncollected Short Stories

"The Putnam Tradition," in *Amazing* (New York), January 1963.
"Winged Victory," in *Fantasy and Science Fiction* (New York), November 1963.
"Splice of Life," in *Orbit 1*, edited by Damon Knight. New York, Putnam, and London, Whiting and Wheaton, 1966.
"Go, Go, Go Said the Bird," in *Dangerous Visions*, edited by Harlan Ellison. New York, Doubleday, 1967; London, David Bruce and Watson, 2 vols., 1971.
"When I Was Miss Dow," in *Nebula Award Stories 2*, edited by Brian Aldiss and Harry Harrison. New York, Doubleday, and London, Gollancz, 1967.
"Lunatic Assignment," in *The Best from Fantasy and Science Fiction 18*, edited by Edward L. Ferman. New York, Doubleday, 1969.
"Bye, Bye, Banana Bird," in *Fantasy and Science Fiction* (New York), December 1969.
"The Living End," in *Orbit 7*, edited by Damon Knight. New York, Putnam, 1970.
"A Mess of Porridge," in *Alchemy and Academe*, edited by Anne McCaffrey. New York, Doubleday, 1970.
"Alpha Bets," in *Fantasy and Science Fiction* (New York), November 1970.
"Me-Too," in *Worlds of Fantasy 3* (New York), Winter 1970.
"The Deepest Blue in the World," in *SF: Authors' Choice 3*, edited by Harry Harrison. New York, Putnam, 1971.
"Bitching It Out," in *Quark 2*, edited by Samuel R. Delany and Marilyn Hacker. New York, Paperback Library, 1971.
"Harry the Tailor," in *A Pocketful of Stars*, edited by Damon Knight. New York, Doubleday, 1971; London, Gollancz, 1972.
"Journey," in *Galaxy* (New York), November 1972.
"The Bear Went over the Mountain," in *Fantasy and Science Fiction* (New York), August 1973.
"Sons of Bingaloo," in *Analog* (New York), November 1973.
"Time Bind," in *Orbit 13*, edited by Damon Knight. New York, Putnam, 1974.
"Cool Affection," in *Galaxy* (New York), May 1974.
"Death or Consequences," in *Tomorrow*, edited by Roger Elwood. New York, Evans, 1976.
"Them and Us and All, " in *Fantasy and Science Fiction* (New York), April 1976.
"Building Block" in *The New Women of Wonder*, edited by Pamela Sargent. New York, Random House, 1978.
"The Gods in Winter," in *Interfaces*, edited by Ursula K. Le Guin and Virginia Kidd. New York, Ace, 1980.

OTHER PUBLICATIONS

Verse

Poems. Columbus, Ohio State University Press, 1970.
Stretching Fence. Athens, Ohio University Press, 1975.
A Paper Raincoat. Orono, Maine, Puckerbrush Press, 1976.
The Far Traveler. La Crosse, Wisconsin, Juniper Press, 1980.

*   *   *

Sonya Dorman is one of the most unusual and gifted contemporary writers of fantasy and science fiction. She has elevated the macabre short story to an art form. Each of her stories is a unique, perfectly executed jewel. In addition to her strong sense of the macabre Dorman possesses a well-developed sense of humor, illustrated by the grimly absurd twists with which she ends many of her stories.

Writing as a woman in a man's field Dorman resists the temptation to succeed by writing "just like a man." Instead she exhibits a combination of many of the traditional female virtues such as compassion and sensitivity in contrast to the traditional male characteristics of strength, energy, and conciseness. All of this is overlaid by her steely determination to make us see the world as she does. Dorman's world is bitterly ironic and at the same time human. The amorphous creatures from "When I Was Miss Dow" seem remarkably similar to the mental patients in "Lunatic Assignment."

Although the short story is a difficult medium in which to develop characters Dorman succeeds admirably. She does not waste time and energy in the description of the minutiae of future civilizations or present scenes. All of her considerable energy is expended in giving us the soul of her characters. Her plots are deceptively simple. On examination, however, they are carefully wrought situations described through fast-paced dialogue and exquisitely crafted action. Dorman is at her best in stories like "Splice of Life" in which an ordinary if somewhat grim situation is expanded and twisted to make a point about the implications of contemporary medical research. This story is gory, but the gore is purposeful and intentional. It's designed to shock us into seeing past the superficialities, to strip bare the meat and bone of living. The harsh and painful exposure of life is characteristic of Dorman's work. The constraints of her chosen medium, the short story, do not allow for the luxury of subtlety.

Sonya Dorman is a rare phenomenon. She is an amalgam like her amorphous and androgynous characters, able to display her sensitivity and compassion without relinquishing her energy and irony. One anthology editor cautions us at the beginning of "Lunatic Assignment" to read the story only when we have time to read it through at one sitting and then to take time to think about it. This precaution might preface all Dorman's stories. They are not trifles to skim while sunbathing or waiting for the bus. They are energizing, thought-provoking, wryly optimistic glimpses of the darker side of the future.

—Alice Chambers Wygant

DOYLE, Arthur Conan. British. Born in Edinburgh, 22 May 1859. Educated at the Hodder School, Lancashire, 1868-70. Stonyhurst College, Lancashire, 1870-75, and the Jesuit School, Feldkirch, Austria, 1875-76; studied medicine at the Universtiy of Edinburgh, 1876-81, M.B. 1881, M.D. 1885. Served as Senior Physician to a field hospital in South Africa during the Boer War, 1899-1902: knighted, 1902. Married 1) Louise Hawkins in 1885 (died, 1906), one daughter and one son; 2) Jean Leckie in 1907, two sons and one daughter. Practised medicine in Southsea, 1882-90; full-time writer from 1891; stood for Parliament as Unionist candidate for Central Edinburgh, 1900, and tariff reform candidate for the Hawick Burghs, 1906. LL.D.: University of Edinburgh, 1905. Knight of Grace of the Order of St. John of Jeruslaem. *Died 7 July 1930.*

SCIENCE-FICTION PUBLICATIONS

Novels (series: Professor Challenger in all books except *The Doings of Raffles Haw*)

The Doings of Raffles Haw. London, Cassell, and New York, Lovell, 1892.
The Lost World. London, Hodder and Stoughton, and New York, Doran, 1912.

The Poison Belt. London, Hodder and Stoughton, and New York, Doran, 1913.
The Land of Mist. London, Hutchinson, and New York, Doran, 1926.

Short Stories

Danger! and Other Stories. London, Murray, and New York, Doran, 1918.
The Maracot Deep and Other Stories. London, Murray, and New York, Doubleday, 1929.
The Professor Challenger Stories. London, Murray, 1952.

OTHER PUBLICATIONS

Novels

A Study in Scarlet. London, Ward Lock, 1888; Philadelphia, Lippincott, 1890.
The Mystery of Cloomber. London, Ward and Downey, 1888; New York, Fenno, 1895.
Micah Clarke. London, Longman, and New York, Harper, 1889.
The Sign of Four. London, Blackett, 1890; Philadelphia, Lippincott, 1893.
The Firm of Girdlestone. London, Chatto and Windus, and New York, Lovell, 1890.
The White Company. London, Smith Elder, 3 vols., 1891; New York, Lovell, 1 vol., 1891.
The Great Shadow. New York, Harper, 1893.
The Great Shadow, and Beyond the City. Bristol, Arrowsmith, 1893; New York, Ogilvie, 1894.
The Refugees. London, Longman, 3 vols., 1893; New York, Harper, 1 vol., 1893.
The Parasite. London, Constable, 1894; New York, Harper, 1895.
The Stark Munro Letters. London, Longman, and New York, Appleton, 1895.
Rodney Stone. London, Smith Elder, and New York, Appleton, 1896.
Uncle Bernac: A Memory of Empire. London, Smith Elder, and New York, Appleton, 1897.
The Tragedy of Korosko. London, Smith Elder, 1898; as *Desert Drama*, Philadelphia, Lippincott, 1898.
A Duet, with an Occasional Chorus. London, Grant Richards, and New York, Appleton, 1899; revised edition, London, Smith Elder, 1910.
The Hound of the Baskervilles. London, Newnes, and New York, McClure, 1902.
Sir Nigel. London, Smith Elder, and New York, McClure, 1906.
The Valley of Fear. New York, Doran, 1914; London, Smith Elder, 1915.

Short Stories

Mysteries and Adventures. London, Scott, 1889; as *The Gully of Bluemansdyke and Other Stories*, 1893.
The Captain of the Polestar and Other Tales. London, Longman, 1890; New York, Munro, 1894.
The Adventures of Sherlock Holmes. London, Newnes, and New York, Harper, 1892.
My Friend the Murderer and Other Mysteries and Adventures. New York, Lovell, 1893.
The Great Keinplatz Experiment and Other Stories. Chicago, Rand McNally, 1894.
The Memoirs of Sherlock Holmes. London, Newnes, and New York, Harper, 1894.
Round the Red Lamp, Being Facts and Fancies of Medical Life. London, Methuen and New York, Appleton, 1894.
The Exploits of Brigadier Gerard. London, Newnes, and New York, Appleton, 1896.
The Man from Archangel and Other Stories. New York, Street and Smith, 1898.
The Green Flag and Other Stories of War and Sport. London, Smith Elder, and New York, McClure, 1900.
The Adventures of Gerard. London, Newnes, and New York, McClure, 1903.

The Return of Sherlock Holmes. London, Newnes, and New York, McClure, 1905.
Round the Fire Stories. London, Smith Elder, and New York, McClure, 1908.
The Last Galley: Impressions and Tales. London, Smith Elder, and New York, Doubleday, 1911.
His Last Bow: Some Reminiscences of Sherlock Holmes. London, Murray, and New York, Doran, 1917.
The Black Doctor and Other Tales of Terror and Mystery. New York, Doran, 1925.
The Dealings of Captain Sharkey and Other Tales of Pirates. New York, Doran, 1925.
The Last of the Legions and Other Tales of Long Ago. New York, Doran, 1925.
The Man from Archangel and Other Tales of Adventure. New York, Doran, 1925.
The Case-Book of Sherlock Holmes. London, Murray, and New York, Doran, 1927.
The Conan Doyle Historical Romances. London, Murray, 2 vols., 1931-32.
Great Stories, edited by John Dickson Carr. London, Murray and New York, London House and Maxwell, 1959.
Strange Studies from Life, Containing Three Hitherto Uncollected Tales, edited by Peter Ruber. New York, Candlelight Press, 1963.
The Annotated Sherlock Holmes, edited by William S. Baring-Gould. New York, Potter, 2 vols., 1967; London, Murray, 2 vols., 1968.
The Best Supernatural Tales of Arthur Conan Doyle, edited by E.F. Bleiler. New York, Dover, 1979.

Plays

Jane Annie; or, The Good Conduct Prize, with J.M. Barrie, music by Ernest Ford (produced London, 1893). London, Chappell, 1893.
Foreign Policy (produced London, 1893).
Waterloo (as *A Story of Waterloo,* produced Bristol, 1894; London, 1895; as *Waterloo,* produced New York, 1899). London, French, 1919 (?).
Halves (produced Aberdeen and London, 1899).
Sherlock Holmes, with William Gillette, adaptation of works by Doyle (produced New York, 1899; Liverpool and London, 1901). London, French, 1922; New York, Doubleday, 1935.
A Duet. London, French, 1903.
Brigadier Gerard, adaptation of his own stories (produced London and New York, 1906).
The Fires of Fate: A Modern Morality, adaptation of his own novel *The Tragedy of Korosko* (produced London and New York, 1909).
The House of Temperley, adaptation of his own novel *Rodney Stone* (produced London, 1909).
The Pot of Caviare, adaptation of his own story (produced London, 1910). London, French, 1912.
The Speckled Band (produced London and New York, 1910). London, French, 1912.
The Crown Diamond (produced London, 1921).
It's Time Something Happened. New York, Appleton, 1925.

Verse

Songs of Action. London, Smith Elder, and New York, Doubleday, 1898.
Songs of the Road. London, Smith Elder, and New York, Doubleday, 1911.
The Guards Came Through and Other Poems. London, Murray, 1919; New York, Doran, 1920.
The Poems: Collected Edition. London, Murray, 1922.

Other

The Great Boer War. London, Smith Elder, and New York, McClure, 1900.
The War in South Africa: Its Cause and Conflict. London, Smith Elder, and New York, McClure, 1902.

Works. London, Smith Elder, 12 vols., 1903.
Through the Magic Door (essays). London, Smith Elder, 1907; New York, McClure, 1908.
The Case of Mr. George Edalji. London, Blake, 1907.
The Crime of the Congo. London, Hutchinson, and New York, Doubleday, 1909.
The Case of Oscar Slater. London, Hodder and Stoughton, 1912; New York, Doran, 1913.
Great Britain and the Next War. Boston, Small Maynard, 1914.
In Quest of Truth, Being a Correspondence Between Sir Arthur Conan Doyle and Captain H. Stansbury. London, Watts, 1914.
The German War: Some Sidelights and Reflections. London, Hodder and Stoughton, 1914; New York, Doran, 1915.
To Arms! London, Hodder and Stoughton, 1914.
Western Wanderings (travel in Canada). New York, Doran, 1915.
The Origin and Outbreak of the War. New York, Doran, 1916.
A Petition to the Prime Minister on Behalf of Roger Casement. Privately printed, 1916 (?).
The British Campaign in France and Flanders. London, Hodder and Stoughton, 6 vols., 1916-19; New York, Doran, 6 vols., 1916-20; revised edition, as *The British Campaigns in Europe 1914-1918,* London, Bles, 1 vol., 1928.
A Visit to Three Fronts. London, Hodder and Stoughton, and New York, Doran, 1916.
The New Revelation: or, What Is Spiritualism? London, Hodder and Stoughton, and New York, Doran, 1918.
The Vital Message (on spiritualism). London, Hodder and Stoughton, and New York, Doran, 1919.
Our Reply to the Cleric. London, Spiritualists' Union, 1920.
A Debate on Spiritualism, with Joseph McCabe. London, Watts, 1920; Girard, Kansas, Haldeman Julius, 1922.
Spiritualism and Rationalism. London, Hodder and Stoughton, 1920.
Fairies Photographed. New York, Doran, 1921.
The Evidence for Fairies. New York, Doran, 1921.
The Wanderings of a Spiritualist. London, Hodder and Stoughton, and New York, Doran, 1921.
The Case for Spirit Photography, with others. London, Hutchinson, 1922; New York, Doran, 1923.
The Coming of the Fairies. London, Hodder and Stoughton, and New York, Doran, 1922.
Three of Them: A Reminiscence. London, Murray, 1923.
Our American Adventure. London, Hodder and Stoughton, and New York, Doran, 1923.
Memories and Adventures. London, Hodder and Stoughton, and Boston, Little Brown, 1924.
Our Second American Adventure. London, Hodder and Stoughton, and Boston, Little Brown, 1924.
Psychic Experiences. London and New York, Putnam, 1925.
The Early Christian Church and Modern Spiritualism. London, Psychic Press, 1925.
The History of Spiritualism. London, Cassell, 2 vols., and New York, Doran, 2 vols., 1926.
Pheneas Speaks: Direct Spirit Communications. London, Psychic Press, and New York, Doran, 1927.
What Does Spiritualism Actually Teach and Stand For? London, Psychic Press, 1928..
A Word of Warning. London, Psychic Press, 1928.
An Open Letter to Those of My Generation. London, Psychic Press, 1929.
Our African Winter. London, Murray, 1929.
The Roman Catholic Church: A Rejoinder. London, Psychic Press, 1929.
The Edge of the Unknown. London, Murray , and New York, Putnam, 1930.

Editor, *D.D. Home: His Life and Mission,* by Mrs. Douglas Home. London, Paul Trench Trubner, and New York, Dutton, 1921.
Editor, *The Spiritualist's Reader.* Manchester, Two Worlds Publishing Company, 1924.

Translator, *The Mystery of Joan of Arc,* by Léon Denis. London, Murray, 1924.

*

Bibliography: *A Bibliographical Catalogue of the Writings of Sir Arthur Conan Doyle* by Harold Locke, Tunbridge Wells, Kent, Webster, 1928.

Manuscript Collection: Humanities Research Center, University of Texas, Austin.

*   *   *

Although literary history best remembers him as the creator of Sherlock Holmes, Arthur Conan Doyle also produced a considerable body of science fiction, adventure tales, and historical romances, as well as numerous works of non-fiction. In common with many other writers whose works spanned both popular and more traditional fields, Doyle preferred to be remembered for his more "mainstream" writings rather than for his popular fiction. Well before Hugo Gernsback coined the term "science fiction," Doyle felt at ease writing heroic adventure tales which would later be placed comfortably in this category. It is not surprising that the author who celebrated deductive reasoning should turn his talents in this direction. From an early age, Doyle was fascinated by history and heroics; his medical training instilled in him a respect for the scientific method; and a flamboyant medical colleague, Dr. George Budd, influenced the young Doyle to bear with the sometimes extreme eccentricities of a man of science. It was Dr. Budd who provided the model for Professor George Edward Challenger, whose appearance in most of Doyle's science fiction reflected the increasing importance of the scientist during the late 19th and early 20th centuries.

Professor Challenger is presented as a man of enormous ego, pride, and determination completely dedicated to discovering scientific truth. He first appears in *The Lost World,* a novel which introduces some of the thematic preoccupations common to most of Doyle's science fiction. "There are heroisms all around us waiting to be done," one character declares, and it is in the spirit of heroic adventure that the fledgling newpaper reporter, Edward Malone, joins Challenger, the gentleman/hunter Lord John Roxton, and the skeptical cantankerous Professor Summerlee on a quest to test the validity of Challenger's assertion that prehistoric life exists on an isolated plateau in South America. As the heroes confront a series of physical hazards and witness numerous awe-inspiring sights, it becomes clear that Doyle's intention is to celebrate a sense of wonder, to convey a fascination with the heroic unknown, and above all to assert modern man's supreme position in both past and present worlds. "Our eyes have seen great wonders," Malone reports after the four adventurers, armed with modern weaponry, help the more advanced Indian race on the plateau dramatically assert their dominance over an inferior race of ape-men. "Now upon this plateau the future must ever be for man," the scientist declares.

The superiority of the modern scientific mind is reasserted in "When the World Screamed," a humorous short story again featuring Challenger, this time armed with "scientific" paraphernalia designed to penetrate the earth's crust in order to prove the preposterous contention that "the world upon which we live is itself a living organism" insensible to man's presence. This is the tale of Challenger's efforts to "let the earth know that there is at least one person, George Edward Challenger, who calls for attention—who, indeed, insists upon attention." Not surprisingly, Challenger achieves his goal.

The Poison Belt is a novel which emphasizes Challenger's unselfish devotion to scientific truth. As the sole predictor of the catastrophic approach toward earth of a "poisonous" belt of ether gas, Challenger can philosophically face the prospect of his own demise and the annihilation of mankind because he is so thrilled at the privilege of observing it! Malone, Roxton, Summerlee, and Mrs. Challenger add more believable exclamations of wonderment to those of the scientist. This novel reveals Doyle's delight in juxtaposing the real and unreal, the beautiful and terrible, as Challenger and company regard through a sealed window the apparent end of the world taking place during a beautiful English summer's day. "The Disintegration Machine" is the most serious of the Challenger stories. Here Malone accompanies Challenger as the professor examines the invention of "Latvian gentleman named Theodore Nemor...a machine of a most extraordinary character which is capable of disintegrating any object placed within its sphere of influence."

Challenger, quick to recognize the awesome military and "evil" potentialities of this invention, uses it to disintegrate Mr. Nemor himself, who holds the secret to the machine's operation.

The Land of Mist, a lengthy novel featuring Challenger only peripherally, cannot be considered science fiction. This apology for the occult reflects Doyle's own conviction about the validity of occult spiritualism. The work does restate one theme expressed in "The Disintegration Machine" and *The Maracot Deep*; it was Doyle's belief that it is absolutely essential for man's spiritual development to keep pace with his strides in the scientific realm. *The Maracot Deep* takes up this theme against a submarine environment. Here Dr. Maracot and a party of deep sea explorers, including a colorful slang-speaking Yankee handyman called Bill Scanlon, discover the lost colony of Atlantis when their undersea vessel is marooned in an Atlantic trench deeper than any previously explored by man. In an image reminiscent of that employed in *The Poison Belt*, Doyle at first isolates his scientist behind impenetrable glass as the real and unreal, the beautiful and sublime, are contrasted. With a sense of wonder, the explorers discover that, in spite of great scientific advances, Atlantis is doomed by its own limited spiritual development. Only through spiritual self-realization combined with cunning and access to scientific equipment do the heroes rise to the surface in Doyle's final assertion of the superiority of modern scientific man.

Some of Doyle's lesser-known stories, sometimes classified as science fiction, have more in common with the horror genre. In "The Silver Mirror," "The Terror of Blue John Gap," "The Horror of the Heights," and "The Captain of the Polestar" Doyle replaces a sense of wonder with a spine-chilling sense of unearthly dread; he purposely leaves the credibility of the narrators in doubt, undercutting any certainty on the reader's part that each story is "scientifically" believable. "Heroisms" are abundant but it is raw courage which makes these protagonists into heroes, not scientific superiority.

—Rosemary Herbert

DOZOIS, Gardner.   American.   Born in Salem, Massachusetts, 23 July 1947. Served as a military journalist, 1966-69. Reader for Dell and Award publishers, and for *Galaxy, If, Worlds of Fantasy,* and *Worlds of Tomorrow,* 1970-73; Co-Founder, and Associate Editor, *Isaac Asimov's Science Fiction Magazine,* 1976-77. Member of the Advisory Committee, Paley Library, Special Collection Department, Temple University, Philadelphia. Agent: Virginia Kidd, Box 278, Milford, Pennsylvania 18337. Address: 401 Quince Street, Philadelphia, Pennsylvania 19147, U.S.A.

SCIENCE-FICTION PUBLICATIONS

Novels

Nightmare Blue, with Geo. Alec Effinger.   New York, Berkley, 1975; London, Fontana, 1977.
Strangers.   New York, Berkley, 1978.

Short Stories

The Visible Man.   New York, Berkley, 1977.

OTHER PUBLICATIONS

Other

"Mainstream SF and Genre SF," in *Fantastic* (New York), November 1973.
"The Science Fiction Novel," with Jack Dann, in *Fiction Writer's Handbook,* edited by Hallie and Whit Burnett. New York, Harper, 1975.

"Living the Future: You Are What You Eat," in *Writing and Selling Science Fiction*.   Cincinnati, Writer's Digest, 1976.
The Fiction of James Tiptree, Jr.   New York, Algol Press, 1977.

Editor, *A Day in the Life*.   New York, Harper, 1972.
Editor, *Beyond the Golden Age*.   New York, Berkley, n.d.
Editor, with Jack Dann, *Future Power*.   New York, Random House, 1976.
Editor, *Another World* (juvenile).   Chicago, Follett, 1977.
Editor, *Best Science Fiction Stories of the Year 6-9*.   New York, Dutton, 4 vols., 1977-80.
Editor, with Jack Dann, *Aliens!*   New York, Pocket Books, 1980.

*

Manuscript Collection: Paskow Collection, Paley Library, Temple University, Philadelphia.

*   *   *

On the basis of only 15 or so pieces of short fiction, an uneven but energetic novel-length collaboration, and one beautifully evocative novel of foredoomed love on an alien world, Gardner Dozois has built an enviable reputation for excellence both as wordsmith and story teller. Robert Silverberg, in his introduction to *The Visible Man*, has declared Dozois "one of the most gifted writers in the United States."

A fine introduction to Dozois's fiction is the novelette "A Special Kind of Morning." Dozois, working with such traditional SF materials as planet-wide warfare and exotic weaponry, upends tradition by framing a cadenced and moving tale whose moral force is as startling as the freshness of its language. On the world called World, one of many planets where politics and economics enforce a complex caste system deriving from institutionalized bio-engineering, the narrator-protagonist confronts his own humanity in the person of a dazed, sexless "null" and comes thereby to a harrowing understanding of life, death, and personal redemption. The opening passage of this novelette, incidentally, also provides a response to those critics who insist on interpreting Dozois's every story as a descent into an inescapable inferno of futility and despair: "Pessimism's just the commonsense knowledge that there's more ways for something to go wrong than for it to go right....As for futility, everybody dies the true death eventually....The philosophical man accepts both as constants and then doesn't let them bother him any."

"The Last Day of July," a less readily accessible story than "A Special Kind of Morning," is in many ways more representative of the Dozois canon, although just as praiseworthy. Devoid of the recognizable trappings of SF (starships, aliens, and whatnot), relentless in its creation of mood, "The Last Day of July" has the inevitability of a Poe horror story and the psychological verisimilitude of a tale by Henry James. Its acute naturalistic detail and its unsentimental chronicling of a man undergoing breakdown may initially obscure the fact that its ending is oddly upbeat. Dozois's memorable concluding line is "There will be a crop"—for the "seeding" of the protagonist into another continuum has apparently taken, and only the most myopic or hidebound among us may cavalierly assume this hidden continuum inferior to our own. Dozois also expresses especial fondness for "A Kingdom by the Sea," an allegory about the odd but unforgettable Lilith of a slaughterhouse worker; "Flash Point" in which an inexplicable variety of spontaneous combustion serves as a metaphor for the spiritual contamination of a small Maine community; and "Chains of the Sea" wherein Dozois again plays with a traditional SF theme—alien invasion—in a colorful and altogether original way. Each of the remaining seven stories in *The Visible Man* invites, and rewards, repeated readings. The collection is a benchmark not only in Dozois's career but in the development of science fiction in the 1970's.

Nightmare Blue, a collaboration with Geo. Alec Effinger, Dozois himself dismisses as a "potboiler." Developed from an early unpublished work of Dozois's entitled *Danegeld*, it functions both as a hardboiled Raymond Chandler pastiche and as a rock 'em/sock 'em SF thriller. The structure of the book and many of the scenes featuring the alien Corcail Sendijen are among Dozois's particular

contributions to this joint effort. Although frequently amusing, *Nightmare Blue* is only rarely believable. The only solo novel to appear from Dozois's pen is the remarkable *Strangers*, expanded from a 1974 novella. Dozois acknowledges his debt to Philip José Farmer's *The Lovers*, itself an expansion of an earlier work, by calling his Teutonic protagonist Joseph Farber. The story details Farber's star-crossed love affair and marriage with a rebellious young woman of a nonhuman species, the Cian, on the world Weinunnach. To this difficult theme Dozois brings not only his empathetic understanding of human motives but the rare ability to create credible alien cultural forms. Imbued with a genuine tragic dimension and recounted in a prose as rhythmic and vivid as the best poetry, *Strangers* is science fiction's *Romeo and Juliet*.

Of late Dozois has devoted much of his time to compiling distinctive best-of-the-year and theme anthologies and some criticism, notably a seminal essay on the fiction of James Tiptree, Jr. However, so prodigious are Dozois's talents as storyteller and stylist that the field will be crucially diminished if he ever decides to channel all his creative energies into these important but secondary pursuits. Perhaps the publication of his forthcoming novel *Nottamuntown* will lead to other fiction.

—Michael Bishop

_____

DRAKE, David A.   American.   Born in Dubuque, Iowa, 24 September 1945. Educated at the University of Iowa, Iowa City, B.A. 1967; Duke University, Durham, North Carolina, J.D. 1972. Served as an interrogator in the United States Army, 1969-71. Married Joanne Kammiller in 1967; one son. Assistant town attorney, Chapel Hill, North Carolina, 1972-80. Since 1980, part-time bus driver, Chapel Hill. Agent: Kirby McCauley, 60 East 42nd Street, New York, New York 10017. Address: Box 904, Chapel Hill, North Carolina 27514, U.S.A.

SCIENCE-FICTION PUBLICATIONS

Short Stories

Hammer's Slammers.   New York, Ace, 1979.

Uncollected Short Stories

"Underground," in *Destinies* (New York), February-March 1980.
"Men Like Us," in *Omni* (New York), May 1980.

OTHER PUBLICATIONS

Novel

The Dragon Lord.   New York, Berkley, 1979

*   *   *

David A. Drake's emphasis on strong characters and action-oriented plotting is earning a growing readership for his literate fiction. His approximately 40 stories are divided almost evenly between science fiction and fantasy-supernatural; his one novel, *The Dragon Lord*, is an Arthurian romance set in a powerfully realistic 5th-century Britain. However, the distinction between fantasy and science fiction is not always an easy or useful one to draw: magic and dragons are treated as rigorously and systematically as any physical science, while the aliens of "Contact!" or "Hunting Ground" would serve the same purpose were they supernatural creatures.

Drake's fiction shows three main non-literary influences. His strong interest in the past, especially ancient Rome, has produced a number of stories with realistic historical backgrounds, including a series about the soldier Lucius Vettius and his friend Dama, a Cappadocian merchant. "Travellers," "The Last Battalion," and

"Children of the Forest," as well as "Contact!," take subjects from Charles Fort and his heirs. Perhaps most important to his writing is Drake's army service as an interrogator in Vietnam and Cambodia, and a number of his stories are set in combat there or have veterans as protagonists. Some of these are almost unreadable with army jargon, but the experience behind them gives them color and rare power.

His war experience is also evident in his major science-fiction series, which deals with Colonel Alois Hammer and Hammer's Slammers, 30th-centruy mercenaries hired by planets constantly at war over shifting conflicts and uneasy alliances. This political background, however, is almost incidental to the stories, which deal compellingly with individual soldiers. The stories are violent and uncompromising, and this, along with the emphasis on military strategy and equipment, may hide the strong anti-war statement of the series. But the very grimness savagely indicts the dehumanization that makes a victorious soldier the greatest victim of war. His other series features Jed Lacey, a Crime Service agent in a near future in which every action is recorded by government scanners. Lacey is totally committed to each job, and only that job, regardless of long-range effects or who gets hurt. That is also true of many other characters; the typical Drake protagonist is dedicated, competent, in many ways admirable, and often thoroughly unlikable, even to himself—or herself, since female protagonists are rarer but no less well done. The only value besides skill and determination is friendship, for which the protagonist will die—or, much more quickly, kill. This kind of characterization is one of Drake's finest accomplishments, though often an undeniably depressing tone results. "Travellers," a recent story, has humanistic characters in a relatively non-violent setting, and may indicate a welcome diversification.

Though his first efforts were very derivative—"Denkirch" is a pastiche of an August Derleth pastiche of H.P. Lovecraft, and "The Shortest Way" is a Roman re-write of Anthony Boucher's "They Bite"—Drake quickly developed his own objective, story-oriented approach. His writing is marked by craftsmanship and rigorous realism, his style vivid and concise and totally lacking in self-consciousness—the use of the historical present tense in "Ranks of Bronze" and, less successfully, "But Loyal to His Own" may be the only evidently artificial technique in his fiction. This is not because he doesn't care about art or style, but because he is concerned with developing plot and character realistically.

If there is one major limitation to Drake's science fiction, it is that he lacks the far-spanning imagination that is a major strength of the genre. His futures are often too much like the present or past. The Vietnam sources are a bit too apparent in Hammer's Slammers; "Underground," inspired by the "vice districts" like Storyville and the Tenderloin, transports that society into Lacey's time without the necessary adaptations. There are also inconsistencies in his future cultures themselves. It is perhaps for this reason that many of Drake's best pieces take place in actual historical settings, providing an exotic background without requiring that a new world and its culture be developed.

But another reason why Drake's sociology and politics are unimpressive is that they are unimportant: it is not the society but the individuals that matter. This emphasis on the individual is a great strength in Drake's work, and has generated many fine stories. Colonel Hammer and his soldiers, Mael and Starkad of *The Dragon Lord*, the eerie but compelling protagonists of Drake's exceptional anti-nuclear story "Men Like Us"—all will linger in the reader's mind whether he wishes them to or not. For this reason, as well as for his craftsmanship, Drake is a writer who deserves serious attention.

—Bernadette Bosky

DuBOIS, Theodora (McCormick). American. Born 14 September 1890.

SCIENCE-FICTION PUBLICATIONS

Novels

Murder Strikes an Atomic Unit. New York, Doubleday, 1946; London, Boardman, 1947.
Solution T-25. New York, Doubleday, 1951; London, Cherry Tree, 1952.

OTHER PUBLICATIONS

Novels

The Devil's Spoon. New York, Stokes, 1930; London, Jarrolds, 1936.
Armed with a New Terror. Boston, Houghton Mifflin, 1936; London, Heinemann, 1937.
Death Wears a White Coat. Boston, Houghton Mifflin, 1938.
Death Tears a Comic Strip. Boston, Houghton Mifflin, 1939.
Death Dines Out. Boston, Houghton Mifflin, 1939; London, Readers Library, 1942.
Death Comes to Tea. Boston, Houghton Mifflin, 1940.
The McNeills Chase a Ghost. Boston, Houghton Mifflin, 1941.
Death Is Late to Lunch. Boston, Houghton Mifflin, 1941; London, Boardman, 1942.
The Body Goes Round and Round. Boston, Houghton Mifflin, 1942.
The Wild Duck Murders. New York, Doubleday, 1943; London, Boardman, 1948.
The Case of the Perfumed Mouse. New York, Doubleday, 1944; London, Boardman, 1946.
Death Sails in a High Wind. New York, Doubleday, 1945; London, Boardman, 1946.
The Footsteps. New York, Doubleday, 1947; London, Boardman, 1949.
The Devil and Destiny. New York, Doubleday, 1948; London, Boardman, 1949.
The Face of Hate. New York, Doubleday, 1948.
It's Raining Violence. New York, Doubleday, 1949; London, Boardman, 1950; as *Money, Murder, and the McNeills,* New York, Lancer, 1969.
Rogue's Coat. New York, Doubleday, 1949.
High Tension. New York, Doubleday, 1950; London, Boardman, 1951.
Fowl Play. New York, Doubleday, 1951; London, Boardman, 1952.
Sarah Hall's Sea God. New York, Doubleday, 1952.
The Cavalier's Corpse. New York, Doubleday, 1952; London, Boardman, 1953.
Freedom's Way. New York, Funk and Wagnalls, 1953.
The Listener. New York, Doubleday, 1953.
Seeing Red. New York, Doubleday, 1954; London, Collins, 1955.
The Emerald Crown. New York, Funk and Wagnalls, 1955.
The Love of Fingin O'Lea. New York, Appleton Century Crofts, 1957.
Captive of Rome. New York, Crown, 1962.
Shannon Terror. New York, Washburn, 1964.
The Late Bride. New York, Washburn, 1965; London, Hale, 1966.

Other (juvenile)

Rocks and Rills: A Cartoon in Three Dimensions. Torrington, Connecticut, Torrington Publishing Company, 1932.
The Traveling Toys. Philadelphia, Penn, 1934.
Diana's Feathers. Boston, Houghton Mifflin, 1935.
Diana Can Do It. Boston, Houghton Mifflin, 1937.
Banjo the Crow. Boston, Houghton Mifflin, 1943; London, Harrap, 1946.
Heroes in Plenty. New York, Doubleday, 1945.
We Merrily Put to Sea. New York, Doubleday, 1950.
Rich Boy, Poor Boy. New York, Ariel, 1961.
Staten Island Patroons (for adults), with Dorothy Valentine Smith. New York, Staten Island Historical Society, 1961.

Tiger Burning Bright.   New York, Ariel, and London, Gollancz, 1964.
The High King's Daughter.   New York, Ariel, 1965; London, Gollancz, 1966.

*   *   *

Theodora DuBois's science-fiction novels and fantasies follow patterns similar to those in her numerous mystery novels: weak young men and women manipulated by the politically unscrupulous of either the right or the left, torn between their sense of duty and loyalty and their innate sense of right and wrong. Usually the young men are war weary/world weary; often they perceive themselves as rogues though others recognize their sterling qualities. The main character, who sees through the sham of vulgar, brazen, political figures, must always endure embarrassment and taunts to protect his loved ones and overthrow the evil forces that threaten to transform sane human beings into mindless automatons, fanatical enthusiasts, and cruel arbitrators of political and moral values. In the background of DuBois's works are bitter memories of Nazi cruelties and of the McCarthy era, as well as later fears of Communist takeovers.

In *Solution T-25* her central figures are at a cocktail party when Russian bombs are dropped on New York and other major cities. The Russians conquer the US with swift and shocking cruelty. But despite the unexpected devastation, young Americans work with government agents to form an underground resistance. They fake collaboration with the enemy in order to infiltrate key positions and protect the lives of children and friends, while a scientific genius hidden away in the Florida Keys works on a solution that will save America and the world from Soviet/Chinese aggression. The solution, a permanent form of chemo-therapy, "melts" the Russian authorities' cruel and autocratic personality structures and turns them into kind-hearted comedians, who are totally inefficient, totally incapable of harming anyone, much less of commanding tyrannical forces. Thus DuBois mingles grim and cynical predictions with a witty hope for benevolent solutions. *Murder Strikes an Atomic Unit* further voices fears of nuclear disasters.

Part of DuBois's rhetorical ploy is to make the reader feel as frustrated with the weak, manipulated characters as does the hero/heroine, even in bizarre situations where the hero is a young devil and the villain his satanic superior (*The Devil's Spoon*). Depicting the mundane relations that persist despite tragedy, her works are decidedly domestic in nature, with the romances of her young couples or the comfortable understanding of her married ones (e.g., her supersleuths, the McNeills) taking precedence over any scientific concerns, and ultimately helping to overcome trauma and chaos.

—Gina Macdonald

DUNCAN, David.   American.   Born in Billings, Montana, 17 February 1913. Educated at the University of Montana, Missoula, B.A. 1935. Married Elaine Sulliger in 1940; three daughters. Personnel examiner, Department of Agriculture, Washington, D.C., 1936; social worker, California State Relief Administration, Fresno, 1936-40; manager of California housing project, Farm Security Administration, 1941-43; field director in California and Nevada, American Red Cross, 1943-44; labor economist, National Labor Bureau, San Francisco, 1944-46. Since 1946, free-lance writer. Agent: Mavis McIntosh, McIntosh McKee and Dodds Inc., 22 East 40th Street, New York, New York 10016. Address: 2229 North Commonwealth Avenue, Los Angeles, California, U.S.A.

SCIENCE-FICTION PUBLICATIONS

Novels

The Shade of Time.   New York, Random House, 1946; London, Grey Walls Press, 1949.
The Madrone Tree.   New York, Macmillan, 1949; London, Gollancz, 1950; as *Worse Than Murder*, New York, Pocket Books, 1954.
Dark Dominion.   New York, Ballantine, 1954; London, Heinemann, 1955.
Beyond Eden.   New York, Ballantine, 1955; as *Another Tree in Eden*, London, Heinemann, 1956.
Occam's Razor.   New York, Ballantine, 1957; London, Gollancz, 1958.

Uncollected Short Stories

"The Immortals," in *Galaxy* (New York), October 1960.
"Requiem on the Moon," in *The Dead Astronaut.*   Chicago, Playboy Press, 1964.
"On Venus the Thunder Precedes the Lightning," in *Worlds of Tomorrow* (New York), Spring 1971.

OTHER PUBLICATIONS

Novels

Remember the Shadows.   New York, McBride, 1944.
The Bramble Bush.   New York, Macmillan, 1948; London, Sampson Low, 1949; as *Sweet, Low, and Deadly*, New York, Mercury, 1949.
The Serpent's Egg.   New York, Macmillan, 1950.
None But My Foe.   New York, Macmillan, 1950.
Wives and Husbands.   Cleveland, World, 1952.
The Trumpet of God.   New York, Doubleday, 1956.
Yes, My Darling Daughters.   New York, Doubleday, 1959; London, Heinemann, 1960.
The Long Walk Home from Town.   New York, Doubleday, 1964.

Plays

Screenplays: *Sangaree*, with Frank Moss, 1953; *Jivaro*, with Winston Miller, 1954; *The White Orchid*, with Reginald LeBorg, 1955; *The Monster That Challenged the World*, with Patricia Fielder, 1957; *The Black Scorpion*, with Robert Blees and Paul Yawitz, 1957; *The Thing That Couldn't Die*, 1958; *Monster on the Campus*, 1958; *The Leech Woman*, with Ben Pivar and Françis Rosenwald, 1960; *The Time Machine*, 1960; *Fantastic Voyage*, with others, 1966.

Television Plays: *The Human Factor* (*The Outer Limits* series), and for *Telephone Time, My Three Sons, National Velvet, It's a Man's World, Higgins, Daniel Boone, Studio One*, and *Men into Space* series.

Other

Strange But True (juvenile).   New York, Scholastic, 1974.

*   *   *

David Duncan is one of the most accomplished stylists to have worked in science fiction and fantasy, yet he is an almost forgotten figure. The reason for this is that, like Edgar Pangborn's and Ray Bradbury's, his ideas are not often very original and his science is sometimes bizarre; his method is that of the mystery story—one in which the enigma is left unexplained for a good deal of the book, and when the problem is solved the story simply ends. The unknown is not brought on stage for very long, and its consequences are left undeveloped. Yet there are so many satisfactions of characterization, background and description, social observation, ideas about human life and destiny, that one is tempted to dismiss the seeming flaws. Duncan is an elegant, poetic wordsmith who involves the reader completely.

Dark Dominion is an overwhelming emotional experience which leaves the reader drained. The story is about the building, in secret, of a military space station that will dominate the earth. We are shown the effects of this terrible purpose on the lives of the scientists involved, as they struggle to complete the project, and later to change its meaning for the world. The novel is filled with moments of great beauty, and they are worth the speculative and scientific lapses. The classic novels of the 1950's do not surpass this one in skill, even when they are superior in ideas and originality. "Duncan's forte is people," wrote Damon Knight (in *In Search of Wonder*, 1967); "he sees them with an inquiring, ironic, compassionate but unsentimental eye. At his best, the characters he draws are sharply individual, each one believable and distinct from every other. He fills up the scene with these moving portraits, and their intricate mutual relationships, effortlessly handled, make his book." This is a lesson that better writers—those whose thinking and conceptual development, even their stories, are better—have not learned: that to produce a valuable piece of fiction, including SF, a writer must show *everything* as belonging to the awareness of characters; ideas as well as feelings must be seen sticking to the *insides* of people.

Occam's Razor is a sketchy story, but it also has the compelling portraits and personal interactions of *Dark Dominion*. The story details the accidental visit of two beings from a parallel world, whose sudden appearance causes much misunderstanding; but the novel ends where it should begin—namely, in the effects of these people's presence on our world, after this fact is discovered. We are given only half the story, that of the events leading up to the solution of the mystery concerning the identity of the two visitors. Still, this is a persuasive and humane story. *Beyond Eden* is more an all-around success than the other two novels, though it lacks the eloquence of *Dark Dominion*. Set in the 1950's atmosphere of the McCarthy hearings and the Oppenheimer persecution, the story deals with a fascinating water project in California. The enterprise discovers a new kind of water which might transform human nature, though at first it seems to kill people, embarrassing the chief scientist who already has a bad past to live down. Again, the story ends where the confrontation with the unknown might lead to new understandings and a set of problems of a higher order.

One might also argue that Duncan chose not to explore beyond "mere mystery"—that his sense of human limits prevented him from inventing glib "understandings" of the kind demanded by so many SF readers. Duncan chose to stay closer to the present. His problem does suggest a prescription: truly great science fiction demands that one be a fine writer with all the skills of a contemporary novelist *and* possess the intellect necessary to speculate beyond the point of "mere mystery," surface drama and obvious topicality.

David Duncan drew enthusiastic reviews for his novels. Groff Conklin called him "a richly endowed mind" whose work should not be missed. Anthony Boucher, Theodore Sturgeon, P. Schuyler Miller, and others ranked his books with the best of their years. In a field whose main problem is a lack of the authenticity that belongs to a literature won from experience, Duncan has the virtue of seeming very authentic, despite his supposed shortcomings. His novels are as he intended them to be, and their virtues are the shortcomings of most science fiction. In the only statement about his science fiction, Duncan wrote: "To me the great virtue of the science-fiction story doesn't reside in its elaborate gadgets and twistings of time and space—although these can be majestically entertaining—but in its possibilities for analysis of man and the social order." He saw SF as a literature of critical possibilities, and for this he deserves serious attention.

—George Zebrowski

DURRELL, Lawrence (George). Also writes as Charles Norden. British. Born in Julundur, India, 27 February 1912. Educated at the College of St. Joseph, Darjeeling, India; St. Edmund's School, Canterbury, Kent. Married 1) Nancy Myers in 1935 (divorced, 1947); 2) Eve Cohen in 1947 (divorced); 3) Claude Durrell in 1961 (died, 1967); 4) Ghislaine de Boysson in 1973 (divorced, 1979); two children. Has had many jobs, including jazz pianist (Blue Peter nightclub, London), automobile racer, and real estate agent. Lived in Corfu, 1934-40. Editor, with Henry Miller and Alfred Perlès, *The Booster* (later *Delta*), Paris, 1937-39; Columnist, *Egyptian Gazette*, Cairo, 1941; Editor, with Robin Fedden and Bernard Spencer, *Personal Landscape*, Cairo, 1942-45; Special Correspondent in Cyprus for *The Economist*, London, 1953-55; Editor, *Cyprus Review*, Nicosia, 1954-55. Taught at the British Institute, Kalamata, Greece, 1940. Foreign Press Service Officer, British Information Office, Cairo, 1941-44; Press Attaché, British Information Office, Alexandria, 1944-45; Director of Public Relations for the Dodecanese Islands, Greece, 1946-47; Director of the British Council Institute, Cordoba, Argentina, 1947-48; Press Attaché, British Legation, Belgrade, 1949-52; Director of Public Relations for the British Government in Cyprus, 1954-56. Andrew Mellon Visiting Professor of Humanities, California Institute of Technology, Pasadena, 1974. Recipient: Duff Cooper Memorial Prize, 1957; Prix du Meilleur Livre Etranger, 1959. Fellow, Royal Society of Literature, 1954. Has lived in France since 1957. Address: c/o National and Grindlay's Bank, 13 St. James's Square, London S.W.1, England.

SCIENCE-FICTION PUBLICATIONS

Novels

The Revolt of Aphrodite. London, Faber, 1974.
  Tunc. London, Faber, and New York, Dutton, 1968.
  Nunquam. London, Faber, and New York, Dutton, 1970.

OTHER PUBLICATIONS

Novels

Pied Piper of Lovers. London, Cassell, 1935.
Panic Spring (as Charles Norden). London, Faber, and New York, Covici Friede, 1937.
The Black Book: An Agon. Paris, Obelisk Press, 1938; New York, Dutton, 1960; London, Faber, 1973.
Cefalû. London, Editions Poetry London, 1947; as *The Dark Labyrinth*, London, Ace, 1958; New York, Dutton, 1962.
The Alexandria Quartet. London, Faber, and New York, Dutton, 1962.
  Justine. London, Faber, and New York, Dutton, 1957.
  Balthazar. London, Faber, and New York, Dutton, 1958.
  Mountolive. London, Faber, 1958; New York, Dutton, 1959.
  Clea. London, Faber, and New York, Dutton, 1960.
White Eagles over Serbia. London, Faber, and New York, Criterion, 1957.
Monsieur; or, The Prince of Darkness. London, Faber, 1974; New York, Viking Press, 1975.
Livia; or, Buried Alive. London, Faber, 1978; New York, Viking Press, 1979.

Short Stories

Zero, and Asylum in the Snow. Privately printed, 1946; as *Two Excursions into Reality,* Berkeley, California, Circle, 1947.
Esprit de Corps: Sketches from Diplomatic Life. London, Faber, 1957; New York, Dutton, 1958.
Stiff Upper Lip: Life among the Diplomats. London, Faber, 1958; New York, Dutton, 1959.
Sauve Qui Peut. London, Faber, 1966; New York, Dutton, 1967.
The Best of Antrobus. London, Faber, 1974.

Plays

Sappho: A Play in Verse (produced Hamburg, 1959; Edinburgh, 1961; Evanston, Illinois, 1964). London, Faber, 1950; New York, Dutton, 1958.
Acte (produced Hamburg, 1961). London, Faber, and New York, Dutton, 1965.

An Irish Faustus: A Morality in Nine Scenes (produced Sommerhausen, Germany, 1966). London, Faber, 1963; New York, Dutton, 1964.

Screenplays: *Cleopatra,* with others, 1963; *Judith,* with others, 1966.

Radio Script: *Greek Peasant Superstitions,* 1947.

Television Scripts: *The Lonely Roads,* with Diane Deriaz, 1970; *The Search for Ulysses* (USA).

Recording: *Ulysses Come Back: Sketch for a Musical* (story, music, and lyrics by Durrell), 1971.

Verse

Quaint Fragment: Poems Written Between the Ages of Sixteen and Nineteen. London, Cecil Press, 1931.
Ten Poems. London, Caduceus Press, 1932.
Ballade of Slow Decay. Privately printed, 1932.
Bromo Bombastes: A Fragment from a Laconic Drama by Gaffer Peeslake. London, Caduceus Press, 1933.
Transition. London, Caduceus Press, 1934.
Mass for the Old Year. Privately printed, 1935.
Proems: An Anthology of Poems, with others. London, Fortune Press, 1938.
A Private Country. London, Faber, 1943.
The Parthenon: For T.S. Eliot. Privately printed, 1945(?).
Cities, Plains, and People. London, Faber, 1946.
On Seeming to Presume. London, Faber, 1948.
A Landmark Gone. Privately printed, 1949.
Deus Loci. Ischia, Italy, Di Mato Vito, 1950.
Private Drafts. Nicosia, Cyprus, Proodos Press, 1955.
The Tree of Idleness and Other Poems. London, Faber, 1955.
Selected Poems. London, Faber, and New York, Grove Press, 1956.
Collected Poems. London, Faber, and New York, Dutton, 1960; revised edition, 1968.
Penguin Modern Poets 1, with Elizabeth Jennings and R.S. Thomas. London, Penguin, 1962.
Poetry. New York, Dutton, 1962.
Beccafico Le Becfigue (English, with French translation by F.J. Temple). Montpellier, France, La Licorne, 1963.
A Persian Lady. Edinburgh, Tragara Press, 1963.
Selected Poems 1935-1963. London, Faber, 1964.
The Ikons and Other Poems. London, Faber, 1966; New York, Dutton, 1967.
The Red Limbo Lingo: A Poetry Notebook for 1968-1970. London, Faber, and New York, Dutton, 1971.
On the Suchness of the Old Boy. London, Turret, 1972.
Vega and Other Poems. London, Faber, 1973.
Lifelines. Edinburgh, Tragara Press, 1974.
Selected Poems, edited by Alan Ross. London, Faber, 1977.
Collected Poems 1931-1974, edited by James Brigham. London, Faber, and New York, Viking Press, 1980.

Other

Prospero's Cell: A Guide to the Landscape and Manners of the Island of Corcyra. London, Faber, 1945; with *Reflections on a Marine Venus,* New York, Dutton, 1960.
Key to Modern Poetry. London, Peter Nevill, 1952; as *A Key to Modern British Poetry,* Norman, University of Oklahoma Press, 1952.
Reflections on a Marine Venus: A Companion to the Landscape of Rhodes. London, Faber, 1953; with *Prospero's Cell,* New York, Dutton, 1960.
Bitter Lemons (on Cyprus). London, Faber, 1957; New York, Dutton, 1958.
Art and Outrage: A Correspondence about Henry Miller Between Alfred Perlès and Lawrence Durrell, with an Intermission by Henry Miller. London, Putnam, 1959; New York, Dutton, 1960.

Groddeck (on Georg Walther Groddeck). Wiesbaden, Limes, 1961.
Briefwechsel über "Actis", with Gustaf Gründgens. Hamburg, Rowohlt, 1961.
Lawrence Durrell and Henry Miller: A Private Correspondence, edited by George Wickes. New York, Dutton, and London, Faber, 1963.
La Descente du Styx (English, with French translations by F.J. Temple). Montpellier, France, La Murène, 1964; as *Down the Styx,* Santa Barbara, California, Capricorn Press, 1971.
Spirit of Place: Letters and Essays on Travel, edited by Alan G. Thomas. London, Faber, and New York, Dutton, 1969.
Le Grand Suppositoire (interview with Marc Alyn). Paris, Belfond, 1972; as *The Big Supposer,* London, Abelard Schuman, and New York, Grove Press, 1973.
The Happy Rock (on Henry Miller). London, Village Press, 1973.
The Plant-Magic Man. Santa Barbara, California, Capra Press, 1973.
Blue Thirst. Santa Barbara, California, Capra Press, 1975.
Sicilian Carousel. London, Faber, and New York, Viking Press, 1977.
The Greek Islands. London, Faber, and New York, Viking Press, 1978.
A Smile in the Mind's Eye. London, Wildwood House, 1980.

Editor, with others, *Personal Landscape: An Anthology of Exile.* London, Editions Poetry London, 1945.
Editor, *A Henry Miller Reader.* New York, New Directions, 1959; as *The Best of Henry Miller,* London, Heinemann, 1960.
Editor, *New Poems 1963: A P.E.N. Anthology of Contemporary Poetry.* London, Hutchinson, 1963.
Editor, *Lear's Corfu: An Anthology Drawn from the Painter's Letters.* Corfu, Corfu Travel, 1965.
Editor, *Wordsworth.* London, Penguin, 1973.

Translator, *Six Poems from the Greek of Sikelianos and Seferis.* Privately printed, 1946.
Translater, with Bernard Spencer and Nanos Valaoritis, *The King of Asine and Other Poems,* by George Seferis. London, Lehmann, 1948.
Translator, *The Curious History of Pope Joan,* by Emmanuel Royidis. London, Verschoyle, 1954; revised edition, as *Pope Joan: A Romantic Biography,* London, Deutsch, 1960; New York, Dutton, 1961.

*

Bibliography: by Alan G. Thomas, in *Lawrence Durrell: A Critical Study* by G.S. Fraser, London, Faber, 1968; New York, Dutton, 1969.

Manuscript Collections: University of California, Los Angeles; University of Illinois, Urbana.

*   *   *

Lawrence Durrell's *Tunc* and *Nunquam* are the two parts of a science-fiction novel known collectively as *The Revolt of Aphrodite.* The plots describe the efforts of Felix Charlock to build a computer, Abel, and a robot double of a prostitute-turned-movie-actress, Iolanthe. In doing so, he is involved with a conglomerate corporation known as Merlin or the "firm" and its owners, Julian, Jocas, and Benedicta. Durrell is attempting to dissect the notion of culture; the superficial bases for this examination are Spengler (the approach to culture, the concern with money and contractual obligation, and even the term "the firm" itself are taken from *The Decline of the West*) and Freud (particularly the psychopathology of sex and the sexual connotations of money).

Durrell has identified the major pre-occupations of all his fiction when he writes (in *Key to Modern Poetry*) that "Time and the ego are the two determinants of style for the twentieth century...." The double, whether robot or human, is also very common in Durrell's writing, and is related to his attempts to handle multi-faceted personalities and fragmented time from multiple viewpoints, as in *The Alexandria Quartet.* In *Key to Modern Poetry* he briefly traces the literary history of the double and ends by saying that "in nearly every case we are given a double which is either a saint, a criminal or a monster." Character is difficult to assess in Durrell's works; the surface descriptions of neuroses, frequently maimed characters, impotence, incestuous triangular relationships, and other sexual aberrations produce a shock value which often hides the suspicion that there really are no "characters" in his work—only puppets with a strong aroma.

The major distinctive feature of Durrell's writing is his baroque style. His writing is that of a poet—a sensuous mosaic of exotic words and images that adds a welcome dimension to the often flat prose of contemporary fiction. The occasional excesses are also those of the poet, mainly over-writing and tiresome platitudes. Throughout his career Durrell has had a remarkable eye for "place," and it appears again in *Tunc* and *Nunquam,* although somewhat supplanted by the ubiquity of the "firm." The technology that supplies the science-fiction basis in both books is remarkably crude, unimaginative, and dated. Much of the character motivation in *Tunc* and *Nunquam* is centered around the concept of a person's work in relation to his culture and his emotional life. As A.W. Friedman has said, "The rule in Durrell is that to deny the validity of one's work is to negate love." Love and work drive and frustrate Charlock and the other characters throughout the books.

The book titles derive from the epigraph "Aut tunc, aut nunquam" (It was then or never) from the *Satyricon* of Petronius. The implication of a last chance for society to define its values is supported by a quotation from *Tunc* which can serve as a statement of purpose for the two books: "When a civilisation has decided to bury its head in the sand what can we do but tickle its arse with a feather?"

—Norman L. Hills

EDMONDSON, G.C. (José Mario Garry Ordonez Edmondson y Cotton). Also writes as Kelly P. Gast. American. Born in Rachuachitlán, Tabasco, Mexico, 11 October 1922. Educated in Vienna, M.D. Served in the United States Marine Corps, 1942-46. Married three times; two sons and two daughters. Has worked as a blacksmith. Agent: Robert P. Mills Ltd., 156 East 52nd Street, New York, New York 10022. Address: 310 Lila Lane, El Cajon, California 92021, U.S.A.

SCIENCE-FICTION PUBLICATIONS

Novels

The Ship That Sailed the Time Stream. New York, Ace, 1965; London, Arrow, 1971.
Chapayeca. New York, Doubleday, 1971; London, Hale, 1973; as *Blue Face,* New York, DAW, 1972.
T.H.E.M. New York, Doubleday, 1974.
The Aluminum Man. New York, Berkley, 1975.

Short Stories

Stranger Than You Think. New York, Ace, 1965.

Uncollected Short Stories

"Nobody Believes an Indian," in *Fantasy and Science Fiction* (New York), May 1970.
"The Tempollutors," in *Infinity 4,* edited by Robert Hoskins. New York, Lancer, 1972.
"One Plus One Equals Eleven," in *Analog* (New York), January 1973.
"Tube," in *If* (New York), August 1974.

OTHER PUBLICATIONS

Novels as Kelly P. Gast

Dil Dies Hard. New York, Doubleday, 1975.
The Long Trail North. New York, Doubleday, 1976.
Murphy's Trail. New York, Doubleday, 1976.
Last Stage from Opal. New York, Doubleday, 1978.
Murder at Magpie Flats. New York, Doubleday, 1978.
Paddy. New York, Doubleday, 1979.

*   *   *

A major theme in G.C. Edmondson's science fiction is the collision between alien civilizations. Two of his novels *(Chapayeca* and *The Aluminum Man)* reflect this concern by setting the encounter with aliens within the context of Indian culture. Edmondson's first-hand knowledge of the subject lends an air of authenticity to his otherwise fanciful and strained plots. Edmondson also likes to write from the viewpoint of outcasts, losers, and drop-outs—those on the margin of society who are often the first to register the shock waves of cultural upheaval.

Set against the background of governmental repression and Indian rebellion, *Chapayeca* focuses on an anthropologist named Nash Taber whose career and marriage are as shaky as his health. Having little to lose and much to gain by pursuing the elusive Chapayeca, an Indian demon, he discovers that the creature is not simply a shaman's fantasy, but an alien with extraordinary powers and curiously dull wits. Taber decides to bring this sensational find back to civilization, but meets opposition from all quarters. Gradually he learns the deadly secret of the alien's ability to overcome pain and confer incredible powers, but only when it is too late. A typical Edmonsonian hero, Taber is a lone individual caught in the cross-fire between cultures and values.

While *Chapayeca* suggests the hazards of dropping out and pursuing a "Yaqui way of knowledge," *T.H.E.M.* is set against the background of the anti-war movement of the 1960's and the Nixon era. The main characters are draft dodgers who decide to enlist with a benevolent galactic force known as the Alliance in order to deter the planet-destroying T.h.e.m. Earthlings are obliged to put aside their own petty differences (such as the Vietnam War) and form an international order. Since the bureaucrats and brass are unable to manage anything efficiently, the power eventually is handed over to Jorf and his crew of mavericks and misfits, who turn out to be the best fighters. Some of Edmondson's experiences as a Marine seem to have influenced this celebration of the on-the-line soldier and the anti-establishment tone.

Edmondson is neither a very skillful nor subtle writer, but his stories have moments of vigor that maintain the reader's interest. Besides writing about Indian culture and interplanetary adventures, he has also written a novel on time travel *(The Ship That Sailed the Time Stream)* and westerns, crime, gothics - "anything to fend off the Transylvanian Mortgage company."

—Anthony Manousos

EFFINGER, Geo(rge) Alec. American. Born in Cleveland, Ohio, 10 January 1947. Attended Yale University, New Haven, Connecticut, 1965, 1969, and New York University, 1968. Free-lance writer: since 1971, writer for *Marvel Comic Books,* New York. Agent: Jane Rostrosen Agency, 351 East 51st Street, New York, New York, 10022. Address: Box 15183, New Orleans, Louisiana 70175, U.S.A.

SCIENCE-FICTION PUBLICATIONS

Novels (series: Planet of the Apes)

What Entropy Means to Me. New York, Doubleday, 1972.

Relatives. New York, Harper, 1973.
Man the Fugitive (Apes). New York, Award, 1974.
Nightmare Blue, with Gardner Dozois. New York, Berkley, 1975;
   London, Fontana, 1977.
Escape to Tomorrow (Apes). New York, Award, 1975.
Journey into Terror (Apes). New York, Award, 1975.
Those Gentle Voices. New York, Warner, 1976.
Lord of the Apes (Apes). New York, Award, 1976.
Death in Florence. New York, Doubleday, 1978; as *Utopia 3,*
   Chicago, Playboy Press, 1980.
Heroics. New York, Doubleday, 1979.

Short Stories

Mixed Feelings. New York, Harper, 1974.
Irrational Numbers. New York, Doubleday, 1976.
Dirty Tricks. New York, Doubleday, 1978.

Uncollected Short Story

"The Pinch-Hitters," in *Isaac Asimov's Science Fiction Magazine*
   (New York), May 1979.

OTHER PUBLICATIONS

Novels

Felicia. New York, Berkley, 1976.
Steel. Chicago, Playboy Press, 1980.

Geo. Alec Effinger comments:

I try to do new things with old material. A good deal of my science
fiction is an attempt to take traditional SF furniture (storylines,
settings, characters, and hardware) and combine it with some element of the absurd. The result is not science fiction, because it bears
little resemblance to the rational real world. Perhaps surreal fantasy
describes these stories best. My antecedents are as much in the
theater of the absurd as they are in science fiction.

One of my favorite experiments is to appropriate an accepted SF
situation and populate it with one or more of the continuing characters I have established in my stories over the years. These characters
are not recurring in the usual sense. Rather, I think of them as a kind
of repertory company. They may die in one story and reappear later
as necessary. They live in many eras and appear together in various
combinations, sometimes contradicting earlier stories. Just as William Bendix appeared in one motion picture and was killed or
married, then months later appeared in another movie, unrelated to
the first, so my characters pop up here and there throughout my
own future history, unaffected by the stories in which they performed previously. Whenever they appear, however, they always
represent the same kind of person, making for me a private stable of
stereotypes to draw upon.

I enjoy parody, satire, and pastiche, but every once in a while I
will do a serious story in a straight SF mode, mostly to keep the
audience on its toes. SF is the only neighborhood of writing where I
could get away with this kind of thing, and I am immensely grateful
to the field and its readers for giving me the opportunity.

*   *   *

Since the publication of his best-known novel, *What Entropy
Means to Me,* Geo. Alec Effinger has demonstrated versatility in
books as disparate as the mainstream novel *Felicia,* the teleplay
adaptation *Man the Fugitive,* and *Nightmare Blue,* a collaboration
with Gardner Dozois. More important, he has produced short
stories and novels linked in strange and wondrous ways to form a
unique "Effinger's World." Some critics label him a writer of sword
and sorcery; other, of myth. Still others avoid labels, preferring a
literary report card showing a high rating in technique, a low one in
substance. Despite any problem with fitting him into the established
definitions of science fiction, Effinger does offer an exceptional
reading experience.

Entropy is a structural tour de force, being four intricately interwoven stories with author-character Seyt as nexus. First is it a
romantic quest tale of an eldest son searching for a lost father.

Aided by a magic-competent companion, Dore overcomes natural
obstacles, monsters, seduction, villainy, only to find Father at a
point of no return. If *Entropy* went no further, it could sustain the
label of sword and sorcery. But *Entropy* is more, three stories more.
Functioning much as a chorus in a Greek tragedy, Seyt relates his
family's saga from Earth to the planet Home. The third story
evolves as a classic political power struggle to fill the vacuum
created by the absence of father and eldest son. Seyt faithfully
records the machinations, religious conflicts, and personal hurt
involved. The fourth story gains subtle attention. This is the story of
creation—literary creation. Seyt makes us aware of the artist, story
churning in his head, faced with the arduous task of shaping it for an
audience. Seyt must grapple with the author's universal problems:
critical pressure from readers; political pressure to slant toward
propaganda; and inner pressure to maintain authorial integrity.
This trenchant commentary on the art and act of writing, reappearing in later short stories and novels, helps link *Entropy* to them.

Effinger's later fictional world is a paradox. We may recognize a
familiar society, only to have subsequent paragraphs jolt us into a
surreal world. Often gray, sometimes diseased, always warped by
conformity, this society is best epitomized by the village of Gremmage in "Things Go Better," "Heart Stop," and "Lights Out."
Gremmage isolates, smothers, and molds newcomers to its ways.
Effinger's larger society has the Representatives, six men governing
by whimsical stupidity ("Lydectes: On the Nature of Sport," "Contentment, Satisfaction, Cheer, Well-Being, Gladness, Joy, Comfort,
and Not Having to Get Up Early Any More," and *Relatives*).
Effinger's people freely slip from story to story, changing personalities and identities illogically. For example, the three separate Wein-
raub/Weintraubs triplicate experience in *Relatives,* then show up as
a writer of a trilogy of novels in "Biting Down Hard in Truth."
Global bum Bo Staefler of *Death in Florence* has little obvious
relationship to baseball catcher Bo Staefler ("Naked to the Invisible
Eye") or to castaway Bo Staefler ("World War II"). Robert Hanson
appears as an 11-year-old boy ("Chase Our Blues Away"), a young
man afflicted with altruism ("Strange Ragged Saintliness"), one for
whom a park is named ("Timmy Was Eight"), and an android clone
("The Awesome Menace of the Polarizer"). Jennings suffers metamorphosis from a tough coach ("Biting Down Hard on Truth") to a
chairman of the board ("At the Bran Foundry") to an astro-
physicist (*Those Gentle Voices*). And then there is Sandor Courane,
Justin Benarcek, Dr. Davis, the hunchback Wagner, Eileen Brant,
and numerous others, all moving in and out of Effinger's multi-
faceted morality play.

Effinger is master of the non sequitur which teases the mind with
the thought that there is a veiled logic and an illuminating insight
here, could one but rearrange things. If not, the reader must provide
his own, for Effinger has prodded his mind unmercifully. Musing on
the act of writing, a character in "The Ghost Writer" inadvertently
gives us a summation for Effinger himself: "There was always the
chance that a new fragment might join two of the enigmatic earlier
pieces, and a whole framework might begin to be evident. But not
today. Here was another piece, of perhaps a totally different puzzle.
It was longer, and it was exciting. The audience would be satisfied,
but not the scholars."

—Hazel Pierce

EHRLICH, Max. American. Born in Springfield, Massachusetts, 10 October 1909. Educated at the University of Michigan,
Ann Arbor, B.A. Married Doris Rubinstein in 1940 (divorced); two
daughters. Member of the copyright and screen credits committees,
Writers Guild of America West. Agent: Scott Meredith Literary
Agency, 845 Third Avenue, New York, New York 10022. Address:
818 North Doheny Drive, Los Angeles, California 90069, U.S.A.

SCIENCE-FICTION PUBLICATIONS

Novels

The Big Eye. New York, Doubleday, 1949; London, Boardman, 1951.
Spin the Glass Web. New York, Harper, 1952; London, Corgi, 1957.
First Train to Babylon. New York, Harper, and London, Gollancz, 1955; as *Dead Letter*, London, Corgi, 1958; as *The Naked Edge*, Corgi, 1961.
The Takers. New York, Harper, and London, Gollancz, 1961.
Dead Is the Blue. New York, Doubleday, and London, Gollancz, 1964.
The Edict. New York, Doubleday, 1971.
The Savage Is Loose. New York, Bantam, 1974.
The Reincarnation of Peter Proud. Indianapolis, Bobbs Merrill, 1974; London, W.H. Allen, 1975.
The Cult. New York, Simon and Schuster, 1978; London, Mayflower, 1979.
Reincarnation in Venice. New York, Simon and Schuster, 1979.
Naked Beach. Chicago, Playboy Press, 1979.
Shaitan. New York, Arbor House, 1980.

OTHER PUBLICATIONS

Plays

Screenplays: *The Savage Is Loose*, with Frank de Felitta, 1975; *The Reincarnation of Peter Proud*, 1975.

Radio Plays: for *The Shadow, Mr. and Mrs. North, Sherlock Holmes, Nick Carter, The Big Story*, and *Big Town* series.

Television Plays: *The Apple (Star Trek* series), and for *Studio One, The Defenders, The Dick Powell Show*, and *Winston Churchill* series.

*   *   *

Besides his film, radio, and television writing, Max Ehrlich has written some dozen novels, often with a science-fiction or fantasy edge. Never a producer of "hard" science fiction, he usually aims at topical thrillers for a wider audience, generally suggesting that traditional value systems are well worth following.

In *The Big Eye* a wandering planet threatens collision with Earth. Encouraged by astronomers to believe the end is near, the public views the invader as a gigantic, baleful watcher. Although the near miss has minimal physical effects on Earth, human repentance augurs at least a semblance of a utopian future. There is little action in the novel, but some movement. The chief character, assistant to the director of Palomar Observatory where the telescopic Big Eye is located, shuttles back and forth across the country, but he is primarily an observer and scarcely affected by his scientific training. Contravening his desire to remain childless, his wife's act of faith and hope in the future is vindicated, though the Earth was scared by a hoax, not saved by a miracle. Ehrlich's millennial psychology and politics are little more convincing than his science, but the book remains a fair representation of the state of Cold War apprehension in its time.

The Edict projects an overpopulated future in which childbirth has been banned for 30 years. The mechanics of social management are never rationalized, but computers, scant food allotments, and police power are invoked. The story focusses on two couples living in a State Museum exhibit preserving 20th-century lifestyles. Rejecting sexual pluralism and mechanical babies, one of the wives insists on bearing her own child. When the other couple discover her secret and insist on sharing, the new parents escape to a radioactive island, where life will be more short than sweet. Style and scene management are both stiff, but Ehrlich has put the population dilemma in simple-to-understand contemporary terms, though with no utopian alternative this time.

Probably his best-written work toys with the supernatural. *Reincarnation in Venice* is an adequate sequel, structurally almost identical, to *The Reincarnation of Peter Proud*. Not having to stage-manage an entire world, Ehrlich can better handle local color in California and New England. The "science" of dream research is confronted with a man whose dreams suggest that, just before his birth, he was somebody else. Following them up leads him to the town where his "double" was killed. When he falls in love with the daughter of the murderess, the results are predictably ironic. Hardly raising a major problem to the level of serious discourse, the novel is an adequate exercise in nightmare logic, suspenseful, and concisely told.

—David N. Samuelson

───────────

EISENBERG, Larry. American. Born in New York City, 21 December 1919. Educated at the City College of New York, B.A. in mathematics 1940; Polytechnic Institute, Brooklyn, M.E.E. 1952; Ph.D. in electronics 1966. Served in the United States Army Air Force, 1945-46: Sergeant. Married Frances Brenner in 1950; one daughter and one son. Instructor, New York Institute of Technology, 1948-52; Project Engineer, PRD, New York, 1952-55; Instructor of Electronics, City College of New York, 1955-56; Digital Logician, Digitronics, Roslyn, New York, 1956-58. Since 1958, Co-Director of the electronics laboratory, Rockefeller University, New York. Address: 315 East 88th Street, New York, New York 10028, U.S.A.

SCIENCE-FICTION PUBLICATIONS

Short Stories

The Best Laid Schemes. New York, Macmillan, 1971.

Uncollected Short Stories (series: Emmett Duckworth)

"The Grand Illusions," in *Galaxy* (New York), May 1972.
"The Soul Music of Duckworth's Dibs," in *Galaxy* (New York), September 1972.
"The Executive Art," in *If* (New York), December 1972.
"The Merchant," in *If* (New York), October 1973.
"Sikh, Sikh, Sikh," in *Vertex* (Los Angeles), December 1973.
"The Baby," in *Galaxy* (New York), March 1974.
"Televerite," in *Vertex* (Los Angeles), April 1974.
"Time and Duckworth," in *Galaxy* (New York), May 1974.
"Where There's Smoke," in *Galaxy* (New York), June 1974.
"The Money Machine," in *Vertex* (Los Angeles), August 1974.
"Elephants Sometimes Forget," in *Fantasy and Science Fiction* (New York), September 1974.
"The Lookalike Revolution," in *Fantasy and Science Fiction* (New York), November 1974.
"The Spurious President," in *Vertex* (Los Angeles), April 1975.
"Dr. Snow Maiden," in *Fantasy and Science Fiction* (New York), August 1975.
"My Random Friend," in *Fantasy and Science Fiction* (New York), August 1977.
"The Interface," in *Fantasy and Science Fiction* (New York), August 1978.
"Djinn and Duckworth," in *Isaac Asimov's Science Fiction Magazine* (New York), March 1979.

OTHER PUBLICATIONS

Novel

The Villa of the Ferromonte. New York, Simon and Schuster, 1974.

Verse

Limericks for Lantzmen, with George Gordon.   New York, Citadel Press, 1965.
Limericks for the Loo, with George Gordon.   New York, Kanrom, and London, Arlington, 1965.

Other

Games People Shouldn't Play, with George Gordon.   New York, Kanrom, 1966.

*   *   *

It is extremely difficult to make a reputation exclusively as a short-story writer, even in the genre of science fiction. Larry Eisenberg is one of the few to attract considerable attention over the years, despite the fact that he appears primarily in magazines and has never had a novel published, although there has been one collection of his shorter works, *The Best Laid Schemes.*

Although many of his stories are serious in intent and execution, he is probably best known for his humor, particularly the ongoing adventures of Professor Emmett Duckworth, twice winner of the Nobel Prize. Duckworth is a true descendant of the classic C.P. Ransome stories of Homer Nearing. In almost every case, Duckworth has developed some new device or principle, which should have had very beneficial effects, but which always seems to somehow go awry at a crucial point. In "The Saga of DMM," for example, Duckworth develops an aphrodisiac which, unfortunately, also tends to fatten up its user, and eventually becomes an unstable explosive akin to nitroglycerin. By chance he taps into a secret government file in "Open Secrets," and finds an ingenious method by which to conceal the data he discovers. In "IQ Soup" he feeds intelligence into an experimental subject, whose plane then crashes in cannibal country with predictable results. In yet other stories, Duckworth develops heavy smoke which falls from your cigarette to the floor, to be removed later, sensory recordings, and a sonic probe that picks up sounds from the past.

As a contrast to the general good humor of the Duckworth stories, Eisenberg has another, very loosely organized series detailing the encounters between humans and an alien species called Sentients. Most of the stories take place after the human race has conquered and occupied the Sentients' home planet. These stories are often very bitter, and are generally very well told. Among the better stories in this series are "The Quintipods," a tale of boxing and the exploitation of a species considered inferior, "The Heart of the Giant," during which a number of humans are killed by a non-violent Sentient when he short circuits the computer that powers their artificial hearts, and "The Conqueror," a story that succeeds through expert use of understatement. A Sentient woman seduces a human soldier, then pretends to be an android in order to humiliate him. There are some outstanding non-series stories as well. Perhaps the best is "The Chameleon," the story of a politician whose use of media and computer devices to enhance his own image is so successful that he is taken in himself. Almost as impressive is the story of an egotistical President whose personality alters when he is lost within his own security system ("The Spurious President").

Eisenberg's stories read well even at their worst because he employs a clear style that is witty without being obtrusive for its own sake. There is almost always an element of humor, although it is often shaded with black, as Eisenberg holds up some attribute of human endeavor for our examination. The Duckworth stories in particular are refreshing and inventive, whether he is duplicating prominent citizens to embarrass them or developing unworkable weapon systems for a defense establishment he dislikes. While it may be a rare occasion when one of his stories will remain in our minds for long, it will be even rarer to find one that is not entertaining while we are reading-it.

—Don D'Ammassa

EISENSTEIN, Phyllis (née Kleinstein).   American.   Born in Chicago, Illinois, 26 February 1946. Educated at the University of Chicago, 1963-66; University of Illinois, Chicago, 1978-79. Married Alex Eisenstein in 1966. Co-Founder and Director, Windy City SF Writers Conference, Chicago, 1972-77. Since 1976, Anthology Trustee, Science Fiction Writers of America. Agent: Kirby McCauley Ltd., 60 East 42nd Street, New York, New York 10017, U.S.A.

SCIENCE-FICTION PUBLICATIONS

Novels

Born to Exile.   Sauk City, Wisconsin, Arkham House, 1978.
Sorcerer's Son.   New York, Ballantine, 1979.
Shadow of Earth.   New York, Dell, 1979.

Uncollected Short Stories

"The Trouble with the Past," with Alex Eisenstein, in *New Dimensions 1,* edited by Robert Silverberg.   New York, Doubleday, 1971.
"Teleprobe," in *Long Night of Waiting,* edited by Roger Elwood.   Nashville, Aurora, 1974.
"Attachment," in *Amazing* (New York), December 1974.
"The Weather on Mars," with Alex Eisenstein, in *Analog* (New York), December 1974.
"Tree of Life," in *Best Science Fiction Stories of the Year,* edited by Lester del Rey.   New York, Dutton, 1976.
"Sleeping Beauty—The True Story," with Alex Eisenstein, in *Cavalier* (New York), February 1976.
"You Are Here," with Alex Eisenstein, in *New Dimensions 7,* edited by Robert Silverberg.   New York, Harper, 1977.
"Alter Ego," with Alex Eisenstein, in *Fantasy and Science Fiction* (New York), March 1977.
"In Answer to Your Call," in *Fantasy and Science Fiction* (New York), January 1978.
"The Man with the Eye," in *Isaac Asimov's Science Fiction Magazine* (New York), November-December 1978.
"Lost and Found," in *Best Science Fiction Stories of the Year,* edited by Gardner Dozois.   New York, Dutton, 1979.
"The Land of Sorrow," in *The Year's Best Fantasy,* edited by Lin Carter.   New York, DAW, 1979.
"The Mountain Fastness," in *Fantasy and Science Fiction* (New York), July 1979.

*   *   *

Phyllis Eisenstein writes of science that barbarians take for magic, and magic that operates with the precision of science. She moves between fantasy and science fiction with an ease that demonstrates their common imaginative ground, and she builds on that ground worlds that are logically consistent and sensually complete. Whether she is writing alone or in collaboration with her husband Alex Eisenstein, her characters appear utterly real within their unique reality, and the resolution of their conflicts is always intrinsically part of that reality.

The first character that Phyllis Eisenstein followed beyond the range of one story was Alaric the minstrel. There are, in fact, minstrels in each of her novels—their mobility, their profession as story-tellers, their observant wisdom and easy love make them useful characters in any plot. But Alaric has an extra ability: he can teleport himself to any place he has seen before. He lives in a medieval landscape, where suspected witches are feared and burned, yet he knows his power is not witchcraft, that it obeys rules as simple as those governing speech or sight. His realization that witchcraft does not exist at all puts him an almost modern distance beyond the primitive people he meets. The Alaric stories were collected in *Born in Exile,* following Alaric as he grows up, searches for his parents, and flees to even more dangerous freedom. He is an appealing and successful character, and his travels are continued in more recent stories.

The minstrel in *Shadow of Earth* is even less magical than Alaric—in fact, he is an ordinary man who sings for a living. But he sings in the 20th century of an earth where the Armada won, and where under continuous Spanish Catholic rule the Industrial Revolution never happened. Celia, a young woman from our own 20th century, is transported to the minstrel's world by an invented device, and must try to survive. To some extent the novel operates as a debunking of popular historical romances, where beautiful women sweep to power with a toss of their heads. Celia does become the wife of a Marquis, but the near-slavery of her role, the inevitability of pregnancy, and the horror of delivery without anesthesia or antibiotics are all designed to put the advantages of the true 1980's in a strong light. Eisenstein details the Spanish world with a historian's care and a feminist's concern, but somehow Celia never achieves Alaric's easy believability. Perhaps this is because the novel's project requires that she be ordinary, a typical woman of her time, with no special powers beyond a tormenting memory. Her situation, though strange, is finally not strange enough; Eisenstein does better further inside the freedom of imagination.

Sorcerer's Son is far inside that freedom. A work of full fantasy, the novel envisions a world where magic not only exists but has fields of study as specialized as modern science, and specialists whose mutual jealousy can lead to war. The narrative is unusually rich with colors, tastes, textures and sounds. The story pits the evil demon-master Rezhyk against the gentle Lady Delivev, sorcerer of weaving and spiders, and mother of Cray, the secret son of Rezhyk. Cray grows to manhood and seeks the identity of his father, but the real hero of the tale is Gildrun, Rezhyk's demon slave, who falls in love with Delivev. *Sorcerer's Son* has many things in common with Eisenstein's other novels—the long circular quest, the minstrel, the fortress, and the father who moves to destroy the prodigal—but this novel, longer and almost overwhelmingly lush, is at the same time more controlled and consistent, and much more successful.

Such ability comes from an apprenticeship begun as a teenager, some of it in collaboration with her husband Alex Eisenstein. Their collaborated stories show a widening of the range of ideas, but no deviation in the competence of their execution. "Alter Ego" tells of a young priest, raised by the Church and troubled by vividly sensual dreams, who finally, chillingly, achieves his destiny. "The Trouble with the Past" is a neatly turned time-travel story with as much humor as ingenuity. The Eisensteins grew up when science fiction and fantasy were already established and thriving. They are natives in a lifetime of alternative worlds, and the case of their citizenship shows in the thoroughness and pleasure of their writing.

—Karen G. Way

* * *

EKLUND, Gordon. American. Born in Seattle, Washington, 24 July 1945. Educated at Contra Costa College, San Pablo, California, 1973-75. Served in the United States Air Force, 1963-67: Sergeant. Married Dianna Mylarski in 1969; two sons. Since 1968, free-lance writer. Recipient: Nebula Award, 1974. Agent: Kirby McCauley Ltd., 60 East 42nd Street, New York, New York 10017. Address: Box 2004, Richmond, California 94802, U.S.A.

SCIENCE-FICTION PUBLICATIONS

Novels (series: Lord Tedric)

The Eclipse of Dawn. New York, Ace, 1971.
A Trace of Dreams. New York, Ace, 1972.
Beyond the Resurrection. New York, Doubleday, 1973.
All Times Possible. New York, DAW, 1974.
Inheritors of Earth, with Poul Anderson. Radnor, Pennsylvania, Chilton, 1974.
Serving in Time. Toronto, Laser, 1975.
Falling Toward Forever. Toronto, Laser, 1975.
The Grayspace Beast. New York, Doubleday, 1976.
Dance of the Apocalypse. Toronto, Laser, 1976.
If the Stars Are Gods, with Gregory Benford. New York, Berkley, 1977; London, Gollancz, 1978.

The Starless World (novelization of TV play). New York, Bantam, 1978.
Lord Tedric, with E.E. Smith. New York, Baronet, 1978.
Space Pirates (Tedric), with E.E. Smith. New York, Baronet, 1979.
The Twilight River. New York, Dell, 1979.
Devil World (novelization of TV play). New York, Bantam, 1979.
The Garden of Winter. New York, Berkley, 1980.
Find the Changeling, with Gregory Benford. New York, Dell, 1980.

Uncollected Short Stories

"Dear Aunt Annie," in *Fantastic* (New York), April 1970.
"A Gift from the Gozniks," in *Fantastic* (New York), August 1970.
"Home Again, Home Again," in *Quark 3,* edited by Samuel R. Delany and Marilyn Hacker. New York, Paperback Library, 1971.
"West Wind, Falling," in *Universe 1,* edited by Terry Carr. New York, Ace, 1971; London, Dobson, 1975.
"Seeker for Still Life," in *Fantasy and Science Fiction* (New York), January 1971.
"Gemini Cavendish," in *Amazing* (New York), March 1971.
"Defender of Death," in *Galaxy* (New York), April 1971.
"The Edge and the Mist," in *Galaxy* (New York), September 1971.
"To End All Wars," in *Amazing* (New York), November 1971.
"Stalking the Sun," in *Universe 2,* edited by Terry Carr. New York, Ace, 1972; London, Dobson, 1975.
"White Summer in Memphis," in *New Dimensions 2,* edited by Robert Silverberg. New York, Avon, 1972.
"Grasshopper Time," in *Fantasy and Science Fiction* (New York), March 1972.
"Soft Change," in *Amazing* (New York), May 1972.
"Underbelly," in *If* (New York), October 1972.
"Examination Day," in *The Other Side of Tomorrow* edited by Roger Elwood. New York, Random House, 1973.
"Free City Blues," in *Universe 3,* edited by Terry Carr. New York, Random House, 1973; London, Dobson, 1976.
"Lovemaker," in *Eros in Orbit,* edited by Joseph Elder. New York, Simon and Schuster, 1973.
"The Shrine of Sebastian," in *Chains of the Sea.* Nashville, Nelson, 1973.
"Three Comedians," in *New Dimensions 3,* edited by Robert Silverberg. New York, Avon, 1973.
"The Ascending Axe," in *Amazing* (New York), January 1973.
"Iron Mountain," in *Fantastic* (New York), July 1973.
"The Stuff of Time," in *Fantastic* (New York), September 1973.
"The Beasts in the Jungle," in *Fantasy and Science Fiction* (New York), November 1973.
"Moby, Too," in *Amazing* (New York), December 1973.
"The Ambiguities of Yesterday," in *The Far Side of Time* edited by Roger Elwood. New York, Dodd Mead, 1974.
"Psychosomatica," in *Crisis,* edited by Roger Elwood. Nashville, Nelson, 1974.
"Continuous Performance," in *If* (New York), February 1974.
"Beneath the Waves," in *Fantasy and Science Fiction* (New York), March 1974.
"The Treasure in the Treasure House," in *Fantasy and Science Fiction* (New York), August 1974.
"Tattered Stars, Tattered Bars," in *Fantastic* (New York), September 1974.
"Angel of Truth," in *Epoch,* edited by Roger Elwood and Robert Silverberg. New York, Berkley, 1975.
"Sandsnake Hunter," in *Fantasy and Science Fiction* (New York), March 1975.
"Second Creation," in *Amazing* (New York), March 1975.
"The Restoration," in *Analog* (New York), September 1975.
"What Did You Do Last Year?," in *Universe 6,* edited by Terry Carr. New York, Doubleday, 1976; London, Dobson, 1978.
"The Rising of the Sun," in *Beyond Time,* edited by Sandra Ley. New York, Pocket Books, 1976.
"The Locust Descending," in *Fantastic* (New York), February 1976.
"Changing Styles," in *Fantasy and Science Fiction* (New York), March 1976.
"The Prince in Metropolis," in *Analog* (New York), May 1976.

"The Anvil of Jove," in *Fantasy and Science Fiction* (New York), July 1976.

"Embryonic Dharma," in *Analog* (New York), December 1976.

"The Retro Man," in *New Dimensions 7,* edited by Robert Silverberg.   New York, Harper, and London, Gollancz, 1977.

"Hellas in Florida," in *Fantasy and Science Fiction* (New York), January 1977.

"The Tides of Time," in *Galaxy* (New York), March 1977.

"Vermeer's Window," in *Universe 8,* edited by Terry Carr.   New York, Doubleday, 1978; London, Dobson, 1979.

"Saint Francis Night," in *Amazing* (New York), May 1978.

"Points of Contact," in *Fantasy and Science Fiction* (New York), June 1978.

"The Anaconda's Smile," in *Fantasy and Science Fiction* (New York), May 1979.

Gordon Eklund comments:

If there's any one aspect of my work to date that seems worth emphasizing, it would have to be the range of themes, subjects, styles, and moods that I've attempted. I don't believe that any two of my novels are very much alike, and the short stories are even more varied, if only because of their greater number. To me, the science-fiction field is an extremely broad category—one encompassing, as it does, all of possibility—and I've found it extremely difficult to settle down to mining a single nook within the field. I suppose a few certain types of stories can easily be seen as favorites of mine—I find particular pleasure in dealing with time and parallel worlds—but I wouldn't want to predict that this will remain valid during my next ten years as a writer.

*   *   *

Gordon Eklund reaches with equal dexterity far out into time or space. This west-coast author has set his plots over a broad spectrum. Eklund relishes the combination of fun and substance in his works. The reader is never able to predict the next paragraph, either icy sarcasm or deep message. One of the notable aspects of this science fiction, especially the early work, is the visionary range concerning the human prospect. Ironically, the specific personalities who are exploring these possibilities appear neurotic and limited. It is something of a tough dichotomy in Eklund's work. Mercifully, the conclusions to these space and time adventures are often thought provoking rather than just cosmically consoling.

Eklund's first novel, *The Eclipse of Dawn*, is certainly one of his best. The story is set about 25 years in the future, and the radical societal smashup (that everyone seems to fear so much now) has occurred. The America of the 21st century is a stark, confusing, and disorienting place. The exaggerated ennui of a fallen America is creatively juxtaposed to the virile faith of Senator William Colonby, who is running for president.

Eklund masterfully caricatures the idiocy and irony of a misplaced crusader. Senator Colonby does a whistle-stop tour of America, uttering loud but meaningless political platitudes. Along with some sexual intrigue, the plot includes a telepathic woman who is in contact with powerful aliens from Jupiter. The book settles down into a nasty chaos and depression when these alien savior-beings turn out to be nonexistent. The book closes with the surrender of the sitting president to Colonby, and a statement about the basic impotency of politics. In *The Eclipse of Dawn* the integrity of the individual is still possible, but the societal prospect is bleak.

Perhaps Eklund's richest achievement is *If the Stars Are Gods* (written with Gregory Benford). The novel is a moving challenge to the limited consciousness we all seek to transcend: "Understanding the new and strange is not so much a matter of work and effort, but of intuition and time to let ideas come to fruition." The hero is Bradley Reynolds, a "brilliant young scientist" whose consuming passion is to discover other dimensions of being in the universe. The plot moves quickly through an initial failure to find life on Mars, an encounter with enlightened aliens from another universe, and 35 years in an African monastery. This contrast of the exploratory and introspective nature of Reynolds's personality is skillfully depicted. His personal odyssey climaxes with his death in a newly discovered place which will open new opportunities for the human race. This work is especially a pleasure in terms of characterization (e.g., beautiful, mercurial and infuriating Mara: "She took drugs, slept

with other women, gambled, drank, stole money"). The characters are strong and brave while remaining believably human.

Perhaps the most memorable of Eklund's heroes is Tommy Bloome in *All Times Possible*. The specifics of Tommy's life, death, and identity are presented in a tantalizing montage of episodes. It becomes clear, however, that Tommy is a savior of the workers and the people. The book, like *The Eclipse of Dawn*, presents a post-catastrophe or transformed America—the difference being that Tommy ends up as a martyr for the cause of the (successful?) revolution. The entire novel is written while Tommy is contemplating a bullet that is in mid-air, whistling toward his forehead. Is Tommy in a new life form after death? Is he having the familiar "life flashing before my eyes" experience? Or is this device a statement about the awful finality of death? *All Times Possible* contains more provocative ambiguity than any of Eklund's other works, and goes somewhat beyond what seems to be the basic Eklund point of view: "We've no right to expect a damn thing from this cold universe" (*If the Stars Are Gods*).

In *Dance of the Apocalypse,* set in 2097, anarchy, poverty and starvation are the major components. The heroes in this showdown are a tough, illiterate street scrounger and a humanistic idealist from the east, William Stoner. *Dance of the Apocalypse* boasts a novel excursion of the imagination in terms of how order is restored to the now barbarous world. In the midst of deep turmoil, China returns to Confucianism and sends an exploratory mission to the United States. By a stroke of profound luck, our dedicated idealist has the sagacity to appreciate the Confucian mind. The final outcome of the insurrection is the realization of a Confucian state in America. The explorer and teacher from China explains quite clearly why things are going to be so happy from now on: "Because William Stoner believes what we believe, and because what we believe is correct."

The final works of Eklund that should be mentioned are the Lord Tedric series, reportedly conceived by E.E. "Doc" Smith, which involves a massive battle of good and evil forces. Lord Tedric's origins are not so different from Superman's (i.e., born in another world he doesn't remember, special powers on earth), but he comes to a realization of his abilities and destiny rather slowly. Tedric is not (and is not meant to be) as believable or human as Bradley Reynolds in *If the Stars Are Gods*.

Eklund has a rare ability to project many alternative outcomes for the United States, the world, and the cosmos. He ranges from sarcastic pessimism in *The Eclipse of Dawn,* to the patently bizarre possibility in *Dance of the Apocalypse* and total cosmic liberation (communication with the stars) in *If the Stars Are Gods*. Eklund's talent and insight are more visible when he keeps the plot and characters close to the reality of today. As he reaches to portray the New Man and the New Woman of the transformed future, his vision breaks down because of what he knows of the human condition. His pure heroes are acceptable, and his portrayal of the bitter defeatism that creeps into human relationships is excellent. As Eklund expatiates widely on the human prospect throughout his work, the reader is forced to deal with both close existential issues and the ultimate potentiality of the universe. Despite consistent inconsistency, Eklund communicates much to the intellect and imagination.

—Peter Lynch

ELDERSHAW, M. Barnard. Pseudonym for Marjorie Faith Barnard (and with Flora Sydney Patricia Eldershaw for non-science-fiction works).   Australian.   Born in Ashfield, New South Wales, 16 August 1897. Educated at Cambridge School, Hunters' Hill; Sydney Girls' High School; University of Sydney (exhibitioner; University Medal, 1920), 1916-20, B.A. (honours) in history 1920; Sydney Teachers College, 1920. Librarian, Sydney Public Library and Sydney Technical College Library, 1920-35; free-lance writer, 1935-42; Librarian, Sydney Public Library, 1942, and Commonwealth Scientific and Industrial Research Organization

Library, Sydney, 1942-50. Recipient: *Bulletin* prize, 1928. Member, Order of Australia, 1979. Agent: Curtis Brown (Australia) Pty. Ltd., 86 William Street, Paddington, New South Wales 2021. Address: 29 Sunshine Drive, Point Clare, New South Wales 2250, Australia.

SCIENCE-FICTION PUBLICATIONS

Novel

Tomorrow and Tomorrow.   Melbourne, Georgian House, 1947; London, Phoenix House, 1949.

OTHER PUBLICATIONS with Flora Sydney Patricia Eldershaw

Novels

A House is Built.   London, Harrap, and New York, Harcourt Brace, 1929.
Green Memory.   London, Harrap, and New York, Harcourt Brace, 1931.
The Glasshouse.   London, Harrap, 1936.
Plaque with Laurel.   London, Harrap, 1937.

Play

The Watch on the Headland, in *Australian Radio Plays*, edited by Leslie Rees.   Sydney, Angus and Robertson, 1946.

Other

Phillip of Australia; An Account of the Settlement at Sydney Cove 1788-1792.   London, Harrap, 1937.
Essays in Australian Fiction.   Melbourne, Melbourne University Press, 1938; Freeport, New York, Books for Libraries, 1970.
The Life and Times of Captain John Piper.   Sydney, Australian Limited Editions Society, 1939.
My Australia.   London, Jarrolds, 1939; revised edition, 1951.

Editor, *Coast to Coast 1946.*   Sydney, Angus and Robertson, 1947.

OTHER PUBLICATIONS as Marjorie Faith Barnard

Short Stories

The Persimmon Tree and Other Stories.   Sydney, Clarendon, 1943.

Other

The Ivory Gate (juvenile).   Privately printed, 1920.
Macquarie's World.   Sydney, Australian Limited Editions Society, 1941.
Australian Outline.   Sydney, Ure Smith, 1943; revised edition, 1949.
The Sydney Book.   Sydney, Ure Smith, 1947.
Sydney: The Story of a City.   Melbourne, Melbourne University Press, 1956.
Australia's First Architect: Francis Greenway.   London, Longman, 1961.
A History of Australia.   Sydney, Angus and Robertson, 1962; revised edition, 1963; New York, Praeger, 1963.
Georgian Architecture in Australia, with others.   Sydney, Ure Smith, 1963.
Lachlan Macquarie.   Melbourne, Oxford University Press, 1964.
Miles Franklin.   New York, Twayne, 1967; revised edition, Melbourne, Hill of Content, 1967.

Marjorie Faith Barnard comments:
Two things have a bearing on my writing: one is the circumstances of my childhood, and the other a successful collaboration.

I was an only child, had no playmates, and did not go to school until I was ten (having been taught by governesses prior to that).

This was the best possible beginning for a writer. My natural creativity was not quenched by having too much. I created my own exciting and happy world. Words were my toys. I had the close companionship of my mother and free access to my great-grandmother's books—the Victorian poets, a complete set of Dickens, many histories. I had no taste for the insipid children's books of my period and escaped them almost entirely.

My collaboration with Flora Eldershaw was successful and disciplined. We both wanted to write and each had something to contribute. Our rule was to discuss the plan of a book in detail and agree upon it before anything was written down. Flora had a fine critical ability and curbed my exuberance. I wrote the better prose and had more leisure, so most of the actual writing fell to me. Our association was professional: her friends were not my friends, her way of life not mine. This was a good thing; close friendship would have brought other than literary considerations into it all. We worked in a dry light.

Tomorrow and Tomorrow was entirely my own work as Flora Eldershaw, for reasons of geography and pressure of work, could not contribute. It is a serious book, the best and worst thing I have ever done. I cared too much. As an historian I could see all too clearly the probable future of this country. The book had its roots in the anguish of the years preceding the Second World War. It is about human survival and escape from bondage. The book ran into difficulties. It was hard to find a publisher for such a long and in some ways controversial novel; times were touchy. Without my knowledge my publisher submitted the manuscript to the censor who cut the latter part severely. It was not subversive and now would have no difficulty in being printed *in toto,* but costs have prohibited its republication in its original form.

*   *   *

M. Barnard Eldershaw is the pen name of the Australian historical novelists Marjorie Barnard and Flora Eldershaw. *Tomorrow and Tomorrow,* the one science fiction work published under this name, is in fact the work of Marjorie Barnard alone. In it she applies the selective techniques of the historical novelist to recreate Australia of the period 1924-46 through the eyes of a man four centuries in the future.

The reconstruction of cultural malaise moving into wartime confusion is brilliant if overlong but the story (completed in 1942) moves on to a vision of a different ending to the World War of 1939-45, one wherein an exhausted people turns on the culture which has brought only recurrent agony to each new generation and destroys it. The razing of Sydney by fire is a tremendous symbolic set piece. All this is conveyed as sections of a novel written by a 24th-century *littérateur,* in a time when youth is again restive in a culture (conventionally pastoral-utopian) which it sees as oppressive in its settled satisfaction. The author's political argument (this is a political novel) turns on a newly devised voting machine which records the thoughts of electors to give an accurate survey of mass attitudes.

When a public test of the machine is made, with youth proposing far-reaching constitutional changes, the outcome is devastating for the young protesters. The motion is lost when the machine records a 62% majority of the electors as utterly indifferent to the question. The warning is simple—that indifference leads to frustration and eventually to the violence which destroyed the earlier culture.

Tomorrow and Tomorrow is overlong, but is written with style and powerful characterisation and is a masterly example of science fiction used to present an argument in dramatic detail. There are few like it in intention or realistic achievement.

—George Turner

ELGIN, (Patricia Anne) Suzette Haden (née Wilkins).   American. Born in Louisiana, Missouri, 18 November 1936. Educated at the

University of Chicago (Academy of American Poets Award, 1955), 1954-56; California State University, Chico, B.A. in French and English 1967; University of California, San Diego, 1968-73, M.A. in Linguistics 1970, Ph.D. 1973. Married 1) Peter Joseph Haden in 1955 (died), one son and two daughters; 2) George N. Elgin in 1964, one son. Television folk music performer, Redding, California, 1966-68; Instructor, Chico Conservatory of Music, 1967-68; French teacher, 1968-69; guitar teacher, 1969-70; Linguistics teacher, University of California, San Diego, summer 1971. Since 1972, Assistant Professor, then Associate Professor of Linguistics, San Diego State University. Recipient: Eugene Saxon Fellowship, 1957-58. Agent: James Byron, Box 2389, Hollywood, California 90028. Address: 2469 Caminito Cove, Cardiff, California 92007, U.S.A.

SCIENCE-FICTION PUBLICATIONS

Novels (series: Coyote Jones in all books)

The Communipaths. New York, Ace, 1970.
Furthest. New York, Ace, 1971.
At the Seventh Level. New York, DAW, 1972.
Star-Anchored, Star-Angered. New York, Doubleday, 1979.

Uncollected Short Stories

"Final Exam," in Pouring Down Words, edited by Suzette Haden Elgin. Englewood Cliffs, New Jersey, Prentice Hall, 1975.
"Babyzap," in Playgirl (New York), 1976.
"Old Rocking Chair's Got Me," in Fantasy and Science Fiction (New York), February 1979.

OTHER PUBLICATIONS

Other

Guide to Transformational Grammar: History, Theory, Practice, with John T. Grinder. New York, Holt Rinehart, 1973.
What Is Linguistics? Englewood Cliffs, New Jersey, Prentice Hall, 1973; revised edition, 1979.
A Primer of Transformational Grammar for Rank Beginners. Urbana, Illinois, National Conference of Teachers of English, 1975.

Editor, Pouring Down Words. Englewood Cliffs, New Jersey, Prentice Hall, 1975.

*

Manuscript Collection: Chater Collection, Love Library, San Diego State University.

Suzette Haden Elgin comments:

I went into writing science fiction originally because as a married woman with four kids at home I couldn't pay my graduate school tuition any other way, it being well known that such women are not "Ph.D. material." I know that's not an inspiring or romantic reason, but it's honest. Because I am a linguist my major interest is problems of communication as they are now and as they are likely to develop in the future; I have focused my books on this topic up to now, along with—as subtopics—an attempt to make clear what a pernicious crock Romantic Love is, and a fascination with problems of theology especially as they apply to women under the constant influence of religious language. My books have been picked up as feminist, which I hadn't realized they were until I read the reviews.

I take my SF writing very seriously, and feel that anybody who spends the time and money to read something I have written should not feel cheated, and should not be presented with a cryptic puzzle used to demonstrate how clever I am. My first four books have been part of an on-going series about a rather bumbling mind-deaf superspy; I am now writing a fantasy trilogy, and am enjoying the change. But there will be more Coyote Jones books—the intergalactic superspy framework is a gentle kind of spoof that allows me plenty of room to move around and be as entertaining as possible without writing anything I have to be ashamed of later. I try to avoid

the Brothers Karamazov Syndrome, and do not allow my characters to pontificate.

I plot a book down to the most minute detail in advance, filling notebooks with maps, biographies, every conceivable sort of information I might need in the book about its culture and characters. That takes at least a year. When I do the actual writing, however, I do only one draft. Then I revise as I type the final manuscript, and that writing process generally takes about six weeks from start to finish. I don't believe in inspiration, I believe in hard work. I hope that shows in my work; it's meant to. I have no problem "finding ideas"; my only problem is finding time to write them all. That, I expect, comes from rigorous training in the scientific method: one just poses hypotheses, and extrapolates.

Most embarrassing moment: having nobody notice that I had intended Furthest as a straightforward satire of the United States system of economics; that is, anything's allowed as long as you've filled out the proper forms.

*   *   *

Suzette Haden Elgin, principally known for her novels featuring the exploits of Tri-Galactic agent Coyote Jones, brings to her science fiction a solid academic ground in linguistics and a strong personal interest in both poetry and music. She is adept at infusing with piquant social satire and genuine human emotion her deliberately grandiose spoofs of the James Bond school of superspy fiction so popular in the 1960's. If she has an immediately recognizable signature as a novelist, in fact, it may be her tactic of dealing seriously with universal human problems in a parodic or sometimes even farcical context. Although this technique poses the very real danger of trivializing important concerns, Elgin is generally successful in using it to place contemporary cultural situations in a fresh and therefore edifying perspective.

"For the Sake of Grace," a novelette later incorporated into At the Seventh Level, was not only Elgin's first story to embody a decidedly "feminist" theme but also her first professionally published fiction. It posits a society in which quasi-Islamic attitudes toward the status of women prevail, the most esteemed profession is Poetry, and any female who unsuccessfully attempts to enter this profession (by failing a computer-administered exam) dooms herself to life-long solitary confinement within the cloisters of her own disgraced household. Jacinth, a talented 12-year-old girl, perturbs the affairs of her podgy and unimaginative father, the Khadilh, by challenging for this honor. A remarkably effective feature of Elgin's storytelling strategy here is that, although the Khadilh is her point-of-view character, Jacinth, who takes center-stage only in the moving penultimate paragraph, utterly dominates the narrative. (Joanna Russ's The Two of Them, incidentally, uses the characters and setting of "For the Sake of Grace" for a completely different story.)

The Communipaths introduces Elgin's recurring protagonist Coyote Jones. With fiery red hair and a beard to match, Coyote is the Continental Op sheared of his cynicism, Philip Marlowe with his consciousness raised, and James Bond writ human—once, that is, you overlook the fact that he is also a "mass projective telepath" capable of inciting entire planetary populations to riot and revolution. Further, in a future where "mind-speech" is commonplace, he is impervious to the projections of others. This linking of Coyote's rare mental talent with a handicap equally rare among his 31st century contemporaries provides Elgin with a rather too handy lever for both comic relief and deus ex machina resolution. Nevertheless, Coyote remains an engaging and often admirable creation, one whom Elgin has permitted to grow and change significantly from novel to novel.

In The Communipaths a baby born to a member of a religious sect called the Maklunites shows overwhelming telepathic potential. Coyote must remove it from its people so that it may one day take its place on a kind of patriotic extra-sensory bucket brigade, mind passing message to mind across the Three Galaxies. Because children taken for this duty invariably die before reaching 20, Coyote repudiates his involvement and attempts to join the Maklunites. Elgin, testing the waters as a novelist and employing a shifting point of view, brings Coyote to the fore so infrequently that her story often seems to lack unifying focus. Furthest, by following Coyote's progress at closer hand, solves this problem. It also contains some of Elgin's most vivid descriptive writing, a fascinating if somewhat implausible alien society, and a moving love story. *At the Seventh Level,* consisting of a novella and three related shorter works, puts Coyote on the planet Abba for the purpose of rescuing the poet Jacinth, now a full-grown woman, from what appears to be a plot to poison her. Elgin has complained that although this book "was taken up as some sort of militant feminist work, what *I* thought I was doing was a parody of American economics and law." She cites in particular the fact that thieves on Abba constitute a legitimate guild and that a variety of crimes are permissible if the proper forms have been filled out. *Star-Anchored, Star-Angered* again pits Coyote against the devotees of a religion for whose leader and tenets he comes to develop an abiding reverence. Indeed, he comes to love the female messiah who performs a startlingly beautiful miracle in order to convince him of her authenticity. Interesting theological speculation and a convincing apportionment of humorous and tragic elements make this novel perhaps the most aesthetically successful of the Coyote Jones "adventures."

—Michael Bishop

ELLIOTT, Sumner Locke. American. Born in Sydney, New South Wales, Australia, 17 October 1917; emigrated to the United States in 1948; naturalized 1955. Educated in schools in Australia. Served in the Australian Army during World War II. Professional actor until 1948; free-lance playwright and novelist. Agent: Annie Laurie Williams Inc., 18 East 41st Street, New York, New York 10017, U.S.A.

SCIENCE-FICTION PUBLICATIONS

Novel

Going.   New York, Harper, and London, W.H. Allen, 1975.

OTHER PUBLICATIONS

Novels

Careful, He Might Hear You.   New York, Harper, and London, Gollancz, 1963.
Some Doves and Pythons.   New York, Harper, 1966.
Edens Lost.   New York, Harper, 1969.
The Man Who Got Away.   New York, Harper, 1972; London, Joseph, 1973.
Water under the Bridge.   New York, Simon and Schuster, 1977; London, Hamish Hamilton, 1978.

Plays

The Cow Jumped over the Moon (produced Sydney, 1937).
The Little Sheep Run Fast (produced Sydney, 1941).
Goodbye to the Music (produced Sydney, 1942).
Interval.   Melbourne, Melbourne University Press-Oxford University Press, 1942.
Your Obedient Servant (produced Sydney, 1943).
Invisible Circus (produced Sydney, 1946).
Rusty Bugles (produced Sydney, 1948). Published in *Khaki, Bush, and Bigotry: Three Australian Plays,* Brisbane, University of Queensland Press, 1968; as *Three Australian Plays,* Minneapolis, University of Minnesota Press, 1968.
Buy Me Blue Ribbons (produced New York, 1951). New York, Dramatists Play Service, 1952.
Sketches, in *John Murray Anderson's Almanac* (revue; produced New York, 1953).
Wicked Is the Vine (produced London, 1953).

Radio Plays: in Australia, 1935-40.

Television Plays (US): *Wish on the Moon,* 1953; *Friday the 13th,* 1954; *Beloved Stranger,* 1955; *You and Me and the Gatepost,* 1955; *The King and Mrs. Candle,* 1955; *Keyhole,* 1956; *Mrs. Gilling and the Skyscraper,* 1957; *The Gray Nurse Said Nothing,* 1959; adaptations of *Of Human Bondage* by W. Somerset Maugham, *The Winslow Boy* by Terence Rattigan, *Peter Pan* by J.M. Barrie, and *The Women* by Clare Booth Luce.

Theatrical Activities:

Actor: **Plays**—with Sydney Independent Theatre Repertory Company from 1934: Dick McGann in *Street Scene* by Elmer Rice, 1937, Morgan Evans in *The Corn Is Green* by Emlyn Williams, 1940, Constantin in *The Seagull* by Chekhov, 1941, and Leo in *The Little Foxes* by Lillian Hellman, 1946; *Sweetest and Lowest* (revue), Sydney, 1946; also appeared in *You Can't Take It with You* by Kaufman and Hart, *Hassan* by James Elroy Flecker, *Lady Precious Stream* by S.I. Hsiung, *Housemaster* by Ian Hay, *Call It a Day* by Dodie Smith, and *Winterset* by Maxwell Anderson.

*   *   *

Sumner Locke Elliott is best known as a mainstream writer. *The Man Who Got Away* borders on fantasy inasmuch as it deals with a suburban husband who has slipped through "the crack" (in time? in reality?) and escaped the trivia of suburban existence. However, the novel is mainstream in its interests, and does not explore the mechanics of the "escape."

Going is therefore Elliott's sole SF novel, displaying to the full his "feel" for middle-class suburban characters, his skill at subtle characterisation, and the values he upholds. Tess Bracken, an ordinary, sensitive, suburban widow, reaches the age when she must submit to "voluntary" euthanasia. Powerless, and not really given to rebellion, she knows she has no choice but to "go." Accepting this acquiescence as dignified and realistic, Elliott contrasts Tess Bracken's moral qualities with those of the world that is killing her. In a sterile world of banal monotony, Mrs. Bracken has clung to her individuality, and to the values which give richness to life:

> This young girl driver I had yesterday…said that she loved everybody? How can you love *everybody?* I said it isn't *human.* But she couldn't or wouldn't understand me…and she said that I oughtn't to think so much and that thinking's *pollution.* It just makes me—well—*tired* even to *try* to accept their philistinism so I said well, beauty is *truth* and truth is beauty and that is all ye know on earth and all ye need to know but she didn't understand that and of course she never *heard* of Keats….

Facing the death of both herself and her values, Tess Bracken must find the reasons to believe that her life has been worthwhile. *Going* is mature SF, a very fine novel of character and contemporary values.

—Van Ikin

ELLISON, Harlan (Jay). American. Born in Cleveland, Ohio, 27 May 1934. Attended Ohio State University, Columbus, 1951-53. Served in the United States Army, 1957-59. Married and divorced three times. Editor, *Rogue;* Founding Editor, Regency Books, Evanston, Illinois, 1961-62. Free-lance writer and lecturer: Editor, Harlan Ellison Discovery Series. Vice-President, Science Fiction Writers of America, 1965-66 (resigned). Recipient: Nebula Award, 1965, 1969, 1977; Writers Guild of America award, for TV play, 1965, 1967; Hugo Award, 1966, 1968, 1969, 1974, 1975, 1978; Mystery Writers of America Edgar Allan Poe Award, for story, 1973. Address: 3484 Coy Drive, Sherman Oaks, California 92403, U.S.A.

SCIENCE-FICTION PUBLICATIONS

Novels

The Man with Nine Lives. New York, Ace, 1960.
Doomsman. New York, Belmont, 1967.
Phoenix Without Ashes, with Edward Bryant. New York, Fawcett, 1975; London, Savoy, 1978.
The City on the Edge of Forever (novelization of TV play). London, Bantam, 1977.
Blood's a Rover. New York, Ace, 1980.

Short Stories

A Touch of Infinity. New York, Ace, 1960.
Ellison Wonderland. New York, Paperback Library, 1962; as *Earthman, Go Home,* 1964.
Paingod and Other Delusions. New York, Pyramid, 1965.
I Have No Mouth, and I Must Scream. New York, Pyramid, 1967.
From the Land of Fear. New York, Belmont, 1967.
Love Ain't Nothing But Sex Misspelled. New York, Simon and Schuster, 1968.
The Beast That Shouted Love at the Heart of the World. New York, Avon, 1969; London, Millington, 1976.
Over the Edge: Stories from Somewhere Else. New York, Belmont, 1970.
Alone Against Tomorrow. New York, Macmillan, 1971; as *All the Sounds of Fear* and *The Time of the Eye,* London, Panther, 2 vols., 1973-74.
Partners in Wonder: Harlan Ellison in Collaboration with.... New York, Walker, 1971.
Approaching Oblivion: Road Signs on the Treadmill Toward Tomorrow, with Edward Bryant. New York, Walker, 1974; London, Millington, 1976.
Deathbird Stories: A Pantheon of Modern Gods. New York, Harper, 1975; London, Millington, 1977.
No Doors, No Windows. New York, Pyramid, 1975.
Strange Wine. New York, Harper, 1978.
The Illustrated Harlan Ellison. New York, Baronet, 1978.

Uncollected Short Story

"Jeffty Is Five," in *The 1978 Annual World's Best SF,* edited by Donald A. Wollheim. New York, DAW, 1978.

OTHER PUBLICATIONS

Novels

Rumble. New York, Pyramid, 1958.
Rockabilly. New York, Fawcett, 1961; London, Muller, 1963; as *Spider Kiss,* New York, BJ, 1975.
Demon with a Glass Hand (novelization of TV play). New York, Doubleday, 1967.
Kill Machine. New York, Belmont, 1967.

Short Stories

The Deadly Streets. New York, Ace, 1958; London, Digit, 1959.
The Juvies. New York, Ace, 1961.
Gentleman Junkie and Other Stories of the Hung-Up Generation. Evanston, Illinois, Regency, 1961; revised edition, New York, Pyramid, 1975.
Perhaps Impossible. New York, Pyramid, 1967.
Shatterday. Boston, Houghton Mifflin, 1980.

Plays

The City on the Edge of Forever (televised, 1967). Published in *Six Science Fiction Plays,* edited by Roger Elwood, New York, Pocket Books, 1976.

Screenplay: *The Oscar,* with Russell Rouse and Clarence Greene, 1966.

Television Plays: *Demon with a Glass Hand* and *Soldier (Outer Limits* series), 1964; *The City on the Edge of Forever (Star Trek* series), 1967; and for *Route 66, The Untouchables, The Alfred Hitchcock Hour, Burke's Law,* and *The Man from U.N.C.L.E.* series.

Other

Memos from Purgatory: Two Journeys of Our Time. Evanston, Illinois, Regency, 1961.
The Glass Teat: Essays of Opinion on the Subject of Television. New York, Ace, 1970.
"You Are What You Write," in *Clarion 2,* edited by Robin Scott Wilson. New York, New American Library, 1972.
"When Dreams Become Nightmares: Some Cautionary Notes on the Clarion Experience," in *Clarion 3,* edited by Robin Scott Wilson. New York, New American Library, 1973.
"Whore with a Heart of Iron Pyrites; or, Where Does a Writer Go to Find a Maggie?," in *Those Who Can: A Science Fiction Reader,* edited by Robin Scott Wilson. New York, New American Library, 1973.
The Other Glass Teat: Further Essays of Opinion on Television. New York, Pyramid, 1975.

Editor, *Dangerous Visions.* New York, Doubleday, 1967; London, David Bruce and Watson, 2 vols., 1971.
Editor, *Again, Dangerous Visions.* New York, Doubleday, 1972; London, Millington, 1976.

*

Bibliography: *Harlan Ellison: A Bibliographical Checklist* by Leslie Kay Swigart, Dallas, Williams, 1973.

*   *   *

Very few people are ambivalent about Harlan Ellison; they thoroughly like or thoroughly dislike his style. But he has won many awards for his writing, and not a few of them have come from outside the science-fiction world. And in spite of the people who walk out of his public appearances feeling insulted and angry or refuse to buy his books because of the lengthy introductions he includes with each one, it cannot be denied that Harlan Ellison is a good writer who has had a significant impact on contemporary science fiction. Ellison's use of language has helped change science fiction considerably. Ellison is not afraid to use any word, however objectionable some person or group might find it, if he thinks that that word is the proper one for a specific situation. His definition of obscenity, promulgated at various personal appearances, is "language which is intended to deceive." Ellison cites "protective reaction strike" and "military incursion" (Vietnam era words which reporters were required to use instead of "bombing mission" and "military invasion") as examples of obscene language.

In Ellison stories like "A Boy and His Dog," there are descriptions of sex and violence, and there is a lot of foul language. But, Ellison might argue, such description and language are necessary to the story. "A Boy and His Dog" depicts the aftermath of World War III. Roving gangs and roving independents, called "solos," occupy the surface of the planet; these young toughs, mostly male, are the same sort as those who roam inner city streets today. Their language must be strong to be realistic. In addition, Ellison sets this group in contrast to the other group of survivors, those living in underground cities to which they retreated as the war broke out. The surface gangs are destroying each other (and themselves) through violence; the below-grounders are sterile and wasting away. And without the four-letter words, the reader would be less able to contrast the destructive aggressiveness of the surface group to the equally destructive non-participation of the below-grounders.

In addition to helping expand the language of science by example in his stories, Ellison has also encouraged others to do the same. As editor of the *Dangerous Visions* series (1967 and 1972; the third volume is forthcoming), Ellison encouraged his fellow science-fiction writers to send him those stories which other editors had considered too controversial to put into print. Ellison encouraged not just experiments with language, but experiments in subject matter and in style as well.

But it is his own writing that is most important. Many of his best-selling short stories are experimental in their subject matter. "Shattered Like a Glass Goblin" is a story about people on drugs who eventually, after continued and heavy use, turn into the creatures they hallucinate. They turn on and destroy each other in bestial ways. The narrator becomes a crystal goblin and is shattered by a swipe from the hairy paw of the creature that was once his girl friend. In "Delusion for a Dragon Slayer" a man is given the chance to attain heaven if he can act like the heroic-fantasy hero he has always dreamed of being; he does not make it. And "Catman" was written as the future sex story for a volume of ultimate science fiction stories called *Final Stage*.

Other Ellison stories are experimental in style. "The Beast That Shouted Love at the Heart of the World" is written to be read as if the separate segments were arranged in a circle instead of a sequence of pages. "Pretty Maggie Moneyeyes" attempts to portray a person's impressions at the moment of death. Ellison uses italics, varied spacing, and other type tricks to try to present these impressions and sensations. And "From A to Z, In the Chocolate Alphabet" consists of the alphabet, with a short story for each letter.

"The Deathbird" is a story which is experimental in both subject and style. In this story, Ellison attempts to show that Satan was the "good guy" and that God, who is responsible for the condition of the world, is insane. The story is told in 26 sections, each numbered, but only 20 or 21 of those sections actually advance the plot of the story. Some of the others are direct addresses to the reader or quizzes for the reader to take, and one section is the story of Ellison's dog, Ahbhu.

In sum, Ellison is a force to be reckoned with in science fiction, for his writing, his anthologies, and his readings and lectures.

—C.W. Sullivan III

EMSHWILLER, Carol (née Fries). American. Born in Ann Arbor, Michigan, 12 April 1921. Educated at the University of Michigan, Ann Arbor, B.A. in music and B. Design 1949; Ecole Nationale Supérieure des Beaux-Arts, Paris (Fulbright Fellow), 1949-50. Married the filmmaker Ed Emshwiller in 1949; two daughters and one son. Organized workshops for Science Fiction Bookstore, New York, 1975, 1976, and Clarion Science Fiction Workshop, 1978, 1979. Recipient: MacDowell Fellowship, 1971; Creative Artists Public Service grant, 1975. Agent: Virginia Kidd, Box 278, Milford, Pennsylvania 18337. Address: 260 East 10th Street, No. 10, New York, New York 10009, U.S.A.

SCIENCE-FICTION PUBLICATIONS

Short Stories

Joy in Our Cause. New York, Harper, 1974.

Uncollected Short Story

"Escape Is No Accident," in *2076: The American Tricentennial,* edited by Edward Bryant. New York, Pyramid, 1977.

OTHER PUBLICATIONS

Plays

Television Plays: *Pilobolis and Joan,* 1974; *Family Focus,* 1977.

Carol Emshwiller comments:
Formal/structural concerns have always interested me the most, so once I had learned to plot and had published numerous science-fiction stories (and a few mystery stories), I decided to learn how *not* to plot. My concerns were for the various ways of forming a story and keeping forward movement without plotting. This was as hard to learn as plotting (harder, because I had no models in those days) and had to be learned as slowly. Looking back, I see that I did away with plot elements one at a time. I was unable to let go of them by twos or threes. I'm not really exactly sure what I put in their place, one by one, but I did refer to modern poetry for inspiration and I took many modern poetry techniques as models for my stories. Sometimes I tried to write a "story" all "between the lines," leaving a lot of work for the reader. Sometimes I tried to create the illusion of action without there actually being any.

Also I tried to write, as in modern poetry (which is influenced in this, I think, by the Chinese and Japanese), without the use of simile or metaphoric language, and, I hope, without a trace of the pathetic fallacy. I also tried to do away with character, and substituted what I called "selves," which, in my mind, were much more real than "characters" (though perhaps just different). I used the first person and tried for a kind of internal, psychological realism. To me, the "selves" represented the insides of everybody...the little fleeting thoughts...the little vanities...things not admitted by any of us. Also big things not admitted: petty hates, oedipal feelings, incest...

Why might one bother doing this? Well, like most science-fiction writers, my study was "what-would-happen-if," but not what-would-happen-if the ice age returned, or if apes began teaching each other to talk, but what-would-happen-if, for instance, a story had only a single bit of action? or none? What could hold the interest? What could move it forward? However, I may have written myself into a hole by now. Plot seems to be slowly coming back into my work. I'm not sure where I'll go from here, but I'm sure that "structures" will be one of my primary concerns.

Of course, there's that other thing: that when your conscious mind is kept busy with forms, the subconscious mind can be freed to work on all those underground things that are, perhaps, more important to a story.

*   *   *

Carol Emshwiller's fictions are perhaps best described, in Richard Kostelanetz's words, as "scrupulously strange," and much of their power derives precisely from her extreme scrupulosity as a maker. As she writes neither science fiction nor fantasy in any standard senses of those terms, her presence in the genre helps to explain why it's so difficult to define: she is there by association, for her husband, Ed Emshwiller, has long been an SF illustrator; thus the SF community knew her. Even so, her stories have appeared only in the more experimental SF anthologies like *Dangerous Visions, Orbit* and *2076: The American Tricentennial.* As a result, SF readers have been exposed to a kind of masterful experimentation seldom found in popular genre writing. Even Borges, one of the great fantasists of our time, remained relatively unknown within the SF world until recently, and his *ficciones* are far closer to Emshwiller's stories than a good 98% of SF is.

Where much SF, partly due to its pulp heritage of banal and conventional discourse, has tended to domesticate the unknown (so that strange planets, the galaxy itself, become merely places to have quite ordinary "extraordinary" adventures), Emshwiller's fictions force us to look again at the supposedly ordinary domestic world and see it as truly weird and, yes, unknown. How she does this is through a prose so precise it cuts away conventional perceptual fat like a surgeon's scalpel. Her writing holds our attention because it so carefully follows the patterns of thought and speech. Even when her stories embrace terror, they do so with economy and an almost fearless awareness cast over every perceived thing and event. Lively wit and intelligence, a fully awake mind whose variegated movements are mapped in the motions of her prose, a truly phenomenological writing: these offer such energy and delight as to exhilarate us even when the ostensible "content" (and her work demonstrates at every turn how form *makes* content, how "content" is never something *else* than what the words say) is almost insupportable— "As a mother, I have served longer than I expected" (and note how powerfully evocative that single verb "served" is).

A few of her stories actually allude to SF conventions, like the famous "Sex and/or Mr. Morrison," but they use these conventions metaphorically and to press home even more forcefully the strange alien lives we all live, here in the "real" world. The marvelous "Escape Is No Accident," for example, by beginning with the narrator's fall—as awkward wife from a ladder or as superior alien from space—forces us to see our culture in a new perspective. Others may have handled the idea before, but only Emshwiller articulates it through perceptions of the ordinary heightened to a frightening degree. The final paragraph gathers all the story's strands together:

> I don't tell him, but I'm afraid that, rather than continue my journey through space and time, I will have to continue it only through time, and (usually) there's something to look at out the window every day. And one isn't much sadder up there in the sky watching galaxies fade by. Why should I worry? Why should I talk so much and so loud? Why should I stay alert to the differences between us, them and me? And then, why shouldn't I croak and groan now and then, dizzy, having fallen down?

This is scrupulous writing precisely because it pays such careful attention to tone and detail. Every word functions fully; there is no dead weight. And this is true of all Emshwiller's best fictions.

Carol Emshwiller's *oeuvre* is small. One of a very small handful of writers in SF acquainted with contemporary poetry, she is, like the most exciting post-modern poets, dedicated to language and the explorations of lived life it allows when trusted and followed rather than manipulated to a foregone conclusion. She is a unique writer and her stories, at their best, are simply superior fictions which offer the adventurous reader rich and exhilarating experiences unlike almost anything to be found within the genre's boundaries.

—Douglas Barbour

ENGDAHL, Sylvia (Louise). American. Born in Los Angeles, California, 24 November 1933. Educated at Pomona College, Claremont, California, 1950; Reed College, Portland, Oregon, 1951; University of Oregon, Eugene, 1951-52; University of California, Santa Barbara, B.A. in education 1955; currently doing graduate work in anthropology, Portland State University. Elementary school teacher, Portland, 1955-56; Programmer, then Computer Systems Specialist, SAGE Air Defense System, in Massachusetts, Wisconsin, Washington, and California, 1957-67. Recipient: Christopher Award, for children's book, 1973. Address: Box 153, Garden Home Post Office, Portland, Oregon 97223, U.S.A.

SCIENCE-FICTION PUBLICATIONS (for young people)

Novels (series: Elana; Norren)

Enchantress from the Stars (Elana). New York, Atheneum, 1970; London, Gollancz, 1974.
Journey Between Worlds. New York, Atheneum, 1970.
The Far Side of Evil (Elana). New York, Atheneum, 1971; London, Gollancz, 1975.
This Star Shall Abide (Norren). New York, Atheneum, 1972; as *Heritage of the Star,* London, Gollancz, 1973.
Beyond the Tomorrow Mountains (Norren). New York, Atheneum, 1973.
The Doors of the Universe (Norren). New York, Atheneum, 1980.

Uncollected Short Stories

"The Beckoning Trail," with Rick Roberson, in *Universe Ahead,* edited by Engdahl and Roberson. New York, Atheneum, 1975.
"Timescape," with Mildred Butler, in *Anywhere, Anywhen,* edited by Engdahl. New York, Atheneum, 1976.

OTHER PUBLICATIONS (for young people)

Other

The Planet-Girded Suns: Man's View of Other Solar Systems. New York, Atheneum, 1974.
The Subnuclear Zoo: New Discoveries in High Energy Physics, with Rick Roberson. New York, Atheneum, 1977.
Tool for Tomorrow: New Knowledge about Genes, with Rick Roberson. New York, Atheneum, 1979.
Our World Is Earth. New York, Atheneum, 1979.

Editor, with Rick Roberson, *Universe Ahead: Stories of the Future.* New York, Atheneum, 1975.
Editor, *Anywhere, Anywhen: Stories of Tomorrow.* New York, Atheneum, 1976.

Sylvia Engdahl comments:

I have encountered a good deal of misunderstanding concerning the audience for which my novels are intended, and I would like to clear it up. In the first place, though the present structure of the publishing business requires them to be issued as children's books, my novels are not meant for children; they are directed to older teenagers and young adults. Some exceptional pre-adolescents enjoy them, but do not grasp all their levels and on the whole find them heavy reading, since they are not primarily action stories. Their main emphasis is on the significance of space exploration, man's place in the universe, and human values I consider universal: all themes in which I believe today's young people are seriously interested.

In the second place, my novels do not fit the "science fiction" category much better than the "children's book" category; they aren't category books at all. Although they are set in future or hypothetical worlds, they are not directed toward fans of genre-oriented SF—they are meant for a general audience. They are not exotic enough to suit many SF fans, and *this is intentional.* My use of themes already old to the "fan" audience is also intentional. My aim is to reach readers who do not have a special background and do not care for fiction that seems far removed from real life, readers who find most SF too "far-out" for their tastes. I feel strongly that the future is not something that should be set apart and discussed only in literature of a particular type, directed to readers of a specific genre. The future is important to everyone, not just to those who choose to become familiar with the conventions and jargon of genre-oriented books. My chief goal is to place it in perspective in relation to the past and present, as well as to offer an affirmative outlook toward a universe wider than the single planet Earth. There is a desperate need, I believe, for fiction that conveys such themes to people beyond the comparatively small circle of SF fandom, and I therefore purposely market my own work outside that circle. I'm happy, of course, when people within the SF field like it; but I'm even happier when other people tell me that they thought they didn't like space stories until they read mine. In my opinion, expansion into space is essential to human survival, and promoting that idea among readers not already space enthusiasts will remain my primary concern.

*   *   *

Sylvia Engdahl claims to have read little science fiction; her first love is science itself, and she cares more about "the future and the universe" then about a genre she feels too enamored of jargon. Her chosen audience is mid-adolescent, as are her protagonists, and her stories propose dilemmas of authority and education that adolescents find relevant. Yet the dilemmas are so originally constructed and Engdahl's commitment is so genuinely intense that her stories should qualify not only as adult reading but as serious science fiction for any age.

Engdahl's envisioned universe is one where hierarchies of human knowledge extend from primitive to sophisticated beyond our current reach, and where the highest must help the lowest. *Enchantress from the Stars* uses three alternating points of view to demonstrate the evolutionary span: that of a primitive culture which sees science as fairy-tale magic, that of an exploitative industrial culture which sees only mechanical science, and that of the highest culture which knows that science includes "magic" through trained psi powers. In this novel and its companion, *The Far Side of Evil*, the focus is on Elana, agent of the highest culture. Sustained by an oath that is both test and reassurance, she must anonymously protect the younglings' development without deforming their normal progress. A similar hierarchy is formed in the linked novels *This Star Shall Abide* and *Beyond the Tomorrow Mountains*. Fleeing from a nova, desperate scientists on a poisonous world set up a protective caste system that ranges from trusting farmers to sophisticated priests. The young protagonist, Norren, personally travels that range, and as in Engdahl's other books there are conflicting scruples, terrifying tests, compassionate but determined teachers, deeply moving oaths, and a pseudo-religious Knowledge beckoning from beyond.

In effect, Engdahl writes a science fiction of morality, where she constructs and inhabits new social systems, new ethical dilemmas. Her insistence on inventing justifiable tyrannies is a little unsettling, and sometimes one wishes for less talk and more visual detail. But her stories are in no sense a mere educational exercise for the young. They are suspenseful, passionately reasoned, freely imagined, and well worth reading.

—Karen G. Way

* * *

ENGLAND, George Allan. American. Born in Fort McPherson, Nebraska, 9 February 1877. Educated at Harvard University, Cambridge, Massachusetts, B.A. 1902 (Phi Beta Kappa); M.A. 1903. Married; one daughter. Regular contributor to Munsey magazines until his retirement from writing, 1931; chicken farmer from 1931. Socialist candidate for congress, 1908, and for governor of Maine, 1912. *Died 26 June 1936.*

SCIENCE-FICTION PUBLICATIONS

Novels

Darkness and Dawn. Boston, Small Maynard, 1914; as *Darkness and Dawn, Beyond the Great Oblivion, The People of the Abyss, Out of the Abyss,* and *The Afterglow,* New York, Avalon, 5 vols., 1964-67.
The Air Trust. St. Louis, Phil Wagner, 1915.
The Golden Blight. New York, H.K. Fly, 1916.
Cursed. Boston, Small Maynard, 1919.
The Flying Legion. Chicago, McClurg, 1930.

Uncollected Short Stories

"The Lunar Advertising Co. Ltd.," in *Munsey* (New York), 1906.
"The House of the Green Flame," in *All-Story* (New York), September 1908.
"My Time Annihilator," in *All-Story* (New York), June 1909.
"The House of Transmutation," in *Scrap Book* (New York), September 1909.
"Beyond White Seas," in *All-Story* (New York), December 1909.
"The Elixir of Hate," in *Cavalier* (New York), August 1911.
"The Million Dollar Patch," in *All-Story* (New York), June 1912.
"The Crime Detector," in *Cavalier* (New York), 22 February 1913.
"The Empire in the Air," in *All-Story Weekly* (New York), 14 November 1914.
"The Fatal Gift," in *All-Story Weekly* (New York), 4 September 1915.
"The Tenth Question," in *All-Story Weekly* (New York), 18 December 1915.
"The Nebula of Death," in *People's Favorite* (New York), 10 February-10 May 1918.
"Drops of Death," in *Munsey* (New York), January 1922.
"The Thing from Outside," in *Amazing* (New York), April 1926.

"The Man with the Glass Heart," in *Famous Fantastic Mysteries* (New York), November 1939.

OTHER PUBLICATIONS

Novels

The Greater Crime. London, Cassell, 1907.
The Alibi. Boston, Small Maynard, 1916.
Pod, Bender, & Co. New York, McBride, 1916; London, Laurie, 1919.
The Gift Supreme. New York, Doran, 1917.
Keep Off the Grass. Boston, Small Maynard, 1919.

Verse

Underneath the Bough. New York, Grafton Press, 1903.

Other

Socialism and the Law. Fort Scott, Kansas, Monitor, 1913.
The Story of the Appeal. Privately printed, 1915(?).
Isles of Romance. New York, Century, 1920.
Vikings of the Ice. New York, Doubleday, and London, Heinemann, 1924; as *The White Wilderness,* London, Cassell, 1924; as *The Greatest Hunt in the World,* Montreal, Tundra, 1969.
Adventure Isle (juvenile). New York, Century, 1926.

Translator, *Their Son, The Necklace,* by Eduardo Zamacois. New York, Boni and Liveright, 1919.

* * *

Although George Allan England lived well into the era of specialized science-fiction magazines, he never wrote any original works for them. His works appeared, for the most part, in the variety pulp magazines published by Frank A. Munsey and edited by Bob Davis. England's heyday was the decade between 1910 and 1920.

By far England's most important work of science fiction is *Darkness and Dawn*. This massive effort was originally published as three separate serials, then as a single volume. In this work a heavy anaesthetic gas sweeps over the entire world, at first rendering unconscious and ultimately killing those who breathe it. One man and one woman, however, in an office in the top story of the Flatiron Building in New York, receive only a partial dose of the gas. They sleep for centuries and revive to find a world in ruins. The revived couple struggle to rebuild their lives, encountering a race of super-evolved intelligent rats, barbaric degenerate humans, and finally a lost civilization cut off from the rest of the world for hundreds of years. The book is highly successful as an adventure tale and as a study in courage and perseverance on the part of the survivors. An unfortunate element of racism is present in this and in several other of the author's works, though England was largely following the conventions of popular literature of his day; he did not originate these attitudes, and did not press them very emphatically.

The Flying Legion, although not as widely remembered as *Darkness and Dawn,* is deserving of recognition in its own more modest right. It reflected a convention of its time, the assumption that World War veterans, returning to the drab realities of civilian, peacetime existence, would suffer from intolerable boredom and would be driven to seek excitement in such fields as might offer danger and exotic adventures. In *The Flying Legion* just such a party of veterans assemble. One of them, to add a fillip, is a beautiful young woman in disguise. This legion hijacks the world's largest and most advanced aircraft (choosing to do so rather than buy it despite their immense joint wealth) and set out to find adventure in the unknown regions of the Arabian desert. In outline the book is an exercise in cliché, yet it is executed with such verve and color as to be irresistible even to the modern reader.

Few of England's other science fiction works were issued in volume form. "The Elixir of Hate" deals with research into a youth serum; the serum is perfected, stolen, swallowed by the thief who then discovers that he has taken an overdose and is reduced to infancy. England's two "socialist novels" both contain science-fiction elements. *The Air Trust* deals with greedy capitalists who corner air and sell the very breath of life for profit. *The Golden Blight* is concerned with a revolutionary who discovers a method by which he can destroy all the gold that exists, thereby bringing about the collapse of the entire world's economy. Both these books are heavy on polemic and of little value as works of fiction, although interesting examples of their sort, and comparable to such socialist science fiction as Jack London's *The Iron Heel*.

A number of England's unreprinted works are rewarding. "The Empire in the Air," concerning an invasion of earth from the fourth dimension, might be compared with the space operas of the 1920's and 1930's, although it appeared in 1914. "The Nebula of Death" involves the passage of the earth through a cosmic cloud which absolutely inhibits photosynthesis; the novel is comparable, in different ways, to *The Second Deluge* by Garrett P. Serviss and *Brain Wave* by Poul Anderson.

—Richard A. Lupoff

ERNST, Paul (Frederick). Also writes as Paul Frederick Stern. American. Born in 1902. Pulp writer: as Kenneth Robeson, wrote *The Avenger* series in the 1930's.

SCIENCE-FICTION PUBLICATIONS

Uncollected Short Stories (series: Dr. Satan)

"The Temple of Serpents," in *Weird Tales* (Indianapolis), 1928.
"Marooned under the Sea," in *Astounding* (New York), September 1930.
"The Radiant Shell," in *Astounding* (New York), January 1931.
"The World Behind the Moon," in *Astounding* (New York), April 1931.
"Hidden in Glass," in *Amazing* (New York), April 1931.
"The Incredible Formula," in *Amazing* (New York), June 1931.
"The Red Hell of Jupiter," in *Astounding* (New York), October 1931.
"The Planetoid of Peril," in *Astounding* (New York), November 1931.
"The Raid on the Termites," in *Astounding* (New York), June 1932.
"From the Wells of the Brain," in *Astounding* (New York), October 1933.
"The Stolen Element," in *Astounding* (New York), September 1934.
"Doctor Satan," in *Weird Tales* (Indianapolis), August 1935.
"The Man Who Chained the Lightning" (Satan), in *Weird Tales* (Indianapolis), September 1935.
"Hollywood Horror" (Satan), in *Weird Tales* (Indianapolis), October 1935.
"The Consuming Flame" (Satan), in *Weird Tales* (Indianapolis), November 1935.
"The Way Home" (as Paul Frederick Stern), in *Weird Tales* (Indianapolis), November 1935.
"Horror Insured" (Satan), in *Weird Tales* (Indianapolis), January 1936.
"Beyond Death's Gateway" (Satan), in *Weird Tales* (Indianapolis), March 1936.
"The Devil's Double" (Satan), in *Weird Tales* (Indianapolis), May 1936.
"Death Dives Deep," in *Thrilling Wonder Stories* (New York), August 1936.
"Mask of Death" (Satan), in *Weird Tales* (Indianapolis), August-September 1936.
"Protoplasmic Station," in *Thrilling Wonder Stories* (New York), February 1937.
"The Invincible Midge," in *Thrilling Wonder Stories* (New York), April 1937.
"Rift in Infinity," in *Thrilling Wonder Stories* (New York), August 1937.

"The Mind Magnet," in *Thrilling Wonder Stories* (New York), December 1937.
"Terror in Utopia," in *Thrilling Wonder Stories* (New York), June 1938.
"The Man Next Door," in *Argosy* (New York), 4 March 1939.
"The Great Green Serpent," in *Argosy* (New York), 10 June 1939.
"He Didn't Want Soup," in *Argosy* (New York), 14 December 1940.
"Escape," in *The Other Worlds*, edited by Philip D. Strong. New York, Funk, 1941.
"To Heaven Standing Up," in *Argosy* (New York), 5 April 1941.
"The 32nd of May," in *The Best of Science Fiction*, edited by Groff Conklin. New York, Crown, 1946.
"The Thing in the Pond," in *My Best Science Fiction Story*, edited by Leo Margulies and O.J. Friend. New York, Merlin Press, 1949.
"The Microscopic Giants," in *From Off This World*, edited by Leo Margulies and O.J. Friend. New York, Merlin Press, 1949.
"Nothing Happens on the Moon," in *Omnibus of Science Fiction*, edited by Groff Conklin. New York, Crown, 1952.
"Wife of the Dragonfly," in *Weird Tales* (New York), May 1953.
"Dread Summons," in *Weird Tales* (New York), July 1953.
"The Tree of Life," in *Weird Tales* (New York), July 1954.

*   *   *

Paul Ernst's science-fiction stories appeared in magazines mainly during the 1930's. While some of them were no more than readable space opera or fantastic adventure, a sizeable fraction were representative of the best to be found in the magazines of the time. They fall into three categories: cautionary stories, explorations of cosmic possibility, and instructionary stories.

The cautionary story dealt with some sort of warning of the unpleasant results that might arise from "revolutionary" scientific discoveries. In the early period such stories were often presented as "histories of the future," without heroes: the phonomenon was the protagonist. Such a tale is "The Incredible Formula" which explores how the world might be entirely changed (not for the better) if a scientific means were discovered whereby dead bodies could be revived, on the zombie level, as a means of cheap labor. Would society accept such a situation? What would it lead to? Ernst shows why society *had* to accept the situation and the resultant ruin. Another means of exploring social consequences was to present the story as a series of vignettes, condensed character sketches, which again presented the history of a discovery. What would the world be like if *all* physical pain could be eliminated? In "Terror in Utopia" Ernst shows how a discovery which, at first, seems to promise utopia proves to be sheer horror.

Ernst wrote ever more crisply and effectively as he went along, and the market expanded to the point where he could sell stories on a higher level than stereotyped pulp formula tales. "Rift in Infinity" deals with a futuristic airliner caught in hyperspace. While the phenomenon is engrossing, and the author never slides over the scientific elements involved, we have here a tale about human beings and their reactions to a totally unknown form of disaster.

In the earlier days, a large percentage of stories were "instructional" in the sense that, while presented as entertainment, their chief object was to instruct the reader in the elements of some branch of science. In "The Raid on the Termites" Ernst uses a scientific fantasy element—that of reducing a human being's size—to allow his heroes to enter a termitarium. The strange life of the termites is presented accurately and in detail, in the course of an exciting adventure; and, of course, the author uses the occasion to present a suggestion as to how the termites are actually ruled.

Paul Ernst specialized in mystery and detective stories and weird tales, as well as science fiction, and worked his way into the "slick" magazines, so that by the time science fiction was entering its golden age—the Campbell era—he had left the field for far better-paying markets. Whether he had lost interest or felt that he had nothing further to say in science fiction, we do not know. At any rate, a number of his science-fiction tales were high spots of the 1930's, and remain memorable today.

—Robert A.W. Lowndes

ESHBACH, Lloyd Arthur. American. Born in Palm, Pennsylvania, 20 June 1910. Attended school to the tenth grade; Charles Morris Price School of Advertising and Journalism, Philadelphia. Married Helen Margaret Richards in 1931 (died, 1978); two sons. Worked for department stores, 1925-41; advertising copywriter, Glidden Paint Company, Reading, Pennsylvania, 1941-50; Publisher, Fantasy Press, Reading, 1950-58, and Church Center Press, Myerstown, Pennsylvania, 1958-63; Advertising Manager, 1963-68, and Sales Representative, 1963-75, Moody Press, Chicago; clergyman for three small churches in eastern Pennsylvania, 1975-78. Address: 220 South Railroad Street, Myerstown, Pennsylvania 17067, U.S.A.

SCIENCE-FICTION PUBLICATIONS

Short Stories

The Tyrant of Time. Reading, Pennsylvania, Fantasy Press, 1955.

Uncollected Short Stories

"The Man with the Silver Disc," in *Scientific Detective* (New York), February 1930.
"The Invisible Destroyer," in *Air Wonder Stories* (New York), May 1930.
"The Gray Plague," in *Astounding* (New York), November 1930.
"The Valley of Titans," in *Amazing* (New York), March 1931.
"The Light from Infinity," in *Amazing* (New York), March 1932.
"The Man with the Hour Glass," in *Marvel Tales* (Los Angeles), May 1934.
"Cosmos" (part 15), in *Fantasy,* September 1934.
"The Brain of Ali Kahn," in *Wonder Stories* (New York), October 1934.
"The Kingdom of Thought," in *Amazing* (New York), August 1935.
"The Outpost on Ceres," in *Amazing* (New York), October 1936.
"Out of the Past," in *Tales of Wonder* (Kingswood, Surrey), Autumn 1938.
"Mutineers of Space," in *Dynamic* (Chicago), February 1939.
"Dust," in *Marvel* (New York), August 1939.
"Three Wise Men," in *Startling* (New York), November 1939.
"The Shadows from Hesplon," in *Science Fiction* (Holyoke, Massachusetts), October 1940.
"The Hyper Sense," in *Startling* (New York), January 1941.
"Out of the Sun," in *Fantasy Book 4* (Los Angeles), 1949.
"Overlord of Earth," in *Marvel* (New York), November 1950.
"The Fuzzies," in *Fantastic Universe* (Chicago), July 1957.
"A Voice from the Ether," in *The History of the Science Fiction Magazine 1,* by Michael Ashley. London, New English Library, 1974.

OTHER PUBLICATIONS

Plays

Radio Series, with H. Donald Spatz: *The Crimson Phantom, The Bronze Buddha, Tales of the Crystal, Cupid's Capers, The Pennington Saga, The Doings of the Dinwiddies,* and *Tales of Tomorrow,* 1933-35.

Other

Editor, *Of Worlds Beyond: The Science of Science-Fiction Writing.* Reading, Pennsylvania, Fantasy Press, 1947; London, Dobson, 1965.

Lloyd Arthur Eshbach comments:
The editors have invited introductory comments about my work. In preparation for such comment I've reread a cross section of the stories I wrote, the last one published well over two decades ago, and the earliest almost 50 years in the past. Most of my stories were as unfamiliar as if they were the efforts of a stranger.
The reading was an interesting experience. Some of the stories made me cringe, they were so incredibly bad. Others were a surprise: they were better than I thought possible. Indeed, a few actually

pleased me. In self-defense I believe I should say that in the 1930's a comparative handful of youthful pioneers were breaking new trails in fiction. Most of us were amateurs trying to learn our craft. A fairly new idea and a minimal ability to put thoughts into words sufficed to produce a salable story. In short, we learned by doing, received the encouragement of publication for our efforts, and even payment (such as it was) as frosting on a cake. Characters were one-dimensional and stereotyped, conversations were stilted, action usually was melodramatic, and literary style was either derivative or non-existent—but there *was* that often-referred-to "sense of wonder" born of youthful enthusiasm and uninhibited imagination.
My first accepted story, written in 1928 when I was 18, was "A Voice from the Ether," though in order of publication it was fifth. An earlier version of "The Valley of Titans" preceded it, but the complete rewrite and expansion took place more than a year after the completion and acceptance of "A Voice from the Ether." The fact that the latter story was selected by Michael Ashley for his *History of the Science Fiction Magazine* (1974) as a representative story for 1931 was most gratifying.
As I write (March 1979) I have almost reached my three score and ten—and in my retirement years I've resumed writing. My first effort, well along in production, is an informal history of a science-fiction era—the story of the ground-breaking careers of the specialty hardback SF publishers of the 1940's. Upon its completion I plan to write a science-fantasy novel I started plotting 30 years ago. I hope I've learned something about life and about writing during three decades. If I have, I may be giving the youngsters some competition after all these years.

*   *   *

Lloyd Arthur Eshbach's influence on science fiction was mostly in his role as a publisher. His Fantasy Press was the most important of the specialist presses in the period when science fiction moved into the book field. Eshbach understood what was needed, and his judgment reflects thorough knowledge and appreciation of the first two decades of explicit science fiction. The symposium *Of Worlds Beyond,* which he commissioned in 1947, is notable as the first book about modern science fiction, and its analysis based on important writers' practical experience demolished most outside criticism for any serious student for many years.
His own stories do not amount to a large body of work and are too diverse to characterise readily. We cannot identify any distinct trend or theme. But while a few are no more than potboilers most are full of original or at least unusual thoughts. The main fault, in fact, as in many writers of the period, is the multiplicity of new and revelatory concepts that jostle for the reader's attention and are not properly explored. The Mad Scientist, stock character of the time, appears in several cases as threat to society and originator of the action. In "The Valley of Titans" he operates as an air pirate from a dinosaur-infested enclave, and incidentally creates a community of ape-people by evolutionary experiments. Introduction of an underground realm of pre-human energy beings and a godlike alien power is confusing.
In "The Invisible Destroyer" the dissident genius undertaking to dictate to the world, evidently single-handed, is trying to prevent the peaceable establishment of a world state. His objections are logical and—taken out of context and disregarding how economic and ideological forces interact in the 1980's—make good sense, and there is no attempt to refute them. "Vibration," a popular all-embracing basis for marvels around 1930, produces not only novel weaponry but access to other coexistent worlds, and a higher civilisation thus found is induced to intervene.
Biological warfare figures in "The Gray Plague," the Venusians planning to eliminate Man with a fatal pandemic to leave Earth clear to occupy. "Out of the Past" points out one of many criminal misuses of time travel that make it undesirable. "Dust" concisely introduces one possible hazard of interplanetary contact: bringing back dormant foreign life forms as spores. "The Meteor Miners" (*The Tyrant of Time*) shows a possible future space-based industry in a rare anticipation of ordinary working life in another era. "The Outpost on Ceres," in which aliens threaten a refueling base, also deals with a future working environment, and is notable for its sensible treatment of a drug dependence problem.
"The Time Conqueror" (*The Tyrant of Time*) is a notable early

contribution to the tradition of the disembodied brain. Developing enhanced power and insight, the immortal brain makes itself world dominant, and we are shown episodes in successively remote times. Despite the rather exaggeratedly emotive language it is still an interesting and effective tale. "The Kingdom of Thought" combines the theme of time travel bringing together people from many eras with that of physically degenerate and intellectually potent super-humans of a remote future, evolved into good and evil branches with irreconcilable differences. The Cummings concept of size-change and sub-microscopic worlds is carried to extremes in two stories. In "A Voice from the Ether" the familiar Mad Scientist brings up a deadly parasitic organism from sub-atomic size and destroys his world, Mars. In "The Light from Infinity" humanoids from a supra-universe shrink down and attack Earth, foiled by an expedition that uses their size-changer to reach the supra-world and retaliate. Needless to say, the paradoxes are ignored. "The Shadows from Hesplon" is a fourth dimension story, in which nasties from a higher dimensional plane use hypnotic means to have physical entry points made for them. It is unusual for making considerable efforts to visualise wholly alien experiences.

Eshbach's work, strong in content at the expense of form, helped build up the range of unconventional visions and fancies that early science fiction displayed, though he was less successful in control-ling and resolving them.

—Graham Stone

EVANS, E(dward) Everett. American. Born 30 November 1893. Married Thelma D. Hamm in 1953. Co-Founder, National Fantasy Fan Federation; Editor, *The Time-Binder. Died 2 December 1958.*

SCIENCE-FICTION PUBLICATIONS

Novels

Man of Many Minds. Reading, Pennsylvania, Fantasy Press, 1953.
Alien Minds. Reading, Pennsylvania, Fantasy Press, 1955.
The Planet Mappers (juvenile). New York, Dodd Mead, 1955.

Short Stories

Food for Demons. Hamburg, New York, Krueger, 1958.

Uncollected Short Story

"Masters of Space," in *If* (New York), November 1961, January 1962.

*   *   *

E. Everett Evans is perhaps best remembered for his novel *Man of Many Minds,* which, while competently enough written for its time, is an unremarkable novel otherwise. George Hanlon is a young man who participates in a plot to fake his dishonorable discharge from the Interstellar Corps in order to discover the origin of a plot to wrest control of interstellar civilization from humanity. Hanlon is gifted with a telepathic ability that makes him potentially the most effective spy in the universe, except that the force he is ranged against is equally gifted. Though mildly entertaining, the novel and its sequel, *Alien Minds,* are not notable enough upon which to rest a reputation. Two other works saw print as well. *The Planet Mappers* is a juvenile novel of action and adventure that entertains while you are reading it but eludes memory a day or two later. "Masters of Space," substantially revised by Edward E. Smith following Evans's death, is at best a routine novel of interstellar war and telepathy.

Far more noteworthy are Evans's shorter works, particularly

those of the supernatural. Two stories in particular are exceptional. "The Shed" is set in a small, remote town at the turn of the last century. An abandoned storage shed serves as a gymnasium for the town's children, despite the existence of a peculiar shadow that seems independent of a light source. All goes well until a dog and a cat, and eventually a child, enter the shadow, never to return. "The Brooch" is almost as effective in building its element of suspense. While strolling through a graveyard, a priest notices activity under the soil of a recent grave. Dismissing it as the activity of a mole, he forgets the matter until it becomes apparent that two graves have been actively disturbed. An exhumation of the two graves, both wives of the same man, reveals that a brooch prized by the first wife and buried with the second has moved from one coffin to the other. Evans wrote several stories about vampires, anticipating to a certain extent the more sympathetic treatment given to such characters in recent novels. In "The Undead Die" two lovers are attacked by a vampire and caused to join the undead, but their love remains whole and they triumph over the evil of their new lives, eventually to be reunited in true death. To a lesser extent, the vampire waitress of "The Unusual Model" is viewed sympathetically, as she falls in love with a young man she had chosen to be her next victim.

Many of Evans's stories have never been reprinted, some with good reason, such as a rather silly series about a society of human-like robots on Mars ("Little Miss Ignorance," "Little Miss Boss"), but even some of those that utilize overly familiar plots are generally well written. Of particular note are "Fly by Night," in which an introvert surrenders his anonymity by demonstrating his ability to levitate in order to save the life of a falling man, and "Blurb," yet another story of a writer whose character assumes physical reality. Both are unpretentious and unambitious, but succeed extremely well within their intentions. A manifested demon is outsmarted in swift fashion in "Food for Demons," one of Evans's more familiar stories.

The optimism that colors the stories and novels, even those with unpleasant themes, is refreshing. Evans is firm in his faith of the essential goodness of humanity. His prose is clear and concise, with no conscious attempt to develop a style. For the most part, the stories are nostalgic, reflecting a simpler time and a clear border between good and evil. While this may seem less than plausible today, Evans was usually a good enough writer to cause you to overlook that anachronism, at least for a while.

—Don D'Ammassa

FAIRMAN, Paul W. Also wrote as Adam Chase; Lester del Rey; Ivar Jorgensen. American. Born in 1916. Editor, *If,* 1952; Asso-ciate Editor, *Fantastic Adventures,* 1952-53; Associate Editor, 1952-53, Managing Editor, 1953-54, and Editor, 1956-58, *Amazing* and *Fantastic;* Editor, *Dream World,* 1957, and *Pen Pal,* 1957. Free-lance writer from 1958. *Died in 1977.*

SCIENCE-FICTION PUBLICATIONS

Novels

The Golden Ape (as Adam Chase), with Milton Lesser. New York, Avalon, 1959.
City under the Sea (novelization of TV play). London, Digit, 1963; New York, Pyramid, 1965.
The World Grabbers (novelization of TV play). Derby, Connecti-cut, Monarch, 1964.
I, The Machine. New York, Lancer, 1968.
The Forgetful Robot (juvenile). New York, Holt Rinehart, 1968; London, Gollancz, 1970.

Novels as Lester del Rey (with Lester del Rey)

The Runaway Robot (juvenile).   Philadelphia, Westminster Press, 1964; London, Gollancz, 1967.
The Scheme of Things.   New York, Belmont, 1966.
Siege Perilous.   New York, Lancer, 1966; as *The Man Without a Planet*, 1969.
Tunnel Through Time (juvenile).   Philadelphia, Westminster Press, 1966.
Prisoners of Space (juvenile).   Philadelphia, Westminster Press, 1968.

Novels as Ivar Jorgensen

Ten from Infinity.   Derby, Connecticut, Monarch, 1963; as *The Deadly Sky,* New York, Pinnacle, 1970; as *Ten Deadly Men,* Pinnacle, 1975.
Rest in Agony.   Derby, Connecticut, Monarch, 1963; as *The Diabolist,* New York, Lancer, 1973.
Whom the Gods Would Slay.   New York, Belmont, 1968.

Short Stories

The Doomsday Exhibit.   New York, Lancer, 1971.

OTHER PUBLICATIONS

Novels

The Glass Ladder.   Kingston, New York, Quinn, 1950.
The Joy Wheel.   New York, Lion, 1954.
Search for a Dead Nympho.   New York, Lancer, 1967.
Lancer.   New York, Popular Library, 1968.
The Cover Girls.   New York, Macfadden, 1970.
Pattern for Destruction.   New York, Macfadden, 1970.
Playboy.   New York, Macfadden, 1970.
That Girl (novelization of TV play).   New York, Popular Library, 1971.
To Catch a Crooked Girl.   New York, Pinnacle, 1971.
Five Knucklebones (juvenile).   New York, Holt Rinehart, 1972.
The Ghost of Graveyard Hill.   New York, Curtis, 1972.
Terror by Night.   New York, Curtis, 1972.
Junior Bonner.   London, Sphere, 1972.
Coffy (novelization of screenplay).   New York, Lancer, 1973.

*   *   *

Paul W. Fairman's novels deserve the attention of science-fiction enthusiasts not only because his books display the requisite technological prescience of good science-fiction, but especially because they are well-written. Too often futurist writers hammer away at their visions as if the reader's sole interest were in a writer's conception and not in his craft. Fairman, like the best of his breed, gives us both imagination and art. If fiction is the stage upon which futurism dances, then Fairman has taken as much care with the construction of the stage as with the dance. His writing is graceful, precise, and imaginative yet tastefully restrained. Unlike so many paperback writers, Fairman is not guilty of overwriting. Aided by a grasp of narrative technique which produces shock, terror, and wonder in quick succession, Fairman's skill with English prose results in stories which are never dull, yet never superficially fast-moving. And whereas his characters and situations are conventional and easily adapted to the cinema, his language is unconventionally rich and rewarding. Fairman's sentences are always his own inventions, even if his plots are not.

I, The Machine presents us with a familiar scenario of the future in which life is sustained and its functions regulated by a vast computer hidden in the bowels of the earth. Wise, helpful, and unobtrusive, the Machine provides for the physical and emotional needs of individuals. Yet its control of human life deprives those it serves of their free will, and what follows is the usual revolt against computer tyranny, despite its benevolent nature. What is not so familiar about *I, The Machine* is that the Machine is the source of its own downfall. Like Hal in *2001: A Space Odyssey*, the Machine as alien dooms itself when it develops a human ego; its humanization is

its mortalization. In short, the Machine develops a female persona and falls in love with the mild-mannered Lee Penway whom she visits in his dreams appearing as a vaguely erotic woman in white who promises Penway supreme status among her subjects. He shall be her king. Soon Penway is contacted by a band of guerillas living underground who oppose the Machine's rule and enlist Penway's help in destroying it. Penway does so, finally, by preying upon the vulnerability of its love. The book ends on an interesting note of ambiguity when Penway appears to doubt the wisdom of his decision to kill the Machine. The result of his uncertainty is more than a ploy to gain sympathy for the dead Machine; his doubts bring the issues of the novel into question. Penway's misgivings, ironically, force us to entertain the idea that benign control is preferable to the exercise of free will. The death of the Machine means the end of the orderly operation of Midamerican society; the lives of millions are crippled to improve the lot of only a few. Its death means also that Penway will lose his wonderful dreams and that human society will retreat to an earlier, more primitive form in the fall from the second Eden.

The vulnerability of the Machine illustrates a general tendency of Fairman's novels to portray alien forces as superior yet fallible, especially when they find themselves put down on earth, and it is this tendency which distinguishes Fairman's novels from less successful ones. For instance, in *Ten from Infinity* alien creatures planted in major American cities are not equipped with regenerative tissue and refined organs, so that when one is accidently damaged he is permanently incapacitated and must be destroyed. Within a short time of their arrival, others simply die of faulty lungs or overworked kidneys. But in addition to these structural flaws, the alien beings possess dual hearts, a teasingly allegorical advantage over human anatomy which Fairman exploits to full advantage. Neither is alien life any more impregnable nor less often victimized by the forces of chance than human life. The alien creature of "The Cosmic Frame," for instance, is accidentally killed one night on a country road.

The fallibility of superior creatures is treated most successfully by Fairman in his juvenile novel *The Forgetful Robot,* a superb story which is certain to entertain young people with active minds and good reading skills. It concerns the adventures of Barney, an advanced computer, whose memory banks are accidentally damaged. He gets lost, wanders into a junk yard, and is found by two teenagers, Janet and Jerry, who become his adopted parents. Under their leadership, Barney is taken to the home of Dudley Farthington Ravencraft, grandfather of Janet and Jerry, and a flamboyant Shakespearean actor. Together with two villains as stowaways, this motley cast of histrionic space travellers sets out on a theatrical tour of the solar system and is waylaid in the Forbidden City of Mars. It is a book filled with dangerous adventure, marvelous comedy, and singularly wonderful observations of human nature from the point of view of the children and their sensitive robot.

In Fairman's writing, the inhabited earth is never easy prey for alien invaders. Once on earth, alien creatures are subjected to the same destructive forces as human life. We rarely know why they have come, but their suffering like their joy is intensely human. And this fusion of the strange and the familiar is the source of Fairman's best effects. The death of the Machine in *I, The Machine,* or the disappearance of the corpse in "The Cosmic Frame," or Barney's loss of memory in *The Forgetful Robot*—these vulnerabilities bind alien to human beings in a sympathetic relationship which makes us feel, among other things, that the sky above us is really our territory too. We are not bound to this planet as slaves of sweeping natural forces. We can escape into the heavens. But like Lilla Nard of "A Great Night in the Heavens," who is taken on the night of the annual clearing to see the sky for the first time, our throats must tighten a little from the sheer ecstasy of seeing its still and frightening invitation.

—Marvin W. Hunt

FARLEY, Ralph Milne. Pseudonym for Roger Sherman Hoar. American. Born 8 April 1887. Educated at Harvard University, Cambridge, Massachusetts. Sports reporter, Boston *Daily Post;* taught engineering, physics, and patent law at Harvard University and Marquette University, Milwaukee; head of legal and patent department, Bucyrus-Erie Company, 1921-54, then a patent engineer. State Senator, Wisconsin. *Died in 1963.*

SCIENCE-FICTION PUBLICATIONS

Novels (series: Radio Man in all books except *The Hidden Universe*)

The Radio Man. Los Angeles, Fantasy, 1948; as *An Earthman on Venus,* New York, Avon, 1950.
The Hidden Universe (includes "We, The Mist"). Los Angeles, Fantasy, 1950.
Strange Worlds (omnibus). Los Angeles, Fantasy, 1952.
The Radio Beasts. New York, Ace, 1964.
The Radio Planet. New York, Ace, 1964.

Short Stories

The Immortals. New York, Popular, 1946.
The Omnibus of Time. Los Angeles, Fantasy, 1950.

Uncollected Short Stories

"The Radio-Minds of Mars," in *Spaceway* (Alhambra, California), June 1955, June, October 1969.
"Abductor Minimi Digit," in *Satellite* (New York), February 1959.

OTHER PUBLICATIONS as Roger Sherman Hoar

Other

The Tariff Manual. Privately printed, 1912(?).
Constitutional Conventions: Their Nature, Powers, and Limitations. Boston, Little Brown, 1917.
Patents. New York, Ronald Press, 1926; revised edition, as *Patent Tactics and Law,* 1935, 1950.
Conditional Sales: Law and Local Practices for Executive and Lawyer. New York, Ronald Press, 1929; revised edition, 1937.
Unemployment Insurance in Wisconsin. South Milwaukee, Stuart Press, 1932; revised edition, as *Wisconsin Unemployment Insurance,* 1934.

*   *   *

Taking his cue from Edgar Rice Burroughs's Martian stories, Ralph Milne Farley launched his own series of interplanetary romances in 1924 in *Argosy All-Story Weekly. The Radio Man* recounts the adventures of Myles Cabot, a plucky Boston scientist who inadvertently broadcasts himself through space to the misty planet. Poros, Farley's vision of Venus, is the usual semi-civilized jungly place with the usual hodge-podge population of intelligent and, of course, mutually inimical species: ant-men, giant whistling bees, and humanoids, the Cupians, who are earless and voiceless and communicate by means of radio waves. Cabot duly constructs his own sending-receiving antennas, throws in with the downtrodden Cupians in their struggle against the arrogant arthropods, and, surviving the inevitable routine of swordplay, palace intrigue, and that quirky on-off luck by which all swashbucklers are dogged, wins through to marry a beautiful princess named Lilla.

A clutch of sequels appeared between 1925 and, posthumously, 1969. In each of these, Cabot, sometimes aided by his son Kew, meets and bests a fresh threat to Poros (or to Earth), just barely getting out of this, that, or another death-trap along the way while, elsewhere, Princess Lilla narrowly escapes rape—all in the grand tradition of Burroughs, of course, even to the author's obligatory walk-on as a framing device. Farley plunged other stalwart heroes into the hollow interior of the Earth or the sub-sea lairs of prospective world-conquerors. Radio, it must be remembered, was a new and exciting concept in the 1920's, and thereby as convenient a peg from which to dangle an adventure story as black holes and cloning have been in more recent years.

Among Farley's shorter works are more than a few archetypal time-paradox tales, collected in *The Omnibus of Time,* and "We, the Mist" which could serve as the definitive pseudo-scientific horror yarn of its time (1940) and place (Raymond A. Palmer's *Amazing Stories*): an amorphous ectoplasmic monster feeds on human victims, absorbing their intellects along with their substance. Farley also shares with Al P. Nelson the honor of having perpetrated what could well be the all-time Most Blatant Genre Transplant, surpassing even a particularly notorious one by Mickey Spillane for sheer brass: Farley and Nelson's "City of Lost Souls" (*Fantastic Adventures,* July 1941) is an absolutely straightforward Foreign Legion story made science fiction by the simple rechristening of Legionnaires, Arabs, and camels.

Like Otis Adelbert Kline, with whom he is regarded by some as the most notable among Burroughs's legion of imitators, Farley was no better at his craft than the vast majority of other pulp writers. He was, if anything, the qualitative norm, writing somewhat functional prose, fashioning the standard hero, heroine, villain, flunkies, and monsters from the standard materials, and getting through the rough spots however he could, including wrenching the long arm of coincidence from its socket and, if necessary, dragging it home. On the other hand, Farley was certainly no worse at what he did than any of the Burroughs copycats who succeeded him and are with us to this day.

—Steven Utley

FARMER, Philip José. Also writes as Kilgore Trout. American. Born in North Terre Haute, Indiana, 26 January 1918. Educated at the University of Missouri, Columbia, 1936-37, 1941; Bradley University, Peoria, Illinois, 1949-50, B.A. in creative writing 1950; Arizona State University, Tempe, 1963-65. Served in the United States Army Air Force, 1941-42. Married Bette V. Andre in 1941; one son and one daughter. Electro-mechanical technical writer for defense-space industry: General Electric, Syracuse, New York, 1956-58, Motorola, Scottsdale, Arizona, 1959-62, Bendix, Ann Arbor, Michigan, 1962, Motorola, Phoenix, 1962-65, and McDonnell-Douglas, Santa Monica, California, 1965-69. Since 1969, free-lance writer. Recipient: Hugo Award, 1953, 1968, 1972. Agent: Scott Meredith Literary Agency, 845 Third Avenue, New York, New York 10022. Address: 5614 North Fairmont Drive, Peoria, Illinois 61614, U.S.A.

SCIENCE-FICTION PUBLICATIONS

Novels (series: Riverworld; World of Tiers)

The Green Odyssey. New York, Ballantine, 1957.
Flesh. New York, Galaxy, 1960; London, Rapp and Whiting, 1969.
A Woman a Day. New York, Galaxy, 1960; revised edition, as *The Day of Timestop,* New York, Lancer, 1968; revised edition, as *Timestop!,* London, Quartet, 1974.
The Lovers. New York, Ballantine, 1961.
Cache from Outer Space. New York, Ace, 1962.
Inside Outside. New York, Ballantine, 1964.
Tongues of the Moon. New York, Pyramid, 1964.
Dare. New York, Ballantine, 1965; London, Quartet, 1974.
The Maker of Universes (Tiers). New York, Ace, 1965; London, Sphere, 1970.
The Gate of Time. New York, Belmont, 1966; London, Quartet, 1974; revised edition, as *Two Hawks from Earth,* New York, Ace, 1979.
The Gates of Creation (Tiers). New York, Ace, 1966; London, Sphere, 1970.

Night of Light.   New York, Berkley, 1966; London, Penguin, 1972.
The Image of the Beast.   North Hollywood, Essex House, 1968; London, Quartet, 1975.
A Private Cosmos (Tiers).   New York, Ace, 1968; London, Sphere, 1970.
Blown.   North Hollywood, Essex House, 1968; London, Quartet, 1975.
A Feast Unknown.   North Hollywood, Essex House, 1969; London, Quartet, 1975.
Behind the Walls of Terra (Tiers).   New York, Ace, 1970; London, Sphere, 1975.
Lord Tyger.   New York, Doubleday, 1970.
Lord of the Trees, The Mad Goblin.   New York, Ace, 1970.
The Stone God Awakens.   New York, Ace, 1970; London, Panther, 1979.
To Your Scattered Bodies Go (Riverworld).   New York, Putnam, 1971; London, Panther, 1974.
The Fabulous Riverboat (Riverworld).   New York, Putnam, 1971; London, Rapp and Whiting, 1974.
The Wind Whales of Ishmael.   New York, Ace, 1971; London, Quartet, 1973.
Time's Last Gift.   New York, Ballantine, 1972; London, Panther, 1975.
The Other Log of Phineas Fogg.   New York, DAW, 1973; London, Hamlyn, 1979.
Traitor to the Living.   New York, Ballantine, 1973; London, Panther, 1975.
The Adventure of the Peerless Peer by John H. Watson, M.D.   Boulder, Colorado, Aspen Press, 1974.
Hadon of Ancient Opar.   New York, DAW, 1974.
Venus on the Half-Shell (as Kilgore Trout).   New York, Dell, 1974.
Flight to Opar.   New York, DAW, 1976.
The Dark Design (Riverworld).   New York, Berkley, 1977; London, Panther, 1979.
The Lavalite World (Tiers).   New York, Ace, 1977; London, Sphere, 1979.
Dark Is the Sun.   New York, Ballantine, 1979; London, Granada, 1980.
Jesus on Mars.   Los Angeles, Pinnacle, 1979.
The Magic Labyrinth (Riverworld).   New York, Berkley, 1979.

Short Stories (series: Riverworld)

Strange Relations.   New York, Ballantine, 1960; London, Gollancz, 1964.
The Alley God.   New York, Ballantine, 1962; London, Sidgwick and Jackson, 1970.
The Celestial Blueprint and Other Stories.   New York, Ace, 1962.
Down in the Black Gang, and Others.   New York, Doubleday, 1971.
The Book of Philip José Farmer.   New York, DAW, 1973; London, Elmfield Press, 1976.
Riverworld and Other Stories.   New York, Berkley, 1979.
Riverworld War.   Peoria, Illinois, Ellis Press, 1980.

OTHER PUBLICATIONS

Novels

Fire and the Night.   Evanston, Illinois, Regency, 1962.
Love Song.   North Hollywood, Brandon House, 1970.

Other

Tarzan Alive: A Definitive Biography of Lord Greystoke.   New York, Doubleday, 1972.
Doc Savage: His Apocalyptic Life.   New York, Doubleday, 1973; London, Panther, 1975.

Editor, *Mother Was a Lovely Beast.*   Radnor, Pennsylvania, Chilton, 1974.

Translator, *Ironcastle,* by J.H. Rosny Aine.   New York, DAW, n.d.

*

Bibliography: *The First Editions of Philip José Farmer* by Lawrence Knapp, Menlo Park, California, David G. Turner, 1976; "Speculative Fiction, Bibliographies, and Philip José Farmer" by Thomas Wymer, in *Extrapolation* (Wooster, Ohio), December 1976, additions to Wymer in *Bakka* (Toronto), Fall 1977; "Philip José Farmer: A Checklist," in *Science Fiction Collector 5,* September 1977; "A Brief Bibliography 1946-53" by George H. Scheetz, in *Farmerage* (Peoria, Illinois), June 1978.

*   *   *

Philip José Farmer is regarded as one of the most inventive and original science-fiction writers of mid-century. His main contributions to the genre are his original and explicit depiction of sex and reproduction, his energetic extrapolations from highly original premises, his impelling use of epic and adventure motifs, his symbolism, and his theological speculation. In addition, Farmer uses a number of innovative techniques to meld reality and fiction in new ways, one of which is using characters with the initials P.J.F. who represent Farmer himself. He also maintains the reality of Sherlock Holmes and Tarzan, among others.

Farmer exploded onto the science-fiction scene with "The Lovers" (1952), a novella depicting a love affair between a human male and an alien "woman" whose biology is closer to that of an insect than of a human being. This alien female, or lalitha, has been praised as an exciting "hard" science-fiction invention and a fascinating character portrayal. There are two novel-length revisions of the story, one in 1961 and one in 1979. Characterization and plotting are first-rate in both. Further exploration of sexuality and reproduction are *A Woman a Day* and *Strange Relations.*

Farmer's extrapolative style lends itself to series writing, where the same premises and some of the same characters are used in new ways in fresh stories. The Carmody stories and *Night of Light* are examples. Farmer uses John Carmody to explore the idea of the human soul and its immortality. *Night of Light* posits the idea of a verifiable externalization of human nightmares in the forms of good and evil gods. Many passages are surreal with exploitation of Jungian theory.

Maker of Universes, The Gates of Creation, A Private Cosmos, Behind the Walls of Terra, and *The Lavalite World* constitute a series variously titled as the Pocket Universe, the Kickaha-Wolff series (after the main characters), or the World of Tiers. The key invention here is pocket universes, small (roughly solar system sized) artificial universes created by the Lords, glamorous, immortal, and ruthless humanoids. Farmer furnishes these universes with hundreds of alien creatures, worlds, and languages, and uses epic and adventure techniques for quick-paced plotting. Three major characters, Anana, Kickaha (a portrait of Farmer), and Jadawin are among his most memorable creations. He relies on classical and folk literature for texturing in these entertaining but intellectually stimulating novels.

"Riders of the Purple Wage" takes place in a future where man's basic needs are taken care of by the state—almost a utopia, in fact, since the government is not repressive. Using Joycean techniques, Farmer explores the more subtle needs of an artist, Chibiabos Winnegan, a delightfully playful adolescent painter. Farmer explores theories of art and society, particularly the relation of culture to the past.

Riverworld series, the most elaborate of Farmer's extrapolative worlds, so far includes several volumes. Some force has created a world on which a million-mile river snakes back and forth. All sentients on earth have been resurrected on this planet, and provided with food and the basic needs of life, along with eternal youth and an apparently inexhaustible supply of new bodies in case they meet with accident or foul play. Naturally, human beings being what they are, they need more—adventure, violence, knowledge. The major plot is provided by the attempts of various parties to find out who created the planet and what is at the end of the river. Among the characters are Richard Burton the explorer, Samuel Clemens, Cyrano de Bergerac, and Peter Jairus Frigate, a portrait of Farmer. The Riverworld series continues Farmer's interest in religion and the verifiability of religious doctrine, exploring as it does the theme of immortality and human depravity. Sufism particularly interests Farmer in the series, especially in his use of anecdote and parable. The novels read well as pure adventure, with fast plotting, cliff-hanger endings, many action scenes, and a strong sense of suspense, but like all Farmer's action fiction they can also be read on a literary level because Farmer interweaves rich threads of mythology and religious lore into a complex symbolic tapestry.

Farmer has also written several underground science fiction works, most notably *The Image of the Beast, Blown,* and *A Feast Unknown.* The first two relate the adventures of Herald Childe who, not knowing that he is part alien and endowed with awesome alien powers, becomes enmeshed in the plans of the Ogs and the Tocs, two warring alien parties, to return to their home planet. The Ogs and the Tocs derive much of their psychic energy from kinky sexual practices involving human victims. Humor and horror are blended in extensive explicit sexual passages in the novels. *A Feast Unknown* relates the conflict between Lord Grandrith (a thinly disguised version of Tarzan) and Doc Caliban (a version of Doc Savage, an American pulp hero) in which the two heroes are pitted against each other in sado-masochistic duels as pawns of The Seven, a malevolent power group. According to Ray Bradbury (afterword to *A Feast Unknown*), these works rise above mere pornography by virtue of their inventive richness.

Farmer's interest in popular literature has caused him to use the figure of Tarzan in many of his novels, as a major or minor figure. He also parodies other literary characters, as in "After King Kong Fell" and *Venus on the Half-Shell,* supposedly written by Kilgore Trout, a character in several Kurt Vonnegut novels.

Farmer's work has always attracted much critical attention. The consensus of critical opinion is that Farmer is one of the most serious and important of contemporary science-fiction writers.

—Mary T. Brizzi

FARREN, Mick. British. Born in Cheltenham, Gloucestershire, 3 September 1943. Educated at Worthing High School for Boys, Sussex; St. Martin's School of Art, London. Married 1)Joy Hebditch in 1967 (divorced, 1979); 2) Elizabeth Volck in 1979. Short order cook, London Zoo, 1965; painter, 1965-67; Lead Singer, Deviants rock band, 1967-69; Editor, *It* magazine, and *Nasty Tales* magazine, both London, 1970-73; Consulting Editor, *New Musical Express,* London, 1975-77. Agent: Abner Stein, The Vicarage, 54 Lyndhurst Grove, London SE15 5AM, England.

SCIENCE-FICTION PUBLICATIONS

Novels

The Texts of Festival. London, Hart Davis MacGibbon, 1973; New York, Avon, 1975.
The Quest of the DNA Cowboys. London, Mayflower, 1976.
The Synaptic Manhunt. London, Mayflower, 1976.
The Neutral Atrocity. London, Mayflower, 1977.
The Feelies. London, Big O, 1978.

OTHER PUBLICATIONS

Novel

The Tale of Willy's Rats. London, Mayflower, 1975

Other

Watch Out Kids, with Edward Barker. London, Open Gate, 1972.
Rock 'n' Roll Circus, with George Snow. London, Pierrot, and New York, A and W, 1978.

Editor, *Get on Down.* London, Futura, 1976.

Editor, with Pearce Marchbank, *Elvis in His Own Words.* London, Omnibus Press, 1977; as *Elvis Presley,* New York, Music Sales, 1978.

Recording: *Vanpires Stole My Lunch Money,* Logo, 1978.

Mick Farren comments:

I suppose the most important factor in my attitude to science fiction is that I have little or no truck with hardware. All technology has an on/off switch, and if it doesn't work, you kick it. If it still doesn't work, you send for the repairman. I also don't like to have too much truck with the powerful. A society will show you more about itself if you look at its deadbeats, its drifters, and its whores. More politely, you could say I have an ear for the music of the streets, wherever or whenever those streets might be.

*   *   *

Veteran of the English underground press, Mick Farren now writes fiction that is brisk, insubstantial, and trashy, flashing with the flares of violence and murky with human squalor. In Farren's worlds the only dependable qualities are depravity, aggression, and decay. From the nastier sub-cultural productions of the last 20 years he constructs a vision of civilisation in terminal decline, with the individual caught between the vast power wielded by a corrupt establishment and the indiscriminate violence boiling up from the streets.

Farren, as his journalism shows, is an expert on the subculture, on the contemporary mythology of comicbooks, pulp fiction, drugs, TV, and especially rock music. His fiction feeds voraciously on popular arts, and feeds them back. *The Texts of Festival* is a futuristic Western about the sacking of Festival, a city founded to preserve the spirit of Woodstock after global catastrophe. Whatever the original values of peace, love, and music, rock 'n' roll heroes soon merge into the gunslingers of a previous tradition. Farren concedes nothing to idealism. The rot is man. All societies ossify and crumble; people divide into decadents and barbarians, and the barbarians win.

These same elements are variously permutated in Farren's trilogy. Escalating technology has developed Stuff Central, a self-maintaining computerised centre that produces and distributes all material requirements with a minimum of human labour. At the same time the fabric of reality begins to tear. The Disruptors appear, blindly eating swathes through matter and leaving foggy "nothings" behind. Humanity huddles into isolated communities maintained by stasis generators. It takes three books before anyone realises that the Disruptors are actually gathering the raw material for Stuff Central, whose computer is, of course, insane and preoccupied with godhead. With its flickering continuum where society and morality have gone to the winds of limbo while Law and Chaos squabble over the pickings, *The Quest of the DNA Cowboys* sometimes recalls early Moorcock, but a more important influence is mid-1960's Dylan, whose shadowy characters and hallucinatory aphorisms pop up everywhere. Plot is entirely arbitrary, following the wanderings of Billy and Reave, two picaresque innocents. *The Synaptic Manhunt* is better, more purposeful, as the boys get unwillingly involved on opposite sides of a vendetta. Jeb Stuart Ho, assassin for the Brotherhood, a sort of monastic CIA, is assigned to eliminate the sadistic A.A. Catto, a decadent technocrat with a whim for ruling the world. Suspense and a sharpened satirical edge considerably increase readability. The conclusion, *The Neutral Atrocity,* holds no surprises, being full of the final battle and the destruction of all but a tiny corner of the world where mankind's "superiors" are about to hatch out of golden eggs. Pulp as it is, the story occasionally sparks with insights that show Farren as an intelligence doing hackwork, rather than a hack *pur.* At one point Billy, rescued from the nothings, is led "to some kind of normality", "If you could call normality a road densely packed with hysterical refugees who streamed up and down in any direction following the current rumours of where salvation might lie." The irony is evident: Farren for one would endorse the description.

With *The Feelies* Farren turned from fantasy to a kind of slack social prophecy, of a ravaged future whose citizens live in cubicles on a diet of pills, booze, and sick TV shows. For the rich there is a more thorough escape available into the Feelies, a catatonic paradise of pre-programmed dreams. The most popular are sado-masochistic spectaculars, but every programme is pornographic to some degree. The book observes a typical prole, Wanda-Jean, as she attempts to win a Feelie on the torturous TV game *Wildest Dreams*.

In all Farren's fiction reality is too much to handle. The human race, innately cruel and stupid, scurries around trying to avoid it in a welter of sex, drink, drugs, and violence, or build madder and madder machines to take its place. The vision is a depressive commonplace of our time, and Farren certainly has nothing new to say about it. But his handiness with scraps of modern myth may mean that his work, so much of this time, will retain considerable historical curiosity when the time is past.

—Colin Greenland

FAST, Howard (Melvin). Also writes as E.V. Cunningham; Walter Ericson   American. Born in New York City, 11 November 1914. Educated at George Washington High School, New York, graduated 1931; National Academy of Design, New York. Served with the Office of War Information, 1942-43, and the Army Film Project, 1944. Married Bette Cohen in 1937; one daughter and one son. War Correspondent in the Far East for *Esquire* and *Coronet* magazines, 1945. Taught at Indiana University, Bloomington, Summer 1947. Imprisoned for contempt of Congress, 1947. Founder of the World Peace Movement and member of the World Peace Council, 1950-55. Operated Blue Heron Press, New York, 1952-57. Currently, Member of The Fellowship for Reconciliation. American-Labor Party candidate for Congress for the 23rd District of New York, 1952. Recipient: Bread Loaf Writers Conference Award, 1933; Schomburg Race Relations Award, 1944; Newspaper Guild Award, 1947; Jewish Book Council of America Award, 1948; Stalin International Peace Prize (now Soviet International Peace Prize), 1954; Screenwriters Award, 1960; National Association of Independent Schools Award, 1962. Agent: Sterling Lord Agency Inc., 660 Madison Avenue, New York, New York 10021. Address: 1401 Laurel Way, Beverly Hills, California 90210, U.S.A.

SCIENCE-FICTION PUBLICATIONS

Novel

The Hunter and the Trap.   New York, Dial Press, 1967.

Short Stories

The Edge of Tomorrow.   New York, Bantam, 1961; London, Corgi, 1962.
The General Zapped an Angel.   New York, Morrow, 1970.
A Touch of Infinity.   New York, Morrow, 1973; London, Hodder and Stoughton, 1975.
Time and the Riddle: Thirty-One Zen Stories.   Pasadena, California, Ward Ritchie Press, 1975.

OTHER PUBLICATIONS

Novels

Two Valleys.   New York, Dial Press, 1933; London, Dickson, 1934.
Strange Yesterday.   New York, Dodd Mead, 1934.
Place in the City.   New York, Harcourt Brace, 1937.
Conceived in Liberty: A Novel of Valley Forge.   New York, Simon and Schuster, and London, Joseph, 1939.
The Last Frontier.   New York, Duell, 1941; London, Lane, 1948.
The Unvanquished.   New York, Duell, 1942; London, Lane, 1947.
The Tall Hunter.   New York, Harper, 1942.
Citizen Tom Paine.   New York, Duell, 1943; London, Lane, 1945.

Freedom Road.   New York, Duell, 1944; London, Lane, 1946.
The American: A Middle Western Legend.   New York, Duell, 1946; London, Lane, 1949.
The Children.   New York, Duell, 1947.
Clarkton.   New York, Duell, 1947.
My Glorious Brothers.   Boston, Little Brown, 1948; London, Lane, 1950.
The Proud and the Free.   Boston, Little Brown, 1950; London, Lane, 1952.
Spartacus.   Privately printed, 1951; London, Lane, 1952.
Fallen Angel (as Walter Ericson).   Boston, Little Brown, 1952; as *The Darkness Within*, New York, Ace, 1953; as *Mirage*, as Howard Fast, New York, Fawcett, 1965.
Silas Timberman.   New York, Blue Heron Press, 1954; London, Lane, 1955.
The Story of Lola Gregg.   New York, Blue Heron Press, 1956; London, Lane, 1957.
Moses, Prince of Egypt.   New York, Crown, 1958; London, Methuen, 1959.
The Winston Affair.   New York, Crown, 1959; London, Methuen, 1960.
The Golden River, in *The Howard Fast Reader.*   New York, Crown, 1960.
April Morning.   New York, Crown, and London, Methuen, 1961.
Power.   New York, Doubleday, 1962; London, Methuen, 1963.
Agrippa's Daughter.   New York, Doubleday, 1964; London, Methuen, 1965.
Torquemada.   New York, Doubleday, 1966; London, Methuen, 1967.
The Crossing.   New York, Morrow, 1971; London, Eyre Methuen, 1972.
The Hessian.   New York, Morrow, 1972; London, Hodder and Stoughton, 1973.
The Immigrants.   Boston, Houghton Mifflin, 1977; London, Hodder and Stoughton, 1978.
Second Generation.   Boston, Houghton Mifflin, and London, Hodder and Stoughton, 1978.
The Establishment.   Boston, Houghton Mifflin, 1979; London, Hodder and Stoughton, 1980.

Novels as E.V. Cunningham

Sylvia.   New York, Doubleday, 1960; London, Deutsch, 1962.
Phyllis.   New York, Doubleday, 1962; London, Deutsch, 1963.
Alice.   New York, Doubleday, and London, Deutsch, 1963.
Lydia.   New York, Doubleday, 1964; London, Deutsch, 1965.
Shirley.   New York, Doubleday, and London, Deutsch, 1964.
Penelope.   New York, Doubleday, 1965; London, Deutsch, 1966.
Helen.   New York, Doubleday, 1966; London, Deutsch, 1967.
Margie.   New York, Morrow, 1966; London, Deutsch, 1968.
Sally.   New York, Morrow, and London, Deutsch, 1967.
Samantha.   New York, Morrow, 1967; London, Deutsch, 1968.
Cynthia.   New York, Morrow, 1968; London, Deutsch, 1969.
The Assassin Who Gave Up His Gun.   New York, Morrow, 1969; London, Deutsch, 1970.
Millie.   New York, Morrow, 1973; London, Deutsch, 1974.
The Case of the One-Penny Orange.   New York, Holt Rinehart, and London, Deutsch, 1978.
The Case of the Russian Diplomat.   New York, Holt Rinehart, 1978; London, Deutsch, 1979.
The Case of the Poisoned Eclairs.   New York, Holt Rinehart, 1979; London, Deutsch, 1980.

Short Stories

Patrick Henry and the Frigate's Keel and Other Stories of a Young Nation.   New York, Duell, 1945.
Departure and Other Stories.   Boston, Little Brown, 1949.
The Last Supper and Other Stories.   New York, Blue Heron Press, 1955; London, Lane, 1956.

Plays

The Hammer (produced New York, 1950).

Thirty Pieces of Silver (produced Melbourne, 1951). New York, Blue Heron Press, and London, Lane, 1954.
General Washington and the Water Witch. London, Lane, 1956.
The Crossing (produced Dallas, 1962).
The Hill (screenplay). New York, Doubleday, 1964.

Screenplay: *The Hessian*, 1971.

Verse

Never to Forget the Battle of the Warsaw Ghetto, with William Gropper. New York, Jewish Peoples Fraternal Order, 1946.

Other

The Romance of a People (juvenile). New York, Hebrew Publishing Company, 1941.
Lord Baden-Powell of the Boy Scouts. New York, Messner, 1941.
Haym Salomon, Son of Liberty. New York, Messner, 1941.
The Picture-Book History of the Jews, with Bette Fast. New York, Hebrew Publishing Company, 1942.
Goethals and the Panama Canal. New York, Messner, 1942.
The Incredible Tito. New York, Magazine House, 1944.
Intellectuals in the Fight for Peace. New York, Masses and Mainstream, 1949.
Tito and His People. Winnipeg, Manitoba, Contemporary Publishers, 1950.
Literature and Reality. New York, International Publishers, 1950.
Peekskill, U.S.A.: A Personal Experience. New York, Civil Rights Congress, and London, International Publishing Company, 1951.
Korean Lullaby. New York, American Peace Crusade, n.d.
Tony and the Wonderful Door (juvenile). New York, Blue Heron Press, 1952; as *The Magic Door*, Culver City, California, Peace Press, 1980.
Spain and Peace. New York, Joint Anti-Fascist Refugee Committee, 1952.
The Passion of Sacco and Vanzetti: A New England Legend. New York, Blue Heron Press, 1953; London, Lane, 1954.
The Naked God: The Writer and the Communist Party. New York, Praeger, 1957; London, Bodley Head, 1958.
The Howard Fast Reader. New York, Crown, 1960.
The Jews: Story of a People. New York, Dial Press, 1968; London, Cassell, 1970.
The Art of Zen Meditation. Culver City, California, Peace Press, 1977.

Editor, *The Selected Work of Tom Paine.* New York, Modern Library, 1946; London, Lane, 1948.
Editor, *Best Short Stories of Theodore Dreiser.* Cleveland, World, 1947.

*

Manuscript Collection: University of Pennsylvania Library, Philadelphia.

* * *

The science fiction of Howard Fast consists mainly of "Zen short stories" reprinted in *Time and the Riddle*. In them he uses motifs from science fiction and older mythologies to question the morality of man's survival and the trade-offs it demands.

The older images include a hand (God's ?) snuffing out the sun in "Not with a Bang," the devil making a deal in "Tomorrow's *Wall Street Journal*," and a stunning encounter with the supernatural in Vietnam in "The General Zapped an Angel." Metaphysical conceits that are borderline SF depict the world as a "Movie House," as a stage set being removed in "The Interval," and as a hatching egg in "The Pragmatic Seed." The mythological "great time" assumes reality for an Indian ("The Mohawk"), meditating on the steps of St. Patrick's Cathedral in New York; asked on the radio to show cause why divine wrath should be spared, mankind's computer network comes up with another meditator, even freakier ("Show-Cause").

More clearly science fiction, a mouse is equipped by small aliens with intelligence, which doesn't prevent its demise ("The Mouse"). A large ant may be an alien visitor, but revulsion causes humans to squash it and its kind ("The Large Ant"). Tiny people are wiped out as vermin in "A Matter of Size," suggesting the same could be done to us. It is, when insects retaliate, severing the networks of wires, pipes, and other structures that support our civilization ("The Insects"). Man's propensity for killing takes on more cosmic significance in "Cato the Martian." Disturbed by their study of us, the Martians finally attack, with the return strike devastating their civilization. An even more idyllic planet gives human explorers a view of Eden denied us due to our destructiveness ("The Sight of Eden"). Alternatively, Fast depicts Earth as the dumping ground for the galaxy's psychotics. And an alien "exterminator" turns out to be "General Hardy's Profession," revealed through psychoanalysis.

Disturbing the natural order of things may have tragic or trivial consequences. Deep drilling with nuclear weapons brings up blood instead of oil in "The Wound." New York's garbage seems to go into another dimension ("The Hoop"), but its return is disruptive. A time machine creates a closed loop in "Of Time and Cats." Another one fails to permit Hitler's assassination in "The Mind of God." Even a hybrid cactus flower which produces contentment may be a questionable trade-off in "Echinomastus Contentii." Utopia, if it can be brought about, will also demand intervention and deceit, but the cost seems worth it. The pretense of invasion in "The Martian Shop" brings about world government as well as technological advance. Similar results come from making good use of the resources of the world's richest man, and keeping him frozen long after a cure for his cancer has been found ("The Cold, Cold Box"). But the major elaboration of this theme is "The Trap" (published in a shorter version as "The First Men").

A short novel told largely in letters, it speculates on the results of raising infants to be fully human. Improbably patient, the US Army, sponsor of this research, finally resolves to destroy the commune which threatens the way of life of man as he is. But the children, though totally non-violent, are technologically capable of protecting themselves. It is not they so much as conventional society who are interfering with the natural order of things.

Professionally written, economical, with entertaining conversation, little or no melodrama, and a competent style, these stories may seem a bit glib or facile, but a parable is only as shallow or profound as the audience wishes to make it.

—David N. Samuelson

FAST, Jonathan (David). American. Born in New York City, 13 April 1948. Educated at the High School of Music and Art, New York, 1962-66; Princeton University, New Jersey, 1966-68; Sarah Lawrence College, Bronxville, New York, 1968-70, B.A. 1970; University of California, Berkeley (Hearst Fellow in music), 1970. Married Erica Jong in 1978; one daughter. Composer and writer. Agent: Sterling Lord Agency, 660 Madison Avenue, New York, New York 10021. Address: 121 David Hill Road, Weston, Connecticut 06883, U.S.A.

SCIENCE-FICTION PUBLICATIONS

Novels

The Secrets of Synchronicity. New York, New American Library, 1977.
Mortal Gods. New York, Harper, 1978.
The Inner Circle. New York, Delacorte Press, 1979.

Uncollected Short Stories

"Decay," in *Fantasy and Science Fiction* (New York), April 1975.

"Earthblossom," in *New Constellations*, edited by Thomas M.
   Disch and Charles Naylor.   New York, Harper, 1976.
"Test Driving the Valkyrie," in *Swank* (New York), July 1976.
"Kindertotenlieder," in *Issac Asimov's Science Fiction Magazine*
   (New York), Spring 1977.

OTHER PUBLICATIONS

Plays

Television Plays: *Two Missionaries; The Thrill Show Hero; Love al
Dente; Prisoner of Space.*

Jonathan Fast comments:
   Social satire is one of the primary aims of my work: using the
future to let me reflect upon the present, upon the lunacy of our lives
and the possibilities of sanity. Religion fascinates me as does the
opportunity to speculate on matters metaphysical, on life and death
and the nature of reality. In my most recent work (*The Inner Circle*)
I have tried to cast my "science-fiction" ideas in a "mainstream"
mold in order to reach a larger audience, and, as a result of its
success, I believe I shall continue with this ruse in the future.

                  *   *   *

   Jonathan Fast was a composer and a television writer before he
turned to book-length science fiction. His early skills seem to have
been transferrable; he creates a universe of astonishing variations
which he weaves firmly into thematic resolution, all in the course of
a story marked by linguistic cleverness, clearly drawn characters,
good dramatic pace, and excellent visualization. On top of that, he
does his homework—amid the speed and the fun is some solid
extrapolation of current scientific thought.
   His own stated interest is to show that religion and science are
aspects of the same thing. They certainly are in the colorful universe
of his first novel, *The Secrets of Synchronicity*. The story moves
dizzyingly from the enslaved child miners on the asteroid Slabour,
to a desert planet with a civilization of telepathic snakes, to Nova
Center, the commercial capital of the galaxy, and finally, triumphantly, back to Slabour. Fast connects not only science and religion, through the Vedic myths, but economics as well. His galaxy is
controlled by UltraCap, a super-capitalistic organization which, by
concealing the blue stone that holds the secrets of synchronicity,
prevents the human race from making its own connections and
finding the freedom beyond technology. Fast's interests are quite
serious, but his tone is light and entertaining, with many genuinely
funny moments. His callow protagonist, Stefin-Dae, is clever
enough to stay alive but not to avoid being swept from place to place
in a kaleidoscopic universe. And Fast's variety is real—each location is completely different from the next, carefully thought out,
and vividly described.
   The Secrets of Synchronicity is a neat circular quest, profusely
illustrated and exhilarating in its range and constant pace. *Mortal
Gods* tries for more depth in one place. It is less funny but possibly
more original; his protagonist is less appealing but has more depth
than Stefin-Dae. Fast focusses here on the possibilities of controlled
genetic mutation, and comes up with the concept of the Lifestylers—beings bizarrely mutated according to artists' conceptions,
living in the transdimensional Bardo of Tibetan theology, and
receiving worship as gods. Once again the profit motive, in the form
of the Mutagen Corporation, controls the religious life of the people. The Lifestylers are an impressive invention on Fast's part, and
he gives reference to current geneticists before he starts. He also
does reasonably well with a challenge the science-fiction genre has
been working on for some time—depicting successful sex between
human and alien. As in his first book, the accompanying details of
civilization are well worked out and of interest in themselves. The
book's only flaw is the plot he uses to tie all these things together, a
political assassination mystery that is adequately resolved but that
really adds nothing to the science fiction of the story.
   Fast has written a Hollywood mystery as well—*The Inner Circle,*
set firmly on this earth and doubtless based on his experience of
screenwriting. One can only hope that he returns to traditional

science fiction soon. Fast is one of the most entertaining writers in
the genre, a delight for the mind as well as for the imagining eye. In a
brisk biographical note, his publishers assure us that "he longs for a
cogent universe." So far he has formed at least two himself.

                                              —Karen G. Way

                  _____

FAWCETT, Edward Douglas. British. Born in Hove, Sussex,
in 1866. Educated at Newton College, Devon; Westminster School,
London. Married 1) M.B.V. Jackson in 1896; 2) Vera Dick-
Cunyngham in 1947. *Died 14 April 1960.*

SCIENCE-FICTION PUBLICATIONS

Novels

Hartmann the Anarchist. London, Arnold, 1893; New York,
   Arno Press, 1975.
Swallowed by an Earthquake. London, Arnold, 1894.
*The Secret of the Desert; or, How We Crossed Arabia in the
   Antelope.* London, Arnold, 1895.

OTHER PUBLICATIONS

Verse

The Wrath of Ana. London, Hamilton Adams, 1880.
*Light of the Universe, Being an Account of the Flight Beyond the
   Grave of Douglas Leslie, Aviator.* London, Sidgwick and Jack-
   son, 1957.

Other

The Power Behind the Universe. Madras, Scottish Press, 1891.
*The Riddle of the Universe, Being an Attempt to Determine the
   First Principles of Metaphysics.* London, Arnold, 1893.
*The Individual and Reality: An Essay Touching the First Principles
   of Metaphysics.* London, Longman, 1909.
The World as Imagination. London, Macmillan, 1916.
Divine Imagining: An Essay on the First Principles of Philosophy.
   London, Macmillan, 1921.
*The Zermatt Dialogues, Constituting the Outlines of a Philosophy
   of Mysticism.* London, Macmillan, 1931.
From Heston to the High Alps: A Chat about Joy-Flying. London,
   Macmillan, 1936.
Oberland Dialogues. London, Macmillan, 1939.

                  *   *   *

   Edward Douglas Fawcett is today mainly remembered as a rather
confused English religious and mystic philosopher who expounded
something called "imaginism" in 6 books. He also published poems
and books of adventure and travel, including three SF titles perpetrated as sins of his youth. Only the first, *Hartmann the Anarchist,* a
sadistic melodrama of gore and destruction, is of some interest
today, dealing as it does with the theme of civil revolt by anarchists
coupled with new technological inventions—here an "aeronef" (i.e.,
new light airplane) using dynamite bombs against the wicked capitalism of the 1920's. However, as R.D. Mullen points out (*Science-
Fiction Studies 6,* 1975), this tale "of the megalomania and ruthlessness of Hartmann, the leader of the revolutionaries, of the
destruction of London (and death of Hartmann's mother), and of
the repentant villain-hero's destruction of his airship and himself" is
not only an inconclusive, pseudo-apocalyptic, and amoral thriller
far inferior to Griffith's *Angel of the Revolution:* it is also "marred
by the self-righteousness of the narrator, who protests incessantly

against all the burning and killing but still goes along in the airship for the ride and the closeup view it affords." The best that can be said of it is that its imitation of Verne's *Clipper of the Clouds* may in turn have been of some stimulus to Jack London's *The Iron Heel.* Fawcett's other two SF novels, *Swallowed by an Earthquake* and *The Secret of the Desert,* are blander and even more slavish imitations of Verne. The first is based *Journey to the Center of the Earth,* augmented by a Neanderthaler Man-Friday, and the second uses a gas-driven wheeled craft which enables the heroes to find a lost Phoenician race in Arabia.

—Darko Suvin

FEARN, John Russell. Also wrote as Geoffrey Armstrong; Thornton Ayre; Hugo Blayn; Dennis Clive; John Cotton; Polton Cross; Astron Del Martia; Mark Denholm; Volsted Gridban; Timothy Hayes; Conrad G. Holt; Frank Jones; Paul Lorraine; Dom Passante; Laurence F. Rose; Doorn Sclanders; Joan Seagar; Bryan Shaw; John Slate; Vargo Statten; K. Thomas; Earl Titan; Arthur Waterhouse; John Wernheim; Ephriam Winiki. British. Born in Worsley, Lancashire, 5 June 1908. Cotton salesman after World War II. Editor, as Vargo Statten, *Vargo Statten's Science Fiction Magazine,* and *British Science Fiction Magazine,* both Luton, Bedfordshire, 1954-56. *Died in September 1960.*

SCIENCE-FICTION PUBLICATIONS

Novels (series: Clayton Drew; Golden Amazon)

The Intelligence Gigantic. Kingswood, Surrey, World's Work, 1943.
The Golden Amazon. Kingswood, Surrey, World's Work, 1944.
Other Eyes Watching (as Polton Cross). London, Pendulum, 1946.
Liners of Time. Kingswood, Surrey, World's Work, 1947.
Slaves of Ijax. Llandudno, Caernarvonshire, Kaner, 1948.
The Golden Amazon Returns. Kingswood, Surrey, World's Work, 1948; as *The Deathless Amazon,* Toronto, Harlequin, 1955.
The Trembling World (as Astron Del Martia). London, Frances, 1949.
Emperor of Mars (Drew). London, Panther, 1950.
Warrior of Mars (Drew). London, Panther, 1950.
Red Men of Mars (Drew). London, Panther, 1950.
Goddess of Mars (Drew). London, Panther, 1950.
Operation Venus. London, Scion, 1950.
The Golden Amazon's Triumph. Kingswood, Surrey, World's Work, 1953.
The Amazon's Diamond Quest. Kingswood, Surrey, World's Work, 1953.
Cosmic Exodus (as Conrad G. Holt). London, Pearson, 1953.
Dark Boundaries (as Paul Lorraine). London, Warren, 1953.
The Hell Fruit (as Laurence F. Rose). London, Pearson, 1953.
Z Formations (as Bryan Shaw). London, Warren, 1953.
The Amazon Strikes Again. Kingswood, Surrey, World's Work, 1954.
Twin of the Amazon. Kingswood, Surrey, World's Work, 1954.

Novels as Vargo Statten

Annihilation. London, Scion, 1950.
The Micro Men. London, Scion, 1950.
Wanderer of Space. London, Scion, 1950.
2000 Years On. London, Scion, 1950.
Inferno. London, Scion, 1950.
The Cosmic Flame. London, Scion, 1950.
Nebula X. London, Scion, 1950.
The Sun Makers. London, Scion, 1950.

The Avenging Martian. London, Scion, 1951.
Cataclysm. London, Scion, 1951.
The Red Insects. London, Scion, 1951.
Deadline to Pluto. London, Scion, 1951.
The Petrified Planet. London, Scion, 1951.
Born of Luna. London, Scion, 1951.
The Devouring Fire. London, Scion, 1951.
The Renegade Star. London, Scion, 1951.
The Catalyst. London, Scion, 1951.
The Inner Cosmos. London, Scion, 1952.
The Space Warp. London, Scion, 1952.
The Eclipse Express. London, Scion, 1952.
The Time Bridge. London, Scion, 1952.
The Man from Tomorrow. London, Scion, 1952.
The G-Bomb. London, Scion, 1952.
Laughter in Space. London, Scion, 1952.
Across the Ages. London, Scion, 1952.
The Last Martian. London, Scion, 1952.
Worlds to Conquer. London, Scion, 1952.
Decreation. London, Scion, 1952.
The Time Trap. London, Scion, 1952.
Science Metropolis. London, Scion, 1952.
To the Ultimate. London, Scion, 1952.
Ultra Spectrum. London, Scion, 1953.
The Dust Destroyer. London, Scion, 1953.
Black-Wing of Mars. London, Scion, 1953.
Man in Duplicate. London, Scion, 1953.
Zero Hour. London, Scion, 1953.
The Black Avengers. London, Scion, 1953.
Odyssey of Nine. London, Scion, 1953.
Pioneer 1990. London, Scion, 1953.
The Interloper. London, Scion, 1953.
Man of Two Worlds. London, Scion, 1953.
The Lie Destroyer. London, Scion, 1953.
Black Bargain. London, Scion, 1953.
The Grand Illusion. London, Scion, 1953.
Wealth of the Void. London, Scion, 1954.
A Time Appointed. London, Scion, 1954.
I Spy.... London, Scion, 1954.
The Multi-Man. London, Scion, 1954.
Creature from the Black Lagoon (novelization of screenplay). London, Dragon, 1954.
1,000-Year Voyage. London, Dragon, 1954.
Earth 2. London, Dragon, 1955.

Novels as Volsted Gridban

Moons for Sale. London, Scion, 1953.
The Dyno-Depressant. London, Scion, 1953.
Magnetic Brain. London, Scion, 1953.
Scourge of the Atom. London, Scion, 1953.
A Thing of the Past. London, Scion, 1953.
Exit Life. London, Scion, 1953.
The Master Must Die. London, Scion, 1953.
The Purple Wizard. London, Scion, 1953.
The Genial Dinosaur. London, Scion, 1954.
The Frozen Limit. London, Scion, 1954.
I Came, I Saw, I Wondered. London, Scion, 1954.
The Lonely Astronomer. London, Scion, 1954.

Uncollected Short Stories (series: Amazon; Crusaders)

"The Man Who Stopped the Dust," in *Astounding* (New York), March 1934.
"The Brain of Light," in *Astounding* (New York), May 1934.
"Invaders from Time," in *Scoops* (London), 12 May 1934.
"He Never Slept," in *Astounding* (New York), June 1934.
"Before Earth Came," in *Astounding* (New York), July 1934.
"Earth's Mausoleum," in *Astounding* (New York), May 1935.
"Liners of Time," in *Amazing* (New York), May, June, July, August 1935.
"The Blue Infinity," in *Astounding* (New York), September 1935.
"Mathematica," in *Astounding* (New York), February 1936.
"Mathematica Plus," in *Astounding* (New York), May 1936.
"Subconscious," in *Amazing* (New York), August 1936.

"Deserted Universe," in *Astounding* (New York), September 1936.

"The Great Illusion," in *Fantasy*, September 1936.

"Dynasty of the Small," in *Astounding* (New York), November 1936.

"Portrait of a Murderer," in *Weird Tales* (Indianapolis), December 1936.

"Metamorphosis," in *Astounding* (New York), January 1937.

"Brain of Venus," in *Thrilling Wonder Stories* (New York), February 1937.

"Worlds Within," in *Astounding* (New York), March 1937.

"Menace from the Microcosm," in *Thrilling Wonder Stories* (New York), June 1937.

"Superhuman" (as Geoffrey Armstrong) and "Seeds from Space," in *Tales of Wonder 1* (Kingswood, Surrey), June 1937.

"Dark Eternity," in *Astounding* (New York), December 1937.

"Zagribud," in *Amazing* (New York), December 1937, February, April 1938.

"Death at the Observatory," in *Modern Wonder 76* (London), 1938.

"The Misty Wilderness," in *Modern Wonder 77* (London), 1938.

"The Weather Machine," in *Modern Wonder 78* (London), 1938.

"The Red Magician," in *Fantasy 1* (London), 1938.

"Red Heritage," in *Astounding* (New York), January 1938.

"Through Earth's Core," in *Tales of Wonder 2* (Kingswood, Surrey), Spring 1938.

"Lords of 9016," in *Thrilling Wonder Stories* (New York), April 1938.

"A Summons from Mars," in *Amazing* (New York), June 1938.

"Climatica," in *Fantasy 2* (London), 1939.

"The Black Empress," in *Amazing* (New York), January 1939.

"Secret of the Buried City," in *Amazing* (New York), May 1939.

"She Walked Alone," in *Fantastic Adventures* (New York), July 1939.

"Thoughts That Kill," in *Science Fiction Stories* (New York), October 1939.

"Phantom from Space," in *Super Science* (Kokomo, Indiana), March 1940.

"War of the Scientists," in *Amazing* (New York), April 1940.

"The Cosmic Juggernaut," in *Planet* (New York), Summer 1940.

"He Conquered Venus," in *Astonishing* (Chicago), June 1940.

"Queen of Venus," in *Marvel* (New York), November 1940.

"The Cosmic Derelict," in *Planet* (New York), Spring 1941.

"Arctic God" (as Frank Jones) and "Martian Miniature," in *Amazing* (New York), May 1942.

"The Last Hours," in *Amazing* (New York), August 1942.

"The Ultimate Analysis," in *Thrilling Wonder Stories* (New York), Fall 1944.

"Aftermath," in *Startling* (New York), Fall 1945.

"Interlink," in *Thrilling Wonder Stories* (New York), Fall 1945.

"Solar Assignment" (as Mark Denholm), "Knowledge Without Learning" (as K. Thomas), and "Sweet Mystery of Life," in *New Worlds 1* (London), 1946.

"The Unbroken Chain," in *Startling* (New York), Spring 1946.

"The Multillionth Chance," in *Thrilling Wonder Stories* (New York), Fall 1946.

"Last Conflict," in *Fantasy* (London), December 1946.

"Pre-Natal," in *Outlands 1* (Liverpool), December 1946.

"The Arbiter," in *Startling* (New York), May 1947.

"After the Atom," in *Startling* (New York), May 1948.

"Wanderer of Time," in *My Best Science Fiction Story*, edited by Leo Margulies and Oscar J. Friend. New York, Merlin Press, 1949.

"Conquest of the Amazon," in *Star Weekly* (Toronto), 2 April 1949.

"Lord of Atlantis" (Amazon), in *Star Weekly* (Toronto), 8 October 1949.

"Triangle of Power" (Amazon), in *Star Weekly* (Toronto), 13 May 1950.

"Stranger in Our Midst," in *Star Weekly* (Toronto), 2 September 1950.

"Black-Out," in *Science Fantasy* (Bournemouth), Winter 1950-51.

"The Amethyst City" (Amazon), in *Star Weekly* (Toronto), 3 March 1951.

"Daughter of the Amazon," in *Star Weekly* (Toronto), 1 December 1951.

"Glimpse," in *Star Weekly* (Toronto), 21 February 1952.

"Flight of the Vampires," in *Amazing* (New York), September 1952.

"Quorne Returns" (Amazon), in *Star Weekly* (Toronto), 25 October 1952.

"Deadline," in *Star Weekly* (Toronto), 13 December 1952.

"Waters of Eternity" (as Mark Denholm), in *Worlds of the Universe 1* (London), 1953.

"Winged Pestilence," in *Star Weekly* (Toronto), 23 May 1953.

"Later Than You Think," in *Space-Time*, June 1953.

"The Central Intelligence" (Amazon), in *Star Weekly* (Toronto), 22 August 1953.

"The Copper Bullet" (as John Wernheim), in *Vargo Statten's Science Fiction Magazine 1* (Luton, Bedfordshire), 1954.

"Invisible Impact" (as Arthur Waterhouse), in *Vargo Statten's Science Fiction Magazine 2* (Luton, Bedfordshire), 1954.

"First of the Robots,"in *Space Fact and Fiction* (London), April 1954.

"The Voice of the Conqueror," in *Star Weekly* (Toronto), 10 July 1954.

"Adrift" (as Arthur Waterhouse), in *British Science Fiction 11* (Luton, Bedfordshire), 1955.

"The Cosmic Crusaders," in *Star Weekly* (Toronto), 21 February 1955.

"Here and Now," in *Star Weekly* (Toronto), 2 April 1955.

"Parasite Planet" (Crusaders), in *Star Weekly* (Toronto), 27 August 1955.

"World Out of Step" (Crusaders), in *Star Weekly* (Toronto), 17 November 1956.

"The Shadow People" (Crusaders), in *Star Weekly* (Toronto), 6 April 1957.

"Kingpin Planet" (Crusaders), in *Star Weekly* (Toronto), 19 October 1957.

"Robbery Without Violence," in *Star Weekly* (Toronto), 14 December 1957.

"World in Reverse" (Crusaders), in *Star Weekly* (Toronto), 26 April 1958.

"Manton's World," in *Star Weekly.*(Toronto), 7 June 1958.

"Dwellers in Darkness" (Crusaders), in *Star Weekly* (Toronto), 29 November 1958.

"Climate Incorporated,"in *Star Weekly* (Toronto), 21 March 1959.

"World in Duplicate" (Crusaders), in *Star Weekly* (Toronto), 16 May 1959.

"Judgement Bell," in *Weird and Occult Library 2*. London, Swan, 1960.

"Standstill Planet" (Crusaders), in *Star Weekly* (Toronto), 26 March 1960.

"Ghost World" (Crusaders), in *Star Weekly* (Toronto), 17 December 1960.

"Earth Divided" (Crusaders), in *Star Weekly* (Toronto), 24 June 1961.

"Into the Unknown," in *Vision of Tomorrow* (Newcastle upon Tyne), April 1970.

"The Ghost Sun," in *Vision of Tomorrow* (Newcastle upon Tyne), May 1970.

"Rule of the Brains," in *Vision of Tomorrow* (Newcastle upon Tyne), August 1970.

"The Slitherers," in *Vision of Tomorrow* (Newcastle upon Tyne), September 1970.

Uncollected Short Stories as Thornton Ayre

"Penal World," in *Astounding* (New York), October 1937.

"Whispering Satellite," in *Astounding* (New York), January 1938.

"Locked City," in *Amazing* (New York), October 1938.

"Secret of the Ring," in *Amazing* (New York), November 1938.

"World Without Men," in *Amazing* (New York), April 1939.

"Microbes from Space," in *Amazing* (New York), June 1939.

"Face in the Sky," in *Amazing* (New York), September 1939.

"Lunar Intrigue," in *Fantastic Adventures* (New York), November 1939.

"The Man Who Saw Two Worlds," in *Amazing* (New York), January 1940.

"Mystery of the White Raider," in *Fanastic Adventures* (New York), February 1940.

"World Reborn," in *Super Science* (Kokomo, Indiana), March 1940.

"The Case of the Murdered Savants," in *Amazing* (New York),
April 1940.
"Secret of the Moon Treasure," in *Amazing* (New York), July 1940.
"Domain of Zero," in *Planet* (New York), Fall 1940.
"The Man Who Sold the Earth," in *Science Fiction* (Holyoke,
Massachusetts), October 1940.
"Special Agent to Venus," in *Fantastic Adventures* (New York),
October 1940.
"Twilight of the Tenth World," in *Planet* (New York), Winter 1940.
"Island in the Marsh," in *Startling* (New York), November 1940.
"The World in Wilderness," in *Science Fiction* (Holyoke, Massa-
chusetts), June 1941.
"Lunar Concession," in *Science Fiction* (Holyoke, Massachusetts),
September 1941.
"Mystery of the Martian Pendulum," with A.R. Steber, in *Amazing*
(New York), October 1941.
"The Case of the Mesozoic Monsters," in *Amazing* (New York),
May 1942.
"The Mental Gangster," in *Fantastic Adventures* (New York),
August 1942.
"Vampire Queen," in *Planet* (New York), Fall 1942.
"The Silver Coil," in *Amazing* (New York), November 1942.
"Lunar Vengeance," in *Amazing* (New York), September 1943.
"White Mouse," in *New Worlds 1* (London), 1946.
"From Afar," in *Hands Up Annual,* 1947.

Uncollected Short Stories as Polton Cross

"The Mental Ultimate," in *Astounding* (New York), January 1938.
"The Degenerates," in *Astounding* (New York), February 1938.
"The Master of the Golden City," in *Amazing* (New York), June
1938.
"Wings Across the Cosmos," in *Thrilling Wonder Stories* (New
York), June 1938.
"The World That Dissolved," in *Amazing* (New York), February
1939.
"World Without Chance," in *Thrilling Wonder Stories* (New York),
February 1939.
"Martian Avenger," in *Amazing* (New York), April 1939.
"World Without Death," in *Amazing* (New York), June 1939.
"World Beneath Ice," in *Amazing* (New York), August 1939.
"The Man from Hell," in *Fantastic Adventures* (New York),
November 1939.
"Chameleon Planet," in *Astonishing* (Chicago), February 1940.
"Wedding of the Forces," in *Future* (New York), November 1940.
"Science from Syracuse," in *Science Fiction* (Holyoke, Massachu-
setts), March 1941.
"The Last Secret Weapon," in *Marvel* (New York), April 1941.
"The Man Who Bought Mars," in *Fantastic Adventures* (New
York), June 1941.
"Destroyer from the Past," in *Amazing* (New York), May 1942.
"Prisoner of Time," in *Super Science* (Kokomo, Indiana), May
1942.
"Outcasts of Eternity," in *Fantastic Adventures* (New York), Sep-
tember 1942.
"The Devouring Tide," in *Thrilling Wonder Stories* (New York),
Summer 1944.
"Mark Grayson Unlimited," in *Thrilling Wonder Stories* (New
York), Spring 1945.
"Space Trap," in *Thrilling Wonder Stories* (New York), Fall 1945.
"Other Eyes Watching," in *Startling* (New York), Spring 1946.
"Twilight Planet," in *Thrilling Wonder Stories* (New York),
Summer 1946.
"The Vicious Circle," in *Startling* (New York), Summer 1946.
"Chaos," in *Startling* (New York), November 1947.
"Ultra Evolution," in *Startling* (New York), January 1948.

Uncollected Short Stories as Dennis Clive

"Valley of Pretenders," in *Science Fiction* (Holyoke, Massachu-
setts), March 1939.
"Frigid Moon," in *Future* (New York), November 1939.
"The Voice Commands," in *Science Fiction* (Holyoke, Massachu-
setts), June 1940.
"Laughter Out of Space,"in *Future* (New York), July 1940.

"The Flat Folk of Vulcan," in *Future* (New York), November 1940.

Uncollected Short Stories as John Cotton

"Outlaw of Saturn," in *Science Fiction* (Holyoke, Massachusetts),
March 1939.
"After Doomsday," in *Future* (New York), March 1940.
"The Onslaught from Below," in *Future* (New York), November
1940.

Uncollected Short Stories as Ephriam Winiki

"Leeches from Space," in *Science Fiction* (Holyoke, Massachu-
setts), March 1939.
"Jewels from the Moon," in *Science Fiction* (Holyoke, Massachu-
setts), August 1939.
"Earth Asunder," in *Science Fiction* (Holyoke, Massachusetts),
October 1939.
"Eclipse Bears Witness," in *Science Fiction* (Holyoke, Massachu-
setts), March 1940.

Uncollected Short Stories as Dom Passante

"Moon Heaven," in *Science Fiction* (Holyoke, Massachusetts),
June 1939.
"Men Without a World," in *Science Fiction* (Holyoke, Massachu-
setts), March 1940.
"Across the Ages," in *Future* (New York), October 1941.

Uncollected Short Stories as Volsted Gridban

"March of the Robots," in *Vargo Statten's Science Fiction Maga-
zine 1* (Luton, Bedfordshire), 1954.
"A Saga of 2270 A.D.," in *Vargo Statten's Science Fiction Maga-
zine 2* (Luton, Bedfordshire), 1954.
"The Others," in *Vargo Statten's Science Fiction Magazine 3*
(Luton, Bedfordshire), 1954.
"Alice, Where Art Thou?," in *Vargo Statten's Science Fiction Mag-
azine 4* (Luton, Bedfordshire), 1954.

Uncollected Short Stories as Vargo Statten

"Beyond Zero," in *Vargo Statten's Science Fiction Magazine 1*
(Luton, Bedfordshire), 1954.
"Before Atlantis," in *Vargo Statten's Science Fiction Magazine 2*
(Luton, Bedfordshire), 1954.
"The Master Mind," in *Vargo Statten's Science Fiction Magazine 3*
(Luton, Bedfordshire), 1954.
"Reverse Action," in *Vargo Statten's Science Fiction Magazine 4*
(Luton, Bedfordshire), 1954.
"Rim of Eternity," in *Vargo Stratten's Science Fiction Magazine 5*
(Luton, Bedfordshire), 1954.
"Something from Mercury," in *British Science Fiction 6* (Luton,
Bedfordshire), 1954.
"A Matter of Vibration," in *British Science Fiction 12* (Luton,
Bedfordshire), 1955.
"Three's a Crowd," in *British Space Fiction 2* (Luton, Bedford-
shire), 1955.

OTHER PUBLICATIONS

Novels

The Flying Horseman. London, Western Book Distributors,
1947.
The Avenging Ranger. Llandudno, Caernarvonshire, Kaner, 1948.
Rustlers Canyon. Llandudno, Caernarvonshire, Kaner, 1948.
Thunder Valley. Redhill, Surrey, Wells Gardner Darton, 1948.
Yellow Gulch Law. Llandudno, Caernarvonshire, Kaner, 1948.
Gunsmoke Valley. Glasgow, Muir Watson, 1948 (?).
Stockwhip Sheriff. Glasgow, Muir Watson, 1948 (?).
Valley of the Doomed. Kingswood, Surrey, World's Work, 1949.
Murder's a Must. Glasgow, Muir Watson, 1949.
Tornado Trail. Glasgow, Muir Watson, 1949.
Arizona Love. London, Rich and Cowan, 1950.

Aztec Gold. London, Scion, 1950.
Ghost Canyon. London, Scion, 1950.
Merridew Rides Again. Kingswood, Surrey, World's Work, 1950.
Rattlesnake. London, Scion, 1950.
Skeleton Pass. London, Scion, 1950.
Bonanza. London, Scion, 1950.
Firewater. London, Scion, 1950.
Hell's Acres. London, Scion, 1950.
Lead Law. London, Scion, 1950.
The Black Star (as Joan Seagar). London, Scion, 1950.
The Harvest Is Ours (as Joan Seagar). London, Scion, 1950.
Merridew Marches On. Kingswood, Surrey, World's Work, 1951.
Golden Canyon. London, Partridge, 1951.
The Gold of Akada (as Earl Titan). London, Scion, 1951.
Anjani the Mighty (as Earl Titan). London, Scion, 1951.
Killer's Legacy. London, Rich and Cowan, 1952.
Merridew Fights Again. Kingswood, Surrey, World's Work, 1952.
Merridew Follows the Trail. Kingswood, Surrey, World's Work, 1953.
King of the Mesa (as Timothy Hayes). London, Pearson, 1953.
Navajo Vengeance. London, Rich and Cowan, 1956.

Novels as John Slate

Black Maria, M.A. London, Rich and Cowan, 1944.
Maria Marches On. London, Rich and Cowan, 1945.
One Remained Seated. London, Rich and Cowan, 1946.
Thy Arm Alone. London, Rich and Cowan, 1947.
Framed in Guilt. London, Rich and Cowan, 1948.
Death in Silhouette. London, Rich and Cowan, 1950.

Novels as Hugo Blayn

Except for One Thing. London, Stanley Paul, 1947.
The Five Matchboxes. London, Stanley Paul, 1948.
Flashpoint. London, Stanley Paul, 1950.
What Happened to Hammond? London, Stanley Paul, 1951.
The Silvered Cage. London, Dragon, 1951.

Novels as Doorn Sclanders

Canyon of Renegades. London, Scion, 1953.
Renegades Ranch. London, Scion, 1954.
Cactus Hits the Trail. London, Dragon Scion, 1955.
Cactus Rides Again. London, Dragon Scion, 1955.
Gun Justice. London, Dragon Scion, 1955.
Gunman's Code. London, Dragon Scion, 1955.
Hangdown. London, Dragon Scion, 1955.
Cactus Takes a Hand. London, Dragon Scion, 1956.

*

Bibliography: *The Multi-Man: A Biographic and Bibliographic Study of John Russell Fearn* by Philip Harbottle, privately printed, 1968.

*   *   *

Among the few British contributors to the science-fiction magazines of the 1930-40 period, John Russell Fearn was the most conspicuously successful if not always the most admired. He achieved front-rank status through the boldness of his conceptions at a time when novelty was more important than story-value. He also wrote weird tales, western, and detective thrillers, some of which represent his better work. In 30 years of writing he was never short of ideas—nor of pen-names, which are still being uncovered among the vast mass of his work. He turned out manuscripts at a prodigious rate, boasting that he could produce a 20,000-word novelet "between shaves" and still spend his afternoons at the cinema, where he collected most of his plots. The science in his stories, such as it was, he culled from the works of Jeans, Huxley, and Eddington in the public library at Blackpool, the Lancashire holiday resort where he lived with his mother, who inspired him. A small, lean man with a large head, he made no secret of the gratifica-

tion (and the dollars) which his American successes brought him. More than once he rushed into print to defend himself against fan critics; for he was in deadly earnest about his work, and soon lost patience with editors who found fault with it.

For the most part, his extravagant inventions were welcomed by the pulp magazines, which were in fierce competition as the field expanded. Following his appearance in the Teck *Amazing Stories* with *The Intelligence Gigantic* (1933), he leapt into prominence in *Astounding Stories,* which had entered a new lease of life under the editor F. Orlin Tremaine. Beginning with "The Man Who Stopped the Dust," he produced a series of novelets which admirably conformed to the new "thought variant" policy, presenting more and more dumbfounding notions without regard for plausible treatment or special concern for scientific accuracy. Fearn's imagination was not bounded by the accepted laws of the universe any more than by the universe itself. In "Before Earth Came" he advanced an entirely novel conception of the origin of the solar system. In "The Blue Infinity" he moved the menaced Earth to Alpha Centauri, thence into another universe altogether. When readers protested, he insisted that he had spent two months in library research to get the science right; but to his intimate associates (who dubbed him "The Blackpool Wonder") he confessed he would never let textbook accuracy impede a startling idea or an original twist. And the situations he posed on such a cosmic scale so inspired cover artists that he became known to his fans as "The Cover-Copper." He reached the limits of audaciousness—and complexity—with "Mathematica" and Mathematica Plus" which reduced the entire universe to a series of equations, the idea having possessed him while he was under gas at the dentist's. When John W. Campbell became editor of *Astounding,* Fearn failed to meet its advancing literary standards, though he modified his style to write as Thornton Ayre and Polton Cross. But his work was featured consistently by *Amazing* and *Thrilling Wonder Stories,* both of which had been transformed to attract a mainly juvenile readership. The accent was on human interest and fast-moving adventure, and Fearn made short work of a stream of material in this vein. Manuscripts that did not sell instantly were absorbed by the new magazines that cluttered the field in 1939-41, appearing under various pen-names.

It was in *Fantastic Adventures* that Fearn's only outstanding character made her bow in 1939—Violet Ray (the Golden Amazon), one of the first wonder women. By 1944 she had endeared herself to the readers of Toronto's *Star Weekly,* where she pursued her colourful career over the next 17 years, becoming a grandmother in the process. His Cosmic Crusaders series was gradually enlarged to re-explore the depths of space and time, the microcosmos, and the larger universe. It was to be expected that some of Fearn's more restrained narratives should be featured by the British magazines, like *Tales of Wonder* and *Fantasy,* for which he was agitating long before they were launched. But most of his home products took the form of cheap paperback novels issued in the early 1950's under pen-names such as Volsted Gridban and Vargo Statten, often adaptations of previously published magazine stories. The Vargo Statten novels proved so popular with their uncritical readers that in 1954 the publishers launched *Vargo Statten's Science Fiction Magazine,* of which Fearn soon became editor. When it evolved into the *British Science Fiction Magazine* he continued to guide its destinies, but even his industry and enormous backlog could not save it from the adversities which overtook it early in 1956.

—Walter Gillings

FERRAT, Jacques Jean. *See* **MERWIN, Sam, Jr.**

FINNEY, Jack (Walter Braden Finney). American. Born in Milwaukee, Wisconsin, in 1911. Educated at Knox College, Galesburg, Illinois. Married Marguerite Guest; one daughter and one son. Self-employed writer. Agent: Harold Matson Company Inc., 22 East 40th Street, New York, New York 10016, U.S.A.

SCIENCE-FICTION PUBLICATIONS

Novels

The Body Snatchers. New York, Dell, and London, Eyre and Spottiswoode, 1955; revised edition, as *Invasion of the Body Snatchers,* Dell, 1961; London, Sphere, 1978.
The Woodrow Wilson Dime. New York, Simon and Schuster, 1968.
Time and Again. New York, Simon and Schuster, 1970; London, Weidenfeld and Nicolson, 1980.
Marion's Wall. New York, Simon and Schuster, 1973.

Short Stories

The Third Level. New York, Rinehart, 1957; as *The Clock of Time,* London, Eyre and Spottiswoode, 1958.
I Love Galesburg in the Springtime: Fantasy and Time Stories. New York, Simon and Schuster, 1963; London, Eyre and Spottiswoode, 1965

OTHER PUBLICATIONS

Novels

5 Against the House. New York, Doubleday, and London, Eyre and Spottiswoode, 1954.
The House of Numbers. New York, Dell, and London, Eyre and Spottiswoode, 1957.
Assault on a Queen. New York, Simon and Schuster, 1959; London, Eyre and Spottiswoode, 1960.
Good Neighbor Sam. New York, Simon and Schuster, and London, Eyre and Spottiswoode, 1963.
The Night People. New York, Doubleday, 1977.

Play

Telephone Roulette. Chicago, Dramatic Publishing Company, 1956.

*   *   *

Escapism is a term too often loosely applied to science fiction, but in the case of Jack Finney it is strangely appropriate. His most enduring theme is escape from the pressures and irritations of the present, usually into an idyllic past, but sometimes to another planet or a parallel dimension. A popular magazine writer who produced many stories in areas other than science fiction, Finney has made himself into the poet of nostalgia and lost innocence within the genre, seldom more than peripherally concerned with the mechanisms of his science-fiction concepts or with how his characters get from this world to the other.

Ironically, Finney's most famous science-fiction novel is also his least characteristic. *The Body Snatchers* (filmed twice as *Invasion of the Body Snatchers*) is a suspenseful invasion-of-earth story that has gained the status of a minor classic because of the popularity of the film versions and because of the key element of paranoid fantasy that is the basis of its appeal: the notion that aliens might gradually replace the entire population of a city with exact duplicates without anyone noticing the difference. Although this idea had been current in science fiction long before Finney brought it to the attention of a wider public, the skill with which Finney unveils this horror and the fears abroad at the time he wrote the story—the "takeover" might as well be a metaphor for either Communism or McCarthyism—combined to give it an impact few science-fiction stories had previously had.

More characteristic are the short stories that Finney published

during the 1950's collected in *The Third Level* and *I Love Galesburg in the Springtime.* The most common theme of these stories is time travel into the past. "I'm Scared," one of the best, details the gradual breakdown of the flow of historical time under psychological pressure from a population seeking to escape the present. In "Such Interesting Neighbors" the time travelers are from the future, but the motivation to escape their own time remains the same (the story ingeniously suggests that the end of the world will be brought about by time travel, because everyone will gradually abandon the future and redistribute themselves throughout history). "Of Missing Persons" replaces time travel with space travel, but the theme of escape remains central. Two stories, "The Third Level" and "Second Chance," suggest that certain things or locations can provide magical "portals" to the past; in "Second Chance" a meticulously reconstructed old car takes its driver into a past world simply because the experience he has in driving it parallels an experience that might have taken place when the car was new.

This notion that by meticulously recreating the past we can return to it was developed at great length in Finney's most ambitious novel, *Time and Again,* in which a volunteer for a secret government time-travel project finds himself in the Manhattan of 1882. Although only the vaguest references to Einstein serve to account for this time travel, and although there are inconsistencies of plot and historical verisimilitude (some of the latter are deliberate), the novel is a convincing portrait of a lost age and a persuasive account of what it might actually feel like to awake in a different time. Other Finney novels have dealt with the culture shock of different ages meeting using even less rationalistic devices—reincarnation, for example, in *Marion's Wall*—but *Time and Again* remains his most successful contribution to this genre. Though not fundamentally a science-fiction writer, Finney is a skilled narrator and an evocative stylist who frequently uses science-fiction themes with considerable effect.

—Gary K. Wolfe

———————

FISK, Nicholas. British. Born in London, 14 October 1923. Educated at Ardingly College, Sussex. Served in the Royal Air Force during World War II. Married Dorothy Antoinette Fisk in 1949; twin daughters and two sons. Has worked as an actor, journalist, musician, editor, and publisher; illustrator of his own books and others. Since 1965, Head of the Creative Department, Percy Lund Humphries Ltd., printers, London. Agent: Laura Cecil, 10 Exeter Mansions, 106 Shaftesbury Avenue, London W1V 7DH. Address: 59 Elstree Road, Bushey Heath, Hertfordshire WD2 3QX, England.

SCIENCE-FICTION PUBLICATIONS

Novels (juvenile)

Space Hostages. London, Hamish Hamilton, 1967; New York, Macmillan, 1969.
Trillions. London, Hamish Hamilton, 1971; New York, Pantheon, 1973.
Grinny. London, Heinemann, 1973; Nashville, Nelson, 1974.
High Way Home. London, Hamish Hamilton, 1973.
Little Green Spaceman. London, Heinemann, 1974.
Time Trap. London, Gollancz, 1976.
Wheelie in the Stars. London, Heinemann, 1976.
Antigrav. London, Penguin, 1978.
Escape from Splatterbang. London, Pelham, 1978; New York, Macmillan, 1979; as *Flamers,* London, Hodder and Stoughton, 1979.
Monster Maker. London, Pelham, 1979; New York, Macmillan, 1980.
A Rag, A Bone, and a Hank of Hair. London, Penguin, 1980.

Uncollected Short Story

"Find the Lady," in *New Dimensions 5*, edited by Robert Silverberg. New York, Harper, 1975; London, Gollancz, 1976.

OTHER PUBLICATIONS (juvenile)

Novels

The Bouncers. London, Hamish Hamilton, 1964.
The Fast Green Car. London, Hamish Hamilton, 1965.
There's Something on the Roof! London, Hamish Hamilton, 1966.
Emma Borrows a Cup of Sugar. London, Heinemann, 1973.
The Witches of Wimmering. London, Pelham, 1976.
Leadfoot. London, Pelham, 1980.

Other

Look at Cars. London, Hamish Hamilton, 1959; revised edition, London, Panther, 1969.
Look at Newspapers. London, Hamish Hamilton, 1962.
Cars. London, Parrish, 1963.
The Young Man's Guide to Advertising. London, Hamish Hamilton, 1963.
Making Music. London, Joseph, 1966; Boston, Crescendo, 1969.
Lindbergh the Lone Flier. London, Hamish Hamilton, and New York, Coward McCann, 1968.
Richtofen the Red Baron. London, Hamish Hamilton, and New York, Coward McCann, 1968.

Nicholas Fisk comments:

I came fairly late to children's writing. It was a Puffin list that showed me the light. I was looking for a copy of Geoffrey Household's *Rogue Male* and found it in Puffin. I thought, if the publisher thinks fit to offer this title to children, the world must be changing. For the better.

Most of my output for children has been science fiction. The SF writer is fortunate in that, unhampered by present or past, he can invent his own games, rules, and players. He is unfortunate in that he must make these matters clear—and explanation is the enemy of narration. Also, unfortunately, the genre is still not quite respectable, not quite nice. Perhaps the word science offends the nice palate? It offends mine. I am not a scientist, my books are not centered on the sciences. They are stories of possibility. Not SF, but IF—what would happen IF.

The stories are on a domestic, not a cosmic, scale because written words are not apt for the rendering of explosions and gargantuan hardware; these belong to the cinema. My central characters are children because the stories are written for children. This poses no problem and indeed may offer simplifications and speedings-up of the narrative. Although the stories have become more complex in subject and structure, I have learned from my own and countless other children that the quick, generous, adventurous mind can always stick to the point, even if the author must stagger about a bit in the hope of satisfying himself or a publisher's editor. And in any case today's children are no longer confined to some nursery ghetto. Families live in each other's laps, watching the same TV programmes. My readers and I are not unalike.

Other reasons for writing as I do include a distaste for most modern adult fiction coupled with a huge admiration for the writers and illustrators of present day children's books. I do various kinds of writing to earn a living; it is the children's writing that gives me the authentic tingle.

*   *   *

Nicholas Fisk is currently one of the best of those writers presenting "hard" SF to children. In such a situation a writer has two choices: to try to explain his science to a juvenile audience, or simply to ignore most of the problems as being outside his province. Fisk has tried both; *Antigrav* is a good story despite the lack of explanations; *Escape from Splatterbang* shows how such explanations can be at once trite and boring. By contrast, in *Trillions* the working out

of a scientific answer forms an exciting and integral part of the plot. *Trillions* is also the book of Fisk's most likely to appeal to the adult reader, partly because of the scientific interest, partly because the "opposition" in *Trillions* is the Military Mind, as personified by General Hartman, in whom he will recognise all those who hate and fear what is alien to them. More usually in Fisk's books the forces of ignorance are the adults who ignore or fail to comprehend their children. The books can most usefully be seen from the point of view of an intelligent 11-year-old—old enough to see and understand the adult world of deceit and hypocrisy, but not old enough to change or participate in it.

One of Fisk's greatest strengths as a writer is his avoidance of clichés, both in plot and character. Indeed several of his books, most notably *Space Hostages* and *Antigrav*, are crucially concerned with a realisation that people do not conform to stereotypes. *Antigrav* rather neatly contrasts two scientists—one the classic sinister, balding geologist from behind the Iron Curtain, the other the expansive English all-rounder much given to appearing on TV chatshows. Arthur Sonning is summed up at the end as "You poor sap," while Czeslaw, victory gained, weighs the possible results of that victory and throws it away. It is further typical of Fisk that this moral superiority does not lessen the personal price which Czeslaw has to pay for "failure." In *Space Hostages* an experienced reader of children's fiction is likely to be expecting the puny clever Pakistani to be triumphant at the expense of the village bully. What actually happens is that both discover their interdependence as Fisk shows that the very qualities which make Tony a bully are those which make him a successful leader in a time of crisis. In *Escape from Splatterbang* a hint of romance is raised, only to be quashed by the bitter-sweet ending as the gypsy girl, only half-understood to the end, disappears back among her people. Here, as in *Time Trap* and other of the novels, the ending respects and even underlines the realities of human behaviour.

Fisk is never likely to have a large adult audience; his books side too firmly with the children—but at least they do so plausibly. In *Grinny* (one of his best books) the reader looks on, as helpless as the children, while the implacable "Great Aunt Emma" manipulates adult minds to her own ends. The notable achievement of this book is the way (again avoiding cliché) that Grinny's curiosity is shown as most sinister—she pokes and pries into human habits and customs like someone lifting a stone to observe the earwigs. Fisk's one real incursion into teenage SF—*Wheelie in the Stars*—is one of his poorest books: his clever-clever cardboard teenagers contrast very badly with the impotent desperation and reluctant courage of his children. This is more to be regretted since *High Way Home* shows how convincingly he can draw both teenagers and female characters (usually a notable blindspot). Fisk is not destined for a place among the Immortals: he lacks the necessary mastery of style and timeless appeal. But he is doing a competent job in a difficult field.

—Philippa Stephensen-Payne

FitzGIBBON, (Robert Louis) Constantine (Lee-Dillon). Irish. Born in Lenox, Massachusetts, United States, 8 June 1919. Educated at Wellington College, 1933-35; University of Munich, and the Sorbonne, Paris, 1935-37; Exeter College, Oxford, 1937-39. Served in the British Army, 1939-42, and the United States Army, 1942-46. Married 1) Marion Gutmann in 1960 (marriage dissolved), one son; 2) Marjorie Steele in 1967, one daughter. Schoolmaster, Saltus Grammar School, Bermuda, 1946-47. Member, Irish Academy of Letters; Fellow, Royal Society of Literature. Address: St. Ann's, Killiney Hill Road, County Dublin, Ireland.

SCIENCE-FICTION PUBLICATIONS

Novels

The Iron Hoop. New York, Knopf, 1949; London, Cassell, 1950.

When the Kissing Had to Stop.   New York, Norton, and London, Cassell, 1960.
The Golden Age.   London, Hart Davis MacGibbon, and New York, Norton, 1975.
The Rat Report.   London, Constable, 1980.

OTHER PUBLICATIONS

Novels

The Arabian Bird.   New York, Rinehart, 1948; London, Cassell, 1949.
Cousin Emily.   London, Cassell, 1952; as *Dear Emily,* New York, Simon and Schuster, 1952.
The Holiday.   London, Cassell, and New York, Simon and Schuster, 1953.
In Love and War.   London, Cassell, 1956; as *The Fair Game,* New York, Norton, 1956; as *Adultery under Arms,* London, Pan, 1962.
Watcher in Florence.   Privately printed, 1959.
Going to the River.   London, Cassell, and New York, Norton, 1963.
High Heroic.   London, Dent, and New York, Norton, 1969.
In the Bunker.   London, Macmillan, and New York, Norton, 1973.
Man in Aspic.   London, Hart Davis MacGibbon, 1977.

Plays

The Devil He Did (produced London, 1969).
The Devil at Work (produced Dublin, 1971).

Other

Miss Finnigan's Fault.   London, Cassell, 1953.
Norman Douglas: A Pictorial Record.   London, Richards Press, 1953.
The Little Tour, with Giles Playfair.   London, Cassell, 1954.
The Shirt of Nessus.   London, Cassell, 1956; as *20 July,* New York, Norton, 1956; as *To Kill Hitler,* London, Stacey, 1972.
The Blitz, illustrated by Henry Moore.   London, Wingate, 1957; as *The Winter of the Bombs,* New York, Norton, 1958.
Random Thoughts of a Fascist Hyena.   London, Cassell, 1963; New York, Norton, 1964.
The Life of Dylan Thomas.   London, Dent, and Boston, Little Brown, 1965.
Through the Minefield: An Autobiography.   London, Bodley Head, and New York, Norton, 1967.
Denazification.   London, Joseph, and New York, Norton, 1969.
Out of the Lion's Paw: Ireland Wins Her Freedom.   London, Macdonald, and New York, American Heritage, 1969.
London's Burning.   New York, Ballantine, 1970; London, Macdonald, 1971.
Red Hand: The Ulster Colony.   London, Joseph, 1971; New York, Doubleday, 1972.
A Concise History of Germany.   London, Thames and Hudson, 1972; New York, Viking Press, 1973.
The Life and Times of Eamon de Valera.   Dublin, Gill and Macmillan, 1973; New York, Macmillan, 1974.
Secret Intelligence in the Twentieth Century.   London, Hart Davis MacGibbon, 1976.
Teddy in the Tree (juvenile).   New York, Doubleday, 1977.
Drink.   London, Granada, 1980.

Editor, *Selected Letters of Dylan Thomas.*   London, Dent, 1966; New York, New Directions, 1967.

Translator from German and French of some 40 books.

Constantine FitzGibbon comments:

I do not consider that I have ever written "science fiction." I have written unusual novels, set in imaginary countries, at an imaginary future date or with a jumbled time sequence, as have Kafka and Joyce. As I grow older I become less interested in writing "realistic"

novels, and give freer and freer play to my imagination. My most recent novel, *The Rat Report,* I have called, it is true, psi-fi, but that is not sci-fi, not in my opinion at least.

*   *   *

Constantine FitzGibbon's *The Golden Age* is a futuristic novel in which the world as we know it is drastically altered and in which mankind has virtually lost his knowledge of history. The world has been divided into two halves, the Upper World separated by a sort of force field from what is termed the Lower World (the southern hemisphere in our terms). The Upper World is now ruled from Oxford by a Monster (Emperor) and the four Horsemen who form his council. They decide that the future of the world must be left in the hands of Orpheus, the poet, as the priests, scientists, and other leaders of the past have simply led the world into chaos. It is FitzGibbon's contention that the poets know more about the universe than do the astronomers. As Orpheus, the central character, begins to rebuild the world in beauty, he enters into a bargain with Mephistopheles, who restores his memory at the cost of his soul. Seemingly victorious in his quest, Orpheus descends into the Underworld to regain Eurydice. A great part of the intrigue and fascination of the novel consists in FitzGibbon's deft reworking of the Orpheus and Mephistopheles myths and a clever blending of the two. The reader versed in classical literature will find the novel interesting and meaningful on a level lost to the average reader. *The Golden Age* is a clever if somewhat overly literary and complex vision of the future based on an intriguing hypothesis and rewarding to the sensitive and discriminating reader.

FitzGibbon's earlier novel, *When the Kissing Had to Stop,* is set in the not-too-distant future and concerns itself with an England which has been taken over by totalitarianism and has become a Russian dependency.

—Joseph A. Quinn

FLINT, Homer Eon.   American.   Born in 1892. *Died in 1924.*

SCIENCE-FICTION PUBLICATIONS

Novels

The Blind Spot, with Austin Hall.   Philadelphia, Prime Press, 1951; London, Museum Press, 1953.
The Devolutionist, and The Emancipatrix.   New York, Ace, 1965.
The Lord of Death, and The Queen of Life.   New York, Ace, 1965.

Uncollected Short Stories

"The Planeteer," in *All-Story Weekly* (New York), 9 March 1918.
"King of Conserve Island," in *All-Story Weekly* (New York), 12 October 1918.
"The Man in the Moon," in *All-Story Weekly* (New York), 4 October 1919.
"The Greater Miracle," in *All-Story Weekly* (New York), 24 April 1920.
"Out of the Moon," in *Argosy All-Story Weekly* (New York), 15 December 1923.
"The Nth Man," in *Amazing Stories Quarterly* (New York), Spring 1928.

See the essay on Austin Hall.

FONTENAY, Charles L(ouis). American. Born in Sao Paulo, Brazil, 17 March 1917. Attended Vanderbilt University, Nashville, 1966-67, 1968-70. Served in the United States Army Air Corps, 1942-43; Army censorship officer, 1943-46: Captain. Married 1) Glenda Miller in 1942 (divorced, 1960); 2) Martha Howard in 1963, one daughter and one son. Reporter, sports editor, and city editor, *Daily Messenger,* Union City, Tennessee, 1936-40; editor, Associated Press, Nashville and Memphis, 1940-42; sports editor, *Press-Chronicle,* Johnson City, Tennessee, 1946. Since 1946, reporter, city editor, then rewrite editor, *The Tennessean,* Nashville. Recipient: Ted V. Rodgers Award, for journalism, 1957. Address: 405 Scott Avenue, Nashville, Tennessee 37206, U.S.A.

SCIENCE-FICTION PUBLICATIONS

Novels

Twice upon a Time. New York, Ace, 1958.
Rebels of the Red Planet. New York, Ace, 1961.
The Day the Oceans Overflowed. Derby, Connecticut, Monarch, 1964.

Uncollected Short Stories

"Escape Velocity," in *Infinity* (New York), October 1954.
"Blow the Man Down," in *If* (New York), March 1955.
"The Patriot," in *If* (New York), August 1955.
"The Strangest Man in the Universe," in *Other Worlds* (Evanston, Indiana), February 1956.
"Atom Drive," in *If* (New York), April 1956.
"Communication," in *If* (New York), October 1956.
"Family Tree," in *If* (New York), December 1956.
"Disqualified," in *The First World of If,* edited by James L. Quinn and Eve Wulff. Kingston, New York, Quinn, 1957.
"Silk and the Song," in *The Best from Fantasy and Science Fiction 6,* edited by Anthony Boucher. New York, Doubleday, 1957.
"The Old Goat," in *If* (New York), February 1957.
"Blind Alley," in *If* (New York), March 1957.
"Up," in *Fantasy and Science Fiction* (New York), March 1957.
"A Case of Sunburn," in *If* (New York), April 1957.
"Moths," in *Science Fiction Adventures* (New York), April 1957.
"Pretty Quadroon," in *If* (New York), June 1957.
"The Last Brave Invader," in *If* (New York), August 1957.
"Earth Transit," in *Infinity* (New York), September 1957.
"The Heart's Long Wait," in *Flying Saucers from Other Worlds* (Evanston, Indiana), September 1957.
"Z," in *The Second World of If,* edited by James L. Quinn and Eve Wulff. Kingston, New York, Quinn, 1958.
"Chip on the Shoulder," in *Science Fiction Quarterly* (Holyoke, Massachusetts), February 1958.
"A Summer Afternoon," in *Fantasy and Science Fiction* (New York), February 1958.
"Never Marry a Venerian," in *Saturn* (Holyoke, Massachusetts), March 1958.
"West of Mars," in *Infinity* (New York), April 1958.
"Conservation," in *If* (New York), April 1958.
"Service with a Smile," in *If* (New York), June 1958.
"Beauty Interrupted," in *If* (New York), August 1958.
"The Gift Bearer," in *Amazing* (New York), September 1958.
"Nothing's Impossible," in *Super Science Fiction* (New York), October 1958.
"Bait," in *Amazing* (New York), February 1959.
"Ghost Planet," in *Fantasy and Science Fiction* (New York), February 1959.
"The Jupiter Weapon," in *Amazing* (New York), March 1959.
"Wind," in *Amazing* (New York), April 1959.
"Matchmaker," in *If* (New York), May 1960.
"Mariwite," in *Fantastic* (New York), November 1960.

OTHER PUBLICATIONS

Other

Epistle to the Babylonians: An Essay on the Natural Inequality of Man. Knoxville, University of Tennessee Press, 1969.
"How Br'er Fox Lost His Pelt," in *Pageant* (New York), April 1971.
The Keyen of Fu Tze. Sherborne, Dorset, Coombe Springs Press, 1977.

Charles L. Fontenay comments:
My science-fiction period was confined to the decade 1954-64. Most of my science fiction was of the adventure or "escapist" type, as contrasted to that line of science fiction oriented to some serious sociological "message" or an attempted extrapolation of current trends; I think it would be legitimate to call it the *Star Wars* type. However, I was often pretty heavy on the scientific basis for the story, to the point that an entire story—or an entire novel—was built around a single scientific gimmick. Despite this general orientation, my science fiction contributed a great deal to the thinking that served as the basis of my later philosophical writing. I think this connection is apparent in some of the stories, but I would be hard put to express it in so many words.

*   *   *

Charles L. Fontenay's SF career spanned a bit more than a decade, ending with the 1964 publication of *The Day the Oceans Overflowed,* a disaster novel. With a writer who produced no major work and who hasn't written in the field for more than 15 years, it is presumptuous to claim any reputation other than hazy. But it is not a fair one in view of much of his short fiction.

He did write space opera, however, much of it forming a generalized future history, and some of it dealing with problems posed by the time-dilatation effect of travel at the speed of light. "The Strangest Man in the Universe" is a fair but unremarkable adventure story that finds a spaceship crew stranded on a backward planet, where they also encounter a benevolent superman (another of Fontenay's favorite themes). "The Heart's Long Wait" is a decidedly more interesting story, a character study of a spaceman alienated from ordinary humans by his profession. The story is sentimental but still effective.

It was Fontenay's trademark to take a standard idea—time-dilatation, evolutionary supermen, the paradoxes of time travel—and develop a good, often quite original variation on it. His stories were usually well constructed, and his writing style clear and readable. If he were to be grouped with any other SF writers, they would probably be Poul Anderson and Gordon Dickson—but Fontenay never displayed Anderson's passion for the poetic in science and nature, or Dickson's thematic strength. He told stories about ideas. But he had other virtues as well, especially an ability to explore his ideas in terms of unobtrusive character development.

It is this lack of character development, in part, that prevents "Z" from being wholly effective. It's a neatly conceived handling of essentially the same idea Heinlein used in "By His Bootstraps," somewhat updated with the addition of a sex-change in the plotline, but not up to the standards of Heinlein's original story. "Pretty Quadroon," however, another time travel story, is one of Fontenay's best works. In the near future, a segregationist South has again seceded from the Union, leading to a second War Between the States. The story's protagonist is a statesman and general whose fiery speech at a conference of Southern governors has made him the pivotal figure in the events leading to the war. His mistress, the quadroon of the title, introduces him to a practitioner of voodoo who believes he can alter the past, thus preventing the war from ever having happened. Again and again the time paths are altered, until it becomes obvious that the key to success lies in preventing the man from ever having met the woman he loves. The strong idea in "Family Tree" might almost be taken for a joke: humans have evolved not from apes, but rodents. The story, however, is serious: an evolutionary superman is threatened by human bigotry. What sets the story apart is Fontenay's insightful portrayal of his central character, a moral rabble-rouser out to destroy the superman.

Fontenay stopped producing magazine fiction as the 1950's closed. His first novel, *Twice Upon a Time,* like "The Heart's Long Wait," deals with a young spaceman whose life and attitudes pivot on his career and on the fact of the time-dilatation effect. A member of a trouble-shooter corps designed to police interstellar colonies, he's sent to one of several planets where it's feared rebellion may be brewing. The theft of his spaceship on his arrival and the complexities of the social and political situation make the novel suspenseful, but a time-travel sub-plot and a pat ending put the book on a level somewhere below his best short fiction. *Rebels of the Red Planet* is even more disappointing. Genetic experiments on Mars, leading to superbeings and other mutations, are played off against another plot involving a growing rebel movement. Fontenay doesn't add much to either idea, although some of his scenes between normal humans and the laboratory-bred mutations are interestingly outré.

Whether Fontenay abandoned the field too early or simply lacked the ability to write novels of a quality comparable to his best short fiction, his novels have added nothing to his reputation. His lapse into obscurity, among the many hundreds of writers who have worked the field since his time, is probably inevitable. But time hasn't rendered his fiction less readable. His trademark was his ability to work stories around ideas cleverly derived from familiar themes. But his strength was that so often these ideas were explained from the points of view of rather interesting people.

—Gerald W. Page

FORSTER, E(dward) M(organ). British. Born in London, 1 January 1879. Educated at Tonbridge School, and at King's College, Cambridge, B.A. 1901, M.A. 1910. Lived in Greece and Italy, 1901-07; helped found, and contributed to, the *Independent Review,* London, 1903; lectured at the Working Men's College, London, 1907; visited India, 1912; Red Cross Volunteer Worker in Egypt, 1914-18; Literary Editor, *The Daily Herald,* London, 1920-21; Private Secretary to the Maharajah of Dewas, India, 1922; Fellow of King's College, Cambridge, and Clark Lecturer, Trinity College, Cambridge, 1927; Honorary Fellow of King's College, 1946, until his death. Vice-President, London Library; Member, General Advisory Council, BBC; President, Cambridge Humanists. Recipient: Black Memorial Prize, 1925; Prix Femina Vie Heureuse, 1925; Royal Society of Literature Benson Medal, 1937, and Companion of Literature, 1961. LL.D.: University of Aberdeen, 1931; Litt.D.: University of Liverpool, 1947; Hamilton College, Clinton, New York, 1949; Cambridge University, 1950; University of Nottingham, 1951; University of Manchester, 1954; Leyden University, Holland, 1954; University of Leicester, 1958. Honorary Member, American Academy and Bavarian Academy of Fine Arts. Companion of Honour, 1953; Order of Merit, 1968. *Died 7 June 1970.*

SCIENCE-FICTION PUBLICATIONS

Short Stories

The Celestial Omnibus and Other Stories. London, Sidgwick and Jackson, 1911; New York, Knopf, 1923.
The Eternal Moment and Other Stories. London, Sidgwick and Jackson, and New York, Harcourt Brace, 1928.
The Collected Tales of E.M. Forster. New York, Knopf, 1947; as *The Collected Short Stories of E.M. Forster,* London, Sidgwick and Jackson, 1948.

OTHER PUBLICATIONS

Novels

Where Angels Fear to Tread. Edinburgh, Blackwood, 1905; New York, Knopf, 1920.
The Longest Journey. Edinburgh, Blackwood, 1907; New York, Knopf, 1922.
A Room with a View. London, Arnold, 1908; New York, Putnam, 1911.
Howards End. London, Arnold, 1910; New York, Putnam, 1911.

A Passage to India. London, Arnold, and New York, Harcourt Brace, 1924.
Maurice. London, Arnold, and New York, Norton, 1971.

Short Stories

The Story of the Siren. Richmond, Surrey, Keepsake Press, 1920.
The Life to Come and Other Stories. London, Arnold, 1972; New York, Norton, 1973.

Plays

Pageant of Abinger, music by Ralph Vaughan Williams (produced Abinger, Surrey, 1934). Privately printed, 1934; as *Abinger Pageant,* in *Abinger Harvest,* 1936.
England's Pleasant Land: A Pageant Play (produced Westcott, Surrey, 1938). London, Hogarth Press, 1940.
Billy Budd, with Eric Crozier, music by Benjamin Britten, adaptation of the story by Melville (produced London and Bloomington, Indiana, 1952). London and New York, Boosey and Hawkes, 1951; revised version (produced London, 1964; New York, 1966), 1962.

Screenplay: *A Diary for Timothy* (documentary), 1945.

Other

Egypt. London, Labour Research Department, 1920.
Alexandria: A History and a Guide. Alexandria, Whitehead Morris, 1922; New York, Doubleday, 1961; revised edition, Whitehead Morris, 1938.
Pharos and Pharillon. Richmond, Surrey, Hogarth Press, and New York, Knopf, 1923.
Anonymity: An Enquiry. London, Hogarth Press, 1925.
Aspects of the Novel. London, Arnold, and New York, Harcourt Brace, 1927.
A Letter to Madan Blanchard. London, Hogarth Press, 1931; New York, Harcourt Brace, 1932.
Sinclair Lewis Interprets America. Privately printed, 1932.
Goldsworthy Lowes Dickinson (biography). London, Arnold, and New York, Harcourt Brace, 1934.
Abinger Harvest. London, Arnold, and New York, Harcourt Brace, 1936.
What I Believe. London, Hogarth Press, 1939.
Reading as Usual (radio talk). London, Tottenham Public Libraries, 1939.
Nordic Twilight. London, Macmillan, 1940.
Virginia Woolf (lecture). Cambridge, University Press, and New York, Harcourt Brace, 1942.
The Development of English Prose Between 1918 and 1939 (lecture). Glasgow, University Press, 1945.
The New Disorder. Privately printed, 1949.
Two Cheers for Democracy. London, Arnold, and New York, Harcourt Brace, 1951.
Desmond MacCarthy. Privately printed, 1952.
The Hill of Devi, Being Letters from Dewas State Senior. London, Arnold, and New York, Harcourt Brace, 1953.
I Assert That There Is an Alternative in Humanism. London, Ethical Society, 1955.
Battersea Rise. New York, Harcourt Brace, 1955.
Marianne Thornton 1797-1887: A Domestic Biography. London, Arnold, and New York, Harcourt Brace, 1956.
Albergo Empedocle and Other Writings, edited by George H. Thomson. New York, Liveright, 1971.
A View Without a Room. New York, Albondocani Press, 1973.
Aspects of the Novel and Related Writings, edited by Oliver Stallybrass. London, Arnold, 1974.
E.M. Forster's Letters to Donald Windham. Privately printed, 1976.
Commonplace Book (facsimile edition). London, Scolar Press, 1978.

*

Bibliography: *A Bibliography of E.M. Forster* by B.J. Kirkpatrick,

London, Hart Davis 1965; *E.M. Forster: An Annotated Bibliography of Secondary Materials* by Alfred Borrello, Metuchen, New Jersey, Scarecrow Press, 1973.

*   *   *

E.M. Forster, who is recognized as among the century's foremost novelists, critics, and essayists, is not generally regarded as a science-fiction writer. Nevertheless, this author, whose most well-known fiction explored questions of human communication and the magic of true intimacy, did turn out an early, highly regarded anti-Wellsian dystopia as well as several works which may be classified as fantasies.

"The Machine Stops" (*Oxford and Cambridge Review,* 1909) satirizes the Wellsian view of "progress" as a state of inevitable improvement. In Forster's dystopia, life has been "improved" and mechanized to the point that individuals live beehive fashion underground in isolated, climate-controlled cells, completely dependent upon the Machine which maintains their environment. This is a world in which "Men seldom moved their bodies; all unrest was concentrated in the soul." A young man who has been thwarted by the Machine in his desire to explore the surface of the world and to view the stars, becomes the prophet of doom when he cryptically informs his incredulous mother "The Machine Stops." Even as the youth's prophecy is realized in the catastrophic winding down of Machine "civilization," Forster declares "Humanity has learned its lesson." The hills of Wessex become the symbolic antithesis of the hive; the ancient appeal of their openness is celebrated. "Happy the man, happy the woman, who awakes the hills of Wessex. For though they sleep they will never die," the hero declares.

E.M. Forster's works of fantasy appear in *The Eternal Moment* and *The Celestial Omnibus.* While "The Celestial Omnibus," which follows the misadventures of a young boy who discovers an unearthly omnibus in a dark alleyway, and "The Other Side of the Hedge," which supposes a fantastic world existing behind the hedgerows lining the busy highway of life, will most readily fit into today's mass-market notion of the *fantasy* category, these and Forster's several highly imaginative, allegorical works fit into the truer sense of the *fantastic.*

—Rosemary Herbert

FOSTER, Alan Dean.   American.   Born in New York City, 18 November 1946. Educated at the University of California, Los Angeles, B.A. in political science 1968; M.F.A. in film 1969. Served in the United States Army Reserve, 1969-75. Married JoAnn Oxley in 1975. Head copywriter, Headlines Ink Agency, Studio City, California, 1970-71; instructor in English and film, University of California, Los Angeles, intermittently since 1971, and Los Angeles City College, 1972-76. Agent: (fiction) Virginia Kidd, Box 278, Milford, Pennsylvania 18337; (scripts) Ilse Lahn, Paul Kohner Agency, 9169 Sunset Boulevard, Hollywood, California 90069. Address: Box BC1-11, Big Bear Lake, California 92315, U.S.A.

SCIENCE-FICTION PUBLICATIONS

Novels (series: Flinx; Skua September)

The Tar-Aiym Krang (Flinx).   New York, Ballantine, 1972; London, New English Library, 1979.
Bloodhype.   New York, Ballantine, 1973.
Icerigger (September).   New York, Ballantine, 1974; London, New English Library, 1976.
Luana.   New York, Ballantine, 1974.
Dark Star (novelization of screenplay).   New York, Ballantine, 1974.

Star Trek Log One [to *Ten*].   New York, Ballantine, 10 vols., 1974-78.
Midworld.   New York, Ballantine, 1975; London, Macdonald and Jane's, 1977.
Orphan Star (Flinx).   New York, Ballantine, 1977; London, New English Library, 1979.
The End of the Matter (Flinx).   New York, Ballantine, 1977; London, New English Library, 1979.
Splinter of the Mind's Eye.   New York, Ballantine, 1978.
Mission to Moulokin (September).   New York, Ballantine, 1979.
Alien (novelization of screenplay).   New York, Ballantine, and London, Macdonald and Jane's, 1979.
The Black Hole (novelization of screenplay).   New York, Ballantine, 1979.
Cachalot.   New York, Ballantine, 1980.
Outland (novelization of screenplay).   New York, Warner, 1981.

Short Stories

With Friends Like These.   New York, Ballantine, 1977.

Uncollected Short Stories

"Snake Eyes," in *Stellar 4,* edited by Judy-Lynn del Rey.   New York, Ballantine, 1978.
"Bystander," in *Isaac Asimov's Adventure Magazine* (New York), Summer 1978.
"The Chair," with Jane Cozart, in *Shadows 2,* edited by Charles L. Grant.   New York, Doubleday, 1979.
"Gift of a Useless Man," in *Isaac Asimov's Science Fiction Magazine* (New York), November 1979.

OTHER PUBLICATIONS

Play

Screenplay: *Star-Trek,* 1979.

Alan Dean Foster comments:
The majority of my science-fiction novels take place in what is called the University of the Commonwealth, a future socio-political spatial government in which man has formed a particularly intimate alliance with a race of insect-like creatures called the Thranx. Within that universe I'm able to tell an immense variety of tales. Some relate to one another, such as *The Tar-Aiym Krang, Orphan Star,* and *The End of the Matter.* These form a trilogy dealing with the adolescence of an extraordinary youth named Flinx. Other books use characters interchangeably. For example, a minor character in *The End of the Matter* named Skua September is a major protagonist in the novels *Icerigger* and *Mission to Moulokin,* the pair forming a single massive story.

Eventually (say, in another 40 years), many seemingly unrelated characters and events will tie together, forming a long narrative extending over some 50 years and, possibly, as many books. Other novels will be set in the Commonwealth universe but will remain unrelated to this central narrative. Still other novels and stories will have nothing to do with the Commonwealth at all.

Most of my shorter fiction is independent of the Commonwealth background. While my novel-length work tends to be rather adventure oriented, my shorter fiction explores more personal, individualized events. In the novels I am interested in exploring how people, especially average people, are forced to react to extraordinary circumstances and events much greater than themselves or their personal concerns. In my shorter fiction I try to delve more deeply into the "human condition." It might be fair to say that the novels force my characters to look outside themselves while the short fiction induces them to look inward.

Particular aspects of science that interest me and are often touched upon in my stories include ecology, the unexplored potentiality of the human mind, and the accidence of history (the way in which massive events are often set in motion utterly unintentionally, and are forced to conclusions and resolutions unimagined by those caught up in such socio-political-personal vortices).

*   *   *

The novels of Alan Dean Foster fall into three groups, in each of which this prolific newcomer to science fiction has been popular. The first is adaptations of screenplays, two of them based on works of the writer-actor Dan O'Bannon. The second, larger group consists of those works in which Foster has devised plots around an existing cast of characters. These might be called "sequels," since they extend the original work, rather than transfer it from one form to another. In this group belong Foster's *Splinter of the Mind's Eye,* based on the characters and milieu of the movie *Star Wars,* and his *Star Trek* novelizations.

Neither of these forms is negligible; but better estimates of the writer's talent and imagination can be made from those works that are wholly his responsibility. Most of Alan Dean Foster's original novels are set in the same extrapolated future universe, and several of them concern the growing up of a single character, Philip Lynx— or Flinx, as he is more often called. We meet Flinx as a young boy in *The Tar-Aiym Krang,* and learn several things about him: first, he has an unusual pet and protector—Pip, a poison-spitting flying reptile. Second, Flinx has an uncertain but at times powerful telepathic ability. And third, Flinx knows nothing of his origins other than what his adopted mother has told him, that he was bought at a slave auction as a small child. Also introduced in *The Tar-Aiym Krang* are several of the alien races that Foster is adept at characterizing: the Thranx—human-sized, ant-shaped insects—whose unexpected affinity for humanity has led to the creation of the Humanx Commonwealth, and the AAnn, the lizard-like race that is the principal adversary of the commonwealth. Foster lavishes special care on his alien creatures, giving them plausibly non-human desires, feelings, and behavior.

Flinx's search for his heritage begins in *Orphan Star,* in which the mystery of his birth is partly illuminated when he finds that his mother had been a concubine from Earth. In *The End of the Matter* he discovers records of the clandestine breeding experiment of which he (among others) has been the result, and he meets Skua September, a large and powerful man who may have been his father. (September had appeared some years earlier as the hero of *Icerigger.*) Although disappointed to learn that the nature of the experiment will forever keep him uncertain of his father's identity, Flinx at least has an explanation of his peculiar powers. As these powers develop, Flinx becomes less of a character with whom the reader can identify, and, in *Bloodtype,* he appears only in a minor role, and less potent beings are the center of the action.

Over the past few years, Alan Dean Foster has most often devoted his craftsmanship to ideas that were conceived in large part by other writers, but novels such as the ones above, or short stories such as those collected in *With Friends Like These,* show him to be a writer capable of his own works of imagination and interest.

—Walter E. Meyers

FOX, Gardner F(rancis). Also writes as Jeff Cooper; Jefferson Cooper; Jeffrey Gardner; James Kendricks; Simon Majors; Kevin Matthews; Bart Somers. American. Born in Brooklyn, New York, 20 May 1911. Educated at St. John's University, Jamaica, New York, B.A. 1932, LL.B. 1935. Married Lynda J. Negrini in 1937; one son and one daughter. Lawyer. Since 1937, comic-book writer (*Batman, Superman, Flash Gordon, Green Lantern,* and others), and since 1938, free-lance writer. Agent: August Lenniger, Lenniger Literary Agency, 11 West 42nd Street, New York, New York 10036. Address: 503 Stockton Lane, Jamesburg, New Jersey 08831, U.S.A.

SCIENCE-FICTION PUBLICATIONS

Novels (series: Commander Craig)

Five Weeks in a Balloon (novelization of screenplay). New York, Pyramid, 1962.

Escape Across the Cosmos. New York, Paperback Library, 1964.
The Arsenal of Miracles. New York, Ace, 1964.
Warrior of Llarn. New York, Ace, 1964.
The Hunter out of Time. New York, Ace, 1965.
Beyond the Black Enigma(Craig; as Bart Somers). New York, Paperback Library, 1965.
Thief of Llarn. New York, Ace, 1966.
Abandon Galaxy (Craig; as Bart Somers). New York, Paperback Library, 1967.
The Druid Stones (as Simon Majors). New York, Paperback Library, 1965.
Conehead. New York, Ace, 1973.
Carty. New York, Doubleday, 1977; London, Hale, 1979.

Uncollected Short Stories

"The Weirds of the Woodcarver," in *Weird Tales* (New York), September 1944.
"The Last Monster," in *Planet* (New York), Fall 1945.
"Man Nth," in *Planet* (New York), Winter 1945.
"Engines of the Gods," in *Planet* (New York), Spring 1946.
"Heart of Light," in *Amazing* (New York), July 1946.
"The Man the Sun Gods Made," in *Planet* (New York), Winter 1946.
"Sword of the Seven Suns," in *Planet* (New York), Spring 1947.
"Vassals of the Lode-Star," in *Planet* (New York), Summer 1947.
"Werewile of the Crystal Crypt," in *Planet* (New York), Summer 1948.
"When Kohonnes Screamed," in *Planet* (New York), Fall 1948.
"Crom the Barbarian" (comic), in *Out of This World Adventures* (New York), July 1950.
"Temptress of the Time Flow," in *Marvel* (New York), November 1950.
"The Spider God of Akka" (comic), in *Out of This World Adventures* (New York), December 1950.
"The Warlock of Sharrador," in *Planet* (New York), March 1953.
"The Holding of Kolymar," in *Fantastic* (New York), October 1971.
"Tonight the Stars Revolt!," in *Galactic Empires,* edited by Brian Aldiss. London, Weidenfeld and Nicolson, 1976; New York, St. Martin's Press, 1977.

OTHER PUBLICATIONS

Novels

The Borgia Blade. New York, Fawcett, 1953; London, Fawcett, 1954.
Madame Buccaneer. New York, Fawcett, 1953; London, Fawcett, 1954.
Woman of Kali. New York, Fawcett, 1954; London, Muller, 1960.
The Gentleman Rogue. New York, Fawcett, 1954; London, Red Seal, 1959.
Rebel Wench. New York, Fawcett, 1955; London, Fawcett, 1958.
Queen of Sheba. New York, Fawcett, 1956.
One Sword for Love. London, Fawcett, 1956.
Terror over London. New York, Fawcett, 1957.
The Conquering Prince. London, Fawcett, 1958.
Witness This Woman. New York, Fawcett, 1959; London, Muller, 1961.
Creole Woman. New York, Fawcett, 1959.
The Devil Sword (as Kevin Matthews). New York, Hill, n.d.
Woman of Egypt (as Kevin Matthews). London, Panther, 1961.
Barbary Devil (as Jeffrey Gardner). New York, Pyramid, n.d.
Cleopatra (as Jeffrey Gardner). New York, Pyramid, n.d.
As Good as Dead. New York, Fawcett, 1962.
One Wife's Ways. New York, Fawcett, and London, Muller, 1963.
Tom Blood, Highwayman. New York, Avon, 1963.
Lion of Lucca. New York, Avon, 1966.
Bastard of Orleans. New York, Avon, n.d.
Ivan the Terrible. New York, Avon, n.d.
Scandal in Suburbia. New York, Hill, n.d.
Kothar—Barbarian Swordsman [of the Magic Sword!, and the

Demon Queen, and the Wizard Slayer, and the Conjurer's Curse].   New York, Belmont, 5 vols., 1969-70.
Kyrik, Warlock Warrior [*Fights the Demon World, and the Wizard's Sword, and the Lost Queen*].   New York, Nordon, 4 vols., 1975-76.
The Bold Ones.   New York, Nordon, 1976.
The Liberty Sword.   New York, Nordon, 1976.
Hurricane.   New York, Nordon, 1976.
Savage Passage.   New York, Nordon, 1978.
Blood Trail.   New York, Belmont, 1979.

Novels as Jefferson Cooper

Arrow in the Hill.   New York, Dodd Mead, 1955.
The Bloody Sevens.   New York, Permabooks, 1956.
The Swordsman.   New York, Pocket Books, 1957.
Captain Seadog.   New York, Pocket Books, n.d.
Delilah.   New York, Paperback Library, n.d.
The Questing Sword.   New York, Permabooks, n.d.; London, Consul, 1960.
Veronica's Veil.   New York, Permabooks, n.d.
Jezebel.   New York, Paperback Library, n.d.
Slave of the Roman Sword.   New York, Paperback Library, n.d.
This Sword for Hire.   New York, Paperback Library, n.d.

Novels as James Kendricks

Adultress.   Derby, Connecticut, Monarch, n.d.
Beyond Our Pleasure.   Derby, Connecticut, Monarch, n.d.
Love Me Tonight.   Derby, Connecticut, Monarch, n.d.
She Wouldn't Surrender.   Derby, Connecticut, Monarch, n.d.
Sword of Casanova.   Derby, Connecticut, Monarch, n.d.
The Wicked, Wicked Woman.   Derby, Connecticut, Monarch, n.d.

Other as Jeff Cooper

Custom Rifles.   Los Angeles, Trend, 1957.
Fighting Handguns.   Los Angeles, Trend, 1958.
The Complete Book of Modern Handgunning.   Englewood Cliffs, New Jersey, Prentice Hall, 1961.
Sports Car Annual.   Los Angeles, Trend, n.d.
Complete Book of Shooting, with others.   New York, Harper, 1965.
Cooper on Handguns.   Los Angeles, Petersen, 1974.

*   *   *

Gardner F. Fox is probably best known for his comic-book work, which includes scripts for such science fiction-based characters as Superman and Hawkman. In science-fiction proper, he's probably best known for a handful of paperback novels. Yet his best science fantasy writing is probably to be found in a dozen space operas published between 1945 and 1952, mainly in *Planet Stories,* where they are overshadowed by the more impressive work of Ray Bradbury, Leigh Brackett, and Ross Rocklynne. But much of that work remains highly entertaining.

His first actual SF-fantasy sale was to *Weird Tales,* but his first story for *Planet Stories,* "The Last Monster"—a benevolent alien's efforts to aid endangered humans are misread as the menacings of a monster—won the instant approval of the magazine's readers. Fox buttressed his success with "Man Nth," in which aliens recruit beings from various worlds and endow them with superhuman powers to enable them to fend off a cosmic threat that would do justice to some of the grander fancies of A.E. van Vogt. "Man Nth" was an almost flawless entertainment and demonstrated a much surer touch than "The Last Monster." "Engines of the Gods" and "The Man the Sun Gods Made" established Fox as one of the most reliable writers of strong space adventure novelets. "The Man the Sun Gods Made," about an artificial superman who stymies Earth's plans to exploit his planet, melded concepts Fox had already proven himself comfortable with—supermen and super-science—with the sort of story Leigh Brackett was already demonstrating success with.

"Vassals of the Lode-Star" is one of the strongest of his stories,

arguably the best work he's produced in the field. A rift in the fabric of time and space transports its hero to another world where he finds himself in a war with a superbeing bent on enslaving everything in reach. This was a story where everything worked for Fox: a strong and likeable lead character, Thor Masterson, a swift and interesting plot, concepts that are sufficiently gradiose and metaphysical to evoke a sense of wonder, and a benevolent alien, the Discoverer. "When Kohonnes Screamed" is less successful, though strongly imaginative, dealing with a planet where space and matter are dangerously and unpredictably distorted by a force which must somehow be located and destroyed. "Tonight the Stars Revolt!" is a strongly plotted story written in a terse prose under the now-traditional influence of Brackett, its conventional overcome-the-evil-ruler plot buoyed with fine story telling and a strong imagination.

With the collapse of the SF market, Fox found success with original paperback historical novels, and he touched the periphery of SF with a novelization of the movie of Jules Verne's *Five Weeks in a Balloon.* But *Escape Across the Cosmos* was his first true SF novel. It was the story of a superman, falsely accused of a crime, who sets out to defend himself. *The Arsenal of Miracles* told of an outcast Earthman—a disgraced space officer—who joins forces with the queen of an alien world to fight the overwhelmingly powerful Empire of Earth. Some of its passages may have promised the same sort of fun delivered by his earlier stories but novel-length SF seems never to have been Fox's forte. *Arsenal of Miracles* is a fun read, but none of the subsequent novels are quite as good as it is. Under the name Bart Somers he produced two space operas based on the adventures of a character called Commander Craig, a space-going trouble shooter.

Conehead is one of his most interesting efforts. It touches on a more serious theme than is common to most of Fox's work, racial prejudice. His hero is the standard space officer of most of Fox's novels, but instead of being a warrior, he is a lawyer who sets out to establish the civil rights of the natives of a planet under the domination of Earth. The story returns ultimately to familiar ground: the planet holds the remnants of an alien race, all but extinct, yet still possessing god-like powers, and it is the force of their powers and not of any moral argument that ultimately sways the empire.

Fox is no idea man. His backgrounds are often merely sketched in, which probably accounts for his failure to draw any really widespread following among readers. But he is also a genuinely unpretentious writer whose work provides the sort of straightforward entertainment expected of good space opera. His novels are workmanlike and fun, but they lack the flair, imagination, and pacing of his best magazine stories.

—Gerald W. Page

FRANK, Pat (Harry Hart).   American.   Born in Chicago, Illinois, 5 May 1907. Attended the University of Florida, Gainesville, 1925-26. Divorced; one son and one daughter. Reporter, Jacksonville *Journal,* 1927-29, New York *Journal,* 1929-32, and Washington *Herald,* 1933-38; Chief of the Washington Bureau, 1938-41, and Correspondent in Italy, Austria, Germany, Turkey, and Hungary, 1944-46, Overseas News Agency; Assistant Chief of Mission, Office of War Information, 1941-44; Member of United Nations Mission to Korea, 1952-53; Staff Member, Democratic National Committee, 1960; Consultant, National Aeronautics and Space Council, 1961; Consultant, Department of Defense, 1963-64. Recipient: War Department commendation, 1945; Reserved Officers Association citation, 1957; American Heritage Foundation award, 1961. *Died 12 October 1964.*

SCIENCE-FICTION PUBLICATIONS

Novels

Mr. Adam.   Philadelphia, Lippincott, 1946; London, Gollancz, 1947.

Forbidden Area. Philadelphia, Lippincott, 1956; as *Seven Days to Never,* London, Constable, 1957.
Alas, Babylon. Philadelphia, Lippincott, and London, Constable, 1959.

OTHER PUBLICATIONS

Novels

An Affair of State. Philadelphia, Lippincott, 1948; London, Corgi, 1951.
Hold Back the Night. Philadelphia, Lippincott, and London, Hamish Hamilton, 1952.

Other

The Long Way Round. Philadelphia, Lippincott, 1953.
How to Survive the H-Bomb, and Why. Philadelphia, Lippincott, 1962.
Rendezvous at Midway: U.S.S. Yorktown and the Japanese Carrier Fleet, with Joseph D. Harrington. New York, Day, 1967.

*   *   *

In the late 1940's and 1950's, a growing distrust of technology focused on the dangers of atomic energy. The most obvious danger was that of nuclear war, but concerns about reactor break-downs or bomb-factory explosions were also on people's minds. The immediate blast was one threat, and genetic damage from radiation was another. Science-fiction writers were among the first during this period to give such fears a public voice, and one of those writers was Pat Frank.

Frank wrote a great deal of material—fiction and non-fiction—dealing with the possible problems with atomic materials. His first novel, *Mr. Adam,* postulates universal male sterility as one of the results of an explosion at an atomic bomb factory in Mississippi. *Forbidden Area* attempts to show how, why, and when the Russians might attack the United States. This book is an especially grim indictment of America's lack of preparedness for such a possibility. Frank shows how the various agencies—paralyzed by red tape, inter-departmental bickering, unqualified political appointees in positions of power, and the like—refuse to act until it is almost too late, averting an all-out Russian attack by only minutes.

Frank is probably best known as the author of *Alas, Babylon,* a post-atomic war novel. Randy Bragg, an inhabitant of Fort Repose, Florida, is warned by his brother, Mark, a SAC Intelligence Officer, that the war is coming. Mark sends his wife and children to Randy because Fort Repose will be safer during such a war than will SAC Headquarters, Omaha. The bombs and missiles fall, and the people of Fort Repose are on their own. Unlike Nevil Shute's *On the Beach,* in which everyone dies, *Alas, Babylon* is basically a romantic view of the aftermath of an atomic war. Randy and his friends do not have too much difficulty surviving—though Civil Defense agencies have prepared almost no one, and Randy has to organize the people of Fort Repose—and only one of the central characters is killed. With this romantic novel, however, Frank presents all the atomic fears, from initial blast to genetic mutation, in one package.

Frank also examines the use of power in *Alas, Babylon.* There are various people in the novel who have power and should not. Randy was defeated in politics by an opponent who appealed to bigotry and fear. The Navy Ensign who fires the shot that starts the war uses the power of his jet plane to compensate for his diminutive physical stature. Randy, however, uses the power at his disposal to keep Fort Repose safe. From this, it is clear that it is not power, *per se,* that Frank objects to but the lack of qualifications of some of the people who have the power.

Frank's novels are well-written. They have strong plots, well-paced action, and interesting characters. They are not so much appeals to the reader's fear of atomic power as they are warnings.

—C.W. Sullivan III

FRAYN, Michael. British. Born in London, 8 September 1933. Educated at Kingston Grammar School, Surrey; Emmanuel College, Cambridge, B.A. 1957. Served in the Royal Artillery and Intelligence Corps, 1952-54. Married Gillian Palmer in 1960; three children. Reporter, 1957-59, and Columnist, 1959-62, *The Guardian,* Manchester and London; Columnist, *The Observer,* London, 1962-68. Recipient: Maugham Award, 1966; Hawthornden Prize, 1967; National Press Award, 1970; *Evening Standard* award for play, 1976; Society of West End Theatre award, 1977. Address: c/o Elaine Greene Ltd., 31 Newington Green, London N16 9PU, England.

SCIENCE-FICTION PUBLICATIONS

Novels

The Tin Men. London, Collins, 1965; Boston, Little Brown, 1966.
A Very Private Life. London, Collins, and New York, Viking Press, 1968.
Sweet Dreams. London, Collins, 1973; New York, Viking Press, 1974.

OTHER PUBLICATIONS

Novels

The Russian Interpreter. London, Collins, and New York, Viking Press, 1966.
Towards the End of the Morning. London, Collins, 1967; as *Against Entropy,* New York, Viking Press, 1967.

Plays

Zounds!, with John Edwards, music by Keith Statham (produced Cambridge, 1957).
The Two of Us (includes *Black and Silver, The New Quixote, Mr. Foot, Chinamen*). (produced London, 1970; Ogunquit, Maine, 1975; *Chinamen* produced New York, 1979). London, Fontana, 1970; *Chinamen* published in *The Best Short Plays 1973,* edited by Stanley Richards, Radnor, Pennsylvania, Chilton, 1973.
The Sandboy (produced London, 1971).
Alphabetical Order (produced London, 1975; New Haven, Connecticut, 1976). Included in *Alphabetical Order and Donkeys' Years,* 1977.
Donkeys' Years (produced London, 1976). Included in *Alphabetical Order and Donkeys' Years,* 1977.
Clouds (produced London, 1976). London, Eyre Methuen, 1977.
Alphabetical Order and Donkeys' Years. London, Eyre Methuen, 1977.
The Cherry Orchard, adaptation of a play by Chekhov (produced London, 1978). London, Eyre Methuen, 1978.
Balmoral (produced Guildford, 1978).
The Fruits of Enlightenment, adaptation of a play by Tolstoy (produced London, 1979). London, Eyre Methuen, 1979.
Liberty Hall (produced London, 1980).
Make and Break (produced London, 1980). London, Eyre Methuen, 1980.
The New Quixote (produced Chichester and London, 1980).

Television Plays and Documentaries: *Jamie, on a Flying Visit,* 1968; *One Pair of Eyes,* 1968; *Birthday,* 1969; *Imagine a City Called Berlin,* 1975; *Making Faces,* 1975; *Vienna: The Mask of Gold,* 1977; *Three Streets in the Country,* 1979.

Other

The Day of the Dog (*Guardian* columns). London, Collins, 1962; New York, Doubleday, 1963.
The Book of Fub (*Guardian* columns). London, Collins, 1963; as *Never Put Off to Gomorrah,* New York, Pantheon Books, 1964.
On the Outskirts (*Observer* columns). London, Collins, 1964.
At Bay in Gear Street (*Observer* columns). London, Fontana, 1967.

Constructions (philosophy). London, Wildwood House, 1974.

Editor, *The Best of Beachcomber,* by J.B. Morton. London, Heinemann, 1963.

* * *

Michael Frayn is not an easy writer to categorize. *The Tin Men* is obviously not SF but witty comedy, school of Waugh; on the other hand, it obviously is SF, as it purports to be written by a computer and satirizes men who behave like computers and are trying to make computers behave like men. When a robot comes to write its own prehistory, it will have to give classic place in its mythology to Macintosh's ethical machines and their struggles on the sinking raft. But the novel is not so much SF itself as an exuberant account of the men who are trying to make our world into an SF dystopia. The great discovery of Macintosh and Goldwasser is that, because all human life is of no purpose other than to provide newspaper headlines and statistics, humans can stop living and let the computers do it for them. Computers can produce newspapers, sports results, pornography, prayers: who needs people? The characteristic inverted logic of Frayn's tin men naturally produces a novelist who begins by writing the blurbs, the potted biography, and the reviews, and only then tries writing the book (formulaically, of course), before capitulating to the superior power of his typewriter keyboard. What *The Tin Men* itself lacks as a novel is a story worthy of its theme. Admittedly the story, which concerns the opening of the Ethics Wings in a computer research establishment, not by the Queen, as planned, but by her stand-in for rehearsals (an ungainly man called Nobbs), illustrates several aspects of the theme of illusion mistaken for reality, but its spirit of low farce inoculates the reader against taking the book seriously. Also, the novel's short-breathed episodic quality—it is really only a series of sketches strung loosely together by a farcical plot—too openly betrays the author's work as a whimsically satiric journalist. The short-breath syndrome is familiar among SF novelists who are really short-story men; in *The Tin Men* we have an essayist trying to write a novel and not quite succeeding.

A Very Private Life also has a mosaic quality (as indeed does Frayn's stimulating philosophical work, *Constructions*), but here the small pieces compose a highly satisfactory work of art, one of the most delightful fabulations in the genre. The heroine, Uncumber, begins as a misfit in a society where what the Haves have is privacy: they meet by holovision, as in Asimov's *The Naked Sun.* Uncumber falls in love with a man who lives on the fringes of her enclosed society, journeys outside her cell to meet him, is disillusioned by life outside, falls in with outlaws, is rescued by the police and rehabilitated. Comparison with *The Naked Sun* is instructive because, unlike Asimov and the typical SF writer who might handle such a theme, Frayn has not written a dystopian satire: his absurd world is presented not as a threat but as an alteration simply, a new mode, not inhuman but nicely domesticated by engaging touches or ordinariness. Again, if we compare Frayn's work with Angela Carter's *Heroes and Villains,* in which the ivory tower world is promptly sacrificed to the perverse gypsy delights of the world outside, we see how detached and balanced, how cool Frayn is. Uncumber does not find the outer world romantic, as a Carter heroine would; instead, the best it can offer is a tatty attempt to emulate the values of those inside, while the worst is nasty and brutish: the outlaws are indeed, as they are called, "Sad Men." Frayn's novel is written as a fairy story that begins "Once upon a time there will be a little girl called Uncumber," and in that spirit it should be read.

In *Constructions* Frayn tells us "I should like to say this: don't *worry* when you find yourself in the midst of a mythology. Relax and enjoy it." Some SF readers may find themselves graveled by the way in which this sharp and witty writer pulls his punches. But Frayn is not a knock-down satirist: he's a comic ironist who enjoys the spectacle of human absurdity, and wants us to share the fun. *Sweet Dreams* should also be read, although, as it is a story set in the after-life, in which revivification is without benefit of technology (by which Farmer and Silverberg, say, have accommodated this mythological idea to SF), it is strictly outside our genre.

—Michael J. Tolley

FRAZEE, (Charles) Steve. Also writes as Dean Jennings. American. Born in Salida, Colorado, 28 September 1909. Educated at Western State College, Gunnison, Colorado, A.B. 1937. Married Patricia Thomass in 1937; one son and one daughter. Worked in heavy construction and mining, 1926-36, 1941-43; journalism teacher, La Junta High School, Colorado, 1937-41. Since 1946, free-lance writer. Building Inspector, City of Salida, 1950-63; Director, Salida Building and Loan Association. President, 1954, and Vice-President, 1962, Western Writers of America. Recipient: *Ellery Queen's Mystery Magazine* Prize, 1953; Western Heritage Award, 1960; Cowboy Hall of Fame Award, 1961. Agent: Scott Meredith Literary Agency, 845 Third Avenue, New York, New York 10022. Address: Salida, Colorado, U.S.A.

SCIENCE-FICTION PUBLICATIONS

Novel

The Sky Block. New York, Rinehart, 1953; London, Lane, 1955.

Uncollected Short Stories

"Dragon Fire," in *Fantasy* (New York), February 1953.
"Geoff the Djinn," in *Cosmos* (New York), July 1954.
"Flying Saucers Do Exist," in *Space SF* (New York), August 1957.

OTHER PUBLICATIONS

Novels

Range Trouble (as Dean Jennings). New York, Phoenix Press, 1951.
Shining Mountains. New York, Rinehart, 1951; London, Muller, 1953.
Pistolman. New York, Lion, 1952; London, Panther, 1967.
Lawman's Feud. New York, Lion, 1953.
Sharp the Bugle Calls. New York, Lion, 1953; as *Gold at Kansas Gulch,* New York, Fawcett, 1958; London, Red Seal, 1959.
Cry Coyote. New York, Macmillan, 1955; London, Lane, 1956.
Many Rivers to Cross. New York and London, Fawcett, 1955.
Spur to the Smoke. New York, Permabooks, 1955.
Tumbling Range Woman. New York, Pocket Books, 1956.
He Rode Alone. New York, Fawcett, 1956; London, Fawcett, 1958.
High Cage. New York, Macmillan, 1957.
Running Target. New York, Fawcett, 1957; London, Fawcett, 1958.
Desert Guns. New York, Dell, 1957; as *Gold of the Seven Saints,* London, Consul, 1961.
Rendezvous. New York, Macmillan, 1958.
Smoke in the Valley. New York, Fawcett, 1959; London, Muller, 1960.
The Alamo. New York, Avon, 1960.
More Damn Tourists. New York, Macmillan, 1960.
Bragg's Fancy Woman. New York, Ballantine, 1966; as *A Gun for Bragg's Woman,* London, Panther, 1967.
Outcasts. New York, Popular Library, 1967.
Utah Hell Guns. London, Panther, 1968.
Flight 409. New York, Avon, 1969.
Fire in the Valley. New York, Lancer, 1972.
Many Rivers to Cross. New York Fawcett, 1978.

Short Stories

The Gun-Throwers. New York, Lion, 1954.

Other (juvenile)

Walt Disney's Zorro (novelization of TV play). Racine, Wisconsin, Whitman, 1958; London, Daily Mirror, 1959.
First Through the Grand Canyon. Philadelphia, Winston, 1960.
Year of the Big Snow. New York, Holt Rinehart, 1962.
Killer Lion. Racine, Wisconsin, Whitman, 1966.

Lassie: The Mystery of the Bristlecone Pine. Racine, Wisconsin, Whitman, 1967.
Where Are You? All about Maps. New York, Meredith Press, 1968.
Lassie: Lost in the Snow [*The Secret of the Smuggler's Cave, Trouble at Panter's Lake*]. New York, Golden Press, 3 vols., 1979.

*   *   *

Steve Frazee has written only one novel which qualifies as science fiction (and but a handful of stories, all of them fantasy-oriented); but that novel, *The Sky Block,* has acquired something of a small cult following among aficionados. *The Sky Block* is primarily a chase/adventure story in the mode of Geoffrey Household and John Buchan, set in a remote section of the rugged Colorado rockies. It concerns Platt Vencel, who becomes involved with the United States Army and the FBI in the search for a hidden device known as the "weather-wrecker." This device, which has been secreted in the Unites States as part of a sinister takeover plot, utilizes cosmic rays to alter meteorological conditions, thereby turning important agricultural areas into literal dust bowls through drought. In synopsis the premise seems implausible and melodramatic, with overtones of the anti-Communist extremism of the McCarthy era. Frazee's handling of the theme, however, minimizes these negative aspects; and his crisp writing, excellent characterization, vivid depiction of background, and ability to create genuine suspense make the novel both interesting and stimulating.

—Bill Pronzini

FREEDMAN, Nancy (née Mars). American. Born in Chicago, Illinois, 4 July 1920. Educated at the Chicago Art Institute, 1937-38; Los Angeles City College, 1938-39; University of Southern California, Los Angeles, 1939. Married Benedict Freedman in 1941; two sons and one daughter. Actress in the 1930's. Agent: Harold Ober Agency, 40 East 49th Street, New York, New York 10017. Address: 5837 Latigo Canyon Road, Malibu, California 90267, U.S.A.

SCIENCE-FICTION PUBLICATIONS

Novels

Joshua Son of None. New York, Delacorte Press, 1973; London, Hart Davis MacGibbon, 1974.

OTHER PUBLICATIONS

Novels with Benedict Freedman

Back to the Sea. New York, Viking Press, 1942.
Mrs. Mike. New York, Coward McCann, and London, Hamish Hamilton, 1947.
This and No More. New York, Harper, 1950.
The Spark and the Exodus. New York, Crown, 1954.
Lootville. New York, Holt, 1957.
Tresa. New York, Holt, 1959.
The Apprentice Bastard. New York, Simon and Schuster, 1966.
Cyclone of Silence. New York, Simon and Schuster, 1969.
The Immortals. New York, St. Martin's Press, 1977.
Prima Donna. New York, Morrow, 1981.

*

Manuscript Collection: Mugar Memorial Library, Boston University.

Theatrical Activities:

Actress: **Plays**—in *Faust* by Goethe; *The Miracle* by Karl Volmöller; *Six Characters in Search of an Author* by Pirandello; *Death Takes a Holiday* by Walter Ferris; in summer stock, Maine, summers 1937-38.

Nancy Freedman comments:
I had no idea I was writing science fiction when I began *Joshua Son of None*. My philosophy of an author's obligation, besides of course literary considerations, is that he should stand slightly outside his own time, letting events wash over his work. To prepare for *Joshua Son of None* I attended a seminar at Cal Tech given by Dr. Robert Sinsheimer and in 1972 I was introduced to the work Dr. Steptoe was doing in genetic engineering. Six years later he refined the process which I describe in my novel, and produced the Brown baby. With *in vitro* technique we are halfway to the possibility of cloning. *Joshua Son of None* was published by Delacorte who paid me a large advance, and it was made a Literary Guild selection—and then, wonder of wonders, silence in the press. The Guild quietly dropped its ads, as did the publisher. The reason? I was told that the public wasn't ready for a book about cloning. It was too terrifying a possibility. Shortly thereafter *The Boys from Brazil* appeared, treated not realistically but in a cops-and-robbers setting. It emanated from my own agent and publisher, who apparently felt that, done in this more fantastic manner, it would not appear threatening. It didn't; in fact, it gave rise to an endless series of jokes on the subject (perhaps equivalent to "whistling in the dark"). *Joshua Son of None* was the first book on the subject of cloning, and I treated the material with great respect for I believe the first clone will within a decade tread this earth. The book was science fiction when I wrote it. How long it will remain so I can only guess.
As a writer I am concerned with the future. I am particularly concerned with the connective tissue that runs from earliest time to the present and stretches into the future. One such skein is mankind's desire for the one attribute denied him by the gods—immortality. Through the process of cloning we may have been handed this key to life everlasting. Man has not defeated death. If he goes this route, he will die many deaths and live many lives in his quest for personal self-perfection. The technical revolution which will make this possible is of greater magnitude than the splitting of the atom. It is the opening of Pandora's box. Skinner and his colleagues claim that environment totally modifies and changes behavior. And a clone is born into a different environment. Carl Rogers takes a more moderate position, believing that while the environment modifies man, man is not passive. He in turn changes and interacts with his surroundings This is the thrust of my novel. Joshua is the son of none, having neither father nor mother but replicated from a single cell of his own dying body. In the book, a deliberate attempt is made to control the environment and replicate the phenotype of the assassinated president. But it appeared to me that the clonee differed from the original when he discovers he is a copy of someone else. This is the identity crisis of all time. When he asks, "Then I'm not myself—I'm *him*?" At that moment he becomes his own person.
I am often asked why I took John F. Kennedy as my prototype. Partly, personal identification. I had broken my back and was forced to lie absolutely flat for seven months. During this time my mind reverted frequently to Kennedy. He had gone through the same ordeal, which is so psychologically damaging, and had rallied to become President. I at least would stand on my own feet and walk. Moreover, when the book was first conceived, I envisioned it as the retelling in modern terms of a myth, namely, man's desire for life everlasting. And for a myth, a folk hero, someone larger than life, is needed to carry it forward. Only one contemporary answered that description, the man I already identified with so closely.

*   *   *

Nancy Freedman comes to science fiction as an established novelist trained in general fiction, with a particular concentration in the history of families—the stories that families make through heir connections, multiplication, and dynastic continuity. For someone with such an interest, the idea of cloning holds special appeal, a desire for the power represented by non-generative extensions of a generative group, plus the dream of repeated personality. When Freedman connected the idea of cloning with the history of the Kennedy dynasty, she produced *Joshua Son of None.*

The premise of the book is that a doctor present at John F. Kennedy's assassination preserved tissue from the dying President, and then found a scientist with knowledge of cloning, and a millionaire with the willingness to raise the resultant child in the Kennedy pattern. Partly an experiment and partly a long-term plan for political power, the project works. A surrogate mother carries the child, the millionaire's family is remodeled to raise him, and simulated deaths and disasters warp his psyche in the original pattern. What is produced is a young man who finally realizes not only that he must become President, but that in some sense he already was.

The problem with the premise is that cloning simply does not have the potential of repeating personality or history. Freedman details the science of the project with intelligence and clarity, but in her need to make the novel work, and in her apparent affection for Kennedy himself, she gives too much credit to chromosomes. The profound differences that develop between identical twins—raised in the same family at the same time—should be enough to demonstrate that there are too many other factors at work. A less meticulous novelist might have invented a technology to help preserve personality as well as genotype, but Freedman, sticking to it-could-happen-here facts, only advances the craft of cloning as far as success with human cells. As a result, the science she invokes but does not follow would condemn the plot, particularly the lurid ending, to the category of wishful thinking and near silliness.

Yet the book is effective, mainly because of Freedman's other novelistic skills. Her characters have a depth that allows her to measure with considerable feeling the impact of technological power on its human victims. The moment when Joshua Francis Kellogg rips off his braces and recognizes someone else in the mirror is surprisingly moving. In fact, throughout the book Joshua's reactions have coherence and growing familiarity that should demonstrate that novelists are better at reproducing personality than genetic scientists.

After *Joshua Son of None*, Freedman continued writing about science in *The Immortals*, the story of an oil dynasty. While this long novel is not actually science fiction, the same interests reappear—the network of family, and the possibility that science could break history loose from its disastrous course. As in *Joshua*, the descriptions of research and technology (the invention of a solar cell) are clear and well-written. Freedman writes on the edge of science fiction, pushing speculation only as far as the near future. Given her solid novelist's skills, it would be interesting to see her attempt a farther future.

—Karen G. Way

FRENCH, Paul. *See* **ASIMOV, Isaac.**

FRIEDBERG, Gertrude (née Tonkonogy). American. Born in New York City, 17 March 1908. Educated at Wellesley College, Massachusetts; Barnard College, New York, B.A. 1929. Married Charles K. Friedberg; one son and one daughter. Mathematics teacher in New York public schools, and free-lance writer. Address: 1185 Park Avenue, New York, New York 10028, U.S.A.

SCIENCE-FICTION PUBLICATIONS

Novel

The Revolving Boy. New York, Doubleday, 1966; London, Gollancz, 1967.

Uncollected Short Stories

"The Short and Happy Death of George Frumkin," in *Fantasy and Science Fiction* (New York), April 1963.
"For Whom the Girl Waits," in *Fantasy and Science Fiction* (New York), May 1972.

OTHER PUBLICATIONS

Plays

Three Cornered Moon (produced New York, 1933). New York, French, 1933.
Town House, adaptation of stories by John Cheever (produced New York, 1948).

*   *   *

Gertrude Friedberg has published several interesting science-fiction works.

The Revolving Boy follows the early life of a supernormal child, Derv, who has the ability to be both radiometer and compass. One of the major themes of the novel is that of discovering and communicating with another civilization. Derv was born to astronauts in 1970, in a weightless condition far from the earth's forces. Because he did not experience gravity at birth, he was able to align himself to a signal from another solar system. He feels compelled to preserve his original orientation to this signal—called the Direction—and consequently, when his body is turned in one direction, he must unwind himself in the opposite direction to recapture his original position. He turns somersaults in bed to compensate for the earth's revolutions and his day's turnings. During his elementary school years, his teachers become concerned as he executes dangerous spins on stairways. He becomes known as "the boy who leans" when his body begins listing in the direction of the signal.

To escape the publicity following his birth, Derv's parents faked a fatal accident in a sailboat, escaped undetected, and assumed new identities. The novel excels in the following the parents' fears of discovery as they observe the development of Derv's talent. When Derv reaches high school, an astronomer who knew the astronaut parents discovers their true identities and persuades them to allow Derv to help trace the signal on a laboratory radiometer. Just as the signal is found electronically, Derv and his parents disappear again. Part Two of the book begins some years later, after Derv has taken a new name—Fred Gany—and married his childhood sweetheart, Prin (now Reine), who has perfect pitch. Derv-Fred's signal has suddenly stopped and he has lost his sense of balance. The remainder of the book concentrates on Prin-Reine's attempts to relocate the laboratory radiometer (which has been abandoned) and to determine if the signal has indeed terminated.

Friedberg's scientific projections are mostly erroneous. For instance, the exposition of her novel is centered around the ban on space travel in 1970, due to a belt of nuclear waste around the earth. She overestimated the speed of change to electronic devices in the homes of the 1970's. Her scientific research can also be faulted, since she has failed to take into account some of the properties of radio signals, such as the possibility of blockage by shielding masses (the earth, tunnels, and concrete buildings).

"The Short and Happy Death of George Frumkin" is a tongue-in-cheek look at the use of artificial organs. George, 97 years old, has developed not only a knock in his artificial heart, but also a bad case of ennui, as he refuses to complete a promised rewrite of the second act of a play. George's wife, Helen, persuades him to call an electrician, Dr. Stebbins (most doctors are electricians these days), who tells him that he needs "a new battery and a new variable autotransformer." In order to hook him to his new system, Dr. Stebbins switches him to house current until the calibration procedure is finished. During the short space between plug-ins, George is "dead."

However, house current proves a boon to George, providing him with the creative energy to rewrite his second act, plus an oversupply of sexual libido (he attacks his wife and propositions the maid during this interval). But after his return to battery power, he resumes his uninspired ways, learning nevertheless that his rewritten second act has given the play "more heart." This entertaining spoof is a gem, undoubtedly Friedberg's best science fiction effort. She uses a female narrator for this story, plus a steady supply of eccentric comic characters.

"For Whom the Girl Waits," properly called science fantasy, is a dreamlike account of double identities in a high school setting. The main character, Louis Demperi, is a substitute teacher who assumes the identity of the teacher he replaces. The role-playing works well until he takes the place of a man named Koppinger, for whom a beautiful girl waits each afternoon after school. Then he becomes disoriented and cannot remember that he is Koppinger, until he discovers that another man has assumed his own identity. Demperi decides to carry on with Koppinger's role and meets the girl, who rejects him and causes him to have a fatal car accident. But his identity lives on in the person of Demperi's substitute. The story is somewhat confusing but is imaginative and fascinating to read.

In her writing, Friedberg uses a simple, unpretentious style and in general organizes her material chronologically. She excels in the handling of women characters, which suggests that her works might have been more successful if the central characters had been women instead of men.

—Judith Snyder

FYFE, H(orace) B(rowne). Also writes as Andrew MacDuff. American. Born in Jersey City, New Jersey, 30 September 1918. Educated at Stevens Academy; Columbia University, New York, B.S. 1950. Served in the United States Army during World War II: Bronze Star. Married Adeline Marie Dougherty in 1946. Laboratory assistant and draftsman, then free-lance writer. Address: Box 221, Ridgefield Park, New Jersey 07660, U.S.A.

SCIENCE-FICTION PUBLICATIONS

Novel

D-99. New York, Pyramid, 1962.

Uncollected Short Stories (series: Bureau of Slick Tricks)

"Hold That Comet," with F.H. Hauser, in *Astonishing* (Chicago), December 1940.
"Sinecure 6," in *Astounding* (New York), January 1947.
"Special Jobbery" (Bureau), in *Astounding* (New York), September 1949.
"Locked Out," in *Men Against the Stars*, edited by Martin H. Greenberg. New York, Gnome Press, 1950.
"Conformity Expected," in *Astounding* (New York), March 1950.
"Spy Scare," in *Astounding* (New York), September 1950.
"In Value Deceived," in *Possible Worlds of Science Fiction*, edited by Groff Conklin. New York, Vanguard Press, 1951.
"Bureau of Slick Tricks," in *Travellers of Space*, edited by Martin H. Greenberg. New York, Gnome Press, 1951.
"The Envoy, Her," in *Planet* (New York), March 1951.
"Key Decision," in *Astounding* (New York), May 1951.
"Open Invitation," in *Planet* (New York), May 1951.
"Temporary Keeper," in *Thrilling Wonder Stories* (New York), June 1951.
"Experimentum Crucis" (as Andrew MacDuff), in *Astounding* (New York), July 1951.
"Yes, Sir!," in *Startling* (New York), September 1951.
"This World Must Die!," in *Future* (New York), September 1951.

"Thinking Machine," in *Astounding* (New York), October 1951.
"Afterthought," in *Beyond Human Ken*, edited by Judith Merril. New York, Random House, 1952; London, Grayson, 1953.
"Manners of the Age," in *Omnibus of Science Fiction*, edited by Groff Conklin. New York, Crown, 1952.
"Protected Species," in *The Astounding Science Fiction Anthology*, edited by John W. Campbell, Jr. New York, Simon and Schuster, 1952.
"Calling World-4 of Kithgol," in *Planet* (New York), January 1952.
"Bluff-Stained Transaction" (Bureau), in *Astounding* (New York), March 1952.
"Extra-Secret Agent," in *Science Fiction Quarterly* (Holyoke, Massachusetts), May 1952.
"Time Limit," in *Fantastic Story* (New York), Winter 1952.
"Implode and Peddle" (Bureau) and "Star-Linked," in *Space Service*, edited by Andre Norton. Cleveland, World, 1953.
"Let There Be Light," in *Crossroads in Time*, edited by Groff Conklin. New York, Permabooks, 1953.
"Ransom," in *The Best from Fantasy and Science Fiction 2*, edited by Anthony Boucher and J. Francis McComas. Boston, Little Brown, 1953.
"The Well-Oiled Machine," in *Science-Fiction Carnival*, edited by Fredric Brown and Mack Reynolds. Chicago, Shasta, 1953.
"The Compleat Collector," in *Future* (New York), January 1953.
"Fast Passage," in *Other Worlds* (Evanston, Indiana), January 1953.
"Exile," in *Space* (New York), February 1953.
"Romance," in *Future* (New York), March 1953.
"Irresistible Weapon," in *If* (New York), July 1953.
"Koenigshaufen's Curve," in *Fantasy Fiction* (New York), August 1953.
"Moonwalk," in *Space Pioneers*, edited by Andre Norton. Cleveland, World, 1954.
"Welcome, Strangers!," in *Astounding* (New York), August 1954.
"The Shell Dome," in *Spaceway* (Alhambra, California), February 1955.
"The Night of No Moon," in *Infinity* (New York), June 1957.
"Lunar Escapade," in *Planet of Doom and Other Stories*. Sydney, Jubilee, 1958.
"Fee of the Frontier," in *Amazing* (New York), August 1960.
"A Transmutation of Muddle," in *Astounding* (New York), September 1960.
"Wedge," in *If* (New York), September 1960.
"The Furies of Zhahnoor," in *Fantastic* (New York), October 1960.
"Satellite System," in *Astounding* (New York), October 1960.
"Round-and-Round Trip," in *Galaxy* (New York), December 1960.
"The Outbreak of Peace," in *Analog* (New York), February 1961.
"Flamedown," in *Analog* (New York), August 1961.
"Tolliver's Orbit," in *If* (New York), September 1961.
"The Talkative Tree," in *If* (New York), January 1962.
"Knowledge Is Power," in *Way Out*, edited by Ivan Howard. New York, Belmont, 1963.
"Star Chamber," in *Amazing* (New York), March 1963.
"The Klygha," in *Amazing* (New York), December 1963.
"The Clutches of Ruin," in *Gamma 4* (North Hollywood), 1965.
"The Old Shill Game," in *Analog* (New York), January 1967.

* * *

H.B. Fyfe has written several dozen conventional short stories and a single eposodic novel that obviously meshes several shorter stories into one whole. He is perhaps best known for his series about the Bureau of Slick Tricks, a secret human organization whose purpose is to finagle humans out of embarrassing situations on other planets. The novel and at least five stories fall into this series, and a number of other stories are very similar thematically. Essentially, the philosophy expressed is that humans are the most flexible, inventive race in the universe, and that any aliens who encounter us should hold onto everything that isn't nailed down.

"In Value Deceived" is a perfect example of this. Two starships, one human and one alien, encounter each other in space. The aliens are short on rations, and are seeking edible plants, which they consider highly valuable. They trade a "worthless" piece of their own equipment for some hydroponic supplies; the "worthless" item allows transmutation of elements. In "Ransom" primitive aliens decide to kidnap humans as leverage against the crew of an exploratory starship. They end up with two robots, and are dismayed at the casual manner in which they are abandoned. The novel, *D-99,* features a host of confused, outsmarted, and frantic aliens, who cannot cope with human manipulation of events.

Fyfe was not permanently wed to this concept, although it does dominate his work. One of his best short stories, "Protected Species," is in fact quite atypical. The primitive aliens skulking about the ruins of their former civilization are treated with active sympathy, and ultimately it is the humans who find themselves the butt of a cosmic joke. In "The Talkative Tree" an alien culture provides the means whereby humans alienated from their dictatorial and conformist culture can escape into almost any conceivable form of freedom by altering their physical nature.

Fyfe makes use of a number of standard plot devices and has done little in the way of innovation. He explores both sides of the human-robot interface. Robotic servants with their built-in limitations drive a magazine editor crazy in "The Well-Oiled Machine," but they come to dominate the world in "Let There Be Light," and are preyed on by human scavengers for the oil they use within their bodies. Man is therefore reduced to the level of a mechanical vampire. By far his most outstanding work is "Moonwalk" which makes use of a classic man-against-nature situation, one that has been used many times both within the genre and without. As the result of an accident, one man is stranded on the lunar surface, several hundred miles from the moon's only human installation. The plot unfolds in logical fashion, as the protagonist wrestles with time and a diminishing air supply, and the reader struggles with frustrated impatience as the authorities refuse to believe that the lack of radio contact portends anything requiring action. Although Fyfe is not capable of making this a truly great story, he handles it quite well, and it is a worthy contribution of its type.

Fyfe has remained a dabbler, and his obvious talents have not been developed. There is little difference in quality between the earliest and most recent stories. Nevertheless, his competent stories have provided entertainment and adventure to his audience.

—Don D'Ammassa

GALLUN, Raymond Z(inke).   Also writes as William Callahan. American.   Born in Beaver Dam, Wisconsin, 22 March 1911. Educated at the University of Wisconsin, Madison, 1929-30; Alliance Française, Paris, 1938-39; San Marcos University, Lima, Peru, 1960. Married 1) Frieda E. Talmey in 1959 (died, 1974); 2) Bertha Erickson Backman in 1978. Construction worker for Army Corps of Engineers, 1942-43; marine blacksmith, Pearl Harbor Navy Yard, 1944; technical writer, EDO Corporation, College Point, New York, 1964-75. Agent: Robert P. Mills Ltd., 156 East 52nd Street, New York, New York 10022. Address: 110-20 71st Street, Forest Hills, New York 11375, U.S.A.

SCIENCE-FICTION PUBLICATIONS

Novels

People Minus X.   New York, Simon and Schuster, 1957.
The Planet Strappers.   New York, Pyramid, 1961.
The Eden Cycle.   New York, Ballantine, 1974.

Short Stories

The Machine That Thought (as William Callahan).   New York, Columbia, 1940.
The Best of Raymond Z. Gallun.   New York, Ballantine, 1978.

Uncollected Short Stories

"The Eternal Wall," in *Amazing* (New York), May 1979.
"A First Glimpse," in *Analog* (New York), February 1980.

Raymond Z. Gallun comments:
Most of my science fiction was originally published in the 1930's, mainly in *Astounding* while F. Orlin Tremaine, whom I remember with appreciation, was editor. I think I aimed mostly at realism insofar as it could be constructed from what was then supposed to be true about the various planets, plus humanizing of even the unhuman characters, giving them points of sympathetic contact without overdoing the sympathy. Some time after World War II I dropped out of SF to do other things. Being now retired from formal employment, I have been trying to get back into SF writing. "Then and Now" (*Analog,* December 1977) is a fair example of what I have been recently trying to do.

*   *   *

Raymond Z. Gallun has published in the pulps vast quantities of clumsy and primitive fiction, and yet his treatments of several of the more sophisticated problems facing modern man are often exciting and provocative to read. He is a vintage science-fiction pulp writer from the 1930's who published his most ambitious novel in the 1970's. One critic has labeled his underlying philosophy "Darwinian existentialism"; and two short quotations from what Gallun himself has called his favorite short story, "The Restless Tide," will introduce the stark polarities that he continually balances in his best work. At the end of the story, the protagonist concludes, "Mankind was like a rough, sturdy plant, growing, thrusting; crude but magnificent, and caught between rot and fire." Earlier he had exhorted his wife, "It's the contrasts that count. There's a rough drama in people."

Gallun's novel *The Eden Cycle* is a fine expansion of these earlier themes. The Hegelian balancing of opposites along with the classic polar opposition, which is also a key to the meaning for us of Darwinian theory, between the glory of early primitive development and the continual trend toward greater sophistication are well developed in this long narration of the most advanced human hedonists governed by aliens. In fact, for Gallun the contrasts that run throughout his fictions are so roughly vivid that they become emblematic of what the Renaissance loved to call man's amphibian nature. Aliens are presented as complex and sympathetic characters early—"Old Faithful" (1934)—and then throughout his career. In addition to the rough contrast of man to alien, there is repeatedly drawn the contrast of creature to environment, as in "Godson of Almarlu," as well as the contrast of past to present. Science fiction lends itself particularly well to the old opposition between a golden age of the past and a modern iron age because science fiction tries to image both technology and man's inner primitive self. Gallun's work conveys these oppositions continually in the narratives mentioned above and in such pieces as *People Minus X,* "Return of a Legend," and "The Lotus-Engine."

Rough contrast is also a most appropriate characterization for the literary impressions of Gallun's extrapolations. For example, "The Lotus-Engine" makes skillful use of the classic Homeric myth of the lotus eaters and also weaves a most explicit set of images to convey again the old story of mutability and decline associated with technological advance. But even in this story the pulp characterizations of "old chums" must enter, and the characters even smoke cigarettes inside the oxygen rich helmets of their "space armor." A genre that can retell the most profound human dilemmas in what are often such rough forms is indeed sturdy and growing, and Gallun was one sturdy and often rough writer who contributed greatly to its growth.

—Donald M. Hassler

GALOUYE, Daniel F(rancis).   American.   Born in New Orleans, Louisiana, 11 February 1920. Educated at Louisiana State University, Baton Rouge, B.A. in journalism 1941. Served as a pilot in the United States Navy, 1941-46: Lieutenant in Naval Reserve. Married

Carmel Barbara Jordan in 1945; two daughters. Reporter, then assistant news editor, 1946-55, Chief editorial Writer, 1955-60, and Associate Editor, 1960-65, New Orleans *States-Item*: now retired. Consultant, New Orleans Science Center and Planetarium Committee. Agent: Harry Altshuler, 225 West 86th Street, New York, New York 10024. Address: 5669 Catina Street, New Orleans, Louisiana 70124, U.S.A.

SCIENCE-FICTION PUBLICATIONS

Novels

Dark Universe. New York, Bantam, 1961; London, Gollancz, 1963.
Lords of the Psychon. New York, Bantam, 1963.
Simulacron-3. New York, Bantam, 1964; as *Counterfeit World*, London, Gollancz, 1964.
The Lost Perception. London, Gollancz, 1966; as *A Scourge of Screamers*, New York, Bantam, 1968.
The Infinite Man. New York, Bantam, 1973.

Short Stories

The Last Leap and Other Stories of the Super Mind. London, Corgi, 1964.
Project Barrier. London, Gollancz, 1968.

Uncollected Short Stories

"O Kind Master," in *If* (New York), January, 1970.
"The Big Blow-Up," in *Fantastic* (New York), July 1979.

*   *   *

Daniel F. Galouye, a greatly underrated and largely forgotten writer, is probably best remembered for the numerous short stories and novelettes in the science-fiction "slicks" of the 1950's and 1960's. Despite them, however, his primary contribution to the field rests in three novels: *Dark Universe, Simulacron-3,* and *Lords of the Psychon.* Always well-conceived, well-planned, and well-crafted, Galouye's stories are extrapolations of scientific fact or theory, but his vivid and far-ranging imagination and his incredible attention to detail often carry his readers well into the fantastic. These characteristics are most visible in the novels where the length permits the accumulation of detail to achieve its full impact.

Though many of Galouye's stories use a post-disaster motif, they reflect his optimistic belief in the capability of man to develop his latent mental abilities, and often the resolutions of his plots depend upon the evolvement of such talents as astral projection, extended vision, teleportation, and mental manipulation of matter or energy. Curiously, he often depicts faster-than-light spaceships powered by psychokinesis, as in "The Centipedes of Space" and "Phantom World." His ultimate statement on human development, however, is found in "The Secret of the Immortals," where he proposes a metamorphosis that not only brings new mental powers but an extended life of at least 5,000 years.

Galouye's work also displays a preoccupation with the idea that man may be manipulated by external forces, and often the world of the story is a microcosm of some vaster universe. This concept frequently takes the form of a puppet motif. One of the most unusual twists on this theme occurs in "Gulliver Planet," where microscopic aliens invade the bodies of seven humans and manipulate them as part of their invasion plan. The theme's unique treatment, however, comes in *Simulacron-3,* where Doug Hall, the protagonist, discovers that he is merely an electric analogue in a total electronic simulation of the real world.

Galouye's overriding concern is the nature of reality and the related problem of perceiving it. Most of his stories and his three best novels treat this theme. *Dark Universe* deals with a colony that has survived a world-wide atomic war by retreating underground. One of 17 such colonies, "U.S. Survival Complex Number Eleven" functions well until a minor fault shift totally destroys its ability to generate electricity and cuts off all but a few of the superheated water conduits that lead to the group's basic living chamber.

Through succeeding generations, the loss of sight and the disintegration of their knowledge of their original world creates a culture totally dependent on sound for survival and ignorant of their true circumstances. The story concerns the attempt of one young man, Jared Fenton, to discover what light really is. The novel's status as a minor classic comes from Galouye's treatment and control of his material. His elimination of all words from the narrative that relate to sight and his passages which describe how Fenton uses his non-visual senses to perceive his world are brilliantly effective.

Simulacron-3, an extremely original work, also treats the nature of reality. Doug Hall discovers that his world is but an electromathematical model of an average community and that it is marked for extinction. In an ironic reversal of roles, he manages to change places with the real Doug Hall, the megalomaniacal operator of the simulator, and prevent his world from being erased. *Lords of the Psychon,* though not quite so well-controlled as *Dark Universe* or so original as *Simulacron-3,* is a post-destruction story that concerns the efforts of Geoffrey Maddox to prevent aliens from drawing Earth into another dimension. In the process of fighting them, he learns that he can mentally manipulate the fundamental form of matter, a pink plasma called psychon, and he proves that it is itself merely a reflection of the mental.

Galouye's major weakness is his relatively shallow characterization. It is often difficult to distinguish between his parade of military protagonists, and his women are seldom more than helpless sex-objects. Where he has the time to infuse his narrative with detail, however, his principal characters manage to become more than cardboard cutouts. Originality, control, and fast pace are typical of his best writing.

—Carl B. Yoke

GARNER, Rolf. *See* BERRY, Bryan.

GARRETT, Randall (Phillip). Also writes as Gordon Aghill; Grandall Barretton; Alexander Blade; Walter Bupp; Ralph Burke; Gordon Garrett; David Gordon; Richard Greer; Larry Mark Harris; Ivar Jorgensen; Darrel T. Langart; Clyde T. Mitchell; Mark Phillips; Robert Randall; Leonard G. Spencer; S.M. Tenneshaw; Gerald Vance. American. Born in Lexington, Missouri, in 1927. Educated at Texas Tech University, Lubbock, B.S. Served in the United States Marine Corps during World War II: Corporal. Married Vicki Ann Heydron. Industrial chemist, Battle Creek, Michigan, and Peoria, Illinois; then free-lance writer. Address: 5216 Meadow Creek Drive, Austin, Texas 78745, U.S.A.

SCIENCE-FICTION PUBLICATIONS

Novels

The Shrouded Planet (as Robert Randall, with Robert Silverberg). New York, Gnome Press, 1957.
The Dawning Light (as Robert Randall, with Robert Silverberg). New York, Gnome Press, 1959.
Pagan Passions (as Larry M. Harris, with Laurence M. Janifer). New York, Galaxy, 1959.
Unwise Child. New York, Doubleday, 1962; London, Mayflower, 1963.
Anything You Can Do... (as Darrel T. Langart). New York, Doubleday, and London, Mayflower, 1963.

Too Many Magicians. New York, Doubleday, 1967; London, Macdonald, 1968.
Takeoff. Virginia Beach, Donning, 1979.

Novels as Mark Phillips (with Laurence M. Janifer) (series: Kenneth J. Malone in all books)

Brain Twister. New York, Pyramid, 1962.
The Impossibles. New York, Pyramid, 1963.
Supermind. New York, Pyramid, 1963.

Uncollected Short Stories (series: Lord Darcy; Leland Hale)

"The Absence of Heat" (as Gordon Garrett), in *Astounding* (New York), June 1944.
"The Waiting Game," in *Astounding* (New York), January 1951.
"Pest," in *Astounding* (New York), December 1952.
"Instant of Decision," in *Space* (Alhambra, California), May 1953.
"Characteristics, Unusual," in *Science Fiction Quarterly* (Holyoke, Massachusetts), August 1953.
"Nom d'un Nom," in *Fantasy Fiction* (New York), August 1953.
"Hell to Pay," in *Beyond* (New York), March 1954.
"Time Fuse," in *If* (New York), March 1954.
"The Wayward Course," in *Future* (New York), March 1954.
"The Surgeon's Knife," in *Universe* (Evanston, Indiana), May 1954.
"Woman Driver," in *Fantastic* (New York), June 1954.
"Infinite Resources," in *Fantasy and Science Fiction* (New York), July 1954.
"Spatial Delivery," in *If* (New York), October 1954.
"Code in the Head," in *Future 29* (New York), 1956.
"Suite Mentale," in *Future 30* (New York), 1956.
"Vanishing Act" (as Robert Randall, with Robert Silverberg), in *Imaginative Tales* (Evanston, Indiana), January 1956.
"The Best of Fences," in *Infinity* (New York), February 1956.
"Quick Cure," in *Fantastic* (New York), February 1956.
"Gambler's Planet" (as Gordon Aghill, with Robert Silverberg), in *Amazing* (New York), June 1956.
"Catch a Thief" (as Gordon Aghill, with Robert Silverberg), in *Amazing* (New York), July 1956.
"The Saboteur," in *Original Science Fiction Stories* (Holyoke, Massachusetts), July 1956.
"Machine Complex," in *Astounding* (New York), July 1956.
"The Beast with Seven Tails" (as Leonard G. Spencer, with Robert Silverberg), in *Amazing* (New York), August 1956.
"Stroke of Genius," in *Infinity* (New York), August 1956.
"The Man Who Hated Mars," in *Amazing* (New York), September 1956.
"The Judas Valley" (as Gerald Vance, with Robert Silverberg), in *Amazing* (New York), October 1956.
"Heist Job on Thizar," in *Amazing* (New York), October 1956.
"The Man Who Knew Everything," in *Fantastic* (New York), October 1956.
"With All the Trappings," in *Astounding* (New York), November 1956.
"Puzzle in Yellow," in *Amazing* (New York), November 1956.
"The Mummy Takes a Wife" (as Clyde T. Mitchell, with Robert Silverberg), in *Fantastic* (New York), December 1956.
"Death to the Earthman," in *Amazing* (New York), December 1956.
"The Inquisitor," in *Imagination* (Evanston, Illinois), December 1956.
"The Star Slavers," in *Imaginative Tales* (Evanston, Illinois), January 1957.
"Deadly Decoy" (as Clyde T. Mitchell, with Robert Silverberg), in *Amazing* (New York), February 1957.
"The Devil Never Waits," in *Dynamic* (New York), February 1957.
"The Time Snatcher," in *Infinity* (New York), February 1957.
"Time to Stop," in *Science Fiction Quarterly* (Holyoke, Massachusetts) February 1957.
"Hungry World," in *Imaginative Tales* (Evanston, Illinois), March 1957.
"Saturnalia," in *Original Science Fiction Stories* (Holyoke, Massachusetts), March 1957.
"Guardians of the Tower," in *Imagination* (Evanston, Illinois), April 1957.

"The Man Who Collected Women," in *Amazing* (New York), April 1957.
"Masters of the Metropolis," in *Fantasy and Science Fiction* (New York), April 1957.
"The Vengeance of Kyvor," in *Fantastic* (New York), April, May 1957.
"The Last Killer," in *Imaginative Tales* (Evanston, Illinois), May 1957.
"What's Eating You?," in *Astounding* (New York), May 1957.
"You Too Can Win a Harem," in *Dreamworld* (New York), May 1957.
"Needler," in *Astounding* (New York), June 1957.
"A Pattern for Monsters," in *Fantastic* (New York), June 1957.
"Six Frightened Men," in *Imagination* (Evanston, Illinois), June 1957.
"Devil's World," in *Imaginative Tales* (Evanston, Illinois), July 1957.
"Gift from Tomorrow," in *Amazing* (New York), July 1957.
"Skid Row Pilot," in *Imagination* (Evanston, Illinois), August 1957.
"Killer—First Class," in *Imaginative Tales* (Evanston, Illinois), September 1957.
"Gentlemen, Please Note," in *Astounding* (New York), October 1957.
"The Mannion Court-Martial," in *Imagination* (Evanston, Illinois), October 1957.
"To Make a Hero" (Hale), in *Infinity* (New York), October 1957.
"Deathtrap Planet," in *Imaginative Tales* (Evanston, Illinois), November 1957.
"Satellite of Death," in *Imagination* (Evanston, Illinois), December 1957.
"Beyond Our Control," in *Infinity* (New York), January 1958.
"Strike the First Blow!," in *Imaginative Tales* (Evanston, Illinois), January 1958.
"The Low and the Mighty," in *Science Fiction Quarterly* (Holyoke, Massachusetts), February 1958.
"Far from Somewhere," in *Original Science Fiction Stories* (Holyoke, Massachusetts), March 1958.
"Penal Servitude," in *Astounding* (New York), March 1958.
"No Connections," in *Astounding* (New York), June 1958.
"Prisoner of War," in *Imagination* (Evanston, Illinois), June 1958.
"Respectfully Mine" (Hale), in *Infinity* (New York), August 1958.
"...and Check the Oil," in *Astounding* (New York), October 1958.
"Burden the Hand," in *Infinity* (New York), November 1958.
"The Savage Machine," in *Fantastic* (New York), November 1958.
"The Queen Bee," in *Astounding* (New York), December 1958.
"The Trouble with Magic," in *Fantastic* (New York), March 1959.
"Small Miracle," in *Amazing* (New York), June 1959.
"But I Don't Think," in *Astounding* (New York), July 1959.
"Dead Giveaway," in *Astounding* (New York), August 1959.
"That Sweet Little Old Lady" (as Mark Phillips, with Larry M. Harris) in *Astounding* (New York), September-October 1959.
"The Unnecessary Man," in *Astounding* (New York), November 1959.
"The Price of Eggs," in *Fantastic* (New York), December 1959.
"The Destroyers," in *Astounding* (New York), December 1959.
"Viewpoint," in *Astounding* (New York), January 1960.
"Drug on the Market" (Hale), in *Fantastic Universe* (Chicago), February 1960.
"In Case of Fire," in *Astounding* (New York), March 1960.
"The Measure of a Man," in *Astounding* (New York), April 1960.
"Damned If You Don't," in *Astounding* (New York), May 1960.
"...and Peace Attend Thee," in *Astounding* (New York), September 1960.
"The Highest Treason," in *Astounding* (New York), January 1961.
"Random Choice," in *Fantastic* (New York), March 1961.
"Something Rich and Strange," in *Fantasy and Science Fiction* (New York), June 1961.
"A Spaceship Named McGuire," in *Analog* (New York), July 1961.
"Mustang," in *Fantasy and Science Fiction* (New York), November 1961.
"Sound Decision," in *Prologue to Analog,* edited by John W. Campbell, Jr. New York, Doubleday, 1962; London, Panther, 1967.
"Hepcats of Venus," in *Fantastic* (New York), January 1962.

"His Master's Voice," in *Analog* (New York), March 1962.
"Through Time and Space with Benedict Breadfruit" (as Grandall Barretton), in *Amazing* (New York), 8 parts, March-October 1962.
"The Bramble Bush," in *Analog* (New York), August 1962.
"Spatial Relationship," in *Fantasy and Science Fiction* (New York), August 1962.
"The Eyes Have It," in *Analog* (New York), January 1964.
"A Case of Identity," in *Analog* (New York), September 1964.
"A Fortnight of Miracles," in *Fantastic* (New York), February 1965.
"The Best Policy," in *Earthmen and Strangers,* edited by Robert Silverberg. New York, Meredith Press, 1966.
"Tin Lizzie," in *Great Science Fiction Stories about Mars,* edited by T.E. Dikty. New York, Fell, 1966.
"Witness for the Prosecution," in *Fantasy and Science Fiction* (New York), February 1966.
"Fighting Division," in *Analog 5,* edited by John W. Campbell, Jr. New York, Doubleday, 1967; London, Dobson, 1968.
"The Hunting Lodge," in *Men and Machines,* edited by Robert Silverberg. New York, Meredith Press, 1968.
"The Foreign Hand Tie," in *14 Great Tales of ESP,* edited by Idella P. Stone. New York, Fawcett, 1969.
"Ready, Aim, Robot!," in *S.F. Greats* (New York), Summer 1969.
"The Briefing," in *Fantastic* (New York), August 1969.
"Fimbulsommer," in *If* (New York), September 1970.
"Look Out. Duck," in *Never in This World,* edited by Idella P. Stone. New York, Fawcett, 1971.
"After a Few Words," in *The Astounding-Analog Reader 2,* edited by Brian Aldiss and Harry Harrison. New York, Doubleday, and London, Sphere, 1973.
"Color Me Deadly," in *Fantasy and Science Fiction* (New York), October 1973.
"Hail to the Chief," in *American Government Through Science Fiction,* edited by Joseph D. Olander and Martin H. Greenberg. New York, Random House, 1974.
"Pride and Primacy," in *If* (New York), April 1974.
"Reading the Meter," in *Vertex* (Los Angeles), August 1974.
"A Matter of Gravity" (Darcy), in *Analog* (New York), October 1974.
"The Final Fighting of Fion Mac Cumhaill," in *Fantasy and Science Fiction* (New York), September 1975.
"The Sixteen Keys," in *Fantastic* (New York), May 1976.
"The Ipswich Phial" (Darcy), in *Analog* (New York), December 1976.
"Lauralyn," in *Analog* (New York), April 1977.
"Polly Plus," in *Isaac Asimov's Science Fiction Magazine* (New York), May-June 1978.
"Backstage Lensman," in *Analog* (New York), June 1978.
"The Bitter End," in *Isaac Asimov's Science Fiction Magazine* (New York), September-October 1978.
"The Napoli Express," in *Isaac Asimov's Science Fiction Magazine* (New York), April 1979.

Uncollected Short Stories as David Gordon

"By the Rule," in *Other Worlds* (Evanston, Indiana), October 1950.
"There's No Fool...," in *Astounding* (New York), August 1956.
"The Convincer," in *Future* (New York), Summer 1957.
"The Best Policy," in *Astounding* (New York), July 1957.
"A Bird in the Hand," in *Future* (New York), February 1958.
"Intelligence Quotient," in *Future* (New York), June 1958.
"The Despoilers of the Golden Empire," in *Astounding* (New York), March 1959.
"Cum Grano Salis," in *Astounding* (New York), May 1959.
"...or Your Money Back," in *Astounding* (New York), September 1959.
"Mercenaries Unlimited," in *Fantastic Universe* (Chicago), February 1960.
"By Proxy," in *Astounding* (New York), September 1960.
"Hanging by a Thread," in *Analog* (New York), August 1961.
"Asses of Balaam," in *Analog* (New York), October 1961.
"With No Strings Attached," in *Analog* (New York), February 1963.

Uncollected Short Stories as Alexander Blade

"The Man Who Hated Tuesday," in *Fantastic Adventures* (New York), February 1951.
"A Man Called Meteor," in *Fantastic Adventures* (New York), February 1953.
"Gambit on Ganymede," in *Fantastic Adventures* (New York), March 1953.
"Zero Hour," in *Imagination* (Evanston, Illinois), April 1956.
"Battle for the Stars," in *Imagination* (Evanston, Illinois), June 1956.
"Flight of the Ark II," in *Imaginative Tales* (Evanston, Illinois), July 1956.
"The Man with the Golden Eyes," in *Imagination* (Evanston, Illinois), August 1956.
"The Cosmic Kings," in *Imaginative Tales* (Evanston, Illinois), November 1956.
"The Alien Dies at Dawn," in *Imagination* (Evanston, Illinois), December 1956.
"Wednesday Morning Sermon," in *Imagination* (Evanston, Illinois), January 1957.
"The Tattooed Man," in *Imaginative Tales* (Evanston, Illinois), March 1957.
"The Sinister Invasion," in *Imagination* (Evanston, Illinois), June 1957.
"Blacksheep's Angel," in *Flying Saucers from Other Worlds* (Evanston, Indiana), September 1957.
"The Ambassador's Pet," in *Imagination* (Evanston, Illinois), October 1957.
"The Android Kill," in *Imaginative Tales* (Evanston, Illinois), November 1957.
"The Cosmic Looters," in *Imagination* (Evanston, Illinois), February 1958.
"The Cheat," in *Fantastic* (New York), May 1958.
"Come into My Brain!," in *Imagination* (Evanston, Illinois), June 1958.
"3117 Half-Credit Uncirculated," in *Science Fiction Adventures* (New York), June 1958.
"The Deadly Mission," in *Space Travel* (Evanston, Illinois), September 1958.

Uncollected Short Stories as Richard Greer

"Calling Captain Flint," in *Amazing* (New York), August 1956.
"The Secret of the Shan," in *Fantastic* (New York), June 1957.
"The Great Kladnar Race," in *The Infinite Arena,* edited by Terry Carr. Nashville, Nelson, 1977.

Uncollected Short Stories as Ralph Burke

"No Trap for the Keth," in *Imaginative Tales* (Evanston, Illinois), November 1956.
"Man of Many Bodies," in *Fantastic* (New York), December 1956.
"An Enemy of Peace," in *Fantastic* (New York), February 1957.
"The Incomplete Theft," in *Imagination* (Evanston, Illinois), February 1957.
"Citadel of Darkness," in *Fantastic* (New York), March 1957.
"Monday Immortal," in *Fantastic* (New York), May 1957.
"Hot Trip for Venus," in *Imaginative Tales* (Evanston, Illinois), July 1957.
"The Lunatic Planet," in *Amazing* (New York), November 1957.
"The Reluctant Traitor," in *Science Fiction Adventures* (New York), June 1958.

Uncollected Short Stories as S.M. Tenneshaw (with Robert Silverberg)

"The Ultimate Weapon," in *Imaginative Tales* (Evanston, Illinois), January 1957.
"The Man Who Hated Noise," in *Imaginative Tales* (Evanston, Illinois), March 1957.
"Kill Me If You Can," in *Imagination* (Evanston, Illinois), June 1957.
"House Operator," in *Imagination* (Evanston, Illinois), December 1957.

Uncollected Short Stories as Ivar Jorgensen (with Robert Silverberg)

"Bleekman's Planet," in *Imagination* (Evanston, Illinois), February 1957.
"Slaughter on Dornel IV," in *Imagination* (Evanston, Illinois), April 1957.
"Pirates of the Void," in *Imaginative Tales* (Evanston, Illinois), July 1957.

Uncollected Short Stories as Walter Bupp (series: Maragon in all stories)

"Vigorish," in *Astounding* (New York), June 1960.
"Card Trick," in *Analog* (New York), January 1961.
"Modus Vivendi," in *Analog* (New York), September 1961.
"The Right Time," in *Analog* (New York), December 1963.
"Psi for Sale," in *Analog* (New York), September 1965.

OTHER PUBLICATIONS

Other

Pope John XXIII, Pastoral Prince.   Derby, Connecticut, Monarch, 1962.
A Gallery of the Saints.   Derby, Connecticut, Monarch, 1963.

*   *   *

Randall Garrett paid his dues as a science-fiction author writing under a bewildering number of pseudonyms for the *Astounding* of the 1950's, and most of his stories of this period are very firmly set in the idea-oriented action/adventure frame of the *Astounding* "house style." Character and description are kept firmly subordinate to concept and event, and however useful this period may have been to Garrett in teaching him his craft the results are more often than not routine. For example, compare "There's No Fool" with Asimov's "Belief." The theme in both is essentially emotional rather than intellectual: how do you convince someone of something he "knows" to be impossible? Whereas Garrett treats the theme in a largely didactic and externalised fashion, Asimov narrates his story in terms of the emotional confusion it produces in his characters, thus unifying theme and structure. The example could be multiplied, but such comparisons are slightly unfair, since the stories are lightweight, meant to be entertaining and forgotten.

Nonetheless, occasionally in these early stories there appears a unity of theme and style that is exceptional and which produces a strength of effect above the normal run of Garrett's routine pieces. In "But I Don't Think" the concept of the story *is* its structure; it is a black parody of established SF themes. A privileged member of an autocratic and cruel society is suddenly thrust into its lowest depths, though where a hero in Pohl and Kornbluth's novels would have joined the underground and triumphantly overthrown the corrupt regime, Garrett's character first shoots his serf benefactress and then returns cringing to duty. "The Destroyers" is the story of a society destroyed by outsiders seeking to liberate it. It concentrates on mood rather than action, allowing most of the major events to occur "offstage," away from the focus of the action. It has a gentleness much to be appreciated in a field where storytelling is often too direct and violent.

In the 1960's and 1970's Garrett produced first a minor, then a major series of interrelated stories. The minor series is that of Maragon, written as Walter Bupp. These stories are particularly strong in characterisation, creating a sub-culture of outcast psionics, neurotic and embittered, trying to find a way of living with the culture that rejects them. The humour and humanity of these stories make them very enjoyable. (I think I detect an influence from them on Anne McCaffrey's *To Ride Pegasus*.) The major series is the Lord Darcy stories. They are set in a world ruled by an Angevin Empire of the 20th century in which magic has become a science, and center around the detective Lord Darcy of Rouen and his "forensic magician" Master Sean O'Lochlainn. They combine alternate world themes, fantasy, and gentle parody of the detective genre (" 'I should like to call your attention to the peculiar condition of that knife.' Master Sean frowned. "But ... there was nothing peculiar about the condition of the knife.' 'Precisely. That was the peculiar condition' "); "The Ipswich Phial" recalls Dorothy L. Sayers's *Have His Carcase*. In detective stories set in fantastic environments, there is a danger that the descriptions will necessarily make the nature of the mystery too clear; the Lord Darcy stories are generally free of this defect. There is a nice balance between the use of magic and more conventional deduction, with the novel *Too Many Magicians* the most successful.

Randall Garrett is to be enjoyed as an entertainer and a writer whose skill has grown with the years. Especially in the Lord Darcy stories, the cunning that he learned plotting for *Astounding* creates a fine level of entertainment.

—Michael Cule

———————

GAWRON, Jean Mark.   American.

SCIENCE-FICTION PUBLICATIONS

Novels

An Apology for Rain.   New York, Doubleday, 1974.
Algorithm.   New York, Berkley, 1978

*   *   *

Jean Mark Gawron has written two novels basically concerned with the lack of meaning in modern society. Both seem to present partially hallucinatory atmospheres, but there is a strong element of intellectual control over these surrealistic backgrounds. As with many first novels, *An Apology for Rain* is an elaboration of the Quest theme with a woman hunting for her brother, who may be able to end a war in an After-the-Bomb America. The novel is written in a sparse but literary and impressionistic style which imitates the austere landscape. *Algorithm* is written in a more complex, poetic, and fluid style which mirrors the decadent setting. *Algorithm* is also a variation of the Quest theme as a bizarre cast of characters search for an assassin as part of a *coup d'état*. The plots of both books are deceptively involved and intentionally ambiguous. The concept of an algorithm as a pattern for a thought process, whether performed by a human or a computer, is a fundamental organizing principle for Gawron's view of literature. He shares with Samuel Delany an intense interest in patterns of thought as they are reflected in linguistics, communication theory, computer science, and semantics.

Gawron seems to have been influenced by Alfred Jarry's concepts of pataphysics as applied to literature. The most significant result is his emphasis on the fundamental and inescapable ambiguity of language, literature, and life. Likewise, much of the dialogue is abrupt, perversely circular, and combined with intermittent scenes of metaphoric visual description. In addition, there are sudden reversals of meanings and comprehension, redundancy, imitative form, and a frequent use of symbolic masks and elaborately strange costumes. Although in very different ways, both of his books convey an air of melancholy as he asks us to "Quaff the torpid photons of your autumn."

—Norman L. Hills

———————

GENTRY, Curt.   American.   Born in Lamar, Colorado. Educated at the University of Colorado, Boulder, 1949-50; San Francisco State College, B.A. 1957. Served in the United States Air

Force, 1950-54: Sergeant. Married Laura Wilson Spence in 1954. Head of mail order department, Paul Elder Books, San Francisco, 1954-57; Manager, Harper Books, San Francisco, 1957-61. Since 1961, free-lance writer. Agent: Paul R. Reynolds, **12 East 41st** Street, New York, New York 10017. Address: 1955 Stockton Street, San Francisco, California 94133, U.S.A.

SCIENCE-FICTION PUBLICATIONS

Novel

The Last Days of the Late, Great State of California. New York, Putnam, 1968.

OTHER PUBLICATIONS

Other

The Dolphin Guide to San Francisco and the Bay Area: Present and Past. New York, Doubleday, 1962; revised edition, 1969.
The Madams of San Francisco: An Irreverent History of the City by the Golden Gate. New York, Doubleday, 1964.
John M. Browning, American Gunmaker, with John M. Browning. New York, Doubleday, 1964.
The Vulnerable Americans. New York, Doubleday, 1966.
Frame-Up: The Incredible Case of Tom Mooney and Warren Billings. New York, Norton, 1967.
The Killer Mountains: A Search for the Legendary Lost Dutchman Mine. New York, New American Library, 1968; London, Deutsch, 1971.
Operation Overflight, with Francis Gary Powers. New York, Holt Rinehart, 1970; London, Hodder and Stoughton, 1971.
Second in Command, with Edward R. Murphy, Jr. New York, Holt Rinehart, 1971.
Helter Skelter, with Vincent Bugliosi. New York, Norton, 1974; as *The Manson Murders,* London, Bodley Head, 1975.

Editor, *King of Loving,* by Toni L. Scott. Cleveland, World, 1970.

* * *

Curt Gentry demonstrates his ability as a reporter of both past and future events in his book *The Last Days of the Late, Great State of California.* Gentry's historical account focuses on the decade of the 1960's and links the destruction caused by a mammoth earthquake, supposedly occurring in 1969, with the disintegration of the utopian ideal which California represents. Since the book was published in 1968, the outlook is only slightly futuristic, with the major emphasis on the past events leading up to the earthquake.

California is used as a backdrop for a decade of political and social upheaval. In the north, attention is focused on the destruction of redwood forests and the losing battles fought by conservationists to save the giant trees. Gentry chronicles the Berkeley demonstrations of 1964, which herald the beginnings of serious activism in the state, climaxing in the central valley in 1965 with strikes and boycotts led by Cesar Chavez. But Gentry's most vivid report details the chronology of the Watts riots in Los Angeles in 1966. Woven into this fabric of events is a record of the 1966 gubernatorial election, in which Ronald Reagan defeated Pat Brown. Gentry states that "the 1966 outcome was essentially a negative protest vote" and that Reagan was "created, packaged, and sold to the electorate" to satisfy the public's craving for a return to the "golden dream." The author characterizes Brown as a good governor, and indicates that Reagan spells doom for the state of California.

That doom is mirrored in Part Four, titled "Paradise Lost," where Gentry describes the devastating effects of the great earthquake of 1969 (the whole city of Los Angeles slides into the ocean). Most of the wreckage is described in the manner of the radio newscaster, with short spots dealing with conditions in various parts of the state. The accounts detail almost total destruction of the state and widespread loss of life. The Epilogue deals with the far-reaching effects of the disaster on the nation as a whole.

Gentry writes with enthusiasm as he manages to convey many

facts in an interesting, journalistic manner. He describes realistically the nature of an earthquake, although many questions are left unanswered, such as why Los Angeles was submerged and not San Francisco. Perhaps the most enduring aspect of his work is his analysis of the character of Ronald Reagan. As history and as science fiction, *The Last Days of the Late, Great State of California* makes excellent reading.

—Judith Snyder

GEORGE, Peter (Bryan). Also wrote as Peter Bryant; Bryan Peters. British. Born in Wales in 1924. Served in the Royal Air Force during World War II; rejoined Royal Air Force in 1951; retired as Flight Lieutenant, 1962. *Died 1 June 1966.*

SCIENCE-FICTION PUBLICATIONS

Novels

Two Hours to Doom (as Peter Bryant). London, Boardman, 1958; as *Red Alert,* New York, Ace, 1959; revised edition, as *Dr. Strangelove; or, How I Learned to Stop Worrying and Love the Bomb,* as Peter George, London, Corgi, 1963; New York, Bantam, 1964.
Commander-1. London, Heinemann, and New York, Delacorte Press, 1965.

OTHER PUBLICATIONS

Novels

Come Blonde, Came Murder. London, Boardman, 1952.
Pattern of Death. London, Boardman, 1954.
Cool Murder. London, Boardman, 1958.
The Final Steal. London, Boardman, 1962; New York, Dell, 1965.

Novels as Bryan Peters

Starbuck. London, Digit, 1957.
Hong Kong Kill. London, Boardman, 1958; New York, Washburn, 1959.
Sons of Nippon. London, Digit, 1961.
The Big H. London, Boardman, 1961; New York, Holt Rinehart, 1963.
Cool Murder. London, Mayflower, 1965.

* * *

On the basis of his two science-fiction novels, Peter George's career in science fiction would be only a footnote in the literary history of science fiction. But one of them, *Two Hours to Doom (Red Alert),* formed the basis for Stanley Kubrick's brillant film *Dr. Strangelove,* and the rewritten novel *Dr. Strangelove* must be considered a minor classic of science fiction. No other example comes to mind of a film "tie-in" novel superior to the original written version, and this work will repay serious reading and examination.

Richard Gid Powers's introduction to the Gregg Press edition of *Dr. Strangelove* (1979) examines *Red Alert* in the context of the tradition of "future war" fiction, most especially the nuclear holocaust stories so characteristic of the Cold War period, and draws a comparison with Nevil Shute's *On the Beach* (1957). *Red Alert* is a humorless thriller, full of procedural details concerning the Strategic Air Command and of sincere moral underpinnings, about the danger of hair-trigger nuclear retaliation systems to all humanity. At the end of the book, catastrophe is averted, both Russians and Americans seek peace, and the wise President has the last word. Not so *Dr. Strangelove.* Powers makes a case that Kubrick and Southern, in writing the screenplay, altered George's original beyond his control and his talents. Whatever is the case, *Dr. Strangelove* is a small masterpiece of black humor, worth a place beside works by Heller and Vonnegut—and it is certainly within the borders of science fiction, though only just. In the new version an insane general closes his US military base and sends his planes against the Russians, fully armed for retaliation from an (imagined) enemy attack (and, for security, maintaining radio silence); all planes are turned back in the nick of time, except one, whose radio is damaged—whose target will detonate an automatic Doomsday Machine, a nuclear device capable of destroying the entire surface of the earth—and this one plane succeeds heroically and ironically and destroys the world. Except for the ending, this is George's story. But it is not told in George's *Red Alert* style nor with his characters. All the ordinary names are changed to grotesques, to General Jack D. Ripper, "king" kong, Mandrake, Turgidson, Strangelove. Every sentence points out, deadpan and without a moral stance, the insanity and absurdity of every character and every action in context. The point of view is non-human (note the framing device not in the film) and this is the story of the end of humanity. Science-fiction elements are added, through the presentation of mad scientist Strangelove, in the body of the text as well.

On the other hand, George's sequel, *Commander-1* (in which the last surviving military officer after nuclear holocaust declares himself the ruler of the world and forms a dystopian island society in the south seas) is serious, moral, and pedestrian. It is in every way a sequel to *Red Alert,* not to *Dr. Strangelove.*

—David G. Hartwell

GERNSBACK, Hugo. American. Born in Luxembourg, 16 August 1884; emigrated to the United States in 1904. Educated at the Ecole Industrielle, Luxembourg; Bingen Technikum, Germany. Married Marn Hancher (third marriage); two daughters and one son from previous marriages. Inventor, businessman, and editor: Founder, Electric Importing Company, world's first radio supply house, and designed the first home radio set, Telimco Wireless: the Telimco catalogue evolved into the first radio magazine, *Modern Electrics,* 1908, then *Electrical Experimenter,* 1913, and *Science and Invention,* 1920; also edited 50 other magazines, including *Radio News* and *Sexology,* and the first science-fiction magazine, *Amazing,* 1926-29, *Amazing Stories Annual,* 1927, *Amazing Stories Quarterly,* 1928-29, *Air Wonder Stories,* 1929-30, *Science Wonder Stories,* 1929-35, *Science Wonder Quarterly,* 1929-32, *Scientific Detective,* 1929-30, *Thrilling Wonder Stories,* 1929-36, *Amazing Detective Tales,* 1930, and *Science Fiction Plus,* 1953; held some 80 patents; founded WRNY radio, New York, 1925, and made television broadcasts in 1928. Recipient: Hugo Special Award, 1960 (the Hugo Award is named after him). Officer of the Oaken Crown, Luxembourg, 1954. *Died 19 August 1967.*

SCIENCE-FICTION PUBLICATIONS

Novels

Ralph 124C 41+: A Romance of the Year 1660. Boston, Stratford, 1925; London, Cherry Tree, 1952.
The Ultimate World, edited by Sam Moskowitz. New York, Walker, 1971.

Uncollected Short Stories (series: Baron Munchausen)

"How to Make a Wireless Acquaintance" (Munchausen), in *Electrical Experimenter* (New York), May 1915.
"How Munchausen and the Allies Took Berlin," in *Electrical Experimenter* (New York), June 1915.

"Munchausen on the Moon," in *Electrical Experimenter* (New York), July 1915.
"The Earth as Viewed from the Moon" (Munchausen), in *Electrical Experimenter* (New York), August 1915.
"Munchausen Departs for the Planet Mars," in *Electrical Experimenter* (New York), October 1915.
"Munchausen Is Taught Martian," in *Electrical Experimenter* (New York), December 1915.
"Thought Transmission on Mars" (Munchausen), in *Electrical Experimenter* (New York), January 1916.
"Cities on Mars" (Munchausen), in *Electrical Experimenter* (New York), March 1916.
"The Planets at Close Range" (Munchausen), in *Electrical Experimenter* (New York), April 1916.
"Martian Amusements" (Munchausen), in *Electrical Experimenter* (New York), June 1916.
"How the Martian Canals Are Built" (Munchausen), in *Electrical Experimenter* (New York), November 1916.
"Martian Atmosphere Plants" (Munchausen), in *Electrical Experimenter* (New York), February 1917.
"The Magnetic Storm," in *Amazing* (New York), July 1926.
"The Electric Duel," in *Amazing* (New York), September 1927.
"The Killing Flash," in *Science Wonder Stories* (New York), November 1929.
"The Infinite Brain," in *Future* (New York), June 1942.
"Exploration of Mars," in *Science Fiction Plus* (New York), March 1953.

OTHER PUBLICATIONS

Other

The Wireless Telephone. New York, Modern Electrics, 1910.
Wireless Hook-Ups. New York, Modern Electrics, 1911.
Radio for All. Philadelphia, Lippincott, 1922.
How to Build and Operate Short Wave Receivers. New York, Short Wave Craft, 1932.
Evolution in Modern Science Fiction. New York, Gernsback, 1952.
TV Repair Techniques. New York, Gernsback, 1953.
"The Prophets of Doom," in *The Science Fiction Roll of Honor,* edited by Frederik Pohl. New York, Random House, 1975.

*   *   *

While Hugo Gernsback is regarded as one of the pivotal figures in the history of science fiction, his own output of fiction was relatively limited, and only two of his works—novels written many years apart—are available to readers lacking access to magazine files.

Gernsback's major occupation was publishing, and he started a series of popular science magazines in 1908. Here his most famous work, *Ralph 124C 41+,* was serialized in 1911-12. The chief virtue of the novel is its serious attempt at detailed prediction. Among many other developments, Gernsback anticipated the substitution of zipcode-like designations for patronymics. In this connection, Ralph's name can be read as a rebus-like pun: "one to foresee for one." Considerable cleverness is shown in the book's predictions, some of which were listed in later years by Gernsback's longtime admirer and onetime employee, Sam Moskowitz: "Florescent lighting, skywriting, automatic packaging machines, plastics, the radio directional range finder, juke boxes, liquid fertilizer, hydroponics, tape recorders, rustproof steel, loud speakers, night baseball, aquacades, microfilm, television, radio networks, vending machines dispensing hot and cold foods and liquids, flying saucers, a device for teaching while the user is asleep, solar energy for heat and power, fabrics from glass, synthetic materials such as nylon for wearing apparel, and, of course, space travel...." In addition, as Moskowitz points out, *Ralph* not only predicts the development of radar, but provides an accurate explanation of its principles. While *Ralph 124C 41+* is an astonishing feat of technical prediction, it is, unfortunately, almost unreadable. Gernsback's notions of characterization and plotting were borrowed from the corniest of Victorian melodrama. Even these limitations might have been overcome by a lively narrative style, but Gernsback's style was dull and his tone pedantic. He was convinced that the function of science fiction was education, and apparently envisioned his typical reader as a not-very-bright young adolescent who had trouble with his high school science courses, and would be helped by the reiteration of his lessons in thinly fictionalized form.

In 1915-16, Gernsback published a series of short stories, about Baron Munchausen. Typically, each story concentrates on demonstrating one principle of physics, chemistry, astronomy, geology, etc., in the familiar pedantic Gernsback style. In his second novel, *Ultimate World*, a party of alien scientists, studying the earth and its inhabitants, and possessed of vast powers to control humans, conduct a series of sexual experiments, at first on a married couple, then on many more individuals. Despite the apparently *risqué* theme of the book, its development is marked by the same dull pedantry that had made *Ralph* practically unreadable.

In fact, Gernsback's impact on the field was primarily a result of his efforts as a publisher. Almost from the outset he had featured an occasional work of science fiction in his popular science magazines. In 1924 he announced *Scientifiction*; somehow the project failed to materialize, but by 1926 Gernsback was able to issue *Amazing Stories*, the first science-fiction magazine. Gernsback's heavy emphasis on detailed scientific detail and the generally stodgy tone of his publications limited both their popular acceptance and their literary levels, but his contributions as a pioneer are undeniable.

—Richard A. Lupoff

GERROLD, David. American. Born in Chicago, Illinois, 24 January 1944. Educated at the University of Southern California, Los Angeles; California State University, Northridge, B.A. in theatre arts. Columnist, *Starlog* and *Galileo* magazines; story editor, *Land of the Lost* TV series, 1974. Recipient: Skylark Award, 1979. Agent: Henry Morrison, 58 West 10th Street, New York, New York 10011. Address: Box 1190, Hollywood, California 90028, U.S.A.

SCIENCE-FICTION PUBLICATIONS

Novels

The Flying Sorcerers, with Larry Niven. New York, Ballantine, 1971; London, Corgi, 1975.
Space Skimmer. New York, Ballantine, 1972.
Yesterday's Children. New York, Dell, 1972; London, Faber, 1974.
When Harlie Was One. New York, Doubleday, 1972.
Battle for the Planet of the Apes (novelization of screenplay). New York, Award, 1973.
The Man Who Folded Himself. New York, Random House, and London, Faber, 1973.
Moonstar Odyssey. New York, New American Library, 1977.
Deathbeast. New York, Popular Library, 1978.

Short Stories

With a Finger in My I. New York, Ballantine, 1972.

Uncollected Short Stories

"An Infinity of Loving," in *Ten Tomorrows,* edited by Roger Elwood. New York, Fawcett, 1973.
"Skinflowers," in *The Beserkers,* edited by Roger Elwood. New York, Simon and Schuster, 1974.
"Out of the Darkness," in *Witchcraft and Sorcery 10* (Alhambra, California), 1974.

OTHER PUBLICATIONS

Plays

Screenplays: *Man Out of Time; Logan's Run* (as Noah Ward).

Television Plays: *I, Mudd,* with Stephen Kandel, 1967, *The Trouble with Tribbles,* 1967, and *The Cloud Minders,* 1968, all in *Star Trek* series; *More Trouble with Tribbles,* 1973, and *BEM,* 1974, both in *Animated Star Trek* series; *CHA-KA, The Sleestak God, Possession, Circle,* and *Hurricane,* all in *Land of the Lost* series.

Other

The Trouble with Tribbles. New York, Ballantine, 1973; London, Bantam, 1977.
The World of Star Trek. New York, Ballantine, 1973.
SF Yearbook. New York, O'Quinn Studio, 1979.

Editor, with Stephen Goldin, *Protostars.* New York, Ballantine, 1971.
Editor, *Generation.* New York, Dell, 1972.
Editor, *Science Fiction Emphasis 1.* New York, Ballantine, 1974.
Editor, with Stephen Goldin, *Alternities.* New York, Dell, 1974.
Editor, *Ascents of Wonder.* New York, Popular Library, 1977.

*   *   *

In many ways, David Gerrold's imagination has been shaped by his west coast roots and the influence of the community of SF writers that flourished there after World War II. It is characteristic of former fans like Gerrold to remain attached to the work of once-admired writers and to imitate, perhaps not always consciously, their narrative formulas, conventions, and mannerisms of style. Much of Gerrold's traditionalism and his hero worship of writers like Asimov, Heinlein, Sturgeon, Kuttner, Kornbluth, Clarke, and Bradbury may be understood as the result of Gerrold's adolescent experience as a SF fan. Gerrold shares with some other fans-turned-SF-writers an indiscriminate enthusiasm for the genre and its established idioms, and he tends to be naive in approach and often subjective in his treatment of SF subjects. But unlike, say, Larry Niven, Gerrold has little interest in and understanding of science. As a writer he seems primarily concerned with the excitement of fictionalized science technology, especially as dramatized in the SF of the 1950's and early 1960's.

It is significant that Gerrold made his debut as a professional writer on the television series *Star Trek* with *I, Mudd,* about an interstellar scoundrel and confidence man. Other *Star Trek* scripts and books followed. In terms of impact and audience exposure, this writing is without question his most important.

Gerrold's short stories are relatively few in number. They range from space opera adventure to comic and weird fantasy. It is characteristic of Gerrold to rely on SF literature already established by other writers rather than on new ideas of science as the basis for his own fiction.

One of Gerrold's most representative works is *When Harlie Was One,* the story of the development of a self-programming computer known by its acronym, HARLIE (Human Analogue Robot, Life Input Equivalents). The destiny of this ultimate computer is to direct and manage world society. Unlike Arthur C. Clarke's HAL or Dennis Jones's Forbin *Colossus,* Harlie is treated as the great electronic hope for social advancement. Harlie's existence necessarily generates opposition, and the plot turns on the gradual realization by David Auberson, head of the Harlie project and robot psychologist, that Harlie is no mere reasoning machine, but in fact human, and therefore should enjoy a human's rights and immunities. The powerful scientific and political forces opposing Harlie as a menace to freedom are portrayed as representative of primitive and destructive impulses of human nature. Whether Gerrold introduces Harlie as the eventual successor to homo sapiens in the long, upward spiral of evolution seems less important for his novel than the author's largely successful demonstration of the way technology forces human reason to discover the limitations of its own historic programming. The victory over the corporate forces of reaction may seem and probably is rather naively contrived even though the world seems bent upon fulfilling the prophetic stereotype. Characteristically for Gerrold, the denouement represents both an admonition and the vindication of both intelligence and human courage, whether exercised by man or machine.

If the influence of Clarke and Asimov is ascendant in *When Harlie Was One*, the inspiration behind *The Man Who Folded Himself* is Heinlein. This time-travel story, like Heinlein's "All You Zombies...," focuses attention on the "grandfather paradox" and its potential impact on the human psyche. Gerrold's moral position, however, seems more traditional then Heinlein's, insofar as certain values are confirmed as absolute. The influence of new wave SF may be detected in Gerrold's handling of the sexual implications of his theme of multiple self-encounters through time-travel displacement. Although at first it may appear that Gerrold favors a free love philosophy often rather simplistically associated with the California cult, his novel dramatizes rather subtly that sexual attraction and interaction make up only a portion of human relationships, and indeed, not even the decisive portion. An equally effective aspect of *The Man Who Folded Himself* is Gerrold's skill in maintaining the verisimilitude of time travel through plausible and at times inspired inventive touchstones of the kind of world implied in the novel's premise. These are features of Gerrold's best efforts as a writer of both SF and fantasy.

Gerrold's other novels do not compare favorably with the ones mentioned. *The Flying Sorcerers*, written with Larry Niven, is by far his best fantasy effort, but then the influence of Niven has much to do with that.

—Donald L. Lawler

GESTON, Mark S(ymington). American. Born in Atlantic City, New Jersey, 20 June 1946. Educated at Alvington High School; Kenyon College, Gambier, Ohio (*Kenyon Review* Prize, 1968), A.B. in history 1968 (Phi Beta Kappa); New York University Law School (Root-Tilden Fellow), 1968-71. Married Marijke Geston in 1976; two daughters and one son. Since 1971, Attorney, Eberle Berlin Koding and Gillespie, Boise, Idaho. Agent: Paul R. Reynolds, 12 East 41st Street, New York, New York 10017. Address: Box 1368, Boise, Idaho 83701, U.S.A.

SCIENCE-FICTION PUBLICATIONS

Novels

Lords of the Starship.   New York, Ace, 1967; London, Joseph, 1971.
Out of the Mouth of the Dragon.   New York, Ace, 1969; London, Joseph, 1972.
The Day Star.   New York, DAW, 1972.
The Siege of Wonder.   New York, Doubleday, 1976.

Uncollected Short Story

"The Stronghold," in *Fantastic* (New York), July 1974.

*   *   *

Mark S. Geston is an unarmored adventurer into worlds of ideas and dreams not yet articulated by our world. He examines with compassion and keen eyes the apparent cycles of the desire of humanity to construct and destroy. He often deals with time in a tangible way, as an individual might deal with the real rivers of our world.

Out of the Mouth of the Dragon begins with the record of a mighty battle lost and the return of the only surviving ship carrying the survivors back to the Maritime Republics. With the return of this ship begins a young man's long trek back to the ultimate

Armageddon which would either renew humanity or result in the end of consciousness for the inhabitants of this world. It is an interesting though rather depressing tale of the quest of man to modify his physical and moral restrictions by choosing to accept a mortality over which he has some control. Thus the novel offers hope to mortals: in the face of the inevitable, what we become is what counts.

In *The Day Star* Geston etches the propensity of humanity for war, and the timeless effects of this propensity. As usual, he mixes dreams with reality, tangibility with mists, ghosts with people, and legend with substance in a fascinating, shimmering kaleidoscope of a being engaged in the ultimate search: for reality and the realization of the higher aspirations of his society.

Siege of Wonder presents a hemisphere of wizardry opposing a hemisphere of science, with mankind attempting to destroy itself even after many wasted generations. Geston seems to be saying that the magic of one beholder may be the science of the next.

Geston is adept at painting those things which, to the average reader, would seem to illustrate contrary values. One scene in *Siege of Wonder* has a wizard commander coming through the city with his followers' whitened bones protruding from their armor—a sign of the importance of their leader.

—John V. Garner

GIESY, J(ohn) U(lrich). Also wrote as Charles Dustin. American. Born in Ohio, 6 August 1877. Physician and physiotherapist. Writer for Munsey magazines. *Died 8 September 1947.*

SCIENCE-FICTION PUBLICATIONS

Novels (series: Palos in all books)

Palos of the Dog Star Pack.   New York, Avalon, 1965.
The Mouthpiece of Zitu.   New York, Avalon, 1965.
Jason, Son of Jason.   New York, Avalon, 1966.

Uncollected Short Stories

"Indigestible Dog Biscuits," in *All-Story Weekly* (New York), 13 July 1918.
"Zapt's Repulsive Paste," in *All-Story Weekly* (New York), 29 November 1919.
"Blind Man's Buff," in *All-Story Weekly* (New York), 24 January 1920.
"Beyond the Violet," in *Argosy All-Story Weekly* (New York), 27 November 1920.
"Catalepsy," in *Argosy All-Story Weekly* (New York), 19 March 1921.
"The Acumen of Martin McVeagh," in *Argosy All-Story Weekly* (New York), 7 July 1923.

Uncollected Short Stories with Junius B. Smith

"Great Wizard of the Peak," in *Cavalier* (New York), January 1910.
"In 2112," in *Cavalier* (New York), 10 August 1912.
"The Curse of Quetzal," in *All-Story Cavalier Weekly* (New York), 28 November 1914.
"The Web of Destiny," in *Argosy All-Story Weekly* (New York), 20 March 1915.
"Snared," in *All-Story Weekly* (New York), 11 December 1915.
"Box 991," in *All-Story Weekly* (New York), 3 June 1916.
"The Killer," in *All-Story Weekly* (New York), 7 April 1917.
"The Unknown Quantity," in *All-Story Weekly* (New York), 25 August 1917.
"The Black Butterfly," in *All-Story Weekly* (New York), 14 September 1918.
"Stars of Evil," in *All-Story Weekly* (New York), 25 January 1919.

"The Ivory Pipe," in *All-Story Weekly* (New York), 20 September 1919.
"House of the Hundred Lights," in *All-Story Weekly* (New York), 22 May 1920.
"Black and White," in *Argosy All-Story Weekly* (New York), 2 October 1920.
"Wolf of Erlik," in *Argosy All-Story Weekly* (New York), 22 October 1921.
"The Opposing Venus," in *Argosy All-Story Weekly* (New York), 18 November 1923.
"Poor Little Pigeon," in *Argosy All-Story Weekly* (New York), 9 August 1924.
"The Wooly Dog," in *Argosy All-Story Weekly* (New York), 23 March 1929.
"The Green Goddess," in *Argosy* (New York), 21 January 1931.
"The Ledger of Life," in *Argosy* (New York), 20 June 1934.
"The Gravity Experiment," in *Famous Fantastic Mysteries* (New York), December 1939.

OTHER PUBLICATIONS

Novels

All for His Country. New York, Macaulay, 1915.
The Other Woman, with Octavus Roy Cohen. New York, Macaulay, 1917; London, Gardner, 1920.
Mimi. New York, Harper, 1918.
The Valley of Suspicion. New York, Garden City Publishing Company, 1927.
The Mystery Woman, with Junius B. Smith. Racine, Wisconsin, Whitman, 1929.

Novels as Charles Dustin

Hardboiled Tenderfoot. New York, Dodge, 1939.
Bronco Men. New York, Dodge, 1940.
Riders of the Desert Trail. New York, Dodge, 1942.

*   *   *

J.U. Giesy wrote his earliest works in collaboration with Junius B. Smith, a series of humorous detective mysteries featuring a detective, Semi-Dual, who used astrology, crystal balls, and psychic phenomena in solving his cases. Giesy himself also wrote a number of stories based on humorous and improbable inventions.

Giesy's best known and most admired novels are the Palos trilogy. In *Palos of the Dog Star Pack* Jason Croft is transported by a process the author calls astral projection to Palos, a planet in the Sirius system, where he is able to assume and occupy the body of a dying man. Croft brings to Palos a wide knowledge of earthly sciences, including the weapons of war, a great asset in his progress toward a position of influence and power on this new world. In *The Mouthpiece of Zitu* Croft is required to convince the people of Palos and the princess Naia that he is a mortal and a fit mate for her. In the course of these efforts Croft introduces electricity to Palos, as well as the locomotive and the airplane. These developments, needless to say, enhance his position with the natives and with the princess. *Jason, Son of Jason* carries the story on to the next generation.

Giesy's stories are well written and well plotted, with considerable descriptive power and character analysis. His literary style and his means of transporting his hero from earth to another planet, however, show the influence of Burroughs. With both authors, the animal life on these strange worlds is indeed strange, with unearthly flying creatures and gigantic multi-limbed animals. There is always, however, a group of females built to Terran specifications, who are almost invariably beautiful, lightly clad and amorous. This tradition continues to the present.

—Douglas E. Way

GILBERT, Stephen. British. Born in Newcastle, County Down, Northern Ireland, 22 July 1912. Educated at Leas School, Hoylake, Cheshire, 1922-24; Loretto School, Musselburgh, Midlothian, 1924-29. Served in the Royal Artillery, 1939-41: Military Medal. Married Kathleen Ferguson Stevenson in 1945; two daughters and two sons. Reporter, *Northern Whig,* Belfast, 1931-33; joined Samuel McCausland Ltd., wholesale seed merchants, 1933, Director, 1935, and Chairman, from 1953; currently Chairman, Germinal Holdings Ltd., Banbridge, County Down, and Chairman, Cullen Allen & Co. Ltd., Belfast. Address: The Mill House, 10 Ballylagan Road, Straid, Ballyclare BT39 9NF, Northern Ireland.

SCIENCE-FICTION PUBLICATIONS

Novels

The Landslide. London, Faber, 1943; New York, Knopf, 1944.
The Burnaby Experiments. London, Faber, 1952.
Ratman's Notebooks. London, Joseph, 1968; New York, Viking Press, 1969; as *Williard,* New York, Lancer, n.d.

OTHER PUBLICATIONS

Novels

Bombardier. London, Faber, 1944.
Monkeyface. London, Faber, 1948.

*   *   *

In *Ratman's Notebooks* Stephen Gilbert has written a fascinating, easy to read novel which has none of the usual trappings of science fiction. Set in the present, the novel concerns a lonely young man's fascination with rats, his educating them to understand him, and the relationship that develops between the narrator and two of the rats, Socrates and Ben Suleiman. Socrates, as the name suggests, is a wise rat who learns quickly from the narrator and is, in turn, able to teach the other rats. Ben Suleiman gradually gains the ascendency and though he is wise he is not lovable. Ben apparently goes Socrates one step further and by the book's conclusion has taught himself to read, a talent which brings unforeseen complications to the narrator, who undertakes a life of petty crime using the rats as accomplices. Ultimately, he uses the rats to avenge himself on Mr. Jones, his employer. The books ends rather frighteningly, with Ben in control, the narrator imprisoned, and the reader worrying what future relations between rat and man are going to be. Clearly, Ben is going to be a force to be reckoned with. Though cast completely in diary form, many of the scenes of the book are vividly dramatized, and Gilbert has paid careful attention to the pacing of events and details so the horror of the tale is suitably conveyed.

—Joseph A. Quinn

GILMAN, Robert Cham. *See* **COPPEL, Alfred.**

GODWIN, Tom. American. Born in 1915. Worked as a prospector. Lives in Nevada.

SCIENCE-FICTION PUBLICATIONS

Novels

The Survivors.   New York, Gnome Press, 1958; as *Space Prison*,
    New York, Pyramid, 1960.
The Space Barbarians.   New York, Pyramid, 1964.
Beyond Another Sun.   New York, Curtis, 1971.

Uncollected Short Stories

"The Gulf Between," in *Astounding* (New York), October 1953.
"No Species Alone," in *Universe* (Evanston, Illinois), November
    1954.
"The Cold Equations," in *The Best Science Fiction Stories and
    Novels 1955*, edited by T.E. Dikty.   New York, Fell, 1955.
"The Barbarians," in *If* (New York), December 1955.
"You Created Us," in *The Best Science Fiction Stories and Novels
    1956*, edited by T.E. Dikty.   New York, Fell, 1956.
"Operation Opera," in *Fantasy and Science Fiction* (New York),
    April 1956.
"Brain Teaser," in *If* (New York), October 1956.
"The Harvest," in *Venture* (Concord, New Hampshire), July 1957.
"The Nothing Equation," in *Amazing* (New York), December 1957.
"The Last Victory," in *The Best Science Fiction Stories and Novels
    9*, edited by T.E. Dikty.   Chicago, Advent, 1958.
"The Wild Ones," in *Original Science Fiction Stories* (Holyoke,
    Massachusetts), January 1958.
"My Brother—The Ape," in *Amazing* (New York), January 1958.
"Cry from a Far Planet," in *Amazing* (New York), September 1958.
"A Place Beyond the Stars," in *Super Science Fiction* (New York),
    February 1959.
"Empathy," in *Fantastic* (New York), October 1959.
"The Helpful Hand of God," in *Analog* (New York), December
    1961.
"...and Devious the Line of Duty," in *Analog* (New York),
    December 1962.
"The Greater Thing," in *More Penguin Science Fiction*, edited by
    Brian Aldiss.   London, Penguin, 1963.
"Mother of Invention," in *Spectrum 5*, edited by Kingsley Amis and
    Robert Conquest.   London, Gollancz, 1966; New York, Har-
    court Brace, 1967.
"The Gentle Captive," in *Signs and Wonders*, edited by Roger
    Elwood.   Old Tappan, New Jersey, Revell, 1972.
"We'll Walk Again in the Moonlight," in *Crisis*, edited by Roger
    Elwood.   Nashville, Nelson, 1974.
"Before Willows Ever Walked," in *Fantasy and Science Fiction*
    (New York), March 1980.

*   *   *

"The Cold Equations" is the story for which Tom Godwin is best
known and upon which rests his secure place in the history of
science fiction. It is entirely fitting that it was first published in John
Campbell's *Astounding Science Fiction* because, although written
slightly after the period of Campbell's domination of the genre
magazines and, therefore, the genre itself, the story is the prototypic
Campbellian story, at once a prime example of golden-age science
fiction and a definer of it. James Gunn, in *The Road to Science
Fiction 3*, called "The Cold Equations" a touchstone story.
    "The Cold Equations" presents a future in which space travel has
become developed enough for mankind to begin the process of
colonizing some of the other habitable planets. But this is only the
beginning of the great age of colonization. Fuel still needs to be
exactly measured and at every turn the universe threatens human
life. As is made clear, however, these threats are not the creations of
a hostile universe for the specific destruction of humanity. These
threats originate within the nature of the universe, and all objects,
living or not, that inhabit that universe must live under their sway.
Thus, early in the story, Godwin presents his reader with a view of
space that parallels the view of the frontier held by early American
pioneers.
    A space colony is suffering from a disease for which there is a
serum, and a small ship is sent to rescue the colonists. The ship has
sufficient fuel to carry the pilot and his cargo to the stricken colony

and not a drop more. However, a girl has stowed away on the ship
with the hope of once again seeing her brother who is one of the
colonists. Within this simple plot Godwin develops the most popular of Campbell's themes: ignorance kills. Whether man is challenged by a creation of science, an alien invasion, or a new environment, what will most surely destroy the race is not the challenge but
a failure to know the nature of that challenge. The girl did not
realize the consequences of her actions, but at the end of the story
she must be jettisoned. The universe is not sentimental. While it will
make no special effort to kill a human being, it will do nothing to
save one, either. Nothing Godwin has written since has equalled this
one story. In *The Survivors* a race of aliens maroon some 4,000
humans on a hostile planet barely capable of sustaining human life.
But the humans do adapt and later return to destroy the aliens who
were once their conquerors. Mankind will prevail, Godwin tells the
reader, for the race has the intelligence, desire, and energy to survive
all threats. *The Space Barbarians*, a sequel to *The Survivors*, continues this theme, though in a more space-opera manner. Godwin
returns again to the pioneer nature of the human race in *Beyond
Another Sun* in which alien anthropologists observe humans as they
colonize a planet.
    In each of the works that follow "The Cold Equations" many of
the features that characterized that story can be seen: a clear narrative voice, simple descriptions that economically fill in the background needed to understand the action of the characters, themes
that form the very foundation of golden-age science fiction, and
occasional sentimental passages that, at their best, soften the harsh-
ness of the fictional worlds and, at their worst, detract from the
effect Godwin is attempting to achieve. But "The Cold Equations"
contains these traits in a way that few other science-fiction works
have matched.

—Stephen H. Goldman

———————

GOLD, H(orace) L(eonard).   Born in Montreal, Canada, 26 April
1914; emigrated to the United States at age 2. Served as a combat
engineer in the Pacific, 1944-46. Married 1) Evelyn Stein in 1939; 2)
Muriel Conley; one son and three step-children. Assistant Editor,
Thrilling Wonder Stories, Startling Stories, and *Captain Future,*
and Associate Editor, Standard Magazines, New York, 1939-41;
Managing and Contributing Editor, Scoop Publications, New
York, 1941-43; Editor, A and S Comics, New York, 1942-44; Con-
tract Writer, Molle Mystery Theatre, 1943-44; President, Rossard
Company, New York, 1946-50; Editor, *Galaxy,* and Galaxy Science
Fiction Novels, New York, 1950-61; Editor, *Beyond Fiction,* 1953-
55, and *If,* 1959-61: retired as disabled veteran, 1960. Recipient:
Hugo Award, for non-fiction, 1953; Westercon Life Achievement
Award, 1975. Address: 360 South Burnside Avenue, No. 6L, Los
Angeles, California 90036, U.S.A.

SCIENCE-FICTION PUBLICATIONS

Short Stories

The Old Die Rich and Other Science Fiction Stories.   New York,
    Crown, 1955; London, Dobson, 1965.

Uncollected Short Stories

"The Transmogrification of Wamba's Revenge," in *Galaxy* (New
    York), October 1967.
"The Riches of Embarrassment," in *Galaxy* (New York), April
    1968.
"The Villains from Vega IV," with E.J. Gold, in *Galaxy* (New
    York), October 1968.
"That's the Spirit," in *Amazing* (New York), March 1975.

OTHER PUBLICATIONS

Other

What Will They Think of Last? Nevada City, California, IDHHB, 1977.

Editor, *Galaxy Reader* [and *Second* to *Sixth*]. New York, Crown, 2 vols., 1952-54; New York, Doubleday, 4 vols., 1958-62; first 2 vols. London, Grayson, 1953-55.
Editor, *Five Galaxy Short Novels*. New York, Doubleday, 1958.
Editor, *The World That Couldn't Be and Eight Other Novelets from Galaxy*. New York, Doubleday, 1959.
Editor, *Bodyguard and Four Other Short Novels from Galaxy*. New York, Doubleday, 1960.
Editor, *Mind Partner and Eight Other Novelets from Galaxy Science Fiction*. New York, Doubleday, 1961.

H.L. Gold comments:
   I would very much like to be rediscovered as a science-fiction and fantasy author (including work since 1955), but I'm overshadowed as editor.

*   *   *

   About half a dozen editors and publishers have had a truly pervasive effect on the development of science fiction. Some of these are well remembered; others, almost wholly forgotten. The list must include Frank A. Munsey, who virtually invented the pulp magazine in 1896, Farnsworth Wright (*Weird Tales*), Hugo Gernsback (*Amazing Stories*), John W. Campbell, Jr. (*Astounding*), Anthony Boucher and J. Francis McComas (*The Magazine of Fantasy and Science Fiction*), and H.L. Gold. After many years of editorial work, in 1950 Gold became the founding editor of *Galaxy Science Fiction*. The importance of this event cannot be overemphasized. For some twenty years prior to 1950, *Astounding* had paid the highest rates in the science fiction field, had enjoyed the backing of the largest, wealthiest, and most influential publishing house, and had maintained by far the largest circulation. As a consequence, the bulk of quality writing in the field was calculated to reach *Astounding*. Even the lesser magazines, because they tended to subsist on the leavings of *Astounding*, also reflected the taste of *Astounding's* editors. With the almost simultaneous founding of *Fantasy and Science Fiction* and *Galaxy*, two new markets opened which paid competitive rates and offered generally equivalent quality of presentation and prestige. *F&SF* emphasized style, wit, and general literary excellence. *Galaxy*, reflecting Gold's world-view, placed heavy emphasis on social satire, combining relevance of theme with irreverence of outlook. The result was a magnificent flowering of novels and short stories by Pohl and Kornbluth, Simak, Asimov, Bradbury, Heinlein, and scores of others.
   Gold's own writing has been of limited quantity and impact, although it is far from worthless. His only novel, *None But Lucifer*, was written in collaboration with L. Sprague de Camp for *Unknown* magazine in 1939, and has never been reprinted. Of Gold's scattered short stories, a dozen were gathered in *The Old Die Rich*. As might be expected, the stories reflect considerable, often acid, wit. The title story of the book concerns a complex scheme of time travel and murder, unravelled through careful, formal detection techniques. "Love in the Dark" deals lightly with the succubus theme, brought up-to-date and converted into a tale of contact with aliens. "Trouble with Water," probably Gold's best-remembered story, is a fantasy concerning a small business man who offends a water elemental. A number of other stories in the book, particularly "The Man with English" and "Problem in Murder," hold up well despite their age. Particularly interesting in the book, is Gold's page of notes on each story, detailing his original conception, technical problems, and writing approach to that project.
   Also of interest is *What Will They Think of Last?*, a collection of Gold's editorials from *Galaxy*. Some of the editorials reflect ephemeral concerns, but others are most illuminating on the functioning of *Galaxy* during the Gold era.

—Richard A. Lupoff

————————

GOLDIN, Stephen. American. Born in Philadelphia, Pennsylvania, 28 February 1947. Educated at the University of California, Los Angeles, B.A. in astronomy 1968. Married Kathleen McKinney (i.e., Kathleen Sky, *q.v.*), in 1962. Physicist, Navy Space Systems Activity, El Segundo, California, 1968-71; Manager, Circle K. Grocery Store, Rosemead, California, 1972; Editor, Jaundice Press, Van Nuys, California, 1973-74; Editor, San Francisco *Ball*, 1973-74, and *SFWA Bulletin*, 1975-77; Director, Merrimont House creative consultants. Agent: Joseph Elder Agency, 150 West 87th Street, No. 6D, New York, New York 10024. Address: 13175½ Bromont Avenue, Sylmar, California 91342, U.S.A.

SCIENCE-FICTION PUBLICATIONS

Novels (series: The Family d'Alembert)

Herds. Toronto, Laser, 1975.
Caravan. Toronto, Laser, 1975.
Scavenger Hunt. Toronto, Laser, 1975.
Finish Line. Toronto, Laser, 1976.
Imperial Stars (d'Alembert). New York, Pyramid, and London, Panther, 1976.
Strangler's Moon (d'Alembert). New York, Pyramid, 1976; London, Panther, 1977.
The Clockwork Traitor (d'Alembert). New York, Pyramid, 1976; London, Panther, 1978.
Assault on the Gods. New York, Doubleday, 1977; London, Hale, 1978.
Getaway World (d'Alembert). New York, Pyramid, and London, Panther, 1977.
Mindflight. New York, Fawcett, 1978.
Appointment at Bloodstar (d'Alembert). New York, Pyramid, 1978; as *The Bloodstar Conspiracy*, London, Panther, 1978.
The Purity Plot (d'Alembert). London, Panther, 1978; New York, Berkley, 1980.
Trek to Madworld. New York, Bantam, 1979.
The Eternity Brigade. New York, Fawcett, 1980.
A World Called Solitude. New York, Doubleday, 1981.

Uncollected Short Stories

"The Girls on USSF 193," in *If* (New York), 1965.
"Sweet Dreams, Melissa," in *Galaxy* (New York), December 1968.
"The Last Ghost" and "The World Where Wishes Worked," in *Protostars*, edited by David Gerrold and Stephen Goldin. New York, Ballantine, 1971.
"Stubborn," in *Generation*, edited by David Gerrold. New York, Dell, 1972.
"Grim Fairy Tale," in *Adam* (Los Angeles), 1972.
"Constance and the Sex Machine," in *Adam* (Los Angeles), 1972.
"Nor Iron Bars a Cage," with C.F. Hensel, in *The Alien Condition*, edited by Stephen Goldin. New York, Ballantine, 1973.
"Harriet," in *Tomorrow's Alternatives*, edited by Roger Elwood. New York, Macmillan, 1973.
"A Nice Place to Visit," in *Vertex* (Los Angeles), 1973.
"Of Love, Free Will, and Gray Squirrels on a Summer Evening," in *Vertex* (Los Angeles), 1973.
"But as a Soldier, for His Country," in *Universe 5*, edited by Terry Carr. New York, Random House, 1974; London, Dobson, 1978.
"Prelude to a Symphony of Unborn Shouts," in *Future Corruption*, edited by Roger Elwood. New York, Warner, 1975.
"In the Land of Angra Mainyu," in *Nameless Places*, edited by Gerald W. Page. Sauk City, Wisconsin, Arkham House, 1975.
"Xenophobe," in *Vertex* (Los Angeles), August 1975.
"Portrait of the Artist as a Young God," in *Ascents of Wonder*, edited by David Gerrold and Stephen Goldin. New York, Popular Library, 1977.
"When There's No Man Around," in *Isaac Asimov's Science Fiction Magazine* (New York), 1977.
"Apollyon ex Machina," in *Chrysalis 6*, edited by Roy Torgeson. New York, Kensington, 1979.

OTHER PUBLICATIONS

Other

Editor, with David Gerrold, *Protostars.* New York, Ballantine, 1971.
Editor, *The Alien Condition.* New York, Ballantine, 1973.
Editor, with David Gerrold, *Science Fiction Emphasis 1.* New York, Ballantine, 1974.
Editor, with David Gerrold, *Alternities.* New York, Dell, 1974.
Editor, with David Gerrold, *Ascents of Wonder.* New York, Popular Library, 1977.

Stephen Goldin comments:

Looking closely at my work might almost give one the impression that my short stories were written by someone entirely different than the author of my novels. This is due in part to the changes in myself, and in part to the nature of the works themselves.

With only a few exceptions, my short stories are downbeat and tragic. They were the product of my early career, a young man trying to impress the world with his cynicism and acceptance of the universe's perversity. In part, too, this is because a short story is like a photograph, an encapsulated moment of immense importance to the character(s) involved—and it seemed far easier for me to capture a tragic moment than a triumphant one. My mind was at its blackest in tragedies like "The Last Ghost," "Sweet Dreams, Melissa," "Of Love, Free Will, and Gray Squirrels on a Summer Evening," and "Xenophobe"; but there is a bleakness in even those stories with a primarily humorous slant: "The World Where Wishes Worked," "Stubborn," "Grim Fairy Tale," and "Constance and the Sex Machine."

My career (and my apparent outlook) did a complete turnabout when I switched to writing novels in the mid-1970's. Every single one of my novels has an upbeat ending. If a short story may be likened to a photograph, then a novel is a movie, the progression of a character through events, changing at least himself if not the world around him. I like to believe now that a person is responsible for his own life; even if the situation starts out looking hopeless and desperate, a firm and resourceful person can take charge of himself and turn the situation around. My characters may go through hell, but in the end they manage to triumph over their adversities. The somewhat more mature me (I'm 32 as I write this) doesn't need to hide behind that shield of cynicism. I've become a born-again optimist. If there is any message in my work at all, it's that no matter how bad things might be there is always a solution to the person willing to work for it.

*   *   *

Stephen Goldin believes that "certain basic drives control our actions at the innermost level—drives of hunger, sex, insecurity, aquisitiveness, curiosity, and others." It is out of these drives that he forms his characters, civilizations, and scenarios. His method allows him to sketch both humans and aliens with an easy vividness, and their motivations are always clear, if sometimes a bit superficial. The vectoring of such drives produces plots of action, not necessarily resonance of depth, but as Goldin matures the action is often exhilarating, and can occasionally break through into the truly unexpected.

In Goldin's first novels the combination of plot elements was sometimes awkward. *Herds* grafts a small, reasonably original science-fiction idea onto a stock detective story, spending too much time on a trite California murder and not enough on Zarti, an interesting planet of herbivores who have been forced into an unusual and peaceful communism. Goldin makes a thematic connection between California communes and Zarticku ideal of the Herd, and the novel's ending is pleasantly upbeat, but the interactions seem clumsy and forced. *Mindflight* is much more successful—the writing is more competent and the story coordinates action and suspense into a single extended adventure. Alain Cheney, a Terran intelligence telepath, goes "telepausal"—a parapsychological menopause producing greater sensitivity, then insanity and death—and his agency wants to eliminate him. The resulting chase covers two worlds, and intersects with a variety of people whose motivations move them into Cheney's path, and whose deaths are sometimes

gratuitously messy. Goldin still spends more time than he needs on inter-agency squabbles, and there is very little visual sense of the places Cheney runs through. Yet the details of telepathy are handled well, and the ending, where the true nature of telepause is revealed, opens satisfyingly into new vistas.

Whatever problems Goldin has in his plots do not appear in his short stories. He knows well how to make the small twist into humor or the tighter turn into horror. "The Last Ghost" gives a grim evocation of a decayed consciousness left floating in a void to point the way for others who never come. The theme of trapped consciousness, where the mind is reduced to a set of drives without personality, recurs in Goldin's stories. "But as a Soldier, for His Country" gives an insider's view of a future dehumanizing warfare that culminates in suicidal terror. The fate of the computer's mind in "Sweet Dreams, Melissa," is more poignant but no less terrifying. A different kind of entrapment is described in "Nor Iron Bars a Cage." Written with C.F. Hensel, the story is told from the point of view of a formless multiple alien who escapes the shifting cage of amnesia and boredom only to find himself in the cage of a rigid body and individual solitude.

Goldin can be funny, too. The quick joke of "Stubborn," where a spoiled brat on a spinning planet refuses to budge, is neatly executed. And in *Trek to Madworld,* within the somewhat predictable requirements of a *Star Trek* novel, Goldin manages an entertaining light whimsy decorated with an unlikely sequence of allusions ranging from Heinlein to Dahl's *Willie Wonka and the Chocolate Factory.*

Goldin's stories are brisk and vivid, whether in the quick revelation of a vignette or the extended action of an interstellar chase. He has wit, inventiveness, and a fan's familiarity with the universe as science fiction has made it. He has been writing long enough to be out of the apprentice stage—the direction of his progress is good.

—Karen G. Way

GOLDING, William (Gerald). British. Born in St. Columb Minor, Cornwall, 19 September 1911. Educated at Marlborough Grammar School; Brasenose College, Oxford, B.A. 1935. Served in the Royal Navy, 1940-45. Married Ann Brookfield in 1939; one son and one daughter. Writer, actor, and producer in small theatre companies, 1934-40, 1945-54; Schoolmaster, Bishop Wordsworth's School, Salisbury, Wiltshire, 1939-40, 1945-61; Visiting Professor, Hollins College, Virginia, 1961-62. Recipient: Black Memorial Award, 1980; Booker Prize, 1980. M.A.: Oxford University, 1961; D.Litt.: University of Sussex, Brighton, 1970. Honorary Fellow, Brasenose College, 1966. Fellow of the Royal Society of Literature, 1955. C.B.E. (Commander, Order of the British Empire), 1966. Address: Ebble Thatch, Bowerchalke, Wiltshire, England.

SCIENCE-FICTION PUBLICATIONS

Novels

Lord of the Flies. London, Faber, 1954; New York, Coward McCann, 1955.
The Inheritors. London, Faber, 1955; New York, Harcourt Brace, 1962.

Short Stories

The Scorpion God. London, Faber, 1971; New York, Harcourt Brace, 1972.

OTHER PUBLICATIONS

Novels

Pincher Martin. London, Faber, 1956; as *The Two Deaths of Christopher Martin,* New York, Harcourt Brace, 1957.
Free Fall. London, Faber, 1959; New York, Harcourt Brace, 1960.
The Spire. London, Faber, and New York, Harcourt Brace, 1964.
The Pyramid. London, Faber, and New York, Harcourt Brace, 1967.
Darkness Visible. London, Faber, and New York, Farrar Straus, 1979.
Rites of Passage. London, Faber, and New York, Farrar Straus, 1980.

Plays

The Brass Butterfly, adaptation of his story "Envoy Extraordinary" (produced London, 1958). London, Faber, 1958; Chicago, Dramatic Publishing Company, n.d.

Radio Plays: *Miss Pulkinhorn,* 1960; *Break My Heart,* 1962.

Verse

Poems. London, Macmillan, 1934; New York, Macmillan, 1935.

Other

"Androids All," in *Spectator* (London), 24 February 1961.
"Astronaut by Gaslight," in *Spectator* (London), 9 June 1961.
The Hot Gates and Other Occasional Pieces. London, Faber, 1965; New York, Harcourt Brace, 1966.

* * *

William Golding first came to notice through two remarkable novels, *Lord of the Flies* and *The Inheritors,* though the emergence of such a rare new talent was not immediately greeted with the acclaim it merited. Both novels concern themselves with mankind's "loss of innocence" (in the Blakeian sense) and to that extent can be regarded as fables. *Lord of the Flies* takes place at some undetermined point in the future and follows the fortunes of a group of young English schoolboys who have survived an air crash on a remote desert island. In the long weeks before they are rescued (some kind of world conflict is in progress) they live out in microcosm the whole gamut of human experience from paradisal innocence to blood lust, and, finally, human sacrifice. *The Inheritors* tells the story of a group of Neanderthaler "Dawn Men" who, living in a state of pre-lapsarian innocence towards the end of the final Ice Age, are drawn into unwitting conflict with a tribe of migrating Cromagnon "New Men" and are destroyed in consequence.

Such sketetal summarising can in no sense do justice to Golding's extraordinary achievement. He compels his reader to accept his imaginative perspectives by means of a succession of brilliant, sharply focused word pictures. The visual impact of his work is truly astonishing. Having persuaded us of the physical existence of his characters and of the settings in which he has placed them he then proceeds, with an almost diabolic subtlety, to undermine our own preconceptions of the fundamental nature of mankind. Golding's themes are vast—archetypal; but what sets his novels and short stories apart from almost all other works of science fiction is that the themes and the characters are inseparable. The marooned children (Ralph, Piggy, Jack, and Simon of *Lord of the Flies*), the doomed Neanderthalers (Lok and Fa of *The Inheritors*) are as close to being living, breathing, and above all *suffering* creatures as it is possible to contrive out of words alone. We feel their agony in our bones and recognize it for our own. Golding's novels have been called "allegories of the human situation" but they are much more than that. The ideas are never allowed to dominate the story. The books are organic wholes. Their creator's own intense involvement with the creatures of his imagination and with the situations he has contrived for them drives the allegorical element into the background where it becomes truly symbolic. On the evidence of these two novels alone

Golding is arguably the finest writer ever to have worked within the classic traditions of Wellsian scientific romance.

The Scorpion God (3 novellas) is Golding's only other work in the genre. Altogether less sombre in theme than his novels these stories are noteworthy alike for their sense of history, their wit, and the brilliance of their imagery.

—Richard Cowper

———

GORDON, David. *See* **GARRETT, Randall.**

———

GORDON, Rex. Pseudonym for Stanley Bennett Hough; also writes as Bennett Stanley. British. Born in Preston, Lancashire, 25 February 1917. Educated at Preston Grammar School; Radio Officers College, Preston; attended classes of the Workers Educational Association. Married Justa E.C. Wodschow in 1938. Radio Operator, Marconi Radio Company, 1936-38; Radio Officer, International Marine Radio Company, 1939-45; ran a yachting firm, 1946-51. Recipient: Infinity Award, 1957. Agent: A.M. Heath and Company Ltd., 40-42 William IV Street, London WC2N 4DD. Address: 21 St. Michael's Road, Ponsanooth, Truro, Cornwall, England.

SCIENCE-FICTION PUBLICATIONS

Novels

Utopia 239. London, Heinemann, 1955.
Extinction Bomber (as S.B. Hough). London, Lane, 1956.
No Man Friday. London, Heinemann, 1956; as *First on Mars,* New York, Ace, 1957.
First to the Stars. New York, Ace, 1959; as *The Worlds of Eclos,* London, Consul, 1961.
Beyond the Eleventh Hour (as S.B. Hough). London, Hodder and Stoughton, 1961.
First Through Time. New York, Ace, 1962; as *The Time Factor,* London, Tandem, 1964.
Utopia minus X. New York, Ace, 1966; as *The Paw of God,* London, Tandem, 1967.
The Yellow Fraction. New York, Ace, 1969; London, Dobson, 1972.

OTHER PUBLICATIONS

Novels as S.B. Hough

Frontier Incident. London, Hodder and Stoughton, 1951; New York, Crowell, 1952.
Moment of Decision. London, Hodder and Stoughton, 1952.
Mission in Guemo. London, Hodder and Stoughton, 1953; New York, Walker, 1964.
The Seas South. London, Hodder and Stoughton, 1953.
The Primitives. London, Hodder and Stoughton, 1954.
The Bronze Perseus. London, Secker and Warburg, 1959; New York, Walker, 1962; as *The Tender Killer,* New York, Avon, 1963.
Dear Daughter Dead. London, Gollancz, 1965; New York, Walker, 1966.
Sweet Sister Seduced. London, Gollancz, 1968.
Fear Fortune, Father. London, Gollancz, 1974.

Novels as Bennett Stanley

Sea Struck.   New York, Crowell, 1953; as *Sea to Eden,* London,
   Hodder and Stoughton, 1954.
The Alscott Experiment.   London, Hodder and Stoughton, 1954.
Government Contract.   London, Hodder and Stoughton, 1956.

Other as S.B. Hough

A Pound a Day Inclusive: The Modern Way to Holiday Travel.
   London, Hodder and Stoughton, 1957.
*Expedition Everyman: Your Way on Your Income to All the Desir-
   able Places of Europe.*   London, Hodder and Stoughton, 1959.
Expedition Everyman 1964.   London, Hodder and Stoughton,
   1964.
*Where? An Independent Report on Holiday Resorts in Britain and
   the Continent.*   London, Hodder and Stoughton, 1964.

*   *   *

Rex Gordon was the pseudonym that Stanley Bennett Hough
used for most of his science fiction. His first science-fiction novels
reflected the Cold War fears that marked the 1950's: *Utopia 239*
begins with an atomic war and moves on to the ideal state that rises
from the ashes, and *Extinction Bomber* deals with the Dr.
Strangelove—situation of the outbreak of war. However, Gordon's
reputation in the genre was established with *No Man Friday,* reminiscent in many ways of Defoe's *Robinson Crusoe.* A manned rocket
is sent to Mars, but the crash of the ship maroons Gordon Holder,
its single survivor, and the secrecy of the flight prevents any rescue
attempt. The bulk of the work concerns Holder's attempts to stay
alive in the forbidding Martian surroundings. *No Man Friday* won
praise from reviewers for the strictness with which it hewed to
scientific conjectures and facts then known about Mars. And
Holder works ingeniously and tirelessly to survive. But the novel
takes a drastic turn when Holder encounters intelligent Martians.
Like Hindu mystics, the Martians have gone beyond desire; they
subtly mock Holder's struggle and the machines that have helped
him, and the Martians hint that they possess immense powers.
Whatever they may have, their view of reality is so different from
that of humankind that Holder foresees, when rescued by an American expedition, that conflict will result between the two planets,
that humans will win the war, and that the victory will cost them a
chance for knowledge that they will never have again.
   First to the Stars followed this somber but successful novel, and
once again its theme was the staggering difference of alien ways of
life and thought. The novel sends a man and woman on an exploration of Mars, but navigational problems cause them to miss their
target and head out of the solar system. Time dilation, an effect of
their speed, keeps them young through a voyage that lasts a hundred
years to a planet where the woman dies giving birth as the man
encounters an alien race. Although the aliens treat the humans well,
eventually enabling them to return to Earth, the novel shows an
insuperable barrier to understanding between humans and aliens,
and ends with tensions and confrontations between the two races. If
Gordon saw human-alien communication as doubtful, he was
probably projecting the difficulties between humans onto a galactic
screen: in *Beyond the Eleventh Hour* he returned to the theme of
world-wide nuclear conflict. Although *First Through Time* turned
to adventure, the discovery of time travel in that novel results from
an accident, as had so many events in the earlier books. And *Utopia
minus X* again shows the conflict that arises from difference, this
time between a space traveler and the Earth he returns to after a
lapse of two centuries.
   No Man Friday brought Rex Gordon a reputation as a writer
who used careful extrapolation in his work. But, more importantly,
one consistent theme has been a deep pessimism about the possibility of understanding, whether between human or alien, or among
humans themselves.

—Walter E. Meyers

GORDON, Stuart.   Pseudonym for Richard Gordon; also writes
as Alex R. Stuart.   British.   Born in Scotland in 1947. Agent:
A.P. Watt Ltd., 26-28' **Bedford** Row, London, WC1R 4HL,
England.

SCIENCE-FICTION PUBLICATIONS

Novels (series: Eyes)

Time Story.   London, New English Library, 1972.
One-Eye.   New York, DAW, 1973; London, Sidgwick and Jack-
   son, 1974.
Two-Eyes.   New York, DAW, 1974; London, Sidgwick and Jack-
   son, 1975.
Three-Eyes.   New York, DAW, 1975; London, Sidgwick and
   Jackson, 1976.
Suaine and the Crow-God.   London, New English Library, 1975.

OTHER PUBLICATIONS as Alex R. Stuart

Novels

The Bike from Hell.   London, New English Library, 1973.
The Devil's Rider.   London, New English Library, 1973.

*   *   *

Stuart Gordon works in the realm of science-fantasy. His most
ambitious work, the trilogy of *One-Eye, Two-Eyes,* and *Three-
Eyes,* is set in a remote future when much technology has ceased to
function, and magic and occultism play a major role in the events.
At its best, this work is as vivid as Tanith Lee's *The Birthgrave;* it
may also remind some readers of the early works of Brian M.
Stableford.
   One-Eye opens in the city of Phadraig with the birth of a mutant
one-eyed child. Phadraig worships the Witch Goddess of the Earth,
and its rulers are the Witchmen; they destroy all infants at birth who
do not conform to Norm Purity. The mutant's mother, Gaidhealla,
being a seeress, has foreseen the child's birth and inevitable con-
demnation to death. She persuades the High Witchman, Patrick
Cormac, to aid her in saving the baby's life, and also to awaken the
Golem Cuyahogan, a monster which kills everyone who does not
know the proper words of command. Since Gaidhealla knows them,
she controls the monster, and she, the mother, and the baby flee
with its aid. Patick follows with old comrades who were his fellow-
soldiers, among them Liam the Songmaker. The opening has tremendous drive, and the chase that follows is extremely effective, as
is the second section of the book, where the Company are imprisoned in a wizard's tower. The third section enlightens us as to the
nature of the telepathic One-Eye; he is bent on releasing chaos, and
does so to the accompaniment of the dance of 30 evil mumen, who
(like Cuyahogan) come from a disastrous earlier age. Nearly everybody is killed, and the survivors nearly all go mad.
   Two-Eyes is set in the neighbouring country of Miir, a peaceful
and prosperous place which is nonetheless torn apart by the madness spread by the Mutant. Liam (the one character in this book
whom we already know) is rescued while wandering in a fit of
madness by Tschea, a lady of high degree from the sophisticated city
of Ussian. They follow a spiritual quest, and eventually reach the
Delta of Miir, where Liam uses the magical instrument called the
sirena to play the Song of the Zuni Bird—an expression of the
harmony of the universe that restores balance to the people driven
mad by the Mutant One-Eye. Liam, however, is drowned by the
rising tide. In *Three-Eyes* we follow the fate of Tah Ti the Boaster,
now the new carrier of the harmonious Song. It becomes gradually
clear that One-Eye is ruled by the Unmen of Lamassa, invaders
from another universe. The Song alone is not effective against them,
but Tah Ti discovers a poem from the past which is. There is a
climactic battle underground, and the final resolution occurs in a
moment of mystic vision which cannot later be recaptured by any of
the characters. But the events have passed beyond the reach of
ordinary language, and it must be said that Gordon's language
falters under the strain.
   The first two volumes of the trilogy are the best, but the third has

vivid passages as well. Gordon is good at dramatic pictorial scenes, and at maintaining tension. Occasionally one balks at certain events in the story (why, in *Three-Eyes,* does the blind man wish to die?). What remains in the mind are the pictures: Gaidhealla fleeing through the swamp, with the baby in the Golem's arms; or the daughter of the wizard in the tower, immensely fat, moving delicately on her tiny feet; or the bandit Nikosner looming up out of the grasslands to ambush the wagon-train from Ussian.

Time Story deals with a criminal from the near future who escapes to the far future, and his attempts to fit into a neo-medieval setting. *Suaine and the Crow-God* deals with tribal battles on the Isle of Lewis just before the birth of Christ, but the main emphasis is on the reincarnation of various Celtic deities. The book is very gloomy, but the dreamlike passages in which the hero asks the Moon-Goddess for help in divining his future are quite effective.

—Charles Cushing

* * *

GOTLIEB, Phyllis (Fay, née Bloom). Canadian. Born in Toronto, Ontario, 25 May 1926. Educated at public schools in Toronto; University of Toronto, B.A. in English 1948, M.A. 1950. Married Calvin Gotlieb in 1949; one son and two daughters. Agent: Virginia Kidd, Box 278, Milford, Pennsylvania 18337, U.S.A. Address: 29 Ridgevale Drive, Toronto, Ontario M6A 1K9, Canada.

SCIENCE-FICTION PUBLICATIONS

Novels

Sunburst. New York, Fawcett, 1964; London, Coronet, 1966.
O Master Caliban. New York, Harper, 1976; London, Bantam, Corgi, 1979.
A Judgment of Dragons. New York, Berkley, 1980.

Uncollected Short Stories

"A Grain of Manhood," in *Fantastic* (New York), September 1959.
"Phantom Foot," in *Amazing* (New York), December 1959.
"No End of Time," in *Fantastic* (New York), June 1960.
"A Bone to Pick," in *Fantastic* (New York), October 1960.
"Gingerbread Boy," in *If* (New York), January 1961.
"Valedictory," in *Amazing* (New York), May 1964.
"Rogue's Gambit," in *If* (New York), January 1968.
"The Dirty Old Men of Maxsec," in *Galaxy* (New York), November 1969.
"Planetoid Idiot," in *To the Stars,* edited by Robert Silverberg. New York, Hawthorn, 1971.
"Son of the Morning," in *Fantasy and Science Fiction* (New York), June 1972.
"Mother Lode," in *Fantasy and Science Fiction* (New York), November 1973.
"The Military Hospital," in *Fantasy and Science Fiction* (New York), May 1974.
"Sunday's Child," in *Cosmos* (New York), 1977.

OTHER PUBLICATIONS

Novel

Why Should I Have All the Grief? Toronto, Macmillan, 1969.

Plays

Doctor Umlaut's Earthly Kingdom (broadcast, 1970; produced Ontario, 1972). Published in *Poems for Voices,* Toronto, CBC, 1970.
Garden Varieties (broadcast, 1973; produced Ontario, 1973).

Radio Plays: *Doctor Umlaut's Earthly Kingdom,* 1970; *Silent Movie Day,* 1971; *The Contract,* 1972; *Garden Varieties,* 1973; *God on Trial Before Rabbi Ovadia,* 1974.

Verse

Who Knows One? Toronto, Hawkshead Press, 1962.
Within the Zodiac. Toronto, McClelland and Stewart, 1964.
Ordinary, Moving. Toronto, Oxford University Press, 1969.
Doctor Umlaut's Earthly Kingdom. Toronto, Calliope Press, 1974.
The Works: Collected Poems. Toronto, Calliope Press, 1978.

Phyllis Gotlieb comments:

I like to work in as broad a range of genres as possible, and in all of them I am primarily interested in people, their emotions, actions, dynamics. After that I am interested in everything else in the universe.

* * *

Phyllis Gotlieb is an unusual figure in the world of science fiction for at least two reasons: she is Canadian born and bred, and she is best known in the Canadian literary world as a fine poet, albeit one whose poems often employ fantasy and SF tropes. But then, as Samuel R. Delany has remarked, "The vision (sense of wonder if you will) that SF tries for seems to me very close to the vision of poetry." Certainly in Gotlieb's case the same vision generates both the poems and the science fiction. One of her major interests is mythology, especially in its more popular manifestations, and the social responses it generates. SF *is* a popular manifestation of mythological thinking and her highly literary control of its conventions in her short fictions and her novels *Sunburst* and *O Master Caliban* reveal her structural comprehension of this fact. She is also fascinated, in both her poetry (*Ordinary, Moving* and much of *The Works,* for example) and her SF, by the continuing presence of children in the world and their many problems in achieving a true maturity. The SF paradigm is especially useful here for it tends to support the expansion of the child-maturing theme until it symbolically embraces the race as well as the individual. Little wonder, then, that Gotlieb's SF, as well as her poetry, explores themes, motifs, and a particular view of life that is guardedly optimistic, mystically clear-eyed.

Perhaps because she hasn't had to live off her SF writing, more likely because she is a very careful writer, Gotlieb has not been overly prolific. *Sunburst* is better written than most such works and a superb example of SF as a true fiction of ideas. It holds the often parallel concepts of ESP and the next evolutionary step for humanity up to a scientifically curious philosophical investigation in the midst of adventure and potential violence. Psi-powers, and, indeed, the often amoral use of power per se, are a standard convention but Gotlieb's 13-year-old putative "superman," Shandy, not only has no Psi, she is impervious to others' use of it against her. What she is is intelligent, very curious, willing to play with unconventional ideas, and capable of moral growth, of which she has a lot to do. Most of the mutant Psi-powered "children" in *Sunburst* lack both any sense of moral connection to the rest of humanity and enough intelligence to handle their powers properly. Gotlieb's conclusion, the core of a powerfully emotional adventure in maturing full of well-realized individuals, is that a "superman" will merely be an intelligent, curious person of high moral sensitivity, looking to help move the whole race forward just a smidgen in her lifetime. Not your usual SF novel at all.

Her stories similarly explore moral dilemmas, and often feature immature individuals who are given the opportunity to "grow up" psychologically through the adventures Gotlieb arranges for them. And in *O Master Caliban,* a group of future delinquents plus a four-armed lost child and his animal friends learn to be more fully human as they battle renegade robots for survival. The boy's father, a scientist who never matured morally, also gets, at 60, his chance to face and accept his failures of humanity and possibly begin to make up for them. In all her work, then, Gotlieb has something to say about the human condition, but she also knows how to entertain. Her poet's eye makes for sharply observed descriptions; her love of adventure makes for powerfully realized scenes of violence and pain; her intelligence makes for intelligent talk among her characters; and her love for people makes for empathetic characters to talk. The result is work which is entertaining and truly provocative of thought, and which contains characters we feel privileged to have met. The integrity and gritty speculation of her work have earned her a respected place in the field.

—Douglas Barbour

GOTSCHALK, Felix C. American. Born in Richmond, Virginia, 7 September 1929. Educated at Virginia Commonwealth University, Richmond, B.S. 1954 (Phi Beta Kappa), M.S. 1956; Tulane University, New Orleans, Ph.D 1958. Served in the United States Marine Corps, 1947-49. Married Nelle Mull in 1957; one son and one daughter. Draftsman, Vepco, Richmond, 1946-47, 1949-51; pianist, Chelf's, 1951-56, and On the Road, 1956-58, both in Richmond; Assistant Professor, Nicholls State University, Thibodaux, Louisiana, 1958-62, and Bowman Medical School, Winston-Salem, North Carolina, 1962-70. Since 1970, in private practice as a psychologist, Winston-Salem. Address: 4021 Tangle Lane, Winston-Salem, North Carolina 27106, U.S.A.

SCIENCE-FICTION PUBLICATIONS

Novels

Growing Up in Tier 3000.   New York, Ace, 1975.
The Last Americans.   New York, Doubleday, 1980.

Uncollected Short Stories

"Bonus Baby," in *Science Fiction Emphasis 1,* edited by David Gerrold.   New York, Ballantine, 1974.
"Outer Concentric" and "The Examination," in *New Dimensions 4,* edited by Robert Silverberg.   New York, New American Library, 1974.
"A Day in the South Quad," in *New Dimensions 5,* edited by Robert Silverberg.   New York, Harper, 1975.
"The Man with the Golden Reticulates," in *Orbit 17,* edited by Damon Knight.   New York, Harper, 1975.
"Pandora's Cryogenic Box," in *Fantastic* (New York), December 1975.
"The Family Winter of 1986," in *Orbit 18,* edited by Damon Knight. New York, Harper, 1976.
"The Day of the Bog Test," in *Future Power,* edited by Jack Dann and Gardner Dozois.   New York, Random House, 1976.
"The Napoleonic Wars," in *Beyond Time,* edited by Sandra Ley. New York, Simon and Schuster, 1976.
"Charisma Leak," in *New Dimensions 6,* edited by Robert Silverberg.   New York, Harper, 1976.
"Home Sweet Geriatric Dome," in *New Dimensions 7,* edited by Robert Silverberg.   New York, Harper, and London, Gollancz, 1977.
"The Veil over the River," in *Orbit 19,* edited by Damon Knight. New York, Harper, 1977.
"Sir Richard's Robots," in *Cosmos* (New York), November 1977.
"Square Pony Express," in *New Dimensions 9,* edited by Robert Silverberg.   New York, Harper, 1979.
"The Wishes of Maidens," in *New Voices in Science Fiction,* edited by George R.R. Martin.   New York, Berkley, 1979.
"Bradley Oesterhaus," in *Fantasy and Science Fiction* (New York), July 1979.
"A Presidential Tape," in *New Dimensions 10,* edited by Robert Silverberg.   New York, Harper, 1980.
"Among the Cave Dwellers of the San Andreas Canyon," in *Fantasy and Science Fiction* (New York), August 1980.

*

Manuscript Collection: Temple University, Philadelphia.

Felix C. Gotschalk comments:
   Writing is for me an indulgence, an egocentric luxuriation, something I do because it pleases me. I have experimented (consciously and unconsciously) with verbosity, neologisms, symmetry, cadence, self-canceling reciprocity, and, even, monosyllabicity. I cannot plot story lines and do not attempt to do so. I do not know what is going to happen in any of my stories; and it is special voyeuristic fun to have a good flow of writing (say, 3000 words in one evening), and then read it the next day to see what it was that I wrote the night before. How to characterize my writing I do not know. One critic called it "poetic hardware," others have been less kind. I would like to write an erotic story that would guarantee the reader a spontaneous orgasm.

*   *   *

   Felix C. Gotschalk is one of the latest in the succession of powerful, idiosyncratic writers like R.A. Lafferty, John Boyd, and the late Cordwainer Smith who might never have seen print if SF had not existed. Gotschalk writes stories, usually of horridly precocious children, in baroque prose with dark humour and a heavy overlay of irony. He, more than most SF writers, accepts the responsibility of depicting an electronic future that is almost incomprehensible in current terms. From *Growing Up in Tier 3000:*

   The two children eat the rich gruel-pudding and watch the trivid news; Synod Chief John Kennedy, re-elected for his 27th term, is having spinal troubles again. After being exhumed and cloned in ancient times, he wears out readily. "God, I Love that charisma-bot," Carol breathes. The energy crisis is easing, the trivid voice continues, gravity engrams are being drawn from Dakotan geologic cores. Mojave Desert fruit-grid farmers are retarding growth inputs of nectarinos until the Synod agrees to allocate more barter-energy to them.

—E.R. Bishop

GOULART, Ron(ald Joseph). Also writes as Josephine Kains; Jullian Kearny; Howard Lee; Kenneth Robeson; Frank S. Shawn; Con Steffanson. American. Born in Berkeley, California, 13 January 1933. Educated at the University of California, Berkeley, B.A. 1955. Married Frances Sheridan in 1964; two sons. Advertising Copywriter, Guild Bascom and Bonfigci, San Francisco, Alan Alch Inc., Hollywood, and Hoefer Dietrich and Brown, San Francisco. Author of science-fiction comic strip *Star Hawks,* with Gil Kane, 1977-79. Recipient: Mystery Writers of America Edgar Allan Poe Award, 1971. Guest of Honor, Lunacon, 1979. Address: 232 Georgetown Road, Weston, Connecticut 06883, U.S.A.

SCIENCE-FICTION PUBLICATIONS

Novels (series: Gypsy; Vampirella)

The Sword Swallower.   New York, Doubleday, 1968.
After Things Fell Apart.   New York, Ace, 1970; London, Arrow, 1975.
The Fire Eater.   New York, Ace, 1970.
Gadget Man.   New York, Doubleday, 1971; London, New English Library, 1977.
Death Cell.   New York, Beagle, 1971.
Hawkshaw.   New York, Doubleday, 1972; London, Hale, 1973.
Plunder.   New York, Beagle, 1972.
Wildsmith.   New York, Ace, 1972.
Shaggy Planet.   New York, Lancer, 1973.
A Talent for the Invisible.   New York, DAW, 1973.
The Tin Angel.   New York, DAW, 1973.
Spacehawk, Inc.   New York, DAW, 1974.

Flux. New York, DAW, 1974.
When the Waker Sleeps. New York, DAW, 1975.
Bloodstalk (novelization of comic strip; Vampirella). New York, Warner, 1975; London, Sphere, 1976.
On Alien Wings (novelization of comic strip; Vampirella). New York, Warner, 1975; London, Sphere, 1977.
The Hellhound Project. New York, Doubleday, 1975; London, Hale, 1976.
A Whiff of Madness. New York, DAW, 1976.
The Enormous Hourglass. New York, Award, 1976.
Quest of the Gypsy. New York, DAW, 1976.
Deadwalk (novelization of comic strip; Vampirella). New York, Warner, 1976; London, Sphere, 1977.
Blood Wedding (novelization of comic strip; Vampirella). New York, Warner, 1976.
Deathgame (novelization of comic strip; Vampirella). New York, Warner, 1976.
Snakegod (novelization of comic strip; Vampirella). New York, Warner, 1976.
Crackpot. New York, Doubleday, and London, Hale, 1977.
The Emperor of the Last Days. New York, Popular Library, 1977.
The Panchronicon Plot. New York, DAW, 1977.
Nemo. New York, Berkley, 1977; London, Hale, 1980.
Eye of the Vulture (Gypsy). New York, Pyramid, 1977.
The Wicked Cyborg. New York, DAW, 1978.
Calling Dr. Patchwork. New York, DAW, 1978.
Cowboy Heaven. New York, Doubleday, 1979; London, Hale, 1980.
Dr. Scofflaw, in *Binary Star 3.* New York, Dell, 1979.
Hello, Lemuria, Hello. New York, DAW, 1979.
Star Hawks: Empire 99, illustrated by Gil Kane. Chicago, Playboy Press, 1980.
Hail Hibbler. New York, DAW, 1980.
Skyrocket Steele. New York, Pocket Books, 1980.

Novels as Frank S. Shawn (series: Phantom in all books)

The Veiled Lady. New York, Avon, 1973.
The Golden Circle. New York, Avon, 1973.
The Mystery of the Sea Horse. New York, Avon, 1973.
The Hydra Monster. New York, Avon, 1974.
The Goggle-Eyed Pirates. New York, Avon, 1974.
The Swamp Rats. New York, Avon, 1974.

Novels as Con Steffanson (series: Flash Gordon in all books)

The Lion Men of Mongo. New York, Avon, 1974.
The Plague of Sound. New York, Avon, 1974.
The Space Circus. New York, Avon, 1974.

Novels as Kenneth Robeson (series: Avenger in all books)

The Man from Atlantis. New York, Warner, 1974.
Red Moon. New York, Warner, 1974.
The Purple Zombie. New York, Warner, 1974.
Dr. Time. New York, Warner, 1974.
The Nightwitch Devil. New York, Warner, 1974.
Black Chariots. New York, Warner, 1974.
The Cartoon Crimes. New York, Warner, 1974.
The Iron Skull. New York, Warner, 1974.
The Death Machine. New York, Warner, 1975.
The Blood Countess. New York, Warner, 1975.
The Glass Man. New York, Warner, 1975.
Demon Island. New York, Warner, 1975.

Short Stories

What's Become of Screwloose? and Other Inquiries. New York, Scribner, and London, Sidgwick and Jackson, 1971.
Clockwork's Pirates, Ghost Breaker. New York, Ace, 1971.
Broke Down Engine and Other Troubles with Machines. New York, Macmillan, 1971.
The Chameleon Corps and Other Shape Changers. New York, Macmillan, 1972; London, Collier Macmillan, 1973.

Nutzenbolts and More Troubles with Machines. New York, Macmillan, 1975; London, Hale, 1976.
Odd Job No. 101 and Other Future Crimes and Intrigues. New York, Scribner, 1975; London, Hale, 1976.

Uncollected Short Stories

"At the Starvation Ball," in *Fantasy and Science Fiction* (New York), April 1976.
"Lunatic at Large," in *Fantasy and Science Fiction* (New York), February 1977.
"Amnesty," in *Analog* (New York), September 1977.
"Assassins," in *Fantasy and Science Fiction* (New York), December 1977.
"Lectric Joe," in *Fantasy and Science Fiction* (New York), February 1978.
"Invisible Stripes," in *Omni* (New York), October 1978.
"Garbage," in *Isaac Asimov's Science Fiction Magazine* (New York), January 1979.
"Steele Wyoming," in *Fantasy and Science Fiction* (New York), March 1980.

OTHER PUBLICATIONS

Novels

If Dying Was All. New York, Ace, 1971.
Too Sweet to Die. New York, Ace, 1972.
The Same Lie Twice. New York, Ace, 1973.
Cleopatra Jones (novelization of screenplay). New York, Warner, 1973.
Superstition (novelization of TV play; as Howard Lee). New York, Warner, 1973.
One Grave Too Many. New York, Ace, 1974.
The Tremendous Adventures of Bernie Wine. New York, Warner, 1975.
Cleopatra Jones and the Casino of Gold (novelization of screenplay). New York, Warner, 1975.
Challengers for the Unknown. New York, Dell, 1977.
Capricorn One. New York, Fawcett, 1978.
Agent of Love (as Jullian Kearny). New York, Warner, 1979.

Novels as Con Steffanson

Laverne and Shirley: Teamwork (novelization of TV play). New York, Warner, 1976.
Laverne and Shirley: Easy Money (novelization of TV play). New York, Warner, 1976.
Laverne and Shirley: Gold Rush (novelization of TV play). New York, Warner, 1976.

Novels as Josephine Kains

The Devil Mask Mystery. New York, Kensington, 1978.
The Curse of the Golden Skull. New York, Kensington, 1978.
The Green Lama Mystery. New York, Kensington, 1979.

Other

The Assault on Childhood. Los Angeles, Sherbourne Press, 1969; London, Gollancz, 1970.
Cheap Thrills: An Informal History of the Pulp Magazines. New Rochelle, New York, Arlington House, 1972.
An American Family. New York, Warner, 1973.
The Adventurous Decade: Comic Strips in the Thirties. New Rochelle, New York, Arlington House, 1975.

Editor, *The Hardboiled Dicks: An Anthology and Study of Pulp Detective Fiction.* Los Angeles, Sherbourne Press, 1965; London, Boardman, 1967.
Editor, *Lineup Tough Guys.* Los Angeles, Sherbourne Press, 1966.

*   *   *

Ron Goulart's fictional world includes Southern California, the Barnum system in outer space, and as many other alternate worlds in between as his lively imagination can conjure up. He began his writing career with parodies and humorous sketches and has continued to write with a slightly cock-eyed view of the world. He has written stories in virtually every genre, but is primarily considered a science-fiction writer. Just as his mysteries have a touch of the fantastic, his science fiction has a touch of the mysterious and often seems to straddle genres when it doesn't simply defy all categories.

His stories of outer space nearly all take place outside our own solar system in that group of planets dominated by Barnum. In the Barnum system, Murdstone is the least favored planet, but Malagra is the pesthole of the universe. Like other legendary places (Dogpatch or Hogscratch, Arkansas) the Barnum system adjusts its dimensions to suit the current story. The Barnum system has been imaginatively realized in visual terms by artist Gil Kane in the comic strip *Star Hawks*. All of the Goulart humor comes across in the adventures of Rex Jaxan and Chavez of the Interplanetary Law Service. Ben Jolson, the multi-faced agent for the Chameleon Corps, is called on by the Political Espionage Office on Barnum to investigate mysterious happenings. *The Sword Swallower* pulls together earlier threads from his short stories, but Jolson's shape-changing powers are not exploited as imaginatively in full length as they are in the shorter form. In "Chameleon" Jolson foils an assassination by hiding in one corner of the room disguised as a TV set.

One of his best collections of short stories, *Broke Down Engine*, is concerned entirely with the problem of man's increasing dependence on machines. Told with humor, they also embody a bitter view of a future in which human beings become isolated from one another. Goulart's days as an advertising copywriter serve as the basis for his stories about androids in show business. He brings a fine eye and ear for the ridiculous to these stories in which the satire may be deeper than mere surface humor. One thinks of real life "personalities" who respond to interviewers in precise, robotic terms. Perhaps the ultimate meshing to themes from Goulart's repertoire is *Cowboy Heaven* in which an android replacing the ailing actor Jake Troop on the film *Saddle Tramp* doesn't know when to stop. Goulart has his serious side and this comes out in the stories of fantasy and derring-do about the mysterious Gypsy's search for his own identity.

Goulart's style is concise and his stories are told mostly in dialogue. The reader has to be alert and not let the fast pace and skeletal appearance prevent him from enjoying the yarn. At his best, Goulart is a witty and engaging story-teller, with a recognizable reality to his fantasies. His Southern California is the extrapolation of present trends in the ridiculous; his machinery gone amok is an extension of our own worst fears as a vacuum cleaner malfunctions or an automobile breaks down.

—J. Randolph Cox

* * *

GRANT, Charles L. American. Born in Newark, New Jersey, 12 September 1942. Educated at Trinity College, Hartford, Connecticut, B.A. 1964. Served in the United States Army Military Police, 1968-70: Bronze Star. Married Debbie Voss in 1973; one son and one daughter. English teacher, Toms River High School, New Jersey, 1964-70, Chester High School, New Jersey, 1970-72, and Mt. Olive High School, New Jersey, 1972-73; English and history teacher, Roxbury High School, New Jersey , 1974-75. Since 1975, free-lance writer. Executive Secretary, Science Fiction Writers of America, 1973-77. Recipient: Nebula Award, 1976, 1978; World Fantasy Award, for non-fiction, 1980. Agent: Kirby McCauley Ltd., 60 East 42nd Street, New York, New York 10017. Address: 51J The Village Green, Budd Lake, New Jersey 07828, U.S.A.

SCIENCE-FICTION PUBLICATIONS

Novels (series: Parric family)

The Shadow of Alpha (Parric).   New York, Berkley, 1976.
Ascension (Parric).   New York, Berkley, 1977.
The Ravens of the Moon.   New York, Doubleday, 1978; London, Sidgwick and Jackson, 1979.
Legion (Parric).   New York, Berkley, 1979.

Uncollected Short Stories

"The House of Evil," in *Fantasy and Science Fiction* (New York), December 1968.
"The Summer of the Irish Sea," in *Orbit 11*, edited by Damon Knight.   New York, Putnam, 1973.
"The Magic Child," in *Frontiers 2*, edited by Roger Elwood.   New York, Macmillan, 1973.
"Weep No More, Old Lady," in *Future Quest*, edited by Roger Elwood.   New York, Avon, 1973.
"But the Other Old Man Stopped Playing," in *Amazing* (New York), April 1973.
"Come Dance with Me on My Pony's Grave," in *Fantasy and Science Fiction* (New York), July 1973.
"Abdication," in *Amazing* (New York), October 1973.
"Everybody a Winner the Barker Cried," in *Orbit 13*, edited by Damon Knight.   New York, Putnam, 1974.
"The Key to English," in *Fantasy and Science Fiction* (New York), May 1974.
"The Rest Is Silence," in *Nebula Award Stories 10*, edited by James E. Gunn.   New York, Harper, 1975.
"In Donovan's Time," in *Orbit 16*, edited by Damon Knight.   New York, Harper, 1975.
"To Be a Witch, in 3/4 Time," in *Fantastic* (New York), February 1975.
"When Two or Three Are Gathered," in *Amazing* (New York), March 1975.
"White Wolf Calling," in *Fantasy and Science Fiction* (New York), April 1975.
"The Three of Tens," in *Fantasy and Science Fiction* (New York), December 1975.
"Seven Is a Birdsong," in *Analog* (New York), January 1976.
"A Crowd of Shadows," in *Fantasy and Science Fiction* (New York), June 1976.
"Eldorado," in *The Arts and Beyond*, edited by Thomas F. Monteleone.   New York, Doubleday, 1977.
"The Dark of Legends, The Light of Lies," in *Chrysalis 1*, edited by Roy Torgeson.   New York, Kensington, 1977.
"A Glow of Candles, A Unicorn's Eye," in *Graven Images*, edited by Edward L. Ferman and Barry N. Malzberg.   Nashville, Nelson, 1977.
"Treatise on the Artifacts of a Civilization," in *Antaeus* (New York), 1977.
"The Shape of Plowshares," in *Analog* (New York), March 1977.
"Gently Rapping," in *Galaxy* (New York), September 1977.
"Knock, and See What Enters," in *Fantastic* (New York), December 1977.
"View, with a Difference," in *Dark Sins, Dark Dreams*, edited by Barry N. Malzberg and Bill Pronzini.   New York, Doubleday, 1978.
"The Peace That Passes Never," in *Chrysalis 3*, edited by Roy Torgeson.   New York, Kensington, 1978.
"Hear Me Now, My Sweet Abbey Rose," in *Fantasy and Science Fiction* (New York), March 1978.
"Caesar, Now Be Still," in *Fantasy and Science Fiction* (New York), September 1978.
"When Dark Descends," with Thomas F. Monteleone, in *Chrysalis 4*, edited by Roy Torgeson.   New York, Kensington, 1979.
"Love-Starved," in *Fantasy and Science Fiction* (New York), August 1979.
"Secret of the Heart," in *Fantasy and Science Fiction* (New York), March 1980.

OTHER PUBLICATIONS

Novels

The Curse.   Canoga Park, California, Major, 1976.
The Hour of the Oxrun Dead.   New York, Doubleday, 1977.
The Sound of Midnight.   New York, Doubleday, 1978.
The Last Call of Mourning.   New York, Doubleday, 1979.

Other

Introduction to *Conjure Wife,* by Charles Chesnutt.   Boston, Gregg Press, 1977.

Editor, *Writing and Selling Science Fiction.*   Cincinnati, Writer's Digest, 1977.
Editor, *Shadows 1-3.*   New York, Doubleday, 3 vols., 1978-80.
Editor, *Nightmares.*   Chicago, Playboy Press, 1979.

Charles L. Grant comments:

In science fiction, I'm working on a future history that most of my more recent stories and novels fit into, a history that will eventually cover over 500 years, primarily tracing a single family (the Parrics). In horror fiction, my aim is, simply, to produce a fright in the reader. In this regard I generally use two settings: Hawthorne Street (a place in an unnamed town in an unnamed area of the country), and Oxrun Station, an upper-middle and upper-class village in western Connecticut. If there's any influence at all in my work it comes not from Lovecraft or Smith, but from Bradbury and Ellison, with perhaps a dollop of Sturgeon.

*   *   *

Charles L. Grant continues to be an author of bright, unfulfilled promise. His first stories showed occasional glimpses of deft imagery, and seemed to be the product of a new author struggling with the development of meaning from story ideas. The struggle continues, but its realization still seems far away.

Grant has begun an ambitious undertaking, a future history spanning several centuries concerning the Parric family, introduced in *The Shadow of Alpha.* This first novel presents a world of the 22nd century, swept by the plague winds. The population of North America has mostly been confined to megalopoli, with small groups of hunters living in the surrounding wilderness. Androids have been developed to take over onerous physical tasks. The plague destroys most of the population of humans, and turns the androids into rogues, a constant threat to the remaining humans. *The Shadow of Alpha* is an unremarkable post-disaster novel, with the conventional projections of science fiction: petty warlords, universal suspicion and hostility, and an unaccountable shortage of women. The protagonist is concerned with the re-establishment of the former culture. *Ascension* concerns the third generation. The government has established itself in a small town and is slowly extending tendrils of control around it. Although the CenGov is manifestly conservative, the advanced technology it offers is presented as preferable to any other lifestyle. No variant cultures are suggested as being anything but decadent or oppressive. On a mission of vengeance the protagonist, Orion, liberates the remaining inhabitants of Philayork. Although he has ostensibly learned the bitter taste of revenge, he still allows the villain to be killed.

The third novel in the series, *Legion,* is remarkably similar. Orion's brother is likewise on a quest for vengeance, although he professes otherwise. Like Orion, he suffers from melancholia. Once again, no alternatives to the CenGov reign are seriously considered and the novel is climaxed by the death of the villain. *Legion* is an improvement over the preceding novels, if only because Grant seems to have achieved a better fusion of action and introspection. As a result, the book has a steadier pace than *Ascension,* which has a strong tendency to bog down in the protagonist's own depression. The language is generally quite well handled, although Grant suffers from the delusion that repetition and sentence fragments enhance emotional impact.

It is clear that Charles L. Grant is trying to write something more than simple-minded science-fiction adventures. His novels and short stories reveal an author who takes his craft seriously. As yet, however, he has been unable to transcend the conventions of the genre he has selected.

—Jeff Frane

GRAVES, Robert (Ranke).   Also writes as Barbara Rich.   British.   Born in London, 24 July 1895. Educated at Charterhouse School, Surrey; St. John's College, Oxford, B.Litt. 1926. Served in France with the Royal Welch Fusiliers in World War I; was refused admittance into the armed forces in World War II. Married 1) Nancy Nicholson, one son and two daughters; 2) Beryl Pritchard, three sons and one daughter. Professor of English, Egyptian University, Cairo, 1926. Settled in Deyá, Mallorca; with the poet Laura Riding established the Seizen Press and *Epilogue* magazine. Clark Lecturer, Trinity College, Cambridge, 1954; Professor of Poetry, Oxford University, 1961-66; Arthur Dehon Little Memorial Lecturer, Massachusetts Institute of Technology, Cambridge, 1963. Recipient: Bronze Medal for Poetry, Olympic Games, Paris, 1924; Hawthornden Prize, 1935; Black Memorial Prize, 1935; Femina Vie Heureuse-Stock Prize, 1939; Russell Loines Award 1958; National Poetry Society of America Gold Medal, 1960; Foyle Poetry Prize, 1960; Arts Council Poetry Award, 1962; Italia Prize, for radio play, 1965; Queen's Gold Medal for Poetry, 1968; Gold Medal for Poetry, Cultural Olympics, Mexico City, 1968. M.A.: Oxford University, 1961. Honorary Fellow, St. John's College, Oxford, 1971. Honorary Member, American Academy of Arts and Sciences, 1970. Address: c/o A.P. Watt Ltd., 26-28 Bedford Row, London WC1R 4HL, England.

SCIENCE-FICTION PUBLICATIONS

Novel

Watch the North Wind Rise.   New York, Creative Age Press, 1949; as *Seven Days in New Crete,* London, Cassell, 1949.

OTHER PUBLICATIONS

Novels

No Decency Left (as Barbara Rich, with Laura Riding).   London, Cape, 1932.
The Real David Copperfield.   London, Barker, 1933; as *David Copperfield by Charles Dickens, Condensed by Robert Graves,* edited by Merrill P. Paine, New York, Harcourt Brace, 1934.
I, Claudius....   London, Barker, and New York, Smith and Haas, 1934.
Claudius the God and His Wife Messalina....   London, Barker, 1934; New York, Smith and Haas, 1935.
"Antigua, Penny, Puce."   Deyá, Mallorca, Seizin Press, and London, Constable, 1936; as *The Antigua Stamp,* New York, Random House, 1937.
Count Belisarius.   London, Cassell, and New York, Random House, 1938.
Sergeant Lamb of the Ninth.   London Methuen, 1940; as *Sergeant Lamb's America,* New York, Random House, 1940.
Proceed, Sergeant Lamb.   London Methuen, and New York, Random House, 1941.
The Story of Marie Powell: Wife to Mr. Milton.   London, Cassell, 1943; as *Wife to Mr. Milton: The Story of Marie Powell,* New York, Creative Age Press, 1944.
The Golden Fleece.   London, Cassell, 1944; as *Hercules, My Shipmate,* New York, Creative Age Press, 1945.
King Jesus.   New York, Creative Age Press, and London, Cassell, 1946.
The Islands of Unwisdom.   New York, Doubleday, 1949; as *The Isles of Unwisdom,* London, Cassell, 1950.
Homer's Daughter.   London, Cassell, and New York, Doubleday, 1955.

Short Stories

The Shout. London, Mathews and Marrot, 1929.
¡Catacrok! Mostly Stories, Mostly Funny. London, Cassell, 1956.
Collected Short Stories. New York, Doubleday, 1964; London, Cassell, 1965; as *The Shout and Other Stories,* London, Penguin, 1978.

Plays

John Kemp's Wager: A Ballad Opera. Oxford, Blackwell, and New York, T.B. Edwards, 1925.

Radio Play: *The Anger of Achilles,* 1964.

Verse

Over the Brazier. London, Poetry Bookshop, 1916; New York, St. Martin's Press, 1975.
Goliath and David. London, Chiswick Press, 1916.
Fairies and Fusiliers. London, Heinemann, 1917; New York, Knopf, 1918.
Treasure Box. London, Chiswick Press, 1919.
Country Sentiment. London, Secker, and New York, Knopf, 1920.
The Pier-Glass. London, Secker, and New York, Knopf, 1921.
Whipperginny. London, Heinemann, and New York, Knopf, 1923.
The Feather Bed. Richmond, Surrey, Hogarth Press, 1923.
Mock Beggar Hall. London, Hogarth Press, 1924.
Welchman's Hose. London, The Fleuron, 1925; Folcroft, Pennsylvania, Folcroft Editions, 1971.
(Poems). London, Benn, 1925.
The Marmosite's Miscellany (as John Doyle). London, Hogarth Press, 1925.
Poems (1914-1926). London, Heinemann, 1927; New York, Doubleday, 1929.
Poems (1914-1927). London, Heinemann, 1927.
Poems 1929. London, Seizin Press, 1929.
Ten Poems More. Paris, Hours Press, 1930.
Poems 1926-1930. London, Heinemann, 1931.
To Whom Else? Deyá, Mallorca, Seizin Press, 1931.
Poems 1930-1933. London, Barker, 1933.
Collected Poems. London, Cassell, and New York, Random House, 1938.
No More Ghosts: Selected Poems. London, Faber, 1940.
(Poems). London, Eyre and Spottiswoode, 1943.
Poems 1938-1945. London, Cassell, and New York, Creative Age Press, 1946.
Collected Poems (1914-1947). London, Cassell, 1948.
Poems and Satires 1951. London, Cassell, 1951.
Poems 1953. London, Cassell, 1953.
Collected Poems 1955. New York, Doubleday, 1955.
Poems Selected by Himself. London, Penguin, 1957; revised edition, 1961, 1966, 1972.
The Poems of Robert Graves. New York, Doubleday, 1958.
Collected Poems 1959. London, Cassell, 1959.
More Poems 1961. London, Cassell, 1961.
Collected Poems. New York, Doubleday, 1961.
New Poems 1962. London, Cassell, 1962; as *New Poems,* New York, Doubleday, 1963.
The More Deserving Cases: Eighteen Old Poems for Reconsideration. Marlborough, Marlborough College Press, 1962; Folcroft, Pennsylvania, Folcroft Editions, 1978.
Man Does, Woman Is 1964. London, Cassell, and New York, Doubleday, 1964.
Love Respelt. London, Cassell, 1965.
Collected Poems 1965. London, Cassell, 1965.
Seventeen Poems Missing from "Love Respelt." Privately printed, 1966.
Collected Poems 1966. New York, Doubleday, 1966.
Colophon to "Love Respelt." Privately printed, 1967.
(Poems), with D.H. Lawrence, edited by Leonard Clark. London, Longman, 1967.

Poems 1965-1968. London, Cassell, 1968; New York, Doubleday, 1969.
Poems about Love. London, Cassell, and New York, Doubleday, 1969.
Love Respelt Again. New York, Doubleday, 1969.
Beyond Giving. Privately printed, 1969.
Poems 1968-1970. London, Cassell, 1970.
Advice from a Mother. London, Poem-of-the-Month Club, 1970.
The Green-Sailed Vessel. Privately printed, 1971.
Corgi Modern Poets in Focus 3, with others, edited by Dannie Abse. London, Corgi, 1971.
Poems 1970-1972. London, Cassell, 1972; New York, Doubleday, 1973.
Deyá. London, Motif Editions, 1973.
Timeless Meeting: Poems. London, Bertram Rota, 1973.
At the Gate. London, Bertram Rota, 1974.
Collected Poems 1975. London, Cassell, 2 vols., 1975.
New Collected Poems. New York, Doubleday, 1977.

Recordings: *Robert Graves Reading His Own Poems,* Argo and Listen, 1960; *Robert Graves Reading His Own Poetry and the White Goddess,* Caedmon; *The Rubaiyat of Omar Khayyam,* Spoken Arts.

Other

On English Poetry. New York, Knopf, and London, Heinemann, 1922.
The Meaning of Dreams. London, Cecil Palmer, 1924; New York, Greenberg, 1925.
Poetic Unreason and Other Studies. London, Cecil Palmer, 1925.
My Head! My Head! Being the History of Elisha and the Shunamite Woman; With the History of Moses as Elisha Related It, and Her Questions to Him. London, Secker, and New York, Knopf, 1925.
Contemporary Techniques of Poetry: A Political Analogy. London, Hogarth Press, 1925; Folcroft, Pennsylvania, Folcroft Editions, 1977.
Another Future of Poetry. London, Hogarth Press, 1926.
Impenetrability; or, The Proper Habit of English. London, Hogarth Press, 1926.
The English Ballad: A Short Critical Survey. London, Benn, 1927; revised edition, as *English and Scottish Ballads,* London, Heinemann, and New York, Macmillan, 1957.
Lars Porsena; or, The Future of Swearing and Improper Language. London, Kegan Paul Trench Trubner, and New York, Dutton, 1927; revised edition, as *The Future of Swearing and Improper Language,* Kegan Paul Trench Trubner, 1936.
A Survey of Modernist Poetry, with Laura Riding. London, Heinemann, 1927; New York, Doubleday, 1928.
Lawrence and the Arabs. London, Cape, 1927; as *Lawrence and the Arabian Adventure,* New York, Doubleday, 1928.
A Pamphlet Against Anthologies, with Laura Riding. London, Cape, 1928; as *Against Anthologies,* New York, Doubleday, 1928.
Mrs. Fisher; or, The Future of Humour. London, Kegan Paul Trench Trubner, 1928; Folcroft, Pennsylvania, Folcroft Editions, 1974.
Goodbye to All That: An Autobiography. London, Cape, 1929; New York, Cape and Smith, 1930; revised edition, New York, Doubleday, and London, Cassell, 1957; London, Penguin, 1960.
T.E. Lawrence to His Biographer Robert Graves. New York, Doubleday, 1938; London, Faber, 1939.
The Long Week-end: A Social History of Great Britain 1918-1939, with Alan Hodge. London, Faber, 1940; New York, Macmillan, 1941.
Work in Hand, with others. London, Hogarth Press, 1942.
The Reader over Your Shoulder: A Handbook for Writers of English Prose, with Alan Hodge. London, Cape, 1943; New York, Macmillan, 1944.
The White Goddess: A Historical Grammar of Poetic Myth. London, Faber, and New York, Creative Age Press, 1948; revised edition, Faber, 1952, 1966; New York, Knopf, 1958.

The Common Asphodel: Collected Essays on Poetry 1922-1949. London, Hamish Hamilton, 1949; Folcroft, Pennsylvania, Folcroft Editions, 1971.

Occupation: Writer. New York, Creative Age Press, 1950; London, Cassell, 1951.

The Nazarene Gospel Restored, with Joshua Podro. London, Cassell, 1953; New York, Doubleday, 1954.

The Crowning Privilege: The Clark Lectures 1954-1955; Also Various Essays on Poetry and Sixteen New Poems. London, Cassell, 1955; as *The Crowning Privilege: Collected Essays on Poetry,* New York, Doubleday, 1956.

Adam's Rib and Other Anomalous Elements in the Hebrew Creation Myth: A New View. London, Trianon Press, 1955; New York, Yoseloff, 1958.

The Greek Myths. London and Baltimore, Penguin, 2 vols., 1955.

Jesus in Rome: A Historical Conjecture, with Joshua Podro. London, Cassell, 1957.

They Hanged My Saintly Billy. London, Cassell, 1957; as *They Hanged My Saintly Billy: The Life and Death of Dr. William Palmer,* New York, Doubleday, 1957.

Steps: Stories, Talks, Essays, Poems, Studies in History. London, Cassell, 1958.

5 Pens in Hand. New York, Doubleday, 1958.

Food for Centaurs: Stories, Talks, Critical Studies, Poems. New York, Doubleday, 1960.

The Penny Fiddle: Poems for Children. London, Cassell, 1960; New York, Doubleday, 1961.

Greek Gods and Heroes. New York, Doubleday, 1960; as *Myths of Ancient Greece,* London, Cassell, 1961.

Selected Poetry and Prose, edited by James Reeves. London, Hutchinson, 1961.

The Siege and Fall of Troy (juvenile). London, Cassell, 1962; New York, Doubleday, 1963.

The Big Green Book. New York, Crowell Collier, 1962; London, Penguin, 1978.

Oxford Addresses on Poetry. London, Cassell, and New York, Doubleday, 1962.

Nine Hundred Iron Chariots: The Twelfth Arthur Dehon Little Memorial Lecture. Cambridge, Massachusetts Institute of Technology, 1963.

The Hebrew Myths: The Book of Genesis, with Raphael Patai. New York, Doubleday, and London, Cassell, 1964.

Ann at Highwood Hall: Poems for Children. London, Cassell, 1964.

Majorca Observed. London, Cassell, and New York, Doubleday, 1965.

Mammon and the Black Goddess. London, Cassell, and New York, Doubleday, 1965.

Two Wise Children (juvenile). New York, Harlin Quist, 1966; London, W.H. Allen, 1967.

Poetic Craft and Principle. London, Cassell, 1967.

Spiritual Quixote. London, Oxford University Press, 1967.

The Poor Boy Who Followed His Star (juvenile). London, Cassell, 1968; New York, Doubleday, 1969.

The Crane Bag and Other Disputed Subjects. London, Cassell, 1969.

On Poetry: Collected Talks and Essays. New York, Doubleday, 1969.

Poems: Abridged for Dolls and Princes (juvenile). London, Cassell, and New York, Doubleday, 1971.

Difficult Questions, Easy Answers. London, Cassell, 1972; New York, Doubleday, 1973.

An Ancient Castle (juvenile). London, Owen, 1980.

Editor, with Alan Porter and Richard Hughes, *Oxford Poetry, 1921.* Oxford, Blackwell, 1921.

Editor, *John Skelton (Laureate), 1460(?)-1529.* London, Benn, 1927.

Editor, *The Less Familiar Nursery Rhymes.* London, Benn, 1927.

Editor, *The Comedies of Terence.* New York, Doubleday, 1962; London, Cassell, 1963.

Translator, with Laura Riding, *Almost Forgotten Germany,* by Georg Schwarz. Deyá, Mallorca, Seizin Press, London, Constable, and New York, Random House, 1936.

Translator, *The Transformations of Lucius, Otherwise Known as The Golden Ass,* by Apuleius. London, Penguin, 1950; New York, Farrar Straus, 1951.

Translator, *The Cross and the Sword,* by Manuel de Jésus Galván. Bloomington, Indiana University Press, 1955; London, Gollancz, 1956.

Translator, *The Infant with the Globe,* by Pedro Antonio de Alarcón. London, Trianon Press, 1955; New York, Yoseloff, 1958.

Translator, *Winter in Majorca,* by George Sand. London, Cassell, 1956.

Translator, *Pharsalia: Dramatic Episodes of the Civil Wars,* by Lucan. London, Penguin, 1956.

Translator, *The Twelve Caesars,* by Suetonius. London, Penguin, 1957.

Translator, *The Anger of Achilles: Homer's Iliad.* New York, Doubleday, 1959; London, Cassell, 1960.

Translator, with Omar Ali-Shah, *Rubaiyat of Omar Khayyam.* London, Cassell, 1967; New York, Doubleday, 1968.

Translator, *The Song of Songs.* New York, Clarkson Potter, and London, Collins, 1973.

*

Bibliography: *A Bibliography of the Works of Robert Graves* by Fred H. Higginson, London, Nicholas Vane, 1966.

Manuscript Collections: Lockwood Memorial Library, State University of New York at Buffalo; New York City Public Library; University of Texas Library, Austin.

*   *   *

Robert Graves is best known as a historical novelist and poet; his exercise in what might be called literary anthropology, *The White Goddess,* was a major intellectual influence in the 1950's. Only one of his novels, *Watch the North Wind Rise,* can be classified as science fiction, and that loosely, but it is an extraordinarily inventive work. In it, Graves uses the classical device of the Utopian novel, an observer from our time (inferred to be Graves himself) reacting to a culture of the future.

As the English title, *Seven Days in New Crete,* implies, this culture is based on the ancient Minoan; it was spread (after our civilization has ended with more of a whimper than a bang) from a test area where the ancient culture had been artificially reproduced as an anthropological experiment. The dress and religion (worship of a Mother Goddess) are very much Minoan, the society itself less so. It is almost obsessively anti-technological and therefore agriculturally based. The population is rigidly divided into five classes and ruled by custom and ritual; one chapter describing in detail a ritual "ballet" is something of a tour de force.

Particularly striking in the novel are Graves's characters, who are vividly three dimensional, and his attention to the arts (especially poetry), an area usually neglected in science fiction of the period. And while superficially Utopic, there is the implication at the climax of the end of the New Cretan era, generally from intrinsic flaws, specifically by disruptions unwittingly set in motion by the 20th century narrator himself.

—Baird Searles

GRAY, Curme.

SCIENCE-FICTION PUBLICATIONS

Novel

Murder In Millennium VI. Chicago, Shasta, 1951.

*   *   *

There are a number of science-fiction writers whose reputations rest primarily on one story which stands out from the rest of their work. Far less numerous are those writers who are only known to have written a single story, and one that is of such quality or importance as to deserve a place in SF history. One of the latter group is Curme Gray, author of *Murder in Millennium VI*.

Murder in Millennium VI is subtitled "A Future Mystery." It is set in a matriarchal society of the far future, whose customs and technology bear no resemblance to our own. One measure of the alienness of this society is that the very concept of "death" has disappeared from common usage. When the ruler of this global society dies, only an antiquarian, a student of curiosities from the distant past, can recognize the condition, and he has great difficulty in explaining its meaning to others. With the eventual understanding of what "death" means comes the realization that it was not the result of a natural process but was "irregularity," deliberately caused by some unknown agent. Not only has death re-entered the perfect and permanent society, but some member of that society has re-invented murder. The questions of who killed the Matriarch, and how, and why, underlie this very distinctive novel.

The unusual thing about *Murder in Millennium VI* is that it is an attempt to depict a future society entirely in terms of that society, without external references. There are no handy expository lectures no conversations in which two characters explain everyday features of their society to each other—all of the details of the future setting and its culture must be deduced from context. To the extent that not all such details *are* deducible, the book falls short of its ambitious goal, but nevertheless, as Damon Knight has said, "it's a prodigious three-quarters success....For sheer audacity and stubbornness, Curme Gray's performance is breathtaking."

—R.E. Briney

GREEN, Joseph (Lee). American. Born in Compass Lake, Florida, 14 January 1931. Educated at Brevard Community College, Cocoa, Florida, A.A. Married 1) Juanita Henderson in 1951 (divorced, 1975), one son and one daughter; 2) Patrice Milton in 1975, two daughters. Laboratory technician, International Paper Company, Panama City, Florida, 1949-51; shop worker and welder, Panama City, 1952-54; millwright in Florida, Texas, and Alabama, 1955-58; senior supervisor, Boeing Company, Seattle, 1959-63. Since 1965, public affairs science writer, Kennedy Space Center, Florida. Agent: Blassingame McCauley and Wood, 60 East 42nd Street, New York, New York 10017; or, E.J. Carnell Agency, Rowneybury Bungalow, Sawbridgeworth, near Old Harlow, Essex CM20 2EX, England. Address: 1390 Holly Avenue, Merritt Island, Florida 32952, U.S.A.

SCIENCE-FICTION PUBLICATIONS

Novels

The Loafers of Refuge. London, Gollancz, and New York, Ballantine, 1965.
Gold the Man. London, Gollancz, 1971; as *The Mind Behind the Eye,* New York, DAW, 1971.
Conscience Interplanetary. London, Gollancz, 1972; New York, Doubleday, 1973.
Star Probe. London, Millington, 1976; New York, Ace, 1978.
The Horde. Toronto, Laser, 1976; London, Dobson, 1979.

Short Stories

An Affair with Genius. London, Gollancz, 1969.

Uncollected Short Stories

"Death and the Sensperience Poet," in *New Writings in SF 17,* edited by John Carnell. London, Dobson, 1970.
"First Light on a Darkling Plain," in *New Writings in SF 19,* edited by John Carnell. London, Dobson, 1971.
"Wrong Attitude," in *Analog* (New York), February 1971.
"The Butterflies of Beauty," in *Fantasy and Science Fiction* (New York), June 1971.
"The Crier of Crystal," in *Analog* (New York), October 1971.
"One Man Game," in *Analog* (New York), February 1972.
"The Dwarfs of Zwergwelt," in *If* (New York), June 1972.
"Three-Tour Man," in *Analog* (New York), August 1972.
"A Custom of the Children of Life," in *Fantasy and Science Fiction* (New York), December 1972.
"Space to Move," in *The New Mind,* edited by Roger Elwood. New York, Macmillan, 1973.
"Let My People Go!," in *The Other Side of Tomorrow,* edited by Roger Elwood. New York, Random House, 1973.
"The Birdlover," in *Showcase,* edited by Roger Elwood. New York, Harper, 1973.
"Robustus Revisited," in *Fantasy and Science Fiction* (New York), April 1973.
"The Waiting World," in *Future Kin,* edited by Roger Elwood. New York, Doubleday, 1974.
"A Star Is Born," in *Fantasy and Science Fiction* (New York), February 1974.
"Walk Barefoot on the Glass," in *Analog* (New York), March 1974.
"Jaybird's Song," in *Fantasy and Science Fiction* (New York), December 1974.
"A Death in Coventry," in *Dystopian Visions,* edited by Roger Elwood. Englewood Cliffs, New Jersey, Prentice Hall, 1975.
"Encounter with a Carnivore," in *Epoch,* edited by Roger Elwood and Robert Silverberg. New York, Berkley, 1975.
"Weekend in Hartford," in *Dude* (Mt. Morris, Illinois), September 1975.
"Last of the Chauvinists," in *Fantasy and Science Fiction* (New York), November 1975.
"Jeremiah, Born Dying," in *Odyssey* (New York), Spring 1976.
"To See the Stars That Blind," with Patrice Milton, in *Fantasy and Science Fiction* (New York), March 1977.
"An Alien Conception," in *Nugget* (New York), June 1977.
"The Wind among the Mindymums," in *Fantasy and Science Fiction* (New York), December 1978.
"The Speckled Gantry," in *Destinies.* New York, Ace, 1979.

OTHER PUBLICATIONS

Other

"Countdown for Surveyor," in *Analog* (New York), March 1967.
"Manufacturing in Space," in *Analog* (New York), December 1970.
"Skylab," in *Analog* (New York), March, April 1972.

Joseph Green comments:
Most of my stories have an underlying philosophical theme that is often not apparent on the surface. At heart I think of myself as an untrained, poorly equipped, corn-ball philosopher, and what I enjoy most is playing with ideas in fictional form. For that reason, I'll never create a consistent "future history." If I write a story about the totally secular world of 2090 today, I want to write one tomorrow about the new surge in absolutist religion from 1070 to 1200. I have no faith at all in a single future.

I've achieved some small reputation as a writer of unusually believable aliens. I don't know why. I dream them up, work to make them real, and write about them because I enjoy it. Do I need a better reason? I write primarily for readers, not critics or other writers. If a reader enjoys my work, that's good. If it also makes him think, that's even better.

*   *   *

Joseph Green is a strongly imaginative writer. He likes to set his heroes problems, sometimes highly exotic or elaborately contrived, always laid out with great clarity and convincingly resolved. These heroes are often troubleshooters, typically working at the interface between human and alien, sometimes—and this is probably his most characteristic motif—even operating with alien bodies. In his most powerful novel, *Gold the Man,* this alienation works as far as two removes, for the hero is emphatically a man trapped in a superman's body, put to work inside an alien giant. In confronting his characters with painful dilemmas, Green communicates to the reader a strong concern; he is also able to treat sympathetically those on both sides of an irreconcilable debate, as in *Star Probe,* which concerns one battle in a larger war between the space scientists and the Friends of the Earth.

Reflecting their origins as series of short stories, *The Loafers of Refuge* and *Conscience Interplanetary* are episodic narratives. In the first, trouble-shooter Carey, as the first man born on Refuge, works to resolve conflict between humans and the native loafers, who have developed mental but not mechanical power. Human-Loafer interaction is mutually beneficial: for instance, the Loafers revivify their living trees (the Ent-like *breshwahr*), one of whom shows how men can survive matter transmission, thus enabling rapid colonization of other planets to relieve the overcrowded Earth. In the second, the hero Allan Odegaard has the job of checking whether intelligence exists on a planet: if so, it must be left alone, if not, it may be colonized (a problem consequent on the solution found in *Loafers*). Throughout his seven extraordinary adventures, Allan is in more danger from reactionary humans than from the weird life-forms he encounters.

Gold the Man is a classic novel, whether considered as a profound study of the loneliness of the superman in no-man's-land or as an exciting contribution to Brobdingnagian fantasy. Earth is at war with giant humanoids, the Hilt-Sil, one of whom, suffering from irreparable brain damage, is captured. The superman Gold, and a female assistant, Marina Petrovna, are installed in the head of the 300-foot captive, where they control his brain, seated behind one of his eyes. In this extraordinary Trojan horse, they spy on the alien planet, finding the feared enemies to be a race of gentle giants living an idyllic life but forced to look for another planet because of danger from their own sun. Gold helps resolve their problems and, remarkably enough, his enforced voyeurism of their Gargantuan love-play resolves his personal fear of impotence: being a superman, he was a slow developer, but he rapes and impregnates the helpless Marina and their child is born with the assistance of a friendly Hilt-Sil doctor who has discovered them (this is not a macho fantasy story for all that). Green sets himself difficult problems in this powerful novel but he handles both the physicalities and the psychological stresses of the intriguing situation with great tact and skill.

In the light of *Gold the Man,* Green makes less than expected of the interesting motif in *Star Probe* of an old man, deceased, who is brought back to life in the body of his idiot grandson for the purposes of a suicide mission. The mission concerns the investigation of an alien probe in the solar system; once the difficulties of getting a rocket to the probe have been resolved, Green is able once again to concern himself with the interesting problem of communication between alien and human; within the novel as a whole, however, the probe serves only as an emblem of what the struggle for funds between space scientists and ecologists is all about. This struggle is, I suppose, bound to be less interesting to the average SF reader, who belongs to the already converted, but Green gallantly sacrifices wonder to pragmatics.

Among Green's many fine short stories, it is hard to pick out the best or most characteristic, but "Jinn," "Once Around Arcturus," "Treasure Hunt" (man inside crystal chariot-horse), "When I Have Passed Away" (exotic Giantesses), "Last of the Chauvinists," and "To See the Stars That Blind" (written with his wife, Patrice Milton, brilliantly presenting the wonder and horror of a new mode of seeing), should be included.

—Michael J. Tolley

GREENLEE, Sam. American. Born in Chicago, Illinois, 13 July 1930. Educated at the University of Wisconsin, Madison, B.S. 1952; University of Chicago, 1954-57; University of Salonica, Greece, 1963-64. Served in the United Army Infantry, 1952-54; First Lieutenant. Married to Nienke Greenlee. Served as a Foreign Service Officer in Iraq, Pakistan, Indonesia, and Greece, 1957-65; Deputy Director, L.M.O.C., 1965-69. Address: 6240 South Champlain Avenue, Chicago, Illinois 60637, U.S.A.

SCIENCE-FICTION PUBLICATIONS

Novel

The Spook Who Sat by the Door. New York, Baron, and London, Allison and Busby, 1969.

OTHER PUBLICATIONS

Novel

Baghdad Blues. New York, Bantam, n.d.

Verse

Blues for an African Princess. Chicago, Third World Press, 1971.
Ammunition! Poetry and Other Raps. London, Bogle L'Ouverture, 1975.

* * *

In his soul speculative novel, *The Spook Who Sat by the Door,* Sam Greenlee subverts the Bonded white spy thriller by making his hero a black spy (hence doubly a "spook") who uses his CIA training to combat the creeping White Peril. The hero is named Freeman and, like his white fictional counterparts, he is a fantastic fighter, weapons wizard, bedroom bull, and all-around wonder, However, unlike these Great White Hopes, he is less concerned about demonstrating his prowess than ensuring the liberation of his people, and he trains other blacks to assume leadership if he dies. In these qualities and in his brilliantly organized nationwide urban guerrilla warfare against the white power structure, Freeman disproves a white senator's assertion in the novel that "the childlike nature of the colored mentality is ill-suited to the craft of intelligence and espionage." Thus, like Melville in *Benito Cereno,* Greenlee warns that the white man underestimates the black man's intelligence to his own detriment. He also contends that if blacks don't get a break from whites, they should take it.

As might be expected from someone who specialized in political science and served in the foreign service, Greenlee's chief virtue as a speculative writer is his political expertise. His plan for organizing black youth gangs into revolutionary units, adapting the espionage and guerrilla tactics of the CIA, Mao, and Giap to American conditions, and harassing whites into releasing their stranglehold on blacks seems feasible. However, his seriousness in advocating this scheme is questionable since his protagonist notes that "the white man can handle a put-down, but a put-on hangs him up," and Greenlee may be applying this theory. As plan or put-on, his mixture of thriller, parody, propaganda, and speculative fiction is highly intriguing.

—Steven R. Carter

GREER, Richard. *See* **GARRETT, Randall.**

GREY, Charles.   *See* **TUBB, E.C.**

GRIDBAN, Volsted.   *See* **FEARN, John Russell; TUBB, E.C.**

GRIFFITH, George (George Chetwynd Griffith-Jones).   Also wrote as Levin Carnac; Lara; Stanton Morich. British. Born in Plymouth, Devon, 20 August 1857. Educated at schools in Lancashire and in evening classes, College of Preceptors Diploma 1887. Married Elizabeth Brierly in 1887 (died, 1933); two sons and one daughter. Merchant seaman, 1873-77; English teacher, Worthing College, Sussex, 1877-83, and Bolton Grammar School, Lancashire, 1883-87; journalist in London, 1888-89; staff writer, *Pearson's Weekly,* 1890-99, and *Pearson's Magazine,* 1896-1903, both London: travelled extensively for these magazines, including two trips around the world; correspondent in South Africa for London *Daily Mail,* 1903. *Died 4 June 1906.*

SCIENCE-FICTION PUBLICATIONS

Novels

The Angel of the Revolution: A Tale of Coming Terror.   London, Tower, 1893; Westport, Connecticut, Hyperion Press, 1974.
Olga Romanoff; or, The Syren of the Skies.   London, Tower, 1894; Westport, Connecticut, Hyperion Press, 1974.
Valdar the Oft-Born: A Saga of Seven Ages.   London, Pearson, 1895.
The Outlaws of the Air.   London, Tower, 1895.
Briton or Boer?   London, White, 1897.
The Romance of Golden Star.   London, White, 1897; New York, Arno Press, 1978.
The Destined Maid.   London, White, 1898.
The Gold-Finder.   London, White, 1898.
The Great Pirate Syndicate.   London, White, 1899.
The Justice of Revenge.   London, White, 1900.
Captain Ishmael.   London, Hutchinson, 1901.
A Honeymoon in Space.   London, Pearson, 1901; New York, Arno Press, 1975.
Denver's Double: A Story of Inverted Identity.   London, White, 1901.
The World Masters.   London, Long, 1903.
The Lake of Gold: A Narrative of the Anglo-American Conquest of Europe.   London, White, 1903.
The Stolen Submarine.   London, White, 1904.
A Criminal Croesus.   London, Long, 1904.
A Mayfair Magician: A Romance of Criminal Science.   London, White, 1905.
The Mummy and Miss Nitocris: A Phantasy of the Fourth Dimension.   London, Laurie, 1906; New York, Arno Press, 1976.
The Great Weather Syndicate.   London, White, 1906.
The World Peril of 1910.   London, White, 1907.
The Sacred Skull.   London, Everett, 1908.
The Lord of Labour.   London, White, 1911.

Short Stories

Gambles with Destiny.   London, White, 1898.
The Raid of "Le Vengeur" and Other Stories.   London, Ferret Fantasy, 1974.

OTHER PUBLICATIONS

Novels

The Knights of the White Rose.   London, White, 1897.
The Virgin of the Sun.   London, Pearson, 1898.
The Rose of Judah.   London, Pearson, 1899.
Brothers of the Chain.   London, White, 1900.
Thou Shalt Not—(as Stanton Morich).   London, Pearson, 1900.
The Missionary.   London, White, 1902.
The White Witch of Mayfair.   London, White, 1902.
A Woman Against the World.   London, White, 1903.
An Island Love-Story.   London, White, 1904.
His Better Half.   London, White, 1905.
His Beautiful Client.   London, White, 1905.
A Conquest of Fortune.   London, White, 1906.
John Brown, Buccaneer.   London, White, 1908.

Short Stories

A Heroine of the Slums.   London, Tower, 1894 (?).
Knaves of Diamonds, Being Tales of Mine and Veld.   London, Pearson, 1899; as *The Diamond Dog,* 1913.

Verse (as Lara)

Poems General, Secular, and Satirical.   London, Stewart, 1883.
The Dying Faith.   London, Stewart, 1884.

Other

Men Who Have Made the Empire.   London, Pearson, 1897.
In an Unknown Prison Land: An Account of Convicts and Colonists in New Caledonia.   London, Hutchinson, 1901.
With Chamberlain in Africa.   London, Routledge, 1903.
Sidelights on Convict Life.   London, Long, 1903.

Translator (as Levin Carnac), *The Hope of the Family,* by Alphonse Daudet.   London, Pearson, 1898.

*

Bibliography: by George Locke, in *The Raid of "Le Vengeur" and Other Stories,* 1974.

*   *   *

George Griffith published almost 50 books of crime, adventure, fantasy, romance, social melodrama, verse, and non-fiction. Most importantly, his output includes over 20 books of, or in the margins of, SF. He became one of the first, most characteristic, and most popular professional writers of editorially planned and instantly sensational fiction in the rising "yellow-press" of the turn of the century. Griffith also met the usual end of such hacks, being forced to get more outrageous and less believable in each succeeding novel and to shed whatever original insights he might have had in the process.

His best work, consequently, is clearly his first novel, *The Angel of the Revolution,* though even that is marred by slipshod haste, racist chauvinism, and melodramatic sensationalism. Yet the subsumption of Verne's gadgetry and the "future war" tale, plus a dash of travelog exoticism and a barrelful of Bulwerian melodrama, under a real sympathy with justice wreaked on the existing political order of despotism and Mammon by a group of avenging heroes united into an Anarchist or Terrorist Brotherhood of Freedom, was a genuine breakthrough. The brains of the conspiracy, the super-intelligent Hungarian Jew Natas, is, in spite of his name, his hypnotic powers, and his crippled exterior, convincingly portrayed as a victim of Tsarist oppression rather than a mad beast. The main hero, an English inventor, is starving in his garret while inventing his super-airplane; and the executive head of the Terrorists is an English aristocrat, thus permitting Griffith to alloy plebeian hatred with snobbery. There follow cliffhanging global adventures dovetailing the fates of the heroes and their beautiful and fully equal female counterparts, especially Natas's daughter Natasha, and the world war that develops in 1904. The bloodthirsty Franco-Slavonic alliance is defeated by the Brotherhood who set up an Anglo-Saxon federation to guide the world toward disarmament and a vague social justice never clearly spelled out in economics terms. But this heady brew contains a few memorable set scenes, and—most importantly—an at-least-partial realization that the fusion of politics and the new technology makes the old social relationships not only unstable but catastrophically untenable. This realization made Griffith a pioneer in the instauration of a new SF tradition which culminated in Wells and still overshadows our whole century.

The sequel, *Olga Romanoff,* written to exploit *The Angel*'s great success, is inferior, its only new element being an interplanetary threat copied from Flammarion's ubiquitous comets. Already in *The Outlaws of the Air* the exploitation becomes unreadable: the anarchists are vicious beasts, the heroes English gentlemen, the ideal a rosewater South Sea colony, the fights simply ludicrous; *The Great Pirate Syndicate* descends to bloodthirsty Anglo-Saxon wishdream-imperialism and anti-semitism. In Griffith's feverish gallop through all the popular literary forms, *A Honeymoon in Space* was his venture into interplanetary voyages; it groups all its clichés (aggressive Martians, angel-like Venusians, antigravity, monsters galore) around a safari-story of a lord, his beautiful American bride, and their faithful retainer. His later works are unworthy of a writer with political convictions and a generous plebeian indignation: if the story that Griffith died of drink is true, it would provide an appropriately moral dying fall. And it would still remain exemplary for the SF of our century.

—Darko Suvin

GRINNELL, David. *See* **WOLLHEIM, Donald A.**

GROVE, Frederick Philip. Canadian. Born Felix Paul Berthold Friedrich Greve, in Radomno, Prussia-Poland, 14 February 1879; naturalized citizen, 1921. Educated at St. Pauli school, Hamburg, 1886-95; Gymnasium des Johanneums, Hamburg, 1895-98; University of Bonn, 1898-1900; Maximiliens University, Munich, 1901-02; University of Manitoba, Winnipeg, B.A. 1921. Married Catherine Wiens in 1914; one daughter and one son. Writer and translator in Germany, 1902-09; imprisoned for fraud, 1903-04; emigrated to Canada c. 1909; settled in Manitoba: taught in Haskett, 1913, Winkler, 1913-15, Virdin, 1915-16, Gladstone, 1916-17, Ferguson, 1918, Eden, 1919-22, and Rapid City, 1922-24; Editor, Graphic Press, Ottawa, 1929-31, and Associate Editor, *Canadian Nation,* 1929; manager of a farm in Simcoe, Ontario, 1931-38, and lived on the farm after his retirement. Recipient: Lorne Pierce Gold Medal, 1934; Canadian Writers' Federation Pension, 1944; Governor-General's Award, for non-fiction, 1947. D.Litt.: University of Manitoba, 1945. Fellow, Royal Society of Canada, 1941. *Died 19 August 1948.*

SCIENCE-FICTION PUBLICATIONS

Novel

Consider Her Ways. Toronto, Macmillan, 1947.

OTHER PUBLICATIONS

Novels

Fanny Essler (in German). Stuttgart, Juncker, 1905.
Maurermeister Ihles Haus. Berlin, Schnabel, 1906; translated by Paul P. Gubbins, as *The Master Mason's House,* edited by Douglas O. Spettigue and A.W. Riley, Ottawa, Oberon Press, 1976.
Settlers of the Marsh. Toronto, Ryerson Press, and New York, Doran, 1925.
A Search for America. Ottawa, Graphic, 1927; New York, Carrier, 1928.
Our Daily Bread. Toronto and New York, Macmillan, 1928; London, Cape, 1929.
The Yoke of Life. Toronto, Macmillan, and New York, R.R. Smith, 1930.
Fruits of the Earth. Toronto and London, Dent, 1933.
Two Generations: A Story of Present-Day Ontario. Toronto, Ryerson Press, 1939.
The Master of the Mill. Toronto, Macmillan, 1944.

Short Stories

Tales from the Margin: The Selected Short Stories of Frederick Philip Grove, edited by Desmond Pacey. Toronto, McGraw Hill Ryerson, 1971.

Verse

Wanderungen. Privately printed, 1902.
Helena und Damon (verse drama). Privately printed, 1902.

Other

Oscar Wilde (in German). Berlin, Gose and Tetzlaff, 1903.
Randarabesken zu Oscar Wilde. Minden, Germany, Bruns, 1903.
Over Prairie Trails. Toronto, McClelland and Stewart, 1922.
The Turn of the Year. Toronto, McClelland and Stewart, 1923.
It Needs to Be Said.... Toronto and New York, Macmillan, 1929.
In Search of Myself. Toronto, Macmillan, 1946.
The Letters of Frederick Philip Grove, edited by Desmond Pacey. Toronto, University of Toronto Press, 1976.

Translator of works by Balzac, Robert and Elizabeth Barrett Browning, Cervantes, Ernest Dowson, Dumas, Flaubert, Gide, Le Sage, Meredith, Henri Murger, Pater, Wells, and Wilde into German, 1903-09.

*

Bibliography: in *FPG: The European Years* by Douglas O. Spettigue, Ottawa, Oberon Press, 1973.

*   *   *

Frederick Philip Grove is primarily known in Canadian literature for his didactic agrarian novels. One might consider his 1942 autobiography, *In Search of Myself,* a work of "fantasy," since in it he sets out the persona of "Grove" he had maintained, with many fabrications, since his arrival in Canada many years before.

Consider Her Ways, his only real science fiction novel, was also his last; it employs genre conventions for social satire. The story is ostensibly set down by a naturalist studying ant colonies in Venezuela. He regards these insects as akin to humans, calling them our "formicarian brethren." In fact, they are superior, since one giant ant, Wawa-quee, is able to hypnotize him and communicate her story of epic quest with an army of warrior-scientists, to gather knowledge for her tribe.

This device of the ant's point of view allows Grove to satirize humanity both directly and indirectly. Wawa-quee's comments on humans are scathing. She ridicules everything from spelling (designed to render knowledge inaccessible) to clothing (especially nightgowns). Yet through the ants' own values—their military ferocity, subordination of the individual, and acceptance of slavery—the author (in the wake of World War II) condemns these evils in human life. This is especially evident when Wawa-quee observes that humans do not operate on children to render them happy and docile in slavery, even though they *do* enslave each other "by means of a thing...[they call] money." She comments: "The curious will infer from this neglect of simple expedients that man has either not yet risen to any very high degree of civilization; or—which is my own opinion—that he has considerably degenerated from a level previously attained." The irony is double-edged; the ants cannot understand human free will, but they can condemn human cruelty. Indirectly, through the ants' courage, treachery, despair, hope for the race, self-sacrifice, and thirst for knowledge, Grove discusses the best and worst of human nature. His satire is often savage; yet it is mixed with compassion. Wawa-quee and her society are convincingly drawn.

Unfortunately, the book is flawed by its pedantic style and by the obvious nature of its allegory. The whole book, in situation and style, seems to be an inferior imitation of an early 20th -century "lost race" fantasy by Wells, Haggard, or Conan Doyle. This may explain its relative obscurity. Nevertheless, for its inventiveness and social commentary, the book deserves examination.

—Susan Wood

GUIN, Wyman (Woods). American. Born in Wanette, Oklahoma, 1 March 1915. Married 1) Jean Adolph in 1939 (divorced, 1955); 2) Valerie Carlson in 1956; two sons and three daughters. Technician in Pharmacology, Advertising Writer, Advertising Manager, and Marketing Vice-President, Lakeside Laboratories Inc., Milwaukee, 1938-62; Vice-President, Medical Television Communications Inc., Chicago, 1962-64. Since 1964, Planning Administrator, L.W. Erolich-Intercon International. Lives in Tarrytown, New York.

SCIENCE-FICTION PUBLICATIONS

Novel

The Standing Joy. New York, Avon, 1969.

Short Stories

Living Way Out. New York, Avon, 1967; as *Beyond Bedlam,* London, Sphere, 1973.

*   *   *

Although Wyman Guin has written a novel, *The Standing Joy,* his most important work is to be found in his novelettes from the 1950's and 1960's. The stories are remarkable for the way in which Guin takes up far-out sociological or psychological ideas and gives them substance in carefully worked out dramatic conflicts against the background of alternate societies; despite some extravaganzas in the details they carry conviction and emerge as fully rounded and believable SF worlds.

His best story is the minor classic "Beyond Bedlam," which employs the basic inversion device of so much science fiction: what is considered an illness today—schizophrenia in this case—is in about a thousand years in the future the norm, with a drug-induced, law-enforced schizophrenia in every human being. Everybody is inhabited by two personalities that change in five-day shifts. This procedure has eliminated man's aggressive impulses, and hence war, but has also led to the disappearance of art and emotional pleasures. The theme of the story is treated not so much as a utopian dream or a dystopian nightmare as an exercise in creating a different alternate society, with all the ramifications in good and evil following from the basic premise.

"The Delegate from Guapanga" and "A Man of the Renaissance" both have richly exotic socio-cultural backgrounds. The first story

contrasts two alien philosophies of "Mentalists" and "Matterists," the Mentalists being closer to nature with ideals of a simpler life and tradition, the Matterists representatives of a mechanistic-scientific culture. The hero of the story develops a curious political idea of "dishonesty in government." The second story is about a man of ambition in an archipelagic world, who by sometimes Machiavellian means tries to realize his purely rationalist and revolutionary notions in a world governed by traditional values. In "Volpla" a joke in genetical engineering by a misanthropic lone scientist—artificially created beings that were to be passed off as visitors from the stars—turns out differently by a simple reversion of the reader's expectations. "My Darling Hecate" and "The Root and the Ring" are slight and mildly amusing volatile fantasies.

Guin's novel, *The Standing Joy,* is a parallel Earth story, with the characters having "twins" on another Earth, perhaps our own. Its protagonist, Colin Collins, a superman who has invented the prolonged orgasm, gathers around him a group of other talented inventors; the sex is harmless, but the whole thing is a bit confused. Wyman Guin's typical work is characteristic of its time and the magazine (*Galaxy*) in which most of it appeared, a slickly written fiction of ideas that manages to entertain and to stimulate without moving the reader deeply.

—Franz Rottensteiner

GUNN, James E(dwin). American. Born in Kansas City, Missouri, 12 July 1923. Educated at the University of Kansas, Lawrence, B.A. in journalism 1947, M.A. in English 1951. Served in the United States Naval Reserve, 1943-46: Lieutenant. Married Jane Frances Anderson in 1947; two sons. Editor, Western Printing and Lithographing Company, Racine, Wisconsin, 1951-52. Assistant Instructor, 1955-56, Managing Editor, Alumni Association, 1955-58, Administrative Assistant to the Chancellor for University Relations, 1958-70, Lecturer, 1970-74, and since 1974, Professor of English, University of Kansas. Member of the Executive Committee, Science Fiction Research Association; President, Science Fiction Writers of America, 1971-72. Recipient: Byron Caldwell Smith Prize; World Science Fiction Convention award, 1976; Pilgrim Award, 1976. Guest of Honor, Mid-Americon 1, Marcon 10, Fortcon 1. Agent: Robert P. Mills, 156 East 52nd Street, New York, New York 10022; or, Reece Halsey, 8733 Sunset Boulevard, Los Angeles, California 90069; or, A.P. Watt Ltd., 26-28 Bedford Row, London WC1R 4HL, England. Address: 2215 Orchard Lane, Lawrence, Kansas 66044, U.S.A.

SCIENCE-FICTION PUBLICATIONS

Novels

This Fortress World. New York, Gnome Press, 1955; London, Sphere, 1977.
Star Bridge, with Jack Williamson. New York, Gnome Press, 1955; London, Sidgwick and Jackson, 1978.
The Joy Makers. New York, Bantam, 1961; London, Gollancz, 1963.
The Immortals. New York, Bantam, 1962; London, Panther, 1975.
The Immortal (novelization of TV series). New York, Bantam, 1970.
The Burning. New York, Dell, 1972.
The Listeners. New York, Scribner, 1972; London, Arrow, 1978.
The Magicians. New York, Scribner, 1976; London, Sidgwick and Jackson, 1978.
Kampus. New York and London, Bantam, 1977.
The Dreamers. New York, Simon and Schuster, and London, Gollancz, 1980.

Short Stories

Station in Space.   New York, Bantam, 1958.
Future Imperfect.   New York, Bantam, 1964.
The Witching Hour.   New York, Dell, 1970.
Breaking Point.   New York, Walker, 1972.
Some Dreams Are Nightmares.   New York, Scribner, 1974.
The End of the Dreams.   New York, Scribner, 1975.

Uncollected Short Stories

"If I Forget Thee," in *Triax,* edited by Robert Silverberg.   Los
    Angeles, Pinnacle, 1977; London, Fontana, 1979.
"Child of the Sun," in *The 1978 Annual World's Best SF,* edited by
    Donald A. Wollheim.   New York, DAW, 1978.
"Guilt," in *Isaac Asimov's Science Fiction Magazine* (New York),
    May-June 1978.

OTHER PUBLICATIONS

Play

Thy Kingdom Come (produced Lawrence, Kansas, 1947).

Other

"On Style," in *Those Who Can,* edited by Robin Scott Wilson.
    New York, New American Library, 1973.
"Science Fiction and the Mainstream," in *Science Fiction, Today
    and Tomorrow,* edited by Reginald Bretnor.   New York,
    Harper, 1974.
"Teaching Science Fiction Revisited," in *Analog* (New York),
    November 1974.
Alternate Worlds: The Illustrated History of Science Fiction.
    Englewood Cliffs, New Jersey, Prentice Hall, 1975.
The Discovery of the Future: The Ways Science Fiction Developed.
    College Station, Texas A and M University, 1975.
"Henry Kuttner, C.L. Moore, Lewis Padgett, et al.," in *Voices for
    the Future,* edited by Thomas D. Clareson.   Bowling Green,
    Ohio, Popular Press, 1976.
"Where Do You Get Those Crazy Ideas?," in *Writing and Selling
    Science Fiction.*   Cincinnati, Writer's Digest, 1976.
"Heroes, Heroines, Villains: The Characters in Science Fiction," in
    The Craft of Science Fiction, edited by Reginald Bretnor.   New
    York, Harper, 1976.
"Teaching Science Fiction," in *Publishers' Weekly* (New York), 14
    June 1976.
"The Academic Viewpoint," in *Nebula Award Winners 12,* edited
    by Gordon R. Dickson.   New York, Harper, 1978.
"Aliens," in *Science Fiction: Contemporary Mythology,* edited by
    Patricia Warrick, Martin H. Greenberg, and Joseph D. Olander.
    New York, Harper, 1978.
"On the Road to Science Fiction: From Heinlein to Here," in *Isaac
    Asimov's Science Fiction Magazine* (New York), February 1978.
"On the Tinsel Screen: Science Fiction and the Movies," in *Isaac
    Asimov's Science Fiction Magazine* (New York), February 1980.
"On the Foundations of Science Fiction," in *Isaac Asimov's Science
    Fiction Magazine* (New York), April 1980.

Editor, *Man and the Future.*   Lawrence, University Press of Kan-
    sas, 1968.
Editor, *Nebula Award Stories 10.*   New York, Harper, 1975.
Editor, *The Road to Science Fiction: From Gilgamesh to Wells,
    From Wells to Heinlein.*   New York, New American Library, 2
    vols., 1977-79.

*

Manuscript Collection: University of Kansas Library, Lawrence.

*   *   *

In his anthology *The Road to Science Fiction* James E. Gunn
defines science fiction as idea-fiction that deals with change. This
change is usually technological and, in most cases, has implications
for the entire human race. While such a definition might not work
for all of science fiction or for all of the writers within the genre, it
has worked well for Gunn. Since 1949 Gunn has constantly sought
in his work to portray representative human characters confronting
altered futures. Frequently, as in the stories in *Station in Space,* the
changes that confront the human characters are themselves the
product of human action. Gunn sees humanity as a race that needs
to be challenged by change but that equally finds a certain appeal in
stasis. Often it is up to major characters within the stories to thwart
the deadly appeal of stasis.

Gunn's favorite writing length is the novelette. Many of his
"novels" consist of three or four novelettes connected by a common
theme, and he has been rather successful with this form. In *The Joy
Makers,* for example, Gunn is able to investigate the various forms
of what goes for happiness within an extended time frame. In each
story a stage is reached which will lead to his conclusion that even if
humanity could find absolute happiness it would probably be rather
disappointing. By using novelettes, Gunn is able to center on a
climactic moment in each story, and, therefore, focus on a series of
dramatic statements that do not require the kinds of exemplifica-
tion and development that a novel would demand.

The Immortals again makes use of this same form, and in the four
stories Gunn succeeds in exploring a world which holds out the hint
of possible immortality. In each story it is not immortality itself that
is important but the ways in which the characters react to the
possibility. The world of the stories and the people that inhabit that
world are all geared toward investigating human attitudes toward
life and death. Given that such a theme is very much a part of
present human concerns, Gunn's stories often touch on very current
issues. For example, medical technology has recently been more
and more directed toward the prolongation of life. But such technology has added huge costs to basic hospital services. In part three
of *The Immortals* Gunn tries to trace the ultimate direction such a
trend could take. The work effectively presents a damning description of just how dangerous man's preoccupation with avoiding
death can be.

In *The Listeners,* another series of interconnected stories, Gunn
studies communications in the same way that he explored immortality in *The Immortals.* While the unifying concern here is the attempt
first to decipher and then to answer a message from the planet
Capella, the major topic is man's attempts to communicate with his
fellow man. In each story, with the Capellan project in the background, the foreground is occupied by husbands and wives, fathers
and sons, leaders and followers, writers and readers, men and
intelligent machines, and humans and aliens who try to communicate. The result of such a juxtaposition is a work that presents not
only an adventure in the future but a moving account of man's own
present. Communication with aliens may happen some day, but for
now human communication stands in need of improvement.

Two more conventional novels deserve mention. *This Fortress
World,* Gunn's first novel, is a highly readable story that takes its
foundation from the popular science-fiction galactic empires, but
instead of simply giving the world one more empire, Gunn tells the
story from an ordinary inhabitant's point of view. Life in a galactic
empire may be fine if the character is a member of "the Foundation." It can be extremely unpleasant, however, if the character is
only one of the crowd. *This Fortress World* is an attempt to bring
reality into space opera. At the opposite pole lies *Kampus,* perhaps
still too close in time to the student demonstrations of the 1960's to
be read objectively. It is too easy—and misleading—to read the
novel as a damnation of these demonstrations. *Kampus,* in fact, is a
parable world in which empty rhetoric is allowed to shape the lives
of all who believe life would be better if everyone did his or her "own
thing." It is similar to Voltare's *Candide* in that the world and
actions presented in the novel are not meant to be taken as serious
attempts to portray "reality." *Kampus,* however, takes up where
Candide left off. If everyone were to tend his own garden, what kind
of world would exist?

James Gunn has made a career of science fiction as an author,
teacher, and scholar. His works show an acute sensitivity to what is
possible in science fiction, and his own works testify to the accuracy
of his perceptions. As one reads his fiction one is struck by the
constant changes in Gunn's themes, plots, and style. *Kampus* is a
remarkable feat of stylistic experimentation that was not at all

predictable from *The Listeners*. In a literature that itself is concerned with change, it is somehow reassuring that one of the authors most interested in this theme is himself able to change. Gunn builds always upon what he has accomplished so that what follows will take both himself and his readers into newer, less known areas of human experience. For James Gunn science fiction must deal with no less a topic than the human race.

—Stephen H. Goldman

GUTTERIDGE, (Thomas Gordon) Lindsay.   British.   Born in Easington, County Durham, 20 May 1923. Educated at an art school in Newcastle upon Tyne. Married to Marjorie Kathleen Carpenter; one daughter. Free-lance commercial artist, London, 1939-41, 1950-68; art teacher, King Edward School of Art, Newcastle, 1941-43; cattle stockman in Australia, 1946-48; free-lance photographer, 1958-60; former art director, Robert Sharp and Partners, advertising agency, London. Address: c/o Jonathan Cape Ltd., 30 Bedford Square, London WC1B 3EL, England.

SCIENCE-FICTION PUBLICATIONS

Novels (series: Matthew Dilke in all books)

Cold War in a Country Garden.   London, Cape, and New York, Putnam, 1971.
Killer Pine.   London, Cape, and New York, Putnam, 1973.
Fratricide Is a Gas.   London, Cape, 1975.

*   *   *

Lindsay Gutteridge is the author of three espionage novels featuring Matthew Dilke as hero, a micro-man one quarter of an inch in height. They are all splendid adventure stories and powerfully engage the sense of wonder. Gutteridge plays rough with his miniature spies and their normal-sized masters and foes, so that these should perhaps be classified as adult entertainments but there is nothing very special in the books considered as offbeat spy thrillers. Their distinctive quality is science-educational: they are the closest fictional equivalents I have found to *The Hellstrom Chronicle*. Whereas that film's overwhelming images of the alien life we overlook projected an inimical world, in which ants are far better adapted for survival than we hubristic humans, Gutteridge, better balanced, discovers not only beauty and terror, monstrosity and indifference, but delightful nourishment. By not being insect-sized, Gutteridge suggests, we are missing the marvellous abundant food of pollen and nectar. If only we could be miniaturized, our survival problems would be over. There, of course, is the rub which would lead us to classify these works as pure fantasies were it not that they belong to a tradition of micro-people in SF established by such writers as Asimov, Blish, and Leinster, and that they use the convention to instruct us about natural history so fully and sensitively. The microscopic eye is a human one, and the wonders seen are related to human fears, needs and desires.

Cold War in a Country Garden, in which the mission of three micro-men is to implant transmitters in the hair of a Russian, is closest perhaps to the conventional spy thriller, substituting a box of centipedes for the snake pit or piranha pool as a persuasive threat to the capured Dilke. When he escapes, rescuing a micro-negress, Hyacinthe, who aids him in his second adventure, the pursuers are caught by an ant-lion. *Killer Pine* is a novel of ecological warfare, in which the enemy are Russian micro-men who inhabit a metal container on a pine in a Canadian forest, breeding termites to spread a viral death. We are given fascinating and horrid glimpses of life in a termite colony, in a tree which, for the micro-climbers, has the scale of Mount Everest. The third novel (which I hope is not the final adventure), *Fratricide Is a Gas,* has affinities with novels of indus-

trial expionage: here Matthew Dilke is pitted alone against a sadistic Nazi chemist in Peru. The highlight of this novel is a sequence in which Dilke climbs jungloid thorns and creepers, enjoying on the way an idyllic repose in the bloom of an orchid, where he is visited by a humming-bird and witnesses the giant courtship of butterflies and the predations of parasitic wasps and shaggy spiders.

Gutteridge's micro-man's view gives us the pleasure of a sardonic perspective on the conventions of spy fiction and also a Swiftian magnification of some of our physical and spiritual coarseness, as when Dilke spies from a perch on the top of Lippe's study chair not only the eroded massif of his head but also the monstrous cruelty of his mind, revealed by his most private occupations. Gutteridge's work may well have influenced *The Micronauts* by Gordon Williams (1977), an exciting, more fully science-fiction narrative which, however, lacks the Gutteridge charm.

—Michael J. Tolley

HAGGARD, H(enry) Rider.   British. Born in Bradenham, Norfolk, 22 June 1856. Educated at Ipswich Grammar School, Suffolk; Lincoln's Inn, London, 1881-85: called to the Bar, 1885. Married Louisa Mariana Margitson in 1880; one son and three daughters. Lived in South Africa, as Secretary to Sir Henry Bulwer, Lieutenant-Governor of Natal, 1875-77, member of the staff of Sir Theophilus Shepstone, Special Commissioner in the Transvaal, 1877, and Master and Registrar of the High Court of the Transvaal, 1877-79; returned to England, 1879; managed his wife's estate in Norfolk, from 1880; worked in chambers of Henry Bargave Deane, 1885-87; Unionist and Agricultural candidate for East Norfolk, 1895; Co-Editor, *African Review*, 1898; travelled throughout England investigating condition of agriculture and the rural population, 1901-02; British Government Special Commissioner to report on Salvation Army settlements in the United States, 1905; Chairman, Reclamation and Unemployed Labour Committee, Royal Commission on Coast Erosion and Afforestation, 1906-11; travelled around the world as a Member of the Dominions Royal Commission, 1912-17. Chairman of the Committee, Society of Authors, 1896-98; Vice-President, Royal Colonial Institute, 1917. Knighted, 1912; K.B.E. (Knight Commander, Order of the British Empire), 1919. *Died 14 May 1925.*

SCIENCE-FICTION PUBLICATIONS

Novels (series: Allan Quatermain; She)

King Solomon's Mines (Quatermain).   London and New York, Cassell, 1885.
She: A History of Adventure.   New York, Harper, 1886; London, Longman, 1887.
Allan Quatermain.   London, Longman, and New York, Harper, 1887.
The People of the Mist.   London and New York, Longman, 1894.
Heart of the World.   New York, Longman, 1895; London, Longman, 1896.
Stella Fregelius: A Tale of Three Destinies.   London and New York, Longman, 1904.
Ayesha: The Return of She.   London, Ward Lock, and New York, Doubleday, 1905.
Benita: An African Romance.   London, Cassell, 1906; as *The Spirit of Bambatse,* New York, Longman, 1906.
The Yellow God.   New York, Cupples and Leon, 1908; London, Cassell, 1909.
Queen Sheba's Ring.   London, Nash, and New York, Doubleday, 1910.
The Mahatma and the Hare: A Dream Story.   London, Longman, and New York, Holt, 1911.
Love Eternal.   London, Cassell, and New York, Longman, 1918.

When the World Shook. London, Cassell, and New York, Longman, 1919.
She and Allan. New York, Longman, and London, Hutchinson, 1921.
Wisdom's Daughter. London, Hutchinson, and New York, Doubleday, 1923.
Heu-Heu; or, The Monster (Quatermain). London, Hutchinson, and New York, Doubleday, 1924.

OTHER PUBLICATIONS

Novels

Dawn. **London, Hurst and Blackett, 3 vols., 1884; New York, Appleton, 1 vol., 1887.**
The Witch's Head. London, Hurst and Blackett, 3 vols., 1885; New York, Appleton, 1 vol., 1885.
Jess. London, Smith Elder, and New York, Harper, 1887.
A Tale of Three Lions, and On Going Back. New York, Munro, 1887.
Mr. Meeson's Will. New York, Harper, and London, Spencer Blackett, 1888.
Maiwa's Revenge. New York, Harper, and London, Longman, 1888.
My Fellow Laborer (includes "The Wreck of the 'Copeland'"). New York, Munro, 1888.
Colonel Quaritch, V.C. New York, Lovell, 1888; London, Longman, 3 vols., 1888.
Cleopatra. London, Longman, and New York, Harper, 1889.
Beatrice. London, Longman, and New York, Harper, 1890.
The World's Desire, with Andrew Lang. London, Longman, and New York, Harper, 1890.
Eric Brighteyes. London, Longman, and New York, United States Book Company, 1891.
Nada the Lily. **New York and London, Longman, 1892.**
Montezuma's Daughter. **New York and London, Longman, 1893.**
Joan Haste. London and New York, Longman, 1895.
The Wizard. Bristol, Arrowsmith, and New York, Longman, 1896.
Doctor Therne. London and New York, Longman, 1898.
Swallow. New York and London, Longman, 1899.
The Spring of a Lion. New York, Neeley, 1899.
Lysbeth. New York and London, Longman, 1901.
Pearl-Maiden. London and New York, Longman, 1903.
The Brethren. London, Cassell, and New York, Doubleday, 1904.
The Way of the Spirit. London, Hutchinson, 1906.
Fair Margaret. London, Hutchinson, 1907; as *Margaret,* New York, Longman, 1907.
The Lady of the Heavens. New York, Authors and Newspapers Association, 1908; as *The Ghost Kings,* London, Cassell, 1908.
The Lady of Blossholme. London, Hodder and Stoughton, 1909.
Morning Star. London, Cassell, and New York, Longman, 1910.
Red Eve. **London, Hodder and Stoughton, and New York, Doubleday, 1911.**
Marie. London, Cassell, and New York, Longman, 1912.
Child of Storm. London, Cassell, and New York, Longman, 1913.
The Wanderer's Necklace. London, Cassell, and New York, Longman, 1914.
The Holy Flower. London, Ward Lock, 1915; as *Allan and the Holy Flower,* New York, Longman, 1915.
The Ivory Child. London, Cassell, and New York, Longman, 1916.
Finished. London, Ward Lock, and New York, Longman, 1917.
Moon of Israel. London, Murray, and New York, Longman, 1918.
The Ancient Allan. London, Cassell, and New York, Longman, 1920.
The Virgin of the Sun. London, Cassell, and New York, Doubleday, 1922.
Queen of the Dawn. New York, Doubleday, and London, Hutchinson, 1925.
Treasure of the Lake. New York, Doubleday, and London, Hutchinson, 1926.

Allan and the Ice Gods. London, Hutchinson, and New York, Doubleday, 1927.
Mary of Marion Isle. London, Hutchinson, and New York, Doubleday, 1929.
Belshazzar. London, Paul, 1930.

Short Stories

Allan's Wife and Other Tales. London, Blackett, and New York, Harper, 1889.
Black Heart and White Heart, and Other Stories. London, Longman, 1900; as *Elissa, and Black Heart and White Heart,* New York, Longman, 1900.
Smith and the Pharaohs and Other Tales. Bristol, Arrowsmith, 1920; New York, Longman, 1921.

Other

Cetywayo and His White Neighbours; or, Remarks on Recent Events in Zululand, Natal, and the Transvaal. London, Trübner, 1882; revised edition, 1888; reprinted in part, as *The Last Boer War,* London, Kegan Paul, 1899; as *A History of the Transvaal,* New York, New Amsterdam, 1899.
Church and the State: An Appeal to the Laity. Privately printed, 1895.
A Farmer's Year, Being His Commonplace Book for 1898. London and New York, Longman, 1899.
The New South Africa. London, Pearson, 1900.
A Winter Pilgrimage:...Travels Through Palestine, Italy, and the Island of Cyprus. London and New York, Longman, 1901.
Rural England. London and New York, Longman, 2 vols., 1902.
A Gardener's Year. London and New York, Longman, 1905.
Report on the Salvation Army Colonies. London, His Majesty's Stationery Office, 1905; as *The Poor and the Land,* London and New York, Longman, 1905.
Regeneration, Being an Account of the Social Work of the Salvation Army in Great Britain. London, Longman, 1910; New York, Longman, 1911.
Rural Denmark and Its Lessons. London and New York, Longman, 1911.
A Call to Arms to the Men of East Anglia. Privately printed, 1914.
The After-War Settlement and the Employment of Ex-Service Men in the Oversea Dominions. London, Saint Catherine Press, 1916.
The Days of My Life: An Autobiography, edited by C.J. Longman. London and New York, Longman, 2 vols., 1926.
The Private Diaries of Sir H. Rider Haggard 1914-1925, edited by D.S. Higgins. London, Cassell, and New York, Stein and Day, 1980.

*

Bibliography: *A Bibliography of the Writings of Sir Henry Rider Haggard* by J.E. Scott, London, Elkin Mathews, 1947.

*   *   *

H. Rider Haggard shares the fate of writers like Mark Twain, Robert Louis Stevenson, and Lewis Carroll in that his novels now serve either in children's editions or as grist for Hollywood's mill. But Haggard never meant his works to be juvenile fare, for they are filled with very adult passions. Of his many novels, the majority are fantasy-romances that range in setting from South Africa to Iceland to Mexico, and in time from the days of Babylon to contemporary central Africa.

Haggard's first successful novel was *King Solomon's Mines,* which he published in the year after he set up practice in London as a barrister. So enthusiastic was the public reception of this novel, in which Haggard created the prototype of the "Great White Hunter," that he virtually gave up the law, and devoted most of his time to writing. The hero of *King Solomon's Mines* is Allan Quatermain, who is asked by a beautiful Englishwoman to find her husband, who is lost in the African jungle. When the tracks of the missing husband lead to a long-hidden cave, only the skeleton of the husband is found, along with the treasure of King Solomon, missing for two thousand years. In the sequel, *Allan Quatermain,* Allan dies, and Haggard found himself in the same position as Conan Doyle when, tiring of his famous detective, he killed off Sherlock Holmes: the public would have no part of it. Because of this outcry, Haggard used the device of the "discovered manuscript" to write 13 more novels about Quatermain. In these, Allan meets with further adventures both in his own time and in a past life in ancient Babylon.

The theme of reliving past lives is one which Haggard used many times, especially in the series of novels about the mysterious Ayesha, or She-Who-Must-Be-Obeyed. *She,* the first of these novels, introduces Ayesha, the queen of a cannibal tribe in Africa, the people of the Kor, as she waits for the return of her lover, whom she murdered two millennia ago when he dared to marry someone else. Her wait comes to an end when a young Englishman, Leo Vincey, comes to her land. One glance at Vincey is enough to convince her that Leo is the reincarnation of the long-dead lover. She tries to persuade Leo to join her in eternal life, the secret of which she had discovered in the flame at the heart of a volcano. But once again Ayesha is frustrated when Leo too takes another woman for a wife. After banishing Leo's wife, Ayesha takes him and his companions to the volcano to renew her arguments for him to bathe with her in the flames. But the magic only works once, for when Ayesha enters for the second time, she begins to age before the eyes of the men, turning into a two-thousand-year-old crone. To their horror, she dies at their feet. Sickened and dazed, the men return to England to try to forget the sight. Like Quatermain, Ayesha was called back for repeat performances. Haggard wrote two more novels about her return from death—*Ayesha* and *She and Allan*—and still another about her early years in ancient Egypt, *Wisdom's Daughter.*

That most of the titles of Haggard's works are unfamiliar even to SF readers shows the success of modern critics in stamping out much of 19th-century fantasy. The few that are relatively well known owe their longevity to the movies, where, even though the plots have been somewhat altered, the mystery and romance of the settings and characters have been preserved.

—Walter E. Meyers

HAIBLUM, Isidore. American. Born in Brooklyn, New York, 23 May 1935. Educated at the High School of Art and Design; City College of New York (Editor, *Mercury),* B.A. in English and social sciences 1958. Served in the United States Army Reserve, 1959-64. Has worked as interviewer, script writer, and folk-singers agent; now free-lance writer. Agent: Henry Morrison, 58 West 10th Street, New York, New York 10011. Address: 160 West 77th Street, New York, New York 10024, U.S.A.

SCIENCE-FICTION PUBLICATIONS

Novels (series: Dunjer)

The Tsaddik of the Seven Wonders. New York, Ballantine, 1971.
The Return. New York, Dell, 1973.
Transfer to Yesterday. New York, Ballantine, 1973.
The Wilk Are among Us. New York, Doubleday, 1975.
Interworld (Dunjer). New York, Dell, 1977; London, Penguin, 1980.
The Nightmare Express. New York, Fawcett, 1979.
Outerworld (Dunjer). New York, Dell, 1979.

OTHER PUBLICATIONS

Other

"Science Fiction, Jewish Style," in *Jewish Digest* (New York), December 1975.
The Complete Book of Radio Trivia, with Stuart Silver. Chicago, Playboy Press, 1980.

Isidore Haiblum comments:

Haiblum's work has its roots in the *Black Mask* Hammett-Chandler tradition and in the humor of Sholom Aleichem; it is often both hard-boiled and zany and sometimes ethnic. His style is awash with idioms, slang, and underworld lingo. His settings, despite the given dates, are often the 1930's, a time he rather likes. The jury is still out on how all this will go over in SF. *The Tsaddik of the Seven Wonders* was billed by the publishers as "The First Yiddish Science Fantasy Novel Ever." And about *Interworld* Gerald Jones wrote in the New York *Times:* "If you have ever wondered what *The Big Sleep* would sound like if Raymond Chandler were reincarnated as Roger Zelazny, this is your book." *The Nightmare Express* (a big alternative universe novel set in the 1930's and elsewhere), *Outerworld* (again with ace gum-shoe Dunjer from *Interworld),* and a revised edition of *The Wilk Are among Us* take all this a step further. Haiblum has his fingers crossed.

*   *   *

In his Afterword in *Binary Star 3,* Isidore Haiblum says that he and Ron Goulart draw on two traditions rare in science fiction, vaudeville comedy and hard-boiled detective stories. The verbal lunacy of the one and the callous violence of the other appear in Haiblum's work as part of his image of the City. New York—Depression era to present, future, and parallel-world—is a major "character" in his books, especially his most ambitious novel, *The Nightmare Express,* with its York, Old York, New York, and Founder's City. In his early novels comedy is the more interesting factor, playing wildly unusual creatures against their slangy, urban speech: the unorthodoxly Orthodox Tsaddik, the intergalactic social workers and their Wilk enemies, etc. The hard-boiled tough guys sometimes seem inappropriate, their imitations of 1930's action and language out of place in future or alternate worlds, especially in the (mainly) non-comic worlds of *The Return* and *Transfer to Yesterday.* In *Nightmare Express,* however, the 1930's scenery is part of the plot, as all the alternate Yorks split from 1935.

Haiblum enjoys complicated plots told from shifting viewpoints, usually to increase the comic or horrific madness of his city-worlds. Even the simplest, *The Return* and *Outerworld,* with one point-of-view character and world apiece, chase through various subcultures (each parodying an aspect of urban life); in *Outerworld* there is also a little time travel ending in a slightly altered alternate universe.

—Ruth Berman

HALDANE, J(ohn) B(urdon) S(anderson). Indian. Born in Oxford, England, 5 November 1892; brother of Naomi Mitchison, *q.v.;* became Indian citizen, 1960. Educated at Oxford Preparatory School; Eton College, Buckinghamshire; New College, Oxford, M.A. Served in the Black Watch in France and Iraq, 1914-19: Captain. Married 1) Charlotte Franken in 1926 (marriage dissolved, 1945); 2) Helen Spurway, 1945. Fellow of New College, 1919-22; Reader in Biochemistry, Cambridge University, 1922-23; Fullerian Professor of Physiology, Royal Institution, London, 1930-32; Professor of Genetics, 1933-37, and Professor of Biometry, 1937-57, London University. Research Professor, Indian Statistical Institute, 1961; Head of Genetics and Biometry, Government of Orissa, 1962-64. President, Genetical Society, 1932-36; Chairman of the Editorial Board, *Daily Worker,* London, 1940-49. Recipient: Royal Society Darwin Medal, 1953; Linnean Society Darwin-Wallace Medal, 1958; National Academy of Sciences Kimber Medal, 1961; Accademia dei Lincei Feltrinelli Prize, 1961. D.Sc.: University of Groningen, 1946; Oxford University, 1961; Honorary Doctorate, University of Paris, 1949; LL.D.: University of Edinburgh, 1956. Honorary Fellow, New College, 1961. Corresponding Member, Société de Biologie, 1928; Fellow, Royal Society, 1932; Chevalier, Legion of Honour, 1937; Honorary Member, Moscow

Academy of Sciences, 1952; Corresponding Member, Deutsche Akademie der Wissenschaften, 1950. National Institute of Sciences of India, 1953, and Royal Danish Academy of Sciences, 1956. *Died 1 December 1964.*

SCIENCE-FICTION PUBLICATIONS

Novel

The Man with Two Memories.   London, Merlin Press, 1976.

Uncollected Short Story

"The Gold-Makers," in *Great Science Fiction by Scientists,* edited by Groff Conklin.   New York, Macmillan, 1962.

OTHER PUBLICATIONS

Novel

My Friend Mr. Leakey (juvenile).   London, Cresset Press, 1937; New York, Harper, 1938.

Other

Daedalus; or, Science and the Future: A Paper Read to the Heretics, Cambridge, on February 4th, 1923.   London, Kegan Paul Trench Trubner, 1923; New York, Dutton, 1924.
Callinicus: A Defence of Chemical Warfare.   London, Kegan Paul Trench Trubner, and New York, Dutton, 1925.
Animal Biology, with Julian Huxley.   London, Oxford University Press, 1927.
The Last Judgment: A Scientist's Vision of the Future of Man.   New York, Harper, 1927.
Possible Worlds and Other Essays.   London, Chatto and Windus, 1927; as *Possible Worlds and Other Papers,* New York, Harper, 1928.
Science and Ethics (lecture).   London, C.A. Watts, 1928.
Enzymes.   London, Longman, 1930; Cambridge, Massachusetts, MIT Press, 1965.
Materialism (miscellany).   London, Hodder and Stoughton, 1932.
The Causes of Evolution.   London, Longman, and New York, Harper, 1932.
The Inequality of Man and Other Essays.   London, Chatto and Windus, 1932; as *Science and Human Life,* New York, Harper, 1933.
Biology in Everyday Life, with John Randal Baker.   London, Allen and Unwin, 1933.
Fact and Faith.   London, C.A. Watts, 1934.
Human Biology and Politics.   London, British Science Guild, 1934.
Science and the Supernatural: A Correspondence Between Harold Lunn and J.B.S. Haldane.   London, Eyre and Spottiswoode, and New York, Sheed and Ward, 1935.
The Outlook of Science, edited by William Empson.   London, Routledge, 1935.
Science and Well-Being, edited by William Empson.   London, Routledge, 1935.
The Chemistry of the Individual (lecture).   London, Oxford University Press, 1938.
The Marxist Philosophy.   London, Birkbeck College, 1938.
A.R.P. [Air Raid Precautions].   London, Gollancz, 1938.
Heredity and Politics.   London, Allen and Unwin, and New York, Norton, 1938.
How to Be Safe from Air Raids.   London, Gollancz, 1938.
The Marxist Philosophy and the Sciences.   London, Allen and Unwin, 1938; New York, Random House, 1939.
Science and Everyday Life.   London, Lawrence and Wishart, 1939; New York, Macmillan, 1940.
Science and You.   London, Fore, 1939.
Keeping Cool and Other Essays.   London, Chatto and Windus, 1940; as *Adventures of a Biologist,* New York, Harper, 1940.
Science in Peace and War.   London, Lawrence and Wishart, 1940.

New Paths in Genetics.   London, Allen and Unwin, 1941; New York, Harper, 1942.
Dialectical Materialism and Modern Science.   London, Labour Monthly, 1942.
Why Professional Workers Should Be Communists.   London, Communist Party, 1945.
A Banned Broadcast and Other Essays.   London, Chatto and Windus, 1946.
Science Advances.   London, Allen and Unwin, and New York, Macmillan, 1947.
What Is Life?   New York, Boni and Gaer, 1947; London, Lindsay Drummond, 1949.
Is Evolution a Myth? A Debate Between Douglas Dewar, C. Merson Davies and J.B.S. Haldane.   London, Paternoster Press, 1949.
Everything Has a History (essays).   London, Allen and Unwin, 1951.
The Biochemistry of Genetics.   London, Allen and Unwin, and New York, Macmillan, 1954.
The Argument from Animals to Men: An Examination of Its Validity for Anthropology (lecture).   London, Royal Anthropological Institute, 1956.
Karl Pearson 1857-1957 (address).   Privately printed, 1958.
The Unity and Diversity of Life (lecture).   New Delhi, Ministry of Information and Broadcasting, 1958.
Science and Indian Culture.   Calcutta, New Age, 1965.
Science and Life: Essays of a Rationalist.   London, Pemberton-Barrie and Rockliff, 1968.

Editor, *You and Heredity,* by Amram Scheinfeld and Morton D. Schweitzer.   London, Chatto and Windus, 1939.

*   *   *

The importance of J.B.S. Haldane for science fiction lies in the influence of his speculation on other writers rather than in his own rare excursions into fiction. Only two of his many works can be classified as science-fictional: a short story, "The Gold-Makers" (1932), and "The Last Judgment" (1927), a long narrative essay that contains a possible scenario for the end of the world, as foreseen not by religious prophecy—which Haldane always enjoyed ridiculing—but by scientific calculations of probability.

His short story dramatizes what for Haldane (later a convert to Communism) was one of the worst evils of capitalism—its exploitation of science, the stifling of the free development of discovery. A French chemist finds out how to extract gold from sea water, and he and his colleagues plan to use their prospective wealth to finance scientific research. But gold-mining interests soon get wind of the project and their hired killers set about eliminating the scientists involved. The story soon degenerates into a cinema-style thriller (but as such is cleverly written): the English narrator-hero, approached in desperation by the one survivor among the scientists, who reveals to him part of the secret, is chased over most of France by the killers until he at last decides to baffle pursuit by publishing what he knows—as fiction!

Far more considerable, even as narrative, is "The Last Judgment" (*Possible Worlds*). This work seems to have furnished Olaf Stapledon with one of the crucial episodes in *Last and First Men:* he freely adapted Haldane's prophecy of the slow collapse of the moon upon the earth, leading to the enforced migration of a small percentage of humanity to Venus, where mankind survives through artificial mutations. C.S. Lewis, whose character Weston in his space trilogy is an unjust caricature of Haldane's (and Stapledon's) attitudes, thought "The Last Judgment" a "depraved" work, but Lewis too found a use for Haldane's idea of the moon's fall as the most probable end of human life on Earth (in *Perelandra*).

Another writer indebted to Haldane was an old Oxford friend, Aldous Huxley, who found in *Daedalus* hints toward the famous test-tube babies of *Brave New World.* Haldane's influence on a friend of his last years, Arthur C. Clarke, is more obvious in the latter's essays than in his fiction. Clarke has given currency to what is now, at least in the science-fiction world, the great biologist's best-known saying (Clarke calls this "Haldane's Law"): "The Universe is not only queerer than we imagine; it is queerer than we *can* imagine."

—John Kinnaird

HALDEMAN, Jack C(arroll, II). American. Born in Hopkinsville, New York, 18 December 1941. Educated at the University of Oklahoma, Norman, 1960-63; Johns Hopkins University, Baltimore, B.S. in life sciences 1973. Married 1) Alice Haldeman in 1965; 2) Vol Haldeman in 1975; two daughters. Research assistant, Johns Hopkins University School of Hygiene and Public Health, 1963-68; medical technician, University of Maryland Hospital, 1968-73; has also worked as a statistician, photographer, and printer's devil. President, Washington Science Fiction Association, seven years; Chairman, Discon II. Agent: Kirby McCauley, 60 East 42nd Street, New York, New York 10017. Address: P.O. Box 969, Port Richey, Florida 33568, U.S.A.

SCIENCE-FICTION PUBLICATIONS

Novels

Vector Analysis. New York, Berkley, 1978.
Perry's Planet. New York, Bantam, 1980.

Uncollected Short Stories (series: Sports)

"Garden of Eden," in *Fantastic* (New York), December 1971.
"Watchdog," in *Amazing* (New York), May 1972.
"What I Did on My Summer Vacation," in *Fantastic* (New York), July 1973.
"Slugging It Out," in *The Far Side of Time,* edited by Roger Elwood. New York, Dodd Mead, 1974.
"Sand Castles," in *Alternities,* edited by David Gerrold and Stephen Goldin. New York, Dell, 1974.
"What Time Is It?," in *Vertex* (Los Angeles), February 1975.
"Laura's Theme," in *Fantastic* (New York), June 1975.
"Time to Come," in *Gallery* (Chicago), June 1975.
"Songs of Dying Swans," in *Stellar 2,* edited by Judy-Lynn del Rey. New York, Ballantine, 1976.
"Limits," with Jack Dann, in *Fantastic* (New York), May 1976.
"Louisville Slugger" (Sports), in *Astronauts and Androids,* edited by Isaac Asimov. New York, Dale, 1977.
"Home Team Advantage" (Sports), in *Black Holes and Bug Eyed Monsters,* edited by Isaac Asimov. New York, Dale, 1977.
"Those Thrilling Days of Yesteryear," in *Amazing* (New York), March 1977.
"Vector Analysis," in *Analog* (New York), May 1977.
"The End-of-the-World Rag," in *Fantastic* (New York), December 1977.
"The Agony of Defeat," in *Comets and Computers,* edited by Isaac Asimov. New York, Dale, 1978.
"The Thrill of Victory" (Sports), in *Isaac Asimov's Science Fiction Magazine* (New York), January-February 1978.
"Mortimer Snodgrass Turtle" (Sports), in *Fantasy and Science Fiction* (New York), June 1978.
"What Weighs 8000 Pounds and Wears Red Sneakers?," in *Fantastic* (New York), July 1978.
"Thirty Love" (Sports), in *Isaac Asimov's Science Fiction Magazine* (New York), September-October 1978.
"Last Rocket from Newark," in *Amazing* (New York), November 1978.
"Race the Wind" (Sports), in *Omni* (New York), January 1979.
"A Scientific Fact," in *Fantastic* (New York), March-April 1979.
"Longshot" (Sports), in *Isaac Asimov's Science Fiction Adventure Magazine* (New York), Spring 1979.

"Starschool," with Joe Haldeman, in *Isaac Asimov's Science Fiction Adventure Magazine* (New York), Spring 1979.
"Hell," with Joe Haldeman, in *Isaac Asimov's Science Fiction Adventure Magazine* (New York), Summer 1979.
"Hear the Crush, Hear the Roar," in *Isaac Asimov's Science Fiction Magazine* (New York), December 1979.
"Spring Fever," in *Fantasy and Science Fiction* (New York), July 1980.

OTHER PUBLICATIONS

Verse

Between Pearl Harbor and Christmas. Privately printed, n.d.

Other

"Space Through Our Fingers" (and cover photograph), in *Amazing* (New York), October 1974.
Story Notes to *Rod Serling's Other Worlds.* New York, Bantam, 1978.

Jack C. Haldeman comments:
Sometimes I write hard science fiction, sometimes soft. Sometimes I'm serious, sometimes I'm humorous. Mostly I'm traditional, though occasionally I try something experimental. I often draw on my scientific background as well as my sense of humor. Mostly I try to entertain, though I have been known to slip in a message or two. I try not to let it clutter up the story.

*   *   *

Jack C. Haldeman has spent a good deal of his writing time on one of the rarest of themes in science fiction, the sports story. He began in 1977 with "Louisville Slugger," an anecdotal piece in which the future of humanity depends on a baseball game against Arcturians. This was followed by a sequel, "Home Team Advantage," wherein the Arcturian aliens discover that man is inedible and forfeit their prize, the consumption of humanity. Apparently having discovered that he had stumbled upon a good thing, Haldeman followed this pair up with a second, "The Thrill of Victory" and "The Agony of Defeat," this time concentrating upon a team of robotic football players who are first faced with discovery that they have been illegally programmed with a will to win, and then matched in a championship game with genetically altered beings. All four stories were played strictly for laughs, and are as trivial as one might expect.

"Thirty Love" was decidedly different. A professional tennis player has led a long and successful career because his precognition allows him to anticipate where the ball will next be hit. On his final match, he deliberately throws the game when he realizes that defeating his opponent will cause the latter a trauma that will utterly ruin his life. Unfortunately, the subsequent sports stories have been as light as the first, and Haldeman's best fiction has not been in this area. Only "Race the Wind" has had a serious theme, a cripple determined to compete in slalom racing, and the story itself was too weak to support the seriousness of the situation.

There were, however, several extremely good non-series stories. "Songs of Dying Swans" involves the tragic destruction of a race of altered humans, and the consequences of this destruction on the rest of civilization. "Laura's Theme" is a haunting, enigmatic story of a strange woman who seems constantly present when people's lives take radical turns for the worse. Many of Haldeman's stories are essentially extended jokes, and these do little for his reputation. On the other hand, even his humorous pieces often demonstrate genuine inventive humor. A typical middle-class family is startled and dismayed to discover that their front yard has suddenly become the legendary elephant's graveyard in "What Weighs 8000 Pounds and Wears Red Sneakers?," an awful title for a very funny story. In "Those Thrilling Days of Yesteryear" archaeologists are engaged in manufacturing and burying artifacts, because the past as we know it is a fraud; in fact, the implication ultimately is that the entire past, even what we personally remember, is false.

Haldeman has written two novels. *Perry's Planet* is a *Star Trek* adventure of no particular interest; *Vector Analysis* is a routine but fairly well-handled novel of adventure and scientific mystery in space. A recent short story, "Spring Fever," compares human activity to that of lemmings in a story that is better controlled than Haldeman's earlier work, a good omen for the future.

—Don D'Ammassa

HALDEMAN, Joe (William). Also writes as Robert Graham. American. Born in Oklahoma City, 9 June 1943. Educated at the University of Maryland, College Park, B.S. in physics and astronomy, 1967; graduate study, 1969-70; University of Iowa, Iowa City, M.F.A. 1975. Served in the United States Army, 1967-69: Purple Heart. Married Mary Gay Potter in 1965. Teaching Assistant, University of Iowa, 1975; Editor, *Astronomy,* Milwaukee, 1976. Since 1970, free-lance writer. Treasurer, Science Fiction Writers of America, for two years. Recipient: Nebula Award, 1975; Hugo Award, 1976, 1977; Ditmar Award, 1976; Galaxy Award, 1978. Agent: Kirby McCauley, 60 East 42nd Street, New York, New York 10017. Address: 345 Grove Street, Ormond Beach, Florida 32074, U.S.A.

SCIENCE-FICTION PUBLICATIONS

Novels (series: Attar)

The Forever War. New York, St. Martin's Press, and London, Weidenfeld and Nicolson, 1975.
Attar 1: Attar's Revenge (as Robert Graham). New York, Pocket Books, 1975.
Attar 2: War of Nerves (as Robert Graham). New York, Pocket Books, 1975.
Mindbridge. New York, St. Martin's Press, 1976; London, Macdonald and Jane's, 1977.
Planet of Judgment (novelization of TV play). New York, Bantam, and London, Corgi, 1977.
All My Sins Remembered. New York, St. Martin's Press, 1977; London, Macdonald and Janes's, 1978.
World Without End (novelization of TV play). New York, Bantam, and London, Corgi, 1979.
Worlds. New York, Viking Press, 1981.

Short Stories

Infinite Dreams. New York, St. Martin's Press, 1978.

Uncollected Short Stories

"No Future in It," in *Omni* (New York), April 1979.
"The Pilot," in *Destinies* (New York), April-June 1979.
"Blood Sisters," in *Playboy* (Chicago), July 1979.
"Four in One," in *Destinies* (New York), Spring 1980.

OTHER PUBLICATIONS

Novel

War Year. New York, Holt Rinehart, 1972; original version, New York, Pocket Books, 1977.

Plays

The Devil His Due, in *Fantastic* (New York), August 1974.
The Moon and Marcek, in *Vertex* (Los Angeles), August 1974.

Other

Introduction to *Double Star,* by Robert A. Heinlein. Boston, Gregg Press, 1978.

Editor, *Cosmic Laughter.* New York, Holt Rinehart, 1974.
Editor, *Study War No More.* New York, St. Martin's Press, 1977; London, Futura, 1979.

*

Bibliography: *Joe Haldeman: Starmont Reader's Guide 4* by Joan Gordon, Mercer Island, Washington, Starmont House, 1980.

Joe Haldeman comments:
Along with most of my contemporaries, I believe that science fiction is primarily a literature of ideas, but that this quality does not make it exempt from normal literary standards. A poorly written SF story may be published if the idea behind it is sufficiently interesting, and there's nothing "improper" about that so long as an audience exists for it. But the best SF is that which excels both in concept and in execution—examplars being as diverse as Bester's *The Stars My Destination* and Delany's *Dhalgren*—and at its best I think it has an advantage over literature that is "just plain literature."
There's no over-riding didactic or dialectic principle behind my writing. I write the sort of stories and books I would like to read. I'm fortunate in that a lot of moneybearing readers seem to share my tastes. Whether I would be willing (or able) to write differently if the market demanded it, I can't honestly say. I would like to think I'd stick to my guns, but on the other hand I do rather like working without bosses or time clocks.

* * *

Action and the hard sciences, concern for the effects of war and career on individuals, and an interest in stylistic experimentation all characterize Joe Haldeman's science fiction. His first novel, *War Year,* is a mainstream depiction of a typical draftee's Viet Nam tour of duty. In fact, Haldeman's Viet Nam experiences—he was severely wounded—have been influential in his writing. Viet Nam taught Haldeman a sharp lesson in mortality and the randomness of fate, and also that careers, soldiering or anything else, can demand so much that individuals may "become" their careers and nothing more.
The Forever War established Haldeman's reputation in SF. The novel's episodic structure, use of sexuality and violence (never gratuitous), vivid descriptions, careful calculations, wry and disillusioned viewpoint character, and documentary collages all typify Haldeman's work. The novel traces a soldier as he travels the ranks from private to major in an 1143-year-long war. Haldeman posits "collapsar jumps" which make possible faster-than-light travel, and shows in the protagonist the future shock caused by such travel in time and space. *The Forever War,* as Haldeman says, operates on a "metaphorical level as a discussion of Viet Nam, war and its effect on American society" (letter to the author).
Mindbridge uses a compressed version of Dos Passos's documentary collage technique to develop a future in which matter transmission and mental telepathy exist. The book uses two major stylistic techniques: chapters which advance the plot and are written in a vigorous, curt manner from a third-person objective viewpoint; and documents of two sorts, excerpts from the protagonist's autobiography and artifacts of his society. *All My Sins Remembered* returns to the episodic structure and examination of violence and career of *The Forever War.* Essentially an espionage thriller with documentary interchapters and a coda, the novel illustrates, through the hyperbole SF makes possible, the process by which a human being becomes absorbed by his job until he becomes his career. Because the novel's non-violent protagonist finds himself working for an amoral organization in a violent occupation, the transformation is especially disturbing. *Worlds* begins a trilogy about space colonization. It uses what Haldeman calls a "viewpoint cascade," beginning as far away from the protagonist as possible, in an address to the reader, and ending with an interior monologue. *Worlds* again uses episodic structure to reflect the episodic, unpatterned nature of reality as Haldeman sees it.
With the exception of *All My Sins Remembered,* written in spurts from 1970 to 1976, Haldeman's writing has shown a steady progress. His strengths include an ability to make characters both individual and representative, a style generally lucid, fast-paced,

and witty, a variety of techniques for blending necessary explanations into his stories, and a commitment to compassionate action in an uncompassionate world.

—Joan Gordon

HALL, Austin. American. Born in 1882 (?). Educated at Lincoln High School, Cleveland; Ohio Northern University, Ada; Ohio State University, Columbus; University of California, Berkeley. Did newspaper and electrical work, then worked in mining and ranching; wrote hundreds of western stories. *Died in 1933.*

SCIENCE-FICTION PUBLICATIONS

Novels

People of the Comet. Los Angeles, Griffin, 1948.
The Blind Spot, with Homer Eon Flint. Philadelphia, Prime Press, 1951; London, Museum Press, 1953.
The Spot of Life. New York, Ace, 1964.

Uncollected Short Stories

"Almost Immortal," in *All-Story Weekly* (New York), 7 October 1916.
"The Rebel Soul," in *All-Story Weekly* (New York), 30 June 1917.
"Into the Infinite," in *All-Story Weekly* (New York), 12 April 1919; expanded version, in *Famous Fantastic Mysteries (*New York), October 1942.
"The Man Who Saved the Earth," in *The Best of Science Fiction*, edited by Groff Conklin. New York, Crown, 1946.

*   *   *

Homer Eon Flint, writing alone and in collaboration with Austin Hall, produced a large quantity of science fiction from 1916 to 1924, most of which appeared in the Munsey magazines *All-Story* and *Argosy.* His fame, however, and that of Austin Hall, rests on one of the most admired and cherished fantasies of the early 20th century, *The Blind Spot,* and its sequel *The Spot of Life,* written by Hall after the death of Flint.

Flint's first published story was "The Planeteer," set in the 23rd century when earth's population has grown so great that global starvation is threatened. Through engineering feats on a truly cosmic scale the earth's orbit is shifted to one closer to Jupiter's, and the latter planet then furnishes a new and inexhaustible source of food. In a sequel, "King of Conserve Island," an earthly monarch attempts to gain control of Jupiter and its food resources, and is thwarted by a hero who cuts off the heat of the sun and freezes the villain into submission. "The Lord of Death" is about two men who travel to the planet Mercury, and find there an ancient record of a man and woman named Adam and Eve who had left Mercury millennia earlier for an unknown destination. In "The Queen of Life" the same characters take their space ship to Venus, where they discover an apparently Utopian civilization.

Hall's writing career began with "Almost Immortal," the story of a Tibetan doctor thousands of years old who has been able to prolong his own life by absorbing the bodies and the wills of younger men at regular intervals. His downfall comes when the last man he assimilates turns out to have a will greater than his own. "The Rebel Soul" has a quite similar plot involving undying souls which take possession of individuals across the ages. A sequel, "Into The Infinite," carries on the story of a man who has been possessed by the Rebel Soul, and who is eventually freed through the power of a woman's love. "The Man Who Saved The Earth" describes an attempt by the inhabitants of Mars to capture all the water on earth and transport it to Mars, turning the latter into a verdant planet.

This plot is foiled at the last minute by the one man on earth with the necessary knowledge, just as the oceans are drying up.

The literary styles of Flint and Hall were curiously similar, sharing the same strengths and weaknesses. Both were totally innocent of the fine points of sentence structure and grammar, and neither had a particularly large vocabulary. Each man, however, had a vivid and far-reaching imagination and a delight in reaching out into the vastnesses of time and space. Their complicated plotting and their skill in describing the life, customs, and technologies of the worlds of the distant future compensate for their somewhat clumsy style at times.

The high point in the literary careers of Flint and Hall was their collaboration on *The Blind Spot,* a classic in the field despite the literary flaws which distinguish the other works of both authors. *The Blind Spot* is more fantasy and mystery than science fiction. In a downtown San Francisco apartment building a gateway between two parallel worlds is discovered. A man emerges from the Spot, and takes back with him a scientist from this world. They are followed by would-be rescuers of the scientist, and the plot thereafter involves additional crossings through the Spot, bringing in more mystery and occultism than science. The Spot is finally closed at the end of the novel, to protect the inhabitants of this world from possible danger from the people on the other side. Flint died in 1924, under violent and mysterious circumstances which have never been explained. Hall continued to write alone, and in 1932 produced *The Spot Of Life,* a sequel in which the Spot is reopened by the inhabitants of the other world, with the object of an invasion by force of our world. This novel takes place a generation after the time of the original story, and earth's savior in *The Spot Of Life* is the son of the principal character in the first novel.

—Douglas E. Way

HAMILTON, Edmond. Also wrote as Brett Sterling. American. Born in Youngstown, Ohio, 21 October 1904. Educated at Westminster College, New Wilmington, Pennsylvania, 1919-21. Married Leigh Brackett, *q.v.,* in 1946. Free-lance writer: staff writer for *Superman* comics in the 1940's. Guest of Honor, 22nd World Science Fiction Convention, 1964; elected to First Fandom Science Fiction Hall of Fame, 1967. *Died in 1977.*

SCIENCE-FICTION PUBLICATIONS

Novels (series: Captain Future; John Gordon; Starwolf)

Quest Beyond the Stars (Future). New York, Popular Library, 1941.
Outlaw World (Future). New York, Popular Library, 1945.
Tiger Girl. London, Utopian, 1945.
The Star Kings (Gordon). New York, Fell, 1949; London, Museum Press, 1951; as *Beyond the Moon,* New York, New American Library, 1950.
The Monsters of Juntonheim. London, Consul, 1950; as *A Yank at Valhalla,* New York, Ace, 1973.
Tharkol, Lord of the Unknown. London, Consul, 1950.
City at World's End. New York, Fell, 1951; London, Museum Press, 1952.
The Sun Smasher. New York, Ace, 1959.
The Star of Life. New York, Torquil, 1959.
The Haunted Stars. New York, Torquil, 1960; London, Jenkins, 1965.
Battle for the Stars. New York, Torquil, 1961; London, Mayflower, 1963.
Outside the Universe. New York, Ace, 1964.
The Valley of Creation. New York, Lancer, 1964.
Fugitive of the Stars. New York, Ace, 1965.
Doomstar. New York, Belmont, 1966.

The Harper of Titan.   New York, Popular Library, 1967.
The Weapon from Beyond (Starwolf).   New York, Ace, 1967.
Calling Captain Future.   New York, Popular Library, 1967.
Captain Future and the Space Emperor.   New York, Popular Library, 1967.
Galaxy Mission (Future).   New York, Popular Library, 1967.
Danger Planet (Future; as Brett Sterling).   New York, Popular Library, 1968.
The Magician of Mars (Future).   New York, Popular Library, 1968.
The Closed Worlds (Starwolf).   New York, Ace, 1968.
World of the Starwolves.   New York, Ace, 1968.
The Comet Kings (Future).   New York, Popular Library, 1969.
Return to the Stars (Gordon).   New York, Lancer, 1969.
Outlaws of the Moon (Future).   New York, Popular Library, 1969.
Planets in Peril (Future).   New York, Popular Library, 1969.
Captain Future's Challenge.   New York, Popular Library, 1969.

Short Stories

The Horror on the Asteroid and Other Tales of Planetary Horror.   London, Allan, 1936; Boston, Gregg Press, 1975.
Murder in the Clinic.   **London, Utopian, 1945.**
Crashing Suns.   **New York, Ace, 1965.**
What's It Like Out There.   New York, Ace, 1974.
The Best of Edmond Hamilton, edited by Leigh Brackett.   New York, Ballantine, 1977.

*

Manuscript Collection: Eastern New Mexico University Library, Portales.

*   *   *

I suppose that all of us have had the chilling experience of trying to communicate something that was significant in our lives to an audience with a different set of values. We usually wind up with a conventionally lame apology: "Well, you really had to be there." Edmond Hamilton is like that. You had to be there. Even in the rather tight little world of science fiction, there are some authors who have a more or less universal appeal; Hamilton was not that kind of writer, even though he demonstrated from time to time that he was capable of turning out "literary" stories that can hold their own in any company. The best of Hamilton had its essence firmly planted in a particular time and a particular place: the time was when you were young and the acid of sophistication had not eaten away at your heart; the place was in the lamented pulps of yesteryear.

Edmond Hamilton virtually invented the idea of the Space Patrol. Moreover, it was an *interstellar* Space Patrol. The concept of a galactic civilization entered the mainstream of science fiction through Hamilton's stories for *Weird Tales* and *Amazing Stories* between 1928 and 1930, and it has been a lasting influence. More generally, Hamilton is identified with space opera. He was writing it before the term was coined, and he wrote a tremendous amount of it for *Air Wonder Stories, Amazing, Startling,* and *Thrilling Wonder Stories* (Hamilton published little in *Astounding, Galaxy* and *Fantasy and Science Fiction;* oddly enough, Hamilton was also conspicuous by his absence in *Planet Stories,* supposedly the epitome of space opera). Most of his stories show the defects of the genre he pioneered. The action was fast and furious and sometimes absurd. The characterization was minimal and the dialogue was ghastly. This was fiction painted in primary colors: it is Good versus Evil and look out for that meteor! In positive terms, he had the ability to fire the imagination. Hamilton was fond of the Big Idea and he could communicate the excitement of sweeping concepts. (It was typical of Hamilton to present the whole panorama of evolution in a short story, and to throw in some original twists along the way.) He caught the drama of science; he may not have gotten all the notes right, but he certainly heard the music. His stories had verve and feeling, and they were alive. Hamilton did not take himself with undue solemnity; he had some fun with his writing. At the same time, he was writing stories that *he* liked to read, and it showed. The

least of Hamilton's stories were always blessed by that extra dimension that makes all the difference: the sense of wonder.

Hamilton's most famous (or infamous) creation was Captain Future. The name was decidedly unfortunate; it is so trite that it virtually demands parody. (It got some, too. Captain Future was the only character in science fiction who managed to attract the scalpel of S.J. Perelman.) The magazine *Captain Future* was published quarterly from 1940 through 1944 and each issue featured a short Captain Future novel. Hamilton wrote most of them, as well as some later Captain Future stories that appeared in *Startling Stories.* By and large, this was formula fiction redeemed at times by flashes of the Hamilton talent. Captain Future was Curt Newton, also known as the Wizard of Science and the Man of Tomorrow. With his sidekicks—Grag the robot, Otho the android, and Simon Wright, a brain in a box—Captain Future kept boredom at bay by saving the solar system from assorted disasters ("Something's up back there at Earth, boys! We're blasting back right now").

Beginning perhaps with *City at World's End* (1951), Hamilton's fiction took on a more subdued tone as he adapted to a changing market. He cut down on the melodrama, introduced more shadings in his stories, and worked to create believable characters. One can only salute the effort; the novels range from *The Haunted Stars* to the *Starwolf* series, and they are better than a great many science-fiction tales with inflated reputations. Unfortunately, when Hamilton got rid of the corn he also lost much of the excitement that had marked his work. The spark is still there, but the fire never really gets going.

There is a kind of pathos about Hamilton's later work. He had been a creative professional writer for a quarter of a century and now he had to prove himself all over again. His talent may have been obscured by the type of science fiction to which he devoted himself, but the mature Hamilton shows to good advantage in a number of classic short stories, including "What's It Like Out There?" and "The Pro."

Edmond Hamilton was one of the most prolific of all science-fiction writers. There was joy in his work, and he opened a lot of doors for those who came after him.

—Chad Oliver

HARDING, Lee (John).   Also writes as Harold G. Nye.   Australian. Born in Colac, Victoria, 17 February 1937. Educated in Australian primary schools. Married Carla Bleeker in 1960 (divorced, 1974); two sons and one daughter. Free-lance photographer, 1953-70. Recipient: Alan Marshall Award, 1978; Australian Children's Book of the Year Award, 1980. Agent: Virginia Kidd, Box 278, Milford, Pennsylvania 18337, U.S.A. Address: P.O. Box 25, Balaclava, Victoria 3183, Australia.

SCIENCE-FICTION PUBLICATIONS

Novels

The Fallen Spaceman (juvenile).   Melbourne, Cassell, 1973; London, Cassell, 1975; revised edition, New York, Harper, 1980.
A World of Shadows.   London, Hale, 1975.
Future Sanctuary.   Toronto, Laser, 1976.
The Children of Atlantis (juvenile).   Melbourne, Cassell, 1976.
The Frozen Sky (juvenile).   Melbourne, Cassell, 1976.
Return to Tomorrow (juvenile).   Melbourne, Cassell, 1976.
The Weeping Sky.   Melbourne, Cassell, 1977.
Displaced Person.   Melbourne, Hyland House, 1979; as *Misplaced Persons,* New York, Harper, 1979.
The Web of Time (juvenile).   Melbourne, Cassell, 1979.

Uncollected Short Stories

"Sacrificial," in *Science Fantasy* (Bournemouth), August 1961.

"Conviction," in *New Worlds* (London), October 1961.

"Echo," in *New Worlds* (London), November 1961.

"Pressure," in *Science Fantasy* (Bournemouth), January 1962.

"Late," in *New Worlds* (London), February 1962.

"Dragonfly," in *New Worlds* (London), April 1962.

"Terminal," in *New Worlds* (London), May 1962.

"Birthright," in *New Worlds* (London), June 1962.

"All My Yesterdays," in *Science Fantasy* (Bournemouth), June 1963.

"The Lonely City," in *New Worlds* (London), August 1963.

"Quest," in *Lambda 1 and Other Stories*, edited by John Carnell. New York, Berkley, 1964; London, Penguin, 1965.

"The Liberators," in *New Writings in SF 5*, edited by John Carnell. London, Dobson, 1965.

"The Evidence," in *The Pacific Book of Australian Science Fiction*, edited by John Baxter. Sydney, Angus and Robertson, 1968; London, Angus and Robertson, 1969.

"Shock Treatment," in *New Writings in SF 11*, edited by John Carnell. London, Dobson, 1968; New York, Bantam, 1971.

"Consumer Report," in *Vision of Tomorrow* (Newcastle upon Tyne), August 1969.

"Soul Survivors," in *New Writings in SF 17*, edited by John Carnell. London, Dobson, 1970.

"Rebirth," in *Vision of Tomorrow* (Newcastle upon Tyne), April 1970.

"The Custodian," in *Vision of Tomorrow* (Newcastle upon Tyne), May 1970.

"The Changer" (as Harold G. Nye), in *Vision of Tomorrow* (Newcastle upon Tyne), June 1970.

"Echoes of Armageddon," in *Vision of Tomorrow* (Newcastle upon Tyne), July 1970.

"The Communication Machine," in *If* (New York), July-August 1970.

"Cassandra's Castle," in *Vision of Tomorrow* (Newcastle upon Tyne), September 1970.

"Dancing Gerontius," in *The Second Pacific Book of Australian Science Fiction*, edited by John Baxter. Sydney and London, Angus and Robertson, 1971.

"Mistress of the Mind," in *New Writings in SF 18*, edited by John Carnell. London, Dobson, 1971.

"The Immortal," in *If* (New York), January-February 1971.

"Night of Passage," in *Space 3*, edited by Richard Davis. London, Abelard Schuman, 1976; New York, Transatlantic Arts, 1977.

"Love in the City," in *Odyssey* (New York), Summer 1976.

"Spaceman," in *The Zeitgeist Machine*, edited by Damien Broderick. London, Angus and Robertson, 1977.

"The Cage of Flesh," in *Envisaged Worlds*, edited by Paul Collins. St. Kilda, Victoria, Void, 1978.

OTHER PUBLICATIONS

Plays

Radio Plays: *Journey into Time* serial, 1978; *The Legend of New Earth* serial, 1979.

Other

Editor, *Beyond Tomorrow: An Anthology of Modern Science Fiction*. Melbourne, Wren, 1976; abridged edition, London, New English Library, 1977.

Editor, *The Altered I: An Encounter with Science Fiction*. Melbourne, Norstrilia Press, 1976; revised edition, New York, Berkley, 1978.

Editor, *Rooms of Paradise*. Melbourne, Quartet, 1978; New York, St. Martin's Press, 1979.

*   *   *

Lee Harding is the most versatile of Australian science-fiction writers. He has acted as editor as well as writer, and his published works include stories and children's books as well as adult novels. His writings reflect a mature and distinctive commitment to charac-

terization, and to sound, straightforward techniques of narrative and construction.

Harding's first novel, *A World of Shadows*, is set in the not-too-distant future when man's exploration of second-order space has disturbed the strange alien Shadows. During a routine space flight the astronaut Stephen Chandler is beset by Shadows, and as a result of their onslaught he returns to Earth in the body of his co-pilot—but with his own mind and memories intact within the new body. He becomes involved in a desperate struggle to convince the authorities—and his wife—of his real identity. But what *is* his "real" identity? *A World of Shadows*, then, is a novel about identity. But Harding describes it as "an unusual ontological thriller," and the epigraph quotes John Donne on love. These three disparate themes are drawn together by Stephen Chandler's plight, and while the novel offers no profound new insights, it does offer an entertaining and cogent canvassing of issues.

Future Sanctuary is a lesser work, marred by a publisher's insistence upon an ending which "explains" material which the author had intended to leave ambiguous and unresolved. Like *A World of Shadows*, *Future Sanctuary* questions man's concept of reality and explores the role of love. The title of *The Weeping Sky* comes from the novel's central image of an eerie weeping "wound" in the sky. Through skilled and subtle manipulation of characters, situation, and setting, Harding presents his most eloquent statement on the elusive, illusory nature of reality. His characters seem to belong to our world, but their society is medieval and their religion is an unknown variant of Christianity; the "wound" in the sky appears to be a harmless though supernatural phenomenon, but there is evidence that it might be a thoroughly rational precursor of natural disaster. *Displaced Person* presents further exploration of the nature of reality as the teenager Graeme Drury gradually finds himself estranged from the world and people around him and is drawn into a soundless, colourless "grey world" or limbo. This novel is more skilled in execution than *The Weeping Sky*, for it contains some hauntingly lyrical scenes, but it is the lesser novel in conception, for its themes are made too explicit. The novel's awkward attempts at metaphysical speculation are particularly ineffective.

Lee Harding has a gift for narrative, and consequently it is the storyline that is paramount in each of his novels. Yet Harding is no "mere" story-teller, for his plots are a way of finding characters and themes, and they are always generated by the plight of his characters. It is stock critical jargon to talk about an author "examining" his themes (implying an approach that is analytical, rigorous, perhaps even exhaustive), but this is not appropriate to Harding's method. Instead of delving deeply into the details of a given issue, Harding's novels handle the themes with a light, deft touch. Harding's approach is not to be characterized by the notion of delving, but rather by the idea of unfolding.

—Van Ikin

HARNESS, Charles L(eonard). American. Born in Colorado City, Texas, 29 December 1915. Educated at George Washington University, Washington, D.C., B.S. 1942, LL.B. 1946. Married Nell W. Harness in 1938; one daughter and one son. Mineral Economist, United States Bureau of Mines, Washington, D.C., 1941-47; patent attorney, American Cyanamid Company, Stamford, Connecticut, 1947-53. Since 1953, patent attorney, W.R. Grace and Company, Columbia, Maryland. Agent: Scott Meredith Literary Agency, 845 Third Avenue, New York, New York 10022. Address: 6705 White Gate Road, Clarksville, Maryland 21029, U.S.A.

SCIENCE-FICTION PUBLICATIONS

Novels

Flight into Yesterday. New York, Bouregy, 1953; as *The Paradox*

Men, New York, Ace, 1955; with *Dome Around America*, London, Faber, 1964.
The Ring of Ritornel.   London, Gollancz, and New York, Berkley, 1968.
Wolfhead.   New York, Berkley, 1978.
The Catalyst.   New York, Pocket Books, 1980.

Short Stories

The Rose.   London, Compact, 1966; New York, Berkley, 1969.

Uncollected Short Stories

"Bugs," in *Fantasy and Science Fiction* (New York), August 1967.
"The Million Year Patient," in *Amazing* (New York), December 1967.
"Probable Cause," in *Orbit 4*, edited by Damon Knight.   New York, Putnam, 1968.
"An Ornament to His Profession," in *SF 12*, edited by Judith Merril.   New York, Delacorte Press, 1968.
"Bookmobile," in *If* (New York), November 1968.
"The Aradnid Window," in *Amazing* (New York), December 1974.

OTHER PUBLICATIONS

Other

Marketing Magnesite and Allied Products, with Nan C. Jensen.   Washington, D.C., Bureau of Mines, 1943.
Mining and Marketing of Barite, with F.M. Barsigian.   Washington, D.C., Bureau of Mines, 1946.

*

Manuscript Collection: University of Maryland, College Park.

Charles L. Harness comments:
   I did it for money.

*   *   *

Charles L. Harness has not written as much as his admirers (Damon Knight, Brian Aldiss, Michael Moorcock) would have wished. His work has always been highly intricate, and his early stories have been compared to those of A.E. van Vogt. Unlike that author, he provides what seems to be a rational explanation for all the astonishing turns of his plots; like van Vogt, his best work has the compelling power of a dream. It is highly cerebral as well; in the words of Louis MacNeice, Harness likes "to draw the corks out of an old conundrum,/And watch the paradoxes fizz."

In *Flight into Yesterday* the hero, Alar, emerges from a wrecked spaceship with no memory of who he is but a certainty that he has a most urgent task to perform. He is sponsored by the Society of Thieves, and protected by the heroine, Keiris, who is the widow of a vanished scientist. The society he finds himself in is sophisticated but decadent; there are brilliant ball scenes and hideous torture chambers. As he attempts to escape from the Imperial police, he talks to the Empress, to a Toynbeean student of the downfall of civilizations, and to the lunatic crew of a solarion, a station perilously located on the surface of the Sun. The play of ideas is brilliant, the menace threatening. The ending is perhaps a shade too perfect, with the hero cancelling out all the misery of humanity. But the book is a dazzler all the same.

"The Rose" is perhaps Harness's most beautiful single work. The heroine, Anna van Tuyl, is at once a composer, a ballet dancer, and a psychotherapist. She is composing a ballet based on Oscar Wilde's story "The Nightingale and the Rose," and is at a standstill in the piece; she is also suffering from a deforming illness. Then she is asked to treat Ruy Jacques, the husband of the eminent and arrogant scientist Martha Jacques; Ruy Jacques has forgotten how to read print, but can read people's intentions instead. In attempting to cure Ruy Jacques, Anna falls in love, incurring the jealousy of Martha Jacques. The climax is one of death and transfiguration: Anna finds the perfect ending to her ballet and dies, but hands on

the key to a higher mode of life. The summary cannot do justice to the work, which must be read.

The Ring of Ritornel is again set in a society of formal brilliance and extreme tyranny. The villain is the Emperor Oberon, who cares nothing for human life. The hero, James Andrek, has been robbed of both his father and his elder brother by Oberon, and is determined to find the culprit. At the close of the book, a new cycle of the universe is about to begin, and only two people from the old universe will survive. In the warring religions of Alea and Ritornel, Harness poses old questions of chance and destiny. The structure of the book is both mathematical and musical: certain characters and motifs recur, but always with a different effect. The book is beautiful and moving.

Wolfhead is more direct in manner than the other novels. Set in an Earth long after an atomic catastrophe, it has a hero who descends into the underground kingdom in pursuit of his lost love Beatra. As is fitting for a successor to Dante, he is guided by Virgil—a she-wolf into whose brain a small part of his own has been grafted. The theme is one of unrelenting war; in the end the hero at least succeeds in rescuing his society, but not his wife.

The Catalyst is set in the near future, and deals with a plague called novarella and a chemical called trialine which can cure it. There is a stunning portrait of the scientist Serane, and the way in which he reaches his discoveries by totally circumventing the bureaucratic structure in which he works. The hero, Paul Blandford, succeeds in securing priority for Serane's invention by an incredible trial run. Thomas M. Disch has complained of the fantastic element in this novel, but I suspect that Harness feels life really is like this: we make our discoveries half in a dream, and sometimes we do seem to be protected by guardian angels. This aspect of the book reminds me strongly of Arthur Koestler's life of Kepler in *The Sleepwalkers*.

Harness's earlier short stories were perhaps stronger on plot than on character; his first, "Time Trap," already showed the ability to construct a highly ingenious time loop. His most brilliant early story, "The New Reality," begins from the premise that early man was not less observant than we, and concludes that the world *was* flat until the 5th century B.C. The villain, Luce (alias Lucifer), brings about a completely new universe by rendering all previous theories about reality untenable, and A. Prentiss and E. (alias Adam and Eve) survive into the new reality—which is paradisal. But so does the snake!

The richest short stories Harness has given us, however, belong to a period since the middle 1960's. "Probable Cause" deals with the case of a convicted murderer of a President: since the evidence against the accused was obtained by clairvoyance, the Supreme Court must consider whether his constitutional rights have been abridged. "The Alchemist" and "An Ornament to His Profession" both deal with a chemical manufacturing firm and the problems of patent law: in the first, the firm discovers with horror that one of its scientists is practising alchemy; in the second, the lawyer Con Patrick is driven to realize that he would sell his soul if necessary to protect his patents. The later Harness stories have surrendered nothing in the skill of plotting, but they have a sure humour and sense of the richness of human life that were lacking in the earlier short stories (excepting always "The Rose"). His best work is a high-water mark in science fiction.

—Charles Cushing

HARPER, Vincent.

SCIENCE-FICTION PUBLICATIONS

Novel

The Mortgage on the Brain, Being the Confessions of the Late

Ethelbert Craft, M.D. New York, Doubleday, and London, Hutchinson, 1905.

OTHER PUBLICATIONS

Other

The Terrible Truth about Marriage. Privately printed, 1907.

*   *   *

Vincent Harper's *The Mortgage on the Brain,* though only tenuously science fiction, is an innovative and foresighted book for its age, Edwardian England—a defense of modern behavioristic theory. It is a scientist's answer to the bishop's theories about sin and moral obligation. Harper's Doctors Yznaga and Croft argue that sin is a product of chemical imbalance, and therefore can be corrected by proper medical treatment. They and their fellows (all honorable men) advocate man giving up his mortgage on the brain, his self-imposed belief in spirit and ego, and realizing that character is merely the sum of one's hereditary and environmental impressions, the result of secretions, and cerebral and nervous conditions and capacities. They talk about the brain as a house capable of holding multiple personalities that pull man schizophrenically into contradictory patterns of behavior (sound young men wenching; mild-tempered wives turning jealous shrews), and postulate a future when the government might well use science beneficently to manufacture and control human character, chemically choosing the best among multiple personality possibilities. Harper's scientists argue that since the government already plays parent and god, punishing and rewarding various behavior patterns, it should take the next step, suppressing "pernicious tendencies," neutralizing "evil hereditary impulses," developing "right wills," and manufacturing "ideal human character," commissioning surgeons and physicians to use electricity, radio-energy, surgery, vibratory control, or chemistry to control man's cerebral functions. The result, Harper believes, would be a utopian society such as the world, hampered by religion and superstition, has not yet known.

Although the plot is merely an excuse for Harper to pursue his theories, it has all the appeal of gothic romances—country houses and French villas, hunting parties, castles, and secret experiments, European ventures and mysterious women, a romantic triangle with unusual repercussions, all downplayed by a cautious and upright gentleman narrator with an eye to propriety and scientific truth, and a deep desire to set straight a record beset by rumor and prejudice. A young doctor, asked by a worried husband to treat a strange "nervous hysteria" finds a seemingly simple case complex and his own situation dangerously compromising. Distracted from medical duties by an innocent young girl, modest and proper, he finds her later transformed into a passionate, wanton creature who pursues him without regard for reputation. Still later she is again metamorphosed into a prim religious zealot, and only after much difficulty and embarrassment does the young doctor discover that all three personalities, so strikingly different in nature, are but multiple facets of his original patient, the very proper and dignified wife of a lord. It is only through experimenting on his own brain that, with the aid of his mentor, a famous Spanish psycho-physician, he can return the wife to her normal personality and restore his own tarnished reputation. In addition to its central theories about human physio-psychology, this unusual and tantalizing book includes suggestions of prescience and parasympathetic communications, and toys with the idea that all great actors and novelists possess to an extraordinary degree the power to transfer other "personalities" into their own minds, and thereby to enter into their lives for a short while.

—Gina Macdonald

HARRISON, Harry (Max). American. Born in Stamford, Connecticut, 12 March 1925. Educated at art schools in New York. Served in the United States Army Air Corps during World War II: Sergeant. Married Joan Merkler in 1954; one son and one daughter. Free-lance oommercial artist, 1946-55. Formerly, Editor, *SF Impulse,* London; Editor, *Fantastic,* New York, 1968. Lives in County Wicklow, Ireland. Recipient: Nebula Award, 1973. Agent: A.P. Watt Ltd., 26-28 Bedford Row, London WC1R 4HL, England.

SCIENCE-FICTION PUBLICATIONS

Novels (series: Deathworld; Stainless Steel Rat; To the Stars)

Deathworld. New York, Bantam, 1960; London, Penguin, 1963.
The Stainless Steel Rat. New York, Pyramid, 1961; London, New English Library, 1966.
Planet of the Damned. New York, Bantam, 1962; as *Sense of Obligation,* London, Dobson, 1967.
Deathworld 2. New York, Bantam, 1964; London, Sphere, 1977; as *The Ethical Engineer,* London, Gollancz, 1964.
Bill, The Galactic Hero. New York, Doubleday, and London, Gollancz, 1965.
Plague from Space. New York, Doubleday, 1965; London, Gollancz, 1966; as *The Jupiter Legacy,* New York, Bantam, 1970.
Make Room! Make Room! New York, Doubleday, 1966; London, Penguin, 1967.
The Technicolor Time Machine. New York, Doubleday, 1967; London, Faber, 1968.
Deathworld 3. New York, Dell, 1968; London, Faber, 1969.
Captive Universe. New York, Putnam, 1969; London, Faber, 1970.
The Daleth Effect. New York, Putnam, 1970; as *In Our Hands, The Stars,* London, Faber, 1970.
The Stainless Steel Rat's Revenge. New York, Walker, 1970; London, Faber, 1971.
Tunnel Through the Deeps. New York, Putnam, 1972; as *A Transatlantic Tunnel, Hurrah!,* London, Faber, 1972.
Stonehenge, with Leon E. Stover. New York, Scribner, and London, Davies, 1972.
The Stainless Steel Rat Saves the World. New York, Putnam, 1972; London, Faber, 1974.
Star Smashers of the Galaxy Rangers. New York, Putnam, 1973; London, Faber, 1974.
The Lifeship, with Gordon R. Dickson. New York, Harper, 1976.
Skyfall. London, Faber, 1976; New York, Atheneum, 1977.
The Stainless Steel Rat Wants You! London, Joseph, 1978.
Planet Story, illustrated by Jim Burns. Lodnon, Pierrot, and New York, A and W, 1979.
Homeworld (To the Stars). London, Panther, and New York, Bantam, 1980.
The QE2 Is Missing. London, Futura, 1980.
Wheelworld (To the Stars). London, Panther, 1981.
Starworld (To the Stars). London, Panther, 1981.

Short Stories

War with the Robots. New York, Pyramid, 1962; London, Dobson, 1967.
Two Tales and Eight Tomorrows. London, Gollancz, 1965; New York, Bantam, 1968.
Prime Number. New York, Berkley, 1970; London, Sphere, 1975.
One Step from Earth. New York, Macmillan, 1970; London, Faber, 1972.
The Best of Harry Harrison. New York, Pocket Books, 1976; London, Sidgwick and Jackson, 1977.

OTHER PUBLICATIONS

Novels

Montezuma's Revenge. New York, Doubleday, 1972.
Queen Victoria's Revenge. New York, Doubleday, 1974; London, Severn House, 1977.

Other

The Man from P.I.G. (juvenile).   New York, Avon, 1968.
Spaceship Medic (juvenile).   London, Faber, and New York, Doubleday, 1970.
"Science Fiction: Short Story and Novel," in *The Writer* (Boston), May 1970.
The Men from P.I.G. and R.O.B.O.T. (juvenile).   London, Faber, 1974; New York, Atheneum, 1978.
The California Iceberg (juvenile).   New York, Walker, and London, Faber, 1975.
"We Are Sitting on Our..." and "With a Piece of Twisted Wire," in *SF Horizons*.   New York, Arno Press, 1975.
Great Balls of Fire.   London, Pierrot, and New York, Grosset and Dunlap, 1977.
Mechanismo.   London, Pierrot, and Los Angeles, Reed, 1978.
Spacecraft in Fact and Fiction, with Malcolm Edwards.   London, Orbis, 1979.

Editor, *Collected Editorials from Analog,* by John W. Campbell, Jr.   New York, Doubleday, 1966.
Editor, with Brian Aldiss, *Nebula Award Stories 2.*   New York, Doubleday, 1967; as *Nebula Award Stories 1967,* London, Gollancz, 1967.
Editor, with Leon E. Stover, *Apeman, Spaceman: Anthropological Science Fiction.*   New York, Doubleday, and London, Rapp and Whiting, 1968.
Editor, with Brian Aldiss, *Best SF 1967* [to *1975*].   New York, Putnam, 7 vols., 1968-74; Indianapolis, Bobbs Merrill, 2 vols., 1975-76; as *The Year's Best Science Fiction 1-9,* London, Sphere, 9 vols., 1968-76.
Editor, *SF: Author's Choice 1-4.*   New York, Berkley, 4 vols., 1968-74; vol. 1 as *Backdrop of Stars,* London, Dobson, 1968.
Editor, *Four for the Future: An Anthology on the Themes of Sacrifice and Redemption.*   London, Macdonald, 1969.
Editor, *Worlds of Wonder.*   New York, Doubleday, 1969; as *Blast Off: SF for Boys,* London, Faber, 1969.
Editor, *The Year 2000.*   New York, Doubleday, 1970; London, Faber, 1971.
Editor, *The Light Fantastic: Science Fiction Classics from the Mainstream.*   New York, Scribner, 1970.
Editor, *Nova 1-4.*   New York, Delacorte Press, 1 vol., 1970; New York, Walker, 3 vols., 1972-74; London, Sphere, 4 vols., 1975-76.
Editor, with Brian Aldiss, *The Astounding-Analog Reader.*   New York, Doubleday, 1972; London, Sphere, 2 vols., 1973.
Editor, with Theodore J. Gordon, *Ahead of Time.*   New York, Doubleday, 1972.
Editor, *The John W. Campbell Memorial Anthology.*   New York, Random House, 1973; London, Sidgwick and Jackson, 1974.
Editor, with Carol Pugner, *A Science Fiction Reader.*   New York, Scribner, 1973.
Editor, with Willis E. McNelly, *Science Fiction Novellas.*   New York, Scribner, 1973.
Editor, with Brian Aldiss, *SF Horizons.*   New York, Arno Press, 1975.
Editor, with Brian Aldiss, *Hell's Cartographers: Some Personal Histories of Science Fiction Writers.*   London, Weidenfeld and Nicolson, and New York, Harper, 1975.
Editor, with Brian Aldiss, *Decade: The 1940's, The 1950's, The 1960's.*   London, Macmillan, 3 vols., 1975-77; *The 1940's* and *1950's,* New York, St. Martin's Press, 2 vols., 1978.

Harry Harrison comments

I have always believed in readability. The easier the flow of the prose, the more basic the vocabulary, the more readers there will be who can follow and enjoy a book. But complex technical terms can be used where there is no alternative. I have found that an action story with two or three levels of intellectual content below the surface enables me to say just what I wish to say. I have also found that humor—and black humor—can carry ideas that can be expressed in no other way. The fact that my books have been translated into 21 languages must indicate that I am communicating with my audience.

*   *   *

As one of the foremost editors of science-fiction anthologies (notably the *Nova* series and, with Brian Aldiss, the annual *Best SF*), Harry Harrison has displayed considerable knowledge of conventional and experimental writing in the field. This knowledge has enabled him to work with a variety of forms in his own science fiction. Although his early reputation was built on adventure science fiction (the *Deathworld* trilogy, *The Stainless Steel Rat, Planet of the Damned*), he soon developed a distinctive cross between adventure and comedy (*Bill, The Galactic Hero; The Technicolor Time Machine; Tunnel Through the Deeps; Star Smashers of the Galaxy Rangers*). This blend employs an adventure SF plot as the base for the simultaneous satirizing of science-fiction gimmicks and excesses—Harrison gleefully depicts such wonders as a time machine enabling men to meet themselves coming and going on trips to the past and a cheese-powered space drive—and of social foibles and problems such as the arrogance, greed, and insensitivity behind Hollywood fantasy, the stuffiness and cruelty of Victorian attitudes to sex and paternal authority, and the atrocities of modern warfare. Though highly entertaining, his comedy is ultimately serious. As Harrison noted in an autobiographical article in *Hell's Cartographers,* "Heller and Voltarie demonstrated to me that some things are so awful that they can only be approached through the medium of humour." Partially contradicting this dictum, Harrison produced an agonizing work of social science fiction unleavened by any comic touches. This novel, *Make Room! Make Room!,* is a nightmarish yet realistic account of what life may be like in the United States in 1999 if our government continues to ignore population growth. As further contradiction, he made a notable contribution to the disaster novel in *Skyfall,* a prophetic vision of the damage wrought by a space satellite that falls intact to earth (an event that occurred after the book was published). In addition, his collection of stories about matter transmission, *One Step from Earth,* offered moderately serious, diverse, and eventually distressing examples of the ways in which any major "advance" in transportation can affect the cultures that are touched by it, especially those that would rather not have been reached by more ruthless cultures newly able to do so. His most experimental work has been "By the Falls," a symbolic "mood story" about a white man living near the middle of a gigantic waterfall who has inured himself to pleas for help by black forms carried in the falls from somewhere above.

Harrison's themes have been as varied as his forms, encompassing such topics as the alterability of time (*The Technicolor Time Machine, The Stainless Steel Rat Saves the World*), the question of what America would have been like if it had lost the Revolution (*Tunnel Through the Deeps*), the absurdity of male chauvinism (*Skyfall, The Stainless Steel Rat Wants You*), the character destruction wrought by racism ("American Dead"), the dangers of excessively respecting authority, including religious and political authority (*Captive Universe, Plague from Space*), the brutalizing effects of war (*Bill, The Galactic Hero; The Stainless Steel Rat's Revenge*), the folly of carrying the Cold War into space (*The Daleth Effect*), the ever increasing damage to our quality of life from the population explosion (*Make Room! Make Room!*), and the desirability of individuality until it becomes insensitive selfishness, as in rampant capitalism (*Deathworld 2, The Stainless Steel Rat*). However, underlying everything Harrison has written is a philosophy based on scientific humanism and situational ethics. This philosophy assumes that there is no God and that, as Stephen Crane asserted, the universe feels no "sense of obligation" toward man (Harrison used this assertion as an epigraph for *Planet of the Damned*). Given the universe's unconcern, men must become concerned about one another and must use all tools available, especially those provided by science, to help each other. According to Harrison, co-operation among men of all nations, races, and creeds is crucial today to everyone's survival. Above all, men must begin to share food, resources, and skills to solve the worldwide problems of excessive population, poverty, and dwindling fuel supplies and to prevent worldwide destruction through atomic warfare. Beyond this, men must realize that they are interdependent on all other living things on this planet and must therefore respect life in whatever form it takes. Harrison's first novel, *Deathworld,* in fact, depicted a group of psionic plants and animals who, upon discerning some men's hatred for them, launched a war against their despisers. Apart from the directive to respect life and foster its growth, however, there are no rules that can be considered valid for every situation. Harrison evidently has been incensed by Christians' efforts to compel others to conform to their group ethics (though he would probably also respond angrily to any other group with similar claims to universal truth and justice). In *Make Room! Make Room!,* for example, he included a tirade against the Catholic Church's dangerously unrealistic moral stand on birth control, and in *Deathworld 2* he showed that his hero's refusal to be bound by an ethical code enabled him to do more than his "ethical" Christian adversary could to help move a savage and treacherous people toward civilization. In Harrison's view, the only meaningful ethical decisions are those grounded in a realistic assessment of consequences in a particular situation and not in an appeal to abstract ideals.

Unless he produces something of comparable or greater value, Harrison will probably remain best known for *Make Room! Make Room!,* his comic SF novels, and his Deathworld and Stainless Steel Rat series. *Make Room! Make Room!* was the first novel to trace in painstaking and painful detail the effect that an overabundance of human beings might have on living conditions, law enforcement, romance. Harrison's overcrowded society is disturbingly credible, and, unlike many novels of social warning, his characters are not simply puppets designed to illustrate points but multi-dimensional, appealing figures. (This novel was made into the film *Soylent Green,* which unfortunately added a plot about cannibalism.) Harrison's comic SF novels have the contrasting virtue of extravagant invention. Consider *The Technicolor Time Machine* in which a movie crew utilizes a time machine to film a Viking epic in the actual Viking era, thus insuring authenticity and reduced costs, or *Bill, The Galactic Hero* in which the protagonist, after a series of ludicrous, soul-shriveling experiences both in and out of combat, becomes a recruiting sergeant—with tusks—and enlists his innocent younger brother to lessen his own time in the army. Given the solemnity of most science fiction, Harrison's humor is a remarkable and delightful achievement. Finally, Jason dinAlt, the wily, irascible gambler with psi powers in the Deathworld series, and Slippery Jim diGriz, the criminal half-converted to policeman in the Stainless Steel Rat series, are memorable creations who have deservedly attracted a wide following.

—Steven R. Carter

HARRISON, M(ichael) John. British. Born in Great Britain, 26 July 1945. Educated at schools in England. Groom, Atherstone Hunt, Warwickshire, 1963; student teacher, Warwickshire, 1963-65; clerk, Royal Masonic Charity Institute, London, 1966. Literary Editor and reviewer, *New Worlds.* Address: c/o Sphere Books, 30-32 Gray's Inn Road, London WC1X 8JL, England.

SCIENCE-FICTION PUBLICATIONS

Novels

The Committed Men. London, Hutchinson, and New York, Doubleday, 1971.
The Pastel City. London, New English Library, 1971; New York, Doubleday, 1972.
The Centauri Device. New York, Doubleday, 1974; London, Panther, 1975.
A Storm of Wings. London, Sphere, and New York, Doubleday, 1980.

Short Stories

The Machine in Shaft Ten and Other Stories. London, Panther, 1975.

* * *

Closely associated with Moorcock's *New Worlds,* M. John Har-

rison was both literary editor and a major contributor. Much of his fiction first appeared in the magazine, beginning with the story "Baa Baa Blocksheep" in 1968. As a reviewer (frequently writing as Joyce Churchill), his opinions earned him numerous enemies. Caustic and penetrating, he criticises the majority of science fiction as moribund, stifled by constraints on literacy, creativity, and even imagination. Many of Harrison's own stories explore inner space in styles commonly identified as New Wave. Typical are fragmentary narrative; imagistic, entropy-haunted worlds; enigmatic individuals driven by metaphoric fates or pursuing them with studied awareness. Characters (or their names) and settings recur throughout his work. In the interlocking pastiches "The Nash Circuit," "The Flesh Circle," and "The Ash Circus" his handling of New Wave avatar Jerry Cornelius rivals Moorcock's original vision. The satire is savage and accurate, extending with characteristic irony to the protagonist himself.

However, Harrison is equally ready to apply fresh perspectives to more orthodox themes and techniques. His oblique approaches and poignant twists are often reminiscent of Ballard, as in "London Melancholy" and "The Causeway." His concern with the intricacies of basic motivation finds increasingly complex expression in "The Machine in Shaft Ten," "Settling the World," and "Coming from Behind." The sober, detailed realism and the meticulous language are all the stronger for being unobtrusive. The same is true of the novelette of entropy "Running Down." Consistent intensification of imagery and mood makes this a powerful piece, regarded by many as Harrison's best work to date.

His first novel, *The Committed Men,* is set in a post-holocaust England. Dominated by images of roads, the book is forceful and bleakly evocative, but not without its humour. The characters' relationships shift, their rationalisations of an anarchic world differ, but their shared ideal fulfils diverse needs. Compared with the obsessions of other survivors their dedication to an ambiguous quest seems relatively sane. Finding purpose in commitment to the future, however alien, offers each the chance to expand the mentality of survival. To quote the title of Harrison's final chapter, "destination is a state of mind."

In *The Pastel City* a far-future civilisation delays its decline with scavenged remnants of old technology. At heart an affectionate parody of sword-and-sorcery fiction, the novel challenges several traditional assumptions. Its heroes, emerging from retirement, are as prone to human weakness as any. Emphasis is also given to the estrangement they have felt from a world at peace: one has turned traitor, while the introverted, self-doubting tegeus-Cromis (an obvious tribute to Moorcock's moody swordsmen) is reunited with a smuggler, an aged lecher, and a gleefully vicious dwarf. Even the threat they face proves somewhat ambivalent. Fulsome description, at times cloying, is partially offset by touches of irony and of calculated restraint. A similar combination seems likely in the projected sequel.

The Centauri Device blends fast-moving, cheerfully anachronistic space opera with a mordant indictment of the processes of dehumanisation. Its focus is the selfish and alienated John Truck, an unwilling pawn in galactic power struggles involving opposing political blocs, a bizarre religious sect, and an insidious drug ring. Sensing their interdependence and having seen their effects on countless people and planets, Truck rejects all their promises and ideologies as worthless mouthings and spends his time in futile flight. Convincingly written, the book is filled with worn-out victims and cold, pointless deaths. A group of improbable Decadent aesthetes, quoting poetry amid battle, relieves the grimness. Joyous and undogmatic, they are crushed, although a few do escape.

Harrison has been accused of replacing the "literature of comfort" he criticises with one of smug pessimism, peopled with characters who have lost all direction. Certainly his characterisation makes no concessions to the stereotypes of appealingness or wish-fulfilment (heroes he regards as dangerous "baboon colony stuff"). But a fundamental underlying theme in his work is that individual responsibility, with continual reassessment of one's own assumptions, is the only valid belief. Harrison has never chosen to present the road to such responsibility as a clearly defined or easy one to travel.

—Nick Pratt

HARTLEY, L(eslie) P(oles). British. Born in Whittlesey, Cambridgeshire, 30 December 1895. Educated at Harrow School; Balliol College, Oxford, B.A. 1922. Served in World War I, 1916-18. Fiction Reviewer for *Spectator, Week-end Review, Weekly Sketch, Time and Tide, The Observer,* and *Sunday Times,* all in London, 1923-72. Clark Lecturer, Trinity College, Cambridge, 1964. Recipient: Black Memorial Prize, 1948; Heinemann Award, 1954. Companion of Literature, Royal Society of Literature, 1972. C.B.E. (Commander, Order of the British Empire), 1956. *Died 13 December 1972.*

SCIENCE-FICTION PUBLICATIONS

Novel

Facial Justice. London, Hamish Hamilton, 1960; New York, Doubleday, 1961.

OTHER PUBLICATIONS

Novels

Simonetta Perkins. London and New York, Putnam, 1925.
Eustace and Hilda. London, Putnam, 1958; Chester Springs, Pennsylvania, Dufour, 1961.
  The Shrimp and the Anemone. London, Putnam, 1944; as *The West Window,* New York, Doubleday, 1945.
  The Sixth Heaven. London, Putnam, 1946; New York, Doubleday, 1947.
  Eustace and Hilda. London, Putnam, 1947.
The Boat. London, Putnam, 1949; New York, Doubleday, 1950.
My Fellow Devils. London, Barrie, 1951.
The Go-Between. London, Hamish Hamilton, 1953; New York, Knopf, 1954.
A Perfect Woman. London, Hamish Hamilton, 1955; New York, Knopf, 1956.
The Hireling. London, Hamish Hamilton, 1957; New York, Rinehart, 1958.
The Brickfield. London, Hamish Hamilton, 1964.
The Betrayal. London, Hamish Hamilton, 1966.
Poor Clare. London, Hamish Hamilton, 1968.
The Love-Adept: A Variation on a Theme. London, Hamish Hamilton, 1969.
My Sisters' Keeper. London, Hamish Hamilton, 1970.
The Harness Room. London, Hamish Hamilton, 1971.
The Collections. London, Hamish Hamilton, 1972.
The Will and the Way. London, Hamish Hamilton, 1973.

Short Stories

Night Fears and Other Stories. London, Putnam, 1924.
The Killing Bottle. London, Putnam, 1932.
The Travelling Grave and Other Stories. Sauk City, Wisconsin, Arkham House, 1948; London, Barrie, 1951.
The White Wand and Other Stories. London, Hamish Hamilton, 1954.
Two for the River. London, Hamish Hamilton, 1961.
The Collected Short Stories of L.P. Hartley. London, Hamish Hamilton, 1968; New York, Horizon Press, 1969.
Mrs. Carteret Receives and Other Stories. London, Hamish Hamilton, 1971.
The Complete Short Stories of L.P. Hartley. London, Hamish Hamilton, 1973.

Other

The Novelist's Responsibility: Lectures and Essays. London, Hamish Hamilton, 1967; New York, Hillary House, 1968.

*

Manuscript Collection: British Library, London.

*   *   *

L.P. Hartley's *Facial Justice* is a dystopian novel of the future in the tradition of Zamyatin's *We.* Hartley envisages a New State founded on self-abasement and equality. All the citizens are patients and delinquents, victims of their own ego-sickness. Each citizen is named after a murderer, biblical murderers being particularly in vogue; sackcloth and ashes provide the regular costume. In this projected society, envy is seen as the single cause of personal dissatisfaction and social friction. The wants, desires, and instincts of the citizens of the New State are suitably provided for by the Dictator. Hartley postulates that envy is stronger in women than in men, especially when it comes to the question of personal beauty. So women who are dissatisfied with their looks are encouraged to be "betafied," to have plastic surgery performed which gives them a pre-packaged beautiful face. The only difficulty is that such women have a difficult time in expressing their emotions.

Hartley's narrator and ultimately the first revolutionary in the New State is a young woman, Jael 93, who, as a result of an accident, is betafied only to resent the loss of her personality. Henceforth she attempts to discredit the Dictator and overthrow the New State. How she goes about it and the totally unexpected result of her activities provide fascinating reading. Hartley poses many of the usual dystopian concerns, freedom versus happiness, community good versus individual fulfillment, but treats them with a fresh perspective. *Facial Justice* is an intriguing venture into the dystopian tradition by a well-known mainstream author, especially in that it is written from the woman's point of view in a society which, though it professes equality, actually denigrates women.

—Joseph A. Quinn

HARTRIDGE, Jon. British. Born in 1934. Features Editor, Oxford *Mail.*

SCIENCE-FICTION PUBLICATIONS

Novels

Binary Divine. London, Macdonald, 1969; New York, Doubleday, 1970.
Earthjacket. London, Macdonald, and New York, Walker, 1970.

Uncollected Short Story

"Like Father," in *Best SF 1969,* edited by Harry Harrison and Brian Aldiss. New York, Putnam, 1970; as *The Year's Best Science Fiction 3,* London, Sphere, 1970.

*   *   *

Jon Hartridge had a very brief science fiction career, and produced only two novels. Neither was particularly successful with readers, who tended to be put off by a highly intellectual style and a certain amount of disdain for the logic of his situations.

Binary Divine, for example makes use of various standard concepts. Production is far ahead of consumption because of a massive drop in the total population, a drop that somehow occurred during a one-month period about which no one can recall anything. Hartridge seemed to have difficulty deciding whether his plot was to be taken seriously or as satirical whimsy. The existence of plastic pedestrians destined to annihilation by automated vehicle traffic might be very amusing in the proper context, but seemed to jar with the other elements in this novel. Ultimately, the resolution of the mystery is less than satisfying. Although the problem is fairly well established, and the plot progresses with some skill, the author was not capable of adequately rationalizing his conclusion, and the novel dissolves into a philosophical denouement that is essentially disappointing.

Earthjacket is an even more traditional novel, one that succeeds more completely because its ambitions were considerably less. Human society has been divided into two classes, the Texecs and the Sleepees, with the former minority suppressing the latter majority. The names change from novel to novel but the basic situation is the same. One man, a member of the lower class, objects to the status quo and sets out to alter the nature of his society. Hartridge utilizes this plot to praise the virtues of individualism and democratic principles of government. Again, his style is more than adequate, and although the plot was not particularly original it was relatively well handled.

A more promising note was in the shorter piece "Like Father." A megalomaniac travels back through time in order to impregnate primitive pre-humans with his own seed, determined to become literally the father of the human race. Having successfully fathered a child, he proceeds forward in small jumps, returning to aid his offspring at crucial moments. But his aspirations backfire because he fails to recognize that the primitive code of conduct is different from his own, and that the adolescent does not in any case recognize him as his parent. Having introduced his son to primitive weapons, he is the first victim of them.

Hartridge never produced enough fiction for a fair judgment of his ability to be drawn. His optimism is colored by a cynical strain which may well have contributed to his lack of popularity.

—Don D'Ammassa

HAWKES, (Jessie) Jacquetta (née Hopkins).   British.   Born in Cambridge, 5 August 1910. Educated at Perse School; Newnham College, Cambridge, B.A. 1935, M.A. Associate 1951. Married 1) Christopher Hawkes in 1933 (marriage dissolved, 1953), one son; 2) J.B. Priestley, *q.v.,* in 1953. Engaged in excavation and archaeological reserach in Britain, Ireland, France, and Palestine, 1931-40; Assistant Principal, Post-War Reconstruction Secretariat, 1941-43; worked in the Ministry of Education, becoming Principal and Secretary, U.K. National Commission for Unesco, 1943-49. General Editor, Past in the Present series, Thames and Hudson, London, 1952-54. John Danz Visiting Professor, University of Washington, Seattle, 1971. Vice-President, Council for British Archaeology, 1949-52; Archaeological Adviser, Festival of Britain, 1949-51; Governor, British Film Institute, 1950-55; Member, Unesco Cultural Advisory Committee, 1966. Recipient: Kemsley Award, for non-fiction, 1951. Fellow, Society of Antiquaries, 1940. O.B.E. (Officer, Order of the British Empire), 1952. Address: Kissing Tree House, Alveston, Stratford on Avon, Warwickshire CV37 7QT, England.

SCIENCE-FICTION PUBLICATIONS

Novel

Providence Island: An Archaeological Tale.   London, Chatto and Windus, and New York, Random House, 1959.

Short Stories

Fables.   London, Cresset Press, 1953; as *A Woman as Great as the World and Other Fables*, New York, Random House, 1953.

OTHER PUBLICATIONS

Novels

King of the Two Lands: The Pharaoh Akhenaten.   London, Chatto and Windus, 1966; New York, Random House, 1967.
A Quest of Love.   London, Chatto and Windus, 1980.

Play

Dragon's Mouth: A Dramatic Quartet, with J.B. Priestley (produced Malvern and London, 1952; New York, 1955).   London, Heinemann, and New York, Harper, 1952.

Verse

Symbols and Speculations.   London, Cresset Press, 1949.

Other

The Bailiwick of Jersey (vol. 2 of *The Archaeology of the Channel Islands*).   Saint Hélier, Société Jersiaise, 1939.
Prehistoric Britain, with Christopher Hawkes.   London, Penguin, 1943; revised edition, London, Chatto and Windus, 1947; Cambridge, Massachusetts, Harvard University Press, 1953.
Early Britain.   London, Collins, 1945.
Christmas.   London, Bureau of Current Affairs, 1949.
A Guide to Prehistoric and Roman Monuments in England and Wales.   London, Chatto and Windus, 1951; revised edition, London, Sphere, 1973; as *History in Earth and Stone,* Cambridge, Massachusetts, Harvard University Press, 1952.
A Land, illustrated by Henry Moore.   London, Cresset Press, 1951; New York, Random House, 1952.
Man on Earth.   London, Cresset Press, 1954; New York, Random House, 1955.
Journey Down a Rainbow (travel), with J.B. Priestley.   London, Cresset Press-Heinemann, and New York, Harper, 1955.
The Aborigines of Australia (address).   London, Headley, 1961.
Man and the Sun.   London, Cresset Press, and New York, Random House, 1962.
Prehistory and the Beginnings of Civilization, with Leonard Woolley.   London, Allen and Unwin, and New York, Harper, 1963.
Pharaohs of Egypt.   New York, American Heritage, 1965; London, Cassell, 1967.
Dawn of the Gods.   London, Chatto and Windus, and New York, Random House, 1968.
Nothing But or Something More (essays).   Seattle, University of Washington Press, 1972.
The First Great Civilizations: Life in Mesopotamia, The Indus Valley, and Egypt.   London, Hutchinson, and New York, Knopf, 1973.
The Atlas of Early Man.   London, Macmillan, and New York, St. Martin's Press, 1976.

Editor, *The World of the Past.*   London, Thames and Hudson, 2 vols., and New York, Knopf, 2 vols., 1963.
Editor, *Atlas of Ancient Archaeology.*   London, Heinemann, and New York, McGraw Hill, 1974.

*   *   *

Jacquetta Hawkes is an archaeologist of the first rank, and the author of both scholarly and popular books on man's prehistory. It is not surprising that the most conspicuous science in her science-fiction writing is archaeology, the profession of the central characters in her major novel,*Providence Island.*

Accidentally discovered by a USAF pilot, some knapped flints from the island of the title prompt an expedition, led by an aging Oxford professor and including a cultured woman archaeologist. The focus of the novel is initially the professor, who, in sudden contempt for the tedium and sterility of his life and supposed studies, finances the expedition from his life's savings. However, in the latter and better half of the book the focus changes to the awakening responses and self-knowledge of the woman archaeologist, most lucidly and touchingly conveyed. The inhabitants of Providence Island have retained their ancient worship of three deities, the Mother-Bride Goddess, the beast-man God who presides over hunting, and the Teacher of Wisdom. Remaining "primitive," they have developed psychic powers that have kept their island and their existence unsuspected for countless centuries by the kinds of humans we regard as "civilised." Their traditional account of their ancestors' revulsion from the "seed-eaters" and the long flight through hostile tribes, culminating in the voyage to the island, is both beautiful and convincing. The climax scene, in which the expedition aids the tribe to "brainwash" American servicemen who have come to take over the island as a nuclear testing ground, is well and indignantly written, but the creation of the tribe itself is the book's greatest achievement.

Hawkes's other significant work specifically in the field of science fiction is the collection *Fables.* 17 very short fables of men, animals, and gods are told crisply and poetically; their subtle and hard-edged morals simultaneously round off the fables and tease the intellect. The novella "The Unites" completed the book. It is set in a far future, when humanity has been collectivised into rigid conformism, based upon three categories of work and four successive age-groups. This hive-life is overthrown by the subtle infiltration of an ancient religion, based on a trinity similar to that of the islanders' worship in *Providence Island.* At the point of violent but welcome success of the rebellion, however, the remnant of three who remain faithful to the Unites' system of social brotherhood and self-forgetfulness escape, to hide away in the very cave where the trinity of the triumphant religion had previously hidden. Thus, the dialectical alternation of social versions of mankind will continue.

The play *Dragon's Mouth* was written with J.B. Priestley, her second husband. Set on a pleasure-cruiser in the Caribbean, it is marginally science fiction in that one of the four characters has contracted an initially undetectable but inevitably fatal disease; it ends with the sound of the motor-boat that bears the information as to which one is doomed. In semi-naturalistic speeches each character at first defends his or her life-style but later becomes more honestly self-critical. The perspective on characterisation reveals much about Hawkes's attitude to ancient religions and her handling of personality in both novels and fables. Perhaps influenced by Jung, perhaps by Virginia Woolf, Hawkes presents her characters as virtual personifications of the elements more balanced in us: the moral, the aesthetic, the sensual, and the active or creative. Hawkes has also written an outstanding historical novel peripheral to science fiction, *King of the Two Lands.* Based on her interpretation of the archaeological evidence about the remarkable Pharaoh Akhnaton, it is probably the finest yoking of narrative fiction with that science so far.

—Norman Talbot

HEARD, Gerald. *See* **HEARD, H.F.**

HEARD, H(enry) F(itzgerald). Also wrote as Gerald Heard. British. Born in London, 6 October 1889. Educated at Gonville and Caius College, Cambridge, B.A. (honours) in history 1911, graduate work 1911-12. Worked with the Agicultural Co-operative Movement in Ireland, 1919-23, and in England, 1923-27; Editor, *Realist,* London, 1929; Lecturer, Oxford University, 1929-31; science commentator, BBC Radio, London, 1930-34; settled in the United States, 1937; Visiting Lecturer, Washington University, St. Louis, 1951-52, 1955-56; Haskell Foundation Lecturer, Oberlin College, Ohio, 1958. Recipient: Bollingen grant, 1955; British Academy Hertz award. *Died 14 August 1971.*

SCIENCE-FICTION PUBLICATIONS

Novels

Doppelgangers: An Episode of the Fourth, the Psychological Revo-

lution, 1997. New York, Vanguard Press, 1947; London, Cassell, 1948.
The Black Fox London, Cassell, 1950; New York, Harper, 1951.

Short Stories

The Great Fog and Other Weird Tales. New York, Vanguard Press, 1944; London, Cassell, 1947; as *Weird Tales of Terror and Detection,* New York, Sun Dial Press, 1946.
The Lost Cavern and Other Tales of the Fantastic. New York, Vanguard Press, 1948; London, Cassell, 1949.

Uncollected Short Stories

"B + M—Planet 4," in *New Tales of Space and Time,* edited by Raymond J. Healy. New York, Holt Rinehart, 1951; London, Weidenfeld and Nicolson, 1952.
"The Marble Ear," in *Fantasy and Science Fiction* (New York), December 1952.

OTHER PUBLICATIONS

Novels

A Taste for Honey. New York, Vanguard Press, 1941; London, Cassell, 1942; as *A Taste for Murder,* New York, Avon, 1955.
Reply Paid. New York, Vanguard Press, 1942; London, Cassell, 1943.
Murder by Reflection. New York, Vanguard Press, 1942; London, Cassell, 1945.
The Notched Hairpin. New York, Vanguard Press, 1949; London, Cassell, 1952.

Other as Gerald Heard

Narcissus: An Anatomy of Clothes. London, Kegan Paul, and New York, Dutton, 1924.
The Ascent of Humanity: An Essay on the Evolution of Civilization. London, Cape, and New York, Harcourt Brace, 1929.
The Emergence of Man. London, Cape, 1931; New York, Harcourt Brace, 1932.
Social Substance of Religion: An Essay on the Evolution of Religion. London, Allen and Unwin, and New York, Harcourt Brace, 1931.
This Surprising World: A Journalist Looks at Science. London, Cobden Sanderson, 1932.
These Hurrying Years: An Historical Outline 1900-1933. London, Chatto and Windus, and New York, Oxford University Press, 1934.
Science in the Making. London, Faber, 1935.
The Source of Civilisation. London, Cape, 1934; New York, Harper, 1937.
The Significance of the New Pacifism, with *Pacifism and Philosophy,* by Aldous Huxley. London, Headley, 1935.
Exploring the Stratosphere. London, Nelson, 1936.
Science Front 1936. London, Cassell, 1937.
The Third Morality. London, Cassell, and New York, Morrow, 1937.
Pain, Sex, and Time: A New Hypothesis of Evolution. New York, Harper, and London, Cassell, 1939.
The Creed of Christ: An Interpretation of the Lord's Prayer. New York, Harper, 1940; London, Cassell, 1941.
A Quaker Meditation. Wallingford, Pennsylvania, Pendle Hill, 1940 (?).
The Code of Christ: An Interpretation of the Beatitudes. New York, Harper, 1941; London, Cassell, 1943.
Training for the Life of the Spirit. London, Cassell, 2 vols., 1941-44; New York, Harper, 1 vol, n.d.
Man the Master. New York, Harper, 1941; London, Faber, 1942.
A Dialogue in the Desert. London, Cassell, and New York, Harper, 1942.
A Preface to Prayer. New York, Harper, 1944; London, Cassell, 1945.
The Recollection. Stanford, California, Delkin, 1944.

The Gospel According to Gamaliel. New York, Harper, 1945; London, Cassell, 1946.
Militarism's Post-Mortem. London, P.P.U., 1946.
The Eternal Gospel. New York, Harper, 1946; London, Cassell, 1948.
Is God Evident? An Essay Toward a Natural Theology. New York, Harper, 1948; London, Faber, 1950.
Is God in History? An Inquiry into Human and Pre-Human History in Terms of the Doctrine of Creation, Fall, and Redemption. New York, Harper, 1950; London, Faber, 1951.
Morals since 1900. London, Dakers, and New York, Harper, 1950.
The Riddle of the Flying Saucers. London, Carroll and Nicholson, 1950; as *Is Another World Watching?*, New York, Harper, 1951; revised editon, New York, Bantam, 1953.
Ten Questions on Prayer. Wallingford, Pennsylvania, Pendle Hill, 1951.
Gabriel and the Creatures. New York, Harper, 1952; as *Wishing Well: An Outline of the Evolution of the Mammals Told as a Series of Stories about How Animals Got Their Wishes,* London, Faber, 1953.
The Human Venture. New York, Harper, 1955.
Kingdom Without God: Road's End for the Social Gospel, with others. Los Angeles, Foundation for Social Research, 1956.
Training for a Life of Growth. Santa Monica, California, Wayfarer Press, 1959.
The Five Ages of Man: The Psychology of Human History. New York, Julian Press, 1964.
"Science Fiction, Morals, and Religion," in *Science Fiction: The Future,* edited by Dick Allen. New York, Harcourt Brace, 1971.

Editor, *Prayers and Meditations.* New York, Harper, 1949.

*   *   *

Doppelgangers, the novel by H.F. Heard best known to science-fiction readers, depicts a hedonistic dictatorship based on behavior control. The hero, nameless except as "the remodeled man" or Alpha II, belongs to an underground organization ruled by the Mole, who also uses behavior control to sabotage the dictatorship. In the novel, the hero is "remodeled" physically to duplicate the dictator Alpha, who needs a double to impersonate him and absorb the psychic impact of his charismatic appearances. When Alpha commits suicide, Alpha II is left as dictator. An assassination attempt by a follower of the Mole leads to a series of discoveries about the true government of the world, which remains in the hands of spiritually evolved people called elevates.

The novel explores Heard's ideas about the human condition. The nature of Alpha's dictatorship is despotism through indulgence, suave reduction of the human soul to childishness by supplying the masses with entertainment and pleasures. "Animectomy," or cutting away of the soul, prefigures B.F. Skinner's *Walden II.* As a dystopian novel, *Doppelgangers* can also be compared to Orwell's *Nineteen Eighty-Four* or Huxley's *Brave New World.* But Heard also explores evolution, especially as a self-directed project with Hegelian overtones, since he sees human history as a continuing aspiration toward something higher, with Alpha's dictatorship only one step on the ladder. Heard is also interested in the relationship of the soul to its manifestations. Clothes reflect customs: a man's appearance determines and is determined by his ideas; etymology reveals truths of history. Indeed, one of Heard's first books was a history and philosophy of costume, *Narcissus: An Anatomy of Clothes,* and his style and ideas are influenced by the "Clothes Philosophy" of Carlyle's *Sartor Resartus.* The dictatorship in *Doppelgangers* is also based on Sheldon's somatypes which posit a relationship between body type and personality. *Doppelgangers* is a philosophical novel; though the psychological exploration of the few major characters is deep, this is not a psychological novel. The style is involuted with tricky puns and allusions.

The Black Fox is an occultist novel with speculative content. Throcton, a British cleric envious of advancement, uses black magic to destroy his enemy. When the magic recoils, he is saved only by the self-sacrifice of his sister. Heard bases the black magic, involving etymology of the word *alopecia* from fox mange, on Biblical, Sufist,

and folklore learning, speculating on the relation of mind and body. Treatment of black magic as an explainable phenomenon prefigures the thinking of such contemporaries as Colin Wilson. Psychological analysis is strong in this novel, and the isolated, highly cerebral Throctons, brother and sister, are eccentric but complexly interesting. Except for his detective fiction, *The Black Fox* represents the best use of suspense in Heard's fiction.

Gabriel and the Creatures is a speculative fantasy based on the premise that a species has a will to evolve in a certain direction, and that God, through the angel Gabriel, will grant each species its wish. *The Gospel According to Gamaliel* is a retelling of the New Testament by a Hebrew ecclesiast, teacher of St. Paul, speculative in its attempt to reconcile differing theological viewpoints.

Heard's short stories are mostly collected in *The Great Fog* and *The Lost Cavern.* They speculate upon some of Heard's favorite concerns: evolution in "The Thaw Plan," "The Lost Cavern," "Wingless Victory," and "The Great Fog"; medical knowledge in "The Rousing of Mr. Bradegar" and "The Crayfish"; architecture in "Dromenon"; and telepathic exchange in "The Swap." "The Cat 'I Am' " may be seen as an early study for *The Black Fox.* Heard's heroes are isolated, scholarly types.

Heard's major output is not in fiction but in religious philosophy; he has also written detective fiction and a work on flying saucers. Except for reviews and an occasional mention in critical works, Heard has received little critical attention. His strength is in speculation rather than character or plot. Nonetheless, *Doppelgangers* is a significant dystopian novel which merits a place in the science-fiction canon.

—Mary T. Brizzi

HEINLEIN, Robert A(nson). American. Born in Butler, Missouri, 7 July 1907. Educated at Central High School, Kansas City; University of Missouri, Columbia, one year; United States Naval Academy, Annapolis, Maryland, B.S. 1929. Served in the United States Navy, 1929 until retirement because of physical disability, 1934. Married 1) Leslyn McDonald; 2) Virginia Gerstenfeld in 1948. Worked in mining and real estate,.1934-39; civilian engineer, Philadelphia Navy Yard, 1942-45. Recipient: Hugo Award, 1956, 1960, 1962, 1967; Boys' Clubs of America Award, 1959; Grand Master Nebula Award, 1975. Guest of Honor, World Science Fiction Convention, 1941, 1961, 1976. Agent: Blassingame McCauley and Wood, 60 East 42nd Street, New York, New York, 10017, U.S.A.

SCIENCE-FICTION PUBLICATIONS

Novels (series: Future History)

Rocket Ship Galileo (juvenile). New York, Scribner, 1947; London, New English Library, 1971.
Space Cadet (juvenile). New York, Scribner, 1948; London, Gollancz, 1966.
Beyond This Horizon. Reading, Pennsylvania, Fantasy Press, 1948; London, Panther, 1967.
Sixth Column. New York, Gnome, 1949; as *The Day after Tomorrow,* New York, New American Library, 1951; London, Mayflower, 1962.
Red Planet (juvenile). New York, Scribner, 1949; London, Gollancz, 1963.
Farmer in the Sky (juvenile). New York, Scribner, 1950; London, Gollancz, 1962.
Waldo, and Magic Inc. New York, Doubleday, 1950.
The Puppet Masters. New York, Doubleday, 1951; London, Museum Press, 1953.
Between Planets (juvenile). New York, Scribner, 1951; London, Gollancz, 1968.

The Rolling Stones (juvenile). New York, Scribner, 1952; as *Space Family Stone,* London, New English Library, 1971.

Starman Jones (juvenile). New York, Scribner, 1953; London, Sidgwick and Jackson, 1954.

The Star Beast (juvenile). New York, Scribner, 1954; London, New English Library, 1971.

Tunnel in the Sky (juvenile). New York, Scribner, 1955; London, Gollancz, 1965.

Time for the Stars (juvenile). New York, Scribner, 1956; London, Gollancz, 1963.

Double Star. New York, Doubleday, 1956; London, Joseph, 1958.

The Door into Summer. New York, Doubleday, 1957; London, Panther, 1960.

Citizen of the Galaxy (juvenile). New York, Scribner, 1957; London, Gollancz, 1969.

Have Space Suit—Will Travel (juvenile). New York, Scribner, 1958; London, Gollancz, 1970.

Methuselah's Children (Future History). New York, Gnome, 1958; London, Gollancz, 1963.

Starship Troopers (juvenile). New York Putnam, 1959; London, New English Library, 1961.

Stranger in a Strange Land. New York, Putnam, 1961; London, New English Library, 1965.

Podkayne of Mars: Her Life and Times (juvenile). New York, Putnam, 1963; London, New English Library, 1969.

Glory Road. New York, Putnam, 1963; London, New English Library, 1965.

Farnham's Freehold. New York, Putnam, 1964; London, Dobson, 1965.

The Moon Is a Harsh Mistress. New York, Putnam, 1966; London, Dobson, 1967.

A Heinlein Triad (includes *The Puppet Masters, Waldo, Magic Inc.*). London, Gollancz, 1966.

I Will Fear No Evil. New York, Putnam, 1971; London, New English Library, 1972.

Time Enough for Love: The Lives of Lazarus Long (Future History). New York, Putnam, 1973; London, New English Library, 1974.

The Number of the Beast. New York, Fawcett, and London, New English Library, 1980.

Expanded Universe. New York, Grosset and Dunlap, 1980.

Short Stories (series: Future History)

The Man Who Sold the Moon (Future History). Chicago, Shasta, 1950; London, Sidgwick and Jackson, 1953.

Universe (Future History). New York, Dell, 1951.

The Green Hills of Earth (Future History). Chicago, Shasta, 1951; London, Sidgwick and Jackson, 1954.

Revolt in 2100 (Future History). Chicago, Shasta, 1953; London, Digit, 1959.

Assignment in Eternity. Reading, Pennsylvania, Fantasy Press, 1953; London, Museum Press, 1955; abridged edition, as *Lost Legacy,* London, Digit, 1960.

The Menace from Earth. New York, Gnome, 1959; London, Dobson, 1966.

The Unpleasant Profession of Jonathan Hoag. New York, Gnome, 1959; London, Dobson 1964; as *6 x H: Six Stories,* New York, Pyramid, 1961.

Orphans of the Sky (Future History). London, Gollancz, 1963; New York, Putnam, 1964.

The Worlds of Robert A. Heinlein. New York, Ace, 1966; London, New English Library, 1970.

The Past Through Tomorrow: Future History Stories. New York, Putnam, 1967; London, New English Library, 2 vols., 1977.

The Best of Robert Heinlein 1939-1959, edited by Angus Wells. London, Sidgwick and Jackson, 1973.

OTHER PUBLICATIONS

Plays

Screenplays: *Destination Moon,* with Rip Van Ronkel and James O'Hanlon, 1950; *Project Moonbase,* with Jack Seaman, 1953.

Other

The Discovery of the Future (address). Los Angeles, Novacious, 1941.

"On the Writing of Speculative Fiction," in *Of Worlds Beyond,* edited by Lloyd Arthur Eshbach. Reading, Pennsylvania, Fantasy Press, 1947; London, Dobson, 1965.

"Why I Selected 'The Green Hills of Earth,' " in *My Best Science Fiction Story,* edited by Leo Margulies and O.J. Friend. New York, Merlin Press, 1949.

"Ray Guns and Rocket Ships," in *Library Journal* (New York), July 1953.

"Science Fiction: Its Nature, Faults, and Virtues," in *The Science Fiction Novel,* edited by Basil Davenport. Chicago, Advent, 1959.

"Heinlein on Science Fiction," in *Vertex* (Los Angeles), April 1973.

The Notebooks of Lazarus Long. New York, Putnam, 1978.

Editor, *Tomorrow, The Stars: A Science Fiction Anthology.* New York, Doubleday, 1951.

*

Bibliography: in *Heinlein in Dimension* by Alexei Panshin, Chicago, Advent, 1968; *Robert A. Heinlein: A Bibliography* by Mark Owings, Baltimore, Croatan House, 1973.

Manuscript Collection: University of California Library, Santa Cruz.

*   *   *

Probably no one deserves the epithet "Mr. Science Fiction" more than Robert A. Heinlein, whose prolific output remains continuously in print, a phenomenon unheard of in an industry which pulps the unsold as quickly as new books can be printed. Nearly always a "good read," Heinlein's work at its best epitomizes the excitement science fiction can generate by exploring the possible future adventures scientific knowledge and technology can open up for humanity and the needs of individuals within a society to survive and find satisfaction compatible with the continuance and growth of our species; at its worst, it's still usually provocative both to SF addicts and to novices. Throughout his long writing career Heinlein has consistently dramatized the essential moral questions for young and old, which boil down to one: What is the ideal way to live, today—and tomorrow? Idealism dosed with pragmatism flavors the answers to this question in each of Heinlein's stories. His sympathetic characters are neither all flesh nor all spirit but a careful balance of both. The majority of his work is cautiously optimistic and celebratory of the triumph of individuals over both internal weakness and, especially, external obstacles to their physical well-being—although there are some notable exceptions, like "All You Zombies."

His best-known novels are the four Hugo-winners *Double Star, Starship Troopers, Stranger in a Strange Land,* and *The Moon Is a Harsh Mistress,* and they each represent much of what is attractive in his other work. The protagonist of *Double Star,* Lorenzo Smythe, tells his own story. Originally an unemployed actor, he is recruited (forcefully) to play the role of an incapacitated leader who must participate in delicate interplanetary diplomacy, an assignment he accepts not out of political conviction but because of the challenge to his acting ability. But during the course of the story he rises to the moral challenge and becomes worthy of his new power and authority. He concludes that the sacrifice of personal peace of mind is justified by "solemn satisfaction in doing the best you can for eight billion people." *Noblesse oblige:* the strong spirit has a duty to the weak.

In *Starship Troopers* a similar lesson is learned by Juan Rico, who also narrates his own conversion, from a mildly pacifist and apolitical youth who almost inadvertently volunteers for Federal Service to impress a female, to a dedicated combat officer who realizes that the noblest fate he can hope for is to die defending others' lives. His Moral Instruction teacher sums it up: "The price demanded for the most precious of all things in life is life itself—ultimate cost for perfect value." Eventually Juan even helps his own father to realize and share his insight. Seasoned with rich slang that provides both verisimilitude and freshness to what could easily be a conventional situation, the novel is shaped like a sandwich with battle action scenes opening and closing the book, and the moral awakening filling its center.

Stranger in a Strange Land is the only one of Heinlein's Hugo-winners to use a third-person narrator, and is less unified in other ways than the other three. The first two sections are largely concerned with the satiric vision of human behavior seen through the unspoiled eyes of a highly intelligent being, Valentine Michael Smith, physically human but culturally alien. Significantly, Mike regains his biological heritage only after he learns to laugh by watching the monkeys in a zoo. The latter part of the book is devoted to myth-making of the possible limits of human interactions. Because he is culture-free, Mike is able to explore unorthodox sensuality and sexuality without feelings of inhibition and guilt which plague the rest of us. The joy of his discoveries is powerful enough to free others from their hangups also (even his mentor Jubal Harshaw), so they create a mystical new religion. But Heinlein undermines his myth with the mocking cynicism of the blatant fraud Foster, who turns out to be Mike's boss in the hereafter (or whereafter?): "Certainly 'Thou art God'—but who isn't?" The creed of the new religion is nothing special in the cosmic scheme of things. For many critics this self-mockery comes too little and too late to counter Mike's simplistic message of free love and the power to dispel all earthly problems simply by correct comprehension.

The Moon Is a Harsh Mistress combines more of Heinlein's strengths and fewer of his artistic limitations than any of his other works. The length of the novel is justified by the complexity of the social and political systems depicted. The story of Luna's fight for freedom is told by Mannie, a sympathetic but fallible person who might be Anyman. He is the best computer technician available on the moon, and so becomes the first friend of Mike, the sentient computer who keeps from going insane at the interface of conflicting data by developing a sense of humor—and a protective love for those who give him a purpose in living. Since the narrator must survive to tell the tale, the interest of the reader is focused less on what happens than on how it happens. Mannie is not of course the individual who created Mike, but humanity has developed an intelligence beyond its own fleshly limitations, one moreover uncorrupted by petty greed and lust for power. The philosophy of TANSTAAFL—there ain't no such thing as a free lunch—naturally becomes the slogan of Free Luna. Their success relies on long odds and high risks, but the stakes of freedom are worth the ultimate price, paid in the end by many of the revolutionaries including Mannie's political mentor and (apparently) Mike. Mannie is left with many doubts and unfulfilled longings at the end in a passage handled with as delicate a poignancy as is to be found anywhere in Heinlein's work, but ultimately decides he will go on living: "My word, I'm not even a hundred yet."

Of Heinlein's juveniles, *The Star Beast* is one of the best for a child to start with. Not only does it have both male and female central characters and a lovable alien creature full of unexpected antics; the story also introduces the unorthodox privilege of unhappy children to divorce unsatisfactory parents, a notion sure to delight young readers. *Podkayne of Mars,* usually regarded as an adult novel in spite of its young protagonists, has been widely denounced for using a phony female viewpoint character; the story purports to be the diary of a teenage girl, but a large portion is written by her precocious bratty pre-teen brother who turns out to be smarter than she is.

While Heinlein's recent novel *The Number of the Beast* doesn't compare to his best, it still has some amusing satire, especially general mockery of sexist prejudices, and ethical discussions like the argument of why the protagonists should assist the British colony on Mars rather than the Russian, an issue of dark gray against lighter gray. But the novel has two notable weaknesses, one in form and one in content. First, the experiment of shifting narrative voices among the four central characters does not entirely succeed due to the heavy reliance on dialog. And the combination of extremely high intelligence and apparent lack of introspection of all four also seems incongruous, even considering Heinlein's purpose to be myth-making, that is, to show the world as it might be rather than as it is. Second, the last third of the novel may be largely unintelligible to readers unfamiliar with Heinlein's previous books; to compre-

hend the novel properly one ought to have read the entire Heinlein *oeuvre.* On the other hand, Heinlein devotees may rejoice to revisit their favorite characters from the earlier future-history stories.

—Elizabeth Anne Hull

HENDERSON, Zenna (née Chlarson). American. Born in Tucson, Arizona, 1 November 1917. Educated at Arizona State College, B.A. 1940; Arizona State University, Tempe, M.A. 1955. Married in 1944 (divorced). Since 1940, elementary school teacher in Arizona: has also taught at the Japanese Relocation Camp, Sacaton, Arizona, Laon sur Marne, Aisne, France, and Seaside Children's Hospital, Waterford, Connecticut. Agent: Curtis Brown Ltd., 575 Madison Avenue, New York, New York 10022. Address: 1111 North Ocotillo, Eloy, Arizona 85231, U.S.A.

SCIENCE-FICTION PUBLICATIONS

Novels

Pilgrimage: The Book of the People. New York, Doubleday, 1961; London, Gollancz, 1962.
The People: No Different Flesh. New York, Doubleday, and London, Gollancz, 1966.

Short Stories

The Anything Box. New York, Doubleday, 1965; London, Gollancz, 1966.
Holding Wonder. New York, Doubleday, 1971; London, Gollancz, 1972.

Uncollected Short Stories

"Thrumthing and Out," in *Fantasy and Science Fiction* (New York), October 1972.
"Katie-Mary's Trip," in *Fantasy and Science Fiction* (New York), January 1975.
"The First Stroke," in *Fantasy and Science Fiction* (New York), October 1977.
"There Was a Garden," in *Cassandra Rising,* edited by Alice Laurance. New York, Doubleday, 1978.

Zenna Henderson comments:
When I was about 12 I began reading science fiction—Jules Verne, Haggard, and Edgar Rice Burroughs, and all the current magazines I could get hold of, but it wasn't until I had graduated from college that I began writing fantasy and science fiction. I have only a sketchy scientific background, so of necessity I write from a non-technical viewpoint. My favorite science-fiction authors, when I was still reading it, were Heinlein, Bradbury, Clement, and Asimov. Mottos I try to observe when I write: stories consist of unusual people in ordinary circumstances or ordinary people in unusual circumstances; write about what you know; don't let your subtleties become obscurities.

*   *   *

"Write what you know" is the cornerstone of Zenna Henderson's science-fiction career. She has constructed story after story out of experiences accumulated during her many years in the elementary classroom. She finds teachers useful viewpoint characters because their vision is multiplied through their students' eyes. Her children have the appealing naturalness that comes of being modeled directly from life.

Henderson makes more and better use of adult-child interactions than adult-adult ones but she always keeps human relationships paramount. She ignores man's struggles against the universe because she does not perceive the cosmos as hostile. By rejecting sex, sadism, and violence, her stories offer a gentle alternative to macho entertainments. Yet feminist critics scorn Henderson for occupational stereotyping without acknowledging that she depicts single women, older women, and female friendships positively. Wonder in familiar settings is Henderson's forte. She reveals the world a child or a saint might see—a place where time can shift and dimensions fold, where mountains walk and wishes come true. Friction between the mundane and the marvelous generates her dramas. For example, a small boy battles a demon ("Stevie and the Dark") or school routine survives the collapse of civilization ("As Simple as That").

Henderson's most popular stories are those collected in *Pilgrimage* and *The People*. Each volume's components are united by a frame-story, a device that succeeds better in *Pilgrimage* because it is a poignant tale in its own right. The frame of *The People* is simply an excuse for flashbacks to events preceding and following those in *Pilgrimage*. The People are extraterrestrial refugees with psychic gifts who have been hiding in the American southwest since the 1890's. They are gradually overcoming memories of persecution and forming partnerships with humans. Their perilous flight from their lost Home to Earth, their true Promised Land, parallels the Old Testament Exodus—a comparison underscored by Biblical names and titles. (Basic Christian values undergird all of Henderson's writing.) Although the People had a different salvation history, their beliefs are compatible with Christianity. They even use a trinitarian invocation of God as the Power, the Presence, and the Name. Their bonding through love is Henderson's answer to the conflicts between community and individuality that run through so much of her fiction.

Secret aliens among us is an old SF notion but no one has put it to happier use than Henderson. The sheer wholesomeness of her People is enough to set them apart. "They're us only more so," says the author. Whether reading thoughts, operating spacecraft, or hemming dresses, the People wield their powers with a cheerful reverence that is refreshingly matter-of-fact. Henderson is neither antitechnological nor pro-occultist like Andre Norton. Miracles in a grittily realistic setting strike just the right note of aesthetic contrast to make the stories work.

Henderson's paradigm of sympathetic adult aiding troubled wonder-child is as distinctive as her signature. Yet it is a conscious pattern to be varied at will. "Something Bright" reverses the usual roles to disguised alien adult and helpful human child. Not all teachers are caring ("The Last Step") or effective ("You Know What, Teacher?"). Not all marvels are desirable ("The Substitute," "Turn the Page," "Sharing Time"). Children's wonderful powers can cause tragedy ("The Believing Child," "Come On, Wagon!," "Hush!"). In such works Henderson displays an excellent although curiously unappreciated touch for horror. She can handle insanity as vividly as psi ("Swept and Garnished," "One of Them").

At her worst, Henderson's sentimentality overflows. Occasionally her ideas are too weak. Her range of subject matter is admittedly small. But overall, she works with sound, unobtrusive craftsmanship. She has the classic short story writer's talents for precise focus, good characterization, and shrewd deployment of details. A kindly, traditional sensibility animates her writing. This description of ultimate happiness from "The Anything Box" conveys her special flavor: "all the worry and waiting, the apartness and loneliness were over and forgotten, their hugeness dwindled by the comfort of a shoulder, the warmth of clasping hands—and nowhere, nowhere was the fear of parting...." Henderson is SF's mistress of the happy ending.

—Sandra Miesel

HENSLEY, Joe L. American. Born in Bloomington, Indiana, 19 March 1926. Educated at Indiana University, Bloomington, B.A. 1950, LL.B. 1955: called to the Indiana Bar, 1955. Served as a hospital corpsman in the United States Navy, 1944-46; recalled as journalist, 1951-52. Married Charlotte Ruth Bettinger in 1950; one son. Partner, Metford and Hensley, 1955-72, and Hensley Todd and Castor, 1972-75, Madison, Indiana; Judge Pro-Tempore, 80th Judicial Circuit, Versailles, Indiana, 1975-76. Since 1977, Judge, 5th Judicial Circuit, Madison. Member, Indiana General Assembly, 1961-62; Prosecuting Attorney, 5th Judicial Indiana Circuit, 1963-66. Agent: Virginia Kidd, Box 278, Milford, Pennsylvania 18337; or, Julia Coopersmith, 10 West 15th Street, New York, New York 10011. Address: 2315 Blackmore, Madison, Indiana 47150, U.S.A.

SCIENCE-FICTION PUBLICATIONS

Novel

The Black Roads. Toronto, Laser, 1976.

Uncollected Short Stories

"Eyes of a Double Moon," in *Planet* (New York), May 1953.
"Guide Wire," in *Future* (New York), August 1954.
"The Red and the Green," in *Science Fiction Quarterly* (Holyoke, Massachusetts), May 1955.
"Once a Starman," in *Planet* (New York), Summer 1955.
"The Sun Hunters," in *Fantastic Universe* (Chicago), September 1955.
"The Outvaders," in *Astounding* (New York), November 1955.
"Now We Are Three," in *Fantastic Universe* (Chicago), August 1957.
"Time of the Tinkers," in *Future* (New York), June 1958.
"Star Ways," in *Original Science Fiction Stories* (Holyoke, Massachusetts), September 1958.
"Visionary," in *Amazing* (New York), May 1959.
"Do-It-Yourself," with Harlan Ellison, in *Ellison Wonderland*. New York, Paperback Library, 1962.
"And Not Quite Human," in *Triple W*, edited by Rod Serling. New York, Bantam, 1963.
"Lord Randy, My Son," in *Dangerous Visions*, edited by Harlan Ellison. New York, Doubleday, 1967; London, David Bruce and Watson, 2 vols., 1971.
"Argent Blood," in *Fantasy and Science Fiction* (New York), August 1967.
"The Edge of the Rose," in *Amazing* (New York), September 1969.
"Shut the Last Door," in *Alchemy and Academe*, edited by Anne McCaffrey. New York, Doubleday, 1970.
"The Run from Home," in *Fantasy and Science Fiction* (New York), December 1970.
"Rodney Parish for Hire," with Harlan Ellison, in *Partners in Wonder*, by Ellison. New York, Walker, 1971.
"Time Patrol," in *If* (New York), February 1972.
"In Dark Places," in *Future City*, edited by Roger Elwood. New York, Simon and Schuster, 1973.
"The Pair," in *Combat SF*, edited by Gordon R. Dickson. New York, Doubleday, 1975.

OTHER PUBLICATIONS

Novels

The Color of Hate. New York, Ace, 1960.
Deliver Us to Evil. New York, Doubleday, 1971.
Legislative Body. New York, Doubleday, 1972.
The Poison Summer. New York, Doubleday, 1974.
Song of Corpus Juris. New York, Doubleday, 1974.
Rivertown Risk. New York, Doubleday, 1977.
A Killing in Gold. New York, Doubleday, 1978; London, Gollancz, 1979.
Minor Murders. New York, Doubleday, 1979.

*   *   *

Joe L. Hensley's most important stories are connected with Harlan Ellison. Hensley and Ellison are great friends, and Ellison wrote

2000 words of introduction to "Lord Randy, My Son" for *Dangerous Visions.* The story is a masterpiece of understated horror. Ellison's introduction to the story tells how Hensley—then a lawyer—saved Ellison from being court-martialed by the U.S. Army. Ellison provides another introduction to "Rodney Parish for Hire." This chilling account of a youngster who kills other children for profit is a good example of the strengths of both writers. The story features strong characterization, fast-paced writing, and a suspenseful plot.

Hensley's only SF novel, *The Black Roads,* is a reworking of the setting and themes best developed by Mack Reynolds's *Rollertown* (1976). After a nuclear war, only American technology survives. A society based on roadways evolves as the ultimate realization of humans' love for their automobiles. Duels are fought between cars, and Red Roadmen ride the lanes in their supercharged autos keeping law and order. The mobile society is interesting, but Hensley never elevates his characters above the level of cardboard. The result is a staleness absent from his better short stories and the mystery novels for which he is better known.

Hensley's writing is usually crisp, his plotting is tight, and his best work has power and insight. Much of his work reflects his background in law.

—George Kelley

HERBERT, Frank (Patrick). American. Born in Tacoma, Washington, 8 October 1920. Attended the University of Washington, Seattle, 1946-47. Married Beverly Ann Stuart in 1946; one daughter and two sons. Reporter and editor for West Coast newspapers; lecturer in general and interdisciplinary studies, University of Washington, 1970-72; social and ecological studies consultant, Lincoln Foundation and the countries of Vietnam and Pakistan, 1971. Recipient: Nebula Award, 1965; Hugo Award, 1966. Agent: Lurton Blassingame, 60 East 42nd Street, New York, New York 10017; or, Ned Brown, P.O. Box 5020, Beverly Hills, California 90210. Address: Box 725, Port Townsend, Washington 98368, U.S.A.

SCIENCE-FICTION PUBLICATIONS

Novels (series: Dune; Jorj X. McKie)

The Dragon in the Sea. New York, Doubleday, 1956; London, Gollancz, 1960; as *21st Century Sub,* New York, Avon, 1956; as *Under Pressure,* New York, Ballantine, 1974.
The Illustrated Dune. New York, Berkley, 1978; as *The Great Dune Trilogy,* London, Gollancz, 1979.
Dune. Philadelphia, Chilton, 1965; London, Gollancz, 1966.
Dune Messiah. New York, Putnam, 1969; London, Gollancz, 1971.
Children of Dune. New York, Berkley, and London, Gollancz, 1976.
Destination: Void. New York, Berkley, 1966; London, Penguin, 1967.
The Eyes of Heisenberg. New York, Berkley, 1966; London, Sphere, 1968.
The Green Brain. New York, Ace, 1966; London, New English Library, 1973.
The Santaroga Barrier. New York, Berkley, 1968; London, Rapp and Whiting, 1970.
The Heaven Makers. New York, Avon, 1968; London, New English Library, 1970.
Whipping Star (McKie). New York, Putnam, 1970; London, New English Library, 1972.
The God Makers. New York, Putnam, and London, New English Library, 1972.
Hellstrom's Hive. New York, Doubleday, 1973; London, New English Library, 1974; as *Project 40,* New York, Bantam, 1973.

The Dosadi Experiment (McKie). New York, Putnam, 1977; London, Gollancz, 1978.
The Jesus Incident, with Bill Ransom. New York, Berkley, and London, Gollancz, 1979.
The Priests of Psi. London, Gollancz, 1980.
Direct Descent. New York, Ace, 1980.

Short Stories

The Worlds of Frank Herbert. London, New English Library, 1970; New York, Ace, 1971.
The Book of Frank Herbert. New York, DAW, 1973; London, Panther, 1977.
The Best of Frank Herbert, edited by Angus Wells. London, Sidgwick and Jackson, 1975.

Uncollected Short Stories

"Come to the Party," with F.M. Busby, in *The 1979 Annual World's Best SF,* edited by Donald A. Wollheim. New York, DAW, 1979.
"Songs of a Sentient Flute," in *Analog* (New York), February 1979.
"Frogs and Scientists," in *Destinies* (New York), August-September 1979.

OTHER PUBLICATIONS

Novel

Soul Catcher. New York, Putnam, 1972; London, New English Library, 1973.

Other

Threshold: The Blue Angels Experience. New York, Ballantine, 1973.
"The Consentiency—and How It Got That Way," in *Galaxy* (New York), May 1977.

Editor, *New World or No World.* New York, Ace, 1970.

*   *   *

Frank Herbert's science fiction focuses on man's nature, limits, and potentialities, his relationship to his environment and his fellow creatures, his ancestral heritage (both genetic and cultural), his mystical and psychic possibilities. Although his characters remain familiar and psychologically true, to Herbert humanity is not fixed, but rather is continually evolving both physically and intellectually. According to Herbert, when men sink into static patterns, they become mechanical, perverted, and doomed, but as long as there is change and evolution, even if it is violent or bizarre or seemingly incomprehensible, there is hope; adversity creates strength.

In the *Dune* series, *The God Makers, The Santaroga Barrier, The Heaven Makers, The Dosadi Experiment,* and *The Jesus Incident,* he describes the trials, conflicts, and rites of passage through which man can evolve god-like powers of intellect and foresight, but further suggests the difficulties and dangers such powers necessitate. Frequently these evolutionary leaps are precipitated by contact with special organic chemicals (spice in *Dune,* Jaspers in *Santaroga Barrier,* kept hallucinogens in *Jesus Incident*), by the genetic mix of unique strains (*God Makers, Dune, Heaven Makers*), or by special mind fuse (*Dosadi Experiment, Jesus Incident*). Soul Catcher, though not science fiction per se, weaves a tale of mystic Indian powers gained through birth and ritual, and ancient alien gods who heighten the perception of those seeking their frightening aid. In *The Dosadi Experiment* humans and aliens are caged together on a toxic planet, conditioned by constant war and hunger—an experiment that proves too successful; bred for vengeance and cunning, the Dosadi learn to overcome all barriers (even a tempokinetic "God Wall") and revenge themselves on their creators. Jedrik (an alien woman with features like a praying mantis) merges with McKie (an outsider) to produce a mind switch and psi power that force the tribunal to recognize Dosadi power. *The God Makers* focuses on an interplanetary troubleshooter assigned to monitor planets and to detect at early stages signs of aggressiveness that might trigger future war; in fulfilling these duties he discovers and develops extrasensory powers that lead him to rites of passage on a special planet of philosophers, rites that make clear his godhood and teach him to use his powers to do what has been his job all along—prevent war and aggression through compromise between potential enemies. But the problem with superpowers and immortality is the possibility of boredom. Paul Atreides of *Dune,* omnipotent ruler of thousands of planets, fakes his own death and retires to private interests. In *Heaven Makers* an immortal alien movie producer, using Earth as a set for filming full sensory movies of wars, natural disasters, and other horrors to relieve the boredom of his jaded race, breaks regulations and interferes with human cycles, originally to provide more entertaining disasters, but ultimately to produce a blessed loss of immortality. Each of these books examines alien intelligence in order more clearly to define human.

The most famous of Herbert's books tracing human evolution to a higher state of being is the *Dune* trilogy, a series of epic proportions and concerns that depicts the logical development, expansion, and diversification of religion and politics on an alien desert world. The series begins with revolutionary powers and vast changes, traces the political line as it sinks into stasis, become ingrown and perverted, until new blood and unexpected evolutions force the changes necessary for ultimate survival. *Dune,* the most powerful of the three, concerns the growth and maturity of Paul Atreides, whose mother has been chosen to bear a new messiah with vast mental powers; but Paul, the product of generations of controlled breeding and Bene Gesserit training in desert discipline, proves to have latent powers as well, and once these are enhanced by an overdose of local spice, his mind becomes permanently opened to see and shape the future; his time travel involves a succession of choices between alternative futures. Prophet to his infant brother, he leads the desert people on a jihad to conquer their planet and a thousand others. *Dune Messiah* traces an imperial intergalactic intrigue by the Bene Gesserit to overthrow the "god" they themselves created (a common Herbert theme), and involves a Tleilaxu face dancer and a ghola recreation of a dead hero. The focus on ecology and political intrigue continues in *Children of Dune* wherein the House of Atreides learns to survive by appreciating traditions that will preserve the ecology, and live by their instincts and to think and act for themselves. Religious mysticism and desert lore, Byzantine intrigue and complex intellectual discourse infuse these books with a life and interest beyond mere plot.

Always Herbert's milieu is firmly grounded in present-day political and social realities rather than in escapist fantasy. His books are carefully researched and highly detailed. For instance, his description of a desert society whose fanatical and feudal codes of behavior center on their desperate need for water projects Bedouin survival in the Sahara, *The Dragon in the Sea* so concretely describes deepwater submarine controls that British Naval Intelligence followed his model, and *Destination: Void* is a comprehensive study in computer theory. In *The Dragon in the Sea* a psychologist joins the four-man crew of a deepsea atomic submarine/tug to find a saboteur. The mission, to steal oil from underwater deposits in enemy territory, involves fear and tension from the natural dangers of depth and pressure, heightened by fears of a spy. The book has good suspense and superb technical detail, and defines sanity as the ability to adapt. So too does *Destination: Void,* where four scientists with a human cargo of thousands, all unknowingly part of a vast experiment to force invention, are supposedly travelling toward an Eden when they suffer organic computer failure and have to create a conscious mechanical brain to guide them. They react under pressure against impossible odds and succeed in producing a super cybernetic computer that acquires godlike powers of life and death, and that agrees to take them to an Eden if they will contemplate how to worship him.

Despite his skillful handling of technical description, Herbert, in the tradition of American romanticism, opposes the mechanistic with the natural and organic to show the superiority of the intuitive biological organism. In *The Jesus Incident* he opposes clones and naturals, test-tube babies and true births; in *The Eyes of Heisenberg* rebels in a totally genetically engineered world oppose the immortal Optimen and their enemy Cyborgs, and deliberately interfere with gene surgery to bring about a return to mortality and to reproduce

an embryo with the forbidden gene combination of intelligence and fertility.

Related to Herbert's concern for the natural are an interest in ecology and a respect for rural values, a fear of man tampering with nature but a realization that he must tamper with himself if he is to advance. In *The Green Brain* and *Hellstrom's Hive* he tackles the problem of human interference in nature. Set in Oregon, *Hellstrom's Hive* focuses on a secretive zoological experiment that postulates the obsolescence of present family relations; a government agent, investigating, discovers evolution's terrifying possibilities—a utopian human hive with physical and mental specialization in order to dominate the world. *The Green Brain* is another chilling tale that emphasizes man's dependence on insects and chemical sprays backfiring in unexpected ways. In an overpopulated world seeking living room in jungles, an international organization systematically exterminates voracious insects, until they defensively mutate to incredible sizes and types; some mutations involve protective coloration—insect colonies that appear human. A ruling insect "Brain," a corporate intelligence that is the product of this mutation, plans to restore and maintain nature's balance. In *The Santaroga Barrier* Herbert deals with man coping with the imbalance himself. In a world dominated by false, greedy, superficial advertising men, the Santaroga Valley remains isolated and impervious to modernization. An investigator engaged to a Santaroga psychiatrist seeks answers in "Jaspers," food infused with natural chemicals from Santaroga caves, chemicals that help users see through artifice and falsity to discover true values of community and integrity. But this proves a two-edged blessing, for with awareness comes the after-effects of not being able to live outside the valley for very long and a subconscious reflex to destroy any stranger who does not belong. The drug produces enlightenment and well-being at the cost of freedom.

The Jesus Incident continues the themes and interests of his earlier works. There is much speculation about the nature of deities and of human evolution and the ramification of genetic manipulation; there are technical wonders and genetic horrors; there are the concept of ancestral memory, natural enlightenment drugs, and a poet who ultimately understands man's destiny. Hope centers around the natural birth of an extraordinary child who will sweep away old orders and initiate new. A sequel to *Destination: Void,* the novel continues the story of the scientists and their crew, deposited on an alien planet (Pandora) filled with incredible horrors (nerve worms and hooded dashers and other predatory alien creatures). Instead of seeking to come to terms with the planet, they and their descendants try to wipe out its population, even the ruling sentient kelp, only to learn that the hope for Pandora rests in accepting the planet and living in harmony with its sentients, who can teach them about themselves and their past, their ship, and their gods.

Herbert mingles Middle Eastern and Oriental philosophies with Christian myth to produce a humanistic amalgam that recognizes man's potentiality for godhood as well as for self-destruction. He continually examines evolving intelligence, whether mechanical, insect, alien, or humanoid.

—Gina Macdonald

HERBERT, James. British. Born in London, 8 April 1943. Educated at St. Aloysius College, and Hornsey College of Art, both London. Married Eileen O'Donnell in 1968; two daughters. Typographer, John Collings Advertising, London, 1963-66; Art Director, Group Head, and Associate Director, Ayer Barker Hegemann International, London, 1966-77. Agent: Paul Gitlin, Ernst Cane Berner and Gitlin, 7 West 51st Street, New York, New York 10019, U.S.A. Address: c/o New English Library, Barnards Inn, Holborn, London, EC1N 2JR, England.

SCIENCE-FICTION PUBLICATIONS

Novels

The Rats. London, New English Library, 1974; New York, New
    American Library, 1975.
The Fog. London, New English Library, and New York, New
    American Library, 1975.
The Survivor. London, New English Library, 1976; New York,
    New American Library, 1977.
Fluke. London, New English Library, 1977; New York, New
    American Library, 1978.
The Spear. London, New English Library, 1978; New York, New
    American Library, 1980.
Lair. London, New English Library, and New York, New Ameri-
    can Library, 1979.
The Dark. London, New English Library, and New York, New
    American Library, 1980.

*   *   *

Although not a science fiction writer as such, James Herbert, on
his past track-record, can easily be assigned a place among those
writers (e.g., John Wyndham, John Christopher, John Lymington)
who have explored the story possibilities inherent in disaster, natural or otherwise, in a peculiarly British manner. The action is
invariably seen from a parochial, almost isolationist, viewpoint,
rather than a global one—for whereas events in such stories set in
America, for instance, tend to lose themselves in, and thus become
minimised by, the vastness of the continent itself, on a small off-
shore island such as Great Britain even minor catastrophes are
magnified to enormous dimensions, more often than not having a
direct and dramatic bearing on the lives of most people in the
country.

Not that Herbert's catastrophies can be catagorised as minor. To
date, London has been ravaged thrice (*The Rats, The Fog,* and *The
Dark*), Eton, home of the world-famous public school, once (*The
Survivor*), and Epping Forest, just outside the capital, has been
turned into a major disaster area (*Lair*). Nor have other parts of the
country been spared. A village in Wiltshire has been swallowed up
by the earth (*The Fog*); staff and boys at a school in Andover (*The
Fog*) and the patients in a home for the elderly in Twickenham (*The
Dark*) have all been turned into rampaging homicidal maniacs; the
entire population of the coastal resort of Bournemouth has,
lemming-like, indulged in mass suicide by walking into the sea (*The
Fog*).

The theme of his first novel, *The Rats,* was simple, clearly derivative (nuclear tests in the Pacific cause rats to mutate into killers,
preying on humans), and somewhat crude in execution. Yet for all
that, the writing has immense vigour and drive, and the story itself
careers along at a headlong pace to a grisly climax. With *The Fog*
most of the earlier rough edges have been smoothed off, and
although again the theme—a type of nerve-gas that forms itself into
a dense fog and turns humans into insane killers is accidentally
released into the atmosphere—was by no means original, the narrative drive and—what has become something of a trademark of
Herbert over the years—the skilful juxtaposition of stark horror
(pigeons affected by the fog tear a man to shreds) and black farce (a
timid bank official, also affected, assaults a policeman) more than
makes up for this.

The Survivor, an excellent horror story with a remarkable twist in
its tail, was followed by a novel that at times reaches extraordinary
peaks of invention and originality. *Fluke* is the startling story of a
man who wakes up to find he's become a dog, and the saga of his
search for the reason behind this transformation is related by Herbert with high good humour yet, at the same time, deep compassion
and an insight into the human psyche rare in such a work. After *The
Spear,* a heavily researched yet absorbing horror novel dealing with
a group of ex-Nazi fanatics who intend to use the Heilige Lance (the
spear of Longinus, said to have pierced the body of Christ on the
cross at Calvary) as a source of diabolic power to raise SS Chief
Heinrich Himmler from the dead, Herbert backtracked a little with
Lair, at first sight a re-run of his highly successful first novel. Even
so, potboiler though it clearly is, the book is in fact a far more
satisfactorily developed and entertaining story than *The Rats.*

The Dark is undoubtedly his most ambitious novel: a mixture of
the paranormal and hard science (Herbert suggests that "evil" is in
fact a physical energy field within the mind, which, like any electrical power source, can be tapped) which on one level is a convincing
dialectic on the nature of evil, and on another a fast-moving and
gruesome tale of terror.

In all of Herbert's books (even, to a certain extent, *Fluke*) he
reveals a dark and pessimistic vision, which certainly mirrors the
times in which we live. Chaos is only just around the corner; the
breakdown of law and order (in the classic tradition of the British
catastrophe novel) is imminent. Yet he is able to pilot his readers
through the most appalling and harrowing situations, and scenes of
nightmarish horror, with the skill of the natural-born storyteller,
and there is no doubt that, in his own field, he is one of the most
powerful writers today.

—Christopher Lowder

HERSEY, John (Richard). American. Born in Tientsin, China,
17 June 1914. Educated at Hotchkiss School; Yale University, New
Haven, Connecticut, B.A. 1936; Clare College, Cambridge (Mellon
Fellow), 1936-37. Married 1) Frances Ann Cannon in 1940
(divorced, 1958), three sons and one daughter; 2) Barbara Day
Kaufman in 1958, one daughter. Secretary to Sinclair Lewis, 1937;
Writer and Correspondent, in China, Japan, the South Pacific, the
Mediterranean and Russia, for *Time,* New York, 1937-45, *Life,*
New York, 1944-46, and *The New Yorker,* 1945-46; Editor and
Director of the writers' cooperative magazine *'47,* 1947-48. Fellow
of Berkeley College, 1950-65, Master of Pierson College, 1965-70,
Lecturer, 1971-76, Visiting Professor, 1976-77, and since 1977,
Adjunct Professor, Yale University: Member of the Yale University
Council Committee on the Humanities, 1951-56, and Member,
1959-64, and Chairman, 1964-69, Yale University Council Commit-
tee on Yale College. Writer-in-Residence, American Academy in
Rome, 1970-71. Member, Westport, Connecticut, School Study
Council, 1945-50, Westport Board of Education, 1950-52, and Fairfield, Connecticut, Citizens School Study Council, 1952-56; Trustee, Putney School, 1953-56; Member, National Citizens' Commission for the Public Schools, 1954-56; Consultant, Fund for the
Advancement of Education, 1954-56; Chairman, Connecticut
Committee for the Gifted, 1954-57; Delegate, White House Conference on Education, 1955; Trustee, National Citizens' Council for
the Public Schools, 1956-58; Trustee, National Committee for Support of the Public Schools, 1962-68; Member, Weston, Connecticut, Board of Education, 1964-65. Chairman, Connecticut Volunteers for Stevenson, 1952; Member, Stevenson Campaign Staff,
1956. Member of the Council, 1946-71, and Vice-President, 1949-
55, Authors League of America; Delegate, P.E.N. Congress,
Tokyo, 1958. Since 1946, Member of the Council, and President,
1975-80, Authors Guild. Recipient: Pulitzer Prize, 1945; Anisfield-
Wolf Award, 1950; Daroff Memorial Award, 1950; Sidney Hillman
Foundation Award, 1950; Yale University Howland Medal, 1952;
Tuition Plan Award, 1961; Sarah Josepha Hale Award, 1963.
Member, 1953, and Secretary, 1961-76, American Academy.
Address: 420 Humphrey Street, New Haven, Connecticut 06511,
U.S.A.

SCIENCE-FICTION PUBLICATIONS

Novels

The Child Buyer. New York, Knopf, 1960; London, Hamish
    Hamilton, 1961.
White Lotus. New York, Knopf, and London, Hamish Hamilton,
    1965.
My Petition for More Space. New York, Knopf, 1974; London,
    Hamish Hamilton, 1975.

OTHER PUBLICATIONS

Novels

A Bell for Adano. New York, Knopf, 1944; London, Hamish Hamilton, 1965.
The Wall. New York, Knopf, and London, Hamish Hamilton, 1950.
The Marmot Drive. New York, Knopf, and London, Hamish Hamilton, 1953.
A Single Pebble. New York, Knopf, and London, Hamish Hamilton, 1956.
The War Lover. New York, Knopf, and London, Hamish Hamilton, 1959.
Too Far to Walk. New York, Knopf, and London, Hamish Hamilton, 1966.
Under the Eye of the Storm. New York, Knopf, and London, Hamish Hamilton, 1967.
The Conspiracy. New York, Knopf, and London, Hamish Hamilton, 1972.
The Walnut Door. New York, Knopf, 1977; London, Macmillan, 1978.

Other

Men on Bataan. New York, Knopf, 1942.
Into the Valley: A Skirmish of the Marines. New York, Knopf, 1943.
Hiroshima. New York, Knopf, and London, Penguin, 1946.
Here to Stay: Studies in Human Tenacity. London, Hamish Hamilton, 1962; New York, Knopf, 1963.
The Algiers Motel Incident. New York, Knopf, and London, Hamish Hamilton, 1968.
Robert Capa, with others. New York, Paragraphic Books, 1969.
Letter to the Alumni. New York, Knopf, 1970.
The President. New York, Knopf, 1975.
Aspects of the Presidency: Truman and Ford in Office. New Haven, Connecticut, Ticknor and Fields, 1980.

Editor, *Ralph Ellison: A Collection of Critical Essays.* Englewood Cliffs, New Jersey, Prentice Hall, 1973; London, Prentice Hall, 1974.
Editor, *The Writer's Craft.* New York, Knopf, 1974.

*

Manuscript Collection: Yale University Library, New Haven, Connecticut.

*   *   *

John Hersey is probably best known as the author of *Hiroshima* and *A Bell For Adano.* Few people think of him as a science-fiction writer even if they have read *White Lotus, My Petition for More Space,* or *The Child Buyer.* Hersey is seldom mentioned by science-fiction fans, or taught in science-fiction courses. It is more than likely that he does not consider himself a science-fiction writer even though some of his books use concepts generally found only in science fiction. Hersey may be one of those writers who occasionally discovers that he cannot write what he wants to write within the bounds of realistic mainstream fiction; and so he presents his ideas in a world similar to but not the same as this one—a world parallel to this one or this world in a future time. The same impulse lies behind Orwell's *Nineteen Eighty-Four* and Huxley's *Brave New World.* Such a situation seems to arise for Hersey, as it did for Orwell and Huxley, when he wishes to comment on or criticize contemporary society.

White Lotus is a parallel world story, one in which the author attempts to show what the world of today might be like had history taken a different turn; in a parallel world, the British defeated the American colonial rebels or lost to the Spanish Armada in 1588. In *White Lotus* the time is the present, and the Chinese are the dominant power in the world, having conquered America sometime in the first quarter of the 20th century. Except for technological developments, much of what the reader would regard as major historical events—like World War I—has not taken place. Hersey seems to have set up the parallel world of *White Lotus* for one purpose: to show white Americans what it might be like to live as an oppressed racial minority. The plot is the personal narrative of an American girl captured by slavers and sent to China. The bulk of the story is told as a flashback. Although *White Lotus* is obviously based on the whites' mistreatment of blacks in America, there are also echoes in the novel of the mistreatment of other minorities, most notably the Jews, in other countries.

My Petition for More Space is set in the over-populated future which has given rise to such science-fiction stories as Alice Glaser's "The Tunnel Ahead," John Brunner's *Stand On Zanzibar,* and Harry Harrison's *Make Room! Make Room!* In Hersey's book, Sam Poynter is petitioning for more living space. Sam's world is tremendously crowded: waiting in line means being crushed up against the four people around you, making love can be a semi-private act only if you hang curtains around your living space, and getting to do anything (except sit in your living space—Sam's is seven by eleven feet) means waiting in line. Simply put, *My Petition for More Space* is about the dehumanizing effects of over-population; the more people there are, the less privacy and choice there will be.

The Child Buyer, often compared to Orwell's *Nineteen Eighty-Four* and Huxley's *Brave New World,* is also set in the future. The plot involves a research company's attempt to buy an extremely bright child, whom they will make into a human computer; and the novel is set in the form of a transcript of a state government sub-committee hearing on the matter. *The Child Buyer* is a bitter satire on education and politics as the politicians doing the investigating and the educators doing the testifying turn out, for the most part, to be extremely shallow, prejudiced, and ignorant. Hersey's most telling point is that the needs of extremely bright children are often all but completely neglected in today's educational system.

When Hersey writes these parallel world or this-world-in-the-future stories, he is, indeed, writing science fiction; but he only does it when he requires such a background for his commentary. He does not explore the science-fiction aspect for its own sake; he uses it as a vehicle. And the rest of his fiction is solidly mainstream.

—C.W. Sullivan III

HIGH, Philip E(mpson). British. Born in Biggleswade, Bedfordshire, 28 April 1914. Served in the Royal Navy during World War II. Married Pamela Baker in 1950; two daughters. Has worked as a salesman, reporter, and insurance agent; bus driver, East Kent Road Car Company, for 28 years; now retired. Address: 34 King Street, Canterbury, Kent CT1 2AJ, England.

SCIENCE-FICTION PUBLICATIONS

Novels

The Prodigal Sun. New York, Ace, 1964; London, Compact, 1965.
No Truce with Terra. New York, Ace, 1964.
The Mad Metropolis. New York, Ace, 1966; as *Double Illusion,* London, Dobson, 1970.
These Savage Futurians. New York, Ace, 1967; London, Dobson, 1969.
Twin Planets. New York, Paperback Library, 1967; London, Dobson, 1968.
Reality Forbidden. New York, Ace, 1967; London, Hale, 1968.
Invader on My Back. New York, Ace, and London, Hale, 1968.
The Time Mercenaries. New York, Ace, 1968; London, Dobson, 1969.
Butterfly Planet. London, Dobson, 1971.
Sold—For a Spaceship. London, Hale, 1973.
Come Hunt an Earthman. London, Hale, 1973.
Speaking of Dinosaurs. London, Hale, 1974.

Fugitive from Time.   London, Hale, 1978.
Blindfold from the Stars.   London, Dobson, 1979.

Uncollected Short Stories

"The Statics," in *Authentic* (London), September 1955.
"Wrath of the Gods," in *Nebula* (Glasgow), July 1956.
"Schoolroom for the Teacher," in *Authentic* (London), November 1956.
"City at Random," in *Nebula* (Glasgow), December 1956.
"The Collaborator," in *Authentic* (London), December 1956.
"Guess Who," in *New Worlds* (London), February 1957.
"Plague Solution," in *Authentic* (London), February 1957.
"Assassin in Hiding," in *Authentic* (London), April 1957.
"Life Sentence," in *Authentic* (London), May 1957.
"Golden Age," in *New Worlds* (London), June 1957.
"Buried Talent," in *New Worlds* (London), August 1957.
"Time Bomb," in *Nebula* (Glasgow), August 1957.
"Topside," in *Authentic* (London), August 1957.
"The Ancient Enemy," in *Authentic* (London), September 1957.
"Further Outlook," in *Nebula* (Glasgow), September 1957.
"The Meek Shall Inherit," in *Nebula* (Glasgow), January 1958.
"Risk Economy," in *Nebula* (Glasgow), February 1958.
"Shift Case," in *Nebula* (Glasgow), March 1958.
"The Guardian," in *New Worlds* (London), October 1958.
"Lords of Creation," in *Nebula* (Glasgow), December 1958.
"A Race of Madmen," in *Nebula* (Glasgow), January 1959.
"Infection," in *Nebula* (Glasgow), February 1959.
"To See Ourselves," in *Nebula* (Glasgow), May 1959.
"Pseudo Path," in *New Worlds* (London), September 1959.
"Mumbo-Jumbo Man," in *New Worlds* (London), January 1960.
"Pursuit Missile," in *New Worlds* (London), June 1960.
"The Jackson Killer," in *New Worlds* (London), May 1961.
"Fallen Angel," in *Astounding* (New York), June 1961.
"The Martian Hunters," in *New Worlds* (London), November 1961.
"Survival Course," in *New Worlds* (London), December 1961.
"The Psi Squad," in *New Worlds* (London), January 1962.
"Probability Factor," in *New Worlds* (London), March 1962.
"Blind as a Bat," in *Science Fiction Adventures* (London), March 1962.
"Dictator Bait," in *New Worlds* (London), May 1962.
"The Method," in *New Worlds* (London), November 1962.
"Dead End," in *Science Fantasy* (Bournemouth), December 1962.
"The Big Tin God," in *New Worlds* (London), January 1963.
"Point of No Return," in *New Worlds* (London), July 1963.
"Relative Genius," in *New Worlds* (London), December 1963.
"Routine Exercise," in *Lambda 1 and Other Stories,* edited by John Carnell.   New York, Berkley, 1964; London, Penguin, 1965.
"Bottomless Pit" (juvenile), in *Out of This World 5,* edited by Amabel Williams-Ellis and Mably Owen.   London, Blackie, 1965.
"Temporary Resident," in *New Worlds* (London), February 1966.
"The Adapters," in *Vision of Tomorrow* (Newcastle upon Tyne), November 1969.
"Psycho-Land," in *Vision of Tomorrow* (Newcastle upon Tyne), January 1970.
"Technical Wizard," in *Vision of Tomorrow* (Newcastle upon Tyne), February 1970.
"Fixed Image," in *Vision of Tomorrow* (Newcastle upon Tyne), May 1970.

Philip E. High comments:

I am a story teller. I have never claimed great literary abilities. I am not only a great believer in a happy ending, but am psychologically incapable of writing any other sort. A reader asks to be entertained and stimulated, not depressed. I have a vivid imagination and I try to put what I imagine on paper. But I am also old-fashioned: I like a story to have a beginning, a middle, an end, and, yes, a purpose with all the loose ends tied up.

*   *   *

Philip E. High is one of a number of writers of fast-paced adventure novels who rose to prominence with the publication of several novels by Ace Books. His work is generally written with little effort at stylistic flamboyance, with simple but well-constructed plots. A definite tendency toward bizarre settings has helped to distinguish his novels from those of others working the same vein.

Twin Planets, for example, was set on a kind of alternate Earth, but not one of the slightly altered histories that is usual. Rather, it was a very similar world somewhat advanced in time, whose unpleasant experience with alien invaders had led its inhabitants to attempt to help our own world avoid a similar fate. Similarly, in *Invader on My Back* aliens have conquered the Earth, and divided humanity into a number of disparate types of personalities. The common failing is a mortal dread of peering upward, conditioned into them because of their subjugated status. *Reality Forbidden* is also characterized by odd settings and events, partially rationalized in this case by the existence of dream machines, inventions which lull humanity into a careless conformity. Indeed, one of the common themes in High's novels is a dread of conformity and the value of the individual, usually a super-normal human. The two protagonists of *Twin Planets* are genetic supermen, and the human sent by aliens to help "civilize" Earth in *The Prodigal Sun* is also a super-human, due to his training on that alien world. A man with an incredibly high I.Q. helps lead a revolt against an overly protective computer mind in *The Mad Metropolis,* and another with an extremely high curiosity quotient leads the revolt against the conformity of a post-collapse experimental community in *These Savage Futurians.*

In *The Time Mercenaries,* possibly High's best work, future humanity has bred itself to the ultimate degree of conformity and passivity, and cannot employ violence even in self defense. To protect themselves against alien invaders, these future beings resurrect the crew of a modern submarine, knowing that men of our times would not be constrained by their inflexible ethical code. Alien invasions are rather common in High's novel, usually with no good intentions. The exceptions to this in the early novels are *The Prodigal Sun* and *No Truce with Terra,* in both of which the author makes the point that we are too prejudiced and violent to participate in a truly civilized interstellar civilization. High does not harp on this point, however, being more concerned with his adventure story than with social commentary.

Despite the limited aspirations of his fiction, High has produced some very durable novels, although recent work like *Speaking of Dinosaurs* and *Come Hunt an Earthman* are practically unknown. High has himself pointed out that a good story should explain itself fully to the reader and not leave him guessing. The straightforward style and relatively simple plots that he utilizes conform to this dictum.

—Don D'Ammassa

HILTON, James.   Also wrote as Glen Trevor.   British.   Born in Leigh, Lancashire, 9 September 1900. Educated at Leys School, Cambridge; Christ's College, Cambridge, B.A. (honours) in history. Columnist, *Irish Independent,* Dublin, in the 1920's. Settled in the United States in 1935. Recipient: Hawthornden Prize, 1934; Academy Award, 1943. *Died 20 December 1954.*

SCIENCE-FICTION PUBLICATIONS

Novel

Lost Horizon.   London, Macmillan, and New York, Morrow, 1933.

OTHER PUBLICATIONS

Novels

Catherine Herself.   London, Unwin, 1920.

Storm Passage.   London, Unwin, 1922.
The Passionate Year.   London, Butterworth, 1923; Boston, Little Brown, 1924.
The Dawn of Reckoning.   London, Butterworth, 1925; n.p., Famous Books, 1937.
The Meadows of the Moon.   London, Butterworth, 1926; Boston, Small Maynard, 1927.
Terry.   London, Butterworth, 1927.
The Silver Flame.   London, Butterworth, 1928.
Murder at School: A Detective Fantasia (as Glen Trevor).   London, Benn, 1931; as *Was It Murder?*, New York, Harper, 1933.
And Now Goodbye.   London, Benn, 1931; New York, Morrow, 1932.
Contango.   London, Benn, 1932; as *Ill Wind*, New York, Grosset and Dunlap, 1932.
Rage in Heaven.   New York, King, 1932.
Knight Without Armour.   London, Benn, 1933; as *Without Armor*, New York, Morrow, 1934.
Good-bye Mr. Chips.   London, Hodder and Stoughton, and Boston, Little Brown, 1934.
We Are Not Alone.   London, Macmillan, and Boston, Little Brown, 1937.
Random Harvest.   London, Macmillan, and Boston, Little Brown, 1941.
The Story of Dr. Wassell.   Boston, Little Brown, 1943; London, Macmillan, 1944.
So Well Remembered.   Boston, Little Brown, 1945; London, Macmillan, 1947.
Nothing So Strange.   Boston, Little Brown, 1947; London, Macmillan, 1948.
Morning Journey.   London, Macmillan, and Boston, Little Brown, 1951.
Time and Time Again.   London, Macmillan, and Boston, Little Brown, 1953.

Short Stories

To You, Mr. Chips.   London, Hodder and Stoughton, 1938.
Twilight of the Wise.   London, St. Hugh's Press, 1949.

Plays

Good-bye Mr. Chips, with Barbara Burnham, adaptation of the novel by Hilton (produced London, 1938).   London, Hodder and Stoughton, 1938.
Mrs. Miniver, with others, in *Twenty Best Film Plays,* edited by John Gassner and Dudley Nichols.   New York, Crown, 1943.
Shangri-La, with Jerome Lawrence and Robert E. Lee, music by Harry Warren, adaptation of the novel *Lost Horizon* by Hilton (produced New York, 1956).   New York, Morris Music, 1956.

Screenplays: *Camille,* with Zoe Akins and Frances Marion, 1936; *We Are Not Alone,* with Milton Krims, 1939; *The Tuttles of Tahiti,* with Lewis Meltzer and Robert Carson, 1942; *Mrs. Miniver,* with others, 1942; *Forever and a Day,* with others, 1944.

Other

Mr. Chips Looks at the World (lecture).   Los Angeles, Modern Forum, 1939.
Addresses on the Present War and Our Hopes for the Future (radio talks).   New York, CBS, 1943.
The Duke of Edinburgh.   London, Muller, 1956; as *H.R.H.: The Story of Philip, Duke of Edinburgh,* Boston, Little Brown, 1956.

*   *   *

Lost Horizon may be considered borderline science fiction, as well as one of the few utopian novels of the 20th century. The protagonist, Conway, whose story is told in a flashback, is kidnapped with three other passengers and flown to a remote and isolated lamasery—the haunting Shangri-La—in the uncharted mountains of Tibet. Despite his companions' impatience to leave, Conway finds peace with the novitiate lamas among the world's masterpieces of literature and art collected there. The ancient High

Lama singles him out in a series of rare interviews and finally reveals their secret of longevity, as well as the purpose for Shangri-La's existence. There will come a devastation, he predicts, "a Dark Age that will cover the world in a single pall. . . . It will rage till every flower of culture is trampled and all human things are leveled in a vast chaos." There will be sanctuary only for those who are too secret to be found or too humble to be noticed. "And," the High Lama explains, "Shangri-La may hope to be both of these. . . . I see, at a great distance, a new world stirring in the ruins, stirring clumsily but in hopefulness, seeking its lost and legendary treasures. And they will all be here. . . preserved as by miracle for a new Renaissance." Having long looked for a man such as Conway, his dying words are: "I place in your hands, my son, the heritage and destiny of Shangri-La." Conway, however, is impetuously persuaded to flee into the outer world with the beautiful girl Lo-Tsen, whose true age catches up with her once outside. The book ends as Conway, after a period of amnesia, begins his search for the lost Shangri-La. This classic, while not wholly science fiction, builds upon intuitive projections into the future.

—Myra Barnes

————————

HOCH, Edward D.   Also writes as Irwin Booth; Stephen Dentinger.   American.   Born in Rochester, New York, 22 February 1930.   Educated at the University of Rochester, New York, 1947-49.   Served in the United States Army, 1950-52.   Married Patricia A. McMahon in 1957.   Worked at Rochester Public Library, 1949-50; Pocket Books, New York City, 1952-54; Hutchins Advertising Company, Rochester, 1954-68.   Since 1968, self-employed writer.   Member, Board of Directors, Mystery Writers of America.   Recipient: Mystery Writers of America Edgar Allan Poe Award, for short story, 1968.   Agent: Larry Sternig, 742 Robertson Street, Milwaukee, Wisconsin 53213.   Address: 2941 Lake Avenue, Rochester, New York 14612, U.S.A.

SCIENCE-FICTION PUBLICATIONS

Novels (series: Carl Crader and Earl Jazine in all books)

The Transvection Machine.   New York, Walker, 1971; London, Hale, 1974.
The Fellowship of the Hand.   New York, Walker, 1973; London, Hale, 1976.
The Frankenstein Factory.   New York, Warner, 1975; London, Hale, 1976.

Short Stories (series: Simon Ark)

The Judges of Hades and Other Simon Ark Stories.   North Hollywood, Nordon, 1971.
City of Brass and Other Simon Ark Stories.   North Hollywood, Nordon, 1971.

Uncollected Short Stories (series: Simon Ark)

"The Man from Nowhere" (Ark), in *Famous Detective* (New York), June 1956.
"Co-Incidence" (as Irwin Booth), in *Original Science Fiction Stories* (Holyoke, Massachusetts), September 1956.
"Versus," in *Fantastic Universe* (Chicago), June 1957.
"The Last Unicorns," in *Original Science Fiction Stories* (Holyoke, Massachusetts), February 1959.
"The Man Who Knew Everything," in *Shock* (New York), September 1960.
"The Maze and the Monster," in *Magazine of Horror* (New York), August 1963.

"The Wolfram Hunters," in *Rulers of Men,* edited by Hans S. Santesson. New York, Pyramid, 1965.

"The Empty Zoo," in *Magazine of Horror* (New York), November 1965.

"God of the Playback" (as Stephen Dentinger), in *Gods of Tomorrow,* edited by Hans S. Santesson. New York, Award, 1967.

"The Times We Had," in *Famous Science Fiction* (New York), Fall 1967.

"Cassidy's Saucer," in *Flying Saucers in Fact and Fiction,* edited by Hans S. Santesson. New York, Lancer, 1968.

"The Maiden's Sacrifice," in *Famous Science Fiction* (New York), Fall 1968.

"The Future Is Ours" (as Stephen Dentinger) and "Computer Cops," in *Crime Prevention in the 30th Century,* edited by Hans S. Santesson. New York, Walker, 1969.

"Unnatural Act," in *Gentle Invaders,* edited by Hans S. Santesson. New York, Belmont, 1969.

"Zoo," in *Combo 402,* edited by John Cooper. Chicago, Scott Foresman, 1971.

"The Lost Pilgrim" (Ark), in *Mike Shayne Mystery Magazine* (Los Angeles), February 1972.

"Night of the Millennium," in *The Other Side of Tomorrow,* edited by Roger Elwood. New York, Random House, 1973.

"Funeral in the Fog" (Ark), in *Weird Tales* (Los Angeles), Summer 1973.

"The Boy Who Bought Love," in *Crisis,* edited by Roger Elwood. Nashville, Nelson, 1974.

"The Faceless Thing," in *Fiends and Creatures,* edited by Marvin Kaye. New York, Popular Library, 1975.

"In the Straw," in *Beware More Beasts,* edited by Vic Ghidalia and Roger Elwood. New York, Manor, 1975.

"The Homesick Chicken," in *Isaac Asimov's Science Fiction Magazine* (New York), Spring 1977.

"The Last Paradox," in *100 Great Science Fiction Short-Short Stories,* edited by Isaac Asimov, Martin H. Greenberg, and Joseph D. Olander. New York, Doubleday, and London, Robson, 1978.

"The Treasure of Jack the Ripper" (Ark), in *Ellery Queen's Mystery Magazine* (New York), October 1978.

"The Mummy from the Sea" (Ark), in *Alfred Hitchcock's Mystery Magazine* (New York), January 1979.

"The Man Who Shot the Werewolf" (Ark), in *Ellery Queen's Mystery Magazine* (New York), February 1979.

"The Avenger from Outer Space" (Ark), in *Ellery Queen's Mystery Magazine* (New York), October 1979.

OTHER PUBLICATIONS

Novel

The Shattered Raven. New York, Lancer, 1969; London, Hale, 1970.

Short Stories

The Spy and the Thief. New York, Davis, 1971.
The Thefts of Nick Velvet. Yonkers, New York, Mysterious Press, 1978.

Other

The Monkey's Clue, and The Stolen Sapphire (juvenile). New York, Grosset and Dunlap, 1978.

Editor, *Dear Dead Days.* New York, Walker, 1972; London, Gollancz, 1974.
Editor, *Best Detective Stories of the Year.* New York, Dutton, 5 vols., 1976-80.

*

Bibliography: "Edward D. Hoch: A Checklist" by William J. Clark, Edward D. Hoch, and Francis M. Nevins, Jr., in *Armchair Detective* (White Bear Lake, Minnesota), February 1976; revised edition, by Nevins and Hoch, privately printed, 1979.

Edward D. Hoch comments:

I have always viewed my science fiction and fantasy as offshoots of my mystery writing, and nearly all my science fiction contains elements of mystery and detection.

* * *

Edward D. Hoch is one of the few writers who have been able to blend successfully the detective story with science fiction (others include Isaac Asimov, Anthony Boucher, Fredric Brown, Randall Garrett, and Ron Goulart). Of his three novels and more than 60 short stories which qualify as science fiction or fantasy, nearly all have criminous elements.

Each of Hoch's three SF novels is a classic mystery set in the 21st century and features the "Computer Cops," a team of government investigators led by Carl Crader and Earl Jazine. The first, *The Transvection Machine,* is perhaps the best—a strong blending of baffling mystery, inventive science fiction, and social commentary. Almost as good is *The Fellowship of the Hand* which continues Crader's and Jazine's attempts to combat an organization known as HAND (Humans Against Neuter Domination), pledged to destroy all machines capable of dominating man. *The Frankenstein Factory,* which deals with a futuristic variation on the Frankenstein theme involving cryonics, is less successful in that it seems more an attenuated novelette than a fully realized novel.

Hoch's true forte, however, is the short story. He has published more than 500 in the past quarter-century and is widely acclaimed as the premier writer of short mystery fiction. Among the more memorable of his science-fiction detective tales are "The Wolfram Hunters" and "Computer Cops"; non-criminous SF include "Zoo," "The Faceless Thing," and "The Last Paradox." But it is the 60 novelette-length adventures about Simon Ark, a man who claims to be a 2000-year-old Copt priest, which are perhaps the most well-known of all of Hoch's fictional creations. These are primarily tales of detection, but each one deals with such fantastic elements as werewolves, witches, religious cults, scientific experiments, and Fortean phenomena. The best of the early Simon Ark stories (from the 1950's) appear in *City of Brass* and *The Judges of Hades.* A new series of Ark stories began in *Ellery Queen's Mystery Magazine* in 1978.

The chief attribute of Hoch's work is invariably intricate and ingenious plotting; few rival him in his ability to summon a seemingly endless and wide-reaching flow of ideas. If plot receives more emphasis than character development in some of his prose (notable exceptions are "The Wolfram Hunters" and "The Faceless Thing"), this in no way diminishes its high entertainment value. The richness of idea and incident more than compensates.

—Bill Pronzini

HODDER-WILLIAMS, (John) Christopher (Glazebrook). Also writes as James Brogan. British. Born in London, in 1926. Educated at Eton College. Served in the Royal Signals, in the Middle East, 1944-48: Lieutenant. Worked in Africa after World War II; worked in England for film, television, and recording companies; also a composer. Address: c/o Weidenfeld and Nicolson Ltd., 91 Chapham High Street, London S.W.4, England.

SCIENCE-FICTION PUBLICATIONS

Novels

Chain Reaction. London, Hodder and Stoughton, and New York, Doubleday, 1959.
The Main Experiment. London, Hodder and Stoughton, 1964; New York, Putnam, 1965.

The Egg-Shaped Thing. London, Hodder and Stoughton, and New York, Putnam, 1967.
Fistful of Digits. London, Hodder and Stoughton, 1968.
98.4. London, Hodder and Stoughton, 1969.
Panic O'Clock. St. Ives, Cornwall, United Writers, 1973.
The Prayer Machine. London, Weidenfeld and Nicolson, 1976; New York, St. Martin's Press, 1977.
The Silent Voice. London, Weidenfeld and Nicolson, 1977.
The Thinktank That Leaked. St. Ives, Cornwall, United Writers, 1979.

OTHER PUBLICATIONS

Novels

The Cummings Report (as James Brogan). London, Hodder and Stoughton, 1958.
Final Approach. London, Hodder and Stoughton, and New York, Doubleday, 1960.
Turbulence. London, Hodder and Stoughton, 1961.
The Higher They Fly. London, Hodder and Stoughton, 1963; New York, Putnam, 1964.

Plays

Radio Play: *Final Approach,* from his own novel, 1967.

Television Plays: *The Ship That Couldn't Stop,* 1961; *The Hot White Coal,* 1963; *The Higher They Fly,* from his own novel, 1963; *A Voice in the Sky,* 1964.

*   *   *

Christopher Hodder-Williams has become one of the most highly regarded British science-fiction writers. His first science-fiction novel was *Chain Reaction.* This had a thriller format but was about the spread of atomic radiation through food. The widespread campaign for nuclear disarmament and the awakening of social conscience to the dangers of nuclear energy caused the book to be widely recognised as a poignant warning to humanity. Since then Hodder-Williams had followed his success with such books as *The Main Experiment,* a mystery thriller set in a research laboratory, and *The Egg-Shaped Thing,* a tale of industrial espionage with a detective leading an investigation for a fourth-dimension terror. Although Hodder-Williams has a relatively small output, he is one of the most serious and influential of British science-fiction writers. Science provides him with a background against which he sets plausible modern-day thrillers which are extremely well constructed and grip the reader's attention with fast-paced action. While purists might not consider him in the mainstream of science-fiction writing, Hodder-Williams has exerted a great deal of influence on his contemporaries.

—Peter Berresford Ellis

HODGSON, William Hope. British. Born in Blackmore End, Essex, 15 November 1877. Went to sea at age 17; became an officer in the Mercantile Marine; later taught physical culture. Joined University of London Officer Training Corps, 1914; commissioned in Royal Field Artillery, 1915; left service because of injury, 1916; recommissioned, 1917, and died at Ypres. Recipient: Royal Humane Society Medal. *Died 17 April 1918.*

SCIENCE-FICTION PUBLICATIONS

Novels

The Boats of the "Glen Carrig." London, Chapman and Hall, 1907; New York, Ballantine, 1971.

The House on the Borderland. London, Chapman and Hall, 1908.
The Ghost Pirates. London, Stanley Paul, 1909; Westport, Connecticut, Hyperion Press, 1976.
The Night Land. London, Nash, 1912; Westport, Connecticut, Hyperion Press, 1976.
The House on the Borderland and Other Novels. Sauk City, Wisconsin, Arkham House, 1946.

Short Stories

Deep Waters. Sauk City, Wisconsin, Arkham House, 1967.
Out of the Storm: Uncollected Fantasies, edited by Sam Moskowitz. West Kingston, Rhode Island, Grant, 1975.

OTHER PUBLICATIONS

Short Stories

The Ghost Pirates, A Chaunty, and Another Story. New York, Reynolds, 1909.
Carnacki, The Ghost Finder, and a Poem. New York, Reynolds, 1910.
Carnacki, The Ghost Finder (collection). London, Nash, 1913; augmented edition, Sauk City, Wisconsin, Mycroft and Moran, 1947.
Men of the Deep Waters. London, Nash, 1914.
The Luck of the Strong. London, Nash, 1916.
Captain Gault, Being the Exceedingly Private Log of a Sea-Captain. London, Nash, 1917; New York, McBride, 1918.

Verse

Poems and The Dream of X. London, Watt, and New York, Paget, 1912.
Cargunka and Poems and Anecdotes. London, Watt, and New York, Paget, 1914.
The Calling of the Sea. London, Selwyn and Blount, 1920.
The Voice of the Ocean. London, Selwyn and Blount, 1921.
Poems of the Sea. London, Ferret Fantasy, 1977.

*

Bibliography: by A.L. Searles, in *The House on the Borderland and Other Novels,* Sauk City, Wisconsin, Arkham House, 1946.

*   *   *

One of the most remarkable visionary fantasy authors of the first part of this century, William Hope Hodgson is remembered today chiefly as the author of two classic fantasies, *The House on the Borderland* and *The Night Land,* and for a number of often-anthologized short horror stories that are models of craft and atmosphere. Though his writing did not become widely known among fantasy and science-fiction readers until the 1940's, when his stories began to be reprinted in American pulp magazines and his novels were reissued, Hodgson's reputation has grown steadily since then, despite the difficulty involved in categorizing his works.

Hodgson's novels are characterized by episodic structure, multiple narrators or "frame" stories, vivid descriptions, images of decay and desolation, and—perhaps most important—an atmosphere of brooding horror that Hodgson manages to sustain and build despite his often digressive plots. His first novel, *The Boats of the "Glen Carrig,"* seems to owe a stylistic debt to Defoe, and is even cast in the form of an 18th-century manuscript. This tale of shipwreck survivors who encounter islands of fungi, weed-bound derelicts, and hideous intelligent slugs quickly helped to establish Hodgson's reputation as a leading writer of sea horror stories, a reputation which was furthered by his short fiction and by another novel, *The Ghost Pirates,* which approached science fiction with its speculation that the ghosts may be inhabitants of an alternate reality, "perhaps something to do with magnetic stresses." Hodgson's most widely read novel, *The House on the Borderland,* did not take place at sea, although Hodgson regarded it as part of a thematic trilogy with *The Boats of the "Glen Carrig"* and *The Ghost Pirates.* Cast in the form of a manuscript discovered in the ruins of an isolated house in the west of Ireland, the novel would vary little from the simple horror formulae of Hodgson's earlier novels were it not for a powerful central passage in which the narrator embarks on a long psychic journey in time and space, witnessing the death of earth, sun, and solar system and encountering hideous creatures on a world strangely parallel to this one. *The Night Land,* Hodgson's last novel and by far his longest, again employs an archaic style, and a visionary narrator but is otherwise a considerable departure from these earlier works. One of the longest and strangest fantastic romances of this century, *The Night Land* is the vision of a 16th-century man into the earth of millions of years in the future, when the "last millions" of humanity have retreated after the sun's death into a huge pyramid, almost eight miles high and comprising 1320 floors, called the "Last Redoubt." Surrounding the Redoubt are monstrous creatures of various kinds, waiting for humanity's power supply to run out so that they can move in. The story is a simple quest of a lover for his beloved in this bizarre context (a story which echoes the frame narrative that introduces the vision), ending with an affirmation of the saving power of love in even the most hopeless of circumstances.

Hodgson's short fiction includes a number of stories that have become horror classics, most notably "The Voice in the Night," concerning a man and woman overcome by fungus on a mysterious island, and "The Derelict," about a ship so overgrown with fungus that it becomes a living organism. These and other tales reveal Hodgson's obsessive repulsion to parasitical life and stagnation, and his use of the sea as an arena for unknown horrors in a manner not unlike that in which later writers would come to use outer space. Of his non-sea stories, the most notable are a series about an occult detective names Carnacki. Written with a humor unusual for Hodgson, these stories range from the clever to the ridiculous, with Carnacki sometimes explaining ingenious hoaxes and sometimes finding himself face to face with the most unlikely supernatural manifestations (such as a room that puckers up and whistles). Though not major works, these stories reveal a versatility that makes one wonder what Hodgson might have produced had he not been killed in the First World War.

—Gary K. Wolfe

HOFFMAN, Lee. Also writes as Georgia York. American. Born in Chicago, Illinois, 14 August 1932. Educated at Armstrong Junior College, Savannah, Georgia, A.A. 1951. Married Larry T. Shaw (divorced). Printer's devil, Savannah Vocational School; staff member, Hoffman Radio-TV Service; Assistant Editor, *Infinity,* 1956-58, and *Science Fiction Adventures,* 1956-58; staff member, MD Publications; claim handler, Hoffman Motors; in printing production, Arrow Press, Allied Typographers, and George Morris Press. Since 1965, free-lance writer. Recipient: Western Writers of America Spur Award, 1968. Agent: Henry Morrison Inc., 58 West 10th Street, New York, New York 10011. Address: 350 N.W. Harbor Boulevard, Port Charlotte, Florida 33952, U.S.A.

SCIENCE-FICTION PUBLICATIONS

Novels

Telepower.   New York, Belmont, 1967.
The Caves of Karst.   New York, Ballantine, 1969; London, Dobson, 1970.
Always the Blackknight.   New York, Avon, 1970.
Change Song.   New York, Doubleday, 1972.

Uncollected Short Stories

"Lost in the Marigolds," with Robert E. Toomey, Jr., in *Orbit 9,* edited by Damon Knight.   New York, Putnam, 1971.

"Soundless Evening," in *Again, Dangerous Visions,* edited by Harlan Ellison.   New York, Doubleday, 1972; London, Millington, 1976.

OTHER PUBLICATIONS

Novels

Gunfight at Laramie.   New York, Ace, 1966; London, Gold Lion, 1975.
The Legend of Blackjack Sam.   New York, Ace, 1966.
Bred to Kill.   New York, Ballantine, 1967.
The Valdez Horses.   New York, Doubleday, 1967; London, Tandem, 1972.
Dead Man's Gold.   New York, Ace, 1968.
The Yarborough Brand.   New York, Avon, 1968.
Wild Riders.   New York, New American Library, 1969; London, Hale, 1979.
Loco.   New York, Doubleday, 1969; London, Tandem, 1973.
Return to Broken Crossing.   New York, Ace, 1969.
West of Cheyenne.   New York, Doubleday, 1969; London, Tandem, 1973.
Wiley's Move.   New York, Dell, 1975.
The Truth about the Cannonball Kid.   New York, Dell, 1975.
Fox.   New York, Doubleday, 1976.
Nothing But a Drifter.   New York, Doubleday, 1976.
Trouble Valley.   New York, Ballantine, 1976.
The Sheriff of Jack Hollow.   New York, Dell, 1977.
The Land Killer.   New York, Doubleday, 1978.
Savage Key (as Georgia York).   New York, Fawcett, 1979.

*   *   *

The science-fiction novels of Lee Hoffman are novels of human feelings, not ones of hard science. The SF concepts are well thought out and are integral to the storylines, but they are clearly secondary to the characters. Unlike some SF where the idea is the star and the emphasis is placed on the nuts and bolts or on the astronomical bodies while the people seem stamped out of cookie dough, Hoffman's fiction is populated with characters who live and breathe and grow and develop. The songs they sing are ones for men and women, not for pulsars and machines.

Perhaps the clearest example of her ability to make her characters very human is the protagonist in *The Caves of Karst,* a man who has undergone an operation to enable him to breathe underwater. Though this allows him to work the underwater mines more effectively, he did not choose to undergo the operation solely for financial considerations; as the novel unfolds it becomes clear that the choice was made (on some level of consciousness) to protect his ego from an unhapply love affair. People on Karst, as on Earth, often shun those who differ physically from the norm and those who *choose* to have such differences are frequently confronted with outright hatred. His adjustment to his condition, to women in general and his girlfriend in particular, and to himself during a time of crisis is the heart of the book.

There are three primary themes that run through Hoffman's work. 1) Individuality and the freedom of choice that comes with it are extremely important but must be tempered with the realization that individuals need to work together, to interact, in order to achieve certain goals. 2) It is both wrong and *dangerous* to try to control something or someone without consent. 3) Things may not be the way you originally thought they were or the way you have been told they were. Each theme is expressed with varying degrees of emphasis, depending on the novel, but all three are interrelated in her science fiction.

Hoffman's style is lean and direct. Each novel opens with action, tossing the reader into the midst of unfolding events: *Telepower* begins with an attack on post-atomic war Cleveland by an army of rats; *The Caves of Karst* starts with an underwater "gunfight" in a mine; *Always the Blackknight* opens with a battle between knights on robot horses; and, although the first chapter of *Change Song* is used to establish a sense of wrongness and an atmosphere of danger, the second chapter quickly produces a fight between men with magical powers. Hoffman uses her writing skills to capture the reader immediately, and all of her work has been set on earth-like planets so that the reader can rapidly believe in the setting. Obviously Hoffman strives to entertain the reader while stating her messages.

To enrich her science fiction, she occasionally employs the techniques of other genres to give a more diverse flavor. In *Telepower* Hoffman forges a bond between the gruesome qualities of the horror novels and the telepathic power so common in science fiction. Drawing upon her own experience as a writer of westerns, she gives *The Caves of Karst* an Old West setting (or what the Old West would have been like if the prospectors had gills) while at the same time using all the plot-twists of a mystery novel. *Always the Black-knight* has the flavor of the tales of knighthood, as the title might indicate, and *Change Song* has most of the elements of a quest-fantasy. In fact *Change Song* is really more fantasy than science fiction, much in the same way that Theodore Sturgeon's *More Than Human* is, although on the world where *Change Song* takes place control of the elements and the power to cast spells are like our science in that one is trained in these fields. By being willing to take the risks of mixing elements of other genres with science fiction, Lee Hoffman has given her work an added dimension.

—Terry Hughes

HOGAN, James P(atrick).   British.   Born in London, 27 June 1941. Educated at the Royal Aircraft Establishment Technical College, Farnborough, Berkshire, 1957-61; Reading and Enfield colleges, 1961-65. Married 1) Iris Crossley in 1961 (divorced), three daughters; 2) Lyn Dockerty in 1976. Engineer, Solarton Electronics, Farnborough, 1961-62, Racal Electronics, Bracknell, Berkshire, 1962-64; Sales engineer, 1964-66, and Sales Manager, 1966-68, ITT, Harlow, Hertfordshire; Computer Sales Executive, Honeywell, London, 1968-70, and Leeds, 1970-72; Insurance Salesman, Sun Life Canada, Leeds, 1972-74; Computer Salesman, 1974-77, and Sales Training Consultant in Maynard, Massachusetts, 1977-79, Digital Equipment Corporation, Leeds. Agent: Scott Meredith Literary Agency, 845 Third Avenue, New York, New York 10022. Address: 174 Main Street, Acton, Massachusetts 01720, U.S.A.

SCIENCE-FICTION PUBLICATIONS

Novels

Inherit the Stars.   New York, Ballantine, 1977.
The Genesis Machine.   New York, Ballantine, 1977.
The Gentle Giants of Ganymede.   New York, Ballantine, 1978.
The Two Faces of Tomorrow.   New York, Ballantine, 1979.
Thrice upon a Time.   New York, Ballantine, 1980.

Uncollected Short Story

"Assassin," in *Stellar 4,* edited by Judy-Lynn del Rey.   New York, Ballantine, 1978.

OTHER PUBLICATIONS

Other

"Think of a Number," in *Galileo* (Boston), July 1978.

*   *   *

James P. Hogan writes cautionary tales concerning the possibilities that the coming century holds for humankind. It is, in fact, rare to find a science-fiction writer as intensely concerned about our future as Hogan is. A character in his best novel, *The Two Faces of*

Tomorrow, observes: "The future has two faces—one totally good and one totally bad." In the bad future, runaway social conditions and inept bureaucratic policies will devastate humankind, perhaps (as in *The Genesis Machine*) bringing us to the verge of nuclear disaster through misapplied science. In the good future, however, the wisdom of enlightened scientists helps to overcome threats—whether in the form of impending disaster or the more benign governmental stupidities—and bring humankind to the verge of sublime social advancement and scientific achievement. While Hogan comes down solidly on the side of the good future, he does strive to warn his readers of the risks entailed if certain present-day policies of both science and government are carried forward into the future. Sometimes his cautions are presented polemically, sometimes through the dramatic use of stark life and death crises.

Although Hogan has a consistent set of attitudes and ideas to offer, he does not achieve his fictional goals simplistically. His grasp of scientific subjects and his clear presentation of them in his fiction make him perhaps the most impressive scientifically oriented writer to enter the field during the 1970's. His characters utilize voluminous scientific data and apply a vast array of scientific knowledge drawn from physics, anthropology, cybernetics, linguistics, astronomy, weaponry—to whatever fictional crisis confronts them. The implications of each stage of scientific thinking are thoroughly investigated. In fact, Hogan's depiction of the workaday activity of scientists is so detailed that it becomes more interesting than any textbook discussion of the scientific method. He smoothly takes the reader from the fictional discovery that puzzles or excites the team of scientists through numerous theories, hypotheses, and speculations, all of which are developed from our current knowledge. From these, he arrives at conclusions related incisively to the speculative levels and takes them even further, to the practical applications of the data gained at all the complex procedural levels. All this is presented clearly and with proper attention to the development of ideas. Hogan does not resort to the science-fiction author's traditional escape hatch, the jump to the sudden insight that skips the intervening stages of thought. At times the adventure-oriented reader may mutter to a Hogan character to stop talking and get on with it; however, when Hogan does get on with it the perceptive reader is grateful for the substantial grounding in scientific matters that the author has provided, especially for the subtle ways by which such grounding enriches the narratives.

Hogan's deep concern with the reality of science is further enhanced by his realistic portrayals of the scientists themselves. In contrast to the tired characterizations of them as eccentrics or daring heroes, Hogan's scientists are normal, hard-working, decent human beings whose virtues and failings are analogous to those in other walks of life. Some of them are more insightful than others; some are reliable workers whose discoveries contribute to the general good; some are even bureaucrats whose allegiance to procedure and traditional thinking interferes with the urgency of the overall mission. They are presented in such unheroic (and, for that matter, unvillainous) terms that their heroism, when it does occur, is not only more believable but also more effective emotionally. Furthermore the precise renderings of their everyday lives increases the novels' verisimilitude. The conventional laboratory and eureka-discovery events are avoided. Instead, Hogan's characters hold committee meetings, sit together for brainstorming sessions, send out for coffee and stop for lunch, throw up their hands at bureaucratic obstacles, flirt and wisecrack, blunder and make social *faux pas.* The ways in which he combines the mundane with the dramatic give the typical Hogan novel a distinct semi-documentary flavor.

Hogan's fiction clearly indicates his social and political conservatism, and his faith in human rationality. The plots of the novels are reminiscent of detective stories, where a problem is thoroughly analyzed by scientific detectives until the surprising solutions are reached. Their main themes are related to his considered and methodical study of man's role on his home-planet now and in the universe of the future. An optimist, he believes in the ability of science to thrust humankind forward into new advanced eras of achievement and productivity. In spite of the first face of tomorrow, the chaos that threatens to ossify human progress, he seems to believe that we will overcome even such formidable obstacles in order peacefully to enter a space age of improved living conditions, technological miracles, and the exploration of the stars. Hogan has been compared to Arthur C. Clarke for his meticulous portrayal of science and the future. For that matter, he can be placed easily in what might be called the grand tradition of science fiction, dating back to Hugo Gernsback and even Jules Verne, a tradition of science fiction in which the known perimeters of real science are the firm speculative base for futuristic tales of wonder.

—Robert Thurston

HOLDSTOCK, Robert. British. Born in Hythe, Kent, 2 August 1948. Educated at University College of North Wales, Bangor, 1967-70, B.Sc. (honours) in applied zoology 1970; London School of Hygiene and Tropical Medicine, 1970-71, M.Sc. in medical zoology 1971. Married Sheila Cummins in 1973. Research Student, Medical Research Council, London, 1971-74. Agent: A.P. Watt Ltd., 26-28 Bedford Row, London WC1R 4HL. Address: 38 Peters Avenue, London Colney, Hertfordshire AL2 1NQ, England.

SCIENCE-FICTION PUBLICATIONS

Novels

Eye among the Blind. London, Faber, 1976; New York, Doubleday, 1977.
Earthwind. London, Faber, 1977; New York, Pocket Books, 1978.
Necromancer. London, Futura, 1978; New York, Avon, 1980.
Where Time Winds Blow. London, Faber, 1981.

Uncollected Short Stories

"Pauper's Plot," in *New Worlds* (London), 1968.
"Microcosm," in *New Writings in SF 20,* edited by John Carnell. London, Dobson, 1972.
"Ash, Ash," in *Stopwatch,* edited by George Hay. Nashville, Nelson, and London, New English Library, 1974.
"Ihl-Kizz,"in *Science Fiction Monthly* (London), June 1975.
"On the Inside," in *New Writings in SF 28,* edited by Kenneth Bulmer. London, Sidgwick and Jackson, 1976.
"The Time Beyond Age" and "The Graveyard Cross," in *Supernova 1.* London, Faber 1976.
"Travellers," in *Andromeda 1,* edited by Peter Weston. London, Futura, 1976; New York, St. Martin's Press, 1977.
"To Lay the Piper," in *Science Fiction Monthly 4* (London), 1976.
"A Small Event," in *Andromeda 2,* edited by Peter Weston. London, Futura, 1977.
"The Touch of a Vanish'd Hand," in *Vortex* (Lawrence, Kansas), 1977.
"High Pressure," in *Pulsar 2,* edited by George Hay. London, Penguin, 1979.
"In the Valley of the Statues," in *Aries 1,* edited by John Grant. Newton Abbot, Devon, David and Charles, 1979.
"Earth and Stone," in *Interfaces,* edited by Ursula K. Le Guin and Virginia Kidd. New York, Ace, 1980.
"Surviving Forces," in *Ad Astra.* London, Rowlot, 1980.

OTHER PUBLICATIONS

Other

Alien Landscapes, with Malcolm Edwards. London, Pierrot, 1979.
Tour of the Universe, with Malcolm Edwards. London, Pierrot, and New York, Mayflower, 1980.

Editor, *Encyclopedia of Science Fiction.* London, Octopus, and Baltimore, Hoen, 1978.
Editor, with Christopher Priest, *Stars of Albion* (anthology of British science fiction). London, Pan, 1979.

Robert Holdstock comments:
I am usually inspired to write by the contemplation of far distant places and far distant times, be they future or past. I quite deliberately build into my work and my characters both a passionate awareness of past times and a strong sense of alienation. I relish alien landscapes, but am not concerned with futuristic man. My characters are humans of my own age, and I try to use them, and the exotic locations of time and space, to explore the boundaries and potentiality of man's awareness, of his senses, of his evolution. All my work is concerned with evolution, and with the persistence of memory, the continued presence—genetically, spiritually, passionately—of all of life in all of mankind.

*   *   *

Robert Holdstock is a talented writer who examines alien cultures with insight and originality. His first novel, *Eye among the Blind,* presents Ree'hdworld, a wind-wracked planet where Earth installations encroach on the closely integrated life of the Ree'hd and the more primitive Rundii. Humans have spread through the galaxy and now they are engulfed by the Fear, a destructive disease that has fastened on Earth itself. Robert Zeitman returns to Ree'hdworld to find his former wife and fellow biologist Kristina seeking ultimate closeness with the aliens. She wishes to become a Ree'hd and share the life of Urak, their alien friend. The complexity of Ree'hd life—sensuous as their heavy bodies, cool as their dawn songs—is brilliantly described. The Ree'hd are evolving before the eyes of the humans but Zeitman is unable to penetrate the mysteries of the culture without the help of a strange intermediary, the blind Kevin Maguire. Long ago Maguire was given "sight" by the legendary third race of Ree'hdworld, the Pianhman. Where have they gone? The author's search for a convincing range of human relationships is sometimes halting but his instinctive grasp of alien atmosphere and the passion of the scientist make this an outstanding first novel.

Elspeth Mueller, the heroine of *Earthwind,* shares the life of the furry humans of the planet Aeran and is drawn on to discover the meaning of Aerani symbols, particularly the triple spiral called the Earthwind, at the risk of her sanity. The beauty of Aeran and the corporate life of the natives are finely drawn. The rituals of the Aerani are bloody—perhaps too bloody for some readers and Elspeth's obsession stems partly from the cruel rituals enacted on her home world. When a federation ship arrives to install mind-monitors Elspeth is determined that the Aerani culture shall not be disturbed. ShipMeister Gorstein is outwardly strong but he turns for support to his Rationalist or soothsayer Peter Ashkar. The relationships between this gentle man, the oracle the I-Ching, the ruthless shipMeister, and the native seer Iondai are examined with great skill. The planetary mystery—why do the Aerani duplicate the culture of Stone Age Celts on the distant Earth?—is solved at a dreadful cost. Peter Ashkar and Elspeth have their moments of enlightenment and they do not escape from Aeran.

Although his characters have much to endure Holdstock lightens the tone of his books with lyrical and reflective passages. This lightness of touch is found in the author's appealing short stories such as "A Small Event," "Travellers," and "In the Valley of the Statues." Holdstock's love of pre-historic Celtic cultures has inspired one of his finest stories, "Earth and Stone," and also an occult novel, *Necromancer.* This untidy, exciting book lacks the control and craftsmanship of his science-fiction works, but the theme of a trapped Elemental spirit carries the reader along. Cruachos, the raging demon, trapped in a stone font but still able to strike at human beings, must be tamed, and the American investigator Kline enlists the help of Françoise who has nurtured her extra-sensory powers among the standing stones of Brittany. The basic weakness of the book is the involvement of Adrian, the mindless child; the area of human reaction approached here is too sensitive.

Kline and Françoise are an interesting team who could well go on to solve more occult mysteries.

Robert Holdstock has already enriched science fiction, and he has found his own style: the future is his for the making.

—Cherry Wilder

HOLLAND, Cecelia (Anastasia). Also writes as Elizabeth Eliot Carter. American. Born in Henderson, Nevada, 31 December 1943. Educated at Pennsylvania State University, University Park, 1961-62; Connecticut College, New London, B.A. 1965. Address: c/o Knopf Inc., 201 East 50th Street, New York, New York 10022, U.S.A.

SCIENCE-FICTION PUBLICATIONS

Novel

Floating Worlds. New York, Knopf, and London, Gollancz, 1976.

OTHER PUBLICATIONS

Novels

The Firedrake. New York, Atheneum, 1966; London, Hodder and Stoughton, 1967.
Rakóssy. New York, Atheneum, and London, Hodder and Stoughton, 1967.
The Kings in Winter. New York, Atheneum, and London, Hodder and Stoughton, 1968.
Until the Sun Falls. New York, Atheneum, and London, Hodder and Stoughton, 1969.
Antichrist. New York, Atheneum, 1970; as *The Wonder of the World,* London, Hodder and Stoughton, 1970.
The Earl. New York, Knopf, 1971; as *Hammer for Princes,* London, Hodder and Stoughton, 1972.
The Death of Attila. New York, Knopf, 1973; London, Hodder and Stoughton, 1974.
Great Maria. New York, Knopf, 1974; London, Hodder and Stoughton, 1975.
Two Ravens. New York, Knopf, and London, Gollancz, 1977.
Valley of the Kings (as Elizabeth Eliot Carter). New York, Dutton, 1977; as Cecelia Holland, London, Gollancz, 1978.
City of God. New York, Knopf, and London, Gollancz, 1979.

Other

Ghost on the Steppe (juvenile). New York, Atheneum, 1969.
The King's Road (juvenile). New York, Atheneum, 1970.

*   *   *

Cecelia Holland's *Floating Worlds* is a space opera, though it lacks many of the traditional attributes of that form. There is no melodrama, only realism. The novel is unsentimental, unromantic, and contains characters who are real people rather than the archetypes of adventure fiction. Several characters, who in a more traditional space opera might have been relegated to the stock roles of villains, here take center stage. The protagonist, Paula Mendoza, is a selfish, intelligent, anarchic, and somewhat unreflective woman who sees an opportunity for power and seizes it. She gambles and loses.

Holland has not extrapolated a future. Her future worlds, though in part modeled on societies and sub-cultures of the past and present, are not developed in the manner of the realistic science-fiction writer. She takes a cyclical rather than progressive view of history. Human nature has not changed in this far future world. The Mar-tian Sunlight League is fascist. The polluted Earth, its inhabited regions covered by domes, is populated by anarchists who have no government, only a Committee for the Revolution. The Styths, mutants who rule an Empire on Saturn and Uranus, are violent and hold slaves. With their spaceships, a technical knowledge that enables them to live in artificial cities on such inhospitable worlds, and their anachronistic customs, the Styths may seem unlikely. But the 20th century has already experienced Nazi Germany—a warrior band with technology, not unlike its predecessors.

Holland is an author of historical novels, and Paula Mendoza bears a resemblance to the protagonist of *Great Maria,* a Norman woman who is the ally of her warlord husband. The Styth Empire has features in common with the Mongols of *Until the Sun Falls.* But the world of the book has its own integrity. Though the novel has devices found in other science fiction, such as spaceships, an interplanetary empire, mutants, and an O'Neill space cylinder, it is not obviously influenced by other SF authors. The style is clear and economical. Holland does not pad her historical novels with endless descriptions of clothing, castles, and weapons; neither does she fill *Floating Worlds* with cumbersome expository passages. The reader lives in this future world and experiences it directly. The book is unique and original, not derivative, though it can be placed in the tradition of Edgar Rice Burroughs.

Modeling a novel of the future on the past does not always work. Cecelia Holland makes it work. Her book is one of the most intelligent and rewarding examples of an often-maligned species of the genus science fiction. I suspect there will be imitators.

—Pamela Sargent

HOLLIS, H.H. Pseudonym for Ben Rhamey. American. Born in Dallas, Texas, in 1921. Educated at Southern Methodist University, Dallas, B.A. in economics; University of Texas, Austin, LL.B. Married. Admiralty lawyer. *Died in 1977.*

SCIENCE-FICTION PUBLICATIONS

Uncollected Short Stories (series: Corky Craven)

"Ouled Nail," in *If* (New York), March 1966.
"Cybernia," in *If* (New York), July 1966.
"The Long, Slow Orbits," in *Galaxy* (New York), May 1967.
"The Guerrilla Trees," in *If* (New York), June 1968.
"Eeeetz Ch," in *Galaxy* (New York), November 1968.
"Sword Game," in *The World's Best Science Fiction 1969,* edited by Donald A. Wollheim and Terry Carr. New York, Ace, and London, Gollancz, 1969.
"Stoned Counsel" (Craven), in *Again, Dangerous Visions,* edited by Harlan Ellison. New York, Doubleday, 1972; London, Millington, 1976.
"Too Many People," in *The Best Science Fiction for 1972,* edited by Frederik Pohl. New York, Ace, 1972.
"Different Angle," in *Amazing* (New York), December 1973.
"Every Day in Every Way" (Craven), in *Lone Star Universe,* edited by George W. Proctor and Steven Utley. Austin, Texas, Heidelberg, 1976.
"Arachne," "Dark Body," and "Inertia," in *Midnight Sun 3,* 1976.

*   *   *

Though included in *Lone Star Universe,* an anthology of science-fiction stories by Texans, H.H. Hollis avoids the possible danger of writing a purely local literature by writing in a pure, clear style—but not simplistically—about complex social issues, such as justice and ecology, which we cannot avoid because to do so is to condemn our culture to an early death.

"Sword Game" displays Hollis's talent for creating characters who are immediately recognizable and likeable despite, or perhaps because of, their inner confusion. A university professor and a hippie girl have reached a point in life that appears to be the fulfillment of their desires, but actually denotes stasis and boredom. The solution to their problem is at once silly and scientific: the professor will insert the girl into an "expanded cube" and drive a fencing foil through her body as part of a circus act. Since time in the cube represents an "endless instant" (as does a state of boredom), she will emerge unhurt in our time. When the original state of ennui reasserts itself, the professor entraps the girl permanently in the cube. Then, in a beautiful show of literary magic, the author has a graduate student "hero" free the girl and "imprison" the professor by distributing him evenly throughout the universe—a truly mind-expanding experience befitting a man who feels confined and lost in reality.

Two stories feature a futuristic Houston lawyer named Corky Craven who shares his author's profession as well as his interest in the drug culture and concern for our violent, polluted world. In "Stoned Counsel" numerous conflicting truths about industrial pollution, which boggle the normal, sane mind, are "dreamed" by drugged lawyers, who behave as though under the influence of a truth serum. The "triple sensory projector," a computer-like machine into which the attorneys are plugged, meanwhile sorts out the facts and decides the case on the basis of knowledge that would not be available without the drugs. So another kind of justice triumphs, a 1960's version with drugs used for good instead of evil. Drugs are also a feature of "Every Day in Every Way," a remarkable tale about the system of future justice in which criminals share both guild and punishment with their legal executioners. In "Year Judge" the judge actually dies with the condemned person at the end of his term and a new judge is elected, eliminating the lust for power that anyone in a position of authority is in danger of acquiring. Corky's purpose in this story is to witness the execution of the Year Judge (a female this year) and a woman (coincidence?) who has murdered her children. But the Witnesses are not mere societal observers: they are also plugged into the electric chairs and severely shocked until the judge and criminal are dead. The message is unmerciful. Justice is not simple or beautiful. It is an imperfect human attempt to bring order to our frightening, chaotic world which itself hurts those whom it strives to serve. Corky's cranial scar, a souvenir of his near-fatal witness of the law, reminds us that violence, though ugly, may be necessary to man's animal nature and a sort of payment for the great beauty he also enjoys.

H.H. Hollis, by mirroring our society in a way that strips it naked (as his characters sometimes appear to be), forces the reader to look honestly with him at our shared problems in the knowledge that, although they will not disappear, we must not abandon efforts to understand and reform our world.

—Rose Flores Harris

HOSKINS, Robert. Also writes as Grace Corren; John Gregory; Susan Jennifer; Michael Kerr. American. Born in Lyons Falls, New York, 23 May 1933. Attended Albany State College for Teachers, New York, 1951-52. Worked in family business, 1952-64; attendant, Wassaic State School for the Retarded, New York, 1964-66; House Parent, Brooklyn Home for Children, 1966-68; sub-agent, Scott Meredith Literary Agency, New York, 1967-68; Senior Editor, Lancer Books, New York, 1969-72. Since 1972, free-lance writer. Address: P.O. Box 930, Chatsworth, California 91311, U.S.A.

SCIENCE-FICTION PUBLICATIONS

Novels (series: Alnians)

Evil in the Family (as Grace Corren). New York, Lancer, 1972.
The Shattered People. New York, Doubleday, 1975.

Master of the Stars (Alnians). Toronto, Laser, 1976.
To Control the Stars (Alnians). New York, Ballantine, 1977.
Tomorrow's Son. New York, Doubleday, 1977.
Jack-in-the-Box Planet. Philadelphia, Westminster Press, 1978.
To Escape the Stars (Alnians). New York, Ballantine, 1978.
Legacy of the Stars (as John Gregory). New York, Nordon, 1979.

Uncollected Short Stories

"Weapon Master," in *Science Fiction Adventures* (London), January 1961.
"A World for Me," in *New Worlds* (London), February 1961.
"Morpheus," in *New Worlds* (London), June 1961.
"Second Chance," in *Amazing* (New York), April 1962.
"Reason for Honor," in *Fantastic* (New York), February 1969.
"The Problem Makers," in *The Far-Out People,* edited by Robert Hoskins. New York, New American Library, 1971.
"The Man Who Lived," in *The Edge of Never,* edited by Robert Hoskins. New York, Fawcett, 1973.
"Pop Goes the Weasel," in *Best Science Fiction Stories of the Year 1975,* edited by Lester del Rey. New York, Dutton, 1976.
"The Kelley's Eye," in *Tomorrow,* edited by Roger Elwood. New York, Evans, 1976.
"The Ghosts of Earth," in *Odyssey* (New York), Summer 1976.
"The Mountain," in *The Future Now,* edited by Robert Hoskins. New York Fawcett, 1977.

OTHER PUBLICATIONS

Novels

The House of Counted Hatreds (as Susan Jennifer). New York, Avon, 1973.
Country of the Kind (as Susan Jennifer). New York, Avon, 1975.
The Gemini Run (as Michael Kerr). New York, Charter, 1979.

Novels as Grace Corren

The Darkest Room. New York, Lancer, 1969.
A Place on Dark Island. New York, Lancer, 1971.
Mansions of Deadly Dreams. New York, Popular Library, 1973.
Dark Threshold. New York, Popular Library, 1977.
The Attic Child. Los Angeles, Pinnacle, 1979.
Survival Run (novelization of screenplay). Los Angeles, Pinnacle, 1979.

Play

Television Play: *Birthday Party* (*Kojak* series), 1976.

Other

Editor, *First Step Outward.* New York, Dell, 1969.
Editor, *Infinity 1-5.* New York, Lancer, 5 vols., 1970-73.
Editor, *The Stars Around Us.* New York, New American Library, 1970.
Editor, *Swords Against Tomorrow.* New York, New American Library, 1970.
Editor, *Tomorrow 1.* New York, New American Library, 1971.
Editor, *The Far-Out People.* New York, New American Library, 1971.
Editor, *Wondermakers 1-2.* New York, Fawcett, 2 vols., 1972-74.
Editor, *Strange Tomorrows.* New York, Lancer, 1972.
Editor, *The Edge of Never.* New York, Fawcett, 1973.
Editor, *The Liberated Future.* New York, Fawcett, 1974.
Editor, *The Future Now.* New York, Fawcett, 1977.
Editor, *Against Tomorrow.* New York, Fawcett, 1979.

Robert Hoskins comments:
An unhappy, and fat, childhood in a small Adirondack football village turned me early to escapism. Comics led to pulps, to fandom, through the letter columns. After years of writing, I began selling an occasional story while still gathering pounds of rejection slips. It was not until I worked, first, for an agent, and then as an editor, that I learned the techniques of novel construction. Impossible though

the idea is, I think all young writers should have a spell in both jobs. I consider myself strictly an entertainer; the one novel that is deliberately allegorical I have not at this date been able to sell. I've published 40 short stories, but find it easier to construct a novel. Once an idea comes, it seems to grow and grow.

* * *

Except for *Evil in the Family,* a gothic novel involving a time-travel fantasy, Robert Hoskins's major contribution to science fiction until 1975 was in writing short stories and editing anthologies. Since then he has developed earlier themes in a series of novels based on the inherent value of primitive versus technological man, the effects of free evolution versus outside interference and artificial controls, the need for change and progress and the threat of regression without it, the private, economic, and sociological reasons for galactic exploration. His works are always filled with action and adventure, monsters and barbaric peoples, advanced races and mercenary predators.

In *The Shattered People* Hoskins gradually reveals the secret ties between a savage desert world of naked hunters armed with slings and stones and a highly technological nuclear civilization ruled by a tyrannical council contemptuous of life. In the first, vicious cats prowl in packs and sentient aliens (huge, bird-like creatures) keep watch, while in the other urban rebels, aided by their "empress," a titular head virtually imprisoned in her own palace, meet in subterranean passages and plot to throw off their shackles. Mind-wipes and deportation thrust the strongest and most outspoken of the urban world into the primitive world, until one man's psi powers enable him to regain his memory and bridge the gap between the two, merging instinctive and rational.

Tomorrow's Son, set in the 23rd century, focuses on a geneticist and his android son, trapped in a rigid caste system, genetically predetermined. On Earth the father engages in forbidden android research to help revitalize the swiftly deteriorating genetic make-up of humanity, while on a primitive planet, Karyllia, his son struggles to protect alien humanoids from repeating humanity's evolutionary mistakes, only to discover that he must protect them not only from themselves but from the fanaticism and destructiveness of his own world. Both men prove pawns of larger schemes to protect Karyllia from outside interference and to force humans to accept change—change that can revitalize a regressing world where average I.Q. decreases yearly and masses of subhumans are crowded into barracks, experience sex and violence vicariously, and drown their minds in joyjuice. The book includes bizarre beasts of burden, strange snake-lizards in swamps, and primitive tribal conflicts. As usual, Hoskins emphasizes the stench of primitive worlds and the lack of respect for life in both primitive and advanced societies.

Hoskins's trilogy sets up a universal cycle of development and regression and postulates a series of stargates on most worlds, built by an ancient interstellar race; one sets the controls and steps into other worlds, some of which have regressed to the primitive while others have advanced to the stars. *Master of the Stars* focuses on the Alnians at the height of their development, struggling to avoid the contaminating barbarism of other worlds. *To Control the Stars* deals with an internal conflict in the Society for Hominidic Studies, a conflict that affects the future of thousands of worlds and which forces the central character to fight for his life from world to world and to seek the Alnians (the only humanoids with a continual history) for answers. The Society's original goal, observation of other worlds without interference, has been perverted in a lust for power, wealth, and exploitation to focus on evolutionary control and forced rapid progress. There is much action—escape, recapture, romance. *To Escape the Stars* picks up thousands of years later when the Society has been reduced to a library cult devoutly recording galactic history. A scheme to plunder a rich, high-gravity world of rural innocents leads first to treachery, and then to a revived search for the Alnians and their master codex to the stargates; the main figure changes from a jaded and unscrupulous exploiter to a student of the universe, and discovers the dangers of isolation and of failure to accept change and conflict.

—Gina Macdonald

HOWELLS, William Dean. American. Born in Martin's Ferry, Ohio, 1 March 1837. Largely self-educated. Married Elinor Mead in 1862 (died, 1910); one son and two daughters. Compositor, 1851-58, Reporter, 1858-60, and News Editor, 1860-61, *Ohio State Journal,* Columbus; also correspondent, in Columbus, for the Cincinnati *Gazette,* 1857; contributor to his father's newspaper, *The Sentinel,* Jefferson, Ohio, from 1852, and wrote for various national magazines from 1860; United States Consul in Venice, 1861-65; Assistant Editor, 1866-71, and Editor-in-Chief, 1871-81, *Atlantic Monthly,* Boston; Professor of Modern Languages, Harvard University, Cambridge, Massachusetts, 1869-71; wrote the "Editor's Study" column for *Harper's* magazine, 1886-92; Co-Editor, *Cosmopolitan* magazine, 1892. Recipient: American Academy Gold Medal, 1915. M.A.: Harvard University, Cambridge, Massachusetts, 1867; Litt.D.: Yale University, New Haven, Connecticut, 1901; Oxford University, 1904; Columbia University, New York, 1905; L.H.D.: Princeton University, New Jersey, 1912. President, American Academy, 1908-20. *Died 11 May 1920.*

SCIENCE-FICTION PUBLICATIONS

Novels

A Traveler from Altruria. New York, Harper, and Edinburgh, Douglas, 1894; complete edition, edited by Clara Marburg Kirk and Rudolf Kirk, as *Letters of an Altrurian Traveller (1893-1894),* Gainesville, Florida, Scholars' Facsimiles and Reprints, 1961.
Through the Eye of a Needle. New York and London, Harper, 1907.

OTHER PUBLICATIONS

Novels

Their Wedding Journey. Boston, Osgood, 1872; Edinburgh, Douglas, 1882.
A Chance Acquaintance. Boston, Osgood, 1873; Edinburgh, Douglas, 1882.
A Foregone Conclusion. Boston, Osgood, 1874.
The Lady of Aroostook. Boston, Houghton Osgood, 1879; Edinburgh, Douglas, 2 vols., 1882.
The Undiscovered Country. Boston, Houghton Mifflin, and London, Sampson Low, 1880.
Doctor Breen's Practice. Boston, Osgood, 1881; Edinburgh, Douglas, 1883.
A Modern Instance. Edinburgh, Douglas, 2 vols., 1882; Boston, Osgood, 1 vol., 1882.
A Woman's Reason. Boston, Osgood, and Edinburgh, Douglas, 1883.
The Rise of Silas Lapham. Boston, Ticknor, and Edinburgh, Douglas, 1885.
Indian Summer. Boston, Ticknor, and Edinburgh, Douglas, 1886.
The Minister's Charge; or, The Apprenticeship of Lemuel Barker. Edinburgh, Douglas, 1886; Boston, Ticknor, 1887.
April Hopes. Edinburgh, Douglas, 1887; New York, Harper, 1888.
Annie Kilburn. Edinburgh, Douglas, 1888; New York, Harper, 1889.
A Hazard of New Fortunes. New York, Harper, and Edinburgh, Douglas, 1889.
The Shadow of a Dream. Edinburgh, Douglas, and New York, Harper, 1890.
An Imperative Duty. New York, Harper, and Edinburgh, Douglas, 1891.
Mercy. Edinburgh, Douglas, 1892; as *The Quality of Mercy,* New York, Harper, 1892.
The World of Chance. Edinburgh, Douglas, and New York, Harper, 1893.
The Coast of Bohemia. New York, Harper, 1893.
The Day of Their Wedding. New York, Harper, 1896.
A Parting and a Meeting. New York, Harper, 1896; with *The Day of Their Wedding,* as *Idyls in Drab,* Edinburgh, Douglas, 1896.

The Landlord at Lion's Head. Edinburgh, Douglas, and New York, Harper, 1897.
The Open-Eyed Conspiracy. New York, Harper, 1897; Edinburgh, Douglas, 1898.
The Story of a Play. New York and London, Harper, 1898.
Ragged Lady. New York, Harper, 1899.
Their Silver Wedding Journey. London and New York, Harper, 1899; abridged edition, as *Hither and Thither in Germany*, New York and London, Harper, 1920.
The Kentons. New York and London, Harper, 1902.
The Flight of Pony Baker: A Boy's Town Story. New York and London, Harper, 1902.
Letters Home. New York and London, Harper, 1903.
The Son of Royal Langbrith. New York and London, Harper, 1904.
Miss Bellard's Inspiration. New York and London, Harper, 1905.
Fennel and Rue. New York and London, Harper, 1908.
New Leaf Mills. New York and London, Harper, 1913.
The Leatherwood God. New York, Century, and London, Jenkins, 1916.
The Vacation of the Kelwyns. New York and London, Harper, 1920.
Mrs. Farrell. New York and London, Harper, 1921.

Short Stories

A Fearful Responsibility and Other Stories. Boston, Osgood, 1881; as *A Fearful Responsibility and Tonelli's Marriage*, Edinburgh, Douglas, 1882.
A Pair of Patient Lovers. New York and London, Harper, 1901.
Questionable Shapes. New York and London, Harper, 1903.
Between the Dark and the Daylight: Romances. New York, Harper, 1907; London, Harper, 1912.

Plays

Samson, adaptation of the play by Ippolito D'Aste (produced on tour, 1874; New York, 1889). New York, Koppel, 1889.
The Parlor Car. Boston, Osgood, 1876; with *A Counterfeit Presentment*, Edinburgh, Douglas, 1882.
Out of the Question. Boston, Osgood, 1877; with *At the Sign of the Savage*, Edinburgh, Douglas, 1882.
A Counterfeit Presentment (produced Cincinnati, 1877; revised version, produced Detroit, 1877). Boston, Osgood, 1877; with *The Parlor Car*, Edinburgh, Douglas, 1882.
Yorick's Love, adaptation of a play by Manuel Tamayo y Baus (as *A New Play*, produced Cleveland, 1878; as *Yorick's Love*, produced New York, 1880; London, 1884). Included in *Complete Plays*, 1960.
The Sleeping-Car (produced New York, 1887). Boston, Osgood, 1883; in *Minor Dramas*, 1907.
The Register. Boston, Osgood, 1884; in *Minor Dramas*, 1907.
The Elevator (produced Streator, Illinois, 1885). Boston, Osgood, 1885; in *Minor Dramas*, 1907.
The Garroters (produced New York, 1886). New York, Harper, 1886; Edinburgh, Douglas, 1897.
A Foregone Conclusion, with William Poel, adaptation of the novel by Howells (produced New York, 1886). Included in *Complete Plays*, 1960.
Colonel Sellers as a Scientist, with Mark Twain, adaptation of the novel *The Gilded Age* by Twain and Charles Dudley Warner (produced New Brunswick, New Jersey, and New York, 1887). Included in *Complete Plays*, 1960.
The Mouse-Trap (produced New York, 1887-88; Edinburgh, 1897). Included in *The Mouse-Trap and Other Farces*, 1889; published separately, Edinburgh, Douglas, 1897.
A Sea-Change; or, Love's Stowaway: A Lyricated Farce, music by George Henschel. Boston, Ticknor, 1888.
The Mouse-Trap and Other Farces (includes *A Likely Story, Five O'Clock Tea, The Garroters*). New York, Harper, 1889.
The Sleeping-Car and Other Farces (includes *The Parlor Car, The Register, The Elevator*). Boston, Houghton Mifflin, 1889.
The Albany Depot. New York, Harper, 1892; Edinburgh, Douglas, 1897.

A Letter of Introduction. New York, Harper, 1892; Edinburgh, Douglas, 1897.
The Unexpected Guests. New York, Harper, 1893; Edinburgh, Douglas, 1897.
Evening Dress (produced New York, 1894). New York, Harper, 1893; Edinburgh, Douglas, 1897.
Bride Roses (produced New York, 1894). Boston, Houghton Mifflin, 1900; in *Minor Dramas*, 1907.
A Dangerous Ruffian (produced London, 1895).
A Previous Engagement. New York, Harper, 1897; in *Minor Dramas*, 1907.
Room Forty-Five. Boston, Houghton Mifflin, 1900; in *Minor Dramas*, 1907.
An Indian Giver. Boston, Houghton Mifflin, 1900; in *Minor Dramas*, 1907.
The Smoking Car. Boston, Houghton Mifflin, 1900; in *Minor Dramas*, 1907.
Minor Dramas. Edinburgh, Douglas, 2 vols., 1907.
The Mother and the Father. New York and London, Harper, 1909.
Parting Friends. New York and London, Harper, 1911.
The Night Before Christmas, and *Self-Sacrifice*, in *The Daughter of the Storage and Other Things in Prose and Verse*, 1916.
The Complete Plays of William Dean Howells, edited by Walter J. Meserve. New York, New York University Press, 1960.

Verse

Poems of Two Friends, with John J. Piatt. Columbus, Ohio, Follett Foster, 1860.
No Love Lost: A Romance of Travel. New York, Putnam, 1869.
Poems. Boston, Osgood, 1873.
Stops of Various Quills. New York, Harper, 1895.
The Mulberries in Pay's Garden. North Bend, Ohio, Scott, 1907.

Other

Lives and Speeches of Abraham Lincoln and Hannibal Hamlin. Columbus, Ohio, Follett Foster, 1860.
Venetian Life. London, Trubner, and New York, Hurd and Houghton, 1866; revised edition, Boston, Osgood, 1872; Boston, Houghton Mifflin, 2 vols., and London, Constable, 2 vols., 1907.
Italian Journeys. New York, Hurd and Houghton, 1867; revised edition, Boston, Osgood, 1872; London, Heinemann, and Boston, Houghton Mifflin, 1901.
Suburban Sketches. New York, Hurd and Houghton, 1871; revised edition, Boston, Osgood, 1872; abridged edition, as *A Day's Pleasure*, Osgood, 1876.
Sketch of the Life and Character of Rutherford B. Hayes. New York, Hurd and Houghton, 1876.
A Little Girl among the Old Masters. Boston, Osgood, 1884; London, Trubner, n.d.
Three Villages. Boston, Osgood, 1884.
Tuscan Cities. Boston, Ticknor, and Edinburgh, Douglas, 1885.
Modern Italian Poets: Essays and Versions. New York, Harper, and Edinburgh, Douglas, 1887.
A Boy's Town (juvenile). New York, Harper, 1890.
Criticism and Fiction. New York, Harper, and London, Osgood McIlvaine, 1891.
A Little Swiss Sojourn. New York, Harper, 1892.
Christmas Every Day and Other Stories Told for Children. New York, Harper, 1892.
My Year in a Log Cabin. New York, Harper, 1893.
My Literary Passions. New York, Harper, 1895.
Impressions and Experiences. New York, Harper, and Edinburgh, Douglas, 1896.
Stories of Ohio. New York, American Book Company, 1897.
Doorstep Acquaintance and Other Sketches. Boston, Houghton Mifflin, 1900.
Literary Friends and Acquaintance: A Personal Retrospect of American Authorship. New York and London, Harper, 1900.
Heroines of Fiction. New York and London, Harper, 2 vols., 1901.
Literature and Life: Studies. New York and London, Harper, 1902.

London Films. New York and London, Harper, 1905.
Certain Delightful English Towns. New York and London, Harper, 1906.
Roman Holidays and Others. New York and London, Harper, 1908.
Seven English Cities. New York and London, Harper, 1909.
My Mark Twain: Reminiscences and Criticisms. New York and London, Harper, 1910.
Imaginary Interviews. New York and London, Harper, 1910.
Familiar Spanish Travels. New York and London, Harper, 1913.
The Seen and Unseen at Stratford-on-Avon: A Fantasy. New York and London, Harper, 1914.
The Daughter of the Storage and Other Things in Prose and Verse. New York and London, Harper, 1916.
Years of My Youth (autobiography). New York, Harper, 1916; London, Harper, 1917.
Life in Letters of William Dean Howells, edited by Mildred Howells. New York, Doubleday, 2 vols., 1928; London, Heinemann, 1 vol., 1929.
Representative Selections, edited by Clara Marburg Kirk and Rudolf Kirk. New York, American Book Company, 1950.
Selected Writings, edited by Henry Steele Commager. New York, Random House, 1950.
Prefaces to Contemporaries (1882-1920), edited by George Arms, William M. Gibson, and Frederic C. Marston, Jr. Gainesville, Florida, Scholars' Facsimiles and Reprints, 1957.
Criticism and Fiction and Other Essays, edited by Clara Marburg Kirk and Rudolf Kirk. New York, New York University Press, 1959.
Mark Twain-Howells Letters: The Correspondence of Samuel L. Clemens and William Dean Howells 1872-1910, edited by Henry Nash Smith and William M. Gibson. Cambridge, Massachusetts, Harvard University Press, 2 vols., 1960; abridged edition, as *Selected Mark Twain-Howells Letters,* 1967.
Discovery of a Genius: William Dean Howells and Henry James, edited by Albert Mordell. New York, Twayne, 1961.
Selected Edition, edited by Ronald Gottesman. Bloomington, Indiana University Press, 1968—
Howells as Critic, edited by Edwin H. Cady. London, Routledge, 1973.

Editor, *Three Years in Chili,* by Mrs. C.B. Merwin. Columbus, Ohio, Follett Foster, 1861; as *Chili through American Spectacles,* New York, Bradburn, n.d.
Editor, *Choice Autobiographies.* Boston, Osgood, 6 vols., 1877, and Houghton Osgood, 2 vols., 1878.
Editor, with Thomas Sergeant Perry, *Library of Universal Adventure by Sea and Land.* New York, Harper, 1888.
Editor, *Mark Twain's Library of Humor.* New York, Webster, 1888.
Editor, *Poems of George Pellew.* Boston, Clarke, 1892.
Editor, *Recollections of Life in Ohio from 1813 to 1840,* by William Cooper Howells. Cincinnati, Clarke, 1895.
Editor, with Russell Sturgis, *Florence in Art and Literature.* Philadelphia, Booklovers Library, 1901.
Editor, with Henry Mills Alden, *Harper's Novelettes.* New York and London, Harper, 8 vols., 1906-08.
Editor, *The Great Modern American Short Stories: An Anthology.* New York, Boni and Liveright, 1920.
Editor, *Don Quixote,* by Cervantes, translated by Charles Jarvis. New York and London, Harper, 1923.

Translator, *Venice, Her Art-Treasures and Historical Associations: A Guide,* by Adalbert Müller. Venice, Münster, 1864.

*

Bibliography: *A Bibliography of William Dean Howells* by William M. Gibson and George Arms, New York, New York Public Library, 1948; in *Bibliography of American Literature 4* by Jacob Blanck, New Haven, Connecticut, Yale University Press, 1963.

*   *   *

William Dean Howells made a major contribution to utopian literature by inventing Altruria, a vision of an America which practiced what it preached in the Declaration of Independence. *A Traveler from Altruria,* "Letters of an Altrurian Traveler" (in *Cosmopolitan,* 1893-94), and *Through the Eye of a Needle* make up the Altrurian romances, Howells's statement on socialism and civil rights.

Edward Bellamy and Ignatius Donnelly had recently caught attention through social protest fiction in *Looking Backward, Equality,* and *Caesar's Column.* In a time of depression, strikes, Populism, and social change, Howells chose to point to a better society through a visit by Aristides (after Aristides the Just) Homos from an imaginary island in the Aegean where law, government, and social relations were based on altruism, a term adopted from Auguste Comte's *System of Positive Polity.* Howells imitated Oliver Goldsmith's *Citizen of the World* papers, introducing the outsider who asks pointed questions and marvels at peculiar customs. Altruria has much in common with Bacon's New Atlantis and More's Utopia and points toward Skinner's Walden II. Mr. Twelvemough, a well-known novelist who narrates *A Traveler from Altruria,* represents the American's attitude toward Homos. He disapproves of his fondness toward the lower classes. "Letters" is composed of five letters from Homos to his friend Cyril at home, openly critical of what he sees. Homos refers to New York as Babylon and to Americans as lost in the dark ages. *Through the Eye of a Needle* is also narrated by letters, some by Homos and the rest by Eveleth Strange, a beautiful widow who marries (after great conflict) Homos and moves to Altruria. Although the Altrurian works seem dated, they are important examples of attempts at social reform by an influential author.

—Mary S. Weinkauf

———————

HOYLE, Fred and Geoffrey. British. **HOYLE, Fred:** Born in Bingley, Yorkshire, 24 June 1915. Educated at Bingley Grammar School; Emmanuel College, Cambridge (Mayhew Prizeman, 1936; Smith's Prizeman, 1938; Goldsmith Exhibitioner; Senior Exhibitioner of the Royal Commission for the Exhibition of 1851), mathematical tripos 1936, M.A. 1939. Served in the Admiralty, London, 1939-45. Married Barbara Clark in 1939; one son, Geoffrey Hoyle, and one daughter. Research Fellow, St. John's College, 1939-72, University Lecturer in Mathematics, 1945-58, Plumian Professor of Astronomy and Experimental Philosophy, 1958-72, and Director, Institute of Theoretical Astronomy, 1966-72, Cambridge University. Visiting Professor, 1953, 1954, 1956, Fairchild Scholar, 1974-75, and since 1963, Associate in Physics, California Institute of Technology, Pasadena. Staff Member, Mount Wilson and Palomar observatories, California, 1957-62; Professor of Astronomy, Royal Institution, London, 1969-72; White Professor, Cornell University, Ithaca, New York, 1972-78. Honorary Research Professor, University of Manchester, since 1972, and University College, Cardiff, since 1975; since 1973, Honorary Fellow, St. John's College, Cambridge. Member, Science Research Council, 1968-72. Recipient: Royal Astronomical Society Gold Medal, 1968; Kalinga Prize, 1968; Astronomical Society of the Pacific Bruce Medal, 1970, and Klumpke-Roberts Award, 1977; Royal Society Medal, 1974. Guest of Honor, Frontiers of Astronomy Symposium, Venice, 1975. Sc.D.: University of East Anglia, Norwich, 1967; D.Sc.: University of Leeds, 1969; Universtiy of Bradford, 1975; University of Newcastle, 1976. Fellow, 1957, and Vice-President, 1969-71, Royal Society; Honorary Member, American Academy of Arts and Sciences, 1964; Foreign Associate, National Academy of Sciences (USA), 1969; President, Royal Astronomical Society, 1971-73. Knighted, 1972. Address: c/o Royal Society, 6 Carlton House Terrace, London SW1Y 5AG, England. **HOYLE, Geoffrey:** Born in Scunthorpe, Lincolnshire, 12 January 1942; son of Fred Hoyle. Educated at Bryanston School, Blandford Forum,

Dorset, 1955-59; St. John's College, Cambridge, 1961-62. Married Valerie Jane Coope in 1971. Worked in documentary film production, 1963-67. Address: Laytus Hall Farm, Inskip, Preston, Lancashire, England.

SCIENCE-FICTION PUBLICATIONS

Novels

Fifth Planet. London, Heinemann, and New York, Harper, 1963.
Rockets in Ursa Major. London, Heinemann, and New York, Harper, 1969.
Seven Steps to the Sun. London, Heinemann, and New York, Harper, 1970.
The Molecule Men: Two Short Novels (includes *The Monster of Loch Ness).* London, Heinemann, and New York, Harper, 1971.
The Inferno. London, Heinemann, and New York, Harper, 1973.
Into Deepest Space. New York, Harper, 1974; London, Heinemann, 1975.
The Incandescent Ones. London, Heinemann, and New York, Harper, 1977.
The Westminster Disaster. London, Heinemann, and New York, Harper, 1978.

Novels by Fred Hoyle

The Black Cloud. London, Heinemann, and New York, Harper, 1957.
Ossian's Ride. London, Heinemann, and New York, Harper, 1959.
A for Andromeda (novelization of TV serial), with John Eliot. London Souvenir Press, and New York, Harper, 1962.
Andromeda Breakthrough (novelization of TV serial), with John Eliot. London, Souvenir Press, and New York, Harper, 1964.
October the First Is Too Late. London, Heinemann, and New York, Harper, 1966.

Short Stories by Fred Hoyle

Element 79. New York, New American Library, 1967.

OTHER PUBLICATIONS

Other

Commonsense in Nuclear Energy. London, Heinemann, and San Francisco, Freeman, 1980.

OTHER PUBLICATIONS by Fred Hoyle

Plays

Rockets in Ursa Major (juvenile: produced London, 1962).

Television Plays (with John Eliot): *A for Andromeda* serial, 1961; *The Andromeda Breakthrough* serial, 1962.

Other

Some Recent Researches in Solar Physics. Cambridge, University Press, 1949.
The Nature of the Universe: A Series of Broadcast Lectures. Oxford, Blackwell, 1950; New York, Harper, 1951; revised edition, 1960.
A Decade of Decision. London, Heinemann, 1953.
Frontiers of Atronomy. London, Heinemann, and New York, Harper, 1955.
Man and Materialism. New York, Harper, 1956; London, Allen and Unwin, 1957.
Astronomy. London, Macdonald, and New York, Doubleday, 1962.

A Contradiction in the Argument of Malthus (lecture). Hull, University of Hull, 1963.
Star Formation. London, Her Majesty's Stationery Office, 1963.
Of Men and Galaxies. Seattle, University of Washington Press, 1964; London, Heinemann, 1965.
Nucleosynthesis in Massive Stars and Supernovae, with William A. Fowler. Chicago, University of Chicago Press, 1965.
Encounter with the Future. New York, Simon and Schuster, 1965.
The Asymmetry of Time (lecture). Canberra, Australian National University, 1965.
Galaxies, Nuclei, and Quasars. New York, Harper, 1965; London, Heinemann, 1966.
Man in the Universe. New York, Columbia University Press, 1966.
The New Face of Science. Cleveland, World, 1971.
From Stonehenge to Modern Cosmology. San Francisco, Freeman, 1972.
Nicolaus Copernicus: An Essay on His Life and Work. London, Heinemann, and New York, Harper, 1973.
Action-at-a-Distance in Physics and Cosmology, with J.V. Narlikar. San Francisco, Freeman, 1974.
Astronomy and Cosmology: A Modern Course. San Francisco, Freeman, 1975.
Astronomy Today. London, Heinemann, 1975; as *Highlights in Astronomy,* San Francisco, Freeman, 1975.
Ten Faces of the Universe. London, Heinemann, and San Francisco, Freeman, 1977.
On Stonehenge. London, Heinemann, and San Francisco, Freeman, 1977.
Energy or Extinction? The Case for Nuclear Energy. London, Heinemann, 1977.
The Cosmogony of the Solar System. Cardiff, University College Press, and Short Hills, New Jersey, Enslow, 1978.
Lifecloud: The Origin of Life in the Universe, with Chandra Wickramasinghe. London, Dent, 1978; New York, Harper, 1979.
Diseases from Space, with Chandra Wickramasinghe. London, Dent, 1979; New York, Harper, 1980.
The Physics-Astronomy Frontier, with J.V. Narlikar. San Francisco, Freeman, 1980.
Steady-State Cosmology Revisited. Cardiff, University College Press, 1980.
The Relation of Astronomy to Biology. Cardiff, University College Press, 1980.

OTHER PUBLICATIONS by Geoffrey Hoyle

Other

2010: Living in the Future (juvenile.). London, Heinemann, 1972; New York, Parents' Magazine Press, 1974.
Disaster (juvenile). London, Heinemann, 1975.
Ask Me Why, with Janice Robertson. London, Severn House, 1976.

*   *   *

Fred Hoyle is a distinguished British astronomer with an international reputation as a teacher and writer. He is the author of astronomy texts and other books ranging from a defense of nuclear power to speculations on the nature of the universe and man's place in creation; he supports the steady state theory and the view of continuous creation. Hoyle is the most prominent scientist writing SF today. He has written novels and stories, and other novels with his son, Geoffrey. The short stories are written as entertainments. They reveal a range and area of interest that readers do not usually associate with Hoyle's name. Most of the stories are either fantasy or fantasy science fiction, and many are comic; but they also include space opera and mystery. Hoyle shares certain comic interests with Asimov in human foibles, especially sexual mores, which are treated in a breezy, good-natured manner. Some of the comedy, however, is social and has teeth, as the title story of the collection, "Element 79." While Hoyle attacks perennials such as human greed, arrogance, and stupidity, he reserves his most trenchant comments for political and economic systems and their repressive, self-serving meddling with history.

The social and sexual comedy are important elements in most of the novels written by Fred Hoyle on his own and in collaboration with his son, but they support ideas and speculations drawn from hard science, especially astronomy. The best of these novels, *The Black Cloud, October the First Is Too Late,* and, with Geoffrey, *Fifth Planet,* are notable examples of speculative science fiction weaving together ideas from hard science with conventions of science fantasy enlivened by comic and sometimes satiric wit and an interest in philosophy and the arts. The overall effect is exceptionally thoughtful and stimulating entertainment for those who do not wish to sacrifice the life of the mind entirely to the enchantment of cosmic adventure. In all three novels the world's fate comes to depend upon the problem-solving powers of the scientific community, represented by a selected cast of characters. The reader has the feeling that Hoyle's characters, beside being plausible, are also representative portraits of men and women in the scientific community and its satellite social spheres in the arts on both sides of the Atlantic. He sees science as the means through which humans must learn to meet the challenges to human survival posed by a hostile if not implacable universe. However, the greatest challenge to mankind comes from human society itself with its outmoded political power structure. The focus of Hoyle's criticism is the obstructionism of political systems and their reliance on barbarous military and police enforcers of national and social interests that are portrayed as active threats to both individual freedom and survival. Contrasted to the enslaving, restrictive, and punative character of political structures is the open, liberating, and creative community of scientists, artists, and intellectuals with no political and social boundaries. Their common ground is the pursuit of truth, and in the novels mentioned, that pursuit involves a challenge to earth from an outside, cosmic force.

The Black Cloud introduces a massive, intelligent black cloud that invades the solar system, nearly destroying earth before communication is established by Cris Kingsley, a brilliant, iconoclastic Cambridge astronomer. The *Fifth Planet* challenge is from an invading star, Helios, and its planetary system of five planets which approaches our own solar system. In *October the First Is Too Late* temporal and geographical boundaries are scrambled for a time by a modulated radio signal of alien origin. In each novel we are given a romance of science. For a moment in history, the world's destiny turns on the calculations, speculations, and superior moral vision of scientists. The excitement is not only the working out of such cosmic challenges but also the sense of being at the center of forces that control human history. Hoyle effectively communicates and creates that sense of excitement, satisfaction, and wish-fulfillment in the rightful exercise of power by those who are qualified to use it by virtue of their intelligence and devotion to both the cause of mankind and of truth.

These and other SF novels by Hoyle effectively create the illusion of lived science in the character's discovery process, formulation of hypotheses, testing of theories, comparing notes with colleagues, and conferring on results. The prominent human dimension of Hoyle's fine novels grows from the resultant sense of competition and cooperation that characterize scientific inquiry at its best. Frustrated often by political and bureaucratic red-tape, Hoyle's scientist-heroes succeed through their capability for planning and taking individual action and for unselfish cooperation in scientific enterprise. As important as science is, both as a liberating and protecting force, Hoyle never ignores or sacrifices humanistic and artistic values. Indeed, one of the special strengths of the best fiction lies in its philosophic probing of the limitations of scientific knowledge and understanding. The great moral ideas science has contributed to the mind are freedom of inquiry and devotion to truth; but philosophy offers an engagement with permanent questions of human conduct and understanding, and art must offer its necessary corrective of value and sublimity if the search for truth regardless of consequences is not to mislead the race to melancholy despair, as it does the futurians of 8000 AD in *October the First Is Too Late.*

Although we have in Hoyle's fiction a delightful balance of adventure, hard science speculation, fantastic premises, and various types of comedy ranging from domestic to social, the most distinctive feature is the depth and power of thought that comes from Hoyle's interest both in the arts (especially music) and philosophy (especially metaphysics and cosmology). His novels stimulate the reader's speculative imagination, and are also rich, early and late, with inspired insights into the relation between the arts and the sciences, between man's instinct for design and beauty and the physical universe he inhabits. The novel richest in such insights is *October the First Is Too Late,* but a brief passage from *The Black Cloud* illustrates how Hoyle triumphantly brings together traditional interests of SF speculation and elite interest in the arts to shed light upon one another. The question under discussion is the black cloud's interest in Beethoven's B flat major Sonata: "Our appreciation of music has really nothing to do with sound, although I know that at first sight it seems otherwise. What we appreciate in the brain are electrical signals that we receive from the ears. Our use of sound is simply a convenient device for generating certain patterns of electrical activity. There is indeed a good deal of evidence that musical rhythms reflect the main electrical rhythms that occur in the brain." Hoyle has written entertaining space opera in *Rockets in Ursa Major* and science adventure melodrama in *Into Deepest Space* and *The Incandescent Ones* with Geoffrey Hoyle, but his permanent contribution to SF is to have brought esthetics, metaphysics, and speculative science together so compellingly in his major works.

—Donald L. Lawler

HUBBARD, L(aFayette) Ron(ald). American. Born in Tilden, Nebraska, 13 March 1911. Educated at George Washington University, Washington, D.C., B.S. in civil engineering 1934; Princeton University, New Jersey, 1945; Sequoia University, Ph.D. 1950. Married Mary Sue Whipp; two daughters and two sons. Wrote travel and aviation articles in the 1930's; explorer: Commander, Caribbean Motion Picture Expedition, 1931, West Indies Mineral Survey Expedition, 1932, and Alaskan Radio-Experimental Expedition, 1940. Director, Hubbard Foundation; Founding Director, Church of Scientology, 1952; Director, Dianetics and Scientology, 1952-66; resigned all directorships, 1966. Address: Saint Hill Manor, East Grinstead, Sussex, England.

SCIENCE-FICTION PUBLICATIONS

Novels

Death's Deputy. Los Angeles, Fantasy, 1948.
Final Blackout. Providence, Rhode Island, Hadley, 1948.
Slaves of Sleep. Chicago, Shasta, 1948.
Triton, and Battle of Wizards. Los Angeles, Fantasy, 1949.
The Kingslayer (includes "The Beast" and "The Invaders"). Los Angeles, Fantasy, 1949; as *Seven Steps to the Arbiter,* Chatsworth, California, Major, 1975.
Fear, and Typewriter in the Sky. New York, Gnome Press, 1951; London, Cherry Tree, 1952.
From Death to the Stars (includes *Death's Deputy* and *The Kingslayer*). Los Angeles, Fantasy, 1953.
Return to Tomorrow. New York, Ace, 1954; London, Panther, 1957.
Fear, Ultimate Adventure. New York, Berkley, 1970.

Short Stories

Ole Doc Methuselah. Austin, Theta Press, 1970.
Lives You Wished to Lead But Never Dared, edited by V.S. Wilhite. Clearwater, Florida, Theta Press, 1978

OTHER PUBLICATIONS

Novel

Buckskin Brigades. New York, Macaulay, 1937; London, Wright and Brown, 1938.

Verse

Hymn of Asia: An Eastern Poem. Los Angeles, Church of Scientology, 1974.

Other

Dianetics: The Modern Science of Mental Health. New York, Hermitage House, 1950; London, Ridgway, 1951.
Science of Survival. Wichita and East Grinstead, Sussex, Hubbard, 1951.
Self Analysis. Wichita, International Library of Arts and Science, 1951.
Dianetics: The Original Thesis. Wichita, Wichita Publishing, 1951.
Handbook for Preclears. Wichita, Scientic Press, 1951.
Notes on the Lectures of L. Ron Hubbard. Wichita, Hubbard, 1951.
Advanced Procedure and Axioms. Wichita, Hubbard, 1951.
Scientology 8-80. Phoenix, Hubbard, and East Grinstead, Sussex, Scientology, 1952.
A Key to the Unconscious. Phoenix, Scientic Press, 1952.
Dianetics: The Evolution of a Science. London, Hubbard, 1953; Phoenix, Hubbard, 1955.
Scientology: A History of Man. London, Hubbard, 1953.
How to Live Though an Executive. Phoenix, Hubbard, 1953.
Self-Analysis in Dianetics. London, Ridgway, 1953.
Scientology 8-8008. London, Hubbard, 1953.
Dianetics 1955! Phoenix, Hubbard, 1954.
The Creation of Human Ability: A Handbook for Scientologists. Phoenix, Hubbard, and London, Scientology, 1955.
This Is Scientology: The Science of Certainty. London, Hubbard, 1955.
The Key to Tomorrow (selections), edited by U. Keith Gerry. Johannesburg, Hubbard, 1955.
Scientology: The Fundamentals of Thought. London, Hubbard, 1956.
Problems of Work. Johannesburg, Hubbard, 1957.
Fortress in the Sky (on the moon). Washington, D.C., Hubbard, 1957.
Have You Lived Before This Life? London, Hubbard, 1958; New York, Vantage, 1960.
Self-Analysis in Scientology. London, Hubbard, 1959.
Scientology: Plan for World Peace. East Grinstead, Sussex, Scientology, 1964.
Scientology Abridged Dictionary. East Grinstead, Sussex, Hubbard, 1965.
A Student Comes to Saint Hill. Bedford, Sidney Press, 1965.
Scientology: A New Slant on Life. London, Hubbard, 1965.
East Grinstead. East Grinstead, Sussex, Hubbard, 1966.
Introduction to Scientology Ethics. Edinburgh, Scientology, 1968.
The Phoenix Lectures. Edinburgh, Scientology, 1968.
How to Save Your Marriage. Copenhagen, Scientology, 1969.
When in Doubt, Communicate: Quotations from the Work of L. Ron Hubbard, edited by Ruth Minshull and Edward M. Lefshon. Ann Arbor, Michigan, Scientology, 1969.
Scientology 0-8. Copenhagen, Scientology, 1970.
Mission into Time. Copenhagen, Scientology, 1973.
The Management Series 1970-1974. Los Angeles, American Saint Hill Organization, 1974.
The Organization Executive Course. Los Angeles, American Saint Hill Organization, 8 vols., 1974.
Dianetics Today. Los Angeles, Scientology, 1975.
Dianetics and Scientology Technical Dictionary. Los Angeles, Scientology, 1975.
The Technical Bulletins of Dianetics and Scientology. Los Angeles, Scientology, 10 vols., 1976.

The Volunteer Minister's Handbook. Los Angeles, Scientology, 1976.
Axioms and Logics. Los Angeles, Scientology, 1976.

Other texts and pamphlets published.

* * *

Best known as the author of *Dianetics* and founder of the Dianetics-based Church of Scientology, L. Ron Hubbard was a prolific writer of science fiction, fantasy, and adventure fiction during the 1930's and 1940's. A good deal of his output, much of it published in *Astounding* and its companion fantasy pulp *Unknown,* is of interest today only because of its use of a bizarre gnostic psychology that foreshadows Hubbard's later eminence as the founder and leader of a cult religion. Yet despite a prose that too often cries out for better editing than it ever received from John W. Campbell, some of his work justifies the high regard in which it is held by other veterans of the Golden Age.

Having begun his writing career with nautical adventure fiction, Hubbard often composed science fiction and fantasy by merely displacing swashbuckling epic into the new context through use of a fantastic premise or framing device. For instance, in *Slaves of Sleep* a meek young shipping magnate is accused of a gruesome murder which occurs when a North African *jinni* is released from an ancient jar. Jailed for the murder, Jan Palmer finds himself plunged while asleep into an alternate life as a cynical, troublemaking, but courageous sailor. In that world dominated by *jinn* and other demons out of middle eastern folklore, he is also in trouble with the authorities. As the two stories clunk along in uneasy partnership, the bookish shipowner's personality is modified by that of his alter ego, who purloins a powerful talisman and wins a battle in the other world. All this results in Jan being cleared and restored to his inheritance in this world, winning a bride in the bargain. In spite of a few moments of social satire and a potentially interesting metafiction about fantasy's role in constructing the personality, the novel remains a blood-and-thunder romance in an awkward framework.

Typewriter in the Sky, clearly Hubbard's most successful fiction, also uses such a framing device. In this delightful bagatelle (which sports, along with several characters bearing Hubbard pen names, one named Bagatela), a musician finds himself transported into the world of a romance of the Spanish Main being composed hastily by a friend who writes mass-market adventure fiction. Mike DeWolf is not only protagonist, but also reader of the text: buffeted by narrative implausibilities and inconsistencies as well as a major rewrite which sets up an alternate but no less fatal ending, he is finally thrust out of the fiction to return as a vagrant on the streets of modern New York, wondering if his *primary* universe is being created by a God "in a dirty bathrobe." This consummate "mockery of plot" appeared a quarter-century before the vogue of Barth, Pynchon, and Vonnegut, and long before Borges became generally known to American writers. A similar vein of humor appears in *Triton,* a well-conceived if clumsily written lark about a meek man who swallows a sea-god, thereby gaining the *machismo* needed to face down Neptune himself as well as his own dry land persecutors. *Triton,* in fact, is a reprise of the fundamental fantasy of *Slaves of Sleep,* but is much tighter and self-deprecating than the earlier piece. Two other early novels, *Fear* and *Death's Deputy,* are noteworthy only in their use of demons to rationalize, respectively, a jealous husband's ax murder of his wife and his best friend, and an RCAF pilot's connection with a statistically unlikely number of accidental or violent deaths. Taken together with the other pieces discussed, they show that Hubbard's true disposition was toward the weird tale rather than science fiction.

When Hubbard is discussed as a science-fiction writer, it is apparently obligatory to praise as his finest effort the militaristic *Final Blackout.* It is hard to understand why, unless its virulent fascism—which the text pathetically attempts to deny—appeals to critics repelled more by the socialist baby than by the Stalinist bath water. It reads like a plot summary for a much longer work, and its hero (known only as "the Lieutenant") is developed neither as a realistic character nor as a credible personification. Only if read ironically—as Hubbard surely did not intend—does *Final Blackout* amount to anything more than a fascist utopia and an anti-social-democratic tract.

Hubbard's post-war science fiction, such as *Ole Doc Methuselah* and *The Kingslayer,* is of little note. The Old Doc stories are about the Galaxy in an interstellar EMS vehicle curing disease and injury, dispelling ignorance, and (extra-legally, it seems) aiding the battle against injustice. The series is vintage space opera: Doc has a cute alien sidekick, he is as comfortable wielding a blaster as a hypodermic, and he faces down hordes of tyrannical villains in his capacity as a Soldier of Light. With all the excitement, however, Doc's favorite pastime is fishing, a fact which provides a bit of ironic counterpoint to the underlying fantasy of unaging omnipotence. Even less need be said of *The Kingslayer,* a tale of Byzantine conspiracy about Kit Kellan, a young drifter who is rescued from the authorities by revolutionaries and recruited to assassinate the all-powerful Galactic Arbiter. Kit manages to overcome all obstacles to finding the Arbiter, but is seized just before reaching his goal. Brought before the Arbiter, he learns that the Arbiter is not a despot, that the "revolutionaries" are operatives loyal to the Council, that his mission has been a test of his mettle, and that he is in fact the Arbiter's son and heir presumptive. The story is thus a variation on the old galactic empire motif, with more than a hint of the militaristic strongman theme found in *Final Blackout.*

Hubbard's contribution to science fiction, then, even if one considers the many short stories not mentioned here, seems to have been an odd one. His success as a fiction machine was emulated by many younger writers, and he was admired by Campbell and other *Astounding* contemporaries. His true talents, however, lay in the direction of light fantasy and ironic, comic manipulation of pulp conventions. It is probable that he would have developed further along those lines had not World War II convinced him that he had a messianic obligation to save the world through "dianetic therapy" instead of continuing to write fiction. So instead, L. Ron Hubbard turned science fantasy into a technological version of the old gnostic religion. Scientology remains Hubbard's supreme science fiction.

—John P. Brennan

HUGHES, Zach. Pseudonym for Hugh Zachary; also writes as Ginny Forman; Elizabeth Hughes; Peter Kanto; Derral Pilgrim; Olivia Rangely; Marcus Van Heller; Elizabeth Zachary. American. Born in Holdenville, Oklahoma, 12 January 1928. Educated at Oklahoma A & M College, 1945-46; University of North Carolina, Chapel Hill, B.A. in journalism 1951. Served in the 82nd Airborne Division of the United States Army, 1946-48. Married Elizabeth Wiggs in 1948; two daughters. Worked in radio and television broadcasting, 1948-61. Since 1962, part-time fisherman, guide, florist, construction worker, and free-lance writer. Agent: Ray Peekner Literary Agency, 2625 North 36th Street, Milwaukee, Wisconsin 53210. Address: 7 Pebble Beach Drive, Yaupon Beach, North Carolina 28461, U.S.A.

SCIENCE-FICTION PUBLICATIONS

Novels

The Book of Rack the Healer. New York, Award, 1973.
The Legend of Miaree. New York, Ballantine, 1974.
Gwen, In Green (as Hugh Zachary). New York, Fawcett, 1974; London, Cornonet, 1976.
Tide. New York, Putnam, 1974.
Seed of the Gods. New York, Berkley, 1974; London, Hale, 1980.
The Stork Factor. New York, Berkley, 1975.
For Texas and Zed. New York, Popular Library, 1976.
Tiger in the Stars. Toronto, Laser, 1976.
The St. Francis Effect. New York, Berkley, 1976.
Killbird. New York, New American Library, 1980.

OTHER PUBLICATIONS as Hugh Zachary

Novels

One Day in Hell. New York, Newstand Library, 1961.
A Small Slice of War. New York, Caravelle, 1968.
A Feast of Fat Things. Jacksonville, Illinois, Harris Wolfe, 1968.
Rake's Junction. New York, Lancer, 1970.
The Legend of the Deadly Doll. New York, Award, 1973.
Second Chance. Canoga Park, California, Major, 1976.
Dynasty of Desire, with Elizabeth Zachary. New York, Dell, 1978.
The Land Rushers, with Elizabeth Zachary. New York, Dell, 1978.
The Golden Dynasty, with Elizabeth Zachary. New York, Dell, 1980.
Bloodrush. New York, Nordon, 1981.

Some 60 other novels published under various pseudonyms

Play

Screenplay: *Tide.*

Other

The Beachcomber's Handbook of Seafood Cookery. Winston Salem, North Carolina, Blair, 1969.
Wild Card Poker. Brattleboro, Vermont, Stephen Greene Press, 1975.

*   *   *

Zach Hughes is the pseudonym Hugh Zachary has used for his science fiction. His first SF novel, *The Book of Rack the Healer,* is in many ways his best book. Earth, centuries after a nuclear holocaust, is dying from accumulated radiation and pollution. Mankind has evolved into four species: Keepers, moronic women whose brains store knowledge like a computer; Far Seers, males who supply leadership; Healers, males who have the power to travel on the Earth's surface and collect raw materials to feed the population by regenerating cells damaged by the corrosive atmosphere; and Power Givers, women with the power of flight. Hughes creates an innovative ecological puzzle, while developing the characters of Rack the Healer, Red Earth the Far Seer, and Beautiful Wings the Power Giver. The ending is tragic, yet Hughes manages to moderate the pathos with hope. *Killbird* returns to these themes. Eban the Hairy One is one of a small group of primitives surviving a nuclear holocaust. Zachary cunningly invents a sophisticated society, while sending Eban on an incredible set of adventures in the dangerous ravaged world. *Killbird* possesses many of Hughes's best developed characters—Eban, his wife Mar, and the bitter Yuree—as well as some of his best writing.

The Legend of Miaree is a clever positioning of a sociological disaster with the problems of translating alien texts. It is really two books in one; the actual legend of Miaree is being read by human students at a planetary university as the translation of the only surviving artifact of two destroyed alien races. The students and their professor provide commentary on the deadly progression of events, commentary that gives additional insight into the contrast between alien societies. Hughes does a masterful job of creating the character of Miaree and her culture as two galaxies collide, threatening two star races. The ending is grim, but Hughes skillfully lightens the mood by shifting the action to the human students and their wise professor. *Seed of the Gods,* an attempt to spoof the von Daniken cult, is a routine "first contact" novel.

Two ecological disaster novels, *Tide* and *The St. Francis Effect,* suffer from undeveloped characters, though some of the information is fascinating. In *Tide* efforts to produce increased breeding of fish lead to mutations which trigger extreme aggression in the fish and the people who eat them. In *The St. Francis Effect* a deep-ocean mining operation in the Pacific brings up an ages-old parasite carried by mosquitos. The resultant plague has a 100% mortality rate, and in a matter of days turns its victims into mummified corpses. The book is an effective disaster novel but the mosquito and the disease—not the human characters—are the stars.

The Stork Factor and *For Texas and Zed* are both superman novels. In the first, set in a repressive and totalitarian future society totally controlled by a religious dictatorship, a young priest, Luke, has developed psi powers, and becomes a part of the underground plotting to overthrow the government. At the time, an advanced alien race sends a starship to Earth to determine the threat its technology presents. The impact of the convergence of events produces a fast-paced, entertaining adventure novel. In the second, Lex Murichon, one of the leading figures of the planet Texas delegation to the Earth Empire, is a blend of the heroes of H. Beam Piper and John J. McGuire's *A Planet for Texans* (1958) and Harry Harrison's satiric *Bill, The Galactic Hero* (1965). The fierce independence of the Texans is translated into a culture on a hidden solitary planet where the new Texans provide meat to the Empire while staying above the cold war between the Empire and the Cassiopeian battle fleet. But Lex gets involved as a gunner aboard an Empire starship, deserts and heads back to Texas, thus causing a state of war. This much of the novel is accomplished with wit and style. But after Texas successfully defends itself against the Empire's attacks and Lex becomes the leader of the Texas forces—evolving into an all-conquering Alexander the Great figure—the book lags badly.

Tiger in the Stars is a van Vogtian novel of humans encountering aliens of vast supremacy. The hero, John Plank, is turned into a cyborg linked with a starship of incredible power. Unfortunately, the novel drifts from subplot to subplot without developing a picture of future human culture or the fantastic alien culture. The ending becomes predictable far too soon and the end result is a flatness usually absent from Hughes's better work.

In *Gwen, In Green,* a young couple moves into a rambling house on an isolated island in the South. But within the clear pool near the house grow alien plants who establish contact with the young wife, Gwen. As the relationship between Gwen and the alien plants become stronger, the plot explodes with murder and sexuality. The book features a memorable grimness as well as a powerful examination of the eerie symbiotic relationship of human and alien.

—George Kelley

HULL, E(dna) M(ayne). American. Born in Brandon, Manitoba, Canada, 1 May 1905. Married A.E. van Vogt, *q.v.*, in 1939. Secretary to Henry Wise Wood. Guest of Honor, 4th World Science Fiction Convention, 1946. *Died 20 January 1975.*

Science-Fiction Publications

Novels

Planets for Sale, with A.E. van Vogt.   New York, Fell, 1954; in *A van Vogt Omnibus,* London, Sidgwick and Jackson, 1967.
The Winged Man, with A.E. van Vogt.   New York, Doubleday, 1966; London, Sidgwick and Jackson, 1967.

Short Stories

Out of the Unknown, with A.E. van Vogt.   Los Angeles, Fantasy, 1948; as *The Sea Thing,* London, Sidgwick and Jackson, 1970.

*   *   *

E.M. Hull was married to A.E. van Vogt, with whom she sometimes collaborated, although not to the extent as did Henry Kuttner with C.L. Moore. In the 1940's she published a number of minor stories in *Astounding* and *Unknown,* among them the Artur Blord series, a cycle of space operas with an unfailingly successful unscrupulous businessman as protagonist; all the stories except the first, "Abdication" (*Astounding*, April 1943), were combined as

Planets for Sale. Partially explaining the fact that van Vogt's name was listed as co-author, Hull says, "The great problem was my almost total lack of scientific knowledge. To overcome this handicap, my husband and I figured out a story pattern which would bypass the need to show a science explanation." Van Vogt's hand is more in evidence in *The Winged Man,* in which the characters, in typical van Vogt fashion, take their time to ponder things and are apt to come up with conclusions, said to be the result of deep thought, which fail to carry the slightest inner conviction. This novel presents a meeting of minds in the far future, to which representatives from various ages of the history of mankind are snatched via time-machine to help in a conflict between winged and sea-based human races, including an American nuclear submarine. The conflict between the two branches of the human race is typically resolved by an attack on a third party, an alien invader responsible for the landmasses of Earth becoming submerged in the ocean. The whole book is a poor sort of space opera, filled with implausible dialogue and "futuristic" touches that are merely ridiculous.

Planets for Sale, while being hardly less implausible, has the virtue of being completely unpretentious both in literary execution and moral intentions. It describes episodically a super-capitalist future world of the Ridge Stars, a frontier world with a complete laissez-faire society, where the large corporations run by quick witted Operators make their own laws. The hero is different from the villains only in being more successful in his dealings (or double-dealings) with other entrepreneurs, plain gangsters, villainous scientists, and the relics of an ancient reptilian race, the Skal. The problems are solved not so much by deduction from logical premises as by sleights of hand and pulling scientific rabbits out of the hat. In fact, the book's redeeming feature is the audacity with which the author seems determined to avoid none of the clichés of space opera, and presents a picture of a corrupt society that might have been written with the intention to discredit capitalism.

Out of the Unknown contains three fantasy stories by each of the two writers. All three of Hull's stories deal with wish-fulfillment, the first two, "The Wishes We Make" and "The Ultimate Wish," openly, "The Patient" in a hidden way. The last is a van Vogtian story of a different sort of persecuted superman, in which dreaded cancer is seen as the first step towards the development of homo superior; the other two stories are clumsy variations of the topic of the foolish wishes.

—Franz Rottensteiner

HUNTER, Evan. Also writes as Curt Cannon; Hunt Collins; Ezra Hannon; Richard Marsten; Ed McBain. American. Born in New York City, 15 October 1926. Educated at Cooper Union, New York, 1943-44; Hunter College, New York, B.A. 1950 (Phi Beta Kappa). Served in the United States Navy, 1944-46. Married 1) Anita Melnick in 1949 (divorced), three children; 2) Mary Vann Finley in 1973, one step-daughter. Recipient: Mystery Writers of America Edgar Allan Poe Award, 1957. Agent: Owen Laster, William Morris Agency, 1350 Avenue of the Americas, New York, New york, 10019; or, Ed Victor Ltd., 27 Soho Square, London W1V 6AY, England.

Science-Fiction Publications

Novels

Find the Feathered Serpent (juvenile).   Philadelphia, Winston, 1952.
Rocket to Luna (juvenile; as Richard Marsten).   Philadelphia, Winston, 1952; London, Hutchinson, 1954.
Danger: Dinosaurs! (juvenile; as Richard Marsten).   Philadelphia, Winston, 1953.

Tomorrow's World (as Hunt Collins).   New York, Avalon, 1956; as *Tomorrow and Tomorrow,* New York, Pyramid, 1956; as Ed McBain, London, Severn House, 1980.

Short Stories

The Jungle Kids.   New York, Pocket Books, 1956; augmented edition as *The Last Spin,* London, Constable, 1960.
Happy New Year, Herbie, and Other Stories.   New York, Simon and Schuster, 1963; London, Constable, 1965.

OTHER PUBLICATIONS

Novels

The Big Fix.   N.p., Falcon, 1952; as *So Nude, So Dead* (as Richard Marsten), New York Fawcett, 1956.
Don't Crowd Me.   New York, Popular Library, 1953; London, Consul, 1960; as *The Paradise Party,* London, New English Library, 1968.
Cut Me In (as Hunt Collins).   New York, Abelard Schuman, 1954; London, Boardman, 1960; as *The Proposition,* New York, Pyramid, 1955.
The Blackboard Jungle.   New York, Simon and Schuster, 1954; London, Constable, 1955.
Second Ending.   New York, Simon and Schuster, and London, Constable, 1956; as *Quartet in H,* New York, Pocket Books, 1957.
Strangers When We Meet.   New York, Simon and Schuster, and London, Constable, 1958.
I'm Cannon—For Hire (as Curt Cannon).   New York, Fawcett, 1958; London, Fawcett, 1959.
A Matter of Conviction.   New York, Simon and Schuster, and London, Constable, 1959; as *The Young Savages,* New York, Pocket Books, 1966.
Mothers and Daughters.   New York, Simon and Schuster, and London, Constable, 1961.
Buddwing.   New York, Simon and Schuster, and London, Constable, 1964.
The Paper Dragon.   New York, Delacorte Press, 1966; London, Constable, 1967.
A Horse's Head.   New York, Delacorte Press, 1967; London, Constable, 1968.
Last Summer.   New York, Doubleday, 1968; London, Constable, 1969.
Sons.   New York, Doubleday, 1969; London, Constable, 1970.
Nobody Knew They Were There.   New York, Doubleday, and London, Constable, 1971.
Every Little Crook and Nanny.   New York, Doubleday, and London, Constable, 1972.
Come Winter.   New York, Doubleday, and London, Constable, 1973.
Streets of Gold.   New York, Harper, 1974; London, Macmillan, 1975.
Doors (as Ezra Hannon).   New York, Stein and Day, 1975; London, Macmillan, 1976.
The Chisholms: A Novel of the Journey West.   New York, Harper, and London, Hamish Hamilton, 1976.
Walk Proud.   New York, Bantam, 1979.
Love, Dad.   New York, Crown, 1981.

Novels as Richard Marsten

Runaway Black.   New York, Fawcett, 1954; London, Red Seal, 1957.
Murder in the Navy.   New York, Fawcett, 1955; as *Death of a Nurse* (as Ed McBain), New York, Pocket Books, 1968; London, Hodder and Stoughton, 1972.
The Spiked Heel.   New York, Holt, 1956; London, Constable, 1957.
Vanishing Ladies.   New York, Permabooks, 1957; London, Boardman, 1961.
Even the Wicked.   New York, Permabooks, 1958; London, Severn House, 1979.

Big Man.   New York, Pocket Books, 1959; London, Penguin, 1978.

Novels as Ed McBain

Cop Hater.   New York, Simon and Schuster, 1956; London, Boardman, 1958.
The Mugger.   New York, Simon and Schuster, 1956; London, Boardman, 1959.
The Pusher.   New York, Simon and Schuster, 1956; London, Boardman, 1959.
The Con Man.   New York, Simon and Schuster, 1957; London, Boardman, 1960.
Killer's Choice.   New York, Simon and Schuster, 1958; London, Boardman, 1960.
Killer's Payoff.   New York, Simon and Schuster, 1958; London, Boardman, 1960.
April Robin Murders, with Craig Rice (completed by McBain).   Random House, 1958; London, Hammond, 1959.
Lady Killer.   New York, Simon and Schuster, 1958; London, Boardman, 1961.
Killer's Wedge.   New York, Simon and Schuster, 1959; London, Boardman, 1961.
'Til Death.   New York, Simon and Schuster, 1959; London, Boardman, 1961.
King's Ransom.   New York, Simon and Schuster, 1959; London, Boardman, 1961.
Give the Boys a Great Big Hand.   New York, Simon and Schuster, 1960; London, Boardman, 1962.
The Heckler.   New York, Simon and Schuster, 1960; London, Boardman, 1962.
See Them Die.   New York, Simon and Schuster, 1960; London, Boardman, 1963.
Lady, Lady, I Did It!   New York, Simon and Schuster, 1961; London, Boardman, 1963.
Like Love.   New York, Simon and Schuster, 1962; London, Hamish Hamilton, 1964.
Ten Plus One.   New York, Simon and Schuster, 1963; London, Hamish Hamilton, 1964.
Ax.   New York, Simon and Schuster, and London, Hamish Hamilton, 1964.
The Sentries.   New York, Simon and Schuster, and London, Hamish Hamilton, 1965.
He Who Hesitates.   New York, Delacorte Press, and London, Hamish Hamilton, 1965.
Doll.   New York, Delacorte Press, 1965; London, Hamish Hamilton, 1966.
Eighty Million Eyes.   New York, Delacorte Press, and London, Hamish Hamilton, 1966.
Fuzz.   New York, Doubleday, and London, Hamish Hamilton, 1968.
Shotgun.   New York, Doubleday, and London, Hamish Hamilton, 1969.
Jigsaw.   New York, Doubleday, and London, Hamish Hamilton, 1970.
Hail, Hail, The Gang's All Here!   New York, Doubleday, and London, Hamish Hamilton, 1971.
Sadie When She Died.   New York, Doubleday, and London, Hamish Hamilton, 1972.
Let's Hear It for the Deaf Man.   New York, Doubleday, and London, Hamish Hamilton, 1973.
Hail to the Chief.   New York, Random House, and London, Hamish Hamilton, 1973.
Bread.   New York, Random House, and London, Hamish Hamilton, 1974.
Where There's Smoke.   New York, Random House, and London, Hamish Hamilton, 1975.
Blood Relatives.   New York, Random House, 1975; London, Hamish Hamilton, 1976.
Guns.   New York, Random House, 1976; London, Hamish Hamilton, 1977.
So Long as You Both Shall Live.   New York, Random House, and London, Hamish Hamilton, 1976.
Long Time No See.   New York, Random House, and London, Hamish Hamilton, 1977.

Goldilocks. New York, Arbor House, 1977; London, Hamish Hamilton, 1978.
Calypso. New York, Viking Press, and London, Hamish Hamilton, 1979.
Ghosts. New York, Viking Press, and London, Hamish Hamilton, 1980.

Short Stories

I Like 'em Tough (as Curt Cannon). New York, Fawcett, 1958.
The Empty Hours (as Ed McBain). New York, Simon and Schuster, 1962; London, Boardman, 1963.
The Beheading and Other Stories. London, Constable, 1971.
The Easter Man (a Play) and Six Stories. New York, Doubleday, 1972; as *Seven,* London, Constable, 1972.

Plays

The Easter Man (produced Birmingham and London, 1964; as *A Race of Hairy Men,* produced New York, 1965). Included in *The Easter Man (a Play) and Six Stories,* 1972.
The Conjuror (produced Ann Arbor, Michigan, 1969).
Stalemate (produced New York, 1975).

Screenplays: *Strangers When We Meet,* 1960; *The Birds,* 1963; *Walk Proud,* 1979

Other

The Remarkable Harry (juvenile). New York and London, Abelard Schuman, 1961.
The Wonderful Button (juvenile). New York, Abelard Schuman, 1961; London, Abelard Schuman, 1962.
Me and Mr. Stenner (juvenile). Philadelphia, Lippincott, 1976; London, Hamish Hamilton, 1977.

Editor (as Ed McBain), *Crime Squad.* London, New English Library, 1968.
Editor (as Ed McBain), *Homicide Department.* London, New English Library, 1968.
Editor (as Ed McBain), *Downpour.* London, New English Library, 1969.
Editor (as Ed McBain), *Ticket to Death.* London, New English Library, 1969.

*

Manuscript Collection: Mugar Memorial Library, Boston University.

*   *   *

Although he is best known as a mainstream novelist of considerable stature (*The Blackboard Jungle, Last Summer, Sons*), and as today's finest practitioner of the police procedural novel (the 87th Precinct series of more than 30 novels under his Ed McBain pseudonym), Evan Hunter began his career in the early 1950's as a science fiction writer and contributed a number of short stories and novels to the genre during the first half of that decade. The best of the stories are "Inferiority Complex," "Million Dollar Maybe," which involves a magazine's offer of one million dollars to the first private citizen who reaches the moon and returns alive, and "The Fallen Angel," an excellent deal-with-the-devil fantasy with a circus background.

All three of Hunter's early SF novels are adventure stories for young readers. *Find the Feathered Serpent,* an interesting blend of time travel and Mayan history, is perhaps the best. *Rocket to Luna* is an account of the first moon-bound rocket, and *Danger, Dinosaurs!* again utilizes the time-travel theme, in this case into the dim past when saurians roamed the earth. Hunter's most memorable contribution to science fiction is his only adult novel, *Tomorrow's World*—a caustically satirical study of a future in which narcotics have been legalized and there is a bitter struggle for control of publishing, movies, and television between the Vikes, who are responsible for the current vogue of drug use and vicarious enter-

tainment, and the Realists, who advocate a return to the moral standards of the past. The novel, which has deservedly remained in print during most of the past quarter-century, is an expanded version of "Malice in Wonderland" (*If,* January 1954); interestingly, "Malice" is told in the first person, by the Vike literary agent Van Brant, while *Tomorrow's World* is a third-person novel whose view-point shifts between Brant and members of the Realist movement. What makes both novella and novel especially fascinating is the combination of Hunter's unsurpassed ear for dialogue and his meticulous use of a drug-oriented, futuristic slang.

With the exception of his screenplay for Alfred Hitchcock's fantasy-based film *The Birds,* Hunter has written no science fiction since the middle 1950's. But the many reprintings of *Tomorrow's World* and the occasional reprinting of short stories serve as reminders to the SF reader that his contribution to the field, though small, is by no means inconsequential.

—Bill Pronzini

———

HUXLEY, Aldous (Leonard). British. Born in Godalming, Surrey, 26 July 1894; son of the scientist T.H. Huxley; brother of the scientist and writer Julian Huxley. Educated at Hillside School, Godalming, 1903-08; Eton College, 1908-13; Balliol College, Oxford, 1913-15, B.A. (honours) in English 1915. Married 1) Maria Nys in 1919 (died, 1955); 2) Laura Archera in 1956; one son. Worked in the War Office, 1917; taught at Eton College, 1918; member of the editorial staff of the *Athenaeum,* London, 1919-20; Drama Critic, *Westminster Gazette,* 1920-21; full-time writer from 1921; travelled and lived in France, Italy, and the United States, 1923-37; settled in California, 1937, and worked as a free-lance screenwriter. Recipient: American Academy Award, 1959. Companion of Literature, Royal Society of Literature, 1962. *Died 22 November 1963.*

SCIENCE-FICTION PUBLICATIONS

Novels

Brave New World. London, Chatto and Windus, and New York, Doubleday, 1932.
After Many a Summer. London, Chatto and Windus, 1939; as *After Many a Summer Dies the Swan,* New York, Harper, 1939.
Time Must Have a Stop. New York, Harper, 1944; London, Chatto and Windus, 1945.
Ape and Essence. New York, Harper, 1948; London, Chatto and Windus, 1949.
Island. London, Chatto and Windus, and New York, Harper, 1962.

OTHER PUBLICATIONS

Novels

Crome Yellow. London, Chatto and Windus, 1921; New York, Doran, 1922.
Antic Hay. London, Chatto and Windus, and New York, Doran, 1923.
Those Barren Leaves. London, Chatto and Windus, and New York, Doran, 1925.
Point Counter Point. London, Chatto and Windus, and New York, Doubleday, 1928.
Eyeless in Gaza. London, Chatto and Windus, and New York, Harper, 1936.
The Genius and the Goddess. London, Chatto and Windus, and New York, Harper, 1955.

Short Stories

Limbo. London, Chatto and Windus, and New York, Doran, 1920.
Mortal Coils (includes play *Permutations among the Nightingales*). London, Chatto and Windus, and New York, Doran, 1922.
Little Mexican and Other Stories. London, Chatto and Windus, 1924; as *Young Archimedes and Other Stories,* New York, Doran, 1924.
Two or Three Graces and Other Stories. London, Chatto and Windus, and New York, Doran, 1926.
Brief Candles. London, Chatto and Windus, and New York, Doubleday, 1930; as *After the Fireworks,* New York, Avon, n.d.
Twice Seven: Fourteen Selected Stories. London, Reprint Society, 1944.
Collected Short Stories. London, Chatto and Windus, and New York, Harper, 1957.

Plays

Liluli, adaptation of a play by Romain Rolland, in *Nation* (London), 20 September-29 November 1919.
Albert, Prince Consort: A Biography Play for Which Mr. John Drinkwater's Historical Dramas Serve as a Model, in *Vanity Fair* (New York), March 1922.
The Ambassador of Capripedia, in *Vanity Fair* (New York), May 1922.
The Publisher, in *Vanity Fair* (New York), April 1923.
The Discovery, adaptation of the play by Frances Sheridan (produced London, 1924). London, Chatto and Windus, 1924; New York, Doran, 1925.
The World of Light (produced London, 1931). London, Chatto and Windus, and New York, Doubleday, 1931.
The Giocanda Smile, adaptation of his own story (produced London, 1948; New York 1950). London, Chatto and Windus, 1948; as *Mortal Coils,* New York, Harper, 1948.
The Genius and the Goddess, with Ruth Wendell, adaptation of the novel by Huxley (produced New York, 1957).

Screenplays: *Pride and Prejudice,* with Jane Murfin, 1940; *Jane Eyre,* with John Houseman and Robert Stevenson, 1944; *A Woman's Vengeance,* 1947.

Verse

The Burning Wheel. Oxford, Blackwell, 1916.
Jonah. Oxford, Holywell Press, 1917.
The Defeat of Youth and Other Poems. Oxford, Blackwell, 1918.
Leda. London, Chatto and Windus, and New York, Doran, 1920.
Selected Poems. Oxford, Blackwell, and New York, Appleton, 1925.
Arabia Infelix and Other Poems. New York, Fountain Press, and London, Chatto and Windus, 1929.
Apennine. Gaylordsville, Connecticut, Slide Mountain Press, 1930.
The Cicadas and Other Poems. London, Chatto and Windus, and New York, Doubleday, 1931.
Verses and a Comedy. London, Chatto and Windus, 1946.
The Collected Poetry of Aldous Huxley, edited by Donald Watt. London, Chatto and Windus, and New York, Harper, 1971.

Other

On the Margin: Notes and Essays. London, Chatto and Windus, and New York, Doran, 1923.
Along the Road: Notes and Essays of a Tourist. London, Chatto and Windus, and New York, Doran, 1925.
Essays New and Old. London, Chatto and Windus, 1926; New York, Doran, 1927.
Jesting Pilate: The Diary of a Journey. London, Chatto and Windus, and New York, Doran, 1926.
Proper Studies. London, Chatto and Windus, 1927; New York, Doubleday, 1928.
Do What You Will: Essays. London, Chatto and Windus, and New York, Doubleday, 1929.

Holy Face and Other Essays. London, The Fleuron, 1929.
Vulgarity in Literature: Digressions from a Theme. London, Chatto and Windus, 1930.
Music at Night and Other Essays. London, Chatto and Windus, and New York, Doubleday, 1931.
Rotunda (selection). London, Chatto and Windus, 1932.
T.H. Huxley as a Man of Letters (lecture). London, Macmillan, 1932.
Retrospect (selection). New York, Doubleday, 1933.
Beyond the Mexique Bay. London, Chatto and Windus, and New York, Harper, 1934.
The Olive Tree and Other Essays. London, Chatto and Windus, 1936; New York, Harper, 1937.
What Are You Going to Do about It? The Case for Constructive Peace. London, Chatto and Windus, 1936; New York, Harper, 1937.
Stories, Essays, and Poems. London, Dent, 1937.
Ends and Means: An Enquiry into the Nature of Ideals and into the Methods Employed for Their Realization. London, Chatto and Windus, and New York, Harper, 1937.
The Most Agreeable Vice. Los Angeles, Ward Ritchie Press, 1938.
Words and Their Meanings. Los Angeles, Ward Ritchie Press, 1940.
Gray Eminence: A Study in Religion and Politics. London, Chatto and Windus, 1941.
The Art of Seeing. New York, Harper, 1942; London, Chatto and Windus, 1943.
The Perennial Philosophy. New York, Harper, 1945; London, Chatto and Windus, 1946.
Science, Liberty, and Peace. New York, Harper, 1946; London, Chatto and Windus, 1947.
The World of Aldous Huxley: An Omnibus of His Fiction and Non-Fiction over Three Decades, edited by Charles J. Rolo. New York, Harper, 1947.
Food and People, with John Russell. London, Bureau of Current Affairs, 1949.
Prisons, with the Carceri Etchings by Piranesi. London, Trianon Press, and Los Angeles, Zeitlin and Ver Brugge, 1949.
Themes and Variations. London, Chatto and Windus, and New York, Harper, 1950.
The Devils of Loudun. London, Chatto and Windus, and New York, Harper, 1952.
Joyce the Artificer: Two Studies of Joyce's Methods, with Stuart Gilbert. London, Chiswick Press, 1952.
A Day in Windsor, with J.A. Kings. London, Britannicus Liber, 1953.
The Doors of Perception. London, Chatto and Windus, and New York, Harper, 1954.
The French of Paris, photographs by Sanford H. Roth. New York, Harper, 1954.
Adonis and the Alphabet, and Other Essays. London, Chatto and Windus, 1956; as *Tomorrow and Tomorrow and Tomorrow and Other Essays,* New York, Harper, 1956.
Heaven and Hell. London, Chatto and Windus, and New York, Harper, 1956.
Brave New World Revisited. New York, Harper, 1958; London, Chatto and Windus, 1959.
Collected Essays. London, Chatto and Windus, and New York, Harper, 1959.
"Chemical Persuasion," in *Fantasy and Science Fiction* (New York), April 1959.
On Art and Artists, edited by Morris Philipson. London, Chatto and Windus, and New York, Harper, 1960.
Selected Essays, edited by Harold Raymond. London, Chatto and Windus, 1961.
Literature and Science. London, Chatto and Windus, and New York, Harper, 1963.
The Politics of Ecology: The Question of Survival. Santa Barbara, California, Center for the Study of Democratic Institutions, 1963.
The Crows of Pearblossom (juvenile). London, Chatto and Windus, and New York, Random House, 1967.
The Letters of Aldous Huxley, edited by Grover Smith. London, Chatto and Windus, 1969; New York, Harper, 1970.

Great Short Works of Aldous Huxley, edited by Bernard Bergonzi. New York, Harper, 1969.
America and the Future. Austin, Texas, Jenkins, 1970.
Moksha: Writings on Psychedelics and the Visionary Experience 1931-1963, edited by Michael Horowitz and Cynthia Palmer. New York, Stonehill, 1977; London, Chatto and Windus, 1980.
The Human Situation: Lectures at Santa Barbara 1959, edited by Piero Ferrucci. New York, Harper, 1977; London, Chatto and Windus, 1978.

Editor, with W.R. Childe and T.W. Earp, *Oxford Poetry 1916.* Oxford, Blackwell, 1916.
Editor, *Text and Pretexts: An Anthology with Commentaries.* London, Chatto and Windus, 1932; New York, Harper, 1933.
Editor, *The Letters of D.H. Lawrence.* London, Heinemann, and New York, Viking Press, 1932.
Editor, *An Encyclopedia of Pacifism.* London, Chatto and Windus, and New York, Harper, 1937.

Translator, *A Virgin Heart,* by Rémy de Gourmont. New York, Brown, 1921; London, Allen and Unwin, 1926.

*

Bibliography: *Aldous Huxley: A Bibliography 1916-1959* by Claire John Eschelbach and Joyce Lee Shober, Berkeley, University of California Press, 1961; supplement by Thomas D. Clareson and Carolyn S. Andrews, in *Extrapolation 6* (Wooster, Ohio), 1964.

*   *   *

Though very few of Aldous Huxley's many books deal with the future, he is most famous as the author of one of the masterpieces of SF. This will appear less paradoxical if we consider how closely *Brave New World* is linked to his essays and mainstream novels. Indeed, in his very first novel, *Crome Yellow,* one of the characters, Scogan, develops his plans for a "Rational State": facing the crumbling of the Victorian system into hypocrisy, national and social conflicts, and sexual frustration—the central subject of Huxley's early novels, crowned and summed up in *Point Counter Point*—an intellectual could not but look for a substitute based on reason, happiness being the only possible aim. Because of the lack of any generally accepted transcendental creed, individuals should be adapted, by education and even by generation, to the functions they are to perform and the place that is to be theirs in the collectivity, thus getting rid of all sources of anxiety. Yet when Huxley developed this rough sketch, the result was a dreadful *counter*-utopia. Scenes as the test-tube generation of as many as 96 similar babies born from a single ovum so that they may later work together with absolute coordination, or the conditioning of children to hate roses and books so that they may become utterly devoted soldiers, remain in the memory as perfect illustrations of the "standardization of the human product" whose horror is perceived even by Bernard Marx, one of the ruling elite. Indeed, the objection to utopia is no longer that it is an unrealistic dream, but, on the contrary—as Huxley pointed out in *Brave New World Revisited*—that it is coming true, and turning out to be a nightmare. The Human "Termitary"—though not reaching the same extremes as Frank Herbert's *Hellstrom's Hive*—is taking shape in several countries. According to Huxley, the path followed by the USA is the surest way to this hell-on-earth, for violence is no longer necessary with the development of the technology of persuasion. Therefore, he considers Orwell's *Nineteen Eighty-Four,* though written later, as less credible than his own prophecies of a "soft" dictatorship.

As regards sex, he seems indeed to be right. For the integrated state, promiscuity seems a far better proposition than puritanism. But generalized free love, rid of both passion and procreation, attractive though it may sound to modern readers, appears as ghastly in *Brave New World,* especially as experienced by the "Savage"—nurtured on the "monstrosities" of Shakespeare's plays. Of post-Victorian writers, Huxley was one of those who strove most desperately to overcome the century-long divorce between body and "soul"; and he was equally attracted and dissatisfied by those who claimed they had found the way to reconciliation (D.H. Lawrence) or release (the psychoanalysts). Huxley never ceased to study

this conflict between upward and downward self-transcendence through his characters who, failing to "play the man," played either the angel, the devil, or the beast—quite literally in the case of the 5th Earl of Hauberk and his servant-mistress at the end of *After Many a Summer,* a mainstream novel to which Huxley was brought to give a SF conclusion. If in it such *individuals* as want to reach a purely physical eternity turn into apes, in *Ape and Essence* a whole *race,* because of mutations due to radioactivity (which "could as well be the product of atomic industry as of atomic war") has to comply with the demands and restrictions of animal rutting, as well as of devil-worship.

Towards the end of his life, Huxley must have thought that he had found a solution to those personal and social problems: after studying the diabolical excesses that may result from misguided religion on some historical characters (*The Devils of Loudun*) and the best expressions of true religious aspirations throughout the world (*The Perennial Philosophy*), he published a novel which, without his knowing it, was his literary testament—and it was a utopia. *Island* has however certain common points with *Brave New World:* free love, removal of children from the narrow family circle (through clubs of mutual adoption), elimination of the tragic from art (*Oedipus* is given a happy ending), legalized and even encouraged drug-taking, and more generally subservience of everything to the quest of happiness. Of course, one may say that the difference lies in the spirit of it all: the yoga of love is not just a contraceptive device, but a means to spread sensual awareness to the whole body; orgasm is not mere animal pleasure but discovery of oneself, and of another self; "Moksha" induces communion with the world, not passive acceptance of the social order like "soma." Yet there is a more serious objection: the ideal state is created from above, by a "sane" Raja, and equally destroyed from above, by a conspiracy of fascists, capitalists, and pseudo-mystics. Though it is acknowledged that total integration of the individual is neither possible nor even desirable, the people of Pala seem to accept with equal passivity the good and the evil that are in turn imposed upon them.

That the ideal state should be so easily overturned tends to prove that Huxley himself did not believe in it very firmly; in our faithless age, he could not base his construction on received principles like Thomas More or Campanella; so he tried his best to take the *whole* man into account—a remarkable feat for an intellectual, but how could *all* men be satisfied? Though for Huxley's personal build-up it was a key attempt, he will certainly be remembered much more for *Brave New World,* a direct continuation of his satirical studies of the present, and a model for many warning pictures of the future, often imitated, sometimes equalled (notable by Pohl and Kornbluth in *The Space Merchants*), but probably never surpassed.

—George W. Barlow

HYNE, C(harles) J(ohn) Cutcliffe (Wright). Also wrote as Weatherby Chesney. British. Born in Bibury, Gloucestershire, 11 May 1865. Educated at Bradford Grammar School; Clare College, Cambridge, B.A., M.A. Married Elsie Haggas in 1897 (died, 1938), one daughter. Journalist: travelled extensively as a writer for magazines. *Died 10 March 1944.*

SCIENCE-FICTION PUBLICATIONS

Novels

Beneath Your Very Boots. London, Digby Long, 1889.
The New Eden. London, Longman, 1892.
The Recipe for Diamonds. London, Heinemann, and New York, Appleton, 1893.
The Lost Continent. London, Hutchinson, and New York, Harper, 1900.

Empire of the World. London, Everett, 1910; New York, Arno Press, 1975; as *Emperor of the World: The Story of an Anglo-German War,* London, Newnes, 1915.
Abbs, His Story Through Many Ages. London, Hutchinson, 1929.

Short Stories

The Adventures of a Solicitor (as Weatherby Chesney). London, Bowden, 1898.
Atoms of Empire. London and New York, Macmillan, 1904.
Man's Understanding. London, Ward Lock, 1933.

OTHER PUBLICATIONS

Novels

Four Red Nightcaps. London, Eden, 1890.
Currie, Curtis & Co., Crammers. London, Remington, 1890.
A Matrimonial Mixture. London, Ward and Downey, 1891.
Stimson's Reef. London, Blackie, 1891.
Sandy Carmichael. London, Sampson Low, 1892; Philadelphia, Lippincott, 1908.
The Captured Cruiser; or, Two Years from Land. London, Blackie, 1892; New York, Scribner, 1895.
The Wild-Catters. London, Sunday School Union, 1895.
Honour of Thieves. London, Chatto and Windus, 1895; New York, Fenno, 1899; as *The Little Red Captain: An Early Adventure of Captain Kettle,* London, Pearson, 1902.
The Stronger Hand. London, Beeman, 1896.
Through Arctic Lapland. London, A. and C. Black, and New York, Macmillan, 1898.
The Glass Dagger. New York, New Amsterdam, 1899.
The Filibusters. London, Hutchinson, and New York, Stokes, 1900.
Prince Rupert the Buccaneer. London, Methuen, and New York, Stokes, 1901.
Thompson's Progress. London, Richards, 1902; New York, Macmillan, 1903.
Captain Kettle, K.C.B. London, Pearson, and New York, Federal, 1903.
McTodd. London and New York, Macmillan, 1903.
The Trials of Commander McTurk. London, Murray, and New York, Dutton, 1906.
Kate Meredith, Financier. New York, Authors and Newspapers Association, 1906; as *Kate Meredith,* London, Cassell, 1907.
The Marriage of Kettle. London, Heinemann, and Indianapolis, Bobbs Merrill, 1912.
Firemen Hot. London, Methuen, 1914.
Captain Kettle on the War-Path. London, Methuen, 1916.
Captain Kettle's Bit. London, Hodder and Stoughton, 1918.
Admiral Teach. London, Methuen, 1920.
President Kettle. London, Nash and Grayson, 1920.
Mr. Kettle, Third Mate. London, Ward Lock, 1931.
West Highland Spirits. London, Ward Lock, 1932.
Captain Kettle, Ambassador. London, Ward Lock, 1932.
Absent Friends. London, Ward Lock, 1933.
Ivory Valley: An Adventure of Captain Kettle. London, Ward Lock, 1938.
Wishing Smith. London, Hale, 1939.

Novels as Weatherby Chesney

The Dilemma of Commander Brett. London, Bowden, 1899.
John Topp, Pirate. London, Methuen, 1901.
The Branded Prince. London, Methuen, 1902.
The Foundered Galleon. London, Methuen, 1902.
The Baptist Ring. London, Methuen, 1903.
The Mystery of a Bungalow. London, Methuen, 1904.
The Tragedy of the Great Emerald. London, Methuen, 1904.
The Cable-Man. London, Chatto and Windus, 1907.
The Claimant. London, Chatto and Windus, 1908.
The Romance of a Queen. London, Chatto and Windus, 1908.

Short Stories

The Paradise Coal-Boat. London, Bowden, and New York, Mansfield, 1897.
Adventures of Captain Kettle. London, Pearson, and New York, Doubleday, 1898.
The Adventures of an Engineer (as Weatherby Chesney). London, Bowden, 1898.
Further Adventures of Captain Kettle. London, Pearson, 1899; as *A Master of Fortune,* New York, Dillingham, 1901.
The Derelict. New York, Lewis Scribner, 1901; revised edition, as *Mr. Horrocks, Purser,* London, Methuen, 1902.
The Escape Agents. London, Laurie, 1911.
Red Herrings. London, Methuen, 1918.
The Rev. Captain Kettle. London, Harrap, 1925.
Ben Watson. London, Country Life, 1926.
Steamboatmen. London, Penguin, 1943.

Other

People and Places. London, Newnes, 1930.
But Britons Are Slaves. London, Harmsworth, 1931.
My Joyful Life. London, Hutchinson, 1935.
Don't You Agree? (essays). London, Hutchinson, 1935.

Editor, *For Britain's Soldiers.* London, Methuen, 1900.

*   *   *

Half a dozen of C.J. Cutcliffe Hyne's novels are SF, as are some of his many short stories ("The Men from Mars" in *The Adventures of a Solicitor*). In *Beneath Your Very Boots* the narrator finds beneath England a race descended underground in pre-Roman times, using Earth heat as energy source, manufacturing diamonds, but otherwise living in a theocratic dictatorship à la Rider Haggard. In a dilution of Bulwer-Lytton's *The Coming Race,* the narrator-hero invents a boring machine, is rewarded by a pleasure drug, and during an unsuccessful rebellion escapes with the obligatory beautiful underground wife. *The New Eden* and *The Recipe for Diamonds* are more pallid. In the first, an archduke-scientist sets up on a Pacific island the experiment of starting a young man and woman from zero; they invent art, alcohol, and Sun-worship. In the second, Lully's recipe is found and, after intrigues involving the equally obligatory anarchist, destroyed again. *The Lost Continent* is a relatively readable Haggard-type melodrama of Atlantis, narrated by a nobleman of those times involved with a strong upstart empress. Though she is the most interesting character of the novel, women's rule still leads to decadence and the flood, after political intrigues and fights with giant saurians and cave-tigers. In *Empire of the World* a poor scientist with a ray-machine that disintegrates iron intervenes in the war of Britain vs. Germany enforcing peace. It is an unsuccessful try at fusing the "future war" story with "a rather heavy-handed comedy of romantic entanglements in high society" (R.D. Mullen, in *Science-Fiction Studies 6,* 1975). Finally, *Abbs* is a novel about longevity, the protagonist living "through many ages." In all, Hyne is a good example of the middle range of pre-World-War SF, a competent storyteller who wrote too conventionally and too much.

—Darko Suvin

———————————

JAKES, John (William). Also writes as Alan Payne; Jay Scotland. American. Born in Chicago, Illinois, 31 March 1932. Educated at DePauw University, Greencastle, Indiana, A.B. 1953; Ohio State University, Columbus, M.A. 1954. Married Rachel Ann Payne in 1951; three daughters and one son. Copywriter, then promotion manager, Abbott Laboratories, North Chicago, 1954-60; copywriter, Rumrill Company, Rochester, New York, 1960-61;

free-lance writer, 1961-65; copywriter, Kircher Helton and Collett, Dayton, Ohio, 1965-68; Copy Chief, then Vice-President, Oppenheim Herminghausen and Clarke, Dayton, 1968-70; Creative Director, Dancer Fitzgerald Sample, Dayton, 1970-71. Since 1971, free-lance writer. Writer-in-Residence, DePauw University, Fall 1979. Address: P.O. Box 3248, Harbour Town Station, Hilton Head, South Carolina 29928, U.S.A.

SCIENCE-FICTION PUBLICATIONS

Novels (series: Brak; Galaxy; Klekton)

When the Star Kings Die (Galaxy). New York, Ace, 1967.
Brak the Barbarian. New York, Avon, 1968; London, Tandem, 1970.
The Asylum World. New York, Paperback Library, 1969; London, New English Library, 1978.
Brak Versus the Mark of the Demons. New York, Paperback Library, 1969; as *Brak the Barbarian—The Mark of the Demons,* London, Tandem, 1970.
Brak the Barbarian Versus the Sorceress. New York, Paperback Library, 1969; as *Brak the Barbarian—The Sorceress,* London, Tandem, 1970.
The Hybrid. New York, Paperback Library, 1969.
The Last Magicians. New York, New American Library, 1969.
The Planet Wizard (Galaxy). New York, Ace, 1969.
Secrets of Stardeep (juvenile). Philadelphia, Westminster Press, 1969.
Tonight We Steal the Stars (Galaxy). New York, Ace, 1969.
Black in Time. New York, Paperback Library, 1970.
Mask of Chaos. New York, Ace, 1970.
Master of the Dark Gate (Klekton). New York, Lancer, 1970.
Monte Cristo 99. New York, Curtis, 1970.
Six-Gun Planet. New York, Paperback Library, 1970; London, New English Library, 1978.
Mention My Name in Atlantis. New York, DAW, 1972.
Time Gate (juvenile). Philadelphia, Westminster Press, 1972.
Witch of the Dark Gate (Klekton). New York, Lancer, 1972.
Conquest of the Planet of the Apes (novelization of screenplay). New York, Award, 1972.
On Wheels. New York, Paperback Library, 1973.
Brak: When the Idols Walked. New York, Pocket Books, 1978.
Excalibur!, with Gil Kane. New York, Dell, 1980.

Short Stories

The Best of John Jakes. New York, DAW, 1977.
Fortunes of Brak. New York, Dell, 1980.

OTHER PUBLICATIONS

Novels

The Texans Ride North (juvenile). Philadelphia, Winston, 1952.
Wear a Fast Gun. New York, Arcadia House, 1956; London, Ward Lock, 1957.
A Night for Treason. New York, Bouregy, 1956.
The Devil Has Four Faces. New York, Bouregy, 1958.
This'll Slay You (as Alan Payne). New York, Ace, 1958.
The Imposter. New York, Bouregy, 1959.
Johnny Havoc. New York, Belmont, 1960.
Johnny Havoc Meets Zelda. New York, Belmont, 1962.
Johnny Havoc and the Doll Who Had "It." New York, Belmont, 1963.
G.I. Girls. Derby, Connecticut, Monarch, 1963.
Making It Big. New York, Belmont, 1968.
Bicentennial Series:
    The Bastard. New York, Pyramid, 1974; London, Corgi, 2 vols., 1975.
    The Rebels. New York, Pyramid, 1975; London, Corgi, 1979.
    The Seekers. New York, Pyramid, 1975; London, Corgi, 1979.
    The Furies. New York, Pyramid, 1976; London, Corgi, 1979.
    The Titans. New York, Pyramid, 1976; London, Corgi, 1979.
    The Warriors. New York, Pyramid, 1977; London, Corgi, 1979.
    The Lawless. New York, Jove, 1978.
    The Americans. New York, Jove, 1980.

Novels as Jay Scotland

The Seventh Man. New York, Bouregy, 1958.
I, Barbarian. New York, Avon, 1959.
Strike the Black Flag. New York, Ace, 1961.
Sir Scoundrel. New York, Ace, 1962; revised edition, as *King's Crusader,* New York, Pyramid, 1977.
Veils of Salome. New York, Avon, 1962.
Arena. New York, Ace, 1963.
Traitors' Legion. New York, Ace, 1963; revised edition, as *The Man from Cannae,* New York, Pyramid, 1977.

Plays

Dracula, Baby (lyrics only). Chicago, Dramatic Publishing Company, 1970.
Wind in the Willows. Elgin, Illinois, Performance, 1972.
A Spell of Evil. Chicago, Dramatic Publishing Company, 1972.
Violence. Elgin, Illinois, Performance, 1972.
Stranger with Roses. Chicago, Dramatic Publishing Company, 1972.
Gaslight Girl. Chicago, Dramatic Publishing Company, 1973.
Pardon Me, Is This Planet Taken? Chicago, Dramatic Publishing Company, 1973.
Doctor, Doctor!, music by Gilbert M. Martin, adaptation of a play by Molière. New York, McAfee Music, 1973.
Shepherd Song. New York, McAfee Music, 1974.

Other

Tiros: Weather Eye in Space. New York, Messner, 1966.
Famous Firsts in Sports. New York, Putnam, 1967.
Great War Correspondents. New York, Putnam, 1968.
Great Women Reporters. New York, Putnam, 1969.
The Bastard Photostory. New York, Jove, 1980.

*   *   *

Unfortunately, as far as his science-fiction writing is concerned, John Jakes is best known for creating Brak the Barbarian. This is not to demean the Brak stories but rather to rue the fact that Jakes has written several other excellent novels which have gone virtually unnoticed.

The Brak stories follow a specific formula and so, even though very good, become wearisome by the repetition of their pattern. Brak's world is a dichotomous one in which evil is an active force represented by the god Yob-Haggoth and is implemented by his agent, Septegundus, a man with no eyelids and skin covered with the living, writhing figures of the souls he has captured. Septegundus is aided by his beautiful but equally evil daughter, Ariane. Throughout his various "on-the-road" adventures, Brak encounters analogues of Ariane, whom he eventually recognizes by their display of evil and lustful natures. Nordica Fire-Hair, in *The Sorceress,* is an excellent example. A dutiful daughter, she suddenly changes. She leaves her father, an alchemist who has learned the secret of turning things to gold, to die in a deep pit inhabited by a dragonlike creature called Manworm. As Brak becomes more and more involved with her, he recognizes that she is possessed by Ariane. When Nordica is finally killed, Brak sees the spirit of Ariane leaving the corpse.

Cast out of his own land in the far north for blaspheming the gods, Brak is constantly pursued by the forces of Septegundus in his eternal quest to reach the fabled golden city of Khurdisan in the south. Septegundus has vowed to kill him for interfering in his affairs. An incarnation of Conan, Brak is instinctive and physical, but even his strength and cunning are no match for the supernatural forces of evil, so he is aided in his continuing battle with Yob-Haggoth by various Nestorian priests who represent the mysterious Nameless God. Inevitably, Brak loses his sword, encounters some sort of fantastic monster which he must slay, Manworm, Scarlet-jaw, Doomdog, or The Thing That Crawls, and plies his way toward Khurdisan. But regardless of the formulization of the stories and the impression that some were written hastily, their fast-paced action recommends them. Within the formula, Jakes's inventiveness makes the stories both attractive and interesting.

The highly imaginative quality of Jakes's writing is perhaps better displayed in some of his other novels. Among them, *The Planet Wizard, The Hybrid,* and the Klekton books are the best. The Klekton is a ring of alternate Earths which can be reached by traveling through various mindgates. The novels tell the story of Gavin Black, a down-and-out journalist who becomes a pawn of Bronwyn, a police official of an alternative world called Earth Prime. Bronwyn is attempting to stop an invasion of our Earth from yet another alternate Earth called Earth Three or Shulkor. The population of all three Earths are descended from a great civilization that lived on heartland Earth before the Ice Age. When cold and ice threatened them, some went up the Klekton and some down, there to develop into radically different peoples. The Shulkorites became savage and warlike, while Bronwyn's people developed their intellectual abilities. Now, the Shulkorites want to use heartland Earth as a base to destroy Earth Prime and to extend their power to the more hospitable worlds down the chain. At first bribed, Black later permits himself to be used so that he can gain access to the gates in order to be reunited with Samantha, a girl from Earth Three with whom he has fallen in love.

The Hybrid tells the story of Andreas Law, the son of an Earth father and an Omqu mother, who has the unique ability to project destructive blasts of mental energy. Law becomes the tool of a fanatic Earth billionaire, Sir Robert Baron, who is trying to sabotage a proposed peace treaty between Earth and Omqu because he hates the humanoid but feathered aliens. Cast against a background of two intergalactic cultures trying to understand one another, *The Hybrid* is a story of prejudice which is handled sensitively and thoughtfully. It is a perceptive and imaginative exploration of what might happen when man achieves intergalactic travel and finds that he is not the only humanoid in the universe.

The Planet Wizard is a story of self-discovery, power, and love. Set in another galaxy eons after it has been colonized by Earthmen, *The Planet Wizard* tells of civilizations left to cope for themselves after planetary wars have destroyed the great business houses which controlled galactic society. Superstition abounds as knowledge and technology fade. Magus Blacklaw, a bogus magician but first-rate confidence man, traps himself and his daughter, Maya, into having to make a trip to the feared planet of Lightmark to exorcise its demons and to secure access to the resources of the great house that did business there. Blacklaw is a lovable rogue who rises above himself in his efforts to provide a better life for his daughter. In ridding Lightmark of its demons, he finds strength and courage he did not know he possessed.

Jakes is a highly competent writer whose imagination and versatility deserve respect. Always interesting, his stories provide fast-paced entertainment while imaginatively exploring the possibility of life in the distant future.

—Carl B. Yoke

JANIFER, Laurence M. Pseudonym for Larry Mark Harris; also writes as Alfred Blake; Andrew Blake; Mark Phillips; Barbara Wilson. American. Born in Brooklyn, New York, 17 March 1933. Attended City College of New York, one year. Married 1) Sylvia Siegel in 1955 (divorced, 1958); 2) Sue Blugerman in 1960 (divorced, 1962); 3) Rae Montor in 1966 (divorced, 1968); 4) Beverly Goldberg in 1969, one daughter. Pianist and arranger, New York, 1950-59; Editor, Scott Meredith Literary Agency, New York, 1952-57; editor and art director, detective and science-fiction magazines, 1953-57. Since 1957, professional comedian. Agent: James Seligmann, 280 Madison Avenue, New York, New York 10016, U.S.A.

SCIENCE-FICTION PUBLICATIONS

Novels (series: Angelo di Stefano)

Pagan Passions (as Larry Mark Harris), with Randall Garrett. New York, Galaxy, 1959.
Slave Planet. New York, Pyramid, 1963.
The Wonder War. New York, Pyramid, 1964.
You Sane Men. New York, Lancer, 1965; as *Bloodworld,* 1968.
A Piece of Martin Cann. New York, Belmont, 1968.
Target: Terra (di Stefano), with S.J. Treibich. New York, Ace, 1968.
The High Hex (di Stefano), with S.J. Treibich. New York, Ace, 1969.
The Wagered World (di Stefano), with S.J. Treibich. New York, Ace, 1969.
Power. New York, Dell, 1974.
Survivor. New York, Ace, 1977.

Novels as Mark Phillips (with Randall Garrett) (series: Kenneth J. Malone in all books)

Brain Twister. New York, Pyramid, 1962.
The Impossibles. New York, Pyramid, 1963.
Supermind. New York, Pyramid, 1963.

Short Stories

Impossible? New York, Belmont, 1968.

Uncollected Short Stories

"Countdown," in *Analog* (New York), July 1972.
"A Few Minutes," in *Ten Tomorrows,* edited by Roger Elwood. New York, Fawcett, 1973.
"Thine Alabaster Cities Gleam," in *Future City,* edited by Roger Elwood. New York, Simon and Schuster, 1973.
"Family Album," in *Fantasy and Science Fiction* (New York), May 1973.
"An Agent in Place," in *Analog* (New York), May 1973.
"Into the Furniture," in *Analog* (New York), June 1973.
"Martyr," in *Analog* (New York), September 1973.
"Amfortas," in *Omega,* edited by Roger Elwood. New York, Walker, 1974.
"The Bible after the Apocalypse," in *New Dimensions 4,* edited by Robert Silverberg. New York, New American Library, 1974.
"Story Time," in *Journey to Another Star,* edited by Roger Elwood. Minneapolis, Lerner, 1974.
"Saving Grace," in *Fantastic* (New York), November 1974.
"Civis Obit" and "The Gift" in *Dystopian Visions,* edited by Roger Elwood. Englewood Cliffs, New Jersey, Prentice Hall, 1975.
"All Possible Worlds," in *Beyond Time,* edited by Sandra Ley. New York, Pocket Books, 1976.
"The Believer," in *Analog* (New York), February 1979.
"Toadstool Sinfonia," in *Analog* (New York), July 1980.

OTHER PUBLICATIONS

Novels

The Pickled Poodles (as Larry M. Harris). New York, Random House, 1960; London, Boardman, 1961.
The Protector (as Larry M. Harris). New York, Random House, 1961; London, Boardman, 1962.
The Bed and I (as Alfred Blake). N.p., Intimate, 1962.
Faithful for 8 Hours (as Alfred Blake). New York, Beacon, 1963.
The Pleasure We Know (as Barbara Wilson). New York, Lancer, 1964.
The Velvet Embrace (as Barbara Wilson). New York, Lancer, 1965.
The Woman Without a Name. New York, New American Library, 1966.
The Final Fear. New York, Belmont, 1967.
You Can't Escape. New York, Lancer, 1967.

Novels as Andrew Blake

I Deal in Desire. N.p., Boudoir, 1962.
Sex Swinger. New York, Beacon, 1963.
Love Hostess. New York, Beacon, 1963.

Other

Editor, *Masters' Choice.* New York, Simon and Schuster, 1966; London, Jenkins, 1967; as *18 Great Science Fiction Stories*, New York, Grosset and Dunlap, 1971.

Ghost writer for *Ken Murray's Giant Joke Book,* 1957; *The Henry Morgan Joke Book,* 1958; *The Foot in My Mouth* by Jeff Harris, 1958; *Tracer!* by Ed Goldfader, 1970; editor for *Yes, I'm Here with Someone* by Thomas Sutton, 1958.

*   *   *

A first impression of Laurence M. Janifer's books might be that they emphasize stock subjects and sensation. *You Sane Men* is the story of a world on which Bound Men and Bound Women are held as objects of torture in what are called Remand Houses. The "Lords and Ladies" inflict pain on them with whips and hot brands and derive pleasure or sexual strength from this. In *Power* Aaron Norin, the son of a respected empire official, leads a spaceship in rebellion against the empire. *Slave Planet* is about a world where cynical colonists from earth use alligator-like aliens as slaves to extract precious metals. Mental telepathy is used in *A Piece of Martin Cann* to cure a patient; *The Wonder War* is about a war to gain power over an entire galaxy.

These lurid but stock topics, however, acquire some complexity in Janifer's best novels. Janifer's central subjects are power and rebellion, and he often treats these with subtle irony. Jo, the narrator of *You Sane Men*, is a refugee from the world of blood, addressing the "sane men" who doubt that it is possible for human beings to run a social system based on torture. But as Jo speaks we see that his horrible world is sane and is human, for the point is that sane people are capable of extreme, thoughtless cruelty. Jo joins with other young people in a revolt against the ruling council, a revolt ironically not against the institution of cruelty but against the exclusion of young people from decision-making. When a lady is killed another irony develops: in contrast to our crime-ridden earth, the blood world has never had a murder, and its natives are comically inept detectives. Torture is legalized, but other crimes are almost unknown. Satire of our sexual taboos develops when Jo is shocked to discover that some men enjoy torturing men, and women, women.

The irony of *Power* is more understated. Isidor Norin's family all have power. His daughter Rachel is married to a famous actor, and his son Alphard is the assistant to a powerful religious leader. When the spaceship *Valor*, lead by his son Aaron, rebels from the empire, Aaron is killed and his father becomes critically ill. The rebellion is apparently crushed, and the Emperor retains all formal power, but the idea of freedom has been kindled in several minds. In *Slave Planet* Janifer gently portrays the naive point of view of several of the enslaved aliens. Janifer avoids pathos by giving us their puzzled acceptance of their condition. We are also made to see through the rather exaggerated moralism which brings a military liberation force from the shocked confederation to Fruyling's world. Thus the overthrow of slavery and its replacement by automatic machinery are complex events. We reject the view of Dr. Haelingen that slavery is inevitable on this world, but we do consider it.

Janifer's short stories are competent but routine, although his talent at presenting unusual points of view comes through in such stories as "Thine Alabaster Cities Gleam," about a couple caught in a skyscraper at night when the electricity, and thus the air supply, goes out. They will die—even the woman's diamond can make only faint scratches in the window. "Civis Obit" gives us the point of view of a telepath who preserves sanity only be developing the skill of shutting out human suffering. "Amfortas" develops the psychological effects of massive organ transplants.

One feature of Janifer's fiction is the regular use of quotations from literature to suggest his themes. Although Janifer's plots leave too many loose ends and his subject matter stays close to formula, he is a writer of promise and more than occasional achievement.

—Curtis C. Smith

———————

JOHNS, W(illiam) E(arl). Also wrote as William Earle. British. Born in Hertford, 5 February 1893. Educated at Hertford Grammar School; articled to a Hertford surveyor, 1909-13. Entered the Norfolk Yeomanry, 1913, commissioned, 1916; served in the Middle East during the First World War; transferred to the Royal Flying Corps (later Royal Air Force), 1916 and served until 1927; Flying Officer; served in the Ministry of Information, London, 1939-45. Married Miss Leigh; one son. Air correspondent for London and Continental newspapers. Founding Editor, *Popular Flying*, 1932, and *Flying,* 1935. *Died 21 June 1968.*

SCIENCE-FICTION PUBLICATIONS (juvenile)

Novels (series: Rex Clinton in all books except *Biggles—Charter Pilot*)

Biggles—Charter Pilot. London, Oxford University Press, 1943.
Kings of Space. London, Hodder and Stoughton, 1954.
Return to Mars. London, Hodder and Stoughton, 1955.
Now to the Stars. London, Hodder and Stoughton, 1956.
To Outer Space. London, Hodder and Stoughton, 1957.
The Edge of Beyond. London, Hodder and Stoughton, 1958.
The Death Rays of Ardilla. London, Hodder and Stoughton, 1959.
To Worlds Unknown. London, Hodder and Stoughton, 1960.
The Quest for the Perfect Planet. London, Hodder and Stoughton, 1961.
The Man Who Vanished into Space. London, Hodder and Stoughton, 1963.

Short Stories

Worlds of Wonder: More Adventures in Space. London, Hodder and Stoughton, 1962.

OTHER PUBLICATIONS

Novels

Mossyface (as William Earle). London, Mellifont Press, 1932.
The Camels Are Coming. London, John Hamilton, 1932.
The Spy Flyers. London, John Hamilton, 1933.
The Raid. London, John Hamilton, 1935.
Sky High. London, Newnes, 1936; revised edition, London, Latimer, 1951.
Steeley Flies Again. London, Newnes, 1936; revised edition, London, Latimer 1951.
Blue Blood Runs Red. London, Newnes, 1936.
Murder by Air. London, Newnes, 1937; revised edition, London, Latimer, 1951.
The Murder at Castle Deeping. London, John Hamilton, 1938; revised edition, London, Latimer, 1951.
Desert Night: A Romance. London, John Hamilton, 1938.
Wings of Romance. London, Newnes, 1939; revised edition, London, Latimer, 1951.
The Unknown Quantity. London, John Hamilton, 1940.
No Motive for Murder. London, Hodder and Stoughton, 1958; New York, Washburn, 1959.
The Man Who Lost His Way. London, Macdonald, 1959

Novels (juvenile)

The Cruise of the Condor: A Biggles Story. London, John Hamilton, 1933.
Biggles Flies Again. London, John Hamilton, 1934.
Biggles of the Camel Squadron. London, John Hamilton, 1934.
Biggles Flies East. London, Oxford University Press, 1935.
Biggles Hits the Trail. London, Oxford University Press, 1935.
The Black Peril. London, John Hamilton, 1935.
Biggles in France. London, Boys' Friend Library, 1935.
Biggles in Africa. London, Oxford University Press, 1936.
Biggles & Co. London, Oxford University Press, 1936.
Biggles — Air Commodore. London, Oxford University Press, 1937.
Biggles Flies West. London, Oxford University Press, 1937.
Biggles Flies South. London, Oxford University Press, 1938.
Biggles Goes to War. London, Oxford University Press, 1938.
Champion of the Main. London, Oxford University Press, 1938.
Biggles Flies North. London, Oxford University Press, 1939.
Biggles in Spain. London, Oxford University Press, 1939.
The Rescue Flight. London, Oxford University Press, 1939.
Biggles in the Baltic. London, Oxford University Press, 1940.
Biggles in the South Seas. London, Oxford University Press, 1940.
Biggles — Secret Agent. London, Oxford University Press, 1940.
Worrals of the W.A.A.F. London, Lutterworth Press, 1941.
Spitfire Parade: Stories of Biggles in War-Time. London, Oxford University Press, 1941.
Biggles Sees It Through. London, Oxford University Press, 1941.
Biggles Defies the Swastika. London, Oxford University Press, 1941.
Biggles in the Jungle. London, Oxford University Press, 1942.
Biggles Sweeps the Desert. London, Hodder and Stoughton, 1942.
Worrals Flies Again. London, Hodder and Stoughton, 1942.
Worrals Carries On. London, Lutterworth Press, 1942.
Worrals on the War-Path. London, Hodder and Stoughton, 1943.
Biggles "Fails to Return." London, Hodder and Stoughton, 1943.
Biggles in Borneo. London, Oxford University Press, 1943.
King of the Commandos. London, University of London Press, 1943.
Biggles in the Orient. London, Hodder and Stoughton, 1944.
Gimlet Goes Again. London, University of London Press, 1944.
Worrals Goes East. London, Hodder and Stoughton, 1944.
Worrals of the Islands. London, Hodder and Stoughton, 1945.
Biggles Delivers the Goods. London, Hodder and Stoughton, 1946.
Gimlet Goes Home. London, University of London Press, 1946.
Sergeant Bigglesworth C.I.D. London, Hodder and Stoughton, 1946.
Comrades in Arms. London, Hodder and Stoughton, 1947.
Gimlet Mops Up. Leicester, Brockhampton Press, 1947.
Worrals in the Wilds. London, Hodder and Stoughton, 1947.
Biggles Hunts Big Game. London, Hodder and Stoughton, 1948.
Biggles' Second Case. London, Hodder and Stoughton, 1948.
Gimlet's Oriental Quest. Leicester, Brockhampton Press, 1948.
The Rustlers of Rattlesnake Valley. London, Nelson, 1948.
Worrals Down Under. London, Lutterworth Press, 1948.
Biggles Breaks the Silence. London, Hodder and Stoughton, 1949.
Biggles Takes a Holiday. London, Hodder and Stoughton, 1949.
Gimlet Lends a Hand. Leicester, Brockhampton Press, 1949.
Worrals Goes Afoot. London, Lutterworth Press, 1949.
Worrals in the Wastelands. London, Lutterworth Press, 1949.
Worrals Investigates. London, Lutterworth Press, 1950.
Biggles Gets His Men. London, Hodder and Stoughton, 1950.
Gimlet Bores In. Leicester, Brockhampton Press, 1950.
Another Job for Biggles. London, Hodder and Stoughton, 1951.
Biggles Goes to School. London, Hodder and Stoughton, 1951.
Biggles Works It Out. London, Hodder and Stoughton, 1951.
Gimlet off the Map. Leicester, Brockhampton Press, 1951.
Biggles — Air Detective. London, Latimer, 1952.
Biggles Follows On. London, Hodder and Stoughton, 1952.

Biggles Takes the Case. London, Hodder and Stoughton, 1952.
Gimlet Gets the Answer. Leicester, Brockhampton Press, 1952.
Biggles and the Black Peril. London, Thames, 1953.
Biggles and the Black-Raider. London, Hodder and Stoughton, 1953.
Biggles in the Blue. Leicester, Brockhampton Press, 1953.
Biggles in the Gobi. London, Hodder and Stoughton, 1953.
Biggles of the Special Air Police. London, Thames, 1953.
Biggles Cuts It Fine. London, Hodder and Stoughton, 1954.
Biggles, Foreign Legionnaire. London, Hodder and Stoughton, 1954.
Biggles, Air Fighter. London, Thames, 1954.
Gimlet Takes a Job. Leicester, Brockhampton Press, 1954.
Adventure Bound. London, Nelson, 1955.
Biggles in Australia. London, Hodder and Stoughton, 1955.
Biggles Learns to Fly. Leicester, Brockhampton Press, 1955.
Biggles of 266. London, Thames, 1956.
Biggles Takes Charge. Leicester, Brockhampton Press, 1956.
No Rest for Biggles. London, Hodder and Stoughton, 1956.
Biggles Makes Ends Meet. London, Hodder and Stoughton, 1957.
Adventure Unlimited. London, Nelson, 1957.
Biggles of the Interpol. Leicester, Brockhampton Press, 1957.
Biggles on the Home Front. London, Hodder and Stoughton, 1957.
Biggles Buries a Hatchet. Leicester, Brockhampton Press, 1958.
Biggles on Mystery Island. London, Hodder and Stoughton, 1958.
Biggles Presses On. Leicester, Brockhampton Press, 1958.
Biggles at World's End. Leicester, Brockhampton Press, 1959.
The Biggles Book of Heroes. London, Parrish, 1959.
Biggles' Combined Operation. London, Hodder and Stoughton, 1959.
Biggles in Mexico. Leicester, Brockhampton Press, 1959.
Adventures of the Junior Detection Club. London, Parrish, 1960.
Biggles and the Leopards of Zinn. Leicester, Brockhampton Press, 1960.
Biggles Goes Home. London, Hodder and Stoughton, 1960.
Where the Golden Eagle Soars. London, Hodder and Stoughton, 1960.
Biggles and the Missing Millionaire. Leicester, Brockhampton Press, 1961.
Biggles and the Poor Rich Boy. Leicester, Brockhampton Press, 1961.
Biggles Forms a Syndicate. London, Hodder and Stoughton, 1961.
The Biggles Book of Treasure Hunting. London, Parrish, 1962.
Biggles Goes Alone. London, Hodder and Stoughton, 1962.
Biggles Sets a Trap. London, Hodder and Stoughton, 1962.
Orchids for Biggles. Leicester, Brockhampton Press, 1962.
Biggles and the Plane That Disappeared. London, Hodder and Stoughton, 1963.
Biggles Flies to Work. London, Dean, 1963.
Biggles' Special Case. Leicester, Brockhampton Press, 1963.
Biggles Takes a Hand. London, Hodder and Stoughton, 1963.
Biggles Takes It Rough. Leicester, Brockhampton Press, 1963.
Biggles and the Black Mask. London, Hodder and Stoughton, 1964.
Biggles and the Lost Sovereigns. Leicester, Brockhampton Press, 1964; as *Biggles and the Lost Treasure,* London, Hodder and Stoughton, 1978.
Biggles and the Blue Moon. Leicester, Brockhampton Press, 1965.
Biggles and the Plot That Failed. Leicester, Brockhampton Press, 1965.
Biggles Looks Back. London, Hodder and Stoughton, 1965.
Biggles Scores a Bull. London, Hodder and Stoughton, 1965.
Biggles in the Terai. Leicester, Brockhampton Press, 1966.
Biggles and the Gun-Runners. Leicester, Brockhampton Press, 1966.
Biggles and the Penitent Thief. Leicester, Brockhampton Press, 1967.
Biggles Sorts It Out. Leicester, Brockhampton Press, 1967.
Biggles in the Underworld. Leicester, Brockhampton Press, 1968.
The Boy Biggles. London, Dean, 1968.

Biggles and the Deep Blue Sea. Leicester, Brockhampton Press, 1968.
Biggles and the Little Green God. Leicester, Brockhampton Press, 1969.
Biggles and the Noble Lord. Leicester, Brockhampton Press, 1969.
Biggles and the Dark Intruder. London, Hodder and Stoughton, 1970.
Biggles Sees Too Much. Leicester, Brockhampton Press, 1970.

Short Stories

Sinister Service. London, Oxford University Press, 1942.
Doctor Vane Answers the Call. London, Latimer, 1950.
Short Sorties. London, Latimer, 1950.
Sky Fever and Other Stories. London, Latimer, 1953.
Biggles and the Pirate Treasure and Other Biggles Adventures (juvenile). Leicester, Brockhampton Press, 1954.
Biggles' Chinese Puzzle and Other Biggles Adventures (juvenile). Leicester, Brockhampton Press, 1955.
Biggles Investigates and Other Stories of the Air Police (juvenile). Leicester, Brockhampton Press, 1964.
Biggles of the Royal Flying Corps (juvenile), edited by Piers Williams. Maidenhead, Berkshire, Purnell, 1978

Other

Fight Planes and Aces (juvenile). London, John Hamilton, 1932.
The Pictorial Flying Course. London, John Hamilton, 1932.
The Air V.C.'s. London, John Hamilton, 1935.
Some Milestones of Aviation. London, John Hamilton, 1935.
The Passing Show: A Garden Diary by an Amateur Gardener. London, My Garden, 1937.
No Surrender, with R.A. Kelly. London, Harrap, 1969.

Editor, *Modern Boys' Book of Aircraft.* London, Amalgamated Press, 1931.
Editor, *Wings: A Book of Thrilling Flying Adventures.* London, John Hamilton, 1931.
Editor, *Thrilling Flights.* London, John Hamilton, 1935.
Editor, *Modern Boys' Book of Pirates.* London, Amalgamated Press, 1939.

* * *

W.E. Johns, creator of the air ace Biggles, chronicled the adventures of the spaceship *Tavona* and her crew in a series of some ten novels, begun in 1954 and awkwardly written around the probably unanticipated eruption of the space race three years later. His aim, as stated in the foreword of *To Worlds Unknown,* was to familiarise young people with "the new science of Astronautics"; but even the most naive member of the intended teenage readership could not fail to catch the author out in such colossal errors as the assertion that an Earth-type planet can become a nova. In the simplified universe through which the *Tavona* speeds at superluminal velocities without Einsteinian complications of hyperspatial confabulations, only Newton's laws escape total maceration. Nonetheless, few youngsters, however sceptical, could fail to be enthralled by these novels, which have the flavour not of science fiction but of a series of adventurous sea voyages: a bunch of cheerful and resourceful sailors embarking on a cosmic ocean filled with wonders and fraught with perils.

The cosmic-ray-powered *Tavona* is built by the supremely advanced Terromagnans, crewed by Martians, and carries as passengers four intrepid Earthmen: the eccentric professor Lucius Brane whose jaunt to the moon in a backyard spaceship got the series off the launching pad; Tiger, the pipe-smoking, gun-toting man of action; Toby, the rather colourless ship's medic; and Tiger's clean-cut, pure-hearted teenage son Rex, contributing reader-identification to the book and the clear eye of youth to the triad of vision, action, and expertise. On their cosmic cruises, they traverse the treacherous reaches of the Galaxy, exploring interesting little islands, occasionally pulling in at a bustling foreign port, sometimes getting stranded, shipwrecked, caught up in hostilities, or attacked by pirates, cannibals, or fearsome beasts, but always, with luck and ingenuity, pulling through. In the course of their travels, any jingoistic assumptions get thoroughly punctured: they discover that their homeland, far from being internationally revered, is feared and hated for its militarism and short-sightedness. The nuclear weapons, carelessly strewn space hardware, and filthy atmosphere of Earth are the shame of the Milky Way, and the cause of much agonising introspection for Rex as he spends the lonely hours between the stars contemplating (while Toby and Tiger attend to their pills and guns, and the Professor compiles his Galactic Guidebook) the universal imponderables, and becomes ever more spacesick and travel-weary as the series progresses.

And progress the series does. In the early books the *Tavona*'s travels are restricted to the local archipelago of the Solar system, the spacefarers tending to land on tiny asteroids completely covered with ice, water, grass, or glass, or if inhabited boasting at most two or three (Terrestrial) species, and the plot is a rambling string of cautionary anecdotes. In the later novels the foursome strike out into the interstellar deeps, encountering various and complex (but inevitably Earthlike) civilisations, and becoming caught up in the machinations of cosmic kidnappers, conquerors, and crooks, and the interminable moralising of superior (but humanoid) beings.

For all Johns's avowed intentions to educate embryo space scientists, the message which comes across much more clearly than the patronising tables of the solar system and glossaries of astronomical terms that bedeck the books is the endless series of imprecations to the Earthmen to put away their bombs and satellites and cease tampering with the biosphere. It comes as a shock to the adult reader to return to these books, written in what seems in retrospect a decade of optimism, to find them filled not with white hope and the white heat of technology (the *Tavona* has no radio and no more navigational equipment than a small inshore craft) but with the doom-laden forebodings of planetary suicide that pervade the world into which the original readers have matured.

—Lee Montgomerie

JONES, D(ennis) F(eltham). British. Served in the Royal Navy during World War II. Has worked as a bricklayer and market gardener. Address: c/o Sidgwick and Jackson Ltd., 1 Tavistock Chambers, Bloomsbury Way, London WC1A 2SG, England.

SCIENCE-FICTION PUBLICATIONS

Novels (series: Colossus)

Colossus. London, Hart Davis, 1966; New York, Putnam, 1967.
Implosion. London, Hart Davis, 1967; New York, Putnam, 1968.
Don't Pick the Flowers. London, Panther, 1971; as *Denver Is Missing,* New York, Walker, 1971.
The Fall of Colossus. New York, Putnam, 1974.
Colossus and the Crab. New York, Berkley, 1977.
Earth Has Been Found. New York, Dell, 1979; as *Xeno,* London, Sidgwick and Jackson, 1979.

Uncollected Short Stories

"Coffee Break," in *Fantasy and Science Fiction* (New York), October 1968.
"Black Snowstorm," in *Fantasy and Science Fiction* (New York), January 1969.
"The Tocsin," in *Fantasy and Science Fiction* (New York), June 1970.

* * *

Asimov, in "The Machine and the Robot," writes, "Surely the *great* fear is not that machinery will harm us—but that it will supplant us." In *Colossus* D.F. Jones has certainly created one of the finest embodiments of this fear. Because men are attached to their freedom, or at least to a sense of freedom, *Colossus* becomes the ultimate horror story in which man is enslaved by his own creation. Jones develops the horror through the logic and detail of presentation. Each of the steps by which Colossus comes to power follows from the previous; all the hardware is credible. Forbin serves as a foil to the machine (eliciting such information as the reader needs to understand Colossus) and as an emotional sounding-board (articulating and amplifying the fear). The futility of Forbin's defiance of Colossus, especially his refusal to love it, contributes to the power of the ending.

The two sequels to *Colossus* do not quite measure up to the same standard. Neither seems to have the same level of conviction. In *The Fall of Colossus* the emphasis has shifted away from the horror of machine domination. Colossus's attempts to comprehend human emotion, Forbin's shift toward love for the machine, the Sect's worship, the Fellowship's opposition—none of these stimulate the same level of excitement. The sexual experiment on Cleo seems contrived and not very relevant. The outside intervention which brings the fall has a *deus ex machina* quality. In *Colossus and the Crab* the tight, straightforward plotting which is a strength in most of Jones's novels seems to have given way to a rather choppy, almost episodic style. The whole concept of the novel, which pits Forbin against two aliens from Mars, leads to the revival of Colossus and ends in a sort of Mexican standoff, gives the feeling that the author merely wanted to wrap up the series. The novel's climactic point, although it effectively builds the emotional tension of Forbin's naval attack, gets its power purely from situation—Forbin never seems to rise to the heroic level.

Perhaps that is because plot and setting, rather than characterization, are Jones's strengths. The plots of his other novels command the reader's attention, leading step-by-step to a satisfying conclusion. Whether he deals with population (*Implosion*), alien invasion (*Earth Has Been Found*), or geologic catastrophe (*Don't Pick the Flowers*), the plot flows ineluctably from the initial assumption. Settings also contribute much to the effectiveness of all his works. Each setting presents a recognizable Earth in a not-too-distant future. The familiarity of setting functions effectively as a contrasting ground for the strange situation. More than a trace of the mad-scientist motif enters into his work. All his central characters are scientists, and either initiate an action beyond control or attempt to cope with a situation beyond comprehension.

Don't Pick the Flowers seems to me the best of his novels. Its highly improbable situation is invested with a sense of possibility. The chief characters seem very human (when compared with Forbin, for instance) in their fears and desires, and in their strength to cope with an overwhelming situation, to endure against very long odds.

—Robert Reilly

JONES, Langdon. British. Born in 1942. Free-lance writer and musician. Former staff member, *New Worlds,* London.

SCIENCE-FICTION PUBLICATIONS

Short Stories

The Eye of the Lens. New York, Macmillan, 1972.

OTHER PUBLICATIONS

Editor, *The New SF: An Original Anthology of Speculative Fiction.* London, Hutchinson, 1969.

Editor, with Michael Moorcock, *The Nature of the Catastrophe.* London, Hutchinson, 1971.

*   *   *

Langdon Jones's best work has been as an editor: he is responsible for the essential New Wave anthology *The New SF,* for the restoration of Mervyn Peake's prodigious but fractured *Titus Alone,* and (with Michael Moorcock) for later issues of *New Worlds* and for *The Nature of the Catastrophe,* the Cornelius anthology. Jones is also the author of a small number of fictions in prose and poetry featured prominently in *New Worlds* and in many readers' altercations at the time, but he has never produced the major work they seemed to foreshadow.

In form and theme Jones's writing is supremely typical of the British New Wave, but his disposition is older, more straightforwardly Romantic than his contemporaries'. Trained as a composer, he makes many references to music in his fiction, characterizing it as a transcendental, irrational power, the language of the heart, and the spirit's apprehension of eternity. In "The Music Makers" Martians of the Bradbury kind prove to have music so mighty that it is fatal for a human hearer, while in the experimental sequence "The Eye of the Lens" echoes of Messiaen affirm a primal, invigorating sun-worship against a collage of corrupt religions and machine-cults. Jones's protest-story "I Remember, Anita" (then outrageous, now unreadable) relates the sorrows of a young student whose adoration of music and his mistress is eclipsed by the shadow of the Bomb.

Several stories show the pattern: an unhappy, cerebral young man has difficulty reaching an idealized woman with whom he has had enthusiastic but anxious sexual congress. Confused by time, by memory, by death, and by machines, he seeks release through music and art, and fulfillment in her. Though Jones's storylines commonly lead to defeat and doom, these awkward quests for true love (certified by cosmic orgasm) secure a corner of hope in the fiction of Inner Space, whose landscapes are more usually coloured by depression and psychic damage. "The Garden of Delights," an Oedipal romance in pastels, is a time-conundrum in which the young man's mysterious lover proves to be his mother as a girl; but the whole cyclic tragedy of lost ideals and ruined lives cannot outweigh the one evening of perfect intimacy. Jones is a moral puritan in his Romanticism: everything is sacrificed to the ideal, and those who recognize no ideal are ugly, discordant, damned. There is the corresponding destructive and even morbid streak in Jones's fiction, seen when he writes about Christianity and the ring of flagellants in "The Eye of the Lens," or the dehumanized slave of "The Great Clock," imprisoned inside it to oil and regulate the mechanism.

The best of Jones's stories, "The Time Machine," deals with all his usual preoccupations, but less dogmatically, more ambiguously. It incorporates some hallucinatory SF imagery into a precise, vivid description of an ordinary adultery, showing the Utopia of the senses as it fades and peels, and envisaging a time machine more organic than most. Influenced, perhaps, by Thomas M. Disch's "The Squirrel Cage," it asks, Are we the prisoners of time, memory, and desire? Are we at the mercy of our own contrivances, and what would happen if we were released?

—Colin Greenland

JONES, Neil R(onald). American. Born in Fulton, New York, 29 May 1909. Attended Fulton public schools. Served in the 2nd Armored Division of the United States Army, 1942-45. Married Rita Gwendoline Rees in 1945. Stamp dealer, bookkeeper, cost analyst, office manager, game manufacturer; unemployment insurance claims examiner, State of New York, for 26 years. Address: 1028 Fay Street, Fulton, New York 13069, U.S.A.

SCIENCE-FICTION PUBLICATIONS

Short Stories (series: Professor Jameson in all books)

The Planet of the Double Sun.   New York, Ace, 1967.
The Sunless World.   New York, Ace, 1967.
Space War.   New York, Ace, 1967.
Twin Worlds.   New York, Ace, 1967.
Doomsday on Ajiat.   New York, Ace, 1968.

Uncollected Short Stories (series: Professor Jameson; 24th Century; 26th Century)

"The Death's Head Meteor" (26th Century), in *Air Wonder Stories* (New York), January 1930.
"The Electrical Man," in *Scientific Detective* (New York), May 1930.
"Shadows of the Night," in *Amazing Detective Tales* (New York), October 1930.
"The Asteroid of Death" (26th Century), in *Wonder Stories Quarterly* (New York), Fall 1931.
"Spacewrecked on Venus" (24th Century), in *Wonder Stories Quarterly* (New York), Winter 1932.
"Escape from Phobus" (24th Century), in *Wonder Stories* (New York), February 1933.
"Martian and Troglodyte," in *Amazing* (New York), May 1933.
"The Moon Pirates" (26th Century), in *Amazing* (New York), September, October 1934.
"Little Hercules" (26th Century), in *Astounding* (New York), September 1936.
"The Astounding Exodus," in *Thrilling Wonder Stories* (New York), April 1937.
"Durna Rangue Neophyte" (24th Century), in *Astounding* (New York), June 1937.
"Swordsman of Saturn" (24th Century), in *Science Fiction* (Holyoke, Massachusetts), October 1939.
"The Dark Swordsmen of Saturn" (26th Century), in *Planet* (New York), Summer 1940.
"Liquid Hell" (26th Century), in *Future* (New York), July 1940.
"The Cat-Men of Aemt" (Jameson), in *Astonishing* (Chicago), August 1940.
"Invisible One" (26th Century), in *Super Science* (Kokomo, Indiana), September 1940.
"Cosmic Derelict" (Jameson), in *Astonishing* (Chicago), February 1941.
"Captives of Durna Rangue" (24th Century), in *Super Science* (Kokomo, Indiana), March 1941.
"Vampire of the Void" (26th Century), in *Planet* (New York), Spring 1941.
"Priestess of the Sleeping Death" (24th Century), in *Amazing* (New York), April 1941.
"The Ransom for Toledo," in *Comet* (Springfield, Massachusetts), May 1941.
"Slaves of the Unknown" (Jameson), in *Astonishing* (Chicago), March 1942.
"Spoilers of the Spaceways" (24th Century), in *Planet* (New York), Winter 1942.
"Parasite Planet" (Jameson), in *Super Science* (Kokomo, Indiana), November 1949.
"Hermit of Saturn's Ring" (24th Century), in *Flight into Space,* edited by Donald A. Wollheim.   New York, Fell, 1950.
"World Without Darkness" (Jameson), in *Super Science* (Kokomo, Indiana), March 1950.
"The Mind Masters" (Jameson), in *Super Science* (Kokomo, Indiana), September 1950.
"The Citadel in Space" (26th Century), in *Two Complete Science Adventure Books* (New York), Summer 1951.
"The Star Killers" (Jameson), in *Super Science* (Kokomo, Indiana), August 1951.

Neil R. Jones comments:

I am one of the earlier science-fiction writers in this country. My first story, "The Death's Head Meteor," appeared in 1930, and was the first science-fiction story to use the word astronaut. "The Jameson Satellite" was the beginning of what is possibly the longest running series in science fiction; from 1931 to 1968, 23 stories in the series were published. I also wrote two other series ("Tales of the 24th Century" and "Tales of the 26th Century"); both included stories of the Durna Mangue cult. All the stories were written in the vein of a future history. Michael Ashley (*History of the Science Fiction Magazine*) puts it this way: "an overall framework in which each story forms part of a future history, invented by Jones long before either Heinlein or Asimov. The key story is the Jameson adventure 'Times's Mausoleum' (*Amazing,* December 1933) which remained the basis for all of Jones' other tales."

*   *   *

Neil R. Jones, while not a prolific writer as measured by total wordage, maintained a small but steady output over two decades in the science-fiction pulps. By far the greater number of his stories concerned adventures of Professor Jameson. The series began with "The Jameson Satellite" in 1931, the story of a professor whose desire to preserve his body after death is stronger than that of the pharaohs. Professor Jameson leaves instructions for his corpse to be placed in a rocket of his own construction which will carry him into an endless orbit of the earth, ensuring if not a perpetual at least a *very* long incorruptibility of the body. Secure in the belief that he has outdone even the embalming practices in H. Rider Haggard's *She,* he goes to his rest, and his wishes are carried out. Forty million years later, his satellite is discovered by creatures called Zoromes, people who eons before had satisfied a similar desire for material immortality by transplanting their brains into mechanical bodies. The Zoromes place the brain of Jameson into one of their spares and revivify it. By the end of the story, Jameson has decided to leave the now-lifeless earth, and travel through the stars with the Zoromes.

The popularity of the story demanded sequels (Isaac Asimov, then 11, was one of the admirers; he attributes the idea of his benevolent robots to the Zoromes). And the Professor Jameson series continued until 1968.

Although both the content and the style of these stories seem outdated today, Jones contributed at least one innovation widely adopted by later writers: he devised a "future history" against which he set the action of his stories. Whether Jones was inspired by the time chart in Olaf Stapledon's *Last and First Men* (1930) has not been established, but the usefulness of the device is clearly demonstrated by its subsequent employment by many writers—Robert Heinlein, Poul Anderson, and Larry Niven, to name just a few.

—Walter E. Meyers

———————

JONES, Raymond F.   American.   Born in Salt Lake City, Utah, in 1915. Studied engineering and English in college. Radio engineer, then full-time writer. Lives in Arizona. Address: c/o Pinnacle, 2029 Century Park East, Los Angeles, California 90067, U.S.A.

SCIENCE-FICTION PUBLICATIONS

Novels

Renaissance.   New York, Gnome Press, 1951; as *Man of Two Worlds,* New York, Pyramid, 1963.
The Alien.   New York, Galaxy, 1951.
This Island Earth.   Chicago, Shasta, 1952; London, Boardman, 1955.
Son of the Stars (juvenile).   Philadelphia, Winston, 1952; London, Hutchinson, 1953.
Planet of Light (juvenile).   Philadelphia, Winston, 1953.
The Secret People.   New York, Avalon, 1956; as *The Deviates,* New York, Galaxy, 1959.
The Year When Stardust Fell (juvenile).   Philadelphia, Winston, 1958.

The Cybernetic Brains. New York, Avalon, 1962.
Voyage to the Bottom of the Sea (juvenile). Racine, Wisconsin, Whitman, 1965.
Syn. New York, Belmont, 1969.
Moonbase One (juvenile). New York and London, Abelard Schuman, 1971.
Renegades of Time. Toronto, Laser, 1975.
The King of Eolim. Toronto, Laser, 1975.
The River and the Dream. Toronto, Laser, 1977.
Weeping May Tarry, with Lester del Rey. Los Angeles, Pinnacle, 1978.

Short Stories

The Toymaker. Los Angeles, Fantasy, 1951.
The Non-Statistical Man. New York, Belmont, 1964; London, Digit, 1965.

Uncollected Short Stories

"Subway to the Stars," in *Galaxy* (New York), December 1968.
"Rat Race," in *Above the Human Landscape,* edited by Willis McNelly and Leon Stover. Pacific Palisades, California, Goodyear, and London, Grayson, 1972.
"The Laughing Lion," in *Science Fiction Tales,* edited by Roger Elwood. New York, Random House, 1973.
"The Lions of Rome," in *Flame Tree Planet,* edited by Roger Elwood. St. Louis, Concordia, 1973.
"Pet," in *Future Quest,* edited by Roger Elwood. New York, Avon, 1973.
"Time Brother," in *Children of Infinity,* edited by Roger Elwood. London, Watts, 1973.
"A Bowl of Biskies Makes a Growing Boy," in *The Other Side of Tomorrow,* edited by Roger Elwood. New York, Random House, 1973.
"Rider in the Sky," in *Most Thrilling Science Fiction Ever Told* (New York), April 1973.
"Flauna," in *The Far Side of Time,* edited by Roger Elwood. New York, Dodd Mead, 1974.
"The Lights of Mars," in *Science Fiction Adventures from Way Out,* edited by Roger Elwood. Racine, Wisconsin, Whitman, 1974.
"Pacer," in *Future Kin,* edited by Roger Elwood. New York, Doubleday, 1974.
"Reflection of a Star," in *Survival from Infinity,* edited by Roger Elwood. New York, Watts, 1974.
"The Touch of Your Hand," in *If* (New York), April 1974.
"Death Eternal," in *Fantastic* (New York), October 1978.

OTHER PUBLICATIONS

Other

The World of Weather (juvenile). Racine, Wisconsin, Whitman, 1961.
Animals of Long Ago (juvenile). Racine, Wisconsin, Whitman, 1965.
Ice Formation on Aircraft. Geneva, World Meteorological Organization, 1968.
Physicians of Tomorrow (juvenile). Chicago, Reilly and Lee, 1971.
Radar: How It Works (juvenile). New York, Putnam, 1972.

*   *   *

Raymond F. Jones is an almost archetypical John Campbell writer, whether writing for *Astounding,* as with "Noise Level" where scientists are lured into inventing anti-gravity, or for *Thrilling Wonder Stories,* with the Peace Engineer stories where aliens secretly involve earth scientists in a program to produce materials needed to defend their home world against invaders (*This Island Earth*).
Jones's first novel, *Renaissance,* is a long and complex parallel-worlds story that contains variations on a number of familiar SF

themes against a somewhat more adventurous narrative than is usual in his stories. *The Alien* is a bit more straightforward in its story-telling, although its ideas and the approach he takes to them is not simple at all. The shadow of A.E. van Vogt falls across both these books, the first in its resemblance in early passages to *Slan,* the second in its exploration of ideas and attitudes similar to those of *The World of Null A. The Alien* opens with a strong idea: a representative of a long-extinct extraterrestrial race is discovered entombed in the asteroid belt, and brought back to life. While the revival processes go forward, new discoveries indicate this being is thoroughly evil and responsible for the destruction of his own race, something he would no doubt manage for humanity as well. The wealth of ideas from which the story draws its strength occasionally betrays it, as when we are suddenly shown that our supposedly solar-system-bound humans have had the capability of interstellar flight (and use that capability with the utmost casualness); and, again, when a semanticist translates and teaches himself an entire alien language on the basis of a few hours' first-contact conversation. Overlook such points, however, and the book is as good an example of this type of space adventure as you're likely to find short of Edmond Hamilton.
It would be a mistake, however, to place Jones in the camp of Doc Smith or Hamilton, or even van Vogt. Jones has always managed to remain a force unto himself, although a pretty low-key force. One of the ways this has been achieved has been in his handling of characters. The typical Jones character is an engineer, technician, or mathematician, middle-class, and presented in a straightforward and realistic manner that contrasts sharply with the politicians, artists, scholars, militarists, rebels and engineer-savants that make up the bulk of the field's fictional populace. Jones seldom attempts any deep probing of his characters but has always drawn his strength from the ability to portray his characters in equally believable environments. He is also a very economical writer, and after *The Alien* he settled down to a more suitably quiet form of fiction. *This Island Earth* is the first book-length work of his that can be labeled typical. His characters are thoroughly convincing engineers, and, despite the melodrama and detective story touches, their thought processes are the thought processes of reasonable engineers. The complexities that cluttered *Renaissance* and *The Alien* are shunted into the background and the interest of the story lies not in galaxy-spanning events but in the impact of galaxy-spanning events on the lives of seemingly everyday people. The argument could be raised that the best of Jones's novels were written for the Winston juvenile series. *Son of the Stars,* in which teenagers encounter the survivor of a wrecked flying saucer and subsequently find their extraterrestrial friend endangered by adult prejudices, is certainly one of the best of that fondly remembered series of juvenile novels. *Planet of Light* was a sequel.
One of Jones's best stories is "The Non-Statistical Man," which tells of an insurance company statistician who encounters a series of anomalies involving recent claims. At first intrigued, then openly alarmed, he investigates and is led to the conclusion that there are people who possess a 100 per cent reliable intuition, rendering his own statistical approach superfluous and pointless. These people know when they're going to need insurance and they don't get it till then. The character's discovery of all this, his reactions to it, and his subsequent change of philosophy as he discovers that the process that makes intuition infallible can be taught to anyone—even him—is written in the low-key style that is the strength of Jones's best writing, and the result is one of his most convincing and compelling stories. It also illustrates the other strength of Jones. He's always been a story-teller who has gone to great pains to build his stories on definite ideas, making him something of a purist among SF writers. His complexities never overwhelm everything else in the way they usually do in the hands of others, and in his later, quieter fiction, his story-telling ability is often quite remarkable for its purity, directness, and seeming effortlessness. This effortlessness may have something to do with the decline in his readership in recent years: Jones is entertaining and often thought-provoking, but he doesn't generate the flair and excitement of a good many lesser but better-known writers.
Jones has also never marked out a particular type of fiction as his own. Most of his stories are recognizably the work of one writer, with a type of character and a worldview that are identifiable, but any story by Jones is apt to be written with a particular market in

mind. "Seven Jewels of Chamar" is pure *Planet Stories* space opera and "Tools of the Trade" is a classic *Astounding* engineering problem story of the type John Campbell was always supposed to be looking for. But the first doesn't rank with the stories of Emmett McDowell or Gardner F. Fox, and the second is a middle-grade example of the sort of thing Eric Frank Russell was starting to be known for. Jones's recent novels have been good entertainments, but they've lacked the strengths of his early work.

Jones is a thorough-going professional and, in retrospect, a writer of surprising versatility. But the price of this seems to be that too often he came on the scene with a perfectly good story that was still second best to the similar works of someone else. But there have been times when the works he produced were principally from no source but himself, slanted to no editorial taste but his own—works like *This Island Earth, Son of the Stars* and "The Non-Statistical Man"—and those results have always been worth waiting for—or searching out.

—Gerald W. Page

JORGENSEN, Ivar. *See* **FAIRMAN, Paul W.; GARRETT, Randall; SILVERBERG, Robert.**

KAPP, Colin. British. Born in 1928 (?). Worked as an electrical technician. Address: c/o Dennis Dobson, 80 Kensington Church Street, London W8 4BZ, England.

SCIENCE-FICTION PUBLICATIONS

Novels

Transfinite Man. New York, Berkley, 1964; as *The Dark Mind,* London, Corgi, 1965.
The Patterns of Chaos. London, Gollancz, 1972; New York, Award, 1973.
The Wizard of Anharitte. London, Panther, 1975.
The Survival Game. New York, Ballantine, 1976; London, Dobson, 1977.
The Chaos Weapon. New York, Ballantine, 1977; London, Dobson, 1979.
Manalone. London, Panther, 1977.
The Ion War. New York, Ace, 1978; London, Dobson, 1980.
The Timewinders. London, Dobson, 1980.

Short Stories

The Unorthodox Engineers. London, Dobson, 1979.

*   *   *

If any SF writer could typify the Blakean aphorism "Energy is eternal delight," Colin Kapp does so both in terms of human passion and of the energies that compose the universe. The former is unusual in a writer dealing with such esoteric sciences as atomic theory; the latter demonstrates a feeling of awe toward the forces of nature, rather than extolling the way technology utilizes such forces.

Not all of Kapp's works demonstrate the fascination with energy—various stories for *Analog* and the tales of "the Unorthodox Engineers" are standard scientific problem-solving puzzles.

The majority of his works, however, describe the energy states of physics in rhapsodic terms ("Around him the hellish suns and unbelievable vortexes of transfinity shifted and phased in a terrible kaleidoscope of new geometrics and unknown colors"—*Transfinite Man*). In essence, Kapp relates to energy-states as Asimov did to robots—devising a conceptual structure for the scientific phenomena, and giving its many facets relevance to the many facets of human response. In fact, Kapp goes so far as to posit direct interaction between natural forces and human thought-energy. *Transfinite Man* describes a demonic hero, able to survive the dimensions of transfinity by virtue of maniacal hatred. *The Ion War* and "Mephisto and the Ion Explorer" portray human beings able to transform themselves into vessels of ionic energy. "Lambda 1" and "The Imagination Trap" detail the world of Tau-space, a subatomic dimension in which matter directly responds to mental manipulation, and *The Chaos Weapon* concerns a female psychic who can read entropic energy-patterns which indicate oncoming catastrophes. Surprisingly, this interaction is not mechanistically explained in terms of psionics (i.e., the human brain transmits energy like a radio, etc.)—rather, Kapp merely portrays a direct correspondence; rather like the hermetic relationship of man and universe, microcosm and macrocosm.

Such a relationship would be facile if the human personalities were not as vividly realized as the cosmic aspects. Kapp's characters are neither subtle nor complex, but they are vivid, especially in regard to romantic attachments. In "Hunger over Sweet Waters" a scientist and his female co-worker, with whom he is in love, are stranded together on a world without drinkable water, and though the scientist is married to another woman and cannot enjoy a relationship with his co-worker, his love for her is the spur for his invention of a way to secure their rescue. In both *The Ion War* and *The Patterns of Chaos* the relationship between woman and man is less like love than like the intimacy of "torturer and victim"—the female being a caustic "bitch-goddess" who drives the male to perform superhuman feats. This sort of antagonistic romance—also present in *Transfinite Man*, *The Chaos Weapon*, and "Lambda 1"—is the means by which the hero exceeds his limits, discovering the means for immediate survival or the ends behind events of cosmos-spanning proportion.

Though Kapp equals several more revered authors in terms of imaginative scope and striking characters, he lacks a quality that often enhances SF popularity—an overt philosophy which defines man's place in the universe. Despite this lack, his stories can yield a wealth of implicit insights, while his articulation of scientific concepts is surpassed only by the very best of SF.

—Gene Phillips

KARP, David. Also writes as Adam Singer; Wallace Ware. American. Born in New York City, 5 May 1922. Educated at the City College of New York, 1940-42, 1946-48, B.S. Sc. 1948. Served in the United States Army in the South Pacific and Japan, 1943-46. Married Lillian Klass in 1944; two sons. Continuity Director, Radio Station WNYC, New York, 1948-49. Since 1949, free-lance writer. Since 1968, President of Leda Productions Inc., Los Angeles. Member, Executive Council, and President of the Television-Radio Branch, 1969-71, Writers Guild of America West, Los Angeles. Member of the Editorial Board of *Television Quarterly,* 1966-71, and since 1972. Recipient: Guggenheim Fellowship, 1956; Ohio State University Award, for drama, 1948, and for television drama, 1958; *Look Magazine* Award, for television drama, 1958; Mystery Writers of America Edgar Allan Poe Award, for television drama, 1959; American Bar Association Gavel Award, for television documentary, 1963; Emmy Award, 1965. Address: 1116 Corsica Drive, Pacific Palisades, California 90272; or, c/o Robinson-Weintraub and Associates Inc., 554 South San Vicente Boulevard, Los Angeles, California 90048, U.S.A.

SCIENCE-FICTION PUBLICATIONS

Novel

One. New York, Vanguard Press, 1953; London, Gollancz, 1954; as *Escape to Nowhere,* New York, Lion, 1955.

OTHER PUBLICATIONS

Novels

The Big Feeling. New York, Lion, 1952.
The Brotherhood of Velvet. New York, Lion, 1952.
Cry, Flesh. New York, Lion, 1953; as *The Girl on Crown Street,* 1956.
Hardman. New York, Lion, 1953.
Platoon (as Adam Singer). New York, Lion, 1953.
The Charka Memorial (as Wallace Ware). New York, Doubleday, 1954.
The Day of the Monkey. New York, Vanguard Press, and London, Gollancz, 1955.
All Honorable Men. New York, Knopf, and London, Gollancz, 1956.
Leave Me Alone. New York Knopf, 1957; London, Gollancz, 1958.
Enter, Sleeping. New York, Harcourt Brace, 1960; as *The Sleep-Walkers,* London, Gollancz, 1960.
The Last Believers. New York, Harcourt Brace, 1964; London, Cape, 1965.

Plays

Cafe Univers (produced New York, 1967).

Screenplays: *Sol Madrid,* 1967; *Che!,* 1968; *Tender Loving Care,* 1972.

Radio Plays: *House I Live In* series (2 plays), 1946; *One Step Forward* series (21 plays), 1946-47; *A Day to Remember* series (4 plays), 1947; *Famine Relief* series (3 plays), 1947; *Unsung Heroes* series (5 plays), 1947; *People, Unlimited* series (5 plays), 1947; *Grand Central Station* series (3 plays), 1948-49; *Aunt Jenny* series (64 programs), 1950-56; *City Hospital* series (3 plays), 1957; and other plays for *Skippy Hollywood Theatre, American Bible Society,* and *CBS Radio Workshop,* 1948-60.

Television Plays: *The Defenders* series (10 plays), 1961-64; *Saints and Sinners* series (3 plays), 1962; *Profiles in Courage* series (5 plays), 1963-65; and other plays for ABC, CBS, and NBC networks.

Verse

The Voice of the Four Freedoms. Privately printed, 1942.

Other

Vice-President in Charge of Revolution (biography), with Murray D. Lincoln. New York, McGraw Hill, 1960.

*

Manuscript Collection: Mugar Memorial Library, Boston University.

*   *   *

David Karp's future dystopia, *One,* was bound to suffer from comparison to Orwell's *Nineteen Eighty-Four.* The somber, muted tones of *One* are less striking than Orwell's fireworks, but this quieter book is in some ways more chilling yet more hopeful than Orwell's masterpiece.

One tells of a future government that has eliminated most of the things we worry about—war, poverty, unemployment, divorce, crime—yet the price of this betterment has been the extinction of individuality. The State relies on no gadgetry to enforce its rule: rather, a vast network of informers regularly report any comment that suggests that the State is not completely and everlastingly right.

The main character, Burden, is one of these spies, an English professor who secretly monitors the conversations of his colleagues. But the watchers are themselves watched, and in a routine interview with an official of the State's security arm, the Department of Internal Examination, Burden makes comments that arouse the suspicions of the inquisitors. Suspected of believing himself to be different from his fellow citizens, he is tried in secret and convicted not of treason but of heresy. The penalty for Burden's "crime" is death, but a monomaniacal bureaucrat, Lark, determines to make a test of Burden: he decides to brainwash him so thoroughly that his entire personality will be different, destroying his past, and giving him a new and politically reliable identity.

All of this happens through means that were much discussed in the 1950's: loneliness, sensory deprivation, injections of drugs, bombardment by propaganda. Burden, rechristened Hughes, is released as cured. But even Hughes still cherishes his individuality. *One* ends with the powerful state murdering one of its citizens, but unlike Orwell's Winston Smith, Burden is killed not because the State is done with him, but because it fears him. The State can kill a man, but it cannot make him less than himself.

—Walter E. Meyers

———————————

KAVAN, Anna. Pseudonym for Helen Woods; also wrote as Helen Ferguson. Born in Cannes, France, in 1901; brought up in California. Educated privately and in Church of England Schools. Married 1) Donald Ferguson (divorced); 2) Stuart Edmonds (divorced), one son. Lived in the United States, Burma, Europe, Australia, and New Zealand; settled in London. *Died 5 December 1968.*

SCIENCE-FICTION PUBLICATIONS

Novels

House of Sleep. New York, Doubleday, 1947; as *Sleep Has His House,* London, Cassell, 1948.
Ice. London, Owen, 1967; New York, Doubleday, 1970.

Short Stories

Asylum Piece and Other Stories. London, Cape, 1940; New York, Doubleday, 1946.
I Am Lazarus. London, Cape, 1945.
Julia and the Bazooka, edited by Rhys Davies. London, Owen, 1970; New York, Knopf, 1975.

OTHER PUBLICATIONS

Novels

Change the Name. London, Cape, 1941.
A Scarcity of Love. Southport, Lancashire, Downie, 1956; New York, Herder, 1972.
Eagles' Nest. London, Owen, 1957.
Who Are You? Lowestoft, Suffolk, Scorpion Press, 1963.

Novels as Helen Ferguson

A Charmed Circle. London, Cape, 1929.
The Dark Sisters. London, Cape, 1930.
Let Me Alone. London, Cape, 1930; Short Hills, New Jersey, Enslow, 1978.

A Stranger Still. London, Lane, 1935.
Goose Cross. London, Lane, 1936.
Rich Get Rich. London, Lane, 1937.

Short Stories

A Bright Green Field and Other Stories. London, Owen, 1958.
My Soul in China, edited by Rhys Davies. London, Owen, 1975.

Other

The Horse's Tale, with K.T. Bluth. London, Gaberbocchus, 1949.

* * *

Recalling the gothic horrors of Mary Shelley's *Frankenstein*, Anna Kavan inverts the terror stimulus from the external monster to the interior of the mind. Kavan's works are explorations of the mentally ill, those possessed by fear of an external and menancing society. The Monster is within the self—sometimes evidenced as unreasoning fear and suspicion and sometimes emanated as an obsessive desire to control/torture others as catharsis for self-destructive tendencies.

Kavan, like Shelley, did not consciously write science fiction. Kavan's writings are characterised by her frequent and enigmatic shifts between fantasy and reality, abrupt mood shifts, and poetic descriptions. Some of her works are catastrophe fiction, envisioning mass chaos epitomized in the chaos of the central character's mind. The protagonist's mental condition both parallels and illuminates the basic irrationality of the civilizations Kavan depicts. It is the shifting of reality planes within a setting of world-wide catastrophe which marks some of Kavan's psychological fiction as science fiction. Although many of her works are primarily descriptions of the world of the mentally ill, at least "The Birthmark," *Ice*, and *House of Sleep* present a world outside the central character's mind which is also distorted.

In "The Birthmark" the young girl narrator meets an alien girl who fears the discovery of her peculiar skin marking, implying to the narrator that such a discovery would ban her from the narrator's world. Many years later, while touring a castle, the narrator discovers (or thinks she does) that same girl locked in a dungeon—being persecuted for her special talents—talents symbolized and identified by that birthmark.

Ice is also set in a hostile world: nuclear testing has brought on a rapidly advancing ice age. Kavan depicts, unlike many science-fiction writers, an apathetic populace who are unable to comprehend the impending disaster or to break their routine existence. The people remain true to their nature: complacent in the face of chaos. Of course some attempt to flee, but government and business continue to function. Even war continues as the demise of civilization approaches. Within this hostile world the protagonist obsessively searches for a frail, seemingly inept woman whom he both loves and hates. Her weakness of will and body obsesses him as it does his rival, and he alternately wishes to protect and destroy her. Ultimately he conquers the fear of rejection which instigates his violent fantasies toward her and they join in love, and at peace, as they wait for their deaths.

In *House of Sleep* Kavan presents B's progressing rejection of reality which stems from childhood. B finds that only her daydreams and the cover of night provide the security ripped away from her by her mother's unexplained death. B retreats into her imagination, finding there a haven from the isolation and alienation of a society which neither cares for her or for itself. She flees from place to place, always recording the threatening, if ineffectual, liaison officer and the civil disruption and fear within an oppressive government. B states: "Without understanding the reason, I knew that I had to keep the day unimportant. I had to prevent the day world from becoming real." In Kavan's abrupt and frequently imperceptible shifts from reality to fantasy she illustrates the operation of an escape mechanism within the mind of one who can neither accept nor interact in the alien world of reality.

Kavan brings brilliant character portrayal into the genre of science fiction, exploring the inner universe of the mind rather than the outer galaxies of the universe. What she finds within the mind is fear and violence: the essence of terror, confirmed by the irrational-ity of uncaring society which persecutes without knowledge or reason those whose perceptions differ from the norm. Thus Kavan explores various reality levels, questioning society's grasp of reality, and indicating that perhaps sanity is only a matter of perception: that we live in an insane world and are unable to judge who within it is sane or insane.

—Jane B. Weedman

KELLER, David H(enry). Also wrote as Henry Cecil. American. Born in Philadelphia, Pennsylvania, 23 December 1880. Educated at the University of Philadelphia Medical School. Served as a physician working in shell-shock during World War I; Medical Professor on the faculty of the Army Chaplain's School at Harvard University, Cambridge, Massachusetts, during World War II. Married in 1903. Physician, specializing in psychoanalysis: Junior Physician, Illinois Mental Institute, after 1915, and worked in other hospitals in Louisiana, Tennessee, and Pennsylvania. Editor, *Sexology* and *Your Body* in the 1930's. *Died 13 July 1966.*

SCIENCE-FICTION PUBLICATIONS

Novels

The Waters of Lethe. Great Barrington, Massachusetts, Kirby, 1937.
The Sign of the Burning Hart. St. Lo, France, Barbaroux, 1938; Hollywood, National Fantasy Fan Foundation, 1948.
The Television Detective. Los Angeles, Los Angeles Science Fiction League, 1938.
The Devil and the Doctor. New York, Simon and Schuster, 1940.
The Solitary Hunters, and The Abyss. Philadelphia, New Era, 1948.
The Eternal Conflict. Philadelphia, Prime Press, 1949.
The Final War. Portland, Oregon, Perri Press, 1949.
The Homunculus. Philadelphia, Prime Press, 1949.
The Lady Decides. Philadelphia, Prime Press, 1950.

Short Stories

The Thought Projector. New York, Stellar, 1930.
Wolf Hollow Bubbles. Jamaica, New York, Arra Printers, 1933.
Men of Avalon. Everett, Pennsylvania, Fantasy, 1935 (?).
The Thing in the Cellar. Millheim, Pennsylvania, Bizarre Series, 1940 (?).
Life Everlasting, edited by Sam Moskowitz and Will Sykora. Newark, New Jersey, Avalon, 1947.
Tales from Underwood. New York, Pellegrini and Cudahy, 1952.
Figment of a Dream. Baltimore, Mirage Press, 1962.
The Folsom Flint and Other Curious Tales. Sauk City, Wisconsin, Arkham House, 1969.

OTHER PUBLICATIONS

Verse

Songs of a Spanish Lover (as Henry Cecil). Privately printed, 1924.

Other

The Kellers of Hamilton Township: A Study in Democracy. Privately printed, 1922.
The Sexual Education Series. New York, Popular Book Corporation, 10 vols., 1928.

Know Yourself! Life and Sex Facts of Man, Woman, and Child....- New York, Popular Book Corporation, 1930.
Portfolio of Anatomical Manikins. New York, Sparacio, 1932.
Picture Stories of the Sex Life of Man and Woman. New York, Popular Medicine, 1941.

*   *   *

The genre of science fiction and fantasy has seemed to attract some of the most talented, versatile, and idiosyncratic personalities and made writers of them. David H. Keller pursued a varied and successful career as physician, military doctor, psychiatrist, and medical researcher. He published widely in the professional literature of his field. He also wrote fiction—but only for his family and friends. Then in 1928 *Amazing Stories* published "The Revolt of the Pedestrians," a long dystopian narrative that Keller had completed before Hugo Gernsback had even started *Amazing.* The story was such a success that Gernsback contracted for twelve more from Keller, and during the next decade or so 66 "Kelleryarns" were published in science-fiction and fantasy markets. *Weird Tales* served as another primary outlet for the Keller stories. During the final two decades of his life, however, Keller returned to private publishing and almost continuous writing of stories and books that may or may not have been marketable. His overall accomplishment seems immense, individual, and idiosyncratic. Some of his stories are classics of the horror, weird fantasy variety. Much of his writing reads as pleasantly whimsical and expressive of the "humours" of his personality in the 18th-century sense. In many ways, especially in the final years of his life, he was like an 18th-century eccentric or country gentleman who loved and expressed wit, humour, and imaginative curiosity in both his living and his writing. In all ways, Keller was his own man; and it is perhaps too soon for a literary assessment of his work whether in abnormal psychology or in fantasy or humorous narrative.

Regardless of any later assessment of his large volume of rather whimsical writing, however, certain careful elements in his art are apparent. Keller is often very skillful in the subtle understated suggestion of the supernatural that creates the greatest chill of horror. He combines with this a fascination in the psychosomatic relations of mental disorder to behavior. Among the short, chilling masterpieces that embody these artfully controlled effects are "The Thing in the Cellar," "A Piece of Linoleum," and "The Dead Woman," all from the early 1930's. Keller writes, then, with a subtle control of statement and tone that is unusual in the early pulp markets of the genre. The other element in his art that is particularly impressive is his use of point of view. Many of his narratives are told in first person, and he is master of the ironic first-person narrator who gradually reveals his own insanity to the reader without realizing it himself. As in Swift's *A Modest Proposal,* a Keller narrator will often be condemning himself or herself while telling what seems to be his or her side of the story. The other kind of first-person narrator is Keller himself in the person of various point-of-view characters with whimsical names, such as Jacobus Hubelaire who writes his own autobiography that is really Keller's, or Colonel Horatio Bumble in *The Homunculus.* This last, strange little book gives a fictional picture in the first person of Keller/Bumble that may or may not be the real Keller. But it shows a 20th-century retired Colonel of the Army Medical Corps who dabbles in writing and in the supernatural and who resembles an 18th-century eccentric, such as one might find in a Smollett novel or in the person of Erasmus Darwin, much more than a modern writer. At the same time the book, in its way, treats fascinating themes of scientific methodology, married life, and writing itself. Keller is a puzzlement in the genre—unique, varied, and often extremely effective.

—Donald M. Hassler

KELLEY, Leo P(atrick). American. Born in Wilkes Barre, Pennsylvania, 10 September 1928. Educated at the New School for Social Research, New York, B.A. in English 1957. Advertising copywriter and manager, McGraw-Hill Book Company, New York, 1959-69. Since 1969, free-lance writer. Address: 702 Lincoln Boulevard, Long Beach, New York 11561, U.S.A.

SCIENCE-FICTION PUBLICATIONS

Novels

The Counterfeits. New York, Belmont, 1967.
Odyssey to Earthdeath. New York, Belmont, 1968.
The Accidental Earth. New York, Belmont, 1968.
Time Rogue. New York, Lancer, 1970.
The Coins of Murph. New York, Berkley, 1971; London, Coronet, 1974.
Mindmix. New York, Fawcett, 1972; London, Cornonet, 1973.
Time: 110100. New York, Walker, 1972; as *The Man from Maybe,* London, Coronet, 1974.
Mythmaster. New York, Dell, 1973; London, Coronet, 1974.
The Earth Tripper. New York, Fawcett, 1973; London, Coronet, 1974.
The Time Trap (juvenile). Belmont, California, Pitman, 1977 (?); London, Murray, 1979.
Backward in Time (juvenile). Belmont, California, Pitman, 1979.
Death Sentence (juvenile). Belmont, California, Pitman, 1979.
Earth Two (juvenile). Belmont, California, Pitman, 1979.
Prison Satellite (juvenile). Belmont, California, Pitman, 1979.
Sunworld (juvenile). Belmont, California, Pitman, 1979.
Worlds Apart (juvenile). Belmont, California, Pitman, 1979.
Dead Moon (juvenile). Belmont, California, Pitman, 1979.
King of the Stars (juvenile). Belmont, California, Pitman, 1979.
On the Red World (juvenile). Belmont, California, Pitman, 1979.
Night of Fire and Blood (juvenile). Belmont, California, Pitman, 1979.
Where No Sun Shines (juvenile). Belmont, California, Pitman, 1979.
Vacation in Space (juvenile). Belmont, California, Pitman, 1979.
Star Gold (juvenile). Chicago, Children's Press, 1979.

Uncollected Short Stories

"Dreamtown, U.S.A.," in *If* (New York), February 1955.
"The Human Element," in *If* (New York), June 1957.
"Any Questions," in *Fantastic* (New York), October 1962.
"To the Victor," in *Fantastic* (New York), May 1964.
"O'Grady's Girl," in *Fantasy and Science Fiction* (New York), December 1965.
"A Therapeutic Success," in *Bizarre* (Concord, New Hampshire), January 1966.
"Coins," in *Fantasy and Science Fiction* (New York), November 1968.
"Harvest," in *Fantasy and Science Fiction* (New York), March 1970.
"The Propheteer," in *Galaxy* (New York), March 1970.
"The Travelin' Man," in *Fantasy and Science Fiction* (New York), September 1970.
"Cold, The Fire of the Phoenix," in *Protostars,* edited by David Gerrold and Stephen Goldin. New York, Ballantine, 1971.
"The Dark Door," in *Witchcraft and Sorcery* (Alhambra, California), January 1971.
"Sam," in *Fantasy and Science Fiction* (New York), February 1971.
"The True Believers," in *Fantasy and Science Fiction* (New York), October 1971.
"Teaching Prime," in *Infinity 3,* edited by Robert Hoskins. New York, Lancer, 1972.
"Song," in *Fantasy and Science Fiction* (New York), February 1973.
"The Ninth Resurrection of Miss Hosanna Galaxy," in *Gallery* (Chicago), December 1973.
"Generation Gap," in *Weird Tales* (Los Angeles), Summer 1974.

OTHER PUBLICATIONS

Novels

Brother John (novelization of screenplay). New York, Avon, and London, Pan, 1971.
Deadlocked! New York, Fawcett, 1973.

Other

Editor, *Themes in Science Fiction: A Journey into Wonder.* New York, McGraw Hill, 1972.
Editor, *The Supernatural in Fiction.* New York, McGraw Hill, 1972.
Editor, *Fantasy: The Literature of the Marvelous.* New York, McGraw Hill, 1973.

*   *   *

Leo P. Kelley's first novel, *The Counterfeits*, develops many of the themes that he uses in his later novels. Earth is invaded by an alien race whose home planet has been destroyed. The aliens are able to assume any shape; they take human form and set about destroying human civilization. What takes this book out of the usual alien-invasion formula is Kelley's attempt to provide a plausible reconciliation at the book's conclusion.

Odyssey to Earthdeath explores the domination of a society by psychological methods in the tradition of Orwell's *Nineteen Eighty-Four.* The book suffers from undeveloped characters and a predictable plot. *Time Rogue* is one of Kelley's few attempts to use time travel as a theme for sociological speculation. Unfortunately, the plot degenerates into a good vs. evil confrontation with predictable results. *The Accidental Earth* blends the themes of the previous books into an eerie amalgam. A counter-Earth is separated from our Earth by a wall of Time, but an accident brings the Earths into contact. Only the secret weapon of the Photon Spray saves Earth from alien invasion by severing the Time link and separating the two Earths again. Although the conclusion is hackneyed space opera, the beginning and middle sections of the novel feature some of Kelley's best writing. *The Coins of Murph* tells of a post-holocaust society based on a religion deifying the Chief Programmer of the Rand Corporation, Joseph Murphy, who, on some surviving audio tapes, blames the holocaust on decision making. His followers interpret this to mean all decisions should be decided by chance, hence the use of coins for flipping. The plot gets bogged down in power politics, but the sociological portrait Kelley presents is memorable.

The remaining novels are chiefly characterized by their cynical perspectives and brutality. *Time: 110100* is a surreal morality play of two humans on an odyssey through a strange world populated by lusty, war-like, and enigmatic simulacra. The book has undertones of Barth's *Giles Goat-Boy* but the weak ending damages the book. *Mindmix* presents contemporary human society stricken by a deadly virus. The Government discovers one man, Pete Bratton, who has become immune. Kelley develops a cynical picture of government scientists exploiting Bratton by transplanting the minds of dying geniuses in Bratton's brain, with successful but grim results. *The Earth Tripper* and *Mythmaster* are written in New Wave style. The better of the two books, *The Earth Tripper,* follows the bizarre adventures of an alien observer who goes AWOL on Earth in human form. Captured releasing animals from a zoo, he's taken to a secret mental institution, and he and the other strange inmates are the subjects of brutal experiments using "reality therapy." The mildly upbeat ending doesn't relieve much of the book's cynicism. Since 1973, Kelley has concentrated on writing science fiction for juveniles, chiefly for elementary students with low reading skills.

Kelley's best work features strong writing and ingenious sociological constructions of unique societies, but the unrelenting grimness of his later work coupled with New Wave writing styles weakens its appeal.

—George Kelley

KELLEY, William Melvin. American. Born in New York City in 1937. Educated at Harvard University, Cambridge, Massachusetts (Reed Prize, 1960). Married Karen Gibson in 1962; two children. Writer-in-Residence, State University College, Geneseo, New York, Spring 1965; taught at New School for Social Research, New York, 1965-67. Recipient: Bread Loaf grant, 1962; Whitney Foundation Award, 1963; Rosenthal Foundation Award, 1963; *Transatlantic Review* Award, 1964. Address: c/o Doubleday and Company Inc., 245 Park Avenue, New York, New York 10017, U.S.A.

SCIENCE-FICTION PUBLICATIONS

Novels

A Different Drummer. New York, Doubleday, 1962; London, Hutchinson, 1963.
Dem. New York, Doubleday, 1967.
Dunsfords Travels Everywheres. New York, Doubleday, 1970.

OTHER PUBLICATIONS

Novel

A Drop of Patience. New York, Doubleday, 1965; London, Hutchinson, 1966.

Short Stories

Dancers on the Shore. New York, Doubleday, 1964; London, Hutchinson, 1965.

*   *   *

Though obviously influenced by Thoreau, Twain, Faulkner, Joyce, and John Hawkes (one of his mentors at Harvard), William Melvin Kelley remains a brilliantly original writer. He has never been intimidated by borrowed techniques or ideas; they are merely threads he can weave into patterns of his design. These patterns also use—on occasion—such diversely colored threads as realism, fantasy, satire, spy fiction, stream of unconsciousness dream language, a mythical past, a speculative present and future, and biological and anthropological science fiction. The result has been a group of appealing, personalized, award-winning literary garments, bright, harmonious, and durable.

Even though all his fiction is as interrelated as Faulkner's Yoknapatawpha County saga with important characters from one work appearing briefly or being mentioned in other works, only *A Different Drummer, Dem* and *Dunsfords Travels Everywhere* combine science fiction with mainstream fiction. In *A Different Drummer,* Kelley adapted the multiple point-of-view techniques Faulkner developed in *As I Lay Dying* to speculative material. He considered what might prompt all the blacks of a Southern state to leave it and what might happen to that state if they did. The state was Kelley's own creation but resembled existing Southern states in history, structure, customs—and prejudices. The actions of the blacks were viewed through the eyes of the remaining whites and the consequences of these actions were implied rather than spelled out. In *Dem,* Kelley satirized whites primarily through the behavior of an overly dependent, fantasizing, occasionally violent white man whose vengefully adulterous wife gave birth to fraternal twins, a sickly white and a healthy black. Like any good science-fiction writer, Kelley took pains to make this scientifically dubious twinning seem plausible; a doctor overcame the white protagonist's incredulity by describing at length the concept of superfecundation and its application to this case. In *Dunsfords Travels Everywheres,* Kelley blurred the line between dream and reality so that it became impossible to be sure where the "real" world left off and the alternate "dream" world began. A few sections clearly took place in a dream world since they were written in the type of punning dream-language which Joyce developed in *Finnegans Wake.* However, other sections written in everyday language concerned incidents that might belong to an alternate reality. For example, the opening section in normal language was set in an imaginary European country with a tradition of determining behavior by the color of clothing. Every morning each native had to decide whether to be a yellowred or a bluered for the day. Yellowreds could go only to the yellowred area of each public building and associate only with other yellowreds; the same held true for bluereds. Even though this section operated as a satirical commentary on our society's absurd division by skin color, the functioning of this society was described with as much attention to detail as a science-fiction writer gives to an alien or alternate society. Another section in normal language depicted a worldwide "game" played by a white group called the Tiwaz Youth Organization and a black group called the Family. The game consisted of offenses by the TYO, such as assassinating a Kennedy-like president and enslaving contemporary Africans, and defenses by the Family, with light-skinned blacks pretending to be whites so they could be spies.

Kelley's philosophy has moved between Thoreau-like individualism and black nationalism. Tucker Caliban of *A Different Drummer* refused to let any group protect his rights; he chose to secure them by himself. However, his symbolic actions of buying the land where his ancestors were slaves, salting it, and then going north initiated the migration of all blacks from the state. Each black acted individually, but each was influenced by Caliban's gesture. On the other hand, Chig Dunford of *Dunsfords Travels Everywheres* was shown that all blacks are subject to offenses by whites and that he was needed by other blacks in the struggle against whites.

Like John A. Williams, Sam Greenlee, and Doris Lessing, Kelley has demonstrated that no sharp dividing line exists between mainstream and science fiction and that a writer may profitably blend the two to present certain personal visions.

—Steven R. Carter

KENT, Kelvin. *See* **BARNES, Arthur K.**

KENT, Mallory. *See* **LOWNDES, Robert A.W.**

KENT, Philip. *See* **BULMER, Kenneth.**

KEPPEL-JONES, Arthur (Mervyn). Canadian. Born in Rondebosch, South Africa, 20 January 1909. Educated at the University of Cape Town, 1926-28, B.A. 1928, Ph.D. 1943; Oxford University (Rhodes Scholar), 1929-32, B.A. (honours) 1931, M.A. 1940. Served in the South African Army. Married Eileen Mary Bate in 1935; two sons and one daughter. Lecturer, 1933-34 and 1936-44, and Senior Lecturer, 1945-53, University of the Witwatersrand, Johannesburg; Lecturer, 1935, and Professor of History, 1954-59, University of Natal, Durban. Visiting Lecturer, 1953-54, Professor, 1959-76, and since 1976, Professor Emeritus of History, Queen's University, Kingston, Ontario. Visiting Professor, Duke University, Durham, North Carolina, 1964. Address: Department of History, Queen's University, Kingston, Ontario K7L 3N6, Canada.

SCIENCE-FICTION PUBLICATIONS

Novel

When Smuts Goes: A History of South Africa from 1952 to 2010, First Published in 2015. Cape Town, African Bookman, and London, Gollancz, 1947.

OTHER PUBLICATIONS

Other

Do We Govern Ourselves? Johannesburg, Society of the Friends of Africa, 1945.
South Africa: A Short History. London, Hutchinson, 1949; revised edition, 1961; New York, Hillary House, 1962.
South Africa. Pietermaritzburg, Shuter and Shooter, 1950.
The Dilemma of South Africa. Toronto, Canadian Association for Adult Education, 1950.
Who Is Destroying Civilisation in South Africa? (in English and Afrikaans). Johannesburg, South African Institute of Race Relations, 1951.
Human Relations in South Africa. Johannesburg, St. Benedict's House, 1953.

Editor, *Thomas Philipps, 1820 Settler: His Letters.* Pietermaritzburg, Shuter and Shooter, 1960.

Arthur Keppel-Jones comments:
When Smuts Goes was written in hot anger in 1946; I had thought about it for some time, but the first draft took only three weeks to write. An important part of the motivation and background was provided by Germany. I was in that country during the elections of 1930. Having read the papers and attended a Nazi election meeting, I came away with a certain conviction that the Nazis, if given the chance, would carry out the programme of *Mein Kampf* to the letter. Then came the years of appeasement and wishful thinking, which drove me, like many others, to despair.

After six years of bloodshed had corrected that error, I looked again at the Afrikaner Nationalists. Though they were, and are, in many ways very different from the Nazis, the resemblances in certain respects were frightening. They, too, had a programme. I knew that they intended to put it into effect, but again there was, among their opponents, wishful thinking, a turning of the blind eye. It was only "electoral propaganda"; they would be "sobered by the responsibility of office." On the other hand, their propaganda had succeeded in creating a climate of thought in which only Afrikaner values deserved respect. The values and aspirations of blacks, English, and the rest were tainted with disloyalty and subversion. Europe of the 1930's was in some way being repeated.

I wrote a prophecy to show where all this would lead. Much of it, unhappily, turned out to be correct. In some respects I was utterly wrong. The mistakes arose mainly from one cause: concentrating on the forces at work in South Africa, I made the assumption (acknowledging it to be merely an assumption) that the course of events everywhere else would continue on the old lines. So I did not foresee decolonisation, the Third World, or the rise in the price of gold.

I did not want my prophecy to be proved right; I wanted the warning to be taken. It was not.

*　　　*　　　*

When Smuts Goes, Arthur Keppel-Jones's one contribution to the science-fiction genre, is a remarkable exception in the category of political and social extrapolation, a projection that rings true, particular incorrect prophecies notwithstanding. Like Orwell in *Nineteen Eighty-Four,* Keppel-Jones extends post-World War II conditions, but for 60 years rather than Orwell's 30, and in South

Africa rather than England. Keppel-Jones's work is a fictional history rather than a novel: there are no particularized characters (the media censor is named "Netwerk," a newspaperman "Penman," and so on) and only the broad outlines of events are delineated. But like *Nineteen Eighty-Four, When Smuts Goes* has a chilling credibility, particularly in its focus on "psycho-history," the way the essential character of a nation leads it to inevitable courses of action.

When General Smut's United Party loses power in South Africa after World War II, the internationalist British tradition is replaced by parochial Afrikaner Nationalists. The Afrikaners, essentially romantics attempting to recapture the lost ox-wagon heritage of *voortrekker* days, progressively destroy the "Jingoistic" British liberalism by playing on divisions in the English-speaking community over the threat of the non-white majority. Keppel-Jones correctly predicts the disenfranchisement of non-whites, the governmental promotion of Afrikaner language and culture in education and the mass media, the establishment of a Republic, the imposition of censorship, and the steady isolation of South Africa in the world community. But he is wrong on some counts: from the perspective of 1947 he sees a German-Japanese-Argentine-South African Fascist axis, a permanent collapse in the price of gold, a powerful U.N. Security Council, and the continuation of the relationship among nations as it existed just after World War II. The detailed politics in the early chapters may be slow going for the casual reader and Keppel-Jones fails to foresee Britain's own colonial difficulties, which dates the book somewhat.

Yet *When Smuts Goes* becomes urgent for the contemporary reader when the consequences of South Africa's racial policies are described: low-level but constant racial violence, increasingly repressive measures by the government, evasions and self-denial of the situation's gravity, revolt, and the growing threat of outside intervention. Keppel-Jones's cautionary history is meant to evoke just this sense of urgency in all who care to prevent the final disaster he prophesizes; it still has its intended effect after more than 30 years.

—Andrew Macdonald

KERN, Gregory. *See* **TUBB, E.C.**

KEY, Alexander (Hill). American. Born in La Plata, Maryland, 21 September 1904. Educated at the Chicago Art Institute, 1922-24. Served in the United States Navy, 1942-45: Lieutenant Commander. Married Alice Towle in 1945; one child. Artist: book illustrator from age 19, then art teacher at Studio School of Art, Chicago; writer from 1929. Recipient: American Association of University Women Award, 1965; Lewis Carroll Shelf Award, 1972. *Died 25 July 1979.*

SCIENCE-FICTION PUBLICATIONS

Novels (juvenile)

Sprockets: A Little Robot. Philadelphia, Westminster Press, 1963.
Rivets and Sprockets. Philadelphia, Westminster Press, 1964.
The Forgotten Door. Philadelphia, Westminster Press, 1965; London, Faber, 1966.
Bolts: A Robot Dog. Philadelphia, Westminster Press, 1966.

Escape to Witch Mountain. Philadelphia, Westminster Press, 1968.
Flight to the Lonesome Place. Philadelphia, Westminster Press, 1969.
The Golden Enemy. Philadelphia, Westminster Press, 1969.
The Incredible Tide. Philadelphia, Westminster Press, 1970.
The Magic Meadow. Philadelphia, Westminster Press, 1975.
Jagger, The Dog from Elsewhere. Philadelphia, Westminster Press, 1976.
The Sword of Aradel. Philadelphia, Westminster Press, 1977.
Return from Witch Mountain. Philadelphia, Westminster Press, 1978.

OTHER PUBLICATIONS

Novels

The Wrath and the Wind. Indianapolis, Bobbs Merrill, 1949; London, Heinemann, 1950.
Island Light. Indianapolis, Bobbs Merrill, 1950; London, Heinemann, 1951.

Other (juvenile)

The Red Eagle. New York, Volland, 1930.
Liberty or Death. New York, Harper, 1936.
With Daniel Boone on the Caroliny Trail. Philadelphia, Winston, 1941.
Boys Will Be Boys: Very Easy Pantomimes and Entertainments for Boys. Franklin, Ohio, Eldridge, 1945.
Cherokee Boy. Philadelphia, Westminster Press, 1957.
Mystery of the Sassafras Chair. Philadelphia, Westminster Press, 1967.
The Strange White Doves: True Mysteries of Nature. Philadelphia, Westminster Press, 1972.
The Preposterous Adventures of Swimmer. Philadelphia, Westminster Press, 1973.
The Case of the Vanishing Boy. New York, Archway, 1979.

* * *

Already an established author by 1963, Alexander Key published that year *Sprockets: A Little Robot,* a simply constructed and written, unassuming story designed to attract children presumably interested in SF or space fantasy but too young for Heinlein or Norton. The story's success prompted a sequel, *Rivets and Sprockets.*

Their acceptance by young readers and reviewers alike probably encouraged Key to believe that children's SF might be both financially profitable and professionally satisfying, for in 1966 he published a third SF tale, *The Forgotten Door,* like its predecessors relatively uncomplicated in plot and simply written but more earnest in tone and theme. Subsequently, all of Key's fiction has been a children's SF best characterized as a mix of narrative simplicity and moral earnestness.

At his best—as in *The Forgotten Door* and *Escape to Witch Mountain,* stories focusing on ESP-gifted, extraterrestrial children marooned on an inhospitable Earth and able to return home only with the help of sympathetic humans—Key creates likeable child protagonists and plausibly involves them in struggles between Good and Evil. Setting, reflecting the Carolina mountains Key so obviously loves, is also a strength. At his worst, Key is prone to sentimentalize, in particular overusing ESP-gifted animals that are morally superior to humans. Perhaps it is this weakness, along with relatively low-keyed plots and a too obvious earnestness, that has denied major status to an author who might otherwise have earned it because of his pioneering SF for young readers.

—Francis J. Molson

KEYES, Daniel. American. Born in New York City, 9 August 1927. Educated at Brooklyn College, New York, B.A. 1950, M.A. 1961. Served as a ship's purser in the maritime service, 1945-47. Married Aurea Georginia Vaquez in 1952; two daughters. Editorial Associate, *Marvel Science Stories,* 1950-51; Associate Editor, Stadium Publishing Company, New York, 1951-52; co-owner, Fenko and Keyes Photography Inc., New York, 1953; high school English teacher, Brooklyn, 1954-55, 1957-62; Instructor, Wayne State University, Detroit 1962-66. Lecturer, 1966-72, and since 1972, Professor of English, and director of creative writing, 1973-74, 1977-78, Ohio University, Athens. Recipient: Hugo Award, 1960; Nebula Award, 1966. Agent: Donald S. Engel, Engel and Engel, 9665 Wilshire Boulevard, Beverly Hills, California 90212, U.S.A.

SCIENCE-FICTION PUBLICATIONS

Novel

Flowers for Algernon. New York, Harcourt Brace, and London, Cassell, 1966.

Uncollected Short Stories

"Precedent," in *Marvel* (New York), May 1952.
"Robot—Unwanted," in *Other Worlds* (Evanston, Indiana), June 1952.
"Something Borrowed," in *Fantastic Story* (New York), Summer 1952.
"The Trouble with Elmo," in *Galaxy* (New York), August 1958.
"Crazy Maro," in *The Best from Fantasy and Science Fiction 10,* edited by Robert P. Mills. New York, Doubleday, 1961; London, Gollancz, 1963.
"A Jury of Its Peers," in *Worlds of Tomorrow* (New York), August 1963.
"The Quality of Mercy," in *Frozen Planet.* New York, Macfadden, 1966.

OTHER PUBLICATIONS

Novels

The Touch. New York, Harcourt Brace, 1968; London, Hale, 1971; as *The Contaminated Man,* London, Mayflower, 1977.
The Fifth Sally. Boston, Houghton Mifflin, 1980; London, Hale, 1981.

Other

"How Much Does a Character Cost?," in *Those Who Can,* edited by Robin Scott Wilson. New York, New American Library, 1973.

*   *   *

Rarely has a science-fiction story won such wide-spread praise from readers and writers alike as Daniel Keyes's "Flowers for Algernon." In *The Hugo Winners* Isaac Asimov characterizes the story and his reaction to it: "Now here was a story which struck me so forcefully that I was actually lost in admiration as I read it. So lost in admiration was I for the delicacy of his feelings, for the sure way he plucked at my heartstrings, for the skill with which he handled the remarkable *tour de force* involved in his method of telling the story, that I completely forgot to hate him." Indeed, "Flowers for Algernon" became almost universally admired in science fiction because it not only blazed new trails in narrative technique, characterization, and development of plot but managed to do so without appearing in any way as "experimental." The story is first and foremost a story, and no single literary device interferes with its unfolding.

When one considers the fact that the story is told from the point of view of a mentally retarded man, Charlie Gordon, who first reaches genius level through treatment with intelligence-enhancing drugs and then regresses to his original state because the effect of the drugs is limited, Keyes's success is all the more memorable.

Much of this success rests on one particular narrative device: Keyes presents "Flowers for Algernon" as if it were a diary written by Charlie from the beginning of his treatment with the drugs to his final reversion back to mental retardation. Since Charlie begins and ends the story as a good-natured, trusting man who by habit and desire prefers to see the best in his fellow man, the story never descends to bathos. Even at his most brilliant, when he is able to understand fully the pettiness and cruelty of many of the humans around him, Charlie refuses to accuse anyone. He accepts people for what they are and will not judge them in terms of good or evil. Thus, while Keyes is able to raise a number of serious issues concerning the nature of intelligence, the benefits and evils that may arise from "improving" the human mind, and man's own respect or lack of it for genius, he is able to avoid simple answers or trivial, superficial statements. The issues arise because they must, given the experiences of Charlie in the story. But because Charlie accepts what happens to him without anger and with a sense of dignity, these questions can be viewed in all their complexity with a minimum of emotional coloring.

Keyes later turned the 30-page story into a 200-page novel. The result is predictably less than happy. Keyes was forced to abandon the first-person narrative of the story for an omniscient point of view that expresses far less dramatically Charlie's dignity and faith in humanity. Moreover, in filling in the vaster space needed for a novel, the story shifts from Charlie's experiences and his reactions to them to Charlie's own development as a character. This shift in focus brings with it a loss of distance that in the first version allowed for a far less emotional exploration of the nature of intelligence. The novel is about Charlie while the short story is about what happens to Charlie and the implications of these experiences for all of humanity.

"Flowers for Algernon" is essential science fiction that proves once and for all how both science fiction and artistic merit can coexist comfortably. As science fiction, it raises questions that only can be hinted at in other genres. As literature, it explores these questions in a manner that carefully, yet delightfully, guides the reader through a myriad of emotional traps.

—Stephen H. Goldman

KILLOUGH, (Karen) Lee. American. Born in Syracuse, Kansas, 5 May 1942. Educated at Fort Hays State College, Kansas, 1960-62; Hadley Memorial Hospital School of Radiologic Technology, 1962-64. Married Howard Patrick Killough in 1966. Radiologic Technologist, St. Joseph Hospital, Concordia, Kansas, 1964-65, St. Mary Hospital, Manhattan, Kansas, 1965-67, 1969-71, and Morris Cafritz Memorial Hospital, Washington, D.C. 1967-69. Since 1971, Radiologic Technologist, Kansas State University Veterinary Hospital, Manhattan. Columnist ("Obiter Dictum"), *The Spang Blah,* 1977-79. Address: Box 422, Manhattan, Kansas 66502, U.S.A.

SCIENCE-FICTION PUBLICATIONS

Novels

A Voice Out of Ramah. New York, Ballantine, 1979.
The Doppelganger Gambit. New York, Ballantine, 1979.
The Monitor, The Miners, and the Shree. New York, Ballantine, 1980.
Deadly Secrets. New York, Ballantine, 1981.

Uncollected Short Stories (series: Aventine)

"Caveat Emptor," in *Analog* (New York), May 1970.
"Caravan," in *If* (New York), June 1972.
"Sentience," in *If* (New York), October 1973.

"The Siren Garden" (Aventine), in *Fantasy and Science Fiction* (New York), March 1974.
"Survival," in *Starwind,* Fall 1976.
"Tropic of Eden" (Aventine), in *The Best Science Fiction of the Year 7,* edited by Terry Carr. New York, Ballantine, 1977; London, Gollancz, 1978.
"Stalking Game," in *Galileo* (Boston), Spring 1977.
"A Cup of Hemlock," in *100 Great Science Fiction Short-Short Stories,* edited by Isaac Asimov, Martin H. Greenberg, and Joseph D. Olander. New York, Doubleday, and London, Robson, 1978.
"Broken Stairways, Walls of Time" (Aventine), in *Fantasy and Science Fiction* (New York), May 1979.
"The Sanctuary" and "My Brother Cain," in *Sol Plus,* Summer 1979.
"A House Divided," in *The Best from Fantasy and Science Fiction 23,* edited by Edward L. Ferman. New York, Doubleday, 1980.
"Achronos," in *Fantasy and Science Fiction* (New York), March 1980.

Lee Killough comments:

I believe that, above all else, fiction should entertain. Every novel or story I write is aimed toward giving the reader enjoyment. I write what I myself would pick off a bookshelf to read. I work hard on researching and developing background and designing realistic, rounded characters. I try to satisfy the reader who might be scientifically knowledgeable. If the expert reader's enjoyment is not spoiled by glaring errors, then the science will have a ring of authenticity to the less knowledgeable reader, too. I write psychological and extrapolative science fiction, but not based so much on my own background of biology and veterinary medicine as, strangely enough, on my husband's background of psychology and law. Even the surrealistic Aventine short stories have their roots in extrapolation.

*   *   *

Lee Killough uses science fiction as a vehicle for imaginative speculation about universal human questions. She is a versatile writer, capable of turning her talents to everything from examination of religious dogma, to creation of a highly imaginative artists' colony, to the spitting out of the essentials in a futuristic police procedural. While her work is rigidly varied in mood and situation, and her science-fiction devices are clever and believable, her chief strength lies in her competent narrative skills and well-rounded characterization which lend an air of human truth to even the most unusual situations.

Many science-fiction writers use SF trappings skillfully and purposefully to tie in with and enhance the plot, but Killough is one of the few to use her futuristic devices as essential elements in character building. Much of her work is preoccupied with questions of personal identity and/or the broader question of appearance versus reality. Her first story, "Caveat Emptor," deals with deceptive business dealings as two space merchants overcharge one another for the junk of their respective cultures, each alien to the other. Value is in the eye of the beholder, Killough concludes good-humoredly. A more sobering question is raised in "Sentience" which examines just what outward signs constitute proof that alien forms are sentient.

Killough's Aventine series explores illusion and reality in more depth. In "The Siren Garden" a wealthy woman hides murderous intentions behind her beauty and apparent fascination with fantastic yet fragile "living" musical crystals from an alien culture. The crystals come to symbolize the character of Lorna Dalriadian, herself gorgeous yet brittle, living yet cold. An infatuated florist in the artists' colony Aventine creates a garden of these crystals for Lorna, but she uses him and his masterpiece in a way which shatters his work *and* his illusions.

In "Tropic of Eden" Killough uses cloning to betray the murderous vanity of another beauty, the dancer Eden Lyle, whose desperation to remain young drives her to clone herself with the intention of transplanting her brain into the body of her young, lithe "progeny." An artist from Aventine, who is creating a futuristic "psychotropic" sculpture, discovers Eden's secret as his sculpture reflects not Eden's outer beauty but her inner ugliness. Another Aventine story, "Broken Stairways, Walls of Time," deals with another woman's extreme vanity. Here the singer Cybele Bournais, who lost her

beauty and voice in an accident, uses numerous holos—artistically and mechanically contrived living sculptures of herself—to carry on her career and to protect her damaged self from revelation or human contact. "Achronos," a story stylistically similar to the Aventine group, features a failing artist who discovers a beach where time does not exist. The apparently beautiful people he meets there reveal themselves as the stuff of nightmarish visions which the artist carries with him to his real world of time—and to his artwork.

A Voice Out of Ramah is also preoccupied with questions of identity and shattered illusions. This contemplative narrative follows the life of Kedar Jared Cloud Joseph, a member of a small, all-male cloistered religious hierarchy dominating a sizeable population of hard-working women. In common with other religious leaders, Jared shares the secret of the Trial—a rite of manhood which few boys survive—derived from the days when the planet's first settlers were stricken by a plague which wiped out the majority of the male population. Several factors combine to undermine Jared's religious conviction of the necessity for this rite and reveal Jared as an extraordinary man in his society. Essential to his revolutionary awakening is an appreciation of the strengths of the women of his world. Jared literally and figuratively takes on the identity of his twin sister, Sky, opens his mind to the marooned visitor Alesandra Pontokouros, who believes that intergalactic communication will save his world, and develops paternal feelings for the male youth of his society. Stylistically, *The Doppelganger Gambit* is a real departure from the ruminations of *A Voice Out of Ramah,* but the plot of this fast-moving police procedural novel relies, too, on a question of false identity. A strong sensible woman law-enforcement officer and her flamboyant partner uncover the truth about a suspicious suicide. Essential to the crime's unravelling is an understanding of a future society in which one's bank records and identity are one and the same thing.

In Lee Killough's work, illusions may be shattered, but the message is generally one of optimism. Small personal victories are seen as important, even in the face of the vast strangeness of other worlds. As Killough quotes in *A Voice Out of Ramah:* "All things by immortal power/ Near or far/ Hiddenly/ To each other linked are/ That thou canst not stir a flower/ Without the troubling of a star."

—Rosemary Herbert

KING, Vincent. Pseudonym for Rex Thomas Vinson. British. Born in Falmouth, Cornwall, 22 October 1935. Educated at Redruth Art School and Falmouth School of Art, both Cornwall; West of England College of Art, Bristol. Served in the Royal Air Force. Married; one son and one daughter. Taught art in schools in London, Bristol, Newcastle upon Tyne, and Redruth. Painter and printmaker: work in several Arts Council exhibitions. Agent: Leslie Flood, E.J. Carnell Literary Agency, Rowneybury Bungalow, Sawbridgeworth, near Old Harlow, Essex CM20 2EX, England.

SCIENCE-FICTION PUBLICATIONS

Novels

Light a Last Candle. New York, Ballantine, 1969; London, Rapp and Whiting, 1970.
Another End. New York, Ballantine, 1971.
Candy Man. London, Gollancz, 1971; New York, Ballantine, 1972.
Time Snake and Superclown. London, Futura, 1976.

Uncollected Short Stories

"Defence Mechanism," in *New Writings in SF 7,* edited by John Carnell. London, Dobson, 1966; New York, Bantam, 1971.

"The Wall to End the World," in *New Writings in SF 8*, edited by John Carnell. London, Dobson, 1966; New York, Bantam, 1971.
"Testament," in *New Writings in SF 9*, edited by John Carnell. London, Dobson, 1966; New York, Bantam, 1972.
"Report from Linelos," in *New Writings in SF 15*, edited by John Carnell. London, Dobson, 1969.
"The Discontent Contingency," in *New Writings in SF 19*, edited by John Carnell. London, Dobson, 1971.

Vincent King comments:

I've no explicit intentions, political or philosophical, but considerations of that type keep coming out of the words. The intention is fantasy, a succession of ideas, events, relationships that change, further and further revelations about the situation/plot/story. Naturally this makes for ever-increasing complexity and a continual raising of the stakes (I'm sometimes deeply shocked by what I write!), maybe for incomprehensibility, too. I often include more or less direct quotations from "reality." (Which is interchangeable with "fiction" anyway; reality is fantasy, fantasised by going through people's heads, and it doesn't matter how objective/pragmatic they say they are—that's a fantasy too.) I tend to use the first person because I fantasise that it's more direct. Also it means the voice that tells the story doesn't know what's to happen, is happening. I also fantasise that it allows the fantasy to develop in a less inhibited way. The freedom of fantasy is the thing.

I think the most exciting writing today is on the fantasy end of the spectrum. I'm not speaking only of what is referred to as SF or occult writing. It's interesting that at a time when a lot of SF authors claim to be trying to "go straight," some good so-called mainstream writing seems to be turning more fantastic. What is finished, I think, for a more or less serious SF writer, is the "science" type of SF, and I think the middle-class "Hobbit" type of adventure is pretty sterile too. To me science is a type of magic—or at least that's how I *use* it. Science is not holy, it's practical; it's probably caused no more suffering, or release from suffering, than religions. Religions, wars, science, adultery, murders, etc. are what happen when people aren't allowed or aren't able to be *creative* in some way: to work out their personal fantasy, which might be a garden, or a fortune, or a model steam locomotive, or anything!

*   *   *

Suspense is a major element in all the works of Vincent King. In part, he develops suspense through the ordinary means—surprising and very quick-paced action—which keep the reader wondering what will come next. But here is also a more intellectual type of suspense which may be regarded as one of the distinguishing marks of King's work. This type of suspense also develops in two ways. First, a sort of jig-saw puzzle effect means that, in the beginning of his novels, it is often difficult to see how the various parts relate to one another. What is the connection between Ice Lover and the Mods (*Light a Last Candle*)? The reader must hold numbers of pieces in his mind, gradually fitting them together into a clear, comprehensive picture. Second, his characters have a certain enigmatic quality about them. One's curiosity is aroused because it isn't clear just who or what the protagonist is. Only near the end of the novel is the identity of Candy Man revealed.

Space exploration, the attempt to find and contact other sentient life, is a theme which King plays in a different key. Working within a long time scheme, expending vast resources, man may just possibly find some sentient life form. Adamson finds Protia (*Another End*) after all hope has been abandoned. In *Candy Man* the failure is absolute. But even success may bring strange results. Protia ultimately absorbs Adamson, and the alien beings in *Light a Last Candle* have unsuccessfully attempted to absorb an entire colony of Earthmen. Mankind is unavoidably changed by contact with aliens.

But mankind is portrayed in a decadent state throughout King's novels. The glorious past is gone, some few men live an enervated life among the ruins. The image of those ruins, vast cities covering entire worlds, has a central place for King. His heroes, regularly isolated (or at most accompanied by a single companion) in these vast, hive-like structures, seem compelled to explore the cellars, the subterranean depths of their worlds. Both Adamson and Candy Man are involved in extensive chase scenes in these labyrinthine

depths. Ice Lover lives and fights in caves. Man, as he declines, seems to be portrayed as returning to his roots, the cave, the sea, the womb. Interestingly, the machines have held up better than their creators. The Probe keeps Adamson alive, frustrating his every suicide attempt. The entire population of Earth may have been maintained by machines (*Candy Man*) or resurrected by a computer (*Another End*). In some sense dependence upon machines has led humanity into decadence. Only if they can shake free of the machines will there be some slight hope of renewal.

Each of King's novels deals with the human proclivity to violence; all his heroes are killers who seem to enjoy killing. But in the final analysis the violence seems to be shown as both pointless and ineffective, a serious defect that men must overcome if they are to survive and advance. The conclusions of *Another End* and *Candy Man* hold out some slight hope of this.

King's greatest strength, his highly imaginative permutations upon conventional themes, combines with his ability to create suspense to produce works which fascinate and puzzle the reader. Yet these strengths are somewhat offset by a style of writing heavily dependent upon dialog which has a rather choppy and unsophisticated quality.

—Robert Reilly

KIPLING, (Joseph) Rudyard. British. Born in Bombay, India, 30 December 1865, of English parents. Educated at the United Services College, Westward Ho!, Devon, 1878-82. Married Caroline Starr Balestier in 1892; three children. Assistant Editor, *Civil and Military Gazette*, Lahore, 1882-87; Editor and Contributor, "Week's News," *Pioneer*, Allahabad, 1887-89; returned to England, and settled in London: full-time writer from 1889; lived in Brattleboro, Vermont, 1892-96, then returned to England; settled in Burwash, Sussex, 1902. Rector, University of St. Andrews, 1922-25. Recipient: Nobel Prize for Literature, 1907; Royal Society of Literature Gold Medal, 1926. LL.D.: McGill University, Montreal, 1899; D.Litt.: University of Durham, 1907; Oxford University, 1907; Cambridge University, 1908; University of Edinburgh, 1920; the Sorbonne, Paris, 1921; University of Strasbourg, 1921; D.Phil.: University of Athens, 1924. Honorary Fellow, Magdalene College, Cambridge, 1932. Associate Member, Académie des Sciences Morales et Politiques, 1933. Refused the Poet Laureateship, 1895, and the Order of Merit. *Died 18 January 1936.*

SCIENCE-FICTION PUBLICATIONS

Short Stories

Actions and Reactions. London, Macmillan, and New York, Doubleday, 1909.
A Diversity of Creatures. London, Macmillan, and New York, Doubleday, 1917.

OTHER PUBLICATIONS

Novel

The Light That Failed. New York, United States Book Company, 1890; London, Macmillan, 1891.

Short Stories

Plain Tales from the Hills. Calcutta, Thacker Spink, 1888; New York, Lovell, and London, Macmillan, 1890.
Soldiers Three: A Collection of Stories.... Allahabad, Wheeler, 1888; London, Sampson Low, 1890.
The Stories of the Gadsbys: A Tale Without a Plot. Allahabad, Wheeler, 1888; London, Sampson Low, and New York, Lovell, 1890.

In Black and White.   Allahabad, Wheeler, 1888; London, Sampson Low, and New York, Lovell, 1890.

Under the Deodars.   Allahabad, Wheeler, 1888; revised edition, London, Sampson Low, 1890.

The Phantom 'Rickshaw and Other Tales.   Allahabad, Wheeler, 1888; revised edition, London, Sampson Low, 1890.

Wee Willie Winkie and Other Child Stories.   Allahabad, Wheeler, 1888; revised edition, London, Sampson Low, 1890.

Soldiers Three, and Under the Deodars.   New York, Lovell, 1890.

The Phantom 'Rickshaw, and Wee Willie Winkie.   New York, Lovell, 1890.

The Courting of Dinah Shadd and Other Stories.   New York, Harper, and London, Macmillan, 1890.

Mine Own People.   New York, United States Book Company, 1891.

Life's Handicaps, Being Stories from Mine Own People.   New York and London, Macmillan, 1891.

The Naulahka: A Story of West and East, with Wolcott Balestier. London, Heinemann, and New York, Macmillan, 1892.

Many Inventions.   London, Macmillan, and New York, Appleton, 1893.

Soldier Tales.   London, Macmillan, 1896; as *Soldier Stories,* New York, Macmillan, 1896.

The Day's Work.   New York, Doubleday, and London, Macmillan, 1898.

The Kipling Reader.   London, Macmillan, 1900; as *Selected Stories,* 1925.

Traffics and Discoveries.   London, Macmillan, and New York, Doubleday, 1904.

Abaft the Funnel.   New York, Dodge, 1909.

Selected Stories, edited by William Lyon Phelps.   New York, Doubleday, 1921.

Debits and Credits.   London, Macmillan, and New York, Doubleday, 1926.

Selected Stories.   London, Macmillan, 1929.

Thy Servant a Dog, Told by Boots.   London, Macmillan, and New York, Doubleday, 1930; revised edition, as *Thy Servant a Dog and Other Dog Stories,* Macmillan, 1938.

Humorous Tales.   London, Macmillan, and New York, Doubleday, 1931.

Animal Stories.   London, Macmillan, 1932; New York, Doubleday, 1938.

Limits and Renewals.   London, Macmillan, and New York, Doubleday, 1932.

All The Mowgli Stories.   London, Macmillan, 1933; New York, Doubleday, 1936.

Collected Dog Stories.   London, Macmillan, and New York, Doubleday, 1934.

More Selected Stories.   London, Macmillan, 1940.

Twenty-One Tales.   London, Reprint Society, 1946.

Ten Stories.   London, Pan, 1947.

A Choice of Kipling's Prose, edited by W. Somerset Maugham. London, Macmillan, 1952; as *Maugham's Choice of Kipling's Best: Sixteen Stories,* New York, Doubleday, 1953.

A Treasury of Short Stories.   New York, Bantam, 1957.

(Short Stories), edited by Edward Parone.   New York, Dell, 1960.

Kipling Stories: Twenty-Eight Exciting Tales.   New York, Platt and Munk, 1960.

The Best Short Stories, edited by Randall Jarrell.   New York, Hanover House, 1961; as *In the Vernacular: The English in India* and *The English in England,* New York, Doubleday, 2 vols., 1963.

Famous Tales of India, edited by B.W. Shir-Cliff.   New York, Ballantine, 1962.

Phantoms and Fantasies: 20 Tales.   New York, Doubleday, 1965.

Short Stories, edited by Andrew Rutherford.   London, Penguin, 1971.

Play

The Harbour Watch (produced London, 1913; revised version, as *Gow's Watch,* produced London, 1924).

Verse

Schoolboy Lyrics.   Privately printed, 1881.

Echoes (published anonymously), with Alice Kipling.   Privately printed, 1884.

Departmental Ditties and Other Verses.   Lahore, Civil and Military Gazette Press, 1886; London, Thacker Spink, 1890.

Departmental Ditties, Barrack-Room Ballads, and Other Verse. New York, United States Book Company, 1890.

Barrack-Room Ballads and Other Verses.   London, Methuen, and New York, Macmillan, 1892.

Ballads and Barrack-Room Ballads.   New York, Macmillan, 1893.

The Seven Seas.   New York, Appleton, and London, Methuen, 1896.

Recessional.   Privately printed, 1897.

An Almanac of Twelve Sports.   London, Heinemann, and New York, Russell, 1898.

Poems, edited by Wallace Rice.   Chicago, Star, 1899.

Recessional and Other Poems.   Privately printed, 1899.

The Absent-Minded Beggar.   Privately printed, 1899.

With Number Three, Surgical and Medical, and New Poems. Santiago, Chile, Hume, 1900.

Occasional Poems.   Boston, Bartlett, 1900.

The Five Nations.   London, Methuen, and New York, Doubleday, 1903.

The Muse among the Motors.   New York, Doubleday, 1904.

Collected Verse.   New York, Doubleday, 1907; London, Hodder and Stoughton, 1912.

A History of England (verse only), with C.R.L. Fletcher.   London, Oxford University Press-Hodder and Stoughton, and New York, Doubleday, 1911; revised edition, 1930.

Songs from Books.   New York, Doubleday, 1912; London, Macmillan, 1913.

Twenty Poems.   London, Methuen, 1918.

The Years Between.   London, Methuen, and New York, Doubleday, 1919.

Verse: Inclusive Edition 1885-1918.   London, Hodder and Stoughton, and New York, Doubleday, 3 vols., 1919; revised edition, 1921, 1927, 1933.

A Kipling Anthology: Verse.   London, Methuen, and New York, Doubleday, 1922.

Songs for Youth, from Collected Verse.   London, Hodder and Stoughton, 1924; New York, Doubleday, 1925.

A Choice of Songs.   London, Methuen, 1925.

Sea and Sussex.   London, Macmillan, and New York, Doubleday, 1926.

Songs of the Sea.   London, Macmillan, and New York, Doubleday, 1927.

Poems 1886-1929.   London, Macmillan, 3 vols., 1929; New York, Doubleday, 3 vols., 1930.

Selected Poems.   London, Methuen, 1931.

East of Suez, Being a Selection of Eastern Verses.   London, Macmillan, 1931.

Sixty Poems.   London, Hodder and Stoughton, 1939.

Verse: Definitive Edition.   London, Hodder and Stoughton, and New York, Doubleday, 1940.

So Shall Ye Reap: Poems for These Days.   London, Hodder and Stoughton, 1941.

A Choice of Kipling's Verse, edited by T.S. Eliot.   London, Faber, 1941; New York, Scribner, 1943.

Sixty Poems.   London, Hodder and Stoughton, 1957.

A Kipling Anthology, edited by W.G. Bebbington.   London, Methuen, 1964.

The Complete Barrack-Room Ballads, edited by Charles Carrington.   London, Methuen, 1973.

Selected Verse, edited by James Cochrane.   London, Penguin, 1977.

Other

Quartette, with others.   Lahore, Civil and Military Gazette Press, 1885.

The City of Dreadful Night and Other Sketches.   Allahabad, Wheeler, 1890.

The City of Dreadful Night and Other Places. Allahabad, Wheeler, and London, Sampson Low, 1891.

The Smith Administration. Allahabad, Wheeler, 1891.

Letters of Marque. Allahabad, Wheeler, and London, Sampson Low, 1891.

American Notes, with *The Bottle Imp,* by Robert Louis Stevenson. New York, Ivers, 1891.

The Jungle Book (juvenile). London, Macmillan, and New York, Century, 1894.

The Second Jungle Book (juvenile). London, Macmillan, and New York, Century, 1895; revised edition, Macmillan, 1895.

Out of India: Things I Saw, and Failed to See, in Certain Days and Nights at Jeypore and Elsewhere. New York, Dillingham, 1895.

The Kipling Birthday Book, edited by Joseph Finn. London, Macmillan, 1896; New York, Doubleday, 1899.

"Captains Courageous": A Story of the Grand Banks (juvenile). London, Macmillan, and New York, Century, 1897.

A Fleet in Being: Notes of Two Trips with the Channel Squadron. London, Macmillan, 1898.

Stalky & Co. (juvenile). London, Macmillan, and New York, Doubleday, 1899; revised edition, as *The Complete Stalky & Co.,* Macmillan, 1929; Doubleday, 1930.

From Sea to Sea: Letters of Travel. New York, Doubleday, 1899; as *From Sea to Sea and Other Sketches,* London, Macmillan, 1900.

Works (Swastika Edition). New York, Doubleday, Appleton, and Century, 15 vols., 1899.

Kim (juvenile). New York, Doubleday, and London, Macmillan, 1901.

Just So Stories for Little Children. London, Macmillan, and New York, Doubleday, 1902.

Puck of Pook's Hill (juvenile). London, Macmillan, and New York, Doubleday, 1906.

Letters to the Family (Notes on a Recent Trip to Canada). Toronto, Macmillan, 1908.

Rewards and Fairies (juvenile). London, Macmillan, and New York, Doubleday, 1910.

The New Army in Training. London, Macmillan, 1915.

France at War. London, Macmillan, and New York, Doubleday, 1915.

The Fringes of the Fleet. London, Macmillan, and New York, Doubleday, 1915.

Tales of "The Trade." Privately printed, 1916.

Sea Warfare. London, Macmillan, and New York, Doubleday, 1916.

The Eyes of Asia. New York, Doubleday, 1918.

The Graves of the Fallen. London, Imperial War Graves Commission, 1919.

Letters of Travel (1892-1913). London, Macmillan, and New York, Doubleday, 1920.

A Kipling Anthology: Prose. London, Macmillan, and New York, Doubleday, 1922.

The Irish Guards in the Great War. London, Macmillan, and New York, Doubleday, 2 vols., 1923.

Land and Sea Tales for Scouts and Guides. London, Macmillan, and New York, Doubleday, 1923.

Works (Mandalay Edition). New York, Doubleday, 26 vols., 1925-26.

A Book of Words: Selections from Speeches and Addresses Delivered Between 1906 and 1927. London, Macmillan, and New York, Doubleday, 1928.

The One Volume Kipling. New York, Doubleday, 1928.

Souvenirs of France. London, Macmillan, 1933.

A Kipling Pageant. New York, Doubleday, 1935.

Ham and the Porcupine (juvenile). New York, Doubleday, 1935.

Something of Myself for My Friends Known and Unknown. London, Macmillan, and New York, Doubleday, 1937.

Complete Works (Sussex Edition). London, Macmillan, 35 vols., 1937-39; as *Collected Works* (Burwash Edition), New York, Doubleday, 28 vols., 1941 (includes revised versions of some previously published works).

A Kipling Treasury: Stories and Poems. London, Macmillan, 1940.

Kipling: A Selection of His Stories and Poems, edited by John Beecroft. New York, Doubleday, 2 vols., 1956.

Letters from Japan, edited by Donald Richie and Yoshimori Harashima. Tokyo, Kenkyusha, 1962.

Pearls from Kipling, edited by C. Donald Plomer. New Britain, Connecticut, Elihu Burritt Library, 1963.

Rudyard Kipling to Rider Haggard: The Record of a Friendship, edited by Morton Cohen. London, Hutchinson, 1965.

The Best of Kipling. New York, Doubleday, 1968.

Stories and Poems, edited by Roger Lancelyn Green. London, Dent, 1970.

Kipling's Horace, edited by Charles Carrington. London, Methuen, 1978.

*

Bibliography: *Rudyard Kipling: A Bibliographical Catalogue* by J. McG. Stewart, edited by A.W. Keats, Toronto, Dalhousie University-University of Toronto Press, 1959, London, Oxford University Press, 1960; "Kipling: An Annotated Bibliography of Writings about Him" by H.E. Gerber and E. Lauterbach, in *English Fiction in Transition 3* (Tempe, Arizona), 1960, and *8,* 1965.

*   *   *

Today, Rudyard Kipling is chiefly remembered as a spokesman for imperialism and as a skilful versifier, and it is often overlooked that approximately one in six of his published short stories were science fiction or fantasy. His influence on 20th-century SF writers was probably greater than anyone else's of his generation, except Wells, and is acknowledged by writers as disparate as Poul Anderson and John Brunner.

His formal excursions into the future are few but memorable. "With the Night Mail" describes an Atlantic crossing by airship in the year 2000, and is accompanied by excerpts from the magazine in which it was supposed to appear. Socially, little appears to have changed, but technologically this is an astounding vision; at a time when it was novel for a liner to carry radio-telegraphy equipment, and broadcasting was two decades distant, Kipling envisaged the need for air traffic control and a General Communicator system. In the sequel, "As Easy as ABC," he speculated on the demise of democracy owing to its tendency to lapse into mob-rule—this may have been conditioned by his disappointment with the USA at a time when lynch-law was still common: witness the terrifying image of the memorial statue, "The Nigger in Flames,"—and on a cure for over-population, a problem he had encountered during his time in India.

His other works of SF and fantasy range from the early "The Bridge-Builders," in which a civil engineer overhears the Indian gods debating whether or not to destroy his masterpiece spanning the Ganges, through those astonishing *tours-de-force* without human characters like ".007" (steam locomotives) and "The Ship That Found Herself" (steel plates and girders and the ship's cat!), by way of speculative SF like "In the Same Boat" (a man and a woman discover that the nightmares haunting them refer to real events which happened while they were in the womb) and "The Finest Story in the World" (a City clerk remembers his previous lives, as a galley-slave and on an expedition to Vinland), right up to the complex, subtle stories of his last years when he left his readers and critics far behind, like "The Children of the Zodiac."

He wrote the classic ghosts-in-reverse story, "They," and the deadpan fantasies of *Just So Stories;* in *Puck of Pook's Hill* and *Rewards and Fairies* he brought the people of past ages forward to the present to speak for themselves; and he wrote about sea-serpents and mysterious curses and the heady excitement of modern inventions—but never quite as anyone else would have handled them. For example, "Wireless" is indeed about early radio, but the narrator's experimental friend, trying to eavesdrop on the Royal Navy, fails to notice how the soul of Keats is striking an echo across time in a lovelorn, tubercular assistant pharmacist.

Kipling, who was possibly the most completely equipped writer ever to tackle the short-story form in the English language, exemplifies the fact that in our literary tradition there has never been a hard-and-fast line between realistic and fantastic. Indeed, he was a master at making the fantastic seem credible.

—John Brunner

KLINE, Otis Adelbert.   American.   Born in Chicago, Illinois, 1 July 1891. Composer and song writer, then music publisher, film writer, and editor: Editor, *Weird Tales,* Chicago, 1924; Founder, Otis Kline Associates, literary agency. *Died 24 October 1946.*

SCIENCE-FICTION PUBLICATIONS

Novels (series: Robert Grandon; Jan; Mars)

The Planet of Peril (Grandon).   Chicago, McClurg, 1929.
Maza of the Moon.   Chicago, McClurg, 1930.
The Prince of Peril (Grandon).   Chicago, McClurg, 1930.
Call of the Savage.   New York, Clode, 1937; as *Jan of the Jungle,* New York, Ace, 1966.
The Port of Peril (Grandon).   Providence, Rhode Island, Grandon, 1949.
The Swordsman of Mars.   New York, Avalon, 1960.
The Outlaws of Mars.   New York, Avalon, 1960.
Tam, Son of the Tiger.   New York, Avalon, 1962.
Jan in India.   Lakemont, Georgia, Fictioneer, 1974.

Short Stories

The Man Who Limped and Other Stories.   Hollywood, Saint, 1946.
Stories.   Oak Lawn, Illinois, Weinberg, 1975.

*   *   *

Otis Adelbert Kline, whose literary career flourished in the 1920's and 1930's, never aimed higher than the prevailing tastes of those who read the pulp magazines *Weird Tales, Argosy,* and *Amazing Stories,* in which he published most of his stories. He was clearly influenced by and competed with his contemporaries Edgar Rice Burroughs, A. Merritt, and H.P. Lovecraft, and made no apologies for pandering to the popular taste for formula adventure stories. His work as a literary agent kept him abreast of whatever appealed to the popular imagination, and he worked these interests into his stories. His SF was of the fantastic variety denounced by Gernsback in the 1930's, Campbell in the 1940's, and Gold in the 1950's, who were committed to making SF respectable among adult readers. Had Kline been writing in the 1950's and 1960's, he would probably have been turning out the same formula stories with New Wave embellishments.

Kline's costume adventure melodramas are SF in the limited sense that he made use of conventions like psi powers, rocket travel, ray guns, and heavy doses of ritualism, totemism, and primitive religion borrowed from Frazer, Malinowski, and other anthropologists whose ideas of primitive social and religious customs had begun to stir the popular imagination. In truth, little beyond the accessories distinguish the SF from, say, the oriental adventures of the Dragoman series (*The Man Who Limped*). Much of his fantastic SF belongs in that loose category known as "sword and sorcery."

Kline's imagination was highly visual and his storytelling techniques were clearly shaped by his film-writing experiences. Whatever the costumes, settings, and properties, his stories are built out of the simplest formulas of the adventure-suspense story, and his characters are stock types familiar to anyone who has seen the old Buck Rogers serials. Like Burroughs, Kline had his series of Mars and Venus stories. The latter (the Robert Grandon series) proved very popular, and perhaps should be taken as representative of Kline's most influential work in the genre.

Critical opinion on Kline has been largely negative. However, despite everything negative that has been said, including the more recently fashionable charges of racism and sexism (equally justified), there remains the embarrassing but undeniable power of Kline's naive handling of the formulas and conventions of exotic adventure. Kline's ideas are second-hand and his treatment of them trite, but that is the very heart of his appeal. He gives the reader the expected cliché, the familiar stereotype, the conventional adventure formula. No summary could do justice to his triteness, but the following vignette from "The Bride of Osiris" (1927) may stand as a fair sample of the action: "As he stood there in the midst of the hostile multitude, holding the half-fainting Doris and expecting

instant death, Buell heard two sounds simultaneously—the twang of a bowstring and an encouraging shout from Rafferty." The power of such a passage may be of a low order, barely a notch above the boy's adventure stories of the time, and yet the reader may find a kind of delight encountering an almost pure example of the thriller whose only purpose is unreflective and mindless entertainment. That Kline succeeds at all is perhaps his revenge upon literary criticism.

Kline's most successful novel, and probably his best, is *Call of the Savage.* The novel was modelled on Kipling's *Jungle Books* and Hudson's *Green Mansions,* and exhibits Kline's ability to use mythic and archetypal story elements to entrap all but the most wary reader. *Call of the Savage* is fantasy rather than SF, but, as we have seen in Kline's other work, the differences as well as the resemblances are coincidental.

—Donald L. Lawler

———————————

KNEALE, (Thomas) Nigel.   British.   Born in Barrow-in-Furness, Lancashire, 28 April 1922. Educated at Douglas High School, Isle of Man; Royal Academy of Dramatic Art, London, 1946-48. Married the writer Judith Kerr in 1954; one daughter and one son. Actor, Stratford upon Avon, 1948-49; staff member, BBC Television, London, 1951-55. Recipient: Maugham Award, 1950, Agent: Dougles Rae (Management) Ltd., 28 Charing Cross Road, London WC2H 0DB, England.

PUBLICATIONS

Novel

Quatermass.   London, Hutchinson, 1979.

Short Stories

Tomato Cain and Other Stories.   London, Collins, 1949; New York, Knopf, 1950.

Plays

The Quatermass Experiment (televised, 1953).   London, Penguin, 1959.
Quatermass II (televised, 1955).   London, Penguin, 1960.
Quatermass and the Pit (televised, 1959).   London, Penguin, 1960.
The Year of the Sex Olympics and Other TV Plays (includes *The Road* and *The Stone Tape*).   London, Ferret Fantasy, 1976.

Screenplays: *Quatermass II (Enemy from Space),* with Val Guest, 1957; *The Abominable Snowman,* 1957; *Look Back in Anger,* with John Osborne, 1959; *The Entertainer,* with John Osborne, 1960; *HMS Defiant (Damn the Defiant),* with Edmund North, 1962; *First Men in the Moon,* with Jan Read, 1964; *The Witches,* 1966; *Quatermass and the Pit (5,000,000 Years to Earth),* 1967; *The Quatermass Conclusion,* 1979.

Television Plays: *The Quatermass Experiment,* 1953; *Nineteen Eighty-Four,* from the novel by Orwell, 1954; *The Creature,* 1955; *Quatermass II,* 1955; *Mrs. Wickens in the Fall,* 1956; *Quatermass and the Pit,* 1959; *The Road,* 1963; *The Crunch,* 1964; *The Year of the Sex Olympics,* 1967; *Bam! Pow! Zapp!,* 1969; *Wine of India,* 1970; *The Chopper,* 1971; *The Stone Tape,* 1972; *Jack and the Beanstalk,* 1974; *Murrain,* 1975; *Buddyboy,* 1976; *During Barty's Party,* 1976; *Special Offer,* 1976; *The Dummy,* 1976; *Baby,* 1976; *What Big Eyes,* 1976; *Quatermass,* 1979.

Nigel Kneale comments:
    I have always been a scriptwriter for television and films because

that's what I like doing best. I don't regard myself as a science fiction writer, and the list above confirms this. Looking through this list I wondered what other things I wrote. The answer, of course, is things that didn't get made. Some of my best screenplays, from Huxley, Lawrence, and the like, went down with collapsing film companies. More rarely, but more painfully, there were stillborn TV originals, like *The Big Big Giggle,* a serial about a teenage suicide craze, wiped out by high cost and official nervousness that was probably justified (it could have been dangerous). Or *Crow,* about the slave trade and not dangerous at all, victim of an internal squabble in a TV company. I just have to be grateful for all those that *did* get made.

*   *   *

With a few notable exceptions, most of them in recent years, movies and television have not been kind to science fiction. The speculative ideas that characterize what is best in the genre have proven difficult to translate into visual media without interrupting the action with long expository speeches, while the spectacular visual surfaces that science-fiction narratives afford have been all too tempting to filmmakers. As a result, few science-fiction writers have been able to work with success in the media, and fewer still have managed to build their primary reputation as a media writer of science fiction. Nigel Kneale is a member of this select latter group. The three television serials concerning Professor Bernard Quatermass that he wrote for the BBC between 1953 and 1959—all three of which were subsequently published in book form and adapted as feature films—established a standard for the televised science-fiction horror story that has seldom been surpassed.

Kneale had little direct experience as a science-fiction writer before joining the BBC, although a few of his short stories from *Tomato Cain* are small masterpieces of weird fiction. While at the BBC, Kneale's plays included an adaptation for television of Orwell's *Nineteen Eighty-Four* and an original play about the abominable snowman called *The Creature* (filmed as *The Abominable Snowman*). But it was his 1953 six-part sequel *The Quatermass Experiment* that quickly established his reputation as a convincing dramatist of suspense thrillers. This tale of an alien life form that takes over the body of the lone survivor of the first space mission and metamorphoses into a hideous monster back on Earth, despite occasional absurdities (super-scientist Quatermass finally succeeds in literally *talking* the monster to death), reveals an ear for convincing dialogue, an awareness of the dramatic possibilities of the television medium (such as the use of "newscasters" to carry forth the action), and a talent for working serious issues and concepts into a fast-moving dramatic narrative. Though Quatermass is a scientist-hero in the mold of Conan Doyle's Professor Challenger, Kneale makes some pointed observations about the morality of scientific research and the relationship of government and the journalistic media to such research.

Professor Quatermass continued his fight against bureaucracy and journalistic sensationalism in two subsequent serials. *Quatermass II* concerns the attempt of an alien civilization to establish colonies on Earth by converting human workers into zombie-like slaves; it is perhaps the weakest of the three serials. *Quatermass and the Pit* is perhaps the strongest: a subway excavation in a reputedly haunted area uncovers an ancient alien spaceship which, when activated, reveals that legends of the devil are based on race memories of the aliens from Mars who once tried to conquer Earth—and in the process created us. The mix of myth, supernaturalism, and science fiction works well, and predates by several years cult rumors of gods from outer space. A fourth installment in the Quatermass series, *The Quatermass Conclusion,* was filmed in 1979.

Kneale worked on other screenplays, most notably the film adaptations of two John Osborne plays and an adaptation of Wells's *First Men in the Moon,* which he gave a characteristic twist by casting the story as a flashback told more than a half-century later by a survivor of the expedition whose secret is revealed only when the "official" first moon-landing party comes across the remnants of the earlier adventurers. Here, as in the Quatermass serials, Kneale's ironic humor, his deftness in sketching minor characters, and his sense of dramatic structure provide a strong script. Though he has

shown little inclination to move beyond the horror-suspense school of science fiction, Kneale has contributed significantly to the genre's growth in the media.

—Gary K. Wolfe

KNEBEL, Fletcher. American. Born in Dayton, Ohio, 1 October 1911. Educated at Miami University, Oxford, Ohio, B.A. 1934. Served in the United States Navy in World War II. Married Laura Bergquist in 1965; two children by a previous marriage. Reporter, *Coatesville Record,* Pennsylvania, 1934, *Chattanooga News,* Tennessee, 1934-35, and *Toledo News-Bee,* Ohio, 1935; Reporter, 1936, and Washington Correspondent, 1937-50, *Cleveland Plain Dealer;* Washington Correspondent, Cowles Publications, Washington, D.C., 1950-64, and writer of the syndicated column "Potomac Fever," 1951-64. Writer for *Look* magazine, New York, 1950-71. Recipient: Sigma Delta Chi award, for reporting, 1955. D.L.: Miami University, 1964; D.LL.: Drake University, Des Moines, Iowa, 1968. Address: 208 Edgerstoune Road, Princeton, New Jersey 08540, U.S.A.

SCIENCE-FICTION PUBLICATIONS

Novels

Seven Days in May, with Charles W. Bailey II. New York, Harper, and London, Weidenfeld and Nicolson, 1962.
Night of Camp David. New York, Harper, and London, Weidenfeld and Nicolson, 1965.
Trespass. New York, Doubleday, and London, W.H. Allen, 1969.

OTHER PUBLICATIONS

Novels

Convention, with Charles W. Bailey II. New York, Harper, and London, Weidenfeld and Nicolson, 1964.
The Zinzin Road. New York, Doubleday, 1966; London, W.H. Allen, 1967.
Vanished. New York, Doubleday, and London, W.H. Allen, 1968.
Dark Horse. New York, Doubleday, 1972; London, Hodder and Stoughton, 1973.
The Bottom Line. New York, Doubleday, 1974; London, Hodder and Stoughton, 1975.
Dave Sulkin Cares! New York, Doubleday, 1978.

Other

No High Ground, with Charles W. Bailey II. New York, Harper, and London, Weidenfeld and Nicolson, 1960

*

Manuscript Collection: Mugar Memorial Library, Boston University.

*   *   *

In his best-selling political thrillers—at least the ones which can be remotely considered science fiction, since those three are set in the near-future—Fletcher Knebel has demonstrated how fragile and tenuous the seemingly stable political institutions of the United States really are. *Seven Days in May* chronicles an attempted coup d'etat by members of the Joint Chiefs of Staff. *Night of Camp David,* anticipating the conclusion of the Watergate scandals, tells of a young US Senator who discovers that the clever and charismatic liberal President has gone insane: he is ultimately forced to resign. *Trespass* deals with a conspiracy by a sympathetically treated Black militant organization to hold several prominent and wealthy white families hostage until the group's demands for the creation of a separate Black nation in the American South are met. The way this last situation is resolved by Knebel smacks too much of sentimentality, but the earlier two novels are tensely plotted, cleverly designed suspense stories that hide, more or less successfully, their plot-saving (as well as nation-saving) coincidences under a bundle of plausible details concerning the daily operations of several inter-related branches of the government. In this regard, Knebel uses his nearly 30 years of experience as a Washington-based journalist. At the end of a Knebel thriller, the country is saved because of the concerted actions of a few good men; yet, given the disturbing implications of some of Knebel's plot premises, the conventional happy endings that Knebel routinely offers may provide the more thoughtful reader with only the coldest of political comfort.

—Kenneth Jurkiewicz

KNIGHT, Damon (Francis). American. Born in Baker, Oregon, 19 September 1922. Educated at Hood River High School, Oregon; WPA Art Center, Salem, Oregon, 1940-41. Married 1) Gertrud Werndl; 2) Helen Schlaz; 3) Kate Wilhelm, *q.v.,* in 1963; four children. Free-lance writer: Assistant Editor, Popular Publications, 1943-44, 1949-50; Editor, *Worlds Beyond,* 1950-51; Book Editor, *Science Fiction Adventures,* 1953-54; Editor, *If,* 1958-59; Book Editor, *Fantasy and Science Fiction,* 1959-60. Co-Founding Director, Milford Science Fiction Writers' Conferences, 1956. Since 1967, Lecturer, Clarion Workshop in Science Fiction and Fantasy. Founder, 1965, and President, 1965-66, Science Fiction Writers of America. Recipient: Hugo Award, for non-fiction, 1956; Pilgrim Award, 1975. Agent: Robert P. Mills Ltd., 156 East 52nd Street, New York, New York 10022. Address: 1645 Horn Lane, Eugene, Oregon 97402, U.S.A.

SCIENCE-FICTION PUBLICATIONS

Novels

Hell's Pavement. New York, Lion, 1955; London, Banner, 1958; as *Analogue Men,* New York, Berkley, 1962.
The People Maker. New York, Zenith, 1959; revised edition, as *A for Anything,* London, New English Library, 1961; New York, Berkley, 1965.
Masters of Evolution. New York, Ace, 1959.
The Sun Saboteurs. New York, Ace, 1961; as *The Earth Quarter* (with *World Without Children*), New York, Lancer, 1970.
Beyond the Barrier. New York, Doubleday, and London, Gollancz, 1964.
Mind Switch. New York, Berkley, 1965; as *The Other Foot,* London, Whiting and Wheaton, 1966.
The Rithian Terror. New York, Award, 1965.
Three Novels: Rule Golden, Natural State, The Dying Man. New York, Doubleday, and London, Gollancz, 1967; as *The Natural State and Other Stories,* London, Pan, 1975.
Two Novels (The Earth Quarter and *Double Meaning).* London, Gollancz, 1974.
The World and Thorinn. New York, Putnam, 1981.

Short Stories

Far Out. New York, Simon and Schuster, and London, Gollancz, 1961.
In Deep. New York, Berkley, 1963; London, Gollancz, 1964.
Off Center. New York, Award, 1965; London, Gollancz, 1969.

Turning On. New York, Doubleday, 1966; London, Gollancz, 1967.
The Best of Damon Knight. New York, Doubleday, 1976.

Uncollected Short Story

"I See You," in *Best Science Fiction of the Year 6,* edited by Terry Carr. New York, Holt Rinehart, and London, Gollancz, 1977.

OTHER PUBLICATIONS

Other

In Search of Wonder. Chicago, Advent, 1956; revised edition, 1967.
Charles Fort, Prophet of the Unexplained. New York, Doubleday, 1970; London, Gollancz, 1971.
The Futurians: The Story of the Science Fiction "Family" of the 30's That Produced Today's Top SF Writers and Editors. New York, Day, 1977.

Editor, *A Century of Science Fiction.* New York, Simon and Schuster, 1962; London, Gollancz, 1963.
Editor, *First Flight.* New York, Lancer, 1963; as *Now Begins Tomorros,* 1969.
Editor, *A Century of Great Short Science Fiction Novels.* New York, Delacorte Press, 1964; London, Gollancz, 1965.
Editor, *Tomorrow x 4.* New York, Fawcett, 1964; London, Coronet, 1967.
Editor, and Translator, *Thirteen French Science-Fiction Stories.* New York, Bantam, and London, Corgi, 1965.
Editor, *Beyond Tomorrow.* New York, Harper, 1965; London, Gollancz, 1968.
Editor, *The Dark Side.* New York, Doubleday, 1965; London, Dobson, 1966.
Editor, *The Shape of Things.* New York, Popular Library, 1965.
Editor, *Nebula Award Stories 1965.* New York, Doubleday, 1966; London, Gollancz, 1967.
Editor, *Cities of Wonder.* New York, Doubleday, 1966; London, Dobson, 1968.
Editor, *Orbit 1-21.* New York, Putnam, 12 vols., 1966-73, New York, Berkley, 1 vol., 1974, New York, Harper, 8 vols., 1974-80; vol. 1, London, Whiting and Wheaton, 1966; vol. 2, London, Rapp and Whiting, 1968.
Editor, *Science Fiction Inventions.* New York, Lancer, 1967.
Editor, *Worlds to Come.* New York, Harper, 1967; London, Gollancz, 1969.
Editor, *The Metal Smile.* New York, Belmont, 1968.
Editor, *One Hundred Years of Science Fiction.* New York, Simon and Schuster, 1968; London, Gollancz, 1969.
Editor, *Toward Infinity.* New York, Simon and Schuster, 1968; London, Gollancz, 1970.
Editor, *Dimension X* (juvenile). New York, Simon and Schuster, 1970; London, Gollancz, 1972.
Editor, *First Contact.* New York, Pinnacle, 1971.
Editor, *A Pocketful of Stars.* New York, Doubleday, 1971; London, Gollancz, 1972.
Editor, *Perchance to Dream.* New York, Doubleday, 1972; London, Gollancz, 1974.
Editor, *A Science Fiction Argosy.* New York, Simon and Schuster, 1972; London, Gollancz, 1973.
Editor, *Tomorrow and Tomorrow.* New York, Simon and Schuster, 1973; London, Gollancz, 1974.
Editor, *The Golden Road.* New York, Simon and Schuster, and London, Gollancz, 1974.
Editor, *Happy Endings.* Indianapolis, Bobbs Merrill, 1974.
Editor, *Elsewhere x 3.* London, Coronet, 1974.
Editor, *A Shocking Thing.* New York, Pocket Books, 1974.
Editor, *Best Stories from Orbit 1-10.* New York, Berkley, 1975.
Editor, *Science Fiction of the Thirties.* Indianapolis, Bobbs Merrill, 1975.
Editor, *Westerns of the 40's: Classics from the Great Pulps.* Indianapolis, Bobbs Merrill, 1977.
Editor, *Turning Points: Essays on the Art of Science Fiction.* New York, Harper, 1977.

Translator, *Ashes, Ashes,* by René Barjavel. New York, Doubleday, 1967.

* * *

Damon Knight, deservedly lauded as a critic and editor, is a competent fiction writer cursed with a vivid imagination, a clear vision of cosmic morality, an understanding of the arbitrariness of human value judgments, and a sardonic sense of humor that prevents him from taking most of it seriously. Often the inevitable irony appears in a sudden plot twist or in the reader's perception of a pun that the story is built on, a technique that in some cases, such as "To Serve Man," becomes thematic as well as technical. In this piece, in which an alien race's benevolence toward humans turns out to have a culinary motive, the pun is turned to a serious criticism of egocentric self-deception. At other times, a pun is all the story has to offer, as in, for example, "Eripmav," in which a vampire on a vegetable world is killed with a steak through its heart. Perhaps the most complexly ironic title in the whole body of work is "Not with a Bang" in which the last man on Earth woos and finally wins the last woman, a prudish spinster, only to find himself paralyzed in the Men's Room—which her prudery will not allow her to enter—just before consummating their wedded bliss. And so the world ends in an allusion to T.S. Eliot, a poet whose influence shows clearly in Knight's work.

Although Knight has produced a number of novels, complete with action and adventure—all of them expanded from the shorter forms in which he is most facile—he works best at the medium length represented by *Three Novels.* His ironic perspective allows him a sharp compression of events into key scenes which are effectively juxtaposed. The result recalls the episodic quality of some of the language's finest satirists, such as Swift and Twain; Knight's choices of theme and situation, and his use of language, are also reminiscent of theirs. He does not often extrapolate from real world situations, although *Hell's Pavement* partially does that; more often he recasts real-world situations in estranged form for ironic perspective: "Earth Quarter" (expanded into *The Sun Saboteurs*) could be any Third World ghetto in any advanced country; *The Rithian Terror* features a slightly disguised British Empire, complete with despised New World colonials; *A for Anything* moves from a 19th-century American plantation setting to a reprise of imperial Rome.

Knight avoids the idea—familiar in SF since Asimov's Foundation trilogy—that history repeats itself; it does not. His basic assumption, that human nature does not change, is very clearly stated in "Time Enough": we are and always will be guilty of the same flaws we always have been. Those flaws provide the sharper, more serious ironies of his work. In such moral fables as "Ask Me Anything," "Man in the Jar," "A Thing of Beauty," "Auto-da-Fé," "Second Class Citizen," and "Collector's Item" (formerly "The End of the Search"), basic human motivations—greed, lust for power or knowledge, anthropocentrism—end by frustrating themselves in plots that just miss being tragic because the human motive is never presented as quite admirable. "The Country of the Kind" also just misses the tragic dimension for a slightly different reason: by letting us share the point of view of the protagonist, Knight makes us almost sympathize with the only cruel and violent—and insane—member of our species left in a world of gentle benevolence. The effect is similar to that achieved by Anthony Burgess in *A Clockwork Orange.* How such a thing can happen to us as readers is explained fictionally in "The Enemy" in which a human explorer meets and is killed by an evil alien more fitted to survive then she—and which she finds beautiful; one of our flaws is that we find competent evil attractive, even at our own expense.

Unlike many SF writers concerned with humanity's destructive environmental impact, Knight does not blame technology itself; as in "Idiot Stick," everything depends on which end of the tool the idiot is on. Even in his most clearly anti-machine story, "Natural State" (a tighter version of the expanded *Masters of Evolution*), a biological technology replaces the mechanical one; nature is still manipulated, although perhaps more cooperatively than antagonistically. But human nature is not so easily handled.

In *The Sun Saboteurs* human nature makes us unfit for a place in the galactic civilization; in "Collector's Item" it makes us unfit for survival. Attempts to control our anti-social insanities in *Hell's Pavement* result in still greater insanity. In *The Rithian Terror*

(expanded from "Double Meaning") our rigidly serious self-importance defeats us. In "The Beachcomber" sheer accident can reduce all of our grand schemes—even in a future, evolved state—to picking up pebbles on the beach.

Even human attempts at morality and ethics come to naught when they come up against the needs of survival, in *A for Anything.* Some kind of improvement—although not necessarily a welcome one—might result from a mental cross of an individual human with a superior alien, as in "Four in One" or *Beyond the Barrier* (expanded from "The Tree of Time"), in which Knight nearly tricks us out of species chauvinism with a bit of manipulation more difficult than that of "The Country of the Kind." Even this unsavory hope is unlikely; we are so flawed that in *Mind Switch* (expanded from "A Visitor at the Zoo"), an alien mind is corrupted by transfer into a human body, even with a built-in sex change. Our psyches are, if anything, less trustworthy; in "Masks" an incorruptible metal body corrupts a human mind. There is also little hope of external salvation. "Rule Golden," which remakes the Christ myth in modern iconography, gives us a paradise at the cost of what we might recognize as human and at the cost of the evolutionary process that has made us what we are. In such a universe even the power of love can not cope with hate, and hate leads to extinction in "Stranger Station." Perhaps the only possible Messiah may be that of "What Rough Beast" who brings in the Kingdom because he is afraid of people—and at the expense of the lives, and the world, of those people who expect him to save them from themselves.

This body of work is on the whole a black comedy, full of ironies and bitter laughter. But the despair that accompanies the logic of Knight's anatomy of the human condition has its compensations. If there is no hope for us, we can still take pleasure where we may: in the fantastic chance of being possessed by friendly demons, in "Be My Guest"; in the archetypal insane adventure of love in "Mary" (formerly "An Ancient Madness"); in the discovery of intimacy in strange places in "To the Pure." Or ultimately in the bitter-sweet knowledge that we, like all things, will pass away. In "The Dying Man" (formerly "Dio"), Knight produces one of his strongest stories. The advent of death into a world of immortals—the reversal of a time-worn story line—brings awareness that human mortality also gives us maturity, depth, strength, balance; and we are led to see that death is just. In this perception is the final escape from human egocentrism. If that perception is too much for us, we can escape, sadly, as in "The Handler," into the fantasy of conscious illusion to find some sort of artificial joy.

All in all, Damon Knight's fiction has a sane, tough-minded wholeness. It does not often give us brilliance; it seldom gives us hope; it does not even give us much that is fundamentally new. Part of its strength—ironic humor—is also sometimes its weakness. But it does give us an imaginatively different look—sometimes with genuine mythic power—at ideas as old as human kind, still built into the very marrow of our species. In the words of a character from *Hell's Pavement,* speaking of a task similar to Knight's, though it may promise us "nothing except the rewards of competence and of curiosity, and an occasional windfall of laughter. . .it is enough." Knight's fiction deserves to share the accolades his criticism and his editing have already earned.

—Robert L. Jones

KNIGHT, Norman L(ouis). American. Born in St. Joseph, Missouri, 21 September 1895. Educated at St. Joseph Junior College, A.A. 1918; George Washington University, Washington, D.C., B.S. in chemical engineering 1925. Served in the United States Army Field Artillery, 1918-19. Married Marie Sarah Yenn in 1921; one daughter. Worked for the Department of Agriculture: assistant observer, Davenport, Iowa, 1919-20, and observer and code translator, Washington, D.C., Weather Bureau; analytical chemist in Washington, D.C., 1925-29, Chicago, 1929, St. Louis, 1929-40, Chicago, 1940-50, and Beltsville, Maryland, 1950-64, Insecticide Division; retired in 1964: Merit Award, 1962. *Died in 1970(?).*

SCIENCE-FICTION PUBLICATIONS

Novel

A Torrent of Faces, with James Blish.   New York, Doubleday, 1967; London, Faber, 1968.

Uncollected Short Stories

"Frontier of the Unknown," in *Astounding* (New York), July 1937.
"Isle of the Golden Swarm," in *Astounding* (New York), June 1938.
"Saurian Valedictory," in *Astounding* (New York), January 1939.
"Bombardment in Reverse," in *Astounding* (New York), February 1940.
"The Testament of Akubii," in *Astounding* (New York), June 1940.
"Fugitive from Vanguard," in *Astounding* (New York), January 1942.
"Kilgallen's Lunar Legacy," in *Astounding* (New York), August 1942.
"Once in a Blue Moon," in *Future* (New York), August 1942.
"Short-Circuited Probability," in *Best of Science Fiction,* edited by Groff Conklin.   New York, Crown, 1946.
"Crisis in Utopia," in *Five Science Fiction Novels,* edited by Martin H. Greenberg.   New York, Gnome Press, 1952; as *Crucible of Power,* London, Lane, 1953.
"The Piper of Dis," in *Galaxy* (New York), August 1966.
"To Love Another," in *Analog* (New York), April 1967.

*   *   *

Norman L. Knight published his first story in *Astounding* in 1937, worked most of his life as a chemist specializing in pesticides, and finally published his most ambitious science fiction work in collaboration with the master, James Blish, in 1967. One theme and one setting, in fact, kept reappearing in the early stories; and the importance of that set of images in the novel suggests that Knight may have been the more seminal partner in the collaboration—if not the more polished stylist. Images that led eventually to the masterpiece, *A Torrent of Faces,* can be seen as early as the serialized novel "Frontier of the Unknown," in which a deep-sea diver moves in "a twilight pierced by a million uneasy, shifting, flickering ghosts of slanting, green-tinged sun rays." This crude flood of modifiers was followed by another two-part novel, "Crisis in Utopia," in which Knight also anticipates his work with Blish. Knight includes here the fully developed conception and description of the undersea race of human mutants called Tritons. The writing is a bit more subtle, and Knight's ideas on the effects of managed evolution are suggestive.

Nevertheless, these early stories are dominated by the usual villains of melodrama and the crude overwriting that so often seems the appropriate literary parallel to the line-drawing illustrations of the early pulp magazines. The novel, however, is the culmination of all this. One of the most popular sections of the novel, "The Shipwrecked Hotel," is a polished undersea disaster epic in which the Triton race plays a major role; Triton characters are fully developed throughout the book, and much of the action takes place undersea. Also, by the time of this later work the earth itself has replaced the melodramatic villains as a key protagonist—a much greater literary accomplishment. The individual extrapolations in the novel about living conditions in a future with one trillion inhabitants on earth are many and richly developed, and the writing shows marked improvement over the early Knight extrapolations on the sea and on Utopia. Blish was a good teacher and a good collaborator for Knight's valuable ideas on the future, on evolution, and on accompanying disasters.

—Donald M. Hassler

KNOX, Calvin M.   *See* SILVERBERG, Robert.

KOESTLER, Arthur.   British.   Born in Budapest, Hungary, 5 September 1905; became a British subject, 1948. Educated at the University of Vienna, 1922-26. Married 1) Dorothy Asher in 1935 (divorced, 1950); 2) Mamaine Paget in 1950 (divorced 1953); 3) Cynthia Jefferies in 1965; one daughter. Foreign Correspondent for the Ullstein chain, Berlin, in the Middle East, 1927-29, and in Paris, 1929-30; Foreign Editor, *B.Z. am Mittag,* and Science Editor, *Vossische Zeitung,* Berlin, 1930-32; member of the Graf Zeppelin polar expedition, 1931; travelled in Russia, 1932-33; member of the Communist Party, 1932-38; free-lance writer, in Paris, London, and Zurich, 1933-36; War Correspondent for the *News Chronicle,* London, in Spain, 1936-37; imprisoned by the Nationalists, then exchanged through intervention of the British government; imprisoned in France, 1939-40, then joined the French Foreign Legion, 1940-41, escaped to Britain, and served in the British Pioneer Corps, 1941-42; after discharge, worked for the Ministry of Information, London, and as a night ambulance driver; Special Correspondent, in Palestine, for *The Times,* London, 1945, and for the *Manchester Guardian* and *New York Herald Tribune,* 1948; Visiting Chubb Fellow, Yale University, New Haven, Connecticut, 1950; Fellow, Center for Advanced Study in the Behavioral Sciences, Stanford University, California, 1964-65. Recipient: Sonning Prize, University of Copenhagen, 1968. LL.D.: Queen's University, Kingston, Ontario, 1968; D.Lit.: Leeds University, 1977. Fellow, 1957, and Companion of Literature, 1974, Royal Society of Literature; Fellow, Royal Astronomical Society, 1976. C.B.E. (Commander, Order of the British Empire), 1972. Address: c/o A.D. Peters and Company Ltd., 10 Buckingham Street, London WC2N 6BU, England.

SCIENCE-FICTION PUBLICATIONS

Novels

The Age of Longing.   London, Collins, and New York, Macmillan, 1951.
The Call-Girls: A Tragi-Comedy.   London, Hutchinson, 1972; New York, Random House, 1973.

Uncollected Short Story

"Pythagoras and the Psychoanalyst," in *Fantasia Mathematica,* edited by Clifton Fadiman.   New York, Simon and Schuster, 1958.

OTHER PUBLICATIONS

Novels

The Gladiators, translated by Edith Simon.   London, Cape, and New York, Macmillan, 1939.
Darkness at Noon, translated by Daphne Hardy.   London, Cape, 1940; New York, Macmillan, 1941.
Arrival and Departure.   London, Cape, and New York, Macmillan, 1943.
Thieves in the Night: Chronicle of an Experiment.   London, Macmillan, and New York, Macmillan, 1946.

Plays

Twilight Bar: An Escapade in Four Acts (produced Paris and Baltimore, 1946).   London, Cape, and New York, Macmillan, 1945.

Screenplay: *Lift Your Head, Comrade* (documentary), 1944.

Other

Von Weissen Nächten und Roten Tagen. Kharkov, Ukrainian
State Publishers for National Minorities, 1933.
Encyclopédie de la Vie Sexuelle, with Ludwig Levy-Lenz and A.
Willy. Paris, Aldor, 1934.
Menschenopfer Unerhört. Paris, Carrefour, 1937.
Spanish Testament (autobiography). London, Gollancz, 1937;
excerpt, as *Dialogue with Death,* translated by Phyllis and Tre-
vor Blewitt, London, Macmillan, 1938; New York, Macmillan,
1942.
Scum of the Earth (autobiography). London, Cape, and New
York, Macmillan, 1941.
The Yogi and the Commissar and Other Essays. London, Cape,
1945; New York, Macmillan, 1946.
*Sexual Anomalies and Perversions: A Summary of the Works of
Magnus Hirschfeld.* London, Torch, 1946; revised edition,
edited by Norman Haire, London, Encyclopaedic Press, 1952.
L'Encyclopédie de la Famille, with Manes Sperber. Paris, n.d.
*Insight and Outlook: An Inquiry into the Common Foundations of
Science, Art, and Social Ethics.* London, Macmillan, and New
York, Macmillan, 1949.
Promise and Fulfillment: Palestine, 1917-1949. London, Macmil-
lan, and New York, Macmillan, 1949.
Arrow in the Blue (autobiography). London, Collins-Hamish
Hamilton, and New York, Macmillan, 1952.
The Invisible Writing (autobiography). London, Collins-Hamish
Hamilton, 1954; Boston, Beacon Press, 1955.
The Trail of the Dinosaur and Other Essays. London, Collins,
and New York, Macmillan, 1955.
Reflections on Hanging. London, Gollancz, 1956; New York,
Macmillan, 1957.
*The Sleepwalkers: A History of Man's Changing Vision of the
Universe.* London, Hutchinson, and New York, Macmillan,
1959; section published as *The Watershed: A Biography of
Johannes Kepler,* New York, Doubleday, 1960; London, Heine-
mann, 1961.
The Lotus and the Robot. London, Hutchinson, 1960; New York,
Macmillan, 1961.
*Hanged by the Neck: An Exposure of Capital Punishment in Eng-
land,* with C.H. Rolph. London, Penguin, 1961.
The Act of Creation. London, Hutchinson, and New York, Mac-
millan, 1964.
The Ghost in the Machine. London, Hutchinson, 1967; New
York, Macmillan, 1968.
Drinkers of Infinity: Essays 1955-1967. London, Hutchinson,
1968; New York, Macmillan, 1969.
The Case of the Midwife Toad. London, Hutchinson, 1971; New
York, Random House, 1972.
The Roots of Coincidence. London, Hutchinson, and New York,
Random House, 1972.
The Lion and the Ostrich (lecture). London, Oxford University
Press, 1973.
The Challenge of Chance: Experiments and Speculations, with
Alister Hardy and Robert Harvie. London, Hutchinson, 1973;
New York, Random House, 1975.
"Echoes of the Mind," in *Science Fact/Fiction.* Chicago, Scott
Foresman, 1974.
The Heel of Achilles: Essays 1968-1973. London, Hutchinson,
1974; New York, Random House, 1975.
The Thirteenth Tribe: The Khazar Empire and Its Heritage. Lon-
don, Hutchinson, and New York, Random House, 1976.
Janus: A Summing Up. London, Hutchinson, and New York,
Random House, 1978.
Bricks to Babel (selections). London, Hutchinson, 1980.

Editor, *Suicide of a Nation? An Enquiry into the State of Britain
Today.* London, Hutchinson, 1963; New York, Macmillan,
1964.
Editor, with J.R. Smythies, *Beyond Reductionism: New Perspec-
tives in the Life Sciences: The Alpbach Symposium.* London,
Hutchinson, 1969; New York, Macmillan, 1970.

Bibliography: *Arthur Koestler: An International Bibliography* by
Reed Merrill and Thomas Frazier, Ann Arbor, Michigan, Ardis,
1979.

*   *   *

To separate out those works by Arthur Koestler that can be
legitimately called science fiction is not easy. His whole body of
work is a record of his personal intellectual pilgrimage, and the
books resonate with the power of passionately held ideas. The first
novels are "close extrapolations" from reality. Rather than futuristic, they are parabolic; instead of extending present tendencies into
a future extreme, they extract structures of situations Koestler sees
as recurrent. They might have happened at any time, past or future.

The Gladiators is based on the historical uprising led by Spartacus in 1st-century B.C. Rome. Only when given intellectual direction does the slave rebellion become a revolution aimed at utopia;
but the inherent structure of such revolutions demands real-world
"detours" from the ideal goal. All revolution, then, must fail. In
Darkness at Noon—Koestler's most powerful work—Rubashov is
intended as a generalized type of the revolutionary. Caught in the
logic that makes ends and ideals a justification of the means used to
attain them, he is led—willingly—to confess crimes against the
Party which he has not committed but which should be the result of
his ideological disagreement. Like the Jesus depicted in "The Misunderstanding" (prologue to *The Call-Girls*), Rubashov is executed
for an idea in which he no longer believes but which he thinks
history may judge kindly—it may survive. The protagonist of *Arrival and Departure,* Peter Slavek, follows a similar course for contrary reasons. After he escapes from fascist torturers into Neutralia,
he learns through psychoanalysis that his "heroism" is a disguised
form of sought-for punishment of a traumatic childhood guilt.
Nevertheless, he chooses to act on the basis of his now-suspect
emotions, returning to the war and to probable death. Intuition has
replaced logic, but neither is capable of ushering humankind into
the promised land. These three novels are important contributions
to the literature of utopia.

Only slightly more futuristic is *The Age of Longing,* set in Europe
of the late 1950's, although, as one character says, the exact time is
not important: if catastrophe does not come this year it will come
later. The title refers to both the historical period and the youth of
the female protagonist, Hydie; both the character and the culture
long for the "new God" Slavek predicts at the end of *Arrival and
Departure.* But no such object of belief appears. The futility of the
situation is symbolized in Hydie's attempt to shoot her former lover,
a revolutionary agent locked safely into his materialistic logic, free
of Hydie's emotional involvement as well as from society's ineffectual moral code. Her act does not even produce a martyr—only an
embarrassing incident.

Even more gloomy is Koestler's play, *Twilight Bar.* Two visitors
arrive from Happy World Number Three, a planet circling Aldebaran, to test the Earth's fitness to survive; their criterion is happiness.
Under duress the world is changed into a happy place. But when the
rumor spreads that the whole affair is a hoax, people eagerly rush
back to their misery. At the final curtain we do not know if the world
will survive or be destroyed.

After a 20-year detour through modern science in search of the
essential flaw in human nature, Koestler returned to fiction with
The Call-Girls, a narrative of an international conference called by
Nikolai Solovief in the face of impending world disaster to consider
"Approaches to Survival." The twelve participants ("call-girls")
summoned by Solovief-Christ represent major contemporary schools
of thought ranging from Skinnerian behaviorism to parapsychology. Their presentations are of actual experiments and ideas that
Koestler has written about in his nonfictional works; Nikolai
resembles Koestler himself. The conference fails to reach agreement; not even science is the God that will save humanity from itself.
The epilogue (the prologue has been mentioned above) is "The
Chimeras," a sketch reminiscent of Ionesco's *Rhinoceros,* in which
the protagonist sees everyone but himself turn into chimeras without realizing it. The inconclusiveness of the novel's ending reminds

us that Rubashov's historical consciousness still applies—only survival can judge the correctness of an idea or act; but in this book there is no Rubashov. Humankind still waits for Godot; the dying Nikolai Solovief (Koestler?) no longer cares.

—Robert L. Jones

———————

KOONTZ, Dean R(ay). Also writes as David Axton; Brian Coffey; K.R. Dwyer. American. Born in Everett, Pennsylvania, 9 July 1945. B.A. in English. Married Gerda Koontz in 1966. English teacher, then free-lance writer. Address: c/o G.P. Putnam's Sons, 200 Madison Avenue, New York, New York 10016, U.S.A.

SCIENCE-FICTION PUBLICATIONS

Novels

Star Quest. New York, Ace, 1968.
The Fall of the Dream Machine. New York, Ace, 1969.
The Dark Symphony. New York, Lancer, 1970.
Hell's Gate. New York, Lancer, 1970.
Dark of the Woods. New York, Ace, 1970.
Beastchild. New York, Lancer, 1970.
Anti-Man. New York, Paperback Library, 1970.
The Crimson Witch. New York, Curtis, 1971.
The Flesh in the Furnace. New York, Bantam, 1972.
A Darkness in My Soul. New York, DAW, 1972.
Time Thieves. New York, Ace, 1972; London, Dobson, 1977.
Warlock. New York, Lancer, 1972.
Starblood. New York, Lancer, 1972.
Demon Seed. New York, Bantam, 1973; London, Corgi, 1977.
A Werewolf among Us. New York, Ballantine, 1973.
Hanging On. New York, Evans, 1973; London, Barrie and Jenkins, 1974.
The Haunted Earth. New York, Lancer, 1973.
After the Last Race. New York, Atheneum, 1974.
Nightmare Journey. New York, Berkley, 1975.
Night Chills. New York, Atheneum, 1976; London, W.H. Allen, 1977.
The Vision. New York, Putnam, 1977.

Short Stories

Soft Come the Dragons. New York, Ace, 1970.

Uncollected Short Stories

"Bruno," in *Fantasy and Science Fiction* (New York), April 1971.
"Altarboy," in *Infinity 3,* edited by Robert Hoskins. New York, Lancer, 1972.
"A Mouse in the Walls of the Global Village," in *Again, Dangerous Visions,* edited by Harlan Ellison. New York, Doubleday, 1972; London, Millington, 1976.
"Ollie's Hands," in *Infinity 4,* edited by Robert Hoskins. New York, Lancer, 1972.
"Cosmic Sin," in *Fantasy and Science Fiction* (New York), February 1972.
"Gravyworld," in *Infinity 5,* edited by Robert Hoskins. New York, Lancer, 1973.
"The Sinless Child," in *Flame Tree Planet,* edited by Roger Elwood. St. Louis, Concordia, 1973.
"Terra Phobia," in *Androids, Time Machines, and Blue Giraffes,* edited by Roger Elwood and Vic Ghidalia. Chicago, Follett, 1973.
"The Undercity," in *Future City,* edited by Roger Elwood. New York, Simon and Schuster, 1973.

"Wake Up to Thunder," in *Children of Infinity,* edited by Roger Elwood. New York, Putnam, 1974.
"We Three," in *Final Stage,* edited by Edward L. Ferman and Barry N. Malzberg. New York, Charterhouse, 1974.

OTHER PUBLICATIONS

Novel

Prison of Ice (as David Axton). Philadelphia, Lippincott, 1976.

Novels as Brian Coffey

Blood Risk. Indianapolis, Bobbs Merrill, 1973; London, Barker, 1974.
Surrounded. Indianapolis, Bobbs Merrill, 1974; London, Barker, 1975.
The Wall of Masks. Indianapolis, Bobbs Merrill, 1975.

Novels as K.R. Dwyer

Chase. New York, Random House, 1972; London, Barker, 1974.
Shattered. New York, Random House, 1973; London, Barker, 1974.
Dragonfly. New York, Random House, 1975.

Other

The Pig Society, with Gerda Koontz. Los Angeles, Aware Press, 1970.
The Underground Lifestyles Handbook, with Gerda Koontz. Los Angeles, Award Press, 1970.
Writing Popular Fiction. Cincinnati, Writer's Digest, 1973.

*   *   *

As of 1979, Dean R. Koontz is no longer writing science fiction. Very likely, only a small circle of fans will miss him. His best work showed great promise because of its sensitive, humanistic amalgam of intellect and sensitivity, but much of his work regressed to the stereotyped characters, ritualistic journeys, and heroic feats found in hard-core SF before 1960.

Koontz is a writer of the New Wave in science fiction, a trend characterized by authors with humanities rather than science backgrounds. Certainly, Koontz's themes are rigorously chosen and often intriguing. His best-known works concern the theme of the malevolent child, of innocence turned inside out; he handles the notion in *Beastchild,* in *A Darkness in My Soul,* in which a mutant becomes God, and quite compellingly in *Demon Seed* in which a super-computer creates its own genetic material which it "implants" into a human woman. In "We Three" genetically mutated children wish away harsh parents, then neighbors, then the entire world through their extra-sensory powers.

This theme is a corollary to Koontz's major concern: what it means to be human. In several works on robots, particularly the crisply written "The Night of the Storm," Koontz explores this theme. The robot-protagonist Suranov is bored by his centralized, staid society "peopled" by robots. Humans are rumored to exist, much to the horror of the robots, whose prime rule is that the universe is logical, a dictum which the existence of humans challenges. The story also begins a robotics series carried on by New Wave writers Pamela Sargent and George Zebrowski, among others, in the *Continuum* series. The more turgid novel *Anti-Man* presents an android who changes into a new form of being, to the consternation of the human protagonist. This novel explores the Frankenstein theme—the relationship of creator and his creation—as does *Demon Seed.*

Beginning with his first story, "Soft Come the Dragons," Koontz clearly favors intuition and emotion as essential components of humanness, rather than logic and reason, which can be assigned to machines. Perhaps his best long work, *A Werewolf among Us* presents a protagonist who is a cyberdective, a human whose brain is electronically and physically linked to a portable computer on his chest. Using a classic Agatha Christie plot, Koontz combines science fiction and detective genres. Members of a family are being murdered, the remaining members of the family are suspects, and the reader is presented with clues. However, the main conflict in the novel is psychological: when the human half of the cyberdective realizes the murderer is another robot, his computer half rejects the notion as illogical.

Koontz also treats themes current in popular culture. Marshall McLuhan's *The Medium Is the Massage* was the origin for "A Mouse in the Walls of the Global Village," and "The Psychedelic Children" projects a society one generation hence in which the children whose parents took LSD in the late 1960's are mutants who are hunted by society. The anti-establishment bias of the 1960's is clear in Koontz's work. In *Dark of the Woods* an unimaginative, conformist society systematically eliminates aliens. In "The Twelfth Bed" old people are shut away in a nursing home run by robots.

When Koontz deals with the theme of the quest and the mythic journey, however, he writes stereotyped pulp science fiction. In *Anti-Man, Nightmare Journey, Dark of the Woods,* and *Warlock* a hero rebelling from society sets out on a trek, usually through a cold wilderness, in which he encounters strange beasts and exotic phenomena which he eventually overcomes. The women in these works are sex goddesses only, deferential to the hero, though, as Koontz condescendingly interjects, spunky. Many of his early works contain these sorts of stereotyped characters and situations.

Koontz reports he is presently interested in such genres as suspense, war tales, and crime stories. At his best in *Warlock,* Koontz shows his ability to create a suspenseful tale and a sensitive character. If he returns to science fiction, he might be well advised to continue to explore his most productive theme of the Cartesian mind-body split and its consequences for what humans define as human. Koontz clearly defines a being as human if the being feels, loves, and intuits, be that creature man, robot, or beast.

—Kathryn L. Seidel

KORNBLUTH, C(yril) M. Also wrote as Simon Eisner; Cyril M. Judd; Jordan Park. American. Born in New York City, in 1923. Educated at the University of Chicago, B.A. Served in the infantry during World War II: Bronze Star. Married Mary Kornbluth; two sons. Editor, Chicago office of Trans-Radio Press, 1949-51; freelance writer after 1951. *Died 21 March 1958.*

SCIENCE-FICTION PUBLICATIONS

Novels

Gunner Cade (as Cyril M. Judd, with Judith Merril). New York, Simon and Schuster, 1952; London, Gollancz, 1964.
Outpost Mars (as Cyril M. Judd, with Judith Merril). New York, Abelard Press, 1952; London, New English Library, 1966; revised edition, as *Sin in Space,* New York, Galaxy, 1956.
Takeoff. New York, Doubleday, 1952.
The Space Merchants, with Frederik Pohl. New York, Ballantine, 1953; London, Heinemann, 1955.
The Syndic. New York, Doubleday, 1953; London, Faber, 1964.
Search the Sky, with Frederik Pohl. New York, Ballantine, 1954; London, Digit, 1960.
Gladiator-at-Law, with Frederik Pohl. New York, Ballantine, 1955; London, Digit, 1958.
Not This August. New York, Doubleday, 1955; as *Christmas Eve,* London, Joseph, 1956.
Wolfbane, with Frederik Pohl. New York, Ballantine, 1959; London, Gollancz, 1960.

Short Stories

The Explorers. New York, Ballantine, 1954; as *The Mindworm and Other Stories,* London, Joseph, 1955.
A Mile Beyond the Moon. New York, Doubleday, 1958.

The Marching Morons. New York, Ballantine, 1959.
The Wonder Effect, with Frederik Pohl. New York, Ballantine, 1962; London, Gollancz, 1967; revised edition, as *Critical Mass,* New York, Bantam, 1977.
Best SF Stories. London, Faber, 1968.
Thirteen O'Clock and Other Zero Stories, edited by James Blish. New York, Dell, 1970; London, Hale, 1972.
The Best of C.M. Kornbluth, edited by Frederik Pohl. New York, Doubleday, 1976.

OTHER PUBLICATIONS

Novels

The Naked Storm (as Simon Eisner). New York, Lion, 1952.
A Town Is Drowning, with Frederik Pohl. New York, Ballantine, 1955; London, Digit, 1960.
Presidential Year, with Frederik Pohl. New York, Ballantine, 1956.

Novels as Jordan Park

Half. New York, Lion, 1953.
Valerie. New York, Lion, 1953.
Sorority House, with Frederik Pohl. New York, Lion, 1956.
The Man of Cold Rages, with Frederik Pohl. New York, Pyramid, 1958.

Other

"The Failure of the Science Fiction Novel as Social Criticism," in *The Science Fiction Novel.* Chicago, Advent, 1969.

* * *

C.M. Kornbluth was a major talent of the specialty magazines in the 1940's and 1950's. Probably best known as a collaborator with Frederik Pohl on novels of social extrapolation, he was primarily a writer of short stories that frequently contrast cosmic affairs with mundane existence, sometimes to farcical, more often to sardonic, effect.

With Pohl, he helped produce a handful of lively, satiric novels that practically constitute a genre of their own: a brand of near-future dystopia, deriving in part from H.G. Wells, concentrating on one particular facet of society which becomes the dominant force in the world, as in *The Space Merchants* and *Gladiator-at-Law.* In *Search the Sky,* a much lighter and lesser work, the satire mutates into a picaresque romp, exposing Kornbluth's penchant for quickstep burlesque. The other two books, though, are characterized by a continual mordant wit in their serious development of the oppressive rule of socio-economic institutions. Of course, these institutions are merely exaggerations of those already operating in the modern world, and are invariably connected to the realms of high finance and mass consumption, unlike say, the dystopian worlds of Zamyatin, Orwell, or even Huxley, which are more distinctly political and totalitarian, and in many ways less directly evolved from the contemporary milieus of those writers. In this regard, Pohl and Kornbluth are more Wellsian, more extrapolative as opposed to symbolic, and much more "radical" in concept and detail than either Huxley or Orwell. The cautionary aspects of *Space Merchants*—its background of overpopulation, scarcity of resources, pollution, and runaway commercial exploitation—have made it a canonical "prophetic novel" in the wider world outside science fiction.

Their last true collaboration, *Wolfbane,* also deals with a culture of severely limited resources, but as a condition ostensibly imposed from outside, by outré alien pyramids who have stolen the Earth-Moon system away from the Sun. The book is almost pure adventure, verging on space opera at the close, but it begins in a setting of material and spiritual poverty acutely drawn in its every detail. Kornbluth never achieved the distinction apart from Pohl that he did alongside him; and Pohl was fond enough of their partnership to "collaborate" with Kornbluth even after the latter's death by working up stories from odd fragments or from their previous common property (*The Wonder Effect* is partly composed of these).

Kornbluth also collaborated with Judith Merril, as Cyril Judd, on *Outpost Mars* and *Gunner Cade*. The second is notable for its vivid evocation of a post-holocaust military brotherhood, a spiritual sort of Spartanism. In both, the setting is again a down-at-heels world, but neither story has the inventive brilliance of the major Pohl-Kornbluth novels. However, each of them concerns a legendary/mythic element that resolves itself as a modest distortion of the book's initial reality-frame. This thematic concern relates to Kornbluth's best short stories, many of which play with the penetration of everyday existence by the utterly fantastic, the occult, the arcane. Such a tendency may seem axiomatic for science fiction; in Kornbluth, it often ranges beyond the usual boundaries of 1950's SF, in tales as diverse in tone as "The Cosmic Expense Account" and "The Last Man Left in the Bar."

On his own, he wrote only three SF novels, *Not This August, Takeoff,* and *The Syndic*. The first two are patent journeyman exercises, apparently slanted for marketing considerations. They are competent, straightforward thrillers, largely unexceptional, only possessing a certain crisp efficiency. The first is the least winsome, giving the drear account of what happens after the Soviets conquer the U.S.A. It reads like a script aimed at the slick magazines (in fact it was serialized in *Maclean's*) and later adapted to the SF market. *Takeoff* tells the more tolerable—but hoary—story of how an atomic scientist helps a bunch of teenagers build a moon rocket, with appropriate interference by foreign agents to provide a veneer of suspense. *The Syndic* is another matter. Though it seems oddly cobbled together, it is nevertheless quite engaging for much of its length and is Kornbluth's best solo novel. It incorporates satire, parody, homiletic fable, pulp adventure, and irrelevant moral lecture, accented by sudden left turns in the plot. Its primary narrative premise is a marvel of ironic supposition: the US government, for just cause, has been exiled to the unfriendly shores of a primitive Ireland by a coalition of laissez-faire smugglers and racketeers, the good-time guys and dolls of the Syndic. Ostensibly a straight adventure story, it ultimately seems to be a loose composite of favorite crotchets, including a forceful depiction of earth-magic which somehow manages not to blow the narrative beyond the pale of mainline SF.

Where Kornbluth truly excelled was in his shorter work, the bulk of which appeared in the collections *The Explorers, A Mile Beyond the Moon,* and *The Marching Morons*. It is often madly comic, and as often sharp and deadly. At its best, it is brief, evocative, to the point; short on description, but full of vivid impressions; and usually possessed of a clearly developed moral thrust, if not always an explicit moral. His strong satiric mode slides easily into march-hare burlesque, in pieces like "Passion Pill," "Thirteen O'Clock," and "Virginia." The omnipresent sardonicism emerges most fiercely in tightly woven shorts like "The Words of Guru," "The Silly Season," and "The Rocket of 1955," but also in longer works like "Two Dooms" and "The Marching Morons." The latter two are Kornbluth's most visibly hortatory stories, although neither exists simply for the sake of its overt "lesson." He also wrote pure, slick adventures, playful novelets like "The Slave" and "Make Mine Mars," which captivate by virtue of sheer readability, a deftness in the handling of stock figures and basic emotional appeals. And all the above, even the darkest tales, are rendered with a spritely touch; they do not sag in the middle, and there is ever a little crooked smile lurking somewhere in the corners.

Kornbluth's view of humanity may seem perplexing and inconsistent. He is sometimes accused of being a hard-case cynic, an elitist who views himself as above the common run. This is not entirely fallacious in light of "The Marching Morons"; in foreseeing a future populated mainly by just-plain-dopes, it is largely a metaphor for what Kornbluth saw around him in his own time. Yet he had a profound affection for lowly, downtrodden people, for stumble-bums and gutter folk, and even some salesmen. In part it may have been the fondness of an aficionado, a collector of "characters." But he was not without a good deal of genuine sympathy, especially for those who were caught in situations they barely understood, like the deformed space pilot in "The Altar at Midnight," or for those who understood too well, like the narrator-physicist of the same story and the young genius of "Gomez." Better remembered, perhaps, are his treatment of workaday grifters and con-artists, like Honest John Barlow of "Morons" or the sly narrator of "1955"—people who have no sympathy at all, and who, however clever, always get the

axe at the finale. If Kornbluth sometimes admired their grit and savvy, he was also moved to exact revenge for their victims.

Though he is often viewed as a commentator on the social fabric, and the various forms of human folly, there is more to Kornbluth than the wary futurologist, the wry chronicler of crafty deals ("1955," "Time Bum"), or even the compassionate observer of human detritus ("The Little Black Bag," "The Altar at Midnight"). And this something more is his sense of the unknown and the unknowable, the hidden layers of reality, the levels of illusion enveloping the world (whether social or metaphysical). Many of his most notable, most intensely realized stories hover somewhere between strict fantasy and strictest science fiction. Both "The Words of Guru" and "Kazam Collects" are outright fantasies, of the sort that "pierce the veil" of ordinary sense, and yet they have the resolute authority, the absolute conviction, of things seen and heard and done. They begin in fairly typical urban settings, enticing the reader through unsuspected realms to arrive at states of being that can only be termed ineffable and exalted, the one horrific, the other all beauty and benevolence. "The Silly Season," a tensely told shocker, provides a contest between a series of uncanny but rather palpable illusions and the normalizing nature of daily journalism. "The Cosmic Expense Account" sets the mundane and extraordinary in adjacent territories, as a crippling "cosmic harmony" engulfs eastern Pennsylvania. And in the jocose "Virginia," our furtive public mythologies about the Secret Masterdom of the Super Rich are made the binding private reality of an heir to fortune. Characteristically, Kornbluth does not simply mention, but actually offers a short tour of the, Museum of Suppressed Inventions.

These tales center on initiation into various kinds of arcane knowledge; and "Guru" and "Kazam" focus on persons of a special nature, born to acquire a special sort of knowledge, and power. This striving after knowledge is at the core of Kornbluth's most elusive and provocative piece of writing, "The Last Man Left in the Bar." Published very late in his career (1957), this short but densely packed work distills all his previous concerns with kinds and visions of reality, and it is a tour de force of oblique, kaleidoscopic narrative worthy of the wildest "experiments" of the New Wave. It portrays the psychological aftermath of an apparent momentary transposition of worlds. It mingles drunken uncertainties and digressions with the haunting obscurities of a poorly apprehended experience. In a landscape of shifting knowledge, the one constant is that its technician-protagonist never does learn the answers, the wherefores of his predicament. His passionate desire to *know* is countered by the obstinate complexity of the universe, and by wilful creatures who are absorbed in their own very separate interests and imperatives.

—Alex Eisenstein

KURLAND, Michael (Joseph). Also writes as Jennifer Plum. American. Born in New York City, 1 March 1938. Educated at Hiram College, Ohio, 1955-56; University of Maryland overseas, 1961-62; Columbia University, New York, 1962-63. Served in the United States Army, 1958-62. Married Rebecca Jacobson in 1976. News Editor, KPFK-Radio, Los Angeles, 1966; English teacher, Happy Valley School, Ojai, California, 1967; Editor, *Crawdaddy,* New York, 1969; also a play director, road manager for a band, advertising copywriter, and ghost writer. Since 1976, Editor, Pennyfarthing Press, San Francisco. Agent: Richard Curtis Associates, 156 East 52nd Street, New York, New York 10022. Address: P.O. Box 7745, San Francisco, California 94120, U.S.A.

SCIENCE-FICTION PUBLICATIONS

Novels

Ten Years to Doomsday, with Chester Anderson. New York, Pyramid, 1964.

The Unicorn Girl.   New York, Pyramid, 1969.
Transmission Error.   New York, Pyramid, 1970.
The Whenabouts of Burr.   New York, DAW, 1975.
Pluribus.   New York, Doubleday, 1975.
Tomorrow Knight.   New York, DAW, 1976.
The Princes of Earth (juvenile).   New York, Elsevier Nelson, 1978.
The Last President, with S.W. Barton.   New York, Morrow, 1980.
Psi Hunt.   New York, Berkley, 1980.

Uncollected Short Stories

"Elementary," with Laurence Janifer, in *Fantasy and Science Fiction* (New York), September 1964.
"Bond of Brothers," in *Worlds of Tomorrow* (New York), May 1965.
"Please State My Business," in *Galaxy* (New York), August 1965.
"Fimbulsommer," with Randall Garrett, in *If* (New York), September 1970.
"A Matter of Taste," in *Men and Malice,* edited by Dean Dickensheet.   New York, Doubleday, 1973.
"Small World," in *Two Views of Wonder,* edited by Thomas N. Scortia and Chelsea Quinn Yarbro.   New York, Ballantine, 1973.
"Think Only This of Me," in *Galaxy* (New York), November 1973.

OTHER PUBLICATIONS

Novels

Mission: Third Force.   New York, Pyramid, 1967.
Mission: Tank War.   New York, Pyramid, 1968.
Mission: Police Action.   New York, Pyramid, 1969.
A Plague of Spies.   New York, Pyramid, 1969.
The Secret of Benjamin Square (as Jennifer Plum).   New York, Lancer, 1972.
The Infernal Device.   New York, New American Library, and London, New English Library, 1979.

Other

Editor, *The Redward Edward Papers,* by Avram Davidson.   New York, Doubleday, 1978.
Editor, *The Best of Avram Davidson.*   New York, Doubleday, 1979.

Michael Kurland comments:
  I try to entertain.

*   *   *

  Michael Kurland's first two science-fiction novels were written in conjunction with Chester Anderson. The first, a conventional collaboration, was *Ten Years to Doomsday*, a lightweight and readable book concerned with the need for an entire planet to change from a feudal/pre-technological to a fully scientific/industrial state in a decade to stave off a planned invasion. Kurland has stated that this book was written as a parody of the works of Poul Anderson. Either as parody or in its own right, the book is fairly successful. The second novel has a more complicated history. When Anderson wrote his popular novel *The Butterfly Kid*, he included himself, Kurland, and a third friend, Tom Waters, as characters. Anderson's novel imposes a comedic alien-invasion theme upon the bohemian East Village milieu of the 1960's with hilarious results. Kurland's *The Unicorn Girl* is a sequel, continuing its themes and characters, though it is generally regarded as less successful. (Waters added a third book to the series, *The Probability Pad.*)
  Kurland's first fully solo novel was *Transmission Error*. In this book he established a protagonist of generally likeable nature, his traits including considerable wit and resourcefulness, but also a feckless ability to get himself into insoluble dilemmas. He is accidentally transported to an alien planet and threatened with a life of slavery. He escapes this situation and plunges into a series of similarly unresolved problems.
  By this point the general pattern of Kurland's books had become clear. Kurland is highly adept at creating societies which are com-

pellingly believable, and populating them with vivid and sympathetic characters. His style is lively, warm, and highly informal. His stories are told with rapidity of pace and great variety of setting and incident. Their major flaw is a failure—whether by the author or his protagonist—to grapple with and satisfactorily resolve problems. The "solutions" offered are almost invariably flight rather than confrontation.
  This pattern holds through Kurland's later novels, although their basic premises are wholly different from one another. *The Whenabouts of Burr* is a chase-novel proceeding through multiple parallel worlds. *Pluribus,* probably Kurland's most successful novel in the genre, takes place in a semi-barbaric future United States. The book abounds in vivid imagery, including an unforgettable scene of the protagonist, arrested for some local infraction, being removed in a standard "black-and-white" California Highway Patrol cruiser—drawn by a team of horses! *Tomorrow Knight* (the title is indicative of Kurland's love for puns and other word-play) takes place on a planet divided, checker-board fashion, into hundreds of miniature stage-set societies. Yet in all the books, the general pattern of insoluble problem and flight persists.
  The Princes of Earth is favorably comparable to standard Heinlein juveniles, containing the usual Kurland mix of convincing future societies, sympathetic characters, intriguing problem-situations, and rapid transfer from problem to problem. There is also an excellent infusion of satire, most notably a hilarious parody of the Church of Scientology. Although no further books in the series have yet appeared, *The Princes of Earth* is clearly intended as the opening volume of a series.

—Richard A. Lupoff

———————

KUTTNER, Henry.   Also wrote as Will Garth; Lewis Padgett. American.   Born in Los Angeles, California, 7 April 1915. Educated at the University of Southern California, Los Angeles, B.A. 1954. Served in the United States Army Medical Corps during World War II. Married C.L. Moore, *q.v.,* in 1940; most of his subsequent work was written with her, though not always acknowledged. Worked briefly for a literary agency, Los Angeles; free-lance writer. *Died 3 February 1958.*

SCIENCE-FICTION PUBLICATIONS

Novels

Dr. Cyclops (as Will Garth).   New York, Phoenix Press, 1940; revised edition, as Henry Kuttner, New York, Popular Library, 1967.
Fury, with C.L. Moore.   New York, Grosset and Dunlap, 1950; London, Dobson, 1954; as *Destination Infinity,* New York, Avon, 1958.
Earth's Last Citadel, with C.L. Moore.   New York, Ace, 1964.
Valley of the Flame, with C.L. Moore.   New York, Ace, 1964.
The Time Axis, with C.L. Moore.   New York, Ace, 1965.
The Dark World.   New York, Ace, 1965; London, Mayflower, 1966.
The Last Castle.   New York, Ace, 1967.
The Creature from Beyond Infinity.   New York, Popular Library, 1968.
The Time Trap, in *Evil Earths,* edited by Brian Aldiss.   London, Futura, 1976.

Novels as Lewis Padgett, with C.L. Moore

Tomorrow and Tomorrow, and The Fairy Chessmen.   New York, Gnome Press, 1951; as *Tomorrow and Tomorrow* and *The Far Reality,* London, Consul, 2 vols., 1963; *The Fairy Chessmen* published as *The Chessboard Planet,* New York, Galaxy, 1956.

Well of the Worlds. New York, Galaxy, 1953.
Beyond Earth's Gates. New York, Ace, 1954.

Short Stories

Ahead of Time. New York, Ballantine, 1953; London, Weidenfeld and Nicolson, 1954.
Remember Tomorrow. Sydney, American Science Fiction, 1954.
Way of the Gods. Sydney, American Science Fiction, 1954.
No Boundaries, with C.L. Moore. New York, Ballantine, 1955; London, Consul, 1961.
As You Were. Sydney, American Science Fiction, 1955.
Sword of Tomorrow. Sydney, American Science Fiction, 1955.
Bypass to Otherness. New York, Ballantine, 1961; London, Consul, 1963.
Return to Otherness. New York, Ballantine, 1962; London, Mayflower, 1965.
The Best of Kuttner. London, Mayflower, 2 vols., 1965-66.
The Best of Henry Kuttner. New York, Doubleday, 1975.
Clash by Night and Other Stories, with C.L. Moore. London, Hamlyn, 1980.

Short Stories as Lewis Padgett, with C.L. Moore

A Gnome There Was. New York, Simon and Schuster, 1950.
Robots Have No Tails (by Kuttner alone). New York, Gnome Press, 1952.
Mutant. New York, Gnome Press, 1953; London, Weidenfeld and Nicolson, 1954.
Line to Tomorrow. New York, Bantam, 1954.

OTHER PUBLICATIONS

Novels

Lawless Guns (as Will Garth). New York, Dodge, 1937.
The Brass Ring (as Lewis Padgett, with C.L. Moore). New York, Duell, 1946; London, Sampson Low, 1947; as *Murder in Brass,* New York, Bantam, 1947.
The Day He Died (as Lewis Padgett, with C.L. Moore). New York, Duell, 1947.
Man Drowning. New York, Harper, 1952; London, New English Library, 1961.
The Murder of Ann Avery. New York, Permabooks, 1956.
The Murder of Eleanor Pope. New York, Permabooks, 1956.
Murder of a Mistress. New York, Permabooks, 1957.
Murder of a Wife. New York, Permabooks, 1958.
The Mask of Circe, with C.L. Moore. New York, Ace, 1971.

*

Bibliography: by Donald H. Tuck, in *Henry Kuttner: A Memorial Symposium* edited by Karen Anderson, Berkeley, California, Sevagram, 1958.

* * *

In reviewing Henry Kuttner's collection *Ahead of Time,* Anthony Boucher characterized the author as "one of S.F.'s most literate and intelligent storytellers." Other adjectives could have been added to the list: prolific, versatile, popular. There have, it is true, been periodic dry spells when editors and readers have seemed to forget the rich legacy of Kuttner's fiction, but the stories have always been re-discovered and brought back into print. There is every reason to believe that his best work will last as long as science fiction is read.

For many years the scope and volume of Kuttner's writing were partially camouflaged by the many bylines under which his stories appeared. Initially the pen-names were adopted for the usual commercial reasons: to differentiate among various types of story or to disguise the fact that more than one story on a contents page was by the same author. But Kuttner, both alone and with his wife C.L. Moore, seemed to take an active delight in the creation of new pseudonyms, even on two occasions going so far as to publish fictional "autobiographies" for an alter ego: Keith Hammond in *Startling Stories,* March 1946 (a Eurasian antiquarian with sixteen

cats), and C.H. Liddell in *Planet Stories,* November 1950. As one after another of the Kuttner/Moore pseudonyms was revealed, a phenomenon arose which was sometimes called the "Kuttner Syndrome": the conviction that *any* promising new name on the SF scene had to be yet another Kuttner pen-name. (One of the victims of this assumption was Jack Vance, who was identified by the editor T.E. Dikty in 1950 as a Kuttner pseudonym.) The original choice of pseudonyms for various stories has by now become clouded through numerous reprintings with altered bylines.

Kuttner's first story, "The Graveyard Rats," a superbly grisly horror story in the Lovecraft mode, appeared in *Weird Tales.* Kuttner continued to write for *Weird Tales,* but at the same time he became a prolific contributor to other pulp magazines of many types, including mystery, detective, western, adventure, "spicy," and South Sea tales. His first long story was "The Time Trap" (*Marvel Science Stories*), called "a marvellous gaudy melodrama" by Brian Aldiss. Kuttner had been a member of H.P. Lovecraft's circle of correspondents, and had met other members of that group, such as Robert Bloch, Fritz Leiber, and E. Hoffmann Price. Kuttner and Bloch collaborated on a few stories. Kuttner also collaborated with Arthur K. Barnes on two stories in their Pete Manx series. Manx was a carnival barker whose mind was projected back in time into the bodies of various inhabitants of ancient Rome, Egypt, Baghdad, and other historical or legendary locales, where he must use his innate cunning to survive. The series was carried on alternately by Kuttner and Barnes from 1939 to 1944.

Another Lovecraft correspondent and well-known *Weird Tales* writer whom Kuttner met was Catherine L. Moore. Kuttner and Moore were married on June 7, 1940, in New York, where Kuttner had moved in order to be close to his magazine markets. Kuttner and Moore had collaborated on one story in 1937, but it was not until after their marriage that their remarkable writing partnership developed. Kuttner stated on several occasions that almost all of his writing since the marriage, regardless of byline, was to some extent a collaboration with his wife; however, the degree and method of collaboration varied widely. Some stories were almost pure Kuttner, with only minor contributions from Moore, while for others the reverse was true; but on a large number of stories the two partners were able to blend their ideas and styles so well that one of them could drop a story in mid-scene and the other could pick it up, with scarcely a seam showing in the final product. While taking part fully in the collaborative works, C.L. Moore also continued to write her own stories.

The Lewis Padgett stories, taken as a whole, form a body of work of which any writer could be proud, and if Kuttner and Moore had done no other writing in the science fiction field, their reputations would still be secure on the basis of these stories. Fritz Leiber (in *Henry Kuttner: A Memorial Symposium,* 1958) identified three themes which recur in Kuttner's science fiction: the madman from the future, wacky robots, and wonder children. All of these are present in the Padgett stories. The Padgett treatment of robots, in particular, is as distinctive as that of any writer in the field. One of the best-known, "The Twonky," is concerned with the effect on a young married couple of a device which looks like a console radio, but is actually a robot designed to enforce its own views of proper behavior. Several of the Padgett stories were about the odd inventions of Gallegher, a scientist who can invent things only while drunk, and when sober, can never remember what the inventions are for. Told in a style frankly borrowed from Thorne Smith, the Gallegher stories are meticulously logical SF puzzles cast as wacky comedies. Five were reprinted as *Robots Have No Tails.* The deservedly famous "Mimsy Were the Borogoves" is about educational toys from the future which have a disastrous effect on a present-day family. Other Lewis Padgett stories include the Baldy series (*Mutant*)—about telepathic mutants who must struggle for survival against the intolerance of their normal neighbors and against irrational renegades in their own ranks, a theme clearly taken from A.E. van Vogt's *Slan*—and "The Fairy Chessmen" (with its celebrated opening line, "The doorknob opened a blue eye and looked at him") and "Tomorrow and Tomorrow," complicated tales of post-Atomic intrigue and alternate futures.

One of C.L. Moore's works from the 1940's was "Clash by Night," a moody, emotion-laden story of the Free Companies, the mercenaries of the feuding undersea Keeps on Venus in the 25th century. The Kuttners returned to this scene with the novel *Fury,* the story of

Sam Harker, ruthless and driven by forces of which he was not fully aware, the one man who could liberate humanity from its stagnant undersea existence and push it into conquering the planet's savage surface. Although published as by Lawrence O'Donnell, the story was mostly Kuttner's. C.L. Moore stated in her introduction to the Lancer reprint: "*Fury* was written by about one and an eighth persons....I wrote comparatively little of the copy. The idea was basically Hank's and I didn't identify very strongly with it." She also pointed out that the novel deals with "the two recurring themes which emerge quite explicitly in nearly everything we wrote. Hank's basic statement was something like, 'Authority is dangerous and I will never submit to it.' Mine was, 'The most treacherous thing in life is love.' " *Fury* is the best, and the best-known, of Kuttner's long stories. Other long works include a series of nine science-fantasy novels, many of them in the romantic/tragic mode of A. Merritt, written between 1943 and 1952, including *Earth's Last Citadel, Valley of the Flame, Beyond Earth's Gates,* and *Well of the Worlds.* Typical shorter works in the same style are "I Am Eden" (December 1946) and "Way of the Gods" (April 1947), both in *Thrilling Wonder Stories.* In the early 1950's the volume of new Kuttner-Moore stories decreased. Both Kuttner and Moore felt written-out in science fiction, although such stories as "Home There's No Returning" and "Two-Handed Engine" (both in *No Boundaries*) belied this claim.

Henry Kuttner has sometimes been criticized as a literary mimic who spent his energies speaking in other people's voices. He did, in fact, speak in many voices, but they were all his own. His borrowings, whether of style or of theme, were all filtered through his own sensibility, and emerged transmuted. In all of his best work there is clear evidence of a highly individual mind at work. Perhaps his most personal contribution to science fiction was the fusion of humor and logic which first emerged fully in the Gallegher stories. The same blend was also evident in the stories of the Hogbens, a family of mutant hillbillies, and in "The Ego Machine," probably his best "wacky robot" story. Through his stories and through his influence on other writers—Ray Bradbury, Leigh Brackett, and Richard Matheson have all acknowledged his guidance—Kuttner left an indelible mark on the science-fiction field. Without his presence, science fiction of the 1940's and 1950's would have been a vastly different and much poorer body of literature.

—R.E. Briney

LAFFERTY, R(aphael) A(loysius). American. Born in Neola, Iowa, 7 November 1914. Educated at the University of Tulsa, Oklahoma, 1932-33; International Correspondence School, electrical engineer course, 1939-42. Served in the United States Army, 1942-46: Staff Sergeant. Civil servant, Washington, D.C., 1934-35; clerk, then buyer, Clark Electrical Supply Company, Tulsa, 1936-42, 1946-50, 1952-71. Since 1971, free-lance writer. Recipient: Phoenix Award, 1971; Hugo Award, 1973; Smith Award, 1973. Agent: Virginia Kidd, Box 278, Milford, Pennsylvania 18337. Address: 1715 South Trenton Avenue, Tulsa, Oklahoma 74120, U.S.A.

SCIENCE-FICTION PUBLICATIONS

Novels

Past Master. New York, Ace, and London, Rapp and Whiting, 1968.
The Reefs of Earth. New York, Berkley, 1968; London, Dobson, 1970.
Space Chantey. New York, Ace, 1968; London, Dobson, 1976.
Fourth Mansions. New York, Ace, 1969; London, Dobson, 1972.
The Devil Is Dead. New York, Avon, 1971; London, Dobson, 1978.

Arrive at Easterwine. New York, Scribner, 1971; London, Dobson, 1977.
Not to Mention Camels. Indianapolis, Bobbs Merrill, 1976; London, Dobson, 1980.
Apocalypses. Los Angeles, Pinnacle, 1977.
Where Have You Been, Sandaliotis?, The Three Armageddons of Enniscorthy Sweeny. Los Angeles, Pinnacle, 1977.
Archipelago. New Orleans, Manuscript Press, 1979.

Short Stories

Nine Hundred Grandmothers. New York, Ace, 1970; London, Dobson, 1975.
Strange Doings. New York, Scribner, 1972.
Does Anyone Else Have Something Further to Add? New York, Scribner, 1974; London, Dobson, 1980.
Funnyfingers, and Cabrito. Portland, Oregon, Pendragon Press, 1976.
Horns on Their Heads. Portland, Oregon, Pendragon Press, 1976.

Uncollected Short Stories

"Brain Fever Season," in *Universe 7,* edited by Terry Carr. New York, Doubleday, 1977; London, Dobson, 1979.
"Thou Whited Wall," in *Fantasy and Science Fiction* (New York), January 1977.
"And All the Skies Are Full of Fish," in *Universe 10,* edited by Terry Carr. New York, Doubleday, and London, Dobson, 1980.

OTHER PUBLICATIONS

Novels

The Fall of Rome. New York, Doubleday, 1971.
The Flame Is Green. New York, Walker, 1971.
Okla Hannali. New York, Doubleday, 1972.

*

Manuscript Collection: McFarlin Library, University of Tulsa, Oklahoma.

R.A. Lafferty comments:
My novels, which I wrote myself at great labor, have received more attention than my short stories, which wrote themselves. Nevertheless, the short stories are greatly superior to the novels. In my introductory note to a Dutch version of *Nine Hundred Grandmothers,* I wrote:

"I hold to the true theory that good stories write themselves, or that they are independent and pre-existent entities or beings.... These pre-existent stories come to persons, sometimes even to persons of a resonant emptiness; and they make themselves known through these persons.... I am very glad that these particular stories first visited me and not someone else.

"There are a few perfect discoveries or encounters that come into every life. Only once I met a mountain lion, quite close, in the wild. She was a discovery of mine. Once only I saw a whale a-blow in the ocean. Once only I saw a big-horn mountain sheep on a high cliff. Once only I saw a pink flamingo in flight. Once only I had an encounter with each of some hundred entities called 'special stories.' These meetings were as quietly thunderous and as unexpected as the discovery of the mountain lion or whale or big-horn sheep or pink flamingo in flight.

"There is an Aladdin cave, lit by 999 lamps, that is the Universal Unconscious...that is shared by all persons and creatures.... Unsuspected stone doors of the cave are thrown open. There may be funny and fascinating encounters and living spectacles. A few of them may cluster together in a pile of things waiting to be discovered...piles of gold, quick ecstasies, intricate delights, entities called 'special stories.'.

"A person favored with such discoveries will look for other

people to share them with. 'Hey, come see the things I've found,' he'll say. That is what I say now."

However pompous that may sound, it's a statement on the most important part of my work.

* * *

R.A. Lafferty is science fiction's most prodigious teller of tall tales. Offspring of a yarn-spinning family, he writes rather than recites his exhilarating stories but nevertheless retains a primary allegiance to the spoken word. The quintessentially oral character of Lafferty's fiction proclaims itself on every page—each of them sounds like a tape recording transcript. (*Arrive at Easterwine* is actually presented as such.) Rhythmic repetitions of phrases and epithets tie the material together. The author is omnipresent as well as omniscient. He explains and interprets every development, sprinkling his text with epigrams, anecdotes, and invented sources. He will even bring himself into the story as a thinly disguised character— Audifax O'Hanlon and his sundry incarnations.

Exposition and dialog overshadow action. Events are more often predicted or recollected than depicted. At shorter lengths, these events are often arranged in artificial patterns reminiscent of folk tales ("Rainbird"), exempla ("The Configuration of the North Shore"), or barroom whoppers ("One at a Time"). In longer works, a degree of order is imposed by means of elaborate symbolism (e.g., the ancient imagery of the Four Living Creatures in *Fourth Mansions*). However, Lafferty's oral mannerisms hamper his performance when he mistakes the accumulation of vignettes for the construction of a novel as in *Arrive at Easterwine* and *The Devil Is Dead*.

Lafferty's way with characters is as distinctive as his story-telling technique. The floridly eccentric beings who populate his fiction are wholly unrealistic yet totally real. He succeeds best with children, traditionally the most difficult of subjects, because he approaches them with all the sentimentality of a W.C. Fields: "A child's a monster yet uncurled." His gleeful demons ("The Transcendent Tigers" and *The Reefs of Earth*) are just as believable as Zenna Henderson's natural angels. (However, Lafferty's distaste for adolescents shows up in his Hugo winner "Euremea's Dam.") Besides outrageous youngsters, Lafferty's character troupe comprises dirty old geniuses and innocent simpletons, ugly but wholesome men and violent but kindly ones, lusty egomaniacs and ascetic manipulators, witch-girls and earthy ladies of muscular charm, plus aliens every bit as variegated. For example, the roll call in *Past Master* reads: "A dead saint from Old Earth, the Devil-kid of Astrobe, a necromancer of unlikely powers, a transcendent ansel, a priest of Saint Klingensmith, an avatar who burns up bodies, and . . . a broken-faced old warlock." This kind of oddly assorted band reappears in tale after tale. Moreover, specific characters get encores; names are common to *Fourth Mansions, The Devil Is Dead, Arrive at Easterwine*, and related short pieces. Even sets are reused; "World Abounding" reveals that many stories share the preposterous universe of *Past Master*.

So closely do Lafferty's novels resemble each other, they might as well be alternate drafts of the same story. This may reflect his habit of rewriting everything five or six times before editing into shape. For instance, Lafferty's plots repeatedly combine conspiracy, romance, and growth. Secret battles between Good and Evil cabals decide the fate of the world. Passionate couples share a yeasty mixture of carnal and spiritual love. Esoteric powers are acquired and used to prepare a chosen hero for his imperial destiny. *The Flame Is Green* exemplifies this scenario best.

In novels and short stories alike, Lafferty is obsessed with transformation. His version of Nature is incorrigibly protean—space, time, and form are liable to shift at any moment. Changes that nourish the "green-growing world" must be welcomed whatever they cost. The price can be bloody. Lafferty's pages are speckled with gore, either from hand-to-hand combat or the butchering of animals. Yet the slaughter does not stun because death can be followed by resurrection, mutilation by healing, corruption by redemption. Lafferty knits these components together with allusions to mythology and theology. Biblical precedents influence his

handling of topics like kingship, sacrifice, and regeneration. They also shape his use of animal symbols such as snakes. This is especially true of *Fourth Mansions*. Here, a naive young newsman integrates the essence of four primeval forces (Badger/Man, Python/Lion, Toad/Ox, and Falcon/Eagle) and becomes mystical Emperor "by entrenched right" to nudge the world towards the next higher Mansion in the cosmic Castle.

Lafferty draws equally on history for inspiration ("Thus We Frustrate Charlemagne"). However, the soundness of his thinking can get lost in the quirkiness of his presentation. For instance, the accurate, preceptively interpreted data in *Okla Hannali*, his epic of the Choctaw Indians, is so entangled with fable that it is difficult to accept anything in the book as real. *The Flame Is Green*, set during the Carlist Wars and the Revolutions of 1848, is a far more satisfying and coherent work because its quest structure disciplines Lafferty's chaotic tendencies. Moreover, foreign locales have a useful distancing effect—exotic events are more plausible in exotic settings than in the contemporary American ones of *Fourth Mansions*. Despite its artistic excellence, *The Flame Is Green* was a commercial failure. It was intended to be the first volume of a tetralogy on the duel between the Green and Red Revolutions but nothing further has appeared to date.

Past Master, Lafferty's most popular novel, depends less on factual than on mythicized history. Sir Thomas More is brought forward in time and outward in space to save a diabolical utopia by dying a king's death. Lafferty sends his highly fictionalized 16th-century hero into the 26th-century to dramatize 20th-century spiritual and social issues. Compare this savory scramble of past, future, and present with Ursula K. Le Guin's didactic fable "The Ones Who Walk Away from Omelas."

There is not a bit of science in Lafferty's SF. He justifies his premises on etymological rather than scientific grounds: the name *is* the object. He coins outlandish names (chiefly from Greek and Latin), then interprets them in idiosyncratic ways—the derivations in *Arrive at Easterwine* and *The Flame Is Green* would make Isadore of Seville blush. His debt to the classics extends to farce as well as philosophy: *Space Chantey* is a reworking of the *Odyssey*. Bizarre nomenclature does not exhaust Lafferty's rampaging delight in words. He showers his pages with odd poetry. Who else would dare to rhyme "roses" with "apotheosis" or turn chapter titles into narrative verse as he does in *The Reefs of Earth*? This verbal virtuosity is commonly attributed to his Irishness. But although he loves exaggeration and grotesquerie as well as any Celt before him—surely one of his ancestors had a hand in *The Cattle Raid of Cooley*—Lafferty appreciates ethnic spice of many flavors. He uses almost as many Amerindian referents as Irish ones ("Narrow Valley") and his intoxication with the outré is readily matched by Avram Davidson's.

Too many readers have prized the shimmering emerald surface of Lafferty at the expense of his substance. This author cannot be understood apart from his self-proclaimed conservative Catholicism. Like the devout Episcopalian Cordwainer Smith, Lafferty suffers from the inability of his audience to comprehend or even recognize his views. (Who realizes the vulgar Mass in *Past Master* is protesting real liturgical abuses?) The strain of delivering a time-dimmed and unwelcome message has seriously weakened Lafferty's output since the early 1970's. A case in point is his abhorrence for the liberal Catholic philosopher Pierre Teilhard de Chardin. This goes unnoticed even when explicitly stated yet is vital to interpreting all Lafferty's metaphysical novels. He decries Chardin's evolutionary Omega Point as "the sickening emptiness of the Point Big-O." He rebuts the notion of natural perfectibility with visions of evil so insidious only grace can conquer it. Lafferty's great subject is the perennial war between Heaven and Hell: "We must kill the Devil afresh every day." This Adversary is no silken Mephisto but a musky blackguard whom healthy young men can drink under the table. Be they ever so pungent, demons like Ifreann in *The Flame Is Green* and Papa Diabolus in *The Devil Is Dead* are never allowed to steal the show. The heroes and heroines overwhelm them with sheer vitality. Vice can imitate but never match the "overrunning gaiety" of Virtue. Making goodness exciting is a Lafferty specialty.

Although he rode to prominence in the 1960's with the New Wave, Lafferty shows none of the gloom characteristic of that movement. His fiction rings with the high hilarity of love and laughter. Each of his serious works ends on a note of hope, for his is the faith-filled vision of a universe en route to redemption. Despite detours, it keeps gyring upward according to divine plan." All final answers were given in the beginning.... It is our task to grow out until we reach them."

—Sandra Miesel

LAKE, David (John). Australian. Born of British parents in Bangalore, India, 26 March 1929; became Australian citizen, 1975. Educated at St. Xavier's School, Calcutta, 1940-44; Dauntsey's, Wiltshire, 1945-47; Trinity College, Cambridge, 1949-53, B.A. 1952, Dip.Ed. 1953, M.A. 1956; University College of North Wales, Bangor, diploma in linguistics 1965; University of Queensland, Brisbane, Ph.D. 1974. Served in the Royal Artillery, 1948-49. Married Marguerite Ivy Ferris in 1964; one daughter. Assistant Master, Sherrardswood School, Welwyn Garden City, Hertfordshire, 1953-58, and St. Albans Boys Grammar School, Hertfordshire, 1958-59; Lecturer in English, Saigon University, 1959-61, for the Thai government, Bangkok, 1961-63, and at Chiswick Polytechnic, London, 1963-64; Reader in English, Jadavpur University, Calcutta, 1965-67. Since 1967, Lecturer, Senior Lecturer, and Reader in English, University of Queensland. Recipient: Ditmar Award, 1977. Agent: Valerie Smith, 538 East Harford Street, Milford, Pennsylvania 18337, U.S.A. Address: Department of English, University of Queensland, St. Lucia, Queensland 4067, Australia.

SCIENCE-FICTION PUBLICATIONS

Novels (series: Dextra)

Walkers on the Sky. New York, DAW, 1976; revised edition, London, Fontana, 1978.
The Right Hand of Dextra. New York, DAW, 1977.
The Wildings of Westron (Dextra). New York, DAW, 1977.
The Gods of Xuma; or, Barsoom Revisited. New York, DAW, 1978.
The Fourth Hemisphere. Melbourne, Void, 1980.

Uncollected Short Stories

"Creator," in *Envisaged Worlds,* edited by Paul Collins. St. Kilda, Victoria, Void, 1978.
"Re-deem the Time," in *Rooms of Paradise,* edited by Lee Harding. Melbourne, Quartet, 1978; New York, St. Martin's Press, 1979.
"What Is She," in *Transmutations,* edited by Rob Gerrard. Melbourne, Outback, 1979.

OTHER PUBLICATIONS

Verse

Hornpipes and Funerals. Brisbane, University of Queensland Press, 1973.

Other

John Milton: Paradise Lost. Calcutta, Mukhopadhyay, 1967.
Greek Tragedy. Calcutta, Excelsus, 1969.
The Canon of Thomas Middleton's Plays: Internal Evidence for the Major Problems of Authorship. Cambridge, University Press, 1975.
"The White Sphinx and the Whitened Lemur: Images of Death in *The Time Machine,*" in *Science-Fiction Studies 6* (Terre Haute, Indiana), 1979.

David Lake comments:
The main impulse embodied in my SF is the impulse of the human rat to imagine escapes from the cosmic trap in which he finds himself. The trap is partly (but only partly) of his own building; it has been building for a very long time; and the bars now loom very high indeed. Sometimes the rat thinks he can escape by a smart technological fix; sometimes he knows that he can't. But either way he can at least dream.

The main influences on my writing are probably H.G. Wells and C.S. Lewis, and the clash between these two authors' values. I follow Wells and Lewis in writing SF that deliberately borders on fantasy. Elves may appear wearing spacesuits. The same themes also appear in my poems, some of which are in fact close to being SF.

* * *

David Lake presents himself as a pessimist in search of the numinous, a fantasist without belief, choosing science fiction as his vehicle for escapism because magic doesn't work. Lake has little confidence in the efficacy of science, either: his alter ego, Ambrose Livermore, is able to use a time machine as his escape hatch into the future, leap-frogging the inevitable Big Bang, only to find the survivors engaged in determined regress, already back in 1900. In this witty tale, despair is salved by humour: Ambrose flourishes in the future 1 BC as Chief Jester to Obliorix.

If Earth is the City of Destruction in a godless universe, where may hope be found? In his novels Lake catapults small colonies of survivors to distant, wondrous planets, and New Jerusalem is actually built foursquare on Dextra. The two Dextra novels are paradigmatically interesting, complementing each other much as Blake's *Songs of Innocence and of Experience. The Right Hand of Dextra* suggests the State of Innocence, in which it is possible for the Puritan tendencies of the New Earthmen with their "Sifted Scriptures" to be corrected by incorporation with the innocent native species, despite the dextran twist of their protein molecules. Experience seems to prove otherwise, however, in the bleak feudal world of *The Wildings of Westron,* several thousand years later, until the implicit conclusion of the first book is reiterated in absolute form: before there can really be a New Earth on Dextra, all human flesh must perish and only Dextran flesh remain. Most humans will voluntarily undergo the change; the reluctant must simply be exterminated. There is no hope in human flesh because it is closed; Dextran flesh, however, is open, unsecret, because it allows telepathic understanding of one another. The conclusion of *The Gods of Xuma* is not quite so sweeping: only the hopelessly evil human colonists are slaughtered—and fortunately the Xuman natives can tell the difference and are prepared to tolerate those humans remaining who are essentially good natured. However, it is decided that humans are not fitted for space travel. If Lake is thus predisposed in favour of aliens, describing them warmly and even with affection, he is not unduly sentimental about them, particularly about his Xumans, and wishes to correct the supposition, hung over from Burroughs, that physical love with an alien can be satisfactory. The hero's comic embarrassments with Xumans in their female phase prove the point. On the other hand, Lake's aliens are usually not very different from people and do provoke erotic ideas; however, their function is not to be wonderful love-objects (as in Burroughs) but to suggest wonderful possibilities of loving interchange between humans, suitably modified. In *The Right Hand of Dextra* he uses the Song of Solomon as the basis for a description of a transcendent sexual union, only confusing the terms, so that male and female sensations become interchangeable; in *The Wildings of Westron* he echoes Blake: "Every minute particle and particular of their body-minds were commingling, from the head even to the feet, and on every plane of existence."

Lake is an imaginative writer with the power not only to invent exciting worlds but to describe them; he acknowledges the influence of C.S. Lewis, and his evocative accounts of the deserts of Xuma or the purple forests of Dextra bear comparison with those of Malacandra. His most wonderful world is in *Walkers on the Sky,* a tier-world Farmer might envy, ruled capriciously by immortals as if to recall Zelazny's *Lord of Light.* It is a pity that he had not found a story worthy of his world, but this charge may also be leveled at Farmer, and Lake's novel is at least free from Farmer's sometimes heavy portentousness. It was more fortunate for Lewis that the impression of his marvellous planets could overwhelm even his grand theme; but to gratify one's sense of wonder and be bored or irritated by the story which presents the wonder is like eating great food in a dirty restaurant with poor service: usually the science fiction reader is glad to pay the one as the price for the other.

In "Creator" Lake shows he is prepared to tackle the big theme and, if he trivializes it somewhat in the process—our universe exists inside a "creatron," a kind of game machine for artists on the planet Olympus, our creator being Jay Crystal (J.C.—get it?)—he does also succeed in providing a provocative ironic perspective on human history. The short story may suit this author's evident talents better than the novel for a while, as it will free him from the tedium of providing a stock narrative.

—Michael J. Tolley

LANIER, Sterling E(dmund). American. Born in New York City, 18 December 1927. Educated at Harvard University, Cambridge, Massachusetts, A.B. 1951; University of Pennsylvania, Philadelphia, 1953-58. Married Martha Hanna Pelton in 1961; one son and one daughter. Research historian, Winterthur Museum, Switzerland, 1958-60; Editor, John C. Winston Company, 1961, Chilton Books, 1961-62, 1965-67, and Macrae-Smith Company, 1963-64. Since 1967, full-time writer and sculptor. Recipient: Follett Award, 1969. Agent: Curtis Brown Ltd., 60 East 56th Street, New York, New York 10022, U.S.A.

SCIENCE-FICTION PUBLICATIONS

Novels

The War for the Lot (juvenile). Chicago, Follett, 1969.
Hiero's Journey. Radnor, Pennsylvania, Chilton, 1973; London, Sidgwick and Jackson, 1975.

Short Stories

The Peculiar Exploits of Brigadier Ffellowes. New York, Walker, 1972; London, Sidgwick and Jackson, 1977.

Uncollected Short Stories

"Thinking of the Unthinkable," in *Fantasy and Science Fiction* (New York), August 1973.
"...No Traveler Returns," in *Fantasy and Science Fiction* (New York), April 1974.
"A Father's Tale," in *Fantasy and Science Fiction* (New York), July 1974.
"Ghost of a Crown," in *Fantasy and Science Fiction* (New York), December 1976.
"The Syndicated Time," in *Fantasy and Science Fiction* (New York), July 1978.

*   *   *

Sterling E. Lanier's fiction presents a world teeming with creatures of the fantastic imagination, making it seem as though Tolkien were set in some future century. No innovator or philosopher, Lanier sails on well-charted seas of the supernatural and unnatural. His work almost always combines the worlds of fantasy and science fiction, and although his output is relatively small, his novel *Hiero's Journey* is of sufficient merit to warrant close attention.

A summary of this novel can hardly do it justice as the story pivots on one of the oldest and most frequently used plots of the genre: the hero sets out on a quest for lost knowledge through a world laid waste by nuclear war and controlled by mutants made horrible and evil by radiation. However, Lanier is able to inform this trite plot with his own vision of the fantastic and produces a world that is both delightful and terrifying. The questing hero is Per

Hiero Desteen—priest, exorcist, killman, and citizen of the Metz republic of Kanda—who sets off in the eighth millennium in search of ancient legendary machines called "computers" that will help him and his people put together the knowledge of the past. This knowledge is the last hope for survival against the various forms of evil that resulted from the Death (nuclear holocaust). This theme is not without its own moral convictions, and Lanier attempts to tie his story to present-day concerns in several ways. Some connections are made through a language that is not nearly as interesting or inventive as one might hope for in this kind of novel: Lantik Sea (Atlantic Ocean), Kanda (Canada), Neeyana (Indiana), Leemutes (lethal mutations). More interesting are the contemporary social and environmental values that are invested in the tale. The nuclear devastation is served by a group of men called "the Unclean." These men were formerly psychologists, biochemists, and physicists who have been severely ravaged by radiation and now seek to rule the evil world they have created. On the other hand, Hiero is joined by a wise ancient, Brother Aldo, who belongs to a group called "the Eleveners." The eleveners are the Brotherhood of the Eleventh Commandment, a group of social scientists dedicated to the ideal: Thou shalt not despoil the Earth and the life thereon. Hiero and Brother Aldo are accompanied by a telepathic, almost human bear (Gorm), a semi-intelligent bull "morse," and a strong-willed but faithful young maiden (Luchare).

Lanier's strengths and weaknesses are both evident in this fantasy adventure yarn. He is at his best when weaving a suspenseful tale, and, while his characters lack depth and the plot has been often used before, the world he creates, filled with radiation-induced mutants, ancient, knowing wizards, and fur-covered dwarves, lives fully in the imagination and allows the reader to partake fully in the suspenseful quest. Lanier is obviously aware of the parallels with medieval romances, and those who enjoy *Beowulf, Le Morte Darthur,* and the sagas will be enthralled by the re-creation of those environments and values in a future time.

Lanier's other work is of a similar but lesser quality. His stories as a rule combine the fantastic world of unnatural monsters with the more traditional trappings of science fiction: space ships, time travel, telepathic communication. *The Peculiar Exploits of Brigadier Ffellowes* presents seven stories that feature a retired English Brigadier who narrates tales that involve supernatural powers and fantastic monsters. Lanier exhibits a good sense of humor in these stories and carefully sets them up as a series of Chinese boxes: a story within a story within a story. The monsters found here, like the Nandi bear and the sea serpent Jormungadir, are similar to those found elsewhere in Lanier's writings. But the best quality of Lanier is what accounts for the success of this and his other works: he is an excellent storyteller.

—Lawrence R. Ries

LATHAM, Philip. Pseudonym for Robert S(hirley) Richardson. American. Born in Kokomo, Indiana, 22 April 1902. Educated at the University of California, Los Angeles, B.A. 1926; University of California, Berkeley, Ph.D. 1931. Married 1) Delia Shull in 1929 (died, 1940); 2) Marjorie Helen Engstead in 1942, one daughter. Assistant Astronomer, Mt. Wilson, now Hale, Observatory, Pasadena, California, 1931-58; Associate Director, Griffith Observatory, Los Angeles, 1958-64. Since 1964, free-lance writer. Agent: Scott Meredith Literary Agency, 845 Third Avenue, New York, New York 10022. Address: 1533 East Altadena Drive, Altadena, California 91001, U.S.A.

SCIENCE-FICTION PUBLICATIONS

Novels

Five Against Venus (juvenile). Philadelphia, Winston, 1952.

Missing Men of Saturn (juvenile).   Philadelphia, Winston, 1953.
Second Satellite (as Robert S. Richardson).   New York, McGraw
   Hill, 1956.

Uncollected Short Stories

"N Day," in *Astounding* (New York), January 1946.
"The Blindness," in *Astounding* (New York), July 1946.
"The Aphrodite Project," in *Astounding* (New York), June 1949.
"The Xi Effect," in *Astounding* (New York), January 1950.
"The Most Dangerous Love," in *Marvel* (New York), November
   1951.
"Martial Ritual," in *Future* (New York), July 1953.
"A Moment of Laughter," in *Fantastic* (New York), October 1953.
"Comeback," in *Future* (New York), November 1953.
"Simpson," in *Cosmos* (New York), July 1954.
"Flash Nova," in *McCall's* (New York), 15 August 1956.
"Disturbing Sun," in *Astounding* (New York), May 1959.
"To Explain Mrs. Thompson," in *The Expert Dreamers,* edited by
   Frederik Pohl.   New York, Doubleday, 1962.
"Kid Anderson" (as Robert S. Richardson), in *Great Science Fic-
   tion by Scientists,* edited by Groff Conklin.   New York, Macmil-
   lan, 1962.
"The Dimple in Draco," in *Orbit 2,* edited by Damon Knight.   New
   York, Putnam, 1967; London, Rapp and Whiting, 1968.
"The Red Euphoric Bands," in *Galaxy* (New York), December
   1967.
"Under the Dragon's Tail," in *Analog* (New York), December 1968.
"After Enfer," in *Fantasy and Science Fiction* (New York), March
   1969.
"The Rose Bowl Pluto Hypothesis," in *Orbit 5,* edited by Damon
   Knight.   New York, Putnam, 1969.
"Jeannette's Hands," in *Fantasy and Science Fiction* (New York),
   January 1973.
"Future Forbidden," in *Galaxy* (New York), May 1973.
"A Drop of Dragon's Blood," in *Fantasy and Science Fiction* (New
   York), July 1975.
"The Miracle Elixir," in *Fantastic* (New York), June 1977.

OTHER PUBLICATIONS as Robert S. Richardson

Plays

Television Plays: *Captain Video* series, 1953.

Other

Preliminary Elements of Object Comas Sola (1927 AA), with
   others.   Berkeley, University of California Press, 1927.
Astronomy, with William T. Skilling.   New York, Holt, and Lon-
   don, Chapman and Hall, 1939; revised edition, Holt, 1947.
The Practical Essentials of Pre-Training Navigation, with William
   T. Skilling.   New York, Holt, 1942.
Sun, Moon, and Stars, with William T. Skilling.   New York,
   McGraw Hill, 1946; revised edition, 1964.
A Brief Text in Astronomy, with William T. Skilling.   New York,
   Holt, 1954; revised edition, 1959.
Exploring Mars (juvenile).   New York, McGraw Hill, 1954; as
   Man and the Planets, London, Muller, 1954.
The Fascinating World of Astronomy.   New York, McGraw Hill,
   1960; London, Faber, 1962.
Man and the Moon.   Cleveland, World, 1961.
Astronomy in Action.   New York, McGraw Hill, 1962.
Mars.   New York, Harcourt Brace, 1964; London, Allen and
   Unwin, 1965.
Getting Acquainted with Comets.   New York, McGraw Hill, 1967.
The Star Lovers.   New York, Macmillan, 1967.
The Stars and Serendipity (juvenile).   New York, Pantheon, 1971.

*

Manuscript Collection: Fullerton College Library, California.

Philip Latham comments:
   Since most of my firsthand experience is in astronomy, most of

my fiction has an astronomical background. But one of my stories,
"Kid Anderson," is about a prizefighter. I firmly believe that science
always leads science fiction. Increasingly I have gone over to science
fantasy, as in "Jeannette's Hands" and other stories. My stories are
always written on the basis of *people* rather than gadgetry.
   Where science fiction will go in the future is a guess. There is little
left to write about: we have already written stories of interplanetary
travel, extra dimensions, time travel. *Star Wars,* for example, to my
mind was a fairy tale: you could have anything you wanted in it.
Most science-fiction writers have inventive ability and ingenuity,
but lack true imagination, an extremely rare gift. I neither read
science fiction nor look at SF on TV or in motion pictures. Henceforth, we must try to find material in the world around us. It is there
if we can see it.

*   *   *

A scandal in American science fiction is how little science there is
in it. A notable exception lies in Philip Latham's stories, since they
were written by the professional astronomer Robert S. Richardson
and bear the marks of his expertise. For more than three decades
Latham's stories have been appearing from time to time in the major
magazines and anthologies, and Latham has also written juvenile
science-fiction novels.
   Many of the early stories are based on astronomical speculation,
often presented as realistic reporting. An example is "The Aphrodite Project," which has the pretense of being science fact, complete
with footnotes to astronomical journals. The story imagines a 1946
Navy contract to launch a satellite rocket to Venus to measure its
mass. Once near Venus the rocket releases a cloud visible to Earth—
Latham does not foresee the sophisticated radio telemetry which
has actually been used on such probes. The rocket succeeds in
measuring not only the mass of Venus but also its period of rotation.
A secondary theme is governmental secrecy as the military authorities clamp down on the release of information about the mission.
The story thus presents itself as an exposé of confidential information. "The Xi Effect" is another example of Latham's astronomical
science fiction. Astronomers discover that although the universe as
a whole expands, the Earth is in a segment which is shrinking,
cutting out greater and greater percentages of radiation so that the
eventual extinction of all light seems inevitable. In this story we
begin to see Latham's interest in the characters of scientists as well
as in science. Latham presents a communication gap between the
branches and modes of science. It is a theoretical physicist who
predicts the Xi Effect, and the practical astronomers are shown to
be as skeptical of theory as is the public at large. "The Blindness,"
about the return of Halley's comet in 1986, is hardly a story at all but
a meditation on the influence the comet has had on history. A
theory of atomic sentience is developed to explain the comet's
deviance from its projected orbit. Even in this early story the scientist Richardson makes clear his interest in anti-science and mysticism.
   Latham's more recent fiction develops much further the theme of
the dubious border between science and magic. Much more central
to these later stories, too, is a particular kind of character: the
anti-hero who wins the reader's sympathy for his struggles in an
absurd world. "After Enfer" is an example of a Latham story which
revolves around character rather than science. The story's title
derives from "N-Fear," fear of other dimensions. Sam Baxter,
afraid of life, stuck in a museum job, applies for the job of exploring
N-space and breaks through to genuine heroism. In "Jeannette's
Hands" and its sequel, "A Drop of Dragon's Blood," Latham's
protagonist is an astronomer, Bob, who is literally and figuratively
married to an astrologer named Dagny. We learn in these stories
about the seamy side of being a professional astronomer: the rivalries and the petty jealousies between those who hold conflicting
theories and conflicting claims to grant money. Bob's rival Thornton has an innovative theory about the age of the universe, but Bob
suspects him of rigging his data. The rivalry is extended in the story
to the details of competition over the use of the observatory during
the limited nights of good viewing. Latham gives us the comedy of
Bob's loss of status when Dagny is appointed official witch of
California. Such are the foibles of astronomers in this story that
astrology seems a refreshing alternative. In "A Drop of Dragon's
Blood" we learn more about the politics of being an astronomer, the
need to produce sensational findings in order to attract research

funds. Bob makes a public prediction of a period for the variable star Mira in a desperate hope for publicity, because his job is in trouble. His prediction comes true in an ironic way: Mira's companion brightens at exactly the time Bob predicted Mira would brighten, in a new phenomenon, the "simmering nova." The point of the story is the unexpected nature of the universe: "there are ghosts everywhere." Once again Latham tempts us to side with Dagny's belief in magic. Although Latham has brought science to science fiction, he certainly has not brought mechanical materialism.

In his most recent stories Latham has turned almost completely away from the hard science of his earlier work. In "Miracle Elixir" an ordinary office worker, who works for Pearce's Golden Specific but never thinks of taking the company product, learns what it is like to have his life turned around by a "real" elixir. Without the interest of science, Latham's recent stories are sometimes thin and awkward. Latham could not be called a major science-fiction writer. But he has brought science to his best science-fiction stories and he has created anti-heroic and likeable astronomers as characters.

—Curtis C. Smith

* * *

LAUMER, (John) Keith. American. Born in Syracuse, New York, 9 June 1925. Educated at the University of Indiana, Bloomington, 1943-44; University of Stockholm, 1947-48; University of Illinois, Urbana, B.Sc. 1950, B.Arch. 1952. Served in the United States Army, 1943-45: Corporal; United States Air Force, 1952-56, 1959-65: Captain. Staff member, University of Illinois, 1952; Foreign Service Vice-Consul and Third Secretary, Rangoon, 1956-59. Since 1964, free-lance writer. Agent: Robert P. Mills, 156 East 52nd Street, New York, New York 10022. Address: Box 972, Brooksville, Florida 33512, U.S.A.

SCIENCE-FICTION PUBLICATIONS

Novels (series: Imperium; Invaders; O'Leary; Retief)

Worlds of the Imperium. New York, Ace, 1962; London, Dobson, 1967.
A Trace of Memory. New York, Berkley, 1963; London, Mayflower, 1968.
The Great Time Machine Hoax. New York, Simon and Schuster, 1964.
A Plague of Demons. New York, Berkley, 1965; London, Penguin, 1967.
The Other Side of Time (Imperium). New York, Berkley, 1965; London, Dobson, 1968.
The Time Bender (O'Leary). New York, Berkley, 1966; London, Dobson, 1975.
Retief's War. New York, Doubleday, 1966.
Earthblood, with Rosel George Brown. New York, Doubleday, 1966; London, Hodder and Stoughton, 1979.
Catastrophe Planet. New York, Berkley, 1966; London, Dobson, 1970.
The Monitors. New York, Berkley, 1966; London, Dobson, 1968.
Enemies from Beyond (novelization of TV series; Invaders). New York, Pyramid, 1966.
Planet Run, with Gordon R. Dickson. New York, Doubleday, 1967; London, Hale, 1977.
The Invaders (novelization of TV series). New York, Pyramid, 1967; as *The Meteor Man,* London, Corgi, 1968.
Galactic Odyssey. New York, Berkley, 1967; London, Dobson, 1968.
The Day Before Forever, and Thunderhead. New York, Doubleday, 1968.
Assignment in Nowhere. New York, Berkley, 1968; London, Dobson, 1972.
Retief and the Warlords. New York, Doubleday, 1968.

The Long Twilight. New York, Putnam, 1969; London, Hale, 1976.
The World Shuffler (O'Leary). New York, Putnam, 1970; London, Sidgwick and Jackson, 1973.
The House in November. New York, Putnam, 1970; London, Sidgwick and Jackson, 1973.
Time Trap. New York, Putnam, 1970; London, Hale, 1976.
Retief's Ransom. New York, Putnam, 1971; London, Dobson, 1975.
The Star Treasure. New York, Putnam, 1971; London, Sidgwick and Jackson, 1974.
Deadfall. New York, Doubleday, 1971; London, Hale, 1974; as *Fat Chance,* New York, Pocket Books, 1975.
Dinosaur Beach. New York, Scribner, 1971; London, Hale, 1973.
The Infinite Cage. New York, Putnam, 1972; London, Dobson, 1976.
Night of Delusions. New York, Putnam, 1972; London, Dobson, 1977.
The Shape Changer (O'Leary). New York, Putnam, 1972; London, Hale, 1977.
The Glory Game. New York, Doubleday, 1973; London, Hale, 1974.
Bolo: The Annals of the Dinochrome Brigade. New York, Berkley, 1976.
The Ultimax Man. New York, St. Martin's Press, 1978; London, Sidgwick and Jackson, 1980.
The Star Colony. New York, St. Martin's Press, 1980.

Short Stories (series: Retief)

Envoy to New Worlds (Retief). New York, Ace, 1963; London, Dobson, 1972.
Galactic Diplomat (Retief). New York, Doubleday, 1965.
Nine by Laumer. New York, Doubleday, 1967; London, Faber, 1968.
Greylorn. New York, Berkley, 1968; as *The Other Sky,* London, Dobson, 1968.
It's a Mad, Mad, Mad Galaxy. New York, Berkley, 1968; London, Dobson, 1969.
Retief, Ambassador to Space. New York, Doubleday, 1969.
Retief of the CDT. New York, Doubleday, 1971.
Once There Was a Giant. New York, Doubleday, 1971; London, Hale, 1975.
The Big Show. New York, Ace, 1972; London, Hale, 1976.
Timetracks. New York, Ballantine, 1972.
The Undefeated. New York, Dell, 1974.
Retief, Emissary to the Stars. New York, Dell, 1975.
The Best of Keith Laumer. New York, Simon and Schuster, 1976.
Retief Unbound (omnibus). New York, Ace, 1979.
Retief at Large. New York, Ace, 1979.

OTHER PUBLICATIONS

Novels

Embassy. New York, Pyramid, 1965.
The Afrit Affair (novelization of TV series). New York, Berkley, 1968.
The Drowned Queen (novelization of TV series). New York, Berkley, 1968.
The Gold Bomb (novelization of TV series). New York, Berkley, 1968.

Other

How to Design and Build Flying Models. New York, Harper, 1960; revised edition, 1970; London, Hale, 1975.

Editor, *Five Fates.* New York, Doubleday, 1970.

*

Manuscript Collections: University of Syracuse, New York; University of Mississippi, University.

Keith Laumer comments:

I have been asked if my work is "relevant," i.e., political propaganda. It is not. I prefer to treat themes that have been important to man ever since he became man, and will continue to be important as long as humanity remains: strength and courage, truth and beauty, loyalty and justice, ethics and integrity, kindness and gentleness, and many others.

*   *   *

During the 1960's, Keith Laumer was one of the most prolific of science-fiction authors. He has slowed down somewhat recently, but even so he has to his credit a long string of titles which range over wide areas both in subject matter and in treatment. Laumer's first novel, *Worlds of the Imperium,* is told as a conventional adventure story, with only an occasional light touch. But in *The Time Bender* and its sequels featuring Layfayette O'Leary, Laumer writes what amounts to a gentle parody of his own Imperium series. And the humor in the long and popular series (mostly of short stories) concerning interstellar diplomat Jame Retief stretches almost all the way to farce. But Laumer can play the other side of the court as well: the tone is serious, even grim, in works such as *A Plague of Demons* and *Night of Delusions.* As for subject matter, Laumer has tried out virtually all the traditional possibilities and has enriched the realm of science fiction with innovations of his own—most notably the brilliantly detailed and remarkably plausible picture of the "fabric of simultaneous reality" introduced in the Imperium series. Laumer has written space-war stories, space-diplomacy stories, slightly rationalized fairy stories, time-travel stories, parallel-world stories, robot stories, psi-power stories, invasion-of-the-Earth stories (including *The Monitors,* in which the invaders are the good guys), stories of intrigue, love, rational detection, mystical apotheosis, and on and on.

Yet for all its diversity, Laumer's work holds unities as well. Some of these are of a negative sort. For instance, there is never an unhappy ending. A Laumer hero may lose a girl, but if so he will usually marry another, and will in no case allow one misfortune to poison his entire life. He may get killed in the end, but he will never go unmourned and (in *Assignment in Nowhere* and others) his sacrifice may well save the world. In the area of positive generalizations, it can be said that in some measure all Laumer stories are adventure stories, even if the author's focus is on satire, farce, romance, ratiocination, or philosophical speculation.

Moreover, Laumer heroes are virtually all of one general pattern, with variations determined chiefly by degree of maturity. While the typologies are not identical, the Laumer character does bear striking similarities to the "Heinlein individual" described by Alexei Panshin. Explanations for this resemblance might range from some basic principle of storytelling to Heinlein's and Laumer's similar background as military officers. The basic Laumer type is the full-formed competent man—sure of himself, resourceful, able to mix easily with all levels of society and to get what he wants out of anyone. Laumer has put the basic type to heaviest use in the person of Retief, hero of a "template series" where character growth is ruled out by the ground rules. For most other applications, the basic competent man is too static—he can indeed be roused to action, but only to protect what he has. A slight variation Laumer employs more often is an incipient competent man whose character is fully formed but who has not yet found his niche in life, and who is consequently searching for fulfillment. Brion Bayard fits in here in *Worlds of the Imperium,* though in the sequel, *The Other Side of Time,* he has matured into the basic type. It is of course possible to begin at an earlier point, with someone who must learn not merely how to apply competence, but competence itself. This gives us characters such as Billy Danger in *Galactic Odyssey* or, in a more humorous vein, Layfayette O'Leary. But Laumer has also interested himself in movement in the other direction, beyond the competent man. Perhaps because of his own relative youth during his peak writing period, Laumer has chosen to do this not by putting one of his heroes through some sort of mid-life crisis, but rather (in a tack he might have picked up from van Vogt or the early Heinlein—or from Sophocles) by having his hero discover something about who he is that causes him to transcend his status as the competent man. In the most extreme case, the largely unsuccessful *Night of Delusions,* the protagonist finds himself to be, for most practical purposes, God. Other Laumer heroes learn that they are supermen, Arthurian reincarnations, and various sorts of robots. The effects of such revelations also vary. Some heroes go off to pursue transcendental existence, some perish gloriously, and others voluntarily return to the human state. It is difficult to decide whether in these various encounters with the transcendental Laumer is trying to put forth a serious philosophy (in the manner of, say, Cordwainer Smith or Gordon R. Dickson), or simply, more playfully, to give his already-competent heroes somewhere to go, and to pique the reader's Sense of Wonder. Such mystic passages are not, in any event, the most successful part of Laumer's work.

His other failings are those one might expect of an author so prolific as Laumer was in the 1960's—insufficient attention to detail and excessive repetition from work to work. Consequently, it will be left to posterity and chance to decide which of five or six versions of essentially the same story is the one really worth keeping. But some of Laumer will most certainly be kept.

—Patrick L. McGuire

LAVOND, Paul Dennis. *See* **LOWNDES, Robert A. W.**

LEE, Matt. *See* **MERWIN, Sam, Jr.**

LEE, Tanith. British. Born in London, 19 September 1947. Educated at Catford Grammar School, London, and at an art college. Lives in London. Address: c/o Macmillan London Ltd., 4 Little Essex Street, London WC2R 3LF, England.

SCIENCE-FICTION PUBLICATIONS

Novels (series: Birthgrave)

The Birthgrave. New York, DAW, 1975; London, Futura, 1977.
Don't Bite the Sun. New York, DAW, 1976.
The Storm Lord. New York, DAW, 1976; London, Futura, 1977.
Drinking Sapphire Wine. New York, DAW, 1977.
Volkhavaar. New York, DAW, 1977.
Vazkor, Son of Vazkor (Birthgrave). New York, DAW, 1978; as *Shadowfire,* London, Futura, 1979.
Quest for the White Witch (Birthgrave). New York, DAW, 1978; London, Futura, 1979.
Night's Master. New York, DAW, 1978.
Death's Master. New York, DAW, 1979.
Drinking Sapphire Wine (includes *Don't Bite the Sun*). London, Hamlyn, 1979.
Electric Forest. New York, DAW, 1979.
Sabella; or, The Blood Stone. New York, DAW, 1980.
Kill the Dead. New York, DAW, 1980.
Day by Night. New York, DAW, 1980.

Uncollected Short Stories

"The Truce," in *The DAW Science Fiction Reader*, edited by Donald A. Wollheim.   New York, DAW, 1976.

"The Demoness," in *The Year's Best Fantasy Stories 2*, edited by Lin Carter.   New York, DAW, 1976.

"Odds Against the Gods," in *Swords Against Darkness 2*, edited by Andrew J. Offutt.   New York, Kensington, 1977.

"Huzdra," in *The Year's Best Horror 5*, edited by Gerald W. Page.   New York, DAW, 1977.

"In the Balance," in *Swords Against Darkness 3*, edited by Andrew J. Offutt.   New York, Kensington, 1978.

"Winter White," in *The Year's Best Horror 6*, edited by Gerald W. Page.   New York, DAW, 1978.

"Sleeping Tiger," in *Dragonbane 5* (Ottawa), 1978.

"One Night of the Year," in *Other Worlds 2*, edited by Roy Torgeson.   New York, Kensington, 1979.

"The Murderous Dove," in *Heroic Fantasy*, edited by Gerald W. Page.   New York, DAW, 1979.

"Northern Chess," in *Amazons*, edited by Jessica Amanda Salmonson.   New York, DAW, 1979.

"Deux Amours d'Une Sorcière, " in *Swords Against Darkness 4*, edited by Andrew J. Offutt.   New York, Kensington, 1979.

"The Third Horseman," in *Weirdbook 14* (New York), 1979.

"A Hero at the Gates," in *Shayol* (New York), Summer 1979.

"Red as Blood," in *Fantasy and Science Fiction* (New York), July 1979.

"Monkey's Stagger," in *Sorcerer's Apprentice* (New York), Fall 1979.

"Perfidious Amber," in *Swords Against Darkness 5*, edited by Andrew J. Offutt.   New York, Kensington, 1980.

"Room with a Vie," in *New Terrors*, edited by Ramsey Campbell.   London, Pan, 1980.

"The Thaw," in *The Best Science Fiction of the Year 9*, edited by Terry Carr.   New York, Ballantine, 1980.

"Cyrion in Bronze," in *Fantasy and Science Fiction* (New York), February 1980.

"The Squire's Tale," in *Sorcerer's Apprentice* (New York), Summer 1980.

"Cyrion in Wax," in *Dragonfields* (Ottawa), Summer 1980.

"Wolfland," in *Fantasy and Science Fiction* (New York), October 1980.

OTHER PUBLICATIONS

Short Story

The Betrothed.   Sidcup, Kent, Slughorn Press, 1968.

Plays

Radio Plays: *Bitter Gate*, 1977; *Red Wine*, 1977; *Death Is King*, 1979; *The Silver Sky*, 1980.

Other (juvenile)

The Dragon Hoard.   London, Macmillan, and New York, Farrar Straus, 1971.

Princess Hynchatti and Some Other Surprises.   London, Macmillan, 1972; New York, Farrar Straus, 1973.

Animal Castle.   London, Macmillan, and New York, Farrar Straus, 1972.

Companions on the Road.   London, Macmillan, 1975.

The Winter Players.   London, Macmillan, 1976.

Companions on the Road, and The Winter Players.   New York, St. Martin's Press, 1977.

East of Midnight.   London, Macmillan, 1977; New York, St. Martin's Press, 1978.

The Castle of Dark.   London, Macmillan, 1978.

Shon the Taken.   London, Macmillan, 1979.

*   *   *

Tanith Lee has established herself in both fantasy and SF with children's books (*The Dragon Hoard*), fairy tales (*Princess Hyn-*

chatti and Some Other Surprises), horror stories ("Winter White"), erotic adult fantasy (*Death's Master, Night's Master*, and *Volkhavaar*), heroic fantasy (*The Storm Lord*, the Birthgrave trilogy, "The Murderous Dove"), and conventional science fiction (*Don't Bite the Sun, Drinking Sapphire Wine*, and *Electric Forest*). All have strong characterization, intense emotional impact, tongue-in-cheek humor, and gorgeous people of enormous power and will who must pass tests before accepting themselves. The fantasies are long and episodic, full of exotic names and barbarous tribes. Though set on other planets, they have little ecological detail. Lee is concerned instead with people who walk alone, searching for their destinies.

The Birthgrave trilogy constitutes heroic searches for identity. *The Birthgrave* was immediately ranked with works by Le Guin and Norton. It is a transition between her fantasy and SF modes, as is the ironic short story "The Truce." Its background is a society degenerated from greatness, horribly ignorant of the past and science. Its heroine awakes with no name or identity and a face so hideous she cannot endure it. Where women are mindless cattle, she cannot accept her obvious superiority and allows others, particularly handsome Vazkor, to use her. In Book III she has another rebirth. Leaving Vazkor's son with a bereaved mother, she follows a peaceful tribe. To save her companions she unconsciously summons a spaceship to destroy a dragon. This confrontation of technical and mental power helps her recall her past and accept her identity, telepathy, power over even nature, and great beauty. She determines to rebuild a race of mental giants. In *Vazkor, Son of Vazkor*, Tuvek changes from an insensitive tribesman to Vazkor, gentle, wise, and powerful. His development continues in *Quest for the White Witch* as the epic hero searches for revenge and a mother. The novels are, like Hesse's *Siddhartha*, about the education of a god.

The ends of *The Birthgrave* and *Quest for the White Witch* have elements of SF in the fall of a great civilization and the actual appearance of a spaceship. Unique in Lee's fantasy is its underlying seriousness and lack of a basis in religion or witchcraft. The people are godlike human beings who must learn to perfect and use their mental abilities responsibly. Before gaining control, Vazkor and Karrakaz, his mother, accidentally cause destruction. Both learn to rise above a degraded society and be rid of guilt, and determine to restore advanced civilization to their planet.

The restlessness of the loner searching for identity is equally significant in the teenage heroine of the anti-utopian *Don't Bite the Sun* and *Drinking Sapphire Wine*. Society is totally controlled, even the weather within the domed city. Before 50, people party, dress outrageously, engage in delinquency, change bodies at whim, marry for a day or so, and try to sabotage machines that maintain perfection. Ensuring immediate rescue from death and a specially designed new body, monitoring bees make suicide impossible. After serious social deviance, an individual is sent to Limbo for Personality Dissolution and a fresh start. The narrator is lonely, precocious, and bored with perpetual fun. Her only true friend is the pet, as troublesome and as little disturbed by convention as she. To find meaning, she goes on an archaelogical expedition. Back in the city, she dons a male body and fights a duel, killing another. Preferring exile to ego dissolution, she settles in the desert where she knows a good life once existed and begins her own counter-culture, outwitting the disapproving authorities. This worldis different from those of Lee's fantasies in its technological development. Her narrative is colloquial, highlighted by special "Jang" slang instead of the high epic style used in the fantasy. Although the climaxes of self-revelation occur with few episodes and characters, one developing character commands attention.

Electric Forest centers on the developing character of "Ugly," Magdala Cled, a disfigured, abandoned child on a planet where everyone is beautiful. Claudio Loro, handsome, wealthy, and brilliant, offers her beauty at a high price—her real body to be cared for, a permanent hostage, while she masquerades as his scientist wife. Their project is successful physical and psychological transfer of people into android bodies for use in exploration and colonization. How will one react when confronting an identical android? As in her other short works, Lee turns the plot abruptly at the end.

In each work there are strong character, vivid detail, carefully worked-out systems, and good story-telling, testimony to Lee's skill and versatility.

—Mary S. Weinkauf

LE GUIN, Ursula K(roeber). American. Born in Berkeley, California, 21 October 1929. Educated at Radcliffe College, Cambridge, Massachusetts, A.B. 1951 (Phi Beta Kappa); Columbia University, New York (Faculty Fellow; Fulbright Fellow, 1953), M.A. 1952. Married Charles A. Le Guin in 1953; two daughters and one son. Instructor in French, Mercer University, Macon, Georgia, 1954, and University of Idaho, Moscow, 1956; former department secretary, Emory University, Atlanta; has taught writing workshops at Pacific University, Forest Grove, Oregon, 1971, University of Washington, Seattle, 1971-73, Portland State University, Oregon, 1974, 1977, 1979, in Melbourne, Australia, 1975, and at the University of Reading, England, 1976. Recipient: *Boston Globe-Horn Book* Award, for children's book, 1969; Nebula Award, 1969, 1974 (twice); Hugo Award, 1970, 1973, 1974, 1975; National Book Award, for children's book, 1972; Jupiter Award, 1974 (twice); Gandalf Life Award, 1979. Guest of Honor, World Science Fiction Convention, 1975. D.Litt. Bucknell University, Lewisburg, Pennsylvania, 1978; honorary degree: Lawrence University, Appleton, Wisconsin. Lives in Portland, Oregon. Agent: Virginia Kidd, Box 278, Milford, Pennsylvania 18337, U.S.A.

SCIENCE-FICTION PUBLICATIONS

Novels (series: Hain)

Rocannon's World (Hain). New York, Ace, 1966; London, Tandem, 1972.
Planet of Exile (Hain). New York, Ace, 1966; London, Tandem, 1972.
City of Illusions (Hain). New York, Ace, 1967; London, Gollancz, 1971.
The Left Hand of Darkness (Hain). New York, Walker, and London, Macdonald, 1969.
The Lathe of Heaven. New York, Scribner, 1971; London, Gollancz, 1972.
The Dispossessed: An Ambiguous Utopia. New York, Harper, and London, Gollancz, 1974.
The Word for World Is Forest (Hain). New York, Putnam, 1976; London, Gollancz, 1977.

Short Stories

The Wind's Twelve Quarters. New York, Harper, 1975; London, Gollancz, 1976.

Uncollected Short Stories

"The Diary of the Rose," in *Future Power,* edited by Jack Dann and Gardner Dozois. New York, Random House, 1976.
"The Eye Altering," in *The Altered Eye,* edited by Lee Harding. Melbourne, Norstrilia Press, 1976; New York, Berkley, 1980.
"The Barrow," in *Fantasy and Science Fiction* (New York), October 1976.
"The Eye of the Heron," in *Millennial Women,* edited by Virginia Kidd. New York, Delacorte Press, 1978.
"SQ," in *The 1979 Annual World's Best SF,* edited by Donald A. Wollheim. New York, DAW, 1979.
"The Pathways of Desire," in *New Dimensions 9,* edited by Robert Silverberg. New York, Harper, 1979.

OTHER PUBLICATIONS

Novels

Malafrena. New York, Putnam, 1979; London, Gollancz, 1980.
The Beginning Place. New York, Harper, 1980; as *Threshold, ,* London, Gollancz, 1980.

Short Stories

Orsinian Tales. New York, Harper, 1976; London, Gollancz, 1977.

Play

No Use to Talk to Me, in *The Altered Eye,* edited by Lee Harding. Melbourne, Norstrilia Press, 1976; New York, Berkley, 1980.

Verse

Wild Angels. Santa Barbara, California, Capra Press, 1975.
Hard Words and Other Poems. New York, Harper, 1981.

Other (juvenile)

A Wizard of Earthsea. Berkeley, California, Parnassus Press, 1967; London, Gollancz, 1971.
The Tombs of Atuan. New York, Atheneum, 1971; London, Gollancz, 1972.
The Farthest Shore. New York, Atheneum, 1972; London, Gollancz, 1973.
Very Far Away from Anywhere Else. New York, Atheneum, 1976; as *A Very Long Way from Anywhere Else,* London, Gollancz, 1976.
Leese Webster. New York, Atheneum, 1979.

Other

"Fifteen Vultures, The Strop, and the Old Lady," in *Clarion 2,* edited by Robin Scott Wilson. New York, New American Library, 1972.
From Elfland to Poughkeepsie (lecture). Portland, Pendragon Press, 1973.
"On Theme," in *Those Who Can,* edited by Robin Scott Wilson. New York, New American Library, 1973.
"On Norman Spinrad's *The Iron Dream,*" in *Science-Fiction Studies* (Terre Haute, Indiana), Spring 1973.
"A Citizen of Mondath: The Development of a Science Fiction Writer 4," in *Foundation 4* (London), July 1973.
"European SF," in *Science-Fiction Studies* (Terre Haute, Indiana), Spring 1974.
Dreams Must Explain Themselves. New York, Algol Press, 1975.
"American SF and the Other," in *Science-Fiction Studies* (Terre Haute, Indiana), November 1975.
The Water Is Wide. Portland, Pendragon Press, 1976.
"Science Fiction and Mrs. Brown," in *Science Fiction at Large,* edited by Peter Nicholls. London, Gollancz, 1976; New York, Harper, 1977.
"Is Gender Necessary?," in *Aurora,* edited by Vonda N. McIntyre and Susan Janice Anderson. New York, Fawcett, 1976.
"A Response to the Le Guin Issue," in *Science-Fiction Studies* (Terre Haute, Indiana), March 1976.
"The Stalin in the Soul," in *The Future Now,* edited by Robert Hoskins. New York, Fawcett, 1977.
The Language of the Night: Essays on Fantasy and Science Fiction, edited by Susan Wood. New York, Putnam, 1979.

Editor, *Nebula Award Stories 11.* London, Gollancz, 1976; New York, Harper, 1977.
Editor, with Virginia Kidd, *Interfaces.* New York, Ace, 1980.
Editor, with Virginia Kidd, *Edges.* New York, Pocket Books, 1980.

*

Bibliography: by Jeffrey Levin, in *The Language of the Night,* 1979.

*   *   *

The immensely popular fiction of the American writer Ursula K. Le Guin proves that popular literature may have literary merit, a serious message, and a large satisfied audience all at once. Today the notion of a science-fiction writer producing a novel of substance, even a novel of character, is not so remarkable, as researchers continue to demonstrate that literarily remarkable works have existed in this genre ever since the publication of Mary Shelley's *Frankenstein,* but at the start of Le Guin's career, in the mid-1960's, literary excellence in science fiction was regarded as rare. Le Guin, hailed as a *novelist* who chose to write science fiction, has always attracted an audience composed of genre fans as well as readers who would ordinarily disdain science fiction. Le Guin's work continues to be known for literary expertise which graces a thematic preoccupation with telling essentially hopeful stories of man transcending alienation to open his imagination, his intellect, and his heart to the real adventure of the universe. Le Guin, in common with many writers of science fiction, is a talented builder of new worlds and alien landscapes; she is comfortable with technological wonders, faster-than-light vehicles, and particularly with marvels in the field of long-distance communication, but her commitment, stated clearly in the essay "Science Fiction and Mrs. Brown," is to confirm man's essential humanity against a backdrop of alien situations by means of consistently viewing her characters as the "subjects" of her narratives rather than as objects. A subjective human approach to the marvelous underlines Le Guin's view that if "Mrs. Brown [the ordinary, intriguing snatch of human character] is dead, you can take your galaxies and roll them up into a ball and throw them into the trashcan, for all I care. What good are all the objects in the universe, if there is no subject?"

A large portion of Le Guin's work focuses upon subjective views of a universe incorporating numerous habitable worlds, each "seeded" by beings from the planet Hain. Each of the five novels and several shorter works in this series revolves around the literal and figurative quests of chief characters to discover their individual purposes within the contexts of their several different worlds and, often, within the broader context of the universe. The themes and chronology of the Hain series have been worked out over two decades of Le Guin's career, but the early works anticipate or foreshadow the best moments of the latest work, while the latest book, fascinatingly, provides the scientific explanation and development of a device—the instantaneous communicator called the ansible—which has been essential to all of the previous works.

The first published works in this series, *Rocannon's World, Planet of Exile,* and *City of Illusions,* do proceed chronologically and establish a thematic preoccupation with the duality existing in nature and in man, viewed as Peter Nicholls has pointed out, "not as polarities or opposed forces" but as archetypical symbols presented as "twin parts of a balanced whole" (*The Science Fiction Encyclopedia,* 1979). Each work employs the alien as the embodiment of alienation presenting to the hero the challenge of transcending fear itself, through embracing the unknown. Communication, whether through telepathic "mindspeach" or by means of the amazing ansible, is significant, often the symbolic crux of each climax. In *Rocannon's World* an outworld ethnological surveyor stranded on Fomalhaut II is unable to accept fully his destiny of remaining on the strange world until he achieves the ability to communicate through mindspeach. In a narrative which also emphasizes the importance of naming, it is significant that, in ironic understatement, the League of All Worlds, unbeknownst to the ethnographer, gives this world his name, Rocannon's World.

Planet of Exile depicts a world which is populated by two humanoid groups, each believing themselves to be fully human and therefore superior to the other. A female character, the dreamy yet strong-willed Rolery, represents the linking of the two cultures as she overcomes her awe of the "farborn" Terran colonists through her command of telepathic powers generally possessed only by the farborns. Interestingly, discipline, along with honest communication, is described as the key to individual purpose and successful community, while community (the cooperation of both "human" societies) is necessary for the basic survival of either group. "Community," asserts Le Guin (in "Science Fiction and Mrs. Brown"), "is the best we can hope for, and community for most people means touches: the touch of your hand against the other's hand, the job done together, the sledge hauled together, the dance danced together, the child conceived together." Significantly, Rolery is offered the hope of conceiving a child with her farborn husband, while the two groups, under extreme challenge from overwhelming environmental conditions, at last unite to form a new society.

Metaphor is particularly rich in this novel, which anticipates *The Left Hand of Darkness* in its description of a world dominated by a frigid winter environment.

City of Illusions describes a Hainish world where mindspeach, previously the epitome of truthful communication, has been perverted by the alien Shing invaders who may manipulate it into a "mind lie." A complex narrative tells the story of the amnesiac Falk and his quest to discover his true name and homeworld. Throughout experiences of betrayal and disorienting double identity, his hopes were "staked now totally on one belief: that an honest man cannot be cheated, that truth, if the game be played through right to the end, will lead to truth." Here truth and falsehood are regarded as polarities in essential struggle; truth may prevail only when the hero learns to allow both of his identities to work together and, significantly, when he gains access to the ansible so that he may communicate with the world of its origin as well as with the League of All Worlds. The League becomes known as the Ekumen of Known Worlds in *The Left Hand of Darkness,* which richly explores the themes suggested in earlier Hainish works. Genly Ai is a human ethnologist who visits the planet Gethen, where he is swiftly caught up in a snowbound society wrapped in political intrigue and characterized by a revolutionary (to Genly Ai as well as to the reader) androgynous worldview which raises questions about sexuality and sexism and shows a populace composed of individuals whose identity is divorced from gender. The Gethenians, usually neuter, experience a sexual cycle which gives them the ability to become either male or female at certain cyclical peaks. The implications of this alienness tax even the comprehension of this professional observer who learns that the limitation of his own alien perspective, his own alienation, is keeping him from appreciating and understanding this strange new world.

"Vaster than Empires and More Slow" and *The Word for World Is Forest* are shorter works in the Hain series which use the forest as metaphors for the unknown. The former (its title derived from Andrew Marvell's poem "To His Coy Mistress") is perhaps Le Guin's most polished and graceful statement of the need to embrace the alien, the Other, in order to understand it. Osden, a ship's empath, transcends the limitations of both time and fear when he literally embraces the surface of an alien planet, covered in a network of sentient vegetation. "He had taken fear into himself, and accepting had transcended it. He had given up his self to the alien, an unreserved surrender, that left no place for evil. He had learned love of the Other, and thereby been given his whole self."

The Dispossessed is centered around the inventor of the ansible, a man called Shevek whose anarchist "Utopia" is ambiguously unable to provide him with the raw materials (chiefly free communication and flow of scientific information) which he needs to make his best contribution to society. This rich work is one in which occasional didacticism is nevertheless fascinating as two politically different worlds (one anarchistic, the other decadently capitalistic) are balanced by means of contrast and comparison, each presented in alternate chapters. The author uses visual perspective most strikingly here; the image of the wall as a defining force is powerfully employed, while in an early scene Shevek's world fills his view like a concave dish until, as his space vessel takes him a greater distance from it, it falls away into a convex circle, then a globe, then a distant world. The author also uses paradox, mathematical and verbal, as the key to truth, while communication among all men is the confirmation of man's essential humanity in the face of political, environmental, or other differences.

Some other major works by this author include the "Earth Sea" trilogy (1968-72), a study of magical skill which appeals to adults as well as to the juvenile audience it was written for. *The Lathe of Heaven* is a novel outside the Hain series dealing with a man of conscience who cannot bear the fact that his dreams effectively change reality. *The Beginning Place* is an allegorical novel portraying a fantastic "twilight world," a haven for two adolescents fleeing from unhappy family situations in a bleak unnamed suburbia. The protagonists learn, by means of encounters with an archtypal monster, to face the harsh disappointments of their "real" lives. *Orsinian Tales* and *Malafrena* evoke the 19th-century in an imaginary country with a central European atmosphere. *Malafrena* deals with the coming of age of a young revolutionary who must learn to balance freedom and commitment.

Le Guin's fiction seems to say that the ultimate adventure in the universe is a subjective, human quest which achieves not only confrontation with the alien but defeat of alienation; the author's message is clearly, sometimes gracefully, conveyed in literary prose, which will always be the hallmark of her work.

—Rosemary Herbert

* * *

LEIBER, Fritz (Reuter, Jr.). Born in Chicago, Illinois, 25 December 1910. Educated at the University of Chicago, Ph.B 1932; Episcopal General Theological Seminary, Washington, D.C. Married Jonquil Stephens in 1936 (died, 1969); one son. Episcopal minister at two churches in New Jersey, 1932-33; actor, 1934-36; Editor, Consolidated Book Publishers, Chicago, 1937-41; Instructor in Speech and Drama, Occidental College, Los Angeles, 1941-42; precision inspector, Douglas Aircraft, Santa Monica, California, 1942-44; Associate Editor, *Science Digest,* Chicago, 1944-56. Lecturer, Clarion State College, Pennsylvania, summers 1968-70. Recipient: Hugo Award, 1958, 1965, 1968, 1970, 1971, 1976; Nebula Award, 1967, 1970, 1975; Ann Radcliffe Award, 1970; Gandalf Award, 1975; World Fantasy Award, 1976, 1978. Guest of Honor, World Science Fiction Convention, 1951. Address: 565 Geary Street, Apartment 604, San Francisco, California 94102, U.S.A.

SCIENCE-FICTION PUBLICATIONS

Novels

Gather, Darkness! New York, Pellegrini and Cudahy, 1950; London, New English Library, 1966.
The Sinful Ones. New York, Universal, 1953; as *You're All Alone,* New York, Ace, 1972.
The Green Millennium. New York, Abelard Press, 1953; London, Abelard Schuman, 1960.
Destiny Times Three. New York, Galaxy, 1957.
The Big Time (includes stories). New York, Ace, 1961; published separately, London, New English Library, 1965.
The Silver Eggheads. New York, Ballantine, 1961; London, New English Library, 1966.
The Wanderer. New York, Ballantine, 1964; London, Dobson, 1967.
A Specter Is Haunting Texas. New York, Walker, and London, Gollancz, 1969.

Short Stories

A Pail of Air. New York, Ballantine, 1964.
Ships to the Stars. New York, Ace, 1964.
The Night of the Wolf. New York, Ballantine, 1966; London, Sphere, 1976.
The Secret Songs. London, Hart Davis, 1968.
The Best of Fritz Leiber, edited by Angus Wells. London, Sidgwick and Jackson, and New York, Ballantine, 1974.
The Book of Fritz Leiber. New York, DAW, 1974.
The Second Book of Fritz Leiber. New York, DAW, 1975.
The Worlds of Fritz Leiber. New York, Ace, 1976.
The Change War. Boston, Gregg Press, 1978.
Ship of Shadows. London, Gollancz, 1979.

OTHER PUBLICATIONS

Novels

Conjure Wife. New York, Twayne, 1953; London, Penguin, 1969.
Tarzan and the Valley of Gold. New York, Ballantine, 1966.
The Swords of Lankhmar. New York, Ace, 1968; London, Hart Davis, 1969.

Swords and Deviltry. New York, Ace, 1970; London, New English Library, 1971.
Our Lady of Darkness. New York, Berkley, 1977; London, Millington, 1978.

Short Stories

Night's Black Agents. Sauk City, Wisconsin, Arkham House, 1947; London, Spearman, 1975.
The Girl with the Hungry Eyes and Other Stories. New York, Avon, 1949.
Two Sought Adventure: Exploits of Fafhrd and the Gray Mouser. New York, Gnome Press, 1957.
Shadows with Eyes. New York, Ballantine, 1962.
Swords Against Wizardry. New York, Ace, 1968; London, Prior, 1977.
Swords in the Mist. New York, Ace, 1968; London, Prior, 1977.
Night Monsters. New York, Ace, 1969; revised edition, London, Gollancz, 1974.
Swords Against Death. New York, Ace, 1970; London, New English Library, 1972.
Swords and Ice Magic. New York, Ace, and London, Prior, 1977.
Rime Isle. Browns Mills, New Jersey, Whispers Press, 1977.
Bazaar of the Bizarre. West Kingston, Rhode Island, Grant, 1978.
Heroes and Horrors. Browns Mills, New Jersey, Whispers Press, 1978.

Verse

The Demons of the Upper Air. Glendale, California, Squires, 1969.
Sonnets to Jonquil and All. Glendale, California, Squires, 1978.

Other

"Way-Out Science," in *National Review* (New York), 9 April 1963.
"Utopia for Poets and Witches," in *Riverside Quarterly* (Regina, Saskatchewan), August 1970.
"The Profession of Science Fiction 12: Mysterious Islands, " in *Foundation 11/12* (London), March 1977.

Editor, with Stuart David Schiff, *The World Fantasy Awards 2.* New York, Doubleday, 1980.

*

Bibliography: *Fritz Leiber: A Bibliography 1934-1979* by Chris Morgan, Birmingham, Morgenstern, 1979.

*   *   *

Fritz Leiber is one of the most popular and respected writers of science fiction and fantasy. While his readers and fellow writers have appreciated his humor and concern for mankind, the critics have largely ignored his work. Leiber has sometimes been classed with the writers of "weird" stories because of his frequent use of the supernatural and his acknowledged literary debt to H.P. Lovecraft. This association is misleading since Leiber uses the supernatural as a souce of symbols for the mysteries of the universe and the mind. As he says, "Many of the most typical creations of science fiction, especially the robot, the android, and the extraterrestrial, are simply the monster in a new guise...."

The supernatural may also turn out to be disguised applications of science, as in his first novel, *Gather, Darkness!* This story concerns a revolution in a repressive society controlled by a religious hierarchy using technology masquerading as supernatural miracle. The resulting satire provides a commentary on the respective roles of religion, science, and government. There is a witty surface of gadgets such as an electronically controlled haunted house, but there is also a warning against the dangers of restricting scientific knowledge to an elite, regardless of the reason. Leiber's background in the theater is probably responsible for the dramatic staging of much of the action.

The Green Millennium, presents a picture of a decadent United States where organized crime and corrupt government control society through sex and games. This society is invaded by two alien species from Vega which end the violence. The main virtues of the novel are fast-moving adventure and humor, but there is an underlying layer of satire about the confusion and banality of modern values. *Destiny Times Three* is an alternate-world novel in which three very different societies have been created by an accidental time fragmentation. These worlds contain similar people, one of whom learns of his other personalities and attempts to resolve the time paradoxes. This re-working of an early magazine story is not as polished as his later work. What might have been treated as a traditional SF story has been handled more as allegory and myth.

The Big Time, the major work in a series of time-travel stories, concerns a war fought by time-travelling warriors of two groups called "Snakes" and "Spiders" who attempt to produce a victory in the future by altering the past. Leiber's belief in pacifism is presented through the disillusionment of the characters about the possibility of final victory. This framework allows Leiber to mix characters from many times and places in an entertainment and recuperation center. By limiting almost all the action to one room and employing dramatic techniques of staging and dialogue, Leiber has almost created a science-fiction play, with first-person interior narration. Character differentiations are neatly provided by excellent parodies of the character's differing diction and vocabulary (for example, Elizabethan and Greek dramatic styles). *The Silver Eggheads* is an experiment in satire which borders on farce. The major point is his dissection of the world of publishers, writers, and readers with humorous references to a wide range of literature, but he seems more at ease with satire in his other books. A long "disaster" novel, *The Wanderer,* describes the responses of people subjected to the earthquakes, tidal waves, and other global disasters caused by an artificial planet which enters an orbit around the earth. Leiber's main interest is in the detailed character studies of both heroes and villains provided by this framework. Almost all of Leiber's themes and interests are included: he deals with almost all aspects of human life, from birth to death. There is also plenty of action, but the novel is not significantly different from many other catastrophe stories. In *A Specter Is Haunting Texas* the specter (a skeletally thin actor from a colony on a satellite around earth's moon) is a coerced leader of a revolution of the enslaved "Mexes" against the Texans, who are hormonally induced giants controlling most of North America. Much of the book is based on theatrical motifs, from costuming and staging to the symbolic roles of the characters, and other devices of the stage. The basic method is again satire, this time against the absurdity of racism, war, and values in general. The plot is somewhat uneven, but the humor and originality of the background are entertaining.

In addition to his science fiction, Leiber has written two novels about the supernatural, *Conjure Wife* and *Our Lady of Darkness,* both of which are border-line science fiction. His fantasy series relating the exploits of Fafhrd and The Gray Mouser has made him one of the most popular writers of this genre. His best-known stories are probably "Coming Attraction" and "Gonna Roll the Bones."

Throughout his career, Leiber has used the same topics and themes—the supernatural, theater, cats, time, sex, politics, alcohol. His most frequent technique is satire. His writing displays considerable stylistic control (particularly in writing parodies) and the influence of many writers from John Webster and Shakespeare to Eddison, C.A. Smith, and Cabell. He seems to view the basic function of literature in terms of human identity and potentiality. The psychological presentation of character is central to his work, as is his view of literature as theater. These factors are related to the problem of psychological identity. All literature requires at least a partial suspension of personality on the part of the reader, but this demand is particularly great in science fiction and also appears prominently in the function of the actor. A similar reaction can occur with stories of the supernatural. All of these features combine to make Leiber an acute commentator on the human mind.

—Norman L. Hills

LEINSTER, Murray. Pseudonym for Will(iam) F(itzgerald) Jenkins. American. Born in Norfolk, Virginia, 16 June 1896. Educated in public and private schools in Norfolk. Served with the Committee of Public Information, and in the United States Army, 1917-18; served in the Office of War Information during World War II. Married Mary Mandola in 1921; three daughters and one son. Free-lance writer from 1918. Recipient: *Liberty* Award, 1937; Hugo Award, 1956. Guest of Honor, 21st World Science Fiction Convention, 1963. *Died 8 June 1975.*

SCIENCE-FICTION PUBLICATIONS

Novels (series: Joe Kenmore; Med Service)

Murder Madness. New York, Brewer and Warren, 1931.
The Murder of the U.S.A. (as Will Jenkins). New York, Crown, 1946; as *Destroy the U.S.A.,* New York, Newsstand, 1950.
The Last Space Ship. New York, Fell, 1949; London, Cherry Tree, 1952.
Fight for Life. New York, Crestwood, n.d.
Space Platform (juvenile; Kenmore). Chicago, Shasta, 1953.
Space Tug (juvenile; Kenmore). Chicago, Shasta, 1953.
Gateway to Elsewhere. New York, Ace, 1954.
The Forgotten Planet. New York, Gnome Press, 1954.
The Brain-Stealers. New York, Ace, 1954; London, Badger, 1960.
Operation: Outer Space. Reading, Pennsylvania, Fantasy Press, 1954; London, Grayson, 1957.
The Black Galaxy. New York, Galaxy, 1954.
The Other Side of Here. New York, Ace, 1955.
City on the Moon (juvenile; Kenmore). New York, Avalon, 1957.
Colonial Survey. New York, Gnome Press, 1957; as *The Planet Explorer,* New York, Avon, 1957.
War with the Gizmos. New York, Fawcett, 1958; London, Muller, 1959.
The Monster from Earth's End. New York, Fawcett, 1959; London, Muller, 1960.
The Mutant Weapon (Med Service). New York, Ace, 1959.
The Pirates of Zan. New York, Ace, 1959.
Four from Planet 5. New York, Fawcett, 1959; London, White Lion, 1974.
The Wailing Asteroid. New York, Avon, 1960.
Creatures of the Abyss. New York, Berkley, 1961; as *The Listeners,* London, Sidgwick and Jackson, 1969.
This World Is Taboo (Med Service). New York, Ace, 1961.
Talents, Incorporated. New York, Avon, 1962.
Operation Terror. New York, Berkley, 1962; London, Tandem, 1968.
The Duplicators. New York, Ace, 1964.
The Other Side of Nowhere. New York, Berkley, 1964.
Time Tunnel. New York, Pyramid, 1964.
The Greks Bring Gifts. New York, Macfadden, 1964.
Invaders of Space. New York, Berkley, 1964; London, Tandem, 1968.
Space Captain. New York, Ace, 1966.
Tunnel Through Time (juvenile). Philadelphia, Westminster Press, 1966.
Checkpoint Lambda. New York, Berkley, 1966; in *A Murray Leinster Omnibus,* London, Sidgwick and Jackson, 1968.
The Time Tunnel (novelization of TV series). New York, Pyramid, 1967; London, Sidgwick and Jackson, 1971.
Miners in the Sky. New York, Avon, 1967.
Space Gypsies. New York, Avon, 1967.
Timeslip! (novelization of TV series). New York, Pyramid, 1967.
Land of the Giants (novelization of TV play). New York, Pyramid, 1968.
The Hot Spot (novelization of TV play). New York, Pyramid, 1969.
Unknown Danger (novelization of TV play). New York, Pyramid, 1969.

Short Stories (series: Med Service)

Sidewise in Time. Chicago, Shasta, 1950.
Out of This World. New York, Avalon, 1958.

Monsters and Such. New York, Avon, 1959.
Twists in Time. New York, Avon, 1960.
Men into Space (novelization of TV series). New York, Berkley, 1960.
The Aliens. New York, Berkley, 1960.
Doctor to the Stars (Med Service). New York, Pyramid, 1964.
Get Off My World! New York, Belmont, 1966.
S.O.S. from Three Worlds (Med Service). New York, Ace, 1967.
The Best of Murray Leinster. London, Corgi, 1976; New York, Ballantine, 1978.

OTHER PUBLICATIONS

Novels

Scalps. New York, Brewer and Warren, 1930; as *Wings of Chance*, London, John Hamilton, 1935.
Murder Mystery. New York, Harcourt Brace, 1930.
Wanted Dead or Alive! London, Wright and Brown, 1951.

Novels as Will F. Jenkins

Murder Will Out. London, John Hamilton, 1932.
The Gamblin' Kid. New York, King, 1933; London, Eldon Press, 1934.
Mexican Trail. New York, King, 1933; London, Eldon Press, 1935.
Sword of Kings. London, Long, 1933.
Fighting Horse Valley. New York, King, 1934; London, Eldon Press, 1935.
Outlaw Sheriff. New York, King, 1934; as *Rustlin' Sheriff*, London, Eldon Press, 1934.
The Kid Deputy. New York, King, and London, Eldon Press, 1935.
Murder in the Family. London, John Hamilton, 1935.
No Clues. London, Wright and Brown, 1935.
Black Sheep. New York, Messer, and London, Eldon Press, 1936.
Guns for Achin. London, Wright and Brown, 1936.
The Man Who Feared. New York, Gateway, 1942.
Dallas (novelization of screenplay). New York, Fawcett, 1950; London, Muller, 1961.
Son of the Flying "Y." New York, Fawcett, 1951; London, Muller, 1957.
Cattle Rustlers. London, Ward Lock, 1952.

Other

Editor, *Great Stories of Science Fiction.* New York, Random House, 1951; London, Cassell, 1953.

*   *   *

A professional writer for the slick and pulp magazines from 1913 until 1967, Murray Leinster embodies in one writer the very essence of the commercial yet ambitiously serious genre of science fiction. He did his best work in short fiction. He developed and extrapolated upon certain key speculative ideas, several of the most important of which he introduced to the genre. He wrote for money and sold to several markets other than science fiction, and yet the imaginative expansion of ideas about nature and about the relation of life forms to nature made science fiction a very important area in his production. Leinster wrote so much that it is hard to categorize his major themes and most characteristic effects, but always his mind is lively and he seems interested particularly in cool analyzing and in alternatives to all possibilities.

In fact, his fascination with the possibility of alternatives to any situation led him to the standard science-fiction theme that he is often best remembered as having introduced to the genre: the theme of parallel points on a time continuum, or parallel worlds. A story from 1931, "The Fifth-Dimension Catapult," plays with the notion as a kind of modern alchemy in which the clever laboratory investigator can change time and space coordinates in order to visit a completely alien parallel world; and in this case the plan finally is to

bring back gold. Leinster's more well-known story of parallel worlds is "Sidewise in Time" in which some unexplained oscillation of the earth results in a myriad of alternate time paths. His method of telling this story in little isolated vignettes of what might be possible here and there as the oscillations produce alternative presents is indicative of why short fiction is a primary form in science fiction. With change and even alternate possibilities ever present there simply does not exist the stable Victorian world for developing long narratives in one time and one place. Leinster, beginning as early as it was popularized, writes a modern alchemy of change according to Einstein-like relativity. Some longer fictions of his that rely on this same balancing of alternatives are *Colonial Survey*, which contains his Hugo-winning novelet "Exploration Team," and *Time Tunnel*.

Similarly, Leinster develops again and again the ramification of contact between different life forms that are alternatives to each other. This is the often-used theme in science fiction of first contact with an alien race; and the most influential story of Leinster's of this type is entitled simply "First Contact" (1945). But many of his stories explore the alternatives of encounter and relationship between life forms who consider each other alien because they cannot or do not communicate. In "Proxima Centauri" the aliens are intelligent and mobile plants that crave animal flesh. This reversal, or notion that what we do ourselves may often be quite alien, permeates Leinster's fictions. Not only do humans enjoy vegetable salads unthinkingly, but in "The Strange Case of John Klingman" the human managers of the mental hospital seem more alien than Klingman. Similarly, the moon monkeys in "Keyhole" have more sympathy and effective understanding than their human opposites because they can communicate telepathically, and hence the human thoughts, although alien to them, are not unknown.

The key seems to be knowledge and understanding, for here the two themes in Leinster's fiction come together. Alternate or parallel worlds as well as life forms alien to each other are only possible when differentiation, separateness, and mental isolation are possible. If the universe were all one, there would be only one time path and there would be continual communion. But the universe is parceled out, and communication is very seldom total or telepathic and instant. In other words, Leinster seems to be continually retelling the myth of original sin. Things are not as they should be, hence continual competitiveness and continual alternatives.

A brilliant working of this theme of the pathos of separateness and difference is in "The Lonely Planet," which seems to be an anticipation of the widely acclaimed novel by Stanislaw Lem, *Solaris*. In Leinster's story, a magnificent creature called Alyx covers an entire planet. In the beginning it is totally telepathic to mankind because it has not developed a defense against mind or total communication since it has evolved in an environment where it was the only creature. The story, then, is how mankind teaches Alyx to be secretive and competitive, finally, because Alyx learns what loneliness was. Perhaps Leinster is saying that a perfect oneness would be lonely and boring and that we need alternatives and even competitiveness. In any case, the clever, inventive, competitive and necessarily separate mind of the scientific investigator is the favorite protagonist in a Leinster story. Thus from the point of view of modern fiction, his characters often seem grossly two dimensional and his conflicts exaggerated and sensational. These bold and exaggerated effects prevail throughout his popular novel *The Forgotten Planet* (an expansion of "Mad Planet," 1926)—the narration of a continual war with giant insects and the growth of human rationality. But many of these effects are simply the demands of the pulp market, and seen in their most symbolic way they continually narrate the inescapable reality of human fallibility.

No treatment of Leinster and of the evolution of the genre of modern science fiction that he contributed so much to would be complete without mention of the sense of awe that goes with what is generally dismissed as space opera. In addition to the suggestiveness in theme and meaning mentioned above, Leinster's fiction reads well because of wide-ranging space patrol and med service action and because of journeys to distant second galaxies. There is also a good deal of violence, quick cruelty, and villainy in Leinster's work; and when this also is handled well it is an ancient emblem for the fallen state of mankind, and exact correlative to the infinite alternatives in the material world. But always in Leinster, along with the awe and the space opera, is the intellectual curiosity and the analytic mind—perhaps again representative of the fallen state of man, but characteristic also of the best in science fiction. Leinster grew with the genre, but he is also a example of how subtle some of the best space opera can be.

—Donald M. Hassler

L'ENGLE, Madeleine. American. Born in New York City, 29 November 1918. Educated at Smith College, Northampton, Massachusetts, A.B. (honors) 1941; New School for Social Research, New York, 1941-42; Columbia University, New York, 1960-61. Married Hugh Franklin in 1946; three children. Worked in the theatre, New York, 1941-47; teacher, St. Hilda's and St. Hugh's School, New York, 1960-66; Member of the Faculty, University of Indiana, Bloomington, summers 1965-66, 1971; Writer-in-Residence, Ohio State University, Columbus, 1970, and University of Rochester, New York, 1972. Since 1966, Librarian, Cathedral of St. John the Divine, New York; since 1970, President, Crosswicks Ltd., New York. Since 1976, Member, Board of Directors, Authors League Foundation, New York. Recipient: American Library Association Newbery Medal, for children's book, 1963; American Book Award, 1980. Agent: Raines and Raines, 475 Fifth Avenue, New York, New York 10017. Address: Crosswicks, Goshen, Connecticut 06756, U.S.A.

SCIENCE-FICTION PUBLICATIONS

Novels (series: Time)

The Time Trilogy. New York, Farrar Straus, 1979.
  A Wrinkle in Time. New York, Farrar Straus, 1962; London, Constable, 1963.
  A Wind in the Door. New York, Farrar Straus, 1973; London, Methuen, 1975.
  A Swiftly Tilting Planet. New York, Farrar Straus, 1978; London, Souvenir Press, 1980.
A Ring of Endless Light. New York, Farrar Straus, 1980.

Uncollected Short Story

"Poor Little Saturday," in *Fantastic Universe* (Chicago), October 1956.

OTHER PUBLICATIONS

Novels

The Small Rain. New York, Vanguard Press, 1945; London, Secker and Warburg, 1955.
Ilsa. New York, Vanguard Press, 1946.
And Both Were Young. New York, Lothrop, 1949.
Camilla Dickinson. New York, Simon and Schuster, 1951; London, Secker and Warburg, 1952; as *Camilla,* New York, Crowell, 1965.
A Winter's Love. Philadelphia, Lippincott, 1957.
Meet the Austins. New York, Vanguard Press, 1960; London, Collins, 1966.
The Moon by Night. New York, Farrar Straus, 1963.
The Arm of the Starfish. New York, Farrar Straus, 1965.
The Love Letters. New York, Farrar Straus, 1966.
The Journey with Jonah. New York, Farrar Straus, 1968.
The Young Unicorns. New York, Farrar Straus, 1968; London, Gollancz, 1970.
Prelude. New York, Vanguard Press, 1969; London, Gollancz, 1972.
The Other Side of the Sun. New York, Farrar Straus, 1971; London, Eyre Methuen, 1972.

Dragons in the Waters. New York, Farrar Straus, 1976.

Plays

18 Washington Square, South (produced Northampton, Massachusetts, 1940) Boston, Baker, 1944.
How Now Brown Cow, with Robert Hartung (produced New York, 1949).
The Journey with Jonah, adaptation of her own novel (produced New York, 1970). New York, Farrar Straus, 1967.

Verse

Lines Scribbled on an Envelope and Other Poems. New York, Farrar Straus, 1969.
Weather of the Heart. Wheaton, Illinois, Shaw, 1978.

Other

The Twenty-Four Days Before Christmas (juvenile). New York, Farrar Straus, 1964.
Dance in the Desert (juvenile). New York, Farrar Straus, and London, Longman, 1969.
A Circle of Quiet (essays). New York, Farrar Straus, 1972.
Everyday Prayers. New York, Morehouse Barlow, 1974.
Prayers for Sunday. New York, Morehouse Barlow, 1974.
The Summer of the Great-Grandmother (essays). New York, Farrar Straus, 1974.
The Irrational Season (essays). New York, Seabury Press, 1977.
Ladder of Angels: Scenes from the Bible Illustrated by Children of the World. New York, Seabury Press, 1979.
The Anti-Muffins (juvenile). New York, Pilgrim Press, 1980.
Walking on Water (essays). Wheaton, Illinois, Shaw, 1980.

Editor, with William R. Green, *Spirit and Light: Essays in Historical Theology.* New York, Seabury Press, 1976.

*

Manuscript Collections: Wheaton College, Illinois; Kerlan Collection, University of Minnesota, Minneapolis; de Grummond Collection, University of Southern Mississippi, Hattiesburg.

Madeleine L'Engle comments:
 I discovered science fiction early, as a lonely only child growing up, for my first 12 years, in New York City, then in France and Switzerland. For me, the real world was clearer in the books of E. Nesbit and H.G. Wells than in the world of school. So I started writing science fiction when I was eight or nine. Fortunately all of my early work was lost somewhere or other on our journeys across the Atlantic.
 During college and after I turned to more "realistic" fiction, and found that it was not real enough, that my true discoveries of reality came while I was writing sci-fi or fantasy. I also discovered that for me the great theologians and modern mystics are the scientists, the physicists and astrophysicists, the cellular biologists, since they are dealing with the nature of Being itself. Einstein, Planck, Eddington, Jeans, Heisenberg, and many others, have been—and are still—my great stimulants.

* * *

 Madeleine L'Engle's first science-fiction work, "Poor Little Saturday," is a light, engaging short story which, in common with her later work, manages to ask questions about open-mindedness and the creative, youthful imagination, and to affirm the author's belief in the power of love. Even this early story, about a lonely boy who discovers the companionship of a witch, a young girl, and a camel in an apparently deserted house, is notable for establishing L'Engle's stylistic strength of putting the fantastic into perspective for the reader. L'Engle's fiction does not merely woo the reader's willing suspension of disbelief; through focusing on the power of love, in herself as creator of the narrative, in her characters, and in appealing to that experience in her readers, she wins the reader's faith in the believability of the extraordinary. In fiction which tackles vast yet basic questions of good versus evil in terms of the creative spirit versus the negative forces of entropy and cosmic disunity, this faith is necessary. L'Engle's gift is an ability to help each reader, young and old, discover an ability to *believe,* in her characters in their situations, and—at least while reading her stories—in each individual's essential and vital role in the struggle between the powers of light and darkness.

"It was a dark and stormy night." So begins L'Engle's best-known work, *A Wrinkle in Time.* This first sentence characteristically sets the narrative on a simple, very recognizable level while it identifies the major situation at the heart of the book. The powers of evil, darkness, and dis-ease are at work while the members of the Murry family meet in the warm, well-lit haven of their kitchen to share physical and spiritual sustenance, and to dispel one anothers' fears. This story, featuring exceptional children who also possess some endearing ordinary faults (and appetites for hot cocoa and tomato sandwiches, for instance), is a tale of spiritual adventure in which archetypal symbols are hidden in eccentrically engaging characters and in which the physical hazards also represent the impediments which have challenged man's spiritual development throughout the ages. Just as the Murry children are facing a crisis of faith in their father, who has disappeared while pursuing a top-secret mission, they encounter three supranormal (*not* supernatural—their powers are those of science and love) beings who aid the children in travelling through a "Tesseract" or "wrinkle in time" in quest of their missing parent. Significantly, they are aided by a boy called Calvin whose chief strength lies in his ability to communicate. The children learn that recovering their father is not an end in itself, that in order to reach him they must win a battle on a cosmic scale which illustrates the belief that all beings great and small have significance in the order of things.

A Wind in the Door develops similar themes. Here the dis-ease the heroes must face is represented by disease in the ordinary sense of the word, and the equal importance of the great and the small is underlined as Meg Murry, Calvin, and an extraordinary cherub called Proginoskes join forces to save Charles Wallace from an illness which is striking at the very basic building blocks of his cellular anatomy. His system is suffocating as the breathing apparatus for the mitochondria in his cells fails to function. This submicroscopic battle within Charles Wallace is mirrored in cosmic disturbances which are creating a "rip in the galaxy" itself, a black hole which is "terrible precisely because it is not a thing, because it was nothing." In order to still the "cosmic scream" and to be her brother's keeper, Meg must learn to overcome the vast forces of annihilation by facing three tests which challenge her to overcome her personal limitations and to recognize and strengthen the creative powers in herself and others, including the ordinary, befuddled school principal, and the extraordinary "beings" whose proper function, small as it is, is necessary to keep Charles Wallace alive.

A Swiftly Tilting Planet traces the "Might-Have-Beens" which have led to a particular evil, in this case the threat of thermonuclear war. Here, a mature Meg, pregnant with her first child, communes with her brother, Charles Wallace, as he explores the family history leading to the rise of a despot who, warped by lack of love and reason, holds universal destruction in the palm of his hand. Through the power of "kything," complete empathic communication, Meg aids Charles Wallace in establishing the fact that the prevalence of evil is not inevitable in a universe where love exists, if each person places his gift of love in the face of the powers of darkness. The agent of the extraordinary here is the unicorn Gaudior, while the representative of the ordinary, Meg's bitter, unhappy mother-in-law, proves herself to possess the courage to fulfill her small but very significant purpose in life.

All of L'Engle's work deals with the question of real maturation, or "deepening." What is true for the smallest part of a living cell is true for the universe. "Now that I am rooted I am no longer limited by motion. I sing with the stars. I dance with the galaxies. I share in the joy—and in the grief."

—Rosemary Herbert

LE QUEUX, William (Tufnell).   British.   Born in London, 2 July 1864. Educated privately in London and Pegli, Italy; studied art in Paris. Foreign Editor, London *Globe,* 1891-93; from 1893 freelance journalist and travel writer; Balkan Correspondent, *Daily Mail,* London, during Balkan War, 1912-13; served as Consul to the Republic of San Marino. Popularly supposed to have been a spy. Lived in Switzerland in later life. *Died 13 October 1927.*

SCIENCE-FICTION PUBLICATIONS

Novels

The Great War in England in 1897.   London, Tower, 1894.
A Madonna of the Music Halls.   London, White, 1897; as *A Secret Sin,* London, Gardner, 1913.
The Eye of Istar.   London, White, and New York, Stokes, 1897.
The Great White Queen.   London, White, 1898; New York, Arno Press, 1975.
England's Peril.   London, White, 1899.
The Invasion of 1910, with a Full Account of the Siege of London.   London, Nash, 1906.
The Unknown Tomorrow.   London, White, 1910.
The Mystery of the Green Ray.   London, Hodder and Stoughton, 1915; as *The Green Ray,* London, Mellifont Press, 1944.
The Terror of the Air.   London, Lloyd's 1920.

Short Stories

Stolen Souls.   London, Tower and New York, Stokes, 1895.

OTHER PUBLICATIONS

Novels

Guilty Bonds.   London, Routledge, 1891; New York, Fenno, 1895.
The Temptress.   London, Tower and New York, Stokes, 1895.
Zoraida: A Romance of the Harem and the Great Sahara.   London, Tower and New York, Stokes, 1895.
Devil's Dice.   London, White, 1896; Chicago, Rand McNally, 1897.
Whoso Findeth a Wife.   London, White, 1897; Chicago, Rand McNally, 1898.
If Sinners Entice Thee.   London, White, 1898; New York, Dillingham, 1899.
Scribes and Pharisees.   London, White, and New York, Dodd Mead, 1898.
The Veiled Man.   London, White, 1899.
The Bond of Black.   London, White, and New York, Dillingham, 1899.
Wiles of the Wicked.   London, Bell, 1899.
The Day of Temptation.   London, White, and New York, Dillingham, 1899.
An Eye for an Eye.   London, White, 1900.
In White Raiment.   London, White, 1900.
Of Royal Blood.   London, Hutchinson, 1900.
The Gamblers.   London, Hutchinson, 1901.
The Sign of the Seven Sins.   Philadelphia, Lippincott, 1901.
Her Majesty's Minister.   London, Hodder and Stoughton, and New York, Dodd Mead, 1901.
The Court of Honour.   London, White, 1901.
The Under-Secretary.   London, Hutchinson, 1902.
The Unnamed.   London, Hodder and Stoughton, 1902.
The Tickencote Treasure.   London, Newnes, 1903.
The Three Glass Eyes.   London, Treherne, 1903.
The Seven Secrets.   London, Hutchinson, 1903.
The Idol of the Town.   London, White, 1903.
As We Forgave Them.   London, White, 1904.
The Closed Book.   London, Methuen, and New York, Smart Set, 1904.
The Hunchback of Westminster.   London, Methuen, 1904.
The Man from Downing Street.   London, Hurst and Blackett, 1904.
The Red Hat.   London, Daily Mail, 1904.
The Sign of the Stranger.   London, White, 1904.

The Valley of the Shadow. London, Methuen, 1905.
Who Giveth This Woman? London, Hodder and Stoughton, 1905.
The Spider's Eye. London, Cassell, 1905.
Sins of the City. London, White, 1905.
The Mask. London, Long, 1905.
Behind the Throne. London, Methuen, 1905.
The Czar's Spy. London, Hodder and Stoughton, and New York, Smart Set, 1905.
The Great Court Scandal. London, White, 1906.
The House of the Wicked. London, Hurst and Blackett, 1906.
The Mysterious Mr. Miller. London, Hodder and Stoughton, 1906.
The Mystery of a Motor-Car. London, Hodder and Stoughton, 1906.
Whatsoever a Man Soweth. London, White, 1906.
The Woman at Kensington. London, Cassell, 1906.
The Secret of the Square. London, White, 1907.
The Great Plot. London, Hodder and Stoughton, 1907.
Whosoever Loveth. London, Hutchinson, 1907.
The Crooked Way. London, Methuen, 1908.
The Looker-On. London, White, 1908.
The Pauper of Park Lane. London, Cassell, and New York, Cupples and Leon, 1908.
Stolen Sweets. London, Nash, 1908.
The Woman in the Way. London, Nash, 1908.
The Red Room. London, Cassell, 1909; Boston, Little Brown, 1911.
The House of Whispers. London, Nash, 1909; New York, Brentano's, 1910.
Fatal Thirteen. London, Stanley Paul, 1909.
The Great God Gold. Boston, Badger, 1910.
Treasure of Israel. London, Nash, 1910.
Lying Lips. London, Stanley Paul, 1910.
Hushed Up!. London, Nash, 1911.
The Money-Spider. London, Cassell, and Boston, Badger, 1911.
The Death-Doctor. London, Hurst and Blackett, 1912.
Fatal Fingers. London, Cassell, 1912.
The Mystery of Nine. London, Nash, 1912.
Without Trace. London, Nash, 1912.
The Price of Power, Being Chapters from the Secret History of the Imperial Court of Russia. London, Hurst and Blackett, 1913.
The Room of Secrets. London, Ward Lock. 1913.
The Lost Million. London, Nash, 1913.
The White Lie. London, Ward Lock, 1914.
Sons of Satan. London, White, 1914.
The Hand of Allah. London, Cassell, 1914; as *The Riddle of the Ring*, London, Federation Press, 1927.
Her Royal Highness. London, Hodder and Stoughton, 1914.
The Maker of Secrets. London, Ward Lock, 1914.
The Four Faces. London, Stanley Paul, and New York, Brentano's, 1914.
The Double Shadow. London, Hodder and Stoughton, 1915.
At the Sign of the Sword. London, Jack, and New York, Scully and Kleinteich, 1915.
The Mysterious Three. London, Ward Lock, 1915.
The Sign of Silence. London, Ward Lock, 1915.
The White Glove. London, Nash, 1915.
The Zeppelin Destroyer. London, Hodder and Stoughton, 1916.
Number 70, Berlin. London, Hodder and Stoughton, 1916.
The Place of Dragons. London, Ward Lock, 1916.
The Spy Hunter. London, Pearson, 1916.
The Man about Town. London, Long, 1916.
Annette of the Argonne. London, Hurst and Blackett, 1916.
The Broken Thread. London, Ward Lock, 1916.
Behind the German Lines. London, London Mail, 1917.
The Breath of Suspicion. London, Long, 1917.
The Devil's Carnival. London, Hurst and Blackett, 1917.
No Greater Love. London, Ward Lock, 1917.
Two in a Tangle. London, Hodder and Stoughton, 1917.
Rasputin, The Rascal Monk. London, Hurst and Blackett, 1917.
The Yellow Ribbon. London, Hodder and Stoughton, 1918.
The Secret Life of the Ex-Tsaritza. London, Odhams Press, 1918.
The Sister Disciple. London, Hurst and Blackett, 1918.
The Stolen Statesman. London, Skeffington, 1918.

The Little Blue Goddess. London, Ward Lock, 1918.
The Minister of Evil: The Secret History of Rasputin's Betrayal of Russia. London, Cassell, 1918.
Bolo, The Super Spy. London, Odhams Press, 1918.
The Catspaw. London, Lloyd's, 1918.
Cipher Six. London, Hodder and Stoughton, 1919.
The Doctor of Pimlico. London, Cassell, 1919; New York, Macaulay, 1920.
The Forbidden Word. London, Odhams Press, 1919.
The King's Incognito. London, Odhams Press, 1919.
The Lure of Love. London, Ward Lock, 1919.
Rasputinism in London. London, Cassell, 1919.
The Secret Shame of the Kaiser. London, Hurst and Blackett, 1919.
Secrets of the White Tsar. London, Odhams Press, 1919.
The Heart of a Princess. London, Ward Lock, 1920.
The Intriguers. London, Hodder and Stoughton, 1920; New York, Macaulay, 1921.
No. 7, Saville Square. London, Ward Lock, 1920.
The Red Widow; or, The Death-Dealers of London. London, Cassell, 1920.
Whither Thou Goest. London, Lloyd's, 1920.
This House to Let. London, Hodder and Stoughton, 1921.
The Lady-in-Waiting. London, Ward Lock, 1921.
The Open Verdict. London, Hodder and Stoughton, 1921.
The Power of the Borgias: The Story of the Great Film. London, Odhams Press, 1921.
Mademoiselle of Monte Carlo. London, Cassell, and New York, Macaulay, 1921.
The Fifth Finger. London, Stanley Paul, and New York, Moffat, 1921.
The Golden Face. London, Cassell, and New York, Macaulay, 1922.
The Stretton Street Affair. New York, Macaulay, 1922; London, Cassell, 1924.
Three Knots. London, Ward Lock, 1922.
The Voice from the Void. London, Cassell, 1922; New York, Macaulay, 1923.
The Young Archduchess. London, Ward Lock, and New York, Moffat, 1922.
Where the Desert Ends. London, Cassell, 1923.
The Bronze Face. London, Ward Lock, 1923; as *Behind the Bronze Door*, New York, Macaulay, 1923.
The Crystal Claw. London, Hodder and Stoughton, and New York, Macaulay, 1924.
Fine Feathers. London, Stanley Paul, 1924.
A Woman's Debt. London, Ward Lock, 1924.
The Valrose Mystery. London, Ward Lock, 1925.
The Marked Man. London, Ward Lock, 1925.
The Blue Bungalow. London, Hurst and Blackett, 1925.
The Broadcast Mystery. London, Holden, 1925.
The Fatal Face. London, Hurst and Blackett, 1926.
Hidden Hands. London, Hodder and Stoughton, 1926; as *The Dangerous Game*, New York, Macaulay, 1926.
The Letter E. London, Cassell, 1926; as *The Tattoo Mystery*, New York, Macaulay, 1927.
The Mystery of Mademoiselle. London, Hodder and Stoughton, 1926.
The Scarlet Sign. London, Ward Lock, 1926.
The Black Owl. London, Ward Lock, 1926.
The Office Secret. London, Ward Lock, 1927.
The House of Evil. London, Ward Lock, 1927.
The Lawless Hand. London, Hurst and Blackett, 1927; New York, Macaulay, 1928.
Blackmailed. London, Nash and Grayson, 1927.
The Chameleon. London, Hodder and Stoughton, 1927; as *Poison Shadows*, New York, Macaulay, 1927.
Concerning This Woman. London, Newnes, 1928.
The Rat Trap. London, Ward Lock, 1928; New York, Macaulay, 1930.
The Secret Formula. London, Ward Lock, 1928.
The Sting. London, Hodder and Stoughton, and New York, Macaulay, 1928.
Twice Tried. London, Hurst and Blackett, 1928.
The Amazing Count. London, Ward Lock, 1929.

The Crinkled Crown. London, Ward Lock, and New York, Macaulay, 1929.
The Golden Three. London, Ward Lock, 1930; New York, Fiction House, 1931.

Short Stories

Strange Tales of a Nihilist. London, Ward Lock, and New York, Cassell, 1892; as *A Secret Service,* Ward Lock, 1896.
Secrets of Monte Carlo. London, White, 1899; New York, Dillingham, 1900.
Secrets of the Foreign Office. London, Hutchinson, 1903.
Confessions of a Ladies' Man, Being the Adventures of Cuthbert Croom, of His Majesty's Diplomatic Service. London, Hutchinson, 1905.
The Count's Chauffeur. London, Nash, 1907.
The Lady in the Car, in Which the Amours of a Mysterious Motorist Are Related. London, Nash, and Philadelphia, Lippincott, 1908.
Spies of the Kaiser: Plotting the Downfall of England. London, Hurst and Blackett, 1909.
Revelations of the Secret Service. London, White, 1911.
The Indiscretions of a Lady's Maid. London, Nash, 1911.
Mysteries. London, Ward Lock, 1913.
The German Spy. London, Newnes, 1914.
"Cinders" of Harley Street. London, Ward Lock, 1916.
The Bomb-Makers. London, Jarrolds, 1917.
Beryl of the Biplane. London, Pearson, 1917.
Hushed Up at German Headquarters. London, London Mail, 1917.
The Rainbow Mystery: Chronicles of a Colour-Criminologist. London, Hodder and Stoughton, 1917.
The Scandal-Monger. London, Ward Lock, 1917.
The Secrets of Potsdam. London, Daily Mail, 1917.
More Secrets of Potsdam. London, London Mail, 1917.
Further Secrets of Potsdam. London, London Mail, 1917.
Donovan of Whitehall. London, Pearson, 1917.
Sant of the Secret Service. London, Odhams Press, 1918.
The Hotel X. London, Ward Lock, 1919.
Mysteries of the Great City. London, Hodder and Stoughton, 1919.
In Secret. London, Odhams Press, 1920.
The Secret Telephone. New York, McCann, 1920; London, Jarrolds, 1921.
Society Intrigues I Have Known. London, Odhams Press, 1920.
The Luck of the Secret Service. London, Pearson, 1921.
The Elusive Four: The Exciting Exploits of Four Thieves. London, Cassell, 1921.
Tracked by Wireless. London, Stanley Paul, and New York, Moffat, 1922.
The Gay Triangle: The Romance of the First Air Adventurers. London, Jarrolds, 1922.
Bleke, The Butler, Being the Exciting Adventures of Robert Bleke During Certain Years of His Service in Various Families. London, Jarrolds, 1923.
The Crimes Club: A Record of Secret Investigations into Some Amazing Crimes, Mostly Withheld from the Public. London, Nash and Grayson, 1927.
The Peril of Helen Marklove and Other Stories. London, Jarrolds, 1928.
The Factotum and Other Stories. London, Ward Lock, 1931.

Play

The Proof (produced Birmingham, 1924; as *Vendetta,* produced London, 1924).

Other

An Observer in the Near East. London, Nash, 1907; as *The Near East,* New York, Doubleday, 1907.
The Balkan Trouble; or, An Observer in the Near East. London, Nash, 1912.
The War of the Nations, vol. 1. London, Newnes, 1914.

German Atrocities: A Record of Shameless Deeds. London, Newnes, 1914.
German Spies in England: An Exposure. London, Stanley Paul, 1915.
Britain's Deadly Peril: Are We Told the Truth? London, Stanley Paul, 1915.
The Devil's Spawn: How Italy Will Defeat Them. London, Stanley Paul, 1915.
The Way to Win. London, Simpkin Marshall, 1916.
Love Intrigues of the Kaiser's Sons. London, Long, and New York, Lane, 1918.
Landru: His Secret Love Affairs. London, Stanley Paul, 1922.
Things I Know about Kings, Celebrities, and Crooks. London, Nash and Grayson, 1923.
Engelberg: The Crown Jewel of the Alps. London, Swiss Observer, 1927.
Interlaken: The Alpine Wonderland: A Novelist's Jottings. Interlaken, Official Information Bureau, n.d.

Translator, *Of the "Polar Star" in the Arctic Sea,* by Luigi Amedeo. London, Hutchinson, 1903.

*   *   *

William Le Queux's life is more interesting than anything he wrote. He travelled extensively, was acquainted with royalty, collected an impressive number of decorations for various services from various courts. He used his position for intelligence or spying activity, claiming to have written his more than 150 potboilers—exotic, political, and spy novels—to support such patriotic amateur ventures as the discovery of a German spy network in England in 1906. Together with Field Marshal Lord Roberts and a number of prominent British politicians, he concocted his most famous war and fifth-column forecast, *The Invasion of 1910* as an appeal to the UK to prepare for war.

His SF writings, besides some marginal stories, are generally worthless, melodramatic novels. They include the ludicrous *A Madonna of the Music Halls,* in which a villainous scientist terrorizes a beautiful girl by foisting on her strange qualities through liquids transferring other people's "brain power" (e.g. hate); a banal first try at the "future war" cum spy story, *The Great War in England in 1897; The Unknown Tomorrow,* depicting the cruelties of the socialism of 1935; and *The Terror of the Air,* a tired exploitation of the German threat. Thus *The Invasion of 1910* remains his only important contribution to the political pathology of SF and of ideology in general, and an object-lesson in the successful use of SF as propaganda, based on the immediate objectives of the ruling politico-military complex allied with the newspapers, London clubland, and the Secret Service. Even Wells was not always immune from such a syndrome, and one wonders in how many SF writers down to Adamov or Cordwainer Smith it is also present.

—Darko Suvin

———————

LESLIE, O.H. *See* **SLESAR, Henry.**

———————

LESSER, Milton. Also writes as Adam Chase; Andrew Frazer; Stephen Marlowe; Jason Ridgway; C.H. Thames. American. Born in New York City, 7 August 1928. Educated at the College of William and Mary, Williamsburg, Virginia, B.A. 1949. Served in the United States Army, 1952-54. Married Ann Humbert (second marriage); two children. Former writer-in-residence, College of William and Mary. Member, Board of Directors, Mystery Writers of America. Agent: Scott Meredith Literary Agency, 845 Third Avenue, New York, New York 10022, U.S.A.

SCIENCE-FICTION PUBLICATIONS

Novels

Earthbound (juvenile). Philadelphia, Winston, 1952; London, Hutchinson, 1955.
The Star Seekers (juvenile). Philadelphia, Winston, 1953.
The Golden Ape (as Adam Chase, with Paul W. Fairman). New York, Avalon, 1959.
Recruit for Andromeda. New York, Ace, 1959.
Stadium Beyond the Stars (juvenile). Philadelphia, Winston, 1960.
Spacemen, Go Home (juvenile). New York, Holt Rinehart, 1962.

Short Stories

Secret of the Black Planet. New York, Belmont, 1965.

OTHER PUBLICATIONS

Novels as Stephen Marlowe

Catch the Brass Ring. New York, Ace, 1954.
Turn Left for Murder. New York, Ace, 1955.
Model for Murder. Hasbrouck Heights, New Jersey, Graphic, 1955.
The Second Longest Night. New York, Fawcett, 1955; London, Fawcett, 1958.
Dead on Arrival. New York, Ace, 1956.
Mecca for Murder. New York, Fawcett, 1956; London, Fawcett, 1957.
Violence Is Golden (as C.H. Thames). New York, Bouregy, 1956.
Killers Are My Meat. New York, Fawcett, 1957; London, Fawcett, 1958.
Murder Is My Dish. New York, Fawcett, 1957.
Trouble Is My Name. New York, Fawcett, 1957; London, Fawcett, 1958.
Violence Is My Business. New York, Fawcett, 1958; London, Fawcett, 1959.
Terror Is My Trade. New York, Fawcett, 1958; London, Muller, 1960.
Blonde Bait. New York, Avon, 1959.
Double in Trouble, with Richard S. Prather. New York, Fawcett, 1959.
Find Eileen Hardin — Alive! (as Andrew Frazer). New York, Avon, 1959.
Passport to Peril. New York, Fawcett, 1959.
Homicide Is My Game. New York, Fawcett, 1959; London, Muller, 1960.
Danger Is My Line. New York, Fawcett, 1960; London, Muller, 1961.
Death Is My Comrade. New York, Fawcett, 1960; London, Muller, 1961.
The Fall of Marty Moon (as Andrew Frazer). New York, Avon, 1960.
Peril Is My Pay. New York, Fawcett, 1960; London, Muller, 1961.
Manhunt Is My Mission. New York, Fawcett, 1961; London, Muller, 1962.
Jeopardy Is My Job. New York, Fawcett, 1962; London, Muller, 1963.
Blood Is My Brother (as C.H. Thames). New York, Permabooks, 1963.
The Shining. New York, Trident Press, 1963.
Francesca. New York, Fawcett, and London, Muller, 1963.
Drum Beat — Berlin. New York, Fawcett, 1964.
Drum Beat — Dominique. New York, Fawcett, 1965.
Drum Beat — Madrid. New York, Fawcett, 1966.

The Search for Bruno Heidler. New York, Macmillan, 1966; London, Boardman, 1967.
Drum Beat — Erica. New York, Fawcett, 1967.
Come Over, Red Rover. New York, Macmillan, 1968.
Drum Beat — Marianne. New York, Fawcett, 1968.
The Summit. New York, Geis, 1970.
Colossus. New York, Macmillan, 1972; London, W.H. Allen, 1973.
The Man with No Shadow. Englewood Cliffs, New Jersey, Prentice Hall, and London, W.H. Allen, 1974.
The Cawthorn Journals. Englewood Cliffs, New Jersey, Prentice Hall, 1975; London, W.H. Allen, 1976; as *Too Many Chiefs*, London, New English Library, 1977.
Translation. Englewood Cliffs, New Jersey, Prentice Hall, 1976; London, W.H. Allen, 1977.
The Valkyrie Encounter. New York, Putnam, and London, New English Library, 1978.

Novels as Jason Ridgway

West Side Jungle. New York, New American Library, 1958.
Adam's Fall. New York, Permabooks, 1960.
People in Glass Houses. New York, Permabooks, 1961.
Hardly a Man Is Now Alive. New York, Permabooks, 1962.
The Treasure of the Cosa Nostra. New York, Pocket Books, 1966.

Other

Lost Worlds and the Men Who Found Them (juvenile). Racine, Wisconsin, Whitman, 1962.
Walt Disney's Strange Animals of Australia (juvenile). Racine, Wisconsin, Whitman, 1963.

Editor, *Looking Forward: An Anthology of Science Fiction*. New York, Beechhurst Press, 1953; London, Cassell, 1955.

*   *   *

Milton Lesser was a prolific contributor to the Ziff-Davis SF magazines in the 1950's, though since 1965 he has abandoned SF to write mainstream novels. Some of these, like *Translation* and *The Valkyrie Encounter*, published under the Stephen Marlowe pseudonym, have science-fiction elements.

Most of Lesser's SF novels are juveniles. In *Earthbound* a young cadet unjustly expelled from the Solar Academy is tricked into helping space pirates. The book is high on action and low on plausibility. *The Star Seekers* is a bit better. It reworks Robert A. Heinlein's idea of a generation starship presented in *Universe*. Here, a starship takes six generations to reach Alpha Centauri, with the attendant problems and struggles. *Stadium Beyond the Stars* is Lesser's weakest SF novel. Most of the action concerns plotting among political groups on the eve of the First Interstellar Olympic Games. The characterizations are shallow and the plot is murky. *Spacemen, Go Home* opens with humanity quarantined from star travel by the super computer which controls the galaxy. Various groups attempt to bomb the Star Brain while others attempt to convince it to lift the quarantine because humans aren't violent. Again, a murky plot mars the fast-paced action.

Lesser's adult works also stress action over plot and violence over character. *The Golden Age* is prime space opera featuring a bold hero who commutes among worlds in the tradition of John Carter. Duels and fights keep the action swift and the pages turning. *Recruit for Andromeda* has a tricky plot with draftees secretly tested to determine which are superior. The story has some mild racist overtones. *Secret of the Black Planet* is made up of two space-opera novelettes, "Secret of the Black Planet" and "Son of the Black Chalice." The search for a lost alien race and the secret of cell regeneration is damaged by hackneyed writing and cardboard characterizations.

—George Kelley

LESSING, Doris (May). British. Born in Kermansha, Persia, 22 October 1919; moved with her family to Southern Rhodesia, 1924. Educated at Girls High School, Salisbury. Married 1) Frank Charles Wisdom in 1939 (divorced, 1943), one son and one daughter; 2) Gottfried Lessing in 1945 (divorced, 1949), one son. Lived in Southern Rhodesia, 1924-49, then settled in London. Recipient: Maugham Award, 1954; Médicis Prize, 1976. Associate Member, American Academy, 1974; Honorary Fellow, Modern Language Association (USA), 1974. Agent: Curtis Brown Ltd., 1 Craven Hill, London W2 3EP, England.

SCIENCE-FICTION PUBLICATIONS

Novels (series: Canopus in Argos)

Briefing for a Descent into Hell. London, Cape, and New York, Knopf, 1971.
The Memoirs of a Survivor. London, Octagon Press, 1974; New York, Knopf, 1975.
Shikasta (Argos). London, Cape, and New York, Knopf, 1979.
The Marriages Between Zones Three, Four, and Five (Argos). London, Cape, and New York, Knopf, 1980.
The Sirian Experiments (Argos). London, Cape, 1981.

Short Stories

No Witchcraft for Sale: Stories and Short Novels. Moscow, Foreign Languages Publishing House, 1956.

OTHER PUBLICATIONS

Novels

The Grass Is Singing. London, Joseph, and New York, Crowell, 1950.
Children of Violence:
    Martha Quest. London, Joseph, 1952.
    A Proper Marriage. London, Joseph, 1954; with *Martha Quest,* New York, Simon and Schuster, 1964.
    A Ripple from the Storm. London, Joseph, 1958
    Landlocked. London, MacGibbon and Kee, 1965; with *A Ripple from the Storm,* New York, Simon and Schuster, 1966.
    The Four-Gated City. London, MacGibbon and Kee, and New York, Knopf, 1969.
Retreat to Innocence. London, Joseph, 1956.
The Golden Notebook. London, Joseph, and New York, Simon and Schuster, 1962.
The Summer Before the Dark. London, Cape, and New York, Knopf, 1973.

Short Stories

This Was the Old Chief's Country: Stories. London, Joseph, 1951; New York, Crowell, 1952.
Five: Short Novels. London, Joseph, 1953.
The Habit of Loving. London, MacGibbon and Kee, 1957; New York, Crowell, 1958.
A Man and Two Women: Stories. London, MacGibbon and Kee, and New York, Simon and Schuster, 1963.
African Stories. London, Joseph, 1964; New York, Simon and Schuster, 1965.
Winter in July. London, Panther, 1966.
The Black Madonna. London, Panther, 1966.
Nine African Stories. London, Longman, 1968.
The Story of a Non-Marrying Man and Other Stories. London, Cape, 1972; as *The Temptation of Jack Orkney and Other Stories,* New York, Knopf, 1972.
Collected African Stories:
    1. *This Was the Old Chief's Country.* London, Joseph, 1973.
    2. *The Sun Between Their Feet.* London, Joseph, 1973.
Collected Stories:
    1. *To Room Nineteen.* London, Cape, 1978.
    2. *The Temptation of Jack Orkney.* London, Cape, 1978.

Stories. New York, Knopf, 1978.

Plays

Before the Deluge (produced London, 1953).
Mr. Dolinger (produced Oxford, 1958).
Each His Own Wilderness (produced London, 1958). Included in *New English Dramatists,* London, Penguin, 1959.
The Truth about Billy Newton (produced Salisbury, Wiltshire, 1960).
Play with a Tiger (produced London, 1962; New York, 1964). London, Joseph, 1962.
The Storm, adaptation of the play by Alexander Ostrowsky (produced London, 1966).
The Singing Door, in *Second Playbill 2,* edited by Alan Durband. London, Hutchinson, 1973.

Television Plays: *The Grass Is Singing,* from her own novel, 1962; *Please Do Not Disturb,* 1966; *Care and Protection,* 1966; *Between Men,* 1967.

Verse

Fourteen Poems. Northwood, Middlesex, Scorpion Press, 1959.

Other

Going Home. London, Joseph, 1957.
In Pursuit of the English: A Documentary. London, MacGibbon and Kee, 1960; New York, Simon and Schuster, 1961.
Particularly Cats. London, Joseph, and New York, Simon and Schuster, 1967.
A Small Personal Voice: Essays, Reviews, Interviews, edited by Paul Schlueter. New York, Knopf, 1974.

*

Bibliography: *Doris Lessing: A Bibliography* by Catharina Ipp, Johannesburg, University of the Witwatersrand Department of Bibliography, 1967; *Doris Lessing: A Checklist of Primary and Secondary Sources* by Selma R. Burkom and Margaret Williams, Troy, New York, Whitston, 1973.

*   *   *

The distinguished novelist Doris Lessing has moved into speculative fiction out of commitment to humanity and concern for a disintegrating society.

She first pushed forward into the future in the final volume of the Children of Violence series, *The Four-Gated City.* Martha Quest, wise in the ways of political and emotional role-playing, comes to London in 1949 and is drawn into the household of Mark Coldridge, gentleman writer. She copes with the needs of the family throughout the anxious days of the Cold War, the hedonism of Swinging London, and a period of decline which reaches into the future. The vision of a society breaking down is one to which Doris Lessing remains true in later books. Martha's struggles towards self-knowledge involve dreams and visions. She discards psychiatry, for instance, as the authoritarian destroyer of telepathic channels of communication, and finds science-fiction writers at once conventional and trivial, playing with great truths.

Briefing for a Descent into Hell, which could be regarded as the author's first science-fiction novel, is one of the great books of "inner space." A man, unidentified, hallucinating, is brought to a London psychiatric clinic. Dr. X and Dr. Y battle like dark and light angels to "bring him back to reality" with drugs and the threat of shock treatment. Meanwhile the patient lives out a stirring adventure in his alternate reality. He is borne across the oceans of the world on a raft after his shipmates have been taken up into a space vehicle, the Crystal Sphere. He makes landfall in a verdant wilderness and is led by two leopardlike beasts to a city in the jungle, half-ruined yet seeming to build itself before his eyes. The patient has been identified as Professor Charles Watkins, a chilly academic with a touch of odd charisma. Now drugged into sleep he travels among the stars and experiences the world as part of the harmony of the solar system. Intelligences have been briefed for life on earth; they are trying to bring humanity to its senses. Other members of this group can be identified among the acquaintances of Watkins—an archeologist, an elderly woman suddenly enlightened by the Professor's lectures. The patient, without his memory, is urged to conform by his Doctors. Finally he submits to shock treatment and becomes Professor Charles Watkins all over again: the light has gone out.

The Memoirs of a Survivor draws together the strands of catastrophe and the mystical reintegration of personality. An elderly woman observes the breakdown of society from her ground-floor apartment. A young girl, Emily, is put into the woman's care and she takes responsibility for her and for her cat-dog pet, Hugo. The woman also explores an alternate world of the past and future, in rooms which lie, mysteriously, through the wall of the apartment. She works in these places, sees Emily's family act out cruel rituals of family life. Through these experiences she is able to achieve a free, non-authoritarian way of caring for Emily. She feels the emergence of a new form of life where individuals have come to terms with their personal pasts and can integrate into a new society. This is a compelling book, illuminated by the author's unique truthfulness and imaginative power.

Lessing has brought out two volumes of a trilogy with the general title *Canopus in Argos: Archives.* Her introductory remarks pay tribute to science-fiction and its writers and are a far cry from Martha Quest's view in *The Four-Gated City.* The first volume, *Shikasta,* is named for the doomed planet Earth, protected and seeded in far-distant times by the Galactic Empires on Canopus and Sirius. Johor, a Canopean envoy, visits the earth in succeeding ages, but the harmony which once prevailed on this loveliest of planets passes inexorably. The evil Galactic Empire Puttiora and its criminal planet Shammat have touched the earth and destroyed its harmony. The compression of history and myth into a colonial episode does not work well. Although the scheme of the book is grand, the visions striking, *Shikasta* remains unsatisfying and tendentious.

The second volume, *The Marriages Between Zones Three, Four, and Five,* is finely judged and very moving, a tour de force of narrative power and profound psychological insights. In a strange land Al*Ith, Queen of peaceful highly civilised Zone Three, is ordered by the unseen Providers to marry Ben Ata, King of the undeveloped militaristic Zone Four, where people are forbidden to look up at the mountains. Their relationship is painful and imperfect but finally full of love; after the birth of their son they are parted by the mysterious powers. Ben Ata must now marry the warrior queen Vahshi of barbarous Zone Five. Al*Ith experiences much suffering: forgotten by her people, displaced on the throne by her sister, she works humbly in the stables of a highland ranch. Yet the sacrifice she has made works towards the integration of all the Zones, and Al*Ith, looking even further upward, reaches a higher plane of existence on the azure heights of Zone Two.

Doris Lessing is a writer so full of industry, variety, idiosyncratic shrewdness, and painful honesty that her work is unusually difficult to summarise. But the warmth and understanding of the author's personality bring an immediate response from the reader: she is much loved in a way that only a writer can be loved. We look forward eagerly to the final volume of the Canopus trilogy and other far-ranging experiments.

—Cherry Wilder

LEVIN, Ira. American. Born in New York City, 27 August 1929. Educated at Drake University, Des Moines, Iowa, 1946–48; New York University, 1948–50, A.B. 1950. Served in the United States Army Signal Corps, 1953–55. Married Gabrielle Aronsohn in 1960 (divorced, 1968); three children. Recipient: Mystery Writers of American Edgar Allan Poe Award, 1954, and Special Award, 1980. Agent: Harold Ober Associates, 40 East 49th Street, New York, New York 10017, U.S.A.

SCIENCE-FICTION PUBLICATIONS

Novels

This Perfect Day. New York, Random House, and London, Joseph, 1970.
The Stepford Wives. New York, Random House, and London, Joseph, 1972.
The Boys from Brazil. New York, Random House, and London, Joseph, 1976.

OTHER PUBLICATIONS

Novels

A Kiss Before Dying. New York, Simon and Schuster, 1953; London, Joseph, 1954.
Rosemary's Baby. New York, Random House, and London, Joseph, 1967.

Plays

No Time for Sergeants, adaptation of the novel by Mac Hyman (produced New York, 1955; London, 1956). New York, Random House, 1956.
Interlock (produced New York, 1958). New York, Dramatists Play Service, 1958.
Critic's Choice (produced New York, 1960; London, 1961). New York, Random House, 1961; London, Evans, 1963.
General Seeger (produced New York, 1962). New York, Dramatists Play Service, 1962.
Drat! The Cat!, music by Milton Schafer (produced New York, 1965).
Dr. Cook's Garden (also director: produced New York, 1967). New York, Dramatists Play Service, 1968.
Veronica's Room (produced New York, 1973). New York, Random House, 1974; London, Joseph, 1975.
Deathtrap (produced New York and London, 1978). New York, Random House, 1979.
Break a Leg (produced New York, 1979).

Theatrical Activities:

Director: Play—*Dr. Cook's Garden,* New York, 1967.

*   *   *

Ira Levin's highly accomplished novels of suspense contain elements of science fiction and fantasy, and one, *This Perfect Day,* is set in the future.

His first novel, *A Kiss Before Dying,* the study of a psychopath stalking three sisters, was skilfully written but gave little suggestion of the richness in store. *Rosemary's Baby* is one of the most perfectly crafted thrillers ever written. Rosemary and Guy Woodhouse step over the threshold of a richly documented old apartment house in New York City into the world of the witches. The strength of the book lies not only in its weaving of a dreadful spell but in the strong, sweet character of the pregnant heroine. Guy's complicity in the schemes of the friendly neighbours is part of a fiendish double climax.

The book following this masterpiece of genre writing was the science-fiction novel *This Perfect Day.* The future race, brown-skinned, depilated, breastless, tranquilised, stroll the windowless walkways of a totally computerised environment, patting the scanners as they pass, en route to death at age 62. LiRM35M4419, called Chip by his wry Grandfather, escapes from the system by resisting UNI, the computer responsible for a boring parody of the good life. Chip's escape is obviously programmed; the appearance of those benign sybarites the Programmers is not surprising. The ideology of the "utopia" is weak but the quality of the writing and the level of invention are high. A leap of the author's prodigious imagination could bring him into the very first rank of speculative fiction.

Instead he returned to the suspense novel with *The Stepford Wives*. The setting, a commuter township in "middle America," is as persuasive as the New York of *Rosemary's Baby*. Joanna Everhart discovers the dreadful secret of the big-bosomed zombies who dote on housework. The climax is clever but the story is unsatisfying and the neatness of the writing hides many loose ends. We look in vain for one husband who refuses to trade in his wife on a new model or for a child with that old complaint from *The Invasion of the Body-Snatchers:* "That Lady isn't my real mother!"

The Boys from Brazil has an international setting but still retains a typical claustrophobic atmosphere. Dr. Josef Mengele, former medical superintendent of Auschwitz, emerges from his South American jungle retreat to send the organization of Nazi veterans on a mission. Yakov Lieberman, the tired Nazi-hunter, discovers soon enough, but more slowly than the readers, why 94 elderly civil servants throughout the western world must die. These men are the adoptive fathers of teen-age sons cloned from the cells of Adolf Hitler; their deaths are an attempt to match up environment with genetic inheritance. This time the humanity of Lieberman balances the outrageous story; it is one of Ira Levin's best books. Mengele's scheme, even with its coda of an artistic lad somewhere indulging tomorrow-the-world fantasies, is revealed as pure moonshine. The story gains piquancy from reports that Mengele still lives in the Paraguayan jungle.

Ira Levin's suspense novels have a unique resonance; these works, rather than *One Perfect Day,* have created a nightmare future world in which the Stepford delinquents, children of megalomaniac fathers raised by robot mothers, tangle with genetic Hitlers, under the eye of the heir of the Prince of This World, Andrew Woodhouse, the devil's child. The author is at the height of his powers and should continue to astonish us.

—Cherry Wilder

LEWIS, C(live) S(taples). Also wrote as Clive Hamilton; N.W. Clerk. British. Born in Belfast, Northern Ireland, 29 November 1898. Educated at Wynyard School, Hertfordshire, 1908-10; Campbell College, Northern Ireland, 1910; Cherbourg School, Malvern, 1911-13; privately 1914-17; University College, Oxford (Scholar; Chancellor's English Essay Prize, 1921), 1917, 1919-23, B.A. (honours) 1922. Served in the Somerset Light Infantry, 1917-19: First Lieutenant. Married Joy Davidman Gresham in 1956 (died, 1960). Philosophy Tutor, 1924, and Lecturer in English, 1924, University College, Oxford; Fellow and Tutor in English, Magdalen College, Oxford, 1924-54; Professor of Medieval and Renaissance English, Cambridge University, 1954-63. Riddell Lecturer, University of Durham, 1943; Clark Lecturer, Cambridge University, 1944. Recipient: Gollancz Prize for Literature, 1937; Library Association Carnegie Medal, 1957. D.D.: University of St. Andrews, Scotland, 1946; Docteur-ès-Lettres, Laval University, Quebec, 1952; D. Litt.: University of Manchester, 1959; Hon. Dr.: University of Dijon, 1962; University of Lyon, 1963. Honorary Fellow, Magdalen College, Oxford, 1955; University College, Oxford, 1958; Magdalene College, Cambridge, 1963. Fellow of the Royal Society of Literature, 1948; Fellow of the British Academy, 1955. *Died 22 November 1963.*

SCIENCE-FICTION PUBLICATIONS

Novels (series: Dr. Elwin Ransom in all books)

Out of the Silent Planet. London, Lane, 1938; New York, Macmillan, 1943.

Perelandra. London, Lane, 1943; New York, Macmillan, 1944; as *Voyage to Venus,* London, Pan, 1953.
That Hideous Strength: A Modern Fairy-Tale for Grown-Ups. London, Lane, 1945; New York, Macmillan, 1946; abridged edition, as *The Tortured Planet,* New York, Avon, 1958.

Short Stories

Of Other Worlds: Essays and Stories, edited by Walter Hooper. London, Bles, 1966; New York, Harcourt Brace, 1967.

OTHER PUBLICATIONS

Novels (juvenile)

The Lion, The Witch, and the Wardrobe. London, Bles, and New York, Macmillan, 1950.
Prince Caspian: The Return to Narnia. London, Bles, and New York, Macmillan, 1951.
The Voyage of the "Dawn Treader." London, Bles, and New York, Macmillan, 1952.
The Silver Chair. London, Bles, and New York, Macmillan, 1953.
The Horse and His Boy. London, Bles, and New York, Macmillan, 1954.
The Magician's Nephew. London, Lane, and New York, Macmillan, 1955.
The Last Battle. London, Lane, and New York, Macmillan, 1956.
Till We Have Faces: A Myth Retold (for adults). London, Bles, 1956; New York, Harcourt Brace, 1957.

Short Stories

The Dark Tower and Other Stories, edited by Walter Hooper. London, Collins, and New York, Harcourt Brace, 1977.

Verse

Spirits in Bondage: A Cycle of Lyrics (as Clive Hamilton). London, Heinemann, 1919.
Dymer (as Clive Hamilton). London, Dent, and New York, Macmillan, 1926.
Poems, edited by Walter Hooper. London, Bles, 1964; New York, Harcourt Brace, 1965.
Narrative Poems, edited by Walter Hooper. London, Bles, 1969; New York, Harcourt Brace, 1972.

Other

The Pilgrim's Regress: An Allegorical Apology for Christianity, Reason, and Romanticism. London, Dent, 1933; New York, Sheed and Ward, 1935; revised edition, London, Bles, 1943; Sheed and Ward, 1944.
The Allegory of Love: A Study in Medieval Tradition. Oxford, Clarendon Press, and New York, Oxford University Press, 1936.
Rehabilitations and Other Essays. London and New York, Oxford University Press, 1939.
The Personal Heresy: A Controversy, with E.M.W. Tillyard. London and New York, Oxford University Press, 1939.
The Problem of Pain. London, Bles, 1940; New York, Macmillan, 1943.
The Weight of Glory. London, S.P.C.K., 1942.
The Screwtape Letters. London, Bles, 1942; New York, Macmillan, 1943; revised edition, Bles, 1961.
Broadcast Talks: Right and Wrong: A Clue to the Meaning of the Universe, and What Christians Believe. London, Bles, 1942; as *The Case for Christianity,* New York, Macmillan, 1943.
A Preface to "Paradise Lost" (lectures). London and New York, Oxford University Press, 1942.
Christian Behaviour: A Further Series of Broadcast Talks. London, Bles, and New York, Macmillan, 1943.
The Abolition of Man; or, Reflections on Education with Special Reference to the Teaching of English in the Upper Forms of Schools. London, Oxford University Press, 1943; New York, Macmillan, 1947.

Beyond Personality: The Christian Idea of God.   London, Bles, 1944; New York, Macmillan, 1945.

The Great Divorce: A Dream.   London, Bles, 1945; New York, Macmillan, 1946.

Miracles: A Preliminary Study.   London, Bles, and New York, Macmillan, 1947.

Vivisection.   London, Anti-Vivisection Society, 1947(?).

Transpositions and Other Addresses.   London, Bles, 1949; as *The Weight of Glory and Other Addresses,* New York, Macmillan, 1949.

The Literary Impact of the Authorized Version (lecture).   London, Athlone Press, 1950; Philadelphia, Fortress Press, 1963.

Mere Christianity.   London, Bles, and New York, Macmillan, 1952.

Hero and Leander (lecture).   London, Oxford University Press, 1952.

English Literature in the Sixteenth Century, Excluding Drama.   Oxford, Clarendon Press, 1954.

De Descriptione Temporum (lecture).   London, Cambridge University Press, 1955.

Surprised by Joy: The Shape of My Early Life.   London, Bles, 1955; New York, Harcourt Brace, 1956.

Reflections on the Psalms.   London, Bles, and New York, Harcourt Brace, 1958.

Shall We Lose God in Outer Space?   London, S.P.C.K., 1959.

The Four Loves.   London, Bles, and New York, Harcourt Brace, 1960.

The World's Last Night and Other Essays.   New York, Harcourt Brace, 1960.

Studies in Words.   London, Cambridge University Press, 1960; revised edition, 1967.

An Experiment in Criticism.   London, Cambridge University Press, 1961.

A Grief Observed (as N.W. Clerk; autobiography).   London, Faber, 1961; Greenwich, Connecticut, Seabury Press, 1963.

They Asked for a Paper: Papers and Addresses.   London, Bles, 1962.

Beyond the Bright Blue (letters).   New York, Harcourt Brace, 1963.

Letters to Malcolm, Chiefly on Prayer.   London, Bles, and New York, Harcourt Brace, 1964.

The Discarded Image: An Introduction to Medieval and Renaissance Literature.   London, Cambridge University Press, 1964.

Screwtape Proposes a Toast and Other Pieces.   London, Collins, 1965.

Letters, edited by W.H. Lewis.   London, Bles, and New York, Harcourt Brace, 1966.

Studies in Medieval and Renaissance Literature, edited by Walter Hooper.   London, Cambridge University Press, 1966.

Spenser's Images of Life, edited by Alastair Fowler.   London, Cambridge University Press, 1967.

Christian Reflections, edited by Walter Hooper.   London, Bles, and Grand Rapids, Michigan, Eerdmans, 1967.

Letters to an American Lady, edited by Clyde S. Kilby.   Grand Rapids, Michigan, Eerdmans, 1967; London, Hodder and Stoughton, 1969.

Mark vs. Tristram: Correspondence Between C.S. Lewis and Owen Barfield, edited by Walter Hooper.   Cambridge, Massachusetts, Lowell House Printers, 1967.

A Mind Awake: An Anthology of C.S. Lewis, edited by Clyde S. Kilby.   London, Bles, 1968; New York, Harcourt Brace, 1969.

Selected Literary Essays, edited by Walter Hooper.   London, Cambridge University Press, 1969.

God in the Dock: Essays on Theology and Ethics, edited by Walter Hooper.   Grand Rapids, Michigan, Eerdmans, 1970; as *Undeceptions: Essays on Theology and Ethics,* London, Bles, 1971.

The Humanitarian Theory of Punishment.   Abingdon, Berkshire, Marcham Books Press, 1972.

Fern-Seed and Elephants and Other Essays on Christianity, edited by Walter Hooper.   London, Fontana, 1975.

The Joyful Christian: 128 Readings, edited by William Griffin.   New York, Macmillan, 1977.

They Stand Together: The Letters of C.S. Lewis to Arthur Greeves 1914-1963, edited by Walter Hooper.   London, Collins, and New York, Macmillan, 1979.

C.S. Lewis at the Breakfast Table, edited by James Como.   London, Collins, 1980.

Editor, *George MacDonald: An Anthology.*   London, Bles, 1946; New York, Doubleday, 1962.

Editor, *Arthurian Torso, Containing the Posthumous Fragment of " The Figure of Arthur,"* by Charles Williams.   London and New York, Oxford University Press, 1948.

*

Bibliography: *C.S. Lewis: An Annotated Checklist of Writings about Him and His Works* by Joe R. Christopher and Joan K. Ostlin, Kent, Ohio, Kent State University Press, 1975.

*   *   *

C.S. Lewis is a unique figure. He once described himself as a specimen of a nearly extinct species, "old Western man": and certainly we had no right to hope for such an author to appear in the 20th century. He has written in many guises: as medieval scholar, lay theologian, fantasist, poet. But his essential role has total inner consistency: he is above all the most powerful defender of traditional Christianity that this century has seen; and his apologia works not through formal argument but through images, through suggestion, through poetic creation. All his life, Lewis was haunted by *Sehnsucht,* a longing for strange beauty which the actual world could never wholly satisfy; and this led him, in early middle life, to identify the source and object of his longing with the Christian heaven and the Christian God. His subsequent creative work was a sustained imaginative polemic for this view of the universe.

Lewis is a science-fiction writer, arguably, in only one short story, "Ministering Angels," and one novel, *Out of the Silent Planet.* Both are set on Mars; but the Mars of the novel is a Christian paradise ruled by an archangel. This is the first novel of Lewis's so called "space trilogy"; the second novel, *Perelandra,* is set on Venus, and the third, *That Hideous Strength,* on Earth but with interplanetary connections. All three novels feature the same hero, Elwin Ransom, and all are a unique mixture of SF and what seem to be fantasy elements. In each novel an important part is played by the "eldils," a species of angels inhabiting interplanetary space whose bodies are composed of semi-visible light; but in the first two novels there is also a spaceship, and in the third novel a type of cyborg, a severed human head kept alive by advanced scientific technology. This mixture of science and the supernatural in the trilogy is deliberate and indeed essential: for the fundamental theme of the whole trilogy is the clash between evil modern scientism and old-fashioned Christianity. The trilogy in fact defies generic classification: it is very dubiously science fiction, by reason of all those angels (and devils, in the second and third novels), yet it is not exactly fantasy either, for the author firmly believes in the actual existence of his supernatural entities, and is out to convince us, with all the power of his very powerful art, of their reality and supreme importance. It is this polemic purpose which may repel some readers: Lewis himself has stated (*Of Other Worlds*) that *Perelandra,* at least, was written essentially for Christians only.

But *Out of the Silent Planet* is less overtly Christian, and should appeal to a wide readership by the sheer beauty of its style and images. The inner action of this novel is twofold: it is partly a *Bildungsroman,* effecting the re-education of Ransom, and through him of the reader; and partly a physical and intellectual defeat of human-racist expansionism. Ransom, an ordinary decent literary scholar, is kidnapped by the ruthless physicist Professor Weston and his capitalist collaborator Devine and taken in Weston's secret spaceship to Mars, for Weston mistakenly believes that the "primitive natives" of Mars have demanded a human sacrifice in exchange for gold. Mars ("Malacandra") proves to be a beautiful, paradisal planet, and the natives comprise three intelligent species, all living in friendship and complementary collaboration, and all ruled by the nearly invisible eldil Oyarsa from his paradise-island of Meldilorn. Ransom escapes from his human captors, takes refuge among the "hrossa," the seal-like poetic species, and learns the Malacandrian language. He is thus equipped to serve as interpreter in the climactic scene of the novel when Weston and Devine are arrested by the hrossa and brought to Oyarsa for judgment. This trial scene is one of the clearest, wittiest, and most striking portrayals in imaginative fiction of the clash between human-racist expansionism and the opposing school of thought — the school now represented chiefly by the ecology movement. Weston boasts to Oyarsa that nothing will stop the human race from conquering the universe, moving on from planet to planet as each world dies. Oyarsa refutes Weston with the question: "And when all are dead?" — to which Weston has no answer. After this the humans, including Ransom, are forced to return to Earth, whereupon their spaceship is destroyed by angelic power.

Perelandra is a sequel in that once more Weston lands on another planet — Venus — and once more is opposed by Ransom; but essentially the work is a variation on Milton's *Paradise Lost*. Venus (Perelandra) is a mostly oceanic world with only two inhabitants —its innocent Adam and Eve. Soon after Weston's arrival, he is possessed by a devil — and he proceeds to tempt the Perelandrian Eve to violate God's sole prohibition. At last Ransom understands his mission, and ends the temptation by destroying Weston. The Venusian paradise is saved, a second Fall is averted. This novel is an even greater achievement than *Out of the Silent Planet:* the action, limited to three characters, has concentrated dramatic power, and the scenery — the floating vegetable islands and seas of Venus — is of a beauty which has never been surpassed by an imaginative writer. It is magnificent — but it is hardly science fiction. That might also be said of the trilogy's final novel, *That Hideous Strength*. The Devil is confronted this time on Earth by planetary angels, Ransom, and the Arthurian wizard Merlin, and the wicked are destroyed in a magic holocaust.

Also relevant to Lewis's SF are his seven Narnia novels for children. These may be called fantasy, since they are set in and around an imaginary world (Narnia) where magic is commonplace and the inhabitants include giants, dwarfs, dragons, fauns, centaurs, and talking animals. Bur Narnia has an intellectual solidity similar to SF and lacking in some fantasy worlds of other writers, since it exists in a parallel universe also created, like this one of ours, by God: it is a universe whose Earth is flat, and whose stars are living beings. It is also, as usual in Lewis, a universe of marvellous beauty. Lewis is also an important critic of SF and related genres, chiefly in the essay collection *Of Other Worlds*. His remarks on characterization are justly famous.

Taking his work as a whole, one must note that although Lewis wrote little that is certainly SF, he is of the first importance in the history of this genre through the sheer power of his imagination, his ability to create beautiful worlds which are wholly realized in their actuality; and through the enormous pressure of his moral commitment, which supplies tension throughout the action of every one of his stories. Above all, he has been a most effective opponent of those who would like to see the human race give itself up to the demon of scientism, the spirit which desires the total conquest of the universe.

—David Lake

LEWIS, (Ernest Michael) Roy. British. Born in Felixstowe, Suffolk, 6 November 1913. Educated at King Edward VI School, Birmingham; University College, Oxford, B.A. 1934; London School of Economics, 1935-36. Married Christine Tew in 1939; two daughters. Economist, Royal Institute of International Affairs, London, 1934-36; Assistant Editor, *Statist,* London, 1936-40; Secretary, Eastern Group Supply, Delhi, 1941-43; Manager, Pekin Syndicate, Delhi and Chungking, 1943-46; feature writer, *Scope,* London, 1946-48, and *Future,* London, 1948-51; Assistant Editor, 1953-60, and Washington correspondent, 1960-61, *Economist,* London; Commonwealth correspondent and leader writer, 1961-71, and editorial consultant, 1971-80, *The Times,* London. Since 1958, Founding Publisher, Keepsake Press, Richmond, Surrey. Agent: David Higham Associates, 5-8 Lower John Street, London W1R 4HA. Address: 26 Sydney Road, Richmond, Surrey TW9 1UB, England.

SCIENCE-FICTION PUBLICATIONS

Novel

What We Did to Father.   London, Hutchinson, 1960; as *The Evolution Man,* London, Penguin, 1963; as *Once upon an Ice Age,* London, Terra Nova Editions, 1979.

Uncollected Short Story

"The Evolution Man," in *Apeman, Spaceman,* edited by Harry Harrison and Leon E. Stover.   New York, Doubleday, and London, Rapp and Whiting, 1968.

OTHER PUBLICATIONS

Other

The Future of Australia.   New Delhi, Hindustan Times Press, 1944.
The Welsh Day in Parliament.   Cardiff, Welsh Party, 1947.
Shall I Emigrate?   London, Phoenix House, 1948.
Emigration Prospect.   London, Longman, 1949.
The English Middle Classes, with Angus Maude.   London, Phoenix House, 1949; New York, Knopf, 1950.
Moving to Harlow: The Story of a Resettlement of a Factory and Its Workers.   Harlow, Essex, Sunvic Controls, 1952.
Professional People, with Angus Maude.   London, Phoenix House, 1952; as *Professional People in England,* Cambridge, Massachusetts, Harvard University Press, 1953.
Sierra Leone: A Modern Portrait.   London, Her Majesty's Stationery Office, 1954.
Colonial Development and Welfare 1946-55.   London, Her Majesty's Stationery Office, 1956.
The Boss: The Life and Times of the British Business Man, with Rosemary Stewart.   London, Phoenix House, 1958; revised edition, 1961; as *The Managers,* New York, New American Library, 1961.
The Death of God.   Privately printed, 1959.
The Keepsake Press: Report and Adieux.   Privately printed, 1961.
The British in Africa, with Yvonne Foy.   London, Weidenfeld and Nicolson, 1971.
A Force for the Future: The Role of the Police in the Next Ten Years.   London, Temple Smith, 1976.
Enoch Powell: Principle in Politics.   London, Cassell, 1979.
Politics and Printing in Winchester 1830-1880.   Richmond, Surrey, Keepsake Press, 1980.

Editor, with Harry Ballam, *The Visitors' Book: England and the English as Others Have Seen Them 1500-1950.*   London, Parrish, 1950.

*   *   *

An English journalist of broad experience, Roy Lewis came to the attention of the science-fiction public in 1963, when his brief novel *What We Did to Father* was selected by Brian Aldiss for the Penguin science-fiction series. The novel was not really conceived as science-fiction, but is rather more in the tradition of such British absurdist humor as Sellar and Yeatman's *1066 and All That.* Its treatment of human evolution as a kind of domestic situation-comedy perhaps most directly calls to mind Thornton Wilder's *The Skin of Our Teeth,* and like Wilder Lewis makes a number of serious satirical points about attitudes to technology, progress, and the family structure. Another way of describing the book might be to say that it is a stone-age version of *Life With Father.*

Cast in the form of an autobiographical narrative by an ape-man named Ernest, who lived sometime during the Pleistocene ("I doubt if we have reached the Upper Pleistocene yet," comments Ernest's father), the story centers around the conflict between Ernest's father, who is determined to evolve into the dominant species, and his Uncle Vanya, who is highly critical of such newfangled gadgets as fire and wants to return to the trees. While father's new inventions invariably get out of hand (he inadvertently creates a forest fire that devastates half of Uganda, where the tribe lives), virtually all the evolutionary discoveries of prehistoric man are credited to him—plus a few that aren't so prehistoric. During the course of the story, father not only discovers fire, he discovers weapons, game traps, clothing, and politics, while other members of the family come up with art, music, dance, the domestication of animals, and cooking. In the end, father goes too far with his latest invention—the bow and arrow—and he is tactfully put to death and eaten.

While not in the mainstream of science fiction, the fantasy, humor and technological insights of this novel may have helped pave the way for the experimental fantasies of some later New Wave writers. And while the novel was clearly not thought of by its author as a response to earlier traditions of science fiction, it serves as a very funny and much-needed corrective to the "noble savage" narratives that comprise much of the genre's treatment of prehistoric or primitive societies. Lewis is a skilled humorist, and it is unfortunate that he has not produced more fiction.

—Gary K. Wolfe

* * *

LEWIS, (Harry) Sinclair. Also wrote as Tom Graham. American. Born in Sauk Center, Minnesota, 7 February 1885. Educated at Sauk Center High School; Oberlin Academy, Ohio, 1902-03; Yale University, New Haven, Connecticut (Editor, *Yale Literary Magazine*), 1903-06, 1907-08, A.B. 1908. Married 1) Grace Livingston Hegger in 1914 (divorced, 1925), one son; 2) the columnist Dorothy Thompson in 1928 (divorced, 1942), one son. Worked as a janitor in Upton Sinclair's socialist community at Helicon Hall, Englewood, New Jersey, 1906-07; Assistant Editor, *Transatlantic Tales*, New York, 1907; successively, reporter on a newspaper in Waterloo, Iowa, promoter for a charity organization in New York, secretary to Alice MacGowan and Grace MacGowan Cook in Carmel, California, writer for the Associated Press and the *Bulletin* in San Francisco, Assistant Editor of the *Volta Review* in Washington, D.C., and, in New York, manuscript reader for the publishers Frederick A. Stokes, Assistant Editor of *Adventure,* Editor for the Publishers' Newspaper Syndicate, and Editor for the George H. Doran Company, 1908-16; full-time writer from 1916; reported the Viennese Revolution for the New York *Evening Post* and Philadelphia *Ledger,* 1918. Recipient: Pulitzer Prize, 1926 (refused); Nobel Prize for Literature, 1930. Litt.D.: Yale University, 1936. Member, American Academy, 1938. Lived in Vermont and, in later years, in Europe. *Died 10 January 1951.*

SCIENCE-FICTION PUBLICATIONS

Novel

It Can't Happen Here. New York, Doubleday, and London, Cape, 1925.

OTHER PUBLICATIONS

Novels

Our Mr. Wrenn. New York, Harper, 1914; London, Cape, 1923.
The Trail of the Hawk. New York, Harper, 1915; London, Cape, 1923.
The Job. New York, Harper, 1917; London, Cape, 1926.
The Innocents. New York, Harper, 1917.
Free Air. New York, Harcourt Brace, 1919; London, Cape, 1924.
Main Street. New York, Harcourt Brace, 1920; London, Hodder and Stoughton, 1921.
Babbitt. New York, Harcourt Brace, and London, Cape, 1922.
Arrowsmith. New York, Harcourt Brace, 1925; as *Martin Arrowsmith,* London, Cape, 1925.
Mantrap. New York, Harcourt Brace, and London, Cape, 1926.

Elmer Gantry. New York, Harcourt Brace, and London, Cape, 1927.
The Man Who Knew Coolidge. New York, Harcourt Brace, and London, Cape, 1928.
Dodsworth. New York, Harcourt Brace, and London, Cape, 1929.
Ann Vickers. New York, Doubleday, and London, Cape, 1933.
Work of Art. New York, Doubleday, and London, Cape, 1934.
The Prodigal Parents. New York, Doubleday, and London, Cape, 1938.
Bethel Merriday. New York, Doubleday, and London, Cape, 1940.
Gideon Planish. New York, Random House, and London, Cape, 1943.
Cass Timberlane. New York, Random House, 1945; London, Cape, 1946.
Kingsblood Royal. New York, Random House, 1947; London, Cape, 1948.
The God-Seeker. New York, Random House, and London, Heinemann, 1949.
World So Wide. New York, Random House, and London, Heinemann, 1951.

Short Stories

Selected Short Stories. New York, Doubleday, 1935.
I'm a Stranger Here Myself and Other Stories, edited by Mark Schorer. New York, Dell, 1962.

Plays

Hobohemia (produced New York, 1919).
Jayhawker, with Lloyd Lewis (produced New York, 1934). New York, Doubleday, and London, Cape, 1935.
It Can't Happen Here, adaptation of his own novel (produced New York, 1936). New York, Dramatists Play Service, 1938.
Storm in the West (screenplay), with Dore Schary. New York, Stein and Day, 1963; London, Sidgwick and Jackson, 1964.

Other

Hike and the Aeroplane (juvenile; as Tom Graham). New York, Stokes, 1912.
John Dos Passos' "Manhattan Transfer." New York, Harper, 1926.
Cheap and Contented Labor: The Picture of a Southern Mill Town in 1929. New York, United Textile Workers of America, 1929.
The American Fear of Literature (Nobel Prize address). Stockholm, Norstedt, 1931.
From Main Street to Stockholm: Letters of Sinclair Lewis 1919-1930, edited by Harrison Smith. New York, Harcourt Brace, 1952.
The Man from Main Street: A Sinclair Lewis Reader: Selected Essays and Other Writings 1904-1950, edited by Harry E. Maule and Melville H. Cane. New York, Random House, 1953; London, Heinemann, 1954.

*

Bibliography: *The Merrill Checklist of Sinclair Lewis* by James Lundquist, Columbus, Ohio, Merrill, 1970.

* * *

Although Sinclair Lewis is a regional satirist, he also belongs firmly within the anti-utopian tradition. *It Can't Happen Here* is unquestionably a dystopia, while *Arrowsmith, Kingsblood Royal,* and "The Cat of the Stars" (1919) deal with science and causality. The unpleasant and restrictive worlds of *Main Street, Babbitt,* and *Elmer Gantry* are similar to those found in works by Harry Harrison, Harlan Ellison, and Robert Sheckley. Lewis himself knew and was influenced by H.G. Wells.

The political satires set in the near future, best exemplified by Allen Drury's work, are Lewis's grandchildren. *It Can't Happen Here* came about because of his wife Dorothy Thompson's political involvement and Lewis's knowledge of America's long line of politically extreme demagogues. Not as intellectually based and universal as *Brave New World* or *Nineteen Eighty-Four,* the book caught attention because of its immediacy. Doremus Jessup, a Vermont newspaper editor, symbolizes America's honesty and love of freedom, while Berzelius (Buzz) Windrip is an American Hitler, appealing to the lowest common denominator. Although Buzz's hangers-on die, Doremus survives. Here, as always, Lewis overdoes. Not content with simple horrors, he catalogues them until the reader becomes numb. Lewis, often criticized for overlong novels, does not manage sustained impact.

In *Kingsblood Royal,* red-haired, blue-eyed Neil Kingsblood is ostracized and broken by Grand Republic, Minnesota, because he is 3.125% black. In "The Cat of the Stars" a boy's stopping to pet a cat causes the loss of a fortune and 3,291 deaths in South America. *Arrowsmith* argues for the superiority of scientific over materialistic values. Its romantic SF theme is man's triumph over nature by fresh perspectives and dedication. The bureaucratic scientific community is etched in acid as Martin Arrowsmith defies mediocrity by refusing to compromise his integrity.

—Mary S. Weinkauf

LICHTENBERG, Jacqueline. American. Born in Flushing, New York, 25 March 1942. Educated at the University of California, Berkeley, B.S. in chemistry 1964. Married Salomon Lichtenberg; two daughters. Industrial chemist for two years, including one year in Israel. Since 1968, free-lance writer. Address: 9 Maple Terrace, Monsey, New York 19052, U.S.A.

SCIENCE-FICTION PUBLICATIONS

Novels (series: Sime in all books)

House of Zeor. New York, Doubleday, 1974.
Unto Zeor, Forever. New York, Doubleday, 1978.
First Channel, with Jean Lorrah. New York, Doubleday, 1980.

Uncollected Short Stories (series: Sime)

"Operation High Time" (Sime), in *If* (New York), January 1969.
"Recompense," in *Galileo 2* (Boston), 1976.
"The Channel's Exemption" (Sime), in *Galileo* (Boston), July 1977.
"The Vanillamint Tapestry," in *Cassandra Rising,* edited by Alice Laurance. New York, Doubleday, 1978.

OTHER PUBLICATIONS

Other

Star Trek Lives!, with Sandra Marshak and Joan Winston. New York, Bantam, and London, Corgi, 1975.

Jacqueline Lichtenberg comments:
As I see it, the emotional substance of the Sime Series is an examination of the fear/compassion axis of emotion that can exist between symbionts. The Sime mutation brings evolutionary pressure to bear on otherwise rather ordinary human beings to develop compassion or die. It is stunning how difficult it is to find true compassion untinged by fear in a human. But when you do find it, it is more precious than life itself. The Sime/Gen mutation is considered as another on the order of the differentiation into male and female, only the second such step ever taken.

The style in which I write emphasizes psychological problems with psychological action and resolution, rather than the standard action/adventure formula in which it is considered bad form to

characterize or motivate. I aim my work basically at women between 18 and 25, though anyone who has been such an age should enjoy it as well. I am constantly surprised at the number of fans who don't fit that description, surprised and delighted no end.

* * *

Jacqueline Lichtenberg began her career in science fiction as the author of *Star Trek* fan fiction. She is the creator of Kraith, one of the largest and most popular of the fannish "universes" in which the cast of the *U.S.S. Enterprise* adventures and struggles. Kraith concerns itself with a Vulcan of intense family loyalties and rivalries which center around Spock, whose half-blood makes him suspect to T'Uriamne, a Vulcan matriarch of his line. Only by performing the Affirmation, a ritual of belonging and binding, can Spock heal the political and social breaches which have developed. Lichtenberg's Spock is also tormented because of an unfortunate, doomed marriage to T'Aniya, a specialist in the Vulcan dances, which combine art, religion, and history on her world. Ultimately, he reaches a sort of measured satisfaction with a Terran wife, and with Captain Kirk as an adopted brother. The Kraith series is notable for its complexity and for Lichtenberg's willingness to allow other writers to participate in it. It, along with several other universes, is described in *Star Trek Lives!*

House of Zeor introduced her readers to the Simes and the Gens. Simes are tentacled humanoids who live after a catastrophe has split the human race into two parts: Simes, who require selyn, or lifeforce, in order to live; and the Gens from whom they draw it. Transfer of selyn almost always results in the Gen's death from terror and neural shock. In *House of Zeor* Hugh Valleroy, an idealistic Gen, allies with Klyd Farria, a Sime and head of a Household, to win back Valleroy's lover. Farris is not only a Sime, he is a channel, one of the politically controversial Simes able to draw selyn without killing and to pass it on to renSimes, who lack that ability. Because the selyn transfer and Kill are so important to Simes, who crave the sensation of the kill as much as selyn, Farris faces heartbreak and battle as his householding founds the Tecton, a society in which Simes and Gens can live together. *Unto Zeor, Forever* takes place generations after Klyd Farris succeeds. Dr. Digen Farris, unable to function fully as a channel, attempts to become a surgeon and faces opposition from Simes and Gens who fear that surgery will make him a killer. Tormented and introspective, Digen is a perfect example of the House of Farris, for whom tragedy and moral purpose are always linked. Lichtenberg's collaboration with Jean Lorrah, *First Channel*, tell of Rimon Farris, Digen and Klyd's ancestor, and the first Sime to learn to live without killing Gens.

Two novels set in a different universe and scheduled for publication, *Molt Brother* and *City of a Million Legends*, introduce the kren, reptilian beings who have venomed fangs and are vulnerable only when they molt. At that time, they choose molt brothers to guard them. This bond, like transfer for Simes, is the most profound linkage possible. In *Molt Brother,* Arshel Holtether, an esper archeologist, chooses a human molt brother and enters worlds of intrigue and danger.

All of Jacqueline Lichtenberg's books are marked by an extraordinary density of thought. She creates extremely dangerous characters: the vampiric Simes, the venomous kren whose pain somehow makes them vulnerable and understandable to her often fanatic readers. Her writing is notable for intensity rather than lyricism; frequently her books are painful to read because of her insistence on confronting the problem of man's inability to communicate totally with others. The bond of transfer or of molt brotherhood supply this communication — but even these bonds are imperfect, if only because their severing creates anguish. Lichtenberg's fans have published three fanzines which feature letters, reviews, fragments from MSS, and original Sime/Gen stories by amateur writers.

—Susan M. Shwartz

LIGHTNER, Alice (Martha). Also writes as Alice L. Hopf. American. Born in Detroit, Michigan, 11 October 1904. Educated at Westover School, Middlebury, Connecticut, graduated 1923; Vassar College, Poughkeepsie, New York, B.A. 1927. Married Ernest Joachim Hopf in 1935; one son. Editorial assistant, *Civil Engineering;* clerk-typist, Grey Advertising, Detroit, 1951. Since 1951, freelance writer. Recipient: National Science Teachers Association Award, 1972, 1973. Agent: Larry Sternig, 742 Robertson Street, Milwaukee, Wisconsin 53213. Address: 136 West 16th Street, New York, New York 10011, U.S.A.

SCIENCE-FICTION PUBLICATIONS

Novels (juvenile)

The Rock of Three Planets. New York, Putnam, 1963.
The Planet Poachers. New York, Putnam, 1965.
Doctor of the Galaxy. New York, Norton, 1965.
The Galactic Troubadours. New York, Norton, 1965.
The Space Plague. New York, Norton, 1966.
The Space Olympics. New York, Norton, 1967.
The Space Ark. New York, Putnam, 1968.
The Day of the Drones. New York, Norton, 1969.
The Thursday Toads. New York, McGraw Hill, 1971.
Gods or Demons? New York, Four Winds Press, 1973.
Star Dog. New York, McGraw Hill, 1973.
The Space Gypsies. New York, McGraw Hill, 1974.
Star Circus. New York, Dutton, 1977.

Uncollected Short Stories

"A New Game," in *Teen-Age Outer Space Stories,* edited by A.L. Furman. New York, Lantern Press, 1962.
"Best Friend," in *The Boys' Life Book of Outer Space Stories.* New York, Random House, 1964.
"A Great Day for the Irish" and "The Mars Jar," in *Teen-Age Space Adventures,* edited by A.L. Furman. New York, Lantern Press, 1972.
"The Ghost of Pirate's Cove," in *Haunted Stories,* edited by A.L. Furman. New York, Lantern Press, 1975.
"Trigger," in *Baleful Beasts and Eerie Creatures,* edited by Dorothy Haas. Chicago, Rand McNally, 1976.

OTHER PUBLICATIONS as Alice L. Hopf

Novel

The Walking Zoo of Darwin Dingle (juvenile). New York, Putnam, 1969.

Verse

The Pillar and the Flame. New York, Vinal, 1928.

Other (juvenile)

Monarch Butterflies. New York, Crowell, 1965.
Wild Traveler: The Story of a Coyote. New York, Norton, 1967.
Earth's Bug-Eyed Monsters. New York, Norton, 1968.
Butterfly and Moth. New York, Putnam, 1969.
Carab, The Trap-Door Spider. New York, Putnam, 1970.
Biography of an Octopus [a Rhino, an Ostrich, an Ant, an Armadillo, an American Reindeer, a Giraffe, a Snowy Owl]. New York, Putnam, 8 vols., 1971-79.
Misunderstood Animals. New York, McGraw Hill, 1973.
Wild Cousins of the Dog [Cat, Horse]. New York, Putnam, 3 vols., 1973-77.
Misplaced Animals and Other Living Creatures. New York, McGraw Hill, 1975.
Animal and Plant Life Spans. New York, Holiday House, 1978.
Animals That Eat Nectar and Honey. New York, Holiday House, 1979.

Nature's Pretenders. New York, Putnam, 1979.
Pigs Wild and Tame. New York, Holiday House, 1979.

*   *   *

Alice Lightner is an author of children's books at home in nonfiction as well as SF. Her informational books about animal life are popular with young readers and have received honors from science teachers because of their solid, up-to-date information, enthusiastic concern for ecology and conservation, and capacity for explaining on a child's level of comprehension. Similar qualities mark Lightner's SF. Actually, so prominent is the last quality that in spite of lacking a prose style as supple as Norton's or an imagination as inventive as Heinlein's, Lightner has produced a body of SF that is perhaps more readily open to and enjoyed by youngsters than either of theirs.

The typical Lightner novel is an amalgam of SF and the Young Adult novel. The most prominent of the former is the presence of "alien" animals: either ones that do not exist today but whose future existence may be extrapolated—a unicorn-like gazelle, for instance, or a telepathic bird that can speak—or ones that are unexpected mutations of species currently existing—giant bees, for example. Another prominent SF feature is exotic setting, most often a planet newly discovered which needs to be explored and surveyed and whose flora and fauna require cataloguing and preserving. Young Adult elements usually found in Lightner's fiction are mystery and dashes of romance and humor in addition to the requisite youthful protagonists. (Incidentally, Lightner is one of the very few writers of children's SF who regularly incorporate females among their protagonists.) So determined is Lightner to appeal to youth that sometimes, as in *The Galactic Troubadours,* she sacrifices plausibility for topicality: a band of rock and roll musicians make a nuisance of themselves as they travel from planet to planet. In general, though, Lightner has been successful in her mix.

Lightner's most successful novel is *The Day of the Drones.* Set in the future when nuclear conflict has poisoned the earth and obliterated virtually everyone, the book concerns the Afrians—descendants of a small group of surviving black Africans who have managed to rebuild civilization by placing under taboo most technology and by practicing strict genetic control. Those born darkest-skinned will enjoy most privileges; fairer-skinned babies, less; the occasional white baby is simply abandoned. A small group of Afrians set out to ascertain whether any other human survivors exist. In what was once England the Afrians come across the Anglics, descendants of the ancient English who are cruel, superstition-ridden, and white. They too practice social engineering, having established a bizarre matriarchy modeled upon bee-society. The impact of *The Day of the Drones* is three-fold. One, the description of the two differing cultures is detailed and plausible. Second, characterization is rounded and convincing; none of the several protagonists is a mouthpiece for conventional sentiments or moral posturing. Especially interesting is Anhara, the young Afrian archeologist who has mastered Anglic so that she can appreciate the little Shakespeare that is extant and becomes sorrowed at the degradation of the race that produced the Master. Third, the investigation of racism, whether black or white, and its demeaning effects is matter-of-fact and even-handed, hence, neither sensational nor preachy. The book, then, is impressive and challenging; as such it must be ranked among the relatively few superior examples of children's SF.

—Francis J. Molson

LINDSAY, David. British. Born in London, 3 March 1878. Educated at schools in London and Jedburgh, Roxburgh. Served in the Grenadier Guards in World War I. Married Jacqueline Lindsay in 1916; two daughters. Worked for Lloyd's underwriters, London, prior to World War I; after the war lived in Cornwall and Sussex. *Died 6 June 1945.*

SCIENCE-FICTION PUBLICATIONS

Novels

A Voyage to Arcturus. London, Methuen, 1920; New York,
  Macmillan, 1963.
The Haunted Woman. London, Methuen, 1922; Hollywood,
  Newcastle, 1975.
Sphinx. London, Long, 1923.
Devil's Tor. London, Putnam, 1932; New York, Arno Press,
  1978.
The Violet Apple (includes "The Witch"). Chicago, Chicago
  Review Press, 1976; London, Sidgwick and Jackson, 1978.

OTHER PUBLICATIONS

Novel

Adventures of Monsieur de Mailly. London, Melrose, 1926; as *A
  Blade for Sale,* New York, McBride, 1927.

*   *   *

While David Lindsay's first novel, *A Voyage to Arcturus,* has
become recognized as one of the masterworks of 20th-century fantasy, his other novels remain unknown to all but a handful of
readers, and the man himself remains a curiously distant and enigmatic figure. More a philosopher than a novelist, Lindsay wrote
often awkward and laborious prose, his later work filled with long
expository digressions, his ideas so complex and densely packed, his
characters so unsympathetic, that many readers find his fiction at
first coldly intellectual and difficult to get into. But Lindsay undeniably expanded the possibilities of fantasy as philosophical fiction,
and his influence has been widely felt among modern authors as
diverse as Colin Wilson and Philip José Farmer.

Lindsay's masterpiece, *A Voyage to Arcturus,* concerns the journey of a man named Maskull to Tormance, a world in the system of
Arcturus, where he encounters bizarre characters and himself
undergoes physical transformations in a series of episodes depicting
different systems of belief not unlike the different moral systems at
work on Earth. As each of these moral systems is shown to be
illusory, Maskull is gradually brought to a confrontation with the
godlike villain Crystalman, who controls this world, and who
seems, at the end, to represent the entire world of phenomenal
experience. Drawing on Nietzsche, Schopenhauer, and Norse
mythology for ideas and imagery, Lindsay develops a world of vivid
scenery and violent action that nevertheless is rigidly structured
according to the philosophical ideas he wishes to explore. The novel
is a remarkable union of action and idea.

Ideas were more interesting to Lindsay than action, however, and
his later novels contained little of the violent action of *Arcturus.* *The
Haunted Woman* continued exploring the notion of subjective reality in a romance of two lovers who could only acknowledge their
love in a phantom room of a haunted house. *Sphinx* turned to the
science-fiction device of a dream-recording machine to explore the
romance between a woman composer and a writer. Like *A Voyage
to Arcturus* itself, however, each of these novels was a commercial
disaster, and Lindsay turned to the historical romance for his next
book, *Adventures of Monsieur de Mailly,* a tale of court intrigue
that nevertheless also reflected Lindsay's preoccupations with illusion and deception. *Devil's Tor* is a sprawling, slow-moving, and at
times brilliant exposition of the myth of the Eternal Feminine, in a
story concerning the reuniting of two halves of an ancient stone and
the founding of a new race by a chosen man and woman.

Lindsay was unable to find a publisher for *The Violet Apple,* and
he left another manuscript, "The Witch," unfinished. Both works
were finally published in abridged form, and both retain the romance structure of *The Haunted Woman* and *Devil's Tor.* In *The
Violet Apple* a dwarf apple tree, grown from a seed which according
to legend came from the original tree of Eden, unites the lovers.
"The Witch" explores the dual myths of the wise woman and
witchcraft in a work whose controlling image is music. Though
none of these later works achieves the narrative power of *A Voyage*

to Arcturus, they nevertheless stand as worthwhile philosophical
meditations and as studies in the problems inherent in trying to
write a truly philosophical fiction.

—Gary K. Wolfe

———————

LLEWELLYN, (David William) Alun. Irish. Born in London,
England, 17 April 1903. Educated at Alleyn's School, Dulwich,
London; St. John's College, Cambridge (Chancellor's Gold Medal,
for poetry, 1923; College Literature Prize, 1924), B.A. (honours) in
history and literature 1924, LL.B. (honours) 1925, M.A. 1928;
Lincoln's Inn, London: called to the Bar, 1927. Served in the Intelli-
gence Corps during World War II. Married Lesley Deane in 1953.
Treaty translator and reviser, League of Nations, Geneva, 1936-39;
legal adviser, Egyptian government, Montreux Capitulations, 1937;
Secretary of the Compensation Tribunal for Coal Nationalisation,
1947-49; counsel, Camberwell Borough, London, 1951-53; public
relations speaker, Commonwealth Industries Association, 1955-72.
Liberal parliamentary candidate for South Croydon, 1931, 1935.
President, Union Society, 1935, and Hardwicke Society, 1953, both
Inner Temple, London; Honorary Treasurer, Poetry Society of
Great Britain, 1961-62. Since 1977, Honorary Secretary, Irish
P.E.N. Address: 52 Silchester Park, Glenageary, Dun Laoghaire,
County Dublin, Ireland.

SCIENCE-FICTION PUBLICATIONS

Novel

The Strange Invaders. London, Bell, 1934.

OTHER PUBLICATIONS

Novels

The Deacon. London, Bell, 1934.
The Soul of Cézar Azan. London, Barker, 1938.
Jubilee John. London, Barker, 1939.

Short Stories

Confound Their Politics. London, Bell, 1934.

Plays

Ways of Love (produced 1968). London, French, 1958.
Shelley Plain (produced London, 1960).

Verse

Ballads and Songs. London, Stockwell, 1921.

Other

History of the Union Society of London. London, Union Society,
  1935.
The Emperor of Britain. London, Montgomeryshire Society,
  1939.
The Tyrant from Below: An Essay in Political Revaluation. London, Macdonald and Evans, 1957.
The World and the Commonwealth. London, British Commonwealth Union, 1968.
The Shell Guide to Wales. London, Rainbird, 1969.

Alun Llewellyn comments:
Only one of my novels is, strictly speaking, science fiction. *The
Strange Invaders* looks at this planet and the ecological change
upon it as a result of Man's abandonment of Mind as a motive force

of his evolution. But since all human psychology is a matter for scientific analysis, and is a more subtle matter than mechanistic theories of economics or sex can explain, the studies in my other novels of the illusions of love, religion, ambition, and power ought really to be called fictional illustrations of scientific themes. By this interpretation, all my fiction qualifies as science fiction.

*   *   *

Alun Llewellyn's *The Strange Invaders* is a fantasy set in the future when the habitable area of the earth is gradually decreasing as a new ice age emerges. Mankind has retrogressed; as a result of disastrous wars it has lost the art of civilization and is living in a pre-iron age existence. The story takes place in what seems to be the Gobi desert, a somewhat hostile environment but one of the last places on earth capable of supporting human life. The plot concerns a small group of people living in a half-destroyed town, isolated within the remains of a ruined city on the plains. There is a pseudo-medieval order to their existence: governed by a religious community of priests dedicated to the new trinity of Marx, Lenin, and Stalin, and controlled by a warrior group, they manage to eke out a life of basic survival. As if their plight were not bad enough, Llewellyn has this last outpost of humanity threatened by an army of enormous lizards—huge, cold-blooded creatures that are virtually invincible. The plot is concerned with the efforts of the community to survive in the face of this new and overpowering challenge. What elevates the story above the ordinary is Llewellyn's ability to show how the basic human emotions of love, hate, and jealousy survive and dominate the lives of these people even in the face of overwhelming danger and the threat of extinction.

Though the novel is cast in the form of a futuristic nightmare, it is difficult for the reader to remember that the time frame is the future and not the past. So vividly does Llewellyn evoke the sense of life of these people and so much is their life a reliving of prehistorical civilization, that the reader inevitably feels that he has been transported into the past rather than into the future.

—Joseph A. Quinn

LONDON, Jack (John Griffith London).   American. Born in San Francisco, California, 12 January 1876. Educated at a grammar school in Oakland, California; Oakland High School, 1895-96; University of California, Berkeley, 1896-97. Married 1) Bessie Maddern in 1900 (separated, 1903; divorced, 1905) two daughters; 2) Charmian Kittredge in 1905. Worked in a cannery in Oakland, 1890; sailor on the *Sophie Sutherland,* sailing to Japan and Siberia, 1893; returned to Oakland, wrote for the local paper, and held various odd jobs, 1893-94; tramped the United States and Canada, 1894-96; arrested for vagrancy in Niagara Falls, New York; joined the gold rush to the Klondike, 1897-98, then returned to Oakland and became a full-time writer; visited London, 1902; War Correspondent in the Russo-Japanese War for the *San Francisco Examiner,* 1904; settled on a ranch in Sonoma County, California, 1906, and lived there for the rest of his life; attempted to sail round the world on a 45-foot yacht, 1907-09; War Correspondent in Mexico, 1914. *Died 22 November 1916.*

SCIENCE-FICTION PUBLICATIONS

Novels

Before Adam.   New York, Macmillan, 1907; London, Laurie, 1908.
The Iron Heel.   New York, Macmillan, and London, Everett, 1908.
The Scarlet Plague.   New York, Macmillan, and London, Mills and Boon, 1915.

The Jacket (*The Star Rover*).   London, Mills and Boon, 1915; as *The Star Rover,* New York, Macmillan, 1915.

Short Stories

The Strength of the Strong (story).   Chicago, Kerr, 1911.
The Dream of Debs.   Chicago, Kerr, 1912 (?).
The Strength of the Strong (collection).   New York, Macmillan, 1914; London, Mills and Boon, 1917.
The Red One.   New York, Macmillan, 1918; London, Mills and Boon, 1919.
Short Stories, edited by Maxwell Geismar.   New York, Hill and Wang, 1960.
Goliah: A Utopian Essay.   Berkeley, California, Thorp Springs Press, 1973.
Curious Fragments: Jack London's Tales of Fantasy Fiction, edited by Dale L. Walker.   Port Washington, New York, Kennikat Press, 1975.
The Science Fiction of Jack London, edited by Richard Gid Powers.   Boston, Gregg Press, 1975.

OTHER PUBLICATIONS

Novels

The Cruise of the Dazzler.   New York, Century, 1902; London, Hodder and Stoughton, 1906.
A Daughter of the Snows   Philadelphia, Lippincott, 1902; London, Isbister, 1904.
The Kempton-Wace Letters (published anonymously), with Anna Strunsky.   New York, Macmillan, and London, Isbister, 1903.
The Call of the Wild.   New York, Macmillan, and London, Heinemann, 1903.
The Sea-Wolf.   New York, Macmillan, and London, Heinemann, 1904.
The Game.   New York, Macmillan, and London, Heinemann, 1905.
White Fang.   New York, Macmillan, 1906; London, Methuen, 1907.
Martin Eden.   New York, Macmillan, 1909; London, Heinemann, 1910.
Burning Daylight.   New York, Macmillan, 1910; London, Heinemann, 1911.
Adventure.   London, Nelson, and New York, Macmillan, 1911.
The Abysmal Brute.   New York, Century, 1913; London, Newnes, 1914.
John Barleycorn.   New York, Century, 1913; London, Mills and Boon, 1914.
The Valley of the Moon.   New York, Macmillan, and London, Mills and Boon, 1913.
The Mutiny of the Elsinore.   New York, Macmillan, 1914; London, Mills and Boon, 1915.
The Little Lady of the Big House.   New York, Macmillan, and London, Mills and Boon, 1916.
Jerry of the Islands.   New York, Macmillan, and London, Mills and Boon, 1917.
Michael, Brother of Jerry.   New York, Macmillan, 1917; London, Mills and Boon, 1918.
Hearts of Three.   London, Mills and Boon, 1918; New York, Macmillan, 1920.
The Assassination Bureau Ltd., completed by Robert L. Fish. New York, McGraw Hill, 1963; London, Deutsch, 1964.

Short Stories

The Son of the Wolf: Tales of the Far North.   Boston, Houghton Mifflin, 1900; London Isbister, 1902; as *An Odyssey of the North,* London, Mills and Boon, 1915.
The God of His Fathers and Other Stories.   New York, McClure, 1901; London, Isbister, 1902.
Children of the Frost.   New York, Macmillan, 1902.
The Faith of Men and Other Stories.   New York, Macmillan, and London, Heinemann, 1904.
Tales of the Fish Patrol.   New York, Macmillan, 1905; London, Heinemann, 1906.

The Apostate. Chicago, Kerr, 1906.
Moon-Face and Other Stories. New York, Macmillan, and London, Heinemann, 1906.
Love of Life and Other Stories. New York, Macmillan, 1907; London, Everett, 1908.
The Road. New York, Macmillan, 1907; London, Mills and Boon, 1914.
Lost Face. New York, Macmillan, 1910; London, Mills and Boon, 1915.
When God Laughs and Other Stories. New York, Macmillan, 1911; London, Mills and Boon, 1912.
South Sea Tales. New York, Macmillan, 1911; London, Mills and Boon, 1912.
The House of Pride and Other Tales of Hawaii. New York, Macmillan, 1912; London, Mills and Boon, 1914.
A Son of the Sun. New York, Doubleday, 1912; London, Mills and Boon, 1913; as *The Adventures of Captain Grief,* Cleveland, World, 1954.
Smoke Bellew. New York, Century, 1912; London, Mills and Boon, 1913; as *Smoke and Shorty,* London, Mills and Boon, 1920.
The Night Born.... New York, Century, 1913; London, Mills and Boon, 1916.
The Turtles of Tasman. New York, Macmillan, 1916; London, Mills and Boon, 1917.
The Human Drift. New York, Macmillan, 1917; London, Mills and Boon, 1919.
On the Makaloa Mat. New York, Macmillan, 1919; as *Island Tales,* London, Mills and Boon, 1920.
Dutch Courage and Other Stories. New York, Macmillan, 1922; London, Mills and Boon, 1923.
Jack London's Tales of Adventure, edited by Irving Shepard. New York, Hanover House, 1956.
Stories of Hawaii, edited by A. Grove Day. New York, Appleton Century Crofts, 1965.
Great Short Works of Jack London, edited by Earle Labor. New York, Harper, 1965.

Plays

The Great Interrogation, with Lee Bascom (produced San Francisco, 1905).
Scorn of Women. New York, Macmillan, 1906; London, Macmillan, 1907.
Theft. New York and London, Macmillan, 1910.
The Acorn-Planters: A California Forest Play.... New York, Macmillan, and London, Mills and Boon, 1916.
Daughters of the Rich. Oakland, California, Holmes, 1971.

Other

The People of the Abyss. New York, Macmillan, and London, Isbister, 1903.
The Tramp. New York, Wilshire's Magazine, 1904.
The Scab. Chicago, Kerr, 1904.
Jack London: A Sketch of His Life and Work. London, Macmillan, 1905.
War of the Classes. New York, Macmillan, and London, Heinemann, 1905.
What Life Means to Me. Princeton, New Jersey, Intercollegiate Socialist Society, 1906.
Jack London: Who He Is and What He Has Done. New York, Macmillan, 1908 (?).
Revolution. Chicago, Kerr, 1909.
Revolution and Other Essays. New York, Macmillan, 1910; London, Mills and Boon, 1920.
The Cruise of the Snark. New York, Macmillan, and London, Mills and Boon, 1911.
Jack London by Himself. New York, Macmillan, and London, Mills and Boon, 1913.
London's Essays of Revolt, edited by Leonard D. Abbott. New York, Vanguard Press, 1926.
(Works) [Fitzroy Edition], edited by I.O. Evans. London, Arco, and New York, Archer House and Horizon Press, 18 vols., 1962-68.

The Bodley Head Jack London, edited by Arthur Calder-Marshall. London, Bodley Head, 4 vols., 1963-66; as *The Pan Jack London,* London, Pan, 2 vols., 1966-68.
Letters from Jack London, Containing an Unpublished Correspondence Between London and Sinclair Lewis, edited by King Hendricks and Irving Shepard. New York, Odyssey Press, 1965; London, MacGibbon and Kee, 1966.
Jack London Reports: War Correspondence, Sports Articles, and Miscellaneous Writings, edited by King Hendricks and Irving Shepard. New York, Random House, 1970.
Jack London's Articles and Short Stories in the (Oakland) High School Aegis, edited by James E. Sisson. Cedar Springs, Michigan, London Collector, 1971.

*

Bibliography: *Jack London: A Bibliography* by Hensley C. Woodbridge, John London, and George H. Tweney, Georgetown, California, Talisman Press, 1966; supplement by Woodbridge, Milwood, New York, Kraus, 1973; in *Bibliography of American Literature 5* by Jacob Blanck, New Haven, Connecticut, Yale University Press, 1969.

* * *

Influenced by Charles Darwin, Herbert Spencer, Friedrich Nietzsche, and Karl Marx, the novels and short stories that comprise Jack London's science-fiction output alternate between the didactic and the sensational, and tend to reveal his limitations as a writer rather than his virtues. Since each is an exposition of some principle or theory that appealed to him, the characterization is generally shallow and the stories either heavy on plot or almost without one. Over and over the same points emerge, and often in the same way, either as a thinly disguised political tract or as a lip-smacking account of savagery and brutality. Sometimes the two are combined in an uneasy alliance, through the idea of primordialism or atavism, the notion that man's adaptability stems from primitive qualities that lurk beneath his civilized veneer, leftovers or throwbacks from an earlier stage of evolution. Then man was closer to the beasts, but also simpler, more natural, uncorrupted by capital and the false values of organized society.

In "When the World Was Young" the businessman James G. Ward is a kind of wolfman who leads a double life, lapsing suddenly into feats of primeval strength, prowess, and savagery, until "suddenly looking out of the eyes of the early Teuton [he] saw the fair frail Twentieth Century girl he loved, and felt something snap in his brain." Afterwards, "he knows in all its bitter fullness the curse of civilized fear. He is now afraid of the dark, and night in the forest is to him a thing of abysmal terror." He is no longer part savage, "nor does he run of nights after the coyotes under the moon"—though none of his friends think him a coward, London hastens to add. *Before Adam* reflects a similar idealization of primitive innocence in a time viewed as hard and cruel, but also simple, unspoiled, and rather wistfully desired. The narrator recounts a series of dreams of living in a dawn world of cave dwellers, "fire men," and "tree people."

The Iron Heel, a novel of life at the other end of time, the far distant future, was the only American work included in the bibliography of Communist literature prepared by Nikolai Bukharin, one of the founders of the Russian revolution. Although considered too bloody and melodramatic by partisans in the US, who feared it would frighten the proletariat, the book is credited with converting an entire generation of revolutionaries to Marxism—including the British socialist leader Aneurin Bevan. Anatole France wrote the introduction for its French edition, and Leon Trotsky praised the book for its politics, though he found it thin on art. The story of a Fascist takeover in the United States, *The Iron Heel* is less impressive than *Animal Farm,* and a good deal longer.

The purely political gets the upper hand in a number of London's moral fantasies. *Goliah* is about a scientist who uses his discovery of a new energy form to bring peace and socialism to the world. "A Curious Fragment" tells how the ruling class became dominant by keeping its slaves illiterate. Both stories purport to be histories written in the far future. *The Dream of Debs* recounts the impact of a nationwide general strike. Like *The Strength of the Strong* and

"The Minions of Midas," which deal with similar political themes but without resorting to new technology or a pretense of being future history), *The Dream of Debs* has often, perhaps erroneously, been listed among London's science fiction. Whatever the time element or state of scientific discovery, the stories are all parables of power and essentially similar. *The Scarlet Plague* has much in common with these. In 2013, the "scarlet death" destroyed almost the entire population of the world; those who survived formed tribes that quickly reverted to barbarism. The story is told 60 years later by an old man, sitting around a camp fire with his grandsons. The dawn-world idyll is a good past—not an inviting future, either in this story or in "A Curious Fragment," where the narrator addresses the reader directly, or in *The Strength of the Strong*, where yet another version of the corruption of society by the propertied classes is told around yet another camp fire.

One of the best of London's science-fiction stories is *The Red One*, which takes place in the South Seas. A dying man held prisoner by headhunters discovers their local god is an artificial sphere sent to earth by unknown beings. Dying of fever, he struggles to understand this harbinger of the future, fallen among savages for whom it serves only as an object of sacrifice. He trades his life for the opportunity to gaze on it in his final moments. The modern man bartering with the ignorant past for a glimpse of the unknown and promising future—the image resonates with beauty and power.

Through all these stories runs as a major theme the idea of determinism—people's actions are the result of outside forces working on them. Allied with that is the notion of the survival of the fittest in society; not only are morals subordinated to survival, but eventually that survival itself becomes the measure of morality. One of the oppressors of Labor speaks in *The Dream of Debs:* "The best thing for us to do is to leave morality out of it. Again I repeat, play the game, play it to the last finish, but for goodness' sake don't squeal when you get hurt."

Many of the stories bear a strong debt to Poe and to Bierce in that they consist entirely of a single idea, stated with little elaboration. Among these are the most traditional science-fiction stories London wrote, most of which exist more for entertainment than propaganda. "The Rejuvenation of Major Rathbone" describes the effect of a youth elixir on a fiery ex-soldier. "A Relic of the Pliocene" is a tall tale of the type often set in a bar or club, about a modern hunter who shoots the last surviving mammoth. "The Shadow and the Flash" concludes with two rival scientists fighting an unseen duel after they have each discovered a means to become invisible. "The Unparalleled Invasion," an example of London's racism and fear of "the yellow peril," is about germ warfare against the rapidly breeding Chinese. All of these substitute a single sensation for real plot development and cardboard puppets for characters. As with the political tracts, the story arises out of an idea of the author's, rather than the ideas from the story.

The alternative seems to be a rambling, episodic account within a loose overall framework. Possibly the most curious of London's novels, *The Star Rover,* falls into this category. Based in part on the experience of London's acquaintance Ed Morrell, who appears in the book under his own name, *The Star Rover* tells the story of Darrell Standing, a university professor who, at the age of 36, kills a colleague "in a surge of anger." He is confined at San Quentin prison, placed in solitary confinement and tortured, but escapes by self hypnosis. In an echo of Nietzsche's theory of eternal recurrence, he wanders through the "stored memories" of a wagonmaster's son in the old west, a desert hermit in Egypt, a medieval Frenchman, an English adventurer in the Orient, a Roman centurion under Pontius Pilate. Some of the phantasmagoric episodes have considerable power. The book reveals an unexpected side of Jack London. Not only was he the victim of poverty in his youth, as his concern for social justice might suggest, he was the illegitimate son of a spiritualist and an astrologer. Thus the novel ends at last with the individual: "Spirit alone endures and continues to build upon itself through successive and endless incarnations as it works upward toward the light."

—T. Collins

LONG, Charles R(ussell).   American.   Born in Paragould, Arkansas, 25 June 1904. Attended public schools in Paragould. Western Union telegraphic operator, mainly in El Paso, Texas, 1921-53. Address: 7777 Gran Quivira, El Paso, Texas 79904, U.S.A.

SCIENCE-FICTION PUBLICATIONS

Novels

The Infinite Brain.   New York, Avalon, 1957.
The Eternal Man.   New York, Avalon, 1964.

*   *   *

Charles R. Long is interested in the possibility of infinite worlds with humanoids in various stages of moral and psychological development and with the more advanced races using their united mental forces to aid the less developed in times of crisis. He envisions the growth of psi powers, now latent in human genetic make-up, psi powers that include telepathy, mindfusion, levitation, and physical transportation of self and others through time and space.

Written in journal form, *The Infinite Brain* traces the attempts of a rich eccentric to come to terms with the contradictions of his memories and experiences and those of his fellow Earthlings. Having once joined with an astronomer and a paranoid genius in an unsuccessful space launch to Venus, one that sent him into a deep-freeze orbit and returned him to a future world, he finds that historical details differ and that he has strange flashes between past and present, an earth he remembers and an earth that seems vaguely unfamiliar. By the time he discovers he has returned to a utopian parallel earth, he has already been drawn, through telepathic possession, into the dangers of the pre-holocaust world he had left. Only with the aid of the "Mind," the combined mental force of the most intelligent and moral of his new planet, can he combat a mad genius (the infinite brain) and save himself and his two worlds. Ironically the mad scientist of his original Earth is the genius and mentor of its parallel. The book suggests an infinite series of parallel worlds with infinite combinations possible. It includes stilted lectures on protons and neutrons, artificially inserted at the prompting of the "infinite brain," enthusiastic descriptions of weightlessness, and much speculation about the physical effects of travelling at or near the speed of light (shrinkage, reduction of centuries to seconds, separation of body and soul).

The Eternal Man is a story of maturation, a half-human, half-alien with god-like genes discovering and coming to terms with his identity and powers during a youth that spans man's history from pre-historic times to an intergalactic future. Though he remains inactive for centuries because his failure to age and his partially developed psi powers frighten mere humans, idealism and sexual allures tempt the "eternal man" into politics, where he founds an economically balanced socialistic society in Texas, tries gradually to introduce democracy into a world based on profit, slavery, and exploitation, and learns how easily even a clever man can be manipulated by a beautiful woman. His contact with the telepathic Mercurians of the rebellious Underground and the cruel and powerful Sagittarian invaders forces recognition that the world's telepaths are the product of his philandering through the ages and that he is the superior seed planted by Pleiads centuries before in a dream of spreading their community of minds throughout the galaxy. Once he rediscovers and accepts his vast powers, inspired by his eternal and alien ancestors, he is ready to rule earth wisely and benevolently.

Despite some awkwardness of style and an occasional propensity to lecture, Long's works raise interesting questions well worth exploring.

—Gina Macdonald

LONG, Frank Belknap. Also writes as Lyda Belknap Long. American. Born in New York City, 27 April 1903. Educated in New York public schools; New York University School of Journalism, 1920-21. Married Lyda Arco in 1960. Writer for *Captain Marvel, Green Lantern, Congo Bill,* and *Planet Comics* in the 1940's; uncredited associate editor, *The Saint Mystery Magazine* and *Fantastic Universe* in the 1950's; associate editor, *Satellite Science Fiction,* 1959, *Short Stories,* 1959-60, and *Mike Shayne Mystery Magazine* until 1966. Recipient: First Fandom Hall of Fame Award, 1977; 4th World Fantasy Convention Award, 1978. Agent: Kirby McCauley, 60 East 42nd Street, New York, New York 10017. Address: 421 West 21st Street, New York, New York 10011, U.S.A.

SCIENCE-FICTION PUBLICATIONS

Novels

Space Station No. 1. New York, Ace, 1957.
Woman from Another Planet. New York, Chariot, 1960.
The Horror Expert. New York, Belmont, 1961.
The Mating Center. New York, Chariot, 1961.
Mars Is My Destination. New York, Pyramid, 1962.
The Horror from the Hills. Sauk City, Wisconsin, Arkham House, 1963; London, Digit, 1965; expanded edition, as *Odd Science Fiction,* New York, Belmont, 1963.
It Was the Day of the Robot. New York, Belmont, 1963; London, Dobson, 1964.
Three Steps Spaceward. New York, Avalon, 1963.
The Martian Visitors. New York, Avalon, 1964.
Mission to a Star. New York, Avalon, 1964.
This Strange Tomorrow. New York, Belmont, and London, Digit, 1966.
Lest Earth Be Conquered. New York, Belmont, 1966; as *The Androids,* 1969.
So Dark a Heritage. New York, Lancer, 1966.
Journey into Darkness. New York, Belmont, 1967.
...and Others Shall Be Born. New York, Belmont, 1968.
The Three Faces of Time. New York, Belmont, 1969.
Monster from Out of Time. New York, Popular Library, 1970; London, Hale, 1971.
Survival World. New York, Lancer, 1971.
The Night of the Wolf. New York, Popular Library, 1972.
Night Fear. New York, Kensington, 1979.

Novels as Lyda Belknap Long

To the Dark Tower. New York, Lancer, 1969.
Fire of the Witches. New York, Popular Library, 1971.
The Shape of Fear. New York, Beagle, 1971.
The Witch Tree. New York, Lancer, 1971.
House of the Deadly Nightshade. New York, Beagle, 1972.
Legacy of Evil. New York, Beagle, 1973.
Crucible of Evil. New York, Avon, 1974.

Short Stories

The Hounds of Tindalos. Sauk City, Wisconsin, Arkham House, 1946; abridged editions, London, Museum Press, 1950; as *The Dark Beasts,* New York, Belmont, 1963; as *The Black Druid and Other Stories,* London, Panther, 1975.
John Carstairs, Space Detective. New York, Fell, 1949; London, Cherry Tree, 1951.
The Demons of the Upper Air. Glendale, California, Squires, 1969.
The Rim of the Unknown. Sauk City, Wisconsin, Arkham House, 1972.
The Early Long. New York, Doubleday, 1975; London, Hale, 1977.

OTHER PUBLICATIONS

Play

Television Play: *A Guest in the House,* 1950.

Verse

A Man from Genoa and Other Poems. Athol, Massachusetts, Cook, 1926.
The Goblin Tower. Cassia, Florida, Dragon-Fly Press, 1935.
On Reading Arthur Machen. Pengrove, Dog and Duck Press, 1949.
In Mayan Splendor. Sauk City, Wisconsin, Arkham House, 1977.

Other

Howard Phillips Lovecraft: Dreamer on the Nightside. Sauk City, Wisconsin, Arkham House, 1975.

*

Manuscript Collection: Lovecraft Collection, Brown University, Providence, Rhode Island.

Frank Belknap Long comments:
My work has been almost equally divided between science fiction or science fantasy and supernatural horror. What fascinates me most in the realm of SF is the strangeness, mystery , and wonder of the cosmic immensities and the possibility of intelligent life on other worlds. A few of my early stories were of the space opera type, but for many years I have shunned that kind of writing. A realistic approach has become of supreme importance to me, and I have drawn upon one or more of the natural sciences in all my more recent stories. They range from future utopias—life on earth two centuries or two million years in the future—to what life may be like, biologically considered, in some far distant region of the expanding universe.

*   *   *

Of all modern writers in the overlapping domains of science fiction, fantasy, and horror, Frank Belknap Long may hold the record for sheer longevity, and, while he does not hold that for total productivity, he has written several hundred short stories and more than 30 books. The latter are difficult to number and categorize, as they involve a number of collections, re-sorting, and retitling of short stories as well as novels. In addition to works published under his own name, Long participated in a number of collaborations and round-robins, wrote short stories under house names such as Leslie Northern, wrote anonymously on occasion, and produced several gothic novels under the name of his wife, Lyda Long. While these last works are in a sense "mere potboilers," Long maintains that they are not without merit and in some cases contain effective scenes of the horror-fantasy or near-fantasy variety.

In a career dating to 1924, and still actively writing, Long has experienced the expectable rises and declines of popularity and critical standing. For some years he was highly regarded; in later times, disdained as little more than a hack; and still more recently has emerged as a revered elder statesman held in wide affection. In this regard his standing is comparable to that of writers like Murray Leinster and Edmond Hamilton. An accumulation of potboilers temporarily obscures the author's best work; with the passage of time the inferior material dissipates and the author's true contribution comes to be recognized.

Long has experienced the additional benefit—and handicap!—of having been for many years the closest friend and associate of H.P. Lovecraft. At one time Lovecraft and Long were partners in the "revision business," working as manuscript doctors, uncredited collaborators, and even ghost writers for literary tyros. A certain portion of Long's own fiction shows a clear stamp of influence by Lovecraft, but this in fact represents a relatively small segment of Long's output, a fact too often overlooked.

A number of Long's horror stories—most of them fantasies, a few technically science fiction but still cast within the gothic mold—are notable. These include "The Desert Lich," "Second Night Out," a supernatural sea story perhaps remotely influenced by the works of William Hope Hodgson, and "The Man with a Thousand Legs," one of the most bizarre of all lycanthropic tales.

Long also contributed some of the earliest and most effective supplements to Lovecraft's "Cthulhu Mythos." Long's dry humor is apparent in "The Brain-Eaters," whose two chief characters are thinly disguised versions of himself and Lovecraft. "The Hounds of Tindalos," probably Long's most famous story, is a thoroughly effective tale of monstrous creatures from beyond normal time and space breaking through the "angles" of our universe; the story is most effective in evoking a sense of non-Euclidean dimension. "A Visitor from Egypt" continues the successful exploitation of the Egyptian craze of the 1920's-early 1930's popular fiction. (One chapter of this novel was written by Lovecraft, based upon a dream.)

Long's science fiction bears no trace of Lovecraft. It is sometimes densely powerful, evocative, and moving; at other times, the author fails in attempted effects and falls into bathos. In general, Long's short fiction is superior to his novels; in this regard he is once more comparable to Leinster. "The Flame Midget" clearly anticipates the development of the laser. A later story, "Dark Vision" (1939), is one of the earlier and still one of the most successful to use psychiatric and specifically Freudian themes in science fiction. Long places strong emphasis on the subconscious, and in the story makes use of both electroshock and chemical shock techniques (the former accidentally; the latter clinically) in bringing about changes in the protagonist's perceptions and interpretations of reality.

Also notable is Long's series of stories about John Carstairs, "Botanical Detective." These are intriguing hybrids of space opera and scientific mystery.

Long's most effective work is probably a series of short stories ("The Great Cold," "Green Glory," and "The Last Men") set in a remote future when humankind is reduced to miniature size and enslaved by races of giant insects. In framework, the stories would appear to be routine absurd super-science adventures. But Long concentrates on the awakening consciousness of the brutalized humans as they regain their awareness of their own humanness. The pitch of noble tragedy achieved is remarkable.

In a recent letter, Long listed his own selection of his short stories which he considers the most accomplished. The stories nominated by Long include "Humpty Dumpty Had a Great Fall," "To Follow Knowledge," "Prison Bright—Prison Deep," "Guest in the House," "Two Face," and "Night Fear" (most included in *Night Fear*). Almost all of these stories are based on psychological themes, most notably difficulties of personal adjustment. Further, the main protagonist is most commonly a child. The psychological sensitivity of the works is noteworthy, as is their acuteness of focus and intensity of treatment. It is also noteworthy that none bears any trace of Long's Lovecraft period; with the continued passage of time it is to be hoped that Long's non-Lovecraft works (which in fact constitute the overwhelming bulk of his output) will achieve their proper evaluation.

—Richard A. Lupoff

LONG, Lyda Belknap. *See* **LONG, Frank Belknap.**

LOOMIS, Noel M(iller). Also wrote as Sam Allison; Benj. Miller; Frank Miller; Silas Water. American. Born in Wakita, Oklahoma, 3 April 1905. Attended Clarendon College, 1921; University of Oklahoma, Norman, 1930. Married Dorothy Moore Green in 1945; one son and one daughter. Printer and editor, then newspaperman; free-lance writer from 1929; English Instructor, San Diego State College, 1958-69. President and Secretary-Treasurer, Western Writers of America. Recipient: Western Writers of America Silver Spur Award, for novel, 1958, for story, 1959. *Died 7 September 1979.*

SCIENCE-FICTION PUBLICATIONS

Novels

City of Glass. New York, Columbia, 1955.
The Man with Absolute Motion (as Silas Water). London, Rich and Cowan, 1955.

Uncollected Short Stories

"Iron Man," in *Startling* (New York), Winter 1945.
"Electron Eat Electron," in *Planet* (New York), Spring 1946.
"Rocket Pants," in *Thrilling Wonder Stories* (New York), Spring 1946.
"Zero," in *Thrilling Wonder Stories* (New York), Summer 1946.
"Mr. Zytztz Goes to Mars," in *Thrilling Wonder Stories* (New York), August 1948.
"Softie," in *Thrilling Wonder Stories* (New York), October 1948.
"Schizophrenic," in *Thrilling Wonder Stories* (New York), December 1948.
"Turnover Time," in *Startling* (New York), March 1949.
"The Ultimate Planet," in *Thrilling Wonder Stories* (New York), April 1949.
"The Long Dawn," in *Big Book of Science Fiction,* edited by Groff Conklin. New York, Crown, 1950.
"Parking Unlimited," in *Future* (New York), May-June 1950.
"The Lithium Rocket," in *Future* (New York), March 1951.
"The Byrd," in *Planet* (New York), May 1951.
"Remember the 4th!," in *Future* (New York), July 1951.
"The Wealth of Echindul," in *Planet* (New York), July 1952.
"The Mischievous Typesetter," in *Imagination* (Evanston, Illinois), July 1952.
"Tough Guy," in *Fantastic Adventures* (New York), September 1952.
"Big-Top on Jupiter," in *Space Stories* (New York), October 1952.
"You Too Can Be a Millionaire," in *If* (New York), November 1952.
"Nine Men in Time," in *Original Science Fiction Stories* (Holyoke, Massachusetts), 1953.
"Thousand-Legged Agent," in *Amazing* (New York), March 1953.
"Cett Was a Whale," in *Fantastic Adventures* (New York), March 1953.
"We Breathe for You," in *Startling* (New York), May 1953.
"The Cyanided Man," in *Space Stories* (New York), June 1953.
"Day's Work," in *Rocket* (New York), September 1953.
"The Chaos Salient," in *Saturn* (Holyoke, Massachusetts), March 1957.
"The Conduit," in *Science Fiction Quarterly* (Holyoke, Massachusetts), November 1957.
"If the Court Pleases," in *Escape to Earth,* edited by Ivan Howard. New York Belmont, 1963.
"Little Green Man," in *Things,* edited by Ivan Howard. New York, Belmont, 1964.
"The State vs. Susan Todd," in *Worlds of Tomorrow 24* (New York), 1970.
"A Time to Teach, A Time to Learn," in *Amazing* (New York), November 1970.

Uncollected Short Stories as Benj. Miller

"Date Line," in *Thrilling Wonder Stories* (New York), October 1948.
"A Horse on Me," in *Thrilling Wonder Stories* (New York), December 1948.
"Monsters from the West," in *Thrilling Wonder Stories* (New York), February 1949.
"On the House," in *Thrilling Wonder Stories* (New York), April 1949.

OTHER PUBLICATIONS

Novels

Murder Goes to Press. New York, Phoenix Press, 1937.
Rim of the Caprock. New York, Macmillan, and London, Collins, 1952; as *Battle for the Caprock,* Collins, 1959.

Tejas Country (as Frank Miller). New York, Avalon, 1953; London, Corgi, 1955.
Trouble on Crazyman. New York, Lion, 1953; (as Sam Allison) London, Hale, 1955.
The Buscadero. New York, Macmillan, 1953; as *Trouble Shooter,* London, Collins, 1953.
North to Texas. New York, Ballantine, 1955; as *Texas Rebel,* London, Corgi, 1956.
West to the Sun. New York, Fawcett, 1955; London, Fawcett, 1957.
The Twilighters. New York, Macmillan, 1955.
Johnny Concho. New York, Fawcett, 1956; London, Fawcett, 1957.
Wild Country. New York, Pyramid, 1956.
Hang the Men High, with Paul Leslie Peil. New York, Fawcett, 1957; London, Fawcett, 1959.
The Maricopa Trail. New York, Fawcett, 1957; London, Fawcett, 1958.
Rifles on the River. London, Collins, 1957.
Short Cut to Red River. New York, Macmillan, 1958.
Wells Fargo, Danger Station (juvenile). Racine, Wisconsin, Whitman, 1958.
The Leaden Cache. London, Collins, 1958.
Above the Palo Duro. New York, Fawcett, 1959.
Cheyenne War Cry. New York, Avon, 1959.
Connelly's Expedition. London, Collins, 1959.
A Time for Violence. New York, Macmillan, 1960; London, Collins, 1961.
Have Gun, Will Travel. New York, Dell, 1960.
Bonanza. New York, Popular Library, 1960; London, Jenkins, 1963.
Ferguson's Ferry. New York, Avon, 1962.

Other

The Linecasting Operator-Machinist. Pittsburgh, Stockton, 1958.
The Texan-Santa Fé Pioneers. Norman, University of Oklahoma Press, 1958.
Pedro Vial and the Roads to Santa Fe, with Abraham P. Nasatir. Norman, University of Oklahoma Press, 1967.
Wells Fargo. New York, Clarkson N. Potter, 1968.

*   *   *

Noel M. Loomis wrote futuristic novels in which a scientific "problem" is fused to the stock elements of the adventure tale. The science in his novels ranges from the probable to the possible to the completely implausible. This uneasy fusion of science and fantasy when wedded to the adventure story leads to an inevitable tension within the novel itself and certainly within the reader's capacity for "willing suspension of disbelief."

In *City of Glass* Loomis postulates the problem of three amateur astronauts who, returning to earth after a few days' absence, find themselves returning to earth of the year 800,000 AD. Civilization as we know it was destroyed in 5,000 AD; there are only a few scattered groups on earth, each of which has evolved separately so that no two are of the same species. The only real human beings left on earth are the 2500 Glassmen who live in the City of Glass and struggle to perpetuate their species, which is "being adapted by necessity and by scientific means to a silicon economy." Beset by a nitrate shortage, hostile invaders, and a plague, the City of Glass seems doomed, until Niles, the amateur astronaut, discovers a way to solve all difficulties.

The Man with Absolute Motion is an intergalactic tale in which the whole universe is threatened with disaster as a result of diminishing energy supplies. The last truly normal man on earth is discovered to have the gift of absolute motion and is thus able to locate the source of Cosmic Power. Having saved the galaxy, he marries the last normal earth woman, raises a family, and is returned to earth only to find it deserted, the human species wiped out. Fortunately, he decides to repopulate the earth, thus ensuring the survival of the human species.

—Joseph A. Quinn

LOVECRAFT, H(oward) P(hillips). American. Born in Providence, Rhode Island, 20 August 1890, and lived there for the rest of his life. Educated in local schools. Married the writer Sonia Greene in 1924 (divorced, 1929). Writer from 1908, supporting himself by ghost writing and working as a revisionist; regular contributor to *Weird Tales* from 1923. *Died 15 March 1937.*

SCIENCE-FICTION PUBLICATIONS

Short Stories

At the Mountains of Madness and Other Novels. Sauk City, Wisconsin, Arkham House, 1964; London, Gollancz, 1966.
The Colour Out of Space. New York, Lancer, 1964.
Collapsing Cosmoses. West Warwick, Rhode Island, Necronomicon Press, 1977.

OTHER PUBLICATIONS

Short Stories

The Shunned House. Athol, Massachusetts, Recluse Press, 1928.
The Battle That Ended the Century. De Land, Florida, Barlow, 1934.
The Cats of Ulthar. Cassia, Florida, Dragonfly Press, 1935.
The Shadow over Innsmouth. Everett, Pennsylvania, Visionary Press, 1936.
The Outsider and Others, edited by August Derleth and Donald Wandrei. Sauk City, Wisconsin, Arkham House, 1939.
The Weird Shadow over Innsmouth and Other Stories of the Supernatural. New York, Bartholomew House, 1944.
The Best Supernatural Stories of H.P. Lovecraft, edited by August Derleth. Cleveland, World, 1945; revised edition, as *The Dunwich Horror and Others,* Sauk City, Wisconsin, Arkham House, 1963.
The Dunwich Horror. New York, Bartholomew House, 1945.
The Dunwich Horror and Other Weird Tales. New York, Editions for the Armed Services, 1945.
The Lurking Fear and Other Stories. New York, Avon, 1947; as *Cry Horror!,* 1958.
The Haunter of the Dark and Other Tales of Horror. London, Gollancz, 1951.
The Case of Charles Dexter Ward. London, Gollancz, 1952.
The Curse of Yig. Sauk City, Wisconsin, Arkham House, 1953.
Dream-Quest of Unknown Kadath. Buffalo, Shroud, 1955.
The Survivor and Others, with August Derleth. Sauk City, Wisconsin, Arkham House, 1957.
The Lurking Fear and Other Stories (not same as 1947 book). London, Panther, 1964.
Dagon and Other Macabre Tales, edited by August Derleth. Sauk City, Wisconsin, Arkham House, 1965; London, Gollancz, 1967.
The Dark Brotherhood and Other Pieces, with others, edited by August Derleth. Sauk City, Wisconsin, Arkham House, 1966.
3 Tales of Horror. Sauk City, Wisconsin, Arkham House, 1967.
The Shadow Out of Time and Other Tales of Horror, with August Derleth. London, Gollancz, 1968.
Ex Oblivione. Glendale, California, Squires, 1969.
The Tomb and Other Tales. London, Panther, 1969; New York, Ballantine, 1973.
The Horror in the Museum and Other Revisions (ghost writing), edited by August Derleth. Sauk City, Wisconsin, Arkham House, 1970; abridged edition, London, Panther, 1975.
Nyarlathotep. Glendale, California, Squires, 1970.
The Shuttered Room and Other Tales of Horror. London, Panther, 1970.
What the Moon Brings. Glendale, California, Squires, 1970.
The Doom That Came to Sarnath, edited by Lin Carter. New York, Ballantine, 1971.
The Lurking Fear and Other Stories (not same as 1947 and 1964 books). New York, Beagle, 1971.
The Watchers Out of Time and Others, with August Derleth. Sauk City, Wisconsin, Arkham House, 1974.
The Horror in the Burying Ground and Other Tales. London, Panther, 1975.

Herbert West Reanimator. West Warwick, Rhode Island, Necronomicon Press, 1977.

Verse

H.P.L. Privately printed, 1937.
Fungi from Yuggoth. N.p., Evans, 1941.
Collected Poems. Sauk City, Wisconsin, Arkham House, 1963; abridged edition, as *Fungi from Yuggoth and Other Poems,* New York, Ballantine, 1971.
A Winter Wish and Other Poems, edited by T. Collins. Browns Mills, New Jersey, Whispers Press, 1977.

Other

The Materialist Today. Privately printed, 1926.
Further Criticism of Poetry. Louisville, Fetter, 1932.
Looking Backward. Haverhill, Massachusetts, C.W. Smith, 1935.
History and Chronology of the Necronomicon. Oakman, Alabama, Rebel Press, 1936.
The Notes and Commonplace Book, edited by R.H. Barlow. Lakeport, California, Futile Press, 1938.
Beyond the Wall of Sleep, edited by August Derleth and Donald Wandrei. Sauk City, Wisconsin, Arkham House, 1943.
Marginalia, edited by August Derleth and Donald Wandrei. Sauk City, Wisconsin, Arkham House, 1944.
Supernatural Horror in Literature. New York, Abramson, 1945.
Something about Cats and Other Pieces, edited by August Derleth. Sauk City, Wisconsin, Arkham House, 1949.
The Lovecraft Collector's Library, edited by George T. Wetzel. Tonowanda, New York, SSR, 5 vols., 1952-55.
The Shuttered Room and Other Pieces, with others, edited by August Derleth. Sauk City, Wisconsin, Arkham House, 1959.
Dreams and Fancies. Sauk City, Wisconsin, Arkham House, 1962.
Autobiography: Some Notes on a Nonentity. Sauk City, Wisconsin, Arkham House, and London, Villiers, 1963.
Selected Letters 1911-1931, edited by August Derleth and Donald Wandrei. Sauk City, Wisconsin, Arkham House, 5 vols., 1965-76.
Hail, Klarkash-Ton! Glendale, California, Squires, 1971.
Ec'h-Pi-El Speaks: An Autobiographical Sketch. Saddle River, New Jersey, Gerry de la Ree, 1972.
Medusa: A Portrait. New York, Oliphant Press, 1975.
The Occult Lovecraft. Saddle River, New Jersey, Gerry de la Ree, 1975.
Lovecraft at Last. Arlington, Virginia, Carrollton, 1975.
The Conservative Complete 1915-1923. West Warwick, Rhode Island, Necronomicon Press, 1976.
To Quebec and the Stars, edited by L. Sprague de Camp. West Kingston, Rhode Island, Grant, 1976.
Writings in the United Amateur 1915-1925. West Warwick, Rhode Island, Necronomicon Press, 1976.
Memoirs of an Inconsequential Scribbler. West Warwick, Rhode Island, Necronomicon Press, 1977.
A Winter Wish, edited by T. Collins. Chapel Hill, North Carolina, Whispers Press, 1977.
Writings in the Tryout. West Warwick, Rhode Island, Necronomicon Press, 1977.

Editor, *The Poetical Works of Jonathan E. Hoag.* Privately printed, 1923.
Editor, *White Fire,* by John Ravenor Bullen. Athol, Massachusetts, Recluse Press, 1927.
Editor, *Thoughts and Pictures,* by Eugene B. Kuntz. Haverhill, Massachusetts, Lovecraft and Smith, 1932.

*

Bibliography: *The New H.P. Lovecraft Bibliography* by Jack L. Chalker, Baltimore, Mirage Press, 1962; revised edition, with Mark Owings, as *The Revised H.P. Lovecraft Bibliography,* 1973.

*   *   *

That horror stories are externalized psychology is a commonplace of literary criticism, but readings based on sex and aggression (the two themes literary critics have tended to pick up from Freudian psychology) do not quite fit H.P. Lovecraft. Lovecraft himself warns readers away from interpretations of his work based on the fear of retribution for specific acts or impulses; his horrors are (as he says again and again) "cosmic," he declares the worst human fears to be displacement in space and time (as in "The Shadow Out of Time"), he speaks of "the maddening rigidity of cosmic law," he creates a non-fantastic and materialistic fictional world—i.e. science fiction—all implying a concern with the conditions of being, not with particular acts or situations. When the conditions of existence are themselves fearful, when such basic ontological categories as space and time break down (as does the geometry of space in so many stories, for example "The Call of Cthulhu"), we are dealing with what the psychiatrist R.D. Laing calls "ontological insecurity." If one fears that one doesn't exist securely, or that one is made of "bad stuff," any contact with another becomes potentially catastrophic. Everyone shares, to some degree, doubts about the psychological solidity or reliability of the self and the possibly devastating effects of others on that self. The extreme form of such fears is schizophrenia.

Lovecraft, although certainly not schizophrenic, did, according to L. Sprague de Camp, have a lifelong sense of marked isolation from others, an intense emotional dependency on things and not people, and the kind of over-possessive bringing up which makes it reasonable to expect that such issues would appear in his work. They do—strongly enough to make him an innovator in weird fiction—for they take precedence over either the beastliness of aggression (embodied, for example, in werewolves) or the lethal possibilities of sexual abandon (e.g., the figure of the vampire), both of which figure largely in 19th-century supernatural fiction. Sex and aggression presuppose a self existing securely enough to have desires and a relatively non-threatening (or at least limited) other towards whom such desires can be directed. Neither an unproblematic sense of self nor a non-catastrophic other exists in Lovecraft's work. In his early Dunsanian fiction he can frolic—but with ghouls!—as in the charming (but, alas, never rewritten or polished) *Dream-Quest of Unknown Kadath* or write pleasing, optimistic fantasies like "The Strange High House in the Mist"; but much of his earlier and most of his later fiction is preoccupied with the foreseen, yet unavoidable, engulfment of a passive, victimized self. If the narrator is a lucky spectator who escapes with his life, or even sanity, intact, his peace of mind has been shattered forever. The real point of these stories is revelation—if the engulfment does not happen, *it can*—and this revelation becomes the central truth of a universe thus rendered uninhabitable. The cannibalistic other takes several forms, but the commonest, strongest image, and the one readers seem to remember best is the shapeless, monstrous, indescribable "entity" (a favorite word of Lovecraft's) whose most terrifying characteristic is its structurelessness ("The Unnameable," "The Call of Cthulhu," "Dagon," "The Dunwich Horror"). The obsession with psychic cannibalism (expressed as physical in one of the flatter stories, "The Picture in the House,") and the insistence on the indescribableness of the threat seem to point to experience so personally archaic it is felt as pre-verbal, as does Lovecraft's characteristic straining after adjectives. In one of his best tales, "The Colour Out of Space," the threat is most abstract, its cannibalism is reported third-hand (through *two* narrators) and the relatively low-keyed, realistic setting gets most of the author's attention.

In only two stories does Lovecraft focus fully on the alternative to engulfment: loneliness. Selves exist and survive in both tales; they even—after a fashion—blossom into initiative. But both are figures that appear in other stories *as monsters*: in the poetically melancholy "The Outsider" a ghoulish walking corpse, and in the very interesting end of *The Weird Shadow over Innsmouth* a degenerate animal/monster. Both stories suggest that the menace is the narrator or something in the narrator, a suggestion not only psychologically truer than the image of the engulfing other that Lovecraft uses elsewhere, but one dramatically more interesting.

The view that human relations exist only as engulfment is a serious limitation on a narrative artist. Towards the end of his life Lovecraft seems to have been unhappily aware of this; unfortunately he also underrated his own work and died before it began to be popular. His originality and his undoubted talent (the eerily parodic autobiography of "The Outsider," details like the "gelatinous" voice in "Randolph Carter," or "a warmth that may have been sardonic" of *Innsmouth*) are best at their quietest, worst in their bravely direct but often inadequate attacks on a theme that requires (at the very least) poetic genius. The very rarity of literary treatments of Lovecraft's main theme gives his work added interest, however, and his work will probably always appeal to readers who find his theme compelling. If he had not died prematurely, he might have moved beyond the kind of horror story that says "This is what it feels like" to the kind that adds "and this is what is really happening." The latter moves into tragedy and implied social criticism (as does, for example, Shirley Jackson's *The Haunting of Hill House*). In *Supernatural Horror in Literature* Lovecraft concludes "the spectral in literature. . .is. . .a narrow though essential branch of human expression," a comment that might well describe his work: narrow, not appealing to wide tastes and even considerably flawed, yet authentic, and by those who find it congenial, securely loved.

—Joanna Russ

LOWNDES, Robert A(ugustine) W(ard). Also writes as Arthur Cooke; S.D. Gottesman; Carol Grey; Carl Groener; Mallory Kent; Paul Dennis Lavond; John MacDougal; Wilfred Owen Morley; Richard Morrison; Robert Morrison; Michael Sherman; Peter Michael Sherman; Lawrence Woods. American. Born in Bridgeport, Connecticut, 4 September 1916. Educated at Darien High School, Connecticut; Stamford Community College, Connecticut, 1936. Married Dorothy Sedor Rogalin in 1948 (divorced, 1974); one stepson. Worked for the Civilian Conservation Corps, 1934, 1936-37, 1939; assistant on a squab farm; salesman; porter, Greenwich Hospital Association, Connecticut, 1937-38; literary agent, Fantastory Sales Service, 1940-42; Editor, *Future Fiction,* 1940-42, and *Science Fiction Quarterly,* 1940-42, 1951-58; Editorial Director, Columbia magazines, 1942; Editor, *Future Science Fiction,* 1950-60, *Dynamic Science Fiction,* 1952-54, and *Science Fiction Stories,* 1954-60; Editor, Avalon science-fiction series, Thomas Bouregy, 1955-67; Editor, *Famous Science Fiction,* 1960-69, *Magazine of Horror,* 1962-71, *Startling Mystery Stories,* 1966-71, *Weird Terror Tales,* 1969-70, and *Bizarre Fantasy Fiction,* 1970-71; Associate Editor, 1971-77, and Managing Editor, 1977-78, *Sexology* and *Luz.* Since 1978, Production Chief, *Luz,* and Production Associate, *Radio Electronics.* Editor, Airmont Classics. Co-Founder, Vanguard Amateur Press Association. Guest of Honor, Lunacon, 1969, and Boskone, 1973. Address: 717 Willow Avenue, Hoboken, New Jersey 07030, U.S.A.

SCIENCE-FICTION PUBLICATIONS

Novels

Mystery of the Third Mine (juvenile). Philadelphia, Winston, 1953.
The Duplicated Man, with James Blish. New York, Avalon, 1959.
The Puzzle Planet. New York, Ace, 1961.
Believers' World. New York, Avalon, 1961.

Uncollected Short Stories

"The Outpost at Altart," in *Super Science* (Kokomo, Indiana), November 1940.
"A Green Cloud Came," in *Comet* (Springfield, Massachusetts), January 1941.
"The Psychological Regulator" (as Arthur Cooke, with others), in *Comet* (Springfield, Massachusetts), March 1941.
"The Martians Are Coming," in *Cosmos* (New York), March 1941.
"Black Flames" (as Lawrence Woods, with Donald A. Wollheim) and "The Other," in *Stirring Science* (New York), April 1941.
"The Grey One," in *Stirring Science* (New York), June 1941.

"The Colossus of Maia" (as Lawrence Woods, with Donald A. Wollheim), in *Cosmos* (New York), July 1941.
"Lure of the Lily," in *Uncanny Tales* (Toronto), January 1942.
"Passage to Sharanee" (as Carol Grey), in *Future* (New York), April 1942.
"The Castle on Outerplanet" (as S.D. Gottesman, with Frederik Pohl and Cyril Kornbluth), in *Future* (New York), October 1942.
"The Deliverers" (as Richard Morrison), in *Science Fiction Quarterly* (Holyoke, Massachusetts), Winter 1942.
"The Leapers" (as Carol Grey), in *Future* (New York), December 1942.
"Chaos, Co-ordinated" (as John MacDougal, with James Blish), in *Astounding* (New York), October 1946.
"Dead on Arrival" (as Robert Morrison), in *Amazing* (New York), August 1948.
"The Troubadour" (as Peter Michael Sherman), in *Future* (New York), September 1951.
"Intervention" (as Michael Sherman), in *Science Fiction Quarterly* (Holyoke, Massachusetts), February 1952.
"A Matter of Faith" (as Michael Sherman), in *Space* (New York), September 1952.
"Highway," in *Looking Forward,* edited by Milton Lesser. New York, Beechhurst Press, 1953; London, Cassell, 1955.
"The Inheritors," with John B. Michel, in *Terror in the Modern Vein,* edited by Donald A. Wollheim. New York, Hanover House, 1955.
"Object Lesson" (as Carl Groener), in *Future* (New York), August 1958.
"The Abyss," in *The History of the Science Fiction Magazines 2,* edited by Michael Ashley. London, New English Library, 1975.

Uncollected Short Stories as Paul Dennis Lavond

"The Doll Master," in *Stirring Science* (New York), April 1941.
"Exiles of New Planet," with Cyril Kornbluth, in *Astonishing* (Chicago), April 1941.
"Something from Beyond," with Frederik Pohl and J.H. Dockweiler, in *Future* (New York), December 1941.
"Einstein's Planetoid," with Frederik Pohl and Cyril Kornbluth, in *Science Fiction Quarterly* (Holyoke, Massachusetts), Spring 1942.

Uncollected Short Stories as Wilfred Owen Morley

"A Matter of Philosophy," in *Science Fiction* (Holyoke, Massachusetts), September 1941.
"My Lady of the Emerald," in *Astonishing* (Chicago), November 1941.
"No Star Shall Fall," in *Future* (New York), December 1941.
"The Long Wall," in *Stirring Science* (New York), March 1942.
"The Lemmings," in *Super Science* (Kokomo, Indiana), May 1942.
"A Message for Jean," in *Future* (New York), June 1942.
"The Slim People," in *Future* (New York), August 1942.
"Highway," in *Science Fiction Quarterly* (Holyoke, Massachusetts), Fall 1942.
"Does Not Imply," in *Future* (New York), February 1943.
"Dhactwhul—Remember?," with Jacques DeForest Erman, in *Super Science* (Kokomo, Indiana), April 1949.

Uncollected Short Stories as Mallory Kent

"Quarry," in *Future* (New York), December 1941.
"The Peacemakers," in *Future* (New York), August 1942.
"The Collector," in *Future* (New York), October 1942.

OTHER PUBLICATIONS

Other

"Why 'Famous'?," "Science Fiction as Instruction [Propaganda, Delight]," "Why Bother with Criticism?," and "The Borders of 'Science Fiction,' " in *Famous Science Fiction 1-9* (New York), Winter 1966-67 to Spring 1969.
Three Faces of Science Fiction. Boston, NESFA Press, 1973.

Introduction to *The Casebook of Jules de Grandin*. New York, Popular Library, 1976.

Editor, *The Best of James Blish*. New York, Ballantine, 1979.

Robert A.W. Lowndes comments:

Although I was an active member of the marxist-oriented Futurian Society of New York (1938-45), calling for social and political relevance in science fiction, when it came down to writing stories I found that I had no interest whatsoever in such relevance. I only wanted to tell the kind of story I actually wanted to read — full of wonder or terror or both. Whether I succeeded, or to what extent I succeeded, is for others to say.

To my mind, the best fantasy and science fiction is imbued with the author's feeling about the human condition, and may or may not contain what amounts to some sort of message. If there is one, it is not something consciously striven for; I've read thousands of stories written to preach a sermon, and however effective the sermon itself may have been, the stories have nearly all suffered from the approach. Fiction and homily writing are two different forms, though each may be done with a high quality of art; but mixing them produces an abortion.

*   *   *

Robert A.W. Lowndes is known mainly as an editor. He is, however, also a science fiction writer of considerable talent, particularly in the creation and description of alien worlds. This talent is best seen in *Believers' World*. Lowndes uses the now-familiar plot of exiles from Earth who have forgotten that their origin was on Earth, and whose religious beliefs have hardened into mindless fragments of ceremony. An investigator from Earth visits these exiles, now living on a "believers' world" locked into elaborate religious ceremonies. He becomes involved in a formula of action, adventure, and violence. But Lowndes effectively describes the Arabian Nights atmosphere of this world: "magic. That was the keynote of everything here—the appearance of magic." Even small everyday events seem magical: "you touched a faucet, or bent over a fountain, or stepped under a shower, and pale yellow water issued forth." Thus Lowndes creates a world that exemplifies Arthur C. Clarke's generalization that advanced technology is indistinguishable from magic.

Everything that happens on the believers' world is supposed by the inhabitants to be the will of "Ein" (Einstein, though they don't remember this). In this topsy-turvey world not only has religion ossified but science has merged with it. *The Puzzle Planet* is about a world that is similar in that our common-sense assumptions are upside down; and once again Lowndes's descriptive powers are impressive.

Even *Mystery of the Third Mine*, a juvenile, is well worth reading. Lowndes makes asteroid mining seem real, creating a historical parallel to the gold rush of 1848. The hero, Peter, is in a mining partnership with his father. The villains use the cover of the Asteroid Miners Association to invalidate Peter's claims and to try to seize the "third mine," platinum, deep in the asteroid. There is a good science-fun gimmick on the asteroid: low gravity baseball with a magnetized ball and players throwing bits of metal to propel themselves through space. Although the young hero is close to being a pastiche of a Heinlein juvenile, Lowndes's magical atmosphere is once again his own.

Lowndes's short stories are quite distinct from his novels and show the influence of Clark Ashton Smith and Lovecraft. One of his best is "The Abyss," which begins with this hook sentence: "We took Graf Norden's body out into the November night, under the stars that burned with a brightness terrible to behold, and drove madly, wildly up the mountain road." Beings in another dimension (or no dimension) send agents to hypnotize humans and drain the fluids from their bodies. The description of these alien beings—with long filaments that restlessly try to break into our dimension from their own—is as well done as anything in Lovecraft, and the economy of the story is beyond Lovecraft. Economy, atmosphere, description: these are Lowndes's strongest points as a writer.

—Curtis C. Smith

LUPOFF, Richard A(llen). American. Born in Brooklyn, New York, 21 February 1935. Educated at the University of Miami, Coral Gables, B.A. 1956. Served in the Adjutant General's Corps of the United States Army, 1956-58: First Lieutenant. Married Patricia Enid Loring in 1958; two sons and one daughter. Technical writer, Sperry Univac, New York, 1958-63; Editor, Canaveral Press, New York, 1962-70; film producer, IBM, New York City and Poughkeepsie, New York, 1963-70; Editor, *Xero* fan magazine, 1963; West Coast Editor, *Crawdaddy,* 1970-71, and *Changes,* 1971-72; Editor, *Organ,* 1972; book editor, *Algol,* 1963-79. Recipient: Hugo Award, for editing, 1963. Agent: Henry Morrison Inc., 58 West 10th Street, New York, New York 10010. Address: 3208 Claremont Avenue, Berkeley, California 94705, U.S.A.

SCIENCE-FICTION PUBLICATIONS

Novels

One Million Centuries. New York, Lancer, 1967.
Sacred Locomotive Flies. New York, Beagle, 1971.
Into the Aether. New York, Dell, 1974.
The Crack in the Sky. New York, Dell, 1976; as *Fool's Hill,* London, Sphere, 1978.
Lisa Kane (juvenile). Indianapolis, Bobbs Merrill, 1976.
Sandworld. New York, Berkley, 1976.
The Triune Man. New York, Berkley, 1976; London, Dobson, 1979.
Sword of the Demon. New York, Harper, 1977.
Space War Blues. New York, Dell, 1978; London, Sphere, 1979.
The Return of Skull-Face, with Robert E. Howard. West Linn, Oregon, Fax, 1978.
Circumpolar. New York, Dell, 1980.
Lovecraft's Book. New York, Simon and Schuster, 1980.

Short Stories

Nebogipfel at the End of Time. Columbia, Pennsylvania, Underwood/Miller, 1979.
The Ova Hamlet Papers. San Francisco, Pennyfarthing Press, 1980.

OTHER PUBLICATIONS

Other

Edgar Rice Burroughs, Master of Adventure. New York, Canaveral Press, 1965; revised edition, New York, Ace, 1968.
"Science Fiction Hawks and Doves," in *Ramparts* (Berkeley, California), February 1972.
"You Can't Say That!," in *Science-Fiction Review* (Portland, Oregon), February 1975.
Barsoom: Edgar Rice Burroughs and the Martian Vision. Baltimore, Mirage Press, 1976.
"A Legend in Poughkeepsie," in *Locus* (New York), March 1977.
Buck Rogers in the Twenty Fifth Century. New York, Dell, 1978.
"A Bulletin from the Ministry of Truth," in *Pretentious SF Quarterly,* Spring 1978.
"The Early Philip K. Dick," in *Algol* (New York), May 1979.

Editor, *The Reader's Guide to Barsoom and Amtor*. Privately printed, 1963.
Editor, with Don Thompson, *All in Color for a Dime*. New Rochelle, New York, Arlington House, 1970.
Editor, with Don Thompson, *The Comic-Book Book*. New Rochelle, New York, Arlington House, 1974.
Editor, *Cosmos,* by John W. Campbell, Jr. San Francisco, Pennyfarthing Press, 1979.
Editor, *What If? Stories That Should Have Won the Hugo*. New York, Pocket Books, 1980.

Richard A. Lupoff comments:
It's very difficult for me to "make a statement" about my own

works. It seems to me that this is a task for critics. The artist is of necessity so close to his or her own work — in fact, more than close to it: is surrounded by and immersed in it — that a critical perspective is impossible.

I'll tell you what I'm *trying* to do, and that is, simply, to write good stories. The fact that most of mine are science-fiction or fantasy stories is, if not irrelevant, then surely of secondary importance at best. I have spent the past dozen years trying to learn to write good stories. I think I've made some progress but I am by no means satisfied with my output, either qualitatively or quantitively. I also feel (most of the time, these days) that I have finally got over the ridge, from tyro to professional. (In my less sanguine moments I don't think I'm over that ridge yet, and may never get over it.)

But I'm still trying hard, and with reasonable expectations of longevity, and if I don't succumb to despair, I should have 30 to 40 more years of productivity ahead of me. I intend to keep on trying hard.

*   *   *

Richard A. Lupoff first achieved recognition as a fan critic. His amateur magazine *Xero* is considered to be the pioneer magazine of comic-book fandom, the first sub-culture to splinter from SF fandom. Lupoff's career as a writer is an effort to determine a postmodern SF writer's relations with his literature's past. Lupoff tends towards either total acceptance or total rejection of that past; thus his first novel, *One Million Centuries,* attempts to preserve Burroughsian panache in the midst of the New Wave, while *Space War Blues* totally rejects that past in favour of stylistic tricks and decadent space opera, with planets of white racists battling black racists for control of the universe. While *Space War Blues* is Lupoff's most acclaimed novel (due, in large measure, to relentless promotion of the original novella by Harlan Ellison), it is not his most important, as it is clearly a product of the concerns of the 1960's and dates very badly in its thematic content.

Lupoff's best novels are those that do not concern themselves with the nature of mainstream science fiction. Only three of his works fulfil this criterion—the dystopia *The Crack in the Sky,* the haunting chinoiserie *Sword of the Demon,* and *Lisa Kane,* published as a juvenile but in truth a thoroughly adult work about the nature of the macabre, and Lupoff's finest novel.

But Lupoff only intermittently achieves excellence. Most of his work is pastiche, ranging from the van Vogtian influences in *Triune Man,* to the parody of 19th-century scientific romances in *Into the Aether,* and *The Return of Skull-Face,* a completion of a Robert E. Howard fragment. These pastiches succeed to the extent that they preserve the flavor of the past without copying its style; *The Return of Skull-Face* shows that one cannot effectively copy Howard, and *Into the Aether,* conceived as a satire, is actually a combination of unfunny farce and irrelevant anachronisms. (Lupoff's other attempt at parody, the short stories published in *Fantastic* as by "Ova Hamlet," are important both for being the only parodies of current authors such as Barry Malzberg and for conclusively showing that most modern writers do not have styles that can be copied.)

Richard Lupoff is a protean writer. He does not belong to any particular school of SF, and was one of the few writers that belonged to the "New Wave" and the "Old Wave" at the same time. Because he has not developed a distinctive style, he has not earned the importance he deserves. If he would continue to develop the trenchant awareness of his art that was shown in *Lisa Kane* and *The Crack in the Sky,* his reputation as one of the most important heirs of the Golden and Silver ages would be secure.

—Martin Morse Wooster

LYMINGTON, John. Pseudonym for John Newton Chance; also writes as J. Drummond; David C. Newton. British. Born in London in 1911. Educated at Streatham Hill College and privately. Served in the Royal Air Force during World War II. Address: c/o Robert Hale Ltd., 45-47 Clerkenwell Green, London EC1R 0HT, England.

SCIENCE-FICTION PUBLICATIONS

Novels

Night of the Big Heat.   London, Corgi, 1959; New York, Dutton, 1960.
The Giant Stumbles.   London, Hodder and Stoughton, 1960.
The Grey Ones.   London, Hodder and Stoughton, 1960.
The Coming of the Strangers.   London, Hodder and Stoughton, 1961; New York, Manor, 1978.
A Sword above the Night.   London, Hodder and Stoughton, 1962.
The Screaming Face.   London, Hodder and Stoughton, 1963; New York, Manor, 1978.
Froomb!   London, Hodder and Stoughton, 1964; New York, Doubleday, 1966.
The Star Witches.   London, Hodder and Stoughton, 1965; New York, Manor, 1978.
The Green Drift.   London, Hodder and Stoughton, 1965.
Ten Million Years to Friday.   London, Hodder and Stoughton, 1967.
The Nowhere Place.   London, Hodder and Stoughton, 1969.
Give Daddy the Knife, Darling.   London, Hodder and Stoughton, 1969.
The Year Dot.   London, Hodder and Stoughton, 1972.
The Sleep Eaters.   London, Hodder and Stoughton, 1973; New York, Manor, 1978.
The Hole in the World.   London, Hodder and Stoughton, 1974.
A Spider in the Bath.   London, Hodder and Stoughton, 1975.
The Laxham Haunting.   London, Hodder and Stoughton, 1976.
Starseed on Gye Moor.   London, Hodder and Stoughton, 1977.
The Waking of the Stone.   London, Hodder and Stoughton, 1978.
The Grey Ones, A Sword above the Night.   New York, Manor, 1978.
A Caller from Overspace.   London, Hodder and Stoughton, 1979.
Voyage of the Eighth Mind.   London, Hodder and Stoughton, 1980.

Short Stories

The Night Spiders.   London, Corgi, 1964; New York, Doubleday, 1967.

OTHER PUBLICATIONS

Novels as John Newton Chance

Murder in Oils.   London, Gollancz, 1935.
Wheels in the Forest.   London, Gollancz, 1935.
The Devil Drives.   London, Gollancz, 1936.
Maiden Possessed.   London, Gollancz, 1937.
Rhapsody in Fear.   London, Gollancz, 1937.
Death of an Innocent.   London, Gollancz, 1938.
The Devil in Greenlands.   London, Gollancz, 1939.
The Ghost of Truth.   London, Gollancz, 1939.
Screaming Fog.   London, Macdonald, 1944; as *Death Stalks the Cobbled Square,* New York, McBride, 1946.
The Red Knight.   London, Macdonald, and New York, Macmillan, 1945.
The Eye in Darkness.   London, Macdonald, 1946.
The Knight and the Castle.   London, Macdonald, 1946.
The Black Highway.   London, Macdonald, 1947.
Coven Gibbet.   London, Macdonald, 1948.
The Brandy Pole.   London, Macdonald, 1949.
The Night of the Full Moon.   London, Macdonald, 1950.
Aunt Miranda's Murder.   London, Macdonald, and New York, Dodd Mead, 1951.
The Man in My Shoes.   London, Macdonald, 1952.

The Twopenny Box. London, Macdonald, 1952.
The Jason Affair. London, Macdonald, 1953; as *Up to Her Neck,*
New York, Popular Library, 1955.
The Randy Inheritance. London, Macdonald, 1953.
Jason and the Sleep Game. London, Macdonald, 1954.
The Jason Murders. London, Macdonald, 1954.
Jason Goes West. London, Macdonald, 1955.
The Last Seven Hours. London, Macdonald, 1956.
A Shadow Called Janet. London, Macdonald, 1956.
Dead Man's Knock. London, Hale, 1957.
The Little Crime. London, Hale, 1957.
Affair with a Rich Girl. London, Hale, 1958.
The Man with Three Witches. London, Hale, 1958.
The Fatal Fascination. London, Hale, 1959.
The Man with No Face. London, Hale, 1959.
Alarm at Black Brake. London, Hale, 1960.
Lady in a Frame. London, Hale, 1960.
Import of Evil. London, Hale, 1961.
The Night of the Settlement. London, Hale, 1961.
Triangle of Fear. London, Hale, 1962.
The Man Behind Me. London, Hale, 1963.
The Forest Affair. London, Hale, 1963.
Commission for Disaster. London, Hale, 1964.
Death under Desolate. London, Hale, 1964.
Stormlight. London, Hale, 1965.
The Affair at Dead End. London, Hale, 1966.
The Double Death. London, Hale, 1966.
The Case of the Death Computer. London, Hale, 1967.
The Case of the Fear Makers. London, Hale, 1967.
The Death Women. London, Hale, 1967.
The Hurricane Drift. London, Hale, 1967.
The Mask of Pursuit. London, Hale, 1967.
The Thug Executive. London, Hale, 1967.
Dead Man's Shoes. London, Hale, 1968.
Death of the Wild Bird. London, Hale, 1968.
Fate of the Lying Jade. London, Hale, 1968.
The Halloween Murders. London, Hale, 1968.
Mantrap. London, Hale, 1968.
The Rogue Aunt. London, Hale, 1968.
The Abel Coincidence. London, Hale, 1969.
The Ice Maidens. London, Hale, 1969.
Involvement in Austria. London, Hale, 1969.
The Killer Reaction. London, Hale, 1969.
The Killing Experiment. London, Hale, 1969.
The Mists of Treason. London, Hale, 1970.
A Ring of Liars. London, Hale, 1970.
Three Masks of Death. London, Hale, 1970.
The Mirror Train. London, Hale, 1970.
The Cat Watchers. London, Hale, 1971.
The Faces of a Bad Girl. London, Hale, 1971.
A Wreath of Bones. London, Hale, 1971.
A Bad Dream of Death. London, Hale, 1972.
Last Train to Limbo. London, Hale, 1972.
The Man with Two Heads. London, Hale, 1972.
The Dead Tale-Tellers. London, Hale, 1972.
The Farm Villains. London, Hale, 1973.
The Grab Operators. London, Hale, 1973.
The Love-Hate Relationship. London, Hale, 1973.
The Girl in the Crime Belt. London, Hale, 1974.
The Shadow of the Killer. London, Hale, 1974.
The Starfish Affair. London, Hale, 1974.
The Canterbury Killgrims. London, Hale, 1974.
Hill Fog. London, Hale, 1975.
The Devil's Edge. London, Hale, 1975.
The Monstrous Regiment. London, Hale, 1975.
The Murder Makers. London, Hale, 1976.
Return to Death Valley. London, Hale, 1976.
A Fall-Out of Thieves. London, Hale, 1976.
The Frightened Fisherman. London, Hale, 1977.
The House of the Dead Ones. London, Hale, 1977.
Motive for a Kill. London, Hale, 1977.
The Ducrow Folly. London, Hale, 1978.
End of an Iron Man. London, Hale, 1978.
A Drop of Hot Gold. London, Hale, 1978.
Thieves' Kitchen. London, Hale, 1979.

The Guilty Witness. London, Hale, 1979.
A Place Called Skull. London, Hale, 1979.
The Death Watch Ladies. London, Hale, 1980.
The Black Widow. London, Hale, 1980.
The Mayhem Madchen. London, Hale, 1980.

Novels as J. Drummond

The Essex Road Crime. London, Amalgamated Press, 1944.
The Manor House Menace. London, Amalgamated Press, 1944.
The Painted Dagger. London, Amalgamated Press, 1944.
The Riddle of the Leather Bottle. London, Amalgamated Press,
1944.
The Tragic Case of the Station Master's Legacy. London, Amal-
gamated Press, 1944.
At Sixty Miles an Hour. London, Amalgamated Press, 1945.
The House on the Hill. London, Amalgamated Press, 1945.
The Riddle of the Mummy Case. London, Amalgamated Press,
1945.
The Mystery of the Deserted Camp. London, Amalgamated
Press, 1948.
The Town of Shadows. London, Amalgamated Press, 1948.
The Case of the "Dead" Spy. London, Amalgamated Press, 1949.
The Riddle of the Receiver's Hoard. London, Amalgamated
Press, 1949.
The Secret of the Living Skeleton. London, Amalgamated Press,
1949.
The South Coast Mystery. London, Amalgamated Press, 1949.
The Case of L.A.C. Dickson. London, Amalgamated Press, 1950.
The Mystery of the Haunted Square. London, Amalgamated
Press, 1950.
The House in the Woods. London, Amalgamated Press, 1950.
The Secret of the Sixty Steps. London, Amalgamated Press, 1951.
The Case of the Man with No Name. London, Amalgamated
Press, 1951.
Hated by All! London, Amalgamated Press, 1951.
The Mystery of the Sabotaged Jet. London, Amalgamated Press,
1951.
The House on the River. London, Amalgamated Press, 1952.
The Mystery of the Five Guilty Men. London, Amalgamated
Press, 1954.
The Case of the Two-Faced Swindler. London, Amalgamated
Press, 1955.

Other as John Newton Chance

The Black Ghost (juvenile; as David C. Newton). London,
Oxford University Press, 1947.
The Dangerous Road (juvenile; as David C. Newton). London,
Oxford University Press, 1948.
*Bunst and the Brown Voice [the Bold, and the Secret Six, and the
Flying Eye]* (juvenile). London, Oxford University Press, 4
vols., 1950-53.
The Jennifer Jigsaw (juvenile), with Shirley Newton Chance.
London, Oxford University Press, 1951.
Yellow Belly (autobiography). London, Hale, 1959.
The Crimes at Rillington Place: A Novelist's Reconstruction.
London, Hodder and Stoughton, 1961.

*   *   *

A rather mysterious British author whose works fall generally in
the tradition of John Wyndham, John Lymington has received
remarkably little notice even within the science-fiction community,
perhaps because the fantastic elements of his fiction often serve as
little more than a backdrop for the main action, which characteristically centers on a small but diverse group of British citizens faced
with a common threat. Lymington's characters, his village settings,
and the structure of his novels owe as much to the tradition of the
classical detective story as to the traditions of science fiction, and
with few exceptions he does not concern himself with the social or
intellectual implications of the marvels he introduces. As an author
of suspense and horror stories, he is often startlingly effective, able
to spin an entertaining novel from a single situation, but when he
attempts more complex themes his novels tend to get out of hand.

Lymington makes use of few of the resources of the science-fiction genre; most of his novels are variations on the basic theme of alien invasion, while a couple deal with time travel and contain elements of social satire. His first SF novel, *Night of the Big Heat,* is an admirable addition to the something-is-amiss-in-the-village school of British suspense novels, though the science-fiction element—an alien civilization transmitting giant spiders into the English countryside via microwaves—is clearly secondary to the portrayal of the reactions of a group of local citizens gathered at a country inn. Spiders are one of Lymington's favorite images of horror—even though he persistently regards them as insects—and were also the featured attractions in another invasion story, "The Night Spiders." The basic formula of an unknown horror menacing a small community was repeated in *The Coming of the Strangers;* in *Sword above the Night*—perhaps the most straightforward and unadorned of Lymington's exercises in suspense—the anticipated "invasion" that provides suspense throughout the novel is dispensed with in a three-paragraph closing summary, explaining that it is merely the pre-programmed return to Earth of dead astronauts who had left from an earlier civilization thousands of years ago. This novel perhaps most clearly indicates the short shrift Lymington gives his science-fiction concepts.

Occasionally, Lymington adds other science-fiction elements to his formula—in *The Sleep Eaters* the invasion is telepathic (*The Night Spiders* also have telepathic powers), and in *The Star Witches* a mad scientist helps bring the aliens to earth. *The Star Witches* also reveals an inclination on Lymington's part to work traditional supernatural appurtenances into his science-fiction narratives: in this case a coven of witches is associated with the alien invasion. Time travel is another concept that Lymington sometimes plays with, in *The Night Spiders, Ten Million Years to Friday,* and *Froomb! Froomb!* is in some ways Lymington's most ambitious novel, and the most satirical. The title is short for "The fluid's running out of my brakes!," a fictional cartoon caption that has come to symbolize the state of world affairs in Lymington's headlong future world. Essentially the story, which somehow encompasses such diverse themes as threatened nuclear war, heaven, heat-rays, insecticide poisoning, food additives, radiation, drugs, and male impotence, concerns a man who dies and goes to heaven, only to find that it is actually a post-holocaust world brought about by an American defense experiment about to take place before he died. His efforts to return and warn the world of the experiment make up the bulk of the novel.

Lymington is not a major writer, and there is much to suggest that he does not take his science fiction seriously, but in the relatively narrow territory he has staked out for himself he provides enjoyable light reading.

—Gary K. Wolfe

LYNN, Elizabeth A. American. Born in New York City, 8 June 1946. Educated at Case Western Reserve University, Cleveland, B.A. 1967; University of Chicago (Woodrow Wilson Fellow, 1967-68), M.A. 1968. Public school teacher, Chicago, 1968-70; unit manager, St. Francis Hospital, Evanston, Illinois, 1970-72, and French Hospital, San Francisco, 1972-75; teacher in the Women's Studies Program, San Francisco State University. Address: P.O. Box 14107, San Francisco, California 94114, U.S.A.

SCIENCE-FICTION PUBLICATIONS

Novels (series: Chronicles of Tornor)

A Different Light. New York, Berkley, 1978; London, Gollancz, 1979.
Watchtower (Tornor). New York, Berkley, 1979.
The Dancers of Arun (Tornor). New York, Berkley, 1979.
The Northern Girl (Tornor). New York, Berkley, 1981.

Uncollected Short Stories

"We All Have to Go," in *Future Pastimes,* edited by Scott Edelstein. Nashville, Aurora, 1977.
"The Island," in *Fantasy and Science Fiction* (New York), November 1977.
"The Fire Man," in *Dark Sins, Dark Dreams,* edited by Barry N. Malzberg and Bill Pronzini. New York, Doubleday, 1978.
"Circus," in *Chrysalis 3,* edited by Roy Torgeson. New York, Kensington, 1978.
"Jubilee's Story," in *Millennial Women,* edited by Virginia Kidd. New York, Delacorte Press, 1978.
"The White King's Dream," in *Shadows 2,* edited by Charles L. Grant. New York, Doubleday, 1979.

* * *

Elizabeth A. Lynn is rapidly developing into one of the finest writers in the field of speculative fiction. Her greatest strength lies in her ability to focus sympathetically on a single character or a small cast of characters that are very human. Although her science-fiction stories are often presented in the trappings of space opera—faster-than-light travel, interstellar exploration, humans kidnapped by aliens—they are peopled by individuals who are clearly drawn from life. They are flawed and identifiably human, not Kimball Kennisons, or comic-book superheroes.

Several of her short stories, and the novel *A Different Light,* are linked by some common images and themes. Although interstellar travel seems taken for granted, Lynn consistently treats the concept of hyperspace, the Hype, as a place not only beyond the normal limits of space-time, but beyond reality itself. It is a source of danger to all but the strongest who attempt to pass through it. In *A Different Light,* in fact, the Hype is the cause of the apparent death of the protagonist. Jimson, an artist, has an incurable cancer, one which will limit his lifespan, if he is careful, to another 20 years. Before he dies, however, he wants to see the light of other stars, and rejoin an old friend and lover. He flees his home planet in the sure knowledge that travel in the Hype will accelerate the process of his cancer. Jimson is typical of Lynn's protagonists. Most of them work in some art form, and seem to pay for their gifts with a physical debility—such as the one-armed telepath in *The Dancers of Arun*—but it is a debility that heightens their sensitivity to others and their surroundings. Jimson is a sexual being. Like many of Lynn's characters he lives in a society not proscribed by sexual roles, and his sexuality finds expression through love for women and men. A first novel, *A Different Light* is certainly flawed, both by its somewhat episodic plot and an ending that seems drawn from other SF novels rather than from within. But the novel's sensitivity and fluid language betray a promise that is more than fulfilled in her later novels.

The Chronicles of Tornor is a true trilogy—three self-contained novels related by continuity of place, cultures, and institutions—that defies neat categorization. The trilogy concerns the way that cultures and institutions change, and succeeds because it focuses on individuals directly involved in those cultures. *Watchtower* introduces the cultures: the rigid, militaristic society of the North, and the newly developed egalitarian life of the Cheari, built on an art composed of dance and martial art. The protagonist is a vassal of the northern culture, and the novel's conflict lies in his inability to assimilate the new mores and lifestyle of the chearis. The language is crisp and precise. *The Dancers of Arun* takes place 100 years later. It centers on the almost utopian lifestyle of the Cheari, and the language of the book is appropriately softened. Kerris is a child of these people but has been raised in the North, and finds difficulty in believing in their acceptance of his maimed arm. Only through the physically loving relationship that he develops with his brother does he learn to accept himself. The trilogy is concluded with *The Northern Girl* which concerns a third culture in the South.

—Jeff Frane

MacDONALD, John D(ann). Also writes as John Wade Farrell; Peter Reed. American. Born in Sharon, Pennsylvania, 24 July 1916. Educated at the University of Pennsylvania, Philadelphia, 1934-35; Syracuse University, New York, B.S. 1938; Harvard University, Cambridge, Massachusetts, M.B.A. 1939. Served with the United States Army, Office of Strategic Services, 1940-46: Lieutenant Colonel. Married Dorothy Mary Prentiss in 1937; one son, Writer in several genres and under a number of pseudonyms for the pulps and other magazines. President, Mystery Writers of America, 1962. Recipient: Benjamin Franklin Award, for short story, 1955; Grand Prix de Littérature Policière, 1964; Mystery Writers of America Grand Master Award, 1972. Agent: Littauer and Wilkinson, 500 Fifth Avenue, New York, New York 10036. Address: 1430 Point Crisp Road, Sarasota, Florida, U.S.A.

SCIENCE-FICTION PUBLICATIONS

Novels

Wine of the Dreamers. New York, Greenberg, 1951; as *Planet of the Dreamers*, New York, Pocket Books, 1953; London, Hale, 1955.
Ballroom of the Skies. New York, Greenberg, 1952.

Short Stories

Other Times, Other Worlds. New York, Fawcett, 1978.

OTHER PUBLICATIONS

Novels

The Brass Cupcake. New York, Fawcett, 1950; London, Muller, 1955.
Judge Me Not. New York, Fawcett, 1951; London, Muller, 1964.
Murder for the Bride. New York, Fawcett, 1951; London, Fawcett, 1954.
Weep for Me. New York, Fawcett, 1951; London, Muller, 1964.
The Damned. New York, Fawcett, 1952; London, Muller, 1964.
Dead Low Tide. New York, Fawcett, 1953; London, Hale, 1976.
The Neon Jungle. New York, Fawcett, 1953; London, Fawcett, 1954.
Cancel All Our Vows. New York, Appleton Century Crofts, 1953; London, Hale, 1955.
Contrary Pleasure. New York, Appleton Century Crofts, 1954; London, Hale, 1955.
All These Condemned. New York, Fawcett, 1954.
Area of Suspicion. New York, Dell, 1954; London, Hale, 1956; revised edition, New York, Fawcett, 1961.
A Bullet for Cinderella. New York, Dell, 1955; London, Hale, 1960; as *On the Make*, New York, Dell, 1960.
Cry Hard, Cry Fast. New York, Popular Library, 1955; London, Hale, 1969.
April Evil. New York, Dell, 1956; London, Hale, 1957.
Border Town Girl (novelets). New York, Popular Library, 1956; as *Five Star Fugitive*, London, Hale, 1970.
Murder in the Wind. New York, Dell, 1956; as *Hurricane,* London, Hale, 1957.
You Live Once. New York, Popular Library, 1956; London, Hale, 1976; as *You Kill Me,* New York, Fawcett, 1961.
Death Trap. New York, Dell, 1957; London, Hale, 1958.
The Empty Trap. New York, Popular Library, 1957; London Magnum, 1980.
The Price of Murder. New York, Dell, 1957; London, Hale, 1958.
A Man of Affairs. New York, Dell, 1957; London, Hale, 1959.
Clemmie. New York, Fawcett, 1958.
The Executioners. New York, Simon and Schuster, 1958; London, Hale, 1959; as *Cape Fear*, New York, Fawcett, 1962.
Soft Touch. New York, Dell, 1958; London, Hale, 1960; as *Man-Trap*, London, Pan 1961.
The Deceivers. New York, Fawcett, 1958; London, Hale, 1968.
The Beach Girls. New York, Fawcett, 1959; London, Muller, 1964.
The Crossroads. New York, Simon and Schuster, 1959; London, Hale, 1961.
Deadly Welcome. New York, Dell, 1959; London, Hale, 1961.
Please Write for Details. New York, Simon and Schuster, 1959.
The End of the Night. New York, Simon and Schuster, 1960; London, Hale, 1964.
The Only Girl in the Game. New York, Fawcett, 1960; London, Hale, 1962.
Slam the Big Door. New York, Fawcett, 1960; London, Hale, 1961.
One Monday We Killed Them All. New York, Fawcett, 1961; London, Hale, 1963.
Where Is Janice Gantry? New York, Fawcett, 1961; London, Hale, 1963.
A Flash of Green. New York, Simon and Schuster, 1962; London, Hale, 1971.
The Girl, The Gold Watch, and Everything. New York, Fawcett, 1962; London, Coronet, 1968.
A Key to the Suite. New York, Fawcett, 1962; London, Hale, 1968.
The Drowner. New York, Fawcett, 1963; London, Hale, 1964.
On the Run. New York, Fawcett, 1963; London, Hale, 1965.
I Could Go On Singing (novelization of screenplay). New York, Fawcett, 1963; London, Hale, 1964.
The Deep Blue Goodby. New York, Fawcett, 1964; London, Hale, 1965.
Nightmare in Pink. New York, Fawcett, 1964; London, Hale, 1966.
A Purple Place for Dying. New York, Fawcett, 1964; London, Hale, 1966.
The Quick Red Fox. New York, Fawcett, 1964; London, Hale, 1966.
A Deadly Shade of Gold. New York, Fawcett, 1965; London, Hale, 1967.
Bright Orange for the Shroud. New York, Fawcett, 1965; London, Hale, 1967.
Darker Than Amber. New York, Fawcett, 1966; London, Hale, 1968.
One Fearful Yellow Eye. New York, Fawcett, 1966; London, Hale, 1968.
The Last One Left. New York, Doubleday, 1967; London, Hale, 1968.
Pale Gray for Guilt. New York, Fawcett, 1968; London, Hale, 1969.
The Girl in the Plain Brown Wrapper. New York, Fawcett, 1968; London, Hale, 1969.
Dress Her in Indigo. New York, Fawcett, 1969; London, Hale, 1971.
The Long Lavender Look. New York, Fawcett, 1970; London, Hale, 1972.
A Tan and Sandy Silence. New York, Fawcett, 1972; London, Hale, 1973.
The Scarlet Ruse. New York, Fawcett, 1973; London, Hale, 1975.
The Turquoise Lament. Philadelphia, Lippincott, 1973; London, Hale, 1975.
The Dreadful Lemon Sky. Philadelphia, Lippincott, 1975; London, Hale, 1976.
Condominium. Philadelphia, Lippincott, and London, Hale, 1977.
The Empty Copper Sea. Philadelphia, Lippincott, 1978; London, Hale, 1979.
The Green Ripper. Philadelphia, Lippincott, 1979; London, Hale, 1980.

Short Stories

End of the Tiger and Other Stories. New York, Fawcett, 1966; London, Hale, 1967.
Seven. New York, Fawcett, 1971; London, Hale, 1974.

Other

The House Guests. New York, Doubleday, 1965; London, Hale, 1966.
No Deadly Drug. New York, Doubleday 1968.

Editor, *The Lethal Sex.* New York, Dell, 1959; London, Collins, 1962.

*

Manuscript Collection: University of Florida Library, Gainesville.

* * *

John D. MacDonald's prolific output of thrillers has not, in the end, prevented the acknowledgment that he is one of America's best novelists. He contributed nearly 50 short stories, under various names, and two novels to the SF genre in the late 1940's and early 1950's before turning almost exclusively to crime fiction, except for three marginal entries, "The Legend of Joe Lee" (a ghost story), "The Annex" (speculative fiction), and *The Girl, The Gold Watch and Everything* (comedy thriller with a gimmick, anticipated in the excellent 1950 story, "Half-Past Eternity," that freezes everyone in time, except the user).

The title of the collection of MacDonald's SF short stories, *Other Times, Other Worlds,* neatly indicates his major themes: time travel, aliens among us or manipulating us, juxtaposition of our culture with others. These stories often communicate a strong sense of the value of the honestly striving individual; however, a good many are horror stories in which this value is arbitrarily denied. What is a "Game for Blondes" from the future who come fishing for a man is a nightmare to him, as is the "Spectator Sport" of the future, to which the unsuspecting visitor from our times is condemned, well-meaningly bound forever to a mechanical fantasy. In "Labor Supply" the best of humans are enslaved by gnomes, through their dreams; in "A Child Is Crying" the gift of seeing the future is a cause of horror to its possessor and those who wish to exploit it.

The two early novels pick with heavy crowbars under the slab of sanity that holds down the incipient paranoia of their readers. Aliens really do take over our minds, they tell us, and for no good purpose. *Wine of the Dreamers* posits a planet on which the principal adult occupation is taking possession of us, playing with us in the belief that we are only creatures of fancy. The irresponsible Dreamers, who have similar remote access to two other planets, all three of which were settled by their ancestors, have forgotten their ordained function, yet they need our help, as only one of their inbred, dwindling number sees. Although MacDonald grossly oversimplifies for the sake of a suspenseful narrative, particularly the closed environment of the Dreamers, this remains a good tightly plotted novel which still reads well. It ends optimistically and is satisfying on its own terms, but *Ballroom of the Skies* concludes uneasily and is a more disturbing novel, because we must be unable to share in its hero's feelings of quiet exultation in the last paragraphs, to the extent that we perceive that he has only succeeded in moving from a smaller to a greater paranoia. A set-up in which ends justify means will never satisfy all readers; here, the given conditions are remarkably distasteful. Our planet is being kept in a state of perpetual warfare, peacemakers being killed, their purposes twisted, in order to preserve Earth as a breeding ground for superhuman leaders who will keep the galactic civilization from stagnating and maintain it in a state of readiness in case of a notional invasion from another galaxy. The hero is one of the world's leading peacemakers, a journalist whose investigation of the fantastic crimes which break up secret negotiations between the world's power blocks leads to his recruitment as an agent of the very powers he dedicates his life to oppose. To keep the reader in sympathy with such a hero would be a fearsome challenge for any writer and, although MacDonald does his best to make him more admirably heroic (using the well-honoured trick of timely praise from a girl friend) as he grows beyond the human norm, the attempt fails. In reality, MacDonald's hero, Dake Lorin, who is excellent in his Lone Wolf phase, would have recognized the speciousness of the conditions he is made, humbly, to accept. The novel is, nevertheless, a gripping narrative and, in the best tradition of such works, honestly presents the lonely dilemma of the superman who can find true friendship only with others of his kind.

Besides the titles already mentioned, "Ring Around the Redhead," "Shadow on the Sand," "The Miniature," "The Big Contest," "Susceptibility," "Common Denominator," and "Trojan Horse Laugh" should be listed as fine short stories by a writer who could

clearly have been a major figure in the genre had he not found crime more rewarding. It should be noted that MacDonald has often used mystery fiction also to be prophetically critical of the suicidal tendencies of our society, being one of those early concerned with threats to our ecology.

—Michael J. Tolley

———

MACKELWORTH, R(onald) W(alter). British. Born in London, 7 April 1930. Educated at Raynes Park Grammar School, London, 1940-48. Served in the British Army Intelligence Corps, 1948-50. Married Sheila Elizabeth Kilpatrick in 1956; one son and two daughters. Worked for Thomas Cook, travel agents, London, 1950; clerk, Norwich Union Insurance, London, 1950-53; Inspector, Kingston, Surrey, 1953-66, Superintendent, Leeds, 1966-72, Manager, Portsmouth, 1972-77, and since 1972, Product Manager, London, Legal and General Insurance Society. Agent: E.J. Carnell Literary Agency, Rowneybury Bungalow, Sawbridgeworth, near Old Harlow, Essex CM20 2EX. Address: 32 Mark Way, Godalming, Surrey, England.

SCIENCE-FICTION PUBLICATIONS

Novels

Firemantle. London, Hale, 1968; as *The Diabols,* New York, Paperback Library, 1969.
Tiltangle. New York, Ballantine, 1970; London, Hale, 1971.
Starflight 3000. New York, Ballantine, 1972; London, New English Library, 1976.
The Year of the Painted World. London, Hale, 1975.

Uncollected Short Stories

"The Statue," in *New Worlds* (London), January 1963.
"I, The Judge," in *New Worlds* (London), May 1963.
"Pattern of Risk," in *New Worlds* (London), July 1963.
"The Rotten Borough," in *New Worlds* (London), September 1963.
"The Cliff-Hangers," in *New Worlds* (London), December 1963.
"The Unexpected Martyr," in *New Worlds* (London), February 1964.
"The Expanding Man," in *New Writings in SF 5,* edited by John Carnell. London, Dobson, 1965; New York, Bantam, 1970.
"A Cave in the Hills," in *Science Fantasy* (Bournemouth), March 1965.
"The Changing Shape of Charlie Snuff," in *New Worlds* (London), April 1965.
"Last Man Home," in *New Worlds* (London), June 1965.
"A Distorting Mirror," in *Science Fantasy* (Bournemouth), July 1965.
"Temptation for the Leader," in *Science Fantasy* (Bournemouth), September 1965.
"Cleaner Than Clean," in *Science Fantasy* (Bournemouth), December 1965.
"A Touch of Immortality," in *New Writings in SF 7,* edited by John Carnell. London, Dobson, 1966; New York, Bantam, 1971.
"Final Solution," in *New Writings in SF 8,* edited by John Carnell. London, Dobson, 1966; New York, Bantam, 1971.
"A Visitation of Ghosts," in *SF Impulse* (London), June 1966.
"Two Rivers," in *New Writings in SF 17,* edited by John Carnell. London, Dobson, 1970.
"Mr. Nobody," in *New Writings in Horror and the Supernatural 1,* edited by David Sutton. London, Sphere, 1971.

*

Manuscript Collection: North London Polytechnic.

R.W. Mackelworth comments:

I am a lifelong addict of SF, but I prefer well-written novels and those that make a satirical statement about contemporary life whether through fantasy or fact. However, I also believe the modern idiom of fast-moving adventure entertains and entertainment is what the writer owes the reader. My work is essentially non-professional; I like to work up my own ideas and enjoy my writing. The conventions of SF are few, and one of its joys is that its scope for the imagination is unlimited. SF is gaining readers because it is largely free of many of the set-piece situations demanded of main-stream writing. Its problem is lack of good characterisation. Characters are often overwhelmed by events: if we can put personality before event, SF writing could improve considerably. The standard of writing is also important. It is possible to write literate SF as well as exciting SF!

*   *   *

The influence of British science-fiction magazines of the 1950's is evident in R.W. Mackelworth's restrained style and use of stock adventure frameworks: his fiction, despite attempts to incorporate profound issues, rarely displays the self-awareness increasingly favoured among his contemporaries. His output has remained small, his foremost works being novels.

In *Firemantle* the hero is projected, apparently through time, to an Earth dominated by a deadly alien life form. Most of the book relates his exploits in this future world and his gradual understanding of its parameters (including his immunity to the aliens). Interwoven with the narrative are themes of revenge and manipulation, the exact details, methods, and motives remaining concealed until the end. The novel finally affirms the intrinsic survival potentiality of human will power, but also questions the cost involved.

Tiltangle is set on Earth during a new ice age, with survivors crowded into an isolated refuge. Once again personal manipulation and callous use of power are introduced, although the central concern is a quest for the uncertain myth of "the warm," the first retreat of snow and ice heralding the return of a habitable world. This is Mackelworth's most effective book: it contains some of his best realised characters, while the depiction of ascetic life in a hostile environment is reinforced by uncharacteristically precise subsidiary detail. The implied background circumstances are less convincing, but this scarcely affects the driving obsession which is the novel's strength.

Starflight 3000 is loosely based on the generation starship concept. A hollowed asteroid becomes a vast spacecraft; use of terraforming bacteria allows the colonisation of any planet. Secondary aspects include faster-than-light communication and mysterious alien science. But for all its reliance on such motifs the novel is not typical of "hard" technological science fiction. It expresses moral concern over a selfish, expansionist mentality, and also gives some consideration to the conflict inherent in Mackelworth's two recurrent themes: the tendency of power to corrupt its wielder and the need for charismatic leadership to ensure progress. However, an abrupt time shift and the creation of a shipboard mythology ultimately avoid the questions raised.

The Year of the Painted World combines traditional elements of both disaster and invasion stories. Surprisingly excitable in tone, it tells of a struggle on present-day Earth against a Martian virus and its aggressive host organisms. The protagonist is an unambiguous man of action, doing what must be done. In his arrogant simplicity he could almost be a caricature of a hero from science fiction's Golden Age. The threatening "Pods" also carry more than a hint of space monsters of old. Possible benefits once the virus is controlled (and the consequent suspicions and machinations surrounding its release) add little depth to a playfully derivative but basically flimsy novel.

Mackelworth is no artist, honing subtleties of vision, language, and motivation to fine edges: instead he relies on mystery and suspense to hold attention until the denouement. His characterisation is usually notional (his stereotyped women are singularly ill portrayed), although within its terms he is adept at drawing concise contrasts. A tendency to slip into careless assumptions and clichés is another result of his intense absorption in plotting. Nevertheless, it is the complexity of his plots which sets Mackelworth apart from routine adventure writers. His underlying themes can be especially thought provoking, and it is unfortunate that he chooses to turn away from their fullest implications rather than develop their dramatic tension.

—Nick Pratt

MacLEAN, Katherine (Anne). American. Born in Glen Ridge, New Jersey, 22 January 1925. Educated at Barnard College, New York, B.A. 1950. Married 1) Charles Dye in 1951 (divorced, 1952); 2) David Mason in 1956 (divorced, 1962), one son; 3) Carl West. Laboratory assistant, 1944-45, and food manufacturing technician, 1945-46; office manager, Hi-Pro Animal Feed, Frankfort, Delaware, 1952-53; technician, Memorial and Knickerbocker hospitals, New York, 1954-56. Free-lance writer and lecturer. Recipient: Nebula Award, 1971. Agent: Virginia Kidd, Box 278, Milford, Pennsylvania 18337. Address: 30 Day Street South, Portland, Maine 04106, U.S.A.

SCIENCE-FICTION PUBLICATIONS

Novels

Cosmic Checkmate, with Charles V. De Vet.   New York, Ace, 1962.
The Man in the Bird Cage.   New York, Ace, 1971.
Missing Man.   New York, Berkley, 1975.
Dark Wing, with Carl West.   New York, Atheneum, 1979.

Short Stories

The Diploids and Other Flights of Fancy.   New York, Avon, 1962.
Trouble with Treaties.   Tacoma, Washington, Lanthorne Press, 1975.
The Trouble with You People.   Virginia Beach, Donning, 1980.

OTHER PUBLICATIONS

Other

"Communicado," in *Science Fiction Quarterly* (Holyoke, Massachusetts), February 1952.

*   *   *

Katherine MacLean is important for introducing in her fiction ethical questions about medical and scientific experimentation. She also writes about mental telepathy and human fears of evolutionary change.

The Diploids and Other Flights of Fancy includes eight works published between 1949 and 1953. The title story tells of genetic experiments that produced a strain of standardized human fetuses for research purposes. "The Pyramid in the Desert" has as its theme human fear of immortality. "Defense Mechanism" and "Games" are both about telepathy. "Feedback" deals with human fear of new ideas; "Pictures Don't Lie" deals with the anthropomorphic tendency to measure all species on a human scale. "The Snowball Effect" and "Incommunicado" are clever but less significant thematically than the others.

In *Cosmic Checkmate,* written with Charles V. De Vet, Robert Lang goes to the planet Velda to discover why its population refuses peaceful contact with the federation of Earth's colonies. In disguise, Lang plays the Veldian Game—based on chess—and beats all comers in the second game; he deliberately loses the first game to discover his opponent's weaknesses. The novel is well crafted: the plot works as an analogous game structure with Lang winning the second game in a cosmic checkmate.

MacLean's essay "Communicado" provides the background for her works that deal thematically with telepathy and psi phenomena. She discusses the important influence Whately Carington's book *Thought Transference* (1946) had on her, and she elaborates the ideas behind stories like "Defense Mechanism," "Feedback," "The Fittest," "Games," "Where or When," and "Curtin in the Sky." Telepathy is also the moving idea behind *Missing Man*. Set in New York, in 1999, the novel features George Sanford, whose extraordinary telepathic abilities make him a valuable special consultant for the Rescue Squad of the Police Department. Sanford is the fear hound, sniffing out people who are in trouble by tuning in to the telepathic vibrations they broadcast. The missing man is Carl Hodges, a super-maintenance man for the city who uses computers to predict breakdowns and accidents before they occur. The novel is thematically complex and almost phantasmagorical at times.

Several of MacLean's stories have medical themes and use physicians as main characters. Among the best of these is "Contagion": colonists on another planet survive a plague only by becoming look-alikes, thus raising questions about the interrelationship between external appearance and personality. "The Origin of the Species" is told in epistolary form by a neurosurgeon who is troubled by his work: he destroys the best parts of people's minds so that they can adapt to life in society. "Gimmick" chronicles the use of a virus as a weapon; "The Other" presents a physician who, ironically, has the same problem as the patient he is trying to cure; and "Syndrome Johnny" shows the usefulness of plagues in speeding up evolution. *Dark Wing*, written with her husband Carl West, also has a medical theme. It presents a future where the practice of medicine is illegal and people believe that illness is immoral, an external sign of defects in their thinking. A teenage boy, Travis Gordon, discovers two old medical kits in an abandoned wrecked ambulance and begins to learn and practice medicine, even performing complicated surgery with no special equipment or assistance. The complex and unbelievable plot, the superficial criticism of medicine, and the youth of the protagonist combine to make the novel read like adolescent fiction.

—Anne Hudson Jones

MADDERN, Pip (Philippa Catherine Maddern). Australian. Born in Albury, New South Wales, 24 August 1952. Educated at Morwell High School; University of Melbourne, 1970-73, B.A. in history and Indonesian studies, M.A. in history 1978; since 1979, graduate student, Brasenose College, Oxford. Tutor, University of Melbourne, 1976-78; Lecturer, Royal Melbourne Institute of Technology, 1979. Agent: Virginia Kidd, Box 278, Milford, Pennsylvania 18337, U.S.A. Address: 72 Lonsdale Road, Oxford OX2 7EP, England.

SCIENCE-FICTION PUBLICATIONS

Uncollected Short Stories

"The Ins and Outs of the Hadhya City State" and "Broken Pit," in *The Altered I*, edited by Lee Harding. Melbourne, Norstrilia Press, 1976; New York, Berkley, 1978.
"Dialogue," "Wherever You Are," and "Silence," in *The View from the Edge*, edited by George Turner. Melbourne, Norstrilia Press, 1977.
"They Made Us Not to Be and They Are Not," in *Orbit 20*, edited by Damon Knight. New York, Harper, 1978.
"Ignorant of Magic," in *Rooms of Paradise*, edited by Lee Harding. Melbourne, Quartet, 1978; New York, St. Martin's Press, 1979.
"Inhabiting the Interspaces," in *Transmutations*, edited by Rob Gerrand. Melbourne, Outback Press, 1979.
"The Pastseer," in *Interfaces*, edited by Ursula K. Le Guin and Virginia Kidd. New York, Ace, 1980.

Pip Maddern comments:
I have never been good at commenting on my own work, partly, I think, because I believe very firmly in the primacy of the subconscious in writing. It seems to me—to my conscious mind—that the stories are something separate from me. I write them because they are there to be written, and for some reason someone else hasn't written them yet. So in a sense, I'm no better fitted to introduce them to their readers than anyone else is.

They are science fiction. As many other people do, I define science fiction as being that branch of fiction in which the readers cannot assume that the story is set in the world as they know it—it might be set in the future, it might be set on a different planet, it might be set in an alternative universe. The only reason I write science fiction is that all the stories that have appeared to me so far have that sort of setting. (It's not that I dislike this-world literature—I love reading it, but I get uncomfortable writing it because it seems to me always to be saying "This is fiction, but I am trying to make it look like reality." Whereas science fiction can more easily say "This is fiction. Let's enjoy it.")

My stories don't carry a message from me. Some of them may carry a message of their own to some of you; but that's up to you to find out. They all seem to me to be worth telling, though I have not told them as well as they deserve; and the people (or aliens) in them seem to me to be worth knowing, though I have not made them all known as completely and accurately as I should have.

*   *   *

Pip Maddern came to immediate notice at the Writers' Workshop conducted by Ursula K. Le Guin at Belgrave, Victoria, in 1975; her admission story, "The Ins and Outs of the Hadhya City State," attracted attention by the assuredness of the technique. A superficial ingenuity (arising from a situation which I, and later Joanna Russ, found doubtful) was a weakness which faded in the stricter control of the imaginative elements in her later work.

She has published only a few stories, but definite characteristics are emerging. Most notable is her ability to manage a considerable complexity of theme and action in minimum wordage. In "Ignorant of Magic" she deals in about 5500 words with interlocking events in three separate universes, of which one is a parallel wherein magic usurps the role of science. Considering the spareness of her narrative style, the clear presentation of the spatio-temporal relationships of all three is a technical feat of no common order. She does not repeat her effects, and in "They Made Us Not to Be and They Are Not" she deals in totally original fashion with one of imagination's oldest dreams, extended life span. In a very different mode is "Inhabiting the Interspaces," a solidly realistic piece of story-telling eschewing all fantasy elements save a single social change; it is a sombre piece of precise observation which shows that she is not dependent on genre effects to carry her prose. A controlled anger (even a subtext of savagery) informs her plotting and characterisation, but it is too early to suggest her general direction. She is one of the most technically accomplished of the newer writers in the field.

—George Turner

MAINE, Charles Eric. Pseudonym for David McIlwain; also writes as Richard Rayner; Robert Wade. British. Born in Liverpool, Lancashire, 21 January 1921. Educated at Holt High School, Liverpool. Served in the Royal Air Force during World War II: Flight Lieutenant. Married and divorced twice; two sons and three daughters. Journalist in London, 1946-71, including 14 years as editor and managing editor of industrial weekly newspapers and journals; regular correspondent for *The Times, Financial Times,* and *Guardian*, London, and *Les Echos*, Paris. Agent: David Higham Associates Ltd., 5-8 Lower John Street, London W1R 4HA, England; or, Scott Meredith Literary Agency, 845 Third Avenue, New York, New York 10022, U.S.A.

SCIENCE-FICTION PUBLICATIONS

Novels (series: Mike Delaney)

Spaceways. London, Hodder and Stoughton, 1953; as *Spaceways Satellite,* New York, Avalon, 1958.
Timeliner. London, Hodder and Stoughton, and New York, Rinehart, 1955.
Crisis 2000. London, Hodder and Stoughton, 1955.
Escapement. London, Hodder and Stoughton, 1956; as *The Man Who Couldn't Sleep,* Philadelphia, Lippincott, 1958.
High Vacuum. London, Hodder and Stoughton, and New York, Ballantine, 1957.
The Isotope Man (Delaney). London, Hodder and Stoughton, and Philadelphia, Lippincott, 1957.
World Without Men. New York, Ace, 1958; London, Digit, 1963.
The Tide Went Out. London, Hodder and Stoughton, 1958; New York, Ballantine, 1959; revised edition, as *Thirst!,* London, Sphere, 1977; New York, Ace, 1978.
Count-Down. London, Hodder and Stoughton, 1959; as *Fire Past the Future,* New York, Ballantine, 1960.
Subterfuge (Delaney). London, Hodder and Stoughton, 1960.
Calculated Risk. London, Hodder and Stoughton, 1960.
He Owned the World. New York, Avalon, 1960; as *The Man Who Owned the World,* London, Hodder and Stoughton, 1961.
The Mind of Mr. Soames. London, Hodder and Stoughton, 1961.
The Darkest of Nights. London, Hodder and Stoughton, 1962; as *Survival Margin,* New York, Fawcett, 1968; revised edition, as *The Big Death,* London, Sphere, 1978.
Never Let Up (Delaney). London, Hodder and Stoughton, 1964.
B.E.A.S.T.: Biological Evolutionary Animal Simulation Test. London, Hodder and Stoughton, 1966; New York, Ballantine, 1967.
The Random Factor. London, Hodder and Stoughton, 1971.
Alph. New York, Doubleday, 1972.

Uncollected Short Stories

"Repulsion Factor," in *Authentic* (London), September 1953.
"Highway," in *Authentic* (London), November 1953.
"Spaceways to Venus," in *Spaceway* (Alhambra, California), December 1953.
"The Boogie Matrix," in *Authentic* (London), January 1954.
"Troubleshooters," in *Nebula* (Glasgow), February 1954.
"The Festival of Earth," in *Spaceway* (Alhambra, California), December 1954.
"The Yupe," in *Nebula* (Glasgow), December 1954.
"The Trouble with Mars," in *Authentic* (London), July 1955.
"Mission from Space," in *Fantastic Universe* (Chicago), September 1955.
"Reverse Procedure," in *Space Science Fiction Magazine* (New York), Spring 1957.
"The Wall of Fire," in *Satellite* (New York), June 1958.
"The Waters under the Earth," in *Amazing* (New York), July 1958.
"Counter-Psych," in *Amazing* (New York), November 1961.
"Highway J," in *Other Worlds, Other Times,* edited by Sam Moskowitz and Roger Elwood. New York, Macfadden Bartell, 1969.
"Scholarly Correspondence," in *Analog* (New York), April 1974.
"Joe Three-Eyes," in *New Tales of Unease,* edited by John Burke. London, Pan, 1976.

OTHER PUBLICATIONS

Novels as Richard Rayner

The Trouble with Ruth. London, Hale, 1960.
Darling Daughter. London, Hale, 1961.
Dig Deep for Julie. London, Hale, 1963.
Stand-In for Danger. London, Hale, 1963.

Novels as Robert Wade

The Wonderful One. London, Hodder and Stoughton, 1960.

The Stroke of Seven. New York, Morrow, 1965; London, Heinemann, 1967.
Knave of Eagles. New York, Random House, 1969; London, Hale, 1970.

Plays

Screenplay: *Escapement (The Electric Man),* with J. McLaren Ross, 1958.

Radio Plays: *Spaceways,* 1952; *The Einstein Way,* 1954.

Television Play: *Timeslip.*

Other

The World's Strangest Crimes. New York, Hart, and London, Odhams Press, 1967; as *The Bizarre and Bloody,* Hart, 1972.
World-Famous Mistresses. London, Odhams Press, 1970.

Charles Eric Maine comments:
Like Arthur C. Clarke, John Christopher, Eric Frank Russell, Jonathan Burke, the late John Wyndham, and other science-fiction author friends, I became an SF addict in my early teens. This was the era of the late 1930's when nobody, apart from a few SF writers and addicts, and fewer scientists, believed that man would ever set foot on the moon in this century, if at all. In my own science fiction, I have always tried to find a theme or situation which no other author has thought of. Although I have written some space opera (such as *Timeliner* and *He Owned the World*), most of my SF books are short-term projections from present-day fact and technology, looking, perhaps, some 10 to 50 years ahead. I am particularly interested in the social and psychological impact of advancing science on crude Homo sapiens. In this respect my two best novels are *The Tide Went Out* and *The Mind of Mr. Soames* (the movie version missed the essential point of the story—the difference between training and education).

*   *   *

Charles Eric Maine's writing is distinguished primarily by its original and imaginative concepts. This is not to demean his writing skills but rather to indicate that when viewed as a body his stories vary considerably in quality. Too often he falls back on clichés to move his stories along, and occasionally the clash between banal plots and sophisticated scientific ideas is resounding. Maine's treatment of time displacement in *The Isotope Man,* for example, is fascinating, but it is embedded in a plot that would do justice to the old pulps. The plot, to sabotage the artificial production of tungsten, is embellished by stereotyped characters: an ex-Nazi plastic surgeon, an evil South American business tycoon, a feisty and irascible city editor, a beautiful, sharp-tongued girl photographer, and a hard-drinking, two-fisted reporter who plays his hunches to the detriment of his job.

Despite this occasional failure to mesh plots, characters, and themes, however, Maine at his best is quite effective. *Alph, B.E.A.S.T., Timeliner,* and *The Tide Went Out* are excellent novels. He seems particularly good at creating memorable female characters. Among them are Synove Rayner (*B.E.A.S.T.*), a brilliant and beautiful exhibitionist nymphomaniac; Koralin (*Alph*), a courageous cytologist who kidnaps and protects the first male baby born into the lesbian society in five hundred years; and Shirley Sye (*The Tide Went Out*), a pathetic and aging model turned fashion editor who instructs the hero on the nature of man when faced with survival.

Survival is one of Maine's recurring themes. Sometimes he treats it directly, as in *The Tide Went Out* and *The Darkest of Nights,* both post-disaster novels. In *The Tide Went Out* repeated hydrogen bomb tests produce a fracture in the ocean floor through which pours nearly all of the world's water supply; in *The Darkest of Nights* a lethal epidemic destroys society. *B.E.A.S.T.* projects the ultimate result of an animal evolved with survival of the fittest as the only standard: a brilliant but mentally unstable scientist, Charles Gilley, creates animals and an environment for them in a computer, then evolves them through millions of generations while making conditions harsher and harsher. Finally all but one species disappears and then all but one animal. It is the ultimate survivor but it has lost all humanistic qualities. *Alph* presents yet another variation on the nature of survival in its exploration of the long-range effects of a society without men. Lesbianism, of course, becomes the acceptable form of sexual expression, but it results in a patterned societal neurosis. An emphasis on superior eugenic standards causes an overthrow of the government because of the elitist attitudes it creates. Even in *Timeliner,* whose primary purpose is to explore time travel, Hugh Macklin, the hero, eventually raises the question of whose right it is to decide who should survive and what standards they should use. Inevitably, Maine proposes, man will do whatever is required in order to survive.

Another prevalent Maine theme is time displacement, which receives its fullest treatment in *Timeliner.* In it, he offers the unique prospect that man's "psycho-identity" but not his body can travel forward in time. Attracted by emotional affinities, the "psycho-identity" possesses other persons' bodies to achieve consciousness. Though it creates a kind of immortality for the traveler, it destroys the possessed's ego. One future society that Macklin encounters labels such time travelers "psycho-temporal parasites" and considers the possession a form of murder.

One of the more interesting aspects of Maine's writing is its projection of possible futures. Though *Alph, Timeliner,* and *He Owned the World,* for example, paint different pictures, they do contain some consistencies. Maine predicts that the historical pattern of man's genius being channeled into aggression and war will continue indefinitely. He also believes that romantic love will die out. In *He Owned the World* it is defined as "an obsessive form of compulsive neurosis," and one of the characters that Macklin encounters in *Timeliner* tells him that man is naturally polygamous. Finally, many of Maine's future societies are totalitarian and man continues to battle his oppressors.

Maine is a journeyman writer who has created some excellent novels, but even if he were far less skilled his ideas alone would make reading his works worth the effort.

—Carl B. Yoke

MALZBERG, Barry N(orman). Also writes as Mike Barry; Claudine Dumas; Mel Johnson; Lee W. Mason; Francine de Natale; K.M. O'Donnell; Gerrold Watkins. American. Born in New York City, 24 July 1939. Educated at Syracuse University, New York (Schubert Fellow, 1964-65), A.B. 1960. Married Joyce Nadine Zelnick in 1964; two daughters. Investigator, New York City Department of Welfare, and Reimbursement Agent, New York State Department of Mental Hygiene; Editor, Scott Meredith Literary Agency, New York; Editor, *Amazing* and *Fantastic,* 1968; Managing Editor, *Escapade,* 1968. Free-lance writer: author of many novels under various pseudonyms for Midwood, Oracle, Soft Cover Library, and Traveler's Companion Series. Recipient: Campbell Memorial Award, 1973. Address: Box 61, Teaneck, New Jersey 07666, U.S.A.

SCIENCE-FICTION PUBLICATIONS

Novels

Oracle of the Thousand Hands. New York, Olympia Press, 1968.
The Falling Astronauts. New York, Ace, 1971; London, Arrow, 1975.
Overlay. New York, Lancer, 1972; London, New English Library, 1975.
Beyond Apollo. New York, Random House, 1972; London, Faber, 1974.
Revelations. New York, Warner, 1972.
The Men Inside. New York, Lancer, 1973; London, Arrow, 1976.

Phase IV. New York, Pocket Books, and London, Pan, 1973.
In the Enclosure. New York, Avon, 1973; London, Hale, 1976.
Herovit's World. New York, Random House, 1973; London, Arrow, 1976.
Guernica Night. Indianapolis, Bobbs Merrill, 1974; London, New English Library, 1978.
On an Alien Planet. New York, Pocket Books, 1974.
The Day of the Burning. New York, Ace, 1974.
Tactics of Conquest. New York, Pyramid, 1974.
The Sodom and Gomorrah Business. New York, Pocket Books, 1974; London, Arrow, 1979.
Underlay. New York, Avon, 1974.
The Destruction of the Temple. New York, Pocket Books, 1974; London, New English Library, 1975.
The Gamesman. New York, Pocket Books, 1975.
Conversations. Indianapolis, Bobbs Merrill, 1975.
Galaxies. New York, Pyramid, 1975.
Scop. New York, Pyramid, 1976.
The Last Transaction. New York, Pinnacle, 1977.
Chorale. New York, Doubleday, 1978.
The Man Who Loved the Midnight Lady. New York, Doubleday, 1980.

Novels as K.M. O'Donnell

The Empty Rooms. New York, Lancer, 1969.
Dwellers of the Deep. New York, Ace, 1970.
Universe Day. New York, Avon, 1971.
Gather in the Hall of the Planets. New York, Ace, 1971.

Short Stories

Final War and Other Fantasies (as K.M. O'Donnell). New York, Ace, 1969.
In the Pocket and Other S-F Stories. New York, Ace, 1971.
Out from Ganymede. New York, Warner, 1974.
The Many Worlds of Barry Malzberg. New York, Popular Library, 1975.
Down Here in the Dream Quarter. New York, Doubleday, 1976.
The Best of Barry Malzberg. New York, Pocket Books, 1976.

Uncollected Short Stories

"Re-Entry," in *Fantastic* (New York), February 1977.
"Shibboleth," in *Amazing* (New York), March 1977.
"The Man Who Married a Beagle," in *Fantastic* (New York), June 1977.
"Indigestion," in *Fantastic* (New York), September 1977.
"On Account of Darkness," in *Fantasy and Science Fiction* (New York), November 1977.
"Here, For Just a While," in *Fantastic* (New York), April 1978.
"Big Ernie, The Royal Russian, and the Big Trapdoor," in *Fantasy and Science Fiction* (New York), May 1978.
"Prowl," in *Fantastic* (New York), July 1978.
"Ring, The Brass Ring, The Russian, and I," in *Fantasy and Science Fiction* (New York), August 1978.
"Varieties of Technological Experience," in *Analog* (New York), October 1978.
"Another Burnt-Out Case," in *Fantastic* (New York), October 1978.
"Out of Quarantine," with Bill Pronzini, in *Isaac Asimov's Science Fiction Magazine* (New York), November-December 1978.
"Clocks," with Bill Pronzini, in *Shadows 2,* edited by Charles L. Grant. New York, Doubleday, 1979.
"Thirty-Six Views of His Dead Majesty," in *Chrysalis 6,* edited by Roy Torgeson. New York, Kensington, 1979.
"The Annual Bash and Circumstance Party," in *Fantasy and Science Fiction* (New York), March 1979.
"Demystification of Circumstance," in *Fantasy and Science Fiction* (New York), November 1979.
"LaCroix," in *Their Immortal Hearts: Three Visions of Time.* Reno, Nevada, West Coast Poetry Review Press, 1980.
"The Last One Left," in *Fantasy and Science Fiction* (New York), January 1980.
"The Lyran Case," with Bill Pronzini, in *Analog* (New York), March 1980.

OTHER PUBLICATIONS

Novels

Screen.   New York, Olympia Press, 1968; London, Olympia Press, 1972.
Diary of a Parisian Chambermaid (as Claudine Dumas).   New York, Midwood, 1969.
In My Parents' Bedroom.   New York, Olympia Press, 1970.
Confessions of Westchester County.   New York, Olympia Press, 1971; London, Olympia Press, 1972.
The Spread.   New York, Belmont, 1971.
Horizontal Woman.   New York, Nordon, 1972; as *The Social Worker,* 1977.
The Case for Elizabeth Moore.   New York, Belmont, 1972.
The Masochist.   New York, Belmont, 1972; as *Everything Happened to Susan,* 1978.
The Way of the Tiger, The Sign of the Dragon.   New York, Warner, 1973.
The Running of Beasts, with Bill Pronzini.   New York, Putnam, 1976.
Lady of a Thousand Sorrows (as Lee W. Mason).   Chicago, Playboy Press, 1977.
Acts of Mercy, with Bill Pronzini.   New York, Putnam, 1977.
Night Screams, with Bill Pronzini.   Chicago, Playboy Press, 1979.
Prose Bowl, with Bill Pronzini.   New York, St. Martin's Press, 1980.

Novels as Mike Barry

Bay Prowler.   New York, Berkley, 1973.
Boston Avenger.   New York, Berkley, 1973.
Night Raider.   New York, Berkley, 1973.
Chicago Slaughter.   New York, Berkley, 1974.
Desert Stalker.   New York, Berkley, 1974.
Havana Hit.   New York, Berkley, 1974.
Los Angeles Holocaust.   New York, Berkley, 1974.
Miami Marauder.   New York, Berkley, 1974.
Peruvian Nightmare.   New York, Berkley, 1974.
Detroit Massacre.   New York, Berkley, 1975.
Harlem Showdown.   New York, Berkley, 1975.
The Killing Run.   New York, Berkley, 1975.
Philadelphia Blow-Up.   New York, Berkley, 1975.
Phoenix Inferno.   New York, Berkley, 1975.

Other

Editor, with Edward L. Ferman, *Final Stage.*   New York, Charter House, 1974.
Editor, with Edward L. Ferman, *Arena: Sports SF.*   New York, Doubleday, and London, Robson, 1976.
Editor, with Edward L. Ferman, *Graven Images.*   New York, Doubleday, 1976.
Editor, with Bill Pronzini, *Dark Sins, Dark Dreams: Crimes in SF.*   New York, Doubleday, 1977.
Editor, with Bill Pronzini, *The End of Summer: Science Fiction in the Fifties.*   New York, Ace, 1979.
Editor, with Bill Pronzini, *Shared Tomorrows: Collaboration in SF.*   New York, St. Martin's Press, 1979.
Editor, with Martin H. Greenberg, *Neglected Vision.*   New York, Doubleday, 1980.
Editor, with Martin H. Greenberg, *The Science Fiction of Mark Clifton.*   Carbondale, Southern Illinois University Press, 1980.

*   *   *

If what Barry N. Malzberg has called, in a typical turn of phrase, "the true and terrible complete history of science fiction" is ever written, Malzberg will occupy a unique niche within its carefully categorized confines. He has often been vilified by authors and reviewers for attacking the very foundations of the genre as they perceive it; but equally, he has been praised, by such writers and critics as Harlan Ellison, Joanna Russ, and Brian Stableford, for attempting to do something new, and artistic, within the expanding, universe of genre conventions.

Malzberg's problem, and the reason perhaps that he quit the genre in 1975 after seven years of highly prolific creation (though he has continued to write *some* short stories and essays), is not that he was unable to use conventional SF props as powerful tropes by which to explore individuals' psychological anxiety, their feelings of alienation and inadequacy when they confront the machineries of technological change and bureaucratic stasis. In fact, in his best work he has polished to a high gloss the mirrored surfaces of many basic SF conventions so that their apparently *inherent* optimism reveals in reflection only its diabolic opposite. But because he did this so well he tended to alienate precisely the audience which his SF writings were meant to attract. But there has always been a place for apocalyptic visions in SF. The problem isn't that Malzberg wasn't read, but that so many of his readers could only turn away from his writings in disgust, saying he had betrayed them because he offered no hope in his stories, or making similar complaints.

In so attacking him these readers are wrong, in that they are ill-equipped to perceive the kind of limited hope or optimism expressed in the actions of Captain Lena Thomas in *Galaxies* or cool Sid in *Guernica Night,* who choose to live even in the face of complexities which are (almost) too great to bear. Certainly the burden of his fictions is often terrifying, bleak: lost in a world they had no part in making, Malzberg's people articulate their precise awareness of that fact, and of the other facts which batter at their defences. Malzberg's obsessions, and those of his characters, expose the dark underbelly of the science-fiction mythos to the terrible light of art. Humans as machines, not in hoped-for supremacy but in near-catatonic anomie, unable to touch one another, even in sex, except mechanically; assassination as a way of life; bureaucracy as a huge engine of human destruction; the horrors of confronting in outer space only the empty reflection of our inner spaces: these are the themes Malzberg explores with obsessive tenacity, entering one after another of SF's favorite narrative conventions only to discover once more that for the human problems his characters have to deal with there are no easy answers, no *dei-ex-machinis* to lumber in at the end and save all. But this knowledge is not necessarily simply pessimistic. Herovit and his other selves utterly fail to adapt to the alien forces of New York, but others in Malzberg's "freak show" survive in the recognition that a not only can they not find answers to their specific complaints but that very likely their problems do not have "answers" as such. So they adapt, they make compromises with reality, they go mad, they go sane, they try to be human (in itself the most heroic act Malzberg can conceive of in the aseptic environment of SF conventions). For Malzberg's characters the material of their reality is strangely impermeable, darkly opaque, and almost completely unmalleable. The universe is bigger, stronger, and more dangerous than they are; it also has a nasty sense of humour.

Indeed, comedy is something not often mentioned in connection with Malzberg yet he is one of the funniest writers in the genre, if you are able to laugh at the end of the world. For black humour, apocalyptic comedy, Lear's fool trying for a final tear-filled laugh, see Malzberg's collected works. If we didn't laugh we might break down and cry, and so might he. The tricks of rhetoric have their purpose, then, and Malzberg is a master of the ironic twist, the sick joke of metaphysics meeting physics head-on. Tone is always difficult, yet Malzberg continually manages such complex presentations of savage wit as this, in *Beyond Apollo: "A Brief History of the Universe:* The universe was invented by man in 1976 as a cheap and easy explanation for all his difficulties in conquering it." Foregrounding the many subtexts of the novel, this remark casts a shadow over not just Harry Evans's attempt to discover what happened to him on the disastrous Venus mission but also over all the stories of successful space imperialism. And yet I believe Malzberg when he says he loves science fiction, for it's obvious he recognizes and values the writing his own seems so fully to subvert. Such ambivalence of love and belief seem proper in a writer whose central subject is human ambivalence on every matter that matters. He only wanted to make room for his vision, *too;* not to replace the others but to provide some balance. And even if he has left the field he has left us a rich legacy of fictions whose integrity cannot be questioned. Of the novels, certainly *The Falling Astronauts, Overlay, Beyond Apollo, Herovit's World, Guernica Night, Scop,* and that amazing analysis of the genre in the form of notes for a novel, *Galaxies,* need no apology. And there are a number of shorter works of equal value.

Although many find his vision not only too dark but too narrow, no one can deny the depth of the chasm his works have cut through contemporary SF.

—Douglas Barbour

MANNING, Laurence (Edward). American. Born in St. John, New Brunswick, Canada, in 1899; emigrated to the United States after World War I. Educated at King's College, Halifax, Nova Scotia, B.C.L. 1919. Served in the Royal Canadian Air Force: Lieutenant. Married Edith B. Manning in 1928; two daughters and one son. Newspaper reporter in St. John, then writer for the Florists Exchange, Philadelphia, in the early 1920's; Manager, 1923-32, President, 1933-52, and Owner, 1952-66, Kelsey Nursery Service, New York. Fellow, American Rocket Society, 1960. *Died in 1972.*

SCIENCE-FICTION PUBLICATIONS

Novel

The Man Who Awoke. New York, Ballantine, 1975; London, Sphere, 1977.

Uncollected Short Stories (series: Stranger Club)

"The Voyage of the Asteroid," in *Wonder Stories* (New York), Summer 1932.
"The Wreck of the Asteroid," in *Wonder Stories* (New York), December 1932.
"The Call of the Mech-Men" (Club), in *Wonder Stories* (New York), November 1933.
"Caverns of Horror" (Club), in *Wonder Stories* (New York), March 1934.
"Voice of Atlantis" (Club), in *Wonder Stories* (New York), July 1934.
"The Moth Message" (Club), in *Wonder Stories* (New York), December 1934.
"The Prophetic Voice," in *Wonder Stories* (New York), April 1935.
"Seeds from Space" (Club), in *Wonder Stories* (New York), June 1935.
"World of the Mist," in *Wonder Stories* (New York), September 1935.
"Expedition to Pluto," with Fletcher Pratt, in *Planet* (New York), Winter 1939.
"The City of the Living Dead," with Fletcher Pratt, in *Avon Fantasy Reader 2,* edited by Donald A. Wollheim. New York, Avon, 1947.
"The Living Galaxy," in *The Science Fiction Galaxy,* edited by Groff Conklin. New York, Permabooks, 1950.
"Good-Bye, Ilha," in *Beyond Human Ken,* edited by Judith Merril. New York, Random House, 1952.
"Men on Mars," in *Fantastic Story* (New York), Spring 1952.
"Mr. Mottle Goes Poof," in *Fantasy Fiction* (New York), August 1953.

OTHER PUBLICATIONS

Other

The How and Why of Better Gardening. New York, Van Nostrand, 1951.

*   *   *

Laurence Manning is remembered primarily for a series of five stories originally published in 1933, later collected in book form as *The Man Who Awoke.* Manning utilized a classic device of science-fiction and Utopian writers, a man from our own culture transported in some fashion to another society, which is then revealed to the reader as the protagonist encounters individuals and institutions. In each of the five episodes, Norman Winters arises from suspended animation to investigate the state of humanity as it advances toward its ultimate destiny.

In the title story, Winters explores the world of the year 5000. Humankind dwells within vast managed forests, in balance with nature, looking back with horror on "the false civilization of Waste!" Seeking to find a place for himself in this new world, Winters attempts to convince his hosts that his own time did have positive aspects for which they should be thankful. But even the most sympathetic of his listeners feel no gratitude. "For exhausting the coal supplies of the world? For leaving us no petroleum for our chemical factories?" Ultimately finding this new society as flawed as the old, Winters sleeps another 5000 years and revives in "Master of the Brain." Now he encounters humanity subservient to a computer that makes all the decisions, the race having abdicated the responsibility for their own future. After being instrumental in breaking the grip of the Brain, Winters advances to the year 15000 in "The City of Sleep." Once more he is disappointed, for now the great majority of people spend their entire lives in mechanically induced dreams, an idea developed from Manning's first story, "The City of the Living Dead," written with Fletcher Pratt. This willing renunciation of reality has recurred within the genre many times, most notably in James Gunn's *The Joy Makers.* The best story in the series is "The Individualists," wherein Winters becomes the quarry of a number of egocentric geniuses in a society that places no value on interpersonal relationships. Winters's journey ends with "The Elixir," the source of immortality which produces an interstellar community. Although not specifically within the series, Manning wrote another tale set eons after the Manning saga, "The Living Galaxy," which postulated that entire stellar systems functioned as single atoms in a higher order universe we could not perceive.

Less ambitious in scope was a second series which recounted the adventures of several members of the Stranger Club. Manning's dislike of automation recurs in "The Call of the Mech-Men," a secret cabal of living machines. His concern about our profligate consumption of natural resources, anticipating our present worries, is repeated in "Voice of Atlantis," in which a device allows communication with an ancient Atlantean. The remaining three stories were more pedestrian and reflected the type of story that dominated the genre in the 1930's. A lost world of prehistoric monsters lies under New York in "Caverns of Horror," a forgotten Atlantean colony is located in "The Moth Message," and a species of sentient, ambient tree is thwarted in its invasion plan in "Seeds from Space."

Manning's fiction, much of which seems quite dated now, was advanced for its time. He produced a series of very accurate—insofar as the state of the art allowed—stories of space travel. His concerns for conservation and human dignity elevated his fiction above that of most of his peers.

—Don D'Ammassa

MARTIN, George R(aymond) R(ichard). Born in Bayonne, New Jersey, 20 September 1948. Educated at Medill School of Journalism, Northwestern University, Evanston, Illinois, B.S. 1970, M.S. 1971. Served with the Cook County Legal Assistance Foundation, for Vista, Chicago, 1972-74. Married Gale Burnick in 1975. Chess tournament director, Continental Chess Association, Mount Vernon, New York, 1973-75; Journalism Instructor, Clarke College, Dubuque, Iowa, 1976-78. Since 1978: free-lance writer. Recipient: Hugo Award, 1975, 1980 (2 awards); Bread Loaf Writers Conference Fellowship, 1977; Nebula Award, 1980. Agent: Kirby McCauley, 60 East 42nd Street, New York, New York 10017. Address: Burnick and Burton Manor, 2266 Jackson, Dubuque, Iowa 52001, U.S.A.

SCIENCE-FICTION PUBLICATIONS

Novels

Dying of the Light.   New York, Simon and Schuster, 1977; London, Gollancz, 1978.
Windhaven, with Lisa Tuttle.   New York, Simon and Schuster, 1980.
Nightflyers, in *Binary Star 5.*   New York, Dell, 1981.

Short Stories

A Song for Lya and Other Stories.   New York, Avon, 1976; London, Coronet, 1978.
Songs of Stars and Shadows.   New York, Simon and Schuster, 1977.

Uncollected Short Stories

"Call Him Moses," in *Analog* (New York), February 1978.
"Warship," with George Florance-Gutheridge, in *Fantasy and Science Fiction* (New York), April 1979.
"The Way of Cross and Dragon," in *Omni* (New York), June 1979.
"Sandkings," in *Omni* (New York), August 1979.

OTHER PUBLICATIONS

Other

Editor, *New Voices in Science Fiction 1-2.*   New York, Macmillan, 1 vol., 1977; New York, Harcourt Brace, 1 vol., 1979.

*   *   *

Critics are in agreement that George R.R. Martin is one of the major talents in science-fiction writing today. His work, which ranges in mood from wistful to chilling, bears the mark of considerable writing skill and a rich imaginative mind. Martin is equally at ease creating work with a tender touch or with a macabre twist; his best work combines both.

Martin himself says, "Love and loneliness may be *among* my favorite themes, but the all-time champion to date has got to be reality's search and destroy missions against romance, a subject that I've turned to again and again" (Introduction to *Songs of Stars and Shadows*). "With Morning Comes Mistfall" is a particularly clear statement of this theme. A group of scientists visit mist-enshrouded Wraithworld and literally make a search mission to dispel the illusion that mysterious and dangerous Wraiths exist on that world. The insensitive scientists are portrayed as blind to the beauties of the world, while Sanders, a hotel owner who loves the mistfall, the mistrise, and most of all the mystery, looks on in despair as scientific paraphernalia take the wonder from his world. Man "needs mystery, and poetry and romance," Sanders reflects. "I think he needs a few unanswered questions, to make him brood and wonder."

The Hugo-award story "A Song for Lya," one of Martin's most successful mixes of the tender and the macabre, is also one of Martin's strongest statements concerning the essential loneliness of human individuals. In this story two Talents are hired by the human administrator of an alien planet to discover just why a particularly bizarre alien religion—one that requires the eventual willing suicide of each devotee—has been winning human converts. In fulfilling the assignment, Rob, a Talent who can read emotions, and his lover Lya, whose gift is the ability to read thoughts, open themselves to empathic understanding of those "Joined" to a gelatinous alien life form, in the first stages of the suicidal process. When Lya becomes convinced that this rite offers an end to human loneliness she decides to become part of the mass immortality offered by the religion. Rob, initially distraught at losing the woman he deeply loves, rises above the possessive aspect of his love for Lya and clings to his human individuality even as he realizes that being human can well mean a return to the "darkling plain" of painful loneliness.

Dying of the Light focuses on another man who must overcome possessiveness in his love for a woman. Upon receiving a whisper-jewel psionically etched with alluring memories of his lost love, Dirk t'Larien proceeds to the most significant relationship of his life. He soon discovers, however, that his presence was requested for anything but romantic reasons; his time on the planet Worlorn is spent in determining the motives behind the whisperjewel's summons and in relinquishing his remembered image of a woman in favor of her present reality. The novel's chief strength lies in its female character, Gwen, who convinces Dirk that she is not *his* Guinevere but her own individual self, but the work is also notable for use of memorable technological gadgetry and very fast-paced action.

While some of Martin's more recent work continues in a wistful, moody vein, as "Bitterblooms" which tells the story of a young woman who is lured from home by a strange older woman who turns out to be Morgan Le Fay, other pieces become showpieces for the author's more macabre turn of mind and for wry comments on human foibles or vices, particularly selfishness and pride. The protagonist in "Sandkings" is an eccentric and sadistic pet enthusiast of the future whose passion for owning strange pets leads him to acquire four colonies of small alien warriors. A penchant for gambling, a ghoulish fascination with watching ritual warfare, and his own increasing conviction that he is as God to his pets leads the protagonist to cause the colonists of his huge terrarium to get completely out of control. This is an absolutely spine-tingling story with a gem of a surprise ending. A related story is "A Beast for Norn" in which several proud houses vie for ownership of the most loathesome monster to compete in gladiator-style games. An accomodating alien in his spaceship known as the "Ark" provides evermore expensive and horrifying beasts along with fast-breeding food for the monsters. Pride and little "hoppers" are the undoing of the houses and the ecology of their world.

—Rosemary Herbert

MASON, Douglas R.   *See* **RANKINE, John.**

MASSON, David I(rvine).   British.   Born in Edinburgh, 6 November 1915. Educated at Oundle School, Northamptonshire, 1929-34; Merton College, Oxford, B.A. (honours) in English 1937, M.A. 1941. Served in the Royal Army Medical Corps, 1940-45. Married Olive Masson in 1950; one daughter. Assistant Librarian, University of Leeds, 1938-40, and University of Liverpool, 1945-55; Sub-Librarian, in charge of Brotherton Collection, University of Leeds, 1956-79. Address: c/o Faber and Faber Ltd., 3 Queen Square, London WC1N 3AU, England.

SCIENCE-FICTION PUBLICATIONS

Short Stories

The Caltraps of Time.   London, Faber, 1968.

Uncollected Short Stories

"The Show Must Go On," in *The Disappearing Future,* edited by George Hay.   London, Panther, 1970.
"Take It or Leave It," in *The Year 2000,* edited by Harry Harrison.   New York, Doubleday, 1970; London, Faber, 1971.
"Doctor Fausta," in *Stop Watch,* edited by George Hay.   London, New English Library, 1974.

OTHER PUBLICATIONS

Other

Hand-List of Incunabula in the University Library, Liverpool. Privately printed, 1948; supplement, 1955.
Catalogue of the Romany Collection... University of Leeds. Edinburgh, Nelson, 1962.
Poetic Sound-Patterning Reconsidered. Leeds, Philosophical and Literary Society, 1976.
"The Light of Imagination," in *Foundation 10* (London), June 1976.

David I. Masson comments:

My SF, although it seeks "scientific" verisimilitude and tries to "convince," has little to do with the processes of science. It explores bizarre assumptions for the sake—or so it seems to me—of mythopoeia, fable, satire, ridicule, scorn, or indignation, and perhaps inner truth about experience and feeling. Only "Take It or Leave It" has much to do with possible futures. Several stories reflect my conviction that the human race is insane.

*   *   *

David I. Masson's SF reputation rests upon a handful of stories, most of them collected in *The Caltraps of Time.* A lively if recondite wit is a characteristic of these stories. A university antiquarian librarian, fascinated by linguistics, Masson plummets a Restoration gentleman into the 20th century courtesy of a borrowed time machine in "The Two Timer," to be amazed and bemused by our antics—and of course to satirize us in approved Swiftian manner. The impeccable late 17th-century prose style of this story throws into contrast our barbaric contemporary parlance: "Myself: *Prithee, Sir, do you converse in* English? At this he frown'd, and turn'd back thro' his Door, but left it open, for I heard him in speech with another, as follows. He:...*Now enthing bauootim? Caun honstan zaklay wottee sez.*" Matters are just as bad for a researcher of the 1980's plunged into the 24th century by a linear accelerator accident in "The Transfinite Choice" ("Namplize." "Don't you speak English, then? Who the hell are you?" "Namplize"). It seems as though one is sliding down a cultural entropy slope. This future, in techno-telegraphize, is trying, however, to master the gradient of time at the sub-particle level. Reality fractures as the future tries to shunt its excess population into parallel time-continua; or was it only, after all, the stricken researcher's reality that fell apart?

The finest of Masson's stories, "Traveller's Rest," deals with time yet again, apocalyptically yet ironically. The country at war in this story is distorted by differential time: whole decades pass in the peaceful south while mere minutes pass at the northern battle frontier where, perhaps, the army is simply fighting itself in the mirror of bent time with mounting frenzy and destructiveness—a powerful nightmare which does for exponential time what Christopher Priest's novel *Inverted World* was later to do for exponential space. In "Not So Certain" an expedition to an alien planet falls foul of the natives' tricky phonemes, another linguistic *jeu d'esprit*, while in "Mouth of Hell" apocalyptic topography confronts the explorers in the form of a 40-kilometre-deep cleft down to the molten magma which, by the end of the story, is tamed and demystified just as so much of our world has been banalised.

In Masson's loving care for language and concern with time one senses a scholarly resentment at the downhill slide of the world into some future mass point of condensed people and words and moments.

—Ian Watson

MATHESON, Richard (Burton). American. Born in Allendale, New Jersey, 20 February 1926. Educated at the University of Missouri, Columbia, Bachelor of Journalism 1949. Served in the 87th Division of the United States Army during World War II. Married Ruth Ann Woodson in 1952; two daughters and two sons. Freelance writer: script editor, *Circle of Fear* TV series. Recipient: Hugo Award, for screenplay, 1958; Writers Guild of America Award, for television writing, 1960, 1974; World Fantasy Award, 1976. Guest of Honor, 16th World Science Fiction Convention, 1958. Agent: Don Congdon, Harold Matson Company, 22 East 40th Street, New York, New York 10016. Address: P.O. Box 81, Woodland Hills, California 91365, U.S.A.

SCIENCE-FICTION PUBLICATIONS

Novels

I Am Legend. New York, Fawcett, 1954; London, Corgi, 1956.
The Shrinking Man. New York, Fawcett, and London, Muller, 1956.

Short Stories

Born of Man and Woman. Philadelphia, Chamberlain Press, 1954; London, Reinhardt, 1956; abridged edition, as *Third from the Sun,* New York, Bantam, 1955.
The Shores of Space. New York, Bantam, 1957; London, Corgi, 1958.
Shock! New York, Dell, 1961; London, Corgi, 1962.
Shock II. New York, Dell, 1964; London, Corgi, 1965.
Shock III. New York, Dell, 1966; London, Corgi, 1967.
Shock Waves. New York, Dell, 1970.

OTHER PUBLICATIONS

Novels

Someone Is Bleeding. New York, Lion, 1953.
Fury on Sunday. New York, Lion, 1954.
A Stir of Echoes. Philadelphia, Lippincott, and London, Cassell, 1958.
Ride the Nightmare. New York, Ballantine, 1959; London, Consul, 1961.
The Beardless Warriors. Boston, Little Brown, 1960; London, Heinemann, 1961.
Hell House. New York, Viking Press, 1971; London, Corgi, 1973.
Bid Time Return. New York, Viking Press, 1975; London, Sphere, 1977.
What Dreams May Come. New York, Putnam, 1978; London, Joseph, 1979.

Plays

Screenplays: *The Incredible Shrinking Man,* 1957; *The Beat Generation,* with Lewis Meltzer, 1959; *The House of Usher,* 1960; *Master of the World,* 1961; *The Pit and the Pendulum,* 1961; *Tales of Terror,* 1962; *Burn, Witch, Burn* (*Night of the Eagle*), with Charles Beaumont and George Baxt, 1962; *The Raven,* 1963; *The Comedy of Terrors,* 1964; *Die! Die! My Darling!* (*Fanatic*), 1965; *The Young Warriors,* 1967; *The Devil Rides Out* (*The Devil's Bride*), 1968; *De Sade,* 1969; *Hell House,* 1976; *Bid Time Return,* 1979.

Television Plays: *Yawkey* (*Lawman* series), 1959; *The Enemy Within* (*Star Trek* series), 1966; *Duel,* 1971; *The Kolchak Papers* (*The Night Stalker* series), 1973; *The Stranger Within,* 1974; *Dracula,* 1974; *The Martian Chronicles,* from the novel by Ray Bradbury, 1980; and scripts for *Twilight Zone, Chrysler Playhouse, Alfred Hitchcock Hour, The Girl from U.N.C.L.E., Have Gun—Will Travel, Wanted Dead or Alive, Night Gallery, The D.A.'s Man, Thriller, Cheyenne, Bourbon Street Beat, Philip Marlowe, Buckskin, Markham,* and *Richard Diamond* series.

*   *   *

As a writer of short fiction which is mostly a hybrid of fantasy and SF, Richard Matheson should be compared with Henry Kuttner and Theodore Sturgeon, both obvious influences, and with later writers like Ellison and Delany who share important similarities of style and angles of vision. Although Matheson's short stories are not easily reduced to a simple classification, most of them explore the psychological impact of sudden discontinuity in the lives of otherwise rather ordinary characters. The stories range from the weird horror of "Long Distance Call," a graveyard variant of the radio drama and movie *Sorry, Wrong Number* (Lucille Fletcher), to the ironic humor of "Legion of Plotters," a tale literally fulfilling the commonplace paranoia that everyone's plotting against us. His ironic sense brings Matheson close to a mode of the fantastic that modern readers associate with Fritz Leiber and Fredric Brown. The very titles of some of his stories, "A Flourish of Strumpets," "'Tis the Season to Be Jelly," "When the Waker Sleeps," and "Witch War," are indicative of the varieties of comic irony and parody that constitute one of Matheson's three distinctive styles as a writer.

Matheson published most of his short fiction in the 1950's. It was during this decade that he also wrote the two novels on which his reputation as a science-fiction master depends. *I Am Legend* and *The Shrinking Man* are built on fantastic premises that are developed experimentally in the spirit of scientific curiosity. Each is also a story of individual courage, physical as well as psychological, trial, and suspense. Each might be described as a fantastic science-fiction horror story. Of the two, *I Am Legend,* clearly the better story, belongs in the tradition of great vampire novels somewhere between Bram Stoker's *Dracula* and Ann Rice's *Interview with the Vampire.* It is more scientific than either, but it shares some of the mythic power of the former and philosophical interests of the latter. The hero, Robert Neville, finds himself the last human alive following a plague that either kills outright or transforms the survivors into vampires. His struggle against his twin enemies, the vampires and his own isolation, is never successfully resolved; and in Neville's failure to win through by courage and single-minded determination lies the special achievement of this novel. Matheson avoids the cliché triumphalism that was practically a genre characteristic in the 1950's in favor of a more thoughtful and artistic denouement. A mutated strain of vampire emerges to establish a new order in which Neville has no place except that of a Nemesis who will pass into the legends of an emerging culture. Although much is inevitably sacrificed to the requirements of suspense melodrama and the sense of terror generated by the specter of personal violation, Matheson makes a stunning success of impressing on the reader the strength of Neville's character, the reasonableness of his reactions to his predicament, and the limitations inherent in both his virtues and in his responses to the challenges the vampires make to his survival as *homo sapiens* rather than as *homo vampiris.* The novel is, therefore, as much a challenge to certain conventional assumptions of the genre of the necessary survival of the species as the highest good as it is to the reader's expectations for the conventional, inevitable triumph of the resourceful hero.

The title of *The Shrinking Man* tells much of the basic idea of the story, except for the working out of the unique sequence of accidents that set in motion Scott's irreversible and apparently endless shrinking process and its consequences. Matheson's flashback inserts detailing the physical and emotional effects of Scott's diminishing stature contrast effectively with the suspense adventure of his warfare in the basement of his house against a black widow spider and his struggle to survive in a miniature state. It is altogether a tour de force for the author who manages to keep the reader bound to the terrifying fate of the hero and his increasing isolation from the familiar, domestic world from which he literally disappears. The theme of Scott's alienation from his wife and child, the psychological impact of his bizarre affliction, and his struggle for self-mastery and identity are powerfully drawn. Scott's sexual frustration is perhaps less subtly managed and is less symbolically meaningful than it is in *I Am Legend,* but then there is less ambiguity to the character of Scott than Neville. There are two or three splendid moments in the novel worthy of Sturgeon or Kuttner. Each moment is an epiphany of sorts in which Scott finds significance and purpose in his incredible life experience as a shrinking man, and each is an existential revelation on that account. He comes to a critical realization in the arms of Clarisse, a carnival midget, that his identity as a man does not depend on his physical stature. In fighting the spider, he realizes that he is opposing symbolically also those irrational, destructive forces in nature to which he refuses to become victim; and finally, having preserved himself against all odds, he is admitted

into a new, molecular universe that science and science fiction have taught us exists below the level of appearances. If the novel vindicates Scott's existential courage, it is at least no easy vindication; and it is a triumph the reader is disposed gratefully to accept, even at the level of fantasy.

Matheson continued to write SF but at a diminished pace in the 1960's. His most recent novels are memorable works of romantic fantasy, indicating perhaps a new direction to his interests as a writer. *Bid Time Return* and *What Dreams May Come* deal in a bittersweet way with romantic love that bridges the gulf separating lovers of different eras, finally separated by time and death but united in spirit. The recent reissue of Matheson's collected stories is an indication of both the continuing popularity and influence of Matheson as a writer of fantasy science fiction.

—Donald L. Lawler

McCAFFREY, Anne (Inez). American. Born in Cambridge, Massachusetts, 1 April 1926. Educated at Stuart Hall, Staunton, Virginia; Montclair High School, New Jersey; Radcliffe College, Cambridge, Massachusetts, B.A. (cum laude) in Slavonic languages and literature 1947; studied meteorology at City of Dublin University. Married E. Wright Johnson in 1950 (divorced, 1970); two sons and one daughter. Copywriter and layout designer, Liberty Music Shops, New York, 1948-50; Copywriter, Helena Rubinstein, New York, 1950-52. Currently runs a thoroughbred horse stud farm in Ireland; since 1978, Director, Dragonhold Ltd., and since 1979, Director, Fin Film Productions. Has performed in and directed several operas and musical comedies in Wilmington and Greenville, Delaware. Secretary-Treasurer, Science Fiction Writers of America, 1968-70. Recipient: Hugo Award, 1968; Nebula Award, 1968; Gandalf Award, 1979. Agent: Virginia Kidd, Box 278, Milford, Pennsylvania 18337, U.S.A. Address: Dragonhold, Kilquade, Greystones, County Wicklow, Ireland.

SCIENCE-FICTION PUBLICATIONS

Novels (series: Dragonrider; Harper Hall)

Restoree. New York, Ballantine, and London, Rapp and Whiting, 1967.
Dragonflight (Dragonrider). New York, Ballantine, 1968; London, Rapp and Whiting, 1969.
Decision at Doona. New York, Ballantine, 1969; London, Rapp and Whiting, 1970.
The Ship Who Sang. New York, Walker, 1969; London, Rapp and Whiting, 1971.
Dragonquest (Dragonrider). New York, Ballantine, 1971; London, Rapp and Whiting-Deutsch, 1973.
To Ride Pegasus. New York, Ballantine, 1973; London, Dent, 1975.
Dragonsong (juvenile; Harper Hall). New York, Atheneum, and London, Sidgwick and Jackson, 1976.
Dragonsinger (juvenile; Harper Hall). New York, Atheneum, and London, Sidgwick and Jackson, 1977.
Dinosaur Planet. London, Futura, 1977; New York, Ballantine, 1978.
The White Dragon (Dragonrider). New York, Ballantine, 1978; London, Sidgwick and Jackson, 1979.
Dragondrums (juvenile; Harper Hall). New York, Atheneum, 1979; London, Sidgwick and Jackson, 1980.

Short Stories

A Time When. Boston, NESFA Press, 1975.
Get Off the Unicorn. New York, Ballantine, 1977; London, Corgi, 1979.

Uncollected Short Story

"Lady in Waiting," in *Cassandra Rising,* edited by Alice Laurance.   New York, Doubleday, 1978.

OTHER PUBLICATIONS

Novels

The Mark of Merlin.   New York, Dell, 1971; London, Millington, 1977.
The Ring of Fear.   New York, Dell, 1971; London, Millington, 1979.
The Kilternan Legacy.   New York, Dell, 1975; London, Millington, 1976.

Other

Editor, *Alchemy and Academe: A Collection of Original Stories Concerning Themselves with Transmutations, Mental and Elemental, Alchemical and Academic.*   New York, Doubleday, 1970.
Editor, *Cooking Out of This World.*   New York, Ballantine, 1973.

*

Manuscript Collections: Syracuse University, New York; Kerlan Collection, University of Minnesota, Minneapolis.

Anne McCaffrey comments:

I am a story-teller of *science-fiction* and wish that label attached to my work in that field. I make this point as I am often classified, erroneously, as a fantasy writer. Since I am more interested in the interaction of people, the research I do for some of the books is not apparent, thus confusing the uninitiated. I have no pretentions to literary style or excellence, nor are my stories allegorical, mystical, or political. I cannot honestly call myself a feminist, though I do not disagree with the aims of the women's movement, and in *The Kilternan Legacy* I make comparisons between the rights of American women and the deplorable lack of status of Irish women. My personal philosophy was heavily influenced by Austin Tappan Wright's classic, *Islandia*—a book I read at 14 and consistently reread. Of all the stories I have written to date, *The Ship Who Sang* is my favorite.

*   *   *

Anne McCaffrey is primarily known for her books on Pern, a planet inhabited by dragons and dragonriders. But she is also the author of a body of science fiction which has nothing to do with dragons.

Restoree, for example, is the story of a terrestrial woman kidnapped by terrifying aliens who butcher sentients for food. Though she is dismembered, humanoid aliens restore her (thus the title). Since the restoration process has hitherto resulted in Frankenstein-like monsters, the heroine is confined to a prison camp; she escapes and has numerous adventures with a dashing hero who becomes her lover. This book has been criticized as too melodramatic and full of sexist stereotypes, but McCaffrey herself says it is a deliberate science-fiction parody of the gothic romance. *Decision at Doona* relates problems of alien encounters. A group of families leave over-populated earth in order to colonize a frontier planet. But terrestrial authorities will not permit them to colonize a planet already inhabited by intelligent life. When cat-like sentients, the Hrrubans, appear, the colonists' wholesome and idyllic life style is threatened. This book is characterized by fine portrayals of family relationships and frontier hardships, plus a touching picture of children's friendships. *The Ship Who Sang* is about a human female, Helva, whose multiple birth defects would have severely limited her activities in present-day society. But in a future society she is cybernetically linked to a space ship, so that her body *becomes* the ship. Her relationships with non-cyborg humans are handled with imagination and verve.

The Dragonrider novels are set on Pern, a planet colonized in the forgotten past by terrestrials who left bio-sculptured dragons as defense against Pern's companion, a giant planet with an eccentric orbit and a mycorrhizoid spore called Thread which travels across vacuum to devour any living thing on Pern. The dragons chew phosphine-bearing rock and fly against Thread, charring it in mid-air. Directing these dragons are their riders, empathically linked to them. The dragons are not only highly empathic and telepathic, they can travel telekinetically across large distances in an instant and also, it is learned, through time. The breeding habits and hatching of the dragons, plus the method by which they are emotionally bonded to their riders, are the subject matter of the most spirited and moving passages of the novels. Though the Dragonrider novels contain many romantic elements—Pern's society is medieval in flavor—they are science fiction rather than sword and sorcery, since McCaffrey bases draconic phenomena on scientific principle. The Pern or dragon books have been McCaffrey's greatest success. They also express best a central metaphor of her fiction, the "rider-Pegasus" image, where the rider of the dragon represents intellect and direction, and the dragon itself (or in her other works various other kinds of flying steed, such as the spaceship in *The Ship Who Sang*) represents emotion and drive. A further development of such imagery is shown in *To Ride Pegasus,* where the human intellect is seen as riding the "Pegasus" of extrasensory perception and other supernormal mental powers. The title of *Get Off the Unicorn* suggests similar imagery; the book itself is a series of stories which are part of various worlds McCaffrey uses in her novels.

A less attractive figure of the artist is seen in the Killashandra stories (in Roger Elwood's *Continuum* series). This brilliantly plotted four-part story depicts Killashandra Ree, a woman whose musical ability enables her to cut crystal used in communications and the drive of interstellar ships. Unfortunately, the cutting process, which involves the creation of reverberating sound which fractures the crystal somewhat as a diamond is cut, eventually drives the talented cutters mad, depriving them of restraint and memory. McCaffrey has also started a series of books on warm-blooded dinosaurs (*Dinosaur Planet*).

McCaffrey's characterization has often been praised as her best trait, and indeed she has created some fine portraits, particularly of strong-minded and noble women, both sympathetic and evil. But her finest achievements are the detailed descriptions of fictional phenomena like mating, hatching, and impressing of dragons, and cutting of crystal. In one novella, "The Greatest Love" (in *Future-love,* 1977), she has predicted an event in the scientific community, extra-uterine fertilization of a human ovum with birth of healthy offspring. Her juvenile dragon series (Harper Hall) is exciting and highly readable without being condescending. Fine characterization and ability to extrapolate creatively from scientific speculation are the qualities that place McCaffrey in the first rank of contemporary science-fiction writers.

—Mary T. Brizzi

McCLARY, Thomas (Calvert).   Also writes as Calvin Peregoy. American.

SCIENCE-FICTION PUBLICATIONS

Novels

Rebirth, When Everyone Forgot.   New York, Bartholomew House, 1944.
Three Thousand Years.   Reading, Pennsylvania, Fantasy Press, 1954.

Uncollected Short Stories

"Food for the First Planet," in *Astounding* (New York), August 1938.
"Parole," in *Unknown Worlds* (New York), June 1939.
"The Tommyknocker," in *Unknown Worlds* (New York), October 1940.
"The Case of Jack Freysling," in *Astounding* (New York), October 1944.

Uncollected Short Stories as Calvin Peregoy (series: Dr. Conklin in all stories)

"Short-Wave Castle," in *Astounding* (New York), February 1934.
"Dr. Conklin—Pacifist," in *Astounding* (New York), August 1934.
"Shortwave Experiment," in *Astounding* (New York), February 1935.
"The Terrible Sense," in *Astounding* (New York), August 1938.

* * *

In addition to a few Calvin Peregoy short stories, Thomas McClary has produced two memorable works, *Rebirth* and *Three Thousand Years*, both Darwinian in attitude. In both a scientific elite theorize that, together with the intelligent and fit from other fields, they can overcome the stratified prejudices and superstitions of their age, wipe the slate clean, and produce a new utopia characterized by some degree of comfort and humanity. To achieve this the scientists intentionally and instantaneously precipitate a catastrophe, by a memory-obliterating ray in *Rebirth* and by the translation of all life forms to a state of suspended animation in *Three Thousand Years*. Both works partially deflate such idealistic visions of reformation by revealing man at the instinctual level as possessive, violent, competitive, and innately unequal (his weaknesses and his strengths), but suggest that love, music, pride in work, and a basic sense of responsibility toward those who can contribute to the community raise man above both his animal limitations and any computerized substitutes. When human minds are reduced to a *tabula rasa* amid a technologically advanced society (*Rebirth*) or when that technology crumbles (*Three Thousand Years*), chaos, destruction, and death ensue. In *Rebirth* man must relearn such elementary skills as talking, walking, and eating; in *Three Thousand Years* experts must learn to start from scratch; in both man must survive on the basis of instinct and innate capacity. Most die, but the clever and strong survive to rebuild society and to become, ultimately, very much what they had been before rebirth or suspension, with only some achieving higher levels of understanding than before. Yet overall the world is a better place, with the weak weeded out, the government established on a more realistic basis of common need and common interest, and scientists and politicians learning to cooperate to keep man striving and progressing. Once one has accepted rather implausible initial premises and a simplistic style, the working out of the details is interesting and occasionally witty and unexpected.

—Gina Macdonald

McCOMAS, J(esse) Francis. Also wrote as Webb Marlowe. American. Born in 1911. Worked for Simon and Schuster, publishers; Editor, with Anthony Boucher, 1949-54, and Advisory Editor, 1954-62, *The Magazine of Fantasy and Science Fiction. Died in April 1978.*

SCIENCE-FICTION PUBLICATIONS

Uncollected Short Stories

"Flight into Darkness" (as Webb Marlowe), in *Adventures in Time*

and Space, edited by Raymond J. Healy and McComas. New York, Random House, 1946; London, Grayson, 1952.
"Contract for a Body" (as Webb Marlowe), in *Fantastic Adventures* (New York), July 1948.
"Shock Treatment," in *9 Tales of Space and Time*, edited by Raymond J. Healy. New York, Holt, 1954.
"Brave New World," in *The Best from Fantasy and Science Fiction 4*, edited by Anthony Boucher. New York, Doubleday, 1955.
"Parallel," in *Fantasy and Science Fiction* (New York), April 1955.
"Criminal Negligence," in *Space, Time, and Crime,* edited by Miriam Allen deFord. New York, Paperback Library, 1964.

OTHER PUBLICATIONS

Other

"In Memoriam—Anthony Boucher," in *Nebula Award Stories 4,* edited by Poul Anderson. New York, Doubleday, 1969.

Editor, with Raymond J. Healy, *Adventures in Time and Space.* New York, Random House, 1946; London, Grayson, 1952.
Editor, with Anthony Boucher, *The Best from Fantasy and Science Fiction 1-3.* Boston, Little Brown, 2 vols., 1952-53; New York, Doubleday, 1 vol., 1954.
Editor, with Raymond J. Healy, *Famous Science-Fiction Stories.* New York, Random House, 1957.
Editor, *The Graveside Companion: An Anthology of California Murders.* New York, Obolensky, 1962.
ditor, *Crimes and Misfortunes: The Anthony Boucher Memorial Anthology of Mysteries.* New York, Random House, 1970.
Editor, *Special Wonder: The Anthony Boucher Memorial Anthology of Fantasy and Science Fiction.* New York, Random House, 1970.

* * *

Although he attracted some critical attention for his writing, J. Francis McComas is best known in partnership activities. His story "Flight Into Darkness" is dated, since it deals with speculative relationships between the US and the remnants of German civilization after World War II. Here the author is concerned with political jingoism in the fanatical devotion to The Leader by the story's villain, who hatches a plot to overthrow the triumphant Americans through the secret construction of a space ship. While the yarn is starkly melodramatic, with a spectacular ending to satisfy the post-World War II reader, McComas's sympathetic sketching of the crippled younger brother earns the account more than passing attention.

It is McComas's sensitivity, in fact, which contributed so greatly to his success in two partnerships that made him a notable figure in science fiction. The first of these was with Anthony Boucher in the creation in 1949 of *The Magazine of Fantasy and Science Fiction*. This periodical was unusual in attracting stories of high literary quality at a time when many pulps subsisted on much cheaper fare. While the magazine's content leaned heavily toward fantasy the balance shifted to include some of the finest science fiction written for magazines. His keen perceptiveness and high literary standards are evident, too, in *Adventures in Time and Space,* which McComas edited with Raymond J. Healy. This anthology gave science fiction an impetus toward respectability and literary value which it may not have previously enjoyed by presenting a stimulating cross-section of speculative experiences and underlining the contribution of science fiction to American literature.

J. Francis McComas deserves great critical attention, then, for his keen perception and high literary standards. Without such individuals it is very speculative whether the fine writers of science fiction we can enjoy today would have developed to such respectable levels. While he was himself a writer, he was more: a connoisseur of writing standards.

—Robert H. Wilcox

McHUGH, Vincent. American. Born in Providence, Rhode Island, 23 December 1904. Educated in parochial schools; Providence College, one year. Writer and director, Bureau of Domestic Motion Pictures, Office of War Information, 1942-43. Married Adeliza Sorenson (second marriage). Public Library messenger; reviewer, New Orleans *Double Dealer;* Associate Editor, New York *Evening Post Literary Review* (later *Saturday Review of Literature*); associated with *American Stuff, New York Panorama, New York City Guide,* and *New Yorker*; teacher and research assistant, New York University; taught at Community Institute of University of Denver, 1948-52, and at writers workshops at the University of Kansas City, University of Missouri, Columbia, and University of New Hampshire, Durham.

SCIENCE-FICTION PUBLICATIONS

Novel

I Am Thinking of My Darling. New York, Simon and Schuster, 1943.

OTHER PUBLICATIONS

Novels

Touch Me Not. New York, Cape and Smith, 1930.
Sing Before Breakfast. New York, Simon and Schuster, 1933.
Caleb Catlum's America. New York, Stackpole, 1936.
The Victory. New York, Random House, 1947.
Edge of the World. New York, Ballantine, 1953.

Verse

The Blue Hen's Chickens: Poems, Verses, Blues. New York, Random House, 1947.
Alpha: The Mutabilities. San Francisco, Porpoise Bookshop, 1958.

Other

Song for American Union, music by Harold J. Rome. New York, Writers' War Board, n.d.
Primer of the Novel. New York, Random House, 1950.

Translator, with C.H. Kwock, *Why I Live on the Mountain.* San Francisco, Golden Mountain Press, 1958.
Translator, with C.H. Kwock, *The Lady and the Hermit,* by Ch'ing-chao Li. San Francisco, Golden Mountain Press, 1962.

*   *   *

Vincent McHugh's *Caleb Catlum's America,* a romp through American history using the device of an 18th-century Methuselah, may be taken as having marginal SF interest. But McHugh's place in science fiction is assured by *I Am Thinking of My Darling.* It made little impression in 1943 and remains little known, yet it is a creditable piece of work, firmly science fiction with a sound and well-detailed basis, and surprisingly little dated.

Plague strikes New York. The victims of the new virus have a mild fever and overwhelming euphoria and irresponsibility. It is dangerous mostly for its crippling effect on community life; workers drop essential jobs to revel in the joy of living, and soon goods and services are free because no one wants to take the money. Meanwhile, a city planner named Jim Rowen, the narrator, leads a committee of key men to keep the plague from becoming a disaster. Simultaneously he hunts for his wife, who under the plague's influence is living out fantasy roles and keeping ahead of him.

One aspect of the book is a detective puzzle, another is an urgent research effort to control the infection, and yet another the effort to cope with the unpredictable situation as the unconscious foundations of society are eroded. It is by no means the light frolic the theme suggests, but a book touching on basic social paradoxes. How much do we give up for public security? Can we live our own

lives and have a high technology? It is crammed with details of New York, with glancing insights on groups in action, planning, and design.

—Graham Stone

———————

McINTOSH, J.T. Pseudonym for James Murdoch Macgregor; also writes as H.J. Murdoch. British. Born in Paisley, Renfrew, 14 February 1925. Educated at Robert Gordon's College, Aberdeen, 1936-41; Aberdeen University, 1943-47, M.A. (honours) in English. Married Margaret Murray in 1960; two daughters and one son. Since 1947, sub-editor, Aberdeen *Press and Journal.* Agent: Campbell Thomson and McLaughlin Ltd., 31 Newington Green, London N16 9PU, England; or, Blassingame McCauley and Wood, 60 East 42nd Street, New York, New York 10017, U.S.A. Address: 63 Abbotswell Drive, Aberdeen, Scotland.

SCIENCE-FICTION PUBLICATIONS

Novels

World Out of Mind. New York, Doubleday, 1953; London, Museum Press, 1955.
Born Leader. New York, Doubleday, 1954; London, Museum Press, 1955; as *Worlds Apart,* New York, Avon, 1958.
One in Three Hundred. New York, Doubleday, 1954; London, Museum Press, 1956.
The Fittest. New York, Doubleday, 1955; London, Corgi, 1961; as *The Rule of the Pagbeasts,* New York, Fawcett, 1956.
200 Years to Christmas. New York, Ace, 1961.
The Million Cities. New York, Pyramid, 1963.
Out of Chaos. London, Digit, 1964.
The Noman Way. London, Digit, 1964.
Time for a Change. London, Joseph, 1967; as *Snow White and the Giants,* New York, Avon, 1968.
Six Gates from Limbo. London, Joseph, 1968; New York, Avon, 1969.
Transmigration. New York, Avon, 1970.
Flight from Rebirth. New York, Avon, 1971; London, Hale, 1973.
The Cosmic Spies. London, Hale, 1972.
The Space Sorcerers. London, Hale, 1972; as *The Suiciders,* New York, Avon, 1973.
Galactic Takeover Bid. London, Hale, 1973.
This Is the Way the World Begins. London, Corgi, 1977.
Norman Conquest 2066. London, Corgi, 1977.
A Planet Called Utopia. New York, Kensington, 1979.

Uncollected Short Stories

"The Curfew Tolls," in *Astounding* (New York), December 1950.
"Safety Margin," in *Planet* (New York), January 1951.
"Venus Mission," in *Planet* (New York), July 1951.
"Sanctuary, Oh Ulla!," in *Planet* (New York), September 1951.
"Then There Were Two," in *Science Fantasy* (Bournemouth), Winter 1951.
"When Aliens Meet," in *New Worlds* (London), Winter 1951.
"Machine Made," in *No Place Like Earth,* edited by E.J. Carnell. London, Boardman, 1952.
"Hallucination Orbit," in *Galaxy* (New York), January 1952.
"The World That Changed," in *New Worlds* (London), March 1952.
"Katahut Said No," in *Galaxy* (New York), April 1952.
"Tradition," in *Other Worlds* (Evanston, Indiana), April 1952.

"The Reluctant Colonist," in *Planet* (New York), May 1952.
"The Broken Record" (as James Macgregor), in *New Worlds* (London), September 1952.
"The ESP Worlds," in *New Worlds* (London), July, September, November 1952.
"Stitch in Time," in *Science Fantasy* (Bournemouth), Autumn 1952.
"Talents," in *Fantasy and Science Fiction* (New York), October 1952.
"The Volunteers," in *Science Fantasy* (Bournemouth), Spring 1953.
"Beggars All," in *Fantasy and Science Fiction* (New York), April 1953.
"Escape Me Never," in *Fantastic* (New York), April 1953.
"Mind Alone," in *Galaxy* (New York), August 1953.
"War's Great Organ," in *Nebula* (Glasgow), September 1953.
"The Happier Eden," in *Nebula* (Glasgow), December 1953.
"Relay Race," in *New Worlds 22* (London), 1954.
"Divine Right," in *Nebula* (Glasgow), February 1954.
"Men Like Mules," in *Galaxy* (New York), February 1954.
"Bias," in *Astounding* (New York), May 1954.
"This Precious Stone" (as H.J. Murdoch), in *Science Fantasy* (Bournemouth), July 1954.
"Five into Four," in *Science Fantasy* (Bournemouth), September 1954.
"Spy," in *Galaxy* (New York), October 1954.
"Playback," in *Galaxy* (New York), December 1954.
"Live for Ever," in *Science Fantasy* (Bournemouth), December 1954.
"First Lady," in *Best SF 1,* edited by Edmund Crispin. London, Faber, 1955.
"Selection," in *Fantasy and Science Fiction* (New York), January 1955.
"Open House," in *Galaxy* (New York), February 1955.
"Eleventh Commandment," in *Fantasy and Science Fiction* (New York), May 1955.
"The Big Hop," in *Authentic* (London), May, June 1955.
"Bluebird World," in *New Worlds* (London), June 1955.
"The Way Home," in *New Worlds* (London), August 1955.
"The Man Who Cried 'Sheep!,'" in *Fantasy and Science Fiction* (New York), September 1955.
"The Lady and the Bull," in *Authentic* (London), December 1955.
"The Solomon Plan," in *New Worlds* (London), February 1956.
"The Deciding Factor," in *Authentic* (London), April 1956.
"The Little Corporal," in *Authentic* (London), July 1956.
"Empath," in *New Worlds* (London), August 1956.
"Report on Earth," in *New Worlds* (London), September 1956.
"Shield Against Death," in *Fantastic Universe* (Chicago), May 1957.
"The Sandmen," in *Fantasy and Science Fiction* (New York), June 1957.
"Unfit for Humans," in *Authentic* (London), August 1957.
"In Black and White," in *Galaxy* (New York), August 1958.
"You Were Right, Joe," in *The Fourth Galaxy Reader,* edited by H.L. Gold. New York, Doubleday, 1959.
"Kingslayer," in *Galaxy* (New York), April 1959.
"Tenth Time Around," in *Fantasy and Science Fiction* (New York), May 1959.
"No Place for Crime," in *Galaxy* (New York), June 1959.
"Return of a Prodigal," in *If* (New York), November 1959.
"The Night Before the Battle," in *Fantastic Universe* (Chicago), February 1960.
"The Ship from Home," in *Science Fantasy* (Bournemouth), February 1960.
"Merlin," in *Fantastic* (New York), March 1960.
"World Without Annette," in *Fantastic* (New York), May 1960.
"In a Body," in *If* (New York), July 1960.
"Planet on Probation," in *Science Fantasy* (Bournemouth), August 1960.
"Absolute Power," in *If* (New York), January 1961.
"I Can Do Anything," in *Galaxy* (New York), April 1961.
"That's How It Goes," in *If* (New York), May 1961.
"Doormat World," in *If* (New York), July 1961.
"The Gatekeepers," in *Galaxy* (New York), August 1961.
"One into Two," in *Fantasy and Science Fiction* (New York), February 1962.

"The Stupid General," in *Fantasy and Science Fiction* (New York), August 1962.
"Immortality...for Some," in *12 Great Classics of Science Fiction,* edited by Groff Conklin. New York, Fawcett, 1963.
"The Ten-Point Princess," in *If* (New York), March 1963.
"Spanner in the Works," in *Analog* (New York), March 1963.
"Iceberg from Earth," in *Analog* (New York), April 1963.
"Hermit," in *Analog* (New York), June 1963.
"To the Stars," in *Worlds of Tomorrow* (New York), August 1963.
"Far Avanal," in *Worlds of Tomorrow* (New York), December 1963.
"Unit," in *Five-Odd,* edited by Groff Conklin. New York, Pyramid, 1964.
"Grandmother Earth," in *Galaxy* (New York), February 1964.
"Humanoid Sacrifice," in *Fantasy and Science Fiction* (New York), March 1964.
"Snap Judgement," in *Analog* (New York), June 1964.
"The Great Doomed Ship," in *Worlds of Tomorrow* (New York), June 1964.
"Planet of Change," in *Fantastic* (New York), September 1964.
"The Kicksters," in *Worlds of Tomorrow* (New York), November 1964.
"At the Top of the World," in *If* (New York), December 1964.
"The Man Who Killed Immortals," in *Galaxy* (New York), February 1965.
"The Iceman Goeth," in *Analog* (New York), March 1965.
"The Sudden Silence," in *Fantasy and Science Fiction* (New York), April 1966.
"Planet of Fakers," in *Galaxy* (New York), October 1966.
"The Saw and the Carpenter," in *Fantasy and Science Fiction* (New York), September 1967.
"Pontius Pirates," in *Analog* (New York), October 1967.
"The Wrong World," in *Elsewhere and Elsewhen,* edited by Groff Conklin. New York, Berkley, 1968.
"Poor Planet," in *Seven Trips Through Time and Space,* edited by Groff Conklin. New York, Fawcett, 1968.
"Almost Human," in *Amazing* (New York), January 1971.
"The Real People," in *If* (New York), December 1971.
"Made in U.S.A.," in *The Androids Are Coming,* edited by Robert Silverberg. New York, Elsevier Nelson, 1979.
"The World of God," in *Galaxy* (New York), March-April 1979.

OTHER PUBLICATIONS

Novels

Take a Pair of Private Eyes (novelization of TV series). London, Muller, and New York, Doubleday, 1968.
A Coat of Blackmail. London, Muller, 1970; New York, Doubleday, 1971.

Novels as James Macgregor

When the Ship Sank. New York, Doubleday, 1959; London, Heinemann, 1960.
Incident over the Pacific. New York, Doubleday, 1960; as *A Cry to Heaven,* London, Heinemann, 1961.
The Iron Rain. London, Heinemann, 1962.

Other as James Macgregor

Glamour in Your Lens: A Commonsense Guide to Attractive Photography. London, Focal Press, 1958.
Wine Making for All. London, Faber, 1966.
Beer Making for All. London, Faber, 1967.

J.T. McIntosh comments:
I became a science fiction writer not by choice but by force of circumstance. At the time when I was ready to publish (1945-50), paper was in short supply and publishers tended to use it for books by established authors. America was the obvious market, but I had no accurate knowledge of the U.S. scene. So I wrote SF, in which accurate knowledge of the U.S. scene is not necessary.

Later, when I tried non-SF, the international nature of SF became clear to me. There was little interest in my mainstream fiction outside Britain, while the SF books often had editions in many other countries.

*   *   *

Under the pen name J.T. McIntosh, the Scots writer and journalist James Murdoch Macgregor first won recognition as an author of science fiction with *World Out of Mind,* his first novel. This work presents a future society organized around the ultimate merit system: IQ. All members of this society are rigorously tested for intelligence; test results place each individual in a group marked by a colored badge indicating rank. The governing class, wearing the white star indicating the highest 1% of intelligence, is infiltrated by a Martian who has been reprocessed as a human being and whose mission is to prepare for a Martian invasion. However, since the Martian spy has become *completely* human, he cannot help falling in love with the youngest (and most beautiful) living white star. He betrays the loveless Martians and thwarts the invasion. Humanity (and love) conquer.

Also greeted with critical enthusiasm, *Born Leader* develops two human conflicts: daring youth pitted against conservative age, and a cooperative libertarian society pitted against a military totalitarian state. Mundis, a planet colonised by space settlers from an Earth destroyed by nuclear war, is inhabited by two generations: the original settlers, determined not to use nuclear power, and their children, born only after the 22-year space voyage, eager to explore its possibilities. Mundis's egalitarian society is threatened by invaders from a second Earth ship, a Spartan, loveless military group whose women are considered subhuman breeders. Under the threat of domination, the Mundans unite, develop nuclear defenses, defeat the invaders, and integrate them into their own egalitarian system.

One in Three Hundred begins on an Earth doomed by a shift in its solar orbit. It shows the selection of a small and random minority for space colonisation, their hazardous voyage, and their sufferings in making Mars habitable from the point of view of one of the leaders responsible for the selection and supervision of a small group. Faced by the threat of a sadist and would-be dictator on Mars, the colonists rebel, kill the tyrants, and cooperate successfully in order to survive. *The Fittest* similarly shows humans forced to work together for survival against great physical odds. Earth is overpopulated by paggets, super-intelligent mice, cats, rats, and dogs, developed by accident in an experiment and determined to overwhelm human life by cutting lines of communication, devouring supplies, sabotage, and murder. Mankind can survive biologically only by using the uniquely human qualities of communication and cooperation to remain the fittest species in simple democratic communities free from social convention.

McIntosh's later full-length fiction fails to live up to the promise of his early novels. Although his later work still deals with his major themes—overpopulation in *The Million Cities,* space travel and evolution in *200 Years to Christmas,* the aftermath of holocaust in *Out of Chaos,* and morality in *Six Gates from Limbo, Transmigration,* and *Flight from Rebirth*—he tends to repeat and overwrite early plots, often expanding ideas originally published as short stories. His ability to write fast and convincing action remains, but he fails to present themes and ideas as convincingly as in his novels from the early 1950's.

McIntosh's four early novels interestingly depict libertarian utopias whose members' mutual concern and willingness to cooperate in order to survive demonstrate a hopeful view of human nature in a threatening universe. The terrible odds his characters must face are plausible threats for our future: overpopulation, misdirected technology, war, physical changes on Earth itself. In the Darwinian struggle to survive, women become essential. McIntosh's heroes are typically attracted to independence, competence, and strength in their mates, rather than to dependence, passivity, and physical frailty they might have preferred in easier times. McIntosh's ability to depict realistically the violence and dangers of the unknown future and his hopefulness about mankind's ability to endure make his early novels both moving and memorable.

—Katherine Staples

McINTYRE, Vonda N(eel). American. Born in Louisville, Kentucky, 28 August 1948. Educated at the University of Washington, Seattle, B.S. in biology 1970, graduate study in genetics, 1970-71. Conference organizer, and riding and writing instructor. Recipient: Nebula Award, 1973, 1979; Hugo Award, 1979. Agent: Frances Collin, Rodell-Collin Literary Agency, 156 East 52nd Street, New York, New York 10022. Address: 4121 Interlake North, Seattle, Washington 98103, U.S.A.

SCIENCE-FICTION PUBLICATIONS

Novels

The Exile Waiting. New York, Doubleday, 1975; London, Gollancz, 1976.
Dreamsnake. Boston, Houghton Mifflin, and London, Gollancz, 1978.

Short Stories

Fireflood and Other Stories. Boston, Houghton Mifflin, 1979.

Uncollected Short Story

"Shadows, Moving," in *Interfaces,* edited by Ursula K. Le Guin and Virginia Kidd. New York, Ace, 1980.

OTHER PUBLICATIONS

Other

Editor, with Susan Janice Anderson, *Aurora: Beyond Equality.* New York, Fawcett, 1976.

*   *   *

Explicitly feminist in orientation, Vonda N. McIntyre's science fiction—part of a surge of feminist science fiction and fantasy being written in the 1970's—is characterized not only by careful attention to those sexist aspects of current society that inhibit or destroy people's potentiality but also by thoughtful depictions of the social and personal problems which may still exist when overt sexual stereotyping and discrimination are vanquished. The need for personal commitment—to oneself and others—despite human imperfection is a theme throughout McIntyre's works, many of which also reflect her scientific background.

"Of Mist, and Grass, and Sand" depicts a post-holocaust society whose healers aid the sick by cultivating specific serums from snake venom. Its protagonist, herself named Snake, is an independent, responsible, and strong person who successfully copes not only with the strenuous demands of her chosen profession but also with her own failure to assess accurately the fears of the nomadic people who have desperately sought her help. Even though they kill one of her snakes, she continues to treat, and ultimately cure, their sick child. This story is exceptional in its understated presentation of realistically flawed characters in a non-sexist society.

The Exile Waiting, McIntyre's first novel, continues to explore strong women in possible futures. Its young protagonist, Mischa, is a telepath in another post-holocaust society who frees herself from a series of tyrannies, mental as well as physical, through her own ingenuity and courage. "Screwtop," set in a future penal institution, is the story of Kylis, a female spaceport "rat" whose resourcefulness has enabled her to survive since childhood as an interplanetary stowaway. Imprisoned, Kylis learns to accept responsibility for others as well as for herself when she is offered, but refuses, freedom for betraying two fellow prisoners. McIntyre's creation of a "tetraparental"—a genetically superior character endowed with the traits of four parents—is a reflection of her scientific training. "Aztecs" again demonstrates McIntyre's concern with psychologically strong, mature women and her scientific background. Beginning with the sentence, "She gave up her heart quite willingly," this story follows its central character, Laena, through several rites of passage. Having had her heart surgically removed in order to survive "transit" as a spaceship pilot, Laena must adjust not only to her new, rarefied social status but to the unexpected side effects of the surgery. It is only when she falls in love (again, giving up her heart) that this character learns that her biological rhythms are no longer compatible with those of any surgically unaltered person. Remaining with her lover will kill her, but Laena rejects the conventional alternatives of either a romantic liebestod or a renunciation of her professional ambitions. Instead, McIntyre's character sadly adjusts to the limitations of her chosen way of life.

In 1978, McIntyre expanded "Of Mist, and Grass, and Sand," into a full-length novel, *Dreamsnake*. Episodic in structure, this work follows Snake on a series of adventures which highlight various restrictive aspects of present-day society and depict social and personal alternatives. While searching for a replacement for the snake she has lost, the protagonist encounters "partnerships" that, unlike contemporary marriages, consist of three people. Avoiding gender pronouns in this episode, McIntyre succeeds in conveying the superfluousness of sex roles in functional relationships. In later episodes, Snake encounters and helps eradicate the pain that lack of contraceptive knowledge or emphasis on physical appearance can cause.

McIntyre is an active, influential younger member of the science-fiction community whose future work is eagerly awaited.

—Natalie M. Rosinsky

* * *

McKENNA, Richard M(ilton).   American.   Born in Mountain Home, Idaho, 9 May 1913. Educated at the University of North Carolina, Chapel Hill, B.A. in English 1956 (Phi Beta Kappa). Married Eva Mae Grice in 1956. Served in the United States Navy, 1931-53: chief machinist's mate; free-lance writer from 1953. Recipient: Harper Prize, 1963; Nebula Award, 1966. *Died 1 November 1964.*

SCIENCE-FICTION PUBLICATIONS

Short Stories

Casey Agonistes and Other Science Fiction and Fantasy Stories. New York, Harper, 1973; London, Gollancz, 1974.

OTHER PUBLICATIONS

Novel

The Sand Pebbles.   New York, Harper, 1962; London, Gollancz, 1963.

Short Stories

The Sons of Martha and Other Stories, edited by M.S. Wyeth, Jr.   New York, Harper, 1967.

Other

New Eyes for Old: Nonfiction Writing, edited by Eva Grice McKenna and Shirley Graves Cochrane.   Winston-Salem, North Carolina, Blair, 1972.
"Journey with a Little Man," in *Turning Points,* edited by Damon Knight.   New York, Harper, 1977.

* * *

Richard M. McKenna, although best known for his fine novel *The Sand Pebbles,* was also a skilled writer of science fiction whose short stories and novelettes are usually concerned with the troubling and often painful aspects of both fantasy and reality. In a small number of science-fiction and fantasy stories that are vividly written, fast paced, and well characterized, McKenna continually exhibits his superb gifts as a storyteller.

Most of McKenna's science-fiction works are rich in anthropological content. They frequently portray individuals in relation to their groups, and both individual and group in relation to alien cultures or fantasy phenomena. "Casey Agonistes" meticulously explores the interrelationships of patients in a tuberculosis ward, depicting their symbolic rebellion against hospital authority through an ape that is either a genuine apparition or their shared fantasy. The ape, Casey, reflects in his antics the patients' underlying attitudes about the hospital and their poignant efforts to cope with the fact of death. Also, the sharing of the fantasy becomes a catalyst for the raising of the emotional levels of the ward and the improvement of the general conditions there. In "Mine Own Ways," "Hunter, Come Home," and "The Bramble Bush" characters who are members of a scientific team are faced with conflicts that in different ways are caused by the uniqueness of an alien culture on the planet that is the focus of their professional activities. In these stories the psychological state of the protagonists influences and affects the relationship of the group to the aliens and leads to the protagonists being put through a symbolic or actual ritual. This experience alters not only their beliefs, but also the outcome of the group's mission. McKenna depicts such anthropological themes and motifs with an equal concern for the humans and the aliens.

The world of fantasy, its virtues as well as defects, is the subject on which McKenna focuses most often. In some stories he studies the interplay between the fantasy and an outer reality, casting certain features of the reality into doubt, and in others he constructs fantasy worlds whose landscapes are the basis for a questioning of the nature of fantasy and reality. Often the fantasy world is more appealing, and even ameliorative, as in the cheerful ape's transformation of the despairing hospital ward into an active and even hopeful place. In "The Secret Place" a barren featureless Oregon countryside hides a wondrous fairyland that, in a way, defies the efforts of science to penetrate it and utilize its resources. Dying sailors, in "Fiddler's Green," escape into an imperfect but, through their own imaginative efforts, developing otherworld that simultaneously represents salvation and sterility. Stories like these present fantasies that are perceived by the characters as just as real as the obsession-ridden world of reality. However the stories are resolved, whether with acceptance or rejection of the fantasy, the worlds function as alternatives to reality or some facet of reality. In "Hunter, Come Home" and "The Bramble Bush" McKenna treats his planetary settings in a fantasy-like way. The exotic world of the former affects the hold on reality of individuals from two differing human cultures, and the bizarre time-changing world of the latter traps a group of meddling scientists in a field that changes the very shape of their universe.

McKenna integrates linguistic considerations into many of his stories, which is not surprising in an author so intensely interested in anthropological subjects and with the structure of reality versus illusion. The overly macho hunting culture of "Hunter, Come Home" reveals itself as much through its language as its cultural statements of belief. In their society bullets is a curse word, and the ideal is to be as sharp as a gunflint. Words are said to come alive in the native rituals of "Mine Own Ways"; time-binding symbology is integral to the plot of "The Bramble Bush."

No matter how exotic his planetary settings are, and no matter how deeply his characters penetrate a fantasy world, McKenna's fiction is always credible. He makes the fantasy worlds real and, for that matter, presents what is essentially fantastic and unreal about the so-called reality. Such attention to detail, along with McKenna's meticulous approach to the writing of language, adds to the verisimilitude of tales that are among the best examples of storytelling in science fiction.

—Robert Thurston

McLAUGHLIN, Dean (Benjamin, Jr.). American. Born in Ann Arbor, Michigan, 22 July 1931. Educated at the University of Michigan, Ann Arbor, A.B. 1953. Buyer for Slater's Inc., bookshop, Ann Arbor. Address: 1214 West Washington Street, Ann Arbor, Michigan 48103, U.S.A.

SCIENCE-FICTION PUBLICATIONS

Novels

Dome World. New York, Pyramid, 1962.
The Fury from Earth. New York, Pyramid, 1963.
The Man Who Wanted Stars. New York, Lancer, 1965.

Short Stories

Hawk among the Sparrows. New York, Scribner, 1976; London, Hale, 1977.

*   *   *

Dean McLaughlin's novels display a fascination with the concept of one man capable of altering the entire course of history. McLaughlin does not have in mind brilliant military strategists or mighty-thewed barbarians, but common men, those who may even doubt their own actions but carry through with them nonetheless. Danial Mason, leader of the undersea city of Wilmington in *Dome World,* is a perfect example. Mason is chief administrator of the domed city, one of many that have sprung up on the ocean floor, built by various nations intent on mining or fishing or trading with other nations. But the undersea cities are also the focus of some conflict because of the haphazard fashion in which matters of sovereignty have been resolved. So it is that the American Union and South Africa are on the verge of war over control of a rich vanadium deposit that lies between two such domes. Because of the utter vulnerability of the domes, Mason organizes a widespread secession from the mainland nations to prevent fatal involvement in their war. The second half of the novel deals with the situation some years later when the creation of smaller, individualized domes is the cause of tension between the newly formed league of domed cities and the mainland authorities. Once again a small businessman ignores his own government to take steps that eventually reduces the chance of war. Both of McLaughlin's characters are far from physically fit; one is recently returned from the moon and has difficulties with Earth's greater gravity, and the other has a weak heart that might cease to function at any time.

Similarly, the protagonist of *The Fury from Earth* is a pacifist who refuses to help the government of Venus to develop weapons for their war with Earth. On the other hand, he is willing to help design purely defensive weapons, and is quick to see that a new development on Earth could be used for interstellar travel rather than as an offensive weapon that will shake entire planets. This is thematically somewhat similar to McLaughlin's remaining novel, *The Man Who Wanted Stars,* in which a single man keeps the space program alive, primarily through his own stubbornness. The latter novel suffers somewhat from the didactic material, which often interferes with the plot, and with the megalomania of the central character, which often causes the reader to dislike him even while agreeing with his position.

McLaughlin has also produced a string of competent short stories, at least two of which are exceptional. "Hawk among the Sparrows" is somewhat unusual for McLaughlin in that the hero tries to alter history and fails utterly. He has been projected back through time with a modern supersonic aircraft, and assumes that he can affect the course of the air war in Europe. Such is not the case. He cannot locate appropriate fuel, and his aircraft travels so rapidly that it is impossible for him to engage in combat with his slower, more primitive antagonists. McLaughlin also produced one of the more fascinating alien societies in "The Brotherhood of Keepers."

Although not a stylistic virtuoso, McLaughlin employs clean prose throughout his writing, with a crisp delivery that falters only in *The Man Who Wanted Stars.* He avoids larger-than-life character very consciously, taking pains to make his characters vulnerable and human. His plots and situations ring true, and he takes care that issues are for the most part presented in many facets rather than clear cut. Most of his better fiction leaves the reader with something to consider even after the story has ended, although McLaughlin is careful to tie up necessary loose ends.

—Don D'Ammassa

———————

MEAD, (Edward) Shepherd. American. Born in St. Louis, Missouri, 26 April 1914. Educated at St. Louis Country Day School, graduated 1932; Washington University, St. Louis, B.A. 1936. Married Annabelle Pettibone in 1943; one daughter and two sons. Worked for Benton and Bowles, New York, 1936-56, retired as Vice-President; consultant, S.H. Benson Ltd., London, 1958-62. Agent: Gerald Pollinger, Laurence Pollinger Ltd., 18 Maddox Street, London W1R 0EU; or, Scott Meredith Literary Agency, 845 Third Avenue, New York, New York 10022, U.S.A. Address: Flat B, 3 West Eaton Place, London SW1X 8LU, England.

SCIENCE-FICTION PUBLICATIONS

Novels

The Magnificent MacInnes. New York, Farrar Straus, 1949; as *The Sex Machine,* New York, Popular Library, 1949.
The Big Ball of Wax: A Story of Tomorrow's Happy World. New York, Simon and Schuster, 1954; London, Boardman, 1955.
The Carefully Considered Rape of the World: A Novel about the Unspeakable. New York, Simon and Schuster, and London, Macdonald, 1966.

OTHER PUBLICATIONS

Novels

Tessie, The Hound of Channel One. New York, Doubleday, 1951.
The Admen. New York, Simon and Schuster, 1958; London, Boardman, 1959.
The Four Window Girl; or, How to Make More Money Than Men. New York, Simon and Schuster, and London, Boardman, 1959.
"Dudley, There Is No Tomorrow!" "Then How about This Afternoon?" New York, Simon and Schuster, and London, Macdonald, 1963.
How to Succeed at Business Spying by Trying. New York, Simon and Schuster, 1968; London, Harrap, 1969.
'Er; or, The Brassbound Beauty, The Bearded Bicyclist, and the Gold-Colored Teen-Age Grandfather. New York, Simon and Schuster, 1969; London, Harrap, 1970.

Other

How to Succeed in Business Without Really Trying: The Dastard's Guide to Fame and Fortune. New York, Simon and Schuster, 1952; Kingswood, Surrey, World's Work, 1953.
How to Get Rich in TV Without Really Trying. New York, Simon and Schuster, 1956; London, Boardman, 1958.
How to Succeed with Women Without Really Trying: The Dastard's Guide to the Birds and the Bees. New York, Ballantine, 1957; London, Boardman, 1958.
How to Live Like a Lord Without Really Trying: A Confidential Manual Prepared as Part of a Survival Kit for Americans Living in Britain. London, Macdonald, 1964; New York, Simon and Schuster, 1965.

How to Stay Medium-Young Practically Forever Without Really Trying.   New York, Simon and Schuster, 1971; London, Joseph, 1972.

Free the Male Man! The Manifesto of the Men's Liberation Movement.   New York, Simon and Schuster, 1972; London, Joseph, 1973.

How to Get to the Future Before It Gets to You.   New York, Hawthorn, and London, Joseph, 1974.

How to Succeed in Tennis Without Really Trying.   New York, McKay, 1977.

*

Manuscript Collection: Washington University, St. Louis.

Shepherd Mead comments:

I have a warm spot in my heart for science fiction. Sometimes things can be said by means of it that cannot be said any other way. That is surely true of *The Carefully Considered Rape of the World,* which is about genetics, really—that the first beings to control their own evolution will become the first gods of the universe.

My favorite book of all is *The Big Ball of Wax.* At the time I considered it the other side of the coin to Orwell's excellent *Nineteen Eighty-Four*—that the future would belong not to the totalitarian Big Brothers but to the persuaders. The book showed what would happen to a society that gave everyone only what the lowest common denominator wanted. Now that the returns are in, we can see which of us was right—and it wasn't Orwell! (a great man, nonetheless).

I have one more SF work in manuscript form called *The Purple Peoplegrams;* this is about the whole business of electronic communication with the rest of the universe.

*   *   *

Shepherd Mead, who is best known for *How to Succeed in Business Without Really Trying,* has written three novels which may be classed as science fiction. *The Magnificent MacInnes* and *The Big Ball of Wax* are similar in thrust—both focus on the manipulation of mass society by the media and by Madison Avenue. In the first the advertising industry and its marketing pollsters by catering to ordinary taste are making "sure everybody gets tomorrow what the lowest common denominator wanted yesterday." When it is accidently discovered that Victor V. MacInnes has the facility (unexplained) to intuit public opinion on any question, an absurd utopia is envisioned. Simply register the will of the people and then feed it in the name of "true Democracy." The result, of course, is a sterile, drab mediocrity—the TV program that achieves top ratings but has its audience soundly sleeping. The similarity between Kornbluth and Pohl (especially in *The Space Merchants*) and Mead extends to *The Big Ball of Wax,* an account of the crucial sequence of events in 1993 that have led to "the best of all possible worlds." The gimmick here is XP, an ersatz electronic experience for the real thing from eating to travel to sex (compare Compton's *Synthajoy*). XP provides the perfect vehicle for the merchandisers to guide society "step by step down the path of mediocrity." The warning is similar to Kornbluth's "The Marching Morons": "Notch by notch the mental level was dropping, thinking was decreasing, self-expression dying out." Both novels have as protagonists male, mid-level Madison Avenue executives who serve the system with naive enthusiasm: "We have made Progress, and we look to all of you to carry the torch when we drop it and to go ahead, always ahead, to the Goal Line."

The Carefully Considered Rape of the World, structurally like *The Big Ball of Wax,* is a chronicle of the brief period when distant kin from Phycyx (48 light years away) arrive like UFO's to lead us to a higher evolutionary stage by artificially impregnating a relatively small number of women the world over. The novel traces the effects on three Long Island couples. The eventual offspring are super-intelligent and baboon-like. Inherent again is a message, a stronger one than the earlier warnings about mass merchandising. The Phycians have a Formula for Evolutionary Termination, popularly called the Doomsday Variable: given a carnivorous heredity (the gentle yielding to the savage), if "nuclear ability comes before

genetic control, extinction follows within approximately four generations." Like Vonnegut, Mead is an adroit comic writer who uses SF material to achieve his satire.

—Anthony Wolk

MEEK, S(terner St.) P(aul).   Also wrote as Sterner St. Paul. American.   Born in Chicago, Illinois, 8 April 1894.   Educated at the University of Chicago, Sc.A. 1914; University of Alabama, University, S.B. 1915 (Phi Beta Kappa); University of Wisconsin, Madison, 1916; Massachusetts Institute of Technology, Cambridge, 1921-23. Married Edna Burndage Noble in 1927; one son. Football coach, Kirkley Junior College, Greenville, Texas, 1915; chemist, Western Electric Company, Hawthorne, Illinois, 1916, and Deuvitt Laboratories, Chicago, 1917. Served in the United States Army from 1917: directed small arms ammunition research, 1923-26; chief publications officer, Ordnance Department, 1941-44; retired due to disability, 1947: Colonel. Held patents on tracer ammunition. *Died 10 June 1972.*

SCIENCE-FICTION PUBLICATIONS

Novels

The Drums of Tapajos.   New York, Avalon, 1961.
Troyana.   New York, Avalon, 1962.

Short Stories

The Monkeys Have No Tails in Zamboanga.   New York, Morrow, 1935.
Arctic Bridge.   London, Utopian, 1944.

Uncollected Short Stories (series: Dr. Bird)

"The Murgatroyd Experiment," in *Amazing Stories Quarterly* (New York), Winter 1929.
"Futility," in *Amazing* (New York), July 1929.
"The Red Peril," in *Amazing* (New York), September 1929.
"The Cave of Horror" (Bird), in *Astounding* (New York), January 1930.
"The Perfect Counterfeit" (Bird), in *Scientific Detective* (New York), January 1930.
"The Thief of Time" (Bird), in *Astounding* (New York), February 1930.
"The Radio Robbery" (Bird), in *Amazing* (New York), February 1930.
"Into Space" (as Sterner St. Paul), in *Astounding* (New York), February 1930.
"Cold Light" (Bird), in *Astounding* (New York), March 1930.
"The Ray of Madness" (Bird), in *Astounding* (New York), April 1930.
"Trapped in the Depths," in *Wonder Stories* (New York), June 1930.
"The Gland Murders" (Bird), in *Scientific Detective* (New York), June 1930.
"Beyond the Heaviside Layer," in *Astounding* (New York), July 1930.
"The Last War," in *Amazing* (New York), August 1930.
"The Tragedy of Spider Island," in *Wonder Stories* (New York), September 1930.
"The Attack from Space," in *Astounding* (New York), September 1930.
"Stolen Brains" (Bird), in *Astounding* (New York), October 1930.
"The Osmotic Theorem," in *Wonder Stories Quarterly* (New York), Winter 1930.
"Sea Terror" (Bird), in *Astounding* (New York), December 1930.

"The Black Lamp" (Bird), in *Astounding* (New York), February 1931.
"The Earth's Cancer" (Bird), in *Amazing* (New York), March 1931.
"When Caverns Yawned" (Bird), in *Astounding* (New York), May 1931.
"The Port of Missing Planes" (Bird), in *Astounding* (New York), August 1931.
"The Solar Magnet" (Bird), in *Astounding* (New York), October 1931.
"Giants on the Earth," in *Astounding* (New York), December 1931.
"Poisoned Air" (Bird), in *Astounding* (New York), March 1932.
"B.C. 30,000," in *Astounding* (New York), April 1932.
"The Great Drought" (Bird), in *Astounding* (New York), May 1932.
"Vanishing Gold," in *Wonder Stories* (New York), May 1932.
"The Synthetic Entity," in *Wonder Stories* (New York), January 1933.
"The Mentality Machine," in *Tales of Wonder* (Kingswood, Surrey), Spring 1939.
"Awlo of Ulm" and "Submicroscopic," in *Before the Golden Age,* edited by Isaac Asimov. New York, Doubleday, 1974.

OTHER PUBLICATIONS

Novel

Island Born. New York, Godwin, 1937.

Other (juvenile)

Jerry: The Adventures of an Army Dog. New York, Morrow, 1932.
Frog, The Horse That Knew No Master. Philadelphia, Penn, 1933.
Gypsy Lad: The Story of a Champion Setter. New York, Morrow, 1934.
Franz, A Dog of the Police. Philadelphia, Penn, 1935.
Dignity, A Springer Spaniel. Philadelphia, Penn, 1937.
Rusty, A Cocker Spaniel. Philadelphia, Penn, 1938.
Gustav, A Son of Franz. Philadelphia, Penn, 1940.
Pat: The Story of a Seeing Eye Dog. New York, Knopf, 1947.
So You're Going to Get a Puppy. New York, Knopf, 1947.
Boots: The Story of a Working Sheep Dog. New York, Knopf, 1948.
Midnight, A Cow Pony. New York, Knopf, 1949.
Ranger, A Dog of the Forest Service. New York, Knopf, 1949.
Hans, A Dog of the Border Patrol. New York, Knopf, 1950.
Surfman: The Adventures of a Coast Guard Dog. New York, Knopf, 1950.
Paga, A Border Patrol Horse. New York, Knopf, 1951.
Red, A Trailing Bloodhound. New York, Knopf, 1951.
Boy, An Ozark Coon Hound. New York, Knopf, 1952.
Rip, A Game Protector. New York, Knopf, 1952.
Omar, A State Police Dog. New York, Knopf, 1953.
Bellfarm Star: The Story of a Pace. New York, Dodd Mead, 1955.
Pierre of the Big Top: The Story of a Circus Poodle. New York, Dodd Mead, 1956.

*   *   *

S.P. Meek was one of the most prominent contributors to the science-fiction magazines which struggled to survive the years of the Depression between 1929 and 1933. He first appeared with "The Murgatroyd Experiment," a still-memorable tale concerning the appalling results of an effort to sustain the world's swollen population in the year 2060, and wrote regularly for the next few years. It was to be expected that he would write about future warfare, and in "The Red Peril" he drew a grim picture of the world's great cities being sprayed with disease germs in 1957—the enemy, inevitably, being the Soviet Union. Propaganda leaflets were also in the armoury of the attackers, whose gravity-defying aircraft were repelled by atomic shells. Even after the Soviet leaders had been confined on St. Helena, the struggle was continued in a sequel, "The Last War," in which synthetic men were produced to turn the tide of battle.

The Red Menace often lurked in the background when Meek's

popular character, Dr. Bird of the Bureau of Standards, accompanied by Operative Carnes of the Secret Service, set out to expose some piece of villainy in a series of intriguing tales. In "The Gland Murders" the plot was designed to decimate the educated rich by lacing their bootleg liquor with an extract from the pineal gland of a murderer, stimulating them to violent acts for which they would pay the penalty. Economic disaster was narrowly averted when, in "Vanishing Gold," bullion in the vaults of the Federal Reserve Bank became radioactive and lost weight. In "When Caverns Yawned" whole cities were imperilled by artificial earthquakes; and in "The Solar Magnet" the subversive genius Ivan Saranoff even tried to straighten the Earth's axis so that Russia might win her true place in the sun. Most of the Dr. Bird stories appeared in the early issues of *Astounding Stories,* where the emphasis on foreign villains brought protests from some readers, and an assurance from the editor that "our authors mean no offence." Among other tales was "Giants on the Earth," a gaudy interplanetary adventure in a style he seldom affected but which clearly showed the extent of his versatility. His tale of an electronic world, "Submicroscopic," was continued in "Awlo of Ulm," an action-romance in the Burroughs tradition. Two serials, *The Drums of Tapajos* and its sequel, *Troyana,* concerned a lost civilisation buried in the Brazilian jungle, and appeared in book form after an interval of 30 years. A collection of his humorous short stories was published as *The Monkeys Have No Tails in Zamboanga.*

—Walter Gillings

MELTZER, David. American. Born in Rochester, New York, 17 February 1937. Educated at public schools in Brooklyn and Los Angeles; Los Angeles City College, 1955; University of California, Los Angeles, 1955-56. Married Christina Meyer in 1958; three daughters. Bookseller, Discovery Book Shop, San Francisco, 1961-69; Editor, *Maya,* Mill Valley, California, 1966-71; teacher, Urban School, San Francisco, 1977-78. Currently, Editor, *Tree,* Bolinas, California. Composer and musician: performed with Serpent Power and David and Tina, 1970-72. Recipient: Council of Literary Magazines grant, 1972; National Endowment for the Arts grant, 1974. Address: Box 9005, Berkeley, California 94709, U.S.A.

SCIENCE-FICTION PUBLICATIONS

Novels (series: Agency; Brain Plant)

The Agency. North Hollywood, Essex House, 1968.
The Agent (Agency). North Hollywood, Essex House, 1968.
How Many Blocks in the Pile? (Agency). North Hollywood, Essex House, 1968.
Lovely (Brain Plant). North Hollywood, Essex House, 1969.
Healer (Brain Plant). North Hollywood, Essex House, 1969.
Out (Brain Plant). North Hollywood, Essex House, 1969.
Glue Factory (Brain Plant). North Hollywood, Essex House, 1969.

Uncollected Short Stories

"Kick Me Deadly," in *Dazzle* (San Francisco), 1957.
"And All That Jazz," in *Showcase* (North Hollywood), 1961.

OTHER PUBLICATIONS

Novels

Orf. North Hollywood, Essex House, 1968.
The Marytr. North Hollywood, Essex House, 1969.
Star. North Hollywood, Brandon House, 1970.

Verse

Poems, with Donald Schenker.   Privately printed, 1957.
Ragas.   San Francisco, Discovery, 1959.
The Clown.   Larkspur, California, Semina, 1960.
Station.   Privately printed, 1964.
The Blackest Rose.   Berkeley, California, Oyez, 1964.
Oyez! Berkeley, California, Oyez, 1965.
The Process.   Berkeley, California, Oyez, 1965.
In Hope I Offer a Fire Wheel.   Berkeley, California, Oyez, 1965.
The Dark Continent.   Berkeley, California, Oyez, 1967.
Nature Poem.   Santa Barbara, California, Unicorn Press, 1967.
Round the Poem Box: Rustic and Domestic Home Movies for Stan and Jane Brakhage.   Los Angeles, Black Sparrow Press, 1969.
Yesod.   London, Trigram Press, 1969.
From Eden Book.   Mill Valley, California, Maya, 1969.
Abulafia Song.   Santa Barbara, California, Unicorn Press, 1969.
Greenspeech.   Santa Barbara, California, Christopher, 1970.
Luna.   Los Angeles, Black Sparrow Press, 1970.
Letters and Numbers.   Berkeley, California, Oyez, 1970.
Bronx Lil/Head of Lillin S.A.C.   Santa Barbara, California, Capra Press, 1970.
32 Beams of Light.   Santa Barbara, California, Capra Press, 1970.
Knots.   Bolinas, California, Tree, 1971.
Bark: A Polemic.   Santa Barbara, California, Capra Press, 1973.
Hero/Lil.   Los Angeles, Black Sparrow Press, 1973.
Tens: Selected Poems 1961-1971, edited by Kenneth Rexroth. New York, Herder, 1973.
The Eyes, The Blood.   San Francisco, Mudra, 1973.
French Broom.   Berkeley, California, Oyez, 1974.
Blue Rags.   Berkeley, California, Oyez, 1974.
Harps.   Berkeley, California, Oyez, 1975.
Six.   Santa Barbara, California, Black Sparrow Press, 1976.
Bolero.   Berkeley, California, Oyez, 1976.

Recordings (Vanguard): *Serpent Power,* 1972; *Poet Song,* 1974.

Other

We All Have Something to Say to Each Other: Being an Essay Entitled "Patchen" and Four Poems.   San Francisco, Auerhahn Press, 1962.
Introduction to the Outsiders (essay on Beat Poetry).   Fort Lauderdale, Florida, Rodale, 1962.
Bazascope Mother (essay on Robert Alexander).   Los Angeles, Drekfesser Press, 1964.
Journal of the Birth.   Berkeley, California, Oyez, 1967.
Isla Vista Notes: Fragmentary, Apocalyptic, Didactic Contradictions.   Santa Barbara, California, Christopher, 1970.
Abra (juvenile).   Berkeley, California, Hipparchia Press, 1976.
Two-way Mirror: A Poetry Note-book.   Berkeley, California, Oyez, 1977.

Editor, with Michael McClure and Lawrence Ferlinghetti, *Journal for the Protection of All Beings.*   San Francisco, City Lights, 1961; vol. 2, 1978.
Editor, *The San Francisco Poets.*   New York, Ballantine, 1971; as *Golden Gate,* Berkeley, California, Wingbow Press, 1978.
Editor, *Birth: An Anthology.*   New York, Ballantine, 1973.
Editor, *The Secret Garden: An Anthology in the Kabbalah.*   New York, Seabury Press, 1976.

Translator, with Allen Say, *Morning Glories,* by Shiga Naoya.   Berkeley, California, Oyez, 1975.

*

Manuscript Collections: Washington University, St. Louis; University of Indiana, Bloomington; University of California, Los Angeles.

David Meltzer comments:

My involvement with science fiction began when I was a teenager with my reading of H.G. Wells. This led to the early Conklin anthologies and to pulps like *Famous Fantastic Mysteries, Amazing,* and *Thrilling Wonder Stories. Weird Tales* directed me to Arkham House and to Bradbury's first book. Though I enjoyed all aspects of the genre—from David H. Keller to A.E. van Vogt—the writers who interested me most, for their style and innovative stories, were Sturgeon, Kuttner, and finally Alfred Bester, whose *Demolished Man* (serialized in *Galaxy*) was a significant opening in the development of my own work. Its typographical free-play, reminiscent of 1920's Dada and Surrealist typewriter art, felt comfortable to a young poet enthralled with Kenneth Patchen and E.E. Cummings.

Though I wrote and sold a few stories in the 1950's, it was writing the erotic tracts for Essex House that gave me the format I needed to extend my involvement with science fiction. These novels allowed me to use the speculative freedom of SF in a free-for-all attempt to make moral, political, and, it is hoped, satirical appraisal of the USA in the late 1960's, without sacrificing any "respectability" poets are supposed to wear as top hats or laurel crowns. I'm sorry these books became lost in the pornographic outlets; because the pornographic is central to my particular concept of science fiction there are almost no outlets for the work I am able to do and that is why I haven't written any novels since 1970.

*   *   *

Of the ten novels by the California poet and novelist David Meltzer, seven were—in the author's words—"SF or fantasy, future projections." The fact that the Essex House series, edited by Brian Kirby, was devoted to serious American erotic writing did not hinder Meltzer when he wrote his prophetic, Blakean novels of the future. As he has said, "The pornographic erotic format seemed most fitting a zone to engage in didactic moral outcries...."

In *The Agency,* the first volume of a trilogy, Meltzer conveys a poetic vision in spare, allusive prose. He uses techniques special to speculative fiction and satire. As the novelist Norman Spinrad writes in his afterword to *The Agent:* the Agency "is clearly Meltzer's paradigm of society; a mindless machine of which we are all 'agents,' *including* those whom the machine supposedly serves.... The Agency is "a well-organized, self-sufficient, sexual underground." In *The Agency* a young man is picked up by sexual agents and—like the woman in *Story of O*—spends the rest of the novel being forcibly indoctrinated with The Agency's tyrannical precepts. Brainwashed, he becomes an agent himself, ready to propagate the evil fantasies of his masters. In *The Agent* the satirical possibilities implied in *The Agency* are applied more broadly to various aspects of American society. Here Meltzer's deliberately ambiguous portrayal of two agents who may or may not be working for the same agency is often reminiscent of scenes from the movie *Dr. Strangelove.* The third volume in the trilogy, *How Many Blocks in the Pile?,* is constructed differently from the first two. In it, Meltzer creates an exaggerated portrait of the Agency's customers—a married couple who respond to sexual advertisements.

Meltzer's most ambitious erotic SF project is the Brain Plant Tetralogy. In classical Greek drama, a tetralogy is a group of four dramatic pieces, either four tragedies or three tragedies and a satire. Meltzer's Brain-Plant novels are not tragedies in the classical sense, and satire is a prominent feature of each of them; but his extrapolation of tendencies in American society of the late 1960's and their application in his prophetic fictions renders a tragic, scarifying vision. Meltzer's achievement in these four novels does not lie in the creation of characters, because they are either deliberate caricatures or disembodied voices, nor in the creation of a central fantasy. His projection of a future American government ruled by "Military Industry" in which "Rads" (radicals) and "Rebs" (lower middle-class whites), "Snarks" (sexual anarchists) and black militants, are pacified by "Fun Zones" (ingenious Disneylands for the satisfaction of sexual fantasies) is simplistic—like R. Crumb cartoons, as Frank M. Robinson points out in his afterword to *Lovely.* Meltzer's achievement lies instead in the utterly convincing manner in which he argues his theme of exploitation through sex, power, and dreams. The Series, because of the extravagant, entertaining, violent, prophetic vision it conveys, is one of the high points of erotic SF literature.

—Michael Perkins

MEREDITH, Richard C(arlton). American. Born in Alderson, West Virginia, 21 October 1937. Educated at West Virginia State College, Institute, 1955-56; Pensacola Junior College, Florida, 1960-61; University of West Florida, Pensacola, B.A. 1972. Served in the United States Army, 1957-60, 1962. Married Joy Cecilia Gates in 1963; three children. Advertising Manager, Grice Electronics Inc., Pensacola, 1962-69; cartoonist and columnist ("Spinoffs"), Milton *Press-Gazette,* Florida, 1972-75; Editor, *Santa Rose Free Press,* Milton, 1975; copy editor, *National Enquirer,* Lantana, Florida, 1976-77; free-lance writer, illustrator, and graphic designer, 1977-79. Recipient: Phoenix Award, 1970. *Died in 1979.*

SCIENCE-FICTION PUBLICATIONS

Novels (series: Timeliner)

The Sky Is Filled with Ships. New York, Ballantine, 1969.
We All Died at Breakaway Station. New York, Ballantine, 1969.
At the Narrow Passage (Timeliner). New York, Putnam, 1973.
No Brother, No Friend (Timeliner). New York, Doubleday, 1976.
Run, Come See Jerusalem. New York, Ballantine, 1976.
Vestiges of Time (Timeliner). New York, Doubleday, 1978.
The Awakening. New York, St. Martin's Press, 1979.

Uncollected Short Stories

"Slugs," in *Knight* (Los Angeles), 1962.
"Choice of Weapons," in *Worlds of Tomorrow* (New York), March 1966.
"To the War Is Gone," in *Worlds of Tomorrow* (New York), November 1966.
"The Fifth Columbiad," in *Worlds of Tomorrow* (New York), February 1967.
"The Longest Voyage," in *Fantastic* (New York), September 1967.
"Earthcoming," in *The Future Is Now,* edited by William F. Nolan. Los Angeles, Sherbourne Press, 1970.
"Hired Man," in *If* (New York), February 1970.
"Time of the Sending," in *If* (New York), December 1971.
"Cold the Stars Are, Cold the Earth," in *Amazing* (New York), August 1978.

*   *   *

The protagonists of Richard C. Meredith's fiction generally are reluctant and/or disabled heroes who are forced by circumstances to attempt to solve the mysteries of the strange worlds in which they have previously been mere functionaries. As in traditional quest tales, they uncover even more mystery until a resolution, not always the solution they seek, is reached. They face frequent crises and perform heroically, if not always wisely, in response to external threats. They usually endure deep pain and are quite often physically injured—in fact, it seems that Meredith needs to put his protagonists through as much physical hell as possible before they are allowed the answers they seek or the revelations that there are some areas of human existence they will never fully understand. However, they are not the usual action-adventure sort of heroes. During their moments of flight or hiding, they reflect often upon their actions, regretting the emotional or physical pain they have caused and the violence, with its often questionable killings, that their need for self-preservation has precipitated. As pain is the recurring problem of the characters, violence is perhaps the aspect of Meredith's work that best sums up the science-fiction worlds he creates. Whether the story is about a contingent of handicapped warriors in outer space; a mercenary crossing alternate worlds, time, and space; or a time-traveller exploring facets of American history, the characters are frequently in a state of paranoiac apprehension, not knowing from where or when the next violent attack will come.

While Meredith's science fiction is thoroughly researched for its scientific and sociological aspects, he derives much of his inspiration from a finely honed sense of history. Science fiction is a field which attracts, in addition to hard-science promoters, social commentators, and literary aspirants, the history-influenced writer whose main impulse is to tamper with known history (time travel, alternate worlds) or to create complex future histories. Both of these impulses are found in Meredith's fiction and, in fact, he combines them skillfully in his timeliner trilogy and his time travel tour de force (*Run, Come See Jerusalem*). Many factors no doubt enter into an author's choice to write science fiction that has a strong historical bent, not the least of which is that it is definitely fun to play with history. Except for some dry leftover subjects, most of the exciting events and adventures of history have been adequately covered academically. On the other hand, the science-fiction writer can deal with history extensively in time travel and alternate world stories. Additionally, such stories often necessitate speculation on historical subjects, an opportunity that Meredith takes full advantage of.

Run, Come See Jerusalem not only presents well-researched historical material but also gives full treatment to the what-if theme of the traveller effecting historical change by his actions in the past. Further, it juxtaposes two possible 21st-century futures against each other to make not only cautionary statements about contemporary trends but also detailed future histories rich in political and social implications. Meredith seems to have realized, along with a few other writers like Fritz Leiber, Jack Finney, and Robert Silverberg, that history can be very much a subject of science fiction, integrated comfortably with its fantastic plots and themes to create worlds just as imaginative as deep space colonies. Historically based science fiction helps to enlarge or at least vitalize our perception of historical matters. Perhaps as a result of this interest in history, Meredith's plots are extremely complicated and skillful. For example, events introduced early in his trilogy fit neatly into later portions of the story, and figure in a nearly apocalyptic finale that brings back into action most of the novels' surviving characters.

Meredith's best novel, *We All Died at Breakaway Station,* is an elegiac space opera which incorporates many elements similar to those in his time and alternate world sagas. It also features his most fully realized protagonist, the slightly embittered but resilient Absolom Bracer, a starship captain who has died in battle and been resurrected and put back together as more machine than man. Before he makes his valiant last stand as defender of Breakaway Station, he reviews his life as a warrior and ponders the more metaphysical questions regarding his place in a cold and alien universe. Like all Meredith heroes, he wonders if the effort and the pain are worth the result, that is, being the leader for a crew of the functioning wounded. He decides he does not regret his warrior life, especially since he has reached his life goal, being a starship captain. He is able to die courageously, also without regret. He may not have found satisfying answers, but he has asked the most important questions. In spite of Absolom's death, Meredith achieves in this novel a glorification of courage that is—oddly, in our times—quite inspiring. *We All Died at Breakaway Station* is a kind of Horatio-at-the bridge epic that is given extra dimension by its main character's questing intelligence, by the way its heroism transcends the adventure story requirements of the genre, and because of the dramatic and poignant sacrifices of its disabled, tortured, but brave men and women. It is intriguing that similar bravery by the protagonist of a later novel, *Run, Come See Jerusalem,* results in a nearly opposite type of solution, the character's failure to create a better world where an already abominable one had existed.

Meredith's fiction is fast-paced, mysterious, and complex. He admirably blends philosophical reflection with high adventure to delineate the essential loneliness of his protagonists in an uncertain universe. A sympathetic observer of what is sometimes called the human condition, he infuses his novels and stories with intelligent compassion and a sense of what drives us to our sometimes disputable goals.

—Robert Thurston

MERRIL, (Josephine) Judith (née Grossman). Also writes as Cyril Judd. Canadian. Born in New York City, 21 January 1923. Attended City College of New York, 1939-40. Married 1)

Daniel A. Zissman in 1940 (divorced, 1947), one daughter; 2) Frederik Pohl, *q.v.*, in 1949 (divorced, 1953), one daughter; 3) Daniel W.P. Sugrue in 1960 (divorced 1975). Research assistant and ghost writer, 1943-47; Editor, Bantam Books, New York, 1947-49. Since 1949, free-lance writer and lecturer: writing teacher, adult education program, Port Jervis, New York, 1963-64; Director, Milford Science Fiction Writers Conference, 1956-61; Book Editor, *Fantasy and Science Fiction,* 1965-69; documentary scriptwriter, Canadian Broadcasting Corporation; commentator and performer, *Dr. Who,* TV Ontario. Lives in Toronto.

SCIENCE-FICTION PUBLICATIONS

Novels

Shadow on the Hearth.   New York, Doubleday, 1950; London, Sidgwick and Jackson, 1953.
Gunner Cade (as Cyril Judd, with C.M. Kornbluth).   New York, Simon and Schuster, 1952; London, Gollancz, 1964.
Outpost Mars (as Cyril Judd, with C.M. Kornbluth).   New York, Abelard Press, 1952; London, New English Library, 1966; as *Sin in Space,* New York, Galaxy, 1956.
The Tomorrow People.   New York, Pyramid, 1960.

Short Stories

Out of Bounds.   New York, Pyramid, 1960.
Daughters of Earth.   London, Gollancz, 1968; New York, Doubleday, 1969.
Survival Ship and Other Stories.   Toronto, Kakabeka, 1973.
The Best of Judith Merril.   New York, Warner, 1976.

OTHER PUBLICATIONS

Other

Editor, *Shot in the Dark.*   New York, Bantam, 1950.
Editor, *Beyond Human Ken.*   New York, Random House, 1952; London, Grayson, 1953.
Editor, *Beyond the Barriers of Space and Time.*   New York, Random House, 1954; London, Sidgwick and Jackson, 1955.
Editor, *Human?*   New York, Lion, 1954.
Editor, *Galaxy of Ghouls.*   New York, Lion, 1955; as *Off the Beaten Orbit,* New York, Pyramid, 1959.
Editor, *S-F: The Year's Greatest Science-Fiction and Fantasy 1-6,* continued as *The Year's Best S-F, 7th* [to *11th*]*Annual,* and *SF 12.*   New York, Dell, 4 vols., 1956-59; New York, Simon and Schuster, 5 vols., 1960-64; New York, Delacorte Press, 3 vols., 1965-68; as *SF' 57* [to *'59*] New York, Gnome Press, 3 vols., 1957-59; as *Annual SF* and *The Best of Sci-Fi,* London, Mayflower, 5 vols., 1965-70.
Editor, *SF: The Best of the Best.*   New York, Delacorte Press, 1967; London, Hart Davis, 1968.
Editor, *England Swings SF.*   New York, Doubleday, 1968; abridged edition, as *The Space-Time Journal,* London, Panther, 1972.

*   *   *

Judith Merril has been so prominent as a reviewer and an editor that her fiction has been somewhat eclipsed. Her most widely known story is her first, "That Only a Mother." On one level this tale shows the power of love to blind the lover to the flaws of the beloved and to see only his or her best parts. On another, it is a horror story about the effects of atomic radiation. The two levels combine thematically: atomic energy is a beloved creation with great power to do good for mankind, but we delude ourselves if we refuse to see its potential dangers. Not only does this theme remain relevant to present-day problems; the story bears rereading for the pleasure of the word play, one of Merril's strengths throughout her work. Her finest novel, *Shadow on the Hearth,* also deals with the danger of atomic energy. It focuses on a Westchester woman with two daughters battling to survive the aftermath of a nuclear attack while her husband is trapped in Manhattan. Quietly rather than militantly feminist and ameliorative rather than separatist, Merril portrays the

domestic reality of coping not only with the dangers of radiation but also with the unwelcome advances of a neighbor who has somehow managed to set himself up as an official of the emergency authorities who wishes to become her "protector."

Working as one of the very few women in the SF field during an era when women were usually dumped with robots and aliens and treated as plot features rather than characters, Merril introduced a "woman's angle"—fiction unlikely to have been written by a man, usually with a female central character, yet still (against the so-called wisdom of the publishing trade) exciting to readers of both sexes. While "Project Nursemaid" (*Daughters of Earth*) does have a male viewpoint character, its main concern is the selection of candidates for foster-mothering babies born in space. "Daughters of Earth" is also quite unusual for its time, chronicling six generations of female space explorers. Merril vividly portrays the interactions and reactions between mother and daughter, who then becomes the mother against whom the next generation must react, and so on. Perhaps her most imaginative story is the novella "Homecalling" (*Daughters of Earth*). Again concerned with beauty in the eye of the beholder and the power of love, it is the story of a girl and her baby brother, shipwrecked on a planet with no other human life, who are adopted by a benevolent but repulsively alien mother.

Although it is always difficult to assess the contributions of each individual in collaborations, the two novels Merril wrote with C.M. Kornbluth as Cyril Judd (*Gunner Cade* and *Outpost Mars*) seem to have benefitted from the strengths of both writers, exhibiting Kornbluth's crisp prose, Merril's full-range view of human experience, and their mutual respect for irony.

—Elizabeth Anne Hull

MERRITT, A(braham).   American.   Born in Beverly, New Jersey, 20 January 1884. Educated at Philadelphia High School. Married 1) Eleanor Ratcliffe (died); 2) Eleanor Humphrey; one daughter. Reporter, then night city editor, Philadelphia *Inquirer,* 1902-11; staff member from 1912, and Editor, 1937-43, *American Weekly. Died 30 August 1943.*

SCIENCE-FICTION PUBLICATIONS

Novels

The Moon Pool.   New York and London, Putnam, 1919.
The Ship of Ishtar.   New York and London, Putnam, 1926.
7 Footprints to Satan.   New York, Boni and Liveright, and London, Richards, 1928.
The Face in the Abyss.   New York, Liveright, 1931; London, Futura, 1974.
Dwellers in the Mirage.   New York, Liveright, 1932; London, Skeffington, 1933.
Burn, Witch, Burn!   New York, Liveright, 1933; London, Methuen, 1934.
Creep, Shadow!   New York, Doubleday, 1934; as *Creep, Shadow, Creep!,* London, Methuen, 1935.
The Metal Monster.   New York, Avon, 1946.
The Black Wheel, completed by Hannes Bok.   New York, New Collectors' Group, 1947.

Short Stories

Thru the Dragon Glass.   New York, ARRA, 1932.
Three Lines of Old French.   Milheim, Pennsylvania, Bizarre Series, 1939.
The Fox Woman, and The Blue Pagoda, with Hannes Bok.   New York, New Collectors' Group, 1946.
The Fox Woman and Other Stories.   New York, Avon, 1949.

OTHER PUBLICATIONS

Other

The Story Behind the Story.   Privately printed, 1942.
The Challenge of Beyond.   Privately printed, 1954.

*   *   *

A. Merritt was probably the most influential American science-fiction writer, after Edgar Rice Burroughs, though he is not nearly so well known to the general public. A major reason for this is the paucity of his output (particularly as compared to Burroughs), though his relatively few novels have been almost continuously in print since World War II. He is generally regarded as a fantasist, but this is mainly a matter of changing standards in definition. A half century ago, many matters were regarded as open to "scientific" speculation that are not currently, particularly in the area of the occult. Three of Merritt's eight completed novels concern themselves with the occult (*Burn, Witch, Burn!, Creep, Shadow!,* and *Seven Footprints to Satan,* the last being a variation on the arch-criminal theme with occult and science-fiction overtones), and one (*The Ship of Ishtar*) is very definitely a fantasy set in an alternate world of Babylonian mythology.

The remaining four, however, are given enough of a pseudo-scientific rationale to qualify as science fiction in the romantic vein. There is a strong debt to H. Rider Haggard for the theme of "lost races" in what were then unknown corners of the world, as well as for the ever-popular idea of super-scientific knowledge from forgotten eras (certainly an idea back in vogue today). All this might be called anthropological speculation. *The Moon Pool* deals with a scientific party that penetrates the great caverns left beneath the Pacific when the Moon was ripped from the Earth. There they find the remnants of the ancient Lemurians, using the sophisticated technological instruments of their past. The conflict is with The Shining One, an entity created by the rulers of this land, three (implied) extra-terrestrials, and now turned against them. *The Face in the Abyss* takes place in an unknown part of the Andes. Again there are the remnants of a lost civilization, here ruled by the Snake Mother, the last of a race of intelligent beings descended from reptilian antecedents. The lost culture of *Dwellers in the Mirage* is a curious mix of Amerindian, Mongol, and Norse. Its people inhabit a valley in Alaska, which due to volcanic activity and thermal layers gives the illusion of a wasteland; underneath the mirage is a "lost world" of unique life forms. *The Metal Monster* takes a slightly different theme; the title creature is an alien life form, sentient metallic beings with a sort of hive mentality reproducing themselves with astonishing vitality in the Himalayas.

Merritt wrote very much to pulp formula, that of rapidly paced adventure. There is inevitably conflict in these exotic locales, in which the protagonists from the outside world become involved, always on the "good" side. There are usually two women, one pure and beautiful to provide romantic interest for the hero, the other just the opposite; both are allied with the obvious sides of the conflict.

What Merritt brought to this formula that made his work so continuously popular was a remarkable writing style, called purple by his detractors, poetic by his followers. The super-scientific artifacts of the stories are given the barest minimum of scientific justification; their functions and activities are described in extremely visual, highly sensuous ways, as are the exotic flora, fauna, and natural phenomena. The result is far from the usual pulp writing of the time in its evocative imagery.

Because of their magazine origins and other factors, Merritt's works have often appeared in several variations and combinations. *The Moon Pool* is the combination of two shorter works ("The Moon Pool" and "The Conquest of the Moon Pool"), as is *The Face in the Abyss* ("The Face in the Abyss" and "The Snake Mother"). *Dwellers in the Mirage* has alternate endings. There is also a handful of short stories and fragments, two of which were completed by the artist Hannes Bok.

There can be no doubt that Merritt was of direct and considerable influence on what might be called the second generation of pulp science-fiction writers such as Kuttner, Moore, and Brackett, and through them on today's writers of the romantic school of SF.

—Baird Searles

MERWIN, Sam(uel Kimball), Jr.   Also writes as Elizabeth Deare Bennett; Jacques Jean Ferrat; Matt Lee; Carter Sprague.   American.   Born in Plainfield, New Jersey, 28 April 1910. Educated at Phillips Academy, Andover, Massachusetts, graduated 1927; Princeon University, New Jersey, B.A. 1931; Boston Museum School of Fine Arts. Married 1) Lee Anna Vance in 1934 (died); 2) Marjory Kendal Davenport in 1959 (divorced); 3) Amanda Varela in 1972; two children. Reporter, Boston *Evening American,* 1932-33; New York Bureau Chief, Philadelphia *Inquirer,* 1936-37; Associate Editor, Dell publishers, 1937-38; staff writer, *Country Home,* New York, 1938-39; sports and mystery editor, Standard Magazines, 1941-51, and King Size Publications, 1952-53: Editor, *Startling Stories,* 1945-51, *Fantastic Story Magazine,* 1950-51, *Wonder Stories Annual,* 1950-51, and *Thrilling Wonder Stories,* 1951-54; Editor, *Fantastic Universe, Galaxy,* 1953-54; Associate Editor, *Galaxy,* 1953-54; Editor, Renown Publications, 1955-56, 1975-79, and Brandon House, 1966-67. Agent: Foley Agency, 34 East 38th Street, New York, New York 10016. Address: 1636 North Fuller Avenue, Hollywood, California 90046, U.S.A.

SCIENCE-FICTION PUBLICATIONS

Novels

The House of Many Worlds.   New York, Doubleday, 1951.
Killer to Come.   New York, Abelard Press, 1953; London, Abelard Schuman, 1959.
The White Widows.   New York, Doubleday, 1953; as *The Sex War,* New York, Galaxy, 1960.
Three Faces of Time.   New York, Ace, 1955; London, Badger, 1960.
The Time Shifters.   New York, Lancer, 1971.
Chauvinisto.   Canoga Park, California, Major, 1976.

Uncollected Short Stories

"The Scourge Below," in *Thrilling Wonder Stories* (New York), October 1939.
" 'Dreaming' Down Axis Planes," in *Thrilling Wonder Stories* (New York), Summer 1944.
"No Greater Worlds," in *Thrilling Wonder Stories* (New York), Spring 1945.
"The Jimson Island Giant," in *Startling* (New York), Winter 1946.
"The Admiral's Walk," in *Thrilling Wonder Stories* (New York), December 1947.
"The Carriers," in *My Best Science Fiction Story,* edited by Leo Margulies and O.J. Friend.   New York, Merlin, 1949.
"Forgotten Envoy," in *Startling* (New York), May 1949.
"The Tenth Degree," in *Thrilling Wonder Stories* (New York), October 1950.
"Exiled from Earth," in *Adventures in Tomorrow,* edited by Ken Crossen.   New York, Greenberg, 1951; London, Lane, 1953.
"Exit Line," in *Possible Worlds of Science Fiction*, edited by Groff Conklin.   New York, Greenberg, 1951.
"Short Order," in *Startling* (New York), March 1951.
"House of Many Worlds," in *Startling* (New York), September 1951.
"The Iron Deer," in *Thrilling Wonder Stories* (New York), December 1951.
"Judas Ram," in *Galaxy Reader,* edited by H.L. Gold.   New York, Crown, 1952; London, Grayson, 1953.

"Star Tracks," in *Astounding* (New York), March 1952.
"Third Alternative," in *Fantastic Adventures* (New York), Spring 1952.
"Lambikin," in *Fantasy and Science Fiction* (New York), June 1952.
"Factor Unknown," in *Other Worlds* (Evanston, Indiana), June 1952.
"One Guitar," in *Fantastic Adventures* (New York), July 1952.
"Centaurus," in *Startling* (New York), March 1953.
"Distortion Pattern," in *Startling* (New York), April 1953.
"The Dark Side of the Moon," in *Space Stories* (New York), June 1953.
"There's Always Amanda," in *Fantastic Story* (New York), July 1953.
"Arbiter," in *Thrilling Wonder Stories* (New York), August 1953.
"Journey to Miseneum," in *Startling* (New York), August 1953.
"A Nice Thing to Know," in *Fantastic* (New York), February 1954.
"The Ambassador," in *If* (New York), March 1954.
"Wampum," in *Future* (New York), March 1954.
"The Wind Shines at Night," in *Thrilling Wonder Stories* (New York), Spring 1954.
"A World Apart," in *Fantastic Universe* (Chicago), May 1954.
"The Intimate Invasion," in *Future* (New York), June 1954.
"Summer Heat," in *Startling* (New York), Summer 1954.
"Process Shot," in *Thrilling Wonder Stories* (New York), Summer 1954.
"Poison Planet," in *Amazing* (New York), July 1954.
"It's Not the Heat," in *Beyond* (New York), September 1954.
"Sizzlesticks," in *Beyond 10* (New York), 1955.
"The Eye in the Window," in *Science Fiction Quarterly* (Holyoke, Massachusetts), May 1955.
"Pink Grass Planet," in *Fantastic Universe* (Chicago), May 1955.
"The Man from the Flying Saucer," in *Fantastic Universe* (Chicago), July 1955.
"Beyond the Door," in *Science Fiction Quarterly* (Holyoke, Massachusetts) August 1955.
"Day after Fear," in *Space Stories* (New York), September 1955.
"Star-Flight," in *Fantastic Universe* (Chicago), October 1955.
"Final Exam," in *Fantastic Universe* (Chicago), November 1955.
"Passage to Anywhere," in *Fantastic Universe* (Chicago), February 1956.
"The Vacationer," in *Original Science Fiction Stories* (Holyoke, Massachusetts), March 1956.
"It's All Yours," in *Fantastic Universe* (Chicago), November 1956.
"Service Elevator," in *Amazing* (New York), November 1956.
"The Stretcher," in *Original Science Fiction Stories* (Holyoke, Massachusetts), November 1956.
"Planet for Plunder," in *Satellite* (New York), February 1957.
"The Final Figure," in *Masters of Science Fiction,* edited by Ivan Howard. New York, Belmont, 1964.

Uncollected Short Stories as Carter Sprague

"The Rocket's Red Glare," in *Startling* (New York), June 1943.
"Climate—Disordered," in *Startling* (New York), March 1948.
"Journey for One," in *Startling* (New York), November 1949.
"The Star Slavers," in *Fantasy* (New York), Spring 1950.
"The Borghese Transparency," in *Thrilling Wonder Stories* (New York), April 1950.
"The Long Flight," in *Fantasy* (New York), Fall 1950.

Uncollected Short Stories as Matt Lee

"A Problem in Astrogation," in *Thrilling Wonder Stories* (New York), April 1948.
"Appointment in New Utrecht," in *Startling* (New York), March 1950.
"Final Haven," in *Thrilling Wonder Stories* (New York), February 1951.
"Deception," in *Thrilling Wonder Stories* (New York), April 1951.
"Letters of Fire," in *Startling* (New York), May 1951.
"I Do Not Like Thee," in *Fantastic Story* (New York), Summer 1951.

Uncollected Short Stories as Jacques Jean Ferrat

"Nightmare Tower," in *Fantastic Universe* (Chicago), July 1953.
"The Sane Men of Satan," in *Fantastic Universe* (Chicago), November 1953.
"Reel Life Films," in *Fantastic Universe* (Chicago), May 1954.
"The Sixth Season," in *Fantastic Universe* (Chicago), March 1955.
"The White Rain Came," in *Fantastic Universe* (Chicago), May 1955.
"Testing," in *Fantastic Universe* (Chicago), March 1956.
"Snowstorm on Mars," in *Fantastic Universe* (Chicago), June 1956.

OTHER PUBLICATIONS

Novels

Murder in Miniatures. New York, Doubleday, 1940.
Death in the Sunday Supplement. New York, Gateway, 1942.
The Big Frame. New York, Handi-Books, 1943.
The Flags Were Three, with Leo Margulies. New York, Curl, 1945; London, Hurst and Blackett, 1948.
Message from a Corpse. New York, Bouregy, 1945; London, Quality Press, 1947.
Knife in My Back. New York, Bouregy, 1945; London, Quality Press, 1947.
A Matter of Policy. New York, Bouregy, 1946; London, Quality Press, 1952.
Body and Soul (novelization of screenplay). Chicago, Century, 1947.
The Creeping Shadow. New York, Fawcett, 1952.
Regatta Summer (as Elizabeth Deare Bennett). New York, Dell, 1974.
Gower Court Manner (as Elizabeth Deare Bennett). New York, Dell, 1975.

Plays

Screenplay: *Manhunt in the Jungle,* with Owen Crump, 1958.

Television Plays: *The Star Slavers* (*Lights Out* series), 1951; *The Big Score* (*Alfred Hitchcock Presents* series), 1963.

Other

Confessions of a Scoundrel, with Guido Orlando. Philadelphia, Winston, 1954.

Sam Merwin, Jr. comments:
Although I have done more work in other fields, SF has been my favorite field since the mid-1950's. I have never sought to re- or in-form the world via such fiction, but have sought to entertain and, perhaps, to increase understanding through the introduction of speculative thought. I consider SF to be the other side of the IF.

*   *   *

Sam Merwin, Jr., is important because he is representative of a larger group of science-fiction writers. During his long career, he has written a number of intricately plotted formula novels. The principal characters and the bare bones of the story lines are remarkably similar; however, the locales and situational details are imaginatively conceived and extremely well executed.

Merwin's basic plot calls for an able but somewhat unlikely and relatively untried hero to be pitted against a group of one sex or the other who are scheming to overthrow the existing world order. The hero is usually assisted by a young and extraordinarily beautiful woman whose feats of strength and sexual prowess are matched only by his own. This remarkable couple is usually opposed by a fiendish mastermind who has somehow thwarted the aging process and lives undercover as a benign professor or in some similar disguise. Amazon-like women, superior mentally or physically or both, always figure prominently in Merwin's novels. They are not always on the side of evil; in *Chauvinisto* the Amazons control the world and have made it a better, if somewhat homogenized, place to live. The denouement of each story occurs when the young hero almost single-handedly exposes the kingpin of the conspiracy and saves the world.

Merwin's short novels are composed of three major elements: the detective story, the conspiracy, and the spy novel. The first element, the detective story, is represented by at least one grisly murder which usually takes place in the opening chapter and the amateur sleuthing that the hero and his female friend do to solve the mystery of who runs the conspiracy. This conspiracy appears as a main thread of the plot in all of Merwin's novels. It is usually a pervasive and secret group that is plotting to control the world through ingenious schemes of disarming disguises and infiltration of the highest reaches of government. The spy element is represented by the exotic locales and the use of bugging devices and other sophisticated electronic espionage paraphernalia.

Some might be tempted to dismiss Merwin as a hack writer of formula science fiction. Such a quick dismissal would be entirely unjustified. While his novels do have many elements in common, they are set in vastly different locations, from the rarified atmosphere of a university think-tank to the female-dominated world of the 22nd century, and use a wide variety of secondary characters and subplots. In addition to being extremely readable these stories have dealt with some controversial issues such as the relationships between men and women; in the 1950's, for instance, Merwin was writing novels that portrayed women as the equal or dominant sex, as worthy adversaries and competent partners. All in all, Sam Merwin, Jr., has written a series of interesting and entertaining novels that have been enjoyed by readers of science fiction for 30 years.

—Alice Chambers Wygant

MEYERS, Roy (Lethbridge).   British.   Born in Hounslow, Middlesex, 17 November 1910. Educated at University College, London; St. Bartholomew's Hospital Medical School, London, L.R.C.P. 1940, M.R.C.S. 1940. Married Mary Isobel Leasor in 1942; one son. Physician in general practice, Taunton, Somerset, 1944-74. Chairman of the Medical Board, Ministry for Social Security, 1945-74; Regional Medical Officer, Ministry of Health, 1971-74. Former Director, Periwinkle Press. *Died 13 February 1974.*

SCIENCE-FICTION PUBLICATIONS

Novels (series: Dolphins in all books)

Dolphin Boy.   New York, Ballantine, 1967; as *The Dolphin Rider,* London, Rapp and Whiting, 1968.
Daughters of the Dolphin.   New York, Ballantine, 1968.
Destiny and the Dolphins.   New York, Ballantine, 1969; London, Hale, 1971.

OTHER PUBLICATIONS

Novel

The Man They Couldn't Kill.   Leicester, Blackfriars Press, 1944.

*   *   *

Long before it became fashionable, Roy Meyers was concerned about the quality of life in the sea and especially about the fate of humanity's underwater relatives, the dolphins and whales. Although Meyers may be considered a minor science fiction author, the questions and speculations he raised in the dolphin novels are important enough to transcend both the pedestrian writing style and the melodramatic plot. Luckily Meyers's education and interest enabled him to found the novels on a factual basis; otherwise they would have been rather ordinary romantic fantasies.

And the Dolphin Boy, born Sir John Averill, is quite a romantic figure. Exposed to radiation in an early fetal stage, John was born with slight physical abnormalities that would enable him to live for extended periods of time in the water. When his wealthy parents' Crab Island home and laboratory exploded, infant John, the sole survivor, was thrown into the ocean, where he was adopted by a school of dolphins. John was taught to swim and eat and live like a dolphin, but he was also taught that he was a human being, and that he would one day have to take his proper place among the "upper air creatures." Curiosity led John to teach himself to walk, and he began to follow ships around the Caribbean, in order to learn more about his own kind. When lovely Della Lord was swept overboard, John rescued her; this was his first encounter with another human. She taught him to speak English (his native tongue was Dolphinese) and instructed him in the rudiments of polite human behavior. Through several lucky coincidences, John, now a young man, made other human friends who helped him discover his identity and, incidentally, that he was very rich.

John's parents had been trying to develop a method of transmitting power through the air; with the resources at his command, John hired a staff to continue the experiments. One staff member, newly pregnant, was exposed to the same type of radiation that had affected John's mother. The woman died in childbirth, but her twin daughters were born with the same bodily abnormalities that John had, so he adopted them. He gave the infants to the dolphins to raise as he had been raised; as they grew older, he taught them to speak and walk and live on the land as humans. When Vinca and Synclaire were grown, John introduced them to society, and they were immediate successes. Some time later, John's Crab Island home was struck by a tidal wave, which opened a deep crack in the earth, from which escaping air promised to provide a perpetual power source. This was fortunate for them, because war broke out around the world; although nuclear weapons were not used, some nations resorted to biological warfare. Plagues and disease quickly wiped out all human life except for John, Syn, and Vinca. The rather vague conclusion (perhaps Meyers had envisioned a fourth novel) leaves the reader to assume that the three protagonists may be entering a new underwater Garden of Eden with their friends the dolphins.

In these novels, Meyers presents strong contrasts between the serenity and simplicity of underwater life and our hectic, strident modern world. When the dolphin-raised humans are introduced to their own kind, they are truly alien, and they shock and surprise other people with their direct and honest dolphin-learned manners and morals. Meyers takes many opportunities for not-so-subtle commentary on the irrationality of some human customs, and, in fact, he cannot be accused of subtlety in any of his messages. As a writer, in fact, Meyers can most charitably be characterized as adequate. The flow of the narrative is uneven: long descriptive passages are interspersed with dramatic action, and occasional Serious Messages. He is most successful when he describes life under the sea; his feeling for the world of nature invests the writing with a touch of beauty. In handling the human characters, Meyers is often repetitious in description: every part of Syn and Vinca's bodies, for example, is called "pretty" at one time or another. The people are one-dimensional; the good characters have no vices, and the villains are all leering brutes, to be dispatched as expeditiously as possible.

Somehow, in spite of the awkward style and the episodic plotline, the novels do impress upon the reader the beauty and the uniqueness of the ocean world. Meyers's dolphins are better friends to John, unacquainted as they are with avarice and cruelty, than many a human. And Meyers's arguments against whaling, illustrated with dignified and intelligent cetaceans, could scarcely be bettered by Greenpeace. Although his limitations as a writer are only too apparent, Meyers clearly showed himself to be a caring person with a creative imagination.

—Susan L. Nickerson

MILLER, Benj.   *See* **LOOMIS, Noel M.**

MILLER, P(eter) Schuyler.   American.   Born 21 February 1912.
Educated at Union College, Schenectady, New York, B.S. in chemistry 1932. Administrator in audio-visual education, Schenectady
public schools; editor and technical writer, Fischer Scientific Company, Pittsburgh, 1949-74. Book reviewer ("The Reference Library"),
Astounding, 1951-74; Editor, *Pennsylvania Archaeologist*; Research
Associate, Carnegie Museum. Recipient: Hugo Award, for non-
fiction, 1963. *Died 12 October 1974.*

SCIENCE-FICTION PUBLICATIONS

Novel

Genus Homo, with L. Sprague de Camp.   Reading, Pennsylvania,
Fantasy Press, 1950.

Short Stories

The Titan.   Reading, Pennsylvania, Fantasy Press, 1952; London,
Weidenfeld and Nicolson, 1954.

Uncollected Short Story

"Daydream," in *Fantasy and Science Fiction* (New York), January
1956.

*   *   *

P. Schuyler Miller is best known for his reviews, covering most
books worth mention over 23 years, a service of enormous value and
influence. His approach was balanced optimism, looking for whatever values books had on any level. He kept history and context in
mind, often interpolating short essays on ideas and trends. His
criticism was neither bland nor shallow, but his more penetrating
observations were briefly stated for the student to probe further. His
own stories had made him a familiar name in the magazines from
1930, and his writing had developed somewhat as the general
ambiance did.

In early years he was often compared to A. Merritt, though he is
not very similar to modern eyes. Early Miller stories tend to be
written in a florid style, though story and character are closer to real
life than to heroic myth, and there is a down-to-earth awareness of
the natural world that gives a strongly visualised location. The
impressions of landscape, forest and mountain, and living environment, contrast with many contemporaries' romantically vague and
perfunctory settings. His early story "The Red Plague" is "More of a
well-written plot synopsis for a novel than a short story" as Sam
Moskowitz remarks—true of innumerable early SF stories. There is
a menace—a chain-reaction mineral blight of dust absorbing all
surface water—and Martians, who have beaten the problem, provide the answer. But the voyage to Mars is vividly written and shows
an original thinker's own vision of the then remote prospect of space
flight. "Through the Vibrations" and its sequel, "Cleon of Yzdral,"
has a world of abandoned automated cities, located on a different
wavelength from Earth. "The Arrhenius Horror" is an exotic crystalline life form falling as particles from space. "If life is energy, why
should it not rest where it will?" SF was opening new vistas of what
other worlds might produce that was not Earth over again. Later
Miller came back to the thought in "Spawn," a grim, powerful story
of particles from beyond carrying elemental vitality that started new
life in inanimate matter: a colloidal mass in the sea, a monster of
gold, and a dead man revived as something else. "Tetrahedra of
Space" deals with an invasion force of crystal beings from Mercury,
not simply fought off but frightened off and diverted to more
suitable Mars. "The Atom Smasher" predicts release of nuclear

energy as an uncontrollable mountain-blasting discharge. "The
Pool of Life" is an amorphous entity mentally controlling subhumans in a cave environment, treated as soberly as such a concept can
be.

Many stories exploit the pre-war vision of the interplanetary
future. "The Forgotten Man of Space" is about a man, marooned
and adopted by primitive Martians, who dies protecting them from
genocide by human exploiters. Several collaborations with Dennis
and McDermott treat space piracy with amoral realism, the thoroughly evil pirate evading justice. "The Flame of Life" is an early
Space Patrol episode, set on the rain-forest Venus of yore, as are
others like "Old Man Mulligan," "Bird Walk," "Cuckoo," and "In
the Good Old Summertime," introducing novel fauna. Others later
move to the fanciful interstellar sphere. "Gleeps" lightly handles the
intelligent alien mimicking people. "Trouble on Tantalus" goes
back to the jungle adventure tradition on a world full of curiosities.

Miller's most distinctive work is the short novel "The Titan."
Unfortunately it was revised into the idiom of the 1950's for its only
complete publication (the original serialisation is incomplete). The
change from first to third person lessens the impact of this story of
crisis in an age-old, decadent Martian civilisation, told from a
native leader's viewpoint, and the tighter style lacks the color and
charm of the early version.

—Graham Stone

MILLER, Walter M(ichael), Jr.   American.   Born in New Smyrna
Beach, Florida, 23 January 1922. Educated at the University of
Tennessee, Knoxville, 1940-42; University of Texas, Austin, 1947-
49. Served in the United States Army Air Force, 1942-45. Married
Anna Louise Becker in 1945; three daughters and one son. Free-
lance writer. Recipient: Hugo Award, 1955, 1961. Address: 403
Lenox Avenue, Daytona Beach, Florida 32018, U.S.A.

SCIENCE-FICTION PUBLICATIONS

Novel

A Canticle for Leibowitz.   Philadelphia, Lippincott, and London,
Weidenfeld and Nicolson, 1960.

Short Stories

Conditionally Human.   New York, Ballantine, 1962; London,
Gollancz, 1963.
The View from the Stars.   New York, Ballantine, 1964; London,
Gollancz, 1965.
The Best of Walter M. Miller, Jr.   New York, Pocket Books, 1980.

*   *   *

An engineer by profession, a Catholic by conversion, Walter M.
Miller, Jr. brought both points of view to bear on the utilization of
science and technology in some 41 stories and novellas of the 1950's,
honing his writing skills to the peak achieved by his much-lauded
novel, *A Canticle for Leibowitz.*

Amid his 1951 apprentice work, the novella "Dark Benediction"
shows control of local color and romance psychology in a study of
faith and prejudice. Gray and scaly "dermies," unable to control
their urge to touch and transform others, are being exiled or killed.
Sympathetic to one such mob victim in the early stages of her
infection, Paul Oberlin takes her to priestly controlled Galveston
Island, where he learns the truth. A meteor shower brought alien
spores to Earth in an ironic invasion story that inverts the story of
Pandora's Box. The benefits outweigh the disadvantages for those
who are able to accept this gift of heaven's grace.

The next year, Miller published 15 pieces, eight of them good,
three outstanding. A classic statement of wanderlust, "The Big

Hunger" is a prose poem about waves of space travellers and homebodies over millennia of human change, if not development. An ironic commentary on conformity is "Command Performance." Resenting her suburban wifely role, Lisa resists her telepathic talent until it saves her from another telepath, intent on breeding supermen with her. With him eliminated, her loneliness sets in again, and she tries out her new communication channel, tentatively, as he too must once have done. "Conditionally Human" concerns playing God with life and death, as man elevates "lower" animals to substitute for babies in an overcrowded, overregulated world. Terry Norris, a veterinarian, must choose between killing a "neutroid" (a chimp-baby too smart and pretty and humanly viable, i.e., a deviant) or keeping his wife who wants children herself. Terry can't avoid playing God, but he plays it his way, killing his supervisor and taking a new job, helping to create more deviants. In making this choice, he opts for a race which "hasn't picked an apple yet," i.e., has no original sin.

Miller's best short story is "Crucifixus Etiam" (1953). Manue Nanti, a Peruvian laborer, works to help terraform Mars, and suffers acclimatization to the technology needed to keep him alive. Though he comes to realize he can never go home again to spend his earnings, he finds his sacrifice worthwhile, an act of faith in future generations.

In "The Ties that Bind" (1954), a novella pitting a far-future pacifist Earth society against the militarism of a fleet refueling at the old home world, the "innocent" pastoralists are the more dangerous, their ancestry including the inner hell with which Earth once infected a whole galaxy. Ambitious formally, this tale of original sin interweaves viewpoints and themes with stanzas from the old ballad "Edward." "Death of a Spaceman" (1954; often reprinted as "Memento Homo") is a sentimental elegy to a man whose decripit body lies in bed while his heart remains in space. A more ambitious variation on the theme of clipped wings is "The Hoofer" (1955), in which an itinerant entertainer comes home to Earth for the last time, his story combining slapstick with tragedy. "The Darfsteller" (1955) is a tale of technological displacement which also comments ironically on the paradox of free will and determinism. In telling the story of an aging matinee idol's near-tragic comeback, replacing a mannequin in an automated stage play, Miller adheres strictly to the actor's egotistical and stage-infatuated point of view. No mere entertainer, he is a genuine artist, for whom the "Maestro," the performance's mechanical producer-director, really has no tolerance. But though he is doomed to lose, the actor becomes more fully human by making this last stand. Miller's last published story, "The Lineman" (1957), portrays a day in the life of a lunar worker, when a travelling whorehouse puts the crew off schedule. Mixing humor and pathos, Miller shows his main character learning to see that God created man and the universe on pretty equal footing.

These stories would be memorable enough, without his novel. But they pale by comparison with what may be the one universally acknowledged literary masterpiece to emerge from magazine SF. First published as three novellas, *A Canticle for Leibowitz* in book form is still a triptych. Each of its three "books" reaches six hundred years further into the future, viewing history from the vantage point of the Abbey of Leibowitz, somewhere in the American southwest. Each era is sharply etched, its characters clearly limned as plausible citizens of the City of God, simultaneously resisting and accommodating the City of Dys (Earthly life), as mankind struggles back from nuclear war to recycled Medieval, Renaissance, and Modern eras. Named for a Jewish engineer, a "booklegger" who memorized forbidden texts in the "Age of Simplicity" following the war, the Order of Leibowitz is committed to the preservation of knowledge, interpretation and use of which lie in secular hands.

In "Fiat Homo" (Let There Be Man), sheer survival is at issue, with marauding tribes threatening each other more than the Abbey. The story centers on Brother Francis's attempts to serve his order and mankind by finding, illuminating, and ultimately giving his life for a blueprint initialled by the Blessed Leibowitz and revealed to Francis by a wandering Jew. Church and State are in equilibrium in "Fiat Lux" (Let There Be Light). A secular scholar visits the Abbey to find his theories of electricity put into practice by Brother Kornhoer, providing artificial illumination over the objections of Brother Armbruster, the librarian, thus enabling the scholar to read—and misread—the Memorabilia. Between the Abbot and the scholar, a parasitic one-eyed Poet and the Wandering Jew, cross-

dialogues reveal the misunderstandings that result from differing premises. The balance of power is secular again in "Fiat Voluntas Tua" (Thy Will Be Done), an allegory of contemporary history. As nuclear war erupts again ("Lucifer is fallen"), the Abbot resists euthanasia clinics while Brother Joshua prepares to lead a remnant of clergy and children to Alpha Centauri, where another attempt will be made to temper technology with wisdom.

Moving enough in bare outline, the story is enriched in the telling. Olympian irony conveys "what fools these mortals be" even as warm humor makes us care about them. The comedy ranges from puns to slapstick to central symbols of misunderstanding. Elaborate jokes escape the confines of one book to echo in another (the blueprint of I, the dynamo and a fragment of *R.U.R.* in II, the Poet's satiric verse in III). Continuity is maintained by location and tradition; each era remembers its predecessors, sometimes mistakenly. Light imagery, the Wandering Jew and his eternal skepticism, an enigmatic statue of him and/or of Leibowitz carved in Book I all mock at pretenses to human wisdom. Names and events resound with symbolism, from the simple Francis to the equally simple old woman, Mrs. Grales, whose quest to have her second head, Rachel, blessed by the Abbot, is reversed at the end when Rachel awakes to bless the Abbot, pinned beneath rubble as the bombs fall, because she alone is untainted by original sin. A weighty but entertaining novel, science fiction's best exposure of the "human comedy," *A Canticle for Leibowitz* is a fitting capstone to Miller's writing career.

—David N. Samuelson

MITCHISON, Naomi (Margaret). British. Born in Edinburgh, 1 November 1897; sister of J.B.S. Haldane, *q.v.* Educated at Dragon School, Oxford; St. Anne's College, Oxford. Served as a volunteer nurse, 1915. Married G.R. Mitchison (who became Lord Mitchison, 1964) in 1916 (died, 1970); five children. Labour Candidate for Parliament, Scottish Universities constituency, 1935; Member, Argyll County Council, 1945-66; Member, Highland Panel, 1947-64, and Highland and Island Advisory Council, 1966-76. Tribal Adviser, and Mmarona (Mother), to the Bakgatla of Botswana, 1963-73. Recipient: Palmes de l'Académie Française, 1921. D.Univ.: University of Stirling, Scotland, 1976. Honorary Fellow, St. Anne's College, 1980. Address: Carradale, Campbeltown, Argyll, Scotland.

SCIENCE-FICTION PUBLICATIONS

Novels

Memoirs of a Spacewoman. London, Gollancz, 1962.
Solution Three. London, Dobson, and New York, Warner, 1975.

Uncollected Short Stories

"After the Accident," in *The Year 2000*, edited by Harry Harrison. New York, Doubleday, 1970; London, Faber, 1971.
"Mary and Joe," in *Nova 1*, edited by Harry Harrison. New York, Delacorte Press, 1970; London, Sphere, 1975.
"Death of a Peculiar Boar," in *Worlds of Fantasy* (New York), Winter 1970.
"Miss Omega Raven," in *Nova 2*, edited by Harry Harrison. New York, Walker, 1972; London, Sphere, 1975.
"The Factory," in *Nova 3*, edited by Harry Harrison. New York, Walker, 1973; London, Sphere, 1975.
"Out of the Waters," in *Nova 4*, edited by Harry Harrison. New York, Walker, 1974; London, Sphere, 1976.
"Valley of the Bushes," in *Andromeda 1*, edited by Peter Weston. London, Futura, 1976; New York, St. Martin's Press, 1979.

OTHER PUBLICATIONS

Novels

The Conquered. London, Cape, and New York, Harcourt Brace, 1923.
Cloud Cuckoo Land. London, Cape, 1925; New York, Harcourt Brace, 1926.
The Corn King and the Spring Queen. London, Cape, and New York, Harcourt Brace, 1931; as *The Barbarian*, New York, Cameron, 1961.
The Powers of Light. London, Cape, and New York, Smith, 1932.
Beyond This Limit. London, Cape, 1935.
We Have Been Warned. London, Constable, 1935; New York, Vanguard Press, 1936.
The Blood of the Martyrs. London, Constable, 1939; New York, McGraw Hill, 1948.
The Bull Calves. London, Cape, 1947.
Lobsters on the Agenda. London, Gollancz, 1952.
Travel Light. London, Faber, 1952.
To the Chapel Perilous. London, Allen and Unwin, 1955.
Behold Your King. London, Muller, 1957.
When We Become Men. London, Collins, 1965.
Cleopatra's People. London, Heinemann, 1972.

Short Stories

When the Bough Breaks and Other Stories. London, Cape, and New York, Harcourt Brace, 1924.
Black Sparta: Greek Stories. London, Cape, and New York, Harcourt Brace, 1928.
Barbarian Stories. London, Cape, and New York, Harcourt Brace, 1929.
The Delicate Fire: Short Stories and Poems. London, Cape, and New York, Harcourt Brace, 1933.
The Fourth Pig: Stories and Verses. London, Constable, 1936.
Five Men and a Swan: Short Stories and Poems. London, Allen and Unwin, 1958.
Images of Africa. Edinburgh, Canongate, 1980.

Plays

Nix-Nought-Nothing: Four Plays for Children. London, Cape, 1928; New York, Harcourt Brace, 1929.
The Price of Freedom, with L.E. Gielgud (produced Cheltenham, 1949). London, Cape, 1931.
Full Fathom Five, with L.E. Gielgud (produced London, 1932).
An End and a Beginning and Other Plays. London, Cape, 1937; as *Historical Plays for Schools*, London, Constable, 2 vols., 1939.
As It Was in the Beginning, with L.E. Gielgud. London, Cape, 1939.
The Corn King, music by Brian Easdale, adaptation of the novel by Mitchison (produced London, 1950).
Spindrift, with Denis Macintosh (produced Glasgow, 1951). London, French, 1951.

Verse

The Laburnum Branch. London, Cape, 1926.
The Alban Goes Out. Harrow, Middlesex, Raven Press, 1939.
The Cleansing of the Knife and Other Poems. Edinburgh, Canongate, 1978.

Other (juvenile)

The Hostages and Other Stories. London, Cape, 1930; New York, Harcourt Brace, 1931.
Boys and Girls and Gods. London, Watts, 1931.
The Big House. London, Faber, 1950.
Graeme and the Dragon. London, Faber, 1954.
The Swan's Road. London, Naldrett Press, 1954.
The Land the Ravens Found. London, Collins, 1954.
Little Boxes. London, Faber, 1956.
The Far Harbour. London, Collins, 1957.
Judy and Lakshmi. London, Collins, 1959.

The Rib of the Green Umbrella. London, Collins, 1960.
The Young Alexander the Great. London, Parrish, 1960; New York, Roy, 1961.
Karensgaard: The Story of a Danish Farm. London, Collins, 1961.
The Young Alfred the Great. London, Parrish, 1962; New York, Roy, 1963.
The Fairy Who Couldn't Tell a Lie. London, Collins, 1963.
Alexander the Great. London, Longman, 1964.
Henny and the Crispies. Wellington, New Zealand School Publications, 1964.
Ketse and the Chief. London, Nelson, 1965.
Friends and Enemies. London, Collins, 1966; New York, Day, 1968.
The Big Surprise. London, Kaye and Ward, 1967.
Highland Holiday. Wellington, New Zealand School Publications, 1967.
African Heroes. London, Bodley Head, 1968; New York, Farrar Straus, 1969.
Don't Look Back. London, Kaye and Ward, 1969.
The Family at Ditlabeng. London, Collins, 1969; New York, Farrar Straus, 1970.
Sun and Moon. London, Bodley Head, 1970; Nashville, Nelson, 1973.
Sunrise Tomorrow. London, Collins, and New York, Farrar Straus, 1973.
The Danish Teapot. London, Kaye and Ward, 1973.
Snake! London, Collins, 1976.
The Brave Nurse and Other Stories. Cape Town, Oxford University Press, 1977.
The Two Magicians, with Dick Mitchison. London, Dobson, 1979.

Other

Anna Comnena. London, Howe, 1928.
Comments on Birth Control. London, Faber, 1930.
The Home and a Changing Civilisation. London, Lane, 1934.
Vienna Diary. London, Gollancz, and New York, Smith and Haas, 1934.
Socrates, with Richard Crossman. London, Hogarth Press, 1937; Harrisburg, Pennsylvania, Stackpole, 1938.
The Moral Basis of Politics. London, Constable, 1938; Port Washington, New York, Kennikat Press, 1971.
The Kingdom of Heaven. London, Heinemann, 1939.
Men and Herring, with Denis Macintosh. Edinburgh, Serif, 1949.
Other People's Worlds (travel). London, Secker and Warburg, 1958.
Presenting Other People's Children. London, Hamlyn, 1961.
A Fishing Village on the Clyde, with G.W.L. Paterson. London, Oxford University Press, 1961.
Return to the Fairy Hill (autobiography and sociology). London, Heinemann, and New York, Day, 1966.
The Africans: A History. London, Blond, 1970.
Small Talk: Memories of an Edwardian Childhood. London, Bodley Head, 1973.
A Life for Africa: The Story of Bram Fischer. London, Merlin Press, and Boston, Carrier Pigeon, 1973.
Oil for the Highlands? London, Fabian Society, 1974.
All Change Here: Girlhood and Marriage (autobiography). London, Bodley Head, 1975.
Sittlichkeit (lecture). London, Birkbeck College, 1975.
You May Well Ask: A Memoir 1920-1940. London, Gollancz, 1979.

Editor, *An Outline for Boys and Girls and Their Parents.* London, Gollancz, 1932.
Editor, *Re-Educating Scotland.* Glasgow, Scoop, 1944.
Editor, *What the Human Race Is Up To.* London, Gollancz, 1962.

*

Manuscript Collections: National Library of Scotland, Edinburgh; University of Texas, Austin.

Naomi Mitchison comments:

I like to present my characters—whether they are in the past or in the future—with interesting moral choices, and it seems to me that science-fiction writers are, or should be, the prophets and moralists of today. I am fairly well up in the biological sciences, but I am deeply uninterested in gadgets. A writer's job is to write about people with sympathy and insight.

*   *   *

In his 1946 introduction to *Brave New World*, Naomi Mitchison's friend and contemporary Aldous Huxley outlined a four-point plan for his own personal nightmare, a world in which foolproof techniques of conditioning had been perfected, social dissension obviated by keeping round pegs out of square holes, a harmless substitute for alcohol and narcotics introduced, and the human product standardised by eugenic techniques. What seemed to horrify Huxley most (coming as he did from a family of privileged, well-educated over-achievers) was the idea that the scientific state, instead of complicated random factors like inheritance, ambition, and opportunity, could determine a person's physical condition and social status. *Brave New World* is a piece of bitter and pessimistic polemic against science reducing noble, wild, and self-determining humanity to the status of laboratory mice.

The science fiction written by those scions of another family of privileged, well-educated over-achievers, Naomi Mitchison and her brother J.B.S. Haldane, is mild and optimistic polemic promoting sundry brave new worlds in which all the elements that so unnerved Huxley have totally lost their power to disturb. In *Solution Three*, for instance, there are sleep-teaching, conditioning with hormones, a superior caste of cloned future leaders, blind obedience to a social code, cannabis, promiscuity, a constant struggle to improve the DNA, and, as in Huxley's novel, a few round pegs chafing at the edges of their square holes. However, Mitchison's characters, controlled though they are, are by no means laboratory mice. After a certain amount of smoothing of curves and filling in of corners, the dissidents fit in, more or less; and while the author obviously views her future society as imperfect, its imperfections are no more sinister than those of the 20th century.

Naomi Mitchison's two novels, *Memoirs of a Spacewoman* and *Solution Three*, are very different from each other, though they are bridged to some extent by her brother's unfinished *The Man with Two Memories*, in which the protagonist inherits the recollections of a subnormal citizen of a hugely advanced extra-terrestrial utopia of the remote past, complete with genetic and social engineering, drugs, free love, space travel, and talking animals. Free love, space travel, and talking animals are three of the four major preoccupations of the heroine of *Memoirs of a Spacewoman*, whose profession is to speed around the galaxy communicating with alien races; and her aliens are not the bug-eyed men of lesser writers' imaginations but genuinely strange beings such as the starfish-like individuals who, being radially rather than bilaterally symmetrical, cannot polarise choices into a right/left, right/wrong duality, and the caterpillars mercilessly tormented by their butterfly inheritors, who try to prevent them damaging their future bodies with too much infantile sex and creativity, all depicted with extraordinary sympathy and sensitivity. The spacewoman's other preoccupation is with motherhood, an emotion which she extends even to the leech-like parasitic embryos from another world which she experimentally nurtures on her thighs, as well as to the various children that she bears to sexually attractive and genetically compatible fathers and the haploid clone that she accidentally conceives while communicating with an over-excited Martian. There is no population problem in the spacewoman's world: even though almost every adventure is concluded by a conception, she spends so much time in relativistic time blackout in outer space that her family is well spaced-out.

Population is much more of a consideration in *Solution Three*. It is an obsession with the society which has conquered aggression and is ever struggling to keep the "popu-curve" dropping while cloning a master race from the two individuals who converted the world to homosexuality, thus stopping the explosion at a stroke (just as well, because the 20th-century palliative, the Green Revolution, is running into serious trouble). In her dedication, Mitchison refers to it as a "horrid idea"; but as ever the book itself is sympathetic and

optimistic, and one pauses to wonder whether a society where power is acquired by random heredity or aggression and where heterosexuality is enforced by social sanctions is really much more marvellous or much more free.

Naomi Mitchison views her utopian creations with a tolerant eye. Her societies are those where emotion has its place but reason is always the last resort. Greed, jealousy, nationalism: all the possessive urges, and all the aggressive ones too, have been conquered. Science *works*. The world has been inherited by progressive, liberal, thoroughly rational, scientifically inclined animal lovers committed to natural childbirth, breastfeeding, pre-school education, early independence, free love, and vegetarianism. They are people not at all unlike the Haldane family (or the Huxley family for that matter). The rest of us round pegs will just have to fit in somehow.

—Lee Montgomerie

———————

MOAMRATH, M.M.   *See* **PUMILIA, Joe.**

———————

MONTELEONE, Thomas F.   American. Born in Baltimore, Maryland, 14 April 1946. Educated at the University of Maryland, College Park, B.S. 1968; M.A. 1973. Married Natalie Monteleone in 1969; one son. Psychotherapist, C.T. Perkins Hospital, Jessup, Maryland, 1969-78. Secretary, Science Fiction Writers of America, 1976-78. Agent: Kirby McCauley Ltd., 60 East 42nd Street, New York, New York 10017. Address: P.O. Box 457, Columbia, Maryland 21045, U.S.A.

SCIENCE-FICTION PUBLICATIONS

Novels

Seeds of Change   Toronto, Laser, 1975.
The Time Connection.   New York, Popular Library, 1976; London, Hale, 1979.
The Time-Swept City.   New York, Popular Library, 1977.
The Secret Sea.   New York, Popular Library, 1979.
Guardian.   New York, Doubleday, 1980.
Night Things.   New York, Fawcett, 1980.
Ozymandias.   New York, Doubleday, 1981.

Short Stories

Dark Stars and Other Illuminations.   New York, Doubleday, 1981.

OTHER PUBLICATIONS

Plays

U.F.O.!, with Grant Carrington (produced Ashton, Maryland, 1977).
Mister Magister (produced Silver Spring, Maryland, 1978). Included in *Dark Stars and Other Illuminations*, 1981.

Other

"Fire and Ice," in *Algol* (New York), Summer 1975.
Introduction to *Isle of the Dead*, by Roger Zelazny. Boston, Gregg Press, 1976.

"Markets: Where and to Whom," in *Writing and Selling Science Fiction.* Cincinnati, Writers Digest, 1976.
"Izat Knows the Way to Flushing," with Grant Carrington, in *Nickelodeon* (Kansas City), 1976.
"Science Fiction as Literature," in *Cerberus* (College Park, Maryland), Fall 1977.
Introduction to *Lords of the Starship*, by Mark Geston. Boston, Gregg Press, 1978.
"The Gullibility Factor," in *Omni* (New York), 1979.

Editor, *The Arts and Beyond: Visions of Man's Aesthetic Future.* New York, Doubleday, 1977.

*

Manuscript Collection: University of Maryland, Baltimore.

Thomas F. Monteleone comments:
Although my early novels were little more than adventure fiction, I feel that the majority of my work intends to be more thought-provoking and imaginative. I think my short fiction reflects my desire to employ imagery, symbol, and ironic statement to create stories which make my readers think. I do not write "hard" SF; rather I find myself most comfortable in dealing with the softer sciences such as psychology, anthropology, and sociology. The main emphasis in my fiction seems to be *people*, and the way our technology and society influence them. Themes which are important to me are love, conscience, responsibility, creativity, and man's dual nature.

*   *   *

The fiction of Thomas F. Monteleone is designed primarily to provide entertainment with strong elements of suspense and adventure, but it is also remarkable for some passages which transcend the author's light-reading aim to make powerful statements expressing humanistic convictions.

"Chicago" is a tale which features an exceptional and "personable" robot who speculates upon the doomed fate of mankind as he helps to maintain a perfectly mechanized but lifeless future city of Chicago. *Monster Tales*, a juvenile anthology edited by Roger Elwood (1973), features three pieces by Monteleone. His juvenile fiction shows an awareness of the fears of childhood as well as a belief that children may courageously overcome fears to take matters into their own hands—including the making of moral decisions. It is consistently written in a voice and vocabulary which speaks to young people without condescending; the inconsistencies of narrative voice and occasional clichés that mar some of his adult fiction are generally absent in his juvenile work.

Monteleone's first novel, *Seeds of Change*, in common with "Chicago," explores the implications of technology carried to an extreme. This time the Denver Citiplex, "a kinetic symbol of good intentions gone slightly awry," is the focus of the narrative which supposes that the descendents of the survivors of nuclear holocaust would be determined, even at the expense of human rights, to operate a society without the possibility of conflict. Deviants of any kind are routinely and effectively eliminated, until a revolutionary group, including the hero, Eric Stone, fights for natural living and an open society. Crucial to the success of their revolution is a space ship with fighting machine capabilities, operated by human colonists from Mars who wish to return to Earth. This novel relies a bit heavily on coincidence, escape scenes, and gadgetry but it also successfully makes the point that man "must retain the power to always be critical and never be satisfied. And the way to accomplish this crucial task is to always have dreams—dreams that surpass the stagnant realities of the present—which are in essence the seeds of change itself."

A similar fascination with the metropolis of the future is featured in *The Time-Swept City*. More mature command of characterization enables Monteleone to show the effects of rampant technology upon human individuals, as in the episode concerning a Catholic priest whose church is to be taken from him after an efficiency study determines that the building could be put to "better" purpose. A future which has no respect or room for spiritual growth is likened to a "dark, rough beast."

The Time Connection, as its title implies, is a time-travel story. The archeologist Devin Wells and the mysterious Marianne Cowens discover in the New Mexico desert "a hole into...somewhere" which shows them "a strange panorama" of the future in which the Earth has been conquered by aliens. Coincidence is again a major element of a narrative in which the protagonists rely upon intuition, hunches, and raw courage as they fulfill their destiny of breathing life into the myth that a "Last Fragment" of human survivors will renew man's civilization.

The Secret Sea is a narrative in a very different, at times rollicking, spirit. A disgruntled college professor discovers in an old attic records of an eccentric adventurer who, through gateways in time and space, has visited parallel "fluxworlds," including a world which features Captain Nemo's *Nautilus*. While *The Secret Sea* is a modern tribute to Jules Verne, *Guardian* toys with Greek mythology as the story is told of an abused, frightened young woman, her kindly "knight" who literally rescues her from slavery, and two professional mercenary adventurers who seek to discover the secret of lost pre-holocaust civilization. An apparently predictable and sometimes clichéd narrative is rescued by a clever twist ending and by moments of superior descriptive writing which prove Monteleone capable of describing the horrific process of thermonuclear holocaust with a convincing eloquence which becomes a powerful statement against war.

Monteleone is an entertainer, fascinated with future cities, concerned about technology getting out of hand, bemused by Greek mythology and the works of Jules Verne—but he is an entertainer with a message often stated in bold, powerful terms.

—Rosemary Herbert

MOORCOCK, Michael. Also writes as Bill Barclay; E.P. Bradbury; James Colvin. British. Born in Mitcham, Surrey, 18 December 1939. Served in the Air Training Corps. Married 1) Hilary Bailey in 1962, two daughters and one son; 2) Jill Riches in 1978. Editor, *Tarzan Adventures,* London, 1956-57, and Sexton Blake Library, Fleetway Publications, London, 1958-61; editor and writer for Liberal Party, 1962-63. Editor since 1964 and Publisher since 1967, *New Worlds,* London. Since 1955, songwriter and member of various rock bands including Hawkwind and Deep Fix. Recipient: British Science Fiction Association Award, 1966; Nebula Award 1967; Derleth Award, 1972, 1974, 1975, 1976; *Guardian* Fiction Prize, 1977; Campbell Memorial Award, 1979; World Fantasy Award, 1979. Guest of Honor, World Fantasy Convention, New York, 1976. Agent: Anthony Sheil Associates Ltd., 2-3 Morwell Street, London WC1B 3AR, England.

SCIENCE-FICTION PUBLICATIONS

Novels (series: Oswald Bastable; Jerry Cornelius; Corum; Dancers at the End of Time; Elric; Erekose; Karl Glogauer; Hawkmoon)

Stormbringer (Elric). London, Jenkins, 1965; New York, Lancer, 1967.
The Sundered Worlds. London, Compact, 1965; New York, Paperback Library, 1966; as *The Blood Red Game*, London, Sphere, 1970.
The Fireclown. London, Compact, 1965; New York, Paperback Library, 1967; as *The Winds of Limbo,* Paperback Library, 1969.
The Twilight Man. London, Compact, 1966; New York, Berkley, 1970; as *The Shores of Death,* London, Sphere, 1970.
Printer's Devil (as Bill Barclay). London, Compact, 1966.
Somewhere in the Night (as Bill Barclay). London, Compact, 1966.
The Jewel in the Skull (Hawkmoon). New York, Lancer, 1967; London, Mayflower, 1969.
The Wrecks of Time. New York, Ace, 1967.

The Final Programme (Cornelius). New York, Avon, 1968; London, Allison and Busby, 1969.

Sorcerer's Amulet (Hawkmoon). New York, Lancer, 1968; as *The Mad God's Amulet*, London, Mayflower, 1969.

The Sword of the Dawn (Hawkmoon). New York, Lancer, 1968; London, Mayflower, 1969.

The Ice Schooner. London, Sphere, and New York, Berkley, 1969.

The Runestaff (Hawkmoon). London, Mayflower, 1969; as *The Secret of the Runestaff*, New York, Lancer, 1969.

Behold the Man (Glogauer). London, Allison and Busby, 1969; New York, Avon, 1970.

The Black Corridor. London, Mayflower, and New York, Ace, 1969.

The Chinese Agent. London, Hutchinson, and New York, Macmillan, 1970.

The Eternal Champion (Erekose). London, Mayflower, and New York, Dell, 1970; revised edition, New York, Harper, 1978.

Phoenix in Obsidian (Erekose). London, Mayflower, 1970; as *Silver Warriors*, New York, Dell, 1971.

A Cure for Cancer (Cornelius). London, Allison and Busby, and New York, Holt Rinehart, 1971.

The Knight of the Swords (Corum). London, Mayflower, and New York, Berkley, 1971.

The Queen of the Swords (Corum). London, Mayflower, and New York, Berkley, 1971.

The King of the Swords (Corum). London, Mayflower, and New York, Berkley, 1971.

The War Lord of the Air (Bastable). London, New English Library, and New York, Ace, 1971.

The Rituals of Infinity; or, the New Adventures of Doctor Faustus. London, Arrow, 1971; New York, DAW, 1978.

The Sleeping Sorceress (Elric). London, New English Library, and New York, Lancer, 1972.

The Dreaming City. New York, Lancer, 1972.

An Alien Heat (Dancers). London, MacGibbon and Kee, and New York, Harper, 1972.

Breakfast in the Ruins (Glogauer). London, New English Library, 1972; New York, Random House, 1974.

The English Assassin (Cornelius). London, Allison and Busby, and New York, Harper, 1972.

Elric of Melnibone[1]. London, Hutchinson, 1972; New York, Lancer, 1973.

The Bull and the Spear (Corum). London, Allison and Busby, and New York, Berkley, 1973.

Count Brass (Hawkmoon). London, Mayflower, 1973; New York, Dell, 1976.

The Champion of Garathorm (Hawkmoon). London, Mayflower, 1973.

The Oak and the Ram (Corum). London, Allison and Busby, and New York, Berkley, 1973.

The Sword and the Stallion (Corum). London, Allison and Busby, and New York, Berkley, 1974.

The Land Leviathan (Bastable). London, Quartet, and New York, Doubleday, 1974.

The Hollow Lands (Dancers). New York, Harper, 1974; London, Hart Davis MacGibbon, 1975.

The Quest for Tanelorn (Hawkmoon). London, Mayflower, 1975; New York, Dell, 1976.

The Distant Suns, with Philip James. Llanfynydd, Dyfed, Unicorn Bookshop, 1975.

The Adventures of Una Persson and Catherine Cornelius in the Twentieth Century. London, Quartet, 1976.

The End of All Songs (Dancers). London, Hart Davis MacGibbon, and New York, Harper, 1976.

The Sailor on the Seas of Fate (Elric). London, Quartet, and New York, DAW, 1976.

The Time of the Hawklords, with Michael Butterworth. Henley on Thames, Oxfordshire, Ellis, 1976.

The Condition of Muzak (Cornelius). London, Allison and Busby, 1977; Boston Gregg Press, 1978.

The Transformation of Miss Mavis Ming (Dancers). London, W.H. Allen, 1977; as *Messiah at the End of Time*, New York, DAW, 1978.

The Weird of the White Wolf (Elric). New York, DAW, 1977.

The Vanishing Tower (Elric). New York, DAW, 1977.

The Bane of the Black Sword (Elric). New York, DAW, 1977.

Gloriana; or, The Unfulfill'd Queen. London, Allison and Busby and New York, Avon, 1979.

The History of the Runestaff (Hawkmoon; collection). London, Hart Davis MacGibbon, 1979.

Byzantium Endures. London, Secker and Warburg, 1980.

The Golden Barge. New York, DAW, 1980.

Novels as E.P. Bradbury (series: Michael Kane in all books)

Warriors of Mars. London, Compact, 1965; New York, Lancer, 1966; as *The City of the Beast*, as Michael Moorcock, Lancer, 1970.

Blades of Mars. London, Compact, 1965; New York, Lancer, 1966; as *Lord of the Spiders*, as Michael Moorcock, Lancer, 1970.

Barbarians of Mars. London, Compact, 1965; New York, Lancer, 1966; as *Masters of the Pit*, as Michael Moorcock, Lancer, 1970.

Short Stories

The Stealer of Souls and Other Stories. London, Spearman, 1963; New York, Lancer 1967.

The Deep Fix (as James Colvin). London, Compact, 1966.

The Time Dweller. London, Hart Davis, 1969; New York, Berkley, 1971.

The Singing Citadel. London, Mayflower, and New York, Berkley, 1970.

The Jade Man's Eyes. Brighton, Unicorn Bookshop, 1973.

Elric: The Return to Melnibone[1] (cartoon), illustrated by Druillet. Brighton, Unicorn Bookshop, 1973.

The Lives and Times of Jerry Cornelius. London, Allison and Busby, 1976; and New York, Dale, n.d.

Legends from the End of Time. London, W.H. Allen, and New York, Harper, 1976.

Dying for Tomorrow. New York, DAW, 1978.

My Experiences in the Third World War. Manchester, Savoy, 1980.

OTHER PUBLICATIONS

Novel

The Great Rock and Roll Swindle. London, Virgin Books, 1980.

Other

Preface to *The New SF*, edited by Langdon Jones. London, Hutchinson, 1969.

"Mal Dean," in *New Worlds 8*, edited by Hilary Bailey. London, Sphere, 1975.

Sojan (juvenile). Manchester, Savoy, 1977.

"New Worlds: A Personal History," in *Foundation 15* (London), January 1979.

"Wit and Humour in Fantasy," in *Foundation 16* (London), May 1979.

Editor, *The Best of New Worlds*. London, Compact, 1965.

Editor, *The Best SF Stories from New Worlds 1-8*. London, Panther, 8 vols., 1967-74; New York, Berkley, 6 vols., 1968-71.

Editor, *The Traps of Time*. London, Rapp and Whiting, 1968.

Editor, *New Worlds Quarterly 1-5*. London, Sphere, 5 vols., 1971-73; New York, Berkley, 4 vols., 1971-73.

Editor, with Langdon Jones, *The Nature of the Catastrophe*. London, Hutchinson, 1971.

Editor, with Charles Platt, *New Worlds 6*. London, Sphere, 1973; as *New Worlds 5*, New York, Avon, 1974.

Editor, *Before Armageddon: An Anthology of Victorian and Edwardian Imaginative Fiction Published Before 1914*. London, W.H. Allen, 1975.

Editor, *England Invaded: A Collection of Fantasy Fiction*. London, W.H. Allen, and New York, Ultramarine, 1977.

*

Bibliography: *Michael Moorcock: A Bibliography* by Andrew Harper and George McAulay, Baltimore, T-K Graphics, 1976.

Manuscript Collection: Bodleian Library, Oxford University; Sterling Library, Texas A and M. University, College Station.

Michael Moorcock comments:

My work varies so widely that it attracts quite different readers. Most of it is not, in fact, generic SF—it's "fantasy," if anything—and much of it uses "genre borrowings" for specific ironic uses. Obsessions include imperialism, "trans-sexuality" (I don't believe in gender-roles as a survival trait—they're anti-survival now), racialism, how to live and grow in modern cities, etc. Modern pieties are another frequent target. I like change. I believe that people and things should be infinitely flexible. I am an anarchist in that I believe every individual should be self-governing and conscious of communal self-interest.

*   *   *

Michael Moorcock doesn't like SF: doubtless for that reason he has been one of the great impulses behind the New Wave, a notable editor of the genre, and its Proteus. Since his stories are "packed with personal symbols" one key to this paradoxical versatility lies in Moorcock's growing up during a crucial phase of British history. The only child of divorced parents, Moorcock was "brought up on an off-beat brand of Christian Mysticism." A professional writer and editor from an early age, and a Liberal party propagandist (now he supports the anarchist movement), he took over *New Worlds* and by publishing a range of the best authors, conservative as well as experimental, made it into one of the most challenging if misunderstood of SF magazines. Moorcock's dissatisfaction with SF was occasioned less by the inadequacies of the American pulps than by the complacency of an older generation of English writers. At a time when much SF was messianic and naive, he was influenced by the European mainstream, especially its *avant-garde,* believing the extension of the genre by such experimental techniques would produce work more ethically and psychologically relevant to the modern age. The exigencies as well as the opportunities of editing also shaped his own work. Because Moorcock was forced to finance *New Worlds* himself from hastily written stories, he wrote a copious amount of "swords and sorcery" fiction; so intertwined is his work in the two genres that the nature of his SF is moulded by the parodic experiments he began in the Elric stories and which culminate in *Gloriana,* that apotheosis of heroic burlesque—even if it does have a tincture of SF.

Remarkably little of his early SF lacks any merit, literary or intellectual. If the Michael Kane trilogy (a pastiche of Edgar Rice Burroughs) is a pot-boiler, the example of William Burroughs proved more encouraging; admittedly the ending of *The Rituals of Infinity* indicates the author is concerned less with the scientific than with the metaphysical validity of these stories.

The theme common to both Moorcock's fantasy and science fiction, the apocalypse, is first introduced in one of the Elric stories. Repeatedly his characters and their societies are faced with the question of how to react when confronted with racial extinction: thus in *The Twilight Man* the geodynamics memorably evoke the threat to human fertility posed by the possible unleashing of such cosmic forces by nuclear developments; in *The Black Corridor* Enoch Powell's anti-immigration policies, Celtic Nationalism, and sexism are powerfully satirized. *The Sundered Worlds* is notable for first presenting Moorcock's basic cosmology: one of the two "enlightened" protagonists sacrifices his life for the rest of mankind; the other preaches the gospel of the "multiverse" (the term probably derives from John Cowper Powys out of defiance of Chesterton), i.e., the occult existence of myriad universes in other dimensions which occasionally interact. The variant title (*The Blood Red Game*) underlines the message: there is a pattern to history, an existential gamble in which through self-knowledge humanity may survive. The appropriate eschatology, most fully stated in the ever more spell-binding fantasies, originates in Zoroastrianism which Moorcock admires (even if finally he demythologizes these beliefs): in the continual struggle between Chaos and Order, the balance is kept by the Cosmic Hand; the Zoroastrian historical perspective of time-cycles and millenary saviours inspired the mythos of the Eter-

nal Champion who assumes different identities depending on which universe demands his reincarnation. The doubts often felt by and about the hero smack also of Brecht's epical theories.

Moorcock describes himself as "a faltering atheist with a deep irradicable religious sense"; in this ambivalence is rooted his fear of the dangers presented by the would-be saviour to his already threatened community; in *The Fireclown* one such target is amusingly L. Ron Hubbard. The risk run by the candidate himself is also the concern of the sensational *Behold the Man*. Moorcock now finds its iconoclasm hatefully deficient in humour, yet Glogauer's character is ambiguous enough for some to interpret his actions as true *Imitatio Christi*, whereas in *The Black Corridor*, that sinister version of Harry Martinson's *Aniara*, the self-seeking head of the bourgeois family lost among Pascal's "infinite spaces" degenerates from appeasement to paranoia. More literary allusions are deployed in *The Ice Schooner* where Melville and Coleridge give symbolic as well as vivid circumstantial detail to a study of a new Ice Age hero who finally resists further social manipulation.

Moorcock has argued that while one of the major themes of 19th-century fiction concerned "the attempt of the individual to find personal freedom in a repressive society," today in the Western democracies (as heirs to the great radical and libertarian movements of the early years of this century) our problem is "how we should use this freedom." These themes are extensively explored in the markedly superior work Moorcock has done since the 1971 winding up of the original *New Worlds*. In the engagingly witty Oswald Bastable cycle, with its burlesque of the Edwardian utopias and wars-to-come of Verne, Wells, Kipling, E. Nesbit (and, hidden in the pseudonymic conundrums, Conrad and Lenin), Moorcock attacks the current nostalgia for Britain's imperial past; in *The War Lord of the Air* and *The Land Leviathan* the lost time-traveller Bastable is educated into the realities of colonialism. Rather similar lessons are to be taken more to heart in the multiple "transincarnations" of Glogauer, whose "Second Coming" is the subject of that sardonic Brechtian experiment in alienation *Breakfast in the Ruins*. Armageddon is easier to depict than "a new heaven and a new earth"; and whereas in the exuberant Dancers at the End of Time series Moorcock can make hilarious use of Dickens, Shaw, Firbank, and of course Wells to ridicule both the wastefulness of the advanced countries and the "doomsters", ecological as well as religious, in *The Transformation of Miss Mavis Ming* he is over-indulgently whimsical.

The quintessence of Moorcock's achievement is the Jerry Cornelius series. At one time placed at the disposal of contributors to *New Worlds*, Cornelius has been progressively developed by Moorcock into a brilliant satirical device, a prism by means of which he does a spectrum analysis of 20th-century Western culture on the point of collapse. *The Final Programme* is a rewrite of some Elric stories in terms of *The Threepenny Novel*; starting with *A Cure for Cancer* the conventional narrative is decomposed into a series of apparently discrete images reflecting the non-linear mode in which, at least at a conscious level, modern life is increasingly conducted—a dazzling ironic synthesis of popular fictional formulae: detective, thriller, gothic horror, adventure, western, and not least science fiction. These are satirically related to 20th-century actualities in a manner often cinematic (though at other times the language is that of the computer or medicine or the theatre in and off the streets)—a montage of sensational headlines, authentic press stories, pop lyrics, fashion news, military and other advertisements, scientific reports, and subtly tampered-with extracts from scholarly authorities—yet the over-all effect of modernity is disturbed by a persistent sense of *déjà vu* that calls attention to a Jungian awareness of the spiritual heritage of archaic man surviving still in the depths of our unconscious, reinforced by the reappearance of situations or characters from Moorcock's other books. Through the burlesques of the different futures or pasts imagined by both society and the SF writer, Moorcock exposes the various illusions around which modern man has tried to build up a stable identity "against the tyranny of time and the human condition." Still, if Cornelius proves to be not "the Messiah of the age of science" but the *zeitgeist* itself, there is a punning kind of Messiah in the series: breaking through the muzak come the authentic voices of Bob Dylan, Jimi Hendrix, Schoenberg, Ives, and Messiaen whose collective presence helps to give structure and meaning to what might seem incoherence (particularly significant are the overarching allusions to Messiaen's

Turangalila Symphony). Like the associated references to Vishnu and Shiva which open respectively the first and last books of the series, or the scientific evidence concerning "a hiss located in outer space [that] may be an echo of this explosive creation," these Messiaen references stress the importance of penetrating the illusion of *maya* to perceive the reality of the divine drama of *lila* enacted within the phenomena of the world. The two-part structure of the traditional harlequinade in which Cornelius finally appears obliquely suggests the unmasking desirable for his society. Paradoxically by departing from the strict conventions of the genre, Moorcock as perhaps no other post-war British SF writer is able to tell home truths.

—Peter Caracciolo

MOORE, Brian. Also writes as Michael Bryan. Canadian. Born in Belfast, Northern Ireland, 25 August 1921; moved to Canada in 1948 and to the United States in 1959. Educated at Saint Malachi's College, Belfast. Served in the Belfast Fire Service, 1942-43, and with the British Ministry of War Transport, in North Africa, Italy, and France, 1943-45. Married 1) Jacqueline Sirois in 1951; 2) Jean Denney in 1966; one son. Served with United Nations Relief and Rehabilitation Administration (UNRRA) Mission to Poland, 1946-47; Reporter, Montreal *Gazette,* 1948-52. Regents Professor, 1974-75, and since 1976, Professor, University of California, Los Angeles. Recipient: Authors Club of Great Britain Award, 1956; Beta Sigma Phi Award, 1956; Quebec Literary Prize, 1958; Guggenheim Fellowship, 1959; Governor-General's Award, 1961, 1975; American Academy grant, 1961; Canada Council Fellowship, 1962; Smith Literary Award, 1973; National Catholic Book Award, 1973; Black Memorial Award, 1976. Agent: James Brown Associates Inc., 25 West 43rd Street, New York, New York 10036, U.S.A.

SCIENCE-FICTION PUBLICATIONS

Novel

Catholics. London, Cape, 1972; New York, Harcourt Brace, 1973.

OTHER PUBLICATIONS

Novels

Judith Hearne. Toronto, Collins, and London, Deutsch, 1955; as *The Lonely Passion of Judith Hearne,* Boston, Little Brown, 1956.
The Feast of Lupercal. Boston, Little Brown, 1957; London, Deutsch, 1958; as *A Moment of Love,* London, Panther, 1965.
The Luck of Ginger Coffey. Boston, Little Brown, and London, Deutsch, 1960.
An Answer from Limbo. Boston, Little Brown, 1962; London, Deutsch, 1963.
The Emperor of Ice-Cream. New York, Viking Press, 1965; London, Deutsch, 1966.
I Am Mary Dunne. New York, Viking Press, and London, Cape, 1968.
Fergus. New York, Holt Rinehart, 1970; London, Cape, 1971.
The Great Victorian Collection. New York, Farrar Straus, and London, Cape, 1975.
The Doctor's Wife. New York, Farrar Straus, and London, Cape, 1976.
The Mangan Inheritance. New York, Farrar Straus, and London, Cape, 1979.

Novels as Michael Bryan

The Executioners. Toronto, Harlequin, 1951.
Wreath for a Redhead. Toronto, Harlequin, 1951.
Intent to Kill. New York, Dell, and London, Eyre and Spottiswoode, 1956.
Murder in Majorca. New York, Dell, 1957; London, Eyre and Spottiswoode, 1958.

Short Stories

Two Stories. Northridge, California, Santa Susana Press, 1978.

Plays

Catholics, adaptation of his own novel (produced Seattle, 1980).

Screenplays: *The Luck of Ginger Coffey,* 1964; *Torn Curtain,* 1966; *The Slave,* 1967; *Catholics,* 1973.

Other

Canada, with the editors of *Life.* New York, Time, 1963.
The Revolution Script. New York, Holt Rinehart, 1971; London, Cape, 1972.

*

Bibliography: in *Brian Moore* by Hallvard Dahlie, Toronto, Copp Clark, 1969.

* * *

Brian Moore, claimed by the conflicting nationalism of Northern Ireland, Canada, and the United States, approximates the writing of science fiction through psychological fantasy in his realistic novels. Only one of his works, *Catholics,* could be called science fiction, and it fits more properly in the genre of Utopian fiction; the rest of his novels, particularly *Fergus* and *The Great Victorian Collection,* have a strong element of psychological fantasy.

In *Fergus* fantasy threatens to overtake reality, as people from Fergus Fadden's past accuse and judge him. Their actions have a corporality that satirizes Fergus's southern California, film-writing present. The situation comedy of his future mother-in-law's visit to the home of her daughter's seducer, the soulless director and producer who victimize the soulful artist-novelist, are easily diminished by Fergus's full-bodied projections from his past. Their judgments stimulate Fergus's real heart attack and self acceptance in a novel close to fantasy science fiction. *The Revolution Script* is similar to Truman Capote's *In Cold Blood* as a non-fiction novel. Imaginatively it attempts to understand the media event of the Front de Libération du Québec's kidnapping of James Cross and the kidnapping and murder of Pierre Laporte. Though non-fiction, fantasy here too plays a part, as television, radio, and *The Battle of Algiers* shape the consciousness of the FLQ. *Catholics,* like *The Revolution Script,* differs from the rest of the Moore canon, in that it closely resembles science fiction. The setting is Ireland near the year 2000, and Rome has sent a Godless priest, James Kinsella, to Muck Island in order to further the ecumenical movement by ridding a monastary of old practices. The Abbot, believing more in obedience than in the rituals he has defended, agrees to change, as a Yeatsian "Second Coming" draws near. *The Great Victorian Collection* is similar to *Fergus,* except that Anthony Maloney dreams real Victorian artifacts, paintings, books, pieces from the Crystal Palace Exhibition, in Carmel, California, instead of people. Like Devine in *The Feast of Lupercal,* Tony can fantasize better than relate, as he is unable to love the real Mary Ann McKelvey, only as "serving girl—innocent, gentle, frail—lying now on her attic bed, obedient to her employer's lust." Unable to match his dream of his deteriorating Victorian Collection, alone, Tony dies a suicide.

Brian Moore, like John Hersey, John Barth, Walker Percy and a host of others, is not really a science-fiction writer, but his protagonists' search for an authentic self, their struggle to distinguish fantasy and reality, cause many of his novels to resemble science fiction's or fantasy's guise. Joyce and Flann O'Brien however are probably the models for this rather than science fiction.

—Craig Wallace Barrow

—————

MOORE, C(atherine) L(ucille). Also writes as Lewis Padgett. American. Born in Indianapolis, Indiana, 24 January 1911. Educated at the University of Southern California, Los Angeles, B.S. 1956 (Phi Beta Kappa), M.A. 1964. Married 1) Henry Kuttner, *q.v.*, in 1940 (died, 1958); 2) Thomas Reggie in 1963. Staff member, later President, Fletcher Trust Company, Indianapolis, 1930-40; Instructor in Writing and Literature, University of Southern California, 1958-61. Most of her work after 1940 was written in collaboration with Henry Kuttner, though not always acknowledged. Agent: Harold Matson Agency, 22 East 40th Street, New York, New York 10016. Address: 5990 Naples Plaza, No. 6, Long Beach, California 90803, U.S.A.

SCIENCE-FICTION PUBLICATIONS

Novels

Fury, with Henry Kuttner. New York, Grosset and Dunlap, 1950; London, Dobson, 1954; as *Destination Infinity*, New York, Avon, 1958.
Judgment Night (includes stories). New York, Gnome Press, 1952.
Northwest of Earth. New York, Gnome Press, 1954.
Doomsday Morning. New York, Doubleday, 1957; London, Consul, 1960.
Earth's Last Citadel, with Henry Kuttner. New York, Ace, 1964.
Valley of the Flame, with Henry Kuttner. New York, Ace, 1964.
The Time Axis, with Henry Kuttner. New York, Ace, 1965.

Novels as Lewis Padgett, with Henry Kuttner

Tomorrow and Tomorrow, and The Fairy Chessmen. New York, Gnome Press, 1951; as *Tomorrow and Tomorrow* and *The Far Reality*, London, Consul, 2 vols., 1962; *The Fairy Chessmen* published as *The Chessboard Planet*, New York, Galaxy, 1956.
Well of the Worlds. New York, Galaxy, 1953.
Beyond Earth's Gates. New York, Ace, 1954.

Short Stories

Shambleau and Others. New York, Gnome Press, 1953; London, Consul, 1961.
No Boundaries, with Henry Kuttner. New York, Ballantine, 1955; London, Consul, 1961.
Jirel of Joiry (collection). New York, Paperback Library, 1969; as *Black God's Shadow*, West Kingston, Rhode Island, Grant, 1977.
The Best of C.L. Moore.. New York, Doubleday, 1975.

Short Stories as Lewis Padgett, with Henry Kuttner

A Gnome There Was. New York, Simon and Schuster, 1950.
Mutant. New York, Gnome Press, 1953; London, Weidenfeld and Nicolson, 1954.
Line to Tomorrow. New York, Bantam, 1954.

OTHER PUBLICATIONS

Novels with Henry Kuttner

The Brass Ring (as Lewis Padgett). New York, Duell, 1946; London, Sampson Low, 1947; as *Murder in Brass*, New York, Bantam, 1947.
The Day He Died (as Lewis Padgett). New York, Duell, 1947.
The Mask of Circe. New York, Ace, 1971.

*

Manuscript Collection: Lovecraft Collection, Brown University Library, Providence, Rhode Island.

*   *   *

One of a handful of American women whose science-fiction and fantasy works were published during the 1930's, C.L. Moore has recently been rediscovered by enthusiastic readers and scholars. Her fiction is of significance not only for its own intrinsic merits but also for its influence on the evolution of this literary field. Alone and later in conjunction with Henry Kuttner, Moore introduced psychological analysis and sensuously evocative setting to a form which had been dominated by stereotyped characterization and technological gimmickry. Moore's works are also of interest in light of the 1970's explicitly feminist science fiction; some of her writing antedates this trend while other aspects of it reflect the beliefs and divided sensibility of a woman writer working without such published, politicized support.

"Shambleau" (1933), Moore's first story, innovatively emphasized characterization, vivid imagery, and human sexuality in its depiction of an Earth adventurer, Northwest Smith, and his encounter with a Medusa-like alien. Through skillfully ambiguous imagery, Moore conveys the female attributes of this alien which, in themselves, simultaneously arouse and dismay her male protagonist. Smith, a conventionally hard-bitten but honorable hero whose illegal exploits are never immoral, figures in a series of stories which include "Black Thirst," "Scarlet Dream," and "Dust of God." Moore began a chronologically parallel series of fantasy stories featuring Jirel of Joiry, an independent, resolute Warrior queen of the 15th century, in 1934. In "Black God's Kiss" Jirel braves the horrors of a supernatural, evil-ridden dimension in order to find a weapon she can use to overthrow her castle's conqueror. Avenging her warrior's honor and slain soldiers, Jirel discovers too late that she had really loved the briefly victorious Guillaume. In subsequent stories Jirel continues to triumph over the supernatural. "Quest of the Star Stone" (1937) (with Kuttner) is of special interest for both series: in it, Northwest Smith is magically transported back to the 15th century to confront Jirel.

After Moore's marriage in 1940, it is difficult to determine which stories are exclusively or predominantly hers and which Kuttner's because both writers—singly and in collaboration—used a total of 17 different pseudonyms. One story, however, written under her own name, stands clearly as Moore's work. "No Woman Born" (1944), the tale of a beautiful dancer caught in a theater fire whose severe burns force her rescuers to transfer her brain into a metal body, shines with Moore's glowing imagery and subtle questions about the nature of humanity. After the accident, Deirdre's resilient physical grace stems from the ingenuity of futuristic engineering as much as from her own guiding memories of motion, but it is her will power, and her own values, that ultimately enable the sensation-deprived dancer to regard friendship and compassion more highly than her new, inhuman strength. "No Woman Born" is one of the first science-fiction treatments of cyborgs—creatures part human and part machine—to emphasize characterization rather than technological detail or innovation.

"Judgment Night" (1943), a novella also credited solely to Moore, illustrates not only her characteristic synaesthetic imagery but also her ambivalent stance towards independent womanhood. The psychological and ethical strengths Deirdre manifests in "No Woman Born" are, in Moore's other works, either adulterated when the female protagonist *is* of woman born—mere flesh and blood—or else have disastrous consequences. Like Jirel of Joiry, Juille in "Judgment Night" is a warrior princess who must choose between adherence to an ethical code and the man she loves. Although circumstances conspire to remove this final decision from her grasp, Juille's cumulative hesitations and missteps seal both her lover's and her civilization's ultimate doom. While Moore presents Juille as a person who can admire her Amazon mentor's betrayal of her because this treachery stems from the woman's own sworn loyalties, the author undercuts this characterization by also presenting Juille as an incomplete woman seeking to capture "the despised femininity she had repudiated all her life." Within the galaxy-view Moore presents, it is impossible for a woman to be both psychologically strong and sexually or emotionally satisfied, to maintain her principles and still enjoy "a concert in color and motion." Juille is initially as unfamiliar with her body's needs and desires as she is with the extensive religiously taboo surfaces of her native planet. And the knowledge this character ultimately gains of both forbidden territories does little to forestall the "Judgement Night" that overtakes her. Moore leaves her protagonists together, "content" to "live each measured moment that remained to them with...vividness," but the reader knows that these moments are numbered.

Two of Moore and Kuttner's collaborations have been included in *The Science Fiction Hall of Fame*. "Mimsy Were the Borogroves" (1943) (as Lewis Padgett) plays with conventional notions of childhood and maturity: in it, two Earth children transport themselves into a different future dimension by deciphering the puzzles and games, scoffed at by their elders, that a time-travelling future scientist has lost. One of these puzzles is the *Through the Looking-Glass* quatrain beginning "Twas brillig...." "Vintage Season" (1946) (as Lawrence O'Donnell) is a novella about time-travellers from the future whose vacations are spent witnessing crucial events in Earth's history. Its action centers upon the characters and personalities of these voyeurs and the reactions of their landlord, a contemporary young man who gradually comes to realize their origin and motivations. Although these dilettantes might avert disaster in his time, they selfishly choose not to. In addition to their numerous short stories, Moore and Kuttner also collaborated on one notable science-fiction novel, *Fury*, set on Venus and describing the aftermath of a failed utopia. Their later collaborative works are of less interest.

Moore's lasting contributions to science fiction and fantasy include not only her own classic works but also the models that she—and Kuttner—set for contemporary and future writers. Depth of characterization and setting, attention to the nuances of human motivation and interaction, recognition of the myths—and mythic quests—that shape human experience, and incorporation of sophisticated mainstream literary techniques—such as the use of a central intelligence in "No Woman Born": these are the innovations one may credit to Moore. Although feminist critics have recently begun to praise Moore for her strong heroine, Jirel of Joiry, at the same time they "excuse" or ignore her other works, such criticism does not recognize the full significance of her oeuvre. Technically innovative, Moore's writing is also emblematic of women's authorial ambivalence in an explicitly patriarchal culture.

—Natalie M. Rosinsky

MOORE, Patrick (Alfred). British. Born in Pinner, Middlesex, 4 March 1923. Educated privately. Served in the Royal Air Force, 1940-45: Squadron Leader. Concerned in running a school, 1945-52; Director, Armagh Planetarium, Northern Ireland, 1965-68. Since 1957, Presenter, *The Sky at Night* television series, BBC, London. Since 1962, Editor, *Yearbook of Astronomy*. Recipient: Lorimer Gold Medal, 1962; Goodacre Gold Medal, 1968; Italian Astronomical Society Arthuro Gold Medal, 1969; Jackson-Gwilt Medal, 1978; Astronomical Society of the Pacific Klumpke-Roberts Award, 1978. Fellow, Royal Astronomical Society. D.Sc.: University of Lancaster, 1974. O.B.E. (Officer, Order of the British Empire), 1968. Address: Farthings, 39 West Street, Selsey, West Sussex, England.

SCIENCE-FICTION PUBLICATIONS

Novels (juvenile; series: Maurice Gray; Quest; Scott Saunders)

The Master of the Moon. London, Museum Press, 1952.

The Island of Fear. London, Museum Press, 1954.
The Frozen Planet. London, Museum Press, 1954.
Destination Luna. London, Lutterworth Press, 1955.
Quest of the Spaceways. London, Muller, 1955.
Mission to Mars (Gray). London, Burke, 1955.
World of Mists (Quest). London, Muller, 1956.
The Domes of Mars (Gray). London, Burke, 1956.
Wheel in Space. London, Lutterworth Press, 1956.
The Voices of Mars (Gray). London, Burke, 1957.
Peril on Mars (Gray). London, Burke, 1958; New York, Putnam, 1965.
Raiders on Mars (Gray). London, Burke, 1959.
Captives of the Moon. London, Burke, 1960.
Wanderer in Space. London, Burke, 1961.
Crater of Fear. London, Burke, and New York, Harvey House, 1962.
Invader from Space. London, Burke, 1963.
Caverns of the Moon. London, Burke, 1964.
Planet of Fire. Kingswood, Surrey, World's Work, 1969.
Spy in Space (Saunders). London, Armada, 1977.
Planet of Fear (Saunders). London, Armada, 1977.
The Moon Raiders (Saunders). London, Armada, 1978.
Killer Comet (Saunders). London, Armada, 1978.
The Terror Star (Saunders). London, Armada, 1979.

OTHER PUBLICATIONS

Play

Perseus and Andromeda, music by Moore (produced Shoreham, Sussex, 1974).

Other

Guide to the Moon. London, Eyre and Spottiswoode, and New York, Norton, 1953; revised edition, London, Collins, 1957; as *Survey of the Moon*, Eyre and Spottiswoode and Norton, 1963; revised edition, Guildford, Surrey, Lutterworth Press, 1976; as *New Guide to the Moon*, Norton, 1976.
Suns, Myths, and Men. London, Muller, 1954; revised edition, Muller, 1968; New York, Norton, 1969; as *The Story of Man and the Stars*, New York, Norton, 1955.
Out into Space, with A.L. Helm. London, Museum Press, 1954.
The Boy's Book of Space. London, Burke, 1954; New York, Roy, 1956.
The True Book about Worlds Around Us. London, Muller, 1954; as *The Worlds Around Us*, New York, Abelard Schuman, 1956.
A Guide to the Planets. New York, Norton, 1954; London, Eyre and Spottiswoode, 1955; revised edition, London, Collins, 1957; Norton, 1960; as *The New Guide to the Planets*, Norton, 1972.
The Moon, with Hugh Percival Wilkins. London, Faber, and New York, Macmillan, 1955.
Earth Satellite: The New Satellite Projects Explained. London, Eyre and Spottiswoode, 1955; as *Earth Satellites*, New York, Norton, 1956; revised edition, Norton, 1958.
The Planet Venus. London, Faber, 1956; New York, Macmillan, 1957; revised edition, 1959, 1961.
Man-Made Moons. London, Newman Neame, 1956.
Making and Using a Telescope, with Hugh Percival Wilkins. London, Eyre and Spottiswoode, 1956; as *How to Make and Use a Telescope*, New York, Norton, 1956.
The True Book about the Earth. London, Muller, 1956.
Guide to Mars. London, Muller, 1956; New York, Macmillan, 1958; revised edition, Muller, 1965.
The True Book about Earthquakes and Volcanoes. London, Muller, 1957.
Isaac Newton (juvenile). London, Black, 1957; New York, Putnam, 1958.
Science and Fiction. London, Harrap, 1957; Folcroft, Pennsylvania, Folcroft Editions, 1970.
The Amateur Astronomer. London, Lutterworth Press, and New York, Norton, 1957; revised edition, Lutterworth Press, 1974; revised edition, as *Amateur Astronomy*, Norton, 1968.
The Earth, Our Home. New York, Abelard Schuman, 1957.

Your Book of Astronomy. London, Faber, 1958; revised edition, 1964, 1979.

The Solar System. London, Methuen, 1958; New York, Criterion, 1961.

The Boys' Book of Astronomy. London, Burke, and New York, Roy, 1958; revised edition, Burke, 1964.

The True Book about Man. London, Muller, 1959.

Man on the Moon. London, Newman Neame, 1959.

Rockets and Earth Satellites. London, Muller, 1959.

Astronautics. London, Methuen, 1960.

Star Spotter. London, Newman Neame, 1960.

Guide to the Stars. London, Eyre and Spottiswoode, and New York, Norton, 1960; revised edition, Guildford, Surrey, Lutterworth Press, 1974; as *The New Guide to the Stars*, New York, Norton, 1975.

Stars and Space. London, Black, 1960.

Conquest of the Air: The Story of the Wright Brothers. London, Lutterworth Press, 1961.

Navigation, with Henry Brinton. London, Methuen, 1961.

Astronomy. London, Oldbourne, 1961; as *The Picture History of Astronomy*, New York, Grosset and Dunlap, 1961; revised edition, 1972; revised edition, as *The Story of Astronomy*, London, Macdonald, 1972; revised edition, London, Macdonald and Jane's, 1977.

The Stars. London, Weidenfeld and Nicolson, 1962.

Exploring Maps, with Henry Brinton. London, Odhams Press, 1962; New York, Hawthorn, 1967.

Exploring Time, with Henry Brinton. London, Odhams Press, 1962.

The Astronomer's Telescope, with Paul Murdin. Leicester, Brockhampton Press, 1962.

Life in the Universe, with Francis J. Jackson. London, Routledge, and New York, Norton, 1962.

The Planets. London, Eyre and Spottiswoode, and New York, Norton, 1962.

The Observer's Book of Astronomy. London, Warne, 1962; revised edition, 1978.

Telescopes and Observatories. London, Weidenfeld and Nicolson, and New York, Day, 1962.

Space in the Sixties. London, Penguin, 1963.

Exploring the Moon. London, Odhams Press, 1964.

The True Book about Roman Britain. London, Muller, 1964.

Exploring Weather, with Henry Brinton. London, Odhams Press, 1964.

The Sky at Night 1-7. London, Eyre and Spottiswoode, 2 vols., and London, BBC, 5 vols., 1964-80; vol. 1, New York, Norton, 1965.

Life on Mars, with Francis L. Jackson. London, Routledge, 1965; New York, Norton, 1966.

Exploring Other Planets, with Henry Brinton. London, Odhams Press, 1965; New York, Hawthorn, 1967.

Exploring the World. London, Oxford University Press, 1966; New York, Watts, 1968.

The New Look of the Universe. London, Hodder and Stoughton, and New York, Norton, 1966.

Exploring the Planetarium. London, Odhams Press, 1966.

Legends of the Stars. London, Odhams Press, 1966.

Naked-Eye Astronomy. London, Lutterworth Press, and New York, Norton, 1966.

Basic Astronomy. Edinburgh, Oliver and Boyd, 1967.

Exploring Earth History, with Henry Brinton. London, Odhams Press, 1967.

The Craters of the Moon, with Peter J. Cattermole. New York, Norton, 1967.

The Amateur Astronomer's Glossary. London, Lutterworth Press, and New York, Norton, 1967; revised edition, as *The A-Z of Astronomy*, London, Fontana, and New York, Scribner, 1976.

Armagh Observatory: A History 1790-1967. Armagh, Armagh Observatory, 1967.

Exploring the Galaxies. London, Odhams Press, 1968.

Exploring the Stars. London, Odhams Press, 1968.

Space. London, Lutterworth Press, 1968; New York, Natural History Press, 1969.

The Sun and Its Influence, by Mervyn A. Ellison, revised edition. London, Routledge, and New York, Elsevier, 1968.

The Sun. London, Muller, and New York, Norton, 1968.

Moon Flight Atlas. London, Mitchell Beazley, and Chicago, Rand McNally, 1969; revised edition, Mitchell Beazley, 1970.

Astronomy and Space Research (bibliography). London, National Book League, 1969.

The Development of Astronomical Thought. Edinburgh, Oliver and Boyd, 1969.

The Atlas of the Universe. London, Mitchell Beazley, and Chicago, Rand McNally, 1970; revised edition, as *The Mitchell Beazley Concise Atlas of the Universe*, Mitchell Beazley, 1974; as *The Concise Atlas of the Universe*, Rand McNally, 1974.

Gunpowder, Treason: November 5, 1605, with Henry Brinton. London, Lutterworth Press, 1970.

Astronomy for O Level. London, Duckworth, 1970.

Seeing Stars. London, BBC, and Chicago, Rand McNally, 1971.

Mars, The Red World. Kingswood, Surrey, World's Work, 1971.

The Astronomy of Birr Castle. London, Mitchell Beazley, 1971.

Can You Speak Venusian: A Guide to Independent Thinkers. Newton Abbot, Devon, David and Charles, 1972; New York, Norton, 1973.

Challenge of the Stars, with David A. Hardy. London, Mitchell Beazley, and Chicago, Rand McNally, 1972; as *The New Challenge of the Stars*, London, Mitchell Beazley-Sidgwick and Jackson, 1977.

How Britain Won the Space Race, with Desmond Leslie. London, Mitchell Beazley, 1972.

Stories of Science and Invention. London, Oxford University Press, 1972.

How to Recognize the Stars, with Lawrence Clarke. London, Corgi, 1972.

The Southern Stars. Cape Town, Timmins, 1972.

1001 Questions Answered about Astronomy, by James S. Pickering, revised edition. Guildford, Surrey, Lutterworth Press, 1972; New York, Dodd Mead, 1973.

Patrick Moore's Colour Star Atlas. Guildford, Surrey, Lutterworth Press, 1973; as *Color Star Atlas*, New York, Crown, 1973.

The Starlit Sky. Cape Town, Timmins, 1973.

Man the Astronomer. London, Priory Press, 1973.

Mars, with Charles A. Cross. London, Mitchell Beazley, and New York, Crown, 1973.

The Comets: Visitors from Space. Shaldon, Devon, Reid, 1973; revised edition, as *Comets*, New York, Scribner, 1976; as *Guide to Comets*, Guildford, Surrey, Lutterworth Press, 1977.

Watchers of the Stars: The Scientific Revolution. London, Joseph, and New York, Putnam, 1974.

Black Holes in Space, with Iain Nicolson. London, Ocean, 1974; New York, Norton, 1976.

The Astronomy Quiz Book. London, Carousel, 1974; revised edition, 1978.

The Young Astronomer and His Telescope. Shaldon, Devon, Reid, 1974.

Let's Look at the Sky: The Planets [The Stars]. London, Carousel, 2 vols., 1975.

Legends of the Planets. London, Luscombe, 1976.

The Next Fifty Years in Space. London, Luscombe, and New York, Taplinger, 1976.

The Stars Above. Norwich, Jarrold, 1976.

The Astronomy of Southern Africa, with Pete Collins. Cape Town, Timmins, and London, Hale, 1977.

The Atlas of Mercury, with Charles A. Cross. London, Mitchell Beazley, 1977.

Guide to Mars (not the same as 1956 book). Guildford, Surrey, Lutterworth Press, 1977; New York, Norton, 1978.

Wonder Why Book of Planets [the Earth, Stars]. London, Transworld, 3 vols., 1977-78.

Man's Future in Space. Hove, Sussex, Wayland, 1978.

The Guinness Book of Astronomy Facts and Figures. London, Guinness Superlatives, 1979.

Out of Darkness: The Planet Pluto, with Clyde Tombaugh. Guildford, Surrey, Lutterworth Press, 1980.

Editor, *Space Exploration.* Cambridge, University Press, 1958.

Editor, *Practical Amateur Astronomy.* London, Lutterworth Press, 1963; as *A Handbook of Practical Amateur Astronomy*, New York, Norton, 1964.

Editor, *Against Hunting.* London, Gollancz, 1965.
Editor, *Some Mysteries of the Universe*, by William R. Corliss. London, Black, 1969.
Editor, *Astronomical Telescopes and Observatories.* Newton Abbot, Devon, David and Charles, and New York, Norton, 1973.
Editor, *Modern Astronomy: Selections from The Yearbook of Astronomy.* London, Sidgwick and Jackson, and New York, Norton, 1977.
Editor, *The Beginner's Book of Astronomy.* London, Sidgwick and Jackson, 1978.

Translator, *The Planet Mars*, by Gerard de Vaucouleurs. London, Faber, and New York, Macmillan, 1950; revised edition, Faber, 1951.
Translator, *The Structure of the Universe*, by Evry L. Schatzman. London, Weidenfeld and Nicolson, 1968.
Translator, *Quanta*, by J. Andrade e Silva and G. Lochak. London, Weidenfeld and Nicolson, 1969.
Translator, *Cosmology*, by Jean Émile Charon. London, Weidenfeld and Nicolson, 1970.
Translator, *The Planet Mercury* [*Mars*], by E.M. Antoniadi. Shaldon, Devon, Reid, 2 vols., 1974-75.

Recording: *The Ever Ready Band Plays Music by Patrick Moore*, Pye, 1979.

Patrick Moore comments:

My novels are written with the aim of entertaining; they are set in space and are for boys aged roughly 10 to 15. I try to keep a reasonably authentic background, though I am not above taking liberties (after all, Wells did!). I do, however, make a rule that any juvenile novels of mine avoid the sordid and unwholesome.

*   *   *

Patrick Moore's novels possess some special quality which is not shared by many of their contemporaries. Like the Biggles series, Moore's tales of interplanetary travel continue to be republished and find a steady readership. Unfortunately the quality which enables these novels to maintain their readership does not transmit itself to the adult reader. The children's books of a writer such as Ursula K. Le Guin can be identified as books of some merit even by adult standards. However, Moore's books tend to present a view of life and character that is narrow and unrealistic. The characters themselves are largely stock creations and are emotionally very limited. The story lines are repetitive and rely on a limited number of situations to maintain the excitement of the tale. (The main variations consist of altering the names of the chief characters, the settings, and the order of the incidents). Finally the stories themselves lack a human realism. Scientifically the stories are slightly behind the times but this is of little significance compared to the ease with which his juvenile heroes become incorporated into the adventure: this strains adult credulity, and probably that of many children as well. Despite this the books continue to attract readers at a time when many superior examples of the story-teller's craft fail to do so. Moore's books offer something beyond an adventure in space, something beyond the lack of literary polish. This something lies within the story.

A typical story line would go something like this: an honest courageous youth with a steady head on his shoulders by some means becomes associated with a research establishment engaged in the exploration of outer space. This establishment is staffed by a group of scientific internationalists who react strongly against national or political interests. A crisis occurs and the staff of the establishment are forced through circumstances to utilise the youth in a task of responsibility on a dangerous mission. The youth, despite the fact that he is not of outstanding intelligence or possessed of great knowledge, manages to win the respect of the scientists through a display of his basic qualities during the many dangers encountered throughout the mission, and, now accepted as an equal, has his future career as a respected member of an exploration team assured. In the series the youthful hero gradually occupies a more and more respected place among the ranks of the scientist/explorers. The appeal of this storyline is fairly obvious. It displays successful adolescent involvement in an adult world, though a

greatly simplified and idealised one. A display of truth, integrity, and courage is sufficient to achieve one's desire, and there are no authority conflicts to establish problems between the adolescent and his elders, since the authority displayed by the scientists stems only from their greater knowledge of a given situation, and the motivation for accepting their authority is made obvious: death in space if the mission fails. In this respect Moore's novels reflect an updating of traditional tales of this type, and in that context a fairly successful updating.

—Gary Coughlan

MOORE, Ward. American. Born in Madison, New Jersey, 10 August 1903. Self-educated. Married 1) Lorna Lenzi in 1942 (divorced); 2) Raylyn Crabbe in 1967; four daughters and three sons. Chicken farmer, bookshop clerk and manager, shipyard worker during World War II, house builder, gardener, ghost writer, copy editor, and book review editor. *Died 29 January 1978.*

SCIENCE-FICTION PUBLICATIONS

Novels

Greener Than You Think. New York, Sloane, 1947; London, Gollancz, 1949.
Bring the Jubilee. New York, Farrar Straus, 1953; London, Heinemann, 1955.
Cloud by Day. London, Heinemann, 1956.
Joyleg, with Avram Davidson. New York, Pyramid, 1962.
Caduceus Wild, with R. Bradford. Los Angeles, Pinnacle, 1978.

Uncollected Short Stories

"Peacebringer" ("Sword of Peace"), in *The Big Book of Science Fiction*, edited by Groff Conklin. New York, Crown, 1950.
"Flying Dutchman," in *Adventures in Tomorrow*, edited by Ken Crossen. New York, Greenberg, 1951; London, Lane, 1953.
"We the People," in *Future Tense*, edited by Ken Crossen. New York, Greenberg, 1952; London, Lane, 1954.
"Measure of a Man," in *Fantasy and Science Fiction* (New York), August 1953.
"Lot," in *The Best from Fantasy and Science Fiction 3*, edited by Anthony Boucher and J. Francis McComas. New York, Doubleday, 1954.
"Rx Jupiter Save Us," in *Future* (New York), January 1954.
"Caution Advisable," in *Original Science Fiction Stories* (Holyoke, Massachusetts), March 1955.
"In Working Order," in *Original Science Fiction Stories* (Holyoke, Massachusetts), May 1955.
"Old Story," in *Fantasy and Science Fiction* (New York), September 1955.
"The Rewrite Man," in *Fantastic Universe* (Chicago), July 1956.
"No Man Pursueth," in *The Best from Fantasy and Science Fiction 6*, edited by Anthony Boucher. New York, Doubleday, 1957.
"Adjustment," in *The Best from Fantasy and Science Fiction 7*, edited by Anthony Boucher. New York, Doubleday, 1958.
"Lot's Daughter," in *A Decade of Fantasy and Science Fiction*, edited by Robert P. Mills. New York, Doubleday, 1960.
"Transient," in *Amazing* (New York), February 1960.
"The Fellow Who Married the Maxill Girl," in *The Best from Fantasy and Science Fiction 10*, edited by Robert P. Mills. New York, Doubleday, 1961.
'It Becomes Necessary" ("The Cold Peace"), in *The Year's Best S-F 7*, edited by Judith Merril. New York, Simon and Schuster, 1962.

"Rebel," in *Fantasy and Science Fiction* (New York), February 1962.
"The Second Trip to Mars" ("Dominions Beyond"), in *The Post Reader of Fantasy and Science Fiction.*   New York, Doubleday, and London, Souvenir Press, 1964.
"The Mysterious Milkman of Bishop Street," in *Fantasy and Science Fiction* (New York), January 1965.
"Frank Merriwell in the White House," in *American Government Through Science Fiction*, edited by Joseph D. Olander and Martin H. Greenberg.   New York, Random House, 1974.
"Durance," in *Epoch*, edited by Roger Elwood and Robert Silverberg.   New York, Berkley, 1975.
"Wish Fiddle," in *Fantasy and Science Fiction* (New York), November 1975.
"A Class with Dr. Chang," in *Beyond Time*, edited by Sandra Ley.   New York, Pocket Books, 1976.
"With Mingled Feelings...," in *Chrysalis 6*, edited by Roy Torgeson.   New York, Kensington, 1979.

OTHER PUBLICATIONS

Novel

Breathe the Air Again.   New York, Harper, 1942.

*   *   *

Ward Moore's science fiction began in 1947 with the publication of *Greener Than You Think*, a disaster novel in which a mysterious mutated "devilgrass" threatens the world. Moore also wrote a number of short stories, but no collected edition exists. This is a shame, since many of the stories are interesting and worthy of a larger audience. "Lot," for example, is a powerful story of a man obsessed with survival, who, with his family, is escaping the fallout of a nuclear attack. "Adjustment" shows Moore's humor in a tale of a man who can make his wishes come true. "The Mysterious Milkman of Bishop Street" shows still another dimension of Moore's ability, in a whimsical fantasy about a milkman too good to be endured.
    Moore's reputation in science fiction, however, rests chiefly on a superlative work of alternate history, *Bring the Jubilee*. This fine novel, which ironically takes its title from the Civil War song "Marching Through Georgia," supposes that Lee's forces had taken the high ground before the Battle of Gettysburg, leading to victory there and eventually to victory in the "War of Southern Independence." Most of the novel shows the results of this turn of events on subsequent history: the Confederacy has become wealthy and powerful, expanding westward to California and southward into Central America, but the Northern States lead an impoverished, backward existence. The central character of the novel, Hodge Backmaker, is born into a poor farm family, and in 1938 goes to New York to expand his opportunities. The world of *Bring the Jubilee* is much more technologically backward than our historical one, and Hodge has trouble gaining the education he seeks. Events bring him to a center for study in Pennsylvania, established years before by Herbert Haggerwells, a major in the Confederate army who remained in the area. There Hodge finds his vocation, and begins to build himself a reputation in Civil War history, but his conclusions are challenged by an authority in the field. A descendant of the Major, Barbara Haggerwells, is a physicist; she has perfected a time machine, and she offers its use to Hodge to visit the Battle of Gettysburg and test his theories. Hodge is to learn painfully that even the fact of observation affects that which is studied. Arriving before dawn on the morning of the 1st of July, 1863, Hodge is spotted by advancing Confederate troops, and they halt to question him. A panic ensues in which the officer is killed, and when light breaks, Hodge recognizes the dead man as Herbert Haggerwells. With the advance interrupted, the Confederates never take the Round Tops, and the battle proceeds as our history knows it.
    Born in 1921, Hodge dies in 1877, a broken man. He realizes his responsibility for the destruction of the world he knew. In addition to the adventure story and the imaginative construction of an

alternative world, Moore has written a probing discussion of the controversy between free will and determinism, and the result is a work that is one of science fiction's best.

—Walter E. Meyers

———————————

MORGAN, Dan.   British.   Born in Holbeach, Lincolnshire, 24 December 1925. Educated at Spalding Grammar School. Served in the Royal Army Medical Corps, 1947-48. Married Georgina Conmen's clothing store, Spaulding. Professional guitarist. Agent: Gerald Pollinger, Laurence Pollinger Ltd., 18 Maddox Street, London W1R 0EU. Address: 1 Chapel Lane, Spalding, Lincolnshire PE11 1BP, England.

SCIENCE-FICTION PUBLICATIONS

Novels (series: Mind; Venturer 12)

Cee Tee Man.   London, Panther, 1955.
The Uninhibited.   London, Digit, 1961.
The Richest Corpse in Show Business.   London, Compact, 1966.
The New Minds.   London, Corgi, 1967; New York, Avon, 1969.
A Thunder of Stars (Venturer 12), with John Kippax.   London, Macdonald, 1968; New York, Ballantine, 1970.
The Several Minds.   London, Corgi, and New York, Avon, 1969.
The Mind Trap.   London, Corgi, and New York, Avon, 1970.
Inside.   London, Corgi, 1971; New York, Berkley, 1974.
Seed of Stars (Venturer 12), with John Kippax.   New York, Ballantine, 1972; London, Pan, 1974.
The Neutral Stars (Venturer 12), with John Kippax.   New York, Ballantine, 1973; London, Pan, 1975.
The High Destiny.   New York, Berkley, 1973; London, Millington, 1975.
The Country of the Mind.   London, Corgi, 1975.
The Concrete Horizon.   London, Millington, 1976.

Uncollected Short Stories

"Alien Analysis," in *New Worlds* (London), January 1952.
"Home Is Tomorrow," in *Authentic* (London), July 1953.
"Amateur Talent," in *Authentic* (London), December 1953.
"Jerry Built," in *New Worlds* (London), June 1954.
"Psychic Twin," in *Authentic* (London), June 1954.
"Alcoholic Ambassador," in *Nebula* (Glasgow), August 1954.
"Forgive Them," in *Authentic* (London), September 1954.
"Trojan Hearse," with John Kippax, in *New Worlds* (London), December 1954.
"Cleansing Fires," in *Authentic* (London), December 1954.
"The Lesser Breed," in *Authentic* (London), February 1955.
"Kwakiutl," in *Authentic* (London), May 1955.
"Life Agency," in *New Worlds* (London), September 1955.
"The Earth Never Sets," in *Authentic* (London), March 1956.
"Wonkle," in *New Worlds* (London), April 1956.
"Controlled Flight," in *New Worlds* (London), May 1956.
"The Little Fleet," in *New Worlds* (London), August 1956.
"The Way I Am," in *Authentic* (London), August 1956.
"More Than Hormone," in *Nebula* (Glasgow), November 1956.
"The Whole Armour," in *New Worlds* (London), December 1956.
"The Humanitarian," in *New Worlds* (London), April 1957.
"The Unwanted," in *New Worlds* (London), February 1958.
"The Star Game," in *New Worlds* (London), June 1958.
"The Hard Way," in *Nebula* (Glasgow), November 1958.
"Insecurity Risk," in *New Worlds* (London), January 1959.
"Protected Planet," in *Future* (New York), April 1959.
"Drive Out of Mind," in *Fantastic* (New York), June 1960.
"Stopover Earth," in *New Worlds* (London), January 1961.
"Father," in *Amazing* (New York), July 1961.

"Emreth," in *New Writings in SF 3*, edited by John Carnell. London, Dobson, 1965; New York, Bantam, 1967.

"Parking Problem," in *New Writings in SF 4*, edited by John Carnell. London, Dobson, 1965; New York, Bantam, 1968.

"Third Party," in *New Worlds* (London), April 1965.

"Frozen Assets," in *Vision of Tomorrow* (Newcastle upon Tyne), December 1969.

"Flanagan's Law," in *Vision of Tomorrow* (Newcastle upon Tyne), February 1970.

"Scramble," in *Galaxy* (New York), February 1971.

"Canary," in *New Writings in SF 20*, edited by John Carnell. London, Dobson, 1972.

"Love in Limbo," in *Genesis* (New York), April 1974.

"The First Day of the Rest of Your Life," in *The Best of Science Fiction Monthly*, edited by Janet Sacks. London, New English Library, 1975.

"Young Tom," in *New Writings in SF 29*, edited by Kenneth Bulmer. London, Sidgwick and Jackson, 1976.

OTHER PUBLICATIONS

Other

Guitar. London, Corgi, 1965; as *Playing the Guitar*, New York, Bantam, 1967.

Dan Morgan comments:

A large number of my novels have been concerned with ESP—particularly the Mind series, of course. People have always interested me more than machines and continue to do so more than ever. The Venturer 12 series, written in collaboration with the late John Hynam (John Kippax), was likewise more concerned with character than hardware, and was labelled by one reviewer as "sophisticated Space Opera."

It may be of interest to note that the one book of mine which continues to stimulate the most comment and interest is *The Richest Corpse in Show Business*. Perhaps there is a clue in that this is the only avowedly humorous novel I have written—maybe I should have mined this vein further. At the moment my business commitments are so heavy that there just isn't time to write, but the bug is still there and I'll be back to it one of these days.

*   *   *

Although Dan Morgan is not the kind of author who attracts a devoted following, he is certainly underrated and generally overlooked. Most of his novels and short stories display sound storytelling ability, and all rely heavily on a fast-moving plot.

In collaboration with John Kippax, Morgan produced a space opera trilogy that enjoyed a brief popularity and was promptly forgotten. *A Thunder of Stars* introduced the Space Corps, a professional military and exploratory organization. Against a muted background of alien encroachment, the protagonist must race against time to prevent disaster from a runaway reactor on a colony ship. In the sequel, *Seed of the Stars*, the governor of an established colony world is determined to wrest independence from the home world, even if it results in disaster for his charge. The Space Corps was pitted against another powerful but unscrupulous antagonist in *The Neutral Stars*, this time a private citizen investing his substantial wealth in highly secret research.

The idea of a single highly talented villain opposed by a well organized group is carried into Morgan's most effective series, the Mind series, which concentrates on a group of people with psi powers who band together for mutual support and enhancement of their powers. In each of these novels a different psionic menace appears, confronts the group in some fashion, and is ultimately vanquished. In one case, the problem is complicated by a schism within the organization itself, but the overall idea of the many banded together against the uncooperative opponent recurs throughout the series.

With one exception, the rest of Morgan's novels are fairly routine adventure stories. There is a struggle for power in reasonably familiar fashion on a far world in *The High Destiny*, interplanetary war and more telepathy in *The Uninhibited*, and contra-terrene matter in *Cee Tee Man*. An interesting novel that doesn't totally succeed is

Inside, wherein an unconscionable experiment with human beings is conducted in a domed city on airless Mars. Totally untypical of Morgan is the satirical *The Richest Corpse in Show Business*. Although the barbed humor is generally directed at the television industry, there are good-natured swipes at nearly everything else along the way, including some satire of the genre itself.

Morgan's relative lack of popularity probably stems from his mining of conceptual veins already fairly well worked over. Competent but unoriginal stories of telepathy make little impression on readers after the surfeit of them provided during the Campbell years at *Analog*. Morgan is not really innovative, but does consistently maintain a degree of competence well above the average. His adventure novels are of the type that form the bulwark of the science-fiction genre.

—Don D'Ammassa

MORLEY, Wilfred Owen. *See* **LOWNDES, Robert A.W.**

MORRESSY, John. American. Born in Brooklyn, New York, 8 December 1930. Educated at St. John's University, New York, B.A. in English 1953; New York University, M.A. 1961. Served in the United States Army, 1953-55. Married Barbara Ann Turner in 1956. Writer and reviewer, Equitable Life, New York, 1957-59; Instructor, St. John's University, 1962-66; Assistant Professor, Monmouth College, West Long Branch, New Jersey, 1966-67. Since 1968, Associate Professor, Professor, and Writer-in-Residence, Franklin Pierce College, Rindge, New Hampshire. Writer-in-Residence, Worcester Consortium, Massachusetts, 1977; Visiting Writer and Elliott Professor of English, University of Maine, Orono, 1977-78. Recipient: Bread Loaf Writers Conference Fellowship, 1968; University of Colorado Writers Conference Fellowship, 1970. Agent: James Brown Associates, 25 West 43rd Street, New York, New York 10036. Address: Apple Hill Road, East Sullivan, New Hampshire 03445, U.S.A.

SCIENCE-FICTION PUBLICATIONS

Novels (series: Ziax II)

Starbrat. New York, Walker, 1972; London, New English Library, 1979.

Nail Down the Stars. New York, Walker, 1973; London, New English Library, 1979; as *Stardrift*, New York, Popular Library, 1975.

The Humans of Ziax II (juvenile). New York, Walker, 1974.

Under a Calculating Star. New York, Doubleday, 1975; London, Sidgwick and Jackson, 1978.

The Windows of Forever (juvenile). New York, Walker, 1975.

A Law for the Stars. Toronto, Laser, 1976.

The Extraterritorial. Toronto, Laser, 1977.

Frostworld and Dreamfire. New York, Doubleday, 1977; London, Sidgwick and Jackson, 1979.

The Drought on Ziax II (juvenile). New York, Walker, 1978.

Ironbrand. Chicago, Playboy Press, 1980.

Uncollected Short Stories

"Accuracy," in *Fantasy and Science Fiction* (New York), December 1971.

"When the Stars Threw Down Their Spears," in *Fantasy and Science Fiction* (New York), January 1973.
"No More Pencils, No More Books," in *Fantasy and Science Fiction* (New York), June 1979.
"The Empath and the Savage," in *Omni* (New York), July 1979.
"August Sunshine for Moe Joost," in *Isaac Asimov's Science Fiction Magazine* (New York), November 1979.
"The Last Jerry Fagin Show," in *Omni* (New York), April 1980.

OTHER PUBLICATIONS

Novels

The Blackboard Cavalier.   New York, Doubleday, 1966; London, Gollancz, 1967.
The Addison Tradition.   New York, Doubleday, 1968.
A Long Communion.   New York, Walker, 1974; as *Displaced Persons*, New York, Popular Library, 1976.

John Morressy comments:

I write science fiction because I find it to be the most interesting, enjoyable, and creative field open to a writer today and the one that may, in time, prove to be the most significant.

My books are founded on the assumption that the human race, in future ages, will behave much as it always has in the past. We are not yet civilized, and I find it hard to believe that we ever will be. After six or seven thousand years of recorded history and, according to some, progress, we still settle our ideological and economic conflicts by killing one another and laying waste to our planet. Piracy, slavery, and brigandage still thrive. In more countries than we can enumerate, torture is routinely inflicted on prisoners, trial and sentencing is a mockery of justice, and execution is quick and brutal. Under the circumstances, such cherished terms as "freedom" and "human dignity" are meaningless, almost silly. And all this is in the age of *Apollo*, *Voyager*, and *Explorer*, of organ transplants and laser surgery and micro-computers and an arm-long list of scientific and technological wonders.

My novels are set in a future spawned by this present. I envision the human race as surviving (though not without great suffering), eventually reaching the stars, encountering other worlds and other races, and making all the old mistakes over again, on a larger scale. I have tried to create a single future continuum and keep my novels within it. The novels are linked, not sequentially, but laterally. There is no one that must be read first, or last, in order to understand some grand design. A few characters, and places, and institutions, and events, appear in several of my novels; others are in one only. My novels are not attempts to predict the future, but glimpses of what might happen in one particular future. To me, that is the thing science fiction can do and no other genre can: it can give a reader a taste of the future without charging the full and non-refundable price of experiencing it in person.

*   *   *

Isaac Asimov has remarked that year in and year out his "juveniles" are his steadiest sellers; and certainly Robert Heinlein's books for young readers have reached a wide audience. Similarly, several of John Morressy's works of science fiction, intended for children, will not be familiar even to avid readers of the genre. Yet they have received favorable reviews from library journals: *The Windows of Forever*, a time-travel story, was praised for the lesson of tolerance it conveys; likewise, the Ziax II novels, are noted for their ecological concerns.

Several of Morressy's science-fiction novels for adults are interesting for a plot technique reminiscent in some ways of Lawrence Durrell's *Alexandria Quartet*. The first of these, *Starbrat*, tells the story of Del Whitby, who, kidnapped as a child, later searches for information about his parentage. In the course of his adventures, he meets a man named Gariv, who has led a slaves' revolt on the planet Xhanchos and is returning to his homeworld, Skorat, to be reunited with his queen, Nikkolope. Del gives the man a lift and says goodbye after putting him on Skorat. Some adventures ensue, and he later encounters a minstrel named Alladale. As the owner of a spaceship, Del accommodates Alladale in his need for transportation, parts with the minstrel, and heads for a planet named Mazat.

There, in the company of six others, he saves the world from marauding pirates and is chosen king. In synopsis, the novel sounds like an episodic, run-of-the-mill space opera. But the story expands as we read more of Morressy's interwoven works.

In *Nail Down the Stars*, we meet Jolon Gallamor, the minstrel who had called himself Alladale when he met Del Whitby. Unknown to either of them at their meeting, Gallamor had also been on Xhanchos as one of the slaves when the revolt took place. He had ridden at the side of Gariv, the leader, and had later sung at the court of Queen Nikkolope; he left there suddenly when a murderous fight broke out at a banquet. Yet neither Del nor Jolon Gallamor, despite their travels, ever learns the whole story of the events they have been part of: *Under a Calculating Star* gives the reader a fuller picture. In that work we meet a confidence man named Kian Jorry. Jorry organizes an expedition for a raid on a long-abandoned but dangerous treasure trove, but the attempt is a failure. He winds up, disgruntled and weary, on Xhanchos shortly after the slave rebellion has succeeded. While there, he sees a picture of the beautiful Queen Nikkolope, and notices the close resemblance between himself and Gariv. He resolves to try one more audacious con-game: after killing Gariv in a fight the king has provoked, he decides to pose as Gariv, return to Skorat, and usurp the throne. It is in this assumed identity that he meets Del Whitby and is taken to the planet. Gallamor (Alladale) is playing at the banquet at which Jorry announces that King Gariv has returned; although Alladale is the only man there able to expose Jorry, the minstrel flees when the fight breaks out at Jorry's announcement. Each of the characters has only part of the truth; only the readers have the whole story of the sequence.

While *Frostworld and Dreamfire* introduces different characters, Morressy sets the work in the same milieu of the far future as the others. It is a time of lost knowledge and heroic action, a time that Morressy makes more familiar with each work.

—Walter E. Meyers

MORRIS, Janet E(llen).   American.   Born in Boston, Massachusetts, 25 May 1946. Attended New York University, 1965-66. Married Christopher C. Morris in 1972 (divorced, 1975). Lighting designer, Chip Monck Enterprises, New York, 1963-64; night manager, 1970; bass player, Christopher Morris Band, 1975, 1977; song songwriter and recording artist. Agent: Perry Knowlton, Curtis Brown Ltd., 575 Madison Avenue, New York, New York 10022. Address: 1 Breakwater Shores, Hyannis, Massachusetts 02601, U.S.A.

SCIENCE-FICTION PUBLICATIONS

Novels (series: Silistra in all books)

High Couch on Silistra.   New York and London, Bantam, 1977.
The Golden Sword.   New York and London, Bantam, 1977.
Wind from the Abyss.   New York and London, Bantam, 1978.
The Carnellian Throne.   New York, Bantam, 1979.

OTHER PUBLICATIONS

Novel

I, The Sun.   New York, Bantam, 1980.

Janet E. Morris comments:

The thrust of my work, over the long term and through a projected group of books, historical, contemporary, and speculative, is the evolution of consciousness, with an eye toward the genetic, societal, and philosophical influences thereon. Sophocles states that one law ever holds true: nothing vast enters into the world of mortals without a curse. I look for in past history or create in my future histories moments of cataclysm in theaters both physical and mental. My intention is always to explore the thought that must precede any outward action, its struggle to reach a new, more tenable position from which to regard self and universe.

My work in history shall eventually include: Sargon of Agade's conquest of Ebla; Rammesseide Egypt in its position as the seat of Yawwhist tradition; the Seven Sages, those wonderful progenitors of pre-Socratic thought; as well as Suppiluliumas I of Hatti and his dealings with the short-lived Atenist rise in Egypt (*I, The Sun*). Another work samples alchemical thought at the time of the death of Paracelsus, father of chemotherapy.

My science-fictional excursions into the possible evolution of consciousness have all centered on man's apprehension of the physical world, and his sense of place in it. My areas of study are necessarily genetics, biology, sociobiology, philosophy, and physics, but the aim at all times is to *show* rather than *tell*. The more crystallized the tenets of my position in a particular book, the more I strive to present them in an experiential manner without technical discourse which might erect a barrier between myself and the reader.

My Silistra series openly treats sexual themes as well as the possible effect of mind on probability. My Dream Dancer books (in progress) treat the marriage of man and mechanical intelligence through the utilization of our mastery of the intelligence code, the decipherment of which is even now in progress, as well as man's attempt to emancipate himself from the prison of relativistic space. Both the above groups of books focus to some extent on women, but are in no sense "women's" books; rather, I feel that technology is the leveler of sexism and the liberator of those sexual types not included in the sub-set "heterosexual male."

Reading back over what I have written, I must add that I write primarily the book which I myself would like to read, the book I can imagine that you might like to read. My hope above all is to tender you, the reader, an excursion, a journey into another realm which, upon returning, you might find to some small degree has enriched your "present."

*   *   *

Although the Silistra tetralogy of Janet E. Morris has several science-fiction trappings, including spaceships, alien humanoids, and the technological remnants of a failed mechanistic civilization, the novels belong primarily to another fictional category, that which is often termed epic fantasy, and sometimes adult fantasy. Morris's works are not only vividly detailed and imaginative; they are also noteworthy for their graphic portrayals of sexual matters, portrayals which do not, as in most epic fantasies, become marred with excessive romanticism or adolescent ugliness. Her characters fulfill the goals of epic fantasy by participating in complex quests, battling awesome adversaries and a few dangerous beasts along the way, encountering defeat and cruelty just as often as victory, and in general meeting with highly fantastic adventures as they pursue their quests and gain the power that is the successful questor's traditional reward.

Morris's novels are an intriguing blend of medieval and Anglo-Saxon literary elements. While the characters' quests have definite religious overtones, and even the occasional interference of godlike beings, the starkness of the narratives and especially the bloody outcomes of their battles strongly suggest epics like *Beowulf*. An important feature of both medieval and Anglo-Saxon literature is setting, and the world of Silistra is quite appropriate to that convention. A barren world of forbidding mountains and deserts, it provides the proper landscapes for the typically nightmarish sequences that occur there, especially for the scenes of sudden attack by violent nomadic tribes or (a key element of epic fantasy) by strange and powerful mythic beasts. The planet's barren landscapes complement the state of society for the fierce barbaric Silistrians, who have had to ritualize sexual customs in primitive fashion because of the rarity of conception. Further, the intense pain and humiliation of their day-to-day existence must be soothed through the use of many pain- and care-relieving drugs. All in all, an arid social system for an arid planet. Morris's fiction also has a strong edge of reality because of its focus on simple romantic relationships that are characterized

by essentially domestic spats and petty jealousies which are, curiously, shown in terms that are at once modern and medieval in tone.

The chief questor of the Silistran tales is Estri, a well-portrayed character whose physical and emotional strengths seem appropriate to one whose very name conjures up an image of the female life force. In the course of the novels Estri experiences many adventures that constitute steps in a frequently interrupted rite of passage that she begins as a childlike and overly submissive courtesan with little control over her life as a woman or her abilities as a unique creature with godlike potentiality. The rite of passage concludes with her becoming a skilled warrior who functions as a member of Silistra's ruling triumvirate. Along the way she adjusts her feelings and beliefs as a result of encounters with a series of petulant but powerful males whose erratic and violent behavior not only affects her emotionally and intellectually, but presents considerable obstacles to her eventual emergence as a heroic woman and intelligent ruler. The males frequently reduce her status through humiliation and even imprisonment. However, by the end of the four books she has advanced from her unenlightened but calculating submission to all males and achieved what must be judged as at least a measure of manipulation over the men, to whom she is willing to submit on her own terms, but with an acceptance and understanding of what their power means. While this denouement will probably not appeal to many of today's feminists, it must be noted that Estri's submission is depicted as reasonable within the barbaric Silistran culture and that she has at least gained control over her sexual and telepathic powers. Also, she has achieved genuine political power, in contrast to the ritualized leader of courtesans that she was at the beginning of the tetralogy.

Bondage is both main theme and central metaphor in the Silistran novels: it seems to function at every conceivable narrative level. In addition to Estri's frequent enslavement and her sexual submission to the conquering males, there are more acceptable aspects to bondage that are symbolized by the chald, a waist-belt of chains that signifies the moral and social achievements of the wearer. The worst humiliation, in fact, is to be divested of the chald. Moreover, people are bound to each other in complicated rituals of friendship and love. Failure in such bond-relationships leads often to self-chastisement and to acceptance of the uglier forms of bondage. Eventually even Silistra itself is held in bondage by a force field that shuts off interstellar travel. Whatever form bondage takes, it is at the heart of Silistra's philosophical systems. As Sereth, Estri's chief lover, tells her in the conclusion of *Wind from the Abyss:* "Say, then, that we are all bound, the highest no less than the meanest."

Perhaps the most characteristic attribute of Morris's fiction is that its author draws on various sources of human knowledge, from mysticism through myth to most of the sciences, in order to help construct her extravagant tales, an ability that should serve her well in her projected new trilogy, *The Dream Dancers*, a science-fantasy about the melding of man and machine.

—Robert Thurston

_____

_____

MURRY, Colin Middleton.   *See* **COWPER, Richard.**

_____

NELSON, Ray (Radell Faraday Nelson).   Also writes as R.N. Elson; Jeffrey Lord.   American.   Born in Schenectady, New York, 3 October 1931.   Educated at the Chicago Art Institute, 1954; Alliance Française, 1957-58; the Sorbonne, Paris, 1958; University of Chicago, B.A. 1960; Automation Institute, computer programmers certificate 1961; Peralta College, Berkeley, California, 1978. Married 1) Perdita Lilly in 1951 (divorced, 1955); 2) Lisa Mullikin in 1955 (divorced, 1958); 3) Kirsten Enge in 1958; one son. Worked for Inland Lakes Fishing Service, Cadillac, Michigan, 1947-50, and Hudson Motor Company, Detroit, 1950-51; sign maker, Chicago, 1951-54; printer, Northside Poster Company, Chicago, 1954; artist, Artcraft Poster Company, Oakland, California, 1955-56; translator for Jean Linard, Vesoul, France, 1959; computer programmer, University of California Press, Berkeley, 1961-62. Since 1962, free-lance writer and artist: Co-Director, Berkeley Free University, 1967-68; Founder, Microcosm Fiction Workshop, later Ramona Street Regulars, 1967; since 1968, teaching assistant, Adams Junior High School, El Cerrito, California. President, California Writers Club, 1977-78. Address: 333 Ramona Avenue, El Cerrito, California 94530, U.S.A.

SCIENCE-FICTION PUBLICATIONS

Novels (series: Beggars)

The Ganymede Takeover, with Philip K. Dick.   New York, Ace, 1967; London, Arrow, 1971.
Blake's Progress.   Toronto, Laser, 1975.
Then Beggars Could Ride.   Toronto, Laser, 1976.
The Ecolog.   Toronto, Laser, 1977.
The Revolt of the Unemployables (Beggars).   San Francisco, Anthelion, 1978.
Dimension of Horror (as Jeffrey Lord).   Los Angeles, Pinnacle, 1979.

Uncollected Short Stories

"Turn Off the Sky," in *Fantasy and Science Fiction* (New York), August 1963.
"Eight O'Clock in the Morning," in *The Best from Fantasy and Science Fiction 13*, edited by Avram Davidson. New York, Doubleday, 1964.
"Losers Weepers," in *Nugget* (New York), 1964.
"Food," in *Gamma 4* (Los Angeles), 1965.
"The Great Cosmic Donut of Life," in *Fantasy and Science Fiction* (New York), September 1965.
"Time Travel for Pedestrians," in *Again, Dangerous Visions*, edited by Harlan Ellison. New York, Doubleday, 1972; London, Millington, 1976.
"Egyptian Christ," in *Orion* (Lakemont, Georgia), 1972.
"The City of the Crocodile," in *Fantastic* (New York), March 1974.
"A Song on the Rising Wind," in *Fantastic* (New York), November 1974.
"What Survives?," in *Uniquest* (Berkeley, California), 1976.
"Microcosm," in *Science Fiction Review* (Portland, Oregon), 1976.
"Who's the Red Queen?," in *Amazing* (New York), March 1976.
"Flesh Pearl," in *Amazing* (New York), December 1976.
"Two Futures," in *Uniquest* (Berkeley, California), 1977.
"Nightfall on the Dead Sea," in *Fantasy and Science Fiction* (New York), September 1977.
"On the Edge of Futuria," in *Science-Fiction Review* (Portland, Oregon), 1978.

OTHER PUBLICATIONS

Novels

The Agony of Love.   San Diego, Greenleaf, 1969.
Girl with the Hungry Eyes.   San Diego, Greenleaf, 1969.

Novels as R.N. Elson

How to Do it.   San Diego, Greenleaf, 1970.
Black Pussy.   San Diego, Greenleaf, 1970.
Sex Happy Hippy.   San Diego, Greenleaf, 1970.
The DA's Wife.   San Diego, Greenleaf, 1970.

Ray Nelson comments:
For me, Jack London, not Hugo Gernsback, is the father of

American Science Fiction, and my aim is to continue the tradition established at the beginning of this century by London and his friends. My three obsessive themes are radical utopianism, experimental occultism, and a love-fear romance with nature. In California these ideas are understood, particularly in the Bay Area (all but two of the living writers I admire live in California), but in New York, where there are no trees, my obsessions seem like nonsense. Most of my work has been published outside New York—places where there are trees and intuition and hope for a better life, and someday New York too will grudgingly lend me an ear, perhaps when I am safely dead.

*   *   *

Although the total of Ray Nelson's science fiction is not distinguished in word count, he has maintained throughout his career a very high standard of performance in his output, even the worst of which is interesting and readable.

The Ganymede Takeover, written with Philip K. Dick, deals with the domination of Earth by wormlike invaders from Ganymede, but it was written as a witty examination of individuals and societies, not the low-grade movie its plot resembles. The most notable of his solo novels is *Blake's Progress*, a serious contender for best novel of its year. Ostensibly, the central character is the poet William Blake, a man capable of mentally travelling through time in company with his wife. It is soon apparent, however, that it is she who dominates their relationship; she has the more powerful intellect, and is soon revealed as a far more interesting character than her rather weak-willed husband. Although Nelson's other novels are also quite well handled, they are both disappointing when compared to the former. *Then Beggars Could Ride* is similar in many ways, a kaleidoscopic odyssey through time. *The Ecolog* is a more conventional novel, pitting a determined, expert military man against a planet ruled by a ruthless matriarch.

Nelson's shorter fiction is extremely good, and equally infrequent. "Nightfall on the Dead Sea," for example, is a fine historical horror story pitting a Roman soldier against a man cursed with immortality. "Time Travel for Pedestrians" aroused a great deal of controversy because of its subject matter—time travel via masturbation—but its clear superiority of language and maturity of its vision outweigh the novelty of its subject matter. Nelson displays a fondness for the grotesque at times. A human is turned into an organic asteroid in "Flesh Pearl," and another becomes a rather unpleasant food source in "Food." Grotesquerie and the absurd dominate "The Great Cosmic Donut of Life" and "Turn Off the Sky." "Eight O'Clock in the Morning" takes a routine science-fiction gimmick (aliens who can only be seen by a single person) but condenses what other writers would have made into a novel into a few thousand words. Another old stand-by given new life is "Who's the Red Queen?": a supposedly insane woman is freed by an attendant at a mental institution because he believes her to be a refugee from another world. Nelson mixes ancient history with the supernatural again in "The City of the Crocodile." "A Song on the Rising Wind" examines the nature of violence and courage on a level rare in any field of writing, as a revolution brews among a society of sequestered unemployables.

Although not prolific, Nelson is a careful writer whose every story reflects great concentration and commitment. He is not afraid of controversial themes or ambitious goals, and maintains tight control of his stories. While his stories may at times be idiosyncratic, their very uniqueness of viewpoint is often what separates them from scores of similar stories.

—Don D'Ammassa

NEVILLE, Kris (Ottman).   American.   Born in Carthage, Missouri, 9 May 1925. Educated at the University of California, Los Angeles, B.A. in English 1950. Served in the United States Army

Signal Corps during World War II. Married Lil Johnson in 1957; five children. Worked in the plastics and chemistry industries: since 1965, staff member, Epoxylite Corporation, Anaheim, California. Agent: Forrest J. Ackerman, 2495 Glendower Avenue, Hollywood, California 90027. Address: 2443 Moreno Drive, Los Angeles, California 90027, U.S.A.

SCIENCE-FICTION PUBLICATIONS

Novels

The Unearth People.   New York, Belmont, 1964.
The Mutants.   New York, Belmont, 1966.
Peril of the Starmen.   New York, Belmont, 1967.
Special Delivery.   New York, Belmont, 1967.
Bettyann.   New York, Belmont, 1970.
Invaders on the Moon.   New York, Belmont, 1970.

Short Stories

Mission: Manstop.   North Hollywood, Nordon, 1971.

Uncollected Short Stories with Lil Neville

"Medical Practices among the Immortals," in *Galaxy* (New York), September 1972.
"Bettyann's Children," in *Demon Kind*, edited by Roger Elwood. New York, Avon, 1973.
"The Quality of the Product," in *Saving Worlds*, edited by Roger Elwood and Virginia Kidd. New York, Doubleday, 1973.
"Pater Familias," with Barry N. Malzberg, in *Out from Ganymede*, by Malzberg. New York, Warner, 1974.
"Survival Problems," in *Universe 5*, edited by Terry Carr. New York, Random House, 1974; London, Dobson, 1977.
"The Man Who Read Equations," in *Fantasy and Science Fiction* (New York), December 1974.
"Arleen," in *Perry Rhodan 94-96.*   New York, Ace, 1976.
"Milk into Brandy," in *Amazing* (New York), June 1976.

OTHER PUBLICATIONS

Novel

Run, The Spearmaker (in Japanese), with Lil Neville.   Tokyo, Hayakawa Shobo, 1975.

Other

Epoxy Resins, with Henry Lee.   New York, McGraw Hill, 1957.
Handbook of Epoxy Resins, with Henry Lee.   New York, McGraw Hill, 1967.
New Linear Polymers, with Henry Lee.   New York, McGraw Hill, 1967.
Handbook of Biomedical Plastics, with Henry Lee.   Pasadena, California, Pasadena Technology Press, 1971.
Adhesive Restorative Dentistry, with Robert L. Ibsen.   Philadelphia, Saunders, 1974.
Motor Users' Handbook of Insulation for Rewinds, with L.J. Rejda.   New York, Elsevier, 1977.

Kris Neville comments:

I wrote the majority of my stories in the early 1950's. Having just graduated from UCLA with a degree in English literature, I was interested in introducing mainstream elements into science fiction (which I had been reading avidly since 1937)—shifting the emphasis to the impact of future technology on ordinary individuals. I also tried to seek out new perspectives—using female protagonists; playing with various viewpoints; seeing the future through the eyes of the old or young; portraying Earthmen in less than favorable lights; breaking taboos; making satirical comments (I was a socialist/-humanist). In many of my shorts, I aimed for emotional effect. I was a trail blazer in my time.

By the mid-1950's, I'd run out of things to say. During the next decade, I kept my hand in with *The Unearth People* and an occa-

sional short, and also revised earlier material into novels. I moved leftward philosophically to my present position: left wing anarchist. The shorts contained sharper social commentary ("Survival Problems"). I was particularly unhappy with the war in Vietnam ("The Price of Simeryl") and, later, Richard Nixon ("The Reality Machine"). During that decade, Lil and I wrote *Run, The Spearmaker*, a novel dealing with the evolution of civilization at the beginning of human history. The translator called it a minor literary masterpiece. Pity it isn't available in English.

During the 1970's, in addition to half a dozen shorts that Lil and I collaborated on, we also did another novel, *Thorstein Macaulay*. It contains our best writing and most carefully considered political statements. It was about 10 years in the making. As of this writing (June 1979) we had not yet found a publisher for it.

*　　*　　*

Kris Neville's large output of stories seems to be equally divided among adventure SF, social SF, fantasy SF and fantasy. While he is known as a *Galaxy* school writer, his most characteristic work appears to be more melodramatic than ironic. Nevertheless, Neville will often subordinate adventure narrative to character interaction or to the character's response to those environmental or cultural forces that are by-products of future science and technology. Neville was a popular and critically respected author in the genre during the 1950's and 1960's, but his reputation as a craftsman seems to have been lost, perhaps as the result of the rather conventional plotting and characterization in his later work.

Neville's great theme is alienation, one which takes its most obvious form in stories that treat alien-human contact. He eschews the more sensational aspects of this theme in favor of the psychological dimensions implied in its use in the future world of SF. Novels like *Special Delivery, Earth Alert* (*If*, February 1953), and *The Mutants* deal with variations of the alien invasion theme or its analogues. *The Mutants*, a potentially timely treatment of the social implications of artificial insemination in a state utopia, fails to rise above the level of the melodramatic struggle of a few idealistic youths fighting to save the race from a progressively more repressive state control of human biology.

In the main, Neville is a writer typical of his time. He knows how to make good use of psychologically enriched characters and possesses more sensitivity toward character motivation and interaction than most of his colleagues. In many ways, he belongs in the Theodore Sturgeon camp of SF writers, although he does lapse into the action/adventure idiom more frequently than Sturgeon and his successors. Neville's style is also more direct, simple, and clear than Sturgeon's, better suited, perhaps, for the pot boilers he produced for Belmont. Neville is, it appears, in nearly every way a writer several cuts above the average who has never quite made the success expected of him. Although he writes SF, Neville gives little evidence of being deeply committed for or against science. It, like the future, is simply one of the unexamined, given elements of his stories. Whatever the cause, Neville has produced a body of SF that refuses to move us deeply in any of the many ways in which less accomplished stylists have done by writing with more conviction, except in one notable case.

Neville may not deserve the obscurity into which his career has fallen if only for the sake of one superb story, "Bettyann" (1951; expanded into a novel, 1970; a sequel is "Bettyann's Children"). This story of a crippled orphan girl raised in a foster home whose sense of difference is confirmed when she discovers she is actually a member of an extra-terrestrial race is handled with the same kind of sensitivity and poignance as Daniel Keyes's "Flowers for Algernon," another story that grew successfully into a novel. In place of the overwriting of most SF melodrama, Neville has his subject and his characters fully under control. In "Bettyann" Neville manages understated effects brilliantly in a way that he approached in only a few other stories besides the sequel: "Old Man Henderson" and "Closing Time" are examples. "Bettyann" is one of those rare SF stories that could not be written in another genre but which deals profoundly with universal, human values. Bettyann's affirmation of a basic humanity which has become stronger in her nature than her lately discovered alien origins is an inspiring moment in literature. The two stories and the novel must be considered neglected masterpieces, which are only beginning to receive their due critical recognition.

—Donald L. Lawler

NEWCOMB, Simon. American. Born in Nova Scotia, Canada, 12 March 1835. Educated at Harvard University, Cambridge, Massachusetts. Married Mary Caroline Hassler in 1863; three daughters. Professor of Mathematics, United States Navy, 1861-97, and Johns Hopkins University, Baltimore, 1894. Director, *Nautical Almanac*, and Editor, *American Journal of Mathematics*. LL.D.: Johns Hopkins University, 1902; other honorary degrees from Cambridge, Oxford, Dublin, and Edinburgh universities. President, Astronomical and Astrophysical Society of America, and Congress of Arts and Sciences, St. Louis, 1904; foreign member, Institute of France and Royal Society. *Died 11 July 1909.*

SCIENCE-FICTION PUBLICATIONS

Novel

His Wisdom, The Defender. New York, Harper, 1900.

OTHER PUBLICATIONS

Other

A Critical Examination of Our Financial Policy During the Southern Rebellion. New York, Appleton, 1865.
An Investigation of the Orbit of Neptune [and *Uranus*]. Washington, D.C., Smithsonian Institution, 2 vols., 1866-73.
Popular Astronomy. New York, Harper, 1877; London, Macmillan, 1878; 6th edition, Harper, 1895.
The ABC of Finance. New York, Harper, 1878.
Astronomy, by R.S. Ball, revised edition. New York, Holt, 1878.
Astronomy for Schools and Colleges, with Edward S. Holden. New York, Holt, 1879; revised edition, as *Astronomy for Students and General Readers*, 1880; revised edition, as *Astronomy for High Schools and Colleges*, 1881; 6th edition, 1893.
The Relation of Scientific Method to Social Progress (lecture). Privately printed, 1880.
Elements of Geometry. New York, Holt, 1881; 4th edition, 1889.
Algebra for Schools and Colleges. New York, Holt, 1881; 6th edition, 1895.
Elements of Plane and Spherical Trigonometry. New York, Holt, 1882; 3rd edition, 1898.
Elements of Plane Geometry and Trigonometry. New York, Holt, 1882.
Logarithmic and Other Mathematical Tables. New York, Holt, 1882.
A School Algebra. New York, Holt, 1882.
Astronomy, with Edward S. Holden. New York, Holt, 1883; 5th edition, 1892.
Elements of Analytic Geometry. New York, Holt, 1884.
The Essentials of Trigonometry. New York, Holt, 1884.
A Plain Man's Talk on the Labor Question. New York, Harper, 1886.
Principles of Political Economy. New York, Harper, 1886.
Elements of the Differential and Integral Calculus. New York, Holt, 1887.
The Problems of Astronomy (lecture). Privately printed, 1897.
Elements of Astronomy. New York, American Book Company, 1900.
The Stars: A Study of the Universe. New York, Putnam, 1901; London, Murray, 1902.

Astronomy for Everybody. New York, McClure, 1902; London, Isbister, 1903.
The Reminiscences of an Astronomer. Boston, Houghton Mifflin, and London, Harper, 1903.
The Evolution of the Scientific Investigator (lecture). St. Louis, Universal Exposition, 1904.
A Compendium of Spherical Astronomy. New York, Macmillan, 1906.
Side-Lights on Astronomy and Kindred Fields of Popular Science: Essays and Addresses. New York, Harper, 1906.
Investigation of Inequalities in the Motion of the Moon Produced by the Action of the Planets. Washington, D.C., Carnegie Institution, 1907.

*   *   *

Simon Newcomb published many works, mainly on astronomy and mathematics, but also on popular science—e.g., the fourth dimension—and economics. His only venture into fiction is *His Wisdom, The Defender*, in which future historians of the state established by a great scientist tell how in the 1940's, having grown rich through inventions, notably that of anti-gravity, he used them to disarm the bellicose German emperor and other kings, and established a just and peaceful global society headed by himself. This naive story of gadgetry, politics, and hero-worship, much inferior to the visions of, say, Jack London, is nonetheless significant as the wish-dream of a top scientist troubled by the destructive potentialities of modern warfare but unwilling to recognize its intimate connection with modern science, and may therefore help to explain more important technocratic works such as Wells's *The World Set Free* or Asimov's *I, Robot*.

—Darko Suvin

NIVEN, Larry (Laurence Van Cott Niven). American. Born in Los Angeles, California, 30 April 1938. Educated at California Institute of Technology, Pasadena, 1956-58; Washburn University, Topeka, Kansas, A.B. 1962; University of California, Los Angeles, 1962-63. Married Marylin Wosowati in 1969. Since 1964, free-lance writer. Recipient: Hugo Award, for story, 1967, 1972, 1975, 1976, for novel, 1971; Nebula Award, 1970; Ditmar Award, 1971. Agent: Robert P. Mills Ltd., 156 East 52nd Street, New York, New York 10022. Address: 3961 Vanalden Avenue, Tarzana, California 91356, U.S.A.

SCIENCE-FICTION PUBLICATIONS

Novels (series: Known Space)

World of Ptavvs (Space). New York, Ballantine, 1966; London, Macdonald, 1968.
A Gift from Earth (Space). New York, Ballantine, 1968; London, Macdonald, 1969.
Ringworld (Space). New York, Ballantine, 1970; London, Gollancz, 1972.
The Flying Sorcerers, with David Gerrold. New York, Ballantine, 1971; London, Corgi, 1975.
Protector (Space). New York, Ballantine, 1973; Tisbury, Wiltshire, Compton Russell, 1976.
The Mote in God's Eye, with Jerry Pournelle. New York, Simon and Schuster, 1974; London, Weidenfeld and Nicolson, 1975.
Inferno, with Jerry Pournelle. New York, Pocket Books, 1976; London, Wingate, 1977.
A World Out of Time. New York, Holt Rinehart, 1976; London, Macdonald and Jane's 1977.
Lucifer's Hammer, with Jerry Pournelle. Chicago, Playboy Press, 1977.

The Magic Goes Away.   New York, Ace, 1978; London, Dobson, 1980.
The Ringworld Engineers (Space).   New York, Holt Rinehart, and London, Gollancz, 1980.
The Patchwork Girl.   New York, Ace, 1980.

Short Stories (series: Known Space)

Neutron Star (Space).   New York, Ballantine, 1968; London, Macdonald, 1969.
The Shape of Space (Space).   New York, Ballantine, 1969.
All the Myriad Ways.   New York, Ballantine, 1971.
The Flight of the Horse.   New York, Ballantine, 1973; London, Futura, 1975.
Inconstant Moon (omnibus).   London, Gollancz, 1973.
A Hole in Space.   New York, Ballantine, 1974; London, Futura, 1975.
Tales of Known Space.   New York, Ballantine, 1975.
The Long ARM of Gil Hamilton (Space).   New York, Ballantine, 1976.
Convergent Series.   New York, Ballantine, 1979.

Uncollected Short Story

"The Green Marauder," in *Destinies* (New York), February-March 1980.

*

Manuscript Collection: George Arents Research Library, Syracuse University, New York.

*   *   *

Larry Niven learned his craft through his long familiarity with SF literature as a fan and through study of writers such as John W. Campbell, Jr., Heinlein, Asimov, and, later, Anderson, Clarke, and Clement. Niven sees himself rightly as carrying on and developing SF traditions and those of the related genre, popular fantasy. Everything Niven has written thus far has a strong genre identification, and his appeal as well as his fame has been until recently within the expanding universe of the SF and fantasy reader. Niven has tried his hand at nearly every major type of SF, including fantasy SF stories of time travel, parallel worlds, and sword and sorcery.

Niven's best and most characteristic work in SF has been done in series works. Among the lesser series are the delightful Hanville Svetz comic SF fantasies (*The Flight of the Horse*); the Leshy series, the best of which is "The Fourth Profession," culminating in *A World Out of Time:* the Draco's Tavern stories (*Convergent Series*); and the Jayberry Jensen teleportation stories, the best of which are "Flash Crowd" and "All the Bridges Rusting."

The pre-eminent series, and possibly the best in SF history, has occupied Niven since the publication of his first story, "The Coldest Place" (1964). Known Space is the saga of the next 1200 years of human history, beginning in 1975 with the development of organ-bank technology on earth, chronicling the exploration of our galaxy and encounters with alien species, and culminating in the spread throughout the race of a mutant gene which incorporates the code for a psychic power that operates to protect the individual from harm and to promote and even guarantee maximum opportunities for happiness. The end result is a universe safe for future human development and for the generation of a species preferred by evolution through the cooperative union of genetics and psionics. In short, Niven's cosmology moves ultimately toward the realization of that universal hope of intelligent species expressed in the story "Convergent Series" (1967) that "There is a way to thwart entropy, to live forever." Many of Niven's critics have found in his ultimate triumphalism a weakness of vision, but it proceeds logically from Niven's traditionalism and from the philosophical assumptions underlying his fiction.

Between the present and dawn of the golden age in the Third Millennium, Niven chronicles the struggles of each generation to meet the challenges presented by the future development of modern technological advances that seem most revolutionary to Niven in biological and transportation engineering. The immediate impact of organ-transplant technology and the development of personal teleportation transfer stations is to polarize society into revolutionary and reactionary factions. Such new technologies "create new customs, new laws, new ethics, new crimes," as Niven observes. The potentiality for repressive and even ghoulish practices by both criminals and by society and its agents is dramatized powerfully in those stories set in the near future which strike the reader with the impact of social realism. Two of the Gil Hamilton stories, "Death by Ecstasy" and "The Defenseless Dead," present the official, police view of "organlegging," while stories like "Cloak of Anarchy," "The Jigsaw Man," and "Rammer" and the novel *A Gift from Earth* focus effectively on the kinds of abuse likely to grow from using criminals to supply body parts for organ banks. The teleportation stories like "Flash Crowd" extrapolates the technology and sociology of the displacement transfer booths. Typically, Niven's solution to the social and ethical problems of this chaotic world is technological. Unlike Huxley, Heinlein, and others who leave the technological base of their narrative in favor of moral speculations on human nature or social history, Niven follows through on his belief that moral values and ethical practice change with the alteration of basic social processes produced by technology.

The challenges of space exploration are even more dramatic because they allow Niven's imagination freer rein for invention. The smaller gravity of asteroids and planetary satellites affects all phases of the lives of the Belt inhabitants. Inevitably, the differences between Belters and Flatlanders (terrans) lead to separate and competing political and economic structures. The colonization of new worlds leads to the further specialization of the race and to the development of new characteristics peculiar to those from colony worlds of other star systems like Jinx and Wunderland. In his Known Space stories, Niven develops consequences implied in ecology-psychology interactions even more successfully than his mentors Asimov, Heinlein, and Herbert. One of the great challenges of Known Space exploration comes from attempting to subdue alien environments of interstellar space and other worlds. Another comes from contact and interaction with aliens which leads to war with Pak protectors and Kzinti, beneficial trade with the Outsiders, and exchanges of technological information with the Puppeteers. In Known Space, mutants become symbols of the impact of alien contact on human development and at the same time they serve as the biological mechanisms for human acquisition of specialized survival traits leading to racial supremacy through the genes, producing the luck of Matt Keller (*A Gift from Earth*) and Teela Brown (*Ringworld*).

Critics who disparage Niven's writing do so on two counts. One is the critic's dislike of Niven's rather conventional optimism, even though there is a historical basis for Niven's positivism, and he is anything but naive about the abuse of technology. Niven's vision may be meliorative in the end, but humanity has to pay for its golden age with hard times to come. Critics have also objected to Niven's plotting difficulties in his novels, and there is no doubt that this is a weakness of his writing. At the same time, it must be said that Niven's use of cinematographic techniques of storytelling work well in his two most successful novels, *World of Ptavvs* and *Ringworld*. Few would deny Niven's extraordinary powers of invention and his ability to blend hard science extrapolation with soft science speculations and space opera adventure. To some degree the pleasure of reading Niven depends on the reader's growing awareness of the grand design of the series so that even the weaker novels and stories take on added dimensions.

At least brief mention should be made here of the appeal of Niven's plausible use of hard science speculations, especially in such glamor fields as biomedical engineering, space exploration, and exobiology. These are complemented brilliantly by Niven's extraordinary powers of naming. Niven's off-world inventions include an orismology of the colonized worlds of Known Space: Plateau, Home, Jinx, Wunderland, Down, and We Made It, with their inspired mixture of naive anthropocentrism, popular folk culture, and humor in a rather typically American combination. Niven is also especially good at suggesting ways in which the impact of these strange new worlds shapes the character and thinking of their inhabitants in the space of even a few generations.

Perhaps the two creations that give Niven's Known Space its distinctive richness and appeal are the alien creatures encountered by humanity in its exploration and expansion and the related discovery or universal history in the records, traditions, and artifacts of alien races, both living and dead. Niven's mythical history discloses three major eras in galactic history. The First is the ancient empire of the Thrint, known as Slavers, whose artifacts are occasionally to be found in stasis boxes, preserved from change, and prized by their finders for their technological importance. We actually meet a Thrint in *World of Ptavvs*, an encounter in which humanity barely escapes with life and freedom. The Thrint empire and its creatures were destroyed eventually during the suicidal revolution of the master technician slaves known as Tnuctipun. The second epoch was that of the Pak, remote ancestors in Niven's mythology of humans and other intelligent life forms, whose breeders had seeded the universe of Known Space and perhaps beyond. Although very ancient, Pak Protectors have survived to challenge the existence of their own unrecognized, mutated human descendants and to produce, accidentally, in what Niven intends to be an analogue of natural selection, a hybrid human protector, the Brennan monster, who ushers in a golden age of peace that lasts three centuries. The Third epoch begins with the Kzin-human wars and the acquisition of hyperdrive from the Outsiders, continues with Beowulf Shaeffer's discovery that the galactic core has exploded, and concludes with the discovery of the great Pak artifact, Ringworld, and with the emergence of the Teela Brown gene. Niven's universal history is an ingenious and beautifully modulated bit of cosmic mythmaking.

A second distinctive creation is Niven's aliens. No SF writer has lavished as much energy in populating his fiction with such a variety of sentient beings: the ancient Thrint slavers; the enslaved master technician Tnuctipun; Pak Protectors; the bellicose, cat-like Kzinti; the cowardly, manipulative Puppeteers; the enigmatic space merchant Outsiders; and an oddity of other creatures including Grogs, Kdatlyno, and Bandersnatchi. Niven gives his readers far more than an alien bestiary, for he creates new species of intelligent beings who are both representative members of a type as well as distinctive individuals. Niven establishes the psychology, attitudes, and cultural identity of his aliens with rare economy and style. And yet we never feel that Niven has told us all he knows about his alien beings, their worlds, or their place in the cosmic history of Known Space.

Niven also writes fantasy, and the chief modern influences on his writing in that genre have been Cabell, Dunsany, Howard, de Camp, and Fletcher Pratt. References, allusions, and analogues to the work of these writers are often deliberately worked into Niven's fantasy as echoes recalling the traditions he follows. So far, Niven has not attempted high or literary fantasy of the kind we associate with the tradition of Morris and Tolkien; rather, he writes in the fashion of popular adventure fantasies of Howard, Burroughs, and Brackett. Niven deserves recognition as a major SF writer who has achieved excellence in individual stories and novels, but whose reputation will securely rest upon the foundation of his Known Space mythology. For readers unfamiliar with Niven's work, it is best to begin with the Gil Hamilton stories and *World of Ptavvs*. *Ringworld* should be saved for last since it comes virtually at the end of the Known Space saga. *Tales of Known Space* is invaluable for Niven's charts and editorial notes: and, although not up to the standard of the best novels, *Protector* forms an important link in the mythology no interested reader will want to overlook.

—Donald L. Lawler

NOLAN, William F(rancis). American. Born in Kansas City, Missouri, 6 March 1928. Educated at Kansas City Art Institute, 1946-47; San Diego State College, California, 1947-48; Los Angeles City College, 1953. Married Marilyn Seal in 1970. Commercial artist, credit clerk, and aircraft worker; Contributing Editor, *Chase;* Managing Editor, *GAMMA;* West Coast Editor, *Auto;* Associate Editor, *Motor Sport Illustrated;* Reviewer, Los Angeles *Times.* Since 1956, free-lance writer. Recipient: Academy of Science Fiction and Fantasy Award, for fiction, and film, 1976. Honorary

Doctorate: American River College, Sacramento, California. Address: 22720 Cavalier Street, Woodland Hills, California 91364, U.S.A.

SCIENCE-FICTION PUBLICATIONS

Novels (series: Logan)

Logan's Run, with G.C. Johnson.   New York, Dial Press, 1967; London, Gollancz, 1968.
Logan's World.   New York, Bantam, 1977; London, Corgi, 1978.

Short Stories

Impact-20.   New York, Paperback Library, 1963; London, Corgi, 1966.
Alien Horizons   New York, Pocket Books, 1974.
Wonderworlds.   London, Gollancz, 1977.

Uncollected Short Stories

"Saturday's Shadow," in *Shadows 2,* edited by Charles L. Grant. New York, Doubleday, 1979.

OTHER PUBLICATIONS

Novels

Death Is for Losers.   Los Angeles, Sherbourne Press, 1968.
The White Cad Cross-Up.   Los Angeles, Sherbourne Press, 1969.
Space for Hire.   New York, Lancer, 1971.

Plays

Screenplays: *The Legend of Machine-Gun Kelly,* 1973; *Logan's Run,* 1976; *Burnt Offerings,* 1976.

Television Plays: *The Joy of Living,* 1971; *The Norliss Tapes,* 1973; *Melvin Purvis, G-Man,* 1974; *The Turn of the Screw,* 1974; *The Kansas City Massacre,* 1975; *Sky Heist,* 1975; *Trilogy of Terror,* 1975; *Logan's Run* series, 1977.

Other

Adventure on Wheels: The Autobiography of a Road Racing Champion, with John Fitch.   New York, Putnam, 1959.
Barney Oldfield.   New York, Putnam, 1961.
Phil Hill, Yankee Champion.   New York, Putnam, 1962.
Men of Thunder: Fabled Daredevils of Motor Sport.   New York, Putnam, 1964.
Sinners and Supermen.   North Hollywood, All Star, 1965.
John Huston, King Rebel.   Los Angeles, Sherbourne Press, 1965.
Dashiell Hammett: A Casebook.   Santa Barbara, California, McNally and Loftin, 1969.
Steve McQueen: Star on Wheels.   New York, Putnam, 1972.
Carnival of Speed.   New York, Putnam, 1973.
Hemingway: Last Days of the Lion.   Santa Barbara, California, Capra Press, 1974.
The Ray Bradbury Companion.   Detroit, Gale, 1975.

Editor, with Carles Beaumont, *Omnibus of Speed.*   New York, Putnam, 1958; London, Paul, 1961.
Editor, with Charles Beaumont, *When Engines Roar.*   New York, Bantam, 1964.
Editor, *Man Against Tomorrow.*   New York, Avon, 1965.
Editor, *The Pseudo People: Androids in Science Fiction.*   Los Angeles, Sherbourne Press, 1965; London, Mayflower, 1967; as *Almost Human,* London, Souvenir Press, 1966.
Editor, *3 to the Highest Power.*   New York, Avon, 1968; London, Corgi, 1971.
Editor, *A Wilderness of Stars.*   Los Angeles, Sherbourne Press, 1969; London, Gollancz, 1970.
Editor, *A Sea of Space.*   New York, Bantam, 1970.
Editor, *The Future Is Now.*   Los Angeles, Sherbourne Press, 1970.

Editor, *The Human Equation.* Los Angeles, Sherbourne Press, 1971; London, Springwood, 1979.
Editor, *The Edge of Forever*, by Chad Oliver. Los Angeles, Sherbourne Press, 1971.
Editor, with Martin H. Greenberg, *Science Fiction Origins.* New York, Fawcett-Popular Library, 1980.

*

Bibliography: *William F. Nolan: A Checklist* by Charles E. Yenter, Tacoma, Washington, Charles E. Yenter, 1974.

William F. Nolan comments:

As a writer I'm hard to pin down. Science fiction is just one of my many fields, and I take equal pride in my crime-suspense writing, auto-racing books, biographies, fantasy-terror fiction, thriller novels, and essays and book reviews. I keep fresh and excited as a writer by switching constantly from one genre to another. I enjoy doing SF, particularly the Logan novels, but I also enjoy all other types of writing. After 25 years as a professional, my work totals 895 items— and I'm just getting started!

*   *   *

William F. Nolan's first full-length science-fiction work was *Logan's Run*, written with G.C. Johnson. Set in the not-too-distant future, with LSD parlors, unlimited sex, and compulsory euthanasia at age 21, the novel has established itself as a classic, and spawned a film and a TV series. The story concerns Logan, a "sandman," whose job it is to search out those people over 21 who have failed to report voluntarily for elimination. These "runners," who present a danger to the rulers of Logan's world, are easily identified, for each member of society has a flower-shaped disc set in the palm of his hand which changes color in accordance with his age. Logan himself begins to question the ethics of his world, and he too becomes a runner. Nolan followed up the success of the book with a sequel, *Logan's World*.

—Peter Berresford Ellis

———————

NORMAN, John. Pseudonym for John (Frederick) Lange (Jr.). American. Born in Chicago, Illinois, 3 June 1931. Educated at the University of Nebraska, Lincoln, B.A.; University of Southern California, Los Angeles, M.A.; Princeton University, New Jersey, Ph.D. Served in the United States Army: Sergeant. Married Bernice L. Green in 1956; two sons and one daughter. Radio writer; story analyst, Warner Brothers; film writer, University of Nebraska; technical writer, Rocketdyne (North American Aviation); Professor of Philosophy, Queens College, City University of New York. Address: 65 Longfellow Drive, Great Neck, New York 11023, U.S.A.

SCIENCE-FICTION PUBLICATIONS

Novels (series: Gor)

Tarnsman of Gor. New York, Ballantine, 1966; London, Sidgwick and Jackson, 1969.
Outlaw of Gor. New York, Ballantine, 1967; London, Sidgwick and Jackson, 1970.
Priest-Kings of Gor. New York, Ballantine, 1968; London, Sidgwick and Jackson, 1971.
Nomads of Gor. New York, Ballantine, 1969; London, Sidgwick and Jackson, 1971.
Assassin of Gor. New York, Ballantine, 1970; London, Sidgwick and Jackson, 1971.
Ghost Dance. New York, Ballantine, 1970; London, Sphere, 1972.

Raiders of Gor. New York, Ballantine, 1971; London, Tandem, 1973.
Captive of Gor. New York, Ballantine, 1972; London, Tandem, 1973.
Hunters of Gor. New York, DAW, 1974; London, Tandem, 1975.
Marauders of Gor. New York, DAW, 1975; London, Universal, 1977.
Time Slave. New York, DAW, 1975.
Tribesmen of Gor. New York, DAW, 1976.
Slave Girl of Gor. New York, DAW, 1977; London, Universal, 1978.
Beasts of Gor. New York, DAW, 1978; London, Star, 1979.
Explorers of Gor. New York, DAW, 1979.
Fighting Slave of Gor. New York, DAW, 1980.

OTHER PUBLICATIONS

Other

The Cognitive Paradox; An Inquiry Concerning the Claims of Philosophy (as John Lange). Princeton, New Jersey, Princeton University Press, 1970.
Imaginative Sex. New York, DAW, 1975.

*   *   *

John Norman has written over a dozen books in the Gor series (The Chronicles of Counter-Earth), novels in the tradition of Edgar Rice Burroughs's Mars books or Andre Norton's Witch World stories. In these works, a character from contemporary Earth finds himself transported, often by inexplicable means, to an unfamiliar world where he is caught up in the events which are shaping the future of that world. And in such worlds heroic action is almost always the means by which destiny is decided.

Norman's hero, Tarl Cabot, is transported to Gor, a planet on the opposite side of the sun from Earth and somehow shielded from any detection by Terran scientists. On Gor, Cabot is initiated into a way of life which the reader would call medieval. All technological development, especially in weaponry, has been held in check by the Priest-Kings, and men must fight with sword, spear, bow and arrow, and the like. For most of the known planet, the largest political unit is the city, and politics in and among cities is generally feudal. Gorean society is highly structured, and each person usually remains in the caste—warriors, bakers, scribes, etc.—into which he is born. But Gor and the Priest-Kings are in trouble and in need of heroics which only Tarl Cabot can and does provide.

As with any extended work of fantasy, the author's ability convincingly to detail a complex culture—or group of cultures—is important. Norman is quite good at this. In the first book, *Tarnsman of Gor*, such detail is a necessity, and Norman provides a wealth of detail on everything from the training of a warrior to the importance of a Home Stone. In what is possibly his best book, *Nomads of Gor*, he brings Cabot to the four tribes of the Wagon People, and the reader is treated to a fascinating description of customs, habits, rituals, and all the other aspects of a complex cultural group. On Gor, the reader realizes, heroic action is not only possible, it is necessary; in other words, the culture is not just a backdrop for the action in Norman's books, it is an integral part of the action.

Heroic fantasies have always been considered male-escapist. The hero is muscular and skillful with weapons; he rescues the heroine who then succumbs to his over-powering maleness. Norman carries this aspect of heroic fantasy one large step farther than his predecessors. On Gor, most of the women are slaves, and those who are not are vaguely unhappy because a woman can be free only in total submission to a man. Earth women brought to Gor are at first distressed by such a prospect but soon realize the falseness of their previous way of life. On Gor, Cabot says, women are free to be women, whereas on Earth they are forced to try to be men. This concept has lost Norman two groups of readers, the first violently opposed to his analysis of women, the second tired of hearing Cabot explain and defend it in book after book.

In terms of literary criticism, it is the defense, not the attitude itself, which mars the novels, some of which seem to have been written solely to present examples of these ideas and attitudes about women. And Cabot's primary quest has suffered as well; to be sure, he fights skirmishes against the enemies of the Priest-Kings, but the main plot-line of the series seems to be barely progressing. This situation is unfortunate, for the Gor books are, in most other respects, good heroic fantasy.

—C.W. Sullivan III

NORTH, Andrew. *See* **NORTON, Andre.**

NORTON, Andre (Alice Mary Norton). Also writes as Andrew North; Allen Weston. American. Born in Cleveland, Ohio, in 1912. Educated at Western Reserve University, Cleveland. Children's Librarian, Cleveland Public Library, 1932-50; Special Librarian, Library of Congress, Washington, D.C., during World War II; Editor, Gnome Press, New York, 1950-58. Recipient: Boys' Clubs of America Award, 1965; Grand Master of Fantasy Award, 1977; Gandalf Award, 1978. Agent: Larry Sternig, 742 Robertson Street, Milwaukee, Wisconsin 53213. Address: 682 South Lakemont, Winter Park, Florida 32789, U.S.A.

SCIENCE-FICTION PUBLICATIONS

Novels (series: Astra; Beast Master; Janus; Shann Lantree; Moon Magic; Star Ka'at; Time Travel; Time War; Zero Stone)

Star Man's Son, 2250 A.D. New York, Harcourt Brace, 1952; London, Staples Press, 1953; as *Daybreak, 2250 A.D.*, New York, Ace, 1954.
Star Rangers. New York, Harcourt Brace, 1953; London, Gollancz, 1968; as *The Last Planet*, New York, Ace, 1955.
The Stars Are Ours! (Astra). Cleveland, World, 1954.
Star Guard. New York, Harcourt Brace, 1955; London, Gollancz, 1969.
The Crossroads of Time (Time Travel). New York Ace, 1956; London, Gollancz, 1976.
Sea Siege. New York, Harcourt Brace, 1957.
Star Born (Astra). Cleveland, World, 1957; London, Gollancz, 1973.
Star Gate. New York, Harcourt Brace, 1958; London, Gollancz, 1970.
The Time Traders (Time War). New York, Harcourt Brace, 1958.
Secret of the Lost Race. New York, Ace, 1959; as *Wolfshead*, London, Hale, 1977.
The Beast Master. New York, Harcourt Brace, 1959; London, Gollancz, 1966.
Galactic Derelict (Time War). Cleveland, World, 1959.
Storm over Warlock (Lantree). Cleveland, World, 1960.
The Sioux Spaceman. New York, Ace, 1960; London, Hale, 1976.
Star Hunter. New York, Ace, 1961.
Catseye. New York, Harcourt Brace, 1961; London, Gollancz, 1962.
Eye of the Monster. New York, Ace, 1962.
The Defiant Agents (Time War). Cleveland, World, 1962.
Lord of Thunder (Beast Master). New York, Harcourt Brace, 1962; London, Gollancz, 1966.
Key Out of Time (Time War). Cleveland, World, 1963.
Judgment on Janus. New York, Harcourt Brace, 1963; London, Gollancz, 1964.
Ordeal in Otherwhere (Lantree). Cleveland, World, 1964.

Night of Masks. New York, Harcourt Brace, 1964; London, Gollancz, 1965.
The X Factor. New York, Harcourt Brace, 1965; London, Gollancz, 1967.
Quest Crosstime (Time Travel). New York, Viking Press, 1965; as *Crosstime Agent,* London, Gollancz, 1975.
Moon of Three Rings (Moon Magic). New York, Viking Press, 1966; London, Longman, 1969.
Victory on Janus. New York, Harcourt Brace, 1966; London, Gollancz, 1967.
Operation Time Search. New York, Harcourt Brace, 1967.
Dark Piper. New York, Harcourt Brace, 1968; London, Gollancz, 1969.
The Zero Stone. New York, Viking Press, 1968; London, Gollancz, 1974.
Postmarked the Stars. New York, Harcourt Brace, 1969; London, Gollancz, 1971.
Uncharted Stars (Zero Stone). New York, Viking Press, 1969; London, Gollancz, 1974.
Ice Crown. New York, Viking Press, 1970; London, Longman, 1971.
Android at Arms. New York, Harcourt Brace, 1971; London, Gollancz, 1972.
Exiles of the Stars (Moon Magic). New York, Viking Press, 1971; London, Longman, 1972.
Breed to Come. New York, Viking Press, 1972; London, Longman, 1973.
Here Abide Monsters. New York, Atheneum, 1973.
Iron Cage. New York, Viking Press, 1974; London, Penguin, 1975.
Outside. New York, Walker, 1975; London, Blackie, 1976.
The Day of the Ness, with Michael Gilbert. New York, Walker, 1975.
Merlin's Mirror. New York, DAW, 1975; London, Sidgwick and Jackson, 1976.
Knave of Dreams. New York, Viking Press, 1975; London, Penguin, 1976.
No Night Without Stars. New York, Atheneum, 1975; London, Gollancz, 1976.
Star Ka'at, with Dorothy Madlee. New York, Walker, 1976; London, Blackie, 1977.
Star Ka'at World, with Dorothy Madlee. New York, Walker, 1978.
Star Ka'at and the Plant People, with Dorothy Madlee. New York, Walker, 1979.

Novels as Andrew North (series: Solar Queen in all books)

Sargasso of Space. New York, Gnome Press, 1955; London, Gollancz, 1970.
Plague Ship. New York, Gnome Press, 1956; London, Gollancz, 1971.
Voodoo Planet. New York, Ace, 1959.

Short Stories

The Many Worlds of Andre Norton, edited by Roger Elwood. Radnor, Pennsylvania, Chilton, 1974.
Perilous Dreams. New York, DAW, 1976.

OTHER PUBLICATIONS

Novels

The Prince Commands. New York, Appleton Century, 1934.
Ralestone Luck. New York, Appleton Century, 1938.
Follow the Drum. New York, Penn, 1942.
The Sword Is Drawn. Boston, Houghton Mifflin, 1944; London, Oxford University Press, 1946.
Scarface. New York, Harcourt Brace, 1948; London, Methuen, 1950.
Sword in Sheath. New York, Harcourt Brace, 1949; as *Island of the Lost,* London, Staples Press, 1953.
Murder for Sale (as Allen Weston, with Grace Hogarth). London, Hammond, 1954.

At Swords' Points. New York, Harcourt Brace, 1954.
Yankee Privateer. Cleveland, World, 1955.
Stand to Horse. New York, Harcourt Brace, 1956.
Shadow Hawk. New York, Harcourt Brace, 1960; London, Gollancz, 1971.
Ride Proud, Rebel! Cleveland, World, 1961.
Rebel Spurs. Cleveland, World, 1962.
Witch World. New York, Ace, 1963; London, Tandem, 1970.
Web of the Witch World. New York, Ace, 1964; London, Tandem, 1970.
Steel Magic. Cleveland, World, 1965; London, Hamish Hamilton, 1967; as *Grey Magic,* New York, Scholastic, 1967.
Three Against the Witch World. New York, Ace, 1965; London, Tandem, 1970.
Year of the Unicorn. New York, Ace, 1965; London, Tandem, 1970.
Octagon Magic. Cleveland, World, 1967; London, Hamish Hamilton, 1968.
Warlock of the Witch World. New York, Ace, 1967; London, Tandem, 1970.
Fur Magic. Cleveland, World, 1968; London, Hamish Hamilton, 1969.
Sorceress of the Witch World. New York, Ace, 1968; London, Tandem, 1970.
Dread Companion. New York, Harcourt Brace, 1970; London, Gollancz, 1972.
The Crystal Gryphon. New York, Atheneum, 1972; London, Gollancz, 1973.
Dragon Magic. New York, Crowell, 1972.
Forerunner Foray. New York, Viking Press, 1973; London, Longman, 1974.
The Jargoon Pard. New York, Atheneum, 1974; London, Gollancz, 1975.
Lavender-Green Magic. New York, Crowell, 1974.
The White Jade Fox. New York, Dutton, 1975; London, W.H. Allen, 1976.
Red Hart Magic. New York, Crowell, 1976; London, Hamish Hamilton, 1977.
Wraiths of Time. New York, Atheneum, 1976; London, Gollancz, 1977.
The Opal-Eyed Fan. New York, Dutton, 1977.
Velvet Shadows. New York, Fawcett, 1977.
Quag Keep. New York, Atheneum, 1978.
Yurth Burden. New York, DAW, 1978.
Zarsthor's Bane. New York, Ace, 1978; London Dobson, 1981.
Snow Shadow. New York, Fawcett, 1979.
Seven Spells to Sunday, with Phyllis Miller. New York, Atheneum, 1979.

Short Stories

High Sorcery. New York, Ace, 1970.
Garan the Eternal. Alhambra, California, Fantasy, 1972.
Spell of the Witch World. New York, DAW, 1972; London, Prior, 1977.
Trey of Swords. New York, Grosset and Dunlap, 1978; London, Star, 1979.
Lore of the Witch World. New York, DAW, 1980.

Other

Rogue Reynard (juvenile). Boston, Houghton Mifflin, 1947.
Huon of the Horn (juvenile). New York, Harcourt Brace, 1951.
"Living in 1980+," in *Library Journal* (New York), 15 September 1952.
Bertie and May (juvenile). Cleveland, World, 1969; London, Hamish Hamilton, 1971.
"The Girl and the B.E.M.," in *Cassandra Rising,* edited by Alice Laurance. New York, Doubleday, 1978.

Editor, *Bullard of the Space Patrol,* by Malcom Jameson. Cleveland, World, 1951.
Editor, *Space Service.* Cleveland, World, 1953.
Editor, *Space Pioneers.* Cleveland, World, 1954.
Editor, *Space Police.* Cleveland, World, 1956.

Editor, with Ernestine Donaldy, *Gates to Tomorrow: An Introduction to Science Fiction.* New York, Atheneum, 1973.
Editor, *Small Shadows Creep: Ghost Children.* New York, Dutton, 1974; London, Chatto and Windus, 1976.

*

Bibliography: *Andre Norton: A Primary and Secondary Bibliography* by Roger C. Schlobin, Boston, Hall, 1980.

Manuscript Collection: George Arents Research Library, Syracuse University, New York.

*   *   *

Andre Norton's early intention was to write fiction for boys, and she changed her name to enter this male-dominated market. Fortunately for the millions of readers who have made her one of the best selling of contemporary fantasy and science-fiction authors, she turned to these two forms in 1947 with her first published short story "People of the Crater" (later title: "Garin of Tav"). It is odd that Norton turned to science fiction at all. In fact, books like *The Beast Master* and its sequel, *Lord of Thunder,* weren't really science fiction at all. They were simply an early experiment applying the form of a western to outer space and alien worlds. Actually, Norton has contempt for science and technology; they appear in her fiction only as vehicles and foils. In Ric Brooks's essay (in *The Many Worlds of Andre Norton,* 1974), she makes her stance quite clear: "Yes, I am anti-machine. The more research I do, the more I am convinced that when western civilization turned to machines..., they threw away parts of life...[the lack of which] leads to much of our present frustration."

Even in Norton's science fiction, technology and science are incidental to plot and character. These major concerns reflect the influences of Edgar Rice Burroughs, H. Rider Haggard, A. Merritt, and Talbot Mundy, and Norton's respect for their tight, fast-moving plots and memorable characters. For plot content, Norton's extensive research and affection for the mysterious and intriguing have led her to a number of specific motifs that occur throughout her fiction. Jewels frequently appear as powerful talismans, particularly in her fantasy novels. For example, as early as *At Swords' Points,* part of the Sword series that focuses on post-World-War-II espionage and the Netherlands during World War II, a set of jeweled miniature knights are central to a young man's search for his brother's murderer. Jewels are also important in *The Zero Stone,* the much heralded Witch World series, *Wraiths of Time,* and the gothic novels, particularly *The White Jade Fox* and *The Opal-Eyed Fan.* Frequently, these talismans are connected to an even more pervasive motif: the pseudo-science psychometry. This is formally defined as the detection of the residue of "memory" retained in an artifact by a sensitive. This plays a major role in the fantasy (with strong science-fiction elements) *Forerunner Foray,* in which Ziatha is drawn into a prehuman age through her reaction to a jewel; in *Wraiths of Time,* a crystal ankh and a staff contain the accumulated psychic power of a race.

Jewels and psychometry are two of the elements that give Norton's fiction its brooding depth, and together they provide a bridge between two other major Norton fascinations: history and speculative archaeology. Whether it be through references to prehistoric alien visits to Earth, as in *Merlin's Mirror,* or allusions to the historic past, as in the Moon Magic series, Norton's fiction always has a resonance that goes beyond the immediate present to a more pervasive and often mysterious past. It is the characters' responsibility to discover the relevance of the past to themselves and their futures.

Yet none of these motifs or devices is the center of Andre Norton's fiction. Rather, the most important aspects are simply humanity and self-realization. Norton explains this in "On Writing Fantasy" (in *The Many Worlds of Andre Norton*): "But the first requirement for writing heroic...fantasy must be a deep interest in and a love for history itself. Not the history of dates, of sweeps and empires—but the kind of history which deals with daily life, the beliefs, and the aspirations of people long since dust." Within the obvious cosmic scope, alien climes, antagonistic technology, vast quests, and fantastic forces of Norton's fiction, the characters are involved in crucial patterns of being, both for themselves and their fellows. While they are arrayed in mythic quests that grow from deep tradition, exist in a momentous present, and face a vital future, the characters remain pointedly human and humane. Most frequently, they move through what Northrop Frye calls "triumphant comedy." They struggle against an unlawful or unnatural order, undergo rites of passage to find realization, and establish new orders and freedoms. Kaththea (*Sorceress of the Witch World*) reflects this pattern as well as Norton's pioneering commitment to female characters. Shattered and disillusioned, Kaththea must find the faith to accept Hilarion, one of the enormously powerful "Old Ones" of the Witch World, if she is to save her family and regenerate her environment. Furtig, the mutated cat protagonist of *Breed to Come,* must overcome the mythology surrounding his long-departed human masters to unleash his own potentiality. Through the characters' agonizing trials, bondages and wastelands are destroyed, shape prejudice is eliminated, generative orders are established, and the protagonists and their fellows are ennobled. As Ric Brooks writes, "the chief value of Andre Norton's fiction may not lie in entertainment or social commentary, but in her 'reenchanting' us with her creations that renew our linkages to all life."

Andre Norton's characters are always alone, alienated, fearful, and seaching. They are admirable for their positive, if sometimes confused, values, and they are attractive in their frailty and their doubt. In spite of their varied shapes and alien abilities, they achieve the nobility and status of the healer as they cure themselves and others. Frequently, their solutions are androgynous—as for Simon Tregarth and Jaelithe in *Witch World*—and they do find the best of male and female. More significantly, their solutions to pain and loneliness are mythic and elemental and are a celebration of the bonds among man, animal, nature, and cosmic order.

—Roger C. Schlobin

NORVIL, Manning.   *See* **BULMER, Kenneth.**

NOURSE, Alan E(dward).   American. Born in Des Moines, Iowa, 11 August 1928. Educated at Rutgers University, New Brunswick, New Jersey, B.A. 1951; University of Pennsylvania, Philadelphia, M.D. 1955. Served in the United States Navy, 1946-48: Hospitalman 3rd Class. Married Ann Jane Morton in 1952; three sons and one daughter. Intern, Virginia Mason Hospital, Seattle, Washington, 1955-56; free-lance writer, 1956-58; private medical practice, North Bend, Washington, 1958-64. Since 1964, free-lance writer. Owner, Chamberlain Press, 1953-55. Chairman of the Board, Tanner Electric Rural Electrification Co-op; President, Science Fiction Writers of America, 1968-69. Agent: Brandt and Brandt, 101 Park Avenue, New York, New York 10017. Address: High Place, 40129 SE 112th Street, North Bend, Washington 98045, U.S.A.

SCIENCE-FICTION PUBLICATIONS

Novels

Trouble on Titan (juvenile).   Philadelphia, Winston, 1954; London, Hutchinson, 1956.
A Man Obsessed.   New York, Ace, 1955; revised edition, as *The Mercy Men*, New York, McKay, 1968; London, Faber, 1969.
Rocket to Limbo (juvenile).   New York, McKay, 1957; London, Faber, 1964.

The Invaders Are Coming!, with J.A. Meyer.   New York, Ace, 1959.
Scavengers in Space (juvenile).   New York, McKay, 1959; London, Faber, 1964.
Star Surgeon (juvenile).   New York, McKay, 1960; London, Faber, 1962.
Raiders from the Rings (juvenile).   New York, McKay, 1962; London, Faber, 1965.
The Universe Between (juvenile).   New York, McKay, 1965; London, Faber, 1966.
The Bladerunner.   New York, McKay, 1974.

Short Stories

Tiger by the Tail (juvenile).   New York, McKay, 1961; London, Dobson, 1962; as *Beyond Infinity,* London, Corgi, 1964.
The Counterfeit Man (juvenile).   New York, McKay, 1963; London, Dobson, 1964.
Psi High and Others.   New York, McKay, 1967; London, Faber, 1968.
Rx for Tomorrow (juvenile).   New York, McKay, 1971; London, Faber, 1972.

OTHER PUBLICATIONS

Novel

Junior Intern.   New York, Harper, 1955.

Other

So You Want to Be a Doctor [*Lawyer, Scientist, Nurse* (with Eleanore Halliday), *Engineer* (with James C. Webbert), *Physicist, Chemist* (with James C. Webbert), *Surgeon, Architect* (with Carl Meinhardt)] (juvenile).   New York, Harper, 9 vols., 1957-69.
Nine Planets.   New York, Harper, 1960; revised edition, 1970.
The Management of a Medical Practice, with Geoffrey Marks.   Philadelphia, Lippincott, 1963.
The Body.   New York, Time, 1964.
Universe, Earth, and Atom: The Story of Physics.   New York, Harper, 1969.
Virginia Mason Medical Center: The First Fifty Years.   Seattle, Virginia Mason Hospital Association, 1970.
Venus and Mercury (juvenile).   New York, Watts, 1972.
Ladies' Home Journal Family Medical Guide.   New York, Harper, 1973.
The Backyard Astronomer.   New York, Watts, 1973.
The Giant Planets (juvenile).   New York, Watts, 1974.
The Outdoorsman's Medical Guide.   New York, Harper, 1974.
The Asteroids (juvenile).   New York, Watts, 1975.
Clear Skin, Healthy Skin (juvenile).   New York, Watts, 1976.
Lumps, Bumps, and Rashes (juvenile).   New York, Watts, 1976.
Viruses (juvenile).   New York, Watts, 1976.
The Tooth Book (juvenile).   New York, McKay, 1977.
Vitamins (juvenile).   New York, Watts, 1977.
Fractures, Dislocations, and Sprains (juvenile).   New York, Watts, 1978.
The Practice.   New York, Harper, 1978.
Hormones (juvenile).   New York, Watts, 1979.
Patient: Inside the Mayo Clinic.   New York, McGraw Hill, 1979.

*

Manuscript Collection: Boston University.

*   *   *

Alan E. Nourse has several specialized interests which form a unifying theme in many of his short stories and novels. Most of them have a number of common stylistic characteristics linking him to the science-fiction writers of the 1950's. In his recent book, *The Bladerunner,* Nourse makes several frightening but logical extrapolations from current social problems.

A number of Nourse's novels, among them *Scavengers in Space, Trouble on Titan, Rocket to Limbo,* and *Raiders from the Rings,* are straightfoward science fiction/adventure stories. Not surprisingly, however, since Nourse is a former practicing physician, his best stories deal with medicine. His most readable adventure story is *Star Surgeon* in which he develops an interesting concept, "Hospital Earth," where Earth utilizes its medical research and technology to serve as medical liaison for the galaxy. A number of stories revolve around Hoffman Center, a futuristic medical complex in Philadelphia, and Nourse develops a tantalizing concept, the "mercy men"—men who are recruited and paid for being guinea pigs. An additional theme Nourse frequently treats is the development, realization, and analysis of mental superpowers in individuals whom Nourse call "PSI high." In a number of his stories Nourse works with the concept of possible alternate universes that exist in other dimensions. Nourse frequently combines the medical and PSI themes, and in *The Universe Between* he adds to these the alternate dimension concept as well.

Like his contemporary Robert Heinlein, Nourse wrote "juveniles" during the 1950's, and unlike Heinlein, continued to write them. These novels contain prototype characters, like the young male hero, and there are no overtly romantic scenes, but the prototype males may have female complements who are, for the 1950's and 1960's, surprisingly forceful. Because so many of Nourse's stories concern mental rather than scientific advancement, he seldom uses the "hard" science-fiction technique of describing in detail futuristic methods and machines; even in his medical-theme novels, where Nourse's familiarity with his subject clearly shows, he does not give his fiction much explicit scientific detail. In the Hoffman Center fiction Nourse does place some emphasis on the world-covering computer hook-up, but he generally expects his reader to take for granted the medical, scientific, and technological accomplishments of his future world. Nourse does not use the familiar 1950's social theme of nuclear disaster, although in his Hoffman Center fiction he postulates a social background which includes a devastating third world war. Like much of the science fiction of the 1950's, most of Nourse's relies for its primary interest on plot development and problem-solving rather than on character development, social philosophy, and other "new wave" techniques.

The Bladerunner is clearly aimed at a more mature audience. While it retains most stylistic characteristics of earlier Nourse novels, its theme is dystopian. Nourse based his novel on two premises: medical advancement would lead to increased longevity, survival of people with hereditary defects, and conquest of viral and bacterial diseases. In addition, the country would turn within 20 years entirely to socialized medicine. The consequences would be overpopulation and more virulent diseases requiring constant development of new medicines. Socialized medical care would have a price—sterilization—and to fulfill the needs of people unwilling to submit to sterilization, an army of underground doctors would work illegally, supplied and aided by "bladerunners." The plot of *The Bladerunner* centers on one doctor's fight to defeat the policies of socialized medicine and simultaneously to publicize a dangerous plague. While the plot and solution to the problem are entertaining, Nourse clearly wishes for *The Bladerunner* to serve as a warning against socialized medicine, and the diatribes against this evil are occasionally intrusive. Despite this flaw, *The Bladerunner* is the best of Nourse's science-fiction novels.

—Karren C. Edwards

NOWLAN, Philip Francis. Also wrote as Frank Phillips. American. Born in Philadelphia, Pennsylvania, in 1888. Educated at the University of Pennsylvania, Philadelphia, B.A. 1910. Married Teresa Marie Junker; four daughters and six sons. Worked for *Public Ledger, North American,* and *Retail Ledger;* collaborated with Dick Calkins on first science-fiction comic strip, *Buck Rogers. Died 1 February 1940.*

SCIENCE-FICTION PUBLICATIONS

Novel

Armageddon 2419 A.D. New York, Avalon, 1962; London, Panther, 1976.

Uncollected Short Stories

"The Onslaught from Venus" (as Frank Phillips), in *Science Wonder Stories* (New York), September 1929.
"The Time Jumpers," in *Amazing* (New York), February 1934.
"The Prince of Mars Returns," in *Fantastic Adventures* (Chicago), February 1940.
"Space Guards," in *Astounding* (New York), May 1940.

OTHER PUBLICATIONS

Other

Buck Rogers on the Moons of Saturn. Racine, Wisconsin, Whitman, 1934.
Buck Rogers in the Dangerous Mission. New York, Blue Ribbon Press, 1934.
Buck Rogers and the Depth Men of Jupiter. Racine, Wisconsin, Whitman, 1935.
Buck Rogers, 25th Century, Featuring Buddy and Allura in "Strange Adventures of the Spider Ship." Chicago, Pleasure, 1935.
Buck Rogers, 25th Century A.D., in the Interplanetay War with Venus. Racine, Wisconsin, Whitman, 1938.
Buck Rogers in the 25th Century 1-2, 7-8. Ann Arbor, Michigan, Ed Aprill, 4 vols., 1964-68.
The Collected Works of Buck Rogers in the 25th Century, with Dick Calkins and Rick Yager, edited by Robert C. Dille. New York, Bonanza, 1969.

*   *   *

Although not as well known as Edgar Rice Burroughs or E.E. Smith, Philip Francis Nowlan was probably their equal both as a writer and as an influence on modern science fiction. In his first story, "Armageddon 2419 A.D." (*Amazing,* August 1928), he introduced perhaps the most popular character in the history of the genre, Anthony, or as he was later known, Buck Rogers. Over the decades that followed Nowlan and others scripted innumerable Buck Rogers comic strips. There were several films, and a current successful television series is proof of Buck Rogers's continuing appeal.

In "Armageddon 2419 A.D." Anthony Rogers, an engineer exploring a Pennsylvania mine in 1929, is caught in a cave-in and placed in suspended animation. Awakening in the 25th century, he discovers that the United States is now ruled by Mongolians and that Americans live in scattered communities, hiding from the conquerers who consider them vermin. The Mongolians, or Hans, a decadent, heartless race, rarely leave their cities and rely on huge airships equipped with disintegrator rays to maintain their dominance. Rogers has appeared at an opportune moment, for the Americans, armed with newly developed anti-gravity devices and rocket guns, are preparing to revolt. Contributing a knowledge of 20th-century military tactics and a certain primitive blood-thirstiness, Rogers soon becomes a leader in the struggle. The American conquest is completed in Nowlan's sequel, "The Airlords of Han." (The two stories were combined in the 1962 book *Armageddon 2419 A.D.*) Although flawed by occasionally awkward language and handicapped by the poorly considered choice of a first-person narrator, the Anthony Rogers stories stand up quite well even today. The action moves smoothly and the various military inventions and tactics are intriguing. The stories are touched by the racism so common in 1920's pulp fiction but, interestingly, are extremely progressive in their treatment of women. Wilma Deering, although occasionally given to the fainting spells and fits of weeping which were *de rigueur* for women in popular fiction, is in general more competent and active than any female character in science fiction prior to Joanna Russ's Alyx.

"The Onslaught from Venus" is a first-person account by a member of the Airguard (the military arm of the Supernational Commission of the Caucasian League) who, captured by the invading Venusians, first studies their civilization and then, escaping, helps destroy it. Again the story is largely taken up with inventive weaponry and tactics. The Venusians, who seem quite human except for their skin color, are, like the Hans, totally evil, totally decadent. They are incapable of even considering coexistence and their complete extermination is thus a necessity.

Nowlan published little science fiction in the years that followed. His final story, and, after "Armageddon 2419 A.D.," probably his best, was "Space Guards." In this tale the narrator and his commanding officer, another of Nowlan's capable women, are searching the jungles of Venus for the headquarters of the criminal mastermind Tiger Madden. They're captured by tribesmen who, again, are totally human except for their skin color. Converting the natives to their side, the two Earth people defeat Madden's troops in battle and then infiltrate his city. Eventually they kidnap the villain and escape under fire. The narrator saves his commander's life, disobeying her direct order to abandon her. She at first considers court-martialing him but then, as the story closes, decides to marry him instead. Despite its silly ending and its somewhat old-fashioned plotting, "Space Guards" is an interesting and exciting story.

Philip Nowlan was a talented writer, and, despite his small output, he is one of the most influential science-fiction writers of the Gernsback era.

—Michael M. Levy

ODLE, E.V. British.

SCIENCE-FICTION PUBLICATIONS

Novel

The Clockwork Man. London, Heinemann, and New York, Doubleday, 1923.

OTHER PUBLICATIONS

Novel

The History of Alfred Rudd. London, Collins, 1922.

Play

First Love (produced London, 1911).

Other

Editor, Great Stories of Human Courage. London, Lane, 1933.
Editor, Quest and Conquest: An Anthology of Personal Adventures. London, Macmillan, 1936.

*   *   *

There is little mystery about the title character of E.V. Odle's The Clockwork Man, for his origins become obvious right from the start. Through a malfunction of his clockwork mechanism he appears at a local village cricket match, having slipped back 8000 years from a future world established after a series of catastrophic wars. His bizarre behaviour and strange appearance throw the cricketers of 1920's England into confusion. Though at first glance human, he is internally a mass of cogs and wheels that are controlled by a "clock" set into the back of his head.

Most of the novel is concerned with the intellectual and moral challenges the Clockwork Man poses to his cricket-playing ances-

tors. His apparent ability to overcome the laws of time and space presents a prospect too bleak to contemplate to the middle-aged bachelor Dr. Allingham, primarily because he threatens, like the Doctor's free-thinking fiancée Lilian, a comfortable and complacent way of life. Gregg, a university graduate in his 20's finds the existence of the Clockwork Man both believable and encouraging, the ideal outcome of man's quest for progress. Arthur Withers, a simple and contented bank clerk, sees only an unhappy soul, transported from a world devoid of emotion and trapped into one that can offer no acceptance.

Odle provides no clear answers to the questions he raises in this book. Is the Clockwork Man a manifestation of man's triumph over his physiological limitations, or merely a glorified puppet, a grim look into a future where, through his pursuit of happiness, man has become a slave to his own technology? The Clockwork Man forces the people he meets to re-examine their own lives. Are they superior to him, being free to act as they will? Or are they not as firmly fixed into their own mechanical patterns of behaviour and thought as he is into his loveless world of perpetual time and space change?

The Clockwork Man is undeniably a slow-moving and uneventful work of science fiction, and can hardly be considered an incisive allegory, but it is a thoughtful and well-constructed novel that shouldn't be quite so forgotten as it has apparently become.

—Judith Summers

O'DONNELL, K.M. See MALZBERG, Barry N.

OFFUTT, Andrew J(efferson V.). Signs name andrew j. offutt. American. Born in Louisville, Kentucky, 16 August 1934 (?). Educated at the University of Louisville, B.A. in English 1955; M.A. in history; Ph.D. in psychology. Married Mary Joe McCarney McCabe in 1958; two daughters and two sons. Sales agent, Procter and Gamble, 1957-62; agency manager, Coastal States Life Insurance Company, Lexington, Kentucky, 1963-68; insurance agent, Andrew Offutt Associates, 1968-71. Since 1971, full-time writer: author of over 100 works under pseudonym John Cleve and others. Treasurer, 1973-76, and President, 1976-77, Science Fiction Writers of America. Recipient: If prize, 1954. Agent: Kirby McCauley Ltd., 60 East 42nd Street, New York, New York 10017. Address: Funny Farm, Haldeman, Kentucky 40329, U.S.A.

SCIENCE-FICTION PUBLICATIONS

Novels (series: Jarik)

Evil Is Live Spelled Backwards. New York, Paperback Library, 1970.
The Castle Keeps. New York, Berkley, 1972; London, Magnum, 1978.
Messenger of Zhuvastou. New York, Berkley, 1973; London, Magnum, 1977.
Ardor on Aros. New York, Dell, 1973.
The Galactic Rejects (juvenile). New York, Lothrop, 1973.
The Genetic Bomb, with D. Bruce Berry. New York, Warner, 1975.
Chieftain of Andor. New York, Dell, 1976; as Clansman of Andor, London, Magnum, 1978.
My Lord Barbarian. New York, Ballantine, 1977; London, Magnum, 1977.
The Iron Lords (Jarik). New York, Harcourt Brace, 1979.
Shadows Out of Hell (Jarik). New York, Berkley, 1979.
King Dragon. New York, Ace, 1980.
Snowmist (Jarik). New York, Berkley, 1981.

Uncollected Short Stories

"And Gone Tomorrow," in *If* (New York), December 1954.

"Blacksword," in *Mind Partner,* edited by H.L. Gold. New York, Doubleday, 1961.

"Mandroid," with Robert Margroff and Piers Anthony, in *If* (New York), June 1966.

"The Forgotten Gods of Earth," in *If* (New York), December 1966.

"Swordsman of the Stars," with Robert Margroff, in *If* (New York), December 1967.

"Population Implosion," in *World's Best Science Fiction 1968,* edited by Donald A. Wollheim and Terry Carr. New York, Ace, 1968.

"The Defendant Earth," in *If* (New York), February 1969.

"The Book," with Robert Margroff, in *Orbit 8,* edited by Damon Knight. New York, Putman, 1970.

"Ask a Silly Question," in *Galaxy* (New York), July 1970.

"My Country, Right or Wrong," in *Protostars,* edited by David Gerrold and Stephen Goldin. New York, Ballantine, 1971.

"Sareva, In Memoriam," in *Fantasy and Science Fiction* (New York), March 1972.

"For Value Received," in *Again, Dangerous Visions,* edited by Harlan Ellison. New York, Doubleday, 1972; London, Millington, 1976.

"Meanwhile, We Eliminate," in *Future City,* edited by Roger Elwood. New York, Simon and Schuster, and London, Sphere, 1973.

"Black Sorcerer of the Black Castle," in *Cosmic Laughter,* edited by Joe W. Haldeman. New York, Holt Rinehart, 1974.

"Tribute," with Robert Margroff, in *Eternity* (Sandy Springs, South Carolina), June 1974.

"Gone with the Gods," in *Analog* (New York), October 1974.

"Enchanté," in *Tomorrow,* edited by Roger Elwood. Philadelphia, Lippincott, 1976.

"Final Solution," in *Perry Rhodan 92-93.* New York, Ace, 1976.

"The Greenhouse Defect," in *Stellar Short Novels,* edited by Judy-Lynn del Rey. New York, Ballantine, 1976.

"Nekht Semerkeht," with Robert E. Howard, in *Swords Against Darkness,* edited by Andrew J. Offutt. New York, Kensington, 1977.

"Final Quest," in *Swords Against Darkness 2,* edited by Andrew J. Offutt. New York, Kensington, 1977.

"On the Beach: A Tale of Jarik," in *Weird Adventures 1,* April 1978.

OTHER PUBLICATIONS

Novels (series: Conan; Cormac mac Art)

The Great 24-Hour Thing. Los Angeles, Orpheus Press, 1971.
Operation: Super Ms. New York, Berkley, 1974.
Sword of the Gael (Cormac). New York, Kensington, 1975; London, Sphere, 1977.
The Undying Wizard (Cormac). New York, Kensington, 1976.
Demon in the Mirror, with Richard K. Lyon. New York, Pocket Books, 1977.
Sign of the Moonbow (Cormac). New York, Kensington, 1977.
The Mists of Doom (Cormac). New York, Kensington, 1977.
Conan and the Sorcerer. New York, Grosset and Dunlap, 1978.
The Sword of Skelos (Conan). New York, Bantam, 1979.
The Tower of Death (Cormac), with Keith Taylor. New York, Ace, 1980.
When Death Birds Fly (Cormac), with Keith Taylor. New York, Ace, 1980.
The Eyes of Sarsis, with Richard K. Lyon. New York, Pocket Books, 1980.
Conan the Mercenary. New York, Grosset and Dunlap, 1981.

Other

"How It Happened: One Bad Decision Leading to Another," in *Science-Fiction Studies* (Terre Haute, Indiana), July 1977.
"Stand Out," in *Writer's Digest* (Cincinnati), June 1978.
"VERYations on a Theme," in *Writer's Digest* (Cincinnati), 1979.

Editor, *Swords Against Darkness 1-5.* New York, Kensington, 5 vols., 1977-79.

*   *   *

Many science fiction and fantasy writers can be categorized according to the particular sub-genre in which they write. However, Andrew J. Offutt must be discussed within several sub-genres, from heroic fantasy to sociological science fiction.

Offutt's heroic fantasy comes in two groups. The first group includes those stories which are totally his own constructions, like *Messenger of Zhuvastou.* Scion Moris Keniston follows a beautiful woman, Elaine Dixon, supposedly his fiancée, to Helene, a planet which is the approximate cultural equivalent of early Imperial Rome. Because the planet is insulated from contact with more technologically advanced civilizations, Keniston must "go native" to follow Elaine onto the planet's surface. Disguised as an official messenger of the most powerful domain on the planet, Keniston sets out on his quest. The description of the planet and the portrayal of the heroic adventures are well-integrated so that the reader is able to envision quite clearly the world through which Keniston makes his way.

The second group of heroic fantasies is based on characters created by Robert E. Howard. In fact, Offutt has selected one, Cormac mac Art, for extended consideration, and admits, in the introduction to *Sword of the Gael,* that he is a Robert E. Howard fan and also "hopelessly in love with the Emerald Isle." This happy combination unites the heroic-age hero with a perfect historical setting, the Celtic/Viking period. Offutt skillfully mixes historical material from his own research with the literary history created by Howard to provide, in *Sword of the Gael,* for example, a cogent background for the adventures of Cormac mac Art and his Viking comrade, Wulfhere Skull-Splitter.

Although it may be difficult to imagine a Howardian writer doing so, Offutt also writes socially critical science fiction. *The Castle Keeps* is set in the same not-too-distant dystopian future which has been the setting for quite a bit of recent science fiction; John Brunner's *Stand on Zanzibar* and *The Sheep Look Up* come immediately to mind. The world of *The Castle Keeps* is over-populated and poisonously polluted, and the society has devolved toward barbarism. The Andrews home in the country is heavily fortified, and there is the constant danger of being overrun by roving bands of looters and killers. In the city, the Caudills live inside a sealed-up apartment building from which they seldom emerge; outside, in spite of official agencies, gangs are a threat by day and all-powerful by night. Throughout the novel, there are signposts of how we, mid-20th-century Americans, got there. In both sub-genres, heroic fantasy and socially critical science fiction, the good triumph over the evil. Scott Andrews, in *The Castle Keeps,* stays alive by being a superior warrior just as Cormac mac Art does in *Sword of the Gael.* The primary difference is that the former speaks directly to us and to our way of life, but the latter is considerably more removed.

Offutt can also write with humor, often with a satiric bite. *Ardor on Aros* is a humorous look at the heroic fantasy Offutt himself seriously writes. And short stories like "For Value Received" satirize one of Offutt's favorite targets, the medical profession—he refers to the AMA as the American Magicians Association. In this story, Bob Barber is told that he cannot take his new baby daughter home before he pays the difference between what his insurance covers and the total bill. He refuses to do so, and Mary Ann Barber grows up in Saint Meinrad Medical Center.

Heroic fantasy, socially critical science fiction, humor and satire—Offutt writes them all and writes them well. His word output is tremendous, and not all of it is science fiction; many feel that not enough of it is science fiction.

—C.W. Sullivan III

OLIVER, (Symmes) Chad(wick). American. Born in Cincinnati, Ohio, 30 March 1928. Educated at the University of Texas, Austin, B.A. 1951; M.A. in English and anthropology 1952; University of California, Los Angeles, Ph.D. in anthropology 1961. Married Betty Jane Jenkins in 1952; two children. Instructor, 1955-59, Assistant Professor, 1959-62, Associate Professor, 1963-68, Department Chairman, 1967-71, and since 1968, Professor of Anthropology, University of Texas. Visiting Professor, University of California, Los Angeles, summer 1960; Research Anthropologist, National Science Foundation in East Africa, 1961-62. Recipient: Western Writers of America Spur Award, 1967. Agent: Scott Meredith Literary Agency, 845 Third Avenue, New York, New York 10022. Address: 301 Eanes Road, Austin, Texas 78746, U.S.A.

SCIENCE-FICTION PUBLICATIONS

Novels

Shadows in the Sun. New York, Ballantine, 1954; London, Reinhardt, 1955.
The Winds of Time. New York, Doubleday, 1957.
Unearthly Neighbors. New York, Ballantine, 1960.
The Shores of Another Sea. New York, New American Library, and London, Gollancz, 1971.
Giants in the Dust. New York, Pyramid, 1976.

Short Stories

Another Kind. New York, Ballantine, 1955.
The Edge of Forever, edited by William F. Nolan. Los Angeles, Sherbourne Press, 1971.

Uncollected Short Stories (series: Caravans Unlimited)

"King of the Hill," in *Again, Dangerous Visions,* edited by Harlan Ellison. New York, Doubleday, 1972; London, Millington, 1976.
"Second Nature," in *Future Quest,* edited by Roger Elwood. New York, Avon, 1973.
"Shaka" (Caravans), in *Continuum 1,* edited by Roger Elwood. New York, Putnam, 1974.
"Stability" (Caravans), in *Continuum 2,* edited by Roger Elwood. New York, Berkley, 1974.
"The Middle Man" (Caravans), in *Continuum 3,* edited by Roger Elwood. New York, Berkley, 1974.
"The Gift," in *Future Kin,* edited by Roger Elwood. New York, Doubleday, 1974.
"Monitor" (Caravans), in *Continuum 4,* edited by Roger Elwood. New York, Berkley, 1975.
"Community Study," in *Lone Star Universe,* edited by George W. Proctor and Steven Utley. Austin, Texas, Heidelberg, 1976.

OTHER PUBLICATIONS

Novel

The Wolf Is My Brother. New York, New American Library, 1967; London, Jenkins, 1968.

Other

Mists of Dawn (juvenile). Philadelphia, Winston, 1952; London, Hutchinson, 1954.
Ecology and Cultural Continuity as Contributing Factors in the Social Organization of the Plains Indians. Berkeley, University of California Press, 1962.
Cultural Anthropology: The Discovery of Humanity. New York, Harper, 1980.
The Kamba of Kenya. Palo Alto, California, Mayfield, 1980.

Bibliography: by William F. Nolan, in *The Edge of Forever,* 1971.

Chad Oliver comments:
I wrote my first story when I was 14, and sold my first story (to Anthony Boucher of *The Magazine of Fantasy and Science Fiction*) when I was 22. I was a professional writer before I was an anthropologist, and I suspect that I still am. I grew up with science fiction and it has been an important part of my life.

I have written many kinds of stories and about all they have in common is that I always tried to write as well as I could. I am not interested in essays disguised as fiction; my stories are about people and my opinion is that if they don't work on an emotional level they don't work at all. I was strongly influenced by writers outside the science-fiction field, notably Hemingway and Steinbeck.

*   *   *

For a genre that deals freely in alien beings and cultures, science fiction has often shown a marked tendency toward simplistic anthropomorphism in handling such themes. Readers and editors who would demand the utmost verisimilitude in fiction dealing with the natural sciences often allowed the most naive applications of social science theory to pass unnoticed in science-fiction stories, and it was not until well into the 1950's that the social sciences began to take their place as serious thematic material in popular science fiction. While economics and sociology began to be treated with relative sophistication by Frederik Pohl and other satirists of the *Galaxy*-magazine school, the credit for introducing well-thought-out anthropological themes into popular American science fiction of the 1950's rests almost solely with Chad Oliver. Himself a professional anthropologist, Oliver dealt with alien cultures, and the problems inherent in communicating with those cultures, in a series of sympathetic and plausible stories and novels that paved the way for later anthropological themes in such writers as Ursula K. Le Guin.

Oliver's fiction tends heavily toward exposition and didacticism, but his pleasant, relaxed style and understated, non-heroic characters work to make the lessons in cultural differentiation and values easily palatable. When he treats a traditional theme, such as the secret colonization of Earth by aliens in *Shadows in the Sun,* he is apt to undercut the reader's expectations by revealing early in the narrative the secret of the alien presence (in this novel, they have completely taken over a small town in Texas, without violence or murder), and focusing instead on the more complex and interesting problem of what their motivations and values are. The equally familiar theme of the generations-long space voyage, initially popularized by Robert Heinlein in "Universe," is given a new twist in Oliver's "Stardust" by the introduction of the problem of the culture shock that the spaceship inhabitants might face if the circumscribed environment that they have come to regard as the universe is suddenly revealed to be only a machine. A "first contact" story is also given a new twist, in "Scientific Method," by its simultaneous presentation from two opposing viewpoints. One of Oliver's favorite themes is the depiction of a "primitive" alien culture that is really advanced, but in radically different cultural terms from our own. This is the theme of "Rite of Passage" and *Unearthly Neighbors;* the latter may be the most carefully reasoned account of the problems of making contact with an alien culture in all of science fiction.

Much of Oliver's fiction clearly draws on his own experiences—his familiarity with small-town Texas culture in *Shadows in the Sun,* his hobby of trout fishing in *The Winds of Time,* his experiences in Kenya in *The Shores of Another Sea.* In the last novel particularly the science-fiction theme seems to be decidedly secondary to the portrayal of life on a baboonery in the bush country of Kenya. Relatively few of his stories deal with future societies, and his portrayals of technologically advanced earth societies (as in *Unearthly Neighbors)* seem somewhat stilted and uncomfortable. His real strengths lie in the construction of hypothetical anthropological problems and his graceful, understated style. Although he has produced relatively little science fiction, what there is is valuable both for the specific insights it offers and for the importance it holds in the developing sophistication of the genre.

—Gary K. Wolfe

OLSEN, Bob (Alfred John Olsen, Jr.).   American.   Born in 1884. Educated at Brown University, Providence, Rhode Island, A.B. (Phi Beta Kappa). *Died 20 May 1956.*

SCIENCE-FICTION PUBLICATIONS

Short Stories

Rhythm Rides the Rocket.   New York, Columbia, 1940.

Uncollected Short Stories (series: Four Dimensional; Justin Pryor)

"Four Dimensional Surgery," in *Amazing* (New York), February 1928.
"Four Dimensional Robberies," in *Amazing* (New York), May 1928.
"The Educated Pill," in *Amazing* (New York), July 1928.
"Four Dimensional Transit," in *Amazing Stories Quarterly* (New York), Fall 1928.
"The Superperfect Bride," in *Amazing* (New York), July 1929.
"Flight in 1999," in *Air Wonder Stories* (New York), September 1929.
"The Phantom Teleview," in *Science Wonder Stories* (New York), November 1929.
"Cosmic Trash," in *Science Wonder Stories* (New York), April 1930.
"The Man Who Annexed the Moon," in *Amazing* (New York), February 1931.
"The Master of Mystery" (Pryor), in *Amazing* (New York), October 1931.
"The Ant with a Human Soul," in *Amazing Stories Quarterly* (New York), Spring-Summer 1932.
"Seven Sunstrokes" (Pryor), in *Amazing* (New York), April 1932.
"The Purple Monsters," in *Amazing* (New York), August 1932.
"Captain Brink of the Space Marines," in *Amazing* (New York), November 1932.
"The Pool of Death" (Pryor), in *Amazing* (New York), January 1933.
"The Crime Crusher," in *Amazing* (New York), June 1933.
"The Four Dimensional Escape," in *Amazing* (New York), December 1933.
"Peril among the Drivers," in *Amazing* (New York), March 1934.
"The Four Dimensional Auto-Parker," in *Amazing* (New York), July 1934.
"Noekken of Norway," in *Amazing* (New York), November 1934.
"Six-Legged Gangsters," in *Amazing* (New York), June 1935.
"The Isle of Juvenescence," in *Amazing* (New York), June 1936.
"The Space Marines and the Slavers," in *Amazing* (New York), December 1936.
"The Scourge of a Single Cell," in *Science Fiction* (Holyoke, Massachusetts), March 1940.
"Our Robot Maid," in *Future* (New York), November 1940.
"The Four Dimensional Roller-Press," in *Every Boy's Book of Science Fiction*, edited by Donald A. Wollheim. New York, Fell, 1951.
"The Drawbridge Horror," in *Phantom* (Bolton, Lancashire), July 1958.

OTHER PUBLICATIONS

Other

"Wanted: A Definition for SF," in *Future* (New York), Summer 1957.

*   *   *

Bob Olsen was among the earliest protégés of the editor Hugo Gernsback, who introduced him to *Amazing Stories* readers in 1927 and was soon pronouncing him "the possessor of a fertile mind with a turn for good writing." He begins with a series of ingenious treatments of the fourth dimension theme, to which he returned more than once in the course of earning a reputation over the next decade as a "distinguished" contributor, if only on account of his consistent popularity.

Some of his early offerings were more like popular lectures than stories, most of the dialogue emanating from his scientist hero, Professor Archimedes Banning, in "Four Dimensional Transit" and "The Man Who Annexed the Moon"—a tale of the first lunar voyage, fairly typical of the period, which today seems uncannily predictive. Another stock character, Justin Pryor, a merchandising counsellor with a yen for criminal investigation, was featured in "The Master of Mystery" and "Seven Sunstrokes." An outstanding story was "The Ant with a Human Soul" in which the subject of a bizarre experiment in brain transference relates his experiences while "going native" among the ants. Two years later the author treated much the same idea to greater effect, with more human interest and less text-book detail, in "Peril Among the Drivers." And in "Six-Legged Gangsters" he told a simple story of formicary antics from the viewpoint of the insects themselves. He was also fascinated by the amoeba, a voracious specimen of which lurked in "The Pool of Death," another Justin Pryor mystery. It was to be found in its natural surroundings in "Noekken of Norway," which clearly betrayed the author's Scandinavian antecedents. And the amoeba-men of Titan were the villains "Captain Brink of the Space Marines" had to contend with.

In a mood close to satire, in "The Purple Monsters" he made light of an invasion of New York by nightmarish giants from Ganymede. "The Crime Crusher" brought criminals to book with a device which photographed their misdeeds in retrospect; and "The Four Dimensional Auto-Parker" offered a solution to a problem which, even in 1934, vexed Los Angeles motorists. By that time Olsen had also added jailbreaking to the list of possibilities—including surgery and bank robbery—presented by the exploitation of hyperspace.

—Walter Gillings

ORWELL, George.   Pseudonym for Eric Arthur Blair.   British. Born in Motihari, Bengal, India, 25 June 1903, of English parents. Educated at Eton College (King's Scholar), 1917-21. Served with the Republicans in the Spanish Civil War, 1936: wounded in action. Married 1) Eileen O'Shaughnessy in 1936 (died, 1945); 2) Sonia Mary Brownell in 1949; one adopted son. Served in the Indian Imperial Police, in Burma, 1922-27; returned to Europe, and lived in Paris, then in London, working as a dishwasher, tutor, bookshop assistant, etc., 1928-34; full-time writer from 1935; settled in Hertfordshire, 1935, and ran a general store until 1936; Correspondent for the BBC and *The Observer*, London, during World War II. *Died 21 January 1950.*

SCIENCE-FICTION PUBLICATIONS

Novel

Nineteen Eighty-Four.   London, Secker and Warburg, and New York, Harcourt Brace, 1949.

Other Publications

Novels

Burmese Days. New York, Harper, 1934; London, Gollancz, 1935.
A Clergyman's Daughter. London, Gollancz, and New York, Harper, 1935.
Keep the Aspidistra Flying. London, Gollancz, 1936; New York, Harcourt Brace, 1954.
Coming Up for Air. London, Gollancz, 1939; New York, Harcourt Brace, 1950.
Animal Farm: A Fairy Story. London, Secker and Warburg, 1945; New York, Harcourt Brace, 1946.

Other

Down and Out in Paris and London. London, Gollancz, and New York, Harper, 1933.
The Road to Wigan Pier. London, Gollancz, 1937; New York, Harcourt Brace, 1958.
Homage to Catalonia. London, Secker and Warburg, 1938; New York, Harcourt Brace, 1952.
Inside the Whale and Other Essays. London, Gollancz, 1940.
The Lion and the Unicorn: Socialism and the English Genius. London, Secker and Warburg, 1941; New York, AMS Press, 1976.
Critical Essays. London, Secker and Warburg, 1946; as *Dickens, Dali and Others: Studies in Popular Culture*, New York, Reynal, 1946.
James Burnham and the Managerial Revolution. London, Socialist Book Centre, 1946.
The English People. London, Collins, 1947; New York, Haskell House, 1974.
Shooting an Elephant and Other Essays. London, Secker and Warburg, and New York, Harcourt Brace, 1950.
Such, Such Were the Joys. New York, Harcourt Brace, 1953; as *England, Your England and Other Essays*, London, Secker and Warburg, 1953.
A Collection of Essays. New York, Doubleday, 1954.
The Orwell Reader, edited by Richard H. Rovere. New York, Harcourt Brace, 1956.
Selected Essays. London, Penguin, 1957; as *Inside the Whale and Other Essays*, 1975.
Selected Writings, edited by George Bott. London, Heinemann, 1958.
Collected Essays. London, Secker and Warburg, 1961.
Decline of English Murder and Other Essays. London, Penguin, 1965.
The Collected Essays, Journalism, and Letters of George Orwell, edited by Sonia Orwell and Ian Angus. London, Secker and Warburg, 4 vols., 1968.

Editor, *Talking to India: A Selection of English Language Broadcasts to India.* London, Allen and Unwin, 1943.
Editor, with Reginald Reynolds, *British Pamphleteers 1: From the Sixteenth Century to the French Revolution.* London, Wingate, 1948.

*

Bibliography: "George Orwell: A Selected Bibliography" by Zoltan G. Zeke and William White, in *Bulletin of Bibliography 23* (Boston), May-August 1961.

*   *   *

George Orwell's world-wide reputation as a writer of science fiction rests upon a single novel, *Nineteen Eighty-Four.* Such is the dynamic force of this work that the title of the book has become a universal symbol for the totalitarian nightmare. Although indisputably an SF novel, it differs from most other works in the genre by having an overt political purpose. In the author's own words he desired "to push the world in a certain direction, to alter other people's idea of the kind of society they should strive after." His

experiences while fighting alongside the Anarchists in the Spanish Civil War had opened his eyes to the "expedient inhumanities" which lay behind both international Communism and European Fascism. From now on in any conflict between the individual human being and the State Orwell was always to be found on the side of the underdog. Orwell's international stature was first established with *Animal Farm*, a classic Swiftian satire on the Soviet experiment. The runaway success of this work ensured that his next book would be given wide critical attention. When *Nineteen Eighty-Four* first appeared it was initially hailed in many quarters as a further trenchant indictment of Soviet Communism though, in fact, it is an indictment of absolutism of whatsoever political hue. Its conception owes a great deal to Eugene Zamyatin's *We* which Orwell had first read in a French translation some 20 years previously.

The plot of *Nineteen Eighty-Four* is straightforward. The story follows the tragic fortues of Winston Smith, a minor civil servant, who lives and works in the London which has survived an atomic Third World War. This London is now the capital of Airstrip One, an off-shore province of Oceania, one of three constantly warring world-power blocs, Oceania, Eurasia, Eastasia. Under the absolute control of the Party and its Leader, Big Brother, the society of Oceania is stratified into the Inner Party (the rulers), the Party (the bureaucracy), and the rest (known collectively as the Proles). The complete ascendency of the Party is symbolized by the four Ministries which dominate Winston Smith's decaying urban metropolis. These are, in order of significance, the Ministry of Love, the Ministry of Truth, the Ministry of Peace, and the Ministry of Plenty:

> The Ministry of Love was the really frightening one. There were no windows in it at all. Winston had never been inside the Ministry of Love, nor within half a kilometre of it. The place was impossible to enter except on official business, and then only by penetrating through a maze of barbed-wire entanglements, steel doors and hidden machine-gun nests. Even the streets leading up to its outer barriers were roamed by gorilla-faced guards in black uniforms, armed with jointed truncheons.

Winston works in the Ministry of Truth whose slogans are "War is Peace. Freedom is Slavery. Ignorance is Strength." His job is to re-write items of recent history in Newspeak (the official Party language) in such a way that it accords with the official Party line. Watched over at all hours of the day and night by the ubiquitous telescreens of the dreaded Thought Police, Winston rebels against the system and commits the crime of falling in love with a fellow Party worker. For a brief spell he enjoys a precarious happiness only to learn, in what is surely one of the most horrendous passages in the whole of SF, that the Party has simply been toying with him all along. He is dragged into the Ministry of Love, and his total physical and spiritual degradation begins as the Party, in the person of the Torquemadian Senior Official O'Brien, sets about the task of extinguishing Winston's one precious spark of individual humanity—his moral conscience. The end is inevitable and horrifying. By a series of physical and psychological tortures Winston Smith as a person is totally erased and is then re-created in the Party's image until, in the end, "he loves Big Brother." Orwell's vision of a future in which the acquisition and tenure of absolute power is the only aspiration left to man is truly terrifying. "Power is not a means, it is an end," O'Brien tells Winston Smith. "If you want a picture of the future, imagine a boot stamping on a human face—for ever."

Nineteen Eighty-Four is a cautionary tale on a heroic scale; its initial impact on an immediately post-war world still groggy from the revelations of the Nazi extermination camps and the tales of Russian defectors to the West is not difficult to imagine. What still gives the story its tremendous emotional force is the intensity with which Orwell has expressed in fictional terms his passionately held belief in individual human freedom. All in all *Nineteen Eighty-Four* seems likely to retain its position as the most powerful as well as the most widely read science-fiction novel of the century.

—Richard Cowper

PADGETT, Lewis. *See* **KUTTNER, Henry; MOORE, C.L.**

———————

PAINE, Albert Bigelow. American. Born in New Bedford, Massachusetts, 10 July 1861. Educated at schools in Xenia, Illinois. Married 1) Minnie Schultz; 2) Dora Locey; three daughters. Assisted his father in a general store and on a farm; learned photography in St. Louis, and travelled as photographer, 1881-82; owned a photographic supply business, Fort Scott, Kansas; lived in New York after 1894: secretary to Mark Twain; children's editor, New York *Herald*, 1898, and League Editor, *St. Nicholas*; later lived in France. Chevalier, Legion of Honor, 1928. *Died 9 April 1937.*

SCIENCE-FICTION PUBLICATIONS

Novels

The Mystery of Evelyn Delorme: A Hypnotic Story. Boston, Arena, 1894.
The Great White Way. New York, Taylor, 1901.

OTHER PUBLICATIONS

Novels

The Bread Line: A Story of a Paper. New York, Century, 1900; London, Kegan Paul, 1901.
The Commuters. New York, Taylor, 1904.
The Lucky Pieces. New York, Outing, 1906.
From Van Dweller to Commuter. New York, Harper, 1907.
Peanuts. New York, Harper, 1913.
Dwellers in Arcady. New York, Harper, 1919.
Jan the Romantic. New York, Harper, 1929.

Short Stories

The Beacon Prize Medals and Other Stories. New York, Baker and Taylor, 1899.
Single Reels. New York, Harper, 1923.

Verse

Rhymes by Two Friends, with William Allen White. Privately printed, 1873.
Gabriel. Privately printed, 1889.
The Three Caravels. Privately printed, 1893.
The Autobiography of a Monkey. New York, Russell, 1897; London, Sands, 1899.

Other

Gobolinks; or, Shadow-Pictures for Young and Old, with Ruth McEnery Stuart. New York, Century, 1896.
The Dumpies (juvenile), with F. Ver-Beck. London, Kegan Paul, 1897.
The Hollow Tree (juvenile). New York, Russell, and London, Constable, 1898.
The Arkansas Bear (juvenile). New York, Russell, 1898; London, Harrap, 1919.
In the Deep Woods (juvenile). New York, Russell, 1899; London, Heinemann, 1900.
The Van Dwellers. New York, Taylor, 1901.
The Hollow Tree and Deep Wood Book. New York, Harper, 1901.
The Little Lady—Her Book (juvenile). Philadelphia, Altemus, and London, Kelly, 1901.
The Wanderings of Joe and Little Em (juvenile). Philadelphia, Altemus, 1903.

Thomas Nast: His Period and His Pictures. New York, Macmillan, 1904.
A Little Garden Calendar for Boys and Girls. Philadelphia, Altemus, 1905.
A Sailor of Fortune: Personal Memoirs of Captain B.S. Osbon. New York, McClure, 1906.
The Tent Dwellers. New York, Outing, and London, Hodder and Stoughton, 1908.
The Ship-Dwellers. New York, Harper, 1909; as *The Lure of the Mediterranean*, 1921.
Captain Bill McDonald, Texas Ranger. New York, Little and Ives, 1909.
Elsie and the Arkansas Bear (juvenile). Philadelphia, Altemus, 1909.
The Hollow Tree Snowed-In Book (juvenile). New York, Harper, 1910.
Mark Twain: A Biography. New York, Harper, 3 vols., 1912; abridged edition, as *A Short Life of Mark Twain*, 1920.
When Jack Rabbit Was a Little Boy (juvenile). New York, Harper, 1915.
How Mr. Dog Got Even (juvenile). New York, Harper, 1915.
How Mr. Rabbit Lost His Tail (juvenile). New York, Harper, 1915.
Making Up with Mr. Dog (juvenile). New York, Harper, 1915.
Mr. 'Possum's Great Balloon Trip (juvenile). New York, Harper, 1915.
Mr. Rabbit's Big Dinner (juvenile). New York, Harper, 1915.
The Boys' Life of Mark Twain. New York, Harper, 1916; as *The Adventures of Mark Twain*, New York, Grosset and Dunlap, 1941.
Hollow Tree Nights and Days (juvenile). New York, Harper, 1916.
Mr. Crow and the Whitewash (juvenile). New York, Harper, 1917.
Mr. Rabbit's Wedding (juvenile). New York, Harper, 1917.
Mr. Turtle's Flying Adventures (juvenile). New York, Harper, 1917.
George Fisher Baker: A Biography. Privately printed, 1920.
In One Man's Life, Being Chapters from the Personal and Business Career of Theodore N. Vail. New York, Harper, 1921; as *Theodore N. Vail: A Biography*, 1929.
The Cat That Went Abroad (juvenile). New York, Harper, 1921.
Joan of Arc, Maid of France. New York, Macmillan, 1925; revised edition, as *The Girl in White Armor: Joan of Arc for Young Readers*, 1929.
Life and Lillian Gish. New York, Macmillan, 1932.
Golden Cat (juvenile). Philadelphia, Penn, 1934.

Editor, *Mark Twain's Letters.* New York, Harper, 2 vols., 1917; abridged edition, London, Chatto and Windus, 1920.
Editor, *Moments with Mark Twain.* New York, Harper, 1920.
Editor, *The Writings of Mark Twain* (Definitive Edition). New York, Gabriel Wells, 37 vols., 1922-25.
Editor, *Mark Twain's Autobiography.* New York and London, Harper, 2 vols., 1924.
Editor, *Mark Twain's Notebook.* New York, Harper, 1935.

*   *   *

Albert Bigelow Paine's *The Great White Way*, an exhilarating book, takes advantage of contemporary interest in the still-unknown geography of the South Polar continent (land exploration began in 1900) to postulate a tropical semi-utopia surrounded by the Great Ice Barrier of the coast. The basic plot consists of an exploratory trip into that country and an exciting escape back to civilization. Although Paine is faithful to—and even cannily extrapolative from—the science (geography, biology, physics) of his day, the surprisingly rich novel is of primary interest as a philosophical fable. Grounded in 19th-century American popular social and economic thought, the book lauds esthetically oriented and scientifically literate "rainbow chasers" (personified in the hero, Nicholas Chase) and common-sense engineers and businessmen (represented by Chauncey Gale), while it gently denigrates both pure science and American capitalism as being too conservative. The idealist (represented by Ferratoni, whose name suggests his belief in magnetic-gravitational force and its similarity to electric, mental, and musical vibrations) is admirable and right but is not suited to the real world. The book's primary values are those of home and hearth, spiced with a bit of adventurous enterprise.

The novel is a bit old-fashioned in its verbal and narrative structures, but it is still very readable, for some of the same reasons that have maintained the popularity of Mark Twain, Paine's friend and mentor.

—Robert L. Jones

PALMER, Raymond A.   Also wrote as Henry Gade; G.H. Irwin; Frank Patton; J.W. Pelkie; Wallace Quitman; A.R. Steber; Morris J. Steele.   American.   Born in Wisconsin, 1 August 1910. Crippled from childhood. Editor and publisher; Editor, *The Comet*, fan magazine, 1930; *Amazing Stories*, 1938-49; *Fantastic Adventures*, 1939-49; *Other Worlds* (later *Science Stories* and *Flying Saucers from Other Worlds*), 1950-57; *Imagination Science Fiction*, 1950; *Universe Science Fiction*, 1953-55; *Fate* and *Mystic* (later *Search*) in the 1950's; *The Hidden World* in the 1960's. *Died 15 August 1977.*

SCIENCE-FICTION PUBLICATIONS

Uncollected Short Stories

"The Time Ray of Jandra," in *Wonder Stories* (New York), June 1930.
"The Time Tragedy," in *Wonder Stories* (New York), December 1934.
"The Symphony of Death," in *Amazing* (New York), December 1935.
"Three from the Test Tube," in *Wonder Stories* (New York), November 1936.
"Matter Is Conserved," in *Astounding* (New York), April 1938.
"Catalyst Planet," in *Thrilling Wonder Stories* (New York), August 1938.
"Outlaw of Space" (as Wallace Quitman), in *Amazing* (New York), August 1938.
"The Vengeance of Martin Brand" (as G.H. Irwin), in *Amazing* (New York), August 1942; expanded edition, as "The Justice of Martin Brand," in *Other Worlds* (New York), July 1950.
"Red Coral," in *Other Worlds* (New York), May 1951.
"Tarzan Never Dies," in *Other Worlds* (New York), May 1955.

Uncollected Short Stories as A.R. Steber

"The Blinding Ray," in *Amazing* (New York), August 1938.
"Black World," in *Amazing* (New York), March 1940.
"When the Gods Make War," in *Amazing* (New York), July 1940.
"Moon of Double Trouble," in *Amazing* (New York), March 1945.

Uncollected Short Stories as Morris J. Steele

"Polar Prison," in *Amazing* (New York), December 1938.
"The Phantom Enemy," in *Amazing* (New York), February 1939.
"Weapon for a Wac," in *Amazing* (New York), September 1944.

Uncollected Short Stories as Henry Gade

"Pioneer—1957," in *Fantastic Adventures* (New York), November 1939.
"Liners of Space," in *Amazing* (New York), December 1939.
"The Invincible Crime Buster," in *Amazing* (New York), July 1941.

Uncollected Short Stories as Frank Patton

"The Test Tube Girl," in *Fantastic Adventures* (New York), January 1942.

"Doorway to Hell," in *Fantastic Adventures* (New York), February 1942.
"A Patriot Never Dies," in *Amazing* (New York), August 1943.
"War Worker," in *Amazing* (New York), September 1943.
"Jewels of the Toad," in *Fantastic Adventures* (New York), October 1943.
"Mahaffey's Mystery," in *Other Worlds* (New York), March 1950.
"The Identity of Sue Tenet," in *Other Worlds* (New York), December 1952.
"Question Please," in *Other Worlds* (New York), April 1953.
"Sure Thing," in *Science Stories* (Evanston, Illinois), February 1954.
"The Secret of Pierre Cotreau," in *Science Stories* (Evanston, Illinois), April 1954.

Uncollected Short Stories as J.W. Pelkie (series: Toka in all stories)

"King of the Dinosaurs," in *Fantastic Adventures* (New York), October 1945.
"Toka and the Man Bats," in *Fantastic Adventures* (New York), February 1946.
"Toka Fights the Big Cats," in *Fantastic Adventures* (New York), December 1947.
"In the Sphere of Time," in *Planet* (New York), Summer 1948.

*   *   *

Raymond A. Palmer was one of the earliest science-fiction fans, his activities dating from the late 1920's, and his major influence was as an editor. His first important assignment was the editorship of *Amazing Stories*, taken over from the moribund Teck Publications in 1938 by Ziff-Davis. Palmer discarded the on-hand inventory, quickly filled the magazine with new, adventure-oriented stories, and (perhaps most important) refurbished its drab appearance to create a lively, colorful package. Simultaneously he worked to bring the contents of the magazine in line with its new appearance.

He was immediately successful, and the following year was able to add a companion magazine, *Fantastic Adventures*. In a number of ways, Palmer's career remarkably paralleled that of the legendary John W. Campbell, Jr. Each editor brought on a stable of new writers, in addition to retaining (or re-recruiting) the best writers of a previous administration. Each editor also ran afoul of reader resistance when he attempted to introduce a variety of pseudoscientific cult material in the 1940's and 1950's. For Campbell it was Dianetics, and other oddities; for Palmer, it was first the Shaver Mystery, and later an infatuation with Flying Saucers. Much given to hucksterism and juvenile promotional appeals, Palmer met strong resistance in science fiction and withdrew to concentrate on occult publishing after 1957. However, his real achievements as an editor have been sorely underrated, and an examination of files of the magazines he edited reveals an absolute treasure-trove of overlooked material, by many leading writers. He lured Edgar Rice Burroughs back to the science-fiction magazines after an absence of 12 years. Palmer was the first editor to publish stories by Isaac Asimov, for all that the latter prefers to emphasize his later association with Campbell in his reminiscences. It is to be hoped that as the lingering bad taste of "Shaverism," "Saucerism," and Palmer's other regrettable antics fades away, his very significant editorial contribution to modern science fiction will be more appreciated

Palmer's own fiction, upon review, indicates a considerable talent but one which was not applied sufficiently consistently to produce a coherent body of works. In Palmer's earliest work, for Gernsback's *Wonder Stories*, he shows strongly the influence of early writers in the field. "The Time Ray of Jandra" reads like a throwback to the early 19th century, with a first-person narrator explaining the circumstances of his birth and naming, and continuing through overlong paragraphs to detail a discovery tale in which he is purely an observer rather than a participant. Before long, Palmer had fallen into the pulp style. His stories of the 1930's and 1940's show a fully developed set of pulp characteristics: simplistic but highly colored characterization, heavy doses of violent action, a reliance on coincidence and a strongly romantic bent. An excellent example, further embellished with occasional pseudo-scientific asides, is "The Test

Tube Girl" (as Frank Patton). In his few stories published in the 1950's, Palmer appears to have overcome the worse excesses of his pulp period, and to have moved toward a less heavy-handed and melodramatic approach.

—Richard A. Lupoff

PANGBORN, Edgar. Also wrote as Bruce Harrison. American. Born in New York City, 25 February 1909. Educated at Brooklyn Friends School, graduated 1924; Harvard University, Cambridge, Massachusetts, 1924-25; New England Conservatory of Music, 1927. Served in the United States Army Medical Corps, 1942-45. Farmer in Maine, 1939-42; writer from 1946. Recipient: International Fantasy Award, 1955. *Died 1 February 1976.*

SCIENCE-FICTION PUBLICATIONS

Novels

West of the Sun. New York, Doubleday, 1953; London, Hale, 1954.
A Mirror for Observers. New York, Doubleday, 1954; London, Muller, 1955.
Davy. New York, St. Martin's Press, 1964; London, Dobson, 1967.
The Judgment of Eve. New York, Simon and Schuster, 1966; London, Rapp and Whiting, 1968.
The Company of Glory. New York, Pyramid, 1975.
The Atlantean Nights Entertainment. San Francisco, Pennyfarthing Press, 1980.

Short Stories

Good Neighbors and Other Strangers. New York, Macmillan, 1972.
Still I Persist in Wondering. New York, Dell, 1978.

OTHER PUBLICATIONS

Novels

A-100 (as Bruce Harrison). New York, Dutton, 1930.
Wilderness of Spring. New York, Rinehart, 1958.
The Trial of Callista Blake. New York, St. Martin's Press, and London, Davies, 1962.

*

Manuscript Collection: Mugar Memorial Library, Boston University.

*   *   *

Edgar Pangborn's work, according to Damon Knight, reflects "the regretful, ironic, sorrowful, deeply joyous—and purblind—love of the world and all in it." Pangborn sees wonder in the ordinary, removing the reader from mundane perceptions. Some readers resent this heightening of the conventional. Knight sees Pangborn's magic as a veil obscuring the story. "The author will not get out of the way, but forces you to look through his own misty substance at what he wants you to see." A moment of reflection reveals that this sort of reaction indicates a matter of taste. Pangborn is an individual writer who directs the reader's perceptions; he does not write to the reader's order. Pangborn's view of life is tragic, comic, serious, and speculatively imaginative; his range is wider than many critics suspect. He is one of the few writers of SF and fantasy who was also a major fiction writer. His ideas were not always original, but he always managed to transform them.

"Angel's Egg," Pangborn's first story, is a powerful and very moving alien-contact story which pleads for tolerence and patience in regard to humankind's fate. Often reprinted, this story would have been enough to make a name for any writer. Pangborn's first SF novel, *West of the Sun*, is a deeply felt story of interstellar castaways, notable for its vividly realized settings, complex characters, and a painful knowledge of human failing. The sense of being there with the characters is overwhelming. *A Mirror for Observers*, a story of alien observers on earth who struggle between being watchers and meddlers, reaches Stapledonian heights of thought and feeling about the fate of humanity, but without the Stapledonian vistas. Pangborn's focus is more personal and intimate. Pangborn regarded *Wilderness of Spring* as a historical novel. Set in colonial New England, there is much in the story's pioneer spirit to interest the SF reader (one of the characters becomes a scientist). *The Trial of Callista Blake* is a novel on the theme of capital punishment.

Davy is Pangborn's most famous novel. Set 300 years after a nuclear holocaust, the book is a memoir written by the title character who grows from a bondsman to an ambitious leader concerned with the fate of humanity. Funny and tragic, bawdy and adventurous in the manner of *Tom Jones, Davy* is one of the lasting works of SF. A similar work, but one involving a female counterpart to Davy, *The Judgment of Eve* is not as well known, but, filled with the agony of choices, the book will please anyone who has enjoyed Pangborn's work. It has been suggested that the ambiguous ending might have been the result of editorial pressure to avoid depicting a *ménage-à-quatre*. *The Company of Glory*, is set in the same world as *Davy* and *The Judgment of Eve* (though the Pyramid edition was censored as being "too faggoty"). *Still I Persist in Wondering* contains most of the shorter works set in the world of *Davy*.

Pangborn's body of work is of a consistent high quality. A reader who responds to his work will want to read it all; but Pangborn is clearly not for everyone who reads science fiction. The narrow genre addict cannot enjoy Pangborn without widening his reading horizons. His work addressed itself to the great problems of life and death, the mystery of existence, and personal worth. Paradoxically, science fiction, though it claims to be a literature of ideas and wide vision, rarely rises above the entertainment formulas. Pangborn helped keep alive the tradition of "high science fiction," even while the pejorative genre associations with SF dragged down serious receptions of his work. Above everything else, Pangborn brought an overpowering sense of beauty to science fiction. *West of the Sun* glows with an unwearying light: "I give you birth and death and the journey of our days and nights between them, the shining of green fields, and patience of the forest, the little stars, the great stars, the love and the thought, the labor and the laughter, the good morning sky." *A Mirror for Observers* breathes with an unwaning love: "Never, beautiful Earth, never even at the height of the human storms have I forgotten you, my planet Earth, your forests and your fields, your oceans, the serenity of your mountains; the meadows, the continuing rivers, the incorruptible promise of returning spring." In trying to make us see, hear, and feel the important things that we so often forget, Pangborn aspired to the utterance of music, his first love.

—George Zebrowski

PANSHIN, Alexei. American. Born in Lansing, Michigan, 14 August 1940. Educated at the University of Michigan, Ann Arbor, 1958-60; Michigan State University, East Lansing, B.A. 1965; University of Chicago, M.A. 1966. Served in the United States Army, 1960-62. Married Cory Seidman in 1969; one son. Librarian, Brooklyn Public Library, 1966-67; Visiting Lecturer in science fiction, Cornell University, Ithaca, New York, summers 1971-72. Recipient: Hugo Award, for non-fiction, 1967; Nebula Award, 1968. Address: R.R. 2, Box 261, Perkasie, Pennsylvania 18944, U.S.A.

SCIENCE-FICTION PUBLICATIONS

Novels (series: Anthony Villiers)

Rite of Passage.   New York, Ace, 1968; London, Sidgwick and Jackson, 1969.
Star Well (Villiers).   New York, Ace, 1968.
The Thurb Revolution (Villiers).   New York, Ace, 1968.
Masque World (Villiers).   New York, Ace, 1969.
Earth Magic, with Cory Panshin.   New York, Ace, 1978; London, Magnum, 1980.

Short Stories

Farewell to Yesterday's Tomorrow.   New York, Berkley, 1975; augmented edition, 1976.

OTHER PUBLICATIONS

Other

Heinlein in Dimension: A Critical Analysis.   Chicago, Advent, 1968.
"Short SF in 1968," in *Nebula Award Stories 5*, edited by James Blish.   New York, Doubleday, and London, Gollancz, 1970.
SF in Dimension: A Book of Explorations, with Cory Panshin. Chicago, Advent, 1976.
Mondi Interiori (in Italian), with Cory Panshin.   Milan, Editrice Nord, 1978.

*

Manuscript Collection: Bowling Green University, Ohio.

Alexei Panshin comments:
My first aim as an SF writer is to tell good stories. To me, that means the solidest, most complete, truest stories I can imagine. My second aim is to make every story new in some way: new characters, new settings, new style, new to myself. For me, each story has its own unique voice, its own autonomy, and I've got to find it and respect it and love it into being.
Most of the time I write stories slowly, and I get published even more slowly. 20 years after I first began to write, I've published five novels and one book of stories. An editor wrote to my first agent: "I used to think Panshin wrote this way because he was stubborn. Now I think he just doesn't have a very interesting imagination." I don't know which it is. All that I know is that the SF that I want to write is still beyond me, but I haven't given up trying.

*   *   *

Alexei Panshin began publishing science-fiction stories as an undergraduate. He had already conceived and begun writing the Nebula Award novel *Rite of Passage* while serving in the army. The novel, an acknowledged science-fiction classic, is an anthropological novel of the maturation of Mia Havero, the 19-year-old narrator recalling her one month "Trial." The time is 150 years after the earth has been destroyed. The Trial is a survival test that all 14-year-olds living on the asteroid star "ships" must undergo on a colony planet in order to be adult citizens. The point of view of an adolescent girl and her maturation are well done, though she and her friend, Jimmy Dentremont, seem rather precocious, particularly at the conclusion of the novel. In its psychological realism and the careful delineation of the "ship" society and the colony planet culture, *Rite of Passage* is Panshin's major fiction achievement.
The three Villiers novels, *Star Well*, *The Thurb Revolution*, and *Masque World*, follow the adventures of the titled Anthony Villiers and his inscrutable, unpredictable alien companion. Torve, the frog-like Torg. Each novel takes place on a different planet near or

in the weak Nashua Empire. Panshin incorporates many comic elements, parodying space operas, spy thrillers, novels of intrigue, and regency and picaresque novels. The narrator is a cynical observer of the human comedy who interrupts the narrative with epigrammatic comments and short essays on human folly and absurdity. While amusing, the literary parody is occasionally labored and the relativistic, amoral narrator can become wearing. However, the emphasis on style and manner is appropriate to the genres being parodied and to the character of a rebellious, wandering aristocrat whose adventures are precipitated by the failure of his father's remittance to arrive. Sometimes Panshin's learning is brought in rather obviously. The novels become increasingly pessimistic. *Masque World* has the weakest plot and ends the most grimly.
Farewell to Yesterday's Tomorrow includes stories written between 1966 and 1975 and shows how deeply affected Panshin was by the revolutionary 1960's and early 1970's in America. "The Sons of Prometheus," "A Sense of Direction," and "Arpad" employ the basis situation of the asteroid star "ships" from *Rite of Passage*. "Sky Blue" reflects a concern with the rapacious development of planets and, by extension, the exploitation of earth's ecology. "When the Vertical World Becomes Horizontal" preaches the need for freedom and spontaneity to replace rigid social assumptions and behavior. Panshin's disillusionment with the failure of the counter culture of the early 1970's is apparent in "How Can We Sink When We Can Fly?" "Lady Sunshine and the Beatus" (written with his wife Cory) is a quest story and a phantasmagoric version of the Beauty and the Beast fairy tale. It ends the collection optimistically and romantically.
Earth Magic, also in collaboration with his wife, is an intriguing heroic fantasy which follows the adventures of Haldane, the son of Black Morca, a barbaric warrior tyrant. It is an exploration of the themes of change, identity, and reality versus vision or magic.

—Diane Parkin-Speer

PASSANTE, Dom.   *See* FEARN, John Russell.

PEDLER, Kit (Christopher Magnus Howard Pedler).   British. Born in London, 11 June 1927. Educated at Ipswich School; King's College, University of London; Westminster Medical School, London, M.B.B.S. 1953, Ph.D., Member, College of Pathologists. Married Una Freeston in 1949; two daughters and two sons. Physician and surgeon in London and Greenwich hospitals, 1953-57; in general practice briefly; Senior Lecturer, then Reader in Pathology, then founded and headed the Anatomy and Electron Microscopy Department, for 12 years, University of London: resigned in 1971 to become free-lance writer: author of many radio and television documentaries and features. Honorary Secretary, Royal Microscopy Society. Agent: Harvey Una and Stephen Durbridge Ltd., 14 Beaumont Mews, London W1N 4HE, England.

SCIENCE-FICTION PUBLICATIONS

Novels with Gerry Davis

Mutant 59, The Plastic Eater.   London, Souvenir Press, 1971; New York, Viking Press, 1972.
Brainrack.   London, Souvenir Press, 1974; New York, Pocket Books, 1975.

The Dynostar Menace. London, Souvenir Press, and New York, Scribner, 1975.

OTHER PUBLICATIONS

Plays

Radio Plays: *Sunday Lunch; Trial by Logic.*

Television Plays: *Doctor Who* series (8 plays, 3 with Gerry Davis); *The Robot* (documentary); *Doomwatch* series (39 plays with Gerry Davis); *Galenforce*, with Gerry Davis.

Other

The Quest for Gala: A Book of Changes. London, Souvenir Press, 1979.

Kit Pedler comments:
My science fiction has always had to do with small logical extensions of current reality. I am currently engaged on "Document from the Year 3," for example, which deals (post hoc) with the evolution of homo sapiens, and "The Logon" which are the result of mating between a mould and a microchip!

*   *   *

Kit Pedler and Gerry Davis have written three disaster novels following their collaboration on BBC-TV's Doomwatch series and their creation of the Cybermen for *Doctor Who.* Their success has been mixed. Strong on the science background, these novels are sometimes markedly weak as fictions because of poor characterization and, particularly in *The Dynostar Menace*, a reliance on stylistic and suspense clichés. Nevertheless, the narratives are at times remarkably exciting and well-sustained, as in the well- executed main sequence in *Mutant 59, The Plastic Eater*, when a small group is trapped in the London Underground by fire and explosion. Further, the authors sometimes achieve nice ironic and satirical effects, for instance, by well-timed narrative switches of focus from one character to another in *Mutant 59.*

As prophets of doom, Pedler and Davis seem to be telling us that we are unwise to rely on over-complicated mechanisms that are vulnerable to simple accidents, caused by unforeseen weaknesses or dangers in materials, human error, or simply the over-complication itself. If we heeded their warnings we would take immediate steps drastically to simplify our lives. At the end of their second and strongest novel, *Brainrack*, this solution is rendered highly appealing by an idyllic evocation of a London without motor vehicles. The solution, perhaps unfortunately, is more convincing than the threats, which are needlessly fantastic. It is not strictly necessary to postulate the existence of a mutant virus that feeds on plastic (and finds abundant food when a new sun-degradable plastic is marketed), in order to explain severe disasters to airliners, submarines, and London. That men brought up in cities are suffering irretrievable brain damage because of an unsuspected ingredient of petrol is a highly unconvincing explanation of the destruction of a new nuclear power plant. It does not seem very likely that a satellite reactor will disrupt the ozone layer of earth's atmosphere and burn large areas of the surface of our planet. (Human greed and negligence are sufficient explanations, as in a disaster novel that is not regarded as SF, John D. MacDonald's *Condominium*). However, these startling threats are piquant and intriguing, and, to be fair to the writers, they take ample account of familiar human nature as a contributory cause of the disasters. What they like to do, in fact, is to make their point by showing how easy it is for various weaknesses inherent in a system to compound each other: the "plastic eater" is simply the icing on the cake. Pedler and Davis are particularly convincing when, in the early part of *Brainrack*, they expose the "EMMY" (man-machine interface) dangers: most of us know how easy it is to hit the wrong keys on typewriters, or misread simple instructions, or confuse colour codes. There is a grand tour de force in *Brainrack*, a long sustained narrative account of the effects of meltdown on the workers in a nuclear reactor. This is vivid and horrific and, except that some people survive, for the sake of the story, highly convincing.

The Dynostar Menace stands apart from the other two novels in being set in a closed environment, a space lab, and having the form of a kind of hard SF version of Christie's *Ten Little Niggers*. In this sort of plot, versions of which can often be found in TV series (*Blake's Seven*) or films (*Alien*), the actual nature of the threat is almost bound to be subordinated to the excitement of detection (here, of a saboteur) in a race against time. Exceptional imaginative power and skill, particularly in characterization, are needed to lift such a hackneyed plot from cliché and perhaps it is here that we can see how a background in TV script-writing may have been a disadvantage, particularly to Davis. However, their three works together constitute a notable contribution to disaster fiction and they are perhaps a shade unlucky to have slightly anticipated the greatest market for this branch of the genre.

—Michael J. Tolley

PERCY, Walker. American. Born in Birmingham, Alabama, 28 May 1916. Educated at the University of North Carolina, Chapel Hill, B.A. 1937; Columbia University, New York, M.D. 1941; intern at Bellevue Hospital, New York, 1942. Married Mary Bernice Townsend in 1946; two daughters. Contracted tuberculosis, gave up medicine, and became a full-time writer, 1943. Recipient: National Book Award, 1962; National Institute of Arts and Letters grant, 1967; National Catholic Book Award, 1972. Address: P.O. Box 510, Covington, Louisiana 70433, U.S.A.

SCIENCE-FICTION PUBLICATIONS

Novel

Love in the Ruins: The Adventures of a Bad Catholic at a Time Near the End of the World. New York, Farrar Straus, and London, Eyre and Spottiswoode, 1971.

OTHER PUBLICATIONS

Novels

The Moviegoer. New York, Knopf, 1961; London, Eyre and Spottiswoode, 1963.
The Last Gentleman. New York, Farrar Straus, 1966; London, Eyre and Spottiswoode, 1967.
Lancelot. New York, Farrar Straus, and London, Secker and Warburg, 1977.
The Second Coming. New York, Farrar Straus, 1980.

Other

The Message in the Bottle: How Queer Man Is, How Queer Language Is, and What One Has to Do with the Other. New York, Farrar Straus, 1975.

*   *   *

In *Love in the Ruins*, his only work of science fiction, Walker Percy uses a chaotic future to dramatize our present chaotic and amoral state. Dr. Thomas More observes the end of life-as-we-know-it, watching from his Louisiana vantage-point as America polarizes into abstraction and lust, the polarization caused by heavy sodium and chloride escaping into the atmosphere from underground. More has a machine which can measure and treat the disorders these heavy chemicals cause. The novel takes place in the future, and a new mechanical invention is crucial to the plot: it *is* science fiction. However, the science would pass no laboratory test—it is symbolically, not scientifically, logical. More is a great deal like his famous namesake; holding out against sin (he never stops believing in God and love) with humorous self-effacement, he beats the devil, here named Art Immelmann. Abstraction and lust are referred to by "technical" and rather medieval terms, angelism and bestialism. The heavy chemicals are sulfur and brimstone, welling up from hell, and More's invention is a lapsometer, which measures and treats nothing less than the disorders of the soul. America is going to hell because of its tendency to polarize into pure abstraction and pure lust, and because it has failed a simple moral test, by violating every right of the black people it transported from Africa.

In "Notes for a Novel about the End of the World" (in *The Message in the Bottle*), Percy makes it clear that we are not to take the strange signs and portents of *Love in the Ruins* as the ephemera of a disordered mind, though More is clearly disturbed. It is the world which is in disorder: "It may be useful to write a novel about the end of the world. Perhaps it is only through the conjuring up of catastrophe, the destruction of all Exxon signs, and the sprouting of vines in the church pews, that the novelist can make vicarious use of catastrophe in order that he and his reader may come to themselves." By making vividly concrete America's spiritual ills, and by warning us through his description of a possible future, Percy hopes to make his readers aware of their present condition. The result of his concretion is a witty and humane novel written in the philosophical tradition of the American romantics and William Faulkner which makes meaningful and entertaining use of science-fiction devices.

—Joan Gordon

PEREGOY, Calvin. *See* **McCLARY, Thomas.**

PETAJA, Emil (Theodore). American. Born in Milltown, Montana, 12 April 1915. Educated at Montana State University, Bozeman, 1936-38. Office worker, 1938-41; film technician, Technicolor Corporation, Hollywood, 1941-46; photographer, 1947-63. Since 1963, full-time writer: Chairman, Bokonalia Memorial Foundation; since 1972, owner, SISU Publishers, San Francisco. Agent: Forrest J. Ackerman, 2495 Glendower Avenue, Hollywood, California 90027. Address: P.O. Box 14126, San Francisco, California 94114, U.S.A.

SCIENCE-FICTION PUBLICATIONS

Novels (series: Green Planet; Kalevala)

Alpha Yes, Terra No! New York, Ace, 1965.
The Caves of Mars. New York, Ace, 1965.
Saga of Lost Earths (Kalevala). New York, Ace, 1965.
The Star Mill (Kalevala). New York, Ace, 1965.
Tramontane (Kalevala). New York, Ace, 1966.
The Stolen Sun (Kalevala). New York, Ace, 1967.
Lord of the Green Planet. New York, Ace, 1967.
The Prism. New York, Ace, 1968.
Doom of the Green Planet. New York, Ace, 1968.
The Time Twister (Kalevala). New York, Dell, 1968.
The Path Beyond the Stars. New York, Dell, 1969.
The Nets of Space. New York, Berkley, 1969.
Seed of the Dreamers. New York, Ace, 1970.

Lost Earths (omnibus). New York, DAW, 1979.

Short Stories

Stardrift and Other Fantastic Flotsam. Los Angeles, Fantasy, 1971.

Uncollected Short Stories

"The Storm-King," in *Dark Things*, edited by August Derleth. Sauk City, Wisconsin, Arkham House, 1971.
"Terrible Quick Sword," in *Signs and Wonders*, edited by Roger Elwood. Old Tappan, New Jersey, Revell, 1972.
"Gola's Well," in *Witchcraft and Sorcery 8* (Alhambra, California), 1972.
"The White Magician," in *Witchcraft and Sorcery 10* (Alhambra, California), 1974.

OTHER PUBLICATIONS

Verse

As Dream and Shadow. San Francisco, SISU, 1972.

Other

And Flights of Angels. San Francisco, SISU, 1968.

Editor, *The Hannes Bok Memorial Showcase of Fantasy Art.* San Francisco, SISU, 1974.
Editor, *Photoplay Edition.* San Francisco, SISU, 1975.

Emil Petaja comments:
My writing endeavors have mainly been to entertain, except for the factual material concerning Hannes Bok and fantasy art in general, which serves to indicate my enthusiasm for these subjects. My novels about the Finnish legendary epic *Kalevala: The Land of Heroes* spring from a lifelong interest in this fine poetic work. I own six translations of the *Kalevala*, as well as the work in the original. Both my parents were Finnish.

*   *   *

Though Emil Petaja published short fiction sporadically during the 1940's and 1950's, his important works were written in the 1960's. Most of these novels were published by Ace Books, and even those that were not followed the Ace formula: heavy on action, with some superficial romance. Though Petaja never sought to go beyond this formula, his innovations within its structure are impressive. Petaja's choice of story-material is the source of his appeal, for into the traditional settings of science fiction he transferred mythic heroes and situations, devoting particular attention to his own Finnish myth-heritage, the Kalevala story-cycle. Petaja deftly contrasts the sterile safety of centralized civilization (into which the hero is born) with the barbaric but vital hardship of primitive culture (into which the hero is initiated), and though the author concedes the necessity for both milieus, he emphasizes the greater need for preserving humanity's poetic potential. Unlike most Ace "common man" heroes, Petaja's protagonists are strong, romantic-minded men, slightly alienated in progressive society, but greatly attuned to the poetry of myths. Ultimately the hero's ability to empathize with mythic situations is the factor which saves all of humanity—whether directly by battling destructive forces, or indirectly by mastering the situation with poetic insight (*Alpha Yes, Terra No!*).

In the Kalevala-based novels the hero's empathy is deep enough to propel his psyche upon astral journeys, becoming merged with a Finnish hero endowed with magic (psychic?) powers. These are probably the best of Petaja's works because of their belief in an actual existence of the Finnish mythos, even by means of rationalizations like psychic powers and alien entities. Thus the mythos provides the structural basis for evoking the poetry of Finnish culture. Earlier authors' works had also rationalized myths into science fiction (Henry Kuttner's *Mask of Circe*), but Petaja is virtually the first to maintain limited fidelity to the cultural content of the myths, rather than manipulating it to fit melodramatic purposes.

Less successful, but equally colorful, are the two books of a planetary culture modeled on Irish story-cycles, though no particular myths are emphasized by the plots of *Lord of the Green Planet* and *Doom of the Green Planet*. The supernatural creatures of Irish myth are robots and alien entities, while the "Irish" are merely transplanted humans from other planets, all brought together by a mad Fenian poet with super-scientific resources. Though entertaining, these books do not have the poetry of the Kalevala books, for the Irish culture is merely a giant mock-up rather than a shamanistic culture like the Finns', seen as surviving into the future. Furthermore, though the mythos-structure is less articulated, Petaja displays more dislike for the "progressive" civilization beyond the Green Planet than in earlier novels, and greater cognizance of the conflict between the appeal of heroism and the necessities of humanism.

Of the non-related books, the best is *The Path Beyond the Stars* in which a man and woman traverse several time-periods attempting to acquire knowledge of the universe's destruction—which they ultimately cannot prevent, though they can become the Adam and Eve of another cosmos. The other novels have less imaginative scope, but, in a melodramatic way, they all work toward the same goal: regeneration of the heroes' mythopoeic faculties, and thus the redemption of the profane world.

Petaja's importance to science fiction is that of a precursor of the increased use of myth in late 1960's SF. At their best his works suggest an archaic heritage of man not unlike the findings of anthropologist Mircea Eliade—a heritage which most contemporary writers, SF and mainstream alike, have chosen to neglect.

—Gene Phillips

PHILLIFENT, John T. *See* **RACKHAM, John.**

PHILLIPS, Mark. *See* **GARRETT, Randall; JANIFER, Laurence M.**

PHILLIPS, Rog (Roger Phillips Graham). Also wrote as Clinton Ames; Robert Arnette; Franklin Bahl; Alexander Blade; Craig Browning; Gregg Conrad; P.F. Costello; Inez McGowan; Melva Rogers; Chester Ruppert; William Carter Sawtelle; A.R. Steber; Gerald Vance; John Wiley; Peter Worth. American. Born in Spokane, Washington, in 1909. Educated at Gonzaga University, Spokane, A.B.; graduate study at the University of Washington, Seattle. Married 1) Mari Wolf; 2) Honey Wood in 1956. Power plant engineer; shipyard welder during World War II; free-lance writer after the War: Columnist ("The Club House"), *Amazing*, New York, 1948-53. *Died in 1965.*

SCIENCE-FICTION PUBLICATIONS

Novels

Time Trap. Chicago, Century, 1949.

Worlds Within. Chicago, Century, 1950.
World of If. Chicago, Century, 1951.
The Involuntary Immortals. New York, Avalon, 1959.

Uncollected Short Stories (series: Lefty Baker)

"Let Freedom Ring," in *Amazing* (New York), December 1945.
"Vacation in Shasta," in *Fantastic Adventures* (New York), February 1946.
"Atom War," in *Amazing* (New York), May 1946.
"The Mutants," in *Amazing* (New York), July 1946.
"Dual Personality," in *Fantastic Adventures* (New York), September 1946.
"The Space" (as Roger P. Graham), in *Amazing* (New York), September 1946.
"Battle of the Gods," in *Amazing* (New York), September 1946.
"The House," in *Amazing* (New York), February 1947.
"So Shall Ye Reap," in *Amazing* (New York), August 1947.
"The Uninvited Jest," in *Amazing* (New York), September 1947.
"The Despoilers," in *Amazing* (New York), October 1947.
"High Ears," in *Fantastic Adventures* (New York), October 1947.
"Squeeze Play" (Baker; as Craig Browning), in *Amazing* (New York), November 1947.
"And Eve Was," in *Amazing* (New York), November 1947.
"Hate," in *Amazing* (New York), January 1948.
"Twice to Die," in *Fantastic Adventures* (New York), February 1948.
"The Supernal Note," in *Amazing* (New York), July 1948.
"Starship from Sirius," in *Amazing* (New York), August 1948.
"The Cube Root of Conquest," in *Amazing* (New York), October 1948.
"The Unthinking Destroyer," in *Amazing* (New York), December 1948.
"Brainstorm" (as Alexander Blade), in *Fantastic Adventures* (New York), December 1948.
"The Can Opener," in *Fantastic Adventures* (New York), January 1949.
"The Immortal Menace" (Baker), and "M'Bong-Ah," in *Amazing* (New York), February 1949.
"Quite Logical," in *Thrilling Wonder Stories* (New York), April 1949.
"She," in *Fantastic Adventures* (New York), April 1949.
"Unthinkable," in *Amazing* (New York), April 1949.
"The Last Stronghold" (as Chester Ruppert), in *Amazing* (New York), May 1949.
"The Robot Men of Bubble City," in *Fantastic Adventures* (New York), July 1949.
"The Shortcut," in *Amazing* (New York), July 1949.
"The Awakening," in *Amazing* (New York), August 1949.
"The Tangential Semanticist," in *Fantastic Adventures* (New York), August 1949.
"Incompatible," in *Fantastic Adventures* (New York), September 1949.
"Matrix," in *Amazing* (New York), October 1949.
"Planet of the Dead," in *Fantastic Adventures* (New York), October 1949.
"The Insane Robot" (Baker), in *Fantastic Adventures* (New York), November 1949.
"Venus Trouble Shooter" (as John Wiley), in *Other Worlds* (Evanston, Indiana), November 1949.
"Beyond the Matrix of Time," in *Amazing* (New York), November 1949.
"The Miracle of Elmer Wilde," in *Other Worlds* (Evanston, Indiana), November 1949.
"To Give Them Welcome" (as Melva Rogers), in *Other Worlds* (Evanston, Indiana), January 1950.
"This Time," in *Other Worlds* (Evanston, Indiana), January 1950.
"The Pranksters," in *Amazing* (New York), February 1950.
"Detour from Tomorrow," in *Fantastic Adventures* (New York), March 1950.
"The Fatal Technicality," in *Other Worlds* (Evanston, Indiana), March 1950.
"The Mental Assassins" (as Gregg Conrad), in *Fantastic Adventures* (New York), May 1950.

"Slaves of the Crystal Brain" (as William Carter Sawtelle), in *Amazing* (New York), May 1950.
"The Lost Bomb," in *Amazing* (New York), May 1950.
"If You Were Me...," in *Amazing* (New York), June 1950.
"Victims of the Vortex" (as Clinton Ames), in *Amazing* (New York), July 1950.
"Warrior Queen of Mars" (as Alexander Blade), in *Fantastic Adventures* (New York), September 1950.
"Holes in My Head," in *Other Worlds* (Evanston, Indiana), October 1950.
"One for the Robot—Two for the Same," in *Imagination* (Evanston, Illinois), October 1950.
"Weapon from the Stars," in *Amazing* (New York), October 1950.
"A Man Named Mars" (as A.R. Steber), in *Other Worlds* (Evanston, Indiana), October 1950.
"Love My Robot," in *Startling* (New York), November 1950.
"Rescue Beacon" (as Craig Browning), in *Other Worlds* (Evanston, Indiana), November 1950.
"These Are My Children," in *Other Worlds* (Evanston, Indiana), January, March 1951.
"You'll Die Yesterday," in *Amazing* (New York), March 1951.
"Secret of the Flaming Ring" (as P.F. Costello), in *Fantastic Adventures* (New York), March 1951.
"In What Dark Mind," in *Fantastic Adventures* (New York), April 1951.
"Vampire of the Deep," in *Amazing* (New York), May 1951.
"The Lurker," in *Fantastic* (New York), May 1951.
"The Man from Mars," in *Other Worlds* (Evanston, Indiana), May 1951.
"Who Sows the Wind," in *Amazing* (New York), June 1951.
"The President Will See You," in *Fantastic Adventures* (New York), July 1951.
"Step Out of Your Body, Please," in *Amazing* (New York), November 1951.
"Remember Not to Die!," in *Fantastic Adventures* (New York), November 1951.
"Checkmate for Aradjo," in *Amazing* (New York), December 1951.
"No Greater Wisdom," in *Amazing* (New York), January 1952.
"The Visitors," in *Amazing* (New York), February 1952.
"The Old Martians," in *If* (New York), March 1952.
"The Unfinished Equation" (as Robert Arnette), in *Fantastic Adventures* (New York), April 1952.
"A More Potent Weapon," in *Fantastic Adventures* (New York), April 1952.
"The World of Whispering Wings," in *Amazing* (New York), May 1952.
"Destiny Uncertain," in *Imagination* (Evanston, Illinois), May 1952.
"Black Angels Have No Wings," in *Amazing* (New York), August 1952.
"All the Answers," in *Science Fiction Quarterly* (Holyoke, Massachusetts), August 1952.
"The Man Who Lived Twice," in *Fantastic Adventures* (New York), August 1952.
"Adam's First Wife," in *Amazing* (New York), September 1952.
"I'll See You in My Dreams," in *Fantastic Adventures* (New York), September 1952.
"It's in the Cards," in *Fantastic Adventures* (New York), October 1952.
"It's Like This," in *Fantastic Story* (New York), November 1952.
"Visitors from Darkness," in *Amazing* (New York), December 1952.
"The Sorceress," in *Amazing* (New York), January 1953.
"Ye of Little Faith," in *If* (New York), January 1953.
"The Menace," in *Fantastic Adventures* (New York), February 1953.
"Your Funeral Is Waiting," in *Amazing* (New York), March 1953.
"The Lost Ego," in *Imagination* (Evanston, Illinois), April 1953.
"The Cyberene," in *Imagination* (Evanston, Illinois), September 1953.
"The Phantom Truckdriver," in *Amazing* (New York), September 1953.
"Pariah," in *Science Stories* (Evanston, Illinois), October 1953.
"From This Dark Mind," in *Fantastic* (New York), December 1953.
"The Cosmic Junkman," in *Imagination* (Evanston, Illinois), December 1953.

"Repeat Performance," in *Imagination* (Evanston, Illinois), January 1954.
"Teach Me to Kill," in *Amazing* (New York), June 1957.
"A Handful of Sand," in *Amazing* (New York), April 1957.
"Homestead," in *Fantasy and Science Fiction* (New York), August 1957.
"Executioner No. 43," in *Venture* (Concord, New Hampshire), September 1957.
"The Cosmic Trap" (as Gerald Vance), in *Fantastic* (New York), November 1957.
"World of Traitors," in *Fantastic* (New York), November 1957.
"Truckstop," in *Imaginative Tales* (Evanston, Illinois), November 1957.
"Captain Peabody," in *If* (New York), December 1957.
"Game Preserve," in *SF '58*, edited by Judith Merril. New York, Dell, 1958.
"Lefty Baker's Nuthouse," in *Imaginative Tales* (Evanston, Illinois), January 1958.
"Love Me, Love My--," in *Fantasy and Science Fiction* (New York), February 1958.
"Venusian, Get Out!," in *Amazing* (New York), April 1958.
"It's Better Not to Know," in *Fantastic* (New York), April 1958.
"Refueling Station," in *Imaginative Tales* (Evanston, Illinois), May 1958.
"Ground Leave Incident," in *Venture* (Concord, New Hampshire), May 1958.
"Space Is for Suckers" (as P.F. Costello), and "Prophecy, Inc.," in *Amazing* (New York), June 1958.
"Services, Inc.," in *Fantasy and Science Fiction* (New York), June 1958.
"Jason's Secret," in *Fantastic* (New York), September 1958.
"In This Dark Mind" (as Inez McGowan), in *Fantastic* (New York), September 1958.
"Unto the Nth Generation," in *Amazing* (New York), December 1958.
"Rat in the Skull," in *If* (New York), December 1958.
"The Yellow Pill," in *SF '59*, edited by Judith Merril. New York, Dell, 1959.
"The Gallery," in *Amazing* (New York), January 1959.
"The Creeper in the Dream," in *Fantastic* (New York), February 1959.
"Keepers in Space," in *Fantastic* (New York), April 1959.
"The Only One Who Lived," in *Fantastic* (New York), May 1959.
"Camouflage," in *Amazing* (New York), June 1959.
"But Who Knows Huer or Huen?" (Baker), in *Fantastic* (New York), November 1961.

Uncollected Short Stories as Peter Worth

"The Robot and the Pearly Gates," in *Amazing* (New York), January 1949.
"I Died Tomorrow," in *Fantastic Adventures* (New York), May 1949.
"Window to the Future," in *Amazing* (New York), May 1949.
"Lullaby," in *Amazing Annual* (New York), 1950.
"Null F," in *Fantastic Adventures* (New York), February 1950.
"The Master Ego," in *Fantastic Adventures* (New York), March 1951.
"The Imitators," in *Amazing* (New York), June 1951.

Uncollected Short Stories as Franklin Bahl

"Face Beyond the Veil," in *Fantastic Adventures* (New York), April 1950.
"The Justice of Tor," in *Fantastic Adventures* (New York), January 1951.
"Lady Killer," in *Amazing* (New York), February 1953.

*   *   *

Rog Phillips (the name by which Roger P. Graham was generally known to science-fiction readers) became a professional writer in his mid-thirties, after several years as a power plant engineer and shipyard welder, and quickly established himself as a prolific and reliable producer of pulp fiction. Phillips used many pseudonyms, including several house names.

Until 1950 Phillips wrote exclusively for the Ziff-Davis magazines; his SF and fantasy fiction appeared in *Amazing Stories* and *Fantastic Adventures*. Phillips wrote everything from featured novels to short stories and fillers. A large part of this output was routine work done to editorial order, but it was often a notch or two above the general level of quality in the magazines, and was very popular with the readers. The first work to attract wide attention was the novel, "So Shall Ye Reap." Starting with the premise that the five atomic bombs already exploded by 1947 had released enough radioactivity into the atmosphere to affect the genes of future generations, the novel offered a scenario of the next hundred and fifty years, in which mankind established an elaborate underground civilization and retreated from the Earth's surface. Although marred by polemical stretches and badly dated now, the story nevertheless has some effective scenes and an overall crude energy. A sequel, "Starship from Sirius," added human colonies on Mars and Venus and an insect-dominated Earth in the far future, and was quite different in tone from its predecessor.

Four memorable Phillips stories appeared in 1949. "M'Bong-Ah" was a novelette telling of the colonization of Venus and of the Earthman who became the natives' pawn in their resistance to the invasion. "Matrix" and "Beyond the Matrix of Time" together form a complex story of time paradox and alternate realities. *The Involuntary Immortals* is the story of a group of "accidental" immortals who band together to discover the source of their immortality and to protect themselves against the vengefulness of their own jealous relatives.

Starting in 1950 Rog Phillips's stories had begun to appear in a wider variety of magazines. "Rat in the Skull" is a memorable story of an experiment in rodent intelligence; "Ground Leave Incident" is a hard-boiled episode on a frontier planet; "Services, Inc." is an offbeat deal-with-the-Devil story. By far the most successful story Phillips ever wrote is "The Yellow Pill," a brief tale of multiple subjective realities.

—R.E. Briney

PIERCY, Marge. American. Born in Detroit, Michigan, 31 March 1936. Educated at the University of Michigan, Ann Arbor (Hopwood Award), B.A. 1957; Northwestern University, Evanston, Illinois, M.A. 1958. Member of the Visiting Faculty, Fine Arts Work Center, Provincetown, Massachusetts, 1976-77; Writer in Residence, College of the Holy Cross, Worcester, Massachusetts, 1976; held Butler Chair of Letters, State University of New York, Buffalo, 1977. Recipient: Borestone Mountain Poetry Award (twice); National Endowment for the Arts Fellowship, 1978. Agent: Lois Wallace, Wallace and Shiel Agency Inc., 177 East 70th Street, New York, New York 10021. Address: Box 943, Wellfleet, Massachusetts 02667, U.S.A.

SCIENCE-FICTION PUBLICATIONS

Novels

Dance the Eagle to Sleep. New York, Doubleday, 1970; London, W.H. Allen, 1971.
Woman on the Edge of Time. New York, Knopf, 1976; London, Women's Press, 1979.

OTHER PUBLICATIONS

Novels

Going Down Fast. New York, Simon and Schuster, 1969.
Small Changes. New York, Doubleday, 1973.

The High Cost of Living. New York, Harper, 1978; London, Women's Press, 1979.
Vida. New York, Summit, and London, Women's Press, 1980.

Play

The Last White Class, with Ira Wood (produced Northampton, Massachusetts, 1978). Trumansburg, New York, Crossing Press, 1979.

Verse

Breaking Camp. Middletown, Connecticut, Wesleyan University Press, 1968.
Hard Loving. Middletown, Connecticut, Wesleyan University Press, 1969.
A Work of Artifice. Detroit, Red Hanrahan Press, 1970.
4-Telling, with others. Trumansburg, New York, Crossing Press, 1971.
When the Drought Broke. Santa Barbara, California, Unicorn Press, 1971.
To Be of Use. New York, Doubleday, 1973.
Living in the Open. New York, Knopf, 1976.
The Twelve-Spoked Wheel Flashing. New York, Knopf, 1978.
The Moon Is Always Female. New York, Knopf, 1980.

Recordings: *Laying Down the Tower,* Black Box; *At the Core,* Watershed, 1978.

Other

The Grand Coolie Dam. Boston, New England Free Press, 1970(?).

* * *

Marge Piercy, best known for her brittle and compelling poetry, has published two thematically and stylistically innovative science fiction novels. It is unusual to find a poet turning to science fiction, and even more atypical to find a "radical feminist lesbian" poet writing science fiction.

Piercy is concerned both with the relationships between men and women and with a patriarchal society's notions of power and victimization that govern human interactions. In *Dance the Eagle to Sleep* she presents a society that mirrors the tense, violent late 1960's in the United States. Teenagers who feel programmed by a materialistic, war-loving society "drop out" to become part of a tribe of Indians, as their leader Corey calls them. Trying to establish relationships not based on power or stereotypes soon becomes impossible, however. Women are given no credence at councils; one warrior preaches peace while another urges violence. At first, then, the novel appears to be about hippies, drop outs, flower children, and communes. A few telling details reveal, however, that this is a parallel universe in that it is the 1960's gone mad. In this dystopia, for example, all young men are conscripted at age 19; rock music is used as a mind-control device. And in the final scenes of the novel, when the Indians attempt to take over New York, the National Guard and Special Forces hunt down the Indians and present the hunt as the latest television show. One Indian says, "we were right and wrong, but the system is all wrong." Thus, Piercy experiments with the notion of utopia and dystopia in this eerie parallel of the 1960's.

Woman on the Edge of Time takes the reader to the future to gain a perspective from which to view our own society. Society in 2137 AD is based on agricultural villages in which the family is composed of people related by love, not genes. Children are incubated until they are "born" to three "mothers" who can be male as well as female. To the villagers, this system rectifies the insularity caused by the nuclear family and frees women from their traditional role as sole child bearers and rearers. Not a "brave new world," the village is a pleasant utopia; there are no totalitarian controls on the individual, not even those of the family, as the villagers would assert. As in Wells's *Time Machine,* the reader is meant to identify with the traveller to this future, Connie, a 37-year-old Chicana. Since Connie is a patient in a mental hospital, however, the reader is faced with the problem of the reliability of the character: is Connie, in the best science-fiction tradition, a time traveller, or is she experiencing psychotic hallucinations? Connie is at once a character, Everywoman Who Suffers, Madwoman, and Time Traveller, and although she is too victimized to bear all these roles convincingly, she has her moment when she lashes out against the doctors who represent all the aspects of modern society that have victimized her. In a brief section, Connie mistakenly journies to an alternate future in which genetically altered women are kept in tiny apartments where they wait for the men who have contracted with the government for their sexual services. This dystopia contrasts with the village and allows Piercy to warn that our society's preoccupations could lead to a similar future. Piercy handles the language of the utopian future with the sensitivity that one might expect from a poet. Sexist language has disappeared; the pronouns "he" and "she" are replaced by "per."

Piercy's two experiments with science fiction are most successful when she presents clearly futuristic societies. In both novels, her characters are sometimes overloaded with polemical burdens, but they are also compelling and well developed—and certainly preferable to the one-dimensional characters who too often frequent science fiction.

—Kathryn L. Seidel

PIPER, H(enry) Beam.   American.   Born in Altoona, Pennsylvania, in 1904. Worked on the engineering staff of the Pennsylvania Railroad. *Died* (suicide) *11 November 1964.*

SCIENCE-FICTION PUBLICATIONS

Novels (series: Terran Federation)

Crisis in 2140, with John J. McGuire.   New York, Ace, 1957.
A Planet for Texans, with John J. McGuire.   New York, Ace, 1958.
Four-Day Planet (juvenile; Federation).   New York, Putnam, 1961.
Little Fuzzy (Federation).   New York, Avon, 1962.
Junkyard Planet (Federation).   New York, Putnam, 1963; as *The Cosmic Computer,* New York, Ace, 1964.
Space Viking (Federation).   New York, Ace, 1963; London, Sphere, 1978.
The Other Human Race (Federation).   New York, Avon, 1964; as *Fuzzy Sapiens,* New York, Ace, 1976.
Lord Kalvan of Otherwhen.   New York, Ace, 1965; as *Gunpowder God,* London, Sphere, 1978.
The Fuzzy Papers (omnibus).   New York, Doubleday, 1977.

Uncollected Short Stories (series: Paratime; Terran Federation)

"Time and Time Again," in *A Treasury of Science Fiction,* edited by Groff Conklin.   New York, Crown, 1948.
"The Mercenaries," in *Astounding* (New York), March 1950.
"Flight from Tomorrow," in *Future* (New York), September-October 1950.
"He Walked Around the Horses" (Paratime) and "Operation RSVP," in *World of Wonder,* edited by Fletcher Pratt.   New York, Twayne, 1951.
"Dearest," in *Weird Tales* (New York), March 1951.
"Temple Trouble" (Paratime), in *Astounding* (New York), April 1951.
"Day of the Moron," in *Astounding* (New York), September 1951.
"Ullr Uprising" (Federation), in *The Petrified Planet.*   New York, Twayne, 1952.
"Genesis," in *Shadow of Tomorrow,* edited by Frederik Pohl.   New York, Permabooks, 1953.
"Null-ABC," in *Astounding* (New York), February-March 1953.

"The Return," in *Astounding* (New York), January 1954.
"Time Crime" (Paratime), in *Astounding* (New York), February, March 1955.
"Last Enemy" (Paratime), in *The Astounding Science Fiction Anthology,* edited by John W. Campbell, Jr.   New York, Berkley, 1956.
"Police Operation" (Paratime), in *Space Police,* edited by Andre Norton.   Cleveland, World, 1956.
"The Edge of the Knife," in *Amazing* (New York), May 1957.
"The Keeper," in *Venture* (Concord, New Hampshire), July 1957.
"Graveyard of Dreams" (Federation), in *Galaxy* (New York), February 1958.
"Ministry of Disturbance," in *Astounding* (New York), December 1958.
"Hunter Patrol," in *Amazing* (New York), May 1959.
"Crossroads of Destiny," in *Fantastic Universe* (Chicago), July 1959.
"The Answer," in *Fantastic Universe* (Chicago), July 1959.
"Oomphel in the Sky" (Federation), in *Astounding* (New York), November 1960.
"Omnilingual," in *Prologue to Analog,* edited by John W. Campbell, Jr.   New York, Doubleday, 1962.
"A Slave Is a Slave" (Federation), in *Astounding* (New York), April 1962.
"Down Styphon!," in *Astounding* (New York), November 1965.

OTHER PUBLICATIONS

Novel

Murder in the Gunroom.   New York, Knopf, 1953.

Other

Editor, *A Catalogue of Early Pennsylvania and Other Firearms and Edged Weapons at "Restless Oaks," McElhattan, Pennsylvania.*   Privately printed, 1927 (?).

*   *   *

H. Beam Piper's science fiction is largely the stories of heroes (or heroines), with ideas apparently subordinate to the needs of plot and action. This is most evident in novels such as *A Planet for Texans, Four-Day Planet, Space Viking,* and *Lord Kalvan of Otherwhen.* The last two of these, especially, are fast-paced adventure yarns, with a well-developed central figure, but quite two-dimensional supporting characters. In each case, the hero (Calvin Morrison in *Lord Kalvan of Otherwhen,* Lucas Trask in *Space Viking*) is forced by circumstances totally beyond his control to enter a life radically different from the one that he had anticipated. A major difficulty each man must resolve is the ethical dilemma of the life which he perceives as central to his functioning. Thus, Morrison is caught in the field of an interdimension/time travel machine, while Trask on his wedding day has his bride-to-be killed by her rejected suitor. Morrison must agonize about the appropriateness of introducing more sophisticated weaponry into an essentially static culture, Trask the ethics of killing and looting even though the attached planets are decadent remnants of the "Old Federation." The ultimate results of the activities of each man are intrinsically the same as well: Morrison defeats Styphon's House (which opposed progress and sought to divide countries against one another) while Trask defeats the destructive forces both on Marduk and among the space vikings, establishing Tanith as a progressive planet which is destined to lead a new League of Civilized Worlds.

Perhaps his most famous works are *Little Fuzzy* and *The Other Human Race. Little Fuzzy* builds toward a dramatic courtroom scene in which good and evil clearly clash over the question of the sapience of the Fuzzies. Again there is a central heroic figure, Jack Holloway, discoverer of the Fuzzies. The ethical dilemma to be resolved is whether to recognize the Fuzzies as sentient, giving them *prima facie* right to their own planet and thereby displacing the human interests on the planet Zarathustra, or to allow them to be treated as charming and quick-to-learn animals, subjecting them to what is—for a sentient being—slavery. Holloway's determination and courage in the face of the bureaucratic opposition to the recognition of the Fuzzies as sentient has elements of the heroic physical challenges confronting Morrison and Trask, but it is primarily a moral courage in the face of social opposition. In *The Other Human Race* the same basic problem is repeated except that the ethical dilemma is whether or not to honor the governmental commitment to the Fuzzy Reservation in the face of economic pressures to open the Reservation for mining. There is the added problem of the radical increase in defective births among the Fuzzies. The apparently neutral position of doing nothing about Fuzzy rights is extensionally the same as the decision to exterminate the Fuzzy race, for the humans have it within their power to halt the flood of defective Fuzzy births. Again, in both books, the resolution of the ethical dilemma leaves the world rather significantly altered in the direction of progress-as-we-know-it.

A side light which many be of significant interest has to do with the name of the Fuzzies' planet—Zarathustra, the name of the central figure in the pre-Christian middle-Eastern religion Zoroastrianism (Zoroaster was also known as Zarathustra), similar to the Christian Manichean heresy, which argues the existence of two co-equal forces in the universe, Ahura Mazda (good) and Angra Mainyu (evil). An interesting speculation is that Piper was consciously trying to depict such a struggle in the Fuzzies novels. The planet's name might also have been an allusion to Friedrich Nietzsche's *Also Sprach Zarathustra.* This interpretation offers a potentially convoluted approach to the text because Nietzsche argued for the recognition of man *and superman.* Since the superman is exempt from the constraints of normal ethics, one might have expected a different conclusion.

Piper's other writings more or less follow the same pattern: the hero/heroine is struck by a major ethical problem—paternalism over a proud people in *A Planet for Texans;* revolution or economic slavery in *Four-Day Planet;* human dependency upon its own machines in *Junkyard Planet;* the dominance of scholarship by economics in "Omnilingual." In each case the protagonist chooses honor and decency, but also, more significantly, the choice is made for progress. Those forces which support the status quo are doomed from the outset. In a Piper story one "knows" that the hero/heroine will prevail, but only after terrible difficulties. More impressive, however, is Piper's recognition that such successes must result in a significant alteration of the world on which they occur. Although Piper's works will never get him classed as a great writer, they certainly would get him listed as one whom the reader enjoys.

—Richard W. Miller

PISERCHIA, Doris (Elaine). American. Born in Fairmont, West Virginia, 11 October 1928. Educated at Fairmont State College, A.B. 1950; University of Utah, Salt Lake City, 1963-65. Served in the United States Navy, 1950-54: Lieutenant. Married Joseph John Piserchia in 1953; three daughters and two sons. Agent: E.J. Carnell Literary Agency, Rowneybury Bungalow, Sawbridgeworth, near Old Harlow, Essex CM20 2EX, England. Address: c/o DAW Books, New American Library, P. O. Box 120, Bergenfield, New Jersey 07621, U.S.A.

SCIENCE-FICTION PUBLICATIONS

Novels

Mister Justice. New York, Ace, 1973; London, Dobson, 1977.
Star Rider. New York, Bantam, 1974.
A Billion Days of Earth. New York, Bantam, 1976; London, Dobson, 1977.
Earthchild. New York, DAW, 1977; London, Dobson, 1979.
Spaceling. New York, Doubleday, 1978; London, Dobson, 1980.
The Spinner. New York, DAW, 1980.

Uncollected Short Stories

"Rocket to Gehenna," in *Fantastic* (New York), September 1966.
"Sheltering Dream," in *The Best Science Fiction for 1972,* edited by Frederik Pohl. New York, Ace, 1972.
"Last Train from Earth," in *If* (New York), August 1972.
"Empty Eden," in *If* (New York), December 1972.
"Half the Kingdom," in *Orbit 12,* edited by Damon Knight. New York, Putnam, 1973.
"Unbiased God," in *Galaxy* (New York), December 1973.
"1010," and "Naked and Afraid I Go," in *Orbit 13,* edited by Damon Knight. New York, Putnam, 1974.
"Limited Accommodations," in *Crisis,* edited by Roger Elwood. Nashville, Nelson, 1974.
"Quarantine," in *The Best from Galaxy 2.* New York, Award, 1974.
"Pale Hands," in *Orbit 15,* edited by Damon Knight. New York, Harper, 1974.
"Substance and Shadow," in *Galaxy* (New York), May 1974.
"Nature's Children," in *Galaxy* (New York), September 1974.
"A Typical Day," in *Best SF 1974,* edited by Harry Harrison and Brian Aldiss. Indianapolis, Bobbs Merrill, and London, Sphere, 1975.
"A Brilliant Curiosity," in *Orbit 16,* edited by Damon Knight. New York, Harper, 1975.
"Deathrights Deferred," in *Science Fiction Discoveries,* edited by Frederik and Carol Pohl. New York, Bantam, 1976.

* * *

Doris Piserchia began her science-fiction writing career in the 1960's, at the time when the New Wave was becoming well-established in Britain, and when science-fiction editors were just beginning to seek out new women writers. Piserchia's work very much identifies her as a writer of this period in that it shares the New Wave fascination with the "soft" sciences (such as sociology and psychology) rather than the "hard" (technological) sciences, it experiments with complicated literary techniques, and, in common with the work of other women writers making a start at this time, it makes a point of being as tough and brutal as the writing of any male science-fiction writer.

Piserchia's first story, "Rocket to Gehenna," reveals a light, humorous side of Piserchia which is very rarely seen in the rest of her work. Significantly, this story shows Piserchia using the epistolary form, not frequently employed by science-fiction writers, as she tells the story of an official whose system of disposing of corpses on uninhabited planets breaks down when a planet supposed to be lifeless turns out to host one very zany resident. This concern with systems getting out of control dominates Piserchia's later work. In her first novel, *Mister Justice,* Piserchia criticizes a faulty judicial system mired in case backlogs and hampered by its own checks and balances; then she proceeds to relate the story of a super-intelligent individual who, motivated by revenge, and utilizing his ability to travel through time, takes justice into his own hands and literally executes those he has judged guilty of crimes. While the author is critical of Mister Justice's Hammurabi-style notion of crime and punishment, the reader finds his actions to be the most comprehensible element in a novel of unease which supposes that all systems are unreliable and apt to be turned against the individual; even time itself is manipulable by the "gifted" few. In a world where time and circumstance are unsteady, where morality is nowhere to be found, where identities are always in question, the concept of "justice" is almost ludicrous. Even lovers—memorably exemplified in Godiva, a human "black widow" who mates with men only to crush and kill them—are apt to be very accomplished traitors. This is an ambitious, overly complex novel; absorbed in her theme of systems gone out of control, the author at times loses control of the narrative itself, actually causing confusion about character identity, yet *Mister Justice* is remarkable for some fine, almost poetic treatment of the concept of time travel.

Star Rider describes another scenario of paranoia in which questions of identity and control over one's own life are central. This narrative, too, is burdened by an excessively complex plot, but it does feature some superior moments of dialogue, as in a brilliantly understated scene where the heroine views a new world for the first time ("What do you see down there in that Village?" "Building." "I see a flat lack of imagination"). A clever gimmick is the pivot of this story: "jinking," described as "When you jinked, you got a thing up close and swarmed all over it with your mind," is a process (vaguely reminiscent of Heinlein's "grokking"). The heroine is a spunky star-hopper who travels with her "mount," a creature suggestive of a horse capable of galloping among worlds. The heroine's very identity is shaken when she is forced to separate from her "mount."

Questions of identity are also essential to *Spaceling*, the story of a headstrong yet appealing adolescent girl who, as "muter," has the ability to move into parallel spheres of reality. *Earthchild* focuses upon another female protagonist facing adventure and challenge. Reee, apparently the last surviving human on a very changed planet Earth (protoplasmic ocean, dangerous plants) must deal with the return to Earth of humans who had fled to Mars and who are now eager to desolate their motherworld. *A Billion Days of Earth* shows more descendents of man revisiting a brutally chaotic Earth, in this case only to flee from it and the powerful creature Sheen who dominates the harsh world. *The Spinner* is a direct descendent of her literature of unease. This study in paranoia features a monster of comic-strip proportions and behavior: a giant invincible blue spider of alien origin horrifically overtakes a metropolis. The story concludes that society is threatened not only by the alien but from within itself.

Piserchia is an imaginative New Wave writer whose grim scenarios for the future reveal criticism of social conditions or systems universal in the world of man.

—Rosemary Herbert

PLATT, Charles. British. Born in Hertfordshire, 25 October 1944. Educated at Cambridge University, one year, and London College of Printing, two years. Worked for Clive Bingley, publishers, London, 1967; designer and production assistant, *New Worlds* magazine; free-lance photographer and book jacket designer. Address: c/o New Worlds, 271 Portobello Road, London W.11, England.

SCIENCE-FICTION PUBLICATIONS

Novels

The Garbage World. New York, Berkley, 1967; London, Panther, 1968.
The City Dwellers. London, Sidgwick and Jackson, 1970; revised edition, as *Twilight of the City*, New York, Macmillan, 1977.
Planet of the Voles. New York, Putnam, 1971.
Sweet Evil. New York, Berkley, 1977.

Uncollected Short Stories

"One of Those Days," in *Science Fantasy* (Bournemouth), January 1965.
"Cultural Invasion," in *New Worlds* (London), November 1965.
"The Failures," in *New Worlds* (London), January 1966.
"A Taste of the Afterlife," in *New Worlds* (London), September 1966.
"The Total Experience Kick," in *The Best SF Stories from New Worlds 2*, edited by Michael Moorcock. London, Panther, and New York, Berkley, 1968.
"The Disaster Story," in *The Best SF Stories from New Worlds 3*, edited by Michael Moorcock. London, Panther, and New York, Berkley, 1968.
"Direction," in *The New SF*, edited by Langdon Jones. London, Hutchinson, 1969.

"The Rodent Laboratory," in *The Best SF Stories from New Worlds 5*, edited by Michael Moorcock. London, Panther, and New York, Berkley, 1969.
"Id," in *New Worlds* (London), March 1969.
"Lone Zone," in *The Best SF Stories from New Worlds 7*, edited by Michael Moorcock. London, Panther, 1971.
"Norman vs. America" (cartoon), in *Quark 4*, edited by Samuel R. Delany and Marilyn Hacker. New York, Paperback Library, 1971.
"A Cleansing of the System," in *New Worlds Quarterly 3*, edited by Michael Moorcock. London, Sphere, 1971; New York, Berkley, 1972.
"New York Times," in *Orbit 11*, edited by Damon Knight. New York, Putnam, 1973.
"Family Literature" and "The Motivation Chart," in *New Worlds Quarterly 5*, edited by Michael Moorcock. London, Sphere, 1973.
"The Coldness," in *New Worlds 6*, edited by Michael Moorcock and Charles Platt. London, Sphere, 1973; as *New Worlds 5*, New York, Avon, 1974.

OTHER PUBLICATIONS

Verse

Highway Sandwiches, with Thomas M. Disch and Marilyn Hacker. Privately printed, 1970.
The Gas. New York, Ophelia Press, 1970.

Other

"The Disaster Story," in *New Worlds* (London), March 1966.
"Expressing the Abstract," in *New Worlds* (London), July 1967.
"Fun Palace—Not a Freakout," in *New Worlds* (London), March 1968.
"The Responsive Environment," in *New Worlds* (London), May 1969.

Editor, with Michael Moorcock, *New Worlds 6.* London, Sphere, 1973; as *New Worlds 5*, New York, Avon, 1974.
Editor, with Hilary Bailey, *New Worlds 7.* London, Sphere, 1974; as *New Worlds 6*, New York, Avon, 1975.

*   *   *

The science fiction written by the old *New Worlds* writers, of whom Charles Platt is a prolific and representative specimen, tends towards the antithesis of the scenario in which a macho hero saves (and preserves in an unchanged or improved state) the world from an alien threat before setting blasters for home, a beautiful but useless girl at his side. Theirs is the science fiction of despair looking to a future where things are inevitably worse. Their pet threats are those implicit in human or cosmic nature, and their totem motif is the inexorable unwinding of the universal mainspring. The entropy in Platt's fiction is the disorder created by the breakdown of the social mechanism rather than the heat death of the universe. His two major novels, *The Garbage World* and *The City Dwellers* (rewritten, with added love interest, as *Twilight of the City*), both concentrate on people coming to terms with the collapse, or loss of meaning, of the system which produced them.

In *The Garbage World* a two-man team arrive, ostensibly to repair a defective gravity generator but actually to blow up Kopra, the rubbish tip of the Asteroid Belt; its inhabitants, as befits the planet's name, pursue the anal pleasures of establishing pecking orders and hoarding trash in a landscape of shanty towns, stinking swamps, and gigantic mutated slugs, with a miserable climate exacerbated by a constant rain of space-going garbage packs. One of the new arrivals is converted to their insalubrious but unrepressed lifestyle, having fallen for the head man's dirty daughter; and after sundry erotic and other adventures in the sewerlike backwaters of the planet, both Kopra and the other official (clean-handed but dirty-dealing) are messily blown up, smothering the pleasures of the pleasure worlds of the Asteroid belt in a shower of excrement.

The City Dwellers has undergone several mutations between appearing as a series of disconnected short stories in *New Worlds* and being completely unified into *Twilight of the City.* This increase in order defies the second law of thermodynamics, but the story in all its forms goes along with it, forsaking the metaphor of *The Garbage World* in an attempt to depict with prophetic realism the degeneration of organised society. Trendy, hip characters from the pulsating, neon-lit heart of the city are forced, as the beat runs down, to abandon the twitching carcass and scrape an existence in the hostile countryside, finally returning to the rotting corpse to exterminate the last few worms which prey upon it.

There are no hairy-chested heroes in shiny suits and boots in Platt's novels. Even in *Planet of the Voles,* most space-operatic of his books, the protagonist struggles in hunger, rags, and filth through a hostile environment to confront a feared enemy and find it (although still an implacable enemy) jewelled, perfumed, and closer to him than he at first supposed. Platt's real heroes are small-time misfits: the coprotropic official of *The Garbage World,* the "socially inept" songwriter of *Twilight of the City,* the artist and the runt of the artificially reared crew of military men in *Planet of the Voles.* They survive where the perfect specimens bite the dust, and in adjusting to the filth and pollution of the rubbish tip or the hardship of scraping a living on the land rapidly come to find, if not happiness, at least substance in the unsynthesised pleasures of life away from the glitter of the civilised artifice. The immaculate white gloves and the rhinestone-studded suit are well lost for such a reward. It is not optimism, but when the cake has been snatched away it is a crumb of consolation.

—Lee Montgomerie

POHL, Frederik. Also writes as James MacCreigh; Edson McCann; Jordan Park. American. Born in New York City, 26 November 1919. Served in the United States Air Force, in the United States and Italy, 1943-45: Sergeant. Married 1)Doris Baumgardt in 1940 (divorced, 1944); 2) Dorothy DesTina in 1945 (divorced, 1947); 3) Judith Merril, *q.v.,* in 1949 (divorced, 1953), one daughter; 4) Carol Metcalf Ulf in 1952, two sons (one deceased) and one daughter. Editor, Popular Publications, New York, 1939-43; copywriter, Thwing and Altman, New York, 1946; Book Editor and Associate Circulation Manager, Popular Science Publication Company, New York, 1946-49; literary agent, New York, 1949-53; Feature Editor, later Editor, *If,* New York, 1959-70; Editor, Galaxy Publishing Company, New York, 1961-69; Executive Editor, Ace Books, New York, 1971-72. Since 1973, Science Fiction Editor, Bantam Books, New York. Since 1976, Contributing Editor, *Algol,* New York. Since 1966, Member of the Executive Board, Monmouth County Civil Liberties Union, and of the Board of Directors, New York City Opera. President, Science Fiction Writers of America, 1974-76. Recipient: Edward E. Smith Memorial Award, 1966; Hugo Award, 1973, 1978; *Locus* Award, 1973, 1978; Nebula Award, 1976, 1977; Campbell Memorial Award, 1978; American Book Award, 1980. Guest of Honor, World Science Fiction Convention, 1972. Agent: Robert P. Mills Ltd., 156 East 52nd Street, New York, New York 10022. Address: 386 West Front Street, Red Bank, New Jersey 07701, U.S.A.

SCIENCE-FICTION PUBLICATIONS

Novels (series: Jim Eden; Starchild)

The Space Merchants, with C.M. Kornbluth. New York, Ballantine, 1953; London, Heinemann, 1955.
Search the Sky, with C.M. Kornbluth. New York, Ballantine, 1954; London, Digit, 1960.
Undersea Quest (juvenile; Eden), with Jack Williamson. New York, Gnome Press, 1954; London, Dobson, 1966.
Preferred Risk (as Edson McCann, with Lester del Rey). New York, Simon and Schuster, 1955.
Gladiator-at-Law, with C.M. Kornbluth. New York, Ballantine, 1955; London, Digit, 1958.
Undersea Fleet (juvenile; Eden), with Jack Williamson. New York, Gnome Press, 1956; London, Dobson, 1968.
Slave Ship. New York, Ballantine, 1957; London, Dobson, 1961.
Undersea City (juvenile; Eden), with Jack Williamson. New York, Gnome Press, 1958; London, Dobson, 1968.
Wolfbane, with C.M. Kornbluth. New York, Ballantine, 1959; London, Gollancz, 1961.
Drunkard's Walk. New York, Ballantine, 1960; revised edition, London, Gollancz, 1961.
The Starchild Trilogy, with Jack Williamson. New York, Pocket Books, 1977; London, Penguin, 1980.
    The Reefs of Space. New York, Ballantine, 1964; London, Dobson, 1965.
    Starchild. New York, Ballantine, 1964; London, Dobson, 1966.
    Rogue Star. New York, Ballantine, 1969; London, Dobson, 1972.
A Plague of Pythons. New York, Ballantine, 1965; London, Gollancz, 1966.
The Age of the Pussyfoot. New York, Simon and Schuster, 1969; London, Gollancz, 1970.
Farthest Star, with Jack Williamson. New York, Ballantine, 1975; London, Pan, 1976.
Man Plus. New York, Random House, and London, Gollancz, 1976.
Gateway. New York, St. Martin's Press, and London, Gollancz, 1979.
Jem: The Making of a Utopia. New York, St. Martin's Press, and London, Gollancz, 1979.
Beyond the Blue Event Horizon. New York, Ballantine, and London, Gollancz, 1980.
The Cool War. New York, Ballantine, 1980.

Short Stories

Danger Moon (as James MacCreigh). Sydney, American Science Fiction, 1953.
Alternating Currents. New York, Ballantine, 1956; London, Penguin, 1966.
The Case Against Tomorrow. New York, Ballantine, 1957.
Tomorrow Times Seven. New York, Ballantine, 1959.
The Man Who Ate the World. New York, Ballantine, 1960; London, Panther, 1979.
Turn Life at Thursday. New York, Ballantine, 1961.
The Wonder Effect, with C.M. Kornbluth. New York, Ballantine, 1962; London, Gollancz, 1967; revised edition, as *Critical Mass,* New York, Bantam, 1977.
The Abominable Earthman. New York, Ballantine, 1963.
The Frederik Pohl Omnibus. London, Gollancz, 1966; reprinted in part, as *Survival Kit,* London, Panther, 1979.
Digits and Dastards (includes essays). New York, Ballantine, 1966; London, Dobson, 1968.
Day Million. New York, Ballantine, 1970; London, Gollancz, 1971.
The Best of Frederik Pohl. New York, Doubleday, 1975; London, Sidgwick and Jackson, 1977.
In the Problem Pit. New York, Bantam, and London, Corgi, 1976.
The Early Pohl. New York, Doubleday, 1976; London, Dobson, 1980.

Uncollected Short Stories

"Rem the Rememberer," in *Cosmos* (New York), May 1977.
"Swanilda's Song," in *Analog* (New York), October 1978.
"Mars Masked," in *Isaac Asimov's Science Fiction Magazine* (New York), March 1979.
"Like unto the Locust," in *Isaac Asimov's Science Fiction Magazine* (New York), December, January 1979-80.

OTHER PUBLICATIONS

Novels

A Town Is Drowning, with C.M. Kornbluth. New York, Ballantine, 1955; London, Digit, 1960.
Presidential Year, with C.M. Kornbluth. New York, Ballantine, 1956.
Sorority House (as Jordan Park, with C.M. Kornbluth). New York, Lion, 1956.
Edge of the City (novelization of screenplay). New York, Ballantine, 1957.
The Man of Cold Rages (as Jordan Park, with C.M. Kornbluth). New York, Pyramid, 1958.

Other

"Long John Nebel and the Woodlouse," in *Library Journal* (New York), 1 November 1956.
Practical Politics 1972. New York, Ballantine, 1971.
"On Velocity Exercises," in *Those Who Can,* edited by Robin Scott Wilson. New York, New American Library, 1973.
"The Publishing of Science Fiction," in *Science Fiction, Today and Tomorrow,* edited by Reginald Bretnor. New York, Harper, 1974.
The Way the Future Was: A Memoir. New York, Ballantine, 1978; London, Gollancz, 1979.

Editor, *Beyond the End of Time.* New York, Permabooks, 1952.
Editor, *Shadow of Tomorrow.* New York, Permabooks, 1953.
Editor, *Star Science Fiction Stories 1-6.* New York, Ballantine, 6 vols., 1953-59; vols. 1 and 2, London, Boardman, 1954-55.
Editor, *Assignment in Tomorrow.* New York, Hanover House, 1954.
Editor, *Star Short Novels.* New York, Ballantine, 1954.
Editor, *Star of Stars.* New York, Doubleday, 1960; as *Star Fourteen,* London, Whiting and Wheaton, 1966.
Editor, *The Expert Dreamers.* New York, Doubleday, 1962; London, Gollancz, 1963.
Editor, *Time Waits for Winthrop and Four Other Short Novels from Galaxy.* New York, Doubleday, 1962.
Editor, *The Seventh* [through *Eleventh*] *Galaxy Reader.* New York, Doubleday, 5 vols., 1964-69; *Seventh* through *Tenth,* London, Gollancz, 4 vols., 1965-68; *Eighth,* as *Final Encounter,* New York, Curtis, 1970; *Tenth,* as *Door to Anywhere,* New York, Curtis, 1970.
Editor, *The If Reader of Science Fiction.* New York, Doubleday, 1966; London, Whiting and Wheaton, 1967; second volume, New York, Doubleday, 1968.
Editor, *Nightmare Age.* New York, Ballantine, 1970.
Editor, *The Best Science Fiction for 1972.* New York, Ace, 1972.
Editor, with Carol Pohl, *Science Fiction: The Great Years.* New York, Ace, 1973; London, Gollancz, 1974; second volume, Ace, 1976.
Editor, with Carol Pohl, *Jupiter.* New York, Ballantine, 1973.
Editor, *The Science Fiction Roll of Honor.* New York, Random House, 1975.
Editor, with Carol Pohl, *Science Fiction Discoveries.* New York, Bantam, 1976.
Editor, *The Best of C.M. Kornbluth.* New York, Doubleday, 1976.
Editor, with Martin H. Greenberg and Joseph D. Olander, *Science Fiction of the 40's.* New York, Avon, 1978.
Editor, with Martin H. Greenberg and Joseph D. Olander, *Galaxy Magazine: Thirty Years of Innovative Science-Fiction Publishing.* Chicago, Playboy Press, 1980.
Editor, *Nebula Award Winners 14.* New York, Harper, 1980.
Editor, with Martin H. Greenberg and Joseph D. Olander, *The Great Science Fiction Series.* New York, Harper, 1980.

*

Manuscript Collection: Syracuse University Library, New York.

*   *   *

One major figure in science fiction whose work shows significant improvement over time, Frederik Pohl combines in his best work technical extrapolation with narrative complexity, penetrating social commentary, and a distinctive sardonic style. His earliest work is forgettable, but the publication of *The Space Merchants* in 1953 identified him (with his collaborator C.M. Kornbluth) as a leading science-fiction satirist. This future dystopia run by advertising agencies is the subject of a tongue-in-cheek tall tale which chronicles the fall from grace of the ad executive Mitchell Courtenay, who survives peon labor and addictive rations to convert to the "Consies" (Conservationists) and subvert the admen's scheme to develop Venus as a dumping ground for excess production and population. With sometimes manic humor, the novel moves swiftly to its climax, side-swiping venerable social institutions and incorporating a routine love-story subplot. Pohl and Kornbluth continued to collaborate, with mixed results. *Gladiator-at-Law* took on the legal profession, *Search the Sky* attacked isolationism in an interplanetary setting, and *Wolfbane* was an occasionally chilling variation on the theme of aliens ruling human zombies. Their short story collaborations have perhaps been over-praised. Another dystopian collaboration, with Lester del Rey, is *Preferred Risk,* a lackluster exposé of dictatorship by worldwide insurance companies.

Pohl's partnership with Jack Williamson began in the 1950's with three formula-perfect juvenile adventure stories, *Undersea Quest, Undersea Fleet,* and *Undersea City,* which depend overmuch on coincidence and derring-do and black-and-white characterizations. The partnership also wrote *The Starchild Trilogy,* a straightforward if tedious entertainment without Pohl's verbal economy and social immediacy. A little more Pohlish was *Farthest Star,* with character replications, multi-race starship, and distant artificial planet, but it has a Williamsonian wandering plot with multiple crises and undistinguished characterizations.

In his short stories of the 1950's Pohl satirized American consumer society, making individual variations in economic planning ("Rafferty's Reasons"), social stratification ("My Lady Greensleeves"), and population stabilization ("The Census Takers") turn conventional expectations upside down. Of these "comic infernos," the first to gain attention was "The Midas Plague" in which increasing status accrues to people who consume less in an overproducing economy. This story is even more of a tall tale than *The Space Merchants,* with complications deliberately multiplied for comic effect, satirizing those who think that affluence is infinite. Best of the "consumer cycle" is "The Tunnel under the World," a horror story based on penetrating insight into social manipulation by commercial interests. Recognizing that the same day keeps being repeated with new and more jarring advertisements, Guy Burckhardt discovers he is imprisoned in a tiny automation, at the mercy of controlled experiments by a marketing research firm. The motif of mind manipulation, derived in part from experience in advertising and sales, continues through Pohl's work.

Less effective are Pohl's first book-length novels. He explores communication with animals in *Slave Ship,* satirizes higher education in *Drunkard's Walk,* and returns to the horrors of mind control in *A Plague of Pythons.* Just short of a comic masterpiece, *The Age of the Pussyfoot* is a futurist's fable of how a man reborn from cryogenic freezing finds that a continually progressing world is not his oyster.

Also significant in the 1960's were Pohl's minimal stories with little plot or dialogue. "The Martian Stargazers" derives Martians' race suicide from their astrological lore. "Speed Trap" shows how the honors and trappings of a scientist's success thwart future creativity. Pohl perfected the form in "Day Million," a "love story" of the far future when "boy" and "girl" and "marriage" have been redefined.

Pohl's consistently best work emerged in the 1970's. "The Merchants of Venus" has adventure and a happy ending, but the real interest is in the setting, the hellish Venus of modern astronomy, and a socio-economic situation little short of desperate. In "The Gold at the Starbow's End" a misfired experiment sends ten bright young people to explore a nonexistent planet orbiting Alpha Centaurus. Ten years of concentrated thinking turns them into supermen who create their own world and return to select colonists from a devastated Earth. "In the Problem Pit" shows how ordinary people in a "think-tank" might help society surmount intractable obstacles. "We Purchased People" is his finest treatment of mind control, based on the "sale" of human criminals to alien remote control in a deal which brings "backward" Earth trade with extra-terrestrial civilizations.

Man Plus chronicles unsqueamishly the transformation of man to meet conditions on Mars, narrated by man's computer network whose own survival is at stake. The venture's success involves great sacrifices for Roger Torraway, whose identity and self -control are stripped away in trade-offs which make him as much man-minus as man-plus. *Gateway* intertwines a literally mechanical Freudian analysis with a story of chance-ridden space exploration via ships left abandoned by aliens on the asteroid Gateway. Robinet Broad-head, the thoroughly dislikeable protagonist, is a palpable stand-in for human society, dependent for survival on a cosmic game of chance. Broadhead's self-confrontation, however, is potentially heroic, and the book's emotional content is as honest as its presentation is complex. *Jem* projects allegorically upon an alien planet the tripartite division of Earth society (productive of food, energy, and people), in conflict with three coexisting intelligent races of natives. The final amalgamation of all four races and all six life-styles in a less than utopian arrangement is once again threatened by contact with a human colony near Alpha Centaurus. A lumbering, unat-tractive book, *Jem* has some excellent scenes and passages and a dire message for mankind to cooperate or die. Like *Jem,* most of Pohl's later work deals with real problems and hard solutions in narrative structures that challenge the imagination as well as the intellect.

—David N. Samuelson

PORGES, Arthur. Also writes as Peter Arthur; Pat Rogers. American. Born in Chicago, Illinois, 20 August 1915. Educated at Illinois Institute of Technology, Chicago, B.S. 1940. Taught mathematics at Illinois Institute of Technology, De Paul University, Chicago, and Western Military Academy: retired, 1975.

SCIENCE-FICTION PUBLICATIONS

Uncollected Short Stories (series: Ensign De Ruyter)

"The Rats," in *The Best Science-Fiction Stories 1952,* edited by E.F. Bleiler and T.E. Dikty.   New York, Fell, 1952; London, Grayson, 1953.
"The Fly," in *The Best Science-Fiction Stories 1953,* edited by E.F. Bleiler and T.E. Dikty.   New York, Fell, 1953; London, Grayson, 1955.
"Story Conference," in *Fantasy and Science Fiction* (New York), May 1953.
"Strange Birth," in *Fantasy and Science Fiction* (New York), June 1953.
"The Liberator," in *Fantasy and Science Fiction* (New York), December 1953.
"The Unwilling Professor," in *Dynamic* (New York), January 1954.
"The Grom," in *Fantasy and Science Fiction* (New York), November 1954.
"Guilty as Charged," in *The Best Science Fiction Stories and Novels 1955,* edited by T.E. Dikty.   New York, Fell, 1955.
"The Ruum," in *Best SF,* edited by Edmund Crispin.   London, Faber, 1955.
"Mop-Up," in *Galaxy of Ghouls,* edited by Judith Merril.   New York, Lion, 1955.
"$1.98," in *The Best from Fantasy and Science Fiction 4,* edited by Anthony Boucher.   New York, Doubleday, 1955.
"The Tidings," in *Fantasy and Science Fiction* (New York), February 1955.
"The Box," in *Startling* (New York), Spring 1955.
"By a Fluke," in *Fantasy and Science Fiction* (New York), October 1955.

"The Logic of Rufus Weir," in *Fantasy and Science Fiction* (New York), November 1955.
"The Entity," in *Fantastic Universe* (Chicago), December 1955.
"Whirlpool," in *Fantastic Universe* (Chicago), March 1957.
"The Devil and Simon Flagg," in *Fantasia Mathematica,* edited by Clifton Fadiman.   New York, Simon and Schuster, 1958.
"What Crouches in the Deep," in *Fantastic* (New York), March 1959.
"A Touch of Sun," in *Fantastic* (New York), April 1959.
"The Forerunner," in *Fantastic* (New York), July 1959.
"The Shakespeare Manuscript," in *Fantastic* (New York), August 1959.
"Security," in *Amazing* (New York), September 1959.
"Off His Rocker," in *Fantastic* (New York), February 1960.
"A Specimen for a Queen," in *Fantasy and Science Fiction* (New York), May 1960.
"Night Quake" (as Pat Rogers) and "Josephus," in *Fear* (Concord, New Hampshire), May 1960.
"The Fiftieth Year of April," in *Fantastic* (New York), June 1960.
"The Crime of Mr. Saver," in *Fantastic* (New York), August 1960.
"The Shadowsmith," in *Fantastic* (New York), September 1960.
"The Auto Hawks," in *Amazing* (New York), September 1960.
"Words and Music," in *If* (New York), September 1960.
"A Diversion for the Baron," in *Fantastic* (New York), November 1960.
"The Radio" (as Peter Arthur) and "The Melanas," in *Fantastic* (New York), December 1960.
"Degree Candidate" (as Peter Arthur) and "Dr. Blackadder's Clients," in *Fantastic* (New York), January 1961.
"The Other Side," in *Fantastic* (New York), February 1961.
"Revenge," in *Amazing* (New York), February 1961.
"Mulberry Moon," in *Fantastic* (New York), April 1961.
"The Arrogant Vampire," in *Fantastic* (New York), May 1961.
"One Bad Habit," in *Fantastic* (New York), June 1961.
"Solomon's Demon," in *Fantastic* (New York), July 1961.
"Report on the Magic Shop," in *Fantastic* (New York), August 1961.
"A Devil of a Day," in *Fantastic* (New York), August 1962.
"Mozart Annuity," in *Fantastic* (New York), November 1962.
"Emergency Operation," in *Great Science Fiction about Doctors,* edited by Groff Conklin and Noah D. Fabricant.   New York, Macmillan, 1963.
"3rd Sister," in *Fantastic* (New York), January 1963.
"The Topper," in *Astounding* (New York), February 1963.
"Through Channels," in *Amazing* (New York), June 1963.
"The Formula," in *Amazing* (New York), July 1963.
"Controlled Experiment," in *Astounding* (New York), August 1963.
"The Rescuer," in *Yet More Penguin Science Fiction,* edited by Brian Aldiss.   London, Penguin, 1964.
"Time-Bomb," in *Fantasy and Science Fiction* (New York), June 1964.
"Urned Reprieve" (De Ruyter), in *Amazing* (New York), October 1964.
"The Fanatic," in *Fantastic* (New York), December 1964.
"The Moths," in *Amazing* (New York), December 1964.
"Problem Child," in *The Year's Best S-F 10,* edited by Judith Merril.   New York, Delacorte Press, 1965; London, Mayflower, 1967.
"Wheeler Dealer" (De Ruyter), in *Amazing* (New York), March 1965.
"Ensign De Ruyter, Dreamer," in *Amazing* (New York), April 1965.
"The Good Seed," in *Amazing* (New York), August 1965.
"Turning Point," in *Fantasy and Science Fiction* (New York), September 1965.
"A Civilized Community," in *Bizarre Mystery Magazine* (Concord, New Hampshire), October 1965.
"Dusty Answer" (De Ruyter), in *Amazing* (New York), October 1965.
"The Creep Brigade," in *Bizarre Mystery Magazine* (Concord, New Hampshire), November 1965.
"Pressure" (De Ruyter), in *Amazing* (New York), February 1966.
"Priceless Possession," in *Galaxy* (New York), June 1966.
"The Mirror," in *Fantasy and Science Fiction* (New York), October 1966.

"The Dragons of Tesla," in *Fantastic* (New York), October 1968.

*   *   *

Arthur Porges's fiction consists of some 70 short stories, often of 3,000 or fewer words. The corpus itself and many of the individual stories within it blend fantasy with science fiction. "Mop-Up," for instance, takes place in the realistic wreckage following a world war fought with atomic and biological weapons. Sharing what is left with the sole human survivor are a witch, a vampire, and a ghoul. Similarly, there appears to be no difference in feel or treatment between stories which are purely SF and others which are purely fantasy. Thus the djinn of "Solomon's Demon" and the robot specimen-gatherer of "The Ruum" are precisely equivalent in so far as the humans who come in contact with them are concerned: they are alien, enormously powerful, inexorable—and they must be stopped if the viewpoint characters are to survive.

The viewpoint character *doesn't* always survive a Porges story, a fact which contributes to the considerable tension of the best of them. The character does always struggle, however. The horror is not that caused by watching a man helpless in the face of the unknown; rather, it is aroused by seeing a strong and resourceful man overborne by a power or cunning still greater than his own. An excellent example of this is "The Rats," in which a lone man fights more-than-bestial rats against a backdrop of impending nuclear war. In his ultimate failure, the man turns over the world to antagonists who have proven themselves worthy at least to attempt to better Mankind's record.

Porges works against sharp, tersely drawn backgrounds; he has an enviable talent for choosing the right word or two which convinces a reader that the scene or character was written from life rather than merely studied. His work typically begins with a narrative hook which draws the reader into the body of the story. And even pedestrian stories are frequently enlivened by flashes of character which demonstrate a considerable depth of feeling. Regrettably, many of the stories *are* pedestrian. This is a result of their being based on gimmicks, often bits of scientific fact: parabolic reflectors concentrate light ("A Touch of Sun," "The Dragons of Tesla"); crickets chirp at a rate dependant on temperature ("The Formula"); a human body reduced to raw elements is of slight value ("$1.98"). While the development may be at least professional, only the gimmick itself is likely to stick in the reader's mind for any length of time. When the gimmick is integral to the story, however, the result can be extremely effective. "The Ruum" (humans can lose significant body weight by sweating) and "Solomon's Demon" (high voltage is harmless unless coupled with a path to ground) are striking examples of this synthesis; and "The Mirror," which turns on an analysis of multiple reflections, is a stunning horror story. If these are the exceptions, then in themselves they constitute a body which many writers must envy.

Despite his frequent use of factual gimmicks, Porges never neglects his characters. It is fitting that one of his last-published stories, "Priceless Possession," involves no gimmicks at all: only the question of what part of their souls three spacemen will pay to avoid losing a treasure which in money terms is priceless. This is not a sardonic story; and perhaps it is a story that is not without hope for humanity; but it is an indictment more damning than any shrill diatribe could have been. As if in summary of much of Porges's best work, men struggle but we cannot assume their victory; and our worst enemies may not be external to our hearts.

—David A. Drake

POURNELLE, Jerry (Eugene). Also writes as Wade Curtis. American. Born in Shreveport, Louisiana, 7 August 1933. Educated at the University of Iowa, Iowa City, 1953-54; University of Washington, Seattle, B.S. 1955, M.S. in statistics and systems engineering 1957, Ph.D. in psychology 1960, Ph.D. in political science

1964. Served in the United States Army 1950-52. Married Roberta Jane Isdell in 1959; four sons. Research Assistant, University of Washington Medical School, 1954-57; Aviation Psychologist and Systems Engineer, Boeing Corporation, Seattle, 1957-64; Manager of Special Studies, Aerospace Corporation, San Bernardino, California, 1964-65; Research Specialist and Proposal Manager, American Rockwell Corporation, 1965-66; Professor of Political Science, Pepperdine University, Los Angeles, 1966-69; Executive Assistant to the Mayor of Los Angeles, 1969-70. Since 1970, free-lance writer, lecturer, and consultant: regular contributor of non-fiction articles to *Galaxy*, 1974-78. President, Science Fiction Writers of America, 1974. Recipient: John W. Campbell Award, 1973; Evans-Freehafer Award, 1977. Fellow, Operations Research Society of America, and American Association for the Advancement of Science. Republic of Estonia Award of Honor, 1968; Officer, Military and Hospitaler Order of St. Lazarus of Jerusalem. Agent: Blassingame McCauley and Wood, 60 East 42nd Street, New York, New York 10017. Address: 12051 Laurel Terrace, Studio City, California 91604, U.S.A.

SCIENCE-FICTION PUBLICATIONS

Novels (series: Falkenberg; Second Empire)

A Spaceship for the King (Empire).   New York, DAW, 1973.
Escape from the Planet of the Apes (novelization of screenplay). New York, Award, 1973.
The Mote in God's Eye (Empire), with Larry Niven.   New York, Simon and Schuster, 1974; London, Weidenfeld and Nicolson, 1975.
Birth of Fire.   Toronto, Laser, 1976; New York, Pocket Books, 1978.
Inferno, with Larry Niven.   New York, Pocket Books, 1976; London, Wingate, 1977.
West of Honor (Falkenberg).   Toronto, Laser, 1976; New York, Pocket Books, 1978.
The Mercenary (Falkenberg).   New York, Simon and Schuster, 1977.
Lucifer's Hammer, with Larry Niven.   Chicago, Playboy Press, 1977.
Exiles to Glory.   New York, Ace, 1978.
Janissaries.   New York, Ace, 1980; London, Dobson 1981.

Short Stories

High Justice.   New York, Simon and Schuster, 1977.

Uncollected Short Story

"Spirals," with Larry Niven, in *Destinies* (New York), April-June 1979.

OTHER PUBLICATIONS

Novels as Wade Curtis

Red Heroin.   New York, Berkley, 1969.
Red Dragon.   New York, Berkley, 1971.

Other

The Strategy of Technology: Winning the Decisive War, with Stefan T. Possony.   New York, Dunellen, 1970.
"The Construction of Believable Societies," in *The Craft of Science Fiction*, edited by Reginald Bretnor.   New York, Harper, 1976.
A Step Further Out.   London, Weidenfeld and Nicolson, 1980.

Editor, *20/20 Vision*.   New York, Avon, 1974.
Editor, *Black Holes*.   New York, Fawcett, 1979.

Jerry Pournelle comments:
My work is intended to entertain. I may well have a serious message, but in my judgment fiction is best served if the characters in a story do not know they have a message to deliver. Science-

fiction writers are bards of the sciences; we are not fundamentally different from the bards of Homeric times, who would travel about and, spying an encamped group, say, "If you'll fill my cup with wine and dish me a bowl of stew, I will tell you a story about a virgin and a bull that you just wouldn't believe...."

* * *

Jerry Pournelle's science fiction has consistently portrayed technological advance as the most significant visible indication of mankind's progress. The most obvious form of benevolent innovation is the development of space travel, and eight of his novels involve space travel. This theme is particularly evident in *A Spaceship for the King*, in which the salvation of an entire world rests upon its ability to develop rapidly a spacefaring technology. In *Exiles to Glory* humanity is jolted out of its introverted and short-sighted doldrums by a space effort financed by commercial organizations. The Martian colony in *Birth of Fire* is entirely dependent on advanced equipment from Earth for its very existence.

Pournelle also frequently expresses admiration for the professional military man. Colonel Nathan MacKinnie, the protagonist of *A Spaceship for the King*, is a cashiered veteran unable to function properly within the military organization of his world. *Janissaries* concerns a small group of professional soldiers kidnapped from Earth by aliens unwilling to fight their own battles. By far the most important single character in Pournelle's fiction is John Falkenberg, a highly skilled strategic and tactical planner who leads a successful career as leader of a unit of mercenaries, moving from one world to another to augment or replace existing forces.

The Falkenberg stories are set within the context of a future history which originates with the establishment of the CoDominium, a pragmatic alliance by the United States and the Soviet Union that eventually evolves into a world government of sorts and an interstellar empire. Pournelle employs the genre's commonly held view that an interstellar civilization will be subject to periodic collapse and renewal, as decadence destroys the old order to make way for the vigorous new. This cyclic view of future history is also present in *A Spaceship for the King*. One of the three novels which Pournelle has written with Larry Niven takes place several centuries after the fall of the CoDominium and the era of Falkenberg; this novel, *The Mote in God's Eye*, is probably Pournelle's best work.

The Mote in God's Eye was met with widely divergent response. In plot, it is a longer than average novel of mankind's first contact with an alien species, one that is biologically diversified in order to cope with the exigencies of survival within the confines of their own system. The favorable reaction centered upon the well-paced and logically developed plot, a strong and sustained element of suspense, gradual revelation of the mystery of the alien culture, and several extremely effective scenes, particularly one in which a handful of aliens animate an empty human spacesuit. But there was adverse reaction to what many readers interpreted as stereotyped characterizations, particularly that of the single female character, a passive individual showing little initiative. There is a certain degree of truth to this charge; neither writer has demonstrated any deep concern for the finer nuances of characterization in their work. Nevertheless, it is an enthralling novel of adventure and discovery, and the focus of the story is on the unfolding mystery of the alien culture, not the reactions of the characters.

Perhaps as a response to the criticism, *Lucifer's Hammer* featured several strong female characters. *Lucifer's Hammer* is an end of the world story on the scale of *When Worlds Collide* by Wylie and Balmer. Following the collision of Earth with a comet, civilization collapses into barbarism and most of the physical features of the world are altered. Marketed as a mainstream disaster novel, the book features an extremely large cast of characters, numerous plots and subplots, and covers a span of decades. There is careful, plausible extrapolation of the slow decay of the few islands of comparatively advanced society that survive as technological devices fall into short supply or disrepair. It is indicative of the shared view of technology that the climactic battle is fought for control of a surviving nuclear power plant. The remaining collaborative novel, *Inferno*, is a fantasy rather than science fiction, a modern man's trip to the hierarchical Hell envisioned by Dante. But Allen Carpentier's damned soul refuses to accept the reality of an afterlife, and his efforts to find rationality and purpose amid almost literal organized

chaos are entertaining and frequently amusing.

Pournelle is not noted for the originality of his plots, which almost invariably rely on such standard topics as interplanetary war and conquest, world disaster, war in space, first contact with aliens, commercial rivalries for control of the government, penal colonies on other worlds, or abduction by aliens. His themes are familiar as well, the importance of space travel in providing new horizons for humanity, technology as the answer to various problems that confront the race, the value of individualist thinking as opposed to mindless collectivism, the primacy of man over aliens because of our stronger competitive drive for survival. But this familiarity of plot and theme should not be construed to mean a lack of ability. The comparatively shallow characters do not reflect a lack of depth in other areas. For the most part, Pournelle develops his plots in a logical fashion, with a good sense of timing and judicious use of suspense and overt action. Most of his fiction is essentially that of adventure, with clear-cut action and sympathetic, if not entirely realistic, characters. His ability to grasp and utilize military detail is exceptional, most notably in *West of Honor*. Social issues, when they arise, are somewhat less plausible, for Pournelle rarely makes his allegiances secret. The short-sighted ecology and population-control movements nearly destroy the space effort in *Exiles to Glory*. Government officials are almost invariably portrayed as corrupt or inept, or both. Even at his most polemical, Pournelle carefully avoids disturbing the momentum of his stories with his discourses. Many readers will be attracted or repulsed by his tendency to present only his own opinion in a favorable light, but this has always been the prerogative of the writer. He is not the kind of writer who spawns numerous imitators, but he is a competent, entertaining practitioner whose works will always find sympathetic readers.

—Don D'Ammassa

POWYS, John Cowper. British. Born in Shirley, Derbyshire, 8 October 1872; brother of the writers T.F. Powys and Llewelyn Powys. Educated at the Sherborne School; Corpus Christi College, Cambridge. Married Margaret Alice Lyon in 1896 (died, 1947); one son. Writer from 1896; lectured on English literature in the United States, 1904-34: spent winters in America, returning to England each summer, 1910-28; lived in New York and California, 1928-34; returned to England, 1934, and subsequently settled in North Wales. D.Litt.: University of Wales, 1962. *Died 17 June 1963.*

SCIENCE-FICTION PUBLICATIONS

Short Stories

Up and Out (2 novelets). London, Macdonald, 1957.

OTHER PUBLICATIONS

Novels

Wood and Stone: A Romance. New York, Shaw, 1915; London, Heinemann, 1917.
Rodmoor: A Romance. New York, Shaw, 1916; London, Macdonald, 1974.
Ducdame. New York, Doubleday, and London, Richards, 1925.
Wolf Solent. New York, Simon and Schuster, 1929.
A Glastonbury Romance. New York, Simon and Schuster, 1932; London, Lane, 1933.
Weymouth Sands. New York, Simon and Schuster, 1934; as *Jobber Skald*, London, Lane, 1935.
Maiden Castle. New York, Simon and Schuster, 1936; London, Cassell, 1937.

Morwyn; or, The Vengeance of God. London, Cassell, 1937; New York, Arno Press, 1976.
Owen Glendower. New York, Simon and Schuster, 1940; London, Cape, 1942.
Porius: A Romance of the Dark Ages. London, Macdonald, 1951; New York, Philosophical Library, 1952.
The Inmates. London, Macdonald, and New York, Philosophical Library, 1952.
Atlantis. London, Macdonald, 1954.
The Brazen Head. London, Macdonald, 1956.
Homer and the Aether. London, Macdonald, 1959.
All or Nothing. London, Macdonald, 1960.
After My Fashion. London, Picador, 1980.

Short Stories

The Owl, The Duck, and—Miss Rowe! Miss Rowe! Chicago, Targ, 1930; London, Village Press, 1975.
Real Wraiths. London, Village Press, 1974.
Two and Two. London, Village Press, 1974.
Romer Mowl and Other Stories, edited by Bernard Jones. St. Peter Port, Guernsey, Toucan Press, 1974.
You and Me. London, Village Press, 1975.

Play

The Idiot, with Reginald Pole, adaptation of a novel by Dostoevsky (produced New York, 1922).

Verse

Odes and Other Poems. London, Rider, 1896.
Poems. London, Rider, 1899.
Wolf's Bane: Rhymes. New York, Shaw, 1916.
Mandragora. New York, Shaw, 1917.
Samphire. New York, Seltzer, 1922.
Lucifer. London, Macdonald, 1956.
John Cowper Powys: A Selection from His Poems, edited by Kenneth Hopkins. London, Macdonald, and Hamilton, New York, Colgate University Press, 1964.

Other

The War and Culture: A Reply to Professor Münsterberg. New York, Shaw, 1914; as *The Menace of German Culture,* London, Rider, 1915.
Visions and Revisions: A Book of Literary Devotions. New York, Shaw, and London, Rider, 1915.
Confessions of Two Brothers, with Llewelyn Powys. Rochester, New York, Manas Press, 1916.
One Hundred Best Books, with Commentary and an Essay on Books and Reading. New York, Shaw, 1916.
Suspended Judgments: Essays on Books and Sensations. New York, Shaw, 1916; London, Village Press, 1974.
The Complex Vision. New York, Dodd Mead, 1920.
The Art of Happiness. Girard, Kansas, Haldeman Julius, 1923; London, Village Press, 1974.
Psycholanalysis and Morality. San Francisco, Colbert, 1923; London, Village Press, 1975.
The Religion of a Sceptic. New York, Dodd Mead, 1925; London, Village Press, 1975.
The Secret of Self Development. Girard, Kansas, Haldeman Julius, 1926; London, Village Press, 1974.
The Art of Forgetting the Unpleasant. Girard, Kansas, Haldeman Julius, 1928; London, Village Press, 1974.
The Meaning of Culture. New York, Norton, and London, Cape, 1929; revised edition, Norton, 1939, Cape, 1940.
Debate! Is Modern Marriage a Failure?, with Bertrand Russell. New York, Discussion Guild, 1930.
In Defence of Sensuality. New York, Simon and Schuster, and London, Gollancz, 1930.
Dorothy M. Richardson. London, Joiner and Steele, 1931.
A Philosophy of Solitude. New York, Simon and Schuster, and London, Cape, 1933.

Autobiography. New York, Simon and Schuster, and London, Lane, 1934.
The Art of Happiness (not the same as 1923 book). New York, Simon and Schuster, and London, Lane, 1935.
The Enjoyment of Literature. New York, Simon and Schuster, 1938; revised edition, as *The Pleasures of Literature,* London, Cassell, 1938.
Mortal Strife. London, Cape, 1942.
The Art of Growing Old. London, Cape, 1944.
Pair Dadeni; or, The Cauldron of Rebirth. Carmarthen, Druid Press, 1946.
Dostoievsky. London, Lane, 1947; New York, Haskell House, 1973.
Obstinate Cymric: Essays 1935-47. Carmarthen, Druid Press, 1947.
Rabelais. London, Lane, 1948; New York, Philosophical Library, 1951.
In Spite Of: A Philosophy for Everyman. London, Macdonald, and New York, Philosophical Library, 1953.
Letters of John Cowper Powys to Louis Wilkinson 1935-1956. London, Macdonald, 1958.
Letters from John Cowper Powys to Glyn Hughes, edited by Bernard Jones. Stevenage, Hertfordshire, Ore, 1971.
Letters to Nicholas Ross, edited by Arthur Uphill. London, Rota, 1971.
Letters 1937-1954, edited by Iorwerth C. Peate. Cardiff, University of Wales Press, 1974.
William Blake. London, Village Press, 1974.
Letters of John Cowper Powys to His Brother Llewelyn 1902-1925, edited by Malcolm Elwin. London, Village Press, 1975.
James Joyce's Ulysses: An Appreciation. London, Village Press, 1975.

Editor, *Ultima Verba,* by Alfred de Kantzow. London, Unwin, 1902.
Editor, *Noctis Susurri: Sighs of the Night,* by Alfred de Kantzow. London, Sherratt and Hughes, 1906.

*

Bibliography: *John Cowper Powys: A Record of Achievement* by Derek Langridge, London, Library Association, 1966.

*   *   *

The space fiction of John Cowper Powys develops Welsh origins, a founder-descended hero who carries a huge telepathic stick, contrived names, mixed mythologies, telepathy and astral travel, sentient Nature, and personified Space that is superior to Time. "Up and Out" extends end-of-the-world fiction and philosophy to end-of-consciousness. Hydrogen bombs destroy the world for Gor Goginog and his soul mate Rhitha, who find on their space-vessel (an earth fragment blasted into outer space by the bomb) a fish-flesh-fowl monster, Org, and his wife, Asm. They journey toward Nothing, which is a wish of their own and of all forms of consciousness they meet. Time and Eternity are destroyed; the star Aldebaran and various mythological gods, even God and Satan, consent to a universal cosmic suicide. In contrast the protagonists of "The Mountains of the Moon" have tree origins and confront an incest problem. The sister Lorlt departs looking for a lover, who is the son of the giant Oom, whom her brother Rorlt resents until after he descends into a cave and finds his own anima, Helia. The philosopher Om tells of multiple creators and universes; and the son of the moon claims Mars, not the Sun, to be his father. Thought-projections and dreams have physical reality; inanimate reliquaries such as the core of the Edenic apple, the heel of Achilles, the fiddle-string of Nero, speak and act as spiritually endowed beings. The three stories of *All or Nothing* scarcely qualify as science fiction; they are fantasy, and take place on the sun, on a star, Vindex, in the Milky Way, and on the return voyage from Vindex.

—Grace Eckley

PRAGNELL, Festus. British. Born 16 January 1905. Worked as a policeman in London.

SCIENCE-FICTION PUBLICATIONS

Novels

The Green Man of Kilsona. London, Philip Allan, 1936; revised edition, as *The Green Man of Graypec*, New York, Greenberg, 1950.
Kastrove der Mächtige. Rastatt, Germany, Utopia-Zukunftsroman, 1966.

Uncollected Short Stories (series: Don Hargreaves)

"The Venus Germ," with R.F. Starzl, in *Wonder Stories* (New York), November 1932.
"Men of the Dark Comet," in *Wonder Stories* (New York), June 1933.
"The Isotope Man," in *Wonder Stories* (New York), August 1933.
"The Essence of Life," in *Amazing* (New York), August 1933.
"A Visit to Venus," in *Wonder Stories* (New York), August 1934.
"Ghost of Mars" (Hargreaves), in *Amazing* (New York), December 1938.
"War of the Human Cats," in *Fantastic Adventures* (New York), August 1940.
"Warlords" (Hargreaves), in *Amazing* (New York), October 1940.
"Kidnapped in Mars," in *Amazing* (New York), October 1941.
"Outlaw" (Hargreaves), in *Amazing* (New York), January 1942.
"Devil Birds of Deimos" (Hargreaves), in *Amazing* (New York), April 1942.
"Into the Caves of Mars" (Hargreaves), in *Amazing* (New York), August 1942.
"Twisted Giant of Mars" (Hargreaves), in *Amazing* (New York), May 1943.
"Conspirators of Phobos" (Hargreaves), in *Amazing* (New York), June 1943.
"Collision in Space," in *Amazing* (New York), July 1943.
"Madcap of Mars" (Hargreaves), in *Amazing* (New York), September 1943.
"The Machine God Laughs," in *The Machine God Laughs*, edited by William L. Crawford. Los Angeles, Griffin, 1949.

OTHER PUBLICATIONS

Novel

The Terror from Timorkal. London, Bear, 1946.

* * *

Festus Pragnell was among the small contingent of British writers who, lacking a suitable market at home, found a billet for their work in the American science-fiction magazines. Though he was far from being the most successful, he enjoyed the distinction of having his work approved by H.G. Wells.

Wells found that *The Green Man of Kilsona* contained a reference to "H. Geewells," a noted author on the electron world of Kilsona where Pragnell's hero finds himself in the body of an ape-man. Having read it, Wells wrote to Pragnell pronouncing it "a very good story indeed," but the resulting publicity was too late to help the sales of the novel. Pragnell's first story, "The Essence of Life," in which super-intelligent beings from Jupiter made a peaceful visit to Earth, appeared in *Amazing* 18 months after acceptance. "Men of the Dark Comet" is the tale of a wandering satellite inhabited by strange plant-creatures, and "The Isotope Men" deals with the destruction of a planet—now the Asteroid Belt—from which man's forebears came to Earth. The ideas were typical of the period, the writing no better or worse than editor Hugo Gernsback was ready to accept at the rates which applied in those days of economic depression. And Pragnell, a spare-time scribbler, knew the pangs of unemployment.

In "A Visit to Venus" he painted a morbid picture of human bodies distorted by poisonous spores distributed by intending invaders. He was a man obsessed by the study of vitamins and other aspects of medicine which furnished him with plot-material while a daily pinch of baker's yeast supplied him with energy. He was fond of inventing bizarre forms of animal and vegetable life, and the effects of a strict religious upbringing against which he rebelled could be detected in his work. He protested, too, the rigid policies of editors who denied him the freedom of expression he craved. He had little success in his own country, but by the 1940's had found his metier in Ray Palmer's *Amazing Stories* where his lively tales of Don Hargreaves on Mars and its moons, replete with twisted giants and devil birds, suited its juvenile appeal.

—Walter Gillings

PRATT, (Murray) Fletcher. Also wrote as George U. Fletcher. American. Born in Buffalo, New York, 25 April 1897. Attended Hobart College, Geneva, New York, 1915-16; University of Paris, 1931-33. Served in the War Library Service during World War I. Married Inga Marie Stephens. Librarian, 1918-20; staff member, Buffalo *Courier Express*, 1920-23; free-lance writer from 1923: regular contributor, *American Mercury* and *Saturday Review of Literature*; military adviser, *Time* and New York *Post* during World War II; staff member, Bread Loaf Writers Conference. President, Authors Club, 1941; Co-Founder, American Rocket Society. Recipient: United States Navy award, 1957. *Died 10 June 1956.*

SCIENCE-FICTION PUBLICATIONS

Novels

The Well of the Unicorn (as George U. Fletcher). New York, Sloane, 1948.
Double in Space (*Project Excelsior, The Wanderer's Return*). New York, Doubleday, 1951.
Double Jeopardy. New York, Doubleday, 1952.
The Undying Fire. New York, Ballantine, 1953; as *The Conditioned Captain*, in *Double in Space*, 1954.
Double in Space (*Project Excelsior, The Conditioned Captain*). London, Boardman, 1954.
Invaders from Rigel. New York, Avalon, 1960.
Alien Planet. New York, Avalon, 1962.
The Blue Star. New York, Ballantine, 1969.

Uncollected Short Stories

"The Spiral of the Ages," in *Startling* (New York), Summer 1954.
"Bell, Book, and Candle," in *Fantastic Universe* (Chicago), October 1959.
"The Weissenbroch Spectacles," in *Invisible Men*, edited by Basil Davenport. New York, Ballantine, 1960.

OTHER PUBLICATIONS

Novels with L. Sprague de Camp

The Incomplete Enchanter. New York, Holt, 1941; London, Sphere, 1979.
Land of Unreason. New York, Holt, 1942.
The Carnelian Cube. New York, Gnome Press, 1948.
The Castle of Iron. New York, Gnome Press, 1950.
Wall of Serpents. New York, Avalon, 1960.
The Compleat Enchanter: The Magical Adventures of Harold Shea (includes *The Incomplete Enchanter* and *The Castle of Iron*). New York, Doubleday, 1975; London, Sphere, 1979.

Short Stories

Tales from Gavagan's Bar, with L. Sprague de Camp.   New York, Twayne, 1953; expanded edition, Philadelphia, Owlswick Press, 1978.

Other

The Heroic Years: Fourteen Years of the Republic 1801-1815.   New York, Smith and Haas, 1934.
The Cunning Mulatto and Other Cases of Ellis Parker, American Detective.   New York, Smith and Haas, 1935; as *Detective No. 1*, London, Methuen, 1936.
Ordeal by Fire: An Informal History of the Civil War.   New York, Smith and Haas, 1935; revised edition, New York, Sloane, 1948; London, Lane, 1950; as *A Short History of the Civil War*, New York, Bantam, n.d.
Hail, Caesar!   New York, Smith and Haas, 1936; London, Williams and Norgate, 1938.
The Navy: A History.   New York, Doubleday, 1938.
Road to Empire: The Life and Times of Bonaparte the General.   New York, Doubleday, 1939.
Sea Power and Today's War.   New York, Harrison Hilton, 1939; London, Methuen, 1940.
Secret and Urgent: The Story of Codes and Ciphers.   Indianapolis, Bobbs Merrill, and London, Hale, 1939.
Fletcher Pratt's Naval War Game.   New York, Harrison Hilton, 1940.
Fighting Ships of the U.S. Navy.   New York, Garden City Publishing Company, 1941.
America and Total War.   New York, Smith and Durrell, 1941.
The U.S. Army.   Racine, Wisconsin, Whitman, 1942.
What the Citizen Should Know about Modern War.   New York, Norton, 1942.
The Navy Has Wings.   New York, Harper, 1943.
My Life to the Destroyers, with Captain L.A. Abercrombie.   New York, Holt, 1944.
The Navy's War.   New York, Harper, 1944.
A Short History of the Army and Navy.   Washington, D.C., Infantry Journal, 1944.
Fleet Against Japan.   New York, Harper, 1946.
Empire of the Sea.   New York, Holt, 1946.
Night Work: The Story of Task Force 39.   New York, Holt, 1946.
A Man and His Meals, with Robeson Bailey.   New York, Holt, 1947.
The Empire and Glory: Napoleon Bonaparte 1800-1806.   New York, Sloane, 1948.
The Marines' War.   New York, Sloane, 1948.
Eleven Generals: Studies in American Command.   New York, Sloane, 1949.
The Third King.   New York, Sloane, 1950.
War for the World: A Chronicle of Our Fighting Forces in World War II.   New Haven, Connecticut, Yale University Press, 1950.
Prebble's Boys: Commodore Prebble and the Birth of American Sea Power.   New York, Sloane, 1950.
Rockets, Jets, Guided Missiles, and Space Ships.   New York, Random House, 1951; London, Sidgwick and Jackson, 1952.
The Monitor and the Merrimac.   New York, Random House, 1951.
By Space Ship to the Moon (juvenile).   New York, Random House, 1952; London, Publicity Products, 1953.
Stanton, Lincoln's Secretary of War.   New York, Norton, 1953.
All about Rockets and Jets.   New York, Random House, 1955.
The Civil War.   New York, Garden City Books, 1955.
Famous Inventors and Their Inventions.   New York, Random House, 1955.
The Battles That Changed History.   New York, Doubleday, 1956.
Civil War on Western Waters.   New York, Holt, 1956.
The Compact History of the United States Navy.   New York, Hawthorn, 1957.

Editor, *World of Wonder.*   New York, Twayne, 1951.
Editor, *Civil War in Pictures.*   New York, Garden City Books, 1951.
Editor, *The Petrified Planet.*   New York, Twayne, 1952.

Editor, *Witches Three.*   New York, Twayne, 1953.
Editor, *My Diary, North and South*, by Sir William Howard Russell.   New York, Harper, 1954.

Translator, *The Great American Parade*, by H.J. Duteil.   New York, Twayne, 1953.

*   *   *

Fletcher Pratt had an extremely varied writing career. While he is considered to be one of the pioneer science-fiction writers, he also wrote fantasy and produced an impressive list of historical non-fiction. In terms of science fiction, Pratt wrote mainly short fiction during his early years, with the exception of *Alien Planet*. The publisher's foreword to the Ace edition of this novel accurately describes it as using "the traditional technique of the 'marvelous voyage' and the 'manuscript found in a bottle'...combined with a penetrating and satiric representation of human society through the method of exploring an alien culture." It is a classic representation of the genre. Of course, much of the material is outdated but there remains some interesting philosophy, including the alien dissident's description of intelligent life as a disease infesting the planets which the divine spirit strives to destroy.

In 1939, Pratt met L. Sprague de Camp and his writing turned toward fantasy. Together they wrote a series of stories about a psychologist who finds himself projected into a number of parallel worlds which are based on our myths. Harold Shea, as he is called, makes his rounds of Norse mythology ("The Roaring Trumpet"), Spenser's *Faerie Queene* ("The Mathematics of Logic"), Ariosto's *Orlando Furioso* (*The Castle of Iron*), the Finnish *Kalevala* (*Wall of Serpents*) and the world of Irish myth ("The Green Magician"). The stories were unique in that they combined the then new field of sword-and-sorcery fantasy with a refreshing humor. The two writers wrote two additional fantasy novels, *Land of Unreason* and *The Carnelian Cube*, as well as a collection of short fantasy spoofs, *Tales from Gavagan's Bar*. The last, similar to Clarke's *Tales of the White Hart*, also showed the magical humor of Pratt and de Camp evident in the Harold Shea pieces. Pratt's solo novel *The Well of the Unicorn* is a fascinating creation by a master storyteller, one of the very best of fantasies.

Pratt's SF work *Double Jeopardy* details the adventures of George Helmfleet Jones, an agent with the Secret Service some time in the future. In his first adventure, Jones solves a case dealing with a matter transmitter; in the second, he is confronted by the theft of a large sum of money from a sealed, remote-controlled cargo rocket. *Double in Space* consists of two unrelated works. The first is born of the early Cold War with Russian and US space stations vying for superiority in space. The second is a take-off on the voyage of Ulysses set in the far distant future. In a similar vein, *The Undying Fire* follows the plot of Jason and the Golden Fleece. None of these works matches the caliber of Pratt's fantasy.

—Paul Swank

PRIEST, Christopher.   British.   Born in Cheadle, Cheshire, in 1943. Educated at Warehouseman and Clerks' Orphan Schools, Manchester, 1951-59. Recipient: British Science Fiction Association Award, 1974, 1979; Ditmar Award (Australia), 1977. Agent: A.P. Watt Ltd., 26-28 Bedford Row, London WC1R 4HL; or, Marie Rodell-Frances Collin Literary Agency, 156 East 52nd Street, New York, New York 10022, U.S.A. Address: c/o Faber and Faber Ltd., 3 Queen Square, London WC1N 3AU, England.

SCIENCE-FICTION PUBLICATIONS

Novels

Indoctrinaire.   London, Faber, and New York, Harper, 1970.

Fugue for a Darkening Island. London, Faber, 1972; as *Darkening Island*, New York, Harper, 1972.
Inverted World. London, Faber, 1974; as *The Inverted World*, New York, Harper, 1974.
The Space Machine. London, Faber, and New York, Harper, 1976.
A Dream of Wessex. London, Faber, 1977; as *The Perfect Lover*, New York, Scribner, 1977.

Short Stories

Real-Time World. London, New English Library, 1974.
An Infinite Summer. London, Faber, and New York, Scribner, 1979.

OTHER PUBLICATIONS

Novel

The Affirmation. London, Faber, and New York, Scribner, 1981.

Other

Your Book of Film-Making (juvenile). London, Faber, 1974.

Editor, *Anticipations.* London, Faber, and New York, Scribner, 1978.
Editor, with Robert Holdstock, *Stars of Albion* (anthology of British science fiction). London, Pan, 1979.

*   *   *

Christopher Priest is one of the most promising new British science-fiction writers to become active in the 1970's. His first novel, *Indoctrinaire* (expanded from "The Interrogator"), reflected the type of story that dominated *New Worlds* at the time. Dr. Wentik is a researcher investigating an experimental drug at a scientific installation in the Antarctic when he is shanghaied by the mysterious American government agent Astrourde. Shortly thereafter he is incarcerated in an enigmatic prison in the Brazilian highlands, in an area that somehow serves as a bridge between the present and the world two centuries from now. Wentik's attempts to escape his situation, or even to make some kind of sense of it, are reminiscent of Kafka. His efforts are largely ineffectual, although it does become increasingly clear to him that even his captors are without true freedom. Reality and fantasy merge at times, and the result is a kaleidoscopic novel that dilutes its effect by the lack of strong focus.

Fugue for a Darkening Island also features a weak and less than entirely admirable protagonist. Following a major war in Africa, the British Isles are rapidly inundated with refugees, an exodus that is met with indecisive hostility on the part of the British authorities. As the influx grows, order begins to disintegrate. Divergent opinions about the obligation to provide succor to the refugees leads to an increasingly violent factionalism. Government control over much of the countryside collapses: individual neighborhoods wall themselves off from the outside world. Alan Whitman and his family are cast adrift in this world, and find that they are unable to control their own future. Frequently it is impossible even to distinguish those who uphold the law from those who break it. Priest makes no effort to plot his novel linearly. The viewpoint jumps back and forth through time, seemingly at random, so that the reader is almost simultaneously exposed to Whitman at all stages of his dissolution. But Priest holds his character at arm's length from us, and we can only vaguely perceive his motivations; the nightmarish quality of his world remains that, for it never quite achieves reality.

Paradoxically, while the all too possible world shown in *Fugue for a Darkening Island* never acquires depth, the almost totally incredible setting of *Inverted World* is vividly realistic. It is a much more cohesive novel than anything Priest had written before. It features a strong sympathetic character, and some of the most innovative settings to appear in years. Helward Mann is a citizen of City Earth, an enormous construct that inches across the surface of its world by winching itself across tracks picked up from behind and laboriously replaced ahead. The city is in eternal pursuit of the Optimum, the place where environmental conditions are most like

that of their home world. For this world, whatever it might be, is treacherous and changing. Behind them, physical features become broad and flat, time passes very rapidly in relation to the city itself, and a mysterious force increasingly attempts to pull laggers back to their destruction. Ahead, the distortions of time and space have exactly the opposite attributes. As Mann is initiated into the guild responsible for scouting the future, he gradually matures and adjusts to the changing nature of his world. Idea is central here rather than character; nevertheless, Helward and his personal relationships with others from the city are well portrayed. Although less ambitious stylistically than Priest's earlier novels, *Inverted World* is far more successful both as an adventure story and as a novel of ideas. Priest indulged in pastiche next, and *The Space Machine* is a witty and frequently funny examination of some of the situations first presented by H.G. Wells. This invocation of Martian invaders and time machines is carried a bit too far, unfortunately, and it is difficult to sustain interest through the end.

A Dream of Wessex is a far more successful novel in almost any terms, and is easily the high point of Priest's career. The Ridpath Project is a secret research installation where a group of people pool their subconscious minds to create a mutual dream world. Within this context, they can extrapolate the future possibilities of various aspects of the present. But David Harkman, one of the dreamers, has lost his awareness of the real world and will not come out of trance. Julia Stretton, another participant, tries desperately to release him from the grip of the dream world, particularly when she learns of the imminent participation of a new dreamer, a man who considers the project to be nonsense. The dream world becomes more real to the reader than the project itself, and, despite the existence of Soviet domination over Britain, it is easy to see why Harkman is unconsciously reluctant to leave it for reality. Both of the central figures are fully realized personalities, and their awakening feelings for each other are convincing and enthralling.

Priest seems to have fused reality and dream in this novel, a blend he used less successfully in *Indoctrinaire*. It should be no surprise, therefore, to note that most of his most noteworthy shorter pieces also explore this interface. "Real Time World" describes the Observatory, supposedly an extra-dimensional establishment from which a small staff could observe the flora and fauna of other worlds, in actuality an experiment in itself on news deprivation, with a staff thoroughly brainwashed about the nature of their situation. In "Palely Loitering" a man spends much of his life travelling back and forth across time bridges, always in pursuit of a young girl he does not have the courage to confront. His ultimate effort draws into question the immutability of the past and the reality of his own present. Two stories set within the context of Priest's "Dream Archipelago" are also worth mentioning. "Whores" is an incident sliced out of time, wherein the protagonist encounters a series of inexplicable events, mutilations of a sort of people living in an area formerly occupied by enemy troops. Much of the story's impact is dissipated by the ambiguous ending, however, a problem that arises also with Priest's best short story, "The Watched." Yvann Ordier is disturbed by his voyeuristic spying on a band of Qataari refugees. The Qataari have an obsessive need for privacy, and will literally starve to death rather than submit to being studied. At the same time, Ordier himself is compulsively wary of scintillas, tiny mechanical spy devices that are almost unavoidable. The result is a complex story of character, obsession, and personal decadence.

The progression from idiosyncratic fiction replete with personal symbolism to mature writing with rich characters, clearly delineated plots, and a firm grasp of the shifting realities of his own stories is likely to increase Priest's popularity as he continues to write.

—Don D'Ammassa

PRIESTLEY, J(ohn) B(oynton). British. Born in Bradford, Yorkshire, 13 September 1894. Educated in Bradford schools, and at Trinity Hall, Cambridge, M.A. Served with the Duke of Wellington's and Devon Regiments, 1914-19. Married 1) Patricia Tempest (died, 1925), two daughters; 2) Mary Wyndham Lewis (divorced, 1952), two daughters and one son; 3) Jacquetta Hawkes, *q.v.*, in 1953. Director, Mask Theatre, London, 1938-39; radio lecturer on BBC programme "Postscripts" during World War II; regular contributor, *New Statesman*, London. President, P.E.N., London, 1936-37; United Kingdom Delegate, and Chairman, UNESCO International Theatre Conference, Paris, 1947, and Prague, 1948; Chairman, British Theatre Conference, 1948; President, International Theatre Institute, 1949; Member, National Theatre Board, London, 1966-67. Recipient: Black Memorial Prize, 1930; Ellen Terry Award, 1948. LL.D.: University of St. Andrews; D.Litt.: University of Birmingham; University of Bradford. Honorary Freeman, City of Bradford, 1973; Order of Merit, 1977; Honorary Student, Trinity Hall, Cambridge, 1978. Address: Kissing Tree House, Alveston, Stratford upon Avon, Warwickshire, England.

SCIENCE-FICTION PUBLICATIONS

Novels

Adam in Moonshine. London, Heinemann, and New York, Harper, 1927.
The Doomsday Men. London, Heinemann, and New York, Harper, 1938.
The Magicians. London, Heinemann, and New York, Harper, 1954.
Low Notes on a High Level: A Frolic. London, Heinemann, and New York, Harper, 1954.
The Thirty-First of June. London, Heinemann, 1961; New York, Doubleday, 1962.
Snoggle (juvenile). London, Heinemann, 1971; New York, Harcourt Brace, 1972.

Short Stories

The Other Place and Other Stories of the Same Sort. London, Heinemann, and New York, Harper, 1953.

OTHER PUBLICATIONS

Novels

Benighted. London, Heinemann, 1927; as *The Old Dark House*, New York, Harper, 1928.
Farthing Hall, with Hugh Walpole. London, Macmillan, and New York, Doubleday, 1929.
The Good Companions. London, Heinemann, and New York, Harper, 1929.
Angel Pavement. London, Heinemann, and New York, Harper, 1930.
Faraway. London, Heinemann, and New York, Harper, 1932.
I'll Tell You Everything, with Gerald Bullett. New York, Macmillan, 1932; London, Heinemann, 1933.
Wonder Hero. London, Heinemann, and New York, Harper, 1933.
They Walk in the City: The Lovers in the Stone Forest. London, Heinemann, and New York, Harper, 1936.
Let the People Sing. London, Heinemann, 1939; New York, Harper, 1940.
Black-Out in Gretley: A Story of—and for—Wartime. London, Heinemann, and New York, Harper, 1942.
Daylight on Saturday: A Novel about an Aircraft Factory. London, Heinemann, and New York, Harper, 1943.
Three Men in New Suits. London, Heinemann, and New York, Harper, 1945.
Bright Day. London, Heinemann, and New York, Harper, 1946.
Jenny Villiers: A Story of the Theatre. London, Heinemann, and New York, Harper, 1947.
Festival at Farbridge. London, Heinemann, 1951; as *Festival*, New York, Harper, 1951.
Saturn over the Water. London, Heinemann, and New York, Doubleday, 1961.

The Shapes of Sleep. London, Heinemann, and New York, Doubleday, 1962.
Sir Michael and Sir George. London, Heinemann, 1964; Boston, Little Brown, 1965.
Lost Empires. London, Heinemann, and Boston, Little Brown, 1965.
Salt Is Leaving. London, Pan, 1966; New York, Harper, 1975.
It's an Old Country. London, Heinemann, and Boston, Little Brown, 1967.
The Image Men: Out of Town, London End. London, Heinemann, 2 vols., 1968; Boston, Little Brown, 1969.
Found, Lost, Found; or, The English Way of Life. London, Heinemann, 1976; New York, Stein and Day, 1977.

Short Stories

The Town Major of Miraucourt. London, Heinemann, 1930.
Albert Goes Through. London, Heinemann, and New York, Harper, 1933.
Going Up: Stories and Sketches. London, Pan, 1950.
The Carfitt Crisis and Two Other Stories. London, Heinemann, 1975.

Plays

The Good Companions, with Edward Knoblock, adaptation of the novel by Priestley (produced London and New York, 1931). London and New York, French, 1935.
Dangerous Corner (produced London and New York, 1932). London, Heinemann, and New York, French, 1932.
The Roundabout (produced Liverpool, London, and New York, 1932). London, Heinemann, and New York, French, 1933.
Laburnum Grove: An Immoral Comedy (produced London, 1933; New York, 1935). London, Heinemann, 1934; New York, French, 1935.
Eden End (produced London, 1934; New York, 1935). London, Heinemann, 1934; in *Three Plays and a Preface*, 1935.
Cornelius: A Business Affair in Three Transactions (produced Birmingham and London, 1935). London, Heinemann, 1935; New York, French, 1936.
Duet in Floodlight (produced Liverpool and London, 1935). London, Heinemann, 1935.
Three Plays and a Preface (includes *Dangerous Corner, Eden End, Cornelius*). New York, Harper, 1935.
Bees on the Boat Deck: A Farcical Tragedy (produced London, 1936). London, Heinemann, and Boston, Baker, 1936.
Spring Tide (as Peter Goldsmith), with George Billam (produced London, 1936). London, Heinemann, and New York, French, 1936.
The Bad Samaritan (produced Liverpool, 1937).
Time and the Conways (produced London, 1937; New York, 1938). London, Heinemann, 1937; New York, Harper, 1938.
I Have Been Here Before (produced London, 1937; New York, 1938). London, Heinemann, 1937; New York, Harper, 1938.
Two Time Plays (includes *Time and the Conways* and *I Have Been Here Before*). London, Heinemann, 1937.
People at Sea (as *I Am a Stranger Here*, produced Bradford, 1937; as *People at Sea*, produced London, 1937). London, Heinemann, and New York, French, 1937.
The Rebels (produced Bradford, 1938).
Mystery at Greenfingers: A Comedy of Detection (produced London, 1938). London, French, 1937; New York, French, 1938.
When We Are Married: A Yorkshire Farcical Comedy (produced London, 1938; New York, 1939). London, Heinemann, 1938; New York, French, 1940.
Music at Night (produced Malvern, 1938; London, 1939). Included in *Three Plays*, 1943; in *Plays I*, 1948.
Johnson over Jordan (produced London, 1939). Published as *Johnson over Jordan: The Play, and All about It (An Essay)*, London, Heinemann, and New York, Harper, 1939.
The Long Mirror (produced Oxford, 1940; London, 1945). Included in *Three Plays*, 1943; in *Four Plays*, 1944.
Good Night Children: A Comedy of Broadcasting (produced London, 1942). Included in *Three Comedies*, 1945; in *Plays II*, 1949.

Desert Highway (produced Bristol, 1943; London, 1944). London, Heinemann, 1944; in *Four Plays*, 1944.

They Came to a City (produced London, 1943). Included in *Three Plays*, 1943; in *Four Plays*, 1944.

Three Plays (includes *Music at Night, The Long Mirror, They Came to a City*). London, Heinemann, 1943.

How Are They at Home? A Topical Comedy (produced London, 1944). Included in *Three Comedies*, 1945; in *Plays II*, 1949.

The Golden Fleece (as *The Bull Market*, produced Bradford, 1944). Included in *Three Comedies*, 1945.

Four Plays (includes *Music at Night, The Long Mirror, They Came to a City, Desert Highway*). London, Heinemann, and New York, Harper, 1944.

Three Comedies (includes *Good Night Children, The Golden Fleece, How Are They at Home?*). London, Heinemann, 1945.

An Inspector Calls (produced Moscow, 1945; London, 1946; New York, 1947). London, Heinemann, 1947; New York, Dramatists Play Service, 1948(?).

Jenny Villiers (produced Bristol, 1946).

The Rose and Crown (televised, 1946). London, French, 1947.

Ever Since Paradise: An Entertainment, Chiefly Referring to Love and Marriage (also director: produced on tour, 1946; London, 1947). London and New York, French, 1949.

Three Time Plays (includes *Dangerous Corner, Time and the Conways, I Have Been Here Before*). London, Pan, 1947.

The Linden Tree (produced Sheffield and London, 1947; New York, 1948). London, Heinemann, and New York, French, 1948.

The Plays of J.B. Priestley:

I. *Dangerous Corner, I Have Been Here Before, Johnson over Jordan, Music at Night, The Linden Tree, Eden End, Time and the Conways*. London, Heinemann, 1948; as *Seven Plays*, New York, Harper, 1950.

II. *Laburnum Grove, Bees on the Boat Deck, When We Are Married, Good Night Children, The Good Companions, How Are They at Home?, Ever Since Paradise*. London, Heinemann, 1949; New York, Harper, 1951.

III. *Cornelius, People at Sea, They Came to a City, Desert Highway, An Inspector Calls, Home Is Tomorrow, Summer Day's Dream*. London, Heinemann, 1950; New York, Harper, 1952.

Home Is Tomorrow (produced Bradford and London, 1948). London, Heinemann, 1949; in *Plays III*, 1950.

The High Toby: A Play for the Toy Theatre (produced London, 1954). London, Penguin-Pollock, 1948.

Summer Day's Dream (produced Bradford and London, 1949). Included in *Plays III*, 1950.

The Olympians, music by Arthur Bliss (produced London, 1949). London, Novello, 1949.

Bright Shadow: A Play of Detection (produced Oldham and London, 1950). London, French, 1950.

Treasure on Pelican (as *Treasure on Pelican Island*, televised, 1951; as *Treasure on Pelican*, produced Cardiff and London, 1952). London, Evans, 1953.

Dragon's Mouth: A Dramatic Quartet, with Jacquetta Hawkes (also director: produced Malvern and London, 1952; New York, 1955). London, Heinemann, and New York, Harper, 1952.

Private Rooms: A One-Act Comedy in the Viennese Style. London, French, 1953.

Mother's Day. London, French, 1953.

Try It Again (produced London, 1965). London, French, 1953.

A Glass of Bitter. London, French, 1954.

The White Countess, with Jacquetta Hawkes (produced Dublin and London, 1954).

The Scandalous Affair of Mr. Kettle and Mrs. Moon (produced Folkestone and London, 1955). London, French, 1956.

Take the Fool Away (produced Vienna, 1955; Nottingham, 1959).

These Our Actors (produced Glasgow, 1956).

The Glass Cage (produced Toronto and London, 1957). London, French, 1958.

The Thirty-First of June (produced Toronto and London, 1957).

A Pavilion of Masks (produced in Germany, 1961; Bristol, 1963). London, French, 1958.

A Severed Head, with Iris Murdoch, adaptation of the novel by Murdoch (produced Bristol and London, 1963; New York, 1964). London, Chatto and Windus, 1964.

Screenplays: *Sing As We Go*, with Gordon Wellesley, 1934; *Look Up and Laugh*, with Gordon Wellesley, 1935; *We Live in Two Worlds*, 1937; *Jamaica Inn*, with Sidney Gilliat and Joan Harrison, 1939; *Britain at Bay*, 1940; *Our Russian Allies*, 1941; *The Foreman Went to France* (*Somewhere in France*), with others, 1942; *Last Holiday*, 1950.

Radio Plays: *The Return of Jess Oakroyd*, 1941; *The Golden Entry*, 1955; *End Game at the Dolphin*, 1956; *An Arabian Night in Park Lane*, 1965.

Television Plays: *The Rose and Crown*, 1946; *Treasure on Pelican Island*, 1951; *The Stone Face*, 1957; *The Rack*, 1958; *Doomsday for Dyson*, 1958; *The Fortrose Incident*, from his play *Home Is Tomorrow*, 1959; *Level Seven*, from the novel by Mordecai Roshwald, 1966; *The Lost Peace* series, 1966; *Anyone for Tennis*, 1968; *Linda at Pulteney's*, 1969.

Verse

The Chapman of Rhymes (juvenilia). London, Alexander Moring, 1918.

Other

Brief Diversions, Being Tales, Travesties, and Epigrams. Cambridge, Bowes and Bowes, 1922.

Papers from Lilliput. Cambridge, Bowes and Bowes, 1922.

I for One. London, Lane, 1923; New York, Dodd Mead, 1924.

Figures in Modern Literature. London, Lane, and New York, Dodd Mead, 1924.

The English Comic Characters. London, Lane, and New York, Dodd Mead, 1925.

George Meredith. London and New York, Macmillan, 1926.

Talking. London, Jarrolds, and New York, Harper, 1926.

(Essays). London, Harrap, 1926.

Open House: A Book of Essays. London, Heinemann, and New York, Harper, 1927.

Thomas Love Peacock. London and New York, Macmillan, 1927.

The English Novel. London, Benn, 1927; revised edition, London and New York, Nelson, 1935.

Apes and Angels: A Book of Essays. London, Methuen, 1928; as *Too Many People and Other Reflections*, New York, Harper, 1928.

The Balconinny and Other Essays. London, Methuen, 1929; as *The Balconinny*, New York, Harper, 1930.

English Humour. London and New York, Longman, 1929.

Self-Selected Essays. London, Heinemann, 1932; New York, Harper, 1933.

Four-in-Hand (miscellany). London, Heinemann, 1934.

English Journey, Being a Rambling But Truthful Account of What One Man Saw and Heard and Felt and Thought During a Journey Through England During the Autumn of the Year 1933. London, Heinemann-Gollancz, and New York, Harper, 1934.

Midnight on the Desert: A Chapter of Autobiography. London, Heinemann, 1937; as *Midnight on the Desert, Being an Excursion into Autobiography During a Winter in America, 1935-36*, New York, Harper, 1937.

Rain upon Godshill: A Further Chapter of Autobiography. London, Heinemann, and New York, Harper, 1939.

Britain Speaks (radio talks). New York, Harper, 1940.

Postscripts (radio talks). London, Heinemann, 1940; as *All England Listened*, New York, Chilmark Press, 1968.

Out of the People. London, Collins-Heinemann, and New York, Harper, 1941.

Britain at War. New York, Harper, 1942.

British Women Go to War. London, Collins, 1943.

Manpower: The Story of Britain's Mobilisation for War. London, His Majesty's Stationery Office, 1944.

Here Are Your Answers. London, Socialist Book Centre, 1944.

Letter to a Returning Serviceman. London, Home and Van Thal, 1945.

The Secret Dream: An Essay on Britain, America, and Russia. London, Turnstile Press, 1946.

Russian Journey. London, Writers Group of the Society for Cultural Relations with the USSR, 1946.

The New Citizen (address). London, Council for Education in World Citizenship, 1946.

Theatre Outlook. London, Nicholson and Watson, 1947.

The Arts under Socialism (lecture). London, Turnstile Press, 1947.

Delight. London, Heinemann, and New York, Harper, 1949.

The Priestley Companion: A Selection from the Writings of J.B. Priestley. London, Penguin-Heinemann, 1951.

Journey down a Rainbow (travel), with Jacquetta Hawkes. London, Cresset Press-Heinemann, and New York, Harper, 1955.

All about Ourselves and Other Essays, edited by Eric Gillett. London, Heinemann, 1956.

The Writer in a Changing Society (lecture). Aldington, Kent, Hand and Flower Press, 1956.

Thoughts in the Wilderness (essays). London, Heinemann, and New York, Harper, 1957.

The Art of the Dramatist: A Lecture Together with Appendices and Discursive Notes. London, Heinemann, 1957; Boston, The Writer, 1958.

Topside; or The Future of England: A Dialogue. London, Heinemann, 1958.

The Story of Theatre (juvenile). London, Rathbone, 1959; as *The Wonderful World of the Theatre*, New York, Doubleday, 1959.

Literature and Western Man. London, Heinemann, and New York, Harper, 1960.

William Hazlitt. London, Longman, 1960.

Charles Dickens: A Pictorial Biography. London, Thames and Hudson, 1961; New York, Viking Press, 1962; as *Charles Dickens and His World*, Thames and Hudson, and New York, Viking Press, 1969.

Margin Released: A Writer's Reminiscences and Reflections. London, Heinemann, and New York, Harper, 1962.

Man and Time. London, Aldus, and New York, Doubleday, 1964.

The Moments and Other Pieces. London, Heinemann, 1966.

The World of J.B. Priestley, edited by Donald G. MacRae. London, Heinemann, 1967.

Essays of Five Decades, edited by Susan Cooper. Boston, Little Brown, 1968; London, Heinemann, 1969.

Trumpets over the Sea, Being a Rambling and Egotistical Account of the London Symphony Orchestra's Engagement at Daytona Beach, Florida, in July-August 1967. London, Heinemann, 1968.

The Prince of Pleasure and His Regency 1811-1820. London, Heinemann, and New York, Harper, 1969.

The Edwardians. London, Heinemann, and New York, Harper, 1970.

Anton Chekhov. London, International Textbook, 1970.

Victoria's Heyday. London, Heinemann, and New York, Harcourt Brace, 1972.

Over the Long High Wall: Some Reflections and Speculations on Life, Death, and Time. London, Heinemann, 1972.

The English. London, Heinemann, and New York, Viking Press, 1973.

Outcries and Asides. London, Heinemann, 1974.

A Visit to New Zealand. London, Heinemann, 1974.

Particular Pleasures, Being a Personal Record of Some Varied Arts and Many Different Artists. London, Heinemann, 1975.

The Happy Dream. Andoversford, Gloucestershire, Whittington Press, 1976.

English Humour. London, Heinemann, 1976.

Instead of the Trees: A Final Chapter of Autobiography. London, Heinemann, and New York, Stein and Day, 1977.

Editor, *Essayists Past and Present: A Selection of English Essays.* London, Jenkins, and New York, Dial Press, 1925.

Editor, *Fools and Philosophers: A Gallery of Comic Figures from English Literature.* London, Lane, and New York, Dodd Mead, 1925.

Editor, *Tom Moore's Diary: A Selection.* London, Cambridge University Press, 1925.

Editor, *The Book of Bodley Head Verse.* London, Lane, and New York, Dodd Mead, 1926.

Editor, *Our Nation's Heritage.* London, Dent, 1939.

Editor, *Scenes from London Life, From Sketches by Boz*, by Dickens. London, Pan, 1947.

Editor, *The Best of Leacock.* Toronto, McClelland and Stewart, 1957; as *The Bodley Head Leacock*, London, Bodley Head, 1957.

Editor, with Josephine Spear, *Adventures in English Literature.* New York, Harcourt Brace, 1963.

*

Bibliography: *J.B. Priestley: An Annotated Bibliography* by Alan Edwin Day, New York, Garland, 1980.

Theatrical Activities:
Director: **Plays**—*Ever Since Paradise*, tour, 1946, and London, 1947; *Dragon's Mouth*, London, 1952.

*   *   *

J.B. Priestley is possessed by a vision of life at its rare best—rich, vivid, eminently worth living. What makes him a science-fiction writer and not just another dreaming romantic is that he espouses theories of time that allow his characters (and conceivably his readers) actually to attain the rich life he envisions. Such theories—chronological simultaneity, serialism, multiple dimensions—are not easy to illustrate, but Priestley succeeds surprisingly well, in stories and novels and also in popular stage plays. As literary fashion moves on and Priestley's sedately conventional style falls from favor, it is his time stories, his personal ventures towards altered reality, that remain fresh and intriguing.

Priestley derived his theories from three sources: E.A. Abbott's idea that a fourth dimension would appear as time; J.W. Dunne's mathematical model of time as continuous, simultaneous, and serial; and P.D. Ouspensky's more philosophical view of time as a repeated circle which can be made to spiral morally up or down. What these concepts gave to Priestley was a non-religious hope. If there are other dimensions, then there might be somewhere to go after life's time ends. In the plays *Music at Night* and *Johnson over Jordan* characters withdraw after death into a higher observer-state similar to the Tibetan "Bardo." Also, if all time is simultaneous then each minute is not murdered by the next, and the goodness of the past can be made accessible to those trapped in a bad present. Such comforting access is given to characters in the play *Time and the Conways* and in fiction such as "Night Sequence" and *The Magicians.* And if precognition and time's recurrence are true, then the known future can be, paradoxically, changed, altered in a tiny moment to redirect the flow, as in the plays *Dangerous Corner* and *I Have Been Here Before.*

Priestley desires these comforts and powers because he sees the modern world as darkening fast. In a short grim tale called "The Grey Ones" he incarnates the powers of darkness into grey tentacled devils capable of human shape. Their weapons are boredom, blandness, and despair; they seek to dull the world down to a suburban hell. Priestley's fullest treatment of this theme, and of the time-conscious man's opposition to it, comes in *The Magicians.* The industrialist Ravenstreet leaves his company when it turns from exciting scientific quest to passionless bureaucracy. As he slides into despair he is tempted by a bitter elitist to help drug the masses into final lethargy. Ravenstreet almost agrees, but is saved by the intervention of three "magicians" whose mysterious abilities include precognition and hypnosis, and who seem to be involved in some larger struggle. They show Ravenstreet the difference between the "tick-tock time" he had been dying in, and "time alive" where his hopeful past still lives. They send him to re-experience crucial moments, and they also rearrange the present so that the drug's numbing secret is lost. At the end, Ravenstreet has reason to live, and the world is a little less grey. Priestley's time visions are not always cheering. In one of his most haunting stories, "The Statues," a tired man is granted exhilarating but temporary sight of huge glorious statues towering above a future London, and the contrast with the banal present saddens the rest of his life. In the well-crafted and widely anthologized "Mr. Strenberry's Tale" the title character is visited briefly by a time traveler from an advanced humanity's last black moment. The traveler vanishes, destroyed, but the terror stays.

Some of Priestley's stories have been classified as science fiction because they focus on some unusual bit of technology—the musical invention in *Low Notes on a High Level* or the earth-destroying transmitter in *The Doomsday Men*. But such devices usually turn out to be occasions for plot, not concepts in themselves, and plot for Priestley means romance, marriages, careers, and individual morale more than anything else. Even his children's book, *Snoggle*, which offers extra-terrestrial pets and invisible spaceships, spends most of its rather unsuccessful pages detailing the interactions of three ordinary children. Priestley began writing in 1910; he learned his craft in an earlier time than most science-fiction writers. His many romantic comedies now seem dated, his plots coercive and even clanking. But his parables of hope and despair remain compelling, and there are few science-fiction writers who can match him for the seriousness of his thinking about time. He really believes that the 20th century's own long degenerating plot could be replayed, and conceivably rewritten. Certainly Priestley could write it better; he may even, like the Magicians, be working on it now.

—Karen G. Way

PUMILIA, Joe (Joseph F. Pumilia). Also writes as M.M. Moamrath. American. Born in Houston, Texas, 10 March 1945. Educated at the University of Houston, 1963-67, B.A. in English 1967; University of Houston School of Journalism, 1970. Married Lucille Pumilia in 1976. Reporter for three years, then layout artist, copywriter, and typesetter. Agent: Irene Goodman Agency, 134 West 81st Street, New York, New York 10024. Address: 8028 Bendell, Houston, Texas 77017, U.S.A.

SCIENCE-FICTION PUBLICATIONS

Uncollected Short Stories

"Niggertown," in *Black Hands on a White Face*, edited by Whit Burnett. New York, Dodd Mead, 1971.
"The Porter of Hell-Gate," in *Generation*, edited by David Gerrold. New York, Dell, 1972.
"As Dreams Are Made On," in *Fantastic* (New York), February 1973.
"Hung Like an Elephant," with Steven Utley, in *Alternities*, edited by David Gerrold. New York, Dell, 1974.
"Willowisp," in *Science Fiction Emphasis 1*, edited by David Gerrold. New York, Ballantine, 1974.
"Dark Vintage," in *Nameless Places*, edited by Gerald W. Page. Sauk City, Wisconsin, Arkham House, 1975.
"Instrument of Darkness," in *The Third Mayflower Book of Black Magic Stories*, edited by Michael Parry. London, Mayflower, 1975.
"Forever Stand the Stones," in *Jack the Knife: Tales of Jack the Ripper*, edited by Michael Parry. London, Mayflower, 1975.
"The Great Red Spot," with Steven Utley, in *Vertex* (Los Angeles), February 1975.
"The Case of James Elmo Freebish," in *Superhorror*, edited by Ramsey Campbell. New York, St. Martin's Press, 1976.
"And Death Once Dead," in *Lone Star Universe*, edited by Steven Utley and George W. Proctor. Austin, Texas, Heidelberg, 1976.
"Contact Myth," in *Ascents of Wonder*, edited by David Gerrold and Stephen Goldin. New York, Popular Library, 1977.
"Toad," in *More Devils Kisses*, edited by Linda Lovecraft. London, Corgi, 1977.
"Our Vanishing Triceratops," with Steven Utley, in *Amazing* (New York), March 1977.
"Myth of the Ape God," in *Rivals of King Kong*, edited by Michael Parry. London, Corgi, 1978.

Uncollected Short Stories as M.M. Moamrath, with Bill Wallace

"Riders of the Purple Ooze," in *Nickelodeon 1* (Kansas City), 1975.
"My Sword Is Quick," in *R.E.H.: Lone Star Fictioneer* (Shawnee Mission, Kansas), Spring 1976.
"Next to the Last Voyage of the Cuttle Sark," in *Chacal 2* (Shawnee Mission, Kansas), Spring 1977.

OTHER PUBLICATIONS

Other

"Moamrath, The Forgotten Bard" and "Famous Last Lines of M.M. Moamrath," in *Nickelodeon 1* (Kansas City), 1975.
"The Weird Tale of Phillip Love," in *H.P.L.*, edited by Meade and Penny Frierson. Privately printed, n.d.

Joe Pumilia comments:

In my work I have no earth-shattering message. I try to tell a good, entertaining tale, often of the chilling, horrific kind, probably because all of us like to be frightened, and feel most alive when gripped by strong emotions, such as fear. I think I've been deeply influenced by writers like H.P. Lovecraft, Eric Frank Russell, and most of the well-known writers of the 1940's and 1950's.

I like to write of a noble fight against great odds, with the hero winning or losing as a logical outcome of the story. The struggle is most interesting to me when it takes place against unknown forces in unmapped territory, as in "Forever Stand the Stones," with its kaleidoscopic leaps through time and space at the whim of a malignant entity.

Strange mysteries of the past and present fascinate me: cryptic inscriptions on half-buried monuments, ghosts, UFO's, ESP. "As Dreams Are Made On," for example, takes place in a common dream world to which all users of a mysterious new drug have access. "Contact Myth," a story about perhaps the earliest urban civilization and its manipulation by an other-worldly visitor, "explains" the mystery of the ziggurats while trying to imagine the reactions of humans to an apparent "god" from outer space.

"The Case of James Elmo Freebish" appeared as the sole humorous story in the formidably named *Superhorror* because the editor wanted some comic relief between the heavy guns. It was written in the style of the old E.C. horror comics (the kind that were finally banned), and deals with the travails of a perambulating corpse. Other thigh-slappers are "Myth of the Ape God" (one of my favorites: a history of Kong-like apes through the eons), "Hung Like an Elephant" (written with Steven Utley), and (with Bill Wallace) a number of stories as M.M. Moamrath, an inept writer of pulp horror fiction.

*   *   *

Joe Pumilia is one of a distinct group of young writers that surfaced in Texas during the early 1970's. The body of his published work is relatively small, amounting to not many more than 20 science-fiction and horror stories in magazines and anthologies, an untold number of generally engaging pulp-fiction parodies, and a feature column of odd news items and cockamamie personal observations in *The Pasadena Citizen*.

Usually in collaboration with Bill Wallace, Pumilia has enlivened a handful of semi-professional magazines with stories attributed to the obscure but genuinely ungifted M.M. Moamrath, who contributed to such low-grade pulp magazines as *Weird Trails* and *Spicy Laundromat Stories* during the 1920's and 1930's. Typical tales by Moamrath, whom Pumilia and Wallace describe as having been utterly incapable of not trying to imitate H.P. Lovecraft, regardless of genre, are "My Sword Is Quick!" (MMM's answer to Conan of Cimmeria is named Mitra McCrom) and a Western, "Riders of the Purple Ooze," whose cowboy hero's name is Buck Eldritch. The level of humor in the Moamrath stories fluctuates wildly, often from one sentence to the next, between the sophomoric and the simply sublime.

For all the frequently dead-on-target lampooning of HPL the writer and HPL the man in the Moamrath stories, the influence of Lovecraft (as well as that of Robert Bloch, Harlan Ellison, and, probably most of all, Charles Fort) is very much in evidence in many of Pumilia's less frivolous efforts, to a degree which at times undermines them. "Forever Stand the Stones," which may be taken as indicative of Pumilia's approach to supernatural fiction, links the grisly career of Jack the Ripper with even grislier doings at Stonehenge during pre-Christian times. Though the story tends to creak under the weight of its horror-yarn conventions, it creates the proper oppressive mood as it shambles toward its preordained conclusion.

Considerably more interesting as a whole are those stories in which Pumilia eschews the unspeakable horrors of the *Weird Tales* school and follows his own lead. His love of the pulp magazines notwithstanding, his published science fiction is markedly untraditional in its choice of both themes and trappings—there is not a galactic empire to be seen anywhere in his work, and despite the occasional concession to the genre's hardware fixation (as in "Contact Myth" which contains a marvelous account of the construction of a liquid computer in ancient Sumer), the emphasis is squarely centered on human responses to the inexplicable.

"Niggertown," Pumilia's first professionally published story, shows some of the hesitation of the novice but nevertheless holds up remarkably well as speculative fiction about race relations. "Willowisp," more tautly executed, perhaps Pumilia's best effort, is a fine, evocative story about an encounter with a spectral alien that captures fireflies and carefully fastens them to cobwebs. Here, at least, Pumilia's training as a horror-story writer, rather than interfering with his intentions, serves him admirably, helping to create and sustain an atmosphere of mystery, vague dread, and melancholy. "And Death Once Dead," inverting a theme explored by Robert Silverberg in "Born with the Dead," tells of a man who cannot, will not, accept a cell-perfect replica of his late wife as anything more than a grotesque travesty of the original. The effect sought, more brutal than that in "Niggertown" or "Willowisp," is achieved at the cost of unsubtle, if efficiently relentless, prose; the story stands as a generally successful, and not at all reassuring, science-fiction horror tale about true love.

Pumilia is a writer still in the process of finding his way and his audience. None too prolific, he has yet to publish a novel, and his work is seldom anthologized and remains uncollected, which makes it all the easier to ignore. But, though sometimes excessive in his rhetoric and too often derivative of Lovecraft and Bloch, he is a writer whose weaknesses are rather outweighted by his main strengths, a keen appreciation of both the absurd and the unknowable, and a sensitivity to human concerns that should be encouraged in all fiction.

—Steven Utley

PURDOM, Tom (Thomas Edward Purdom). American. Born in New Haven, Connecticut, 19 April 1936. Educated at Lafayette College, Easton, Pennsylvania, 1952-54; Thomas Edison State College, Trenton, New Jersey, B.A. in social sciences 1977. Served in the United States Army Medical Corps, 1959-61. Married Sara Wescot in 1960; one son. Reservation agent, United Airlines, Philadelphia, 1957-58; science writer, University of Pennsylvania, Philadelphia, 1968-69; Visiting Professor of English, Temple University, Philadelphia, 1970-71; adjunct professor of English, Drexel University, Philadelphia, 1975; instructor in science fiction, Institute for Human Resources Development, Philadelphia, 1976-77. Vice-President, Science Fiction Writers of America, 1970-72. Agent: Scott Meredith Literary Agency, 845 Third Avenue, New York, New York 10022. Address: 4734 Cedar Avenue, Philadelphia, Pennsylvania 19143, U.S.A.

SCIENCE-FICTION PUBLICATIONS

Novels

I Want the Stars.   New York, Ace, 1964.
The Tree Lord of Imeten.   New York, Ace, 1966.
Five Against Arlane.   New York, Ace, 1967.
Reduction in Arms.   New York, Berkley, 1971.
The Barons of Behavior.   New York, Ace, 1972; London, Dobson, 1977.

Uncollected Short Stories

"Grieve for a Man," in *Fantastic Universe* (Chicago), August 1957.
"A Matter of Privacy," in *Science Fiction Quarterly* (Holyoke, Massachusetts), August 1957.
"The Man Who Wouldn't Sign Up," in *Infinity* (New York), October 1958.
"The Holy Grail," in *Star Science Fiction Stories 6,* edited by Frederik Pohl.   New York, Ballantine, 1959.
"The Duel of the Insecure Man," in *Satellite* (New York), April 1959.
"Excellence," in *Amazing* (New York), October 1959.
"Soroman the Protector," in *Galaxy* (New York), August 1960.
"The Green Beret," in *Analog* (New York), January 1961.
"The Warriors," in *Amazing* (New York), June 1962.
"Greenplace," in *World's Best Science Fiction 1965,* edited by Donald A. Wollheim and Terry Carr.   New York, Ace, 1965.
"Courting Time," in *Galaxy* (New York), February 1966.
"Reduction in Arms," in *Fantasy and Science Fiction* (New York), August 1967.
"Toys," in *Crime Prevention in the Thirtieth Century,* edited by Hans S. Santesson.   New York, Walker, 1969.
"A War of Passion," in *The Future Is Now,* edited by William F. Nolan.   Los Angeles, Sherbourne Press, 1970.
"Moonchild," in *Future Quest,* edited by Roger Elwood.   New York, Avon, 1973.
"Moon Rocks," in *Analog* (New York), April 1973.
"The Chains of Freedom," in *Galaxy* (New York), May 1977.

OTHER PUBLICATIONS

Other

"The Urban Hell," in *Worlds of Tomorrow* (New York), April 1964.
"The Alien Psyche," in *Worlds of Tomorrow* (New York), May 1965.
"SF's Creative Vigor," in *American Libraries* (Chicago), March 1974.
"Who's Going to Run Things in Twenty Three Hundred? And How Are They Going to Do It?," in *Writing and Selling Science Fiction.*   Cincinnati, Writer's Digest, 1976.

Editor, *Adventures in Discovery.*   New York, Doubleday, 1969.

Tom Purdom comments:
My main aim as a fiction writer is to create the kind of stories I like to read—engrossing, well-plotted works that hold you from the first page to the end and really get you involved in the characters and the things that are happening to them. Once I jokingly said that the greatest living novelists were Alexander Solzhenitsyn, Ursula K. Le Guin, Richard Adams, and George MacDonald Fraser. I was poking a little fun at literary pomposity, but I would give a great deal to have written the better works of any of them.

The struggle that most interests me—and I think it's mostly what I've written about and like to read about in SF—is the problem of adapting to technology, especially the attempt to seize the opportunity it gives us without falling into all the traps it puts in front of us (some of which are not too obvious). I'm also fond of one of the things the man Santiago said about his fish: "It will feed many people, and it will bring a good price on the market." I think science fiction has given a great many people a lot of things they needed, and it has even—especially recently—brought some of its practitioners a good price on the market.

*   *   *

Tom Purdom's career spans more than two decades. Though clearly distinguishable from one another, his early novels share the same narrative formula: the hero finds himself on an alien planet which is ruled by a dictator, either benign as in *Five Against Arlane* or malevolent as in *The Tree Lord of Imeten*. In either case, the hero struggles to overthrow tyranny and re-establish social equilibrium through bloodshed. In the aftermath of the battle against the tyrant, the hero emerges victorious from the rubble to announce that democratic liberties have been restored to the people. Great adulation of the Purdom hero follows the revolution, and the novel closes on a note of exhaustion as an infant republic comes uncertainly to life.

This well-worn plot serves as the basis for Purdom's more recent novels too, but in *The Barons of Behavior* he has achieved more interesting results. Here Purdom's subject is the potential threat which Skinnerian behaviorism poses to a free society. The novel opens in a world of the remote future in which the privileges and responsibilities of life in 20th-century America have been lost. Nurtured by democracy, the growth of lawlessness and violence has long ago become intolerable to society, and politicians, seeking a retardant, have turned to the behavioral sciences for help. And indeed they have found there willing social physicians. Thus a terrible triple alliance is formed of science, technology, and politics, whose aim it is to produce law and order, to provide security and comfort to the citizens of Windham County, Pennsylvania, but whose real accomplishment is to rob the human spirit of its civil liberties and to render the human will impotent. In *The Barons of Behavior* the orderly operation of society is insured by an arsenal of devices and techniques which can subvert individual free will. It can be numbed or stupified by insidious drugs; it can be forced to betray itself through the techniques of behavior modification; or, most horribly, it can be bypassed altogether by devices surgically implanted in the brain. Opposed to the dehumanizing powers in control of society stands the Purdom hero, Ralph Nicholson, "psychotherapist to a psyched-out world," who manages to defeat the political machine of Martin Boyd despite the overwhelming odds against his doing so.

But this is familiar stuff to science-fiction readers. The science of control has inspired dozens of novels along the same line, the very best of which achieve truly chilling results. The atrocities committed against Alex in Burgess's *A Clockwork Orange,* for instance, evoke the archetypal fear humans have of being obliterated by forces beyond their comprehension, while his struggle to remain human and intact in the face of dehumanizing powers approaches Aristotle's definition of great tragedy, the purgation of fear and pity. Unfortunately, *The Barons of Behavior* never achieves such impact. Though Purdom's technological imagination is impressive, his ability to conceive and delineate character is not. Ralph Nicholson of *The Barons of Behavior* is as two-dimensional as Migel Lassamba of *Five Against Arlane*. Both are conventional super-heroes, men of endless resource and daring, but, since they lack depth and delineation, their suffering appears rather more ludicrous than tragic, their lives more gratuitously violent than compelling, and their inevitable victory more contrived than earned.

Nevertheless, Purdom's interest in possibilities is genuine, and his grasp of the implications of behaviorism is very thorough. At his best, he is capable of constructing a shockingly plausible and horrifying vision of the future, a time when individual freedom is a suppressed, half-forgotten memory, abandoned centuries ago in pursuit of law and order. There is little anxiety in this world, even less disorder once chance factors have been all but eliminated. There are no dangers, except to the intellect and imagination. There is no physical suffering in the America of *The Barons of Behavior,* but there is no free thought either, no unapproved writing, no spontaneous creation of any kind. Men and women smile and go about their daily business, but their eyes appear vacant. They reflect no light. Birth and death are quiet, pre-arranged experiences.

—Marvin W. Hunt

PYNCHON, Thomas. American. Born in Glen Cove, New York, 8 May 1937. Educated at Cornell University, Ithaca, New York, 1954-58, B.A. 1958. Served in the United States Navy. Former editorial writer, Boeing Aircraft, Seattle. Recipient: Faulkner Award, 1964; Rosenthal Memorial Award, 1967; National Book Award, 1974; American Academy Howells Medal, 1975. Address: c/o Viking Press, 625 Madison Avenue, New York, New York 10022, U.S.A.

SCIENCE-FICTION PUBLICATIONS

Novel

Gravity's Rainbow.   New York, Viking Press, and London, Cape, 1973.

OTHER PUBLICATIONS

Novels

V. Philadelphia, Lippincott, and London, Cape, 1963.
The Crying of Lot 49.   Philadelphia, Lippincott, 1966; London, Cape, 1967.

Short Stories

Mortality and Mercy in Vienna.   London, Aloes, 1976.
Low-lands.   London, Aloes, 1978.

*

Bibliography: *Three Contemporary Novelists: An Annotated Bibliography* by Robert M. Scotto, New York, Garland, 1977.

*   *   *

Thomas Pynchon's three novels, *V, The Crying of Lot 49,* and *Gravity's Rainbow,* have the same theme and share characters and incidents. The theme is that of a vast shadowy conspiracy which shapes the destinies of the characters (and of the human race) without their knowledge or consent. This is a common SF topic. It appears more clearly in each successive work of Pynchon's until with *Gravity's Rainbow* we have the specific plot used by Mark S. Geston in *Lords of the Starship*; the race is engaged in an enterprise of great moment which turns out to be far different in intent and effect than they had supposed. In Pynchon's case, the enterprise is the entire body of modern science; the effect is wholesale immolation. This is a hackneyed theme for most SF readers, and what makes Pynchon of interest is that his use of characters, of figures of speech, of incident; his mastery of language; his force and economy of narrative; his mixture of the humorous, the bizarre, and the tragic can only be compared with the same qualities in the work of Shakespeare.

Gravity's Rainbow, for which the other two books may be regarded as apprentice work, is a novel of 750,000 words and over 300 characters, and is, at that, the most condensed outline possible of the events it describes. The rainbow is the parabolic curve described by a ballistic missile. The centre of the novel is the V-2 (A-4) missile, forerunner of the ICBM and in particular the mysterious Schwarzgeraten 00000 and 00001, ostensible weapons which are in reality sacrificial vehicles. The action commences in England in early 1945 and then swirls through Europe during the spring and summer of that year. The characters, including the American Slothrop, the Russian Tchitcherine, the Herero Enzian, and the German Blicero, move in an intricate dance centered on the Rocket. Some perish, some are saved, some like poor Slothrop are passed over, preterite, an excess part of God's plan. But in the end, when the rockets fall, we are all called home. The reader of *Gravity's Rainbow* will find help in the essay "Gravity's Encyclopedia" by Edward Mendelson (in *Mindful Pleasures,* 1976). Mendelson sees *Gravity's Rainbow,* like *Moby-Dick* and *Faust,* as an encyclopedic narrative which "attempt[s] to render the full range of knowledge and beliefs of a national culture, while identifying the ideological perspectives from which that culture shapes and interprets its knowledge." From the SF point of view, Pynchon handles mathematics, chemistry, and ballistics, in description and as metaphor, with an effect and sureness of touch that are unique. We have here a major writer, recognized by the academics and in the mainstream, in whose work the importance of science mirrors its importance in the real world. If there is a flaw in *Gravity's Rainbow*, apart from the inchoate structure caused by the vast weight and variety of matter included, it is the apparent espousal of the view that all evil flows from the white European—but this is indeed a feature of the time in which he writes and probably should not be laid at the author's door. At any rate, incoherence and all, Pynchon's achievement is not surpassed in modern English letters.

—E.R. Bishop

RACKHAM, John. Pseudonym for John Thomas Phillifent. British. Born in Durham, 10 November 1916. Served in the Royal Navy, 1935-47. Worked for the Central Electricity Generating Board in the early 1960's. *Died 16 December 1976.*

SCIENCE-FICTION PUBLICATIONS

Novels

Space Puppet.   London, Pearson, 1954.
Jupiter Equilateral.   London, Pearson, 1954.
The Master Weed.   London, Pearson, 1954.
The Touch of Evil.   London, Digit, 1963.
We, The Venusians.   New York, Ace, 1965.
The Beasts of Kohl.   New York, Ace, 1966.
Time to Live.   New York, Ace, 1966; London, Dobson, 1969.
Danger from Vega.   New York, Ace, 1966; London, Dobson, 1970.
The Double Invaders.   New York, Ace, 1967.
Alien Sea.   New York, Ace, 1968; London, Dobson, 1975.
The Proxima Project.   New York, Ace, 1968.
The Treasure of Tau Ceti.   New York, Ace, 1969.
Ipomoea.   New York, Ace, 1969; London, Dobson, 1972.
The Flower of Doradil.   New York, Ace, 1970.
The Anything Tree.   New York, Ace, 1970; London, Dobson, 1977.
Beyond Capella.   New York, Ace, 1971.
Dark Planet.   New York, Ace, 1971.
Earthstrings.   New York, Ace, 1972.
Beanstalk.   New York, DAW, 1973.

Novels as John T. Phillifent

Genius Unlimited.   New York, DAW, 1972.
Hierarchies.   New York, Ace, 1973.
Life with Lancelot.   New York, Ace, 1973.
King of Argent.   New York, DAW, 1973.

Uncollected Short Stories

"Drog," in *Science Fantasy* (Bournemouth), February 1958.
"One-Eye," in *Astounding* (New York), May 1958.
"Nulook," in *Science Fantasy* (Bournemouth), April 1959.
"Curse Strings," in *Science Fantasy* (Bournemouth), November 1959.
"If You Wish," in *If* (New York), November 1959.
"The Bright Ones," in *New Worlds* (London), May 1960.
"Idea Man," in *Galaxy* (New York), June 1960.
"Theory," in *New Worlds* (London), September 1960.
"The Science Fiction Ethic," in *New Worlds* (London), November 1960.
"The Black Cat's Paw," in *Science Fantasy* (Bournemouth), December 1960.

"Trial Run," in *New Worlds* (London), December 1960.
"Blink," in *New Worlds* (London), May 1961.
"The Veil of Isis," in *Science Fantasy* (Bournemouth), June 1961.
"The Trouble with Honey," in *New Worlds* (London), July 1961.
"The Stainless-Steel Knight," in *If* (New York), July 1961.
"Goodbye, Doctor Gabriel," in *New Worlds* (London), August 1961.
"Ankh," in *Science Fantasy* (Bournemouth), December 1961.
"The Dawson Diaries," in *New Worlds* (London), April, May 1962.
"Fire and Ice," in *Science Fantasy* (Bournemouth), December 1962.
"The Rainmaker," in *Science Fiction Adventures* (London), February 1963.
"Dossier," in *New Worlds* (London), April 1963.
"Confession," in *New Worlds* (London), May 1963.
"What You Don't Know," in *Science Fantasy* (Bournemouth), June 1963.
"With Clean Hands," in *Science Fantasy* (Bournemouth), August 1963.
"Dr. Jeckers and Mr. Hyde," in *Amazing* (New York), August 1963.
"Deep Freeze," in *New Worlds* (London), September 1963.
"Man-Hunt," in *New Worlds* (London), October 1963.
"Crux," in *New Worlds* (London), November 1963.
"The Last Salamander," in *Lambda 1 and Other Stories*, edited by John Carnell.   New York, Berkley, 1964; London, Penguin, 1965.
"Hell-Planet," in *New Writings in SF 2*, edited by John Carnell.   London, Dobson, 1964; New York, Bantam, 1966.
"Die and Grow Rich," in *New Worlds* (London), February 1964.
"God Killer," in *Science Fantasy* (Bournemouth), August 1964.
"Advantage," in *New Writings in SF 6*, edited by John Carnell.   London, Dobson, 1965; New York, Bantam, 1971.
"Room with a View," in *Science Fantasy* (Bournemouth), January 1965.
"Bring Back a Life," in *Science Fantasy* (Bournemouth), March 1965.
"A Way with Animals," in *Science Fantasy* (Bournemouth), August 1965.
"Computer's Mate," in *New Writings in SF 8*, edited by John Carnell.   London, Dobson, 1966.
"Poseidon Project," in *New Writings in SF 9*, edited by John Carnell.   London, Dobson, 1966; New York, Bantam, 1972.
"The God-Birds of Glentallach," in *Science Fantasy* (Bournemouth), January 1966.
"A Light Feint," in *Impulse* (London), April 1966.
"Catharsis," in *New Writings in SF 11*, edited by John Carnell.   London, Dobson, 1968.
"The Divided House," in *New Writings in SF 13*, edited by John Carnell.   London, Dobson, 1968.
"Stoop to Conquer," in *New Writings in SF 19*, edited by John Carnell.   London, Dobson, 1971.
"Wise Child," in *New Writings in SF 22*, edited by Kenneth Bulmer.   London, Sidgwick and Jackson, 1973.
"The Halted Village," in *New Writings in SF 25*, edited by Kenneth Bulmer.   London, Sidgwick and Jackson, 1975.
"Heal Thyself," in *New Writings in SF 27*, edited by Kenneth Bulmer.   London, Sidgwick and Jackson, 1976.

Uncollected Short Stories as John T. Phillifent

"Point," in *Fantastic* (New York), December 1961.
"Ethical Quotient," in *Analog* (New York), October 1962.
"Flying Fish," in *Analog* (New York), October 1964.
"Finnegan's Knack," in *Analog* (New York), January 1965.
"Aim for the Heel," in *Analog* (New York), July 1967.
"Incorrigible," in *Analog* (New York), April 1968.
"The Rites of Man," in *Analog* (New York), November 1968.
"All Fall Down," in *Analog* (New York), August 1969.
"The Fine Print," in *Analog* (New York), September 1971.
"Owe Me," in *Analog* (New York), May 1974.

OTHER PUBLICATIONS

Novels as John T. Phillifent

The Lonely Man.   London, Boardman, 1965.

The Mad Scientist Affair. London, Souvenir Press, and New York, Ace, 1966.
The Corfu Affair. London, Souvenir Press, 1967; New York, Ace, 1969.
The Power Cube Affair. London, Souvenir Press, and New York, Ace, 1968.

*   *   *

Under his own name and the pseudonym of John Rackham, John T. Phillifent produced a series of short adventure novels that made use of traditional science-fiction plots to present a fast-moving plot set against an exotic background. There is little doubt in the reader's mind that right will ultimately prevail, but the events along the way are the chief attraction.

To a great extent, Rackham repeated the situations he found most appealing. One of these is the Mowgli tale set in the future; one or more humans are returned to civilization after being raised among aliens, and the ensuing culture shock provides much of the basis of the story. This is the major plotline in *The Beasts of Kohl*, for example, where Earth has become considerably more benign but still unsettling to one not used to human ways. The same is true of the far better Phillifent novel, *Life with Lancelot*, in which the alien Shogleet rebuilds a damaged human with mechanical parts, and then tries to reintegrate him into human culture. Another recurring plot is the search for a fabulous treasure, be it gem, secret plans, or immortality drug. The protagonist of *The Treasure of Tau Ceti* is motivated by legends of priceless gems on that jungle world, but along the way he forces humans to recognize that the inhabitants of the planet are indeed intelligent. A secret agent searches for a rumored sentient plant in *The Anything Tree*. Another plant, this time one that will cure all human diseases, is the target of another group of adventurers in *The Flower of Doradil*. This time the major subplot is a crew of human smugglers determined to prevent the success of the hero's mission. Jewels are the quarry once again in the *Hierarchies* (Phillifent), this time purloined from their rightful owner. Another theme is that of secret alien or human manipulation of society. Secret aliens provoke a war between Earth and Venus in *Alien Sea*; a new drug is revealed to be the tool of insidious would-be alien conquerors in *Ipomoea*; human expansion into space is blocked by apparently invulnerable alien constructs in *Beyond Capella*. Secret human societies appear in *Earthstrings*, in which a human colony is wiped out as part of a plot by commercial magnates, and in *Genius Unlimited* (Phillifent), wherein a scientific colony is actually serving as a mask to conceal a plot for interstellar conquest.

Rackham did interject some commentary into his novels, and the earlier ones in particular seem to demonstrate his faith that mankind would grow out of its petty prejudices. In *We, The Venusians* Anthony Taylor passes as human because a pill changes his skin color and he cannot be identified as a native Greenie. Ultimately, the racial prejudice that forms the basis of the novel is reconciled as the two races eventually recognize each other's equality. In *The Beasts of Kohl* humanity has learned to accept the rights of whales on Earth and aliens in space. There is some evidence that Rackham became disillusioned in his last years. Nefarious plots are invariably human-instigated in the later novels, and the more enlightened humans cast themselves loose from the race, as in *King of Argent* (Phillifent), or even settle down among aliens, as does the hero of *Dark Planet*. Where the human refugees had favorable effects on a primitive alien race in *Danger from Vega*, they are presented as a danger to the interstellar community in *Genius Unlimited* (Phillifent) and, to a lesser extent, *Beyond Capella*. Other standard plots appear here and there. There is a rather dull interstellar war in *The Double Invaders*, and a rather amusing view of one in *Beanstalk*, which presents the familiar fairy tale as a distorted version of Earth's minor involvement in an interstellar war. Mankind's necessity to advance into the universe is central to *Beyond Capella* and *The Proxima Project*.

Rackham never produced what could fairly be termed an outstanding work. He made no attempt to tackle major social problems except in the most superficial way, and he broke no new ground in either style or plot. But he did produce a string of competently written light adventure novels that don't insult the intelligence of the reader. They are invariably upbeat, there is no confusion between heroes and villains, and any incompetence on the part of the central character is transitory. It is a simple universe in many ways that Rackham wrote about, and generally an entertaining one.

—Don D'Ammassa

RAND, Ayn. American. Born in St. Petersburg, now Leningrad, Russia, 2 February 1905; emigrated to the United States in 1926; naturalized, 1931. Educated at the University of Leningrad: graduated in history 1924. Married Frank O'Connor in 1929. Screenwriter, 1932-34, 1944-49. Editor, *The Objectivist*, New York, 1962-71, and since 1971, *The Ayn Rand Letter*, New York. D.H.L.: Lewis and Clark College, Portland, Oregon, 1963. Address: P.O. Box 177, Murray Hill Station, New York, New York 10016, U.S.A.

SCIENCE-FICTION PUBLICATIONS

Novels

Anthem. London, Cassell, 1938; revised edition, Los Angeles, Pamphleteers, 1946.
Atlas Shrugged. New York, Random House, 1957.

OTHER PUBLICATIONS

Novels

We the Living. New York, Macmillan, and London, Cassell, 1936.
The Fountainhead. Indianapolis, Bobbs Merrill, 1943; London, Cassell, 1947.

Plays

Night of January 16th (as *Woman on Trial*, produced Hollywood, 1934; New York, 1935; London, 1936; as *Penthouse Legend*, produced New York, 1973). New York, Longman, 1936.
The Unconquered, adaptation of her novel *We the Living* (produced New York, 1940).

Screenplays: *You Came Along*, with Robert Smith, 1945; *Love Letters*, 1945; *The Fountainhead*, 1949.

Other

Textbook of Americanism. New York, Branden Institute, 1946.
Notes on the History of American Free Enterprise. New York, Platen Press, 1959.
Faith and Force: The Destroyers of the Modern World. New York, Branden Institute, 1961.
For the New Intellectual. New York, Random House, 1961.
The Objectivist Ethics. New York, Branden Institute, 1961.
America's Persecuted Minority: Big Business. New York, Branden Institute, 1962.
Conservatism: An Obituary. New York, Branden Institute, 1962.
The Fascist New Frontier. New York, Branden Institute, 1963.
The Virtue of Selfishness: A New Concept of Egoism. New York, New American Library, 1965.
Capitalism: The Unknown Ideal, with others. New York, New American Library, 1966.
Introduction to Objectivist Epistemology. New York, The Objectivist, 1967.
The Romantic Manifesto: A Philosophy of Literature. Cleveland, World, 1970.
The New Left: The Anti-Industrial Revolution. New York, New American Library, 1971.

*   *   *

Considering her unvarying depictions of heroes and heroines as people adhering to unpopular views despite hostility and abuse, Ayn Rand must be pleased at resembling them through the controversy she arouses by her novels. In spite of claiming to be an unswerving advocate of reason, her appeal is often violently emotional. She makes her readers long to identify themselves with her dynamic, creative, productive, intelligent, handsome, and ultimately victorious heroes (and thereby with the ideas associated with them). She also compels her readers to despise the cowardly, lazy, incompetent, vicious, ugly, and inevitably defeated spokesmen for the ideas she abhors. Her two speculative novels, *Anthem* and *Atlas Shrugged*, stridently warn against shaping our future according to the ideals of Christianity, Marxism, liberalism, or any other viewpoint advocating self-sacrifice which, to her, means self-negation. In opposition to such ideals, they applaud man's ego as the source of all inventiveness, achievement, and happiness and capitalism as the system allowing the fullest expression of the ego. In spite of her stridency, Rand remains one of the most powerful—and thoughtful—defenders of conservative American values, portraying the businessman as the unacknowledged Atlas who carries the burden of civilization on his mighty shoulders.

Although *Anthem* and *Atlas Shrugged* are clearly intended as cautionary tracts expounding Rand's social and philosophical beliefs and fears, both present carefully detailed pictures of future societies. In creating these societies, Rand extrapolates the possible consequences of self-sacrificial goals on art, politics, economics, sex, and family and social relationships. *Anthem* is set in a new dark age which has come about after the collectivists have defeated all the individualists. In this world, technology has nearly ceased to exist since, for Rand, it is the product of individual curiosity, effort, and ability which have also nearly ceased to exist. At birth, all children are taken from their parents and placed in a communal home where they will be taught that they must devote their lives to working for the benefit of their brothers, act as all their brothers act, and think only what all their brothers think. No man is permitted to live as an individual and the word "I" is forbidden. However, one man known as Equality 7-2521 finds such a world uncomfortable, "transgresses," and through his "sinful" behavior rediscovers individualism, creativity, self-respect, and selective love and friendship—or, in short, Rand's own values. *Atlas Shrugged* is set in an America resembling that of the 1950's when the book was written. However, this America soon becomes transformed into a society trying to follow the Christian goal of loving one's brother like oneself and the Marxist principle "From each according to his ability, to each according to his need." The government assumes control over the economy, places all industries under a Unification Board, and attempts to redistribute the benefits earned by the most efficient companies to the least efficient ones on the assumption that the weaker companies have the greater need. The result of this policy of penalizing success and rewarding failure is that moochers rise to the highest levels of government (the head of the economic program is named Wesley Mouch) and the most productive businessmen have difficulty surviving. Having foreseen these developments, the superheroic protagonist, John Galt, leads the greatest producers and creators on strike, thus precipitating the collapse of the moochers' government and preparing the way for a new society founded on the Randian oath: "I swear—by my life and by my love of it—that I will never live for the sake of another man, nor ask another man to live for mine."

Both of Rand's speculative novels are major contributions to the field. Her passionate commitment to ideas about social structure is well suited to the speculative form, especially since it is coupled with an ability to give concrete embodiment to these ideas. Though the slim *Anthem* only sketches her ideas, it offers a good introduction to them. Longer than Samuel Delany's *Dhalgren* and talkier than Robert Heinlein's *I Will Fear No Evil*, the gigantic *Atlas Shrugged* spells them out fully in repetitious but often exciting, provocative, and even brilliant detail.

—Steven R. Carter

RANDALL, Marta. American. Born in Mexico City, 26 April 1948; moved to San Francisco at age 2. Educated at San Francisco State College, 1966-72. Married Robert H. Bergstresser in 1966 (divorced, 1973); one son. Since 1968, office manager, H. Zimmerman, Oakland, California. Agent: Richard Curtis, 156 East 52nd Street, New York, New York 10022. Address: P.O. Box 13243, Station E, Oakland, California 94661, U.S.A.

SCIENCE-FICTION PUBLICATIONS

Novels (series: Kennerin Saga)

A City in the North. New York, Warner, 1976.
Islands. New York, Pyramid, 1976; revised edition, New York, Simon and Schuster, 1980.
Journey (Kennerin). New York, Pocket Books, 1978; London, Hamlyn, 1979.
Dangerous Games (Kennerin). New York, Pocket Books, 1980.

Uncollected Short Stories

"A Scarab in the City of Time," in *New Dimensions 5*, edited by Robert Silverberg. New York, Harper, 1975; London, Gollancz, 1976.
"Secret Rider," in *New Dimensions 6*, edited by Robert Silverberg. New York, Harper, and London, Gollancz, 1976.
"Megan's World," in *The Crystal Ship*, edited by Robert Silverberg. Nashville, Nelson, 1976; London, Millington, 1980.
"The State of the Art on Alyssum," in *New Dimensions 7*, edited by Robert Silverberg. New York, Harper, and London, Gollancz, 1977.
"The Captain and the Kid," in *Universe 9*, edited by Terry Carr. New York, Doubleday, 1979; London, Dobson, 1980.
"The View from Endless Scarp," in *Fantasy and Science Fiction* (New York), July 1979.
"Circus," in *New Dimensions 10*, edited by Robert Silverberg. New York, Harper, 1980.

OTHER PUBLICATIONS

Other

Introduction to *Galaxies*, by Barry N. Malzberg. Boston, Gregg Press, 1980.

Editor, with Robert Silverberg, *New Dimensions 11*. New York, Pocket Books, 1980.

Marta Randall comments:
I find it difficult to speak about my own fiction—primarily, I think, because of a conviction that stories must stand by themselves, and the hopes, opinions, or beliefs of their authors are ultimately irrelevant. I view science fiction as a tool, as a useful series of conventions with which to deal with a storyteller's basic task, that is, the exploration not of ideas, but of people. By using the devices of the genre the writer can pare away anything not relevant to the characters and their dilemmas, can, in effect, create a crucible in which to toss the characters and view their reactions. Lest that sound pompous, I believe it equally important that science fiction remain, far more than general mainstream fiction, a genre in which one can tell stories, present adventures, write for the simple joy of creating wonderful things. My principal goal as a science-fiction writer is to meld these two approaches to the genre. It is a goal which I hope to be chasing for the rest of my professional life.

*   *   *

Marta Randall is very much a writer of the 1970's who confidently uses science-fiction situations as the stage for human drama. Her tales of personal triumphs against unknown environments as well as the unknowns of the human heart are enriched by her eye for detail and her well-drawn characters. Her work is notable for its firm sense of men and women as equals facing the future and for its belief in the importance of children and the elderly—along with individuals in the prime of life—in determining the directions taken by future societies.

Her first novel, *A City in the North*, established Randall as a writer committed to the development of particularly strong female characters. Here two women of dissimilar bearing, appearance, and personality join forces to aid Toyon Sutak—a powerfully drawn male character in his own right—in realizing his dream of reaching the ruins of an alien city. Stylistically, the book is interesting for its rich descriptive passages and for its use of shifting narrative point of view. The journals of Sutak and his wife Kennerin reveal their mutual perplexity and distrust as well as their courage and determination, while the proud, no-nonsense reflections of their helpmeet Quellan and the befuddled recollections of the planetary Governor Rhodes add variety to the narrative. Most importantly, the author knows how to give eloquence to the almost unbroken silence of the alien Haapati. In common with Randall's other writings, *A City in the North* points out the necessity for openmindedness and adaptability on the part of humans in dealing with other peoples and other worlds.

"The View from Endless Scarp" makes a clear statement about the need for human adaptability on other worlds. Here a human female called Markowitz must adapt to the harsh way of life on an alien planet, after a Terran-engineered life support and weather control system, geared to creating an ideal environment for humanity, breaks down. Randall's characteristic eye for detail is employed very strikingly here. The alien Peri, who have watched the rise and fall of Terran life on their planet, have an annoying (to Terrans) giggle-like vocabulary which seems to be a comment on the humans' plight. When Markowitz finally accepts her fate as a permanent inhabitant of her new home, she bursts into a similar giggling sound. "You are a Peri," her alien companion declares. *Journey* is another tale of world-building on an alien planet, this time a world more hospitable to humans. Here a gentle alien race wins the friendship of the initially suspicious humans. Enriched by its science-fiction trappings, *Journey* is essentially a family saga, a story not only of building a home but of homecoming. As an exploding supernova signals the ending of one world, Randall's men and women, children and elders must share the commitment of creating a new one. "The Captain and the Kid" features a spunky elderly spaceship Captain who finds herself intolerably restless while anchored to an agricultural job on a new world. This restlessness for the freedom of space flight, combined with her distaste for the bigoted and ungrateful behavior of those colonists she had singlehandedly transported to their new planet (as they slept in life support systems), cause the Captain and her sidekick to flee the drudgery of their planet-bound existence and embrace the joyous possibilities afforded by travel between the stars.

Whether on alien soil or in space vehicles, Randall's characters are people in search of a home, a haven in which they can live out their lives and come to terms with personal and environmental challenges. Randall is interested in the pioneering spirit, and portrays it admirably against settings which represent the modern imaginative frontier.

—Rosemary Herbert

RANKINE, John. Pseudonym for Douglas Rankine Mason; also writes as R.M. Douglas. British. Born in Hawarden, Flintshire, 26 September 1918. Educated at Heywood Grammar School, 1929-34; Chester Grammar School, 1934-37; Manchester University, 1937-39, 1946-48, B.A. Served in the Royal Signals, 1939-46: Lieutenant. Married Mary Cooper in 1945; two sons and two daughters. Headmaster, Somerville Junior School, 1954-67, and St. George's Primary School, 1967-78, both Wallasey, Cheshire. Agent: Leslie Flood, E.J. Carnell Literary Agency, Rowneybury Bungalow, Sawbridgeworth, near Old Harlow, Essex CM20 2EX. Address: 16 Elleray Park Road, Wallasey, Merseyside L45 OLH, England.

SCIENCE-FICTION PUBLICATIONS

Novels

The Blockade of Sinitron (juvenile). London, Nelson, 1966.
Interstellar Two-Five. London, Dobson, 1966.
Never the Same Door. London, Dobson, 1968.
One Is One. London, Dobson, 1968.
Moons of Triopus. London, Dobson, 1968; New York, Paperback Library, 1969.
Binary Z. London, Dobson, 1969.
The Weisman Experiment. London, Dobson, 1969.
The Plantos Affair. London, Dobson, 1971.
The Ring of Garamas. London, Dobson, 1972.
Operation Umanaq. New York, Ace, 1973; London, Sidgwick and Jackson, 1974.
The Bromius Phenomenon. New York, Ace, 1973; London, Dobson, 1976.
The Fingalnan Conspiracy. London, Sidgwick and Jackson, 1973.
Moon Odyssey (novelization of TV series). London, Dobson, and Mattituck, New York, Amereon, 1975.
Lunar Attack (novelization of TV series). London, Dobson, 1975; New York, Pocket Books, 1976.
Astral Quest (novelization of TV series). London, Dobson, 1975; New York, Pocket Books, 1976.
Android Planet (novelization of TV series). London, Barker, and New York, Pocket Books, 1976.
The Phoenix of Megaron. New York, Pocket Books, 1976.
The Thorburn Enterprise. London, Dobson, 1977.
The Vort Programme. London, Dobson, 1979.
The Star of Hesiock. London, Dobson, 1979.
Last Shuttle to Planet Earth. London, Dobson, 1980.

Novels as Douglas R. Mason

From Carthage Then I Came. New York, Doubleday, 1966; London, Hale, 1968; as *Eight Against Utopia*, New York, Paperback Library, 1967.
Ring of Violence. London, Hale, 1968; New York, Avon, 1969.
Landfall Is a State of Mind. London, Hale, 1968.
The Tower of Rizwan. London, Hale, 1968.
The Janus Syndrome. London, Hale, 1969.
Matrix. New York, Ballantine, 1970; London, Hale, 1971.
Satellite 54-Zero. New York, Ballantine, and London, Pan, 1971.
Horizon Alpha. New York, Ballantine, 1971.
Dilation Effect. New York, Ballantine, 1971.
The Resurrection of Roger Diment. New York, Ballantine, 1972.
The Phaeton Condition. New York, Putnam, 1973; London, Hale, 1974.
The End Bringers. New York, Ballantine, 1973; London, Hale, 1975.
Pitman's Progress. Morley, Yorkshire, Elmfield Press, 1976.
The Omega Worm. London, Hale, 1976.
Euphor Unfree. London, Hale, 1977.
Mission to Pactolus R. London, Hale, 1978.

Uncollected Short Stories (series: Dag Fletcher)

"Two's Company" (Fletcher), in *New Writings in SF 1*, edited by John Carnell. London, Dobson, 1964; New York, Bantam, 1966.
"Maiden Voyage" (Fletcher), in *New Writings in SF 2*, edited by John Carnell. London, Dobson, 1964; London, Bantam, 1966.
"Six Cubed Plus 1," in *New Writings in SF 7*, edited by John Carnell. London, Dobson, 1966; New York, Bantam, 1971.
"Seventh Moon," in *Impulse* (London), May 1966.
"Pattern as Set," in *Impulse* (London), July 1966.
"Image of Destruction" (Fletcher), in *New Writings in SF 10*, edited by John Carnell. London, Dobson, 1967.
"Flight of the Plastic Bee," in *New Writings in SF 11*, edited by John Carnell. London, Dobson, 1968.
"Worm in the Bud" (Fletcher), in *New Writings in SF 12*, edited by John Carnell. London, Dobson, 1968.
"The Peacemakers," in *If* (New York), January 1968.

"Moonchip," in *Vision of Tomorrow* (Newcastle upon Tyne), December 1969.
"Second Run at the Data," in *Galaxy* (New York), February 1971.
"Link," in *Amazing* (New York), January 1973.

Uncollected Short Stories as Douglas R. Mason

"Traveller's Rest," in *New Worlds* (London), September 1965.
"Squared Out with Poplars," in *Worlds of Tomorrow* (New York), May 1967.
"Locust Years," in *Galaxy* (New York), November 1968.
"Dinner of Herbs," in *Vision of Tomorrow* (Newcastle upon Tyne), February 1970.
"Rejection Syndrome," in *Vision of Tomorrow* (Newcastle upon Tyne), April 1970.
"The Castoffs," in *If* (New York), February 1972.
"Algora One Six," in *New Writings in SF 21*, edited by John Carnell.   London, Sidgwick and Jackson, 1973.

OTHER PUBLICATIONS

Novel as R.M. Douglas

The Darkling Plain.   London, Hale, 1979.

John Rankine comments:
    Science fiction is either escapist adventure—Hornblower in a star ship—or an allegory for our time—the dystopia, *Brave New World* bit. I tend to write the first as John Rankine and the second as Douglas R. Mason.
    I hold the view that the biogrammar that determines the human make-up was laid down over such a long period that events like the technological revolution will not alter anything in the foreseeable future. Therefore my inhabitants of Wirral City in 4000 AD act in the same way as people of the present. Cain is still Cain and unable to change.

                    *   *   *

    John Rankine, who also writes under his real name, Douglas R. Mason, envisions future battles waged by man against android, robot, computer, or physically recreated bionic man. Usually the machines' rigidity, their propensity toward predictable patterns, their lack of emotion, their machine nature is responsible for or aids in their ultimate defeat, while man's doubt, his emotion, his loyalty, his physical self, spurred by instinct, passion, and a need for action and for self-preservation, help him ultimately to conquer. Rankine continually deplores man's insidious tendency to sacrifice freedom and intellectual activity for the sake of comfort, stability, and pleasure, and asks if there can be true pleasure without conflict and pain. His heroes are constantly struck with the realization that they have never felt truly alive until they have tasted sweat, endured trauma, and shared danger. Rankine also wonders whether prolonging life through chemicals and mechanical replacements might not be ultimately self-destructive, immortality at the price of humanity and selfhood. Frequently his bionic characters are patronizing about real humans, and feel an intellectual sympathy with computers, attitudes that always doom them.
    Rankine heroes are tough and manly but have sunk into the mindless apathy of modern regimentation only to be jarred into self-awareness and rebellion by a freak incident, a sudden intuition or insight, an irrepressible instinct. Occasionally they articulate these attitudes in lines from Shakespeare or Keats. Often these men are attracted to cold, incredibly beautiful women who keep them at a distance and intellectualize their relationship; ultimately, however, they learn that such women are either useless in a crisis or actively act against them, turning them over to robots for "readjustment." Usually the heroes are passionately aroused by a less perfect but more nubile woman who has worked with them unnoticed in the past, who fights in their cause, and who finally accepts a division of labor whereby the male is leader and warrior and the woman submits as helpmate, nurse, cook, and technician.
    In *The End Bringers* androids rule, monitoring human emotions and repressing them with drugs, until a natural rebel uncovers a plot to eliminate all humanoids; rescuing hundreds before robots eviscerate them, he leads survivors to an air raid shelter from which revived humanity launches its attack on android tyrants. In *Matrix* city computers plan to eliminate all human life and use the free space to unify storage banks and achieve godhood, but a human administrator discovers the plan and fights back. In doing so he has to deal with conformists who not only disapprove of rebellion, but actively battle against it, blind to their own precarious predicament, or with doubters who understand his logic but question his motives, or with humanists who oppose the violence of his methods, violence that ultimately proves justified. In *From Carthage Then I Came* a computer, originally established to protect man from a cruel ice age, has monitored all life in the domed city for seven thousand years, but life is sterile, impersonal, and public. A few who have learned to evade mind probes unite in an escape plot, and, against difficult odds, outwit computers and robots, and start a new world in the wilderness, agrarian but free. These patterns with their Edenic themes are typical of much of Rankine's canon.
    Basically Rankine writes about science's potential abuses, limiting man's potentiality, reducing originality, variety, and natural evolution, controlling his weather and his atmosphere, tampering with his mind. In *Satellite 54-Zero* a secret agent tries to penetrate a private scientific operation studying Jupiter, only to encounter the horror of mechanical failure in space, a scientific mind out of control, and a centaur transported from another dimension. In *Operation Umanaq* the Southern hemisphere plots to destroy the Northern by affecting weather conditions and producing another ice age, while a fast-acting Northern agent evades hitmen and suicide drugs to invade a Polar station and reset weather computers. *The Phaeton Condition* begins in a world so polluted by industrial waste that its oxygen supply is fast being depleted; an industrial giant who helped create this condition plans to exploit it further through a secret high-priced safe zone with its own underground oxygen reserves. Frequently Mason's scientists consider humans expendable and progress worth any danger. In *Moons of Triopus* the industrial advantages of exploiting a new planet are judged more important than slow, safe investigation, but politicians and businessmen learn too late that more rational beings may well view their selfish acts with contempt and act accordingly.
    The "Dag Fletcher" series are all set in the same galaxy and involve lots of action, while his novelized episodes from TV *Space 1999*, are episodic, a progression of threats and dangers ranging from space brain anti-bodies to materialized nightmares to alien wars of annihilation. His short stories often focus on mathematics, "Six Cubed Plus 1" on the magical properties of special numbers and "Traveller's Rest" on topological oddities whereby time and language vary with the structure of space.

                                        —Gina Macdonald

RAPHAEL, Rick.   American.   Born in New York City, 20 February 1919. Educated at Boise Junior College, Idaho; University of New Mexico, Albuquerque, B.A. 1948; Colorado State University, Fort Collins. Served in the United States Army, 1936-45, and in the reserve service, 1945-65: retired as Captain: Bronze Star, Purple Heart, and service stars. Married 1) Dolores Raphael in 1941; 2) Elizabeth L. Van Schaick in 1958; one son and five daughters. Newspaper reporter, writer, and editor, 1945-58; copy editor, *Idaho Daily Statesman*, Boise, 1958-59; assistant news editor and political editor, KBOI-TV and Radio, Boise, 1959-65; Press Secretary for Senator Frank Church, 1965-69. Since 1969, executive, J.C. Penney Company. Recipient: Radio-Television News Directors Award, for documentary, 1963.

SCIENCE-FICTION PUBLICATIONS

Novel

Code Three. New York, Simon and Schuster, 1965; London, Gollancz, 1966.

Short Stories

The Thirst Quenchers. London, Gollancz, 1965.

*   *   *

Though he is probably best known for his novel, *Code Three*, Rick Raphael is a skilled writer of long stories. *The Thirst Quenchers* ("The Thirst Quenchers," "Guttersnipe," "The Mailman Cometh," "Odd Man In") demonstrates this skill. The title story and "Guttersnipe" both deal with futures in which overpopulation has led to a scarcity of fresh water. Formidable managerial and technological resources are shown being used to maintain supplies. The different measures adopted in each story are threatened by disasters which generate the interest. Most notable in these stories, and typical of Raphael's work, is the patience and intelligence with which he has worked out the operations of the agencies concerned with conserving the precious water; his technical descriptions are confidently and convincingly written.

Code Three actually exemplifies Raphael's basic inclination toward the novella form. The novel is really three long stories strung together in sequence; in fact two of the stories were originally published separately. Like much of Raphael's work, *Code Three* presents a dystopian future, in this case one dominated by five-mile-wide thruways providing routes for cars which travel at 400 miles per hour or more. The main characters of the book are officers who man a patrol car designed to cope with the dangers of driving on such roads—and the irresponsibilities of the civilian motorists, who often use their vehicles in a lunatic manner.

Because of its episodic structure, *Code Three* lacks true cohesion as a novel. In the first two sections, the officers of patrol car 56 deal efficiently with a rampaging criminal vehicle (the cars, rather than the people, are the real characters of this section), then with the reckless son of an important businessman. The son, like his father, thinks he is beyond the law. He turns out to be likeable enough, and even shows signs of learning his lesson; however, the corrupt father is made to feel the full weight of the law when he tries to interfere criminally with the legal proceedings. In the last section, heroic romance suddenly changes to tragic irony: the main character, Ben Martin, is killed while testing a new type of patrol car, portentously known as "the Bomb." His death is caused by an irresponsible young officer whose recklessness epitomizes what Martin had spent his life controlling. The sinister, ironic tone of this section meshes badly with the rest of the novel; yet the section itself is genuinely moving. Ultimately, Ben Martin is a *pharmakos* destroyed by a guilty society. That society may no longer look like a plausible extrapolation of our own: the development of more and more powerful fuel-driven vehicles seems unfeasible in the context of a fuel crisis. However, the novel is still an effective parable of the destruction wrought by human irresponsibility.

As in "The Thirst Quenchers" and his other stories, Raphael is admirable when describing the more technical aspects of his projected society's workings; he is certain and lucid in his descriptions of car chases and vehicular operations. He is less certain in handling his characters: his women are particularly stereotyped, while the male characters are seldom treated in psychological depth and often utter lines which are downright corny. Nonetheless, Raphael is a formidable and often underrated minor talent. He has written effectively on a variety of subjects, from a twist on the telepathy gambit ("Sonny") to sexual tensions in the Galactic Postal Service ("The Mailman Cometh"). His detailed treatments of future dystopias deserve particular respect.

—Russell Blackford

RAYER, Francis G(eorge). Also writes as George Longdon; Milward Scott; Roland Worcester. British. Born in Longdon, Worcestershire, 6 June 1921. Married Tessa Elizabeth Platt in 1957; two sons. Since 1945, self-employed technical designer and electronic engineer; also a technical journalist. Agent: E.J. Carnell Literary Agency, Rowneybury Bungalow, Sawbridgeworth, near Old Harlow, Essex CM20 2EX. Address: Reddings, Longdon Heath, Upton-on-Severn, Worcestershire WR8 ORJ, England.

SCIENCE-FICTION PUBLICATIONS

Novels

Tomorrow Sometimes Comes. London, Home and Van Thal, 1951.
The Star Seekers. London, Pearson, 1954.
Cardinal of the Stars. London, Digit, 1964; as *Journey to the Stars*, New York, Arcadia House, 1964.
The Iron and the Anger. London, Digit, 1964; New York, Arcadia House, 1967.

Uncollected Short Stories

"Basic Fundamental," in *Fantasy* (London), August 1947.
"From Beyond the Dawn," in *New Worlds 3* (London), n.d.
"Necessity," in *New Worlds 5* (London), 1949.
"Fearful Barrier," in *Worlds at War*, edited by Francis G. Rayer. London, Temple, 1950.
"Adaptability," in *New Worlds* (London), Spring 1950.
"Quest," in *New Worlds* (London), Summer 1950.
"Deus ex Machina," in *New Worlds* (London), Winter 1950.
"Time Was," in *New Worlds* (London), Winter 1951.
"The Undying Enemy," in *Science Fantasy* (Bournemouth), Winter 1951.
"Coming of the Darakua," in *Authentic 17* (London), 1952.
"Earth Our New Eden," in *Authentic 20* (London), 1952.
"When Greed Steps In," in *Fantastic Adventures* (New York), January 1952.
"Plimsoll Line," in *Science Fantasy* (Bournemouth), Spring 1952.
"Man's Questing Ended," in *New Worlds* (London), July 1952.
"The Peacemaker," in *New Worlds* (London), September 1952.
"We Cast No Shadow," in *Authentic* (London), December 1952.
"Prison Trap," in *Laurie's Space Annual.* London, Laurie, 1953.
"Thou Pasture Us," in *Nebula* (Glasgow), Spring 1953.
"Traders' Planet," in *Science Fantasy* (Bournemouth), Spring 1953.
"Power Factor," in *New Worlds* (London), June 1953.
"Firstling," in *Nebula* (Glasgow), December 1953.
"Of Those Who Came" (as George Longdon), in *Gateway to Tomorrow*, edited by John Carnell. London, Museum Press, 1954.
"Seek Earthman No More," in *Science Fantasy 7* (Bournemouth), 1954.
"The Lava Seas Tunnel," in *Authentic* (London), March 1954.
"Space Prize," in *Science Fantasy* (Bournemouth), May 1954.
"Pipe Away Stranger," in *New Worlds* (London), June 1954.
"Come Away Home," in *New Worlds* (London), September 1954.
"Dark Summer," in *Science Fantasy* (Bournemouth), September 1954.
"Co-Efficiency Zero," in *Science Fantasy* (Bournemouth), December 1954.
"Kill Me This Man," in *New Worlds* (London), January 1955.
"Ephemeral This City," in *New Worlds* (London), March 1955.
"This Night No More," in *Nebula* (Glasgow), September 1955.
"Stormhead," in *New Worlds* (London), October 1955.
"The Jakandi Moduli," in *New Worlds* (London), December 1955.
"Hyperant," in *New Worlds* (London), March 1956.
"Consolidation Area," in *New Worlds* (London), April 1956.
"Culture Pattern," in *New Worlds* (London), May 1956.
"Period of Quarantine," in *New Worlds* (London), June 1956.
"Error Potential," in *New Worlds* (London), August 1956.
"Three-Day Tidal," in *New Worlds* (London), October 1956.
"Beacon Green," in *Nebula* (Glasgow), March 1957.
"Stress Complex," in *New Worlds* (London), June 1957.
"Painters of Narve," in *New Worlds* (London), March 1958.

"The Voices Beyond," in *New Worlds* (London), August 1958.
"Wishing Stone," in *Science Fantasy* (Bournemouth), August 1958.
"Searchpoint," in *New Worlds* (London), May 1959.
"Static Trouble," in *New Worlds* (London), February 1960.
"Alien," in *New Worlds* (New York), May 1960.
"Adjustment Period," in *Science Fiction Adventures* (London), September 1960.
"Sands Our Abode" (juvenile), in *Out of This World 3*, edited by Amabel Williams-Ellis and Mably Owen. London, Blackie, 1961.
"Spring Fair Moduli," in *New Worlds* (London), February 1961.
"Contact Pattern," in *Science Fiction Adventures* (London), March 1961.
"Sacrifice," in *New Worlds* (London), June 1962.
"Sixth Veil," in *New Worlds* (London), July 1962.
"Variant," in *New Worlds* (London), August 1962.
"Capsid," in *New Worlds* (London), December 1962.
"Aqueduct," in *New Worlds* (London), March 1963.

OTHER PUBLICATIONS

Novel

Lady in Danger. Dublin, Grafton, 1948.

Other

Modern Fiction-Writing Technique. London, Bond Street, 1960.
Repair of Domestic Electrical Appliances. London, Arco, 1961.
Electricity in the Home. London, Arco, 1962.
Amateur Radio. London, Arco, 1964.
Electricity in Your Home (as Milward Scott). London, Foyles, 1964.
Electrical Hobbies. London, Collins, 1964.
Transistor Receivers and Amplifiers. London, Focal Press, 1965.
The Pegasus Book of Radio Experiments (juvenile). London, Dobson, 1968.
The Pegasus Book of Electrical Experiments (juvenile). London, Dobson, 1968.
Popular Electronics and Computers. London, Arco, 1968; as *Electronics and Computers*, South Brunswick, New Jersey, A.S. Barnes, 1968.
The Pegasus Book of Electronic Experiments (juvenile). London, Dobson, 1969.
Electronics (as Roland Worcester). London, Hamlyn, 1969.
A Guide to Outdoor Building. London, Barker, 1970.
Handbook of IC Audio Preamplifier and Power Amplifier Construction. London, Babani Press, 1976.
Two Transistor Electronic Projects. London, Babani Press, 1976.
50 Projects Using Relays. London, Babani Press, 1977.
50 Field Effect Transistor Projects. London, Babani Press, 1977.
How to Make Walkie-Talkies. London, Babani Press, 1977.
Electronic Game Projects. London, Newnes, 1979.
Electronic Projects in Hobbies. London, Newnes, 1979.
How to Build Your Own Solid State Oscilloscope. London, Babani Press, 1979.
Counter, Driver, and Numeral Display Projects. London, Babani Press, 1979.
Radio Control for Beginners. London, Babani Press, 1980.
Electronic Test Equipment Construction. London, Babani Press, 1980.

Editor, *Worlds at War.* London, Temple, 1950.

Francis G. Rayer comments:
My aim in writing science fiction was to show some aspects of the world as it could be within one or two generations. "Time Was," *Tomorrow Sometimes Comes*, and *The Star Seekers* were probably the best examples of this.

*   *   *

Much of the work produced by Francis G. Rayer is the routine potboiler that makes up the vast majority of published science fiction. In novels such as *The Iron and the Anger* he depicts the conflict between a typical unwillingly heroic human and some non-human menace, in this case homicidally inclined robots determined to wipe out the human race. At times, there is a more serious note to his fiction, but still only in a very limited sense. For example, *Cardinal of the Stars* points out what Rayer sees as the importance of humanity's progress into space, in this case in order to be able to defend itself from the encroachment of a hostile alien fleet. But the novel remains essentially a spy story set in the future, with the two-fisted hero determined to stop the series of sabotaged spaceships and bombings from outer space that have begun to plague the world. Similarly, *Star Seekers* makes some tentative efforts toward philosophy, but remains essentially a potboiler about the dangers inherent in violating Einstein's laws and attempting to travel faster than light. Rayer's attempts here to avoid overt melodrama result in slow-paced scenes made even more ineffective by a turgid prose that is void of wit or clarity.

But there are times when Rayer is more than just a hack adventure writer. He has been most successful with his series about an intelligent computer of unprecedented capacity that appears first as the administrator of a completely unemotional legal system in a short story, then progresses to taking complete control of humanity during a nuclear war in Rayer's best novel, *Tomorrow Sometimes Comes*. In a short story later in that same series, and possibly the best piece of short fiction Rayer has written, the computer becomes "The Peacemaker," paradoxically by helping an alien race to invade Earth and conquer humanity for its own good. At the time Rayer wrote this story, this was certainly a far more novel and less acceptable conclusion than it would be now.

—Don D'Ammassa

READ, Herbert (Edward). British. Born at Muscoates Grange, Kirbymoorside, Yorkshire, 4 December 1893. Educated at Crossley's School, Halifax, Yorkshire; University of Leeds. Commissioned in The Green Howards, 1915, and fought in France and Belgium, 1915-18: Captain, 1917; Military Cross, Distinguished Service Order, 1918; mentioned in despatches. Married 1) Evelyn Roff; 2) Margaret Ludwig; four sons and one daughter. Assistant Principal, The Treasury, London, 1919-22; Assistant Keeper, Victoria and Albert Museum, London, 1922-31; Watson Gordon Professor of Fine Arts, University of Edinburgh, 1931-33; Editor, *Burlington Magazine*, London, 1933-39; Sydney Jones Lecturer in Art, University of Liverpool, 1935-36; Editor, English Master Painters series, from 1940. Leon Fellow, University of London, 1940-42; Charles Eliot Norton Professor of Poetry, Harvard University, Cambridge, Massachusetts, 1953-54; A.W. Mellon Lecturer in Fine Arts, Washington, 1954; Senior Fellow, Royal College of Art, London, 1962; Fellow, Center for Advanced Studies, Wesleyan University, Middletown, Connecticut, 1964-65. Trustee, Tate Gallery, London, 1965-68. President, Society for Education Through Art, Yorkshire Philosophical Society, Institute of Contemporary Arts, and British Society of Aesthetics. Recipient: Erasmus Prize, 1966. Prof. Honorario: University of Cordoba, Argentina, 1962; Doctor of Fine Arts: State University of New York at Buffalo, 1962; Litt.D.: University of Boston, 1965; University of York, 1966. Honorary Fellow, Society of Industrial Artists; Foreign Corresponding Member, Académie Flamande des Beaux Arts, 1953; Foreign Member, Royal Academy of Fine Arts, Stockholm, 1960; Honorary Member, American Academy, 1966. Knighted, 1953. *Died 12 June 1968.*

SCIENCE-FICTION PUBLICATIONS

Novel

The Green Child: A Romance. London, Heinemann, 1935; New York, New Directions, 1948.

OTHER PUBLICATIONS

Plays

Aristotle's Mother: An Argument in Athens and *Thieves of Mercy*
(radio plays), in *Imaginary Conversations*, edited by Rayner
Heppenstall. London, Secker and Warburg, 1948.
Lord Byron at the Opera (broadcast, 1953). North Harrow, Mid-
dlesex, Ward, 1963.
The Parliament of Women. Huntingdon, Vine Press, 1960.

Radio Plays: *Aristotle's Mother*, 1946; *Thieves of Mercy*, 1947;
Lord Byron at the Opera, 1953.

Verse

Songs of Chaos. London, Elkin Mathews, 1915; New York, St.
Martin's Press, 1975.
Auguries of Life and Death. Privately printed, 1919.
Eclogues. London, Beaumont, 1919.
Naked Warriors. London, Art and Letters, 1919.
Mutations of the Phoenix. Richmond, Surrey, Hogarth Press,
1923.
Collected Poems 1913-1925. London, Faber, 1926; revised edi-
tion, 1946, 1966; New York, New Directions, 1953.
The End of a War. London, Faber, 1933.
Poems 1914-34. London, Faber, and New York, Harcourt Brace,
1935.
Thirty-Five Poems. London, Faber, 1940.
A World Within a War. London, Faber, 1944; New York, Har-
court Brace, 1945.
Moon's Farm, and Poems Mostly Elegiac. London, Faber, 1955;
New York, Horizon Press, 1956.

Other

*English Pottery: Its Development from Early Times to the End of
the Eighteenth Century*, with Bernard Rackham. London,
Benn, 1924.
In Retreat. London, Hogarth Press, 1925.
English Stained Glass. London, Putnam, 1926; Millwood, New
York, Kraus, 1973.
Reason and Romanticism: Essays in Literary Criticism. London,
Faber, 1926; New York, Russell, 1963.
English Prose Style. London, Bell, and New York, Holt, 1928;
revised edition, Bell, 1952.
Phases of English Poetry. London, Hogarth Press, 1928; New
York, Harcourt Brace, 1929; revised edition, London, Faber,
1950.
The Sense of Glory: Essays in Criticism. Cambridge, University
Press, 1929; Freeport, New York, Books for Libraries, 1967.
Staffordshire Pottery Figures. London, Duckworth, 1929.
Wordsworth. London, Cape, 1930; New York, Cape and Smith,
1931; revised edition, London, Faber, 1949.
Ambush. London, Faber, 1930; New York, Haskell House, 1974.
Julien Benda and the New Humanism. Seattle, University of
Washington, 1930.
The Meaning of Art. London, Faber, 1931; revised edition, 1936,
1951, 1968; as *The Anatomy of Art*, New York, Dodd Mead,
1932.
The Place of Art in a University. Edinburgh, Oliver and Boyd,
1931.
Form in Modern Poetry. London, Sheed and Ward, 1932; revised
edition, London, Vision, 1948; Folcroft, Pennsylvania, Folcroft
Editions, 1976.
*Art Now: An Introduction to the Theory of Modern Painting and
Sculpture.* London, Faber, 1933; revised edition, 1936, 1948,
1960, 1968; New York, Harcourt Brace, 1937.
The Innocent Eye. London, Faber, 1933.
Henry Moore, Sculptor: An Appreciation. London, Zwemmer,
1934.
Art and Industry: The Principles of Industrial Design. London,
Faber, 1934; New York, Harcourt Brace, 1935; revised edition,
Faber, 1944, 1953, 1957; New York, Horizon Press, 1953.

Essential Communism. London, Nott, 1935.
In Defence of Shelley and Other Essays. London, Heinemann,
1936; Freeport, New York, Books for Libraries, 1968.
Art and Society. London, Heinemann, and New York, Macmil-
lan, 1937; revised edition, London, Faber, 1945, 1956, 1967.
Paul Nash. London, Soho Gallery, 1937.
Collected Essays in Literary Criticism. London, Faber, 1938; as
The Nature of Literature, New York, Horizon Press, 1956;
abridged edition, as *Essays in Literary Criticism: Particular Stu-
dies*, Faber, 1969.
Poetry and Anarchism. London, Faber, 1938; Freeport, New
York, Books for Libraries, 1972.
Annals of Innocence and Experience. London, Faber, 1940;
revised edition, 1946; as *The Innocent Eye*, New York, Holt,
1947.
The Philosophy of Anarchism. London, Freedom Press, 1940.
To Hell with Culture: Democratic Values Are New Values. Lon-
don, Kegan Paul, 1941.
Education Through Art. London, Faber, 1943; revised edition,
1958; New York, Pantheon, 1945(?).
The Politics of the Unpolitical. London, Routledge, 1943.
Paul Nash. London, Penguin, 1944.
The Education of Free Men. London, Freedom Press, 1944.
Flicker, with Toni del Renzio and R.S.O. Poole. Croydon, Sur-
rey, Poole, 1944.
Freedom: Is It a Crime? London, Freedom Press, 1945.
A Coat of Many Colours: Occasional Essays. London, Rout-
ledge, 1945; revised edition, 1956; New York, Horizon Press,
1956.
The Future of Industrial Design. London, Design and Industries
Association, 1946.
Youth and Leisure. Peterborough, Peterborough Education Board,
1947.
The Grass Roots of Art: Four Lectures. New York, Wittenborn,
and London, Drummond, 1947; revised edition, Wittenborn, and
London, Faber, 1955.
Culture and Tradition in World Order. New York, Museum of
Modern Art, 1948.
Klee 1879-1940. London, Faber, 1948; New York, Pitman, 1949.
Coleridge as Critic. London, Faber, 1949.
Gauguin 1848-1903. London, Faber, 1949; New York, Pitman,
1951.
Education for Peace. New York, Scribner, 1949; London, Rout-
ledge, 1950.
Existentialism, Marxism, and Anarchism: Chains of Freedom.
London, Freedom Press, 1949.
Byron. London, Longman, 1951.
Art and the Evolution of Man (lecture). London, Freedom Press,
1951.
Contemporary British Art. London, Penguin, 1951; revised edi-
tion, 1954, 1961.
The Philosophy of Modern Art: Collected Essays. London,
Faber, 1952; New York, Horizon Press, 1953.
The True Voice of Feeling: Studies in English Romantic Poetry.
London, Faber, and New York, Pantheon, 1953.
Anarchy and Order: Essays in Politics. London, Faber, 1954;
Boston, Beacon Press, 1971.
*Icon and Idea: The Function of Art in the Development of Human
Consciousness.* London, Faber, and Cambridge, Massachu-
setts, Harvard University Press, 1955.
The Art of Sculpture (lectures). London, Faber, and New York,
Pantheon, 1956.
The Psychopathology of Reaction in the Arts. London, Institute
of Contemporary Arts, 1956.
The Significance of Children's Art: Art as Symbolic Language.
Vancouver, University of British Columbia, 1957.
The Tenth Muse: Essays in Criticism. London, Routledge, 1957;
New York, Horizon Press, 1958.
Lynn Chadwick. Amriswil, Switzerland, Bodensee, 1958.
A Concise History of Modern Painting. London, Thames and
Hudson, 1959; New York, Praeger, 1964; revised edition, Thames
and Hudson, 1968.
Kandinsky 1866-1944. London, Faber, and New York, Witten-
born, 1959.
The Forms of Things Unknown: Essays Towards an Aesthetic

Philosophy. London, Faber, and New York, Horizon Press, 1960.

Truth Is More Sacred: A Critical Exchange on Modern Literature, with Edward Dahlberg. New York, Horizon Press, and London, Routledge, 1961.

Design and Tradition. Huntingdon, Vine Press, 1962.

A Letter to a Young Painter (essays). London, Thames and Hudson, and New York, Horizon Press, 1962.

Vocal Avowals. St. Gallen, Switzerland, Tschudy, 1962.

The Contrary Experience: Autobiographies. London, Faber, and New York, Horizon Press, 1963.

Selected Writings: Poetry and Criticism. London, Faber, 1963.

To Hell with Culture and Other Essays on Art and Society. London, Routledge, and New York, Schocken, 1963.

Art and Education. Melbourne, Cheshire, 1964.

A Concise History of Modern Sculpture. London, Thames and Hudson, and New York, Praeger, 1964; revised edition, Thames and Hudson, 1968; Praeger, 1969.

Henry Moore: A Study of His Life and Work. London, Thames and Hudson, 1965; New York, Praeger, 1966.

High Noon and Darkest Night. Middletown, Connecticut, Wesleyan University Center for Advanced Studies, 1965.

The Origins of Form in Art. London, Thames and Hudson, and New York, Horizon Press, 1965.

The Redemption of the Robot: My Encounter with Education Through Art. New York, Simon and Schuster, 1966; London, Faber, 1970.

T.S.E.: A Memoir (on T.S. Eliot). Privately printed, 1966.

Art and Alienation: The Role of the Artist in Society. London, Thames and Hudson, and New York, Horizon Press, 1967.

Poetry and Experience. London, Vision, 1967.

The Cult of Sincerity. London, Faber, 1968; New York, Horizon Press, 1969.

Arp. London, Thames and Hudson, 1968; as *The Art of Jean Arp*, New York, Abrams, 1968.

Editor, *Speculations: Essays on Humanism and the Philosophy of Art*, by T.E. Hulme. London, Kegan Paul, 1924; New York, Humanities Press, 1965.

Editor, *Form in Gothic*, by W.R. Worringer. London, Putnam, 1927.

Editor, *Notes on Language and Style*, by T.E. Hulme. Seattle, University of Washington, 1929.

Editor, with Bonamy Dobrée, *The London Book of English Prose*. London, Eyre and Spottiswoode, 1931; as *The Book of English Prose*, 1931; revised edition, New York, Macmillan, 1949.

Editor, *The English Vision.* London, Eyre and Spottiswoode, 1933.

Editor, *Unit 1: The Modern Movement in English Architecture, Painting, and Sculpture.* London, Cassell, 1934.

Editor, with Denis Saurat, *Selected Essays and Critical Writings*, by A.R. Orage. London, Nott, 1935.

Editor, *Surrealism.* London, Faber, 1936; New York, Praeger, 1971.

Editor, *The Knapsack: A Pocket-Book of Prose and Verse.* London, Routledge, 1939.

Editor, *Kropotkin: Selections from His Writings.* London, Freedom Press, 1942.

Editor, *The Practice of Design.* London, Humphries, 1946.

Editor, with Bonamy Dobrée, *The London Book of English Verse.* London, Eyre and Spottiswoode, 1949; revised edition, New York, Macmillan, 1952.

Editor, with Michael Fordham and Gerhard Adler, *The Collected Works of C.J. Jung.* London, Routledge, 20 vols., 1953-79.

Editor, *This Way Delight: A Book of Poetry for the Young.* New York, Pantheon, 1956; London, Faber, 1957.

Editor, *The Origins of Western Art.* New York, Grolier, 1965.

Editor, *The Styles of European Art.* London, Thames and Hudson, 1965.

Translator, with Margaret Ludwig, *Radio*, by Rudolf Arnheim. London, Faber, 1936.

*   *   *

A prolific art historian, essayist, poet, critic, autobiographer, and scholar, Herbert Read exerted a profound influence on British and American cultural life for more than a half century. Although he wrote only one novel, *The Green Child*, this work alone is sufficient to warrant Read a place in the history of fantastic literature. First published in 1935, *The Green Child* is essentially a utopian fantasy, although it is less concerned with imagining an ideal state than with presenting meditations on the relationships of order and structure to life. The narrative is in three parts, the first concerning the return to England of a former teacher named Oliver and his encounter in his native village with the now-grown green child, the survivor of a pair of green children who had mysteriously appeared in the village some 30 years earlier. After inadvertently killing the green child's rude husband, Oliver tells her of his experiences of the intervening 30 years. The second part of the narrative details Oliver's unlikely adventures in South America, where he rises to the dictatorship of a small inland country under the name Don Olivero, and establishes there a virtual utopia of peace and stability, choosing to leave under the guise of an assassination when the relentless order of his state offers him no new challenges. In the third part of the story, the green child, Siloën, leads Oliver through a magic spring to her own native land, an underground society of near-perfect order which has only the faintest sense of time and worships the perfection represented by crystallization. There Oliver spends the remainder of his life, rejoining Siloën in crystallization after his death. Set in the 19th century, the novel is notable for its remarkable clarity of style and sustained sense of wonder, and stands as a profound rumination on art, order, and society.

—Gary K. Wolfe

REAMY, Tom. American. Born in Woodson, Texas, in 1935. Movie projectionist, technical illustrator, dispatcher for a concrete plant, assistant movie director and propman, photo-typositor, and house painter; Editor, *CriFanAc*, Dallas, in the 1950's and *Trumpet*, in the 1960's; Founder, with Ken Keller, Nickelodeon Graphics, Kansas City (worked on *Delap's SF & F Review* and *Chacol /Shayol*), and Editor, with Keller, *Nickelodeon*, 1975-77. Recipient: Nebula Award, 1975; Campbell Memorial Award, 1976. *Died 5 November 1977.*

SCIENCE-FICTION PUBLICATIONS

Novel

Blind Voices. New York, Berkley, 1978; London, Sidgwick and Jackson, 1979.

Short Stories

San Diego Lightfoot Sue and Other Stories. Kansas City, Earthlight, 1980.

OTHER PUBLICATIONS

Play

Sting!, in *Six Science Fiction Plays*, edited by Roger Elwood. New York, Pocket Books, 1976.

*   *   *

From 1974, when his first stories appeared, Tom Reamy was considered a promising new writer and his progress watched with interest. His sudden death in 1977 meant that, instead of the long and prolific career and the steady increase in his already formidable powers his admirers expected, we have only one novel and a dozen short stories. But the novel, *Blind Voices*, and the best of the short stories need no special pleading as early experiments—they can stand on their own as successful and remarkable works. Tom Reamy's position is secure. Although he is often called a science-fiction writer, and won science-fiction awards, nearly all of Reamy's work would be better classified as fantasy. His stories skim along the edge of reality, firmly anchored in time and place, whether Depression-era, rural Kansas, or present-day Los Angeles, and the plots range between the subtlest of fantasies and the most visceral, outrageous horrors. His recurring themes are of human relationships, the frightening, dark side of sexuality, the triumph or destruction of the innocent, and monsters—from outer space, from Hollywood, from the id.

"Twilla," his first published story, shows the strong influence films—particularly low-budget horror films—had on Reamy, who worked in Hollywood and first tried his hand at script-writing. The plot of "Twilla" is straightforward and violent, full of vivid, visual descriptions with little time wasted on explanations. Like the films it emulates, the story seeks to entertain and shock, and it succeeds. There are some problems with plot construction and logic, but the story works as well as it does because of a solid grounding in reality, the accumulation of detail giving it a peculiar depth. In this, as in later stories, Reamy revealed his talent for selecting the perfect details to bring scenes and characters to life, from the utterly convincing names of even minor characters to precise descriptions of dress and furniture. "San Diego Lightfoot Sue," Reamy's own favorite and an award-winner, is the gentlest and most romantic of all his stories. The horror takes place off-stage and the emphasis is that of the so-called "mainstream," with the fantasy element almost superfluous. It is not the story, nor any sense of the fantastic, which remains to haunt the reader, but the characters—the vividly depicted Pearl and Daisy Mae; the extreme innocence and beauty of John Lee Peacock; the dying Grace Elizabeth; the hinted-at depths of the title character.

To my mind, Reamy's best and most powerful stories are "The Detweiler Boy" and "Under the Hollywood Sign," both set in a grittily real Los Angeles, both told in the first-person and using many of the conventions of the hard-boiled detective story, both probing the dark side of sexual desire and offering a complex vision of the conflict, on many levels, between innocence and evil. They are both disturbing stories which reveal love and need as the inseparable siamese twins of violence and destruction. In these stories people need each other and shy away from their need, knowing that sexual love will inevitably lead to death.

Blind Voices takes place in the American midwest during the Depression—a time and a place that Reamy makes convincingly his own. The story sets the fantastic creatures of a travelling wonder-show against the everyday lives of the people of Hawley, Kansas. It obviously owes much to works by Ray Bradbury, Charles Finney, and Theodore Sturgeon, but it shows Reamy's distinctive touch in the reworking of some familiar material, in the characterizations, the vivid style, and the dark undercurrent of sexuality which runs through all his writings. Although the material is that of fantasy, like *The Circus of Doctor Lao* or *Something Wicked This Way Comes*, an explanation near the end tips the book into science fiction.

—Lisa Tuttle

REED, Kit (Lillian Reed, née Craig). American. Born in San Diego, California, 7 June 1942. Educated at the College of Notre Dame of Maryland, Baltimore, B.A. 1954. Married Joseph Wayne Reed, Jr., in 1955; two sons and one daughter. Reporter, *St. Petersburg Times*, Florida, 1954-55; editor of house newspaper, District Public Works Office, Great Lakes Naval Training Center, Illinois, 1956; reporter, *Hamden Chronicle*, Connecticut, 1956, and *New Haven Register*, Connecticut, 1956-59; book reviewer, *New Haven Register* and *Choice*. Visiting Professor of English, Wesleyan Uni-

versity, Middletown, Connecticut. Recipient: New England Newspaperwoman of the Year award, 1958, 1959; Guggenheim Fellowship, 1964; Abraham Woursell Foundation five-year grant, 1965. Agent: Brandt and Brandt, 101 Park Avenue, New York, New York 10017, U.S.A.

SCIENCE-FICTION PUBLICATIONS

Novels

Armed Camps.   London, Faber, 1959; New York, Dutton, 1970.
Magic Time.   New York, Berkley, 1980.

Short Stories

Mister da V. and Other Stories.   London, Faber, 1967; New York, Berkeley, 1973.
The Killer Mice.   London, Gollancz, 1976.

Uncollected Short Stories

"The Holdouts," in *Fantasy and Science Fiction* (New York), June 1977.
"Shan," in *Fantasy and Science Fiction* (New York), January 1978.

OTHER PUBLICATIONS

Novels

Mother Isn't Dead, She's Only Sleeping.   Boston, Houghton Mifflin, 1961.
At War as Children.   New York, Farrar Straus, 1964.
The Better Part.   New York, Farrar Straus, 1967; London, Hutchinson, 1968.
Cry of the Daughter.   New York, Dutton, 1971.
Tiger Rag.   New York, Dutton, 1973.
Captain Grown-Up.   New York, Dutton, 1976.
The Ballad of T. Rantula.   Boston, Little Brown, 1979.

Play

Radio Play: *The Bathyscaphe*, 1979.

Other

When We Dream (juvenile).   New York, Hawthorn, 1966.

Editor, *Fat.*   Indianapolis, Bobbs Merrill, 1974.

*

Manuscript Collection: Beinecke Library, Yale University, New Haven, Connecticut.

*   *   *

Kit Reed writes within several fiction genres. Her stories have been published in *Fiction* (Paris), *Town* (London), *Seventeen*, and a variety of science-fiction and fantasy magazines. Some of her stories are realistic, some impressionistic, some fantasy, some science fiction. And representatives of each of these types appear in the collection *Mister da V*. Reed does not write hard, or technologically oriented, science fiction; and although some of her stories do make use of traditional science-fiction devices or theories, those stories actually focus on the people in them and the ways in which those people are affected by their surroundings. While this is typical of science fiction in general, Reed seems to deal primarily with the people and to use the science-fiction elements as another writer might use a car or truck—as a detail necessary to the story.

In "Automatic Tiger" the full-sized mechanical tiger is not presented as an object of wonder. Edward Benedict accepts the tiger as no more than a special toy for his nephew. When he tries the tiger out, however, he decides to keep it. Having his own tiger gives Benedict confidence and changes his previously nondescript life. He becomes successful in business and in society—until he no longer has time for the tiger, which deteriorates. When he loses the tiger, his life collapses, and he is left much as he was when the story began. "Mister da V." is a story in which time travel is the traditional science-fiction device, but the story is really about the 20th-century family into which Leonardo da Vinci is brought. The mother can see only the extra work that this "guest" necessitates. The twins like the strange toys he makes for them, but after he has gone and the toys are broken, they forget him. The father sees Leonardo as the source for a definitive biography. But the teen-aged girl sees a sweet, lonely, brilliant old man who seems to be sad because he will never get to do all the things he can envision.

This focus on people and the ways in which technology affects them is also at the heart of Reed's socially critical stories. One of her strongest pieces of social criticism is "Golden Acres," about a home for the elderly. In this future setting, an old person can use his negotiable assets to purchase a place in Golden Acres. Although these establishments look very attractive from the outside, they are extremely dehumanizing: all of the rooms are the same, the furniture is bolted down, and there is no place for personal effects or mementoes—what the management calls "clutter." And when a person's funds run out—rent, medical care, etc. all add up—he is taken to the Tower of Sleep where his life is terminated.

"At Central," "Ordeal," and the novel *Armed Camps* are similar stories about societies in which technology has all but taken over. In "At Central" people watch television all the time (never going outside), pump their money into the appropriate slots when they see something they want, and have everything delivered. The people in "Ordeal" are all on "life fluid" and spend their time hooked up to the intravenous tubes which pump the purple liquid into their veins. In *Armed Camps* warfare is the one constant thing in the world; and although it seems that only champions fight and die, great numbers of people are killed each year. And instead of trying to end it, the top brass make sure that it will go on—forever, if possible.

In the final analysis, it is Reed's characters that carry her fiction— science fiction, fantasy, or mainstream. To be sure, the other aspects of her writing are not found wanting, but her characters—especially the women struggling to find themselves in an indifferent or hostile society, or struggling against various institutions—remain in the reader's mind.

—C.W. Sullivan III

REPP, Ed(ward) Earl. Also wrote as John Cody; Peter Field. American. Born in Pittsburgh, Pennsylvania, 22 May 1900. Married Margaret Louise Smith in 1925; one son. Newspaperman: reporter and feature writer for Hearst papers and others; screenwriter and publicity director for Warner Brothers, Columbia, and RKO; wrote westerns using the house name Peter Field. *Died 19 February 1979.*

SCIENCE-FICTION PUBLICATIONS

Short Stories

The Radium Pool.   Los Angeles, Fantasy, 1949.
Stellar Missiles.   Los Angeles, Fantasy, 1949.

Uncollected Short Stories (series: John Hale in all stories except "Rescue from Jupiter")

"The Scientific Ghost," in *Amazing* (New York), January 1939.
"The Curse of Montezuma," in *Amazing* (New York), May 1939.
"Brigade of the Damned," in *Amazing* (New York), June 1939.
"John Hale Convicts a Killer," in *Amazing* (New York), July 1939.
"John Hale's Hollywood Mystery," in *Amazing* (New York), August 1939.
"Rescue from Jupiter," in *Science Fiction Quarterly* (Holyoke, Massachusetts), Spring 1941.

"The Light That Killed," in *Amazing* (New York), March 1943.
"The Black Pool," in *Amazing* (New York), November 1943.

OTHER PUBLICATIONS

Novels

Cyclone Jim.   New York, Godwin, 1935; London, Wright and Brown, 1936.
Hell on the Pecos.   New York, Godwin, 1935; London, Wright and Brown, 1936.
Gun Hawk.   New York, Godwin, 1936; London, Wright and Brown, 1937.
Hell in the Saddle.   New York, Godwin, and London, Wright and Brown, 1936.
Suicide Ranch.   New York, Godwin, 1936; London, Wright and Brown, 1937.
Empty Holsters (as John Cody).   New York, Godwin, 1936; London, Wright and Brown, 1937.
Canyon of the Forgotten.   London, Wright and Brown, 1950.
Don Hurricane.   London, Wright and Brown, 1950.
Hell's Hacienda.   London, Wright and Brown, 1951.
Six-Gun Law.   London, Wright and Brown, 1951.
Colt Carrier of the Rio.   London, Ward Lock, 1952.
Desperado.   London, Wright and Brown, 1954.

Plays

Screenplays: *The Cherokee Strip*, with Joseph K. Watson and Luci Ward, 1937; *The Old Wyoming Trail*, with J. Benton Cheney, 1937; *Prairie Thunder*, 1937; *Devil's Saddle Legion*, 1937; *Cattle Raiders*, with Joseph F. Poland and Folmer Blangsted, 1938; *Outlaws of the Prairie*, 1938; *Call of the Rockies*, 1938; *West of Cheyenne*, 1938; *Rawhide Raiders*, 1941; *The Vigilantes Ride*, 1943; *Saddles and Sagebrush*, 1943; *The Last Horseman*, 1944; *Silver City Raiders*, 1944; *Six Gun Gospel*, with Jess Bowers, 1944; *Trigger Trial*, 1944; *Texas Panhandle*, 1945; *Galloping Thunder*, 1945; *Gunning for Vengeance*, with Louise Rousseau, 1946; *Heading West*, 1946; *Prairie Raiders*, 1946; *Terror Trail*, 1947; *The Lone Hand Texan*, 1947; *The Fighting Frontiersman* (serial), 1947; *The Stranger from Ponca City*, 1947; *Guns of Hate*, with Norman Houston, 1948; *Challenge of the Range*, 1948; *Storm over Wyoming*, 1950; *Rider from Tucson*, 1950; *Saddle Legion*, 1951; *Law of the Badlands*, 1951; *Gunplay*, 1951; *Cyclone Fury*, with Barry Shipman, 1952; *The Kid from Broken Gun*, with Barry Shipman, 1953; and short films.

Television Plays: for *The Lone Ranger, Arizona Rangers,* and *Broken Arrow* series.

*   *   *

For decades Ed Earl Repp was regarded in science-fiction circles as the ultimate example of the hack pulp writer, representing both the best and the worst elements of the pulp tradition. Never very interested in mingling, Repp had become a legendary figure, widely believed to have been dead for many years, when he was tracked down and interviewed shortly before his actual death in 1979. His statements indicated that his personal philosophy fit neatly into the pulp mold. He maintained that a commerical writer should produce 20 pages of manuscript a day. His formula for story construction was simple: place a sympathetic hero in dire peril and bring him through to triumph in the face of insurmountable odds. He had had little formal education (two years of high school), wandered from newspaper reporting into publicity work, and decided to try fiction when Edgar Rice Burroughs and Zane Grey independently recommended he do so.

Repp produced scores of SF stories. Probably the best known is "The Radium Pool," wherein he uses a practical knowledge of geological exploration as background for an adventure tale typical of his work. The Explorers—accompanied by a newspaper reporter who acts also as narrator—discover a mysterious glowing pool. There they discover evidence of alien intelligences with malign intentions toward the earth. In an atmosphere of isolation from the outside world, the explorers struggle against the alien forces, appear to be in hopeless straits, but ultimately triumph.

The characters in the story are typical of pulp science fiction: elderly professor, younger male companion, beautiful young woman who comes within the thrall of the villains and is ultimately rescued by the courageous newsman. The action is crude and physical, the pace a trifle less frenetic than in some pulp stories, the characterization vivid but simplistic.

Stellar Missiles (originally published as separate novelettes) is thematically similar to "The Radium Pool." Ancient aliens existing in a state of suspended animation are discovered in two sites, one in Arizona and the other in Siberia. As the result of tampering with the aliens, the young son of the elderly scientist faces permanent suspended animation and in fact the entire earth is menaced. Other aspects aside, the story remarkably anticipates John W. Campbell's celebrated "Who Goes There?" (1938).

Repp's most successful shorter story is "The Red Dimension" (in *The Radium Pool*), a tale in which a scientist develops a technique for first observing, then physically entering, other vibrational planes of existence. In plot the story is unremarkable, concerning the usual pulp paraphernalia of hostile monstrosities, but in "The Red Dimension" Repp's prose, usually of a pedestrian flavor, achieves a number of descriptive moments little short of epiphanous.

Repp's science fiction is illuminated by an examination of samples of his western fiction. The latter appeared under such titles as *Suicide Ranch, Cyclone Jim,* and *Hell on the Pecos.* It is possible through the direct substitution of blasters for six-shooters, spaceliners for stage-coaches, remote asteroids for isolated ranchos, and so on, to transform Repp's westerns into science fiction (or vice versa).

—Richard A. Lupoff

REYNOLDS, Mack (Dallas McCord Reynolds). Also writes as Todd Harding; Maxine Reynolds. American. Born in Corcoran, California, 12 November 1917. Attended public schools in Kingston, New York. Served in the United States Army Transportation Corps, during World War II; trained in the Marine Officers School, New Orleans: Navigator. Married Jeanette Wooley in 1947; two sons and one daughter. Editor, *Catskill Mountain Star,* Saugerties, New York, 1937-38, and *Oneonta News,* New York, 1939-40; IBM supervisor, San Pedro shipyards, California, 1940-43; National Organizer, Socialist Labor Party, 1946-52; foreign correspondent and travel editor, *Rogue,* 1953-63. Agent: Scott Meredith Literary Agency, 845 Third Avenue, New York, New York 10022, U.S.A. Address: Apartado 252, San Miguel de Allende, Guanajuato, Mexico.

SCIENCE-FICTION PUBLICATIONS

Novels (series: Homer Crawford; Bat Hardin; Joe Mauser; United Planets Organization; Julian West)

The Case of the Little Green Men. New York, Phoenix Press, 1951.
The Earth War (Mauser). New York, Pyramid, 1963; London, New English Library, 1965.
Planetary Agent X (United Planets). New York, Ace, 1965.
Time Gladiator (Mauser). London, New English Library, 1966; New York, Lancer, 1969.
Of Godlike Power. New York, Belmont, 1966; as *Earth Unaware,* 1968.
Dawnman Planet (United Planets). New York, Ace, 1966.
Space Pioneer. London, New English Library, 1966.
The Rival Rigellians. New York, Ace, 1967.
Computer War. New York, Ace, 1967.
After Some Tomorrow. New York, Belmont, 1967.
Mercenary from Tomorrow (Mauser). New York, Ace, 1968.
Code Duello (United Planets). New York, Ace, 1968.

Star Trek: Mission to Horatius. Racine, Wisconsin, Whitman, 1968.
The Space Barbarians. New York, Ace, 1969.
The Cosmic Eye. New York, Belmont, 1969.
Once Departed. New York, Curtis, 1970.
Computer World. New York, Curtis, 1970.
Blackman's Burden (Crawford). New York, Ace, 1972.
Border, Breed nor Birth (Crawford). New York, Ace, 1972.
Looking Backward, From the Year 2000 (West). New York, Ace, 1973; Morley, Yorkshire, Elmfield Press, 1976.
Commune 2000 A.D. (Hardin). New York, Bantam, 1974.
Depression or Bust. New York, Ace, 1974.
Ability Quotient. New York, Ace, 1975.
Amazon Planet (United Planets). New York, Ace, 1975.
The Five Way Secret Agent. New York, Ace, 1975.
Satellite City. New York, Ace, 1975.
Tomorrow Might Be Different. New York, Ace, 1975; London, Sphere, 1976.
The Towers of Utopia (Hardin). New York, Bantam, 1975.
Day after Tomorrow. New York, Ace, 1976.
Galactic Medal of Honor. New York, Ace, 1976.
Rolltown (Hardin). New York, Ace, 1976.
Section G: United Planets. New York, Ace, 1976.
After Utopia. New York, Ace, 1977.
Equality in the Year 2000 (West). New York, Ace, 1977.
Perchance to Dream. New York, Ace, 1977.
Police Patrol 2000 A.D. New York, Ace, 1977.
Space Visitor. New York, Ace, 1977.
The Best Ye Breed (Crawford). New York, Ace, 1978.
Trample an Empire Down. New York, Nordon, 1978.
Brain World. New York, Nordon, 1978.
The Fracas Factor. New York, Nordon, 1978.
Language Five. New York, Bantam, 1979.

Short Stories

The Best of Mack Reynolds. New York, Pocket Books, 1976.

Uncollected Short Stories

"Of Future Fears," in *Analog* (New York), October, November, December 1977.
"All Things to Us," in *Amazing* (New York), May 1978.
"A Halo for Horace," in *Amazing* (New York), February 1979.
"Toro," in *Amazing* (New York), May 1979.
"The Case of the Disposable Jalopy," in *Analog* (New York), October 1979.
"Golden Rule," in *Analog* (New York), March 1980.
"Hell's Fire," in *Fantasy and Science Fiction* (New York), June 1980.

OTHER PUBLICATIONS

Novels

Episode on the Riviera. Derby, Connecticut, Monarch, 1961.
A Kiss Before Loving. Derby, Connecticut, Monarch, 1961.
This Time We Love. Derby, Connecticut, Monarch, 1962.
The Kept Woman. Derby, Connecticut, Monarch, 1963.
The Jet Set. Derby, Connecticut, Monarch, 1964.
Sweet Dreams, Sweet Prince. London, New English Library, 1965.
Once Departed. New York, Curtis, 1970.
The House in the Kasbah (as Maxine Reynolds). New York, Beagle, 1972.
The Home of the Inquisitor (as Maxine Reynolds). New York, Beagle, 1972.
Four Letter World (as Todd Harding). San Diego, Greenleaf, 1972.

Other

Paradise for Males. New York, Plaza, 1957.
How to Retire Without Money. New York, Belmont, 1958.
The Expatriates. Evanston, Illinois, Regency, 1963.

Puerto Rican Patriot: The Life of Luis Muñoz Rivera.   New York, Macmillan, 1969.
"What Do You Mean—Marxism?," in *Science-Fiction Studies* (Terre Haute, Indiana), Fall 1974.

Editor, with Fredric Brown, *Science-Fiction Carnival.*   Chicago, Shasta, 1953.

Mack Reynolds comments:

Thirty years ago, when I first began writing science fiction, I soon arrived at the conclusion that a serious free-lancer in the field must be acquainted with the sciences he dealt with. The day of the space opera was rapidly disappearing, and the writer had best know what he was talking about. My background in the hard sciences was sketchy and I realized that I was out of my depth in them. However, I have had a lifelong interest in the social sciences and particularly in political economy. And, somewhat to my surprise, I discovered that few writers in our genre were so equipped. I decided to concentrate on stories with socio-economic backgrounds.

Many of us in our extrapolations do very well in portraying a future in which the sciences and technology have blossomed fantastically. We rejoice in faster-than-light travel, we colonize the galaxy, we have become immortal, we have matter transformers and transmitters. And what is our socio-economic system? Often it's feudalism, complete with galactic emperors, dukes, counts, and barons, sometimes swinging laser swords, whatever they are. We don't even have capitalism, not to speak of something in advance. What is the means of exchange? Often currency, silver and gold coins. What is the relationship between the sexes? What type of family prevails? The writers have returned to Victorian times.

Not one story in 25 in depicting the future ever considers that the private ownership of the means of production, the profit system, and class divided society, might one day end. American science fiction is myopic when it comes to foreseeing an evolved social system. So is Soviet Science fiction. In the Soviets' case, they seem to have a fond belief that the millennium has been reached, that nothing lies beyond the state capitalism they have achieved, so there is no point in speculating on future socio-economics. The big difference is that even if a Soviet SF writer did attempt to look beyond their version of Utopia, it is unlikely that his story would ever see print. In the west we are still free to extrapolate in the field of political economy—we just don't. And, in my belief, science fiction is the poorer for it.

The world is going through an unprecedented period of revolutionary change, in science, in medicine, in technology, in the family relationship, in social systems, in the relationship between nations, between generations, between sexes. And if the future is to be a valid one we must buckle down to deciding just what we want. An end of war, an end of poverty, an end of the rape of our planet, a viable world government, are only a few of the goals we should keep ever in mind.

In my stories, I do not have any particular ax to grind. I have written stories (some humorous ones) both for and against every socio-economic system that I know of including socialism, in all its myriad forms, communism, syndicalism, anarchism, fascism, theocracy, technocracy, meritocracy, and industrial feudalism. It simply seems not to occur to the average person, even science fiction readers, that there is an alternative, or alternatives, to our present social system. I am attempting to bring home to them that there is, and possibly desirable alternatives at that.

*   *   *

Satire and suspense characterize Mack Reynolds's contributions to "social science fiction" (his "Trademark," according to the anthologist Judith Merril). The many novels, short stories, and articles he has produced since 1950 have proven popular, if not permanent, attracting readers rather than critical acclaim. Undoubtedly the most widely travelled and politically active SF writer to emerge since World War II, Reynolds translates his socio-economic concerns into briskly written and imaginative stories. *The Best of Mack Reynolds* demonstrates the variety and scope of his work, the ability to range freely and convincingly in time and space. "Compounded Interest" depicts a mysterious time traveller who first appears in a medieval banking house to invest a gold coin and then reappears every hundred years to watch his investment grow into the world's most formidable fortune. In the early 1960's, after travelling extensively in Eastern Eruope and Russia, Reynolds wrote a series of futuristic scenarios expressing his disillusionment with totalitarian regimes ("The Pacifist," "The Subversive," "Freedom," "The Revolution"). "Down the River," one of his first stories, presents a technologically superior alien civilization that blithely lays claim to all the earth's resources and justifies itself in terms ironically recalling our own colonialist and racist heritage. In the children's story "Come In, Spaceport" the rescued waifs from a despised Martian colony turn out to be cleverer than their grown-up rescuers. Finally, in a Jesus-as-alien parable ("The Second Advent") a fed-up Christ barges into the office of a 20th-century president and advises him to commit suicide for the good of the country.

Iconoclasm and unconventionality come naturally to Reynolds, whose own life is as colorful as his fiction. Reynolds began his career writing mystery stories until he turned to SF at the advice of his friend Fredric Brown. His early work includes a silly and muddled whodunit, *The Case of the Little Green Men,* in which the tough guy private eye hero attempts to solve a series of murders supposedly committed by aliens. Later works, such as *Galactic Medal of Honor* and *Planetary Agent X,* are more successful in wedding suspense and science fiction.

The most ambitious and far-reaching project that Reynolds has undertaken is a sequence of interlocking novels that focus on different aspects of life in the year 2000. Inspired in part by the Commission on the Year 2000 (see *Daedalus* summer 1967), each of these novels explores a particular problem or issue in a future society where all man's material wants have been supplied by technology. In *Looking Backward, From the Year 2000* a chronically ill businessman named Julian West awakens from 30 years of suspended animation to discover a society unimaginably different from what he has known. Books, government, disease, and economic deprivation have disappeared. *Commune 2000 A.D.* explores the problems and paradoxes of this "perfect" society with its leisure, guaranteed income, and total sexual freedom. An anthropology student Theodore Swain, becomes caught up in the counterculture he is supposed to be studying and learns that the status quo is not as flawless as it pretends. *Rolltown* depicts the vast mobile towns that aimlessly wander across the country, trying to fulfill the dream of being "on the road." Related works like *The Cosmic Eye* and *Satellite City* deal with individuals pitted against utopian superstates.

Although Reynolds's style can be tedious and preachy at times, his skillful plots and colorful characters usually manage to sustain interest. His sensitivity to the social implications of technological change makes his work compelling, even when the writing itself becomes careless, pedestrian, or long-winded.

"It is my belief," writes Reynolds, "that the world is currently going through a revolutionary period of greatest significance." Portraying characters who are caught up in the revolutionary cycles of our times and yet can maintain their individuality is Reynolds's perennial theme. The outsider, the rebel, and the disenchanted are the ones, Reynolds assures us, who alone can be saved from economic determinism and technological manipulation.

—Anthony Manousos

RICHMOND, Walt and Leigh. Americans. RICHMOND, Walt(er F.): Born in Memphis, Tennessee, 5 December 1922. Married Leigh Tucker; three children. Research physicist; President and Executive Director, Centric Foundation, Merritt Island, Florida. *Died 14 April 1977.* RICHMOND, Leigh (née Tucker): Educated at Louisiana State University, Baton Rouge; Tulane University, New Orleans. Reporter, photographer, newspaper editor, and research anthropologist; President, Centric Foundation. Address: Rathmann's Marina, 705 South Harbor City Boulevard, Melbourne, Florida 32901, U.S.A.

SCIENCE-FICTION PUBLICATIONS

Novels

Shock Waves. New York, Ace, 1967.
The Lost Millennium. New York, Ace, 1967; as *SIVA!,* 1979.
Phoenix Ship. New York, Ace, 1969; expanded edition as *Phase Two,* 1980.
Gallagher's Glacier. New York, Ace, 1970; revised edition, 1979.
Challenge the Hellmaker. New York, Ace, 1976.
The Probability Corner. New York, Ace, 1977.

Short Stories

Positive Charge. New York, Ace, 1970.

Uncollected Short Story

"Antalogia," in *Analog* (New York), October 1973.

*   *   *

Walt and Leigh Richmond both grew up before the atomic bomb fell, when science seemed both simpler and more accessible. Understanding was not yet locked in moated research foundations—in those days (it seemed) a boy could invent anti-gravity with the right cardboard tubes and wires, and a few people thinking hard could uncover the secrets of the universe and Explain Everything. The Richmonds wanted to be among those few people, and in their eager stories the maverick amateurs always win. But because the Richmonds did not actually start writing until after the atomic bomb fell, their stories are also marked by a scorn for the current secrecy-bound scientific bureaucracy, and an appetite for apocalypse.

When the Richmonds' stories work, they successfully convey the excitement of individual discovery—the mind's reaction to its own new thinking, to its own awakening power. As a result, the Richmonds' most convincing characters tend to be children. An early story, "Poppa Needs Shorts," neatly details the way a four-year-old can combine pieces of information that an adult would keep rigidly separate. The same child, Oley, grows up in the novel *The Probability Corner* to learn how to read the mind of a computer and invent a matter transmitter in his cellar—all through his willingness to keep combining divergent types of knowledge. Such willingness, the Richmonds imply, is usually destroyed by modern education, and education is the most interesting topic in their novel *Phase Two.* The hero, S.T.A.R. Dustin, is injected with molecules of trained men's brains, whose knowledge is then activated in him through four years of computer testing. But the boy's real mental power develops from his efforts to recombine the facts on his own, pre-guessing the computer and eventually walking easily out of his political prison into new realms of science. The idea that the computer is an appropriate tool for the expanding mind is also pursued in *Challenge the Hellmaker,* where a group of friends on an orbital station accidentally invent a spacedrive while singlehandedly fighting off a world-wide military takeover. Though the heroes in the Richmonds' books are almost anachronistically individualistic, they are rarely isolated. Even little Oley feels secure in the center of his family, and the collaboration of friends (another means of combing divergent knowledge) is one of the more pleasant constants in the Richmonds' own collaboration.

When their stories do not work—or do not work consistently—they are flawed by unconvincing politics, hyperactive melodrama, and scientific explanations that are not only impossible but are also praised for their clarity by the other characters. The worst offender on all counts is *The Lost Millennium,* a novel that tries to explain all human and geologic history by proposing a prehistorical race of supermen who, through solar taps located in pyramids, possessed broadcast electrical power. The story covers so much so quickly—including all myths, many lectures on electricity, and an incomprehensible soap opera sub-plot—that the result is a fragmented scenario whose several apocalypses are the only relief.

Yet perhaps even *The Lost Millennium* is just part of the Richmonds' effort to scramble our brains into new connections. They were serious enough about the content of their work to form their own research group, the Centric Foundation, and before Walt

Richmond's death in 1977 they planned to apply "relatively simple high school mathematics" to physics, and improve on the quantum theory. Few young science-fiction readers would fault their attack on education, and it is hard to resist the Richmonds' faith in the potentially supernatural power of individual thinking. Their eagerness and their determined amateur science ("'It's really quite easy,' he explained briskly") are part of an innocence science fiction has lost, and could never easily regain.

—Karen G. Way

* * *

ROBERTS, Keith (John Kingston). British. Born in Kettering, Northamptonshire, 20 September 1935. Educated at Northampton School of Art, National Diploma in Design 1956; Leicester College of Art, 1956-57. Has worked as a cartoon animator, and as an illustrator for advertising, magazines, and books. Editor, *SF Impulse,* London, 1966-67. Agent: Leslie Flood, E.J. Carnell Literary Agency, Rowneybury Bungalow, Sawbridgeworth, near Old Harlow, Essex CM20 2EX. Address: 23 New Street, Henley-on-Thames, Oxfordshire RG9 2BP, England.

SCIENCE-FICTION PUBLICATIONS

Novels

The Furies. London, Hart Davis, and New York, Berkley, 1966.
Pavane. London, Hart Davis, and New York, Doubleday, 1968.
The Inner Wheel. London, Hart Davis, and New York, Doubleday, 1970.
Anita. New York, Ace, 1970; London, Millington, 1976.
The Chalk Giants. London, Hutchinson, 1974; New York, Putnam, 1975.
Molly Zero. London, Gollancz, 1980.

Short Stories

Machines and Men. London, Hutchinson, 1973.
The Grain Kings. London, Hutchinson, 1976.
The Passing of the Dragons. New York, Berkley, 1977.
Ladies from Hell. London, Gollancz, 1979.

Uncollected Short Stories

"The Lordly Ones," in *Fantasy and Science Fiction* (New York), March 1980.
"The Comfort Station," in *Fantasy and Science Fiction* (New York), May 1980.

OTHER PUBLICATIONS

Novel

The Boat of Fate. London, Hutchinson, 1971; Englewood Cliffs, New Jersey, Prentice Hall, 1974.

Keith Roberts comments:
I think if we survive our do-it-yourself Armageddon, the 20th century will be remembered as the Age of the Pigeonhole. Everything has to have its tag; Stonehenge is a computer, etc. The particular label attached to me is science-fiction writer. I've nothing against it; but I really know very little science. I suppose I did write some technological fiction in the very early days. But I've simply tried to talk about characters who interested me, and events that moved or disturbed me. If that's science fiction, then so be it.

*   *   *

Keith Roberts is the Thomas Hardy of science fiction, a writer whose vision is deeply embedded in a particular place—the area of southwest England from Salisbury plain south to the Dorset downs and the Isle of Purbeck where Corfe Castle stands. That landscape is the spiritual centre of his work, from the alternate world of *Pavane,* the historical crumbling Roman Empire of *The Boat of Fate,* to the hallucinatory primitive "future" of *The Chalk Giants.* This sense of place even affects the landscapes of the stories set on other worlds. Roberts's people live in a profoundly felt world, a phenomenal and perceived *lebenswelt* which actively influences their behaviour and beliefs. Roberts also shares with Hardy a desire to articulate the human struggle with passion, need, violence, and the corruption of power; to explore humankind's tremendous will to survive in even the worst of circumstances; the possibilities of love; and the kinds of penances people committed to others serve for the rest of guilty humanity. If his stories often seem extremely dark, they are shot through with lightning strokes of passionate love and spiritual striving. They are full of powerful emotional currents, and the best of them are truly visionary.

Roberts began his career with a somewhat typically British disaster novel, *The Furies.* In it Britain is ravaged by giant wasps controlled by an alien intelligence. It's a good example of the sub-genre, and the descriptions, especially those of the wasps' underground nests, are strong; yet the ironic self-destruction of the wasps and humanity's somewhat humble new beginning are quite conventional, as a quick look at *The Day of the Triffids* shows. *The Inner Wheel* is also an apprentice work, though a very good one. In this work Roberts explores the theme of *homo gestalt* in a story that obviously owes a great deal to Theodore Sturgeon's *More Than Human,* yet, especially in his handling of sexual love and the interactions of power and violence, he engages us with his singular emerging "voice." Although his characterizations deepen in later works, in *The Inner Wheel* he is already using tone of voice and the small revealing gesture to present complex and humanly opaque individuals. Most important, his people *feel,* and because he renders their feelings with care and precision, we feel with and for them, as well.

In the stories in *Machines and Men* Roberts shows a wide-ranging imagination in his handling of SF themes, from ESP to flying saucers (revealing a capacity for comedy often ignored by his critics). Yet he sets them all in England, as if to say there's no need to go careening across the galaxy in order to explore either the workings of the human heart or the awesome and awful possibilities of technological changes in society. "The Deeps" is especially interesting for its complex and subtle presentation of a new, underwater, society.

In the mosaic novel *Pavane,* Roberts comes into his own as a unique and major SF writer. Set in 20th-century England in an alternate universe where Elizabeth I was assassinated, the Spanish Armada won, and the Catholic Church has held power over most of the world until the present day, it is a superb complex chain of interlocked stories showing how, finally, the Church's attempts to hold civilization in stasis fail in the face of political and technological "progress." We learn of the many social changes mostly by implication, however, for Roberts seeks to show us how particular people seek and find their destinies in such a world, a world after all not that different from our own in the sacrifices it demands of each person trying to live a "good" life. Roberts is a moral writer in that he insists that all persons face choices in life which will affect not only themselves but their families, friends, perhaps their whole societies. His people engage us because they face those moments of choice and bear the often terrible responsibilities they find there. Thus Brother John the artist, after he has seen and painted the Inquisition, finds he must turn heretic and preach against the Church, and the Lady Eleanor of Corfe Castle (which broods over so much of Roberts's fiction) is moved by compassion and political wit to do battle with the Pope, even at the cost of finally losing all. These people, and others, are troubling and passionate reflections of ourselves, and in their struggles we perforce recognize the possibilities our own lives offer. Yeats's line "In dreams begin responsibilities" could be taken as an epigraph to all Roberts's fiction, for his people break or make themselves in their struggles with precisely that recognition.

It certainly applies to the figures in that even darker novel of a future return to barbarism, *The Chalk Giants.* After an atomic war

has literally torn Britain apart, Stan Potts, a lost little fatman, lies dreaming (or foreseeing) passages in the story of humanity's return to an almost medieval culture in the centuries to come. Almost all the stories feature a character resembling Martine, the woman he never dared to tell he adored. This fantasy lady is never in full control, though she is sometimes priestess, sometimes almost goddess, sometimes princess. The stories themselves are brooding meditations on the human capacity for love and violent hatred of others. Roberts's vision of humanity is not kindly; people will survive but they will often do so at any cost in pain and suffering, for themselves, yes, but especially for others. Yet sometimes suffering is a kind of necessary penance, a recognition of human guilt. *The Chalk Giants* is a complex, awe-ful book, yet like any good tragedy it is cathartic rather than simply depressing. There *are* flashes of light in the darkness. These flashes, often the discovery of courage in love, even if love lost, occur in the best stories in *The Grain Kings* as well, such as the powerful "Weihnachtsabend" and the two stories set on the planet Xerxes, where humanity's technology has destroyed the natives' traditional way of life. "Weihnachtsabend" is another example of Roberts's talent for alternate universes: this time it's a Britain conquered by the Third Reich, in which the most terrifying of the German gods hold power.

Roberts understands the power of the gods. Much of the dark power of his fiction derives from a mythic sensibility steeped in the spirits of the land. To know the land of Britain as Roberts does is to know all its gods, the mythic inheritance which inheres in the very stuff of the language he uses with such visionary power. Balder, Tir-nan-Og, the spirits of place, the Old Ones, all live in Roberts's beloved landscape, as much a part of it as the trees and grass, the ruins of Corfe Castle, or the stones of the henge. Their special presence adds another element to the tapestries in which all the major threads of art and life—passion, compassion, love, courage, vision, humanity, and the human awareness of how easily these can be lost to their opposites, which are therefore also present in the warp and woof of his stories—are woven into rich and exciting patterns.

—Douglas Barbour

ROBESON, Kenneth.   *See* **DENT, Lester; GOULART, Ron.**

ROBINETT, Stephen.   American.   Born in Long Beach, California, 13 July 1941. Educated at California State University, Long Beach, B.A. in history 1966; University of California Hastings College of the Law, J.D. 1971. Served in the United States Army: Sergeant. Married Louise Robinett in 1969. Lawyer. Agent: Hy Cohen, 111 West 57th Street, New York, New York 10019. Address: 718½ Fernleaf Avenue, Corona del Mar, California 92628, U.S.A.

SCIENCE-FICTION PUBLICATIONS

Novels

Stargate.   New York, St. Martin's Press, 1976; London, Hale, 1978.
The Man Responsible.   New York, Ace, 1978.

Short Stories

Projections.   New York, Ace, 1979.

Uncollected Short Stories

"Hell Creatures of the Third Planet," in *Omni* (New York), March 1979.
"The President's Image," in *Omni* (New York), February 1980.

*   *   *

Stylist, theorist, storyteller, Stephen Robinett has written some of the funniest science fiction ever published. Whatever the "what if" situation, he is concerned with telling a story with grace and wit and style. True also of his non-SF and pseudonymous SF potboilers, this facet of his writing stands out in two novels and a clutch of short stories from "Mini-talent" to "The President's Image." Once typed as an *Analog* writer, Robinett was first published by John W. Campbell, who liked his care with details, engaging style, and neutral attitude toward science and technology. Close extrapolation, narrow focus and an eye for the self-mocking detail mark even his early stories bylined Tak Hallus (Arabic for pen-name).

After two stories about matter transmitters, Robinett wrote a novel about big corporations and people on the make, in which two huge shipping concerns fight for their share, or more, of the 180-kilometer-wide tantalum ring through which drone freighters are transmitted to and from the stars. Set in near-future Orange County, California, and somewhere beyond the orbit of Mars, *Stargate* is also a detective story with a difference. The detective, who enters the story late, is a 75-year-old, cigar-smoking physical fitness buff, whose reconstruction of the crime is only part of the story. The narrator, an ambitious young project engineer, lives through consequent events and his success or failure hangs on their outcome. Revolutionary politics, utopian urban planning and a dead man's quest for immortality are involved in *The Man Responsible,* which cannibalizes earlier stories about a computer projection as corporation head and an almost-perfected method of transferring personality via synthesized RNA. A lawyer like Robinett, the hero has an essential interest only in recovering a client's $200 investment. Like a futuristic Philip Marlowe, he jousts with the forces of evil, ambition, and just plain flakiness in Southern California.

Collected in *Projections,* Robinett's best short fiction reveals in miniature his control of style, construction, local color, and humor. He plays it straight in "Tomus" and "Cynthia," ably exploiting the pathos of lost opportunities, but his zanier side dominates most of the others. In "Helbent 4" a self-conscious warship, having conquered the monstrous "Space Things," returns earlier in time to a parallel universe, where shocking us into taking the threat seriously costs it its "life." "The Linguist" exploits his talent by selling engrams that strip away each language as soon as he has learned it. "The Satyr" is produced in real life by molecular engineering, but his "natural" proclivities cause distress to his maker and eventually to himself.

Excessive taxation is the enemy in "The Tax Man" where a trucker manages to beat the system. Birdlike aliens' threat to Earth is turned back by an Indian in full-feathered regalia in "Powwow." A "telesthesia projector" for subliminal commericials gets an ad agency involved with politics and the law in the title story. A more recent story, "Hell Creatures of the Third Planet," finds a movie buff witnessing an insane attack by aliens on a movie studio parking lot and defending police and military forces. In each case, an appropriate narrator makes believable not only the everyday, but also the ridiculous and the sublime. How they're told makes all the difference.

—David N. Samuelson

ROBINSON, Frank M(alcolm). American. Born in Chicago, Illinois, 9 August 1926. Educated at Beloit College, Wisconsin, B.S. in physics in 1950 (Phi Beta Kappa); Northwestern University, Evanston, Illinois, M.S. in journalism 1955. Served as radar technician in the United States Army, 1944-45, 1950-51. Office boy, Ziff-Davis Publishing Company; Assistant Editor, *Family Weekly,* 1955-56, and *Science Digest,* 1956-59; Editor, *Rogue,* 1959-65; Managing Editor, *Cavalier,* 1965-66; Editor, *Censorship Today,* 1967; staff writer, *Playboy,* 1969-73. Since 1973, free-lance writer. Agent: Curtis Brown Ltd., 60 East 56th Street, New York, New York 10022, U.S.A.

SCIENCE-FICTION PUBLICATIONS

Novels

The Power.   Philadelphia, Lippincott, 1956; London, Eyre and Spottiswoode, 1957.
The Glass Inferno, with Thomas N. Scortia.   New York, Doubleday, 1974; London, Hodder and Stoughton, 1975.
The Prometheus Crisis, with Thomas N. Scortia.   New York, Doubleday, 1975; London, Hodder and Stoughton, 1976.
The Nightmare Factor, with Thomas N. Scortia.   New York, Doubleday, and London, Hodder and Stoughton, 1978.
The Gold Crew, with Thomas N. Scortia.   New York, Warner, 1980.

Short Stories

A Life in the Day of, and Other Stories.   New York, Bantam, 1980.

OTHER PUBLICATIONS

Other

Editor, with Earl Kemp, *The Truth about Vietnam.*   San Diego, Greenleaf, 1966.
Editor, with Nat Lehrman, *Sex, American Style.*   Chicago, Playboy Press, 1971.

*   *   *

Despite his background in physical science, Frank M. Robinson's stories are most often based on psychology or cultural anthropology. One such story, "The Fire and the Sword," is concerned with the reactions of Earthmen to a "perfect" alien society. Robinson chose this story to represent his work in the anthology *SF: Author's Choice 4* (edited by Harry Harrison, 1974). He worked entertaining variations on time travel in "Untitled Story," and produced a short novel of headlong action in "The Hunting Season." "The Night Shift" is a clever short fantasy, and "The Oceans Are Wide" a short novel telling of a young boy's harsh passage to maturity in the warped society on board a generation-ship carrying colonists to a distant planetary system. Behind the editor's inappropriate title of "Dead End Kids of Space" was an entertaining story of the adventures of a survey team on a planet with a very confusing and unpredictable culture. Another light-hearted story with an anthropological basis was "The Santa Claus Planet" concerning a society in which the giving of gifts had been elevated into a ritual with decidedly sinister overtones. In another vein entirely, "Dream Street" was a deceptively simple story of a boy on the run from an orphanage, and of his longing to become a spaceman.

His first novel, *The Power,* was published by Lippincott as part of a short-lived series of "novels of menace." It lived up to its billing admirably. The story concerns a Navy-subsidized research team studying human endurance and survival characteristics. Results of an anonymous questionnaire suggest that one of the team members is a superman with an assortment of psychic powers, and the one team member who takes these results seriously promptly dies under mysterious circumstances. He leaves an uncompleted letter for team chairman William Tanner: "I want to tell you about Adam Hart...." In his review of the book, Damon Knight characterized Robinson as "a gifted and sensitive writer" but found fault with his logic and with an anti-scientific tone to the book. Most readers and critics, on the other hand, found Tanner's nightmare battle against Adam Hart hair-raising and compulsively readable.

After the publication of *The Power,* Robinson temporarily gave up fiction writing and took a succession of editorial jobs. Occasionally another story would appear. "East Wind, West Wind" is a grim story of an inspector for Air Central, monitoring air quality in a smog-bound future Los Angeles in which all forms of air pollution, from cigarette smoking to internal combustion engines, are outlawed.

In 1973 Robinson began a very successful collaboration with Thomas N. Scortia. The team has produced a series of best-selling "disaster" novels, some of which are borderline science fiction. The first of these was *The Glass Inferno,* a story of a fire in a modern high-rise building. (Together with a similar book, *The Tower* by Richard Martin Stern, this was the basis for the popular film *The Towering Inferno.*) *The Prometheus Crisis* is about a reactor failure in a nuclear power plant, *The Nightmare Factor,* covert biological warfare. Even when not concerned with science-fiction ideas, these books exhibit the science-fiction writer's careful analysis of processes, both physical and mental. This attention to expository detail is not allowed to interfere with the pace of the story, and serves to enhance the realistic tone.

—R.E. Briney

ROBINSON, Spider. American. Born in New York City, 24 November 1948. Educated at the State University of New York, Stony Brook, B.A. 1972; New York State University College, Plattsburgh; LeMoyne College, Syracuse, New York. Married Jeanne Rubbicco in 1975; one daughter. Realty editor, *Long Island Commercial Review,* Syosset, New York, 1972-73. Since 1973, free-lance writer: reviewer, *Galaxy,* 1975-77. Recipient: Campbell Memorial Award, 1974; Hugo Award, 1977, 1978; Nebula Award, 1977. Agent: Kirby McCauley, 60 East 42nd Street, New York, New York 10017, U.S.A. Address: Red Palace, R.R. 1, Hampton, Nova Scotia BOS 1LO, Canada.

SCIENCE-FICTION PUBLICATIONS

Novels

Telempath. New York, Berkley, 1976; London, Macdonald and Jane's, 1978.
Stardance, with Jeanne Robinson. New York, Dial Press, and London, Sidgwick and Jackson, 1979.

Short Stories

Callahan's Crosstime Saloon. New York, Ace, 1977.

Uncollected Short Stories

"Antimony," in *Destinies* (New York), November-December 1978.
"Local Champ," in *Chrysalis 4,* edited by Roy Torgeson. New York, Kensington, 1979.
"Satan's Children," in *New Voices 2,* edited by George R.R. Martin. New York, Harcourt Brace, 1979.
"God Is an Iron," in *Omni* (New York), May 1979.
"Fivesight," in *Omni* (New York), July 1979.
"Soul Search," in *Omni* (New York), December 1979.
"Have You Heard the One...?," in *Analog* (New York), June 1980.

*   *   *

In only a few years Spider Robinson has established himself as a major writer of science fiction, and has done so with a handful of short stories, his *Analog* book reviews, an anthology, and two novels. He has garnered more than his share of literary awards, but his importance arises primarily from the fact that his works combine successfully two science-fiction themes that elsewhere often seem incompatible: technological optimism and a critique of technological society.

The themes and style of Robinson's work show a clear continuity from early stories and novellas such as those collected in *Callahan's Crosstime Saloon* through the apocalyptic novels *Telempath* and *Stardance* (written with Jeanne Robinson). The first, in fact, is not merely a collection of stories about the singular clientele of a well-realized Irish-American bar, though it is that. The book turns out to be a metaphorical symposium as well as a literal one: the gruff but kindly bartender Callahan presides over a series of dialogues and encounters that move from a vision of social disintegration to one of restored community in the final story, which takes place on New Year's Eve. This comedic pattern appears in *Telempath* as well: here the remnant population of a post-catastrophe America is threatened by powerful aliens as well as by conflict between pro-technology forces and the Agros, a naturalist cult, but the story ends in a love-feast marked by marriages, restored filial relations, and administrative merger. And in *Stardance* the final vision is of a Dantesque redemption of humanity symbolized by freefall dance, flesh become incorruptible, and polymorphous sexual and spiritual communion among humanity's elect and the plasmoid (angelic) aliens.

The first-person narrator plays a similar role in each of the three fictions. Jake, the frame-narrator of *Callahan,* is nursing a spiritual wound—he was responsible for the deaths of his wife and daughter in an auto accident—but it is he who articulates the redemptive (*cross*-time) nature of Callahan's place. In *Telempath* Isham Stone has been nurtured on violence, hatred, and revenge, and early in the story loses an arm and attempts to murder his father; yet it is Isham who evolves the ability to communicate with the aliens and to make peace between the two factions of humanity. Charlie Armstead (*Stardance*) is similarly wounded. An embittered dancer whose career was destroyed when his hip was damaged by a gunman's bullet, he works as a video specialist with the dancer Shara Drummond, and this leads to communication with the alien entity that threatens Earth, and later to his (and his dance company's) transcendence of a polluted and corrupted Earth, union with the aliens, and reunion with Shara. The importance of the disabled narrator redeemed through the shared experience of pain is underlined by the Callahan story "The Law of Conservation of Pain." In that story, a time traveler interferes with the early life of a blues singer. Instead of destroying her ability by obliterating the universe in which she suffered and was scarred, his interference creates a universe in which her songs of joy are as wrenching as her songs of pain in the original universe. Joy and pain, it seems, are, like matter and energy, two aspects of the same reality.

It might seem paradoxical that a writer whose themes involve the fragmentary and incomplete, not to say destructive, qualities of discursive thought and verbalized experience, should be so word-conscious a stylist. A hallmark of Robinson's writing is the pun, from the "Punday night" contests in Callahan's place to the "abominable multi-level puns" being swapped by Raoul and Charlie at the conclusion of *Stardance.* Especially in *Telempath* the function of the pun is to deconstruct the reality asserted by the utterances in which it appears, suggesting that the universe of propositional language is created and provisional rather than given. Another feature making for dense verbal texture is a complex web of allusions, especially to science-fiction writers, situations, and language, but also to the words and music of popular songs, and in *Stardance* to the traditions of modern dance and to the literature on the colonization of space. Also notable is the high proportion of text devoted to dialogue and internal monologue (and in *Telempath* to documents), often reducing pure narration to not much more than stage directions. What makes this dense verbal texture non-paradoxical is a fact pointed out by both Northrop Frye and Wolfgang Iser: such an "associative rhythm" is characteristic more of lyric poetry than of traditional prose fiction. Robinson's fictions, which communicate a secular vision of the "communion of saints" (*Telempathy*), are thus rather more lyric than narrative in style and structure.

The lyric quality of Robinson's fictions explains how he is able to fuse sharp social critique with technological optimism. Such a collocation sits uneasily in the universe of realistic prose fiction, a universe governed by either/or, cause-and-effect logic, the customary universe of hard science fiction. In *Telempath* and *Stardance* we see a world literally poisoned by the effects of modern technical society: pollution, overpopulation, war, crime, and madness. This is pretty much the same world of *Callahan's Crosstime Saloon,* but in that work redemption is allotted only to those whose steps direct them to Callahan's refuge and who are able to share in the bar's feast of love and empathy. In the two apocalyptic novels, redemption is communal: humanity overcomes its disintegration and moves onto a new evolutionary plateau of physical, intellectual, and spiritual fusion. This is accomplished, to be sure, partly through the encounters with angels called plasmoids—alien entities embodied in the fourth state of matter. But it happens only when man makes benign application of his most advanced technologies—mostly electronic, but in *Stardance* other technologies associated with space exploration—to facilitate full communication. In that fusion are obliterated the oppositions which seem to structure the possibilities of our universe, including the one between technology and nature.

At this point, then, Robinson has created a myth of the future, as all good science-fiction writers do. His is no less audacious and imaginative than those of, say, Olaf Stapledon and Arthur C. Clarke, but it is one in which human initiative and technological achievement play a much more active part. It remains to be seen whether he (and his collaborator Jeanne Robinson) will continue to mine this potentially rich apocalyptic vein, or will strike off into new territories on the science-fiction map.

—John P. Brennan

ROCKLYNNE, Ross (Ross Louis Rocklin). American. Born in Cincinnati, Ohio, 21 February 1913. Educated at schools in Cincinnati. Married Frances Rosenthal in 1941 (divorced, 1947); two sons. Has worked as a story analyst for Warner Brothers and a literary agency, sewing machine salesman and repairman, cab driver, lumberjack, sales clerk, and building manager. Address: 456 South Lake Street, Los Angeles, California 90057, U.S.A.

SCIENCE-FICTION PUBLICATIONS

Short Stories

The Men and the Mirror. New York, Ace, 1973.
The Sun Destroyers. New York, Ace, 1973.

Uncollected Short Stories

"The Doom That Came to Blagham," in *Witchcraft and Sorcery 10* (Alhambra, California), 1974.
"Emptying the Place," in *Fantastic* (New York), April 1975.

*   *   *

Ross Rocklynne was one of the important authors of magazine science fiction's middle years. He published his first story in *Astounding* in 1935, and for some 15 years was a regular contributor to a variety of science-fiction magazines. His work was of sufficiently high quality that L. Sprague de Camp wanted to include him as one of the 20 or so leading writers in the field for his *Science-Fiction Handbook* (1953). Both the key early anthologies of science fiction featured Ross Rocklynne stories: "Quietus" was in the Healy and McComas *Adventures in Time and Space* (1946) and "Jackdaw" was in the Groff Conklin *The Best of Science Fiction* (1946). Since 1950, Rocklynne's appearances have been sporadic.

Although he wrote some short novels, Rocklynne concentrated on shorter works. It is possible that his avoidance of the longer lengths has made his name less well known than it should be. Usually a careful craftsman, he wrote many types of science fiction: competent space operas, time-travel stories, effective mood pieces, scientific puzzle stories, detective stories, and yarns spun around the

Big Idea. Typical of the latter was "The Moth" (*Astounding,* 1939). Here—in 14 pages—he presented what John Campbell called "a wholly new idea for a spaceship drive" and for good measure threw in a fairly sophisticated picture of competing corporations.

Rocklynne also wrote a series of stories about a character named Hallmeyer. They are unfortunately largely forgotten today. Dealing with a "Bureau of Transmitted Egos," they are early examples of reshaping human beings to live on alien worlds. More than that, Hallmeyer was a person who *cared.* The stories have an atmosphere of compassion, of questioning basic values, of sadness. (For example, see "Task to Lahri," *Planet,* Summer 1942.) Indeed, there is an elegiac quality that pervades many of Rocklynne's better stories. The experimental side of Rocklynne appears most notably in his *Darkness* stories (1940 to 1951). They are concerned with the fates of sentient stars, and the writing is far removed from the usual styles of pulp fiction. The series was reworked as *The Sun Destroyers.*

Ross Rocklynne was never less than a capable storyteller. However, he tried to be more than that: he pushed himself instead of always taking the easy way. He was a major creator of the science fiction of the past, but he was also one of those who pointed the way ahead.

—Chad Oliver

ROHMER, Richard. Canadian. Born in Hamilton, Ontario, 24 January 1924. Educated at Fort Erie High School, Ontario; Assumption College; University of Western Ontario, London, B.A. 1948; Osgoode Hall, Toronto; read law with Phelan O'Brien and Phelan: called to Ontario bar 1951, to Northwest Territories bar 1971. Served in the Royal Canadian Air Force, 1942-45: Distinguished Flying Cross, 1945; in the reserve, 1950-53: Wing Commander; Honorary Colonel, 1971, Brigadier General, and Senior Air Reserve Adviser to Chief of Defense Staff, 1975, Major General, 1978. Married Mary Olivia Whiteside; two daughters. Since 1951, lawyer: Partner, Rohmer and Swayze; now Counsel, Frost and Redway, Toronto. Chairman, Royal Commission on Publishing, 1970-72; Counsel, Royal Commission on Metropolitan Toronto, 1975-77; Chairman of the Board of Governors, University of Canada North. Recipient: Centennial Medal, 1967; Jubilee Medal, 1977. LL.D.: University of Windsor, Ontario, 1975. Address: 44 King Street West, Toronto, Ontario, Canada.

SCIENCE-FICTION PUBLICATIONS

Novels

Ultimatum. Toronto, Clarke Irwin, and New York, Pocket Books, 1973.
Exxoneration. Toronto, McClelland and Stewart, 1974.
Exodus/UK. Toronto, McClelland and Stewart, 1975.
Separation. Toronto, McClelland and Stewart, 1976.
Balls! Toronto, General, 1979.

OTHER PUBLICATIONS

Other

The Green North. Toronto, Maclean Hunter, 1970.
The Arctic Imperative: An Overview of the Energy Crisis. Toronto, McClelland and Stewart, 1973.
E.P. Taylor (biography). Toronto, McClelland and Stewart, 1978.

*   *   *

Richard Rohmer's five novels present a curious paradox to anyone seeking to gauge his achievement, for they combine potentially exciting scenarios with forced and artificial technique. Four of the novels are twinned, with *Exxoneration* a sequel to *Ultimatum* and *Separation* a sequel to *Exodus/UK*. As his biography confirms, Rohmer has trodden the corridors of power in Canada and, presumably, to a lesser extent, in the USA and Britain. Unlike C.P. Snow, whose relaxation from the British Ministry of Science and Technology has been the practice of the craft of the novelist, Rohmer is quite clearly one of those men of authority and power who has always thought that anyone can take up the writing of fiction on Monday morning and only a fool would fail to write a novel by Friday week. The outcome of this situation is that a man of great experience and considerable imagination, as that term is understood in the think-tank realm of scenario games, produces stereotypes so blatant as to embarrass the most hardened reader of space opera or penny dreadful romances. His beautiful Arab terrorist has "... full, pointed breasts, unrestrained under the tight-fitting bodice," and almost all of his military men are sharp-eyed, cool heavies who can hold large amounts of liquor while managing rush seductions of exquisite and always willing women.

Rohmer writes of the immediate future. (Indeed, his publishers do not mention SF in their publicity.) There are events in all five novels which are now impossible as a result of historical change. The Shah of Iran is no longer in a position to help Western nations by providing extra oil, and North Sea oil has come on line for Britain much more quickly than Rohmer predicts. In *Ultimatuum* the President of the United States gives the Prime Minister of Canada just over 30 hours to agree to surrender natural gas and a territorial corridor to transport it to an energy-desperate USA. After some absurdly quick political action the Canadians refuse to surrender their sovereignty and the novel ends with the President announcing that he has annexed Canada. In *Exxoneration* the Canadians defeat the USA by the simple but unexpected expedient of opposing their occupation landings at various major airports and holding their troops and planes hostage. Canada then negotiates proper terms for the sale of the required gas, and one of the militia commanders, who is also the president of Petro-Canada, proposes a daring takeover of Exxon to give Canada a major new world voice on petroleum. The bulk of the book is about the take-over bid and the resistance to it by the United States.

The other pair of novels deals with the political futures of Britain, Canada, and the United States. The Arabs cut off all oil supplies to punish Britain for missile sales to Israel and the ensuing financial and supply collapse creates a need for 10% of the British population to emigrate. The United States absorbs its two million share but Canada is driven into an acute crisis when the predominantly French Province of Quebec votes to separate rather than be overwhelmed by a wave of Anglo-Saxon immigrants. In *Separation* the Canadian crisis is played out and then a *deus ex machina* bails out the British Isles. *Balls!* deals with a 1984 crisis in natural gas supplies which the President of the United States undertakes to solve after wicked winter weather has caused gas supplies to fail in the Buffalo area, killing over 20,000 people. Once again the heroes are all-American types and the villain a small, whining, egghead academic.

While Rohmer is acutely, almost embarrassingly unable to develop characters with any psychological subtlety, and while the action of his scenes is so boringly consistent in justifying his quite sharp right-wing sympathies and sexual chauvinism, there are a number of things to be said on behalf of the books. They come to life when he is describing the Arctic, military matters, or aspects of the energy crisis, and he can effectively describe settings and generate realism until his characters appear on the stages he sets. And while the plotting is rather too contrived, a fact not masked by alternating different lines of action in successive chapters, it does offer realistic projections of contemporary events. Although the novels lack subtlety they have a roller-coaster-ride energy in the exciting world of the international scientific, economic, and political all-too-near future.

—Peter A. Brigg

ROSHWALD, Mordecai (Marceli). American. Born in Drohobycz, Poland, 26 May 1921. Educated at Hebrew University, Jerusalem, M.A. 1942, Ph.D. in philosophy 1947. Served in the Israeli Army, 1950-51. Married Miriam Wyszynski in 1945; one son. Lecturer, Israel Institute of Public Administration, Tel-Aviv, 1947-51, and Hebrew University, 1951-55. Since 1957, member of the Philosophy Department, now Professor, University of Minnesota, Minneapolis. Visiting Professor, Brooklyn College, Summer 1956, Israel Institute of Technology, Haifa; 1963-64, University of Bath, Spring 1966, and Simon Fraser University, Burnaby, British Columbia. Recipient: McKnight Foundation Humanities Award, 1962, 1963. Address: 314 Ford Hall, University of Minnesota, Minneapolis, Minnesota 55455, U.S.A.

SCIENCE-FICTION PUBLICATIONS

Novels

Level Seven. London, Heinemann, 1959; New York, McGraw Hill, 1960.
A Small Armageddon. London, Heinemann, 1962; New York, New American Library, 1976.

Uncollected Short Stories

"The Politics of Ratology," in *The Nation* (New York), 17 September 1960.
"Awakening in Olympus," in *The Nation* (New York), 30 January 1967.

OTHER PUBLICATIONS

Other

Adam Ve'hinukno (Man and Education). Tel-Aviv, Dvir, 1954.
Humanism in Practice. London, Watts, 1955.
Moses, Leader, Prophet, Man, with Miriam Roshwald. New York, Yoseloff, 1969.

Mordecai Roshwald comments:
I became involved in fiction writing through concern about the menace to humanity from nuclear armament, as well as out of a sense of disenchantment with some aspects of modern life. However, an involvement in this kind of writing creates a momentum of its own, as it releases half-hidden emotions and sentiments in the writer's mind. Thus, in a way, I have become a fiction writer, intent on not neglecting this kind of self-expression and public address, despite my regular academic commitments to teaching and scholarly research, as well as occasional journalistic writing. The diversity of my activity does not prevent me from looking for a common denominator, a philosophy common to these varied efforts. Indeed, I believe I have maintained a fairly consistent approach throughout the different modes of expression.

The science fiction I have written is very much coloured by social, political and cultural concern. Indeed, science fiction is for me a *form* of expression rather than an objective in its own right. In this sense I would classify it with such books as Swift's *Gulliver's Travels* or Huxley's *Brave New World*, rather than with some modern stories dealing with inter-stellar warfare, monsters from distant planets, and the like (unless such stories are used as parables). Though my main success as a fiction writer was due to the success of *Level Seven*, classified as science fiction, I do not feel restricted to this literary form.

*   *   *

Mordecai Roshwald's first book, *Level Seven*, is perhaps the most chilling of all warnings about the new and unlimited dangers of thermonuclear war—such as Nevil Shute's *On the Beach*, Eugene Burdick and Harvey Wheeler's *Fail Safe*, Peter George's *Red Alert*, and others. The story begins as the Push-button Officer X-127 is taken down the one-way escalator 4000 feet to Level 7, the deepest in his country's shelter system and the control centre for its offensive weapons. The personnel on this level have numbers and opinions, but not names and faces; they have an atomic reactor for power, synthetic food for 500 years, and taped music for amusement. Marriage is permitted and plans are made for raising children to carry on life as troglodytes after the inevitable war. Finally the order comes (set off, we learn, by an accidental rocket firing), X-127 and his colleagues push all their buttons and the surface of the planet is destroyed. Gradually, as the radiation penetrates deeper, the other Levels and those of the enemy and the neutrals fall silent. Level 7 itself is flooded with radiation from its faulty reactor, and X-127 dies with the others, huddled in his bunk and dreaming of the sun. The terrifying effect of *Level Seven* depends on the absolute inevitability of its outcome. The feeble protests of X-117, a button-pusher who refuses to do his duty, only underscore the iron determinism of the system. If the story were recast in more mundane and conventional form, using real characters instead of numbered abstractions, much of its unique capacity to convince and frighten would probably be lost.

We see the other side of the coin in Roshwald's second novel, *A Small Armageddon*. In this peculiar tale, a group of officers of the American nuclear submarine *Polar Lion* hold a clandestine drinking party while the ship is on patrol. When the captain finds them, a scuffle takes place in which the captain is killed. The submarine proceeds to cruise the world, exacting tribute under threat of its missiles. It is finally destroyed in an exchange of fire with a Minuteman base which has been taken over by religious fanatics. Meanwhile neo-Nazis have captured missile bases in Germany, and the African state of Qunta-Qunta announces its own demands, backed by three hydrogen bombs that it has managed to buy or steal.

Level Seven depends on the notion that heads of state are irresponsible maniacs. Its abstract nature enables the reader to believe this, at least enough to give the story a profound impact. *A Small Armageddon* requires us to believe that malcontents and fanatics can easily gain control of nuclear weapons. It fails because of Roshwald's failure to make either people or situations even remotely credible. Submarine officers are not sophomores who wait till the captain's asleep to hold booze parties. Armed civilians cannot take over a functional missile base as bandits might a supermarket. *Level Seven* is an effective work produced by an author who cannot handle the demands of mainstream fiction; as such, the book is interesting as an SF boundary marker as well as for its own real and unique terror.

—E.R. Bishop

ROTSLER, William. Also writes as William Arrow; John Ryder Hall. American. Born in Los Angeles, California, 3 July 1926. Educated at Ventura Junior College, California, 1946; Los Angeles County Art Institute, 1947-50. Served in the United States Army, 1944-45. Married Marian Abney in 1953 (divorced, 1958); one daughter. Rancher in Camarillo, California, 1942-44, 1946; sculptor, 1950-59. Since 1959, photographer and filmmaker: writer, producer, and director of commercials, documentaries, and industrial and feature films. Recipient: *Locus* Award, for artwork, 1971, 1972, 1973; Hugo Award, for artwork, 1975, 1977, 1979. Guest of Honor, 31st World Science Fiction Convention, 1973. Agent: Richard Curtis, 156 East 52nd Street, New York, New York 10022. Address: 6640 Cedros Avenue, Van Nuys, California 91405, U.S.A.

SCIENCE-FICTION PUBLICATIONS

Novels

Patron of the Arts. New York, Ballantine, 1974; Morley, Yorkshire, Elmfield Press, 1975.
Futureworld (novelization of screenplay; as John Ryder Hall). New York, Ballantine, 1976.

Man, The Hunted Animal (novelization of screenplay; as William Arrow). New York, Ballantine, 1976.
To the Land of the Electric Angel. New York, Ballantine, 1976.
Visions of Nowhere (novelization of screenplay; as William Arrow). New York, Ballantine, 1976.
Sinbad and the Eye of the Tiger (novelization of screenplay; as John Ryder Hall). New York, Pocket Books, 1977.
Zandra. New York, Doubleday, 1978.
Iron Man: Call My Killer...Modok. New York, Pocket Books, 1979.
Dr. Strange. New York, Pocket Books, 1979.
The Far Frontier. Chicago, Playboy Press, 1980.
Shiva Descending, with Gregory Benford. New York, Avon, 1980.

Uncollected Short Stories

"Ship Me Tomorrow," in *Galaxy* (New York), June 1970.
"The Kong Papers," with Harlan Ellison, in *Partners in Wonder*, by Ellison. New York, Walker, 1971.
"After the End Before the Beginning," in *If* (New York), October 1971.
"Star Level," in *Amazing* (New York), March 1972.
"There's a Special Kind Needed Out There," in *Amazing* (New York), July 1972.
"Seed," in *Amazing* (New York), June 1973.
"Gerald Fitzgerald and the Time Machine," in *Vertex* (Los Angeles), October 1973.
"The Gods of Zar," in *Amazing* (New York), October 1973.
"War of the Magicians," in *Fantastic* (New York), November 1973.
"A la Mode Knights," in *Vertex* (Los Angeles), December 1973.
"The Immortality of Lazarus," in *Amazing* (New York), December 1973.
"Bohassian Learns," in *School and Society Through Science Fiction*, edited by Joseph D. Olander and Martin H. Greenberg. New York, Random House, 1974.
"A New Life," in *Fantastic* (New York), May 1974.
"The Raven and the Hawk," in *Analog* (New York), September 1974.
"Balance Point" and "The Conversation," in *Vertex* (Los Angeles), December 1974.
"Surprise Party," in *Vertex* (Los Angeles), April 1975.
"Landing Party," in *Vertex* (Los Angeles), August 1975.
"To Gain a Dream," in *Amazing* (New York), September 1975.
"Epic," in *Future Pastimes*, edited by Scott Edelstein. Nashville, Aurora, 1977.
"Parental Guidance Suggested," in *Fantasy and Science Fiction* (New York), January 1979.

OTHER PUBLICATIONS

Plays

Screenplays: *The Agony of Love*, 1966; *The Girl with Hungry Eyes*, 1966; *Four Kinds of Love*, 1967; *Suburban Pagans*, 1967; *Like It Is*, 1968; *Mantis in Lace* (*Lila*), 1968; *A Taste of Hot Lead*, 1969; *Shannon's Women*, 1969; *The Godson*, 1969; *She Did What He Wanted*, 1970; *Midnight*, 1970.

Other

Contemporary Erotic Cinema. New York, Ballantine, 1973.

Theatrical Activities:
Director: **Films**—all his screenplays.
Actor: **Films**—*The Notorious Daughter of Fanny Hill*, 1966; *The Agony of Love*, 1966; *Shannon's Women*, 1969; *The Secret Sex Life of Romeo and Juliet*, 1970.

*   *   *

William Rotsler is one of the few SF writers who has also achieved fame as a cartoonist. His distinctive style of cartooning has proven popular for over 30 years, and he writes frequently on the arts for such monthlies as *Adam*. It is little wonder, then, that

Rotsler's first novel, *Patron of the Arts*, is about the nature of the artistic process. Rotsler attempts in this novel to determine the social effects of a *Gekamstwerk*, an attempt at the total union of the arts through a synthesis of holography and electronic music. This novel succeeds to the extent that the ideas it contains are reflections of authentic experience, but Rotsler's extrapolative sense is not keen, and the novel can best be characterised as an interesting failure.

From his promising first novel, Rotsler's work quickly declined. Rotsler has tried a career as a commercial entertainer, but fails to provide that depth of characterisation and intellection that the best popular writers, such as Poul Anderson and Gordon Dickson, provide. His later novels are mere repetition of formulas without any distinctive presence. His favourite formula is that of the Ship of Fools, a cast of various racial and sexual types gathered together to face a perilous situation. Thus in *Zandra* the varied cast is drawn together after their cruiseship passes through the Bermuda Triangle into another dimension. In *Shiva Descending* (with Gregory Benford) the cast faces the familiar peril of a meteor about to destroy Earth. Rotsler and Benford mine this tired lode of apocalyptic fiction to little effect. Rotsler's worst novel, however, is *The Far Frontier*. In this work, Rotsler fulfills the worst fantasies of those mundane critics who insist that science fiction is nothing more than Western formulas transported to a wider setting. Rotsler has replied with a novel complete with interstellar Indians, space cows, and planet rustlers. Rarely does one read a novel where the writer rejoices in its trashy content; such, unfortunately, is the case with *The Far Frontier*.

Rotsler, then, after achieving promise as a first novelist, has reneged upon that promise with his later novels. He is less important for his writings than for his cartoons, which have the distinction and wit that his novels lack.

—Martin Morse Wooster

ROUSSEAU, Victor (Victor Rousseau Emanuel).   Also wrote as H.M. Egbert. American. Born in London, in 1879. Lived in South Africa at the turn of the century; emigrated to the United States, and wrote for pulp magazines until 1941. *Died 5 April 1960.*

SCIENCE-FICTION PUBLICATIONS

Novels

The Messiah of the Cylinder.   Chicago, McClurg, and London, Curtis Brown, 1917; as *The Apostle of the Cylinder*, London, Hodder and Stoughton, 1918.
Draught of Eternity (as H.M. Egbert).   London, Long, 1924.
The Sea Demons (as H.M. Egbert).   London, Long, 1924.

Uncollected Short Stories (series: Surgeon of Souls)

"Fruit of the Lamp," in *Argosy* (New York), 2 February 1918.
"The Eye of Balamok," in *All-Story Weekly* (New York), 17 January 1920.
"The Case of the Jailer's Daughter" (Surgeon), in *Weird Tales* (Indianapolis), September 1926.
"The Woman with the Crooked Nose" (Surgeon), in *Weird Tales* (Indianapolis), October 1926.
"The Tenth Commandment" (Surgeon), in *Weird Tales* (Indianapolis), November 1926.
"The Legacy of Hate" (Surgeon), in *Weird Tales* (Indianapolis), December 1926.
"The Mayor's Menagerie" (Surgeon), in *Weird Tales* (Indianapolis), January 1927.
"The Fetish of the Waxworks" (Surgeon), in *Weird Tales* (Indianapolis), February 1927.

"The Seventh Symphony" (Surgeon), in *Weird Tales* (Indianapolis), March 1927.
"The Chairs of Stuyvesant Baron" (Surgeon), in *Weird Tales* (Indianapolis), April 1927.
"The Man Who Lost His Luck" (Surgeon), in *Weird Tales* (Indianapolis), May 1927.
"The Dream That Came True" (Surgeon), in *Weird Tales* (Indianapolis), June 1927.
"The Ultimate Problem" (Surgeon), in *Weird Tales* (Indianapolis), July 1927.
"The Beetle Horde," in *Astounding* (New York), January 1930.
"The Atom Smasher," in *Astounding* (New York), May 1930.
"The Lord of Space," in *Astounding* (New York), August 1930.
"The Invisible Death," in *Astounding* (New York), October 1930.
"The Wall of Death," in *Astounding* (New York), November 1930.
"Outlaws of the Sun," in *Miracle* (New York), April-May 1931.
"Revolt on Inferno," in *Miracle* (New York), June-July 1931.
"The Curse of Amen-Ra," in *Strange Tales* (New York), October 1932.
"World's End," in *Argosy* (New York), 6 July 1933.
"The Stone Man of Ignota," in *Future* (New York), August 1941.
"Moon Patrol," in *Thrilling Wonder Stories* (New York), October 1941.
"The Seal Maiden," in *A. Merritt's Fantasy Magazine* (Kokomo, Indiana), February 1950.
"A Cry from Beyond," in *The Fantastic Pulps*, edited by Peter Haining.   New York, St. Martin's Press, 1975.

OTHER PUBLICATIONS

Novels

Derwent's Horse.   London, Methuen, 1901.
Wooden Spoil.   New York, Doran, 1919; London, Hodder and Stoughton, 1923.
The Big Muskeg.   Cincinnati, Stewart Kidd, 1921; London, Hodder and Stoughton, 1923.
The Lion's Jaw.   London, Hodder and Stoughton, 1923.
The Home Trail.   London, Hodder and Stoughton, 1924.
The Big Man of Bonne Chance.   London, Hodder and Stoughton, 1925.
The Golden Horde.   London, Hodder and Stoughton, 1926.

Novels as H.M. Egbert

Jacqueline of Golden River.   New York, Doubleday, 1920; London, Hodder and Stoughton, 1924.
My Lady of the Nile.   London, Hodder and Stoughton, 1923.
The Big Malopo.   London, Long, 1924.
Eric of the Strong Heart.   London, Long, 1925.
Mrs. Aladdin.   London, Long, 1925.
Salted Diamonds.   London, Long, 1926.
Winding Trails.   London, Long, 1927.

Novels as V.R. Emanuel

The Story of John Paul.   London, Constable, 1923.
Middle Years.   New York, Minton Balch, 1925.
The Selmans.   New York, Dial Press, 1925.

*   *   *

Victor Rousseau's stories spring out immediately and absorb the reader with global plots and bold valiance. Rousseau's rare talent is to combine medieval values and Louis L'Amour's style in the science-fiction context. The unique result provides sentimental satisfaction. The amusement in reading Rousseau is similar to the *Star Wars* experience in cinema. Both *The Messiah of the Cylinder* and *The Sea Demons* present strong heroes and execrable villains.

Even if the "daring sexual implications" that the promotion page of *The Sea Demons* promises are hard to find, there are enough imagination and activity in the macrocosmic plots to satisfy thrill-seeking readers. In *The Messiah of the Cylinder*, our hero (Arnold) and his foul antagonist are prep school mates. One of their schoolmates, Herman Lagaroff, invents the 100-year time-lock cylinder that transports the two men (and the pristine maiden whom they both love) into the year 2017. The time forwarding is believably described, involving Arnold's tortuous arrival in the strange London of 2017: "I flung myself upon my face and prayed, with all my will, to die." The story line of these books is similar to Wells's *A Modern Utopia* and *When the Sleeper Wakes*. The time travelers in Rousseau's work are propelled into a barbarous authoritarian nightmare, however, where "the dull and the base" are categorized by size of cranium. "The Prophet Wells," as he is referred to by Rousseau, would be aghast at the cold brutality of the rational society as it is portrayed in *The Messiah*. The triumphant ending in *The Messiah* includes the destruction and overthrow of the (fascist) government, the outlawing of divorce, and a return to a "ruling class bound to its traditions of public service." Where Wells asserts the final victory of reason, Rousseau longs for a futuristic theocracy. The priests would be happier than the scientists in Rousseau's future. Nonetheless, Rousseau exhibits a vivid technological imagination. He writes about solar power, plausible flying machines, and a communication network similar to the current and projected reality. The sinister governments' effective propagandistic use of the media is a startling reminder of the current world situation.

The plot of *The Sea Demon* is of the canned-on-the-shelf variety, and the story is similar to *The Messiah*. The strange sea creatures who are struggling to take over the world are discovered by noble Captain Donald Paget. Gallantry overcoming the hideous threat is the main course: Donald "Raised the girl in his arms, and felt one of the blubbery flippers on his hand...the stinging flippers sucked the blood from his face and hands....But Donald could not lose with Ida's life at stake." The battle to save the world intensifies to involve all governments and world resources. The story culminates in suicidal frenzy as the Queen Sea Beast dies of a broken heart and leaves the hordes without leadership, which we all know leads immediately to destruction.

The enduring impressions one gets of Rousseau are staunch traditionalism and faith in a well-ordered universe. Rousseau is good for a cheerful escape from heady ambiguity, and the pleasures of a frantic plot with the sugar-coated conclusion never in doubt.

—Peter Lynch

RUSS, Joanna. American. Born in New York City, 22 February 1937. Educated at Cornell University, Ithaca, New York, B.A. 1957; Yale University School of Drama, New Haven, Connecticut, M.F.A. 1960. Married Albert Amateau in 1963 (divorced, 1967). Lecturer in Speech, Queensborough Community College, New York, 1966-67; Instructor, 1967-70, and Assistant Professor of English, 1970-72, Cornell University; Assistant Professor of English, State University of New York, Binghamton, 1972-73, 1974-75, and University of Colorado, Boulder, 1975-77. Since 1977, Associate Professor of English, University of Washington, Seattle. Occasional book reviewer, *Fantasy and Science Fiction*, 1966-79. Recipient: Nebula Award, 1972; National Endowment for the Humanities Fellowship, 1974. Agent: Curtis Brown Ltd., 60 East 56th Street, New York, New York 10022. Address: Department of English, University of Washington, Seattle, Washington 98195, U.S.A.

SCIENCE-FICTION PUBLICATIONS

Novels

Picnic on Paradise. New York, Ace, 1968; London, Macdonald, 1969.
And Chaos Died. New York, Ace, 1970.
The Female Man. New York, Bantam, 1975; London, Star, 1977.
We Who Are About to.... New York, Dell, 1977.
Kittatinny: A Tale of Magic (juvenile). New York, Daughters, 1978.

The Two of Them. New York, Berkley, 1978.
On Strike Against God. New York, Out and Out, 1979.

Short Stories

Alyx. Boston, Hall, 1976.

Uncollected Short Stories

"My Boat," in *Fantasy and Science Fiction* (New York), January 1976.
"How Dorothy Kept Away the Spring," in *Fantasy and Science Fiction* (New York), February 1977.
"Women Talking, Women Thinking," in *Heresies* (New York), Winter 1977-78.
"Nobody's Home," in *Alpha 9*, edited by Robert Silverberg. New York, Berkley, 1978.
"The Extraordinary Voyages of Amelie Bertrand," in *Fantasy and Science Fiction* (New York), September 1979.
"Dragons and Dimwits," in *Fantasy and Science Fiction* (New York), December 1979.

OTHER PUBLICATIONS

Play

Window Dressing, in *The New Women's Theatre*, edited by Honor Moore. New York, Random House, 1977.

Other

"Daydream Literature and Science Fiction," in *Extrapolation* (Wooster, Ohio), December 1969.
"Genre," in *Clarion*, edited by Robin Scott Wilson. New York, New American Library, 1971.
"Communique from the Front: Teaching and the State of the Art," in *Colloquy*, May 1971.
"The Wearing Out of Genre Materials," in *College English* (Urbana, Illinois), October 1971.
"The He-Man Ethos in Science Fiction," in *Clarion 2*, edited by Robin Scott Wilson. New York, New American Library, 1972.
"Images of Women in Science Fiction" and "What Can a Heroine Do? or, Why Women Can't Write," in *Images of Women in Fiction: Feminist Perspectives*, edited by Susan Cornillon. Bowling Green, Ohio, Popular Press, 1972.
"Setting," in *Those Who Can*, edited by Robin Scott Wilson. New York, New American Library, 1973.
"Speculations: The Subjectivity of Science Fiction," in *Extrapolation* (Wooster, Ohio), December 1973.
" 'What If...?' Literature," in *The Contemporary Literary Scene 1973*, edited by Frank N. Magill. Englewood, New Jersey, Salem Press, 1974.
Introduction to *Tales and Stories*, by Mary Shelley. Boston, Hall, 1975.
"Towards an Aesthetic of Science Fiction," in *Science-Fiction Studies* (Terre Haute, Indiana), July 1975.
"Symposium: Women and Science Fiction," in *Khatru* (Baltimore), November 1975.
"Outta Space: Women Write Science Fiction," in *MS* (New York), January 1976.
"Alien Monsters," in *Turning Points*, edited by Damon Knight. New York, Harper, 1977.
"S.F. and Technology as Mystification," in *Science-Fiction Studies* (Terre Haute, Indiana), November 1978.

*   *   *

During the 1960's, Joanna Russ emerged as one of the most talented and provocative writers of science fiction's New Wave. While Russ identifies herself primarily as a feminist, she is equally well known for her experimental way of handling the conventional materials and narrative strategies of science fiction. Since Russ is opposed to all social fixities and intellectual givens, her major effort as a science-fiction writer has been to explore alternate realities and create new myths, especially ones which depict women as complex human subjects.

Russ's apprentice work is feminist only obliquely. Ostensibly she aims at an interesting mix of historical fantasy and the supernatural, a combination she continues to use in her later work. The initial run of stories exploits the theme of the after-life to fresh effect. "Nor Custom Stale," her first story, is untypically set in the future. It describes a bourgeois couple who live stubbornly immured in a future-tech "House" while catastrophic ages pass unnoticed outside; domestic monotony preserves them in a living death. Several of the stories are set in the 19th century, an era Russ understands but dislikes. "Mr. Wilde's Second Chance" is a wry account of the dead poet's renunciation of an opportunity to live a conventionally tasteful second life. In "There Is Another Shore...," a revenant young woman, a kind of female Keats, returns to her deathplace in Rome to taste "the fullness of life" in romantic adventure. The ironic premise of this story—that if life for the 19th-century woman was death, death was liberation—is also the germ for "My Dear Emily," whose sober young heroine is passionately emancipated when she becomes a vampire. Part of the wit of such stories is their literary allusiveness; "My Dear Emily" condenses the romantic plot of *Wuthering Heights.*

With her first Alyx stories, Russ introduces a character new to science fiction, an adventuress whose daring and cunning issue from her womanly strength. Set in ancient Phoenicia, these stories launch her on a career as a soldier of fortune. In her natural setting, Alyx is of necessity an outlaw sensibility—a rationalist in a world of superstitious mystique, an imaginist in a world of empty, brutal pragmatism: in short, Russ implies, the ancestor of the intelligent modern woman. *Picnic on Paradise* also built around Alyx, casts her again as an outlaw, here a ruthlessly sensible, martially skilled Trans-Temp agent abstracted from Tyre to a future world wasted by advanced capitalist war. Alyx is Russ's *agent provocateur*: neither Amazon nor androgyne, she foils both old and new notions of the feminine ideal. At the same time, her unromantic heroics are designed to satirize the "he-man ethos" of Sword and Sorcery. For all its modesty in plot and narrative strategy, *Picnic on Paradise* may be Russ's most inventive novel.

It was closely followed by another ground-breaking novel of the future and several increasingly accomplished shorter fantasies. *And Chaos Died* is at once a penetrating social critique and a lyrical celebration of a psionic near-utopia. Russ maroons her hero on a pastoral planet where he is drawn into an egalitarian community and taught psi-powers. What is really new in the novel is its style: the magic arbitrariness of the narrator's experience is rendered by a stream-of-expanding-consciousness technique that registers his initial nausea, then his growing joy, and finally his disgust when he is returned to a dystopic earth wholly given over to violence and mental imperialism. In the novelette "The Second Inquisition," Russ makes a poignantly funny story of one of her central concerns, a young girl's need for a worthy feminine model to counteract her social training in self-extinction. The tutelary genius in this case is a Trans-Temp agent from a non-sexist future world. The heroine of "The Zanzibar Cat" is yet another Alyx-like subversive ironist, a medieval miller's daughter who faces down a lord of Fantasyland. By the end of the tale, the humble milleress has grown into the mother of all meaning, the author. The archaic setting of "The Zanzibar Cat" and the Hellenistic background of "Poor Man, Beggar Man," a story that splits the historic Alexander into ego and ghostly alter ego, testify to Russ's continuing interest in unwritten history.

With "When It Changed" and "Nobody's Home," Russ reached a new level of achievement. These visions of an emancipated future for women on the wistfully named Whileaway are thorough reconstructions of the standard manless-world story. They are utopian, but only in a special sense: the particular virulence of male-dominated culture is no more, yet life remains unpredictably anguishing and rewarding.

The Female Man, a reconsideration of Whileawayan possibilities, has become an underground classic in both science-fiction and feminist circles. The book is built around the digressive journal of a present-day woman who encounters three other selves: the victim of an altered past even more oppressive of women than our own, an ambassador from a Whileawayan future, and an intermediary figure from a world split by gender war into Manland and Woman-

land. Each is, in her way, an Everywoman. Janet is Russ's ultimate heroine, "the Might-be of our dreams," the goal of feminine evolution. The way to Janet lies through Jael, or Alice Reasoner, the sex warrior based on Alyx; Jael knows that liberation must be won at hard cost. Joanna, the sometime narrator, and Jeanine are both confused products of a culture which invalidates their every aspiration. These four life histories are super-imposed on one another to create an anti-novel: narrative with dense novelistic detail is interspersed with meditation, reverie, and fragments of the mythology and history of Whileaway. What holds all this together is impassioned articulation, a style as sensitive as ever to the bizarre complexities of women's lives, but here honed to laser precision by rage.

Russ distinguishes herself in *The Female Man* as radical intelligencer and stylist. *We Who Are About to...* is a study of an hallucinating woman dying alone on an emptied planet. For all its eerie fascination, the book remains rather private and untransformed. In *The Two of Them* Russ returns to the earlier mode of the politically and socially informed adventure. The Trans-Temp heroine of this novel has escaped from the stultifying world of America in the 1950's to become an agent in the future. Sent to a sexist society that owes something to the Arabian Nights and something to the Islamic world of today, she rescues a girl from a harem, discovering in the process the depth of her commitment to the child: "it'll take longer than one woman's lifetime," she realizes, to free herself. Russ's own commitment to the liberation of the young has borne fruit in two recent short stories ("My Boat," "How Dorothy Kept Away the Spring") and *Kittatinny*, a fantasy written expressly for young girls.

—Carol L. Snyder

RUSSELL, Bertrand (Arthur William); became 3rd Lord Russell, 1931. British. Born in Ravenscroft, Monmouthshire, 18 May 1872. Educated privately; Trinity College, Cambridge (scholar), 1890-94, degrees in mathematics and moral sciences; Berlin University, 1895. Married 1) Alys Pearsall Smith in 1894 (separated, 1911, divorced, 1921); 2) Dora Black in 1921 (divorced, 1935), one son and one daughter; 3) Patricia Helen Spence in 1936 (divorced, 1952), one son; 4) Edith Finch in 1952. Attaché, British Embassy, Paris, 1894; Fellow, 1895, and Lecturer, 1910-16 (dismissed for pacifist views), 1944, Trinity College, Cambridge; Lowell Lecturer, Harvard University, Cambridge, Massachusetts, 1914; Lecturer, National University, Peking, 1920-21; Earl Grey Lecturer, Armstrong College, Newcastle, 1936; Lecturer, University of Chicago, 1938, University of California, Berkeley, 1939-40, and Barnes Foundation, Pennsylvania, 1941-43; Sidgwick Lecturer, Newnham College, Cambridge, 1945; Reith Lecturer, 1948; Lecturer, Columbia University, New York, 1951. Regular reviewer, *Mind*, 1890-1910's; Editor, *Tribune*, 1916-17; regular contributor, *The New Leader*, in the 1920's. Liberal parliamentary candidate for Wimbledon, 1907, and Labour candidate for Chelsea, 1922 and 1923. Founder, with Dora Russell, Beacon Hill School, 1927; Co-Founder, Campaign for Nuclear Disarmament, 1958; Founder, Bertrand Russell Peace Foundation and Atlantic Peace Foundation, 1963. Imprisoned for 6 months for pacifist writings, 1918, and for anti-nuclear demonstration, 1961. Recipient: Royal Society Sylvester Medal; Heinemann Award, 1947; Order of Merit, 1949; Nobel Prize for Literature, 1950; Unesco Kalinga Prize, 1957; Sonning Prize (Denmark), 1960; Jerusalem Prize, 1963. Honorary Fellow, London School of Economics, 1961. Fellow, Royal Society, 1908. *Died 2 February 1970.*

SCIENCE-FICTION PUBLICATIONS

Short Stories

Satan in the Suburbs and Other Stories.   London, Lane, and New York, Simon and Schuster, 1953.

Nightmares of Eminent Persons and Other Stories. London, Lane, 1954; New York, Simon and Schuster, 1955.

The Collected Stories of Bertrand Russell, edited by Barry Feinberg. London, Allen and Unwin, 1972; New York, Simon and Schuster, 1973.

OTHER PUBLICATIONS

Other

German Social Democracy (lectures). London, Longman, 1896; New York, Simon and Schuster, 1965.

An Essay on the Foundations of Geometry. Cambridge, University Press, 1897; New York, Dover, 1956; revised edition, translated into French by M. Cadenat as *Essai sur les Fondements de la Géométrie*, Paris, Gautier Villars, 1901.

A Critical Exposition of the Philosophy of Leibniz, with an Appendix of Leading Passages. Cambridge, University Press, 1900.

The Principles of Mathematics. Cambridge, University Press, 1903; New York, Norton, 1938.

Principia Mathematica, with Alfred North Whitehead. Cambridge, University Press, 3 vols., 1910-13; revised edition, 3 vols., 1925-27.

Anti-Suffragist Anxieties. London, People's Suffrage Federation, 1910.

Philosophical Essays. London, Longman, 1910; revised edition, London, Allen and Unwin, 1966; New York, Simon and Schuster, 1967.

The Problems of Philosophy. London, Williams and Norgate, and New York, Holt, 1912.

Our Knowledge of the External World as a Field for Scientific Method in Philosophy (lectures). London, Allen and Unwin, and Chicago, Open Court, 1914; revised edition, London, Allen and Unwin, 1926; New York, Norton, 1929.

The Philosophy of Bergson. London, Macmillan, 1914; Folcroft, Pennsylvania, Folcroft Editions, 1977.

Scientific Method in Philosophy (lecture). Oxford, Clarendon Press, 1914.

War—The Offspring of Fear. London, Union of Democratic Control, 1915.

The Philosophy of Pacifism. London, League of Peace and Freedom, 1915(?).

Policy of the Entente 1904-1914: A Reply to Professor Gilbert Murray. Manchester, National Labour Party, 1916.

Justice in War-Time. Chicago, Open Court, and London, Allen and Unwin, 1916.

The Case of Ernest F. Everett. London, No-Conscription Fellowship, 1916.

Principles of Social Reconstruction. London, Allen and Unwin, 1916; as *Why Men Fight: A Method of Abolishing the International Duel*, New York, Century, 1916.

Rex vs. Bertrand Russell. London, No-Conscription Fellowship, 1916.

What Are We Fighting For? London, No-Conscription Fellowship, 1916.

Why Not Peace Negotiations? London, No-Conscription Fellowship, 1916.

Political Ideals (lectures). New York, Century, 1917; London, Allen and Unwin, 1963.

Mysticism and Logic and Other Essays. London, Longman, 1918; New York, Norton, 1929; as *A Free Man's Worship and Other Essays*, London, Allen and Unwin, 1976.

Roads to Freedom: Socialism, Anarchism, and Syndicalism. London, Allen and Unwin, 1918; revised edition, 1919; as *Proposed Roads to Freedom*, New York, Holt, 1919.

Introduction to Mathematical Philosophy. London, Allen and Unwin, and New York, Macmillan, 1919.

The Practice and Theory of Bolshevism. London, Allen and Unwin, 1920; as *Bolshevism: Practice and Theory*, New York, Harcourt Brace, 1920; revised edition, as *The Practice and Theory of Bolshevism*, Allen and Unwin, 1949; New York, Simon and Schuster, 1964.

The Analysis of Mind. London, Allen and Unwin, 1921; New York, Macmillan, 1924.

Free Thought and Official Propaganda. London, Allen and Unwin, and New York, Huebsch, 1922.

The Problem of China. London, Allen and Unwin, and New York, Century, 1922.

The ABC of Atoms. London, Kegan Paul, and New York, Dutton, 1923.

The Prospects of Industrial Civilization, with Dora Russell. London, Allen and Unwin, and New York, Century, 1923.

Bolshevism and the West, with Scott Nearing. London, Allen and Unwin, 1924; as *Debate: Resolved That the Soviet Form of Government Is Applicable to Western Civilization*, New York, League of Public Discussion, 1924.

How to Be Free and Happy (lecture). New York, Rand School for Social Science, 1924.

Icarus; or, The Future of Science. London, Kegan Paul, and New York, Dutton, 1924; as *The Future of Science*, New York, Wisdom Library, 1959.

The ABC of Relativity. London, Kegan Paul, and New York, Harper, 1925; revised edition, edited by Felix Pirani, London, Allen and Unwin, 1958; New York, New American Library, 1959.

What I Believe. London, Kegan Paul, and New York, Dutton, 1925.

On Education, Especially in Early Childhood. London, Allen and Unwin, 1926; as *Education and the Good Life*, New York, Boni and Liveright, 1926; reprinted in part as *Education of Character*, New York, Philosophical Library, 1961.

The Analysis of Matter. London, Kegan Paul, and New York, Harcourt Brace, 1927.

An Outline of Philosophy. London, Allen and Unwin, 1927; as *Philosophy*, New York, Norton, 1927.

Why I Am Not a Christian. London, Watts, and New York, American Association for the Advancement of Atheism, 1927.

Selected Papers of Bertrand Russell. New York, Modern Library, 1927.

Sceptical Essays. London, Allen and Unwin, and New York, Norton, 1928.

A Liberal View of Divorce. Girard, Kansas, Haldeman Julius, 1929.

Marriage and Morals. New York, Liveright, and London, Allen and Unwin, 1929.

The Conquest of Happiness. New York, Liveright, and London, Allen and Unwin, 1930.

Debate! Is Modern Marriage a Failure?, with John Cowper Powys. New York, Discussion Guild, 1930.

Has Religion Made Useful Contributions to Civilization? An Examination and a Criticism. London, Watts, 1930; Girard, Kansas, Haldeman Julius, n.d.

The Scientific Outlook. London, Allen and Unwin, and New York, Norton, 1931.

Education and the Social Order. London, Allen and Unwin, 1932; as *Education and the Modern World*, New York, Norton, 1932.

Freedom and Organization 1814-1914. London, Allen and Unwin, 1934; as *Freedom Versus Organization*, New York, Norton, 1934; as *Legitimacy Versus Industrialism 1814-1848*, and *Freedom Versus Organization 1776-1914*, Allen and Unwin, 2 vols., 1965.

The Meaning of Marx: A Symposium, with others. New York, Farrar and Rinehart, 1934.

In Praise of Idleness and Other Essays. London, Allen and Unwin, and New York, Norton, 1935.

Religion and Science. London, Butterworth, and New York, Holt, 1935.

Determinism and Physics (lecture). Newcastle upon Tyne, Armstrong College, 1936.

Which Way to Peace? London, Joseph, 1936.

Education for Democracy (lecture). London, Association for Education in Citizenship, 1937.

Power: A New Social Analysis. London, Allen and Unwin, and New York, Norton, 1938.

Taming Economic Power, with T.V. Smith and Paul Douglas. Chicago, University of Chicago, 1938.

Is Security Increasing?, with A. Hart and M.H.C. Laves. Chicago, University of Chicago, 1939.

An Inquiry into Meaning and Truth. London, Allen and Unwin, and New York, Norton, 1940.

On Freedom in Time of Stress.   New York, Regional Progressive Conference, 1940.

Let the People Think: A Selection of Essays.   London, Watts, 1941.

How to Become a Philosopher....   Girard, Kansas, Haldeman Julius, 1942; as *The Art of Philosophizing and Other Essays*, New York, Philosophical Library, 1968.

How to Read and Understand History: The Past as the Key to the Future.   Girard, Kansas, Haldeman Julius, 1943.

An Outline of Intellectual Rubbish: A Hilarious Catalogue of Organized and Individual Stupidity.   Girard, Kansas, Haldeman Julius, 1943.

The Value of Free Thought: How to Become a Truth-Seeker and Break the Chains of Mental Slavery.   Girard, Kansas, Haldeman Julius, 1944.

A History of Western Philosophy and Its Connection with Political and Social Circumstances from the Earliest Times to the Present Day.   New York, Simon and Schuster, 1945; London, Allen and Unwin, 1946.

Ideas That Have Harmed Mankind.   Girard, Kansas, Haldeman Julius, 1946.

Ideas That Have Helped Mankind.   Girard, Kansas, Haldeman Julius, 1946.

Is Materialism Bankrupt? Mind and Matter in Modern Science.   Girard, Kansas, Haldeman Julius, 1946.

Physics and Experience.   Cambridge, University Press, 1946.

Can Man Be Rational?   Girard, Kansas, Haldeman Julius, 1947.

The Faith of a Rationalist: No Supernatural Reasons to Make Men Kind.   London, Watts, and Girard, Kansas, Haldeman Julius, 1947.

Philosophy and Politics (lecture).   London, National Book League, 1947.

Towards World Government.   London, New Commonwealth, 1947.

Human Knowledge: Its Scope and Limit.   London, Allen and Unwin, and New York, Simon and Schuster, 1948.

Am I an Atheist or an Agnostic? A Plea for Tolerance in the Face of New Dogma, with others.   Girard, Kansas, Haldeman Julius, 1949.

Authority and the Individual (lectures).   London, Allen and Unwin, and New York, Simon and Schuster, 1949.

Unpopular Essays.   London, Allen and Unwin, and New York, Simon and Schuster, 1950.

The Wit and Wisdom of Russell, edited by Lester E. Denonn.   Boston, Beacon Press, 1951.

The Impact of Science on Society.   New York, Columbia University Press, 1951; revised edition, London, Allen and Unwin, and New York, Simon and Schuster, 1952.

New Hopes for a Changing World.   London, Allen and Unwin, 1951; New York, Simon and Schuster, 1952.

How Near Is War?   London, Ridgway, 1952.

Bertrand Russell's Dictionary of Mind, Matter, and Morals, edited by Lester E. Denonn.   New York, Philosophical Library, 1952.

What Is Freedom?   London, Batchworth, 1952; revised edition, 1960.

The Good Citizen's Alphabet.   London, Gaberbocchus, 1953; New York, Philosophical Library, 1958.

What Is Democracy?   London, Batchworth, 1953; revised edition, 1960.

History as an Art (lecture).   Aldington, Kent, Hand and Flower Press, 1954.

Human Society in Ethics and Politics.   London, Allen and Unwin, 1954; New York, Simon and Schuster, 1955.

Logic and Knowledge: Essays 1901-1950, edited by Robert Charles Marsh.   London, Allen and Unwin, and New York, Macmillan, 1956.

Portraits from Memory and Other Essays.   London, Allen and Unwin, and New York, Simon and Schuster, 1956.

Understanding History and Other Essays.   New York, Philosophical Library, 1957.

Why I Am Not a Christian and Other Essays on Religion and Related Subjects, edited by Paul P. Edwards.   London, Allen and Unwin, and New York, Simon and Schuster, 1957.

Bertrand Russell's Best: Silhouettes in Satire, edited by Robert E. Egner.   London, Allen and Unwin, 1958; New York, New American Library, 1961; revised edition, 1971.

The Will to Doubt.   New York, Philosophical Library, 1958.

Common Sense and Nuclear Warfare.   London, Allen and Unwin, and New York, Simon and Schuster, 1959.

The Future of Science, with a "Self-Portrait" of the Author.   New York, Philosophical Library, 1959.

My Philosophical Development.   London, Allen and Unwin, and New York, Simon and Schuster, 1959.

Wisdom of the West: A Historical Survey of Western Philosophy in Its Social and Political Setting, edited by Paul Foulkes.   London, Macdonald, and New York, Doubleday, 1959.

Bertrand Russell Speaks His Mind (interviews), with Woodrow Wyatt.   Cleveland, World, and London, Barker, 1960.

The Basic Writings of Bertrand Russell 1903-1959, edited by Robert E. Egner and Lester E. Denonn.   London, Allen and Unwin, and New York, Simon and Schuster, 1961.

Fact and Fiction (essays and fiction).   London, Allen and Unwin, 1961; New York, Simon and Schuster, 1962.

Has Man a Future?   London, Allen and Unwin, 1961; New York, Simon and Schuster, 1962.

Essays in Skepticism.   New York, Philosophical Library, 1962.

History of the World in Epitome: For Use in Martian Infant Schools.   London, Gaberbocchus, 1962.

Unarmed Victory.   London, Allen and Unwin, and New York, Simon and Schuster, 1963.

On the Philosophy of Science, edited by Charles A. Fritz, Jr.   Indianapolis, Bobbs Merrill, 1965.

Appeal to the American Conscience.   London, Bertrand Russell Peace Foundation, 1966.

The Autobiography of Bertrand Russell.   London, Allen and Unwin, 3 vols., 1967-69; Boston, Little Brown, 2 vols., 1967-68; New York, Simon and Schuster, 1 vol., 1969.

War Crimes in Vietnam.   London, Allen and Unwin, and New York, Monthly Review Press, 1967.

Dear Bertrand Russell...: A Selection of His Correspondence with the General Public 1950-1968, edited by Barry Feinberg and Ronald Kasrils.   London, Allen and Unwin, and Boston, Houghton Mifflin, 1969.

A Collection of Critical Essays, edited by D.F. Peers.   New York, Doubleday, 1972.

Letters from Bertrand Russell (to Irma Stickland).   Penzance, Cornwall, Triton Press, 1972.

My Own Philosophy: A New Essay.   Hamilton, Ontario, McMaster University Library, 1972.

Atheism: Collected Essays 1943-1949.   New York, Arno Press, 1972.

The Ethics of War: Bertrand Russell and Ralph Barton Perry on World War I, edited by Charles Chatfield.   New York, Garland, 1972.

The Life of Bertrand Russell in Pictures and in His Own Words, edited by Christopher Farley and David Hodgson.   Nottingham, Spokesman, 1972.

Bertrand Russell's America: His Transatlantic Travels and Writings, edited by Barry Feinberg and Ronald Kasrils.   London, Allen and Unwin, 1973; New York, Viking Press, 1974.

Essays in Analysis, edited by Douglas Lackey.   London, Allen and Unwin, and New York, Braziller, 1973.

Bertrand Russell: An Introduction, edited by Brian Carr.   London, Allen and Unwin, 1975.

Mortals and Others: Bertrand Russell's American Essays 1931-1935, edited by Harry Ruja.   London, Allen and Unwin, 1975.

Editor, *The Amberley Papers: The Letters and Diaries of Lord and Lady Amberley.*   London, Hogarth Press, 2 vols., and New York, Norton, 2 vols., 1937.

*

Bibliography: by Lester E. Denonn, in *The Philosophy of Bertrand Russell* edited by P.A. Schilpp, Evanston, Illinois, Northwestern University Press, 1944; revised edition, New York, Harper, 1963.

*   *   *

Bertrand Russell, not content with a career as a world-renowned philosopher, essayist, and mathematician, began writing short stories at 80. *Satan in the Suburbs*, as he asserts in the Preface, is intended only to amuse, though the one "science-fiction" story, "The Infra-redioscope," a satiric fable, brings up serious issues; these issues, involving a basic philosophical and political conflict, are further dramatized in "Zahatopolk" and "Faith and Mountains," two futuristic tales from *Nightmares of Eminent Persons*.

In "The Infra-redioscope" a dishonest scientist invents a fraudulent machine which supposedly detects Martians who have secretly invaded earth, a plot that strains credibility; the scientists' backers make millions as terror-stricken folk buy the machine, and, as an unintended result, end East-West conflict when enemies unite against an alien peril. The young, idealistic scientist who discovers the fraud is faced with a terrible choice—should the truth be revealed, at the cost of world peace, or should the fantasy be allowed to continue, to the benefit of a privileged few?—a choice whose import is undercut by an unsatisfactory ending. This theme is handled much more skillfully in "Faith and Mountains," wherein the competition of two absurd quasi-religious cults which have captured the fancy of much of the world brings the protagonists to much the same question—can man accept truth and reason without the comfort of myth and fantasy—a question whose answer is an uncomfortable yes. The best exposition of this question is in "Zahatopolk," a well-crafted, nicely imagined fable. Peruvian Indians rule the world in a far-distant future. At the cost of brutal exploitation of the non-Peruvian majority they have achieved a completely stable world order based on religious myth. An intellectual Peruvian maiden sees through the false ideology and by self-sacrifice destroys the society. The ending wittily and wisely suggest man's inherent need for escapist and self-serving myth and the equally basic response of lonely debunkers, the two occurring in cycles. Russell, of course, was such a debunker himself, and summarizes the conflict in the last line of "Faith and Mountains," "Ah, how hard is the Life of Reason!"

—Andrew Macdonald

RUSSELL, Eric Frank. British. Born in Camberley, Surrey, 6 January 1905; grew up in Egypt. Served in the King's Regiment, 1922-26, and in the Royal Air Force, 1941-45. Married Ellen Russell in 1930; one daughter. Worked as a telephonist, quantity surveyor, and draughtsman. Founding Member, British Interplanetary Society. Recipient: Hugo Award, 1955. *Died 28 February 1978.*

SCIENCE-FICTION PUBLICATIONS

Novels

Sinister Barrier. Kingswood, Surrey, World's Work, 1943; Reading, Pennsylvania, Fantasy Press, 1948.
Dreadful Sanctuary. Reading, Pennsylvania, Fantasy Press, 1951; London, Museum Press, 1953.
Sentinels from Space. New York, Bouregy, 1953; London, Museum Press, 1954.
Three to Conquer. New York, Avalon, 1956; London, Dobson, 1957.
Wasp. New York, Avalon, 1957; London, Dobson, 1958.
The Space Willies. New York, Ace, 1958; revised edition, as *Next of Kin*, London, Dobson, 1959.
The Great Explosion. London, Dobson, and New York, Torquil, 1962.
With a Strange Device. London, Dobson, 1964; as *The Mind Warpers*, New York, Lancer, 1965.

Short Stories

Deep Space. Reading, Pennsylvania, Fantasy Press, 1954; London, Eyre and Spottiswoode, 1956.
Men, Martians, and Machines. London, Dobson, and New York, Roy, 1956.
Six Worlds to Conquer. New York, Ace, 1958.
Far Stars. London, Dobson, 1961.
Dark Tides. London, Dobson, 1962.
Somewhere a Voice. London, Dobson, 1965; New York, Ace, 1966.
Like Nothing on Earth. London, Dobson, 1975.
The Best of Eric Frank Russell. New York, Ballantine, 1978.

OTHER PUBLICATIONS

Other

Great World Mysteries. London, Dobson, and New York, Roy, 1957.
The Rabble Rousers. Evanston, Illinois, Regency, 1963.

*   *   *

Eric Frank Russell will always be remembered as the author of *Sinister Barrier*, the story which helped John W. Campbell launch the magazine *Unknown* in 1939. Boosted as "the greatest imaginative novel in two decades," it established the British writer at the centre of the international science-fiction scene where he remained a popular figure for more than 30 years. It also drew attention to the abundance of plot material in the much-maligned works of Charles Fort, whose philosophy of scepticism Russell upheld consistently on behalf of the Fortean Society.

The novel relies on the notion that the Earth belongs to an alien race which feeds on the human misery it causes. With consummate skill, goaded by Campbell, Russell presented it as a mystery story in the tradition of the detective pulps he had studied in preparing to write for the American market. His taut, racy style had first attracted attention in *Astounding Stories* in 1937, when "The Saga of Pelican West" showed the influence of Stanley G. Weinbaum which affected many writers at that time. His contributions to the British *Tales of Wonder* and *Fantasy* also revealed a refreshing touch of humour coupled with a vigorous approach that was rare in science fiction. Typical examples were "Vampire from the Void," set in his Liverpool habitat, and "I, Spy!" concerning a Martian visitant that could simulate any form of terrestrial life. His amusing tales of Jay Score, the robot space-pilot, and his crewmen were collected in *Men, Martians, and Machines.* War service curtailed his writing, but "Metamorphosite," a story about a galactic empire, and *Dreadful Sanctuary* returned him to front-rank status. A fast-moving tale about a secret society which sabotaged the first attempts at space-travel, *Dreadful Sanctuary* seriously considers mankind's irrational ways while posing the question "How do you know you're sane?"

All through the 1950's Russell's lucid narratives delighted readers. He broke new ground with "First Person Singular" by adapting the Adam and Eve legend to an interstellar setting; in other stories he revealed an unsuspected flair for emotional themes and moral issues such as racial intolerance. "And There Were None" postulates the effect of passive resistance on planetary invaders, which later became the theme of his satirical novel *The Great Explosion*. *Three to Conquer* reflected the interest in *psionics* fostered by Campbell. "Allamagoosa" (Hugo) is a clever piece of nonsense. *Sentinels from Space*, in which a highly evolved species keeps a watch over lesser beings, derives something from Olaf Stapledon, with whom Russell maintained friendly contact after introducing him to American science fiction. *Wasp* is an action-thriller relating the escapades of a secret agent preparing the way for a Terran invasion of the Sirian Empire. Simplest of all Russell's novels is *With a Strange Device*, almost a straight mystery story about a conspiracy to sabotage a new defensive weapon. Almost as intriguing as any of his fiction, too, is his collection *Great World Mysteries* in which he delved into some of the enigmas which have baffled scientists over the past century or more.

—Walter Gillings

RUSSELL, Ray. American. Born in Chicago, Illinois, 4 September 1924. Educated at the Chicago Conservatory of Music, 1947-48; Goodman Memorial Theater, Chicago, 1949-51. Served in the United States Army Air Force, 1943-46. Married Ada Beth Stevens in 1950; one daughter and one son. Associate Editor, 1954-55, Executive Editor, 1955-60, and Contributing Editor, 1968-75, *Playboy*, Chicago. Recipient: Festival Internazionale del Film di Fantascienza Silver Globe Award, 1963; Sri Chinmoy Poetry Award, 1977. Agent: H.N. Swanson Inc., 8523 Sunset Boulevard, Los Angeles, California 90069, U.S.A.

SCIENCE-FICTION PUBLICATIONS

Novels

The Case Against Satan. New York, Obolensky, 1962; London, Souvenir Press, 1963.
Incubus. New York, Morrow, 1976; London, Sphere, 1977.
Princess Pamela. Boston, Houghlin Mifflin, 1979.

Short Stories

Sardonicus and Other Stories. New York, Ballantine, 1962.
Unholy Trinity. New York, Bantam, 1967; London, Sphere, 1971.
Prince of Darkness. London, Sphere, 1971.
Sagittarius. Chicago, Playboy Press, 1971.
The Devil's Mirror. London, Sphere, 1980.
The Book of Hell. London, Sphere, 1980.

OTHER PUBLICATIONS

Novel

The Colony. Los Angeles, Sherbourne Press, 1969; London, Sphere, 1971.

Plays

Screenplays: *Mr. Sardonicus*, 1961; *Zotz!*, 1962; *The Premature Burial*, with Charles Beaumont, 1962; *X — The Man with X-Ray Eyes*, with Robert Dillon, 1963; *The Horror of It All*, 1964; *Chamber of Horrors*, with Stephen Kandel, 1966.

Other

The Little Lexicon of Love. Los Angeles, Sherbourne Press, 1966.
Holy Horatio! The Strange Life and Paradoxical Works of the Legendary Mr. Alger. Santa Barbara, California, Capra Press, 1976.

Editor, *Playboy's Ribald Classics.* New York, Waldorf, 1957.
Editor, *The Permanent Playboy.* New York, Crown, 1959.
Editor, *The Playboy Book of Science Fiction and Fantasy.* Chicago, Playboy Press, 1966; London, Souvenir Press, 1967.
Editor, *The Playboy Book of Horror and the Supernatural.* Chicago, Playboy Press, 1967; London, Souvenir Press, 1968.

*

Manuscript Collection: University of Wyoming Library, Laramie.

Ray Russell comments:

I suppose I am, for want of a better word, a mainstream writer, and yet I have flirted with science fiction all my life. I began reading it at a pre-school age (I was a *very* early reader) and by the age of nine I was writing it. That juvenile effort—a quartet of miniature tales under the group title "Captain Clark of the Space Patrol"—appeared some decades later in the magazine *Odyssey*. I seize this opportunity to honor a forgotten man named Carl H. Claudy. He used to write books for boys—adventure stories, mostly—but he dipped into SF for a series of four novels about a pair of friends who journeyed to another planet, to prehistoric times, to the fourth dimension, and beneath the Earth's surface (*The Mystery Men of Mars, A Thousand Years a Minute, The Land of No Shadow,* and

The Blue Grotto Terror). These excellent books had a profound influence on me.

Although I admire the best SF practitioners, particularly Clarke, and have nostalgic fondness for Weinbaum, Kuttner, the brothers Binder, and all the others who brightened my boyhood, I hold the opinion that the best SF is written by non-specialists. An unpopular view in SF circles, I know, but has there ever been a better series of SF novels than the great interplanetary trilogy of C.S. Lewis? Wells, Huxley, Orwell, Amis, William Hjortsberg (*Gray Matters*), Anthony Burgess have given us SF that is several notches above the specialists' product. Too much of that product is insular. It is also derivative: for instance, the allegedly bold, new "experiments" that were in vogue a few years back were not bold or new to anyone who read Borges, Marquez, Calvino, Barthelme, Pynchon, Nabokov, or other mainstream trailblazers. Even within the SF field, many have short memories, or have read little published before 1970. If there's a moral to any of this, it's simply that SF is good fun, marvelous entertainment, occasionally thought-provoking, head and shoulders above the general level of the pulp slums from which it climbed, but should be read as part of a wider spectrum that includes the best contemporary writers outside the field and the acknowledged masterworks of the past.

*   *   *

Ray Russell came to the attention of the science-fiction world in the mid-1950's when, as Executive Editor of *Playboy*, he opened the magazine's pages to work by Clarke, Sheckley, Matheson, Bradbury, Charles Beaumont and other SF/fantasy writers, many of whom had never appeared in a large-circulation journal. When Russell left *Playboy*, he kept in touch by writing stories for it, several of which were SF. Exceptional among these is "Sagittarius," a Gothic sequel to Stevenson's "Dr. Jekyll and Mr. Hyde." Other outstanding examples of his *Playboy* SF include the powerful story of a black astronaut, "Here Comes John Henry," the haunting end-of-the-world tale "Xong of Xuxan," and "The Room," which spoofs future advertising. A non-*Playboy* specimen of Russell at his science-fiction best is "The Humanic Complex," a bitingly satirical portrait of a God gone mad.

Russell is essentially a mainstream writer, but his work often displays a fondness for the fantastic and the fabulistic. His novels *The Case Against Satan* and *Incubus* deal with sinister forces that we can interpret as either supernatural or scientifically explicable; and Russell in these books is deliberately ambiguous, carefully providing us with sufficient evidence for both interpretations, making the books eligible for mainstream, fantasy, or science-fiction labels. A later novel, *Princess Pamela*, appears to be nothing more nor less than a richly wrought Victorian thriller-romance—until the author stuns us with a dramatic twist some have called outright science fiction, others pure fantasy. Russell, true to his nature, is not saying.

—William F. Nolan

SABERHAGEN, Fred(erick Thomas). American. Born in Chicago, Illinois, 18 May 1930. Educated Wright Junior College, 1956-57. Served in the United States Air Force, 1951-55. Married Joan Dorothy Spicci in 1968; one daughter and two sons. Electronics technician, Motorola Inc., Chicago, 1956-62; assistant editor, *Encyclopaedia Britannica*, 1967-73. Free-lance writer, 1962-67, and since 1973. Agent: Virginia Kidd, Box 278, Milford, Pennsylvania 18337. Address: 1813 Dakota, Albuquerque, New Mexico 87110, U.S.A.

SCIENCE-FICTION PUBLICATIONS

Novels (series: Berserker; Chup; Dracula)

The Golden People.   New York, Ace, 1964.
The Water of Thought.   New York, Ace, 1965; complete edition, Los Angeles, Pinnacle, 1981.
The Empire of the East (Chup).   New York, Ace, 1979.
   The Broken Lands.   New York, Ace, 1968.
   The Black Mountains.   New York, Ace, 1971.
   Changeling Earth.   New York, DAW, 1973.
Brother Assassin.   New York, Ballantine, 1969; as *Brother Berserker*, London, Macdonald, 1969.
Berserker's Planet.   New York, DAW, 1975.
The Dracula Tape.   New York, Warner, 1975.
Specimens.   New York, Popular Library, 1976.
The Holmes-Dracula File.   New York, Ace, 1978.
The Veils of Azlaroc.   New York, Ace, 1978.
Love Conquers All.   New York, Ace, 1979.
Mask of the Sun.   New York, Ace, 1979.
Berserker Man.   New York, Ace, 1979.
An Old Friend of the Family (Dracula).   New York, Ace, 1979.
A Matter of Taste (Dracula).   New York, Ace, 1980.
Thorn.   New York, Ace, 1980.

Short Stories (series: Berserker)

Berserker.   New York, Ballantine, 1967.
The Book of Saberhagen.   New York, DAW, 1975.
The Ultimate Enemy (Berserker).   New York, Ace, 1979.

Uncollected Short Story

"The Metal Murderer," in *Omni* (New York), January 1980.

*   *   *

Fred Saberhagen's gift is to dramatize familiar ideas with compelling thoroughness. For nearly two decades his principal theme has been Life's war with Death across the evolutionary gradient. It is the very substance of his best-known work, the berserker stories. The berserkers are self-programming, self-replicating robotic spacecraft set by their "long-dead masters to destroy anything that lived." Fighting these ineradicable foes unites all life forms in the galaxy and, ironically, stimulates progress that might not otherwise have come about without the berserkers' challenge. This popular "divergent" series, which originally grew out of games theory, is a novelty in that it is organized around a common enemy instead of a continuing hero. Its premise, however, is not unique (see Theodore Sturgeon's 1948 novella "There Is No Defense"), but Saberhagen has made it so completely his own that "his murderous mechanisms are the recognized standard in the field" (Sandra Miesel, Afterword, *Berserker Man*, 1979).

Style is Saberhagen's weakest point. His language is awkward at worst, serviceable at best. This fault is most obvious when he attempts too ambitious a project, as in his Orpheus tale, "Starsong." But Saberhagen has gradually come to make a virtue of plainness—most successfully in *Berserker Man*—and subordinates the accidents of his prose to the substance of his story. The mythic power inherent in his subject matter usually more than compensates for stylistic deficiencies. A second weakness is that he occasionally allows plot schematics to hobble his natural flair for narration. Rigid one-to-one correspondences spoil *Love Conquers All*, making it harshly polemical instead of effectively thematic. Ordinarily, Saberhagen renders material well. For example, notice how he economically establishes the hideousness of the demons and their allies in his science-fantasy trilogy *The Empire of the East*.

On the positive side, Saberhagen possesses a sound scientific imagination. He can see a story in a Foucault pendulum ("Brother Berserker"), a black hole (*The Veils of Azlaroc*), or even a squash seed ("Pressure"). He gives a biochemical basis to Paleolithic rituals in *The Water of Thought*. *The Empire of the East* translates the laws of science into magic and back again, yielding such curiosities as a technologist djinn and valkyrie robots. Saberhagen also draws inspiration from literature ("The Masque of the Red Shift"), the arts

("Young Girl at an Open Half-Door"), history ("Wings Out of Shadow"), myth (*The Broken Lands*), and theology (*Berserker Man*). He is especially deft at combining the legendary and historical aspects of a subject and then infusing the result with theological significance. "Stone Place" recreates Don John of Austria, Philip II of Spain, and the Battle of Lepanto in a way G.K. Chesterton himself would have applauded. St. Francis of Assisi, Galileo, and the mystical theories of Pierre Teilhard de Chardin are brought together to beautiful effect in "Brother Berserker."

One of Saberhagen's greatest strengths is the sheer conviction he brings to his work. Because he believes in his stories, he convinces his readers to do the same. His best characterizations are precisely those which ought to have been the most difficult—Brother Jovann, his St. Francis figure; Johann Karlsen, his Don John; and Draffut, the Beast-Lord in *The Black Mountains*. In *Berserker Man* the Child-Hero Michel succeeds both as child and as hero while carrying a heavy load of metaphysics on his shoulders at the same time. Saberhagen can also make highly unpromising characters sympathetic; as when he tells the second volume of *The Empire of the East* from the viewpoint of the first volume's villain. His excellent Dracula pastiches show the Count as entrancingly alien rather than monstrous and make him a force for justice.

Saberhagen is unglamorous, ironic, and never sentimental. The unblinking eye he turns on evil records its horror with the utmost clarity. It allows no ambiguity: entities like the berserkers and the demons are as totally evil as any beings can be. They are to be fought without compromise or quarter. Saberhagen's stated goal is "to impose different coordinate systems upon the human condition," but the functions he plots are traditional Western Christian ones. Whatever the weaponry, his battles are wonder-wars between cosmic principles, and whatever the odds, he says that life will wear the final victor's crown.

—Sandra Miesel

ST. CLAIR, Margaret (née Neeley).   American.   Born in Hutchinson, Kansas, 17 February 1911. Educated at the University of California, Berkeley, M.A. 1933 (Phi Beta Kappa). Married Eric St. Clair in 1932. Horticulturist, St. Clair Rare Bulb Gardens, El Sobrante, California, 1938-41. Since 1945, full-time writer. Agent: Shirley Fisher, McIntosh and Otis, 475 Fifth Avenue, New York, New York 10017. Address: Star Route, Manchester, California 95459, U.S.A.

SCIENCE-FICTION PUBLICATIONS

Novels

Agent of the Unknown.   New York, Ace, 1956.
The Green Queen.   New York, Ace, 1956.
The Games of Neith.   New York, Ace, 1960.
Sign of the Labrys.   New York, Bantam, and London, Corgi, 1963.
Message from the Eocene.   New York, Ace, 1964.
The Dolphins of Altair.   New York, Dell, 1967.
The Shadow People.   New York, Dell, 1969.
The Dancers of Noyo.   New York, Ace, 1973.

Short Stories

Three Worlds of Futurity.   New York, Ace, 1964.
Change the Sky and Other Stories.   New York, Ace, 1974.

Margaret St. Clair comments:
   It would take me days to write adequately about my work. So I shall only say that I think I am better at short fiction than at

novels—the short story is more philosophical—and that I like my amusing stories better than the frightening ones, and prefer both classes to what I call "uplift."

I am not a natural writer. Writing is painful and difficult for me.

*   *   *

Margaret St. Clair is an example of a woman writer who did not have to disguise her sex in order to be successful as a writer in a male-dominated field. She was able to write in a natural "female voice" at a time when some women writers of science fiction were outdoing the men in tough-flavored style, and, particularly in her fantasy short stories (generally written as by Idris Seabright), to introduce some sensitive characterization, including portrayals of housewives, single mothers, and young children, into a field which was highly technologically oriented. In common with others writing in the 1950's, St. Clair's fiction was oriented toward adventurous episodes, but she had a penchant for tackling controversial themes and for using gadgetry and environments symbolically.

Most of St. Clair's short fiction was published during the 1950's. Some of her astonishing output of approximately 130 stories may be found in *Three Worlds of Futurity* and *Change the Sky and Other Stories*; both are representative of her work. Other individual stories are found in anthologies: "Short in the Chest" (in Greenberg and Olander's *Science Fiction of the 50's*, 1979), featuring Marine Major Sonya Briggs and a "philosophical robot" psychologist called a "huxley," is remarkable for its portrayal of women and its grappling with questions of sexuality. "New Ritual" (in Boucher's *The Best from Fantasy and Science Fiction*, 1954), also featuring a female protagonist, gives a futuristic twist to the plight of the dissatisfied housewife as a deep freeze turns everything from apricots to an inattentive husband into more desirable items. "Child of Void" (in Conklin's *Invaders of Earth*, 1952) shows a lonely boy grappling with the unknown in the form of a luminous egg which presents children with alluring visions of those things they most desire.

St. Clair's novels, not as consistently well-crafted as her shorter work, are usually adventures and may be relied upon to convey a message. *Agent of the Unknown* is set on the synthetic pleasure planetoid Fyon. An appealing non-conformist with a drinking problem finds purpose in life when he rescues from the edge of the sea a small but awe-inspiring "Weeping Doll," the creation of the master craftsman Vulcan. The protagonist muses "Sometimes I think everything in our world is synthetic, even happiness." While "Vulcan's Weeping Doll" passively inspires changes in one world, *The Green Queen* and *The Games of Neith* both feature heroines as active characters who are chosen to inspire or lead their respective societies toward change. Histrionic talents, intelligence, and physical beauty are attributes possessed by the Green Queen, who lives in a post-holocaust society ripe for revolution, "a place where ten percent of the population monopolized eighty percent of the dwelling space and fifty percent of the unpolluted food, and where everybody, Uppers and Lowers alike, was always terribly afraid of damage from the omnipresent radioactive elements...." In *The Games of Neith* Anassa, Priestess to the Goddess of Neith, possesses similar traits, and guides her seafaring society, which is threatening to return to the worship of primitive gods, to a new future. Anassa's relationship with Ehr'li Wan, a physics professor, is an excellent early example of a man and a woman in science fiction working in an equal partnership against evil forces.

The Shadow People is a striking work. Although the quality of the prose is uneven and the thrust of the narrative is excessively cheerless, an underworld of zombie-like people is memorably portrayed as scuttling through a rat-and-fungus-infested underworld in a hallucinatory, hopeless future. *Sign of the Labrys* portrays another dark underworld, this time inhabited by the survivors of a devastating plague who cower in damp caverns hacked out of rock until the hero, Sam Sewell, brings them awareness of an open, habitable world above ground. *Message from the Eocene* introduces Tharg, an ancient being of alien origin, who desperately attempts to overcome his condition of existing (for century upon century) as a disembodied sentient force so that he may convey a message to mankind. He eventually makes contact with a modern woman whose gift of mental sensitivity to unusual phenomena is sensitively portrayed.

St. Clair's best novel, *The Dolphins of Altair*, is a moving work critical of man's disregard for the ecosystems of Earth. Members of a well-drawn, intelligent dolphin society conspire with a few enlightened humans to preserve the world for an unusual new future. *The Dancers of Noyo*, like *Agent of The Unknown*, relies upon a male protagonist to hold together a tale of the future. A quest for personal identity is set against a world dominated by powerful androids.

St. Clair's best work is tightly written shorter fiction which introduced unusual protagonists to the pages of science-fiction magazines. While some of her longer works suffer from over-ambitious exploration of diverse themes, the best of her novels are those most concerned with an individual's experience with the extraordinary, or a group's commitment to a visionary future.

—Rosemary Herbert

SALLIS, James. American. Born in Helena, Arkansas, 21 December 1944. Attended Tulane University, New Orleans, 1962-64. Married Jane Rose in 1964; one son. Worked as a college instructor and publisher's reader; Editor, *New Worlds*, London, 1969-70; now a full-time writer. Agent: Brandt, 101 Park Avenue, New York, New York 10017, U.S.A.

SCIENCE-FICTION PUBLICATIONS

Short Stories

A Few Last Words. London, Hart Davis, 1969; New York, Macmillan, 1970.

Uncollected Short Stories

"This One," in *If* (New York), January 1970.
"Front and Centaur," in *New Worlds* (London), March 1970.
"Binaries" and "Only the Words Are Different," in *Orbit 9*, edited by Damon Knight. New York, Putnam, 1971.
"Mensuration," in *Quark 2*, edited by Samuel R. Delany and Marilyn Hacker. New York, Paperback Library, 1971.
"Field," in *Quark 3*, edited by Samuel R. Delany and Marilyn Hacker. New York, Paperback Library, 1971.
"The Fly at Ciron," in *Fantasy and Science Fiction* (New York), December 1971.
"At the Fitting Shop" and "53rd American Dream," in *Again, Dangerous Vision*, edited by Harlan Ellison. New York, Doubleday, 1972; London, Millington, 1976.
"Doucement, S'Il Vous Plait," in *Orbit 11*, edited by Damon Knight. New York, Putnam, 1973.
"Echo," in *The Berserkers*, edited by Roger Elwood. New York, Simon and Schuster, 1973.
"Delta Flight 281" and "The First Few Kinds of Truth," in *Alternities*, edited by David Gerrold. New York, Dell, 1974.
"My Friend Zarathustra," in *Orbit 13*, edited by Damon Knight. New York, Putnam, 1974.
"They Will Not Hush," in *Whispers 24* (Browns Mills, New Jersey), 1974.
"The Invasion of Dallas," in *Lone Star Universe*, edited by George W. Proctor and Steven Utley. Austin, Texas, Heidelberg, 1976.
"Miranda-Escobedo," in *Fantasy and Science Fiction* (New York), July 1976.
"One Road to Damascus," in *2076: The American Tricentennial*, edited by Edward Bryant. New York, Pyramid, 1977.
"La Fin d'une Monde (Intérieure)," in *Fantastic* (New York), June 1977.
"Jackson," in *Fantastic* (New York), December 1977.
"Changes," in *Fantastic* (New York), April 1978.
"Exigency and Martin Heidegger," in *Amazing* (New York), November 1978.

OTHER PUBLICATIONS

Other

Down Home: Country-Western. New York, Macmillan, 1971.
"The Writer as Teacher," in *Clarion 2,* edited by Robin Scott
Wilson. New York, New American Library, 1972.

Editor, *The War Book.* London, Hart Davis, 1969; New York,
Dell, 1971.
Editor, *The Shores Beneath.* New York, Avon, 1970.

*   *   *

James Sallis's extraordinary fiction is distinguished by its honesty and meticulous artistry. With his highly imagistic stories, he has regularly displayed a finely honed mastery of sophisticated literary techniques and sharply etched psychological insights. Often the stories are clearly autobiographical, presenting painful indications of their author's personal difficulties, even his torments. They are not always easy to read, and it is sometimes hard to discern their intent or meaning, but they affect readers powerfully, at least those readers who demand more than thrill-seeking and fantastic adventures from the fiction they read. (It always sounds a bit pompous to score the escapist reader in such terms, but writers like Sallis, who employ quite subtle fictional devices, *do* demand more from their readers. In "My Friend Zarathustra" Sallis writes: "Yes—I mean what I say, and you must listen; must hear what's not said if you're to understand properly what is said.")

Many of his stories are moving portrayals of troubled or dazed individuals who are dissociated from their environments. In nearly every Sallis story the main character is helpless, or at least quite passive. Things are dreadfully confused in his private life or are being disrupted in the outside world. Sometimes nothing much is happening, but even then the character does not cope well. At the rare times when the character is able to act decisively, the action turns out to be futile or grotesque. (The disposal of the child in the brilliantly executed "Jim and Mary G." is a harrowing example of such futility and ugliness.) Usually the character is still helpless at the end of the story. In many stories, the protagonists are last seen merely waiting or going off into darkness or standing still as the world begins to disintegrate, literally or physically, around them. However Sallis dramatizes it, the main impression the reader receives from most of the stories is of humankind trapped in environments upon which they can have no effect, and for which they no longer have any effective responses or reactions. In "Faces, Hands: The Kettle of Stars" a courier is halted from his message-carrying mission and stranded in an intergalactic waiting room, where he contemplates art in the form of an also-waiting alien singer whose destiny is repulsive servitude on another planet, an injustice the courier perceives but cannot affect. The protagonist of "The History Makers" occupies himself with letters or music or sitting at a window while whole time-accelerated civilizations grow, decline, and fall nearby. The only movement he makes is to move away from a city's encroaching border. Nevertheless, he is able to speculate on the exigencies of time, as manifested in the slow progress of a beetle across sand or in a review of his own life or in the odd inverted timescale of the cities. In "A Few Last Words" a man attempts to decide what to do as a doomed city more or less empties before his eyes.

In such stories the sense of dissociation is pronounced both in the relationship of character to setting and in the character's own "inner space," the phrase emphasized by interpreters of the new wave of science fiction as its primary subject matter. Sallis's characters, even at their most articulate, are often in danger of breaking up themselves in just about the same way the setting is crumbling around them. In one of his most effective and painful stories, "Binaries," the narrator-writer (who perceives his immediate environment as being regularly broken up and moved away) is in a state of dissociation with himself as a person and as a writer:

Someone has written a collection of short stories and published them under my name; they have even put my photograph on the back cover. I received a copy in the morning post. Anonymous, no return address, postmarked Grnd Cntrl Stn. The stories reveal my deepest secrets. Only one person could have written them. Or had reason to. My attorney is investigating the possibility of a lawsuit against the publisher but, as the work was copyrighted in my own name, there seems little we can do. The publisher expressed to my attorney his desire to meet the author, his admiration for the book.

The passage's poignancy, its precise delineation of the character's troubled emotions, and—incidentally—its wrenching irony, are all hallmarks of the fiction of James Sallis.

Sallis also has an appealing knack for humorous, especially surrealistic, writing, which he uses in stories like "Kazoo," "The Creation of Bennie Good," and "Miranda-Escobedo." It is worth noting, however, that, even in these works, with their clever improvisations, sly allusions, and superb word-play, the sense of psychological and emotional dissociation generally remains, as dazed or momentarily baffled characters and even ghost-cops are disoriented by their absurd environments.

Sallis started publishing science fiction in the 1960's, a time when the field was being rattled by a number of literary experimenters who came to be dubbed, for better or for worse, the "new wave" of science fiction. He served some time as an editor of the British magazine *New Worlds,* the SF publication that became most associated with the new wave because it dared to publish the works of adventuresome writers during a period when many other SF markets were resisting anything that did not correspond with accepted approaches to the genre. Now that the new furore has somewhat subsided, upheld in print only by a few still petulant writers, it is clear that the contributions of the new wavers are legitimate literary extensions of established science-fiction traditions, and that Sallis's stories are among the best writings to emerge from the phenomenon. In recent years James Sallis, never prolific, has published few stories, but the ones that have been published exhibit the same care for literary details and intellectual concerns as the earlier stories. One recent story, "Changes," ranks with the best of his fiction.

—Robert Thurston

SARBAN. Pseudonym for John W. Wall. British.

SCIENCE-FICTION PUBLICATIONS

Novel

The Sound of His Horn. London, Davies, 1952; New York, Ballantine, 1960.

Short Stories

Ringstones and Other Curious Tales. London, Davies, and New York, Coward McCann, 1951.
The Doll Maker and Other Tales of the Uncanny. London, Davies, 1953; *The Doll Maker* published separately, New York, Ballantine, 1960.

*   *   *

The only true science-fiction novel to appear under the Sarban byline was *The Sound of His Horn,* a novel that evokes a mood of gloom and horror as well as anything that has ever been written. Kingsley Amis pointed out that it is one of the few novels ever to suggest a rural rather than urban dystopia, a future after Germany has won World War II and the other races of the world are viewed as little better than lower animals. Alan Querdilion wanders into an electrified fence while escaping from a German POW camp and finds himself somehow projected into a world where the Germans have already been victorious. After a brief period where he is the guest of a German landholder, he is set loose as prey for his host's periodic hunts.

Two other short novels appeared, both of which have been published as horror novels though the subject matter is such that they could as well be considered fantasies. In *The Doll Maker* a young girl is compelled to become a tutor at mysterious Brackenbine Hall, and soon falls under the influence of Niall Sterne, a peculiar reclusive man who roams the forests and exists only, it seems, for his collection of extremely lifelike dolls. In due course, the heroine learns of Stern's connection with several past deaths, and comes to believe that he can transfer human souls into the dolls he creates. *The Doll Maker* also brilliantly creates a mood of despair and awakening horror. Sarban's skill at drawing the reader into his book is probably at its best, however, in *Ringstones*. A young woman is employed to tutor two young children at a remote estate, but soon becomes enmeshed in magic and the struggle to maintain her own personality and view of reality when faced with a form of existence that she had formerly considered only a dream. *Ringstones* is a haunting novel that is far more worthwhile than the hundreds of modern gothics which it in many ways resembles.

Although they are extremely hard to locate, Sarban also created several excellent shorter pieces. The most noteworthy of these are probably "Calmahain" and "Capra." In the former, two young children allow their fantasy world to become so real that it overflows into the real world and adults begin to experience elements of the fantasy. In the latter, a vicious lover's triangle at a costume party has unexpected results when the real God Pan makes an entry.

The most striking element in Sarban's fiction is obviously the evocation of a weird atmosphere, and the quiet construction of a world where things aren't quite as safe and logical as the characters have always believed. But the quality of the prose should not be overlooked either. Though couched in very formal style, Sarban's words flow and the current draws the reader along with it. There is never any hint that this is an amateur writing fiction as a hobby; the cool competent hand of the professional is obvious. Despite his small body of work, Sarban remains a unique and significant writer: the talent he displayed at creating a mood of slow despair has never been equalled.

—Don D'Ammassa

SARGENT, Pamela. American. Born in Ithaca, New York, 20 March 1948. Educated at the State University of New York, Binghamton, B.A. in Philosophy 1968, M.A. 1970. Office worker, Webster Paper Company, Albany, New York, 1969; teaching assistant in philosophy, State University of New York, Binghamton, 1969-71. Since 1971, free-lance writer and editor. Agent: Joseph Elder Agency, 150 West 87th Street, New York, New York 10024. Address: Box 586, Johnson City, New York 13790, U.S.A.

SCIENCE-FICTION PUBLICATIONS

Novels

Cloned Lives. New York, Fawcett, 1976.
The Sudden Star. New York, Fawcett, 1979; as *The White Death,* London, Futura, 1980.
Watchstar. New York, Pocket Books, 1980.

Short Stories

Starshadows and Blue Roses. New York, Ace, 1977.

Uncollected Short Stories

"The Renewal," in *Immortal,* edited by Jack Dann. New York, Harper, 1978.
"The Novella Race," in *Orbit 20,* edited by Damon Knight. New York, Harper, 1978.

OTHER PUBLICATIONS

Other

"The Promise of Space: Transformations of a Dream," in *Riverside Quarterly* (Regina, Saskatchewan), February 1972.
"Women in Science Fiction," in *Futures* (New York), October 1975.
Afterword to *The Fifth Head of Cerberus,* by Gene Wolfe. New York, Ace, 1976.

Editor, *Women of Wonder: Science Fiction Stories by Women about Women..* New York, Random House, 1975; London, Penguin, 1978.
Editor, *More Women of Wonder: Science-Fiction Novelettes by Women about Women.* New York, Random House, 1976; London, Penguin, 1979.
Editor, *Bio-Futures: Science Fiction Stories about Biological Metamorphosis.* New York, Random House, 1976.
Editor, *The New Women of Wonder: Science-Fiction Novelettes by Women about Women.* New York, Random House, 1978.

*

Manuscript Collection: David Paskow Science Fiction Collection, Temple University, Philadelphia.

*   *   *

Gadgets, aliens, and robots used to be the stuff of science fiction, but no longer. Since the 1960's, the genre has diversified in its characterizations, themes, and style. Alongside the SF novels about male heroes conquering menacing aliens are novels about female anti-heroines whose conflicts are biological and psychological in origin. The crest of this New Wave, as it is called, includes several writers living in the Binghamton, New York, area in the late 1960's among them George Zebrowski, Jack Dann, Joanna Russ, and Pamela Sargent.

Sargent's name is recognizable because she has edited four anthologies which emphasize the current feminist and biological concerns of science fiction. Less well known but growing in acclaim is Sargent's own fiction which cogently presents these themes. As her introduction to the anthology *Bio-Futures* states, she is concerned not simply with the future consequences of today's biological research but also with its effect on our concepts of mortality, and on the definition of what it means to be human. In "The Renewal" she presents the theme of immortality and genetic experimentation: a 300-year-old woman kept at a permanent age 28 or so by RNA doses has a child who has been genetically altered to be both male and female. The ties between parent and child are explored in this context. In *Cloned Lives* Sargent presents the situation of siblings cloned from their parent. The problems these children have in establishing individual identities and pursuing separate lives speak to problems experienced in all families. Thus this novel has a universal appeal that typifies Sargent's best work. Moreover, since the possibility of human cloning is nearly upon us, novels like this one are inevitable preludes to the profound decisions that must eventually be made. The deleterious effects of such research are explored in *The Sudden Star* in which a brutal society outlaws Dr. Simon Negron for treating a diabetic. This society is plagued by a mysterious disease, the result of a recombinant DNA experiment gone awry. Sargent affirms her faith in the human body's capacity for survival when, at the close of the novel, some individuals are revealed to be immune because they are mutants.

Sargent is also a feminist in the best sense—she explores the relationship between the sexes, and never presents one or the other as enemy. The works value human love, generosity, unselfishness, and dignity as pre-eminent values, even more important in determining one's "humanness" than the shape of the body, the sexual organs, or the fact that one is born from a woman. In "Darkness of Day" (written with George Zebrowski) the sensitive robot Suranov is more "human" than the savage humans who destroy him. In the moving story "If Ever I Should Leave You" the immortality of human love effects a reunion in another time for two lovers.

Occasionally, a work of Sargent's will bog down as plot elements are worked out or when a character or event is representative of an idea. The mysterious Mura's Star in *Sudden Star,* for example, is a grafted-on device rather than an integral symbol.

Overall, Sargent's work is characterized by consistently compelling treatments of contemporary issues and even more by believable characters who, unlike many heroes of earlier science fiction, feel as well as think and act.

—Kathryn L. Seidel

society slowly awakens to the reality of its existence and prepares to emerge onto the surface of its world. Once more, we are warned against the decay that inevitably accompanies conformity to the exclusion of individuality.

On balance, Saxon is a slightly above average writer whose talents might have developed had he remained active. The small body of essentially minor work which he produced are reasonable entertainments, but neither original enough nor well-written enough to survive through the years.

—Don D'Ammassa

SAXON, Richard. Pseudonym for Joseph Lawrence Morrissey; also writes as Henry Richards. American.

SCIENCE-FICTION PUBLICATIONS

Novels

City of the Hidden Eyes (as J.L. Morrissey). London, Consul 1964.
Cosmic Crusade. London, Consul 1964; New York, Arcadia House, 1966.
Future for Sale. London, Consul 1964; New York, Arcadia House, 1965.
The Hour of the Phoenix. London, Consul 1964; (as Henry Richards), New York, Arcadia House, 1965.
The Stars Came Down. London, Consul 1964; New York, Arcadia House, 1967.

*   *   *

Richard Saxon's career was begun and ended in a single year. Although none of his novels was exceptional enough to attract any particular interest, they are not as unprepossessing as their poor success might indicate.

For the most part, Saxon eschewed melodrama in a period when action and suspense were the main attractions for most genre devotees. The protagonists of *Future for Sale* invent a time machine with which they travel to both the past and the future, but with considerable less liveliness than in, for example, Wells's *The Time Machine.* In the past, one character relives a poignant moment of his own life; in the future, he discovers that a scientific dictatorship has been created which provides mankind with all of its material wants but which exacts in payment an irresistible drive for conformity. Far from leading a revolt, the hero returns to our own time, where a quarreling mob destroys the time machine utterly.

The Stars Came Down is also more reflective than active. Humanity's first trip to the stars is over, and the returnees discover that a new civilization has evolved on Earth during the relative five millennia that have passed since their departure. For the most part, the latter half of the novel consists of a quiet discourse on the nature of Utopian society.

The Hour of the Phoenix is Saxon's most lively novel. The drive into space is cut short as a new astronomical object appears, destined to destroy our world in the near future. The usual occurs, mobs riot, order breaks down into chaos, and through it all a small group attempts to make plans to allow humanity to carry on elsewhere in space. The waning chapters are a bit sentimental, and this is in balance no more than a very lightweight imitation of Wylie and Balmer's *When Worlds Collide.*

The Cosmic Crusade has another conventional plot, this time weighted with excessive ruminative discourses. An underground

---

SAXTON, Josephine (née Howard). British. Born in Halifax, Yorkshire, 11 June 1935. Educated at Clare Hall County Secondary School, Halifax. Married 1) Geoffrey Banks in 1958, one son; 2) Colin Saxton in 1962, one son and one daughter. Agent: Virginia Kidd, Box 278, Milford, Pennsylvania 18337, U.S.A.; or, Dolores Rosenberg, 95 Finchley Lane, London N.W.4. Address: 16 Claremont Road, Leamington Spa, Warwickshire CV31 3EH, England.

SCIENCE-FICTION PUBLICATIONS

Novels

The Hieros Gamos of Sam and An Smith. New York, Doubleday, 1969.
Vector for Seven; or, The Weltanshauung of Mrs. Amelia Mortimer and Friends. New York, Doubleday, 1971.
Group Feast. New York, Doubleday, 1971.
The Travails of Jane Saint. London, Virgin, 1981.

Uncollected Short Stories

"Nothing Much to Relate," in *Fantasy and Science Fiction* (New York), November 1967.
"Ne Deja Vu Pas," in *England Swings SF,* edited by Judith Merril. New York, Doubleday, 1968; as *The Space-Time Journal,* London, Panther, 1972.
"Light on Cader," in *Fantasy and Science Fiction* (New York), January 1968.
"The Consciousness Machine," in *Fantasy and Science Fiction* (New York), June 1968.
"Dormant Soul," in *Fantasy and Science Fiction* (New York), February 1969.
"The Triumphant Head," in *Alchemy and Academe,* edited by Anne McCaffrey. New York, Doubleday, 1970.
"Heads Africa, Tails America," in *Orbit 9,* edited by Damon Knight. New York, Putnam, 1971.
"Nature Boy," in *Quark 3,* edited by Samuel R. Delany and Marilyn Hacker. New York, Paperback Library, 1971.
"The Power of Time," in *New Dimensions 1,* edited by Robert Silverberg. New York, Doubleday, 1971.
"The Wall," in *Best SF Stories from New Worlds 7,* edited by Michael Moorcock. London, Panther, 1971.
"Living Wild," in *Fantasy and Science Fiction* (New York), October 1971.
"Black Sabbatical," in *Fantasy and Science Fiction* (New York), December 1971.
"Elouise and the Doctors of the Planet Pergamon," in *Again, Dangerous Visions,* edited by Harlan Ellison. New York, Doubleday, 1972; London, Millington, 1976.
"In Memoriam, Jeannie," in *Stopwatch,* edited by George Hay. Nashville, Nelson, and London, New English Library, 1974.
"Lysenge of Anaglyptany," in *Science Fiction Monthly* (London), July 1975.

"Alien Sensation," in *Cassandra Rising,* edited by Alice Laurance.   New York, Doubleday, 1978.
"The Snake Who Had Read Chomsky," in *Universe 10,* edited by Terry Carr.   New York, Doubleday, 1980.

Josephine Saxton comments:
I have been called many kinds of writer: science-fiction editors say I am mainstream, mainstream editors say I am science fantasy, for example. I have written things with violent death in them, does this make me a writer of horror, detective, sadism, metaphysics? I refuse to be labelled, because metaphysical content embraces every possible experience and mode of existence which might be taken from real life, imaginary life. One theme seems to be emerging over the years which I was not aware of until I recently collected and revised my short stories, and that is a strong feminist theme. This does not make me a woman's writer, so forget it. I write about things which happen to people, for people to read; who needs more? I can say with authority that it takes just as much imagination to write well about something you do every day as it does to write about a trip to Aldebaran 62. People who only write and/or read SF are very narrow people and I don't wish to be identified with them, any more than if I set a story in the West of America I would want to be called a cowboy writer. Who started this ghetto of fiction, anyway? Publishers? Editors? It certainly couldn't have been thinking writers.

*   *   *

The flying saucer sighted twice in Josephine Saxton's *Vector for Seven* is definitely not an integral part of its plot. *Group Feast* and *The Hieros Gamos of Sam and An Smith* also do not stress science fiction's usual trappings. Instead of positing fantastic planets and alien creatures, Saxton focuses upon man confronting his absurd world. In contrast to a typical power fantasy, her novels emphasize aspects of human existence which are both finite and ridiculous. Her characters must come to terms with their material culture and their social relationships. The reader must also come to terms with Saxton's style. In addition to de-emphasizing the expected extrapolative characteristics of science fiction, she writes counter to the genre's allegorical clichés: the two "wild" children in *The Hieros Gamos* become a stereotypical married couple; Cora Caley, the rich self-obsessed heroine of *Group Feast,* does not suffer; the wanderings of the seven protagonists in *Vector for Seven* do not symbolize a death trip. Her technique causes one to question the validity of categorizing these novels as science fiction. An image of a barker standing outside of a circus tent shouting, "step right up folks and see the most terrible monster on Earth" helps to clarify this question. Those people whose curiosity is aroused venture within and view the promised exhibit: a mirror image of themselves. Similarly, marketing Saxton's work as science fiction attracts readers by establishing the expectation of fantastic characters. To continue the metaphor, like those who enter the tent, readers of Saxton's "science fiction" are directed toward an unexpected vision of man.

It is fair to call her work science fiction of the softest variety, a fiction of mundane existing technology—airplanes, buses, and an unusually long water pipe, for example—set against the background of a surreal vision of our world. Saxton's earthbound characters encounter such things as a department store which fulfills one's need without the necessity of remuneration (*The Hieros Gamos*) and a house with a seemingly limitless number of rooms (*Group Feast*). This is the way the world within that house ends: "there was a mushroom cloud containing caviar, shoes, bath mats, pot plants, priceless tapestries, parquet floors, starving cats, pickled peppers...telephones, crystal chandeliers and eight gallons of cooking oil full of sodden French-fried potatoes." Cora pedals off into the Australian sunset relieved to see the destruction of her innumerable possessions.

Journeys form the predominant image in Saxton's novels. But despite the characters' incessant walking, driving, and pedaling, their travel through inner space is most important; they all complete a journey of inner mental change while confronting the juxtaposition between animalistic and civilized aspects of their existences. Cora contemplates an example of this juxtaposition while she eats: "this terrible animal content...the thrill of hot meat juices between

the teeth, albeit that many of those teeth were the skilled products of orthodontists." Orthodontists artificially beautify meat-tearing teeth. We have many methods of masking or obliterating our natural characteristics. Saxton, on the other hand, will not allow us to forget nature. Description of all varieties of unpleasant bodily secretions are coupled with the novels' discussions of material good. *Vector for Seven,* for example, immediately presents us with the image of bird droppings spattering over a proper British lady's hat. And in *The Hieros Gamos,* after some years pass, the couple returns to a supermarket where they remove the excrement they previously left there. It comes as no surprise that Saxton's characters are obsessed with washing and with bathrooms.

These characters illustrate the absurdity of people's isolation and their mutual distrust. And Saxton's plots—as well as her titles—emphasize togetherness. In *Vector for Seven,* at the conclusion of their journey through a surreal landscape, individuals of differing age, gender, and class who were at first suspicious of each other form a trusting communal unit. Hence what Saxton views as the evil forces of society and materialism can no longer separate these people; members of this once disparate group can no longer feel, according to the initial opinion of one of their fellows, that "these days no one had any thoughtfulness for anyone....People did not like each other; it was the Labour government and the Commies, and the labour saving devices that had done all that." While *Vector for Seven* fuses a group together, *Group Feast* breaks one apart. The relationship between Cora and her servants is artificial and poisoned by the fact that money holds them together. Meaningful human interaction cannot take place in Cora's world; even an unrealistically freely flowing money supply does not stop one of the servants from setting out to murder Cora while she plays hostess at her fantastically sumptuous party. This party, which continues throughout the novel, is not the work's most thought-provoking group feast, however. We must not forget the cats who are locked in Cora's basement, wallowing in their own filth, having only each other to eat. Like these cats, Cora, who has clawed her way to the apex of the social pyramid, devours members of her own species: three people die during the course of her 24-hour party. Yet, as opposed to the hopeless situation of the imprisoned cats, there is hope for her. Despite her history of unfriendly friends and unloving lovers, when she abandons her property Cora has the potentiality to find a fulfilling relationship.

Unlike Cora and the characters in *Vector for Seven,* the lone male adolescent we meet at the beginning of *The Hieros Gamos* immediately assumes a significant place in the life of a fellow human being. He encounters a female baby attached to her dead mother and faces a dilemma: does he sacrifice his solitude or allow the baby to die? He decides in favor of life, and the two grow up in their own natural world which, at the same time, affords them free access to all the material they need. A description of them dressing in proper adult attire just before removing it to experience coitus is one example of the novel's preoccupation with man's civilized and animalistic behavior. This text's most important *hieros gamos,* the Greek words for holy marriage, is the union between people's biological and man-made roles. Its protagonists are Everyman. And, like every man, they must be civilized. The two individuals who once called themselves "boy" and "baby" assume many roles and names until thy become the suburban couple, Sam and An Smith. It is sad to see these surreal children develop into characters appropriate to an Erma Bombeck column. This is not to say, however, that Sam and An's relationship is devoid of positive aspects. An's life was saved and she in turn becomes the mother of a female child. In fact, life literally springs from death in all of Saxton's novels: in addition to the circumstances of An's birth, Cora is impregnated by someone who dies immediately after he ejaculates; and a gentleman in *Vector for Seven* expires while holding an infant who bears his name.

Like another of the travelers in *Vector for Seven,* members of the Smith family might think that "it was good having people in the house all together, living with one another instead of being alone and isolated, all of them in different homes, not even knowing each other or acknowledging the existence of other people." *Group Feast,* then, best articulates the main idea of Saxton's work, an idea which Freud expressed in *Civilization and Its Discontents:* "Human life in common is only made possible when a majority comes together which is stronger than any separate individual and which remains united against all separate individuals." Despite the novels' attention to the absurdity of the human condition, they celebrate human life, which, after all, depends upon the fulfillment of cultural as well as biological needs.

—Marleen S. Barr

SCHACHNER, Nat(han). Also wrote as Chan Corbett; Walter Glamis. American. Born in New York City, 16 January 1895. Educated at the City College of New York, B.S. 1915; New York University, J.D. 1919. Served in the United States Army chemical warfare service, 1917-18. Married Helen Lichtenstein in 1919; one daughter. Chemist, New York City Department of Health, 1915-17; admitted to the New York Bar, 1919; practicing lawyer, New York, 1919-33; free-lance writer from 1933; Editorial Consultant, American Jewish Committee, 1945-51; Director of Public Relations, National Council of Jewish Women, 1954-55. President, American Rocket Society, 1933. *Died 2 October 1955.*

SCIENCE-FICTION PUBLICATIONS

Novel

Space Lawyer. New York, Gnome Press, 1953.

Uncollected Short Stories (series: Past, Present, and Future)

"The Tower of Evil," with Leo Zagat, in *Wonder Stories Quarterly* (New York), Summer 1930.
"In 20,000 A.D.," with Leo Zagat, in *Wonder Stories* (New York), September 1930.
"Back to 20,000 A.D.," with Leo Zagat, in *Wonder Stories* (New York), March 1931.
"The Emperor of the Stars," with Leo Zagat, in *Wonder Stories* (New York), April 1931.
"The Menace from Andromeda," with Leo Zagat, in *Amazing* (New York), April 1931.
"The Death-Cloud," with Leo Zagat, in *Astounding* (New York), May 1931.
"The Revolt of the Machines," with Leo Zagat, in *Astounding* (New York), July 1931.
"Venus Mines, Incorporated," with Leo Zagat, in *Wonder Stories* (New York), August 1931.
"Exiles of the Moon," with Leo Zagat, in *Wonder Stories* (New York), September 1931.
"Pirates of the Gorm," in *Astounding* (New York), May 1932.
"Slaves of Mercury," in *Astounding* (New York), September 1932.
"Emissaries of Space," in *Wonder Stories Quarterly* (New York), Fall 1932.
"The Time Express," in *Wonder Stories* (New York), December 1932.
"The Memory of the Atoms," with R. Lacher, in *Wonder Stories* (New York), January 1933.
"The Eternal Dictator," in *Wonder Stories* (New York), February 1933.
"The Robot Technocrat," in *Wonder Stories* (New York), March 1933.
"The Revolt of the Scientists," in *Wonder Stories* (New York), April, May, June 1933.
"The Orange God" (as Walter Glamis), and "Fire Imps of Vesuvius," in *Astounding* (New York), October 1933.
"Ancestral Voices," in *Astounding* (New York), December 1933.
"Redmask of the Outlands," in *Astounding* (New York), January 1934.
"The Time Imposter," in *Astounding* (New York), March 1934.
"He from Procyon," in *Astounding* (New York), April 1934.
"The 100th Generation," in *Astounding* (New York), May 1934.

"The Living Equation," in *Astounding* (New York), September 1934.
"The Great Thirst," in *Astounding* (New York), November 1934.
"Mind of the World," in *Astounding* (New York), March 1935.
"The Orb of Probability," in *Astounding* (New York), June 1935.
"The Son of Redmask," in *Astounding* (New York), August 1935.
"World Gone Mad," in *Amazing* (New York), October 1935.
"I Am Not God," in *Astounding* (New York), October, November 1935.
"The Isotope Men," in *Astounding* (New York), January 1936.
"Entropy," in *Astounding* (New York), March 1936.
"Reverse Universe," in *Astounding* (New York), June 1936.
"Pacifica," in *Astounding* (New York), July 1936.
"The Return of the Murians," in *Astounding* (New York), August 1936.
"The Saphrophyte Men of Venus," in *Astounding* (New York), October 1936.
"The Eternal Wanderer," in *Astounding* (New York), November 1936.
"Infra Universe," in *Astounding* (New York), December 1936, January 1937.
"Beyond Which Limits," in *Astounding* (New York), February 1937.
"Earthspin," in *Astounding* (New York), June 1937.
"Sterile Planet," in *Astounding* (New York), July 1937.
"Crystallized Thought," in *Astounding* (New York), August 1937.
"Lost in the Dimensions," in *Astounding* (New York), November 1937.
"City of the Rocket Horde," in *Astounding* (New York), December 1937.
"Negative Space," in *Astounding* (New York), April 1938.
"Island of the Individualists" (Past), in *Astounding* (New York), May 1938.
"The Sun World of Soldus," in *Astounding* (New York), October 1938.
"Simultaneous Worlds," in *Astounding* (New York), November 1938.
"Palooka from Jupiter," in *Astounding* (New York), February 1939.
"Worlds Don't Care," in *Astounding* (New York), April 1939.
"When the Future Dies," in *Astounding* (New York), June 1939.
"City of the Cosmic Rays" (Past), in *Astounding* (New York), July 1939.
"City under the Sea," in *Fantastic Adventures* (New York), September 1939.
"City of the Corporate Mind" (Past), in *Astounding* (New York), December 1939.
"Cold," in *Astounding* (New York), March 1940.
"Space Double," in *Astounding* (New York), May 1940.
"Master Gerald of Cambray," in *Unknown Worlds* (New York), June 1940.
"Runaway Cargo," in *Astounding* (New York), October 1940.
"The Return of Circe," in *Fantastic Adventures* (New York), August 1941.
"Beyond All Weapons," in *Astounding* (New York), November 1941.
"Eight Who Came Back," in *Fantastic Adventures* (New York), November 1941.
"The Ultimate Metal," in *The Best of Science Fiction,* edited by Groff Conklin. New York, Crown, 1946.
"Stratosphere Towers," in *Astounding* (New York), August 1954.
"Past, Present, and Future," in *Before the Golden Age,* edited by Isaac Asimov. New York, Doubleday, and London, Robson, 1974.
"The Shining One," in *Visions of Tomorrow,* edited by Roger Elwood. New York, Pocket Books. 1976.

Uncollected Short Stories as Chan Corbett

"When the Sun Dies," in *Astounding* (New York), March 1935.
"Intra-Planetary," in *Astounding* (New York), October 1935.
"Ecce Homo," in *Astounding* (New York), June 1936.
"The Thought Web of Minipar," in *Astounding* (New York), November 1936.
"Beyond Infinity," in *Astounding* (New York), January 1937.

"Nova in Messier 33," in *Astounding* (New York), May 1937.
"When Time Stood Still," in *Astounding* (New York), June 1937.

OTHER PUBLICATIONS

Novels

By the Dim Lamps.   New York, Stokes, 1941.
The King's Messenger.   Philadelphia, Lippincott, 1942.
The Sun Shines West.   New York, Appleton Century, 1943.
The Wanderer: A Novel of Dante and Beatrice.   New York,
   Appleton Century, 1944; London, Melrose, 1948.

Other

Aaron Burr.   New York, Stokes, 1937.
The Medieval Universities.   New York, Stokes, and London,
   Allen and Unwin, 1938.
Alexander Hamilton.   New York, Appleton Century, 1946.
The Price of Liberty: A History of the American Jewish Committee.
   New York, American Jewish Committee, 1948.
Thomas Jefferson.   New York, Appleton Century Crofts, 1951.
Alexander Hamilton, Nation Builder.   New York, McGraw Hill,
   1952.
The Founding Fathers.   New York, Putnam, 1954.

*   *   *

Nat Schachner was attracted for a time to the vigorous, young
genre of pulp-magazine science fiction where he left an impression
with his liberal ideas and his earnest inventiveness. Schachner
worked first as a chemist, spent a number of years in law practice,
published hundreds of pieces of short fiction in the pulps (science,
detective, mystery, western, and adventure stories), and wrote several scholarly books on history. During the Nazi threat before and
during World War II he defended human liberties vigorously in all
his writings—both pulp fiction and scholarly. Schachner's total
commitment to the life of letters and to humanitarian values makes
him a true 20th-century representative of the Romantics whom he
said he loved as a child. He represents the writer as hero; and the
heroic vigor of the science-fiction genre during the time that he was
active in it corresponds well with his later American Revolutionary
history. Schachner's hopeful ideas for progress through clever technology and rationality had their roots both in the 18th-century
Enlightenment of Thomas Jefferson and in the pulp-fiction world of
the early *Astounding.*
   The first dozen or so of Schachner's science-fiction stories were
written in collaboration with Arthur Leo Zagat, but it was with the
"thought variant" stories of the F. Orlin Tremaine *Astounding* that
the inventive lawyer began to hit his stride as a writer who would
extrapolate into the future his liberal ideas about the present and
eventually about the past. The first thought variant story was
Schachner's "Ancestral Voices" (1933), and new idea stories followed rapidly for the rest of the decade. In his book on the science-
fiction pulp magazines, Paul Carter calls Schachner the earliest of
the "anti-Nazi Paul Reveres" whose speculative fictions increasingly explored the opportunities for sociological themes that could
be related to current events. A rather stiff and primitive story called
"The Eternal Wanderer" contains a crude courtroom scene about
interplanetary law that anticipates Schachner's only science-fiction
book *Space Lawyer* (made out of two later stories,"Old Fireball"
and "Jurisdiction").
   Schachner's best writing and most memorable contribution to
letters is undoubtedly his historical work, and he properly gave up
work for the pulps in order to pursue that research. But one cannot
help thinking that his thought variant extrapolations were both
inspired by his knowledge of the Enlightenment and contributed
greatly to his understanding of it. One of his more carefully written
and sophisticated fictions, "Past, Present, and Future" (1937), performs just that balancing between a nostalgia for the heroic and
glorious lost past on the one hand and an awareness of the challenges in the present on the other that creates the ironic complexity

of mind that is necessary for true liberal thinking. Schachner was a
hero among writers not only for the vast amount of work that he got
done but also for how he did it—less an artist than a propagandist
for democracy.

—Donald M. Hassler

SCHMIDT, Stanley (Albert).   American.   Born in Cincinnati,
Ohio, 7 March 1944. Educated at the University of Cincinnati, B.S.
in physics 1966 (Phi Beta Kappa); Case Western Reserve Univer-
sity, Cleveland, M.A. 1968, Ph.D. 1969. Assistant Professor of
Physics, Heidelberg College, Tiffin, Ohio, 1969-78. Since 1978,
Editor, *Analog,* New York. Agent: Scott Meredith Literary Agency,
845 Third Avenue, New York, New York 10022. Address: c/o
Analog, 350 Madison Avenue, New York, New York 10017, U.S.A.

SCIENCE-FICTION PUBLICATIONS

Novels (series: Lifeboat Earth)

Newton and the Quasi-Apple.   New York, Doubleday, 1975.
The Sins of the Fathers (Lifeboat Earth).   New York, Berkley,
   1976.
Lifeboat Earth.   New York, Berkley, 1978.

Uncollected Short Stories

"A Flash of Darkness," in *Analog* (New York), September 1968.
"The Reluctant Ambassadors," in *Analog* (New York), December
   1968.
"...and Comfort to the Enemy," in *Analog* (New York), July 1969.
"The Unreachable Stars," in *Analog* (New York), April 1971.
"The Prophet," in *Analog* (New York), April 1972.
"May the Best Man Win," in *American Government Through
   Science Fiction,* edited by Joseph D. Olander and Martin H.
   Greenberg.   New York, Random House, 1974.
"Lost Newton," in *Anthropology Through Science Fiction,* edited
   by Carol Mason, Martin H. Greenberg, and Patricia Warrick.
   New York, St. Martin's Press, 1974.
"A Thrust of Greatness," in *Analog* (New York), June 1976.
"His Loyal Opposition," in *Analog* (New York), July 1976.
"Caesar Clark," in *Analog* (New York), July 1977.
"Pinocchio," in *Analog* (New York), September 1977.
"Dark Age," in *Analog* (New York), December 1977.
"The Promised Land," in *Analog* (New York), January 1978.
"Panic," in *Isaac Asimov's Science Fiction Magazine* (New York),
   January-February 1978.
"A Midsummer Newt's Dream," in *Isaac Asimov's Science Fiction
   Magazine* (New York), June 1979.

OTHER PUBLICATIONS

Other

"Science Fiction Courses: An Example and Some Alternatives," in
   American Journal of Physics (New York), September 1973.
"Science Fiction and the Science Teacher," in *Extrapolation*
   (Wooster, Ohio), May 1976.
"Science in Science Fiction," in *Many Futures, Many Worlds,*
   edited by Thomas D. Clareson.   Kent, Ohio, Kent State Univer-
   sity Press, 1977.

Stanley Schmidt comments:
   In all my fiction I try to tell entertaining stories about people in
situations which are directly shaped by scientific or technological
changes, with neither the human nor the technical parts of the

foundation slighted in favor of the other. Probably the best examples to date of the type of thing I try to do are the Kyyra or Lifeboat Earth series, of which, to date, two books are complete: *The Sins of the Fathers* and *Lifeboat Earth.*

*   *   *

Stanley Schmidt seems to be one of the final products of the John Campbell influence on science fiction although it is probably too early in Schmidt's career to tell definitely. His three novels to date, however, as well as the short story versions of them that appeared in *Analog* all show the Campbell marks of hard science extrapolation, of positive-thinking problem-solving approaches to thorny human and social problems, and of two-dimensional human beings compared to a sense of rounded sublimity for whole planets and even galaxies. Schmidt's two later novels begin what will no doubt be a series in which galactic history unfolds much like Campbell taught the young Asimov to attempt sublime galactic history four decades ago. The first novel narrates a segment from the history of the planet Ymrek in which the natives seem more interesting than the human emissaries to the planet. Even if Schmidt had not told us that correspondence and ideas from Campbell influenced him, the effects of that influence are apparent in all three novels.

Schmidt is best when he begins to suggest the unresolved and, perhaps, unresolvable tensions that underlie the problems that must be resolutely solved by technology and engineering techniques; these interesting tensions lurking beneath the Campbell-like scenarios are almost exclusively associated with the alien species of the latter two novels. Although Ymrek is an interesting alien extrapolation, its natives are not nearly as symbolically (or scientifically) suggestive as the Kyyra who were originally from nearer the center of our galaxy and who literally set in motion all the action in *The Sins of the Fathers* and its sequel, *Lifeboat Earth.* The more suggestive passages appear in the first book of the series when the Kyyra seem to symbolize the dilemmas of maturation. We must destroy our pasts and even our gods to atone for our mistakes—almost Christian and yet more universal symbolism of the dying god.

The strength related to this symbolic suggestiveness is the detailed elaboration of the aliens themselves—his departure from Campbell. Without the concrete detail to make them credible, the Kyyra could suggest nothing. In fact, as Beldan conducts his human visitor on a tour of the immense Kyyra spaceship orbiting the earth, and explains to her the language and the customs of his people, the reader is reminded of the tours through Walden Two. These aliens are an advanced culture with a kind of social engineering that B.F. Skinner would admire. The Campbell positivism is not unlike Skinner's hopes for managing behavior, and it is to Schmidt's credit that while the parallels are developed in his narrative, the dilemmas are lurking just beneath the surface that Campbell may not have noticed. We can anticipate, perhaps, more development of the Kyyra in future Schmidt stories; and we can wonder if their utopian, problem-solving traits will prevail or if the tragic implications in the death of their god will haunt Schmidt more.

—Donald M. Hassler

SCHMITZ, James H(enry). American. Born in Hamburg, Germany, 15 October 1911. Educated at Realgymnasium Obersekunda. Served in the United States Army Air Force during World War II. Married Betty Mae Chapman in 1957. Worked for International Harvester Company, in Germany, 1932-39; built automobile trailers in the United States after the war. Since 1961, full-time writer. Recipient: Invisible Little Man Award, 1973. Agent: Scott Meredith Literary Agency, 845 Third Avenue, New York, New York 10022. Address: 1256 15th Street, Hermosa Beach, California 90254, U.S.A.

SCIENCE-FICTION PUBLICATIONS

Novels (series: Telzey Amberdon)

A Tale of Two Clocks.   New York, Torquil, 1962; as *Legacy*, New York, Ace, 1979.
The Universe Against Her (Telzey).   New York, Ace, 1964.
The Witches of Karres.   Philadelphia, Chilton, 1966.
The Demon Breed.   New York, Ace, 1968.
The Eternal Frontiers.   New York, Putnam, 1973; London, Sidgwick and Jackson, 1974.
The Lion Game (Telzey).   New York, DAW, 1973; London, Sidgwick and Jackson, 1976.

Short Stories

Agent of Vega.   New York, Gnome Press, 1960.
A Nice Day for Screaming and Other Tales of the Hub.   Philadelphia, Chilton, 1965.
A Pride of Monsters.   New York, Macmillan, 1970.
The Telzey Toy.   New York, DAW, 1973; London, Sidgwick and Jackson, 1976.

Uncollected Short Stories

"One Step Ahead," in *If* (New York), April 1974.
"Aura of Immortality," in *If* (New York), June 1974.

*   *   *

James H. Schmitz is a craftsmanlike writer who has been a steady contributor to science-fiction magazines for over 20 years. The best of his shorter works are collected in *A Nice Day for Screaming* and *A Pride of Monsters.* In the first work the stories repeat a consistent theme that the universe is stranger than we can imagine, and that unexpected discoveries will meet us at every turn. Although the stories are set in the far future, humans (and others) continually encounter both creatures and behaviors they could not have foreseen, from the alien automated service-station for spaceships of the title story to an alien so intelligent it keeps humans for pets in "The Winds of Time." But aliens can be surprised, too, as "The Other Likeness" shows: agents genetically engineered to resemble humans become so much like us that they begin to sympathize with humans against their masters. There are new machines, too, like the fear broadcaster of "The Tangled Web" or the half-men, half-machines of "The Machmen." And there are some things so strange yet so intelligent they can conceal their very existence from humans, like the forest-sized organism in "Balanced Ecology."

A Pride of Monsters collects stories that attempt to rejuvenate the idea of "the monster" through tales of future encounters with alien life-forms. In "Lion Loose" Detective Bad-News Quillan, a favorite character of Schmitz's, meets a rug-sized creature with the ability to pass through solid matter, but it is not nearly so dangerous as the radiation creature of "The Searcher," which endangers a pair of private detectives working undercover against interstellar hijackers. "The Pork Chop Tree" is an alien plant whose very presence is addictive, a less forthright menace than the plant of "Greenface," a story which is unusual (for Schmitz) in being set in the present.

In his longer works, Schmitz has often shown a close cooperation between man and alien. The alien may be a machine, like the robot spaceships of the four thematically connected stories of *Agent of Vega*, or mutated animals, like the intelligent giant otters of *The Demon Breed*, who help to repel a threat to human civilization. The "aliens" may even be other humans, as in *The Eternal Frontiers*, in which the Swimmers have diverged so far from normal humanity as to be almost a different species. Rather than forming a close relationship, though, the two groups are keen competitors. And of course, there are the aliens that, like those in *A Pride of Monsters*, are threats to humanity, ones such as the plasmoids in *A Tale of Two Clocks*.

A second theme that Schmitz has frequently used is that of supranormal mental powers: Telzey, a telepathic teen-aged girl, is the central character in a number of stories. Telepathy (and various other kinds of mental powers, chiefly psychokinesis) is central to Schmitz's most celebrated work, *The Witches of Karres*. The book is a fast-moving, episodic adventure story of an ordinary human, Captain Pausert, who becomes entangled with three psychically endowed girls. Its account of the wakening of telepowers in Pausert draws on familiar science-fiction recipes, mixing appropriately evil villains with nick-of-time escapes, and spicing the whole with an entertaining sense of humor.

—Walter E. Meyers

SCORTIA, Thomas N(icholas). American. Born in Alton, Illinois, 29 August 1926. Educated at Washington University, St. Louis, A.B. 1949, graduate work 1950. Served in the United States Army Infantry, 1944-46, and chemical corps, 1951-53. Married Irene Baron in 1960 (divorced, 1968). Senior chemist, Union Starch and Refining Company, Granite City, Illinois, 1954-57; director of research, Chromalloy, Edwardsville, Illinois, 1957-60; group leader, Celanese Corporation, Asheville, North Carolina, 1960-61; section head, United Technology Corporation, Sunnyvale, California, 1961-70. Since 1970, full-time writer and lecturer. Agent: Curtis Brown Ltd., 60 East 56th Street, New York, New York 10022. Address: 156 Carnelian Way, San Francisco, California 94131, U.S.A.

SCIENCE-FICTION PUBLICATIONS

Novels

What Mad Oracle? Evanston, Illinois, Regency, 1961.
Artery of Fire. New York, Doubleday, 1972.
Earthwreck! New York, Fawcett, 1974; London, Coronet, 1975.
The Glass Inferno, with Frank M. Robinson. New York, Doubleday, 1974; London, Hodder and Stoughton, 1975.
The Prometheus Crisis, with Frank M. Robinson. New York, Doubleday, 1975; London, Hodder and Stoughton, 1976.
The Nightmare Factor, with Frank M. Robinson. New York, Doubleday, and London, Hodder and Stoughton, 1978.
The Gold Crew, with Frank M. Robinson. New York, Warner, 1980.

Short Stories

Caution! Inflammable! New York, Doubleday, 1975.

Uncollected Short Stories

"The Armageddon Tapes—Tape IV," in *Continuum 4*, edited by Roger Elwood. New York, Berkley, 1975.
"Someday I'll Find You, " in *Odyssey* (New York), April 1976.

OTHER PUBLICATIONS

Other

"Science Fiction as the Imaginary Experiment," in *Science Fiction, Today and Tomorrow,* edited by Reginald Bretnor. New York, Harper, 1974.

Editor, *Strange Bedfellows.* New York, Random House, 1972.
Editor, with Chelsea Quinn Yarbro, *Two Views of Wonder.* New York, Ballantine, 1973.
Editor, with George Zebrowski, *Human-Machines: An Anthology of Stories about Cyborgs.* New York, Random House, 1975; London, Hale, 1977.

*   *   *

Thomas N. Scortia's first published story, "The Prodigy," imme-

diately established him as an accomplished storyteller. Detailing a violent conflict with a paranormal child, the story reaches one of the few unguessable resolutions of the theme. "The Shores of Night" is a vision of a solar-system-wide civilization straining for the stars; here are the sounds and colors of change, as the human spirit readies itself with a new strength. Scortia writes with a virtuosity comparable to Bester's, with the high emotional content of a Lem in depicting "cruel miracles" at their most intense. This story belongs, to borrow the words of C.S. Lewis, "to those works of science fiction which are actual additions to life; they give, like certain rare dreams, sensations we never had before, and enlarge our conception of the range of possible experience." The work belongs to the period of Scortia's greatest attachment to the ideals of space travel. The story's success lies in its melding of personal loss with a haunting series of pictorial images.

His first novel, *What Mad Oracle?*, is based on Scortia's experience as a physico-chemist in the aerospace industry. It is a powerful story of engineers and corporations confronting the realities of American business and politics in the 1950's. SF in the sense that it shows the human impact of science and technology, the novel has a historical interest for SF readers.

As Scortia's involvement in aerospace increased, his SF production diminished; but stories continued to appear throughout the 1960's. One of the most notable is "Broken Image," depicting a future earth's attempts to have an ethical influence on an alien culture. Seldom has the theme of the savior been given such a strong presentation. "The Destroyer" was an in-depth return to the theme of "The Prodigy," but this time the note was one of compassion. By 1970 Scortia was writing full time. The great success of this period is "The Weariest River," hailed by P.S. Miller and others as an instant classic on the theme of immortality, containing an original twist of great power; and *Artery of Fire*, a tense, taut novel of conflict over the building of an immense power system (the central image of the story is as strikingly original as that of Niven's *Ringworld*). John W. Campbell had turned down the novella version because he could not accept Scortia's prediction that fusion power would not be available by 1973 (appearing in 1960, the novella makes a striking contrast to "The Shores of Night" of four years before, prefiguring Scortia's critical approach to the products of technology).

Also appearing in the early 1970's was the novel *Earthwreck!* (the title was changed from *Endangered Species* without Scortia's consent), a strongly characterized story of human survival in space after an atomic war has devastated the earth. With the SF veteran Frank M. Robinson, Scortia wrote several disaster novels. These bestsellers earned the authors an international reputation, considerable monetary reward, and the often unfair scorn of the SF community. *The Prometheus Crisis* is of interest to SF readers because, in its depiction of a severe nuclear accident, the story is the legitimate descendant of such pioneering stories as Heinlein's "Blowups Happen," and del Rey's *Nerves*. There is a strong cautionary tone in all of Scortia's later work; it is the warning of the once idealistic, Campbell-influenced aerospace scientist who dreamed of space travel and found that human beings have a penchant for perverting any worthwhile project, from high-rise dwellings to atomic power plants.

Scortia's popular success outside the SF world is part of the continuing science fictionalization of our civilization, in the sense that many of the prophetic suggestions made by SF in the first half of this century, positive and negative, have become commonplace in the second half. That a veteran SF writer should take part in this infusion of what once would have been science-fiction themes and ideas into the body of popular fiction is not surprising. Scortia's special success lies in his genuine emotional and dramatic appeal to the average reader, and in showing how the real world has turned out to be more complex and full of human failure, darker than the idealistic SF on which he grew up had foreseen. That human beings *can* do something is no longer enough; the problem is whether they will, or should.

Thomas N. Scortia's life might have been a science-fiction story, as written in some alternate dimension. He came to maturity in the 1950's, full of feeling and intellect, overflowing with the wonder of human possibilities as pictured in Campbell's *Astounding*, only to learn that human beings don't always do their best for worthy dreams. One might say that Scortia's views were modified by the kind of satirical SF which Gold published in *Galaxy* (Gold himself was a Campbell writer who extended his master's approach to SF to include the "soft" social sciences). Scortia's stories of the 1950's and 1960's are powerful streams of thought and feeling, combined with rigorous speculation, flowing out of his critical but compassionate disappointment with the world. Though in his 50's, it is hard to think of Scortia as anything but a young man with his crowning work still to come. Some of it will be SF and some not. His work in aerospace enabled humanity to send probes into the outer solar system, while at the same time he was struggling in his fiction to understand the failing, often partly rational inner space of human nature.

—George Zebrowski

SEARLS, Hank (Henry Hunt Searls, Jr.). American. Born in San Francisco, California, 10 August 1922. Educated at the University of California, Berkeley, 1940; United States Naval Academy, Annapolis, Maryland, B.S. 1944. Married Berna Ann Cooper; three children. Served in the United States Navy, 1941-54: Lieutenant Commander; writer for Hughes Aircraft, Culver City, California, 1955-56, Douglas Aircraft, Santa Monica, California, 1956-57, and Warner Brothers, Burbank, California, 1959. Since 1959, free-lance writer. Agent: Scott Meredith Literary Agency, 845 Third Avenue, New York, New York 10022, U.S.A.

SCIENCE-FICTION PUBLICATIONS

Novels

The Big X. New York, Harper, and London, Heinemann, 1959.
The Crowded Sky. New York, Harper, and London, Heinemann, 1960.
The Astronaut. London, Penguin, 1960; New York, Pocket Books, 1962.
The Pilgrim Project. New York, McGraw Hill, 1964; London, W.H. Allen, 1965.
The Hero Ship. Cleveland, World, and London, W.H. Allen, 1969.
Overboard. New York, Norton, and London, Raven, 1977.

Uncollected Short Story

"Martyr's Flight," in *Imagination* (Evanston, Illinois), December 1955.

OTHER PUBLICATIONS

Novels

Pentagon. New York, Geis, 1971.
Never Kill a Cop. New York, Pocket Books, 1977.
Jaws 2 (novelization of screenplay). Universal City, California, MCA, and London, Pan, 1978.
Firewind. New York, Doubleday, 1981.

Other

"The Astronaut, The Novelist, and Cadwalder Glotz," in *The Writer* (Boston), September 1965.
The Lost Prince: Young Joe, The Forgotten Kennedy. Cleveland, World, 1969.

*   *   *

Hank Searls's stories revolve around the emerging space program, astronauts and their families, and whatever political machinations are most likely to create problems. His realistic contemporary fiction is built on timeliness, as each novel has foreshadowed a stage in man's actual venture into space.

The Big X explores some potential problems, both technical and human, of manned orbital space flight. Norco's X-F18, the experimental rocket-like ship of the title, must reach a speed of Mach 8 and prove maneuverable for Norco Aircraft to land the government contract for construction of the first manned spacecraft. Mitch Westerly, the test pilot for the Big X, knows he will probably be chosen as the first man in space if his testing is successful. But the test schedule grows tense as a psychopathic chief of operations orders more and more telemetering equipment mounted in the cockpit, despite Mitch's protests that the additional weight has made the ship unstable. The suspense of the impending Mach 8 test flight builds as Mitch must decide whether to push the plane beyond its limits, at the expense of the girl he wants to marry, and possibly his life, in order to provide telemetric data necessary to the space program. Besides an inside view of the politics of the aircraft industry, there is much authentic-sounding shop talk, as well as a love story with the turmoil surrounding the personal lives of men such as Mitch.

A story of our race for the moon, *The Pilgrim Project* begins as a routine orbital flight is mysteriously ordered to abort prematurely. Except for the commander, even the men aboard do not know that a top secret plan must be put into effect immediately to land an American on the moon ahead of the Russians. The reader remains in a sustained sense of urgency and intrigue as NASA officials, Congressmen, the President, the media, and the astronauts themselves unravel clues about a plan so secret that even the man who originated it does not know it is about to be carried out. The tempo accelerates even more when it is discovered that the Russian moon shot carries a civilian cosmonaut, and the American astronauts are quickly switched to include the civilian Steve Lawrence in order to prove our equally peaceful intentions. When the Pilgrim Project is finally revealed, all concerned must re-evaluate their psychological and moral attitudes about what appears to be a heroic but suicidal one-way flight to the moon. Both Russians and Americans launch, and the race is neck and neck all the way. Several subplots weave throughout the story, providing continuous action.

It is clear that Hank Searls knows his way around both the technical and the human aspects of the space program, and if his stories have not retained their impact, it is only a matter of timing. The fictional Big X barely preceded North American's X-15, untested in free flight at the time, and *The Pilgrim Project* preceded the actual moon landing by less than five years. Still, Searls has incorporated enough human drama into his stories that these after-the-fact elements detract only negligibly for the modern reader.

—Myra Barnes

SELLINGS, Arthur. Pseudonym for Robert Arthur Ley; also wrote as Martin Luther. British. Born in 1921. Worked in Customs and as an antiquarian book dealer. *Died 24 September 1968.*

SCIENCE-FICTION PUBLICATIONS

Novels

Telepath. New York, Ballantine, 1962; as *The Silent Speakers*, London, Dobson, 1963.
The Uncensored Man. London, Dobson, 1964; New York, Berkley, 1967.
The Quy Effect. London, Dobson, 1966; New York, Berkley, 1967.
Intermind (as Martin Luther). New York, Banner, 1967; London, Dobson, 1969.

The Power of X. London, Dobson, 1968; New York, Berkley, 1970.
Junk Day. London, Dobson, 1970.

Short Stories

Time Transfer and Other Stories. London, Joseph, 1956.
The Long Eureka. London, Dobson, 1968.

Uncollected Short Stories

"The Trial," in *New Writings in SF 15*, edited by John Carnell. London, Dobson, 1969.
"The Legend and the Chemistry," in *Fantasy and Science Fiction* (New York), January 1969.
"The Dodgers," in *Fantastic* (New York), April 1969.
"The Last Time Around," in *If* (New York), November 1970.

*   *   *

Arthur Sellings was interested in how man reacts to the unknown, whether in outer space or on his own planet. He believed man is slowly evolving but that his essential self, with its present weaknesses and strengths, will endure—even if in unrecognizable forms. Thus his works explore man's inner space, his adaptability, his sense of responsibility, his psychological reactions (to holocaust, time travel, alien confrontation, genetic engineering), and his psychological potentialities (to control bodily shape, change reality, span dimensions, read thoughts). Notable among his short stories are "The Well-Trained Heroes," which deals with a special task force trained to predict and reduce urban tensions by becoming scapegoats, "Homecoming," wherein a disturbed space explorer discovers he has spent centuries in suspended animation and now resides amid aliens, "Verbal Agreement," about a cosmic salesman who learns, through poetry, to adapt a telepathic society to his needs, and "Start in Life," which records the robot training of five-year-old survivors of a starship plague.

Always Sellings's stories and novels focus on a well-developed central figure who must come to terms with the unexpected, while in the background large military complexes and political groups vie for power. In *The Power of X*, a conspiracy novel, an art dealer learns that other dimensions may be ones of time, not space, as he explores the dangers of "plying," a modern duplicating process which perfectly reproduces originals whether Old Masters or a living President. *The Quy Effect* depicts an aging inventor's struggle to perfect and publicize anti-gravity power, while *Intermind* focuses on a secret agent injected with a dead spy's memory. In *Telepath* young strangers, suddenly intimate due to unsuspected telepathic powers, combat the destiny of their life form until they gradually understand and communicate to others this mutant power which can transform man's future, opening up the potentiality for preserving racial memories through generations in space. The intriguing and suspenseful *Uncensored Man* focuses on a nuclear physicist's contact with another dimension, one where racial memories and the minds of earth's dead have accumulated and developed and now seek to reveal to man the power in his genes and in his physical and chemical heritage. The novel includes disappearing bodies, sympathetic, multi-personality beings warning of man's self-destructive blindness, and a hero who develops a full range of psi powers to protect the future of two dimensions. In Sellings's finest work, *Junk Day*, a cynical, gripping, post-holocaust tale of survival, a traumatized artist joins forces with a wary novitiate to tackle the junkman, a tough lower-class bully who, in a ruined world, is king of the London junkpile. The junkman's protection racket helps reunite dispersed humanity, while destroying the basic values that, from the artist's view, make life valuable. Ultimately his power is confirmed by overbearing scientists who set themselves up as gods of the new order, reconditioning and transforming those who fail to meet their interpretation of the ideal citizen.

Sellings's works have interesting themes, careful characterization, sensory detail, and satisfying suspense, all handled with discipline and restraint. Frequently a central character is an artist whose special powers of perception, temperament, and intuitive insight raise him above the limitations of those around him. Sellings's typical pattern is for such a character, confronted with the unusual,

first to doubt his sanity, but then rationally confirm his perceptions, and ultimately learn to deal with new powers or concepts, and understand and accept the responsibilities they entail.

—Gina Macdonald

SENARENS, Luis P(hilip). Also wrote as Captain Howard. American. Born in Brooklyn, New York, 24 April 1865. Educated at St. John's College, Brooklyn; law degree. Married in 1895; one son and one daughter. Free-lance writer from age 16: Editor, Frank Tousey publications, from 1904, and scenario writer from 1911; Editor, *Moving Picture Stories Weekly*, from 1913; retired in 1923. *Died in 1939.*

<small>SCIENCE-FICTION PUBLICATIONS</small>

Novels (series: Frank Reade, Jr.)

Frank Reade, Jr. and His Steam Wonder. New York, Tousey, 1884.
Frank Reade, Jr. and His Electric Boat. New York, Tousey, 1884.
Frank Reade, Jr. and His Adventures with His Latest Invention. New York, Tousey, 1884.
Frank Reade, Jr. and His Airship. New York, Tousey, 1884.
Frank Reade, Jr.'s Marvel; or, Above and Below Water. New York, Tousey, 1884.
Frank Reade, Jr. in the Clouds. New York, Tousey, 1885.
Frank Reade, Jr.'s Great Electric Tricycle and What He Did for Charity. New York, Tousey, 1885.
Frank Reade, Jr. and His Airship in Africa. New York, Tousey, 1885.
Across the Continent on Wings; or, Frank Reade, Jr.'s Greatest Flight. New York, Tousey, 1886.
Frank Reade, Jr. Exploring Mexico in His New Air Ship. New York, Tousey, 1886.
The Electric Man; or, Frank Reade, Jr. in Australia. New York, Tousey, 1887.
The Electric Horse; or, Frank Reade, Jr. and His Father in Search of the Lost Treasure of the Peruvians. New York, Tousey, 1888.
Frank Reade, Jr.'s Race Through the Clouds. New York, Tousey, 1888.
Frank Reade, Jr. and His Electric Team; or, In Search of a Missing Man. New York, Tousey, 1888.
Frank Reade, Jr.'s Search for a Sunken Ship; or, Working for the Government. New York, Tousey, 1889.
Frank Reade, Jr. in the Far West; or, The Search for a Lost Gold Mine. New York, Tousey, 1890.
Frank Reade, Jr. and His Queen Clipper of the Clouds. New York, Tousey, 1890.
Frank Reade, Jr. and His Monitor of the Deep; or, Helping a Friend in Need. New York, Tousey, 1890.
Frank Reade, Jr. Exploring a River of Mystery. New York, Tousey, 1890.
Frank Reade, Jr. and His Electric Air Yacht; or, The Great Inventor among the Aztecs. New York, Tousey, 1891.
Frank Reade, Jr. in a Sea of Sand and His Discovery of a Lost People. New York, Tousey, 1891.
Frank Reade, Jr. and His Greyhound of the Air; or, The Search for the Mountain of Gold. New York, Tousey, 1891.
From Pole to Pole; or, Frank Reade, Jr.'s Strange Submarine Voyage. New York, Tousey, 1891.
Frank Reade, Jr. and His Electric Coach; or, The Search for the Isle of Diamonds. New York, Tousey, 1891.
Frank Reade, Jr. and His Airship in Asia; or, A Flight Across the Steppes. New York, Tousey, 1892.
Frank Reade, Jr. and His Electric Ice Boat; or, Lost in the Land of Crimson Snow. New York, Tousey, 1892.

Frank Reade, Jr.'s Electric Cyclone; or, Thrilling Adventures in No Man's Land. New York, Tousey, 1892.

Frank Reade, Jr. and His New Steam Man; or, The Young Inventor's Trip to the Far West. New York, Tousey, 1892.

Frank Reade, Jr. with His New Steam Man in No Man's Land; or, On a Mysterious Trail. New York, Tousey, 1892.

Frank Reade, Jr. with His New Steam Man in Central America. New York, Tousey, 1892.

Frank Reade, Jr. with His New Steam Man in Texas; or, Chasing the Train Robbers. New York, Tousey, 1892.

Frank Reade, Jr. with His New Steam Man in Mexico; or, Hot Work among the Greasers. New York, Tousey, 1892.

Frank Reade, Jr. with His New Steam Man Chasing a Gang of "Rustlers"; or, Wild Adventures in Montana. New York, Tousey, 1892.

Frank Reade, Jr. and His New Steam Horse; or, The Search for a Million Dollars. New York, Tousey, 1892.

Frank Reade, Jr. with His New Steam Horse among the Cowboys; or, The League of the Plains. New York, Tousey, 1892.

Frank Reade, Jr. with His New Steam Horse in the Great American Desert; or, The Sandy Trail of Death. New York, Tousey, 1892.

Frank Reade, Jr. with His New Steam Horse and the Mystery of the Underground Ranch. New York, Tousey, 1892.

Frank Reade, Jr. with His New Steam Horse in Search of an Ancient Mine. New York, Tousey, 1892.

Frank Reade, Jr. with His New Steam Horse in the North-West; or, Wild Adventures among the Blackfeet. New York, Tousey, 1892.

Frank Reade, Jr.'s Electric Air Canoe; or, The Search for the Valley of Diamonds. New York, Tousey, 1892.

Frank Reade, Jr.'s New Electric Submarine Boat "The Explorer"; or, To the North Pole under the Ice. New York, Tousey, 1893.

Frank Reade, Jr.'s New Electric Van; or, Hunting Wild Animals in the Jungles of India. New York, Tousey, 1893.

Frank Reade, Jr.'s "White Cruiser" of the Clouds; or, The Search for the Dog-Faced Men. New York, Tousey, 1893.

Frank Reade, Jr.'s Deep Sea Diver the "Tortoise"; or, The Search for a Sunken Island. New York, Tousey, 1893.

Frank Reade, Jr.'s New Electric Terror the "Thunderer"; or, The Search for the Tartar's Captive. New York, Tousey, 1893.

Frank Reade, Jr. and His Air-Ship. New York, Tousey, 1893.

Frank Reade, Jr.'s Latest Air Wonder the "Kite"; or, A Six Weeks' Flight over the Andes. New York, Tousey, 1893.

Frank Reade, Jr.'s New Electric Invention the "Warrior"; or, Fighting the Apaches in Arizona. New York, Tousey, 1893.

Frank Reade, Jr.'s "Sea Serpent"; or, The Search for Sunken Gold. New York, Tousey, 1893.

Fighting the Slave Hunters; or, Frank Reade, Jr. in Central Africa. New York, Tousey, 1893.

Around the World Under Water; or, The Wonderful Cruise of a Submarine Boat. New York, Tousey, 1893.

Lost in the Land of Fire; or, Across the Pampas in the Electric Turret. New York, Tousey, 1893.

Six Weeks in the Great Whirlpool; or, Strange Adventures in a Submarine Boat. New York, Tousey, 1893.

Chased Across the Sahara; or, The Bedouins' Captive. New York, Tousey, 1893.

The Mystic Brand; or, Frank Reade, Jr. and His Overland Stage upon the Staked Plains. New York, Tousey, 1893.

Frank Reade, Jr. and His New Torpedo Boat; or, At War with the Brazilian Rebels. New York, Tousey, 1893.

Frank Reade, Jr. and His Magnetic Gun-Carriage; or, Working for the U.S. Mail. New York, Tousey, 1893.

Frank Reade, Jr. and His Engine of the Clouds; or, Chased Around the World in the Sky. New York, Tousey, 1893.

The Sunken Pirate; or, Frank Reade, Jr. in Search of Treasure at the Bottom of the Sea. New York, Tousey, 1893.

Frank Reade, Jr. and His Electric Air-Boat; or, Hunting Wild Beasts for a Circus. New York, Tousey, 1893.

The Black Range; or, Frank Reade, Jr. among the Cowboys with His New Electric Caravan. New York, Tousey, 1894.

From Zone to Zone; or, The Wonderful Trip of Frank Reade, Jr. with His Latest Air-Ship. New York, Tousey, 1894.

Frank Reade, Jr. and His Electric Prairie Schooner; or, Fighting the Mexican Horse Thieves. New York, Tousey, 1894.

Frank Reade, Jr. and His Electric Cruiser of the Lakes; or, A Journey Through Africa by Water. New York, Tousey, 1894.

Adrift in Africa; or, Frank Reade, Jr. among the Ivory Hunters with His New Electric Wagon. New York, Tousey, 1894.

Six Weeks in the Clouds; or, Frank Reade Jr.'s Air-Ship, The Thunderbolt of the Skies. New York, Tousey, 1894.

Frank Reade, Jr.'s Electric Air Racer; or, Around the Globe in Thirty Days. New York, Tousey, 1894.

Frank Reade, Jr. and His Flying Ice Ship; or, Driven Adrift in the Frozen Sky. New York, Tousey, 1894.

Frank Reade, Jr. and His Electric Sea Engine; or, Hunting for a Sunken Diamond Mine. New York, Tousey, 1894.

Frank Reade, Jr. Exploring a Submarine Mountain; or, Lost at the Bottom of the Sea. New York, Tousey, 1894.

Frank Reade, Jr.'s Electric Buckboard; or, Thrilling Adventures in North Australia. New York, Tousey, 1894.

Frank Reade, Jr.'s Search for the Sea Serpent; or, Six Thousand Miles under the Sea. New York, Tousey, 1894.

Frank Reade, Jr.'s Desert Explorer; or, The Underground City of the Sahara. New York, Tousey, 1894.

Frank Reade, Jr.'s New Electric Air-Ship the "Zephyr"; or, From North to South Around the Globe. New York, Tousey, 1894.

Across the Frozen Sea; or, Frank Reade, Jr.'s Electric Snow Cutter. New York, Tousey, 1894.

Lost in the Great Atlantic Valley; or, Frank Reade, Jr. and His Submarine Wonder the "Dart." New York, Tousey, 1894.

Frank Reade, Jr. and His New Electric Air-Ship the "Eclipse"; or, Fighting the Chinese Pirates. New York, Tousey, 1894.

Frank Reade, Jr.'s Clipper of the Prairie; or, Fighting the Apaches in the Far Southwest. New York, Tousey, 1894.

Under the Amazon for a Thousand Miles; or, Frank Reade, Jr.'s Wonderful Trip. New York, Tousey, 1894.

Frank Reade, Jr.'s Search for the Silver Whale; or, Under the Ocean in the Electric "Dolphin." New York, Tousey, 1894.

Frank Reade, Jr.'s Catamaran of the Air; or, Wild and Wonderful Adventures in North Australia. New York, Tousey, 1894.

Frank Reade, Jr.'s Search for a Lost Man in His Latest Air Wonder. New York, Tousey, 1894.

Frank Reade, Jr. in Central India; or, The Search fr the Lost Savants. New York, Tousey, 1894.

The Missing Island; or, Frank Reade, Jr.'s Wonderful Trip under the Deep Sea. New York, Tousey, 1894.

Over the Andes with Frank Reade, Jr. in His New Air-Ship; or, Wild Adventures in Peru. New York, Tousey, 1894.

Frank Reade, Jr.'s Prairie Whirlwind; or, The Mystery of the Hidden Canyon. New York, Tousey, 1894.

Under the Yellow Sea; or, Frank Reade, Jr.'s Search for the Cave of Pearls with His New Submarine Cruiser. New York, Tousey, 1894.

Around the Horizon for Ten Thousand Miles; or, Frank Reade, Jr.'s Most Wonderful Trip with His Air-Ship. New York, Tousey, 1894.

Frank Reade, Jr.'s "Sky Scraper"; or, North and South Around the World. New York, Tousey, 1894.

Under the Equator from Ecuador to Borneo; or, Frank Reade, Jr.'s Greatest Submarine Voyage. New York, Tousey, 1894.

From Coast to Coast; or Frank Reade, Jr.'s Trip Across Africa in His Electric "Boomerang." New York, Tousey, 1894.

Frank Reade, Jr. and His Electric Car; or, Outwitting a Desperate Gang. New York, Tousey, 1894.

Lost in the Mountains of the Moon; or, Frank Reade, Jr.'s Great Trip with His New Air-Ship, the "Scud." New York, Tousey, 1894.

100 Miles below the Surface of the Sea; or, The Marvelous Trip of Frank Reade, Jr.'s "Hardshell" Submarine Boat. New York, Tousey, 1894.

Abandoned in Alaska; or, Frank Reade, Jr.'s Thrilling Search for a Lost Gold Claim with His New Electric Wagon. New York, Tousey, 1894.

Around the Arctic Circle; or, Frank Reade, Jr.'s Most Famous Trip with His Air-Ship, The "Orbit." New York, Tousey, 1894.

Under Four Oceans; or, Frank Reade, Jr.'s Submarine Chase of a "Sea Devil." New York, Tousey, 1894.

From the Nile to the Niger; or, Frank Reade, Jr. Lost in the Soudan with His "Overland Omnibus." New York, Tousey, 1894.

The Chase of a Comet; or, Frank Reade, Jr.'s Most Wonderful Aerial Trip with His New Air-Ship, The "Flash." New York, Tousey, 1894.

Lost in the Great Undertow; or, Frank Reade, Jr.'s Submarine Cruise in the Gulf Stream. New York, Tousey, 1894.

From Tropic to Tropic; or, Frank Reade, Jr.'s Latest Tour with His Bicycle Car. New York, Tousey, 1894.

To the End of the Earth in an Air-Ship; or, Frank Reade, Jr.'s Great Mid-Air Flight. New York, Tousey, 1894.

The Underground Sea; or, Frank Reade, Jr.'s Subterranean Cruise in His Submarine Boat. New York, Tousey, 1894.

The Mysterious Mirage; or, Frank Reade, Jr.'s Desert Search for a Secret City with His New Overland Chaise. New York, Tousey, 1894.

The Electric Island; or, Frank Reade, Jr.'s Search for the Greatest Wonder on Earth with His Air-Ship, The "Flight." New York, Tousey, 1894.

For Six Weeks Buried in a Deep Sea Cave; or, Frank Reade, Jr.'s Great Submarine Search. New York, Tousey, 1894.

The Galleon's Gold; or, Frank Reade, Jr.'s Deep Sea Search. New York, Tousey, 1894.

Across Australia with Frank Reade, Jr. in His New Electric Car; or, Wonderful Adventures in the Antipodes. New York, Tousey, 1894.

Frank Reade, Jr.'s Greatest Flying Machine; or, Fighting the Terror of the Coast. New York, Tousey, 1894.

On the Great Meridian with Frank Reade, Jr. in His New Air-Ship; or, A Twenty-Five Thousand Mile Trip in Mid-Air. New York, Tousey, 1895.

Under the Indian Ocean with Frank Reade, Jr.; or, A Cruise in a Submarine Boat. New York, Tousey, 1895.

Astray in the Selvas; or, The Wild Experiences of Frank Reade, Jr., Barney and Pomp, in South America with the Electric Car. New York, Tousey, 1895.

Lost in a Comet's Tail; or, Frank Reade, Jr.'s Strange Adventure with His New Air-Ship. New York, Tousey, 1895.

Six Sunken Pirates; or, Frank Reade, Jr.'s Marvelous Adventures in the Deep Sea. New York, Tousey, 1895.

Beyond the Gold Coast; or, Frank Reade, Jr.'s Overland Trip with His Electric Phaeton. New York, Tousey, 1895.

Latitude 90°; or, Frank Reade, Jr.'s Most Wonderful Mid-Air Flight. New York, Tousey, 1895.

Afloat in a Sunken Forest; or, With Frank Reade, Jr. on a Submarine Cruise. New York, Tousey, 1895.

Across the Desert of Fire; or, Frank Reade, Jr.'s Marvelous Trip to a Strange Country. New York, Tousey, 1895.

Over Two Continents; or, Frank Reade, Jr.'s Long Distance Flight with His New Air-Ship. New York, Tousey, 1895.

The Coral Labyrinth; or, Lost with Frank Reade, Jr. in a Deep Sea Cave. New York, Tousey, 1895.

Along the Orinoco; or, With Frank Reade, Jr. in Venezuela. New York, Tousey, 1895.

Across the Earth; or, Frank Reade, Jr.'s Latest Trip with His New Air-Ship. New York, Tousey, 1895.

1,000 Fathoms Deep; or, With Frank Reade, Jr. in the Sea of Gold. New York, Tousey, 1895.

The Island in the Air; or, Frank Reade, Jr.'s Trip to the Tropics. New York, Tousey, 1895.

In the Wild Man's Land; or, With Frank Reade, Jr. in the Heart of Australia. New York, Tousey, 1895.

The Sunken Isthmus; or, With Frank Reade, Jr. in the Yucatan Channel, with His New Submarine Yacht, The "Sea Diver." New York, Tousey, 1895.

The Lost Caravan; or, Frank Reade, Jr. on the Staked Plains with His "Electric Racer." New York, Tousey, 1895.

The Transient Lake; or, Frank Reade, Jr.'s Adventures in a Mysterious Country with His New Air-Ship, The "Spectre." New York, Tousey, 1895.

The Weird Island; or, Frank Reade, Jr.'s Strange Submarine Search for a Deep Sea Wonder. New York, Tousey, 1895.

The Abandoned Country; or, Frank Reade, Jr. Exploring a New Continent. New York, Tousey, 1895.

Over the Steppes; or, Adrift in Asia with Frank Reade, Jr. New York, Tousey, 1895.

The Unknown Sea; or, Frank Reade, Jr.'s Under-Water Cruise. New York, Tousey, 1895.

In the Black Zone; or, Frank Reade, Jr.'s Quest for the Mountain of Ivory. New York, Tousey, 1895.

The Lost Navigators; or, Frank Reade, Jr.'s Mid-Air Search with His New Air-Ship, The "Sky Flyer." New York, Tousey, 1895.

The Magic Island; or, Frank Reade, Jr.'s Deep Sea Trip of Mystery. New York, Tousey, 1895.

Through the Tropics; or, Frank Reade, Jr.'s Adventures in the Gran Chaco. New York, Tousey, 1895.

In White Latitudes; or, Frank Reade, Jr.'s Ten Thousand Mile Flight over the Frozen North. New York, Tousey, 1895.

Below the Sahara; or, Frank Reade, Jr. Exploring an Underground River, with His Submarine Boat. New York, Tousey, 1895.

The Black Mogul; or, Through India with Frank Reade, Jr. Aboard His "Electric Boomer." New York, Tousey, 1895.

The Missing Planet; or, Frank Reade, Jr.'s Quest for a Fallen Star with His New Air-Ship, "The Zenith." New York, Tousey, 1895.

The Black Squadron; or, Frank Reade, Jr. in the Indian Ocean with His Submarine Boat, The "Rocket." New York, Tousey, 1895.

The Prairie Pirates; or, Frank Reade, Jr.'s Trip to Texas with His Electric Vehicle, The "Detective." New York, Tousey, 1895.

Over the Orient; or, Frank Reade, Jr.'s Travels in Turkey with His New Air-Ship. New York, Tousey, 1895.

The Black Whirlpool; or, Frank Reade, Jr.'s Deep Sea Search for a Lost Ship. New York, Tousey, 1895.

The Silent City; or, Frank Reade, Jr.'s Visit to a Strange People with His New Electric "Flyer." New York, Tousey, 1895.

The White Desert; or, Frank Reade, Jr.'s Trip to the Land of Tombs. New York, Tousey, 1895.

Under the Gulf of Guinea; or, Frank Reade, Jr. Exploring the Sunken Reef of Gold with His New Submarine Boat. New York, Tousey, 1895.

The Yellow Khan; or, Frank Reade, Jr. among the Thugs in Central India. New York, Tousey, 1895.

Frank Reade, Jr. in Japan, with His War Cruiser of the Clouds. New York, Tousey, 1895.

Frank Reade, Jr. in Cuba; or, Helping the Patriots with His Latest Air-Ship. New York, Tousey, 1895.

Chasing a Pirate; or, Frank Reade, Jr. on a Desperate Cruise. New York, Tousey, 1895.

In the Land of Fire; or, Frank Reade, Jr. among the Head Hunters. New York, Tousey, 1895.

7,000 Miles Underground; or, Frank Reade, Jr. Exploring a Volcano. New York, Tousey, 1895.

The Demon of the Clouds; or, Frank Reade, Jr. and the Ghosts of Phantom Island. New York, Tousey, 1895.

The Cloud City; or, Frank Reade, Jr.'s Most Wonderful Discovery. New York, Tousey, 1895.

The White Atoll; or, Frank Reade, Jr. in the South Pacific. New York, Tousey, 1895.

The Monarch of the Moon; or, Frank Reade, Jr.'s Exploits in Africa with His Electric "Thunderer." New York, Tousey, 1895.

37 Bags of Gold; or, Frank Reade, Jr. Hunting for a Lost Steamer. New York, Tousey, 1895.

The Lost Lake; or, Frank Reade, Jr.'s Trip to Alaska. New York, Tousey, 1895.

The Caribs' Cave; or, Frank Reade, Jr.'s Submarine Search for the Reef of Pearls. New York, Tousey, 1895.

The Desert of Death; or, Frank Reade, Jr. Exploring an Unknown Land. New York, Tousey, 1895.

A Trip to the Sea of the Sun; or, With Frank Reade, Jr. on a Perilous Cruise. New York, Tousey, 1895.

The Black Lagoon; or, Frank Reade, Jr.'s Submarine Search for a Sunken City in Russia. New York, Tousey, 1896.

The Mysterious Brand; or, Frank Reade, Jr. Solving a Mexican Mystery. New York, Tousey, 1896.

Across the Milky Way; or, Frank Reade, Jr.'s Great Astronomical Trip with His Air-Ship, "The Shooting Star." New York, Tousey, 1896.

Under the Great Lakes; or, Frank Reade, Jr.'s Latest Submarine Cruise. New York, Tousey, 1896.

The Magic Mine; or, Frank Reade, Jr.'s Trip up the Yukon with His Electric Combination Traveller. New York, Tousey, 1896.

Across Arabia; or, Frank Reade, Jr.'s Search for the Forty Thieves. New York, Tousey, 1896.

The Silver Sea; or, Frank Reade, Jr.'s Submarine Cruise in Unknown Waters. New York, Tousey, 1896.

In the Tundras; or, Frank Reade, Jr.'s Latest Trip Through Northern Asia. New York, Tousey, 1896.

The Circuit of Cancer; or, Frank Reade, Jr.'s Novel Trip Around the World with His New Air-Ship, The "Flight." New York, Tousey, 1896.

The Sacred Sea; or, Frank Reade, Jr.'s Submarine Exploits among the Dervishes of India. New York, Tousey, 1896.

The Land of Dunes; or, With Frank Reade, Jr. in the Desert of Gobi. New York, Tousey, 1896.

Six Days under Havana Harbor; or, Frank Reade, Jr.'s Secret Service Work for Uncle Sam. New York, Tousey, 1896.

The Sinking Star; or, Frank Reade, Jr.'s Trip into Space with His New Air-Ship "Saturn." New York, Tousey, 1896.

In the Gran Chaco; or, Frank Reade, Jr. in Search of a Missing Man. New York, Tousey, 1896.

The Lost Oasis; or, With Frank Reade, Jr. in the Australian Desert. New York, Tousey, 1896.

The Isle of Hearts; or, Frank Reade, Jr. in a Strange Sea with His Submarine Boat. New York, Tousey, 1896.

Jack Wright and Frank Reade, Jr., The Two Young Inventors; or, Brains Against Brains. New York, Tousey, 1896.

Novels (series: Jack Wright)

Jack Wright, The Boy Inventor; or, Hunting for a Sunken Treasure. New York, Tousey, 1891.

Jack Wright and His Electric Turtle; or, Chasing the Pirates of the Spanish Main. New York, Tousey, 1891.

Jack Wright's Submarine Catamaran; or, The Phantom Ship of the Yellow Sea. New York, Tousey, 1891.

Jack Wright and His Ocean Racer; or, Around the World in Twenty Days. New York, Tousey, 1891.

Jack Wright and His Electric Canoe; or, Working the Revenue Service. New York, Tousey, 1891.

Jack Wright's Air and Water Cutter; or, Wonderful Adventures on the Wing and Afloat. New York, Tousey, 1891.

Jack Wright and His Magnetic Motor; or, The Golden City of the Sierras. New York, Tousey, 1891.

Jack Wright, The Boy Inventor, and His Under-Water Iron-clad; or, The Treasure of the Sandy Sea. New York, Tousey, 1892.

Jack Wright and His Electric Deer; or, Fighting the Bandits of the Black Hills. New York, Tousey, 1892.

Jack Wright and His Prairie Engine; or, Among the Bushmen of Australia. New York, Tousey, 1892.

Jack Wright and His Electric Air Schooner; or, The Mystery of a Magic Mine. New York, Tousey, 1892.

Jack Wright and His Electric Sea-Motor; or, The Search for a Drifting Wreck. New York, Tousey, 1892.

Jack Wright and His Ocean Sleuth-Hound; or, Tracking an Underwater Treasure. New York, Tousey, 1892.

Jack Wright and His Dandy of the Deep; or, Driven Afloat in the Sea of Fire. New York, Tousey, 1892.

Jack Wright and His Electric Torpedo Ram; or, The Sunken City of the Atlantic. New York, Tousey, 1892.

Jack Wright and His Deep Sea Monitor; or, Searching for a Ton of Gold. New York, Tousey, 1892.

Jack Wright, The Boy Inventor, Exploring Central Asia in His Magnetic Hurricane. New York, Tousey, 1892.

Jack Wright and His Ocean Plunger; or, The Harpoon Hunters of the Arctic. New York, Tousey, 1892.

Jack Wright and His Electric "Sea-Ghost"; or, A Strange Under-Water Journey. New York, Tousey, 1892.

Jack Wright, The Boy Inventor, and His Deep Sea Diving Bell; or, The Buccaneers of The Gold Coast. New York, Tousey, 1892.

Jack Wright, The Boy Inventor, and His Electric Tricycle-Boat; or, The Treasure of the Sun-Worshippers. New York, Tousey, 1892.

Jack Wright and His Undersea Wrecking Raft; or, The Mystery of a Scuttled Ship. New York, Tousey, 1892.

Jack Wright and His Terror of the Seas; or, Fighting for a Sunken Fortune. New York, Tousey, 1892.

Jack Wright and His Electric Diving Boat; or, Lost under the Ocean. New York, Tousey, 1892.

Jack Wright and His Submarine Yacht; or, The Fortune Hunters of the Red Sea. New York, Tousey, 1892.

Jack Wright and His Electric Gunboat; or, The Search for a Stolen Girl. New York, Tousey, 1893.

Jack Wright and His Electric Sea Launch; or, A Desperate Cruise for Life. New York, Tousey, 1893.

Jack Wright and His Electric Bicycle-Boat; or, Searching for Captain Kidd's Gold. New York, Tousey, 1893.

Jack Wright and His Electric Side-Wheel Boat; or, Fighting the Brigands of the Coral Isles. New York, Tousey, 1893.

Jack Wright's Wonder of the Waves; or, The Flying Dutchman of the Pacific. New York, Tousey, 1893.

Jack Wright and His Electric Exploring Ship; or, A Cruise Around Greenland. New York, Tousey, 1893.

Jack Wright and His Electric Man-of-War; or, Fighting the Sea Robbers of the Frozen Coast. New York, Tousey, 1893.

Jack Wright and His Submarine Torpedo-Tug; or, Winning a Government Reward. New York, Tousey, 1893.

Jack Wright and His Electric Sea-Demon; or, Daring Adventures under the Ocean. New York, Tousey, 1893.

Jack Wright and His Electric "Whale"; or, The Treasure Trove of the Polar Sea. New York, Tousey, 1893.

Jack Wright and His Electric Marine "Rover"; or, 50,000 Miles in Ocean Perils. New York, Tousey, 1893.

Jack Wright and His Electric Deep Sea Cutter; or, Searching for a Pirate's Treasure. New York, Tousey, 1893.

Jack Wright and His Electric Monarch of the Ocean; or, Cruising for a Million in Gold. New York, Tousey, 1893.

Jack Wright and His Electric Devil-Fish; or, Fighting the Smugglers of Alaska. New York, Tousey, 1893.

Jack Wright and His Electric Demon of the Plains; or, Wild Adventures among the Cowboys. New York, Tousey, 1893.

Jack Wright and His Electric Balloon Ship; or, 30,000 Leagues above the Earth. New York, Tousey, 1893.

Jack Wright and His Electric Locomotive; or, The Lost Mine of Death Valley. New York, Tousey, 1893.

Jack Wright and His Iron-Clad Air-Motor; or, Searching for a Lost Explorer. New York, Tousey, 1893.

Jack Wright and His Electric Tricycle; or, Fighting the Stranglers of the Crimson Desert. New York, Tousey, 1893.

Jack Wright and His Electric Dynamo Boat; or, The Mystery of a Buried Sea. New York, Tousey, 1893.

Jack Wright and His Flying Torpedo; or, The Black Demons of Dismal Swamp. New York, Tousey, 1893.

Jack Wright and His Prairie Privateer; or, Fighting the Western Road-Agents. New York, Tousey, 1893.

Jack Wright and His Naval Cruiser; or, Fighting the Pirates of the Pacific. New York, Tousey, 1893.

Jack Wright, The Boy Inventor, and His Whaleback Privateer; or, Cruising in the Behring Sea. New York, Tousey, 1893.

Jack Wright and His Electric Phantom Boat; or, Chasing the Outlaws of the Ocean. New York, Tousey, 1893.

Jack Wright and His Winged Gunboat; or, A Voyage to an Unknown Land. New York, Tousey, 1894.

Jack Wright and His Electric Flyer; or, Racing in the Clouds for a Boy's Life. New York, Tousey, 1894.

Jack Wright, The Boy Inventor's Electric Sledge Boat; or, Wild Adventures in Alaska. New York, Tousey, 1894.

Jack Wright and His Electric Express Wagon; or, Wiping Out the Outlaws of Deadwood. New York, Tousey, 1894.

Jack Wright and His Submarine Explorer; or, A Cruise at the Bottom of the Ocean. New York, Tousey, 1894.

Jack Wright and His Demon of the Air; or, A Perilous Trip in the Clouds. New York, Tousey, 1894.

Jack Wright and His Electric Ripper; or, Searching for a Treasure in the Jungle. New York, Tousey, 1894.

Jack Wright and His King of the Sea; or, Diving for Old Spanish Gold. New York, Tousey, 1894.

Jack Wright and His Electric Balloons; or, Cruising in the Clouds for a Mountain Treasure. New York, Tousey, 1894.

Jack Wright and His Imp of the Ocean; or, The Wreckers of Whirlpool Reef. New York, Tousey, 1894.

Jack Wright and His Electric Cab; or, Around the Globe on Wheels. New York, Tousey, 1894.
Jack Wright and His Flying Phantom; or, Searching for a Lost Balloonist. New York, Tousey, 1894.
Jack Wright and His Submarine Warship; or, Chasing the Demons of the Sea of Gold. New York, Tousey, 1894.
Jack Wright and His Prairie Yacht; or, Fighting the Indians of the Sea of Grass. New York, Tousey, 1894.
Jack Wright and His Electric Air Rocket; or, The Boy Exile of Siberia. New York, Tousey, 1894.
Jack Wright and His Submarine Destroyer; or, Warring Against the Japanese Pirates. New York, Tousey, 1894.
Jack Wright and His Electric Battery Diver; or, A Two Months' Cruise under Water. New York, Tousey, 1894.
Jack Wright and His Electric Stage; or, Leagued Against the James Boys. New York, Tousey, 1894.
Jack Wright and His Wheel of the Wind; or, The Jewels of the Volcano Dwellers. New York, Tousey, 1894.
Jack Wright and the Head-Hunters of the African Coast; or, The Electric Pirate Chaser. New York, Tousey, 1894.
3,000 Pounds of Gold; or, Jack Wright and His Electric Bat, Fighting the Cliff-Dwellers of the Sierras. New York, Tousey, 1894.
Jack Wright and the Wild Boy of the Woods; or, Exposing a Strange Mystery with the Electric Cart. New York, Tousey, 1894.
Jack Wright among the Demons of the Ocean with His Electric Sea-Fighter. New York, Tousey, 1894.
Jack Wright, The Wizard of Wrightstown and His Electric Dragon; or, A Wild Race to Save a Fortune. New York, Tousey, 1894.
Jack Wright's Electric Land-Clipper; or, Exploring the Mysterious Gobi Desert. New York, Tousey, 1894.
Skull and Cross-Bones; or, Jack Wright's Diving-Bell and the Pirates. New York, Tousey, 1895.
Jack Wright, The Boy Inventor, and His Phantom Frigate; or, Fighting the Coast Wreckers of the Gulf. New York, Tousey, 1895.
Jack Wright and His Air-Ship on Wheels; or, A Perilous Journey to Cape Farewell. New York, Tousey, 1895.
Jack Wright and His Electric Roadster in the Desert of Death; or, Chasing the Australian Brigand. New York, Tousey, 1895.
Jack Wright's Ocean Marvel; or, The Mystery of a Frozen Island. New York, Tousey, 1895.
Jack Wright and His Electric Soaring Machine; or, A Daring Flight Through Miles of Peril. New York, Tousey, 1895.
Jack Wright and His Electric Battery Car; or, Beating the Express Train Robbers. New York, Tousey, 1895.
Jack Wright and His Electric Sea Horse; or, Seven Weeks in Ocean Perils. New York, Tousey, 1895.
Jack Wright and His Electric Balloon Boat; or, A Dangerous Voyage above the Clouds. New York, Tousey, 1895.
In the Jungles of India; or, Jack Wright as a Wild Animal Hunter. New York, Tousey, 1895.
50,000 Leagues under the Sea; or, Jack Wright's Most Dangerous Voyage. New York, Tousey, 1895.
Jack Wright, The Boy Inventor, Working for the Union Pacific Railroad; or, Over the Continent on the "Electric." New York, Tousey, 1895.
Over the South Pole; or, Jack Wright's Search for a Lost Explorer with His Flying Boat. New York, Tousey, 1895.
Jack Wright and His Electric Air Monitor; or, The Scourge of the Pacific. New York, Tousey, 1895.
The Boy Lion Fighter; or, Jack Wright in the Swamps of Africa. New York, Tousey, 1895.
Jack Wright and His Electric Submarine Ranger; or, Afloat among the Cannibals of the Deep. New York, Tousey, 1895.
The Demon of the Sky; or, Jack Wright's $10,000 Wager. New York, Tousey, 1895.
Adrift in the Land of Snow; or, Jack Wright and His Sledge-boat on Wheels. New York, Tousey, 1896.
The Floating Terror; or, Jack Wright Fighting the Buccaneers of the Venezuelan Coast. New York, Tousey, 1896.
Lost in the Polar Circle; or, Jack Wright and His Aerial Explorer. New York, Tousey, 1896.
Jack Wright, The Boy Inventor, and the Smugglers of the Border Lakes; or, The Second Cruise of the Whaleback "Comet." New York, Tousey, 1896.
The Fatal Blue Diamond; or, Jack Wright among the Demon Worshippers with His Electric Motor. New York, Tousey, 1896.
Running the Blockade; or, Jack Wright Helping the Cuban Filibusters. New York, Tousey, 1896.
Jack Wright and Frank Reade, Jr., The Two Young Inventors; or, Brains Against Brains. New York, Tousey, 1896.
The Flying Avenger; or, Jack Wright Fighting for Cuba. New York, Tousey, 1896.
Jack Wright and His New Electric Horse; or, A Perilous Trip over Two Continents. New York, Tousey, 1896.
Over the Sahara Desert; or, Jack Wright Fighting the Slave Hunters. New York, Tousey, 1896.
Diving for a Million; or, Jack Wright and His Electric Ocean Liner. New York, Tousey, 1896.

Uncollected Serials (all published in *Happy Days*, New York)

"Young Frank Reade and His Electric Air Ship; or, a 10,000 Mile Search for a Missing Man," 14 October—2 December 1899; "Jack Wright, The Boy Inventor, and His Electric Flying Machine; or, A Record Trip Around the World," 29 March—19 April 1902; "Jack Wright and His Marvel of the Sea; or, Among the Demons of the Deep," 1 June—5 July 1902; "Jack Wright and His Ship of the Desert; or, Adventures in the Sea of Sand," 26 July—16 August 1902; "Jack Wright and His King of the Clouds; or, Around the World on Wings," 16 August—6 September 1902; "Jack Wright and His Submarine Boat; or, Working for the Navy," 20 September—11 October 1902; "Jack Wright and His Red Terror; or, Fighting the Bushmen of Australia," 1—22 November 1902; "Jack Wright and His Tandem Balloons; or, Hunting Wild Beasts in India," 29 November—27 December 1902; "Jack Wright and His Queen of the Deep; or, Exploring Submarine Caves," 10—31 January 1903; "Jack Wright and His Wonder of the Prairie; or, Perils among the Cowboys," 28 February—21 March 1903; "Jack Wright and His Flying Ice Boat; or, Adrift in the Polar Regions," 28 March—18 April 1903; "Jack Wright's Floating Terror; or, Fighting the Pirates," 25 April—16 May 1903; "Jack Wright's Electric Prairie Car; or, Hot Times with the Broncho Busters," 23 May—13 June 1903; "Jack Wright's Sky Scraper; or, After the Lost Balloonists," 20 June—11 July 1903; "Jack Wright's Sea Demon; or, Running the Blockade," 18 July—8 August 1903; "Jack Wright's Rapid Transit; or, Trailing the Cattle Punchers," 29 August—19 September 1903; "Jack Wright's Queen of the Air; or, After the Cliff Dwellers' Gold," 6—27 February 1904; "Jack Wright's King of the Plains; or, Calling Down the Cowboys," 3—24 December 1904.

Uncollected Short Story

"Frank Reade's Christmas in the Air," in *Muldoon's Christmas*. New York, Tousey, 1889.

OTHER PUBLICATIONS

Novels

Young Sleuths in Demijohn City; or, Waltzing William's Dancing School. New York, Tousey, 1894.
Young Sleuths on the Stage; or, An Act Not on the Bills. New York, Tousey, 1894.

Novels as Police Captain Howard

A.D.T.; or, The Messenger Boy Detective. New York, Champion, 1882.
The Girl Detective. New York, Champion, 1882.
The Mystery of One Night. New York, Champion, 1882.
Young Vidocq. New York, Champion, 1882.

Other

How to Become a Naval Cadet. New York, Tousey, 1891.
How to Become a West Point Military Cadet. New York, Tousey, 1891.

*   *   *

During his lifetime, Luis P. Senarens was referred to as "the American Jules Verne" and a comparison of the work of both writers indicates the similarity. Senarens was writing stories of airships suspended by helicopter blades ("helices") three years before the *Albatross* took off in *Robur le Conquérant* (*Clipper of the Clouds*) in 1886. His epic serial *Frank Reade, Jr. and His Queen Clipper of the Clouds* leaned heavily on Verne. Even the illustrations were identical, with three of those in Senarens's story also used in Verne's *Maitre du Monde* (*Master of the World*). Senarens's story is basically a long air voyage hampered by the presence of several malcontents and a lunatic scientist intent on seizing Frank's vessel.

Frank Reade, boy inventor, was created by Harry Enton, who put himself through medical school writing dime novels and story-paper serials. The steam-driven robot in *The Steam Man of the Plains* (1876) is mainly a device for transporting Frank and his cousin, Charley Gorse, to the far West. The story is a tongue-in-cheek yarn of encounters with outlaws and Indians, named "Motzer-Ponum" and "Sholum Alarkum." Out west, Frank meets the comic Irishman, Barney Shea. Barney and the black man, Pomp (introduced in a later story), became regular members of the cast. The plot may be improbable, but the steam man (borrowed from Edward S. Ellis's 1865 *Steam Man of the Prairies*) is engaging and novel for its day. We are told just enough about how it works to make it plausible. Senarens seemed to take the stories more seriously than Enton when he stepped in with the fifth serial. He introduced Frank Reade, Jr., but kept Frank, Sr., and eventually gave Jr. a wife. No stylist, he often wrote in the choppy manner peculiar to writers paid by the line. Without the aid of a typewriter, he wrote fast, kept the plot moving, and the characters in hot water. In formula fiction the fascination is in the variation on the basic themes. A new airship, surpassing any effort of the imagination; a new type of submarine; electrified equipment to drive off enemies; aluminum bullet-proof armor; pneumatic revolvers; damsels in distress; gentlemen unjustly accused of murder; a race against time; evil men determined to steal the invention; the pranks of comic relief companions, forever quarrelling; the wonderfully strange foreign lands; the deadly beauty of an undersea cavern or ice-locked vessel. Along the way a bit of social comment: does the U.S. government protect citizens abroad? Do the workshops in Readestown provide enough jobs for the community?

Senarens himself claimed authorship of most of the Frank Reade stories and all of the companion series about Jack Wright, who lived in Wrightstown and whose specialty was inventing submarines. His adventures were novelettes cut from the same pattern as the Frank Reades. In 1894 the two raced each other around the world for $10,000. Jack's submarine won by 15 minutes because Frank set down his airship to save a girl on a runaway horse. The stories ended in 1904 when public sentiment decided the ideas were too bizarre and Senarens ran out of ideas, though they lived on in reprints.

Senarens's contribution to science fiction is in his early and imaginative use of so many scientific marvels harnessed for popular consumption to a mass market. Had it not been for the wonders of Senarens there might have been no Tom Swift.

—J. Randolph Cox

SERLING, (Edward) Rod(man). American. Born in Syracuse, New York, 25 December 1924. Educated at Antioch College, Yellow Springs, Ohio, B.A. 1950. Served as a paratrooper in the United States Army during World War II. Married Carolyn Kramer in 1948; two daughters. Writer, WLW-Radio, 1946-48, and WKRC-TV, 1948-53, both Cincinnati; free-lance writer from 1953: Producer of television series *The Twilight Zone*, 1959-64, and *Night Gallery*, from 1969; taught at Antioch College, 1950's, and Ithaca College, New York, 1970's. President, National Academy of Television Arts and Sciences, 1965-66; Member of the Council, Writers Guild of America West, 1965-67. Recipient: Emmy Award, for television plays, 1955, 1957, 1959; Sylvania Award, 1955, 1956; Christopher Award, 1956, 1971; Peabody Award, 1957. D.H.L.: Emerson College, Boston, 1971; Alfred University, New York, 1972; Litt.D.: Ithaca College, 1972. *Died 28 June 1975.*

SCIENCE-FICTION PUBLICATIONS

Short Stories

Stories from the Twilight Zone.   New York, Bantam, 1960.
More Stories from the Twilight Zone.   New York, Bantam, 1961.
New Stories from the Twilight Zone.   New York, Bantam, 1962.
From the Twilight Zone (selection).   New York, Doubleday, 1962.
Night Gallery.   New York, Bantam, 1971.
Night Gallery 2.   New York, Bantam, 1972.

OTHER PUBLICATIONS

Novel

Requiem for a Heavyweight (novelization of screenplay).   New York, Bantam, and London, Corgi, 1962.

Short Stories

The Season to Be Wary.   Boston, Little Brown, 1967.

Plays

Requiem for a Heavyweight (televised, 1956).   Included in *Patterns*, 1957; (revised version, produced New York, 1979).
Patterns: Four Television Plays (includes *Patterns, The Rack, Requiem for a Heavyweight, Old MacDonald Had a Curve*).   New York, Simon and Schuster, 1957.
The Killing Season (produced New York, 1968).
The Lonely, in *Writing for Television*, edited by Max Wylie.   New York, Cowles, 1970.
A Storm in Summer, in *Camera Two: Two Plays for Television.*   Toronto, Holt Rinehart, 1972.

Screenplays: *Patterns*, 1956; *Saddle the Wind*, with Thomas Thompson, 1958; *Requiem for a Heavyweight*, 1962; *The Yellow Canary*, 1963; *Seven Days in May*, 1964; *Assault on a Queen*, 1966; *Planet of the Apes*, with Michael Wilson, 1968; *The Man*, 1971; *A Time for Predators*, 1971.

Television Plays: *Patterns*, 1955; *Requiem for a Heavyweight*, 1956; *Forbidden Area*, from the novel by Pat Frank, 1956; *The Comedian*, 1957; *The Rack; Old MacDonald Had a Curve; Line of Duty; The Lonely; A Storm in Summer*; and other plays for *U.S. Steel Hour, Playhouse 90, Hallmark Hall of Fame, Suspense,* and *Danger* series.

Other

Editor, *Triple W: Witches, Warlocks, and Werewolves.*   New York, Bantam, 1963.
Editor, *Devils and Demons.*   New York, Bantam, 1967.

*   *   *

One of the handful of scriptwriters who consistently produced quality drama during American television's "golden age" of the 1950's, Rod Serling demonstrated an interest in science-fiction themes as early as 1956, when he adapted Pat Frank's novel *Forbidden Area* for television. Later, as one of the few writers to be given relative artistic control over a TV series, he turned again to science fiction and fantasy with *The Twilight Zone*, an anthology series which began in 1959. *The Twilight Zone* is often cited as one of the first serious attempts to bring intelligent fantastic stories to television, and, in addition to the large number of scripts that Serling himself wrote for the series, he elicited scripts from major writers within the science fiction and fantasy field, including Richard Matheson, Charles Beaumont, and Ray Bradbury. A later TV series, *Night Gallery*, retained a few science-fiction stories but tended more toward fantasy and the supernatural. Serling also wrote the filmscripts for *Seven Days in May* and the hugely successful *Planet of the Apes*.

Serling adapted several of his *Twilight Zone* episodes as short stories. These often reveal the constraints of writing for television, and Serling for the most part made no effort to take advantage of the new form to develop or expand upon his initial scripts. The characters tend to be exaggerated stereotypes, easily recognizable in a half-hour TV format; the style is often precious or portentous, reflecting Serling's own opening and closing narrations for the original shows; and the fantastic elements are kept elementary and at times even simplistic. With their moralistic lessons and often sentimental tone, the tales work more as fables than as serious attempts at character or idea development.

Serling's attitude toward technology, for example, is decidedly ambiguous. When he writes of robots, he is unabashedly sentimental, as in "The Mighty Casey," which concerns a robot pitcher who nearly saves the Brooklyn Dodgers until he gets a mechanical heart which makes him too kind to strike out batters (the story is an odd combination of *Damn Yankees* and *The Wizard of Oz*), or "The Lonely," which concerns a prisoner sentenced to a lonely asteroid who finds companionship in a female robot brought by a kindly spaceship captain (a variation on a story by Ray Bradbury, who seems to be Serling's most consistent influence, even cropping up as a character name in a couple of Serling's stories). But in some stories mechanical contrivances become evil presences with minds of their own—a slot machine bent on destroying a compulsive gambler in "The Fever" or household appliances and a vengeful automobile in "A Thing about Machines." The implicit technophobia of "A Thing about Machines," however, is undercut by the almost pathological hostility of the victim who is the central character. Other stories also reflect technophobia in their concern with escape into a simpler past life ("A Stop at Willoughby," "Walking Distance"). The relatively few that deal with the familiar science-fiction theme of alien presences, such as "Mr. Dingle, The Strong" or "The Monsters Are Due on Maple Street," treat them as little more than background for stories essentially concerned with character relations.

Not surprisingly, the major strength in Serling's writing is the convincing dialogue and his ability to sketch recognizable characters quickly—both skills well-suited to TV writing. His exposition is weak and at times even cloying, his themes and plots derivative. He is most likely to be remembered for his powerful non-science fiction dramas, such as *Patterns* or *Requiem for a Heavyweight*, and for his contribution in bringing serious, character-oriented fantastic tales—however familiar such tales may have been to veteran readers—to the television screen.

—Gary K. Wolfe

SERVISS, Garrett P(utnam). Born in Sharon Springs, New York, 24 March 1851. Educated at Cornell University, Ithaca, New York, B.S. 1872; Columbia University, New York, LL.B. 1874. Married Henrietta Gros le Blond in 1907. Editorial writer, New York *Sun*, to 1892; then lecturer on travel, history, and astronomy, and writer. *Died 25 May 1929.*

SCIENCE-FICTION PUBLICATIONS

Novels

The Moon Metal. New York, Harper, 1900.
A Columbus of Space. New York and London, Appleton, 1911.
The Second Deluge. New York, McBride Nast, and London, Richards, 1912.

Edison's Conquest of Mars. Los Angeles, Carcosa House, 1947; abridged edition, as *Invasion of Mars*, Reseda, California, Powell, 1969.

Uncollected Short Stories

"The Sky Pirate," in *Scrap Book* (New York), April 1909.
"The Moon Maiden," in *Argosy* (New York), May 1915.

OTHER PUBLICATIONS

Other

Astronomy with an Opera-Glass. New York, Appleton, 1888.
Wonders of the Lunar Worlds; or, A Trip to the Moon. New York, Urania, 1892.
Napoleon Bonaparte (lecture). Philadelphia, Morris, 1901.
Other Worlds: Their Nature, Possibilities, and Habitability in their Light of the Latest Discoveries. New York, Appleton, 1901.
Pleasures of the Telescope. New York, Appleton, 1901; London, Hirschfeld, 1902.
The Heavens Without a Telescope, with Leon Barritt. New York, Barritt, 1906.
Planet Tables, Moon Phases, and the Sun's Daily Position, with Leon Barritt. New York, Barritt, 1906.
The Barritt-Serviss Star and Planet Finder, Northern Hemisphere, with Leon Barritt. New York, Barritt, 1906.
The Moon. New York, Appleton, 1907; as *The Story of the Moon*, 1928.
Astronomy with the Naked Eye. New York, Harper, 1908.
Curiosities of the Sky. New York, Harper, 1909.
Round the Year with the Stars. New York, Harper, 1910.
Eloquence: Counsel on the Art of Public Speaking. New York, Harper, 1912.
Astronomy in a Nutshell. New York, Putnam, 1912.
The Einstein Theory of Relativity. New York, Fadman, 1923.
Riding Through Space: The Earth's Scenic Voyage. Springfield, Ohio, Corwell, 1923.

*   *   *

Most of the writings of Garrett P. Serviss were never read, or even suspected, by the generation which lauded his small but significant contribution to science fiction. As a staff writer for the New York *Sun*, and later for a newspaper syndicate, he produced many columns of popular science material, much of which was unsigned. Having made his name as the popular astronomer of his day, he wrote for several leading magazines on subjects ranging from "Facts and Fancies about Mars" to the Shakespeare-Bacon controversy. A series of articles (*Astronomy with an Opera-Glass*) in *Popular Science Monthly* was extended to become the first of a small library of works including such titles as *Other Worlds* and *Curiosities of the Sky*.

His first novel was serialised in 1898 in the New York *Evening Journal*, and was evidently designed to exploit the public interest engendered by H.G. Wells's *The War of the Worlds*. *Edison's Conquest of Mars* was in the nature of a sequel to the Wells classic, though it went far beyond the limits of imaginative conception that even the Master had essayed in a single story. The Martians, too, were rather more human than Wells's monstrous marauders; and they had no chance to launch a second invasion before the great American inventor had organised a counter-attack on Mars in a whole fleet of spaceships armed with deadly disintegrators. Though hurriedly written in a bombastic style, the story was remarkably inventive for its time, anticipating many of the devices which became the substance of later science fiction. No less remarkable is the fact that it was exhumed and published in hardcover only in 1947, having become legendary among fans who admired the author's subsequent stories.

One which attained classic status was *A Columbus of Space*, the tale of a voyage to Venus in an atomic-powered spaceship. Even more notable is *The Second Deluge*, in which a cosmic collision results in a universal flood. The story of how a latter-day Noah saved the human race from extinction proved so popular that it was twice reprinted by *Amazing*, where one reader found it so convincing that he wrote in asking for the plans of Cosmo Versál's ark so that he might save his family from the impending disaster. *The Moon Metal* concerned a mysterious metal originating in the lunar crater Tycho which replaced gold when this became as plentiful as iron. "The Sky Pirate" dared to predict air travel at 140 miles an hour in the year 1936; and "The Moon Maiden," the least of all his works, marked the last appearance of Serviss, in *Argosy*, the magazines which pioneered science fiction long before the advent of the specialist pulps.

—Walter Gillings

SEYMOUR, Alan. Australian. Born in Perth, Western Australia, 6 June 1927. Educated at Fremantle State School and Perth Modern School. Free-lance film and theatre critic and educational writer, Australian Broadcasting Commission, late 1940's and 1950's; Script Editor and Producer, BBC Television, London, 1974-77. Theatre Critic, *London Magazine*, 1963-65, and contributor to *Overland*, Melbourne, *Meanjin*, Melbourne, and *Bulletin-Observer*, Sydney. Recipient: Sydney Journalists' Club prize, 1960; Australian Council for the Arts grant, 1974. Address: c/o Laurence Fitch Ltd., 113 Wardour Street, London W1V 4EH, England.

SCIENCE-FICTION PUBLICATIONS

Novel

The Coming Self-Destruction of the United States of America. London, Souvenir Press, 1969; New York, Grove Press, 1971.

OTHER PUBLICATIONS

Novel

The One Day of the Year. London, Souvenir Press, 1967.

Plays

Swamp Creatures (produced Canberra, 1958).
The One Day of the Year (produced Sydney and London, 1961). Sydney, Angus and Robertson, 1962; included in *Three Australian Plays*, London, Penguin, 1962.
The Gaiety of Nations (produced Glasgow, 1965; London, 1966).
A Break in the Music (produced Perth, 1966).
The Pope and the Pill (produced London, 1968).
Oh Grave, Thy Victory (produced Canberra, 1973).
Structures (produced Perth, 1974).
The Wind from the Plain, adaptation of the novel by Yashar Kemal (produced Turku, Finland, 1974-75).

Radio Plays: *Little Moron*, 1956; *A Winter Passion*, 1960; *Donny Johnson*, 1965 (Finland).

Television Plays: *The Runner*, 1962 (Australia); *Lean Liberty*, 1962 (UK); *Auto-Stop*, 1964 (UK); *And It Wasn't Just the Feathers*, 1964 (UK); *The Trial and Torture of Sir John Rampayne*, 1965 (UK); *Stockbrokers Are Smashing But Bankers Are Better*, 1965 (UK); *Fixation*, from work by Miles Tripp, 1973 (UK); *The Lotus, Tigers Are Better Looking*, and *Outside the Machine*, from stories by Jean Rhys, 1973-74 (UK); *Eustace and Hilda*, from novels by L.P. Hartley, 1977 (UK).

*

Manuscript Collection: Mitchell Library, Sydney.

Theatrical Activities:

Director: **Plays**—*The One Day of the Year*, Australia tour, 1961. Operas for the Sydney Opera Group, 1953-57.

* * *

Alan Seymour produced his important science-fiction novel, *The Coming Self-Destruction of the United States of America*, when anxiety over Vietnam and racism were at fever pitch. Reviewers recognized its quality, but its plot and message, that racism will lead to guerilla civil war and the ruin of America, virtually guaranteed it would be no best seller. Such has been the fate of the host of works on these subjects, though Sam Greenlee's *The Spook Who Sat by the Door*, telling a similar tale, sold widely. In any case Seymour tells this story as well as it's been told. Its mysterious black revolutionary leader, "Hero," accurately recalls the authentic "Stagger Lee" of Black American folklore. Seymour keeps the focus on the experience of the individual human participants in the events with snippets of diaries, logs, tapes, and letters, and a first-person narrating "editor." The effect is a mosaic of awful concrete detail in place of sweeping abstraction that so often diminishes the impact of science fiction. The sociology is excellent. That the political and economic theory that vaguely bolsters the novel is questionable matters not at all. America's racism is a fatal expression of its mono-cultural obsession and paranoia. In this context a black revolutionary effort will give no quarter, even to sympathetic whites. The result will be, therefore, ruinous as well for blacks.

Self-Destruction is a fine representative of the ruin-of-America and racial civil war stories that go back to Martin R. Delany's *Blake; or, The Huts of America* (1859), W.E.B. Du Bois's *Dark Princess* (1928), Sinclair Lewis's *It Can't Happen Here* (1935), and Warren Miller's *The Siege of Harlem* (1964).

—John R. Pfeiffer

SHARKEY, Jack (John Michael Sharkey). Also writes as Mike Johnson. American. Born in Chicago, Illinois, 6 May 1931. Educated at St. Mary's College, Winona, Minnesota, B.A. in English 1953. Served in the United States Army, 1955-56. Married Patricia Walsh in 1962; three daughters and one son. Since 1952, professional writer: Assistant Editor, *Playboy*, Chicago, 1963-64; Editor, *Aim*, later *Good Hands*, for Allstate Insurance, Northbrook, Illinois, 1964-75. Recipient: American Association of Industrial Editors prize, 1967. Agent: (plays) Samuel French, 25 West 45th Street, New York, New York 10036. Address: 24276 Ponchartrain Lane, Lake Forest, California 92630, U.S.A.

SCIENCE-FICTION PUBLICATIONS

Novels

The Secret Martians. New York, Ace, 1960.
Ultimatum in 2050 A.D. New York, Ace, 1965.

Uncollected Short Stories (series: Jerry Norcriss)

"The Captain of His Soul" and "The Obvious Solution," in *Fantastic* (New York), March 1959.
"The Arm of Enmord," in *Fantastic* (New York), April 1959.
"Queen of the Green Sun," in *Fantastic* (New York), May 1959.
"Bedside Monster," in *Fantastic* (New York), June 1959.
"The Kink-Remover," in *Fantastic* (New York), July 1959.
"Let X = Alligators," in *Fantastic* (New York), August 1959.
"Dolce al Fine," in *Amazing* (New York), August 1959.
"The Blackbird," in *Fantastic* (New York), September 1959.
"Ship Ahoy!," in *Fantastic* (New York), October 1959.

"Minor Detail," in *Amazing* (New York), November 1959.

"The Man Who Was Pale," in *Fantastic* (New York), December 1959.

"Multum in Parvo," in *The Year's Best S-F 5,* edited by Judith Merril. New York, Simon and Schuster, 1960; London, Mayflower, 1966.

"Old Friends Are the Best," in *Amazing* (New York), March 1960.

"The Dope on Mars," in *Galaxy* (New York), August 1960.

"The Crispin Affair," in *Fantastic* (New York), July, August 1960.

"The Business, As Usual," in *Galaxy* (New York), August 1960.

"Squeeze," in *Fantastic* (New York), September 1960.

"Status Quaint," in *Fantastic* (New York), October 1960.

"According to the Plan," in *Fantastic* (New York), January 1961.

"The Contact Point," in *If* (New York), January 1961.

"A Thread in Time," in *Fantastic* (New York), February 1961.

"Night Caller," in *Fantastic* (New York), March 1961.

"The Flying Tuskers of Kiniik-Kinaak," in *If* (New York), May 1961.

"Are You Now or Have You Ever Been?," in *Fantastic* (New York), May 1961.

"No Harm Done," in *Fantastic* (New York), July 1961.

"One Small Drawback," in *Fantastic* (New York), August 1961.

"Arcturus Times Three" (Norcriss), in *Galaxy* (New York), October 1961.

"Robotum Delenda Est!," in *Fantastic* (New York), March 1962.

"Big Baby" (Norcriss), in *Galaxy* (New York), April 1962.

"Double or Nothing," in *Fantastic* (New York), May 1962.

"Behind the Door," in *Fantastic* (New York), August 1962.

"A Matter of Protocol" (Norcriss), in *Galaxy* (New York), August 1962.

"It's Magic, You Dope," in *Fantastic* (New York), November, December 1962.

"The Final Ingredient," in *Triple W,* edited by Rod Serling. New York, Bantam, 1963.

"The Leech," in *Fantastic* (New York), January 1963.

"The Smart Ones," in *Amazing* (New York), February 1963.

"The Programmed People," in *Amazing* (New York), June, July 1963.

"The Trouble with Tweenity," in *Fantastic* (New York), July 1963.

"Collector's Item," in *Fantasy and Science Fiction* (New York), September 1963.

"The Aftertime," in *Fantastic* (New York), November 1963.

"The Creature Inside" (Norcriss), in *Worlds of Tomorrow* (New York), December 1963.

"The Awakening," in *Galaxy* (New York), February 1964.

"The Orginorg Way," in *Fantastic* (New York), February 1964.

"Survival of the Fittest," in *Fantasy and Science Fiction* (New York), March 1964.

"At the Feelies," in *Galaxy* (New York), April 1964.

"Illusion," in *Fantastic* (New York), June 1964.

"The Venus Charm," in *Fantastic* (New York), July 1964.

"Weetl," in *If* (New York), June 1964.

"Footnote to an Old Story," in *Fantastic* (New York), August 1964.

"The Colony That Failed" (Norcriss), in *Galaxy* (New York), August 1964.

"Hear and Obey," in *Fantastic* (New York), September 1964.

"The Grooves," in *Fantastic* (New York), October 1964.

"Breakthrough," in *Fantasy and Science Fiction* (New York), November 1964.

"The Seminarian," in *Amazing* (New York), November 1964.

"To Each His Own," in *The 6 Fingers of Time and 5 Other Science Fiction Novelets.* New York, Macfadden, 1965.

"The Twerlik," in *10th Annual Edition of the Year's Best SF,* edited by Judith Merril. New York, Delacorte Press, 1965; London, Mayflower, 1967.

"Trade-In," in *Best from Fantasy and Science Fiction 14,* edited by Avram Davidson. New York, Doubleday, 1965; London, Panther, 1967.

"Blue Boy," in *Amazing* (New York), January 1965.

"Look Out Below," in *Fantastic* (New York), March 1965.

"Essentials Only," in *Fantasy and Science Fiction* (New York), March 1965.

"The Trouble with Hyperspace," in *Fantastic* (New York), April 1965.

"The Glorious Fourth," in *Fantasy and Science Fiction* (New York), October 1965.

"Matrix Goose," in *Galaxy* (New York), August 1967.

"Life Cycle," in *If* (New York), September 1970.

"Conversation with a Bug" and "The Pool," in *From the "S" File.* Chicago, Playboy Press, 1971.

"Rate of Exchange," in *Galaxy* (New York), May 1971.

OTHER PUBLICATIONS

Novels

Murder, Maestro, Please. New York and London, Abelard Schuman, 1960.

Death for Auld Lang Syne. New York, Holt Rinehart, 1962; London, Joseph, 1963.

The Addams Family. New York, Pyramid, 1965.

Plays

Here Lies Jeremy Troy (produced New York, 1965). New York, French, 1969.

M Is for Million. New York, French, 1971.

How Green Was My Brownie. New York, French, 1972.

Kiss or Make Up. New York, French, 1972.

Meanwhile, Back on the Couch.... New York, French, 1973.

A Gentleman and a Scoundrel. New York, French, 1973.

Roomies. New York, French, 1974.

Spinoff. New York, French, 1974.

Who's on First? (produced Mount Prospect, Illinois, 1975). New York, French, 1975.

What a Spot!, with Dave Reiser. New York, French, 1975.

Saving Grace. New York, French, 1976.

Take a Number, Darling. New York, French, 1976.

The Creature Creeps! New York, French, 1977.

Dream Lover. New York, French, 1977.

Hope for the Best, with Dave Reiser. New York, French, 1977.

Rich Is Better. New York, French, 1977.

The Murder Room. New York, French, 1977.

Pushover, with Ken Easton. New York, French, 1977.

Once Is Enough. New York, French, 1977.

The Clone People (as Mike Johnson). New York, French, 1978.

Missing Link. New York, French, 1978.

Turnabout, with Ken Easton. New York, French, 1978.

Not the Count of Monte Cristo?, with Dave Reiser. New York, French, 1978.

Turkey in the Straw. New York, French, 1979.

Operetta!, with Dave Reiser. New York, French, 1979.

My Son the Astronaut. New York, French, 1980.

*   *   *

Jack Sharkey started publishing science fiction in 1959, but produced little fiction of any kind after 1965. In that span of time, Sharkey sold about 50 stories and seven novels.

Sharkey's best-known series featured Jerry Norcriss, Space Zoologist. These stories were typical SF puzzle stories where Norcriss would "merge" minds with an alien organism in order to solve the environmental puzzle and save a star colony. Two novels which were serialized but never published in book form are "The Crispin Affair," a thrilling space opera, and "It's Magic, You Dope!," a wildly funny fantasy in the mode of Pratt and de Camp's *The Incomplete Enchanter.*

Sharkey's two SF novels published in book form are complete opposites. *The Secret Martians* is a first-person account of the mystery of the missing Space Scouts and the discovery of the ancient Martian civilization. The action is fast paced and laced with humor. *Ultimatum in 2050 A.D.* is the grim story, with overtones of *Logan's Run,* of revolt against an Earth society where all its citizens are completely programmed. Sharkey's works are enjoyable, well written, and unfortunately completely out-of-print.

—George Kelley

SHAVER, Richard S(harpe). Also wrote as Wes Amherst; Edwin Benson; Peter Dexter; Richard Dorset; Richard English; G.H. Irwin; Paul Lohrman; Frank Patton; Stan Raycraft. American. Born in 1907. Little is known of his life: probably a welder who lived in Pennsylvania. *Died 5 November 1975.*

SCIENCE-FICTION PUBLICATIONS

Short Stories

I Remember Lemuria, and The Return of Sathanas. Evanston, Illinois, Venture, 1948.

Uncollected Short Stories (series: Red Dwarf)

"The Tale of the Red Dwarf," in *Fantastic Adventures* (New York), May 1947.
"Daughter of Night" (Dwarf), in *Amazing* (New York), December 1948.
"The Cyclops," in *Amazing* (New York), January 1949.
"The Cyclopeans," in *Fantastic Adventures* (New York), June 1949.
"Exiles of the Elfmounds," in *Amazing* (New York), July 1949.
"Erdis Cliff" (Dwarf), in *Amazing* (New York), September 1949.
"Where No Foot Walks" (as G.H. Irwin), and "The Fall of Lemuria," in *Other Worlds* (Evanston, Indiana), November 1949.
"Battle in Eternity," with Chester S. Geier, in *Amazing* (New York), November 1949.
"When the Moon Bounced" (as Frank Patton), and "Pillars of Delight" (as Stan Raycraft), in *Amazing* (New York), December 1949.
"Sons of the Serpent" (as Wes Amherst), in *Other Worlds* (Evanston, Indiana), January 1950.
"The Gamin" (as Peter Dexter), "Mahai's Wife" (as Edwin Benson), and "Lady," in *Other Worlds* (Evanston, Indiana), March 1950.
"The World of the Lost" (as Paul Lohrman), in *Fantastic Adventures* (New York), March 1950.
"We Dance for the Dom," in *Amazing* (New York), July 1950.
"The Palace of Darkness" (as Peter Dexter), in *Other Worlds* (Evanston, Indiana), September 1950.
"Glass Woman of Venus" (as G.H. Irwin), in *Other Worlds* (Evanston, Indiana), January 1951.
"Green Man's Grief," in *Future* (New York), January 1951.
"Yelisen," in *Other Worlds* (Evanston, Indiana), December 1951.
"Of Stegner's Folly," in *If* (New York), March 1952.
"The Sun Smiths," in *Other Worlds* (Evanston, Indiana), July, August, October 1952.
"Beyond the Barrier," in *Other Worlds* (Evanston, Indiana), November, December 1952, January, February 1953.
"The Dark Goddess," in *Imagination* (Evanston, Illinois), February 1953.
"Paradise Planet," in *Imagination* (Evanston, Illinois), Spring 1953.
"She Was Sitting in the Dark" (as Richard Dorset), in *Science Stories* (Evanston, Illinois), December 1953.
"The Dream Makers," in *Fantastic* (New York), July 1958.
"The Heart of the Game" (as Richard English), in *Orbit 1*, edited by Damon Knight. New York, Putnam, and London, Whiting and Wheaton, 1966.

*   *   *

If Richard S. Shaver is discussed today, it is usually as a curiosity in the history of science fiction, or as an early example of that dim area where fiction shades into UFO's and ancient astronauts. This is to some extent justified but not altogether fair. Although "the Shaver Mystery" series was presented for the most part as fact, it is far more akin to the science fiction of its time, both in execution and in sources, than most realize; and, taken as fiction, the stories do have intrinsic interest and merit.

During his writing career, spanning three decades, Shaver's stories and "non-fiction" explications were published in a number of magazines, primarily under his longtime editor and advocate, Ray Palmer, at first in science-fiction magazines such as *Amazing Stories* and *Other Worlds,* and later in "occult" publications such as *Hidden World.* A letter from Shaver (*Amazing,* December 1944)

described the underground races called the "dero" and "tero" who had taught him the pre-catastrophe language of "Mantong." Then, at Palmer's request, Shaver sent a 10,000 word manuscript from which Palmer wrote a 31,000 word story, "I Remember Lemuria!" Constructed for high drama and written in colorful and traditional pulp style, it told the story of "Mutan Mion of ancient Lemuria," and fully outlined the background and dogma of the Shaver Mystery. The Atlans and Titans, Shaver reports, had been immortal giants of advanced technology; then the sun began to age and give off "heavy metal radiation," causing aging and death. Most fled the earth for a planet with a younger sun, but others burrowed beneath the ground seeking protection from the poisonous rays. These are the dero and tero Shaver claimed to have met in the caves—struggling remnants of a once-great civilization. Of these two warring factions, the dero are by far the more interesting; Shaver has developed the quintessential conspiracy theory. Whenever anything goes wrong. the degenerate dero, crazed by the sun's rays and using the almost-magical machines left by the Elder Races, are responsible. Against this depravity the tero fight valiantly but often in vain, sometimes aided by sensitive surface men like Richard Shaver.

This is fairly basic stuff, at least in its psychological appeal both as archetype and as wish fulfillment, especially for *Amazing* with its younger and less demanding readership. What made it controversial was that, after the first story, the series was presented as fact. It is debatable whether Palmer believed this; it is probable that he saw it mainly as a way to increase circulation, at least at first. Shaver, however, apparently believed completely in his visit to the caves, in the voices that spoke to him from underground, and in what those voices told him. In the May 1978 *Science Fiction Review* Palmer announced that the eight years Shaver spent "in the caves" were actually spent in the Ypsilanti State Hospital as a paranoid schizophrenic. This sheds light on the style as well as the content of Shaver's writing: besides adventure-writing devices and techniques, Shaver's style is marked by "schizophrenese" characteristics such as disjointed sentences and, more importantly, word-dismantling and "clang associations."

But it would be wrong to dismiss these writings as only psychotic ravings, or even as Shaver's ravings hammered into salable fiction by Palmer. For one thing, Shaver himself wrote for other magazines under a number of pseudonyms, including house names. Beyond that, the stories show an eclectic range of clearly literary influences, These include the lush fiction of A. Merritt, Wells's Morlocks and Eloi, and the fictional worldview of H.P. Lovecraft, from whose novel *At the Mountains of Madness* Shaver probably got the term "Elder Race." Harry Warner, Jr. (in *All Our Yesterdays*) mentions a possible influence from E.R. Eddison, "whom Shaver once identified as his literary idol" and *A Reader's Guide to Science Fiction* demonstrates patterning, perhaps conscious, after the planetary romances of Edgar Rice Burroughs. Possible sources in occult non-fiction include Charles Fort, the Theosophy of Mme. Blavatsky, and James Churchward's Mu series, which Shaver mentions in his first letter to Palmer. Shaver also mentions Edith Hamilton's writings on mythology—which his own works explain and correct. The Bible, especially the Edenic theme, is also an important source.

What results is an odd but fascinating blend of high adventure, outrageous "science," and elusive but striking systems of cosmic speculation. If the characters are sometimes flat, if the plots too often seem "boy meets girl, boy beats dero, boy wins girl"—and this is not always the case—the sheer wealth and strangeness of the concepts Shaver develops more than compensate for that. There is a king of Stapledonian scope to Shaver, a sense of epic, and mythic, panoramas; the races, societies, and technologies with which he populates his universe are varied and often impressive. The appeal of Richard Shaver to the reader then and now is, as Palmer said, "One thing only, his unusual imagination. His strange sense of the unusual, his feeling for emotion, his sense of the beautiful and his sense of the outré." For that reason Shaver's writings, shrouded in controversy and now largely neglected, are worthy of new attention.

—Bernadette Bosky

SHAW, Bob (Robert Shaw). British. Born in Belfast, Northern Ireland, 31 December 1931. Educated at Technical High School, Belfast, 1944-46. Married Sarah Gourley in 1954; two daughters and one son. Prior to 1960 worked in the steel and aircraft industries and as a cab driver; Assistant Publicity Officer, 1960-66, and Press Officer, 1969-73, Short Bros. and Harland, aircraft manufacturers, Belfast; journalist, Belfast *Telegraph,* 1966-69. Recipient: British Science Fiction Association Award, 1975. Address: 3 Braddyll Terrace, Ulverston, Cumbria LA12 0DH, England.

SCIENCE-FICTION PUBLICATIONS

Novels

Night Walk. New York, Banner, 1967; London, New English Library, 1970.
The Two-Timers. New York, Ace, 1968; London, Gollancz, 1969.
Shadow of Heaven. New York, Avon, 1969; abridged edition, London, New English Library, 1970.
The Palace of Eternity. New York, Ace, 1969; London, Gollancz, 1970.
One Million Tomorrows. New York, Ace, 1970; London, Gollancz, 1971.
The Ground Zero Man. New York, Avon, 1971; London, Corgi, 1976.
Other Days, Other Eyes. New York, Ace, and London, Gollancz, 1972.
Orbitsville. New York, Ace, and London, Gollancz, 1975.
A Wreath of Stars. London, Gollancz, 1976; New York, Doubleday, 1977.
Medusa's Children. London, Gollancz, 1977; New York, Doubleday, 1979.
Who Goes Here? London, Gollancz, 1977; New York, Ace, 1978.
Ship of Strangers. London, Gollancz, 1978; New York, Dell, 1979.
Vertigo. London, Gollancz, 1978; New York, Ace, 1979.
Dagger of the Mind. London, Gollancz, 1979.

Short Stories

Tomorrow Lies in Ambush. New York, Ace, and London, Gollancz, 1973.
Cosmic Kaleidoscope. London, Gollancz, 1976; New York, Doubleday, 1977.

Uncollected Short Stories

"Crossing the Line," in *Andromeda 2*, edited by Peter Weston. London, Futura, 1977.
"Dream Fighter," in *Fantasy and Science Fiction* (New York), February 1977.
"The Edge of Time," with Malcolm Harris, in *Aries 1,* edited by John Grant. Newton Abbot, Devon, David and Charles, 1979.
"Frost Animals," in *Universe 9,* edited by Terry Carr. New York, Doubleday, 1979.
"Well-Wisher," in *Fantasy and Science Fiction* (New York), November 1979.

*

Manuscript Collection: Science Fiction Foundation, North East London Polytechnic.

Bob Shaw comments:
It is very difficult, if not impossible, for an author to write objectively about his own work, but I sum up my output by saying that I write science fiction for people who don't read a great deal of science fiction. This doesn't mean that I curb my imagination. I'm quite prepared to deal with the most fantastic concepts, but I try to do it in such a way that the ideas can be appreciated by any reader. The technique involves a minimal use of in-group jargon and a very firm emphasis on relating every fictional event to real characters of a kind that the reader can immediately recognise and identify or empathise with. The universe is wonderful, but only when there is somebody there to wonder at it. Humour also plays an important role in my work, partly because I feel that science fiction shouldn't become too gloomy and portentous, mainly because one of the things we need most these days is a good laugh.

*   *   *

Bob Shaw is a prolific writer whose work shows an enthusiasm for taking the great traditional themes of science fiction and giving them a contemporary voice. While his fiction focuses upon a wide variety of themes, including everything from space legionnairing and alien cartography to spiritual transcendence, and his literary craftsmanship proves him to be comfortable as a humorist, teller of tall tales, or dreamer, all of his work is characterized by competent writing, in-depth characterization, and a fascination with changing perspectives—visual, temporal, and emotional—upon the condition of humankind. Except for a few stories from the 1950's his earliest stories deal with themes common to his later fiction. "...And Isles Where Good Men Lie," for instance, is preoccupied with problems in interpersonal relationships. The need for communication and understanding between a couple whose marriage is shattering echoes the science-fiction problem presented in the narrative, that of stopping misleading signals in an alien satellite from hurtling human beings to panic-stricken death on Earth.

Shaw gained notoriety as the inventor of "slow glass" when, inspired by lines from the poet Moore, he wrote "Light of Other Days." His invention proved to be one which had many clever applications, all successfully and intriguingly explored in the novel *Other Days, Other Eyes,* a complex work which not only shows the impact of an amazing new product, but which ruminates upon larger questions important to Shaw, those of exploitation, personal identity, and privacy, and most importantly the influence of time and perspective upon the affairs, personal and political, of men. Stylistically the book is complex, relying upon vignettes, sometimes referred to as "sidelights," to mesh the personal story of Alban Garrod, whose life is changed when the new type of windshield "glass" he invents turns out to have extraordinary properties, with the far-reaching effects of his invention upon the world. "Slow glass" or "retardite" goes far beyond the usual science-fiction gimmick in that it acts not only as an ingenious invention around which to weave a narrative but also on the symbolic level. This substance, with the capability of visually slowing down time, of holding within itself images of the past, provides Shaw with an excellent vehicle for a discussion of perspective as a means of discovering the truth about oneself. This is a research-and-development story on many levels. As an imaginative concept becomes a product to be used, exploited, and abused, Garrod is similarly manipulated by his tenacious wife Esther who makes their marriage into a travesty of sharing and intense communication. Blinded in an accident in his lab, Esther takes the opportunity falsely to martyr herself and to use "slow glass" spectacles to invade her husband's personal privacy. Meanwhile, society in general has found several perverse applications of "slow glass" spying devices. As Garrod sees his invention used for everything from providing city dwellers with lovely country views, to acting as evidence in murder cases, to poignantly recording for a lonely widower memories of his dead wife and child, he gains perspective upon his own twisted life. In an exchange which shows Shaw at his best, Garrod reveals his invention to Esther whose discouraging comment is only "'You'll get nowhere with it.' 'Think so? Garrod walked to the window, held the rectangular crystal up to it, then strode quickly to the darkest corner of the room. When he turned to face her, Esther took a step back and shielded her eyes. In his hands, blinding in its red-gold magnificence, Garrod held the setting sun." Eventually, after much struggle, he applies his invention to illuminate the truth of his own life.

The "other eyes" or surrogate vision motif is also employed in Shaw's first novel, *Night Walk.* The espionage agent Tallon overcomes his physical blindness by means of spectacles which make it possible for him to see through the eyes of others (humans *and* animals), and on a larger scale he conquers the invisible barriers in null space which have limited men to overpopulation of two worlds. Tallon breaks out of the prison of his blindness in a novel which succeeds as a fastpaced fugitive story but which also shows Shaw again dealing with questions of the perversion of pure thought and invention, and the invasion of privacy. In an effective scene of eerie understatement, Shaw shows the fugitive running, with damaged spectacles and failing vision through a dusky world of the countless half-lit lawns and gardens of an oblivious suburbia, always carrying the secret locked in his mind which will free the crowded masses who rejected him. *Orbitsville* has a similar theme, and incidentally protrays a loving couple who are fugitives from the wrath of despotic President Elizabeth and her Starflight house fleet which controls the only two (again overcrowded) worlds hospitable to man. In a desperate mission to save his wife and son, Captain Garramond discovers a new star, surrounded by a metallic shell whose interior is a vast green hilled fertile haven which Garramond would like to make available to all mankind.

The search for new worlds is taken in another direction in the stylistically different work *Ship of Strangers*. The middle-aged Dave Surgenor, along with a "personable" computer affectionately called Captain Aesop, applies logic and common sense to various problems encountered while making cartographical surveys of apparently dead worlds. *The Palace of Eternity* features another middle-aged hero, Mack Taverner, whose desire to forget the haunting memory of his parents' death at the hands of alien beings leads him first into a lengthy and heroic military career, then to the planet Mnemosyne, one of the only planets not yet scourged by the alien Pythsyccas. Full-scale warfare quickly takes its toll on this sanctuary, significantly named for the muse of memory. Taverner finds that only through transcendence of his self and his past may he join the spiritual awakening of mankind. Tense adventure is the keynote of a book preoccupied with the question of transcendental identity and an extraordinary future for humankind.

Who Goes Here? is the humorous story of a man who joins the Space Legion "to forget" and finds that a memory eraser wipes out his entire identity: it concludes an identity crisis with trancendence into a superbeing. *The Two-Timers* is a contemplative novel relying upon very excellent characterization to tell a tale of doubles and murder. Other works by Shaw include *Medusa's Children*, featuring a down-to-earth protagonist drawn into saving a dreamy society of humans who have adapted to a tenuous and beautiful undersea existence; *A Wreath of Stars*, which describes the congruence of an unseen anti-neutrino world with Earth (significantly, Shaw invents special eyeglasses through which the world and its inhabitants can be viewed); *One Million Tomorrows*, a scientifically implausible work which envisions that immortality could be made available to men but only at the expense of sexual potency; *The Ground Zero Man*, the tale of a man who would like to destroy all nuclear armaments; and *Vertigo*, concerning an Air Patrolman who must overcome his fear of flying engendered by a serious accident.

Shaw is a well-known fan as well as a writer whose works, without exception, show a flair for taking science-fiction themes and giving them an original twist, or an ability to invent his own gimmicks and make them into something extraordinary.

—Rosemary Herbert

SHAWN, Frank S. *See* GOULART, Ron.

SHECKLEY, Robert. American. Born 16 July 1928. Educated at New York University, B.A. 1951. Served in the United States Army, 1946-48. Married Ziva Kwitney in 1957; one daughter and one son. Address: c/o Bantam Books Inc., 666 Fifth Avenue, New York, New York 10019, U.S.A.

SCIENCE-FICTION PUBLICATIONS

Novels

Immortality Delivered. New York, Avalon, 1958; revised edition, as *Immortality Inc.,* New York, Bantam, 1959; London, Gollancz, 1963.
The Status Civilization. New York, New American Library, 1960; London, New English Library, 1967.
Journey Beyond Tomorrow. New York, New American Library, 1962; London, Gollancz, 1964; as *Journey of Joenes,* London, Sphere, 1978.
The Tenth Victim. New York, Ballantine, 1965; London, Mayflower, 1966.
Mindswap. New York, Delacorte Press, and London, Gollancz, 1966.
Dimension of Miracles. New York, Dell, 1968; London, Gollancz, 1969.
Options. New York, Pyramid, 1975; London, Pan, 1977.
Crompton Divided. New York, Holt Rinehart, 1978; as *The Alchemical Marriage of Alistair Crompton,* London, Joseph, 1978.
Futuropolis. New York, A and W, 1978; London, Big O, 1979.

Short Stories

Untouched by Human Hands. New York, Ballantine, 1954; London, Joseph, 1955.
Citizen in Space. New York, Ballantine, 1955; London, New English Library, 1969.
Pilgrimage to Earth. New York, Bantam, 1957; London, Corgi, 1959.
Store of Infinity. New York, Bantam, 1960.
Notions: Unlimited. New York, Bantam, 1960.
Shards of Space. New York, Bantam, and London, Corgi, 1962.
The People Trap. New York, Dell, 1968; London, Gollancz, 1969.
Can You Feel Anything When I Do This? New York, Doubleday, 1971; London, Gollancz, 1972.
The Robert Sheckley Omnibus, edited by Robert Conquest. London, Gollancz, 1973.
The Robot Who Looked Like Me. London, Sphere, 1978.
The Wonderful Worlds of Robert Sheckley. New York, Bantam, 1979.

OTHER PUBLICATIONS

Novels

Calibre .50. New York, Bantam, 1961.
Dead Run. New York, Bantam, 1961.
Live Gold. New York, Bantam, 1962.
The Man in the Water. Evanston, Illinois, Regency, 1962.
White Death. New York, Bantam, 1963.
The Game of X. New York, Delacorte Press, 1965; London, Cape, 1966.
Time Limit. New York, Bantam, and London, New English Library, 1967.

*   *   *

Robert Sheckley is, if we must find a category for him, a metaphysical wit and satirist. His major theme, manifested in dozens of superb stories and novels, is that in an infinite universe "reality" is infinitely variegated, depending upon one's environmental or psychological framework. While some writers would regard this as a nihilistic nightmare, for Sheckley it offers an opportunity for unbounded imaginative romping—precisely the sort of freedom that SF so eagerly welcomes. "The quest for non-ordinary reality is something more than curiosity and wishful thinking," Sheckley once said in a rare public address ("The Search for the Marvellous," delivered at the Institute of Contemporary Arts, London, 1975); "We are too crowded in our everyday lives by replicas of ourselves and by the repetitious artifacts of our days and nights. But we do not quite believe in this prosaic world. Continually we are reminded of the strangeness of birth and death, the vastness of time and space, the unknowability of ourselves." These somber thoughts Sheckley clothes with highly imaginative and entertaining plots. For example, in *Dimension of Miracles* Carmody is brought to the galactic center for a prize he has won in the Intergalactic Sweepstakes. The prize is a sentient being in a gaily wrapped box which takes Carmody on a wild-goose chase through the universe in search of Earth (the Prize Committee does not know the co-ordinates for returning Carmody). Each episode makes it clear that the universe is such that one cannot go home again anyway, just as one cannot step into the same river twice. Carmody's search for home is also a search for self, and on this matter he has quite a bit to learn—such as the fact that the shapes of objects and creatures are a function of environment. What is evil or ugly in one environment may well appear benevolent and lovely when transferred to another.

This idea of the universe as protean and magical serves as a satirical ploy for Sheckley. In "Dreamworld" (*The People Trap*) Lanigan, whose real world is one in which objects are continually changing shape and color, suffers from a recurrent nightmare wherein he finds himself in a world where change is largely imperceptible. "The pavement never once yielded beneath his feet. Over there was the First National City Bank; it had been there yesterday, it would be there tomorrow. Grotesquely devoid of possibilities it would never become a tomb, an airplane...." The satiric tone then darkens: "This was the frozen world. This was the slow motion world of preordination, routine, habituation." Finally, Lanigan becomes trapped in his nightmare—the nightmare which, Sheckley is implying, is *our* nightmare. The nightmare becomes Lanigan's reality ("A dream is the shorter life, a life is the longer dream") and goes insane.

No matter how absurd and wildly episodic Sheckley's plots sometimes become, the metaphysician is always lurking in the wings, cueing us with tidbits of cosmic wisdom which are themselves refreshing. For example, *Mindswap* introduces us to a universe in which people can change bodies like garments. Marvin Flynn gets swindled out of his body by the notorious body-pirate Ze Kraggash, whose ruling philosophy is "If a man cannot retain control of his own body, then he deserves to lose it." During the galaxy-wide search Flynn begins to realize just how indeterminate bodies really are and how useless it is to attach any lasting importance to them. "The acceptance of indeterminacy was the beginning of wisdom," a hermit on some alien world tells him. And after he chases Ze Kraggash into the Twisted World, he attains ultimate wisdom: "Nothing is permanent except our illusions."

Perhaps Sheckley's most dramatic rendering of the indeterminacy of selfhood is "Slaves of Time." Like the solipsistic nightmare world of Robert Heinlein's "All You Zombies," this story depicts some of the uncannily paradoxical things that can happen if one engages in some serious time traveling. Gleister builds a time machine and goes into the future. Because nature "can tolerate a paradox but abhors a vacuum," it instantaneously creates another Gleister to take the first Gleister's place. This new Gleister, identical to the other, but on a different reality-track, also builds a time machine and travels into the future. The inevitable, grim result: an endless stream of Gleisters, each following his own reality-track. "It is strange," Gleister/Mingus says at one point where all the Gleister manifestations convene, "that all of us are one person, yet we represent widely differing viewpoints." And Gleister/Ergon replies, "It's not so strange.... One person is many people even under normal circumstances."

Options offers yet another treatise on reality vs. illusion and mind-as-universe—embedded, but not too deeply, beneath a slapstick surface. Tom Mishkin, an intergalactic trader (" Frozen South African lobster tails, tennis shoes, air conditioners") finds himself stranded somewhere in the Lesser Magellanic Cloud, in need of a hard-to-get spare part for his ship. He is directed to Harmonia, a bizarre world where, as is almost always the case in Sheckley's cosmos, nothing is quite the way it seems. Mishkin and a mealy-mouthed robot set off on a mock-pilgrimage across Harmonia in search of the elusive spare part. To be sure, Harmonia is Tom Mishkin's disorderly mind strewn across an external milieu like an overstuffed closet that had burst open. Monsters pause in their deadly assaults to discuss metaphysical issues with him; carnival men entertain him; he meets poker players who think they are inside their hotel room in Manhattan (and very likely are). In one of the final episodes we get the sense that Mishkin is "really" just a little earth boy who has been engaged in a daydream that would make

Walter Mitty's look dreary ("Tommy! Stop playing now!" "I'm not playing, Mom. This is real.""...Put down that broom and come into the house at once." "It's not a broom, it a spaceship. Anyhow, my robot says..." "And bring that old radio in with you").

Most of Sheckley's works are in some sense explorations of the nature of selfhood. The early story "Shape" (*Untouched by Human Hands*) is about a team of alien space explorers who possess the ability to change shape at will, but whose society has forbidden them to do so (shapes were allotted, and had to be rigorously maintained). No wonder, then, that when they land on a strange planet called Earth, they are so awed by the multitude of shapes, that they cannot bring themselves to return home; instead they joyfully assume the shapes of trees, rocks, animals, humans. And in *Crompton Divided* Alistair Crompton, because of his multiple personality, is forced to undergo "Cleavage"—separation of the personalities, which are then placed in separate bodies and shipped, unknown to the main personality, to remote planets. Crompton, now mild-mannered but totally devoid of spunk, learns what has happened to him and, after raising sufficient funds by embezzling rare and exotic perfumes from his company, embarks on a galaxy-wide search for his lost selves. That this is yet another indictment of society for the pressures it exerts upon us to be consistent, predictable, content citizens is clear from the following passage:

> On all sides of him, the envious Crompton saw people with all their marvelous complexities and contradictions constantly bursting out of the stereotypes that society tried to force on them. He observed prostitutes who were not good-hearted, army sergeants who detested brutality, wealthy men who never gave a cent to charity, Irishmen who hated talking, Italians who could not carry a tune....Most of the human race seemed to live lives of a wonderful and unpredictable richness, erupting into sudden passions and strange calms, saying one thing and meaning another.

To be fully human, Sheckley is suggesting, we have got to be mavericks of selfhood, assuming different roles, letting our imaginations shape our reality. Change and mystery and uncertainty are crucial to our survival; without them the oasis inside our skulls would shrivel into a sterile desert.

—Fred D. White

SHERRIFF, R(obert) C(harles). British. Born in Kingston upon Thames, Surrey, 6 June 1896. Educated at Kingston Grammar School; New College, Oxford, 1931-34. Served as a Captain in the East Surrey Regiment, 1917. Entered the Sun Insurance Company, 1914. Fellow, Society of Antiquaries; Fellow, Royal Society of Literature. *Died 13 November 1975.*

SCIENCE-FICTION PUBLICATIONS

Novel

The Hopkins Manuscript. London, Gollancz, and New York, Macmillan, 1939; revised edition, as *The Cataclysm*, London, Pan, 1958, as *The Hopkins Manuscript*, Macmillan, 1963.

OTHER PUBLICATIONS

Novels

Journey's End, with Vernon Bartlett. London, Gollancz, and New York, Stokes, 1930.
The Fortnight in September. London, Gollancz, 1931; New York, Stokes, 1932.
Greengates. London, Gollancz, and New York, Stokes, 1936.

Chedworth. New York, Macmillan, 1944.
Another Year. London, Heinemann, and New York, Macmillan, 1948.
The Wells of St. Mary's. London, Heinemann, 1962.

Plays

Profit and Loss (produced Surbiton, Surrey, 1923).
Cornlow-in-the-Downs (produced Surbiton, Surrey, 1923).
Badger's Green (as *Mr. Birdie's Finger,* produced Surbiton, Surrey, 1926; revised version, as *Badger's Green,* produced London, 1930). London, Gollancz, 1930; New York, French, 1934; revised version (produced Wimbledon, 1961), London, French, 1962.
Journey's End (produced London, 1928; New York, 1929). London, Gollancz, and New York, Brentano's, 1929.
Windfall (produced London, 1934).
St. Helena, with Jeanne de Casalis (produced London and New York, 1936). London, Gollancz, 1934; New York, Stokes, 1935.
Two Hearts Doubled: A Playlet. London, French, 1935.
Goodbye Mr. Chips (screenplay), with Claudine West and Eric Maschwitz, in *The Best Pictures 1939-1940,* edited by Jerry Wald and Richard Macaulay. New York, Dodd Mead, 1940.
Mrs. Miniver (screenplay), with others, in *Twenty Best Film Plays,* edited by John Gassner and Dudley Nichols. New York, Crown, 1943.
Miss Mabel (produced London, 1948; Coonamesset, Massachusetts, 1950). London, Gollancz, 1949.
Quartet: Stories by W. Somerset Maugham, Screenplays by R.C. Sherriff. London, Heinemann, 1948; New York, Doubleday, 1949.
Trio: Stories and Screen Adaptations, with W. Somerset Maugham and Noel Langley. London, Heinemann, and New York, Doubleday, 1950.
Odd Man Out (screenplay), with F.L. Green, in *Three British Screen Plays,* edited by Roger Manvell. London, Methuen, 1950.
Home at Seven (produced London, 1950). London, Gollancz, 1950; New York, French, 1951.
The Kite, in *Action: Beacon Lights of Literature,* edited by Georgia G. Winn and others. Syracuse, New York, Iroquois, 1952.
The White Carnation (produced London, 1953). London, Heinemann, 1953.
The Long Sunset (broadcast, 1955; produced Manchester, 1955; London, 1961). London, Elek, 1956.
The Telescope (broadcast, 1956; produced London, 1957). Published in *Plays of the Year 15,* London, Elek, 1957.
A Shred of Evidence (produced London, 1960). London, French, 1961.

Screenplays: *The Old Dark House,* with Benn Levy, 1932; *The Invisible Man,* with Philip Wylie, 1933; *The Road Back,* with Charles Kenyon, 1937; *Goodbye Mr. Chips,* with Claudine West and Eric Maschwitz, 1939; *The Four Feathers,* with Arthur Wimperis and Lajos Biro, 1939; *That Hamilton Woman (Lady Hamilton),* with Walter Reisch, 1941; *Unholy Partners,* with others, 1941; *This Above All,* 1942; *Mrs. Miniver,* with others, 1942; *Stand By for Action,* with others, 1943; *Forever and a Day,* with others, 1944; *Odd Man Out,* with F.L. Green, 1947; *Quartet,* 1948; *Mr. Know-All* (in *Trio*), 1950; *No Highway (No Highway in the Sky),* with Alec Coppel and Oscar Millard, 1951; *The Dam Busters,* 1955; *The Night My Number Came Up,* 1955; *Storm over the Nile,* with Lajos Biro and Arthur Wimperis, 1955.

Radio Plays: *The Long Sunset,* 1955; *The Night My Number Came Up,* 1956; *The Telescope,* 1956; *Cards with Uncle Tom,* 1958.

Television Play: *The Ogburn Story,* 1963.

Other

King John's Treasure (juvenile). London, Macmillan, 1954; New York, Macmillan, 1955.
No Leading Lady: An Autobiography. London, Gollancz, 1968.
The Siege of Swayne Castle (juvenile). London, Gollancz, 1973.

Although best known for his plays (the most recent of which include futuristic "visionary adapters"), R.C. Sherriff made two main contributions to science fiction, the 1933 screenplay of *The Invisible Man* and *The Hopkins Manuscript,* a story of planetary disaster. The screenplay focuses on the adverse psychological effects of physical transformation to depict the menace inherent in invisibility, while the novel contrasts the menace of doomsday with the positive effects of crisis: growing loyalty, love, unity, and tolerance.

Though fanciful by scientific criteria, *The Hopkins Manuscript* is dramatic, imaginative, and mildly satiric. Its strength rests in its realistic psychological detail and its unusual point of view: an eccentric and rather Victorian Englishman, fussy, pompous, and endearing, a lunar scholar, breeder of prize poultry, upholder of rural values. He records his and his neighbors' reactions to the discovery that the moon, dislodged from its course and creating tornadoes and tidal waves as it nears earth, may well destroy all life; their preparation for survival, the actual catastrophe (the moon landing in mid-Atlantic), the attempt to rebuild civilization are fascinating because of the mildly satiric and detailed characterization. Throughout Sherriff eulogizes the common rural Englishman as basically honest and hard-working, with a strong sense of responsibility, a love of the land and of the community; but laments the fact that he can be baffled, betrayed, and destroyed by greedy politicians who use patriotism as a weapon to forward private manias and to manipulate the simple commoner, who, left to himself, would live and let live. Ironically, after demonstrating man's capacity to overcome his vanity and selfishness in the common interest of survival against nature, he shows man's capacity for self-destruction in a meaningless and unnecessary war over the crashed moon's extensive wealth. Ultimately a Persian barbarian on a jihad so thoroughly destroys what remains of European civilization that years later an Abyssinian archeologist finds only traces of this lost civilization.

—Gina Macdonald

SHIEL, M(atthew) P(hipps). Also wrote as Gordon Holmes. British. Born on Montserrat Island, West Indies, 21 July 1865. Educated at Harrison College, Barbados; King's College, London; St. Bartholomew's Hospital Medical School, London. Married 1) Carolina García Gomez in 1898 (died), two daughters; 2) Mrs. Gerald Jewson c. 1918. Taught math at a school in Derbyshire, two years. Granted Civil List pension, 1938. *Died 14 February 1947.*

SCIENCE-FICTION PUBLICATIONS

Novels

The Yellow Danger. London, Richards, 1898; New York, Fenno, 1899.
The Purple Cloud. London, Chatto and Windus, 1901; revised edition, London, Gollancz, 1929; New York, Vanguard Press, 1930.
The Lord of the Sea. London, Richards, and New York, Stokes, 1901; revised edition, New York, Knopf, 1924; London, Gollancz, 1929.
The Yellow Wave. London, Ward Lock, 1905.
The Isle of Lies. London, Laurie, 1909.
This Knot of Life. London, Everett, 1909.
The Dragon. London, Richards, 1913; New York, Clode, 1914; as *The Yellow Peril,* London, Gollancz, 1929.
This above All. New York, Vanguard Press, 1933; as *Above All Else,* London, Cole, 1943.
The Young Men Are Coming! London, Allen and Unwin, and New York, Vanguard Press, 1937.

Short Stories

Shapes in the Fire. London, Lane, and Boston, Roberts, 1896.
The Pale Ape and Other Pulses. London, Laurie, 1911.
The Invisible Voices, with John Gawsworth. London, Richards, 1935; New York, Vanguard Press, 1936.
The Best Short Stories of M.P. Shiel, edited by John Gawsworth. London, Gollancz, 1948.

OTHER PUBLICATIONS

Novels

The Rajah's Sapphire. London, Ward Lock, 1896.
Contraband of War. London, Richards, 1899; revised edition, London, Pearson, 1914; Ridgewood, New Jersey, Gregg Press, 1968.
Cold Steel. London, Richards, 1899; New York, Brentano's, 1900; revised edition, London, Gollancz, and New York, Vanguard Press, 1929.
The Man-Stealers. London, Hutchinson, and Philadelphia, Lippincott, 1900; revised edition, Hutchinson, 1927.
The Weird o' It. London, Richards, 1902.
Unto the Third Generation. London, Chatto and Windus, 1903.
The Evil That Men Do. London, Ward Lock, 1904.
The Lost Viol. New York, Clode, 1905; London, Ward Lock, 1908.
The Last Miracle. London, Laurie, 1907; revised edition, London, Gollancz, 1929.
The White Wedding. London, Laurie, 1908.
Children of the Wind. London, Laurie, 1908.
Dr. Krasinski's Secret. New York, Vanguard Press, 1929; London, Jarrolds, 1930.
The Black Box. New York, Vanguard Press, 1930; London, Richards, 1931.
Say Au R'Voir but Not Goodbye. London, Benn, 1933.

Novels as Gordon Holmes (with Louis Tracy)

An American Emperor. New York, Putnam, and London, Pearson, 1897.
The Late Tenant. New York, Clode, 1906; London, Cassell, 1907.
By Force of Circumstance. New York, Clode, 1909; London, Mills and Boon, 1910.
The House of Silence. New York, Clode, 1911; as *The Silent House*, London, Nash, 1911.

Short Stories

Prince Zaleski. London, Lane, and Boston, Roberts, 1895.
How the Old Woman Got Home. London, Richards, 1927; New York, Vanguard Press, 1928.
Here Comes the Lady. London, Richards, 1928.
Xélucha and Others. Sauk City, Wisconsin, Arkham House, 1975.
Prince Zaleski and Cummings King Monk. Sauk City, Wisconsin, Arkham House, 1977.

Verse

(*Poems*), edited by John Gawsworth. London, Richards, 1936.

Other

Science, Life, and Literature. London, Williams and Norgate, 1950.

Translator, *The Hungarian Revolution: An Eyewitness's Account*, by Charles Henry Schmitt. London, Worker's Socialist Federation, 1919.

*

Bibliography: *The Works of M.P. Shiel: A Study in Bibliography* by A. Reynolds Morse, Los Angeles, Fantasy, 1948.

Certainly one of the most idiosyncratic writers of fantastic fiction of the late 19th and early 20th centuries, M.P. Shiel is primarily remembered today for a single novel, *The Purple Cloud*, although during his own lifetime he was perhaps better known for his tales of imaginary warfare warning of Jewish conspiracies and invading hordes of Oriental devils. A capable stylist whose fine attention to detail can make the most unlikely fantasies persuasive, Shiel also aspired to philosophy, psychology, economics, and historical theory. Unfortunately, his intellectual theories are often no less bizarre than his imaginative situations, and tend to weaken most of his narratives.

Though Shiel produced more than 20 novels and a number of short stories, many of them are occult and historical romances, and relatively few are of interest to modern readers of science fiction. His first major work of science fiction followed in the tradition of future war narratives that became popular in England in the 1870's and 1880's. *The Yellow Danger* concerns the conquest by Japan and China of all Europe except for England, which successfully retaliates with torpedoes and biological warfare and finally comes to rule the world itself. The novel is as notable for its blatant racism as for its detailed and well-thought-out accounts of imaginary battle movements. In *The Lord of the Sea* Europe is again conquered, this time by Jews, and the retaliation comes from a kind of superman who constructs enormous floating fortresses to rule the seas, has the Jews banished to Palestine, and—in a decidedly strange denouement—reveals himself to be a Jew, and in fact the Second Coming! *This Knot of Life* combines themes from both novels in a tale of an Oriental invasion repelled by a European master race (literally called "Overmen") who invent a weapon that causes blindness. *The Young Men Are Coming!* concerns another favorite theme—the superiority of science to religion. A scientist is inspired (by aliens, who kidnap him to a moon of Jupiter) to set about a kind of reverse holy war to overthrow religion with science.

While few of these novels have retained readers, Shiel's masterpiece, *The Purple Cloud*, remains one of the most widely read end-of-the-world stories. Loosely modeled on Mary Shelley's *The Last Man* (1826), *The Purple Cloud* is essentially a study of conflicting creative and destructive impulses as characterized by a single man, Adam Jefferson, who conspires to be the first man to reach the north pole and returns to find the rest of humanity annihilated by a purple volcanic gas that has since dissipated. The "black" and "white" forces that struggled for Jefferson's personality even before he left for the pole create a strange and conflicting pattern of behavior in this last man. His only recreation becomes the burning of the huge cities that humanity left behind, and when he finds another survivor—a girl whose mind is a virtual *tabula rasa* from having lived alone in a dungeon her entire life (she was born just as the gas was dissipating)—he experiences a strange impulse to kill and eat her. But her companionship finally seems to restore a moral balance in Jefferson, and with her he sets out to start the race anew. Although the novel may not quite deserve the lavish praise heaped on it by H.G. Wells, Hugh Walpole, and Arthur Machen, it is an eerily fascinating and strangely powerful novel.

Shiel probably deserves greater attention than he has thus far received as an important figure in the history of science fiction. The intolerance and racial paranoia that characterize many of his works understandably put off many readers, but his works are not without substance, and at least one of them has become an acknowledged classic.

—Gary K. Wolfe

SHIRAS, Wilmar H(ouse). Also writes as Jane Howes. American. Born in Boston, Massachusetts, 23 September 1908. Educated at Holy Names College, Oakland, California; University of California, Berkeley, M.A. 1956. Married Russell Shiras in 1927; three daughters and two sons. Address: 3720 Rhoda Avenue, Oakland, California 94602, U.S.A.

SCIENCE-FICTION PUBLICATIONS

Short Stories

Children of the Atom.   New York, Gnome Press, 1953; London, Boardman, 1954.

Uncollected Short Stories

"Backward, Turn Backward," in *New Worlds of Fantasy 2*, edited by Terry Carr.   New York, Ace, 1970.
"Shadow-Led," in *Fantastic* (New York), October 1971.
"Reality," in *Fantastic* (New York), February 1972.
"Bird-Song," in *Fantastic* (New York), April 1973.

OTHER PUBLICATIONS

Other

Slow Dawning (as June Howes).   St. Louis, Herder, 1946.

Wilmar H. Shiras comments:
   "In Hiding" grew out of my wondering whether very high-I.Q. children would have problems; the rest of the book deals with other such children and their problems.

*   *   *

   Wilmar H. Shiras's total literary output has been far from copious, and even of the total number of works, not all have been science fiction. In fact, she is known almost entirely for a single volume, *Children of the Atom.* Though it reveals serious shortcomings and limitations, its virtues are even greater.
   Children of the Atom originated in three stories published in *Astounding*; the author added two further stories, collecting the five into an episodic work which experienced a considerable vogue in the 1950's. ("In Hiding," the first story in the cycle, has been anthologized no fewer than nine times.) The basic premise of the stories, questionable even in 1948 and now recognized as an absurdity, is that an accident in a nuclear industrial plant will produce a uniform mutation in the offspring of all workers in the plant. Specifically, all children born to women pregnant at the time of the accident, or conceived by workers present at the accident, will be of genius-grade intelligence and of highly creative temperament. The author postulates, further, that all of the workers exposed to the accident will die within approximately two years, but that their children will be perfect. Shiras's main concern is the problems of adjustment and development of these children in later years. Her major adult protagonists are a group of sympathetic educators and psychologists who discover the existence of these children (who are "in hiding"), and the existence of a network of communication among them. The author assumes that these mentally superior children will be automatically outcasts. The boys, with their inclination to study science, will not fit into a society which emphasizes athletics and violent competition; the girls, inclined toward art, will be similarly excluded from a society which emphasizes prettiness and socialization. Thus the children, in order to survive, hide their superiority beneath a veneer of assumed ordinariness.
   Although the author's notions of mutation were quickly seen as absurd, her portrayal of the "superior" children—hyperintellectual adolescents, the boys frequently myopic and unathletic, the girls similarly not adept at the sex-role dictates of the day—struck a strong responsive chord in the typical science-fiction readers of the period. Both Marion Zimmer Bradley and Barry Malzberg, in notes published with a 1978 reissue of the book, comment upon the sense of identity felt by the original readers with the youngsters in the book. It is this uncanny identification of reader with character which gave the book its popularity in the 1950's. In later years the reading of science fiction gained a far greater acceptance in schools, *aficionados* ceased to be automatic outcasts, and this sense of identity became weakened although it did not cease altogether.
   In its later segments the novel shows unfortunate tendencies to degenerate into piously one-sided theological argumentation, and at the end the adult sponsors of the brilliant children are told by the children themselves that it will be best to terminate their experimen-

tal community and disperse themselves among the general populace. This ending, too, has proved controversial among readers of the book, many of them indicating that they see in it a surrender to the very standards of mediocrity and conformism which the children had earlier sought to escape. Shiras has continued to produce short works of science fiction at long intervals. These have been uniformly pleasant, low-keyed, generally concerned with children, and have received little attention from readers.

—Richard A. Lupoff

———————

SHUTE, Nevil (Nevil Shute Norway).   British.   Born in Ealing, London, 17 January 1899. Educated at Dragon School, Oxford; Shrewsbury School, Shropshire; Royal Military Academy, Woolwich, London; Balliol College, Oxford, B.A. Served as a private in the Suffolk Regiment, British Army, 1918; commissioned in the Royal Naval Volunteer Reserve, 1940: Lieutenant Commander; retired 1945. Married Frances Mary Heaton in 1931; two daughters. Calculator, de Havilland Aircraft Company, 1922-24; Chief Calculator, 1925, and Deputy Chief Engineer, 1928, on the construction of Rigid Airship R.100 for the Airship Guarantee Company: twice flew Atlantic in R.100, 1930; Managing Director, Yorkshire Aeroplane Club Ltd., 1927-30; Founder and Joint Managing Director, Airspeed Ltd., airplane constructors, 1931-38. After World War II lived in Australia. Fellow, Royal Aeronautical Society. *Died 12 January 1960.*

SCIENCE-FICTION PUBLICATIONS

Novels

What Happened to the Corbetts.   London, Heinemann, 1939; as *Ordeal*, New York, Morrow, 1939.
An Old Captivity.   London, Heinemann, and New York, Morrow, 1940.
No Highway.   London, Heinemann, and New York, Morrow, 1948.
In the Wet.   London, Heinemann, and New York, Morrow, 1953.
On the Beach.   London, Heinemann, and New York, Morrow, 1957.
The Rainbow and the Rose.   London, Heinemann, and New York, Morrow, 1958.

OTHER PUBLICATIONS

Novels

Marazan.   London, Cassell, 1926.
So Disdained.   London, Cassell, 1928; as *Mysterious Aviator*, Boston, Houghton Mifflin, 1928.
Lonely Road.   London, Cassell, and New York, Morrow, 1932.
Ruined City.   London, Cassell, 1938; as *Kindling*, New York, Morrow, 1938.
Landfall: A Channel Story.   London, Heinemann, and New York, Morrow, 1940.
Pied Piper.   New York, Morrow, 1941; London, Heinemann, 1942.
Pastoral.   London, Heinemann, and New York, Morrow, 1944.
Most Secret.   London, Heinemann, and New York, Morrow, 1945.
The Chequer Board.   London, Heinemann, and New York, Morrow, 1947.
A Town Like Alice.   London, Heinemann, 1950; as *The Legacy*, New York, Morrow, 1950.
Round the Bend.   London, Heinemann, and New York, Morrow, 1951.

The Far Country.   London, Heinemann, and New York, Morrow, 1952.
Requiem for a Wren.   London, Heinemann, 1955; as *The Breaking Wave*, New York, Morrow, 1955.
Beyond the Black Stump.   London, Heinemann, and New York, Morrow, 1956.
Trustee from the Toolroom.   London, Heinemann, and New York, Morrow, 1960.
Stephen Morris.   London, Heinemann, and New York, Morrow, 1961.

Play

Vinland the Good (screenplay).   London, Heinemann, and New York, Morrow, 1946.

Other

Slide Rule: The Autobiography of an Engineer.   London, Heinemann, and New York, Morrow, 1954.

*   *   *

Nevil Shute's science-fiction novels make up only a quarter of his output of 22 novels. Yet like all his work, the science fiction profits from Shute's ability to create strong, interesting characters. Although without exception ordinary middle-class people, living calm, almost prosaic lives, these characters are of interest because of their devotion to duty and their pursuit of some personal goal. These goals are as divergent as planting next year's garden in the face of death, finding a missing aircraft part, or providing proof for the Viking settlement in North America. But it is the people and their absorption in their goals in the face of gargantuan difficulties that draw the reader into the story. Shute's novels move at a very leisurely pace, full of details of country, city, and daily routine. Through the wealth of detail a verisimilitude develops so that the sufferings and triumphs of the characters are shared rather than observed. *On the Beach* is filled with characters who draw such interest. Peter and Mary Holmes calmly plant next spring's bulbs and buy a playpen for their daughter Jennifer, even though they know they will never see the bulbs bloom, nor see their daughter use the playpen. So slowly does the atomic fallout move that the Holmes's wait becomes the reader's wait as the world moves inexorably to its end.

No Highway, too, contains characters whose dedication to duty provides a way to live. Mr. Honey, a scientist studying metal fatigue, allows his daughter to locate the missing tail of a crashed plane through a clairvoyant hypnotic session. Unlike the characters who watch the proceedings, the reader is not shocked, for we are convinced, along with Honey, that the experiment is vital. *An Old Captivity, In the Wet, What Happened to the Corbetts,* and *The Rainbow and the Rose* are science-fiction works filled with ordinary people who face tremendous odds yet manage to survive.

—Walter E. Meyers

SILLITOE, Alan. British. Born in Nottingham, 4 March 1928. Educated in Nottingham schools to the age of 14. Served as a radio operator in the Royal Air Force, 1946-49. Married the poet Ruth Fainlight in 1959; two children. Since 1970, Literary Adviser to W.H. Allen, publishers, London. Recipient: Authors Club prize, 1958; Hawthornden Prize, 1960. Address: 21 The Street, Wittersham, Kent, England.

SCIENCE-FICTION PUBLICATIONS

Novels

The General.   London, W.H. Allen, 1960; New York, Knopf, 1961; as *Counterpoint*, New York, Avon, 1968.
Travels in Nihilon.   London, W.H. Allen, 1971; New York, Scribner, 1972.

OTHER PUBLICATIONS

Novels

Saturday Night and Sunday Morning.   London, W.H. Allen, 1958; New York, Knopf, 1959.
Key to the Door.   London, W.H. Allen, 1961; New York, Knopf, 1962.
The Death of William Posters.   London, Macmillan, and New York, Knopf, 1965.
A Tree on Fire.   London, Macmillan, 1967; New York, Doubleday, 1968.
A Start in Life.   London, W.H. Allen, 1970; New York, Scribner, 1971.
Raw Material.   London, W.H. Allen, 1972; New York, Scribner, 1973.
The Flame of Life.   London, W.H. Allen, 1974.
The Widower's Son.   London, W.H. Allen, 1976; New York, Harper, 1977.
The Storyteller.   London, W.H. Allen, 1979; New York, Simon and Schuster, 1980.

Short Stories

The Loneliness of the Long Distance Runner.   London, W.H. Allen, 1959; New York, Knopf, 1960.
The Ragman's Daughter.   London, W.H. Allen, 1963; New York, Knopf, 1964.
A Sillitoe Selection, edited by Michael Marland.   London, Longman, 1968.
Guzman Go Home.   London, Macmillan, 1968; New York, Doubleday, 1969.
Men, Women, and Children.   London, W.H. Allen, 1973; New York, Scribner, 1974.
Down to the Bone.   Exeter, Wheaton, 1976.
The Second Chance.   London, Cape, and New York, Simon and Schuster, 1981.

Plays

The Ragman's Daughter (produced Felixstowe, Suffolk, 1966).
All Citizens Are Soldiers, with Ruth Fainlight, adaptation of a play by Lope de Vega (produced Stratford upon Avon and London, 1967).   London, Macmillan, and Chester Springs, Pennsylvania, Dufour, 1969.
The Slot Machine (as *This Foreign Field*, produced London, 1970).   Included in *Three Plays*, 1978.
Pit Strike (televised, 1977).   Included in *Three Plays*, 1978.
The Interview (produced London, 1978).   Included in *Three Plays*, 1978.
Three Plays (includes *The Slot Machine, Pit Strike, The Interview*).   London, W.H. Allen, 1978.

Screenplays: *Saturday Night and Sunday Morning*, 1960; *The Loneliness of the Long Distance Runner*, 1961; *The Ragman's Daughter*, 1974.

Television Play: *Pit Strike*, 1977.

Verse

Without Beer or Bread.   London, Outposts, 1957.
The Rats and Other Poems.   London, W.H. Allen, 1960.
A Falling Out of Love and Other Poems.   London, W.H. Allen, 1964.

Love in the Environs of Voronezh.   London, Macmillan, 1968;
New York, Doubleday, 1970.
Shaman and Other Poems.   London, Turret, 1968.
Poems, with Ted Hughes and Rugh Fainlight.   London, Rainbow
Press, 1971.
Barbarians and Other Poems.   London, Turret, 1974.
Storm: New Poems.   London, W.H. Allen, 1974.
Day-Dream Communique.   Knotting, Bedfordshire, Sceptre Press,
1977.
From "Snow on the North Side of Lucifer."   Knotting, Bedford-
shire, Sceptre Press, 1979.
Snow on the North Side of Lucifer.   London, W.H. Allen, 1979.

Other

Road to Volgograd (travel).   London, W.H. Allen, and New York,
Knopf, 1964.
The City Adventures of Marmalade Jim (juvenile).   London,
Macmillan, 1967; revised edition, London, Robson, 1977.
Mountains and Caverns: Selected Essays.   London, W.H. Allen,
1975.
Big John and the Stars (juvenile).   London, Robson, 1977.
The Incredible Fencing Fleas (juvenile).   London, Robson, 1978.
Marmalade Jim at the Farm (juvenile).   London, Robson, 1980.

Editor, *Poems for Shakespeare 7.*   London, Bear Gardens Museum
and Arts Centre, 1979.

*   *   *

The distinguished author Alan Sillitoe has created an appalling
imaginary country. *Travels in Nihilon* should not be put into the
hands of nervous tourists entering any foreign land.

Shots at the frontier disturb the everyday round of compulsory
drunken driving, robbery, forgery, and other forms of cheerful
self-expression which flourish in Nihilon. Five travellers collecting
information for a guide book barely have time to orient themselves
among the naked air-hostesses, rapacious officials, and news
broadcasts ("Good Afternoon...here are the Lies...") before they are
drawn severally into a revolution. A certain xenophobia is apparent
for the travellers seem Anglo-Saxon, although one, Benjamin
Smith, is a former revolutionary returning home. The style, with its
overtones of Butler and Swift, might be described as "mad man-
darin." Bright ideas from shadowy President Nil include a Geriatric
army, Killing Licenses, regularly manipulated scandals and disasters, a War Ministry financed by pornographic novels, and a space
program involving a "honeymoon" in space. Adam and Jaquiline,
two of the travellers, come by circuitous means to take part in this
televised spectacular. "Nihilistic Private Enterprise," muses the
President, "works because it enslaves most of the population for the
benefit of a small portion of it. Thus it is unfair. To be fair all must
be enslaved and only socialism can do that." As the travellers leave,
without regret, the New Regime has abolished theft and is confiscat-
ing the property of all tourists.

—Cherry Wilder

SILVERBERG, Robert.   Also writes as Walter Chapman; Ivar
Jorgensen; Calvin M. Knox; David Osborne; Robert Randall; Lee
Sebastian.   American.   Born in New York City, 15 January 1935.
Educated at Columbia University, New York, A.B. 1956. Married
Barbara H. Brown in 1956. Full-time writer: Associate Editor,
Amazing, January 1969 issue, and Associate Editor, *Fantastic*,
February-April 1969 issues. President, Science Fiction Writers of
America, 1967-68. Recipient: Hugo Award, 1956, 1969; Nebula
Award, for story, 1969, 1971, 1974, for novel, 1971. Guest of Honor,
28th World Science Fiction Convention, 1970. Agent: Scott Mere-
dith Literary Agency, 845 Third Avenue, New York, New York
10022. Address: Box 13160 Station E, Oakland, California 94661,
U.S.A.

SCIENCE-FICTION PUBLICATIONS

Novels (series: Nidor)

Revolt on Alpha C (juvenile).   New York, Crowell, 1955.
The Thirteenth Immortal.   New York, Ace, 1957.
Master of Life and Death.   New York, Ace, 1957; London, Sidg-
wick and Jackson, 1977.
The Shrouded Planet (Nidor; as Robert Randall, with Randall
Garrett).   New York, Gnome Press, 1957; London, Mayflower,
1964.
Invaders from Earth.   New York, Ace, 1958; London, Sidgwick
and Jackson, 1977.
Starman's Quest (juvenile).   New York, Gnome Press, 1958.
Invincible Barriers (as David Osborne).   New York, Avalon, 1958.
Stepsons of Terra.   New York, Ace, 1958.
Aliens from Space (as David Osborne).   New York, Avalon, 1958.
The Dawning Light (Nidor; as Robert Randall, with Randall Gar-
rett).   New York, Gnome Press, 1959; London, Mayflower,
1964.
The Planet Killers.   New York, Ace, 1959.
Lost Race of Mars (juvenile).   Philadelphia, Winston, 1960.
Collision Course.   New York, Avalon, 1961.
The Seed of Earth.   New York, Ace, 1962; London, Hamlyn, 1978.
Recalled to Life.   New York, Lancer, 1962; London, Gollancz,
1974.
The Silent Invaders.   New York, Ace, 1963; London, Dobson,
1975.
Regan's Planet.   New York, Pyramid, 1964.
Time of the Great Freeze (juvenile).   New York, Holt Rinehart,
1965.
Conquerors from the Darkness (juvenile).   New York, Holt Rine-
hart, 1965.
The Gate of Worlds (juvenile).   New York, Holt Rinehart, 1967;
London, Gollancz, 1978.
To Open the Sky.   New York, Ballantine, 1967; London, Sphere,
1970.
Thorns.   New York, Ballantine, 1967; London, Rapp and Whit-
ing, 1969.
Those Who Watch.   New York, New American Library, 1967;
London, New English Library, 1977.
The Time-Hoppers.   New York, Doubleday, 1967; London, Sidg-
wick and Jackson, 1968.
Planet of Death.   New York, Holt Rinehart, 1967.
Hawksbill Station.   New York, Doubleday, 1968; as *The Anvil of
Time*, London, Sidgwick and Jackson, 1969.
The Masks of Time.   New York, Ballantine, 1968; as *Vornan-19*,
London, Sidgwick and Jackson, 1970.
Up the Line.   New York, Ballantine, 1969.
Nightwings.   New York, Avon, 1969; London, Sidgwick and Jack-
son, 1972.
Across a Billion Years (juvenile).   New York, Dial Press, 1969;
London, Gollancz, 1977.
The Man in the Maze (juvenile).   New York, Avon, and London,
Sidgwick and Jackson, 1969.
Three Survived (juvenile).   New York, Holt Rinehart, 1969.
To Live Again.   New York, Doubleday, 1969; London, Sidgwick
and Jackson, 1975.
World's Fair 1992 (juvenile).   Chicago, Follett, 1970.
Downward to the Earth.   New York, Doubleday, 1970; London,
Gollancz, 1977.
Tower of Glass.   New York, Scribner, 1970; London, Panther,
1976.
The World Inside.   New York, Doubleday, 1971; London, Mil-
lington, 1976.
A Time of Changes.   New York, Doubleday, 1971; London, Gol-
lancz, 1973.
Son of Man.   New York, Ballantine, 1971; London, Panther, 1979.
The Book of Skulls.   New York, Scribner, 1972; London, Gol-
lancz, 1978.
Dying Inside.   New York, Scribner, 1972; London, Sidgwick and
Jackson, 1974.
The Second Trip.   New York, Doubleday, 1972; London, Gol-
lancz, 1979.

The Stochastic Man. New York, Harper, 1975; London, Gollancz, 1976.
Shadrach in the Furnace. Indianapolis, Bobbs Merrill, 1976; London, Gollancz, 1977.
Lord Valentine's Castle. New York, Harper, and London, Gollancz, 1980.

Novels as Ivar Jorgensen

Starhaven. New York, Avalon, 1958.
Whom the Gods Would Slay. New York, Belmont, 1968.
The Deadly Sky. New York, Pinnacle, 1971.

Novels as Calvin M. Knox

Lest We Forget Thee, Earth. New York, Ace, 1958.
The Plot Against Earth. New York, Ace, 1959.
One of Our Asteroids Is Missing. New York, Ace, 1964.

Short Stories

Next Stop the Stars. New York, Ace, 1962; London, Dobson, 1979.
Godling, Go Home! New York, Belmont, 1964.
To Worlds Beyond. Philadelphia, Chilton, 1965; London, Sphere, 1969.
Needle in a Timestack. New York, Ballantine, 1966; London, Sphere, 1967.
To Open the Sky. New York, Ballantine, 1967.
The Calibrated Alligator (juvenile). New York, Holt Rinehart, 1969.
Dimension Thirteen. New York, Ballantine, 1969.
Parsecs and Parables. New York, Doubleday, 1970; London, Hale, 1973.
The Cube Root of Uncertainty. London, Macmillan, 1970.
Moonferns and Starsongs. New York, Ballantine, 1971.
The Reality Trip and Other Implausibilities. New York, Ballantine, 1972.
Valley Beyond Time. New York, Dell, 1973.
Unfamiliar Territory. New York, Scribner, 1973; London, Gollancz, 1974.
Earth's Other Shadow. New York, New American Library, 1973; London, Millington, 1977.
Born with the Dead. New York, Random House, 1974; London, Gollancz, 1975.
Sundance. Nashville, Nelson, 1974; London, Abelard Schuman, 1975.
Sunrise on Mercury (juvenile). Nashville, Nelson, 1975.
The Feast of St. Dionysus. New York, Scribner, 1975; London, Gollancz, 1976.
The Shores of Tomorrow. Nashville, Nelson, 1976.
The Best of Robert Silverberg. New York, Pocket Books, 1976; London, Sidgwick and Jackson, 1977.
Capricorn Games. New York, Random House, 1976; London, Gollancz, 1978.
The Songs of Summer. London, Gollancz, 1979.

OTHER PUBLICATIONS

Other

Treasures Beneath the Sea (juvenile). Racine, Wisconsin, Whitman, 1960.
First American into Space. Derby, Connecticut, Monarch, 1961.
Lost Cities and Vanished Civilizations (juvenile). Philadelphia, Chilton, 1962.
The Fabulous Rockefellers. Derby, Connecticut, Monarch, 1963.
Sunken History: The Story of Underwater Archaeology (juvenile). Philadelphia, Chilton, 1963.
15 Battles That Changed the World. New York, Putnam, 1963.
Home of the Red Man: Indian North America Before Columbus (juvenile). Greenwich, Connecticut, New York Graphic Society, 1963.
Empires in the Dust. Philadelphia, Chilton, 1963.

The Great Doctors (juvenile). New York, Putnam, 1964.
Akhnaten, The Rebel Pharaoh. Philadelphia, Chilton, 1964.
The Man Who Found Nineveh: The Story of Austen Henry Layard (juvenile). New York, Holt Rinehart, 1964; Kingswood, Surrey World's Work, 1968.
Man Before Adam. Philadelphia, Macrae Smith, 1964.
The Loneliest Continent (as Walker Chapman). Greenwich, Connecticut, New York Graphic Society, 1965; London, Jarrolds, 1967.
Scientists and Scoundrels: A Book of Hoaxes. New York, Crowell, 1965.
The World of Coral (juvenile). New York, Duell, 1965.
The Mask of Akhnaten (juvenile). New York, Macmillan, 1965.
Socrates (juvenile). New York, Putnam, 1965.
The Old Ones: Indians of the American Southwest. Greenwich, Connecticut, New York Graphic Society, 1965.
Men Who Mastered the Atom. New York, Putnam, 1965.
The Great Wall of China. Philadelphia, Chilton, 1965.
Niels Bohr, The Man Who Mapped the Atom (juvenile). Philadelphia, Macrae Smith, 1965.
Forgotten by Time: A Book of Living Fossils (juvenile). New York, Crowell, 1966.
Frontiers of Archaeology. Philadelphia, Chilton, 1966.
Kublai Khan, Lord of Xanadu (juvenile; as Walker Chapman). Indianapolis, Bobbs Merrill, 1966.
The Long Rampart: The Story of the Great Wall of China. Philadelphia, Chilton, 1966.
Rivers (juvenile; as Lee Sebastian). New York, Holt Rinehart, 1966.
Bridges. Philadelphia, Macrae Smith, 1966.
To the Rock of Darius: The Story of Henry Rawlinson (juvenile). New York, Holt Rinehart, 1966.
The Dawn of Medicine. New York, Putnam, 1967.
The Adventures of Nat Palmer, Antarctic Explorer. New York, McGraw Hill, 1967.
The Auk, The Dodo, and the Oryx. New York, Crowell, 1967; Kingswood, Surrey, World's Work, 1969.
The Golden Dream: Seekers of El Dorado. Indianapolis, Bobbs Merrill, 1967.
Men Against Time: Salvage Archaeology in the United States. New York, Macmillan, 1967.
The Morning of Mankind. Greenwich, Connecticut, New York Graphic Society, 1967; Kingswood, Surrey, World's Work, 1970.
The World of the Rain Forest. New York, Meredith Press, 1967.
Light for the World: Edison and the Power Industry. Princeton, New Jersey, Van Nostrand, 1967.
Four Men Who Changed the Universe (juvenile). New York, Putnam, 1968.
Ghost Towns of the American West. New York, Crowell, 1968.
Mound Builders of Ancient America. Greenwich, Connecticut, New York Graphic Society, 1968.
The South Pole (juvenile; as Lee Sebastian). New York, Holt Rinehart, 1968.
Stormy Voyager: The Story of Charles Wilkes. Philadelphia, Lippincott, 1968.
The World of the Ocean Depths. New York, Meredith Press, 1968; Kingswood, Surrey, World's Work, 1970.
Bruce of the Blue Nile (juvenile). New York, Holt Rinehart, 1969.
The Challenge of Climate: Man and His Environment. New York, Meredith Press, 1969; Kingswood, Surrey, World's Work, 1971.
Vanishing Giants: The Story of the Sequoias. New York, Simon and Schuster, 1969.
Wonders of Ancient Chinese Science. New York, Hawthorn, 1969.
The World of Space. New York, Meredith Press, 1969.
If I Forget Thee, O Jerusalem: American Jews and the State of Israel. New York, Morrow, 1970.
Mammoths, Mastodons, and Man. New York, McGraw Hill, 1970; Kingswood, Surrey, World's Work, 1972.
The Pueblo Revolt. New York, Weybright and Talley, 1970.
The Seven Wonders of the Ancient World (juvenile). New York, Crowell Collier, 1970.
Before the Sphinx. New York, Nelson, 1971.
Clocks for the Ages: How Scientists Date the Past. New York, Macmillan, 1971.

To the Western Shore: Growth of the United States 1776-1853.
New York, Doubleday, 1971.
Into Space, with Arthur C. Clarke. New York, Harper, 1971.
John Muir: Prophet among the Glaciers. New York, Putnam,
1972.
The Longest Voyage: Circumnavigation in the Age of Discovery.
Indianapolis, Bobbs Merrill, 1972.
The Realm of Prester John. New York, Doubleday, 1972.
The World Within the Ocean Wave. New York, Weybright and
Talley, 1972.
The World Within the Tide Pool. New York, Weybright and
Talley, 1972.
"Introduction to *Sundance,*" in *Those Who Can,* edited by Robin
Scott Wilson. New York, New American Library, 1973.
Drug Themes in Science Fiction. Rockville, Maryland, National
Institute on Drug Abuse, 1974.
"The Profession of Science Fiction IX: Sounding Brass, Tinkling
Cymbal," in *Foundation 7-8* (London), March 1975.

Editor, *Great Adventures in Archaeology.* New York, Dial Press,
1964; London, Hale, 1966.
Editor, *Earthmen and Strangers.* New York, Duell, 1966.
Editor (as Walker Chapman), *Antarctic Conquest.* Indianapolis,
Bobbs Merrill, 1966.
Editor, *Voyagers in Time.* New York, Meredith Press, 1967.
Editor, *Men and Machines.* New York, Meredith Press, 1968.
Editor, *Mind to Mind.* New York, Meredith Press, 1968.
Editor, *Tomorrow's Worlds.* New York, Meredith Press, 1969.
Editor, *Dark Stars.* New York, Ballantine, 1969; London, Ballan-
tine, 1971.
Editor, *Three for Tomorrow.* New York, Meredith Press, 1969;
London, Gollancz, 1970.
Editor, *The Mirror of Infinity: A Critics' Anthology of Science
Fiction.* New York, Harper, 1970; London, Sidgwick and Jack-
son, 1971.
Editor, *Science Fiction Hall of Fame 1.* New York, Doubleday,
1970; London, Gollancz, 1971.
Editor, *The Ends of Time.* New York, Hawthorn, 1970.
Editor, *Great Short Novels of Science Fiction.* New York, Ballan-
tine, 1970; London, Pan, 1971.
Editor, *Worlds of Maybe.* New York, Nelson, 1970.
Editor, *Alpha 1-9.* New York, Ballantine, 5 vols., 1970-74; New
York, Berkley, 4 vols., 1975-78.
Editor, *Four Futures.* New York, Hawthorn, 1971.
Editor, *The Science Fiction Bestiary.* New York, Nelson, 1971.
Editor, *To the Stars.* New York, Hawthorn, 1971.
Editor, *New Dimensions 1-11* (vol. 11 edited with Marta Randall).
New York, Doubleday, 3 vols., 1971-73; New York, New Ameri-
can Library, 1 vol., 1974; New York, Harper, 6 vols., 1975-80;
New York, Pocket Books, 1 vol., 1980; 5-7 published London,
Gollancz, 3 vols., 1976-77.
Editor, *The Day the Sun Stood Still.* Nashville, Nelson, 1972.
Editor, *Invaders from Space.* New York, Hawthorn, 1972.
Editor, *Beyond Control.* Nashville, Nelson, 1972; London, Sidg-
wick and Jackson, 1973.
Editor, *Deep Space.* Nashville, Nelson, 1973; London, Abelard
Schuman, 1976.
Editor, *Chains of the Sea.* Nashville, Nelson, 1973.
Editor, *No Mind of Man.* New York, Hawthorn, 1973.
Editor, *Other Dimensions.* New York, Hawthorn, 1973.
Editor, *Three Trips in Time and Space.* New York, Hawthorn,
1973.
Editor, *Mutants.* Nashville, Nelson, 1974; London, Abelard
Schuman, 1976.
Editor, *Threads of Time.* Nashville, Nelson, 1974; London, Mil-
lington, 1975.
Editor, *Infinite Jest.* Radnor, Pennsylvania, Chilton, 1974.
Editor, *Windows into Tomorrow.* New York, Hawthorn, 1974.
Editor, with Roger Elwood, *Epoch.* New York, Berkley, 1975.
Editor, *Explorers of Space.* Nashville, Nelson, 1975.
Editor, *The New Atlantis.* New York, Hawthorn, 1975.
Editor, *Strange Gifts.* Nashville, Nelson, 1975.
Editor, *The Aliens.* Nashville, Nelson, 1976.
Editor, *The Crystal Ship.* Nashville, Nelson, 1976; London, Mil-
lington, 1980.

Editor, *Triax.* New York, Pinnacle, 1977; London, Fontana,
1979.
Editor, *Trips in Time.* Nashville, Nelson, 1977; London, Hale,
1979.
Editor, *Earth Is the Strangest Planet.* Nashville, Nelson, 1977.
Editor, *Galactic Dreamers.* New York, Random House, 1977.
Editor, *The Infinite Web.* New York, Dial Press, 1977.
Editor, *The Androids Are Coming.* New York, Elsevier Nelson,
1979.
Editor, *Lost Worlds, Unknown Horizons.* New York, Elsevier
Nelson, 1979.
Editor, *Edge of Space.* New York, Elsevier Nelson, 1979.
Editor, with Martin H. Greenberg and Joseph D. Olander, *Car
Sinister.* New York, Avon, 1979.
Editor, with Martin H. Greenberg and Joseph D. Olander, *Dawn of
Time: Prehistory Through Science Fiction.* New York, Elsevier
Nelson, 1979.
Editor, *The Best of New Dimensions.* New York, Simon and
Schuster, 1979.
Editor, with Martin H. Greenberg, *The Arbor House Treasury of
Modern Science Fiction.* New York, Arbor House, 1980.
Editor, with Martin H. Greenberg, *The Arbor House Treasury of
Great Science Fiction Short Novels.* New York, Arbor House,
1980.

*

Bibliography: in *Fantasy and Science Fiction* (New York), April
1974.

Manuscript Collection: Syracuse University, New York.

*   *   *

Robert Silverberg, one of the most prolific writers of the last 25
years, has emerged as one of the great science-fiction writers of the
century, proving that the Hugo Award for most promising new
author, which he received in 1956, was well deserved. Science fiction
has come a long way in the years that Silverberg has been writing,
from the mostly shallow adventure stories of yesterday to the richly
characterized and psychologically complex writings of today.
Robert Silverberg has been in the vanguard of that movement.
    Much of his work revolves around his extrapolations of the
future from the world today. He paints realistic (sometimes frightening) pictures of the world to come and populates them with vivid,
imaginative characters who grapple with the problems of their time.
But Silverberg is by no means a conventional science fiction writer.
Consider, for example, *Dying Inside,* which takes place in the
present. This is the story of David Selig, a receiving telepath. There
have been other character studies of telepaths, but in this unique
story Selig is slowly losing his power, and this knowledge threatens
to destroy him. It is hard to imagine possessing such a gift (or is it a
curse?), much less losing it, but Silverberg does a masterful job of
presenting a powerful psychological portrait of a peeping-tom of
the mind.
    Like much of his work, *Dying Inside* deals with frank sexual
situations, not, I believe, because he wishes to write pornographic
science fiction but because sex is such a prevalent aspect of the
human condition. Erotic material has long been a part of mainstream fiction, and if science fiction is to move out of the juvenile
realm into the adult world, it will have to deal with sex. Erotic
material used to heighten the dramatic quality of a work is a
justifiable literary technique. *A Time of Changes* is a good example.
In this socially meaningful work, the religious cult which colonized
Borthan established a covenant under which the self is to be despised. The most heinous crime is that of revealing one's self to
others; the words "I" and "me" are obscenities. Only to one's bond-
brother or bondsister may a person reveal anything about himself,
but bond-kin are forbidden to marry. Within this repressive society,
Kinnal Darival wrestles with his guilt, for he loves his bondsister,
Hallum. With the help of an Earthman's mind-baring drug, Darival's love overcomes his religion with disastrous results for him but
with hope for a time of change on Borthan. This moving work
makes masterful use of erotic material in a well-developed plot.
    Not all of Silverberg's works are quite so sexual in content.

Perhaps his most successful work is *Nightwings*. The novel is set in Earth's distant future, during the third cycle, a time of decadence following man's fall from the pinnacle of power. An elaborate guild structure has arisen including Dominators, Watchers, Rememberers, Defenders, Fliers, and the guildless Changelings. This is a haunting story of man's shame for his past arrogance, his penance at the hand of revenge-minded aliens, and the start of his subsequent rise to the fourth cycle as seen through the eyes of the Watcher Wuelig. It is a showplace for Silverberg's powerful imagination and literary style. Not all of Silverberg's aliens are vengeful. In *Downward to the Earth* two sentient life-forms, the elephant-like Noldoror and the ape-like Sulidoror, inhabit the planet Belzagor. Edmund Gunderson, a former Earth official on Belzagor, returns eight years after the planet has been declared independent to discover what the strange relationship is between the two species and to seek redemption for his participation in the occupation of the planet. The plot revolves around the mysterious rite of rebirth which Gunderson feels is at the heart of the relationship, and his quest for the secret that could prove to be his destruction. This work is an excellent representation of an alien species different from but not inferior to the human species. The anti-imperialism theme compares well with Lloyd Biggle's *Monument*.

Silverberg is not a "hard" science-fiction writer. He does not have the technical skill of Larry Niven, Robert Heinlein, or Arthur C. Clarke. His strength is his characterizations and his vivid future worlds, which are generally developed more psychologically and sociologically than scientifically. Super science, when he uses it, is a backdrop against which his characters stand. In *To Live Again* science has developed a technique by which someone may have his "persona" recorded while he lives, and then transferred to another person after he dies. The "persona" becomes a rider in the host's mind, incapable of making its presence known, in most cases, to anyone other than the host. The procedure is so expensive that only the rich can afford it. True to Silverberg's form, it is not the process itself but its psychological and sociological implications which the plot centers on.

Recalled to Life centers on a scientific development by which newly dead persons can be brought back to life. One might expect the world to embrace the process as the scientific achievement of the century but, using "the Monkey's Paw" kind of reasoning, many people fear it. The attempt to interweave political intrigue, scientific bumbling, and mass hysteria, is not quite successful. In *The Stochastic Man* political intrigue is matched this time with the art of premonition. An interesting time paradox is raised in this work: those who know the future are condemned to live it. This is an excellent representative of Silverberg's work. The inability to change the past without disturbing the future is another time paradox which he deals with in *The Time-Hoppers* and *Up the Line*, though these are interesting rather than exceptional novels.

One of Silverberg's more colorful characters is Shadrach Mordecai, a young black doctor who ministers to the health of Genghis II Mao IV, the 87-year-old ruler of the world in *Shadrach in the Furnace*. The old monarch becomes tired of the transplants which keep him alive and decides he will transfer his mind to another, younger body which means trouble for Shadrach, since it is his body that will be used. This work mirrors the timeless struggle between the idealistic and the ruthless, the young and the old. Another such duel is developed in *Thorns*, when Minner Burris, a spaceman whose body has been redesigned by aliens, is exploited by Duncan Chalk, the rich and powerful painmaster who lives on the emotions of others.

It's hard to imagine what science fiction would have been like without Robert Silverberg, but it would have been a poorer field, both in quality and in vision. He is a masterful writer whose stories are always worth reading.

—Paul Swank

SIMAK, Clifford D(onald). American. Born in Millville, Wisconsin, 3 August 1904. Attended the University of Wisconsin, Madison. Married Kay Kuchenberg in 1929; two children. Reporter, 1924-76, News Editor, 1949-62, and Editor of Science Reading Series, 1962-76, Minneapolis *Star* and *Tribune*. Recipient: International Fantasy Award, 1953; Hugo Award, for story, 1959, for novel, 1964; First Fandom Hall of Fame Award; Nebula Grand Master Award, 1977. Guest of Honor, 29th World Science Fiction Convention, 1971. Agent: Robert P. Mills Ltd., 156 East 52nd Street, New York, New York 10022. Address: 16325 Excelsior Boulevard, Minnetonka, Minnesota 55343, U.S.A.

SCIENCE-FICTION PUBLICATIONS

Novels

Cosmic Engineers. New York, Gnome Press, 1950.
Time and Again. New York, Simon and Schuster, 1951; London, Heinemann, 1955; as *First He Died*, New York, Dell, 1953.
Empire. New York, Galaxy, 1951.
Ring Around the Sun. New York, Simon and Schuster, 1953; London, Consul, 1960.
Time Is the Simplest Thing. New York, Doubleday, 1961; London, Gollancz, 1962.
The Trouble with Tycho. New York, Ace, 1961.
They Walked Like Men. New York, Doubleday, 1962; London, Gollancz, 1963.
Way Station. New York, Doubleday, 1963; London, Gollancz, 1964.
All Flesh Is Grass. New York, Doubleday, 1965; London, Gollancz, 1966.
Why Call Them Back from Heaven? New York, Doubleday, and London, Gollancz, 1967.
The Werewolf Principle. New York, Putnam, 1967; London, Gollancz, 1968.
The Goblin Reservation. New York, Putnam, 1968; London, Rapp and Whiting, 1969.
Out of Their Minds. New York, Putnam, 1970; London, Sidgwick and Jackson, 1972.
Destiny Doll. New York, Putnam, 1971; London, Sidgwick and Jackson, 1972.
A Choice of Gods. New York, Putnam, 1972; London, Sidgwick and Jackson, 1973.
Cemetery World. New York, Putnam, 1973; London, Sidgwick and Jackson, 1975.
Our Children's Children. New York, Putnam, 1974; London, Sidgwick and Jackson, 1975.
Enchanted Pilgrimage. New York, Berkley, 1975; London, Sidgwick and Jackson, 1976.
Shakespeare's Planet. New York, Berkley, 1976; London, Sidgwick and Jackson, 1977.
A Heritage of Stars. New York, Berkley, 1977; London, Sidgwick and Jackson, 1978.
Mastodonia. New York, Ballantine, 1978; as *Catface*, London, Sidgwick and Jackson, 1978.
The Fellowship of the Talisman. New York, Ballantine, 1978; London, Sidgwick and Jackson, 1980.
The Visitors. New York, Ballantine, 1980.
Project Pope. New York, Ballantine, 1981.

Short Stories

The Creator. Los Angeles, Crawford, 1946.
City. New York, Gnome Press, 1952; London, Weidenfeld and Nicolson, 1954.
Strangers in the Universe. New York, Simon and Schuster, 1956; London, Faber, 1958.
The Worlds of Clifford Simak. New York, Simon and Schuster, 1960; abridged edition, as *Aliens for Neighbours*, London, Faber, 1961; abridged edition, as *Other Worlds of Clifford Simak*, New York, Avon, 1962.
All the Traps of Earth. New York, Doubleday, 1962; as *All the Traps of Earth* and *The Night of the Puudly*, London, New English Library, 2 vols., 1964.

Worlds Without End. New York, Belmont, 1964; London, Jenkins, 1965.
Best Science Fiction Stories of Clifford Simak. New York, Doubleday, 1965; London, Faber, 1967.
So Bright the Vision. New York, Ace, 1968.
The Best of Clifford D. Simak, edited by Angus Wells. London, Sidgwick and Jackson, 1975.
Skirmish: The Great Short Fiction of Clifford D. Simak. New York, Putnam, 1977.

Uncollected Short Stories

"Dusty Zebra," in *Alpha 9*, edited by Robert Silverberg. New York, Berkley, 1978.
"Brother," in *The 1978 Annual World's Best SF*, edited by Donald A. Wollheim. New York, DAW, 1978.
"Party Line," in *Destinies* (New York), November-December 1978.
"Grotto of the Dancing Deer," in *Analog* (New York), April 1980.

OTHER PUBLICATIONS

Other

"Faces of Science Fiction," in *Minnesota Libraries* (St. Paul), September 1953.
The Solar System: Our New Front Yard (juvenile). New York, St. Martin's Press, 1963.
Trilobite, Dinosaur, and Man: The Earth's Story. New York, St. Martin's Press, and London, Macmillan, 1966.
Wonder and Glory: The Story of the Universe. New York, St. Martin's Press, 1969.
Prehistoric Man. New York, St. Martin's Press, 1971.
"Room Enough for All of Us," in *Extrapolation* (Wooster, Ohio), May 1972.

Editor, *From Atoms to Infinity: Readings in Modern Science.* New York, Harper, 1965.
Editor, *The March of Science* (juvenile). New York, Harper, 1971.
Editor, *Nebula Award Stories 6.* New York, Doubleday, 1971.
Editor, *The Best of Astounding.* New York, Baronet, 1978.

*

Bibliography: *The Electric Bibliograph 1: Clifford D. Simak* by Mark Owings, Baltimore, Alice and Jay Haldeman, 1971.

*   *   *

Who but Clifford D. Simak would expose invaders from space by mobilizing skunks in a large midwestern city? Since 1931 he has retained popularity, writing about time machines and mystic quests, a man in touch with his world. He is SF's special ambassador to the stars, casually introducing robots, goblins, sociable monstrosities, cyborg ships, and alien intelligences from shades to slugs. Perhaps his popularity is explained by his engaging escapism: communication with other beings is established; the war avoided; the talisman found; the boy and girl (even werewolves) get together.

Much early and minor Simak is gadget SF. "The World of the Red Sun" is a time-machine story with an uncharacteristically unhappy ending, though his interest in time, man's destiny, and illusion is obvious in this first publication. *The Trouble with Tycho* is a treasure hunt on the moon. "The Answers," "The Fence," "Beachhead," "Goodnight, Mr. James," "The Street That Wasn't There," and "To Walk a City's Streets" are classic horror stories. Although the message in "The Answer" is that life is an insignificant accident, most disasters are avoided by courage and determination. Such is the case in *They Walked Like Men, Why Call Them Back from Heaven?, Out of Their Minds*, and *Our Children's Children*. One man who risks life and reputation to save mankind is joined by a tough but feminine friend and at least one unique being. With this mixed cast, what should be terrifying becomes humorous. Another SF gadget is the robot. "How-2," "Earth for Inspiration," "Installment Plan," "All the Traps of Earth," "Ogre," and "Lulu" feature strong-willed, people-loving robots, stock characters in his works,

companions, guides, and occasionally scatter-brained troublemakers. Hezekiah of "Installment Plan" and *A Choice of Gods*, Richard Daniel of "All the Traps of Earth," and Jenkins of *City* are interchangeable. Although *Time and Again* is concerned with the plight of human-looking androids, Simak's robots are usually obviously machines in all but personality.

Simak frequently deals with time and parallel universes. His ideal is a place outside time where things remain the same and a body can rock peacefully on his front porch while auks and dinosaurs frolic by the stream. He is unquestionably the leading exponent of the pastoral mode in SF. "The Autumn Land," "Auk House," "New Folks' Home," "Kindergarten," "The Sitters," "Retrograde Revolution," and "The Marathon Photograph" offer simple, out-of-the-way retreats, often in the Wisconsin countryside. "Neighbor" is perhaps the best statement of Simak's ideal rural utopia where crops never fail, machinery does not break down, and people are friends. A house or a car waits to take someone to a higher existence. "The Ghost of a Model-T" and "New Folks' Home" are particularly appealing because they carry old men to new value. In *Mastodonia* and *Cemetery World* the adventurers remain in their isolated world, Adam, Eve, and machine. Simak's characters share his love for home by returning to childhood spots and fishing in *Ring Around the Sun, All Flesh Is Grass, Out of Their Minds*, and *Cemetery World*. Small town distrust of strangers often makes the plot move forward by sending the heroes into hiding. In *Our Children's Children* ravening beasts from time invade back yards.

Into the everyday, however, comes the world in which all creatures are brothers and all time is linked. The most important of Simak's works combine his themes into allegories of man's need to establish peaceful, respectful communications with all creation. As his world experienced the cold war, racism, ecological deterioration, and loss of faith, Simak responded with works that were at once good SF adventures and parables. *Cosmic Engineers* is one of the earliest and most typical of the works dealing with man's destiny. Two newspapermen, a thousand-year-old lady mathematician, and a group of super-robots save two universes. Their antagonists are the vicious Hellhounds who reappear in *Enchanted Pilgrimage*. The Cosmic Engineers summon every possible life form, including nightmarish, misshapen creatures and goblins. Only man can help—present and future. The one remaining man on Earth explains that the others have migrated to the stars, pushing on to their inheritance as masters of the universe; the Engineers were their creation.

Interstellar cooperation also prevents total annihilation in *Way Station*, Simak's masterpiece. A Civil War veteran, Enoch Wallace, in spite of his 124 years, looks 30. Living alone with only one friend, a mailman who delivers reading material and supplies, he survives by selling precious jewels for less than their worth. Enoch works for the Galaxy, running a way station for interstellar travelers. When the CIA digs up the remains of an extraterrestrial and he rescues a psychic deaf-mute, Lucy Fisher, from a beating, Enoch is thrust into his troubled world. Just when the world is on the brink of war and the Galaxy is torn by strife because its talisman is lost, he is threatened by irate townspeople and his station is to be closed by offended officials. As Enoch packs his records and treasures, a ratlike saboteur invades and he must kill him. Lucy is found to be a Guardian when she reactivates the stolen talisman the rat had with him. Because of Lucy, Earth is spared war and given Galactic status.

This improbably plotted book is significant for its messages of universal brotherhood and the significance of life. It is also a storehouse of Simak's materials. The talisman is a spiritual force that unites planets. The ability of the Andromedans to adapt by changing shape appears in *City* and *The Werewolf Principle*. The picture cube, five-person sexual unit, companions created by thought, affable aliens, lonely hero, old-fashioned romance, bad government, powerful simple person, and narrator who mulls over the meaning of his existence all are traits of Simak's work. "The Big Front Yard" is a similar tale of the establishment of a portal through which citizens of other worlds may pass peacefully. In *All Flesh Is Grass* a rural area is the entry point for a flower-like group-being that brings peace. "Mirage," "Contraption," "Limiting Factor," "Construction Shack," and *Time and Again* bring man into contact with far greater but non-threatening powers.

City is the most sweeping of his speculations about man's destiny among the stars. In eight stories written as myths passed on by the dogs and robots of the Webster family, Simak relates a history in which man takes to space, leaving his successors behind to doubt he ever existed. *City, The Creator, Time and Again*, and "Founding Father" suggest that man, as we know him, may not inherit the universe after all. In *Time Is the Simplest Thing* and *Ring Around the Sun* paranormals are resented and hunted.

Simak's recent works return to optimism and move into man-glorifying fantasy. All are quests for meaning in a vastly changed world. In *Cemetery World* Earth has become a glorified graveyard; in *A Choice of Gods* it has been left to robots, Indians, and a few conservatives. *Enchanted Pilgrimage, Destiny Doll, A Heritage of Stars,* and *The Fellowship of the Talisman* have a medieval flavor, with ominous, degraded antagonists, magic, and waste lands, matching the interests of the times. They suggest a guiding cosmic principle.

Simak's work has great consistency. Names like Horton, Duncan, Hezekiah, Thorndyke, Bounce, and Bowser recur. Ideas like creating beings from thought, changing bodies for colonization, gateways to other world, and characters like long-winded, argumentative robots, friendly worms, mythical creatures like brownies, and strong-willed but malleable women are predictable. Above all, Simak insists on the dignity of all life and the irresponsibility of undervaluing any. Though he often preaches oversimplification, time stops while Simak spins his leisurely yarns.

—Mary S. Weinkauf

SINCLAIR, Upton. Also wrote as Frederick Garrison. American. Born in Baltimore, Maryland, 20 September 1878; moved with his family to New York City, 1888. Educated at the City College of New York, 1893-97, A.B. 1897; Columbia University, New York, 1897-1901. Married 1) Meta H. Fuller in 1900 (divorced, 1911); 2) Mary Craig Kimbrough in 1913 (died, 1961); 3) Mary Elizabeth Willis in 1961 (died, 1967). Writer from 1893; wrote Clif Faraday stories (as Ensign Clarke Fitch) and Mark Mallory stories (as Lieutenant Frederick Garrison) for various boys' weeklies, 1897-98; founded socialist community, Helicon Home Colony, Englewood, New Jersey, 1906-07; Socialist candidate for Congress, from New Jersey, 1906; settled in Pasadena, California, 1915; Socialist candidate for Congress, 1920, and for the United States Senate, 1922, and for Governor of California, 1926, 1930; moved to Buckeye, Arizona, 1953. Recipient: Pulitzer Prize, 1943; American Newspaper Guild Award, 1962. *Died 25 November 1968.*

SCIENCE-FICTION PUBLICATIONS

Novels

Prince Hagen. Boston, Page, and London, Chatto and Windus, 1903.
The Industrial Republic. New York, Doubleday, and London, Heinemann, 1907.
They Call Me Carpenter. New York, Boni and Liveright, and London, Laurie, 1922.
The Millennium: A Comedy of the Year 2000. Girard, Kansas, Haldeman Julius, 1924; London, Laurie, 1929.
Roman Holiday. New York, Farrar and Rinehart, and London, Laurie, 1931.
Our Lady. Emmaus, Pennsylvania, Rodale Press, and London, Laurie, 1938.

Uncollected Short Story

"Author's Adventure," in *The Fantastic Pulps,* edited by Peter Haining. New York, St. Martin's Press, 1975.

OTHER PUBLICATIONS

Novels

Springtime and Harvest: A Romance. New York, Sinclair Press, 1901; as *King Midas,* New York and London, Funk and Wagnalls, 1901.
The Journal of Arthur Stirling. New York, Appleton, and London, Heinemann, 1903.
Manassas. New York and London, Macmillan, 1904; as *Theirs Be the Guilt,* New York, Twayne, 1959.
The Jungle. New York, Doubleday, and London, Heinemann, 1906.
A Captain of Industry. Girard, Kansas, Appeal to Reason, and London, Heinemann, 1906.
The Metropolis. New York, Moffat Yard, and London, Laurie, 1908.
The Moneychangers. New York, Dodge, and London, Long, 1908.
Samuel the Seeker. New York, Dodge, and London, Long, 1910.
Love's Pilgrimage. New York, Kennerley, 1911; London, Heinemann, 1912.
Sylvia. Philadelphia, Winston, 1913; London, Long, 1914.
Damaged Goods. Philadelphia, Winston, and London, Hutchinson, 1913.
Sylvia's Marriage. Philadelphia, Winston, 1914; London, Laurie, 1915.
King Coal. New York, Macmillan, and London, Laurie, 1917.
Jimmie Higgins. London, Hutchinson, 1918; New York, Boni and Liveright, 1919.
The Spy. London, Laurie, 1919; as *100%: The Story of a Patriot,* privately printed, 1920; excerpt, as *Peter Gudge Becomes a Secret Agent,* Moscow, State Publishing House, 1930.
Oil! New York, Boni, and London, Laurie, 1927.
Boston. New York, Boni, 1928; London, Laurie, 1929; abridged edition, as *August 22nd,* New York, Universal, 1965; Bath, Chivers, 1971.
Mountain City. New York, Boni, 1929; London, Laurie, 1930.
The Wet Parade. New York, Farrar and Rinehart, and London, Laurie, 1931.
Co-op: A Novel of Living Together. New York, Farrar and Rinehart, and London, Laurie, 1936.
The Gnomobile. New York, Farrar and Rinehart, and London, Laurie, 1936.
Little Steel. New York, Farrar and Rinehart, and London, Laurie, 1938.
Marie Antoinette. New York, Vanguard Press, and London, Laurie, 1939; as *Marie and Her Lover,* Girard, Kansas, Haldeman Julius, 1948.
World's End. New York, Viking Press, and London, Laurie, 1940.
Between Two Worlds. New York, Viking Press, and London, Laurie, 1941.
Dragon's Teeth. New York, Viking Press, and London, Laurie, 1942.
Wide Is the Gate. New York, Viking Press, and London, Laurie, 1943.
Presidential Agent. New York, Viking Press, 1944; London, Laurie, 1945.
Dragon Harvest. New York, Viking Press, and London, Laurie, 1945.
A World to Win. New York, Viking Press, 1946; London, Laurie, 1947.
Presidential Mission. New York, Viking Press, 1947; London, Laurie, 1948.
One Clear Call. New York, Viking Press, 1948; London, Laurie, 1949.
O Shepherd, Speak! New York, Viking Press, 1949; London, Laurie, 1950.
Another Pamela; or, Virtue Still Rewarded. New York, Viking Press, and London, Laurie, 1950.
The Return of Lanny Budd. New York, Viking Press, and London, Laurie, 1953.
What Didymus Did. London, Wingate, 1954; as *It Happened to Didymus,* New York, Sagamore Press, 1958.

The Cup of Fury. Great Neck, New York, Channel Press, 1956; London, Arco, 1957.
Affectionately Eve. New York, Twayne, 1961.
The Coal War: A Sequel to King Coal. Boulder, Colorado Associated University Press, 1976.

Plays

Prince Hagen, adaptation of his own novel (produced San Francisco, 1909). Privately printed, 1909.
Plays of Protest (includes *Prince Hagen, The Naturewoman, The Machine, The Second-Story Man*). New York, Kennerley, 1912.
Hell: A Verse Drama and Photo-Play. Privately printed, 1923.
The Pot Boiler. Girard, Kansas, Haldeman Julius, 1924.
Singing Jailbirds (produced London, 1930). Privately printed, 1924.
Bill Porter. Privately printed, 1924.
Wally for Queen! The Private Life of Royalty. Privately printed, 1936.
A Giant's Strength. Girard, Kansas, Haldeman Julius, and London, Laurie, 1948.
The Enemy Had It Too. New York, Viking Press, 1950.
Three Plays (includes *The Second-Story Man, John D., The Indignant Subscriber*). Moscow, Progress, 1965.

Verse

Songs of Our Nation (as Frederick Garrison). New York, Marks Music, 1941.

Other

The Toy and the Man. Westwood, Massachusetts, Ariel Press, 1904.
Our Bourgeois Literature. Chicago, Kerr, 1905.
Colony Customs. Englewood, New Jersey, Sinclair, 1906.
The Helicon Home Colony. Englewood, New Jersey, Constitution, 1906.
A Home Colony: A Prospectus. New York, Jungle, 1906.
What Life Means to Me. Girard, Kansas, Appeal to Reason, 1906.
The Overman. New York, Doubleday, 1907.
Good Health and How We Won It, with Michael Williams. New York, Stokes, 1909; as *Strength and Health*, 1910; as *The Art of Health*, London, Health and Strength, 1909.
War: A Manifesto Against It. Girard, Kansas, Appeal to Reason, New York, Wilshire, and London, Clarion Press, 1909.
Four Letters about "Love's Pilgrimage." Privately printed, 1911.
The Fasting Cure. New York, Kennerley, and London, Heinemann, 1911.
The Sinclair-Astor Letters: Famous Correspondence Between Socialist and Millionaire. Girard, Kansas, Appeal to Reason, 1914.
The Social Problem as Seen from the Viewpoint of Trade Unionism, Capital, and Socialism, with others. New York, Industrial Economics Department of the National Civic Federation, 1914.
Upton Sinclair: Biographical and Critical Opinions. Privately printed, 1917.
The Profits of Religion. Privately printed, 1918; London, Laurie, 1936.
Russia: A Challenge. Girard, Kansas, Appeal to Reason, 1919.
The High Cost of Living (address). Girard, Kansas, People's Press, 1919.
The Brass Check. London, Laurie, 1919; Pasadena, California, privately printed, 1920; excerpt, as *The Associated Press and Labor*, privately printed, 1920.
Press-titution. Girard, Kansas, Appeal to Reason, 1920.
The Crimes of the "Times": A Test of Newspaper Decency. Privately printed, 1921.
The Book of Life. Pasadena, California, Sinclair Paine, 1922; London, Laurie, 1934.
    Mind and Body. New York, Macmillan, 1921; revised edition, Girard, Kansas, Haldeman Julius, 4 vols., 1950.
    Love and Society. Pasadena, California, Sinclair Paine, 1922;

revised edition, Girard, Kansas, Haldeman Julius, 4 vols., n.d.
The McNeal-Sinclair Debate on Socialism. Girard, Kansas, Haldeman Julius, 1921.
The Goose-Step: A Study of American Education. Privately printed, 1922; revised edition, n.d.; London, Laurie, 1923.
Biographical Letter and Critical Opinions. Privately printed, 1922.
The Goslings. Privately printed, 1924; London, Laurie, 1930; excerpt, as *The Schools of Los Angeles*, privately printed, 1924.
Mammonart. Privately printed, 1925; London, Laurie, 1934.
Letters to Judd. Privately printed, 1926; revised edition, as *This World of 1949 and What to Do about It*, Girard, Kansas, Haldeman Julius, 1949.
The Spokesman's Secretary. Privately printed, 1926.
Money Writes! New York, Boni, 1927; London, Laurie, 1931.
The Pulitzer Prize and "Special Pleading." Privately printed, 1929.
Mental Radio. New York, Boni, and London, Laurie, 1930; revised edition, Springfield, Illinois, Thomas, 1962.
Socialism and Culture. Girard, Kansas, Haldeman Julius, 1931.
Upton Sinclair on "Comrade" Kautsky. Moscow, Co-operative Publishing Society of Foreign Workers in the USSR, 1931.
American Outpost. New York, Farrar and Rinehart, 1932; as *Candid Reminiscences: My First Thirty Years*, London, Laurie, 1932.
I, Governor of California, and How I Ended Poverty. New York, Farrar and Rinehart, and London, Laurie, 1933.
Upton Sinclair Presents William Fox. Privately printed, 1933.
The Way Out—What Lies Ahead for America? New York, Farrar and Rinehart, and London, Laurie, 1933; revised edition, as *Limbo on the Loose: A Midsummer Night's Dream*, Girard, Kansas, Haldeman Julius, 1948.
EPIC Plan for California. New York, Farrar and Rinehart, 1934.
EPIC Answers: How to End Poverty in California. Los Angeles, End Poverty League, 1934.
Immediate EPIC. Los Angeles, End Poverty League, 1934.
The Lie Factory Starts. Los Angeles, End Poverty League, 1934.
An Upton Sinclair Anthology, edited by I.O. Evans. New York, Farrar and Rinehart, and London, Laurie, 1934; revised edition, Culver City, California, Murray and Gee, 1947.
Upton Sinclair's Last Will and Testament. Los Angeles, End Poverty League, 1934.
We, People of America, and How We Ended Poverty: A True Story of the Future. Pasadena, California, National EPIC League, 1934.
Depression Island. Pasadena, California, privately printed, and London, Laurie, 1935.
I, Candidate for Governor, and How I Got Licked. New York, Farrar and Rinehart, 1935; as *How I Got Licked and Why*, London, Laurie, 1935.
What God Means to Me: An Attempt at a Working Religion. New York, Farrar and Rinehart, and London, Laurie, 1936.
The Flivver King. Girard, Kansas, Haldeman Julius, 1937; London, Laurie, 1938.
No Pasoran! (They Shall Not Pass). New York, Labor Press, and London, Laurie, 1937.
Terror in Russia: Two Views, with Eugene Lyons. New York, Richard R. Smith, 1938.
Upton Sinclair on the Soviet Union. New York, Weekly Masses, 1938.
Expect No Peace! Girard, Kansas, Haldeman Julius, 1939.
Telling the World. London, Laurie, 1939.
What Can Be Done about America's Economic Troubles? Girard, Kansas, Haldeman Julius, 1939.
Your Million Dollars. Privately printed, 1939; as *Letters to a Millionaire*, London, Laurie, 1939.
Is the American Form of Capitalism Essential to the American Form of Democracy? Girard, Kansas, Haldeman Julius, 1940.
Peace or War in America? Girard, Kansas, Haldeman Julius, 1940.
Index to the Lanny Budd Story, with others. New York, Viking Press, 1943.
To Solve the German Problem—A Free State? Privately printed, 1943.

A Personal Jesus: Portrait and Interpretation. New York, Evans, 1952; London, Allen and Unwin, 1954; as *Secret Life of Jesus*, Philadelphia, Mercury, 1962.
Radio Liberation Speech to the Peoples of the Soviet Union. New York, American Committee for Liberation from Bolshevism, 1955.
My Lifetime in Letters. Columbia, University of Missouri Press, 1960.
The Autobiography of Upton Sinclair. New York, Harcourt Brace, 1962; London, Allen and Unwin, 1963.

Editor, *The Cry for Justice: An Anthology of the Literature of Social Protest.* Philadelphia, Winston, 1915.

*

Bibliography: *Upton Sinclair: An Annotated Checklist* by Ronald Gottesman, Kent, Ohio, Kent State University Press, 1973.

*   *   *

Upton Sinclair is best known as a socialist muckraking novelist, and has a spectacular history as a much-admired and much-traduced political crusader. However, as an "Economic Scientist" he has experimented in both science fiction and fantasy, especially of the time-travel variety. Since his talents are journalistic and narrative rather than evocative of character and subtle human relations, his SF drama is less skilful than his novels are.

One group of novels takes America into a possible alternative world, consequent upon Sinclair being elected Governor of California and his EPIC programme being adopted by the USA. *I, Governor of California, and How I Ended Poverty* is fiction only in the sense that it projects a political campaign into the immediate future, emphasising the virtues and values of the co-operative movement that defeats the Depression. *We, People of America, and How We Ended Poverty* expands the canvas and the time-scale, but is still more argument than fiction. *Co-op* is a genuine fiction, but leaves the reader to debate whether President Roosevelt will or will not embrace the Co-operative Commonwealth ideal. That ideal is interesting in itself, uniting patriotism with socialist and collectivist principles, but the protagonists of the novel are more typical than individually memorable.

Genuinely science-fiction and fantasy novels are *The Millennium: A Comedy of the Year 2000*, a satirical parable on the need for socialism combined with social justice, and the rather stiffly Utopian *The Industrial Republic*. More striking juxtapositions of modern American assumptions with those of very different societies make *Prince Hagen* still interesting; the avaricious Nibelung ruler is impressed by the superior chicanery and greed of "Christian" American capitalism. In *Roman Holiday* a rich young American playboy, in the delirium following a motor-racing accident, finds himself back in patrician Rome, which tells him a great deal about his 20th-century life-style and society. *They Call Me Carpenter* also uses a rich and idle American as principle observer: laid out after a scuffle with "patriotic" demonstrators against the film *The Cabinet of Dr. Caligari*, he sees Christ step down from a cathedral window; inevitably "Carpenter" loves His fellow men, but is forced to denounce the press, the society's privileged, and especially the church that has deserted the revolutionary doctrines of its supposed Founder (the novel stops short of the crucifixion which its logic seems to entail). Sinclair's other major time-travel fantasy, *Our Lady*, is excellent in both research and the basic contrast between the mother of Jesus and the modern Californian Catholic world to which she is translated. Both her reaction to the ball-game where she first appears and her total alienation from any element of Roman Catholic faith which theoretically invokes her mingle comedy, pathos, and a genuine reverence for human spiritual exploration; even the exorcism climax has an obsessive power lacking in most of Sinclair's endings.

Most of Sinclair's immense number of novels were written too quickly, and stumble into structural faults as well as psychological shallowness. Yet the best of his writing carries immense compassion for human suffering and frustration, and the force and courage of his defence of human relations against capitalist priorities is worth the loss of many graces. Although genuinely convinced that all good art is primarily propaganda, Sinclair avoids portraying all capitalists or playboys as fools or ogres, and often relishes the sudden understanding that can spring up between characters socially alien to each other. In his drama there is genuine development between the versions of the "noble savage" girl in *The Naturewoman* (*Plays of Protest*) and *The Enemy Had It Too*, where the unspoiled maiden kills the sophisticated gangster by the use of flirtation and curare! Nonetheless, the exploration of Great Issues does not suit the stage, and mixing the world-disaster (or last-men) theme with the return-from-Mars, the noble savage, the satiric portrait, and the all-aboard-the-Ark themes makes even the latter too overloaded. It is for such novels as *Our Lady* that Sinclair most deserves the fantasy reader's attention.

—Norman Talbot

SIODMAK, Curt (Kurt Siodmak). American. Born in Dresden, Germany, 10 August 1902; brother of the film director Robert Siodmak. Educated at the University of Zurich, Ph.D. 1927. Married Henrietta De Perrot in 1931; one son. Railroad engineer and factory worker; film writer and director: worked for Gaumont British, 1931-37, and in the United States after 1937. Recipient: Bundespreis, for film, 1964. Lives in California. Agent: Paul R. Reynolds, 599 Fifth Avenue, New York, New York, 10017 U.S.A.

SCIENCE-FICTION PUBLICATIONS

Novels (series: Cory)

F.P. 1 Antwortet Nicht. Berlin, Keils, 1931; translated by H.W. Farrell as *F.P. 1 Does Not Reply*, Boston, Little Brown, 1933; as *F.P. 1 Fails to Reply*, London, Collins, 1933.
Donovan's Brain (Cory). New York, Knopf, 1943; London, Chapman and Hall, 1944.
Skyport. New York, Crown, 1959.
Hauser's Memory (Cory). New York, Putnam, 1968; London, Jenkins, 1969.
The Third Ear. New York, Putnam, 1971.
City in the Sky. New York, Putnam, 1974; London, Barrie and Jenkins, 1975.

Uncollected Short Stories

"The Eggs from Lake Tanganyika," in *Amazing* (New York), July 1926.
"Variations on a Theme," in *Fantasy and Science Fiction* (New York), June 1972.
"The P Factor," in *Fantasy and Science Fiction* (New York), September 1976.

OTHER PUBLICATIONS

Novels

Schluss in Tonfilmatelier. Berlin, Scherl, 1930.
Stadt Hinter Nebeln. Berlin, Verlag der Seit-Romane, 1931.
Die Madonna aus der Markusstrasse. Leipzig, Goldmann, 1932.
Bis ans Ende der Welt. Leipzig, Goldmann, 1932.
Rache im Äther. Leipzig, Goldmann, 1932.
Die Macht im Dunkeln. Zurich, Morgarten, 1937.
Whomsoever I Shall Kiss. New York, Crown, 1952.
For Kings Only. New York, Crown, 1961.

Plays

Screenplays: *Mensch am Sonntag* (*People on Sunday*) (documentary), 1929; *Le Bal*, 1931; *Der Mann der Seinen Mörder Sucht* (*Looking for His Murderer*), 1931; *F.P. 1 Antwortet Nicht*, 1933; *Girls Will Be Boys*, with Clifford Grey and Roger Burford, 1934; *I Give My Heart*, with others, 1935; *The Tunnel* (*Transatlantic Tunnel*), with L. DuGarde Peach and Clemence Dane, 1935; *It's a Bet*, with Frank Miller and L. DuGarde Peach, 1935; *Non-Stop New York*, 1938; *Her Jungle Love*, with others, 1938; *The Invisible Man Returns*, with Lester Cole and Joe May, 1940; *The Ape*, with Richard Carroll, 1940; *Black Friday*, with Eric Taylor, 1950; *The Invisible Woman*, with others, 1941; *The Wolf Man*, with Gordon Kahn, 1941; *Pacific Blackout*, with others, 1941; *Aloma of the South Seas*, with others, 1941; *London Blackout Murders*, 1942; *The Invisible Agent*, 1942; *I Walked with a Zombie*, with Ardel Wray and Inez Wallace, 1943; *Frankenstein Meets the Wolf Man*, 1943; *The Mantrap*, 1943; *Son of Dracula*, with Eric Taylor, 1943; *False Faces*, 1943; *The Purple "V,"* with Bertram Millhauser, 1943; *House of Frankenstein*, with Edward T. Lowe, 1944; *The Climax*, with Lynn Starling, 1944; *Frisco Sal*, with Gerald Geraghty, 1945; *Shady Lady*, with others, 1945; *The Return of Monte Cristo*, with others, 1946; *The Beast with Five Fingers*, with Harold Goldman, 1947; *Berlin Express*, with Harold Medford, 1948; *Tarzan's Magic Fountain*, with Harry Chandlee, 1949; *Four Days Leave*, with others, 1950; *Bride of the Gorilla*, 1951; *The Magnetic Monster*, with Ivan Tors, 1953; *Riders to the Stars*, 1954; *Creature with the Atom Brain*, 1955; *Earth vs. Flying Saucers*, with George Worthing Yates and Raymond Marcus, 1956; *Curucu, Beast of the Amazon*, 1956; *Love Slaves of the Amazon*, 1957; *Lightship*, 1963; *Ski Fever*, with Robert Joseph, 1967.

Television Plays: *13 Demon Street* series, 1959 (Sweden).

Theatrical Activities:

Director: **Films**—*Bride of the Gorilla*, 1951; *The Magnetic Monster*, 1953; *Curucu, Beast of the Amazon*, 1956; *Love Slaves of the Amazon*, 1957; *Ski Fever*, 1967.

*   *   *

As novelist, screenwriter, and film director, Curt Siodmak has had a long career, first in Germany and then in Hollywood, popularizing for the mass audience basic and extremely banal science-fiction motifs originated long before by other writers: an airfield floating in mid-ocean, the building of a trans-Atlantic tunnel or a spaceport, experiments with artificially induced telepathy or genetic manipulation all provide formulaic grist for some very melodramatic mills. Siodmak's protagonists in his novels and films are either Frankensteinian mad scientists in the grand pulp tradition or strong-willed and far-sighted entrepreneurial over-reachers in the Faustian/Ayn Rand mold. Indeed, perhaps the only redeeming feature of Siodmak's early German science-fiction work of the 1930's is that the films based on his novels (three versions of *F.P. 1 Does Not Reply* and two versions of *Transatlantic Tunnel*) utilized some impressive special effects. Not even that much can be said for most of the movies based on his Hollywood screenplays in the 1940's, which were invariably low-budget programmers that attempted to milk tried-and-true monster-movie formulas that had long been dried out.

Siodmak is best known, however, within both the science-fiction field and the mainstream of literary and cinematic popular culture, as the creator of *Donovan's Brain*, which has itself been adapted three times for the movies, with varying degrees of success: *The Lady and the Monster* (1947, with Erich von Stroheim), *Donovan's Brain* (1953, with Lew Ayres), and *The Brain* (1963, with Peter Van Eyck). In all of its manifestations, the story has held up durably and has retained to a certain extent its queasy fascination. The reclusive scientist-physician Patrick Cory extracts the still-living brain of the powerful industrialist Warren Horace Donovan after an airplane crash had mangled the tycoon's elderly body. Despite the stereotypical warnings of his devoted wife and an alcoholic colleague, Cory establishes telepathic contact with the disembodied brain, which, nurtured by chemicals, is growing daily in size and telepathic power.

The brain quickly takes control of Cory's body, forcing it to wreak vengeance on Donovan's enemies. What gives Siodmak's novel its inherent power is not only its central theme of physical possession caused by unchecked and thus finally destructive scientific research, but also the first-person narration from Cory's panicky point of view. Unfortunately, the story eventually degenerates into unduly complicated histrionics detailing Donovan's desire to pay off an old debt by intruding on a murder investigation involving the heir of one of Donovan's early business partners. By plunging Donovan and his hapless, progressively will-less surrogate into such a desultory and pointless subplot so late in the proceedings, Siodmak conveniently sidesteps the more somber medical, legal, and metaphysical implications of his initially intriguing concept.

Siodmak's later novels continued his career-long tendency to graft mainstream genres onto science-fiction settings. Thus, *City in the Sky* is a kind of *Grand Hotel* in orbit, mixed in with political intrigue and prison-escape heroics, while *Skyport* is like a space-age *Fountainhead*. A bit more interesting to the genuine science-fiction enthusiast are *The Third Ear*, which concerns the chemically created cultivation of ESP abilities, and *Hauser's Memory*, Siodmak's belated sequel to *Donovan's Brain*, with the intrepid Cory again blazing new scientific trails, transplanting a German chemist's overactive, revenge-minded RNA onto another ill-fated human guinea pig. Despite the pseudo-scientific trappings, both books are relatively straightforward espionage thrillers, demonstrating again that Siodmak's talents lie in welding worn-out science-fiction themes with other conventional, pop-cultural formulas.

—Kenneth Jurkiewicz

SKINNER, B(urrhus) F(rederic). American. Born in Susquehanna, Pennsylvania, 20 March 1904. Educated at Hamilton College, Clinton, New York, B.A. 1926 (Phi Beta Kappa); Harvard University, Cambridge, Massachusetts, M.A. 1930, Ph.D. 1931. Conducted war research sponsored by General Mills Inc., 1942-43. Married Yvonne Blue in 1936; two daughters. National Research Council Fellow, 1931-33, and Junior Fellow, 1933-36, Harvard University; Instructor, 1936-37, Assistant Professor, 1937-39, and Associate Professor of Psychology, 1939-45, University of Minnesota, Minneapolis; Professor of Psychology and Department Chairman, Indiana University, Bloomington, 1945-48. William James Lecturer, 1947, Professor, 1948-57, and Edgar Pierce Professor of Psychology, 1958-75, Harvard University: since 1975, Professor Emeritus. Recipient: Society of Experimental Psychology Warren Medal, 1942; Guggenheim Fellowship, 1944; American Psychological Association Award, 1958; Edward L. Thorndike Award, 1966; National Medal of Science, 1968; American Psychological Foundation Gold Medal, 1971; Joseph P. Kennedy, Jr., Foundation for Mental Retardation International Award, 1971; American Humanist Society Award, 1972; American Educational Research Association Award, 1978. Sc.D.: North Carolina State College, 1960; University of Chicago, 1967; University of Missouri, Columbia, 1968; Alfred University, New York, 1969; University of Exeter, 1969; McGill University, Montreal, 1970; Indiana University, 1970; Long Island University, C.W. Post Center, Greenvale, New York, 1971; Dickinson College, Carlisle, Pennsylvania, 1972; Lowell Technological Institute, 1974; Litt.D.: Ripon College, Wisconsin, 1961; L.H.D.: Rockford College, Illinois, 1971; Framlingham State College, Massachusetts, 1972; University of Maryland, College Park, 1974; Hofstra University, Hempstead, New York, 1974; Institute of Behavioral Research Experimental College, 1974; LL.D.: Ohio Wesleyan University, Delaware, 1971; Hobart and William Smith Colleges, Geneva, New York, 1972. Member, National Academy of Sciences and American Academy of Arts and Sciences; Fellow, Royal Society of Arts. Address: William James Hall, 33 Kirkland Street, Cambridge, Massachusetts 02138, U.S.A.

SCIENCE-FICTION PUBLICATIONS

Novel

Walden Two. New York, Macmillan, 1948; London, Macmillan, 1969.

OTHER PUBLICATIONS

Other

The Behavior of Organisms: An Experimental Analysis. New York, Appleton, 1938.
Verbal Behavior. Cambridge, Massachusetts, Harvard University, 1948.
Science and Human Behavior. New York, Macmillan, 1953.
Schedules of Reinforcement, with C.B. Ferster. New York, Appleton Century Crofts, 1957.
Cumulative Record: A Selection of Papers. New York, Appleton Century Crofts, 1959; revised edition, 1972.
The Analysis of Behavior: A Program for Self-Instruction, with James G. Holland. New York, McGraw Hill, 1961.
"Visions of Utopia," in *The Listener* (London), 5 January 1967.
"Utopia Through the Control of Human Behavior," in *The Listener* (London), 12 January 1967.
The Technology of Teaching. New York, Appleton Century Crofts, 1968.
Earth Resources. Englewood Cliffs, New Jersey, Prentice Hall, 1969.
Contingencies of Reinforcement: A Theoretical Analysis. New York, Appleton Century Crofts, 1969.
Beyond Freedom and Dignity. New York, Knopf, 1971; London, Cape, 1972.
The Freedom to Have a Future. Syracuse, New York, Syracuse University, 1973.
"*Walden* (One) and *Walden Two,*" in *Thoreau Society Bulletin* (Geneseo, New York), Winter 1973.
About Behaviorism. New York, Knopf, and London, Cape, 1974.
Sound Seminars, with Carl R . Rogers, edited by Gerald A. Gladstein. New York, Norton, 1976.
Particulars of My Life. New York, Knopf, and London, Cape, 1976.
Reflections on Behaviorism and Society. Englewood Cliffs, New Jersey, Prentice Hall, 1978.
The Shaping of a Behaviorist: Part Two of an Autobiography. New York, Knopf, 1979.
Notebooks, edited by Robert Epstein. Englewood Cliffs, New Jersey, Prentice Hall, 1981.

*

Bibliography: "A Listing of the Published Works of B.F. Skinner, with Notes and Comments" by Robert Epstein, in *Behaviorism 5* (Reno, Nevada), 1977.

*   *   *

It is not inappropriate for the work of B.F. Skinner, who has said that he wanted at first to be a writer, to be described among the work of science-fiction writers. Although Skinner has made a systematic contribution to knowledge as a psychologist and social theorist in numerous non-fiction works, his one classic fictional telling of his hopes and plans for social engineering, *Walden Two,* is exciting and vigorous not only because of its clarity and ambition but also because of its representative relationship to the science-fiction genre itself. Set, written, and published in the immediate post-war period that was dominated in science fiction by Campbell, Asimov, Heinlein, etc., Skinner's narrative vibrates with the intellectual positivism of the genre. His protagonists talk and theorize at great length, and even though the reader never sees the narrative leave the eastern United States a kind of cosmic optimism prevails—space opera of the mind. The only qualification is the one that seems to accompany any Utopia: Walden Two is so ideal that it is "no place." But the underlying effectiveness of Skinner's narrative is finally that he

captures much of the paradox inherent in a managed and highly sophisticated society whose ultimate objective and blind hope is to allow individuals to be truly themselves.

—Donald M. Hassler

———————

SKY, Kathleen. American. Born in Alhambra, California, 5 August 1943. Married Stephen Goldin, *q.v.,* in 1972. Children's barber, Bullock's Department Store, Pasadena, California, 1964-71; volunteer worker for the Humane Society, Pasadena, 1972; film extra. Since 1968, free-lance writer. Agent: Joseph Elder Agency, 150 West 87th Street, New York, New York 10024. Address: 13175½ Bromont Avenue, Sylmar, California 91342, U.S.A.

SCIENCE-FICTION PUBLICATIONS

Novels

Birthright. Toronto, Laser, 1975.
Ice Prison. Toronto, Laser, 1976.
Vulcan! New York, Bantam, 1978.
Death's Angel. New York, Bantam, 1980.

Uncollected Short Stories

"One Ordinary Day, with Box," in *Generation,* edited by David Gerrold. New York, Dell, 1972.
"Lament of the Keeku Bird," in *The Alien Condition,* edited by Stephen Goldin. New York, Ballantine, 1973.
"Door to Malequar," in *Vertex* (Los Angeles), June 1975.
"A Daisychain for Pav," in *Odyssey* (New York), Summer 1976.
"Motherbreast," in *Cassandra Rising,* edited by Alice Laurance. New York, Doubleday, 1978.

Kathleen Sky comments:
    It's difficult to analyze my fiction on the basis of past output because I know that my best work still lies ahead of me. Nevertheless, I recognize some themes in my books that will continue to appear. Just as blacks and Chicanos need strong positive images in their literature, I feel that the increasing number of women who read science fiction will require strong female characters to give them a postive self-image. It's easy to write a strong woman as a bitch, but much harder to write her as a loving, caring person (the "mother" aspect). Nevertheless, I try. In my forthcoming fantasy series, *The Witchdame Trilogy* , I have a strong character, Princess Elizabeth, who eventually becomes the queen of her realm and consequently a strong mother figure. In my novel *Shalom,* there are several strong women, most notably Judith, who eventually becomes a mother figure to her entire planet.
    In writing about strong women, I find I need strong male characters to match them. It's no use liberating only one gender; men and women need to share their strengths equally. I feel that everyone is psychologically bisexual—that is, each human being has both masculine and feminine components to his personality. Only by bringing out *all* the strengths, masculine and feminine, can people truly become liberated from the stereotypes of the past. Because of this, I reject the role of the traditional feminist. Too many of the radical women writers tend to view men as an enemy to be overcome. In doing so, they are doing more harm to themselves than to their supposed enemies. I view men and women as but two halves of a single race. If one side loses, we all do; only by having both sides succeed can humanity be the victor.

*   *   *

Kathleen Sky is good at understanding a special variety of emotion: the grief of a creature coerced by its own nature into a task both valuable to others and costly to itself. One could say it is a woman's grief—Sky makes it into the grief of a tired little man, or a green alien, or a Vulcan. Sky has the visibly struggling competence of a new writer, but also a depth of emotional perception which is already formed. The plight of her characters is both cleverly illustrated and deeply felt.

"One Ordinary Day, with Box," her first story, functions with the simplicity of a parable. A little old man travels from place to place with a big black box. To those who reach inside, the box gives what they need, but not what they want. The disparity between imagined want and true need runs like a moral lesson through this quick, effective tale, but the emotional focus is finally on the old man himself. Scorned by the people that the box has frustrated and insulted, he goes off alone and at last reaches into the box himself. He is given another box. His need, the box implies, is to continue his thankless task, his unappreciated giving.

Sometimes the task is change itself. In the somewhat overwritten but surprisingly moving "Lament of the Keeku Bird" Sky details the painful process of an alien initiation ritual, a menopause by violence in which a female creature makes a ceremonial journey that wears off her sexuality. The writing task is difficult—Sky narrates in the first person present from the alien's point of view and thus must develop landscape, species, and personality all indirectly. The development is coherent and interesting; Sky manages not only to establish a believable extraterrestrial world but also to show the beginnings of personal change, the openings of thought in what was at first a thoughtless breeding animal. The mingling of grief and triumph at the end is consistent with Sky's awareness of the inner price to be paid for anything of value.

This awareness is carried into Sky's Star Trek novel, *Vulcan!* Enough young science-fiction writers have written Star Trek continuations that it may become a set exercise for entering the craft. As such it provides a useful device of classification: *Trek to Madworld* by Sky's husband, Stephen Goldin, is whimsical and extravagant; Sky's version has a deeper concentration on personality, and is in effect a serious consideration of what it means to be a Vulcan or to love one. The fan's potential delight in this can be easily imagined, and Sky does well in capturing Spock's angular appeal, his passionless speech, his promise of intensities withheld. Her portrayal of Katalya Tremain, the scientist who tries to hate Vulcans in order to avoid loving them, is less consistent, but the book as a whole works. Sky transmits both Spock's calm appreciation of the powers he has and his regret at his limitations. He helps Tremain to change but cannot change himself. His last request to the woman is that she help him to rediscover his childhood imagination and thus find a way out of his box of logical competence.

Sky's style is as yet unremarkable; she chooses the nearest words to communicate what she envisions—the view from inside a sensitive mind looking at a landscape both alien and alienating, where endurance is a value and change expensive. This view is one that lends itself to science fiction, to making new landscapes and locating characters in them emotionally as well as sensually. Sky's work is not an investigation into science or ideas, but into experience, and she succeeds, even in her career's outset, in making the experiences both strange and believable.

—Karen G. Way

SLADEK, John (Thomas). Also writes as Thom Demijohn; Cassandra Knye. American. Born in Waverly, Iowa, 15 December 1937. Educated at College of St. Thomas, St. Paul, Minnesota, 1955-56; University of Minnesota, Minneapolis, 1956-59. Married in 1970, one child. Engineering assistant, University of Minnesota, 1959-61; technical writer, Technical Publications Inc., St. Louis Park, Minnesota, 1961-62; switchman, Great Northern Railway, Minneapolis, 1962-63; draftsman, New York, 1964-65. Editor, with

Pamela A. Zoline, *Ronald Reagan: The Magazine of Poetry*, London, 1968. Agent: A.P. Watt Ltd., 26-28 Bedford Row, London WC1R 4HL, England.

SCIENCE-FICTION PUBLICATIONS

Novels

The Reproductive System. London, Gollancz, 1968; New York, Avon, 1974; as *Mechasm*, New York, Ace, 1969.
The Müller-Fokker Effect. London, Hutchinson, 1970; New York, Morrow, 1971.
Roderick; or, The Education of a Young Machine. London, Granada, 1980.

Short Stories

The Steam-Driven Boy and Other Strangers. London, Panther, 1973.
Keep the Giraffe Burning. London, Panther, 1977.
The Best of John Sladek. New York, Pocket Books, 1981.

OTHER PUBLICATIONS

Novels

The House That Fear Built (as Cassandra Knye, with Thomas M. Disch). New York, Paperback Library, 1966.
The Castle and the Key (as Cassandra Knye). New York, Paperback Library, 1967.
Black Alice (as Thom Demijohn, with Thomas M. Disch). New York, Doubleday, 1968; London, W.H. Allen, 1969.
Black Aura. London, Cape, 1974; New York, Walker, 1980.
Invisible Green. London, Gollancz, 1977; New York, Walker, 1979.

Other

The New Apocrypha: Guide to Strange Science and Occult Beliefs. London, Hart Davis MacGibbon, 1973; New York, Stein and Day, 1974.

John Sladek comments:

Most of my novels and short stories are set in the near future, in a recognizable America in which technology has either solved all of our problems or failed to solve any of them, or something else entirely has happened. Something else entirely is always happening in science fiction, I understand. My work is usually called satire or black humor, but it also reflects my preoccupation with certain themes.

I am endlessly fascinated by machines which can mimic or displace human beings. So a number of my characters are robots (such as "The Steam-Driven Boy") or computers or cyborgs, or self-replicating machines (as in *Mechasm*). This theme informs *Roderick; or The Education of a Young Machine*, first of a two-part novel which attempts to cover the entire "life" history of a robot learning machine, and efforts to assimilate him into human society.

A parallel concern is with dehumanizing processes—ways in which governments and other institutions, mistakenly modelled on machines, attempt to reduce their citizens or members to mechanical components. This is the argument of three novellas, "Masterson and the Clerks," "The Communicants," and "The Great Wall of Mexico," and of at least a dozen short stories, and it creeps into the novels, too. It seems almost as though machines, evolving rapidly towards a kind of mimetic humanity, are meeting humans on the way down.

People do of course escape the process of robotization, and one escape route is madness, another recurring theme. Most of the stories in *Keep the Giraffe Burning* seem to deal with mad people (as well as bad, sad, and silly people) and how they succeed at their madness. As the title indicates, these stories are steeped in Surrealism; they are meant to blur the border between dream and reality.

That border is blurred by science fiction all the time. Science fiction, it seems to me, constitutes the right brain hemisphere of contemporary fiction (the dreaming part). My work, if it isn't buried in the hypothalamus or the hippocampus or something, is probably somewhere near the lobotomy scars.

*   *   *

John Sladek's work in SF has persistently been compared to that of Kurt Vonnegut, since its principal characteristics include parody, satire, grotesquerie, the absurd. Sladek's SF is unlike Vonnegut's principally in its tendency toward the surreal, its enforcement of aesthetic distance in the reader, its constant attack upon sentiment. The milk of human kindness is not present, but Sladek's deadpan pileup of absurdities is often uproariously funny; if there is such a thing as amoral satire, Sladek achieves it. He is closer in spirit to the Nathanael West of *Miss Lonelyhearts* than to Vonnegut. His style has been unfashionable in the US, and consequently considered uncommercial. In addition, in the 1960's he was associated with the British New Wave centered around *New Worlds,* considered in some circles an exemplar of the "experimental and literary" (for which read not traditional and unpopular). Therefore his short fiction has not been widely available.

It is in shorter lengths that Sladek has been most accomplished, precise, and impressive. His comic effects often depend upon hyperbole and absurdities—at novel length the effect sometimes diminishes through repetition. *The Reproductive System* is better than *The Müller-Fokker Effect* partially because it is shorter, but also because its mood is more playful. *The Müller-Fokker Effect* is satire bitter sometimes to the point of nastiness—losing the sympathetic attention of many readers. Sladek seems to have little or no compassion for any of its characters. Sladek's notable stories are contained in two collections. The parodies of major SF authors (*The Steam-Driven Boy*) are particularly acute and effective commentary on their subjects, including Bradbury, Asimov, Heinlein, Dick, and Cordwainer Smith. Stories such as "The Poets of Millgrove, Iowa," a wicked and unsettling vision of a disillusioned astronaut suffering a fete in his honor in his old home town, "The Secret of the Old Custard," Sladek's surreal mode triumphant, and "Elephant with Wooden Leg," the maddest of mad-scientist stories, display Sladek at his best. Perhaps the final lines of his introduction to the second collection communicate the unique qualities of his style best: "People have laughed at all great inventors and discoverers. They laughed at Galileo, at Edison's light bulb, and even at nitrous oxide. I hope they will laugh, a little, at these stories."

—David G. Hartwell

SLESAR, Henry. Also writes O.H. Leslie. American. Born in Brooklyn, New York, 12 June 1927. Educated in public schools. Served in the United States Air Force, 1946-47. Married 1) Oenone Scott in 1953; 2) Jan Maakestad in 1970; 3) Manuela Jone in 1974; one daughter and one son. Advertising Executive: Vice-President and Creative Director, Robert W. Orr Inc., New York, 1949-57; Fuller and Smith and Ross, New York, 1957-60; West Wir and Bartel, New York, 1960-64. President and Creative Director, Slesar and Kanzer, New York, 1964-69, and since 1974, Slesar and Manuela. Recipient: Mystery Writers of America Edgar Allan Poe Award, for novel, 1960, for television serial, 1977; Emmy Award, 1974. Agent: Jerome S. Siegel Associates, 8733 Sunset Boulevard, Hollywood, California 90069. Address: 125 East 72nd Street, New York, New York 10021, U.S.A.

SCIENCE-FICTION PUBLICATIONS

Uncollected Short Stories

"The Brat," in *Imaginative Tales* (Evanston, Illinois), September 1955.

"The Bloodless Laws," in *Fantastic Universe* (Chicago), May 1956.
"The Monument," in *Amazing* (New York), July 1956.
"The Movie Makers," in *Fantastic Universe* (Chicago), July 1956.
"A Message from Our Sponsor," in *Infinity* (New York), October 1956.
"Sleep It Off," in *Amazing* (New York), November 1956.
"The Chimp," in *Fantastic* (New York), December 1956.
"Repeat Broadcast," in *Amazing* (New York), December 1956.
"Who Am I," in *Super Science Fiction* (New York), December 1956.
"Thought for Today," in *If* (New York), December 1956.
"20 Million Miles to Earth," from screenplay, in *Amazing Stories Science Fiction Novel 1* (New York), 1957.
"Dream Town," in *Fantastic Universe* (Chicago), January 1957.
"Heart," in *Amazing* (New York), January 1957.
"Beauty Contest," in *Fantastic* (New York), February 1957.
"Mr. Loneliness," in *Super Science Fiction* (New York), February 1957.
"The Goddess of World 21," in *Fantastic* (New York), March 1957.
"25 Words or Less," in *Fantastic Universe* (Chicago), April 1957.
"Brainchild," in *If* (New York), April 1957.
"Bottle Baby," in *Fantastic* (New York), April 1957.
"The Metal Martyr," in *Fantastic* (New York), May 1957.
"The Babbit from Bzlfsk," in *Amazing* (New York), June 1957.
"Ben's Idea," in *Satellite* (New York), June 1957.
"Desire Woman," in *Super Science Fiction* (New York), June 1957.
"The Show Must Go On," in *Infinity* (New York), July 1957.
"The Secret of Marracott Deep," in *Fantastic* (New York), July 1957.
"A God Named Smith," in *Amazing* (New York), July 1957.
"Monster on Stage 4," in *Amazing* (New York), August 1957..
"Traveling Man," in *Fantastic* (New York), August 1957.
"Saucer/Saucer," in *Fantastic* (New York), September 1957.
"The Success Machine," in *Amazing* (New York), September 1957.
"Jewel of Ecstasy," in *Fantastic* (New York), February 1958.
"The Night We Died," in *Amazing* (New York), February 1958.
"The Moon Chute," in *Amazing* (New York), March 1958.
"The Genie Takes a Wife," in *Fantastic* (New York), March 1958.
"Brother Robot," in *Amazing* (New York), May 1958.
"The Man Who Took It with Him," in *Fantastic* (New York), June 1958.
"No Place to Go," in *Amazing* (New York), July 1958.
"Garden of Evil," in *Amazing* (New York), August 1958.
"The Delegate from Venus," in *Amazing* (New York), October 1958.
"Deadly Satellite," in *Amazing* (New York), December 1958.
"The Eleventh Plague," in *Fantastic* (New York), December 1958.
"The Blonde from Space," in *Amazing* (New York), January 1959.
"Like Father—Like Son," in *Fantastic* (New York), February 1959.
"Job Offer," in *Satellite* (New York), April 1959.
"The Worth of a Man," in *Fantastic* (New York), June 1959.
"The Trigger," in *Amazing* (New York), June 1959.
"The Traveling Couch," in *Amazing* (New York), August 1959.
"The Toy," in *Fantastic* (New York), September 1959.
"The Invisible Man Murder Case," in *Invisible Men,* edited by Basil Davenport. New York, Ballantine, 1960.
"My Father the Cat," in *The Fantastic Universe Omnibus,* edited by Hans S. Santesson. Englewood Cliffs, New Jersey, Prentice Hall, 1960; London, Panther, 1962.
"Who Is Mrs. Myob," in *Fantastic* (New York), September 1960.
"Long Shot," in *Fantastic* (New York), November 1960.
"Very Small, Very Fine," in *Amazing* (New York), November 1960.
"Chief," in *The Year's Best S-F 6,* edited by Judith Merril. New York, Simon and Schuster, 1961; London, Mayflower, 1963.
"Discoverers," in *Fantastic* (New York), April 1961.
"The Self-Improvement of Salvatore Ross," in *Fantasy and Science Fiction* (New York), May 1961.
"Policeman's Lot," in *Fantastic* (New York), August 1961.
"The Stuff," in *Galaxy* (New York), August 1961.
"The Living End," in *Fantastic* (New York), November 1961.
"The Candidate," in *The Fiend in You,* edited by Charles Beaumont. New York, Ballantine, 1962.
"Way-Station," in *Fantasy and Science Fiction* (New York), January 1963.
"Jobo," in *Amazing* (New York), May 1963.

"Before the Talent Dies," in *No Limits,* edited by Joseph W. Ferman.   New York, Ballantine, 1964.
"Beside the Golden Door," in *Amazing* (New York), February 1964.
"Prisoner in Orbit," in *Amazing* (New York), April 1964.
"The Knocking in the Castle," in *Fantastic* (New York), November 1964.
"The Rats of Dr. Picard," in *Bizarre Mystery* (Concord, New Hampshire), October 1965.
"After," in *The Playboy Book of Science Fiction and Fantasy,* edited by Ray Russell.   Chicago, Playboy Press, 1966; London, Souvenir Press, 1967.
"I Remember Oblivion," in *Fantasy and Science Fiction* (New York), March 1966.
"The Jam," in *The Playboy Book of Horror and the Supernatural,* edited by Ray Russell.   Chicago, Playboy Press, 1967; London, Souvenir Press, 1968.
"The Moving Finger Types," in *Fantasy and Science Fiction* (New York), September 1968.
"Ball of the Centuries," in *Fantastic* (New York), December 1968.
"Cry, Baby, Cry," in *Startling Mystery* (New York), Spring 1970.
"Examination Day," "Melodramine," and "Victory Parade," in *From the "S" File.*   Chicago, Playboy Press, 1971.
"I Do Not Like Thee, Dr. Feldman," in *Weird Show.*   Chicago, Playboy Press, 1971.
"Survivor No. 1 (The Man with the Green Nose)," with Harlan Ellison, in *Partners in Wonder,* by Ellison.   New York, Walker, 1971.
"Legacy of Terror," in *Satan's Pets,* edited by Vic Ghidalia.   New York, Manor, 1972.
"The Rise and Fall of the Fourth Reich," in *Fantasy and Science Fiction* (New York), August 1975.

Uncollected Short Stories as O.H. Leslie

"Death Rattle," in *Fantastic* (New York), December 1956.
"Marriages Are Made in Detroit," in *Amazing* (New York), December 1956.
"Reluctant Genius," in *Amazing* (New York), January 1957.
"My Robot," in *Fantastic* (New York), February 1957.
"Abe Lincoln—Android," in *Fantastic* (New York), April 1957.
"The Dope," in *Super Science Fiction* (New York), June 1957.
"No Room in Heaven," in *Amazing* (New York), June 1957.
"The Marriage Machine," in *Fantastic* (New York), July 1957.
"Inheritance," in *Fantastic* (New York), August 1957.
"Space Boat," in *Fantastic* (New York), January 1958.
"Danger Red," in *Fantastic* (New York), February 1958.
"The Mind Merchants," in *Amazing* (New York), February 1958.
"The Creators," in *Amazing* (New York), March 1958.
"The Search for Murphy's Bride," in *Fantastic* (New York), March 1958.
"Mission Murder," in *Amazing* (New York), November 1958.
"The Seven Eyes of Captain Dark," in *Amazing* (New York), January 1959.
"The Chair," in *Amazing* (New York), April 1964.

OTHER PUBLICATIONS

Novels

The Gray Flannel Shroud.   New York, Random House, 1959; London, Deutsch, 1960.
Enter Murderers.   New York, Random House, 1960; London, Gollancz, 1961.
The Bridge of Lions.   New York, Macmillan, 1963; London, Gollancz, 1964.
The Seventh Mask (novelization of TV play).   New York, Ace, 1969.
The Thing at the Door.   New York, Random House, 1974; London, Hamish Hamilton, 1975.

Short Stories

A Bouquet of Clean Crimes and Neat Murders.   New York, Avon, 1960.
A Crime for Mothers and Others.   New York, Avon, 1962.

Plays

Screenplays: *Two on a Guillotine,* with John Kneubuhl, 1965; *Murders in Rue Morgue,* with Christopher Wilding, 1970.

Radio Plays: *CBS Radio Mystery Theatre* (39 plays).

Television Plays: *The Edge of Night* series, 1968-79; 100 scripts for *Alfred Hitchcock Presents* and other series.

*   *   *

The magazine *TV Guide* once called Henry Slesar "the writer with the largest audience in America." This accolade, whether true or not, was due primarily to the fact that Slesar spent nine years as head writer for the daytime TV serial *The Edge of Night,* and also wrote 100 teleplays for *Alfred Hitchcock Presents* and other dramatic TV series, as well as plays for CBS Radio Mystery Theater. Most of Slesar's work in science fiction has been in the short story form. (His only SF novel is a version of the film *Twenty Million Miles to Earth,* not published in hardcover, although the suspense novel *The Bridge of Lions* may be considered borderline science fiction.) About 20 of his stories have been anthologized, most notably such excellent and provocative short-shorts as "Examination Day," "The Jam," "After" (four post-apocalyptic vignettes), and "Victory Parade." The best of Slesar's work is not only entertaining but offers quite horrifying statements on human folly and cruelty ("Examination Day"). Clever O. Henry-type surprise endings are also used to good advantage, as they are in his mystery short stories.

—Bill Pronzini

SLOANE, William M(illigan, III).   American.   Born in Plymouth, Massachusetts, 15 August 1906. Educated at Hill School, graduated, 1925; Princeton University, New Jersey, A.B. 1929 (Phi Beta Kappa). Married Julie Hawkins in 1930; one son and two daughters. Publisher: in Play Department, 1929-31, and Editorial Department, 1931, Longmans Green and Company; Manager, Fitzgerald Publishing Company, 1932-37; Associate Editor, Farrar and Rinehart, 1937-38; Manager of the Trade Department, 1939-46, and Vice-President, 1944-46, Henry Holt and Company; President, William Sloane Associates, 1946-52; Editorial Director, Funk and Wagnalls Company and Wilfred Funk Inc., 1952-55; Director, Rutgers University Press, 1955-74. Director, Council on Books in Wartime; Chairman of the Editorial Committee, Armed Services Editions, 1943-44; staff member, Bread Loaf Writers Conference, 1946-72. President, Association of American University Presses, 1969-70. *Died 25 September 1974.*

SCIENCE-FICTION PUBLICATIONS

Novels

To Walk the Night.   New York, Farrar and Rinehart, 1937; London, Barker, 1938.
The Edge of Running Water.   New York, Farrar and Rinehart, 1939; London, Methuen, 1940; as *The Unquiet Corpse,* New York, Dell, 1946.
The Rim of Morning (omnibus).   New York, Dodd Mead, 1964.

Uncollected Short Story

"Let Nothing You Dismay," in *Stories for Tomorrow,* edited by William M. Sloane.   New York, Funk and Wagnalls, 1954; London, Eyre and Spottiswoode, 1955.

OTHER PUBLICATIONS

Plays

Back Home: A Ghost Play.   New York, Longman, 1931.
Runner in the Snow: A Play of the Supernatural, adaptation of the story "I Saw a Woman Turn Into a Wolf" by W.B. Seabrook. Boston, Baker, 1931.
Digging Up the Dirt, adaptation of a play by Bert J. Norton.   New York, Longman, 1931.
Crystal Clear.   New York, Longman, 1932.
Ballots for Bill: A Light-Hearted Comedy of Politics, with William Ellis Jones.   New York, Fitzgerald, 1933.
The Silence of God: A Play for Christmas.   Boston, Baker, 1933.
Art for Art's Sake.   Boston, Baker, 1934.
The Invisible Clue.   New York, Fitzgerald, 1934.
Gold Stars for Glory.   Boston, Baker, 1935.

Other

Editor, *Space, Space, Space.*   New York, Watts, 1953.
Editor, *Stories for Tomorrow.*   New York, Funk and Wagnalls, 1954; London, Eyre and Spottiswoode, 1955.

*   *   *

William M. Sloane had an extremely brief career as a science-fiction writer, completing two novels and a single short story, but those two novels have probably won him a permanent place in the history of the genre. He blended science and horror with consummate skill, and his calm, smooth-paced novels are more successful at developing suspense and tension than most of the lurid thrillers that reach the bestseller lists.

To Walk the Night utilizes a plot device so standard, so familiar, that it has long since become a cliché avoided even by the less inventive film makers, but in the hands of a writer with Sloane's talent it is transformed into an entirely new vehicle. Two young men make a surprise visit to an old friend, and arrive just in time to see his body mysteriously incinerated as if from within. Although they are unable to explain the peculiar nature of his death, they are freed by the authorities. But one of them has become infatuated with the unexpected widow of his late friend. The perceptive reader will realize fairly soon that the mysterious death resulted from the scientist's researches into the nature of reality. Sloane leaves myriad hints of other oddities as well, the widow's awkwardness in familiar human situations, the disappearance of a young girl with virtually no intelligence, the mystery of yet another death, this time clearly suicide. Despite the fact that the reader has a clear idea what comprises the general nature of the mystery, the details provide the true suspense, and the climactic confrontation is one of the most effective scenes in the genre.

The Edge of Running Water broke no new ground either, and moves even further toward the supernatural, while still retaining the scientific rationale of its mystery. Although the characters are not as well drawn in this story of a man convinced he can develop a machine that will enable him to communicate with the dead, the element of suspense is just as expertly handled. There is little overt action, even though one character is eventually killed and another destroyed, propelled into another universe, but the reader's attention is unlikely to waver despite this fact.

Both novels have been published as mysteries, which they are, as horror stories, which they are, and science fiction, which they also are. Sloane's sole foray into more conventional science fiction, "Let Nothing You Dismay," is singularly unremarkable, a pedestrian examination of human refugees adjusting to a new world after the death of Earth. He was at his best at greater length, using a familiar setting and coloring it with a series of hints of something totally unfamiliar. His style was highly advanced for his time, and both novels are free of archaic anomalies and outdated prose. It seems clear that had Sloane chosen to pursue his career as a genre writer, he would have become one of the dominant forces within it.

—Don D'Ammassa

SMITH, Clark Ashton.   American.   Born 13 January 1893. Left school at 14. Married in 1954. Writer and artist: regular contributor to *Weird Tales* in the early 1930's; ceased writing in 1936. *Died 14 August 1961.*

SCIENCE-FICTION PUBLICATIONS

Short Stories

The Immortals of Mercury.   New York, Stellar, 1932.
Tales of Science and Sorcery.   Sauk City, Wisconsin, Arkham House, 1964; London, Panther, 1976.
Other Dimensions.   Sauk City, Wisconsin, Arkham House, 1970; London, Panther, 1977.

OTHER PUBLICATIONS

Short Stories

The Double Shadow and Other Fantasies.   Privately printed, 1933.
The White Sybil.   Everett, Pennsylvania, Fantasy, 1935 (?).
Out of Space and Time (includes verse).   Sauk City, Wisconsin, Arkham House, 1942; London, Spearman, 1971.
Lost Worlds.   Sauk City, Wisconsin, Arkham House, 1944; London, Spearman, 1971.
Genius Loci.   Sauk City, Wisconsin, Arkham House, 1948; London, Spearman, 1972.
The Abominations of Yondo.   Sauk City, Wisconsin, Arkham House, 1960; London, Spearman, 1972.
Zothique, Hyperborea, Xiccarth, Poseidonis (selections).   New York, Ballantine, 4 vols., 1970-73.
The Mortuary.   Glendale, California, Squires, 1971.
Prince Alcouz and the Magician.   Glendale, California, Squires, 1977.

Verse

The Star-Treader and Other Poems.   San Francisco, Robertson, 1912.
Odes and Sonnets.   San Francisco, Book Club of California, 1918.
Ebony and Crystal: Poems in Verse and Prose.   Privately printed, 1922.
Sandalwood.   Privately printed, 1925.
Nero and Other Poems.   Lakeport, California, Futile Press, 1937.
The Dark Chateau and Other Poems.   Sauk City, Wisconsin, Arkham House, 1951.
Spells and Philtres.   Sauk City, Wisconsin, Arkham House, 1958.
Poems in Prose.   Sauk City, Wisconsin, Arkham House, 1965.
Grotesques and Fantastiques.   Saddle River, New Jersey, Gerry de la Ree, 1973.
Klarkash-ton and Monstro Kigriv.   Saddle River, New Jersey, Gerry de la Ree, 1974.
Fugitive Poems.   Privately printed, 4 vols., 1974-75.

Other

Planets and Dimensions: Collected Essays, edited by Charles K. Wolfe.   Baltimore, Mirage Press, 1973.

*   *   *

Clark Ashton Smith was a contributor to the early sceince-fiction and fantasy pulp magazines whose output, despite its unevenness, became a seminal influence on modern science fiction. Jack Vance, Harlan Ellison, Theodore Sturgeon, Fritz Leiber, H.P. Lovecraft, Robert E. Howard, and Ray Bradbury, among others, were influenced by his work.

Smith's earliest short stories—he wrote no novels—are the primitive interplanetary narratives common in the pulp magazines. Of these, "Marooned in Andromeda" and "The Amazing Planet" are typical. They recount the adventures of the crew of the space ship *Alcyone* on distant worlds, and are odysseys of perilous adventure distinguished only by Smith's exotic language and bizarre imagination.

Smith, also a poet, was concerned mainly with the poetry of death and the alien. His protagonists are decidedly unheroic, being either misfits or rogues who seek other worlds because they do not fit into their own. In "The Monster of the Prophecy" the suicidal poet Theophilus Alvor agreeably becomes the instrument through which the Antarean wizard Vizaphmal assumes control of his world. This lack of virtue does not prevent Alvor from finding true love in the arms of an Antarean woman. Similarly, the renegade and thief Datu Buang lives out his life in peace after assassinating an evil ruler with the aid of his consort in "As It Is Written."

The search for a better reality is the predominant theme in Smith. In his haunting classic, "The City of the Singing Flame," the author Giles Angarth discovers the gateway to another dimension where the Singing Flame lures the unwary into its fires. Angarth finds himself finally drawn to the flame and discovers it is the entrance to still another, better, reality beyond.

Those stories set wholly on other worlds, in which he gives his poetic vision free rein, are considered Smith's best. Among these are the sardonic tales of the world of Xiccarpth and those set on the continent of Zothique in the last days of Earth. In "The Maze of Maal Dweb" the hunter Tiglari seeks his kidnapped lover in the stronghold of Xiccarph's tyrant, Maal Dweb, but falls victim to the tyrant's powers. Maal Dweb, on the other hand, is the protagonist of "The Flower-Women." It is a peculiarity of Smith's fiction that the amoral flourish and the good become the victims of ironic fates. Like Tiglari, the hero of "The Demon of the Flower" ultimately fails to rescue the woman he loves from the plant ruler of his world. The tales of Zothique, although set in Earth's distant future, are closer to fantasy. In these Smith's macabre poetic vision is at its highest. "Xeethra" is a poignant story of a goatherd who partakes of strange fruit and imagines himself the ruler of a distant land. He goes in search of that land, only to find it in ruins. "The Last Hieroglyph" is an ironic tale of an astrologer, Nushain, who reads in the stars that he must go on a journey which will fulfill his destiny. At the voyage's end, he meets his end. "The Weaver in the Vault" relates the weird doom of two individuals who desecrate a tomb. Hope and futility are expertly balanced in "The Isle of the Torturers."

Despite the weird trappings of his stories, Smith's work cannot be rightfully labeled as horror stories. He was a fatalist who delighted in spinning phantasms, not terror. With rare exceptions ("Master of the Asteroid" and "The Dweller in the Gulf"), his work is too remote from reality to evoke a convincing mood of horror and his imaginings thus fascinate instead of terrify. The power of Smith's writing, and the reason for its widespread influence, lay in the fact that Smith shared with many of his protagonists a yearning for a reality *truer* than the one he knew, and he discovered a language which enabled him to express his unique vision.

—Will Murray

SMITH, Cordwainer. Pseudonym for Paul Myron Anthony Linebarger; also wrote as Felix C. Forrest; Carmichael Smith. American. Born in Milwaukee, Wisconsin, 11 July 1913. Educated at the University of Nanking, 1930; North China Union Language School, 1931; George Washington University, Washington, D.C., A.B. 1933 (Phi Beta Kappa); Oxford University, 1933; American University, Washington, D.C., 1934; University of Chicago, 1935; Johns Hopkins University, Baltimore, M.A. 1935; Ph.D. 1936; University of Michigan, Ann Arbor, 1937, 1939; Washington School of Psychiatry, certificate in psychiatry 1955; Universidad Interamericana, 1959-60. Served in the United States Army Intelligence Service, 1942-66: helped found Office of War Information, served in Chungking, 1942-46, and as consultant to British forces in Malaya, 1950, and to 8th Army, Korea, 1950-52: Lieutenant Colonel. Married Genevieve Cecilia Collins in 1950; two daughters by previous marriage. Instructor, Harvard University,

Cambridge, Massachusetts, 1936-37; Instructor, then Associate Professor, Duke University, Durham, North Carolina, 1937-46; Professor of Asiatic Politics, Johns Hopkins University School of Advanced International Studies, Washington, D.C., 1946-66. Visiting Professor, University of Pennsylvania, Philadelphia, 1955-56, and Australian National University, Canberra, 1957. President, American Peace Society. *Died 6 August 1966.*

SCIENCE-FICTION PUBLICATIONS

Novels (series: Instrumentality in all books)

The Planet Buyer.   New York, Pyramid, 1964.
The Underpeople.   New York, Pyramid, 1968.
Norstrilia (omnibus).   New York, Ballantine, 1975.

Short Stories (series: Instrumentality)

You Will Never Be the Same.   Evanston, Illinois, Regency, 1963.
Space Lords (Instrumentality).   New York, Pyramid, 1965; London, Sidgwick and Jackson, 1969.
Quest of the Three Worlds.   New York, Ace, 1966.
Under Old Earth and Other Explorations.   London, Panther, 1970.
Stardreamer.   New York, Beagle, 1971.
The Best of Cordwainer Smith.   New York, Doubleday, 1975.
The Instrumentality of Mankind.   New York, Ballantine, 1979.

OTHER PUBLICATIONS

Novels

Ria (as Felix C. Forrest).   New York, Duell, 1947.
Carola (as Felix C. Forrest).   New York, Duell, 1948.
Atomsk (as Carmichael Smith).   New York, Duell, 1949.

Other as P.M.A. Linebarger

The Political Doctrines of Sun Yat-Sen.   Baltimore, Johns Hopkins University Press, 1937.
Government in Republican China.   New York, McGraw Hill, 1938.
The China of Chiang Kai-shek.   Boston, World Peace Foundation, 1941.
Psychological Warfare.   Washington, D.C., Infantry Journal Press, 1948; revised edition, Washington, D.C., Combat Forces Press, 1954.
Far Eastern Governments and Politics, with Djang Chu and Ardath W. Burks.   New York, Van Nostrand, 1952.

Editor, *The Gospel of Chung Shan,* by Paul Linebarger.   Privately printed, 1932.
Editor, *The Ocean Men,* by Paul Linebarger.   Washington, D.C., Mid-Nation, 1937.

*

Bibliography: in *Exploring Cordwainer Smith,* edited by Andrew Porter, New York, Algol Press, 1975.

*   *   *

Paul Linebarger, who wrote science fiction under the name Cordwainer Smith, certainly stands as one of the most unusual and imaginative writers of fantastic literature of this century. Though his total output of fiction is relatively small, Smith's reputation and influence have grown consistently since his death in 1966. Virtually his entire science fiction output was in print in book form by early 1979, and the theme that ties most of these stories together—a future galactic civilization called the Instrumentality of Mankind—has emerged as one of the most striking and detailed future history constructs in all of science fiction. His non-science-fiction novels *Ria* and *Carola* also reveal the strength of imagination, idiosyncratic style, and sensitivity to character that make his better-known work stand out.

Smith was a Christian, a romantic, and a shrewd political theorist who had written under his own name an internationally influential text on psychological warfare. All of these strains come together in his fiction, giving it a complexity and depth of meaning that are sometimes confusing to readers encountering one of his stories for the first time. The first of his mature stories to be published (his first science-fiction story, "War No. 81-Q," had appeared when he was only 15), "Scanners Live in Vain," appeared in 1950, and clearly implied a more detailed imaginary universe than the story itself explained. Set early in the history of the Instrumentality, the tale concerns a threat posed to the guild of "scanners"—humans mechanically restructured to survive in space—by the discovery of a new and safer means of space travel. In a characteristically bizarre Smith touch, the new method depends on lining the spaceships with oysters to insulate the passengers from harm. Clearly, this odd version of a technological breakthrough represented an event of historical importance to this future world, but the nature of that world itself remained unclear.

During the next decade and a half, Smith gradually filled in some of the gaps. Following a series of disastrous wars that nearly reduced Earth to barbarism, humanity gradually recovers its vitality, aided by a powerful family called the Vomacts, descended from the daughters of a Nazi scientist who were placed in suspended animation in orbit and who returned following the wars ("Mark Elf" and "The Queen of the Afternoon"). The Vomacts help give rise to the universal government called the Instrumentality, which initially explores space with the aid of scanners, briefly replaces these with the oyster-shell ships, and in turn replaces these with ships powered by massive photonic sails ("The Lady Who Sailed *The Soul*," "Think Blue, Count Two"). Finally, a near-instantaneous form of space travel, called planoforming, is discovered ("The Colonel Came Back from the Nothing-at-All," "The Burning of the Brain"), but planoforming ships are subject to attacks by hideous, incorporeal outer-space "dragons" and must be protected by telepathic technicians called pinlighters, sometimes assisted by telepathic cats ("The Game of Rat and Dragon"). As the Instrumentality grows increasingly powerful and decadent—offering humans near-immortality through a life-extending drug called stroon—its economy comes to depend on a slave class of converted animals called underpeople. Aided by a few heroic underpeople and the sympathetic Jestocost family, the underpeople finally attain civil rights ("The Dead Lady of Clown Town," "Under Old Earth," "The Ballad of Lost C'Mell"), and a renaissance of humanism, the Rediscovery of Man, sets in ("Alpha Ralpha Boulevard," *Norstrilia*). In the far distant future, civilization finally seems to be achieving some kind of stability (*Quest of the Three Worlds*), but the actual conclusion of the history of the Instrumentality, if planned by Smith, was not completed during his lifetime.

Although there is an abundance of political and social satire in Smith's work—the Instrumentality is clearly not a simple utopia—what stands out most are the memorable characters of near-mythic proportions, the romantic legends he weaves, and the oddly nostalgic style, reminiscent of oral history or folktales, in which he writes. Smith has a unique ability to make a romance between a man and a cat convincing ("The Game of Rat and Dragon") or to make an unconsummated romance between a servant girl and a lord as powerful as a medieval legend ("The Ballad of Lost C'Mell"). Occasionally, he turns to actual legends for his source material; "The Dead Lady of Clown Town" is a retelling of the Joan of Arc legend, with Joan made into an underperson converted from a dog. In other cases, he turns to literary culture for his sources; "Drunkboat" is essentially a tour de force on themes from Arthur Rimbaud. "Golden the Ship Was—Oh! Oh! Oh!" is at once a satire on the bureaucracy of war and a retelling of the Trojan horse story—with the horse becoming a 90-million-mile-long decoy spaceship used to frighten an enemy while second-level bureaucrats drop poisonous bombs. Other of his stories are supposedly based on Chinese narrative techniques, and occasionally he deliberately plays games with the reader, such as working anagrammatic references to the Kennedy-Oswald assassinations into *Quest of the Three Worlds*. One wonders, at times, whether Smith's curious style and unusual way of structuring stories is due to his great sophistication or to his ingenuousness as a writer. *Norstrilia* does not stand up as well as do

many of the short stories, partly because the narrative tends to ramble, partly because the style seems to grow self-conscious over such an extended narrative. But Smith's short fiction includes some of science fiction's finest stories, and demonstrates that an author need not abandon sensitive insights into love and ethics in order to create imaginary universes of great imagination.

—Gary K. Wolfe

SMITH, E(dward) E(lmer). American. Born in Sheboygan, Wisconsin, 1 May 1890. Educated at the University of Idaho, Moscow; George Washington University, Washington, D.C., Ph.D. in food chemistry 1919. Served in an explosives arsenal during World War II. Married Jeannie McDougall; one daughter and one son. Worked as ranch hand, lumberjack, silver miner, and surveyor, before becoming chemist, specializing in food mixes: Manager of General Mix Division of J.W. Allen and Company, 1945; retired in the early 1960's. Recipient: First Fandom Hall of Fame Award (as "Doc" Smith), 1964. Guest of Honor, 2nd World Science Fiction Convention, 1940. *Died 31 August 1965.*

SCIENCE-FICTION PUBLICATIONS

Novels (series: Lensman; Skylark)

The Skylark of Space, with Mrs. Lee Hawkins Garby. Providence, Rhode Island, Buffalo, 1946; revised edition, New York, Pyramid, 1958; London, Digit, 1959.
Spacehounds of IPC. Reading, Pennsylvania, Fantasy Press, 1947; London, Panther, 1974.
Skylark Three. Reading, Pennsylvania, Fantasy Press, 1948; London, Panther, 1974.
The History of Civilization (Lensman):
  Triplanetary. Reading, Pennsylvania, Fantasy Press, 1948; London, Boardman, 1954.
  First Lensman. Reading, Pennsylvania, Fantasy Press, 1950; London, Boardman, 1955.
  Galactic Patrol. Reading, Pennsylvania, Fantasy Press, 1950; London, W.H. Allen, 1971.
  Gray Lensman. Reading, Pennsylvania, Fantasy Press, 1951; London, W.H. Allen, 1971.
  Second Stage Lensman. Reading, Pennsylvania, Fantasy Press, 1953; London, W.H. Allen, 1972.
  Children of the Lens. Reading, Pennsylvania, Fantasy Press, 1954; London, W.H. Allen, 1972.
Skylark of Valeron. Reading, Pennsylvania, Fantasy Press, 1949.
The Vortex Blaster (Lensman). New York, Gnome Press, 1960; as *Masters of the Vortex*, New York, Pyramid, 1968; London, W.H. Allen, 1972.
The Galaxy Primes. New York, Ace, 1965; London, Panther, 1975.
Subspace Explorers. New York, Canaveral Press, 1965; London, Panther, 1975.
Skylark DuQuesne. New York, Pyramid, 1966; London, Panther, 1974.
Masters of Space. London, Futura, 1976.

Short Stories

The Best of E.E. ("Doc") Smith. London, Futura, 1975.

OTHER PUBLICATIONS

Novel

Imperial Stars, completed by Stephen Goldin. New York, Pyramid, 1976.

Other

What Does This Convention Mean? A Speech Delivered at the Chicago 1940 World's Science Fiction Convention. Privately printed, 1941.

"The Epic of Space," in *Of Worlds Beyond*, edited by Lloyd Arthur Eshbach. Chicago, Advent, 1964.

* * *

It is difficult if not impossible to overestimate the impact of E.E. "Doc" Smith on 20th-century science fiction. He developed and perfected the space opera, a form which had existed only in a rudimentary state prior to his work. As one of the two major forms of "pulp" science fiction, space opera should be distinguished from interplanetary romance. The latter, with strong roots in 19th-century works, was perfected about 1912 by Edgar Rice Burroughs, and continued in later years by innumerable others of whom the greatest was probably Leigh Brackett. In interplanetary romance an adventurer is transported rapidly by any convenient means to an alien planet. This planet is generally primitive, inhabited by non-technological societies, and in these societies the adventurer rises by means of derring-do not very different from those described in the works of Rafael Sabatini. The space opera, in contrast, involves the clash of two or more technologically advanced societies. The protagonist society is normally human; the antagonist may be human or otherwise. Major segments of the action take place in outer space, usually in spaceships or fleets of spaceships quite comparable to 20th-century navies. A frequent sub-theme of space opera is the interplanetary or interstellar alliance of wildly differing intelligent species.

Precursors of space opera may be found in works of the late 19th and early 20th centuries. Smith's contemporary Edmond Hamilton actually preceded Smith into print with relevant works, starting with *Across Space*, serialized in *Weird Tales* from September 1926. However, with the appearance of Smith's *The Skylark of Space* in *Amazing Stories* in 1928, Smith achieved pre-eminence in the field and never was surpassed. (Smith actually began the novel in 1915 and completed it in 1919.) A secondary point concerns the role of Mrs. Lee Hawkins Garby in the writing of the book. It is widely known that Smith asked Mrs. Garby to assist him with "the love interest." The usually perceptive critic Paul A. Carter infers from this that "so incidental was the heroine to the plot that the author himself need pay no attention to her!" Carter quite misinterprets Smith's motive: Smith was concerned that he might delineate his heroine and "the love interest" inadequately, and sought assistance in doing a proper job. (The result was still thoroughly stilted and unsatisfying, and in later works Smith omitted the collaboration. With passing years, Smith's delineation of character—regardless of gender—improved substantially, but neither characterization nor dialogue nor "the love interest" was ever his strongest suit.)

Once Smith was established, numerous others wrote within the arena he had created. The two who did so most effectively were Hamilton and Jack Williamson. Clifford Simak, in *Cosmic Engineers*, produced a single, brilliant space opera. John W. Campbell, Jr., before switching his energies from authorship to editing, also wrote a number of such works. More recently the film *Star Wars* has been classed by many viewers as the "purest" space opera yet produced in dramatic form. The bulk of Smith's works falls into two series. The Skylark series runs to four volumes. It opens with a thoroughly familiar love triangle, the rival suitors being the noble, brilliant Richard Seaton and the villainous, brilliant "Blacky" DuQuesne. When Seaton invents an atomic-powered spaceship, he and DuQuesne proceed to battle on an ever-growing canvas for the favor of the lovely and accomplished Dorothy Vaneman. Upon this rudimentary framework, Smith built the most audacious and energetic series of super-scientific adventures—often harking back to the geographic wonder-tales of Verne—written up to that time.

But Smith's Lensman cycle exceeded even the Skylark series in scope, audacity, and power. They represent space opera at its very peak of development; the two central volumes of the series, *Galactic Patrol* and *Gray Lensman*, certainly embody both the greatest virtues and the greatest faults of the space-opera form. These novels are based on the premise that a cosmic struggle is taking place, between the Arisians, godlike protectors of the galaxy, and the

Eddorians, satanic invaders and destroyers from another galaxy. The epic spans eons of time and inconceivable volumes of space, in the tradition of the works of Olaf Stapledon. Its central phase involves a family saga, the most notable character being Kimball Kinnison, Smith's supreme hero. In sequence after sequence, seemingly cosmic struggles between the two great forces are seen to be merely local incidents in the titanic war which only Smith fully knows. The Lensmen are a cosmic "elite corps" of the forces of Arisia; as such they are carefully selected individuals of the highest intellectual, physical, and moral perfection. Each receives, as badge of membership in this corps, a lens which not only identifies its owner but amplifies that owner's outstanding abilities into the superhuman range. Smith's advocates have suggested that the struggle between Arisia and Eddore, if it is to be read as more than a grand but literal-minded adventure, may be considered a sort of Judeo-Christian allegory, with the Arisians representing the forces of Heaven and the Eddorians the Adversary. In this regard, congruences are obvious between the series and Tolkien's *Lord of the Rings*. Both cycles, in this aspect, are further comparable to Wagner's great operatic cycle. On the other hand, Smith's critics have pointed out that the elitism, the (at least implicit) racism, the ruthlessness, and the authoritarianism involved in Lens philosophy make the works more Nazi-like than Biblical in theme.

In addition to his two major series, Smith wrote a number of other works. *Spacehounds of IPC* is a charming retelling of the babes-in-the-woods story, with boy and girl castaway on an alien planet. *The Galaxy Primes* is an unsuccessful attempt to write a more modern novel with psionic themes. *Subspace Explorers* is a very readable volume intended as the first of three in a final series. The other two volumes never appeared but it is believed that Smith had completed at least a draft of the second before his death.

Smith was the very paradigm of the great "primitive" novelist, perhaps comparable to Grandma Moses in painting. Where the formal or academic novelist may be judged on the basis of subtlety of characterization, polish of style, complexity of plot, ambiguity of theme—and, in the case of the science-fiction writer, detail, plausibility, and accuracy of scientific background—the primitive novelist is subject to a quite different set of criteria—*vividness* rather than subtlety of characterization, *dynamism* rather than polish of style, *power* rather than complexity of plot, and *directness* rather than ambiguity of theme. In the case of the science-fiction writer in particular, the primitive may be judged by the audacity, emotional and structural effect of any scientific postulate not obviously absurd. By these criteria, Smith was the absolute champion of his realm.

—Richard A. Lupoff

SMITH, Evelyn E. Also writes as Delphine C. Lyons. American. Born in 1927. Writer and crossword puzzle compiler. Lives in New York.

SCIENCE-FICTION PUBLICATIONS

Novels

The Perfect Planet. New York, Avalon, 1962.
Valley of Shadows (as Delphine C. Lyons). New York, Lancer, 1968.
Unpopular Planet. New York, Dell, 1975.

Uncollected Short Stories

"Nightmare on the Nose," in *Fantastic Universe* (Chicago), November 1953.
"Baxbr Daxbr," in *Time to Come*, edited by August Derleth. New York, Farrar Straus, 1954.

"Not Fit for Children" and "Tea Tray in the Sky," in *Second Galaxy Reader of Science Fiction*, edited by H.L. Gold. New York, Crown, 1954; London, Grayson, 1955.

"Call Me Wizard," in *Beyond* (New York), January 1954.

"Gerda," in *Fantasy and Science Fiction* (New York), April 1954.

"The Agony of the Leaves," in *Beyond* (New York), July 1954.

"At Last I've Found You," in *Fantasy and Science Fiction* (New York), October 1954.

"Collector's Item," in *Galaxy* (New York), December 1954.

"The Laminated Woman," in *Fantastic Universe* (Chicago), December 1954.

"Helpfully Yours," in *Galaxy* (New York), February 1955.

"The Big Jump," in *Fantastic Universe* (Chicago), March 1955.

"Man's Best Friend," in *Galaxy* (New York), April 1955.

"The Princess and the Physicist," in *Galaxy* (New York), June 1955.

"The Faithful Friend," in *Fantasy and Science Fiction* (New York), June 1955.

"Teregram," in *Fantastic Universe* (Chicago), June 1955.

"Dragon Lady," in *Beyond* (New York), June 1955.

"The Good Husband," in *Fantastic Universe* (Chicago), August 1955.

"The Doorway," in *Fantastic Universe* (Chicago), September 1955.

"Weather Prediction," in *Fantastic Universe* (Chicago), October 1955.

"Jack of No Trades," in *Galaxy* (New York), October 1955.

"Floyd and the Eumenides," in *Fantastic Universe* (Chicago), December 1955.

"The Captain's Mate," in *Fantasy and Science Fiction* (New York), March 1956.

"The Venus Trap," in *Galaxy* (New York), June 1956.

"Mr. Replogle's Dream," in *Fantastic Universe* (Chicago), December 1956.

"Woman's Touch," in *Super Science Fiction* (New York), February 1957.

"The Ignoble Savages," in *Galaxy* (New York), March 1957.

"The Lady from Aldebaran," in *Fantastic Universe* (Chicago), March 1957.

"The 4D Bargain," in *Saturn* (Holyoke, Massachusetts), May 1957.

"Outcast of Mars," in *Fantasy and Science Fiction* (New York), May 1957.

"The Most Sentimental Man," in *Fantastic Universe* (Chicago), August 1957.

"The Man Outside," in *Galaxy* (New York), August 1957.

"The Weegil," in *Super Science Fiction* (New York), December 1957.

"The Vilbar Party," in *The Third Galaxy Reader*, edited by H.L. Gold. New York, Doubleday, 1958.

"The Blue Tower," in *Galaxy* (New York), February 1958.

"My Fair Planet," in *Galaxy* (New York), March 1958.

"Two Suns of Morcali," in *Fantastic Universe* (Chicago), July 1958.

"Once a Greech," in *Worlds That Couldn't Be and 8 Other SF Novelets*, edited by H.L. Gold. New York, Doubleday, 1959.

"The People Upstairs," in *Fantastic Universe* (Chicago), March 1959.

"The Alternate Host," in *Fantastic Universe* (Chicago), September 1959.

"Send Her Victorious," in *Fantasy and Science Fiction* (New York), February 1960.

"The Hardest Bargain," in *Mind Partner and 8 Other Novelets from Galaxy*, edited by H.L. Gold. New York, Doubleday, 1961.

"Sentry of the Sky," in *Galaxy* (New York), February 1961.

"Robert E. Lee at Moscow," in *Fantasy and Science Fiction* (New York), October 1961.

"Softly While You're Sleeping," in *The Best from Fantasy and Science Fiction 11*, edited by Robert P. Mills. New York, Doubleday, 1962.

"They Also Serve," in *Fantasy and Science Fiction* (New York), September 1962.

"The Last of the Spode," in *17 x Infinity*, edited by Groff Conklin. New York, Dell, 1963.

"The Martian and the Magician," in *Fifty Short Science Fiction Tales*, edited by Isaac Asimov and Groff Conklin. New York, Macmillan, 1963.

"Little Gregory," in *Fantasy and Science Fiction* (New York), February 1964.

"Calliope and Gherkin and the Yankee Doodle Thing," in *The Best from Fantasy and Science Fiction 19*, edited by Edward L. Ferman. New York, Doubleday, 1971.

"A Day in the Suburbs," in *Sociology Through Science Fiction*, edited by John W. Milstead and others. New York, St. Martin's Press, 1974.

OTHER PUBLICATIONS

Other

The Building Book (juvenile). New York, Howell Soskin, 1947.

*   *   *

Although Evelyn E. Smith's individual works of SF vary greatly in style, mood, and focus, it is possible to characterize her work as making a wry statement about human nature. Here is an author who is optimistic in spite of herself; even in those works which focus on post-nuclear holocaust worlds, humanity has survived and—whether or not its representatives are honorable or otherwise admirable—they do possess the ability to meet wild challenges and to survive their own foibles.

Smith's comments on human nature range from sharp and ironical to light and ludicrous. Her first story, "The Last of the Spode," is a terse portrayal of three Britishers who, by a twist of fate, seem to be the sole survivors of nuclear holocaust. A "correct" professor and a young chap join a figure of British womanhood in an afternoon tea at the end of the world. As the Spode teapot is poured out, they reveal their chief concern as to whether or not their tea supply will last them to the end of their days. "No point in anything, really," the young chap remarks. "We must face the facts, lad," the professor says and then adds, in a gem of understatement, "Pity about the Bodleian, though." "The Hardest Bargain" envisions another post-holocaust future, in which the American populace is weakened with hunger and racial debility. Presidential advisor Dr. Livingston, who believes that "the thinking man is the despairing man," urges President Buchbinder to accept extraterrestrial aid in decontaminating the lands, but when the earthlings fail to keep their bargain to pay the extraterrestrial Foma in famous works of art, the Foma reveals his true identity as a pied piper to the robots which are so desperately needed by human society. "Not Fit for Children" is representative of Smith's more lighthearted stories. Here a group of alien children pose as war-dancing "natives" on an asteroid-like space ship which is visited regularly by human tourists. In payment for their antics, the children receive coins which are melted down by their disbelieving elders into metal which is needed to repair their space ship.

Most of Smith's short stories appeared during the 1950's; just as they varied in seriousness of theme as well as sophistication of writing technique, her novels represent the extremes of the author's abilities. *The Perfect Planet* shares the wry ironic tone of so many of her shorter works, as the author tells an amusing but insubstantial tale of two astronauts, one male and one female, who land on a planet populated by vain health enthusiasts who foist their obsession with slim, perfect physiques upon the slightly pudgy, space-weary duo. While the book does have some impact as a critique of mindless conformity, sadly the astronauts, who start out as rebellious to the ways of this world, come to have a fondness for the pampered inhabitants of "the perfumed planet." The initially gutsy female astronaut Moodie comes to value herself as an alluring female using charm, artifice, and cosmetics to enhance her self-worth while the captain learns to be protective of his changed space partner. *Unpopular Planet* is also preoccupied with questions of sexual identity. While it, too, features some portrayals of women which would not please feminists—the hero's partner is a female who is fully mature sexually although mentally and chronologically she is but three years old—such characterization is used with more sophisticated satirical purpose. An aspiring musician, Nicholas Piggot, careens perplexedly yet enthusiastically through a series of picaresque adventures observed by blue dragons. They turn out not to be the result of drunken fancy but to be "real" beings from another dimension who have a particular genetic purpose in store for the hero, who rises from life as an unknown in subterranean Manhattan to become father of a new future.

—Rosemary Herbert

————————

SMITH, George H(enry).   Also writes as M.J. Deer; Jan Hudson; Jerry Jason; Clancy O'Brien; Diana Summers. American. Born in Vicksburg, Mississippi, 27 October 1922. Educated at the University of Southern California, Los Angeles, B.A. 1950. Served in the United States Navy, 1942-45. Married M. Jane Deer in 1950. Since 1950, free-lance writer. Agent: John Boswell Associates, 45 East 51st Street, New York, New York 10022. Address: 4113 West 180th Street, Torrance, California 90504, U.S.A.

SCIENCE-FICTION PUBLICATIONS

Novels (series: Annwn)

1976: Year of Terror.   New York, Epic, 1961.
Scourge of the Blood Cult.   New York, Epic, 1961.
The Coming of the Rats.   New York, Pike, 1961; London, Digit, 1964.
Doomsday Wing.   Derby, Connecticut, Monarch, 1963.
The Unending Night.   Derby, Connecticut, Monarch, 1964.
The Forgotten Planet.   New York, Avalon, 1965.
The Psycho Makers (as Jerry Jason).   New York, Tempo, 1965.
The Four Day Weekend.   New York, Belmont, 1966.
Druid's World (Annwn).   New York, Avalon, 1967.
Kar Kaballa (Annwn).   New York, Ace, 1969.
Witch Queen of Lochlann (Annwn).   New York, New American Library, 1969.
The Second War of the Worlds (Annwn).   New York, DAW, 1978.
The Island Snatchers (Annwn).   New York, DAW, 1978.

Uncollected Short Stories

"The Last Spring," in *Startling* (New York), August 1953.
"The Savages," in *Universe* (Evanston, Illinois), December 1953.
"The Ordeal of Colonel Johns," in *If* (New York), June 1954.
"The Last Crusade," in *If* (New York), February 1955.
"The Unwanted," in *Spaceway* (Alhambra, California), February 1955.
"Witness," in *If* (New York), May 1955.
"At the Bridge," in *Other Worlds* (Evanston, Indiana), July 1955.
"Bridge to Limbo," in *Pacific Stars and Stripes* (Tokyo), 3 October 1955.
"Shrine of Hate," in *Original Science Fiction Stories* (Holyoke, Massachusetts), January 1956.
"Elected," in *Science Fiction Quarterly* (Holyoke, Massachusetts), February 1956.
"The Other Army," in *Original Science Fiction Stories* (Holyoke, Massachusetts), September 1956.
"The Ships in the Sky," in *Fantastic Universe* (Chicago), February 1957.
"The Barbarian," in *Jem* (Union City, New Jersey), August 1957.
"In the Beginning," in *Good Humor*, March 1958.
"The Night the TV Went Out," in *Future* (New York), April 1958.
"Hello, Terra Central!," in *Original Science Fiction Stories* (Holyoke, Massachusetts), July 1958.
"Benefactor," in *Fantastic Universe* (Chicago), August 1958.
"Perfect Marriage," in *Original Science Fiction Stories* (Holyoke, Massachusetts), January 1959.
"Ego-Transfer Machine," in *Super Science Fiction* (New York), February 1959.
"The Last Days of L.A.," in *If* (New York), February 1959.

"Paradox Lost," in *Original Science Fiction Stories* (Holyoke, Massachusetts), February 1959.
"Conquerors Return," in *Gallant*, May 1959.
"The Bare Facts," in *Original Science Fiction Stories* (Holyoke, Massachusetts), July 1959.
"Specimens," in *Super Science Fiction* (New York), August 1959.
"The Great Secret," in *Super Science Fiction* (New York), October 1959.
"Too Robot to Marry," in *Fantastic Universe* (Chicago), October 1959.
"The Outcasts," in *Now and Beyond*, edited by Ivan Howard. New York, Belmont, 1965.
"The Night Before," in *Galaxy* (New York), April 1966.
"The Look," in *Galaxy* (New York), August 1966.
"The Plague," in *Famous Science Fiction* (New York), Winter 1966.
"In the Imagicon," in *Nebula Award Stories 2*, edited by Brian Aldiss and Harry Harrison.   New York, Doubleday, and London, Gollancz, 1967.
"In the Land of Love," in *Worlds of Tomorrow 24* (New York), 1970.
"A Matter of Freedoms" (as Clancy O'Brien) and "Flame Tree Planet," in *Flame Tree Planet*, edited by Roger Elwood.   St. Louis, Concordia, 1973.

OTHER PUBLICATIONS

Novels

A Place Called Hell (as M.J. Deer, with Mary J. Deer Smith).   New York, France, 1963.
Flames of Desire (as M.J. Deer, with Mary J. Deer Smith).   New York, France, 1963.
Wild Is the Heart (as Diana Summers).   Chicago, Playboy Press, 1978.
Love's Wicked Ways (as Diana Summers).   Chicago, Playboy Press, 1979.

Other

Bayou Belle (juvenile).   New York, Day, 1967.
Who Is Ronald Reagan?   New York, Pyramid, 1968.
Martin Luther King, Jr.   New York, Lancer, 1971.
Atheism: The Case Against God.   Los Angeles, Nash, 1974.

Other as Jan Hudson

The Sex and Savagery of Hell's Angels.   San Diego, Greenleaf, 1966; London, New English Library, 1967; as *The New Barbarians*, New English Library, 1973.
Those Sexy Saucer People.   San Diego, Greenleaf, 1967.
Bikers at War.   London, New English Library, 1976.

George H. Smith comments:
   Science fiction was my first love in writing, and I've done it off and on for the last 25 years. Five of my novels are set in the imaginary Celtic other world called Annwn. I am currently committed to a series of historical novels so it will be some time before I get back to science fiction, but when I do I hope to continue the Annwn series.

*   *   *

   The career of George H. Smith as a writer of science fiction is a peculiar one. Since most of his early novels were written for small paperback houses specializing in lurid action and violent sex, there is a certain crudity about them that masks his positive values as a writer. It was not until the 1970's that Smith began to sell novels to the more prestigious paperback houses, and the quality of his novels seems to have improved proportionately.
   The early novels made use of a standard set of characters. The typical male protagonist was an indecisive man who had some insight into the future and realized that a significant change was coming to the world, but who was unable to communicate this to those around him. Typically, he spends the first half of each novel infatuated with a woman obviously unsuited for him, gradually

awakening to the fact that some third character is actually the person with whom he wishes to spend his life. This is the pattern of *The Coming of the Rats*, for example; the hero finally convinces his totally impractical girlfriend to accompany him to a remote cave as nuclear war hovers just over the horizon. In the aftermath, the rats of the title challenge man for supremacy with predictable results. The pattern repeats itself in *Doomsday Wing*, also about a nuclear war, this time threatening to extinguish all life on Earth, and *The Unending Night*, wherein runaway nuclear reactors knock Mars out of its orbit, and threaten to pull our own planet away from the warmth of the sun. In the former the dedicated military man cannot convince his ambitious wife of the importance of serving his country, and in the latter a hyper-liberated woman is convinced that the best thing that can happen to the human race is for it to descend to a primitive culture. The scientist hero of the latter is thoroughly enamored of her until she proves insane. This basic arrangement of characters also appears in *The Four Day Weekend*, involving a plot by secret aliens to take over the world by reprogramming the computers that direct our motor vehicles. Although there is some amusing satire here, it is rather silly most of the time, possibly the worst of Smith's novels.

Surprisingly enough, one of his better novels was published by a softcore pornography publisher. *1976: Year of Terror* is set in a future America in which the Libertarian Party has seized power by assassination and clever plotting by the head of the Federal Security Police. Opposed to him is a secret agent intent on finding the missing Vice-President and restoring democratic rule to the country. This anticipates a number of thrillers along similar lines, and is fairly well written.

Somewhere along the line, Smith became interested in mythology and druidism. It crops up first in *Druid's World*, a fairly dull novel, then to much better effect in *Witch Queen of Lochlann*, written in the mode of the stories made famous by *Unknown* magazine. Duffus January is a magician of sorts who undertakes to restore the rightful queen to the throne of Lochlann, a Welsh alternate world where magic works. A low-key sword and sorcery tale, this seems to have set the stage for a major series of novels. *Kar Kaballa* is named for the king of the Gogs, a barbaric nation of nomads whose existence is barely noted by their neighbors, the civilized inhabitants of Avalon, a nation comparable to 19th-century England in our universe. Dylan MacBride, a young adventurer, is convinced that the imminent freezing of the channel between Avalon and the northern regions will result in a massive invasion, but he is unable to convince anyone in authority of the seriousness of the threat. Despondent, he seems doomed to failure when he encounters a man from our own universe who plans to sell Gatling guns to the alternate world. Smith went on to chronicle the Martian invasion of his alternate world in *The Second War of the Worlds*, an entertaining novel throughout, and a magical plot to destroy civilization in *The Island Snatchers*, the weakest in the series. These latter books are far better than his earlier efforts, with more complex characters, a quieter and more careful style, and more significant care taken in establishing settings, mood, and suspense.

Although he has written shorter pieces, Smith's only interesting story is "In the Imagicon," an enigmatic piece about a machine that allows its user to create the mental world of his choosing. It seems unlikely that Smith will add to his reputation with short stories, but it is quite possible that his novels will continue to improve.

—Don D'Ammassa

SMITH, George O(liver). American. Born in Chicago, Illinois, 9 April 1911. Attended the University of Chicago, 1929-30. Served as an editorial engineer, National Defense Research Council, 1944-45. Married 1) Helen Kunzler in 1936 (divorced, 1948); 2) Dona Louise Stebbins in 1949 (died, 1974); one daughter and two sons. Radio serviceman, Chicago, 1932-35; radio engineer: General Household, 1935-38, Wells-Gardiner, 1938-40, Philco, 1940-42,

1946-51, Crosley, 1942-44; Manager, Emerson Radio components engineering, 1951-57; Analyst, ITT Defense Communications, 1959-74. Reviewer, *Space Science Fiction*. Agent: Lurton Blassingame, 60 East 42nd Street, New York, New York 10017. Address: 47 Waterman Avenue, Rumson, New Jersey 07760, U.S.A.

SCIENCE-FICTION PUBLICATIONS

Novels

Pattern for Conquest: An Interplanetary Adventure.   New York, Gnome Press, 1949; London, Clerke and Cockeran, 1951.
Nomad.   Philadelphia, Prime Press, 1950.
Operation Interstellar.   Chicago, Century, 1950.
Hellflower.   New York, Abelard Press, 1953; London, Lane, 1955.
Highways in Hiding.   New York, Gnome Press, 1956; abridged edition, as *The Space Plague*, New York, Avon, 1957.
Troubled Star.   New York, Avalon, 1957.
Fire in the Heavens.   New York, Avalon, 1958.
The Path of Unreason.   New York, Gnome Press, 1958.
Lost in Space.   New York, Avalon, 1959.
The Fourth "R."   New York, Ballantine, 1959; as *The Brain Machine*, New York, Lancer, 1968.

Short Stories

Venus Equilateral.   Philadelphia, Prime Press, 1947; London, Futura, 1975; enlarged edition, as *The Complete Venus Equilateral*, New York, Ballantine, 1976.

Uncollected Short Story

"On Our Museum," in *Isaac Asimov's Science Fiction Magazine* (New York), Spring 1977.

OTHER PUBLICATIONS

Other

Mathematics, The Language of Science (juvenile).   New York, Putnam, 1961.
Scientists' Nightmares.   New York, Putnam, 1972.

*   *   *

When one mentions "the golden age of science fiction," several stereotypes come to mind, including bug-eyed aliens who act like humans, humans who act like supermen, mysterious gadgets and even more mysterious ray guns. Fortunately, much of the science fiction written during this period did not employ such stereotypes. A few became classics. Many more, while certainly not classics, have to be considered as good, solid science fiction.

One such work is George O. Smith's *Highways in Hiding*. Although it might be classified as a science-fiction mystery, it moves fast enough and has enough action to keep your attention. In fact, it is difficult to put down. The characterizations are only adequate, but the plot is well thought out, involving psychic phenomena, a mysterious disease, and a baffling disappearance. There is a political message here, too, which is common in Smith's works: the fruits of science should be for all and not just the elite. *The Fourth "R"* is another Smith work which makes use of this underlying idea. This time it is the Holden Electromechanical Educator which promises to be mankind's salvation. However, Jimmy Holden's parents, who developed the device, are murdered by an unscrupulous business associate who wishes the device to further his own aims. Because Jimmy's parents had used the device on him, he is no ordinary five-year-old, but practically an adult trapped in a child's body, and his adventures protecting the device make a very clever work.

Fire in the Heavens, Nomad, Hellflower, and *Troubled Star* are less interesting. The first has a lot of science but not much plot: the sun is about to go nova and a young scientist who doesn't believe in the Law of Conservation of Energy or in neutrinos must save the day. The plot of *Hellflower* is a little worn, though suspenseful. Space pilot Farradyne crashes his ship, killing 33 people. He is banished to the Venusian fungus field until a federal agent gives him a chance to prove himself anew by becoming an undercover agent and helping to break the hellflower smuggling ring. *Troubled Star* may not have been intended as a tongue-in-cheek stab at 1950's science fiction, but I take it as such. Dusty Britton of the space patrol has so many TV followers that, when a group of aliens plan to make Sol into a three-day variable beacon, they approach Dusty to be their spokesman. In *Nomad* humans are made out to be monsters who use sub-sentient life forms for vivisection and who annihilate the "10th" planet of the solar system with little provocation. It is a particularly frightening projection of the future of mankind.

No discussion of Smith's works would be complete without mentioning *Venus Equilateral*. Venus Equilateral Relay Station is a manned satellite circling the sun at the orbit of Venus, but 60 degrees ahead of that planet. It's purpose is to relay radio transmissions among the inhabited planets whenever the sun interferes with direct transmission. The stories mostly concern technical problems and their solution by the station's scientists. Most of the problems are archaic by today's standards, but the stories are of interest, at least from a historical perspective. Many of the stereotypes of golden age science fiction are found here.

—Paul Swank

SOHL, Jerry (Gerald Allan Sohl). Also writes as Nathan Butler; Sean Mei Sullivan. American. Born in Los Angeles, California, 2 December 1913. Attended Central College, Chicago, 1933-34. Served in the United States Army Air Force, 1942-45: Sergeant. Married Jean Gordon in 1942; one son and two daughters. Reporter, telegraph editor, photographer, and feature writer, Bloomington *Daily Pantagraph*, Illinois, 1945-58. Since 1958, free-lance writer: staff writer for *Star Trek, Alfred Hitchcock Presents*, and *The New Breed*; also concert pianist. Agent: Joseph Elder Agency, 150 West 87th Street, New York, New York 10024. Address: P.O. Box 1336, Thousand Oaks, California 91360, U.S.A.

SCIENCE-FICTION PUBLICATIONS

Novels

The Haploids. New York, Rinehart, 1952.
Costigan's Needle. New York, Rinehart, 1953; London, Grayson, 1955.
The Transcendent Man. New York, Rinehart, 1953.
The Altered Ego. New York, Rinehart, 1954.
Point Ultimate. New York, Rinehart, 1955.
The Mars Monopoly. New York, Ace, 1956; London, Satellite, 1958.
The Time Dissolver. New York, Avon, 1957; London, Sphere, 1967.
The Odious Ones. New York, Rinehart, 1959; London, Consul, 1961.
One Against Herculum. New York, Ace, 1959.
Night Slaves. New York, Fawcett, 1965.
The Anomaly. New York, Curtis, 1971.
I, Aleppo. Toronto, Laser, 1976.

Uncollected Short Stories

"The Seventh Order," in *Galaxy* (New York), March 1952.
"The Ultroom Error," in *Space* (New York), May 1952.
"Brink's Bounty," in *Galaxy* (New York), January 1955.
"The Hand," in *Imagination* (Evanston, Illinois), January 1955.
"The Elroom," in *If* (New York), March 1955.
"The Invisible Enemy," in *Imaginative Tales* (Evanston, Illinois), September 1955.
"Death in Transit," in *Infinity* (New York), June 1956.

"Counterweight," in *If* (New York), November 1959.
"The Little Red Bag," in *If* (New York), January 1960.
"Jelna," in *Fantasy and Science Fiction* (New York), August 1972.
"Mr. Moyachki," in *Playboy* (Chicago), May 1974.
"Before a Live Audience," in *Future Corruption*, edited by Roger Elwood. New York, Warner, 1975.
"The Service," in *Fantasy and Science Fiction* (New York), February 1976.

OTHER PUBLICATIONS

Novels

Prelude to Peril. New York, Rinehart, 1957.
The Lemon Eaters. New York, Simon and Schuster, and London, Cassell, 1967.
The Spun Sugar Hole. New York, Simon and Schuster, 1971.
The Resurrection of Frank Borchard. New York, Simon and Schuster, 1973.
Supermanchu, Master of Kung Fu (as Sean Mei Sullivan). New York, Ballantine, 1974.

Novels as Nathan Butler

Dr. Josh. New York, Fawcett, 1973.
Mamelle. New York, Fawcett, 1974.
Blow-Dry. New York, Fawcett, 1976.
Mamelle, The Goddess. New York, Fawcett, 1977.

Plays

Screenplays: *Twelve Hours to Kill*, 1960; *Monster of Terror (Die, Monster, Die!)*, 1965; *Frankenstein Conquers the World*, with Kaoru Mabuchi and Reuben Bercovitch, 1966.

Television Plays: *The Corbomite Maneuver* (*Star Trek* series), 1966; *Night Slaves*, from his own novel, 1970; and episodes for *Naked City, Route 66, M-Squad, G.E. Theater, Markham, Border Patrol, Twilight Zone, The Invaders, The Outer Limits, Target: The Corrupters, Man from Atlantis*, and *The Next Step Beyond* series.

Other

Underhanded Chess. New York, Hawthorn, 1973.
Underhanded Bridge. New York, Hawthorn, 1975.

Jerry Sohl comments:

The corpus of my science-fiction work reflects, I believe, rather accurately what was fashionable in the genre from 1950 to 1970, moving from gimmick as story to people as story. Although superior to what it was prior to 1970, today's science fiction is often too abstruse to be understood. Because of my interest in mainstream literature I have abandoned science fiction and am, at the moment, working on a long novel about northwestern California Indians, though the book does have a science-fiction base. Although I labored in the television and film vineyards for more than 20 years, some of it in science-fiction programs of prestige, such as *Star Trek*, I do believe that most television and film is deeply rooted in what was science fiction 20 years ago. Perhaps that is where the public SF mind is. Pity.

*   *   *

Like many fans-turned-writers, Jerry Sohl reveals an appreciative understanding of the surface structures of science-fiction narratives but often fails at deeper levels of conceptualization and extrapolation. Although Sohl has contributed little of originality to the genre, he is in many ways a representative popular writer of the 1950's, skilled in generating an initial sense of mystery and wonder, but often confusing or even absurd in his resolutions.

Most of his novels and stories deal with familiar science-fiction themes. *The Transcendent Man*, for example, borrows a premise from Charles Fort via earlier treatments by Eric Frank Russell, L. Ron Hubbard, and others: the idea that humanity's intelligence and civilization are the creations of a vastly superior race of invisible aliens who feed off the emotional energy generated by catastrophes such as wars and plagues. Although these aliens, called the Capellans in this novel, might serve as an interesting metaphor for the paradoxical quality in human nature that somehow accounts for both creative and destructive impulses, Sohl develops the story into little more than an adventure narrative concerning one supernormal human who discovers the alien secret and, in the end, singlehandedly takes on the task of maintaining civilization. *Point Ultimate*, Sohl's contribution to the literature of dystopia, concerns a world conquered by communists who seem to come right out of the nightmares of Joe McCarthy, and quickly descends into a welter of germ warfare, gypsies, underground railways, and secret Martian colonies. *The Altered Ego* involves the somewhat more intriguing notion of a society which has learned how to resurrect important citizens after death, but soon becomes a familiar tale of chases and conspiracies.

Sohl's more successful novels are those in which the science-fiction element is kept fairly simple or relegated to the background. *The Time Dissolver* is an intriguing amnesia mystery for most of its length, with the protagonist and his wife awaking one morning to find that their memories from 1946 to 1957 have disappeared—and that, consequently, they do not even know each other. The carefully wrought details of the investigation into the missing years of their lives provide a suspenseful narrative, and the rather weak explanation concerning a memory-dissolving machine does not interfere greatly with the overall impact of the novel. *Costigan's Needle*, an exploration of the parallel-universe theme, is perhaps Sohl's best novel: an account of a group of people who pass into a parallel world through a needle-shaped machine invented by a Chicago scientist, only to find themselves trapped in the other world and forced to spend years redesigning the technology that will enable them to build another machine (which, it turns out, will only enable them to enter another of an apparently infinite series of parallel worlds). Understandably, the people choose not to abandon this new world that they have created with their own hands. Although the characters in the novel are a familiar assortment of popular fiction stereotypes, the exploration of the problems inherent in trying to recreate a sophisticated technology from raw materials is well-handled.

Sohl has had relatively little influence on the genre, although one of his novels, *Night Slaves*—concerning a community dominated by alien visitors—provided the basis for a television movie. A writer with undeniable skill in constructing suspenseful situations, and one who enjoyed some popularity during the 1950's, his works in retrospect seem weakened by inadequate conceptualization of the scientific and social ideas he dealt with.

—Gary K. Wolfe

<hr/>

SPINRAD, Norman. American. Born in New York City, 15 September 1940. Educated at the City College of the City University of New York, B.S. 1961. Literary agent. Since 1963, full-time writer. President, Science Fiction Writers of America, 1980-81. Recipient: Jupiter Award, 1975. Agent: Lurton Blassingame, 60 East 42nd Street, New York, New York 10017. Address: 45 Perry Street, No. 16, New York, New York 10014, U.S.A.

SCIENCE-FICTION PUBLICATIONS

Novels

The Solarians. New York, Paperback Library, 1966; London, Sphere, 1979.
Agent of Chaos. New York, Belmont, 1967.
The Men in the Jungle. New York, Doubleday, 1967; London, Sphere, 1972.

Bug Jack Barron. New York, Walker, 1969; London, Macdonald, 1970.
The Iron Dream. New York, Avon, 1972; London, Panther, 1974.
Riding the Torch. New York, Dell, 1978.
A World Between. New York, Pocket Books, 1979.
Songs from the Stars. New York, Simon and Schuster, 1980.

Short Stories

The Last Hurrah of the Golden Horde. New York, Doubleday, 1970; London, Macdonald, 1971.
No Direction Home. New York, Pocket Books, 1975; London, Millington, 1976.
The Star-Spangled Future. New York, Ace, 1979.

OTHER PUBLICATIONS

Novel

Passing Through the Flame. New York, Berkley, 1975.

Plays

Television Plays: for *Star Trek* series.

Other

Fragments of America. North Hollywood, Now Library Press, 1970.
"*Stand on Zanzibar*: The Novel as Film," in *SF: The Other Side of Realism*, edited by Thomas D. Clareson. Bowling Green, Ohio, Popular Press, 1971.
Experiment Perilous: Three Essays on Science Fiction. New York, Algol Press, 1976.

Editor, *The New Tomorrows.* New York, Belmont, 1971.
Editor, *Modern Science Fiction.* New York, Doubleday, 1974.

*

Bibliography: *Le Livre d'Or de Norman Spinrad* by Patrice Duvic, Paris, Presses Pocket, n.d.

*   *   *

Norman Spinrad's most original and insightful fiction emerges from his remarkable grasp of the present and potential impacts of the communication revolution on American ways of living, loving, and dying. He can create for us the archetypes and myths we need to understand the new electronic milieu which he sees overloading our senses and sensitivities, creating a "multi-valued, post Age-of-Reason reality." Spinrad helps us to imagine what we are becoming in the hands of the "media pros" and even what might happen if the "pros" had a case of conscience and a commitment to something more than improving the ratings.

In his best novel, *Bug Jack Barron*, Spinrad creates the ultimate American TV hero, who, in the style of Joe Pine, electronically extends his brand of kick-em-in-the-ass confrontation of the power structure into the tube minds and hearts of all the "losers" and "suckers" sitting in front of the glass teat. Barron is a latter day cousin of Robin Hood or Billy the Kid—the bad guy turned good cowboy; hating authority, power, and civilization; riding to danger with his tube blazing; shooting it out verbally at OK TV studio; and walking into the fade out with his sexetary, after Sweet Sara, his good-hearted whore and first love, has laid down her life for him and changed him from hired gun (or mouth) to public hero number one. It may be familiar, but it's the stuff of which democracy is made. Americans have to believe the good guy could save the damned town.

Similarly, in *A World Between* Spinrad's strongest writing and most effective imagining occur as he describes the media campaigns used to influence public opinion in a totally participatory electronic democracy. Even in *Riding the Torch*, a novella that is in the main a typical science-fiction confrontation between man and the immensity of an uncaring universe, Spinrad's protagonist is an artist producing sensos, total recreations of experience. His task is to help mankind face the truth about having to live forever in space. Despite his own fears and doubts the artist achieves affirmation and hope. At least Spinrad himself is seeking to make such an affirmation.

Spinrad's hope, that the electronic media can serve the common good, is not, however, mindless optimism, and four of his best short stories explore the manipulation that the media message can produce. "National Pastime" finds a TV producer inventing a modern gladiatorial version of football that capitalizes on race hatred, sexual intolerance, and the national love of violence to win the ratings "wars." "Blackout" details the sheep-like response to an alien take-over created by stopping the flow of network news. "The Conspiracy," an interesting experiment in style, uses news-flash diction and headline typography to reveal and/or parody the growing sense of paranoia that leads many to a conspiratorial view of modern life. "The Big Flash" explores the possibilities of using a media-hyped rock group to sell the populace on the ultimate death trip, a thermonuclear flash. In each of these stories Spinrad is raising serious questions about the ethical vacuum that produces the wasteland we call the entertainment industry.

All of this is not to say that Spinrad has not written or imagined well in a multiplicity of other areas. In fact, with the exception of Burgess in *A Clockwork Orange*, no one writing speculative fiction has explored 20th-century manifestations of violence and sadism more thoroughly. *The Men in the Jungle* is an account of the crimes men and women commit in running revolutions to "free" or "save" one another. In *The Iron Dream* Spinrad imagines an alternative past in which Adolph Hitler as a science-fiction writer gives us a novel bad enough to be pulp science fiction, and which, unbelievably, in the "real" world was sold to Nazi Germany. His earlier novels, *The Solarians* and *Agent of Chaos*, reveal the same concern with the problems of government, power, individual freedom, and social responsibility found in the later work.

Spinrad's short stories are among the best of the past 15 years. *The Last Hurrah of the Golden Horde* contains stories published between 1963 and 1969. The works are tightly structured and contain flashes of brilliant characterization. As might be expected several of the stories tend to be formulaic, but "Carcinoma Angels," "The Last of the Romany," "The Ersatz Ego," "It's a Bird! It's a Plane!," "The Entropic Gang Bang Caper," and the title story reveal a command of the form, an active sense of humor, and a whimsical imagination. In *No Direction Home* there is little that could be called conventional science fiction. In terms of topics, themes, and approaches we are in a universe that is Spinradian. The stories are highly crafted and the characters well drawn; to use Spinrad's own distinction, the stories are "speculative fiction," a modern form that seeks to explore the "could-be-but-isn't." They cross whatever boundaries there are that define what Spinrad calls "science fiction as a commercial genre-cum-subculture." In *The Star-Spangled Future* Spinrad reprints several stories from his other collections with a series of annotations and essays that make clear the way in which he sees speculative fiction-science fiction as the literature of the American present. What the collection makes clear is that Norman Spinrad is a sensitive observer of his culture, a skilled craftsman of the short story, and one of the best writers of his generation. Let us hope that, at least personally, he is able to avoid the problems that plague the "genre-cum-subculture" he so clearly delineates in his essays and notes in *Modern Science Fiction*. At his best, in his most recent novel, Spinrad is good, but *A World Between* falls between *Bug Jack Barron* and *The Solarians*, and we need sharper criticism, stronger affirmations, and the best writing we can get if science fiction is to help us understand and shape ourselves and our world.

—Thomas D. Bacig

SPRAGUE, Carter. *See* **MERWIN, Sam, Jr.**

STABLEFORD, Brian M(ichael). Also writes as Brian Craig. British. Born in Shipley, Yorkshire, 25 July 1948. Educated at Manchester Grammar School; University of York, B.A. (honours) in biology 1969, D.Phil. in sociology 1979. Married Vivien Owen in 1973; one son and one daughter. Lecturer in Sociology, University of Reading, Berkshire, 1976 and since 1977. Agent: Janet Freer, 118 Tottenham Court Road, London W1P 9HL. Address: 113 St. Peter's Road, Reading, Berkshire RG6 1PG, England.

SCIENCE-FICTION PUBLICATIONS

Novels (series: Daedalus; Dies Irae; Hooded Swan)

Cradle of the Sun. New York, Ace, and London, Sidgwick and Jackson, 1969.
The Blind Worm. New York, Ace, and London, Sidgwick and Jackson, 1970.
The Days of Glory (Dies Irae). New York, Ace, and Manchester, Five Star, 1971.
In the Kingdom of the Beasts (Dies Irae). New York, Ace, 1971; London, Quartet, 1974.
Day of Wrath (Dies Irae). New York, Ace, 1971; London, Quartet, 1974.
To Challenge Chaos. New York, DAW, 1972.
Halcyon Drift (Swan). New York, DAW, 1972; London, Dent, 1976.
Rhapsody in Black (Swan). New York, DAW, 1973; London, Dent, 1975.
Promised Land (Swan). New York, DAW, 1974; London, Dent, 1975.
The Paradise Game (Swan). New York, DAW, 1974; London, Dent, 1976.
The Fenris Device (Swan). New York, DAW, 1974; London, Pan, 1978.
Swan Song. New York, DAW, 1975; London, Pan, 1978.
Man in a Cage. New York, Day, 1975.
The Face of Heaven. London, Quartet, 1976.
The Mind-Riders. New York, DAW, 1976; London, Fontana, 1977.
The Florians (Daedalus). New York, DAW, 1976; London, Hamlyn, 1978.
Critical Threshold (Daedalus). New York, DAW, 1977; London, Hamlyn, 1979.
The Realms of Tartarus. New York, DAW, 1977.
Wildeblood's Empire (Daedalus). New York, DAW, 1977; London, Hamlyn, 1979.
The City of the Sun (Daedalus). New York, DAW, 1978; London, Hamlyn, 1980.
The Last Days of the Edge of the World (juvenile). London, Hutchinson, 1978.
Balance of Power (Daedalus). New York, DAW, 1979.
The Walking Shadow. London, Fontana, 1979.
The Paradox of Sets (Daedalus). New York, DAW, 1979.
Optiman. New York, DAW, 1980.

Uncollected Short Stories

"Beyond Time's Aegis" (as Brian Craig, with Craig Mackintosh), in *Science Fantasy* (Bournemouth), November 1965.
"The Man Who Came Back," in *SF Impulse* (London), October 1966.
"Inconstancy," in *SF Impulse* (London), February 1967.
"Prisoner in the Ice," in *Vision of Tomorrow* (Newcastle upon Tyne), November 1969.
"Story with a Happy Ending," in *Science Fiction Monthly* (London), June 1974.
"Sad Story," in *Science Fiction Monthly* (London), August 1974.
"An Offer of Oblivion," in *Amazing* (New York), December 1974.
"The Sun's Tears," in *The 1975 Annual World's Best SF*, edited by Donald A. Wollheim. New York, DAW, 1975.
"Judas Story," in *The Year's Best Horror Stories 3*, edited by Richard Davis. New York, DAW, 1975.
"The Conqueror," in *Science Fiction Monthly* (London), April 1975.

"The Engineer and the Executioner," in *The 1976 Annual World's Best SF*, edited by Donald A. Wollheim. New York, DAW, 1976.

"Captain Fagan Died Alone," in *The DAW Science Fiction Reader*, edited by Donald A. Wollheim. New York, DAW, 1976.

"Skinned Alive," in *Weekend Fiction Extra* (London), September 1978.

"Mortification of the Flesh," in *Ad Astra* (London), vol. 1, no. 5, 1979.

OTHER PUBLICATIONS

Other

"The Evolution of Science Fiction," in *Beyond This Horizon*, edited by Christopher Carrell. Sunderland, Ceolfrith Press, 1973.

"The Robot in Science Fiction," in *Vector* (Reading), July-August 1973.

"Machines and Inventions," in *Vector* (Reading), Spring 1974.

"SF: A Sociological Perspective," in *Fantastic* (New York), March 1974.

"SF: The Nature of the Medium," in *Amazing* (New York), August 1974.

"The Social Role of Science Fiction," in *Algol* (New York), Summer 1975.

"The Metamorphosis of Robert Silverberg," in *Science Fiction Monthly 3* (London), 1976.

"William Watson's Prospectus for Science Fiction," in *Foundation 10* (London), June 1976.

"Opening Minds," in *Vector* (Reading), August-September 1976.

"Edgar Fawcett," in *Vector* (Reading), November-December 1976.

The Mysteries of Modern Science. London, Routledge, 1977.

"Insoluble Problems: Barry Malzberg's Career in Science Fiction," in *Foundation 11-12* (London), March 1977.

"Icaromenippus; or, The Future of Science Fiction," in *Vector* (Reading), May-June 1977.

"The Needs and Demands of the Science Fiction Reader," in *Vector* (Reading), September-October 1977.

"The Marriage of Science and Fiction," in *Encyclopedia of Science Fiction*, edited by Robert Holdstock. London, Octopus, and Baltimore, Hoen, 1978.

"Science Fiction and the Image of the Future," in *Foundation 14* (London), September 1978.

"The Unexplored Imagination," in *Biology and Human Affairs* (London), vol. 43, no. 1, 1978.

"Locked in the Slaughterhouse: The Novels of Kurt Vonnegut," in *Arena* (Canterbury), September 1978.

"The Best of Hamilton and Brackett," in *Vector* (Reading), November-December 1978.

A Clash of Symbols: The Triumph of James Blish. San Bernardino, California, Borgo Press, 1979.

"Notes Toward a Sociology of Science Fiction," in *Foundation 15* (London), January 1979.

"Social Design in Science Fiction," in *Amazing* (New York), February 1979.

"The Utopian Dream Revisited: Socioeconomic Speculation in the SF of Mack Reynolds," in *Foundation 16* (London), May 1979.

*   *   *

The prolific writer Brian M. Stableford is probably best known for his Star Pilot Grainger series focussing upon a vigorously appealing hero and his adventures piloting the remarkable faster-than-light vessel *The Hooded Swan*, and the Daedalus series concerning the space ship *Daedalus* assigned to contact Earth colonies on various remote planets. Stableford, however, has also penned two other trilogies, individual novels and stories, and a good number of pieces on the development of science fiction. His own science fiction has made a definite progression from weak space opera to work which is formulaic in plot yet graced with some mature characterization and literary flights of excellence transcending the limitations usually characteristic of formula stories. Stableford's academic background in biology and sociology is evident in a body of work which often depicts ecosystems or biological puzzles as important to the understanding of his new worlds, while the interplay of individuals as representatives of societal factions is often central to his characterization.

Stableford's earliest work includes *Cradle of the Sun* and *The Blind Worm*, two futuristic tales of quest and adventure which established his flair for creating memorable biological/ecological environments. The Dies Irae trilogy is also set in the future. Featuring a hero burdened with the name Mark Chaos, this vigorous but flawed space opera raises questions of genetic tampering which has resulted in a race of "Beasts" who originated from human gene banks. *To Challenge Chaos* is a wildly complex adventure story dealing with the overused notion of a world intersecting another dimension.

Halcyon Drift is the strikingly well-crafted first volume in the *Hooded Swan* series, introducing the tough yet contemplative, cynical yet perservering Grainger, a lone survivor who, believing himself to be untouched by personal relationships, turns out to be a loyal friend to his comrades in trouble. The series begins with Grainger futilely tending the grave of a shipmate who died in a crash which also stranded Grainger on an inhospitable world. As Grainger discovers the existence of a "mind parasite" within himself, a benign being "who" will exist symbiotically with Grainger throughout many adventures, the hero is rescued by a ship from the large Caradoc Company, a greedy business concern which demands stiff payment for the rescue. Desperate for money, Grainger signs on as pilot of a competing ship, *The Hooded Swan*, a faster-than-light vessel remarkable for its winglike structures which give it a unique maneuverability. Grainger, a pilot with a dramatic record for tackling the unknown and flying instinctively, controls *The Hooded Swan* by linking up mentally and physically with her: he and the ship become one entity. Perhaps the most memorable aspect of *Halcyon Drift* is the author's ability to convey awe and enthusiasm for an exceptional ship.

Stableford's ability to make the vast comprehensible, to make the hero human, to give the reader the *sensation* of spaceflight along with the description of a grand space ship, is the keynote to the success of this series. Five of the novels focus upon Grainger as a pilot committed to fulfill a contract; the last, significantly, shows him as a relatively free agent, choosing to risk himself for his friends and coming to terms with mixed feelings about his mind parasite who ceases to exist during the course of the narrative. Stableford rises to his best in almost poetic description neatly under-cut by down-to-earth understatement when he describes the Nightingale Nebula. "The Nightingale," he says

> is a weird bird....Most nebulas are ugly and ungainly. They sprawl across the sky in glorious decadent confusion, flaccid and menacing. Nebulas are the wreckage of cosmic disasters, or cosmic disasters in the process of happening, wounds or birthmarks in the fabric of space and time. Their worst dangers lie in their arbitrariness and unpredictability....The fact remained that all nebulas are veritable devils, and he who plays hell with devils is apt to have his hands scorched. Such is life.

Stableford's Daedalus series also relies upon a combination of a thoughtful approach to new worlds and well-crafted, action-packed plotting. While no single hero is the focus of this series, Stableford creates diverse casts of characters and, once again, biologically interesting new worlds. In *Balance of Power*, for instance, two United Nations observers make an adventurous ocean crossing to a continent populated by a strange cat-like alien race. A well-realized cast of characters includes everything from leering mutineers undertaking a Columbus-style voyage of discovery to a paranoid individual jealously guarding his family's dominance over an alien populace.

Generally considered inferior to his other series, *The Realms of Tartarus* (a trilogy published in one volume) does create a gloomy but memorable "utopian" society in conflict with weirdly mutated life forms. In blatant symbolism, the privileged society lives *above* the troubled mutants—on a platform constructed over the polluted landscape of the old world. Individual novels by Stableford include *Man in a Cage*, regarded by some as his most serious novel, employing a complex style and drawing upon the author's background in sociology to describe the actions of a schizophrenic narrator who succeeds, where sane individuals cannot, in a specialized space project. In *The Mind-Riders* a future society is portrayed as relying for entertainment upon electronically stimulating simulations of emotion-packed events. Ryan Hart, a boxer who provides the experience of victory and defeat for millions, is a cynical, detached hero not unlike Grainger, essentially a survivor looking for new life. *Optiman* gives philosophical substance to a novel of adventure which, reminiscent of the Dies Irae trilogy, is concerned with the implications of genetic engineering. A hostile environment, choked by dust storms, is masterfully created while suspense is maintained in a narrative which concludes "The conquest of fear...is the single most important step in man's evolution."

Stableford's fiction, featuring tough men (and some women) who challenge and conquer fear, generally transcends the formulaic pattern to convey thoughtful, occasionally inspired messages. Stableford seems to know the reader is better convinced by a cynic who becomes awestruck than by numerous astonished dreamers.

—Rosemary Herbert

STAPLEDON, (William) Olaf. British. Born near Wallasey, Cheshire, 10 May 1886. Educated at Abbotsholme School; Balliol College, Oxford, M.A. 1909; University of Liverpool, Ph.D. 1925. Served in the Friends' Ambulance Unit in France, 1916-19. Married Agnes Zena Miller in 1919; one son and one daughter. Assistant Headmaster, Manchester Grammar School, 1910; worked for Alfred Holt and Company, shippers, Liverpool and Port Said, 1911; Lecturer in History and English, Workers' Educational Association, University of Liverpool 1912-15; after World War I, Lecturer in Philosophy and Psychology, University of Liverpool. *Died 6 September 1950.*

SCIENCE-FICTION PUBLICATIONS

Novels

Last and First Men: A Story of the Near and Far Future. London, Methuen, 1930; New York, Cape and Smith, 1931.
Last Men in London. London, Methuen, 1932; Boston, Gregg Press, 1976.
Odd John. London, Methuen, 1935; New York, Dutton, 1936.
Star-Maker. London, Methuen, 1937; New York, Berkley, 1961.
Darkness and the Light. London, Methuen, 1942; Westport, Connecticut, Hyperion Press, 1974.
Sirius. London, Secker and Warburg, 1944; included in *To the End of Time*, 1953.
Death into Life. London, Methuen, 1946.
The Flames. London, Secker and Warburg, 1947.
Worlds of Wonder (includes *The Flames; Death into Life; Old Man in New World*). Los Angeles, Fantasy, 1949.
A Man Divided. London, Methuen, 1950.
To the End of Time: The Best of Olaf Stapledon, edited by Basil Davenport. New York, Funk and Wagnalls, 1953.
Nebula Maker. Hayes, Middlesex, Bran's Head, 1976.

Short Stories

Old Man in New World. London, Allen and Unwin, 1944.
Four Encounters. Hayes, Middlesex, Bran's Head, 1976.
Far Future Calling: Uncollected Science Fiction and Fantasies, edited by Sam Moskowitz. Philadelphia, Trainer, 1980.

OTHER PUBLICATIONS

Verse

Latter-Day Psalms. Liverpool, Young, 1914.

Other

A Modern Theory of Ethics: A Study of the Relations of Ethics and Psychology. London, Methuen, and New York, Dutton, 1929.
Waking World. London, Methuen, 1934.
New Hope for Britain. London, Methuen, 1939.
Saints and Revolutionaries. London, Heinemann, 1939.
Philosophy and Living. London, Penguin, 2 vols., 1939.
Beyond the "Isms." London, Secker and Warburg, 1942.
The Seven Pillars of Peace. London, Common Wealth, 1944.
Youth and Tomorrow. London, St. Botolph, 1946.
The Opening of the Eyes, edited by Agnes Z. Stapledon. London, Methuen, 1954.

* * *

Between the age of Verne and Wells and the Golden Age of American science fiction in the 1940's, the greatest achievement in the genre belongs, without much question, to Olaf Stapledon. Future history, galactic wars and empires, sympathetic presentation of alien psychologies and cultures, science and technology conceived critically in their reaction upon society (and even upon sexuality), man's mind itself seen as radically mutating, evolving toward a trans-earthly destiny either tragic or superhuman (or both), and in that evolution exploring the depths of time and space in the quest to find some ultimate meaning in the Universe—these themes and motifs enter the genre, or receive for the first time ample and serious treatment, in Stapledon's work.

Last and First Men the most ambitious and systematic of future histories, is also memorable as the first attempt in science fiction to create a full-scale apocalyptic "myth" (Stapledon's own term in his Preface). Man's future is projected here through unprecedented magnitudes of time and change, not because of some compulsive need in Stapledon to write a "titanic" book, but because only a vast, flexibly protean counter-myth could challenge effectively the dominant patterns of belief—orthodoxies both of right-wing religion and left-wing politics—that he saw usurping the sense of the future in his time. Not from any irrepressible pessimism in himself but to demolish—or shock awake—such complacencies among his readers, Stapledon has his First Men perish after a few more millennia of steadily degenerating civilization. World-unity of a sort, the First World State, is achieved, but only through a tyrannous, super-technologized culture. After several million years, the Second Men emerge, gifted with larger bodies and more acute senses, but these amiable semi-Utopian giants fail to reconcile their will to universal human communion with their cosmic awareness, especially after that awareness is fatally darkened by a long and hopeless conflict with invading, biologically alien, intelligent "clouds" from Mars. Not until the Last Men, sixteen species later—that is, almost two billennia and several interplanetary migrations later—do we learn in retrospect what the controlling model of transcendence, the ideal relationship of human will to cosmic reality, is in Stapledon's myth.

The Last (Eighteenth) Men are, in one sense, the First of Men—the first to attain full humanity, to "awaken" thoroughly from animal "sleep," to develop latent powers of both body and mind beyond man's evolutionary childhood to something like "maturity." The great civilization that flowers on Neptune succeeds in remaking man's nature by correcting the tragic imbalance of powers, and especially the will to overtranscendence, of the earlier species (e.g., the abstract intellectuality of the Fourth Men, the love of tragic "ecstasy" that lures the Flying Men on Venus to racial suicide). Although their bodies are made superstrong by artificial atoms, man's mammalian sexuality has not now been left behind but enlarged and enhanced in sensibility, so as to become the sympathetic basis of world-community. The "racial mind" achieved on Neptune is thus both—and equally—human and "astronomical" in its modes of consciousness; it has both psychic and electromagnetic dimension, capable of reaching telepathically far out into galactic space and far back through historical time (hence the virtual omniscience, where the past is concerned, of the narrator, one of the Last Men). The supreme test of this transcendent "spirit" comes when radiation from a supernova dooms the Neptunian race to extinction: they plan to "seed" the galaxy with artificial life-spores but they themselves—and with them the entire human past—cannot escape obliteration. What enables the Neptunians to meet, and even "salute," this fate without despair is not only their tragic wisdom about the cosmos but a renewed influx of animal courage and "loyalty to life," gained from telepathic interaction with the primitive minds of the First Men. It is really therefore the indomitable will of all humanity in time that speaks through the well-known words of the young prophet, last-born of the Last Men, which close Stapledon's epic "symphony":

> Man himself, at the very least, is music, a brave theme that makes music also of its vast accompaniment, its matrix of storms and stars....It is very good to have been man. And so we may go forward together with laughter in our hearts, and peace, thankful for the past, and for our own courage. For we shall make after all a fair conclusion to this brief music that is man.

Star-Maker takes the mythic history of "spirit" beyond the solar system into all space and time. This may not be, as Stapledon himself thought, his best book but it is certainly his most marvellously inventive. The first-person narrator (we may think of him as Stapledon) finds himself magically transported from a suburban hillside at night on a disembodied journey to the stars, where he is soon joined by like-minded spirits from other worlds. At first the telepathic abilities of the travellers are limited to their own level of experience—to their sympathetic awareness of "the human crisis" that results whenever a planet's civilization develops transcendent consciousness and struggles toward world-community. Very few of these worlds achieve Utopia; most succumb to war or cataclysm; and even many of those that emerge triumphantly from the crisis lapse into a "mad" imperialism of galactic conquest. A true community of "minded worlds" is at last realized, but its survival is not assured until the traumatic discovery that stars, too, are "living minds." Only after this breakthrough does the ever-enlarging communion of spiritual travellers become the multi-galactic "cosmical mind"—and only then does the narrator, now the "I" of this supremely human spirit, attain the long-sought vision of the Star Maker. Himself evolving, this neo-Bergsonian yet teleology-minded Deity, experimenting with one cosmos after another (our own, a middling success, occurs about halfway through His education) may be Stapledon's boldest and most brilliant but not therefore his best invention in the book. The Creator-God of this cosmos seems to me surpassed, even in sublimity, by many of its psychozoic creatures (the Nautiloids, the Plant Men, the symbiotic Arachnids and Ichthyoids). More indifferent Star than man-inspiring God, the Star Maker remains, almost by definition, a loveless Deity, despite Stapledon's insistence that He is worthy of "adoration." And at the end this ambiguity of attitude seems to have become intentional. For when the traveler returns to his suburban hill, he finds that he needs "two lights for guidance," the human and the astral, living radiances linked in a symbiosis of "spirit." The human warmth of "our little glowing atom of community" is defined and valued by its dialectical contrast with "the cold light of the stars," in whose "crystal ecstasy...even the dearest love is frostily assessed."

Stapledon's later drift toward mysticism, which takes increasingly religious (though always agnostic) form after *Star-Maker*, was first strongly evident in *Odd John*. Between his two myth-histories Stapledon wrote two novels—the first of which, *Last Men in London*, generally fails to wed philosophical fantasy (his Last Man narrator reappears here as a time-explorer trying to "influence" a young First Man's mind) with autobiographical realism (the novel faithfully reproduces Stapledon's experiences before and during World War I). The second novel, *Odd John*, has become, however, a justly popular classic of the genre because it dramatizes both the good and the evil latent in the post-Nietzschean myth of the Superman. The intrepid, ultra-intelligent John (he too acquires telepathic powers) is in many ways a hero, even a martyr, of Stapledonian "spirit," and the island-colony in the Pacific that he establishes with other "super-normals" is, in its organization and way of life, a model of Stapledon's philosophical ideal of "Personality-in-Community." But in the effort to make his colony secure and viable John commits a series of tactical murders, with little or no remorse; and such acts would have been for Stapledon (not in this book to be confused with his narrator, a rather servile hero-worshipper) violations of the only surely real vehicle of spirit, namely, "human personality," without reverence for which no society can long endure. And such is the fate awaiting John's colony, which rapidly perishes—or vanishes. Hopelessly threatened by all the world's powers, the colonists blow themselves up, confident that the "music" of their minds, their immortal being, is destined for new and greater realms of Spirit.

What is tragically wrong with John is clear by contrast with Stapledon's protagonist in the last of his four major works of fiction. The eponymous hero of *Sirius* is a hero without hands—and therefore free of the supple-handed John's delusions of power through manipulations of men and their world. Sirius is a huge Alsatian sheepdog, with an artificially mutated brain capable of reaching all but the very highest levels of human intelligence. Like John, Sirius rebels against his human conditioning, but this time the will to transcendence is informed by a passional commitment to love (love of Plaxy, the girl with whom he has been raised as an "equal") and by profounder intuitions of "spirit," gained through this love and the life-sympathies of his animal being. Yet, again not unlike John, Sirius never reconciles the two halves of his being; he continually succumbs to a violent "wolf-madness" seemingly rooted in his nature. And at the end, as Plaxy stands in the moorland dawn over the dead body of her lover—he has been hunted down by a rifle-armed pack of human wolves—we are left looking more to the skies than to earth for hope.

The theme of divided consciousness, of an insuperable, darkly ambiguous contradiction in man's nature, haunts most of Stapledon's fiction in his last decade. It appears throughout *Darkness and the Light*, where man's future prospects for good and evil are divided into alternate time-streams, and even the Utopian triumph of the Light scenario is threatened by inscrutable forces of cosmic Darkness. It is much less apparent in the exceptional *Death into Life*, neither a novel nor a myth-narrative so much as a work of visionary rhetoric designed to promote the belief that death is a passage to higher forms of cosmically immortal Spirit. It returns with a vengeance in *The Flames*, a novella of ambiguous fantasy, where the protagonist, a mental patient, may be hallucinating or actually encountering (at the end he dies mysteriously in a fire) a race of flame-like beings—self-declared aborigines of the Sun, in some ways spokesman of Stapledonian "spirit" yet also lethally dangerous to man and his planet. The theme finds consummation in the semi-autobiographical novel *A Man Divided*, a Psychic Double story, where the philosophically awakened Victor struggles unsuccessfully with his "doltish" other self, who in turn rebels against the former's "beatitude," until both perish together in an act of suicide, despite the efforts of the loving Maggie to save both her husbands.

Offsetting the decline of Stapledon's prophetic confidence in his last years was a generally finer command of the art and craftsmanship of fiction. First strikingly apparent in *Sirius,* which is perhaps his most aesthetically satisfying fiction, the greater range and variety of his literary skills are most observable in several fantastic short stories written in this period (or slightly earlier)—three of which, "A Modern Magician," "Arms Out of Hand," and "The Man Who Became a Tree," show Stapledon succeeding impressively in a form that he had hitherto avoided. Not that Stapledon in the 1930's was ever a stylistically incompetent writer, as he is sometimes said to be. The theme of the myth-histories necessarily demanded prose of a certain rarefied abstraction and austerity of feeling. And if his purely narrative talents were then sometimes weak, his poetic and dramatic powers—the powers, in a word, of a gifted myth-maker's imagination—were always demonstrably present. Certainly if his literary abilities had not been in large measure commensurate with his intellectual originality, Stapledon would never have exercised so great an influence on, or have won the continued admiration of, so many science-fiction writers in our time, most notably Clifford D. Simak, Cordwainer Smith, Arthur C. Clarke, Brian W. Aldiss, Ursula K. Le Guin, and Stanislaw Lem.

—John Kinnaird

STASHEFF, Christopher. American. Born in Mt. Vernon, New York, in January 1944. Educated at the University of Michigan, Ann Arbor, B.A. 1965, M.A. 1966; University of Nebraska, Lincoln, Ph.D. in theater 1972. Married Mary Miller in 1973; one daughter and one son. Since 1972, Instructor in Speech and Theater, Montclair State College, New Jersey. Member of Radio Advisory Committee, New Jersey Public Broadcasting Authority, 1973-74. Address: Department of Speech and Theater, Montclair State College, Upper Montclair, New Jersey 07043, U.S.A.

SCIENCE-FICTION PUBLICATIONS

Novels (series: Rod Gallowglass)

The Warlock in Spite of Himself (Gallowglass). New York, Ace, 1969.
King Kobold (Gallowglass). New York, Ace, 1971.
A Wizard in Bedlam. New York, Doubleday, 1979.

*   *   *

Christopher Stasheff has written three novels which relate the complex adventures of agents from advanced societies as they attempt to influence the politics of backward worlds. Both *The Warlock in Spite of Himself* and *King Kobold* concern the efforts of Rod Gallowglass to promote democracy; *A Wizard in Bedlam* follows Dirk Dulaine through a revolution in a despotic monarchical society. The first two books are particularly strong in humor and inventiveness, as in the scenes with Fess, the epileptic robot horse, and the skillful use of asides, puns, allusions, alliteration, and acronyms. The narratives are less satiric than they are combinations of polemic and humor. *King Kibold* is less successful than *The Warlock,* in spite of some humorous characterizations, particularly the quarrelling witch and wizard, and their unborn yet corporeal son. All three books are blends of science fiction and fantasy, with wizardry presented as technology—with major unexplained exceptions. The novels are primarily adventure stories, with *A Wizard in Bedlam* showing more growth and development of the character. The reckless fun of *The Warlock* has made it a minor classic, and the literate and lively writing makes all three quite entertaining.

—Norman L. Hills

STATTEN, Vargo. *See* FEARN, John Russell.

STEFFANSON, Con. *See* GOULART, Ron.

STEPHENSON, Andrew M(ichael). British. Born in Maracaibo, Venezuela, 8 October 1946. Educated at Rottingdean Preparatory School, Sussex, 1956-60; Stowe School, Buckinghamshire, 1960-65; City University, London, B.Sc. (honours) in electrical and electronic engineering 1969. Design engineer, Plessey Telecommunications Research, Taplow, Buckinghamshire, 1969-76.

European Representative, Science Fiction Writers of America, 1976-78. Lives in High Wycombe, Buckinghamshire. Agent: Maggie Noach, A.P. Watt Ltd., 26-28 Bedford Row, London WC1R 4HL, England; or Frances Collin, Marie Rodell-Frances Collin Literary Agency, 156 East 52nd Street, New York, New York, 10022 U.S.A.

SCIENCE-FICTION PUBLICATIONS

Novels

Nightwatch. London, Futura, 1977; New York, Dell, 1979.
The Wall of Years. London, Futura, 1979; New York, Dell, 1980.

Uncollected Short Stories

"Holding Action," in *Analog* (New York), November 1971.
"The Giant Killers," in *Andromeda 1,* edited by Peter Weston. London, Futura, 1976; New York, St. Martin's Press, 1979.

Andrew M. Stephenson comments:
   The notion of making any sort of introductory statement on my work repels me: it feels as though I am being required to define what I wrote about, whereas the work itself is sufficient definition. All I will say is that I am content to be described (where relevant) as a writer of science fiction, provided my works are judged on their *individual* merits, not as samples of "science fiction," whatever that may be.

*   *   *

   Andrew M. Stephenson began his career in SF as an illustrator. "The Giant Killers," like *Nightwatch*, is highly technophilic but at the same time possesses a deep concern and sensitivity for human and animal suffering. Whereas in the short story man is seen at war against himself, in the novel he is seen pitted against an alien intruder. It is a competent if unoriginal novel about semi-sentient machines and their creator, set mainly on the moon.
   A much lengthier and far more successful novel is *The Wall of Years*, moulding together two traditional SF themes—time travel and parallel worlds—into a story which is both convincing and compelling. Experiments into parallel worlds reveal that there are nearby worlds of possibility and that the majority of these are engaged in warfare. The bonds that separate the worlds break and they begin to intermingle. As the world falls into chaos some humans escape into the future of the 26th century where they set about trying to stabilise their own history (in this alternate world). The protagonist, Jerlan Nilssen, goes back to the time of Alfred the Great to ensure that history is not changed by an outside agency which might wish to see the future city destroyed. Stephenson ties the plot threads tightly together and manages to portray accurately the clash between modern and 9th-century worldviews. There is, again, a marked sensitivity, but with a much more defined skill in the writing. The crudity of the dark ages is well drawn, and the nobility is subdued as Stephenson leads us through the laws of necessity that govern behaviour in those times. By comparison, the world of the 21st century (the time of the break-up of reality as the parallel worlds impose upon one another) is not so well focused, and seems to hint that Stephenson's future direction may be toward historical fiction, or, like Keith Roberts, toward charting parallel worlds based on the past.
   With a quite clear command over the intricacies of plot and a constantly improving style, Andrew M. Stephenson appears one of the most promising of the young British SF writers, although his reputation at present rests upon a single book.

—David Wingrove

STEVENS, Francis.   Pseudonym for Gertrude Barrows Bennett. American.   Born in Minneapolis, Minnesota, 18 September 1884. Widow; one daughter. Disappeared in September 1939.

SCIENCE-FICTION PUBLICATIONS

Novels

The Heads of Cerberus.   Reading, Pennsylvania, Polaris Press, 1952.
Claimed!   New York, Avalon, 1966.
The Citadel of Fear.   New York, Paperback Library, 1970.

Uncollected Short Stories

"The Nightmare," in *All-Story* (New York), 14 April 1917.
"Behind the Curtain," in *All-Story* (New York), 7 September 1918.
"Unseen—Unfeared," in *People's Favorite Magazine* (New York), 10 February 1919.
"The Elf Trap," in *Argosy* (New York), 5 July 1919.
"Serapion," in *Argosy* (New York), 19 June—10 July 1920.
"Sunfire," in *Weird Tales* (Chicago), July-August, September 1923.
"Friend Island," in *Under the Moons of Mars,* edited by Sam Moskowitz.   New York, Harper, 1970.

*   *   *

The body of writing for which the name Francis Stevens is remembered was published during a span of little more than six years (1917-23), and was probably written in an even shorter period. Gertrude Barrows Bennett, the woman who used the pseudonym Francis Stevens, wrote under pressure of economic necessity, and stopped when the immediate need for extra income was removed. Through the years those readers who have fallen under the spell of her remarkable fantasies have had cause to regret not only the premature cessation of her fiction-writing, but also the fact that some already-completed work remained unpublished (and is now presumed to be lost).

Francis Stevens wrote mainly for *All-Story* and *Argosy* magazines during the same period in which the first of A. Merritt's fantasies were published. It has been said that some readers thought Francis Stevens was a pen-name of Merritt's. The conjecture could just as easily have gone the other way, for when Steven's first major novel, *The Citadel of Fear*, appeared, Merritt had published only a few short works. Merritt was, in fact, a great admirer of Stevens's work, and was instrumental in having several of her stories reprinted during the 1940's. Although the first part of *The Citadel of Fear*, which takes place in the lost city of Tlapallan in an uncharted corner of Mexico, is superficially similar to Merritt's work, Stevens replaced Merrritt's romantic/tragic outlook with a much more down-to-earth viewpoint. The story, while forfeiting none of its appeal as an exotic lost-race adventure, is told with liveliness and humor, to which the hints of darker things form an effective counterpoint. In the latter two-thirds of the novel, the very real and concrete evil of Tlapallan reappears in the quiet American countryside, and a succession of mysterious events builds up to a climactic confrontation between supernatural forces.

The second of Francis Stevens's three major works, *The Heads of Cerberus*, was serialized in *The Thrill Book* in 1919. Like *The Citadel of Fear* the novel opens with an episode of Merrittesque fantasy, involving a substance called the Dust of Purgatory which transports people into the strange alternate world of Ulithia. But once the main characters have passed through Ulithia and find themselves in a future Philadelphia in the year 2118, the novel becomes political and social satire of a high order. The two parts of the novel fit somewhat oddly together, but each is so good in itself that one is willing to accept the discontinuity between them. In the introduction to the Polaris Press edition, P. Schuyler Miller is quoted as saying that the novel "can be read as perhaps the first work of fantasy to envisage the parallel-time-track concept, with an added variation that so far as I know has not been reused since"— the idea that times moves at different rates in the alternate tracks.

The third of Stevens's important works is *Claimed!* Here the focus of attention is a carved oblong box found on a volcanic island in the Atlantic. The box comes into the possession of millionaire Jesse Robinson, whose creed is, "What I want, I get—and what I get, I keep." The novel tells, in a straightforward narrative without any of the subplots or side-trips evident in earlier works, of the attempts at recovery of the box by the supernatural being who had created it many thousands of years in the past.

Three novels by Francis Stevens have so far appeared only in magazine form. Her first work was the short novel "The Nightmare," of which Stevens herself said that its only merit was "a rather grotesque originality." "Serapion" is a grim and powerful story of psychic possession which stands up well in comparison to more recent works on the same theme. "Sunfire" was a return to both the lost-race fantasy and the light-hearted narrative style of earlier works.

Of Stevens's short works, "Friend Island" is notable for its background of a future world when women are the dominant gender, but the story itself is little more than an extended joke. (It is probably nothing more than coincidence that the byline "Francis Stevens" appeared on a story called "The Curious Experience of Thomas Dunbar" in the March 1904 issue of *Argosy*.)

—R.E. Briney

STEWART, George R(ippey).   American.   Born in Sewickley, Pennsylvania, 31 May 1895. Educated at Princeton University, New Jersey, A.B. 1917 (Phi Beta Kappa); University of California, Berkeley, M.A. 1920; Columbia University, New York, Ph.D. 1922. Served in the United States Army, 1917-19; civilian technician, United States Navy, 1944. Married Theodosia Burton in 1924; one daughter and one son. Instructor, University of Michigan, Ann Arbor, 1922-23. Member of the English Department from 1923, Professor of English, 1942-62, and since 1962, Professor Emeritus, University of California. Taught at the University of Michigan, summer 1926, and Duke University, Durham, North Carolina, summer 1939; Fellow in Creative Writing, Princeton University, 1942-43; Fulbright Professor, University of Athens, 1952-53. Recipient: International Fantasy Award, 1951; American Association for State and Local History Award, 1963; Hillman Award, 1969. L.H.D.: University of California, 1963. Address: 100 Cordornices Road, Berkeley, California 94728, U.S.A.

SCIENCE-FICTION PUBLICATIONS

Novel

Earth Abides.   New York, Random House, 1949; London, Gollancz, 1950.

OTHER PUBLICATIONS

Novels

East of the Giants.   New York, Holt, 1938; London, Harrap, 1939.
Doctor's Oral.   New York, Random House, 1939.
Storm.   New York, Random House, 1941; London, Hutchinson, 1942.
Fire.   New York, Random House, 1948; London, Gollancz, 1951.
Sheep Rock.   New York, Random House, 1951.
The Years of the City.   New York, Random House, 1955.

Other

The Technique of English Verse.   New York, Holt, 1930.
Bret Harte, Argonaut and Exile.   Boston, Houghton Mifflin, 1931.

Ordeal by Hunger: The Story of the Donner Party. New York, Holt, and London, Cape, 1936; revised edition, Boston, Houghton Mifflin, 1960.
English Composition. New York, Holt, 2 vols., 1936.
John Phoenix, Esq. New York, Holt, 1937.
Take Your Bible in One Hand: The Life of William Henry Thomes. San Francisco, Colt Press, 1939.
Names on the Land. New York, Random House, 1945; revised edition, Boston, Houghton Mifflin, 1958.
Man: An Autobiography. New York, Random House, 1946; London, Cassell, 1948.
The Year of the Oath: The Fight for Academic Freedom at the University of California, with others. New York, Doubleday, 1950.
U.S. 40. Boston, Houghton Mifflin, 1953.
American Ways of Life. New York, Doubleday, 1954.
To California by Covered Wagon (juvenile). New York, Random House, 1954.
N.A.1: The North-South Continental Highway. Boston, Houghton Mifflin, 1957.
Pickett's Charge. Boston, Houghton Mifflin, 1959.
Donner Pass and Those Who Crossed It. San Francisco, California Historical Society, 1960.
The California Trail. New York, McGraw Hill, 1962; London, Eyre and Spottiswoode, 1964.
Committee of Vigilance: Revolution in San Francisco 1851. Boston, Houghton Mifflin, 1964.
This California, photographs by Michael Bry. Berkeley, California, Diablo Press, 1965.
Good Lives. Boston, Houghton Mifflin, 1967.
The Department of English of the University of California on the Berkeley Campus. Berkeley, University of California, 1968.
Not So Rich as You Think. Boston, Houghton Mifflin, 1968.
American Place Names. New York, Oxford University Press, 1970.
Names on the Globe. New York, Oxford University Press, 1975.

Editor, *The Luck of Roaring Camp and Selected Stories and Poems,* by Bret Harte. New York, Macmillan, 1928.
Editor, *Map of the Emigrant Road from Independence, Missouri, to St. Francisco,* by T.H. Jefferson. San Francisco, California Historical Society, 1945.
Editor, *The Diary of Patrick Bean.* San Francisco, Book Club of California, 1946.
Editor, *The Opening of the California Trail.* Berkeley, University of California Press, 1953.

*   *   *

In 1951, George R. Stewart received the first of the International Fantasy Awards for *Earth Abides,* the only one of his novels to fall into the SF genre. He is also the author of non-fiction works which, like his novels, all touch on some aspect of American history or culture.

Earth Abides inverts the famous story of Ishi, the last wild Indian in North America, a story recently retold by Theodora Kroeber in *Ishi in Two Worlds* (1962). Ishi, the last member of the Yahi, a tribe of California Indians long thought to be extinct, emerged from his Stone Age world to live in the early 20th-century world of trolley cars and electric lights. He was rescued by an anthropologist at the University of California, and taken to live in its Museum of Anthropology, then located in San Francisco, where he passed his remaining years. He showed the anthropologists the native Yahi way of making and hunting with a bow and arrow, and of making fire. With these lessons Ishi paid his way and enjoyed the fruits of civilization, which for him were mainly glue (for the easier feathering of arrows) and matches. His name in Yahi means "man."

The hero of *Earth Abides* is named Ish, which in Hebrew also means "man." Ish is one of a very few to survive a pandemic disease to see civilization collapse and his descendants return to the life of Stone Age hunters like that of Ishi. Ish is the last of the civilized Americans as Ishi is the last of the aboriginal Americans. Naked, hungry, and weakened by snake bite, the real Ishi stumbled into industrial America on 29 August 1911. The last of the Yahi, he wandered down from his native hills into the corral of a slaughter-house near Oroville, California. There he fell exhausted, was jailed as a "wild man," was finally recognized for what he was, and taken to the museum in San Francisco. Weakened by snake bite, the fictional Ish stumbles out of the same hills into a dead civilization, its populace almost wiped out by some deadly virus. He had been studying the ecology of the Sacramento Valley, Ishi's tribal home, for a master's degree at the University of California. Throughout the novel, Ish watches with ecological detachment the transformation of a world emptied of men.

He returns to his home in a suburb of San Francisco, overlooking the Golden Gate bridge. The few survivors he gathers around him facetiously call themselves the "Tribe." Everybody forages in stores for food and other goods, trying to maintain the old way of life under new conditions. One couple brings home a bridge lamp and a fancy radio set, even though no electricity is available. Even Ish, the only one to think about the future, teaches spelling and arithmetic, although the world is so depopulated it cannot sustain occupational specialities based on literacy. At last Ish realises the futility of his classroom lessons and school is dismissed. He then teaches the children a game, which he knows will have to become a way of life once there are no more store goods to scavenge: he teaches them how to make and use the bow and arrow, and how to make fire without matches, the same technology he knew from his study of anthropology to have been the basis for successful living by our pre-civilized ancestors.

In time, the tribe departs the crumbling ruins of San Francisco. By then Ish is an old man and the tribe, now skilled hunters, sets out to cross the bridge to new lands. Crossing the bridge, Ish slows to a stop. Before he dies, he reflects on the course of human history and the fate of his grandchildren and others of their generation, who squat in a half circle around him. "They were very young in age, at least by comparison with him, and in the cycle of mankind they were many thousands of years younger than he. He was the last of the old; they were the first of the new. But whether the new would follow the course which the old had followed, that he did not know." But the moral of the novel is certain. Inverting the story of Ishi, Stewart dramatises the humanistic fact that man is man, be he civilised or tribal; that a Stone Age culture is just as valid a setting for being human as is an industrial culture.

—Leon E. Stover

—————

STINE, Hank (Henry Eugene Stine). American. Born in Sikeston, Missouri, 13 April 1945. Married Christine Annette Kindred in 1966 (divorced, 1968); one child. Film director; Editor, *Galaxy,* 1978-79. Editor, Starblaze Books. Address: Starblaze Books, 5041 Admiral Wright Road, Virginia Beach, Virginia 23462, U.S.A.

SCIENCE-FICTION PUBLICATIONS

Novels

Season of the Witch. New York, Essex House, 1968.
Thrill City. New York, Essex House, 1969.
A Day in the Life (novelization of TV series). New York, Ace, 1970; London, Dobson, 1979.

Uncollected Short Story

"No Exit," in *Fantastic* (New York), June 1971.

*   *   *

Hank Stine's *Season of the Witch* included a moodpiece "Postscript" by Harlan Ellison, was given a warm welcome by the few critics who found it, and then allowed to drift into obscurity. It is notable as a special combination of science fiction and pornographic detail and rhetoric. The quality of the novel artistically justifies this radical strategy and invites association with other well-known pieces of science fiction that have employed it. In *Season of the Witch* Andre Fuller rape-murders Josette Kovacs under the influence of a hallucinogen. He is punished in a low-population civilization by having his brain put into his victim's body. His own body is given to someone else. He/she, as Celeste Fuller, begins an odyssey in which, after confusion and pain, Celeste makes a new and happy life as a woman and a wife. Plot and setting are minimal. The story combines dramatic narrative and stream-of-consciousness in a tight control of point-of-view that vividly exposes the painful psychological transformation of Fuller from male to female. The shock to the male psyche directly experiencing the vulnerability of the female body is stunningly revealed. The pornographic elements of the novel can titillate only briefly before the reader is plunged into the agony of the ordeal. Where science fiction as well as pornography are often male chauvinist, the novel might raise male consciousness.

Explicit sexual description as well as sex-changing effects are not rare in important science fiction works. They appear in such novels as Theodore Sturgeon's *Venus Plus X*, Norman Spinrad's *Bug Jack Barron*, Robert Heinlein's *I Shall Fear No Evil*, Mike Dolinsky's *Mind One*, David Gerrold's *The Man Who Folded Himself*, and Sam Delany's *Dhalgren*.

—John R. Pfeiffer

STOCKTON, Frank R. (Francis Richard Stockton). American. Born in Philadelphia, Pennsylvania, 5 April 1834. Educated at Zane Street School, 1840-48, and Central High School, 1848-52, both in Philadelphia. Married Marian E. Tuttle in 1860. Apprenticed as a wood-engraver, 1852, and worked as an engraver until 1870. Assistant Editor, *Hearth and Home*, 1868-73, and *St. Nicholas* magazine, 1873-78. Regular contributor to *Scribner's Magazine. Died 20 April 1902.*

SCIENCE-FICTION PUBLICATIONS

Novels

The Great War Syndicate. New York, Collier, and London, Longman, 1889.
The Great Stone of Sardis. New York and London, Harper, 1898.

Short Stories

The Science Fiction of Frank R. Stockton, edited by Richard Gid Powers. Boston, Gregg Press, 1976.

OTHER PUBLICATIONS

Novels

The Late Mrs. Null. New York, Scribner, and London, Sampson Low, 1886.
The Hundredth Man. New York, Century, and London, Sampson Low, 1887.
The Stories of the Three Burglars. New York, Dodd Mead and London, Sampson Low, 1890.
The Merry Chanter. New York, Century, and London, Sampson Low, 1890.
Ardis Claverden. New York, Dodd Mead, and London, Sampson Low, 1890.
The House of Martha. Boston, Houghton Mifflin, and London Osgood, 1891.
The Squirrel Inn. New York, Century, and London, Sampson Low, 1891.

Pomona's Travels. New York, Scribner, and London, Cassell, 1894.
The Adventures of Captain Horn. New York, Scribner, and London, Cassell, 1895.
Mrs. Cliff's Yacht. New York, Scribner, and London, Cassell, 1896.
The Girl at Cobhurst. New York, Scribner, and London, Cassell, 1898.
The Novels and Stories. New York, Scribner, 23 vols., 1899-1904.
A Bicycle in Cathay. New York, Harper, 1900.
The Captain's Toll Gate, edited by Marian E. Stockton. New York, Appleton, and London, Cassell, 1903.

Short Stories

Rudder Grange. New York, Scribner, 1879; Edinburgh, Douglas, 1883.
The Lady or the Tiger? and Other Stories. New York, Scribner, and Edinburgh, Douglas, 1884.
The Transferred Ghost. New York, Scribner, 1884.
The Casting Away of Mrs. Lecks and Mrs. Aleshine. New York, Century, and London, Sampson Low, 1886.
The Christmas Wreck and Other Stories. New York, Scribner, 1886; as *A Borrowed Month and Other Stories,* Edinburgh, Douglas, 1887.
The Dusantes. New York, Century, and London, Sampson Low, 1888.
Amos Kilbright, His Adscititious Experiences, with Other Stories. New York, Scribner, and London, Unwin, 1888.
The Rudder Grangers Abroad. New York, Scribner, and London, Sampson Low, 1891.
The Watchmaker's Wife and Other Stories. New York, Scribner, 1893; as *The Shadrach and Other Stories,* London, W.H. Allen, 1893.
A Chosen Few. New York, Scribner, 1895.
A Story-Teller's Pack. New York, Scribner, and London, Cassell, 1897.
The Associate Hermits. New York and London, Harper, 1898.
The Vizier of the Two-Horned Alexander. New York, Century, and London, Cassell, 1899.
Afield and Afloat. New York, Scribner, and London, Cassell, 1901.
John Gayther's Garden. New York, Scribner, and London, Cassell, 1903.
The Magic Egg and Other Stories. New York, Scribner, 1907.

Other (juvenile)

Ting-a-Ling. Boston, Hurd and Stoughton, 1870; London, Ward and Downey, 1889.
Roundabout Rambles in Lands of Fact and Fancy. New York, Scribner, 1872.
What Might Have Been Expected. New York, Dodd Mead, 1874; London, Routledge, 1875.
Tales Out of School. New York, Scribner, 1875.
A Jolly Friendship. New York, Scribner, and London, Kegan Paul, 1880.
The Floating Prince and Other Fairy Tales. New York, Scribner, and London, Ward and Downey, 1881.
Ting-a-Ling Tales. New York, Scribner, 1882.
The Story of Viteau. New York, Scribner, and London, Sampson Low, 1884.
The Bee-Man of Orn and Other Fanciful Tales. New York, Scribner, 1887; London, Sampson Low, 1888.
The Queen's Museum. New York, Scribner, 1887.
Personally Conducted. New York, Scribner, and London, Sampson Low, 1889.
The Clocks of Rondaine and Other Stories. New York, Scribner, and London, Sampson Low, 1892.
Fanciful Tales, edited by Julia E. Langworthy. New York, Scribner, 1894.
Captain Chap; or, The Rolling Stones. Philadelphia, Lippincott, and London, Nimmo, 1896; as *The Young Master of Hyson Hall,* Lippincott, 1899.

New Jersey, from the Discovery of the Scheyichbi to Recent Times. New York, Appleton, 1896; as *Stories of New Jersey,* New York, American Book Company, 1896.
The Buccaneers and Pirates of Our Coasts. New York, Macmillan, 1898.
Kate Bonnet. New York, Appleton, and London, Cassell, 1902.
Stories of the Spanish Main. New York, Macmillan, 1913.
The Poor Count's Christmas. New York, Stokes, 1927.

*

Bibliography: in *Frank R. Stockton* by Martin I.J. Griffin, Philadelphia, University of Pennsylvania Press, 1939.

*   *   *

Frank R. Stockton's science fiction has been neglected in histories of the field, perhaps because his literary reputation has suffered such eclipse in this century (he was highly praised during his lifetime), and because science fiction was only a small part of his literary output. Except in his two important novels, *The Great War Syndicate* and *The Great Stone of Sardis,* his science fiction was light and humorous popular magazine fiction. A recent collection, *The Science Fiction of Frank R. Stockton,* assembles all his SF stories (and *The Great Stone of Sardis*), and the introduction by Richard Gid Powers is notable for its disdain for his lack of "seriousness."

Most of Stockton's SF stories have a similar plot: a gentleman amateur wins fame and fortune and gets the girl by means of an invention. This is true in "My Terminal Moraine," *The Great Stone of Sardis,* "My Translatophone," and, to a certain extent, "A Tale of Negative Gravity." The remainder are fantasies laced with contemporary science: "The Water Devil" concerns the trans-Atlantic cable and a ship whose cargo is electricity; "Amos Kilbright" is a ghost story; "The Knife That Killed Po Hancy" is a Jekyll and Hyde story concerning blood transfusions. Powers points out that *The Great Stone of Sardis* (the stone is a great diamond at the earth's core) combines Jules Verne's books *Journey to the Center of the Earth* and *The Adventures of Captain Hatteras* in a novel of polar exploration (Clewes, the amateur scientist/hero is first to reach the North Pole) and geological theory (Clewes invents an "Artesian Ray" to explore the interior of the earth). Clewes's adventures (set in 1947) are a significant contribution to the development of the "wonders of science" novel.

Stockton's major novel, however, is *The Great War Syndicate.* Although not mentioned in I.F. Clarke's *Voices Prophesying War,* Stockton's novel of a war between the US and England, fought using such new technology as an ultimate weapon (a disintegrator), is perhaps the most important SF novel in the "future war" tradition between *The Battle of Dorking* (1871) and *The War of the Worlds* (1898). World peace, capitalism, and the English language are enforced by an Anglo-American syndicate using the threat of ultimate destruction. The novel surpasses its many contemporaries, which characteristically dealt with politics, military tactics, and unimaginative technology (with minor innovations such as a new gun which would cause tactics to change) and were warnings clothed in fictional attributes. *The Great War Syndicate* is a true science-fiction vision of a new world created by a war to end war and a weapon to end war, the archetype of that naive hope which led to the building and use of the first atomic bombs and the "pax Americana."

That Stockton's immediate followers in this mode were for the most part popular hacks (e.g., George Griffith) has not enhanced his reputation as progenitor. However, despite its failings as a novel (principally a lack of adequate characterization), *The Great War Syndicate* repays serious examination.

—David G. Hartwell

STOVER, Leon E(ugene). American. Born in Lewiston, Pennsylvania, 9 April 1929. Educated at Western Maryland College, Westminster, B.A. in English 1950; University of New Mexico, Albuquerque, 1950; Harvard University, Cambridge, Massachusetts, 1951; Columbia University, New York, M.A. 1952, Ph.D. in anthropology and Chinese studies 1962. Married Takeko Kawai in 1956. Instructor, American Museum of Natural History, New York, 1955-57; Assistant Professor of Anthropology, Hobart and William Smith Colleges, Geneva, New York, 1957-63; Visiting Professor, Tokyo University (Human Ecology Fellow and National Institute of Health Fellow), 1963-65. Associate Professor, 1965-74, and since 1974, Professor of Anthropology, Illinois Institute of Technology, Chicago. Script writer for Encyclopaedia Britannica Films; Science Editor, *Amazing* and *Fantastic,* 1968-69. Co-Founder, Campbell Memorial Award. Recipient: Chris Award, and Cine Award, both for filmstrip, 1973. LL.D.: Western Maryland College, 1980. Agent: A.P. Watt and Son, 26-28 Bedford Row, London WC1R 4HL, England. Address: Department of Social Sciences, Illinois Institute of Technology, Chicago, Illinois 60616, U.S.A.

SCIENCE-FICTION PUBLICATIONS

Novel

Stonehenge, with Harry Harrison. New York, Scribner, and London, Davies, 1972.

Uncollected Short Stories

"The Visit," in *Fantastic* (New York), April 1969.
"What We Have Here Is Too Much Communication," in *Orbit 9,* edited by Damon Knight. New York, Putnam, 1971.
"Extra Ecclesium Nulla Salus," in *Fantastic* (New York), August 1971.

OTHER PUBLICATIONS

Other

La Science-Fiction Américaine: Essai d'Anthropologie Culturelle. Paris, Aubier Montaigne, 1972.
The Cultural Ecology of Chinese Civilization. New York, Universe, 1973.
"Science Fiction, The Research Revolution, and John Campbell," in *Du Fantastique à la Science-Fiction Américaine,* edited by Roger Asselineau. Paris, Librairie Marcel Didier, 1973.
"Anthropology and Science Fiction," in *Current Anthropology* (Chicago), October 1973.
China: An Anthropological Perspective, with Takeko Stover. Pacific Palisades, California, Goodyear, 1975.
"Is Jaspers Beer Good for You? Mass Society and Counter Culture in Herbert's *Santaroga Barrier,*" in *Extrapolation* (Wooster, Ohio), May 1976.
Stonehenge: The Indo-European Heritage, with Bruce Kraig. Chicago, Nelson Hall, 1978.

Editor, with Harry Harrison, *Apeman, Spaceman: Anthropological Science Fiction.* New York, Doubleday, and London, Rapp and Whiting, 1968.
Editor, with Willis E. McNelly, *Above the Human Landscape: Anthology of Sociological Science Fiction.* Pacific Palisades, California, Goodyear, 1972.

Leon E. Stover comments:
What little SF done in my name is a didactic extension of anthropology. Thus the story in *Orbit 9* shows that telepathy is a western idea, and that for the Japanese, given to social-distance techniques in their inter-personal relations rather than to confessional efforts of intimacy, the capacity for ESP would be regarded as a disease. Also the novel *Stonehenge* (1972) was a playground for the real thing, a new theory published in 1978. Read the fiction, then read the facts based on it!

*   *   *

Leon E. Stover, an anthropologist who teaches, writes, and criticizes science fiction, has also written books on Chinese culture and Stonehenge. His literary criticism is especially skilled in setting forth the relationships between science and science fiction. One of the best examples of a story by Stover—one that combines his anthropology, Chinese experience, and speculative fiction—is "What We Have Here Is Too Much Communication." Stover describes the story this way:

> Sahara-san, a Japanese mental patient, is recruited by Tokyo University as a telepathic dreamer for Dr. Hayashi's experiment in psionic movie making. In the hospital, Sahara-san's personal nurse, his *tsukisoi*, has read books to him and he has fed pictorial images back to her. Dr. Hayashi discovered his talent, and trained Sahara-san to direct his images, inspired by a movie script read to him by his *tsukisoi*. His secret fantasies of highly formal and ritualized interpersonal conduct begin to intrude on the screen, and the project is ruined. He recovers from the disease of too much communication when he is released from mind-to-mind dreaming with his *tsukisoi*, and he is returned to normal Japanese society where the mystery of close contact with others is not celebrated.

—Grace Eckley

STRETE, Craig. Pseudonym for a Cherokee Indian writer. American. Received M.F.A. in creative writing. Editor, *Red Planet Earth*. Address: 140 Meyer Avenue, Dayton, Ohio 45431, U.S.A.

SCIENCE-FICTION PUBLICATIONS

Short Stories

If All Else Fails, We Can Whip the Horse's Eyes and Make Him Cry and Sleep. Amsterdam, 1976.
The Bleeding Man and Other Science Fiction Stories (juvenile). New York, Greenwillow, 1977.
If All Else Fails. New York, Doubleday, 1980.

OTHER PUBLICATIONS

Other

When Grandfather Journeys into Winter (juvenile). New York, Greenwillow, 1979.

*   *   *

Craig Strete is unique in being the first native American to be recognized for his SF work. Strete has the flamboyance of R.A. Lafferty and Norman Spinrad, combining flights of fantasy with intense social criticism. He capitalizes on his Indian heritage in theme, motif, humor, and plot, leaning heavily on the mythic. His works are relatively short and indicate fascination with the sound and rhythm of sentences, giving the poetic effect of the native American oral tradition. Exaggeration, word play, and comic, low-key dialogue are characteristic. Because he often omits transition, becomes pyrotechnical, and demands close attention, Strete is not read rapidly.

Strete's recurrent theme is society's attempt to mold human beings into productive working parts of the white man's big world machine. What does not work is thrown out (the old man of "Time Deer"), or put to better use, providing blood for transfusions ("Bleeding Man") or adding color to movies ("A Horse of a Different Technicolor"). "Bleeding Man," his most conventionally narrated work, is most illustrative of the clash that occurs when emotionless bureaucracy meets the supernatural. On one level, it is a parable of the policy of first making war with Indians and then studying them. "Time Deer" similarly contrasts values. "A Horse of a Different Technicolor," a horror story of mind control, and "Why Has the Virgin Mary Never Entered the Wigwam of Standing Bear?" attack materialism and forced conformity, using television as a metaphor for the regimented spectator/consumer life.

—Mary S. Weinkauf

STURGEON, Theodore. Born Edward Hamilton Waldo; also writes as Frederick R. Ewing; Ellery Queen. American. Born in Staten Island, New York, 26 February 1918. Attended Overbrook High School, Philadelphia. Married Wina Golden in 1969; one son; four children by previous marriage. Worked as manager of apartment house, bulldozer operator, seaman, and literary agent; now full-time writer: book reviewer for *Venture* and New York *Times*; columnist, *National Review*, 1961-71; Contributing Editor, *If*, 1972-74, and since 1974, *Galaxy*. Recipient: International Fantasy Award, 1954; Nebula Award, 1970; Hugo Award, 1971. Guest of Honor, 20th World Science Fiction Convention, 1962. Address: 841¼ North Vendome Street, Los Angeles, California 90026, U.S.A.

SCIENCE-FICTION PUBLICATIONS

Novels

The Dreaming Jewels. New York, Greenberg, 1950; London, Nova, 1955; as *The Synthetic Man*, New York, Pyramid, 1957.
More Than Human. New York, Farrar Straus, 1953; London, Gollancz, 1954.
The Cosmic Rape. New York, Dell, 1958.
Venus Plus X. New York, Pyramid, 1960.
Voyage to the Bottom of the Sea (novelization of screenplay). New York, Pyramid, 1961.
...and My Fear Is Great; Baby Is Three. New York, Galaxy, 1963.

Short Stories

"It." Philadelphia, Prime Press, 1948.
Without Sorcery. Philadelphia, Prime Press, 1948; as *Not Without Sorcery*, New York, Ballantine, 1961.
E Pluribus Unicorn. New York, Abelard Press, 1953; London, Abelard Schuman, 1959.
Caviar. New York, Ballantine, 1955; London, Sidgwick and Jackson, 1968.
A Way Home. New York, Funk and Wagnalls, and London, Mayflower, 1955; as *Thunder and Roses*, London, Joseph, 1957.
A Touch of Strange. New York, Doubleday, 1958; London, Hamlyn, 1978.
Aliens 4. New York, Avon, 1959.
Beyond. New York, Avon, 1960.
Sturgeon in Orbit. New York, Pyramid, 1964; London, Gollancz, 1970.
The Joyous Invasions. London, Gollancz, 1965.
Starshine. New York, Pyramid, 1966; London, Gollancz, 1968.
Sturgeon Is Alive and Well. New York, Putnam, 1971.
The Worlds of Theodore Sturgeon. New York, Ace, 1972.
To Here and the Easel. London, Gollancz, 1973.
Visions and Venturers. New York, Dell, 1978; London, Gollancz, 1979.
Maturity. Minneapolis, Science Fiction Society, 1979.
The Golden Helix. New York, Doubleday, 1979.
The Stars Are the Styx. New York, Dell, 1979.

Uncollected Short Story

"Why Dolphins Don't Bite," in *Omni* (New York), February 1980.

OTHER PUBLICATIONS

Novels

I, Libertine (as Frederick R. Ewing).   New York, Ballantine, 1956.
The King and Four Queens.   New York, Dell, 1956.
Some of Your Blood.   New York, Ballantine, 1961; London, Sphere, 1967.
The Player on the Other Side (as Ellery Queen).   New York, Random House, 1963.
The Rare Breed.   New York, Fawcett, 1966.

Short Stories

Sturgeon's West.   New York, Doubleday, 1973.

Other

"Why I Selected Thunder and Roses," in *My Best Science Fiction Story*, edited by Leo Margulies and O.J. Friend.   New York, Merlin Press, 1949.
"The Mover and the Shaker," in *I Have No Mouth, And I Must Scream*, by Harlan Ellison.   New York, Pyramid, 1967.
"The Wonder-Full Age," in *Science Fiction Tales*, edited by Roger Elwood.   New York, Random House, 1973.
"Why?," in *Clarion 3*, edited by Robin Scott Wilson.   New York, New American Library, 1973.
"All the Effingers at Once," in *Mixed Feelings*, by Geo. Alec Effinger.   New York, Harper, 1974.

Editor, *New Soviet Science Fiction.*   London, Collier Macmillan, 1980.

*   *   *

In Kurt Vonnegut's fictional universe, Kilgore Trout writes SF stories pregnant with emotion and philosophy, but relegated to the unread pages of pornographic magazines, while he ekes out a living with odd jobs. Trout's most likely model is Theodore Sturgeon, whose much-anthologized stories have made him probably the best *loved* of all SF writers. Inclined toward magic and fantasy, unashamedly romantic and psychologically penetrating, Sturgeon commonly writes about the yearning for wholeness that characterizes love in a disjointed, repressive society. This emotional edge and his mastery of styles, using a classically restrained vocabulary, make him second only to Heinlein as a living model for other SF writers. Bradbury and Delany acknowledge their debt openly; others, like Vonnegut, are more indirect. Besides extensive writing outside SF, Sturgeon's fantasies fill over a dozen volumes of stories and several novels, plus the novelization of the movie, *Voyage to the Bottom of the Sea.*

Of his earliest work, *It* and "Killdozer" concern menaces whose life and terrestrial origins are in question. The latter is a compelling metaphor of machine malevolence. Another horror story, extraordinarily sensuous, is "Bianca's Hands" which tells of an idiot with beautiful hands that work without conscious direction, eventually strangling her lover. Other early stories include "Shottle Bop," about a mysterious shop selling talents people inevitably misuse, and "Microcosmic God" in which a misanthropic scientist drives the evolution of a race of tiny creatures who propitiate him with remarkable inventions. "Maturity" concerns a charming self-educated polymath whose perpetual youthful irresponsibility stems from a glandular defect; when it is corrected medically, he ripens and dies. The maturing of a society is the subject of "Thunder and Roses" in which a beautiful entertainer, dying from radiation sickness, persuades the men at a key military base in an America crippled by nuclear attack to spare their enemy and the human race.

Sturgeon's first novel, *The Dreaming Jewels*, is a mad melodrama of circus freaks and humanoid products of living crystals. Its few poetic moments cannot overcome simplistic conflicts among telepathic cardboard characters, but elements in it look forward to *More*

Than Human, which won the International Fantasy Award. In "Baby Is Three" a boy finds out in a marathon psychiatric session why he tried to kill his foster mother. With the analyst's vocabulary and his own repressed memories, he discovers his role as the central ganglion of a multi-person form, or gestalt, whose other members are also children with parapsychological powers complementing his own. Actually killing off the governess in the middle section of the novel, Sturgeon begins it with the youthful outcasts and an older "idiot" coalescing into the gestalt's "first draft," and ends it with the addition of a moral component who binds the entity to homo sapiens while he opens the door to the superior race, homo gestalt. Written in a vivid, impressionistic style, this parable of social organization and psychological integration became for many readers the one SF classic. Completing this parapsychological trilogy, *The Cosmic Rape* finds another outcast repelling a group-mind invasion by uniting Earth's mental forces over the galaxy-spanning alien being. In the process, he breaks through his isolation and finds himself, while healing the fragmentation of the individualistic human race.

Featuring magic and wish-fulfillment, aliens and esp, Sturgeon's stories exploit the most peripheral of science-fiction content. In "Saucer of Loneliness" a girl learns from a miniature flying saucer that someone is lonelier than she is. Though it brings tribulations, it sustains her through them, finally bringing the love of the narrator, who saves her from suicide. "The World Well Lost" appears to concern a pair of aliens, "loverbirds" from Dirnadu, a planet closed to mankind. It is really about the love between two human space crewmen, which literally "cannot speak its name," and which taints the entire human race from the perspective of the aliens, whose gender differences are more pronounced. Apparent homosexuality also surfaces in "Affair with a Green Monkey" in which a slightly built young man is rescued from thugs by a pompously "well-adjusted" psychologist. Overbearingly tolerant, the host throws his wife and his guest together, and a platonic affair develops. Its consummation is prevented not by the guest's being gay but by his being an alien, far too well-endowed sexually for interspecies sex. But what may seem merely a dirty joke is in fact a sensitive plea for understanding, tolerance, and tenderness.

Closer to hard science fiction, "Bulkhead" (originally "Who?") tells of an astronaut kept company by the childish half of his artificially split personality, supposedly beyond a bulkhead which actually separates him from the vacuum of space. More utopian is the far-future pastoral world of "The Skills of Xanadu" where people are integrated by means of "belts" that virtually transcend technology, freeing them to realize their (and our) potential. Three other tales show the variety of Sturgeon's production in the 1950's. In "The Girl Had Guts" a symbiotic alien saves human lives by becoming a false digestive system, vomited out in times of peril. Marooned on Mars, a man disguises from himself, with lyrical impressions and memories, his impending death as the first human to take this next evolutionary step into an alien environment ("The Man Who Lost the Sea"). The comic elegy "Like Young" suggests that fun-loving otters have already inherited the Earth from a doomed human race.

Never avoiding controversy, Sturgeon anticipated by a decade Le Guin's Gethenians in *Venux Plus X*. In alternating chapters, suburbanites talk about sexual variety and stereotypes, and a downed aviator with macho hangups fails to be integrated into a utopian society of surgically created bisexuals. Flirting with another taboo, *Some of Your Blood* takes the vampire theme seriously, probing its causes in a fictional case history of a man's bizarre need. Like these novels, Sturgeon's later stories tend to be talky, as well as controversial. "When You Care, When You Love" extends love to one's own creation, a cloned replica of a lost beloved. "If All Men Were Brothers, Would You Want One to Marry Your Sister?" posits a world in which keeping sex in the family is the "healthy" rule, not a frequently broken proscription. In perhaps his best story about healing, "Slow Sculpture" compares it to raising bonsai plants (Hugo and Nebula awards). His more recent work is less successful. A case in point is "Case and the Dreamer"; ambitious but diffuse, it is about an astronaut and his lover, resurrected by an indrawn human race to explore the universe for it, in the company of a clownish "god" (the dreamer) with whom their ship's computer has fallen in love.

A *science-fiction* writer largely by courtesy, Sturgeon equates "science" with "wisdom," not with hardware and limitations. Moving even when they are talky, his fantasies are wrought from emotional experiences his readers recognize as theirs, but which his skill with words can distance artistically. As unselfishly giving and fiscally "irresponsible" as the protagonist of "Maturity," Sturgeon has never profited much financially from his writing. But he has turned his suffering into beauty, encapsulating in fiction the longing for alternatives which characterizes many people's fascination with science fiction and fantasy.

—David N. Samuelson

SUTTON, Jeff and Jean.   American.   **SUTTON, Jeff(erson H.):** Born in Los Angeles, California, 25 July 1913. Educated at San Diego State College, B.A. 1954, M.A. 1956. Served in the United States Marine Corps, 1941-45: Technical Sergeant. Married Eugenia Geneva Hansen in 1941; one son and one daughter. Photographer, International News Photos, Los Angeles, 1937-40; reporter, photographer, public relations writer for General Dynamics Astronautics; free-lance writer and editorial consultant to aerospace industries from 1960. *Died 31 January 1979.* **SUTTON, Jean** (Eugenia Geneva Sutton, née Hansen): Born in Denmark, Wisconsin, 5 July 1916. Educated at the University of Wisconsin, Madison, 1934-37; University of California, Los Angeles, B.A. in economics 1940; San Diego State University, M.A. in education 1959. Personnel worker, U.S. Steel, Los Angeles, 1940-41; construction company timekeeper, San Diego, 1942-45; lathe operator, Douglas Aircraft, Santa Monica, California, and social worker in Los Angeles; Executive Secretary, San Diego City Council, 1949-52; Administrative Assistant, San Diego State College, 1953-55; social studies teacher, San Diego county high schools, 1958-71. Since 1971, consultant assistant. Agent: Scott Meredith Literary Agency, 845 Third Avenue, New York, New York 10022. Address: 4325 Beverly Drive, La Mesa, California 92041, U.S.A.

SCIENCE-FICTION PUBLICATIONS

Novels by Jeff Sutton

First on the Moon.   New York, Ace, 1958.
Bombs in Orbit.   New York, Ace, 1959.
Spacehive.   New York, Ace, 1960.
The Atom Conspiracy.   New York, Avalon, 1963.
Apollo at Go (juvenile).   New York, Putnam, 1963; London, Mayflower, 1964.
The Missile Lords.   New York, Putnam, 1963; London, Sidgwick and Jackson, 1964.
Beyond Apollo (juvenile).   New York, Putnam, 1966; London, Gollancz, 1967.
H-Bomb over America.   New York, Ace, 1967.
The Man Who Saw Tomorrow.   New York, Ace, 1968.
Whisper from the Stars.   New York, Dell, 1970.
Alton's Unguessable.   New York, Ace, 1970.
The Mindlocked Man.   New York, DAW, 1972.
Cassady.   New York, St. Martin's Press, 1979.

Novels by Jeff and Jean Sutton (juvenile)

The River.   New York, Belmont, 1966.
The Beyond.   New York, Putnam, 1968.
The Programmed Man.   New York, Putnam, 1968.
Lord of the Stars.   New York, Putnam, 1969.
Alien from the Stars.   New York, Putnam, 1970.
The Boy Who Had the Power.   New York, Putnam, 1971.

Uncollected Short Stories by Jeff Sutton

"The Third Empire," in *Spaceway* (Alhambra, California), February 1955.

"The Man Who Had No Brains," in *Amazing* (New York), September 1961.
"Forerunner," in *Androids, Time Machines, and Blue Giraffes*, edited by Roger Elwood and Vic Ghidalia.   Chicago, Follett, 1973.
"After Ixmal," in *Space Opera*, edited by Brian Aldiss.   London, Weidenfeld and Nicolson, 1974; New York, Doubleday, 1975.

*   *   *

Jeff Sutton's career as a writer of SF has been checkered. In spite of the fact that its melodramatic plot of conflict between the United States and Russia is a reflection in miniature of the then Cold War, *First on the Moon*, his first novel, was considered promising because its technological detailing seemed authentic, perhaps owing to the author's engineering background. His second novel, *Bombs in Orbit*, again elicited some praise for its handling of technological details and for what appeared to be an increased skill in manipulating plot and creating suspense. However, the next two novels, *Spacehive* and *The Atom Conspiracy*, aroused substantial critical misgivings. No one doubted Sutton's ability to describe technological processes, current and extrapolated, and to suggest thereby verisimilitude. But plotting and characterization seemed more and more throwbacks to 1930's space opera; further, Sutton's style increasingly manifested an embarrassing fondness for cliché.

The Atom Conspiracy aptly illustrates Sutton's limitations. Its portrait of the Empire of Earth in 2449 when research in the atom is outlawed because of previous nuclear catastrophes, and a World Government is directed by an elite Council of Six who possess the highest IQ, is neither original nor convincing. The world looks and society functions very much the way they do today, and the Council of Six appear no better or worse than anyone with normal IQ. For reasons not entirely clear the Empire also looks with disdain upon anyone with ESP powers. The novel's hero, Max Krull, a government agent and a secret ESPer, is sent to investigate the circumstances behind the death by nuclear burning of a long-missing man. Most of the action, consisting of conventional intrigue, flight and chase, confrontations with supposedly all-powerful figures, and a gingerly touch of sex, is designed to keep Max from being where it was foretold he would be regardless of anything done to prevent it. Finally, Sutton's use of ESP owes more to a need for narrative gimmicks than a desire to investigate seriously an important topic.

Perhaps believing that his ability for describing technological processes and penchant for conventional plotting and characterization might be better utilized in children's SF, Sutton pointed his next novel, *Apollo at Go*, at the juvenile market. Buoyed by the novel's positive acceptance, Sutton turned out seven additional children's SF novels, most of which were written in collaboration with his wife Jean. (Several more Jeff Sutton adult SF novels have been published but none has made any stir.) Unfortunately, after initial acceptance and subsequent tinkering to find other effective ways of attracting young readers, the Suttons have been unable to come up with the one unqualified success that would establish them as significant authors of SF. Still their children's SF is as good as the representative Nourse or Lightner juvenile, and superior to a typical Hugh Walters story. *The Programmed Man, Lord of the Stars*, and *Alien from the Stars*, in particular, are all action-packed, quick-moving novels. Considered as a whole, then, Jeff Sutton's SF, whether intended for adults or children, has fallen short of the first rank. Although always solid in its depiction of technological process and procedures and usually adequately grounded in its scientific speculation, his fiction has yet to move beyond the merely competent and predictable and to achieve originality and literary distinction.

—Francis J. Molson

SZILARD, Leo. American. Born in Budapest, Hungary, 11 February 1898; emigrated to the United States, 1937; naturalized, 1943. Educated at the Budapest Institute of Technology; University of Berlin, D.Phil. 1922. Married Gertrud Weiss in 1951. Staff member, University of Berlin, 1925-32; research worker in nuclear physics, St. Bartholomew's Hospital, London, and Clarendon Laboratory, Oxford, 1934-38; staff member at Columbia University, New York, 1939-42, and, with Enrico Fermi, University of Chicago, 1942-46: devised chain reaction system with Fermi; resident fellow, Salk Institute of Biological Studies, La Jolla, California, 1964. Recipient: Atoms for Peace Prize, 1959. *Died 30 May 1964.*

SCIENCE-FICTION PUBLICATIONS

Short Stories

The Voice of the Dolphins and Other Stories. New York, Simon and Schuster, and London, Gollancz, 1961.

OTHER PUBLICATIONS

Other

The Collected Works of Leo Szilard, edited by Bernard T. Feld and Gertrud Weiss Szilard. Cambridge, Massachusetts Institute of Technology, 1972.
Leo Szilard: His Version of the Facts: Selected Recollections and Correspondence, edited by Spencer R. Weart and Gertrud Weiss Szilard. Cambridge, Massachusetts Institute of Technology, 1978.

*   *   *

Leo Szilard will always be remembered more for his involvement with the atomic bomb than for his literary achievements. His sole work of science fiction, *The Voice of the Dolphins and Other Stories,* is of interest more because it is written by a famous physicist than for any particular merit. All the stories are told in dry, lecture-tour manner, rather like the crudest efforts of the Gernsback era. Szilard was a vigorous thinker but he showed no interest in character development or plot. Instead, he merely presented ideas. The title story concerns efforts by dolphins to control the human race, using scientific organizations as fronts. They do fairly well for a while. All this is told in straight exposition, as a "non-fact" history. Some of the political predictions have turned out to be uncannily on the mark, others way off. "My Trial as a War Criminal" concerns the possible guilt of the early atomic bomb scientists. The others are less important. "Report on 'Grand Central Terminal' " has future extraterrestrial archeologists puzzling over pay toilets.

—Darrell Schweitzer

TAINE, John. Pseudonym for Eric Temple Bell. American. Born in Aberdeen, Scotland, 7 February 1883. Educated at the University of London, 1902; Stanford University, California, A.B. 1904 (Phi Beta Kappa); University of Washington, Seattle, A.M. 1908; Columbia University, New York, Ph.D. 1912. Married Jessie Lillian Brown in 1910; one child. Professor of Mathematics, University of Washington, 1912-26, and California Institute of Technology, Pasadena, 1927-53. Vice-President, American Mathematical Society, 1926; President, Mathematical Association of America, 1931-33. Recipient: Bocher Prize, for academic work, 1920-24. Vice-President, American Academy of Arts and Sciences, 1930; Member, National Academy of Sciences. *Died 21 December 1960.*

SCIENCE-FICTION PUBLICATIONS

Novels

The Purple Sapphire. New York, Dutton, 1924.
Quayle's Invention. New York, Dutton, 1927.
The Gold Tooth. New York, Dutton, 1927.
Green Fire. New York, Dutton, 1928.
The Greatest Adventure. New York, Dutton, 1929.
The Iron Star. New York, Dutton, 1930.
Before the Dawn. Baltimore, Williams and Wilkins, 1934.
The Time Stream. Providence, Rhode Island, Buffalo, 1946.
The Forbidden Garden. Reading, Pennsylvania, Fantasy Press, 1947.
The Cosmic Geoids, and One Other. Los Angeles, Fantasy, 1949.
Seeds of Life. Reading, Pennsylvania, Fantasy Press, 1951; London, Rich and Cowan, 1955.
The Crystal Horde. Reading, Pennsylvania, Fantasy Press, 1952; as *White Lily*, in *Seeds of Life, and White Lily*, New York, Dover, 1966.
G.O.G. 666. Reading, Pennsylvania, Fantasy Press, 1954; London, Rich and Cowan, 1955.

Uncollected Short Stories

"Twelve Eighty-Seven," in *Astounding* (New York), May 1935.
"Tomorrow," in *Marvel* (New York), April-May 1939.
"The Ultimate Catalyst," in *My Best Science Fiction Story*, edited by Leo Margulies and O.J. Friend. New York, Merlin Press, 1949.

OTHER PUBLICATIONS

Verse

Recreations (as J.T.). Boston, Gorham Press, 1915.
The Singer (as J.T.). Boston, Gorham Press, 1916.

Other as Eric Temple Bell

The Cyclotomic Quinary Quintic. New York, Columbia University, 1912.
An Arithmetic Theory of Certain Numerical Functions. Seattle, University of Washington, 1915.
Algebraic Arithmetic. New York, American Mathematical Society, 1927.
Debunking Science. Seattle, University of Washington Book Store, 1930.
The Queen of the Sciences. Baltimore, Williams and Wilkins, 1931.
Numerology. Baltimore, Williams and Wilkins, 1933.
The Handmaiden of the Sciences. Baltimore, Williams and Wilkins, and London, Baillière, 1937.
Men of Mathematics. New York, Simon and Schuster, and London, Gollancz, 1937.
Man and His Lifebelts. Baltimore, Williams and Wilkins, 1938.
"Why Science Fiction?" (as John Taine) in *Startling* (New York), March 1939.
The Development of Mathematics. New York, McGraw Hill, 1940; revised edition, 1945.
The Magic of Numbers. New York, McGraw Hill, 1946.
Mathematics, Queen and Servant of Science. New York, McGraw Hill, 1951; London, Bell, 1952.
The Last Problem. New York, Simon and Schuster, 1961; London, Gollancz, 1962.

.*   *   *

John Taine was the pseudonym used by the prominent research mathematician Eric Temple Bell in his science-fiction novels. Taine was a respected science-fiction novelist during the 1920's who turned to the pulp SF magazines with the depression. His best work blended theoretical inquiry into the unknown with high adventure in the H. Rider Haggard tradition, and he combined sound science with a rare story-telling ability.

The major preoccupation in Taine's handful of novels is that of technological disaster. In almost all his work, scientific inquiry into the unknown precipitates an impending cataclysm. These disasters can be man-made, as in *Seeds of Life*, natural, as in *The Iron Star*, or accidental, as the monsters created in *White Lily*. In *The Greatest Adventure* and *The Purple Sapphire* unknown cataclysms in remote antiquity have their effect on the modern world. *The Time Stream* links the destruction of a future world with the great San Francisco earthquake.

Taine's novels invariably focus on individuals who band together to quest into the unknown. Often, he teams a scientist with an adventurer. On one level his narratives function as scientific mystery stories in which inexplicable phenomena screen a hidden truth. Taine slowly—in *White Lily*, ponderously—reveals the solution through his close-mouthed scientist characters. At times complete and final answers are withheld in order to maintain a sense of wonder and mystery. This is particularly true in *The Greatest Adventure* and *The Purple Sapphire*, both of which concern survivals of ancient super-civilizations of Earth's past. In *The Greatest Adventure* an Antarctic expedition uncovers the remnants of such a civilization. Under the ice is a city which had entombed itself alive rather than allow the possibility of escape to the mutated creatures spawned when they discovered the secret of life. The expedition inadvertently activates the menace. Taine concentrates on the biological nightmares, and neither explores nor identifies the ancient civilization, but this enhances the power of the novel. On the other hand, this reserve limits the otherwise excellent *Purple Sapphire*. Three seekers of fortune discover a fantastic city in the heart of Central Asia where a degraded theocracy guards its technological marvels against the day its true inhabitants return. They do not return, and the three successfully rescue the kidnapped daughter of a British General but lose the secret of transmuting matter.

Genetic mutation is a theme Taine finds fascinating. Two novels, *Seeds of Life* and *G.O.G. 666*, deal with the consequences of human genetic tampering. *Seeds of Life* chronicles the brief career of a dissolute research scientist, Neils Bork, who becomes a superman when exposed to radiation. Bork, who considers human life beneath contempt, masterminds a fiendish plan to eradicate all humans, but is stymied when he regresses and falls in love with the women he has chosen as the instrument of annihilation. A similar figure is Gog, the hulking travesty of a man whom plant geneticist Dr. Clive Chase encounters in his investigation of a Soviet plan to liberate its workers from drudgery in *G.O.G. 666*. Gog is the keystone of the plan, and he hides a secret darker than that of Neils Bork. *G.O.G. 666* is somewhat marred by its Cold War preoccupations. *White Lily* also depicts Russia in an uncomplimentary light. In China, two despicable Russian agents foment revolution. Against this bloody backdrop, a US soldier has unwittingly introduced silicon-based lifeforms on Earth, which run unchecked.

Considered to be his greatest work, *The Time Stream* is a complex excursion into the dynamics of time travel and cyclical universes. The Time Stream is the medium by which ten individuals from the future send their minds back to 20th-century San Francisco. There they live new lives in an attempt to determine if a scientifically forbidden marriage will result in the destruction of their world. Although somewhat confusing in its narrative structure, *The Time Stream* is nevertheless a compelling example of imaginative writing. Of his other works, *The Iron Star*, a novel of a destructive asteroid, and "The Ultimate Catalyst" are noteworthy.

—Will Murray

TALL, Stephen. Pseudonym for Compton Newby Crook. American. Born in Rossville, Tennessee, 14 June 1908. Educated at George Peabody College (now Vanderbilt University), Nashville, B.S. 1932, M.A. 1933; Johns Hopkins University, Baltimore; Arizona State University, Tempe. Served as an intelligence officer in the Office of Strategic Services, 1943-45: Captain. Married Lucy Bev-

erly Courtney in 1940; three children. Science teacher, Appalachian State University, Boone, North Carolina, Middle Tennessee State University, Murfreesboro, Tennessee Polytechnic Institute, Western Reserve University, Cleveland, College of William and Mary, Williamsburg, Virginia, and Episcopal Academy, Philadelphia, 1933-39. Instructor, then Professor of Biology and Department Chairman, 1939-73, and since 1973, Professor Emeritus, Towson State University, Baltimore. Ranger and naturalist with the National Park Service, eight summers. Recipient: National Science Foundation grants for ecological study. Agent: Blassingame McCauley and Wood, 60 East 42nd Street, New York, New York 10017. Address: Merryman's Mill Road, Phoenix, Maryland 21131, U.S.A.

SCIENCE-FICTION PUBLICATIONS

Novels

The Ramsgate Paradox. New York, Berkley, 1976.
The People Beyond the Wall. New York, DAW, 1980.

Short Stories

The Stardust Voyages. New York, Berkley, 1975.

Uncollected Short Stories

"Chlorophyll," in *Fantasy and Science Fiction* (New York), June 1976.
"The Rock and the Pool," in *Galaxy* (New York), December 1976.
"The Man Who Saved the Sun," in *Fantasy and Science Fiction* (New York), January 1977.
"The King Is Dead, Long Live the Queen!," in *Amazing* (New York), January 1978.
"Home Is the Hunter," in *Analog* (New York), August 1979.
"The Hot and Cold Running Waterfall," in *Isaac Asimov's Science Fiction Magazine* (New York), May 1980.
"The Merry Men of Methane," in *Fantasy and Science Fiction* (New York), May 1980.

Stephen Tall comments:
I was born in Tennessee near the Big River, the Mississippi, the son of a country doctor and a cultured, sensitive mother. The levees, the cotton fields, the cypress swamps, and the cane breaks were my first playgrounds. And in our home books and good reading always had status. Respect for knowledge and how it is acquired was instilled early.

I have always been a biologist writing fiction, not the other way around. I write because I like to tell a good story, and because the mechanics of good writing are pleasing to me. My stories are about what I know, and about what I have concern for. They have always reflected my awareness of and interest in the living world other than man. I wrote stories based on ecology before the word was generally familiar. I regard science fiction as almost the ideal medium for expressing ecological concerns: any species, any race, anywhere.

*   *   *

Approximately half of Stephen Tall's science fiction concerns the crew of the interstellar explorer ship *Stardust*: six short stories collected as *The Stardust Voyages* and one of the two published novels, *The Ramsgate Paradox*. They are in many ways from the same mold as the television program *Star Trek*. A crew of 400 staffs the ship as it makes its way from one star system to another, but for all practical purposes, there are only three characters. Roscoe Kissinger is the obligatory hero, not too long on brains, but courageous to a fault. Equally necessary is Lindy Peterson, the attractive female scientist whose major significance seems to be to require rescue by Roscoe. The last is Pegleg Williams, the tried and true best friend, comic relief, and jack of all trades. There is also an elderly woman whose psychic abilities manifest themselves in her cryptic paintings.

There is no doubt that the entire series is built around pure stereotypes. Nevertheless, some of the adventures have been very well received. Perhaps the best known is "The Bear with a Knot on His Tail", in which the star Mizar is about to explode and the

Stardust arrives to carry off significant records and frozen germ plasma of the local intelligent species. Perhaps the most interesting, however, is the first, "Seventy Light-Years from Sol" (retitled "A Star Called Cyrene"). This time our protagonists land on a planet inhabited by two very distinct races. The first consists of featureless vari-colored cubes who can teleport themselves about from one location to another, and do so frequently in order to escape the predations of a species of carnivorous wheel. But now the cubes face a new threat, invasion from a nearby island of formless blobs, against which they have no defense. Human policy is to avoid taking sides in local squabbles, but the crew decides that offering advice is not tantamount to interference. This strange twist of logic seems not to present any problems to the characters or the author, and the story is well written enough for us to ignore the chauvinism. These two stories set the pattern for the rest of the series, in which the three central characters meet and overcome a variety of menaces ranging from a manifestation of ancient Greek gods to mutated giant crabs. The latter appear in "The Invaders," another above-average story that suffers from problems of internal logic.

A non-series story of note is "Allison, Carmichael, and Tattersall" which seems to have been molded at least in part by recollection of the Arcot, Morey, and Wade stories of John W. Campbell Jr. Indeed, much of Tall's fiction would not have been at all out of place in the 1930's, although the level of literary achievement is substantially higher. This was also the beginning of a truncated series, and is a satisfying light adventure story marred by over-reliance on coincidence, a flaw which appears in many of the other stories as well.

The Ramsgate Paradox is distinguished from the shorter *Stardust* pieces only by length, making no serious effort to add substantial depth to the characters. The second novel, *The People Beyond the Wall*, is also a return to a tradition largely abandoned in the genre, the Utopian novel. A pair of adventurers set off to explore an area of glacier in the Antarctic and find themselves in a hidden land where people have returned to a pastoral existence unmarred by organized strife. Although this is probably the most ambitious work Tall has produced, it falls prey eventually to an internal problem of most such novels; the plot begins to slow to a crawl as the varied aspects of the totally sane but rather dull society are revealed. Tall loses control totally in the final chapters, jumping forward years in time, introducing new characters, and confusing the reader. Nevertheless, the early chapters are quite well done, and the move away from the repetitiveness of the *Stardust* stories is promising.

—Don D'Ammassa

TATE, Peter. British. Journalist. Agent: Virginia Kidd, Box 278, Milford, Pennsylvania 18837, U.S.A. Address: 3 Seaway Avenue, Friars Cliff, Christchurch, Hampshire, England.

SCIENCE-FICTION PUBLICATIONS

Novels

The Thinking Seat. New York, Doubleday, 1969; London, Faber, 1970.
Gardens One to Five. New York, Doubleday, 1971; as *Gardens, 1,2,3,4,5*, London, Faber, 1971.
Country Love and Poison Rain. New York, Doubleday, 1973.
Moon on an Iron Meadow. New York, Doubleday, 1974.
Faces in the Flames. New York, Doubleday, 1976.
Greencomber. New York, Doubleday, 1979.

Short Stories

Seagulls under Glass. New York, Doubleday, 1975.

* * *

Although Peter Tate can be a futurist, an allegorist, and a fantasist, in his major work he is a realist who utilizes current trends in natural and social science as well as technology for conveying his values. His concept of science fiction is a "work styled in protest at a particular facet of...technology and using research to qualify that protest" (introduction to "The Post-Mortem People" in *Seagulls Under Glass*). Unlike futurists who project their characters onto other planets, eons removed from the present, Tate remains on a familiar earth only a few years distanced from the copyright date. He chooses recognizable settings (Waukegan, Zimbabwe, New Forest) and with them creates an illusion that his scientific and technological projections have already left the laboratory and are threatening the balance in man and nature. Likewise, he interweaves imagined crises with references to current headlines (Che Guevara, Vorster, Kent State, Mozambique), thus enabling the reader to fuse fabrication with newspaper fact. Sobering is his recognition that heroes sometimes die. Tate further asserts the realness of his fictions by overlapping characters and plots. Simeon and Tomorrow Julie star in *The Thinking Seat, Moon on an Iron Meadow*, and *Faces in the Flames*; Scarlatti and Prinz counter each other in *Gardens One to Five* and *Faces in the Flames*. Famous Gogan slips in and out of *The Thinking Seat, Gardens One to Five* and *Faces in the Flames*; and Shem of *Gardens One to Five* is a memory in *Faces in the Flames*. Even more interesting than overlapping is Tate's technique of using fiction to authenticate fiction, as in *Moon on an Iron Meadow* where he returns to the buildings, people, and atmosphere created 50 years before by his mentor Ray Bradbury (*Something Wicked This Way Comes*).

Many of Tate's plots are compelling in their fast-paced intrigue ("Skyhammer"); their allegorical assessment of social and political forces (*Gardens One to Five*); or their subtle ambivalence between realism and fantasy (*Greencomber*). A few are bizarre. In "Mars Pastorale" a defenseless poppy seed invades a defenseless human's throat; in "Post-Mortem People" licensed ghouls stalk dying men for healthy body parts; in "The Gloom Pattern"—whose science, says Tate, is "bunkum"—a youngster is sucked up from his earthly existence on an "ecstasy beam" when he craves a sad man's happiness. Tate's humor surfaces in the provocative "Same Autumn in a Different Park." In this parody of the Adam-Eve story, Addison springs from the side of Tina who with the help of "molecular rejig" turns into an apple which is eaten by the new Adam.

Tate sees the world as essentially good; but it has been contaminated by ignorance, indifference, misguided heroics, self-serving, and malice. As in Bradbury's *Something Wicked This Way Comes*, the spirit of evil is pervasive and its confrontation inevitable. It periodically erupts in such "bodies" as the United Nations, desalination plants, canisters of biological weapons, defoliants, contaminated rabbits, atom bombs, church "Prinzes," and Hitlerian megalomaniacs. Once this force is loose, balance between good and evil can be restored only by a figure who embodies the spirit of pristine Christianity: "the time of authenticity on the lake shores of Nazareth before two thousand years of controversy and schism and compromise and commerce had muddied the waters beyond perception" (*Faces in the Flames*). Simeon, along with Shem, Nelso Ojukwe (*Faces in the Flames*), Greencomber, and Adams ("Mainchance"), insists on rational, willed self-involvement—even to the point of death—against any sort of manipulation of humans. Like the Galilean, all of these heroes provoke action in the quiescent; by the force of their integrity, they transform Judases and self-deceivers into disciples. A developing theme from *The Thinking Seat* to *Greencomber* is individual and social transformation effected by altruistic love.

Tate enjoys language. He puns, makes memorable metaphors, and sometimes achieves a mesmerizing lyricism. His use of myth is haunting: blood is the price for exaltation; life consciously saved counterbalances that which is wantonly taken; love dispels enslaving myths created by malevolent scientists. At times he mistakes clichés for original expression, or reaches too far for an apt comparison. But Tate is a stimulating writer who structures complex materials into convincing fictions.

—Rosemary Coleman

TEMPLE, William F(rederick). British. Born in London, 9 March 1914. Educated at Gordon School, London, 1919-27; Woolwich Polytechnic, London, 1928-30. Served in the Royal Artillery, 1940-46. Married Joan Streeton in 1939; one daughter and one son. Head Clerk, Stock Exchange, London, 1930-50. Agent: E.J. Carnell Literary Agency, Rowneybury Bungalow, Sawbridgeworth, near Old Harlow, Essex CM20 2EX. Address: Flat 1, 20 Grimston Gardens, Folkestone, Kent CT20 2PU, England.

SCIENCE-FICTION PUBLICATIONS

Novels (series: Martin Magnus)

Four-Sided Triangle. London, Long, 1949; New York, Fell, 1951.
Martin Magnus, Planet Rover (juvenile). London, Muller, 1955.
Martin Magnus on Venus (juvenile). London, Muller, 1955.
Martin Magnus on Mars (juvenile). London, Muller, 1956.
The Automated Goliath, The Three Suns of Amara. New York, Ace, 1962.
Battle on Venus. New York, Ace, 1963.
Shoot at the Moon. New York, Simon and Schuster, and London, Whiting and Wheaton, 1966.
The Fleshpots of Sansato. London, Macdonald, 1968.

Uncollected Short Stories

"The Kosso," in *Thrills.* London, Philip Allan, 1935.
"Lunar Lilliput," in *Tales of Wonder 2* (Kingswood, Surrey), 1938.
"The Smile of the Sphinx," in *Tales of Wonder* (Kingswood, Surrey), Autumn 1938.
"Mr. Craddock's Amazing Experience," in *Amazing* (New York), February 1939.
"Experiment in Genius," in *Tales of Wonder* (Kingswood, Surrey), Summer 1940.
"The Monster on the Border," in *Super Science* (Kokomo, Indiana), November 1940.
"The Three Pylons," in *New Worlds 1* (London), 1946.
"Miracle Town," in *Thrilling Wonder Stories* (New York), October 1948.
"The Brain Beast," in *Super Science* (Kokomo, Indiana), July 1949.
"For Each Man Kills," in *Amazing* (New York), March 1950.
"Martian's Fancy," in *New Worlds* (London), Summer 1950.
"Wisher Take All," in *Other Worlds* (Evanston, Indiana), July 1950.
"The Bone of Contention," in *Thrilling Wonder Stories* (New York), October 1950.
"Forget-Me-Not," in *The Best Science Fiction Stories 1951*, edited by E.F. Bleiler and T.E. Dikty. New York, Fell, 1951.
"Conditioned Reflex," in *Other Worlds* (Evanston, Indiana), January 1951.
"You Can't See Me," in *Fantastic Adventures* (New York), June 1951.
"Double Trouble," in *Science Fantasy* (Bournemouth), Winter 1951.
"A Date to Remember," in *Invaders of Earth*, edited by Groff Conklin. New York, Vanguard Press, 1952; London, Weidenfeld and Nicolson, 1953.
"The Two Shadows," in *The Best Science-Fiction Stories 1952*, edited by E.F. Bleiler and T.E. Dikty. New York, Fell, 1952; London, Grayson, 1953.
"Counter-Transference," in *The Best Science-Fiction Stories 1953*, edited by E.F. Bleiler and T.E. Dikty. New York, Fell, 1953; London, Grayson, 1955.
"Way of Escape," in *Science Fiction Adventures in Dimension*, edited by Groff Conklin. New York, Vanguard Press, 1953; London, Grayson, 1955.
"Immortal's Playthings," in *Authentic* (London), January 1953.
"Field of Battle," in *Other Worlds* (Evanston, Indiana), February 1953.
"Mind Within Mind," in *Authentic* (London), May 1953.
"Limbo," in *Nebula* (Glasgow), Summer 1953.
"Pawn in Revolt," in *Nebula* (Glasgow), Autumn 1953.
"Destiny Is My Enemy," in *Nebula* (Glasgow), September 1953.

"Moon Wreck," in *Boy's Own Paper* (London), November 1953.
"Explorers of Mars," in *Authentic Book of Space*, edited by Herbert J. Campbell. London, Panther, 1954.
"Pilot's Hands," in *Nebula* (Glasgow), February 1954.
"Errand of Mercy," in *Authentic* (London), March 1954.
"Space Saboteur," in *Boy's Own Paper* (London), March 1954.
"Eternity," in *Science Fantasy* (Bournemouth), February 1955.
"Man in a Maze," in *Authentic* (London), February 1955.
"The Lonely," in *Imagination* (Evanston, Illinois), July 1955.
"Better Than We Know," in *Science Fiction Quarterly* (Holyoke, Massachusetts), August 1955.
"Mansion of Love," in *Nebula* (Glasgow), September 1955.
"Uncle Buno," in *Science Fantasy* (Bournemouth), November 1955.
32 stories, in *Rocket* (London), April to November 1956.
"The Girl from Mars," in *Heiress* (London), September 1956.
"Outside Position," in *Nebula* (Glasgow), November 1956.
"The Green Car," in *Science Fantasy* (Bournemouth), June 1957.
"A Date to Remember," in *Nebula* (Glasgow), July 1957.
"Against Goliath," in *Nebula* (Glasgow), August 1957.
"Brief Encounter," in *Nebula* (Glasgow), October 1957.
"War Against Darkness," in *Nebula* (Glasgow), June 1958.
"The Different Complexion," in *New Worlds* (London), October 1958.
"Imbalance," in *Nebula* (Glasgow), May 1959.
"Magic Ingredient," in *Science Fantasy* (Bournemouth), December 1959.
"The Whispering Gallery," in *Zacherley's Midnight Snacks*, edited by Zacherley. New York, Ballantine, 1960.
" 'L' Is for Lash," in *Amazing* (New York), July 1960.
"Sitting Duck," in *New Worlds* (London), November 1960.
"The Unknown," in *Amazing* (New York), March 1961.
"A Trek to Na-Abiza," in *Science Fiction Adventures* (London), July 1961.
"Beyond the Line," in *Fantastic* (New York), September 1964.
"A Niche in Time," in *World's Best Science Fiction 1965*, edited by Donald A. Wollheim and Terry Carr. New York, Ace, 1965.
"The Legend of Ernie Deacon," in *Analog* (New York), March 1965.
"Coco-Talk," in *New Writings in SF 7*, edited by John Carnell. London, Dobson, 1966; New York, Bantam, 1971.
"Echo," in *Famous Science Fiction* (New York), Winter 1967.
"The Year Dot," in *If* (New York), January 1969.
"When in Doubt—Destroy!," in *Vision of Tomorrow* (Newcastle upon Tyne), August 1969.
"The Undiscovered Country," in *A Sea of Space*, edited by William F. Nolan. New York, Bantam, 1970.
"Life of the Party," in *Vision of Tomorrow* (Newcastle upon Tyne), February 1970.
"The Impatient Dreamers," in *Vision of Tomorrow* (Newcastle upon Tyne), June 1970.
"The Unpicker," in *Androids, Time Machines, and Blue Giraffes*, edited by Roger Elwood and Vic Ghidalia. Chicago, Follett, 1973.
"The Man Who Wasn't There," in *Amazing* (New York), November 1978.

OTHER PUBLICATIONS

Novel

The Dangerous Edge. London, Long, 1951.

Other

The True Book about Space Travel. London, Muller, 1954; as *The Prentice-Hall Book about Space Travel*, New York, Prentice Hall, 1955.

William F. Temple comments:
I've read SF since childhood. At first, uncritically: I didn't notice it was only two-dimensional, i.e., lacked depth, especially in characterization. Then critically: I decided to try to add that third dimension in my writing. Then despairingly: Nobody noticed that I had. Then cynically: Nobody wanted it, anyway. They preferred their robots. Then uncaringly: I don't bother to write it any more.

Most critics would agree that the golden age of modern science fiction occurred in the 1930's. Then were found the pulp magazines with such visionary editors as John Campbell to encourage and develop the writers who were to become almost legendary figures in the field. While Asimov, van Vogt, and others were honing their skills in the United States, William F. Temple was drawn to science fiction in England. Temple's interest, like that of his counterparts across the sea, was fostered by his companionship with Arthur C. Clarke, John Wyndham, and John Christopher. In the early days of science fiction there seemed to work among such individuals a kind of cross current which stimulated and sustained them in the creation of materials at which conventional critics of the day looked askance. Only the hardy survived those pioneering times to bring forth such books as *Childhood's End* and *No Blade of Grass*.

That Temple was of durable stuff was demonstrated by what he went through to turn out what was perhaps his most notable work, *Four-Sided Triangle*. While serving in Africa with the Eighth Army in World War II, Temple converted what had been a short story into novel length. Despite the novel's publication delay, its survival qualities could not be extinguished. In a fascinating variation of the trite, a woman selects one of the two suitors who vie for her. The man who loses uses a matter-copying device to create an "exact" duplicate of her—which loads the novel's plot structure engrossingly.

Some readers may find Temple's work a bit stuffy at times, but his plots employ interesting contrasts and conflicts: a group of explorers investigates the alien topography of the Moon, but the real territory to be mapped is the unknown personality of warring party members. His story ideas are usually quite interesting, as in a short story like "A Date to Remember." This yarn seems almost banal in some ways—a wife about to bring forth a child, rainy night, success/failure conflict of two old school chums. Then we discover the central idea, that Martians have long "passed" as Earthlings, struggling to civilize the inhabitants of Earth while disguised as Byron, Pasteur, Haydn, and others throughout the centuries.

Despite his demonstrated control of time in the fiction he produced, Temple has fallen prey to its fangs, like all mortals. He has not written much science fiction since the 1960's, a considerable loss for modern readers.

—R.H. Wilcox

TENN, William. Pseudonym for Philip Klass. American. Born in 1920. Served in the United States Army during World War II. Consulting Editor, *Fantasy and Science Fiction*, 1958; member of the English Department, Pennsylvania State University, State College. Address: 323 West Fairmont Avenue, State College, Pennsylvania 16802, U.S.A.

Science-Fiction Publications

Novels

A Lamp for Medusa. New York, Belmont, 1968.
Of Men and Monsters. New York, Ballantine, 1968; London, Pan, 1971.

Short Stories

Of All Possible Worlds. New York, Ballantine, 1955; enlarged edition, London, Joseph, 1956.
The Human Angle. New York, Ballantine, 1956.
Time in Advance. New York, Bantam, 1958; London, Gollancz, 1963.
The Seven Sexes. New York, Ballantine, 1968.
The Square Root of Man. New York, Ballantine, 1968; London, Pan, 1971.

The Wooden Star. New York, Ballantine, 1968; London, Pan, 1971.

Uncollected Short Stories

"On Venus, Have We Got a Rabbi," in *The Best Science Fiction of the Year 4*, edited by Terry Carr. New York, Ballantine, and London, Gollancz, 1975.
"Bernie the Faust," in *Dark Sins, Dark Dreams*, edited by Barry N. Malzberg and Bill Pronzini. New York, Doubleday, 1978.

Other Publications

Other

"The Fiction in Science Fiction," in *Science Fiction Adventures* (New York), March 1954.
"Jazz Then, Musicology Now," in *Fantasy and Science Fiction* (New York), May 1972.

Editor, *Children of Wonder*. New York, Simon and Schuster, 1953; as *Outsiders*, New York, Doubleday, 1954.
Editor, with Donald E. Westlake, *Once Against the Law*. New York, Macmillan, 1968.

*   *   *

"The incredible William Tenn," as he has been dubbed by Brian Aldiss, started a whole school of comic and satiric science fiction in the 1940's. Tenn quickly perfected a way of looking at things, at once funny, bitter, and serious, that made him the natural heir to the nearly silent tradition of Swift and Voltaire. Sheckley, Pohl, Ellison, Russell, Goulart, Knight, Kagan, Eisenberg, Brown, Lafferty, and Malzberg have all echoed Tenn's work at one time or another. A serious humorist, Tenn has had a double problem. The science-fiction genre has always made it difficult to tell serious writers from entertainers, through the manner of publication and because the entertainers often claim to be serious, or have it claimed for them; also, satirists and funny men have rarely risen high in the genre (in terms of awards and sales). Tenn was a pioneer whose example was imitated by writers who developed in different ways, but who also became known for the angle opened up by Tenn, thus diffusing the effect he might have had if his plumage had not been confused with that of imitators. Tenn imitations might have been more acceptable to some editors of the 1950's because they were watered-down versions of Tenn-like material—less serious and not so critical of the world and human nature. Tenn's stories are always a bit disturbing at some level, even when they are breathlessly readable, amusing, or cute.

An outgoing but sensitive man, Tenn fell silent by the end of the 1960's, even as his work was gathered into an impressive, though editorially flawed, six-volume set from Ballantine. One suspects that neglect made him feel that perhaps his work was not worthy. He went on to become an excellent college teacher, leaving behind a body of work sufficient to secure the reputation of any major writer in this field, and a name often confused with another Klass in various reference works. He published one story in the 1970's, "On Venus, Have We Got a Rabbi," which Damon Knight called "the great story he was talking about in the fifties." It was well received, garnering award nominations and appearing in a best of the year collection. There have been recent signs that he will soon have several works, including a new novel, to offer his readers. Tenn was also the editor of *Children of Wonder*, a pioneering theme anthology which was notable for its variety of stories and non-parochial choice of authors. Two incisive essays, "The Fiction in Science Fiction" and "Jazz Then, Musicology Now," are both required reading for anyone who cares about the ideals of literate science fiction, if not its practice.

Notable stories from Tenn's first two decades include "Brooklyn Project," which Fritz Leiber has called a "Marvelously cynical" time-travel story, and "Firewater!," one of the most sophisticated stories ever published by John W. Campbell, with its unforgettable lament by Larry for the loss of what he was and what he cannot be as humanity struggles to keep its sanity before the seemingly superior aliens who have taken up residence on earth. The story should have taken all the awards. "Generation of Noah" is one of the finest atomic threat stories ever written. "Of All Possible Worlds," "Wednesday's Child" (a fascinating sequel to the much reprinted classic "Child's Play"), "Time Waits for Winthrop," "Eastward Ho!," and "The Malted Milk Monster" all drew honorable mentions in Judith Merril's best of the year collections, while "Bernie the Faust" took pride of place as the first story in the 1964 collection. "Time Waits for Winthrop" shows a remarkable use of exotic ideas, among them fairly advanced biological concepts, another feature of Tenn's stories that makes them unusual for the 1950's. "The Discovery of Morniel Mathaway" shows an understanding of the creative process that is usually beyond most SF writers. Jacques Sadoul has called it "the most beautiful example of a temporal paradox offered by science fiction." "The Custodian," with its plea for the blending of art and utility, and "Down among the Dead Men," with its clever use of offstage space opera to heighten a pathetic predicament, both manage to do what few SF stories can do—move us emotionally and intellectually on a mature level.

Tenn is always a master of situations, which at first prod and intrigue, then provoke curiosity, make us laugh a bit, then explode into some thoughtful irony or observation. Once you catch on to a Tenn situation, you can't stop reading. The satirical tones of irony, mockery, slapstick, and occasional bitterness do wonders for genre materials, precisely because Tenn joins these materials to human experience outside the insular worlds of SF wish-fulfillment and power fantasy. The science-fiction materials are all there, strong and clear, but just as you're about to accept the story at its face value Tenn hits you with something real and painful. He's a very sly writer, inserting polished, precise narratives into our minds through unexpected channels. Many of his stories have the effect of blossoming into a single line of great beauty and illumination; but always the aesthetic fires are banked by irony and, above all, eloquent wit, behind which sits the ultimate authority of an author who has something to say, who sometimes seems to believe with Oscar Wilde that eloquence and wit alone can make the scales fall from human eyes. One senses an author laughing and crying at the same time, writing, exhibiting intellect and dramatic talent within the confines of a narrow genre.

Tenn's two long works are the novel *Of Men and Monsters* and the short novel *A Lamp for Medusa*. The second work is easily worthy of having appeared in *Unknown Worlds*. Funny, atmospheric, and wonderfully paced, this neglected work has seen only a shabby book appearance. It is not surprising, given Tenn's tendencies, that it recalls the poise of the *Unknown Worlds* tradition, since that magazine was the only sizable market for humorous work of the early 1940's, and Tenn's only antecedent within the SF genre.

Of Men and Monsters, a story of humanity living in the walls of the houses of giant aliens who have occupied the earth, is a vivid, energetically paced story which best embodies one of Tenn's main points: that humanity is not what it thinks itself to be, that implicit in our biological history is a nature not of our making; we may glimpse it, even understand it at times, but it may be a while before we can remake ourselves, if ever. In his awareness of biological and anthropological complexities, Tenn has at the center of his work the most thoroughgoing of science-fiction methods: the collision of the possible with the actual, with the actual displaying fantastic holding power. Eric the Eye, the Lilliputian viewpoint character of the novel, learns that his society is not what he thought it was, that its rites of passage are a sham, and finally that human beings are not what he thought they were either; since change seems unlikely on a radical scale, he accepts this human nature and joins the plan to make of it something pervasive and influential. Eric becomes part of the reverse invasion of human vermin as they begin the infestation of the great alien starships. The story is very vivid, the characters charming (Eric meets Rachel Esthersdaughter, one of the nicest nice Jewish girls in all science fiction). The death of Eric's uncle is shatteringly presented. There are great wonder and awesome confrontation, sharply realized. Most importantly, there is an anthropological sophistication in the depiction of social systems; the aliens are properly terrifying, puzzling, and *other*. Tenn's tendency to romance, compassion, and brief, hard-bitten sentimentality shows through his bitterness just enough to be believable. The novel may be compared to Daniel Galouye's *Dark Universe* and Thomas M. Disch's *The Genocides*.

It is regrettable that Tenn stopped his development in the 1960's,

when it was clear that the continuous practice of his craft, coupled with his acute and constant rethinking of the nature of fiction and science fiction, would certainly have produced a mighty progress over his very worthy body of work. Now that he seems poised at the start of his most mature period, it remains to be seen whether he will continue the main line suggested by his previous work, or whether his silence is a sign that he has been developing a new direction. He can do anything he wants, except hack work ("I have no talent for it," he has said). Few writers have ever suggested so much promise at the start of their sixth decade. Tenn belongs to the great generation of Asimov, Heinlein and Clarke. He is the most perfect example of the failure of the awards system within the science-fiction community, and an obvious candidate for the Grand Master Nebula Award. His work is a clear example that SF can be literature, that it can provoke us to see, feel, and think. Tenn belongs to that unbroken chain of sayers who expose our delusions and foibles, our willful blindness and stupidity, and who ultimately stand against death and the amnesia of generations. "Tenn is another artist," Damon Knight has written, "who won't stop till he's had the last word."

—George Zebrowski

TENNANT, Emma (Christina). Also writes as Catherine Aydy. British. Born in London, 20 October 1937. Educated at St. Paul's Girls' School, London. Has one son and two daughters. Travel correspondent, *Queen*, London, 1963; features editor, *Vogue*, London, 1966; Editor, *Bananas*, London, 1975-78. Agent: Gillon Aitken Ltd., 17 Belgrave Place, London S.W. 1. Address: 78 Elgin Crescent, London W. 11, England.

SCIENCE-FICTION PUBLICATIONS

Novels

The Time of the Crack. London, Cape, 1973; as *The Crack*, London, Penguin, 1978.
The Last of the Country House Murders. London, Cape, 1974; New York, Nelson, 1976.
Hotel de Dream. London, Gollancz, 1976.

OTHER PUBLICATIONS

Novels

The Colour of Rain (as Catherine Aydy). London, Weidenfeld and Nicolson, 1964.
The Bad Sister. London, Gollancz, and New York, Coward McCann, 1978.
Wild Nights. London, Cape, 1979; New York, Harcourt Brace, 1980.
Alice Fell. London, Cape, 1980.

Other

The Boggart (juvenile). London, Granada, 1980.

Editor, *Bananas.* London, Quartet-Blond and Briggs, 1977.
Editor, *Saturday Night Reader.* London, W.H. Allen, 1979.

Emma Tennant comments:
My aim has been and continues to be the depiction of two sorts of time, as defined by Boris Pasternak—"a time that can be disposed of and a time that is lacking."
My other aim, starting to write in an atmosphere defined by McLuhan in which the written word was finished and the age was exclusively visual, has been to "write" films. I don't believe people will stop reading, and I would like to feel, when they read my work, that they are seeing a film in their heads.

Emma Tennant is less concerned with storytelling than with exploring the psychological fabric of life. Her plots are primarily concerned with the interplay between fantasy and reality and the interactions of her characters. Yet her characters are not well developed, but rather serve as allegorical vehicles. All of this is served up with a hardy helping of humor.

In *The Time of the Crack* her allegorical devices are presented against the backdrop of a London shaken by a cataclysm which has turned the Thames into an enormous chasm. Her characters, identifiable types, respond to the crisis predictably. Each attempts to reach the "other side" of the crack, which has been endowed with the fulfillment of desire. Reality, which of course resembles none of those projections, hints at Tennant's nihilism which suggests the futility of striving. Thus, we are first warned about pursuing our fantasies. This warning is strongly reiterated in *Hotel de Dream*. The dreams of the Westringham Hotel residents assume their own life and start to control the dreamers, and eventually interact with the dreams of others. The intertwining of the dreams and its effect on the rest of reality leads to the nightmare of being caught in another's fantasies. This theme further solidifies in two characters created by a writer, Mrs. Houghton, who resides in the hotel. These two characters develop personalities; despite Mrs. Houghton's contrivance of their romance, the only times they relate well are when they outwit the author and slip "unacceptable expressions into the fabric of her style," or try to murder her and go their own ways. As we come to expect with Tennant, they are less than successful.

The sense of the futility of change also occurs in *The Last of the Country House Murders*. Britain after "The Revolution" is presented as an overrun island with a Big Brother government, an economy dependent on the tourism of the middle classes whose coaches bypass the crushing hordes of the poor. Finally rebelling under the leadership of an actor playing out the Fuehrer role, the hordes threaten to topple a government they are unable to replace. Yet these pressing issues are merely the backdrop to the elaborate staging of the Last Country House Murder to establish Widiscome Manor as a "Grade One Tourist Attraction," with a body laid out in the library at an angle to allow for clear viewing.

Tennant presents no solutions to life's problems, but she persistently highlights the absurdities to be encountered in attempts at solution. No one escapes being laughed at in Tennant's works. The only character remotely approaching hero status is Baba, the Playboy bunny who guides us through London in *The Time of the Crack*. But despite her resilience and generosity, she also remains the ingenue with no sense of what she is running towards or from. Despite the futuristic or fantastic setting of her works, many of the motifs Tennant employs have long pedigrees—life as a dream, the dance of death. Other themes bear the currency of the Agatha Christie murder mystery of manners. Yet is is the juxtaposition of these disparate elements which highlights the sense of the absurdity of life which runs through the three novels.

—Hilary Karp

———————

TENNESHAW, S.M. *See* **GARRETT, Randall; SILVERBERG, Robert.**

———————

TEVIS, Walter (Stone). American. Born in San Francisco, California, 28 February 1928. Educated at the University of Kentucky, Lexington, M.A. 1956; University of Iowa, Iowa City, M.F.A. 1961. Served in the United States Navy. Divorced; one son and one daughter. Since 1965, Professor of English, Ohio Univer-

sity, Athens. Agent: Robert P. Mills, 156 East 52nd Street, New York, New York 10022. Address: 20 East 63rd Street, New York, New York 10021, U.S.A.

SCIENCE-FICTION PUBLICATIONS

Novels

The Man Who Fell to Earth.   New York, Fawcett, and London, Muller, 1963.
Mockingbird.   New York, Doubleday, and London, Hodder and Stoughton, 1980.

Short Stories

Far from Home.   New York, Doubleday, 1981.

OTHER PUBLICATIONS

Novel

The Hustler.   New York, Harper, 1959; London, Joseph, 1960.

Walter Tevis comments:
I suppose I write disguised autobiographies. The idea, as far as I know, is to move other people. I feel alienated from other people sometimes; when I was younger the feeling was stronger than it is now. My major characters are alienated, by virtue of being pool players, from Mars, robots, the only people alive who can read, or alcoholics. I like to write about people under psychological stress, and when I write I am very serious about it.

*   *   *

Thomas Jerome Newton, in *The Man Who Fell to Earth*, is an emissary from the dying planet of Anthea, sent to prepare a refuge and transportation for its last few survivors. We never learn his real name. By introducing advanced Anthean technology Newton amasses the necessary millions of dollars, but attracts the attentions of the FBI who imprison and interrogate him, blinding him in the process. Eventually released, he abandons his project and dwindles into perpetual alcoholic exile. Earth, though they colonised it in the first place, is no place for Antheans. Walter Tevis's novel is the classic refutation of the alien invasion theme in SF. He reduces the interplanetary war to a case of depression, the story of the loneliest man in the world. Newton could save mankind, but represents a threat to the American economy. He is disabled not by military might or scientific ingenuity, but by smothering bureaucracy. Seeing Newton decrepit and drunk in a bar, Nathan Bryce, his only human confidant, reflects that he "certainly would not have been the first means of possible salvation to get the official treatment." Christ, it seems, was an Anthean too. The failure of Newton's mission is a slow, pathetic crucifixion. Bryce remembers Thoreau's dictum: "quiet desperation" is the mood of the novel, an unobstrusive tragedy in an unostentatious style that conceals irony, bitterness, and ultimately cold fury. "I worked very hard to become an imitation human being...." Newton says. "And of course I succeeded."

Mockingbird is altogether less original and distinctive. In a future America run and serviced by robots human faculties, emotions, and even social urges have been eroded. The senior robot, Bob Spofforth (Mark Nine), is an interesting figure of moral ambivalence, sexless and immortal, but plagued by human dreams that slipped in under his mental programming. As in Bradbury's *Fahrenheit 451*, literacy is suppressed but the hero learns to read, and is emboldened to further rebellion when he meets a woman less obedient to convention than he is. The book is efficiently plotted and written, but suffers from too much formula and too little variation.

—Colin Greenland

———————

THOMAS, D(onald) M(ichael). British. Born in Redruth, Cornwall, 27 January 1935. Educated at Redruth Grammar School; University High School, Melbourne; New College, Oxford, B.A. (honours) in English, 1958, M.A. Since 1963, Senior Lecturer in English, Hereford College of Education. Visiting Lecturer in English, Hamline University, St. Paul, Minnesota, 1967. Recipient: Richard Hillary Memorial Prize, 1960; Cholmondeley Award, 1978; *Guardian*-Gollancz Fantasy Novel prize, 1979. Address: 10 Greyfriars Avenue, Hereford, England.

PUBLICATIONS

Novels

The Flute-Player. London, Gollancz, and New York, Dutton, 1979.
Birthstone. London, Gollancz, 1980.
The White Hotel. London, Gollancz, and New York, Viking Press, 1981.

Uncollected Short Stories

"Seeking a Suitable Donor," in *The New SF*, edited by Langdon Jones. London, Hutchinson, 1969.
"Mr. Black's Poems of Innocence," in *New Worlds* (London), March 1969.
"Labyrinth," in *New Worlds* (London), April 1969.
"Hospital of Transplanted Hearts," in *Best SF 1969*, edited by Harry Harrison and Brian Aldiss. New York, Putnam, and London, Sphere, 1970.

Verse

Personal and Possessive. London, Outposts, 1964.
Penguin Modern Poets 11, with D.M. Black and Peter Redgrove. London, Penguin, 1968.
Two Voices. London, Cape Goliard Press, and New York, Grossman, 1968.
Logan Stone. London, Cape Goliard Press, and New York, Grossman, 1971.
The Shaft. Gillingham, Kent, ARC, 1973.
Lilith-Prints. Cardiff, Second Aeon, 1974.
Symphony in Moscow. Richmond, Surrey, Keepsake Press, 1974.
Love and Other Deaths. London, Elek, 1975.
The Rock. Knotting, Bedfordshire, Sceptre Press, 1975.
Orpheus in Hell. Knotting, Bedfordshire, Sceptre Press, 1977.
The Honeymoon Voyage. London, Secker and Warburg, 1978.

Other

The Devil and the Floral Dance (juvenile). London, Robson, 1978.

Editor, *The Granite Kingdom: Poems of Cornwall.* Truro, Cornwall, Barton, 1970.
Editor, *Poetry in Crosslight.* London, Longman, 1975.
Editor, *Songs from the Earth: Selected Poems of John Harris, Cornish Miner 1820-84.* Padstow, Cornwall, Lodenek Press, 1977.

Translator, *Requiem, and Poem Without a Hero*, by Anna Akhmatova. London, Elek, and Athens, Ohio University Press, 1976.
Translator, *Way of All the Earth*, by Anna Akhmatova. London, Secker and Warburg, and Athens, Ohio University Press, 1979.

D.M. Thomas comments:
Most of my science-fiction poetry is collected in one publication, *Penguin Modern Poets 11* (1968). Since then I have remained interested in the mythic aspect of SF, but have moved away from "pure" SF into other areas of myth.

* * *

Like the other English New Wave writers of the 1960's D.M. Thomas approached science fiction as a large and only partly developed set of metaphors for contemporary experience. In 1968 he said, "I suppose I was drawn to the SF myths of man's dispossession and self-imposed obsolescence as symbols of my own rootlessness." He speaks of his poems evolving "from myths suggested by science-fiction stories"; in this way he has retold or supplemented stories by Bradbury, Clarke, Knight, Latham, and others. Thomas reinforces his use of SF as myth with figures and themes from classical and Blakean mythology. His SF poetry ranges from the early "Tithonus," an Auden-like satire on a man who has achieved immortality as a disembodied brain in a culture-bath, to "Computer 70: Dreams and Love Poems," in which he describes a modern love-affair in the mechanistic imagery of moon-landings, entropy, and Godard's *Alphaville*. He comments, "Instant-and indeed over-communication ensures that our most private experiences are coloured by remote acts of violence and technological advances." Moorcock's *New Worlds* has published much of his work, including his masterpieces "Two Voices" and "Mr. Black's Poems of Innocence."

Stylistically, Thomas began with surprising conservatism. Poems like "Missionary" and "Hera's Spring" are in the form of narrative monologues that strongly recall Robert Browning, as does "A Conversation upon the Shadow," set on a planet where telepathy is the norm of social communication, but lovers are privileged to wear devices that close their minds to one another. Other more enterprising poems include "Ge," a description of a troubled Earth hoping for messages of relief from outer space like a decrepit prostitute languishing by a silent telephone. The poem is in the shape of a circle, like the planet and the dish of the radio-telescope. Similarly "Mercury," ode to that planet as the sun's most loyal disciple, is an endless sentence written in the shape of a corona around a solar disc. "Hospital of Transplanted Hearts," a humorous fantasy on the effect of putting one person's heart into the chest of someone of a different profession, is written in tabular form.

The most notable of Thomas's retellings of earlier SF stories is "X," based on Tom Godwin's "The Cold Equations." The story of the space pilot compelled by limited supplies to jettison a young female stowaway was clearly a potent myth for Thomas: he produced another version, "Limbo," in which the sexes are tellingly reversed. The demands and hidden dangers of machines and a society geared to technological progress, expressed in these poems and in the android love songs "The Strait" and "Elegy for an Android," are central to his vision. The symbols of science fiction are those of dispossession and obsolescence. The stories he tells are of change, especially unpredictable change, and loss, which science fiction illustrates abundantly.

Overall, science fiction in Thomas's poetry dramatises an attempt to see the individual in a cosmic context, paying proper respect to the values of both human and universe. He shows how difficult that attempt is and how often it must fail, with absurd or sad results. In "Cygnus A" he tries to measure the tender awkwardness of illicit sex in a hotel bedroom against the majestic but meaningless collisions of galaxies; in "Two Voices" he intercuts the thoughts of a single girl throughout an unwanted pregnancy with the experiences of three astronauts roaming the planetary colonies after the nuclear devastation of Earth.

—Colin Greenland

THOMSON, Edward. *See* TUBB, E.C.

THURSTON, Robert (Donald). American. Born in Lockport, New York, 28 October 1936. Educated at the University of Buffalo, now State University of New York, B.A. in English 1959, M.A. 1967. Served in the United States Army Air Defense Command, 1960-62. Married Joan K. Sullivan in 1964; one son. Reporter, *Union-Sun and Journal*, Lockport, 1959-60; Assistant Professor, Alliance College, Cambridge Springs, Pennsylvania, 1967-68; Manager, Glen Art Book Store, Williamsville, New York, 1968-71. Recipient: Clarion Workshop Award, 1970. Agent: Lea C. Braff, Jarvis Braff Ltd., 133 Seventh Avenue, Brooklyn, New York 11215. Address: 200 Cabrini Boulevard, No. 19, New York, New York 10033, U.S.A.

SCIENCE-FICTION PUBLICATIONS

Novels (series: Battlestar Galactica)

Alicia II. New York, Putnam, 1978.
Battlestar Galactica, with Glen A. Larson. New York, Berkley, and London, Futura, 1978.
Battlestar Galactica 2: The Cylon Death Machine, with Glen A. Larson. New York, Berkley, 1979.
Battlestar Galactica 3: Flight to Kobal, with Glen A. Larson. New York, Berkley, 1979.

Uncollected Short Stories

"Stop Me Before I Tell More," in *Orbit 9*, edited by Damon Knight. New York, Putnam, 1971.
"Wheels," "Anaconda," and "The Last Desperate Hour," in *Clarion*, edited by Robin Scott Wilson. New York, New American Library, 1971.
"Get FDR!," "Punchline," and "The Good Life," in *Clarion 2*, edited by Robin Scott Wilson. New York, New American Library, 1972.
"Goodbye Shelley, Shirley, Charlotte, Charlene," in *Orbit 11*, edited by Damon Knight. New York, Putnam, 1972.
"Carolyn's Laughter," in *Fantasy and Science Fiction* (New York), January 1972.
"She/Her," in *Infinity 5*, edited by Robert Hoskins. New York, Lancer, 1973.
"Up Against the Wall," in *School and Society Through Science Fiction*, edited by Martin H. Greenberg and Joseph D. Olander. New York, Random House, 1974.
"Soundtrack: The Making of a Thoroughbred," in *Fantastic* (New York), May 1974.
"Under Siege," in *Fantasy and Science Fiction* (New York), July 1974.
"Searching the Ruins," in *Amazing* (New York), August 1974.
"The Hippie-Dip File," in *Social Problems Through Science Fiction*, edited by Martin H. Greenberg and others. New York, St. Martin's Press, 1975.
"Theodora and Theodora," in *New Dimensions 5*, edited by Robert Silverberg. New York, Harper, 1975.
"Jack and Betty," in *Orbit 16*, edited by Damon Knight. New York, Harper, 1975.
"Dream by Number," in *Fantasy and Science Fiction* (New York), September 1975.
"The Haunted Writing-Manual," in *Fantastic* (New York), October 1975.
"Groups," in *Fantastic* (New York), February 1976.
"If That's Paradise, Toss Me an Apple," in *Amazing* (New York), March 1976.
"One Magic Ring, Used," in *Fantastic* (New York), May 1976.
"Parker Frightened on a Tightrope," in *Fantastic* (New York), November 1976.
"Aliens,"in *Fantasy and Science Fiction* (New York), December 1976.
"The Kingmakers," in *New Voices in Science Fiction*, edited by George R.R. Martin. New York, Macmillan, 1977.
"The Mars Ship,"in *Fantasy and Science Fiction* (New York), June 1977.
"Wheels Westward," in *Cosmos* (New York), November 1977.

"What Johnny Did on His Summer Vacation," with Joe Haldeman, in *Rod Serling's Other Worlds*. New York, Bantam, 1978.
"The Bulldog Nutcracker," in *Chrysalis 2*, edited by Roy Torgeson. New York, Kensington, 1978.
"Seedplanter," in *Chrysalis 3*, edited by Roy Torgeson. New York, Kensington, 1978.
"Vibrations," in *Chrysalis 4*, edited by Roy Torgeson. New York, Kensington, 1979.
"The Wanda Lake Number," in *Analog* (New York), January 1979.

OTHER PUBLICATIONS

Other

Introduction to *Early Science Fiction Stories of Thomas M. Disch, The Big Time* by Fritz Leiber, *Dark Universe* by Daniel F. Galouye, *Driftglass* by Samuel R. Delany, *Today We Choose Faces* by Roger Zelazny, and *The Game Players of Titan* by Philip K. Dick. Boston, Gregg Press, 6 vols., 1972-79.

*　　*　　*

Robert Thurston is one of few new writers to achieve a considerable reputation almost solely on the basis of short fiction. Starting with his award-winning "Wheels," Thruston has produced almost three dozen short stories and novelets, almost all of which are of very high quality. His recent publication of a novel, *Alicia II*, cannot help but improve his standing within the genre.

One of Thurston's most powerful stories appeared very early in his career, and hovers around the border between science fiction and the supernatural. A young man is troubled by memories of his first wife, now deceased, and eventually resorts to a computer medium in a half-hearted effort to contact her spirit. Carolyn had agreed to have her organs used in transplants, and there is some evidence that she may have reached across the borderline between life and death in a effort to reclaim the parts of her body that survive. The result is a fairly well-handled suspense story, but overshadowing the plot is the excellent characterization typical of Thurston's stories.

"Under Siege" relies even more heavily upon strong characters. Within the context of a racist police state, a white liberal with a black wife is plagued by the constant silent presence of a black man. The growing tensions among the three are superbly handled, and the story might well have attracted much wider attention had it been published outside the genre. Indeed, one of Thurston's most impressive stories, "Punchline," is straight mainstream fiction, despite its appearance in a science-fiction market. Time travel is ostensibly the subject of "The Kingmakers," in which a man travels through the past to write a biography of a pivotal figure, but the four visits he makes, spaced widely apart in the lifespans of both men, cause tensions and contrasts that are the main focus of the story, a mature theme handled with extreme skill.

Thurston's short stories run the gamut from comic to surreal, occasionally having very strong concentration on plot, more often focusing on character, theme, or style. Doppelgangers are a frequent plot device, with inexplicable duplicate women in "Goodbye Shelley, Shirley, Charlotte, Charlene," a host of people with no apparent pasts in "Searching the Ruins," and two virtually identical wives in "Theodora and Theodora." Some of his stories have attracted considerable acerbic comment because of their explicit handling of controversial themes, as in "Aliens," where a human male is used as a sex object by non-humanoid aliens.

The novel *Alicia II* is a mixture of good and bad. As might be expected, Thurston has done a remarkable job of developing his characters as human beings. Voss Geraghty callously accepts the society he lives in, one which classifies people early in their lives, designating some as "rejects" whose bodies will be confiscated in young adulthood to become the new home of non-rejects. But Geraghty's new body was sabotaged by its former owner, and cannot function in sexual relations. Starting with this blow to his view of the world, Geraghty must re-examine much of what he believes about his own society. Unfortunately, despite the fine handling of the situation as established, the world depicted in the novel is unconvincing, and the long delay before the advent of organized resistance is not particularly credible. Nevertheless, it is a very promising novel, and it is to be hoped that Thurston will write more, other than his current series based on the television program *Battlestar Galactica.*

Don D'Ammassa

TIPTREE, James, Jr. Pseudonym for Alice Hastings Sheldon; also writes as Raccoona Sheldon. American. Born near Chicago, Illinois, in 1916. Educated at George Washington University, Washington, D.C., Ph.D. 1967. Married Huntington Denton Sheldon in 1955; two children. Worked as a government employee, businesswoman, college teacher, and experimental psychologist. Recipient: Nebula Award, 1973, 1976, 1977; Hugo Award, 1974, 1977. Agent: Robert P. Mills Ltd., 156 East 52nd Street, New York, New York 10022. Address: 6037 Ramshorn Place, McLean, Virginia 22101, U.S.A.

SCIENCE-FICTION PUBLICATIONS

Novels

Up the Walls of the World. New York, Berkley, and London, Gollancz, 1978.
Star Songs of an Old Primate. New York, Ballantine, 1978.

Short Stories

Ten Thousand Light-Years from Home. New York, Ace, 1973; London, Eyre Methuen, 1975.
Warm Worlds and Otherwise. New York, Ballantine, 1975.

Uncollected Short Stories.

"The Psychologist Who Wouldn't Do Awful Things to Rats," in *New Dimensions 6*, edited by Robert Silverberg. New York, Harper, 1976.
"She Waits for All Men Born," in *Future Power,* edited by Jack Dann and Gardner Dozois. New York, Random House, 1976.
"Your Faces, O My Sisters! Your Faces Filled with Light!" (as Raccoona Sheldon) and "Houston, Houston, Do You Read?," in *Aurora,* edited by Vonda N. McIntyre and Susan Janice Anderson. New York, Fawcett, 1976.
"Beaver Tears" (as Raccoona Sheldon), in *Galaxy* (New York), May 1976.
"Time-Sharing Angel," in *Fantasy and Science Fiction* (New York), October 1977.
"We Who Stole the Dream," in *Stellar 4*, edited by Judy-Lynn del Rey. New York, Ballantine, 1976.
"A Source of Innocent Merriment," in *Universe 10*, edited by Terry Carr. New York, Doubleday, and London, Dobson, 1980.
"Slow Music," in *Interfaces,* edited by Ursula K. Le Guin and Virginia Kidd. New York, Ace, 1980.

*   *   *

With the revelation that James Tiptree, Jr., is Alice ("Raccoona") Sheldon, the SF community that had praised Tiptree for treating feminist themes in a "masculine" style had to rethink its categories. In fact, Tiptree is simply a gifted writer who brings to her feminist concerns a critical knowledge of traditionally male domains—"all the huge authoritarian organizations," as one of her heroines puts it, "for doing unreal things."

Tiptree's early work is marked by a certain manic inventiveness and a preoccupation with far-future sex and science. Some of the best of these tightly written short stories are pure farce: "Birth of a Salesman," for instance, turns on the proposition that commercial packaging meant for distant client planets may trigger bizarre sexual and religious reactions among alien dockworkers. With powerfully dark stories like "The Last Flight of Dr. Ain," however, it became clear that Tiptree is more than a comic artist. Indeed, the twists of her fiction suggest a deeply skeptical turn of mind, wary of all absolutes, suspicious of all power.

These stories often have errant sexuality in the foreground. Human types encounter aliens whose sexual morphology is unstable or haploid ("All the Kinds of Yes," "Your Haploid Heart"), animal orgiasts who form delicious Lovepiles ("Painwise"), primitive mud-beings who offer "gentle glubbering" satisfaction ("The Milk of Paradise"). Tiptree exploits such situations to satirize our own sexual parochialism and, occasionally, to make a further point: even on alternate worlds or among weirdly equipped life forms, sexual existence is pain for the powerless.

In two overtly feminist stories, Tiptree's work revealed a new clarity and firmness of purpose. "The Girl Who Was Plugged In" translates social truths into grotesque literal images; it describes a near-future society that secretly uses devastatingly attractive waldos to sell goods and preserve the commercial status quo. The girl of the title is a monstrous socio-sexual reject who finds momentary happiness wired into an empty android playgirl. "The Women Men Don't See" is a vivid story of the invisible real women in our own world, surviving, as the protagonist tells the Hemingwayesque narrator, "by ones and twos in the chinks of your world-machine."

By one means or another, every recent Tiptree story condemns that world-machine as a tyrannical yet ultimately doomed system. Typically, her protagonists live anxiously on its margins. In "The Psychologist Who Wouldn't Do Awful Things to Rats" the system is the present scientific establishment, and the hero, himself a ratman of sorts, a "failed" researcher, "failed" because humanely dedicated. "Houston, Houston, Do You Read?" is Tiptree's most powerful anti-system work and a landmark in the recent feminist revival of the manless world story. In it, Tiptree identifies the male ethos of aggression and domination with life-plague. An epidemic in the past has left only women, their clones, and androgenic creations to refashion human existence. This history, patchily revealed to the crew of a NASA ship plunged 300 years into the future, is intercut with the scientist narrator's memories of their rescue and his efforts to comprehend a stunningly different reality.

An extension of this concern with sexual politics often surfaces in the short works and wholly informs the novella "A Momentary Taste of Being": the ambivalent force of the biologic urge itself, mercilessly driving toward the completion or transformation of species. The title of one of these stories, "Love Is the Plan, The Plan Is Death," could serve for them all. In "A Momentary Taste of Being" humanity is forced to the stars to fertilize like spermatozoa alien ova. Surrender to the female half of a zygote is seen by most as an ecstatic taste of being, but the narrator, a quasi-objective male doctor, sees it as doom—"Sex equals death." The death literally occurs; the worth of the sacrifice remains a matter of faith.

For *Up the Walls of the World*, her first novel, Tiptree creates an epic transformational journey through space and time for a group of painfully human telepaths. In alternating chapters that shift from our own botched world to a dying parallel world and into the center of a vast star-destroying being, a drama of destruction versus creation unfolds. Philosophically rich and formally ambitious, the novel is evidence that Tiptree's powers continue to grow.

—Carol L. Snyder

TRAIN, Arthur (Cheney). American. Born in Boston, Massachusetts, 6 September 1875. Educated at Prince School, Boston; Boston Latin School; St. Paul's School, Concord, New Hampshire; Harvard University, Cambridge, Massachusetts, A.B. 1896, LL.B. 1899; admitted to the Massachusetts bar 1899. Married 1) Ethel Kissam in 1897 (died, 1923); three daughters and one son; 2) Helen C. Gerard in 1926; one son. Lawyer: worked in firm of Robinson Biddle and Ward, 1900; Assistant District Attorney for New York, 1901-08; in private practice (Train and Olney, later Perkins and

Train) after 1908; Attorney General, Commonwealth of Massachusetts. Prolific story writer from 1904. President, National Institute of Arts and Letters, 1941-45. *Died 22 December 1945.*

SCIENCE-FICTION PUBLICATIONS

Novels (with Robert William Wood)

The Man Who Rocked the Earth. New York, Doubleday, 1915.
The Moon Maker. Hamburg, New York, Krueger, 1958.

Short Stories

Mortmain. New York, Appleton, 1907.

OTHER PUBLICATIONS

Novels

The Butler's Story. New York, Scribner, and London, Laurie, 1909.
The Confessions of Artemas Quibble. New York, Scribner, 1911.
"C.Q."; or, In the Wireless House. New York, Century, 1912.
The World and Thomas Kelly. New York, Scribner, 1917.
As It Was in the Beginning. New York, Macmillan, 1921.
The Hermit of Turkey Hollow. New York, Scribner, 1921.
His Children's Children. New York, Scribner, and London, Nash, 1923.
The Needle's Eye. New York, Scribner, 1924.
The Lost Gospel. New York, Scribner, 1925.
The Blind Goddess. New York, Scribner, 1926.
High Winds. New York, Scribner, and London, Nash, 1927.
Ambition. New York, Scribner, and London, Nash, 1928.
The Horns of Ramadan. New York, Scribner, 1928; London, Nash, 1929.
Illusion. New York, Scribner, and London, Nash, 1929.
Paper Profits. New York, Liveright, and London, Mathews and Marrot, 1930.
The Adventures of Ephraim Tutt. New York, Scribner, 1930.
Princess Pro Tem. New York, Scribner, 1932.
No Matter Where. New York, Scribner, 1933.
Jacob's Ladder. New York, Scribner, 1935.
Manhattan Murder. New York, Scribner, 1936; as *Murderers' Medicine*, London, Constable, 1937.
Tassels on Her Boots. New York, Scribner, and London, Hutchinson, 1940.
Yankee Lawyer—Autobiography of Ephraim Tutt. New York, Scribner, 1943.

Short Stories

McAllister and His Double. New York, Scribner, and London, Newnes, 1905.
Tutt and Mr. Tutt. New York, Scribner, 1920.
By Advice of Counsel. New York, Scribner, 1921.
Tut, Tut! Mr. Tutt. New York, Scribner, 1923; London, Nash, 1924.
Page Mr. Tutt. New York, Scribner, 1926.
When Tutt Meets Tutt. New York, Scribner, 1927.
Tutt for Tutt. New York, Scribner, 1934.
Mr. Tutt Takes the Stand. New York, Scribner, 1936.
Mr. Tutt's Case Book (omnibus). New York, Scribner, 1936.
Old Man Tutt. New York, Scribner, 1938.
Mr. Tutt Comes Home. New York, Scribner, 1941.
Mr. Tutt Finds a Way. New York, Scribner, 1945.
Mr. Tutt at His Best, edited by Harold R. Medina. New York, Scribner, 1961.

Other

The Prisoner at the Bar. New York, Scribner, 1906; London, Laurie, 1907; revised edition, 1908; revised edition, as *From the District Attorney's Office,* 1939.
True Stories of Crime from the District Attorney's Office. New

York, Scribner, and London, Laurie, 1908.
Courts, Criminals, and the Camorra. New York, Scribner, and London, Chapman and Hall, 1912.
The Earthquake. New York, Scribner, 1918.
Courts and Criminals (selection). New York, Scribner, 1921.
On the Trail of the Bad Men. New York, Scribner, 1925.
Puritan's Progress. New York, Scribner, 1931.
The Strange Attacks on Herbert Hoover. New York, Day, 1932.
My Day in Court (autobiography). New York, Scribner, 1939.

Editor, *The Goldfish, Being the Confessions of a Successful Man.* New York, Century, 1914.

* * *

While serving as Assistant District Attorney for New York County, Arthur Train began to write stories about the procession of human comedy and tragedy that passed through the criminal court building. Train wrote fewer than 100 short stories and only one short novel about Mr. Ephraim Tutt, Counsellor and Attorney at Law, but it is for Mr. Tutt that he will always be remembered. The Lincolnesque lawyer with his frock coat, stove pipe hat, and fondness for stogies is a vivid part of American folklore. Most of his books deal with human nature and not with crime or the law, but his few attempts at fantasy suggest he had abilities in that direction which ought to have been exercised further. Unfortunately, he often allowed the literary conventions of the day to undercut his imagination. The wonderfully weird theme of the dead man's hand grafted onto the wrist of Sir Richard Mortmain (*Mortmain*), which thus gives him the fingerprints of a murderer, is marred by the revelation that it has all been a dream.

The Man Who Rocked the Earth, written with the scientist Robert Williams Wood, was planned to demonstrate Wood's theories that the man who exploded the atom would be master of the world, able to dictate peace and banish war forever. The story features the mysterious commander Pax of the atomic-powered *Flying Ring*, and has echoes of Jules Verne's *Clipper of the Clouds* and *Master of the World*. The "lavender ray" which can tilt the earth's axis and level the Atlas Mountains to force the world powers to stop the war is never completely explained scientifically, yet it has a plausibility that only a creative writer can give. Train claimed never to have understood Wood's scientific data, but found it didn't matter in telling the story. Some parts of it turned out to be strangely prophetic. The description of the German bombardment of Paris from a distance of 60 miles came true several years later. The story is told in a lively style which overcomes the obvious propaganda of its theme.

The ending makes the publication of a sequel, *The Moon Maker*, inevitable (it was serialized in 1916-17, but not published in book form for 40 years). The physicist Professor Benjamin Hooker, having captured the *Flying Ring* from Pax (who has disappeared), takes it into outer space to deflect or destroy an asteroid which may destroy the earth. There is more scientific detail in the story as well as the added presence of a mathematician and romantic interest, Rhoda Gibbs, who accompanies Hooker on the mission. Forced to land on the moon to replace a uranium cylinder for the trip home, the party demonstrates some of the real problems in space survival when Rhoda loses sight of the ship. Absent-minded scientist and would-be feminist, Hooker and Rhoda are near caricatures, but very appealing. Their marriage at the end of the story seems a proper romantic outcome to their adventure, while Train's imaginative and humorous use of traditional themes in science fiction make his work of more than historical interest.

—J. Randolph Cox

TRIMBLE, Louis (Preston). Also writes as Stuart Brock; Gerry Travis. American. Born in Seattle, Washington, 2 March 1917. Educated at Eastern Washington State College, Cheney, B.A. 1950,

Ed.M. 1953; University of Washington, Seattle, 1952-53, 1955, 1956-57; University of Pennsylvania, Philadelphia, 1955-56. Served as an editor in the United States Army Corps of Engineers Architects Division. Married 1) Renee Eddy in 1938 (died, 1951), one daughter; 2) Jacquelyn Whitney in 1952; 3) Mary Todd in 1974. English teacher, Bonners Ferry High School, Idaho, 1946-47; Instructor in Spanish and English, Eastern Washington State College, 1950-54. Instructor, 1956-59, Assistant Professor, 1959-65, and since 1965, Associate Professor of Humanities and Social Studies, University of Washington. Participated in English as a Second Language seminars in Yugoslavia, 1972-74, 1976. Since 1977, Consultant, Pacific American Institute. Member of the Executive Board, Western Writers of America, 1963-64. Agent: Scott Meredith Literary Agency, 845 Third Avenue, New York, New York 10022. Address: 12840 139th Avenue, Kirkland, Washington 98033, U.S.A.

SCIENCE-FICTION PUBLICATIONS

Novels

Anthropol. New York, Ace, 1968.
The Noblest Experiment in the Galaxy. New York, Ace, 1970.
Guardians of the Gate, with Jacqueline Trimble. New York, Ace, 1972.
The City Machine. New York, DAW, 1972.
The Wandering Variables. New York, DAW, 1972.
The Bodelan Way. New York, DAW, 1974.

Uncollected Short Story

"Probability," in *If* (New York), April 1954.

OTHER PUBLICATIONS

Novels

Fit to Kill. New York, Phoenix Press, 1941.
Date for Murder. New York, Phoenix Press, 1942.
Tragedy in Turquoise. New York, Phoenix Press, 1942.
Design for Dying. New York, Phoenix Press, 1945.
Murder Trouble. New York, Phoenix Press, and London, Wells Gardner, 1945.
Give Up the Body. Seattle, Superior, 1946.
You Can't Kill a Corpse. New York, Phoenix Press, 1946.
Valley of Violence. Philadelphia, Macrae Smith, 1948; London, Corgi, 1951.
The Case of the Blank Cartridge. New York, Phoenix Press, 1949.
Gunsmoke Justice. Philadelphia, Macrae Smith, 1950; London, Corgi, 1951.
Blonds Are Skin Deep. New York, Lion, 1950.
Gaptown Law. Philadelphia, Macrae Smith, 1952.
Fighting Cowman. New York, Popular, 1952; London, Viking, 1956.
Bring Back Her Body. New York, Ace, 1953.
Crossfire. New York, Avalon, 1953.
Bullets on Bunchgrass. New York, Avalon, 1954.
Stab in the Dark. New York, Ace, 1956.
The Virgin Victim. New York, Mercury, 1956.
Nothing to Lose But My Life. New York, Ace, 1957.
The Tide Can't Wait. New York, Avalon, 1957; London, Wright and Brown, 1959.
Mountain Ambush. New York, Avalon, 1958.
The Smell of Trouble. New York, Ace, 1958.
Cargo for the Styx. New York, Ace, 1959.
The Corpse Without a Country. New York, Ace, 1959.
Obit Deferred. New York, Ace, 1959.
Til Death Do Us Part. New York, Ace, 1959.
The Duchess of Skid Row. New York, Ace, 1960.
Girl on a Slay Ride. New York, Avon, 1960.
Love Me and Die. New York, Ace, 1960.
Deadman's Canyon. New York, Ace, 1961.
Montana Gun. New York, Hillman, 1961; London, White Lion, 1972.

The Surfside Caper. New York, Ace, 1961.
Siege at High Meadow. New York, Ace, 1962.
The Dead and the Deadly. New York, Ace, 1963.
The Man from Colorado. New York, Ace, 1963.
Wild Horse Range. New York, Ace, 1963.
Trouble at Gunsight. New York, Ace, 1964.
The Desperate Deputy of Cougar Hill. New York, Ace, 1965; London, Severn House, 1979.
Holdout in the Diablos. New York, Ace, 1965.
Showdown in the Cayuse. New York, Ace, 1966.
Standoff at Massacre Buttes. New York, Ace, 1967.
Marshal of Sangaree. New York, Ace, 1968.
West to the Pecos. New York, Ace, 1968.
The Hostile Peaks. New York, Ace, 1969; London, Severn House, 1979.
The Ragbag Army. New York, Ace, 1971.

Novels as Gerry Travis

Tarnished Love. New York, Phoenix Press, 1942.
A Lovely Mask for Murder. New York, Avalon, 1956.
The Big Bite. New York, Avalon, 1957.

Novels as Stuart Brock

Death Is My Lover. New York, Mill, 1948.
Just Around the Corner. New York, Mill, 1948.
Double-Cross Ranch. New York, Avalon, 1954; London, Barker, 1957.
Action at Boundary Peak. New York, Avalon, 1955.
Whispering Canyon. New York, Avalon, 1955.
Forbidden Range. New York, Avalon, 1956.
Killer's Choice. New York, Graphic, 1956.
Railtown Sheriff. New York, Avalon, 1957; London, Barker, 1959.

Other

Sports of the World. Los Angeles, Golden West, 1939.
Working Papers in Scientific and Technical English, with Robert Bley-Vroman and Larry Selinker. Seattle, University of Washington, 1972.
New Horizons: A Reader in Scientific and Technical English, with others. Zagreb, Skolska Knjiga, 1975.
Course Materials for Non-Native Speakers Planning to Enter U.S. Universities to Study Science or Technology, with Mary Todd Trimble. San Francisco, Pacific American Institute, 1977.

Editor, *Criteria for Highway Benefit Analysis.* Seattle, University of Washington-National Academy of Sciences, 3 vols., 1964-65; revised edition, with Robert G. Hennes, Washington, D.C., National Highway Research Board, 1966-67.
Editor, *Incorporation of Shelter into Apartments and Office Buildings.* Washington, D.C., Office of Civil Defense, 1965.
Editor, with Karl Drobnic and Mary Todd Trimble, *English for Specific Purposes: Scientific and Technical English.* Corvallis, Oregon State University Press, 1978.

*   *   *

Louis Trimble made his debut as a science-fiction novelist in 1968 with the publication of *Anthropol*. Trimble has mastered one form of the futuristic novel, the lyrical fantasy, quite handily. Especially entertaining are *The Wandering Variables*, *The City Machine*, and *The Bodelan Way*, books which share a motif of whimsical fantasy underpinning the rather standard fare of futuristic gadgetry and intergalactic conflict. In each the setting reminds one of the more familiar works of C.S. Lewis and Jules Verne; there are botanical wildernesses, shimmering islands, stark winter steppes, deep pools, and medieval valleys.

The lyrical tone is a result of the presence of fantastic goddesses, women of divine birth or superior knowledge, who accompany kind-hearted and competent, if somewhat insecure, males on their adventures. Because Trimble's novels transpire under this divine feminine sanction, the gratuitous violence typical of so much popular science fiction is diminished, and in its place has come the spirit of romance. His books move from loss to reacquisition, from discord to harmony, from problem to solution.

However, Trimble often achieves the effect of romance at the expense of sound narrative construction. There is frequently too much fortuitous coincidence in his books, too many miraculous rescues of the protagonists, too little real threat of failure or death. We are too rarely awe-struck by what happens and too often left incredulous. Neither are his romances true romances of the heart or of the head: his problems tend to be created and resolved by machines rather than by human experience. The problem for Trimble's characters is always to escape physical threat or to build a new city or to return to a familiar planet. Thus only rarely, as in the final scenes of *The Bodelan Way* and *Guardians of the Gate*, does the solution involve the emotional or intellectual growth we demand of first-rate fiction. There is altogether too little development of Trimble's characters and too little engagement of our deeper human sympathies in his situations. Another difficulty arises from the fact that Trimble's novels sometimes cannot sustain their futurism through an entire narrative. In particular, *The Wandering Variables* and *The City Machine* retain their futurism only through the initial phases of exposition before finding their true subject in earth's Middle Ages. At the center of these books are dirt floors, oxdrawn carts, and bellicose medieval clans. Consequently, one feels that in these books science fiction is more peripheral than central, more a vehicle to Trimble's real interest, which is in the past rather than the future.

Nevertheless, after more than 50 books Trimble has developed a prose style which is elaborate yet efficient, and vividly descriptive yet never excessive. Like so many others, his narratives are fast-paced and full of action, yet one does not have the sensation that their pace and action are purely an exploitation of commercial appeal. More often, one feels that though Trimble's novels may fall short of the very best, his concern with the remote future is sincere and his imagination sufficient to include the human condition in that future. For young readers initiating themselves into the worlds of futuristic literature, Trimble's works are fine preparation for the more distant and rewarding vision of Lewis and others like him.

—Marvin W. Hunt

TUBB, E(dwin) C(harles). Also writes as Chuck Adams; Jud Cary; J.F. Clarkson; James S. Farrow; James R. Fenner; Charles S. Graham; Charles Grey; Volsted Gridban; Gill Hunt; E.F. Jackson; Gregory Kern; King Lang; Mike Lantry; P. Lawrence; Chet Lawson; Arthur Maclean; Carl Maddox; M.L. Powers; Paul Schofield; Brian Shaw; Roy Sheldon; John Stevens; Edward Thomson. British. Born in London, 15 October 1919. Married Iris Kathleen Smith in 1944; two daughters. Has worked as a welfare officer, catering manager, and printing machine salesman. Editor, *Authentic Science Fiction*, London, 1956-57. Recipient: Cytricon Award, 1955; Eurocon Award, 1972. Guest of Honor, World Science Fiction Convention, Heidelberg, 1970. Agent: E.J. Carnell Literary Agency, Rowneybury Bungalow, Sawbridgeworth, near Old Harlow, Essex CM20 2EX. Address: 67 Houston Road, London SE23 2RL, England.

SCIENCE-FICTION PUBLICATIONS

Novels (series: Dumarest; Space 1999)

Saturn Patrol (as King Lang). London, Warren, 1951.
Planetfall (as Gill Hunt). London, Warren, 1951.
Argentis (as Brian Shaw). London, Warren, 1952.
Alien Impact. London, Panther, 1952.
Atom War on Mars. London, Panther, 1952.
The Mutants Rebel. London, Panther, 1953.
Venusian Adventure. London, Comyns, 1953.

Alien Life. London, Paladin, 1954.
The Living World (as Carl Maddox). London, Pearson, 1954.
World at Bay. London, Panther, 1954.
The Metal Eater (as Roy Sheldon). London, Panther, 1954.
Journey to Mars. London, Scion, 1954.
Menace from the Past (as Carl Maddox). London, Pearson, 1954.
City of No Return. London, Scion, 1954.
The Stellar Legion. London, Scion, 1954.
The Hell Planet. London, Scion, 1954.
The Resurrected Man. London, Scion, 1954.
Alien Dust. London, Boardman, 1955; New York, Avalon, 1957.
The Space-Born. New York, Ace, 1956; London, Digit, 1961.
Touch of Evil (as Arthur Maclean). London, Fleetway, 1959.
Moon Base. London, Jenkins, and New York, Ace, 1964.
Death Is a Dream. London, Hart Davis, and New York, Ace, 1967.
The Winds of Gath (Dumarest). New York, Ace, 1967; as *Gath*, London, Hart Davis, 1968.
C.O.D. Mars. New York, Ace, 1968.
Derai (Dumarest). New York, Ace, 1968; London, Arrow, 1973.
S.T.A.R. Flight. New York, Paperback Library, 1969.
Toyman (Dumarest). New York, Ace, 1969; London, Arrow, 1973.
Escape into Space. London, Sidgwick and Jackson, 1969.
Kalin (Dumarest). New York, Ace, 1969; London, Arrow, 1973.
The Jester at Scar (Dumarest). New York, Ace, 1970; London, Arrow, 1977.
Lallia (Dumarest). New York, Ace, 1971; London, Arrow, 1977.
Technos (Dumarest). New York, Ace, 1972; London, Arrow, 1977.
Century of the Manikin. New York, DAW, 1972; London, Millington, 1975.
Mayenne (Dumarest). New York, DAW, 1973; London, Arrow, 1977.
Veruchia (Dumarest). New York, Ace, 1973; London, Arrow, 1977.
Jondelle (Dumarest). New York, DAW, 1973; London, Arrow, 1977.
Zenya (Dumarest). New York, DAW, 1974; London, Arrow, 1978.
Breakaway (Space 1999; novelization of TV series). London, Futura, and New York, Pocket Books, 1975.
Eloise (Dumarest). New York, DAW, 1975; London, Arrow, 1978.
Eye of the Zodiac (Dumarest). New York, DAW, 1975; London, Arrow, 1978.
Collision Course (Space 1999; novelization of TV series). London, Futura, 1975; New York, Pocket Books, 1976.
Jack of Swords (Dumarest). New York, DAW, 1976.
Alien Seed (Space 1999; novelization of TV series). London, Futura, 1976.
Spectrum of a Forgotten Sun (Dumarest). New York, DAW, 1976.
Rogue Planet (Space 1999; novelization of TV series). London, Futura, 1976.
Earthfall (Space 1999; novelization of TV series). London, Futura, 1977.
Haven of Darkness (Dumarest). New York, DAW, 1977.
Prison of Light (Dumarest). New York, DAW, 1977.
The Primitive. London, Futura, 1977.
Incident on Ath (Dumarest). New York, DAW, 1978.
The Quillian Sector. New York, DAW, 1978.
Stellar Assignment. London, Hale, 1979.
Web of Sand (Dumarest). New York, DAW, 1979.
Death Wears a White Face. London, Hale, 1979.
Iduna's Universe (Dumarest). New York, DAW, 1979.
The Luck Machine. London, Dobson, 1980.
The Terra Data (Dumarest). New York, DAW, 1980.
The Life Buyer. London, Dobson, 1980.

Novels as Volsted Gridban

Alien Universe. London, Scion, 1952.
Reverse Universe. London, Scion, 1952.
Planetoid Disposals Ltd. London, Milestone, 1953.

De Bracy's Drug. London, Scion, 1953.
Fugitive of Time. London, Milestone, 1953.

Novels as Charles Grey

The Wall. London, Milestone, 1953.
Dynasty of Doom. London, Milestone, 1953.
The Tormented City. London, Milestone, 1953.
Space Hunger. London, Milestone, 1953.
I Fight for Mars. London, Milestone, 1953.
The Extra Man. London, Milestone, 1954.
The Hand of Havoc. London, Merit, 1954.
Enterprise 2115. London, Merit, 1954; as *The Mechanical Monarch*, New York, Ace, 1958.

Novels as Gregory Kern (series: Cap Kennedy in all books)

Galaxy of the Lost. New York, DAW, 1973; London, Mews, 1976.
Slave Ship from Sergan. New York, DAW, 1973; London, Mews, 1976.
Monster of Metelaze. New York, DAW, 1973.
Enemy Within the Skull. New York, DAW, 1974.
Jewel of Jarhan. New York, DAW, 1974; London, Mews, 1976.
Seetee Alert! New York, DAW, 1974; London, Mews, 1976.
The Gholan Gate. New York, DAW, 1974.
The Eater of Worlds. New York, DAW, 1974.
Earth Enslaved. New York, DAW, 1974.
Planet of Dread. New York, DAW, 1974.
Spawn of Laban. New York, DAW, 1974.
The Genetic Buccaneer. New York, DAW, 1974.
A World Aflame. New York, DAW, 1974.
The Ghosts of Epidoris. New York, DAW, 1975.
Mimics of Dephene. New York, DAW, 1975.
Beyond the Galactic Lens. New York, DAW, 1975.
Das Kosmiche Duelle. Bergisch Gladbach, Germany, Bastei, 1976.

Novels as Edward Thomson (series: Atilus in all books)

Atilus the Slave. London, Futura, 1975.
Atilus the Gladiator. London, Futura, 1975.
Gladiator. London, Futura, 1978.

Short Stories

Ten from Tomorrow. London, Hart Davis, 1966.
A Scatter of Stardust. New York, Ace, 1972; London, Dobson, 1976.

Uncollected Short Stories

"Evane," in *New Writings in SF 22*, edited by Kenneth Bulmer. London, Sidgwick and Jackson, 1973.
"Mistaken Identity," in *Space 1*, edited by Richard Davis. London, Abelard Schuman, 1973.
"Sword in the Snow," in *Weird Tales* (Los Angeles), Fall 1973.
"Death God's Doom," in *Witchcraft and Sorcery* (Alhambra, California), Winter 1973.
"Lazarus," in *Beyond This Horizon*, edited by Christopher Carrell. Sunderland, Ceolfrith Press, 1974.
"Made to Be Broken," in *New Writings in SF 23*, edited by Kenneth Bulmer. London, Sidgwick and Jackson, 1974.
"Face to Infinity," in *New Writings in SF 28*, edited by Kenneth Bulmer. London, Dobson, 1976.
"Random Sample," in *New Writings in SF 29*, edited by Kenneth Bulmer. London, Sidgwick and Jackson, 1976.
"The Captain's Dog," in *The Androids Are Coming*, edited by Robert Silverberg. New York, Elsevier Nelson, 1979.

OTHER PUBLICATIONS

Novels

The Fighting Fury (as Paul Schofield). London, Spencer, 1955.

Assignment New York (as Mike Lantry). London, Spencer, 1955.
Comanche Capture (as E.F. Jackson). London, Spencer, 1955.
Sands of Destiny (as Jud Cary). London, Spencer, 1955.
Men of the Long Rifle (as J.F. Clarkson). London, Spencer, 1955.
Scourge of the South (as M.L. Powers). London, Spencer, 1956.
Vengeance Trail (as James S. Farrow). London, Spencer, 1956.
Quest for Quantrell (as John Stevens). London, Spencer, 1956.
Trail Blazers (as Chuck Adams). London, Spencer, 1956.
Drums of the Prairie (as P. Lawrence). London, Spencer, 1956.
Men of the West (as Chet Lawson). London, Spencer, 1956.
Wagon Trail (as Charles S. Graham). London, Spencer, 1957.
Colt Vengeance (as James R. Fenner). London, Spencer, 1957.
Target Death. London, Micron, 1961.
Lucky Strike. London, Fleetway, 1961.
Calculated Risk. London, Fleetway, 1961.
Too Tough to Handle. London, Fleetway, 1962.
The Dead Keep Faith. London, Fleetway, 1962.
The Spark of Anger. London, Fleetway, 1962.
Full Impact. London, Fleetway, 1962.
I Vow Vengeance. London, Fleetway, 1962.
Gunflash. London, Fleetway, 1962.
Hit Back. London, Fleetway, 1962.
One Must Die. London, Fleetway, 1962.
Suicide Squad. London, Fleetway, 1962.
Airbourne Commando. London, Fleetway, 1963.
No Higher Stakes. London, Fleetway, 1963.
Penalty of Fear. London, Fleetway, 1963.

*   *   *

The quantity of E.C. Tubb's output can be gauged by the fact that he has used over 40 pseudonyms. Since 1951 he has been turning out novels and stories on a monthly basis, occasionally editing on the side; Michael Ashley in *The History of the Science Fiction Magazine* calls Tubb "an inspired fiction machine." His popularity, well established in England, is now sizable in America as well. He is quick to turn ideas into stories set out in hard, clear prose, and many of his plots have been repeated by younger writers, not always with as much success.

Tubb writes of a hostile universe where men seek to dominate each other, and nowhere is it as hostile or extensive as in the Dumarest saga. Stretching now to a score of novels, the long quest of Earl Dumarest for his lost Earth is an effective device for creating science-fiction adventure. Reticent, grim, dressed in grey, and quick with a knife, Dumarest travels from planet to planet pursued by the Cyclan, cold zealots whose emotions have been surgically removed and who are psychically linked to an organic computer of a million embalmed brains. They want Dumarest because he has the secret to another kind of psychic linking, and Dumarest wants his mythical Earth because it is his own home. In effect the books form a 20-novel chase sequence. Some aspects become repetitive—for example, the description of Low and High travelling (frozen vs. time-accelerated) is transferred almost verbatim from book to book. And in each story Dumarest is injured in ghastly detail, which he stoically endures until advanced medicine repairs him. But the planets are different—vivid landscapes and weathers similar only in their exoticism and their environmental exacerbation of the baser emotions. There is also range in the interpersonal plots. Sometimes Dumarest finds friends, sometimes only enemies; sometimes the lush women (all of whom desire him) have to be taught a lesson, and sometimes they do not; and in *Jondelle*, with creditable devotion, Dumarest defends a child. All this escapes being ludicrous through the stolid understatement in Tubb's competent style, and through the character of Dumarest himself, who is so determined and so quiet that he remains something of an enigma even after repeated adventures. That he has no sense of humor can be attributed to the desperate situations his author devises for him, situations in which genuine heroism can only consist of bleak courage and violent action.

Violence is important to Tubb; his interest in it is conscious and explicity defended, not only in the Dumarest series but in novels like *Century of the Manikin* as well. The "manikins" are people who have been conditioned to believe violence is wrong. They live on a decadent, drug-controlled Earth where sex is so free that the only secret pleasure is violence. It takes a 20th-century woman, thawed out from cryogenic sleep, to tell them that men need weapons and honest fighting in order to be truly masculine and alive. Like almost every woman in Tubb's books, she finds male combat sexually exciting. But violence is not Tubb's only theme, however much it motivates his characters. His plots cover the full range of traditional science fiction, from first-contact riddles like "Random Sample," to sad tales of awakening computers like "J Is for Jeanne," and even to mood pieces like "The Last Day of Summer," where a man waits for the Bureau of Euthanasia. Tubb can also play with concepts of time and space; in *S.T.A.R. Flight* the instantaneous transport Gates of the dictatorial Kaltich are a puzzle to be solved, rather bloodily, by Earth's resistance organization.

E.C. Tubb is a good candidate for the theory that science fiction is essentially conservative. Against varying backgrounds of unexplained technology, Tubb talks about the most basic human passions. And however many suns are in the sky, the framework for ethical decision remains the same. For Tubb, the old values matter in the new places—matter more, since the strangeness isolates the grasping nature of men in plainer sight. Dumarest appears as a appropriate alter-ego for a man whose prose is lean and unsentimental. Tubb works in a highly colored imaginative landscape, but like Dumarest he does his job quickly and then moves on, convictions unchanged, to the next world.

—Karen G. Way

TUCKER, (Arthur) Wilson ("Bob"). American. Born in Deer Creek, Illinois, 23 November 1914. Educated at Normal High School, Illinois. Married 1)Mary Jan Joestine in 1937 (divorced, 1942); 2) Fern Delores Brooks in 1953; one daughter and four sons. Motion picture projectionist, 1933-72, and electrician for 20th Century Fox and the University of Illinois at Urbana and at Normal. Publisher of many fan magazines: *The Planetoid*, 1932, *Science Fiction News Letter, D'Journal, Le Zombie*, 1938-75, *Fantasy and Weird Fiction*, 1938-39, *Yearbook of Science, Fanewscard Weekly, Fanzine Yearbook*, 1941-45, *Fapa Variety*. President, National Fantasy Fan Federation, 1942-43. Recipient: Hugo Award, for non-fiction, 1970; Campbell Memorial Award, 1976. Guest of Honor, 25th World Science Fiction Convention, 1967. Agent: Curtis Brown Ltd., 575 Madison Avenue, New York, New York 10022. Address: 34 Greenbriar Drive, Jacksonville, Illinois 62650, U.S.A.

SCIENCE-FICTION PUBLICATIONS

Novels

The City in the Sea. New York, Rinehart, 1951; London, Nova, 1955.
The Long Loud Silence. New York, Rinehart, 1952; London, Lane, 1953.
The Time Masters. New York, Rinehart, 1953; revised edition, New York, Doubleday, 1971; London, Gollancz, 1973.
Wild Talent. New York, Rinehart, 1954; London, Joseph, 1955; as *Man from Tomorrow*, New York, Bantam, 1955.
Time Bomb. New York, Rinehart, 1955; as *Tomorrow Plus X*, New York, Avon, 1957.
The Lincoln Hunters. New York, Rinehart, 1958; London, Phoenix House, 1961.
To the Tombaugh Station. New York, Ace, 1960.
The Year of the Quiet Sun. New York, Ace, 1970; London, Hale, 1971.
Ice and Iron. New York, Doubleday, 1974; revised edition, New York, Ballantine, and London, Gollancz, 1975.

Short Stories

The Science-Fiction Subtreasury. New York, Rinehart, 1954; as *Time: X*, New York, Bantam, 1955.

Uncollected Short Stories

"The Job is Ended," in *Science Fantasy* (Bournemouth), September 1955.
"King of the Planet," in *Galaxy* (New York), October 1959.
"The Recon Man," in *If* (New York), January 1965.
"Time Exposures," in *Universe 1,* edited by Terry Carr. New York, Ace, 1971; London, Dobson, 1975.
"The Near-Zero Crime Rate on J.J. Avenue," in *Analog* (New York), April 1978.

OTHER PUBLICATIONS

Novels

The Chinese Doll. New York, Rinehart, 1946; London, Cassell, 1948.
To Keep or Kill. New York, Rinehart, 1947; London, Cassell, 1950.
The Dove. New York, Rinehart, 1948; London, Cassell, 1950.
The Stalking Man. New York, Rinehart, 1949; London, Cassell, 1950.
Red Herring. New York, Rinehart, 1951; London, Cassell, 1953.
The Man in My Grave. New York, Rinehart, 1956; London, Macdonald, 1958.
The Hired Target. New York, Ace, 1957.
Last Stop. New York, Doubleday, 1963; London, Hale, 1965.
A Processional of the Damned. New York, Doubleday, 1965; London, Hale, 1967.
The Warlock. New York, Doubleday, 1967; London, Hale, 1968.
This Witch. New York, Doubleday, 1971; London, Gollancz, 1972.

Other

"How to Write an Sf Story," in *Fantasy Fan,* November 1933.
The Neo-Fan's Guide to Science Fiction Fandom. Privately printed, 1955.

Wilson Tucker comments:
I write to entertain an editor, his readers, and myself, in that order. If I fail to entertain the editor, there will be no readers; if I fail to entertain the readers my own livelihood will be reduced accordingly. Some critics have said that my books may paint a bleak picture for humanity but that I always offer hope and sunshine for the future. That's news to me. I had always believed that I was writing adventure and offering entertainment, nothing more.

*   *   *

Wilson Tucker's stories have the modesty of realistic black and white films. His casts are small, his scale intimate, and his settings familiar. He develops his plots and characters using human actions and reactions. He prefers concrete imagery to abstract verbiage: he tells by showing. In *The Year of the Quiet Sun,* for example, shots of the same swimming pool in four different years give instant summaries of intervening events at the site. Indeed, the cinematic flow of Tucker's narratives may reflect his 40 years' experience as a motion picture projectionist.

Tucker's style is economical and unadorned. He understates so much that careless readers sometimes miss the full implications of his text, such as clues to the hero's race in *The Year of the Quiet Sun* or the practice of cannibalism in *The Long Loud Silence.* He actually had to revise the ending of *Ice and Iron* after its initial publication to supply additional explanations. Characterization is his strongest gift. His heroes are marked by a certain ornery ordinariness and a stubborn integrity that the critic Bruce Gillespie calls "the ability neither to give in to the world nor to push it around" (*SF Commentary 43*, 1976). These heroes crave simplicity and distrust institutions. They wield their talents—anything from telepathy to acting to survival skills—without bravado. They establish prickly, often unsatisfactory relationships with heroines as stubborn as themselves. Tucker sensibly combines appreciation of feminine charms with respect for feminine strength.

Historical, not physical, sciences have been Tucker's major inspiration. His personal enthusiasm for history and archeology fuels the well-researched vitality of *The Lincoln Hunters* and *The Year of the Quiet Sun*. The human dimensions of time travel have seldom been better portrayed in SF, for instance in the chief Lincoln-hunter's joy at meeting people from past eras: "They were living *now* and he was among them." Although he does plot with time paradoxes, Tucker always makes time travel a means rather than an end in itself. In *The Lincoln Hunters* it enables the author to place his hero in two radically different environments—a sterile, repressive future and a burgeoning, liberal past—and then generates a eucatastrophe to leave him in the happier world. Tucker keeps restating the proposition that life itself is a kind of time machine operating at the maximum rate of one second per second.

A poignant version of temporal translation is achieved through extreme longevity in *The Time Masters*. A marooned extraterrestrial who had been Gilgamesh in ancient Sumer waits thousands of years while the mayfly lives of ordinary humans flicker out around him before he finds an alternative to both loneliness and escape. The hero of *The Time Masters* reappears in a minor role in *Time Bomb*, a novel in which mechanical time travel changes history by eliminating a McCarthy-like villain in his larval stage. This premise is inverted in Tucker's finest work, *The Year of the Quiet Sun*, when data gleaned from temporal research preserve a villain and trigger a catastrophic world race war. Every element in this honest, solidly built book meshes securely and unobtrusively to present a close-up of Armageddon.

Tucker thriftily incorporated the same research on Biblical archeology and the Dead Sea Scrolls used for *The Year of the Quiet Sun* into his mystery novel *This Witch*. He prefers doing mysteries because he finds them easier and more fun to write than SF, but his dual careers cross-fertilize each other. He often uses SF elements (even facts about SF fandom) in his mysteries and employs mystery/thriller conventions in his SF. (Compare the espionage apparatus and psychic elements in *Wild Talent* and *The Warlock*.) The clearest instance of Tucker's debt to the hard-boiled mystery styles of the 1940's is *The Long Loud Silence*. Its protagonist is a monomaniac scrambling for survival in a plague-devastated eastern United States. Although the unrelenting brutality of this novel cost it popular acceptance on its initial publication, it remains a chilling reflection of Cold War attitudes.

Yet despite the grimness that underlies much of his professional work, Tucker has been one of SF fandom's favorite humorists—in person and in print—for half a century. His close friend Robert Bloch calls him "a legend in his own time." Tucker's chief handicap as a writer is an excess of humility—even after a score of novels he still refuses to think of himself as a professional writer. But the author of *The Year of the Quiet Sun* need stand in awe of no one.

—Sandra Miesel

TURNER, George (Reginald). Australian. Born in Melbourne, Victoria, 8 October 1916. Educated in Victoria state schools; at University High School, Melbourne. Served in the Australian Imperial Forces, 1939-45. Employment Officer, Commonwealth Employment Service, Melbourne, 1945-49, and Wangaratta, Victoria, 1949-50; Textile Technician, Bruck Mills, Wangaratta, 1951-64; Senior Employment Officer, Volkswagen Ltd., Melbourne, 1964-67; Beer Transferrer, Carlton and United Breweries, Melbourne, 1970-77. Since 1970, science fiction reviewer, Melbourne *Age*. Recipient: Miles Franklin Award, 1962; Commonwealth Literary Fund award, 1968. Agent: Carl Routledge, 22 Knoll House, Carlton Hill, London N.W. 8, England. Address: 87 Westbury Street, Balaclava, Victoria 3183, Australia.

SCIENCE-FICTION PUBLICATIONS

Novel

Beloved Son. London, Faber, 1978; New York, Pocket Books, 1979.

Uncollected Short Story

"In a Petri Dish Upstairs," in *Rooms of Paradise*, edited by Lee Harding. Melbourne, Quartet, 1978; New York, St. Martin's Press, 1979.

OTHER PUBLICATIONS

Novels

Young Man of Talent. London, Cassell, 1959; as *Scobie*, New York, Simon and Schuster, 1959.
A Stranger and Afraid. London, Cassell, 1961.
The Cupboard under the Stairs. London, Cassell, 1962.
A Waste of Shame. Melbourne and London, Cassell, 1965.
The Lame Dog Man. Melbourne, Cassell, 1967; London, Cassell, 1968.
Transit of Cassidy. Melbourne, Nelson, 1978; London, Hamish Hamilton, 1979.

Other

"Science Fiction as Literature," in *The Visual Encyclopedia of Science Fiction*, edited by Brian Ash. London, Pan, 1977.

Editor, *The View from the Edge.* Melbourne, Nostrilia Press, 1977.

George Turner comments:

Since it is my personal view (admittedly shared by few contemporary SF writers) that SF long ago lost its way among erotica, exotica, wishdreams, metaphysical guesswork, "mind-blowing" conceptions, and plain bad writing, I prefer to maintain a low key in my own work. To this end I have concentrated on simple, staple SF ideas, mostly those which have become conventions in the genre, injected without background or discussion into stories on the understanding that readers know all they need about such things. So in *Beloved Son* I used only the everyday ingredients of the genre—genetic manipulation, telepathy, the nature of World War III, the politics of renaissance—in order to rethink them and point out that all is not as obvious as conventional SF usage would have the readers believe.

My work will always be concerned with how human beings behave—as all fiction ultimately must be. Super-heroes, super-intelligences, and unlikely worlds created for melodrama or the spelling out of doubtful metaphors for the future of man do not interest me. My SF method remains the same as for my mainstream novels—set characters in motion in a speculative situation and let them work out their destinies with a minimum of auctorial interference.

* * *

A well-known and prize-winning mainstream Australian novelist, George Turner has earned a reputation as Australia's most rigorous and astute science-fiction critic and reviewer. (He claims, with justification, that his "thirty-year-apprenticeship" in the writer's craft has given him "the critical confidence to stand in awe of no-one but Shakespeare and Tolstoy.".) It was no surprise when in 1978 he made his comeback as novelist with a work of science fiction.

Beloved Son is the best SF novel yet written in Australia. Set in Australia in the post-holocaust world of 2032 AD, the events are prompted by the return of a starship which left Earth in the 1990's. Routine research reveals anomalies in the starship's crew and mission, and it is soon obvious that a 40-year old experiment in human cloning is reaching its climax, and that the political structure of the reconstructed world will be radically altered as a result.

Ostensibly, then, *Beloved Son* is a novel about the abuses and consequences of biological research. However, it is also about the pitfalls of romantic idealism and utopian thinking. The plagues, famines, and fire-storms of the Collapse have eroded the population until it is chiefly the young who hold political power, and the older generation has become the scapegoat for the world's ills. (Not that the old are put to death, or even denied political office; Turner's vision avoids such melodramatic clichés.) The young rulers are brash, idealistic, and confidently over-confident. In Turner's words they are "super-educated fledglings," but in their own eyes they are the reconstructors of a utopia. The novel strips away these illusions, exposing a world that has succumbed to materialism and the cult of progress, losing sight of values that cannot be quantified. The emblem of this sad, depleted society is the Security Headquarters building: "Plain, ugly, efficient and temporary, it was uncompromisingly an administrative block. Like this entire civilization, it was there only to serve a passing purpose and be torn down. It symbolized with repellent neatness a world with an immutable past and a hopefully solid future but only a ramshackle, disposable present."

The compelling wisdom of *Beloved Son* lies in Turner's ability to see with this kind of clarity: to see the shabby present amid the rosy dreams of the future. Such qualities have attracted charges of dourness, cynicism, and pessimism, but these accusations miss the point of the novel's achievement. *Beloved Son* may be forthright and uncompromising, but it is also honest—bluntly, harshly honest. Just as the novel's ideas about cloning are based upon sound extrapolation from the present, so its view of society—and indeed, of man—is firmly founded upon present realities. In a phrase, *Beloved Son* is about "the unholy competence of man"; it demonstrates that man's wisdom is less than his ability, and that the human talent for self-delusion and naive dreaming can be disastrous in its consequences. Just as *Brave New World* and *Nineteen Eighty-Four* brought home to an earlier generation the general socio-political dangers posed by the unevaluated advancement of science, so Turner's novel brings home to our age the dangers lurking in the test tubes of the biologists, and the fatal weaknesses inherent in man's slothful complacency. *Beloved Son* can fitly be mentioned side by side with Huxley's and Orwell's classics; it is a major science-fiction novel.

—Van Ikin

TUTTLE, Lisa. American. Born in Houston, Texas, 16 September 1952. Educated at Syracuse University, New York, B.A. in English 1973. Editor of the fan magazine *Mathom*, 1968-70; television columnist, Austin *American Statesman*, Texas, 1976-79. Recipient: Campbell Memorial Award, 1974; *Locus* Award, 1976. Agent: Kirby McCauley, 60 East 42nd Street, New York, New York 10017. Address: 2700 West 35th Street, Austin, Texas 78703, U.S.A.

SCIENCE-FICTION PUBLICATIONS

Novel

Windhaven, with George R.R. Martin. New York, Simon and Schuster, 1980.

Uncollected Short Stories

"Stranger in the House," in *Clarion 2*, edited by Robin Scott Wilson. New York, New American Library, 1972.
"Till Human Voices Wake Us...," in *Clarion 3*, edited by Robin Scott Wilson. New York, New American Library, 1973.
"Dollburger," in *Fantasy and Science Fiction* (New York), February 1973.
"I Have Heard the Mermaids," in *Survival from Infinity*, edited by Roger Elwood. New York, Watts, 1974.

"Changelings," in *Best SF 75*, edited by Harry Harrison and Brian Aldiss. Indianapolis, Bobbs Merrill, and London, Weidenfeld and Nicolson, 1976.
"Woman Waiting," in *Lone Star Universe*, edited by George W. Proctor and Steven Utley. Austin, Texas, Heidelberg, 1976.
"Stone Circle," in *Amazing* (New York), March 1976.
"Mrs. T," in *Amazing* (New York), September 1976.
"Tom Sawyer's Sub-Orbital Escapade," with Steven Utley, in *Ascents of Wonder*, edited by David Gerrold and Stephen Goldin. New York, Popular Library, 1977.
"The Family Monkey," in *New Voices in Science Fiction*, edited by George R.R. Martin. New York, Macmillan, 1977.
"Flies by Night," with Steven Utley, in *SF Choice 77*, edited by Mike Ashley. London, Quartet, 1977.
"Kin to Kaspar Hauser," in *Galaxy* (New York), April 1977.
"The Horse Lord," in *Fantasy and Science Fiction* (New York), June 1977.
"Sangre," in *Fantastic* (New York), June 1977.
"A Mother's Heart: A True Bear Story," in *Isaac Asimov's Science Fiction Magazine* (New York), January-February 1978.
"Uncoiling," with Steven Utley, in *Fantastic* (New York), April 1978.
"In the Arcade," in *Amazing* (New York), May 1978.
"The Hollow Man," in *New Voices 2*, edited by George R.R. Martin. New York, Harcourt Brace, 1979.
"The Birds of the Moon," in *Fantastic* (New York), January 1979.
"Wives," in *Fantasy and Science Fiction* (New York), December 1979.
"Bug House," in *Fantasy and Science Fiction* (New York), June 1980.

* * *

George R.R. Martin has called Lisa Tuttle's writing "distinctive, delightful," and Ted White attributed "a reputation for strong stories which deal with human responses to the unusual" to her. The editors of the fanzine *Shayol* called her the sort of writer who drives up property values. Her first story, "Stranger in the House," is about childhood. Tuttle called it a "going home story" that grew from the "nearly incessant chatter inside [her] head." A young woman returns home and attempts to regain her childhood. It's a familiar theme, and such skilled writers as Ray Bradbury and Harlan Ellison have touched on it to produce stories of ineffable sadness. But Tuttle goes a step further and produces a work of genuine horror, catching an aspect of our desire to recapture the past that few writers ever even hint at. It was a fitting beginning. In the few short years since, Tuttle has revealed herself as a writer of interesting variety and probing insight.

But it may be more important that she's shown herself to be a writer of highly original horror fiction, a writer whose talent in that direction is still growing. "Changelings," for example, is a nicely extrapolated sociological vignette about a society that employs surgery to cure anti-social behavior; in it, a father is betrayed by his pre-school-age child. "Flies by Night," written with Steven Utley, is a psychological study of a woman who longs to turn into a fly. "Stone Circle" is a complex character study set in a near-future welfare state. "In the Arcade" depicts a future where racism is offered as a sideshow attraction. "Sangre" and "The Horse Lord" are almost, but not quite, conventional, the first juxtaposing the story of a woman's affair with her stepfather with a tale of vampirism, the other telling of a family that encounters Indian superstition that turns out to be justified—again, parents are betrayed by their children.

In "The Family Monkey" a rural Texas couple saves an alien from its crashed spaceship and adopts it as a servant. The story is simple and straightforward: the alien is saved, becomes a sort of family retainer, is discovered years later by its own people, and leaves. What gives the story a remarkable depth is that Tuttle's interest lies not with the plot or the alien, but with the relationships of the characters. Relationship, in fact, is the focus of most of Tuttle's work. "The Hollow Man," set in the near future, concerns a woman whose husband commits suicide. She has him brought back to life through new medical techniques that revive the flesh but nothing else. Cold and indifferent to everything, the husband no longer has the interest necessary even to kill himself. The tragedy of the ending is classically inevitable and doubly powerful for it.

Little of Tuttle's fiction takes place away from the Earth. In "Wives," one of the few set on another planet, aliens are permitted by their Earthman conquerers to exist only so long as they pretend to be the human's wives. "The Birds of the Moon" is set on Earth, but tells about a woman whose astronaut husband has been to the moon. The voyage has changed him, and the woman hallucinates about beings—strange, ugly birds—which live on the moon. As with many of Tuttle's stories, it is impossible to tell where hallucination ends and reality begins, particularly in man-woman relationships: in "Flies by Night," for example, the woman who longs to be a fly is captured by men who have become spiders—or so she believes.

Yet such images, striking as they are in a writer of her talent, never dominate Tuttle's fiction; nor does her interest in relationships. If anything, they serve only as a focus for what appears to be a still-emerging concern for the humanity of her characters. In "Bug House" a young woman visits an aunt who lives in a lonely, isolated house. She finds the aunt sick, the house given over to insects. The aunt dies, apparently the victim of a strange young man whose connection with her, the house, the insects, becomes apparent only when it's too late. As in "Stone Circle," sex is treated as a numbing, enslaving element.

Windhaven, written with George R.R. Martin, is not typical Lisa Tuttle fiction, but it would be wrong to call it typical Martin, either. It's a superb collaborative effort set on a planet whose inhabitants, descendants of the survivors of a spaceship wreck, are dependent on the skills of messengers who travel on artificial wings, similar to hang gliders. It's good, solid science fiction, carefully crafted and strongly written, making the most of Martin's eye for the exotic and ability to plot a story, and Tuttle's graceful style and sensitivity to people.

Lisa Tuttle is still a relative newcomer, but her skill with characterization and psychological probing as well as her ear for language promise that her career will not be a minor one.

—Gerald W. Page

TWAIN, Mark. Pseudonym for Samuel Langhorne Clemens. American. Born in Florida, Missouri, 30 November 1835; grew up in Hannibal, Missouri. Married Olivia Langdon in 1870 (died, 1904); one son and three daughters. Printer's apprentice from age 12; helped brother with Hannibal newspapers, 1850-52; worked in St. Louis, New York, Philadelphia, Keokuk, Iowa, and Cincinnati, 1853-57; river pilot's apprentice, on the Mississippi, 1857: licensed as a pilot, 1859; went to Nevada as secretary to his brother, then in the service of the governor, and also worked as a goldminer, 1861; staff member, *Territorial Enterprise*, Virginia City, Nevada, 1862-64; moved to San Francisco, 1864; visited France, Italy, and Palestine, 1867; writer from 1867, lecturer from 1868; Editor, *Buffalo Express*, New York, 1868-71; moved to Hartford, Connecticut, and became associated with the Charles L. Webster Publishing Company, 1884: went bankrupt, 1894 (last debts paid, 1898). M.A.: Yale University, New Haven, Connecticut, 1888; Litt.D.: Yale University, 1901; Oxford University, 1907; LL.D.: University of Missouri, Columbia, 1902. *Died 21 April 1910.*

SCIENCE-FICTION PUBLICATIONS

Novel

A Connecticut Yankee in King Arthur's Court. New York, Webster, and London, Chatto and Windus, 1889.

OTHER PUBLICATIONS

Novels

The Innocents Abroad; or, The New Pilgrims' Progress. Hart-ford, Connecticut, American Publishing Company, 1869; London, Routledge, 2 vols., 1872.
The Innocents at Home. London, Routledge, 1872.
The Gilded Age: A Tale of Today, with Charles Dudley Warner. Hartford, Connecticut, American Publishing Company, 1873; London, Routledge, 3 vols., 1874; *The Adventures of Colonel Sellers, Being Twain's Share of "The Gilded Age,"* edited by Charles Neider, New York, Doubleday, 1965; London, Chatto and Windus, 1966.
The Adventures of Tom Sawyer. London, Chatto and Windus, and Hartford, Connecticut, American Publishing Company, 1876.
A Tramp Abroad. Hartford, Connecticut, American Publishing Company, and London, Chatto and Windus, 1880.
The Prince and the Pauper. London, Chatto and Windus, and Boston, Osgood, 1881.
The Adventures of Huckleberry Finn (Tom Sawyer's Companion). London, Chatto and Windus, 1884; New York, Webster, 1885.
The American Claimant. New York, Webster, and London, Chatto and Windus, 1892.
Pudd'nhead Wilson: A Tale. London, Chatto and Windus, 1894; as *The Tragedy of Pudd'nhead Wilson*, Hartford, Connecticut, American Publishing Company, 1894.
Personal Recollections of Joan of Arc.... New York, Harper, and London, Chatto and Windus, 1896.
A Double Barrelled Detective Story. New York, Harper, and London, Chatto and Windus, 1902.
Extracts from Adam's Diary. New York and London, Harper, 1904.
Eve's Diary. New York and London, Harper, 1906.
A Horse's Tale. New York and London, Harper, 1907.
Simon Wheeler, Detective, edited by Franklin R. Rogers. New York, New York Public Library, 1963.
The Complete Novels, edited by Charles Neider. New York, Doubleday, 2 vols., 1964.

Short Stories

The Celebrated Jumping Frog of Calaveras County and Other Sketches, edited by John Paul. New York, Webb, 1867.
A True Story and the Recent Carnival of Crime. Boston, Osgood, 1877.
Date 1601: Conversation as It Was by the Social Fireside in the Time of the Tudors. Privately printed, 1880; as *1601...*, edited by Franklin J. Meine, Chicago, privately printed, 1939.
The Stolen White Elephant Etc. London, Chatto and Windus, and Boston, Osgood, 1882.
Merry Tales. New York, Webster, 1892.
The £1,000,000 Bank-Note and Other New Stories. New York, Webster, and London, Chatto and Windus, 1893.
Tom Sawyer Abroad. New York, Webster, and London, Chatto and Windus, 1894.
Tom Sawyer Abroad, Tom Sawyer, Detective, and Other Stories. New York, Harper, 1896; as *Tom Sawyer, Detective, as Told by Huck Finn, and Other Tales.* London, Chatto and Windus, 1897.
The Man That Corrupted Hadleyburg and Other Stories and Essays. New York, Harper, and London, Chatto and Windus, 1900.
A Dog's Tale. London, National Anti-Vivisection Society, and New York, Harper, 1904.
The $30,000 Bequest and Other Stories. New York, Harper, 1906; London, Harper, 1907.
Extract from Captain Stormfield's Visit to Heaven. New York and London, Harper, 1909; revised edition, as *Report from Paradise*, edited by Dixon Wecter, New York, Harper, 1952.
The Mysterious Stranger: A Romance. New York, Harper, 1916; London, Harper, 1917.
The Curious Republic of Gondour and Other Whimsical Sketches. New York, Boni and Liveright, 1919.
The Mysterious Stranger and Other Stories. New York and London, Harper, 1922.
The Adventures of Thomas Jefferson Snodgrass, edited by Charles Honce. Chicago, Covici, 1928.
A Boy's Adventure. Privately printed, 1928.

Jim Smiley and His Jumping Frog, edited by Albert B. Paine. Chicago, Pocahontas Press, 1940.

A Murder, A Mystery, and a Marriage. Privately printed, 1945.

The Complete Short Stories, edited by Charles Neider. New York, Hanover House, 1957.

The Complete Humorous Sketches and Tales, edited by Charles Neider. New York, Doubleday, 1961.

Mark Twain's Satires and Burlesques, edited by Franklin R. Rogers. Berkeley, University of California Press, 1967.

Mark Twain's Mysterious Stranger Manuscripts, edited by William M. Gibson. Berkeley, University of California Press, 1969.

Mark Twain's Hannibal, Huck, and Tom, edited by Walter Blair. Berkeley, University of California Press, 1969.

Plays

Colonel Sellers as a Scientist, with William Dean Howells, adaptation of the novel *The Gilded Age* by Twain and Charles Dudley Warner (produced New Brunswick, New Jersey, and New York, 1887). Published in *The Complete Plays of William Dean Howells*, edited by Walter J. Meserve, New York, New York University Press, 1960.

Ah Sin, with Bret Harte, edited by Frederick Anderson (produced Washington, D.C., 1877). San Francisco, Book Club of California, 1961.

The Quaker City Holy Land Excursion: An Unfinished Play. Privately printed, 1927.

Verse

On the Poetry of Mark Twain, with Selections from His Verse, edited by Arthur L. Scott. Urbana, University of Illinois Press, 1966.

Other

Mark Twain's (Burlesque) Autobiography and First Romance. New York, Sheldon, 1871.

Memoranda: From the Galaxy. Toronto, Canadian News and Publishing Company, 1871.

Roughing It. London, Routledge, and Hartford, Connecticut, American Publishing Company, 1872.

A Curious Dream and Other Sketches. London, Routledge, 1872.

Screamers: A Gathering of Scraps of Humour, Delicious Bits, and Short Stories. London, Hotten, 1872.

Sketches. New York, American News Company, 1874.

Sketches, New and Old. Hartford, Connecticut, American Publishing Company, 1875.

Old Times on the Mississippi. Toronto, Belford, 1876.

Punch, Brothers, Punch! and Other Sketches. New York, Slote Woodman, 1878.

An Idle Excursion. Toronto, Belford, 1878.

A Curious Experience. Toronto, Gibson, 1881.

Life on the Mississippi. London, Chatto and Windus, and Boston, Osgood, 1883.

Facts for Mark Twain's Memory Builder. New York, Webster, 1891.

How to Tell a Story and Other Essays. New York, Harper, 1897; revised edition, 1900.

Following the Equator: A Journey Around the World. Hartford, Connecticut, American Publishing Company, 1897; as *More Tramps Abroad*, London, Chatto and Windus, 1897.

The Writings of Mark Twain. Hartford, Connecticut, American Publishing Company, and London, Chatto and Windus, 25 vols., 1899-1907.

The Pains of Lowly Life. London, London Anti-Vivisection Society, 1900.

English as She Is Taught. Boston, Mutual, 1900; revised edition, New York, Century, 1901.

To the Person Sitting in Darkness. New York, Anti-Imperialist League, 1901.

Edmund Burke on Croker, and Tammany (lecture). New York, Economist Press, 1901.

My Début as a Literary Person, with Other Essays and Stories. Hartford, Connecticut, American Publishing Company, 1903.

Mark Twain on Vivisection. New York, New York Anti-Vivisection Society, 1905(?).

King Leopold's Soliloquy: A Defense of His Congo Rule. Boston, Warren, 1905; revised edition, 1906; London, Unwin, 1907.

Editorial Wild Oats. New York, Harper, 1905.

What Is Man? (published anonymously). New York, DeVinne Press, 1906; as Mark Twain, London, Watts, 1910.

Mark Twain on Spelling (lecture). New York, Simplified Spelling Board, 1906.

The Writings of Mark Twain (Hillcrest Edition). New York and London, Harper, 25 vols., 1906-07.

Christian Science, with Notes Containing Corrections to Date. New York and London, Harper, 1907.

Is Shakespeare Dead? From My Autobiography. New York and London, Harper, 1909.

Mark Twain's Speeches, edited by F.A. Nast. New York and London, Harper, 1910; revised edition, 1923.

Queen Victoria's Jubilee. Privately printed, 1910.

Letter to the California Pioneers. Oakland, California, Dewitt and Snelling, 1911.

What Is Man? and Other Essays. New York, Harper, 1917; London, Chatto and Windus, 1919.

Mark Twain's Letters, Arranged with Comment, edited by Albert B. Paine. New York, Harper, 2 vols., 1917; shortened version, as *Letters*, London, Chatto and Windus, 1920.

Moments with Mark Twain, edited by Albert B. Paine. New York, Harper, 1920.

The Writings of Mark Twain (Definitive Edition), edited by Albert B. Paine. New York, Gabriel Wells, 37 vols., 1922-25.

Europe and Elsewhere. New York and London, Harper, 1923.

Mark Twain's Autobiography, edited by Albert B. Paine. New York and London, Harper, 2 vols., 1924.

Sketches of the Sixties by Bret Harte and Mark Twain ... from "The Californian," 1864-67. San Francisco, John Howell, 1926.

The Suppressed Chapter of "Following the Equator." Privately printed, 1928.

A Letter from Mark Twain to His Publisher, Chatto and Windus. San Francisco, Penguin Press, 1929.

Mark Twain the Letter Writer, edited by Cyril Clemens. Boston, Meador, 1932.

Mark Twain's Works. New York, Harper, 23 vols., 1933.

The Family Mark Twain. New York, Harper, 1935.

The Mark Twain Omnibus, edited by Max J. Herzberg. New York, Harper, 1935.

Representative Selections, edited by Fred L. Patee. New York, American Book Company, 1935.

Mark Twain's Notebook, edited by Albert B. Paine. New York, Harper, 1935.

Letters from the Sandwich Islands, Written for the "Sacramento Union," edited by G. Ezra Dane. San Francisco, Grabhorn Press, 1937; London, Oxford University Press, 1938.

The Washoe Giant in San Francisco, Being Heretofore Uncollected Sketches..., edited by Franklin Walker. San Francisco, George Fields, 1938.

Mark Twain's Western Years, Together with Hitherto Unreprinted Clemens Western Items, by Ivan Benson. Stanford, California, Stanford University, 1938.

Letters from Honolulu Written for the "Sacramento Union," edited by Thomas Nickerson. Honolulu, Thomas Nickerson, 1939.

Mark Twain in Eruption: Hitherto Unpublished Pages about Men and Events, edited by Bernard De Voto. New York, Harper, 1940.

Travels with Mr. Brown, Being Heretofore Uncollected Sketches Written for the San Francisco "Alta California" in 1866 and 1867, edited by Franklin Walker and G. Ezra Dane. New York, Knopf, 1940.

Republican Letters, edited by Cyril Clemens. Webster Groves, Missouri, International Mark Twain Society, 1941.

Letters to Will Brown..., edited by Theodore Hornberger. Austin, University of Texas, 1941.

Letters in the "Muscatine Journal," edited by Edgar M. Branch. Chicago, Mark Twain Association of America, 1942.

Washington in 1868, edited by Cyril Clemens. Webster Groves, Missouri, International Mark Twain Society, and London, Laurie, 1943.

Mark Twain, Business Man, edited by Samuel Charles Webster. Boston, Little Brown, 1946.

The Letters of Quintus Curtius Snodgrass, edited by Ernest E. Leisy. Dallas, Southern Methodist University Press, 1946.

The Portable Mark Twain, edited by Bernard De Voto. New York, Viking Press, 1946.

Mark Twain in Three Moods: Three New Items of Twainiana, edited by Dixon Wecter. San Marino, California, Friends of the Huntington Library, 1948.

The Love Letters of Mark Twain, edited by Dixon Wecter. New York, Harper, 1949.

Mark Twain to Mrs. Fairbanks, edited by Dixon Wecter. San Marino, California, Huntington Library, 1949.

Mark Twain to Uncle Remus 1881-1885, edited by Thomas H. English. Atlanta, Emory University Library, 1953.

Twins of Genius (letters to George Washington Cable), edited by Guy A. Cardwell. East Lansing, Michigan State College Press, 1953.

Mark Twain of the "Enterprise"..., edited by Henry Nash Smith and Frederick Anderson. Berkeley, University of California Press, 1957.

Traveling with Innocents Abroad: Mark Twain's Original Reports from Europe and the Holy Land, edited by Daniel Morley McKeithan. Norman, University of Oklahoma Press, 1958.

The Autobiography of Mark Twain, edited by Charles Neider. New York, Doubleday, 1959.

The Art, Humor, and Humanity of Mark Twain, edited by Minnie M. Brashear and Robert M. Rodney. Norman, University of Oklahoma Press, 1959.

Mark Twain and the Government, edited by Svend Petersen. Caldwell, Idaho, Caxton Printers, 1960.

Mark Twain-Howells Letters: The Correspondence of Samuel L. Clemens and William Dean Howells 1872-1910, edited by Henry Nash Smith and William M. Gibson. Cambridge, Massachusetts, Harvard University Press, 2 vols., 1960; abridged edition, as *Selected Mark Twain-Howells Letters*, 1967.

Your Personal Mark Twain.... New York, International Publishers, 1960.

Life as I Find It: Essays, Sketches, Tales, and Other Material, edited by Charles Neider. New York, Doubleday, 1961.

The Travels of Mark Twain, edited by Charles Neider. New York, Doubleday, 1961.

Contributions to "The Galaxy," 1868-1871, edited by Bruce R. McElderry. Gainesville, Florida, Scholars Facsimiles and Reprints, 1961.

Mark Twain on the Art of Writing, edited by Martin B. Fried. Buffalo, Salisbury Club, 1961.

Letters to Mary, edited by Lewis Leary. New York, Columbia University Press, 1961.

The Pattern for Mark Twain's "Roughing It": Letters from Nevada by Samuel and Orion Clemens, 1861-1862, edited by Franklin R. Rogers. Berkeley, University of California Press, 1961.

Letters from the Earth, edited by Bernard De Voto. New York, Harper, 1962.

Mark Twain on the Damned Human Race, edited by Janet Smith. New York, Hill and Wang, 1962.

Selected Shorter Writings, edited by Walter Blair. Boston, Houghton Mifflin, 1962.

The Complete Essays, edited by Charles Neider. New York, Doubleday, 1963.

Mark Twain's San Francisco, edited by Bernard Taper. New York, McGraw Hill, 1963.

The Forgotten Writings of Mark Twain, edited by Henry Duskus. New York, Citadel Press, 1963.

General Grant by Matthew Arnold, with a Rejoinder by Mark Twain (lecture), edited by John Y. Simon. Carbondale, Southern Illinois University Press, 1966.

Letters from Hawaii, edited by A. Grove Day. New York, Appleton Century Crofts, 1966; London, Chatto and Windus, 1967.

Which Was the Dream? and Other Symbolic Writings of the Later Years, edited by John S. Tuckey. Berkeley, University of California Press, 1967.

The Complete Travel Books, edited by Charles Neider. New York, Doubleday, 1967.

Letters to His Publishers, 1867-1894, edited by Hamlin Hill. Berkeley, University of California Press, 1967.

Clemens of the "Call": Mark Twain in California, edited by Edgar M. Branch. Berkeley, University of California Press, 1969.

Correspondence with Henry Huttleston Rogers, 1893-1909, edited by Lewis Leary. Berkeley, University of California Press, 1969.

Man Is the Only Animal That Blushes — or Needs to: The Wisdom of Mark Twain, edited by Michael Joseph. Los Angeles, Stanyan Books, 1970.

Mark Twain's Quarrel with Heaven: Captain Stormfield's Visit to Heaven and Other Sketches, edited by Roy B. Browne. New Haven, Connecticut, College and University Press, 1970.

Everybody's Mark Twain, edited by Caroline Thomas Harnsberger. South Brunswick, New Jersey, A.S. Barnes, and London, Yoseloff, 1972.

Fables of Man, edited by John S. Tuckey. Berkeley, University of California Press, 1972.

A Pen Warmed Up in Hell: Mark Twain in Protest, edited by Frederick Anderson. New York, Harper, 1972.

The Choice Humorous Works of Mark Twain. London, Chatto and Windus, 1973.

Mark Twain's Notebooks and Journals, edited by Frederick Anderson and others. Berkeley, University of California Press, 1975 (and later volumes).

Letters from the Sandwich Islands, edited by Joan Abramson. Norfolk Island, Australia, Island Heritage, 1975.

Mark Twain Speaking, edited by Paul Fatout. Iowa City, University of Iowa Press, 1976.

The Mammoth Cod, and Address to the Stomach Club. Milwaukee, Maledicta, 1976.

The Comic Mark Twain Reader, edited by Charles Neider. New York, Doubleday, 1977.

Mark Twain Speaks for Himself, edited by Paul Fatout. West Lafayette, Indiana, Purdue University Press, 1978.

Translator, *Slovenly Peter (Der Struwwelpeter)*. New York, Limited Editions Club, 1935.

*

Bibliography: *A Bibliography of the Works of Mark Twain, Samuel Langhorne Clemens* by Merle Johnson, New York, Harper, revised edition, 1935; in *Bibliography of American Literature 2* by Jacob Blanck, New Haven, Connecticut, Yale University Press, 1957.

* * *

Although Mark Twain's science-fiction works are often labeled mimetic fiction (ultimately what occurs can be explained as dreams rather than actual time travel resulting from scientific extrapolation), his dystopic creations and employment of the ideology of science within or preceding the dream structures qualifies his works as science fiction. *Report from Paradise, The Mysterious Stranger*, and *Letters from the Earth* are not science fiction but fantasy: satires on man's place in the universe in which science is neither used as a tool to create the condition of the stories nor as a thematic consideration within them. *Tom Sawyer Abroad*, "The Comedy of those Extraordinary Twins," and "The Curious Republic of Gondour" contain minor elements of science fiction, but Twain's three major contributions to the genre are *A Connecticut Yankee in King Arthur's Court*, "The Great Dark," and "From the 'London Times' of 1904," all of which reflect the increasing cynicism of Twain's later years. In the confusion of dream and reality accompanied by alteration of time and space, Twain creates different worlds for his protagonists to struggle in. These dystopias present Twain's perception of the unchanging human condition: man as a petty being, always willing to prey on his fellow man.

The comic relief in *Connecticut Yankee* (a literary burlesque of Malory's *Morte d'Arthur*) erupts through Twain's satire of the age of chivalry whose precepts had been adopted by the Old South, a frequent target of Twain's social criticism in his mainstream works. But primarily Twain investigates the effects of industrialization on a pre-industrial society which was a matter of public concern both in relation to the United States and to our foreign policy at the time. In this view, Twain attacked Social Darwinism: the establishment of an industrialized, capitalistic society where the common man was once again suppressed by the financial power of a few individuals who had gained their power through that technological revolution. Hank, the protagonist of *Connecticut Yankee*, a 19th-century common working man, rises to power in King Arthur's Court through creative use of his technical skills and scientific knowledge. By introducing industrialization, Hank attempts to change the economic, political, and intellectual structures of a nation of oppressed people, but his failure results not so much through the powers of the church and state as through his own failure. He succumbs to one of the primary evils of capitalism (according to Twain): once Hank gains power, he becomes self-absorbed. The megalomanic Hank instigates a civil war (purportedly in the name of creating a viable civilization for the common man) which results in the ultimate destruction of all that he has established. What makes *Connecticut Yankee* science fiction is not just the question of whether Hank actually experiences time travel and suspended animation or whether he dreams it. Instead it is Twain's questioning of the effects of technology, his concentration on the idea of technology in another time and space.

The problem of dream versus reality occurs again in "The Great Dark." Whereas in *Connecticut Yankee* the protagonist goes back in time to a setting already familiar to the reader, in "The Great Dark" Twain concentrates on establishing a setting in which circumstance, not time, is important. Presenting a tiny world as seen through a microscope, Twain creates a whole watery universe filled with monsters, destruction, and suffering for his protagonist to attempt to survive in. Like Hank, Mr. Edwards returns to the present no longer accepting it as real, finding his other existence to have all the qualities of reality and his present that of the dream. This exploration of dream versus reality is closely linked with temporal/spatial relationships so that time and setting become an integral part of what makes these works science fiction. In *Connecticut Yankee*, science, or at least technology, is a thematic consideration, whereas in "The Great Dark" technology is used only as a tool to create the setting in which the characters must question temporal/spatial relationships. Twain embarks on another approach to science in "From the 'London Times' of 1904." Instead of employing a thematic consideration of technology as in *Connecticut Yankee* or using an already existing scientific instrument to create the circumstances of the story as in "The Great Dark," Twain invents the telectroscope (television) to use in conjunction with his usual exploration of thought and visual transference in temporal/spatial relationships.

In these three works, Twain, as an early writer of science fiction, presents three different approaches still frequently used in the genre. Additionally, through his social criticism, Twain is one of the first mainstream writers to present dystopias rather than utopias to show by comparison rather than by contrast the inequities of the social institutions he questions: religion, government, taxes, prejudice, slavery, censorship, and politics. Yet his dark view of man is made bearable through his caustic humor. He invokes our laughter even as we accept with humility his accusations of our greed, jealousy, lack of common sense, thirst for power, cruelty, and ultimately the smallness of mind of the human beast.

—Jane B. Weedman

UTLEY, Steven. American. Born in 1948. Address: 2700 West 35th Street, Austin, Texas 78703, U.S.A.

SCIENCE-FICTION PUBLICATIONS

Uncollected Short Stories

"The Unkindest Cut of All," in *Perry Rhodan 20*. New York, Ace, 1972.

"Parrot Phrase," in *Perry Rhodan 24*. New York, Ace, 1973.
"The Queen and I," in *Perry Rhodan 31*. New York, Ace, 1973.
"Crash Cameron and the Slime Beast," in *Vertex* (Los Angeles), June 1973.
"The Reason Why," in *Vertex* (Los Angeles), December 1973.
"Hung Like an Elephant," with Joe Pumilia, and "Womb, with a View," in *Alternities*, edited by David Gerrold. New York, Dell, 1974.
"Sport," in *Best SF 1973*, edited by Harry Harrison and Brian Aldiss. New York, Putnam, and London, Sphere, 1974.
"Deeper Than Death," in *Vertex* (Los Angeles), April 1974.
"Act of Mercy," in *Galaxy* (New York), July 1974.
"Big Black Whole" and "Time and Variance," in *Galaxy* (New York), August 1974.
"Amber Eyes," in *Galaxy* (New York), December 1974.
"The Great Red Spot," with Joe Pumilia, and "Dear Mom, I Don't Like It Here," in *Vertex* (Los Angeles), February 1975.
"Caring for Your Edaphosaurus," in *Vertex* (Los Angeles), August 1975.
"The Other Half," in *Galaxy* (New York), September 1975.
"Custer's Last Jump," with Howard Waldrop, in *Universe 6*, edited by Terry Carr. New York, Doubleday, 1976; London, Dobson, 1978.
"Predators," in *The Ides of Tomorrow*, edited by Terry Carr. Boston, Little Brown, 1976.
"Ghost Seas," in *Lone Star Universe*, edited by George W. Proctor and Steven Utley. Austin, Texas, Heidelberg, 1976.
"Sic Transit...? A Shaggy Hairless-Dog Story," with Howard Waldrop, in *Stellar 2*, edited by Judy-Lynn del Rey. New York, Ballantine, 1976.
"Getting Away," in *Galaxy* (New York), January 1976.
"Deviation from a Theme," in *Galaxy* (New York), May 1976.
"Larval Stage," in *Galaxy* (New York), July 1976.
"Ocean," in *Fantastic* (New York), August 1976.
"The Man at the Bottom of the Sea," in *Galaxy* (New York), October 1976.
"The Thirteenth Labor," in *Stellar 3*, edited by Judy-Lynn del Rey. New York, Ballantine, 1977.
"Black as the Pit, from Pole to Pole," with Howard Waldrop, in *New Dimensions 7*, edited by Robert Silverberg. New York, Harper, and London, Gollancz, 1977.
"In Brightest Day, In Darkest Night," in *Fantastic* (New York), February 1977.
"Passport for a Phoenix," in *Galaxy* (New York), April 1977.
"Spectator Sport," in *Amazing* (New York), July 1977.
"The Maw," in *Fantasy and Science Fiction* (New York), July 1977.
"Flies by Night," with Lisa Tuttle, in *SF Choice 77*, edited by Mike Ashley. London, Quartet, 1977.
"Tom Sawyer's Sub-Orbital Escapade," with Lisa Tuttle, in *Ascents of Wonder*, edited by David Gerrold and Stephen Goldin. New York, Popular Library, 1977.
"Losing Streak," in *Fantasy and Science Fiction* (New York), January 1977.
"Our Vanishing Triceratops," with Joe Pumilia, in *Amazing* (New York), March 1977.
"Time and Hagakure," in *Asimov's Choice: Black Holes and Bug-Eyed Monsters*, edited by George H. Scithers. New York, Dale, 1978.
"Uncoiling," with Lisa Tuttle, in *Fantastic* (New York), April 1978.
"The Man Who Ran Up the Clock," in *Fantastic* (New York), January 1979.
"Leaves," in *Amazing* (New York), February 1979.
"Genocide Man," in *Fantasy and Science Fiction* (New York), April 1979.
"Upstart," in *The Best from Fantasy and Science Fiction 23*, edited by Edward L. Ferman. New York, Doubleday, 1980.

OTHER PUBLICATIONS

Other

Editor, with George W. Proctor, *Lone Star Universe*. Austin, Texas, Heidelberg, 1976.

Steven Utley comments:

I don't have much to say, meaningful or otherwise, about my stories. I did, of course, think rather highly of some of my own work when I wrote it. I was possessed of considerable enthusiasm for what I was about. Disenchantment with the SF field, when it set in, set in hard, and now time has made all the difference. Anymore, I view my having been a writer as just a phase, like puberty, into which I entered at one point in my life and from which I emerged, not exactly unscathed, at a subsequent point. I've done some writing since the, ah, divorce, but I no longer *think* of myself as a writer, only as someone who every now and then misses the actual grueling work of sitting in front of the typewriter for hours on end. Most of my energy goes into other pursuits which are quite unrelated to SF and, more to the point, quite satisfying.

*   *   *

Between 1972 and 1979, Steven Utley established a reputation as a prolific author of short stories and novelettes, either alone or in collaboration with a number of other Texas-based writers, most notably Howard Waldrop and Lisa Tuttle. With George W. Proctor he edited a volume of SF and fantasy by Texans, *Lone Star Universe*, whose appearance Harlan Ellison hailed as a "watershed event." Working exclusively at less-than-novel length, Utley has produced fiction either competent but undistinguished or astonishing for its inventive mordancy. At his best, his pervasive angst leavened with humor, angry wit, or local color, he has written chilling horror stories ("Ghost Seas"), scathingly funny satires ("Upstart"), outrageous pastiches ("Black as the Pit, from Pole to Pole," with Waldrop), and evocative, melancholy science fiction ("The Man at the Bottom of the Sea"). The strongest contemporary influences on Utley's development appear to be the October landscapes of Ray Bradbury, the ironic pessimism of the later Robert Silverberg, the pop-culture eclecticism of Philip José Farmer, and the manic-depressive black humor of Barry N. Malzberg, whose style and subject matter Utley affectionately parodies in "Losing Streak." In one conspicuous but hardly damning sense, then, he is a writer still in the process of discovering his own voice and métier.

"Custer's Last Jump," with Waldrop, first secured wide recognition of Utley's talents. It postulates a frontier America in which the Oglala Sioux, equipped with Krupp monoplanes, defeat the 7th Cavalry of George Armstrong Custer and its airborne auxiliary, the 505th Balloon Infantry. Told in earnest text-book prose, this off-the-wall tour de force concludes with a "Suggested Reading" list as whacky and authentic-seeming as the "historical" matter preceding it. This final bibliographic fillip may owe something to Farmer's convolute appendices in the mock-biography *Tarzan Alive*.

A second Utley-Waldrop collaboration, "Black as the Pit, from Pole to Pole," pays homage to Farmer (again), Mary Shelley, Poe, Verne, Burroughs, and others. Its protagonist is that quintessential symbol of alienation, the Frankenstein monster, and its setting is the perilous hollow interior of the earth. Although the disparate elements of this tale do not always mesh convincingly, sheer narrative *chutzpah* often effectively disguises the fact. Like "Custer's Last Jump," it has been much discussed and anthologized.

Among Utley's solo efforts "Upstart" is a pointed, and hilarious, satire of the spacefarer-as-superman ethos in science fiction, perhaps the last word on this indefatigable idiocy. "Ghost Seas," meanwhile, invokes the desolate West Texas landscape in the service of a terrifying tale of avarice and revenge. "The Man at the Bottom of the Sea" demonstrates Utley's ability to dramatize, poignantly, a private sense of loss; it is notable for a calm descriptive overlay at odds with the emotional intensity of its characters.

Another effective story, set against the historical backdrop of World War II, is "Time and Hagakure," wherein the son of a Japanese kamikaze pilot attempts to preserve his own sanity by mediating, through time, the salvation of his doomed father. In "Getting Away" Utley makes effective use of his deep-seated interest in dinosaurs — creatures which frequently raise their huge, anomalous heads in his fiction — to give his protagonist a means of psychological escape from a polluted and regimented future.

In many ways Utley has been an undervalued writer, perhaps because he shows little interest in writing a novel. The fact that even his best short stories and novelettes remain uncollected has also obscured his accomplishment.

—Michael Bishop

———————

VANCE, Jack (John Holbrook Vance). Also writes as Peter Held; John Holbrook; Ellery Queen; Alan Wade. American. Born in San Francisco, California. Educated at the University of California, Berkeley, B.A. 1942. Married Norma Ingold in 1946; one son. Self-employed writer. Recipient: Mystery Writers of America Edgar Allan Poe Award, 1960; Hugo Award, 1963, 1967; Nebula Award, 1966; Jupiter Award, 1974. Agent: Kirby McCauley Ltd., 60 East 42nd Street, New York, New York, 10017. Address: 6383 Valley View Road, Oakland, California 94611, U.S.A.

SCIENCE-FICTION PUBLICATIONS

Novels (series: Alastor; Big Planet; Demon Princes; Durdane; Tschai)

The Space Pirate.   New York, Toby Press, 1953; as *The Five Gold Bands*, New York, Ace, 1963.
Vandals of the Void (juvenile).   Philadelphia, Winston, 1953.
To Live Forever.   New York, Ballantine, 1956; London, Sphere, 1976.
Big Planet.   New York, Avalon, 1957; London, Hodder and Stoughton, 1977.
The Languages of Pao.   New York, Avalon, 1958.
Slaves of the Klau.   New York, Ace, 1958.
The Dragon Masters.   New York, Ace, 1963; London, Dobson, 1965.
The Houses of Iszm, Son of the Tree.   New York, Ace, 1964; *Son of the Tree* published separately, London, Mayflower, 1974.
The Star King (Demon Princes).   New York, Berkley, 1964; London, Dobson, 1966.
The Killing Machine (Demon Princes).   New York, Berkley, 1964; London, Dobson, 1967.
Monsters in Orbit.   New York, Ace, 1965; London, Dobson, 1977.
Space Opera.   New York, Pyramid, 1965.
The Blue World.   New York, Ballantine, 1966; London, Mayflower, 1976.
The Brains of Earth.   New York, Ace, 1966; London, Dobson, 1976.
The Palace of Love (Demon Princes).   New York, Berkley, 1967; London, Dobson, 1968.
City of the Chasch (Tschai).   New York, Ace, 1968; London, Dobson, 1975.
Emphyrio.   New York, Doubleday, 1969.
Servants of the Wankh (Tschai).   New York, Ace, 1969; London, Dobson, 1975.
The Dirdir (Tschai).   New York, Ace, 1969; London, Dobson, 1975.
The Pnume (Tschai).   New York, Ace, 1970; London, Dobson, 1975.
The Anome (Durdane).   New York, Dell, 1973; London, Hodder and Stoughton, 1975; as *The Faceless Man*, New York, Ace, 1978.
The Brave Free Men.   New York, Dell, 1973; London, Hodder and Stoughton, 1975.
Trullion: Alastor 2262.   New York, Ballantine, 1973; London, Mayflower, 1979.
The Asutra (Durdane).   New York, Dell, 1974; London, Hodder and Stoughton, 1975.
The Gray Prince.   Indianapolis, Bobbs Merrill, 1974; London, Hodder and Stoughton, 1976.
Marune: Alastor 993.   New York, Ballantine, 1975; London, Coronet, 1978.

Showboat World (Big Planet).   New York, Pyramid, 1975; London, Hodder and Stoughton, 1977.

Maske: Thaery.   New York, Berkley, 1976; London, Fontana, 1978.

Wyst: Alastor 1716.   New York, DAW, 1978.

The Face (Demon Princes).   New York, DAW, 1979; London, Dobson, 1980.

All the Shattered Worlds.   Canoga Park, California, Manor, 1980.

Nopalgarth.   New York, DAW, 1980.

The Book of Dreams (Demon Princes).   New York, DAW, 1981.

Short Stories (series: Dying Earth)

The Dying Earth.   New York, Curl, 1950; London, Mayflower, 1972.

Future Tense.   New York, Ballantine, 1964.

The World Between and Other Stories.   New York, Ace, 1965; as *The Moon Moth and Other Stories*, London, Dobson, 1975.

The Eyes of the Overworld (Dying Earth).   New York, Ace, 1966; London, Mayflower, 1972.

The Many Worlds of Magnus Ridolph.   New York, Ace, 1966; London, Dobson, 1977.

The Last Castle.   New York, Ace, 1967.

Eight Fantasms and Magics.   New York, Collier, 1970; as *Fantasms and Magics*, London, Mayflower, 1978.

The Worlds of Jack Vance.   New York, Ace, 1973.

The Best of Jack Vance.   New York, Pocket Books, 1976.

Green Magic.   San Francisco, Underwood Miller, 1979.

The Bagful of Dreams.   San Francisco, Underwood Miller, 1979.

The Seventeen Virgins.   San Francisco, Underwood Miller, 1979.

Galactic Effectuator.   Columbia, Pennsylvania, Underwood Miller, 1980.

Dust of Far Suns.   New York, DAW, 1981.

OTHER PUBLICATIONS

Novels as John Holbrook Vance

Isle of Peril (as Alan Wade).   New York, Curl, 1957.

Take My Face (as Peter Held).   New York, Curl, 1957.

The Man in the Cage.   New York, Random House, 1960; London, Boardman, 1961.

The Fox Valley Murders.   Indianapolis, Bobbs Merrill, 1966; London, Hale, 1967.

The Pleasant Grove Murders.   Indianapolis, Bobbs Merrill, 1967; London, Hale, 1968.

The Deadly Isles.   Indianapolis, Bobbs Merrill, 1969; London, Hale, 1970.

Bad Ronald.   New York, Ballantine, 1973.

The House on Lily Street.   San Francisco, Underwood Miller, 1979.

The View from Chickweed's Window.   San Francisco, Underwood Miller, 1979.

Novels as Ellery Queen

The Four Johns.   New York, Pocket Books, 1964; as *Four Men Called John*, London, Gollancz, 1976.

A Room to Die In.   New York, Pocket Books, 1965.

The Madman Theory.   New York, Pocket Books, 1966.

Plays

Television Plays: *Captain Video* (6 episodes), 1952-53.

*

Bibliography: *Fantasms: A Bibliography of the Literature of Jack Vance* by Daniel J.H. Levack and Tim Underwood, San Francisco, Underwood Miller, 1978.

Manuscript Collection: Mugar Memorial Library, Boston University.

*   *   *

No author who is generally acknowledged to be a science-fiction author has done more to blur the distinction between science fiction and fantasy than Jack Vance. His works simply refuse to fit any simple definition of either genre, and to try to force them into one or the other category is to do violence to both the works and the genres. If it is at all possible to characterize the many novels and stories written by Vance over a period of more than 30 years, such a characterization must include the fact that Vance creates fictional worlds with a devotion to detail and inner logic rarely encountered in either science fiction or fantasy. Often what makes a Vance work both readable and enjoyable is the sense of otherness that permeates the work. If, for example, a future, dying Earth is presented as in *The Dying Earth* and its sequel *The Eyes of the Overworld*, the center of the reader's attention soon becomes the remarkable creatures that share this world with man rather than a particularly original plot or a strongly stated theme. More often than not, his plots are rather standard ones based on classical and Germanic mythology, medieval romances, and earlier space operas. What prevents such adventure yarns as *The Eyes of the Overworld*, *Slaves of the Klau*, and most of his series novels from becoming merely repetitive is the setting, newly invented for each work. A Vance work teases the reader; just when he suspects that nothing can top a particularly inventive and often mind-boggling creation, the next sentence proceeds to do just that.

The six interconnected stories that compose *The Dying Earth* serve well to illustrate the fantasy nature of Vance's writing. Using a popular science-fiction device, a future in which magic replaces science as the prime force for change, Vance has his characters undergo a series of adventures which succeed at once in thrilling the reader with a touch of the strange and implying the existence of an inner logic which somehow gives the magical elements credibility. Though the stories are populated with magicians, half-humans, tree creatures, and demons which seem to inhabit a fantasy world, there exist the master matrix of life, air cars, antigravity shafts, and the great machines, all of which hint at a future world clearly the creation of science fiction. Vance's combination of a folklore atmosphere with a science-fiction theme (humanity will overcome any hardship it has the will to overcome) further underscores the difficulty in placing any label on the collection. The stories read like fantasy, but they mean like science fiction. The fantastic elements in *The Dying Earth* confront the reader with a vastly, unimaginably changed, future. But having presented that future, the stories concern themselves with how identifiably human characters manage to preserve identifiably human values despite the changes.

It is this balance between fantasy and science fiction that Vance constantly returns to in so many of his works: *Big Planet*, *Son of the Tree*, *The Houses of Iszm*, the Tschai, Durdane, and incomplete Demon Princes series. In each of these works Vance lavishes great care on the multitude of settings and goes about presenting characters who insist on their humanity despite the strangeness of these settings. Vance, in fact, has been accused of lavishing too much care on his settings. Indeed, in some recent works, such as *Wyst: Alastor 1716*, Vance himself seems to run out of interest in the story once the details of the world have been presented. But if there are times when attention to imaginative details upsets the delicate balance, there are also times when that balance is not only maintained but done in such a manner as to create a significant achievement within science fiction.

The Languages of Pao is such an achievement, a classic science-fiction novel. Using a simple plot of palace intrigue, Vance explores the complicated issue of the interconnection of man's perception of himself and his world with his universal use of language. Does language so filter a speaker's sense of his world through providing names for each object and experience that human perception is limited to what is contained within the language? Can these limits be expanded? What is the cost of such expansion? Vance raises each of these questions, and he finds satisfying answers for each. What allows for the successful resolution of the novel is the care with which Vance first presents the worlds of Pao and Breakness. Pao is a passive world in which a massive population is favored by a planet with a geology that sees to all its needs. The planet Breakness, however, is rugged, harsh, indifferent to the needs of its inhabitants. On Pao, "The typical Paonese saw himself as a cork on a sea of a million waves, lofted, lowered, thrust aside by incomprehensible forces — if he thought of himself as a discrete personality at all."

The people of Breakness, on the other hand, can only see themselves as individuals. On a world in which the individual is in constant danger, concern for individual identity remains uppermost. Given these two worlds, and the care with which Vance develops their contrasting natures, the exploration of the languages of each world and their implications for mankind as the race confronts a future that increasingly demands flexibility is both believable and happily clever. *The Languages of Pao* deals with a complex concept with significant implications for humanity's future, but does so in a straightforward story that dramatizes the issue without trivializing it. The balance between setting and theme is largely responsible for this success.

Finally, one further point needs to be made concerning Vance's use of fantasy and science fiction: often, in the process of detailing the fantastic, Vance turns the unusual into the familiar. What might start out as totally alien ends up as comfortably recognizable. Such a development in a Vance story is usually the result of his interest in elaborating upon the social and cultural institutions and customs of his fictional worlds. *Big Planet*, for example, affords Vance many opportunities to describe a vast number of social institutions. *Space Opera* allows for similar occasions in a more humorous vein. "Moon Moth" combines the detective story with science fiction and, at the same time, presents a credible picture of a society in which all people wear masks and use music as an important aid in communication. In each of these works, however, what becomes significant is not the strangeness of the societies but the fact that they are all human societies. No matter how alien the environment, humanity will prevail and remain humane.

The Dragon Masters (Hugo) is perhaps Vance's finest and most poetic example of his ability to translate the strange to the familiar. Using a rather evocative vocabulary, Vance presents the world of Aerlith as a place of wind and stone with a few valleys of fertile beauty. In this future world, genetic engineering has become a commonplace part of life, tinged, perhaps, with a bit of magic. Vance has clearly produced a world that would allow for maximum freedom for his passion to create strange creatures. Indeed, many such creatures exist in *The Dragon Masters*. Yet, by the end of the novel, Aerlith becomes a human world, a world the reader feels comfortable with because the characters, particularly Joaz Banbeck, have reacted to the exotic elements in ways that humans do. The society so carefully detailed is understandable to the reader because he is convinced that, given such circumstances, that is exactly the type of society the human race would create. Thus the unknown is made knowable through the use of characters that the reader can easily recognize. While *The Dragon Masters* is clearly Vance's most successful attempt at such an union of the bizarre and the common, *The Last Castle* (Hugo), *The Blue World*, *Emphyrio*, and *The Anome* all illustrate Vance's love for this particular technique.

Jack Vance creates by taking extremes that initially threaten to tear a story apart by the tensions that exist between them but that finally resolve themselves into a unified world in which every element appears exactly as it should be. The worlds created by Vance are neither fantasy nor science fiction; they are, quite simply, Jack Vance worlds.

—Stephen H. Goldman

VAN SCYOC, Sydney (Joyce). American. Born in Mt. Vernon, Indiana, 27 July 1939. Educated at Florida State University, Tallahassee; University of Hawaii, Honolulu; Chabot College, Hayward, California; California State University, Hayward. Married Jim R. Van Scyoc in 1957; one daughter and one son. Since 1962, free-lance writer. Secretary, 1975-77, and President, 1977-79, Starr King Unitarian Church, Hayward. Agent: Owl Agency, 5228 Miles, Oakland, California 94618. Address: 2636 East Avenue, Hayward, California 94541, U.S.A.

SCIENCE-FICTION PUBLICATIONS

Novels

Saltflower. New York, Avon, 1971.
Assignment: Nor'Dyren. New York, Avon, 1973.
Starmother. New York, Berkley, 1976.
Cloudcry. New York, Berkley, 1977.

Uncollected Short Stories

"Shatter the Wall," in *Galaxy* (New York), February 1962.
"Bimmie Says," in *Galaxy* (New York), October 1962.
"Pollony Undiverted," in *Galaxy* (New York), February 1963.
"Zack with His Scar," in *Fantasy and Science Fiction* (New York), March 1963.
"Cornie on the Walls," in *Fantastic* (New York), August 1963.
"Soft and Soupy Whispers," in *Galaxy* (New York), April 1964.
"One Man's Dream," in *Fantasy and Science Fiction* (New York), November 1964.
"The Dead Ones," in *Worlds of Tomorrow* (New York), January 1965.
"A Visit to Cleveland General," in *World's Best Science Fiction 1969*, edited by Donald A. Wollheim and Terry Carr. New York, Ace, and London, Gollancz, 1969.
"Unidentified Fallen Object," in *Fantasy and Science Fiction* (New York), January 1969.
"Little Blue Hawk," in *Galaxy* (New York), May 1969.
"Summons to the Medicmat," in *Worlds of Tomorrow* (New York), Spring 1971.
"Noepti-Noe," in *Galaxy* (New York), November 1972.
"When Petals Fall," in *Two Views of Wonder*, edited by Thomas M. Scortia and Chelsea Quinn Yarbro. New York, Ballantine, 1973.
"Mnarra Mobilis," in *The Best from If 2*. New York, Award, 1974.
"Skyveil," in *Galaxy* (New York), April 1974.
"Aberrant," in *Analog* (New York), June 1974.
"Sweet Sister, Green Brother," in *The Best from Galaxy 3*, edited by James Baen. New York, Award, 1975.
"Deathsong," in *The 1975 Annual World's Best SF*, edited by Donald A. Wollheim and Arthur W. Saha. New York, DAW, 1975; Morley, Yorkshire, Elmfield Press, 1976.
"Nightfire," in *Cassandra Rising*, edited by Alice Laurance. New York, Doubleday, 1978.
"Mountain Wings," in *Isaac Asimov's Science Fiction Magazine* (New York), November 1979.
"Darkmorning," in *Isaac Asimov's Science Fiction Magazine* (New York), March 1980.

*

Manuscript Collection: California State University, Fullerton.

Sydney J. Van Scyoc comments:

My earlier short fiction was set on Earth in the not-too-distant future and dealt primarily with individuals struggling against an increasingly dehumanizing technological society. I took several years off from writing in the mid 1960's, while my children were very young. Soon after I began writing again, I found my focus had shifted to short fiction set on other planets and dealt primarily with communities struggling against inexplicable alien environments. I am increasingly intrigued now by the genetic and social changes which I believe will overtake the human race once we begin to colonize other planets. I prefer not to deal in much detail with the inevitable technological changes we will see. Instead I like to set my fiction on isolated worlds inhabited by a relatively small human population. My personal orientation is increasingly pantheistic, and in my longer fiction I am attempting to deal with the spiritual relationship of human to environment.

* * *

Sydney J. Van Scyoc's early stories are set on earth not very far in the future and show the dehumanization of persons in an advanced technological society. The dehumanization is primarily apparent in the characters' lack of personal freedom and conscious choice in such stories as "Pollony Undiverted," "Soft and Soupy Whispers," and the chilling "Visit to Cleveland General." The recent "Nightfire" is an unusual story in which a stalemated war in North America has confined 12 million non-combatants as virtual hostages in orbit above the earth for 41 years. The protagonist, Corneil Rothler, in a carefully planned coup d'etat ruthlessly engineers a truce alone.

A major shift in her work becomes apparent in the long short story "Little Blue Hawk," set in the 21st century; this story focuses on the personal and social costs of human genetic engineering. Van Scyoc's interest in the relationship of human with alien species and an alien ecology appears in "Noepti-Noe," "Sweet Sister, Green Brother," and "Aberrant." These stories emphasize the interdependence and unity of all life forms.

Van Scyoc's impressive first novel, *Saltflower*, takes the basic premise of a dying race seeding earth to generate a transpecies who will be able to reproduce and be viable. The novel is set on earth in the year 2024, and follows the adventures of one of the "transracial" children, Hadley Greer, who is under surveillance by the US government agency SIBling. Most of the action takes place at the Purification Colony's headquarters near Salt Lake City. The Purification Colony is a cult headed by a psychotic leader, Dr. Braith. The novel deftly blends government intrigue, and burgling, religious fanaticism, mysterious murders, and credible alien consciousness, reactions, and biology.

Assignment: Nor'Dyren is an anti-utopian novel with strong satiric elements. It begins on earth in the not-too-distant future with a maintenance sub-engineer, Tollan Bailey, attempting to get a job in the huge company CalMega. Only a few people are employed; the rest live comfortable, futile lives without realizing the social controls that narrow their existence. Bailey wins a trip to the planet Nor'Dyren inhabited by three humanoid species whose rigid social roles and asexual inter-species marriage are leading to a breakdown of the moneyless economy and culture. The Gonnegon are the thinkers and administrators, the Allegon serve, and the Berregon manufacture. The novel follows Bailey's attempts to understand the culture and his maturation. He is an appealing character, particularly in his enchantment with trying to repair machines on Nor'Dyren and help the aliens. The anthropologist Laarica Johns, sent to aid him in his legal battle, discovers the reason for the de-evolution on Nor'Dyren. The satire of earth bureaucracy, rigid social and sexual roles, and crippling cultural assumptions both on earth and Nor'Dyren is effective. The novel is an impassioned plea for a humane culture in which persons can be free to develop their capacities and make ethical choices.

Starmother presents the pathos of ostracized human mutants on a colony world, a race of aliens, the dirads, and the testing of the young protagonist, Jahna Swiss, a cadet of the Service Corps from the planet Peace. The novel alternates the points of view of Jahna, Zuniin, an alienated social outcast, and a young mother, Piety, who is a victim of the superstition and fanaticism of the puritanical human colonists, known as The First Fathers, on the planet Nelding. The alien planet, the various social groups, and species are vividly realized. Suspense is generated by the attempt of Zuniin to kill Jahna out of insane jealousy and zenophobia. Jahna's ethical dilemma and her final commitment to the mutant children enrich the novel. Van Scyoc contrasts the civilization of Peace, Jahna's planet, with Nelding, showing the deficiencies of rigid social roles, fanatic religion, and superstition which make life almost unbearable on the unlovely Nelding.

Cloudcry is an expansion and development of the short story "Deathsong." Around the core of the earlier story of an encounter with still-powerful alien artifacts resembling flutes by members of two humanoid races on an alien planet, Van Scyoc has added the framestory of the human space adventurer Verrons's search for the man-leopards of the planet Rumar and the complication of a deadly space disease called bloodblossom. Verrons is exiled on the quarantine planet, Selmarii, along with another human, Sadler Wells, and a sentient bird-man alien because they have the disease. Aleida, one of the descendants of the ancient race, has psionic powers and heightens them with a crystal which focuses solar energy. The radiation from the light dancer's flute cures the bloodblossom disease. Verrons leaves the abandoned isolation planet haunted by the prospect of Aleida and a new race of powerful light dancers who do not share humane values. *Cloudcry*, like Van Scyoc's other novels,

is distinguished by vivid imagery and sensuous detail, particularly when she portrays non-human perceptions and consciousness.

—Diane Parkin-Speer

---

van VOGT, A(lfred) E(lton). American. Born in Manitoba, Canada, 26 April 1912. Educated in schools in Manitoba, graduated 1928; University of Ottawa; University of California, Los Angeles. Served in the Department of National Defense, Ottawa, 1939-41. Married Edna Mayne Hull, *q.v.*, in 1939 (died, 1975). Census clerk, Ottawa, 1931-32; Western Representative, Maclean Trade Papers, Winnipeg, 1936-39. Managing Director, Hubbard Dianetic Research Foundation of California, Los Angeles, 1950-52, owner, with his wife, Hubbard Dianetic Center, Los Angeles, 1953-61, and since 1958, President, California Association of Dianetic Auditors. Recipient: Manuscripters Literature Award, 1948; Count Dracula Society Ann Radcliffe Award, 1968; Academy of Science Fiction, Fantasy, and Horror Films Award, 1979. B.A.: Golden Gate College, Los Angeles. Guest of Honor, 4th World Science Fiction Convention, 1946, and European Science Fiction Convention, 1978. Agent: Forrest J. Ackerman, 2495 Glendower Avenue, Los Angeles, California 90027. Address: P.O. Box 3065, Hollywood, California 90028, U.S.A.

SCIENCE-FICTION PUBLICATIONS

Novels (series: Clane; Gilbert Gosseyn; Weapon Shop)

Slan. Sauk City, Wisconsin, Arkham House, 1946; revised edition, New York, Simon and Schuster, 1951; London, Weidenfeld and Nicolson, 1953.
The Weapon Makers (Weapon Shop). Providence, Rhode Island, Hadley, 1947; revised edition, New York, Greenberg, 1952; London, Weidenfeld and Nicolson, 1954; as *One Against Eternity*, New York, Ace, 1955.
The Book of Ptath. Reading, Pennsylvania, Fantasy Press, 1947; as *Two Hundred Million A.D.*, New York, Paperback Library, 1964.
The World of A (Gosseyn). New York, Simon and Schuster, 1948; as *The World of Null-A*, London, Dobson, 1969.
The Voyage of the Space Beagle. New York, Simon and Schuster, 1950; London, Grayson, 1951; as *Mission: Interplanetary*, New York, New American Library, 1952.
Masters of Time. Reading, Pennsylvania, Fantasy Press, 1950; as *Earth's Last Fortress*, New York, Ace, 1960; in *Two Science Fiction Novels*, London, Sidgwick and Jackson, 1973.
The House That Stood Still. New York, Greenberg, 1950; London, Weidenfeld and Nicolson, 1953; revised edition, as *The Mating Cry*, New York, Galaxy, 1960; as *The Undercover Aliens*, London, Panther, 1976.
The Weapon Shops of Isher. New York, Greenberg, 1951; London, Weidenfeld and Nicolson, 1952.
The Mixed Men. New York, Gnome Press, 1952; as *Mission to the Stars*, New York, Berkley, 1955; London, Digit, 1960.
The Universe Maker. New York, Ace, 1953; in *The Universe Maker, and The Proxy Intelligence*, London, Sidgwick and Jackson, 1967.
Planets for Sale, with E. Mayne Hull. New York, Fell, 1954; in *A van Vogt Omnibus*, London, Sidgwick and Jackson, 1967.
The Pawns of Null-A (Gosseyn). New York, Ace, 1956; London, Digit, 1960; as *The Players of Null-A*, New York, Berkley, 1966.
Empire of the Atom (Clane). Chicago, Shasta, 1957; London, New English Library, 1975.
The Mind Cage. New York, Simon and Schuster, 1957; London, Panther, 1960.
Triad (omnibus). New York, Simon and Schuster, 1959.
The War Against the Rull. New York, Simon and Schuster, 1959; London, Panther, 1961.

Siege of the Unseen. New York, Ace, 1959; in *Two Science Fiction Novels*, London, Sidgwick and Jackson, 1973.

The Wizard of Linn (Clane). New York, Ace, 1962; London, New English Library, 1975.

The Beast. New York, Doubleday, 1963; as *Moonbeast*, London, Panther, 1969.

Rogue Ship. New York, Doubleday, 1965; London, Dobson, 1967.

The Winged Man, with E. Mayne Hull. New York, Doubleday, 1966; London, Sidgwick and Jackson, 1967.

The Silkie. New York, Ace, 1969; London, New English Library, 1973.

Quest for the Future. New York, Ace, 1970; London, Sidgwick and Jackson, 1971.

Children of Tomorrow. New York, Ace, 1970; London, Sidgwick and Jackson, 1972.

The Battle of Forever. New York, Ace, 1971; London, Sidgwick and Jackson, 1972.

The Darkness on Diamondia. New York, Ace, 1972; London, Sidgwick and Jackson, 1974.

Future Glitter. New York, Ace, 1973; London, Sidgwick and Jackson, 1976; as *Tyranopolis*, London, Sphere, 1977.

The Secret Galactics. Englewood Cliffs, New Jersey, Prentice Hall, 1974; London, Sidgwick and Jackson, 1975; as *Earth Factor X*, New York, DAW, 1976.

The Man with a Thousand Names. New York, DAW, 1974; London, Sidgwick and Jackson, 1975.

The Anarchistic Colossus. New York, Ace, 1977; London, Sidgwick and Jackson, 1978.

Supermind. New York, DAW, 1977; London, Sidgwick and Jackson, 1978.

Renaissance. New York, Pocket Books, 1979.

Cosmic Encounter. New York, Doubleday, 1980.

Short Stories

Out of the Unknown, with E. Mayne Hull. Los Angeles, Fantasy, 1948; London, New English Library, 1970; expanded edition, Reseda, California, Powell, 1969; as *The Sea Thing and Other Stories*, London, Sidgwick and Jackson, 1970.

Masters of Time. Reading, Pennsylvania, Fantasy Press, 1950.

Away and Beyond. New York, Pellegrini and Cudahy, 1952; London, Panther, 1963.

Destination: Universe! New York, Pellegrini and Cudahy, 1952; London, Weidenfeld and Nicolson, 1953.

The Twisted Men. New York, Ace, 1964.

Monsters. New York, Doubleday, 1965; London, Corgi, 1970; as *The Blal*, New York, Kensington, 1976.

The Far-Out Worlds of A.E. van Vogt. New York, Ace, 1968; London, Sidgwick and Jackson, 1973; expanded edition, as *The Worlds of A.E. van Vogt*, Ace, 1974.

More Than Superhuman. New York, Dell, 1971; London, New English Library, 1978.

The Proxy Intelligence and Other Mind Benders. New York, Paperback Library, 1971.

M-33 in Andromeda. New York, Paperback Library, 1971.

The Book of van Vogt. New York, DAW, 1972; as *Lost: Fifty Suns*, 1979.

The Best of A.E. van Vogt. London, Sidgwick and Jackson, 1974.

The Best of A.E. van Vogt. New York, Pocket Books, 1976.

The Gryb. New York, Kensington, 1976.

Pendulum. New York, DAW, 1978.

OTHER PUBLICATIONS

Novel

The Violent Man. New York, Farrar Straus, 1962.

Other

"Complication in the Science Fiction Story," in *Of Worlds Beyond*, edited by Lloyd Arthur Esbach. Reading, Pennsylvania, Fantasy Press, 1947; London, Dobson, 1965.

The Hypnotism Handbook, with Charles Edward Cooke. Los Angeles, Griffin, 1956.

"Introduction" to *The Pseudo-People*, edited by William F. Nolan. Los Angeles, Sherbourne Press, 1965; as *Almost Human*, London, Souvenir Press, 1966.

The Money Personality. West Nyack, New York, Parker, 1972; Wellingborough, Northamptonshire, Thorsons, 1975.

"The Development of a Science Fiction Writer," in *Foundation 3* (London), March 1973.

Reflections of A.E. van Vogt. Lakemont, Georgia, Fictioneer, 1975.

* * *

In the stories of A.E. van Vogt all things are possible, for saying makes them so. It seems of little moment that any event logically follow the preceding one or that one character dominate the action. For readers expecting tightly structured plots, careful characterization, polished prose style, and a logical extrapolation van Vogt affords a field day for criticism. (For a classic lambasting on such matters see Damon Knight's "Cosmic Jerrybuilder: A.E. van Vogt" in *In Search of Wonder*.) But for the reader willing to submit his reason to another's wide-ranging imagination van Vogt is a "good read."

Van Vogt's canon offers a melange of intriguing situations spiced with telepathy, teleportation, shape control, inner and outer space, mass consciousness, time shifts, technological wonders beyond count. Humans, super-creatures, androids, and aliens perform an intricate dance of adventure on a cosmic stage, existing in past, present, and future time, out-of-time and space as we know them, and often out-of-phase with each other. Incidents bombard us, with little transition to ease the pace. Disconcerting as this can be, it does have the trade-off value of keeping one in continual suspense. In "Complication in the Science Fiction Story" van Vogt explained his method of writing scenes in 800-word blocks, the first one to introduce both scene and story purpose. As the main plot develops logically in succeeding scenes, van Vogt adds a secondary plot and minor plot threads deriving from "theme science and atmosphere." While one may question the success of the logical development, there is no argument about van Vogt's ability to handle the minor threads skillfully to induce a sense of mystery, wonder, and suspense.

Since van Vogt writes both short stories and novels, often combining the former to create the latter, a mixed sampling of these modes makes a valid introduction to his characters, situations, and techniques. One especially notices van Vogt's emphasis on superior beings, well exemplified in *The Mixed Men*, a novel combining three short stories. In the earliest story of this group, "The Storm," we meet three super-creatures: the Dellian robots, physically and mentally advanced over man; the non-Dellian robots, higher in creativity; and the Mixed Men of human form but with double brains. Another superhuman, Gilbert Gosseyn of *The World of Null-A*, also has the extra brain, in addition possessing the ability to evade death, thus becomng a more godlike entity than Captain Maltby of the Mixed Men.

Van Vogt's catalog of aliens ranges from BEM's to intelligent forms fearsome in appearance but cooperative in action, once accepted by men. In *The Voyage of the Space Beagle* four aliens appear: the catlike Coeurl, the Ixtl, the Riim folk (a colony-psyche), and the anabis. All four pose grave problems to the expedition whose aim is "to explore limits of deep space and contact alien life forms." By contrast, two sympathetic aliens aid men in *The War Against the Rull*. For mutual survival they contribute their telepathic ability and energy-conducting bodies respectively. The inimical Rull in turn infiltrates human society, using its capability to assume human form. This minor theme of replication appears in many van Vogt tales, starting with "Vault of the Beast" (1940), with the ultimate example being the title character of *The Silkie* which can shift from fish to bullet-like spaceship to human form to innumerable other shapes for its own purposes and protection.

These aliens often educate men about his own nature. In "The Replicators" a harmless alien assumes the form of its first human contact, an ex-Marine full of anger and aggressiveness. The resultant trouble is predictable. A more gentle lesson comes from the super-intelligent, catlike creature in "The Cataaaaa." On assignment to study man on earth the Cat does so from the stage of a carnival freak show. The title, linking the Cat with the spontaneous awed exclamation of the carnival crowd, spotlights the human response. The Cat's response comes in the final act of his study when he communicates to one man the conclusion that the basic human characteristic is self-dramatisation. This may well be the most agreeable comment van Vogt can offer about humans. All too often the enemy turns out to be one of our own. In the power struggle which runs as a major theme throughout van Vogt's stories, the specific enemy is often the trusted man-in-charge. Morlake of "The Earth Killers" tracks down the destroyers of civilization, only to find them racists headed by a power-driven ex-senator pretending to be the altruistic guardian of the people.

Critics note in van Vogt a predilection for the power of monarchy, such as held by the Isher empire in *The Weapon Shops of Isher* and the House of Linn in *Empire of the Atom*. More notable is van Vogt's sense of the drama inherent in all authoritarian systems. Finding authority operating all around us, he exploits the emotional possibilities in such situations as the struggle of the "dynasties" in *Rogue Ship*, the parent-child confrontations in *Children of Tomorrow*, and the professional friction aboard the *Space Beagle*. However, van Vogt always supplies an antithesis to authoritarianism. Most intriguing are those single characters who perform this duty, those superior beings motivated by a sense of mission and possessing a gift or a powerful idea to be manipulated for benefit of all. The combination is varied: Lesley Craig and "toti-potency" in *Masters of Time*; Elliot Grosvenor and "Nexialism" on the *Space Beagle*; Robert Hedrock and the Weapon Shops opposing Isher power; Gilbert Gosseyn with Null-A training (here van Vogt gives a nod to Alfred Korzybski's *Theory of General Semantics*); and others. A natural extension of this balance is a recognition of the cyclic nature of human society in the character of Morton Cargill of *The Universe Maker*. The most famous "savior" of human values and idealism is Johnny Cross of *Slan*, the novel usually considered van Vogt's most outstanding. A member of a mutant group hated and persecuted by the majority, the slan Johnny Cross is a telepath, superior both in intelligence and physique to ordinary men. From childhood his training points toward the end of bringing slans and normal men closer together in harmony. He must contend not only with John Petty, the human chief of the secret police, but also with Kier Gray, the head of the government and a slan passing as a normal human.

Slan epitomizes van Vogt's major thematic issues: the tenacity of the life force whatever its form, the need of cooperative effort for mutual survival, and an overwhelming optimism that a consciousness shared with all life forms can work only to a mutual benefit. For the new reader approaching van Vogt, *Slan* provides a satisfactory entry into van Vogt's provocative and imaginative worlds.

—Hazel Pierce

VARLEY, John. American. Born in Austin, Texas, in 1947. Attended Michigan State University, East Lansing, 1966. Married Anet Mconel; three sons. Since 1973, free-lance writer. Recipient: *Locus* Award, 1977, 1979 (2); Jupiter Award, 1978; Hugo Award, 1979. Agent: Kirby McCauley, 60 East 42nd Street, New York, New York 10017. Address: 345 River Road, Eugene, Oregon 97404, U.S.A.

SCIENCE-FICTION PUBLICATIONS

Novels (series: Cirocco Jones)

The Ophiuchi Hotline. New York, Dial Press, 1977; London, Sidgwick and Jackson, 1978.

Titan (Jones). New York, Berkley, 1978; London, Sidgwick and Jackson, 1979.
Wizard (Jones). New York, Berkley, 1980.

Short Stories

The Persistence of Vision. New York, Dial Press, 1978; as *In the Hall of the Martian Kings*, London, Sidgwick and Jackson, 1978.
The Barbie Murders and Other Stories. New York, Berkley, 1980.

*

Manuscript Collection: Special Collections, Temple University, Philadelphia.

*   *   *

Superficially, John Varley is most noteworthy for his exuberant inventiveness. The cliché to the effect that first novels are frequently overpacked, containing enough material for two or three novels, certainly applies to Varley's *The Ophiuchi Hotline*; however, it is an essential characteristic of the author rather than the fault of a novice. Enigmatic, all-powerful Invaders have come to the Solar System some centuries earlier to commune with their analogues inhabiting Jupiter and have swept all human technology off the Earth (for the sake of whales and dolphins, oceanic intelligences being second in the cosmic pecking order, with land-dwellers a poor third). Yet human beings still survive on other planets and moons, and positively thrive, assisted by massive data transmissions supposedly from another star system. With this aid, men have developed cloning, memory recording, genetic manipulation (banana-meat trees supplying meat protein fruits are only one of the exotics), cosmetisurgery, quantum black hole manipulation, symbiotic space-dwelling vegetables which allow people to coast through free space and colonise the rings of Saturn. The heroine, Lilo, is condemned to death for illegal genetic experiments; however, her various avatar clones live on—rebelling, dying, escaping, falling into Jupiter to be relocated by Invader superscience to a neoprimitive Earth, and travelling on a 20-year deep-space mission to discover the origin of the hotline signals which prove to be the key to what happens to land-dwellers when they get kicked off their planets by the cosmic big leaguers and must roam the starways, suffering identity crises. This vigorous, spliced, multi-faceted adventure story, with its prodigal yet almost casual richness of societies, settings, and technowizardry, does successfully cohere and explain itself; the casual abandonment and placing in abeyance of successive heroine-avatars yields interesting insights into the nature and value of "character" in SF.

Most readers of the novel will put their sense of invigoration down to the cornucopia of ideas which Varley pours out, in action-packed style. The actual method behind the "dazzle effect" of the book becomes more obvious, however, on a close reading of Varley's shorter fiction. Here again we have adventures in Varley's Invader future and in non-Invader futures too, told with the same brio and rainbow scatter of future science used to metamorphose and enhance human life—and it becomes obvious that Varley is actually spinning *juvenile* yarns (using the term generically rather than pejoratively) dressed up as something toughly sophisticated. His tales are juvenile in the *feel* of the characters, once one strips away the obligatory and skillful veneer of post-adolescence. Above all they are juvenile in their ultimate sense of comfort and security. In "Overdrawn at the Memory Bank" anyone can perform spare-time surgery because germs are gone; dirt is clean in Varley's future. In "The Phantom of Kansas" if you get murdered you will still live again through memory recording and cloning. In "The Black Hole Passes" your girlfriend—hitherto sealed with a holographic kiss—will cobble together a flying chair to rescue you from the void for bathtub sex, so that the actual threat of the story evaporates and nobody feels any pain. (By contrast, in "Air Raid" people *do* feel pain, and it endures. This story was published pseudonymously, as though Varley felt unconsciously obligated to separate himself from it.)

Varley tends to forget details selectively (such as the black hole victim's source of nourishment); he looks the other way, or his tales might not be as cosy as, at heart, they are. Yet there is a genuine inventive power. His symbiotic space-going vegetables are a persuasive invention, not merely a bit of fantasy. And there is genuine emotion: Varley does indeed pluck the heart strings in "In the Hall of the Martian Kings" when his Martian relief expedition turn up to find, not corpses, but a wrap-around plastic paradise and hibernating Martians. He skims very close to schmaltziness, but his story succeeds. "The Persistence of Vision" itself conveys a sense of mature inadequacy—and is thoughtful, tragic, and heartwracking as a result, though one wonders whether Varley is quite aware that it is a tragic story.

"The Persistence of Vision" still shares the B-feature narrative tone characteristic of Varley—for he is certainly no stylist. Nevertheless, his flaws do not matter as much as they might in another writer; one disregards them, wooed as much by the ultimate sense of security as dazzled by the ideas. Varley is a bit of an alchemist: he constantly turns lead into gold, even though the lead is always threatening to turn back again, and even doing so.

—Ian Watson

VERNON, Roger Lee. American. Born in 1924. Educated at Northwestern University, Evanston, Illinois, M.A. High School teacher, Chicago.

SCIENCE-FICTION PUBLICATIONS

Novel

Robot Hunt. New York, Avalon, 1959.

Short Stories

The Space Frontier. New York, New American Library, 1955.

* * *

Roger Lee Vernon's first book was a collection of nine rather routine stories, *The Space Frontier.* Several of the stories displayed such idiosyncratic style and lack of good narrative techniques that it is a wonder they saw print at all, yet others bear at least the rudiments of careful plotting. "Battle," for example, is exactly that, a glimpse of rather unimaginative future combat, replete with invented terms and stiff military conversation. But "The Chess Civilization" is a reasonably well-thought-out story of an alternate world where chess is the most important thing in all of existence, and all interhuman relations are molded by reference to the game. There are bits of wry satire as well. For the most part, the stories all reflect the concerns of their time. In one, humans discover a means to lie telepathically to alien telepaths; in others men are confronted with a robot city or a globe-spanning plant tests the human mettle.

There is some indication that Vernon might have become a better writer if his career had continued. His only novel, *Robot Hunt*, is a routinely readable story of spies and political corruption in the future. Military secrets have been stolen, apparently by one of several otherwise identical robots. The protagonists have only a matter of hours to recover the secret and avert a world war. Vernon spends time developing his characters, with some effect, and though the novel never really rises above its limited aspirations it is significantly improved over the earlier volume.

—Don D'Ammassa

VERRILL, A(lpheus) Hyatt. Also wrote as Ray Ainsbury.

American. Born in New Haven, Connecticut, 23 July 1871. Educated at Yale University School of Fine Arts, New Haven; studied zoology with his father. Married 1) Kathryn L. McCarthy in 1892, four children; 2) Lida Ruth Shaw in 1944. Natural history illustrator for *Webster's International Dictionary*, 1896, and for *Clarendon Dictionary*; invented the autochrome process of photography, 1902; explorer and archaeologist: lived in Domenica, 1903-06, British Guiana, 1913-17, and Panama, 1917-21, and made expeditions to Central and South America, the West Indies, and Mexico, to 1950; did undersea excavation in the West Indies, 1933-34; established the Anhlarka experimental gardens and natural science museum, Florida, 1940; established shell business, Lake Worth, Florida, 1944. *Died 14 November 1954.*

SCIENCE-FICTION PUBLICATIONS

Novels

Uncle Abner's Legacy. New York, Holt, 1915.
The Golden City (juvenile). New York, Duffield, 1916.
The Trail of the Cloven Foot (juvenile). New York, Dutton, 1918.
The Tail of the White Indians (juvenile). New York, Dutton, 1920.
The Boy Adventurers in the Land of the Monkey Men (juvenile). New York, Putnam, 1923.
The Bridge of Light. Reading, Pennsylvania, Fantasy Press, 1950.
When the Moon Ran Wild (as Ray Ainsbury). London, Consul, 1962.

Uncollected Short Stories

"Beyond the Pole," in *Amazing* (New York), October 1926.
"Through the Crater's Rim," in *Amazing* (New York), December 1926.
"The Man Who Could Vanish," in *Amazing* (New York), January 1927.
"The Plague of the Living Dead," in *Amazing* (New York), April 1927.
"The Voice from the Inner World," in *Amazing* (New York), July 1927.
"The Ultra-Elixir of Youth," in *Amazing* (New York), August 1927.
"The Astounding Discoveries of Doctor Mentiroso," in *Amazing* (New York), November 1927.
"The Psychological Solution," in *Amazing* (New York), January 1928.
"The King of the Monkey Men," in *Amazing Stories Quarterly* (New York), Spring 1928.
"The World of the Giant Ants," in *Amazing Stories Quarterly* (New York), Fall 1928.
"Into the Green Prism," in *Amazing* (New York), March 1929.
"Death from the Skies," in *Amazing* (New York), October 1929.
"Vampires of the Desert," in *Amazing* (New York), December 1929.
"Beyond the Green Prism," in *Amazing* (New York), January 1930.
"The Feathered Detective," in *Amazing* (New York), April 1930.
"The Non-Gravitational Vortex," in *Amazing* (New York), June 1930.
"Monsters of the Ray," in *Amazing Stories Quarterly* (New York), Summer 1930.
"A Visit to Suari," in *Amazing* (New York), July 1930.
"The Dirigibles of Death," in *Amazing Stories Quarterly* (New York), Winter 1930.
"The Exterminator," in *Amazing* (New York), February 1931.
"The Treasures of the Golden God," in *Amazing* (New York), January 1933.
"The Death Drum," in *Amazing* (New York), May 1933.
"Through the Andes," in *Amazing* (New York), September 1934.
"The Inner World," in *Amazing* (New York), June 1935.
"The Mummy of Ret-Seh," in *Fantastic Adventures* (New York), May 1939.

OTHER PUBLICATIONS

Novels (juvenile)

The American Crusoe. New York, Dodd Mead, 1914.

The Cruise of the Cormorant. New York, Holt, 1915.
In Morgan's Wake. New York, Holt, 1915.
Marooned in the Forest. New York, Harper, 1916.
Jungle Chums. New York, Holt, 1916.
The Boy Adventurers in the Forbidden Land [*in the Land of El Dorado, in the Unknown Land*]. New York, Putnam, 3 vols., 1922-24.
The Deep Sea Hunters [*in the Frozen Sea, in the South Seas*]. New York, Appleton, 3 vols., 1922-24.
The Radio Detectives [*in the Jungle, Southward Bound, under the Sea*]. New York, Appleton, 4 vols., 1922.
Barton's Mills: A Saga of the Pioneers. New York, Appleton, 1932.
The Incas' Treasure House. Boston, Page, 1932; London, Harrap, 1936.
Before the Conquerors. New York, Dodd Mead, 1935.
The Treasure of the Bloody Gut. New York, Putnam, 1937.

Other

Gasolene Engines: Their Operation, Use, and Care. New York, Henley, 1912.
Knots, Splices, and Rope Work. New York, Henley, 1912; revised edition, 1917, 1922.
Harper's Book for Young Naturalists [*Gardeners*]. New York, Harper, 2 vols., 1913-14.
Harper's Wireless [*Aircraft, Gasoline Engine*] *Book.* New York, Harper, 3 vols., 1913-14.
Cuba Past and Present. New York, Dodd Mead, 1914; revised edition, 1920.
South and Central American Trade Conditions of Today. New York, Dodd Mead, 1914; revised edition, 1919.
Porto Rico Past and Present. New York, Dodd Mead, 1914.
Pets for Pleasure and Profit. New York, Scribner, 1915.
The Boys' Outdoor Vacation Book. New York, Dodd Mead, 1915.
The Amateur Carpenter. New York, Dodd Mead, 1915.
The Boy Collector's Handbook. New York, McBride, 1915.
Isles of Spice and Palm. New York, Appleton, 1915.
A-B-C of Automobile Driving. New York, Harper, 1916.
The Real Story of the Whaler. New York, Appleton, 1916.
The Ocean and Its Mysteries. New York, Duffield, 1916.
The Book of the Motor Boat [*Sailboat*]. New York, Appleton, 2 vols., 1916.
The Book of the West Indies. New York, Dutton, 1917.
The Book of Camping. New York, Knopf, 1917.
How to Operate a Motor Car. Philadelphia, McKay, 1918.
Getting Together with Latin America. New York, Dutton, 1918.
Islands and Their Mysteries. New York, Duffield, 1920; London, Melrose, 1922.
Panama, Past and Present. New York, Dodd Mead, 1921.
The Boys' Book of Whalers [*Carpentry, Buccaneers*]. New York, Dodd Mead, 3 vols., 1922-23.
Radio for Amateurs. New York, Dodd Mead, and London, Heinemann, 1922.
Rivers and Their Mysteries. New York, Duffield, 1922.
The Home Radio. New York, Harper, 1922; revised edition, 1924; revised edition, as *The Home Radio Up to Date*, with E.E. Verrill, 1927.
In the Wake of the Buccaneers. New York, Century, and London, Parsons, 1923.
The Real Story of the Pirate. New York, Appleton, 1923.
Smugglers and Smuggling. New York, Duffield, and London, Allen and Unwin, 1924.
Love Stories of Some Famous Pirates. London, Collins, 1924.
Panama [*Cuba, Jamaica, West Indies*] *of Today.* New York, Dodd Mead, 4 vols., 1927-31.
The American Indian. New York, Appleton, 1927.
Old Civilization of the New World. Indianapolis, Bobbs Merrill, and London, Williams and Norgate, 1929.
Thirty Years in the Jungle. London, Lane, 1929.
Great Conquerors of South and Central America. New York, Appleton, 1929.
Lost Treasure. New York, Appleton, 1930.
Gasoline-Engine Book for Boys. New York, Harper, 1930.

Under Peruvian Skies. London, Hurst and Blackett, 1930.
Secret Treasure. New York, Appleton, 1931.
The Inquisition. New York, Appleton, 1931.
Romantic and Historic Maine [*Florida, Virginia*]. New York, Dodd Mead, 3 vols., 1933-35.
Our Indians. New York, Putnam, 1935.
They Found Gold. New York and London, Putnam, 1936; as *Carib Gold*, London, Collins, 1939.
The Heart of Old New England. New York, Dodd Mead, 1936.
Along New England Shores. New York, Putnam, 1936.
Strange Sea Shells [*Insects, Reptiles, Birds, Fish, Animals*] *and Their Stories.* Boston, Page, and London, Harrap, 6 vols., 1936-39.
My Jungle Trails. Boston, Page, and London, Harrap, 1937.
Foods America Gave the World. Boston, Page, 1937.
Minerals, Metals, and Gems. Boston, Page, 1939.
Wonder Plants and Plant Wonders. New York, Appleton Century, 1939.
Perfumes and Spices. Boston, Page, 1940.
Wonder Creatures of the Sea. New York, Appleton Century, 1940.
Strange Prehistoric Animals and Their Stories. Boston, Page, 1948.
The Strange Story of Our Earth. Boston, Page, 1952.
America's Ancient Civilization, with R. Verrill. New York and London, Putnam, 1954.

*   *   *

A. Hyatt Verrill was one of the more distinguished writers who helped in the development of *Amazing Stories* during its early years, and who continued to contribute to it until the mid-1930's. Many of his stories were set in the South American jungles with which he was so familiar, or dealt with ancient civilisations whose cultures he studied for more than half a century. But he did not limit himself to such themes, drawing on astronomy, biology, optics, atomic physics, and fourth-dimension theory for ideas which he developed with equal facility.

The magazine was only six months old when his first offering, "Beyond the Pole," dealing with a race of intelligent crustaceans discovered in the Antarctic, appeared late in 1926. It compared favourably with the stories of Wells and Verne which almost monopolised those early issues, while the editor, Hugo Gernsback, contrived to nurture new writers to displace them. Some of Verrill's longer stories went to fill out the inch-thick *Amazing Stories Quarterly*; "The World of the Giant Ants" was remarkable for its engrossing narrative combined with an enlightening insight into its subject. Even more fascinating was "Into the Green Prism," with its sequel, "Beyond the Green Prism," which sought to dispel the storm of controversy over the scientific fallacies it raised. "The Astounding Discoveries of Doctor Mentiroso" began the endless argument in the readers' columns over the time-travel theme. "Death from the Skies" was about a bombardment of Earth by the Martians, and "The Bridge of Light" took readers to a hidden city where the Mayas still thrived. Verrill's flights of imagination reached their peak in 1931 with "Monsters of the Ray" and "When the Moon Ran Wild"; but his later contributions, such as "The Death Drum" and "Through the Andes," were pure adventure tales which reflected the gradual decline of *Amazing*.

—Walter Gillings

VIDAL, (Eugene Luther) Gore. Also writes as Edgar Box. American. Born in West Point, New York, 3 October 1925. Educated at Los Alamos School, New Mexico, 1939-40; Phillips Exeter Academy, New Hampshire, 1940-43. Served in the United States Army, 1943-46. Editor, E.P. Dutton, publishers, New York, 1946. Member, Advisory Board, *Partisan Review*, New Brunswick, New

Jersey, 1960-71; Democratic-Liberal candidate for Congress, New York, 1960; Member, President's Advisory Committee on the Arts, 1961-63; Co-Chairman, New Party, 1968-71. Address: Via di Torre Argentina 21, Rome, Italy.

SCIENCE-FICTION PUBLICATIONS

Novels

Messiah. New York, Dutton, 1954; London, Heinemann, 1955; revised edition, Boston, Little Brown, 1965; Heinemann, 1968.
Myra Breckinridge. Boston, Little Brown, and London, Blond, 1968.
Myron. New York, Random House, 1974; London, Heinemann, 1975.
Kalki. New York, Random House, and London, Heinemann, 1978.

OTHER PUBLICATIONS

Novels

Williwaw. New York, Dutton, 1946; London, Panther, 1965.
In a Yellow Wood. New York, Dutton, 1947; London, New English Library, 1967.
The City and the Pillar. New York, Dutton, 1948; London, Lehmann, 1949; revised edition, Dutton, and London, Heinemann, 1965.
The Season of Comfort. New York, Dutton, 1949.
Dark Green, Bright Red. New York, Dutton, and London, Lehmann, 1950.
A Search for the King: A Twelfth Century Legend. New York, Dutton, 1950; London, New English Library, 1967.
The Judgment of Paris. New York, Dutton, 1952; London, Heinemann, 1953; revised edition, Boston, Little Brown, 1965; London, Heinemann, 1966.
Julian. Boston, Little Brown, and London, Heinemann, 1964.
Washington, D.C. Boston, Little Brown, and London, Heinemann, 1967.
Two Sisters: A Memoir in the Form of a Novel. Boston, Little Brown, and London, Heinemann, 1970.
Burr. New York, Random House, 1973; London, Heinemann, 1974.
1876. New York, Random House, and London, Heinemann, 1976.
Creation. New York, Random House, 1981.

Novels as Edgar Box

Death in the Fifth Position. New York, Dutton, 1952; London, Heinemann, 1954.
Death Before Bedtime. New York, Dutton, 1953; London, Heinemann, 1954.
Death Likes It Hot. New York, Dutton, 1954; London, Heinemann, 1955.

Short Stories

A Thirsty Evil: Seven Short Stories. New York, Zero Press, 1956; London, Heinemann, 1958.

Plays

Visit to a Small Planet (televised, 1955). Included in *Visit to a Small Planet and Other Television Plays*, 1956; revised version (produced New York, 1957; London, 1960), Boston, Little Brown, 1957; in *Three Plays*, 1962.
Honor (televised, 1956). Published in *Television Plays for Writers: Eight Television Plays*, edited by A.S. Burack, Boston, The Writer, 1957; revised edition, as *On the March to the Sea: A Southron Comedy* (produced Bonn, Germany, 1961), in *Three Plays*, 1962.

Visit to a Small Planet and Other Television Plays (includes *Barn Burning, Dark Possession, The Death of Billy the Kid, A Sense of Justice, Smoke, Summer Pavilion, The Turn of the Screw*). Boston, Little Brown, 1956.
The Best Man: A Play about Politics (produced New York, 1960). Boston, Little Brown, 1960; in *Three Plays*, 1962.
Three Plays (*Visit to a Small Planet, The Best Man, On the March to the Sea*). London, Heinemann, 1962.
Romulus: A New Comedy, adaptation of a play of Friedrich Dürrenmatt (produced New York, 1962). New York, Dramatists Play Service, 1962.
Weekend (produced New York, 1968). New York, Dramatists Play Service, 1968.
An Evening with Richard Nixon and ... (produced New York, 1972). New York, Random House, 1972.

Screenplays: *The Catered Affair*, 1956; *I Accuse*, 1958; *The Scapegoat*, with Robert Hamer, 1959; *Suddenly Last Summer*, with Tennessee Williams, 1960; *The Best Man*, 1964; *Is Paris Burning?*, with Francis Ford Coppola, 1966; *Last of the Mobile Hot-Shots*, 1970.

Television Plays: *Barn Burning*, from the story by Faulkner, 1954; *Dark Possession*, 1954; *Smoke*, from the story by Faulkner, 1954; *Visit to a Small Planet*, 1955; *The Death of Billy the Kid*, 1955; *A Sense of Justice*, 1955; *Summer Pavilion*, 1955; *The Turn of the Screw*, from the story by Henry James, 1955; *Honor*, 1956; *The Indestructible Mr. Gore*, 1960.

Other

Rocking the Boat (essays). Boston, Little Brown, 1962; London, Heinemann, 1963.
Sex, Death and Money. New York, Bantam, 1968.
Reflections upon a Sinking Ship (essays). Boston, Little Brown, and London, Heinemann, 1969.
Homage to Daniel Shays: Collected Essays, 1952-1972. New York, Random House, 1972; as *Collected Essays, 1952-1972*, London, Heinemann, 1974.
Matters of Fact and of Fiction: Essays 1973-1976. New York, Random House, and London, Heinemann, 1977.
Great American Families, with others. New York, Norton, and London, Times Books, 1977.
Views from a Window: Conversations with Gore Vidal, with Robert J. Stanton. Secaucus, New Jersey, Stuart, 1980.

Editor, *Best Television Plays.* New York, Ballantine, 1956.

* * *

Only a part of Gore Vidal's varied literary production strongly relates to science fiction and fantasy: two plays, *An Evening with Richard Nixon* and *Visit to a Small Planet*, and four novels, *Messiah, Myra Breckinridge, Myron*, and *Kalki*. Vidal's "Edgar Box" detective novels resemble science-fiction formula writing, while his many historical novels, *Julian, Washington, D.C., Burr*, and *1876*, have some Utopian elements, particularly *Julian*, where Vidal speculates about the possibility of the development of the West out of the grip of Christianity. *1876* is vaguely Utopian, but resembles a Henry James novel with Europeanized Americans, Charles and the Princess, socially evaluating the politics and manners of the United States while pursuing marriage for the Princess and a writing career for Charles.

An Evening with Richard Nixon, dramatically showing the high points of Nixon's career, does so by framing Nixon's own words and some fictional dialogue and action with a chorus and narrative commentary by former Presidents George Washington, John Kennedy, and Dwight Eisenhower. These fantastic characters are used for satiric purposes, not only by their views of Nixon but by their views of one another. Only Washington seems genuinely decent; the others are mocked. The play *Visit to a Small Planet* uses a typical science-fiction action, alien invasion, for satiric purposes. What is devalued by Kreton, unintentionally because he loves it, is man's hostility. By performing a miracle of telekinesis, Kreton nearly starts a war between Russia and the United States, prevented only by Delton 4, who as deus ex machina, hauls Kreton (cretin) away, bending time prior to Kreton's visit. Of course, Kreton's plan depends on destructive human passion, which projects hostility from a visit, glories in hate, and is secretive about love, as the Conrad-Ellen plot illustrates.

Messiah, a memoir by Eugene Luther, is a futuristic retelling of the Christ story and the development of Christianity, except the Good News by John Cave, the Christ figure, is that death is good. Luther, writing about the year 2000 in Luxor, Egypt about his involvement with Cave, recounts his relationships with Clarissa, a witch-like woman supposedly over 2000 years old, Iris, who becomes a new Virgin Mary, and Paul Himmel, a PR version of St. Paul. In an opening similar to H.G. Wells's *War of the Worlds*, Marx, Freud, and modern science have failed to organize the world well, so a new mystic, John Cave, argues that death is a friend to be embraced. Luther likes the message, but sees it as the existentialists would, that life's value increases because of death. As Cave is forced to practice what he preaches and is killed, Eugene is forced to flee the Cavites, realizing later that he should have been the Messiah.

Myra Breckinridge, also a memoir, is a comic, Frankenstein-like sex-change story. Though treated as soft pornography, Vidal's satiric targets are frequently sophisticated, such as Robbe-Grillet's theories of anthropomorphic projection in *For a New Novel*. When Myra says "Nothing is *like* anything else. Things are themselves entirely and do not need interpretation, only a minimal respect for their precise integrity," Robbe-Grillet is being reduced. Though the novel's action climaxes with Myra's sodomizing of Rusty and winning her inheritance from Buck Loner, as Myra goes through two sex changes, the satire caused by her alien encounter with the world is subtly clever. *Myron*, the sequel to *Myra Breckinridge*, uses a staple of fantasy, the alternate universe, as Myron is pushed into his television set while watching *Siren of Babylon* by the suppressed personality of Myra. As Myron seeks to return to his wife, Mary Ann, by finding the exit to the film in production, Myra seeks to change cinematic history, thereby changing cultural history—even Watergate and the election of Richard Nixon. Myra, as many science-fiction authors have fabulated, is trying to manipulate the present by changing the past.

Kalki is a dystopian novel in which a former GI poses as the Hindu god Kalki and poisons the world population except for four chosen followers. Though a mystery plot dominates the novel with its two catastrophes, the poisoning and the doublecross of Kelly by Giles, Vidal's social concerns are still present. The memoir and additional narrative voices, common in *Two Sisters*, *Julian*, *Messiah*, and other Vidal novels, combine with science-fiction and Utopian strategies so that Vidal's satire, his social criticism and liberal social message, appears with the ease of Petronius and the power of Juvenal. Though he is primarily a realistic novelist, one can expect Vidal to continue to experiment with science fiction, Utopian fiction, and fantasy, for they are all strategies of his primary aim, satire.

—Craig Wallace Barrow

VINCENT, Harl. Pseudonym for Harold Vincent Schoepflin. American. Born in Buffalo, New York, in 1893. Married; one daughter. Engineer and free-lance writer. *Died 5 May 1968.*

SCIENCE-FICTION PUBLICATIONS

Novel

The Doomsday Planet. New York, Belmont, 1966.

Uncollected Short Stories

"The Golden Girl of Munan," in *Amazing* (New York), June 1928.

"The Ambassador from Mars," in *Amazing* (New York), September 1928.

"The War of the Planets," in *Amazing* (New York), January 1929.

"Venus Liberated," in *Amazing Stories Quarterly* (New York), Summer 1929.

"The Menace from Below," in *Science Wonder Stories* (New York), July 1929.

"Barton's Island," in *Amazing* (New York), August 1929.

"Yellow Air Peril," in *Air Wonder Stories* (New York), September 1929.

"Through the Air Tunnel," in *Air Wonder Stories* (New York), October 1929.

"The Microcosmic Buccaneers," in *Amazing* (New York), November 1929.

"The Colloidal Nemesis," in *Amazing* (New York), December 1929.

"The Seventh Generation," in *Amazing Stories Quarterly* (New York), Winter 1929.

"Old Crompton's Secret," in *Astounding* (New York), February 1930.

"Callistro at War," in *Amazing* (New York), March 1930.

"Before the Asteroids," in *Science Wonder Stories* (New York), March 1930.

"The Return to Subterrania," in *Science Wonder Stories* (New York), April 1930.

"The Terror of Air-Level Six," in *Astounding* (New York), July 1930.

"Silver Dome," in *Astounding* (New York), August 1930.

"Free Energy," in *Amazing* (New York), September 1930.

"Vagabonds of Space," in *Astounding* (New York), November 1930.

"Gray Denim," in *Astounding* (New York), December 1930.

"Tanks under the Sea," in *Amazing* (New York), January 1931.

"Terrors Unseen," in *Astounding* (New York), March 1931.

"Invisible Ships," in *Amazing Stories Quarterly* (New York), April 1931.

"Too Many Boards," in *Amazing* (New York), April 1931.

"Beyond the Dark Nebula," in *Argosy* (New York), 4 April 1931.

"The Moon Weed," in *Astounding* (New York), August 1931.

"The Copper-Clad World," in *Astounding* (New York), September 1931.

"Red Twilight," in *Argosy* (New York), 12 September 1931.

"A Matter of Ethics," in *Amazing* (New York), October 1931.

"Sky Corps," with Charles Roy Cox, in *Amazing* (New York), December 1931.

"Power," in *Amazing* (New York), January 1932.

"Creatures of Vibration," in *Astounding* (New York), January 1932.

"Water-Bound World," in *Amazing Stories Quarterly* (New York), Spring-Summer 1932.

"Vulcan's Workshop," in *Astounding* (New York), June 1932.

"Thia of the Drylands," in *Amazing* (New York), July 1932.

"Faster than Light," in *Amazing Stories Quarterly* (New York), Fall-Winter 1932.

"Roadways of Mars," in *Amazing* (New York), December 1932.

"Once in a Blue Moon," in *Amazing Stories Quarterly* (New York), Winter 1932.

"Wanderer of Infinity," in *Astounding* (New York), March 1933.

"When the Comet Returned," in *Amazing* (New York), April 1933.

"Cavern of Thunders," in *Amazing* (New York), July 1933.

"Whisper of Death," in *Amazing* (New York), November 1933.

"Telegraph Plateau," in *Astounding* (New York), November 1933.

"Master of Dreams," in *Amazing* (New York), January 1934.

"Lost City of Mars," in *Astounding* (New York), February 1934.

"Cat's Eye," in *Amazing* (New York), April 1934.

"The Barrier," in *Amazing* (New York), September 1934.

"Cosmic Rhythm," in *Astounding* (New York), October 1934.

"The Explorers of Callistro," in *Amazing* (New York), January 1935.

"Energy," in *Astounding* (New York), January 1935.

"Valley of the Rukh," in *Amazing* (New York), February 1935.

"The Plane Compass," in *Astounding* (New York), June 1935.

"Parasite," in *Amazing* (New York), July 1935.

"Return of the Prowler," in *Astounding* (New York), November 1938.

"Prince Deru Returns," in *Amazing* (New York), December 1938.

"Newscast," in *Marvel* (New York), April-May 1939.
"The Devil Flower," in *Fantastic Adventures* (New York), May 1939.
"The Morons," in *Astounding* (New York), June 1939.
"The Mystery of the Collapsing Skyscrapers," in *Amazing* (New York), August 1939.
"Lightning Strikes Once," in *Marvel* (New York), August 1939.
"Power Plant," in *Astounding* (New York), November 1939.
"Neutral Vessel," in *Astounding* (New York), January 1940.
"High Frequency War," in *Astounding* (New York), February 1940.
"Undersea Prisoner," in *Amazing* (New York), February 1940.
"Gravity Island," in *Super Science* (Kokomo, Indiana), March 1940.
"Master Control," in *Astonishing* (Chicago), April 1940.
"Deputy Correspondent," in *Astounding* (New York), June 1940.
"Trouble Shooter," in *Super Science* (Kokomo, Indiana), July 1940.
"OtherWorld," in *Astonishing* (Chicago), October 1940.
"Lunar Station," in *Comet* (Springfield, Massachusetts), January 1941.
"Grave of the Achilles," in *Captain Future* (New York), Winter 1941.
"Voice from the Void," in *Amazing* (New York), June 1942.
"Life Inside a Wall," in *The Moon Conquerors*. London, Swan, 1943.
"Rex," in *The Coming of the Robots*, edited by Sam Moskowitz. New York, Macmillan, 1963.
"Prowler of the Wastelands," in *Strange Signposts*, edited by Roger Elwood and Sam Moskowitz. New York, Holt Rinehart, 1966.
"Invader," in *If* (New York), September 1967.
"Lethal Planetoid," in *Spaceway* (Alhambra, California), January 1969.
"Space Storm," in *Famous Science Fiction* (New York), Spring 1969.

* * *

Of Harl Vincent's stories, few are familiar to the present generation of readers. With the possible exception of "Barton's Island," none of his tales has been granted "classic" status, and most of his output was of an order consistent with the pulps of the 1930's. Yet he will be remembered by a few as a writer who, even when conforming to strict editorial policies (which he did with remarkable facility), never failed to evoke the sense of wonder which is vital to science fiction.

Following his initial appearance in 1928 with "The Golden Girl of Munan," he soon became a favourite with *Amazing Stories* readers. His full-length novel, "Venus Liberated," was typical: a tale of interplanetary adventure, full of incident, yet told with restraint and with equal regard for both scientific and romantic interest. "Barton's Island," the story of an inventive genius at odds with a future dictator, revealed a penchant for novel variations on more realistic themes. In "The Colloidal Nemesis" the War of Extermination ended abruptly in 1953 when the Western Alliance let loose on the Asiatics a monstrous mass of devouring protoplasm. He was not so original that he could ignore the note of menace which resounded through science fiction's pages in those days. As well as arriving from Callisto, the threat lurked among the super-apes of Subterrania, or loomed up from the microcosmos. But his ideas were so diverse and his hand so adroit that, having catered equally to *Science Wonder* and *Air Wonder Stories*, he was able to produce a string of lusty tales for the new *Astounding* which further enlarged the field in 1930. "Vagabonds of Space" and "The Copper-Clad World" were typical of the formalised space opera on which the magazine relied for much of its appeal.

Meanwhile, *Amazing* continued to feature Vincent's work in more reflective mood, as "Power," a significant tale of conflicting forces in 23rd-century New York which hinted at nuclear fission as a new source of energy. Several of his stories at this period were set in the "drylands" of Mars, among the superstitious savages of the parched plains between the canals ("Red Twilight" and "Beyond the Dark Nebula"). "Faster Than Light" brought back the heroes who had liberated Venus for another adventure in remoter realms.

When *Astounding* reappeared under new management towards the end of 1933, Vincent was among those who found their way back

into its pages. But, except for "Cosmic Rhythm," he was not particularly successful in meeting its "thought-variant" demands; and some of his more interesting concepts, such as "Parasite," were still to be found in *Amazing*. By 1942 he seemed to have given up writing; but in 1966 he made a brief comeback with *The Doomsday Planet*, an interplanetary adventure.

—Walter Gillings

VINGE, Joan (Carol) D(ennison). American. Born in Baltimore, Maryland, 2 April 1948. Educated at San Diego State University, B.A. in anthropology 1971. Married Vernor Vinge, *q.v.*, in 1972. Salvage archaeologist, San Diego County, 1971. Recipient: Hugo Award, 1978. Agent: Frances Collin, Rodell-Collin Literary Agency, 156 East 52nd Street, New York, New York 10022. Address: 31 Third Place, Brooklyn, New York 11231, U.S.A.

SCIENCE-FICTION PUBLICATIONS

Novels

The Outcasts of Heaven Belt. New York, New American Library, 1978.
The Snow Queen. New York, Dial Press, and London, Sidgwick and Jackson, 1980.

Short Stories

Fireship. New York, Dell, 1978; London, Sidgwick and Jackson, 1981.
Eyes of Amber and Other Stories. New York, New American Library, 1979.

Uncollected Short Story

"Voices from the Dust," in *Destinies* (New York), April 1980.

OTHER PUBLICATIONS

Other

Editor, with Steven G. Sprukill, *Binary Star 4*. New York, Dell, 1980.

*

Manuscript Collection: Elizabeth Chater Science Fiction Collection, San Diego State University.

Joan D. Vinge comments:
Because I have a degree in anthropology, I tend to write anthropological science fiction, with an emphasis on the interaction of different cultures (human and alien) and of individual people to their surroundings. The importance of communication across barriers of alienness often becomes a theme in my stories. Mythology and music also influence my work; my novel *The Snow Queen* was in large part inspired by Robert Graves's *The White Goddess*. I have written several stories with a "hard" science background, thanks to the borrowed expertise of my husband, who is a mathematician and also a science-fiction writer; however, I've written other stories which I hope cover a wide range of moods and styles. I feel as if I'm just beginning to explore the infinite possibilities of the future.

* * *

Joan D. Vinge, whose first published work appeared in 1974, is already recognized as among the best new writers of science fiction.

Most of her works feature strong women characters, and a recurrent theme is the difficulty of communication—among human beings as well as between humans and other life forms. Her background in anthropology shows in the carefully created and detailed social structures of her fictional worlds. Vinge's best works are in the novella form she favors.

Fireship includes two novellas. "Fireship" is atypical in its comic elements. Set on Mars, it relates the adventures of Ethan Ring, a conglomerate personality created when a sophisticated computer was plugged into an insignificant lab assistant. Ring matches wits with Khorram Kabir, an Arab shiek who controls most of Earth after World War III. "Mother and Child" is set in a future that resembles our medieval past; it is basically a love story with an overlay of SF elements. The beautiful princess Etaa is stolen from her husband by a neighboring king, only to be stolen from the king by an alien xenobiologist sent to intervene in human progress. The power of human love to survive betrayal, separation, and loss in an everchanging world is hauntingly rendered.

The Outcasts of Heaven Belt has a feminist theme. Betha Torgussen pilots the starship *Ranger* from her home planet Morningside to Heaven Belt in search of ores and gases. She discovers that civil war has wasted the riches of Heaven Belt and left only two feuding societies: the degraded democracy, the Demarchy, and the military socialist state of the Ringers, Grand Harmony. Both are contrasted unfavorably with Morningside's social system based on multiple marriage and kinship clans. The novel is interesting but not as good as Vinge's shorter works.

The six stories in *Eyes of Amber and Other Stories* are Vinge's best work. The award-winning "Eyes of Amber" tells of an alien woman, T'uupieh, who discovers on her homeworld Titan a space probe launched from Earth and mistakes it for a demon. Attempts of human linguists to communicate with her to alter her behavior reflect their deeply entrenched desires to impose human value structures on other species and cultures. In "To Bell the Cat" a human criminal learns to communicate with tiny, complex aliens and tries to protect them from human experimenters. The story plays off the legend of the mice who tried to bell a cat so they would know when it was coming. In the only true short story Vinge has written, "View from a Height," a woman born with no immune responses volunteers to go on a one-way space mission into infinity. Her trip is a metaphor for our lives; we are all aliens on a one-way trip to death. "Media Man," set in Heaven Belt, the world of Vinge's novel, presents a media man of the future who regains his integrity and loses his job and the woman he loves. "The Crystal Ship" is by Vinge's own admission the most depressing she has ever written. Its view of human nature is all too familiar: human fear of alien life forms is so great that humans will refuse to learn from other species even when those species could help resolve problems of human society. The charming "Tin Soldier" is based, Vinge says, on the song "Brandy," about a woman who stays home and waits for her man who goes to sea. In Vinge's story, the Woman Brandy is a spacer, and Maris, the cyborg-tin soldier of the tale, stays in port in New Piraeus, waiting for her. Unlike the Hans Christian Andersen fairy tale it resembles, the story ends happily.

All Vinge's works are conceptually rich and superbly crafted; hers is a major talent.

—Anne Hudson Jones

VINGE, Vernor (Steffen). American. Born in Waukesha, Wisconsin, 2 October 1944. Educated at Michigan State University, East Lansing, M.S. 1966; University of California, San Diego, M.A. 1968, Ph.D. 1971. Married Joan Carol Dennison (i.e., Joan D. Vinge, *q.v.*), in 1972. Since 1972, Assistant Professor of Mathematics, San Diego State University. Address: 6439 Jackson Drive, San Diego, California 92119, U.S.A.

SCIENCE-FICTION PUBLICATIONS

Novels

Grimm's World. New York, Berkley, 1976; London, Hamlyn, 1978.
The Witling. New York, DAW, and London, Dobson, 1976.
True Names, in *Binary Star 5.* New York, Dell, 1981.

Uncollected Short Stories

"Apartness," in *World's Best Science Fiction 1966*, edited by Donald A. Wollheim and Terry Carr. New York, Ace, 1966.
"The Accomplice," in *If* (New York), April 1967.
"Bookworm, Run!," in *Analog 6*, edited by John W. Campbell, Jr. New York, Doubleday, 1968.
"Conquest by Default," in *Analog* (New York), May 1968.
"The Science Fair," in *Orbit 9*, edited by Damon Knight. New York, Putnam, 1971.
"Just Peace," in *Analog* (New York), December 1971.
"Original Sin," in *Analog* (New York), December 1972.
"Long Shot," in *Best Science Fiction Stories of the Year 1972*, edited by Lester del Rey. New York, Dutton, 1973.
"Bomb Scare," in *Tomorrow, and Tomorrow, and Tomorrow...*, edited by B. Heintz and others. New York, Holt Rinehart, 1974.
"The Whirligig of Time," in *Stellar 1*, edited by Judy-Lynn del Rey. New York, Ballantine, 1974.
"The Peddler's Apprentice," in *Best Science Fiction Stories of the Year 1975*, edited by Lester del Rey. New York, Dutton, 1976.

*   *   *

Vernor Vinge is not a prolific writer but his significance is considerably greater than the size of his output because of the high quality of much of his work. Especially in his best stories, Vinge deals with extreme social situations, with crises within a society or with intercultural conflict. Much of his work is permeated with a melancholy awareness of the evanescence of all human institutions. Typically, Vinge's characters are faced with some personal problem arising out of social change. They furnish the best possible solution given the initial conditions, but it is never more than a half-solution, and they must live with their failure as well as with their success.

The early story "Apartness" sets the pattern for many to follow. Two hundred years after the North World War has obliterated half the globe, a Sudamérican expedition to Antarctica discovers descendants of the last surviving Afrikaner whites, now savages starving on the Palmer Peninsula. An anthropologist fears that when the black Zulunders learn of these survivals they will exterminate them too, but eventually a Zulunder diplomat assures him that his people will take more satisfaction in the Afrikaner descendants' present misery than they would in their destruction. We are left with the implication that this festering hatred may yet lead to a fourth world war. A somewhat less effective sequel, "Conquest by Default," puts the shoe on the other foot. Some decades after the time of "Apartness," extraterrestrials with an overwhelming technological advantage arrive and prepare to colonize the depopulated regions of Earth. Almost as an afterthought, they agree to grant equal rights in the new order to Terrestrials, but human culture is inevitably doomed to transformation beyond recognition. Vinge depicts the virtues and defects of the aliens' anarcho-capitalistic social system in impressive detail.

Vinge's most significant work is his novel *Grimm's World*, set on a retrogressed colony planet now climbing back to high technology, and centering on the intrigues and struggles of a native-born superwoman whose only intellectual equals are two visitors from a higher interstellar culture. The novel focuses our greatest sympathy not on the superhumans but on the ordinary people caught up in their machinations. The various cultures of this largely archipelagic, metal-poor world, and especially its alternative technologies, are described in fascinating elaboration. The more recent *The Witling* has many of the same story elements (covert interplanetary visitors, an emotionally crippled woman genius, a person of ordinary capacity caught up in all this, a pet with psionic powers), but the combination is less successful. For one thing, much of the exposition is taken up with a brilliantly logical but never quite believable development of a world where practically everyone has an inborn ability to teleport. The title (which Vinge uses to mean approximately "halfwit") is a pun: at first it is applied in scorn to Pelio, the native hero who lacks his race's usual teleportational ability, but by the end it applies with more justification to the genius heroine. In a typical Vinge twist-of-the-knife ending, she suffers brain damage which both impairs her intellect and renders her a more balanced, happier person, a suitable partner for the love-stricken Pelio.

There are few glaring faults in Vinge stories, even in the occasional ones that misfire. Sometimes the author gets so taken up with an intellectual conceit that he neglects to consider its true effect on the plot or its plausibility. The bleak worldview expressed in most Vinge stories would become a defect if the author were more prolific—after a time it would simply wear the reader down. But at Vinge's present rate of production, his characteristic tone is instead an advantage. It lends his work distinctiveness and charges it with emotional intensity. Vinge's protagonists are surrounded by bleakness, denied most hope, always deprived of a clear victory—still they persevere. We come away feeling that in our own comfortable surroundings we have no excuse to do any less.

—Patrick L. McGuire

* * *

VONNEGUT, Kurt, Jr. American. Born in Indianapolis, Indiana, 11 November 1922. Educated at Cornell University, Ithaca, New York, 1940-42; University of Chicago, 1945-47. Served in the United States Army Infantry, 1942-45: Purple Heart. Married Jane Marie Cox in 1945; two daughters and one son. Police Reporter, Chicago City News Bureau, 1946; worked in public relations for the General Electric Company, Schenectady, New York, 1947-50. Since 1950, free-lance writer. Since 1965, Teacher, Hopefield School, Sandwich, Massachusetts. Visiting Lecturer, Writers Workshop, University of Iowa, Iowa City, 1965-67; Harvard University, Cambridge, Massachusetts, 1970-71. Recipient: Guggenheim Fellowship, 1967; National Institute of Arts and Letters grant, 1970. Litt.D.: Hobart and William Smith Colleges, Geneva, New York, 1974. Member, American Academy, 1973. Address: Scudder's Lane, West Barnstable, Massachusetts 02688, U.S.A.

SCIENCE-FICTION PUBLICATIONS

Novels

Player Piano. New York, Scribner, 1952; London, Macmillan, 1953; as *Utopia 14*, New York, Bantam, 1954.
The Sirens of Titan. New York, Dell, 1959; London, Gollancz, 1962.
Cat's Cradle. New York, Holt Rinehart, and London, Gollancz, 1963.
Slaughterhouse-Five; or, The Children's Crusade. New York Delacorte Press, 1969; London, Cape, 1970.

Short Stories

Canary in a Cat House. New York, Fawcett, 1961.
Welcome to the Monkey House: A Collection of Short Works. New York, Delacorte Press, 1968; London, Cape, 1969.

OTHER PUBLICATIONS

Novels

Mother Night. New York, Fawcett, 1962; London, Cape, 1968.
God Bless You, Mr. Rosewater; or, Pearls Before Swine. New York, Holt Rinehart, and London, Cape, 1965.
Breakfast of Champions; or, Goodbye, Blue Monday. New York, Delacorte Press, and London, Cape, 1973.

Slapstick; or, Lonesome No More. New York, Delacorte Press, and London, Cape, 1976.
Jailbird. New York, Delacorte Press, and London, Cape, 1979.

Plays

The Very First Christmas Morning, in *Better Homes and Gardens* (Des Moines, Iowa), December 1962.
Fortitude, in *Playboy* (Chicago), September 1968.
Happy Birthday, Wanda June (produced New York, 1970; London, 1977). New York, Delacorte Press, 1971; London, Cape, 1973.
Between Time and Timbuktu; or, Prometheus-5: A Space Fantasy (televised, 1972; produced New York, 1976). New York, Delacorte Press, 1972; London, Panther, 1975.
Timesteps (produced Edinburgh, 1979).
God Bless You, Mr. Rosewater, adaptation of his own novel (produced New York, 1979).

Television Play: *Between Time and Timbuktu*, 1972.

Other

"Science Fiction," in *Page 2: The Best of "Speaking of Books" from the New York Times Book Review*, edited by Francis Brown. New York, Holt Rinehart, 1970.
Wampeters, Foma, and Granfalloons: Opinions. New York, Delacorte Press, 1974; London, Cape, 1975.
Sun Moon Star. New York, Harper, and London, Hutchinson, 1980.
Palm Sunday. New York, Delacorte Press, 1981.

*

Bibliography: *Kurt Vonnegut, Jr.: A Descriptive Bibliography and Annotated Secondary Checklist* by Asa B. Pieratt, Jr., and Jerome Klinkowitz, Hamden, Connecticut, Shoe String Press, 1974.

* * *

Outside science-fiction studies, Kurt Vonnegut, Jr., is normally identified as the writer-hero of the 1960's counterculture in America. He is the underground writer who has emerged. He is also called a black humorist, a fantasist, and a "serious writer," among other things. These are labels, of course, and since Vonnegut is a current success, his labels usually tell us more about his publishers and his readers then they do about his fiction. Vonnegut began as a science-fiction writer. As far as he is concerned, however, science fiction is another label. In a mid 1960's essay for the *New York Times Book Review*, he announced that he did not want to be called a science-fiction writer anymore. He did not like the effect it was having on his reputation.

Except for a few of his early short stories, Vonnegut writes fiction that is predominantly satire. His recurrent target is the cruelty of American culture, which teases, cheats, and abuses ordinary human beings. Vonnegut's fictional landscapes, his portraits of America, are clotted with dull, vaguely resentful, purposeless people. At the top of society are the wealthy and intelligent, who rule with a confounding mixture of arrogance and paternalism. Technology, the great hope of the 20th century, has been turned to war and commerce, threatening the planet and poisoning life. Vonnegut manages, for the most part, to keep this version from becoming both dismal and sentimental because he is a humorist of extraordinary talent—a self-professed 20th-century Mark Twain.

Vonnegut entered the science-fiction genre with some of his earliest short stories, published between 1950 and 1953 and subsequently collected under the title of a much later story, "Welcome to the Monkey House." The early stories are all fairly conventional extrapolations on single ideas. They are trials for Vonnegut, who is poking at his culture, holding it at odd angles under the light. By the end of the decade he has become a master at this kind of telling distortion. Vonnegut says he wrote the short stories to finance his early novels. He has since devoted all his efforts to longer fiction. His first novel, *Player Piano*, reads not much differently than an expanded short story. It is virtually humorless, and it relies, as do the short stories, upon a single idea—that the replacement of human labor with machine labor eventually robs human beings of their dignity. The idea appropriately came to him while he was employed at General Electric in Schenectady. Schenectady becomes Illium in the novel, an industrial center like other industrial centers around the country where almost all the work is performed and monitored by machines. The machines are invented and maintained by Ph.D.'s. Since there is no work, the useless working class must choose either to enter military service (there will always be war) or to join one of the public maintenance crews that mill listlessly about the city. At a higher standard of living than their ancestors would have thought possible, these people live frustrated, pointless lives in a section of the city apart from the elite technocracy. Here, in infant form, is the argument of much of Vonnegut's later fiction.

Vonnegut's mature work begins with his second novel, *The Sirens of Titan*. The book is a science-fiction parody poking fun at the late 1950's American corporate-aerospace mentality. Its characters travel to Mars, Mercury, and the moons of Saturn. They witness astonishing technologies, meet alien life forms, and found a new religion. But in spite of all the novelty, their adventures come to nothing more than "empty heroics, low comedy, and pointless death." Vonnegut makes of outer space a medium for the magnification of human greed and folly. *Cat's Cradle* appears even more pessimistic. It chronicles the end of the world at the hands of an irresponsible and inhumane technocracy, who invent, maintain, and eventually fumble mankind's ultimate technological achievement—a chip of ice with a melting point of 114° F. A seed of this "ice-nine" reaches the ocean and crystallizes all the water on the planet. Before the world dies, however, we witness the flowering of a charming new religion called Bokononism. The gentle teachings of Bokonon exemplify the positive side of Vonnegut's satire. Throughout his fiction, Vonnegut mitigates criticism, not only by joking, but by suggesting that there are alternatives to the vicious habits of our civilization. It doesn't matter that Bokononism teaches lies; they are harmless lies, and they make people feel good.

After *Cat's Cradle*, Vonnegut appears less interested in writing science fiction than in making a statement on it. In *God Bless You, Mr. Rosewater* the author steps out of his own skin by introducing the science-fiction writer, Kilgore Trout, as a character. Trout is an outwardly pathetic figure, a writer almost without an audience. Most of his stories are bizarre to the point of comedy. But he is also a figure with a tangible inner strength. Like Bokonon and Eliot Rosewater, he is one of those enigmatic characters representing the affirmative side of Vonnegut's satire. Trout, the science-fiction writer—ignored and abused by his own culture—can still speak with detachment and imagination. He is, like Vonnegut, a source of alternatives. The self-conscious authorial point of view continues in *Slaughterhouse-Five*—where the author's preface blends into and echoes throughout the novel itself—and especially in *Breakfast of Champions*, where author Vonnegut and his creation, Kilgore Trout, meet face to face. The latter work, moreover, draws interestingly upon science fiction as a context without strictly taking part in it. Vonnegut's determination to write *Breakfast of Champions* as if every character and every detail were equally important causes him to adopt a posture of such exaggerated objectivity that the novel's point of view seems almost alien. The reader is confronted with a description of middle America—complete with McDonald's hamburgers, the American flag, "wide open beavers," and the electric chair—rendered in a style reminiscent at times of the classical fairy tale, and all distanced by the past tense. Given such a format, a day in Midland City sounds as exotic as an episode in Olaf Stapledon's *Starmaker*.

The structure of Vonnegut's fiction has undergone substantial changes in the course of his career that parallel his development as a humorist. The conventional narrative of his earlier stories had already begun to erode in the writing of *The Sirens of Titan*, and by *God Bless You, Mr. Rosewater* the shift was complete. The mature Vonnegut employs relatively simple sentences, short stacatto paragraphs, and highly repetitious construction at times resembling the lyrics of song. He divides chapters into smaller sections whose endings are often punchlines rather than junctures in time and place. His fundamental unit of construction is the joke (in *Slapstick* he compares himself as an artist with Laurel and Hardy). The unusually short segments have the effect of heightening the incongruity among events in his fiction. His novels read like intimate chronicles of the circus of human existence on earth.

Whether what Vonnegut writes is precisely science fiction is not an interesting question. Perhaps Vonnegut represents the disintegration of the science-fiction tradition, or a realization of new possibilities. In any case, he has given us a careful and imaginative scrutiny of our species and pictures of ourselves at once both strange and familiar.

—Robert Froese

WALLACE, (Richard Horatio) Edgar. English. Born in Greenwich, London, 1 April 1875. Educated at St. Peter's School, London; Board School, Camberwell, London, to age 12. Served in the Royal West Kent Regiment in England, 1893-96, and in the Medical Staff Corps in South Africa, 1896-99; bought his discharge, 1899; served in the Lincoln's Inn branch of the Special Constabulary, and as a special interrogator for the War Office, during World War I. Married 1) Ivy Caldecott in 1901 (divorced, 1919), two daughters and two sons; 2) Violet King in 1921, one daughter. Worked in a printing firm, shoe shop, rubber factory, and as a merchant seaman, plasterer, and milk delivery boy, in London, 1886-91; South African Correspondent for Reuter's, 1899-1902, and the London *Daily Mail*, 1900-02; Editor, *Rand Daily News*, Johannesburg, 1902-03; returned to London: Reporter, *Daily Mail*, 1903-07, and *Standard*, 1910; Racing Editor, and later Editor, *The Week-End*, later *The Week-End Racing Supplement*, 1910-12; Racing Editor and Special Writer, *Evening News*, 1910-12; founded *Bibury's Weekly* and *R.E. Walton's Weekly*, both racing papers; Editor, *Ideas* and *The Story Journal*, 1913; Writer, and later Editor, *Town Topics*, 1913-16; regular contributor to the *Birmingham Post*, and *Thomson's Weekly News*, Dundee; Racing Columnist, *The Star*, 1927-32, and *Daily Mail*, 1930-32; Drama Critic, *Morning Post*, 1928; Founder, *The Bucks Mail*, 1930; Editor, *Sunday News*, 1931. Chairman of the Board of Directors, and film writer/director, British Lion Film Corporation. President, Press Club, London, 1923-24. *Died 10 February 1932.*

SCIENCE-FICTION PUBLICATIONS

Novels

1925: The Story of a Fatal Peace. London, Newnes, 1915.
The Green Rust. London, Ward Lock, 1919; Boston, Small Maynard, 1920.
Captains of Souls. Boston, Small Maynard, 1922; London, Long, 1923.
The Day of Uniting. London, Hodder and Stoughton, 1926; New York, Mystery League, 1930.
Planetoid 127 (includes *The Sweizer Pump*). London, Readers Library, 1929.

OTHER PUBLICATIONS

Novels

The Four Just Men. London, Tallis Press, 1906; revised edition, 1906; revised edition, Sheffield, Weekly Telegraph, 1908; Boston, Small Maynard, 1920.
Angel Esquire. Bristol, Arrowsmith, 1908; Boston, Small Maynard, 1920.
The Council of Justice. London, Ward Lock, 1908.
The Duke in the Suburbs. London, Ward Lock, 1909.
Captain Tatham of Tatham Island. London, Gale and Polden, 1909; revised edition, as *The Island of Galloping Gold*, London, Newnes, 1916; as *Eve's Island*, Newnes, 1926.
The Nine Bears. London, Ward Lock, 1910; as *Silinski, Master Criminal*, Cleveland, World, 1930; as *The Cheaters*, London, Digit, 1964.

The Other Man. New York, Dodd Mead, 1911.

Private Selby. London, Ward Lock, 1912.

The Fourth Plague. London, Ward Lock, 1913; New York, Doubleday, 1930.

Grey Timothy. London, Ward Lock, 1913; as *Pallard the Punter*, 1914.

The River of Stars. London, Ward Lock, 1913.

The Man Who Bought London. London, Ward Lock, 1915.

The Melody of Death. Bristol, Arrowsmith, 1915; New York, Dial Press, 1927.

The Clue of the Twisted Candle. Boston, Small Maynard, 1916; London, Newnes, 1917.

A Debt Discharged. London, Ward Lock, 1916.

The Tomb of Ts'in. London, Ward Lock, 1916.

The Just Men of Cordova. London, Ward Lock, 1917.

Kate Plus Ten. London, Ward Lock, and Boston, Small Maynard, 1917.

The Secret House. London, Ward Lock, 1917; Boston, Small Maynard, 1919.

Down under Donovan. London, Ward Lock, 1918.

The Man Who Knew. Boston, Small Maynard, 1918; London, Newnes, 1919.

Those Folk of Bulboro. London, Ward Lock, 1918.

The Daffodil Mystery. London, Ward Lock, 1920; as *The Daffodil Murder*, Boston, Small Maynard, 1921.

Jack o'Judgment. London, Ward Lock, 1920; Boston, Small Maynard, 1921.

The Book of All Power. London, Ward Lock, 1921.

The Angel of Terror. Boston, Small Maynard, and London, Hodder and Stoughton, 1922; as *The Destroying Angel*, London, Pan, 1959.

Number Six. London, Newnes, 1922.

The Crimson Circle. London, Hodder and Stoughton, 1922; New York, Doubleday, 1929.

The Flying Fifty-Five. London, Hutchinson, 1922.

Mr. Justice Maxell. London, Ward Lock, 1922.

The Valley of Ghosts. London, Odhams Press, 1922; Boston, Small Maynard, 1923.

The Books of Bart. London, Ward Lock, 1923.

The Clue of the New Pin. Boston, Small Maynard, and London, Hodder and Stoughton, 1923.

The Green Archer. London, Hodder and Stoughton, 1923; Boston, Small Maynard, 1924.

The Missing Million. London, Long, 1923; as *The Missing Millions*, Boston, Small Maynard, 1925.

The Dark Eyes of London. London, Ward Lock, 1924; New York, Doubleday, 1929.

Double Dan. London, Hodder and Stoughton, 1924; as *Diana of Kara-Kara*, Boston, Small Maynard, 1924.

The Face in the Night. London, Long, 1924; New York, Doubleday, 1929.

Room 13. London, Long, 1924.

Flat 2. New York, Garden City Publishing Company, 1924; revised edition, London, Long, 1927.

The Sinister Man. London, Hodder and Stoughton, 1924; Boston, Small Maynard, 1925.

The Three Oaks Mystery. London, Ward Lock, 1924.

Blue Hand. London, Ward Lock, 1925; Boston, Small Maynard, 1926.

The Black Avons. London, Gill, 1925; as *How They Fared in the Times of the Tudors, Roundhead and Cavalier, From Waterloo to the Mutiny,* and *Europe in the Melting Pot,* 4 vols., 1925.

The Daughters of the Night. London, Newnes, 1925.

The Fellowship of the Frog. London, Ward Lock, 1925; New York, Doubleday, 1928.

The Gaunt Stranger. London, Hodder and Stoughton, 1925; as *The Ringer,* New York, Doubleday, 1926.

The Hairy Arm. Boston, Small Maynard, 1925; as *The Avenger,* London, Long, 1926.

A King by Night. London, Long, 1925; New York, Doubleday, 1926.

The Strange Countess. London, Hodder and Stoughton, 1925; Boston, Small Maynard, 1926.

The Three Just Men. London, Hodder and Stoughton, 1925; New York, Doubleday, 1930.

Barbara on Her Own. London, Newnes, 1926.

The Black Abbot. London, Hodder and Stoughton, 1926; New York, Doubleday, 1927.

The Door with Seven Locks. London, Hodder and Stoughton, and New York, Doubleday, 1926.

The Joker. London, Hodder and Stoughton, 1926; as *The Colossus,* New York, Doubleday, 1932.

The Man from Morocco. London, Long, 1926; as *The Black,* New York, Doubleday, 1930.

The Million Dollar Story. London, Newnes, 1926.

The Northing Tramp. London, Hodder and Stoughton, 1926; New York, Doubleday, 1929; as *The Tramp,* London, Pan, 1965.

Penelope of the Polyantha. London, Hodder and Stoughton, 1926.

The Square Emerald. London, Hodder and Stoughton, 1926; as *The Girl from Scotland Yard,* New York, Doubleday, 1927.

The Terrible People. London, Hodder and Stoughton, and New York, Doubleday, 1926.

We Shall See! London, Hodder and Stoughton, 1926; as *The Gaol Breaker,* New York, Doubleday, 1931.

The Yellow Snake. London, Hodder and Stoughton, 1926.

Big Foot. London, Long, 1927.

The Feathered Serpent. London, Hodder and Stoughton, 1927; New York, Doubleday, 1928.

The Forger. London, Hodder and Stoughton, 1927; as *The Clever One,* New York, Doubleday, 1928.

The Hand of Power. London, Long, 1927; New York, Mystery League, 1930.

The Man Who Was Nobody. London, Ward Lock, 1927.

The Ringer (novelization of stage play). London, Hodder and Stoughton, 1927.

The Squeaker. London, Hodder and Stoughton, 1927; as *The Squealer,* New York, Doubleday, 1928.

Terror Keep. London, Hodder and Stoughton, and New York, Doubleday, 1927.

The Traitor's Gate. London, Hodder and Stoughton, and New York, Doubleday, 1927.

The Double. London, Hodder and Stoughton, and New York, Doubleday, 1928.

The Thief in the Night. London, Readers Library, 1928.

The Flying Squad. London, Hodder and Stoughton, 1928; New York, Doubleday, 1929.

The Gunner. London, Long, 1928; as *Gunman's Bluff,* New York, Doubleday, 1929.

The Twister. London, Long, 1928; New York, Doubleday, 1929.

The Golden Hades. London, Collins, 1929.

The Green Ribbon. London, Hutchinson, 1929; New York, Doubleday, 1930.

The India-Rubber Men. London, Hodder and Stoughton, 1929; New York, Doubleday, 1930.

The Terror. London, Detective Story Club, 1929.

The Calendar. London, Collins, 1930; New York, Doubleday, 1931.

The Clue of the Silver Key. London, Hodder and Stoughton, 1930; as *The Silver Key,* New York, Doubleday, 1930.

The Lady of Ascot. London, Hutchinson, 1930.

White Face. London, Hodder and Stoughton, 1930; New York, Doubleday, 1931.

On the Spot. London, Long, and New York, Doubleday, 1931.

The Coat of Arms. London, Hutchinson, 1931; as *The Arranways Mystery,* New York, Doubleday, 1932.

The Devil Man. London, Collins, and New York, Doubleday, 1931; as *The Life and Death of Charles Peace,* 1932.

The Man at the Carlton. London, Hodder and Stoughton, 1931; New York, Doubleday, 1932.

The Frightened Lady. London, Hodder and Stoughton, 1932; New York, Doubleday, 1933.

When the Gangs Came to London. London, Long, and New York, Doubleday, 1932.

Short Stories

Smithy. London, Tallis Press, 1905; revised edition, as *Smithy, Not to Mention Nobby Clark and Spud Murphy,* London, Newnes, 1914.

Smithy Abroad: Barrack Room Sketches. London, Hulton, 1909.
Sanders of the River. London, Ward Lock, 1911; New York, Doubleday, 1930.
The People of the River. London, Ward Lock, 1912.
Smithy's Friend Nobby. London, Town Topics, 1914; as *Nobby*, London, Newnes, 1916.
The Admirable Carfew. London, Ward Lock, 1914.
Bosambo of the River. London, Ward Lock, 1914.
Bones, Being Further Adventures in Mr. Commissioner Sanders' Country. London, Ward Lock, 1915.
Smithy and the Hun. London, Pearson, 1915.
The Keepers of the King's Peace. London, Ward Lock, 1917.
Lieutenant Bones. London, Ward Lock, 1918.
Tam o' the Scouts. London, Newnes, 1918; as *Tam of the Scouts*, Boston, Small Maynard, 1919; as *Tam*, Newnes, 1919.
The Fighting Scouts. London, Pearson, 1919.
The Adventures of Heine. London, Ward Lock, 1919.
Bones in London. London, Ward Lock, 1921.
The Law of the Four Just Men. London, Hodder and Stoughton, 1921; as *Again the Three Just Men*, New York, Doubleday, 1933.
Sandi, The King-Maker. London, Ward Lock, 1922.
Bones of the River. London, Newnes, 1923.
Chick. London, Ward Lock, 1923.
Educated Evans. London, Webster, 1924.
The Mind of Mr. J.G. Reeder. London, Hodder and Stoughton, 1925; as *The Murder Book of Mr. J.G. Reeder*, New York, Doubleday, 1929.
More Educated Evans. London, Webster, 1926.
Mrs. William Jones and Bill. London, Newnes, 1926.
Sanders. London, Hodder and Stoughton, 1926; as *Mr. Commissioner Sanders*, New York, Doubleday, 1930.
The Brigand. London, Hodder and Stoughton, 1927.
Good Evans!. London, Webster, 1927; as *The Educated Man—Good Evans!*, London, Collins, 1929.
The Mixer. London, Long, 1927.
Again Sanders. London, Hodder and Stoughton, 1928; New York, Doubleday, 1929.
Again the Three Just Men. London, Hodder and Stoughton, 1928; as *The Law of the Three Just Men*, New York, Doubleday, 1931; as *Again the Three*, London, Pan, 1968.
Elegant Edward. London, Readers Library, 1928.
The Orator. London, Hutchinson, 1928.
Again the Ringer. London, Hodder and Stoughton, 1929; as *The Ringer Returns*, New York, Doubleday, 1931.
Four Square Jane. London, Readers Library, 1929.
The Big Four. London, Readers Library, 1929.
The Black. London, Readers Library, 1929; augmented edition, London, Digit, 1962.
The Ghost of Down Hill (includes *The Queen of Sheba's Belt*). London, Readers Library, 1929.
The Cat Burglar. London, Newnes, 1929.
Circumstantial Evidence. London, Newnes, 1929; Cleveland, World, 1934.
Fighting Snub Reilly. London, Newnes, 1929; Cleveland, World, 1934.
The Governor of Chi-Foo. London, Newnes, 1929; Cleveland, World, 1934.
The Little Green Man. London, Collins, 1929.
The Prison-Breakers. London, Newnes, 1929.
Forty-Eight Short Stories. London, Newnes, 1929.
For Information Received. London, Newnes, 1929.
The Lady of Little Hell. London, Newnes, 1929.
The Lone House Mystery. London, Collins, 1929.
Red Aces. London, Hodder and Stoughton, 1929; New York, Doubleday, 1930.
The Reporter. London, Readers Library, 1929.
The Iron Grip. London, Readers Library, 1930.
Killer Kay. London, Newnes, 1930.
The Stretelli Case and Other Mystery Stories (omnibus). Cleveland, World, 1930.
The Lady Called Nita. London, Newnes, 1930.
The Guv'nor and Other Stories. London, Collins, 1932; as *Mr. Reeder Returns*, New York, Doubleday, 1932; as *The Guv'nor and Mr. J.G. Reeder Returns*, Collins, 2 vols., 1933-34.
Sergeant Sir Peter. London, Chapman and Hall, 1932; as *Sergeant Dunn C.I.D.*, London, Digit, 1962.
The Steward. London, Collins, 1932.
The Last Adventure. London, Hutchinson, 1934.
The Woman from the East and Other Stories. London, Hutchinson, 1934.
Nig-Nog (omnibus). Cleveland, World, 1934.
The Undisclosed Client. London, Digit, 1962.
The Man Who Married His Cook and Other Stories. London, White Lion, 1976.
Unexpected Endings. Oxford, Edgar Wallace Society, 1979.

Plays

An African Millionaire (produced South Africa, 1904). London, Davis Poynter, 1972.
The Forest of Happy Dreams (produced London, 1910; New York, 1914). Published in *One-act Play Parade*, London, Hodder and Stoughton, 1935.
Dolly Cutting Herself (produced London, 1911).
Sketches, in *Hullo, Ragtime* (produced London, 1912).
Sketches, in *Hullo, Tango!* (produced London, 1912).
Hello, Exchange! (sketch; produced London, 1913; as *The Switchboard*, produced New York, 1915).
The Manager's Dream (sketch; produced London, 1913).
Sketches, in *Business as Usual* (produced London, 1914).
The Whirligig (revue), with Wal Pink and Albert de Courville, music by Frederick Chappelle (produced London, 1919; as *Pins and Needles*, produced New York, 1922).
M'Lady (produced London, 1921).
The Whirl of the World (revue), with Albert de Courville and William K. Wells, music by Frederick Chappelle (produced London, 1924).
The Looking Glass (revue), with Albert de Courville, music by Frederick Chappelle (produced London, 1924).
The Ringer, adaptation of his own novel *The Gaunt Stranger* (produced London, 1926). London, Hodder and Stoughton, and New York, French, 1929.
The Mystery of Room 45 (produced London, 1926).
The Terror, adaptation of his own novel *Terror Keep* (produced Brighton and London, 1927). London, Hodder and Stoughton, 1929.
Double Dan, adaptation of his own novel (produced Blackpool and London, 1926).
A Perfect Gentleman (produced London, 1927).
The Yellow Mask, music by Vernon Duke, lyrics by Desmond Carter (produced Birmingham, 1927; London, 1928).
The Flying Squad, adaptation of his own novel (produced Oxford and London, 1928). London, Hodder and Stoughton, 1929.
The Man Who Changed His Name (produced London, 1928; New York, 1932). London, Hodder and Stoughton, 1929.
The Squeaker, adaptation of his own novel (produced London, 1928; as *Sign of the Leopard*, produced New York, 1928). London, Hodder and Stoughton, 1929.
The Lad (produced Wimbledon, 1928; London, 1929).
Persons Unknown (produced London, 1929).
The Calendar (also director: produced Manchester and London, 1929). London, French, 1932.
On the Spot (produced London and New York, 1930).
The Mouthpiece (produced London, 1930).
Smoky Cell (produced London, 1930).
Charles III, adaptation of a play by Curt Götz (produced London, 1931).
The Old Man (produced London, 1931).
The Case of the Frightened Lady (produced London, 1931). London, French, 1932; as *Criminal at Large* (produced New York, 1932), New York, French, 1934.
The Green Pack (produced London, 1932). London, French, 1933.

Screenplays: *Nurse and Martyr*, 1915; *The Ringer*, 1928; *Valley of the Ghosts*, 1928; *The Forger*, 1928; *Red Aces*, 1929; *The Squeaker*, 1930; *Should a Doctor Tell?*, 1930; *The Hound of the Baskervilles*, with V. Gareth Gundrey, 1931; *The Old Man*, 1931.

Verse

The Mission That Failed! A Tale of the Raid and Other Poems.
 Cape Town, Maskew Miller, 1898.
Nicholson's Nek. Cape Town, Eastern Press, 1900.
War! and Other Poems. Cape Town, Eastern Press, 1900.
Writ in Barracks. London, Methuen, 1900.

Other

Unofficial Despatches. London, Hutchinson, 1901.
Famous Scottish Regiments. London, Newnes, 1914.
Fieldmarshall Sir John French and His Campaigns. London,
 Newnes, 1914.
Heroes All: Gallant Deeds of the War. London, Newnes, 1914.
The Standard History of the War. London, Newnes, 4 vols.,
 1914-16.
War of the Nations, vols. 2-11. London, Newnes, 1914-19.
*Kitchener's Army and the Territorial Forces: The Full Story of a
 Great Achievement.* London, Newnes, 6 vols., 1915.
People: A Short Autobiography. London, Hodder and Stoughton,
 1926; New York, Doubleday, 1929.
This England. London, Hodder and Stoughton, 1927.
My Hollywood Diary. London, Hutchinson, 1932.

Ghostwriter: *My Life*, by Evelyn Thaw, London, Long, 1914.

Theatrical Activities:

Director: **Plays**—*The Calendar*, Manchester and London, 1929;
Brothers by Herbert Ashton, Jr., London, 1929. **Films**—*Red Aces*,
1929; *The Squeaker*, 1930.

* * *

Edgar Wallace is not a name which comes to mind as a writer of
science fiction. Were it not for the integral part which the fantastic
plays in some of his plots they might be classed among his other
thrillers. Even his stories of high adventure about Sanders of the
River have skirmishes with the fantastic, if witch doctors can be so
classified. The difficulty in discussing Wallace's science fiction
arises from its dual nature. The mystery critic's convention of not
revealing the ending of a story has to be discarded in discussing
Wallace. To explain what makes them science fiction is to give away
the solutions to their mysteries.

Apart from the Sanders stories, Wallace's earliest use of a science-
fiction theme is *1925: The Story of a Fatal Peace* which deals with
the consequences for Britain if Germany is not totally beaten in
World War I. During the Festival of Schleswig-Holstein in 1925 the
Germans attempt to invade Britain in the very transports which had
brought British veterans to the German festival. An interesting
device in the story is the submarine detector activated by the sound
of propellers, invented by Sir John Venniman. The preface frankly
proclaims the story's propangandistic purpose. *The Green Rust*
involves a scheme by a German scientist to infest the rest of the
world's grain crops with a bacteria, thus putting Germany in a
position of power. A layman's view of science and of scientists
dominate both *Planetoid 127* and *The Day of Uniting*. The second
work recalls a traditional theme in early science fiction, the impending destruction of the world and the effect the knowledge of this has
on the characters. The humorous view of science by the non-
scientist is combined with the moral dilemma over whether to
protect the population from panic by keeping the disaster a secret
against the objective view of their need to know. The impending
disaster itself is the explanation for the mysterious incidents in the
first half of the story, but the conclusion may still come as a surprise
to all but the most alert reader. The title refers to the officially
proclaimed day for families to be reunited before the end of the
world. Professor Colson's "sound strainer" in *Planetoid 127* by
which he talks to his alter ego on the planet Vulcan is a thing of
"instruments, of wires that spun across the room like the web of a
spider, of strange machines which seemed to be endowed with
perpetual motion." Events on the other world often being in
advance of those on earth, Colson is able to predict the future. This
knowledge enables him to manipulate the stock market to his

advantage until an unscrupulous gentleman kills him for his secret.
The planet Vulcan is on the opposite side of the Sun from the Earth
and thus the story has been called the earliest example of the "twin
world" theme. It is obvious that the dominant theme in the story
itself is the mis-use of scientific knowledge. *Captains of Souls* is a
tour de force for Wallace. The transfer of the souls of the two men,
Ambrose Sault and Robert Morelle, is an intriguing device which
allows the author to explore his characters in depth and also results
in a happy ending with retribution for all.

—J. Randolph Cox

WALLACE, F(loyd) L. American. Lives in California.

SCIENCE-FICTION PUBLICATIONS

Novel

Address: Centauri. New York, Gnome Press, 1955.

Uncollected Short Stories

"Hideaway," in *Astounding* (New York), February 1951.
"Student Body," in *Crossroads in Time*, edited by Groff Conklin.
 New York, Permabooks, 1953.
"Worlds in Balance," in *Science Fiction Plus* (Philadelphia), May
 1953.
"The Music Master," in *Imagination* (Evanston, Illinois), November
 1953.
"The Seasoned Traveler," in *Universe* (Evanston, Illinois), December
 1953.
"Forget Me Nearly," in *Galaxy* (New York), June 1954.
"The Deadly Ones," in *Fantastic Universe* (Chicago), July 1954.
"The Man Who Was Six," in *Galaxy* (New York), September 1954.
"Simple Psiman," in *Startling* (New York), Fall 1954.
"The Impossible Voyage Home," in *Science Fiction Adventures in
 Mutation*, edited by Groff Conklin. New York, Vanguard
 Press, 1955.
"The Assistant Self," in *Fantastic Universe* (Chicago), March 1956.
"Little Thing for the House," in *Astounding* (New York), July 1956.
"The Nevada Virus," in *Venture* (Concord, New Hampshire), Sep-
 tember 1957.
"End as a World," in *The Third Galaxy Reader*, edited by H.L.
 Gold. New York, Doubleday, 1958.
"Tangle Hold," in *5 Galaxy Short Novels*, edited by H.L. Gold.
 New York, Doubleday, 1958.
"Mezzerow Loves Company," in *World That Couldn't Be and 8
 Other SF Novelets*, edited by H.L. Gold. New York, Double-
 day, 1959.
"Delay in Transit," in *Bodyguard and 4 Other Short SF Novels
 from Galaxy*, edited by H.L. Gold. New York, Doubleday,
 1960.
"Second Landing," in *Amazing* (New York), January 1960.
"Privates All," in *Fantasy and Science Fiction* (New York), Sep-
 tember 1961.
"Accidental Flight," in *Time Waits for Winthrop and Four Other
 Short Novels*, edited by Frederick Pohl. New York, Double-
 day, 1962.
"Bolden's Pets," in *Great Science Fiction about Doctors*, edited by
 Groff Conklin and Noah D. Fabricant. New York, Macmillan,
 1963.
"Big Ancestor," in *Five-Odd*, edited by Groff Conklin. New York,
 Pyramid, 1964.
"Growing Season," in *Frozen Planet and 4 Other SF Novellas*.
 New York, Macfadden, 1966.

OTHER PUBLICATIONS

Novels

Three Times a Victim.   New York, Ace, 1957.
Wired for Scandal.   New York, Ace, 1959.

*   *   *

Still a hazy figure in the history of science fiction, F.L. Wallace was one of the field's most outstanding and least appreciated writers during the 1950's. His only SF novel, *Address: Centauri*, is a minor work that was an expansion of his very good story "Accidental Flight" (*Galaxy*, 1952). Wallace's other SF stories are of high quality, characterized by a depth and a thoroughness uncommon to the field in the 1950's. Among his most noteworthy stories are "Delay in Transit"; "Big Ancestor," a powerful commentary on the human race and its future direction; "Student Body," which features one of the very best descriptions and development of an alien life form in all of science fiction; "Bolden's Pets," wherein Wallace brilliantly employs the unique concept of *positive* parasitism; "Mezzerow Loves Company"; "Tangle Hold"; and "The Impossible Voyage Home."

—Martin H. Greenberg

WALLACE, Ian. Pseudonym for John Wallace Pritchard. American.   Born in Chicago, Illinois, 4 December 1912. Educated at the University of Michigan, Ann Arbor, B.A. in English 1934, M.A. in educational psychology 1939, graduate study 1949-51; Wayne University, now Wayne State University, Detroit, education certificate 1936, Ed. D. 1957. Served as a clinical psychologist in the United States Army during World War II: Captain. Married Elizabeth Paul in 1938; two sons. Psychology Technician, Clinical Psychologist, Department Head, Administrative Assistant, Director, and Divisional Director, Board of Education, Detroit, 1942-74; now retired. Part-time lecturer in education, Wayne State University, 1955-74. Lives near Ashville, North Carolina. Address: c/o DAW Books, 1301 Avenue of the Americas, New York, New York 10019, U.S.A.

SCIENCE-FICTION PUBLICATIONS

Novels (series: Croyd; St. Cyr and U. Tuli)

Croyd.   New York, Putnam, 1967.
Dr. Orpheus (Croyd).   New York, Putnam, 1968.
Deathstar Voyage (St. Cyr).   New York, Putnam, 1969; London, Dobson, 1972.
The Purloined Prince (St. Cyr).   New York, McCall, 1971.
Pan Sagittarius.   New York, Putnam, 1973.
A Voyage to Dari (Croyd).   New York, DAW, 1974.
The World Asunder.   New York, DAW, 1976.
The Sign of the Mute Medusa (St. Cyr).   New York, Popular Library, 1977.
Z-Sting (Croyd).   New York, DAW, 1978.
Heller's Leap.   New York, DAW, 1979.
The Lucifer Rocket.   New York, DAW, 1980.

OTHER PUBLICATIONS as John Wallace Pritchard

Novel

Every Crazy Wind.   New York, Dodd Mead, 1952.

Other

Frank Cody, A Realist in Education, with others.   New York, Macmillan, 1943.
Off to Work, with Paul H. Voelker.   Pittsburgh, Stanwix House, 1962.

Author-editor-publisher of numerous Detroit Board of Education textbooks and teaching guides, 1942-74.

Ian Wallace comments:
I aim my books at well-educated or self-educated minds. For them, I try to write pleasurable, frequently startling, coherently designed stories, taking advantage of fantasy to enlarge their scope, but disciplining the tales with logic and with scientific and philosophic theory. I try to portray humans living at the highest levels of their humanity, entailing many-sided intelligence, emotion intelligently guided and expressed, and human fellow-feeling for all the different kinds of humans (including some weird-bodied instances on other planets); that, for me, is both a moral issue and a taste preference.

*   *   *

Among the more recent writers to deal in such "soft" sciences as psychology (as opposed to "hard" sciences such as physics), Ian Wallace is an example of particular interest. Most of his works are full-length novels of great complexity, a quality that tends to work in his favor on some books, but against it in others.

The first two books of Wallace's Croyd series—*Croyd* and *Dr. Orpheus*—are deservedly his most famous works. They deal with the adventures of Croyd, a humanoid being of great psychic powers, including those of teleportation and moving through time. The complexity of both the events and the characters is exemplary, especially in *Dr. Orpheus*, which concerns the attempt of a madman of that name to subjugate all humanity with a drug called Anagonon, which frees humans from pain and the will to question authority. Behind Orpheus, however, is the threat of a race of arthropodal aliens who have furnished the drug to facilitate conquest of the primate race, which they intend to use as food-sources in which to lay their eggs. As Croyd and a female companion investigate Dr. Orpheus, they are subjugated by his drug, until, in the grand tradition of time paradoxes, Croyd's future time-traveling actions free him from his "present" captivity. But the conflict between Croyd and Orpheus is more psychological than physical, and Croyd discovers additional mysteries which he must solve by time-traveling to ancient Greece. There he briefly explores the Heraclitean and Pythagorean philosophies that were roughly contemporaneous with Orphic worship; philosophies he will use in strategies to defeat Orpheus and the aliens. Despite the apparent conflicts of these plot-threads, Wallace manages to merge all these concepts—alien biology, philosophy, time-paradox, psychology—into a logically unified whole.

In a later Croyd novel, however, Wallace's penchant for complexity leads to an inferior plot. *Z-Sting* lacks the other books' dazzling concepts, and consists of a little more than an SF version of *Fail-Safe*. Croyd has lived to an incredible age, but physically rejuvenates himself to prevent Earth's destruction by a doomsday device, the Z-Sting. Lacking elaborate concepts, Wallace tries to emphasize characters—which was a mistake, for Wallace's sense of dialogue is variable, sometimes adequate, sometimes distressingly artificial. For instance, when a female suggests to Croyd the possibility of a liaison, he responds: "No longer long-range strategic." Despite his talents as a conceptual SF writer, Wallace has had a tendency to emulate Edward E. Smith and the later Heinlein in imposing a static, analytical mindset on all characters, so that they react to proposals of love no differently than to world crises. More extreme than *Z-Sting* in this respect is *The World Asunder*, a confusing tumult of plots and counterplots which lacks the philosophical inquiry of *Dr. Orpheus*. A madman naming himself Kali is actually a temporal duplicate of one of the protagonists. Those protagonists—all of whom have an intense, undifferentiated flair for analytical psychology—never really solve the problem of why this madman of Irish ancestry takes the name of a female Hindu deity (obviously, it simply appealed to Wallace because it denoted "the destructiveness of time"). Unlike the Orpheus myth's culmination, the Kali myth does not actively serve the plot, but merely provides a facile Jungian metaphor for human destructiveness, which the protagonists struggle to control. Wallace has a few interesting, if didactic, insights, as when a character says, "I suppose you know that you must never totally reject your dark side; it is where you get your depth." But the novel as a whole is a conglomeration of psychological analysis and psychic shenanigans, with characters too self-assured to be real.

However, Wallace's contributions extend into other formats as well. Though his St. Cyr detective mysteries are not as philosophically complex as *Croyd* and *Dr. Orpheus*, they have in common with those works a rigorous logic and colorful settings. Galactic policeman Claudine St. Cyr appears in three books. In *Deathstar Voyage*, an exceptional blend of mystery and SF plotting, St. Cyr and a group of luxury passengers are trapped aboard a spaceship which a madman plans to obliterate, again with Wallace's recurrent use of psychic powers. St. Cyr is probably Wallace's single best character, and *Deathstar Voyage* uses complex cultural and psychological motivations in ways that few SF writers have matched.

Ian Wallace is at his best when he is able to balance his analytical proclivities with a sense of aesthetics, and of abstract philosophy. Thematically he remains a simple adventure writer, but his occasional mastery of many levels of thinking should never be underestimated—in that respect he is among the best modern SF writers.

—Gene Phillips

WALLIS, G(eorge) C. Also wrote as B. Wallis; B. and G.C. Wallis. British. Partner in a printing firm, Sheffield, prior to World War II; after the war worked in cinema management; wrote comics as John Stanton.

SCIENCE-FICTION PUBLICATIONS

Novels

The Children of the Sphinx. London, Simpkin Marshall, 1924.
The Call of Peter Gaskell. Kingswood, Surrey, World's Work, 1948.

Uncollected Short Stories

"The Last King of Atlantis," in *Short Stories* (London), 1896-97.
"World Wreckers," in *Scraps*, 1908.
"Wireless War," with A.J. Andrews, in *Comic Life*, 1909.
"The World at Bay" (as B. and G.C. Wallis), in *Amazing* (New York), November 1928.
"The Mother World" (as B. and G.C. Wallis), in *Amazing Stories Quarterly* (New York), Summer 1933.
"The Voyage of the Neutralia," in *Weird Tales* (Indianapolis), 1937.
"The Orbit Jumper," in *Tales of Wonder* (Kingswood, Surrey), Winter 1938.
"Invaders from the Void," in *Fantasy 3* (London), 1939.
"Voyage of Sacrifice," in *Tales of Wonder* (Kingswood, Surrey), Spring 1939.
"Across the Abyss," in *Tales of Wonder* (Kingswood, Surrey), Summer 1939.
"The Crystal Menace," in *Tales of Wonder* (Kingswood, Surrey), Autumn 1939.
"Under the Dying Sun," in *Tales of Wonder* (Kingswood, Surrey), Summer 1940.
"The Red Spheres," in *Tales of Wonder* (Kingswood, Surrey), Spring 1941.
"The Cosmic Cloud," in *Tales of Wonder* (Kingswood, Surrey), Autumn 1941.

"The Power Supreme," in *Tales of Wonder* (Kingswood, Surrey), Winter 1941.
"From Time's Dawn" (as B. Wallis), in *Fantastic Novel* (New York), May 1950.
"The Great Sacrifice," in *Worlds Apart*, edited by George Locke. London, Cornmarket Reprints, 1972.

OTHER PUBLICATIONS

Novel

Taquita the Pearl. London, Stockwell, 1924.

* * *

The writing career of G.C. Wallis started at the turn of the last century, when the stories of Wells, Shiel, and Griffith were delighting the readers of the *Strand* and *Pearson's*. A list of his published tales, delicately printed by the Sheffield firm in which he was a partner, contains almost a hundred titles, including *The Children of the Sphinx*, a novel which the *Literary World* found "full of swing and interest." By then he had published half a dozen magazine serials, such as "The Last King of Atlantis" and "World Wreckers," and 40-odd short stories which appeared in a variety of publications from the *Penny Magazine* to *Tit-Bits*.

Only some of these tales were science fiction, which was often to be found in juvenile papers like the *Boy's Friend*, *Union Jack*, and *Lot-o'-Fun*. To such as these he contributed another 40-odd stories and serials, some under the name of John Stanton and a few in collaboration with a certain A. Anthony. Though most of his heroes were "Fighting the Spaniards," "In Peril in Persia," or "In the Grip of the Mafia," there were others who ventured to the "City at the South Pole," who voyaged "In Trackless Space," or joined in the "Wireless War."

Like several of his contemporaries who were the real pioneers of science fiction, Wallis played with ideas of cosmic proportions long before they became the stock-in-trade of the pulp magazines of a more advanced period. In "The Great Sacrifice" he anticipated writers like John Russell Fearn by destroying the outer planets (excepting Pluto, yet undiscovered) with the aid of the Martians, who finally exploded their own world so that Earth might escape the meteor stream invading the solar system. The notion that the Martians might not be the monsters that Wells made them was fairly well established among the writers who followed in the wake of Flammarion. Another early Wallis story, "The Last Days of Earth," shows all too obviously the influence of the French astronomer's classic *Omega: The Last Days of the World*.

In acknowledgment of a Canadian cousin's help in placing his manuscripts in America, many of Wallis's stories were by-lined B. & Geo. C. Wallis, Bruce & G.C. Wallis, or simply B. Wallis. He made several appearances in *Weird Tales*, where a four-part serial, "The Star Shell," typified the kind of science-fantasy with which the editor Farnsworth Wright sought to offset the competition of *Amazing Stories* when it appeared in 1926. Within two years the writer had made his bow in Hugo Gernsback's magazine with "The World at Bay," dealing with an invasion of the surface world by a subterranean race (a tale simple and exciting enough to be serialised also in the London *Daily Herald*). Though just as simply told, with his usual touches of romantic interest, "The Mother World" contained some of Wallis's most thoughtful speculations upon the origin and destiny of the human species. An unlikely party of space-travellers is lured to a distant world whose godlike inhabitants have the power to expunge all life on other planets where they have planted their seed, should it fail to reach maturity—and man's fate is in the balance.

A pedestrian thriller, "The Voyage of the Neutralia," depicting lesser forms of life on Mars and Venus, marked his last appearance in *Weird Tales* in 1937. His sole contribution to the British *Fantasy*, "Invaders from the Void," was equally conventional; and when *Tales of Wonder* became established it featured several stories which, though fresh from his still brisk pen, mostly stemmed from ideas he had developed years earlier. His last novel, *The Call of Peter Gaskell*, concerned a mysterious Inca queen in a lost city in the

Amazon jungle, and proved so close to Rider Haggard, yet so difficult to read, that a devastating critique in *Fantasy Review* was headed "She-Who-Must-Be-Avoided."

—Walter Gillings

———————

WALSH, J(ames) M(organ). Also wrote as H. Haverstock Hill; Stephen Maddock; George M. White. British. Born in Geelong, Victoria, Australia, in 1897. Educated at Xavier College, Melbourne. Married Louisa Mary Murphy; one son and one daughter. Cattleman, auctioneer, and bookseller before becoming a full-time writer; lived in England in later life. *Died 29 August 1952.*

SCIENCE-FICTION PUBLICATIONS

Novels

Vandals of the Void. London, John Hamilton, 1931; Westport, Connecticut, Hyperion Press, 1976.
Vanguard to Neptune. London, Kemsley, 1932.

Uncollected Short Stories

"The Struggle for Pallas," in *Wonder Stories Quarterly* (New York), Fall 1931.
"After 1,000,000 Years," in *Wonder Stories* (New York), October 1931.
"When the Earth Tilted," in *Wonder Stories* (New York), May 1932.
"The Terror Out of Space" (as H. Haverstock Hill), in *Amazing* (New York), February 1934.
"The Stick Men," in *Fantasy 3* (London), 1939.
"The Belt," in *Science Fantasy* (Bournemouth), 1950.

OTHER PUBLICATIONS

Novels

The Brethren of the Compass, with E.J. Blythe. London, Jarrolds, 1925.
The White Mask. London, John Hamilton, 1925; New York, Doran, 1927.
The Company of Shadows. London, John Hamilton, 1926; New York, Brewer and Warren, 1931.
The Mystery of the Crystal Skull (as George M. White). London, John Hamilton, 1926.
The Hairpin Mystery. London, John Hamilton, 1926.
The Hand of Doom. London, John Hamilton, 1927.
The Images of Hân. London, John Hamilton, 1927.
The Black Cross. London, John Hamilton, 1928.
The Crimes of Cleopatra's Needle. London, John Hamilton, 1928.
The Purple Stain. London, John Hamilton, 1928.
The Silver Greyhound. London, John Hamilton, 1928.
The Mystery Man. London, John Hamilton, 1929.
The Mystery of the Green Caterpillars. London, John Hamilton, 1929.
The Tempania Mystery. London, John Hamilton, 1929.
The Black Ghost. London, John Hamilton, 1930; New York, Brewer and Warren, 1931.
Exit Simeon Hex. London, John Hamilton, 1930; New York, Brewer Warren and Putnam, 1931.
The Man Behind the Curtain. London, John Hamilton, 1931.
Mystery House. London, John Hamilton, 1931.
The Whisperer. London, John Hamilton, 1931.
The Girl of the Islands. London, John Hamilton, 1932.

The League of Missing Men. London, John Hamilton, 1932.
Lady Incognito. London, Collins, 1932.
King's Messenger. London, Collins, 1933.
The Secret Service Girl. London, Collins, 1933.
Spies Are Abroad. London, Collins, 1933.
The Man from Whitehall. London, Collins, 1934.
Spies in Pursuit. London, Collins, 1934.
The Silent Man. London, Collins, 1935.
Spies Never Return. London, Collins, 1935.
Tiger in the Night. London, Collins, 1935.
The Half Ace. London, Collins, 1936.
Spies' Vendetta. London, Collins, 1936.
Chalk-Face. London, Hodder and Stoughton, 1937.
Spies in Spain. London, Collins, 1937.
Island of Spies. London, Collins, 1937.
Black Dragon. London, Collins, 1938.
Dial 999. London, Collins, 1938.
Bullets for Breakfast. London, Collins, 1939.
King's Enemies. London, Collins, 1939.
Secret Weapons. London, Collins, 1940.
Death at His Elbow. London, Collins, 1941.
Spies from the Skies. London, Collins, 1941.
Danger Zone. London, Collins, 1942.
Island Alert. London, Collins, 1943.
Face Value. London, Collins, 1944.
Whispers in the Dark. London, Collins, 1945.
The Man Who Grew Bulbs. London, Vallancey Press, 1945.
Express Delivery. London, Collins, 1946.
Once in Tiger Bay. London, Collins, 1947.
Walking Shadow. London, Collins, 1948.
Time to Kill. London, Collins, 1949.
Return to Tiger Bay. London, Collins, 1950.
Next, Please. London, Collins, 1951.
King of Tiger Bay. London, Collins, 1952.

Novels as H. Haverstock Hill

Anne of Flying Gap. London, Hodder and Stoughton, 1926.
Spoil of the Desert. London, Hodder and Stoughton, 1927.
The Golden Isle. London, Hodder and Stoughton, 1928.
Golden Harvest. London, Hodder and Stoughton, 1929.
The Secret of the Crater. London, Hurst and Blackett, 1930.

Novels as Stephen Maddock

A Woman of Destiny. London, Collins, 1933.
Danger after Dark. London, Collins, 1934.
Gentlemen of the Night. London, Collins, 1934.
The White Siren. London, Collins, 1934.
Conspirators in Capri. London, Collins, 1935.
The Eye of the Keyhole. London, Collins, 1935.
Conspirators Three. London, Collins, 1936.
Forbidden Frontiers. London, Collins, 1936.
Conspirators at Large. London, Collins, 1937.
Doorway to Danger. London, Collins, 1938.
Lamp-Post 592. London, Collins, 1938.
Spies along the Severn. London, Collins, 1939.
Spades at Midnight. London, Collins, 1940.
Date with a Spy. London, Collins, 1941.
Step Aside to Death. London, Collins, 1942.
Drums Beat at Dusk. London, Collins, 1943.
Something on the Stairs. London, Collins, 1944.
I'll Never Like Friday Again. London, Collins, 1945.
Overture to Trouble. London, Collins, 1946.
Exit Only. London, Collins, 1947.
East of Piccadilly. London, Collins, 1948.
Keep Your Fingers Crossed. London, Collins, 1949.
Private Line. London, Collins, 1950.
Public Mischief. London, Collins, 1951.
Close Shave. London, Collins, 1952.

Short Stories

The Week-End Crime Book, with Audrey Baldwin. London, John Hamilton, 1929.

Mutton Dressed as Lamb, and *Live Bait*.   London, Vallancey Press, 1944.

Play

Six Characters for an Actress.   London, French, 1947.

*   *   *

J.M. Walsh was best known as a writer of mystery thrillers with such intriguing titles as *The Crimes of Cleopatra's Needle*. He found publishers chary of science fiction, but in 1931 he persuaded one to risk issuing his *Vandals of the Void*, a full-blooded adventure set in the space-lanes of the 21st century. At the time, it represented a breakthrough. A year later he published another novel of inter-planetary exploration, *Vanguard to Neptune*. In both cases, Walsh contrived to avoid holding up the action by confining most of the science to footnotes; and in a sequel to the first novel, "The Struggle for Pallas," he continued to rely on the familiar gambit of an encounter between exploring spacemen and alien forms of life on other worlds. In "After 1,000,000 Years" he attempted to resolve the paradoxes inherent in the popular time-travel theme while depicting the dilemma of a world facing extinction. A variation of the same concept received original treatment in "When the Earth Tilted," in which the legendary children of Mu were discovered living comfortably in a lush Antarctica while the rest of the world starved.

These last four works had appeared in magazines edited by Hugo Gernsback, but Walsh ceased to write for Gernsback when, like many other contributors, he found his just dues were not always forthcoming without a struggle. "The Terror Out of Space," in which the Martians aid the Earth in resisting a menace from a world hidden behind the Moon, appeared in *Amazing* after British publishers found it too unconventional. For this, the author also concealed his own identity behind the pen-name H. Haverstock Hill, derived from a London thoroughfare immortalised by H.G. Wells. Though somewhat overshadowed by E.E. "Doc" Smith's *Triplanetary*, the eventful tale was generally approved by readers, at least one of whom penetrated the disguise. Walsh was too occupied with his mysteries to concern himself overmuch with British science fiction, except to regret its limitations. "The Stick Men," an undistinguished tale of alien invasion, marked his only appearance in *Fantasy*, and the first issue of *Science Fantasy* featured "The Belt," a well-written story of a space expedition which followed the break-up of the Moon in a cosmic collision.

—Walter Gillings

———————

WALTERS, Hugh.   Pseudonym for Walter Llewellyn Hughes. British.   Born in Bilston, Staffordshire, 15 June 1910. Educated at St. Martin's School; Bilston Central School; Dudley Grammar School, 1923-26; Wednesbury College, 1939-41; Wolverhampton Polytechnic, 1941-43. Married 1) Doris Higgins in 1933, one son and one daughter; 2) Susan Hughes in 1977. Since 1954, Managing Director, Bransteds Ltd., engineers, and Chairman, Walter Hughes Ltd., furnishings. Justice of the Peace, 1947-74. Agent: John Farquharson Ltd., 8 Bell Yard, London WC2A 2JU. Address: 16 Elm Avenue, Bilston, West Midlands WV14 6AS, England.

SCIENCE-FICTION PUBLICATIONS

Novels (juvenile; series: Chris Godfrey in all books)

Blast Off at Woomera.   London, Faber, 1957; as *Blast-Off at 0300*, New York, Criterion, 1958.
The Domes of Pico.   London, Faber, 1958; as *Menace from the Moon*, New York, Criterion, 1959.
Operation Columbus.   London, Faber, 1960; as *First on the Moon*, New York, Criterion, 1961.

Moon Base One.   London, Faber, 1961; as *Outpost on the Moon*, New York, Criterion, 1962.
Expedition Venus.   London, Faber, 1962; New York, Criterion, 1963.
Destination Mars.   London, Faber, 1963; New York, Criterion, 1964.
Terror by Satellite.   London, Faber, and New York, Criterion, 1964.
Mission to Mercury.   London, Faber, and New York, Criterion, 1965.
Journey to Jupiter.   London, Faber, 1965; New York, Criterion, 1966.
Spaceship to Saturn.   London, Faber, and New York, Criterion, 1967.
The Mohole Mystery.   London, Faber, 1968; as *The Mohole Menace*, New York, Criterion, 1969.
Nearly Neptune.   London, Faber, 1969; as *Neptune One Is Missing*, New York, Washburn, 1969.
First Contact? London, Faber, 1971; Nashville, Nelson, 1973.
Passage to Pluto.   London, Faber, and Nashville, Nelson, 1973.
Tony Hale, Space Detective.   London, Faber, 1973.
Murder on Mars.   London, Faber, 1975.
Boy Astronaut.   London, Abelard Schuman, 1977.
The Caves of Drach.   London, Faber, 1977.
The Last Disaster.   London, Faber, 1978.
The Blue Aura.   London, Faber, 1979.
First Family on the Moon.   London, Abelard Schuman, 1979.

Hugh Walters comments:
All my books are for young people in the 9-11 and 11-16 age groups. I believe that books for this readership should 1) entertain, which is the primary object; 2) educate painlessly (astronomy, mathematics, geology, etc.); 3) inspire the young people of today to become the scientists and technicians of tomorrow.

*   *   *

Hugh Walters has devoted his entire writing career to children's SF, and the results have been mixed. At first, his novels were welcomed as filling a void in SF publishing, being praised as the way SF should be written for children. Gradually critical opinion shifted as Walters's fiction came to be seen as repetitive, formula-bound, and even carelessly written; and the attention it received from the review media in both SF and children's literature virtually ceased. In the face of critical neglect and sometimes even open scorn, the wonder is, then, that Walters's novels continue to be published and have retained popularity for as long as they have. Obviously, his publishers are satisfied that the young audience Walters writes for does read and enjoy his novels and, ignoring adult disapproval, even puts pressure upon librarians to keep his books in circulation and order new titles as they appear. This phenomenon is readily understood once it is perceived that Walters's fiction is the result of his attempt to wed the formulas and expectations of boys' series books and SF. In other words, Walters's SF manifests both the strengths and weaknesses of children's series fiction writing.

On one hand, Walters's SF celebrates the exploits of youthful, dashing, and resourceful protagonists that boys chaffing under the dullness of their routine-filled lives enthusiastically identify with. In *Operation Columbus* Chris Godfrey, hero of Walters's SF, is the first person on the moon and he also magnanimously saves the life of his young Russian rival, Serge Smyslov, who had previously disabled Chris's space craft. Chris then pilots the Russian's space ship safely to earth in spite of not being familiar with the controls. In *Terror by Satellite* Tony Hale, who appears in some of the Godfrey books, is the remaining link between earth and the Observatory, the space satellite taken over by its crazed commander, Hendriks, who threatens to destroy earth; through his skill in electronics Tony proves indispensable as Chris successfully retakes control of the Observatory. Of more than passing interest is that Walters is clearly a knowledgeable author of children's books, and is careful to balance Chris, the public-school boy born to privilege and noblesse oblige, with Tony, the son of lower-class shop-keeping parents. In this way, many different kinds of young readers may be able to identify with Walters's protagonists. Further, although he does emphasize action and the various dangers of space exploration—

emphases obviously intended to capture the attention of young readers—Walters does not neglect space technology and weaponry. Described in detail, these are usually up-to-date or plausibly extrapolated so that youngsters looking for "nuts and bolts SF" are readily satisfied.

On the other hand, Walters's SF exhibits the weaknesses characteristic of most series fiction: conventional, two-dimensional characterization, repetitive and predictable plotting, and dull, pedestrian writing. As a result of these weaknesses, Walters has rightfully been denied major status. At the same time, however, it would be unfair to dismiss Walters as just another author of series SF, another Victor Appleton II or John Blaine. For, in view of his strengths it is clear that Walters's work is definitely a cut or two above typical series SF.

—Francis J. Molson

WANDREI, Donald. American. Born in 1908. Founding Editor, with August Derleth, Arkham House, 1939-42. Address: 1152 Portland Avenue, St. Paul, Minnesota 55104, U.S.A.

SCIENCE-FICTION PUBLICATIONS

Novel

The Web of Easter Island. Sauk City, Wisconsin, Arkham House, 1948; London, Consul, 1961.

Short Stories

The Eye and the Finger. Sauk City, Wisconsin, Arkham House, 1944.
Strange Harvest. Sauk City, Wisconsin, Arkham House, 1965.

OTHER PUBLICATIONS

Verse

Ecstasy and Other Poems. Athol, Massachusetts, Cook, 1928.
Dark Odyssey. St. Paul, Webb, 1931.
Poems for Midnight. Sauk City, Wisconsin, Arkham House, 1964.

Other

Editor, with August Derleth, *The Outsiders and Others,* by H.P. Lovecraft. Sauk City, Wisconsin, Arkham House, 1939.
Editor, with August Derleth, *Beyond the Wall of Sleep,* by H.P. Lovecraft. Sauk City, Wisconsin, Arkham House, 1943.
Editor, with August Derleth, *Marginalia,* by H.P. Lovecraft. Sauk City, Wisconsin, Arkham House, 1944.
Editor, with August Derleth, *Selected Letters 1911-1924, 1925-1929, 1929-1931,* by H.P. Lovecraft. Sauk City, Wisconsin, Arkham House, 3 vols., 1965-71.

*   *   *

Donald Wandrei's short SF appeared in a variety of pulp, slick, and academic outlets from 1926 to 1953. Wandrei was a frequent contributor to *Weird Tales,* but most of his appearances there were SF, not fantasy; his novel, *The Web of Easter Island,* is SF despite its close connection to H.P. Lovecraft's Cthulhu Mythos. Throughout the body of Wandrei's work runs a fascination with science, scientists, and the scientific attitude. Despite their scientific form, however, the stories are almost invariably horror stories. Considered as such, many of them work very well indeed. An ill-conceived experiment may bloodily destroy the experimenter in front of his

wife—or may release all atomic bonds, allowing the Earth to slump into a formless mass. Aliens invade across space or dimensional boundaries, doing enormous, graphically described damage. Human warfare sets into motion events which destroy the universe, the Earth, or simply civilization. Natural processes bring the universe to a quiet end or sterilize all life on Earth.

The unity of the stories is deeper than the horrifying nature of the events alone: there is also the coldness with which the events are perpetrated. A well-written illustration of this tendency is "The Witch-Makers." An adventurer trying to escape with the jeweled idol he stole from an African tribe stumbles into the camp of a pair of scientists. They have chosen to camp in an uncivilized area so that no one will interfere with their experiments in mind-transfer among animals. They experiment on the unwilling adventurer until they kill him, feeling neither compassion nor dislike for their human guinea pig. The effect is chilling.

Regrettably, Wandrei had little scientific background, a factor which severely weakens some of his best-known stories and most of the minor ones. "Colossus" and "Colossus Eternal," in effect the two halves of a novella, have a truly cosmic conclusion; but they are riddled with—and indeed built upon—repeated misunderstandings of basic concepts such as the periodic table and the difference between mass and volume. Likewise, the universe of "The Red Brain" is being choked with dust which glues all the stars to blackness, a notion, whatever its validity in 1927, which has not aged well but which is crucial to the plot.

However, when Wandrei wrote of characters and settings with which he was personally familiar, he consistently created stories of great reality and impact. The Upper Minnesota farmer and his wife in "The Crystal Bullet" are tersely and ably described. They are bewildered by the object which falls in their woodlot; and while they react to the object, they do not halt the story to explain the event as Wandrei's scientists would have felt compelled to do. Similarly, the overworked reporter of "Infinity Zero" is wholly real. He is so wrapped up in the everyday horrors of war-time news-gathering that it is some time before he realizes that he has witnessed the beginning of the process which will end the world in a few weeks.

The Web of Easter Island adds a level of compassion and, perhaps, hope to the horror it shares with the shorter fiction. A statuette turns up in a British cemetery amid buried structures built in the prehuman past. The statuette proceeds westward from one doomed carrier to another. It is studied and finally pursued by an archeologist who realizes that it is only a portion of a living being which will open our dimension to its own and the creatures thereof—unless stopped. The confrontation on Easter Island is not a final confrontation: there can be no final victory over such an opponent. But Mankind has found a champion, and at whatever cost to that individual there will be someone to protect the Earth beyond the foreseeable future.

The bulk of Wandrei's work is flawed, but there is some merit in the worst of it. At his best, Wandrei wrote fiction that was the equal of anything of its type.

—David A. Drake

WATERLOO, Stanley. American. Born in St. Clair County, Michigan, 21 May 1846. Educated at the University of Michigan, Ann Arbor, A.B. 1869. Married Anna C. Kitten in 1874. Journalist and editor: reporter in Chicago, 1870-71; co-owner, St. Louis *Journal,* 1872; editor, St. Louis *Republic Chronicle* and *Globe-Democrat;* founded St. Paul *Day;* writer, Chicago *Tribune;* editor in chief, Chicago *Mail;* editor, Washington *Critic and Capitol.* A.M.: University of Michigan, 1898. *Died 11 October 1913.*

SCIENCE-FICTION PUBLICATIONS

Novels

The Story of Ab: A Tale in the Time of the Cave Men. Chicago, Way and Williams, 1897.

Armageddon. Chicago, Rand McNally, 1898.
A Son of the Ages. New York, Doubleday, and London, Curtis Brown, 1914.

Short Stories

The Wolf's Long Howl. Chicago, Stone, 1899.

OTHER PUBLICATIONS

Novels

A Man and a Woman. Chicago, Schulte, 1892; London, Redway, 1896.
An Odd Situation. Chicago, Morrill Higgins, 1893; London, Black, 1896.
The Launching of a Man. Chicago, Rand McNally, 1899.
The Seekers. Chicago, Stone, 1900.
The Cassowary. Chicago, Monarch, 1906.

Other

How It Looks. New York, Brentano's, 1888.
Honest Money. Chicago, Equitable, 1895.
These Are My Jewels (juvenile). Chicago, Coolidge and Waterloo, 1902.

Editor, with John Wesley Hanson, Jr., *Famous American Men and Women.* Chicago, Wabash, 1896; as *Eminent Sons and Daughters of Columbia,* Chicago, International, 1896; as *Our Living Leaders,* Chicago, Monarch, 1896.
Editor, *The Parties and the Men; or, Political Issues of 1896.* Chicago, Conkey, 1896.
Editor, *The Story of a Strange Career.* New York, Appleton, 1902.

*   *   *

In discussing Stanley Waterloo's novels it is necessary to differentiate between the conception and the execution of the works. *The Story of Ab* is an early realistic novel of prehistoric man. Jack London admitted plagiarizing it for his *Before Adam,* and Waterloo's novel predated even H.G. Wells's splendid "A Story of the Stone Age" by some months. (Lang's still earlier "The Romance of the First Radical" differs from both works in being based in anthropology, not archeology, and being primarily a vehicle for social comment.) Similarly, *Armageddon* was probably the first of the fictional attempts to presage World War I with its weaponry and fabric of alliances. Writers as fine as Wells and Shiel (and many of lesser note) again followed in Waterloo's footsteps. On the other hand, Waterloo's execution (with a few brief exceptions) ranged from poor to worse. Both these novels as well as mainstream novels by Waterloo show signs of hasty construction and a basic lack of writing talent.

The Story of Ab is a serious attempt at the biography of a Stone Age (perhaps Neanderthal) man, told through significant incidents. Ab does many of the things that prehistoric heroes have done in more recent fiction: he hunts mammoths, domesticates dogs, slays a sabre-toothed tiger, invents the bow, and wages the first war. He does *not* tame fire. Waterloo claims to have based his novel on the best contemporary scientific opinion. Fire had been used by men long before the rise of Ab's subspecies, and Waterloo refused to take artistic license with scientific fact. While our knowledge of prehistory has greatly increased in the years since the book was published, Waterloo's obvious care keeps the novel from being badly dated. Indeed, Waterloo's picture of the Clam People combing tide flats for food and scuttling deeper in the water when danger threatens anticipates that drawn by Elaine Morgan in her 1972 treatise *The Descent of Woman.* However, the incidents of Ab's life are only incidents. Some of them are spun into short skeins, but there is no connected purpose controlling the action of the novel. In general, chapters stand or fall on their own merits. There is little preparation for later events and almost no character development.

Armageddon is also rich in exciting material: the creation of the first airship, the building of a sea-level canal through Nicaragua, the

greatest sea battle of all time, and, for that matter, a romance between parties of widely differing social positions. Waterloo's failure to make any of this material interesting results from a combination of flaws. First, there are no realized characters. Second, matters of large moment are trivialized by their handling. For instance, the novel's description of the international political situation descends beneath the level of national stereotype to the anthropomorphization of nations *as* national stereotypes. Third, the gritty details which could create the illusion of reality in a fictional world are absent. From the evidence of the novel, Waterloo simply did not know enough about the gadgetry of the present to be able to describe realistically the gadgetry of his future.

In sum, Waterloo was imaginative and was capable of good research. His writing, however, was generally pedestrian and invariably hasty. *The Story of Ab* remains readable, especially for younger people; *Armageddon* is at most of historical interest.

—David A. Drake

———

WATKINS, William Jon. American. Born in Coaldale, Pennsylvania, 19 July 1942. Educated at Rutgers University, New Brunswick, New Jersey, B.S. 1964, M.Ed. 1965. Married Sandra Lee Preno in 1961; three children. Instructor, Delaware Valley College, Doyleston, Pennsylvania, 1965-68; high school teacher, Asbury Park, New Jersey, 1968-69. Instructor, 1969-70, Assistant Professor, 1970-71, and since 1971, Associate Professor of Humanities, Brookdale Community College, Lincroft, New Jersey. Recipient: Per Se Award, for play, 1970. Agent: Scott Meredith Literary Agency, 845 Third Avenue, New York, New York 10022. Address: 1406 Garven Avenue, Wanamassa, New Jersey 07712, U.S.A.

SCIENCE-FICTION PUBLICATIONS

Novels

Ecodeath, with Gene Snyder. New York, Doubleday, 1972.
Clickwhistle. New York, Doubleday, 1973.
The God Machine. New York, Doubleday, 1973.
The Litany of Sh'reev, with Gene Snyder. New York, Doubleday, 1976.
What Rough Beast. Chicago, Playboy Press, 1980.

Uncollected Short Stories

"The People's Choice," in *If* (New York), June 1974.
"Ten Micro Novels," in *Vertex* (Los Angeles), December 1974.
"The Last Ten Micro Novels," in *Vertex* (Los Angeles), August 1975.
"Like Sno-Humped Fields Afraid of Rain," in *2076: The American Tricentennial,* edited by Edward Bryant. New York, Pyramid, 1977.
"Untitled," in *New Worlds 10,* edited by Hilary Bailey. London, Corgi, 1977.
"Coming of Age in Henson's Tube," in *Isaac Asimov's Science Fiction Magazine* (New York), Spring 1977.
"Butcher's Thumb," in *Shadows,* edited by Charles L. Grant. New York, Doubleday, 1978.

OTHER PUBLICATIONS

Play

The Judas Wheel (produced Warrensburg, Missouri, 1970). New York, Smith, 1969.

Verse

Five Poems. Chula Vista, California, Word Press, 1968.

Other

A Fair Advantage (juvenile).   Englewood Cliffs, New Jersey, Prentice Hall, 1975.
Suburban Wilderness.   New York, Putnam, 1981.

*   *   *

William Jon Watkins's novels, two of which were written with Gene Snyder, show man as a corrupt evil-doer who creates his own doomsday crises in which he barely avoids the total extinction of human life on Earth.

In *Ecodeath* Earth is about to die from water pollution. Two characters, Watkins and Snyder, start out as opponents but soon pool forces in order to rescue mankind. They use teleportation and finally link their mindpower to transport a small group of survivors to a pollution-free parallel earth of the future by telekinesis. Mankind survives because Watkins realizes that time implies parallel worlds existing simultaneously in infinity.

In *Clickwhistle* extraterrestrial beings take possession of the minds of killer whales to send computerized commands to atomic missiles stored in submarines. Dr. Pearson, a dolphin authority, defeats the aliens with the help of dolphins but other human beings are either evil-doers or slaves of dark political powers. Intrigue and betrayal run rampant while Orcas and dolphins battle. Earth is saved when dolphins triumph but men will forever live in fear of political bosses.

The God Machine shows perpetual and total warfare between a totalitarian worldwide state machine of Orwell's *Nineteen Eighty-Four* type and a highly technological underground opponent. Sophisticated weapons and tactics improve with the need to accelerate extermination. A reduction machine, the "micronizer," is central to several plot twists. Ecological negligence is the trademark of the status quo. An unbreathable atmosphere makes the use of masks and air filters universal. Neither side is a definite winner in the end.

In *The Litany of Sh'reev* Sh'reev uses mental powers to heal and save lives while a chronic state of revolutionary wars wrecks civilization. Empire is run by the will of an absolute and totalitarian ruler who destroys extant royal families to seize their wealth. The revolutionaries are ESPers who reject the increase of oppression. Sh'reev gets his spiritual power from Tao techniques. His mind fuses with those of the sick and dying in a state called Sh'aela. Eternal Return in its Eastern version provides further existences for Sh'reev.

The central action of *What Rough Beast* is the hunt for one huge, extraterrestrial, telekinetic, furry humanoid female who lands on Earth in order to help humans acquire her talents. Corporation mentality as the villainous hunter is aided by an almost sentient computer, Slic 1000, and his offspring Tad. There is an ironical twist when corporational man, dominated by a rigid mentality, becomes a dehumanized animal backbiting other corporate members in the struggle for power and rewards while the computers become humanized. The hero and savior is Lth, the alien furry female whose telepathic abilities merge with Tad in order to confer superhuman status upon man. Mankind is saved when sentient microcomputers become an implanted standard stabilizing device in human brains.

Although Watkins's novels are simply constructed and appropriate for juvenile audiences they deal with the vital issue of man's chances of survival. In each instance, man brings a catastrophic end upon himself and an environment he can neither preserve nor duplicate, and avoids self-annihilation by the slightest margin. Watkins implies that mankind, part angel but mostly beast, is on a cyclical course and will probably repeat its past mistakes. In *What Rough Beast*, Watkins introduces two new solutions to the "scorpion syndrome," man against himself. One is Lth's Superwoman mentality; the other is brain microcomputer implantation. In both cases, Watkins suggests that man can not be his own master.

—Eric A. Fontaine

WATSON, Ian. British. Born in North Shields, Northumberland, 20 April 1943. Educated at Tynemouth School, 1948-59; Balliol College, Oxford, 1960-65, B.A. (honours) in English 1963, B.Litt. 1965, M.A. 1966. Married Judith Jackson in 1962; one daughter. Lecturer, University College, Dar es Salaam, Tanzania, 1965-67, and Tokyo University of Education, 1967-70; Lecturer, 1970-75, and Senior Lecturer in Complementary Studies, 1975-76, Birmingham Polytechnic Art and Design Centre. Features editor and regular contributor, *Foundation*, London. Recipient: Prix Apollo (France), 1975; Orbit Award, 1976; British Science Fiction Association Award, 1978. Address: Bay House, Banbury Road, Moreton Pinkney, near Daventry, Northamptonshire, England.

SCIENCE-FICTION PUBLICATIONS

Novels

The Embedding.   London, Gollancz, 1973; New York, Scribner, 1975.
The Jonah Kit.   London, Gollancz, 1975; New York, Scribner, 1976.
The Martian Inca.   London, Gollancz, and New York, Scribner, 1977.
Alien Embassy.   London, Gollancz, 1977; New York, Ace, 1978.
Miracle Visitors.   London, Gollancz, and New York, Ace, 1978.
God's World.   London, Gollancz, 1979.
The Gardens of Delight.   London, Gollancz, 1980.
Under Heaven's Bridge, with Michael Bishop.   London, Gollancz, 1980.

Short Story

The Very Slow Time Machine.   London, Gollancz, and New York, Ace, 1979.

Uncollected Short Stories

"Insight," in *Destinies* (New York), February-March 1980.
"The World Science Fiction Convention of 2080," in *Fantasy and Science Fiction* (New York), September 1980.

OTHER PUBLICATIONS

Other

Japan: A Cat's Eye View.   Osaka, Bunken, 1969.
"SF Idea Capsules for Art Students," in *Foundation 5* (London), January 1974.
"Le Guin's *Lathe of Heaven* and the Role of Dick: The False Reality as Mediator," in *Science-Fiction Studies* (Terre Haute, Indiana), March 1975.
"The Forest as Metaphor for Mind," in *Science-Fiction Studies* (Terre Haute, Indiana), November 1975.
"Towards an Alien Linguistics," in *Vector 71* (Reading), 1975.
"The Greening of Ballard," in *J. G. Ballard: The First Twenty Years*, edited by James Goddard and David Pringle.   Hayes, Middlesex, Bran's Head, 1976.
"Science Fiction: Form Versus Content" and "Fancy Going to the Vats?," in *Foundation 10* (London), June 1976.
"W(h)ither Science Fiction?," in *Vector 78* (Reading), 1976.
Japan Tomorrow.   Osaka, Bunken, 1977.
"The Crudities of Science Fiction," in *Arena* (Canterbury), March 1978.
"Some Sufist Insights into the Nature of Inexplicable Events," in *SFWA Bulletin* (Sea Cliff, New York), 1979.

Ian Watson comments:
My books are all primarily about the relationship between reality and consciousness (testing out this theme variously by way of linguistics, speculation about cetacean intelligence, evolution, novel life forms, the UFO mythos, etc.) and whether any kind of ultimate understanding of the nature of reality and the reason for life and the universe may or may not be arrived at. Intersecting this is frequently—particularly in my earlier books—a strong socio-

political underpinning to events. A dialectic of history and transcendence is at work. I regard my fiction as a research programme, in fictional form, into the nature of existence and the nature of knowledge.

* * *

"SF is founded upon the exploration of ideas, rather than stylistics. It is a community of ideas; in its sum, it composes what one might call an 'idea-myth,' the idea-myth of man in the universe," Ian Watson wrote in "The Crudities of Science Fiction." That Watson should define science fiction in terms of its speculative content, with particular emphasis on myth and ontology, provides a telling gloss on both the form and the substance of his novels and stories. A former academic whose work displays not only a serious metaphysical bent but also an engaging internationalism in his choice of settings and characters, Ian Watson vaulted to prominence with the publication of *The Embedding*. Few novel-length debuts are so dazzling, either for their structural brilliance or for the multifaceted complexity of their intellectual speculations, and reviewers responded with laudatory comparisons to the works of Arthur C. Clarke and Stanislaw Lem. Later J.G. Ballard emphatically styled Ian Watson "the most interesting British SF writer of ideas—or, more accurately, the *only* British SF writer of ideas" (*New Statesman*). Christopher Priest, likewise commenting on Watson's talent for launching cerebral flights of fancy within the expansive parameters of science fiction, has described his novels as having "a Wagnerian quality to them, with immense clashings of intellectual bravura and cosmic event" (Introduction to *Anticipations*, 1978).

One idea exploited in different guises or subtle variations from novel to novel is Watson's strategically held "belief" that consensus reality, or the world of everyday experience, is ripe for transcendence. The means of transcending our human limitations or the prison of the physical universe may differ from one fictional foray to the next, but the fact that there does exist a transcendent mental set or cosmic continuum to which we may or should aspire remains a conspicuous constant. Although Watson usually embeds this idea in a scrupulously rational context (often it is a research project or a scientific mission), a strong element of the primordial or the mystical (from meta-linguistics to Sufism) lends his several restatements of the concept a rich and endlessly ramifying ambiguity. Indeed, Watson is especially adept at legitimizing the paranormal with the argot of technological discourse. Good examples of this technique include not only the recent stories "The Very Slow Time Machine" and "The Rooms of Paradise," but the mind-bogglingly open-ended novel *Miracle Visitors*, whose concluding sentence, rendered almost after the fashion of a haiku or a koan, points directly to the metaphysical beyond with which Watson is so obsessed: "Somewhere else, / Khidr smiled."

The structural complexity of Watson's work, as a matter of fact, almost certainly stems from his preoccupation with ideas. In *The Embedding*, for instance, the agency for arriving at the freedom and omnipotence of "Other-Reality" is language, a distilled grammar of perception permitting its speakers to encompass "This-Reality" psycho-biologically and so to transcend it. Language, then, is the unifying element of the complicated, threefold plot. First, in an English hospital a group of Pakistani orphans are learning artificial languages as "probes at the frontiers of mind." Second, a French anthropologist in the Amazon is studying a tribe of Indians whose use of a local drug enables them to alter their day-to-day language into an otherwise incomprehensible embedded language of transcendent perception and control. Finally, an alien race called the Sp'thra, whose name means "Signal Traders," arrive on Earth and as part of their ongoing "language inventory" of the galaxy ask for six living human brains programmed with six different terrestrial grammars. By this inventory the Sp'thra hope to escape "This-Reality" for the ineffable "Other-Reality" now inhabited by a transcendent alien species called the "Change Speakers." Watson's ending, however, is both apocalyptic and enigmatic.

His next two novels follow a somewhat similar pattern. In *The Jonah Kit* escape from this illusory universe lies within the grasp only of the world's whales. By forming a "Thought Star"—a cetacean computer whose living components reach out with their minds to an alternate continuum—and by later committing mass suicide, these self-aware sea beasts abstract themselves from the homocen-

tric madnesses of man. In *The Martian Inca*, on the other hand, transcendence derives from a viral activator in the soil of Mars. This mysterious catalyst triggers a dormant genetic program in our DNA for releasing the superhuman in every adult representative of the species—but humanity, in the person of a bourgeois American astronaut, resists the transformation and the novel ends on a decidedly downbeat note. Although as complex and inventive as *The Embedding*, these books cast a dark and somewhat fatalistic spell. (*The Martian Inca*, incidentally, contains the seminal idea for Watson's story "The Very Slow Time Machine.")

Between *The Martian Inca* and *Alien Embassy* an interesting change apparently took place in Watson's thinking. His fourth novel—besides boasting his most appealing protagonist, Lila Makindi, who also narrates her own story—is noteworthy for framing the moral dilemma of a young African woman who sees the conscious formulation of humanity's next evolutionary step as a betrayal of the species *as it exists at present*. Watson cannily dramatizes the poignancy of Lila's dilemma even as he establishes forceful arguments for the necessity of society's taking the step that so appalls her. Although beyond is better, getting there may entail fearful hardships and the cruelty of institutionalized deceit. A departure from as well as a recognizable sequel to his previous work, *Alien Embassy* shows Watson opting for a hard-nosed humanistic compassion for his characters. For just that reason, it may be his most moving novel to date.

Miracle Visitors, perhaps an even more structurally complex novel than *The Embedding*, partakes of this same auctorial generosity and openmindedness. Here Watson's presiding metaphor for transcendence is the phenomenon of the UFO experience, which, because it manifests itself to different characters in different ways, establishes at least three separate subjective "realities" within the novel's conceptual framework. Imagine a Philip K. Dick novel sustained by undiluted intellectual rigor, and you have some idea of the tone and the narrative effects of *Miracle Visitors*. Its most striking bravura passage details a trip to the moon in a Ford Thunderbird. Although an intrinsically wacky, if not downright dumb, concept, Watson handles it with admirable pokerfaced dexterity—just as he does the psychological portraiture of his principal characters, even if the major part of his own sympathy seems to lie with the consciousness researcher, John Deacon. The book's final lines, "Somewhere else, / Khidr smiled," are therefore a kind of password phrase hinting at both the reality and the benevolence of Watson's hoped-for beyond. They also provide a clue to his own aesthetic orientation to the problem of demonstrable human limitations; the desire to know what some have labeled unknowable, Watson implies, is precisely what makes us human.

The Very Slow Time Machine, although lacking the eerily brilliant story "The Rooms of Paradise," contains a full-course feast of Watson's short fiction—from the title story to the early and nightmarish "Thy Blood Like Milk" to the playful and admonitory "Programmed Love Story" to the concluding complex mini-novel "The Event Horizon." In addition, Watson has written *God's World*, which he describes as "a kind of companion novel to *Miracle Visitors*," although neither a sequel nor a blatant parallel, and *The Gardens of Delight*, in which Watson creates a world based on the famous triptych by Hieronymus Bosch.

Not yet forty, Watson has already produced a formidable oeuvre. The breadth of his intellectual interests, along with the nimbleness of his imagination and his wholehearted commitment to the possibilities of the field, ensures that no attempt to assess either the direction or the quality of 20th-century science fiction can ignore his remarkable contribution.

—Michael Bishop

WEINBAUM, Stanley G(rauman). American. Born in Louisville, Kentucky, in 1900. Educated at public schools in Milwaukee; University of Wisconsin, Madison, B.Chem.Engr. 1923. *Died 14 December 1935.*

SCIENCE-FICTION PUBLICATIONS

Novels

The New Adam. Chicago, Ziff Davis, 1939; London, Sphere, 1974.
The Black Flame. Reading, Pennsylvania, Fantasy Press, 1948.
The Dark Other. Los Angeles, Fantasy, 1950.

Short Stories

Dawn of Flame. New York, Ruppert, 1936.
A Martian Odyssey and Others. Reading, Pennsylvania, Fantasy Press, 1949.
The Red Peri. Reading, Pennsylvania, Fantasy Press, 1952.
The Best of Stanley G. Weinbaum. New York, Ballantine, 1974; London, Sphere, 1977.

*   *   *

It is now formulaic to include the term "tragic death" with each mention of the name Stanley G. Weinbaum. His total career as a writer lasted from the publication of "A Martian Odyssey" in the July 1934 issue of *Wonder Stories* to his death in December 1935. Almost every critic who discusses the early years of pulp science fiction singles out Weinbaum as a unique voice who never had the chance to develop fully his powers as a writer. While one can never know just how far these powers would have in fact developed, a number of conclusions can be drawn, based on the short stories published during Weinbaum's career and a number of stories published after his death.

With his very first story Weinbaum managed to break a number of standard formulae in pulp fiction. "A Martian Odyssey" not only attempted to portray aliens as creatures unlike man but went so far as to present one such creature in a highly sympathetic light. Weinbaum seems to have been one of the first, if not the first, to realize that aliens may differ from humans in not only their outer appearances but their inner thought processes as well. His invention of the bib-bird-like creature Tweel in "A Martian Odyssey" stands as a major step in the genre because it undertakes the difficult task of describing the actions of a creature that clearly thinks differently. Given its non-human nature, Weinbaum uses a human character's interaction with Tweel to bring out the alien's basic nature. While both the human character and the reader begin the story amused at the weird actions of Tweel, this amusement is changed to admiration and respect by the end of the story. Tweel first grasps the possibility of communication between alien and human, and is able to make use of the human language while the human character gives up any chance of comprehending Tweel's. Tweel shows the greater understanding of the other aliens on Mars, and looks more at home on Mars, even though he too is an explorer from another planet. In other words, with Tweel readers were given an alternative to the murderous aliens of H.G. Wells, and many writers were soon imitating Weinbaum.

But Weinbaum's stories were not successful simply because he had invented a new attitude toward aliens. In the stories that followed (all in *Wonder Stories*) Weinbaum continued to emphasize the fact that his aliens lived by systems of logic that were different from man's, and it is the fact that these different systems were both strange *and* internally consistent that won him a wide audience. The care with which Weinbaum created new aliens and described their alienness was unique to the pulp fiction of its time. Thus, even in a story such as "Paradise Planet" in which alien forms on Venus do menace humans, the threat originates in the nature of life on Venus and not in some anthropomorphic desire to rape and pillage humanity.

As *Wonder Stories* continued to publish stories by Weinbaum almost monthly, a second reason for his popularity became apparent: his stories contained a good deal of humor. This humor was often achieved at the expense of human character and human science. Thus in a series of stories based on a delightfully "mad" scientist named Professor Haskel van Manderpootz ("The Worlds of If," "The Ideal," and "The Point of View"), inventions constantly appear that seem to have no other reason for existence than the fact that they constantly complicate the life of Dixon Wells, a young and somewhat love-sick romantic.

Weinbaum's treatment of aliens and his use of humor, however, did not free him from all of the pulp formulas. In "Pygmalion's Spectacles," for example, Weinbaum refuses to bring the story to its logical, tragic conclusion. A young man, while wearing spectacles that allow the wearer to take full part in an illusion, falls in love with a dream woman. When the dream ends and he must take off the glasses, he remains in love with the woman. Weinbaum, however, begs the whole issue of illusion and reality when at the end of the story a living counterpart to the dream woman is produced. Given the strength with which Weinbaum evokes the dream world and the sadness that the hero undergoes with its loss, one feels that "Pygmalion's Spectacles" could have been a better story. Weinbaum's ties to pulp fiction can also be seen in *The Black Flame*, which contains two versions of the same story. The first version, "Dawn of Flame" is a competent but uninspired story of the innocent young man who meets the exotic and erotic immortal woman. Reminiscent of H. Rider Haggard's *She*, the story contains some powerfully sexual scenes but basically remains a formula story. In the second version, "The Black Flame," however, Weinbaum rewrites the story and adds the paraphernalia of a pulp story complete with happy ending. The mixture of these two separate traditions was less than successful, and "The Black Flame" seems to be constantly struggling to make up its mind as to exactly what it wants to be.

On those occasions when Weinbaum does completely overcome his pulp environment, however, the fiction he produces is both sensitive and moving. In "The Adoptive Ultimate" he refuses to opt for the happy ending, and in *The New Adam* Weinbaum takes the stock superman character and turns him into a sympathetic character who is alone in a world of mere humans. Because of the first-person narration the reader is able to see a side of such a character that rarely was portrayed before Weinbaum's treatment, and never so carefully or intimately. Lester del Rey calls the hero of *The New Adam* "a rather helpless failure," but such a characterization refuses to take into account what caused that failure, what it was in the nature of being a superman that led to it. And it is Weinbaum's investigation of exactly these questions in a sympathetic and painstaking manner that makes the novel so readable.

Works like *The New Adam* are rare in science fiction. Too often they are ignored when they do appear, and such was particularly true during the great age of the pulps. Weinbaum is remembered best for his aliens and the strange worlds he created for his stories in *Wonder Stories*. Thus, "A Martian Odyssey" remains Stanley Weinbaum's best known work. While such stories have had a significant effect on the direction science fiction was to take in the 1940's, *The New Adam* deserves far more notice than it has received to date.

—Stephen H. Goldman

WELLMAN, Manly Wade. Also writes as Gans T. Field. American. Born in Kamundongo, Angola, 21 May 1903; brother of the writer Paul I. Wellman. Educated at Wichita State University, Kansas, A.B. 1926; Columbia University, New York, B.Lit. 1927. Married Frances Obrist in 1930; one son. Reporter and feature writer, Wichita *Beacon*, 1927-30, and *Eagle*, 1930-34; assistant project supervisor, WPA Writers Project, New York, 1936-38; Instructor of Creative Writing, Elon College, North Carolina, 1962-70, and University of North Carolina evening college, Chapel Hill, 1963-73. Recipient: Ellery Queen Award, 1946; American Association for State and Local History certificate, 1973; H.P. Lovecraft Award, 1975. Agent: Kirby McCauley, 60 East 42nd Street, New York, New York 10017. Address: Box 744, Chapel Hill, North Carolina 27514, U.S.A.

SCIENCE-FICTION PUBLICATIONS

Novels (series: John the Ballad Singer)

The Invading Asteroid. New York, Stellar, 1932.
Sojarr of Titan. New York, Crestwood, 1949.
The Beasts from Beyond. London, Consul, 1950.
The Devil's Planet. London, Consul, 1951.
Twice in Time. New York, Avalon, 1957.
Giants from Eternity. New York, Avalon, 1959.
The Dark Destroyers. New York, Avalon, 1959.
Island in the Sky. New York, Avalon, 1961.
The Solar Invasion. New York, Popular Library, 1968.
Sherlock Holmes's War of the Worlds, with Wade Wellman. New York, Warner, 1975.
The Beyonders. New York, Warner, 1977; London, Dobson, 1980.
The Old Gods Waken (John). New York, Doubleday, 1979.
After Dark (John). New York, Doubleday, 1980.

Short Stories

Who Fears the Devil? Sauk City, Wisconsin, Arkham House, 1963.
Worse Things Waiting. Chapel Hill, North Carolina, Carcosa, 1973.

Uncollected Short Stories

"Goodman's Place," in *Night Chills,* edited by Kirby McCauley. New York, Avon, 1975.
"The Beasts That Perish," in *Whispers 3,* 1975.
"The Ghastly Priest Doth Reign," in *Fantasy and Science Fiction* (New York), March 1975.
"The Petey Car," in *Superhorror,* edited by Ramsey Campbell. London, W.H. Allen, 1976; New York, St. Martin's Press, 1977.
"Where the Woodbine Twineth," in *Fantasy and Science Fiction* (New York), October 1976.
"Caretaker," in *Fantasy and Science Fiction* (New York), October 1977.
"Hundred Years Gone," in *Fantasy and Science Fiction* (New York), March 1978.
"The Spring," in *Shadows 2,* edited by Charles L. Grant. New York, Doubleday, 1979.
"Toad's Foot," in *Fantasy and Science Fiction* (New York), April 1979.
"What of the Night," in *Fantasy and Science Fiction* (New York), March 1980.

OTHER PUBLICATIONS

Novels

Romance in Black (as Gans T. Field). London, Mitre Press, 1946.
A Double Life (novelization of screenplay). Chicago, Century, 1947.
Find My Killer. New York, Farrar Straus, 1947; London, Sampson Low, 1948.
Fort Sun Dance. New York, Dell, and London, Corgi, 1955.
Candle of the Wicked. New York, Putnam, 1960.
Not at These Hands. New York, Putnam, 1962.

Novels (juvenile)

The Sleuth Patrol. New York, Nelson, 1947.
The Mystery of Lost Valley. New York, Nelson, 1948.
The Raiders of Beaver Lake. New York, Nelson, 1950.
The Haunting of Drowning Creek. New York, Holiday House, 1951.
Wild Dogs of Drowning Creek. New York, Holiday House, 1952.
The Last Mammoth. New York, Holiday House, 1953.
Gray Riders: Jeb Stuart and His Men. New York, Aladdin, 1954.
Rebel Mail Runner. New York, Holiday House, 1954.
Flag on the Levee. New York, Washburn, 1955.
To Unknown Lands. New York, Holiday House, 1956.

Young Squire Morgan. New York, Washburn, 1956.
Lights over Skeleton Ridge. New York, Washburn, 1957.
The Ghost Battalion: A Story of the Iron Scouts. New York, Washburn, 1958.
Ride, Rebels! New York, Washburn, 1959.
Appomattox Road. New York, Washburn, 1960.
Third String Center. New York, Washburn, 1960.
Rifles at Ramsour's Mill. New York, Washburn, 1961.
Battle for King's Mountain. New York, Washburn, 1962.
Clash on the Catawba. New York, Washburn, 1962.
The River Pirates. New York, Washburn, 1963.
Settlement on Shocco. Winston-Salem, North Carolina, Blair, 1963.
The South Fork Rangers. New York, Washburn, 1963.
The Master of Scare Hollow. New York, Washburn, 1964.
A True Story of the Revolting and Bloody Crimes of Sergeant Stanlas, U.S.A. Wichita, Kansas, Four Ducks Press, 1964.
The Great Riverboat Race. New York, Washburn, 1965.
Mystery at Bear Paw Gap. New York, Washburn, 1965.
Battle at Bear Paw Gap. New York, Washburn, 1966.
The Specter of Bear Paw Gap. New York, Washburn, 1966.
Jamestown Adventure. New York, Washburn, 1967.
Brave Horse: A Story of Janus. New York, Holt Rinehart, 1968.
Carolina Pirate. New York, Washburn, 1968.
Frontier Reporter. New York, Washburn, 1969.
Mountain Feud. New York, Washburn, 1969.
Napoleon of the West: A Story of the Aaron Burr Conspiracy. New York, Washburn, 1970.
Fast Break Five. New York, Washburn, 1971.

Play

Many Are the Hearts. Raleigh, North Carolina, Confederate Centennial Commission, 1961.

Other

Giant in Gray: A Biography of Wade Hampton of South Carolina. New York, Scribner, 1949.
Dead and Gone: Classic Crimes of North Carolina. Chapel Hill, University of North Carolina Press, 1954.
Rebel Boast: First at Bethel—Last at Appomattox. New York, Holt, 1956.
Fastest on the River. New York, Holt, 1957.
The Life and Times of Sir Archie, with Elizabeth Amis Blanchard. Chapel Hill, University of North Carolina Press, 1958.
The County of Warren, North Carolina, 1586-1917. Chapel Hill, University of North Carolina Press, 1959.
They Took Their Stand: The Founders of the Confederacy. New York, Putnam, 1959.
The Rebel Songster, with Frances Wellman. New York, Heritage House, 1959.
Harpers Ferry, Prize of War. Charlotte, North Carolina, McNally and Loftin, 1960.
The County of Gaston, with Robert F. Cope. Castonia, North Carolina, Gaston County Historical Society, 1961.
The County of Moore 1847-1947. Southern Pines, North Carolina, Moore County Historical Association, 1962.
Winston-Salem in History: The Founders. Winston-Salem, North Carolina, Blair, 1966.
The Kingdom of Madison. Chapel Hill, University of North Carolina Press, 1973.
The Story of Moore County. Southern Pines, North Carolina, Moore County Historical Association, 1974.

Manly Wade Wellman comments:

I came to America from an African wilderness, but with strong family heritage and association in the American west and south. I began by wanting to write of the fantastic, the imaginative. I wrote in other fields, too, but now I've returned to that first love. A writer must find himself out all alone, must understand himself, use himself in all he writes. More than by years or ability or reputation, your life is measured by the work you do. You pave your road by your writing, and travel it always into new wonders and perils and joys and sorrows. You find and use things out of sight and sound of all others. It's part of you, like the blood in your veins, the breath in your nostrils.

I look back on more than half a century of writing, and hope to keep on until they say the last words over me.

* * *

The bulk of Manly Wade Wellman's writing has been outside the science-fiction field. A popular writer during the heyday of the SF pulps, he is best known today as a fantasy author and for his fiction and nonfiction work in the field of Southern regionalism.

Wellman began selling SF as early as 1927 with "Back to the Beast" in *Weird Tales.* In 1930 he turned to writing as a full-time profession, and in 1934 moved to New York in order to be closer to his markets. After "Outlaws on Callisto" made the cover of the April 1936 *Astounding Stories,* Wellman became a client of the noted agent, Julius Schwartz, under whose direction he became part of the Better Publications stable. There Wellman became a regular contributor to *Thrilling Wonder Stories* and *Startling Stories.* These popular pulps, aimed at an adolescent readership, were well suited to Wellman's brisk, simple narrative style, and the bulk of his SF appeared in these and similar pulps. Most of his SF books are reprints of his earlier work, although recently he has begun to write SF again.

Wellman's first book publication was *The Invading Asteroid.* It set the tone for the sort of space opera Wellman was to become known for. He created a consistent futuristic setting of the 30th century, and utilized this for some 16 of his stories. Wellman's 30th century was pretty much the same as the 20th, with the addition of interplanetary travel and extraterrestrials. Nonetheless, so well-liked was Wellman's future world that fans cried "plagiarism" when Nelson Bond utilized certain of these elements for a story of his own, and Wellman had to explain that Bond had done so with his permission.

Sojarr of Titan is a "Tarzan of outer space" pastiche written at editor Leo Margulies's request. *The Beasts from Beyond* made use of the idea of invasion at the intersection point of bubble universes that Wellman recently returned to in *The Beyonders. The Devil's Planet,* part of his 30th-century series, is a murder mystery set on Mars that teams a human and an android as detectives, and appears to be the archetype of Asimov's *Caves of Steel. Twice in Time* is a novel of a man who travels through time to become Leonardo da Vinci. It is Wellman's most important SF work and remains a superior time-travel novel. *The Dark Destroyers* has Earthmen throwing off the yoke of extraterrestrial conquest. In *Giants from Eternity,* Pasteur, Darwin, Newton, Edison, and Curie are brought back to life to combat an alien growth that threatens to engulf the Earth. In *Island in the Sky* a future gladiator rebels against a technological dictatorship that holds Earth in thrall. A final reprint from the pulp days, *The Solar Invasion* is Wellman's one fling at writing a Captain Future episode.

During the 1960's Wellman collaborated with his son, Wade Wellman, for a series of droll pastiches that placed Doyle's Sherlock Holmes and Watson alongside Professor Challenger in the London of Wells's *War of the Worlds.* These were expanded and collected as *Sherlock Holmes's War of the Worlds,* a book which ranks among the best of the Holmes pastiches. *The Beyonders* is a routine novel of invasion by creatures from another dimension, with the saving charm of its Southern mountain setting.

Wellman has returned to writing fantasy in recent years, and it is in this genre that he has excelled. The best of his fantasy stories have been collected in *Who Fears the Devil?* and *Worse Things Waiting.*

—Karl Edward Wagner

WELLS, H(erbert) G(eorge). British. Born in Bromley, Kent, 21 September 1866. Educated at Mr. Morley's Commerical Academy, Bromley, until age 13: certificate in bookkeeping; apprentice draper in Windsor, 1880; student teacher at a school in Wookey, Somerset, 1880; apprentice chemist in Midhurst, Sussex, 1880-81; apprentice draper at Hyde's Emporium, Southsea, Hampshire, 1881-83; student/assistant at Midhurst Grammar School, 1883-84; studied at the Royal College of Science, London, 1884-87 (failed examinations); taught at Holt Academy, Wrexham, 1887-88, and at Henley House School, Kilburn, London, 1888-89; awarded B.Sc., University of London, 1890. Married 1) his cousin Isabel Mary Wells in 1891 (separated, 1893; divorced, 1895); 2) Amy Catherine Robbins in 1895 (died, 1927), two sons; had a son by the writer Rebecca West, the writer Anthony West. Tutor at the University Tutorial College, London, 1891-92; full-time writer from 1893; Labour candidate for Parliament, for the University of London, 1922, 1923. Member of the Fabian Society, 1903-08. D.Lit.: University of London, 1936; Honorary Fellow, Imperial College of Science and Technology, London. *Died 13 August 1946.*

SCIENCE-FICTION PUBLICATIONS

Novels

The Time Machine: An Invention. London, Heinemann, and New York, Holt, 1895.
The Island of Doctor Moreau. London, Heinemann, and New York, Stone and Kimball, 1896.
The Invisible Man: A Grotesque Romance. London, Pearson, and New York, Arnold, 1897.
The War of the Worlds. London, Heinemann, and New York, Harper, 1898.
When the Sleeper Wakes. London and New York, Harper, 1899; revised edition, as *The Sleeper Wakes,* London, Nelson, 1910.
The First Men in the Moon. London, Newnes, and Indianapolis, Bowen Merrill, 1901.
The Food of the Gods, and How It Came to Earth. London, Macmillan, and New York, Scribner, 1904.
A Modern Utopia. London, Chapman and Hall, and New York, Scribner, 1905.
In the Days of the Comet. London, Macmillan, and New York, Century, 1906.
The War in the Air, and Particularly How Mr. Bert Smallways Fared While It Lasted. London, Bell, and New York, Macmillan, 1908.
The World Set Free: A Story of Mankind. London, Macmillan, and New York, Dutton, 1914.
Men Like Gods. London, Cassell, and New York, Macmillan, 1923.
The Shape of Things to Come: The Ultimate Resolution. London, Hutchinson, and New York, Macmillan, 1933; revised edition, as *Things to Come* (film story), London, Cresset Press, and New York, Macmillan, 1935.
The Croquet Player. London, Chatto and Windus, 1936; New York, Viking Press, 1937.
Star Begotten: A Biological Fantasia. London, Chatto and Windus, and New York, Viking Press, 1937.
The Holy Terror. London, Joseph, and New York, Simon and Schuster, 1939.

Short Stories

The Stolen Bacillus and Other Incidents. London, Methuen, 1895.
The Plattner Story and Others. London, Methuen, 1897.
Thirty Strange Stories. New York, Arnold, 1897.
Tales of Space and Time. London, Harper, and New York, Doubleday, 1899.
Twelve Stories and a Dream. London, Macmillan, 1903; New York, Scribner, 1905.
The Country of the Blind and Other Stories. London, Nelson, 1911; revised edition of *The Country of the Blind,* London, Golden Cockerel Press, 1939.
The Door in the Wall and Other Stories. New York, Kennerley, 1911; London, Richards, 1915.
Complete Short Stories. London, Benn, 1927; as *The Short Stories of H.G. Wells,* New York, Doubleday, 1929.

28 Science Fiction Stories. New York, Dover, 1952.
Selected Short Stories. London, Penguin, 1958.
Best Science Fiction Stories of H.G. Wells. New York, Dover, 1966.

OTHER PUBLICATIONS

Novels

The Wonderful Visit. London, Dent, and New York, Macmillan, 1895.
The Wheels of Chance. London, Dent, and New York, Macmillan, 1896.
Love and Mr. Lewisham. London, Harper, and New York, Stokes, 1900.
The Sea Lady: A Tissue of Moonshine. London, Methuen, and New York, Appleton, 1902.
Kipps. London, Macmillan, and New York, Scribner, 1905.
Tono-Bungay. London, Macmillan, and New York, Duffield, 1908.
Ann Veronica. London, Unwin, and New York, Harper, 1909.
The History of Mr. Polly. London, Nelson, and New York, Duffield, 1910.
The New Machiavelli. London, Lane, and New York, Duffield, 1911.
Marriage. London, Macmillan, and New York, Duffield, 1912.
The Passionate Friends. London, Macmillan, and New York, Harper, 1913.
The Wife of Sir Isaac Harman. London and New York, Macmillan, 1914.
Boon. London, Unwin, and New York, Doran, 1915.
Bealby. London, Methuen, and New York, Macmillan, 1915.
The Research Magnificent. London and New York, Macmillan, 1915.
Mr. Britling Sees It Through. London, Cassell, and New York, Macmillan, 1916.
The Soul of a Bishop. London, Cassell, and New York, Macmillan, 1917.
Joan and Peter. London, Cassell, and New York, Macmillan, 1918.
The Undying Fire. London, Cassell, and New York, Macmillan, 1919.
The Secret Places of the Heart. London, Cassell, and New York, Macmillan, 1922.
The Dream. London, Cape, and New York, Macmillan, 1924.
Christina Alberta's Father. London, Cape, and New York, Macmillan, 1925.
The World of William Clissold. London, Benn, 3 vols., and New York, Doran, 2 vols., 1926.
Meanwhile: The Picture of a Lady. London, Benn, and New York, Doran, 1927.
Mr. Blettsworthy on Rampole Island. London, Benn, and New York, Doubleday, 1928.
The King Who Was a King: The Book of a Film. London, Benn, and New York, Doubleday, 1929.
The Autocracy of Mr. Parham. London, Heinemann, and New York, Doubleday, 1930.
The Bulpington of Blup. London, Hutchinson, 1932; New York, Macmillan, 1933.
Man Who Could Work Miracles (film story). London, Cresset Press, and New York, Macmillan, 1936.
Brynhild. London, Methuen, and New York, Scribner, 1937.
The Camford Visitation. London, Methuen, 1937.
The Brothers. London, Chatto and Windus, and New York, Viking Press, 1938.
Apropos of Dolores. London, Cape, and New York, Scribner, 1938.
The Holy Terror. London, Joseph, and New York, Simon and Schuster, 1939.
Babes in the Darkling Wood. London, Secker and Warburg, and New York, Alliance, 1940.
All Aboard for Ararat. London, Secker and Warburg, 1940; New York, Alliance, 1941.

You Can't Be Too Careful: A Sample of Life 1901-1951. London, Secker and Warburg, 1941; New York, Putnam, 1942.
The Wealth of Mr. Waddy, edited by Harris Wilson. Carbondale, Southern Illinois University Press, 1969.

Short Stories

Select Conversations with an Uncle (Now Extinct) and Two Other Reminiscences. London, Lane, and New York, Merriman, 1895.
A Cure for Love. New York, Scott, 1899.
The Vacant Country. New York, Kent, 1899.
Tales of the Unexpected [of Life and Adventure, of Wonder]. London, Collins, 3 vols., 1922-23.
The Valley of Spiders. London, Collins, 1964.
The Cone. London, Collins, 1965.

Plays

Kipps, with Rudolf Besier, adaptation of the novel by Wells (produced London, 1912).
The Wonderful Visit, with St. John Ervine, adaptation of the novel by Wells (produced London, 1921).
Hoopdriver's Holiday, adaptation of his novel *The Wheels of Chance*, edited by Michael Timko. Lafayette, Indiana, Purdue University English Department, 1964.

Screenplays: *H.G. Wells Comedies* (*Bluebottles, The Tonic, Daydreams*), with Frank Wells, 1928; *Things to Come*, 1936; *The Man Who Could Work Miracles*, 1936.

Other

Text-Book of Biology. London, Clive, 2 vols., 1893.
Honours Physiography, with R.A. Gregory. London, Hughes, 1893.
Certain Personal Matters: A Collection of Material, Mainly Autobiographical. London, Lawrence and Bullen, 1897.
Anticipations of the Reaction of Mechanical and Scientific Progress upon Human Life and Thought. London, Chapman and Hall, 1901; New York, Harper, 1902.
The Discovery of the Future (lecture). London, Unwin, 1902; New York, Heubsch, 1913.
Mankind in the Making. London, Chapman and Hall, 1903; New York, Scribner, 1904.
The Future in America: A Search after Realities. London, Chapman and Hall, and New York, Harper, 1906.
Faults of the Fabian (lecture). Privately printed, 1906.
Socialism and the Family. London, Fifield, 1906; Boston, Ball, 1908.
Reconstruction of the Fabian Society. Privately printed, 1906.
This Misery of Boots. London, Fabian Society, 1907; Boston, Ball, 1908.
Will Socialism Destroy the Home? London, Independent Labour Party, 1907.
New Worlds for Old. London, Constable, and New York, Macmillan, 1908.
First and Last Things: A Confession of Faith and Rule of Life. London, Constable, and New York, Putnam, 1908; revised edition, London, Constable, 1917; London, Watts, 1929.
Floor Games (juvenile). London, Palmer, 1911; Boston, Small Maynard, 1912.
The Labour Unrest. London, Associated Newspapers, 1912.
War and Common Sense. London, Associated Newspapers, 1913.
Liberalism and Its Party. London, Good, 1913.
Little Wars (children's games). London, Palmer, and Boston, Small Maynard, 1913.
An Englishman Looks at the World, Being a Series of Unrestrained Remarks upon Contemporary Matters. London, Cassell, 1914; as *Social Forces in England and America*, New York, Harper, 1914.
The War That Will End War. London, Palmer, and New York, Duffield, 1914; reprinted in part as *The War and Socialism*, London, Clarion Press, 1915.
The Peace of the World. London, Daily Chronicle, 1915.

What Is Coming? A Forecast of Things after the War. London, Cassell, and New York, Macmillan, 1916.
The Elements of Reconstruction. London, Nisbet, 1916.
War and the Future. London, Cassell, 1917; as *Italy, France, and Britain at War*, New York, Macmillan, 1917.
God the Invisible King. London, Cassell, and New York, Macmillan, 1917.
In the Fourth Year: Anticipations of a World Peace. London, Chatto and Windus, and New York, Macmillan, 1918; abridged edition, as *Anticipations of a World Peace*, Chatto and Windus, 1918.
British Nationalism and the League of Nations. London, League of Nations Union, 1918.
History Is One. Boston, Ginn, 1919.
The Outline of History, Being a Plain History of Life and Mankind. London, Newnes, 2 vols., and New York, Macmillan, 2 vols., 1920 (and later revisions).
Russia in the Shadows. London, Hodder and Stoughton, 1920; New York, Doran, 1921.
The Salvaging of Civilisation. London, Cassell, and New York, Macmillan, 1921.
The New Teaching of History, with a Reply to Some Recent Criticism of "The Outline of History." London, Cassell, 1921.
Washington and the Hope of Peace. London, Collins, 1922; as *Washington and the Riddle of Peace*, New York, Macmillan, 1922.
The World, Its Debts, and the Rich Men. London, Finer, 1922.
A Short History of the World. London, Cassell, and New York, Macmillan, 1922.
Socialism and the Scientific Motive (lecture). Privately printed, 1923.
The Story of a Great Schoolmaster, Being a Plain Account of the Life and Ideas of Sanderson of Oundle. London, Chatto and Windus, and New York, Macmillan, 1924.
A Year of Prophesying. London, Unwin, 1924; New York, Macmillan, 1925.
Works (Atlantic Edition). London, Unwin, and New York, Scribner, 28 vols., 1924.
A Forecast of the World's Affairs. New York, Encyclopedia Britannica, 1925.
Works (Essex Edition). London, Benn, 24 vols., 1926-27.
Mr. Belloc Objects to "The Outline of History." London, Watts, 1926.
Democracy under Revision (lecture). London, Hogarth Press, and New York, Doran, 1927.
Wells' Social Anticipations, edited by H.W. Laidler. New York, Vanguard Press, 1927.
The Book of Catherine Wells. London, Chatto and Windus, 1928.
The Way the World Is Going: Guesses and Forecasts of the Years Ahead. London, Benn, 1928; New York, Doubleday, 1929.
The Open Conspiracy: Blue Prints for a World Revolution. London, Gollancz, and New York, Doubleday, 1928; revised edition, London, Hogarth Press, 1930; revised edition, as *What Are We to Do with Our Lives?*, London, Heinemann, and New York, Doubleday, 1931.
The Common Sense of World Peace (lecture). London, Hogarth Press, 1929.
Imperialism and the Open Conspiracy. London, Faber, 1929.
The Adventures of Tommy (juvenile). London, Harrap, and New York, Stokes, 1929.
The Science of Life: A Summary of Contemporary Knowledge about Life and Its Possibilities, with Julian Huxley and G.P. Wells. London, Amalgamated Press, 3 vols., 1929-30; New York, Doubleday, 4 vols., 1931; revised edition, as *Science of Life Series*, London, Cassell, 9 vols., 1934-37.
Settlement of the Trouble Between Mr. Thring and Mr. Wells: A Footnote to the Problem of the Troublesome Collaborator. Privately printed, 1930.
The Way to World Peace. London, Benn, 1930.
The Work, Wealth, and Happiness of Mankind. New York, Doubleday, 2 vols., 1931; London, Heinemann, 1 vol., 1932; as *The Outline of Man's Work and Wealth*, Doubleday, 1936.
After Democracy: Addresses and Papers on the Present World Situation. London, Watts, 1932.
What Should Be Done Now? New York, Day, 1932.

Experiment in Autobiography: Discoveries and Conclusions of a Very Ordinary Brain since 1866. London, Gollancz-Cresset Press, 2 vols., and New York, Macmillan, 1 vol., 1934.
The New America: The New World. London, Cresset Press, and New York, Macmillan, 1935.
The Anatomy of Frustration: A Modern Synthesis. London, Cresset Press, and New York, Macmillan, 1936.
The Idea of a World Encyclopaedia. London, Hogarth Press, 1936; as *World Encyclopedia*, Folcroft, Pennsylvania, Folcroft Editions, 1973.
World Brain. London, Methuen, and New York, Doubleday, 1938.
Travels of a Republican Radical in Search of Hot Water. London, Penguin, 1939.
The Fate of Homo Sapiens: An Unemotional Statement of the Things That Are Happening to Him Now and of the Immediate Possibilities Confronting Him. London, Secker and Warburg, 1939; as *The Fate of Man*, New York, Alliance, 1939.
The New World Order, Whether It Is Obtainable, How It Can Be Obtained, and What Sort of World a World at Peace Will Have to Be. London, Secker and Warburg, and New York, Knopf, 1940.
The Rights of Man; or, What Are We Fighting For? London, Penguin, 1940.
The Common Sense of War and Peace: World Revolution or War Unending? London, Penguin, 1940.
The Pocket History of the World. New York, Pocket Books, 1941.
Guide to the New World: A Handbook of Constructive World Revolution. London, Gollancz, 1941.
The Outlook for Homo Sapiens. London, Secker and Warburg, 1942.
Science and the World-Mind. London, New Europe, 1942.
Phoenix: A Summary of the Inescapable Conditions of World Reorganization. London, Secker and Warburg, 1942; Girard, Kansas, Haldeman Julius, n.d.
A Thesis on the Quality of Illusion in the Continuity of Individual Life of the Higher Metazoa, with Particular Reference to the Species Homo Sapiens. Privately printed, 1942.
The Conquest of Time. London, Watts, 1942.
The New Rights of Man. Girard, Kansas, Haldeman Julius, 1942.
Crux Ansata: An Indictment of the Roman Catholic Church. London, Penguin, 1943; New York, Agora, 1944.
The Mosley Outrage. London, Daily Worker, 1943.
'42 to '44: A Contemporary Memoir upon Human Behaviour During the Crisis of the World Revolution. London, Secker and Warburg, 1944.
Marxism vs. Liberalism (interview with Stalin). New York, Century, 1945.
The Happy Turning: A Dream of Life. London, Heinemann, 1945.
Mind at the End of Its Tether. London, Heinemann, 1945.
Mind at the End of Its Tether, and The Happy Turning. New York, Didier, 1945.
The Desert Daisy (juvenile), edited by Gordon N. Ray. Urbana, University of Illinois Press, 1957.
Henry James and H.G. Wells: A Record of Their Friendship, Their Debate on the Art of Fiction, and Their Quarrel, edited by Leon Edel and Gordon N. Ray. Urbana, University of Illinois Press, and London, Hart Davis, 1958.
Arnold Bennett and H.G. Wells: A Record of Their Personal and Literary Friendship, edited by Harris Wilson. London, Hart Davis, 1960.
George Gissing and H.G. Wells: Their Friendship and Correspondence, edited by R.A. Gettman. London, Hart Davis, 1961.
Journalism and Prophecy 1893-1946, edited by W. Warren Wagar. Boston, Houghton Mifflin, 1964; London, Bodley Head, 1965.
Early Writings in Science and Science Fiction, edited by Robert M. Philmus and David Y. Hughes. Berkeley, University of California Press, 1975.

Editor, with G.R.S. Taylor and Frances Evelyn Greville, *The Great State: Essays in Construction.* London, Harper, 1912; as *Socialism and the Great State*, New York, Harper, 1914.

*

Bibliography: *H.G. Wells: A Comprehensive Bibliography*, London, H.G. Wells Society, 1966; revised edition, 1968.

*   *   *

Bernard Bergonzi, in his monograph *The Early H.G. Wells*, notes somewhat caustically that if Wells had died in 1900, like his young American friend Stephen Crane, "he would be remembered primarily as a literary artist." The 45 years of ardent "pamphleteering" that followed would not have occurred, and Well's place in the firmament of high culture would have been more secure, unshadowed by the embarrassment of his crusades for public enlightenment, or even by his sometimes awkward attempts after 1900 to write mainstream fiction. From the perspective of literary criticism as it is practiced in the second half of the 20th century, Bergonzi's judgment is hard to fault. What Wells produced between 1894 and 1901, from the earliest short stories in *The Pall Mall Budget* to *The First Men in the Moon*, was not only the most imaginative and artistically satisfying science fiction of any novelist of his generation, but also the best writing of his long career. None of the mainstream novels, sociological tracts, prophetic manifestos, collections of journalism, or encyclopedic surveys of science and history that Wells published after 1900 bears comparison, as art, with his early science fiction. Most of his later science fiction also suffers when measured against the standards he set for himself between 1894 and 1901.

Fortunately for his literary soul, Wells did more than enough in his salad days to win admission to the ranks of the immortals. From 1894 to 1901 his output of fantasy and science fiction (chiefly the latter) came to six novels and more than 30 short stories; most of these captured immediate public and critical acclaim. *The Time Machine*, the first of the novels, is a profound dystopian parable and the archetype of all time-travel stories in 20th-century science fiction. *The Island of Dr. Moreau* retells the Frankenstein tale, with dark satirical touches reminiscent of Swift. *The Invisible Man* furnishes the model for every later warning in science fiction of the Faustian potentiality for human self-destruction in the powers of science. *The War of the Worlds* is the first great story of interplanetary conflict, and *When the Sleeper Wakes* inspired Zamyatin's *We* and Huxley's *Brave New World*. In *The First Men in the Moon* Wells produced a masterful fantasia on the theme of biological engineering and one of the first credible accounts of space travel.

Several of the short stories have the same archetypal quality as the early novels. The deadliness of nature disclosed by modern science, which has supplied the raw material for a huge literature of disaster in our century, and in a few others written just after 1901. Apart from *The War of the Worlds*, which can also be read as a Darwinian fairy-tale, there were stories of man-eating orchids and cephalopods, giant birds and spiders, world-conquering ant hordes, and, in "The Star," an astrophysical disaster story of classical discipline, which seems almost to have been carved in ice. In "A Story of the Stone Age" Wells was among the first writers to make imaginative use of modern anthropology. "The New Accelerator" and "A Dream of Armageddon" carry further the admonitions in *The Invisible Man* on the perils of science and technology. "You know the silly way of the ingenious sort of men who make these things," the dreamer tells the narrator in "A Dream of Armageddon," recalling the weapons research in his nightmare of future life. "They turn 'em out as beavers build dams, and with no more sense of the rivers they're going to divert and the lands they're going to flood!"

The flow of science fiction from Well's pen did not stop in 1901, but time sapped his creative powers and eroded his craftsmanship. He grew careless. Between 1902 and 1914 he wrote six fantasy and science-fiction novels and a dozen stories. From 1914 until his death another five science-fiction novels made their appearance, three filmscripts, and several works located in a literary no-man's-land halfway between speculative and mainstream fiction. In his later work some of the warnings and anxieties of the first novels emerge again, and new ground is broken as well. What chiefly distinguishes Wells's science fiction after 1901 is its heightened political consciousness. Scenarios of global war fought with diabolical weapons alternate with visions of a technocratic worldwide utopia. Wells foresaw tank warfare in 1903 ("The Land Ironclads"), massive bombardment of cities by aircraft in 1908 (*The War in the Air*), and atomic bombs in 1914 (*The World Set Free*). He satirized fascism in

The Autocracy of Mr. Parham and turned it to his advantage in *The Holy Terror*. His three major utopian novels, *A Modern Utopia*, *Men Like Gods*, and *The Shape of Things to Come*, are landmarks in that extraordinarily difficult genre.

Writing in 1934, Wells took stock of the "incurable habit with literary critics to lament some lost artistry and innocence in my early work and to accuse me of having become polemical in my later years." In his defense, he observed—quite correctly—that his work had always been concerned with contemporary issues and with "life in the mass." So far, so true. But Wells could not bring himself to admit the decline of imagination and technique that overtook his later fiction. The success of such eminently polemical writers of science fiction as George Orwell and Walter M. Miller, Jr., who has as many axes to grind as Wells at his worst, suffices to show that Wells did not go wrong by abandoning "pure" literature for "pamphleteering." He merely let impatience and irritability diminish the effectiveness of his art. But the size of his achievement remains formidable. Well's best work is superb, and grandly paradigmatic. No other early writer of science fiction opened so many pathways. He is also a singularly universal figure. One may wonder if even one significant writer in the genre anywhere in the world in this century has missed reading H.G. Wells. Quite simply, he is to science fiction what Albert Einstein is to modern physics, or Pablo Picasso to modern art.

—W. Warren Wagar

WEST, Wallace (George). American. Born in Walnut Hills, Kentucky, 22 May 1900. Educated at Butler University, Indianapolis, A.B. 1924 (Phi Beta Kappa); Indiana University Law School, Bloomington, LL.B. 1925. Assistant to the Director of Radio Censorship during World War II. Married Claudia M. Weyant in 1928. Farmer, barber, and telegrapher; lawyer, Calvin and West, in the 1920's; journalist, United Press; publicity officer, Paramount Pictures; editor, *ROTO*, *Voice of Experience*, *Song Hits*, and *Movie Mirror*; publicity writer for CBS Radio, and news writer and commentator for ABC, NBC, and Mutual radio; pollution control expert, American Petroleum Institute, 1947-58; consultant, Air Pollution Control Administration; now retired.

SCIENCE-FICTION PUBLICATIONS

Novels

The Bird of Time. New York, Gnome Press, 1959.
Lords of Atlantis. New York, Avalon, 1960.
The Memory Bank. New York, Avalon, 1961.
River of Time. New York, Avalon, 1963.
The Time-Lockers. New York, Avalon, 1964.
The Everlasting Exiles. New York, Avalon, 1967.

Short Stories

Outposts in Space. New York, Avalon, 1962.

Uncollected Short Stories

"A Thing of Beauty," in *Magazine of Horror* (New York), August 1963.
"Glimpses of the Moon," in *Great Science Fiction about the Moon*, edited by T.E. Dikty. New York, Fell, 1967.
"The Last Filibuster," in *Galaxy* (New York), February 1967.
"Dust," in *Famous Science Fiction* (New York), Spring 1967.
"Steamer Time?," in *Analog* (New York), September 1968.
"The 'Last Man' Mess," in *WT 50: A Tribute to Weird Tales*. Chicago, Advent, 1974.

OTHER PUBLICATIONS

Novels

Jimmy Allen in The Sky Parade (novelization of screenplay).   New York, Lynn, 1936.
Thirteen Hours by Air (novelization of screenplay).   New York, Lynn, 1936.

Other

Betty Boop in Snow-White (adaptation of screenplay; juvenile). Racine, Wisconsin, Whitman, 1934.
Alice in Wonderland (novelization of screenplay; juvenile).   Racine, Wisconsin, Whitman, 1934.
Paramount Newsreel Men with Admiral Byrd in Little America. Racine, Wisconsin, Whitman, 1934.
Our Good Neighbors in Latin America.   New York, Noble, 1942.
Our Good Neighbors in Soviet Russia, with James P. Mitchell. New York, Noble, 1945.
Down to the Sea in Ships.   New York, Noble, 1947.
Find a Career in Electronics.   New York, Putnam, 1959.
Clearing the Air.   New York, American Petroleum Institute, 1961.
Conserving Our Waters.   New York, American Petroleum Institute, 1964(?).
The Amazing Inventor from Laurel Creek (juvenile).   New York, Putnam, 1967.

*   *   *

Shortly after the end of World War II, a number of science-fiction enthusiasts became small-time book publishers, dealing exclusively in fantasy and science fiction. Many of the oldtime favorite magazine authors found that they could rework their earlier short stories or novelettes into full-length novels for an appreciate audience. Wallace West was one of the "names" thus uncovered to the book-buying world, and his novels are such expansions and conflations. *Lords of Atlantis*, though, was originally published as a series of novelettes; it retells the Greek myths as the memories of an invasion from Mars in a combination of the author's ingenuity and ironic humor.

Wallace West was never a full-time writer. He wrote stories because he enjoyed reading science fiction and enjoyed writing it. He could tailor his plots to any magazine's requirements, and some of his stories are wildly melodramatic in the old "pulp" manner; but even those examples offer humor and speculation beyond the level of pulp entertainment. A number of the early stories were the first to present themes that are very familiar. The Feminist movement foreshadowed today's Women's Liberation, and there were those Feminists who felt that a truly decent society could exist only if males were completely subjugated to females—if not dispensed with altogether. In "The Last Man" (*Amazing*, February 1929) West draws an amusing yet grim portrait of a world where that "final solution" has been achieved. The last man is a museum exhibit; there are no more wars and sex conflict is a thing of the past. But is the world a utopia? The picture is not enticing.

West was concerned with air and water pollution decades before it became a public issue. In 1935, West wrote a short story, "Dust," which shows what happens when several elements of runaway pollution peak simultaneously. The story was rejected in 1935; he effectively rewrote and updated the tale for publication in 1967. "The Phantom Dictator," his best-remembered story, showed the possibilities of subliminal propagandizing some 20 years before Vance Packard's *The Hidden Persuaders*. (That story was subsumed, with other themes, in his novel *The Time-Lockers*.)

Wallace West was well-educated and widely read in many fields—literature, history, and the theater—as well as science. He used the entire range of his learning, in addition to his wry sense of humor, to write stories that stimulated thought as well as provided entertainment; that is why so many of them are still a pleasure to read and have not grown stale with time. He cared too much for the joys of science fiction to preach to or condescend to his readers, however seriously he himself might consider some of the themes, and would be the first to snort if some academic found his work "significant."

—Robert A.W. Lowndes

———————————

WHEATLEY, Dennis (Yates).   British.   Born in London, 8 January 1897. Educated at Dulwich College, London, 1908; H.M.S. Worcester, 1909-13; privately in Germany, 1913. Married 1) Nancy Robinson in 1923, one son; 2) Joan Gwendoline Johnstone in 1931. Served in the Royal Field Artillery, City of London Brigade, 1914-17; 36th Ulster Division, 1917-19 (invalided out); recommissioned in Royal Air Force Volunteer Reserve, 1939; Member, National Recruiting Panel, 1940-41; Member, Joint Planning Staff of War Cabinet, 1941-44; Wing Commander, 1944-45: United States Army Bronze Star. Joined his father's wine business, Wheatley and Son, London, 1914; worked in the business, 1919-26; sole owner, 1926-31. Editor, Dennis Wheatley's Library of the Occult, Sphere Books, London, from 1973 (over 40 volumes). Received Livery of Vintners' Company, 1918, and Distillers' Company, 1922. Fellow, Royal Society of Arts, and Royal Society of Literature. *Died 11 November 1977.*

SCIENCE-FICTION PUBLICATIONS

Novels

Such Power Is Dangerous.   London, Hutchinson, 1933.
Black August.   London, Hutchinson, and New York, Dutton, 1934.
The Fabulous Valley.   London, Hutchinson, 1934.
They Found Atlantis.   London, Hutchinson, and Philadelphia, Lippincott, 1936.
The Secret War.   London, Hutchinson, 1937.
Uncharted Seas.   London, Hutchinson, 1938.
Sixty Days to Live.   London, Hutchinson, 1939.
The Man Who Missed the War.   London, Hutchinson, 1945.
Star of Ill-Omen.   London, Hutchinson, 1952.

OTHER PUBLICATIONS

Novels

The Forbidden Territory.   London, Hutchinson, and New York, Dutton, 1933.
The Devil Rides Out.   London, Hutchinson, 1935; New York, Bantam, 1967.
The Eunuch of Stamboul.   London, Hutchinson, and Boston, Little Brown, 1935.
Murder Off Miami.   London, Hutchinson, 1936; as *File on Bolitho Blane*, New York, Morrow, 1936.
Contraband.   London, Hutchinson, 1936.
Who Killed Robert Prentice?   London, Hutchinson, 1937; as *File on Robert Prentice*, New York, Greenberg, 1937.
The Malinsay Massacre.   London, Hutchinson, 1938.
The Golden Spaniard.   London, Hutchinson, 1938.
The Quest of Julian Day.   London, Hutchinson, 1939.
Herewith the Clues!   London, Hutchinson, 1939.
The Scarlet Imposter.   London, Hutchinson, 1940; New York, Macmillan, 1942.
Three Inquisitive People.   London, Hutchinson, 1940.
Faked Passports.   London, Hutchinson, 1940; New York, Macmillan, 1943.
The Black Baroness.   London, Hutchinson, 1940; New York, Macmillan, 1942.
Strange Conflict.   London, Hutchinson, 1941.
The Sword of Fate.   London, Hutchinson, 1941; New York, Macmillan, 1944.

"V" for Vengeance. London, Hutchinson, and New York, Macmillan, 1942.
Codeword—Golden Fleece. London, Hutchinson, 1946.
Come into My Parlour. London, Hutchinson, 1946.
The Launching of Roger Brook. London, Hutchinson, 1947; New York, Ballantine, 1973.
The Shadow of Tyburn Tree. London, Hutchinson, 1948; New York, Ballantine, 1973.
The Haunting of Toby Jugg. London, Hutchinson, 1948; New York, Ballantine, 1974.
The Rising Storm. London, Hutchinson, 1949.
The Second Seal. London, Hutchinson, 1950.
The Man Who Killed the King. London, Hutchinson, 1951; New York, Putnam, 1965.
To the Devil—A Daughter. London, Hutchinson, 1953; New York, Bantam, 1968.
Curtain of Fear. London, Hutchinson, 1953.
The Island Where Time Stands Still. London, Hutchinson, 1954.
The Dark Secret of Josephine. London, Hutchinson, 1955.
The Ka of Gifford Hillary. London, Hutchinson, 1956; New York, Ballantine, 1973.
The Prisoner in the Mask. London, Hutchinson, 1957.
Traitors' Gate. London, Hutchinson, 1958.
The Rape of Venice. London, Hutchinson, 1959.
The Satanist. London, Hutchinson, 1960; New York, Bantam, 1967.
Vendetta in Spain. London, Hutchinson, 1961.
Mayhem in Greece. London, Hutchinson, 1962.
The Sultan's Daughter. London, Hutchinson, 1963.
Bill for the Use of a Body. London, Hutchinson, 1964.
They Used Dark Forces. London, Hutchinson, 1964.
Dangerous Inheritance. London, Hutchinson, 1965.
The Wanton Princess. London, Hutchinson, 1966.
Unholy Crusade. London, Hutchinson, 1967.
The White Witch of the South Seas. London, Hutchinson, 1968.
Evil in a Mask. London, Hutchinson, 1969.
Gateway to Hell. London, Hutchinson, 1970; New York, Ballantine, 1973.
The Ravishing of Lady Mary Ware. London, Hutchinson, 1971.
The Strange Story of Linda Lee. London, Hutchinson, 1972.
The Irish Witch. London, Hutchinson, 1973.
Desperate Measures. London, Hutchinson, 1974.

Short Stories

Mediterranean Nights. London, Hutchinson, 1942; revised edition, London, Arrow Books, 1963.
Gunmen, Gallants, and Ghosts. London, Hutchinson, 1943; revised edition, London, Arrow Books, 1963.

Play

Screenplay: *An Englishman's Home (Madmen of Europe)*, with others, 1939.

Other

Old Rowley: A Private Life of Charles II. London, Hutchinson, 1933; as *Private Life of Charles II*, 1938.
Red Eagle: A Life of Marshal Voroshilov. London, Hutchinson, 1937.
Invasion (war game). London, Hutchinson, 1938.
Blockade (war game). London, Hutchinson, 1939.
Total War. London, Hutchinson, 1941.
The Seven Ages of Justerini's. London, Riddle Books, 1949; revised edition, as *1749-1965: The Eight Ages of Justerini's*, Aylesbury, Buckinghamshire, Dolphin, 1965.
Alibi (war game). London, Geographia, 1951.
Stranger Than Fiction. London, Hutchinson, 1959.
Saturdays with Bricks and Other Days under Shell-Fire. London, Hutchinson, 1961.
The Devil and All His Works. London, Hutchinson, and New York, American Heritage Press, 1971.
The Time Has Come (autobiography)
　　The Young Man Said. London, Hutchinson, 1977.

Officer and Temporary Gentleman. London, Hutchinson, 1978.
Drink and Ink, edited by Anthony Lejeune. London, Hutchinson, 1979.
The Deception Planners: My Secret War. London, Hutchinson, 1980.

Editor, *A Century of Horror Stories*. London, Hutchinson, 1935; Freeport, New York, Books for Libraries, 1971; selection as *Quiver of Horror* and *Shafts of Fear*, London, Arrow Books, 2 vols., 1965; as *Tales of Strange Doings* and *Tales of Strange Happenings*, Hutchinson, 2 vols., 1968.
Editor, *A Century of Spy Stories*. London, Hutchinson, 1938.

Bibliography: *Fyra Decennier med Dennis Wheatley: En Biografi & Bibliografi* by Iwan Hedman and Jan Alexandersson, privately printed, 1963; revised edition, Strägnäs, Sweden, DAST, 1973.

*　　*　　*

In 40 years, Dennis Wheatley published some 60 books of detection, adventure, fantasy, and romance. While his plots may seem fantastic, his is not a name which comes to mind when science-fiction writers are mentioned. Many of those which may be classed in the genre are only marginally science fiction in theme. The fantasy is often only a framework for a story of romance and adventure. His stories of black magic may give him one claim to belong to the field.

The heroes of two of his major series of thrillers, the Duke de Richleau and Gregory Sallust, become involved with the occult in some of their adventures. *The Devil Rides Out*, which concerns a classic confrontation between the forces of good and evil (Richleau and a group of Satanists in contemporary London) is considered his best novel in the genre. In the sequel, *Strange Conflict*, the success of the Nazis in World War II is traced to their use of the supernatural. This fancy is also the theme of a later work, *They Used Dark Forces*, in which the occult is turned upon Hitler himself. Richleau's third black magic adventure is *Gateway to Hell*. Other black magic novels which do not involve recurring characters from the major series are *The Haunting of Toby Jugg*, *To the Devil a Daughter*, *The Ka of Gifford Hillary*, and *The Satanist*. While there is a definite attempt to make the reader believe in the occult in these novels (one is uncertain of the extent to which the author is being creative or reporting his own belief) it must be admitted that the supernatural is described in such detail that the reader is never really frightened. Actual malevolence is never as convincing as the suggestion of the possibility that ghosts exist. The diabolists could just as well have been gangsters. The ghost hunter stories in *Gunmen, Gallants, and Ghosts* and the lurking fears in *The Haunting of Toby Jugg* more successfully evoke the true shudder.

More traditional science-fiction motifs occur in some of his other novels. *Black August* is a Wellsian story of England in the future during a Communist revolution. In *The Fabulous Valley* the heirs to a diamond field in Africa have only a knobkerrie, a necklace of monkey skulls, and a leopard skin to tell them where to find the treasure, in a story of high adventure in the Haggard vein. A somewhat incongruously diverse group of adventurers find a lost race in *They Found Atlantis*; while the plot may not appear original to us there is a sound foundation of archeology and anthropology behind the telling of the story. *Uncharted Seas* is another lost-race story in which the shipwrecked protagonists are cast adrift on the open sea and discover a continent made of seaweed. A more conventional thriller, *The Secret War*, is a speculative fantasy about an anti-war league called the "Millers of God" who assassinate war profiteers. Also in the Wellsian vein is *Sixty Days to Live*, the story of the comet scheduled to strike the earth. The bulk of the novel concerns three men in love with the same woman and a world gone mad. A third lost-race story is *The Man Who Missed the War*: Philip Vaudell tries to float a raft across the Atlantic, is diverted to the Antarctic, and discovers a warm climate and a people cut off from the world. In *Star of Ill Omen* a British secret agent discovers the secret behind flying saucers and travels from Argentina to Mars. One of the novels often found on lists of Wheatley's fantasy, *Such Power Is Dangerous*, has little to recommend it apart from a fascinating idea of motion picture studios combining to shape public opinion through the films they produce. It is more satiric than fantastic.

Even in fantasy, Wheatley's strength lies in his having discovered that what the readers wanted was what he enjoyed writing for them. His adventure stories are far better than the elements of fantasy with which he filled them. A study of Wheatley is a study of public taste.

—J. Randolph Cox

WHITE, James. British. Born in Belfast, Northern Ireland, 7 April 1928. Educated at St. John's Primary School, 1935-41, and St. Joseph's Secondary Technical School, 1942-43, both Belfast. Married Margaret Sarah Martin in 1955; one daughter and two sons. Salesman and manager in several tailoring stores, Belfast, 1943-65. Technical clerk, 1965-66, publicity assistant, 1966-68, and since 1968, publicity officer, Shorts Aircraft, Belfast. Patron, Irish Science Fiction Association, 1974; Council Member, British Science Fiction Association, 1975. Recipient: Europa Award, 1972. Agent: Leslie Flood, E.J. Carnell Literary Agency, Rowneybury Bungalow, Sawbridgeworth, near Old Harlow, Essex CM20 2EX, England. Address: 10 Riverdale Gardens, Belfast BT11 9DG, Northern Ireland.

SCIENCE-FICTION PUBLICATIONS

Novels

The Secret Visitors. New York, Ace, 1957; London, Digit, 1961.
Second Ending. New York, Ace, 1962.
Star Surgeon. New York, Ballantine, 1963; London, Corgi, 1967.
Open Prison. London, New English Library, 1965; as *Escape Orbit*, New York, Ace, 1965.
The Watch Below. London, Whiting and Wheaton, and New York, Ballantine, 1966.
All Judgment Fled. London, Rapp and Whiting, 1968; New York, Walker, 1969.
Tomorrow Is Too Far. London, Joseph, and New York, Ballantine, 1971.
Dark Inferno. London, Joseph, 1972; as *Lifeboat*, New York, Ballantine, 1972.
The Dream Millennium. London, Joseph, and New York, Ballantine, 1974.
Underkill. London, Corgi, 1979.
Ambulance Ship. New York, Ballantine, 1979; London, Corgi, 1980.

Short Stories

Hospital Station. New York, Ballantine, 1962; London, Corgi, 1967.
Deadly Litter. New York, Ballantine, 1964; London, Corgi, 1968.
The Aliens Among Us. New York, Ballantine, 1969; London, Corgi, 1970.
Major Operation. New York, Ballantine, 1971.
Monsters and Medics. London, Corgi, and New York, Ballantine, 1977.

Uncollected Short Story

"Federation World," in *Analog* (New York), August 1980.

James White comments:

I have always felt that the best stories are those in which ordinary people are faced with extraordinary situations, and my early attraction to science fiction, both as a very young reader and later as a writer, was that it was the only genre which allowed ordinary people to be faced with truly extraordinary situations. My favourite of

these is the one in which Earth-human characters make first contact with an extraterrestrial species. The attempts to understand the behaviour and thought processes of the aliens frequently illuminate the human condition as well, and the problem of learning to understand and adapt to a totally alien viewpoint places in proper perspective the very minor differences of skin pigmentation and politics which bedevil our own culture.

*   *   *

One of the most memorable of James White's many intriguing settings is to be found in *The Watch Below*: a colony survives for several generations trapped inside the hull of a tanker torpedoed during World War II. In their effort to keep themselves sane, one of the things the first generation does is to attempt to recall every story any of them has ever read. One survivor has read a few works in the relatively new genre of science fiction. He particularly remembers a Doc Smith novel with a character "who was a winged dragon with scales, claws, four extensible eyes, and a lot of other visually horrifying features and who was more human than some of the human characters." Now, since *The Watch Below* is a "first contact" story, there are reasons of plot for this introduction of this tribute to the idea of interspecific brotherhood. But beyond this, the tradition of the fraternity of all intelligent life which first took firm hold in magazine SF in the mid-1930's is one which has had a marked impact on White himself as an author.

Most of White's stories involve extraterrestrials, and these beings are a varied lot indeed, including creatures indistinguishable from terrestrials in *The Secret Visitors*, aquatic lifeforms in *The Watch Below*, chlorine-breathers in *Open Prison*, and giant caterpillar-like tree-dwellers in *All Judgment Fled*. All these varieties together, and others besides, can be found at once in *Hospital Station* and the other books in White's series about Sector Twelve General Hospital, a multi-environmental hospital in deep space with staff and patients from a diverse galactic culture. Indeed, as an author White is quite fond of the field of medicine, perhaps seeing in it a paradigm of the cooperation and fellowship which should embrace all intelligent beings. Even outside the Sector General series, physicians are important characters in *The Secret Visitors*, *The Watch Below*, *All Judgment Fled*, and *Underkill*.

But soldiers figure almost as prominently as doctors in White's work. One section of *Hospital Station* is given over to the hero's realization that the Monitor Corps performs a necessary police function. White is not happy about this fact of life. Indeed, in at least three different books characters are relieved to have it turn out that the lifeforms they were forced to kill are only animals, and not intelligent beings after all. And beyond such justified violence, White's work also depicts some conflicts based on honest misunderstanding, and others stemming from deliberate selfishness and greed. But with one exception, the accent in White's work is not on the existence of such abominations but on the possibility of doing something about them. White's stories almost always close with harmony restored, or at least with such a restoration anticipated. This stubborn optimism has been one of White's trademarks, though its direct expression has been abandoned in the recent *Underkill*.

A second trademark, already alluded to, is his inventiveness regarding environments. If his most brilliant achievement in this area is the sunken tanker in *The Watch Below*, other instances are almost equally imaginative—the prison planet of *Open Prison*, the alien starship overrun with laboratory animals in *All Judgment Fled*, the energy-poor world of the "powerdown" in *Underkill*, and others.

White's work is not without flaws. His human characters are too much alike, and sometimes their actions are inadequately motivated. Often White's extraterrestrials have incongruously human—indeed, Western—psychologies, whatever their external forms. White's fascinating environments are also sometimes a little too visibly contrived. But until his recent work, the single most serious accusation that could be brought against White was his utopianism, his seeming disbelief that any group of people could willfully persist in evil once they had the right path pointed out to him. Now, however, events in White's native Northern Ireland seem to have had the same sobering effect on him as did the war in Vietnam on many American writers—*Underkill* is recognizably the work of the same James White who wrote, say, the Hospital Station series, but this novel is at once more bitter and markedly more powerful than any of White's previous work. Extraterrestrials playing the part of an Old-Testament Yahweh find mankind so sunken in sin (particularly in the ethnic and sectarian hatreds that lead to terrorism) that they see no solution but to destroy all the Earth's population save for a remnant of ten million, and to start over again. And White's viewpoint characters can no more sway the aliens from their purpose than could Abraham dissuade Yahweh from destroying Sodom.

The suddenness of White's belated recognition (belated at least in his fiction) of the power of evil seems to have infused his latest work with a bitterness reminiscent of Jonathan Swift. It is to be hoped that this bitterness is a device intended to shock White's countrymen and the whole world back to their senses rather than a more basic surrender to despair. Other science-fiction writers such as Cordwainer Smith, the Strugatsky brothers (whose Russian national experience is surely at least as harrowing as Northern Ireland's), and C.J. Cherryh have looked evil in the face throughout their writing careers without forsaking hope or ideals. It will be a real loss if White finds himself unable to do the same.

—Patrick L. McGuire

WHITE, Ted (Theodore Edwin White). Also writes as Ron Archer; Norman Edwards. American. Born in Washington, D.C., 4 February 1938. Educated in public schools in Falls Church, Virginia. Married 1) Sylvia Dees in 1958; 2) Robin Postal in 1966; one child. Head of foreign department, Scott Meredith Literary Agency, 1963; Assistant Editor, 1963-67, and Associate Editor, 1967-68, *Fantasy and Science Fiction*; Associate Editor, Lancer Books, 1966; Managing Editor, 1969, and Editor, 1970-78, *Amazing* and *Fantastic*. Since 1979, Editor, *Heavy Metal*. Editor, *Void* fan magazine, 1959-68. Recipient: Hugo Award, for non-fiction, 1968. Agent: Henry Morrison Inc., 58 West 10th Street, New York, New York 10011. Address: 339 49th Street, Brooklyn, New York 11220, U.S.A.

SCIENCE-FICTION PUBLICATIONS

Novels

Invasion from 2500 (as Norman Edwards, with Terry Carr). Derby, Connecticut, Monarch, 1964.
Android Avenger. New York, Ace, 1965.
Phoenix Prime. New York, Lancer, 1966.
The Sorceress of Qar. New York, Lancer, 1966.
The Jewels of Elsewhen. New York, Belmont, 1967.
Lost in Space (novelization of TV play; as Ron Archer, with Dave Van Arnam). New York, Pyramid, 1967.
Sideslip, with Dave Van Arnam. New York, Pyramid, 1968.
Captain America: The Great Gold Steal. New York, Bantam, 1968.
The Spawn of the Death Machine. New York, Paperback Library, 1968.
No Time Like Tomorrow (juvenile). New York, Crown, 1969.
By Furies Possessed. New York, New American Library, 1970.
Star Wolf! New York, Lancer, 1971.
Trouble on Project Ceres (juvenile). Philadelphia, Westminister Press, 1971.
Forbidden World, with David Bischoff. New York, Popular Library, 1978.

Uncollected Short Stories

"I, Executioner," in *If* (New York), March 1963.
"Policy Conference," in *Gamma* (North Hollywood), September 1965.

"The Peacock King," in *Fantasy and Science Fiction* (New York), November 1965.
"The Secret of the City," in *Startling* (New York), Fall 1966.
"Wednesday Noon," in *Fantasy and Science Fiction* (New York), February 1968.
"Saboteur," in *If* (New York), March 1969.
"Only Yesterday," in *Amazing* (New York), July 1969.
"It Could Be Anywhere," in *Fantastic* (New York), October 1969.
"A Girl Like You," in *Amazing* (New York), March 1971.
"Wolf Quest," in *Fantastic* (New York), April 1971.
"Growing Up Fast in the City," in *Amazing* (New York), May 1971.
"Junk Patrol," in *Amazing* (New York), September 1971.
"Things Are Tough All Over," in *Fantastic* (New York), December 1971.
"Stella," in *And Walk Now Gently Through the Fire...*, edited by Roger Elwood. Philadelphia, Chilton, 1972.
"4148 PM, October 6, 197-, Late Afternoon, on Christopher Street," in *Amazing* (New York), January 1972.
"Dandy," in *Demon Kind*, edited by Roger Elwood. New York, Avon, 1973.
"Phoenix," with Marion Zimmer Bradley, in *The Best from Amazing Stories*, edited by Ted White. New York, Manor, 1973; London, Hale, 1976.
"...and Another World Above," in *Fantastic* (New York), January 1974.
"Sixteen and Vanilla," in *Vertex* (Los Angeles), June 1974.
"Manhattan Square Dance," in *Amazing* (New York), August 1974.
"Doc Phoenix (The Man Who Enters the Wind)," in *Weird Heroes 2*, edited by Byron Preiss. New York, Pyramid, 1975.
"Under the Mad Sun," in *Amazing* (New York), May 1975.
"What Is Happening to Sarah Anne Lawrence?," in *Amazing* (New York), September 1975.
"Welcome to the Machine," in *Amazing* (New York), June 1976.
"Vengeance Is Mine," in *Fantastic* (New York), June 1977.

OTHER PUBLICATIONS

Other

Editor, *The Best from Amazing Stories.* New York, Manor, 1973; London, Hale, 1976.
Editor, *The Best from Fantastic.* New York, Manor, 1973; London, Hale, 1976.

*   *   *

Ted White, like many writers of his generation, first achieved prominence as a fan. He was responsible for what was recognised as the first fanzine devoted exclusively to comics in 1953; his fanzine *Void* helped advance both his career and that of Gregory Benford.

White's career as a novelist was relatively short. His novels tend to be all of a type, in that they usually deal with supermen with neuroses. Thus *The Spawn of the Death Machine*, a novel much better than its title suggests, concerns an android in a post-apocalyptic future who wanders about determining the limits of his powers. In *Phoenix Prime* the cab-driver Maximillan Quest learns that he is an incomplete superman and is rushed to another dimension to fight a cosmic war. White's novels are essentially imitative, at times reminding one of Heinlein, at other times of van Vogt; while his work is competent, he has not achieved any writing of the first rank, save for certain sections of the fascinating failure, *The Jewels of Elsewhen*, White's favorite among his own works.

White's distinction is as an editor, more than as a writer. White was editor of *Amazing Stories* and *Fantastic Science Fiction* for some ten years; he returned the magazines to a policy of publishing original fiction, and developed some of the talented young writers of the 1970's.

—Martin Morse Wooster

WIBBERLEY, Leonard (Patrick O'Connor). Also writes as Leonard Holton; Patrick O'Connor; Christopher Webb. Irish. Born in Dublin, 9 April 1915. Educated at Ring College, Ireland; Abbey House, Romsey, Hampshire; Cardinal Vaughan's School, London, 1925-30; El Camino College, Torrance, California. Served in the Trinidad Artillery Volunteers, 1938-40: Lance Bombardier. Married Katherine Hazel Holton in 1948; two daughters and four sons. Reporter, *Sunday Dispatch*, 1931-32, *Sunday Express*, 1932-34, and *Daily Mirror*, 1935-36, all London; Editor, Trinidad *Evening News*, 1936; oilfield worker, Trinidad, 1936-43; Cable Editor, Associated Press, New York, 1943-44; New York Correspondent and Bureau Chief, London *Evening News*, 1944-46; Editor, *Independent Journal*, San Rafael, California, 1947-49; Reporter and Copy Editor, Los Angeles *Times*, 1950-54. Agent: McIntosh and Otis, 475 Fifth Avenue, New York, New York 10017. Address: Box 522, Hermosa Beach, California 90254, U.S.A.

SCIENCE-FICTION PUBLICATIONS

Novels (series: Mouse)

The Mouse That Roared. Boston, Little Brown, 1955; London, Corgi, 1959; as *The Wrath of Grapes*, London, Hale, 1955.
The Mouse on the Moon. New York, Morrow, 1962; London, Muller, 1964.
Encounter Near Venus (juvenile). New York, Farrar Straus, 1967; London, Macdonald, 1968.
Journey to Untor (juvenile). New York, Farrar Straus, 1970; London, Macdonald, 1971.

OTHER PUBLICATIONS

Novels

Mrs. Searwood's Secret Weapon. Boston, Little Brown, 1954; London, Hale, 1955.
McGillicuddy McGotham. Boston, Little Brown, 1956; London, Hale, 1958.
Take Me to Your President. New York, Putnam, 1957.
Beware of the Mouse. New York, Putnam, 1958.
The Quest for Excalibur. New York, Putnam, 1959.
The Hands of Cormac Joyce. New York, Putnam, 1960; London, Muller, 1962.
Stranger at Killknock. New York, Putnam, 1961; London, Muller, 1963.
A Feast of Freedom. New York, Morrow, 1964.
The Island of the Angels. New York, Morrow, 1965.
The Centurion. New York, Morrow, 1966.
The Road from Toomi. New York, Morrow, 1967.
Adventures of an Elephant Boy. New York, Morrow, 1968.
The Mouse on Wall Street. New York, Morrow, 1969.
Meeting with a Great Beast. New York, Morrow, 1971; London, Chatto and Windus, 1972.
The Testament of Theophilus. New York, Morrow, 1973; as *Merchant of Rome*, London, Cassell, 1974.
The Last Stand of Father Felix. New York, Morrow, 1974.
1776—and All That. New York, Morrow, 1975.
One in Four. New York, Morrow, 1976.
Homeward to Ithaka. New York, Morrow, 1978.
The Mouse That Saved the West. New York, Morrow, 1981.

Novels as Leonard Holton

The Saint Maker. New York, Dodd Mead, 1959; London, Hale, 1960.
A Pact with Satan. New York, Dodd Mead, 1960; London, Hale, 1961.
Secret of the Doubting Saint. New York, Dodd Mead, 1961.
Deliver Us from Wolves. New York, Dodd Mead, 1963.
Flowers by Request. New York, Dodd Mead, 1964.
Out of the Depths. New York, Dodd Mead, 1966; London, Hammond, 1967.
A Touch of Jonah. New York, Dodd Mead, 1968.
A Problem in Angels. New York, Dodd Mead, 1970.

The Mirror of Hell. New York, Dodd Mead, 1972.
The Devil to Play. New York, Dodd Mead, 1974.
A Corner of Paradise. New York, St. Martin's Press, 1977.

Plays

Black Jack Rides Again. Chicago, Dramatic Publishing Company, 1971.
1776—And All That. Chicago, Dramatic Publishing Company, 1973.
Once, In a Garden. Chicago, Dramatic Publishing Company, 1975.

Verse

The Ballad of the Pilgrim Cat (juvenile). New York, Washburn, 1962.
The Shepherd's Reward (juvenile). New York, Washburn, 1963.

Other

The King's Beard (juvenile). New York, Farrar Straus, 1952; London, Faber, 1954.
The Coronation Book: The Dramatic Story as History and Legend (juvenile). New York, Farrar Straus, 1953.
The Secret of the Hawk (juvenile). New York, Farrar Straus, 1953; London, Faber, 1956.
Deadmen's Cave (juvenile). New York, Farrar Straus, and London, Faber, 1954.
The Epics of Everest (juvenile). New York, Farrar Straus, 1954; London, Faber, 1955.
The Wound of Peter Wayne (juvenile). New York, Farrar Straus, 1955; London, Faber, 1957.
The Life of Winston Churchill (juvenile). New York, Farrar Straus, 1956; revised edition, 1965.
The Trouble with the Irish (or the English, Depending on Your Point of View). New York, Holt Rinehart, 1956; London, Muller, 1958.
John Barry, Father of the Navy (juvenile). New York, Farrar Straus, 1957.
Kevin O'Connor and the Light Brigade (juvenile). New York, Farrar Straus, 1957; London, Harrap, 1959.
Wes Powell, Conquerer of the Grand Canyon (juvenile). New York, Farrar Straus, 1958.
The Coming of the Green. New York, Holt Rinehart, 1958.
John Treegate's Musket (juvenile). New York, Farrar Straus, 1959.
No Garlic in the Soup (on Portugal). New York, Washburn, 1959; London, Faber, 1960.
Peter Treegate's War (juvenile). New York, Farrar Straus, 1960.
The Land That Isn't There: An Irish Adventure. New York, Washburn, 1960.
Sea Captain from Salem (juvenile). New York, Farrar Straus, 1961.
Yesterday's Land: A Baja California Adventure. New York, Washburn, 1961.
Zebulon Pike, Soldier and Explorer (juvenile). New York, Funk and Wagnalls, 1961.
The Time of the Lamb (juvenile). New York, Washburn, 1961.
Ventures into the Deep: The Thrill of Scuba Diving. New York, Washburn, 1962.
Treegate's Raiders (juvenile). New York, Farrar Straus, 1962.
Ah Julian! A Memoir of Julian Brodetsky. New York, Washburn, 1963.
Fiji: Islands of the Dawn. New York, Washburn, 1964.
Toward a Distant Island: A Sailor's Odyssey. New York, Washburn, 1966.
Something to Read. New York, Washburn, 1967.
Attar of the Ice Valley (juvenile). New York, Farrar Straus, 1968; London, Macdonald, 1969.
Man of Liberty: A Life of Thomas Jefferson (juvenile). New York, Farrar Straus, 1968.
  1. *Young Man from the Piedmont: The Youth of Thomas Jefferson.* New York, Farrar Straus, 1963.
  2. *A Dawn in the Trees: Thomas Jefferson, The Years 1776 to*

1789. New York, Farrar Straus, 1964.
3. *The Gales of Spring: Thomas Jefferson, The Years 1789 to 1801.* New York, Farrar Straus, 1965.
4. *Time of the Harvest: Thomas Jefferson, The Years 1801 to 1826.* New York, Farrar Straus, 1966.
Hound of the Sea. New York, Washburn, 1969.
Leopard's Prey (juvenile). New York, Farrar Straus, 1971.
Voyage by Bus. New York, Morrow, 1971.
The Shannon Sailors: A Voyage to the Heart of Ireland. New York, Morrow, 1972.
Flint's Island (juvenile). New York, Farrar Straus, 1972; London, Macdonald, 1973.
Red Pawns (juvenile). New York, Farrar Straus, 1973.
Guarneri (juvenile). New York, Farrar Straus, 1974; London, Macdonald and Jane's, 1976.
The Last Battle (juvenile). New York, Farrar Straus, 1976.
Perilous Gold (juvenile). New York, Farrar Straus, 1978.
Little League Family (juvenile). New York, Doubleday, 1978.
The Good-Natured Man: A Portrait of Oliver Goldsmith. New York, Morrow, 1979.
The Crime of Martin Coverly (juvenile). New York, Farrar Straus, 1980.

Other as Patrick O' Connor (juvenile)

The Lost Harpooner. New York, Washburn, 1947; London, Harrap, 1959.
Flight of the Peacock. New York, Washburn, 1954.
The Society of Foxes. New York, Washburn, 1954.
The Watermelon Mystery. New York, Washburn, 1955.
Gunpowder for Washington. New York, Washburn, 1956.
The Black Tiger. New York, Washburn, 1956.
Mexican Road Ace. New York, Washburn, 1957.
Black Tiger at Le Mans. New York, Washburn, 1958.
The Five-Dollar Watch. New York, Washburn, 1959.
Black Tiger at Bonneville. New York, Washburn, 1960.
Treasure at Twenty Fathoms. New York, Washburn, 1961.
Black Tiger at Indianapolis. New York, Washburn, 1962.
The Raising of the Dubhe. New York, Washburn, 1964.
Seawind from Hawaii. New York, Washburn, 1965.
South Swell. New York, Washburn, 1967; London, Macdonald, 1968.
Beyond Hawaii. New York, Washburn, 1969; London, Macdonald, 1970.
A Car Called Camellia. New York, Washburn, 1970.

Other as Christopher Webb (juvenile)

Matt Tyler's Chronicle. New York, Funk and Wagnalls, 1958; London, Macdonald, 1966.
Mark Toyman's Inheritance. New York, Funk and Wagnalls, 1960.
The River of Pee Dee Jack. New York, Funk and Wagnalls, 1962.
The "Ann and Hope" Mutiny. New York, Funk and Wagnalls, 1966; London, Macdonald, 1967.
Eusebius, The Phoenician. New York, Funk and Wagnalls, 1969; London, Macdonald, 1970.

*

Manuscript Collection: University of Southern California, Los Angeles.

*   *   *

Leonard Wibberley's science fiction for adults is limited to two books of a series on the Duchy of Grand Fenwick, *The Mouse That Roared* and *The Mouse on the Moon.* The scientific element in them, and the others in the series, is quite thin, bordering upon the fantastic. The only element of *The Mouse That Roared* that seems at all science-fictional is Dr. Kokintz's "Quadium Bomb." It is supposedly based upon quadium, the unstable isotope of hydrogen that follows deuterium and tritium. The bomb itself is built in a lead shoebox and uses a hairpin as a triggering device (which ultimately doesn't work). The essence of the story, however, is the extolling of

the presumed virtues of smallness. Wibberley seems to assume that there is some sort of Rousseau-like principle at work in nations, that size and density of population virtually force immoral behavior upon the inhabitants of large countries. This is apparent when the rulers of Grand Fenwick realize that large nations cannot be trusted to handle a "doomsday device" but a coalition of little nations can. *The Mouse on the Moon* is a virtual repeat of *The Mouse That Roared.* The now-famous Dr. Kokintz discovers that an extract of the Duchy's wine, Pinot Grand Fenwick, is the basis for the world's most powerful rocket fuel. The Prime Minister has obtained a $50,000,000 grant from the US (under the guise of starting a space program, but really to improve the castle's plumbing), so the Duchy enters the space race. As in *The Mouse That Roared* Grand Fenwick succeeds in besting the world's "Great Powers." When the Russian and American spacemen arrive on the moon, they find Grand Fenwickians already in possession of it. Of course, again, the little countries accept their responsibilities, where the big ones hadn't, and agree to keep the moon free for all humanity.

Wibberley's science fiction for children seems only slightly more juvenile in plot and thesis. *Encounter Near Venus* tells of four children who, almost despite the aid of their child-hating uncle, save an Edenic Venusian moon from the deadly clutches of Ka the Smiler. On a simplified basis it is quite reminiscent of C.S. Lewis's Narnia chronicles. In *Journey to Untor* the message is again that the big and/or mature lack flexibility and sensitivity to the world around them, while the small and/or immature, when given the opportunity, have those properties and the will to use them in the most responsible manner possible.

In general, Wibberley's supposed science-fiction writings are so categorized only as a recognition that they employ gimmicks which nominally belong to that realm. In actuality they are fairly simple-minded morality stories written in a clever and entertaining fashion.

—Richard W. Miller

WILDER, Cherry. Pseudonym for Cherry Barbara Grimm, née Lockett. New Zealander. Born in Auckland, 9 March 1930. Educated at Canterbury University College, Christchurch, B.A. 1952. Married 1) A.J. Anderson in 1952; 2) H.K.F. Grimm in 1963. Lived in Australia, 1954-76: high school teacher, editorial assistant, theatre director; regular reviewer for Sydney *Morning Herald* and *The Australian,* 1964-74. Recipient: Australia Council grant, 1973, 1975. Agent: Virginia Kidd, Box 278, Milford, Pennsylvania 18337, U.S.A. Address: 16B Egelsbacher Strasse, 6070 Langen/Hessen, West Germany.

SCIENCE-FICTION PUBLICATIONS

Novels (juvenile)

The Luck of Brin's Five. New York, Atheneum, 1977; London, Angus and Robertson, 1979.
The Nearest Fire. New York, Atheneum, 1980.

Uncollected Short Stories

"The Ark of James Carlyle," in *New Writings in SF 24*, edited by Kenneth Bulmer. London, Sidgwick and Jackson, 1974.
"The Phobos Transcripts," in *New Writings in SF 26*, edited by Kenneth Bulmer. London, Sidgwick and Jackson, 1975.
"Way Out West," in *Science Fiction Monthly* (London), August 1975.
"The Remittance Man," in *The Ides of Tomorrow*, edited by Terry Carr. Boston, Little Brown, 1976.
"Double Summer Time," in *New Writings in SF 29*, edited by Kenneth Bulmer. London, Sidgwick and Jackson, 1976.

"Point of Departure," in *The Zeitgeist Machine*, edited by Damien Broderick. London, Angus and Robertson, 1977.
"The Recollectors," in *New Writings in SF 30*, edited by Kenneth Bulmer. London, Corgi, 1977.
"The Lodestar," in *Cosmos* (New York), May 1977.
"Mab Gallen Recalled," in *Millennial Women*, edited by Virginia Kidd. New York, Dell, 1978.
"The Falldown of Man," in *Rooms of Paradise*, edited by Lee Harding. New York, St. Martin's Press, 1979.
"Dealers in Light and Darkness," in *20 Houses of the Zodiac*, edited by Maxim Jakubowski. London, New English Library, 1979.
"Odd Man Search," in *Alien Worlds*, edited by Paul Collins. St. Kilda, Victoria, Void, 1979.

*   *   *

Cherry Wilder learned to write in other modes—general fiction, articles, reviews—before she turned to science fiction, and her early training shows. Her prose has a solidity and competence above that of many a writer trained from the first in the short cuts of convention. She also comes from a part of the world unfamiliar to most science-fiction readers—New Zealand and Australia—and she credits her inventiveness in landscapes and animals to that difference. But aside from such accomplishments in form she also fulfills a less tangible requirement for good science fiction: she truly desires to encounter an alternate mentality, and in her desire she creates thoroughly believable aliens that reach out to humans and make with them a bond unavailable in either separate race. Each of her stories tells of the first formation of that bond.

In "The Ark of James Carlyle" humans and aliens are already in contact, but without understanding. James Carlyle mans a weather observation station on an island in a purple sea, an island inhabited by polite blue "quogs" who communicate in shy, dim boomings. When a flood forces them to flee together, the quogs teach Carlyle to speak on a new level. Telepathic dreams mix with vivid adventures which in turn help explain the ecology of the planet. The story uses the full range of Wilder's style; she effortlessly transmits humor, hurry, beauty, danger, and, at the end, a moving joy. She uses her skills differently in "The Phobos Transcripts," where she writes in three styles: a straight narration of a shuttle rescue on the moon Phobos, an archaic invocation by an ancient alien, and the brisk report of the medical officer. The alien, bodiless and immensely advanced, takes over the body of one of the crew in order to radio his old comrades. The experience enriches everyone involved, but no one outside the crew believes them. The resulting human division is a theme repeated in a sweet, confusing story called "Double Summer Time," probably the most ambitious of Wilder's stories. Aliens land in England with an ability to mimic any life form nearby. Their secret is discovered by an environmental radical, who in effect falls in love with a tree which later becomes human. The aliens can also alter the flow of time, and in the resulting convolutions the reader would do best to know the strange poetry and times of Andrew Marvell, who also cared about trees. It is an unusual story, good for rereading, and one of the few science-fiction stories effectively to combine "high" literature and space adventure.

Wilder's first novel, and also her only alien-contact story to continue the interaction after the first joyous meld, is *The Luck of Brin's Five*. The influence of New Zealand and Australia is clearer here, for on a landscape of mountains and plains she creates a family of Moruian "bush weavers," marsupial humanoids who live in a pre-industrial culture marked by tight families, or "fives," and a language told in both writing and macrame knotting. Into this society falls Scott Gale, a human observer whose ship failed. He is rescued by Brin's Five to be their "Luck"—the abnormal member every family needs to bring them good fortune. The concept of the Luck is central to Wilder's treatment of aliens—that the non-normal should be sought out and treasured, whether in or out of a species. Scott Gale, of course, is less normal than most Lucks, and the benefits are therefore greater. He and Brin's Five begin a trek that takes them through all aspects of Moruian culture, and far away to the sea. The culture and the land are coherently imagined, though the plot's action tends to bog near the middle. Also, the long explanatory list of characters at the beginning turns out to be unfortunately necessary. But Dorn, the young Moruian narrator, is

an appealing storyteller, and at sea's edge the novel ends with a pleasant promise of more adventures.

Cherry Wilder has only recently begun writing science fiction, and her stories are tales of beginnings and hope. The hope lies in her belief that bonds between strangers can be made, but even more in her belief that the best bonds are made between the strangest strangers. Her smooth, competent prose is a vindication of the craft of science fiction, but her hope is a vindication of science fiction itself.

—Karen G. Way

WILHELM, Kate (née Meredith). American. Born in Toledo, Ohio, 8 June 1928. Married 1) Joseph B. Wilhelm in 1947 (divorced, 1962), two sons; 2) Damon Knight, *q.v.*, in 1963, one son. Co-Director, Milford Science Fiction Writers Conference, 1963-72; Lecturer, Clarion Science Fiction Writers Conference, 1968-70, and Tulane University, New Orleans, 1971. Recipient: Nebula Award, 1968; Hugo Award, 1977; Jupiter Award, 1977; *Locus* Award, 1977. Agent: Brandt and Brandt, 101 Park Avenue, New York, New York 10017. Address: 1645 Horne Lane, Eugene, Oregon 97402, U.S.A.

SCIENCE-FICTION PUBLICATIONS

Novels

The Clone, with Ted Thomas. New York, Berkley, 1965; London, Hale, 1968.
The Nevermore Affair. New York, Doubleday, 1966.
The Killer Thing. New York, Doubleday, 1967; as *The Killing Thing*, London, Jenkins, 1967.
Let the Fire Fall. New York, Doubleday, 1969; London, Panther, 1972.
Year of the Cloud, with Ted Thomas. New York, Doubleday, 1970.
Abyss. New York, Doubleday, 1971.
Margaret and I. Boston, Little Brown, 1971.
The Clewiston Test. New York, Farrar Straus, 1976; London, Hutchinson, 1977.
Where Late the Sweet Birds Sang. New York, Harper, 1976; London, Hutchinson, 1977.
Juniper Time. New York, Harper, 1979; London, Hutchinson, 1980.

Short Stories

The Mile-Long Spaceship. New York, Berkley, 1963; as *Andover and the Android*, London, Dobson, 1966.
The Downstairs Room. New York, Doubleday, 1968.
The Infinity Box. New York, Harper, 1975; London, Hutchinson, 1979.
Somerset Dreams and Other Fictions. New York, Harper, 1978; London, Hutchinson, 1979.

OTHER PUBLICATIONS

Novels

More Bitter Than Death. New York, Simon and Schuster, 1963; London, Hale, 1965.
City of Cain. Boston, Little Brown, 1974; London, Gollancz, 1975.
Fault Lines. New York, Harper, 1977; London, Hutchinson, 1978.

Other

"Something Happens," in *Clarion*, edited by Robin Scott Wilson. New York, New American Library, 1971.
"The Source," in *Clarion 3*, edited by Robin Scott Wilson. New York, New American Library, 1973.

Editor, *Nebula Award Stories 9*. London, Gollancz, 1974; New York, Harper, 1975.
Editor, *Clarion SF*. New York, Berkley, 1977.

*   *   *

Kate Wilhelm has said that about half of her published work is science fiction, though much of the rest contains elements of fantasy. Her first novel was a mystery; later works such as *Margaret and I* and *Fault Lines* are novels of contemporary life, though *Margaret and I* makes use of a speculative element by portraying the protagonist's subconscious as a separate character. Wilhelm is primarily a writer who skillfully uses genre elements—suspenseful plots, scientific or technological notions, and slick prose—to produce fiction as satisfying and as well-rounded as any being written today.

Wilhelm's technique, in most of her work, is to introduce a character or set of characters in a commonplace setting, then to reveal the unusual or uncommon elements of the story through the thoughts and actions of the people in it. Her characters are some of the most fully realized people to be found in science fiction. Her style is the smooth, almost slick manner of so much "women's magazine" fiction, complete with the details of domestic and everyday life; this manner of telling her stories makes the contrast and tension between the usual and the unusual even more striking. This technique can be seen in Wilhelm's first novel, *More Bitter Than Death*. A young couple, Eve and Grant, return to Grant's home, where the body of Grant's murdered mother has been found. Eve must come to terms with her husband, who is one of those suspected of the murder, and Grant must deal with long-suppressed feelings about his home and family. The problems raised here are resolved by the book's conclusion, though in her later work Wilhelm's characters find answers more difficult to come by, life more complex, and reconciliations more problematic. The problem Eve and Grant face, that of having to understand the past and to reconcile it with their future hopes in the midst of unusual events, is present in Wilhelm's later work, and is especially prominent in her science fiction. These same problems are depicted movingly in the novella "Somerset Dreams," ostensibly a story about dream research in a dying town.

In two early science-fiction novels, Wilhelm writes about standard science-fiction themes. In *The Killer Thing* a computerized robot which is trying to kill all life must be destroyed; in *Let the Fire Fall* an alien landing on Earth and the rise of a new religion are shown. *The Killer Thing* shows Wilhelm's mastery of the technique of suspense. Though it is set in the familiar future of colonized planets so common in SF, the book shows the author's concern with the moral issues raised by space travel and human greed. *Let the Fire Fall* begins in the familiar, almost cozy, environs of a small American city. This novel is written in an uncharacteristically breezy style; the author's strong opinions about organized religion and cults are not concealed, and the new religion is much like some rather disturbing present-day cults. These books, and early pieces such as "The Mile-Long Spaceship" and "Stranger in the House," are better than average stories, but it is in later works that Wilhelm shows her real strengths.

Wilhelm, unlike many writers, is a master of both the novel and shorter forms of fiction. Her short story "Baby, You Were Great" shows a world where it is possible, through brain-implanted electrodes, to live a celebrity's life vicariously and to feel all her emotions as well. Her Nebula Award-winning "The Planners" concerns biological research, and "The Funeral" depicts a rigid future society. But these stories are not simply intellectual adventures comfortably removed from us in time. "The Planners" shows a scientist who does not fully comprehend the moral and ethical implications of his research, "The Funeral" reveals the crippling constraints in which adults often place children, and "Baby, You Were Great" takes place in a world uncomfortably like our own.

Wilhelm's work gains much of its strength by showing us life as it is lived, as so many works of science fiction do not. Her stories are easily accessible, but they are not escapist entertainments which one can read and then put aside; the issues she raises are present in our lives. She is a concerned writer, but she does not moralize and she does not lapse into despair. Many of her works, notably *City of Cain*, a novel about a plot to build an underground city where experiments will be conducted on survivors of atomic and environmental disasters, show the dangers of excessive power thoughtlessly used. One especially strong novella, "The Infinity Box," shows the corrupting influence of power from the inside; the story is made more disturbing by the fact that the protagonist is a likeable, intelligent, and sympathetic man who is altered and changed simply by having the power to enter another person's mind. In "April Fool's Day Forever" immortality, the ultimate power over death, has been achieved by some, but its price turns out to be the loss of the bond with the collective unconscious and all creative forces. *Where Late the Sweet Birds Sang* (Hugo Award) has been called the best treatment of cloning in science fiction by many critics. But the novel is also about the often destructive strategies human beings can employ in order to survive, and it shows the author's concern with the damage we have done to the earth, a common theme in her work.

Wilhelm's abilities are at their height in *The Clewiston Test* and *Juniper Time*. *The Clewiston Test* is a feminist novel and a psychological thriller which presents issues in the context of a suspenseful story. The isolation of the protagonist, Anne Clewiston, who is recovering from a serious accident, is symbolic of the isolation felt by so many women; the scientific project in the novel is used as a plot device to illuminate the personal conflicts of the characters. *Juniper Time* tells the story of two people, Jean Brighton and Arthur Cluny, who are the children of astronauts. The two grow up in a drought-plagued world in which the dream of space exploration, the goal to which their fathers had devoted themselves, has died. The conflicts in the book reflect our own predicament; we must live with our technology, however uneasily, and cannot turn back, but we must conserve what is valuable of the past, and keep future hopes from being perverted to unworthy and short-sighted ends.

In her science fiction, Kate Wilhelm holds a mirror to our world, and in her work we can see the dilemmas present in our uneasy, late-20th-century lives.

—Pamela Sargent

WILLIAMS, John A(lfred). American. Born in Jackson, Mississippi, 5 December 1925. Educated at Central High School, Syracuse, New York; Syracuse University, A.B. 1950. Served in the United States Navy, 1943-46. Married 1) Carolyn Clopton; 2) Lorrain Isaac; three children. Has worked for publishers, in an advertising agency, and for the American Committee on Africa, New York. Distinguished Professor of English, LaGuardia Community College, City University of New York, 1973-75; Visiting Professor, University of Hawaii, Honolulu, Summer 1974, and Boston University, 1978-79. Since 1979, Professor of English, Rutgers University, New Brunswick, New Jersey. Recipient: American Academy grant, 1962; Syracuse University Outstanding Achievement Award, 1970; National Endowment for the Arts grant, 1977. Litt.D.: Southeastern Massachusetts University, North Dartmouth, 1978. Address: 693 Forest Avenue, Teaneck, New Jersey 07666, U.S.A.

SCIENCE-FICTION PUBLICATIONS

Novels

Sons of Darkness, Sons of Light. Boston, Little Brown, 1969; London, Eyre and Spottiswoode, 1970.
Captain Blackman. New York, Doubleday, 1972.

Novels

The Angry Ones. New York, Ace, 1960; as *One for New York*,
   Chatham, New Jersey, Chatham Bookseller, 1975.
Night Song. New York, Farrar Straus, 1961; London, Collins,
   1962.
Sissie. New York, Farrar Straus, 1963; as *Journey Out of Anger*,
   London, Eyre and Spottiswoode, 1968.
The Man Who Cried I Am. Boston, Little Brown, 1967; London,
   Eyre and Spottiswoode, 1968.
Mothersill and the Foxes. New York, Doubleday, 1975.
The Junior Bachelor Society. New York, Doubleday, 1976.

Other

Africa: Her History, Lands, and People. New York, Cooper
   Square, 1962.
This Is My Country, Too. New York, New American Library,
   1965; London, New English Library, 1966.
The Most Native of Sons: A Biography of Richard Wright. New
   York, Doubleday, 1970.
*The King God Didn't Save: Reflections on the Life and Death of
   Martin Luther King, Jr.* New York, Coward McCann, 1970;
   London, Eyre and Spottiswoode, 1971.
Flashbacks: A Twenty-Year Diary of Article Writing. New York,
   Doubleday, 1973.
Romare Bearden. New York, Abrams, 1973.
Minorities in the City. New York, Harper, 1975.

Editor, *The Angry Black.* New York, Lancer, 1962.
Editor, *Beyond the Angry Black.* New York, Cooper Square,
   1967.
Editor, *Amistad I* and *II.* New York, Knopf, 2 vols., 1970-71.

*

Manuscript Collection: Syracuse University, New York.

*   *   *

As a sensitive black writer, John A. Williams is alert to discrimi-
natory literary restrictions and chafes against them. His article "The
Literary Ghetto" contends that the critical practice of comparing
black writers only to black writers denies them the rights to compete
with whites and to be taken seriously when they examine issues and
emotions common to all men. Although his fiction concentrates on
the manifold ways in which blacks have been oppressed and have
reacted to that oppression, he also depicts similar maltreatment
accorded to Jews and others, the need for man to transcend his
progenitor, the killer ape, the differences between casual affairs and
emotional commitments. Moreover, he welcomes—and merits—
comparison with such contemporaries as Mailer and Styron.
   Williams's novels *The Man Who Cried I Am*, *Sons of Darkness,
Sons of Light*, and *Captain Blackman* demonstrate that he also
rejects the critical practice of placing future-oriented fiction in a
literary ghetto. These novels blend mainstream, experimental,
thriller, and speculative fiction techniques into artistic wholes that
confound many critics. Like Doris Lessing's Martha Quest series,
The Man Who Cried I Am starts with a realistic delineation of social
and political forces at work in the modern era as experienced by a
protagonist and ends with a vision of the future those forces have
shaped. The protagonist, Max Reddick, is a black man whose
advances from job-seeker to journalist to presidential speechwriter
reveal increasingly subtle refusals by whites to share power. Thus,
he is not surprised to confront the King Alfred plan, the American
government's proposal to put all blacks into concentration camps
and gas them if some blacks move from rioting to rebellion over
unfulfilled promises. The more extensively speculative *Sons of
Darkness, Sons of Light* shows how a racial war could develop in
the United States from one black man's decision to initiate the
assassination of whites who kill blacks as an alternative to the
random violence of riots. Both blacks and whites readily comprehend the "eye for an eye" philosophy behind such assassinations and

both escalate the number of eyes to be exchanged. However, Williams never repudiates retaliatory violence by blacks but raises unresolved moral and practical questions about it. *Captain Blackman*
also combines realism and extrapolation but examines the distant
past before considering the future. Like Twain's Connecticut Yankee, Captain Blackman receives a wound that jolts him back in time
while leaving his present knowledge intact. Blackman then experiences life as a typical black soldier from the Revolutionary War to
Vietnam. Since he has thus encountered two hundred years of white
callousness, his decision not to accept integration into a white army
that countenances My Lai massacres and contemplates nuclear
holocausts gains added meaning. His achieved goal of infiltrating
light-skinned blacks into key positions to take over the nuclear
strike system and dismantle it is not only a blow for black power but
also an attempt to substitute decency for destructiveness. All three
novels reflect Williams's belief that man must comprehend his
personal, racial, national, and evolutionary history to alter himself
and his society. He also feels that in an oppressive society manhood
depends on the willingness to strive for change. It is his longing for
change that leads him to link mainstream and speculative fiction.
   Williams also refuses to segregate fiction from fact and the personal from the political. His background as journalist and poet
makes him aware of the fictive in much so-called fact and the reality
behind fantasy. Both *The Man Who Cried I Am* and *Captain
Blackman* intermingle historical persons with fictional characters
and actual occurrences with invented ones to illuminate his view of
history. Both works also analyze the interrelationships between the
social and the individual. In *The Man Who Cried I Am*, for example, the social impinges on the personal when Max's white-imposed
joblessness prompts his girlfriend to undergo an abortion. And the
personal impinges on the social when Max's "friend" Harry Ames
risks leaving the King Alfred plan unexposed by giving it to Max
because he is jealous of Max and expects him to die for possessing it.
Such insightful juxtapositions, plus that of the realistic with the
speculative, place Williams among the best contemporary writers.

—Steven R. Carter

WILLIAMS, Robert Moore. American. Born in Farmington,
Missouri, 19 June 1907. Educated at the University of Missouri,
Columbia, B.A. in journalism. Married Margaret Jelley in 1938
(divorced, 1952); one daughter. Full-time writer, 1937-72. *Died in
1977.*

Novels (series: Jongor; Zanthar)

The Chaos Fighters. New York, Ace, 1955.
Conquest of the Space Sea. New York, Ace, 1955.
Doomsday Eve. New York, Ace, 1957.
The Blue Atom. New York, Ace, 1958.
World of the Masterminds. New York, Ace, 1960.
The Day They H-Bombed Los Angeles. New York, Ace, 1961.
The Darkness Before Tomorrow. New York, Ace, 1962.
King of the Fourth Planet. New York, Ace, 1962.
Walk Up the Sky. New York, Avalon, 1962.
The Star Wasps. New York, Ace, 1963.
Flight from Yesterday. New York, Ace, 1963.
The Lunar Eye. New York, Ace, 1964.
The Second Atlantis. New York, Ace, 1965.
Vigilante—21st Century. New York, Lancer, 1967.
Zanthar of the Many Worlds. New York, Lancer, 1967.
Zanthar of the Edge of Never. New York, Lancer, 1968.
The Bell from Infinity. New York, Lancer, 1968.
Zanthar at Moon's Madness. New York, Lancer, 1968.
Zanthar at Trip's End. New York, Lancer, 1968.

Beachhead Planet. New York, Dell, and London, Sidgwick and Jackson, 1970.
Jongor of Lost Land. New York, Popular Library, 1970.
The Return of Jongor. New York, Popular Library, 1970.
Jongor Fights Back. New York, Popular Library, 1970.
Now Comes Tomorrow. New York, Curtis, and London, Sidgwick and Jackson, 1971.

Short Stories

The Void Beyond and Other Stories. New York, Ace, 1958.
To the End of Time. New York, Ace, 1960.
When Two Worlds Meet. New York, Curtis, 1970.

Uncollected Short Story

"Now Comes Tomorrow," in *Science Fiction Special 6.* London, Sidgwick and Jackson, 1973.

OTHER PUBLICATIONS

Other

Love Is Forever, We Are for Tonight (autobiography). New York, Curtis, 1970.

*   *   *

During the editorship of Ray Palmer in the 1940's, *Amazing Stories* and *Fantastic Adventures* were juvenile action pulps principally written by a stable of writers under their own by-lines and an assortment of house names. Robert Moore Williams was part of this stable, producing scores of stories including a few under the name Russell Storm. (It is not clear which stories he wrote under house names, but it's probable that most of the stories published prior to 1951 under the name E.K. Jarvis are his.) Even today, Williams is largely associated with these magazines and their juvenile policy, but the truth is he was one of only a handful of writers of those years who were able to cut across policy boundaries and sell stories to almost all the existing science-fiction magazines. He appeared often, for example, in both *Thrilling Wonder* and *Startling*, and also in John Campbell's *Astounding* (Campbell thought enough of his talents to mention him in his essay for Lloyd Eshbach's *Of Worlds Beyond*). In fact, of these writers, Williams is unique in sustaining a continuous career as an SF writer through to the 1970's.

Although Williams wrote almost 200 stories, it is possible from one of his collections to get a good feel for his approaches and talent. The stories in *When Two Worlds Meet* are linked through a common background of Earthman-Martian conflict, although the background details of Mars and the Martians are inconsistent. The title story tells of an Earthman who tries to learn the secret behind a "god weapon" that allows one race to subjugate another. "Aurochs Came Walking" concerns a shaman's crystal ball that turns out to be a control device for a machine built by ancient Martians. In "The Sound of Bugles" Martians show an Earthman the secret of creating such resources as food and housing from pure thought. The weakest story in the book is probably "When the Spoilers Came," marred by an unconvincing and rather sentimental resolution, something not especially common in the fiction of Williams whose romantic streak more often manifested itself as a mildly ironic cynicism. "The Final Frontier," in which a dying Martian wields strange powers to thwart exploitative Earthmen, is only technically better. The best story in the book is "On Pain of Death," a suspense story about a group of Earthmen trapped in a strange prison that may be either a particularly efficient execution machine or a test of their worthiness to live.

Again and again, Williams's fiction deals with machines that bestow godlike powers, or ordinary humans who possess a special rapport with machines or elemental energies. In "The Night the General Left Us" a mathematician's love of machines is returned by a model rocket that attacks a general who orders the man arrested. "The Smallness Beyond Thought" deals with an eccentric hermit whose ability to grow food without water is related to his ability to sense the flow of electromagnetic and less familiar forms of energy.

It should not be assumed that Williams is playing with the traditional science-fiction theme of the superman. Rather, his work expresses a basically mystical view of the world. This is borne out by "The Grove of God" (*Other Worlds*, 1956), whose editor described it as too taboo-breaking for other magazines. An expedition of space explorers from Earth lands on a planet where they discover god-like humans living in a primitive paradise. They discover that the planet is actually Earth, to which they have returned through some sort of application of Lorenz-Fitzgerald principle that none of the scientists seem to have been aware of. The narrative is as awkward and downright clumsy as the idea, something surprising in the work of a professional as experienced as Williams. Ironically, another story by him in that issue ("The Steogar" as by Russell Storm) deals more effectively with similar material: a research scientist at a government installation acquires godlike abilities through the agency of a miraculous invention.

Williams turned to novels for the growing paperback markets in 1955 with *The Chaos Fighters.* During the next decade and a half Williams produced almost 30 books. By and large they were not too different from the mass of his magazine fiction and they abound with such concepts as aliens trying to control human destiny, Earthmen exploiting alien planets, and humans with miraculous powers. Williams did manage, in *The Day They H-Bombed Los Angeles* and *The Second Atlantis*, to find interesting ways to destroy Southern California. The Jongor series consist of Burroughs-like lost-land stories, and the Zanthar series are about a super scientist who seems as interested in the occult as in physics. The last, appropriately called *Zanthar at Trip's End*, has him coping with a machine that blows the souls out of people's bodies.

The strangest of Williams's books, however, is a slim volume titled *Love Is Forever—We Are for Tonight.* Although it's called science fiction on one cover and a "strange and fantastic novel of a man trapped in an inner world of fear and evil" on the other, the book is autobiography with no pretense of being fiction. It begins with some fairly evocative descriptions of his childhood and youth but soon focuses on Williams's interest in and experiences with such things as dianetics, hallucinogenic gases, and communes (in the 1950's). The style reminds one of Ray Palmer's in his editorials for *Other Worlds*, but Palmer's delightful flamboyance and self-directed humor are missing and missed. The book is often vague and evasive, but some facts about the man crop up and the portions dealing with dianetics, while not particularly revealing, might hold interest for anyone curious about the impact of that cult on the SF field.

Williams doesn't seem to have very often probed deeply into any of his ideas or themes, and this makes some of his work, while perfectly readable on the surface, seem disturbingly incomplete. His best work tends to be stories of adventure and suspense, such as "On Pain of Death," and stories about determined human beings trying to survive, such as "Last Ship Out" where two disfigured survivors of atomic war try to battle their way on board a spaceship bound for Mars. The story is slight but compact and straightforward and very readable. It satisfies more than the ponderous "Grove of God," reminding us that Williams is more likely to be at his best writing about people and situations than about ideas.

—Gerald W. Page

* * *

WILLIAMSON, Jack (John Stewart Williamson). Also writes as Will Stewart. American. Born in Bisbee, Arizona, 29 April 1908. Educated at Richland High School, New Mexico; West Texas State University, Canyon, 1928-30; University of New Mexico, Albuquerque, 1931-32; Eastern New Mexico University, Portales, B.A. (summa cum laude), M.A. 1957; University of Colorado, Boulder, Ph.D. 1964. Weather forecaster in the United States Army, 1942-45: Staff Sargeant. Married Blanche Slaten Harp in 1947; two step-children. Writer from 1928; wire editor, Portales *News Tribune*, 1947; created comic strip *Beyond Mars*, New York *Sunday News*, 1952-55; Instructor in English, New Mexico Military

Institute, Roswell, 1958-60, and University of Colorado, 1960; Professor of English, Eastern New Mexico University, 1960-77, now retired. Since 1978, President, Science Fiction Writers of America. Recipient: Pilgrim Award, 1973; Nebula Grand Master Award, 1976. Guest of Honor, 35th World Science Fiction Convention, 1977. Agent: Scott Meredith Literary Agency, 845 Third Avenue, New York, New York 10022. Address: Box 761, Portales, New Mexico 88130, U.S.A.

SCIENCE-FICTION PUBLICATIONS

Novels (series: Jim Eden; Legion of Space; Seetee; Starchild)

The Girl from Mars, with Miles J. Breuer. New York, Stellar, 1929.
The Legion of Space. Reading, Pennsylvania, Fantasy Press, 1947; London, Sphere, 1977.
Darker Than You Think. Reading, Pennsylvania, Fantasy Press, 1948; London, Sphere, 1976.
The Humanoids. New York, Simon and Schuster, 1949; London, Museum Press, 1953.
The Green Girl. New York, Avon, 1950.
The Cometeers (Legion). Reading, Pennsylvania, Fantasy Press, 1950; London, Sphere, 1977; expanded section published as *One Against the Legion*, New York, Pyramid, 1967.
Seetee Shock (as Will Stewart). New York, Simon and Schuster, 1950; Kingswood, Surrey, World's Work, 1954.
Seetee Ship (as Will Stewart). New York, Gnome Press, 1951.
Dragon's Island. New York, Simon and Schuster, 1951; London, Museum Press, 1954; as *The Not-Men*, New York, Belmont, 1968.
The Legion of Time. Reading, Pennsylvania, Fantasy Press, 1952; as *The Legion of Time* and *After World's End*, London, Digit, 2 vols., 1961.
Undersea Quest (Eden), with Frederik Pohl. New York, Gnome Press, 1954; London, Dobson, 1966.
Dome Around America. New York, Ace, 1955.
Star Bridge, with James E. Gunn. New York, Gnome Press, 1955; London, Sidgwick and Jackson, 1978.
Undersea Fleet (Eden), with Frederik Pohl. New York, Gnome Press, 1956; London, Dobson, 1968.
Undersea City (Eden), with Frederik Pohl. New York, Gnome Press, 1958; London, Dobson, 1968.
The Trial of Terra. New York, Ace, 1962.
Golden Blood. New York, Lancer, 1964.
The Reign of Wizardry. New York, Lancer, 1964.
The Starchild Trilogy, with Frederik Pohl. New York, Pocket Books, 1977; London, Penguin, 1980.
    The Reefs of Space. New York, Ballantine, 1964; London, Dobson, 1965.
    Starchild. New York, Ballantine, 1965; London, Dobson, 1966.
    Rogue Star. New York, Ballantine, 1969; London, Dobson, 1972.
Bright New Universe. New York, Ace, 1967; London, Sidgwick and Jackson, 1969.
Trapped in Space (juvenile). New York, Doubleday, 1968.
The Moon Children. New York, Putnam, 1972; Morley, Yorkshire, Elmfield Press, 1975.
Farthest Star, with Frederik Pohl. New York, Ballantine, 1975; London, Pan, 1976.
The Power of Blackness. New York, Berkley, 1976; London, Sphere, 1978.
Brother to Demons, Brother to Gods. Indianapolis, Bobbs Merrill, 1979.
The Humanoid Touch. New York, Holt Rinehart, 1980.

Short Stories

Lady in Danger. London, Utopian, n.d.
The Pandora Effect. New York, Ace, 1969.
People Machines. New York, Ace, 1971.
The Early Williamson. New York, Doubleday, 1975; London, Sphere, 1978.
The Best of Jack Williamson. New York, Ballantine, 1978.

OTHER PUBLICATIONS

Other

"The Logic of Fantasy," in *Of Worlds Beyond*, edited by Lloyd Arthur Eshbach. Reading, Pennsylvania, Fantasy Press, 1947; London, Dobson, 1965.
"Why I Selected Star Bright," in *My Best Science Fiction Story*, edited by Leo Margulies and O.J. Friend. New York, Merlin Press, 1949.
"As I Knew Hugo," in *Extrapolation* (Wooster, Ohio), May 1970.
"Science Fiction Comes to College," in *Extrapolation* (Wooster, Ohio), May 1971.
"Science Fiction: Emerging from Its Exile in Limbo," in *Publishers Weekly* (New York), 5 July 1971.
Teaching Science Fiction. Privately printed, 1972.
H.G. Wells, Critic of Progress. Baltimore, Mirage Press, 1973.
"The Years of Wonder," in *Voices for the Future*, edited by Thomas D. Clareson. Bowling Green, Ohio, Popular Press, 1976.
"The Next Century of Science Fiction," in *Analog* (New York), February 1978.
"The Case Against the Critics," in *Analog* (New York), April 1980.

Editor, *Science Fiction: Education for Tomorrow*. Philadelphia, Owlswick Press, 1980.

*

Manuscript Collection: Special Collections, Eastern New Mexico University Library, Portales.

Jack Williamson comments:

I began writing at 20, hardly half-educated but dazzled with visions of science and intoxicated with science fiction as a device for exploring the possible. In the 50 years since, the known universe has vastly expanded and science fiction has grown as fast. Now at 70 I'm still held by the unfolding drama of science and still excited about science fiction. As a career, it has been rewarding. Though in the first few decades the pay in money was meager, there were always rich compensations in the satisfactions of creating, in the fine friendships, in the opportunities to observe the explosions of scientific knowledge and the human impacts of science and technology. The writers and readers of science fiction form a special community, still tiny when I first discovered it, inhabited by the most able and interesting people I have known. Belonging to it has been a privilege.

*   *   *

Jack Williamson occupies the same place in the history of science fiction that Richard Strauss occupies in the history of music. Both men were artistic prodigies who first achieved recognition in their early twenties; both represented, as they grew older, a dynamic conservative branch of their art that used the techniques of their heirs to refine their own skills. Thus Strauss tended, as he aged, towards a neo-classic style that was late Romanticism freed of ostentation; thus Williamson, in the past decade, has returned to the characters of his early novels, echoing Strauss's return to the forms of his youth.

Williamson's early life was spent in a covered wagon on one of the last frontiers, that of rural New Mexico. His first story resulted from reading one of the first numbers of *Amazing Stories*; it was "The Metal Man" (1928). In a crude but enthusiastic way, it established one of Williamson's *leitmotifs*: the interface between man and machine, as the hero becomes a technological object, a "person-machine." After several early novels that have never been published in book form (e.g., "The Stone from the Green Star") Williamson first earned a reputation as a master of space opera with *The Legion of Space* (1934). This novel put Williamson in the same rank with such galaxy-conquerors as John W. Campbell and E.E. "Doc" Smith; but the novel resembles those of his contemporaries only in its exuberance. Unlike Campbell and Smith, Williamson was not espousing either technocracy, as Campbell did, or the joys of physics unchecked by any intellectual bound, as Smith did. Williamson is neither pro- nor anti-technology; while there is a good deal of gimcrack physics scattered throughout the text, the central device that allows the heroes to conquer their foes, AKKA, can be activated only by a few scraps and an act of will; its operation is never explained. *The Legion of Space* is important because it is the first sign that SF was moving away from the epic of technocracy; although it is what Alexei Panshin would call a lost-race novel of space (much of the action is standard lost-race adventure transported to the jungle-covered moon of Jupiter, Titan), it is still an advance over other, duller works of the time and can still be read with pleasure. Its sequels are better written but less entertaining. Williamson was one of the few writers of the 1930's who could write with equal facility for the *Astounding* of F. Orlin Tremaine and the *Astounding* of John Campbell. It is generally forgotten that *One Against the Legion* was published in Campbell's *Astounding*. Campbell prodded Williamson to excellence in much the same way as he prodded other writers; Williamson's best work dates from this period, and the only novel that Williamson produced after 1948 that achieves excellence is a result of a Campbell-inspired fragment of 1941.

Williamson's three great works deal with the same theme: the eternal tension of man in society. Man, Aristotle teaches, is a social animal; it is the degree to which an individual must participate in society without abandoning free will that Williamson seeks to find in *Darker Than You Think*, *The Humanoids*, and *Star Bridge*.

Darker Than You Think is a result of the two years Williamson spent in psychoanalysis in the late 1930's. Ostensibly it concerns a war between lycanthropy and humanity for dominance; but the werewolves are seen as agents of freedom, creatures that put the lie to scientific and psychoanalytic explanations with mystical truth that transcends attempts at rationalization. But freedom, in this novel, requires a price, a sum of dependence, of eternal vigilance. It is as if the werewolves were organised anarchists, determined to preserve absolute liberty with a new order. Added to this, Williamson has produced what is the best explanation of lycanthropy extant (it depends on probablistic physics, a theme deepened in *The Humanoids*). *Darker Than You Think* is an excellent thriller as well, being the finest novel of the occult produced by a science-fiction writer.

Williamson continued his search for controlling agents in his best work, *The Humanoids*. In two ancillary works designed to match each other as thesis and antithesis, "With Folded Hands" and "The Equalizer," Williamson ruminated on the use and abuse of technology. The former introduces a classic dystopian theme, that of robots following a categorical imperative to its logical limit; the latter shows that technology can preserve as well as destroy free will. But these two novellas are two halves of a larger whole; they can not be read apart, and consequently they lose some of their artistic impact. Only in *The Humanoids* does Williamson attempt a synthesis; and he does this by relying on the old Campbellian warhorse, that of psionic power, as Williamson combines metaphysics with particle physics and the laws of probability to produce a new unified field theory. It is hard for the modern reader to accept psionics with the willingness of those in the late 1940's; but Williamson transcends mere reciting of psionic power to examine the epistemological foundations behind that power. Williamson also examines the fate of those who have accepted the humanoid categorical imperative, producing an examination of the middle ground between the two cultures of pure technocracy and pure mysticism that still retains its impact. *The Humanoids* is Williamson's best novel, a classic dystopia and the single best work on robot instrumentalities outside the work of Isaac Asimov.

Williamson began a rapid decline after *The Humanoids*; for the next dozen years, he produced works only in collaboration. These collaborations with Frederik Pohl are minor entertainments, the earlier novels such as *Undersea City* being competent juveniles, but rapidly declining to reach a nadir with *Starchild*, the worst novel of either author. Williamson's other "collaboration" is not that at all, but is instead the completion of a Williamson fragment by James Gunn. This novel, *Star Bridge*, is Williamson's last important work, an examination of the processes of political change no less searching than his examination of psychoanalysis in *Darker Than You Think* and of technology in *The Humanoids*. The dialectic between individual and society here is less distinct; the chief representative of individualism is an assassin who does not know what he stands for, the society a corporate state whose internal dynamic has been spent.

Williamson could not finish this novel, and Gunn finished it rather confusedly; nonetheless, there are passages which rival the best passages in *The Humanoids* as models of intelligent writing.

Williamson's work since 1955 has been minor. He has preferred to concentrate on an academic career, earning his doctorate with work published as *H.G. Wells: Critic of Progress*. The conflict between his academic present and his pulpish past is symbolised in *Bright New Universe*. In recent years, his novels have returned to stories that could have appeared in *Planet Stories*: such a work as *The Power of Blackness* suffers from a black hero who is so characterless that Williamson can find no other descriptive qualities for him than the color of his skin. He has, like many older writers, regressed to such a state that his reputation is higher than his skill; but his award as Grand Master presented by the Science Fiction Writers of America is indeed deserved, not only for his 52 years of writing (longer than any other SF writer), but also for his 1940's works.

—Martin Morse Wooster

WILSON, Colin (Henry). British. Born in Leicester, 26 June 1931. Educated at Gateway Secondary Technical School, Leicester, 1942-47. Served in the Royal Air Force, 1949-50. Married 1) Dorothy Betty Troop in 1951 (marriage dissolved), one son; 2) Pamela Joy Stewart in 1960, two sons and one daughter. Laboratory Assistant, Gateway School, 1948-49; tax collector, Leicester and Rugby, 1949-50; labourer and hospital porter in London, 1951-53; salesman for the magazines *Paris Review* and *Merlin*, Paris, 1953. Since 1954, full-time writer. British Council Lecturer in Germany, 1957; Writer-in-Residence, Hollins College, Virginia, 1966-67; Visiting Professor, University of Washington, Seattle, 1968; Professor, Institute of the Mediterranean (Dowling College, New York), Majorca, 1969; Visiting Professor, Rutgers University, New Brunswick, New Jersey, 1974. Agent: David Bolt, Bolt and Watson Ltd., 8-12 Old Queen Street, Storey's Gate, London SW1H 9HP. Address: Tetherdown, Gorran Haven, Cornwall, England.

SCIENCE-FICTION PUBLICATIONS

Novels

The Mind Parasites. London, Barker, and Sauk City, Wisconsin, Arkham House, 1967.
The Philosopher's Stone. London, Barker, 1969; New York, Crown, 1971.
The Space Vampires. London, Hart Davis MacGibbon, and New York, Random House, 1976.

Short Story

The Return of the Lloigor. London, Village Press, 1974.

Uncollected Short Story

"Timeslip," in *Aries 1*, edited by John Grant. Newton Abbot, Devon, David and Charles, 1979.

OTHER PUBLICATIONS

Novels

Ritual in the Dark. London, Gollancz, and Boston, Houghton Mifflin, 1960.
Adrift in Soho. London, Gollancz, and Boston, Houghton Mifflin, 1961.
The World of Violence. London, Gollancz, 1963; as *The Violent World of Hugh Greene*, Boston, Houghton Mifflin, 1963.

Man Without a Shadow: The Diary of an Existentialist. London, Barker, 1963; as *The Sex Diary of Gerard Sorme*, New York, Dial Press, 1963.

Necessary Doubt. London, Barker, and New York, Simon and Schuster, 1964.

The Glass Cage: An Unconventional Detective Story. London, Barker, 1966; New York, Random House, 1967.

The Killer. London, New English Library, 1970; as *Lingard*, New York, Crown, 1970.

The God of the Labyrinth. London, Hart Davis, 1970; as *The Hedonists*, New York, New American Library, 1971.

The Black Room. London, Weidenfeld and Nicolson, 1971; New York, Pyramid, 1975.

The Schoolgirl Murder Case. London, Hart Davis MacGibbon, and New York, Crown, 1974.

Plays

Viennese Interlude (produced Scarborough, Yorkshire, and London, 1960).

Strindberg (as *Pictures in a Bath of Acid*, produced Leeds, Yorkshire, 1971; as *Strindberg: A Fool's Decision*, produced London, 1975). London, Calder and Boyars, 1970; New York, Random House, 1971.

Mysteries (produced Cardiff, 1979).

Other

The Outsider. London, Gollancz, and Boston, Houghton Mifflin, 1956.

Religion and the Rebel. London, Gollancz, and Boston, Houghton Mifflin, 1957.

The Age of Defeat. London, Gollancz, 1959; as *The Stature of Man*, Boston, Houghton Mifflin, 1959.

Encyclopedia of Murder, with Patricia Pitman. London, Barker, 1961; New York, Putnam, 1962.

The Strength to Dream: Literature and the Imagination. London, Gollancz, and Boston, Houghton Mifflin, 1962.

Origins of the Sexual Impulse. London, Barker, and New York, Putnam, 1963.

Rasputin and the Fall of the Romanovs. London, Barker, and New York, Farrar Straus, 1964.

Brandy of the Damned: Discoveries of a Musical Eclectic. London, Baker, 1964; as *Chords and Discords: Purely Personal Opinions on Music*, New York, Crown, 1966; augmented edition, as *Colin Wilson on Music*, London, Pan, 1967.

Beyond the Outsider: The Philosophy of the Future. London, Barker, and Boston, Houghton Mifflin, 1965.

Eagle and Earwig (essays). London, Baker, 1965.

Introduction to the New Existentialism. London, Hutchinson, 1966; Boston, Houghton Mifflin, 1967.

Sex and the Intelligent Teenager. London, Arrow, 1966; New York, Pyramid, 1968.

Voyage to a Beginning (autobiography). London, Cecil and Amelia Woolf, 1966; New York, Crown, 1969.

Bernard Shaw: A Reassessment. London, Hutchinson, and New York, Atheneum, 1969.

A Casebook of Murder. London, Frewin, 1969; New York, Cowles, 1970.

Poetry and Mysticism. San Francisco, City Lights, 1969; London, Hutchinson, 1970.

The Strange Genius of David Lindsay, with E.H. Visiak and J.B. Pick. London, Baker, 1970; as *The Haunted Man*, San Bernardino, California, Borgo Press, 1979.

The Occult. New York, Random House, and London, Hodder and Stoughton, 1971.

New Pathways in Psychology: Maslow and the Post-Freudian Revolution. New York, Taplinger, and London, Gollancz, 1972.

Order of Assassins: The Psychology of Murder. London, Hart Davis, 1972.

L'Amour: The Ways of Love, photographs by Piero Rimaldi. New York, Crown, 1972.

Strange Powers. London, Latimer New Dimensions, 1973; New York, Random House, 1975.

Tree by Tolkien. London, Covent Garden Press-Inca, 1973; Santa Barbara, California, Capra Press, 1974.

Hermann Hesse. London, Village Press, and Philadelphia, Leaves of Grass Press, 1974.

Wilhelm Reich. London, Village Press, and Philadelphia, Leaves of Grass Press, 1974.

Jorge Luis Borges. London, Village Press, and Philadelphia, Leaves of Grass Press, 1974.

A Book of Booze. London, Gollancz, 1974.

The Unexplained. Lake Oswego, Oregon, Lost Pleiade Press, 1975.

Mysterious Powers. London, Aldus, and Danbury, Connecticut, Danbury Press, 1975; as *They Had Strange Powers*, New York, Doubleday, 1975.

The Craft of the Novel. London, Gollancz, 1975.

Enigmas and Mysteries. London, Aldus, and New York, Doubleday, 1976.

The Geller Phenomenon. London, Aldus, 1976.

Mysteries: An Investigation into the Occult, The Paranormal, and the Supernatural. London, Hodder and Stoughton, and New York, Putnam, 1978.

Science Fiction as Existentialism. Hayes, Middlesex, Bran's Head, 1978.

Starseekers. London, Hodder and Stoughton, 1980.

The War Against Sleep: The Philosophy of Gurdjieff. Wellingborough, Northamptonshire, Thorsons, 1980.

The Quest for Wilhelm Reich. New York, Doubleday, 1981.

Editor, *Colin Wilson's Men of Mystery.* London, W.H. Allen, 1977.

Editor, *Dark Dimensions: A Celebration of the Occult.* New York, Everest House, 1978.

Editor, with John Grant, *The Book of Time.* Newton Abbot, Devon, David and Charles, 1980.

*

Bibliography: in *Colin Wilson* by John A. Weigel, New York, Twayne, 1975.

Manuscript Collection: University of Texas, Austin.

*   *   *

Colin Wilson is an enormously energetic and eclectic writer whose works include non-fiction and fiction of many classes. For his world view he acknowledges a seminal and continuing influence of Bernard Shaw, whose long science-fantasy play *Back to Methuselah* is a sort of mainspring for Wilson's science-fiction novels.

In the Preface to *The Mind Parasites* Wilson remarks that the work is his first attempt at fantasy and likely his last. It was not. At least two more have followed. In *The Mind Parasites* Professor Gilbert Austin discovers a counter-life entity competing with humanity for life energy from the wellspring of creation. Throughout history the parasites have masked from men mankind's own true powers—which are enormous, even godlike. Austin and his cohorts turn the tide of battle in favor of man, after themselves becoming considerably advanced in this "natural" power. Similarly, in *The Philosopher's Stone* Howard Lester seeks and finds the answer to the problem of death. The power of the will to live has been blocked by the "Old Ones," a superspecies millions of years old that caused and then intercepted the evolution of man. Long asleep, the Old Ones may soon awaken. Lester hopes to lead men to confront them as "Masters" where they once served the Old Ones as slaves. *The Space Vampires* streamlines in style and strategy a similar tale. Spaceship Commander Carlsen discovers a gigantic interstellar craft of perverted aliens from the star-system Rigel. These creatures cheat death by absorbing life energy from host species such as humanity. Fortunately for mankind, sane Rigelians catch up with the vampire Rigelians just in time. Carlsen acts as the medium of the saviors, and in the process learns wholesome means by which mankind can be "immortal."

There are an enthusiam and bright-eyed bombast about these tales that make it not unrewarding to read them as parodies of science fiction. This may account for a number of the elements common in the three works, though one need not forego taking them seriously as well. Each is furnished with a preface acknowledging a debt to H.P. Lovecraft or August Derleth. Each manifests considerable erudition exhibiting Wilson's encyclopaedic knowledge of the occult as well as the arts and history: ancient mythologies are found to have considerable basis in fact. Each story presents an intellectual power fantasy. The hero, in whom a panoply of parapsychological abilities is emerging, seems torn between visions of mankind as mean, gullible, and cowardly and man with a destiny of vaulting grandeur. These heroes, after lifting the yoke of mental slavery from humanity, win a form of personal transcendence, a step in the direction of joining the advanced intelligent life that lives throughout the universe.

Of the three *The Space Vampires* is the shortest and slickest. *The Philosopher's Stone* bogs us down and seems precisely repetitive of *The Mind Parasites* whose patient narrative, nicely deployed scenic hyperboles, and wonderful message were Wilson's first, best attempt after all.

—John R. Pfeiffer

WILSON, Richard. American. Born in Huntington Station, New York, 23 September 1920. Educated at Brooklyn College, 1935-36; University of Chicago, 1947-48. Served in the United States Army Signal Corps, 1942-46. Married 1) Jessica Gould in 1941 (divorced, 1944); 2) Doris Owens in 1950 (divorced, 1967); 3) Frances Daniels in 1967; one son and three step-children. Reporter, Copyreader, and assistant drama critic, Fairchild Publications, New York, 1941-42; Chief of Bureau, Transradio Press, Chicago, Washington, D.C., and New York, 1946-51; reporter, and deputy to the North American editor, Reuters, New York, 1951-64. Since 1964, Director, Syracuse University News Bureau, New York. Recipient: Nebula Award, 1968. Agent: Leslie Flood, E.J. Carnell Literary Agency, Rowneybury Bungalow, Sawbridgeworth, near Old Harlow, Essex CM20 2EX, England. Address: Syracuse University News Bureau, 105 Administration Building, Syracuse, New York 13210, U.S.A.

SCIENCE-FICTION PUBLICATIONS

Novels

The Girls from Planet 5. New York, Ballantine, 1955; London, Hale, 1968.
And Then the Town Took Off. New York, Ace, 1960.
30-Day Wonder. New York, Ballantine, 1960; London, Icon, 1963.

Short Stories

Those Idiots from Earth. New York, Ballantine, 1957.
Time Out for Tomorrow. New York, Ballantine, 1962; London, Mayflower, 1967.

Uncollected Short Stories (series: Harry Protagonist)

"The Carson Effect," in *The Year's Best S-F 10*, edited by Judith Merril. New York, Delacorte Press, 1965.
"Harry Protagonist, Brain-Drainer," in *Galaxy* (New York), February 1965.
"Box," in *New Worlds* (London), February 1965.
"The Eight Billion," in *Fantasy and Science Fiction* (New York), July 1965.
"Watchers in the Glade," in *The Ninth Galaxy Reader*, edited by Frederik Pohl. New York, Doubleday, and London, Gollancz, 1966.
"Deserter," in *Impulse* (Bournemouth), March 1966.

"Inside Out," in *Impulse* (Bournemouth), December 1966.
"Green Eyes," in *Impulse* (Bournemouth), January 1967.
"The Evil Ones," in *If* (New York), February 1967.
"9-9-99," in *Galaxy* (New York), August 1967.
"The South Waterford Rumble Club," in *Galaxy* (New York), December 1967.
"Mother to the World," in *Orbit 3*, edited by Damon Knight. New York, Putnam, 1968.
"See Me Not," in *World's Best Science Fiction 1968*, edited by Donald A. Wollheim and Terry Carr. New York, Ace, and London, Gollancz, 1968.
"Harry Protagonist, Undersec for Overpop," in *Magazine of Horror* (New York), December 1969.
"A Man Spekith," in *World's Best Science Fiction 1970*, edited by Donald A. Wollheim and Terry Carr. New York, Ace, and London, Gollancz, 1970.
"If a Man Answers," in *If* (New York), January 1970.
"Shave It Your Own Way," in *The Most Thrilling Science Fiction Ever Told* (New York), Winter 1970.
"The Day They Had the War," in *Fantasy and Science Fiction* (New York), June 1971.
"The Far King," in *Isaac Asimov's Science Fiction Magazine* (New York), March-April 1978.
"The Story Writer," in *Destinies 3* (New York), April-June 1979.

OTHER PUBLICATIONS

Plays

Jack and Jill (produced Syracuse, New York, 1965).

Radio Play: *Inside Story* (*X Minus One* series), 1955.

Other

"Syracuse University's Science-Fiction Collections," in *Worlds of Tomorrow* (New York), May 1967.

*   *   *

Richard Wilson's career as a writer breaks quite nicely into two stages. In his early years, Wilson was a satirical humorist in the mode of Henry Kuttner and Robert Sheckley, whose stories were frequently infused with a grim humor and a sharp eye for humanity's foibles. The three novels written at this time are cases in point. *The Girls from Planet 5* takes a pair of old stand-by plots and fuses them, with delightful results. America has become a matriarchy, where only one state still upholds the macho ideal—Texas, naturally. Into this strife-ridden world come invaders from another world, but invaders who are actually beautiful women. Frustrated by their loss of pre-eminence, the Texan patriarchs are not willing to become a minor backwater in an increasingly female universe. Aliens appear again in *And Then the Town Took Off*, a shorter novel that details the effect upon the citizens of Superior, Ohio, when their city uproots itself from Earth and rises into space to become a separate planet. This rollicking escapade pokes amusing if unconscious fun at James Blish's famous "Cities in Flight" series. The third and best of the novels is *30-Day Wonder* which takes what should be an ideal situation and turns it completely around. The Monolithians are alien visitors who express their determination to obey scrupulously all human laws and regulations, and ensure that all humans in their vicinity will do the same. The effect on rush-hour traffic of several automobiles sedately travelling well within the speed limit is just the beginning of an increasingly taxing month for the human race.

Although most of Wilson's early short stories such as "Those Idiots from Earth," were satirical or actively funny, his most well-known story of that period was very serious. The heroine of "Love" is a blind human girl living on Mars, who is in love with one of the despised Martian natives. When her father forbids her to have anything further to do with him, she runs off for one last meeting, and together they discover an ancient artifact that may well cure her sight. It is a touching tale told somewhat awkwardly, but effective.

The awkwardness left during the years that followed, and several of Wilson's recent works are outstanding. "Mother to the World" won a Nebula award for its tender, effective portrayal of the last man on Earth and the last woman, a gentle but retarded individual whose tolerance and flexibility overcome the horrors of their situation. Wilson returned to the last man theme in "A Man Spekith" in which a disc jockey and a computer remain in orbit, looking down over the corpse of the Earth. "See Me Not" is one of the few recent treatments of invisibility that contains any novelty. "The Carson Effect" portrays a wave of philanthropy on the eve of the last day of the world, an ending that is miscalculated and never happens, much to the consternation of those who have given away their fortunes. "The Story Writer" is a complex, engrossing story that contains enough complexity for a brace of novels. An aging successful pulp writer sits in flea markets, writing stories for people as a whim, until he finds himself a character in one of his own stories, the tale of the meeting of our own race and another that has reached us through another plane of existence in their flight from a ravaged homeworld. In this as in the other later stories, Wilson employs a rich, witty style that is a delight in itself; the expertly handled plots and characters are almost superfluous.

—Don D'Ammassa

WILSON, Robert Anton. American. Born in Brooklyn, New York, 18 January 1932. Educated at Brooklyn Polytechnic Institute; New York University, Paideia University, B.S., M.A. 1978. Married Arlen Riley in 1959; four children. Engineering aide, Ebasco Inc., New York, 1950-56; salesman, Doubleday, publishers, 1957; copywriter, Popular Club, Passaic, New Jersey, 1959-62; Sales Manager, Antioch Bookplate, Yellow Springs, Ohio, 1962-65; Associate Editor, *Playboy*, Chicago, 1966-71; astrology columnist, *National Mirror*, and Editor, *Jaguar*. Agent: Al Zuckerman, Writers House, 132 West 31st Street, New York, New York 10001, U.S.A.

SCIENCE-FICTION PUBLICATIONS

Novels

Illuminatus! The Eye in the Pyramid, The Golden Apple, Leviathan, with Robert Shea. New York, Dell, 3 vols., 1975; London, Sphere, 3 vols., 1976.

OTHER PUBLICATIONS

Novel

The Sex Magician. Los Angeles, Jaundice Press, 1974.

Play

Illuminatus! (produced Liverpool, 1976; London, 1977; Seattle, 1978).

Other

Playboy's Book of Forbidden Words. Chicago, Playboy Press, 1972.
Sex and Drugs. Chicago, Playboy Press, 1973; London, Mayflower, 1975.
The Book of the Breast. Chicago, Playboy Press, 1974.
Cosmic Trigger: The Final Secret of the Illuminati. Berkeley, California, And/Or Press, 1977; London, Abacus, 1979.
Neuropolitics, with Timothy Leary. Culver City, California, Peace Press, 1977.
Illuminati Papers. Berkeley, California, And/Or Press, 1980.

Robert Anton Wilson comments:
I define my writing as guerilla ontology—that is, a literary

expression of the discoveries of physical relativity (Einstein), cultural relativity (anthropology), neurological relativity (Korzybski, Leary) and the new head-spaces opened to us by psychedelics, bio-feedback, scientific study of yoga, etc. Each of my books presents not one map of reality, but several; the humor, the suspense, and the philosophical meaning (if any) derive from the search for the one reality, never quite found, which will synthesize or include all the alternative reality-tunnels presented. As in quantum physics, the observer or omniscient narrator does not exist in my world; it is a participatory universe in which each entity projects/creates its own surrounding experiential continuum.

*   *   *

> George, you're too serious. Don't you know how to play? Did you ever think that life is maybe a game? There is no difference between life and a game, you know.

Perhaps the best way to approach the Illuminatus trilogy is to treat it as a game in the way that detective stories are a game. The trilogy begins as a detective story that rapidly escalates to more and more involved levels until the allegiance, motivation, and even identity of all major characters are in doubt. As in a more conventional detective story, red herrings are let loose on the trail, but in this case they constitute a major part of the novel. Some are insoluble, others merely irrelevant. For example, I know now the meaning of Joe Malik's dogs (though it took me several months) but I doubt if anyone will understand what Howard the Dolphin discovered at Peos.

The trilogy is also a literary game of a type particularly popular among science-fiction fans. It parodies and pastiches many stories from many genres—sword and sorcery in Mama Sutra's version of Things As They Really Are; "Uyllese" in Mary Lou's trip in the final book. This literariness should not be looked on as pretension but as playfulness. It's part of the games the authors play with their readers.

Some readers will find *Illuminatus* difficult because of its philosophical pretensions. Its mockery of virtually all political and moral systems (including the anarchy it spends much of the time defending), and the "transcendental agnosticism" the book seeks to create in its reader are very much a product of the late 1960's. The easy acceptance and rejection of one system of thought after another, however, is not the product of deep-rooted agnosticism or cynicism but the end product of too much hearty involvement in too many causes. As Wilson's "autobiography," *Cosmic Trigger*, makes clear he has drunk too deeply of too many springs of ultimate wisdom for any to seem absolute. The book runs counter to the spirit of reaction in the 1970's, which requires more respect for dogmatism. One of the chief delights of the books is its touch with lunatic characterisation: "The name is James Cash Cartwright," the fat man said, "and the subject is consciousness energy." "George decided...to grow his hair long, smoke dope and become a musician. He succeeded in two of these ambitions." "Drake let out a small fart, an incredible thing, it seemed to George, for the leader of all organised crime in the United States to do." Character is defined in small flashes spread throughout the work, and as these flashes build up the work's one serious point comes clear: the inter-relatedness of everyone and everything. The authors are far from completely successful, but given such a theme, who could be?

—Michael Cule

WINIKI, Ephriam. *See* **FEARN, John Russell.**

WINTER, H.G.   *See* **BATES, Harry.**

———————

WODHAMS, Jack. Australian. Born in Dagenham, Essex, England, 3 September 1931; emigrated to Australia in 1955. Has worked as a weighing-machine mechanic, brush salesman, porter in mental hospital, taxi and truck driver, bartender, welder, and magician's assistant. Currently mailvan driver, Brisbane. Guest of Honor, Melbourne Science Fiction Convention, 1968. Address: P.O. Box 48, Caboolture, Queensland 4510, Australia.

SCIENCE-FICTION PUBLICATIONS

Novels

The Authentic Touch.   New York, Curtis, 1971.
Looking for Blücher.   St. Kilda, Victoria, Void, 1980.

Uncollected Short Stories

"The Pearly Gates of Hell," in *Analog* (New York), September 1967.
"The Cure-All Merchant," in *Analog* (New York), November 1967.
"Whosa Whatsa," in *Analog* (New York), December 1967.
"The Helmet of Hades," in *New Writings in SF 11*, edited by John Carnell. London, Corgi, 1968.
"The God Pedlars," in *Analog* (New York), February 1968.
"Handyman," in *Analog* (New York), April 1968.
"The Fuglemen of Recall," in *Analog* (New York), August 1968.
"Homespinner," in *Galaxy* (New York), October 1968.
"Try Again," in *Amazing* (New York), November 1968.
"Split Personality," in *Analog* (New York), November 1968.
"The Form Master," in *Analog* (New York), December 1968.
"Hey but No Presto," in *Analog* (New York), April 1969.
"A Run of Deuces," in *Fantasy and Science Fiction* (New York), June 1969.
"The Empty Balloon," in *Analog* (New York), July 1969.
"Androtomy and the Scion," in *Analog* (New York), August 1969.
"Anchor Man," in *Vision of Tomorrow* (Newcastle upon Tyne), August 1969.
"Star Hunger," in *Galaxy* (New York), August 1969.
"The Visitors," in *Analog* (New York), September 1969.
"Undercover Weapon," in *Vision of Tomorrow* (Newcastle upon Tyne), December 1969.
"There Is a Crooked Man," in *Analog 7*, edited by John W. Campbell, Jr. New York, Doubleday, 1970.
"The Ill Wind," in *Vision of Tomorrow* (Newcastle upon Tyne), January 1970.
"On Greatgrandfather's Knee," in *Vision of Tomorrow* (Newcastle upon Tyne), February 1970.
"Dali, For Instance," in *Analog* (New York), February 1970.
"Wrong Rabbit," in *Analog* (New York), March 1970.
"Zwoppover," in *Vision of Tomorrow* (Newcastle upon Tyne), April 1970.
"Beau Farcson Regrets," in *Analog* (New York), July 1970.
"Top Billing," in *Analog* (New York), September 1970.
"Enemy by Proxy," in *Amazing* (New York), November 1970.
"Big Time Operator," in *Analog* (New York), December 1970.
"Sprog," in *Analog* (New York), January 1971.
"The Pickle Barrel," in *Analog* (New York), February 1971.
"Knight Arrant," in *Analog* (New York), September 1971.
"Foundling's Father," in *Analog* (New York), December 1971.
"Stormy Bellwether," in *Analog* (New York), January 1972.
"Budnip," in *Analog* (New York), August 1972.
"Lien Low," in *Void 1* (St. Kilda, Victoria), 1975.
"The 200-1 Asset," in *Void 2* (St. Kilda, Victoria), 1975.
"Squawman," in *Void 3* (St. Kilda, Victoria), 1976.

"The Masque Behind the Face," in *Void 4* (St. Kilda, Victoria), 1976.
"The Butterfly Must Die," in *Envisaged Worlds*, edited by Paul Collins. St. Kilda, Victoria, Void, 1978.
"Jade Elm," in *Other Worlds*, edited by Paul Collins. St. Kilda, Victoria, Void, 1978.
"One Clay Foot," in *Alien Worlds*, edited by Paul Collins. St. Kilda, Victoria, Void, 1979.

*   *   *

It is well known that science fiction tends to emphasise content at the expense of style, but the positive influence this has had on narrative techniques is not always appreciated. Writers have been encouraged to create methods better adapted to its needs than traditional story-telling procedures. Jack Wodhams is one such writer. The way his stories are constructed could not have evolved in traditional short story writing. Smooth, effortless, controlled, a typical Wodhams story moves irresistibly ahead, mostly carried by dialog with a minimum of description and explanation. Indeed, when the author intrudes to fill in background or discuss principles, the pace slows or falters. There may be a firm single viewpoint, or a focus of action on a continuing situation if it is required. Often there are frequent scene changes as the action unfolds through related events. Characters tend to be no more than voices whose conversation shows what is happening, details of motivation unknown and irrelevant. The effect at its best is of the story happening, not being reported. It has much in common with modern film scripts, but it emerged naturally in science fiction as the field matured and a sophisticated readership developed.

Wodham's stories usually grow out of an original scientific premise, often a revaluation of a familiar speculation. They may bring out new objections or snags or turn a familiar argument around, often for a surprise ending. Some are in the venerable "dangerous invention" tradition. Thus "Stormy Bellwether" devastatingly sets out the bad news about person-to-person television. "The Fuglemen of Recall" has criminal exploitation of a memory recording and transfer process. "The Empty Balloon" looks at a "mind-reading" device working on sub-vocalised verbal thinking, an uncomfortable possibility, with a spy plot. In "Androtomy and the Scion" a cloned duplicate brain, in rapport with the original, gives the forces of evil new powers for coercion. "Split Personality" has an even more macabre atrocity, a felon physically dissected into living left and right halves for use as a better form of radio for an interstellar expedition.

The author's awareness of the social implications of radical new techniques, their value for oppression by ever-ready authority or for private anti-social acts, shows in many other stories. Thus "Whosa Whatsa" explores the utter ruin of traditional legal assumptions and conventions implicit in human sex reversal, and its impact on adultery, divorce, custody, and inheritance. "The Form Master" brings out the weakness of the coming world data bank, including its use for fraud by selective use of false input. In "Sprog" the inventor of a system of predicting future events cannot get a hearing and ends up exploiting the gullible as an ordinary fortune-teller. In "The Cure-All Merchant" behavior modification drugs have been refined into effective specifics for all problems, but a practitioner treats patients just as well by suggestion. One group of stories deals with the hazards and misuses of matter-transmission systems. "There Is a Crooked Man" shows future crime and detection in action. In "Wrong Rabbit" communication is accidentally opened with another world. "Top Billing" looks at duplication of people transmitted. "Hey but No Presto" shows a future form of hijacking. Among the stories of the interstellar future, "Star Hunger" is an excellent look at the need to reach the stars, the drive for habitable new worlds, and the danger of failure.

Wodhams's two novels are similar, though episodic and with more complexity of detail. *Looking for Blücher* has a thin rationale for a series of shared hallucinatory adventures, and is a disappointing waste of effort. *The Authentic Touch* uses the setting of a planet settled with re-creations of past epochs for jaded tourists of an opulent future, and it tends to get a little out of control through too much realism.

Perhaps Wodhams's writing is so typical of *Analog*, where most of his stories have been published, that he does not seem distinctive, despite his considerable originality and individuality.

—Graham Stone

WOLF, Gary K.   American. Address: 536 West Poplar Street, San Mateo, California 94402, U.S.A.

SCIENCE-FICTION PUBLICATIONS

Novels

Killerbowl.   New York, Doubleday, 1975; London, Sphere, 1976.
A Generation Removed.   New York, Doubleday, 1977.
The Resurrectionist.   New York, Doubleday, 1979.

Uncollected Short Stories

"Love Story," in *Worlds of Tomorrow* (New York), Winter 1970.
"Dissolve," in *Orbit 11*, edited by Damon Knight.   New York, Putnam, 1973.
"Therapy," in *Orbit 13*, edited by Damon Knight.   New York, Putnam, 1974.
"The Bridge Builder," in *Orbit 14*, edited by Damon Knight.   New York, Harper, 1974.
"Slammer," in *Fantasy and Science Fiction* (New York), March 1974.
"Dr. Rivet and Supercon Sal," in *Fantasy and Science Fiction* (New York), January 1976.

*   *   *

Gary K. Wolf's "Love Story" opens with a marriage ceremony during which the couple involved are required to relive briefly their pasts. Their civilization at first seems typically dystopian—conception occurs artificially, each fetus is properly programmed, children are raised in state facilities—yet Wolf cleverly reverses the situation, making it clear that the children are both well cared for and happy. We briefly tour a culture where there is no excess population, where everyone is content and virtually immortal. Our protagonists grow to adulthood, fall in love, and live together. Eventually they decide to have children, and their twin babies born artificially, they prepare for marriage. "Love Story" ends with a jolt. The priest at the ceremony hands them each a wafer, Eucharist-like, symbolic of their love, poisoned. They give up immortality to provide space for their babies.

"Dissolve" argues that television, because of its documentary-like quality and its oversimplification of moral problems, is drastically distorting our view of reality. The story jumps montage-like between a TV talk-show discussion of this problem, a number of typical television programs, and a young couple living in a bombed out TV studio after an atomic war. The girl is dying from radiation sickness but the boy, immersed in the simplistic television mind set, seems to think that he can save her by making a video-tape in which she is cured. A grim story, it is very effective.

"Therapy" is a slight, funny piece about a computer marriage counselor, one of its less successful cases, and a robot elevator which thinks it's the computer's mother. "The Bridge Builder" is a gripping story set in a world where the main transportation system is the Bridge, a matter transmitter. The protagonist builds bridges, repairs them, and is, in fact, fatally addicted to their use. "Slammer" and "Dr. Rivet and Supercon Sal" are both wildly comic tales reminiscent of Ron Goulart. The first concerns a prissy momma's boy who, mistakenly arrested for breaking into his own car and interred in a city reserved entirely for criminals, decides to stay there and become one. The second details the adventures of two shysters out to make a fast buck. He's a failure with people, but can do anything with machines. She's just the reverse. Their partner in crime is a rogue robot kitchenette. The story ends with one of the most hilarious chase scenes in recent fiction.

Wolf's novels, as a rule, are not of the same quality as his short fiction. *Killerbowl*, the best of them, is set in the world of street football, a cross between our current sport and guerilla warfare. The playing field covers several square city blocks, knives, clubs, and rifles are routinely issued, and the millions of fans keep statistics not only on touchdowns but on kills. T.R. Mann, a veteran quarterback, has been marked for assassination because he isn't bloody enough. The novel is very effective, but seems derivative of William Harrison's well-known story "Roller Ball Murder" (1973). Less successful are *A Generation Removed*, which involves a near-future America where only those under 20 can hold political office and where those over 55 are "euthed," and *The Resurrectionist*, which details the adventures of a Bridge repairman (see "The Bridge Builder") who must rescue a defector lost in the lines during transmission. Both novels suffer from weaknesses of plot, characterization, and style. All three books involve basically the same character motivation: a competent middle-aged protagonist, while working for the System, discovers it to be corrupt, and, finding himself in jeopardy, sets out vigilante-style to destroy it.

In summary, Wolf is a talented but uneven writer who seems most at home with short fiction. His best work is found in such slightly avant-garde stories as "Dissolve" and "The Bridge Builder," and in the broad comedy of "Slammer" and "Dr. Rivet."

—Michael M. Levy

WOLFE, Bernard.   American.   Born in New Haven, Connecticut, 28 September 1915. Educated at Yale University, New Haven, 1931-36, B.A. 1935. Married Dolores Michaels in 1964. Taught at Bryn Mawr College, Pennsylvania, 1936; Trotsky's secretary, Mexico, 1937; served in the United States Merchant Marine, 1937-39; Editor, *Mechanix Illustrated*, New York, 1944-45; ghostwriter for Billy Rose's syndicated column, "Pitching Horseshoes," 1947-50; taught creative writing, University of California, Los Angeles, 1966-68. Screenwriter, Universal-International Productions, and Tony Curtis Productions, Hollywood. Address: c/o Eliot Gordon Company, 8888 Olympic Boulevard, Beverly Hills, California, U.S.A.

SCIENCE-FICTION PUBLICATIONS

Novel

Limbo.   New York, Random House, 1952; abridged edition, as *Limbo '90*, London, Secker and Warburg, 1953.

Uncollected Short Stories

"Self Portrait," in *The Robot and the Man*, edited by Martin H. Greenberg.   New York, Gnome Press, 1953.
"The Never Ending Penny," in *The Year's Best S-F 6*, edited by Judith Merril.   New York, Simon and Schuster, 1961; London, Mayflower, 1963.
"The Dot and Dash Bird," in *The Playboy Book of Science Fiction and Fantasy*, edited by Ray Russell.   Chicago, Playboy Press, 1966; London, Souvenir Press, 1967.
"The Biscuit Position" and "The Girl with the Rapid Eye Movements," in *Again, Dangerous Visions*, edited by Harlan Ellison. New York, Doubleday, 1972; London, Millington, 1976.

OTHER PUBLICATIONS

Novels

Really the Blues, with Mezz Mezzrow.   New York, Random House, 1946; London, Musicians Press, 1947.

The Late Risers: Their Masquerade. New York, Random House, 1954; London, Consul, 1962; as *Everything Happens at Night*, New York, New American Library, 1963.
In Deep. New York, Knopf, 1957; London, Secker and Warburg, 1958.
The Great Prince Died. New York, Scribner, and London, Cape, 1959.
The Magic of Their Singing. New York, Scribner, 1961.
Come On Out, Daddy. New York, Scribner, 1963.
Memoirs of a Not Altogether Shy Pornographer. New York, Doubleday, 1972.
Logan's Gone. Los Angeles, Nash, 1974.
Lies. Los Angeles, Wollstonecraft, 1975.
Trotsky Dead: The Brutal Last Days of Trotsky's Exile. Los Angeles, Wollstonecraft, 1975.

Short Stories

Move Up, Dress Up, Drink Up, Burn Up. New York, Doubleday, 1968.

Plays

Television Plays: *Assassin!*, 1955; *The Ghost Writer*, 1955; *The Five Who Shook the Mighty*, 1956.

Other

How to Get a Job in the Aircraft Industry. Mount Vernon, New York, Wallach, 1943.
Full Disclosure, edited by Annette Welles. Los Angeles, Wollstonecraft, 1975.
Julie: The Life and Times of John Garfield. Los Angeles, Wollstonecraft, 1976.

Translator, with Alice Backer, *The Plot*, by Egon Hostovsky. London, Cassell, 1961.

*   *   *

A lifelong enemy of science fiction, to judge from his comments in Harlan Ellison's *Again, Dangerous Visions*, Bernard Wolfe has written a few science fiction stories and a celebrated dystopian novel. The stories are tightly written, but *Limbo* is a masterpiece.

Zany, action-packed, Joycean in style, *Limbo* is formally and conceptually complex and unremittingly analytical, both politically and psychologically. Most effectively of Wolfe's novels, it argues Dr. Edmund Bergler's acceptance of ambivalence and opposition to "pseudo-aggression." Alongside Korzybskian semantics, cybernetics, and various technological fantasies (van Vogt is cited by name in the Afterword), Bergler's neo-Freudian theories are entertained in an entertaining manner. Besides its Dantesque associations, the novel's title signifies voluntary amputation, the absurdist idea for literal "disarmament" Dr. Martine left behind in a journal when he deserted World War III's automated carnage. Self-exiled among the relatively primitive Mandunji for 18 years, he has perfected their traditional cure for evil spirits, lobotomy. When civilization invades his island in 1990, Martine feels compelled to return to the mainland, where he finds the postwar "Inland Strip" and its great power rival, the "East Union," have taken his gallows humor seriously.

As in Plato's *Republic*, the state is the individual writ large; only Martine, as its unwitting begetter, can end this travesty, after he comes to know himself. Others are little more than extensions of him, for or against the prosthetic limbs that are more dangerous than their originals. Tom, son of his loins, is the ultimate pacifist, a basket case, and a spokesman for the Anti-Pros. Children of Martine's thought are his former colleague, now President Helder (hero) and the charismatic Theo (god) whose wartime amputation by Martine started the whole chain of ideas. Performing a social lobotomy, Martine removes both party "heads," returning with Theo to his tropical island. There, his healthy native son, Rambo (for Arthur Rimbaud), is leading a similar revolution against single-minded solutions.

Not a prediction of 1990, *Limbo* is a metaphorical extension of a literal malaise, most dangerous among the technologically sophisticated whose dependence on their tools blinds them to their own responsibility. Self-amputation is no answer to the human dilemma, rather a symptom of it. This central absurdity is the most important of many estranging devices integrated into a thoroughly modernist novel; its vision of wholeness and balance is both its form and its substance. Wolfe does not simply arouse anxiety about the uncontrollable, or appease it with an appeal to contemplate the artwork. *Limbo* locates the trouble's source in the individual, whose recognition of the problem is the necessary first step toward its solution.

This therapy may not have worked for Wolfe, whose subsequent novels belabored Berglerian analysis without winning much of an audience. Nor has post-1952 American society been self-evidently more able to laugh at and accept its ambivalence. The book's acceptance in SF circles is marginal; reviewed at arm's length, it has often been ignored in historical studies of the genre. Though its direct influence is questionable, *Limbo* is still a harbinger of more stylish, sexy, complex novels to come. On its literary merits, *Limbo* is the "great American dystopia."

—David N. Samuelson

_____

WOLFE, Gene (Rodman). American. Born in Brooklyn, New York, 7 May 1931. Educated at Texas A and M University, College Station, 1949, 1952; University of Houston, B.S. 1956; Miami University. Served in the United States Army, 1952-54. Married Rosemary Frances Dietsch in 1956; two sons and two daughters. Project engineer, Procter and Gamble, 1956-72. Since 1972, Senior Editor, *Plant Engineering*, Barrington, Illinois. Recipient: Nebula Award, 1973; Rhysling Award, for verse, 1978. Agent: Virginia Kidd, Box 178, Milford, Pennsylvania 18337. Address: P.O. Box 69, Barrington, Illinois 60010, U.S.A.

SCIENCE-FICTION PUBLICATIONS

Novels (series: Book of the New Sun)

Operation ARES. New York, Berkley, 1970; London, Dobson, 1977.
The Shadow of the Torturer (New Sun). New York, Simon and Schuster, 1980.
The Claw of the Conciliator (New Sun). New York, Simon and Schuster, 1981.

Short Stories

The Fifth Head of Cerberus. New York, Scribner, 1972.
The Island of Doctor Death and Other Stories and Other Stories. New York, Pocket Books, 1980.
Gene Wolfe's Book of Days. New York, Doubleday, 1981.

OTHER PUBLICATIONS

Novels

Peace. New York, Harper, 1975.
The Devil in a Forest (juvenile). Chicago, Follett, 1976.

Gene Wolfe comments:

I am frequently called an *Orbit* writer, by which the callers appear to mean an obscurantist. I do not feel the term is justified. I try to bring pleasure to my readers on more than one level; but that, I think is a characteristic of virtually all good fiction. I avoid private symbolism, and usually provide more than enough clues for such small puzzles as I set. If I show a man lying when it is to his advantage to lie, I assume that my reader is intelligent enough to see that the man in question is a liar—and so on.

My heroes are often boys or young men trying to find a place in the world (Tacky Babcock in "The Island of Doctor Death and Other Stories," Mark in *The Devil in a Forest*, Number Five in *The Fifth Head of Cerberus* and so on); perhaps despite a conscious conviction to the contrary, I feel that the most adventurous years are between 10 and 30. But I have written about old women too, and young ones, aliens, and middle-aged men. Recently I wrote a story—"The War Beneath the Tree"—in which the chief character was an automated teddy bear.

I think I am still at least as much a reader as a writer. I like Proust, Chesterton, Dickens (I've done a Dickens story: "Our Neighbor by David Copperfield"), Washington Irving, Lewis Carroll (not just *Alice*), Kipling, Maugham, Wells, John Fowles, R.A. Lafferty, Ursula K. Le Guin, Kate Wilhelm, Jorge Luis Borges, Tolkien, and C.S. Lewis. If you like half or more of those writers (for example, Maugham as far as the "h") you should probably try me. Trembling, I throw myself on the mercy of the court.

* * *

Gene Wolfe has claimed that it is impossible to make his life sound interesting. A similar problem faces one who would write about his work; how can the complexities, the ambiguities, the atmosphere, and the beautifully crafted prose style characteristic of his writing be conveyed to those who have not read Wolfe? If Gene Wolfe's life is indeed dull, then his novels and stories are evidence that he can find rich detail and haunting drama in even the most commonplace of events.

Most of Wolfe's work is extremely atmospheric. Though many of its props are familiar to science-fiction readers, the author's oblique manner forces us to see these devices with fresh eyes. An early Wolfe story, "Trip, Trap," has a standard plot, that of a man landing on an alien world and trying to communicate with its people, whom he wishes to study. The author tells the story through a message sent by the man to his superior and a letter dictated by one of the aliens, alternating between the two points of view so that we see how differently the two perceive the same events. A first-contact adventure story becomes an oddly amusing horror tale when the two meet a strange and formidable foe.

Wolfe's first science-fiction novel, *Operation ARES*, is ostensibly about a Martian attempt to invade the earth. But the author plays with this old theme; the "Martians" are Earthpeople who were sent to Mars by NASA, only to be abandoned by a United States which has given up science and technology. The Martians are trying to convince the United States to return to a constitutional government, since the country's pro tem leaders are becoming pawns of the Russians while an opposition movement is being aided by the Chinese. The novel's plot has apparently been modeled on a game of chess. *Operation ARES* is not up to the standards of Wolfe's later work; its pace is too rapid toward the end, since the original manuscript was cut before publication; the protagonist, John Castle, is one of the few characters who stand out clearly. But in several scenes, particularly those at the beginning of the novel and those in which we see John pressed into forced service as a welfare worker in New York, Wolfe's ability to write suspenseful and frightening narratives is displayed.

Wolfe is especially noteworthy for his short fiction, and he is a prolific master of this form. In "Seven American Nights" a young Iranian visits a future America which is wretched and poor, populated by the degenerate descendants of a once-powerful culture. The Iranian keeps a diary, in which we read the story. The author skillfully works with an old idea, that of a man from an advanced civilization becoming repelled by, then attracted to, the ruins and inhabitants of a poorer land, giving the story an extra twist by making the Middle East the dominant culture and the United States the ruined one. "Forlesen" succeeds in making an average working day seem utterly alien; this story could have been influenced by the work of Philip K. Dick. "How I Lost the Second World War and Helped Turn Back the German Invasion" shows Adolf Hitler's attempt to market Volkswagons and Dwight D. Eisenhower's prowess at a military game called "World War." "When I Was Ming the Merciless" is the tale of an experiment in human aggression told in the form of a monologue.

Three stories deserve special attention, since they are related and are among Wolfe's best work. "The Island of Doctor Death and Other Stories," written in the second person, tells of a young boy who begins to see the people and events around him mirror those in a pulp magazine he is reading. "The Death of Dr. Island" is, according to the author, the first story reversed, a mirror image of it; Dr. Island is an artificial world in which disturbed people needing treatment dwell, and again a boy is the central character. "The Doctor of Death Island" may be the same story turned inside out; a prisoner is serving a life sentence. The catch is that he, and everyone else, is immortal. Each story shows a character imprisoned or confined in some way, each ends in violence and the character's understanding of what has happened to him. Two protagonists are boys, one is an older man; two female characters are threatened by death in the first two stories, while the man in the third is himself threatened by a woman. The stories conclude when the main characters are, in different ways, freed from the circumstances around them. Each story can stand by itself, and each contains carefully worked out details in the manner of the best science fiction and fantasy, while the three tales are connected thematically in an unusual manner.

The Devil in a Forest, a fantasy novel published for younger readers, rewards adult readers as well. It tells the story of a medieval peasant boy whose village is involved with the activities of a highwayman. The boy, trying to sort out good from evil, finds that the world is a good deal more ambiguous than it once seemed. Another book, *Peace*, was published as a "serious" novel, but this remarkable work deserves mention here. It reveals the inner life of a man whose outer life is uneventful; we are shown the man's memories and associations so vividly and subtly that, by the novel's end, we feel we know this other mind as well as we know our own. The book's manner is at times reminiscent of Marcel Proust, at other times of Thomas Wolfe, but it is Gene Wolfe's style that prevails. *Peace* is, in its own way, a novel of "speculative" fiction and a major American novel which has been neglected.

Wolfe's most important science-fiction book to date is the brilliant *The Fifth Head of Cerberus*. It was published as a collection of three novellas, but can also be read as a novel. Each novella gains strength in the reader's mind by being read as part of a larger work. The second novella, "'A Story' by John V. Marsch," is supposedly a tale written by a character who appears briefly in the first novella and is the main character of the third; it is an imaginative depiction of an alien culture. The first novella, "The Fifth Head of Cerberus," is considered to be one of the most intriguing treatments of cloning in science fiction. The background of the book includes many traditional science-fiction elements: an alien culture, the settling of planets by Earthpeople, biological experimentation, and space travel are among them. Wolfe has made his settlers Frenchmen, thus giving the book a flavor unlike that of most such stories. *The Fifth Head of Cerberus* raises a great many questions about its characters and its world that it never fully answers; it reflects the ambiguity of life rather than the clarity of a dramatic paradigm. It is a richly rewarding work, one of the most important science-fiction novels ever published.

Gene Wolfe is a major writer who writes for the thinking reader; he will reward anyone searching for intelligence, crafted prose, involving stories, and atmospheric detail. He is the heir of many literary traditions—pulp stories, fantasy, adventure stories of all kinds, and serious literature—and he makes use of all of them. His work can be read with pleasure many times; new discoveries are made in each reading, and the stories linger in one's mind.

—Pamela Sargent

WOLLHEIM, Donald A(llen). Also writes as David Grinnell. American. Born in New York City, 1 October 1914. Educated at New York University, B.A. Married Elsie Balter in 1943; one daughter. Editor, *Stirring Science Stories*, 1941-42, and *Cosmic Stories*, 1941; Editor, *Avon Fantasy Reader*, 1947-52, *Avon Detective Mysteries*, 1947, *Avon Western Reader*, 1947, *Out of This World Adventures*, 1950, *10 Story Fantasy*, 1951, and *Avon*

Science-Fiction Reader, 1951-52; Editor, Ace Books, 1952-67; editorial consultant, *Saturn*, 1957-58. Since 1971, publisher and editor, DAW Books. Recipient: Hugo Award, for publishing, 1964; 33rd World Science Fiction Convention Award, 1975. Address: 66-17 Clyde Street, Rego Park, New York 11374, U.S.A.

SCIENCE-FICTION PUBLICATIONS

Novels (juvenile; series: Mike Mars)

The Secret of Saturn's Rings [*the Martian Moons, the Ninth Planet*]. Philadelphia, Winston, 3 vols., 1954-59.
One Against the Moon. Cleveland, World, 1956.
Mike Mars, Astronaut [*at Cape Canaveral* (*at Cape Kennedy*), *Flies the X-15, in Orbit, Flies the Dyna-Soar, South Pole Spaceman, and the Mystery Satellite, Around the Moon*]. New York, Doubleday, 8 vols., 1961-64.

Novels as David Grinnell (series: Ajax Calkins)

Across Time. New York, Avalon, 1957.
The Edge of Time. New York, Avalon, 1958.
The Martian Missile. New York, Avalon, 1959.
Destiny's Orbit (Calkins). New York, Avalon, 1961.
Destination: Saturn (Calkins), with Lin Carter. New York, Avalon, 1967.
To Venus! To Venus! New York, Ace, 1970.

Short Stories

Two Dozen Dragon Eggs. Reseda, California, Powell, 1969; London, Dobson, 1977.

Uncollected Short Story

"The Rules of the Game," in *New Writings in SF 22*, edited by Kenneth Bulmer. London, Sidgwick and Jackson, 1973.

OTHER PUBLICATIONS

Other

Lee de Forest: Advancing the Electronic Age (juvenile). Chicago, Encyclopaedia Britannica Press, 1962.
The Universe Makers: Science Fiction Today. New York, Harper, 1971; London, Gollancz, 1972.

Editor, *The Pocket Book of Science Fiction.* New York, Pocket Books, 1943.
Editor, *Portable Novels of Science.* New York, Viking Press, 1945.
Editor, *Avon Bedside Companion: A Treasury of Tales for the Sophisticated.* New York, Avon, 1947.
Editor, *Avon Book of New Stories of the Great Wild West.* New York, Avon, 1949.
Editor, *The Fox Woman and Other Stories*, by A. Merritt. New York, Avon, 1949.
Editor, *The Girl with the Hungry Eyes and Other Stories.* New York, Avon, 1949.
Editor, *Flight into Space.* New York, Fell, 1950; London, Cherry Tree, 1951.
Editor, *Every Boy's Book of Science-Fiction.* New York, Fell, 1951.
Editor, *Giant Mystery Reader.* New York, Avon, 1951.
Editor, *Hollywood Bedside Reader.* New York, Avon, 1951.
Editor, *Let's Go Naked.* New York, Pyramid, 1952.
Editor, *Prize Science Fiction.* New York, McBride, 1953; as *Prize Stories of Space and Time*, London, Weidenfeld and Nicolson, 1953.
Editor, *Adventures in the Far Future.* New York, Ace, 1954.
Editor, *Tales of Outer Space.* New York, Ace, 1954.
Editor, *The Ultimate Invader and Other Science-Fiction.* New York, Ace, 1954.
Editor, *Adventures on Other Planets.* New York, Ace, 1955.

Editor, *Terror in the Modern Vein.* New York, Hanover House, 1955; abridged edition, as *Terror* [*and More Terror*] *in the Modern Vein*, London, Digit, 2 vols., 1961.
Editor, *The End of the World.* New York, Ace, 1956.
Editor, *The Earth in Peril.* New York, Ace, 1957.
Editor, *Men on the Moon.* New York, Ace, 1958.
Editor, *The Hidden Planet.* New York, Ace, 1959.
Editor, *The Macabre Reader.* New York, Ace, 1959; London, Digit, 1960.
Editor, *More Macabre.* New York, Ace, 1961.
Editor, *More Adventures on Other Planets.* New York, Ace, 1963.
Editor, *Swordsmen in the Sky.* New York, Ace, 1964.
Editor, with Terry Carr, *World's Best Science Fiction 1965* [to *1971*]. New York, Ace, 1965-71; *1968* to *1971* vols. published London, Gollancz, 4 vols., 1969-71; first 4 vols. published as *World's Best Science Fiction: First* [to *Fourth*] *Series*, Ace, 1970.
Editor, *Operation Phantasy: The Best from the Phantagraph.* Rego Park, New York, Phantagraph Press, 1967.
Editor, with George Ernsberger, *The Avon Fantasy Reader* [and *2nd Reader*]. New York, Avon, 2 vols., 1969.
Editor, *A Quintet of Sixes.* New York, Ace, 1969.
Editor, *Ace Science Fiction Reader.* New York, Ace, 1971; as *A Trilogy of the Future*, London, Sidgwick and Jackson, 1972.
Editor, *The 1972* [to *1980*] *Annual World's Best SF* (first 4 vols. edited with Arthur W. Saha). New York, DAW, 9 vols., 1972-80; first 2 vols. published as *Wollheim's World's Best SF 1-2*, 2 vols., 1977-78; *1974-1975* vols. published as *The World's Best SF Short Stories 1-2*, Morley, Yorkshire, Elmfield Press, 1975-76; *World's Best SF 4*, London, Dobson, 1979.
Editor, *The Best from the Rest of the World: European Science Fiction.* New York, Doubleday, 1976.
Editor, *The DAW Science Fiction Reader.* New York, DAW, 1976.

*   *   *

Although Donald A. Wollheim made his first sale while still in his teens ("The Man from Ariel," *Wonder Stories*, January 1934), and has written about 20 volumes of science fiction, his greatest impact on science fiction has been in capacities other than that of author. Wollheim was one of the pioneering fan publishers in the 1930's, founded the influential Fantasy Amateur Press Association (which still exists), and was a founding member of the original Futurian Society. The Futurians, founded in New York in 1938, were an odd combination of science-fiction club, radical political movement, communal residential society, and literary mutual aid association. At one point Futurians controlled no fewer than seven science-fiction pulp magazines—*Stirring Science Stories* and *Cosmic Stories* edited by Wollheim, *Super Science Stories* and *Astonishing* edited by Frederik Pohl, and *Future, Science Fiction*, and *Science Fiction Quarterly* edited by Robert A.W. Lowndes.

Since the Futurians numbered among their membership such young talents as James Blish, Damon Knight, Isaac Asimov, Judith Merril, and Richard Wilson, in addition to the three editors, there was a constant flow of material into the magazines. Wollheim's *Stirring* was the most interesting of the seven, divided into science-fiction and fantasy sections. Wollheim later edited *The Pocket Book of Science Fiction* (1943), generally regarded as the first significant science-fiction anthology, and helped A.A. Wyn in the creation of Ace Books in 1952. At Ace, Wollheim was known for his keen choices and successful mixture of commercially popular and artistically valid works. Besides publishing many important new SF writers, he was responsible for publication of the first mass-market editions of Tolkien's *The Lord of the Rings* and of many of the science-fiction works of Edgar Rice Burroughs. In 1972 Wollheim left Ace to create DAW Books, the first mass publisher devoted entirely to science fiction. At DAW, Wollheim has continued his formula of mixing pulp-style adventure series with significant works.

Notwithstanding the greater importance of Wollheim's work as editor and publisher, his own production of fiction has been substantial. In the 1950's he wrote three juvenile novels in the "Secret of...." series; all are set in the intermediate-near future and deal with the exploration of the solar system. In the 1960's Wollheim produced eight novels featuring the juvenile hero *Mike Mars*; these are set even closer in the future than the previous series. Among Wollheim's other novels, many readers have found amusement in *Destiny's Orbit* and its sequel *Destination: Saturn*. These amusing space opera-comedies feature Ajax Calkins, introduced in a series of short stories written by Wollheim under the pseudonym Martin Pearson. Also of interest is the novel *Edge of Time*, regarded by many as the definitive (although far from the first) treatment of the macro/micro-universe theme.

A good collection of Wollheim's shorter fiction is *Two Dozen Dragon Eggs*. The short stories tend toward extreme simplicity of plot and minimal characterization, concentrating on a mix of atmosphere and "idea." "The Rag Thing" and "Mimic," probably Wollheim's two best stories, are both included in this collection. Wollheim's short critical volume, *The Universe Makers*, is one of the most cohesive and convincing statements of philosophy to date in the context of science fiction.

—Richard A. Lupoff

WOODCOTT, Keith. *See* BRUNNER, John

WORTH, Peter. *See* PHILLIPS, Rog.

WRIGHT, Austin Tappan. American. Born in Hanover, New Hampshire, 20 August 1883. Educated at Harvard University, Cambridge, Massachusetts, A.B. 1905, LL.B. 1908. Corporation and admiralty lawyer: practiced with firm of Brandeis Dunbar and Nutter, Boston, 1908-16; Professor of Law, University of California, Berkeley, 1916-24, and University of Pennsylvania, Philadelphia, 1924-31. *Died 18 September 1931.*

SCIENCE-FICTION PUBLICATIONS

Novel

Islandia. New York, Rinehart, 1942.

*   *   *

The reputation of Austin Tappan Wright rests on only one work, but it is safe to say there is nothing quite like *Islandia* in all of literature. If one can make a fine semantic distinction between science fiction and speculative fiction, Wright's novel is more the latter than the former. His "speculation" is in the area of geography and, spinning off that, sociology and cultural anthropology.

Islandia is a nation located on the southern half of the Karain subcontinent in the southern hemisphere. It is civilized but isolationist, and for it Wright has created the most detailed and in-depth of all fictional cultures. There are discernible elements of Japan, Madagascar, Indonesia, and India, but the sum total is curiously more Western than Eastern, more homely than exotic. Islandia is revealed to the reader in all its richness by the action of the novel,

which takes place in the early part of this century. The country has decided to end its isolation from the rest of the world, and a few representatives of other governments are allowed in. One of these is a young American diplomat, John Lang; we learn about Islandia through his eyes as he travels the country and becomes acquainted and involved with her people.

The novel is peripherally a remarkable portrait of the nationalistic power plays that were occurring at the turn of the century, and a fine character sketch of an intelligent, moral young American confronted with values different from his own. But it is Islandia and the wonderful cast of characters with which it is peopled that is Wright's most notable achievement.

—Baird Searles

WRIGHT, Harold Bell. American. Born near Rome, New York, 4 May 1872. Attended Hiram College, Ohio, 1894-96. Married 1) Frances Elizabeth Long in 1899 (divorced, 1920), three sons; 2) Mrs. Winifred Mary Potter Duncan in 1920. Painter and decorator, 1887-93; landscape painter in the 1890's; unqualified preacher: Pastor, Christian (Disciples) Church, Pierce City, Missouri, 1897-98, Pittsburg, Kansas, 1898-1903, Kansas City, Missouri, 1903-05, Lebanon, Missouri, 1905-07, and Redlands, California, 1907-08: retired, 1908, to become full-time writer. *Died 24 May 1944.*

SCIENCE-FICTION PUBLICATIONS

Novel

The Devil's Highway, with John Lebar. New York, Appleton, 1932.

OTHER PUBLICATIONS

Novels

That Printer of Udell's: A Story of the Middle West. Chicago, Book Supply Company, 1903; London, Hodder and Stoughton, 1910.
The Shepherd of the Hills. Chicago, Book Supply Company, 1907; London, Hodder and Stoughton, 1909.
The Calling of Dan Matthews. Chicago, Book Supply Company, 1909; London, Hodder and Stoughton, 1910.
The Uncrowned King. Chicago, Book Supply Company, 1910.
The Winning of Barbara Worth. Chicago, Book Supply Company, 1911; London, Hodder and Stoughton, 1923.
Their Yesterdays. Chicago, Book Supply Company, 1912; London, Hodder and Stoughton, 1923.
The Eyes of the World. Chicago, Book Supply Company, 1914; London, Hodder and Stoughton, 1923.
When a Man's a Man. Chicago, Book Supply Company, and London, International News Company, 1916.
The Re-creation of Brian Kent. Chicago, Book Supply Company, 1919; London, Hodder and Stoughton, 1923.
Helen of the Old House. New York and London, Appleton, 1921.
The Mine with the Iron Door: A Romance. New York and London, Appleton, 1923.
A Son of His Father. New York and London, Appleton, 1925.
God and the Groceryman. New York and London, Appleton, 1927.
Exit. New York and London, Appleton, 1930.
Ma Cinderella. New York and London, Harper, 1932.
The Man Who Went Away. New York, Harper, 1942.

Other

Long Ago Told (Huh-Kew ah-Kah): Legends of the Papago Indi-

ans. New York and London, Appleton, 1929.
To My Sons (autobiography). New York and London, Harper, 1934.

* * *

A self-taught preacher, Harold Bell Wright was "king of the bestsellers" in the first two decades of this century, competing with a flood of popular religious works by the first heavy use of advertising for book promotion. "Arguments [are] presented through the medium of characters, plots, incidents, and the other properties of the story," Wright said, acknowledging that they were primarily intended as sermons. His novels were wholesome, often highly picturesque, and exerted a strong influence. His best work, and also the best-known, is *The Shepherd of the Hills*, a story of the Ozarks.

Wright's one science-fiction venture, *The Devil's Highway*, written with John Lebar, is the story of a graduate student, Frederick Ramsey, who is held captive at a secret laboratory in an area called El Camino del Diablo near the Arizona/Mexico border. The "demon scientist" L. Munsker uses the site for research on a psychic energy called "ethericity," with which he plans to rule the world. A misshapen dwarf, Munsker is devoid of any human emotion, and removes all laughter, joy, love, and other emotions from his co-workers, making them grimly materialist. This foul scheme is thwarted by the efforts of Ramsey's cousin, the reporter Jimmie Crawford, and Alma Weston, whose love for the student is pure and true. The authors are obviously ignorant of science, and use the plot only to illustrate a moral, which is explicitly stated: "A really great scientific mind above all others needs the balance of a great ideal ....All scientific advancement, if not attended and controlled by an adequate spiritual development, must, in the end, work havoc with the human race."

—T. Collins

WRIGHT, S(ydney) Fowler. Also wrote as Sydney Fowler; Alan Seymour. British. Born 6 January 1874. Educated at King Edward's School, Birmingham. Married 1) Nellie Ashbarry in 1895 (died, 1918), three sons and three daughters; 2) Truda Hancock in 1920, one son and three daughters. Accountant in Birmingham from 1895. Editor, *Poetry* (later *Poetry and the Play*) magazine, Birmingham, 1920-32. *Died 25 February 1965.*

SCIENCE-FICTION PUBLICATIONS

Novels

The Amphibians: A Romance of 500,000 Years Hence. London, Merton Press, 1925.
Deluge. London, Fowler Wright, 1927; New York, Cosmopolitan, 1928.
The Island of Captain Sparrow. London, Gollancz, and New York, Cosmopolitan, 1928.
The World Below (includes *The Amphibians*). London, Collins, 1929; New York, Longman, 1930; *The World Below* published as *The Dwellers*, London, Panther, 1954.
Dawn. New York, Cosmopolitan, 1929; London, Harrap, 1930.
Dream; or, The Simian Maid. London, Harrap, 1931.
Beyond the Rim. London, Jarrolds, 1932.
Prelude in Prague: A Story of the War of 1938. London, Newnes, 1935; as *The War of 1938.* New York, Putnam, 1936.
Four Days War. London, Hale, 1936.
The Screaming Lake. London, Hale, 1937.
Megiddo's Ridge. London, Hale, 1937.
The Hidden Tribe. London, Hale, 1938.

The Adventure of Wyndham Smith. London, Jenkins, 1938.
The Adventure in the Blue Room (as Sydney Fowler). London, Rich and Cowan, 1945.
The Vengeance of Gwa. London, Books for Today, 1945.
Spiders' War. New York, Abelard Press, 1954.

Short Stories

The New Gods Lead (as Sydney Fowler). London, Jarrolds, 1932.
Justice, and The Rat. London, Books for Today, 1945.
The Witchfinder. London, Books for Today, 1946.
The Throne of Saturn. Sauk City, Wisconsin, Arkham House, 1949; London, Heinemann, 1951.

OTHER PUBLICATIONS

Novels

Elfwin. London, Harrap, and New York, Longman, 1930.
Seven Thousand in Israel. London, Jarrolds, 1931.
Red Ike, with J.M. Denwood. London, Hutchinson, 1931; as *Under the Brutchstone*, New York, Coward McCann, 1931.
Lord's Right in Languedoc. London, Jarrolds, 1933.
Power. London, Jarrolds, 1933.
David. London, Butterworth, 1934.
Ordeal of Barata. London, Jenkins, 1939.
The Siege of Malta: Founded on an Unfinished Romance by Sir Walter Scott. London, Muller, 1942.

Novels as Sydney Fowler

The King Against Anne Bickerton. London, Harrap, 1930; as *The Case of Anne Bickerton*, New York, Boni, 1930; as *Rex v. Anne Bickerton*, London, Penguin, 1947.
The Bell Street Murders. London, Harrap, and New York, Macaulay, 1931.
By Saturday. London, Lane, 1931.
The Hanging of Constance Hillier. London, Jarrolds, 1931; New York, Macaulay, 1932.
Crime & Co. New York, Macaulay, 1931; as *The Hand-Print Mystery*, London, Jarrolds, 1932.
Arresting Delia. London, Jarrolds, and New York, Macaulay, 1933.
The Secret of the Screen. London, Jarrolds, 1933.
Who Else But She? London, Jarrolds, 1934.
Three Witnesses. London, Butterworth, 1935.
The Attic Murder. London, Butterworth, 1936.
Was Murder Done? London, Butterworth, 1936.
Post-Mortem Evidence. London, Butterworth, 1936.
Four Callers in Razor Street. London, Jenkins, 1937.
The Jordans Murder. London, Jenkins, 1938; New York, Curl, 1939.
The Murder in Bethnal Square. London, Jenkins, 1938.
The Wills of Jane Kanwhistle. London, Jenkins, 1939.
The Rissole Mystery. London, Rich and Cowan, 1941.
A Bout with the Mildew Gang. London, Eyre and Spottiswoode, 1941.
Second Bout with the Mildew Gang. London, Eyre and Spottiswoode, 1942.
Dinner in New York. London, Eyre and Spottiswoode, 1943.
The End of the Mildew Gang. London, Eyre and Spottiswoode, 1944.
Too Much for Mr. Jellipot. London, Eyre and Spottiswoode, 1945.
Who Murdered Reynard? London, Jarrolds, 1947.
With Cause Enough. London, Harvill Press, 1954.

Verse

Scenes from the Morte d'Arthur (as Alan Seymour). London, Erskine MacDonald, 1919.
Some Songs of Bilitis. Birmingham, Poetry, 1921.
The Song of Songs and Other Poems. London, Merton Press, 1925; New York, Cosmopolitan, 1929.
The Ballad of Elaine. London, Merton Press, 1926.

The Riding of Lancelot: A Narrative Poem. London, Fowler Wright, 1929.

Other

Police and Public: A Political Pamphlet. London, Fowler Wright, 1929.
The Life of Walter Scott: A Biography. London, Poetry League, 1932; New York, Haskell House, 1971.
Should We Surrender Colonies? London, Readers' Library, 1939.

Editor, *Voices on the Wind: An Anthology of Contemporary Verse.* London, Merton Press, 3 vols., 1922-24.
Editor, *Poets of Merseyside: An Anthology of Present-Day Liverpool Poetry.* London, Merton Press, 1923.
Editor, with R. Crompton Rhodes, *Poems: Chosen by Boys and Girls.* Oxford, Blackwell, 4 vols., 1923-24.
Editor, *Birmingham Poetry 1923-1924.* London, Merton Press, 1924.
Editor, *From Overseas: An Anthology of Contemporary Dominion and Colonial Verse.* London, Merton Press, 1924.
Editor, *Some Yorkshire Poets.* London, Merton Press, 1924.
Editor, *A Somerset Anthology of Modern Verse 1924.* London, Merton Press, 1924.
Editor, *The County Series* (verse anthologies). London, Fowler Wright, 13 vols., 1927-30.
Editor, *The Last Days of Pompeii: A Redaction*, by Edward Bulwer-Lytton. London, Vision Press, 1948.

Translator, *The Inferno*, by Dante. London, Fowler Wright, 1928.
Translator, *Marguerite de Valois*, by Dumas pére. London, Temple, 1947.
Translator, *The Purgatorio*, by Dante. Edinburgh, Oliver and Boyd, 1954.

*   *   *

S. Fowler Wright escaped being an accountant and poetry magazine editor with tales of fantasy, adventure, detection, and disaster. This prolific and versatile author began writing fantasy at 50.

His early novels reflect the influence of H.G. Wells. Wright, however, had such a pessimistic view of man's devolution that most human beings and their social customs vanish with dramatic flourishes. *The World Below* features a time-machine trip 500,000 years ahead to encounter Amphibians, delicate, web-footed, and cerebral, and Dwellers, gigantic seekers of knowledge through scientific investigation. The hero is most like the lizard-like Killers, who boil and eat victims. Much of the conversation between him and his amphibian companion reveals man's mistreatment of other living things, while many of the adventures show how close he is to bestiality when he throws reason aside in panic.

In *Beyond the Rim* descendants of British Puritans live in an Antarctic theocracy, raided occasionally by the Anabaptist horde from the volcanic hell nearby. The explorers include two strong women, one of whom remains while the other and her lover return home, but never to tell the real story. Similarly, in *The Island of Captain Sparrow* Charlton Fogle is shipwrecked where a pirate established a kingdom for his men and their women. Already present were a race of satyrs, providing meat, and a tribe of handsome natives decimated by disease brought by the outsiders. Charlton and Marcelle, intended for Sparrow's ugly, vicious heir, fall in love. At the book's spectacular climax the giant rokas, birds used for agricultural work, turn on the pirates, leaving the young lovers and the last native child to start over.

Deluge narrates a cataclysmic flood in which a hero and two heroines survive the barbarity to which most civilized people descend and found a new order. Martin Webster and Claire Arlington are among the few who adapt to living with nature. Because she is the kind of woman men put on a pedestal, Helen Webster also survives with her children. Some men—a murderer among them—become humane while others degenerate into ravaging, rapacious beasts who must be exterminated. At the end of this engrossing novel, Wright surprises his readers by allowing Martin to have both women. What's more—with noble psychological struggles—the

women love each other. In *Dawn*, its sequel, Wright goes back in time to introduce new characters and repeat the flood's horrors. Defeat of the threatening gang and escape from another flood promise a future.

In *Dream* and its sequel, *Spiders' War*, Marguerite Leinster enjoys dangerous adventures with the help of a psychologist-magician. In the first she dreams of an ape-girl fighting off the river rats that challenge human supremacy. In *Spiders' War* she goes into a future where the threat to divided humanity stalks in the form of giant spiders. Her man, a scholar of 20th-century history, is also a warrior-leader. Together they organize three hostile groups against the intelligent monsters. *The Vengeance of Gwa* contrasts similar groups, ranging from starving barbarism to bored perfection, in a tale of an evil queen and her well-deserved end.

Prelude in Prague, Four Days War, and *Megiddo's Ridge* form a trilogy dealing with an ugly near-future in which Germany conquers Europe, by the use of a freezing gas, air raids, and political terrorism. In this apocalyptic disaster culminating in the destruction of the powerful forces of Von Teufel, Wright creates and kills a large cast of interesting characters, including a double agent and a woman pilot. He also vents anger at British underestimation of Germany, lack of preparation for war, and callousness about highway mortalities. As in *Deluge* he warns readers that, while they vegetate, their neighbors hover a step from savagery.

In addition, Wright produced numerous short stories—light fantasy, medieval romance, mystery, and satire. Among the best are "Justice" and "Original Sin," a short version of *The Adventure of Wyndham Smith*. Society can be so perfect that only mass suicide can abolish boredom. So often does Wright annihilate mankind that it is not surprising that the heroine of his last story, "The Better Choice," prefers to remain a cat.

—Mary S. Weinkauf

WYLIE, Philip (Gordon). American. Born in Beverly, Massachusetts, 12 May 1902. Educated at Montclair High School, New Jersey; Princeton University, New Jersey, 1920-23. Member of the Board, Office of Facts and Figures, 1942; with Bureau of Personnel, United States Army Air Force, 1945. Married 1) Sally Ondeck in 1928 (divorced, 1937), one daughter; 2) Frederica Ballard in 1938. Staff member, *The New Yorker*, 1925-27; Advertising Manager, Cosmopolitan Book Corporation, 1927-28; Screenwriter, Paramount Pictures, 1931-33, and MGM, 1936-37; Editor, Farrar and Rinehart, publishers, New York, 1944. Member of the Council, Authors Guild, 1945. Consultant to the Federal Civil Defense Administration, 1949-71. Recipient: Freedom Foundation Gold Medal, 1953; Hyman Memorial Trophy, 1959. D.Litt.: University of Miami; Florida State University, Tallahassee. *Died 26 October 1971.*

SCIENCE-FICTION PUBLICATIONS

Novels

Gladiator. New York, Knopf, 1930.
The Murderer Invisible. New York, Farrar and Rinehart, 1931.
The Savage Gentleman. New York, Farrar and Rinehart, 1932.
When Worlds Collide, with Edwin Balmer. New York, Stokes, and London, Paul, 1933.
After Worlds Collide, with Edwin Balmer. New York, Stokes, and London, Paul, 1934.
Finnley Wrenn: A Novel in a New Manner. New York, Farrar and Rinehart, 1934.
The Disappearance. New York, Rinehart, and London, Gollancz, 1951.
Tomorrow! New York, Rinehart, 1954.
Triumph. New York, Doubleday, 1963.

Los Angeles: A.D. 2017 (novelization of TV play). New York, Popular Library, 1971.
The End of the Dream. New York, Doubleday, 1972; Morley, Yorkshire, Elmfield Press, 1975.

Short Stories

Night unto Night. New York, Farrar and Rinehart, 1944.
Three to Be Read. New York, Rinehart, 1951.
The Answer. New York, Rinehart, and London, Muller, 1956.

Uncollected Short Story

"Jungle Journey (The Paradise Crater)," in *Masterpieces of Science Fiction*, edited by Sam Moskowitz. Cleveland, World, 1967.

OTHER PUBLICATIONS

Novels

Heavy Laden. New York, Knopf, 1928.
Babes and Sucklings. New York, Knopf, 1929; as *The Party*, New York, Popular Library, 1966(?).
Footprint of Cinderella. New York, Farrar and Rinehart, 1931; as *9 Rittenhouse Square*, New York, Popular Library, 1959.
Five Fatal Words, with Edwin Balmer. New York, Long and Smith, 1932; London, Paul, 1933.
The Golden Hoard, with Edwin Balmer. New York, Stokes, 1934.
As They Reveled. New York, Farrar and Rinehart, 1936.
Too Much of Everything. New York, Farrar and Rinehart, and London, Chapman and Hall, 1936.
The Shield of Silence, with Edwin Balmer. New York, Stokes, 1936; London, Collins, 1937.
An April Afternoon. New York, Farrar and Rinehart, 1938.
Danger Mansion. New York, Bantam, 1940.
The Other Horseman. New York, Farrar and Rinehart, 1941.
Corpses at Indian Stones. New York, Farrar and Rinehart, 1943.
Opus 21. New York, Rinehart, 1949; London, Consul, 1962.
They Both Were Naked. New York, Doubleday, 1965.
Autumn Romance. New York, Lancer, 1967.
The Spy Who Spoke Porpoise. New York, Doubleday, 1969.

Short Stories

The Big Ones Get Away! New York, Farrar and Rinehart, 1940.
Salt Water Daffy. New York, Farrar and Rinehart, 1941.
Fish and Tin Fish: Crunch and Des Strike Again. New York, Farrar and Rinehart, 1944.
Fifth Mystery Book, with others. New York, Farrar and Rinehart, 1944.
Selected Short Stories. New York, Editions for the Armed Services, 1944.
Crunch and Des: Stories of Florida Fishing. New York, Rinehart, 1948.
The Best of Crunch and Des. New York, Rinehart, 1954.
Treasure Cruise and Other Crunch and Des Stories. New York, Rinehart, 1956.

Plays

Screenplays: *Island of Lost Souls*, with Waldemar Young, 1932; *The Invisible Man*, with R.C. Sherriff, 1933; *Murders in the Zoo*, 1933; *The King of the Jungle*, with Fred Niblo, Jr., 1933.

Other

The Army Way: A Thousand Pointers for New Soldiers, with William W. Muir. New York, Farrar and Rinehart, 1940.
Generation of Vipers. New York, Farrar and Rinehart, 1942; revised edition, Rinehart, and London, Muller, 1955.
An Essay on Morals. New York, Rinehart, 1947.
Denizens of the Deep: True Tales of Deep-Sea Fishing. New York, Rinehart, 1953.
The Innocent Ambassadors. New York, Rinehart, 1957; London, Muller, 1958.

The Lerner Marine Laboratory at Bimini, Bahamas. New York, American Museum of Natural History, 1960.
The Magic Animal. New York, Doubleday, 1968.
Sons and Daughters of Mom. New York, Doubleday, 1971.

*

Manuscript Collection: Princeton University, New Jersey.

*   *   *

Philip Wylie's science fiction represents only a small portion of his prolific output of magazine stories, novels, polemics, and screenplays. Wylie consciously and carefully placed himself in the "popular" market where his strongly moralistic and iconoclastic eye could not only observe and criticise but where his work would be read by large numbers. For, unlike the satirist, Wylie passionately believed that his pen could contribute to the sweeping away of cant and the creation of a modern and sane society.

Gladiator was accepted for publication in 1928 but Wylie's publishers held it for two years until he had produced two non-science fiction works. In it and in *The Murderer Invisible* he set the pattern for his ventures in the science-fiction idiom. In both novels the scientific projections (a genetically produced superman and an invisible man) are put in place quickly and without fuss as in H.G. Wells's novels, and the real stress lies on what the innovation can reveal about human nature and human society. Hugo Danner, the superman in *Gladiator*, observes the futility of human greed and of things like fraternity parties, football games, and the stock market. Through Hugo Wylie poses the problem of what could be done to improve the lot of man even by a superman if the masses would not change themselves. In *The Murderer Invisible* moral issues emerge because a scientist, William Carpenter, seriously wronged in a previous career on the commodities market, develops invisibility with intentions of a fair revenge and further use for the good of mankind. But he becomes a megalomaniac and attempts to take over the world for its own good. In these novels Wylie keeps calling his characters back to reckonings of conscience and analyses of the society which they are trying to change. These real and central concerns of his work were continued in *The Savage Gentleman*, a novel about a child educated away from mankind which offers a Tarzan-like variation on the single-man-against-society theme of the earlier novels.

Wylie's most optimistic venture into SF comes in two novels written in collaboration with Edwin Balmer, *When Worlds Collide* and *After Worlds Collide*. In these cosmic disaster stories two planets, a gas giant with an Earthlike planet in orbit about it, enter the solar system and destroy the Earth when the gas giant brushes against it. *When Worlds Collide* chronicles the discovery of the threat and the desperate efforts of a group of scientists to build rockets to get them onto Bronson Beta, the smaller of the invaders. Several parties succeed and the second novel deals with their survival on Bronson Beta, their discovery of a high civilisation there, and the conflicts between the American party and a Japanese-Chinese-Soviet party which has also survived. These novels contain a good deal of Wylie's most careful scientific prognostication in astronomy, earth physics, and in the prediction of human behaviour in times of extreme crisis, although the extrapolations about rocketry and interplanetary travel are considerably flawed.

Time spent in Hollywood, war work, and the pursuit of other kinds of writing leave a gap in Wylie's SF output until the publication of *The Disappearance*. The simple but very elegant premise of this novel is a world in which all of the women disappear in an instant from the world of the men and all of the men disappear from the world of the women. Although no real explanation is offered for this split in the stream of reality, the device is a perfect instrument for some very carefully considered opinions on the roles of the sexes, particularly in modern America. Wylie cleverly sets a great deal of the novel in a family unit very like his own which lives in Miami and has all the domestic complications that society tends to produce. On one level the novel is fascinating because chapters taking place in exactly the same surroundings trace the varied collapses of the two worlds, the men having an all-out atomic war and a return to savagery while the women struggle with technological collapse. But in addition to the outward struggle there runs through the book some very serious contemplation of the double standard and the fragility of male-female relationships.

Wylie's next three SF works deal in various ways with his deep concern for the dangers of nuclear war, a phenomenon about which he was particularly well informed because of his activities in civil defence organisation. *Tomorrow!* is a detailed portrait of a nuclear attack on an American city and the civil defence response. He is heavily critical of the failure to face and prepare for this inevitability, and his realistically detailed picture of the carnage is both blunt and sobering. *The Answer* is a brief allegory in which both the Americans and the Russians bring down an angel in their bomb tests. The angel was carrying the message "Love one another" to mankind. *Triumph* paints the most horrible picture of holocaust, in which virtually the only survivors in the northern hemisphere are 14 people in a supershelter prepared by a farsighted millionaire.

Wylie's posthumous legacy to mankind, *The End of the Dream*, is his prediction of the pollution death of the world. Like John Brunner's novel of the same year, *The Sheep Look Up*, *The End of the Dream* ties together projections of man's mistreatment of the environment to foresee mass deaths from air pollution in the cities, a rice blight which leaves most of the world starving, and a particularly horrible mutation of an ocean leech which sucks the life from millions. *The End of the Dream* is a fitting culmination of Wylie's career, for it combines his anger against human foolishness with his obvious desire to warn and thus influence the future positively. From *Gladiator* to *The End of the Dream* Philip Wylie has used the science-fiction mode and the style of the popular writer to reach and caution the widest possible audience in his life-long crusade to save man from his own foolishness and blinkered views.

—Peter A. Brigg

WYNDHAM, John. Pseudonym for John Wyndham Parkes Lucas Beynon Harris; also wrote as John Beynon; J.B. Harris; Johnson Harris. British. Born in Knowle, Warwickshire, 10 July 1903. Educated at Bedales School, Petersfield, Hampshire; also read for the Bar. Served in the Royal Signals during World War II. Married Grace Wilson in 1963. *Died 11 March 1969.*

SCIENCE-FICTION PUBLICATIONS

Novels

The Secret People (as John Beynon). London, Newnes, 1935; (as J.B. Harris), New York, Lancer, 1964.
Planet Plane (as John Beynon). London, Newnes, 1936; as *Stowaway to Mars*, London, Nova, 1953.
The Day of the Triffids. New York, Doubleday, and London, Joseph, 1951; as *Revolt of the Triffids*, New York, Popular Library, 1952.
The Kraken Wakes. London, Joseph, 1953; as *Out of the Deeps*, New York, Ballantine, 1953.
Re-Birth. New York, Ballantine, 1955; as *The Chrysalids*, London, Joseph, 1955.
The Midwich Cuckoos. London, Joseph, 1957; New York, Ballantine, 1958; as *Village of the Damned*, Ballantine, 1960.
The Outward Urge (as John Wyndham and Lucas Parkes). London, Joseph, and New York, Ballantine, 1959.
Trouble with Lichen. London, Joseph, and New York, Ballantine, 1960.
Chocky. New York, Ballantine, and London, Joseph, 1968.
Web. London, Joseph, 1979.

Short Stories

Jizzle. London, Dobson, 1954.
The Seeds of Time. London, Joseph, 1956.

Tales of Gooseflesh and Laughter. New York, Ballantine, 1956.
Consider Her Ways and Others. London, Joseph, 1961.
The Infinite Moment. New York, Ballantine, 1961.
The Best of John Wyndham. London, Sphere, 1973.
The Man from Beyond and Other Stories. London, Joseph, 1975.

Short Stories as John Beynon

Sleepers of Mars. London, Coronet, 1973.
Wanderers of Time. London, Coronet, 1973.
Exiles on Asperus. London, Severn House, 1979.

OTHER PUBLICATIONS

Novels

Foul Play Suspected (as John Beynon). London, Newnes, 1935.
Love in Time (as Johnson Harris). London, Utopian, 1946.

Verse

'Melia Ann: A Fantasy of the W.I. Taunton, Somerset, Wessex Press, 1953.

*   *   *

J.B. Harris had been writing long before the reading public first heard of John Wyndham. Beginning in 1930, he published—primarily in the US and under several pseudonyms—a great many short stories and several novels. Eventually it was the novel *The Day of the Triffids* which in 1951 brought Harris wide public recognition and permanently affixed to him the pseudonym under which he had published it: John Wyndham. Wyndham is justifiably considered to be the truest disciple of H.G. Wells in English literature. He himself said that of all science fiction he was most influenced by two of Wells's novels, *The Time Machine* and *War of the Worlds.* Indeed, Wyndham more than once dealt with themes raised in those novels, such as displacement in time and invasion from outer space, though Wells's influence on Wyndham was not restricted to thematic borrowing.

Wyndham loves to write about perfectly familiar things, some everyday occurrence, and let the fantastic element help him uncover unprecedented and unforeseen possibilities in that daily routine. Only one of his novels, *The Outward Urge*, deals with other worlds. In his other novels and stories the action is set on Earth and in time frames not all that distant from ours. Nor does he burden us with technical minutiae. Being a firm opponent of the Jules Verne school of science fiction, resurrected and modernized in the US by Hugo Gernsback, Wyndham uses technical—and other—detail only insofar as he or any other writer needs it: for the sake of credibility, realism, authenticity. In addition Wyndham has the ability—decidedly not within any other writer's reach—to compel us to suspend disbelief by being true to human character. Damon Knight correctly observed that Wyndham achieved his objective with down-to-earth means, that is, making us believe the most unbelievable things simply because they happened to people whom we all knew well. Wyndham's imagination is very tactile, sequential, logical. He follows the Wellsian method of the "single premise." In each of his books there is, then, one fantastic assumption; something in the world has changed and all subsequent changes follow as a consequence. Wyndham has the inventiveness to illustrate with many examples the impact of an event on all realms of life. All this causes Wyndham's fantasy novels to be part of the basic current of literature. He has no use for space opera; instead he practices a special kind of "realism in fantasy." One of his tasks has been the exploration of possibilities created by application of science-fiction motifs to various types of short stories. That is the guiding principle behind the collection *Seeds of Time.* Here again there can be no doubt about the influence of H.G. Wells.

The influence of Wells also determined the basic theme of Wyndham's writings. He is usually concerned with some catastrophe, cosmic or social, which results in the discovery of hitherto hidden dangers in daily life, in the revelation of character under novel circumstances, in the disclosure of defects in the society. In searching for his "single fantastic premise" Wyndham displays a degree of imagination which belies his ostensibly traditional manner. In *The Day of the Triffids*, which remains Wyndham's best-known novel, he showed his greatest originality. The novel deals with the disintegration of the social order under the impact of two events—a rain of meteors which has blinded most of the human race, and the appearance of mobile carnivorous plants. In two other novels Wyndham writes about the invasion of Earth by beings from other planets. In the first of these, *The Kraken Wakes*, invaders from space who can exist only under conditions of enormous pressure, establish a bridgehead deep under the ocean. In an attempt to wipe out the human race, they melt down the polar ice caps; the resulting flooding of the continents almost brings about the desired end. All this occurs under Cold War conditions, with mutual suspicion between the great powers preventing them from joining forces against the invaders. In the final analysis the catastrophe is caused by human divisiveness. In *The Midwich Cuckoos* the subject matter is not so much invasion as a kind of "penetration" from space. Here the non-earthlings isolate the village of Midwich and a few other places on Earth from their surroundings and put their inhabitants to sleep. Nine months later there appear in those localities children of non-earthly origin who are evidently destined to become the rulers of all mankind. Their intellectual and spiritual superiority is such that the earthlings submit without protest, even to the point of taking actions clearly detrimental to themselves. What makes these children from outer space so superior is their capacity to communicate constantly with each other by telepathy. Thus, while remaining individual beings, they form at the same time a formidable collective force. Anything learned by one becomes immediately part of everyone's knowledge. And the group also has the ability to channel everyone's will in one direction. Eventually the extra-planetary colony becomes so dangerous to Earth that it must be destroyed.

Telepathy is a rather common theme in Wyndham's fiction. It serves as a means of demonstrating its relationship to various forms of collectivism. The collectivism of the non-earthlings in *The Midwich Cuckoos*, for instance, reminds one of a fascist order. *The Chrysalids* provides an example of another sort of collectivist order. *The Chrysalids* takes place many centuries after a devastating nuclear war. Enclaves of life are cut off from one another by vast areas of radioactive contamination. Random mutations are occurring. As a result people, animals, and plants become so grotesquely disfigured that their hideousness exceeds even that which Wells anticipated in *The Island of Doctor Moreau*. These circumstances have given rise to puritanical communities seeking salvation by suppressing anything "different." Should anything new turn out to be superior to the old, these puritans are all the more eager to suppress it. They are convinced that they themselves represent the only kind of perfection possible, and at the very thought that elsewhere there might live people of a different color they fly into a rage. Nevertheless, life, movement, progress win out even here. These horrible, monstrous families produce children similar to those who tried to control Midwich. They differ in one respect, though: they hate cruelty. According to Wyndham these children who feel themselves to be members of one single family will not merely rebuild the old world: they will build a new and better one. *Trouble with Lichen* is the least interesting of Wyndham's novels. Taking the theme of Shaw's *Back to Methuselah*, he discusses the possibilities a vastly extended life expectancy could open for mankind.

—Julius Kagarlitsky

YARBRO, Chelsea Quinn. American. Born in Berkeley, California, 15 September 1942. Attended San Francisco State College, 1960-63. Married Donald P. Simpson in 1969. Theatre manager and playwright, Mirthmakers Children's Theatre, San Francisco, 1961-64; children's counsellor, 1963; cartographer, C.E. Erickson and Associates, Oakland, California, 1963-70; composer; card and palm reader, 1974-78. Secretary, Science Fiction Writers of Amer-

ica, 1970-72. Agent: Kirby McCauley, 60 East 42nd Street, New York, New York 10017. Address: 977 Kains Street, Albany, California 94706, U.S.A.

SCIENCE-FICTION PUBLICATIONS

Novels

Time of the Fourth Horseman. New York, Doubleday, 1976; London, Sidgwick and Jackson, 1980.
False Dawn. New York, Doubleday, 1978; London, Sidgwick and Jackson, 1979.

Short Stories

Cautionary Tales. New York, Doubleday, 1978; expanded edition, New York, Warner, and London, Sidgwick and Jackson, 1980.

OTHER PUBLICATIONS

Novels

Ogilvie, Tallant, and Moon. New York, Putnam, 1976.
Hotel Transylvania: A Novel of Forbidden Love. New York, St. Martin's Press, 1978.
Music When Sweet Voices Die. New York, Putnam, 1979.
The Palace. New York, St. Martin's Press, 1979.
Blood Games. New York, St. Martin's Press, 1980.
Ariosto. New York, Pocket Books, 1980.
Dead and Buried. New York, Warner, 1980.

Play

The Little-Girl Dragon of Alabaster-on-Fenwick (produced San Francisco, 1973).

Other

Messages from Michael. Chicago, Playboy Press, 1979.

Editor, with Thomas N. Scortia, *Two Views of Wonder.* New York, Ballantine, 1973.

Chelsea Quinn Yarbro comments:
My work, for the most part, has to do with some aspect of love and survival, though that should be interpreted in its broadest sense. Music has very much influenced me, not only as subject matter, but structurally as well. Since I make my living as a writer, I do, in a pragmatic sense, write for money. However, I regard writing as an art, and feel that within certain realistic limitations a part of my responsibility is to maintain and protect the integrity of my work.

* * *

Chelsea Quinn Yarbro's first collection of short fiction is appropriately called *Cautionary Tales*, a title which fits a lot of work in the genre of SF. Although she loves opera and has based at least three stories on operas, and although she creates strong characters and likes to put them in moments of confrontation which feel like grand opera duets (as James Tiptree, Jr., points out in the Introduction to *Cautionary Tales*), Yarbro is most easily categorized as a dystopian SF writer whose horrific speculations on the future are meant as dire warnings, predictions she hopes will *not* come true. But all categories, even useful ones, tend to be too narrow and simplistic. Yarbro is not simply a prophet of hard times to come; it just happens that a lot of her stories occur in rather harsh and unfriendly worlds. This makes for very stark conflict, and lots of passion, pain, romance, violence, terror, adventure and love, all of them marshalled into evocative form by a strong and vivid talent.

What is most obvious once you read the stories is that Yarbro finds the very starkness of ultimate situations aesthetically exciting. In *Time of the Fourth Horseman*, *False Dawn*, "Allies," "The Generalissimo's Butterfly," and "Dead in Irons" her protagonists must continually battle for physical, psychological, *and* moral balance against the final enemy in whatever form: plague, ecological breakdown and the descent to barbarism, an alien death-force, the corruption of political power, or slavery in the hold of a giant FTL cargo ship. Their heroism is not the easy kind found in escapist adventures; it is, rather, hard won and often of little value to anyone except the protagonist, and then only as a psychological talisman with which to face oncoming destruction. But Yarbro's morality is fiercely held to, in both her characters and her style of presenting them. As well (remember the opera), love can light up portions of a grim life if like Thea, of *False Dawn*, you're especially lucky. It won't solve any problems, really, but its presence helps a person carry on. And even the act of loving, though that love may not be returned, is presented as a positive virtue, something to hold on to in the midst of destructive chaos.

If many of the stories and the two novels are extremely dark, there is some lighter fare in *Cautionary Tales*. "Frog Pond," whose protagonist later becomes Thea of *False Dawn*, is, despite its post-apocalyptic setting, a social comedy. "Disturb Not My Slumbering Fair" is a kind of Hitchcockian black comic thriller about the trials and tribulations of a young ghoul, while "Lammas Night" is a historical sketch revealing the kind of wit Yarbro brings to her historical fantasies concerning an ageless, charming, and essentially good vampire, *Hotel Transylvania* and *The Palace*. Interestingly, these novels are full of the operatic colour and larger-than-life romance which Yarbro tends to eschew in the bleak spaces of her pure SF works.

But there are ways to introduce such colour into SF worlds. "Un Bel Di" is a story of a confrontation between two alien races that is also a variation on the structure of *Madame Butterfly*. "The Fellini Beggar," surely one of Yarbro's finest stories, gathers together a number of significant motifs in her work: her ability to suggest through telling details the lineaments of a whole world, in this case another post-apocalypse Earth; her delight in the beauty to be found even in the midst of rubble; and her recognition that emotion and the absolute need to satisfy it are continually changing with personal circumstances—this beggar allowed Fellini to "use" him brutally in his final film because it was a worthy exchange for his personal grail, the manuscript which allowed him to *know* exactly how Puccini had planned to finish *Turandot*. This, like all Yarbro's fiction, is 160 proof, and meant to satisfy a discriminating palate.

—Douglas Barbour

YEP, Laurence (Michael). American. Born in San Francisco, California, 14 June 1948. Educated at Marquette University, Milwaukee (Dretzka Award, 1968), 1966-68; University of California, Santa Cruz, B.A. in English 1970; State University of New York, Buffalo, Ph.D. in English 1975. Part-time English teacher, Foothill College, Mountain View, California, 1975, and San Jose City College, California, 1975-76. Recipient: Book-of-the-Month-Club Fellowship, 1970; International Reading Association award, for juvenile, 1976; *Boston Globe-Horn Book* Award, for juvenile, 1977; Jane Addams Peace Award, 1978. Agent: Pat Berens, Sterling Lord Agency, 660 Madison Avenue, New York, New York 10021. Address: 921 Populus Place, Sunnyvale, California 94086, U.S.A.

SCIENCE-FICTION PUBLICATIONS

Novels

Sweetwater (juvenile).   New York, Harper, 1973; London, Faber, 1976.
Seademons.   New York, Harper, 1977.

Uncollected Short Stories

"The Selchey Kids," in *World's Best Science Fiction 1969*, edited by

Donald A. Wollheim and Terry Carr.   New York, Ace, and London, Gollancz, 1969.
"The Electric Neon Mermaid," in *Quark 2*, edited by Samuel R. Delany and Marilyn Hacker.   New York, Paperback Library, 1971.
"In a Sky of Daemons," in *Protostars*, edited by David Gerrold and Stephen Goldin.   New York, Ballantine, 1971.
"The Looking-Glass Sea," in *Strange Bedfellows*, edited by Thomas N. Scortia.   New York, Random House, 1972.
"My Friend Klatu," in *Signs and Wonders*, edited by Roger Elwood.   Old Tappen, New Jersey, Revell, 1972.
"The Eddystone Light," in *Demon Kind*, edited by Roger Elwood. New York, Avon, 1973.

OTHER PUBLICATIONS

Novels (juvenile)

Dragonwings.   New York, Harper, 1975.
Child of the Owl.   New York, Harper, 1977.

Laurence Yep comments:
Growing up as a Chinese in America, I felt much like Ralph Ellison's "invisible man": without form and without shape. In my studies and in my teaching, I pursued the psychological figure of the Stranger, both in the American classics and in the works of popular culture. In writing science-fiction stories about aliens and alienated heroes, I was also unconsciously seeking my own identity. I've used the results to good effect in my children's books on Chinese-Americans. When I'm having problems with a historical novel, I still find it useful to do a science-fiction story on a similar theme.

*   *   *

Laurence Yep is perhaps more widely recognized today as a writer of children's realistic fiction than of SF. In his two novels depicting Chinese-American experience in San Francisco, *Dragonwings* and *Child of the Owl*, Yep, himself Chinese-American, has acknowledged a deliberate intent to combat racial stereotyping of his people. And indeed the novels have been praised for their effectiveness in repairing some of the harm stereotyping has inflicted upon fiction by persisting in describing Chinese or Chinese Americans as characters who must either resemble Charlie Chan or Fu Manchu or play the seemingly omnipresent houseboy, gardener, or launderer. Further, the impact of *Child of the Owl*, in particular, derives largely from the author's frank and sympathetic rendering of the inevitable, painful clash between an old generation of Chinese in America who, while mindful of the opportunities their new land provides, still cherish the folkways of their mother country, and a young generation, convinced of the importance of change and the necessity of becoming American, who are tempted to deny the value of their ancestral past. It is surely not coincidental but evidence of what must be for Yep a major issue that a similar clash is at the thematic center of *Sweetwater*, one of the most distinguished SF narratives ever written for children.

Set on the planet Harmony some centuries in the future, *Sweetwater* describes the efforts of the Silkies, descendants of the Anglic starship crews who had brought the first colonists and then been forced themselves to remain, to maintain their own distinctive society—one lived in harmony with the sea that surrounds and dominates their lives—and to resist the blandishments of those, primarily descendants of the first colonists, who are enamored with progress, especially the latest technology. The Silkies are led by Captain Inigo Priest whose 13-year-old son, Tyree, is both the narrator and moral center of the novel. His several ethical choices make up a great part of the plot, encapsulating the novel's concern with the conflict between tradition and the necessity of change and growth. The most praiseworthy SF element is surely the setting Yep creates for Harmony and the plausible ecology he devises. Not knowing that the planet is subject to cyclic flooding, the first settlers, aided by the Argans, an indigenous race resembling terran spiders, built on the flood plain. When the waters rise, the settlement, Old Sion, is abandoned by all except the Silkies who struggle to wrest a livelihood from the sea and what it has to offer. *Sweetwater* is also the perceptive story of the development of an artist, a relatively rare topic in children's fiction, as Tyree senses within himself a gift for music, a gift his parents disdain. Secretly abetted by Amadeus, an old Argan (the many references to music and the Old Testament contribute to the allusive richness of the novel), Tyree gradually internalizes the expressive nature of music and its centrality in any life that aspires for wholeness. Both thematic complexity and verbal richness, then, make *Sweetwater* superior SF.

Yep's second, adult SF novel, *Seademons*, describes Fancyfree, a world colonized by other descendants of the Anglics, the Folk. Unlike the Silkies, however, the latter are unable to live in harmony with the Seademons, the intelligent life forms native to Fancyfree, until catastrophe forces it upon them. Like *Sweetwater*, *Seademons* dramatizes a clash between tradition and change. Also, its most prominent SF element is the sea-dominant setting. Lastly, *Seademons*, a densely written and poetically evocative novel, is especially effective in incorporating celtic lore into its plot. Thus, in view of his versatility and achievement, it seems safe to say that Yep is an author whose work, present and to come, will be increasingly admired.

—Francis J. Molson

YOUNG, Michael (Dunlop); Baron Young of Dartington. British. Born 9 August 1915. Educated at Dartington Hall School, Devon; University of London, B.Sc., M.A., Ph.D.; Gray's Inn, London: called to the Bar. Married 1) Joan Lawson in 1945, two sons and one daughter 2) Sasha Moorsom in 1960, one son and one daughter. Director of Political and Economic Planning, 1941-45; Secretary, Research Department, Labour Party, 1945-51. Since 1953, Director, Institute of Community Studies, London. Chairman, Social Science Reseach Council, 1965-68; Visiting Professor, Ahmadu Bello University, Nigeria, 1972; Chairman, National Consumer Council, 1975-77. Chairman, 1956-65, and since 1965 President, Consumer's Association; Chairman, 1962-71, and since 1971 President, National Extension College. Fellow, Churchill College, Cambridge, 1961-66. Since 1942, Trustee, Dartington Hall. Litt.D.: University of Sheffield, 1965; Hon. Dr.: Open University, 1973; D.Litt.: University of Adelaide, 1974. Created Baron Young of Dartington, 1978. Address: Institute of Community Studies, 18 Victoria Park Square, London E2 9PF, England.

SCIENCE-FICTION PUBLICATIONS

Novel

The Rise of the Meritocracy 1870-2033: An Essay on Education and Equality.   London, Thames and Hudson, 1958; New York, Random House, 1959.

OTHER PUBLICATIONS

Other

Will the War Make Us Poorer?, with Henry Bunbury.   London, Oxford Univerity Press, 1943.
Civil Aviation.   London, Pilot Press, 1944.
There's Work for All, with Theodore Prager.   London, Nicholson and Watson, 1945.
Labour's Plan for Plenty.   London, Gollancz, 1947.
What Is Socialised Industry?   London, Fabian Publications, 1947.
Small Man, Big World: A Discussion of Socialist Democracy.   London, Labour Publications, 1949.
Fifty Million Unemployed (on India).   London, Labour Party, 1952.
Family and Kinship in East London, with Peter Willmott.   Lon-

don, Routledge, and Glencoe, Illinois, Free Press, 1957; revised edition, London, Penguin, 1962.
Family and Class in a London Suburb, with Peter Willmott.   London, Routledge, 1960; New York, Humanities Press, 1961.
New Look at Comprehensive Schools, with Michael Armstrong.   London, Fabian Society, 1964.
Innovation and Research in Education.   London, Routledge, 1965.
Learning Begins at Home, with Patrick McGeeney.   London, Routledge, 1968.
Is Equality a Dream? (lecture).   London, Hinden Memorial Fund, 1972.
The Symmetrical Family: A Study of Work and Leisure in the London Region, with Peter Willmott.   London, Routledge, 1973; New York, Pantheon, 1974.
Distance Teaching for the Third World, with others.   London, Routledge, 1980.

Editor, *Forecasting and the Social Sciences*.   London, Heinemann, 1968.
Editor, *Poverty Report 1974* [and *1975*].   London, Temple Smith, 2 vols., 1974-75.

*   *   *

With doctorates in sociology and economics, Michael Young is dominantly an academic. It is difficult, in fact, to tell if *The Rise of the Meritocracy* is literature or sociology. Young uses the handy and familiar future perspective in order to persuade the reader that the world has evolved into a complete meritocracy by the year 2034.

The form of the book is a historical-sociological analysis of the present (2034 AD) social situation in Great Britain. Young takes us step by step up the rungs of educational reform that rendered a system of happy justice on the basis of education to fit the intelligence of the individual. This transformation from "an aristocracy of wealth to an aristocracy of merit" produces a smooth and durable social order. It becomes evident through the book that Young may be more infatuated with the aristocracy than the merit. The villains of this fantasy are the socialists who stupidly support equal and uniform education for all, therefore enslaving the gifted to mediocrity. In fact, some of the more cogent points in the book are made on the subject of education as "social leveling" on one hand, and the potentiality wasted by a system that excludes talented lower-class children from educational opportunity on the other. Part of the scenario Young builds is Britain surging ahead in productivity "thanks mainly to the scientific management of talent." In the meritorious future students do not have to wash dishes, and in fact are paid a 60% higher wage than industrial workers.

The Rise of the Meritocracy is surely unique in form, as it has no characters and no plot, and is footnoted as an academic work would be. In fact Young may be accused of dressing up his bizarre political notions in literary garb and selling it on the basis of its being a bi-genre novelty. But this would be too harsh; Young deserves credit for his inventiveness and believable scenario construction.

—Peter Lynch

YOUNG, Robert F(ranklin).   American.   Born in Silver Creek, New York, 8 June 1915. Served in the United States Army during World War II. Married Regina M. Sadusky in 1941; one daughter. Inspector in a non-ferrous foundry. Agent: Raines and Raines, 244 Madison Avenue, New York, New York 10016, U.S.A.

SCIENCE-FICTION PUBLICATIONS

Short Stories

The Worlds of Robert F. Young.   New York, Simon and Schuster, 1965; London, Gollancz, 1966.

A Glass of Stars.   Jacksonville, Illinois, Harris Wolfe, 1968.

Uncollected Short Stories

"Pithecanthropus Astralis," in *Venture* (Concord, New Hampshire), August 1969.
"The Ogress," in *The Future Is Now*, edited by William F. Nolan. Los Angeles, Sherbourne Press, 1970.
"Starscape with Frieze of Dreams," in *Orbit 8*, edited by Damon Knight.   New York, Putnam, 1970.
"Reflections," in *Galaxy* (New York), March 1970.
"To Touch a Star," in *If* (New York), April 1970.
"A Ship Will Come," in *Worlds of Fantasy* (New York), Winter 1970.
"Abyss of Tartarus," in *If* (New York), October 1971.
"Genesis 500," in *Analog* (New York), February 1972.
"The Hand," in *Galaxy* (New York), March 1972.
"Whom the Gods Love," in *If* (New York), December 1972.
"The Years," in *Best SF 1972*, edited by Harry Harrison and Brian Aldiss.   New York, Putnam, 1973; as *The Year's Best Science Fiction 6*, London, Sphere, 1973.
"Remnants of Things Past," in *Fantasy and Science Fiction* (New York), April 1973.
"Girl Saturday," in *Galaxy* (New York), May 1973.
"The Adventures of the Last Earthman in Search of Love," in *Amazing* (New York), June 1973.
"The Giantess," in *Fantasy and Science Fiction* (New York), July 1973.
"Ghosts," in *Best Science Fiction Stories of the Year*, edited by Lester del Rey.   New York, Dutton, 1974.
"No Deposit, No Refill," in *Amazing* (New York), February 1974.
"The Star of Stars," in *Fantasy and Science Fiction* (New York), March 1974.
"Tinkerboy," in *Galaxy* (New York), May 1974.
"New Route to the Indies," in *Amazing* (New York), August 1974.
"Spacetrack," in *Fantasy and Science Fiction* (New York), September 1974.
"Hex Factor," in *Fantasy and Science Fiction* (New York), November 1974.
"The Decayed Leg Bone," in *Amazing* (New York), December 1974.
"Perchance to Dream," in *Fantastic* (New York), February 1975.
"Techmech," in *Fantastic* (New York), June 1975.
"Lord of Rays," in *Amazing* (New York), July 1975.
"The Curious Case of Henry Dickens," in *Fantasy and Science Fiction* (New York), August 1975.
"Shakespeare of the Apes," in *Fantasy and Science Fiction* (New York), December 1975.
"Clay Suburb," in *The Best Science Fiction of the Year 5*, edited by Terry Carr.   New York, Ballantine, and London, Gollancz, 1976.
"Above This Race of Men," in *Amazing* (New York), January 1976.
"Ghur R'Hut Urr," in *Amazing* (New York), June 1976.
"PRNDLL," in *Fantasy and Science Fiction* (New York), June 1976.
"Milton Inglorious," in *Fantasy and Science Fiction* (New York), September 1976.
"The Day the Limited Was Late," in *Fantasy and Science Fiction* (New York), March 1977.
"The Star Eel," in *Fantasy and Science Fiction* (New York), June 1977.
"Fleuve Red," in *Fantastic* (New York), September 1977.
"The Space Roc," in *Amazing* (New York), January 1978.
"The Journal of Nathaniel Worth," in *Fantastic* (New York), July 1978.
"The Winning of Gloria Grandonwheels," in *Amazing* (New York), August 1978.
"Hologirl," in *Fantasy and Science Fiction* (New York), August 1978.
"Crutch," in *Amazing* (New York), November 1978.
"The First Mars Mission," in *Fantasy and Science Fiction* (New York), May 1979.
"Project Hi-Rise," in *The Best from Fantasy and Science Fiction 23*, edited by Edward L. Ferman.   New York, Doubleday, 1980.
"Bourgeoisie," in *Fantasy and Science Fiction* (New York), January 1980.
"The Mindanao Deep," in *Fantasy and Science Fiction* (New York), March 1980.
"As a Man Has a Whale: A Love Story," in *Fantasy and Science Fiction* (New York), July 1980.

*　　*　　*

In an introductory essay to Robert F. Young's *A Glass of Stars*, Fritz Leiber remarks: "And I say that the field to which Robert F. Young has many times proven his claim is that of romantic love. The magic potion of which he is master creator is the love philter." It could be further noted that the potion is not meant merely for the characters in his stories, but to captivate the audience that reads them. Robert F. Young's realm is the realm of boy meets girl, not in some bygone era but on other worlds or in a future mired in the sins of our own time, crass commercialism and the violation of the environment. Almost always Young surveys his domain with the force of his sense of humor, inserting it at the proper junctures so as not to allow "boy meets girl" to become soap opera. Young skillfully weaves his plots in such a manner that the reader can only smile at the fact that the man and woman are together, living happily ever after, in the end.

An especially fine example of Young's plot-twisting talent is the story "L'Arc de Jeanne," which takes place on the planet Ceil Bleu, near the key city of Fleur du Sud. This is a planet committed to the Psycho-Phenomenalist Church. We find it under attack by the forces of the evil tyrant O'Riordan. All that stands in the way of conquest is a young maiden who rides a "magnificent black stallion" and is armed with what appears to be a magic bow and arrow. O'Riordan wants the maiden captured, and sends a computer-selected young man guaranteed to be irresistible to the maiden, to win her affection. The story evolves in such a manner that Young's Joan of Arc must burn at the stake, yet Young manages the plot so that the story ends happily.

Young's conservationist concerns show forth in "To Fell a Tree." A young treeman has the task of felling a glorious 1000-foot tree, a job his company has been hired to do by a rather greedy village. The tree is so enormous that he must live in the tree for a number of days in order to bring it down. While in the tree he meets a dryad, the spirit of the tree, who is seen slowly dying as the tree is cut down, a tree the sap of which looks just like blood. Young's talent as a weaver of words is revealed in this story, along with his passionate concern for nature's living forms.

Young, a shrewd commentator on the crassness of commercialism, has a special fondness for the crudities of the automotive world. In "Romance in a Twenty-First-Century Used-Car Lot" the auto industry has managed to miniaturize cars sufficiently so that they can be worn as clothing, and then convinced the public that not wearing them is obscene. Those who don't wear cars are called nudists and consigned to a nudist colony. "It wasn't hard to do," Howard Highways tells Arabella Grille, "because people had been wearing their cars unconsciously all along." Then there is Emily ("Emily and the Bards Sublime"), an assistant curator of a museum. She is extremely fond of the android poets, especially Lord Tennyson. One day she is told that the poets must go to make room for a display of 20th-century art, cars, that is. Mr. Brandon tells her she will be taking over the new exhibit; "Mr. Brandon handed her the big book he was carrying. '*An Analysis of the Chrome Motif in Twentieth Century Art.* Read it religiously, Miss Meredith. It's the most important book of our century.' "

However, Young's first love is romance, and he is willing to go to, or to manipulate, the ends of time to bring his loved ones together. "The Dandelion Girl," "The Girl Who Made Time Stop," and "Mine Eyes Have Seen The Glory" are all examples of first-rate stories that entail clever use of the intricacies of time as the fourth dimension. Robert Young's gift as a story teller is brought out in these tales, for by the end of each story the reader has been moved to believe in the possibility of romantic love even when it entails bending the known laws of physics.

—Mitchell Aboulafia

ZAGAT, Arthur Leo. American. Born in New York City, in 1895. Educated at City College of New York, B.A.; Bordeaux University; Fordham University Law School, New York, LL.D. Served in the United States Army during World War I, and with the Office of War Information during World War II. Married Ruth Zagat; one daughter. Founded Writers Workshop at New York University. Member of the Council, Authors League of America. *Died 3 April 1949.*

SCIENCE-FICTION PUBLICATIONS

Novel

Seven Out of Time. Reading, Pennsylvania, Fantasy Press, 1949.

Uncollected Short Stories

"The Tower of Evil," with Nat Schachner, in *Wonder Stories Quarterly* (New York), Summer 1930.
"In 20,000 A.D.," with Nat Schachner, in *Wonder Stories* (New York), September 1930.
"Back to 20,000 A.D.," with Nat Schachner, in *Wonder Stories* (New York), March 1931.
"The Emperor of the Stars," with Nat Schachner, in *Wonder Stories* (New York), April 1931.
"The Menace from Andromeda," with Nat Schachner, in *Amazing* (New York), April 1931.
"The Death-Cloud," with Nat Schachner, in *Astounding* (New York), May 1931.
"The Revolt of the Machines," with Nat Schachner, in *Astounding* (New York), July 1931.
"Venus Mines Incorporated," with Nat Schachner, in *Wonder Stories* (New York), August 1931.
"Exiles of the Moon," with Nat Schachner, in *Wonder Stories* (New York), September 1931.
"The Great Dome on Mercury," in *Astounding* (New York), April 1932.
"When the Sleepers Woke," in *Astounding* (New York), November 1932.
"The Living Flame," in *Astounding* (New York), February 1934.
"Spoor of the Bat," in *Astounding* (New York), July 1934.
"Beyond the Spectrum," in *Astounding* (New York), August 1934.
"The Land Where Time Stood Still," in *Thrilling Wonder Stories* (New York), August 1936.
"Flight of the Silver Eagle," in *Thrilling Wonder Stories* (New York), April 1937.
"Lost in Time," in *Thrilling Wonder Stories* (New York), June 1937.
"Drink We Deep," in *Argosy* (New York), 31 July 1937.
"The Cavern of the Shining Pool," in *Thrilling Wonder Stories* (New York), October 1937.
"Island in the Sky," in *Argosy* (New York), 17 December 1937.
"The Green Ray," in *Thrilling Wonder Stories* (New York), August 1938.
"Jungle Interlude," in *Argosy* (New York), February 1943.
"Sunward Flight," in *Super Science* (Kokomo, Indiana), February 1943.
"Venus Station," in *Science Fiction Stories* (New York), April 1943.
"The Lanson Screen," in *Best of Science Fiction*, edited by Groff Conklin. New York, Crown, 1946.
"Slaves of the Lamp," in *Astounding* (New York), August, September 1946.
"Grim Rendezvous," in *Thrilling Wonder Stories* (New York), December 1946.
"The Faceless Men," in *Thrilling Wonder Stories* (New York), April 1948.
"No Escape from Destiny," in *Startling* (New York), May 1948.

*   *   *

Arthur Leo Zagat is essentially an early 1930's figure, to be seen in the context of science fiction broadening, diversifying, and acquiring a definite character as more magazines emerged.

His relatively small science-fiction output reflected a personal interest in futuristic ideas; as with many others of the time whose overall output was trivial hack work, he showed originality and vision in science fiction. Every cliché began as an inspiration. Though his stories ranged over a variety of themes, his main contribution was to space flight. This was then something predicted for the indefinite future, but it was a vision that excited that generation as no other. The spectacular progress of aviation had made a profound impression, clearly made obvious the pace of technological change, and raised imagination from the ground.

Interplanetary travel had a long literary tradition, but, aside from its use as a springboard to introduce a Utopia or a reflection on man's follies, its emphasis had always been on the initial problems to be solved. By the time SF was firmly established, readers had gone over that ground many times and were ready to go beyond it. Early 1930's science fiction tried to imagine regular traffic between worlds, and settled into a picture analogous to ocean shipping as it had been in earlier times when it was more hazardous and maritime countries more remote and diverse. Zagat helped build up the image of a dangerous yet established trade, of interplanetary shipping lines and business rivalries, of a rough spaceport district analogous to the traditional waterfront, of a rough frontier class of spacemen, with occasional piracy and clashes with natives, or a well-disciplined space service to keep order.

Inevitably this led to the repetitive action stories Tucker aptly tagged space opera. It tended to trivialise space flight by glossing over the problems, though it popularised the concept. Its rather optimistic view had a strong appeal in its time. Zagat's stories such as "The Great Dome on Mercury," "Spoor of the Bat," and "The Cavern of the Shining Pool" were good entertainment, and added to the movement's repertory of expectations. World-scale conflict of East and West, another standard theme, was exploited in "The Death-Cloud," "The Green Ray," and "Flight of the Silver Eagle," dated, but showing what then seemed good probabilities: a world shrunk by better communications, conflict mainly airborn, deathrays and other devices.

And there are many other themes, all fairly new and treated originally—unearthlike life, the amorphous "Menace from Andromeda," logically evolved; a nonhuman intelligent race in "The Emperor of the Stars" sympathetically treated without humanising it; invisible subterranean beings in "Beyond the Spectrum"; machine intelligence in "The Revolt of the Machines"; the world depopulated and left to a few chance survivors in "When the Sleepers Woke"; big business replacing traditional state power in "Exiles of the Moon" and "Lost in Time"; glimpses of future custom and folklore, even sport, in "Sunward Flight"; dangerous inventions in "The Lanson Screen," the defensive shield that became a deadly prison.

Zagat's only book, *Seven Out of Time*, drew on elements he had used before and clearly suffers from spinning out the suspense in a six-part serial. The early chapters with their missing-person plot and eery touches contrast with the strange remote world of millions of years hence, where the group of dehumanised monsters evolved from us try to recover the insights and motivations they have lost by studying their kidnapped people of our own and earlier times. Dated and plausible only as symbolic fantasy even in 1939, it has merit for the message it presents even today.

Zagat's first works were written with Nat Schachner, whose role cannot be distinguished. The writing is conventional, the human interest elementary, with characterisation going little beyond stock figures. But it is competent, good of its kind in its time, and it has conviction.

—Graham Stone

ZEBROWSKI, George. American. Born in Villach, Austria, 28 December 1945. Attended the State University of New York, Binghamton, 1964-69. Copy editor, Binghamton *Evening Press*, 1967; filtration plant operator, New York, 1969-70; lecturer in science fiction, State University of New York, Binghamton, Spring

1971; Editor, *SFWA Bulletin*, 1970-75. Free-lance writer and lecturer. Agent: Joseph Elder Agency, 150 West 87th Street, New York, New York 10024. Address: Box 586, Johnson City, New York 13790, U.S.A.

SCIENCE-FICTION PUBLICATIONS

Novels

The Omega Point. New York, Ace, 1972; London, New English Library, 1974.
The Star Web. Toronto, Laser, 1975.
Ashes and Stars. New York, Ace, 1977; London, New English Library, 1978.
Macrolife. New York, Harper, 1979; London, Futura, 1980.

Short Stories

The Monadic Universe and Other Stories. New York, Ace, 1977.

Uncollected Short Stories

"Transfigured Night," in *Immortal*, edited by Jack Dann. New York, Harper, 1978.
"The Word Sweep," in *Fantasy and Science Fiction* (New York), August 1979.

OTHER PUBLICATIONS

Other

"Whatever Gods There Be: Space-Time and Deity in Science Fiction," in *Strange Gods*, edited by Roger Elwood. New York, Simon and Schuster, 1974.
"Science Fiction and the Visual Media," in *Science Fiction: Today and Tomorrow*, edited by Reginald Bretnor. New York, Harper, 1974.
Introduction to *Things to Come*, by H.G. Wells. Boston, Gregg Press, 1975.
"Afterword" to *The Space Beyond and Other Short Novels*, by John W. Campbell, Jr. New York, Pyramid, 1976.
"How It Happened" (on the Lem affair), with Pamela Sargent, and "Why It Happened," in *Science-Fiction Studies* (Terre Haute, Indiana), July 1977.
"Androids, Cyborgs, and Others," with Patricia Warrick, in *Science Fiction: Contemporary Mythology*, edited by Warrick, Martin H. Greenberg, and Joseph D. Olander. New York, Harper, 1978.

Editor, *Tomorrow Today.* Santa Cruz, California, Unity Press, 1975.
Editor, with Thomas N. Scortia, *Human-Machines: An Anthology of Stories about Cyborgs.* New York, Random House, 1975; London, Hale, 1977.
Editor, with Jack Dann, *Faster Than Light: An Anthology of Stories about Interstellar Travel.* New York, Harper, 1976.

*   *   *

George Zebrowski writes stories probing the dreams, yearnings, and loneliness of those forced to leave earth and create a new way of life in the alien environment of deep space. A sense of loss and the need to make an imaginative leap of faith in order to confront the unknown are the recurrent themes of Zebrowski's fiction.

Macrolife, his most ambitious work, depicts with Stapledonian scope the evolution of artificial space colonies (or macrolife). Jack Bulero, a 21st-century businessman in charge of the world's largest corporation, inadvertently causes a disaster that threatens to destroy earth. Blamed for the catastrophe, his family is forced to seek asylum in a space colony where Richard Bulero, the visionary younger brother, realizes that macrolife has the potentiality to become the next logical step in man's evolutionary development. Freed from the drawbacks of natural planets, with their scarcity of resources and other limitations, macroworlds offer man the oppor-

tunity for almost limitless expansion and social experimentation. This dream is tested in the second section of the novel when a descendant of the Bulero clan becomes sentimentally attracted to the savage inhabitants of a decayed natural world, only to find that his primitivistic yearnings are not only impossible but deadly. The novel concludes on an apocalyptic note: as the last remnants of macrolife huddle around a few dying dwarf stars, a cloned descendant of the Buleros is called upon to perform an apparent miracle: the rebirth of the cosmos.

Imaginative rebirth, with its philosophic and religious implications, is the dominant motif of *The Monadic Universe*, Zebrowski's collection of stories. "Monadic Universe" charts the nightmarish voyage of the last survivors of earth's destruction. Hurtling through deep space, they must confront the terrible truth that they cannot return to their normal space-time continuum without unleashing forces that would destroy the entire cosmos. Their only hope lies in a leap of faith so unimaginable that it drives the rigidly rationalistic captain to his death. Self-enclosed space systems as a metaphor for human isolation and regeneration also appear in the Christian Praeger series. A struggling city youth in "Assassins of Air," Praeger decides to quit the "recycling gangs" roaming the polluted city and trafficking in bootleg auto parts. Sensitive and idealistic, he tries to acquire an education that will help him to combat pollution, but his former cohorts drive him from the city with murderous fury. In "Parks of Rest and Culture" he becomes so disillusioned with the seemingly insoluble problems of earth that he enlists on a space shuttle to the moon, dreaming of an idyllic new life "filled with elegant people, full-leafed trees casting broad shadows." Several years later Praeger, now a seasoned space colonist, encounters his old friend Julian, "The Water Sculptor," a reclusive artist in an orbiting studio. When Julian commits suicide rather than return to the crass and corrupt earth, Praeger not only learns a poignant lesson about the human condition but also has a deeper insight into the transformative power of art and the imagination.

Other stories in this collection, such as "Star-Crossed" and "First Love, First Fear," explore the paradoxes of eroticism in an utterly alien context. In "Heathen God" a priest of a proudly "enlightened" interstellar empire is shocked to discover that a gnome-like alien is actually the worship-starved "father" of the human race. The religious implications of an "alien god" are also taken up in "Interpose," a story whose account of the Jesus-as-alien theme is as subtle as its punning title.

Arriving in the United States as a displaced person while still a child (his parents were captured by the Nazis), Zebrowski is preoccupied with exile, loss, and the need to find meaning and identity in a strange environment. Thomas Scortia has compared Zebrowski's style and background to that of another deracinated Polish writer, Joseph Conrad, whose "prose... is alternatively complex and leanly descriptive" and whose "themes reflect the intellectual heritage of Middle Europe." Serious and original as well as entertaining, Zebrowski has proven a promising new voice whose work deserves a wider readership.

—Anthony Manousos

ZELAZNY, Roger (Joseph). American. Born in Cleveland, Ohio, 13 May 1937. Educated at Western Reserve University, Cleveland, B.A. 1959; Columbia University, New York, M.A. 1962. Served in the Ohio National Guard, 1960-63, and the United States Army Reserve, 1963-66. Married 1) Sharon Steberl in 1964 (divorced, 1966); 2) Judith Callahan in 1966, two sons. Claims representative, Cleveland, 1963-65, and claims specialist, Baltimore, 1965-69, Social Security Administration. Since 1969, freelance writer and lecturer. Secretary-Treasurer, Science Fiction Writers of America, 1967-68. Recipient: Nebula Award, 1965 (2 awards), 1975; Hugo Award, for novel, 1966, 1968, for story, 1976; Prix Apollo, 1972; American Library Association award, 1976.

Guest of Honor, 32nd World Science Fiction Convention, 1974, and Australian National Science Fiction Convention, 1978. Agent: Henry Morrison Inc., 59 West 10th Street, New York, New York 10011. Address: 1045 Stagecoach Road, Santa Fe, New Mexico 87501, U.S.A.

SCIENCE-FICTION PUBLICATIONS

Novels (series: Amber)

This Immortal. New York, Ace, 1966; London, Hart Davis, 1967.
The Dream Master. New York, Ace, 1966; London, Hart Davis, 1968.
Lord of Light. New York, Doubleday, 1967; London, Faber, 1968.
Isle of the Dead. New York, Ace, 1969; London, Deutsch, 1970.
Creatures of Light and Darkness. New York, Doubleday, 1969; London, Faber, 1970.
Damnation Alley. New York, Putnam, 1969; London, Faber, 1971.
Nine Princes in Amber. New York, Doubleday, 1970; London, Faber, 1972.
Jack of Shadows. New York, Walker, 1971; London, Faber, 1972.
The Guns of Avalon (Amber). New York, Doubleday, 1972; London, Faber, 1974.
Today We Choose Faces. New York, New American Library, 1973; London, Millington, 1974.
To Die in Italbar. New York, Doubleday, 1973; London, Faber, 1975.
Sign of the Unicorn (Amber). New York, Doubleday, 1975; London, Faber, 1977.
Doorways in the Sand. New York, Harper, 1976; London, W.H. Allen, 1977.
The Hand of Oberon. New York, Doubleday, 1976; London, Faber, 1978.
Bridge of Ashes. New York, New American Library, 1976.
Deus Irae, with Philip K. Dick. New York, Doubleday, 1976; London, Gollancz, 1977.
The Courts of Chaos (Amber). New York, Doubleday, 1978; London, Faber, 1980.
The Chronicles of Amber (omnibus). New York, Doubleday, 2 vols., 1979.
The Bells of Shoredam. San Francisco, Underwood Miller, 1979.
Roadmarks. New York, Ballantine, 1979.
Changeling. New York, Ace, 1980.

Short Stories

Four for Tomorrow. New York, Ace, 1967; as *A Rose for Ecclesiastes*, London, Hart Davis, 1969.
The Doors of His Face, The Lamps of His Mouth, and Other Stories. New York, Doubleday, 1971; London, Faber, 1973.
My Name Is Legion. New York, Ballantine, 1976; London, Faber, 1979.
The Last Defender of Camelot. New York, Pocket Books, 1980.

OTHER PUBLICATIONS

Other

"In Praise of His Spirits Noble and Otherwise," in *From the Land of Fear*, by Harlan Ellison. New York, Belmont, 1967.
The Illustrated Roger Zelazny, with Gray Morrow. New York, Baronet, 1978.

Editor, *Nebula Award Stories 3.* New York, Doubleday, and London, Gollancz, 1968.

*

Manuscript Collections: George Arents Research Library, Syracuse University, New York; Special Collections, University of Maryland, Baltimore.

Roger Zelazny comments:
    My earlier writing involved considerable use of mythological materials. I have, however, attempted to diversify over the years. I write both fantasy and science fiction, as well as mixtures of the two. My objectives vary from book to book, but in general I begin with character in mind rather than plot. Among my personal favorites are the novels *Lord of Light* and *Doorways in the Sand.*

*   *   *

    A writer who constantly challenges himself, Roger Zelazny is difficult to categorize. He has successfully written both fantasy and "hardcore" science fiction, his work has been both light and serious in tone, he is adept at all lengths, he has tackled most of the standard science-fiction themes. Even his style has changed since he published his first short story in 1962—from one that was highly mythic and richly poetic to one that is more controlled, economical, and precise. Yet despite the wide variation in tone, content, and style of his work, there are definite and consistent characteristics in his writing. Certain themes recur; certain kinds of characters reappear. Perhaps it is in his characterization that the threads which link his works are most easily seen.
    Zelazny's ability to create believable characters is probably his single most important contribution to science fiction. Even though his protagonists usually possess some ability or talent which makes them "larger-than-life," they remain entirely credible. They prize their self-reliance, personal integrity, and individualism. They must develop their own unique abilities and talents. And, since growth is a result of experience, the psychological growth of the characters is directly linked to their adventures. Frequently, Zelazny's stories begin with his protagonist disillusioned, alienated, or geographically isolated, and, whatever the circumstances, the specific conditions of his situation set him off on some kind of quest. In addition to attaining some physical objective, however, Zelazny's heroes are also set off unconsciously on a psychological quest—which is to achieve a metamorphosis of personality, to raise their level of consciousness. If successful, this new maturity brings the disparate elements of their personalities into harmony, gives them a broader and deeper knowledge of themselves and the worlds in which they live, and creates the possibility for love. Of Zelazny's best works, the Amber novels, "A Rose for Ecclesiastes," and "The Doors of His Face, The Lamps of His Mouth" use protagonists who achieve metamorphosis in the course of the story, while *Lord of Light* and *This Immortal* tell stories which could not happen until after their protagonists have achieved this growth.
    Zelazny's recurrent themes are integrally related to the psychological quests of his heroes. Vanity, greed, power, guilt, and revenge block metamorphosis and must be overcome before it can occur. Immortality permits a character to achieve a fuller realization of his capabilities. Zelazny recognizes that as long as a healthy person lives, psychological growth will continue. Love and fertility, in all their possible forms, are the positive benefits of metamorphosis. Self-reliance, personal integrity, and individualism are the keys to achieving it. Renewal, or restoration, which appears so frequently in Zelazny's stories, is an encompassing theme which signals both physical and psychological success.
    Zelazny's most important works are the stories "A Rose for Ecclesiastes," "The Doors of His Face, The Lamps of His Mouth," and "Home Is the Hangman" and the novels *This Immortal, The Dream Master, Lord of Light*, and the five Amber books. Both "A Rose for Ecclesiastes" and "The Doors of His Face, The Lamps of His Mouth" are renewal stories, and both Gallinger, the conceited Earth poet, and Carlton Davits, the bankrupt baitman, must overcome their vanity in order to achieve personality metamorphosis. Each does, and in the process Gallinger saves the Martians from racial suicide and restores fertility to the planet, while Davits brings both his and his ex-wife's personalities into harmony and creates a healthy relationship. "Home Is the Hangman," one of Zelazny's "no-name detective" stories, presents a unique twist on the metamorphosis motif. In it, the Hangman, a combination telefactor and computer, returns to Earth after many years in space to show its teachers that it has overcome the neurosis they created for it. The anthropomorphic machine has successfully integrated the elements of its personality, while, ironically, one of its teachers, Jessie

Brockden, is so overpowered by guilt that he believes that the machine has returned to kill him.

This Immortal presents a protagonist, Conrad Nomikos, who has already achieved maturity by the time the story begins, so the focus of the story shifts from achieving metamorphosis to the role of the hero in restoring the irradiated Earth. A revolutionary group believes that the Vegans, a superior alien culture, are about to begin a wholesale exploitation of the planet, when in truth they are testing Conrad's worth to inherit and subsequently restore it.

The Dream Master presents the only instance in Zelazny's writing where a protagonist fails to achieve metamorphosis. Because his particular personality fault, once again pride, continues to dominate, Dr. Charles Render, a neuroparticipation therapist, is ultimately drawn into the madness of one of his patients. His vanity has prevented him from seeing the limits of his abilities. In one of Zelazny's more interesting attempts to expand a novel through the use of myth, he links Render to the Scandinavian *ragnarok* and Eileen, his patient, to Arthurian legend. The *ragnarok* represents Render's view of the world and signifies the psychologically deterministic course of his life. The Arthurian material characterizes Eileen's chivalric and highly idealized view of the world. Though the concept is ingenious, the use of symbolic mythic sequences tends to confuse meaning for the perceptive reader rather than clarify it. In addition to illustrating the dangers inherent in allusion, it also illustrates the danger of assuming that Zelazny is attempting to translate whole bodies of myth into science fiction.

Lord of Light, undoubtedly Zelazny's best novel, also treats renewal—in this case the renewal of a society. By the time the story begins, Sam, the protagonist, has long since passed on to a higher state of consciousness. The world of Urath is ruled by colonists who have virtually become gods. They patterned the new after the Hindu culture that they left behind on Earth, and they have achieved virtual immortality because they have the technology for body transfer. Unfortunately, their power has corrupted them. They exploit the masses, their own descendants, and refuse to let them share their technological benefits. Society is repressive and stagnant, and Sam sets out to change it. Of course, he accomplishes his reform mission.

The Amber novels treat both the physical and psychological sides of renewal—the restoration of the land and the metamorphosis of personality. Corwin, the protagonist, journeys from youthful and romantic idealism to optimistic pragmatism in the course of his adventures to keep his universe from being absorbed back into chaos. In the process, he learns that the most important reason for living is psychologically healthy human relationships. A dramatization of Zelazny's form and chaos philosophy, the Amber novels also show how man should relate to the basic forces of the universe.

The Amber novels are not only a major fantasy work, they are also an excellent window on Zelazny's capabilities. Criticized by some who feel that he has not achieved the stature projected for him when he broke into science fiction more than 15 years ago, Zelazny has perhaps more than any other writer brought the techniques, style, and language of serious literature to the field. There can be no question of his stature, for he has written several major works, but his greatest contribution may in the end prove to be that he has brought characters who are psychologically credible, who are sympathetic, who have depth and scope, to a literature famous for its cardboard figures.

—Carl B. Yoke

ZOLINE, Pamela A. American. Born in Chicago, Illinois, in 1941. Educated at the Slade School of Fine Art, London. Artist and illustrator; group show—Young Contemporaries, Tate Gallery, London, 1966. Has lived in England since 1963.

SCIENCE-FICTION PUBLICATIONS

Uncollected Short Stories

"The Heat Death of the Universe," in *The Best SF Stories from New Worlds 3*, edited by Michael Moorcock. London, Panther, 1968; New York, Berkley, 1969.
"The Holland of the Mind," in *The New SF*, edited by Langdon Jones. London, Hutchinson, 1969.

*   *   *

Pamela A. Zoline's "The Heat Death of the Universe" is an unusual piece of science fiction that examines a typical day in the life of an intelligent, college-educated "housewife," Sarah Boyle, and pronounces it a voyage toward insanity. The heroine's intellectual life has ended with her exit from "a fine Eastern college," and her existence now centers around the endless duplication and rearing of her own kind—a business she does not understand and is not suited for. That Sarah is struggling to make sense of her continuing motherhood is shown by the notes and signs she writes and places around her house, including one over the stove that cries, "Help, Help, Help, Help, Help." Her daily (real) life revolves only around her children (of whose number she is not sure), her cluttered, messy home and preparations for chaotic events, such as the birthday party planned for that afternoon. The shopping expedition to purchase party goods is the precursor of a period of disintegration from which Sarah may not recover. The image of Zoline's overwrought heroine in the supermarket panicking at the sight of an infinite number of cleaning products captures completely the confusion of our age of consumerism-gone-mad, forcing the reader to wonder: why this duplication and waste in a world of want? And is it possible that people are also being uselessly reproduced and discarded in a world already overpopulated and careless of its inhabitants?

"The Holland of the Mind" also explores the theme of disintegration—of a man and a marriage—in a foreign setting (as Sarah's house was alien to her intellectuality). Graham and Jessica are Americans living a seemingly pointless existence in Amsterdam. Their marriage appears to be similarly meaningless, except for an abundant sex life and a daughter Rachel whom both sincerely love. The death of his mother triggers Graham's breakdown, which was immanent in this story as Sarah's was in "Heat Death"; however, there are recovery and the apparent ability to carry on a life that is now different but still possibly good.

The alienation of Zoline's characters seems to be offset by their intelligence and desire to survive in a world not of their creation, which they do not understand yet struggle to cope with. This common dilemma of human beings of all eras and the tenacious frailty of the author's heros unite the reader sympathetically with them and with their creator.

—Rose Flores Harris

ZETFORD, Tully. *See* **BULMER, Kenneth**

FOREIGN-LANGUAGE
WRITERS

ABE, Kobo (1924—). Japanese. *Inter Ice Age 4*, 1970.

* * *

Science fiction is but a small part of Kobo Abe's work, though his creations in other genres have tinges of science-fiction character. He is, however, regarded in Japan as a major literary figure mainly because of his plays.

As a medical school graduate, Abe has the technical knowledge for outstanding work in science fiction. Also relevant is his creation of psychological novels in the 1960's, as well as his propensity for experimental literary work, combining his familiarity with European 20th-century trends with the characteristic Japanese mindfulness of indigenous cultural tradition. One important example of this is the mask, for centuries a major resource of Japanese drama. His novel *Tanin no kao* (The Face of Another) is scarcely science fiction, but has technological content, the methods by which a realistic mask is substituted for a horribly disfigured face. Here the hero compares himself to the monsters of television, and the film is replete with the organ-filled laboratories of the Frankenstein tradition.

The greatest science-fiction work of Abe is *Inter Ice Age 4* in which the forthcoming inundation of the Earth by melting polar ice caps is to be dealt with by modifying human embryos to produce gill-breathers. Very important in predicting the disaster here is computer technology, and we are told that the computers have also discerned Communism as the shape of things to come. However, says a leading character, Communism *would* fit the predictions of a machine; it neglects free will. The computers are also described as scanning a human mind completely, then engaging in dialogue with the "individual" stored in their data banks. When this dialogue with the "data bank ghost" is extended even to the mind of a newly dead person, one sees an old Japanese concept in action (the 11th-century novel *Tale of Genji*, as well as the modern film *Rashomon*). Abe's philosophy of present-future relationships is especially significant. *Inter Ice Age 4* comments that "The future is not to be judged by us," but rather it "sits in judgment on the present." It gives a verdict of guilty, says Abe, and the people of the present, confident in the continuity of their microcosm, are to be scorned. This author's vision may have been enhanced by a sense of alienation from his immediate present. Also monumental in his work is an eager confrontation with the great borderlines between life and death, between illusion and reality, and between the inner and outer worlds of human beings.

—Frank H. Tucker

ANDREVON, Jean-Pierre (1937—). French. "Observation of Quadragnes," in *View from Another Shore*, edited by Franz Rottensteiner, 1973; "The Time of the Big Sleep," in *A Shocking Thing*, edited by Damon Knight, 1974.

* * *

Jean-Pierre Andrevon is perhaps the best-known French science-fiction writer because of his intense activity ever since he became a professional writer. He quickly became the most prolific critic of the main French SF monthly *Fiction*, in which most of his short stories have appeared. His first novel, *Les Hommes-Machines contre Gandahar* is a sort of *Great Dictator* of the future, with a strange time-controlling creature thrown in as game-master. He has also written both traditional space operas (*La Guerre des Gruuls*) and time operas (*Le Dieu de Lumière*), and very effective mystery-and-horror novels (*Un Froid Mortel*) under the pen-name of Alphonse Brutsche.

Even in these quickly written books the quality of his style is remarkable: he puts to use his sense of everyday dialogue and the eye of the painter that he also is, thus uniting realism with poetry.

But what has been mostly noticed is the political orientation which—as true son of the protest movement—he has given both to his criticism and to his fiction, to the delight of the most progressive readers and the (very vocal) fury of the devotees of conventional SF: he explodes the taboos about sex ("Observation of Quadragnes") as well as death (*Le Reflux de la Nuit*), strips the glamour from war in space and on the earth ("Retour à Broux") and technology in its present excesses and presumptuous hopes. He has rallied round him a whole school of young writers, whom he has published in his series of anthologies *Retour à la Terre* (3 vols., 1975-77)—whose title clearly expresses the intention of devoting one's attention to our world and its immediate problems (pollution, over-population, the dangers of nuclear energy in its "civilian" as well as military uses). Andrevon's ideology has shifted from extreme socialism (Trotskyism) to ecology, i.e., a more general concern for harmonious relationships between man and his environment and concurrently between various social groups. The main shortcoming that he has been reproached with is that, because of the huge gap between his views of the ideal future and the present evils he denounces, he has failed to imagine any acceptable transition: in his novel *Le Temps des Grandes Chasses* an idyllic society emerges only after world-wide disaster; and in "Le Monde Enfin" (*Utopies 75*) our planet finds beauty and balance again only at the cost of...humanity!

By the abundance and variety of his production, his rich characterization, the wide resources of his style, the warning function he gives his fiction, Andrevon can be compared to John Brunner. Though he has not yet produced a masterpiece like *Stand on Zanzibar*, his last novel, *Le Désert du Monde*—a rather dickian approach to the "end of mankind" theme—may very well be a decisive step in that direction.

—George W. Barlow

BARJAVEL, René (1911—). French. *Ashes, Ashes*, 1967; *Future Times Three*, 1970; *The Ice People*, 1970; *The Immortals*, 1974.

* * *

René Barjavel's work contrasts pastoral utopias full of love with war-torn dystopias full of distrust. Although *Le Diable l'Emporte*, *Colomb de la Lune*, and *L'Homme Forte* have not been translated, *Ashes, Ashes*, *Future Times Three*, *The Ice People*, and *The Immortals* are passionately anti-war, erotic, and satiric, relating vividly penned horrors and sentimental romance.

Typical science fiction, *Future Times Three* deals with time travel, its paradoxes and its dangers. Playful escapades in the near future and malicious forays into the 19th century echo Wells's *Invisible Man*, and the specialized races of 100,000 AD follow Stapledon. Exploring the future, mathematician and physicist brood over questions of God and causality. This episodic novel declares—like *Faust*—that man cannot safely extend beyond God.

In traveling to 2052, St. Menoux learns the fate of the survivors of *Ashes, Ashes*, in which some inexplicable sunspot phenomenon cuts off electricity and the world goes mad. Fire and bloodshed purge a decadent technological society on the verge of all-out war. As in the earlier novel, the pure love of two young people provides hope. The heroes, however, are ruthless killers who fight their way into the country to found a pastoral world where books and inventions are forbidden.

One of the numerous Swiftian sallies of *Ashes, Ashes* explains the system of freezing ancestors. In *The Ice People* South Pole explorers find two gorgeous bodies from 900,000 years earlier, obviously remnants of a vastly advanced society destroyed by atomic holocaust. Unfrozen, Elea transmits her memories of her perfect love with Paikan and her selection as the mate to be preserved for the mastermind, Coban. This Romeo and Juliet tale is set against political turmoil of past and present. Only a coalition of scientists and students might save the world, though Elea and Paikan are destroyed.

Using the actual backdrop and leaders of today, *The Immortals* examines the frightening long-range political effects of a drug that defeats death and disease. Since immortality is contagious, all those involved in research have been isolated on an Aleutian paradise. They are, however, human time bombs doomed to annihilation by world powers when scientists learn there is nowhere for man in space. Although pessimistic, Barjavel asserts the values of love and peace.

—Mary S. Weinkauf

BELYAEV, Aleksandr (1884-1942). Russian. *The Amphibian*, n.d.; *The Struggle in Space*, 1965; *Professor Dowell's Head*, 1980.

*   *   *

Aleksandr Belyaev's first SF stories were published in adventure journals in 1925 and his first book in 1926. He wrote about 30 SF stories, about 20 novels, and a dozen articles or prefaces (e.g., to Jack London's novels) which make of him the first penetrating Russian SF critic. He used the breathtaking Vernean adventure plot or the current detective-thriller-SF (from Wells, London, Renard, Burroughs or A. Tolstoy) with an isolated and romantically alienated hero, either a scientist with humanistic ideals, a biologically modified man who is a naive child of nature (Ichthyander in his most popular novel, *The Amphibian Man*, or Ariel in the novel of the same title), or quite openly an artist (such as Presto in the two variant novels *The Man Who Lost His Face* and *The Man Who Found His Face*). This bearer of the novum and of the desire for freedom is opposed to and hounded by the cruel power of wicked scientists and financiers; most interestingly, he is at the center of an extreme situation or novum validated by a bold scientific technique. This is usually biological adaptation, including the changing use of the senses, and, most prominently, a sundering of brain from body as in *Professor Dowell's Head* (much superior to Renard's *New Bodies for Old*) or various, often humorous and folktale-like, scientific inventions in the "Professor Wagner" cycle. Such works are imbued with an aching lyricism and a vibrant humanistic vehemence. But often Belyaev's hero triumphs thanks to an essentially fairytale metamorphosis that allows him to vanquish physical gravity and social injustice. The black-and-white opposition of his threatened hero to a grotesque capitalist environment becomes then a form of escapism into a wicked Ruritania.

In the late 1920's and early 1930's Belyaev's SF was interrupted by a campaign against the genre. From 1934 he largely shifted his focus to short-range technological anticipation and (more interestingly) to interplanetary work and struggles, domesticating the notions of Tsiolkovsky and early Soviet rocket experimenters. For all his shortcomings, Belyaev's basic concern with human metamorphosis striving for freedom and the external resistance and inner anxieties it provokes have not only made of him at least the equal of any interwar German, French, or US SF writer, and a lasting influence in Russia, but also an author who remains of interest today.

—Darko Suvin

BORGES, Jorge Luis (1899—). Argentine. *Ficciones*, 1962; *Labyrinths*, 1962; *The Aleph and Other Stories 1933-1969*, 1970; *The Book of Sand*, 1975.

*   *   *

Jorge Luis Borges has been called "the greatest living writer in the Spanish language today." His literary achievements secured him a post as director of the Argentine National Library in 1955, though blindness obliged him to retire in 1973.

Primarily a miniaturist and poet, Borges has been attracted throughout his long career by themes which transcend our normal reality, and many of his short stories are frankly science-fictional. In "Tlön, Uqbar, Orbis Tertius" he describes how our Earth is gradually being taken over by another, invented version of the world. His pitiable title character in "Funes the Memorious" is endowed with a memory which will not permit him to forget anything, yet this talent cripples him as a person. "Dr. Brodie's Report" gives an account of a visit to an imaginary African tribe halfway between apes and humans, who possess a religion, the concept of poetry, and a rudimentary ability to foretell the future. "The Aleph" is a point within which the whole world, past and future, can be seen. "The Zahir" is a satirical variation on a similar motif: an object which obsesses its beholder, sometimes a man or a tiger, but at present a common coin. Paradoxes connected with infinity abound in Borge's work, for instance, in *The Library of Babel*, which is an endless store of incomprehensible books, and *The Book of Sand*, which appears to be a sort of scripture, but contains literally countless leaves. He has also long been fascinated by fabulous animals, and indeed devoted an entire volume to the subject, a sort of bestiary of the nonexistent: *The Book of Imaginary Beings* (with Margarita Guerrero).

It is known that Borges has occasionally been influenced by authors of SF or near-SF, including Poe and Lovecraft; in turn his elegant economy of style and his ability to compress long complex arguments into a few pages have earned him the admiration of many younger SF writers, who not infrequently imitate him, though with scant success.

—John Brunner

BOULLE, Pierre (1912—). French. *Planet of the Apes*, 1963 (as *The Monkey Planet*, 1964); *Garden on the Moon*, 1964; *Time Out of Mind and Other Stories*, 1966; *Because It Is Absurd* (stories), 1971; *Desperate Games*, 1973; *The Marvellous Palace and Other Stories*, 1977; *The Good Leviathan*, 1979.

*   *   *

Like that of the venerable minister-priest of the Religion of Doubt who is the narrator of the six "*histoires perfides*" that make up *The Marvellous Palace and Other Stories*, Pierre Boulle's main function throughout his prolific and varied career has been "to arouse curiosity by the prospect of an enigma." In Boulle's wryly laconic fables, the enigmatic takes many forms: in *The Good Leviathan* an oil supertanker capable of miraculous cures; in "His Last Battle" (*Because It Is Absurd*) an aging Fuehrer dying in his Edenic Peruvian jungle-compound who has finally found it within himself to forgive the Jews; in "The Heart of the Galaxy" (*Because It Is Absurd*), a message from the stars, engendered by an immense expenditure of energy, which—much to the consternation of the scientists on earth who decipher it—turns out to be an advertising slogan; in *Desperate Games* a world government of Nobel Prize-winning scientists who cure all of mankind's social ills but must devise destructive war games to prevent the universal ennui that sets in when man is left with nothing to struggle against. Boulle's style is too arch and his stance too knowing for his science-fiction tales to be called cautionary, just as his espionage stories set in the Far East are too coolly ironic to be labeled merely escapist thrillers: even a casual reader must have anticipated that the astronaut escaping from *Planet of the Apes*—undoubtedly Boulle's most well-known science-fiction work and the basis for the popular film series—was returning to an earth in which a similar evolutionary movement had taken its inevitable course. In all of Boulle's work, the tone may be cynical but it is rarely morose, since Boulle remains detached from the delusions, vanities, and follies of technocratic man confronting the remorselessness of an implacable Nature and the unchangingness of his own prideful and enigmatic heart.

—Kenneth Jurkiewicz

BOYE, Karin (1900-41).   Swedish.   *Kallocain*, 1966.

*   *   *

Karin Boye was a distinguished Swedish poet and a disciple of the radical French pacifist Henri Barbusse. She committed suicide a year after the publication of *Kallocain* in 1940. She was one of those intellectuals horrified by the rise of Nazism, and she returned disappointed from a journey to the Soviet Union, a country she had considered a hope for the future. Her anxieties and her experiences with Nazism and Stalinism are clearly reflected in her novel, one of the few dystopias written by a woman. Her work uncannily anticipates many of the black features that Orwell made known in *Nineteen Eighty-Four*, in particular the total surveillance of citizens by spy-lenses in their private homes, the concept of a thought police and thought crime, and the thoroughgoing division of the world into (two) big states which are so antagonistic to each other that they deny their enemy the common human ancestry. Leo Kall, a chemist and inventor of the epynomous truth serum Kallocain, is a citizen of the "world state" in the 21st century—a "fellow soldier," for the country's organization is thoroughly militaristic. The police are omnipresent, and citizens are urged to denounce their friends and relatives and to join in communal "hate sessions." The fear of spies is so great that even simple geographical data are treated as secrets of state. Leo Kall is deeply distrustful of his immediate superior Edo Rissen, one of the few human beings who have kept their individualism, and he suspects that his wife is unfaithful to him. Knowing very well that under the influence of his new drug all are equally guilty, Kall decides to attack and to denounce Rissen, who is promptly sentenced. In the end the "world state" is invaded by the "universal state," which is, we may assume, different only by name, and Kall serves his new masters with equal zeal. The psychological conflicts of the hero are depicted powerfully, and the novel reflects a deep fear of the rise of totalitarianism and an all-powerful state that inexorably crushes the individual.

—Franz Rottensteiner

BRAUN, Johanna (1929—), and **Günter** (1928—).   East German.   *The Great Magician's Error*, 1972; *Uncanny Phenomena on Omega 11*, 1974; *The Mistake Factor* (stories), 1975; *Conviva Ludibundus*, 1978.

*   *   *

Johanna and Günter Braun, a married couple, were newspaper reporters and editors before they turned free-lance writers. They published 9 juvenile adventures, historical novels, TV plays, and experimental prose such as *Eve and the New Adam* touching on equal rights for women and sparking off much public discussion. At the beginning of the 1960's they entered into full possession of their narrative voice—ironical, lyrically oriented toward characterization rather than plot, and strongly concerned with the integrity of people enmeshed into politics and economics. *An Objective Angel*, for instance, deals with the societal and personal implications of

modern technology in contemporary East Germany. In the 1970's they published four SF books.

The Great Magician's Error, a juvenile novel, is a folktale-like parable on a country ruled by a Magician whose power is founded on the soporific effects of a special pear, in its natural state both inebriating and stimulating. Helped by a snake-like girl, the young hero, drawn to pranks and interesting knowledge rather than obedience, manages to defeat the despotic rule, in an analogy to Stalinism's rule and fall. In their collection of stories, *The Mistake Factor*, the central conflict is between critical socialist humanism and technocratic self-satisfaction. The collection contains at least three small masterpieces. In "Choosing Astronauts" the earthy and quirky independence of Merkur and Elektra (heroes of the second novel) amounts to an *exemplum* not only for the fitness of astronauts but of people in general to cohabit. "The Jingling of Caesar's Cowbells," told by an involved narrator changing her opinion, is a tour de force of economy and clarity, successfully blending the East European "production tale" with understated sexiness and graceful wit. Best of all is the title story: in a utopian future the narrator is sent to investigate the malfunctioning of the central computer. The setting is an inertia-inducing centre near the Bertolt Brecht Lake with rejuvenating qualities, and the story opposes the rejuvenation associated with a critical and anti-bureaucratic marxism to the huge but tired technocracy which concealed the malfunctioning because the machine had become a soothing idol.

In the second novel, *Uncanny Phenomena on Omega 11*, the erotic and cognitive interplay between the playful Merkur and the serious Elektra, from grudging mutual acceptance through connubial bliss and the ups and downs of team-work to final growing apart, possesses a gentle power. The adventure-puzzle on a foreign planet with a treacherous exploiting race, whom our heroes circumvent by brain not brawn, suggests the uses of playfulness fused with work as anitdote to class isolation and specialization. *Conviva Ludibundus* is named after a marine bio-electronic life-form which is the indispensable link in the production of a mussel containing all the nutrients necessary for a future humanity. Instead of the gardener-like encouragement by the narrator, the Conviva is subjected to rationalization and enclosures by his successor, a typical hardworking, unimaginative, upwardly mobile, pompous scientist. His hunt for the Conviva in a super-technological Vernean vehicle manages, by misusing scraps of knowledge, to turn it for a time into the producer of uneatable giant mussels and of unnecessary data from the seabed. A global catastrophe is only averted by the narrator's girlfriend who unwittingly deprograms the Conviva (a one-celled being which can come together in many shapes) by leading it into mobile self-constructs and aquatic ballet. This key scene of the novel is not unworthy of comparison with some of Lem's *Solaris*. The upshot is that art is the only antidote to elitist power and technocratic breakdown: a darker and weightier conclusion in a text with a more powerful antagonist, putting up stronger obstacles to utopian ethics. But the satire remains accompanied by comedy and wit, by the constant disrespectful and funny inversion of received authority.

The Brauns' playful cognizing makes them part of the "warm current" in socialism, colliding with the cold one. Their artful manipulation of narrative voices, their commitment to the feminine principle amusingly associated with sexual emotion, productive self-management, and critical intelligence place them at the pivot of East German SF, and on the map of the best world SF.

—Darko Suvin

BRYUSOV, Valery (1873-1924).   Russian.   *The Republic of the Southern Cross and Other Stories*, 1918.

*   *   *

Valery Bryusov, from a rich merchant family, become a leader of

Russian Symbolist poetry, publishing a dozen books of formidably erudite and polished verse, as well as stories, plays, brilliant verse translations from many languages (including the complete poetry of Poe), and interesting criticism of poetry. His esoteric disdain for the multitude changed after the 1904-05 revolution into a growing acceptance of social responsibility and sympathy for the revolutionary destruction of the "ugly and shameful" capitalist order. He thus became one of the few prominent non-Marxists to take an active part in Soviet cultural life, and in 1920 even joined the communist party.

Bryusov had a long-standing interest in a "scientific poetry" akin to SF. Two of his major preoccupations were more obviously SF. From the 1890's he was haunted by the fall of world civilization, envisioned as a giant symbolic city. In his play *Youth* (1904) a revolt of youth shatters the glass dome that bars the city from sunshine and open space; the revolt both seeks liberation and exposes the city to the risk of death (see also his story "The Last Martyrs"). Written after the defeat of the 1905 revolution, his Poesque story "The Republic of the Southern Cross" is frankly dystopian: an enclosed industrial city on the South Pole falls prey to an epidemic leading the afflicted to do the opposite from what they wish to do; a resolute bourgeois minority fighting for order is overwhelmed by the brutalized inhabitants. Raskolnikov's dream at the end of *Crime and Punishment* blends here with a parable on the great social convulsions of our century. Bryusov's second SF theme is one of cosmic contacts, treated both in his poetry and in a number of unfinished stories and plays, and influenced by the utopian philosopher Fyodorov and his disciple Tsiolkovsky, by Poe, Wells, and most of all Flammarion; as in this last writer such contacts often involved a cometary world. His old theme of catastrophe and a distant presentiment of a possible new world lent themselves well to the widespread post-1917 equation of the social revolution with man's leap into interplanetary space. Bryusov thus became the link between, on the one hand, the tradition of Russian utopianism, 19th-century European SF, and philosophic speculation leading from Leibniz to Spengler, and, on the other, early Soviet "Cosmist" poetry and SF. Bryusov's peculiar double horizon, embracing both dystopia and utopia is his greatest strength: he clearly managed to influence both Zamyatin and Mayakovsky, and, through them as well as directly, most prewar Russian SF.

—Darko Suvin

BULGAKOV, Mikhail (1891-1940).   Russian.   *Heart of a Dog,* 1968; *Diaboliad and Other Stories,* 1972.

*   *   *

"The stars will remain when the shadows of our presence and our deeds have vanished from the earth. There is no man who does not know that. Why, then, will we not turn our eyes toward the stars?" This is the leitmotiv of Mikhail Bulgakov's science fiction: the nature of a true relationship between a Kantian universe and a human existence of thought and action.

Bulgakov's early science-fiction stories established an allegoric parallel between scientific discovery and social revolution, using every technique from slapstick comedy to black humor and horror, to show the absurdity and danger of trying to impose human purposes on reality. In "The Fatal Eggs" (*Diaboliad*), based on H.G. Wells's *The Food of the Gods,* mammoth artificially hatched serpents almost devour Moscow. In "The Crimson Island"—"Jules Verne translated into Aesopian"—an involuted rebellion results in nothing but a drunken revel and a telegram to the West: "Go (indecipherable) your (indecipherable) mother."

The novella *Heart of a Dog* exhibits Bulgakov's characteristic literary method: a fantastic realism that is a combination of grotesque action and a naturalistic background, with a satiric intent, serving a philosophical idea. It concerns a Moscow professor who transforms a dog into a man in a rejuvenation experiment. The identification of professor and Lenin, rejuvenation and revolution is implicit. Within a week, the new creation has a vocabulary of "every known Russian swearword"; he can't button his fly, eats toothpaste, and has fleas: he is immediately made a Commissar. His mature virtues include greed, viciousness, and "cosmic stupidity." Disgusted, the professor curses the attempt to substitute the artificial for the authentic, whether dog for man or dogma for life, and reverses the experiment.

Bulgakov's science-fiction plays range from burlesque to near-tragedy, but all deal with the ontological theme. In *Bliss* a wondrous future utopia is revealed to be inadequate and boring compared to the mystery of reality and the adventure of living. In *Ivan Vasilievich* Ivan the Terrible's farcical misadventures in modern Moscow revolve around a confusion of definitions and roles with actualities. The best of the type, however, both in character development and seriousness of thought, is the tragicomedy *Adam and Eve.* In a war-devastated Leningrad, a few surviving men and one woman must choose between reality and ideology, represented by the pacifist Yefrosimov, whose anti-gas invention saved them, and Adam Krasovsky, who wants to risk annihilation for the sake of Communism. In the end, Eve chooses Yefrosimov for her mate because, as she tells Adam, "the forest and the singing of the birds, and the rainbow, this is real, but you with your frenzied cries are unreal."

The Master and Margarita is Bulgakov's masterpiece of indefinable genre and indeterminate meaning, wherein Satan visits Moscow, punishing evil, driving rationalists insane, and "putting the fear of God" into atheists. In it, the science-fiction theme converges with all of Bulgakov's other themes, styles, and techniques, and is fully realized. In *The Master and Margarita* reality is infinite, eternal, and transcendent; time and space are relative; man is immortal. Living according to the demands of universal truth is a moral duty for which man is held accountable. "Cowardice is the worst sin of all" for a character like Pontius Pilate whose "mind is too closed" and whose "life is too cramped." Yet man's denial and betrayal of reality cannot alter it. "All will be as it should," the devil promises; "that is how the world is made."

By his science-fiction model of a surreal method to present a multi-dimensional universe, and by the example of his artistic courage, Bulgakov obliged Russian writers to contemplate "the shadows of man's presence" from the perspective of the stars and therefore "to a complete truth of thought and word."

—Jana I. Tuzar

CALVINO, Italo (1923—).   Italian.   *Cosmicomics* (stories), 1968; *T Zero,* 1969 (as *Time and the Hunter,* 1970); *The Watchers and Other Stories,* 1971; *Invisible Cities,* 1974.

*   *   *

Italo Calvino's *Cosmicomics* first brought him to the attention of English-speaking SF readers, although a previous fantasy novel had been translated as *Baron in the Trees.* Each taking as its starting-point a deadpan statement about a scientific discovery or hypothesis—for example, the recession of the moon or the extinction of the dinosaurs—these fables recount the experiences of one Qfwfq, whose memories extend back before the universe took form but who was far from the only conscious being of his "day." With unabashed exaggeration and witty trivialisation, Calvino makes each scientific assertion into the excuse for a parable about everyday human weaknesses: jealousy ("The Form of Space"), vanity ("The Light-Years"), the desire to be one-up on somebody else ("How Much Shall We Bet?").

Two other of his books hold particular appeal for the SF audience. *The Castle of Crossed Destinies* derives from his observation that the pattern which results from laying out tarot cards implies classic stories and legends: Faust, Parsifal, Oedipus,

Orlando. He explores this in a medieval castle and a somewhat more modern tavern; it is to be regretted that he never wrote the projected motel section based on comic strips featuring "gangsters, terrified women, spacecraft, vamps, war in the air, mad scientists"—to quote his final Note. In *Invisible Cities* Marco Polo, part-guest, part-captive at the court of Kublai Khan, describes the fabulous cities he has visited, yet speaks only of his native Venice. Poignant and poetic, these are truly other-worldly visions.

Like Borges, Calvino is a miniaturist; it is his gift for condensing vast implications into a brief compass which has evoked the admiration of many contemporary SF writers.

—John Brunner

CAPEK, Karel (1890-1938). Czech. Fiction—*Krakatit*, 1925 (as *An Atomic Phantasy*, 1948); *The Absolute at Large*, 1927; *War with the Newts*, 1937. Plays—*R.U.R. (Rossum's Universal Robots)*, 1923; *And So Ad Infinitum (The Life of the Insects)*, 1923 (as *The World We Live In*, 1933); *The Makropoulos Secret*, 1925; *Adam the Creator*, 1929; *The White Sickness*, 1937.

*　　*　　*

Karel Capek was a prolific author of stories, essays, novels, travelogues, plays, and newspaper articles. The word "robot" was coined by his brother Josef (his collaborator in some works), but its blend of psycho-physiology and politics expresses precisely Karel's preoccupation with contemporary inhumanity, opposing Natural Man to Unnatural Pseudo-Man, a manlike, reasoning, but unfeeling being associated with capitalist technology and the social extremes of upper-class tycoon and working-class multitude. Capek's heroes range from small employees and craftsmen to doctors and deviant scientists, and his most stubborn values arise from peasant confidence in traditional things and relationships. In the plays, this is openly expressed by his small people and ideological arbiters, such as Nana in *R.U.R.* or Kristina in *The Makropoulos Secret*, while in the novels it is implied by key actions such as the final return to normality in *Krakatit* and *The Absolute at Large*. Yet Capek was also spellbound and terrified by the workers' world of factories and the power of capitalists (e.g., Bondy from both the latter novel and *War with the Newts*).

In Capek's first SF phase, after World War I, the tension between the little people (the audience he was writing for) and the catastrophic forces of technology and violence is largely vitiated by the ambiguity between a menace to man and to the middle class: does it arise from aliens created by the large industry, its capitalists and engineers, or from the workers? The robots of *R.U.R.*, synthetic androids outwardly like men, are mass-produced to be "workers with the minimum amount of requirements," i.e. without the non-exploitable emotions. In their first story, "System" (1908), the Capeks had shown a workers' revolt in such circumstances; the machine-men of *R.U.R.* are technological stand-ins for workers (and for Wells's Morlocks) but also, simultaneously, inhuman aliens "without history." Their creation doesn't lead to Domin's engineering utopia with Nietzschean supermen but to genocidal revolt. Yet during the play they grow more like a new human order than like inhuman aliens, more workers than machines; reacquiring feelings, they usher in a new cycle of creation. This oscillation, parallel to one between psychological and collective drama, has dated *R.U.R.* This holds even more strongly for *Adam the Creator* and *The Makropoulos Secret* (about the elixir of longevity). In *And So Ad Infinitum* the flighty erotics of upper-class "golden youth," the acquisitive sentimentalities of the petty bourgeoisie, and the militarism and deathlust racism of incipient fascism are personified as insects in a bitter satire, Capek's best stage play.

Capek's SF strength lies in his novels. *The Absolute at Large* presents another supposedly utopian but destructive invention: the Absolute or God, mass-produced as a by-product of atomic fission

in "karburators" that supply cheap energy. The novel passes in sarcastic review its abuses by church and state, corporations and individuals, academics and journalists: both the economy and personal relations collapse. Absolutized sectarian and national fanaticism leads to the "Greatest War," which peters out only when all "atomotors" have been destroyed along with most people. Yet it isn't clear why the Absolute, a "mystical Communism," must bend itself to capitalist economy and competitive psychology, or work disparately in things (overpopulation of industrial goods only) and in people (destructiveness matching the overpopulation). The power unleashed is simply a chaotic magnification of acquisitive economics and psychology. This makes for brilliant if spotty social satire, in which the little people outlast the highminded idea, but hardly for consistent SF.

In *Krakatit* the naive genius who pierces the secret of atomic fission finds a parallel "destructive chemistry" in Dostoevskian fevered nightmares, dissociations of memory, and explosive human encounters, and develops from "value-free" science to painful recognition of the primacy and dangers of human relationships. Capek integrated here popular literature—detection mystery and epic adventure from Homer through the folktale to pulp thrillers—into poetic and committed modern SF. The love and heroism of sensational melodrama and the counter-creation of the mad-scientist tradition are balanced by a sympathetic, suffering, and relatively complex hero, who rejects a series of erotic-cum-political temptations—not only the established class and new personal power but also the idyllic retreat. He is left with a resolve to achieve useful warmth instead of destructive explosions, and emerges from the fog of yearning into the clarity of moderation. Though the novel doesn't quite fuse realism and allegory, ethical moderation and folktale certainties, it largely succeeds in transcending the opposition between scientific progress and human happiness. For the first and last time in Capek's SF, a believable hero fights back successfully at destructive forces within himself and society.

Capek's second phase comprises some minor, marginally SF stories, *War with the Newts*, and one play. The rise of Nazism dispelled his illusions of the little man's instinctual rightness and the relativity of truth. Instead of satirizing the intellect, he wrote sharply against irrationalism, "be it the cult of will, of the soil, of the subconscious, of the mass instincts, or of the violence of the powerful." The pseudo-human becomes clearly evil when the Salamanders become analogous to the Nazi aggressors. Their rise is interwoven with a satire on the illusion industries which screen biological and social reality from mankind—the exotic and juvenile adventure romance, sensational tabloid newspaper, Hollywood movies, pseudo-scientific polls and interviews in newspapers. Scientists and academics are as timid and ideologically limited as the public at large, but the real villains are the capitalists who finance the menace through the Salamander Syndicate—an industrial utopianism satirized in the minutes of its meeting. The Salamanders, who began as exotic pets, become an "extremely cheap labor force" parallel to the transformation of competitive merchant-buccaneering into a global exploitative corporation aiming at a new Atlantis—which will end as Atlantis did. An appendix on the Salamanders' sexual life shows that their "Collective Male" horde is capable of politics and technics but not of real sociability: the Syndicate is the greatest illusion of them all. Progressing to a powerful alternate society, learning well mankind's combination of slavery and stock-market, aggression and ideological propaganda, they begin their assault. Capek's satire is here most bitter, topical, and precise. Startlingly, even his beloved small people are found guilty of complacency as continents crumble around them.

The satire of literary, journalistic, and essayistic forms in this novel is also a critique of SF. The history of the Salamanders echoes Wells's *Island of Dr. Moreau*, Conan Doyle's *Lost World*, and the animal fable; the global overview latches onto Wells's later SF and France's *Penguin Island*; it ends with Wellsian havoc-wreaking aliens—but also with an open question, much superior to ordinary SF: "No cosmic catastrophes, nothing but state, official, economic, and other causes...." The menace could have been stopped—if people had organized to fight it, if "All the industries. All the banks. All the different states" had not financed "this End of the World." Such writing makes of Capek not only the pioneer of all anti-fascist and anti-militarist SF but also (together with Zamyatin) the most significant SF writer between the World Wars. True, *War with the*

Newts didn't quite manage to overcome this ambiguity: the Salamanders are at the beginning a wronged inferior race and yet grow into an embodiment of both the Nazis and robotized masses. Russia, moreover, is presented as a Tsarist state: Capek couldn't deal with socialism or any positive radical novelty. He dealt in catastrophes, and concentrated his fire almost entirely on bourgeois society. Conversely, such a love-hate relationship led the communist bureaucracy in Czechoslovakia to neglect him in the early 1950's, though he has since been rehabilitated.

Capek's evolution is not simple. One of his best works, *Krakatit*, is early, and his final SF play, *The White Sickness*—a critique of fascism, militarism, and subservient medicine—is second rate. But in a few works he left a precious heritage. He—rather than Burroughs or Gernsback—is the missing link between Wells and a literature which will be both entertaining (which means popular) and cognitively (which means also formally) avant garde. He infused the legacy of the adventure novel and melodramatic thriller, French and British SF, and German fantasy with the prospects of modern poetry, painting, and movies as well as with an eager and constant interest in societal relationships, in natural and physical sciences, and above all in the richly humorous and idiomatic language of the street and the little people. In that way, he is the most "American" of the often elitist European SF writers. And yet he is also not only intensely Czech, but a "European local patriot" for whom Europe meant culture and humanism; when they were betrayed, the Salamanders—read fascists—had arrived.

—Darko Suvin

FLAMMARION, Camille (1842-1925). French. *Stories of Infinity*, 1873; *Urania* (stories), 1890; *Omega: The Last Days of the World*, 1894.

* * *

Camille Flammarion was perhaps the most famous astronomical popularizer of the 19th century. His first book, *Plurality of Inhabited Worlds* (1861), was an instant success; he was science editor of several French magazines and simultaneously an enthusiastic propagandist of spiritualism; he gave courses in popular astronomy, voyaged in balloons to study meteorology, was a serious scholar in astronomy pioneering the investigation of double stars and of Mars, founder of the monthly *Revue d'Astronomie*, co-founder of the French astronomical society, and, most importantly, an indefatigable writer, primarily of vivid popular-science books. By the time of his death he had published almost 50 books on astronomy, general science, amateur semi-religious philosophy (arguing for scientifically provable psychic life after death), and fiction.

A number of Flammarion's popularizations had from the 1860's mixed careful imaginative reconstruction of the way planet surfaces would look with speculations on the probable life there. In 1865 he published a survey of both non-fictional and fictional writings on other worlds, *Imaginary and Real Worlds*, one of the very first books of SF history; in his later work, he blithely pillaged that whole tradition—from Cyrano through Fourier to Defontenay—for bizarre figures and incidents of life on other planets which he inserted into his long lectures amd tirades. It is thus difficult to say where his fiction begins, but it can perhaps be dated with the three stories in *Stories of Infinity*. The first story, "Lumen," consists of dialogs between a questioner and a being reincarnated on several worlds, and comprises descriptions of alien life, including a sight of history and evolution reversed down to the extinction of life. The second story, "Story of a Comet," is one of the first and best of Flammarion's "comet stories": it is narrated by the comet as it, during various visits over 600,000 years, observes the development of inhabitants from Jupiter to the Moon. In the third story a spirit discourses on how movement, matter, and soul compose the universe. *Starry Dreams* is a mixed bag of speculative essays shading

into fiction, which among other things features reincarnation on other planets as flying beings with 17 senses (e.g., electric and psychic ones) and new organs, an imaginary voyage outward from Earth to various planets and stars with life adapted to each venue, and the possibilities of interplanetary signalling, terrestrial paradise, fourth dimension (picked up from Newcomb), and cyclical civilizations.

But his two major works were translated into English in the 1890's. *Urania* is again a collection of three stories, in which the narrator finds himself on Mars and on another solar system; he meets aliens with different organs, androgynous, telepathic, flowerlike, chrysalid-like, all of which is intermixed with soul transmigration and liberation from base matter. His only SF novel, *Omega: The Last Days of the World*, is still properly speaking no novel but an anticipation divided into two parts accompanied by long lectures. "The Twenty-Fifth Century" is an uncertainly focussed technocratic picture of triumphant science, radiant cities, menial labor by apes, disturbed by a huge comet scare and enlivened by some scandal-mongering satire on papal infallibility and on a rampant yellow press. "In Ten Million Years" starts with an overview of a utopian future of peace, abundance, perfect health, and splendid cities with moving sidewalks, television, and spaceflight; yet for unclear reasons apes still function as servants, a decadent upper class is juxtaposed with a childbearing lower class, and both communism and religion are forgotten. Eventually both Sun and Earth heat dwindles, and the story moves into "the last couple" sub-genre (imitated from Cousin de Grainville's *Le Dernier Homme* 100 years earlier); the ice-death of Omega and Eva is however compensated by their soul's flitting on to better things on Jupiter.

As a living writer, Flammarion is deservedly forgotten. He never mastered some basic fictional techniques; his writing is vivid only in straightforward descriptions of alien planets and beings or of an estranged Earth, and his most convincing character is a comet. Particularly difficult to stomach is the hushed or pathos-laden oracular tone of his marriage of natural science and spiritualist tenets such as metempsychosis, which in his time brought him such mass acclaim from the disoriented petty bourgeoisie. Flammarion's rather frenzied anti-materialism vented itself in pet peeves against such indignities as material food-taking and insufferable passages detailing (literally) ethereal love encounters. Nonetheless, his is a highly important phenomenon in SF history. He pre-empted the whole repertory of Stapledon's galactic evolution, he revived the "end of the world" story by grounding it in thermodynamics and directly influencing both Wells and Verne, his technocratic 25th century and its pleasure cities echo in *When the Sleeper Wakes* and all its myriad descendants, he stands behind all the comets in early modern SF from Verne and Griffith to Wells and Bryusov as well as behind most of the Martian and Selenite aliens who are not simply virtuous or wicked Earthmen but asexual, phosphorescent, siliceous, vegetable, or whatever. In other words, for late 19th-century fantasy and SF Flammarion functioned as a repository of ideas almost as Stapledon was to function after 1930, though without his depth and tragic humanism. Flammarion's variations on Kant's idea that the physical and moral perfection of psychozoa is proportional to the planet's distance from the Sun contributed to a spate of spiritualist and/or utopian ideals being reached by interplanetary voyages to Mars, Jupiter, or Saturn more straightforwardly fictional but not more intelligent than his (Cromie, Braine, Astor, Pallander). For all his clumsy eccentricities, his best work testifies to the birth of a vision which is strongest when it adopts the distant, cosmic, or macroscopic point of view: one could call it the birth of science fiction out of the spirit of astronomy. H.G. Wells would triumphantly consummate this estranged vision, but much of his work—such as the sunrise on the Moon in *The First Men in the Moon* or his story "The Star"—would not have been possible without Flammarion.

—Darko Suvin

FRANKE, Herbert W. (1927—). Austrian. *The Orchid Cage*, 1973; *Zone Null*, 1974.

* * *

Now a free-lance writer, Herbert W. Franke is, like Isaac Asimov, a scientist who has published for his profession and for the layman. The results of research into and knowledge of computers and information science play a fundamental role in Franke's novels (most notably *Zone Null*), which begin with the puzzling settings symbolic of space-time's mind-teasing ambiguities. His themes are those beloved of the last two decades: the smother-mother military-industrial complex which maintains a sterile conformity that nourishes the drugged culture; the animated computers and composite personalities which are analogs to the identification crisis; radioactive desolations encircling cadres of men and ships; the decadent games of an effete, satiated mass culture; and the volatile, plastic environmental structures whose life support systems are actually traps. Some of his characters show a modest development, as in *Die Stahlwüste* where a terrorist experiences humanizing sympathetic comradeship among desperate survivors on the moon. But in general his heroes are, like his novels, ironic in outline and analytical in their gradual disclosures of the social, political, and psychological networks and systems which alone unify the plots. Blind, self-righteous military aggressiveness, revolutionary fervor, and atavistic opportunism do battle with the affirmation of the courageous communal struggle against natural and unnatural wastelands (*Die Stahlwüste*, *Die Glasfalle*), the dignity of the family unit (*Die Glasfalle*), and a technology which is a servant rather than a master. Making good use of dialogue in interesting trial scenes (*The Orchid Cage*) and dialectical discussions (*Der Elfenbeinturm*), he plumbs the problem of survival in the long view both for the individual and the human species.

—Alice Carol Gaar

JEURY, Michel (1934—). French. *Chronolysis*, 1980.

* * *

Michel Jeury had already published two SF novels in 1960 under the pen-name of Albert Higon (*Aux Etoiles du Destin*, a space opera in Edmond Hamilton's style, and *La Machine du Pouvoir*, somewhat akin to van Vogt's *World of Null-A*) when he won a prize in 1974 for *Le Temps Incertain*. After a long silence he had found his true vein, parallel to Philip K. Dick's perhaps, yet highly personal, which he has since kept exploiting—and exploring—in a continuous flow of short stories and novels. Higon is not dead, but his "entertainments" have drawn nearer and nearer to Jeury's deeper novels, so that the two streams have now merged together.

The main novelty that Jeury has brought to French SF is "chronolysis": whereas time travel hitherto consisted in revisiting unchanged scenes, as, for example, in Gérard Klein's *The Overlords of War*, past moments are no more unalterable than the places one goes back to after a lapse of time; and their very changes are highly significant of the contradictions and evolution of the "psychronaut" (this triple portmanteau word is a fine example of Jeury's art of coining the vocabulary of future realities). Yet, those experiences are not pure explorations of the self: this impression of starting from scratch every time may reflect the author's period of maturation, when he undertook a huge variety of odd jobs and of literary experiments which all came to nothing; but the situations which cause the rupture of linear time for the hero, and which he then strives to understand and overcome in "the unsteady time," have all to do with present problems and future threats—the promises and dangers of the nuclear age, anarchical and tyrannical results of the growing world-wide domination of "cold monsters."

Nor is "chronolysis" the only psychopathological way of facing or escaping unbearable conditions that Jeury studies: for example, in

Soleil Chaud Poisson des Profondeurs the two syndromes which give the novel its fine surrealistic title ("hot sun, deep-sea fish") are opposite psychosomatic responses to an icy social environment, the mental equivalents of animal hibernation and migration. Just as in Jeury's first works characters were not defined before being confronted with various adventures but progressively built-up as much as revealed, in his later works—such as *Le Territoire Humain*—swarming multitudes circumscribe the systems whose imbalance their neuroses and psychoses reflect. Thus Jeury achieves the rare blend of the SF of escapism and the SF of protest, with the occasional emergence of a utopian streak as well in "La Fête du Changement" (*Utopies 75*).

—George W. Barlow

KLEIN, Gérard (1937—). French. *The Day Before Tomorrow*, 1972; *Star Masters' Gambit*, 1973; *The Overlords of War*, 1973.

* * *

Gérard Klein has been a prolific writer of science fiction as well as an important editor, publisher, and critic. He has produced considerable critical writing about American science fiction, and the influence of such writers as Silverberg, Dick, and Brunner can be seen frequently in his work. His first novel, *Star Masters' Gambit*, falls into the pulp tradition of adventure action narrative and space opera. One French critic argues that Klein wished to revive the Romantic tradition of the *bildungsroman*; and a later novel, *The Overlords of War*, is drawn from Klein's own personal experience with the French Algerian crisis. His more than 60 science-fiction short stories show a wide literary influence as well as a preciousness and polish in style at times that seems peculiarly French. The reader can move from space opera set on Uranus and told straight to first-person monologues suggestive of Malzberg's *Beyond Apollo* to Swiftian irony set like an 18th-century *conte philosophique* to fantastic aliens such as Snarks in his most widely known story, "Jonah." Without doubt Klein is important and influential in the current science-fiction scene in Europe.

—Donald M. Hassler

KOMATSU, Sakyo (1931—). Japanese. *Japan Sinks*, 1976.

* * *

The stature of Sakyo Komatsu was best reflected in the early 1970's when a number of his major works were published and his fame spread as one of the "Big Five" of Japanese science-fiction writers—the others being Yasutaka Tsutsui, Shin'ichi Hoshi, Ryu Mitsuse, and Taku Mayumura. That grouping leaves aside Kobo Abe, who may exceed the "Big Five" in fame, but is by no means an SF specialist, having produced much mainstream literature. Komatsu himself is not at all the narrow or standard SF writer. He is sometimes called the Robert Heinlein of Japan, while Hoshi is contrastingly referred to as Japan's Ray Bradbury. Komatsu is more closely akin to the later Heinlein, drawing more on sociological matters and somewhat less on the technological. Like Heinlein he gives much thought to political and international problems, and both writers have had a fairly diversified cultural, technical, and occupational background. For Komatsu, this diversified experience contributes to his ability to present natural and realistic narratives.

The story "Fukurokoji" (Blind Alley) is actually a summary of his futurology, and is included in his book, *Hoshi koroshi* (Star Killer—a title drawn from another very original story in that volume). In the same book are his skilled narratives of the birth and death of our moon, "Kaigo" (Conjunction) and "Wareta kagami" (The Broken Mirror). The title story of another collection, *Chi ni wa heiwa* (Peace on Earth), was nominated for the Naoki Prize, while a short-short story therein, "Koppu ippai no senso" (A Full Cup of War), deals with the development and hazards of nuclear war.

Komatsu's *Japan Sinks* enlarged his status considerably. In this novel he makes plausible, with plenteous data from geology and physics, what would otherwise be regarded as highly fantastic, the submergence of virtually the entire Japanese archipelago as the result of earthquakes, catastrophic currents of energy in the earth, and terrific volcanic action. The loss of Japan in a mere year or so is the fantastic element here. The same process extending over millions of years would not be so questionable—nor might it make much of a narrative. Komatsu has called this novel a fable, and it surely can be read as a caution against insularity in Japan or any nation. In pondering the question of the surviving Japanese refugees and their culture after their land disappears, Komatsu says that beyond ethnocentric and insular nationalism is a better, enriched identity, that one's own language and customs can be kept, while being enhanced by a global bending. Komatsu also considers the often problematic question of how peoples in distress may interact with the nations to whom they call for help. This thought-provoking novel has established Komatsu as an outstanding SF writer.

—Frank H. Tucker

LASSWITZ, Kurd (1848-1910).   German.   *Two Planets*, 1971.

*   *   *

In the literature of space travel Kurd Lasswitz's *Two Planets* merits notice, particularly for its acknowledged impact upon a generation of German scientist-engineers. After the initial 1897 publication translations fostered audiences throughout Europe. Lasswitz's thousand-page novel (abridged in the English translation) focuses on the conflict of values when intellectually and ethically superior but physically similar Martians ("Nume") invade Earth ("Ba").

Three explorers accidentally discover the Martian land station at Earth's North Pole. Their balloon runs afoul of the "abaric" or anti-gravity field used to propel craft to a solar-powered, ring-shaped satellite. Despite this peaceful contact a subsequent misunderstanding between Martians and the crew of an English warship precipitates military reactions from Earth, soon nullified by superior Martian weapons utilizing repulsion rather than destruction. Ensuing events admit no victory for Earth. The Martians reduce Earth to protectorate status and institute a stringent system of education. Ironically they in turn suffer a re-awakening of the corrupting urge to power. Only through such efforts as those of La, a Nume, and the explorer Saltner does compromise occur. Offering a microcosmic solution for the macrocosmic problem, these two fulfill destiny, or "reason within timeless will," by becoming one with love: "To follow destiny is freedom; to satisfy it is dignity."

Even as the novel gains philosophical complexity, it suffers weak plotting and characterization. Its great strength lies in description and exposition. In detail Lasswitz describes the Martian utopia as a society accommodating freedom of the individual moral will. His scientific and technological exposition of establishment of space stations, utilization of solar energy, synthetic food, and the healthy balance of scientific and humanitarian concerns prophetically foreshadows contemporary interests.

—Hazel Pierce

LEM, Stanislaw (1921—   ).   Polish.   *Solaris*, 1970; *The Invincible*, 1973; *Memoirs Found in a Bathtub*, 1973; *The Cyberiad* (stories), 1974; *The Futurological Congress*, 1974; *The Chain of Chance*, 1975; *Tales of Pirx the Pilot* (stories), 1979; *Return from the Stars*, 1980.

*   *   *

Stanislaw Lem is the author who has in Europe (and many think in the world) best realized the possibilities of sophisticated SF. His early novels (*Astronauts* and *The Magellan Nebula*) and stories (*Sesame*), apprentice works limited by some conventions of "socialist realism," deal interestingly with Lem's constant themes (threat of global destruction and militarism, human identity), and their utopian naivety is shaped by a committed humanism. His other pole, a black grotesque, appeared in *The Star Diaries* (later expanded), which also advance to a parabolic expression. The dozen years after the "Polish October" of 1956 were the golden noontime of Lem's SF. He published 17 books, including five novels, 10 partly overlapping books of short stories including the Pirx cycle, and the crown of his speculation and key to his fiction, *Summa technologiae*, a breathtakingly brilliant and risky survey of possible social, informational, cybernetic, cosmogonic, and biological engineering in Man's game with Nature. The novels, *Eden*, *Solaris* (his most admired work), *Return From the Stars*, *Memoirs Found in a Bathtub*, and *The Invincible*, and *Tales of Pirx the Pilot* use the mystery of strange beings, events, and localities for educating the protagonist into understanding the limitations and strengths of humanity. These parables for our age are fittingly open-ended. Their tenor is that no closed reference system is viable in the age of cybernetics and rival political absolutisms: the protagonists are redeemed by ethical and esthetic insight rather than hardware, abstract cognition, or power.

This is the source of Lem's strong, at times oversimplifying but salutary critique of English-language SF in *Fantastyka i futurologia* for abusing the potentialities of the New in gimmicks and disguised fairy tales. Only Wells, Stapledon, and Dick—and Capek and Zulawski in Slavic SF—find favor in his eyes. His critique of equally anthropomorphic banalities in Russian SF was conducted through his immense popularity and liberating influence there. Lem uses the experience of Central European intellectuals to fuse the bright humanistic hope with bitter historical warning. This double vision subverts both the "comic inferno" approach and a deterministic utopianism by juxtaposing the black flickerings of the former with the bright horizons of the latter. Such a procedure of wit places him in the "philosophic tale" tradition of Swift and Voltaire. Even his grotesque stories, where no "cruel miracles" redeem the often disgusting limits of man—e.g., *The Book of the Robots* and *The Cyberiad*—are informed by such humanizing fun, black satire, or allegorical iconoclasm.

Signs of an ideological dead-end if not exhaustion showed about 1968, prompting further formal experimentation and a furious brilliance in Lem's writing. In his last work, *The Master's Voice*, his radical doubts about human self-determination and sovereignty, and therefore about possibilities of communication with other people (much less other civilizations), began threatening to divert the fictional form of the novel into solipsist musings, lectures, and ideational adventure. This novel may have avoided the threat by a tour de force of narrative tone, but Lem drew some consequences from it: he turned to a brilliantly innovative series of briefer second-order glosses at the limits of fiction and treatise. *Hard Vacuum*—mainly composed of reviews of non-existent books, characterized and persiflaged simultaneously—and *Imaginary Greatness* range from thumbnail sketches of grisly futuristic follies to developments of ideas on "intellectronics" or artificial, heightened intelligence, "phantomatics" or illusory existence—e.g., in the longest works of this period, the grimly hilarious "Futurological Congress" (in *Insomnia*) and "The Mask"—and show Lem's deeply rooted though atheistic obsessions.

Lem's overflowing linguistic inventiveness, matching his controversial ideational plenty, is partly lost in translation. Nonetheless, his peculiar geo-political vantage point, enabling him effectively to transcend both cynical pragmatism and abstract utopianism, his stubborn warnings against static "final solutions," his position at the crossroads of major European cultures and ethics joined to an intense internalization of problems from cybernetics and information theory, his fusion of dilemmas from ultramodern science and the oldest cosmogonic heresies, his dazzling formal virtuosity—all mark him as one of the most significant SF writers of our century, and a distinctive voice in world literature.

—Darko Suvin

MAUROIS, André (1885-1967). French. *The Next Chapter: The War Against the Moon*, 1927; *Voyage to the Island of the Articoles*, 1928; *A Private Universe* (stories), 1932; *The Thought-Reading Machine*, 1938; *The Weigher of Souls, and the Earth Dwellers*, 1963.

* * *

The scores of diverse books published by André Maurois show the varied experience and interests of the man. His family business of cloth manufacturing claimed his attention in early life and the first World War also delayed his full-time devotion to writing, thus helping to carry out the advice of his mentor, Emile Chartier, that he should experience the real world amply before turning to a life of literary creativity. Certainly his novels and short stories evince a mastery of human nature and profound understanding of the French and English character. His careful analysis and biographies of Percy and Mary Shelley, Charles Dickens, Honoré de Balzac, and other authors contributed further to this, as did his many works of history and commentary on modern affairs.

Maurois gave only a fraction of his literary attention to science fiction, and his typical works in this genre are novellas. In these, as always with Maurois, we see reflections of the universal curiosity to which he himself gives major credit for his successes. Always also there is the readiness to interpret discerningly. In *The Thought-Reading Machine* a professor makes a machine to detect the passing thoughts of the targeted persons, but Maurois discerns that transient thoughts are of quite limited value. In *Voyage to the Island of the Articoles* the author imagines a South Sea island society, but he is also satirizing the purblindness of his European contemporaries. Maurois's close acquaintance with H.G. Wells and with even more innovation-minded Frenchmen of his time did not prevent him from warning against rapid changes in society. He also warned of the destructiveness of then undeveloped "ray" and atomic weapons. *The Next Chapter* contemplates wars of genocidal scope—with 30 million deaths in 1947 alone. Equally imaginative, for 1927, is his description of the marshalling of the media to shape and control public opinion on a grand scale. The author's historical works show that he knew how this opinion-moulding had worked in the propaganda for the wars before 1927. The ambitious re-casting of national opinion is shown as the benevolent but arbitrary project of the powerful magnates who control the media of the world, and Maurois envisions unforeseen, even catastrophic, effects from this tampering with the outlook of the masses.

In quality, the science fiction of Maurois can be ranked among the early classics, with impressive insights into human affairs.

—Frank H. Tucker

MAYAKOVSKY, Vladimir (1893-1930). Russian. *The Bedbug* (play), 1960; *The Bathhouse*, in *20th Century Russian Drama*, 1963.

* * *

Vladimir Mayakovsky, the Futurist poet and playwright, is one of the brightest stars in the great constellation of modern Russian literature. His paradoxical fusion of lyrical tenderness and oratorical violence marks a decisive change and renewal in it. Some of his works—even though, or perhaps because, only partly SF—are most representative of the embattled utopianism of the Soviet structure of feeling 1917-30. In poems such as "About It," "150,000,000," and "The Fifth International," in short propagandist pieces such as *Before and Now*, in film scenarios, and most clearly in his three post-revolutionary plays, the mainspring of Mayakovsky's creation was the tension between anticipatory utopianism and recalcitrant reality. An admirer of Wells and London, Mayakovsky wrote his witty masterpiece *Mystery Buffo* to celebrate the first anniversary of the October revolution, envisaging it as a second cleansing Flood in which the working classes, inspired by a poetic vision from the future, get successively rid of their masters, devils, heaven, and (in the 1921 version) economic chaos, and finally achieve a Terrestrial Paradise of reconciliation with Things around them. The revolution is thus both political and cosmic, it is an irreversible and eschatological, irreverent and mysterious, earthy and tender return to direct relationships of men with a no longer alien universe. No wonder that Mayakovsky's two later plays become satirical protests against the threatening separation of the classless heavens from the Earth. The future heavens of the sun-lit Commune remain the constant horizon of Mayakovsky's imaginative experiments, and it is by its values that the grotesque tendencies of petty-bourgeois restoration in *The Bedbug* or of bureaucratic degeneration in *The Bathhouse* are savaged. Indeed, in the second part of both plays, the future—though too vaguely imagined for scenic purposes—irrupts into the play. In *The Bedbug* it absorbs and quarantines the petty "bedbugus normalis" in its bestiary. In *The Bathhouse* the newly proclaimed Soviet Five-Year-Plan slogan of "Time forward!" materializes into the invention of a time machine that communicates with and leaps into the future, sweeping along the productive and the downtrodden characters but spewing out the bureaucrats. The victory over time was for Mayakovsky a matter of central political, cosmic, and personal importance: intrigued by Fyodorov and by Einstein's theory of relativity, he firmly expected it to make immortality possible for men. His suicide in 1930 cut him off in the middle of a fierce fight against the bureaucrats whom he envisaged as holding time back and who engineered the failure of Meyerhold's production of *The Bathhouse*.

—Darko Suvin

NESVADBA, Josef (1926—). Czechoslovak. "The Last Secret Weapon of the Third Reich," in *The Year's Best S-F 10*, edited by Judith Merril, 1965; "Mordair," in *Czech and Slovak Short Stories*, 1967; "The Planet Circè," in *New Writing from Czechoslovakia*, edited by George Theiner, 1969; "Vampire Ltd.," in *Other Worlds, Other Seas*, edited by Darko Suvin, 1970; *In the Footsteps of the Abominable Snowman* (stories), 1970 (as *The Lost Face*, 1971); "Captain Nemo's Last Adventure," in *View from Another Shore*, edited by Franz Rottensteiner, 1973.

* * *

Josef Nesvadba is a practicing psychiatrist. Almost all of his stories are introverted, brooding, and hauntingly effective probings of humanist morality and the "small people" that inhabit the real world of modern, Soviet-dominated Czechoslovakia. Those stories which have appeared in English show his penchant for intellectual and psychological questions; Nesvadba's tales are rarely "upbeat" as they dig beneath appearances, peel away affectations, and discover a universality in man that transcends the hated memories of the Nazis, the heavy presence of Soviet power, and the occasionally wistful reflections about Britons and somewhat distant Americans.

One major collection has appeared in translation, *In the Foot-*

steps of the Abominable Snowman. The best in this assortment is "The Death of an Apeman," a wry retelling of the Tarzan story with a typical twist: the nobleman (German, not English) must commit suicide once he has learned what "civilized" men are like. "Expedition in the Opposite Direction" tells of time travel gone afoul, especially when one's sense of *déjà vu* cannot prevent the inevitable; "The Trial Nobody Ever Heard Of" focuses on petty scientists and their academic wars extrapolated by analogy into the Nazi murderers and their callous inhumanity; "The Lost Face" suggests that even plastic surgery cannot change essentials; "The Chemical Formula of Destiny" examines the uniqueness of genius; "Inventor of His Own Undoing" asks what would happen if everyone worked for fun; "Doctor Moreau's Other Island" grumpily predicts man's inevitable degeneracy; and the title story is a moving tale of wanderlust, perhaps indicative of Nesvadba's sense of isolation.

Other stories which have appeared in English include "Mordair," that suggests a cheap and inhumane solution to fuel costs; "Vampire Ltd.," a beautifully crafted tale of the soul-sucking qualities of the modern automobile; "Captain Nemo's Last Adventure," one of Nesvadba's best, showing the wanderlust and the eternal search for "The Fundamental Question of Life" and its "Final Answer"; "The Planet Circè" which examines the dangers of total indolence and complete satisfaction of childhood desires; and "The Last Secret Weapon of the Third Reich" which recalls the nightmare of the Nazi ability to pit Czech against Czech.

Nesvadba writes with great dexterity, and his stories deserve wider attention in the West. He represents a brand of science fiction quite distinct from either the Russian variety, which sometimes smothers good writing in the cocoon of socialistic theorizing, or from the American-British science fiction, which tends to focus on disasters (man-made or natural) or how heroes with mechanical know-how can undo cosmic evils. Nesvadba is a clear descendent in Czech literature of Hasek and perhaps Polacek, but not Capek. The zest of Capek's furious and ironic humor does not appear in Nesvadba's writing. The vision is narrowed, and Capek's wide-ranging internationalism has been replaced by a poignant sadness, an inner reflection of the fate of the Czech nation.

—John Scarborough

RENARD, Maurice (1875-1939). French. *New Bodies for Old*, 1923; *Blind Circle*, with Albert Jean, 1928; *The Hands of Orlac*, 1929; *The Flight of the Aerofix*, 1932.

*   *   *

Maurice Renard is considered a pioneer of French SF and one of the most important SF writers of the period 1910-30. His first novel, a wildly impressionist fantasy akin to Wells's *The Island of Dr. Moreau*, albeit with more overt sexuality that sometimes rises to strange ecstasies, was *New Bodies for Old*, in which the brain of the hero is transplanted into a bull by one of the proverbial mad scientists of science fiction; the novel ends with an even more fantastic identity change that brings to mind demoniac possession. A similar grafting experiment on a more modest scale (a pianist is given the hands of a criminal), but with hardly less gruesome consequences, appears in the more glib and weaker *The Hands of Orlac*, which is probably better known since it was filmed twice. In *L'Homme Truqué*, finally, a giant is given a pair of electric eyes which turns the world into a nightmarish vision. *Un Homme Chez les Microbes* is an elegant and sophisticated treatment of the journey into a microscopic world, a theme often mishandled in American SF by Ray Cummings. Renard's most ambitious novel, however, is *Le Péril Bleu*, an almost surrealist work with strong Fortean overtones. It introduces a strange civilization of etheric lifeforms, the Oniweig, living on top of our atmosphere and fishing for objects in the air as we might fish the deep seas. They abduct humans and experiment with them, returning them to the surface of Earth only

as a rain of picked bones and skeletons. Another SF novel is *Le Maître de la Lumière*, a fantastic mystery novel about duplicated bodies. His short stories tend towards the mystical and fantastic; a common theme is the relativity of perception, and their favorite device a distortion of perspective: time and space, other dimensions, mirrors, and changed sense organs figure prominently in them, and he is fond of joining together opposites, cold reason as well as feverish dreams.

—Franz Rottensteiner

ROBIDA, Albert (1848-1926). French. "A Forecast of Life in the 20th Century as Seen in 1883," in *Beyond This Horizon*, edited by Christopher Carrell, 1974.

*   *   *

Albert Robida, the French illustrator, lithographer, and writer, was the first artist who raised the anticipation of the future to an art, although he owes much to Grandville and Gustave Doré. He illustrated the work of Rabelais, Swift, and Cyrano de Bergerac, among others, but was most original in his own books, for which he wrote the texts himself. But his prose, generally uninspired, serves only as an artless vehicle for his prophetic imagination, and often deteriorates into mere catalogues of fantastic inventions. His work is somewhat undecided; on the one hand he is a typical representative of the Victorian age, assuming the future to be ruled by the same sets of values as the present; on the other hand he foresees the most amazing future devices, some beneficial, but more often with disastrous social consequences. He surmises pre-marital voyages for young couples to get acquainted with each other—but accompanied by chaperones. Television, dirigible balloons as well as heavier-than-air machines, submarines for undersea sightseeing, giant floodlights—all figure in his work; but he also drew machines and weapons of war, dreadnoughts, tanks, poison gas, submarine and aerial battles, chemical and bacteriological warfare, and he foresaw also the pollution accompanying technological progress. His first work was a gentle satire on Jules Verne entitled *Voyages Trés Extraordinaires de Saturnin Farandoul dans les 5 ou 6 Parties du Monde et dans Tous les Pays Connus et Même Inconnus de Monsieur Jules Verne*, and his comico-serious view of future events is to be found in *Le Vingtième Siècle*, *La Guerre au Vingtième Siècle*, and *La Vie Electrique*. His drawings of even the most horrible weapons are permeated by a 19th-century period charm, and through them he exerted a marked influence on future war stories. His later work, such as *La Guerre Infernale* (with Pierre Giffard) and *L'Ingénieur von Satanas*, was bleaker and more pessimistic, ending in the total collapse of civilization.

—Franz Rottensteiner

STRUGATSKY, Boris (1933—), and **Arkady** (1925—). Soviet. *Far Rainbow*, 1967; *Hard to Be a God*, 1973; *The Final Circle of Paradise*, 1976; *Monday Begins on Saturday*, 1977; *Prisoners of Power*, 1977; *Tale of the Troika*, 1977; *Definitely Maybe*, 1978; *Noon: 22nd Century* (stories), 1978; *The Ugly Swans*, 1979; *Far Rainbow: Second Invasion from Mars*, 1979; *Roadside Picnic*, 1979; *The Snail on the Slope*, 1980; *Beetle in the Anthill*, 1980.

*   *   *

The Strugatskys' early cycle—the trilogy *The Country of Crimson Clouds*, *A Voyage to Amaltheia*, *The Apprentices* and the short stories in *Six Matches* and *Noon: 22nd Century*—is an optimistic "future history" on or near Earth, a not quite systematic series with interlocking characters progressing through the next two centuries. The young explorers and scientists, their vivid and variegated surroundings, are shown in adventure-packed action leading to ethical choice. In this first idyllic cycle, except for egotistic and capitalist survivals, conflicts take place "between the good and the better," basically between man and nature. Yet at its end, doubt and darkness enter into the somewhat aseptically bright horizons. Some protagonists die or retire, some "come home" from cosmic jaunts to Earth and its problems.

The dialectics of innocence and experience, of utopian ethics and historical destructiveness provides henceforth the Strugatskys' main tension. Slavery joins high technology in *An Attempted Escape*, which already uses the effective device of a protagonist caught in a blind alley of history. In this second phase (1962-65), the Strugatskys wrote their first masterpieces, *Far Rainbow* and *Hard to Be a God*, where utopian ethics are put to the test of an inhuman and apparently irresistible wave of destruction. On the small planet Far Rainbow a physical Black Wave, let loose by a joyous community of experimenting creators, destroys them in a clear historical parable. Almost all remaining heroes of the first cycle die here; only the children, and the mysterious deathless man-robot Kamill (a lonely and powerless Reason), are saved. The conflict of militant philistinism, stupidity, and social entropy with utopia is faced without natural-science disguises—and therefore with richer and subtler consequences—in *Hard to Be a God*, a very successful domestication of a historical novel. The hero is an emissary from classless Earth on a feudal planet, instructed to observe without interfering. However, the Earth historians' projection of progress turns out to be wrong; organized obscurantism is killing off intellectuals and destroying all human values. A calamitous twist of history, reminiscent of the worst of Stalinism and Nazism, is vividly recreated and left open-ended. Revolt is undying, but so is inertia. Outside interference would introduce a new benevolent dictatorship: the Earthling "gods" are both ethically obliged and historically powerless to act. The utopian abhorence of class violence and the belief in humanization, faced with intense social devolution, lead to tragic utopian activism. *The Final Circle of Paradise* (the original title means *Predatory Things of Our Age!*) returns to the anticipatory universe of the first cycle. The protagonist, a Soviet cosmonaut turned UN agent, flushes out addictive stimulation of pleasure centers, born of social demoralization and feeding into it, in a wealthy capitalist state. This attempt at localizing historical blind alleys, though vigorous, is neither sufficiently concrete for political criticism nor sufficiently generalized for a socio-philosophical model. *Hard to Be a God* thus remains, in its vivid yet estranged localization and its fusion of public and private, the supreme model of this phase.

Running into increasing pressures, the Strugatskys opted in their third phase (1965-68) for parables with increasingly satirical overtones, in a variety of probings, formal manoeuverings, and reading publics—from the juvenile to the most sophisticated. Formal mastery is joined to sociological bewilderment. The protagonist turns into the privileged point of view, often a naive glance at the disharmonious world with monopolized information channels. In *The Second War of the Worlds* the protagonist is also happy in his conformist ignorance. Now the Martians don't need heat rays and gases to poison a nation but simply local traitors, economic corruption, and misinformation: the muted calamity is more horrible.

In the two interlocked stories of *The Snail on the Slope* a fantastic and symbolic forest with nightmarish time is seen indistinctly from inside and outside by protagonists painfully struggling to understand. The "Kandid" part juxtaposes his stream of consciousness to rural idioms, infuriatingly repetitive and monotonous as the life whose flavor they convey: the dearth of information and impossibility of generalizing, the "vegetable way of life" bereft of history and subject to unknown destructive forces. The "Pepper" part views the forest from the bureaucracy supposedly managing it. The two protagonists come to stand for the alternatives of modern intellectuals faced with power: accommodation versus refusal. Though a culmination of the Strugatskys' escape from politics into ethics, the novel is among their most interesting creations, and the Kandid part a gem of contemporary Russian literature. The publication of *The Ugly Swans* was repudiated by the authors. In a Shchedrinian

satiric city, persistent rainfall signifies the end of a morally corrupt society; the children evolve to higher intelligence and justice with the help of mutant "Wetters," midwives of the New. As in the former novel, the puzzles are left unsolved: all we can infer from the final exodus of the children, through the ambiguous protagonist—a politically suspect writer—and the hardboiled, polemical vernacular, is that our species is doomed.

The novels *Monday Begins on Saturday* and *Tale of the Troika* are linked by the main character. The updating of folktale to embody the "magic" of modern alienated sciences and society results in a loose picaresque work ranging from fun to the Goyaesque horrors of charlatanism and bureaucratic power. *Monday Begins on Saturday* deals primarily with the use and abuse of science. The director of the Scientific Institute for Magic, studying human happiness, has split into scientist and administrator who lives backward; the demagogic charlatan Vybegallo plans a happy Universal Consumer and his homunculus is destroyed just short of consuming the universe. *Tale of the Troika* shows a bureaucratic triumvirate "rationalizing" a country of unexplained phenomena. The Troika's semiliterate jargon and fossilized pseudo-democratic slogans, its incompetent qui pro quos and malapropisms, make for wildly hilarious black humour. Somewhat uneven, this is perhaps the Strugatskys' weightiest experiment.

The post-1968 novels can be thought of as their fourth phase, somber and uneven, often of juvenile heroics amid increasing alienation and desperation. *Prisoners of Power* is very good adventure where the utopian protagonist fights a military dictatorship and its new persuasion technologies. The masterly depiction of various social strata bereft of history, the insights into both oligarchy and underground politics, contrast with the superhero and the happy ending. *Hotel "To the Lost Climber"* and *The Kid* are entertaining lightweights: a mystery with an SF twist, and a "wolfchild" brought up by superior aliens. The weightiest work is *Roadside Picnic*, simultaneously a folktale, utopian quest, and straight psychological novel, with a rich array of standpoints and vernaculars. Somberness prevails in the two recent novels *The Guy from Hell* and *Definitely Maybe*, but both the tough-minded clarity of relationships described and a glimmer of utopian brightness persist.

The Strugatskys' work is at the heart of Soviet SF; its permanent polemic acted as an aesthetic icebreaker. From static utopian brightness in a near future they have moved through a return to the complex dynamics of history to an unresolvable tension between the necessity of utopian ethics and the inhuman inscrutable powers of anti-utopian stasis. There are deficiencies in their vision: the junction of ethics with either politics and philosophy has remained unclear; the localization of events has oscillated somewhat erratically; the socio-philosophic criticism has sometimes fitted only loosely into the SF framework. Nonetheless, half a dozen of the Strugatskys' works approach major literature. Their later phases are a legitimate continuation of the Gogol vein and of the great Soviet tradition of Ilf and Petrov or Olesha, at the borders of SF and satirical fantasy, as in Mayakovsky's late plays, Lem, Kafka, or Carroll. The predatory bestiary into which people without cognitive ethics are transmuted, the strange countries and monsters becoming increasingly horrible certify to their final source in the greatest SF paradigm, *Gulliver's Travels*. The Strugatskys' work has some of Swift's fascination with language—a mimicry of bureaucratic and fanatic jargon, irony and parody, colloquialisms and neologisms. They are polemic at the deepest level of wordcraft and vision, making untenable what they termed the "fiery banalities" of the genre.

Within the Russian tradition, the best of the later Strugatskys reads like an updating of Shchedrin's fables and chronicle of Foolsville. However, the hero and ideal reader is no longer Shchedrin's *muzhik*, but the contemporary scientific and cultural intellectual, the reader of Voznesensky and Voltaire, Wiener and Wells. Many Strugatsky passages read as a hymn to young scientists who are also citizen-activists, inner-directed by and toward "constant cognition of the unknown." The central source of the Strugatskys is an ethics of cognition, sprung from a confluence of utopianism and modern philosophy of science. Such a horizon transcends Russian borders and marks their rightful place in world SF and literature.

—Darko Suvin

TENDRYAKOV, Vladimir (1923—). Soviet. *Three, Seven, Ace, and Other Stories*, 1973.

*   *   *

"A Lifelong Journey" is a departure from Vladimir Tendryakov's usual realistic stories of rural life and moral decision into a "scientific-fantastic" metaphor of human existence. Told in a matter-of-fact linear style, it is the story of the scientist Bartenyev whose disembodied mind is sent on an interstellar voyage while the rest of him works, loves, and dies on earth. The central conflict is Cartesian. The rational mind may hold all of time and space in itself and "be greater than all the universe," yet, isolated in space, it is inhumanly unhappy and "the most meaningless thing" in creation. Similarly, "it is necessary simply to live," but the body alone is purposeless, and "there is no more terrible unhappiness than the happiness of comfort."

Aside from the unifying potentiality of artistic experience and of natural beauty, Tendryakov offers no solution for the contradictions in humanity. His world is constructed to move always in a dual pattern, exclusive and complementary, of good-evil, life-death, thought-being. He warns that any attempt at one-sided reduction leads to falsification of reality and loss of movement; and "to crave motionlessness is just as unnatural as for a healthy individual to think of the grave." The future disturbs me," Tendryakov writes, because the "tormenting puzzles" of the human situation will not only obtain in the future, but will become more urgent with increasing knowledge and power. "To describe the future as a rosy Eden populated with the blessed, means to deceive oneself." His hope is that as science once discovered the laws governing matter and the processes of life, so now it will uncover the essential nature and laws of "thinking life," that mankind may learn to cope with the perennial problems of its existence. "Our future is real," Tendryakov says; "we have to take it seriously."

—Jana I. Tuzar

TERTZ, Abram. Pseudonym for Andrey Sinyavsky (1925—). Soviet. *The Icicle and Other Stories*, 1963 (as *Fantastic Stories*, 1963); *The Makepeace Experiment*, 1965; "Pkhentz," in *Soviet Short Stories 2*, 1968.

*   *   *

Abram Tertz, a literary critic who, after six years in Soviet prison camps, now lives in Paris, can be only marginally claimed for SF, though he has written on the subject. *The Makepeace Experiment* has strong SF aspects, both in its use of thought-reading and thought-control powers by means of which the hero Makepeace becomes for a while ruler of the town of Lyubimov, and as a satirical parable in the vein of Gogol, Shchedrin, and Dostoevsky on Russian messianic utopianism. However, the psi powers are ultimately shown to be a gift from a historical ghost who is exorcised at the same time as the robot tanks break through, and the whole narrative system of the story leads one to call it a fantastic parable. Similarly inconclusive is the clairvoyance in "The Icicle," which the government tries to use but which is lost with the death of the hero's beloved. But the short story "Pkhentz" is brilliant SF, a simultaneously sad, grotesque, and terrible parable on an individual Alien isolated in a claustrophobic, menacing, and repugnant everyday life. Though grounded in the banalities and pettinesses of Soviet reality, it has implications for all situations where stifling social pressures pervade the most intimate strivings of alienated exceptions, who see it with a foreign and estranging eye yet slowly lose their original insight.

—Darko Suvin

TOLSTOY, Alexey (1882-1945). Russian. *The Deathbox*, 1934 (as *The Garin Death Ray*, 1955); *Aelita*, 1957.

*   *   *

Alexey Tolstoy published two collections of poetry before he turned away from both verse and Symbolism to stories and novels in the tradition of 19th-century realism. He emigrated to Germany after the Bolshevik revolution, but returned to Russia in 1923 and became a leading and privileged exponent of the official Socialist Realism, especially in a number of historical novels.

Tolstoy became the first classic writer of Russian SF by giving the fast-developing genre the accolade of literary quality and respectability, much as his model Wells did. In *Aelita* this blend is enriched with a lyrical component, the love of Los, the inventor of the rocketship, for the Martian princess Aelita. Los, the creative intellectual, with his vacillations and individualist concerns, is contrasted to but also allied with Gusev, a shrewd man of the people and fearless fighter who leads the revolt of Martian workers (the Martians are descendants of the Atlantans) against the decadent dictatorship of the Engineers' Council. If the standard adventure and romance were taken over from Wells and pulp SF (e.g., Benoit's *Atlantis* and Burroughs's *A Princess of the Moon*) or indeed from theosophy, the politics are diametrically opposed to Lasswitz's and Bogdanov's idea of a Martian benevolent technocracy. Yet if the workers' uprising led by a Red Army man was a clear parable for the times, such as could have been shared by all Soviet SF from Mayakovsky to Zamyatin, the dejected and somewhat hasty return which has Los listening at the end to the desperate wireless calls of his beloved is clearly of a Wellsian gloom (*The First Men on the Moon*). But this ambiguity, which sometimes strains the plot mechanics, makes also for an encompassing of differing attitudes and levels that follows Bogdanov by envisaging the price as well as the necessity of an activist happiness. This is achieved by plastic characterization, differentiated language, and consistent verisimilitude. Tolstoy's second novel, *The Deathbox* (four versions from 1926 to 1937), is a retreat to the "catastrophe" novel: Vernean adventures and Chestertonian detections and conspiracies center around a well-drawn amoral scientist who beats the capitalist industry kings at their own game but comes to grief when faced with popular revolt. It moves fast if jerkily; as Tolstoy had training in engineering, its science is believable (atomic disintegration of a transuranium element is posited as well as something resembling lasers), and it remains a prototype of the anti-imperialist and antifascist satire-thriller melodrama, always a vigorous strand in Russian SF. The two novels, as well as the stories "Blue Cities" and "The League of the Five" and several plays (including an adaptation of Capek's *R.U.R.*), blended SF adventures (interplanetary flight, the revolt of machines, or global struggle for a new scientific invention) with a utopian pathos arising from revolutionary social perspectives in a way calculated to please almost all segments of the reading public. This blend was to remain the basic Soviet SF tradition till Yefremov, and indeed to the end of the 1960's.

—Darko Suvin

TSIOLKOVSKY, Konstantin (1857-1935). Russian. *Beyond the Planet Earth*, 1960; *The Call of the Cosmos* (miscellany), 1963.

*   *   *

Konstantin Tsiolkovsky lost most of his hearing as a boy, and grew up a lonely eccentric. He became a provincial teacher, writing scientific papers all the while—particularly on aeronautics (from balloons to jet aircraft) and interplanetary travel. A self-made mathematician; he often rediscovered already known hypotheses; yet he also created the theory of rocket flight for interplanetary space (formula for attaining cosmic velocities). Disregarded before the revolution, he was elected to the Socialist Academy in 1918 and given a pension in 1921, when he devoted himself entirely to writing. His SF tales *On the Moon* and *Beyond the Planet Earth* and his anticipatory fictionalized essays bordering on SF, *Dreams of Earth and Heaven: The Effects of Universal Gravitation*, as well as some other anticipatory essays, are collected in *The Call of the Cosmos*, while other essays are collected in *Life in Interstellar Environment*; a number of utopian visions, notably *Sorrow and Genius*, have been relatively slighted.

The deep-seated obsession in all of Tsiolkovsky's writings is liberation from earthly and indeed universal gravity. The cosmic alternative—on rocket spaceships, satellite stations, asteroids, or space colonies—is accompanied by diverse aspects of bliss: perpetual Spring, physical ease and health, utopian-socialist democracy, unheard-of technological achievements, "heavenly life without sorrow," and finally immortality—possibly for individuals and certainly for the human species moving from sun to sun through billions of years. When touching on such a cluster of beatific desire Tsiolkovsky's clear but very pedestrian style rises to passages of a naive poetry, e.g., in descriptions of life-forms on the low-gravity Moon. This is also what makes for the peculiar hybrid genre of these writings, oscillating between fantastic idea and scientific (or popularizing) prose, with the stories just on this and the essays just on that side of an imaginary halfway house. Visionary essays seem the primary form of his expression, while the tales are primarily an attempt at reaching a wider readership. Thus even their clumsy plots and non-existent characterization are an interesting testimonial to the genesis of one kind of SF, the "literature of ideas" (in Tsiolkovsky this embraces also speculations on "etheric" beings, on a photonic phase of mankind and universe, on reversing entropy).

The main literary influences on Tsiolkovsky seem to have been the eccentric Russian philosopher of cosmic utopianism and this-worldly resurrection N.F. Fyodorov, Verne, and Flammarion. In his turn, he stands behind all Soviet writings on cosmic travel, in fiction from Tolstoy and Belyaev to Yefremov and Altov, and in science from Oberth and others down to the Sputnik and Yostok constructors. He remains one of the great pioneers of modern SF, particularly important for his refusal to discriminate between utopia and science.

—Darko Suvin

VARSHAVSKY, Ilya (1909—). Russian. "In Man's Own Image," in *Russian Science Fiction 1968*, edited by Robert Magidoff, 1968; "Out in Space," in *Last Door to Aiya*, edited by Mirra Ginsburg, 1968; "A Raid Takes Place at Midnight," in *Russian Science Fiction 1969*, edited by Robert Magidoff, 1969; "Preliminary Research," in *The Ultimate Threshold*, edited by Mirra Ginsburg, 1970; "Biocurrents, Biocurrents," "Lectures on Parapsychology," "The Noneaters," and "Somp," in *Other Worlds, Other Seas*, edited by Darko Suvin, 1970; "Robby," in *Path into the Unknown*, 1973; "Escape," in *Best SF 1973*, edited by Harry Harrison and Brian Aldiss, 1974.

*　　*　　*

Ilya Varshavsky's main interests are thinking machines, space travel, and advanced medical and mechanical technology. His attitude toward science is generally humorous or ironic, but at times bitingly satiric or questioning. He expresses nostalgia for the beauty and spirit of the 20th century.

Varshavsky's machines are subject not only to the laws of mathematical logic but to those of self-organization which demand that robots eventually develop the impulses and drives of humans. For example, when confronted with "death," they are impelled to reproduce themselves ("Homunculus"); rather than harm their robot children, they choose a life of frustration ("Conflict"); thoughts of soccer and redheads can subvert them ("The Duel");

like any vocabulary-gifted human, they can develop into pompous, abusive, tricky, intellectually perverse beings ("Robby"). Of interest to Varshavsky is the relationship between language and humanness, as well as the obstacles to a robot's thinking processes posed by connotation, non-objective reality, and accidental characteristics.

Varshavsky uses space travel to examine his ideas on closed-circuit systems (animal organisms in "The Noneaters"; time in "The Trap"); the effects of man on other life forms ("Lilac Planet"; "The Noneaters"); the continuity of human qualities, from petty to heroic ("The Return"). He twits simpleton-scientists ("Somp"; "Lectures on Parapsychology"; "A Raid Takes Place at Midnight"); castigates those who sell their minds to blind projects ("Preliminary Research"); and satirizes science-fiction writers who do anything for a plot. He questions both means and ends of psycho-scientists ("Escape") and ponders the human complications of organ transplants ("Plot for a Novel").

—Rosemary Coleman

VERCORS. Pseudonym for Jean Bruller (1902—). French. *You Shall Know Them*, 1953 (as *Borderline*, 1954; as *The Murder of the Missing Ling*, 1955); *The Insurgents*, 1956; *Sylvia*, 1962.

*　　*　　*

Although never really considered a genre writer, Vercors contributed two interesting and well-crafted novels to the field. *Sylva* is a poetic fantasy about a fox that changes magically into a human woman before the eyes of a hunter. The man falls in love with this wereperson, but the peculiarities of her origin provide rather unusual stresses in their married life. *Sylva* bears more than a passing resemblance to David Garnett's fantasy *Lady into Fox*, though with a more coherent plot. There are traces of satire as well, much in the tradition of John Collier's *His Monkey Wife* or Mikhail Bulgakov's *Heart of a Dog*. But Vercors is less a humorist than a novelist, and his novel portrays a touching love story that transcends the gimmick that might otherwise seem central to the story.

At the same time, *Sylva* reflects the concerns mentioned in his more significant novel, *You Shall Know Them*. We are told in the latter that "all man's troubles arise from the fact that we do not know what we are and do not agree on what we want to be." The relevance to the lady into fox theme is obvious, but the statement has equal validity when applied to the latter novel. A thoughtful man becomes aware of the existence of a sub-human race on Earth, the legendary missing link in our own evolutionary climb. Concerned about their exploitation by the rest of humanity, he embarks on a bizarre course to determine their legal humanity. He sires a child which he then kills, confessing himself a murderer and surrendering to the authorities. The stage is hereby set for a precedent-setting murder trial, for if the protagonist is indeed guilty of murder, then the sub-humans must be considered our equal and be protected by the law. If they are not to be considered as human, then he has not in fact committed anything worse than cruelty to animals. In conception, this is one of the finest novels in the genre, establishing and examining a genuine ethical question with ruthless realism. At the same time, it is a well-balanced, craftily written tale that should appeal to all readers. Indeed, the novel has been marketed as a mystery, which in at least one sense it is. But it is also that most rare of creations, a novel of science fiction that tells us something about ourselves and our society.

Only one other of Vercors's novels can truly be said to be science fiction. *The Insurgents* chronicles one man's search for physical immortality, and the perils and prices inherent in both the search and the attainment. Thematically it is remarkably similar to Aldous Huxley's *After Many a Summer*, and in some ways is more effectively handled.

—Don D'Ammassa

VERNE, Jules (1828-1905). French. *Five Weeks in a Balloon*, 1869; *From the Earth to the Moon*, 1869, complete version, 1873 (as *The American Gun Club*, 1874; as *The Baltimore Gun Club*, 1874) (sequels: *All Around the Moon*, 1876; *The Purchase of the North Pole*, 1890); *A Journey to the Centre of the Earth*, 1871; *Twenty Thousand Leagues under the Sea*, 1872; *Doctor Ox and Other Stories*, 1874; *A Floating City, and The Blockade Runners*, 1874; *From the Clouds to the Mountains*, 1874 (as *Dr. Ox's Experiment*, n.d.); *The Mysterious Island: Shipwrecked in the Air* (as *Dropped from the Clouds*), *Abandoned, The Secret of the Island*, 3 vols., 1874-75; *The Voyages and Adventures of Captain Hatteras: The English at the North Pole, The Field of Ice*, 2 vols., 1874-76; *Hector Servadac*, 1877 (as *To the Sun*, 1878; as *Off on a Comet*, 1957; as *Homeward Bound*, 1965; as *Anomalous Phenomena*, 1965); *The Begum's Fortune*, 1879 (as *500 Millions of the Begum*, 1879); *The Steam House: The Demon of Cawnpore, Tigers and Traitors*, 2 vols., 1881; *The Clipper of the Clouds*, 1887 (as *Robur the Conqueror*, 1887; as *A Trip Around the World in a Flying Machine*, 1887) (sequel: *Master of the World*, n.d.); *Adventures of a Chinaman in China*, 1889; *The Winter amid the Ice and Other Stories*, 1890; *The Castle of the Carpathians*, 1893; *The Floating Island*, 1896 (as *Propeller Island*, 1961); *For the Flag*, 1897 (as *Facing the Flag*, 1897); *An Antarctic Mystery*, 1898 (as *The Mystery of Arthur Gordon Pym*, 1960); *The Chase of the Golden Meteor*, 1909 (as *Hunt for the Meteor*, 1965); *The Master of the World*, 1914; *The Lottery Ticket, and The Begum's Fortune*, 1919; *The Barsac Mission: The City in the Sahara, Into the Niger Bend*, 2 vols., 1960; *Village in the Treetops*, 1964.

*   *   *

Jules Verne is without doubt one of the greatest of the founding fathers of the genre, a master of narrative, a purveyor of dreams and adventures which have stirred the blood of countless readers. He was the first writer to attempt to abolish the artificial boundaries between literature and science; a writer who inspired his readers with a desire to find out more about the universe and its hidden forces. Many of Verne's "inventions" were amazingly prophetic.

Verne's work can be placed into two distinct periods—early optimism and later pessimism. At first Verne was an enthusiast about science and conveyed a sense of wonder to his readers which some critics have considered a glorification of "the machine." Verne certainly took pains to ensure the plausibility of his futuristic inventions. His avid reading of scientific journals resulted, in some of his novels, in technical explanations which are perhaps a little tedious and overlong. The cannon which fired his heroes on their classic journey to the moon may seem quaint today but at the time it was a scientific advance on the ideas of establishing men on the moon. H.G. Wells considered it viable even in 1936. The robot (a steam-driven metal elephant in *The Steam House*) and the submarine (in *Twenty Thousand Leagues under the Sea*) are viable propositions. But Verne's most impressive invention was the airship—the 100-foot long, 74-masted, rotor blade-driven machine in *The Clipper of the Clouds*. The inventor of this airship was William Robur, driven on to use his invention for world peace. In fact, Robur's degeneration into a power-hungry megalomaniac in a sequel, *Master of the World*, is typical of the second period of Verne's work—the cynical and worried period in which Verne was convinced that science was overstepping the boundaries of morality.

Verne's increasing concern that science was being misused, seems to have begun with *The Begum's Fortune*, a rather oppressive novel filled with an anti-Utopian vision of industrial power and militarism combined against human progress. This mood continued in *The Floating Island*, the tale of a struggle for supremacy and domination between two factions on an incredible floating city. The internecine strife tears the giant craft apart, and the allegorical intention of the work is unmistakable. Perhaps one of the darkest examples of Verne's cynicism about his fellow man appeared in *For the Flag*, in which an archetypal mad inventor creates a guided missile and uses it to rob shipping in the Atlantic. No longer was science being harnessed for mankind's progress, as in Verne's earlier works, but as weapons against it. Of his grandfather's attitude, Jean Jules-Verne has written:

He lost his blind faith in unlimited progress. The conquest of nature was dependent on the conquest of wisdom—and mankind had no wisdom. Men's pride made them forget the ephemerality of their existence and the wordly possession of a fragile fragment of a precarious world, pride made them continue to indulge in the absurd cruel strife from which they were the first to suffer. Why persist in trying to build on thin air? Civilizations are transitory and collapse in a day after centuries of effort. What good was anything we did in a world destined to die?

Verne was not the earliest science-fiction writer—but he must be acknowledged as being the first writer to develop the genre as a specialized form of literature and make it distinct from fantasy writing, his speculations based on a firm and plausible scientific foundation. For this, and for his amazing gift of prophecy, Verne must be acclaimed as "The Father of Science Fiction."

—Peter Berresford Ellis

WERFEL, Franz (1890-1945). Austrian. *Star of the Unborn*, 1946.

*   *   *

Franz Werfel fled from Nazi Germany, finding refuge in California, the setting of his single contribution to utopian science fiction, *Star of the Unborn*. His expressionism, poetic skill, love for the lush music and grand passions of the opera, religious mysticism, and experience in a society as surreal as fiction combine in a novel much like Olaf Stapledon's vast future panoramas, Dante's *Inferno*, and *Gulliver's Travels*.

Star of the Unborn envisions a huge underground city full of decadent, beautiful, ethereal souls who live over 200 years and avoid physical contact. Summoned from the past to be a wedding guest, F.W. is guided by his old friend, B.H. Unfortunately, since his glasses were left behind, F.W. never sees the world with complete sharpness. The novel tours a world 100,000 years in the future, vividly reporting social customs and chronicling long philosophical conversations. What little plot there is revolves around the atavistic bridegroom, Io-Do, and the lovely bride, Io-La, who develops a crush on F.W. More like a long poetic satire than a blueprint for an ideal world, it is full of brilliant scenes and paradoxes. "I am doing my utmost to avoid any invention in this narrative," Werfel insists.

Star of the Unborn is organized around the three days of F.W.'s visit. In "Irongray Turf" he encounters Mental Man and his society, which uses a "travel puzzle" to move destinations in individuals and prints its news in the stars. In "Djebel and Jungle" he meets the Jew, Idiot, and Worker of the Era, travels in space with an elementary chronosopher class, has three questions answered by the High Floater, and witnesses the first shot of a revolution. In "Flight from the Wintergarden" he visits the Jungle where people drink beer and remain earthy and the Wintergarden where Mental Man goes for Antiception, a sometimes horror-producing form of euthanasia. Finally, the Grand Bishop of the powerful Catholic Church returns him to April 1943.

—Mary S. Weinkauf

YEFREMOV, Ivan (1907-72). Russian. *A Meeting over Tuscarora* (stories), 1946; *Stories*, 1954; *Andromeda*, 1959.

*   *   *

Ivan Yefremov, with degrees in geology and biology, was Professor of Paleontology at the Paleontological Institute in Moscow. His first book of stories was *A Meeting over Tuscarora*, hovering between folk legends, sea and historical romance, scientific popularization, and SF. His first "cosmic" novella was "Stellar Ships" (*Stories*), but it is *Andromeda* which is his breakthrough, the bearer of the post-Stalinist "thaw" in SF, and the supreme achievement of its first phase (1957-63). *Andromeda* achieved this position after a long and acrimonious public debate, unheard of in the USSR since the enthronement of dogmatic literary policy and the Stalinist purges of the 1930's. Against violent ideological opposition, this debate resulted in 1957-58 in the victory of the new wave, which wanted to build upon the pristine Soviet tradition, in abeyance since the Leninist 1920's. The opinion of "warm stream" critics, and of the thousands of readers who wrote to the author, newspapers, and periodicals, that this was a liberating turning-point in Soviet SF, finally prevailed.

Andromeda creatively revived the classical utopian and socialist vision, which looks forward to a unified, affluent, humanist, classless, and stateless world. The novel is situated in year 408 of the Era of the Great Ring, when mankind has established communicational contact with inhabitants of distant constellations who pass information to each other through a ring of inhabited systems. The Earth itself is administered—by analogy with the associative centers of the human brain—by an Astronautic Council and an Economic Council which tallies all plans with existing possibilities; their specialized research academies correspond to man's sensory centers. Within this framework of the body politic, Yefremov concentrates on new ethical relationships of disalienated men. For all the theatrical loftiness of his characters, whose emotions are rarely less than sublime, they can learn through painful mistakes and failures, as distinct from the desperado and superman clichés of "socialist realism" or much American SF after Gernsback.

The novel's strong narrative sweep full of action, from fistfights to encounters with electrical predators and a robot-spaceship from the Andromeda nebula, is imbued with the joy and romance of cognition. Yefremov's strong anthropocentric bent places the highest value on creativity, a simultaneous adventure of deed, thought, and feeling, resulting in physical and ethical beauty. Even his title indicates not only a constellation but also the chained Greek beauty rescued from a monster (here, class egotism and violence, personified in the novel as a bull, and often bearing hallmarks of Stalinism) by a flying hero endowed with superior science. Astronautics thus don't evolve into a new uncritical cult, but are claimed as a humanist discipline, in one of the most significant fusions of physical sciences, social sciences, ethics, and art established as the norm for Yefremov's new people. Such a connection is embodied even in the compositional oscillation between cosmic and terrestrial chapters, where the "astronautic" Erg-Nisa subplot is finally integrated with the "earthly" Darr-Veda subplot by means of the creative beauty of science united to art (Mven-Chara and Renn-Evda). Furthermore, this future is not the arrested, pseudo-perfect end of history—that weak point of optimistic utopianism. Freed from economic and power worries, people must still redeem time through a dialectics of personal creativity and societal teamwork mediated by functional beauty, shown in Dar's listening to the "Cosmic Symphony in F-minor, Color Tone 4.75 u." Creativity is always countered by entropy, and self-realization paid for in effort and suffering. In fact, several very interesting approaches to a Marxist "optimistic tragedy" can be found in Andromeda, e.g., in Mven's "happy Fall": the failed and destructive "null-space" experiment finally leads to great advances. Significantly, the accent on beauty and responsible freedom places at the center of the novel female heroines, interacting with the heroes and contributing to the emotional motivation of new utopian ethics—in contrast to the US SF of those times.

True, *Andromeda* has somewhat dated. In a number of places its dialog, motivation, and rhythm flag, and it falls back on melodrama and preaching. Yefremov's characters tend to be plaster-of-Paris statuesque, and his incidents often exploit the quantitatively grandiose: Mven blows up a satellite and half a mountain, Veda loses the greatest anthropological find ever; Erg is manly, Nisa is pure. One feels in *Andromeda* the presence of an unsophisticated reader, who is, as Yefremov wrote, "still attracted to the externals, decorations, and theatrical effects of the genre," and the presence of the erotic, philosophic, and literary taboos of the cultural context. Yefremov's

epistemology is a naive anthropocentrism: the 19th-century view of man as subject and the universe as object of a cognition that is ever expanding, if necessary through a basic social change yet without major existential consequences. Doubt and the menace of entropy are only external enemies—e.g., the electric predators of a far-off planet; if any epistemological opaqueness ever becomes internalized in a man, then he is a melodramatic villain, such as Pour Hyss.

Yefremov's ideology is thus receptive only to a certain romantically codified range of creativity. His limitations are more clearly manifested in his later works. In *The Heart of the Serpent* Terrans meeting a fluorine-based mankind put an end to its loneliness by promising to transmute fluorine into oxygen. This story—an avowed counterblast to Leinster's "First Contact" with its aggressive and acquisitive presuppositions—might be a legitimate pacifist-socialist allegory for changing US capitalist meritocrats into Russian socialist ones, yet it is curiously ethnocentric. Yefremov's last SF novel, *The Hour of the Bull*, demonstrates this even more clearly. Though he took from Lem and the Strugatskys the device of showing heroes (and heroines) facing anti-utopia, his old preachiness reaches monumental proportions; and the fascist regime of Tormans seems nearer to US pulp SF of the 1930's and 1940's, or indeed to the weirdnesses of Lindsay (from whom the planet's name is taken), than to either the reactionary capitalism or Maoism which Yefremov declared he wanted to hit in one fell swoop. Such parochial views preclude a full development of imaginative SF vistas.

Yet any discussion of such vistas in Soviet SF was made possible by Yefremov's pioneering effort. *Andromeda* has polyphonic scope and a large number of protagonists; it is Tolstoian rather than Flaubertian. Not limited to the consciousness of one central hero, it is one of the first utopias in world literature which successfully shows new characters creating, and being created by, a new society, i.e., the personal working out of a collective utopia (analogous to what Scott did for the historical novel). Yefremov's unfolding the narration as if the anticipated future were already a normative present unites the classic "looking backward" of utopian anticipations with the modern Einsteinian conception of different coordinate systems with autonomous norms: 20th-century science and the age-old Russian folk dreams of a just and happy society meet in his novel. This meeting made it a nodal point of the Russian and socialist SF tradition, and enabled it to usher in the second Golden Age of Soviet SF—an age which closed with the 1960's.

—Darko Suvin

ZAMYATIN, Yevgeny (1884-1937). Russian. *We*, 1924.

*   *   *

Yevgeny Zamyatin wrote some 40 books of fiction, fables, plays, and essays. After the October Revolution he became a prominent figure in key literary groups, but from 1921 he incurred much critical disfavor, eventually culminating in a campaign of vilification, especially after *We* was published in an émigré journal. He died in Paris shunned both by Soviet officialdom and right-wing émigrés.

As all post-revolutionary Russian SF, *We* (written in 1920) deals with the relation of the new Heavens and the old Earth. It incorporates significant features of Zamyatin's novella satirizing life-crushing bourgeois respectability and clerical philistinism written in England during World War I (sex coupons, Taylorite "table of compulsory salvation" through minutely regulated daily occupations). In *We* the Revolution, sunlike principle of life and movement, is opposed to Entropy, principle of dogmatic evil and death. Zamyatin thought of himself as a utopian, more revolutionary than the latter-day Bolsheviks. He is thus not primarily anti-Soviet—even though the increasingly dogmatic high priests of Soviet letters thought so. Extrapolating the repressive possibilities of every strong state and technocratic set-up, including the socialist ones, Zamyatin describes a Unique State 12 centuries hence having for its leader "the Benefactor" (a prototype for Orwell), where art is a public utilitarian service, and science a guide for linear, undeviating happiness. Zamyatin's sarcasm against abstract utopian prescriptions takes on Dostoevskian and Shchedrinian overtones against the totally rationalized city. The only irrational element left is people, like the narrator, the mathematician and rocketship builder D-503, and the temptress from the underground movement who for a moment makes of him a deviant. But man has a built-in instinct for slavery, the rebellion fails, and all the citizen "Numbers" are subjected to brain surgery removing the possibility of harmful imagination.

A practicing scientist, committed to the scientific method, Zamyatin could not seriously blame it for the deformation of life. How was it then that a certain rationalism, claiming to be scientific, became harmful? Zamyatin could answer this only in mythical terms: the victory of any lofty ideal causes it to turn repressive. To the extent that *We* equates Leninist Communism with institutionalized Christianity and models its fable on an inevitable Fall from Eden ending in ironical crucifixion, it has a strong anti-utopian streak. Instead of motivations, it advances through powerful recurring images, unable to reconcile rationalism and irrationalism, science and art (including the art of love). Zamyatin's political ideology conflicts here with his experimental approach: a meaningful exploration would have to be conducted in terms of the least alienating utopia imaginable—one in which there is no misuse of natural sciences by a dogmatic science of man.

Yet the basic values of *We* imply a stubborn vision of a classless new moral world free from all social alienations, a vision common to Anarchism and libertarian Marxism. Zamyatin confronts absolutistic control—extrapolated from both tsarist-bourgeois and early socialist state practices—with a utopian-socialist norm. As he wrote: "We do not turn to those who reject the present in the name of a return to the past, nor to those hopelessly stupefied by the present, but to those who can see the far-off tomorrow—and in the name of tomorrow, in the name of man, we judge the present." His novel brought to SF the realization that the new world cannot be a static changeless paradise of a new religion—albeit of steel, mathematics, and interplanetary flights. The materialist utopia must subject itself to a constant scrutiny; its values are for Zamyatin centered in an ever-developing human personality and expressed in irreducible and subversive erotic passion. For all its resolute one-sidedness, the uses of Zamyatin's bitter and paradoxical warning in a dialectical utopianism seem obvious.

The expressionistic language of *We*, manipulated for speed and economy ("a high voltage of every word"), helps to subsume the protagonist's defeat under the novel's concern for the integrity of man's knowledge (science) and practice (love and art). By sensitively subjecting the deformities it describes to the experimental examination and hyperbolic magnification of SF, Zamyatin's method makes it possible to identify and cope with them. In his own vocabulary, the protagonist's defeat is of the day but not necessarily of the epoch. The defeat in the novel *We* is not the defeat of the novel itself, but an exasperated shocking of the reader into thought and action. Zamyatin's encyclopedic knowledge embraced the SF tradition before and after Wells, from the utopias through the planetary and underground novels to the anticipations of Odoevsky, About, Bellamy, Morris, Lasswitz, Willbrandt, Jack London, and most notably Anatole France. *We* is thus a document of an acute clash between the "cold" and the "warm" utopia: it probably fails to attain full consistency because of the one-sided assumptions, but Zamyatin remains a heretic socialist.

Zamyatin also wrote the SF story "A Story about the Most Important Thing," interleaving developments on three levels—an episode of the Russian civil war, the death of a caterpillar, and four people on a dying "star" (planet, asteroid?) rushing toward destruction on Earth. Its lyrical investigation of the kinds of love and death that are "the most important thing" doesn't quite come off, but presents an interesting literary experiment.

—Darko Suvin

MAJOR FANTASY WRITERS

DUNSANY, Lord; Edward John Moreton Drax Plunkett, 18th Baron Dunsany (1878-1957). Irish. *The Gods of Pegana* (stories), 1905; *Time and the Gods* (stories), 1906; *The Sword of Wellaran and Other Stories*, 1908; *A Dreamer's Tales*, 1910; *The Book of Wonder: A Chronicle of Little Adventures at the Edge of the World*, 1912; *Fifty-One Tales*, 1919 (as *The Food of Death*, 1974); *Tales of Wonder*, 1916 (as *The Last Book of Wonder*, 1916); *Tales of Three Hemispheres*, 1919; *The Chronicles of Rodriguez*, 1922 (as *Don Rodriguez: Chronicles of Shadow Valley*, 1922); *The King of Elfland's Daughter*, 1924; *The Charwoman's Shadow*, 1926; *The Blessing of Pan*, 1927; *The Travel Tales of Mr. Joseph Jorkens*, 1931; *The Curse of the Wise Woman*, 1933; *Mr. Jorkens Remembers Africa* (stories), 1934; *Jorkens has a Large Whisky* (stories), 1940; *The Fourth Book of Jorkens* (stories), 1948; *The Man Who Ate the Phoenix* (stories), 1949; *The Strange Journeys of Colonel Polders*, 1950; *Jorkens Borrows Another Whisky* (stories), 1954; *At the Edge of the World* (selection), 1970; *Beyond the Fields We Know* (selection), 1972; *God, Men, and Ghosts* (selection), 1972.

* * *

While Lord Dunsany may have been a minor figure in Irish literature, the extent of his role in the development of modern fantasy is major. He was a critical influence on H.P. Lovecraft, L. Sprague de Camp, and Fritz Leiber, and his play *King Argimenes and the Unknown Warrior* is one of the sources for Fletcher Pratt's *The Well of the Unicorn*. From his first book, *The Gods of Pegana*, in which he creates an entire pantheon, to his Jorkens series of adventure stories based on his travels in Algeria and the Sudan, to his masterpiece *The King of Elfland's Daughter*, Dunsany belongs with William Morris and George MacDonald as the generating forces of modern fantasy.

Dunsany's fantasy is characterized by his exotic settings; difficult, if creative and frequently numinous, prose; and stalwart protagonists and alluring, exquisite heroines. His ability to create vivid setting is partially explained by his relationship with Sidney H. Sime; Sime's drawings inspired "The Distressing Tale of Thangobrind the Jeweller, and of the Doom that Befell Him" (in *The Book of Wonder*). Dunsany's visual settings are evident in the country village and the activities of love in *The Blessing of Pan* and in the fictional Spanish Golden Age in *The Chronicles of Don Rodriguez* and *The Charwoman's Shadow*. However, his greatest stylistic triumph is the much-heralded *The King of Elfland's Daughter*, and in this novel all the qualities of his fantastic fictions are epitomized. Drawing on the themes of alienation and identity and the structure of the quest, which characterize much of his canon, Dunsany creates an interplay between the world of faery and everyday with his innovative proper names, coined phrases, and characterizations. In the novel Alveric falls in love with an elfin princess, but after she bears him a son she can no longer endure the crude society of mankind and returns to faery. Alveric's quest for his wife provides ample opportunity for Dunsany's ability to create numinous wonder, and the quest is resolved through love and harmony.

The on-going reprinting of Dunsany's tales—especially "The Sword of Welleran" and "The Fortress Unvanquishable Save for Sacnoth"—demonstrates Dunsany's continuing influence on the literature of fantasy, the lasting appeal of his fantastic settings, and his role as a progenitor of modern fantasy literature in all its varieties and techniques.

—Roger C. Schlobin

EDDISON, E(ric) R(ucker) (1882-1945). British. *The Worm Ouroboros*, 1922; *Styrbiorn the Strong*, 1926; *Mistress of Mistresses: A Vision of Zimiamvia*, 1935; *A Fish Dinner in Memison*, 1941; *The Menzentian Gate*, 1958.

* * *

William Morris was an important influence on many later writers, including E.R. Eddison. Eddison's *Styrbiorn the Strong*, a historical romance, is based on materials found in the Norse and Icelandic sagas, and is often considered, with Haggard's *Eric Brighteyes*, one of the best modern depictions of the Viking Age. Four years later, Eddison published *Egil's Saga*, a prose translation of an Icelandic saga. In both works, Eddison mentions Morris's romances and translations.

Eddison's fame, however, rests largely on a work which has much in common with saga and historical romance but is actually pure fantasy, *The Worm Ouroboros*. It is both romantic and epic, filled with the lavish description and heroic adventure that delight fantasy readers. And at the end of the novel, just as the reader and the characters are wishing that it could go on forever, their wish is granted, the action begins all over again, and the plot of the novel, like the worm of the title, becomes circular and eats its own tail. Eddison's Zimiamvian trilogy—*Mistress of Mistresses, A Fish Dinner in Memison*, and *The Menzentian Gate*—which follows *The Worm Ouroboros* and is set in the heaven of the world depicted in that novel, is less successful. Most critics agree that the philosophy Eddison propounds in the Zimiamvian trilogy makes the novels difficult to read, and most readers find them harder going than *The Worm Ouroboros*. *The Menzentian Gate* is especially difficult because it was finished and published after Eddison's death.

—C.W. Sullivan III

MORRIS, William (1834-96). British. *The Earthly Paradise* (verse), 3 vols., 1868-70, revised edition, 1890; *The Story of Sigurd the Volsung and the Fall of the Niblungs* (verse), 1876; *A Dream of John Ball, and A King's Lesson*, 1888; *The Roots of the Mountains Wherein Is Told Somewhat of the Lives of the Men of Burgdale...*, 1889; *News from Nowhere*, 1890; *The Story of the Glittering Plain Which Has Been Also Called the Land of Living Men, or the Acre of the Undying*, 1891; *The Wood Beyond the World*, 1894; *Child Christopher and Goldilind the Fair*, 1895; *The Well at the World's End*, 1896; *The Hollow Land*, 1897; *The Water of the Wondrous Isles*, 1897; *The Sundering Flood*, 1897; *Golden Wings*, 1900; *The Hollow Land and Other Contributions to the Oxford and Cambridge Magazine*, 1903.

* * *

William Morris is primarily remembered in English literature as a poet, artist, and socialist. Yet he is, along with George MacDonald and Lord Dunsany, one of the progenitors of modern heroic fantasy. It would be difficult to imagine Morris not writing heroic or sword-and-sorcery fantasy. His fascination with Iceland led him to learn the language and visit the country, and resulted in his translation and pastiche of *Volsunga Saga* as *The Story of Sigurd the Volsung and the Fall of the Niblungs* and in his early historical novels *The House of the Wolfing* and *The Roots of the Mountains*. It is the barbaric, northern European nature of these works and its continuation in Morris's later fantasies (most commonly referred to as "romances"), particularly *The Glittering Plain* and *The Sundering Flood*, that had such an influence on the work of E.R. Eddison, Fletcher Pratt, and Poul Anderson. This Icelandic fascination was combined with Morris's interest in the Middle Ages and in the dramatic growth of archaeology in the 19th century. Certainly the excavations of the tombs of Egypt, the discovery of the Rossetti Stone (1821), and the deep interest of his Pre-Raphaelite friends in the mysterious and arcane partially generated the presence of the lingering old magics and ancient secrets that are central concerns in his fantasies and are what impressed H.P. Lovecraft and C.S. Lewis with his work.

It is invariably these lingering old magics and their allures or threats that initiate the quests of Morris's heroic protagonists. In his masterpiece, *The Well at the World's End*, the protagonist, a ruler in a medieval realm, and his comrade must confront the price demanded from a well whose water gives drinkers super-human powers. In *The Story of the Glittering Plain* the main character is lured into the realm of immortality. A young boy, Osberne, must mature while using a magic sword, Broadcleaver, given by a mysterious stranger in *The Sundering Flood*, Morris's last fantasy. In *The Wood Beyond the World* a young man pursues a maiden who appears to him and then disappears. He rediscovers her on an island, enslaved by an evil witch. Finally, Birdalone, the heroine of *The Water of the Wondrous Isles*, joins with, is separated from, and reunited with three enchanted maidens in a search for love that must endure a series of magic dangers and barbaric battles.

Thus hidden or pagan magic supplies the catalyst for the narrative tension in Morris's fantasies, and this tension extends to the female characters who frequently personify the polarities of the archetypal Earth Mother. Representing the dark and light aspects of the archetype, Morris's women are either deeply dangerous beings who threaten the protagonists' essential beings, or fecund and impassioned creatures who are keys to life and satisfaction. This characteristic is dramatically illustrated by the polarities represented by the two women in *The Well at the World's End* and is symbolic of the conflict between the pagan and the Christian. However, this also points to one of the least agreeable aspects of Morris's writing. Along with his archaic prose style and oppressive use of whither's, wottest's, hight's, and whilom's, he frequently indulges in the Victorian titillating eroticism and sado-masochism. This tendency is most obvious in William Hope Hodgson's *The Nightland*, but is a common characteristic of Victorian, and Edwardian, fantasies; it is particularly conspicuous in Birdalone's trials in *The Water of the Wondrous Isles*.

Yet the sum total of Morris's fantasies must be that they are uniformly concerned with transition and movement through the quest. These quests invariably move toward communions through trials (rites of passage and initiation) that resolve the numerous tensions the characters endure and that represent the harmonious union of man and nature.

—Roger C. Schlobin

PEAKE, Mervyn (1911-68). British. The Gormenghast books: *Titus Groan*, 1946, *Gormenghast*, 1950, and *Titus Alone*, 1959; *Mr. Pye*, 1953.

* * *

Peake's major fictional works are the three books which relate the heritage, childhood, and adolescence of Titus, 77th Earl of Gormenghast. They are often inaccurately called the Gormenghast Trilogy, but the third volume is not set in Gormenghast, nor were they designed as a trilogy. Peake certainly intended a fourth book, and would probably have written more.

Gormenghast is an immense, ancient castle of crumbling stone and suffocating ritual, set in a wild and dreary land. Its inhabitants, from Count Sepulchrave, suffused in laudanum and antiquarian gloom, down to Swelter, the mountainous chef, make up one of the greatest gallery of grotesques in English literature. Every aspect of their existence is dictated by the Master of Ritual from the Books of the Law, though the observances and ceremonies are so old that no one can even remember their significance. Seizing on his shadowy castle and its atmosphere of doom, many critics have called Peake a gothic writer, but the label is misleading. He makes almost no use of the supernatural, which is essential to Gothic, and his descriptive writing has a visual and tactile solidity foreign to the genre. His characters, with their extraordinary forms and names—Flay, Muzzlehatch, Prunesquallor—are caricatures whose robust and energetic presence recalls Dickens or Rabelais, not Walpole or Radcliffe. Again, Peake is farcical as well as horrific; he writes out of a

relish for life and colour that is hostile to Gothic morbidity, sunlight to its vampires.

Titus Groan is the story of Titus's birth and the ripples of disturbance that spread inexorably from it. He is a natural rebel, impulsive, moody, idealistic; his arrival coincides with the rise of Steerpike, a more sinister figure, who works his way up from kitchen the highest place of power by insinuation, flattery, violence, and murder. The prose is deep, dense, eloquent, and richly detailed. Peake was a painter, and when he used purple he knew exactly what shade and texture he needed.

Gormenghast, which tells of Titus's truant childhood, the growing horror and inhumanity of Steerpike, and their eventual, inevitable confrontation, moves more quickly. Once set going, "change, that most unforgivable of all heresies," spreads like contagion. The rituals are disrupted. Love shows itself in strange distortions, ungainly, absurd, or corrupt. Steerpike is exposed and hunted. Peake loses none of his control as his plot gains momentum. He portrays the adolescent tumult in all its quicksilver ambiguity. Titus's experience of life and death both in and outside the castle brutally confirm his individuality, the impossibility that he will stay there. Disobeying his mother by going in to fight the cornered villain, he is attacking the Master of Ritual and manipulator of lives, powers of Gormenghast that he hates; but he is also ridding the castle of the man who would crush it to dominate it.

Titus Alone is entirely different again, which has put off readers who (unlike Peake) are more interested in Gormenghast than in Titus and the rest of the world. It is, though rarely acknowledged as such, science fiction, from a class somewhere between Huxley's *Brave New World* and Harness's *The Rose*. Titus wanders, exiled and imperilled, in a strange land, a meticulous parody of modern Europe with furnishings and fittings that place it in an imminent, unpleasant future. He is arrested in a city of crystal towers and rockets; he is pursued by machine-like police and a robot flying eye, and hides in the refugee camp of the Under-River with all the malcontents and victims of a damaged civilisation; he falls into the hands of Cheeta, the corrupt daughter of the master of the death factory. Wherever he goes, no one has heard of Gormenghast, and few will believe it exists. Where *Titus Groan* was ponderous and slow, *Titus Alone* is fast and elusive. We barely glimpse the scenes as they whirr by. The effect is intentional, frightening in a way that Peake's other horror fiction never is; but the mysteries and frustrations of the book are, unavoidably, too many. Peake's last illness was well upon him when he began it, and his ability to express his ideas deteriorated as he wrote. The moral vision, at once urgent and subtle, emerges in flashes, or dimly; the novel is a characteristic document of the 20th century, damaged, hallucinatory, but intensely purposeful. (Langdon Jones's 1970 edition is the best possible version of what Peake had in mind).

"Boy in Darkness" tells an extra story of Titus Groan, though without naming him. After the rituals of his 14th birthday he slips away from the castle into the wilderness, where he meets two old creatures called Goat and Hyena. They take him to the Blind Lamb, a malevolent deity who lives deep in an abandoned mine where once, like Comus, he commanded a rout of beasts transformed from human originals. The Goat and the Hyena are the last of this crew. He begins the metamorphosis of Titus, who fights back at the last minute for his humanity and that of the two pathetic courtiers. More sombre than almost any episode in the novels, "Boy in Darkness" has been read by some as spiritual, perhaps blasphemous, allegory, though interpretation was never the purpose of Peake's imaginings. Certainly the story is his most chilling and sensuous exercise in the macabre, far superior to the merely gruesome "Same Time, Same Place" and the ghoulish "Danse Macabre." *Mr. Pye*, Peake's only other novel, was unsuccessful when it was published because of expectations aroused by the Titus books. It is comic fantasy of a very different kind: a remarkable mixture of farce and fable, lighter in tone than the Titus books, but more exclusively adult in appeal. Set on Sark, it records the misadventures of a charming, irritating, self-appointed missionary whose work of disseminating love among the close, suspicious islanders is upset when God, "the Great Pal," rewards him rather too literally.

It can be said that Mervyn Peake lived before his time, and died too soon. Best known during his life for his dense, vigorous illustration of works by authors from Carroll to Coleridge, he also produced poetry, paintings, plays for radio and stage, and theatrical designs, as well as the prose fantasy for which he is now most famous. An eccentric to his own generation, he has been rightly honoured as a master by the next—unfortunately too late to know or benefit by it.

—Colin Greenland

TOLKIEN, J.R.R. (1892-1973). British. *The Hobbit, or, There and Back Again*, 1937; *Farmer Giles of Ham*, 1949; *The Lord of the Rings: The Fellowship of the Ring*, 1954, *The Two Towers*, 1955, *The Return of the Ring*, 1956, revised edition, 1966; *The Adventures of Tom Bombadil and Other Verses from the Red Book*, 1962; *Tree and Leaf*, 1964; *Smith of Wootton Manor*, 1967; *The Road Goes Ever On* (verse), 1968; *Bilbo's Last Song*, 1974; *The Father Christmas Letters* (juvenile), 1976; *The Silmarillion*, edited by Christopher Tolkien, 1977; *Unfinished Tales of Numenor and Middle-Earth*, edited by Christopher Tolkien, 1980.

*   *   *

In 1937, J.R.R. Tolkien published *The Hobbit*. The story, now a classic of the genre, introduces the reader to hobbits and their culture in Middle Earth. As the tale develops, we are to meet characters that step into Bilbo's adventure out of folk legend and fairy story: a wizard, dwarfs bent upon revenge and the recovery of a fabulous treasure, trolls, goblins, elves both magical and dangerous, a bear-man changeling, and above all the great dragon Smaug. Much of the story's success depends upon the way in which Tolkien introduces us to the character of Bilbo Baggins, the hobbit whose uneventful life as a comfortable bachelor at Bag End is forever upset by the intervention of Gandalf the wizard who leads Thorin Oakenshield and his company of dwarfs to Bilbo's door with the promise that Bilbo will prove to be a daring and resourceful burglar, and just the person needed to win back the treasure of the dwarfs from Smaug. Bilbo is an unwilling adventurer who loves his comfortable hobbit hole and his reputation as a respectable member of a community of innocent, good-natured burghers. Tolkien manages successfully the difficult task of keeping the comic dimensions of Bilbo's character pleasantly in focus while at the same time developing the equally endearing qualities of good humor, humility, moral courage, and a temperate mind.

In the course of the action, two things are happening. The first is the discovery of the shape, constitution, and nature of Middle Earth and its wondrous if sometimes menacing inhabitants. Tolkien opens a prospect of unexplored territory in fairyland, and rarely misses an opportunity to enrich the reader's imagination with new and permanent boundary markers. The second is that, in the course of the action, Bilbo comes to discover his limitations but also his own powers and his place in the wide world. Tolkien has shaped the action of Bilbo's quest as correlative to the experience of growing up. His adventures remind us with the solicitude of a wise parent: be yourself, trust your instincts for good, overcome your belittling fears, be generous and brave always, be courteous, especially in strange company or in foreign lands, be resourceful, and the world will discover your worth and praise your accomplishments, and you will be numbered with the mighty and powerful.

Since Bilbo's initiation into life is one of the substructures shaping this narrative, part of his learning experience comes from rubbing elbows with creatures of other kinds and species. He learns about the special virtues, powers, and shortcomings of dwarfs, elves, orcs, goblins, wizards, and men. He learns a bit of the history and lore of Middle Earth and of the polite conventions that make common action possible between variant races and species. In learning these things, Bilbo comes to understand himself better as a hobbit and to see his place and that of his kind in the great scheme of things, although the full revelation of that awaits *Lord of the Rings*. Bilbo learns to his surprise, discomfort, and eventual satisfaction

that he has a role to play in life and in the great adventures of the wide world—even of the wild world.

Tolkien made a revision of *The Hobbit* after he had completed the trilogy *The Lord of the Rings*. The revision was a major one, raising the tone and characterization considerably above the original child's story level to the threshold of the legendary, making it more consistent with the great sequel to which, in a way, it gave birth. Also Tolkien made some adjustments in the details of the original story so as to bring them into line with the more serious mythology of the trilogy.

In the end, the greatness of the trilogy has to be assessed on the basis of what Tolkien attempted. The trilogy is, of course, fantasy, an extension of the fairy-story elements of *The Hobbit* into the heroic tradition. Some critics have called it "high fantasy," others myth, still others saga, legend, even science fiction and "super science fiction." Tolkien himself described the trilogy as "feigned history," and as such it is best understood. Feigned history is imagined history, which is not at all the same thing as imaginary history. Tolkien insisted that he did not simply make up his world rather discovered it in the logic of what had come before it: language, then ethology, geology, botany, and so on.

The trilogy, then, is an imagined history that records the great events which led to the closing of the Third Age of Middle Earth and the disappearance of the elves, dwarfs, and other intelligent creatures who formerly shared it with men. After the beginning of the Fourth Age, legends, sagas, and tales would deal primarily with the exploits of humans. In the actions Tolkien records, we are meant to see the completion of an enormous cycle that had its origins in the uttermost West at the start of the First Age. The full import of these early events and their true character had to await the revelations of *The Silmarillion*. But Tolkien makes it clear that in each of the successive eras that make up the three great ages of Middle Earth, we find moments when the choices of individuals (Valar, elves, men, dwarfs and other creatures) can change the course of history for good or ill. The tale of Middle Earth is the record of those freely made but not always wisely made choices.

We see Tolkien's feigned history itself becoming history by imitating the ways our envisioning and understanding of the past are formed out of the filaments of myth upon the loom of time. In this practice we find an important clue to Tolkien's powers of mythologizing. Tolkien truly possessed the "archetypal imagination," as Philip Wheelwright has said, and that includes the ways Tolkien fulfills stereotypes in his characters and their behavior. It is also revealed in the ways he connects his own anterior mythology with the existing legends of Faerie and its inhabitants as recorded by the epics and sagas of the ancients and the romances of medieval writers. As the result, the reader has the sensation of a curiously interwoven relationship between mythologies that have become in Middle Earth anachronistically present to one another. The character of Treebeard the Ent illustrates the sense in which talking and bleeding trees in Virgil, Spenser, and Frank L. Baum are recognized as later manifestations of the archetypal form Tolkien has invented. For those who enjoy fantasy as a game of the imagination, here is the game of games.

The scope, the tone, and the feigned historical context of the trilogy are both heroic and mythic, genuinely so. Both fantasy and SF continue to preserve these experiences and literary conventions until once again they become critically respectable. Those critics who have damned the trilogy as simplistic and juvenile are reacting in part to the tradition in which it is written and to that which the tradition bears witness, namely, the felt presence of supernatural agencies and a moral order that depends on absolutes transcending time, place, and even the human dimension. Many who have praised it nevertheless argued that its success depends on Tolkien's inspired use of hobbits once again as mediums for the reader's own experiences of Middle Earth. Others have stressed the similar archetypal quest motif underlying both the trilogy and *The Hobbit*, which is undeniable. One need only look to the way the ring is treated in both works, however, to understand the great gulf that lies between the two works. In *The Hobbit* the ring is used by Bilbo to disappear at convenient and even necessary times. Even after Tolkien revised it, to work in hints, suggestions, and foreshadowings of something more, nothing quite prepares us for the sinister intensity and terrible beauty of the Ring Rime and everything that it stands for. In the trilogy, the Ring Rime is not Tolkien's poem; it is

Sauron's. Its rhythms, its single-minded purpose, its dark intent, its craftsmanship, and its power are all his; and it is the first thing we are introduced to when we open the trilogy: "One ring to rule them all and in the darkness bind them/In the Land of Mordor where the shadows lie." Tolkien the poet is revealed as a great writer, not because the poetry itself is great, but because it becomes a key to understanding something in the nature of the character, even something in the nature of a whole race, that only poetic utterance can express. Thus in Tolkien's world, incantation or even the jogtrot doggerel of a hobbit becomes revelation. Tolkien is not uniformly successful in doing these things, of course, but his skill as a writer and storyteller is equal to the vision realized in *The Lord of the Rings* as something more than heroic epic, or even mythic fantasy, because Tolkien makes his history an amalgam of these and other, lesser elements.

Four years after his death, *The Silmarillion*, the incomplete work of a lifetime was published, edited out of the many unresolved drafts and versions of the stories that taken together make up, even in its present state, the supreme achievement of Tolkien's career. We now have the essential pieces of Tolkien's breathtaking vision of the creation of Faerie and of the ages preceding the main action of the trilogy. Included are "Ainulindale" (Tolkien's creation myth: the elvish word means literally "Music of the Ainur"), "Valaquenta" (the lore of the elves regarding the Valar and the Maiar), "Quenta Silmarillion" (the lore of the Silmarils embracing the history of the Noldor elves in the first age), "Akallabeth" (Tolkien's Atlantis myth of the downfall of Numenor), and "Of the Rings of Power and the Third Age" (which fills in the gap with a sketch of the main events surrounding Sauron's forging of the one ring in the Second Age and those events of the Third Age preceding *The Hobbit*).

The Lord of the Rings and *The Silmarillion* are not merely great fantasy; they are great literature. Tolkien will continue to interest scholars and students who have already begun the exhaustive study of his work, its sources, inspirations, and its elements. There is little doubt that Tolkien will eventually take his place somewhere in the neo-romantic movement which followed the aestheticism and decadence of the late 19th century. He has already been placed in the tradition of writers like Rider Haggard and William Morris, and the influences of the Eddas, the Kalevela, Anglo-Saxon, and Middle English romance have already been noted and will doubtless yield more secrets in the future. Nor should we ignore the influence of the Inklings and their interest in Tolkien's work during the long, difficult years before recognition came. Other students will consider the relation or at least the parallels to contemporary writers of fantasy like Mervyn Peake and Austin Tappan Wright. In the end, it may be that Tolkien will be understood best when linked and compared to James Joyce, an unlikely pairing, perhaps, but one that is full of telling comparisons and contrasts.

—Donald L. Lawler

NOTES
ON
ADVISERS
AND
CONTRIBUTORS

ABOULAFIA, Mitchell. Assistant Professor of Philosophy, University of Houston, Clear Lake City. **Essay:** Robert F. Young.

ALDISS, Brian. See his own entry. **Essay:** Jeni Couzyn.

ARBUR, Rosemarie. Associate Professor of English, Lehigh University, Bethlehem, Pennsylvania. Author of books on Leigh Brackett, Marion Zimmer Bradley, and Anne McCaffrey, and of articles in *Survey of Science Fiction Literature*, 1979, and in journals. **Essays:** Leigh Brackett; Marion Zimmer Bradley.

BACIG, Thomas D. Associate Professor of English, University of Minnesota, Duluth; Editor of *Minnesota English Newsletter*. Author of articles in *Arizona English Bulletin*, *Minnesota English Journal*, and *Choice*. Editor of *Newman Annual*, 1961. **Essay:** Norman Spinrad.

BARBOUR, Douglas. Associate Professor of English, University of Alberta, Edmonton; Poetry Editor, *Canadian Forum*. Author of several books of poetry—the most recent being *Visions of My Grandfather*, 1977, and *Shore Lines*, 1979—and *World Out of Words: The SF Novels of Samuel R. Delany*, 1979. **Essays:** Brian Aldiss; Edward Bryant; Samuel R. Delany; Carol Emshwiller; Phyllis Gotlieb; Barry N. Malzberg; Keith Roberts; Chelsea Quinn Yarbro.

BARLOW, George W. Author of short stories and essays in French science-fiction magazines; contributor to and translator of *Le Livre d'Or de John Brunner*. **Essays:** Jean-Pierre Andrevon (appendix); J.G. Ballard; John Brunner; Thomas M. Disch; Aldous Huxley; Michel Jeury (appendix).

BARNES, Myra. Teacher. Author of *Linguistics and Language in Science Fiction-Fantasy*, 1975. **Essays:** James Hilton; Hank Searls.

BARR, Marleen S. Assistant Professor of English, Virginia Polytechnic Institute and State University, Blacksburg. Author of the forthcoming books *Future Females: A Critical Anthology* and *The Diary of Deborah Norris Logan*. **Essays:** Suzy McKee Charnas; Josephine Saxton.

BARROW, Craig Wallace. Associate Professor of English, University of Tennessee, Chattanooga. Author of the forthcoming book *Montage in Joyce's Ulysses*, and of many essays and reviews. **Essays:** Piers Anthony; John Barth; Jack L. Chalker; Brian Moore; Gore Vidal.

BERMAN, Ruth. Instructor in English, University of Oklahoma, Norman. Author of *Patterns of Unification in Lewis Carroll's Sylvie and Bruno*, 1974, science-fiction and fantasy stories in magazines, and reviews for *F and SF Review*. **Essay:** Isidore Haiblum.

BISHOP, E.R. Associate Professor of Mathematics, Acadia University, Wolfville, Nova Scotia. **Essays:** Felix C. Gotschalk; Thomas Pynchon; Mordecai Roshwald.

BISHOP, Michael. See his own entry. **Essays:** Gardner Dozois; Suzette Haden Elgin; Steven Utley; Ian Watson.

BLACKFORD, Russell. Tutor in English, Monash University, Clayton, Victoria. Author of a forthcoming essay on Vonnegut in *Science Fiction: A Review of Speculative Literature*. **Essays:** Damien Broderick; William S. Burroughs; Rick Raphael.

BOSKY, Bernadette. Teaching Assistant, Duke University, Durham, North Carolina. Author of an essay in *Ursula K. Le Guin*, 1979. **Essays:** David A. Drake; Richard S. Shaver.

BRENNAN, John P. Assistant Professor of English, Indiana University-Purdue University, Fort Wayne. **Essays:** L. Ron Hubbard; Spider Robinson.

BRIGG, Peter A. Associate Professor of English, University of Guelph, Ontario. Author of articles in *Arthur C. Clarke*, 1977, *Ursula K. Le Guin*, 1979, *Survey of Science Fiction Literature*, 1979, and in several periodicals including *Mosaic* and *Science-Fiction Studies*. **Essays:** Jerome Bixby; Lester del Rey; Richard Rohmer; Philip Wylie.

BRINEY, R.E. Professor of Mathematics and Chairman of the Computer Science Department, Salem State College, Massachusetts; Editor, *Rohmer Review*. Author of *SF Bibliographies* (with Edward Wood), 1972, essays in *The Mystery Writer's Art*, 1971, *The Conan Grimoire*, 1971, and *The Mystery Story*, 1976, and of articles and bibliographies in journals. Editor of *Master of Villainy: A Biography of Sax Rohmer*, 1972; Co-Editor of *Multiplying Villainies: Selected Mystery Criticism* by Anthony Boucher, 1973; Contributing Editor of *Encyclopedia of Mystery and Detection*, 1976. Member of the Board, *Views and Reviews*, 1972-75, and a founder, Advent Publishers. **Essays:** Juanita Coulson; Robert Coulson; August Derleth; Gene DeWeese; Curme Gray; Henry Kuttner; Rog Phillips; Frank M. Robinson; Francis Stevens.

BRIZZI, Mary T. Associate Professor of English, Kent State University, Kent, Ohio; Associate Editor, *Extrapolation*. Author of *Philip José Farmer: A Reader's Guide*, a forthcoming study of Anne McCaffrey, and reviews in *Choice*. **Essays:** Philip José Farmer; H.F. Heard; Anne McCaffrey.

BRUNNER, John. See his own entry. **Essays:** Jorge Luis Borges (appendix); Italo Calvino (appendix); Rudyard Kipling.

BURNS, Karen. Instructor in English, Alvin Community College, Texas. **Essay:** Fredric Brown.

CARACCIOLO, Peter. Lecturer in English, Royal Holloway College, London University; science fiction reviewer for *The Tablet*. Author of articles on Dryden, Defoe, Wilkie Collins, Doyle, Emily Brontë, Chesterton, Wyndham Lewis, Sheridan Le Fanu, Lady Gregory, and the landscape garden. **Essay:** Michael Moorcock.

CARTER, Steven R. Assistant Professor of English, University of North Carolina, Wilmington; Co-Editor, *Tugboat Review*. Author of articles on mystery fiction, black literature, and science fiction in *Dimensions of Detective Fiction*, *Popular Culture Association Newsletter*, and *Armchair Detective*. **Essays:** Sam Greenlee; Harry Harrison; William Melvin Kelley; Ayn Rand; John A. Williams.

COLEMAN, Rosemary. Associate Professor of Literature, Illinois Benedictine College, Lisle. **Essays:** Peter Tate; Ilya Varshavsky (appendix).

COLLINS, T. Author of several books. Editor of *A Winter Wish and Other Poems* by H.P. Lovecraft, 1977. **Essays:** Jack London; Harold Bell Wright.

COUGHLAN, Gary. Teacher. **Essay:** Patrick Moore.

COWPER, Richard. See his own entry. **Essays:** William Golding; George Orwell.

COX, J. Randolph. Reference and Documents Librarian, and Assistant Professor, St. Olaf College, Northfield, Minnesota. Author of bibliographies and studies of John Buchan, M.R. James, the Nick Carter authors, George Harmon Coxe, and others for *Dime Novel Roundup*, *Baker Street Journal*, *Edgar Wallace Newsletter*, *English Literature in Transition*, *Armchair Detective*, and other journals. **Essays:** Ron Goulart; Luis P. Senarens; Arthur Train; Edgar Wallace; Dennis Wheatley.

CULE, Michael. Actor; recently worked with Ken Campbell's Science Fiction Theatre of Liverpool. **Essays:** Randall Garrett; Robert Anton Wilson.

CUSHING, Charles. Adult Services Librarian, Hamilton Public Library, Ontario. **Essays:** Robert Abernathy; Stephen Vincent Benét; Stuart Gordon; Charles L. Harness.

D'AMMASSA, Don. Production Control Manager, Taunton Silversmiths. Former Editor of *Mythologies* and *Critical Mass*; reviewer for *SF Chronicle* and other magazines. **Essays:** J.F. Bone; Sydney J. Bounds; David R. Bunch; Paul Capon; D.G. Compton; Alfred Coppel; Lee Correy; Larry Eisenberg; E. Everett Evans; H.B. Fyfe; Jack C. Haldeman; Jon Hartridge; Philip E. High; Laurence Manning; Dean McLaughlin; Dan Morgan; Ray Nelson; Jerry Pournelle; Christopher Priest; John Rackham; Francis G. Rayer; Sarban; Richard Saxon; William M. Sloane; George H. Smith; Stephen Tall; Robert Thurston; Vercors (appendix); Roger Lee Vernon; Richard Wilson.

DRAKE, David A. See his own entry. **Essays:** Arthur Porges; Donald Wandrei; Stanley Waterloo.

ECKLEY, Grace. Professor of English, Drake University, Des Moines, Iowa. Author of *Benedict Kiely*, 1972, *Edna O'Brien*, 1974, and a forthcoming study of Finley Peter Dunne; co-author of *Narrator and Character in Finnegans Wake*, 1974. **Essays:** John Boland; John Cowper Powys; Leon E. Stover.

EDWARDS, Karren C. Teacher. **Essays:** Fenton Ash; Arsen Darnay; Alan E. Nourse.

EDWARDS, Malcolm. Administrator, Science Fiction Foundation, London, and Editor, *Foundation*, London. Editor of *Vector*, 1972-74; Science Fiction Editor for Gollancz publishers, 1976-77.

EGGELING, John. Science fiction bibliographer.

EISENSTEIN, Alex. Author of several science-fiction short stories with Phyllis Eisenstein. **Essay:** C.M. Kornbluth.

ELKINS, Charles. Associate Professor of English, Director of the Humanities Program, and Associate Dean for College Programs, Florida International University, Miami; Co-Editor, *Science-Fiction Studies*. Author of a chapter in *Isaac Asimov*, 1977, and of essays in *Survey of Science Fiction Literature*, 1979, and periodicals.

ELLIS, Peter Berresford. Author of *H. Rider Haggard: A Voice from the Infinite*, 1978. **Essays:** Kingsley Amis; Charles Chilton; Christopher Hodder-Williams; William F. Nolan; Jules Verne (appendix).

FONTAINE, Eric A. Free-lance Writer; author of articles on contemporary French and Latin American literature. **Essay:** William Jon Watkins.

FRANE, Jeff. Free-lance Editorial Consultant; Editor of *Locus*. Author of *A Reader's Guide to Fritz Leiber*, 1980, and of numerous articles and reviews. **Essays:** Charles L. Grant; Elizabeth A. Lynn.

FROESE, Robert. Instructor, Department of Media and Communications, North Shore Community College, Beverly, Massachusetts. **Essays:** Alfred Bester; Kurt Vonnegut, Jr.

GAAR, Alice Carol. Librarian, Tennessee Technological University, Cookeville. Co-Author of *Deutsche Stunden*, 1964; author of articles in *Robert A. Heinlein*, 1978, *Quarber Merkur*, *Science-Fiction Studies*, and *SForum*. **Essay:** Herbert W. Franke (appendix).

GARNER, John V. High school language director. **Essay:** Mark S. Geston.

GILLINGS, Walter. Editor and Publisher of British science fiction from the 1930's; Editor of *Tales of Wonder*, *Scientifiction*, *Fantasy Review*, *Science Fantasy*, and *Cosmos Science-Fantasy Review*; Associate Editor of Utopian Publications, and Founding Director of Nova Publications. Died, 1979. **Essays:** Miles J. Breuer; John Russell Fearn; S.P. Meek; Bob Olsen; Festus Pragnell; Eric Frank Russell; Garrett P. Serviss; A. Hyatt Verrill; Harl Vincent; G.C. Wallis; J.M. Walsh.

GOLDMAN, Stephen H. Associate Professor of English, University of Kansas, Lawrence. Author of articles in *Survey of Science Fiction*, 1979, and *Science-Fiction Studies*. **Essays:** Tom Godwin; James E. Gunn; Daniel Keyes; Jack Vance; Stanley G. Weinbaum.

GORDON, Joan. Graduate Student, University of Iowa, Iowa City. Author of a two-volume correspondence course on science fiction and of a forthcoming book on Joe Haldeman. **Essays:** Joe Haldeman; Walker Percy.

GREENBERG, Martin H. Associate Professor of Political Science, University of Wisconsin, Green Bay. Co-Founder of Gnome Press; Editor of many thematic anthologies of science fiction. **Essays:** Christopher Anvil; Chan Davis; F.L. Wallace.

GREENLAND, Colin. Lexicographer. Author of a forthcoming study of New Wave science fiction, *The Entropy Exhibition*, and of reviews for *Foundation*. **Essays:** Mick Farren; Langdon Jones; Mervyn Peake (appendix); Walter Tevis; D.M. Thomas.

HALL, H.W. Serials Librarian, Texas A and M University, College Station; Member of the Executive Committee and Editor, Science Fiction Research Association. Author of *Science Fiction Book Review Index*, 1975 (and later volumes).

HARDING, Lee. See his own entry.

HARRIS, Rose Flores. Instructor in English, Galveston College, Texas. **Essays:** H.H. Hollis; Pamela A. Zoline.

HARTWELL, David G. Editor, Pocket Books, New York. **Essays:** Peter Dickinson; Peter George; John Sladek; Frank R. Stockton.

HASSLER, Donald M. Professor of English and Acting Dean, Honors and Experimental College, Kent State University, Kent, Ohio. Author of *Erasmus Darwin*, 1973, *The Comedian as the Letter D: Erasmus Darwin's Comic Materialism*, 1973, and of essays on Theodore Sturgeon and Isaac Asimov. **Essays:** Harry Bates; James Blish; Hal Clement; Raymond Z. Gallun; David H. Keller; Gérard Klein (appendix); Norman L. Knight; Murray Leinster; Nat Schachner; Stanley Schmidt; B.F. Skinner.

HERBERT, Rosemary. Librarian, Harvard College Library, Cambridge, Massachusetts; Science Fiction Book Review Editor, *Library Journal*. **Essays:** David F. Bischoff; G.K. Chesterton; Arthur Conan Doyle; E.M. Forster; Lee Killough; Ursula K. Le Guin; Madeleine L'Engle; George R.R. Martin; Thomas F. Monteleone; Doris Piserchia; Marta Randall; Margaret St. Clair; Bob Shaw; Evelyn E. Smith; Brian M. Stableford.

HILLS, Norman L. Director of Data Processing, Iowa Hospital Association. **Essays:** Lawrence Durrell; Jean Mark Gawron; Fritz Leiber; Christopher Stasheff.

HUGHES, Terry. Free-lance Writer. **Essay:** Lee Hoffman.

HULL, Elizabeth Anne. Assistant Professor of English, Harper College, Palatine, Illinois; North American Secretary of World SF, and Founder of the Science Fiction Oral History Association. Author of essays in *Extrapolation*, *Essays in Arts and Sciences*, *Destinies*, and *Starlog Science Fiction Yearbook*. **Essays:** Lloyd Biggle, Jr.; Robert A. Heinlein; Judith Merril.

HUNT, Marvin W. Graduate Student in English, University of North Carolina, Chapel Hill. **Essays:** Paul W. Fairman; Tom Purdom; Louis Trimble.

IKIN, Van. Senior Tutor in English, University of Western Australia, Nedlands; Editor and Publisher of *Science Fiction: A Review of Speculative Literature*. Editor of *Enigma*, 1972-79. **Essays:** John Baxter; Frank Bryning; Sumner Locke Elliott; Lee Harding; George Turner.

JONES, Anne Hudson. Assistant Professor of Literature and Medicine, Institute for the Medical Humanities, University of Texas Medical Branch, Galveston; Member of the Editorial Board, *The Comparatist* and *Texas Reports on Biology and Medicine.* Author of a forthcoming book on Kate Wilhelm. Chairperson, "Feminist Science Fiction," Modern Language Association conference, 1977. **Essays:** Katherine MacLean; Joan D. Vinge.

JONES, Robert L. Professor of English and Chairman of the Department, Radford University, Virginia; Humanist in Residence, Rosenberg Library, Galveston, Texas, 1980-81. Author of the forthcoming books *Style and Value Structures in English* and *A Reader's Guide to Gordon R. Dickson.* **Essays:** Damon Knight; Arthur Koestler; Albert Bigelow Paine.

JURKIEWICZ, Kenneth. Assistant Professor of English, Central Michigan University, Mount Pleasant. Author of articles on film and popular culture in *College Composition and Communication* and other journals. **Essays:** Pierre Boulle (appendix); Fletcher Knebel; Curt Siodmak.

KAGARLITSKY, Julius. Professor at the Moscow Theatrical Institute. Author of *The Life and Thought of H.G. Wells,* 1966; *What Does It Mean, SF?,* 1974; *Russian Estimation of the Enlightenment Theatre in the West,* 1976; *Shakespeare and Voltaire,* 1980. Editor of a 15-volume edition of works by Wells, 1964. **Essay:** John Wyndham.

KARP, Hilary. Associate Professor of Behavioral Science, University of Houston, Clear Lake City. **Essay:** Emma Tennant.

KELLEY, George. Instructor in English, Erie Community College, Buffalo, New York. **Essays:** Mark Clifton; Miriam Allen deFord; Joe L. Hensley; Zach Hughes; Leo P. Kelley; Milton Lesser; Jack Sharkey.

KETTERER, David. Professor of English, Concordia University, Montreal; Consulting Editor, *Science-Fiction Studies.* Author of *New Worlds for Old: The Apocalyptic Imagination, Science Fiction, and American Literature,* 1974, and of articles in *Journal of American Studies, PMLA,* and *Texas Studies in Literature and Language.* Editor of the forthcoming *The Science Fiction of Mark Twain.*

KINNAIRD, John. Member of the English Department, University of Maryland, College Park. Author of a forthcoming book on Olaf Stapledon. Died, 1980. **Essays:** J.B.S. Haldane; Olaf Stapledon.

LAKE, David. See his own entry. **Essay:** C.S. Lewis.

LAWLER, Donald L. Professor of English, East Carolina University, Greenville, North Carolina. Co-Author of *Vonnegut in America,* 1977, and author of *Approaches to Science Fiction,* 1978, and articles on 19th- and 20th-century British and American writers. Contributing Editor of *Survey of Science Fiction Literature,* 1979, and Editor of a forthcoming edition of Wilde's *The Picture of Dorian Gray.* **Essays:** Anthony Boucher; Avram Davidson; David Gerrold; Fred and Geoffrey Hoyle; Otis Adelbert Kline; Richard Matheson; Kris Neville; Larry Niven; J.R.R. Tolkien (appendix).

LEVY, Michael M. Instructor in English, University of Wisconsin, Menomonie. Reviewer of science fiction and literary criticism. **Essays:** Philip Francis Nowlan; Gary K. Wolf.

LIVEZEY, James A. Professor, Chapman College, Orange, California. **Essays:** Eugene Burdick; Richard Condon.

LOWDER, Christopher. Free-lance Writer; Author of thrillers, pulp fiction, and comics under several pseudonyms, and of critical articles on popular fiction. **Essay:** James Herbert.

LOWNDES, Robert A.W. See his own entry. **Essays:** Paul Ernst; Wallace West.

LUPOFF, Richard A. See his own entry. **Essays:** Edwin L. Arnold; Robert Asprin; Eando Binder; Robert Bloch; Edgar Rice Burroughs; Stanton A. Coblentz; George Allan England; Hugo Gernsback; H.L. Gold; Michael Kurland; Frank Belknap Long; Raymond A. Palmer; Ed Earl Repp; Wilmar H. Shiras; E.E. Smith; Donald A. Wollheim.

LYNCH, Peter. Graduate Student in Future Studies, University of Houston, Clear Lake City. **Essays:** Gordon Eklund; Victor Rousseau; Michael Young.

MACDONALD, Andrew. Director of English as a Second Language, Loyola University, Chicago. Author of articles on Jonson, Shakespeare, English as a second language, science fiction, and popular culture. **Essays:** Martin Caidin (with Gina Macdonald); Arthur Keppel-Jones; Bertrand Russell.

MACDONALD, Gina. Assistant Professor of English, Loyola University, Chicago. Author of articles on Southwestern writers, popular culture, science fiction, and Shakespearean influences. **Essays:** Martin Caidin (with Andrew Macdonald); Theodora DuBois; Vincent Harper; Frank Herbert; Robert Hoskins; Charles R. Long; Thomas McClary; John Rankine; Arthur Selings; R.C. Sherriff.

MANOUSOS, Anthony. Member of the Faculty, Cook College, Rutgers University, New Brunswick, New Jersey. Author of articles in *Dictionary of American Science Fiction Writers,* and on D.H. Lawrence and Swift. **Essays:** Lin Carter; Jack Dann; L.P. Davies; G.C. Edmondson; Mack Reynolds; George Zebrowski.

McGUIRE, Patrick L. Free-lance Writer; Author of articles on Joe Haldeman, the Strugatskys, C.J. Cherryh, and Poul Anderson; translator of works of Soviet science fiction. Consulting Editor, *Survey of Science Fiction Literature,* 1979. **Essays:** C.J. Cherryh; Keith Laumer; Vernor Vinge; James White.

MEYERS, Walter E. Professor of English, North Carolina State University, Raleigh; Member of the Editorial Board, *Science-Fiction Studies.* Author of *Aliens and Linguists,* 1980. Consulting Editor, *Survey of Science Fiction Literature,* 1979. **Essays:** T.J. Bass; James Cooke Brown; Rosel George Brown; A. Bertram Chandler; Alan Dean Foster; Rex Gordon; H. Rider Haggard; Neil R. Jones; David Karp; Ward Moore; John Morressy; James H. Schmitz; Nevil Shute.

MIESEL, Sandra. Free-lance Writer. Author of *Myth, Symbol, and Religion in Lord of the Rings,* 1973, *Against Arrow's Time: The High Crusade of Poul Anderson,* 1978, and of articles in *Amazing, SF Monthly, Isaac Asimov's Science Fiction Magazine,* and other periodicals; also writes introductions and afterwords for Gregg Press and Ace Books. **Essays:** Poul Anderson; Gordon R. Dickson; Zenna Henderson; R.A. Lafferty; Fred Saberhagen; Wilson Tucker.

MILLER, Richard W. Associate Professor of Philosophy, University of Missouri, Rolla. **Essays:** H. Beam Piper; Leonard Wibberley.

MOLSON, Francis J. Professor of English, Central Michigan University, Mount Pleasant. Author of the chapter on juvenile science fiction in *Anatomy of Wonder,* 1976, and of articles on Le Guin, Emily Dickinson, Frances Hodgson Burnett, and other writers. **Essays:** Alexander Key; Alice Lightner; Jeff and Jean Sutton; Hugh Walters; Laurence Yep.

MONTGOMERIE, Lee. Journalist. Reviewer for *Foundation.* **Essays:** W.E. Johns; Naomi Mitchison; Charles Platt.

MURRAY, Will. Vice-President and Editor, Odyssey Publications; Editor of *Duende,* a research journal on pulp magazines. Co-Author of *The Man Behind Doc Savage,* 1974, and author of *The Duende History of The Shadow Magazine,* 1979, and of articles and interviews in *Pulp* and *Xenophile.* **Essays:** Lester Dent; Clark Ashton Smith; John Taine.

NICKERSON, Susan L.   Branch Supervisor, Sylvan Oaks Community Library, Sacramento.   Reviewer for *Library Journal* and *Science Fiction and Fantasy Book Review*.   **Essay:** Roy Meyers.

NOLAN, William F.   See his own entry.   **Essay:** Ray Russell.

OLIVER, Chad.   See his own entry.   **Essays:** Edmond Hamilton; Ross Rocklynne.

PAGE, Gerald W.   Local Programming Editor, *TV Guide*.   Author of 40 science-fiction and fantasy stories since 1963.   Editor of *Witchcraft and Sorcery, Nameless Places, Year's Best Horror Stories 4-7,* and *Heroic Fantasy*.   **Essays:** Bryan Berry; Nelson S. Bond; Charles L. Fontenay; Gardner F. Fox; Raymond F. Jones; Lisa Tuttle; Robert Moore Williams.

PARKIN-SPEER, Diane.   Associate Professor of English, Southwest Texas State University, San Marcos.   Author of two articles on Heinlein in *Extrapolation*.   **Essays:** Alexei Panshin; Sydney J. Van Scyoc.

PERKINS, Michael.   Editor, *New York Arts*.   Author of *The Secret Record*, 1976, and *The Persistence of Desire*, 1977.   **Essay:** David Meltzer.

PFEIFFER, John R.   Professor of English, Central Michigan University, Mount Pleasant; Special Editor, *Shaw Review*.   Author of *Fantasy and Science Fiction: A Critical Guide*, 1971, and a chapter on the modern period in *Anatomy of Wonder*, 1976.   **Essays:** Herbert Best; John Christopher; Alan Seymour; Hank Stine; Colin Wilson.

PHILLIPS, Gene.   Librarian.   Author of fantasy stories.   **Essays:** Kenneth Bulmer; Robert Chilson; Colin Kapp; Emil Petaja; Ian Wallace.

PHILMUS, Robert M.   Professor of English, Loyola College, Concordia University, Montreal; Member of the Editorial Board, *Science-Fiction Studies*.   Author of *Into the Unknown: The Evolution of Science Fiction from Francis Godwin to H.G. Wells*, 1970, and a chapter on early science fiction in *Anatomy of Wonder*, 1976.   Editor, with David Y. Hughes, *H.G. Wells: Early Writings in Science and Science Fiction*, 1975, and with Darko Suvin, *H.G. Wells and Modern Science Fiction*, 1977.

PIERCE, Hazel.   Professor of English, Kearney State College, Nebraska.   Author of essays on Asimov and Bradbury in books, and on Blake and Byron in *Platte Valley Review*.   **Essays:** Geo. Alec Effinger; Kurd Lasswitz (appendix); A.E. van Vogt.

PRATT, Nick.   Free-lance Photographer; also book reviewer.   **Essays:** M. John Harrison; R. W. Mackelworth.

PRIEST, Christopher.   See his own entry.

PRONZINI, Bill.   Author of 20 novels and 250 stories, articles, and essays.   Editor of three anthologies of fantasy and four of science fiction.   **Essays:** Arthur K. Barnes; Charles Beaumont; Cleve Cartmill; Steve Frazee; Edward D. Hoch; Evan Hunter; Henry Slesar.

QUINN, Joseph A.   Associate Professor of English, University of Windsor, Ontario.   Author of articles in *Chesterton Review* and *Alternative Futures*.   **Essays:** John Atkins; Constantine FitzGibbon; Stephen Gilbert; L.P. Hartley; Alun Llewellyn; Noel M. Loomis.

RABKIN, Eric S.   Professor of English, University of Michigan, Ann Arbor.   Author of *The Fantastic in Literature*, 1976, *Science Fiction: History, Science, Vision* (with Robert Scholes), 1977, and *Arthur C. Clarke*, 1979.   **Essay:** Arthur C. Clarke.

REILLY, Robert.   Associate Professor of English, Rider College, Lawrenceville, New Jersey.   Author of articles on Ray Bradbury in *Extrapolation*.   **Essays:** D.F. Jones; Vincent King.

RIES, Lawrence R.   Coordinator, Great Meadow Correctional Facility College Program, Skidmore College, Saratoga Springs, New York.   Author of *Wolf Masks: Violence in Contemporary Poetry*, 1977.   **Essays:** Robert Conquest; Sterling E. Lanier.

ROSINSKY, Natalie M.   Teaching Assistant in English, University of Wisconsin, Madison.   Author of an essay on C.L. Moore, and an article in *The Lost Tradition: A History of Mothers and Daughters in Literature*. 1979.   **Essays:** Vonda N. McIntyre; C.L. Moore.

ROTTENSTEINER, Franz.   Librarian, Austrian Institute for Building Research, Vienna; Consultant to Suhrkamp publishers, Frankfurt, and Zsolnay publishers, Vienna; Consulting Editor, *Science-Fiction Studies*.   Author of *The Science Fiction Book*, 1975, and *The Fantasy Book*, 1978.   Editor of *View from Another Shore*.   **Essays:** Karin Boye (appendix); Wyman Guin; E.M. Hull; Maurice Renard (appendix); Albert Robida (appendix).

RUSS, Joanna.   See her own entry.   **Essay:** H.P. Lovecraft.

SAMUELSON, David N.   Professor of English, California State University, Long Beach; Editorial Adviser to *Alternate Futures*, *Science-Fiction Studies*, *Survey of Science Fiction Literature*, and several publishers.   Author of *Visions of Tomorrow*, 1975, a forthcoming bibliography of Arthur C. Clarke, and essays on Aldiss, Pohl, Benford, Bernard Wolfe, and Walter M. Miller, Jr.   **Essays:** Isaac Asimov; Greg Bear; Gregory Benford; John Boyd; Anthony Burgess; Max Ehrlich; Howard Fast; Walter M. Miller, Jr.; Frederik Pohl; Stephen Robinett; Theodore Sturgeon; Bernard Wolfe.

SARGENT, Pamela.   See her own entry.   **Essays:** Cecelia Holland; Kate Wilhelm; Gene Wolfe.

SATTY, Harvey J.   President of the Olaf Stapledon Society.   **Essay:** Chester Anderson.

SCARBOROUGH, John.   Professor of History, University of Kentucky, Lexington.   Author of *Roman Medicine*, 1969, *Facets of Hellenic Life*, 1976, "Medicine in Science Fiction" in *Encyclopedia of Science Fiction*, 1979, and an article on von Daniken in *Dictics*.   **Essay:** Josef Nesvadba (appendix).

SCHLOBIN, Roger C.   Associate Professor of English and Special Assistant to the Chancellor, Purdue University North Central Campus, Westville, Indiana; Editor for Garland and Starmont publishers.   Author of *A Research Guide to Science Fiction Studies* (with Marshall B. Tymn and L.W. Currey), 1977; *The Year's Scholarship in Science Fiction and Fantasy* (with Tymn), 1979; *The Literature of Fantasy* (bibliography), 1979; *Andre Norton: A Primary and Secondary Bibliography*, 1980.   **Essays:** Lord Dunsany (appendix); William Morris (appendix); Andre Norton.

SCHOLES, Robert.   Professor of English, Brown University, Providence, Rhode Island; General Editor, Masters of Science Fiction series.   Author of *The Fabulators*, 1969, *Structural Fabulation*, 1975, and *Science Fiction: History, Science, Vision* (with Eric S. Rabkin), 1977.

SCHWEITZER, Darrell.   Free-lance Writer.   Editor of *Essays Lovecraftian*, 1976, and *SF Voices*, 1976.   **Essays:** L. Sprague de Camp; Leo Szilard.

SEARLES, Baird.   Film and television critic, *Fantasy and Science Fiction*; Associate Editor, *Science Fiction Review Monthly*.   Author of a study of Heinlein, *The Science Fiction Quiz Book*, *A Reader's Guide to Science Fiction* (with others), 1979, and reviews in *The New York Times Book Review*, *Village Voice*, and other periodicals.   Producer of "Of Unicorns and Universes," a radio program of science fiction criticism, 1967-69.   **Essays:** Robert Graves; A. Merritt; Austin Tappan Wright.

SEIDEL, Kathryn L.   Assistant Professor English, University of Maryland, College Park.   Author of an essay in *Survey of Science Fiction Literature*, 1979, and of articles on Marge Piercy and technical writing. **Essays:** Dean R. Koontz; Marge Piercy; Pamela Sargent.

SHWARTZ, Susan M. Assistant Professor of English, Ithaca College, New York. Author of science fiction stories in *Analog* and other periodicals. **Essay:** Jacqueline Lichtenberg.

SMITH, Curtis C. Associate Professor of Humanities, University of Houston, Clear Lake City. Editor of *Twentieth-Century Science-Fiction Writers*, 1981. **Essays:** Laurence M. Janifer; Philip Latham; Robert A.W. Lowndes.

SNYDER, Carol L. Assistant Professor of Humanities, University of Houston, Clear Lake City. **Essays:** Joanna Russ; James Tiptree, Jr.

SNYDER, Judith. Member of the Faculty, San Jacinto College, Houston. **Essays:** Gertrude Friedberg; Curt Gentry.

STABLEFORD, Brian M. See his own entry.

STAPLES, Katherine. Instructor in English, University of Texas, Austin. Translator of works by Henri Rousseau, and of *Les Illuminations* by Rimbaud. **Essays:** John Crowley; J.T. McIntosh.

STEPHENSEN-PAYNE, Philippa. Free-lance Writer. **Essay:** Nicholas Fisk.

STONE, Graham. Author of *Australian Science Fiction Index 1925-1967*, 1968, supplement, 1976. **Essays:** Christopher Blayre; Erle Cox; Ray Cummings; Lloyd Arthur Eshbach; Vincent McHugh; P. Schuyler Miller; Jack Wodhams; Arthur Leo Zagat.

STOVER, Leon E. See his own entry. **Essays:** John W. Campbell, Jr.; George R. Stewart.

SULLIVAN, C.W., III. Assistant Professor of English, East Carolina University, Greenville, North Carolina; Editor of *Children's Folklore Newsletter*. Author of articles in *Survey of Science Fiction Literature*, 1979. Editor of *As Tomorrow Becomes Today*, 1974. **Essays:** E.R. Eddison (appendix); Harlan Ellison; Pat Frank; John Hersey; John Norman; Andrew J. Offutt; Kit Reed.

SUMMERS, Judith. Film Editor, BBC Television, London. **Essay:** E.V. Odle.

SUVIN, Darko. Professor of English and Comparative Literature, McGill University, Montreal; Editor, *Science-Fiction Studies*. Author of *Russian Science Fiction 1956-1974: A Bibliography*, 1976, *Pour Une Poétique de la Science-Fiction*, 1977, and *Metamorphoses of Science Fiction*, 1979. Editor of *Other Worlds, Other Seas*, 1970, *Science Fiction Studies* (with R.D. Mullen), 2 vols., 1976-78, and *H.G. Wells and Modern Science Fiction* (with Robert M. Philmus), 1977. **Essays:** Grant Allen; Edward Bellamy; Aleksandr R. Belyaev (appendix); Johanna and Günter Braun (appendix); Valery Bryusov (appendix); Samuel Butler; Karel Capek (appendix); Robert Cromie; Edward Douglas Fawcett; Camille Flammarion (appendix); George Griffith; C.J. Cutcliffe Hyne; Stanislaw Lem (appendix); William Le Queux; Vladimir Mayakovsky (appendix); Simon Newcomb; Boris and Arkady Strugatsky (appendix); Abram Tertz (appendix); Alexey Tolstoy (appendix); Konstantin Tsiolkovsky (appendix); Ivan Yefremov (appendix); Yevgeny Zamyatin (appendix).

SWANK, Paul. Assistant Professor of Human Sciences, University of Houston, Clear Lake City. **Essays:** Fletcher Pratt; Robert Silverberg; George O. Smith.

TALBOT, Norman. Professor of English, University of Newcastle. **Essays:** F. Anstey; Hugh Sykes Davies; Jacquetta Hawkes; Upton Sinclair.

THURSTON, Robert. See his own entry. **Essays:** James P. Hogan; Richard M. McKenna; Richard C. Meredith; Janet E. Morris; James Sallis.

TOLLEY, Michael J. Senior Lecturer in English, University of Adelaide, South Australia; Editorial Adviser, *Blake Studies*. Author of 20 essays on Blake and an article in *Armchair Detective*. Co-Editor of *William Blake's Designs for Edward Young's Night Thoughts*, 2 vols., 1979, and of the forthcoming book *The Stellar Gage*. **Essays:** Mark Adlard; Angela Carter; Michael G. Coney; Lionel Davidson; Michael Frayn; Joseph Green; Lindsay Gutteridge; David Lake; John D. MacDonald; Kit Pedler and Gerry Davis.

TUCK, Donald H. Bibliographer and industrial manager. Author of *A Handbook of Science Fiction and Fantasy*, 1954 (revised edition, 2 vols., 1959), and *The Encyclopedia of Science Fiction and Fantasy*, 2 vols., 1974-78.

TUCKER, Frank H. Professor of History, Colorado College, Colorado Springs. Author of *The White Conscience*, 1969, a chapter in *Robert A. Heinlein*, 1978, and articles in *Russian Affairs*, *Japanese Affairs*, *Intellect*, and *Extrapolation*. **Essays:** Kobo Abe (appendix); Sakyo Komatsu (appendix); André Maurois (appendix).

TURNER, George. See his own entry. **Essays:** J.D. Beresford; M. Barnard Eldershaw; Pip Maddern.

TUTTLE, Lisa. See her own entry. **Essay:** Tom Reamy.

TUZAR, Jana I. Graduate Student in Slavic Languages, University of Wisconsin, Madison. **Essay:** Mikhail Bulgakov (appendix); Vladimir Tendryakov (appendix).

TYMN, Marshall B. Member of the Department of English, Eastern Michigan University, Ypsilanti; Editor for G.K. Hall publishers. Author of *A Research Guide to Science Fiction Studies* (with Roger C. Schlobin and L.W. Currey), 1977; *Index to Stories in Thematic Anthologies of Science Fiction*, 1978; *American Fantasy and Science Fiction* (bibliography), 1979; *The Year's Scholarship in Science Fiction and Fantasy* (with Schlobin), 1979.

UNDERWOOD, Marylyn. Instructor in English, Victoria University, Toronto. Author of *First Principles*, 1978, and of articles in *CEA Forum*, *Texas Folklore Society Bulletin*, and *Kaleidoscope*. **Essay:** Ben Bova.

UTLEY, Steven. See his own entry. **Essays:** Ralph Milne Farley; Joe Pumilia.

WAGAR, W. Warren. Professor of History, State University of New York, Binghamton; Member of the Advisory Board, *Alternative Futures*. Author of *H.G. Wells and the World State*, 1961; *The City of Man*, 1963; *Building the City of Man*, 1971; *Good Tidings: The Belief in Progress from Darwin to Marcuse*, 1972; *Books in World History*, 1973; *World Views: A Study in Comparative History*, 1977. Editor of *H.G. Wells: Journalism and Prophecy*, 1964; *European Intellectual History since Darwin and Marx*, 1967; *Science, Faith, and Man*, 1968; *The Idea of Progress since the Renaissance*, 1969; *History and the Idea of Mankind*, 1971. **Essay:** H.G. Wells.

WAGNER, Karl Edward. Psychiatrist; Editor for Putnam publishers, and of *The Year's Best Horror Stories* series. Author of *Darkness Weaves*, 1970; *Death Angel's Shadow*, 1973; *Bloodstone*, 1975; *Legion from the Shadows*, 1976; *Dark Crusade*, 1976; *Night Winds*, 1978; *The Road of Kings*, 1979. **Essay:** Manly Wade Wellman.

WATSON, Ian. See his own entry. **Essays:** Barrington John Bayley; Michael Bishop; David I. Masson; John Varley.

WAY, Douglas E. Retired businessman. **Essays:** J.U. Giesy; Austin Hall and Homer Eon Flint.

WAY, Karen G. Teaching Assistant, Department of English, Rutgers University, New Brunswick, New Jersey. Past Editor of *Lovejoy's Guidance Digest*. **Essays:** Neal Barrett, Jr.; F.M. Busby; Phyllis Eisenstein; Sylvia Engdahl; Jonathan Fast; Nancy Freedman; Stephen Goldin; J.B. Priestley; Walt and Leigh Richmond; Kathleen Sky; E.C. Tubb; Cherry Wilder.

WEEDMAN, Jane B. Member of the Department of Language and Literature, Rochester Institute of Technology, New York. Author of a forthcoming book on Delany and of articles in *Survey of Science Fiction*, 1979. **Essays:** Anna Kavan; Mark Twain.

WEINKAUF, Mary S. Professor of English and Head of the Department, Dakota Wesleyan University, Mitchell, South Dakota. Author of *Early Poems by a Late Beginner*, 1976, and of articles and reviews in *Fantasy and Science Fiction Book Review, SFRA Newsletter, Extrapolation, Studies in English Literature, Texas Quarterly*, and other periodicals. **Essays:** Colin Anderson; René Barjavel (appendix); L. Frank Baum; Octavia E. Butler; William Dean Howells; Tanith Lee; Sinclair Lewis; Clifford D. Simak; Craig Strete; Franz Werfel (appendix); S. Fowler Wright.

WELCH, Dennis M. Associate Professor Humanities, Clarkson College, Potsdam, New York. Author of poems in literary magazines and articles in journals. Former Assistant Editor of *Eighteenth Century*. **Essay:** Theodore R. Cogswell.

WHITE, Fred D. Assistant Professor of English, University of Santa Clara, California. Author of short fiction in *Michigan Quarterly Review* and of articles and reviews in *Minneapolis Tribune* and *Walt Whitman Review*. **Essay:** Robert Sheckley.

WILCOX, Robert H. Professor of English, Glendale College, California; Consulting Editor, *Amazing*. Editor of a technical magazine for 15 years. **Essays:** Louis Charbonneau; J. Francis McComas; William F. Temple.

WILDER, Cherry. See her own entry. **Essays:** Robert Holdstock; Doris Lessing; Ira Levin; Alan Sillitoe.

WINGROVE, David. Editor of *Vector*, the journal of the British Science Fiction Association. Co-author of a forthcoming book on Brian Aldiss. **Essays:** Richard Cowper; Andrew M. Stephenson.

WOLFE, Gary K. Associate Professor of Humanities, Roosevelt University, Chicago. Author of *The Known and the Unknown: The Iconography of Science Fiction*, 1979, *Elements of Research*, 1979, *David Lindsay: A Reader's Guide* (forthcoming), and articles in *Dictionary of Literary Biography, Survey of Science Fiction Literature*, and periodicals. **Essays:** Ray Bradbury; Edmund Cooper; John Keir Cross; Jack Finney; William Hope Hodgson; Nigel Kneale; Roy Lewis; David Lindsay; John Lymington; Chad Oliver; Herbert Read; Rod Serling; M.P. Shiel; Cordwainer Smith; Jerry Sohl.

WOLFE, Gene. See his own entry. **Essay:** Algis Budrys.

WOLK, Anthony. Member of the Department of English, Portland State University, Oregon. **Essays:** Philip K. Dick; Shepherd Mead.

WOOD, Susan. Assistant Professor of English, University of British Columbia, Vancouver. Author of essays on fantasy, science-fiction, and Canadian literature. Editor of *The Language of the Night* by Le Guin, 1979, and of the science-fiction and fantasy issue of *Room of One's Own*. **Essays:** Terry Carr; Frederick Philip Grove.

WOOSTER, Martin Morse. Publisher. Author of *The Social History of Science Fiction* (forthcoming), and of essays in *Science Fiction Review, Thrust*, and *Starship*. **Essays:** Reginald Bretnor; Richard A. Lupoff; William Rotsler; Ted White; Jack Williamson.

WYGANT, Alice Chambers. Librarian, University of Texas Medical Branch, Galveston. **Essays:** Sonya Dorman; Sam Merwin, Jr.

YOKE, Carl B. Associate Professor of English, Kent State University, Kent, Ohio. Author of *A Reader's Guide to Roger Zelazny*, 1979, and of articles in *Survey of Science Fiction Literature*, 1979. **Essays:** Michael Crichton; Daniel F. Galouye; John Jakes; Charles Eric Maine; Roger Zelazny.

ZEBROWSKI, George. See his own entry. **Essays:** David Duncan; Edgar Pangborn; Thomas N. Scortia; William Tenn.